THE ARDEN SHAKESPEARE THIRD SERIES COMPLETE WORKS

Edited by Richard Proudfoot, Ann Thompson, David Scott Kastan
and H.R. Woudhuysen

THE ARDEN SHAKESPEARE

LONDON · NEW YORK · OXFORD · NEW DELHI · SYDNEY

THE ARDEN SHAKESPEARE
Bloomsbury Publishing Plc
50 Bedford Square, London, WC1B 3DP, UK
1385 Broadway, New York, NY 10018, USA

BLOOMSBURY, THE ARDEN SHAKESPEARE and the Arden Shakespeare logo are trademarks
of Bloomsbury Publishing Plc

First published in Great Britain 2021

The general editors of the Arden Shakespeare have been W.J. Craig and R.H. Case (first series 1899–1944)
Una Ellis-Fermor, Harold F. Brooks, Harold Jenkins and Brian Morris (second series 1946–82)
Present general editors (third series)
Richard Proudfoot, Ann Thompson, David Scott Kastan and H.R. Woudhuysen

Cover design by Charlotte Daniels
Cover image: Curtain with large flower and leaf motifs, England, seventeenth century
(© Victoria and Albert Museum, London)

A catalogue record for this book is available from the British Library.

A catalog record for this book is available from the Library of Congress.

ISBN: HB: 978-1-4742-9638-0
         PB: 978-1-4742-9636-6
         ePDF: 978-1-4742-9640-3
         eBook: 978-1-4742-9639-7

Series: The Arden Shakespeare Third Series

Typeset by RefineCatch Limited, Bungay, Suffolk
Printed and bound in India

To find out more about our authors and books visit www.bloomsbury.com
and sign up for our newsletters.

CONTENTS

LIST OF ILLUSTRATIONS

General Editors' Preface

This volume marks a milestone: the completion of the Third Series of the Arden Shakespeare. From the first volume of the First Series, Edward Dowden's edition of *Hamlet*, published in 1899, the Arden Shakespeare has been widely acknowledged as the pre-eminent Shakespeare edition, valued by scholars, teachers, students, actors and 'the great variety of readers' alike. The Third Series (Arden 3; General Editors: Richard Proudfoot, Ann Thompson, David Scott Kastan and H.R. Woudhuysen) began publication in 1995 and was completed early in 2020. This volume is the first collected edition of an entire series of Arden texts. The earlier 'complete' edition of the Arden Shakespeare included mixtures of Arden 2 and Arden 3 texts.

The third series of the Arden Shakespeare consists of 44 individual volumes, somewhat more, that is, than the 36 plays that appear in the 1623 Folio or even than the 37 or 38 plays usually claimed as Shakespeare's. Least controversial is the inclusion of edited versions of *The Sonnets* and Shakespeare's other *Poems*, most notably the two long narrative poems published separately in Shakespeare's lifetime, *Venus and Adonis* and *The Rape of Lucrece*. Two collaborative plays written late in Shakespeare's career are included in the series, as has become common in other complete Shakespeares: *Pericles*, written with George Wilkins, and *The Two Noble Kinsmen*, written with John Fletcher. In this volume, those texts that have been corrected or revised since their first publication are printed in their most recent form.

Hamlet is the only play to appear in this volume in more than one text. The Prince says that 'a man's life is no more than to say "one"', but the text of Shakespeare's most complex play cannot adequately be represented singularly. We offer edited versions of all three early texts: Q1 (1603), Q2 (1604–5) and F (1623). There are various theories about the relationships between these: Q1, the shortest of the three, has often been dismissed as a shortened bootleg version, a 'memorial reconstruction' put together by actors or audience members, so despite being published first it would have been derived from one of the longer texts. In recent years, however, scholars have revived the notion that it represents Shakespeare's first draft. Q2, the longest text, appeared soon after Q1 and claims to be 'enlarged . . . according to the true and perfect Coppie'. F, the last text to be published, omits some 230lines that are

present in Q2 but adds some 70 of its own; it has recently been regarded as an authorial revision. Most editors, like most theatre practitioners, offer a 'conflated' text, usually combining elements from Q2 and F, but in the absence of a consensus about the precise relationship between the texts it seems preferable to treat each as if it were an independent entity.

More controversial is the inclusion of three plays in which, if they are in some sense 'by' Shakespeare, his role is different from that in the collaborative plays which are now conventionally included in the canon. The editors of *Sir Thomas More*, *Edward III* and *Double Falsehood* each make the case for their play's inclusion in the Arden series. *Sir Thomas More*, a collaboration that was never published and exists in a unique manuscript now in the British Library, contains material now widely agreed to be by Shakespeare and likely written in his own hand. *Edward III*, published anonymously in 1596, was first identified as possibly by Shakespeare by Edward Capell in 1760, and increasingly scholars have agreed that the play was written by two collaborators, one of whom might well be Shakespeare on the basis of various kinds of stylistic analysis; and for the putatively Shakespearean portions there is no better candidate.

Double Falsehood has a more complex relationship to Shakespeare. This play was first performed in December 1727 and published early the next year. The title-page of the published version claims that it was 'Written Originally by *W. Shakespeare*' and is 'now Revised and Adapted to the Stage' by Lewis Theobald. The plot is based on the story of Cardenio, a character in *Don Quixote*, which was published in English in 1612. A play known as *Cardenio* (or *Cardenno* or *Cardenna*) was played at court twice in 1613 by the King's Men, Shakespeare's company. In 1653 Humphrey Moseley registered a large group of plays as his property, including 'The History of Cardenio, by Mr. Fletcher. and Shakespeare'. Although some have claimed *Double Falsehood* is a forgery, more likely it is what it claims to be: an eighteenth-century adaptation of a probably revised seventeenth-century play, which Shakespeare seems to have written in collaboration with John Fletcher. How far Shakespeare's contribution is buried beneath layers of revision is hard to know with certainty, but the likelihood of that contribution justifies its inclusion here.

If the understanding of the Shakespeare canon is thus expansive, the editorial work of the Arden texts is for the most part conservative: modernizing the spelling and punctuation of the early editions, normalizing capitalization, removing superfluous italics, regularizing (and not abbreviating) the names of characters, and rationalizing entrances and exits. Clarity and consistency are the goals of these procedures.

In certain play-texts there are typographical conventions specific to the textual understanding of the play. Superscript indicators are used in a number of plays to indicate the use of different source texts. In *King Lear*, the Arden 3 editor presents a single edited text based on the 1623 Folio, which incorporates words and passages present only in the 1608 Quarto. The conventions used to signal the differences between the two early texts are explained in the note on p. 751. Similar conventions are used for three passages in *Titus Andronicus* (see note on p. 1271). The various hands involved in the manuscript of *Sir Thomas More* are indicated according to the system described on p. 1160.

For the most part, however, the goal of Arden 3 has been to present scrupulously edited texts designed to be accessible to modern readers. If there is some inescapable loss of the historical feel of the early printed texts resulting from the adoption of these modernizing editorial principles and conventions, it is justified by the removal of obstacles to understanding that Shakespeare never could have intended for his readers.

Mr. WILLIAM
SHAKESPEARES

COMEDIES,
HISTORIES, &
TRAGEDIES.

Published according to the True Originall Copies.

Martin Droeshout sculpsit London

LONDON
Printed by Isaac Iaggard, and Ed. Blount. 1623.

1 Title-page, with a portrait of Shakespeare engraved by Droeshout, from the First Folio edition of Shakespeare's plays, edited by John Heminges and Henry Condell and printed by Isaac Jaggard and Edward Blount, published in 1623

Introduction

WHY SHAKESPEARE?

What is 'Shakespeare'? A worldwide cultural phenomenon, a brand-name, a logo, an image that appears on T-shirts and credit cards, a mainstay of theatre, film and video production, a compulsory component of education, a label that sells thousands of books, a household name. Also an individual human being, born in a small English country town in 1564, a man who went to London and had a successful career as an actor, playwright and shareholder in the theatre. By all accounts an agreeable and modest man who did not seek to draw attention to himself, even by publishing his plays, though he does seem to have hoped that the fame of his *Sonnets* would outlive him. His surname has nevertheless become so familiar that his first name, William, does not need to be mentioned – is not indeed mentioned on the covers or title-pages of his works as published in 'The Arden Shakespeare': a person from another planet might work carefully through an entire volume in our series without discovering the first name of the author, but on our planet 'everyone' knows who he is. It has even become a kind of perverse tribute to him that periodically people attempt to prove that he didn't write anything after all, that the works ascribed to him were in fact written by somebody else entirely.

The names of some of this man's works have become so familiar themselves that we can even drop 'Shakespeare' without fear of being misunderstood when we talk of 'Orson Welles's *Othello*' or 'Kenneth Branagh's *Henry V*'. Certain images have become instantly recognizable: a man dressed in black holding a skull 'means' *Hamlet*, a man talking to a woman above him on a moonlit balcony 'means' *Romeo and Juliet*. We quote Shakespeare all the time, sometimes unconsciously, using phrases that have dropped into common usage: 'to have one's pound of flesh' (*The Merchant of Venice* 1.3.147–8 and subsequently); 'to the manner born' (*Hamlet* Q2 1.4.15); 'more honoured in the breach than the observance' (*Hamlet* Q2 1.4.16); 'at one fell swoop' (*Macbeth* 4.3.222). Compilers of crossword puzzles and quiz games routinely rely on Shakespearean quotations and references.

Words and phrases from the plays and poems have provided the titles of hundreds of novels, plays and films:

one might cite Edith Wharton's *The Glimpses of the Moon* (*Hamlet* Q2 1.4.53), William Faulkner's *The Sound and the Fury* (*Macbeth* 5.5.26), Aldous Huxley's *Brave New World* (*The Tempest* 5.1.183), Vladimir Nabokov's *Pale Fire* (*Timon of Athens* 4.3.434) and Christopher Isherwood's *All the Conspirators* (*Julius Caesar* 5.5.70), Agatha Christie's *By the Pricking of My Thumbs* – Ray Bradbury completed the rhyme with his *Something Wicked This Way Comes* (*Macbeth* 4.1.44–5) – and H.E. Bates's *The Darling Buds of May* (Sonnet 18.3). The plays are still being performed live all over the world, and film and video versions have made them accessible to millions of people who never go to the theatre. They continue to inspire adaptations and spin-offs such as Peter Greenaway's film *Prospero's Books* (1991), Gus Van Sant's film *My Own Private Idaho* (1991) and Alan Isler's novel *The Prince of West End Avenue* (1994), all of which assume a prior knowledge of a work by Shakespeare on the part of their viewers or readers.

How and why has this happened? Four hundred years after the heyday of Shakespeare's own dramatic career we find ourselves arguing about whether his extraordinary fame and influence were somehow inevitable, a direct result of the intrinsic qualities of his works themselves, or a piece of sustained hype, the manipulation of a myth by those with a personal stake in its perpetuation – performers, teachers, publishers, Stratford-upon-Avon hoteliers – and by those with a more general interest in promoting British 'high' culture: Shakespeare has been adopted as 'the Swan of Avon', the ultimate canonical figure who is taken to represent the genius and values of an entire nation.

Shakespeare did do well during his lifetime out of what was the nearest thing Elizabethan and Jacobean London had to a mass entertainment industry. Unlike other dramatists of the time, he did most of his work for a single theatrical company, the Lord Chamberlain's Men, under Elizabeth I, who became the King's Men under James I. This stability in itself probably provided him with reasonably good working conditions and the opportunity to develop his projects with known performers and business associates; it made it relatively easy for his plays to be collected and published after he died. Other dramatists, such as Thomas Middleton, who wrote for a number of different companies, had less chance of having their work collected or even identified.

The First Folio of Shakespeare's plays was published in 1623, seven years after his death, and reprinted in 1632, but in 1642 the theatres were closed, and were to remain closed for nearly twenty years during the Civil War and Commonwealth period, potentially jeopardizing the chances of Shakespeare or any other dramatist achieving lasting fame. With the Restoration of the monarchy in 1660, however, the theatres reopened and Shakespeare's plays came back into the repertory, albeit in truncated and altered versions. During the eighteenth century his reputation was consolidated by the publication of a number of scholarly editions and monographs, the erection of a monument in Westminster Abbey (1741) and the promotion of Stratford-upon-Avon as his birthplace and the site of David Garrick's festival or 'Jubilee' (1769). While the plays were often rewritten wholesale for the contemporary stage, their texts were simultaneously being 'restored' with great care (and even more ingenuity) by editors who contributed largely to the 'canonization' of the author. This has essentially been the story of Shakespeare's reception and cultural survival ever since: we still (in the absence of manuscripts other than the possible contribution by Shakespeare to the manuscript of *Sir Thomas More*) pursue the chimaera of 'what Shakespeare really wrote', while on the other hand treating his texts as endlessly adaptable, available for rewriting, rereading and reinterpreting by each generation.

The plays have turned out to be equally suitable for export, and Shakespeare has been enthusiastically appropriated by many countries around the world. In Germany, for example, Ferdinand Freiligrath's 1844 poem beginning '*Deutschland ist Hamlet*' ('Germany is Hamlet') spelt out a long-lasting identification of the character of Hamlet with the German Romantic self-image of a people capable of profound reflection but incapable of action. In the United States, on the other hand, Shakespeare became a kind of symbol of racial and cultural integration and democracy, perhaps especially during the period when silent films made his work accessible to people who did not know English. In Japan, which imported Shakespeare relatively late in the nineteenth century, he quickly came to represent the essence of westernization and modernization. All these countries now have thriving Shakespeare industries of their own.

The globalization of Shakespeare was of course assisted by the political and economic spread of the British Empire in the nineteenth century and by the continuing dominance of English as a worldwide language after the decline of that Empire. What remains remarkable is that Shakespeare is actually quite a difficult writer linguistically – much harder to read today than most of his contemporaries such as Ben Jonson, Thomas Middleton or John Fletcher. His syntax is often complex, his figures of speech are elaborate and his ideas hard to grasp. Some of this may be offset by the larger patterns of satisfaction we find in his plots and characters, and indeed it could be said that the difficulty itself leaves room for our explanations and interpretations. Shakespeare still 'works' in the theatre, but at school we have to be taught to 'appreciate' Shakespeare: is this indoctrination or something more benign – an educational process involving the 'recognition' of intrinsic merit?

In his essay *Of the Standard of Taste*, written in 1742, the philosopher David Hume argued that there is such a thing as intrinsic excellence in literature and that it is the continuity of a work's reputation that proves it. What he calls 'catholic and universal beauty' in various art forms is demonstrated by 'the durable admiration which attends those works that have survived all the caprices of mode and fashion, all the mistakes of ignorance and envy'. To support this he claims that 'The same Homer who pleased at Athens and Rome two thousand years ago, is still admired at Paris and London'. Shakespeare can be said to have passed the survival test, but perhaps it is not 'the same Shakespeare' now as 400 years ago, and not 'the same Shakespeare' in Berlin, New York or Tokyo as in London or Stratford-upon-Avon. One of the secrets of Shakespeare's success may be his changeability, the openness of his works to take on new meanings in contexts he cannot have anticipated.

SHAKESPEARE: THE LIFE

William Shakespeare was a successful man of the emerging entertainment industry of Elizabethan England. He was an actor, a 'sharer' in the acting company (that is, no mere hireling, but a partner entitled to share in its profits) and, of course, a leading playwright and poet.

He began, however, more humbly. We know a remarkable amount, for this period, about Shakespeare and his family. He was born late in April 1564 in Stratford-upon-Avon, in Warwickshire. The parish church records his baptism on 26 April; his unrecorded birthdate is conventionally set three days earlier on 23 April, St George's Day (and also, apparently, the date of Shakespeare's death). He was the third of eight children; his father was John Shakespeare, a glover and later a wool merchant, and his mother was Mary Arden, daughter of a well-established farmer in the nearby village of Wilmcote. Though the records have not survived, we can safely assume that he attended the King's New School, the Stratford grammar school with its strenuous classically based curriculum, but we know for certain that at the age of eighteen he married Anne Hathaway, also of Stratford, and that a daughter, Susanna, was born to them, as the parish records note, on 26 May 1583. On 2 February 1585 the register records the birth of twins, Hamnet and Judith.

Shakespeare was well established in London by the early 1590s as an actor and as a playwright. In 1592 a book appeared in which Robert Greene criticized an unnamed actor, 'an upstart Crow', for his presumption in writing plays, supposing himself 'as well able to bombast out a blanke verse' as any and imagining himself 'the onely Shake-scene in a countrey'. Since Greene's attack contains a parody of a line from *King Henry VI, Part 3*, it seems certain that it is Shakespeare that he aims at. By 1592, then, Shakespeare had already established himself in the theatre and drawn the ire of a jealous rival. In 1594, Court records indicate payments to Shakespeare and two other sharers in the Lord Chamberlain's Men for 'twoe severall comedies or Enterludes shewed by them before her Majesty in Christmas tyme laste'. References to Shakespeare's activity in the theatre abound, and in 1598 Francis Meres claimed that Shakespeare could be compared with Seneca for the writing of tragedy and with Plautus for comedy, indeed that among English writers he was 'the most excellent in both kinds for the stage'. But he wrote nondramatic poetry as well. When a severe outbreak of plague beginning in the summer of 1592 forced the closing of the theatres until the spring of 1594, Shakespeare wrote two narrative poems, *Venus and Adonis* and *The Rape of Lucrece*, both dedicated to Henry Wriothesley, the 3rd Earl of Southampton, and printed by a former fellow-resident of Stratford, Richard Field, in 1593 and 1594, respectively; and an edition of *Shakespeare's Sonnets* was published by Thomas Thorpe in 1609.

But Shakespeare's primary work was in the theatre, and it was the theatre that made him a wealthy man. His money, however, came neither from commissions nor from royalties for his plays, but from his position as a sharer in the Lord Chamberlain's Men (who, with the accession of James to the throne in 1603, became the King's Men), by which he was entitled to one-tenth of the company's profits, a share handsome enough to permit him considerable investment in property. In 1597 he bought for £60 the substantial freehold house in Stratford known as New Place, the second largest dwelling in the town; in 1602, he purchased 107 acres of land in the manorial fields to the north of Stratford for £320, and later that year a cottage in Stratford in Chapel Lane; in 1605 he bought a half-interest in a Stratford tithe farm for an additional £440; and in 1613, with three other investors, he acquired a 'tenement' in Blackfriars for £140.

If Shakespeare's business dealings can be traced in the Stratford Court Rolls, his family's lives and deaths can be followed in the parish register. His son, Hamnet, died at the age of eleven and was buried on 11 August 1596. Shakespeare's father died in September 1601, his mother in 1608. Shakespeare's elder daughter, Susanna, married John Hall, a well-respected Stratford physician, in Holy Trinity church on 5 June 1607. His younger daughter, Judith, married Thomas Quiney on 10 February 1616. Shakespeare's wife, Anne, died on 6 August 1623; she had lived to see a monument to her husband installed in Holy Trinity, but died just before the publication of the First Folio of his plays, the more lasting monument to his memory.

Shakespeare himself had died in late April of 1616, and was buried on the north side of the chancel of Holy Trinity, having left a will written that January. He bequeathed ten pounds to 'the Poore of Stratford', remembered local friends and his extended family, and allotted 26*s*. 8*d*. each for memorial rings for his theatrical colleagues Richard Burbage, John Heminges and Henry Condell. He left £150 to his daughter Judith, and another £150 to be paid if 'shee or Anie issue of her bodie be Lyvinge' three years from the execution of the will, but the bulk of the estate was left to Susanna. His wife is mentioned only once, in an apparent afterthought to the document: 'Item I gyve unto my wief my second best bed with the furniture.' The bequest of the bed and bedding has led many to speculate that this was a deliberate slight, but English customary law provided the widow with a third of the estate, and the 'second best bed' was almost certainly their own, the best being saved for guests.

Yet in spite of the detailed records that remain, allowing us to trace major and minor events in the lives of Shakespeare and his family, as well as to see his vital presence in the life of the London stage, some critics have passionately held that the author of the plays was someone other than 'the man from Stratford'. It was not until the eighteenth century that anyone questioned Shakespeare's authorship, but since then many, including Mark Twain, Henry James and Sigmund Freud, have been attracted to the anti-Stratfordian heresy. Various candidates have been proposed. Christopher Marlowe, Francis Bacon, Edward de Vere, 17th Earl of Oxford, Queen Elizabeth, even Daniel Defoe (who was not born until 1660) have all been suggested as the 'real' author of 'Shakespeare's' plays and poems. The controversy, however, has little to recommend it except its unintended humour; anti-Stratfordian champions have sometimes had unfortunate names, including Looney, Battey and Silliman. Although usually energetically asserted, the belief that someone other than Shakespeare wrote the plays seemingly derives from simple, if unattractive, social snobbery: a certainty that only someone educated at university, the Inns of Court or at the Court would be capable of such artistry. The desire to give the plays a more socially distinguished origin than they in fact had at least attests to the importance they have come to assume in our culture. All in all, however, there seems little doubt that William Shakespeare, the glover's son from Stratford, wrote the plays that bear his name, though their greatness can hardly be illuminated or intensified by the evidence of the life of their author.

SHAKESPEARE AND THE THEATRE

At an unknown date between 1585 and 1591, William Shakespeare left Stratford-upon-Avon and became an actor and playwright. Early tradition holds that he was for a few years before this a country schoolmaster (which might help to explain his close knowledge of some Latin texts, including plays by Plautus and Seneca). In 1587 the Queen's Men visited Stratford shortly after they lost a leading actor, William Knell, killed in a duel at Thame in Oxfordshire. Whether or not this may be imagined as Shakespeare's opportunity to join the players, plays from the Queen's Men's repertoire were, on the evidence of later allusions in his plays, well known to him. His name is, however, more often associated with two other companies, Lord Strange's (Derby's) Men and its offshoot the Earl of Pembroke's Men, which collapsed in the summer of 1593. A new play, called 'harey the vj' and usually identified as *King Henry VI, Part 1*, was performed by Strange's Men at the Rose playhouse on 3 March 1592 and thereafter. *Titus Andronicus*, played by the Earl of Sussex's Men, followed on 23 January 1594: in

June two more performances of it were given by the Lord Admiral's Men and the Lord Chamberlain's Men. By June 1594 Shakespeare had become a leading member of a newly formed company, the Lord Chamberlain's Men. He would remain with them for the rest of his career. Of his repertoire as an actor we know almost nothing. His name heads the list of 'Principall Actors in all these Playes' prefaced to the First Folio in 1623. It had earlier appeared in the similar lists for Ben Jonson's *Every Man in His Humour* (1598) and *Sejanus, His Fall* (1603), printed in the Jonson Folio of 1616. Beyond this, we have only late seventeenth-century traditions that he played Adam in *As You Like It* and the Ghost in *Hamlet*.

1594 saw the stabilization in London of the leading playing companies. The Admiral's Men, led by Edward Alleyn, under the management of Philip Henslowe, were at Henslowe's theatre, the Rose, on Bankside in Southwark (whose foundations were partially revealed by archaeologists in the spring of 1989, before being covered once more for the construction above them of an office block). The Chamberlain's Men, led by Richard Burbage and managed by his father, James, acted at the Theatre, north of the Thames, in Finsbury (not far from the modern Barbican Centre). The Theatre, built in 1576 for James Burbage, was the first building to be erected in the suburbs of London expressly for the presentation of plays. Henslowe's Rose followed in 1587; after it came the Swan (1595); the Globe (1599), replacing the Theatre and built with its structural timbers, bodily removed through London and across the River Thames from Finsbury to Southwark; the Fortune (1600), built in north London to replace the Rose; the Red Bull (1605); and the Hope

3 The Globe Theatre, as recreated in the 1990s on London's Bankside

(1614). The building of the Globe was an important event for Shakespeare, and we can see in the first plays he wrote for it, perhaps *As You Like It* and *King Henry V*, more surely *Julius Caesar* and *Hamlet*, a renewed awareness of the propositions that 'all the world's a stage' and that every man and woman is a performer in the wider theatre of the world. Not for nothing was it called the Globe.

Before 1576 plays had been performed, as they continued to be throughout the lifetime of Shakespeare, in a wide variety of locations, indoors and out. In London, the yards of coaching inns were used as theatres (and sometimes adapted for the purpose at considerable expense). Throughout the country the halls of schools, towns, colleges and noble houses were used for occasional performances by visiting players. Models for the public playhouses in London included inn yards as well as the baiting rings on the south bank used for bull- and bear-baiting. A large auditorium (with 20 sides and a diameter of 100 feet in the case of the Globe) had seats arranged in three galleries, and contained within it the separate structure of a stage and backstage building. The stage was covered by a canopy, or 'heavens', which could house winding-gear for lowering large properties or descending gods, and it was accessible from below through a trapdoor. At the back of the stage, behind a wall with two or three large doors in it, lay the 'tiring-house' (dressing rooms and wings combined), above which was a gallery, reached by a stair and divided into a number of 'rooms' or boxes, where the most important members of the audience could sit to see and to be seen. When necessary, one or more of these boxes could be used to represent a window, or walls, if required by action 'above' or 'aloft', and they may also have housed the musicians.

Indoor acting continued throughout the period at smaller 'private' playhouses, of which the earliest were set up in the halls of former monastic buildings within the city of London. Holding an audience of some 600 or 700 (against the 2,500–3,000 capacity attributed to the public playhouses) these theatres were used for plays appealing to a more restricted and wealthier audience. While you could stand in the yard at the Globe for a penny, the cheapest seat at the Blackfriars or St Paul's theatre would cost sixpence. The indoor playhouses were associated

2 Portrait of Richard Burbage, 1567–1619, leading actor of the Lord Chamberlain's Men, theatre owner, entrepreneur, painter, business associate and friend of William Shakespeare

4 View of London, engraving by Claes Jansz. Visscher, seventeenth century

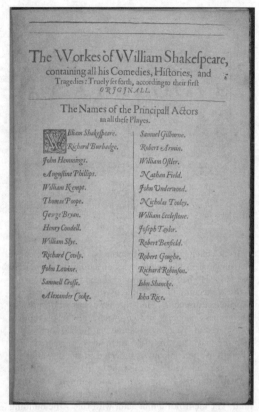

The Workes of William Shakespeare, containing all his Comedies, Histories, and Tragedies: Truely set forth, according to their first *ORIGINALL*

The Names of the Principall Actors in all these Playes.

William Shakespeare.
Richard Burbadge.
John Hemmings.
Augustine Phillips.
William Kempt.
Thomas Poope.
George Bryan.
Henry Condell.
William Slye.
Richard Cowly.
John Lowine.
Samuell Crosse.
Alexander Cooke.

Samuel Gilburne.
Robert Armin.
William Ostler.
Nathan Field.
John Underwood.
Nicholas Tooley.
William Ecclestone.
Joseph Taylor.
Robert Benfield.
Robert Goughe.
Richard Robinson.
John Shancke.
John Rice.

5 The principal actors in the King's Men, as listed in the First Folio of 1623

with companies of boy players, composed of choristers of the Chapel Royal and of St Paul's Cathedral. The playhouses Shakespeare wrote for were the Theatre (and its substitute the Curtain), the Globe and, after 1608 or 1609, the Blackfriars private theatre.

During the lifetime of Shakespeare adult playing companies grew to a size and achieved a stability which justified the expense of building permanent theatres around London. Such companies consisted of some dozen to fifteen men and three to five boys, who trained as the apprentices of leading members and played female and juvenile roles. Earlier in the century, companies were much smaller – sometimes as small as three men and a boy – and playwrights had developed writing techniques to allow a cast of five to double in up to seventeen roles. Survival of such techniques accounts for the very large number of roles for Shakespeare's histories and tragedies, where most actors would have played two or more parts, some of them appearing for no more than a scene or two.

In sixteenth- and early seventeenth-century Europe the prohibition of public acting by women and the convention of all-male casting were peculiar to England. Though easily accepted by audiences, the playing of female roles by boys led writers to emphasize the femininity of the women in their plays to an extent that the use of female performers would have rendered unnecessary. Shakespeare had much to do with the popularity of female roles in which a girl spends much of the action in male disguise. While this may have been an easier convention to accept when the role was played by a boy, it also meant that the performer's skill was required, not to impersonate a young man, but to keep the audience aware that 'he' was 'really' a girl under the male costume.

In the early Jacobean years the King's Men evidently had a boy or young man of exceptional talent, if we assume that the roles of Lady Macbeth, Cleopatra and Volumnia in *Coriolanus* may have been written for the same actor; the same must be true of such roles as Queen Margaret in the *King Henry VI* plays and Katherine in *The Taming of the Shrew* in the early 1590s, and of the comic heroines of *Much Ado About Nothing, As You Like It* and *Twelfth Night* around the turn of the century.

As the plays indicate, the skills demanded of an actor included singing, dancing and sword-fighting as well as the rhetorician's arts of speech and significant gesture. We know little, however, about acting styles in the period; nevertheless, it is not fanciful to suppose that the changing style of the plays written between 1590 and 1620 reflects a change by actors from a broad style, dependent on resonant vocal delivery and confident use of expansive gesture, such as suited open-air playhouses, to a subtler and more intimate manner, less dependent on emphatic speech and allowing a wider range of gesture and even facial expression, which could register with most of the audience in the smaller space of a private playhouse. The contrast is clear if *The Tempest* is compared with the *King Henry VI* plays or *Titus Andronicus*.

6 The earliest illustration of a work by Shakespeare: a scene from *Titus Andronicus*, attributed to Henry Peacham, *c*. 1595, 1605 or 1615

It is likely that Shakespeare's own plays were instrumental in changing styles of acting between 1590 and 1614. He had the unparalleled good fortune to work in the same company for some twenty years, as actor and as principal dramatist. He wrote for actors who were also his business partners and co-owners of the playhouses they played in. We must presume that he had some say in how the plays he wrote for them were presented. The strength of the company is reflected in the demands his plays make on actors. The Jacobean plays, in particular, regularly require strong performances in ten or a dozen significant roles – a hard requirement for any company to fulfil. The identification of actor with role – the building of a 'character' – is a commonplace of modern theatre. In Shakespeare's time it seems to have been something of an innovation: indeed a 'character' would have been understood to mean a stock or stereotyped stage figure such as the old man, the melancholy lover or the country clown. Richard Burbage, Shakespeare's leading actor, attracted comment for (exceptionally) remaining in character when he came offstage during a performance. Not the least of Shakespeare's achievements was the writing of dramatic roles a few hundred lines in length which can reward close and subtle verbal, moral or psychological analysis, three-dimensional fictions which create the illusion of the authentically recognizable inconsistency of human individuals.

Career and chronology
We do not know the dates of composition of all of Shakespeare's plays. Such evidence as there is is circumstantial: dates when they (or works on which they are certainly based) were published, or dated references to, and comments on, early performances can narrow the limits for many of them, while a very few allude to datable events of the time. On such evidence, supported by internal features of style, metre and subject, the plays can be arranged, with varying degrees of certainty, in groups relating to five phases of his theatrical career.

First come the plays Shakespeare had probably already written before the forming of the Chamberlain's Men in the summer of 1594. These are *The Two Gentlemen of Verona* (perhaps written for their first season), *The Taming of the Shrew* and possibly *The Comedy of Errors*, the three parts of *King Henry VI*, *King Richard III* and *Titus Andronicus* and possibly *King Edward III*. Plays written for the new company at the Theatre in the five years from 1594 until the opening of the Globe in the autumn of 1599, in possible sequence of composition, are *Romeo and Juliet*, *Love's Labour's Lost*, *A Midsummer Night's Dream*, *King Richard II*, *King John*, *The Merchant of Venice*, the two parts of *King Henry IV*, *Much Ado About Nothing*, *The Merry Wives of Windsor* and (at some date before summer 1598) the lost *Love's Labour's Won*. *As You Like It* and *King Henry V* may belong in this group, though both show signs of having been written with the Globe in mind.

Plays for the Globe from 1599 until the death of Queen Elizabeth I in the spring of 1603 are *Julius Caesar*, *Hamlet*, *Twelfth Night*, *Troilus and Cressida*, *Othello* and possibly *All's Well That Ends Well*. As a leading member of the King's Men, Shakespeare seems to have reduced his output from the previous average of two plays per year. His new plays from 1603 to 1608 were: *Measure for Measure*, *Timon of Athens*, *King Lear*, *Macbeth*, *Antony and Cleopatra*, *Pericles* and *Coriolanus*. He seems also to have revised *Sir Thomas More*. The final period, from the company's recovery of the indoor Blackfriars theatre for winter use in 1608–9 to 1613–14, saw composition of *The Winter's Tale*, *Cymbeline*, *The Tempest* and three plays written in collaboration with John Fletcher: *King Henry VIII*, the lost *Cardenio* (traces of which may survive in *Double Falsehood*) and *The Two Noble Kinsmen*.

SHAKESPEARE IN PRINT

Shakespeare's literary career in his own lifetime appears strikingly to resist the very notions of artistic autonomy and authority that his name has come to represent. He had little direct financial interest in his plays. He wrote scripts to be performed, scripts that once they were turned over to the acting company no longer belonged to him in any legal sense and immediately escaped his artistic control, as staging requirements and actors' temperaments inevitably enforced their changes upon them. He involved himself with the printing and publication of none of them, and held no copyrights. In the absence of anything like modern copyright law, which in Britain dates only from 1709, the scripts belonged to the acting company (whose actors could exercise artistic control over them and sought to keep their property current).

Except that, as an experienced actor and sharer in his company, he could no doubt influence productions in a way that an independent playwright could not, Shakespeare's relation to the plays he wrote was in no way unusual. Like all playwrights, he wrote so that his plays could be acted; his words were intended in the first instance to be heard, not read. In spite of Ben Jonson's efforts to establish his own plays as a form of high culture, plays remained sub-literary, the piece-work of an emerging entertainment industry. Thomas Bodley called them 'baggage books' in 1612, and ordered his librarian not to collect such 'riff-raff' or 'idle' books in order to protect his Oxford library against the 'scandal' that would be caused by their presence.

A play was generally written on demand for an acting company, and the completed script then belonged to the company that had commissioned and paid for it. Under certain circumstances, and with no necessary regard for the author's wishes or interests, the companies would sell their rights in a play to a publisher, who would have it printed in an edition of about 800 copies, usually in quarto format and selling for sixpence. The author would receive no money from the sale of the play manuscript or from any subsequent sale of books. Neither were the literary ambitions of the playwrights usually a factor in publication. Ben Jonson's aggressive effort to fashion himself as a literary figure is, of course, the exception that proves the rule; his 1616 Folio's characteristic 'The Author, B.I.' on the individual title-pages of plays in the volume is revealingly anomalous.

Shakespeare displayed no similarly proprietary artistic impulses. At the time of his death, eighteen plays had reached print (many in more than one edition), but he had prepared none of the texts for publication and had seen none through the press. The eighteen play-texts each appeared in a printed quarto or octavo volume; none has a dedication or an epistle from the author; none displays any sign of Shakespeare's direct interest or involvement in its printing. On the other hand, his two long poems, *Venus and Adonis* (1593) and *The Rape of Lucrece* (1594), printed by his fellow-Stratfordian Richard Field, were obviously produced with care, and each was published with a signed dedication to the Earl of Southampton. The texts of the plays show nothing comparable.

In the course of Shakespeare's lifetime twenty different publishers brought forth editions of individual plays, but not one took any unusual care to ensure that the text was authoritative or the printing exact. The texts are of varied quality and provenance, some seemingly printed from manuscripts that appear authorial, others apparently from copy showing the inevitable cuts and interpolations of the theatre, still others printed from transcripts, as his fellow-playwright Thomas Heywood claimed, 'corrupt and mangled, (coppied onely by the eare)', reported texts reconstructing performances witnessed or acted. In any case, no manuscript of a Shakespeare play certainly survives (unless the contribution of the so-called 'Hand D' in the manuscript of *The Booke of Sir Thomas More* is indeed Shakespeare's own, in which case it bears witness to his work as collaborator, one of five playwrights involved in writing the play).

Though today Shakespeare's literary pre-eminence has made the publication of his plays a thriving cultural industry, his earliest publishers did not seem much to care about his authorship. The 1594 edition of *Titus Andronicus* omits Shakespeare's name from the title-page, giving information rather about the printer and where the play could be bought. The play was advertised – and title-pages were explicitly forms of advertising, pasted on posts and walls – not as by William Shakespeare but by the acting company that performed it: 'As it was Plaide by the Right Honourable the Earle of *Darbie*, Earle of *Pembrooke*, and Earle of *Sussex* their Seruants.' When it was reprinted, first in 1600 and then in 1611, neither bibliographical scruple nor thought of commercial advantage led the publisher to add Shakespeare's name to the title-page.

Indeed, until 1598 none of Shakespeare's plays that appeared in print identified Shakespeare as its author. Not merely *Titus* or the early texts of *King Henry VI*, *Parts 2* and *3*, which could be thought immature efforts of a young playwright whose achievement did not yet merit nor permit a publisher to capitalize on his name on the title-page, but even his later and more successful plays failed to acknowledge or exploit Shakespeare's authorship of them. *Romeo and Juliet* appeared in 1597, identified only 'As it hath been often (with great applause) plaid publiquely, by the right Honourable the L. of *Hunsdon* his Seruants'; and its next two printings, in 1599 and 1609, while claiming that the text has now been '*Newly corrected, augmented, and amended*', still made no mention of its author (or corrector), again only identifying the acting company that performed it as the source of its authority. *King Richard II* and *King Henry IV*, *Part 1* similarly first appeared with no mention of Shakespeare on the title-page, or anywhere else for that matter.

In fact, seven plays appeared before one was issued with Shakespeare's name. In 1598 Cuthbert Burby

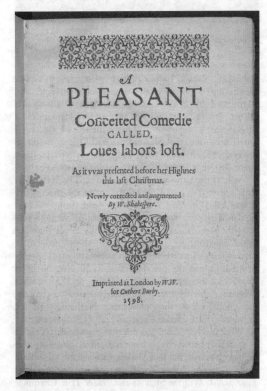

7 Title-page of the First Quarto of *Love's Labour's Lost*, 1598, the earliest edition of a play to bear Shakespeare's name

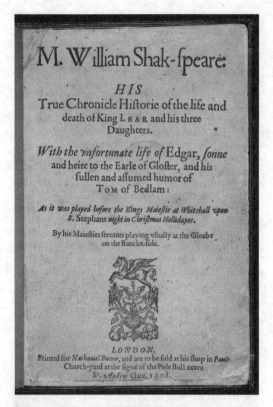

8 Title-page of the First Quarto of *King Lear*, 1608

published *Love's Labour's Lost* with the title-page identifying the play in small type as 'Newly corrected and augmented *By W. Shakespere*'. Whatever this assertion meant, it was certainly no ardent proclamation of Shakespeare's authorship. The evidence of the early Quartos is, then, that Shakespeare had little or no direct interest in their publication and, what is perhaps more surprising, that his publishers had as little interest in him.

At least the latter would soon change. The 1608 'Pide Bull' Quarto (so called after the name of the shop where it was sold) of *King Lear* does indeed proudly assert Shakespeare's authorship, emblazoning his name across the title-page in a typeface substantially larger than any other. But the text, it must be said, shows no sign of Shakespeare's involvement in its publication. It is poorly printed. (It was the first play that its printer, Nicholas Okes, had attempted, and noticeably so.) An author overseeing the printing would have insisted on changes, but nonetheless the publisher, Nathaniel Butter, unmissably identified the printed play as Shakespeare's.

What had happened was not that Shakespeare's rights as an author had suddenly been recognized and were here being celebrated, but that Shakespeare's name was now of value to the publisher. For Butter, identifying his *King Lear* as '*M. William Shak-speare: HIS* True Chronicle Historie of the life and death of King LEAR' served to differentiate his property from another play about King Lear (*The True Chronicle History of King Leir*) that had been published in 1605 and was available on the bookstalls. Shakespeare's name functioned on the title-page at least as much to identify the play*book* as the play*wright*, though already it was becoming evident that Shakespeare's name could sell books. As the publisher of *Othello* in 1622 later asserted: 'the Authors name is sufficient to vent his worke'.

But in truth it was only in 1623 with the publication of the First Folio edition of his plays that Shakespeare truly entered English literature as an author, though this, of course, was neither his own idea nor of any direct benefit to him. He had died in 1616, seven years before the Folio appeared, and to the end showed no sign of any literary ambition for his plays. But the Folio assumes that Shakespeare was indeed an author to be read and not merely the provider of scripts to be acted. The play-texts in the Folio are stripped of their theatrical association. Unlike the early Quartos, there is no mention in the Folio that any text is 'as it was played'. Indeed, though 'The Names of the Principall Actors in all these Playes' are listed, Shakespeare's own at the head of them, no acting company is ever mentioned by name; rather the texts are described, no doubt too confidently, as perfect and purely authorial, presented here exactly 'as he conceived them'.

It is not clear whose idea the collected volume was or even what was the precise motivation for it (beyond a general hope of making some money). The volume's two principal publishers, Edward Blount and Isaac Jaggard, apparently negotiated with two of Shakespeare's old friends and fellow-actors, John Heminges and Henry Condell, for the rights to the plays that had not been printed, and they then worked to secure the publishing rights to those that had. Eventually, they acquired them all (except for *Pericles*, which had been published in a Quarto in 1609 as the work of Shakespeare, and *The Two Noble Kinsmen*, not published until 1634 but identified then as the work of Shakespeare and John Fletcher), and the Folio was published in 1623. It includes thirty-six plays, eighteen of which had never before appeared in print, a dedication and an epistle, prefatory verses and an engraved title-page with a three-quarter-page portrait of Shakespeare and a facing poem.

Printing had begun early in 1622 and took about twenty-one months to complete. The volume sold for £1 with a plain calf binding, for somewhat less when more cheaply bound; and unbound, as many books were sold, it could be bought for 15*s*. Its very appearance in folio, a format usually reserved for theological or historical works or for collected editions of canonical authors, itself marked a major shift in the cultural positioning of Shakespeare – a shift confirmed within a few months of publication when Sir Thomas Bodley's library received a copy of the Folio from the Stationers' Company, had it bound in calf and placed it, chained, on a shelf.

Today it seems obvious that the Folio published by Blount and Jaggard was a necessary and appropriate memorial to England's greatest playwright, but at the time all that was clear to the publishers was that they had undertaken a complex and expensive project with no guarantee of recovering their considerable investment. In

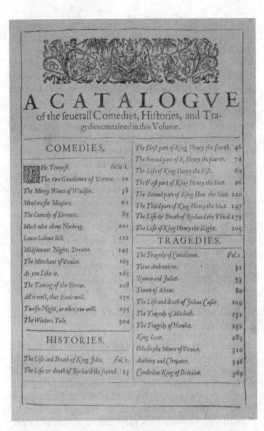

9 The catalogue of thirty-five of Shakespeare's plays as listed in the First Folio, 1623

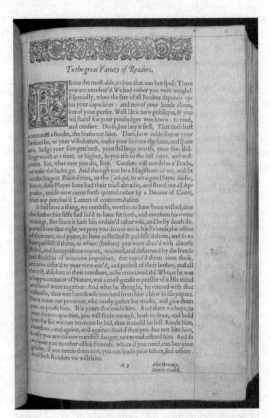

10 The second epistle, 'To the great Variety of Readers', prefacing the First Folio, 1623, and signed by John Heminges and Henry Condell

the event, of course, they did. The book sold well, and a second edition appeared only nine years later, remarkable evidence of its popularity. For later generations, with no financial stake, the book is of even greater value. Without the Folio the eighteen plays that first appeared in it might well have been lost; and without the Folio, Shakespeare might never have emerged as the singular figure of English literature he has become, for it is that book that first established Shakespeare as the author he never aspired to be.

The second epistle to the First Folio

By the autumn of 1623 John Heminges and Henry Condell were the senior surviving members of the King's Men. In April 1616 they and their colleague, Richard Burbage, who died in 1619, had been left small bequests in the will of William Shakespeare to buy memorial rings. The publication of the First Folio was a different kind of memorial to *'so worthy a Friend, & Fellow . . . as . . . our* SHAKESPEARE', as the dead dramatist is described in the first of two epistles prefaced to the volume and signed with the names of Heminges and Condell. In that epistle the book is dedicated to William Herbert, Earl of Pembroke and Lord Chamberlain, and his brother Philip, Earl of Montgomery, and calls on them to act as guardians

to Shakespeare's orphaned plays. The second epistle (reproduced here in facsimile) urged 'the great Variety of Readers' to buy 'these Playes', which 'have had their triall alreadie, and stood out all Appeales' in the theatre.

The second paragraph made several claims that have important implications for actors, readers and editors of Shakespeare. Heminges and Condell asserted that they had done the best they could, in the absence of their dead friend, to collect and verify the texts of his plays for publication. Three of their claims have been the source of dispute and controversy, and need some qualification. The mention of adding 'all the rest' to the plays already in print leads readers to expect the Folio to contain the complete plays of Shakespeare. It does not. Not only are two collaborative late plays, *Pericles* and *The Two Noble Kinsmen*, omitted, but the volume initially went on sale without *Troilus and Cressida* (as its absence from the 'Catalogue', or table of contents, testifies). *Troilus* was soon added to the volume – though not to the catalogue: its late arrival is best explained as the result of difficulties experienced by Edward Blount and Isaac Jaggard, the principal publishers, in obtaining permission to reprint it from the copyright holder, Henry Walley. Exclusion from the Folio is accordingly not conclusive evidence that a play may not have had Shakespeare's hand in it.

More teasing is the warning to readers against previous editions of the plays (half of which were already in print in quarto). What Heminges and Condell meant by 'diverse stolne, and surreptitious copies, maimed, and deformed by the frauds and stealthes of injurious impostors, that expos'd them' has been much debated. They were clearly aware that some earlier quarto editions of plays by Shakespeare differed radically from the texts they were printing. Among those, a handful are conspicuous by the extent to which they differ from the texts printed in the Folio in length, wording, names and natures of characters, and even scenic sequence or particulars of action. They are *The Taming of a Shrew* (1594), *The First Part of the Contention* (i.e. *King Henry VI, Part 2*) (1594), *The True Tragedy of Richard, Duke of York* (i.e. *King Henry VI, Part 3*) (1595), *Romeo and Juliet* (1597), *King Henry V* (1600), *Sir John Falstaff* (i.e. *The Merry Wives of Windsor*) (1602) and *Hamlet* (1603). Modern scholarship (unhappily) has dubbed these the 'bad' Quartos. They do seem, however, to merit the description 'maimed, and deformed', at least in relation to their Folio counterparts (or to later 'good' Quartos in the cases of *Romeo* and *Hamlet*).

Variation in a further group of Quartos is less radical, though often pervasive. These are *King Richard III* (1597), *King Henry IV, Part 2* (1600), *Hamlet* (1604–5), *King Lear* (1608), *Troilus and Cressida* (1609) and *Othello* (1622). Where the seven 'bad' Quartos seem to demand exceptional circumstances of textual transmission, such as someone's attempt to reconstruct them from memory, to account for their very approximate resemblance to the equivalent 'good' texts, the other six may be adequately accounted for as products of the various usual processes of stage abridgement or adaptation, or of authorial revision, to which they may have been subjected.

What is clear is that Heminges and Condell cannot have intended a blanket condemnation of all earlier published versions, but that their focus must have been on the 'bad' texts and, to a lesser degree, on those plays which they could offer in texts reflecting a later stage in their evolution than that represented by the Quartos. They had no qualms about simply reprinting Quartos they found reliable, like *The Merchant of Venice* or *Much Ado About Nothing*, with the minimum of editorial intervention.

The myth of Shakespeare's fluency in composition originated in the Folio's second epistle. Where Heminges and Condell saw that fluency as a virtue, others, and especially Ben Jonson, demurred. Jonson was later to respond to the claim that Shakespeare rarely 'blotted' a line – that is, deleted and revised it – with the wish that he 'had blotted a thousand'. In his own contribution to the preliminary matter of the Folio, his verses 'To the memory of my beloved, the Author, Mr. William Shakespeare: and what he hath left us', Jonson took pains to offer an alternative view of Shakespeare as a conscious and painstaking poetic craftsman, ready to:

> strike the second heat
> Upon the *Muses* anvile: turne the same
> (And himselfe with it) that he thinkes to frame;
> Or for the lawrell, he may gaine a scorne;
> For a good *Poet's* made, as well as borne;
> And such wert thou.

Although nearly half of his plays had been printed in his lifetime, Shakespeare only became an author to be read as well as a dramatist to be performed seven years after his death, with the publication of his comedies, histories and tragedies in the First Folio. During the eighteen-year period between the closure of the theatres in 1642 and the Restoration of Charles II in 1660, his plays could only be read. The first published criticism of his work, in Margaret Cavendish's *Sociable Letters* (1664), reflects this shift, claiming that 'those that could Read his Playes, could not be so Foolish to Condemn them'. The shift was radical and irreversible. By 1660, the theatrical company Shakespeare wrote for was long dispersed, though survivors would act again and some had distant or second-hand memories of him. The split between progressive revision and adaptation of the plays for theatres with new facilities and constantly changing audiences, and an increasingly conservative scholarly concern to preserve or restore the plays as reading texts had begun. Shakespeare the book and Shakespeare the dramatist were set on their divergent paths.

SHAKESPEARE'S READING AND READING SHAKESPEARE

Elizabethan playwrights worked in a repertory system which constantly demanded new plays. Their sensible practice, encouraged by a literary climate which set store by creative imitation of existing models, was to base many, even most, of their plays on familiar stories. Shakespeare was no exception, other than in the range of subjects he dramatized. Almost all his plays can be shown to follow, broadly or closely, what scholars have designated as his 'sources' – that is, earlier works he had read or otherwise knew of. Often he combined material from two or more sources into a single play, particularly in his comedies. His reading was wide and multifarious: history – Greek, Roman and British; prose fiction (chiefly translated into English from continental originals); earlier plays, ancient and modern, in Latin, Italian and English; pamphlets and other ephemera – all were grist to his mill. He had favourite authors, such as Chaucer, Spenser and Sir Philip Sidney among English writers, or Michel de Montaigne, whose essays he seems to have known by the time he wrote *Hamlet* (about 1600). His Latin favourites were Ovid's *Metamorphoses* and the comedies of Plautus, but he also knew Virgil, Seneca and Horace, and Plutarch's *Lives of the Noble Grecians and Romans*, written originally in Greek, were well known to him in Thomas North's English translation published in 1579. Playwrights of his own and the previous generation, notably John Lyly, Thomas Kyd, Robert Greene and Christopher Marlowe, had much to offer him by way of example, and he must also have learned from his interaction with such rivals as Ben Jonson and from his collaborators, John Fletcher and (less certainly) Thomas Middleton. And it goes without saying that he knew the plays that he had written. In many ways Shakespeare is his own most important source.

Reading Shakespeare 400 years later, we encounter the English language of a period now described as Early

Modern, before any notion of correctness of usage, whether of grammar, syntax, spelling or punctuation, had acquired wide currency, let alone authority. The primary language of education, both in schools and universities, was still Latin, a language which required the formal understanding of its rules and structures. Shakespeare had his own schooling in Latin, a schooling which included the standard subjects of grammar, logic and (most important of the three for an aspiring poet) rhetoric, the art of appropriate use of language for all practical and literary purposes. The fluidity of English in the late sixteenth century was a gift to a linguistically inventive generation of writers. Shakespeare did as much as any to exploit and extend the wide range of literary styles and linguistic registers available to him. His characters speak in all styles, from the artificial rhyming verse of *Love's Labour's Lost* or *Romeo and Juliet* to the uneducated prose of Dogberry or the regional dialect of Fluellen. It was to his plays that Samuel Johnson turned, while compiling his great *Dictionary* (1755), for illustrations of 'the diction of common life'.

Blank verse, already the norm of dramatic language in the 1580s, was adopted by Shakespeare and developed into the flexible and versatile medium of his Jacobean plays. The forging of a dramatic prose which could range from low comedy to Hamlet's philosophical musings or the inexhaustible improvisations of Falstaff was among his major stylistic achievements. The conciseness which is so marked a feature of his dramatic writing was learned, in part, from the experience of writing sonnets.

Readers of Shakespeare have long needed the assistance of a glossary to help with the unfamiliar vocabulary or idiom and the semantic changes that constitute one initial obstacle to full enjoyment and understanding. The glossary in this volume is based on the commentaries in the Arden editions whose texts are reprinted in it. It aims at giving answers to readers' most likely questions about meaning but makes no attempt at full explanation of the difficulty. Readers should always remember that Shakespeare's plays were written to be heard, not read – least of all silently read. The attempt at full understanding of linguistic detail and subtlety (if such an aim were attainable) should always be seen as secondary to the experience of the play as a whole. Fuller comprehension of detail will follow with subsequent rereadings. This is what Shakespeare's two friends and fellow actors, John Heminges and Henry Condell advised when, in the prefatory material to the 1623 Folio, they advised 'the great Variety of Readers' to "Reade him, therefore; and againe, and againe: And if then you doe not like him, surely you are in some manifest danger, not to understand him'.

AFTERLIFE

While 'Shakespeare' has been a stable element in English culture for 400 years, and has been successfully exported to numerous other cultures, there is considerable variation in the reputation and influence of individual works. Each generation seems able to find something (its own image?) in 'Shakespeare', but it has always been possible to choose a different work or a different interpretation. Some plays, such as *Julius Caesar*, *Romeo and Juliet* and *The Taming of the Shrew*, have an almost continuous history of performance and appear regularly on school and college syllabuses; others, such as *Timon of Athens*, *Troilus and Cressida* and *Pericles*, are rarely either performed or set for study; others again, such as *Cymbeline*, *King John* and *King Henry VIII*, were far more popular in the past than they are today. During his lifetime it would seem that Shakespeare's most highly esteemed tragedy was *Titus Andronicus*; for the next 350 years it was *Hamlet*; since about 1960 it has been *King Lear*, but *Othello* and *Macbeth* are becoming strong contenders. There is a similar degree of variation in the extent to which works have been adapted, translated and filmed. Broadly speaking, the 'afterlife' of the plays and poems has depended on and can be measured by four things: publication, performance, criticism, and adaptation and creative influence.

Publication

Publication is taken first as even performers need to read plays before they stage them. About half of Shakespeare's plays were published during his lifetime as single pocket-size volumes known from their method of printing and small size as Quartos. All the plays in the present volume apart from *Double Falsehood*, *King Edward III*, *Pericles*, *Sir Thomas More* and *The Two Noble Kinsmen* were printed (or reprinted) after his death in the large-format 1623 First Folio. Until 1709 two separate traditions of publication continued independently of each other: the First Folio was followed by the Second (1632), Third (1663) and Fourth (1685) Folios – 'literary' collections of the almost-complete works which found their way into the libraries of individuals and institutions – while many of the Quartos were reprinted as play-texts, used by actors and bought by playgoers.

In 1709 Nicholas Rowe published *The Works of Mr William Shakespear, Revised and Corrected* in eight volumes, the first of a line of eighteenth-century edited texts. He based his text on the Folio but also began the tradition of including passages which had previously appeared only in the Quartos. He and later eighteenth-century editors also provided commentaries in which they often disagreed with each other over variant readings, emendations and interpretations. These editions were usually published by subscription and were relatively expensive, but cheap acting editions continued to be available, for example the rival sets published in the 1730s by Robert Walker and Jacob Tonson or Bell's Shakespeare (1773–4). The nineteenth century saw the publication of cheaper mass-market texts and, after the Bowdlers' *Family Shakespeare* (1807), a proliferation of expurgated texts explicitly aimed at women and children. In the twentieth century, Shakespeare continued to be big business for publishers and editors, with hot competition for school, college and university markets, and the consequent provision both of popular versions of Shakespeare and of increasingly specialist series such as the Cambridge *Shakespeare in Performance*, which provides detailed annotation of stage business, the Arden *Performance Editions*, which offer specific advice to theatre practitioners, and the Harvester *Shakespearean Originals*, which offer reprints of the earliest texts.

Shakespeare has also, of course, been translated into many languages. Some translations have become 'classics' in their own right – François-Victor Hugo's translations into French, August Wilhelm Schlegel's translations into German and Boris Pasternak's translations into Russian – but it has also seemed necessary for each generation to produce new translations (sometimes specifically commissioned for performance), just as each generation of English speakers produces new editions.

Performance

Our records of performances in Shakespeare's lifetime are poor, possibly because of the fire which destroyed the first Globe theatre (and presumably its papers) in 1613. The title-pages of play-texts sometimes give misleading information about whether plays were (or were not) performed and where; sometimes we have to rely on chance diary entries or on what we can deduce from passing references by contemporaries – evidence for pre-1623 performances is provided in the introductions to individual plays in this volume. We do know that no plays were performed from 1642, when the theatres were closed during the Civil War and the Commonwealth period, until they returned as staple fare when the theatres reopened at the Restoration of the monarchy in 1660. At this time Shakespeare was popular but not as popular as the Jacobean dramatists Francis Beaumont and John Fletcher. Two significant innovations in 1660 were the use of stage scenery and the introduction of female performers; before 1640 women's roles had been played by young male actors.

The Restoration theatres were relatively small, indoor and expensive, attracting patrons from upper- and middle-class circles. In this they were like the Blackfriars theatre, used by the King's Men before the Civil War, and unlike the large outdoor Globe which had cheap standing room for those who could not afford a seat. Attendance at a Shakespearean performance had thus become more of a minority pursuit, though touring companies continued to flourish in the British provinces and abroad in the eighteenth, nineteenth and indeed twentieth centuries. Shakespeare reached a mass market again with the invention of film and video in the twentieth century. The versions performed in the Restoration and in the eighteenth century were regularly cut (partly in order to allow time for changing the scenery and trimming the candles) and often substantially rewritten. Despite a first attempt by the famous actor David Garrick in the mid-eighteenth century to restore more of Shakespeare's lines, the performance tradition continued to give audiences far less of the texts than was available in published versions.

A fashion for historical accuracy and heavily pictorial staging in the nineteenth century further weighted the plays with unnecessary baggage, and it was not until the 1880s that, under the influence of William Poel, a serious attempt was made to return to fluid 'Elizabethan' staging with minimal props and scenery. In Britain in the twentieth century the performance of Shakespeare became institutionalized with the foundation of the Shakespeare Memorial Theatre (originally built 1879, rebuilt after a fire in 1932) and later, in 1961, of the Royal Shakespeare Company, which currently performs in three

theatres in Stratford-upon-Avon (the main house having been redesigned again in 2007–10) and transfers some productions to London. It also undertakes national and international tours. Shakespeare's Globe, reconstructed on London's Bankside, offers outdoor performances in summer in its main space and indoor performances in

11 Antony Sher's *Richard III*, directed by Bill Alexander, Royal Shakespeare Company, 1984

12 Titania (Sarah Kestelman), Bottom (David Waller) and fairies in Peter Brook's production of *A Midsummer Night's Dream*, Royal Shakespeare Company, 1970

13 Graeme Rose as Horatio and Sally Mortemore as the Queen in Scene 14 of the Red Shift production by Jonathan Holloway of Q1 *Hamlet*, London and on tour, 1999–2000

14 Adrian Lester (Othello) and Olivia Vinall (Desdemona) in Nicholas Hytner's production of *Othello* at the National Theatre in London, 2013

winter in its smaller space, the Sam Wanamaker Playhouse (a reconstruction of a theatre like the Blackfriars). Other performances are offered by London's National Theatre and by numerous other houses in London and elsewhere in Britain. Some of these are made available by live broadcasts to cinemas, both nationally and internationally.

Shakespeare's plays were widely performed in Europe from the very beginning (English actors toured to Germany, Poland and other countries), and a strong acting tradition grew up in America in the nineteenth century, but the silent cinema brought a new and powerful means of internationalization. Dozens of silent versions were made, in America, England, Germany, France and Italy, usually abbreviating the plots but often finding inventive ways of replacing Shakespeare's language with visual images. This tradition continued into the sound period after 1929 when, perhaps ironically, it has been precisely those films which have not been 'hampered' by Shakespeare's text which have been seen as the most successful screen versions: Akira Kurosawa's Japanese *Macbeth* (*Throne of Blood*, 1957), for example,

and Grigori Kozintsev's Russian *Hamlet* (1964) and *King Lear* (1970). A few English-language directors have nevertheless managed to make creditable films, notably Laurence Olivier (*Henry V*, 1944; *Hamlet*, 1948; *Richard III*, 1955), Orson Welles (*Macbeth*, 1948; *Othello*, 1952; *Chimes at Midnight* (the Falstaff plays), 1966) and Kenneth Branagh (*Henry V*, 1989; *Much Ado About Nothing*, 1993; *Hamlet*, 1996). Many Shakespeare films are commercially available on video and DVD.

Criticism

The first person to publish a critical essay on Shakespeare was Margaret Cavendish, Duchess of Newcastle, in 1664. A poet, dramatist and essayist, in effect she inaugurated a tradition of critical writing on Shakespeare by people who were themselves creative writers: John Dryden, Samuel Johnson, William Hazlitt, Samuel Taylor Coleridge and T.S. Eliot are examples of such influential critics whose work is still read today. While from the beginning Shakespeare was highly praised for his dramatic skills, particularly in the construction of lifelike characters, late seventeenth- and eighteenth-century writers were often critical of what they saw as his grammatical incorrectness, his undisciplined elaboration of metaphors and his carelessness with plotting and historical accuracy. During the nineteenth century the general tone became more adulatory and the focus on character increased: many studies treated Shakespeare's men and women as if they were real people or at least characters in realistic novels. The publication by famous performers of their reminiscences enhanced this tendency. At the same time, the introduction of English Literature as a subject for study at universities brought about a professionalization of criticism and resulted in the situation we have today where most Shakespeare criticism is written by people with full-time academic posts in university departments of English or Drama.

Modern criticism is diverse and alarmingly prolific: the journal *Shakespeare Quarterly* publishes listings which show that around 200 items (editions, translations, books and essays) are currently published every year on *King Lear*, and around 400 on *Hamlet*. As in the past, critics today aim in various ways to elucidate Shakespeare for audiences and readers. They study his language and the literary and dramatic conventions of his time. They explore the circumstances in which the texts were originally produced – how and where they were performed, how they were copied and printed. They are also perhaps more attentive than their predecessors were to the circumstances in which the texts are continually reproduced – how and why we keep rereading and even rewriting Shakespeare for our own purposes. Dominant in criticism in the late twentieth century were issues of power and gender: 'power' in the sense of Shakespeare's relation to and analysis of early modern political structures and also in the sense of the power of 'Shakespeare' as a cultural artefact; 'gender' in the sense of his representations of gender identity and sexual relations when seen from the perspective of the continuing struggle of women, gay men and lesbians for acceptance and equality. The twenty-first century has seen an increasing focus on issues of racial identity and on the significance of Shakespeare in colonial and post-colonial contexts.

Adaptation and creative influence

While he was still alive, some of Shakespeare's works were already exerting an influence on other writers. John Fletcher's play *The Woman's Prize, or The Tamer Tamed* (1611) is a 'sequel' to *The Taming of the Shrew*, and Fletcher and Francis Beaumont's *Philaster* (1609) could not have been written without *Hamlet*; if we read the plays of the next generation of dramatists such as John Ford, Philip Massinger, Thomas Middleton and John Webster, we keep encountering echoes of Shakespeare in characters, situations, lines and phrases. In the Restoration period playwrights 'adapted' his plays for their own stage by cutting them and 'improving' the language, correcting Shakespeare's grammar and clarifying his difficult metaphors. They also began to rewrite the plays substantially, producing hybrids which are clearly dependent on their Shakespearean originals but sometimes very different in their handling of the plots. John Dryden and William Davenant's 1667 *The Enchanted Island*, for example, a version of *The Tempest*, introduces a sister for Miranda and Hippolito, a man who has never seen a woman; Dryden's 1678 *All for Love* is a version of *Antony and Cleopatra* in which Antony's wife Octavia confronts Cleopatra (who never wavers in her commitment to Antony); Nahum Tate's 1681 *King Lear* leaves Lear and Gloucester alive at the end and Cordelia about to marry Edgar.

In later centuries, the plays inspired works in other genres: operas, novels, films and musicals. Neither Henry Purcell's opera *The Fairy Queen* (1692) nor Benjamin Britten's opera (1960) would exist without *A Midsummer Night's Dream*; *Hamlet* inspired countless works in the nineteenth century, from Johann Wolfgang von Goethe's novel *Wilhelm Meister's Apprenticeship* (1795) and Charles Dickens's *Great Expectations* (1860–1) to Anton Chekhov's play *The Seagull* (1896); Cole Porter's musical *Kiss Me Kate* (1948) and Jerome Robbins's and Leonard

16 Natalie Wood and Richard Beymer perform the balcony scene in the 1961 film *West Side Story*, directed by Jerome Robbins and Robert Wise

17 Akira Kurosawa's Japanese film version of *Macbeth*, *Throne of Blood*, 1957

Bernstein's *West Side Story* (1957) depend on *The Taming of the Shrew* and *Romeo and Juliet* respectively. Looser cinematic adaptations include Kurosawa's *The Bad Sleep Well* (*Hamlet*, 1960) and Gus Van Sant's *My Own Private Idaho* (the Henry IV plays, 1991).

In the late twentieth century *King Lear* inspired Kurosawa's film *Ran* (1984) and Jane Smiley's novel *A Thousand Acres* (1991); *The Tempest* inspired Suniti Namjoshi's poem sequence *Snapshots of Caliban* (1984) and Marina Warner's novel *Indigo* (1992). More recently, the Hogarth Press commissioned a series of retellings of Shakespeare's plays by well-known novelists, including *The Gap of Time* (*The Winter's Tale*) by Jeanette Winterson (2015), *Hag-Seed* (*The Tempest*) by Margaret Atwood (2016) and *Macbeth* by Jo Nesbo (2018). Outside this sequence, Ian McEwan's novel *Nutshell* (2016) is a retelling of *Hamlet*, while John Updike's *Gertrude and Claudius* (2000) is a prequel to the same play.

Shakespeare's fame and influence began early and show no sign of abating. In the volume of his notebooks covering the years 1661–3, John Ward, vicar of Stratford-upon-Avon from 1662 to 1681, wrote of his most famous deceased parishioner:

15 Petruccio (Howard Keel) whipping Katherina (Kathryn Grayson) in *Kiss Me Kate*, directed by George Sidney (MGM, 1953)

I have heard that Mr. Shakespeare was a natural wit without any art at all. hee frequented the plays all his younger time, but in his elder days livd at Stratford: and supplied the stage with 2 plays every year and for that had an allowance so large that hee spent att the Rate of a thousand pounds 1000^l a yeer as I have heard.

He continued with a note to himself: 'Remember to peruse Shakespeare's plays, and bee versed in them, that I may not bee ignorant in that matter'. We can think of no better advice to give our readers, and to repeat with it the encouragement of his first editors inviting the public to 'read, and censure' their volume of the collected works. 'Do so', they exhort frankly, 'but buy it first':

> Then, how odde soever your braines be, or your wisedomes, make your licence the same,

and spare not. Judge your sixe-pen'orth, your shillings worth, your five shillings worth at a time, or higher, so you rise to the just rates, and welcome. But, what ever you do, Buy. Censure will not drive a Trade, or make the Jacke go. And though you be a Magistrate of wit, and sit on the Stage at *Black-Ffriers*, or the *Cock-pit*, to arraigne Playes dailie, know, these Playes have had their triall alreadie, and stood out all Appeales, and do now come forth quitted rather by a Decree of Court than any purchas'd Letters of commendation.

Like Heminges and Condell and all our distinguished predecessor editors, we urge you to buy and read or reread Shakespeare, confident that 'if then you doe not like him, surely you are in some manifest danger, not to understand him'.

THE HOUSES OF YORK AND LANCASTER

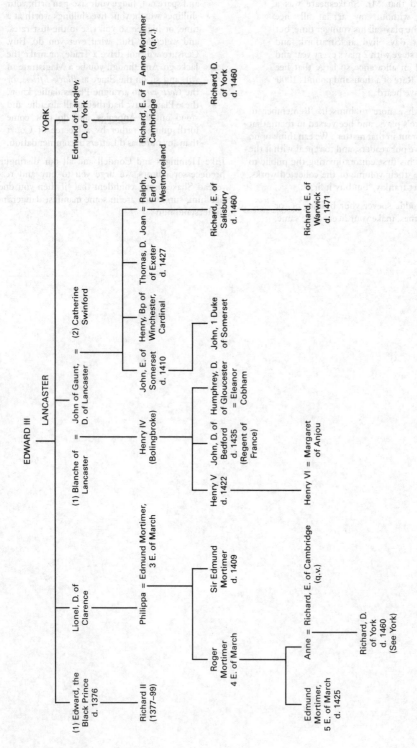

18 Genealogical table showing the houses of York and Lancaster

Shakespeare's Sonnets and A Lover's Complaint

On the evidence of Francis Meres in *Palladis Tamia*, by 1598 Shakespeare was known to have written 'sugared sonnets' and to have circulated them among his 'private friends'. In 1599 four sonnets by him were printed in *The Passionate Pilgrim* together with a further collection of lyrical poems, several of which, despite a general title-page attribution of the small book to 'W. Shakespeare', are known to be the work of other poets. Two of those sonnets had already been printed in 1598, in the Quarto of *Love's Labour's Lost*, and the other two were to be numbered 138 and 144 in *Shakespeare's Sonnets*, printed together with *A Lover's Complaint* in 1609. Surviving manuscript copies of various sonnets probably all date from later than Shakespeare's death in 1616 and none is earlier than the 1609 edition. The celebrated dedication of the *Sonnets* by their publisher T[homas] T[horpe] to 'Mr. W.H.' as 'the only begetter of these ensuing sonnets' will continue to provoke conjecture and controversy. The most plausible identifications of 'W.H.' are: William Herbert, Earl of Pembroke, which fits if the poems are of early seventeenth-century date; Henry Wriothesley, Earl of Southampton, which only makes sense if they were written in the early 1590s; and William Shakespeare – assuming that the 'H' is a misprint for 'S'.

Though other views have long prevailed, the *Sonnets* can be seen as an authorized publication in which the 154 sonnets appear in a significant order determined by Shakespeare, and the *Complaint* (whose characters and situation bear some resemblance to those in *Troilus*, *Othello*, *All's Well* and *Measure for Measure*) is also a planned feature of the volume. Few of the sonnets admit of certain dating, but 138 and 144 were written before 1599 and 107 may well relate to the death of Queen Elizabeth I in the spring of 1603 and to the coronation of King James I in the following spring. This likelihood is a caution against too ready an assumption that all the sonnets must have been written in the mid-1590s, at the height of the sonneteering vogue. The final line of 94 occurs also in *King Edward III* (2.617), printed in 1596, but it remains unclear which was the debtor, and the possibility of common authorship cannot be ruled out.

The relationships and narrative implicit in Shakespeare's sonnets contrast strongly with the conventional pattern in which courtship of a woman by a male lover leads to acceptance (as in Edmund Spenser's *Amoretti* (1595)), or to a final rejection (as in Philip Sidney's *Astrophil and Stella* (1591)), or to the death of the lady and the continuation of celebration by her lover (as in the *Canzoniere* of Petrarch (1358–74)). Shakespeare's sonnets are poems of introspection in which no character but the poet has a name, which makes it easy for the reader to identify with him. Sonnets 1–126 are mainly addressed to a man younger and of higher social standing than the poet; sonnets 127–52 to an unfaithful mistress, whose other lovers include the young man. The last two sonnets, on the traditional theme of Cupid and Diana, stand apart from this pattern. In the *Complaint*, a young woman abandoned by a lying and faithless lover recounts her story to a stranger, re-enacting the seduction to which she concludes that she would still be vulnerable.

The earliest reprint of the sonnets, in the volume of Shakespeare's poems published by John Benson in 1640, rearranged them, changed many male pronouns to their female equivalents and added titles describing them in terms of address to a mistress. Interest in the sonnets waned until 1780, when Edmond Malone republished them in an influential edition. Nineteenth-century attempts to read them as Shakespeare's amatory autobiography have persisted throughout the twentieth and twenty-first centuries, but without reaching any stable conclusions. To Wordsworth's claim that 'With this key, Shakespeare unlocked his heart', Robert Browning's rejoinder was, 'Did Shakespeare? If so, the less Shakespeare he!'. Oscar Wilde's notorious interest in the sonnets as homosexual love poems articulated a source of unease felt by many scholars and readers since 1780 and led to half a century of nervous evasion of any such unseemly possibility. The question that will always divide opinion is whether or not, and if so in what sense, these poems reflect the lived experience of their playwright-poet.

The Arden text is based on the 1609 First Quarto.

TO. THE. ONLY. BEGETTER. OF.
THESE. ENSUING. SONNETS.
Mr. W.H. ALL. HAPPINESS.
AND. THAT. ETERNITY.
PROMISED.
BY.
OUR. EVER-LIVING. POET.
WISHETH.
THE. WELL-WISHING.
ADVENTURER. IN.
SETTING.
FORTH.

T.T.

1

From fairest creatures we desire increase,
That thereby beauty's rose might never die,
But as the riper should by time decease
His tender heir might bear his memory:
But thou, contracted to thine own bright eyes,
Feed'st thy light's flame with self-substantial fuel,
Making a famine where abundance lies,
Thyself thy foe, to thy sweet self too cruel.
Thou that art now the world's fresh ornament,
And only herald to the gaudy spring,
Within thine own bud buriest thy content,
And, tender churl, mak'st waste in niggarding.
  Pity the world, or else this glutton be,
  To eat the world's due, by the grave and thee.

2

When forty winters shall besiege thy brow,
And dig deep trenches in thy beauty's field,
Thy youth's proud livery, so gazed on now,
Will be a tattered weed of small worth held:
Then being asked, where all thy beauty lies,
Where all the treasure of thy lusty days,
To say, within thine own deep-sunken eyes,
Were an all-eating shame and thriftless praise.
How much more praise deserved thy beauty's use
If thou couldst answer, 'This fair child of mine
Shall sum my count, and make my old excuse',
Proving his beauty by succession thine:
  This were to be new made when thou art old,
  And see thy blood warm when thou feel'st it cold.

3

Look in thy glass, and tell the face thou viewest
Now is the time that face should form another,
Whose fresh repair if now thou not renewest
Thou dost beguile the world, unbless some mother.
For where is she so fair whose uneared womb
Disdains the tillage of thy husbandry?
Or who is he so fond will be the tomb
Of his self-love, to stop posterity?
Thou art thy mother's glass, and she in thee
Calls back the lovely April of her prime:
So thou through windows of thine age shalt see,
Despite of wrinkles, this thy golden time.
  But if thou live remembered not to be,
  Die single, and thine image dies with thee.

4

Unthrifty loveliness, why dost thou spend
Upon thyself thy beauty's legacy?
Nature's bequest gives nothing, but doth lend,
And being frank, she lends to those are free:
Then, beauteous niggard, why dost thou abuse
The bounteous largesse given thee to give?
Profitless usurer, why dost thou use
So great a sum of sums, yet canst not live?
For having traffic with thyself alone,
Thou of thyself thy sweet self dost deceive;
Then how, when nature calls thee to be gone,
What acceptable audit canst thou leave?
  Thy unused beauty must be tombed with thee,
  Which used, lives th'executor to be.

5

Those hours that with gentle work did frame
The lovely gaze where every eye doth dwell
Will play the tyrants to the very same,
And that unfair which fairly doth excel.
For never-resting time leads summer on
To hideous winter, and confounds him there,
Sap checked with frost and lusty leaves quite gone,
Beauty o'er-snowed and bareness everywhere;
Then were not summer's distillation left,
A liquid prisoner pent in walls of glass,
Beauty's effect with beauty were bereft,
Nor it, nor no remembrance what it was.
  But flowers distilled, though they with winter
    meet,
  Leese but their show; their substance still lives
    sweet.

6

Then let not winter's ragged hand deface
In thee thy summer, ere thou be distilled:
Make sweet some vial, treasure thou some place
With beauty's treasure, ere it be self-killed.
That use is not forbidden usury
Which happies those that pay the willing loan;
That's for thyself to breed another thee,
Or ten times happier, be it ten for one:
Ten times thyself were happier than thou art,
If ten of thine ten times refigured thee;
Then what could death do if thou shouldst depart,
Leaving thee living in posterity?
  Be not self-willed, for thou art much too fair
  To be death's conquest and make worms thine
    heir.

7

Lo, in the orient when the gracious light
Lifts up his burning head, each under eye
Doth homage to his new appearing sight,
Serving with looks his sacred majesty;
And having climbed the steep-up heavenly hill,
Resembling strong youth in his middle age,
Yet mortal looks adore his beauty still,
Attending on his golden pilgrimage:
But when from high-most pitch with weary car
Like feeble age he reeleth from the day,
The eyes, fore-duteous, now converted are
From his low tract, and look another way:
  So thou, thyself out-going in thy noon,
  Unlooked on diest, unless thou get a son.

8

Music to hear, why hear'st thou music sadly?
Sweets with sweets war not, joy delights in joy;
Why lov'st thou that which thou receiv'st not gladly,
Or else receiv'st with pleasure thine annoy?
If the true concord of well-tuned sounds
By unions married, do offend thine ear,
They do but sweetly chide thee, who confounds
In singleness the parts that thou shouldst bear:
Mark how one string, sweet husband to another,
Strikes each in each by mutual ordering,
Resembling sire, and child, and happy mother,
Who all in one, one pleasing note do sing:
  Whose speechless song being many, seeming one,
  Sings this to thee: 'Thou single wilt prove none.'

9

Is it for fear to wet a widow's eye
That thou consum'st thyself in single life?
Ah, if thou issueless shalt hap to die,
The world will wail thee like a makeless wife;
The world will be thy widow, and still weep
That thou no form of thee hast left behind,
When every private widow well may keep,
By children's eyes, her husband's shape in mind:
Look what an unthrift in the world doth spend,
Shifts but his place, for still the world enjoys it;
But beauty's waste hath in the world an end,
And kept unused the user so destroys it:
  No love toward others in that bosom sits
  That on himself such murd'rous shame commits.

10

For shame deny that thou bear'st love to any,
Who for thyself art so unprovident;
Grant, if thou wilt, thou art beloved of many,
But that thou none lov'st is most evident:
For thou art so possessed with murd'rous hate
That 'gainst thyself thou stick'st not to conspire,
Seeking that beauteous roof to ruinate
Which to repair should be thy chief desire:
O change thy thought, that I may change my mind;
Shall hate be fairer lodged than gentle love?
Be as thy presence is, gracious and kind;
Or to thyself at least kind-hearted prove,
  Make thee another self for love of me,
  That beauty still may live in thine or thee.

11

As fast as thou shalt wane, so fast thou grow'st
In one of thine, from that which thou departest;
And that fresh blood which youngly thou bestow'st
Thou mayst call thine, when thou from youth
    convertest;
Herein lives wisdom, beauty and increase;
Without this, folly, age and cold decay.
If all were minded so, the times should cease,
And threescore year would make the world away:
Let those whom nature hath not made for store,
Harsh, featureless and rude, barrenly perish;
Look whom she best endowed, she gave the more,
Which bounteous gift thou shouldst in bounty cherish:
  She carved thee for her seal, and meant thereby
  Thou shouldst print more, not let that copy die.

12

When I do count the clock that tells the time,
And see the brave day sunk in hideous night;
When I behold the violet past prime,
And sable curls all silvered o'er with white:
When lofty trees I see barren of leaves,
Which erst from heat did canopy the herd,
And summer's green all girded up in sheaves
Borne on the bier with white and bristly beard:
Then of thy beauty do I question make,
That thou among the wastes of time must go,
Since sweets and beauties do themselves forsake,
And die as fast as they see others grow,
   And nothing 'gainst time's scythe can make defence
   Save breed to brave him, when he takes thee hence.

13

O that you were yourself! But, love, you are
No longer yours, than you yourself here live;
Against this coming end you should prepare,
And your sweet semblance to some other give:
So should that beauty which you hold in lease
Find no determination; then you were
Yourself again after yourself's decease,
When your sweet issue your sweet form should bear.
Who lets so fair a house fall to decay,
Which husbandry in honour might uphold
Against the stormy gusts of winter's day
And barren rage of death's eternal cold?
   O none but unthrifts, dear my love you know:
   You had a father; let your son say so.

14

Not from the stars do I my judgement pluck;
And yet, methinks, I have astronomy,
But not to tell of good or evil luck,
Of plagues, of dearths, or seasons' quality;
Nor can I fortune to brief minutes tell,
Pointing to each his thunder, rain and wind;
Or say with princes if it shall go well
By aught predict that I in heaven find;
But from thine eyes my knowledge I derive,
And, constant stars, in them I read such art
As truth and beauty shall together thrive
If from thyself, to store thou wouldst convert:
   Or else of thee this I prognosticate,
   Thy end is truth's and beauty's doom and date.

15

When I consider everything that grows
Holds in perfection but a little moment;
That this huge stage presenteth naught but shows
Whereon the stars in secret influence comment;
When I perceive that men as plants increase,
Cheered and checked even by the self-same sky,
Vaunt in their youthful sap, at height decrease,
And wear their brave state out of memory:
Then the conceit of this inconstant stay
Sets you, most rich in youth, before my sight,
Where wasteful time debateth with decay
To change your day of youth to sullied night:
   And all in war with time for love of you
   As he takes from you, I engraft you new.

16

But wherefore do not you a mightier way
Make war upon this bloody tyrant, time,
And fortify yourself in your decay
With means more blessed than my barren rhyme?
Now stand you on the top of happy hours,
And many maiden gardens, yet unset,
With virtuous wish would bear your living flowers,
Much liker than your painted counterfeit:
So should the lines of life that life repair,
Which this, time's pencil or my pupil pen,
Neither in inward worth nor outward fair,
Can make you live yourself in eyes of men:
   To give away yourself keeps yourself still,
   And you must live drawn by your own sweet skill.

17

Who will believe my verse in time to come,
If it were filled with your most high deserts?
Though yet, heaven knows, it is but as a tomb,
Which hides your life, and shows not half your parts:
If I could write the beauty of your eyes,
And in fresh numbers number all your graces,
The age to come would say, 'This poet lies;
Such heavenly touches ne'er touched earthly faces.'
So should my papers (yellowed with their age)
Be scorned, like old men of less truth than tongue,
And your true rights be termed a poet's rage,
And stretched metre of an antique song;
   But were some child of yours alive that time,
   You should live twice: in it, and in my rhyme.

18

Shall I compare thee to a summer's day?
Thou art more lovely and more temperate:
Rough winds do shake the darling buds of May,
And summer's lease hath all too short a date:
Sometime too hot the eye of heaven shines,
And often is his gold complexion dimmed;
And every fair from fair sometime declines,
By chance, or nature's changing course, untrimmed:
But thy eternal summer shall not fade,
Nor lose possession of that fair thou ow'st,
Nor shall death brag thou wander'st in his shade
When in eternal lines to time thou grow'st:
   So long as men can breathe or eyes can see,
   So long lives this, and this gives life to thee.

19

Devouring time, blunt thou the lion's paws,
And make the earth devour her own sweet brood;
Pluck the keen teeth from the fierce tiger's jaws,
And burn the long-lived Phoenix in her blood;
Make glad and sorry seasons as thou fleet'st,
And do whate'er thou wilt, swift-footed time,
To the wide world and all her fading sweets:
But I forbid thee one most heinous crime,
O carve not with thy hours my love's fair brow,
Nor draw no lines there with thine antique pen;
Him in thy course untainted do allow
For beauty's pattern to succeeding men.
   Yet do thy worst, old Time, despite thy wrong,
   My love shall in my verse ever live young.

20

A woman's face with nature's own hand painted
Hast thou, the master mistress of my passion;
A woman's gentle heart, but not acquainted
With shifting change, as is false women's fashion;
An eye more bright than theirs, less false in rolling,
Gilding the object whereupon it gazeth;
A man in hue, all hues in his controlling,
Which steals men's eyes and women's souls amazeth;
And for a woman wert thou first created,
Till nature as she wrought thee fell a-doting,
And by addition me of thee defeated,
By adding one thing to my purpose nothing:
   But since she pricked thee out for women's pleasure,
   Mine be thy love, and thy love's use their treasure.

21

So is it not with me as with that Muse,
Stirred by a painted beauty to his verse,
Who heaven itself for ornament doth use,
And every fair with his fair doth rehearse,
Making a couplement of proud compare
With sun and moon, with earth and sea's rich gems;
With April's first-born flowers and all things rare
That heaven's air in this huge rondure hems;
O let me true in love but truly write,
And then believe me: my love is as fair
As any mother's child, though not so bright
As those gold candles fixed in heaven's air:
   Let them say more that like of hearsay well,
   I will not praise, that purpose not to sell.

22

My glass shall not persuade me I am old
So long as youth and thou are of one date;
But when in thee time's furrows I behold,
Then look I death my days should expiate:
For all that beauty that doth cover thee
Is but the seemly raiment of my heart,
Which in thy breast doth live, as thine in me;
How can I then be elder than thou art?
O therefore love be of thyself so wary
As I not for myself, but for thee will,
Bearing thy heart, which I will keep so chary
As tender nurse her babe from faring ill:
   Presume not on thy heart when mine is slain;
   Thou gav'st me thine not to give back again.

23

As an unperfect actor on the stage,
Who with his fear is put besides his part;
Or some fierce thing, replete with too much rage,
Whose strength's abundance weakens his own heart;
So I, for fear of trust, forget to say
The perfect ceremony of love's right,
And in mine own love's strength seem to decay,
O'ercharged with burden of mine own love's might:
O let my books be then the eloquence
And dumb presagers of my speaking breast,
Who plead for love, and look for recompense,
More than that tongue that more hath more
    expressed:
   O learn to read what silent love hath writ!
   To hear with eyes belongs to love's fine wit.

24

Mine eye hath played the painter, and hath steeled
Thy beauty's form in table of my heart;
My body is the frame wherein 'tis held,
And perspective it is best painter's art;
For through the painter must you see his skill,
To find where your true image pictured lies,
Which in my bosom's shop is hanging still,
That hath his windows glazed with thine eyes:
Now see what good turns eyes for eyes have done:
Mine eyes have drawn thy shape, and thine for me
Are windows to my breast, wherethrough the sun
Delights to peep, to gaze therein on thee;
    Yet eyes this cunning want to grace their art:
    They draw but what they see, know not the heart.

25

Let those who are in favour with their stars
Of public honour and proud titles boast,
Whilst I, whom fortune of such triumph bars,
Unlooked for joy in that I honour most;
Great princes' favourites their fair leaves spread
But as the marigold at the sun's eye,
And in themselves their pride lies buried,
For at a frown they in their glory die.
The painful warrior famoused for worth,
After a thousand victories once foiled,
Is from the book of honour razed quite,
And all the rest forgot for which he toiled:
    Then happy I, that love and am beloved
    Where I may not remove, nor be removed.

26

Lord of my love, to whom in vassalage
Thy merit hath my duty strongly knit:
To thee I send this written embassage,
To witness duty, not to show my wit;
Duty so great, which wit so poor as mine
May make seem bare, in wanting words to show it;
But that I hope some good conceit of thine
In thy soul's thought (all naked) will bestow it:
Till whatsoever star that guides my moving
Points on me graciously with fair aspect,
And puts apparel on my tattered loving,
To show me worthy of thy sweet respect;
    Then may I dare to boast how I do love thee;
    Till then, not show my head where thou mayst
        prove me.

27

Weary with toil, I haste me to my bed,
The dear repose for limbs with travail tired;
But then begins a journey in my head
To work my mind, when body's work's expired:
For then my thoughts, from far where I abide,
Intend a zealous pilgrimage to thee,
And keep my drooping eyelids open wide,
Looking on darkness which the blind do see;
Save that my soul's imaginary sight
Presents thy shadow to my sightless view,
Which like a jewel hung in ghastly night
Makes black night beauteous, and her old face new:
    Lo, thus by day my limbs, by night my mind,
    For thee, and for myself, no quiet find.

28

How can I then return in happy plight
That am debarred the benefit of rest?
When day's oppression is not eased by night,
But day by night and night by day oppressed,
And each, though enemies to either's reign,
Do in consent shake hands to torture me,
The one by toil, the other to complain
How far I toil, still farther off from thee.
I tell the day to please him, thou art bright,
And dost him grace, when clouds do blot the
        heaven;
So flatter I the swart-complexioned night,
When sparkling stars twire not thou gild'st the even;
    But day doth daily draw my sorrows longer,
    And night doth nightly make grief's length seem
        stronger.

29

When in disgrace with fortune and men's eyes
I all alone beweep my outcast state,
And trouble deaf heav'n with my bootless cries,
And look upon myself, and curse my fate,
Wishing me like to one more rich in hope,
Featured like him, like him with friends possessed,
Desiring this man's art and that man's scope,
With what I most enjoy contented least;
Yet in these thoughts myself almost despising,
Haply I think on thee, and then my state,
Like to the lark at break of day arising,
From sullen earth sings hymns at heaven's gate;
    For thy sweet love remembered such wealth brings
    That then I scorn to change my state with kings.

30

When to the sessions of sweet silent thought
I summon up remembrance of things past,
I sigh the lack of many a thing I sought,
And with old woes new wail my dear time's waste;
Then can I drown an eye (unused to flow)
For precious friends hid in death's dateless night,
And weep afresh love's long since cancelled woe,
And moan th'expense of many a vanished sight.
Then can I grieve at grievances foregone,
And heavily from woe to woe tell o'er
The sad account of fore-bemoaned moan,
Which I new pay, as if not paid before;
    But if the while I think on thee, dear friend,
    All losses are restored, and sorrows end.

31

Thy bosom is endeared with all hearts
Which I, by lacking, have supposed dead;
And there reigns love, and all love's loving parts,
And all those friends which I thought buried.
How many a holy and obsequious tear
Hath dear religious love stol'n from mine eye,
As interest of the dead, which now appear
But things removed that hidden in thee lie:
Thou art the grave where buried love doth live,
Hung with the trophies of my lovers gone,
Who all their parts of me to thee did give;
That due of many, now is thine alone.
    Their images I loved, I view in thee,
    And thou, all they, hast all the all of me.

32

If thou survive my well-contented day,
When that churl death my bones with dust shall
        cover,
And shalt by fortune once more re-survey
These poor rude lines of thy deceased lover:
Compare them with the bett'ring of the time,
And though they be outstripped by every pen,
Reserve them for my love, not for their rhyme,
Exceeded by the height of happier men.
O then vouchsafe me but this loving thought:
'Had my friend's Muse grown with this growing age,
A dearer birth than this his love had brought,
To march in ranks of better equipage:
    But since he died and poets better prove,
    Theirs for their style I'll read, his for his love.'

33

Full many a glorious morning have I seen
Flatter the mountain tops with sovereign eye,
Kissing with golden face the meadows green,
Gilding pale streams with heavenly alchemy;
Anon permit the basest clouds to ride
With ugly rack on his celestial face,
And from the forlorn world his visage hide,
Stealing unseen to west with this disgrace:
Even so my sun one early morn did shine
With all triumphant splendour on my brow;
But out alack, he was but one hour mine,
The region cloud hath masked him from me now.
    Yet him for this, my love no whit disdaineth:
    Suns of the world may stain, when heaven's sun
        staineth.

34

Why didst thou promise such a beauteous day
And make me travail forth without my cloak,
To let base clouds o'ertake me in my way,
Hiding thy brav'ry in their rotten smoke?
'Tis not enough that through the cloud thou break,
To dry the rain on my storm-beaten face,
For no man well of such a salve can speak
That heals the wound and cures not the disgrace;
Nor can thy shame give physic to my grief;
Though thou repent, yet I have still the loss;
Th'offender's sorrow lends but weak relief
To him that bears the strong offence's loss.
    Ah, but those tears are pearl which thy love sheds,
    And they are rich, and ransom all ill deeds.

35

No more be grieved at that which thou hast done;
Roses have thorns, and silver fountains mud;
Clouds and eclipses stain both moon and sun,
And loathsome canker lives in sweetest bud.
All men make faults, and even I, in this,
Authorizing thy trespass with compare,
Myself corrupting, salving thy amiss,
Excusing these sins more than these sins are:
For to thy sensual fault I bring in sense;
Thy adverse party is thy advocate,
And 'gainst myself a lawful plea commence:
Such civil war is in my love and hate
    That I an accessory needs must be
    To that sweet thief which sourly robs from me.

36

Let me confess that we two must be twain,
Although our undivided loves are one;
So shall those blots that do with me remain,
Without thy help, by me be borne alone.
In our two loves there is but one respect,
Though in our lives a separable spite;
Which, though it alter not love's sole effect,
Yet doth it steal sweet hours from love's delight.
I may not evermore acknowledge thee,
Lest my bewailed guilt should do thee shame,
Nor thou with public kindness honour me,
Unless thou take that honour from thy name:
   But do not so; I love thee in such sort,
   As thou being mine, mine is thy good report.

37

As a decrepit father takes delight
To see his active child do deeds of youth,
So I, made lame by fortune's dearest spite,
Take all my comfort of thy worth and truth:
For whether beauty, birth, or wealth, or wit,
Or any of these all, or all, or more,
Entitled in thy parts do crowned sit,
I make my love engrafted to this store:
So then I am not lame, poor, nor despised,
Whilst that this shadow doth such substance give
That I in thy abundance am sufficed,
And by a part of all thy glory live:
   Look what is best, that best I wish in thee;
   This wish I have, then ten times happy me.

38

How can my Muse want subject to invent
While thou dost breathe, that pour'st into my verse
Thine own sweet argument, too excellent
For every vulgar paper to rehearse?
O give thyself the thanks, if aught in me
Worthy perusal stand against thy sight:
For who's so dumb, that cannot write to thee,
When thou thyself dost give invention light?
Be thou the tenth Muse, ten times more in worth
Than those old nine which rhymers invocate;
And he that calls on thee, let him bring forth
Eternal numbers to outlive long date.
   If my slight Muse do please these curious days,
   The pain be mine, but thine shall be the praise.

39

O how thy worth with manners may I sing,
When thou art all the better part of me?
What can mine own praise to mine own self bring,
And what is't but mine own, when I praise thee?
Even for this, let us divided live,
And our dear love lose name of single one,
That by this separation I may give
That due to thee which thou deserv'st alone.
O absence, what a torment wouldst thou prove,
Were it not thy sour leisure gave sweet leave
To entertain the time with thoughts of love,
Which time and thoughts so sweetly dost deceive,
   And that thou teachest how to make one twain
   By praising him here who doth hence remain.

40

Take all my loves, my love; yea, take them all;
What hast thou then more than thou hadst before?
No love, my love, that thou mayst true love call;
All mine was thine, before thou hadst this more:
Then if for my love thou my love receivest,
I cannot blame thee, for my love thou usest;
But yet be blamed, if thou thyself deceivest
By wilful taste of what thyself refusest.
I do forgive thy robb'ry, gentle thief,
Although thou steal thee all my poverty;
And yet love knows it is a greater grief
To bear love's wrong, than hate's known injury.
   Lascivious grace, in whom all ill well shows,
   Kill me with spites; yet we must not be foes.

41

Those pretty wrongs that liberty commits
When I am sometime absent from thy heart,
Thy beauty and thy years full well befits;
For still temptation follows where thou art.
Gentle thou art, and therefore to be won;
Beauteous thou art, therefore to be assailed;
And when a woman woos, what woman's son
Will sourly leave her till he have prevailed?
Ay me, but yet thou mightst my seat forbear,
And chide thy beauty and thy straying youth
Who lead thee in their riot even there
Where thou art forced to break a twofold truth:
   Hers by thy beauty tempting her to thee,
   Thine by thy beauty being false to me.

42

That thou hast her it is not all my grief,
And yet it may be said I loved her dearly;
That she hath thee is of my wailing chief,
A loss in love that touches me more nearly.
Loving offenders, thus I will excuse ye:
Thou dost love her, because thou knowst I love
    her,
And for my sake even so doth she abuse me,
Suff'ring my friend for my sake to approve her;
If I lose thee, my loss is my love's gain,
And losing her, my friend hath found that loss;
Both find each other, and I lose both twain,
And both for my sake lay on me this cross:
    But here's the joy, my friend and I are one;
    Sweet flattery! Then she loves but me alone.

43

When most I wink, then do mine eyes best see;
For all the day they view things unrespected,
But when I sleep, in dreams they look on thee,
And darkly bright, are bright in dark directed.
Then thou whose shadow shadows doth make
    bright,
How would thy shadow's form form happy show
To the clear day with thy much clearer light,
When to unseeing eyes thy shade shines so?
How would (I say) mine eyes be blessed made
By looking on thee in the living day,
When in dead night thy fair imperfect shade
Through heavy sleep on sightless eyes doth stay?
    All days are nights to see till I see thee,
    And nights bright days when dreams do show
      thee me.

44

If the dull substance of my flesh were thought,
Injurious distance should not stop my way;
For then, despite of space, I would be brought
From limits far remote, where thou dost stay;
No matter then although my foot did stand
Upon the farthest earth removed from thee,
For nimble thought can jump both sea and land
As soon as think the place where he would be.
But ah, thought kills me, that I am not thought,
To leap large lengths of miles when thou art gone,
But that so much of earth and water wrought,
I must attend time's leisure with my moan;
    Receiving naughts by elements so slow
    But heavy tears, badges of either's woe.

45

The other two, slight air, and purging fire,
Are both with thee, wherever I abide:
The first my thought, the other my desire,
These, present absent, with swift motion slide;
For when these quicker elements are gone
In tender embassy of love to thee,
My life being made of four, with two alone
Sinks down to death, oppressed with melancholy,
Until life's composition be recured
By those swift messengers returned from thee
Who even but now come back again assured
Of thy fair health, recounting it to me.
    This told, I joy; but then no longer glad,
    I send them back again and straight grow sad.

46

Mine eye and heart are at a mortal war
How to divide the conquest of thy sight;
Mine eye, my heart thy picture's sight would bar;
My heart, mine eye the freedom of that right;
My heart doth plead that thou in him dost lie,
A closet never pierced with crystal eyes;
But the defendant doth that plea deny,
And says in him thy fair appearance lies.
To find this title is empanelled
A quest of thoughts, all tenants to the heart,
And by their verdict is determined
The clear eyes' moiety, and the dear heart's part:
    As thus, mine eyes' due is thy outward part,
    And my heart's right, thy inward love of heart.

47

Betwixt mine eye and heart a league is took,
And each doth good turns now unto the other;
When that mine eye is famished for a look,
Or heart in love with sighs himself doth smother,
With my love's picture then my eye doth feast,
And to the painted banquet bids my heart;
Another time mine eye is my heart's guest,
And in his thoughts of love doth share a part.
So either by thy picture or my love,
Thyself away, art present still with me:
For thou no further than my thoughts canst move,
And I am still with them, and they with thee;
    Or if they sleep, thy picture in my sight
    Awakes my heart to heart's and eye's delight.

48

How careful was I, when I took my way,
Each trifle under truest bars to thrust,
That to my use it might unused stay
From hands of falsehood, in sure wards of trust;
But thou, to whom my jewels trifles are,
Most worthy comfort, now my greatest grief,
Thou best of dearest, and mine only care,
Art left the prey of every vulgar thief.
Thee have I not locked up in any chest,
Save where thou art not, though I feel thou art,
Within the gentle closure of my breast,
From whence at pleasure thou mayst come and part;
    And even thence thou wilt be stol'n, I fear;
    For truth proves thievish for a prize so dear.

49

Against that time, if ever that time come,
When I shall see thee frown on my defects;
Whenas thy love hath cast his utmost sum,
Called to that audit by advised respects;
Against that time when thou shalt strangely pass,
And scarcely greet me with that sun, thine eye;
When love, converted from the thing it was,
Shall reasons find of settled gravity;
Against that time do I ensconce me here,
Within the knowledge of mine own desert,
And this my hand against myself uprear,
To guard the lawful reasons on thy part:
    To leave poor me, thou hast the strength of laws,
    Since why to love, I can allege no cause.

50

How heavy do I journey on the way
When what I seek, my weary travel's end,
Doth teach that ease and that repose to say,
'Thus far the miles are measured from thy friend.'
The beast that bears me, tired with my woe,
Plods dully on to bear that weight in me,
As if by some instinct the wretch did know
His rider loved not speed being made from thee:
The bloody spur cannot provoke him on
That sometimes anger thrusts into his hide,
Which heavily he answers with a groan,
More sharp to me than spurring to his side,
    For that same groan doth put this in my mind:
    My grief lies onward and my joy behind.

51

Thus can my love excuse the slow offence
Of my dull bearer, when from thee I speed:
From where thou art, why should I haste me
    thence?
Till I return, of posting is no need.
O what excuse will my poor beast then find,
When swift extremity can seem but slow?
Then should I spur, though mounted on the wind;
In winged speed no motion shall I know;
Then can no horse with my desire keep pace;
Therefore desire, of perfect'st love being made,
Shall neigh no dull flesh in his fiery race,
But love, for love, thus shall excuse my jade:
    Since from thee going he went wilful slow,
    Towards thee I'll run, and give him leave to go.

52

So am I as the rich, whose blessed key
Can bring him to his sweet up-locked treasure,
The which he will not every hour survey,
For blunting the fine point of seldom pleasure;
Therefore are feasts so solemn and so rare,
Since, seldom coming, in the long year set,
Like stones of worth they thinly placed are,
Or captain jewels in the carcanet.
So is the time that keeps you as my chest,
Or as the wardrobe which the robe doth hide,
To make some special instant special blessed
By new unfolding his imprisoned pride.
    Blessed are you, whose worthiness gives scope,
    Being had, to triumph; being lacked, to hope.

53

What is your substance, whereof are you made,
That millions of strange shadows on you tend?
Since every one hath every one one shade,
And you, but one, can every shadow lend;
Describe Adonis, and the counterfeit
Is poorly imitated after you;
On Helen's cheek all art of beauty set
And you in Grecian tires are painted new;
Speak of the spring, and foison of the year:
The one doth shadow of your beauty show,
The other as your bounty doth appear,
And you in every blessed shape we know.
    In all external grace you have some part,
    But you like none, none you, for constant heart.

54

O how much more doth beauty beauteous seem
By that sweet ornament which truth doth give!
The rose looks fair, but fairer we it deem
For that sweet odour which doth in it live;
The canker blooms have full as deep a dye
As the perfumed tincture of the roses,
Hang on such thorns, and play as wantonly,
When summer's breath their masked buds discloses;
But for their virtue only is their show
They live unwooed, and unrespected fade,
Die to themselves. Sweet roses do not so;
Of their sweet deaths are sweetest odours made;
   And so of you, beauteous and lovely youth;
   When that shall vade, by verse distils your truth.

55

Not marble, nor the gilded monuments
Of princes, shall outlive this powerful rhyme;
But you shall shine more bright in these contents
Than unswept stone, besmeared with sluttish time.
When wasteful war shall statues overturn
And broils root out the work of masonry,
Nor Mars his sword, nor war's quick fire, shall burn
The living record of your memory:
'Gainst death, and all oblivious enmity,
Shall you pace forth; your praise shall still find room
Even in the eyes of all posterity
That wear this world out to the ending doom.
   So till the judgement that yourself arise,
   You live in this, and dwell in lovers' eyes.

56

Sweet love, renew thy force; be it not said
Thy edge should blunter be than appetite,
Which but today by feeding is allayed,
Tomorrow sharpened in his former might;
So, love, be thou; although today thou fill
Thy hungry eyes even till they wink with fullness,
Tomorrow see again, and do not kill
The spirit of love with a perpetual dullness;
Let this sad interim like the ocean be
Which parts the shore, where two contracted new
Come daily to the banks, that when they see
Return of love, more blessed may be the view;
   Or call it winter, which being full of care
   Makes summer's welcome thrice more wished,
      more rare.

57

Being your slave, what should I do but tend
Upon the hours and times of your desire?
I have no precious time at all to spend,
Nor services to do, till you require;
Nor dare I chide the world-without-end hour
Whilst I, my sovereign, watch the clock for you,
Nor think the bitterness of absence sour
When you have bid your servant once adieu;
Nor dare I question with my jealous thought
Where you may be, or your affairs suppose,
But like a sad slave stay and think of naught,
Save, where you are, how happy you make those.
   So true a fool is love, that in your will,
   Though you do anything, he thinks no ill.

58

That god forbid, that made me first your slave,
I should in thought control your times of pleasure,
Or at your hand th'account of hours to crave,
Being your vassal bound to stay your leisure.
O let me suffer, being at your beck,
Th'imprisoned absence of your liberty,
And patience tame, to sufferance bide each check,
Without accusing you of injury.
Be where you list, your charter is so strong
That you yourself may privilege your time
To what you will; to you it doth belong
Yourself to pardon of self-doing crime.
   I am to wait, though waiting so be hell,
   Not blame your pleasure be it ill or well.

59

If there be nothing new, but that which is
Hath been before, how are our brains beguiled,
Which, labouring for invention, bear amiss
The second burden of a former child?
O that record could with a backward look
Even of five hundred courses of the sun
Show me your image in some antique book,
Since mind at first in character was done,
That I might see what the old world could say
To this composed wonder of your frame;
Whether we are mended, or whe'er better they,
Or whether revolution be the same.
   O sure I am, the wits of former days
   To subjects worse have given admiring praise.

60

Like as the waves make towards the pebbled shore,
So do our minutes hasten to their end,
Each changing place with that which goes before,
In sequent toil all forwards do contend.
Nativity, once in the main of light,
Crawls to maturity; wherewith being crowned
Crooked eclipses 'gainst his glory fight,
And time, that gave, doth now his gift confound.
Time doth transfix the flourish set on youth,
And delves the parallels in beauty's brow;
Feeds on the rarities of nature's truth,
And nothing stands but for his scythe to mow.
    And yet to times in hope my verse shall stand,
    Praising thy worth, despite his cruel hand.

61

Is it thy will thy image should keep open
My heavy eyelids to the weary night?
Dost thou desire my slumbers should be broken
While shadows like to thee do mock my sight?
Is it thy spirit that thou send'st from thee
So far from home into my deeds to pry,
To find out shames and idle hours in me,
The scope and tenor of thy jealousy?
O no, thy love, though much, is not so great;
It is my love that keeps mine eye awake,
Mine own true love that doth my rest defeat,
To play the watchman ever for thy sake.
    For thee watch I, whilst thou dost wake elsewhere,
    From me far off, with others all too near.

62

Sin of self-love possesseth all mine eye,
And all my soul, and all my every part;
And for this sin there is no remedy,
It is so grounded inward in my heart.
Methinks no face so gracious is as mine,
No shape so true, no truth of such account,
And for myself mine own worth do define
As I all other in all worths surmount.
But when my glass shows me myself indeed,
Beated and chopped with tanned antiquity,
Mine own self-love quite contrary I read;
Self, so self-loving, were iniquity;
    'Tis thee (myself) that for myself I praise,
    Painting my age with beauty of thy days.

63

Against my love shall be as I am now,
With time's injurious hand crushed and o'erworn;
When hours have drained his blood, and filled his brow
With lines and wrinkles; when his youthful morn
Hath travailed on to age's steepy night,
And all those beauties whereof now he's king
Are vanishing, or vanished out of sight,
Stealing away the treasure of his spring;
For such a time do I now fortify
Against confounding age's cruel knife,
That he shall never cut from memory
My sweet love's beauty, though my lover's life.
    His beauty shall in these black lines be seen,
    And they shall live, and he in them still green.

64

When I have seen by time's fell hand defaced
The rich proud cost of outworn buried age;
When sometime lofty towers I see down razed,
And brass eternal slave to mortal rage;
When I have seen the hungry ocean gain
Advantage on the kingdom of the shore,
And the firm soil win of the wat'ry main,
Increasing store with loss, and loss with store;
When I have seen such interchange of state,
Or state itself confounded, to decay,
Ruin hath taught me thus to ruminate:
That time will come and take my love away.
    This thought is as a death, which cannot choose
    But weep to have that which it fears to lose.

65

Since brass, nor stone, nor earth, nor boundless sea,
But sad mortality o'er-sways their power,
How with this rage shall beauty hold a plea,
Whose action is no stronger than a flower?
O how shall summer's honey breath hold out
Against the wrackful siege of batt'ring days
When rocks impregnable are not so stout,
Nor gates of steel so strong, but time decays?
O fearful meditation! Where, alack,
Shall time's best jewel from time's chest lie hid?
Or what strong hand can hold his swift foot back,
Or who his spoil o'er beauty can forbid?
    O none, unless this miracle have might:
    That in black ink my love may still shine bright.

66

Tired with all these for restful death I cry:
As to behold desert a beggar born,
And needy nothing trimmed in jollity,
And purest faith unhappily forsworn,
And gilded honour shamefully misplaced,
And maiden virtue rudely strumpeted,
And right perfection wrongfully disgraced,
And strength by limping sway disabled,
And art made tongue-tied by authority,
And folly, doctor-like, controlling skill,
And simple truth miscalled simplicity,
And captive good attending captain ill:
   Tired with all these, from these would I be gone,
   Save that to die I leave my love alone.

67

Ah, wherefore with infection should he live,
And with his presence grace impiety,
That sin by him advantage should achieve,
And lace itself with his society?
Why should false painting imitate his cheek,
And steal dead seeing of his living hue?
Why should poor beauty indirectly seek
Roses of shadow, since his rose is true?
Why should he live, now nature bankrupt is,
Beggared of blood to blush through lively veins?
For she hath no exchequer now but his,
And proud of many, lives upon his gains.
   O, him she stores, to show what wealth she had
   In days long since, before these last so bad.

68

Thus is his cheek the map of days outworn,
When beauty lived and died as flowers do now,
Before these bastard signs of fair were borne,
Or durst inhabit on a living brow;
Before the golden tresses of the dead,
The right of sepulchres, were shorn away,
To live a second life on second head;
Ere beauty's dead fleece made another gay:
In him those holy antique hours are seen,
Without all ornament, itself and true,
Making no summer of another's green,
Robbing no old to dress his beauty new;
   And him as for a map doth nature store
   To show false art what beauty was of yore.

69

Those parts of thee that the world's eye doth view
Want nothing that the thought of hearts can mend;
All tongues, the voice of souls, give thee that due,
Utt'ring bare truth, even so as foes commend:
Thy outward thus with outward praise is crowned.
But those same tongues that give thee so thine own
In other accents do this praise confound,
By seeing further than the eye hath shown;
They look into the beauty of thy mind,
And that in guess they measure by thy deeds;
Then churls their thoughts (although their eyes were
    kind)
To thy fair flower add the rank smell of weeds.
   But why thy odour matcheth not thy show,
   The soil is this, that thou dost common grow.

70

That thou art blamed shall not be thy defect,
For slander's mark was ever yet the fair;
The ornament of beauty is suspect,
A crow that flies in heaven's sweetest air.
So thou be good, slander doth but approve
Thy worth the greater, being wooed of time;
For canker vice the sweetest buds doth love,
And thou present'st a pure unstained prime.
Thou hast passed by the ambush of young days,
Either not assailed, or victor, being charged;
Yet this thy praise cannot be so thy praise,
To tie up envy, evermore enlarged:
   If some suspect of ill masked not thy show
   Then thou alone kingdoms of hearts shouldst owe.

71

No longer mourn for me when I am dead
Than you shall hear the surly sullen bell
Give warning to the world that I am fled
From this vile world, with vilest worms to dwell:
Nay, if you read this line, remember not
The hand that writ it, for I love you so
That I in your sweet thoughts would be forgot,
If thinking on me then should make you woe.
O if (I say) you look upon this verse,
When I, perhaps, compounded am with clay,
Do not so much as my poor name rehearse,
But let your love even with my life decay;
   Lest the wise world should look into your moan,
   And mock you with me after I am gone.

72

O, lest the world should task you to recite
What merit lived in me that you should love,
After my death (dear love) forget me quite,
For you in me can nothing worthy prove;
Unless you would devise some virtuous lie
To do more for me than mine own desert,
And hang more praise upon deceased I
Than niggard truth would willingly impart;
O, lest your true love may seem false in this,
That you for love speak well of me untrue,
My name be buried where my body is,
And live no more to shame nor me, nor you:
    For I am shamed by that which I bring forth,
    And so should you, to love things nothing worth.

That time of year thou mayst in me behold,
When yellow leaves, or none, or few do hang
Upon those boughs which shake against the cold,
Bare ruined choirs where late the sweet birds sang;
In me thou seest the twilight of such day
As after sunset fadeth in the west,
Which by and by black night doth take away,
Death's second self that seals up all in rest;
In me thou seest the glowing of such fire
That on the ashes of his youth doth lie,
As the deathbed, whereon it must expire,
Consumed with that which it was nourished by;
    This thou perceiv'st, which makes thy love more
        strong,
    To love that well, which thou must leave ere long.

But be contented when that fell arrest
Without all bail shall carry me away;
My life hath in this line some interest,
Which for memorial still with thee shall stay.
When thou reviewest this, thou dost review
The very part was consecrate to thee;
The earth can have but earth, which is his due,
My spirit is thine, the better part of me;
So then thou hast but lost the dregs of life,
The prey of worms, my body being dead,
The coward conquest of a wretch's knife,
Too base of thee to be remembered:
    The worth of that, is that which it contains,
    And that is this, and this with thee remains.

75

So are you to my thoughts as food to life,
Or as sweet seasoned showers to the ground;
And for the peace of you I hold such strife
As 'twixt a miser and his wealth is found:
Now proud as an enjoyer, and anon
Doubting the filching age will steal his treasure;
Now counting best to be with you alone,
Then bettered that the world may see my pleasure;
Sometime all full with feasting on your sight,
And by and by clean starved for a look,
Possessing or pursuing no delight
Save what is had, or must from you be took.
    Thus do I pine and surfeit day by day,
    Or gluttoning on all, or all away.

Why is my verse so barren of new pride,
So far from variation or quick change?
Why with the time do I not glance aside
To new-found methods and to compounds
    strange?
Why write I still all one, ever the same,
And keep invention in a noted weed,
That every word almost doth tell my name,
Showing their birth, and where they did proceed?
O know, sweet love, I always write of you,
And you and love are still my argument:
So all my best is dressing old words new,
Spending again what is already spent:
    For as the sun is daily new and old,
    So is my love still telling what is told.

Thy glass will show thee how thy beauties wear,
Thy dial how thy precious minutes waste,
The vacant leaves thy mind's imprint will bear,
And of this book, this learning mayst thou taste:
The wrinkles which thy glass will truly show
Of mouthed graves will give thee memory;
Thou by thy dial's shady stealth mayst know
Time's thievish progress to eternity;
Look what thy memory cannot contain,
Commit to these waste blanks, and thou shalt find
Those children nursed, delivered from thy brain,
To take a new acquaintance of thy mind.
    These offices, so oft as thou wilt look,
    Shall profit thee, and much enrich thy book.

78

So oft have I invoked thee for my Muse,
And found such fair assistance in my verse,
As every alien pen hath got my use,
And under thee their poesy disperse.
Thine eyes, that taught the dumb on high to sing,
And heavy ignorance aloft to fly,
Have added feathers to the learned's wing,
And given grace a double majesty. —
Yet be most proud of that which I compile,
Whose influence is thine, and born of thee:
In others' works thou dost but mend the style,
And arts with thy sweet graces graced be;
    But thou art all my art, and dost advance,
    As high as learning, my rude ignorance.

79

Whilst I alone did call upon thy aid
My verse alone had all thy gentle grace;
But now my gracious numbers are decayed,
And my sick Muse doth give another place.
I grant, sweet love, thy lovely argument
Deserves the travail of a worthier pen;
Yet what of thee thy poet doth invent
He robs thee of, and pays it thee again;
He lends thee virtue, and he stole that word
From thy behaviour; beauty doth he give,
And found it in thy cheek; he can afford
No praise to thee, but what in thee doth live:
    Then thank him not for that which he doth say,
    Since what he owes thee, thou thyself dost pay.

80

O how I faint when I of you do write,
Knowing a better spirit doth use your name,
And in the praise thereof spends all his might,
To make me tongue-tied speaking of your fame.
But since your worth, wide as the ocean is,
The humble as the proudest sail doth bear,
My saucy bark, inferior far to his,
On your broad main doth wilfully appear.
Your shallowest help will hold me up afloat,
Whilst he upon your soundless deep doth ride;
Or, being wracked, I am a worthless boat,
He of tall building, and of goodly pride.
    Then if he thrive, and I be cast away,
    The worst was this: my love was my decay.

81

Or I shall live, your epitaph to make;
Or you survive, when I in earth am rotten;
From hence your memory death cannot take,
Although in me each part will be forgotten.
Your name from hence immortal life shall have,
Though I, once gone, to all the world must die;
The earth can yield me but a common grave,
When you entombed in men's eyes shall lie.
Your monument shall be my gentle verse,
Which eyes not yet created shall o'er-read,
And tongues to be your being shall rehearse,
When all the breathers of this world are dead.
    You still shall live, such virtue hath my pen,
    Where breath most breathes, even in the mouths
      of men.

82

I grant thou wert not married to my Muse,
And therefore mayst without attaint o'erlook
The dedicated words which writers use
Of their fair subject, blessing every book.
Thou art as fair in knowledge as in hue,
Finding thy worth a limit past my praise,
And therefore art enforced to seek anew
Some fresher stamp of the time-bettering days,
And do so love; yet when they have devised
What strained touches rhetoric can lend,
Thou, truly fair, wert truly sympathized
In true plain words, by thy true-telling friend;
    And their gross painting might be better used
    Where cheeks need blood; in thee it is abused.

83

I never saw that you did painting need,
And therefore to your fair no painting set;
I found (or thought I found) you did exceed
The barren tender of a poet's debt;
And therefore have I slept in your report,
That you yourself, being extant, well might show
How far a modern quill doth come too short,
Speaking of worth, what worth in you doth grow.
This silence for my sin you did impute,
Which shall be most my glory, being dumb;
For I impair not beauty, being mute,
When others would give life, and bring a tomb.
    There lives more life in one of your fair eyes
    Than both your poets can in praise devise.

84

Who is it that says most? Which can say more,
Than this rich praise: that you alone are you,
In whose confine immured is the store
Which should example where your equal grew?
Lean penury within that pen doth dwell
That to his subject lends not some small glory;
But he that writes of you, if he can tell
That you are you, so dignifies his story.
Let him but copy what in you is writ,
Not making worse what nature made so clear,
And such a counterpart shall fame his wit,
Making his style admired everywhere.
  You to your beauteous blessings add a curse,
  Being fond on praise, which makes your praises
    worse.

85

My tongue-tied Muse in manners holds her still,
While comments of your praise richly compiled
Reserve your character with golden quill,
And precious phrase by all the Muses filed;
I think good thoughts, whilst other write good
    words,
And like unlettered clerk still cry 'Amen'
To every hymn that able spirit affords
In polished form of well-refined pen.
Hearing you praised, I say, ''Tis so, 'tis true',
And to the most of praise add something more;
But that is in my thought, whose love to you
(Though words come hindmost) holds his rank
    before;
  Then others for the breath of words respect,
  Me for my dumb thoughts, speaking in effect.

86

Was it the proud full sail of his great verse,
Bound for the prize of all-too-precious you,
That did my ripe thoughts in my brain in-hearse,
Making their tomb the womb wherein they grew?
Was it his spirit, by spirits taught to write
Above a mortal pitch, that struck me dead?
No, neither he, nor his compeers by night,
Giving him aid, my verse astonished.
He, nor that affable familiar ghost
Which nightly gulls him with intelligence,
As victors of my silence cannot boast;
I was not sick of any fear from thence.
  But when your countenance filled up his line,
  Then lacked I matter, that enfeebled mine.

87

Farewell, thou art too dear for my possessing,
And like enough thou knowst thy estimate;
The charter of thy worth gives thee releasing;
My bonds in thee are all determinate.
For how do I hold thee but by thy granting,
And for that riches where is my deserving?
The cause of this fair gift in me is wanting,
And so my patent back again is swerving.
Thyself thou gav'st, thy own worth then not
    knowing,
Or me, to whom thou gav'st it, else mistaking;
So thy great gift upon misprision growing
Comes home again, on better judgement making.
  Thus have I had thee as a dream doth flatter,
  In sleep a king, but waking no such matter.

88

When thou shalt be disposed to set me light
And place my merit in the eye of scorn,
Upon thy side, against myself, I'll fight,
And prove thee virtuous, though thou art
    forsworn:
With mine own weakness being best acquainted,
Upon thy part I can set down a story
Of faults concealed, wherein I am attainted,
That thou, in losing me, shall win much glory;
And I by this will be a gainer too,
For bending all my loving thoughts on thee,
The injuries that to myself I do,
Doing thee vantage, double vantage me:
  Such is my love, to thee I so belong,
  That for thy right myself will bear all wrong.

89

Say that thou didst forsake me for some fault,
And I will comment upon that offence;
Speak of my lameness, and I straight will halt,
Against thy reasons making no defence.
Thou canst not, love, disgrace me half so ill,
To set a form upon desired change,
As I'll myself disgrace, knowing thy will;
I will acquaintance strangle and look strange,
Be absent from thy walks, and in my tongue
Thy sweet beloved name no more shall dwell,
Lest I, too much profane, should do it wrong,
And haply of our old acquaintance tell.
  For thee, against myself I'll vow debate;
  For I must ne'er love him whom thou dost hate.

90

Then hate me when thou wilt, if ever, now,
Now, while the world is bent my deeds to cross,
Join with the spite of fortune, make me bow,
And do not drop in for an after-loss.
Ah, do not, when my heart hath 'scaped this sorrow,
Come in the rearward of a conquered woe;
Give not a windy night a rainy morrow,
To linger out a purposed overthrow.
If thou wilt leave me, do not leave me last,
When other petty griefs have done their spite;
But in the onset come, so shall I taste
At first the very worst of fortune's might;
   And other strains of woe, which now seem woe,
   Compared with loss of thee, will not seem so.

91

Some glory in their birth, some in their skill,
Some in their wealth, some in their bodies' force,
Some in their garments, though new-fangled ill,
Some in their hawks and hounds, some in their horse,
And every humour hath his adjunct pleasure,
Wherein it finds a joy above the rest;
But these particulars are not my measure;
All these I better in one general best.
Thy love is better than high birth to me,
Richer than wealth, prouder than garments' cost,
Of more delight than hawks or horses be;
And having thee, of all men's pride I boast –
   Wretched in this alone, that thou mayst take
   All this away, and me most wretched make.

92

But do thy worst to steal thyself away;
For term of life thou art assured mine,
And life no longer than thy love will stay,
For it depends upon that love of thine.
Then need I not to fear the worst of wrongs,
When in the least of them my life hath end;
I see a better state to me belongs
Than that which on thy humour doth depend.
Thou canst not vex me with inconstant mind,
Since that my life on thy revolt doth lie.
O what a happy title do I find,
Happy to have thy love, happy to die!
   But what's so blessed fair that fears no blot?
   Thou mayst be false, and yet I know it not.

93

So shall I live, supposing thou art true,
Like a deceived husband; so love's face
May still seem love to me, though altered new,
Thy looks with me, thy heart in other place;
For there can live no hatred in thine eye,
Therefore in that I cannot know thy change.
In many's looks, the false heart's history
Is writ in moods and frowns and wrinkles strange;
But heaven in thy creation did decree
That in thy face sweet love should ever dwell;
Whate'er thy thoughts or thy heart's workings be,
Thy looks should nothing thence but sweetness tell.
   How like Eve's apple doth thy beauty grow,
   If thy sweet virtue answer not thy show.

94

They that have power to hurt, and will do none,
That do not do the thing they most do show,
Who, moving others, are themselves as stone,
Unmoved, cold, and to temptation slow:
They rightly do inherit heaven's graces,
And husband nature's riches from expense;
They are the lords and owners of their faces,
Others, but stewards of their excellence.
The summer's flower is to the summer sweet,
Though to itself it only live and die,
But if that flower with base infection meet,
The basest weed outbraves his dignity:
   For sweetest things turn sourest by their deeds;
   Lilies that fester smell far worse than weeds.

95

How sweet and lovely dost thou make the shame
Which like a canker in the fragrant rose
Doth spot the beauty of thy budding name:
O in what sweets dost thou thy sins enclose!
That tongue that tells the story of thy days,
Making lascivious comments on thy sport,
Cannot dispraise; but in a kind of praise,
Naming thy name, blesses an ill report.
O what a mansion have those vices got,
Which for their habitation chose out thee,
Where beauty's veil doth cover every blot,
And all things turns to fair that eyes can see!
   Take heed, dear heart, of this large privilege;
   The hardest knife ill used doth lose his edge.

96

Some say thy fault is youth, some wantonness;
Some say thy grace is youth and gentle sport;
Both grace and faults are loved of more and less;
Thou mak'st faults graces, that to thee resort:
As on the finger of a thronèd queen
The basest jewel will be well esteemed,
So are those errors that in thee are seen
To truths translated, and for true things deemed.
How many lambs might the stern wolf betray
If like a lamb he could his looks translate?
How many gazers mightst thou lead away
If thou wouldst use the strength of all thy state?
    But do not so; I love thee in such sort,
    As thou being mine, mine is thy good report.

97

How like a winter hath my absence been
From thee, the pleasure of the fleeting year!
What freezings have I felt, what dark days seen,
What old December's bareness everywhere!
And yet this time removed was summer's time,
The teeming autumn big with rich increase
Bearing the wanton burden of the prime,
Like widowed wombs after their lords' decease:
Yet this abundant issue seemed to me
But hope of orphans, and unfathered fruit;
For summer and his pleasures wait on thee,
And thou away, the very birds are mute;
    Or if they sing, 'tis with so dull a cheer
    That leaves look pale, dreading the winter's near.

98

From you have I been absent in the spring,
When proud pied April, dressed in all his trim,
Hath put a spirit of youth in everything,
That heavy Saturn laughed, and leaped with him.
Yet nor the lays of birds, nor the sweet smell
Of different flowers in odour and in hue,
Could make me any summer's story tell,
Or from their proud lap pluck them where they grew;
Nor did I wonder at the lily's white,
Nor praise the deep vermilion in the rose;
They were but sweet, but figures of delight,
Drawn after you, you pattern of all those.
    Yet seemed it winter still, and, you away,
    As with your shadow I with these did play.

99

The forward violet thus did I chide:
'Sweet thief, whence didst thou steal thy sweet that
    smells,
If not from my love's breath? The purple pride
Which on thy soft cheek for complexion dwells
In my love's veins thou hast too grossly dyed.'
The lily I condemned for thy hand,
And buds of marjoram had stol'n thy hair;
The roses fearfully on thorns did stand,
One blushing shame, another white despair;
A third, nor red, nor white, had stol'n of both,
And to his robb'ry had annexed thy breath;
But for his theft, in pride of all his growth,
A vengeful canker ate him up to death.
    More flowers I noted, yet I none could see,
    But sweet, or colour, it had stol'n from thee.

100

Where art thou, Muse, that thou forget'st so long
To speak of that which gives thee all thy might?
Spend'st thou thy fury on some worthless song,
Dark'ning thy power to lend base subjects light?
Return, forgetful Muse, and straight redeem,
In gentle numbers, time so idly spent;
Sing to the ear that doth thy lays esteem,
And gives thy pen both skill and argument.
Rise, resty Muse: my love's sweet face survey,
If time have any wrinkle graven there;
If any, be a satire to decay,
And make time's spoils despised everywhere:
    Give my love fame faster than time wastes life,
    So thou prevent'st his scythe and crooked knife.

101

O truant Muse, what shall be thy amends
For thy neglect of truth in beauty dyed?
Both truth and beauty on my love depends;
So dost thou, too, and therein dignified:
Make answer, Muse, wilt thou not haply say,
'Truth needs no colour with his colour fixed,
Beauty no pencil, beauty's truth to lay,
But best is best if never intermixed'?
Because he needs no praise, wilt thou be dumb?
Excuse not silence so, for't lies in thee
To make him much outlive a gilded tomb,
And to be praised of ages yet to be.
    Then do thy office, Muse: I teach thee how
    To make him seem long hence as he shows now.

102

My love is strengthened, though more weak in
    seeming;
I love not less, though less the show appear.
That love is merchandised, whose rich esteeming
The owner's tongue doth publish everywhere.
Our love was new, and then but in the spring,
When I was wont to greet it with my lays,
As Philomel in summer's front doth sing,
And stops her pipe in growth of riper days.
Not that the summer is less pleasant now
Than when her mournful hymns did hush the night;
But that wild music burdens every bough,
And sweets grown common lose their dear delight:
    Therefore, like her, I sometime hold my tongue,
    Because I would not dull you with my song.

103

Alack, what poverty my Muse brings forth,
That, having such a scope to show her pride,
The argument all bare is of more worth
Than when it hath my added praise beside.
O blame me not if I no more can write!
Look in your glass, and there appears a face
That overgoes my blunt invention quite,
Dulling my lines, and doing me disgrace.
Were it not sinful, then, striving to mend,
To mar the subject that before was well?
For to no other pass my verses tend
Than of your graces and your gifts to tell;
    And more, much more, than in my verse can sit
    Your own glass shows you, when you look in it.

104

To me, fair friend, you never can be old;
For as you were when first your eye I eyed,
Such seems your beauty still: three winters cold
Have from the forests shook three summers' pride;
Three beauteous springs to yellow autumn turned
In process of the seasons have I seen;
Three April perfumes in three hot Junes burned,
Since first I saw you fresh, which yet art green.
Ah, yet doth beauty, like a dial hand,
Steal from his figure, and no pace perceived;
So your sweet hue, which methinks still doth stand,
Hath motion, and mine eye may be deceived;
    For fear of which, hear this, thou age unbred,
    Ere you were born was beauty's summer dead.

105

Let not my love be called idolatry,
Nor my beloved as an idol show,
Since all alike my songs and praises be,
To one, of one, still such, and ever so.
Kind is my love today, tomorrow kind,
Still constant in a wondrous excellence;
Therefore my verse, to constancy confined,
One thing expressing, leaves out difference.
Fair, kind and true is all my argument;
Fair, kind and true, varying to other words,
And in this change is my invention spent,
Three themes in one, which wondrous scope affords.
    Fair, kind and true have often lived alone,
    Which three, till now, never kept seat in one.

106

When in the chronicle of wasted time
I see descriptions of the fairest wights,
And beauty making beautiful old rhyme,
In praise of ladies dead, and lovely knights;
Then in the blazon of sweet beauties best,
Of hand, of foot, of lip, of eye, of brow,
I see their antique pen would have expressed
Even such a beauty as you master now:
So all their praises are but prophecies
Of this our time, all you prefiguring;
And for they looked but with divining eyes
They had not skill enough your worth to sing;
    For we which now behold these present days
    Have eyes to wonder, but lack tongues to praise.

107

Not mine own fears, nor the prophetic soul
Of the wide world, dreaming on things to come,
Can yet the lease of my true love control,
Supposed as forfeit to a confined doom.
The mortal moon hath her eclipse endured,
And the sad augurs mock their own presage;
Uncertainties now crown themselves assured,
And peace proclaims olives of endless age.
Now with the drops of this most balmy time
My love looks fresh, and death to me subscribes,
Since 'spite of him I'll live in this poor rhyme,
While he insults o'er dull and speechless tribes;
    And thou in this shalt find thy monument,
    When tyrants' crests and tombs of brass are spent.

108

What's in the brain that ink may character
Which hath not figured to thee my true spirit?
What's new to speak, what new to register,
That may express my love, or thy dear merit?
Nothing, sweet boy; but yet, like prayers divine,
I must each day say o'er the very same,
Counting no old thing old; thou mine, I thine,
Even as when first I hallowed thy fair name:
So that eternal love, in love's fresh case,
Weighs not the dust and injury of age,
Nor gives to necessary wrinkles place
But makes antiquity for aye his page,
    Finding the first conceit of love there bred,
    Where time and outward form would show it dead.

109

O never say that I was false of heart,
Though absence seemed my flame to qualify;
As easy might I from myself depart
As from my soul which in thy breast doth lie:
That is my home of love; if I have ranged,
Like him that travels I return again,
Just to the time, not with the time exchanged,
So that myself bring water for my stain;
Never believe, though in my nature reigned
All frailties that besiege all kinds of blood,
That it could so preposterously be stained,
To leave for nothing all thy sum of good:
    For nothing this wide universe I call,
    Save thou, my rose; in it thou art my all.

110

Alas, 'tis true, I have gone here and there,
And made myself a motley to the view,
Gored mine own thoughts, sold cheap what is most
    dear,
Made old offences of affections new.
Most true it is that I have looked on truth
Askance and strangely; but by all above,
These blenches gave my heart another youth,
And worse essays proved thee my best of love.
Now all is done, save what shall have no end;
Mine appetite I never more will grind
On newer proof, to try an older friend,
A god in love, to whom I am confined:
    Then give me welcome, next my heaven the best,
    Even to thy pure and most most loving breast.

111

O, for my sake do you with Fortune chide,
The guilty goddess of my harmful deeds,
That did not better for my life provide
Than public means, which public manners breeds;
Thence comes it that my name receives a brand,
And almost thence my nature is subdued
To what it works in, like the dyer's hand;
Pity me, then, and wish I were renewed,
Whilst like a willing patient I will drink
Potions of eisell 'gainst my strong infection;
No bitterness that I will bitter think,
Nor double penance to correct correction.
    Pity me then, dear friend, and I assure ye,
    Even that your pity is enough to cure me.

112

Your love and pity doth th'impression fill
Which vulgar scandal stamped upon my brow;
For what care I who calls me well or ill
So you o'er-green my bad, my good allow?
You are my all-the-world, and I must strive
To know my shames and praises from your tongue;
None else to me, nor I to none, alive,
That my steeled sense o'er-changes right or wrong.
In so profound abysm I throw all care
Of others' voices, that my adder's sense
To critic and to flatterer stopped are.
Mark how with my neglect I do dispense:
    You are so strongly in my purpose bred
    That all the world besides me thinks you're dead.

113

Since I left you, mine eye is in my mind,
And that which governs me to go about
Doth part his function, and is partly blind;
Seems seeing, but effectually is out:
For it no form delivers to the heart
Of bird, of flower, or shape which it doth latch;
Of his quick objects hath the mind no part,
Nor his own vision holds what it doth catch:
For if it see the rud'st or gentlest sight,
The most sweet-favoured or deformed'st creature,
The mountain, or the sea, the day, or night,
The crow, or dove, it shapes them to your feature.
    Incapable of more, replete with you,
    My most true mind thus maketh mine untrue.

114

Or whether doth my mind, being crowned with you,
Drink up the monarch's plague, this flattery?
Or whether shall I say mine eye saith true,
And that your love taught it this alchemy,
To make of monsters and things indigest
Such cherubins as your sweet self resemble,
Creating every bad a perfect best
As fast as objects to his beams assemble?
O, 'tis the first, 'tis flatt'ry in my seeing,
And my great mind most kingly drinks it up:
Mine eye well knows what with his gust is greeing,
And to his palate doth prepare the cup.
    If it be poisoned, 'tis the lesser sin,
    That mine eye loves it and doth first begin.

115

Those lines that I before have writ do lie,
Even those that said I could not love you dearer;
Yet then my judgement knew no reason why
My most full flame should afterwards burn clearer.
But reckoning time, whose millioned accidents
Creep in 'twixt vows, and change decrees of kings,
Tan sacred beauty, blunt the sharp'st intents,
Divert strong minds to th' course of alt'ring things;
Alas, why, fearing of time's tyranny,
Might I not then say, 'Now I love you best',
When I was certain o'er uncertainty,
Crowning the present, doubting of the rest?
    Love is a babe; then might I not say so,
    To give full growth to that which still doth grow?

116

Let me not to the marriage of true minds
Admit impediments; love is not love
Which alters when it alteration finds,
Or bends with the remover to remove.
O no, it is an ever-fixed mark,
That looks on tempests and is never shaken;
It is the star to every wand'ring bark,
Whose worth's unknown, although his height be
    taken.
Love's not Time's fool, though rosy lips and cheeks
Within his bending sickle's compass come;
Love alters not with his brief hours and weeks,
But bears it out even to the edge of doom.
    If this be error and upon me proved,
    I never writ, nor no man ever loved.

117

Accuse me thus: that I have scanted all
Wherein I should your great deserts repay,
Forgot upon your dearest love to call,
Whereto all bonds do tie me day by day;
That I have frequent been with unknown minds,
And given to time your own dear-purchased right;
That I have hoisted sail to all the winds
Which should transport me farthest from your
    sight.
Book both my wilfulness and errors down,
And on just proof surmise accumulate;
Bring me within the level of your frown,
But shoot not at me in your wakened hate:
    Since my appeal says I did strive to prove
    The constancy and virtue of your love.

118

Like as, to make our appetites more keen,
With eager compounds we our palate urge;
As, to prevent our maladies unseen,
We sicken to shun sickness when we purge;
Even so, being full of your ne'er-cloying sweetness,
To bitter sauces did I frame my feeding,
And, sick of welfare, found a kind of meetness
To be diseased ere that there was true needing.
Thus policy in love, t'anticipate
The ills that were not, grew to faults assured,
And brought to medicine a healthful state
Which, rank of goodness, would by ill be cured;
    But thence I learn, and find the lesson true,
    Drugs poison him that so fell sick of you.

119

What potions have I drunk of siren tears
Distilled from limbecks foul as hell within,
Applying fears to hopes, and hopes to fears,
Still losing when I saw myself to win?
What wretched errors hath my heart committed,
Whilst it hath thought itself so blessed never?
How have mine eyes out of their spheres been fitted
In the distraction of this madding fever?
O benefit of ill: now I find true
That better is by evil still made better,
And ruined love when it is built anew
Grows fairer than at first, more strong, far greater:
    So I return rebuked to my content,
    And gain by ills thrice more than I have spent.

120

That you were once unkind befriends me now,
And for that sorrow, which I then did feel,
Needs must I under my transgression bow,
Unless my nerves were brass or hammered steel:
For if you were by my unkindness shaken,
As I by yours, you've passed a hell of time,
And I, a tyrant, have no leisure taken
To weigh how once I suffered in your crime.
O that our night of woe might have remembered
My deepest sense how hard true sorrow hits,
And soon to you, as you to me then, tendered
The humble salve which wounded bosoms fits!
   But that your trespass now becomes a fee;
   Mine ransoms yours, and yours must ransom me.

121

'Tis better to be vile than vile esteemed,
When not to be, receives reproach of being,
And the just pleasure lost, which is so deemed
Not by our feeling, but by others' seeing.
For why should others' false adulterate eyes
Give salutation to my sportive blood?
Or on my frailties why are frailer spies,
Which in their wills count bad what I think good?
No, I am that I am, and they that level
At my abuses, reckon up their own;
I may be straight, though they themselves be bevel.
By their rank thoughts my deeds must not be shown,
   Unless this general evil they maintain:
   All men are bad, and in their badness reign.

122

Thy gift, thy tables, are within my brain
Full charactered with lasting memory,
Which shall above that idle rank remain
Beyond all date, even to eternity;
Or at the least, so long as brain and heart
Have faculty by nature to subsist;
Till each to razed oblivion yield his part
Of thee, thy record never can be missed.
That poor retention could not so much hold,
Nor need I tallies thy dear love to score;
Therefore to give them from me was I bold,
To trust those tables that receive thee more;
   To keep an adjunct to remember thee
   Were to import forgetfulness in me.

123

No! Time, thou shalt not boast that I do change;
Thy pyramids, built up with newer might,
To me are nothing novel, nothing strange;
They are but dressings of a former sight:
Our dates are brief, and therefore we admire
What thou dost foist upon us that is old,
And rather make them born to our desire
Than think that we before have heard them told:
Thy registers and thee I both defy,
Not wond'ring at the present, nor the past,
For thy records, and what we see doth lie,
Made more or less by thy continual haste:
   This I do vow, and this shall ever be,
   I will be true despite thy scythe and thee.

124

If my dear love were but the child of state
It might, for fortune's bastard, be unfathered,
As subject to time's love or to time's hate,
Weeds among weeds, or flowers with flowers
   gathered.
No, it was builded far from accident;
It suffers not in smiling pomp, nor falls
Under the blow of thralled discontent,
Whereto th'inviting time our fashion calls:
It fears not policy, that heretic,
Which works on leases of short-numbered hours,
But all alone stands hugely politic,
That it nor grows with heat, nor drowns with
   showers.
   To this I witness call the fools of time,
   Which die for goodness, who have lived for crime.

125

Were't ought to me I bore the canopy,
With my extern the outward honouring,
Or laid great bases for eternity,
Which proves more short than waste or ruining?
Have I not seen dwellers on form and favour
Lose all, and more, by paying too much rent,
For compound sweet forgoing simple savour,
Pitiful thrivers, in their gazing spent?
No, let me be obsequious in thy heart,
And take thou my oblation, poor but free,
Which is not mixed with seconds, knows no art,
But mutual render, only me for thee.
   Hence, thou suborned informer, a true soul
   When most impeached, stands least in thy control.

126

O thou my lovely Boy, who in thy power
Dost hold time's fickle glass, his sickle hour,
Who hast by waning grown, and therein show'st
Thy lover's withering, as thy sweet self grow'st;
If nature, sovereign mistress over wrack,
As thou goest onwards still will pluck thee back,
She keeps thee to this purpose: that her skill
May time disgrace, and wretched minute kill.
Yet fear her, O thou minion of her pleasure:
She may detain, but not still keep, her treasure!
Her audit, though delayed, answered must be,
And her quietus is to render thee.
    (   )
    (   )

127

In the old age black was not counted fair,
Or if it were, it bore not beauty's name;
But now is black beauty's successive heir,
And beauty slandered with a bastard shame:
For since each hand hath put on nature's power,
Fairing the foul with art's false borrowed face,
Sweet beauty hath no name, no holy bower,
But is profaned, if not lives in disgrace.
Therefore my mistress' eyes are raven black,
Her eyes so suited, and they mourners seem
At such who, not born fair, no beauty lack,
Sland'ring creation with a false esteem;
    Yet so they mourn, becoming of their woe,
    That every tongue says beauty should look so.

128

How oft when thou, my music, music play'st
Upon that blessed wood whose motion sounds
With thy sweet fingers, when thou gently sway'st
The wiry concord that mine ear confounds,
Do I envy those jacks that nimble leap,
To kiss the tender inward of thy hand,
Whilst my poor lips, which should that harvest reap,
At the wood's boldness by thee blushing stand?
To be so tickled they would change their state
And situation with those dancing chips,
O'er whom thy fingers walk with gentle gait,
Making dead wood more blessed than living lips.
    Since saucy jacks so happy are in this,
    Give them thy fingers, me thy lips to kiss.

129

Th'expense of spirit in a waste of shame
Is lust in action; and till action, lust
Is perjured, murd'rous, bloody, full of blame,
Savage, extreme, rude, cruel, not to trust;
Enjoyed no sooner but despised straight;
Past reason hunted, and no sooner had,
Past reason hated as a swallowed bait,
On purpose laid to make the taker mad;
Mad in pursuit, and in possession so,
Had, having, and in quest to have, extreme;
A bliss in proof, and proved, a very woe;
Before, a joy proposed; behind, a dream.
    All this the world well knows, yet none knows well
    To shun the heaven that leads men to this hell.

130

My mistress' eyes are nothing like the sun;
Coral is far more red than her lips' red;
If snow be white, why then her breasts are dun;
If hairs be wires, black wires grow on her head;
I have seen roses damasked, red and white,
But no such roses see I in her cheeks;
And in some perfumes is there more delight
Than in the breath that from my mistress reeks.
I love to hear her speak, yet well I know
That music hath a far more pleasing sound;
I grant I never saw a goddess go;
My mistress when she walks treads on the ground.
    And yet, by heaven, I think my love as rare
    As any she belied with false compare.

131

Thou art as tyrannous, so as thou art,
As those whose beauties proudly make them cruel;
For well thou knowst, to my dear doting heart
Thou art the fairest and most precious jewel.
Yet in good faith some say, that thee behold,
Thy face hath not the power to make love groan;
To say they err, I dare not be so bold,
Although I swear it to myself alone;
And to be sure that is not false, I swear
A thousand groans but thinking on thy face;
One on another's neck do witness bear
Thy black is fairest in my judgement's place.
    In nothing art thou black save in thy deeds,
    And thence this slander, as I think, proceeds.

132

Thine eyes I love, and they, as pitying me,
Knowing thy heart torment me with disdain,
Have put on black, and loving mourners be,
Looking with pretty ruth upon my pain;
And truly, not the morning sun of heaven
Better becomes the grey cheeks of the East,
Nor that full star that ushers in the even
Doth half that glory to the sober West
As those two mourning eyes become thy face:
O let it then as well beseem thy heart
To mourn for me, since mourning doth thee grace,
And suit thy pity like in every part:
    Then will I swear beauty herself is black,
    And all they foul that thy complexion lack.

133

Beshrew that heart that makes my heart to groan
For that deep wound it gives my friend and me;
Is't not enough to torture me alone,
But slave to slavery my sweet'st friend must be?
Me from myself thy cruel eye hath taken,
And my next self thou harder hast engrossed:
Of him, myself and thee I am forsaken,
A torment thrice threefold thus to be crossed.
Prison my heart in thy steel bosom's ward;
But then my friend's heart let my poor heart bail.
Whoe'er keeps me, let my heart be his guard;
Thou canst not then use rigour in my jail.
    And yet thou wilt, for I being pent in thee,
    Perforce am thine, and all that is in me.

134

So now I have confessed that he is thine,
And I myself am mortgaged to thy will,
Myself I'll forfeit, so that other mine
Thou wilt restore to be my comfort still;
But thou wilt not, nor he will not be free,
For thou art covetous, and he is kind;
He learned but surety-like to write for me,
Under that bond that him as fast doth bind.
The statute of thy beauty thou wilt take,
Thou usurer, that put'st forth all to use,
And sue a friend, came debtor for my sake:
So him I lose through my unkind abuse.
    Him have I lost; thou hast both him and me;
    He pays the whole, and yet am I not free.

135

Whoever hath her wish, thou hast thy Will,
And Will to boot, and Will in overplus;
More than enough am I, that vex thee still,
To thy sweet will making addition thus.
Wilt thou, whose will is large and spacious,
Not once vouchsafe to hide my will in thine?
Shall will in others seem right gracious,
And in my will no fair acceptance shine?
The sea, all water, yet receives rain still,
And in abundance addeth to his store;
So thou, being rich in Will, add to thy Will
One will of mine, to make thy large Will more:
    Let no unkind, no fair beseechers kill;
    Think all but one, and me in that one Will.

136

If thy soul check thee that I come so near,
Swear to thy blind soul that I was thy Will,
And will, thy soul knows, is admitted there;
Thus far for love my love-suit sweet fulfil.
Will will fulfil the treasure of thy love,
Ay, fill it full with wills, and my will one;
In things of great receipt with ease we prove
Among a number one is reckoned none.
Then in the number let me pass untold,
Though in thy store's account I one must be.
For nothing hold me, so it please thee hold
That nothing, me, a something sweet to thee.
    Make but my name thy love, and love that still;
    And then thou lov'st me, for my name is Will.

137

Thou blind fool love, what dost thou to mine eyes,
That they behold, and see not what they see?
They know what beauty is, see where it lies,
Yet what the best is, take the worst to be.
If eyes, corrupt by over-partial looks,
Be anchored in the bay where all men ride,
Why of eyes' falsehood hast thou forged hooks,
Whereto the judgement of my heart is tied?
Why should my heart think that a several plot
Which my heart knows the wide world's common
    place?
Or mine eyes, seeing this, say this is not,
To put fair truth upon so foul a face?
    In things right true my heart and eyes have erred,
    And to this false plague are they now transferred.

138

When my love swears that she is made of truth,
I do believe her, though I know she lies,
That she might think me some untutored youth
Unlearned in the world's false subtleties.
Thus vainly thinking that she thinks me young,
Although she knows my days are past the best,
Simply I credit her false-speaking tongue;
On both sides thus is simple truth suppressed.
But wherefore says she not she is unjust?
And wherefore say not I that I am old?
O love's best habit is in seeming trust,
And age in love loves not t' have years told:
   Therefore I lie with her, and she with me,
   And in our faults by lies we flattered be.

139

O call not me to justify the wrong
That thy unkindness lays upon my heart;
Wound me not with thine eye, but with thy tongue;
Use power with power, and slay me not by art.
Tell me thou lov'st elsewhere; but in my sight,
Dear heart, forbear to glance thine eye aside.
What need'st thou wound with cunning, when thy
     might
Is more than my o'er-pressed defence can bide?
Let me excuse thee: ah, my love well knows
Her pretty looks have been mine enemies,
And therefore from my face she turns my foes
That they elsewhere might dart their injuries.
   Yet do not so, but since I am near slain,
   Kill me outright with looks, and rid my pain.

140

Be wise as thou art cruel, do not press
My tongue-tied patience with too much disdain,
Lest sorrow lend me words, and words express
The manner of my pity-wanting pain.
If I might teach thee wit, better it were,
Though not to love, yet love to tell me so,
As testy sick men, when their deaths be near,
No news but health from their physicians know:
For if I should despair, I should grow mad,
And in my madness might speak ill of thee;
Now this ill-wresting world is grown so bad,
Mad slanderers by mad ears believed be.
   That I may not be so, nor thou belied,
   Bear thine eyes straight, though thy proud heart go
     wide.

141

In faith, I do not love thee with mine eyes,
For they in thee a thousand errors note;
But 'tis my heart that loves what they despise,
Who in despite of view is pleased to dote.
Nor are mine ears with thy tongue's tune delighted,
Nor tender feeling to base touches prone,
Nor taste, nor smell, desire to be invited
To any sensual feast with thee alone:
But my five wits, nor my five senses, can
Dissuade one foolish heart from serving thee,
Who leaves unswayed the likeness of a man,
Thy proud heart's slave and vassal wretch to be:
   Only my plague thus far I count my gain,
   That she that makes me sin, awards me pain.

142

Love is my sin, and thy dear virtue hate,
Hate of my sin, grounded on sinful loving;
O but with mine compare thou thine own state,
And thou shalt find it merits not reproving;
Or if it do, not from those lips of thine,
That have profaned their scarlet ornaments,
And sealed false bonds of love as oft as mine,
Robbed others' beds' revenues of their rents.
Be it lawful I love thee as thou lov'st those
Whom thine eyes woo, as mine importune thee,
Root pity in thy heart, that when it grows,
Thy pity may deserve to pitied be.
   If thou dost seek to have what thou dost hide,
   By self-example mayst thou be denied.

143

Lo, as a careful housewife runs to catch
One of her feathered creatures broke away,
Sets down her babe, and makes all swift dispatch
In pursuit of the thing she would have stay;
Whilst her neglected child holds her in chase,
Cries to catch her whose busy care is bent
To follow that which flies before her face,
Not prizing her poor infant's discontent:
So run'st thou after that which flies from thee,
Whilst I, thy babe, chase thee afar behind.
But if thou catch thy hope, turn back to me,
And play the mother's part, kiss me, be kind:
   So will I pray that thou mayst have thy Will,
   If thou turn back and my loud crying still.

144

Two loves I have, of comfort and despair,
Which, like two spirits, do suggest me still:
The better angel is a man right fair,
The worser spirit a woman coloured ill.
To win me soon to hell my female evil
Tempteth my better angel from my side,
And would corrupt my saint to be a devil,
Wooing his purity with her foul pride;
And whether that my angel be turned fiend
Suspect I may, yet not directly tell;
But being both from me both to each friend,
I guess one angel in another's hell.
  Yet this shall I ne'er know, but live in doubt,
  Till my bad angel fire my good one out.

145

Those lips that love's own hand did make
Breathed forth the sound that said 'I hate',
To me, that languished for her sake;
But when she saw my woeful state,
Straight in her heart did mercy come,
Chiding that tongue that, ever sweet,
Was used in giving gentle doom,
And taught it thus anew to greet:
'I hate' she altered with an end
That followed it as gentle day
Doth follow night, who like a fiend
From heaven to hell is flown away.
  'I hate' from 'hate' away she threw,
  And saved my life, saying 'not you'.

146

Poor soul, the centre of my sinful earth,
Feeding these rebel powers that thee array,
Why dost thou pine within and suffer dearth,
Painting thy outward walls so costly gay?
Why so large cost, having so short a lease,
Dost thou upon thy fading mansion spend?
Shall worms, inheritors of this excess,
Eat up thy charge? Is this thy body's end?
Then soul, live thou upon thy servant's loss,
And let that pine to aggravate thy store;
Buy terms divine in selling hours of dross,
Within be fed, without be rich no more:
  So shalt thou feed on death, that feeds on men,
  And death once dead, there's no more dying then.

147

My love is as a fever, longing still
For that which longer nurseth the disease,
Feeding on that which doth preserve the ill,
Th'uncertain sickly appetite to please:
My reason, the physician to my love,
Angry that his prescriptions are not kept,
Hath left me, and I, desperate, now approve
Desire is death, which physic did except.
Past cure I am, now reason is past care,
And frantic mad with ever more unrest;
My thoughts and my discourse as madmen's are,
At random from the truth vainly expressed:
  For I have sworn thee fair, and thought thee bright,
  Who art as black as hell, as dark as night.

148

O me! What eyes hath love put in my head,
Which have no correspondence with true sight?
Or if they have, where is my judgement fled,
That censures falsely what they see aright?
If that be fair whereon my false eyes dote,
What means the world to say it is not so?
If it be not, then love doth well denote,
Love's eye is not so true as all men's: no,
How can it? O how can love's eye be true,
That is so vexed with watching and with tears?
No marvel then though I mistake my view:
The sun itself sees not, till heaven clears.
  O cunning love, with tears thou keep'st me blind,
  Lest eyes well seeing thy foul faults should find.

149

Canst thou, O cruel, say I love thee not,
When I against myself with thee partake?
Do I not think on thee, when I forgot
Am of myself, all, tyrant, for thy sake?
Who hateth thee that I do call my friend?
On whom frown'st thou that I do fawn upon?
Nay, if thou lour'st on me, do I not spend
Revenge upon myself with present moan?
What merit do I in myself respect
That is so proud thy service to despise,
When all my best doth worship thy defect,
Commanded by the motion of thine eyes?
  But, love, hate on; for now I know thy mind:
  Those that can see thou lov'st, and I am blind.

150

O from what power hast thou this powerful might,
With insufficiency my heart to sway,
To make me give the lie to my true sight,
And swear that brightness doth not grace the day?
Whence hast thou this becoming of things ill,
That in the very refuse of thy deeds
There is such strength and warrantise of skill
That in my mind thy worst all best exceeds?
Who taught thee how to make me love thee more,
The more I hear and see just cause of hate?
O, though I love what others do abhor,
With others thou shouldst not abhor my state:
    If thy unworthiness raised love in me,
    More worthy I to be beloved of thee.

151

Love is too young to know what conscience is:
Yet who knows not conscience is born of love?
Then, gentle cheater, urge not my amiss,
Lest guilty of my faults thy sweet self prove;
For, thou betraying me, I do betray
My nobler part to my gross body's treason;
My soul doth tell my body that he may
Triumph in love; flesh stays no further reason,
But rising at thy name doth point out thee
As his triumphant prize, proud of this pride:
He is contented thy poor drudge to be,
To stand in thy affairs, fall by thy side.
    No want of conscience hold it that I call
    Her 'love', for whose dear love I rise and fall.

152

In loving thee thou knowst I am forsworn;
But thou art twice forsworn to me love swearing,
In act thy bed-vow broke and new faith torn,
In vowing new hate after new love bearing.
But why of two oaths' breach do I accuse thee,
When I break twenty? I am perjured most,
For all my vows are oaths but to misuse thee,
And all my honest faith in thee is lost:
For I have sworn deep oaths of thy deep kindness,
Oaths of thy love, thy truth, thy constancy,
And to enlighten thee gave eyes to blindness,
Or made them swear against the thing they see:
    For I have sworn thee fair: more perjured eye,
    To swear against the truth so foul a lie.

153

Cupid laid by his brand, and fell asleep;
A maid of Dian's this advantage found,
And his love-kindling fire did quickly steep
In a cold valley-fountain of that ground,
Which borrowed from this holy fire of love
A dateless lively heat still to endure,
And grew a seething bath, which yet men prove
Against strange maladies a sovereign cure:
But at my mistress' eye love's brand new fired,
The boy for trial needs would touch my breast;
I, sick withal, the help of bath desired,
And thither hied, a sad distempered guest,
    But found no cure; the bath for my help lies
    Where Cupid got new fire: my mistress' eye.

154

The little love-god lying once asleep,
Laid by his side his heart-inflaming brand,
Whilst many nymphs, that vowed chaste life to keep,
Came tripping by; but in her maiden hand
The fairest votary took up that fire
Which many legions of true hearts had warmed;
And so the general of hot desire
Was, sleeping, by a virgin hand disarmed.
This brand she quenched in a cool well by,
Which from love's fire took heat perpetual,
Growing a bath and healthful remedy
For men diseased; but I, my mistress' thrall,
    Came there for cure, and this by that I prove:
    Love's fire heats water, water cools not love.

A Lover's Complaint

From off a hill whose concave womb reworded
A plaintful story from a sist'ring vale,
My spirits t'attend this double voice accorded,
And down I laid to list the sad-tuned tale;
Ere long espied a fickle maid full pale,   5
Tearing of papers, breaking rings a-twain,
Storming her world with sorrow's wind and rain.

Upon her head a plaited hive of straw,
Which fortified her visage from the sun,
Whereon the thought might think sometime it saw   10
The carcass of a beauty spent and done;
Time had not scythed all that youth begun,
Nor youth all quit, but spite of heaven's fell rage
Some beauty peeped through lattice of seared age.

Oft did she heave her napkin to her eyne,   15
Which on it had conceited characters,
Laund'ring the silken figures in the brine
That seasoned woe had pelleted in tears,
And often reading what contents it bears;
As often shrieking undistinguished woe,   20
In clamours of all size, both high and low.

Sometimes her levelled eyes their carriage ride,
As they did batt'ry to the spheres intend;
Sometime, diverted, their poor balls are tied
To th'orbed earth; sometimes they do extend   25
Their view right on; anon their gazes lend
To every place at once, and nowhere fixed,
The mind and sight distractedly commixed.

Her hair, nor loose, nor tied in formal plait,
Proclaimed in her a careless hand of pride;   30
For some untucked descended her sheaved hat,
Hanging her pale and pined cheek beside;
Some in her threaden fillet still did bide,
And, true to bondage, would not break from thence,
Though slackly braided in loose negligence.   35

A thousand favours from a maund she drew,
Of amber, crystal and of beaded jet,
Which, one by one, she in a river threw,
Upon whose weeping margent she was set,
Like usury, applying wet to wet,   40
Or monarch's hands, that lets not bounty fall
Where want cries 'Some!', but where excess begs, 'All!'.

Of folded schedules had she many a one,
Which she perused, sighed, tore and gave the flood;
Cracked many a ring of posied gold and bone,   45
Bidding them find their sepulchres in mud;
Found yet moe letters, sadly penned in blood,
With sleided silk, feat and affectedly
Enswathed and sealed to curious secrecy.

These often bathed she in her fluxive eyes,   50
And often kissed, and often gave to tear;
Cried, 'O false blood, thou register of lies,
What unapproved witness dost thou bear!
Ink would have seemed more black and damned here.'
This said, in top of rage the lines she rents,   55
Big discontent so breaking their contents.

A reverend man, that grazed his cattle nigh,
Sometime a blusterer, that the ruffle knew
Of court, of city, and had let go by
The swiftest hours observed as they flew,   60
Towards this afflicted fancy fastly drew,
And, privileged by age, desires to know
In brief the grounds and motives of her woe.

So slides he down upon his grained bat,
And comely distant sits he by her side,   65
When he again desires her, being sat,
Her grievance with his hearing to divide:
If that from him there may be aught applied
Which may her suffering ecstasy assuage,
'Tis promised in the charity of age.   70

'Father,' she says, 'though in me ye behold
The injury of many a blasting hour,
Let it not tell your judgement I am old:
Not age, but sorrow, over me hath power.
I might as yet have been a spreading flower,   75
Fresh to myself, if I had self-applied
Love to myself, and to no love beside.

'But woe is me! Too early I attended
A youthful suit; it was to gain my grace;
O, one by nature's outwards so commended   80
That maidens' eyes stuck over all his face;
Love lacked a dwelling, and made him her place;
And when in his fair parts she did abide
She was new-lodged and newly deified.

'His browny locks did hang in crooked curls,   85
And every light occasion of the wind
Upon his lips their silken parcels hurls;
What's sweet to do, to do will aptly find;
Each eye that saw him did enchant the mind:
For on his visage was in little drawn   90
What largeness thinks in paradise was sawn.

'Small show of man was yet upon his chin;
His phoenix down began but to appear,
Like unshorn velvet, on that termless skin,
Whose bare out-bragged the web it seemed to wear;   95
Yet showed his visage by that cost more dear,
And nice affections wavering stood in doubt
If best were as it was, or best without.

'His qualities were beauteous as his form:
For maiden-tongued he was, and thereof free;
Yet if men moved him, was he such a storm
As oft 'twixt May and April is to see,
When winds breathe sweet, unruly though they be.
His rudeness so with his authorized youth
Did livery falseness in a pride of truth.

'Well could he ride, and often men would say,
"That horse his mettle from his rider takes,
Proud of subjection, noble by the sway,
What rounds, what bounds, what course, what stop
    he makes!"
And controversy hence a question takes,
Whether the horse by him became his deed,
Or he his manage, by th' well-doing steed.

'But quickly on this side the verdict went:
His real habitude gave life and grace
To appertainings and to ornament,
Accomplished in himself, not in his case;
All aids, themselves made fairer by their place,
Came for additions; yet their purposed trim
Pieced not his grace, but were all graced by him.

'So on the tip of his subduing tongue
All kind of arguments and question deep,
All replication prompt, and reason strong,
For his advantage still did wake and sleep,
To make the weeper laugh, the laugher weep:
He had the dialect and different skill,
Catching all passions in his craft of will.

'That he did in the general bosom reign
Of young, of old, and sexes both enchanted
To dwell with him in thoughts, or to remain
In personal duty, following where he haunted;
Consent's bewitched, ere he desire have granted,
And dialogued for him what he would say,
Asked their own wills, and made their wills obey.

'Many there were that did his picture get
To serve their eyes, and in it put their mind,
Like fools, that in th'imagination set
The goodly objects which abroad they find,
Of lands and mansions, theirs in thought assigned,
And labouring in moe pleasures to bestow them
Than the true gouty landlord which doth owe them.

'So many have, that never touched his hand,
Sweetly supposed them mistress of his heart:
My woeful self that did in freedom stand,
And was my own fee-simple, not in part,
What with his art in youth, and youth in art,
Threw my affections in his charmed power,
Reserved the stalk and gave him all my flower.

'Yet did I not, as some, my equals, did,
Demand of him; nor, being desired, yielded,
Finding myself in honour so forbid:
With safest distance I mine honour shielded.
Experience for me many bulwarks builded
Of proofs new-bleeding, which remained the foil
Of this false jewel and his amorous spoil.

'But ah! Who ever shunned by precedent
The destined ill she must herself assay,
Or forced examples 'gainst her own content,
To put the by-passed perils in her way?
Counsel may stop a while what will not stay:
For when we rage, advice is often seen
By blunting us to make our wits more keen.

'Nor gives it satisfaction to our blood
That we must curb it upon others' proof,
To be forebode the sweets that seems so good,
For fear of harms that preach in our behoof:
O appetite, from judgement stand aloof!
The one a palate hath that needs will taste,
Though reason weep and cry, "It is thy last!"

'For further, I could say, "This man's untrue",
And knew the patterns of his foul beguiling;
Heard where his plants in others' orchards grew;
Saw how deceits were gilded in his smiling;
Knew vows were ever brokers to defiling;
Thought characters and words merely but art,
And bastards of his foul adulterate heart.

'And long upon these terms I held my city,
Till thus he 'gan besiege me: "Gentle maid,
Have of my suffering youth some feeling pity
And be not of my holy vows afraid:
That's to ye sworn to none was ever said,
For feasts of love I have been called unto,
Till now, did ne'er invite, nor never woo.

'"All my offences that abroad you see
Are errors of the blood, none of the mind:
Love made them not; with acture they may be
Where neither party is nor true nor kind;
They sought their shame that so their shame did find,
And so much less of shame in me remains,
By how much of me their reproach contains.

'"Among the many that mine eyes have seen,
Not one whose flame my heart so much as warmed,
Or my affection put to th' smallest teen,
Or any of my leisures ever charmed:
Harm have I done to them, but ne'er was harmed;
Kept hearts in liveries, but my own was free,
And reigned commanding in his monarchy.

"'Look here what tributes wounded fancies sent me,
Of pallid pearls and rubies red as blood,
Figuring that they their passions likewise lent me
200   Of grief and blushes, aptly understood,
In bloodless white and the encrimsoned mood,
Effects of terror and dear modesty,
Encamped in hearts, but fighting outwardly.

"'And lo! Behold these talons of their hair,
205   With twisted metal amorously empleached,
I have received from many a several fair,
Their kind acceptance weepingly beseeched,
With th'annexions of fair gems enriched,
And deep-brained sonnets, that did amplify
210   Each stone's dear nature, worth and quality.

"'The diamond? Why, 'twas beautiful and hard,
Whereto his invised properties did tend:
The deep green emerald, in whose fresh regard
Weak sights their sickly radiance do amend;
215   The heaven-hued sapphire and the opal blend
With objects manifold; each several stone
With wit well-blazoned smiled, or made some moan.

"'Lo, all these trophies of affections hot,
Of pensived and subdued desires the tender,
220   Nature hath charged me that I hoard them not,
But yield them up where I myself must render,
That is, to you, my origin and ender:
For these of force must your oblations be;
Since I their altar, you empatron me.

225   "'O then advance of yours that phraseless hand,
Whose white weighs down the airy scale of praise;
Take all these similes to your own command,
Hallowed with sighs that burning lungs did raise:
What me, your minister for you, obeys,
230   Works under you; and to your audit comes
Their distract parcels in combined sums.

"'Lo, this device was sent me from a nun,
Or sister sanctified, of holiest note,
Which late her noble suit in court did shun,
235   Whose rarest havings made the blossoms dote;
For she was sought by spirits of richest coat,
But kept cold distance, and did thence remove
To spend her living in eternal love.

"'But O, my sweet, what labour is't to leave
240   The thing we have not, mast'ring what not strives,
Planing the place which did no form receive,
Playing patient sports in unconstrained gyves;
She that her fame so to herself contrives
The scars of battle 'scapeth by the flight,
245   And makes her absence valiant, not her might.

"'O pardon me, in that my boast is true;
The accident which brought me to her eye
Upon the moment did her force subdue,
And now she would the caged cloister fly,
Religious love put out religion's eye;   250
Not to be tempted would she be immured,
And now to tempt all liberty procured.

"'How mighty then you are, O hear me tell!
The broken bosoms that to me belong
Have emptied all their fountains in my well,   255
And mine I pour your ocean all among:
I strong o'er them, and you o'er me being strong,
Must for your victory us all congest,
As compound love, to physic your cold breast.

"'My parts had power to charm a sacred nun,   260
Who, disciplined, I dieted in grace,
Believed her eyes, when they t'assail begun,
All vows and consecrations giving place.
O most potential love! Vow, bond, nor space,
In thee hath neither sting, knot, nor confine,   265
For thou art all and all things else are thine.

"'When thou impressest, what are precepts worth
Of stale example? When thou wilt inflame,
How coldly those impediments stand forth,
Of wealth, of filial fear, law, kindred, fame?   270
Love's arms are peace, 'gainst rule, 'gainst sense,
    'gainst shame,
And sweetens in the suff'ring pangs it bears
The aloes of all forces, shocks and fears.

"'Now all these hearts that do on mine depend,
Feeling it break, with bleeding groans they pine,   275
And supplicant their sighs to you extend,
To leave the batt'ry that you make 'gainst mine,
Lending soft audience to my sweet design
And credent soul to that strong-bonded oath
That shall prefer and undertake my troth."   280

'This said, his wat'ry eyes he did dismount,
Whose sights till then were levelled on my face;
Each cheek a river running from a fount
With brinish current downward flowed apace.
O how the channel to the stream gave grace,   285
Who glazed with crystal gate the glowing roses
That flame through water which their hue encloses!

'O father, what a hell of witchcraft lies
In the small orb of one particular tear!
But with the inundation of the eyes   290
What rocky heart to water will not wear?
What breast so cold that is not warmed here?
O cleft effect! Cold modesty, hot wrath,
Both fire from hence and chill extincture hath.

295 'For lo, his passion, but an art of craft,
Even there resolved my reason into tears;
There my white stole of chastity I daffed,
Shook off my sober guards and civil fears,
Appeared to him as he to me appears,
300 All melting, though our drops this diff'rence bore:
His poisoned me, and mine did him restore.

'In him a plenitude of subtle matter,
Applied to cautels, all strange forms receives,
Of burning blushes, or of weeping water,
305 Or swooning paleness; and he takes and leaves
In either's, aptness, as it best deceives,
To blush at speeches rank, to weep at woes,
Or to turn white and swoon at tragic shows.

'That not a heart which in his level came
310 Could 'scape the hail of his all-hurting aim,
Showing fair nature is both kind and tame;
And veiled in them, did win whom he would maim.
Against the thing he sought he would exclaim;
When he most burned in heart-wished luxury
315 He preached pure maid, and praised cold chastity.

'Thus, merely with the garment of a grace,
The naked and concealed fiend he covered,
That th'unexperient gave the tempter place
Which, like a cherubin, above them hovered.
Who, young and simple, would not be so lovered? 320
Ay me, I fell, and yet do question make
What I should do again for such a sake.

'O, that infected moisture of his eye!
O, that false fire which in his cheek so glowed!
O, that forced thunder from his heart did fly! 325
O, that sad breath his spongy lungs bestowed!
O, all that borrowed motion, seeming owed,
Would yet again betray the fore-betrayed,
And new pervert a reconciled maid.'

Venus and Adonis; The Rape of Lucrece; The Passionate Pilgrim; 'The Phoenix and Turtle'

The first published works to name William Shakespeare as their author were two long narrative poems. *Venus and Adonis* was entered in the Stationers' Register in April 1593, a few days before its author's twenty-ninth birthday, *Lucrece* (or *The Rape of Lucrece*), a year later. Their printer, Richard Field, was, like Shakespeare, a native of Stratford-upon-Avon. Both poems were dedicated to Henry Wriothesley (probably pronounced 'Ris-ly', 'Rise-ly' or 'Rose-ly'), Earl of Southampton, a prominent member of the circle that surrounded Robert Devereux, second Earl of Essex, the rising star of the 1590s. The dedicatory epistle to *Venus and Adonis* describes it as 'the first heir of my invention' and vows to Southampton that if he likes it, it will be followed by 'some graver labour' as a more fitting gift. That 'graver labour', *Lucrece*, had gone through nine editions by 1655: *Venus and Adonis* – on this evidence the most popular of all Shakespeare's works in his own time – went through sixteen editions by 1640. A marginal note by Gabriel Harvey, made no later than February 1601, records that while *Venus and Adonis* delights 'The younger sort', *Lucrece* and *Hamlet* 'have it in them, to please the wiser sort'.

The poems complement each other. *Venus and Adonis* rewrites the classical myth, best known from Ovid's version in Book 10 of his *Metamorphoses*, turning it into a contest between Venus' passion for a sulky, adolescent Adonis and his greater passion for hunting the boar (which leads to his death). The poem has been interpreted as an erotic celebration of love, a satire on the indignities of sex or a platonic myth. What can safely be claimed is that it offers, in the predicament of Venus, a sharply defined embodiment of the urgency, perversity and contrariety of love – 'She's Love, she loves, and yet she is not loved' (610) – as well as justifying her prophecy that love will always be attended by disaster and that 'They that love best, their loves shall not enjoy' (1164).

Lucrece handles a crucial episode from early Roman history, in which the rape of the chaste wife of the Roman general Collatinus by the king's son, Sextus Tarquinius, and her subsequent suicide became the flint to fire the republican rebellion which expelled the Tarquin kings from Rome. This story, known to Shakespeare from Chaucer, Ovid and Livy, provided him with his first serious tragic theme, and his poem is replete with ideas and images that were to remain in his imagination for the rest of his career. Tarquin is his first self-destructive self-deceiver, whose lust destroys him as surely as it destroys his victim. The lengthy complaint of Lucrece is written in a familiar tradition of poems of female lamentation. After it, she likens her situation to the siege and fall of Troy, as represented in a picture, in Shakespeare's first extended treatment of that most familiar *topos* of tragic deceit, loss and suffering. The poem has provoked new interest and has found a new readership among modern feminists.

William Jaggard's unauthorized anthology *The Passionate Pilgrim*, 'By W. Shakespeare' (1599), contains only five poems which are certainly by him (three from *Love's Labour's Lost* (3, 5 and 16) and *Sonnets* 138 and 144 (1 and 2)). Shakespeare is known to have been displeased by the publication, as another author, Thomas Heywood (himself misappropriated by Jaggard in a later edition), has left on record.

'The Phoenix and Turtle' is Shakespeare's most enigmatic work. It was published in a book entitled *Love's Martyr* (1601), compiled and largely written by Robert Chester, who also commissioned contributions from other poets. Shakespeare's poem relates to the subject-matter of Chester's book and may call to mind the 'metaphysical' manner of John Donne, but it also belongs in a long tradition of bird poems whose most famous English examples include Chaucer's *The Parliament of Fowls* and the closing songs of Shakespeare's own *Love's Labour's Lost*.

The Arden text is based on the first editions of *Venus and Adonis* (1593), *The Rape of Lucrece* (1594), *The Passionate Pilgrim* (1599) and Robert Chester's *Love's Martyr* (1601).

Venus and Adonis

Vilia miretur vulgus; mihi flavus Apollo
Pocula Castalia plena ministret aqua.

To the Right Honourable Henry Wriothesley,
Earl of Southampton and Baron of Titchfield

Right Honourable

I know not how I shall offend in dedicating my unpolished
5   lines to your lordship, nor how the world will censure me
for choosing so strong a prop to support so weak a burden:
only if your honour seem but pleased, I account myself
highly praised, and vow to take advantage of all idle hours,
till I have honoured you with some graver labour. But if
10 the first heir of my invention prove deformed, I shall be
sorry it had so noble a godfather, and never after ear so
barren a land, for fear it yield me still so bad a harvest. I
leave it to your honourable survey, and your honour to
your heart's content; which I wish may always answer
15 your own wish and the world's hopeful expectation.

> Your honour's in all duty,
> William Shakespeare

Even as the sun with purple-coloured face
Had ta'en his last leave of the weeping morn,
Rose-cheeked Adonis hied him to the chase;
Hunting he loved, but love he laughed to scorn.
5   Sick-thoughted Venus makes amain unto him,
     And like a bold-faced suitor 'gins to woo him.

'Thrice fairer than myself,' thus she began,
'The field's chief flower, sweet above compare,
Stain to all nymphs, more lovely than a man,
10 More white and red than doves or roses are;
     Nature that made thee, with herself at strife,
     Saith that the world hath ending with thy life.

'Vouchsafe, thou wonder, to alight thy steed,
And rein his proud head to the saddle-bow;
15 If thou wilt deign this favour, for thy meed
A thousand honey secrets shalt thou know.
     Here come and sit, where never serpent hisses,
     And being set, I'll smother thee with kisses;

'And yet not cloy thy lips with loathed satiety,
20 But rather famish them amid their plenty,
Making them red and pale with fresh variety.
Ten kisses short as one, one long as twenty:
     A summer's day will seem an hour but short,
     Being wasted in such time-beguiling sport.'

25 With this she seizeth on his sweating palm,
The precedent of pith and livelihood,
And trembling in her passion, calls it balm,
Earth's sovereign salve to do a goddess good.
     Being so enraged, desire doth lend her force
30   Courageously to pluck him from his horse.

Over one arm the lusty courser's rein,
Under her other was the tender boy,
Who blushed and pouted in a dull disdain,
With leaden appetite, unapt to toy;
     She red and hot as coals of glowing fire,   35
     He red for shame, but frosty in desire.

The studded bridle on a ragged bough
Nimbly she fastens – O, how quick is love!
The steed is stalled up, and even now
To tie the rider she begins to prove: 40
     Backward she pushed him, as she would be
        thrust,
     And governed him in strength, though not in
        lust.

So soon was she along as he was down,
Each leaning on their elbows and their hips;
Now doth she stroke his cheek, now doth he frown,   45
And 'gins to chide, but soon she stops his lips,
     And kissing speaks, with lustful language broken,
     'If thou wilt chide, thy lips shall never open.'

He burns with bashful shame: she with her tears
Doth quench the maiden burning of his cheeks;   50
Then with her windy sighs and golden hairs
To fan and blow them dry again she seeks.
     He saith she is immodest, blames her miss;
     What follows more she murders with a kiss.

Even as an empty eagle, sharp by fast,   55
Tires with her beak on feathers, flesh and bone,
Shaking her wings, devouring all in haste,
Till either gorge be stuffed or prey be gone,
     Even so she kissed his brow, his cheek, his chin,
     And where she ends she doth anew begin.   60

Forced to content, but never to obey,
Panting he lies and breatheth in her face;
She feedeth on the steam as on a prey,
And calls it heavenly moisture, air of grace,
     Wishing her cheeks were gardens full of flowers,   65
     So they were dewed with such distilling showers.

Look how a bird lies tangled in a net,
So fastened in her arms Adonis lies;
Pure shame and awed resistance made him fret,
Which bred more beauty in his angry eyes.   70
     Rain added to a river that is rank
     Perforce will force it overflow the bank.

Still she entreats, and prettily entreats,
For to a pretty ear she tunes her tale.
Still is he sullen, still he lours and frets,   75
'Twixt crimson shame and anger ashy pale.
     Being red, she loves him best, and being white,
     Her best is bettered with a more delight.

Look how he can, she cannot choose but love;
80 And by her fair immortal hand she swears
From his soft bosom never to remove
Till he take truce with her contending tears,
    Which long have rained, making her cheeks all wet;
    And one sweet kiss shall pay this countless debt.

85 Upon this promise did he raise his chin,
Like a dive-dapper peering through a wave,
Who, being looked on, ducks as quickly in;
So offers he to give what she did crave.
    But when her lips were ready for his pay,
90   He winks, and turns his lips another way.

Never did passenger in summer's heat
More thirst for drink than she for this good turn.
Her help she sees, but help she cannot get;
She bathes in water, yet her fire must burn.
95   'O, pity,' 'gan she cry, 'flint-hearted boy!
    'Tis but a kiss I beg; why art thou coy?

'I have been wooed, as I entreat thee now,
Even by the stern and direful god of war,
Whose sinewy neck in battle ne'er did bow,
100 Who conquers where he comes in every jar;
    Yet hath he been my captive and my slave,
    And begged for that which thou unasked shalt have.

'Over my altars hath he hung his lance,
His battered shield, his uncontrolled crest,
105 And for my sake hath learned to sport and dance,
To toy, to wanton, dally, smile and jest,
    Scorning his churlish drum and ensign red,
    Making my arms his field, his tent my bed.

'Thus he that overruled I overswayed,
110 Leading him prisoner in a red-rose chain;
Strong-tempered steel his stronger strength obeyed,
Yet was he servile to my coy disdain.
    O, be not proud, nor brag not of thy might,
    For mast'ring her that foiled the god of fight!

115 'Touch but my lips with those fair lips of thine –
Though mine be not so fair, yet are they red –
The kiss shall be thine own as well as mine.
What seest thou in the ground? Hold up thy head.
    Look in mine eyeballs, there thy beauty lies;
120   Then why not lips on lips, since eyes in eyes?

'Art thou ashamed to kiss? Then wink again,
And I will wink; so shall the day seem night.
Love keeps his revels where there are but twain;
Be bold to play, our sport is not in sight.
125   These blue-veined violets whereon we lean
    Never can blab, nor know not what we mean.

'The tender spring upon thy tempting lip
Shows thee unripe; yet mayst thou well be tasted.
Make use of time, let not advantage slip;
Beauty within itself should not be wasted. 130
    Fair flowers that are not gathered in their prime
    Rot and consume themselves in little time.

'Were I hard-favoured, foul, or wrinkled-old,
Ill-nurtured, crooked, churlish, harsh in voice,
O'erworn, despised, rheumatic and cold, 135
Thick-sighted, barren, lean and lacking juice,
    Then mightst thou pause, for then I were not for thee;
    But having no defects, why dost abhor me?

'Thou canst not see one wrinkle in my brow,
Mine eyes are grey and bright and quick in turning, 140
My beauty as the spring doth yearly grow,
My flesh is soft and plump, my marrow burning;
    My smooth moist hand, were it with thy hand felt,
    Would in thy palm dissolve, or seem to melt.

'Bid me discourse, I will enchant thine ear, 145
Or, like a fairy, trip upon the green,
Or, like a nymph, with long dishevelled hair,
Dance on the sands, and yet no footing seen.
    Love is a spirit all compact of fire,
    Not gross to sink, but light, and will aspire. 150

'Witness this primrose bank whereon I lie:
These forceless flowers like sturdy trees support me;
Two strengthless doves will draw me through the sky
From morn till night, even where I list to sport me.
    Is love so light, sweet boy, and may it be 155
    That thou should think it heavy unto thee?

'Is thine own heart to thine own face affected?
Can thy right hand seize love upon thy left?
Then woo thyself, be of thyself rejected,
Steal thine own freedom, and complain on theft. 160
    Narcissus so himself himself forsook,
    And died to kiss his shadow in the brook.

'Torches are made to light, jewels to wear,
Dainties to taste, fresh beauty for the use,
Herbs for their smell, and sappy plants to bear: 165
Things growing to themselves are growth's abuse.
    Seeds spring from seeds and beauty breedeth beauty;
    Thou wast begot: to get it is thy duty.

'Upon the earth's increase why shouldst thou feed,
Unless the earth with thy increase be fed? 170
By law of nature thou art bound to breed,
That thine may live when thou thyself art dead;
    And so in spite of death thou dost survive,
    In that thy likeness still is left alive.'

175 By this the love-sick queen began to sweat,
For where they lay the shadow had forsook them,
And Titan, tired in the midday heat,
With burning eye did hotly overlook them,
   Wishing Adonis had his team to guide,
180   So he were like him and by Venus' side.

And now Adonis, with a lazy sprite,
And with a heavy, dark, disliking eye,
His louring brows o'erwhelming his fair sight
Like misty vapours when they blot the sky,
185   Souring his cheeks, cries, 'Fie, no more of love!
   The sun doth burn my face; I must remove.'

'Ay me,' quoth Venus, 'young, and so unkind?
What bare excuses mak'st thou to be gone!
I'll sigh celestial breath, whose gentle wind
190 Shall cool the heat of this descending sun.
   I'll make a shadow for thee of my hairs;
   If they burn too, I'll quench them with my tears.

'The sun that shines from heaven shines but warm,
And lo, I lie between that sun and thee;
195 The heat I have from thence doth little harm,
Thine eye darts forth the fire that burneth me;
   And were I not immortal, life were done
   Between this heavenly and earthly sun.

'Art thou obdurate, flinty, hard as steel?
200 Nay, more than flint, for stone at rain relenteth.
Art thou a woman's son, and canst not feel
What 'tis to love, how want of love tormenteth?
   O, had thy mother borne so hard a mind,
   She had not brought forth thee, but died unkind!

205 'What am I, that thou shouldst contemn me this?
Or what great danger dwells upon my suit?
What were thy lips the worse for one poor kiss?
Speak, fair, but speak fair words, or else be mute.
   Give me one kiss, I'll give it thee again,
210   And one for int'rest, if thou wilt have twain.

'Fie, lifeless picture, cold and senseless stone,
Well-painted idol, image dull and dead,
Statue contenting but the eye alone,
Thing like a man, but of no woman bred!
215   Thou art no man, though of a man's complexion,
   For men will kiss even by their own direction.'

This said, impatience chokes her pleading tongue
And swelling passion doth provoke a pause;
Red cheeks and fiery eyes blaze forth her wrong;
220 Being judge in love, she cannot right her cause.
   And now she weeps, and now she fain would speak,
   And now her sobs do her intendments break.

Sometime she shakes her head, and then his hand,
Now gazeth she on him, now on the ground.
Sometime her arms enfold him like a band: 225
She would, he will not in her arms be bound.
   And when from thence he struggles to be gone,
   She locks her lily fingers one in one.

'Fondling,' she saith, 'since I have hemmed thee here
Within the circuit of this ivory pale, 230
I'll be a park, and thou shalt be my deer;
Feed where thou wilt, on mountain or in dale:
   Graze on my lips, and if those hills be dry,
   Stray lower, where the pleasant fountains lie.

'Within this limit is relief enough, 235
Sweet bottom-grass and high delightful plain,
Round rising hillocks, brakes obscure and rough,
To shelter thee from tempest and from rain:
   Then be my deer, since I am such a park;
   No dog shall rouse thee, though a thousand bark.' 240

At this Adonis smiles as in disdain,
That in each cheek appears a pretty dimple:
Love made those hollows, if himself were slain
He might be buried in a tomb so simple;
   Foreknowing well, if there he came to lie, 245
   Why, there love lived, and there he could not die.

These lovely caves, these round enchanting pits,
Opened their mouths to swallow Venus' liking.
Being mad before, how doth she now for wits?
Struck dead at first, what needs a second striking? 250
   Poor queen of love, in thine own law forlorn,
   To love a cheek that smiles at thee in scorn!

Now which way shall she turn? What shall she say?
Her words are done, her woes the more increasing;
The time is spent, her object will away, 255
And from her twining arms doth urge releasing.
   'Pity,' she cries, 'some favour, some remorse!'
   Away he springs, and hasteth to his horse.

But lo, from forth a copse that neighbours by,
A breeding jennet, lusty, young and proud, 260
Adonis' trampling courser doth espy;
And forth she rushes, snorts and neighs aloud.
   The strong-necked steed, being tied unto a tree,
   Breaketh his rein, and to her straight goes he.

Imperiously he leaps, he neighs, he bounds, 265
And now his woven girths he breaks asunder;
The bearing earth with his hard hoof he wounds,
Whose hollow womb resounds like heaven's thunder;
   The iron bit he crusheth 'tween his teeth,
   Controlling what he was controlled with. 270

His ears up-pricked, his braided hanging mane
Upon his compassed crest now stand on end;
His nostrils drink the air, and forth again,
As from a furnace, vapours doth he send;
275   His eye which scornfully glisters like fire
    Shows his hot courage and his high desire.

Sometime he trots, as if he told the steps,
With gentle majesty and modest pride;
Anon he rears upright, curvets and leaps,
280 As who should say, 'Lo, thus my strength is tried,
    And this I do to captivate the eye
    Of the fair breeder that is standing by.'

What recketh he his rider's angry stir,
His flatt'ring 'Holla' or his 'Stand, I say'?
285 What cares he now for curb or pricking spur,
For rich caparisons or trappings gay?
    He sees his love, and nothing else he sees,
    For nothing else with his proud sight agrees.

Look when a painter would surpass the life
290 In limning out a well-proportioned steed,
His art with nature's workmanship at strife,
As if the dead the living should exceed:
    So did this horse excel a common one
    In shape, in courage, colour, pace and bone.

295 Round-hoofed, short-jointed, fetlocks shag and long,
Broad breast, full eye, small head and nostril wide,
High crest, short ears, straight legs and passing strong,
Thin mane, thick tail, broad buttock, tender hide:
    Look what a horse should have he did not lack,
300   Save a proud rider on so proud a back.

Sometime he scuds far off and there he stares;
Anon he starts at stirring of a feather.
To bid the wind a base he now prepares,
And whe'er he run or fly they know not whether;
305   For through his mane and tail the high wind sings,
    Fanning the hairs, who wave like feathered wings.

He looks upon his love and neighs unto her,
She answers him as if she knew his mind;
Being proud, as females are, to see him woo her,
310 She puts on outward strangeness, seems unkind,
    Spurns at his love and scorns the heat he feels,
    Beating his kind embracements with her heels.

Then, like a melancholy malcontent,
He vails his tail that, like a falling plume,
315 Cool shadow to his melting buttock lent;
He stamps, and bites the poor flies in his fume.
    His love, perceiving how he was enraged,
    Grew kinder, and his fury was assuaged.

His testy master goeth about to take him,
When lo, the unbacked breeder, full of fear,   320
Jealous of catching, swiftly doth forsake him,
With her the horse, and left Adonis there.
    As they were mad, unto the wood they hie them,
    Outstripping crows that strive to overfly them.

All swoln with chafing, down Adonis sits,   325
Banning his boist'rous and unruly beast.
And now the happy season once more fits
That love-sick love by pleading may be blest;
    For lovers say the heart hath treble wrong
    When it is barred the aidance of the tongue.   330

An oven that is stopped, or river stayed,
Burneth more hotly, swelleth with more rage;
So of concealed sorrow may be said,
Free vent of words love's fire doth assuage.
    But when the heart's attorney once is mute,   335
    The client breaks, as desperate in his suit.

He sees her coming, and begins to glow,
Even as a dying coal revives with wind,
And with his bonnet hides his angry brow,
Looks on the dull earth with disturbed mind,   340
    Taking no notice that she is so nigh,
    For all askance he holds her in his eye.

O, what a sight it was, wistly to view
How she came stealing to the wayward boy!
To note the fighting conflict of her hue,   345
How white and red each other did destroy!
    But now her cheek was pale, and by and by
    It flashed forth fire, as lightning from the sky.

Now was she just before him as he sat,
And like a lowly lover down she kneels;   350
With one fair hand she heaveth up his hat,
Her other tender hand his fair cheek feels:
    His tend'rer cheek receives her soft hand's print,
    As apt as new-fall'n snow takes any dint.

O, what a war of looks was then between them!   355
Her eyes petitioners to his eyes suing,
His eyes saw her eyes as they had not seen them;
Her eyes wooed still, his eyes disdained the wooing;
    And all this dumb play had his acts made plain
    With tears which chorus-like her eyes did rain.   360

Full gently now she takes him by the hand,
A lily prisoned in a gaol of snow,
Or ivory in an alabaster band:
So white a friend engirts so white a foe.
    This beauteous combat, wilful and unwilling,   365
    Showed like two silver doves that sit a-billing.

Once more the engine of her thoughts began:
'O fairest mover on this mortal round,
Would thou wert as I am, and I a man,
370   My heart all whole as thine, thy heart my wound;
    For one sweet look thy help I would assure thee,
    Though nothing but my body's bane would cure
      thee!'

'Give me my hand,' saith he; 'why dost thou feel it?'
'Give me my heart,' saith she, 'and thou shalt have it:
375 O, give it me, lest thy hard heart do steel it,
  And being steeled, soft sighs can never grave it;
    Then love's deep groans I never shall regard,
    Because Adonis' heart hath made mine hard.'

'For shame,' he cries, 'let go, and let me go;
380 My day's delight is past, my horse is gone,
And 'tis your fault I am bereft him so.
I pray you hence, and leave me here alone;
    For all my mind, my thought, my busy care,
    Is how to get my palfrey from the mare.'

385 Thus she replies: 'Thy palfrey, as he should,
Welcomes the warm approach of sweet desire.
Affection is a coal that must be cooled;
Else, suffered, it will set the heart on fire.
    The sea hath bounds, but deep desire hath none;
390   Therefore no marvel though thy horse be gone.

'How like a jade he stood, tied to the tree,
Servilely mastered with a leathern rein!
But when he saw his love, his youth's fair fee,
He held such petty bondage in disdain,
395   Throwing the base thong from his bending crest,
    Enfranchising his mouth, his back, his breast.

'Who sees his true-love in her naked bed,
Teaching the sheets a whiter hue than white,
But, when his glutton eye so full hath fed,
400 His other agents aim at like delight?
    Who is so faint that dares not be so bold
    To touch the fire, the weather being cold?

'Let me excuse thy courser, gentle boy;
And learn of him, I heartily beseech thee,
405 To take advantage on presented joy.
Though I were dumb, yet his proceedings teach
    thee.
    O, learn to love; the lesson is but plain,
    And once made perfect, never lost again.'

'I know not love,' quoth he, 'nor will not know it,
410 Unless it be a boar, and then I chase it.
'Tis much to borrow, and I will not owe it;
My love to love is love but to disgrace it,
    For I have heard it is a life in death,
    That laughs and weeps, and all but with a breath.

'Who wears a garment shapeless and unfinished?   415
Who plucks the bud before one leaf put forth?
If springing things be any jot diminished,
They wither in their prime, prove nothing worth.
    The colt that's backed and burdened being young
    Loseth his pride, and never waxeth strong.   420

'You hurt my hand with wringing; let us part,
And leave this idle theme, this bootless chat.
Remove your siege from my unyielding heart;
To love's alarms it will not ope the gate.
    Dismiss your vows, your feigned tears, your flatt'ry,   425
    For where a heart is hard they make no batt'ry.'

'What, canst thou talk?' quoth she, 'Hast thou a tongue?
O, would thou hadst not, or I had no hearing!
Thy mermaid's voice hath done me double wrong;
I had my load before, now pressed with bearing: 430
    Melodious discord, heavenly tune harsh sounding,
    Ears' deep sweet music, and heart's deep sore
      wounding.

'Had I no eyes but ears, my ears would love
That inward beauty and invisible;
Or were I deaf, thy outward parts would move   435
Each part in me that were but sensible.
    Though neither eyes nor ears, to hear nor see,
    Yet should I be in love by touching thee.

'Say that the sense of feeling were bereft me,
And that I could not see, nor hear, nor touch,   440
And nothing but the very smell were left me,
Yet would my love to thee be still as much;
    For from the stillatory of thy face excelling
    Comes breath perfumed, that breedeth love by
      smelling.

'But O, what banquet wert thou to the taste,   445
Being nurse and feeder of the other four!
Would they not wish the feast might ever last,
And bid Suspicion double-lock the door,
    Lest Jealousy, that sour unwelcome guest,
    Should by his stealing in disturb the feast?'   450

Once more the ruby-coloured portal opened,
Which to his speech did honey passage yield;
Like a red morn, that ever yet betokened
Wrack to the seaman, tempest to the field,
    Sorrow to shepherds, woe unto the birds,   455
    Gusts and foul flaws to herdmen and to herds.

This ill presage advisedly she marketh:
Even as the wind is hushed before it raineth,
Or as the wolf doth grin before he barketh,
Or as the berry breaks before it staineth,   460
    Or like the deadly bullet of a gun,
    His meaning struck her ere his words begun.

And at his look she flatly falleth down,
For looks kill love, and love by looks reviveth:
465 A smile recures the wounding of a frown;
But blessed bankrupt that by loss so thriveth!
　　The silly boy, believing she is dead,
　　Claps her pale cheek, till clapping makes it red;

And all amazed brake off his late intent,
470 For sharply he did think to reprehend her,
Which cunning love did wittily prevent:
Fair fall the wit that can so well defend her!
　　For on the grass she lies as she were slain,
　　Till his breath breatheth life in her again.

475 He wrings her nose, he strikes her on the cheeks,
He bends her fingers, holds her pulses hard,
He chafes her lips: a thousand ways he seeks
To mend the hurt that his unkindness marred.
　　He kisses her, and she by her good will
480 　　Will never rise, so he will kiss her still.

The night of sorrow now is turned to day:
Her two blue windows faintly she upheaveth,
Like the fair sun, when in his fresh array
He cheers the morn and all the earth relieveth;
485 　　And as the bright sun glorifies the sky,
　　So is her face illumined with her eye,

Whose beams upon his hairless face are fixed,
As if from thence they borrowed all their shine.
Were never four such lamps together mixed,
490 Had not his clouded with his brow's repine;
　　But hers, which through the crystal tears gave
　　　　light,
　　Shone like the moon in water seen by night.

'O, where am I?' quoth she, 'In earth or heaven,
Or in the ocean drenched, or in the fire?
495 What hour is this? Or morn or weary even?
Do I delight to die, or life desire?
　　But now I lived, and life was death's annoy;
　　But now I died, and death was lively joy.

'O, thou didst kill me: kill me once again!
500 Thy eyes' shrewd tutor, that hard heart of thine,
Hath taught them scornful tricks, and such disdain
That they have murdered this poor heart of mine;
　　And these mine eyes, true leaders to their queen,
　　But for thy piteous lips no more had seen.

505 'Long may they kiss each other, for this cure!
O, never let their crimson liveries wear!
And as they last, their verdure still endure,
To drive infection from the dangerous year,
　　That the star-gazers, having writ on death,
510 　　May say, the plague is banished by thy breath.

'Pure lips, sweet seals in my soft lips imprinted,
What bargains may I make, still to be sealing?
To sell myself I can be well contented,
So thou wilt buy, and pay, and use good dealing;
　　Which purchase if thou make, for fear of slips   515
　　Set thy seal-manual on my wax-red lips.

'A thousand kisses buys my heart from me;
And pay them at thy leisure, one by one.
What is ten hundred touches unto thee?
Are they not quickly told and quickly gone?   520
　　Say for non-payment that the debt should double,
　　Is twenty hundred kisses such a trouble?'

'Fair queen,' quoth he, 'if any love you owe me,
Measure my strangeness with my unripe years.
Before I know myself, seek not to know me;   525
No fisher but the ungrown fry forbears.
　　The mellow plum doth fall, the green sticks fast,
　　Or being early plucked is sour to taste.

'Look, the world's comforter with weary gait
His day's hot task hath ended in the west.   530
The owl, night's herald, shrieks: 'tis very late.
The sheep are gone to fold, birds to their nest,
　　And coal-black clouds that shadow heaven's light
　　Do summon us to part and bid good-night.

'Now let me say good-night, and so say you;   535
If you will say so, you shall have a kiss.'
'Good-night', quoth she, and ere he says adieu,
The honey fee of parting tendered is:
　　Her arms do lend his neck a sweet embrace;
　　Incorporate then they seem: face grows to face.   540

Till breathless he disjoined, and backward drew
The heavenly moisture, that sweet coral mouth,
Whose precious taste her thirsty lips well knew,
Whereon they surfeit, yet complain on drouth.
　　He with her plenty pressed, she faint with
　　　　dearth,   545
　　Their lips together glued, fall to the earth.

Now quick desire hath caught the yielding prey,
And glutton-like she feeds, yet never filleth.
Her lips are conquerors, his lips obey,
Paying what ransom the insulter willeth;   550
　　Whose vulture thought doth pitch the price so high
　　That she will draw his lips' rich treasure dry.

And having felt the sweetness of the spoil,
With blindfold fury she begins to forage;
Her face doth reek and smoke, her blood doth boil,   555
And careless lust stirs up a desperate courage,
　　Planting oblivion, beating reason back,
　　Forgetting shame's pure blush and honour's wrack.

Hot, faint and weary, with her hard embracing,
Like a wild bird being tamed with too much handling,
Or as the fleet-foot roe that's tired with chasing,
Or like the froward infant stilled with dandling,
 He now obeys, and now no more resisteth,
 While she takes all she can, not all she listeth.

What wax so frozen but dissolves with temp'ring,
And yields at last to every light impression?
Things out of hope are compassed oft with vent'ring,
Chiefly in love, whose leave exceeds commission:
 Affection faints not like a pale-faced coward,
 But then woos best when most his choice is froward.

When he did frown, O, had she then gave over,
Such nectar from his lips she had not sucked.
Foul words and frowns must not repel a lover:
What though the rose have prickles? Yet 'tis plucked.
 Were beauty under twenty locks kept fast,
 Yet love breaks through, and picks them all at last.

For pity now she can no more detain him;
The poor fool prays her that he may depart.
She is resolved no longer to restrain him,
Bids him farewell, and look well to her heart,
 The which by Cupid's bow she doth protest
 He carries thence encaged in his breast.

'Sweet boy,' she says, 'this night I'll waste in sorrow,
For my sick heart commands mine eyes to watch.
Tell me, love's master, shall we meet tomorrow?
Say, shall we? Shall we? Wilt thou make the match?'
 He tells her, no; tomorrow he intends
 To hunt the boar with certain of his friends.

'The boar!' quoth she, whereat a sudden pale,
Like lawn being spread upon the blushing rose,
Usurps her cheek; she trembles at his tale,
And on his neck her yoking arms she throws.
 She sinketh down, still hanging by his neck,
 He on her belly falls, she on her back.

Now is she in the very lists of love,
Her champion mounted for the hot encounter.
All is imaginary she doth prove:
He will not manage her, although he mount her;
 That worse than Tantalus' is her annoy,
 To clip Elysium, and to lack her joy.

Even so poor birds, deceived with painted grapes,
Do surfeit by the eye and pine the maw;
Even so she languisheth in her mishaps,
As those poor birds that helpless berries saw.
 The warm effects which she in him finds missing
 She seeks to kindle with continual kissing.

But all in vain, good queen, it will not be.
She hath assayed as much as may be proved;
Her pleading hath deserved a greater fee;
She's Love, she loves, and yet she is not loved.
 'Fie, fie,' he says, 'you crush me, let me go;
 You have no reason to withhold me so.'

'Thou hadst been gone,' quoth she, 'sweet boy, ere this,
But that thou told'st me thou wouldst hunt the boar.
O, be advised: thou knowst not what it is
With javelin's point a churlish swine to gore,
 Whose tushes never sheathed he whetteth still,
 Like to a mortal butcher bent to kill.

'On his bow-back he hath a battle set
Of bristly pikes that ever threat his foes;
His eyes like glow-worms shine when he doth fret;
His snout digs sepulchres where'er he goes:
 Being moved, he strikes whate'er is in his way,
 And whom he strikes his crooked tushes slay.

'His brawny sides, with hairy bristles armed,
Are better proof than thy spear's point can enter.
His short thick neck cannot be easily harmed:
Being ireful, on the lion he will venture.
 The thorny brambles and embracing bushes,
 As fearful of him, part; through whom he rushes.

'Alas, he naught esteems that face of thine,
To which love's eyes pays tributary gazes;
Nor thy soft hands, sweet lips and crystal eyne,
Whose full perfection all the world amazes;
 But having thee at vantage – wondrous dread! –
 Would root these beauties as he roots the mead.

'O, let him keep his loathsome cabin still;
Beauty hath naught to do with such foul fiends.
Come not within his danger by thy will;
They that thrive well take counsel of their friends.
 When thou didst name the boar, not to dissemble,
 I feared thy fortune, and my joints did tremble.

'Didst thou not mark my face? Was it not white?
Sawest thou not signs of fear lurk in mine eye?
Grew I not faint, and fell I not down right?
Within my bosom, whereon thou dost lie,
 My boding heart pants, beats, and takes no rest,
 But like an earthquake shakes thee on my breast.

'For where Love reigns, disturbing Jealousy
Doth call himself Affection's sentinel;
Gives false alarms, suggesteth mutiny,
And in a peaceful hour doth cry, "Kill, kill!"
 Distemp'ring gentle Love in his desire,
 As air and water do abate the fire.

'This sour informer, this bate-breeding spy,   655
This canker that eats up Love's tender spring,
This carry-tale, dissentious Jealousy,
That sometime true news, sometime false doth bring,
     Knocks at my heart and whispers in mine ear
     That if I love thee, I thy death should fear.   660

'And more than so, presenteth to mine eye
The picture of an angry chafing boar,
Under whose sharp fangs on his back doth lie
An image like thyself, all stained with gore;
     Whose blood upon the fresh flowers being shed   665
     Doth make them droop with grief and hang the head.

'What should I do, seeing thee so indeed,
That tremble at th'imagination?
The thought of it doth make my faint heart bleed,
And fear doth teach it divination: 670
     I prophesy thy death, my living sorrow,
     If thou encounter with the boar tomorrow.

'But if thou needs wilt hunt, be ruled by me:
Uncouple at the timorous flying hare,
Or at the fox which lives by subtlety,   675
Or at the roe which no encounter dare.
     Pursue these fearful creatures o'er the downs,
     And on thy well-breathed horse keep with thy hounds.

'And when thou hast on foot the purblind hare,
Mark the poor wretch, to overshoot his troubles,   680
How he outruns the wind, and with what care
He cranks and crosses with a thousand doubles.
     The many musits through the which he goes
     Are like a labyrinth to amaze his foes.

'Sometime he runs among a flock of sheep,   685
To make the cunning hounds mistake their smell,
And sometime where earth-delving conies keep,
To stop the loud pursuers in their yell;
     And sometime sorteth with a herd of deer:
     Danger deviseth shifts, wit waits on fear.   690

'For there his smell with others being mingled,
The hot scent-snuffing hounds are driven to doubt,
Ceasing their clamorous cry till they have singled
With much ado the cold fault cleanly out.
     Then do they spend their mouths; Echo replies,   695
     As if another chase were in the skies.

'By this, poor Wat, far off upon a hill,
Stands on his hinder legs with list'ning ear,
To hearken if his foes pursue him still.
Anon their loud alarums he doth hear;   700
     And now his grief may be compared well
     To one sore sick that hears the passing-bell.

'Then shalt thou see the dew-bedabbled wretch
Turn, and return, indenting with the way.
Each envious briar his weary legs do scratch,   705
Each shadow makes him stop, each murmur stay:
     For misery is trodden on by many,
     And being low never relieved by any.

'Lie quietly, and hear a little more;
Nay, do not struggle, for thou shalt not rise.   710
To make thee hate the hunting of the boar,
Unlike myself thou hear'st me moralize,
     Applying this to that, and so to so,
     For love can comment upon every woe.

'Where did I leave?' 'No matter where,' quoth he,   715
'Leave me, and then the story aptly ends.
The night is spent.' 'Why, what of that?' quoth she.
'I am', quoth he, 'expected of my friends;
     And now 'tis dark, and going I shall fall.'
     'In night', quoth she, 'desire sees best of all.   720

'But if thou fall, O, then imagine this:
The earth, in love with thee, thy footing trips,
And all is but to rob thee of a kiss.
Rich preys make true men thieves; so do thy lips
     Make modest Dian cloudy and forlorn,   725
     Lest she should steal a kiss and die forsworn.

'Now of this dark night I perceive the reason:
Cynthia for shame obscures her silver shine
Till forging Nature be condemned of treason
For stealing moulds from heaven that were divine;   730
     Wherein she framed thee in high heaven's despite,
     To shame the sun by day and her by night.

'And therefore hath she bribed the Destinies
To cross the curious workmanship of nature,
To mingle beauty with infirmities,   735
And pure perfection with impure defeature,
     Making it subject to the tyranny
     Of mad mischances and much misery;

'As burning fevers, agues pale and faint,
Life-poisoning pestilence and frenzies wood,   740
The marrow-eating sickness whose attaint
Disorder breeds by heating of the blood,
     Surfeits, imposthumes, grief and damned despair,
     Swear Nature's death for framing thee so fair.

'And not the least of all these maladies   745
But in one minute's fight brings beauty under.
Both favour, savour, hue and qualities,
Whereat th'impartial gazer late did wonder,
     Are on the sudden wasted, thawed and done,
     As mountain snow melts with the midday sun.   750

'Therefore, despite of fruitless chastity,
Love-lacking vestals and self-loving nuns,
That on the earth would breed a scarcity
And barren dearth of daughters and of sons,
    Be prodigal: the lamp that burns by night
    Dries up his oil to lend the world his light.

'What is thy body but a swallowing grave,
Seeming to bury that posterity
Which by the rights of time thou needs must have,
If thou destroy them not in dark obscurity?
    If so, the world will hold thee in disdain,
    Sith in thy pride so fair a hope is slain.

'So in thyself thyself art made away;
A mischief worse than civil home-bred strife,
Or theirs whose desperate hands themselves do slay,
Or butcher sire that reaves his son of life.
    Foul cank'ring rust the hidden treasure frets,
    But gold that's put to use more gold begets.'

'Nay, then,' quoth Adon, 'you will fall again
Into your idle overhandled theme.
The kiss I gave you is bestowed in vain,
And all in vain you strive against the stream;
    For, by this black-faced night, desire's foul nurse,
    Your treatise makes me like you worse and worse.

'If love have lent you twenty thousand tongues,
And every tongue more moving than your own,
Bewitching like the wanton mermaid's songs,
Yet from mine ear the tempting tune is blown.
    For know, my heart stands armed in mine ear,
    And will not let a false sound enter there,

'Lest the deceiving harmony should run
Into the quiet closure of my breast;
And then my little heart were quite undone,
In his bedchamber to be barred of rest.
    No, lady, no; my heart longs not to groan,
    But soundly sleeps, while now it sleeps alone.

'What have you urged that I cannot reprove?
The path is smooth that leadeth on to danger.
I hate not love, but your device in love,
That lends embracements unto every stranger.
    You do it for increase: O, strange excuse,
    When reason is the bawd to lust's abuse!

'Call it not love, for Love to heaven is fled
Since sweating Lust on earth usurped his name,
Under whose simple semblance he hath fed
Upon fresh beauty, blotting it with blame;
    Which the hot tyrant stains and soon bereaves,
    As caterpillars do the tender leaves.

'Love comforteth like sunshine after rain,
But Lust's effect is tempest after sun.
Love's gentle spring doth always fresh remain;
Lust's winter comes ere summer half be done.
    Love surfeits not; Lust like a glutton dies.
    Love is all truth, Lust full of forged lies.

'More I could tell, but more I dare not say;
The text is old, the orator too green.
Therefore, in sadness, now I will away;
My face is full of shame, my heart of teen:
    Mine ears that to your wanton talk attended
    Do burn themselves for having so offended.'

With this, he breaketh from the sweet embrace
Of those fair arms which bound him to her breast,
And homeward through the dark laund runs apace;
Leaves Love upon her back deeply distressed.
    Look how a bright star shooteth from the sky,
    So glides he in the night from Venus' eye,

Which after him she darts, as one on shore
Gazing upon a late-embarked friend,
Till the wild waves will have him seen no more,
Whose ridges with the meeting clouds contend;
    So did the merciless and pitchy night
    Fold in the object that did feed her sight.

Whereat amazed, as one that unaware
Hath dropped a precious jewel in the flood,
Or 'stonished as night-wand'rers often are,
Their light blown out in some mistrustful wood,
    Even so confounded in the dark she lay,
    Having lost the fair discovery of her way.

And now she beats her heart, whereat it groans,
That all the neighbour caves, as seeming troubled,
Make verbal repetition of her moans;
Passion on passion deeply is redoubled:
    'Ay me!' she cries, and twenty times, 'Woe, woe!'
    And twenty echoes twenty times cry so.

She marking them begins a wailing note
And sings extemporally a woeful ditty,
How love makes young men thrall, and old men dote;
How love is wise in folly, foolish witty.
    Her heavy anthem still concludes in woe,
    And still the choir of echoes answer so.

Her song was tedious and outwore the night,
For lovers' hours are long, though seeming short:
If pleased themselves, others, they think, delight
In suchlike circumstance, with suchlike sport.
    Their copious stories, oftentimes begun,
    End without audience, and are never done.

755
760
765
770
775
780
785
790
795
800
805
810
815
820
825
830
835
840
845

For who hath she to spend the night withal
But idle sounds resembling parasites,
Like shrill-tongued tapsters answering every call,
850 Soothing the humour of fantastic wits?
    She says, ''Tis so'; they answer all ''Tis so',
    And would say after her if she said 'No'.

Lo, here the gentle lark, weary of rest,
From his moist cabinet mounts up on high,
855 And wakes the morning, from whose silver breast
The sun ariseth in his majesty;
    Who doth the world so gloriously behold
    That cedar tops and hills seem burnished gold.

Venus salutes him with this fair good-morrow:
860 'O thou clear god, and patron of all light,
From whom each lamp and shining star doth
      borrow
The beauteous influence that makes him bright,
    There lives a son that sucked an earthly mother
    May lend thee light, as thou dost lend to other.'

865 This said, she hasteth to a myrtle grove,
Musing the morning is so much o'erworn
And yet she hears no tidings of her love.
She hearkens for his hounds and for his horn:
    Anon she hears them chant it lustily,
870   And all in haste she coasteth to the cry.

And as she runs, the bushes in the way
Some catch her by the neck, some kiss her face,
Some twined about her thigh to make her stay;
She wildly breaketh from their strict embrace,
875   Like a milch-doe, whose swelling dugs do ache,
    Hasting to feed her fawn hid in some brake.

By this she hears the hounds are at a bay;
Whereat she starts, like one that spies an adder
Wreathed up in fatal folds just in his way,
880 The fear whereof doth make him shake and shudder.
    Even so the timorous yelping of the hounds
    Appals her senses and her spirit confounds.

For now she knows it is no gentle chase,
But the blunt boar, rough bear or lion proud,
885 Because the cry remaineth in one place,
Where fearfully the dogs exclaim aloud;
    Finding their enemy to be so curst,
    They all strain court'sy who shall cope him first.

This dismal cry rings sadly in her ear,
890 Through which it enters to surprise her heart;
Who, overcome by doubt and bloodless fear,
With cold-pale weakness numbs each feeling part:
    Like soldiers when their captain once doth yield,
    They basely fly and dare not stay the field.

Thus stands she in a trembling ecstasy, 895
Till, cheering up her senses all dismayed,
She tells them 'tis a causeless fantasy,
And childish error, that they are afraid;
    Bids them leave quaking, bids them fear no more.
    And with that word she spied the hunted boar, 900

Whose frothy mouth, bepainted all with red,
Like milk and blood being mingled both together,
A second fear through all her sinews spread,
Which madly hurries her she knows not whither:
    This way she runs, and now she will no further, 905
    But back retires to rate the boar for murther.

A thousand spleens bear her a thousand ways;
She treads the path that she untreads again.
Her more than haste is mated with delays,
Like the proceedings of a drunken brain, 910
    Full of respects, yet naught at all respecting,
    In hand with all things, naught at all effecting.

Here kennelled in a brake she finds a hound,
And asks the weary caitiff for his master;
And there another licking of his wound, 915
'Gainst venomed sores the only sovereign plaster;
    And here she meets another sadly scowling,
    To whom she speaks, and he replies with howling.

When he hath ceased his ill-resounding noise,
Another flap-mouthed mourner, black and grim, 920
Against the welkin volleys out his voice;
Another and another answer him,
    Clapping their proud tails to the ground below,
    Shaking their scratched ears, bleeding as they go.

Look how the world's poor people are amazed 925
At apparitions, signs and prodigies,
Whereon with fearful eyes they long have gazed,
Infusing them with dreadful prophecies;
    So she at these sad signs draws up her breath,
    And sighing it again exclaims on Death. 930

'Hard-favoured tyrant, ugly, meagre, lean,
Hateful divorce of love,' – thus chides she Death –
'Grim-grinning ghost, earth's worm, what dost thou
    mean
To stifle beauty and to steal his breath,
    Who when he lived, his breath and beauty set 935
    Gloss on the rose, smell to the violet?

'If he be dead – O no, it cannot be,
Seeing his beauty, thou shouldst strike at it –
O yes, it may; thou hast no eyes to see,
But hatefully at random dost thou hit. 940
    Thy mark is feeble age, but thy false dart
    Mistakes that aim and cleaves an infant's heart.

'Hadst thou but bid beware, then he had spoke,
And hearing him thy power had lost his power.
945 The Destinies will curse thee for this stroke;
They bid thee crop a weed, thou pluck'st a flower.
  Love's golden arrow at him should have fled,
  And not Death's ebon dart, to strike him dead.

'Dost thou drink tears, that thou provok'st such
      weeping?
950 What may a heavy groan advantage thee?
Why hast thou cast into eternal sleeping
Those eyes that taught all other eyes to see?
  Now Nature cares not for thy mortal vigour,
  Since her best work is ruined with thy rigour.'

955 Here overcome, as one full of despair,
She vailed her eyelids, who like sluices stopped
The crystal tide that from her two cheeks fair
In the sweet channel of her bosom dropped;
  But through the floodgates breaks the silver rain
960   And with his strong course opens them again.

O, how her eyes and tears did lend and borrow!
Her eye seen in the tears, tears in her eye:
Both crystals, where they viewed each other's sorrow,
Sorrow that friendly sighs sought still to dry;
965   But like a stormy day, now wind, now rain,
  Sighs dry her cheeks, tears make them wet again.

Variable passions throng her constant woe,
As striving who should best become her grief.
All entertained, each passion labours so
970 That every present sorrow seemeth chief,
  But none is best. Then join they all together,
  Like many clouds consulting for foul weather.

By this, far off she hears some huntsman hallow;
A nurse's song ne'er pleased her babe so well.
975 The dire imagination she did follow
This sound of hope doth labour to expel;
  For now reviving joy bids her rejoice,
  And flatters her it is Adonis' voice.

Whereat her tears began to turn their tide,
980 Being prisoned in her eye like pearls in glass;
Yet sometimes falls an orient drop beside,
Which her cheek melts, as scorning it should pass
  To wash the foul face of the sluttish ground,
  Who is but drunken when she seemeth drowned.

985 O hard-believing love, how strange it seems
Not to believe, and yet too credulous!
Thy weal and woe are both of them extremes;
Despair and hope makes thee ridiculous:
  The one doth flatter thee in thoughts unlikely,
990   In likely thoughts the other kills thee quickly.

Now she unweaves the web that she hath wrought:
Adonis lives, and Death is not to blame;
It was not she that called him, all to naught.
Now she adds honours to his hateful name:
  She clepes him king of graves, and grave for
      kings,   995
  Imperious supreme of all mortal things.

'No, no,' quoth she, 'sweet Death, I did but jest;
Yet pardon me, I felt a kind of fear
Whenas I met the boar, that bloody beast,
Which knows no pity but is still severe.   1000
  Then, gentle shadow – truth I must confess –
  I railed on thee, fearing my love's decease.

''Tis not my fault: the boar provoked my tongue;
Be wreaked on him, invisible commander.
'Tis he, foul creature, that hath done thee wrong; 1005
I did but act, he's author of thy slander.
  Grief hath two tongues, and never woman yet
  Could rule them both without ten women's wit.'

Thus hoping that Adonis is alive,
Her rash suspect she doth extenuate;   1010
And that his beauty may the better thrive,
With Death she humbly doth insinuate:
  Tells him of trophies, statues, tombs, and stories
  His victories, his triumphs and his glories.

'O Jove,' quoth she, 'how much a fool was I   1015
To be of such a weak and silly mind
To wail his death who lives and must not die
Till mutual overthrow of mortal kind!
  For he being dead, with him is beauty slain,
  And, beauty dead, black chaos comes again.   1020

'Fie, fie, fond love, thou art as full of fear
As one with treasure laden, hemmed with thieves;
Trifles unwitnessed with eye or ear
Thy coward heart with false bethinking grieves.'
  Even at this word she hears a merry horn,   1025
  Whereat she leaps that was but late forlorn.

As falcons to the lure, away she flies:
The grass stoops not, she treads on it so light,
And in her haste unfortunately spies
The foul boar's conquest on her fair delight;   1030
  Which seen, her eyes, as murdered with the view,
  Like stars ashamed of day, themselves withdrew.

Or as the snail, whose tender horns being hit,
Shrinks backward in his shelly cave with pain,
And there, all smothered up, in shade doth sit,   1035
Long after fearing to creep forth again:
  So at his bloody view her eyes are fled
  Into the deep-dark cabins of her head,

60

Where they resign their office and their light
1040 To the disposing of her troubled brain;
Who bids them still consort with ugly night,
And never wound the heart with looks again;
    Who, like a king perplexed in his throne,
    By their suggestion gives a deadly groan,

1045 Whereat each tributary subject quakes,
As when the wind, imprisoned in the ground,
Struggling for passage, earth's foundation shakes,
Which with cold terror doth men's minds confound.
    This mutiny each part doth so surprise
1050   That from their dark beds once more leap her eyes;

And being opened, threw unwilling light
Upon the wide wound that the boar had trenched
In his soft flank, whose wonted lily white
With purple tears, that his wound wept, was drenched:
1055   No flower was nigh, no grass, herb, leaf or weed
    But stole his blood and seemed with him to bleed.

This solemn sympathy poor Venus noteth;
Over one shoulder doth she hang her head.
Dumbly she passions, franticly she doteth;
1060 She thinks he could not die, he is not dead.
    Her voice is stopped, her joints forget to bow;
    Her eyes are mad that they have wept till now.

Upon his hurt she looks so steadfastly
That her sight, dazzling, makes the wound seem
    three;
1065 And then she reprehends her mangling eye
That makes more gashes where no breach should be:
    His face seems twain, each several limb is doubled;
    For oft the eye mistakes, the brain being troubled.

'My tongue cannot express my grief for one,
1070 And yet,' quoth she, 'behold two Adons dead!
My sighs are blown away, my salt tears gone,
Mine eyes are turned to fire, my heart to lead:
    Heavy heart's lead, melt at mine eyes' red fire!
    So shall I die by drops of hot desire.

1075 'Alas, poor world, what treasure hast thou lost!
What face remains alive that's worth the viewing?
Whose tongue is music now? What canst thou boast
Of things long since, or anything ensuing?
    The flowers are sweet, their colours fresh and trim;
1080   But true sweet beauty lived and died with him.

'Bonnet nor veil henceforth no creature wear!
Nor sun nor wind will ever strive to kiss you.
Having no fair to lose, you need not fear;
The sun doth scorn you, and the wind doth hiss you.
1085   But when Adonis lived, sun and sharp air
    Lurked like two thieves to rob him of his fair.

'And therefore would he put his bonnet on,
Under whose brim the gaudy sun would peep;
The wind would blow it off and, being gone,
Play with his locks. Then would Adonis weep; 1090
    And straight, in pity of his tender years,
    They both would strive who first should dry his
    tears.

'To see his face the lion walked along
Behind some hedge, because he would not fear him;
To recreate himself when he hath sung, 1095
The tiger would be tame and gently hear him;
    If he had spoke, the wolf would leave his prey,
    And never fright the silly lamb that day.

'When he beheld his shadow in the brook,
The fishes spread on it their golden gills; 1100
When he was by, the birds such pleasure took
That some would sing, some other in their bills
    Would bring him mulberries and ripe-red cherries:
    He fed them with his sight, they him with berries.

'But this foul, grim and urchin-snouted boar, 1105
Whose downward eye still looketh for a grave,
Ne'er saw the beauteous livery that he wore;
Witness the entertainment that he gave.
    If he did see his face, why then I know
    He thought to kiss him, and hath killed him so. 1110

''Tis true, 'tis true; thus was Adonis slain:
He ran upon the boar with his sharp spear,
Who did not whet his teeth at him again,
But by a kiss thought to persuade him there;
    And nuzzling in his flank, the loving swine 1115
    Sheathed unaware the tusk in his soft groin.

'Had I been toothed like him, I must confess,
With kissing him I should have killed him first.
But he is dead, and never did he bless
My youth with his; the more am I accurst.' 1120
    With this, she falleth in the place she stood,
    And stains her face with his congealed blood.

She looks upon his lips, and they are pale;
She takes him by the hand, and that is cold;
She whispers in his ears a heavy tale, 1125
As if they heard the woeful words she told.
    She lifts the coffer-lids that close his eyes,
    Where lo, two lamps, burnt out, in darkness lies:

Two glasses, where herself herself beheld
A thousand times, and now no more reflect; 1130
Their virtue lost wherein they late excelled,
And every beauty robbed of his effect.
    'Wonder of time,' quoth she, 'this is my spite,
    That, thou being dead, the day should yet be light.

1135 'Since thou art dead, lo, here I prophesy:
Sorrow on love hereafter shall attend.
It shall be waited on with jealousy,
Find sweet beginning, but unsavoury end;
Ne'er settled equally, but high or low,
1140 That all love's pleasure shall not match his woe.

'It shall be fickle, false and full of fraud,
Bud, and be blasted, in a breathing while;
The bottom poison, and the top o'erstrawed
With sweets that shall the truest sight beguile;
1145 The strongest body shall it make most weak,
Strike the wise dumb, and teach the fool to speak.

'It shall be sparing, and too full of riot,
Teaching decrepit age to tread the measures;
The staring ruffian shall it keep in quiet,
1150 Pluck down the rich, enrich the poor with treasures;
It shall be raging-mad and silly-mild,
Make the young old, the old become a child.

'It shall suspect where is no cause of fear;
It shall not fear where it should most mistrust;
1155 It shall be merciful, and too severe,
And most deceiving when it seems most just;
Perverse it shall be where it shows most toward,
Put fear to valour, courage to the coward.

'It shall be cause of war and dire events,
1160 And set dissension 'twixt the son and sire;
Subject and servile to all discontents,
As dry combustious matter is to fire.
Sith in his prime death doth my love destroy,
They that love best their loves shall not enjoy.'

By this the boy that by her side lay killed   1165
Was melted like a vapour from her sight,
And in his blood that on the ground lay spilled
A purple flower sprung up, chequered with white,
Resembling well his pale cheeks and the blood
Which in round drops upon their whiteness stood.   1170

She bows her head the new-sprung flower to smell,
Comparing it to her Adonis' breath,
And says within her bosom it shall dwell,
Since he himself is reft from her by death.
She crops the stalk, and in the breach appears   1175
Green-dropping sap, which she compares to tears.

'Poor flower,' quoth she, 'this was thy father's guise –
Sweet issue of a more sweet-smelling sire –
For every little grief to wet his eyes.
To grow unto himself was his desire,   1180
And so 'tis thine; but know, it is as good
To wither in my breast as in his blood.

'Here was thy father's bed, here in my breast;
Thou art the next of blood, and 'tis thy right.
Lo, in this hollow cradle take thy rest,   1185
My throbbing heart shall rock thee day and night;
There shall not be one minute in an hour
Wherein I will not kiss my sweet love's flower.'

Thus weary of the world, away she hies,
And yokes her silver doves, by whose swift aid   1190
Their mistress, mounted through the empty skies
In her light chariot quickly is conveyed,
Holding their course to Paphos, where their queen
Means to immure herself and not be seen.

The Rape of Lucrece

To the Right Honourable Henry Wriothesley,
Earl of Southampton and Baron of Titchfield

The love I dedicate to your lordship is without end;
whereof this pamphlet without beginning is but a
superfluous moiety. The warrant I have of your honourable
disposition, not the worth of my untutored lines, makes it
assured of acceptance. What I have done is yours; what I
have to do is yours; being part in all I have, devoted yours.
Were my worth greater, my duty would show greater;
meantime, as it is, it is bound to your lordship, to whom I
wish long life, still lengthened with all happiness.

Your lordship's in all duty,
William Shakespeare

THE ARGUMENT

Lucius Tarquinius, for his excessive pride surnamed
Superbus, after he had caused his own father-in-law Servius
Tullius to be cruelly murdered, and, contrary to the Roman
laws and customs, not requiring or staying for the people's
suffrages, had possessed himself of the kingdom, went,
accompanied with his sons and other noblemen of Rome, to
besiege Ardea. During which siege the principal men of the
army meeting one evening at the tent of Sextus Tarquinius,
the king's son, in their discourses after supper every one
commended the virtues of his own wife; among whom
Collatinus extolled the incomparable chastity of his wife
Lucretia. In that pleasant humour they all posted to Rome;
and intending by their secret and sudden arrival to make trial
of that which every one had before avouched, only Collatinus
finds his wife, though it were late in the night, spinning
amongst her maids: the other ladies were all found dancing
and revelling, or in several disports. Whereupon the
noblemen yielded Collatinus the victory, and his wife the
fame. At that time Sextus Tarquinius being inflamed with
Lucrece' beauty, yet smothering his passions for the present,
departed with the rest back to the camp; from whence he
shortly after privily withdrew himself and was, according to
his estate, royally entertained and lodged by Lucrece at
Collatium. The same night he treacherously stealeth into her
chamber, violently ravished her and early in the morning
speedeth away. Lucrece, in this lamentable plight, hastily
dispatcheth messengers, one to Rome for her father, another
to the camp for Collatine. They came, the one accompanied
with Junius Brutus, the other with Publius Valerius; and
finding Lucrece attired in mourning habit, demanded the
cause of her sorrow. She, first taking an oath of them for her
revenge, revealed the actor and whole manner of his dealing
and withal suddenly stabbed herself. Which done, with one
consent they all vowed to root out the whole hated family of
the Tarquins; and, bearing the dead body to Rome, Brutus
acquainted the people with the doer and manner of the vile
deed, with a bitter invective against the tyranny of the king:
wherewith the people were so moved that, with one consent
and a general acclamation, the Tarquins were all exiled, and
the state government changed from kings to consuls.

From the besieged ARDEA all in post,
Borne by the trustless wings of false desire,
Lust-breathed TARQUIN leaves the ROMAN host,
And to COLLATIUM bears the lightless fire
Which, in pale embers hid, lurks to aspire   5
    And girdle with embracing flames the waist
    Of COLLATINE's fair love, LUCRECE the chaste.

Haply that name of 'chaste' unhapp'ly set
This bateless edge on his keen appetite;
When COLLATINE unwisely did not let   10
To praise the clear unmatched red and white
Which triumphed in that sky of his delight,
    Where mortal stars as bright as heaven's beauties
    With pure aspects did him peculiar duties.

For he the night before in TARQUIN's tent   15
Unlocked the treasure of his happy state:
What priceless wealth the heavens had him lent
In the possession of his beauteous mate;
Reck'ning his fortune at such high-proud rate
    That kings might be espoused to more fame,   20
    But king nor peer to such a peerless dame.

O happiness enjoyed but of a few
And, if possessed, as soon decayed and done
As is the morning silver melting dew
Against the golden splendour of the sun,   25
An expired date, cancelled ere well begun!
    Honour and beauty, in the owner's arms,
    Are weakly fortressed from a world of harms.

Beauty itself doth of itself persuade
The eyes of men without an orator.   30
What needeth then apology be made
To set forth that which is so singular?
Or why is COLLATINE the publisher
    Of that rich jewel he should keep unknown
    From thievish ears, because it is his own?   35

Perchance his boast of LUCRECE' sov'reignty
Suggested this proud issue of a king,
For by our ears our hearts oft tainted be.
Perchance that envy of so rich a thing,
Braving compare, disdainfully did sting   40
    His high-pitched thoughts, that meaner men
        should vaunt
    That golden hap which their superiors want.

But some untimely thought did instigate
His all-too-timeless speed, if none of those.
His honour, his affairs, his friends, his state,   45
Neglected all, with swift intent he goes
To quench the coal which in his liver glows.
    O rash false heat, wrapped in repentant cold,
    Thy hasty spring still blasts and ne'er grows old!

50 When at COLLATIUM this false lord arrived,
Well was he welcomed by the ROMAN dame,
Within whose face beauty and virtue strived
Which of them both should underprop her fame.
When virtue bragged, beauty would blush for shame;
55   When beauty boasted blushes, in despite
   Virtue would stain that o'er with silver white.

But beauty, in that white intituled
From VENUS' doves, doth challenge that fair field.
Then virtue claims from beauty beauty's red,
60 Which virtue gave the golden age to gild
Their silver cheeks, and called it then their shield;
   Teaching them thus to use it in the fight,
   When shame assailed, the red should fence the
     white.

This heraldry in LUCRECE' face was seen,
65 Argued by beauty's red and virtue's white.
Of either's colour was the other queen,
Proving from world's minority their right.
Yet their ambition makes them still to fight,
   The sov'reignty of either being so great
70   That oft they interchange each other's seat.

This silent war of lilies and of roses
Which TARQUIN viewed in her fair face's field
In their pure ranks his traitor eye encloses;
Where, lest between them both it should be killed,
75 The coward captive vanquished doth yield
   To those two armies that would let him go
   Rather than triumph in so false a foe.

Now thinks he that her husband's shallow tongue,
The niggard prodigal that praised her so,
80 In that high task hath done her beauty wrong,
Which far exceeds his barren skill to show.
Therefore that praise which COLLATINE doth owe
   Enchanted TARQUIN answers with surmise,
   In silent wonder of still-gazing eyes.

85 This earthly saint, adored by this devil,
Little suspecteth the false worshipper;
"For unstained thoughts do seldom dream on evil";
"Birds never limed no secret bushes fear."
So guiltless she securely gives good cheer
90   And reverent welcome to her princely guest,
   Whose inward ill no outward harm expressed.

For that he coloured with his high estate,
Hiding base sin in pleats of majesty;
That nothing in him seemed inordinate,
95 Save sometime too much wonder of his eye,
Which, having all, all could not satisfy;
   But, poorly rich, so wanteth in his store
   That, cloyed with much, he pineth still for more.

But she that never coped with stranger eyes
Could pick no meaning from their parling looks, 100
Nor read the subtle-shining secrecies
Writ in the glassy margents of such books.
She touched no unknown baits, nor feared no hooks,
   Nor could she moralize his wanton sight
   More than his eyes were opened to the light. 105

He stories to her ears her husband's fame
Won in the fields of fruitful Italy,
And decks with praises COLLATINE's high name
Made glorious by his manly chivalry
With bruised arms and wreaths of victory. 110
   Her joy with heaved-up hand she doth express,
   And wordless so greets heaven for his success.

Far from the purpose of his coming thither
He makes excuses for his being there.
No cloudy show of stormy blust'ring weather 115
Doth yet in his fair welkin once appear;
Till sable Night, mother of dread and fear,
   Upon the world dim darkness doth display,
   And in her vaulty prison stows the day.

For then is TARQUIN brought unto his bed, 120
Intending weariness with heavy sprite;
For after supper long he questioned
With modest LUCRECE, and wore out the night.
Now leaden slumber with life's strength doth fight,
   And every one to rest himself betakes, 125
   Save thieves and cares and troubled minds that
     wakes.

As one of which doth TARQUIN lie revolving
The sundry dangers of his will's obtaining;
Yet ever to obtain his will resolving,
Though weak-built hopes persuade him to abstaining. 130
Despair to gain doth traffic oft for gaining,
   And when great treasure is the meed proposed,
   Though death be adjunct, there's no death supposed.

Those that much covet are with gain so fond
That what they have not, that which they possess, 135
They scatter and unloose it from their bond,
And so by hoping more they have but less;
Or, gaining more, the profit of excess
   Is but to surfeit, and such griefs sustain,
   That they prove bankrupt in this poor-rich gain. 140

The aim of all is but to nurse the life
With honour, wealth and ease in waning age;
And in this aim there is such thwarting strife
That one for all or all for one we gage:
As life for honour in fell battle's rage; 145
   Honour for wealth; and oft that wealth doth cost
   The death of all, and all together lost.

So that in vent'ring ill we leave to be
The things we are for that which we expect,
150 And this ambitious foul infirmity,
In having much, torments us with defect
Of that we have; so then we do neglect
  The thing we have, and all for want of wit
  Make something nothing by augmenting it.

155 Such hazard now must doting TARQUIN make,
Pawning his honour to obtain his lust;
And for himself himself he must forsake.
Then where is truth, if there be no self-trust?
When shall he think to find a stranger just
160   When he himself himself confounds, betrays
  To sland'rous tongues and wretched hateful days?

Now stole upon the time the dead of night,
When heavy sleep had closed up mortal eyes.
No comfortable star did lend his light,
165 No noise but owls' and wolves' death-boding cries;
Now serves the season that they may surprise
  The silly lambs. Pure thoughts are dead and still,
  While lust and murder wakes to stain and kill.

And now this lustful lord leaped from his bed,
170 Throwing his mantle rudely o'er his arm,
Is madly tossed between desire and dread.
Th'one sweetly flatters, th'other feareth harm,
But honest fear, bewitched with lust's foul charm,
  Doth too-too oft betake him to retire,
175   Beaten away by brainsick rude desire.

His falchion on a flint he softly smiteth,
That from the cold stone sparks of fire do fly,
Whereat a waxen torch forthwith he lighteth,
Which must be lodestar to his lustful eye,
180 And to the flame thus speaks advisedly:
  'As from this cold flint I enforced this fire,
  So LUCRECE must I force to my desire.'

Here, pale with fear, he doth premeditate
The dangers of his loathsome enterprise,
185 And in his inward mind he doth debate
What following sorrow may on this arise.
Then, looking scornfully, he doth despise
  His naked armour of still-slaughtered lust,
  And justly thus controls his thoughts unjust:

190 'Fair torch, burn out thy light, and lend it not
To darken her whose light excelleth thine;
And die, unhallowed thoughts, before you blot
With your uncleanness that which is divine.
Offer pure incense to so pure a shrine.
195   Let fair humanity abhor the deed
  That spots and stains love's modest snow-white
    weed.

'O shame to knighthood and to shining arms!
O foul dishonour to my household's grave!
O impious act including all foul harms!
A martial man to be soft fancy's slave!
200 True valour still a true respect should have;
  Then my digression is so vile, so base,
  That it will live engraven in my face.

'Yea, though I die the scandal will survive
And be an eyesore in my golden coat. 205
Some loathsome dash the herald will contrive
To cipher me how fondly I did dote,
That my posterity, shamed with the note,
  Shall curse my bones, and hold it for no sin
  To wish that I their father had not been. 210

'What win I if I gain the thing I seek?
A dream, a breath, a froth of fleeting joy.
Who buys a minute's mirth to wail a week?
Or sells eternity to get a toy?
For one sweet grape who will the vine destroy? 215
  Or what fond beggar, but to touch the crown,
  Would with the sceptre straight be strucken down?

'If COLLATINUS dream of my intent,
Will he not wake, and in a desp'rate rage
Post hither, this vile purpose to prevent? 220
This siege that hath engirt his marriage,
This blur to youth, this sorrow to the sage,
  This dying virtue, this surviving shame,
  Whose crime will bear an ever-during blame.

'O, what excuse can my invention make 225
When thou shalt charge me with so black a deed?
Will not my tongue be mute, my frail joints shake,
Mine eyes forgo their light, my false heart bleed?
The guilt being great, the fear doth still exceed;
  And extreme fear can neither fight nor fly, 230
  But coward-like with trembling terror die.

'Had COLLATINUS killed my son or sire,
Or lain in ambush to betray my life,
Or were he not my dear friend, this desire
Might have excuse to work upon his wife, 235
As in revenge or quittal of such strife.
  But as he is my kinsman, my dear friend,
  The shame and fault finds no excuse nor end.

'Shameful it is: ay, if the fact be known.
Hateful it is: there is no hate in loving. 240
I'll beg her love: but she is not her own.
The worst is but denial and reproving:
My will is strong, past reason's weak removing.
  Who fears a sentence or an old man's saw
  Shall by a painted cloth be kept in awe.' 245

Thus graceless holds he disputation
'Tween frozen conscience and hot-burning will,
And with good thoughts makes dispensation,
Urging the worser sense for vantage still;
250 Which in a moment doth confound and kill
    All pure effects, and doth so far proceed
    That what is vile shows like a virtuous deed.

Quoth he, 'She took me kindly by the hand,
And gazed for tidings in my eager eyes,
255 Fearing some hard news from the warlike band,
Where her beloved COLLATINUS lies.
O, how her fear did make her colour rise!
    First red as roses that on lawn we lay,
    Then white as lawn, the roses took away.

260 'And how her hand, in my hand being locked,
Forced it to tremble with her loyal fear!
Which struck her sad, and then it faster rocked
Until her husband's welfare she did hear,
Whereat she smiled with so sweet a cheer
265   That had NARCISSUS seen her as she stood
    Self-love had never drowned him in the flood.

'Why hunt I then for colour or excuses?
All orators are dumb when beauty pleadeth;
Poor wretches have remorse in poor abuses;
270 Love thrives not in the heart that shadows dreadeth.
Affection is my captain, and he leadeth;
    And when his gaudy banner is displayed,
    The coward fights and will not be dismayed.

'Then childish fear avaunt! debating die!
275 Respect and reason wait on wrinkled age!
My heart shall never countermand mine eye:
Sad pause and deep regard beseems the sage.
My part is youth, and beats these from the stage.
    Desire my pilot is, beauty my prize.
280   Then who fears sinking where such treasure lies?'

As corn o'ergrown by weeds, so heedful fear
Is almost choked by unresisted lust.
Away he steals with open list'ning ear,
Full of foul hope and full of fond mistrust;
285 Both which, as servitors to the unjust,
    So cross him with their opposite persuasion
    That now he vows a league, and now invasion.

Within his thought her heavenly image sits,
And in the self-same seat sits COLLATINE.
290 That eye which looks on her confounds his wits,
That eye which him beholds, as more divine,
Unto a view so false will not incline,
    But with a pure appeal seeks to the heart,
    Which once corrupted takes the worser part;

And therein heartens up his servile powers, 295
Who, flattered by their leader's jocund show,
Stuff up his lust, as minutes fill up hours;
And as their captain, so their pride doth grow,
Paying more slavish tribute than they owe.
    By reprobate desire thus madly led, 300
    The ROMAN lord marcheth to LUCRECE' bed.

The locks between her chamber and his will,
Each one by him enforced, retires his ward;
But as they open they all rate his ill,
Which drives the creeping thief to some regard. 305
The threshold grates the door to have him heard;
    Night-wand'ring weasels shriek to see him there:
    They fright him, yet he still pursues his fear.

As each unwilling portal yields him way,
Through little vents and crannies of the place 310
The wind wars with his torch to make him stay,
And blows the smoke of it into his face,
Extinguishing his conduct in this case.
    But his hot heart, which fond desire doth scorch,
    Puffs forth another wind that fires the torch; 315

And being lighted, by the light he spies
LUCRETIA's glove, wherein her needle sticks.
He takes it from the rushes where it lies,
And, griping it, the needle his finger pricks,
As who should say, 'This glove to wanton tricks 320
    Is not inured. Return again in haste;
    Thou seest our mistress' ornaments are chaste.'

But all these poor forbiddings could not stay him;
He in the worst sense consters their denial:
The doors, the wind, the glove that did delay him 325
He takes for accidental things of trial;
Or as those bars which stop the hourly dial,
    Who with a ling'ring stay his course doth let
    Till every minute pays the hour his debt.

'So, so,' quoth he, 'these lets attend the time, 330
Like little frosts that sometime threat the spring
To add a more rejoicing to the prime,
And give the sneaped birds more cause to sing.
Pain pays the income of each precious thing.
    Huge rocks, high winds, strong pirates, shelves and
      sands 335
    The merchant fears, ere rich at home he lands.'

Now is he come unto the chamber door
That shuts him from the heaven of his thought,
Which with a yielding latch, and with no more,
Hath barred him from the blessed thing he sought. 340
So from himself impiety hath wrought,
    That for his prey to pray he doth begin,
    As if the heavens should countenance his sin.

But in the midst of his unfruitful prayer,
345   Having solicited th'eternal power
That his foul thoughts might compass his fair fair,
And they would stand auspicious to the hour,
Even there he starts. Quoth he, 'I must deflower.
350   The powers to whom I pray abhor this fact;
How can they then assist me in the act?

'Then love and fortune be my gods, my guide!
My will is backed with resolution.
Thoughts are but dreams till their effects be tried;
355   The blackest sin is cleared with absolution;
Against love's fire fear's frost hath dissolution.
        The eye of heaven is out, and misty night
Covers the shame that follows sweet delight.'

This said, his guilty hand plucked up the latch,
And with his knee the door he opens wide.
360   The dove sleeps fast that this night-owl will catch.
Thus treason works ere traitors be espied.
Who sees the lurking serpent steps aside,
        But she, sound sleeping, fearing no such thing,
Lies at the mercy of his mortal sting.

365   Into the chamber wickedly he stalks,
And gazeth on her yet unstained bed.
The curtains being close, about he walks,
Rolling his greedy eyeballs in his head.
By their high treason is his heart misled,
370   Which gives the watchword to his hand full soon
To draw the cloud that hides the silver moon.

Look as the fair and fiery-pointed sun
Rushing from forth a cloud bereaves our sight;
Even so, the curtain drawn, his eyes begun
375   To wink, being blinded with a greater light:
Whether it is that she reflects so bright
        That dazzleth them, or else some shame
            supposed,
But blind they are and keep themselves enclosed.

O, had they in that darksome prison died,
380   Then had they seen the period of their ill;
Then COLLATINE again by LUCRECE' side
In his clear bed might have reposed still.
But they must ope, this blessed league to kill,
        And holy-thoughted LUCRECE to their sight
385   Must sell her joy, her life, her world's delight.

Her lily hand her rosy cheek lies under,
Coz'ning the pillow of a lawful kiss;
Who, therefore angry, seems to part in sunder,
Swelling on either side to want his bliss;
390   Between whose hills her head entombed is,
        Where like a virtuous monument she lies,
To be admired of lewd unhallowed eyes.

Without the bed her other fair hand was,
On the green coverlet, whose perfect white
Showed like an April daisy on the grass,   395
With pearly sweat resembling dew of night.
Her eyes, like marigolds, had sheathed their light,
        And canopied in darkness sweetly lay
Till they might open to adorn the day.

Her hair, like golden threads, played with her breath,   400
O modest wantons, wanton modesty!
Showing life's triumph in the map of death,
And death's dim look in life's mortality.
Each in her sleep themselves so beautify,
        As if between them twain there were no strife,   405
But that life lived in death, and death in life.

Her breasts like ivory globes circled with blue,
A pair of maiden worlds unconquered,
Save of their lord no bearing yoke they knew,
And him by oath they truly honoured.   410
These worlds in TARQUIN new ambition bred,
        Who like a foul usurper went about
From this fair throne to heave the owner out.

What could he see but mightily he noted?
What did he note but strongly he desired?   415
What he beheld, on that he firmly doted,
And in his will his wilful eye he tired.
With more than admiration he admired
        Her azure veins, her alabaster skin,
Her coral lips, her snow-white dimpled chin.   420

As the grim lion fawneth o'er his prey,
Sharp hunger by the conquest satisfied,
So o'er this sleeping soul doth TARQUIN stay,
His rage of lust by gazing qualified,
Slacked, not suppressed; for standing by her side,   425
        His eye, which late this mutiny restrains,
Unto a greater uproar tempts his veins.

And they, like straggling slaves for pillage fighting,
Obdurate vassals fell exploits effecting,
In bloody death and ravishment delighting,   430
Nor children's tears nor mothers' groans respecting,
Swell in their pride, the onset still expecting.
        Anon his beating heart, alarum striking,
Gives the hot charge, and bids them do their
            liking.

His drumming heart cheers up his burning eye,   435
His eye commends the leading to his hand;
His hand, as proud of such a dignity,
Smoking with pride, marched on to make his stand
On her bare breast, the heart of all her land,
        Whose ranks of blue veins, as his hand did scale,   440
Left their round turrets destitute and pale.

They, must'ring to the quiet cabinet
Where their dear governess and lady lies,
Do tell her she is dreadfully beset,
And fright her with confusion of their cries.
445 She, much amazed, breaks ope her locked-up eyes,
    Who, peeping forth this tumult to behold,
    Are by his flaming torch dimmed and controlled.

Imagine her as one in dead of night
450 From forth dull sleep by dreadful fancy waking,
That thinks she hath beheld some ghastly sprite,
Whose grim aspect sets every joint a-shaking:
What terror 'tis! But she in worser taking,
    From sleep disturbed, heedfully doth view
455 The sight which makes supposed terror true.

Wrapped and confounded in a thousand fears,
Like to a new-killed bird she trembling lies.
She dares not look; yet, winking, there appears
Quick-shifting antics, ugly in her eyes.
460 "Such shadows are the weak brain's forgeries,
    Who, angry that the eyes fly from their lights,
    In darkness daunts them with more dreadful sights."

His hand that yet remains upon her breast –
Rude ram, to batter such an ivory wall! –
465 May feel her heart, poor citizen, distressed,
Wounding itself to death, rise up and fall,
Beating her bulk, that his hand shakes withal.
    This moves in him more rage and lesser pity,
    To make the breach and enter this sweet city.

470 First, like a trumpet doth his tongue begin
To sound a parley to his heartless foe,
Who o'er the white sheet peers her whiter chin,
The reason of this rash alarm to know,
Which he by dumb demeanour seeks to show.
475 But she with vehement prayers urgeth still
    Under what colour he commits this ill.

Thus he replies: 'The colour in thy face,
That even for anger makes the lily pale
And the red rose blush at her own disgrace,
480 Shall plead for me and tell my loving tale.
Under that colour am I come to scale
    Thy never-conquered fort. The fault is thine,
    For those thine eyes betray thee unto mine.

'Thus I forestall thee, if thou mean to chide:
485 Thy beauty hath ensnared thee to this night,
Where thou with patience must my will abide,
My will that marks thee for my earth's delight,
Which I to conquer sought with all my might.
    But as reproof and reason beat it dead,
490 By thy bright beauty was it newly bred.

'I see what crosses my attempt will bring,
I know what thorns the growing rose defends;
I think the honey guarded with a sting:
All this beforehand counsel comprehends.
But Will is deaf, and hears no heedful friends;   495
    Only he hath an eye to gaze on Beauty,
    And dotes on what he looks, 'gainst law or duty.

'I have debated even in my soul
What wrong, what shame, what sorrow I shall breed;
But nothing can affection's course control,   500
Or stop the headlong fury of his speed.
I know repentant tears ensue the deed,
    Reproach, disdain and deadly enmity;
    Yet strive I to embrace mine infamy.'

This said, he shakes aloft his ROMAN blade,   505
Which like a falcon tow'ring in the skies
Coucheth the fowl below with his wings' shade,
Whose crooked beak threats if he mount he dies:
So under his insulting falchion lies
    Harmless LUCRETIA, marking what he tells   510
    With trembling fear, as fowl hear falcons' bells.

'LUCRECE,' quoth he, 'this night I must enjoy thee.
If thou deny, then force must work my way,
For in thy bed I purpose to destroy thee.
That done, some worthless slave of thine I'll slay   515
To kill thine honour with thy life's decay;
    And in thy dead arms do I mean to place him,
    Swearing I slew him, seeing thee embrace him.

'So thy surviving husband shall remain
The scornful mark of every open eye;   520
Thy kinsmen hang their heads at this disdain,
Thy issue blurred with nameless bastardy;
And thou, the author of their obloquy,
    Shalt have thy trespass cited up in rhymes
    And sung by children in succeeding times.   525

'But if thou yield, I rest thy secret friend:
The fault unknown is as a thought unacted.
"A little harm done to a great good end
For lawful policy remains enacted."
"The poisonous simple sometime is compacted   530
    In a pure compound; being so applied,
    His venom in effect is purified."

'Then, for thy husband and thy children's sake
Tender my suit: bequeath not to their lot
The shame that from them no device can take,   535
The blemish that will never be forgot,
Worse than a slavish wipe or birth-hour's blot;
    For marks descried in men's nativity
    Are Nature's faults, not their own infamy.'

540 Here with a cockatrice' dead-killing eye
He rouseth up himself, and makes a pause,
While she, the picture of pure piety,
Like a white hind under the gripe's sharp claws,
545 Pleads in a wilderness where are no laws
    To the rough beast that knows no gentle right,
    Nor aught obeys but his foul appetite.

But when a black-faced cloud the world doth threat,
In his dim mist th'aspiring mountains hiding,
From earth's dark womb some gentle gust doth get,
550 Which blow these pitchy vapours from their biding,
Hind'ring their present fall by this dividing;
    So his unhallowed haste her words delays,
    And moody PLUTO winks while ORPHEUS plays.

Yet, foul night-waking cat, he doth but dally
555 While in his hold-fast foot the weak mouse panteth;
Her sad behaviour feeds his vulture folly,
A swallowing gulf that even in plenty wanteth.
His ear her prayers admits, but his heart granteth
    No penetrable entrance to her plaining:
560   "Tears harden lust, though marble wear with raining."

Her pity-pleading eyes are sadly fixed
In the remorseless wrinkles of his face;
Her modest eloquence with sighs is mixed,
Which to her oratory adds more grace.
565 She puts the period often from his place,
    And midst the sentence so her accent breaks
    That twice she doth begin ere once she speaks.

She conjures him by high almighty JOVE,
By knighthood, gentry and sweet friendship's oath,
570 By her untimely tears, her husband's love,
By holy human law and common troth,
By heaven and earth, and all the power of both,
    That to his borrowed bed he make retire,
    And stoop to honour, not to foul desire.

575 Quoth she, 'Reward not hospitality
With such black payment as thou hast pretended;
Mud not the fountain that gave drink to thee;
Mar not the thing that cannot be amended;
End thy ill aim before thy shoot be ended.
580   He is no woodman that doth bend his bow
    To strike a poor unseasonable doe.

'My husband is thy friend: for his sake spare me;
Thyself art mighty: for thine own sake leave me;
Myself a weakling: do not then ensnare me;
585 Thou look'st not like deceit: do not deceive me.
My sighs like whirlwinds labour hence to heave thee.
    If ever man were moved with woman's moans,
    Be moved with my tears, my sighs, my groans:

'All which together, like a troubled ocean,
590 Beat at thy rocky and wrack-threat'ning heart,
To soften it with their continual motion;
For stones dissolved to water do convert.
O, if no harder than a stone thou art,
    Melt at my tears, and be compassionate!
595   Soft pity enters at an iron gate.

'In TARQUIN's likeness I did entertain thee.
Hast thou put on his shape to do him shame?
To all the host of heaven I complain me.
Thou wrong'st his honour, wound'st his princely
    name.
600 Thou art not what thou seem'st, and if the same,
    Thou seem'st not what thou art, a god, a king;
    For kings like gods should govern everything.

'How will thy shame be seeded in thine age
When thus thy vices bud before thy spring?
605 If in thy hope thou dar'st do such outrage,
What dar'st thou not when once thou art a king?
O, be remembered, no outrageous thing
    From vassal actors can be wiped away;
    Then kings' misdeeds cannot be hid in clay.

610 'This deed will make thee only loved for fear,
But happy monarchs still are feared for love.
With foul offenders thou perforce must bear,
When they in thee the like offences prove.
If but for fear of this, thy will remove;
615   For princes are the glass, the school, the book,
    Where subjects' eyes do learn, do read, do look.

'And wilt thou be the school where Lust shall learn?
Must he in thee read lectures of such shame?
Wilt thou be glass wherein it shall discern
620 Authority for sin, warrant for blame,
To privilege dishonour in thy name?
    Thou back'st reproach against long-living laud,
    And mak'st fair reputation but a bawd.

'Hast thou command? By him that gave it thee,
625 From a pure heart command thy rebel will.
Draw not thy sword to guard iniquity,
For it was lent thee all that brood to kill.
Thy princely office how canst thou fulfil
    When patterned by thy fault foul Sin may say
630   He learned to sin, and thou didst teach the way?

'Think but how vile a spectacle it were
To view thy present trespass in another.
Men's faults do seldom to themselves appear;
Their own transgressions partially they smother.
635 This guilt would seem death-worthy in thy brother.
    O, how are they wrapped in with infamies
    That from their own misdeeds askance their eyes!

'To thee, to thee, my heaved-up hands appeal,
Not to seducing lust, thy rash relier.
640 I sue for exiled majesty's repeal;
Let him return, and flatt'ring thoughts retire.
His true respect will prison false desire,
 And wipe the dim mist from thy doting eyne,
 That thou shalt see thy state, and pity mine.'

'Have done,' quoth he. 'my uncontrolled tide
645 Turns not, but swells the higher by this let.
Small lights are soon blown out; huge fires abide,
And with the wind in greater fury fret.
The petty streams that pay a daily debt
 To their salt sovereign, with their fresh falls'
650   haste
 Add to his flow, but alter not his taste.'

'Thou art', quoth she, 'a sea, a sovereign king,
And lo, there falls into thy boundless flood
Black lust, dishonour, shame, misgoverning,
655 Who seek to stain the ocean of thy blood.
If all these petty ills shall change thy good,
 Thy sea within a puddle's womb is hearsed,
 And not the puddle in thy sea dispersed.

'So shall these slaves be king, and thou their slave;
660 Thou nobly base, they basely dignified;
Thou their fair life, and they thy fouler grave;
Thou loathed in their shame, they in thy pride.
The lesser thing should not the greater hide:
 The cedar stoops not to the base shrub's foot,
665 But low shrubs wither at the cedar's root.

'So let thy thoughts, low vassals to thy state –'
'No more,' quoth he. 'By heaven, I will not hear thee!
Yield to my love. If not, enforced hate
Instead of love's coy touch shall rudely tear thee.
670 That done, despitefully I mean to bear thee
 Unto the base bed of some rascal groom
 To be thy partner in this shameful doom.'

This said, he sets his foot upon the light,
For light and lust are deadly enemies:
675 Shame folded up in blind concealing night,
When most unseen, then most doth tyrannize.
The wolf hath seized his prey, the poor lamb cries,
 Till with her own white fleece her voice controlled
 Entombs her outcry in her lips' sweet fold.

680 For with the nightly linen that she wears
He pens her piteous clamours in her head,
Cooling his hot face in the chastest tears
That ever modest eyes with sorrow shed.
O, that prone lust should stain so pure a bed!
685 The spots whereof could weeping purify,
 Her tears should drop on them perpetually.

But she hath lost a dearer thing than life,
And he hath won what he would lose again.
This forced league doth force a further strife;
This momentary joy breeds months of pain; 690
This hot desire converts to cold disdain:
 Pure Chastity is rifled of her store,
 And lust, the thief, far poorer than before.

Look as the full-fed hound or gorged hawk,
Unapt for tender smell or speedy flight, 695
Make slow pursuit, or altogether balk
The prey wherein by nature they delight,
So surfeit-taking TARQUIN fares this night:
 His taste delicious, in digestion souring,
 Devours his will that lived by foul devouring. 700

O deeper sin than bottomless conceit
Can comprehend in still imagination!
Drunken Desire must vomit his receipt
Ere he can see his own abomination.
While lust is in his pride, no exclamation 705
 Can curb his heat or rein his rash desire,
 Till like a jade Self-will himself doth tire.

And then with lank and lean discoloured cheek,
With heavy eye, knit brow and strengthless pace,
Feeble Desire, all recreant, poor and meek, 710
Like to a bankrupt beggar wails his case.
The flesh being proud, Desire doth fight with Grace,
 For there it revels, and when that decays,
 The guilty rebel for remission prays.

So fares it with this faultful lord of ROME, 715
Who this accomplishment so hotly chased;
For now against himself he sounds this doom,
That through the length of times he stands disgraced.
Besides, his soul's fair temple is defaced,
 To whose weak ruins muster troops of cares, 720
 To ask the spotted princess how she fares.

She says her subjects with foul insurrection
Have battered down her consecrated wall,
And by their mortal fault brought in subjection
Her immortality, and made her thrall 725
To living death and pain perpetual;
 Which in her prescience she controlled still,
 But her foresight could not forestall their will.

Ev'n in this thought through the dark night he
 stealeth,
A captive victor that hath lost in gain; 730
Bearing away the wound that nothing healeth,
The scar that will, despite of cure, remain;
Leaving his spoil perplexed in greater pain.
 She bears the load of lust he left behind,
 And he the burden of a guilty mind. 735

He like a thievish dog creeps sadly thence;
She like a wearied lamb lies panting there.
He scowls, and hates himself for his offence;
She, desperate, with her nails her flesh doth tear.
740 He faintly flies, sweating with guilty fear;
    She stays, exclaiming on the direful night;
    He runs, and chides his vanished loathed delight.

He thence departs, a heavy convertite;
She there remains, a hopeless castaway.
745 He in his speed looks for the morning light;
She prays she never may behold the day.
'For day', quoth she, 'night's scapes doth open lay,
    And my true eyes have never practised how
    To cloak offences with a cunning brow.

750 'They think not but that every eye can see
The same disgrace which they themselves behold;
And therefore would they still in darkness be,
To have their unseen sin remain untold.
For they their guilt with weeping will unfold,
755   And grave, like water that doth eat in steel,
    Upon my cheeks what helpless shame I feel.'

Here she exclaims against repose and rest,
And bids her eyes hereafter still be blind.
She wakes her heart by beating on her breast,
760 And bids it leap from thence, where it may find
Some purer chest to close so pure a mind.
    Frantic with grief thus breathes she forth her
        spite
    Against the unseen secrecy of night:

'O comfort-killing Night, image of hell,
765 Dim register and notary of shame,
Black stage for tragedies and murders fell,
Vast sin-concealing chaos, nurse of blame,
Blind muffled bawd, dark harbour for defame,
    Grim cave of death, whisp'ring conspirator
770   With close-tongued treason and the ravisher!

'O hateful, vaporous and foggy Night!
Since thou art guilty of my cureless crime,
Muster thy mists to meet the eastern light,
Make war against proportioned course of time;
775 Or if thou wilt permit the sun to climb
    His wonted height, yet ere he go to bed,
    Knit poisonous clouds about his golden head.

'With rotten damps ravish the morning air;
Let their exhaled unwholesome breaths make sick
780 The life of purity, the supreme fair,
Ere he arrive his weary noontide prick;
And let thy musty vapours march so thick
    That in their smoky ranks his smothered light
    May set at noon and make perpetual night.

785 'Were TARQUIN Night, as he is but Night's child,
The silver-shining queen he would distain;
Her twinkling handmaids too, by him defiled,
Through Night's black bosom should not peep again.
So should I have co-partners in my pain;
790   And fellowship in woe doth woe assuage,
    As palmers' chat makes short their pilgrimage.

'Where now I have no one to blush with me,
To cross their arms and hang their heads with mine,
To mask their brows and hide their infamy;
795 But I alone, alone must sit and pine,
Seasoning the earth with showers of silver brine,
    Mingling my talk with tears, my grief with groans,
    Poor wasting monuments of lasting moans.

'O Night, thou furnace of foul-reeking smoke,
800 Let not the jealous Day behold that face
Which underneath thy black all-hiding cloak
Immodestly lies martyred with disgrace!
Keep still possession of thy gloomy place,
    That all the faults which in thy reign are made
805   May likewise be sepulchred in thy shade!

'Make me not object to the tell-tale Day!
The light will show, charactered in my brow,
The story of sweet chastity's decay,
The impious breach of holy wedlock vow.
810 Yea, the illiterate, that know not how
    To cipher what is writ in learned books,
    Will quote my loathsome trespass in my looks.

'The nurse to still her child will tell my story,
And fright her crying babe with TARQUIN's name.
815 The orator to deck his oratory
Will couple my reproach to TARQUIN's shame.
Feast-finding minstrels, tuning my defame,
    Will tie the hearers to attend each line,
    How TARQUIN wronged me, I COLLATINE.

820 'Let my good name, that senseless reputation,
For COLLATINE's dear love be kept unspotted.
If that be made a theme for disputation,
The branches of another root are rotted,
And undeserved reproach to him allotted,
825   That is as clear from this attaint of mine
    As I ere this was pure to COLLATINE.

'O unseen shame, invisible disgrace!
O unfelt sore, crest-wounding private scar!
Reproach is stamped in COLLATINUS' face,
830 And TARQUIN's eye may read the mot afar,
"How he in peace is wounded, not in war."
    "Alas, how many bear such shameful blows,
    Which not themselves but he that gives them
        knows!"

'If, COLLATINE, thine honour lay in me, 835
From me by strong assault it is bereft;
My honey lost, and I, a drone-like bee,
Have no perfection of my summer left,
But robbed and ransacked by injurious theft.
 In thy weak hive a wand'ring wasp hath crept, 840
 And sucked the honey which thy chaste bee kept.

'Yet am I guilty of thy honour's wrack;
Yet for thy honour did I entertain him.
Coming from thee, I could not put him back,
For it had been dishonour to disdain him.
Besides, of weariness he did complain him, 845
 And talked of virtue: O, unlooked-for evil,
 When virtue is profaned in such a devil!

'Why should the worm intrude the maiden bud?
Or hateful cuckoos hatch in sparrows' nests?
Or toads infect fair founts with venom mud? 850
Or tyrant folly lurk in gentle breasts?
Or kings be breakers of their own behests?
 "But no perfection is so absolute
 That some impurity doth not pollute."

'The aged man that coffers up his gold 855
Is plagued with cramps and gouts and painful fits,
And scarce hath eyes his treasure to behold;
But like still-pining TANTALUS he sits,
And useless barns the harvest of his wits,
 Having no other pleasure of his gain 860
 But torment that it cannot cure his pain.

'So then he hath it when he cannot use it,
And leaves it to be mastered by his young,
Who in their pride do presently abuse it.
Their father was too weak and they too strong 865
To hold their cursed-blessed fortune long.
 "The sweets we wish for turn to loathed sours
 Even in the moment that we call them ours."

'Unruly blasts wait on the tender spring;
Unwholesome weeds take root with precious
 flowers; 870
The adder hisses where the sweet birds sing;
What virtue breeds iniquity devours.
We have no good that we can say is ours,
 But ill-annexed opportunity
 Or kills his life or else his quality. 875

'O Opportunity, thy guilt is great:
'Tis thou that execut'st the traitor's treason;
Thou sets the wolf where he the lamb may get;
Whoever plots the sin, thou point'st the season.
'Tis thou that spurn'st at right, at law, at reason; 880
 And in thy shady cell, where none may spy him,
 Sits Sin, to seize the souls that wander by him.

'Thou mak'st the vestal violate her oath;
Thou blow'st the fire when temperance is thawed;
Thou smother'st honesty, thou murd'rest troth; 885
Thou foul abettor, thou notorious bawd!
Thou plantest scandal and displacest laud:
 Thou ravisher, thou traitor, thou false thief,
 Thy honey turns to gall, thy joy to grief!

'Thy secret pleasure turns to open shame, 890
Thy private feasting to a public fast,
Thy smoothing titles to a ragged name,
Thy sugared tongue to bitter wormwood taste;
Thy violent vanities can never last.
 How comes it then, vile Opportunity, 895
 Being so bad, such numbers seek for thee?

'When wilt thou be the humble suppliant's friend,
And bring him where his suit may be obtained?
When wilt thou sort an hour great strifes to end,
Or free that soul which wretchedness hath chained? 900
Give physic to the sick, ease to the pained?
 The poor, lame, blind, halt, creep, cry out for
  thee,
 But they ne'er meet with opportunity.

'The patient dies while the physician sleeps;
The orphan pines while the oppressor feeds; 905
Justice is feasting while the widow weeps;
Advice is sporting while infection breeds.
Thou grant'st no time for charitable deeds:
 Wrath, envy, treason, rape, and murder's rages,
 Thy heinous hours wait on them as their pages. 910

'When Truth and Virtue have to do with thee,
A thousand crosses keep them from thy aid:
They buy thy help, but Sin ne'er gives a fee;
He gratis comes, and thou art well apaid
As well to hear as grant what he hath said. 915
 My COLLATINE would else have come to me
 When TARQUIN did, but he was stayed by thee.

'Guilty thou art of murder and of theft,
Guilty of perjury and subornation,
Guilty of treason, forgery and shift, 920
Guilty of incest, that abomination:
An accessory by thine inclination
 To all sins past and all that are to come,
 From the creation to the general doom.

'Misshapen Time, copesmate of ugly Night, 925
Swift subtle post, carrier of grisly care,
Eater of youth, false slave to false delight,
Base watch of woes, sin's pack-horse, virtue's snare;
Thou nursest all, and murd'rest all that are:
 O, hear me then, injurious shifting Time, 930
 Be guilty of my death, since of my crime!

'Why hath thy servant Opportunity
Betrayed the hours thou gav'st me to repose,
Cancelled my fortunes, and enchained me
935   To endless date of never-ending woes?
Time's office is to fine the hate of foes,
    To eat up errors by opinion bred,
    Not spend the dowry of a lawful bed.

'Time's glory is to calm contending kings,
940   To unmask falsehood and bring truth to light,
To stamp the seal of time in aged things,
To wake the morn and sentinel the night,
To wrong the wronger till he render right,
    To ruinate proud buildings with thy hours,
945   And smear with dust their glitt'ring golden towers;

'To fill with worm-holes stately monuments,
To feed oblivion with decay of things,
To blot old books and alter their contents,
To pluck the quills from ancient ravens' wings,
950   To dry the old oaks' sap and cherish springs,
    To spoil antiquities of hammered steel,
    And turn the giddy round of fortune's wheel;

'To show the beldam daughters of her daughter,
To make the child a man, the man a child,
955   To slay the tiger that doth live by slaughter,
To tame the unicorn and lion wild,
To mock the subtle in themselves beguiled,
    To cheer the ploughman with increaseful crops,
    And waste huge stones with little water-drops.

960 'Why work'st thou mischief in thy pilgrimage,
Unless thou couldst return to make amends?
One poor retiring minute in an age
Would purchase thee a thousand thousand friends,
Lending him wit that to bad debtors lends.
    O, this dread night, wouldst thou one hour come
965   back,
    I could prevent this storm and shun thy wrack!

'Thou ceaseless lackey to eternity,
With some mischance cross TARQUIN in his flight.
Devise extremes beyond extremity
970   To make him curse this cursed crimeful night.
Let ghastly shadows his lewd eyes affright,
    And the dire thought of his committed evil
    Shape every bush a hideous shapeless devil.

'Disturb his hours of rest with restless trances;
975   Afflict him in his bed with bedrid groans;
Let there bechance him pitiful mischances
To make him moan, but pity not his moans.
Stone him with hardened hearts harder than stones,
    And let mild women to him lose their mildness,
980   Wilder to him than tigers in their wildness.

'Let him have time to tear his curled hair,
Let him have time against himself to rave,
Let him have time of Time's help to despair,
Let him have time to live a loathed slave,
Let him have time a beggar's orts to crave,   985
    And time to see one that by alms doth live
    Disdain to him disdained scraps to give.

'Let him have time to see his friends his foes,
And merry fools to mock at him resort;
Let him have time to mark how slow time goes   990
In time of sorrow, and how swift and short
His time of folly and his time of sport;
    And ever let his unrecalling crime
    Have time to wail th'abusing of his time.

'O Time, thou tutor both to good and bad,   995
Teach me to curse him that thou taught'st this ill!
At his own shadow let the thief run mad,
Himself himself seek every hour to kill!
Such wretched hands such wretched blood should spill,
    For who so base would such an office have   1000
    As sland'rous deathsman to so base a slave?

'The baser is he, coming from a king,
To shame his hope with deeds degenerate;
The mightier man, the mightier is the thing
That makes him honoured or begets him hate;   1005
For greatest scandal waits on greatest state.
    The moon being clouded presently is missed,
    But little stars may hide them when they list.

'The crow may bathe his coal-black wings in mire,
And unperceived fly with the filth away;   1010
But if the like the snow-white swan desire,
The stain upon his silver down will stay.
Poor grooms are sightless night, kings glorious day;
    Gnats are unnoted wheresoe'er they fly,
    But eagles gazed upon with every eye.   1015

'Out, idle words, servants to shallow fools,
Unprofitable sounds, weak arbitrators!
Busy yourselves in skill-contending schools,
Debate where leisure serves with dull debaters;
To trembling clients be you mediators: 1020
    For me, I force not argument a straw,
    Since that my case is past the help of law.

'In vain I rail at Opportunity,
At Time, at TARQUIN, and uncheerful Night,
In vain I cavil with mine infamy,   1025
In vain I spurn at my confirmed despite:
This helpless smoke of words doth me no right.
    The remedy indeed to do me good
    Is to let forth my foul-defiled blood.

1030 'Poor hand, why quiver'st thou at this decree?
Honour thyself to rid me of this shame.
For if I die, my honour lives in thee;
But if I live, thou liv'st in my defame.
Since thou couldst not defend thy loyal dame,
1035　　And wast afeard to scratch her wicked foe,
　　Kill both thyself and her for yielding so.'

This said, from her betumbled couch she starteth,
To find some desp'rate instrument of death.
But this, no slaughterhouse, no tool imparteth
1040 To make more vent for passage of her breath,
Which thronging through her lips so vanisheth
　　As smoke from ETNA that in air consumes,
　　Or that which from discharged cannon fumes.

'In vain', quoth she, 'I live, and seek in vain
1045 Some happy mean to end a hapless life.
I feared by TARQUIN's falchion to be slain,
Yet for the self-same purpose seek a knife.
But when I feared I was a loyal wife;
　　So am I now – O no, that cannot be:
1050　　Of that true type hath TARQUIN rifled me.

'O, that is gone for which I sought to live,
And therefore now I need not fear to die.
To clear this spot by death, at least I give
A badge of fame to slander's livery,
1055 A dying life to living infamy.
　　Poor helpless help, the treasure stol'n away,
　　To burn the guiltless casket where it lay!

'Well, well, dear COLLATINE, thou shalt not know
The stained taste of violated troth;
1060 I will not wrong thy true affection so
To flatter thee with an infringed oath.
This bastard graff shall never come to growth:
　　He shall not boast who did thy stock pollute,
　　That thou art doting father of his fruit.

1065 'Nor shall he smile at thee in secret thought,
Nor laugh with his companions at thy state;
But thou shalt know thy int'rest was not bought
Basely with gold, but stol'n from forth thy gate.
For me, I am the mistress of my fate,
1070　　And with my trespass never will dispense,
　　Till life to death acquit my forced offence.

'I will not poison thee with my attaint,
Nor fold my fault in cleanly coined excuses;
My sable ground of sin I will not paint
1075 To hide the truth of this false night's abuses.
My tongue shall utter all; mine eyes, like sluices,
　　As from a mountain spring that feeds a dale
　　Shall gush pure streams to purge my impure tale.'

By this, lamenting PHILOMEL had ended
The well-tuned warble of her nightly sorrow, 1080
And solemn night with slow sad gait descended
To ugly hell, when lo, the blushing morrow
Lends light to all fair eyes that light will borrow;
　　But cloudy LUCRECE shames herself to see,
　　And therefore still in night would cloistered be. 1085

Revealing day through every cranny spies,
And seems to point her out where she sits weeping;
To whom she sobbing speaks: 'O eye of eyes,
Why pry'st thou through my window? Leave thy
　　　peeping,
Mock with thy tickling beams eyes that are sleeping, 1090
　　Brand not my forehead with thy piercing light,
　　For day hath naught to do what's done by night.'

Thus cavils she with everything she sees:
True grief is fond and testy as a child
Who, wayward once, his mood with naught agrees. 1095
Old woes, not infant sorrows, bear them mild:
Continuance tames the one; the other wild,
　　Like an unpractised swimmer plunging still,
　　With too much labour drowns for want of skill.

So she, deep drenched in a sea of care, 1100
Holds disputation with each thing she views,
And to herself all sorrow doth compare;
No object but her passion's strength renews,
And as one shifts, another straight ensues.
　　Sometime her grief is dumb and hath no words, 1105
　　Sometime 'tis mad and too much talk affords.

The little birds that tune their morning's joy
Make her moans mad with their sweet melody,
"For mirth doth search the bottom of annoy;
Sad souls are slain in merry company; 1110
Grief best is pleased with grief's society:
　　True sorrow then is feelingly sufficed
　　When with like semblance it is sympathized."

"'Tis double death to drown in ken of shore;
He ten times pines that pines beholding food; 1115
To see the salve doth make the wound ache more;
Great grief grieves most at that would do it good;
Deep woes roll forward like a gentle flood
　　Who, being stopped, the bounding banks oerflows;
　　Grief dallied with nor law nor limit knows." 1120

'You mocking birds,' quoth she, 'your tunes entomb
Within your hollow-swelling feathered breasts,
And in my hearing be you mute and dumb:
My restless discord loves no stops nor rests.
"A woeful hostess brooks not merry guests." 1125
　　Relish your nimble notes to pleasing ears;
　　"Distress likes dumps when time is kept with tears."

'Come, PHILOMEL, that sing'st of ravishment,
Make thy sad grove in my dishevelled hair.
1130 As the dank earth weeps at thy languishment,
So I at each sad strain will strain a tear,
And with deep groans the diapason bear;
 For burden-wise I'll hum on TARQUIN still,
 While thou on TEREUS descants better skill.

1135 'And whiles against a thorn thou bear'st thy part,
To keep thy sharp woes waking, wretched I,
To imitate thee well, against my heart
Will fix a sharp knife to affright mine eye,
Who if it wink shall thereon fall and die.
1140 These means, as frets upon an instrument,
 Shall tune our heart-strings to true languishment.

'And for, poor bird, thou sing'st not in the day,
As shaming any eye should thee behold,
Some dark deep desert, seated from the way,
1145 That knows not parching heat nor freezing cold,
Will we find out, and there we will unfold
 To creatures stern sad tunes to change their kinds:
 Since men prove beasts, let beasts bear gentle
  minds.'

As the poor frighted deer that stands at gaze,
1150 Wildly determining which way to fly,
Or one encompassed with a winding maze
That cannot tread the way out readily,
So with herself is she in mutiny,
 To live or die which of the twain were better,
1155 When life is shamed and death reproach's debtor.

'To kill myself,' quoth she, 'alack, what were it,
But with my body my poor soul's pollution?
They that lose half with greater patience bear it
Than they whose whole is swallowed in confusion.
1160 That mother tries a merciless conclusion
 Who, having two sweet babes, when death takes one
 Will slay the other and be nurse to none.

'My body or my soul, which was the dearer,
When the one pure the other made divine?
1165 Whose love of either to myself was nearer,
When both were kept for heaven and COLLATINE?
Ay me! The bark pilled from the lofty pine,
 His leaves will wither and his sap decay;
 So must my soul, her bark being pilled away.

1170 'Her house is sacked, her quiet interrupted,
Her mansion battered by the enemy,
Her sacred temple spotted, spoiled, corrupted,
Grossly engirt with daring infamy.
 Then let it not be called impiety,
1175 If in this blemished fort I make some hole
 Through which I may convey this troubled soul.

'Yet die I will not till my COLLATINE
Have heard the cause of my untimely death,
That he may vow in that sad hour of mine
Revenge on him that made me stop my breath. 1180
My stained blood to TARQUIN I'll bequeath,
 Which by him tainted shall for him be spent,
 And as his due writ in my testament.

'My honour I'll bequeath unto the knife
That wounds my body so dishonoured. 1185
'Tis honour to deprive dishonoured life;
The one will live, the other being dead.
So of shame's ashes shall my fame be bred,
 For in my death I murder shameful scorn;
 My shame so dead, mine honour is new born. 1190

'Dear lord of that dear jewel I have lost,
What legacy shall I bequeath to thee?
My resolution, love, shall be thy boast,
By whose example thou revenged mayst be.
How TARQUIN must be used, read it in me: 1195
 Myself, thy friend, will kill myself, thy foe,
 And for my sake serve thou false TARQUIN so.

'This brief abridgement of my will I make:
My soul and body to the skies and ground;
My resolution, husband, do thou take; 1200
Mine honour be the knife's that makes my wound;
My shame be his that did my fame confound;
 And all my fame that lives disbursed be
 To those that live and think no shame of me.

'Thou, COLLATINE, shalt oversee this will. 1205
How was I overseen that thou shalt see it!
My blood shall wash the slander of mine ill;
My life's foul deed, my life's fair end shall free it.
Faint not, faint heart, but stoutly say "So be it."
 Yield to my hand; my hand shall conquer thee: 1210
 Thou dead, both die, and both shall victors be.'

This plot of death when sadly she had laid
And wiped the brinish pearl from her bright eyes,
With untuned tongue she hoarsely calls her maid,
Whose swift obedience to her mistress hies; 1215
"For fleet-winged duty with thought's feathers flies."
 Poor LUCRECE' cheeks unto her maid seem so
 As winter meads when sun doth melt their snow.

Her mistress she doth give demure good-morrow
With soft slow tongue, true mark of modesty, 1220
And sorts a sad look to her lady's sorrow,
For why her face wore sorrow's livery,
But durst not ask of her audaciously
 Why her two suns were cloud-eclipsed so,
 Nor why her fair cheeks overwashed with woe. 1225

But as the earth doth weep, the sun being set,
Each flower moistened like a melting eye,
Even so the maid with swelling drops 'gan wet
Her circled eyne, enforced by sympathy
1230   Of those fair suns set in her mistress' sky,
    Who in a salt-waved ocean quench their light,
    Which makes the maid weep like the dewy night.

A pretty while these pretty creatures stand,
Like ivory conduits coral cisterns filling.
1235   One justly weeps, the other takes in hand
No cause but company of her drops' spilling:
Their gentle sex to weep are often willing,
    Grieving themselves to guess at others' smarts,
    And then they drown their eyes or break their hearts.

1240   For men have marble, women waxen minds,
And therefore are they formed as marble will.
The weak oppressed, th'impression of strange kinds
Is formed in them by force, by fraud or skill.
Then call them not the authors of their ill,
1245   No more than wax shall be accounted evil
    Wherein is stamped the semblance of a devil.

Their smoothness, like a goodly champaign plain,
Lays open all the little worms that creep;
In men, as in a rough-grown grove, remain
1250   Cave-keeping evils that obscurely sleep.
Through crystal walls each little mote will peep.
    Though men can cover crimes with bold stern looks,
    Poor women's faces are their own faults' books.

No man inveigh against the withered flower,
1255   But chide rough winter that the flower hath killed;
Not that devoured, but that which doth devour,
Is worthy blame. O, let it not be hild
Poor women's faults that they are so fulfilled
    With men's abuses: those proud lords, to blame,
1260   Make weak-made women tenants to their shame.

The precedent whereof in LUCRECE view,
Assailed by night with circumstances strong
Of present death, and shame that might ensue
By that her death to do her husband wrong.
1265   Such danger to resistance did belong
    That dying fear through all her body spread;
    And who cannot abuse a body dead?

By this, mild patience bid fair LUCRECE speak
To the poor counterfeit of her complaining:
1270   'My girl,' quoth she, 'on what occasion break
Those tears from thee that down thy cheeks are
      raining?
If thou dost weep for grief of my sustaining,
    Know, gentle wench, it small avails my mood:
    If tears could help, mine own would do me good.

'But tell me, girl, when went' – and there she stayed   1275
Till after a deep groan – 'TARQUIN from hence?'
'Madam, ere I was up,' replied the maid,
'The more to blame my sluggard negligence.
Yet with the fault I thus far can dispense:
    Myself was stirring ere the break of day,   1280
    And ere I rose was TARQUIN gone away.

'But lady, if your maid may be so bold,
She would request to know your heaviness.'
'O, peace!' quoth LUCRECE: 'If it should be told,
The repetition cannot make it less;   1285
For more it is than I can well express,
    And that deep torture may be called a hell
    When more is felt than one hath power to tell.

'Go, get me hither paper, ink and pen;
Yet save that labour, for I have them here.   1290
What should I say? One of my husband's men
Bid thou be ready by and by to bear
A letter to my lord, my love, my dear.
    Bid him with speed prepare to carry it;
    The cause craves haste, and it will soon be writ.'   1295

Her maid is gone, and she prepares to write,
First hovering o'er the paper with her quill.
Conceit and grief an eager combat fight;
What wit sets down is blotted straight with will.
This is too curious-good, this blunt and ill: 1300
    Much like a press of people at a door,
    Throng her inventions, which shall go before.

At last she thus begins: 'Thou worthy lord
Of that unworthy wife that greeteth thee,
Health to thy person! Next, vouchsafe t'afford –   1305
If ever, love, thy LUCRECE thou wilt see –
Some present speed to come and visit me.
    So I commend me, from our house in grief:
    My woes are tedious, though my words are brief.'

Here folds she up the tenor of her woe,   1310
Her certain sorrow writ uncertainly.
By this short schedule COLLATINE may know
Her grief, but not her grief's true quality.
She dares not thereof make discovery,
    Lest he should hold it her own gross abuse,   1315
    Ere she with blood had stained her stained excuse.

Besides, the life and feeling of her passion
She hoards, to spend when he is by to hear her;
When sighs and groans and tears may grace the
    fashion
Of her disgrace, the better so to clear her   1320
From that suspicion which the world might bear her.
    To shun this blot she would not blot the letter
    With words, till action might become them better.

To see sad sights moves more than hear them told,
For then the eye interprets to the ear
The heavy motion that it doth behold,
When every part a part of woe doth bear.
'Tis but a part of sorrow that we hear:
 Deep sounds make lesser noise than shallow fords,
 And sorrow ebbs, being blown with wind of words.

Her letter now is sealed, and on it writ
'At ARDEA to my lord with more than haste.'
The post attends, and she delivers it,
Charging the sour-faced groom to hie as fast
As lagging fowls before the northern blast.
 Speed more than speed but dull and slow she deems:
 Extremity still urgeth such extremes.

The homely villain curtsies to her low,
And blushing on her with a steadfast eye
Receives the scroll without or yea or no,
And forth with bashful innocence doth hie.
But they whose guilt within their bosoms lie
 Imagine every eye beholds their blame;
 For LUCRECE thought he blushed to see her shame,

When, silly groom, God wot, it was defect
Of spirit, life and bold audacity.
Such harmless creatures have a true respect
To talk in deeds, while others saucily
Promise more speed, but do it leisurely.
 Even so this pattern of the worn-out age
 Pawned honest looks, but laid no words to gage.

His kindled duty kindled her mistrust,
That two red fires in both their faces blazed;
She thought he blushed as knowing TARQUIN's lust,
And blushing with him, wistly on him gazed.
Her earnest eye did make him more amazed:
 The more she saw the blood his cheeks replenish,
 The more she thought he spied in her some blemish.

But long she thinks till he return again,
And yet the duteous vassal scarce is gone.
The weary time she cannot entertain,
For now 'tis stale to sigh, to weep and groan:
So woe hath wearied woe, moan tired moan,
 That she her plaints a little while doth stay,
 Pausing for means to mourn some newer way.

At last she calls to mind where hangs a piece
Of skilful painting made for PRIAM's TROY,
Before the which is drawn the power of GREECE,
For HELEN's rape the city to destroy,
Threat'ning cloud-kissing ILION with annoy;
 Which the conceited painter drew so proud
 As heaven, it seemed, to kiss the turrets bowed.

A thousand lamentable objects there,
In scorn of nature, art gave lifeless life;
Many a dry drop seemed a weeping tear
Shed for the slaughtered husband by the wife:
The red blood reeked, to show the painter's strife,
 And dying eyes gleamed forth their ashy lights,
 Like dying coals burnt out in tedious nights.

There might you see the labouring pioneer
Begrimed with sweat and smeared all with dust;
And from the towers of TROY there would appear
The very eyes of men through loop-holes thrust,
Gazing upon the GREEKS with little lust.
 Such sweet observance in this work was had
 That one might see those far-off eyes look sad.

In great commanders grace and majesty
You might behold, triumphing in their faces;
In youth, quick bearing and dexterity;
And here and there the painter interlaces
Pale cowards marching on with trembling paces,
 Which heartless peasants did so well resemble
 That one would swear he saw them quake and
  tremble.

In AJAX and ULYSSES, O, what art
Of physiognomy might one behold!
The face of either ciphered either's heart;
Their face their manners most expressly told:
In AJAX' eyes blunt rage and rigour rolled;
 But the mild glance that sly ULYSSES lent
 Showed deep regard and smiling government.

There, pleading, might you see grave NESTOR stand,
As 'twere encouraging the GREEKS to fight,
Making such sober action with his hand
That it beguiled attention, charmed the sight.
In speech it seemed his beard, all silver white,
 Wagged up and down, and from his lips did fly
 Thin winding breath, which purled up to the sky.

About him were a press of gaping faces,
Which seemed to swallow up his sound advice,
All jointly list'ning, but with several graces,
As if some mermaid did their ears entice,
Some high, some low, the painter was so nice;
 The scalps of many, almost hid behind,
 To jump up higher seemed, to mock the mind.

Here one man's hand leaned on another's head,
His nose being shadowed by his neighbour's ear;
Here one being thronged bears back, all boll'n and red;
Another, smothered, seems to pelt and swear;
And in their rage such signs of rage they bear
 As, but for loss of NESTOR's golden words,
 It seemed they would debate with angry swords.

1325
1330
1335
1340
1345
1350
1355
1360
1365
1370
1375
1380
1385
1390
1395
1400
1405
1410
1415
1420

For much imaginary work was there:
Conceit deceitful, so compact, so kind,
That for ACHILLES' image stood his spear,
1425 Griped in an armed hand; himself behind
Was left unseen, save to the eye of mind:
 A hand, a foot, a face, a leg, a head,
 Stood for the whole to be imagined.

And from the walls of strong-besieged TROY
When their brave hope, bold HECTOR, marched to
1430 field,
Stood many TROJAN mothers, sharing joy
To see their youthful sons bright weapons wield;
And to their hope they such odd action yield
That through their light joy seemed to appear,
1435 Like bright things stained, a kind of heavy fear.

And from the strand of DARDAN where they fought
To SIMOIS' reedy banks the red blood ran,
Whose waves to imitate the battle sought
With swelling ridges; and their ranks began
1440 To break upon the galled shore, and than
 Retire again, till meeting greater ranks
 They join, and shoot their foam at SIMOIS' banks.

To this well-painted piece is LUCRECE come,
To find a face where all distress is stelled.
1445 Many she sees where cares have carved some,
But none where all distress and dolour dwelled
Till she despairing HECUBA beheld,
 Staring on PRIAM's wounds with her old eyes,
 Which bleeding under PYRRHUS' proud foot lies.

1450 In her the painter had anatomized
Time's ruin, beauty's wrack and grim care's reign.
Her cheeks with chaps and wrinkles were disguised;
Of what she was no semblance did remain.
Her blue blood changed to black in every vein,
1455 Wanting the spring that those shrunk pipes had fed,
 Showed life imprisoned in a body dead.

On this sad shadow LUCRECE spends her eyes,
And shapes her sorrow to the beldam's woes,
Who nothing wants to answer her but cries
1460 And bitter words to ban her cruel foes:
The painter was no god to lend her those,
 And therefore LUCRECE swears he did her wrong
 To give her so much grief and not a tongue.

'Poor instrument' quoth she, 'without a sound,
1465 I'll tune thy woes with my lamenting tongue
And drop sweet balm in PRIAM's painted wound,
And rail on PYRRHUS that hath done him wrong,
And with my tears quench TROY that burns so long,
 And with my knife scratch out the angry eyes
1470 Of all the GREEKS that are thine enemies.

'Show me the strumpet that began this stir,
That with my nails her beauty I may tear.
Thy heat of lust, fond PARIS, did incur
This load of wrath that burning TROY doth bear:
Thy eye kindled the fire that burneth here, 1475
 And here in TROY, for trespass of thine eye,
 The sire, the son, the dame and daughter die.

'Why should the private pleasure of some one
Become the public plague of many moe?
Let sin, alone committed, light alone 1480
Upon his head that hath transgressed so;
Let guiltless souls be freed from guilty woe:
 For one's offence why should so many fall,
 To plague a private sin in general?

'Lo, here weeps HECUBA, here PRIAM dies, 1485
Here manly HECTOR faints, here TROILUS swounds,
Here friend by friend in bloody channel lies,
And friend to friend gives unadvised wounds,
And one man's lust these many lives confounds.
 Had doting PRIAM checked his son's desire, 1490
 TROY had been bright with fame, and not with fire.'

Here feelingly she weeps TROY's painted woes:
For sorrow, like a heavy-hanging bell,
Once set on ringing, with his own weight goes;
Then little strength rings out the doleful knell. 1495
So LUCRECE, set a-work, sad tales doth tell
 To pencilled pensiveness and coloured sorrow;
 She lends them words, and she their looks doth
 borrow.

She throws her eyes about the painting round,
And who she finds forlorn she doth lament. 1500
At last she sees a wretched image bound,
That piteous looks to PHRYGIAN shepherds lent:
His face, though full of cares, yet showed content.
 Onward to TROY with the blunt swains he goes,
 So mild that patience seemed to scorn his woes. 1505

In him the painter laboured with his skill
To hide deceit, and give the harmless show
An humble gait, calm looks, eyes wailing still,
A brow unbent that seemed to welcome woe,
Cheeks neither red nor pale, but mingled so 1510
 That blushing red no guilty instance gave,
 Nor ashy pale the fear that false hearts have.

But like a constant and confirmed devil
He entertained a show so seeming just,
And therein so ensconced his secret evil 1515
That jealousy itself could not mistrust
False creeping craft and perjury should thrust
 Into so bright a day such black-faced storms,
 Or blot with hell-born sin such saintlike forms.

1520 The well-skilled workman this mild image drew
For perjured SINON, whose enchanting story
The credulous old PRIAM after slew;
Whose words like wildfire burnt the shining glory
Of rich-built ILION, that the skies were sorry,
1525   And little stars shot from their fixed places,
        When their glass fell wherein they viewed their
        faces.

This picture she advisedly perused,
And chid the painter for his wondrous skill,
Saying some shape in SINON's was abused:
1530 So fair a form lodged not a mind so ill.
And still on him she gazed, and gazing still,
        Such signs of truth in his plain face she spied,
        That she concludes the picture was belied.

'It cannot be', quoth she, 'that so much guile' –
1535 She would have said 'can lurk in such a look'.
But TARQUIN's shape came in her mind the while,
And from her tongue 'can lurk' from 'cannot' took.
'It cannot be' she in that sense forsook,
        And turned it thus: 'It cannot be, I find,
1540   But such a face should bear a wicked mind.

'For even as subtle SINON here is painted,
So sober-sad, so weary and so mild,
As if with grief or travail he had fainted,
To me came TARQUIN armed to beguild
1545 With outward honesty, but yet defiled
        With inward vice. As PRIAM him did cherish,
        So did I TARQUIN, so my TROY did perish.

'Look, look, how list'ning PRIAM wets his eyes
To see those borrowed tears that SINON sheds!
1550 PRIAM, why art thou old and yet not wise?
For every tear he falls a TROJAN bleeds:
His eye drops fire, no water thence proceeds;
        Those round clear pearls of his that move thy pity
        Are balls of quenchless fire to burn thy city.

1555 'Such devils steal effects from lightless hell;
For SINON in his fire doth quake with cold,
And in that cold hot-burning fire doth dwell.
These contraries such unity do hold
Only to flatter fools and make them bold;
1560   So PRIAM's trust false SINON's tears doth flatter
        That he finds means to burn his TROY with water.'

Here, all enraged, such passion her assails,
That patience is quite beaten from her breast.
She tears the senseless SINON with her nails,
1565 Comparing him to that unhappy guest
Whose deed hath made herself herself detest.
        At last she smilingly with this gives o'er:
        'Fool, fool!' quoth she, 'his wounds will not be sore.'

Thus ebbs and flows the current of her sorrow,
And time doth weary time with her complaining. 1570
She looks for night, and then she longs for morrow,
And both she thinks too long with her remaining.
Short time seems long in sorrow's sharp sustaining:
        Though woe be heavy, yet it seldom sleeps,
        And they that watch see time how slow it creeps. 1575

Which all this time hath overslipped her thought
That she with painted images hath spent,
Being from the feeling of her own grief brought
By deep surmise of others' detriment,
Losing her woes in shows of discontent. 1580
        It easeth some, though none it ever cured,
        To think their dolour others have endured.

But now the mindful messenger come back
Brings home his lord and other company,
Who finds his LUCRECE clad in mourning black, 1585
And round about her tear-distained eye
Blue circles streamed, like rainbows in the sky:
        These water-galls in her dim element
        Foretell new storms to those already spent.

Which when her sad-beholding husband saw, 1590
Amazedly in her sad face he stares:
Her eyes, though sod in tears, looked red and raw,
Her lively colour killed with deadly cares.
He hath no power to ask her how she fares.
        Both stood like old acquaintance in a trance, 1595
        Met far from home, wond'ring each other's
        chance.

At last he takes her by the bloodless hand,
And thus begins: 'What uncouth ill event
Hath thee befall'n, that thou dost trembling stand?
Sweet love, what spite hath thy fair colour spent? 1600
Why art thou thus attired in discontent?
        Unmask, dear dear, this moody heaviness,
        And tell thy grief, that we may give redress.'

Three times with sighs she gives her sorrow fire,
Ere once she can discharge one word of woe. 1605
At length addressed to answer his desire,
She modestly prepares to let them know
Her honour is ta'en prisoner by the foe;
        While COLLATINE and his consorted lords
        With sad attention long to hear her words. 1610

And now this pale swan in her wat'ry nest
Begins the sad dirge of her certain ending:
'Few words', quoth she, 'shall fit the trespass best,
Where no excuse can give the fault amending.
In me moe woes than words are now depending, 1615
        And my laments would be drawn out too long
        To tell them all with one poor tired tongue.

'Then be this all the task it hath to say:
Dear husband, in the interest of thy bed
1620 A stranger came, and on that pillow lay
Where thou wast wont to rest thy weary head;
And what wrong else may be imagined
    By foul enforcement might be done to me,
    From that, alas, thy LUCRECE is not free.

1625 'For in the dreadful dead of dark midnight,
With shining falchion in my chamber came
A creeping creature with a flaming light,
And softly cried, "Awake, thou ROMAN dame,
And entertain my love; else lasting shame
1630   On thee and thine this night I will inflict,
    If thou my love's desire do contradict.

'"For some hard-favoured groom of thine,"
        quoth he,
"Unless thou yoke thy liking to my will,
I'll murder straight, and then I'll slaughter thee,
1635 And swear I found you where you did fulfil
The loathsome act of lust, and so did kill
    The lechers in their deed: this act will be
    My fame, and thy perpetual infamy."

'With this I did begin to start and cry;
1640 And then against my heart he set his sword,
Swearing, unless I took all patiently,
I should not live to speak another word.
So should my shame still rest upon record,
    And never be forgot in mighty ROME
1645   Th'adulterate death of LUCRECE and her groom.

'Mine enemy was strong, my poor self weak,
And far the weaker with so strong a fear.
My bloody judge forbade my tongue to speak;
No rightful plea might plead for justice there.
1650 His scarlet lust came evidence to swear
    That my poor beauty had purloined his eyes;
    And when the judge is robbed, the prisoner dies.

'O, teach me how to make mine own excuse!
Or, at the least, this refuge let me find:
1655 Though my gross blood be stained with this abuse,
Immaculate and spotless is my mind;
That was not forced, that never was inclined
    To accessory yieldings, but still pure
    Doth in her poisoned closet yet endure.'

1660 Lo, here the hopeless merchant of this loss,
With head declined and voice dammed up with woe,
With sad-set eyes and wreathed arms across,
From lips new waxen pale begins to blow
The grief away that stops his answer so.
1665   But, wretched as he is, he strives in vain:
    What he breathes out his breath drinks up again.

As through an arch the violent roaring tide
Outruns the eye that doth behold his haste,
Yet in the eddy boundeth in his pride
Back to the strait that forced him on so fast, 1670
In rage sent out, recalled in rage, being past;
    Even so his sighs, his sorrows make a saw,
    To push grief on, and back the same grief draw.

Which speechless woe of his poor she attendeth,
And his untimely frenzy thus awaketh: 1675
'Dear lord, thy sorrow to my sorrow lendeth
Another power; no flood by raining slaketh.
My woe too sensible thy passion maketh
    More feeling-painful. Let it then suffice
    To drown one woe, one pair of weeping eyes. 1680

'And for my sake, when I might charm thee so,
For she that was thy LUCRECE, now attend me:
Be suddenly revenged on my foe –
Thine, mine, his own. Suppose thou dost defend me
From what is past, the help that thou shalt lend me 1685
    Comes all too late, yet let the traitor die;
    "For sparing justice feeds iniquity."

'But ere I name him, you fair lords', quoth she,
Speaking to those that came with COLLATINE,
'Shall plight your honourable faiths to me, 1690
With swift pursuit to venge this wrong of mine;
For 'tis a meritorious fair design
    To chase injustice with revengeful arms:
    Knights, by their oaths, should right poor ladies'
      harms.'

At this request with noble disposition 1695
Each present lord began to promise aid,
As bound in knighthood to her imposition,
Longing to hear the hateful foe bewrayed.
But she, that yet her sad task hath not said,
    The protestation stops. 'O, speak,' quoth she, 1700
    'How may this forced stain be wiped from me?

'What is the quality of my offence,
Being constrained with dreadful circumstance?
May my pure mind with the foul act dispense,
My low-declined honour to advance? 1705
May any terms acquit me from this chance?
    The poisoned fountain clears itself again;
    And why not I from this compelled stain?'

With this they all at once began to say
Her body's stain her mind untainted clears; 1710
While with a joyless smile she turns away
The face, that map which deep impression bears
Of hard misfortune, carved in it with tears.
    'No, no,' quoth she, 'no dame hereafter living
    By my excuse shall claim excuse's giving.' 1715

Here, with a sigh as if her heart would break,
She throws forth TARQUIN's name: 'He, he', she says,
But more than 'he' her poor tongue could not speak;
Till, after many accents and delays,
Untimely breathings, sick and short assays,
    She utters this: 'He, he, fair lords, 'tis he
    That guides this hand to give this wound to me.'

Even here she sheathed in her harmless breast
A harmful knife, that thence her soul unsheathed:
That blow did bail it from the deep unrest
Of that polluted prison where it breathed.
Her contrite sighs unto the clouds bequeathed
    Her winged sprite, and through her wounds doth fly
    Life's lasting date from cancelled destiny.

Stone-still, astonished with this deadly deed,
Stood COLLATINE and all his lordly crew,
Till LUCRECE' father, that beholds her bleed,
Himself on her self-slaughtered body threw;
And from the purple fountain BRUTUS drew
    The murd'rous knife, and as it left the place,
    Her blood in poor revenge held it in chase;

And bubbling from her breast, it doth divide
In two slow rivers, that the crimson blood
Circles her body in on every side,
Who like a late-sacked island vastly stood
Bare and unpeopled in this fearful flood.
    Some of her blood still pure and red remained,
    And some looked black, and that false TARQUIN
      stained.

About the mourning and congealed face
Of that black blood a wat'ry rigol goes,
Which seems to weep upon the tainted place;
And ever since, as pitying LUCRECE' woes,
Corrupted blood some watery token shows,
    And blood untainted still doth red abide,
    Blushing at that which is so putrefied.

'Daughter, dear daughter,' old LUCRETIUS cries,
'That life was mine which thou hast here deprived.
If in the child the father's image lies,
Where shall I live now LUCRECE is unlived?
Thou wast not to this end from me derived.
    If children predecease progenitors,
    We are their offspring, and they none of ours.

'Poor broken glass, I often did behold
In thy sweet semblance my old age new born;
But now that fair fresh mirror, dim and old,
Shows me a bare-boned death by time outworn.
O, from thy cheeks my image thou hast torn,
    And shivered all the beauty of my glass,
    That I no more can see what once I was.

'O time, cease thou thy course and last no longer,
If they surcease to be that should survive.
Shall rotten death make conquest of the stronger,
And leave the falt'ring feeble souls alive?
The old bees die, the young possess their hive.
    Then live, sweet LUCRECE, live again and see
    Thy father die, and not thy father thee!'

By this, starts COLLATINE as from a dream,
And bids LUCRETIUS give his sorrow place;
And then in key-cold LUCRECE' bleeding stream
He falls, and bathes the pale fear in his face,
And counterfeits to die with her a space,
    Till manly shame bids him possess his breath,
    And live to be revenged on her death.

The deep vexation of his inward soul
Hath served a dumb arrest upon his tongue,
Who, mad that sorrow should his use control,
Or keep him from heart-easing words so long,
Begins to talk; but through his lips do throng
    Weak words, so thick come in his poor heart's aid
    That no man could distinguish what he said.

Yet sometime 'TARQUIN' was pronounced plain,
But through his teeth, as if the name he tore.
This windy tempest, till it blow up rain,
Held back his sorrow's tide, to make it more.
At last it rains, and busy winds give o'er;
    Then son and father weep with equal strife
    Who should weep most, for daughter or for wife.

The one doth call her his, the other his,
Yet neither may possess the claim they lay.
The father says 'She's mine.' 'O, mine she is,'
Replies her husband: 'do not take away
My sorrow's interest; let no mourner say
    He weeps for her, for she was only mine,
    And only must be wailed by COLLATINE.'

'O,' quoth LUCRETIUS, 'I did give that life
Which she too early and too late hath spilled.'
'Woe, woe,' quoth COLLATINE, 'she was my wife;
I owed her, and 'tis mine that she hath killed.'
'My daughter' and 'My wife' with clamours filled
    The dispersed air, who, holding LUCRECE' life,
    Answered their cries, 'My daughter' and 'My wife'.

BRUTUS, who plucked the knife from LUCRECE' side,
Seeing such emulation in their woe,
Began to clothe his wit in state and pride,
Burying in LUCRECE' wound his folly's show.
He with the ROMANS was esteemed so
    As silly jeering idiots are with kings,
    For sportive words and utt'ring foolish things.

But now he throws that shallow habit by,
1815 Wherein deep policy did him disguise,
And armed his long-hid wits advisedly,
To check the tears in COLLATINUS' eyes.
'Thou wronged lord of ROME,' quoth he, 'arise;
    Let my unsounded self, supposed a fool,
1820   Now set thy long-experienced wit to school.

'Why, COLLATINE, is woe the cure for woe?
Do wounds help wounds, or grief help grievous
        deeds?
Is it revenge to give thyself a blow
For his foul act by whom thy fair wife bleeds?
1825 Such childish humour from weak minds proceeds.
    Thy wretched wife mistook the matter so,
    To slay herself, that should have slain her foe.

'Courageous ROMAN, do not steep thy heart
In such relenting dew of lamentations,
1830 But kneel with me and help to bear thy part
To rouse our ROMAN gods with invocations
That they will suffer these abominations –
    Since ROME herself in them doth stand disgraced –
    By our strong arms from forth her fair streets
        chased.

'Now by the CAPITOL that we adore,   1835
And by this chaste blood so unjustly stained,
By heaven's fair sun that breeds the fat earth's store,
By all our country rights in ROME maintained,
And by chaste LUCRECE' soul that late complained
    Her wrongs to us, and by this bloody knife,   1840
    We will revenge the death of this true wife.'

This said, he struck his hand upon his breast,
And kissed the fatal knife to end his vow;
And to his protestation urged the rest,
Who, wond'ring at him, did his words allow.   1845
Then jointly to the ground their knees they bow,
    And that deep vow which BRUTUS made before
    He doth again repeat, and that they swore.

When they had sworn to this advised doom
They did conclude to bear dead LUCRECE thence,   1850
To show her bleeding body thorough ROME,
And so to publish TARQUIN's foul offence;
Which being done, with speedy diligence,
    The ROMANS plausibly did give consent
    To TARQUINS' everlasting banishment.   1855

The Passionate Pilgrim

[1]

When my love swears that she is made of truth,
I do believe her (though I know she lies),
That she might think me some untutored youth,
Unskilful in the world's false forgeries.
5   Thus vainly thinking that she thinks me young,
Although I know my years be past the best,
I, smiling, credit her false-speaking tongue,
Outfacing faults in love with love's ill rest.
But wherefore says my love that she is young?
10 And wherefore say not I that I am old?
O, love's best habit's in a soothing tongue,
And age, in love, loves not to have years told.
    Therefore I'll lie with love, and love with me,
    Since that our faults in love thus smothered be.

[2]

Two loves I have, of comfort and despair,
That like two spirits do suggest me still:
My better angel is a man (right fair),
My worser spirit a woman (coloured ill).
5   To win me soon to hell, my female evil
Tempteth my better angel from my side,
And would corrupt my saint to be a devil,
Wooing his purity with her fair pride.
And whether that my angel be turned fiend,
10 Suspect I may (yet not directly tell):
For being both to me, both to each, friend,
I guess one angel in another's hell.
    The truth I shall not know, but live in doubt,
    Till my bad angel fire my good one out.

[3]

Did not the heavenly rhetoric of thine eye,
'Gainst whom the world could not hold argument,
Persuade my heart to this false perjury?
Vows for thee broke deserve not punishment.
5   A woman I forswore; but I will prove,
Thou being a goddess, I forswore not thee:
My vow was earthly, thou a heavenly love;
Thy grace being gained cures all disgrace in me.
My vow was breath, and breath a vapour is;
10 Then thou, fair sun, that on this earth doth shine,
Exhale this vapour vow; in thee it is.
If broken, then it is no fault of mine.
    If by me broke, what fool is not so wise
    To break an oath, to win a paradise?

[4]

Sweet Cytherea, sitting by a brook
With young Adonis, lovely, fresh and green,
Did court the lad with many a lovely look,
Such looks as none could look but beauty's queen.
She told him stories to delight his ear;   5
She showed him favours to allure his eye;
To win his heart, she touched him here and there –
Touches so soft still conquer chastity.
But whether unripe years did want conceit,
Or he refused to take her figured proffer,   10
The tender nibbler would not touch the bait,
But smile and jest at every gentle offer.
    Then fell she on her back, fair queen, and toward:
    He rose and ran away; ah, fool too froward!

[5]

If love make me forsworn, how shall I swear to love?
O, never faith could hold, if not to beauty vowed:
Though to myself forsworn, to thee I'll constant prove;
Those thoughts, to me like oaks, to thee like osiers
        bowed.
Study his bias leaves, and makes his book thine eyes,   5
Where all those pleasures live that art can comprehend.
If knowledge be the mark, to know thee shall suffice;
Well learned is that tongue that well can thee
        commend;
All ignorant that soul that sees thee without wonder;
Which is to me some praise, that I thy parts admire: 10
Thine eye Jove's lightning seems, thy voice his
        dreadful thunder,
Which (not to anger bent) is music and sweet fire.
    Celestial as thou art, O, do not love that wrong
    To sing heaven's praise with such an earthly tongue.

[6]

Scarce had the sun dried up the dewy morn,
And scarce the herd gone to the hedge for shade,
When Cytherea (all in love forlorn)
A longing tarriance for Adonis made,
Under an osier growing by a brook,   5
A brook where Adon used to cool his spleen.
Hot was the day; she hotter that did look
For his approach that often there had been.
Anon he comes and throws his mantle by,
And stood stark naked on the brook's green brim. 10
The sun looked on the world with glorious eye,
Yet not so wistly as this queen on him.
    He, spying her, bounced in whereas he stood;
    'O Jove,' quoth she, 'why was not I a flood?'

[7]

Fair is my love, but not so fair as fickle;
Mild as a dove, but neither true nor trusty;
Brighter than glass, and yet as glass is brittle;
Softer than wax, and yet as iron rusty:
5   A lily pale, with damask dye to grace her,
     None fairer, nor none falser to deface her.

Her lips to mine how often hath she joined,
Between each kiss her oaths of true love swearing.
How many tales to please me hath she coined,
10   Dreading my love, the loss whereof still fearing.
     Yet in the midst of all her pure protestings
     Her faith, her oaths, her tears and all were jestings.

She burned with love as straw with fire flameth;
She burned out love as soon as straw out-burneth;
15   She framed the love, and yet she foiled the framing;
     She bade love last, and yet she fell a-turning.
     Was this a lover, or a lecher whether?
     Bad in the best, though excellent in neither.

[8]

If music and sweet poetry agree,
As they must needs (the sister and the brother),
Then must the love be great 'twixt thee and me,
Because thou lov'st the one, and I the other.
5   Dowland to thee is dear, whose heavenly touch
Upon the lute doth ravish human sense;
Spenser to me, whose deep conceit is such
As passing all conceit needs no defence.
Thou lov'st to hear the sweet melodious sound
10   That Phoebus' lute (the queen of music) makes;
And I in deep delight am chiefly drowned
When as himself to singing he betakes.
     One god is god of both (as poets feign)
     One knight loves both, and both in thee remain.

[9]

Fair was the morn when the fair queen of love,
Paler for sorrow than her milk-white dove,
For Adon's sake, a youngster proud and wild,
Her stand she takes upon a steep-up hill.
5   Anon Adonis comes with horn and hounds;
She, silly queen, with more than love's good will,
Forbade the boy he should not pass those grounds:
'Once', quoth she, 'did I see a fair sweet youth
Here in these brakes deep wounded with a boar,
10   Deep in the thigh, a spectacle of ruth.
See in my thigh,' quoth she, 'here was the sore.'
     She showed hers; he saw more wounds than one,
     And blushing fled, and left her all alone.

[10]

Sweet rose, fair flower, untimely plucked, soon vaded,
Plucked in the bud, and vaded in the spring;
Bright orient pearl, alack too timely shaded,
Fair creature, killed too soon by Death's sharp sting!
5   Like a green plum that hangs upon a tree,
     And falls (through wind) before the fall should be.

I weep for thee, and yet no cause I have;
For why thou left'st me nothing in thy will.
And yet thou left'st me more than I did crave,
For why I craved nothing of thee still:
10   O yes, dear friend, I pardon crave of thee:
     Thy discontent thou didst bequeath to me.

[11]

Venus with Adonis sitting by her
Under a myrtle shade began to woo him.
She told the youngling how god Mars did try her,
And as he fell to her, she fell to him.
'Even thus', quoth she, 'the warlike god embraced me.'   5
And then she clipped Adonis in her arms;
'Even thus', quoth she, 'the warlike god unlaced me,'
As if the boy should use like loving charms.
'Even thus', quoth she, 'he seized on my lips,'
And with her lips on his did act the seizure.   10
And as she fetched breath, away he skips,
And would not take her meaning nor her pleasure.
     Ah, that I had my lady at this bay,
     To kiss and clip me till I run away!

[12]

Crabbed age and youth cannot live together:
Youth is full of pleasance, age is full of care;
Youth like summer morn, age like winter weather;
Youth like summer brave, age like winter bare.
Youth is full of sport, age's breath is short;   5
Youth is nimble, age is lame;
Youth is hot and bold, age is weak and cold;
Youth is wild, and age is tame.
     Age I do abhor thee, youth I do adore thee;
     O my love, my love is young.   10
     Age I do defy thee. O, sweet shepherd, hie thee,
     For methinks thou stays too long.

[13]

Beauty is but a vain and doubtful good,
A shining gloss that vadeth suddenly,
A flower that dies when first it gins to bud,
A brittle glass that's broken presently,
5   A doubtful good, a gloss, a glass, a flower,
    Lost, vaded, broken, dead within an hour.

And as goods lost are seld or never found,
As vaded gloss no rubbing will refresh,
As flowers dead lie withered on the ground,
10 As broken glass no cement can redress,
    So beauty blemished once, for ever lost,
    In spite of physic, painting, pain and cost.

[14]

Good-night, good rest, ah, neither be my share.
She bade good-night that kept my rest away
And daffed me to a cabin hanged with care,
To descant on the doubts of my decay.
5   'Farewell,' quoth she, 'and come again tomorrow.'
    Fare well I could not, for I supped with sorrow.

Yet at my parting sweetly did she smile,
In scorn or friendship, nill I conster whether;
'T may be she joyed to jest at my exile,
10 'T may be again to make me wander thither:
    'Wander', a word for shadows like myself,
    As take the pain but cannot pluck the pelf.

Lord, how mine eyes throw gazes to the east!
My heart doth charge the watch; the morning rise
15 Doth cite each moving sense from idle rest,
Not daring trust the office of mine eyes.
    While Philomela sits and sings, I sit and mark,
    And wish her lays were tuned like the lark.

For she doth welcome daylight with her ditty,
20 And drives away dark-dreaming night:
The night so packed, I post unto my pretty.
Heart hath his hope, and eyes their wished sight;
    Sorrow changed to solace, and solace mixed with
      sorrow;
    For why she sighed and bade me come tomorrow.

25 Were I with her, the night would post too soon,
But now are minutes added to the hours.
To spite me now, each minute seems a moon;
Yet not for me, shine sun to succour flowers!
    Pack night, peep day; good day, of night now
      borrow;
30   Short night tonight, and length thyself tomorrow.

SONNETS

To Sundry Notes of Music

[15]

It was a lording's daughter, the fairest one of three,
That liked of her master, as well as well might be,
Till looking on an Englishman, the fairest that eye
    could see
    Her fancy fell a-turning.
Long was the combat doubtful, that love with love did
    fight   5
To leave the master loveless, or kill the gallant knight;
To put in practice either, alas it was a spite
    Unto the silly damsel.
But one must be refused; more mickle was the pain,
That nothing could be used to turn them both to
    gain,   10
For of the two the trusty knight was wounded with
    disdain,
    Alas, she could not help it.
Thus art with arms contending was victor of the day,
Which by a gift of learning did bear the maid away.
Then, lullaby, the learned man hath got the lady gay,   15
    For now my song is ended.

[16]

    On a day (alack the day)
    Love, whose month was ever may,
    Spied a blossom passing fair,
    Playing in the wanton air.
    Through the velvet leaves the wind   5
    All unseen, gan passage find;
    That the lover (sick to death)
    Wished himself the heaven's breath.
    'Air,' quoth he, 'thy cheeks may blow;
    Air, would I might triumph so.   10
    But (alas) my hand hath sworn
    Ne'er to pluck thee from thy thorn:
    Vow (alack) for youth unmeet;
    Youth, so apt to pluck a sweet.
    Thou for whom Jove would swear   15
    Juno but an Ethiope were,
    And deny himself for Jove,
    Turning mortal for thy love.'

[17]

My flocks feed not, my ewes breed not,
My rams speed not, all is amiss:
Love is dying, faith's defying,
Heart's denying, causer of this.
5   All my merry jigs are quite forgot,
All my lady's love is lost (God wot),
Where her faith was firmly fixed in love
There a nay is placed without remove.
    One silly cross wrought all my loss;
10   Oh frowning fortune, cursed fickle dame,
    For now I see inconstancy
    More in women than in men remain.

In black mourn I, all fears scorn I;
Love hath forlorn me, living in thrall:
15   Heart is bleeding, all help needing,
O cruel speeding, fraughted with gall.
My shepherd's pipe can sound no deal,
My wether's bell rings doleful knell,
My curtal dog that wont to have played
20   Plays not at all, but seems afraid:
    With sighs so deep, procures to weep,
    In howling wise, to see my doleful plight.
    How sighs resound through heartless ground,
    Like a thousand vanquished men in bloody fight.

25   Clear wells spring not, sweet birds sing not,
Green plants bring not forth their dye;
Herds stands weeping, flocks all sleeping,
Nymphs back peeping fearfully.
All our pleasure known to us poor swains,
30   All our merry meetings on the plains,
All our evening sport from us is fled,
All our love is lost, for love is dead.
    Farewell, sweet love, thy like ne'er was
    For a sweet content, the cause of all my woe.
35   Poor Corydon must live alone;
    Other help for him I see that there is none.

[18]

When as thine eye hath chose the dame,
And stalled the deer that thou shouldst strike,
Let reason rule things worthy blame,
As well as fancy, partial might.
5   Take counsel of some wiser head,
    Neither too young, nor yet unwed.

And when thou com'st thy tale to tell,
Smooth not thy tongue with filed talk,
Lest she some subtle practice smell –
10   A cripple soon can find a halt –
    But plainly say thou lov'st her well,
    And set her person forth to sale.

And to her will frame all thy ways;
Spare not to spend, and chiefly there
Where thy desert may merit praise   15
By ringing in thy lady's ear:
    The strongest castle, tower and town,
    The golden bullet beats it down.

Serve always with assured trust,
And in thy suit be humble true;   20
Unless thy lady prove unjust,
Press never thou to choose anew:
    When time shall serve, be thou not slack
    To proffer, though she put thee back.

What though her frowning brows be bent,   25
Her cloudy looks will calm ere night:
And then too late she will repent
That thus dissembled her delight;
    And twice desire, ere it be day,
    That which with scorn she put away.   30

What though she strive to try her strength
And ban and brawl, and say thee nay,
Her feeble force will yield at length,
When craft hath taught her thus to say:
    'Had women been so strong as men,   35
    In faith, you had not had it then.'

The wiles and guiles that women work,
Dissembled with an outward show,
The tricks and toys that in them lurk,
The cock that treads them shall not know.   40
    Have you not heard it said full oft,
    A woman's 'nay' doth stand for naught?

Think women still to strive with men
To sin, and never for to saint;
There is no heaven: be holy then   45
When time with age shall them attaint.
    Were kisses all the joys in bed,
    One woman would another wed.

But soft, enough – too much, I fear –
Lest that my mistress hear my song;   50
She will not stick to round me on the ear,
To teach my tongue to be so long.
    Yet will she blush, here be it said,
    To hear her secrets so bewrayed.

[19]

Live with me and be my love,
And we will all the pleasures prove
That hills and valleys, dales and fields,
And all the craggy mountains yield.

5 There will we sit upon the rocks,
And see the shepherds feed their flocks,
By shallow rivers, by whose falls
Melodious birds sing madrigals.

There will I make thee a bed of roses,
10 With a thousand fragrant posies,
A cap of flowers and a kirtle
Embroidered all with leaves of myrtle.

A belt of straw and ivy buds,
With coral clasps and amber studs;
15 And if these pleasures may thee move,
Then live with me, and be my love.

Love's Answer

If that the world and love were young,
And truth in every shepherd's tongue,
These pretty pleasures might me move
20 To live with thee and be thy love.

[20]

As it fell upon a day,
In the merry month of May,
Sitting in a pleasant shade
Which a grove of myrtles made,
5 Beasts did leap, and birds did sing,
Trees did grow, and plants did spring.
Every thing did banish moan,
Save the nightingale alone.
She (poor bird) as all forlorn,
10 Leaned her breast up-till a thorn,
And there sung the dolefull'st ditty,
That to hear it was great pity.
'Fie, fie, fie', now would she cry;

'Tereu, Tereu', by and by;
That to hear her so complain,
Scarce I could from tears refrain,   15
For her griefs so lively shown
Made me think upon mine own.
Ah, thought I, thou mourn'st in vain,
None takes pity on thy pain: 20
Senseless trees, they cannot hear thee;
Ruthless bears, they will not cheer thee.
King Pandion, he is dead,
All thy friends are lapped in lead.
All thy fellow birds do sing,   25
Careless of thy sorrowing.
Whilst as fickle fortune smiled,
Thou and I were both beguiled.
Everyone that flatters thee
Is no friend in misery.   30
Words are easy, like the wind;
Faithful friends are hard to find.
Every man will be thy friend
Whilst thou hast wherewith to spend;
But if store of crowns be scant,   35
No man will supply thy want.
If that one be prodigal,
Bountiful they will him call,
And with suchlike flattering:
'Pity but he were a king.'   40
If he be addict to vice,
Quickly him they will entice.
If to women he be bent,
They have at commandment;
But if Fortune once do frown,   45
Then farewell his great renown:
They that fawned on him before
Use his company no more.
He that is thy friend indeed,
He will help thee in thy need;   50
If thou sorrow, he will weep;
If thou wake, he cannot sleep;
Thus of every grief in heart
He with thee doth bear a part.
These are certain signs to know   55
Faithful friend from flattering foe.

['The Phoenix and Turtle']

Let the bird of loudest lay
On the sole Arabian tree,
Herald sad and trumpet be:
To whose sound chaste wings obey.

5 But thou shrieking harbinger,
Foul precurrer of the fiend,
Augur of the fever's end,
To this troop come thou not near.

From this session interdict
10 Every fowl of tyrant wing,
Save the eagle, feathered king:
Keep the obsequy so strict.

Let the priest in surplice white,
That defunctive music can,
15 Be the death-divining swan,
Lest the requiem lack his right.

And thou treble-dated crow,
That thy sable gender mak'st
With the breath thou giv'st and tak'st,
20 'Mongst our mourners shalt thou go.

Here the anthem doth commence:
Love and constancy is dead,
Phoenix and the Turtle fled,
In a mutual flame from hence.

25 So they loved as love in twain
Had the essence but in one,
Two distincts, division none:
Number there in love was slain.

Hearts remote, yet not asunder;
30 Distance and no space was seen,
'Twixt this Turtle and his queen,
But in them it were a wonder.

So between them love did shine
That the Turtle saw his right
35 Flaming in the Phoenix' sight;
Either was the other's mine.

Property was thus appalled
That the self was not the same:
Single nature's double name
Neither two nor one was called. 40

Reason in itself confounded,
Saw division grow together,
To themselves yet either neither,
Simple were so well compounded,

That it cried, 'How true a twain 45
Seemeth this concordant one;
Love hath reason, Reason none,
If what parts can so remain.'

Whereupon it made this threne
To the Phoenix and the Dove, 50
Co-supremes and stars of love,
As chorus to their tragic scene.

Threnos

Beauty, truth and rarity,
Grace in all simplicity,
Here enclosed, in cinders lie. 55

Death is now the Phoenix' nest,
And the Turtle's loyal breast
To eternity doth rest.

Leaving no posterity,
'Twas not their infirmity, 60
It was married chastity.

Truth may seem, but cannot be;
Beauty brag, but 'tis not she;
Truth and beauty buried be.

To this urn let those repair 65
That are either true or fair,
For these dead birds sigh a prayer.

All's Well That Ends Well

The only early text of *All's Well That Ends Well* is that of the 1623 Folio. Judging from stylometric analyses and the repeated invocation of God, forbidden on stage after 1606, it was probably written 1605–6. On 8 November 1623, along with fifteen other plays 'not formerly entered to other men', it was entered in the Stationers' Register to the Folio's principal publishers, Edward Blount and Isaac Jaggard. There is no record of early performance, but the play has been successful onstage in the late twentieth and early twenty-first centuries.

Although *All's Well* appears as the twelfth of the comedies in the Folio, its genre has been a principal source of debate. A combination of fairy tale, romance, prodigal son play and sexual comedy, it was labelled a 'problem play' in 1896 by F.S. Boas, who classed it with *Measure for Measure* and *Troilus and Cressida* as of one a group of plays where 'the issues raised preclude a completely satisfactory outcome'. A persistent question for readers and viewers has been whether the play does, in fact, 'end well'. The main plot, the story of the curing of the king and the satisfying of apparently impossible conditions by the young heroine, is the stuff of folklore. Shakespeare seems to have read it in William Painter's *The Palace of Pleasure*, a translation of Giovanni Boccaccio's *Decameron*, where it appears as the ninth story on the third day. The heroine, Giletta of Narbonne, cures the French king of a painful fistula and demands, as her reward, the hand of Beltramo, Count of Rossiglione. The Count flees this unwanted marriage, but Giletta finds him and 'by policy' gets pregnant by him, 'which known to her husband, he received her again, and afterwards he lived in great honour and felicity'.

Shakespeare darkens the outline of this plot and sharpens the social particularity of its characters. Count Bertram, a fatherless adolescent proud of his nobility and determined to prove his manhood at war, away from his mother and her ward, who loves him, is callow and unwilling to marry 'a poor physician's daughter', while Helen's pursuit of the hostile Count, and especially her participation in the bed-trick she arranges, have seemed too overt about female desire in periods when virginal young women were expected to be less assertive. In general, reactions to the play over time have reflected the surrounding culture; the Victorians were distressed by its sexual content, but modern feminists have been attracted to its activist heroine.

Shakespeare's distinctive additions to the story include a fuller portrayal of the older generation: the dowager Countess, her friend Lord Lafeu and the King, who all support Helen. The action follows Helen's successive quests, first to cure the King and then to fulfil Bertram's challenge once he refuses to consummate the marriage, demanding that she 'get the ring upon my finger, which never shall come off' and show him 'a child begotten of thy body that I am father to' (3.2.56–8), before she can call him husband.

The second plot, the exposure of Bertram's overly talkative follower, the significantly named Paroles, is entirely Shakespeare's. The scenes of Paroles's unmasking have traditionally been played as farce; in the eighteenth and nineteenth centuries they often dominated productions. Paroles is a foil to the Countess's Fool Lavatch, but more psychological readings of his relation to Bertram see him serving as a substitute father like Falstaff or even as a homoerotic companion. In any case, Bertram cannot accept Helen until he recognizes his follower as the knave he is and rejects him.

As the play ends, the heroine, presumed dead, reappears with Bertram's ring and 'quick' or pregnant. The King has been cured, and Bertram asks 'pardon'. Yet the happy ending is hedged with qualifications and uncertainties. In the final scene, Bertram lies repeatedly and only conditionally promises to love Helen, who describes herself as 'the shadow of a wife . . . The name and not the thing' (5.3.303–4). Even the King's apparently generous offer to Diana, 'Choose thou thy husband, and I'll pay thy dower' (323), repeats the arbitrary imposition that caused Bertram's earlier flight. Hence the Epilogue can only acknowledge a final 'if': 'All yet seems well, and if it end so meet, / The bitter past, more welcome is the sweet' (328–9). This uncertainty is one source of the play's interest, as it complicates the wish-fulfilling logic of comedy itself.

The Arden text is based on the 1623 First Folio.

COUNTESS of Roussillon	*a recent widow*
BERTRAM	*Count of Roussillon, her son*
HELEN	*her young gentlewoman*
RINALDO	*her steward*
LAVATCH	*a Clown in her household*
PAROLES	*companion to Bertram*
PAGE	
KING of France	
LAFEU	*an old French lord*
LORD G.	*the Dumaine brothers, lords at*
LORD E.	*the French court*
AUSTRINGER	*a gentleman of the French court*
Four LORDS	*at the French court*
DUKE of Florence	
WIDOW	*of Florence*
DIANA	*her daughter*
MARIANA	*her neighbour*
FIRST SOLDIER	*acting as interpreter*
SERVANT	*to Bertram*

Attendants, French Lords leaving for Florence, Soldiers,
Drummer, Trumpeter, Citizens of Florence

1.1   *Enter young* BERTRAM, *Count of Roussillon,*
     his Mother the COUNTESS *of Roussillon,*
     HELEN *and Lord* LAFEU, *all in black.*

COUNTESS   In delivering my son from me, I bury a
second husband.

BERTRAM   And I in going, madam, weep o'er my
father's death anew; but I must attend his majesty's
command, to whom I am now in ward, evermore in   5
subjection.

LAFEU   You shall find of the King a husband, madam;
you, sir, a father. He that so generally is at all times
good must of necessity hold his virtue to you, whose
worthiness would stir it up where it wanted rather than   10
lack it where there is such abundance.

COUNTESS   What hope is there of his majesty's
amendment?

LAFEU   He hath abandoned his physicians, madam,
under whose practices he hath persecuted time with   15
hope, and finds no other advantage in the process but
only the losing of hope by time.

COUNTESS   This young gentlewoman had a father – O,
that 'had', how sad a passage 'tis! – whose skill was
almost as great as his honesty. Had it stretched so far,   20
would have made nature immortal, and death should
have play for lack of work. Would for the King's sake
he were living! I think it would be the death of the
King's disease.

LAFEU   How called you the man you speak of, madam?   25

COUNTESS   He was famous, sir, in his profession, and it
was his great right to be so: Gérard de Narbonne.

LAFEU   He was excellent indeed, madam. The King
very lately spoke of him admiringly and mourningly.
He was skilful enough to have lived still, if knowledge   30
could be set up against mortality.

BERTRAM   What is it, my good lord, the King languishes
of?

LAFEU   A fistula, my lord.

BERTRAM   I heard not of it before.   35

LAFEU   I would it were not notorious. – Was this
gentlewoman the daughter of Gérard de Narbonne?

COUNTESS   His sole child, my lord, and bequeathed to
my overlooking. I have those hopes of her good that
her education promises her dispositions she inherits,   40
which makes fair gifts fairer; for where an unclean
mind carries virtuous qualities, there commendations
go with pity: they are virtues and traitors too. In her
they are the better for their simpleness. She derives
her honesty and achieves her goodness.   45

LAFEU   Your commendations, madam, get from her tears.

COUNTESS   'Tis the best brine a maiden can season her
praise in. The remembrance of her father never
approaches her heart but the tyranny of her sorrows
takes all livelihood from her cheek. – No more of this,   50
Helena. Go to, no more, lest it be rather thought you
affect a sorrow than to have –

HELEN   I do affect a sorrow indeed, but I have it too.

LAFEU   Moderate lamentation is the right of the dead,
excessive grief the enemy to the living.   55

COUNTESS   If the living be enemy to the grief, the
excess makes it soon mortal.

BERTRAM   Madam, I desire your holy wishes.

LAFEU   How understand we that?

COUNTESS
Be thou blessed, Bertram, and succeed thy father   60
In manners, as in shape. Thy blood and virtue
Contend for empire in thee, and thy goodness
Share with thy birthright. Love all, trust a few,
Do wrong to none. Be able for thine enemy
Rather in power than use, and keep thy friend   65
Under thy own life's key. Be checked for silence,
But never taxed for speech. What heaven more will,
That thee may furnish and my prayers pluck down,
Fall on thy head. [*to Lafeu*] Farewell, my lord.
'Tis an unseasoned courtier. Good my lord,   70
Advise him.

LAFEU   He cannot want the best
That shall attend his love.

COUNTESS   Heaven bless him! – Farewell, Bertram.

BERTRAM   The best wishes that can be forged in your
thoughts be servants to you.   *Exit Countess.*   75
[*to Helen*] Be comfortable to my mother, your mistress,
and make much of her.

LAFEU   Farewell, pretty lady. You must hold the credit
of your father.   *Exeunt Bertram and Lafeu.*

HELEN   O, were that all! I think not on my father,   80
And these great tears grace his remembrance more
Than those I shed for him. What was he like?
I have forgot him. My imagination
Carries no favour in't but Bertram's.
I am undone: there is no living, none,   85
If Bertram be away. 'Twere all one
That I should love a bright particular star
And think to wed it, he is so above me.
In his bright radiance and collateral light
Must I be comforted, not in his sphere.   90
Th'ambition in my love thus plagues itself:
The hind that would be mated by the lion
Must die for love. 'Twas pretty, though a plague,
To see him every hour, to sit and draw
His arched brows, his hawking eye, his curls   95
In our heart's table – heart too capable
Of every line and trick of his sweet favour.
But now he's gone, and my idolatrous fancy
Must sanctify his relics. Who comes here?

           Enter PAROLES.

One that goes with him. I love him for his sake,   100
And yet I know him a notorious liar,
Think him a great way fool, solely a coward.
Yet these fixed evils sit so fit in him
That they take place when virtue's steely bones
Looks bleak i'th' cold wind. Withal, full oft we see   105
Cold wisdom waiting on superfluous folly.

PAROLES   Save you, fair queen.
HELEN   And you, monarch.
PAROLES   No.
110   HELEN   And no.
PAROLES   Are you meditating on virginity?
HELEN   Ay. You have some stain of soldier in you. Let
me ask you a question. Man is enemy to virginity; how
may we barricado it against him?
115   PAROLES   Keep him out.
HELEN   But he assails, and our virginity, though valiant,
in the defence yet is weak. Unfold to us some warlike
resistance.
PAROLES   There is none. Man, setting down before you,
120   will undermine you and blow you up.
HELEN   Bless our poor virginity from underminers and
blowers-up. Is there no military policy how virgins
might blow up men?
PAROLES   Virginity being blown down, man will
125   quicklier be blown up. Marry, in blowing him down
again, with the breach yourselves made, you lose your
city. It is not politic in the commonwealth of nature to
preserve virginity. Loss of virginity is rational increase,
and there was never virgin got till virginity was first
130   lost. That you were made of is metal to make virgins.
Virginity, by being once lost, may be ten times found;
by being ever kept, it is ever lost. 'Tis too cold a
companion. Away with't!
HELEN   I will stand for't a little, though therefore I die a
135   virgin.
PAROLES   There's little can be said in't; 'tis against the
rule of nature. To speak on the part of virginity is
to accuse your mothers, which is most infallible
disobedience. He that hangs himself is a virgin:
140   virginity murders itself, and should be buried in
highways out of all sanctified limit, as a desperate
offendress against nature. Virginity breeds mites, much
like a cheese, consumes itself to the very paring, and so
dies with feeding his own stomach. Besides, virginity is
145   peevish, proud, idle, made of self-love, which is the
most inhibited sin in the canon. Keep it not; you cannot
choose but lose by't. Out with't! Within t'one year it
will make itself two, which is a goodly increase, and the
principal itself not much the worse. Away with't!
150   HELEN   How might one do, sir, to lose it to her own
liking?
PAROLES   Let me see. Marry, ill, to like him that ne'er it
likes. 'Tis a commodity will lose the gloss with lying;
the longer kept, the less worth. Off with't while 'tis
155   vendible. Answer the time of request. Virginity, like an
old courtier, wears her cap out of fashion, richly
suited, but unsuitable, just like the brooch and the
toothpick, which wear not now. Your date is better in
your pie and your porridge than in your cheek. And
160   your virginity, your old virginity, is like one of our
French withered pears: it looks ill, it eats drily; marry,
'tis a withered pear. It was formerly better, marry, yet
'tis a withered pear. Will you anything with it?

HELEN   Not my virginity yet –
There shall your master have a thousand loves,   165
A mother, and a mistress, and a friend,
A phoenix, captain, and an enemy,
A guide, a goddess, and a sovereign,
A counsellor, a traitress, and a dear;
His humble ambition, proud humility,   170
His jarring concord, and his discord dulcet,
His faith, his sweet disaster; with a world
Of pretty, fond, adoptious christendoms
That blinking Cupid gossips. Now shall he –
I know not what he shall. God send him well!   175
The court's a learning place, and he is one –
PAROLES   What one, i'faith?
HELEN   That I wish well. 'Tis pity.
PAROLES   What's pity?
HELEN
That wishing well had not a body in't
Which might be felt, that we the poorer born,   180
Whose baser stars do shut us up in wishes,
Might with effects of them follow our friends
And show what we alone must think, which never
Returns us thanks.

Enter Page.

PAGE   Monsieur Paroles, my lord calls for you.   *Exit.*   185
PAROLES   Little Helen, farewell. If I can remember
thee, I will think of thee at Court.
HELEN   Monsieur Paroles, you were born under a
charitable star.
PAROLES   Under Mars, I.   190
HELEN   I especially think, under Mars.
PAROLES   Why under Mars?
HELEN   The wars hath so kept you under that you must
needs be born under Mars.
PAROLES   When he was predominant.   195
HELEN   When he was retrograde, I think rather.
PAROLES   Why think you so?
HELEN   You go so much backward when you fight.
PAROLES   That's for advantage.
HELEN   So is running away when fear proposes the safety.   200
But the composition that your valour and fear makes in
you is a virtue of a good wing, and I like the wear well.
PAROLES   I am so full of businesses I cannot answer thee
acutely. I will return perfect courtier, in the which my
instruction shall serve to naturalize thee, so thou wilt   205
be capable of a courtier's counsel and understand what
advice shall thrust upon thee; else thou diest in thine
unthankfulness, and thine ignorance makes thee away.
Farewell. When thou hast leisure, say thy prayers;
when thou hast none, remember thy friends. Get thee a   210
good husband, and use him as he uses thee. So, farewell.
Exit.

HELEN   Our remedies oft in ourselves do lie
Which we ascribe to heaven. The fated sky
Gives us free scope, only doth backward pull
Our slow designs when we ourselves are dull.   215

What power is it which mounts my love so high,
That makes me see, and cannot feed mine eye?
The mightiest space in fortune nature brings
To join like likes, and kiss like native things.
220 Impossible be strange attempts to those
That weigh their pains in sense and do suppose
What hath been cannot be. Who ever strove
To show her merit that did miss her love?
The King's disease – my project may deceive me,
225 But my intents are fixed and will not leave me.   *Exit.*

1.2   *Flourish cornetts. Enter the* KING *of France*
with letters, LORDS G. *and* E. *and*
divers Attendants.

KING   The Florentines and Senois are by th'ears,
Have fought with equal fortune, and continue
A braving war.
LORD G.   So 'tis reported, sir.
KING   Nay, 'tis most credible. We here receive it
5   A certainty vouched from our cousin Austria,
With caution that the Florentine will move us
For speedy aid; wherein our dearest friend
Prejudicates the business, and would seem
To have us make denial.
LORD G.   His love and wisdom,
10   Approved so to your majesty, may plead
For amplest credence.
KING   He hath armed our answer,
And Florence is denied before he comes.
Yet for our gentlemen that mean to see
The Tuscan service, freely have they leave
To stand on either part.
15 LORD E.   It well may serve
A nursery to our gentry, who are sick
For breathing and exploit.
KING   What's he comes here?

Enter BERTRAM, LAFEU *and* PAROLES.

LORD G.   It is the Count Roussillon, my good lord,
Young Bertram.
KING   Youth, thou bear'st thy father's face;
20   Frank nature, rather curious than in haste,
Hath well composed thee. Thy father's moral parts
Mayst thou inherit too! Welcome to Paris.
BERTRAM   My thanks and duty are your majesty's.
KING   I would I had that corporal soundness now
25   As when thy father and myself in friendship
First tried our soldiership. He did look far
Into the service of the time, and was
Disciped of the bravest. He lasted long,
But on us both did haggish age steal on,
30   And wore us out of act. It much repairs me
To talk of your good father. In his youth
He had the wit which I can well observe
Today in our young lords; but they may jest
Till their own scorn return to them unnoted

Ere they can hide their levity in honour.   35
So like a courtier, contempt nor bitterness
Were in his pride or sharpness; if they were,
His equal had awaked them, and his honour,
Clock to itself, knew the true minute when
Exception bid him speak, and at this time   40
His tongue obeyed his hand. Who were below him,
He used as creatures of another place,
And bowed his eminent top to their low ranks,
Making them proud of his humility,
In their poor praise he humbled. Such a man   45
Might be a copy to these younger times,
Which, followed well, would demonstrate them now
But goers backward.
BERTRAM   His good remembrance, sir,
Lies richer in your thoughts than on his tomb.
So in approof lives not his epitaph   50
As in your royal speech.
KING   Would I were with him! He would always say –
Methinks I hear him now; his plausive words
He scattered not in ears, but grafted them
To grow there and to bear. 'Let me not live' –   55
This his good melancholy oft began
On the catastrophe and heel of pastime,
When it was out – 'Let me not live', quoth he,
'After my flame lacks oil, to be the snuff
Of younger spirits, whose apprehensive senses   60
All but new things disdain, whose judgements are
Mere fathers of their garments, whose constancies
Expire before their fashions.' This he wished.
I, after him, do after him wish too,
Since I nor wax nor honey can bring home,   65
I quickly were dissolved from my hive
To give some labourers room.
LORD E.   You're loved, sir.
They that least lend it you shall lack you first.
KING   I fill a place, I know't. – How long is't, Count,
Since the physician at your father's died?   70
He was much famed.
BERTRAM   Some six months since, my lord.
KING   If he were living, I would try him yet.
– Lend me an arm. – The rest have worn me out
With several applications. Nature and sickness
Debate it at their leisure. Welcome, Count;   75
My son's no dearer.
BERTRAM   Thank your majesty.
Flourish. Exeunt.

1.3   *Enter* COUNTESS, RINALDO *and* LAVATCH.

COUNTESS   I will now hear. What say you of this
gentlewoman?
RINALDO   Madam, the care I have had to even your
content I wish might be found in the calendar of my
past endeavours, for then we wound our modesty and   5
make foul the clearness of our deservings, when of
ourselves we publish them.

COUNTESS What does this knave here? [*to Lavatch*]
Get you gone, sirrah. The complaints I have heard of
you I do not all believe. 'Tis my slowness that I do not,
for I know you lack not folly to commit them and have
ability enough to make such knaveries yours.

LAVATCH 'Tis not unknown to you, madam, I am a
poor fellow.

COUNTESS Well, sir.

LAVATCH No, madam, 'tis not so well that I am poor,
though many of the rich are damned, but if I may have
your ladyship's good will to go to the world, Isbel the
woman and I will do as we may.

COUNTESS Wilt thou needs be a beggar?

LAVATCH I do beg your good will in this case.

COUNTESS In what case?

LAVATCH In Isbel's case and mine own. Service is no
heritage, and I think I shall never have the blessing of
God till I have issue o'my body; for they say bairns are
blessings.

COUNTESS Tell me thy reason why thou wilt marry.

LAVATCH My poor body, madam, requires it: I am
driven on by the flesh, and he must needs go that the
devil drives.

COUNTESS Is this all your worship's reason?

LAVATCH Faith, madam, I have other holy reasons,
such as they are.

COUNTESS May the world know them?

LAVATCH I have been, madam, a wicked creature, as
you and all flesh and blood are, and indeed I do marry
that I may repent.

COUNTESS Thy marriage sooner than thy wickedness.

LAVATCH I am out o'friends, madam, and I hope to
have friends for my wife's sake.

COUNTESS Such friends are thine enemies, knave.

LAVATCH You're shallow, madam, in great friends, for
the knaves come to do that for me which I am aweary
of. He that ears my land spares my team, and gives me
leave to in the crop. If I be his cuckold, he's my drudge.
He that comforts my wife is the cherisher of my flesh
and blood; he that cherishes my flesh and blood loves
my flesh and blood; he that loves my flesh and blood is
my friend: *ergo*, he that kisses my wife is my friend. If
men could be contented to be what they are, there were
no fear in marriage; for young Chairbonne the puritan
and old Poisson the papist, howsome'er their hearts are
severed in religion, their heads are both one: they may
jowl horns together like any deer i'th' herd.

COUNTESS Wilt thou ever be a foul-mouthed and
calumnious knave?

LAVATCH A prophet I, madam, and I speak the truth
the next way:
[*Sings.*] For I the ballad will repeat,
　　　Which men full true shall find:
　　　Your marriage comes by destiny,
　　　Your cuckoo sings by kind.

COUNTESS Get you gone, sir. I'll talk with you more
anon.

RINALDO May it please you, madam, that he bid Helen
come to you. Of her I am to speak.

COUNTESS Sirrah, tell my gentlewoman I would speak
with her – Helen, I mean.

LAVATCH [*Sings.*]
'Was this fair face the cause', quoth she,
　'Why the Grecians sacked Troy?
Fond done, done fond,
　Was this King Priam's joy?'
With that she sighed as she stood,
With that she sighed as she stood,
　And gave this sentence then:
'Among nine bad if one be good,
Among nine bad if one be good,
　There's yet one good in ten.'

COUNTESS What, one good in ten? You corrupt the
song, sirrah.

LAVATCH One good woman in ten, madam, which is a
purifying o'th' song. Would God would serve the
world so all the year! We'd find no fault with the tithe-
woman if I were the parson. One in ten, quoth 'a? An
we might have a good woman born but or every blazing
star, or at an earthquake, 'twould mend the lottery
well. A man may draw his heart out ere 'a pluck one.

COUNTESS You'll be gone, sir knave, and do as I
command you!

LAVATCH That man should be at woman's command,
and yet no hurt done! Though honesty be no puritan,
yet it will do no hurt; it will wear the surplice of
humility over the black gown of a big heart. I am going,
forsooth. The business is for Helen to come hither.
　　　　　　　　　　　　　　　　　Exit.

COUNTESS Well, now.

RINALDO I know, madam, you love your gentlewoman
entirely.

COUNTESS Faith, I do. Her father bequeathed her to
me, and she herself, without other advantage, may
lawfully make title to as much love as she finds. There
is more owing her than is paid, and more shall be paid
her than she'll demand.

RINALDO Madam, I was very late more near her than I
think she wished me. Alone she was, and did
communicate to herself, her own words to her own
ears. She thought, I dare vow for her, they touched not
any stranger sense. Her matter was, she loved your son.
Fortune, she said, was no goddess, that had put such
difference betwixt their two estates; Love no god, that
would not extend his might only where qualities were
level; Dian no queen of virgins, that would suffer her
poor knight surprised without rescue in the first
assault or ransom afterward. This she delivered in the
most bitter touch of sorrow that e'er I heard virgin
exclaim in, which I held my duty speedily to acquaint
you withal, sithence in the loss that may happen it
concerns you something to know it.

COUNTESS You have discharged this honestly; keep it
to yourself. Many likelihoods informed me of this

120 before, which hung so tottering in the balance that I
could neither believe nor misdoubt. Pray you, leave
me. Stall this in your bosom; and I thank you for your
honest care. I will speak with you further anon.

Exit Rinaldo.

Enter HELEN.

[*aside*] Even so it was with me when I was young.
125 If ever we are nature's, these are ours: this thorn
Doth to our rose of youth rightly belong.
Our blood to us, this to our blood is born;
It is the show and seal of nature's truth,
Where love's strong passion is impressed in youth.
130 By our remembrances of days foregone,
Such were our faults, or then we thought them none.
Her eye is sick on't; I observe her now.
HELEN What is your pleasure, madam?
COUNTESS You know, Helen, I am a mother to you.
HELEN Mine honourable mistress.
135 COUNTESS Nay, a mother.
Why not a mother? When I said 'a mother',
Methought you saw a serpent. What's in 'mother'
That you start at it? I say I am your mother,
And put you in the catalogue of those
140 That were enwombed mine. 'Tis often seen
Adoption strives with nature, and choice breeds
A native slip to us from foreign seeds.
You ne'er oppressed me with a mother's groan,
Yet I express to you a mother's care.
145 God's mercy, maiden! Does it curd thy blood
To say I am thy mother? What's the matter,
That this distempered messenger of wet,
The many-coloured Iris, rounds thine eye?
– Why, that you are my daughter?
HELEN That I am not.
COUNTESS I say I am your mother.
150 HELEN Pardon, madam;
The Count Roussillon cannot be my brother.
I am from humble, he from honoured name;
No note upon my parents, his all noble.
My master, my dear lord he is, and I
155 His servant live and will his vassal die.
He must not be my brother.
COUNTESS Nor I your mother?
HELEN You are my mother, madam; would you were –
So that my lord your son were not my brother –
Indeed my mother! Or were you both our mothers
160 I care no more for than I do for heaven,
So I were not his sister. Can 't no other
But, I your daughter, he must be my brother?
COUNTESS
Yes, Helen, you might be my daughter-in-law.
God shield you mean it not! 'Daughter' and 'mother'
165 So strive upon your pulse! What, pale again?
My fear hath catched your fondness. Now I see
The mystery of your loneliness and find
Your salt tears' head, now to all sense 'tis gross:

You love my son. Invention is ashamed
Against the proclamation of thy passion 170
To say thou dost not. Therefore tell me true,
But tell me then 'tis so – for look, thy cheeks
Confess it t'one to th'other, and thine eyes
See it so grossly shown in thy behaviours
That in their kind they speak it. Only sin 175
And hellish obstinacy tie thy tongue,
That truth should be suspected. Speak: is't so?
If it be so, you have wound a goodly clew;
If it be not, forswear't. Howe'er, I charge thee,
As heaven shall work in me for thine avail, 180
To tell me truly.
HELEN Good madam, pardon me.
COUNTESS Do you love my son?
HELEN Your pardon, noble mistress.
COUNTESS Love you my son?
HELEN Do not you love him, madam?
COUNTESS Go not about. My love hath in't a bond
Whereof the world takes note. Come, come, disclose 185
The state of your affection, for your passions
Have to the full appeached.
HELEN Then I confess,
Here on my knee, before high heaven and you,
That before you, and next unto high heaven,
I love your son. 190
My friends were poor but honest, so's my love.
Be not offended, for it hurts not him
That he is loved of me. I follow him not
By any token of presumptuous suit,
Nor would I have him till I do deserve him, 195
Yet never know how that desert should be.
I know I love in vain, strive against hope;
Yet in this captious and intenable sieve
I still pour in the waters of my love
And lack not to lose still. Thus, Indian-like, 200
Religious in mine error, I adore
The sun that looks upon his worshipper,
But knows of him no more. My dearest madam,
Let not your hate encounter with my love
For loving where you do; but if yourself, 205
Whose aged honour cites a virtuous youth,
Did ever in so true a flame of liking
Wish chastely and love dearly, that your Dian
Was both herself and Love, O then give pity
To her whose state is such that cannot choose 210
But lend and give where she is sure to lose;
That seeks not to find that her search implies,
But riddle-like lives sweetly where she dies.
COUNTESS
Had you not lately an intent – speak truly –
To go to Paris?
HELEN Madam, I had.
COUNTESS Wherefore? Tell true. 215
HELEN I will tell truth, by grace itself I swear.
You know my father left me some prescriptions
Of rare and proved effects, such as his reading

And manifest experience had collected
220 For general sovereignty; and that he willed me
In heedfull'st reservation to bestow them,
As notes whose faculties inclusive were
More than they were in note. Amongst the rest,
There is a remedy, approved, set down,
225 To cure the desperate languishings whereof
The King is rendered lost.

COUNTESS
This was your motive for Paris, was it? Speak.

HELEN   My lord your son made me to think of this;
Else Paris, and the medicine, and the King
230 Had from the conversation of my thoughts
Haply been absent then.

COUNTESS   But think you, Helen,
If you should tender your supposed aid,
He would receive it? He and his physicians
Are of a mind: he that they cannot help him,
235 They that they cannot help. How shall they credit
A poor unlearned virgin, when the schools,
Embowelled of their doctrine, have left off
The danger to itself?

HELEN   There's something in't
More than my father's skill, which was the great'st
240 Of his profession, that his good receipt
Shall for my legacy be sanctified
By th' luckiest stars in heaven; and would your honour
But give me leave to try success, I'd venture
The well-lost life of mine on his grace's cure
By such a day, an hour.

245 COUNTESS   Dost thou believe't?

HELEN   Ay, madam, knowingly.

COUNTESS
Why, Helen, thou shalt have my leave and love,
Means and attendants, and my loving greetings
To those of mine in court. I'll stay at home
250 And pray God's blessing into thy attempt.
Be gone tomorrow, and be sure of this:
What I can help thee to, thou shalt not miss.   *Exeunt.*

2.1   *Enter the* KING, LORDS G. *and* E., *with
divers young* Lords *taking leave for the
Florentine war;* BERTRAM *and* PAROLES;
Attendants. Flourish cornetts.

KING   Farewell, young lords; these warlike principles
Do not throw from you. And you, my lords, farewell.
Share the advice betwixt you; if both gain all,
The gift doth stretch itself as 'tis received,
And is enough for both.

5 LORD G.   'Tis our hope, sir,
After well-entered soldiers, to return
And find your grace in health.

KING   No, no, it cannot be; and yet my heart
Will not confess he owes the malady
10 That doth my life besiege. Farewell, young lords;
Whether I live or die, be you the sons

Of worthy Frenchmen. Let higher Italy
(Those bated that inherit but the fall
Of the last monarchy) see that you come
Not to woo honour but to wed it, when   15
The bravest questant shrinks. Find what you seek,
That fame may cry you loud. I say farewell.

LORD G.   Health at your bidding serve your majesty!

KING   Those girls of Italy, take heed of them.
They say our French lack language to deny   20
If they demand. Beware of being captives
Before you serve.

LORDS G. AND E.   Our hearts receive your warnings.

KING   Farewell. [*to Attendants*] Come hither to me.
        [*Withdraws with Attendants.*]

LORD G. [*to Bertram*]
O my sweet lord, that you will stay behind us!

PAROLES   'Tis not his fault, the spark.

LORD E.   O 'tis brave wars.   25

PAROLES   Most admirable. I have seen those wars.

BERTRAM   I am commanded here, and kept a coil with:
'Too young', and 'the next year', and ''tis too early'.

PAROLES
An thy mind stand to't, boy, steal away bravely.

BERTRAM   I shall stay here the forehorse to a smock,   30
Creaking my shoes on the plain masonry,
Till honour be bought up, and no sword worn
But one to dance with. By heaven, I'll steal away!

LORD G.   There's honour in the theft.

PAROLES   Commit it, Count.

LORD E.   I am your accessory, and so farewell.   35

BERTRAM
I grow to you, and our parting is a tortured body.

LORD G.   Farewell, captain.

LORD E.   Sweet Monsieur Paroles.

PAROLES   Noble heroes, my sword and yours are kin,
good sparks and lustrous. A word, good mettles.
You shall find in the regiment of the Spinii one   40
Captain Spurio with his cicatrice, an emblem of war,
here on his sinister cheek. It was this very sword
entrenched it. Say to him I live, and observe his reports
for me.

LORD G.   We shall, noble captain.   45

PAROLES   Mars dote on you for his novices.
                              Exeunt Lords G. and E.
[*to Bertram*] What will ye do?

BERTRAM   Stay the King.

PAROLES   Use a more spacious ceremony to the noble
lords. You have restrained yourself within the list of   50
too cold an adieu. Be more expressive to them; for they
wear themselves in the cap of the time, there do muster
true gait; eat, speak and move under the influence of
the most received star, and though the devil lead the
measure, such are to be followed. After them, and take   55
a more dilated farewell.

BERTRAM   And I will do so.

PAROLES   Worthy fellows, and like to prove most sinewy
swordmen.   *Exeunt Bertram and Paroles.*

Enter LAFEU. *The King comes forward.*

LAFEU [*Kneels.*]
60   Pardon, my lord, for me and for my tidings.
KING   I'll fee thee to stand up.
LAFEU [*Stands.*]
     Then here's a man stands that has bought his pardon.
     I would you had kneeled, my lord, to ask me mercy,
     And that at my bidding you could so stand up.
65   KING   I would I had, so I had broke thy pate
     And asked thee mercy for't.
LAFEU   Good faith, across!
     But, my good lord, 'tis thus: will you be cured
     Of your infirmity?
KING   No.
LAFEU   O, will you eat
     No grapes, my royal fox? Yes, but you will
70   My noble grapes, an if my royal fox
     Could reach them. I have seen a medicine
     That's able to breathe life into a stone,
     Quicken a rock and make you dance canary
     With sprightly fire and motion; whose simple touch
75   Is powerful to araise King Pépin, nay,
     To give great Charlemagne a pen in's hand,
     And write to her a love-line.
KING   What 'her' is this?
LAFEU
     Why, Doctor She! My lord, there's one arrived,
     If you will see her. Now, by my faith and honour,
80   If seriously I may convey my thoughts
     In this my light deliverance, I have spoke
     With one that in her sex, her years, profession,
     Wisdom and constancy, hath amazed me more
     Than I dare blame my weakness. Will you see her –
85   For that is her demand – and know her business?
     That done, laugh well at me.
KING   Now, good Lafeu,
     Bring in the admiration, that we with thee
     May spend our wonder too, or take off thine
     By wondering how thou took'st it.
LAFEU   Nay, I'll fit you,
90   And not be all day neither.   [*Lafeu goes to the door.*]
KING   Thus he his special nothing ever prologues.
LAFEU   Nay, come your ways.

Enter HELEN.

KING   This haste hath wings indeed.
LAFEU   Nay, come your ways.
     This is his majesty, say your mind to him.
95   A traitor you do look like, but such traitors
     His majesty seldom fears. I am Cressid's uncle,
     That dare leave two together. Fare you well.
                         Exeunt all but the King and Helen.
KING   Now, fair one, does your business follow us?
HELEN   Ay, my good lord.
100   Gérard de Narbonne was my father,
     In what he did profess, well found.

KING   I knew him.
HELEN   The rather will I spare my praises towards him:
     Knowing him is enough. On's bed of death
     Many receipts he gave me, chiefly one
     Which as the dearest issue of his practice,   105
     And of his old experience th'only darling,
     He bade me store up as a triple eye,
     Safer than mine own two, more dear. I have so,
     And hearing your high majesty is touched
     With that malignant cause wherein the honour   110
     Of my dear father's gift stands chief in power,
     I come to tender it and my appliance
     With all bound humbleness.
KING   We thank you, maiden,
     But may not be so credulous of cure,
     When our most learned doctors leave us, and   115
     The congregated college have concluded
     That labouring art can never ransom nature
     From her inaidable estate. I say we must not
     So stain our judgement, or corrupt our hope,
     To prostitute our past-cure malady   120
     To empirics, or to dissever so
     Our great self and our credit, to esteem
     A senseless help, when help past sense we deem.
HELEN   My duty then shall pay me for my pains.
     I will no more enforce mine office on you,   125
     Humbly entreating from your royal thoughts
     A modest one to bear me back again.
KING   I cannot give thee less, to be called grateful.
     Thou thought'st to help me, and such thanks I give
     As one near death to those that wish him live.   130
     But what at full I know, thou knowst no part;
     I knowing all my peril, thou no art.
HELEN   What I can do can do no hurt to try,
     Since you set up your rest 'gainst remedy.
     He that of greatest works is finisher   135
     Oft does them by the weakest minister.
     So holy writ in babes hath judgement shown
     When judges have been babes: great floods have flown
     From simple sources, and great seas have dried
     When miracles have by the greatest been denied.   140
     Oft expectation fails, and most oft there
     Where most it promises; and oft it hits
     Where hope is coldest, and despair most fits.
KING   I must not hear thee. Fare thee well, kind maid.
     Thy pains not used must by thyself be paid: 145
     Proffers not took reap thanks for their reward.
HELEN   Inspired merit so by breath is barred.
     It is not so with Him that all things knows
     As 'tis with us that square our guess by shows;
     But most it is presumption in us when   150
     The help of heaven we count the act of men.
     Dear sir, to my endeavours give consent.
     Of heaven, not me, make an experiment.
     I am not an impostor that proclaim
     Myself against the level of mine aim,   155
     But know I think, and think I know most sure,

My art is not past power, nor you past cure.

KING   Art thou so confident? Within what space
Hop'st thou my cure?

HELEN   The greatest grace lending grace,
160   Ere twice the horses of the sun shall bring
Their fiery torcher his diurnal ring;
Ere twice in murk and occidental damp
Moist Hesperus hath quenched her sleepy lamp;
Or four and twenty times the pilot's glass
165   Hath told the thievish minutes, how they pass,
What is infirm from your sound parts shall fly,
Health shall live free, and sickness freely die.

KING   Upon thy certainty and confidence
What dar'st thou venture?

HELEN   Tax of impudence,
170   A strumpet's boldness, a divulged shame;
Traduced by odious ballads, my maiden's name
Seared otherwise; nay, worse of worst, extended
With vilest torture let my life be ended.

KING   Methinks in thee some blessed spirit doth speak
175   His powerful sound within an organ weak.
And what impossibility would slay
In common sense, sense saves another way.
Thy life is dear, for all that life can rate
Worth name of life in thee hath estimate:
180   Youth, beauty, wisdom, courage, all
That happiness and prime can happy call.
Thou this to hazard needs must intimate
Skill infinite, or monstrous desperate.
Sweet practiser, thy physic I will try,
185   That ministers thine own death if I die.

HELEN   If I break time, or flinch in property
Of what I spoke, unpitied let me die,
And well deserved. Not helping, death's my fee;
But if I help, what do you promise me?

KING   Make thy demand.

190   HELEN   But will you make it even?

KING   Ay, by my sceptre and my hopes of heaven.

HELEN   Then shalt thou give me with thy kingly hand
What husband in thy power I will command.
Exempted be from me the arrogance
195   To choose from forth the royal blood of France,
My low and humble name to propagate
With any branch or image of thy state;
But such a one, thy vassal, whom I know
Is free for me to ask, thee to bestow.

200   KING   Here is my hand. The premises observed,
Thy will by my performance shall be served.
So make the choice of thy own time, for I,
Thy resolved patient, on thee still rely.
More should I question thee, and more I must,
205   Though more to know could not be more to trust:
From whence thou cam'st, how tended on – but rest
Unquestioned welcome and undoubted blest.
– Give me some help here, ho! – If thou proceed
As high as word, my deed shall match thy deed.

                     Flourish. Exeunt.

2.2   *Enter* COUNTESS *and* LAVATCH.

COUNTESS   Come on, sir, I shall now put you to the
height of your breeding.

LAVATCH   I will show myself highly fed and lowly
taught. I know my business is but to the court.

COUNTESS   To the court? Why, what place make you   5
special, when you put off that with such contempt: 'but
to the court'?

LAVATCH   Truly, madam, if God have lent a man any
manners, he may easily put it off at court. He that
cannot make a leg, put off 's cap, kiss his hand and say   10
nothing, has neither leg, hands, lip, nor cap; and
indeed such a fellow, to say precisely, were not for
the court. But for me, I have an answer will serve all
men.

COUNTESS   Marry, that's a bountiful answer that fits all   15
questions.

LAVATCH   It is like a barber's chair that fits all buttocks:
the pin-buttock, the quatch-buttock, the brawn-
buttock or any buttock.

COUNTESS   Will your answer serve fit to all questions?   20

LAVATCH   As fit as ten groats is for the hand of an
attorney, as your French crown for your taffeta punk,
as Tib's rush for Tom's forefinger, as a pancake for
Shrove Tuesday, a Morris for May Day, as the nail to
his hole, the cuckold to his horn, as a scolding quean to   25
a wrangling knave, as the nun's lip to the friar's mouth,
nay, as the pudding to his skin.

COUNTESS   Have you, I say, an answer of such fitness
for all questions?

LAVATCH   From below your duke to beneath your   30
constable, it will fit any question.

COUNTESS   It must be an answer of most monstrous
size that must fit all demands.

LAVATCH   But a trifle neither, in good faith, if the
learned should speak truth of it. Here it is, and all that   35
belongs to't. Ask me if I am a courtier: it shall do me
no harm to learn.

COUNTESS   To be young again, if we could! I will be a
fool in question, hoping to be the wiser by your answer.
I pray you, sir, are you a courtier?   40

LAVATCH   O Lord, sir! – There's a simple putting off.
More, more, a hundred of them.

COUNTESS   Sir, I am a poor friend of yours that loves
you.

LAVATCH   O Lord, sir! – Thick, thick, spare not me.   45

COUNTESS   I think, sir, you can eat none of this homely
meat.

LAVATCH   O Lord, sir! – Nay, put me to't, I warrant
you.

COUNTESS   You were lately whipped, sir, as I think.   50

LAVATCH   O Lord, sir! – Spare not me.

COUNTESS   Do you cry 'O Lord, sir!' at your whipping,
and 'Spare not me'? Indeed your 'O Lord, sir!' is very
sequent to your whipping; you would answer very well
to a whipping, if you were but bound to't.   55

LAVATCH   I ne'er had worse luck in my life in my 'O Lord,
  sir!' I see things may serve long, but not serve ever.
COUNTESS   I play the noble housewife with the time,
  To entertain it so merrily with a fool.
60 LAVATCH   O Lord, sir! Why, there's serves well again.
COUNTESS
  An end, sir! To your business: [*giving him a letter*] give
    Helen this,
  And urge her to a present answer back.
  Commend me to my kinsmen and my son.
  This is not much.
65 LAVATCH   Not much commendation to them.
COUNTESS   Not much employment for you. You
  understand me?
LAVATCH   Most fruitfully. I am there before my legs.
COUNTESS   Haste you again.   *Exeunt.*

2.3   *Enter* BERTRAM, LAFEU *and* PAROLES.

LAFEU   They say miracles are past, and we have our
  philosophical persons to make modern and familiar,
  things supernatural and causeless. Hence is it that we
  make trifles of terrors, ensconcing ourselves into
5   seeming knowledge, when we should submit ourselves
  to an unknown fear.
PAROLES   Why, 'tis the rarest argument of wonder that
  hath shot out in our latter times.
BERTRAM   And so 'tis.
10 LAFEU   To be relinquished of the artists –
PAROLES   So I say, both of Galen and Paracelsus.
LAFEU   Of all the learned and authentic fellows –
PAROLES   Right, so I say.
LAFEU   That gave him out incurable –
15 PAROLES   Why, there 'tis; so say I too.
LAFEU   Not to be helped.
PAROLES   Right, as 'twere, a man assured of a –
LAFEU   Uncertain life, and sure death.
PAROLES   Just, you say well; so would I have said.
20 LAFEU   I may truly say it is a novelty to the world.
PAROLES   It is indeed. If you will have it in showing, you
  shall read it in what-do-ye-call there.
LAFEU [*Reads.*]   'A showing of a heavenly effect in an
  earthly actor.'
25 PAROLES   That's it; I would have said the very same.
LAFEU   Why, your dolphin is not lustier. 'Fore me, I
  speak in respect –
PAROLES   Nay, 'tis strange, 'tis very strange; that is the
  brief and the tedious of it, and he's of a most facinorious
30   spirit that will not acknowledge it to be the –
LAFEU   Very hand of heaven.
PAROLES   Ay, so I say.
LAFEU   In a most weak –
PAROLES   And debile minister, great power, great
35   transcendence, which should indeed, give us a further
  use to be made than alone the recovery of the King, as
  to be –
LAFEU   Generally thankful.

Enter KING, HELEN *and Attendants.*

PAROLES   I would have said it; you say well. Here comes
  the King.   40
LAFEU   *Lustig*, as the Dutchman says. I'll like a maid the
  better whilst I have a tooth in my head. Why, he's able
  to lead her a coranto.
PAROLES   *Mort du vinaigre!* Is not this Helen?
LAFEU   'Fore God, I think so.   45
KING   Go call before me all the lords in court.
                                          Exit Attendant.
  Sit, my preserver, by thy patient's side,
  And with this healthful hand, whose banished sense
  Thou hast repealed, a second time receive
  The confirmation of my promised gift,   50
  Which but attends thy naming.

Enter four Lords.

  Fair maid, send forth thine eye. This youthful parcel
  Of noble bachelors stand at my bestowing,
  O'er whom both sovereign power and father's voice
  I have to use. Thy frank election make;   55
  Thou hast power to choose, and they none to forsake.
HELEN   To each of you one fair and virtuous mistress
  Fall, when love please; marry, to each but one.
LAFEU   I'd give bay curtal and his furniture,
  My mouth no more were broken than these boys',   60
  And writ as little beard.
KING   Peruse them well:
  Not one of those but had a noble father.
  [*She addresses her to a Lord.*]
HELEN   Gentlemen,
  Heaven hath through me restored the King to health.
LORDS   We understand it, and thank heaven for you.
HELEN   I am a simple maid, and therein wealthiest   65
  That I protest I simply am a maid.
  – Please it your majesty, I have done already.
  The blushes in my cheeks thus whisper me,
  'We blush that thou shouldst choose; but, be refused,
  Let the white death sit on thy cheek for ever,   70
  We'll ne'er come there again.'
KING   Make choice and see.
  Who shuns thy love shuns all his love in me.
HELEN   Now, Dian, from thy altar do I fly,
  And to imperial Love, that god most high,
  Do my sighs stream. [*to 1 Lord*] Sir, will you hear my
    suit?   75
1 LORD   And grant it.
HELEN   Thanks, sir; all the rest is mute.
LAFEU [*aside*]   I had rather be in this choice than throw
  ambs-ace for my life.
HELEN [*to 2 Lord*]
  The honour, sir, that flames in your fair eyes
  Before I speak too threateningly replies.   80
  Love make your fortunes twenty times above
  Her that so wishes, and her humble love.
2 LORD   No better, if you please.

HELEN   My wish receive,
Which great Love grant, and so I take my leave.

85   LAFEU [*aside*]   Do all they deny her? An they were sons
of mine, I'd have them whipped, or I would send them
to th' Turk to make eunuchs of.

HELEN [*to 3 Lord*]
Be not afraid that I your hand should take,
I'll never do you wrong for your own sake.
90   Blessing upon your vows, and in your bed
Find fairer fortune, if you ever wed.

LAFEU [*aside*]   These boys are boys of ice, they'll none
have her. Sure, they are bastards to the English; the
French ne'er got 'em.

HELEN [*to 4 Lord*]
95   You are too young, too happy and too good
To make yourself a son out of my blood.

4 LORD   Fair one, I think not so.

LAFEU [*aside*]   There's one grape yet. I am sure thy
father drunk wine. But if thou be'st not an ass, I am a
100   youth of fourteen. I have known thee already.

HELEN [*to Bertram*]   I dare not say I take you; but I give
Me and my service, ever whilst I live,
Into your guiding power. – This is the man.

KING
Why then, young Bertram, take her: she's thy wife.

BERTRAM
105   My wife, my liege? I shall beseech your highness
In such a business give me leave to use
The help of mine own eyes.

KING   Knowst thou not, Bertram,
What she has done for me?

BERTRAM   Yes, my good lord,
But never hope to know why I should marry her.

KING
110   Thou knowst she has raised me from my sickly bed.

BERTRAM   But follows it, my lord, to bring me down
Must answer for your raising? I know her well:
She had her breeding at my father's charge.
A poor physician's daughter my wife? Disdain
115   Rather corrupt me ever.

KING   'Tis only title thou disdain'st in her, the which
I can build up. Strange is it that our bloods,
Of colour, weight and heat, poured all together,
Would quite confound distinction, yet stands off
120   In differences so mighty. If she be
All that is virtuous – save what thou dislik'st,
'A poor physician's daughter' – thou dislik'st
Of virtue for the name. But do not so.
From lowest place when virtuous things proceed,
125   The place is dignified by th' doer's deed.
Where great additions swell 's, and virtue none,
It is a dropsied honour. Good alone
Is good, without a name. Vileness is so:
The property by what it is should go,
130   Not by the title. She is young, wise, fair;
In these to Nature she's immediate heir,
And these breed honour. That is honour's scorn

Which challenges itself as honour's born
And is not like the sire. Honours thrive
When rather from our acts we them derive   135
Than our foregoers. The mere word's a slave
Debauched on every tomb, on every grave
A lying trophy, and as oft is dumb
Where dust and damned oblivion is the tomb
Of honoured bones indeed. What should be said?   140
If thou canst like this creature as a maid,
I can create the rest. Virtue and she
Is her own dower; honour and wealth from me.

BERTRAM   I cannot love her, nor will strive to do't.

KING
Thou wrong'st thyself, if thou shouldst strive to choose.   145

HELEN   That you are well restored, my lord, I'm glad.
Let the rest go.

KING   My honour's at the stake, which to defeat
I must produce my power. Here, take her hand,
Proud scornful boy, unworthy this good gift,   150
That dost in vile misprision shackle up
My love and her desert; that canst not dream
We, poising us in her defective scale,
Shall weigh thee to the beam; that wilt not know
It is in us to plant thine honour where   155
We please to have it grow. Check thy contempt;
Obey our will, which travails in thy good.
Believe not thy disdain, but presently
Do thine own fortunes that obedient right
Which both thy duty owes and our power claims;   160
Or I will throw thee from my care forever
Into the staggers and the careless lapse
Of youth and ignorance, both my revenge and hate
Loosing upon thee, in the name of justice,
Without all terms of pity. Speak, thine answer.   165

BERTRAM   Pardon, my gracious lord; for I submit
My fancy to your eyes. When I consider
What great creation and what dole of honour
Flies where you bid it, I find that she, which late
Was in my nobler thoughts most base, is now   170
The praised of the King who, so ennobled,
Is as 'twere born so.

KING   Take her by the hand,
And tell her she is thine; to whom I promise
A counterpoise, if not to thy estate
A balance more replete.

BERTRAM   I take her hand.   175

KING   Good fortune and the favour of the King
Smile upon this contract, whose ceremony
Shall seem expedient on the now-born brief,
And be performed tonight. The solemn feast
Shall more attend upon the coming space,   180
Expecting absent friends. As thou lov'st her,
Thy love's to me religious; else, does err.
                    Exeunt all but Paroles and Lafeu who
                    stay behind, commenting of this wedding.

LAFEU   Do you hear, monsieur? A word with you.

PAROLES   Your pleasure, sir?

185 LAFEU Your lord and master did well to make his recantation.

PAROLES Recantation? My lord? My master?

LAFEU Ay. Is it not a language I speak?

PAROLES A most harsh one, and not to be understood
190 without bloody succeeding. My master?

LAFEU Are you companion to the Count Roussillon?

PAROLES To any count; to all counts; to what is man.

LAFEU To what is count's man. Count's master is of another style.

195 PAROLES You are too old, sir. Let it satisfy you, you are too old.

LAFEU I must tell thee, sirrah, I write man; to which title age cannot bring thee.

PAROLES What I dare too well do, I dare not do.

200 LAFEU I did think thee for two ordinaries to be a pretty wise fellow. Thou didst make tolerable vent of thy travel; it might pass. Yet the scarves and the bannerets about thee did manifoldly dissuade me from believing thee a vessel of too great a burden. I have now found thee.
205 When I lose thee again, I care not. Yet art thou good for nothing but taking up, and that thou'rt scarce worth.

PAROLES Hadst thou not the privilege of antiquity upon thee –

LAFEU Do not plunge thyself too far in anger, lest thou
210 hasten thy trial; which if – Lord have mercy on thee for a hen. So, my good window of lattice, fare thee well. Thy casement I need not open, for I look through thee. Give me thy hand.

PAROLES My lord, you give me most egregious
215 indignity.

LAFEU Ay, with all my heart, and thou art worthy of it.

PAROLES I have not, my lord, deserved it.

LAFEU Yes, good faith, every dram of it, and I will not bate thee a scruple.

220 PAROLES Well, I shall be wiser.

LAFEU Even as soon as thou canst, for thou hast to pull at a smack o'th' contrary. If ever thou be'st bound in thy scarf and beaten, thou shall find what it is to be proud of thy bondage. I have a desire to hold my
225 acquaintance with thee, or rather my knowledge, that I may say in the default, 'He is a man I know'.

PAROLES My lord, you do me most insupportable vexation.

LAFEU I would it were hell-pains for thy sake, and my
230 poor doing eternal. For doing I am past, as I will by thee, in what motion age will give me leave. *Exit.*

PAROLES Well, thou hast a son shall take this disgrace off me, scurvy, old, filthy, scurvy lord. Well, I must be patient, there is no fettering of authority. I'll beat him,
235 by my life, if I can meet him with any convenience, an he were double and double a lord. I'll have no more pity of his age than I would have of – I'll beat him, an if I could but meet him again.

Enter LAFEU.

LAFEU Sirrah, your lord and master's married. There's
240 news for you. You have a new mistress.

PAROLES I most unfeignedly beseech your lordship to make some reservation of your wrongs. He is my good lord; whom I serve above is my master.

LAFEU Who? God?

PAROLES Ay, sir. 245

LAFEU The devil it is that's thy master. Why dost thou garter up thy arms o'this fashion? Dost make hose of thy sleeves? Do other servants so? Thou wert best set thy lower part where thy nose stands. By mine honour, if I were but two hours younger, I'd beat thee. 250 Methink'st thou art a general offence, and every man should beat thee. I think thou wast created for men to breathe themselves upon thee.

PAROLES This is hard and undeserved measure, my lord.

LAFEU Go to, sir; you were beaten in Italy for picking a 255 kernel out of a pomegranate. You are a vagabond and no true traveller. You are more saucy with lords and honourable personages than the commission of your birth and virtue gives you heraldry. You are not worth another word, else I'd call you knave. I leave you. *Exit.* 260

PAROLES Good, very good. It is so then. Good, very good. Let it be concealed awhile.

Enter BERTRAM.

BERTRAM Undone, and forfeited to cares for ever!

PAROLES What's the matter, sweet heart?

BERTRAM
Although before the solemn priest I have sworn, 265
I will not bed her.

PAROLES   What? What, sweet heart?

BERTRAM O my Paroles, they have married me!
I'll to the Tuscan wars, and never bed her.

PAROLES France is a dog-hole, and it no more merits
The tread of a man's foot. To th' wars! 270

BERTRAM There's letters from my mother. What
th'import is, I know not yet.

PAROLES Ay, that would be known. To th' wars, my boy,
to th' wars!
He wears his honour in a box unseen 275
That hugs his kicky-wicky here at home,
Spending his manly marrow in her arms,
Which should sustain the bound and high curvet
Of Mars's fiery steed. To other regions!
France is a stable, we that dwell in't jades. 280
Therefore, to th' war!

BERTRAM It shall be so. I'll send her to my house,
Acquaint my mother with my hate to her
And wherefore I am fled, write to the King
That which I durst not speak. His present gift 285
Shall furnish me to those Italian fields
Where noble fellows strike. Wars is no strife
To the dark house and the detested wife.

PAROLES Will this capriccio hold in thee, art sure?

BERTRAM Go with me to my chamber, and advise me. 290
I'll send her straight away. Tomorrow,
I'll to the wars, she to her single sorrow.

PAROLES
Why, these balls bound; there's noise in it. 'Tis hard:

A young man married is a man that's marred.
295 Therefore away, and leave her bravely. Go!
The King has done you wrong; but hush, 'tis so.
                                          Exeunt.

2.4   *Enter* HELEN *reading a letter and* LAVATCH.

HELEN   My mother greets me kindly. Is she well?

LAVATCH   She is not well, but yet she has her health.
She's very merry, but yet she is not well. But, thanks be
given, she's very well, and wants nothing i'th' world.
5 But yet she is not well.

HELEN   If she be very well, what does she ail that she's
not very well?

LAVATCH   Truly, she's very well indeed, but for two things.

HELEN   What two things?

10 LAVATCH   One, that she's not in heaven, whither God
send her quickly. The other, that she's in earth, from
whence God send her quickly.

Enter PAROLES.

PAROLES   Bless you, my fortunate lady.

HELEN   I hope, sir, I have your good will to have mine
15 own good fortunes.

PAROLES   You had my prayers to lead them on, and to
keep them on have them still. [*to Lavatch*] O my knave,
how does my old lady?

LAVATCH   So that you had her wrinkles and I her money,
20 I would she did as you say.

PAROLES   Why, I say nothing.

LAVATCH   Marry, you are the wiser man; for many a
man's tongue shakes out his master's undoing. To say
nothing, to do nothing, to know nothing and to have
25 nothing is to be a great part of your title, which is
within a very little of nothing.

PAROLES   Away, thou'rt a knave.

LAVATCH   You should have said, sir, 'Before a knave
thou'rt a knave'; that's, 'Before me thou'rt a knave'.
30 This had been truth, sir.

PAROLES   Go to, thou art a witty fool. I have found thee.

LAVATCH   Did you find me in yourself, sir, or were you
taught to find me?

PAROLES   In myself.

35 LAVATCH   The search, sir, was profitable, and much fool
may you find in you, even to the world's pleasure and
the increase of laughter.

PAROLES   A good knave, i'faith, and well fed.
Madam, my lord will go away tonight.
40 A very serious business calls on him.
The great prerogative and rite of love,
Which as your due time claims, he does acknowledge,
But puts it off to a compelled restraint;
Whose want and whose delay is strewed with sweets,
45 Which they distil now in the curbed time
To make the coming hour o'erflow with joy
And pleasure drown the brim.

HELEN   What's his will else?

PAROLES
That you will take your instant leave o'th' King
And make this haste as your own good proceeding,
Strengthened with what apology you think   50
May make it probable need.

HELEN   What more commands he?

PAROLES   That, having this obtained, you presently
Attend his further pleasure.

HELEN   In everything I wait upon his will.

PAROLES   I shall report it so.   *Exit.*   55

HELEN   I pray you. – Come, sirrah.   *Exeunt.*

2.5   *Enter* LAFEU *and* BERTRAM.

LAFEU   But I hope your lordship thinks not him a
soldier.

BERTRAM   Yes, my lord, and of very valiant approof.

LAFEU   You have it from his own deliverance.

BERTRAM   And by other warranted testimony.   5

LAFEU   Then my dial goes not true. I took this lark for a
bunting.

BERTRAM   I do assure you, my lord, he is very great in
knowledge, and accordingly valiant.

LAFEU   I have then sinned against his experience and   10
transgressed against his valour; and my state that way
is dangerous, since I cannot yet find in my heart to
repent. Here he comes. I pray you, make us friends; I
will pursue the amity.

Enter PAROLES.

PAROLES [*to Bertram*]   These things shall be done, sir. 15

LAFEU   Pray you, sir, who's his tailor?

PAROLES   Sir!

LAFEU   O, I know him well, ay, 'Sir'. He, sir, 's a good
workman, a very good tailor.

BERTRAM [*aside to Paroles*]   Is she gone to the King?   20

PAROLES   She is.

BERTRAM   Will she away tonight?

PAROLES   As you'll have her.

BERTRAM   I have writ my letters, casketed my treasure,
Given order for our horses, and tonight,   25
When I should take possession of the bride,
End ere I do begin.

LAFEU   A good traveller is something at the latter end of
a dinner; but one that lies three-thirds and uses a known
truth to pass a thousand nothings with should be once   30
heard and thrice beaten. God save you, captain.

BERTRAM   Is there any unkindness between my lord and
you, monsieur?

PAROLES   I know not how I have deserved to run into
my lord's displeasure.   35

LAFEU   You have made shift to run into't, boots and
spurs and all, like him that leaped into the custard; and
out of it you'll run again, rather than suffer question
for your residence.

BERTRAM   It may be you have mistaken him, my lord.   40

LAFEU   And shall do so ever, though I took him at's

prayers. Fare you well, my lord, and believe this of me:
there can be no kernel in this light nut. The soul of this
man is his clothes. Trust him not in matter of heavy
45 consequence. I have kept of them tame, and know their
natures. [*to Paroles*] Farewell, monsieur: I have spoken
better of you than you have wit or will to deserve at my
hand; but we must do good against evil.   *Exit.*
PAROLES An idle lord, I swear.
50 BERTRAM I think not so.
PAROLES Why, do you not know him?
BERTRAM Yes, I do know him well, and common speech
Gives him a worthy pass. Here comes my clog.

Enter HELEN.

HELEN   I have, sir, as I was commanded from you,
55 Spoke with the King, and have procured his leave
For present parting; only he desires
Some private speech with you.
BERTRAM   I shall obey his will.
You must not marvel, Helen, at my course,
Which holds not colour with the time, nor does
60 The ministration and required office
On my particular. Prepared I was not
For such a business; therefore am I found
So much unsettled. This drives me to entreat you
That presently you take your way for home,
65 And rather muse than ask why I entreat you,
For my respects are better than they seem
And my appointments have in them a need
Greater than shows itself at the first view
To you that know them not. This to my mother.
    [*Gives a letter.*]
70 'Twill be two days ere I shall see you, so
I leave you to your wisdom.
HELEN   Sir, I can nothing say,
But that I am your most obedient servant –
BERTRAM Come, come, no more of that.
HELEN   – And ever shall
With true observance seek to eke out that
75 Wherein toward me my homely stars have failed
To equal my great fortune.
BERTRAM   Let that go.
My haste is very great. Farewell; hie home.
HELEN   Pray, sir, your pardon.
BERTRAM   Well, what would you say?
HELEN   I am not worthy of the wealth I owe,
80 Nor dare I say 'tis mine, and yet it is;
But, like a timorous thief, most fain would steal
What law does vouch mine own.
BERTRAM   What would you have?
HELEN
Something, and scarce so much; nothing, indeed.
I would not tell you what I would, my lord.
85 Faith, yes:
Strangers and foes do sunder and not kiss.
BERTRAM I pray you stay not, but in haste to horse.
HELEN   I shall not break your bidding, good my lord.

– Where are my other men? Monsieur, farewell. *Exit.*
BERTRAM
Go thou toward home, where I will never come   90
Whilst I can shake my sword or hear the drum.
Away, and for our flight.
PAROLES   Bravely. *Coraggio!* *Exeunt.*

3.1   *Flourish. Enter the* DUKE *of Florence, the two*
       French LORDS G. *and* E., *with a troop of Soldiers.*

DUKE   So that from point to point now have you heard
The fundamental reasons of this war,
Whose great decision hath much blood let forth
And more thirsts after.
LORD G.   Holy seems the quarrel
Upon your grace's part; black and fearful   5
On the opposer.
DUKE   Therefore we marvel much our cousin France
Would in so just a business shut his bosom
Against our borrowing prayers.
LORD E.   Good my lord,
The reasons of our state I cannot yield   10
But like a common and an outward man
That the great figure of a council frames
By self-unable motion; therefore dare not
Say what I think of it, since I have found
Myself in my incertain grounds to fail   15
As often as I guessed.
DUKE   Be it his pleasure.
LORD G. But I am sure the younger of our nation,
That surfeit on their ease, will day by day
Come here for physic.
DUKE   Welcome shall they be;
And all the honours that can fly from us   20
Shall on them settle. You know your places well:
When better fall, for your avails they fell.
Tomorrow to the field.   *Flourish. Exeunt.*

3.2   *Enter* COUNTESS *holding a letter*
       and LAVATCH.

COUNTESS It hath happened all as I would have had it,
save that he comes not along with her.
LAVATCH By my troth, I take my young lord to be a very
melancholy man.
COUNTESS By what observance, I pray you?   5
LAVATCH Why, he will look upon his boot and sing;
mend the ruff and sing; ask questions and sing; pick
his teeth and sing. I know a man that had this trick of
melancholy sold a goodly manor for a song.
COUNTESS [*opening the letter*] Let me see what he   10
writes, and when he means to come.
LAVATCH I have no mind to Isbel since I was at court.
Our old ling and our Isbels o'th' country are nothing
like your old ling and your Isbels o'th' court. The
brains of my Cupid's knocked out, and I begin to love   15
as an old man loves money, with no stomach.

COUNTESS   What have we here?

LAVATCH   E'en that you have there.   *Exit.*

COUNTESS [*Reads.*]   *I have sent you a daughter-in-law.*
20   *She hath recovered the King, and undone me. I have*
wedded her, not bedded her, and sworn to make the 'not'
eternal. You shall hear I am run away; know it before the
report come. If there be breadth enough in the world, I will
hold a long distance. My duty to you.

25   *Your unfortunate son,*
                                    Bertram.

This is not well, rash and unbridled boy,
To fly the favours of so good a king,
To pluck his indignation on thy head
30   By the misprizing of a maid too virtuous
For the contempt of empire.

Enter LAVATCH.

LAVATCH   O madam, yonder is heavy news within
between two soldiers and my young lady.

COUNTESS   What is the matter?

35   LAVATCH   Nay, there is some comfort in the news, some
comfort: your son will not be killed so soon as I thought
he would.

COUNTESS   Why should he be killed?

LAVATCH   So say I, madam, if he run away, as I hear he
40   does. The danger is in standing to't; that's the loss of
men, though it be the getting of children. Here they
come will tell you more. For my part, I only hear your
son was run away.   *Exit.*

Enter HELEN *holding a letter and the*
two French LORDS G. *and* E.

LORD E.   Save you, good madam.

45   HELEN   Madam, my lord is gone, for ever gone.

LORD G.   Do not say so.

COUNTESS
Think upon patience. Pray you, gentlemen.
I have felt so many quirks of joy and grief
That the first face of neither on the start
50   Can woman me unto't. Where is my son, I pray you?

LORD G.
Madam, he's gone to serve the Duke of Florence.
We met him thitherward, for thence we came,
And, after some dispatch in hand at court,
Thither we bend again.

HELEN
55   Look on his letter, madam; here's my passport:
[*Reads.*] *When thou canst get the ring upon my finger,*
which never shall come off, and show me a child begotten
of thy body that I am father to, then call me husband. But
in such a 'then', I write a 'never'.
60   This is a dreadful sentence.

COUNTESS   Brought you this letter, gentlemen?

LORD G.   Ay, madam, and for the contents' sake are
sorry for our pains.

COUNTESS   I prithee, lady, have a better cheer.
65   If thou engrossest all the griefs are thine,

Thou robb'st me of a moiety. He was my son,
But I do wash his name out of my blood,
And thou art all my child. Towards Florence is he?

LORD G.   Ay, madam.

COUNTESS   And to be a soldier?

LORD G.   Such is his noble purpose; and believe't,   70
The Duke will lay upon him all the honour
That good convenience claims.

COUNTESS   Return you thither?

LORD E.   Ay, madam, with the swiftest wing of speed.

HELEN [*Reads.*]
Till I have no wife, I have nothing in France.
'Tis bitter.

COUNTESS   Find you that there?

HELEN   Ay, madam.   75

LORD E.   'Tis but the boldness of his hand, haply,
Which his heart was not consenting to.

COUNTESS
Nothing in France until he have no wife!
There's nothing here that is too good for him
But only she, and she deserves a lord   80
That twenty such rude boys might tend upon
And call her, hourly, mistress. Who was with him?

LORD E.   A servant only, and a gentleman
Which I have sometime known.

COUNTESS   Paroles, was it not?   85

LORD E.   Ay, my good lady, he.

COUNTESS
A very tainted fellow, and full of wickedness.
My son corrupts a well-derived nature
With his inducement.

LORD E.   Indeed, good lady,
The fellow has a deal of that too much   90
Which holds him much to have.

COUNTESS   You're welcome, gentlemen.
I will entreat you, when you see my son,
To tell him that his sword can never win
The honour that he loses. More I'll entreat you
Written to bear along.

LORD G.   We serve you, madam,   95
In that and all your worthiest affairs.

COUNTESS   Not so, but as we change our courtesies.
Will you draw near?   *Exit with the Lords G. and E.*

HELEN
'Till I have no wife, I have nothing in France.'
Nothing in France until he has no wife.   100
Thou shalt have none, Roussillon, none in France;
Then hast thou all again. Poor lord, is't I
That chase thee from thy country and expose
Those tender limbs of thine to the event
Of the none-sparing war? And is it I   105
That drive thee from the sportive court, where thou
Wast shot at with fair eyes, to be the mark
Of smoky muskets? O you leaden messengers
That ride upon the violent speed of fire,
Fly with false aim, move the still-piecing air   110
That sings with piercing; do not touch my lord.

Whoever shoots at him, I set him there.
Whoever charges on his forward breast,
I am the caitiff that do hold him to't,
115 And though I kill him not, I am the cause
His death was so effected. Better 'twere
I met the ravin lion when he roared
With sharp constraint of hunger; better 'twere
That all the miseries which nature owes
120 Were mine at once. No, come thou home, Roussillon,
Whence honour but of danger wins a scar,
As oft it loses all. I will be gone:
My being here it is that holds thee hence.
Shall I stay here to do't? No, no, although
125 The air of paradise did fan the house
And angels officed all. I will be gone,
That pitiful rumour may report my flight
To consolate thine ear. Come, night; end, day;
For with the dark, poor thief, I'll steal away.   *Exit.*

3.3   *Flourish. Enter the* DUKE *of Florence,*
       BERTRAM, *Drum and Trumpets, Soldiers,* PAROLES.

DUKE   The general of our horse thou art, and we,
       Great in our hope, lay our best love and credence
       Upon thy promising fortune.
BERTRAM   Sir, it is
       A charge too heavy for my strength, but yet
5   We'll strive to bear it for your worthy sake
       To th'extreme edge of hazard.
DUKE   Then go thou forth;
       And Fortune play upon thy prosperous helm
       As thy auspicious mistress.
BERTRAM   This very day,
       Great Mars, I put myself into thy file.
10   Make me but like my thoughts, and I shall prove
       A lover of thy drum, hater of love.   *Exeunt.*

3.4   *Enter* COUNTESS *and* RINALDO *her Steward.*

COUNTESS   Alas! And would you take the letter of her?
       Might you not know she would do as she has done
       By sending me a letter? Read it again.
RINALDO [*Reads.*]
       I am Saint Jacques' pilgrim, thither gone.
5   *Ambitious love hath so in me offended*
       That barefoot plod I the cold ground upon,
           With sainted vow my faults to have amended.
       Write, write, that from the bloody course of war
           My dearest master, your dear son, may hie.
10   *Bless him at home in peace, whilst I from far*
           His name with zealous fervour sanctify.
       His taken labours bid him me forgive.
           I, his despiteful Juno, sent him forth
       From courtly friends, with camping foes to live,
15   *Where death and danger dogs the heels of worth.*
       He is too good and fair for death and me,
       Whom I myself embrace to set him free.

COUNTESS
       Ah, what sharp stings are in her mildest words!
       Rinaldo, you did never lack advice so much
       As letting her pass so. Had I spoke with her,   20
       I could have well diverted her intents,
       Which thus she hath prevented.
RINALDO   Pardon me, madam.
       If I had given you this at overnight,
       She might have been o'erta'en; and yet she writes
       Pursuit would be but vain.
COUNTESS   What angel shall   25
       Bless this unworthy husband? He cannot thrive,
       Unless her prayers, whom heaven delights to hear
       And loves to grant, reprieve him from the wrath
       Of greatest justice. Write, write, Rinaldo,
       To this unworthy husband of his wife.   30
       Let every word weigh heavy of her worth
       That he does weigh too light. My greatest grief,
       Though little he do feel it, set down sharply.
       Dispatch the most convenient messenger.
       When haply he shall hear that she is gone,   35
       He will return, and hope I may that she,
       Hearing so much, will speed her foot again,
       Led hither by pure love. Which of them both
       Is dearest to me, I have no skill in sense
       To make distinction. Provide this messenger.   40
       My heart is heavy, and mine age is weak;
       Grief would have tears, and sorrow bids me speak.
                                           Exeunt.

3.5   *A tucket afar off. Enter an old* WIDOW *of*
           Florence, her daughter DIANA *and*
           MARIANA, *with other Citizens.*

WIDOW   Nay, come, for if they do approach the city, we
       shall lose all the sight.
DIANA   They say the French count has done most
       honourable service.
WIDOW   It is reported that he has taken their greatest   5
       commander, and that with his own hand he slew the
       Duke's brother. [*Tucket*] We have lost our labour: they
       are gone a contrary way. Hark, you may know by their
       trumpets.
MARIANA   Come, let's return again, and suffice   10
       ourselves with the report of it. Well, Diana, take heed
       of this French earl. The honour of a maid is her name,
       and no legacy is so rich as honesty.
WIDOW   I have told my neighbour how you have been
       solicited by a gentleman, his companion.   15
MARIANA   I know that knave, hang him! One Paroles, a
       filthy officer he is in those suggestions for the young
       earl. Beware of them, Diana; their promises,
       enticements, oaths, tokens and all these engines of lust
       are not the things they go under. Many a maid hath   20
       been seduced by them; and the misery is example that
       so terrible shows in the wrack of maidenhood cannot
       for all that dissuade succession, but that they are limed

with the twigs that threatens them. I hope I need not to
25   advise you further, but I hope your own grace will keep
you where you are, though there were no further
danger known but the modesty which is so lost.
DIANA   You shall not need to fear me.

         Enter HELEN *dressed as a pilgrim.*

WIDOW   I hope so. Look, here comes a pilgrim. I know
30   she will lie at my house; thither they send one another.
I'll question her.
    God save you, pilgrim! Whither are you bound?
HELEN   To Saint Jacques le Grand.
    Where do the palmers lodge, I do beseech you?
35   WIDOW   At the Saint Francis here beside the port.
HELEN   Is this the way?   [*A march afar*]
WIDOW   Ay, marry, is't. Hark you, they come this way.
If you will tarry, holy pilgrim,
But till the troops come by,
40   I will conduct you where you shall be lodged,
The rather for I think I know your hostess
As ample as myself.
HELEN   Is it yourself?
WIDOW   If you shall please so, pilgrim.
HELEN   I thank you, and will stay upon your leisure.
WIDOW   You came, I think, from France?
45   HELEN   I did so.
WIDOW   Here you shall see a countryman of yours
That has done worthy service.
HELEN   His name, I pray you?
DIANA   The Count Roussillon. Know you such a one?
HELEN   But by the ear, that hears most nobly of him.
His face I know not.
50   DIANA   Whatsome'er he is,
He's bravely taken here. He stole from France,
As 'tis reported, for the King had married him
Against his liking. Think you it is so?
HELEN   Ay, surely, mere the truth. I know his lady.
55   DIANA   There is a gentleman that serves the count
Reports but coarsely of her.
HELEN   What's his name?
DIANA   Monsieur Paroles.
HELEN   O, I believe with him.
In argument of praise, or to the worth
Of the great count himself, she is too mean
60   To have her name repeated. All her deserving
Is a reserved honesty, and that
I have not heard examined.
DIANA   Alas, poor lady.
'Tis a hard bondage to become the wife
Of a detesting lord.
65   WIDOW   I warrant, good creature, wheresoe'er she is,
Her heart weighs sadly. This young maid might do
    her
A shrewd turn, if she pleased.
HELEN   How do you mean?
May be the amorous count solicits her
In the unlawful purpose.

WIDOW   He does indeed,
And brokes with all that can in such a suit   70
Corrupt the tender honour of a maid.
But she is armed for him, and keeps her guard
In honestest defence.

         Drum and colours.
   Enter BERTRAM, PAROLES *and the whole Army.*

MARIANA   The gods forbid else!
WIDOW   So, now they come:
That is Antonio, the Duke's eldest son;   75
That, Escalus.
HELEN   Which is the Frenchman?
DIANA   He,
That with the plume; 'tis a most gallant fellow.
I would he loved his wife. If he were honester,
He were much goodlier.
Is't not a handsome gentleman?
HELEN   I like him well.   80
DIANA
'Tis pity he is not honest. Yond's that same knave
That leads him to these places. Were I his lady,
I would poison that vile rascal.
HELEN   Which is he?
DIANA   That jackanapes with scarves. Why is he
melancholy?   85
HELEN   Perchance he's hurt i'th' battle.
PAROLES   Lose our drum? Well!
MARIANA   He's shrewdly vexed at something. Look, he
has spied us.
WIDOW [*to Paroles*]   Marry, hang you!   90
MARIANA [*to Paroles*]   And your curtsy, for a ring-
carrier!   *Exeunt Bertram, Paroles and Army.*
WIDOW
The troop is passed. Come, pilgrim, I will bring you
Where you shall host. Of enjoined penitents
There's four or five, to great Saint Jacques bound, 95
Already at my house.
HELEN   I humbly thank you.
Please it this matron and this gentle maid
To eat with us tonight, the charge and thanking
Shall be for me. And, to requite you further,
I will bestow some precepts of this virgin   100
Worthy the note.
BOTH   We'll take your offer kindly.   *Exeunt.*

3.6   *Enter* BERTRAM *and the French*
        LORDS G. *and* E., *as at first.*

LORD E.   Nay, good my lord, put him to't; let him have
his way.
LORD G.   If your lordship find him not a hilding, hold
me no more in your respect.
LORD E.   On my life, my lord, a bubble.   5
BERTRAM   Do you think I am so far deceived in him?
LORD E.   Believe it, my lord. In mine own direct
knowledge, without any malice, but to speak of him as

my kinsman, he's a most notable coward, an infinite
and endless liar, an hourly promise-breaker, the owner
of no one good quality worthy your lordship's
entertainment.

LORD G.   It were fit you knew him, lest, reposing too far
in his virtue, which he hath not, he might at some great
and trusty business in a main danger fail you.

BERTRAM   I would I knew in what particular action to
try him.

LORD G.   None better than to let him fetch off his drum,
which you hear him so confidently undertake to do.

LORD E.   I, with a troop of Florentines, will suddenly
surprise him. Such I will have, whom I am sure he
knows not from the enemy. We will bind and hoodwink
him so that he shall suppose no other but that he is
carried into the leaguer of the adversary's when we
bring him to our own tents. Be but your lordship
present at his examination. If he do not, for the
promise of his life, and in the highest compulsion of
base fear, offer to betray you and deliver all the
intelligence in his power against you, and that with the
divine forfeit of his soul upon oath, never trust my
judgement in anything.

LORD G.   O, for the love of laughter, let him fetch his
drum. He says he has a stratagem for't. When your
lordship sees the bottom of his success in't, and to
what metal this counterfeit lump of ore will be melted,
if you give him not John Drum's entertainment, your
inclining cannot be removed. Here he comes.

Enter PAROLES.

LORD E.   [*to Bertram and Lord G.*]   O, for the love of
laughter, hinder not the honour of his design. Let him
fetch off his drum in any hand.

BERTRAM   How now, monsieur? This drum sticks sorely
in your disposition.

LORD G.   A pox on't! Let it go; 'tis but a drum.

PAROLES   But a drum? Is't but a drum? A drum so lost!
There was excellent command, to charge in with our
horse upon our own wings, and to rend our own
soldiers.

LORD G.   That was not to be blamed in the command of
the service. It was a disaster of war that Caesar himself
could not have prevented, if he had been there to
command.

BERTRAM   Well, we cannot greatly condemn our success.
Some dishonour we had in the loss of that drum, but it
is not to be recovered.

PAROLES   It might have been recovered.

BERTRAM   It might, but it is not now.

PAROLES   It is to be recovered. But that the merit of
service is seldom attributed to the true and exact
performer, I would have that drum or another, or *hic
iacet*.

BERTRAM   Why, if you have a stomach, to't, monsieur!
If you think your mystery in stratagem can bring this
instrument of honour again into his native quarter, be

magnanimous in the enterprise and go on. I will grace
the attempt for a worthy exploit. If you speed well in it,
the Duke shall both speak of it and extend to you what
further becomes his greatness, even to the utmost
syllable of your worthiness.

PAROLES   By the hand of a soldier, I will undertake it.

BERTRAM   But you must not now slumber in it.

PAROLES   I'll about it this evening, and I will presently
pen down my dilemmas, encourage myself in my
certainty, put myself into my mortal preparation; and
by midnight look to hear further from me.

BERTRAM   May I be bold to acquaint his grace you are
gone about it?

PAROLES   I know not what the success will be, my lord,
but the attempt I vow.

BERTRAM   I know thou'rt valiant, and to the possibility
of thy soldiership will subscribe for thee. Farewell.

PAROLES   I love not many words.   *Exit.*

LORD E.   No more than a fish loves water. Is not this a
strange fellow, my lord, that so confidently seems to
undertake this business, which he knows is not to be
done; damns himself to do, and dares better be damned
than to do't?

LORD G.   You do not know him, my lord, as we do.
Certain it is that he will steal himself into a man's
favour and for a week escape a great deal of discoveries;
but when you find him out, you have him ever after.

BERTRAM   Why, do you think he will make no deed at all
of this that so seriously he does address himself unto?

LORD E.   None in the world, but return with an
invention and clap upon you two or three probable lies.
But we have almost embossed him. You shall see his
fall tonight; for indeed he is not for your lordship's
respect.

LORD G.   We'll make you some sport with the fox ere we
case him. He was first smoked by the old Lord Lafeu.
When his disguise and he is parted, tell me what a
sprat you shall find him, which you shall see this very
night.

LORD E.   I must go look my twigs. He shall be caught.

BERTRAM   [*to Lord G.*]   Your brother, he shall go along
with me.

LORD G.   As't please your lordship, I'll leave you.
                                                        Exit.

BERTRAM
Now will I lead you to the house and show you
The lass I spoke of.

LORD E.   But you say she's honest.

BERTRAM
That's all the fault. I spoke with her but once
And found her wondrous cold. But I sent to her
By this same coxcomb that we have i'th' wind
Tokens and letters, which she did re-send.
And this is all I have done. She's a fair creature.
Will you go see her?

LORD E.   With all my heart, my lord.
                                                        Exeunt.

3.7   *Enter* HELEN *and the* WIDOW.

HELEN   If you misdoubt me that I am not she,
    I know not how I shall assure you further
    But I shall lose the grounds I work upon.
WIDOW   Though my estate be fall'n, I was well born,
5   Nothing acquainted with these businesses,
    And would not put my reputation now
    In any staining act.
HELEN   Nor would I wish you.
    First, give me trust the count he is my husband,
    And what to your sworn counsel I have spoken
10   Is so from word to word. And then you cannot,
    By the good aid that I of you shall borrow,
    Err in bestowing it.
WIDOW   I should believe you,
    For you have showed me that which well approves
    You're great in fortune.
HELEN   Take this purse of gold,
15   And let me buy your friendly help thus far,
    Which I will over-pay and pay again
    When I have found it. The count he woos your
       daughter,
    Lays down his wanton siege before her beauty,
    Resolves to carry her. Let her in fine consent,
20   As we'll direct her how 'tis best to bear it.
    Now his important blood will naught deny
    That she'll demand. A ring the county wears
    That downward hath succeeded in his house
    From son to son some four or five descents
25   Since the first father wore it. This ring he holds
    In most rich choice; yet, in his idle fire,
    To buy his will it would not seem too dear,
    Howe'er repented after.
WIDOW   Now I see
    The bottom of your purpose.
30 HELEN   You see it lawful then. It is no more
    But that your daughter, ere she seems as won,
    Desires this ring; appoints him an encounter;
    In fine, delivers me to fill the time,
    Herself most chastely absent. After,
35   To marry her, I'll add three thousand crowns
    To what is passed already.
WIDOW   I have yielded.
    Instruct my daughter how she shall persever
    That time and place with this deceit so lawful
    May prove coherent. Every night he comes
40   With musics of all sorts, and songs composed
    To her unworthiness. It nothing steads us
    To chide him from our eaves, for he persists
    As if his life lay on't.
HELEN   Why then, tonight
    Let us assay our plot, which if it speed,
45   Is wicked meaning in a lawful deed,
    And lawful meaning in a wicked act,
    Where both not sin, and yet a sinful fact.
    But let's about it.   *Exeunt.*

4.1   *Enter* LORD G., *with five or six other*
                      Soldiers *in ambush.*

LORD G.   He can come no other way but by this hedge-
    corner. When you sally upon him, speak what terrible
    language you will. Though you understand it not
    yourselves, no matter; for we must not seem to
5   understand him, unless some one among us, whom we
    must produce for an interpreter.
1 SOLDIER   Good captain, let me be th'interpreter.
LORD G.   Art not acquainted with him? Knows he not
    thy voice?
10 1 SOLDIER   No, sir, I warrant you.
LORD G.   But what linsey-woolsey hast thou to speak to
    us again?
1 SOLDIER   E'en such as you speak to me.
LORD G.   He must think us some band of strangers i'th'
15   adversary's entertainment. Now he hath a smack of all
    neighbouring languages; therefore we must every one
    be a man of his own fancy, not to know what we speak
    one to another. So we seem to know, is to know straight
    our purpose: choughs' language, gabble enough and
20   good enough. As for you, interpreter, you must seem
    very politic. But couch, ho! Here he comes, to beguile
    two hours in a sleep, and then to return and swear the
    lies he forges.

                Enter PAROLES.

PAROLES   Ten o'clock. Within these three hours 'twill be
25   time enough to go home. What shall I say I have done?
    It must be a very plausive invention that carries it. They
    begin to smoke me, and disgraces have of late knocked
    too often at my door. I find my tongue is too foolhardy,
    but my heart hath the fear of Mars before it, and of his
30   creatures, not daring the reports of my tongue.
LORD G. [*aside*]   This is the first truth that e'er thine
    own tongue was guilty of.
PAROLES   What the devil should move me to undertake
    the recovery of this drum, being not ignorant of the
35   impossibility, and knowing I had no such purpose? I
    must give myself some hurts and say I got them in
    exploit. Yet slight ones will not carry it. They will
    say, 'Came you off with so little?' And great ones I dare
    not give. Wherefore, what's the instance? Tongue, I must
40   put you into a butter-woman's mouth and buy myself
    another of Bajazet's mute if you prattle me into these
    perils.
LORD G. [*aside*]   Is it possible he should know what he
    is, and be that he is?
45 PAROLES   I would the cutting of my garments would
    serve the turn, or the breaking of my Spanish sword.
LORD G. [*aside*]   We cannot afford you so.
PAROLES   Or the baring of my beard, and to say it was in
    stratagem.
50 LORD G. [*aside*]   'Twould not do.
PAROLES   Or to drown my clothes, and say I was
    stripped.

LORD G. [*aside*]   Hardly serve.

PAROLES   Though I swore I leaped from the window of
55   the citadel –

LORD G. [*aside*]   How deep?

PAROLES   Thirty fathom.

LORD G. [*aside*]   Three great oaths would scarce make
that be believed.

60   PAROLES   I would I had any drum of the enemy's. I
would swear I recovered it.

LORD G. [*aside*]   You shall hear one anon.

PAROLES   A drum now of the enemy's –

                                        [*Alarum within*]

LORD G.   *Throca movousus, cargo, cargo, cargo.*

65   ALL   *Cargo, cargo, cargo, villianda par corbo, cargo.*

       [*They seize Paroles and blindfold him.*]

PAROLES   O, ransom, ransom! Do not hide mine eyes.

1 SOLDIER   *Boskos thromuldo boskos.*

PAROLES   I know you are the Muskos' regiment,
And I shall lose my life for want of language.

70   If there be here German or Dane, Low Dutch,
Italian or French, let him speak to me:
I'll discover that which shall undo the Florentine.

1 SOLDIER   *Boskos vauvado.* I understand thee and can
speak thy tongue. *Kerelybonto*, sir, betake thee to thy
75   faith, for seventeen poniards are at thy bosom.

PAROLES   O!

1 SOLDIER   O, pray, pray, pray! *Manka revania dulche.*

LORD E.   *Oscorbidulchos volivorco.*

1 SOLDIER   The general is content to spare thee yet,
80   And hoodwinked as thou art, will lead thee on
To gather from thee. Haply thou mayst inform
Something to save thy life.

PAROLES   O, let me live,
And all the secrets of our camp I'll show,
Their force, their purposes. Nay, I'll speak that
Which you will wonder at.

85   1 SOLDIER   But wilt thou faithfully?

PAROLES   If I do not, damn me.

1 SOLDIER   *Acordo linta.* Come on, thou art granted
space.   *Exit with Paroles guarded.*

                                        [*A short alarum within*]

LORD G.   Go tell the Count Roussillon and my brother,
We have caught the woodcock, and will keep him
90   muffled
Till we do hear from them.

2 SOLDIER   Captain, I will.

LORD G.   'A will betray us all unto ourselves:
Inform on that.

2 SOLDIER   So I will, sir.

LORD G.   Till then I'll keep him dark and safely locked.

                                        Exeunt.

4.2   *Enter* BERTRAM *and the maid called* DIANA.

BERTRAM
They told me that your name was Fontybell.

DIANA   No, my good lord, Diana.

BERTRAM   Titled goddess,
And worth it, with addition. But, fair soul,
In your fine frame hath love no quality?
If the quick fire of youth light not your mind,   5
You are no maiden but a monument.
When you are dead, you should be such a one
As you are now, for you are cold and stern,
And now you should be as your mother was
When your sweet self was got.   10

DIANA   She then was honest.

BERTRAM   So should you be.

DIANA   No.
My mother did but duty, such, my lord,
As you owe to your wife.

BERTRAM   No more o'that!
I prithee do not strive against my vows.
I was compelled to her, but I love thee   15
By love's own sweet constraint, and will for ever
Do thee all rights of service.

DIANA   Ay, so you serve us
Till we serve you. But when you have our roses,
You barely leave our thorns to prick ourselves
And mock us with our bareness.

BERTRAM   How have I sworn!   20

DIANA   'Tis not the many oaths that makes the truth,
But the plain single vow that is vowed true.
What is not holy, that we swear not by,
But take the high'st to witness. Then pray you tell me,
If I should swear by Jove's great attributes   25
I loved you dearly, would you believe my oaths
When I did love you ill? This has no holding,
To swear by him whom I protest to love
That I will work against him. Therefore your oaths
Are words and poor conditions, but unsealed,   30
At least in my opinion.

BERTRAM   Change it, change it!
Be not so holy-cruel. Love is holy,
And my integrity ne'er knew the crafts
That you do charge men with. Stand no more off,
But give thyself unto my sick desires,   35
Who then recovers. Say thou art mine, and ever
My love as it begins shall so persever.

DIANA   I see that men may rope 's in such a snare
That we'll forsake ourselves. Give me that ring.

BERTRAM   I'll lend it thee, my dear, but have no power   40
To give it from me.

DIANA   Will you not, my lord?

BERTRAM   It is an honour 'longing to our house,
Bequeathed down from many ancestors,
Which were the greatest obloquy i'th' world
In me to lose.

DIANA   Mine honour's such a ring.   45
My chastity's the jewel of our house,
Bequeathed down from many ancestors,
Which were the greatest obloquy i'th' world
In me to lose. Thus your own proper wisdom
Brings in the champion honour on my part   50

Against your vain assault.
BERTRAM   Here, take my ring.
My house, mine honour, yea, my life be thine,
And I'll be bid by thee.
DIANA
When midnight comes, knock at my chamber
          window;
55   I'll order take my mother shall not hear.
Now will I charge you in the band of truth,
When you have conquered my yet maiden bed,
Remain there but an hour, nor speak to me.
My reasons are most strong, and you shall know
          them
60   When back again this ring shall be delivered.
And on your finger in the night I'll put
Another ring, that what in time proceeds
May token to the future our past deeds.
Adieu till then; then fail not. You have won
65   A wife of me, though there my hope be done.
BERTRAM
A heaven on earth I have won by wooing thee.   *Exit.*
DIANA
For which live long to thank both heaven and me!
You may so in the end.
My mother told me just how he would woo,
70   As if she sat in's heart. She says all men
Have the like oaths. He had sworn to marry me
When his wife's dead; therefore I'll lie with him
When I am buried. Since Frenchmen are so braid,
Marry that will, I live and die a maid.
75   Only in this disguise I think't no sin
To cozen him that would unjustly win.   *Exit.*

4.3   *Enter the two French* LORDS G. *and* E.
          and some two or three Soldiers.

LORD G.   You have not given him his mother's letter?
LORD E.   I have delivered it an hour since. There is
   something in't that stings his nature, for on the reading
   it he changed almost into another man.
5   LORD G.   He has much worthy blame laid upon him for
   shaking off so good a wife and so sweet a lady.
LORD E.   Especially, he hath incurred the everlasting
   displeasure of the King, who had even tuned his
   bounty to sing happiness to him. I will tell you a thing,
10   but you shall let it dwell darkly with you.
LORD G.   When you have spoken it, 'tis dead, and I am
   the grave of it.
LORD E.   He hath perverted a young gentlewoman here
   in Florence of a most chaste renown, and this night he
15   fleshes his will in the spoil of her honour. He hath
   given her his monumental ring, and thinks himself
   made in the unchaste composition.
LORD G.   Now, God delay our rebellion! As we are
   ourselves, what things are we!
20   LORD E.   Merely our own traitors. And as in the
   common course of all treasons, we still see them reveal

themselves till they attain to their abhorred ends, so he
that in this action contrives against his own nobility, in
his proper stream o'erflows himself.
25   LORD G.   Is it not meant damnable in us to be
   trumpeters of our unlawful intents? We shall not then
   have his company tonight?
LORD E.   Not till after midnight, for he is dieted to his
   hour.
30   LORD G.   That approaches apace. I would gladly have
   him see his company anatomized that he might take a
   measure of his own judgements, wherein so curiously
   he had set this counterfeit.
LORD E.   We will not meddle with him till he come, for
35   his presence must be the whip of the other.
LORD G.   In the meantime, what hear you of these wars?
LORD E.   I hear there is an overture of peace.
LORD G.   Nay, I assure you, a peace concluded.
LORD E.   What will Count Roussillon do then? Will he
40   travel higher, or return again into France?
LORD G.   I perceive by this demand you are not
   altogether of his counsel.
LORD E.   Let it be forbid, sir. So should I be a great deal
   of his act.
45   LORD G.   Sir, his wife some two months since fled from
   his house. Her pretence is a pilgrimage to Saint
   Jacques le Grand, which holy undertaking with most
   austere sanctimony she accomplished. And there
   residing, the tenderness of her nature became as a prey
50   to her grief; in fine, made a groan of her last breath,
   and now she sings in heaven.
LORD E.   How is this justified?
LORD G.   The stronger part of it by her own letters,
   which makes her story true even to the point of her
55   death. Her death itself, which could not be her office to
   say is come, was faithfully confirmed by the rector of
   the place.
LORD E.   Hath the count all this intelligence?
LORD G.   Ay, and the particular confirmations, point
60   from point, to the full arming of the verity.
LORD E.   I am heartily sorry that he'll be glad of this.
LORD G.   How mightily sometimes we make us comforts
   of our losses!
LORD E.   And how mightily some other times we drown
65   our gain in tears! The great dignity that his valour hath
   here acquired for him shall at home be encountered
   with a shame as ample.
LORD G.   The web of our life is of a mingled yarn, good
   and ill together. Our virtues would be proud, if our
70   faults whipped them not; and our crimes would
   despair, if they were not cherished by our virtues.

Enter a Servant.

How now? Where's your master?
SERVANT   He met the Duke in the street, sir, of whom
   he hath taken a solemn leave. His lordship will next
75   morning for France. The Duke hath offered him letters
   of commendations to the King.

LORD E.   They shall be no more than needful there, if they were more than they can commend.

Enter BERTRAM.

80 LORD G.   They cannot be too sweet for the King's tartness. Here's his lordship now. How now, my lord, is't not after midnight?

BERTRAM   I have tonight dispatched sixteen businesses, a month's length apiece. By an abstract of success: I have congeed with the Duke, done my adieu with his nearest,
85 buried a wife, mourned for her, writ to my lady mother I am returning, entertained my convoy, and between these main parcels of dispatch effected many nicer needs. The last was the greatest, but that I have not ended yet.

LORD E.   If the business be of any difficulty, and this
90 morning your departure hence, it requires haste of your lordship.

BERTRAM   I mean the business is not ended, as fearing to hear of it hereafter. But shall we have this dialogue between the fool and the soldier? Come, bring forth
95 this counterfeit model, h'as deceived me like a double-meaning prophesier.

LORD E.   Bring him forth.   *Exeunt Soldiers.*
H'as sat i'th' stocks all night, poor gallant knave.

BERTRAM   No matter; his heels have deserved it in
100 usurping his spurs so long. How does he carry himself?

LORD E.   I have told your lordship already: the stocks carry him. But to answer you as you would be understood, he weeps like a wench that had shed her milk. He hath confessed himself to Morgan, whom he
105 supposes to be a friar, from the time of his remembrance to this very instant disaster of his setting i'th' stocks. And what think you he hath confessed?

BERTRAM   Nothing of me, has 'a?

LORD E.   His confession is taken, and it shall be read to
110 his face. If your lordship be in't, as I believe you are, you must have the patience to hear it.

Enter PAROLES *blindfold with*
1 Soldier *as his interpreter.*

BERTRAM   A plague upon him! Muffled! He can say nothing of me.

LORD G.   Hush, hush! Hoodman comes. – [*aloud*]
115 *Portotartarossa.*

1 SOLDIER   He calls for the tortures. What will you say without 'em?

PAROLES   I will confess what I know without constraint. If ye pinch me like a pasty, I can say no more.

120 1 SOLDIER   *Bosko chimurcho.*

LORD G.   *Boblibindo chicurmurco.*

1 SOLDIER   You are a merciful general. – Our general bids you answer to what I shall ask you out of a note.

PAROLES   And truly, as I hope to live.

125 1 SOLDIER [*Reads.*]   *First, demand of him, how many horse the Duke is strong.* What say you to that?

PAROLES   Five or six thousand, but very weak and unserviceable. The troops are all scattered, and the commanders very poor rogues, upon my reputation and credit, and as I hope to live.   130

1 SOLDIER   Shall I set down your answer so?

PAROLES   Do. I'll take the sacrament on't, how and which way you will.

BERTRAM [*aside*]   All's one to him. What a past-saving slave is this!   135

LORD G.   You're deceived, my lord: this is Monsieur Paroles, the gallant militarist – that was his own phrase – that had the whole theoric of war in the knot of his scarf, and the practice in the chape of his dagger.

LORD E.   I will never trust a man again for keeping his   140
sword clean, nor believe he can have everything in him by wearing his apparel neatly.

1 SOLDIER   Well, that's set down.

PAROLES   Five or six thousand horse, I said – I will say true – or thereabouts, set down, for I'll speak truth.   145

LORD G. [*to Bertram*]   He's very near the truth in this.

BERTRAM   But I con him no thanks for't, in the nature he delivers it.

PAROLES   Poor rogues, I pray you, say.

1 SOLDIER   Well, that's set down.   150

PAROLES   I humbly thank you, sir. A truth's a truth: the rogues are marvellous poor.

1 SOLDIER [*Reads.*]   *Demand of him, of what strength they are afoot.* What say you to that?

PAROLES   By my troth, sir, if I were to live this present   155
hour, I will tell true. Let me see: Spurio, a hundred and fifty, Sebastian so many, Corambus so many, Jacques so many; Guiltian, Cosmo, Lodowick and Gratii, two hundred fifty each; mine own company, Chitopher, Vaumond, Bentii, two hundred fifty each. So that the   160
muster file, rotten and sound, upon my life, amounts not to fifteen thousand poll, half of which dare not shake the snow from off their cassocks, lest they shake themselves to pieces.

BERTRAM [*to Lord G.*]   What shall be done to him?   165

LORD G.   Nothing, but let him have thanks. – Demand of him my condition, and what credit I have with the Duke.

1 SOLDIER   Well, that's set down. [*Reads.*] *You shall demand of him whether one Captain Dumaine be i'th'*   170
camp, a Frenchman: what his reputation is with the Duke, what his valour, honesty and expertness in wars; or whether he thinks it were not possible with well-weighing sums of gold, to corrupt him to a revolt. What say you to this? What do you know of it?   175

PAROLES   I beseech you let me answer to the particular of the inter'gatories. Demand them singly.

1 SOLDIER   Do you know this Captain Dumaine?

PAROLES   I know him. 'A was a botcher's 'prentice in Paris, from whence he was whipped for getting the   180
sheriff's fool with child, a dumb innocent that could not say him nay.

BERTRAM [*to Lord G.*]   Nay, by your leave, hold your hands – though I know his brains are forfeit to the next tile that falls.   185

1 SOLDIER Well, is this captain in the Duke of Florence's camp?

PAROLES Upon my knowledge, he is, and lousy.

LORD G. [*to Bertram*] Nay, look not so upon me; we
190   shall hear of your lordship anon.

1 SOLDIER What is his reputation with the Duke?

PAROLES The Duke knows him for no other but a poor officer of mine, and writ to me this other day to turn him out o'th' band. I think I have his letter in my
195   pocket.

1 SOLDIER Marry, we'll search.

PAROLES In good sadness, I do not know. Either it is there or it is upon a file with the Duke's other letters in my tent.

200 1 SOLDIER Here 'tis, here's a paper. Shall I read it to you?

PAROLES I do not know if it be it or no.

BERTRAM [*to Lord G.*] Our interpreter does it well.

LORD G. Excellently.

1 SOLDIER [*Reads.*]
205   *Dian, the count's a fool, and full of gold.*

PAROLES That is not the Duke's letter, sir. That is an advertisement to a proper maid in Florence, one Diana, to take heed of the allurement of one Count Roussillon, a foolish idle boy, but for all that very
210   ruttish. I pray you, sir, put it up again.

1 SOLDIER Nay, I'll read it first, by your favour.

PAROLES My meaning in't, I protest, was very honest in the behalf of the maid. For I knew the young count to be a dangerous and lascivious boy, who is
215   a whale to virginity, and devours up all the fry it finds.

BERTRAM [*aside*] Damnable both-sides rogue!

1 SOLDIER [*Reads the letter.*]
    When he swears oaths, bid him drop gold, and take it.
      After he scores, he never pays the score.
220   *Half-won is match well made; match, and well make it.*
      He ne'er pays after-debts; take it before.
    And say a soldier, Dian, told thee this:
    Men are to mell with, boys are not to kiss.
    For count of this, the count's a fool, I know it,
225   *Who pays before, but not when he does owe it.*
      Thine, as he vowed to thee in thine ear,
                          Paroles.

BERTRAM He shall be whipped through the army with this rhyme in's forehead.

230 LORD E. This is your devoted friend, sir, the manifold linguist and the armipotent soldier.

BERTRAM I could endure anything before but a cat, and now he's a cat to me.

1 SOLDIER [*to Paroles*] I perceive, sir, by the general's
235   looks we shall be fain to hang you.

PAROLES My life, sir, in any case! Not that I am afraid to die, but that, my offences being many, I would repent out the remainder of nature. Let me live, sir, in a dungeon, i'th' stocks or anywhere, so I may live.

240 1 SOLDIER We'll see what may be done, so you confess

freely. Therefore once more to this Captain Dumaine: you have answered to his reputation with the Duke, and to his valour. What is his honesty?

PAROLES He will steal, sir, an egg out of a cloister. For
245   rapes and ravishments he parallels Nessus. He professes not keeping of oaths; in breaking 'em he is stronger than Hercules. He will lie, sir, with such volubility that you would think truth were a fool. Drunkenness is his best virtue, for he will be swine-drunk, and in his sleep
250   he does little harm, save to his bed-clothes about him; but they know his conditions and lay him in straw. I have but little more to say, sir, of his honesty. He has everything that an honest man should not have; what an honest man should have, he has nothing.

255 LORD G. [*to Bertram*] I begin to love him for this.

BERTRAM For this description of thine honesty? A pox upon him. For me, he's more and more a cat.

1 SOLDIER What say you to his expertness in war?

PAROLES Faith, sir, h'as led the drum before the English
260   tragedians. To belie him I will not, and more of his soldiership I know not, except in that country he had the honour to be the officer at a place there called Mile End, to instruct for the doubling of files. I would do the man what honour I can, but of this I am not certain.

265 LORD G. [*to Bertram*] He hath out-villained villainy so far that the rarity redeems him.

BERTRAM A pox on him; he's a cat still.

1 SOLDIER His qualities being at this poor price, I need not to ask you if gold will corrupt him to revolt.

270 PAROLES Sir, for a *quart d'écu* he will sell the fee-simple of his salvation, the inheritance of it, and cut th'entail from all remainders, and a perpetual succession for it perpetually.

1 SOLDIER What's his brother, the other Captain
    Dumaine?   275

LORD E. Why does he ask him of me?

1 SOLDIER What's he?

PAROLES E'en a crow o'th' same nest: not altogether so great as the first in goodness, but greater a great deal in evil. He excels his brother for a coward, yet his brother   280
    is reputed one of the best that is. In a retreat he outruns any lackey; marry, in coming on he has the cramp.

1 SOLDIER If your life be saved, will you undertake to betray the Florentine?

PAROLES Ay, and the captain of his horse, Count   285
    Roussillon.

1 SOLDIER I'll whisper with the general and know his pleasure.

PAROLES I'll no more drumming; a plague of all drums! Only to seem to deserve well, and to beguile the   290
    supposition of that lascivious young boy the count, have I run into this danger. Yet who would have suspected an ambush where I was taken?

1 SOLDIER There is no remedy, sir, but you must die. The general says you that have so traitorously   295
    discovered the secrets of your army, and made such pestiferous reports of men very nobly held, can serve

the world for no honest use. Therefore you must die.
Come, headsman, off with his head.

300 PAROLES O Lord, sir, let me live, or let me see my death!

LORD G. That shall you, and take your leave of all your
friends. [*Removes the blindfold.*] So, look about you.
Know you any here?

BERTRAM Good morrow, noble captain.

305 LORD E. God bless you, Captain Paroles.

LORD G. God save you, noble captain.

LORD E. Captain, what greeting will you to my Lord
Lafeu? I am for France.

LORD G. Good captain, will you give me a copy of the
310 sonnet you writ to Diana in behalf of the Count
Roussillon? An I were not a very coward, I'd compel it
of you, but fare you well.

Exeunt Bertram and Lords G. and E.

1 SOLDIER You are undone, captain – all but your scarf,
that has a knot on't yet.

315 PAROLES Who cannot be crushed with a plot?

1 SOLDIER If you could find out a country where but
women were that had received so much shame, you
might begin an impudent nation. Fare ye well, sir, I am
for France too. We shall speak of you there.

Exit with Soldiers.

320 PAROLES Yet am I thankful. If my heart were great,
'Twould burst at this. Captain I'll be no more,
But I will eat and drink and sleep as soft
As captain shall. Simply the thing I am
Shall make me live. Who knows himself a braggart,
325 Let him fear this; for it will come to pass
That every braggart shall be found an ass.
Rust sword, cool blushes, and Paroles live
Safest in shame. Being fooled, by fool'ry thrive.
There's place and means for every man alive.
330 I'll after them. *Exit.*

4.4 *Enter* HELEN, *the* WIDOW *and* DIANA.

HELEN
That you may well perceive I have not wronged you,
One of the greatest in the Christian world
Shall be my surety, 'fore whose throne 'tis needful,
Ere I can perfect mine intents, to kneel.
5 Time was, I did him a desired office,
Dear almost as his life, which gratitude
Through flinty Tartar's bosom would peep forth
And answer thanks. I duly am informed,
His grace is at Marseilles, to which place
10 We have convenient convoy. You must know
I am supposed dead. The army breaking,
My husband hies him home, where, heaven aiding,
And by the leave of my good lord the King,
We'll be before our welcome.

WIDOW   Gentle madam,
15 You never had a servant to whose trust
Your business was more welcome.

HELEN   Nor you, mistress,

Ever a friend whose thoughts more truly labour
To recompense your love. Doubt not but heaven
Hath brought me up to be your daughter's dower,
20 As it hath fated her to be my motive
And helper to a husband. But O, strange men,
That can such sweet use make of what they hate,
When saucy trusting of the cozened thoughts
Defiles the pitchy night! So lust doth play
25 With what it loathes for that which is away –
But more of this hereafter. You, Diana,
Under my poor instructions yet must suffer
Something in my behalf.

DIANA   Let death and honesty
Go with your impositions, I am yours
Upon your will to suffer.

HELEN   Yet, I pray you:
30 But with the word the time will bring on summer,
When briars shall have leaves as well as thorns,
And be as sweet as sharp. We must away.
Our wagon is prepared, and time revives us.
All's well that ends well; still the fine's the crown.
35 Whate'er the course, the end is the renown. *Exeunt.*

4.5 *Enter* LAVATCH, COUNTESS *and* LAFEU.

LAFEU No, no, no, your son was misled with a snipped-
taffeta fellow there, whose villainous saffron would
have made all the unbaked and doughy youth of a
nation in his colour. Your daughter-in-law had been
5 alive at this hour, and your son here at home, more
advanced by the King than by that red-tailed humble-
bee I speak of.

COUNTESS I would I had not known him. It was the
death of the most virtuous gentlewoman that ever
10 nature had praise for creating. If she had partaken of
my flesh, and cost me the dearest groans of a mother, I
could not have owed her a more rooted love.

LAFEU 'Twas a good lady, 'twas a good lady. We may pick
a thousand salads ere we light on such another herb.

15 LAVATCH Indeed, sir, she was the sweet marjoram of
the salad, or rather the herb of grace.

LAFEU They are not herbs, you knave, they are
nose-herbs.

LAVATCH I am no great Nebuchadnezzar, sir; I have not
20 much skill in grass.

LAFEU Whether dost thou profess thyself, a knave or a
fool?

LAVATCH A fool, sir, at a woman's service, and a knave
at a man's.

25 LAFEU Your distinction?

LAVATCH I would cozen the man of his wife and do his
service.

LAFEU So you were a knave at his service, indeed.

LAVATCH And I would give his wife my bauble, sir, to
30 do her service.

LAFEU I will subscribe for thee, thou art both knave and
fool.

LAVATCH At your service.

LAFEU No, no, no.

35 LAVATCH Why, sir, if I cannot serve you, I can serve as great a prince as you are.

LAFEU Who's that? A Frenchman?

LAVATCH Faith, sir, 'a has an English name, but his phys'nomy is more hotter in France than there.

40 LAFEU What prince is that?

LAVATCH The black prince, sir, alias the prince of darkness, alias the devil.

LAFEU Hold thee, there's my purse. I give thee not this to suggest thee from thy master thou talk'st of. Serve

45 him still.

LAVATCH I am a woodland fellow, sir, that always loved a great fire, and the master I speak of ever keeps a good fire. But sure he is the prince of the world; let his nobility remain in's court. I am for the house with the

50 narrow gate, which I take to be too little for pomp to enter. Some that humble themselves may, but the many will be too chill and tender, and they'll be for the flowery way that leads to the broad gate and the great fire.

55 LAFEU Go thy ways. I begin to be aweary of thee, and I tell thee so before, because I would not fall out with thee. Go thy ways. Let my horses be well looked to, without any tricks.

LAVATCH If I put any tricks upon 'em, sir, they shall be

60 jades' tricks, which are their own right by the law of nature. *Exit.*

LAFEU A shrewd knave and an unhappy.

COUNTESS So 'a is. My lord that's gone made himself much sport out of him. By his authority he remains

65 here, which he thinks is a patent for his sauciness, and indeed he has no pace but runs where he will.

LAFEU I like him well, 'tis not amiss. And I was about to tell you, since I heard of the good lady's death and that my lord your son was upon his return home, I moved the

70 King my master to speak in the behalf of my daughter, which in the minority of them both, his majesty, out of a self-gracious remembrance, did first propose. His highness hath promised me to do it; and to stop up the displeasure he hath conceived against your son, there is

75 no fitter matter. How does your ladyship like it?

COUNTESS With very much content, my lord, and I wish it happily effected.

LAFEU His highness comes post from Marseilles, of as able body as when he numbered thirty. 'A will be here

80 tomorrow, or I am deceived by him that in such intelligence hath seldom failed.

COUNTESS It rejoices me that I hope I shall see him ere I die. I have letters that my son will be here tonight. I shall beseech your lordship to remain with me till they

85 meet together.

LAFEU Madam, I was thinking with what manners I might safely be admitted.

COUNTESS You need but plead your honourable privilege.

LAFEU Lady, of that I have made a bold charter; but, I 90
thank my God, it holds yet.

Enter LAVATCH.

LAVATCH O madam, yonder's my lord your son with a patch of velvet on's face. Whether there be a scar under't or no, the velvet knows, but 'tis a goodly patch of velvet. His left cheek is a cheek of two pile and a 95
half, but his right cheek is worn bare.

LAFEU A scar nobly got, or a noble scar, is a good livery of honour. So belike is that.

LAVATCH But it is your carbonadoed face.

LAFEU Let us go see your son, I pray you. I long to talk 100
with the young noble soldier.

LAVATCH Faith, there's a dozen of 'em with delicate fine hats, and most courteous feathers which bow the head and nod at every man. *Exeunt.*

5.1 *Enter* HELEN, *the* WIDOW *and* DIANA,
with two Attendants.

HELEN But this exceeding posting day and night
Must wear your spirits low. We cannot help it.
But since you have made the days and nights as one
To wear your gentle limbs in my affairs,
Be bold you do so grow in my requital 5
As nothing can unroot you.

Enter a gentle AUSTRINGER.

In happy time!
This man may help me to his majesty's ear,
If he would spend his power. – God save you, sir.

AUSTRINGER And you.

HELEN Sir, I have seen you in the court of France. 10

AUSTRINGER I have been sometimes there.

HELEN I do presume, sir, that you are not fallen
From the report that goes upon your goodness,
And therefore, goaded with most sharp occasions
Which lay nice manners by, I put you to 15
The use of your own virtues, for the which
I shall continue thankful.

AUSTRINGER What's your will?

HELEN That it will please you
To give this poor petition to the King,
And aid me with that store of power you have 20
To come into his presence.

AUSTRINGER The King's not here.

HELEN Not here, sir?

AUSTRINGER Not, indeed.
He hence removed last night, and with more haste
Than is his use.

WIDOW Lord, how we lose our pains!

HELEN All's well that ends well yet, 25
Though time seem so adverse and means unfit.
I do beseech you, whither is he gone?

AUSTRINGER Marry, as I take it, to Roussillon,
Whither I am going.

HELEN   I do beseech you, sir,
Since you are like to see the King before me,
Commend the paper to his gracious hand,
Which I presume shall render you no blame
But rather make you thank your pains for it.
I will come after you with what good speed
Our means will make us means.
AUSTRINGER   This I'll do for you.
HELEN
And you shall find yourself to be well thanked,
Whate'er falls more. [*to Attendants*] We must to horse
    again.
Go, go, provide.   *Exeunt.*

5.2   *Enter* LAVATCH *and* PAROLES.

PAROLES   Good Monsieur Lavatch, give my Lord
    Lafeu this letter. I have ere now, sir, been better known
    to you, when I have held familiarity with fresher
    clothes. But I am now, sir, muddied in Fortune's mood,
    and smell somewhat strong of her strong displeasure.
LAVATCH   Truly, Fortune's displeasure is but sluttish if
    it smell so strongly as thou speak'st of. I will henceforth
    eat no fish of Fortune's buttering. Prithee allow the
    wind.
PAROLES   Nay, you need not to stop your nose, sir; I
    spake but by a metaphor.
LAVATCH   Indeed, sir, if your metaphor stink, I will stop
    my nose, or against any man's metaphor. Prithee get
    thee further.
PAROLES   Pray you, sir, deliver me this paper.
LAVATCH   Foh! Prithee stand away. A paper from
    Fortune's close-stool, to give to a nobleman! Look,
    here he comes himself.

Enter LAFEU.

Here is a purr of Fortune's, sir, or of Fortune's cat –
    but not a musk cat – that has fallen into the unclean
    fishpond of her displeasure and, as he says, is muddied
    withal. Pray you, sir, use the carp as you may, for he
    looks like a poor, decayed, ingenious, foolish, rascally
    knave. I do pity his distress in my similes of comfort,
    and leave him to your lordship.   *Exit.*
PAROLES   My lord, I am a man whom Fortune hath
    cruelly scratched.
LAFEU   And what would you have me to do? 'Tis too late
    to pare her nails now. Wherein have you played the knave
    with Fortune that she should scratch you, who of herself
    is a good lady, and would not have knaves thrive
    long under her? There's a *quart d'écu* for you. Let the
    justices make you and Fortune friends; I am for other
    business.
PAROLES   I beseech your honour to hear me one single
    word.
LAFEU   You beg a single penny more. Come, you shall
    ha't. Save your word.
PAROLES   My name, my good lord, is Paroles.

LAFEU   You beg more than one word then. Cock's my
    passion! Give me your hand. How does your drum?
PAROLES   O my good lord, you were the first that found
    me.
LAFEU   Was I, in sooth? And I was the first that lost thee.
PAROLES   It lies in you, my lord, to bring me in some
    grace, for you did bring me out.
LAFEU   Out upon thee, knave! Dost thou put upon me
    at once both the office of God and the devil? One
    brings thee in grace, and the other brings thee out.
                                [*Trumpets sound.*]
The King's coming; I know by his trumpets. Sirrah,
    enquire further after me. I had talk of you last night;
    though you are a fool and a knave, you shall eat. Go to,
    follow.
PAROLES   I praise God for you.   *Exeunt.*

5.3   *Flourish. Enter* KING, COUNTESS, LAFEU, *the
          two French* LORDS G. *and* E., *with* Attendants.

KING   We lost a jewel of her, and our esteem
Was made much poorer by it. But your son,
As mad in folly, lacked the sense to know
Her estimation home.
COUNTESS   'Tis past, my liege,
And I beseech your majesty to make it
Natural rebellion done i'th' blade of youth,
When oil and fire, too strong for reason's force,
O'erbears it, and burns on.
KING   My honoured lady,
I have forgiven and forgotten all,
Though my revenges were high bent upon him,
And watched the time to shoot.
LAFEU   This I must say –
But first I beg my pardon – the young lord
Did to his majesty, his mother and his lady
Offence of mighty note; but to himself
The greatest wrong of all. He lost a wife
Whose beauty did astonish the survey
Of richest eyes, whose words all ears took captive,
Whose dear perfection hearts that scorned to serve
Humbly called mistress.
KING   Praising what is lost
Makes the remembrance dear. Well, call him hither.
We are reconciled, and the first view shall kill
All repetition. Let him not ask our pardon.
The nature of his great offence is dead,
And deeper than oblivion we do bury
Th'incensing relics of it. Let him approach
A stranger, no offender; and inform him
So 'tis our will he should.
ATTENDANT   I shall, my liege.   *Exit.*
KING
What says he to your daughter? Have you spoke?
LAFEU   All that he is hath reference to your highness.
KING
Then shall we have a match. I have letters sent me

That sets him high in fame.

Enter BERTRAM.

LAFEU   He looks well on't.

KING   I am not a day of season,
        For thou mayst see a sunshine and a hail
        In me at once. But to the brightest beams
35   Distracted clouds give way. So stand thou forth;
        The time is fair again. So stand thou forth;

BERTRAM   My high-repented blames,
        Dear sovereign, pardon to me.

KING   All is whole.
        Not one word more of the consumed time.
        Let's take the instant by the forward top;
40   For we are old, and on our quick'st decrees
        Th'inaudible and noiseless foot of time
        Steals ere we can effect them. You remember
        The daughter of this lord?

BERTRAM   Admiringly, my liege. At first
45   I stuck my choice upon her, ere my heart
        Durst make too bold a herald of my tongue;
        Where the impression of mine eye infixing,
        Contempt his scornful perspective did lend me,
        Which warped the line of every other favour,
50   Scorned a fair colour or expressed it stolen,
        Extended or contracted all proportions
        To a most hideous object. Thence it came
        That she whom all men praised, and whom myself,
        Since I have lost, have loved, was in mine eye
        The dust that did offend it.

55 KING   Well excused.
        That thou didst love her strikes some scores away
        From the great count. But love that comes too late,
        Like a remorseful pardon slowly carried,
        To the great sender turns a sour offence,
60   Crying, 'That's good that's gone.' Our rash faults
        Make trivial price of serious things we have,
        Not knowing them until we know their grave.
        Oft our displeasures, to ourselves unjust,
        Destroy our friends and after weep their dust.
65   Our own love, waking, cries to see what's done,
        While shameful hate sleeps out the afternoon.
        Be this sweet Helen's knell, and now forget her.
        Send forth your amorous token for fair Maudlin.
        The main consents are had, and here we'll stay
70   To see our widower's second marriage day.

COUNTESS
        Which better than the first, O dear heaven, bless!
        Or, ere they meet, in me, O nature, cease!

LAFEU   Come on, my son, in whom my house's name
        Must be digested; give a favour from you
75   To sparkle in the spirits of my daughter,
        That she may quickly come. [*Bertram gives a ring.*]
                                    By my old beard,
        And ev'ry hair that's on't, Helen that's dead
        Was a sweet creature. Such a ring as this,
        The last that e'er I took her leave at court,

I saw upon her finger.

BERTRAM   Hers it was not.   80

KING   Now pray you let me see it, for mine eye,
        While I was speaking, oft was fastened to't.
        This ring was mine, and when I gave it Helen,
        I bade her if her fortunes ever stood
        Necessitied to help, that by this token   85
        I would relieve her. Had you that craft to reave her
        Of what should stead her most?

BERTRAM   My gracious sovereign,
        Howe'er it pleases you to take it so,
        The ring was never hers.

COUNTESS   Son, on my life,
        I have seen her wear it, and she reckoned it   90
        At her life's rate.

LAFEU   I am sure I saw her wear it.

BERTRAM   You are deceived, my lord, she never saw it.
        In Florence was it from a casement thrown me,
        Wrapped in a paper, which contained the name
        Of her that threw it. Noble she was, and thought   95
        I stood engaged; but when I had subscribed
        To mine own fortune, and informed her fully
        I could not answer in that course of honour
        As she had made the overture, she ceased
        In heavy satisfaction, and would never   100
        Receive the ring again.

KING   Plutus himself,
        That knows the tinct and multiplying medicine,
        Hath not in nature's mystery more science
        Than I have in this ring. 'Twas mine, 'twas Helen's,
        Whoever gave it you. Then if you know   105
        That you are well acquainted with yourself,
        Confess 'twas hers, and by what rough enforcement
        You got it from her. She called the saints to surety
        That she would never put it from her finger
        Unless she gave it to yourself in bed,   110
        Where you have never come, or sent it us
        Upon her great disaster.

BERTRAM   She never saw it.

KING   Thou speak'st it falsely, as I love mine honour,
        And mak'st conjectural fears to come into me
        Which I would fain shut out. If it should prove   115
        That thou art so inhuman – 'twill not prove so.
        And yet I know not. Thou didst hate her deadly,
        And she is dead, which nothing but to close
        Her eyes myself could win me to believe
        More than to see this ring. Take him away.   120
        My fore-past proofs, howe'er the matter fall,
        Shall tax my fears of little vanity,
        Having vainly feared too little. Away with him.
        We'll sift this matter further.

BERTRAM   If you shall prove
        This ring was ever hers, you shall as easy   125
        Prove that I husbanded her bed in Florence,
        Where yet she never was.   *Exit guarded.*

Enter AUSTRINGER.

KING I am wrapped in dismal thinkings.

AUSTRINGER   Gracious sovereign,
  Whether I have been to blame or no, I know not.
130 Here's a petition from a Florentine
  Who hath for four or five removes come short
  To tender it herself. I undertook it,
  Vanquished thereto by the fair grace and speech
  Of the poor suppliant, who by this I know
135 Is here attending. Her business looks in her
  With an importing visage, and she told me,
  In a sweet verbal brief, it did concern
  Your highness with herself.

KING [*Reads a letter.*] *Upon his many protestations to*
140 *marry me when his wife was dead, I blush to say it, he won*
  me. Now is the Count Roussillon a widower, his vows are
  forfeited to me and my honour's paid to him. He stole from
  Florence, taking no leave, and I follow him to his country
  for justice. Grant it me, O King! In you it best lies.
145 *Otherwise a seducer flourishes, and a poor maid is undone.*
                                    Diana Capilet

LAFEU I will buy me a son-in-law in a fair, and toll for
  this. I'll none of him.

KING The heavens have thought well on thee, Lafeu,
150 To bring forth this discovery. Seek these suitors.
  Go speedily, and bring again the count.
                    Exeunt Austringer and other Attendants.
  I am afeard the life of Helen, lady,
  Was foully snatched.

COUNTESS   Now, justice on the doers!

Enter BERTRAM *guarded.*

KING I wonder, sir, sith wives are monsters to you
155 And that you fly them as you swear them lordship,
  Yet you desire to marry.

Enter the WIDOW *and* DIANA.

                              What woman's that?

DIANA I am, my lord, a wretched Florentine,
  Derived from the ancient Capilet.
  My suit, as I do understand, you know,
160 And therefore know how far I may be pitied.

WIDOW I am her mother, sir, whose age and honour
  Both suffer under this complaint we bring,
  And both shall cease without your remedy.

KING Come hither, Count. Do you know these women?

165 BERTRAM My lord, I neither can nor will deny
  But that I know them. Do they charge me further?

DIANA Why do you look so strange upon your wife?

BERTRAM She's none of mine, my lord.

DIANA   If you shall marry,
  You give away this hand, and that is mine;
170 You give away heaven's vows, and those are mine;
  You give away myself, which is known mine;
  For I by vow am so embodied yours
  That she which marries you must marry me,
  Either both or none.

LAFEU [*to Bertram*] Your reputation comes too short for   175
  my daughter; you are no husband for her.

BERTRAM [*to the King*]
  My lord, this is a fond and desperate creature,
  Whom sometime I have laughed with. Let your highness
  Lay a more noble thought upon mine honour
  Than for to think that I would sink it here.   180

KING
  Sir, for my thoughts, you have them ill to friend
  Till your deeds gain them. Fairer prove your honour
  Than in my thought it lies.

DIANA   Good my lord,
  Ask him upon his oath, if he does think
  He had not my virginity.   185

KING What sayst thou to her?

BERTRAM   She's impudent, my lord,
  And was a common gamester to the camp.

DIANA He does me wrong, my lord. If I were so,
  He might have bought me at a common price.
  Do not believe him. O, behold this ring,   190
  Whose high respect and rich validity
  Did lack a parallel. Yet for all that
  He gave it to a commoner o'th' camp,
  If I be one.

COUNTESS   He blushes, and 'tis hit.
  Of six preceding ancestors, that gem,   195
  Conferred by testament to th' sequent issue,
  Hath it been owed and worn. This is his wife:
  That ring's a thousand proofs.

KING   Methought you said
  You saw one here in court could witness it.

DIANA I did, my lord, but loath am to produce   200
  So bad an instrument. His name's Paroles.

LAFEU I saw the man today, if man he be.

KING
  Find him, and bring him hither.   *Exit Attendant.*

BERTRAM   What of him?
  He's quoted for a most perfidious slave,
  With all the spots o'th' world taxed and debauched,   205
  Whose nature sickens but to speak a truth.
  Am I or that or this for what he'll utter,
  That will speak anything?

KING   She hath that ring of yours.

BERTRAM I think she has. Certain it is I liked her,
  And boarded her i'th' wanton way of youth.   210
  She knew her distance, and did angle for me,
  Madding my eagerness with her restraint,
  As all impediments in fancy's course
  Are motives of more fancy; and in fine,
  Her infinite cunning with her modern grace   215
  Subdued me to her rate. She got the ring,
  And I had that which any inferior might
  At market price have bought.

DIANA   I must be patient.
  You that have turned off a first so noble wife
  May justly diet me. I pray you yet –   220

Since you lack virtue, I will lose a husband –
Send for your ring, I will return it home,
And give me mine again.
BERTRAM   I have it not.
KING   What ring was yours, I pray you?
DIANA   Sir, much like
225   The same upon your finger.
KING   Know you this ring? This ring was his of late.
DIANA   And this was it I gave him, being abed.
KING   The story then goes false, you threw it him
        Out of a casement.
DIANA   I have spoke the truth.

Enter PAROLES.

230   BERTRAM   My lord, I do confess the ring was hers.
        KING   You boggle shrewdly; every feather starts you.
        Is this the man you speak of?
        DIANA   Ay, my lord.
        KING   Tell me, sirrah – but tell me true, I charge you,
        Not fearing the displeasure of your master,
235   Which on your just proceeding I'll keep off –
        By him and by this woman here, what know you?
        PAROLES   So please your majesty, my master hath been
        an honourable gentleman. Tricks he hath had in him,
        which gentlemen have.
240   KING   Come, come, to th' purpose: did he love this woman?
        PAROLES   Faith, sir, he did love her; but how?
        KING   How, I pray you?
        PAROLES   He did love her, sir, as a gentleman loves a
        woman.
245   KING   How is that?
        PAROLES   He loved her, sir, and loved her not.
        KING   As thou art a knave and no knave. What an
        equivocal companion is this!
        PAROLES   I am a poor man, and at your majesty's
250   command.
        LAFEU   He's a good drum, my lord, but a naughty orator.
        DIANA   Do you know he promised me marriage?
        PAROLES   Faith, I know more than I'll speak.
        KING   But wilt thou not speak all thou know'st?
255   PAROLES   Yes, so please your majesty. I did go between
        them as I said; but more than that he loved her, for
        indeed he was mad for her, and talked of Satan and of
        limbo and of furies, and I know not what. Yet I was in
        that credit with them at that time that I knew of their
260   going to bed, and of other motions, as promising her
        marriage, and things which would derive me ill will to
        speak of. Therefore I will not speak what I know.
        KING   Thou hast spoken all already, unless thou canst
        say they are married, but thou art too fine in thy
265   evidence; therefore stand aside.
        This ring, you say, was yours.
        DIANA   Ay, my good lord.
        KING   Where did you buy it? Or who gave it you?
        DIANA   It was not given me, nor I did not buy it.
        KING   Who lent it you?
        DIANA   It was not lent me neither.

KING   Where did you find it, then?
DIANA   I found it not.   270
KING   If it were yours by none of all these ways,
        How could you give it him?
DIANA   I never gave it him.
LAFEU   This woman's an easy glove, my lord; she goes
        off and on at pleasure.
KING   This ring was mine; I gave it his first wife.   275
DIANA   It might be yours or hers for aught I know.
KING   Take her away, I do not like her now.
        To prison with her; and away with him.
        Unless thou tell'st me where thou hadst this ring,
        Thou diest within this hour.
DIANA   I'll never tell you.   280
KING   Take her away.
DIANA   I'll put in bail, my liege.
KING   I think thee now some common customer.
DIANA   By Jove, if ever I knew man, 'twas you.
KING   Wherefore hast thou accused him all this while?
DIANA   Because he's guilty, and he is not guilty.   285
        He knows I am no maid, and he'll swear to't.
        I'll swear I am a maid, and he knows not.
        Great King, I am no strumpet, by my life;
        I am either maid, or else this old man's wife.
KING   She does abuse our ears. To prison with her!   290
DIANA   Good mother, fetch my bail.   *Exit the Widow.*
                                        Stay, royal sir.
        The jeweller that owes the ring is sent for,
        And he shall surety me. But for this lord,
        Who hath abused me as he knows himself,
        Though yet he never harmed me, here I quit him.   295
        He knows himself my bed he hath defiled,
        And at that time he got his wife with child.
        Dead though she be, she feels her young one kick.
        So there's my riddle: one that's dead is quick.
        And now behold the meaning.

Enter HELEN *and the* WIDOW.

KING   Is there no exorcist   300
        Beguiles the truer office of mine eyes?
        Is't real that I see?
HELEN   No, my good lord;
        'Tis but the shadow of a wife you see,
        The name and not the thing.
BERTRAM   Both, both. O, pardon!
HELEN   O my good lord, when I was like this maid,   305
        I found you wondrous kind. There is your ring,
        And look you, here's your letter. This it says:
        When from my finger you can get this ring
        And are by me with child, etc. This is done.
        Will you be mine, now you are doubly won?   310
BERTRAM
        If she, my liege, can make me know this clearly,
        I'll love her dearly, ever, ever dearly.
HELEN   If it appear not plain, and prove untrue,
        Deadly divorce step between me and you.
        O my dear mother, do I see you living?   315

LAFEU   Mine eyes smell onions, I shall weep anon.
     [*to Paroles*] Good Tom Drum, lend me a handkerchief.
     So I thank thee; wait on me home, I'll make sport with
     thee. Let thy curtsies alone, they are scurvy ones.
320 KING   Let us from point to point this story know,
     To make the even truth in pleasure flow.
     [*to Diana*] If thou be'st yet a fresh uncropped flower,
     Choose thou thy husband, and I'll pay thy dower,
     For I can guess that by thy honest aid
325 Thou kept'st a wife herself, thyself a maid.
     Of that and all the progress, more and less,
     Resolvedly more leisure shall express.
     All yet seems well, and if it end so meet,
     The bitter past, more welcome is the sweet.   [*Flourish*]

EPILOGUE

The king's a beggar, now the play is done.
All is well ended, if this suit be won,
That you express content; which we will pay
With strife to please you, day exceeding day.
Ours be your patience, then, and yours our parts;   5
Your gentle hands lend us, and take our hearts.
                                        Exeunt.

Antony and Cleopatra

Antony and Cleopatra was first published in the Folio of 1623, as the tenth of the tragedies. Along with 'The booke of Pericles prynce of Tyre', it had previously been entered by Edward Blount in the Stationers' Register on 20 May 1608. Both Barnabe Barnes's *The Devil's Charter* (performed at Court on 2 February 1607) and Samuel Daniel's 'newly altered' fourth edition of his tragedy *Cleopatra* (published in 1607) show knowledge of Shakespeare's play. It was therefore probably completed sometime in 1606, roughly contemporaneously with the writing of *Macbeth* and shortly before *Coriolanus*.

The story of the tragic love affair was, of course, well known; literary references go back as far as Virgil and Horace, and Chaucer includes Cleopatra in his *Legend of Good Women*. Shakespeare almost certainly knew several Renaissance versions of the story, most notably the Countess of Pembroke's tragedy *Antonius* (1592), adapted from Robert Garnier's *Marc Antoine*, and Samuel Daniel's *Cleopatra*, first published in 1594 and dedicated to the Countess of Pembroke. However, he depended mainly upon 'The Life of Marcus Antonius' in Plutarch's *Lives of the Noble Grecians and Romans*, translated from Greek into French by Jacques Amyot, from French into English by Thomas North, and published in London in 1579. Shakespeare often follows North's Plutarch closely – verbal borrowings are frequent – but he shapes the story to his own purposes, as the action constantly shifts location, ranging quickly back and forth across the Mediterranean.

Rome and Egypt are not merely the geographical poles of the action, but become powerful symbols of competing emotional and ethical values. Rome is a world of measure, Egypt of excess; Rome of pragmatism, Egypt of passion; Rome of political ambition, Egypt of emotional desire. Even stylistically the differences are marked: Roman speech is 'Attic', spare and direct; Egyptian speech is 'Asiatic', ornate and sensuous. However, the competing values are not wholly consistent, nor do they admit of easy judgements. If Roman values, judged on their own terms, appear disciplined and high-minded, by Egyptian standards they seem cold and inhuman; similarly, Egyptian values, judged on Egyptian terms as generous and life-affirming, by Roman standards appear self-indulgent and irresponsible. The play never allows an audience a secure and stable moral vantage-point from which to judge the action or the characters, giving us instead multiple perspectives and inviting constant reassessment of our responses.

Even death partakes at once of tragic loss and of a paradoxical victory and transcendence. Plutarch's Antony seeks his own death in despair, 'sith spiteful fortune hath taken from thee the only joy thou hadst'; Shakespeare's Antony rather seeks death, to be reunited with his queen: 'I will o'ertake thee, Cleopatra, and / Weep for my pardon' (4.14.45–6). Antony would be 'A bridegroom in [his] death' (4.14.101), and Cleopatra dies with a final magnificent claim to Antony, 'Husband, I come!' (5.2.285). For them, at least, love does overcome death. From Cleopatra's viewpoint indeed ''Tis paltry to be Caesar' (5.2.2). But, of course, Caesar survives to become Emperor of the world, and Rome will not 'in Tiber melt' (1.1.34).

The moral contents of the play are projected in a succession of scenes, many of them brief, which exploit to the full the fluid staging practices of early Jacobean theatres. The proscenium stages and the realistic props and scenery which developed after 1660 ensured that Shakespeare's play was superseded for a century or more by John Dryden's neoclassical rewriting of the story as *All for Love, or the World Well Lost* (1678). When *Antony and Cleopatra* returned to the theatres of the nineteenth and early twentieth centuries, productions became ever more opulent and operatic. Spectacle disrupted the play's own dramatic structure, and critics and reviewers regularly decried its apparent lack of unity. Simply set and played with the staccato rhythms marked by the text, the play has achieved notable, though infrequent, success on the modern stage, its principle of construction clear and effective, its moral design complex and compelling.

The Arden text is based on the 1623 First Folio.

Mark ANTONY	
Octavius CAESAR	*triumvirs*
LEPIDUS	
CLEOPATRA	*Queen of Egypt*
Sextus Pompeius *or* POMPEY	*rebel against the triumvirs*
DEMETRIUS	
PHILO	
Domitius ENOBARBUS	
VENTIDIUS	
SILIUS	*followers of Antony*
EROS	
CANIDIUS	
SCARUS	
DERCETUS	
A Schoolmaster, Antony's AMBASSADOR	
OCTAVIA	*sister of Octavius Caesar*
MAECENAS	
AGRIPPA	
TAURUS	
DOLABELLA	*followers of Caesar*
THIDIAS	
GALLUS	
PROCULEIUS	
CHARMIAN	
IRAS	
ALEXAS	*attendants on Cleopatra*
MARDIAN, *a eunuch*	
DIOMEDES	
SELEUCUS	
MENAS	
MENECRATES	*followers of Pompey*
VARRIUS	
MESSENGERS	
SOOTHSAYER	
SERVANTS	*of Pompey*
BOY SINGER	
CAPTAIN	*in Antony's army*
SENTRIES *and* GUARDS	
CLOWN	

Eunuchs, Attendants, Captains, Soldiers, Servants

Antony and Cleopatra

1.1   *Enter* DEMETRIUS *and* PHILO.

PHILO   Nay, but this dotage of our general's
O'erflows the measure. Those his goodly eyes,
That o'er the files and musters of the war
Have glowed like plated Mars, now bend, now turn
5   The office and devotion of their view
Upon a tawny front. His captain's heart,
Which in the scuffles of great fights hath burst
The buckles on his breast, reneges all temper
And is become the bellows and the fan
To cool a gipsy's lust.

> *Flourish. Enter* ANTONY, CLEOPATRA, *her Ladies*
> CHARMIAN *and* IRAS, *the train, with Eunuchs fanning her.*

10   Look where they come!
Take but good note, and you shall see in him
The triple pillar of the world transformed
Into a strumpet's fool. Behold and see.
CLEOPATRA   If it be love indeed, tell me how much.
ANTONY
15   There's beggary in the love that can be reckoned.
CLEOPATRA   I'll set a bourn how far to be beloved.
ANTONY
Then must thou needs find out new heaven, new earth.

> *Enter a* Messenger.

MESSENGER   News, my good lord, from Rome.
ANTONY   Grates me! The sum.
20   CLEOPATRA   Nay, hear them, Antony.
Fulvia perchance is angry, or who knows
If the scarce-bearded Caesar have not sent
His powerful mandate to you: 'Do this, or this;
Take in that kingdom and enfranchise that.
Perform't, or else we damn thee.'
25   ANTONY   How, my love?
CLEOPATRA   Perchance? Nay, and most like.
You must not stay here longer; your dismission
Is come from Caesar; therefore hear it, Antony.
Where's Fulvia's process? – Caesar's, I would say.
Both?
30   Call in the messengers! As I am Egypt's Queen,
Thou blushest, Antony, and that blood of thine
Is Caesar's homager; else so thy cheek pays shame
When shrill-tongued Fulvia scolds. The messengers!
ANTONY   Let Rome in Tiber melt, and the wide arch
35   Of the ranged empire fall! Here is my space!
Kingdoms are clay! Our dungy earth alike
Feeds beast as man. The nobleness of life
Is to do thus, when such a mutual pair
And such a twain can do't, in which I bind,
40   On pain of punishment, the world to weet
We stand up peerless.
CLEOPATRA   Excellent falsehood!
Why did he marry Fulvia and not love her?
I'll seem the fool I am not. Antony
Will be himself.

ANTONY   But stirred by Cleopatra.
Now, for the love of Love and her soft hours,   45
Let's not confound the time with conference harsh.
There's not a minute of our lives should stretch
Without some pleasure now. What sport tonight?
CLEOPATRA   Hear the ambassadors.
ANTONY   Fie, wrangling queen,
Whom everything becomes – to chide, to laugh,   50
To weep; whose every passion fully strives
To make itself, in thee, fair and admired!
No messenger but thine, and all alone
Tonight we'll wander through the streets and note
The qualities of people. Come, my queen!   55
Last night you did desire it. [*to the Messenger*] Speak
not to us.
> *Exeunt Antony and Cleopatra with the train.*
DEMETRIUS   Is Caesar with Antonius prized so slight?
PHILO   Sir, sometimes, when he is not Antony,
He comes too short of that great property
Which still should go with Antony.
DEMETRIUS   I am full sorry   60
That he approves the common liar who
Thus speaks of him at Rome, but I will hope
Of better deeds tomorrow. Rest you happy!   *Exeunt.*

1.2   *Enter* ENOBARBUS *and other Roman Officers,*
a Soothsayer, CHARMIAN, IRAS, MARDIAN *the*
Eunuch and ALEXAS.

CHARMIAN   Lord Alexas, sweet Alexas, most anything
Alexas, almost most absolute Alexas, where's the
soothsayer that you praised so to th' Queen? O, that I
knew this husband which you say must charge his
horns with garlands!   5
ALEXAS   Soothsayer!
SOOTHSAYER   Your will?
CHARMIAN   Is this the man? Is't you, sir, that know
things?
SOOTHSAYER   In nature's infinite book of secrecy   10
A little I can read.
ALEXAS   Show him your hand.
ENOBARBUS
Bring in the banquet quickly; wine enough
Cleopatra's health to drink.

> *Enter Servants with wine and other*
> *refreshments and exeunt.*

CHARMIAN [*Gives her hand to the Soothsayer.*]   Good sir,
give me good fortune.   15
SOOTHSAYER   I make not, but foresee.
CHARMIAN   Pray then, foresee me one.
SOOTHSAYER   You shall be yet far fairer than you are.
CHARMIAN   He means in flesh.
IRAS   No, you shall paint when you are old.   20
CHARMIAN   Wrinkles forbid!
ALEXAS   Vex not his prescience. Be attentive.

CHARMIAN Hush!

SOOTHSAYER You shall be more beloving than beloved.

25 CHARMIAN I had rather heat my liver with drinking.

ALEXAS Nay, hear him.

CHARMIAN Good now, some excellent fortune! Let me be married to three kings in a forenoon and widow them all. Let me have a child at fifty to whom Herod of
30 Jewry may do homage. Find me to marry me with Octavius Caesar and companion me with my mistress.

SOOTHSAYER
You shall outlive the lady whom you serve.

CHARMIAN O, excellent! I love long life better than figs.

SOOTHSAYER
You have seen and proved a fairer former fortune
35 Than that which is to approach.

CHARMIAN Then belike my children shall have no names. Prithee, how many boys and wenches must I have?

SOOTHSAYER If every of your wishes had a womb, And fertile every wish, a million.

40 CHARMIAN Out, fool! I forgive thee for a witch.

ALEXAS You think none but your sheets are privy to your wishes.

CHARMIAN Nay, come, tell Iras hers.

ALEXAS We'll know all our fortunes.

45 ENOBARBUS Mine, and most of our fortunes tonight, shall be drunk to bed.

IRAS [*Holds out her hand.*] There's a palm presages chastity, if nothing else.

CHARMIAN E'en as the o'erflowing Nilus presageth famine.

50 IRAS Go, you wild bedfellow, you cannot soothsay!

CHARMIAN Nay, if an oily palm be not a fruitful prognostication, I cannot scratch mine ear. Prithee, tell her but a workaday fortune.

SOOTHSAYER Your fortunes are alike.

55 IRAS But how? But how? Give me particulars!

SOOTHSAYER I have said.

IRAS Am I not an inch of fortune better than she?

CHARMIAN Well, if you were but an inch of fortune better than I, where would you choose it?

60 IRAS Not in my husband's nose.

CHARMIAN Our worser thoughts heavens mend! Alexas – come, his fortune, his fortune! O, let him marry a woman that cannot go, sweet Isis I beseech thee, and let her die too, and give him a worse, and let worse
65 follow worse, till the worst of all follow him laughing to his grave, fiftyfold a cuckold! Good Isis, hear me this prayer, though thou deny me a matter of more weight; good Isis, I beseech thee!

IRAS Amen. Dear goddess, hear that prayer of the
70 people! For as it is a heartbreaking to see a handsome man loose-wived, so it is a deadly sorrow to behold a foul knave uncuckolded. Therefore, dear Isis, keep decorum and fortune him accordingly!

CHARMIAN Amen.

75 ALEXAS Lo now, if it lay in their hands to make me a cuckold, they would make themselves whores, but they'd do't.

Enter CLEOPATRA.

ENOBARBUS Hush, here comes Antony.

CHARMIAN Not he, the Queen.

CLEOPATRA Saw you my lord? 80

ENOBARBUS No, lady.

CLEOPATRA Was he not here?

CHARMIAN No, madam.

CLEOPATRA
He was disposed to mirth, but on the sudden
A Roman thought hath struck him. Enobarbus! 85

ENOBARBUS Madam?

CLEOPATRA
Seek him and bring him hither.   *Exit Enobarbus.*
                    Where's Alexas?

ALEXAS Here, at your service. My lord approaches.

Enter ANTONY *with a* Messenger.

CLEOPATRA We will not look upon him. Go with us.
                    Exeunt all but Antony and Messenger.

MESSENGER Fulvia thy wife first came into the field. 90

ANTONY Against my brother Lucius?

MESSENGER Ay,
But soon that war had end, and the time's state
Made friends of them, jointing their force 'gainst Caesar,
Whose better issue in the war from Italy 95
Upon the first encounter drave them.

ANTONY Well, what worst?

MESSENGER The nature of bad news infects the teller.

ANTONY When it concerns the fool or coward. On!
Things that are past are done with me. 'Tis thus: 100
Who tells me true, though in his tale lie death,
I hear him as he flattered.

MESSENGER   Labienus –
This is stiff news – hath with his Parthian force
Extended Asia. From Euphrates
His conquering banner shook, from Syria 105
To Lydia, and to Ionia,
Whilst –

ANTONY 'Antony', thou wouldst say –

MESSENGER   O, my lord!

ANTONY
Speak to me home; mince not the general tongue;
Name Cleopatra as she is called in Rome;
Rail thou in Fulvia's phrase, and taunt my faults 110
With such full licence as both truth and malice
Have power to utter. Oh, then we bring forth weeds
When our quick minds lie still, and our ills told us
Is as our earing. Fare thee well awhile.

MESSENGER At your noble pleasure. *Exit Messenger.* 115

Enter another Messenger.

ANTONY From Sicyon how the news? Speak there!

2 MESSENGER The man from Sicyon –

ANTONY   Is there such a one?

2 MESSENGER He stays upon your will.

ANTONY   Let him appear.
                    Exit Second Messenger.

These strong Egyptian fetters I must break,
Or lose myself in dotage.

Enter another Messenger *with a letter.*

120   What are you?
MESSENGER   Fulvia thy wife is dead.
ANTONY   Where died she?
3 MESSENGER   In Sicyon.
Her length of sickness, with what else more serious
Importeth thee to know, this bears.
     [*Gives him the letter.*]
125 ANTONY   Forbear me.
                    Exit Third Messenger.
There's a great spirit gone! Thus did I desire it.
What our contempts doth often hurl from us
We wish it ours again. The present pleasure,
By revolution lowering, does become
130 The opposite of itself. She's good, being gone.
The hand could pluck her back that shoved her on.
I must from this enchanting queen break off.
Ten thousand harms, more than the ills I know,
My idleness doth hatch. How now, Enobarbus!

Enter ENOBARBUS.

135 ENOBARBUS   What's your pleasure, sir?
ANTONY   I must with haste from hence.
ENOBARBUS   Why then we kill all our women. We see
how mortal an unkindness is to them. If they suffer our
departure, death's the word.
140 ANTONY   I must be gone.
ENOBARBUS   Under a compelling occasion let women
die. It were pity to cast them away for nothing, though
between them and a great cause they should be
esteemed nothing. Cleopatra, catching but the least
145 noise of this, dies instantly. I have seen her die twenty
times upon far poorer moment. I do think there is
mettle in death which commits some loving act upon
her, she hath such a celerity in dying.
ANTONY   She is cunning past man's thought.
150 ENOBARBUS   Alack, sir, no; her passions are made of
nothing but the finest part of pure love. We cannot call
her winds and waters sighs and tears; they are greater
storms and tempests than almanacs can report. This
cannot be cunning in her. If it be, she makes a shower
155 of rain as well as Jove.
ANTONY   Would I had never seen her!
ENOBARBUS   O, sir, you had then left unseen a
wonderful piece of work, which not to have been blest
withal would have discredited your travel.
160 ANTONY   Fulvia is dead.
ENOBARBUS   Sir?
ANTONY   Fulvia is dead.
ENOBARBUS   Fulvia?
ANTONY   Dead.
165 ENOBARBUS   Why, sir, give the gods a thankful sacrifice.
When it pleaseth their deities to take the wife of a man
from him, it shows to man the tailors of the earth;

comforting therein, that when old robes are worn out,
there are members to make new. If there were no more
women but Fulvia, then had you indeed a cut, and the   170
case to be lamented. This grief is crowned with
consolation: your old smock brings forth a new
petticoat, and indeed the tears live in an onion that
should water this sorrow.
ANTONY   The business she hath broached in the state   175
Cannot endure my absence.
ENOBARBUS   And the business you have broached here
cannot be without you, especially that of Cleopatra's,
which wholly depends on your abode.
ANTONY   No more light answers. Let our officers   180
Have notice what we purpose. I shall break
The cause of our expedience to the Queen
And get her leave to part. For not alone
The death of Fulvia, with more urgent touches,
Do strongly speak to us, but the letters too   185
Of many our contriving friends in Rome
Petition us at home. Sextus Pompeius
Hath given the dare to Caesar and commands
The empire of the sea. Our slippery people,
Whose love is never linked to the deserver   190
Till his deserts are past, begin to throw
Pompey the Great and all his dignities
Upon his son, who, high in name and power,
Higher than both in blood and life, stands up
For the main soldier; whose quality going on,   195
The sides o'th' world may danger. Much is breeding
Which, like the courser's hair, hath yet but life
And not a serpent's poison. Say our pleasure,
To such whose place is under us, requires
Our quick remove from hence.   200
ENOBARBUS   I shall do't.   *Exeunt.*

1.3   *Enter* CLEOPATRA, CHARMIAN,
                ALEXAS *and* IRAS.

CLEOPATRA   Where is he?
CHARMIAN   I did not see him since.
CLEOPATRA [*to Alexas*]
See where he is, who's with him, what he does.
I did not send you. If you find him sad,
Say I am dancing; if in mirth, report   5
That I am sudden sick. Quick, and return.
                    Exit Alexas.
CHARMIAN
Madam, methinks if you did love him dearly,
You do not hold the method to enforce
The like from him.
CLEOPATRA   What should I do I do not?
CHARMIAN
In each thing give him way; cross him in nothing.   10
CLEOPATRA
Thou teachest like a fool: the way to lose him.
CHARMIAN   Tempt him not too so far; I wish, forbear.
In time we hate that which we often fear.

Enter ANTONY.

But here comes Antony.

CLEOPATRA   I am sick and sullen.

15 ANTONY   I am sorry to give breathing to my purpose –

CLEOPATRA   Help me away, dear Charmian! I shall fall!
It cannot be thus long; the sides of nature
Will not sustain it.

ANTONY   Now, my dearest queen –

CLEOPATRA   Pray you, stand farther from me!

ANTONY   What's the matter?

CLEOPATRA

20 I know by that same eye there's some good news.
What, says the married woman you may go?
Would she had never given you leave to come!
Let her not say 'tis I that keep you here.
I have no power upon you; hers you are.

25 ANTONY   The gods best know –

CLEOPATRA   O, never was there queen
So mightily betrayed! Yet at the first
I saw the treasons planted.

ANTONY   Cleopatra –

CLEOPATRA

Why should I think you can be mine and true –
Though you in swearing shake the throned gods –
30 Who have been false to Fulvia? Riotous madness,
To be entangled with those mouth-made vows
Which break themselves in swearing!

ANTONY   Most sweet queen –

CLEOPATRA

Nay, pray you seek no colour for your going,
But bid farewell and go. When you sued staying,
35 Then was the time for words; no going then.
Eternity was in our lips and eyes,
Bliss in our brows' bent; none our parts so poor
But was a race of heaven. They are so still,
Or thou, the greatest soldier of the world,
Art turned the greatest liar.

40 ANTONY   How now, lady?

CLEOPATRA

I would I had thy inches! Thou shouldst know
There were a heart in Egypt!

ANTONY   Hear me, queen.
The strong necessity of time commands
Our services awhile, but my full heart
45 Remains in use with you. Our Italy
Shines o'er with civil swords; Sextus Pompeius
Makes his approaches to the port of Rome;
Equality of two domestic powers
Breed scrupulous faction; the hated, grown to strength,
50 Are newly grown to love; the condemned Pompey,
Rich in his father's honour, creeps apace
Into the hearts of such as have not thrived
Upon the present state, whose numbers threaten;
And quietness, grown sick of rest, would purge
55 By any desperate change. My more particular,
And that which most with you should safe my going,
Is Fulvia's death.

CLEOPATRA
Though age from folly could not give me freedom,
It does from childishness. Can Fulvia die?

ANTONY   She's dead, my queen.   [*Gives her the letters.*]   60
Look here, and at thy sovereign leisure read
The garboils she awaked. At the last, best,
See when and where she died.

CLEOPATRA   O most false love!
Where be the sacred vials thou shouldst fill
With sorrowful water? Now I see, I see,   65
In Fulvia's death how mine received shall be.

ANTONY   Quarrel no more, but be prepared to know
The purposes I bear; which are, or cease,
As you shall give th'advice. By the fire
That quickens Nilus' slime, I go from hence   70
Thy soldier, servant, making peace or war
As thou affects.

CLEOPATRA   Cut my lace, Charmian, come!
But let it be; I am quickly ill and well –
So Antony loves.

ANTONY   My precious queen, forbear,
And give true evidence to his love, which stands 75
An honourable trial.

CLEOPATRA   So Fulvia told me.
I prithee, turn aside and weep for her,
Then bid adieu to me, and say the tears
Belong to Egypt. Good now, play one scene
Of excellent dissembling, and let it look   80
Like perfect honour.

ANTONY   You'll heat my blood. No more.

CLEOPATRA   You can do better yet, but this is meetly.

ANTONY   Now by my sword –

CLEOPATRA   And target. Still he mends,
But this is not the best. Look, prithee, Charmian,
How this Herculean Roman does become   85
The carriage of his chafe.

ANTONY   I'll leave you, lady.

CLEOPATRA   Courteous lord, one word:
Sir, you and I must part, but that's not it;
Sir, you and I have loved, but there's not it;   90
That you know well. Something it is I would –
Oh, my oblivion is a very Antony,
And I am all forgotten!

ANTONY   But that your royalty
Holds idleness your subject, I should take you
For idleness itself.

CLEOPATRA   'Tis sweating labour   95
To bear such idleness so near the heart
As Cleopatra this. But, sir, forgive me,
Since my becomings kill me when they do not
Eye well to you. Your honour calls you hence;
Therefore be deaf to my unpitied folly,   100
And all the gods go with you! Upon your sword
Sit laurel victory, and smooth success
Be strewed before your feet!

ANTONY   Let us go. Come.
Our separation so abides and flies

105   That thou, residing here, goes yet with me,
        And I, hence fleeting, here remain with thee.
        Away!   *Exeunt.*

1.4   *Enter* OCTAVIUS CAESAR *reading a*
          letter, LEPIDUS *and their train.*

CAESAR   You may see, Lepidus, and henceforth know,
    It is not Caesar's natural vice to hate
    Our great competitor. From Alexandria
    This is the news: he fishes, drinks, and wastes
5   The lamps of night in revel; is not more manlike
    Than Cleopatra, nor the Queen of Ptolemy
    More womanly than he; hardly gave audience, or
    Vouchsafed to think he had partners. You shall find there
    A man who is the abstract of all faults
    That all men follow.
10 LEPIDUS   I must not think there are
    Evils enough to darken all his goodness.
    His faults, in him, seem as the spots of heaven,
    More fiery by night's blackness; hereditary
    Rather than purchased; what he cannot change
15   Than what he chooses.
    CAESAR   You are too indulgent. Let's grant it is not
    Amiss to tumble on the bed of Ptolemy,
    To give a kingdom for a mirth, to sit
    And keep the turn of tippling with a slave,
20   To reel the streets at noon, and stand the buffet
    With knaves that smells of sweat. Say this becomes him –
    As his composure must be rare indeed
    Whom these things cannot blemish – yet must Antony
    No way excuse his foils, when we do bear
25   So great weight in his lightness. If he filled
    His vacancy with his voluptuousness,
    Full surfeits and the dryness of his bones
    Call on him for't. But to confound such time
    That drums him from his sport, and speaks as loud
30   As his own state and ours, 'tis to be chid
    As we rate boys who, being mature in knowledge,
    Pawn their experience to their present pleasure
    And so rebel to judgement.

            Enter a Messenger.

LEPIDUS   Here's more news.
MESSENGER
    Thy biddings have been done, and every hour,
35   Most noble Caesar, shalt thou have report
    How 'tis abroad. Pompey is strong at sea,
    And it appears he is beloved of those
    That only have feared Caesar. To the ports
    The discontents repair, and men's reports
    Give him much wronged.
40 CAESAR   I should have known no less.
    It hath been taught us from the primal state
    That he which is was wished until he were,
    And the ebbed man, ne'er loved till ne'er worth love,

    Comes deared by being lacked. This common body,
    Like to a vagabond flag upon the stream,   45
    Goes to and back, lackeying the varying tide,
    To rot itself with motion.

          Enter another Messenger.

2 MESSENGER   Caesar, I bring thee word
    Menecrates and Menas, famous pirates,
    Makes the sea serve them, which they ear and wound   50
    With keels of every kind. Many hot inroads
    They make in Italy – the borders maritime
    Lack blood to think on't – and flush youth revolt.
    No vessel can peep forth but 'tis as soon
    Taken as seen; for Pompey's name strikes more   55
    Than could his war resisted.
CAESAR   Antony,
    Leave thy lascivious wassails! When thou once
    Was beaten from Modena, where thou slew'st
    Hirtius and Pansa, consuls, at thy heel
    Did famine follow, whom thou fought'st against,   60
    Though daintily brought up, with patience more
    Than savages could suffer. Thou didst drink
    The stale of horses and the gilded puddle
    Which beasts would cough at. Thy palate then did deign
    The roughest berry on the rudest hedge.   65
    Yea, like the stag when snow the pasture sheets,
    The barks of trees thou browsed. On the Alps,
    It is reported, thou didst eat strange flesh
    Which some did die to look on. And all this –
    It wounds thine honour that I speak it now –   70
    Was borne so like a soldier that thy cheek
    So much as lanked not.
LEPIDUS   'Tis pity of him.
CAESAR   Let his shames quickly
    Drive him to Rome. 'Tis time we twain
    Did show ourselves i'th' field, and to that end   75
    Assemble we immediate council. Pompey
    Thrives in our idleness.
LEPIDUS   Tomorrow, Caesar,
    I shall be furnished to inform you rightly
    Both what by sea and land I can be able
    To front this present time.
CAESAR   Till which encounter,   80
    It is my business too. Farewell.
LEPIDUS
    Farewell, my lord. What you shall know meantime
    Of stirs abroad, I shall beseech you, sir,
    To let me be partaker.
CAESAR   Doubt not, sir.
    I knew it for my bond.   *Exeunt by different doors.*   85

1.5   *Enter* CLEOPATRA, CHARMIAN,
          IRAS *and* MARDIAN.

CLEOPATRA   Charmian!
CHARMIAN   Madam?

CLEOPATRA [*Yawns.*] Ha, ha.
   Give me to drink mandragora.

CHARMIAN   Why, madam?

CLEOPATRA

5   That I might sleep out this great gap of time
   My Antony is away.

CHARMIAN   You think of him too much.

CLEOPATRA   O, 'tis treason!

CHARMIAN   Madam, I trust not so.

CLEOPATRA   Thou, eunuch Mardian!

MARDIAN   What's your highness' pleasure?

CLEOPATRA

10   Not now to hear thee sing. I take no pleasure
   In aught an eunuch has. 'Tis well for thee
   That, being unseminared, thy freer thoughts
   May not fly forth of Egypt. Hast thou affections?

MARDIAN   Yes, gracious madam.

15 CLEOPATRA   Indeed?

MARDIAN   Not in deed, madam, for I can do nothing
   But what indeed is honest to be done.
   Yet have I fierce affections, and think
   What Venus did with Mars.

CLEOPATRA   O, Charmian,

20   Where think'st thou he is now? Stands he, or sits he?
   Or does he walk? Or is he on his horse?
   O happy horse, to bear the weight of Antony!
   Do bravely, horse, for wot'st thou whom thou mov'st?
   The demi-Atlas of this earth, the arm

25   And burgonet of men! He's speaking now,
   Or murmuring 'Where's my serpent of old Nile?'
   For so he calls me. Now I feed myself
   With most delicious poison. Think on me
   That am with Phoebus' amorous pinches black

30   And wrinkled deep in time? Broad-fronted Caesar,
   When thou wast here above the ground, I was
   A morsel for a monarch; and great Pompey
   Would stand and make his eyes grow in my brow;
   There would he anchor his aspect, and die

35   With looking on his life.

Enter ALEXAS *from Antony.*

ALEXAS   Sovereign of Egypt, hail!

CLEOPATRA   How much unlike art thou Mark Antony!
   Yet, coming from him, that great medicine hath
   With his tinct gilded thee.

40   How goes it with my brave Mark Antony?

ALEXAS   Last thing he did, dear queen,
   He kissed – the last of many doubled kisses –
   This orient pearl. His speech sticks in my heart.

CLEOPATRA   Mine ear must pluck it thence.

ALEXAS   'Good friend,' quoth he,

45   'Say the firm Roman to great Egypt sends
   This treasure of an oyster, at whose foot,
   To mend the petty present, I will piece
   Her opulent throne with kingdoms. All the East,
   Say thou, shall call her mistress.' So he nodded

50   And soberly did mount an arm-gaunt steed

Who neighed so high that what I would have spoke
Was beastly dumbed by him.

CLEOPATRA   What, was he sad or merry?

ALEXAS
   Like to the time o'th' year between the extremes
   Of hot and cold, he was nor sad nor merry.   55

CLEOPATRA   O well-divided disposition! Note him,
   Note him, good Charmian, 'tis the man; but note him!
   He was not sad, for he would shine on those
   That make their looks by his; he was not merry,
   Which seemed to tell them his remembrance lay   60
   In Egypt with his joy; but between both.
   O heavenly mingle! Be'st thou sad or merry,
   The violence of either thee becomes,
   So does it no man else. Met'st thou my posts?

ALEXAS   Ay, madam, twenty several messengers.   65
   Why do you send so thick?

CLEOPATRA   Who's born that day
   When I forget to send to Antony
   Shall die a beggar. Ink and paper, Charmian!
   Welcome, my good Alexas! Did I, Charmian,
   Ever love Caesar so?

CHARMIAN   O that brave Caesar!   70

CLEOPATRA   Be choked with such another emphasis!
   Say, 'the brave Antony'.

CHARMIAN   The valiant Caesar!

CLEOPATRA   By Isis, I will give thee bloody teeth
   If thou with Caesar paragon again
   My man of men!

CHARMIAN   By your most gracious pardon,   75
   I sing but after you.

CLEOPATRA   My salad days,
   When I was green in judgement, cold in blood,
   To say as I said then. But come, away,
   Get me ink and paper!
   He shall have every day a several greeting   80
   Or I'll unpeople Egypt!   *Exeunt.*

2.1   *Enter* POMPEY, MENECRATES *and*
            MENAS *in warlike manner.*

POMPEY   If the great gods be just, they shall assist
   The deeds of justest men.

MENECRATES   Know, worthy Pompey,
   That what they do delay they not deny.

POMPEY   Whiles we are suitors to their throne, decays
   The thing we sue for.

MENECRATES   We, ignorant of ourselves,   5
   Beg often our own harms, which the wise powers
   Deny us for our good; so find we profit
   By losing of our prayers.

POMPEY   I shall do well.
   The people love me, and the sea is mine;
   My powers are crescent, and my auguring hope   10
   Says it will come to th' full. Mark Antony
   In Egypt sits at dinner, and will make
   No wars without doors; Caesar gets money where

He loses hearts; Lepidus flatters both, 15
Of both is flattered; but he neither loves,
Nor either cares for him.

MENAS   Caesar and Lepidus
Are in the field. A mighty strength they carry.

POMPEY   Where have you this? 'Tis false.

MENAS   From Silvius, sir.

POMPEY
He dreams. I know they are in Rome together, 20
Looking for Antony. But all the charms of love,
Salt Cleopatra, soften thy waned lip!
Let witchcraft join with beauty, lust with both;
Tie up the libertine in a field of feasts;
Keep his brain fuming. Epicurean cooks
Sharpen with cloyless sauce his appetite 25
That sleep and feeding may prorogue his honour
Even till a Lethe'd dullness –

Enter VARRIUS.

                              How now, Varrius?

VARRIUS   This is most certain that I shall deliver:
Mark Antony is every hour in Rome
Expected. Since he went from Egypt 'tis 30
A space for farther travel.

POMPEY   I could have given less matter
A better ear. Menas, I did not think
This amorous surfeiter would have donned his helm
For such a petty war. His soldiership 35
Is twice the other twain. But let us rear
The higher our opinion, that our stirring
Can from the lap of Egypt's widow pluck
The ne'er-lust-wearied Antony.

MENAS   I cannot hope
Caesar and Antony shall well greet together. 40
His wife that's dead did trespasses to Caesar;
His brother warred upon him, although I think
Not moved by Antony.

POMPEY   I know not, Menas,
How lesser enmities may give way to greater.
Were't not that we stand up against them all, 45
'Twere pregnant they should square between
        themselves,
For they have entertained cause enough
To draw their swords. But how the fear of us
May cement their divisions, and bind up
The petty difference, we yet not know. 50
Be't as our gods will have't! It only stands
Our lives upon to use our strongest hands.
Come, Menas.   *Exeunt.*

2.2   *Enter* ENOBARBUS *and* LEPIDUS.

LEPIDUS   Good Enobarbus, 'tis a worthy deed,
And shall become you well, to entreat your captain
To soft and gentle speech.

ENOBARBUS   I shall entreat him
To answer like himself. If Caesar move him,

Let Antony look over Caesar's head 5
And speak as loud as Mars. By Jupiter,
Were I the wearer of Antonio's beard,
I would not shave't today!

LEPIDUS   'Tis not a time
For private stomaching.

ENOBARBUS   Every time
Serves for the matter that is then born in't. 10

LEPIDUS
But small to greater matters must give way.

ENOBARBUS   Not if the small come first.

LEPIDUS   Your speech is passion;
But pray you stir no embers up. Here comes
The noble Antony.

Enter ANTONY *and* VENTIDIUS.

ENOBARBUS   And yonder Caesar.

Enter CAESAR, MAECENAS *and* AGRIPPA.

ANTONY   If we compose well here, to Parthia. 15
Hark, Ventidius.

CAESAR   I do not know, Maecenas. Ask Agrippa.

LEPIDUS   Noble friends,
That which combined us was most great, and let not
A leaner action rend us. What's amiss, 20
May it be gently heard. When we debate
Our trivial difference loud, we do commit
Murder in healing wounds. Then, noble partners,
The rather for I earnestly beseech,
Touch you the sourest points with sweetest terms, 25
Nor curstness grow to th' matter.

ANTONY   'Tis spoken well.
Were we before our armies, and to fight,
I should do thus.   [*Flourish*]

CAESAR   Welcome to Rome.

ANTONY   Thank you. 30

CAESAR   Sit.

ANTONY   Sit, sir.

CAESAR   Nay then. [*Caesar sits, then Antony.*]

ANTONY   I learn you take things ill which are not so,
Or being, concern you not.

CAESAR   I must be laughed at 35
If, or for nothing or a little, I
Should say myself offended, and with you
Chiefly i'th' world; more laughed at that I should
Once name you derogately when to sound your name
It not concerned me.

ANTONY   My being in Egypt, Caesar, 40
What was't to you?

CAESAR   No more than my residing here at Rome
Might be to you in Egypt. Yet if you there
Did practise on my state, your being in Egypt
Might be my question.

ANTONY   How intend you, 'practised'? 45

CAESAR   You may be pleased to catch at mine intent
By what did here befall me. Your wife and brother
Made wars upon me, and their contestation

Was theme for you; you were the word of war.

ANTONY
50 You do mistake your business. My brother never
Did urge me in his act. I did enquire it,
And have my learning from some true reports
That drew their swords with you. Did he not rather
Discredit my authority with yours,
55 And make the wars alike against my stomach,
Having alike your cause? Of this my letters
Before did satisfy you. If you'll patch a quarrel,
As matter whole you have to make it with,
It must not be with this.

CAESAR   You praise yourself
60 By laying defects of judgement to me, but
You patched up your excuses.

ANTONY   Not so, not so!
I know you could not lack – I am certain on't –
Very necessity of this thought, that I,
Your partner in the cause 'gainst which he fought,
65 Could not with graceful eyes attend those wars
Which fronted mine own peace. As for my wife,
I would you had her spirit in such another.
The third o'th' world is yours, which with a snaffle
You may pace easy, but not such a wife.

ENOBARBUS
70 Would we had all such wives, that the men
might go to wars with the women!

ANTONY   So much uncurbable, her garboils, Caesar,
Made out of her impatience – which not wanted
Shrewdness of policy too – I grieving grant
75 Did you too much disquiet. For that, you must
But say I could not help it.

CAESAR   I wrote to you
When rioting in Alexandria. You
Did pocket up my letters, and with taunts
Did gibe my missive out of audience.

ANTONY   Sir,
80 He fell upon me ere admitted, then.
Three kings I had newly feasted, and did want
Of what I was i'th' morning. But next day
I told him of myself, which was as much
As to have asked him pardon. Let this fellow
85 Be nothing of our strife; if we contend,
Out of our question wipe him.

CAESAR   You have broken
The article of your oath, which you shall never
Have tongue to charge me with.

LEPIDUS   Soft, Caesar!

ANTONY
90 No, Lepidus, let him speak.
The honour is sacred which he talks on now,
Supposing that I lacked it. But on, Caesar:
'The article of my oath –'

CAESAR
To lend me arms and aid when I required them,
The which you both denied.

ANTONY
95   Neglected, rather;
And then when poisoned hours had bound me up
From mine own knowledge. As nearly as I may

I'll play the penitent to you, but mine honesty
Shall not make poor my greatness, nor my power
Work without it. Truth is that Fulvia,   100
To have me out of Egypt, made wars here,
For which myself, the ignorant motive, do
So far ask pardon as befits mine honour
To stoop in such a case.

LEPIDUS   'Tis noble spoken.

MAECENAS   If it might please you to enforce no further   105
The griefs between ye; to forget them quite
Were to remember that the present need
Speaks to atone you.

LEPIDUS   Worthily spoken, Maecenas.

ENOBARBUS   Or, if you borrow one another's love for
the instant, you may, when you hear no more words of   110
Pompey, return it again. You shall have time to wrangle
in when you have nothing else to do.

ANTONY   Thou art a soldier only. Speak no more.

ENOBARBUS   That truth should be silent, I had almost
forgot.   115

ANTONY
You wrong this presence; therefore speak no more.

ENOBARBUS   Go to, then! Your considerate stone.

CAESAR   I do not much dislike the matter but
The manner of his speech; for't cannot be
We shall remain in friendship, our conditions   120
So differing in their acts. Yet, if I knew
What hoop should hold us staunch, from edge to edge
O'th' world I would pursue it.

AGRIPPA   Give me leave, Caesar.

CAESAR   Speak, Agrippa.

AGRIPPA   Thou hast a sister by the mother's side,   125
Admired Octavia. Great Mark Antony
Is now a widower.

CAESAR   Say not so, Agrippa.
If Cleopatra heard you, your reproof
Were well deserved of rashness.

ANTONY   I am not married, Caesar. Let me hear   130
Agrippa further speak.

AGRIPPA   To hold you in perpetual amity,
To make you brothers, and to knit your hearts
With an unslipping knot, take Antony
Octavia to his wife; whose beauty claims   135
No worse a husband than the best of men;
Whose virtue and whose general graces speak
That which none else can utter. By this marriage
All little jealousies which now seem great,
And all great fears which now import their dangers   140
Would then be nothing. Truths would be tales,
Where now half-tales be truths. Her love to both
Would each to other, and all loves to both
Draw after her. Pardon what I have spoke,
For 'tis a studied, not a present thought,   145
By duty ruminated.

ANTONY   Will Caesar speak?

CAESAR   Not till he hears how Antony is touched
With what is spoke already.

ANTONY   What power is in Agrippa,
150   If I would say, 'Agrippa, be it so',
    To make this good?
CAESAR   The power of Caesar, and
    His power unto Octavia.
ANTONY   May I never,
    To this good purpose that so fairly shows,
    Dream of impediment! Let me have thy hand.
155   Further this act of grace, and from this hour
    The heart of brothers govern in our loves
    And sway our great designs!
CAESAR   There's my hand.
        [*They clasp hands.*]
    A sister I bequeath you, whom no brother
    Did ever love so dearly. Let her live
160   To join our kingdoms and our hearts; and never
    Fly off our loves again!
LEPIDUS   Happily, amen!
ANTONY
    I did not think to draw my sword 'gainst Pompey,
    For he hath laid strange courtesies and great
    Of late upon me. I must thank him, only
165   Lest my remembrance suffer ill report;
    At heel of that, defy him.
LEPIDUS   Time calls upon's.
    Of us must Pompey presently be sought
    Or else he seeks out us.
ANTONY   Where lies he?
170   CAESAR   About the Mount Misena.
ANTONY   What is his strength by land?
CAESAR   Great and increasing, but by sea
    He is an absolute master.
ANTONY   So is the fame.
    Would we had spoke together! Haste we for it.
175   Yet, ere we put ourselves in arms, dispatch we
    The business we have talked of.
CAESAR   With most gladness,
    And do invite you to my sister's view,
    Whither straight I'll lead you.
ANTONY   Let us, Lepidus, not lack your company.
180   LEPIDUS   Noble Antony, not sickness should detain me.
        Flourish. Exeunt all except Enobarbus,
                    Agrippa, Maecenas.
MAECENAS   Welcome from Egypt, sir.
ENOBARBUS   Half the heart of Caesar, worthy Maecenas!
    My honourable friend, Agrippa!
AGRIPPA   Good Enobarbus!
185   MAECENAS   We have cause to be glad that matters are so
    well digested. You stayed well by't in Egypt.
ENOBARBUS   Ay, sir, we did sleep day out of countenance
    and made the night light with drinking.
MAECENAS   Eight wild boars roasted whole at a
190   breakfast, and but twelve persons there. Is this
    true?
ENOBARBUS   This was but as a fly by an eagle. We had
    much more monstrous matter of feast, which worthily
    deserved noting.

MAECENAS   She's a most triumphant lady, if report be   195
    square to her.
ENOBARBUS   When she first met Mark Antony, she
    pursed up his heart upon the river of Cydnus.
AGRIPPA   There she appeared indeed! Or my reporter
    devised well for her.   200
ENOBARBUS   I will tell you.
    The barge she sat in, like a burnished throne,
    Burned on the water; the poop was beaten gold;
    Purple the sails, and so perfumed that
    The winds were love-sick with them; the oars were
        silver,   205
    Which to the tune of flutes kept stroke, and made
    The water which they beat to follow faster,
    As amorous of their strokes. For her own person,
    It beggared all description: she did lie
    In her pavilion, cloth-of-gold of tissue,   210
    O'erpicturing that Venus where we see
    The fancy outwork nature. On each side her
    Stood pretty dimpled boys, like smiling cupids,
    With divers-coloured fans, whose wind did seem
    To glow the delicate cheeks which they did cool,   215
    And what they undid did.
AGRIPPA   O, rare for Antony!
ENOBARBUS   Her gentlewomen, like the Nereides,
    So many mermaids, tended her i'th' eyes,
    And made their bends adornings. At the helm
    A seeming mermaid steers. The silken tackle   220
    Swell with the touches of those flower-soft hands
    That yarely frame the office. From the barge
    A strange invisible perfume hits the sense
    Of the adjacent wharfs. The city cast
    Her people out upon her, and Antony,   225
    Enthroned i'th' market-place, did sit alone,
    Whistling to th'air, which, but for vacancy,
    Had gone to gaze on Cleopatra, too,
    And made a gap in nature.
AGRIPPA   Rare Egyptian!
ENOBARBUS   Upon her landing, Antony sent to her;   230
    Invited her to supper. She replied
    It should be better he became her guest,
    Which she entreated. Our courteous Antony,
    Whom ne'er the word of 'No' woman heard speak,
    Being barbered ten times o'er, goes to the feast,   235
    And, for his ordinary, pays his heart
    For what his eyes eat only.
AGRIPPA   Royal wench!
    She made great Caesar lay his sword to bed.
    He ploughed her, and she cropped.
ENOBARBUS   I saw her once
    Hop forty paces through the public street   240
    And, having lost her breath, she spoke and panted,
    That she did make defect perfection,
    And, breathless, pour breath forth.
MAECENAS   Now Antony must leave her utterly.
ENOBARBUS   Never! He will not.   245
    Age cannot wither her, nor custom stale

Her infinite variety. Other women cloy
The appetites they feed, but she makes hungry
Where most she satisfies; for vilest things
250 Become themselves in her, that the holy priests
Bless her when she is riggish.

MAECENAS   If beauty, wisdom, modesty can settle
The heart of Antony, Octavia is
A blessed lottery to him.

AGRIPPA   Let us go.
255 Good Enobarbus, make yourself my guest
Whilst you abide here.

ENOBARBUS   Humbly, sir, I thank you.
                                                              Exeunt.

2.3   *Enter* ANTONY, CAESAR; OCTAVIA
                         between them.

ANTONY
The world and my great office will sometimes
Divide me from your bosom.

OCTAVIA   All which time
Before the gods my knee shall bow my prayers
To them for you.

ANTONY   Good night, sir. My Octavia,
5   Read not my blemishes in the world's report.
I have not kept my square, but that to come
Shall all be done by th' rule. Good night, dear lady.

OCTAVIA   Good night, sir.

CAESAR   Good night.   *Exeunt Caesar and Octavia.*

              Enter Soothsayer.

10 ANTONY   Now, sirrah! You do wish yourself in Egypt?

SOOTHSAYER
Would I had never come from thence, nor you thither!

ANTONY   If you can, your reason?

SOOTHSAYER
I see it in my motion; have it not in my tongue.
But yet hie you to Egypt again.

ANTONY   Say to me,
15   Whose fortunes shall rise higher, Caesar's or mine?

SOOTHSAYER   Caesar's.
Therefore, O Antony, stay not by his side.
Thy daemon – that thy spirit which keeps thee – is
Noble, courageous, high unmatchable,
20   Where Caesar's is not. But near him, thy angel
Becomes afeard, as being o'erpowered; therefore
Make space enough between you.

ANTONY   Speak this no more.

SOOTHSAYER
To none but thee; no more but when to thee.
If thou dost play with him at any game,
25   Thou art sure to lose; and of that natural luck
He beats thee 'gainst the odds. Thy lustre thickens
When he shines by. I say again, thy spirit
Is all afraid to govern thee near him;
But, he away, 'tis noble.

ANTONY   Get thee gone.
Say to Ventidius I would speak with him.   30
                                              Exit Soothsayer.
He shall to Parthia. Be it art or hap,
He hath spoken true. The very dice obey him,
And in our sports my better cunning faints
Under his chance. If we draw lots, he speeds;
His cocks do win the battle still of mine   35
When it is all to naught, and his quails ever
Beat mine, inhooped, at odds. I will to Egypt;
And though I make this marriage for my peace,
I'th' East my pleasure lies.

              Enter VENTIDIUS.

                              O come, Ventidius.
You must to Parthia. Your commission's ready.   40
Follow me and receive't.   *Exeunt.*

2.4   *Enter* LEPIDUS, MAECENAS *and* AGRIPPA.

LEPIDUS
Trouble yourselves no further. Pray you hasten
Your generals after.

AGRIPPA   Sir, Mark Antony
Will e'en but kiss Octavia, and we'll follow.

LEPIDUS   Till I shall see you in your soldiers' dress,
Which will become you both, farewell.

MAECENAS   We shall,   5
As I conceive the journey, be at the Mount
Before you, Lepidus.

LEPIDUS   Your way is shorter;
My purposes do draw me much about.
You'll win two days upon me.

MAECENAS, AGRIPPA   Sir, good success!   10

LEPIDUS   Farewell.   *Exeunt.*

2.5   *Enter* CLEOPATRA, CHARMIAN,
                       IRAS *and* ALEXAS.

CLEOPATRA   Give me some music – music, moody food
Of us that trade in love.

ALL   The music, ho!

              Enter MARDIAN *the Eunuch.*

CLEOPATRA
Let it alone. Let's to billiards. Come, Charmian.

CHARMIAN   My arm is sore. Best play with Mardian.

CLEOPATRA   As well a woman with an eunuch played   5
As with a woman. Come, you'll play with me, sir?

MARDIAN   As well as I can, madam.

CLEOPATRA
And when good will is showed, though't come too short,
The actor may plead pardon. I'll none now.
Give me mine angle; we'll to th' river. There,   10
My music playing far off, I will betray
Tawny-finned fishes. My bended hook shall pierce

Their slimy jaws, and, as I draw them up,
I'll think them every one an Antony,
And say 'Ah, ha! You're caught!'

15 CHARMIAN   'Twas merry when
You wagered on your angling; when your diver
Did hang a salt fish on his hook, which he
With fervency drew up.

CLEOPATRA   That time? O times!
I laughed him out of patience, and that night

20 I laughed him into patience, and next morn,
Ere the ninth hour, I drunk him to his bed,
Then put my tires and mantles on him, whilst
I wore his sword Philippan.

Enter a Messenger.

Oh, from Italy!
Ram thou thy fruitful tidings in mine ears,
That long time have been barren!

25 MESSENGER   Madam, madam –

CLEOPATRA   Antonio's dead! If thou say so, villain,
Thou kill'st thy mistress; but well and free,
If thou so yield him, there is gold, and here
My bluest veins to kiss, a hand that kings

30 Have lipped, and trembled, kissing.

MESSENGER   First, madam, he is well.

CLEOPATRA   Why, there's more gold.
But sirrah, mark, we use
To say the dead are well. Bring it to that,
The gold I give thee will I melt and pour
Down thy ill-uttering throat.

35 MESSENGER   Good madam, hear me.

CLEOPATRA   Well, go to, I will.
But there's no goodness in thy face if Antony
Be free and healthful. So tart a favour
To trumpet such good tidings! If not well,
Thou shouldst come like a Fury crowned with

40   snakes,
Not like a formal man.

MESSENGER   Will't please you hear me?

CLEOPATRA
I have a mind to strike thee ere thou speak'st.
Yet if thou say Antony lives, is well,
Or friends with Caesar, or not captive to him,

45 I'll set thee in a shower of gold and hail
Rich pearls upon thee.

MESSENGER   Madam, he's well.

CLEOPATRA   Well said!

MESSENGER   And friends with Caesar.

CLEOPATRA   Thou'rt an honest man!

MESSENGER
Caesar and he are greater friends than ever.

CLEOPATRA   Make thee a fortune from me!

MESSENGER   But yet, madam –

50 CLEOPATRA   I do not like 'But yet'. It does allay
The good precedence. Fie upon 'But yet'!
'But yet' is as a gaoler to bring forth
Some monstrous malefactor. Prithee, friend,

Pour out the pack of matter to mine ear,
The good and bad together. He's friends with Caesar,   55
In state of health, thou sayst, and, thou sayst, free.

MESSENGER   Free, madam? No. I made no such report.
He's bound unto Octavia.

CLEOPATRA   For what good turn?

MESSENGER   For the best turn i'th' bed.

CLEOPATRA   I am pale, Charmian.

MESSENGER   Madam, he's married to Octavia.   60

CLEOPATRA   The most infectious pestilence upon thee!
[*Strikes him down.*]

MESSENGER   Good madam, patience!

CLEOPATRA   What say you?
[*Strikes him.*]   Hence,
Horrible villain, or I'll spurn thine eyes
Like balls before me! I'll unhair thy head!
[*She hales him up and down.*]
Thou shalt be whipped with wire and stewed in brine,   65
Smarting in lingering pickle!

MESSENGER   Gracious madam,
I that do bring the news made not the match.

CLEOPATRA   Say 'tis not so, a province I will give thee,
And make thy fortunes proud. The blow thou hadst
Shall make thy peace for moving me to rage,   70
And I will boot thee with what gift beside
Thy modesty can beg.

MESSENGER   He's married, madam.

CLEOPATRA   Rogue, thou hast lived too long!
[*Draws a knife.*]

MESSENGER   Nay then, I'll run.
What mean you, madam? I have made no fault.   *Exit.*

CHARMIAN
Good madam, keep yourself within youself.   75
The man is innocent.

CLEOPATRA
Some innocents 'scape not the thunderbolt.
Melt Egypt into Nile, and kindly creatures
Turn all to serpents! Call the slave again!
Though I am mad, I will not bite him. Call!   80

CHARMIAN   He is afeard to come.

CLEOPATRA   I will not hurt him.
Exit Charmian.
These hands do lack nobility that they strike
A meaner than myself, since I myself
Have given myself the cause.

Enter the Messenger *again with* CHARMIAN.

Come hither, sir.
Though it be honest, it is never good   85
To bring bad news. Give to a gracious message
An host of tongues, but let ill tidings tell
Themselves when they be felt.

MESSENGER   I have done my duty.

CLEOPATRA   Is he married?
I cannot hate thee worser than I do   90
If thou again say 'Yes'.

MESSENGER   He's married, madam.

CLEOPATRA
The gods confound thee! Dost thou hold there still?
MESSENGER   Should I lie, madam?
CLEOPATRA   Oh, I would thou didst,
So half my Egypt were submerged and made
A cistern for scaled snakes! Go, get thee hence!
Hadst thou Narcissus in thy face, to me
Thou wouldst appear most ugly. He is married?
MESSENGER   I crave your highness' pardon.
CLEOPATRA   He is married?
MESSENGER
Take no offence that I would not offend you.
To punish me for what you make me do
Seems much unequal. He's married to Octavia.
CLEOPATRA
Oh, that his fault should make a knave of thee
That act not what thou'rt sure of! Get thee hence!
The merchandise which thou hast brought from
        Rome
Are all too dear for me. Lie they upon thy hand
And be undone by 'em.   *Exit Messenger.*
CHARMIAN   Good your highness, patience.
CLEOPATRA
In praising Antony, I have dispraised Caesar.
CHARMIAN   Many times, madam.
CLEOPATRA   I am paid for't now.
Lead me from hence;
I faint! O Iras, Charmian! 'Tis no matter.
Go to the fellow, good Alexas, bid him
Report the feature of Octavia, her years,
Her inclination; let him not leave out
The colour of her hair. Bring me word quickly.
                            Exit Alexas.
Let him for ever go! Let him not, Charmian.
Though he be painted one way like a Gorgon,
The other way's a Mars. [*to Iras*] Bid you Alexas
Bring me word how tall she is. Pity me, Charmian,
But do not speak to me. Lead me to my chamber.
                            Exeunt.

2.6   *Flourish. Enter* POMPEY *and* MENAS
        at one door with drum and trumpet;
            at another CAESAR, LEPIDUS,
        ANTONY, ENOBARBUS, MAECENAS,
        AGRIPPA, *with Soldiers marching.*

POMPEY   Your hostages I have, so have you mine,
And we shall talk before we fight.
CAESAR   Most meet
That first we come to words, and therefore have we
Our written purposes before us sent,
Which if thou hast considered, let us know
If 'twill tie up thy discontented sword
And carry back to Sicily much tall youth
That else must perish here.
POMPEY   To you all three,
The senators alone of this great world,

Chief factors for the gods: I do not know   10
Wherefore my father should revengers want,
Having a son and friends, since Julius Caesar,
Who at Philippi the good Brutus ghosted,
There saw you labouring for him. What was't
That moved pale Cassius to conspire? And what   15
Made the all-honoured, honest Roman, Brutus,
With the armed rest, courtiers of beauteous
        freedom,
To drench the Capitol, but that they would
Have one man but a man? And that is it
Hath made me rig my navy, at whose burden   20
The angered ocean foams, with which I meant
To scourge th'ingratitude that despiteful Rome
Cast on my noble father.
CAESAR   Take your time.
ANTONY
Thou canst not fear us, Pompey, with thy sails.
We'll speak with thee at sea. At land thou know'st   25
How much we do o'ercount thee.
POMPEY   At land indeed
Thou dost o'ercount me of my father's house;
But since the cuckoo builds not for himself,
Remain in't as thou mayst.
LEPIDUS   Be pleased to tell us –
For this is from the present – how you take   30
The offers we have sent you.
CAESAR   There's the point.
ANTONY
Which do not be entreated to, but weigh
What it is worth embraced.
CAESAR   And what may follow
To try a larger fortune.
POMPEY   You have made me offer
Of Sicily, Sardinia; and I must   35
Rid all the sea of pirates; then to send
Measures of wheat to Rome. This 'greed upon,
To part with unhacked edges, and bear back
Our targes undinted.
CAESAR, ANTONY, LEPIDUS   That's our offer.
POMPEY   Know, then,
I came before you here a man prepared   40
To take this offer, but Mark Antony
Put me to some impatience. Though I lose
The praise of it by telling, you must know
When Caesar and your brother were at blows,
Your mother came to Sicily and did find   45
Her welcome friendly.
ANTONY   I have heard it, Pompey,
And am well studied for a liberal thanks
Which I do owe you.
POMPEY   Let me have your hand.
    [*They shake hands.*]
I did not think, sir, to have met you here.
ANTONY
The beds i'th' East are soft; and thanks to you   50
That called me timelier than my purpose hither,

For I have gained by't.

CAESAR   Since I saw you last,
There is a change upon you.

POMPEY   Well, I know not
What counts harsh Fortune casts upon my face,
55 But in my bosom shall she never come
To make my heart her vassal.

LEPIDUS   Well met here!

POMPEY
I hope so, Lepidus. Thus we are agreed.
I crave our composition may be written
And sealed between us.

CAESAR   That's the next to do.

60 POMPEY We'll feast each other ere we part, and let's
Draw lots who shall begin.

ANTONY   That will I, Pompey.

POMPEY No, Antony, take the lot.
But, first or last, your fine Egyptian cookery
Shall have the fame. I have heard that Julius Caesar
Grew fat with feasting there.

65 ANTONY   You have heard much.

POMPEY I have fair meanings, sir.

ANTONY   And fair words to them.

POMPEY Then so much have I heard.
And I have heard Apollodorus carried –

ENOBARBUS No more of that! He did so.

POMPEY   What, I pray you?

70 ENOBARBUS A certain queen to Caesar in a mattress.

POMPEY I know thee now. How far'st thou, soldier?

ENOBARBUS   Well;
And well am like to do, for I perceive
Four feasts are toward.

POMPEY   Let me shake thy hand.
[*They shake hands.*]
I never hated thee. I have seen thee fight
When I have envied thy behaviour.

75 ENOBARBUS   Sir,
I never loved you much, but I ha' praised ye
When you have well deserved ten times as much
As I have said you did.

POMPEY   Enjoy thy plainness;
It nothing ill becomes thee.
80 Aboard my galley I invite you all.
Will you lead, lords?

CAESAR, ANTONY, LEPIDUS Show's the way, sir.

POMPEY   Come.

Exeunt all but Enobarbus and Menas.

MENAS [*aside*] Thy father, Pompey, would ne'er have
made this treaty. [*to Enobarbus*] You and I have known,
sir.

85 ENOBARBUS At sea, I think.

MENAS We have, sir.

ENOBARBUS You have done well by water.

MENAS And you by land.

ENOBARBUS I will praise any man that will praise me,
90 though it cannot be denied what I have done by land.

MENAS Nor what I have done by water.

ENOBARBUS Yes, something you can deny for your own
safety: you have been a great thief by sea.

MENAS And you by land.

ENOBARBUS There I deny my land service. But give me   95
your hand, Menas! [*They shake hands.*] If our eyes had
authority, here they might take two thieves kissing.

MENAS All men's faces are true, whatsome'er their
hands are.

ENOBARBUS But there is never a fair woman has a true   100
face.

MENAS No slander. They steal hearts.

ENOBARBUS We came hither to fight with you.

MENAS For my part, I am sorry it is turned to a
drinking. Pompey doth this day laugh away his fortune.   105

ENOBARBUS If he do, sure he cannot weep't back again.

MENAS You've said, sir. We looked not for Mark Antony
here. Pray you, is he married to Cleopatra?

ENOBARBUS Caesar's sister is called Octavia.

MENAS True, sir. She was the wife of Caius Marcellus.   110

ENOBARBUS But she is now the wife of Marcus
Antonius.

MENAS Pray ye, sir?

ENOBARBUS 'Tis true.

MENAS Then is Caesar and he for ever knit together.   115

ENOBARBUS If I were bound to divine of this unity, I
would not prophesy so.

MENAS I think the policy of that purpose made more in
the marriage than the love of the parties.

ENOBARBUS I think so too. But you shall find the band   120
that seems to tie their friendship together will be the
very strangler of their amity. Octavia is of a holy, cold
and still conversation.

MENAS Who would not have his wife so?

ENOBARBUS Not he that himself is not so; which is   125
Mark Antony. He will to his Egyptian dish again.
Then shall the sighs of Octavia blow the fire up in
Caesar, and, as I said before, that which is the strength
of their amity shall prove the immediate author of
their variance. Antony will use his affection where it is.   130
He married but his occasion here.

MENAS And thus it may be. Come, sir, will you
aboard? I have a health for you.

ENOBARBUS I shall take it, sir. We have used our throats   135
in Egypt.

MENAS Come, let's away.   *Exeunt.*

2.7   *Music plays. Enter two or three*
                Servants with a banquet.

1 SERVANT Here they'll be man. Some o' their plants
are ill-rooted already; the least wind i'th' world will
blow them down.

2 SERVANT Lepidus is high-coloured.

1 SERVANT They have made him drink alms-drink.   5

2 SERVANT As they pinch one another by the
disposition, he cries out 'No more', reconciles them to
his entreaty, and himself to th' drink.

1 SERVANT   But it raises the greater war between him
10   and his discretion.

2 SERVANT   Why, this it is to have a name in great men's
fellowship. I had as lief have a reed that will do me no
service as a partisan I could not heave.

1 SERVANT   To be called into a huge sphere and not to be
15   seen to move in't, are the holes where eyes should be,
which pitifully disaster the cheeks.

A sennet sounded. Enter CAESAR, ANTONY, POMPEY,
LEPIDUS, AGRIPPA, MAECENAS, ENOBARBUS,
MENAS *with other captains and a* Boy Singer.

ANTONY
Thus do they, sir: they take the flow o'th' Nile
By certain scales i'th' pyramid. They know
By th'height, the lowness, or the mean, if dearth
20   Or foison follow. The higher Nilus swells,
The more it promises. As it ebbs, the seedsman
Upon the slime and ooze scatters his grain,
And shortly comes to harvest.

LEPIDUS   You've strange serpents there?
25   ANTONY   Ay, Lepidus.

LEPIDUS   Your serpent of Egypt is bred, now, of your
mud by the operation of your sun; so is your crocodile.

ANTONY   They are so.

POMPEY   Sit, and some wine! A health to Lepidus!
[They sit and drink.]

30   LEPIDUS   I am not so well as I should be, but I'll ne'er
out.

ENOBARBUS *[aside]*   Not till you have slept. I fear me
you'll be in till then.

LEPIDUS   Nay, certainly, I have heard the Ptolemies'
35   pyramises are very goodly things. Without contradiction
I have heard that.

MENAS *[aside to Pompey]*   Pompey, a word.

POMPEY *[aside to Menas]*   Say in mine ear what is't.

MENAS *[Whispers in his ear.]*
Forsake thy seat, I do beseech thee, captain,
And hear me speak a word.

POMPEY *[aside to Menas]*
40   Forbear me till anon. – This wine for Lepidus!

LEPIDUS   What manner o' thing is your crocodile?

ANTONY   It is shaped, sir, like itself, and it is as broad as
it hath breadth. It is just so high as it is, and moves
with it own organs. It lives by that which nourisheth it,
45   and the elements once out of it, it transmigrates.

LEPIDUS   What colour is it of?

ANTONY   Of it own colour too.

LEPIDUS   'Tis a strange serpent.

ANTONY   'Tis so, and the tears of it are wet.

50   CAESAR   Will this description satisfy him?

ANTONY   With the health that Pompey gives him, else
he is a very epicure. *[Menas whispers again.]*

POMPEY *[aside to Menas]*
Go hang, sir, hang! Tell me of that? Away!
Do as I bid you. – Where's this cup I called for?

MENAS *[aside to Pompey]*

If for the sake of merit thou wilt hear me,   55
Rise from thy stool.

POMPEY *[aside to Menas]*
                      I think thou'rt mad. The matter?
[Rises and walks aside with Menas.]

MENAS   I have ever held my cap off to thy fortunes.

POMPEY
Thou hast served me with much faith. What's else to
say? –
Be jolly, lords.

ANTONY   These quicksands, Lepidus,
Keep off them, for you sink.   60

MENAS   Wilt thou be lord of all the world?

POMPEY   What sayst thou?

MENAS   Wilt thou be lord of the whole world?
That's twice.

POMPEY   How should that be?

MENAS   But entertain it,
And, though thou think me poor, I am the man
Will give thee all the world.

POMPEY   Hast thou drunk well?   65

MENAS   No, Pompey, I have kept me from the cup.
Thou art, if thou dar'st be, the earthly Jove,
Whate'er the ocean pales or sky inclips
Is thine, if thou wilt ha't.

POMPEY   Show me which way.

MENAS   These three world-sharers, these competitors,   70
Are in thy vessel. Let me cut the cable,
And when we are put off, fall to their throats.
All then is thine.

POMPEY   Ah, this thou shouldst have done
And not have spoke on't. In me 'tis villainy;
In thee't had been good service. Thou must know   75
'Tis not my profit that does lead mine honour;
Mine honour, it. Repent that e'er thy tongue
Hath so betrayed thine act. Being done unknown,
I should have found it afterwards well done,
But must condemn it now. Desist and drink.   80
[Returns to the others.]

MENAS *[aside]*   For this,
I'll never follow thy palled fortunes more.
Who seeks and will not take, when once 'tis offered,
Shall never find it more.

POMPEY   This health to Lepidus!

ANTONY
Bear him ashore. I'll pledge it for him, Pompey.   85

ENOBARBUS   Here's to thee, Menas!

MENAS   Enobarbus, welcome!

POMPEY
Fill till the cup be hid.

ENOBARBUS   There's a strong fellow, Menas.
[Points to the Attendant who carries off Lepidus.]

MENAS   Why?

ENOBARBUS
'A bears the third part of the world, man. Seest not?   90

MENAS
The third part then he is drunk. Would it were all,

That it might go on wheels!

ENOBARBUS   Drink thou! Increase the reels!

MENAS   Come!

95 POMPEY   This is not yet an Alexandrian feast.

ANTONY   It ripens towards it. Strike the vessels, ho!
Here's to Caesar!

CAESAR   I could well forbear't.
It's monstrous labour when I wash my brain
And it grows fouler.

ANTONY   Be a child o'th' time.

100 CAESAR   'Possess it', I'll make answer.
But I had rather fast from all, four days,
Than drink so much in one.

ENOBARBUS [*to Antony*]   Ha, my brave emperor,
Shall we dance now the Egyptian Bacchanals
And celebrate our drink?

POMPEY   Let's ha't, good soldier.

105 ANTONY   Come, let's all take hands
Till that the conquering wine hath steeped our sense
In soft and delicate Lethe.

ENOBARBUS   All take hands.
Make battery to our ears with the loud music,
The while I'll place you; then the boy shall sing.

110 The holding every man shall beat as loud
As his strong sides can volley.
     [*Music plays. Enobarbus places them hand in hand.*]
                    The Song.

BOY   Come, thou monarch of the vine,
                 Plumpy Bacchus with pink eyne!
                 In thy vats our cares be drowned;

115   With thy grapes our hairs be crowned.

ALL   Cup us till the world go round!
                 Cup us till the world go round!

CAESAR
What would you more? Pompey, good night. Good
     brother,
Let me request you off. Our graver business

120 Frowns at this levity. Gentle lords, let's part.
You see we have burnt our cheeks. Strong Enobarb
Is weaker than the wine, and mine own tongue
Splits what it speaks. The wild disguise hath
     almost
Anticked us all. What needs more words? Good night.

125 Good Antony, your hand.

POMPEY   I'll try you on the shore.

ANTONY   And shall, sir. Give's your hand.

POMPEY   O, Antony, you have my father's house.
But what? We are friends! Come down into the boat.

ENOBARBUS   Take heed you fall not.
                    Exeunt all but Enobarbus and Menas.
                         Menas, I'll not on shore.

130 MENAS
No, to my cabin! These drums, these trumpets, flutes!
     What!
Let Neptune hear we bid a loud farewell
To these great fellows. Sound and be hanged!
Sound out!   [*Sound a flourish with drums.*]

ENOBARBUS   Hoo, says 'a! There's my cap! [*Flings his
cap in the air.*]

MENAS   Hoo! Noble captain, come!   *Exeunt.*   135

3.1   *Enter* VENTIDIUS *as it were in triumph, with*
          SILIUS *and other Romans, Officers and Soldiers,*
          the dead body of Pacorus borne before him.

VENTIDIUS
Now, darting Parthia, art thou struck, and now
Pleased Fortune does of Marcus Crassus' death
Make me revenger. Bear the King's son's body
Before our army. Thy Pacorus, Orodes,
Pays this for Marcus Crassus.

SILIUS   Noble Ventidius,   5
Whilst yet with Parthian blood thy sword is warm,
The fugitive Parthians follow. Spur through Media,
Mesopotamia, and the shelters whither
The routed fly. So thy grand captain Antony
Shall set thee on triumphant chariots and   10
Put garlands on thy head.

VENTIDIUS   O Silius, Silius,
I have done enough. A lower place, note well,
May make too great an act. For learn this, Silius:
Better to leave undone than, by our deed,
Acquire too high a fame when him we serve's away.   15
Caesar and Antony have ever won
More in their officer than person. Sossius,
One of my place in Syria, his lieutenant,
For quick accumulation of renown,
Which he achieved by th' minute, lost his favour.   20
Who does i'th' wars more than his captain can,
Becomes his captain's captain; and ambition,
The soldier's virtue, rather makes choice of loss
Than gain which darkens him.
I could do more to do Antonius good,   25
But 'twould offend him, and in his offence
Should my performance perish.

SILIUS
Thou hast, Ventidius, that
Without the which a soldier and his sword
Grants scarce distinction. Thou wilt write to
     Antony?   30

VENTIDIUS   I'll humbly signify what in his name,
That magical word of war, we have effected;
How, with his banners and his well-paid ranks,
The ne'er-yet-beaten horse of Parthia
We have jaded out o'th' field.

SILIUS   Where is he now?   35

VENTIDIUS
He purposeth to Athens, whither, with what haste
The weight we must convey with's will permit,
We shall appear before him. On there! Pass along!
                         Exeunt.

3.2   *Enter* AGRIPPA *at one door,*
               ENOBARBUS *at another.*

AGRIPPA   What, are the brothers parted?
ENOBARBUS
       They have dispatched with Pompey; he is gone.
       The other three are sealing. Octavia weeps
       To part from Rome; Caesar is sad, and Lepidus
5   Since Pompey's feast, as Menas says, is troubled
       With the green-sickness.
       AGRIPPA   'Tis a noble Lepidus.
ENOBARBUS   A very fine one. O, how he loves Caesar!
AGRIPPA   Nay, but how dearly he adores Mark Antony!
ENOBARBUS   Caesar? Why he's the Jupiter of men!
10   AGRIPPA   What's Antony? The god of Jupiter!
ENOBARBUS   Spake you of Caesar? Hoo! The nonpareil!
AGRIPPA   O Antony! O thou Arabian bird!
ENOBARBUS
       Would you praise Caesar, say 'Caesar'. Go no further.
AGRIPPA
       Indeed, he plied them both with excellent praises.
ENOBARBUS
15   But he loves Caesar best. Yet he loves Antony.
       Hoo! Hearts, tongues, figures, scribes, bards, poets,
             cannot
       Think, speak, cast, write, sing, number – hoo! –
       His love to Antony! But as for Caesar,
       Kneel down, kneel down, and wonder!
AGRIPPA   Both he loves.
ENOBARBUS
20   They are his shards and he their beetle.
                                    [*Trumpet within.*]
                                    So,
       This is to horse. Adieu, noble Agrippa.
AGRIPPA   Good fortune, worthy soldier, and farewell.

       Enter CAESAR, ANTONY, LEPIDUS *and* OCTAVIA.

ANTONY   No further, sir.
CAESAR   You take from me a great part of myself.
25   Use me well in't. Sister, prove such a wife
       As my thoughts make thee, and as my farthest bond
       Shall pass on thy approof. Most noble Antony,
       Let not the piece of virtue which is set
       Betwixt us, as the cement of our love
30   To keep it builded, be the ram to batter
       The fortress of it. For better might we
       Have loved without this mean, if on both parts
       This be not cherished.
ANTONY   Make me not offended
       In your distrust.
CAESAR   I have said.
ANTONY   You shall not find,
35   Though you be therein curious, the least cause
       For what you seem to fear. So the gods keep you,
       And make the hearts of Romans serve your ends.
       We will here part.
CAESAR   Farewell, my dearest sister, fare thee well.

       The elements be kind to thee, and make   40
       Thy spirits all of comfort! Fare thee well.
OCTAVIA   My noble brother! [*She weeps.*]
ANTONY   The April's in her eyes; it is love's spring
       And these the showers to bring it on. Be cheerful.
OCTAVIA   Sir, look well to my husband's house, and –   45
CAESAR   What, Octavia?
OCTAVIA   I'll tell you in yur ear.
       [*She whispers to Caesar.*]
ANTONY   Her tongue will not obey her heart, nor can
       Her heart inform her tongue – the swan's-down feather
       That stands upon the swell at full of tide,
       And neither way inclines.   50
ENOBARBUS [*aside to Agrippa*]
       Will Caesar weep?
AGRIPPA [*aside to Enobarbus*]   He has a cloud in's face.
ENOBARBUS [*aside to Agrippa*]
       He were the worse for that were he a horse;
       So is he, being a man.
AGRIPPA [*aside to Enobarbus*]   Why, Enobarbus,
       When Antony found Julius Caesar dead,
       He cried almost to roaring, and he wept   55
       When at Philippi he found Brutus slain.
ENOBARBUS [*aside to Agrippa*]
       That year, indeed, he was troubled with a rheum.
       What willingly he did confound he wailed,
       Believe't, till I wept too.
CAESAR   No, sweet Octavia,
       You shall hear from me still. The time shall not   60
       Outgo my thinking on you.
ANTONY   Come, sir, come,
       I'll wrestle with you in my strength of love.
       Look, here I have you [*embracing him*]; thus I let you
             go,
       And give you to the gods.
CAESAR   Adieu. Be happy!
LEPIDUS   Let all the number of the stars give light   65
       To thy fair way!
CAESAR   Farewell, farewell!   [*Kisses Octavia.*]
ANTONY   Farewell!
                          Trumpets sound. Exeunt.

3.3   *Enter* CLEOPATRA, CHARMIAN,
               IRAS *and* ALEXAS.

CLEOPATRA   Where is the fellow?
ALEXAS   Half afeard to come.
CLEOPATRA
       Go to, go to.

                  Enter the Messenger *as before.*

                      Come hither, sir.
ALEXAS   Good majesty,
       Herod of Jewry dare not look upon you
       But when you are well pleased.
CLEOPATRA   That Herod's head

I'll have! But how, when Antony is gone,
Through whom I might command it? – Come thou
   near.
MESSENGER   Most gracious majesty!
CLEOPATRA   Didst thou behold
Octavia?
MESSENGER   Ay, dread queen.
CLEOPATRA   Where?
MESSENGER   Madam, in Rome.
I looked her in the face, and saw her led
Between her brother and Mark Antony.
CLEOPATRA   Is she as tall as me?
MESSENGER   She is not, madam.
CLEOPATRA
Didst hear her speak? Is she shrill-tongued or low?
MESSENGER
Madam, I heard her speak; she is low-voiced.
CLEOPATRA
That's not so good. He cannot like her long.
CHARMIAN   Like her? O Isis! 'Tis impossible.
CLEOPATRA
I think so, Charmian. Dull of tongue and dwarfish.
What majesty is in her gait? Remember,
If e'er thou look'dst on majesty.
MESSENGER   She creeps.
Her motion and her station are as one.
She shows a body rather than a life,
A statue than a breather.
CLEOPATRA   Is this certain?
MESSENGER
Or I have no observance.
CHARMIAN   Three in Egypt
Cannot make better note.
CLEOPATRA   He's very knowing;
I do perceiv't. There's nothing in her yet.
The fellow has good judgement.
CHARMIAN   Excellent.
CLEOPATRA   Guess at her years, I prithee.
MESSENGER   Madam,
She was a widow –
CLEOPATRA   Widow? Charmian, hark!
MESSENGER   And I do think she's thirty.
CLEOPATRA
Bear'st thou her face in mind? Is't long or round?
MESSENGER   Round, even to faultiness.
CLEOPATRA
For the most part, too, they are foolish that are so.
Her hair, what colour?
MESSENGER   Brown, madam, and her forehead
As low as she would wish it.
CLEOPATRA   There's gold for thee.
Thou must not take my former sharpness ill.
I will employ thee back again; I find thee
Most fit for business. Go, make thee ready;
Our letters are prepared.   *Exit Messenger.*
CHARMIAN   A proper man.
CLEOPATRA   Indeed, he is so. I repent me much

That so I harried him. Why methinks, by him,
This creature's no such thing.
CHARMIAN   Nothing, madam.
CLEOPATRA
The man hath seen some majesty, and should know.
CHARMIAN   Hath he seen majesty? Isis else defend,
And serving you so long!
CLEOPATRA
I have one thing more to ask him yet, good Charmian.
But 'tis no matter; thou shalt bring him to me
Where I will write. All may be well enough.
CHARMIAN   I warrant you, madam.   *Exeunt.*

3.4   *Enter* ANTONY *and* OCTAVIA.

ANTONY   Nay, nay, Octavia, not only that.
That were excusable – that, and thousands more
Of semblable import – but he hath waged
New wars 'gainst Pompey; made his will, and read it
To public ear;
Spoke scantly of me; when perforce he could not
But pay me terms of honour, cold and sickly
He vented them; most narrow measure lent me;
When the best hint was given him, he not took't,
Or did it from his teeth.
OCTAVIA   O, my good lord,
Believe not all, or if you must believe,
Stomach not all. A more unhappy lady,
If this division chance, ne'er stood between,
Praying for both parts.
The good gods will mock me presently
When I shall pray 'O, bless my lord and husband!';
Undo that prayer by crying out as loud
'O, bless my brother!' Husband win, win brother,
Prays and destroys the prayer; no midway
'Twixt these extremes at all.
ANTONY   Gentle Octavia,
Let your best love draw to that point which seeks
Best to preserve it. If I lose mine honour,
I lose myself; better I were not yours
Than yours so branchless. But, as you requested,
Yourself shall go between's. The meantime, lady,
I'll raise the preparation of a war
Shall stain your brother. Make your soonest haste,
So your desires are yours.
OCTAVIA   Thanks to my lord.
The Jove of power make me, most weak, most weak,
Your reconciler! Wars 'twixt you twain would be
As if the world should cleave, and that slain men
Should solder up the rift.
ANTONY   When it appears to you where this begins,
Turn your displeasure that way, for our faults
Can never be so equal that your love
Can equally move with them. Provide your going;
Choose your own company, and command what cost
Your heart has mind to.   *Exeunt.*

3.5 *Enter* ENOBARBUS *and* EROS, *meeting.*

ENOBARBUS   How now, friend Eros?

EROS   There's strange news come, sir.

ENOBARBUS   What, man?

EROS   Caesar and Lepidus have made wars upon
5   Pompey.

ENOBARBUS   This is old. What is the success?

EROS   Caesar, having made use of him in the wars 'gainst
     Pompey, presently denied him rivality; would not let
     him partake in the glory of the action, and, not resting
10   here, accuses him of letters he had formerly wrote to
     Pompey; upon his own appeal, seizes him. So the poor
     third is up, till death enlarge his confine.

ENOBARBUS
     Then, world, thou hast a pair of chaps, no more,
     And throw between them all the food thou hast,
15   They'll grind the one the other. Where's Antony?

EROS   He's walking in the garden, thus, and spurns
     The rush that lies before him; cries, 'Fool Lepidus!',
     And threats the throat of that his officer
     That murdered Pompey.

ENOBARBUS   Our great navy's rigged.

20 EROS   For Italy and Caesar. More, Domitius:
     My lord desires you presently. My news
     I might have told hereafter.

ENOBARBUS   'Twill be naught,
     But let it be. Bring me to Antony.

EROS   Come, sir.   *Exeunt.*

3.6   *Enter* AGRIPPA, MAECENAS *and* CAESAR.

CAESAR
     Contemning Rome, he has done all this, and more
     In Alexandria. Here's the manner of 't:
     I'th' market-place, on a tribunal silvered,
     Cleopatra and himself in chairs of gold
5   Were publicly enthroned. At the feet sat
     Caesarion, whom they call my father's son,
     And all the unlawful issue that their lust
     Since then hath made between them. Unto her
     He gave the stablishment of Egypt; made her
10   Of lower Syria, Cyprus, Lydia,
     Absolute Queen.

MAECENAS   This in the public eye?

CAESAR   I'th' common showplace where they exercise.
     His sons he there proclaimed the kings of kings:
     Great Media, Parthia and Armenia
15   He gave to Alexander; to Ptolemy he assigned
     Syria, Cilicia and Phoenicia. She
     In th'habiliments of the goddess Isis
     That day appeared, and oft before gave audience,
     As 'tis reported, so.

20 MAECENAS   Let Rome be thus informed.

AGRIPPA   Who, queasy with his insolence already,
     Will their good thoughts call from him.

CAESAR   The people knows it, and have now received

His accusations.

AGRIPPA   Who does he accuse?

CAESAR   Caesar; and that having in Sicily   25
     Sextus Pompeius spoiled, we had not rated him
     His part o'th' isle. Then does he say he lent me
     Some shipping, unrestored. Lastly, he frets
     That Lepidus of the triumvirate
     Should be deposed and, being that we detain   30
     All his revenue.

AGRIPPA   Sir, this should be answered.

CAESAR
     'Tis done already, and the messenger gone.
     I have told him Lepidus was grown too cruel,
     That he his high authority abused
     And did deserve his change. For what I have conquered, 35
     I grant him part; but then in his Armenia
     And other of his conquered kingdoms, I
     Demand the like.

MAECENAS   He'll never yield to that.

CAESAR   Nor must not then be yielded to in this.

Enter OCTAVIA *with her train.*

OCTAVIA
     Hail, Caesar, and my lord! Hail, most dear Caesar!   40

CAESAR   That ever I should call thee castaway!

OCTAVIA
     You have not called me so, nor have you cause.

CAESAR
     Why have you stolen upon us thus? You come not
     Like Caesar's sister. The wife of Antony
     Should have an army for an usher, and   45
     The neighs of horse to tell of her approach
     Long ere she did appear. The trees by th' way
     Should have borne men, and expectation fainted,
     Longing for what it had not. Nay, the dust
     Should have ascended to the roof of heaven,   50
     Raised by your populous troops. But you are come
     A market maid to Rome, and have prevented
     The ostentation of our love which, left unshown,
     Is often left unloved. We should have met you
     By sea and land, supplying every stage   55
     With an augmented greeting.

OCTAVIA   Good my lord,
     To come thus was I not constrained, but did it
     On my free will. My lord, Mark Antony,
     Hearing that you prepared for war, acquainted
     My grieved ear withal, whereon I begged   60
     His pardon for return.

CAESAR   Which soon he granted,
     Being an abstract 'tween his lust and him.

OCTAVIA   Do not say so, my lord.

CAESAR   I have eyes upon him,
     And his affairs come to me on the wind.
     Where is he now?

OCTAVIA   My lord, in Athens.

CAESAR   No,   65
     My most wronged sister. Cleopatra hath

Nodded him to her. He hath given his empire
Up to a whore, who now are levying
The kings o'th' earth for war. He hath assembled
70   Bocchus the King of Libya, Archelaus
Of Cappadocia, Philadelphos King
Of Paphlagonia, the Thracian King Adallas,
King Manchus of Arabia, King of Pont,
Herod of Jewry, Mithridates King
75   Of Comagene, Polemon and Amyntas,
The Kings of Mede and Lycaonia,
With a more larger list of sceptres.
OCTAVIA   Ay me, most wretched,
That have my heart parted betwixt two friends
That does afflict each other!
80   CAESAR   Welcome hither.
Your letters did withhold our breaking forth
Till we perceived both how you were wrong led
And we in negligent danger. Cheer your heart.
Be you not troubled with the time, which drives
85   O'er your content these strong necessities,
But let determined things to destiny
Hold unbewailed their way. Welcome to Rome,
Nothing more dear to me! You are abused
Beyond the mark of thought, and the high gods,
90   To do you justice, makes his ministers
Of us and those that love you. Best of comfort,
And ever welcome to us.
AGRIPPA   Welcome, lady.
MAECENAS   Welcome, dear madam.
Each heart in Rome does love and pity you.
95   Only th'adulterous Antony, most large
In his abominations, turns you off
And gives his potent regiment to a trull
That noises it against us.
OCTAVIA   Is it so, sir?
CAESAR   Most certain. Sister, welcome. Pray you
100 Be ever known to patience. My dear'st sister! *Exeunt.*

3.7   *Enter* CLEOPATRA *and* ENOBARBUS.

CLEOPATRA   I will be even with thee, doubt it not.
ENOBARBUS   But why, why, why?
CLEOPATRA
Thou hast forspoke my being in these wars
And say'st it is not fit.
ENOBARBUS   Well, is it, is it?
CLEOPATRA
5   Is't not denounced against us? Why should not we
Be there in person?
ENOBARBUS   Well, I could reply
If we should serve with horse and mares together,
The horse were merely lost. The mares would bear
A soldier and his horse.
CLEOPATRA   What is't you say?
10   ENOBARBUS   Your presence needs must puzzle Antony,
Take from his heart, take from his brain, from's time
What should not then be spared. He is already

Traduced for levity, and 'tis said in Rome
That Photinus, an eunuch and your maids
Manage this war.
CLEOPATRA   Sink Rome, and their tongues rot   15
That speak against us! A charge we bear i'th' war,
And, as the president of my kingdom, will
Appear there for a man. Speak not against it!
I will not stay behind.

Enter ANTONY *and* CANIDIUS.

ENOBARBUS   Nay, I have done.
Here comes the Emperor.
ANTONY   Is it not strange, Canidius,   20
That from Tarentum and Brundusium
He could so quickly cut the Ionian sea
And take in Toryne? You have heard on't, sweet?
CLEOPATRA   Celerity is never more admired
Than by the negligent.
ANTONY   A good rebuke,   25
Which might have well becomed the best of men,
To taunt at slackness. Canidius, we
Will fight with him by sea.
CLEOPATRA   By sea – what else?
CANIDIUS   Why will my lord do so?
ANTONY   For that he dares us to't.
ENOBARBUS   So hath my lord dared him to single fight.   30
CANIDIUS   Ay, and to wage this battle at Pharsalia,
Where Caesar fought with Pompey. But these offers,
Which serve not for his vantage, he shakes off,
And so should you.
ENOBARBUS   Your ships are not well manned,
Your mariners are muleteers, reapers, people   35
Engrossed by swift impress. In Caesar's fleet
Are those that often have 'gainst Pompey fought;
Their ships are yare, yours heavy. No disgrace
Shall fall you for refusing him at sea,
Being prepared for land.
ANTONY   By sea, by sea.   40
ENOBARBUS   Most worthy sir, you therein throw away
The absolute soldiership you have by land;
Distract your army, which doth most consist
Of war-marked footmen; leave unexecuted
Your own renowned knowledge; quite forgo   45
The way which promises assurance; and
Give up yourself merely to chance and hazard
From firm security.
ANTONY   I'll fight at sea.
CLEOPATRA   I have sixty sails, Caesar none better.
ANTONY   Our overplus of shipping will we burn,   50
And with the rest full-manned, from th'head of Actium
Beat th'approaching Caesar. But if we fail,
We then can do't at land.

Enter a Messenger.

             Thy business?
MESSENGER   The news is true, my lord; he is descried.
Caesar has taken Toryne.   55

ANTONY   Can he be there in person? 'Tis impossible;
Strange that his power should be. Canidius,
Our nineteen legions thou shalt hold by land
And our twelve thousand horse. We'll to our ship.
Away, my Thetis!

Enter a Soldier.

60   How now, worthy soldier?
SOLDIER   O noble Emperor, do not fight by sea.
Trust not to rotten planks. Do you misdoubt
This sword and these my wounds? Let th'Egyptians
And the Phoenicians go a-ducking; we
65   Have used to conquer standing on the earth
And fighting foot to foot.
ANTONY   Well, well, away!

Exeunt Antony, Cleopatra and Enobarbus.

SOLDIER   By Hercules, I think I am i'th' right.
CANIDIUS
Soldier, thou art. But his whole action grows
Not in the power on't. So our leader's led,
And we are women's men.
70   SOLDIER   You keep by land
The legions and the horse whole, do you not?
CANIDIUS   Marcus Octavius, Marcus Justeius,
Publicola and Caelius are for sea,
But we keep whole by land. This speed of Caesar's
Carries beyond belief.
75   SOLDIER   While he was yet in Rome,
His power went out in such distractions as
Beguiled all spies.
CANIDIUS   Who's his lieutenant, hear you?
SOLDIER   They say one Taurus.
CANIDIUS   Well I know the man.

Enter a Messenger.

MESSENGER   The Emperor calls Canidius.
CANIDIUS
80   With news the time's in labour, and throws forth
Each minute some.   *Exeunt.*

3.8   *Enter* CAESAR *and* TAURUS *with his
army, marching.*

CAESAR   Taurus!
TAURUS   My lord?
CAESAR
Strike not by land; keep whole; provoke not battle
Till we have done at sea. Do not exceed
The prescript of this scroll.   [*Gives him a scroll.*]
5   Our fortune lies
Upon this jump.   *Exeunt.*

3.9   *Enter* ANTONY *and* ENOBARBUS.

ANTONY   Set we our squadrons on yond side o'th' hill
In eye of Caesar's battle, from which place

We may the number of the ships behold
And so proceed accordingly.   *Exeunt.*

3.10   CANIDIUS *marcheth with his land army one
way over the stage, and* TAURUS, *the lieutenant
of Caesar, the other way. After their going in, is
heard the noise of a sea fight.*

Alarum. Enter ENOBARBUS.

ENOBARBUS
Naught, naught, all naught! I can behold no longer!
Th'Antoniad, the Egyptian admiral,
With all their sixty, fly and turn the rudder.
To see't mine eyes are blasted.

Enter SCARUS.

SCARUS   Gods and goddesses!
All the whole synod of them!
ENOBARBUS   What's thy passion?   5
SCARUS   The greater cantle of the world is lost
With very ignorance. We have kissed away
Kingdoms and provinces.
ENOBARBUS   How appears the fight?
SCARUS   On our side, like the tokened pestilence
Where death is sure. Yon ribaudred nag of Egypt –   10
Whom leprosy o'ertake! – i'th' midst o'th' fight
When vantage like a pair of twins appeared
Both as the same – or, rather, ours the elder –
The breeze upon her, like a cow in June,
Hoists sails and flies.   15
ENOBARBUS   That I beheld.
Mine eyes did sicken at the sight and could not
Endure a further view.
SCARUS   She once being loofed,
The noble ruin of her magic, Antony,
Claps on his sea-wing and, like a doting mallard, 20
Leaving the fight in height, flies after her.
I never saw an action of such shame.
Experience, manhood, honour, ne'er before
Did violate so itself.
ENOBARBUS   Alack, alack!

Enter CANIDIUS.

CANIDIUS   Our fortune on the sea is out of breath   25
And sinks most lamentably. Had our general
Been what he knew – himself – it had gone well.
Oh, he has given example for our flight
Most grossly by his own!
ENOBARBUS   Ay, are you thereabouts?
Why then, good night indeed.   30
CANIDIUS   Toward Peloponnesus are they fled.
SCARUS   'Tis easy to't, and there I will attend
What further comes.
CANIDIUS   To Caesar will I render
My legions and my horse. Six kings already
Show me the way of yielding.

ENOBARBUS   I'll yet follow
The wounded chance of Antony, though my reason
Sits in the wind against me.

Exit at one door Canidius, at the other
Scarus and Enobarbus.

3.11   *Enter* ANTONY *with Attendants.*

ANTONY
Hark! The land bids me tread no more upon't;
It is ashamed to bear me. Friends, come hither.
I am so lated in the world that I
Have lost my way for ever. I have a ship
Laden with gold. Take that, divide it. Fly
And make your peace with Caesar.

ALL   Fly? Not we.

ANTONY
I have fled myself and have instructed cowards
To run and show their shoulders. Friends, be gone.
I have myself resolved upon a course
Which has no need of you. Be gone.
My treasure's in the harbour. Take it. O,
I followed that I blush to look upon.
My very hairs do mutiny, for the white
Reprove the brown for rashness, and they them
For fear and doting. Friends, be gone. You shall
Have letters from me to some friends that will
Sweep your way for you. Pray you, look not sad
Nor make replies of loathness; take the hint
Which my despair proclaims. Let that be left
Which leaves itself. To the sea-side straightway.
I will possess you of that ship and treasure.
Leave me, I pray, a little – pray you, now;
Nay, do so; for indeed I have lost command;
Therefore, I pray you. I'll see you by and by.

Exeunt Attendants. Antony sits down.

Enter CLEOPATRA *led by* CHARMIAN, IRAS *and* EROS.

EROS   Nay, gentle madam, to him! Comfort him.
IRAS   Do, most dear queen.
CHARMIAN   Do? Why, what else?
CLEOPATRA   Let me sit down. O, Juno!
ANTONY   No, no, no, no, no!
EROS   See you here, sir?
ANTONY   O fie, fie, fie!
CHARMIAN   Madam!
IRAS   Madam! O, good empress!
EROS   Sir, sir!
ANTONY   Yes, my lord, yes. He at Philippi kept
His sword e'en like a dancer, while I struck
The lean and wrinkled Cassius, and 'twas I
That the mad Brutus ended. He alone
Dealt on lieutenantry, and no practice had
In the brave squares of war. Yet now – no matter.
CLEOPATRA   Ah, stand by.
EROS   The Queen, my lord! The Queen!
IRAS   Go to him, madam; speak to him.

He is unqualited with very shame.
CLEOPATRA   Well then, sustain me. Oh!
EROS   Most noble sir, arise. The Queen approaches.
Her head's declined, and death will seize her but
Your comfort makes the rescue.
ANTONY   I have offended reputation,
A most unnoble swerving.
EROS   Sir, the Queen!
ANTONY   O, whither hast thou led me, Egypt? See
How I convey my shame out of thine eyes
By looking back what I have left behind
'Stroyed in dishonour.
CLEOPATRA   O, my lord, my lord,
Forgive my fearful sails! I little thought
You would have followed.
ANTONY   Egypt, thou knewst too well
My heart was to thy rudder tied by th' strings
And thou shouldst tow me after. O'er my spirit
Thy full supremacy thou knewst, and that
Thy beck might from the bidding of the gods
Command me.
CLEOPATRA   O, my pardon!
ANTONY   Now I must
To the young man send humble treaties; dodge
And palter in the shifts of lowness, who
With half the bulk o'th' world played as I pleased,
Making and marring fortunes. You did know
How much you were my conqueror, and that
My sword, made weak by my affection, would
Obey it on all cause.
CLEOPATRA   Pardon, pardon!
ANTONY   Fall not a tear, I say; one of them rates
All that is won and lost. Give me a kiss.   [*They kiss.*]
Even this repays me.
We sent our schoolmaster. Is a come back?
Love, I am full of lead. Some wine
Within there and our viands! Fortune knows
We scorn her most when most she offers blows.

Exeunt.

3.12   *Enter* CAESAR, AGRIPPA, DOLABELLA
and THIDIAS *with others.*

CAESAR   Let him appear that's come from Antony.
Know you him?
DOLABELLA   Caesar, 'tis his schoolmaster;
An argument that he is plucked, when hither
He sends so poor a pinion of his wing,
Which had superfluous kings for messengers
Not many moons gone by.

Enter Ambassador *from Antony.*

CAESAR   Approach, and speak.
AMBASSADOR   Such as I am, I come from Antony.
I was of late as petty to his ends
As is the morn-dew on the myrtle leaf
To his grand sea.

10   CAESAR   Be't so. Declare thine office.

       AMBASSADOR   Lord of his fortunes he salutes thee, and
          Requires to live in Egypt; which not granted,
          He lessens his requests and to thee sues
          To let him breathe between the heavens and earth,
15   A private man in Athens. This for him.
          Next, Cleopatra does confess thy greatness,
          Submits her to thy might, and of thee craves
          The circle of the Ptolemies for her heirs,
          Now hazarded to thy grace.

       CAESAR   For Antony,
20   I have no ears to his request. The Queen
          Of audience nor desire shall fail, so she
          From Egypt drive her all-disgraced friend
          Or take his life there. This if she perform,
          She shall not sue unheard. So to them both.

       AMBASSADOR   Fortune pursue thee!

25   CAESAR   Bring him through the bands.
                           Exit Ambassador, attended.
       [*to Thidias*] To try thy eloquence now 'tis time.
          Dispatch.
       From Antony win Cleopatra; promise,
       And in our name, what she requires; add more,
       From thine invention, offers. Women are not
30   In their best fortunes strong, but want will perjure
       The ne'er-touch'd vestal. Try thy cunning, Thidias;
       Make thine own edict for thy pains, which we
       Will answer as a law.

       THIDIAS   Caesar, I go.

       CAESAR   Observe how Antony becomes his flaw,
35   And what thou think'st his very action speaks
       In every power that moves.

       THIDIAS   Caesar, I shall.   *Exeunt.*

       3.13   *Enter* CLEOPATRA, ENOBARBUS,
                  CHARMIAN *and* IRAS.

       CLEOPATRA   What shall we do, Enobarbus?

       ENOBARBUS   Think, and die.

       CLEOPATRA   Is Antony or we in fault for this?

       ENOBARBUS   Antony only, that would make his will
       Lord of his reason. What though you fled
5   From that great face of war, whose several ranges
       Frighted each other? Why should he follow?
       The itch of his affection should not then
       Have nicked his captainship, at such a point,
       When half to half the world opposed, he being
10   The mered question. 'Twas a shame no less
       Than was his loss, to course your flying flags
       And leave his navy gazing.

       CLEOPATRA   Prithee, peace.

          Enter the Ambassador *with* ANTONY.

       ANTONY   Is that his answer?

       AMBASSADOR   Ay, my lord.

15   ANTONY   The Queen shall then have courtesy, so she
       Will yield us up.

       AMBASSADOR   He says so.

       ANTONY   Let her know't.
       To the boy Caesar send this grizzled head,
       And he will fill thy wishes to the brim
       With principalities.

       CLEOPATRA   That head, my lord?

       ANTONY   To him again! Tell him he wears the rose   20
       Of youth upon him, from which the world should note
       Something particular. His coin, ships, legions,
       May be a coward's, whose ministers would prevail
       Under the service of a child as soon
       As i'th' command of Caesar. I dare him therefore   25
       To lay his gay caparisons apart
       And answer me declined, sword against sword,
       Ourselves alone. I'll write it. Follow me.
                    Exeunt Antony and Ambassador.

       ENOBARBUS [*aside*]
       Yes, like enough high-battled Caesar will
       Unstate his happiness, and be staged to th' show   30
       Against a sworder! I see men's judgements are
       A parcel of their fortunes, and things outward
       Do draw the inward quality after them
       To suffer all alike. That he should dream,
       Knowing all measures, the full Caesar will   35
       Answer his emptiness! Caesar, thou hast subdued
       His judgement too.

                 Enter a Servant.

       SERVANT   A messenger from Caesar.

       CLEOPATRA
       What, no more ceremony? See, my women,
       Against the blown rose they may stop their nose   40
       That kneeled unto the buds. Admit him, sir.
                    Exit Servant.

       ENOBARBUS [*aside*]
       Mine honesty and I begin to square.
       The loyalty well held to fools does make
       Our faith mere folly. Yet he that can endure
       To follow with allegiance a fallen lord   45
       Does conquer him that did his master conquer,
       And earns a place i'th' story.

                   Enter THIDIAS.

       CLEOPATRA   Caesar's will?

       THIDIAS   Hear it apart.

       CLEOPATRA   None but friends. Say boldly.   50

       THIDIAS   So haply are they friends to Antony.

       ENOBARBUS   He needs as many, sir, as Caesar has,
       Or needs not us. If Caesar please, our master
       Will leap to be his friend. For us, you know,
       Whose he is we are, and that is Caesar's.

       THIDIAS   So.   55
       Thus then, thou most renowned: Caesar entreats
       Not to consider in what case thou stand'st
       Further than he is Caesar.

       CLEOPATRA   Go on; right royal.

THIDIAS   He knows that you embrace not Antony
As you did love, but as you feared him.

60 CLEOPATRA   Oh!

THIDIAS   The scars upon your honour, therefore, he
Does pity as constrained blemishes,
Not as deserved.

CLEOPATRA   He is a god and knows
What is most right. Mine honour was not yielded
65 But conquered merely.

ENOBARBUS [*aside*]
To be sure of that, I will ask Antony.
Sir, sir, thou art so leaky
That we must leave thee to thy sinking, for
Thy dearest quit thee.   *Exit Enobarbus.*

THIDIAS   Shall I say to Caesar
70 What you require of him? For he partly begs
To be desired to give. It much would please him
That of his fortunes you should make a staff
To lean upon. But it would warm his spirits
To hear from me you had left Antony
75 And put yourself under his shroud,
The universal landlord.

CLEOPATRA   What's your name?

THIDIAS   My name is Thidias.

CLEOPATRA   Most kind messenger,
Say to great Caesar this in deputation:
I kiss his conqu'ring hand. Tell him I am prompt
80 To lay my crown at's feet, and there to kneel
Till from his all-obeying breath I hear
The doom of Egypt.

THIDIAS   'Tis your noblest course.
Wisdom and fortune combating together,
If that the former dare but what it can,
85 No chance may shake it. Give me grace to lay
My duty on your hand.

CLEOPATRA [*Offers him her hand.*]
Your Caesar's father oft,
When he hath mused of taking kingdoms in,
Bestowed his lips on that unworthy place
As it rained kisses.

Enter ANTONY *and* ENOBARBUS.

90 ANTONY   Favours? By Jove that thunders!
What art thou, fellow?

THIDIAS   One that but performs
The bidding of the fullest man and worthiest
To have command obeyed.

ENOBARBUS [*aside*]   You will be whipped.

ANTONY [*Calls for Servants.*]
Approach there! – Ah, you kite! – Now, gods and devils,
95 Authority melts from me. Of late when I cried 'Ho!',
Like boys unto a muss, kings would start forth
And cry 'Your will?'

Enter Servants.

Have you no ears? I am
Antony yet. Take hence the jack and whip him!

ENOBARBUS [*aside*]
'Tis better playing with a lion's whelp
Than with an old one dying.

ANTONY   Moon and stars!   100
Whip him! Were't twenty of the greatest tributaries
That do acknowledge Caesar, should I find them
So saucy with the hand of she here – what's her name
Since she was Cleopatra? Whip him, fellows,
Till like a boy you see him cringe his face   105
And whine aloud for mercy. Take him hence!

THIDIAS   Mark Antony –

ANTONY   Tug him away! Being whipped,
Bring him again. The jack of Caesar's shall
Bear us an errand to him.

Exeunt Servants with Thidias.
You were half blasted ere I knew you. Ha?   110
Have I my pillow left unpressed in Rome,
Forborne the getting of a lawful race,
And by a gem of women, to be abused
By one that looks on feeders?

CLEOPATRA   Good my lord –

ANTONY   You have been a boggler ever.   115
But when we in our viciousness grow hard –
Oh, misery on't! – the wise gods seel our eyes,
In our own filth drop our clear judgements, make us
Adore our errors, laugh at's while we strut
To our confusion.

CLEOPATRA   Oh, is't come to this?   120

ANTONY   I found you as a morsel, cold upon
Dead Caesar's trencher – nay, you were a fragment
Of Gnaeus Pompey's, besides what hotter hours,
Unregistered in vulgar fame, you have
Luxuriously picked out. For I am sure,   125
Though you can guess what temperance should be,
You know not what it is.

CLEOPATRA   Wherefore is this?

ANTONY   To let a fellow that will take rewards
And say 'God quit you!' be familiar with
My playfellow, your hand, this kingly seal   130
And plighter of high hearts! O that I were
Upon the hill of Basan, to outroar
The horned herd! For I have savage cause,
And to proclaim it civilly were like
A haltered neck which does the hangman thank   135
For being yare about him.

Enter a Servant *with* THIDIAS.

                  Is he whipped?

SERVANT   Soundly, my lord.

ANTONY   Cried he? And begged 'a pardon?

SERVANT   He did ask favour.

ANTONY [*to Thidias*]
If that thy father live, let him repent
Thou wast not made his daughter; and be thou sorry   140
To follow Caesar in his triumph, since
Thou hast been whipped for following him. Henceforth
The white hand of a lady fever thee;

Shake thou to look on't. Get thee back to Caesar;
145 Tell him thy entertainment. Look thou say
He makes me angry with him. For he seems
Proud and disdainful, harping on what I am,
Not what he knew I was. He makes me angry,
And at this time most easy 'tis to do't,
150 When my good stars that were my former guides
Have empty left their orbs and shot their fires
Into th'abysm of hell. If he mislike
My speech and what is done, tell him he has
Hipparchus, my enfranched bondman, whom
155 He may at pleasure whip or hang or torture,
As he shall like to quit me. Urge it thou.
Hence with thy stripes! Be gone!

           Exit Thidias with Servant.

CLEOPATRA   Have you done yet?
ANTONY Alack, our terrene moon is now eclipsed
And it portends alone the fall of Antony.
160 CLEOPATRA I must stay his time.
ANTONY To flatter Caesar would you mingle eyes
   With one that ties his points?
CLEOPATRA   Not know me yet?
ANTONY Cold-hearted toward me?
CLEOPATRA   Ah, dear, if I be so,
From my cold heart let heaven engender hail
165 And poison it in the source, and the first stone
Drop in my neck; as it determines, so
Dissolve my life! The next Caesarion smite,
Till by degrees the memory of my womb,
Together with my brave Egyptians all,
170 By the discandying of this pelleted storm
Lie graveless, till the flies and gnats of Nile
Have buried them for prey!
ANTONY   I am satisfied.
Caesar sets down in Alexandria, where
I will oppose his fate. Our force by land
175 Hath nobly held; our severed navy too
Have knit again, and fleet, threat'ning most sea-like.
Where hast thou been, my heart? Dost thou hear, lady?
If from the field I shall return once more
To kiss these lips, I will appear in blood.
180 I and my sword will earn our chronicle.
There's hope in't yet.
CLEOPATRA That's my brave lord!
ANTONY I will be treble-sinewed, hearted, breathed,
And fight maliciously. For when mine hours
185 Were nice and lucky, men did ransom lives
Of me for jests. But now, I'll set my teeth
And send to darkness all that stop me. Come,
Let's have one other gaudy night. Call to me
All my sad captains. Fill our bowls once more.
Let's mock the midnight bell.
190 CLEOPATRA   It is my birthday.
I had thought t'have held it poor, but since my lord
Is Antony again, I will be Cleopatra.
ANTONY We will yet do well.
CLEOPATRA *[to Charmian and Iras]*

Call all his noble captains to my lord!
ANTONY
  Do so, we'll speak to them; and tonight I'll force   195
The wine peep through their scars. Come on, my queen,
There's sap in't yet! The next time I do fight
I'll make Death love me, for I will contend
Even with his pestilent scythe.

        Exeunt all but Enobarbus.

ENOBARBUS
  Now he'll outstare the lightning. To be furious   200
Is to be frighted out of fear, and in that mood
The dove will peck the estridge; and I see still
A diminution in our captain's brain
Restores his heart. When valour preys on reason,
It eats the sword it fights with. I will seek   205
Some way to leave him.   *Exit.*

4.1   *Enter CAESAR, AGRIPPA and MAECENAS,*
    with his army, Caesar reading a letter.

CAESAR He calls me boy, and chides as he had power
To beat me out of Egypt. My messenger
He hath whipped with rods; dares me to personal
   combat,
Caesar to Antony. Let the old ruffian know
I have many other ways to die; meantime   5
Laugh at his challenge.
MAECENAS   Caesar must think,
When one so great begins to rage, he's hunted
Even to falling. Give him no breath, but now
Make boot of his distraction. Never anger   10
Made good guard for itself.
CAESAR   Let our best heads
Know that tomorrow the last of many battles
We mean to fight. Within our files there are,
Of those that served Mark Antony but late,
Enough to fetch him in. See it done,   15
And feast the army. We have store to do't
And they have earned the waste. Poor Antony!

            Exeunt.

4.2   *Enter ANTONY, CLEOPATRA, ENOBARBUS,*
    CHARMIAN, IRAS, ALEXAS with others.

ANTONY He will not fight with me, Domitius?
ENOBARBUS   No.
ANTONY Why should he not?
ENOBARBUS
  He thinks, being twenty times of better fortune,
He is twenty men to one.
ANTONY   Tomorrow, soldier,
By sea and land I'll fight. Or I will live,   5
Or bathe my dying honour in the blood
Shall make it live again. Woo't thou fight well?
ENOBARBUS I'll strike, and cry 'Take all!'
ANTONY   Well said! Come on!

Call forth my household servants.   *Exit Alexas.*
                                   Let's tonight
Be bounteous at our meal.

                    Enter three or four Servitors.

10   Give me thy hand.
Thou hast been rightly honest; so hast thou,
Thou, and thou, and thou. You have served me well
And kings have been your fellows.
CLEOPATRA [*aside to Enobarbus*]   What means this?
ENOBARBUS [*aside to Cleopatra*]
'Tis one of those odd tricks which sorrow shoots
Out of the mind.
ANTONY   And thou art honest too.
15 I wish I could be made so many men,
And all of you clapped up together in
An Antony, that I might do you service
So good as you have done.
ALL THE SERVANTS   The gods forbid!
20 ANTONY   Well, my good fellows, wait on me tonight;
Scant not my cups, and make as much of me
As when mine empire was your fellow too
And suffered my command.
CLEOPATRA [*aside to Enobarbus*] What does he mean?
ENOBARBUS [*aside to Cleopatra*]
To make his followers weep.
ANTONY   Tend me tonight.
25 May be it is the period of your duty.
Haply you shall not see me more, or if,
A mangled shadow. Perchance tomorrow
You'll serve another master. I look on you
As one that takes his leave. Mine honest friends,
30 I turn you not away, but, like a master
Married to your good service, stay till death.
Tend me tonight two hours – I ask no more –
And the gods yield you for't!
ENOBARBUS   What mean you, sir,
To give them this discomfort? Look, they weep,
35 And I, an ass, am onion-eyed. For shame!
Transform us not to women!
ANTONY   Ho, ho, ho!
Now the witch take me if I meant it thus!
Grace grow where those drops fall! My hearty friends,
You take me in too dolorous a sense,
40 For I spake to you for your comfort, did desire you
To burn this night with torches. Know, my hearts,
I hope well of tomorrow, and will lead you
Where rather I'll expect victorious life
Than death and honour. Let's to supper, come,
45 And drown consideration.   *Exeunt.*

4.3   *Enter through one door,* First Soldier *and his*
      Company, through the other door, Second Soldier.

1 SOLDIER   Brother, good night. Tomorrow is the day.
2 SOLDIER   It will determine one way. Fare you well.

Heard you of nothing strange about the streets?
1 SOLDIER   Nothing. What news?
2 SOLDIER   Belike 'tis but a rumour. Good night to you.   5
1 SOLDIER   Well sir, good night.

      Other Soldiers *enter and join Second Soldier.*

2 SOLDIER   Soldiers, have careful watch.
3 SOLDIER   And you. Good night, good night.
            [*They place themselves in every corner of the stage.*]
2 SOLDIER   Here we. And if tomorrow
Our navy thrive, I have an absolute hope   10
Our landmen will stand up.
1 SOLDIER   'Tis a brave army and full of purpose –
            [*Music of the hautboys is under the stage.*]
2 SOLDIER   Peace! What noise?
1 SOLDIER   List, list!
2 SOLDIER   Hark!   15
1 SOLDIER   Music i'th' air.
3 SOLDIER   Under the earth.
4 SOLDIER   It signs well, does it not?
3 SOLDIER   No.
1 SOLDIER   Peace, I say! What should this mean?   20
2 SOLDIER   'Tis the god Hercules whom Antony loved
Now leaves him.
1 SOLDIER   Walk. Let's see if other watchmen
Do hear what we do.
2 SOLDIER   How now, masters? [*Speak together.*]
ALL   How now? How now? Do you hear this?   25
1 SOLDIER   Ay. Is't not strange?
3 SOLDIER   Do you hear, masters? Do you hear?
1 SOLDIER   Follow the noise so far as we have quarter.
Let's see how it will give off.
ALL   Content. 'Tis strange.
                                             Exeunt.

4.4   *Enter* ANTONY *and* CLEOPATRA *with*
       CHARMIAN *and others.*

ANTONY   Eros! Mine armour, Eros!
CLEOPATRA   Sleep a little.
ANTONY
No, my chuck. Eros! Come, mine armour, Eros!

                Enter EROS *with armour.*

Come, good fellow, put thine iron on.
If fortune be not ours today, it is
Because we brave her. Come!
CLEOPATRA   Nay, I'll help too.   5
What's this for?
ANTONY   Ah, let be, let be! Thou art
The armourer of my heart. False, false! This, this!
CLEOPATRA   Sooth, la, I'll help. Thus it must be.
ANTONY   Well, well!
We shall thrive now. Seest thou, my good fellow?
Go put on thy defences.
EROS   Briefly, sir.   10

147

CLEOPATRA   Is not this buckled well?
ANTONY   Rarely, rarely!
  He that unbuckles this, till we do please
  To doff 't for our repose, shall hear a storm.
  Thou fumblest, Eros, and my queen's a squire
15 More tight at this than thou. Dispatch. O love,
  That thou couldst see my wars today and knewst
  The royal occupation, thou shouldst see
  A workman in't.

                Enter an armed Soldier.

                  Good morrow to thee! Welcome!
  Thou look'st like him that knows a warlike charge.
20 To business that we love we rise betime
  And go to't with delight.
SOLDIER   A thousand, sir,
  Early though 't be, have on their riveted trim
  And at the port expect you.
                [*Shout. Trumpets flourish.*]

                Enter Captains *and* Soldiers.

CAPTAIN   The morn is fair. Good morrow, General!
ALL THE SOLDIERS   Good morrow, General!
25 ANTONY   'Tis well blown, lads!
  This morning, like the spirit of a youth
  That means to be of note, begins betimes.
  [*to Cleopatra*] So, so. Come, give me that. This way.
    Well said.
  Fare thee well, dame. Whate'er becomes of me,
30 This is a soldier's kiss. [*Kisses her.*] Rebukable
  And worthy shameful check it were, to stand
  On more mechanic compliment. I'll leave thee
  Now like a man of steel. – You that will fight,
  Follow me close, I'll bring you to't. Adieu.
              Exeunt all but Cleopatra and Charmian.
CHARMIAN   Please you retire to your chamber?
35 CLEOPATRA   Lead me.
  He goes forth gallantly. That he and Caesar might
  Determine this great war in single fight!
  Then Antony – but now –. Well, on.   *Exeunt.*

4.5   *Trumpets sound. Enter* ANTONY *and*
          EROS, *a Soldier meeting them.*

SOLDIER   The gods make this a happy day to Antony!
ANTONY
  Would thou and those thy scars had once prevailed
  To make me fight at land!
SOLDIER   Hadst thou done so,
  The kings that have revolted and the soldier
5 That has this morning left thee would have still
  Followed thy heels.
ANTONY   Who's gone this morning?
SOLDIER   Who?
  One ever near thee. Call for Enobarbus,
  He shall not hear thee, or from Caesar's camp
  Say 'I am none of thine.'

ANTONY   What sayest thou?
SOLDIER   Sir,
  He is with Caesar.
EROS   Sir, his chests and treasure   10
  He has not with him.
ANTONY   Is he gone?
SOLDIER   Most certain.
ANTONY   Go, Eros, send his treasure after. Do it.
  Detain no jot, I charge thee. Write to him –
  I will subscribe – gentle adieus and greetings.
  Say that I wish he never find more cause   15
  To change a master. Oh, my fortunes have
  Corrupted honest men! Dispatch. – Enobarbus!
                                        Exeunt.

4.6   *Flourish. Enter* AGRIPPA, CAESAR, *with*
              ENOBARBUS *and* DOLABELLA.

CAESAR   Go forth, Agrippa, and begin the fight.
  Our will is Antony be took alive.
  Make it so known.
AGRIPPA   Caesar, I shall.   *Exit.*
CAESAR   The time of universal peace is near.   5
  Prove this a prosp'rous day, the three-nooked world
  Shall bear the olive freely.

              Enter a Messenger.

MESSENGER   Antony
  Is come into the field.
CAESAR   Go charge Agrippa
  Plant those that have revolted in the van
  That Antony may seem to spend his fury   10
  Upon himself.   *Exeunt all but Enobarbus.*
ENOBARBUS   Alexas did revolt and went to Jewry on
  Affairs of Antony; there did dissuade
  Great Herod to incline himself to Caesar
  And leave his master Antony. For this pains   15
  Caesar hath hanged him. Canidius and the rest
  That fell away have entertainment but
  No honourable trust. I have done ill,
  Of which I do accuse myself so sorely
  That I will joy no more.   20

              Enter a Soldier *of Caesar's.*

SOLDIER   Enobarbus, Antony
  Hath after thee sent all thy treasure, with
  His bounty overplus. The messenger
  Came on my guard, and at thy tent is now
  Unloading of his mules.
ENOBARBUS   I give it you.   25
SOLDIER   Mock not, Enobarbus.
  I tell you true. Best you safed the bringer
  Out of the host. I must attend mine office
  Or would have done't myself. Your emperor
  Continues still a Jove.   *Exit.*   30
ENOBARBUS   I am alone the villain of the earth,
  And feel I am so most. O Antony,

Thou mine of bounty, how wouldst thou have
    paid
My better service, when my turpitude
35 Thou dost so crown with gold! This blows my heart.
If swift thought break it not, a swifter mean
Shall outstrike thought, but thought will do't, I feel.
I fight against thee? No, I will go seek
Some ditch wherein to die; the foul'st best fits
40 My latter part of life.   *Exit.*

4.7   *Alarum. Drums and Trumpets. Enter*
          AGRIPPA *and others.*

AGRIPPA   Retire! We have engaged ourselves too far.
Caesar himself has work, and our oppression
Exceeds what we expected.   *Exeunt.*

     Alarums. Enter ANTONY, *and*
         SCARUS *wounded.*

SCARUS   O, my brave emperor, this is fought indeed!
5 Had we done so at first, we had droven them home
With clouts about their heads.
ANTONY   Thou bleed'st apace.
SCARUS   I had a wound here that was like a T
But now 'tis made an H.   [*Sound retreat far off.*]
ANTONY   They do retire.
SCARUS   We'll beat 'em into bench-holes. I have yet
10 Room for six scotches more.

         Enter EROS.

EROS   They're beaten, sir, and our advantage serves
For a fair victory.
SCARUS   Let us score their backs
And snatch 'em up as we take hares – behind!
'Tis sport to maul a runner.
ANTONY   I will reward thee
15 Once for thy sprightly comfort, and tenfold
For thy good valour. Come thee on!
SCARUS   I'll halt after.   *Exeunt.*

4.8   *Alarum. Enter* ANTONY *again in a march;*
         SCARUS *with others.*

ANTONY
We have beat him to his camp. Run one before
And let the Queen know of our gests.   *Exit a Soldier.*
                     Tomorrow,
Before the sun shall see's, we'll spill the blood
That has today escaped. I thank you all,
5 For doughty-handed are you, and have fought
Not as you served the cause, but as't had been
Each man's like mine. You have shown all Hectors.
Enter the city; clip your wives, your friends;
Tell them your feats, whilst they with joyful tears
10 Wash the congealment from your wounds, and kiss
The honoured gashes whole.

         Enter CLEOPATRA.

[*to Scarus*]   Give me thy hand.
To this great fairy I'll commend thy acts,
Make her thanks bless thee.
[*to Cleopatra*]   O thou day o'th' world,
Chain mine armed neck! Leap thou, attire and all,
Through proof of harness to my heart, and there   15
Ride on the pants triumphing!   [*They embrace.*]
CLEOPATRA   Lord of lords!
O infinite virtue! Com'st thou smiling from
The world's great snare uncaught?
ANTONY   My nightingale,
We have beat them to their beds. What, girl! Though
    grey
Do something mingle with our younger brown, yet
    have we   20
A brain that nourishes our nerves and can
Get goal for goal of youth. Behold this man.
Commend unto his lips thy favouring hand.
  [*She offers Scarus her hand.*]
Kiss it, my warrior. He hath fought today
As if a god in hate of mankind had   25
Destroyed in such a shape.
CLEOPATRA   I'll give thee, friend,
An armour all of gold. It was a king's.
ANTONY   He has deserved it, were it carbuncled
Like holy Phoebus' car. Give me thy hand.
Through Alexandria make a jolly march;   30
Bear our hacked targets like the men that owe them.
Had our great palace the capacity
To camp this host, we all would sup together
And drink carouses to the next day's fate
Which promises royal peril. Trumpeters,   35
With brazen din blast you the city's ear;
Make mingle with our rattling taborins
That heaven and earth may strike their sounds together,
Applauding our approach.   *Trumpets sound. Exeunt.*

4.9   *Enter a* Sentry *and his Company of*
        Watch. ENOBARBUS *follows.*

SENTRY   If we be not relieved within this hour,
We must return to th' court of guard. The night
Is shiny, and they say we shall embattle
By th' second hour i'th' morn.
1 WATCH   This last day was a shrewd one to's.   5
ENOBARBUS   O bear me witness, night –
2 WATCH   What man is this?
1 WATCH   Stand close and list him.   [*They stand aside.*]
ENOBARBUS   Be witness to me, O thou blessed moon,
When men revolted shall upon record   10
Bear hateful memory, poor Enobarbus did
Before thy face repent.
SENTRY   Enobarbus?
2 WATCH   Peace! Hark further.
ENOBARBUS   O sovereign mistress of true melancholy,   15

The poisonous damp of night disponge upon me,
That life, a very rebel to my will,
May hang no longer on me. Throw my heart
Against the flint and hardness of my fault,
20   Which, being dried with grief, will break to powder
And finish all foul thoughts. O Antony,
Nobler than my revolt is infamous,
Forgive me in thine own particular,
But let the world rank me in register
25   A master-leaver and a fugitive.
O Antony! O Antony! [*He sinks down.*]

1 WATCH   Let's speak to him.
SENTRY   Let's hear him, for the things he speaks may
concern Caesar.
30   2 WATCH   Let's do so. But he sleeps.
SENTRY   Swoons rather, for so bad a prayer as his was
never yet for sleep.
1 WATCH   Go we to him.
2 WATCH   Awake sir! Awake! Speak to us!
35   1 WATCH   Hear you, sir?
SENTRY   The hand of death hath raught him.

[*Drums afar off*]
Hark! The drums
Demurely wake the sleepers. Let us bear him
To th' court of guard. He is of note. Our hour
Is fully out.
40   2 WATCH   Come on, then. He may recover yet.
Exeunt with the body.

4.10   *Enter* ANTONY *and* SCARUS *with their army.*

ANTONY   Their preparation is today by sea;
We please them not by land.
SCARUS   For both, my lord.
ANTONY
I would they'd fight i'th' fire or i'th' air;
We'd fight there too. But this it is: our foot
5   Upon the hills adjoining to the city
Shall stay with us – order for sea is given;
They have put forth the haven –
Where their appointment we may best discover
And look on their endeavour.   *Exeunt.*

4.11   *Enter* CAESAR *and his army.*

CAESAR   But being charged we will be still by land,
Which, as I take't, we shall, for his best force
Is forth to man his galleys. To the vales,
And hold our best advantage.   *Exeunt.*

4.12   *Alarum afar off, as at a sea fight. Enter*
ANTONY *and* SCARUS.

ANTONY
Yet they are not joined. Where yond pine does stand
I shall discover all. I'll bring thee word

Straight how 'tis like to go.   *Exit.*
SCARUS   Swallows have built
In Cleopatra's sails their nests. The augurs
Say they know not, they cannot tell; look grimly,   5
And dare not speak their knowledge. Antony
Is valiant and dejected, and by starts
His fretted fortunes give him hope and fear
Of what he has and has not.

Enter ANTONY.

ANTONY   All is lost!
This foul Egyptian hath betrayed me.   10
My fleet hath yielded to the foe, and yonder
They cast their caps up and carouse together
Like friends long lost. Triple-turned whore! 'Tis thou
Hast sold me to this novice, and my heart
Makes only wars on thee. Bid them all fly!   15
For when I am revenged upon my charm,
I have done all. Bid them all fly! Be gone!

Exit Scarus.
O sun, thy uprise shall I see no more.
Fortune and Antony part here; even here
Do we shake hands. All come to this! The hearts   20
That spanieled me at heels, to whom I gave
Their wishes, do discandy, melt their sweets
On blossoming Caesar, and this pine is barked
That overtopped them all. Betrayed I am.
O this false soul of Egypt! This grave charm   25
Whose eye becked forth my wars and called them
    home,
Whose bosom was my crownet, my chief end,
Like a right gipsy hath at fast and loose
Beguiled me to the very heart of loss.
What, Eros, Eros!

Enter CLEOPATRA.

                                    Ah, thou spell! Avaunt!   30
CLEOPATRA   Why is my lord enraged against his love?
ANTONY   Vanish, or I shall give thee thy deserving
And blemish Caesar's triumph. Let him take thee
And hoist thee up to the shouting plebeians!
Follow his chariot like the greatest spot   35
Of all thy sex; most monster-like be shown
For poor'st diminutives, for dolts, and let
Patient Octavia plough thy visage up
With her prepared nails!   *Exit Cleopatra.*
                                    'Tis well thou'rt gone
If it be well to live. But better 'twere   40
Thou fell'st into my fury, for one death
Might have prevented many. Eros, ho!
The shirt of Nessus is upon me. Teach me
Alcides, thou mine ancestor, thy rage;
Let me lodge Lichas on the horns o'th' moon,   45
And with those hands that grasped the heaviest club
Subdue my worthiest self. The witch shall die.
To the young Roman boy she hath sold me, and I fall
Under this plot. She dies for't. Eros, ho!   *Exit.*

4.13   *Enter* CLEOPATRA, CHARMIAN,
              IRAS, MARDIAN.

CLEOPATRA   Help me, my women! Oh, he's more mad
  Than Telamon for his shield; the boar of Thessaly
  Was never so embossed.
CHARMIAN   To th' monument!
  There lock yourself and send him word you are dead.
  The soul and body rive not more in parting
  Than greatness going off.
CLEOPATRA   To th' monument!
  Mardian, go tell him I have slain myself.
  Say that the last I spoke was 'Antony',
  And word it, prithee, piteously. Hence, Mardian,
  And bring me how he takes my death. To th'
      monument!   *Exeunt.*

4.14   *Enter* ANTONY *and* EROS.

ANTONY   Eros, thou yet behold'st me?
EROS   Ay, noble lord.
ANTONY   Sometime we see a cloud that's dragonish,
  A vapour sometime like a bear or lion,
  A towered citadel, a pendent rock,
  A forked mountain, or blue promontory
  With trees upon't that nod unto the world
  And mock our eyes with air. Thou hast seen these signs?
  They are black vesper's pageants.
EROS   Ay, my lord.
ANTONY
  That which is now a horse, even with a thought
  The rack dislimns and makes it indistinct
  As water is in water.
EROS   It does, my lord.
ANTONY   My good knave Eros, now thy captain is
  Even such a body. Here I am Antony,
  Yet cannot hold this visible shape, my knave.
  I made these wars for Egypt, and the Queen –
  Whose heart I thought I had, for she had mine,
  Which, whilst it was mine, had annexed unto't
  A million more, now lost – she, Eros, has
  Packed cards with Caesar, and false-played my glory
  Unto an enemy's triumph.
  Nay, weep not, gentle Eros. There is left us
  Ourselves to end ourselves.

              Enter MARDIAN.

                      O thy vile lady!
  She has robbed me of my sword.
MARDIAN   No, Antony,
  My mistress loved thee and her fortunes mingled
  With thine entirely.
ANTONY   Hence, saucy eunuch! Peace!
  She hath betrayed me and shall die the death.
MARDIAN   Death of one person can be paid but once,
  And that she has discharged. What thou wouldst do
  Is done unto thy hand. The last she spake

Was 'Antony! Most noble Antony!'   30
  Then, in the midst, a tearing groan did break
  The name of Antony; it was divided
  Between her heart and lips. She rendered life,
  Thy name so buried in her.
ANTONY   Dead, then?
MARDIAN   Dead.
ANTONY   Unarm, Eros. The long day's task is done   35
  And we must sleep. [*to Mardian*] That thou depart'st
      hence safe
  Does pay thy labour richly. Go.   *Exit Mardian.*
  Off! Pluck off!   [*Eros unarms him.*]
  The sevenfold shield of Ajax cannot keep
  The battery from my heart. O, cleave, my sides!   40
  Heart, once be stronger than thy continent;
  Crack thy frail case! Apace, Eros, apace!
  No more a soldier; bruised pieces go;
  You have been nobly borne. From me awhile.
                              Exit Eros.
  I will o'ertake thee, Cleopatra, and   45
  Weep for my pardon. So it must be, for now
  All length is torture; since the torch is out,
  Lie down and stray no farther. Now all labour
  Mars what it does – yea, very force entangles
  Itself with strength. Seal then, and all is done.   50
  Eros! – I come, my queen. – Eros! – Stay for me.
  Where souls do couch on flowers we'll hand in hand
  And with our sprightly port make the ghosts gaze.
  Dido and her Aeneas shall want troops,
  And all the haunt be ours. Come Eros! Eros!   55

              Enter EROS.

EROS   What would my lord?
ANTONY   Since Cleopatra died,
  I have lived in such dishonour that the gods
  Detest my baseness. I, that with my sword
  Quartered the world and o'er green Neptune's back
  With ships made cities, condemn myself to lack   60
  The courage of a woman; less noble mind
  Than she which, by her death, our Caesar tells
  'I am conqueror of myself.' Thou art sworn, Eros,
  That when the exigent should come – which now
  Is come indeed – when I should see behind me   65
  Th'inevitable prosecution of
  Disgrace and horror, that on my command
  Thou then wouldst kill me. Do't. The time is come.
  Thou strik'st not me; 'tis Caesar thou defeat'st.
  Put colour in thy cheek.
EROS   The gods withhold me!   70
  Shall I do that which all the Parthian darts,
  Though enemy, lost aim and could not?
ANTONY   Eros,
  Wouldst thou be windowed in great Rome and see
  Thy master thus with pleached arms, bending down
  His corrigible neck, his face subdued   75
  To penetrative shame, whilst the wheeled seat
  Of fortunate Caesar, drawn before him, branded

His baseness that ensued?

EROS   I would not see't.

ANTONY
80   Come, then! For with a wound I must be cured.
Draw that thy honest sword which thou hast worn
Most useful for thy country.

EROS   O sir, pardon me!

ANTONY
When I did make thee free, swor'st thou not then
To do this when I bade thee? Do it at once,
Or thy precedent services are all
85   But accidents unpurposed. Draw, and come!

EROS   Turn from me then that noble countenance
Wherein the worship of the whole world lies.

ANTONY [*Turns from him.*]   Lo thee!

EROS   My sword is drawn.

ANTONY   Then let it do at once
The thing why thou hast drawn it.

90   EROS   My dear master,
My captain and my emperor, let me say,
Before I strike this bloody stroke, farewell.

ANTONY   'Tis said, man, and farewell.

EROS   Farewell, great chief. Shall I strike now?

ANTONY   Now, Eros.

EROS   Why, there then!   [*Kills himself.*]
95   Thus I do escape the sorrow
Of Antony's death.

ANTONY   Thrice nobler than myself!
Thou teachest me, O valiant Eros, what
I should and thou couldst not! My queen and
    Eros
Have by their brave instruction got upon me
100   A nobleness in record. But I will be
A bridegroom in my death and run into't
As to a lover's bed. Come then! And, Eros,
Thy master dies thy scholar. To do thus
    [*Falls on his sword.*]
I learned of thee. How? Not dead? Not dead?
The guard, ho! O, dispatch me.

Enter a Company of the Guard, *one of them* DERCETUS.

105   1 GUARD   What's the noise?

ANTONY
I have done my work ill, friends. O make an end
Of what I have begun.

2 GUARD   The star is fallen.

1 GUARD   And time is at his period.

ALL THE GUARD   Alas and woe!

ANTONY   Let him that loves me strike me dead.

1 GUARD   Not I!

110   2 GUARD   Nor I!

3 GUARD   Nor any one!

       Exeunt all the Guard but Dercetus.

DERCETUS
Thy death and fortunes bid thy followers fly.
This sword but shown to Caesar with this tidings
Shall enter me with him.   [*Takes up Antony's sword.*]

Enter DIOMEDES.

DIOMEDES   Where's Antony?   115

DERCETUS   There, Diomed, there!

DIOMEDES   Lives he? Wilt thou not answer, man?
     Exit Dercetus with the sword of Antony.

ANTONY
Art thou there, Diomed? Draw thy sword and give me
Sufficing strokes for death.

DIOMEDES   Most absolute lord,
My mistress Cleopatra sent me to thee.   120

ANTONY   When did she send thee?

DIOMEDES   Now, my lord.

ANTONY   Where is she?

DIOMEDES
Locked in her monument. She had a prophesying fear
Of what hath come to pass, for when she saw –
Which never shall be found – you did suspect
She had disposed with Caesar, and that your rage   125
Would not be purged, she sent you word she was
    dead,
But fearing since how it might work, hath sent
Me to proclaim the truth, and I am come,
I dread, too late.

ANTONY
Too late, good Diomed. Call my guard, I prithee.   130

DIOMEDES
What ho! The Emperor's guard! The guard, what ho!
Come, your lord calls!

Enter four or five of the Guard *of Antony.*

ANTONY
Bear me, good friends, where Cleopatra bides.
'Tis the last service that I shall command you.

1 GUARD
Woe, woe are we, sir! You may not live to wear   135
All your true followers out.

ALL THE GUARD   Most heavy day!

ANTONY
Nay, good my fellows, do not please sharp fate
To grace it with your sorrows. Bid that welcome
Which comes to punish us, and we punish it,
Seeming to bear it lightly. Take me up.   140
I have led you oft; carry me now, good friends,
And have my thanks for all.

     Exeunt, bearing Antony and Eros.

4.15   *Enter* CLEOPATRA *and her Maids aloft,*
       with CHARMIAN *and* IRAS.

CLEOPATRA   O Charmian, I will never go from hence.

CHARMIAN   Be comforted, dear madam.

CLEOPATRA   No, I will not.
All strange and terrible events are welcome,
But comforts we despise. Our size of sorrow,
Proportioned to our cause, must be as great   5
As that which makes it.

Enter DIOMEDES *below.*

How now? Is he dead?

DIOMEDES His death's upon him, but not dead.
Look out o'th' other side your monument;
His guard have brought him thither.

Enter below ANTONY *borne by the* Guard.

10 CLEOPATRA O sun,
Burn the great sphere thou mov'st in! Darkling stand
The varying shore o'th' world! O Antony,
Antony, Antony! Help, Charmian! Help, Iras, help!
Help, friends below! Let's draw him hither.

ANTONY Peace!
15 Not Caesar's valour hath o'erthrown Antony,
But Antony's hath triumphed on itself.

CLEOPATRA So it should be that none but Antony
Should conquer Antony, but woe 'tis so.

ANTONY I am dying, Egypt, dying. Only
20 I here importune death awhile until
Of many thousand kisses the poor last
I lay upon thy lips.

CLEOPATRA I dare not, dear.
Dear my lord, pardon. I dare not
Lest I be taken. Not th'imperious show
25 Of the full-fortuned Caesar ever shall
Be brooched with me. If knife, drugs, serpents, have
Edge, sting or operation, I am safe.
Your wife Octavia, with her modest eyes
And still conclusion, shall acquire no honour
30 Demuring upon me. But come, come Antony –
Help me, my women – we must draw thee up.
Assist, good friends! [*They begin lifting.*]

ANTONY O quick, or I am gone!

CLEOPATRA
Here's sport indeed! How heavy weighs my lord!
Our strength is all gone into heaviness;
35 That makes the weight. Had I great Juno's power,
The strong-winged Mercury should fetch thee up
And set thee by Jove's side. Yet come a little;
Wishers were ever fools. O come, come, come,
[*They heave Antony aloft to Cleopatra.*]
And welcome, welcome! Die when thou hast lived;
40 Quicken with kissing. Had my lips that power,
Thus would I wear them out. [*Kisses him.*]

ALL THE GUARD Ah, heavy sight!

ANTONY I am dying, Egypt, dying.
Give me some wine and let me speak a little –

45 CLEOPATRA No, let me speak, and let me rail so high
That the false huswife Fortune break her wheel,
Provoked by my offence –

ANTONY One word, sweet queen:
Of Caesar seek your honour with your safety. Oh!

CLEOPATRA They do not go together.

ANTONY Gentle, hear me.
50 None about Caesar trust but Proculeius.

CLEOPATRA My resolution and my hands I'll trust;

None about Caesar.

ANTONY The miserable change now at my end,
Lament nor sorrow at, but please your thoughts
In feeding them with those my former fortunes 55
Wherein I lived the greatest prince o'th' world,
The noblest; and do now not basely die,
Not cowardly put off my helmet to
My countryman; a Roman by a Roman
Valiantly vanquished. Now my spirit is going; 60
I can no more.

CLEOPATRA Noblest of men, woo't die?
Hast thou no care of me? Shall I abide
In this dull world, which in thy absence is
No better than a sty? O see, my women,
The crown o'th' earth doth melt. My lord! 65
[*Antony dies.*]
O withered is the garland of the war,
The soldier's pole is fallen; young boys and girls
Are level now with men; the odds is gone
And there is nothing left remarkable
Beneath the visiting moon. [*She faints.*]

CHARMIAN O quietness, lady! 70

IRAS She's dead too, our sovereign.

CHARMIAN Lady!

IRAS Madam!

CHARMIAN O madam, madam, madam!

IRAS Royal Egypt! Empress! [*Cleopatra stirs.*] 75

CHARMIAN Peace, peace, Iras.

CLEOPATRA
No more but e'en a woman, and commanded
By such poor passion as the maid that milks
And does the meanest chares. It were for me
To throw my sceptre at the injurious gods 80
To tell them that this world did equal theirs
Till they had stolen our jewel. All's but naught;
Patience is sottish, and impatience does
Become a dog that's mad. Then is it sin
To rush into the secret house of death 85
Ere death dare come to us? How do you, women?
What, what, good cheer! Why, how now, Charmian?
My noble girls! Ah, women, women! Look,
Our lamp is spent, it's out. Good sirs, take heart.
We'll bury him, and then what's brave, what's noble, 90
Let's do't after the high Roman fashion
And make death proud to take us. Come, away.
This case of that huge spirit now is cold.
Ah, women, women! Come, we have no friend
But resolution and the briefest end. 95
Exeunt, bearing off Antony's body.

5.1 *Enter* CAESAR *with his Council of War:* AGRIPPA,
DOLABELLA, MAECENAS, PROCULEIUS, GALLUS.

CAESAR Go to him, Dolabella, bid him yield.
Being so frustrate, tell him, he mocks
The pauses that he makes.

DOLABELLA Caesar, I shall. *Exit.*

Enter DERCETUS *with the sword of Antony.*

CAESAR
  Wherefore is that? And what art thou that dar'st
  Appear thus to us?

DERCETUS   I am called Dercetus.
  Mark Antony I served, who best was worthy
  Best to be served. Whilst he stood up and spoke
  He was my master, and I wore my life
  To spend upon his haters. If thou please
  To take me to thee, as I was to him
  I'll be to Caesar. If thou pleasest not,
  I yield thee up my life.

CAESAR   What is't thou say'st?

DERCETUS   I say, O Caesar, Antony is dead.

CAESAR   The breaking of so great a thing should make
  A greater crack. The round world
  Should have shook lions into civil streets
  And citizens to their dens. The death of Antony
  Is not a single doom; in the name lay
  A moiety of the world.

DERCETUS   He is dead, Caesar,
  Not by a public minister of justice,
  Nor by a hired knife, but that self hand
  Which writ his honour in the acts it did
  Hath, with the courage which the heart did lend it,
  Splitted the heart. This is his sword;
  I robbed his wound of it. Behold it stained
  With his most noble blood.

CAESAR [*Points to the sword.*]   Look you, sad friends.
  The gods rebuke me, but it is tidings
  To wash the eyes of kings.

AGRIPPA   And strange it is
  That nature must compel us to lament
  Our most persisted deeds.

MAECENAS   His taints and honours
  Waged equal with him.

AGRIPPA   A rarer spirit never
  Did steer humanity; but you gods will give us
  Some faults to make us men. Caesar is touched.

MAECENAS
  When such a spacious mirror's set before him,
  He needs must see himself.

CAESAR   O Antony,
  I have followed thee to this; but we do launch
  Diseases in our bodies. I must perforce
  Have shown to thee such a declining day
  Or look on thine. We could not stall together
  In the whole world. But yet let me lament
  With tears as sovereign as the blood of hearts
  That thou, my brother, my competitor
  In top of all design, my mate in empire,
  Friend and companion in the front of war,
  The arm of mine own body, and the heart
  Where mine his thoughts did kindle, that our stars,
  Unreconciliable, should divide
  Our equalness to this. Hear me, good friends –

Enter an Egyptian.

  But I will tell you at some meeter season.
  The business of this man looks out of him;
  We'll hear him what he says. Whence are you?

EGYPTIAN
  A poor Egyptian yet. The Queen, my mistress,
  Confined in all she has, her monument,
  Of thy intents desires instruction,
  That she preparedly may frame herself
  To th' way she's forced to.

CAESAR   Bid her have good heart.
  She soon shall know of us, by some of ours,
  How honourable and how kindly we
  Determine for her. For Caesar cannot lean
  To be ungentle.

EGYPTIAN   So the gods preserve thee!   *Exit.*

CAESAR   Come hither, Proculeius. Go and say
  We purpose her no shame. Give her what comforts
  The quality of her passion shall require,
  Lest, in her greatness, by some mortal stroke
  She do defeat us. For her life in Rome
  Would be eternal in our triumph. Go,
  And with your speediest bring us what she says
  And how you find of her.

PROCULEIUS   Caesar, I shall.

CAESAR   Gallus, go you along.

                 Exeunt Proculeius and Gallus.
                 Where's Dolabella
  To second Proculeius?

ALL BUT CAESAR   Dolabella!

CAESAR   Let him alone, for I remember now
  How he's employed. He shall in time be ready.
  Go with me to my tent, where you shall see
  How hardly I was drawn into this war,
  How calm and gentle I proceeded still
  In all my writings. Go with me and see
  What I can show in this.   *Exeunt.*

5.2   *Enter* CLEOPATRA, CHARMIAN *and* IRAS.

CLEOPATRA   My desolation does begin to make
  A better life. 'Tis paltry to be Caesar.
  Not being Fortune, he's but Fortune's knave,
  A minister of her will. And it is great
  To do that thing that ends all other deeds,
  Which shackles accidents and bolts up change,
  Which sleeps and never palates more the dung,
  The beggar's nurse and Caesar's.

Enter PROCULEIUS.

PROCULEIUS
  Caesar sends greeting to the Queen of Egypt,
  And bids thee study on what fair demands
  Thou mean'st to have him grant thee.

CLEOPATRA   What's thy name?

PROCULEIUS   My name is Proculeius.

CLEOPATRA   Antony
Did tell me of you, bade me trust you, but
I do not greatly care to be deceived
15 That have no use for trusting. If your master
Would have a queen his beggar, you must tell him
That majesty, to keep decorum, must
No less beg than a kingdom. If he please
To give me conquered Egypt for my son,
20 He gives me so much of mine own as I
Will kneel to him with thanks.
PROCULEIUS   Be of good cheer.
You're fallen into a princely hand; fear nothing.
Make your full reference freely to my lord,
Who is so full of grace that it flows over
25 On all that need. Let me report to him
Your sweet dependency, and you shall find
A conqueror that will pray in aid for kindness
Where he for grace is kneeled to.
CLEOPATRA   Pray you tell him
I am his fortune's vassal and I send him
30 The greatness he has got. I hourly learn
A doctrine of obedience, and would gladly
Look him i'th' face.
PROCULEIUS   This I'll report, dear lady.
Have comfort, for I know your plight is pitied
Of him that caused it.

Enter GALLUS and Roman Soldiers.

35 [*to the Soldiers*] You see how easily she may be surprised.
Guard her till Caesar come.
IRAS   Royal queen!
CHARMIAN   O Cleopatra, thou art taken, queen!
CLEOPATRA   Quick, quick, good hands.
       [*Draws a dagger.*]
PROCULEIUS   Hold, worthy lady, hold!
       [*Disarms her.*]
Do not yourself such wrong, who are in this
Relieved, but not betrayed.
40 CLEOPATRA   What, of death too,
That rids our dogs of languish?
PROCULEIUS   Cleopatra,
Do not abuse my master's bounty by
Th'undoing of yourself. Let the world see
His nobleness well acted, which your death
Will never let come forth.
45 CLEOPATRA   Where art thou, Death?
Come hither, come! Come, come and take a queen
Worth many babes and beggars!
PROCULEIUS   O temperance, lady!
CLEOPATRA   Sir, I will eat no meat; I'll not drink, sir;
If idle talk will once be necessary,
50 I'll not sleep neither. This mortal house I'll ruin,
Do Caesar what he can. Know, sir, that I
Will not wait pinioned at your master's court,
Nor once be chastised with the sober eye
Of dull Octavia. Shall they hoist me up
55 And show me to the shouting varletry

Of censuring Rome? Rather a ditch in Egypt
Be gentle grave unto me! Rather on Nilus' mud
Lay me stark naked, and let the water-flies
Blow me into abhorring! Rather make
My country's high pyramides my gibbet   60
And hang me up in chains!
PROCULEIUS   You do extend
These thoughts of horror further than you shall
Find cause in Caesar.

Enter DOLABELLA.

DOLABELLA   Proculeius,
What thou hast done thy master Caesar knows,
And he hath sent for thee. For the Queen,   65
I'll take her to my guard.
PROCULEIUS   So, Dolabella,
It shall content me best. Be gentle to her.
[*to Cleopatra*] To Caesar I will speak what you shall
   please,
If you'll employ me to him.
CLEOPATRA   Say I would die.
       Exit Proculeius with Gallus and Soldiers.
DOLABELLA
Most noble empress, you have heard of me?   70
CLEOPATRA   I cannot tell.
DOLABELLA   Assuredly you know me.
CLEOPATRA
No matter, sir, what I have heard or known.
You laugh when boys or women tell their dreams;
Is't not your trick?
DOLABELLA   I understand not, madam.
CLEOPATRA   I dreamt there was an emperor Antony.   75
O, such another sleep, that I might see
But such another man!
DOLABELLA   If it might please ye –
CLEOPATRA
His face was as the heavens, and therein stuck
A sun and moon which kept their course and lighted
The little O, the earth.
DOLABELLA   Most sovereign creature –   80
CLEOPATRA   His legs bestrid the ocean; his reared arm
Crested the world; his voice was propertied
As all the tuned spheres, and that to friends;
But when he meant to quail and shake the orb,
He was as rattling thunder. For his bounty,   85
There was no winter in't; an autumn it was
That grew the more by reaping. His delights
Were dolphin-like: they showed his back above
The element they lived in. In his livery
Walked crowns and crownets; realms and islands were   90
As plates dropped from his pocket.
DOLABELLA   Cleopatra –
CLEOPATRA
Think you there was or might be such a man
As this I dreamt of?
DOLABELLA   Gentle madam, no.
CLEOPATRA   You lie up to the hearing of the gods!

95   But if there be nor ever were one such,
       It's past the size of dreaming. Nature wants stuff
       To vie strange forms with fancy; yet t'imagine
       An Antony were nature's piece 'gainst fancy,
       Condemning shadows quite.
       DOLABELLA   Hear me, good madam.
100   Your loss is as yourself, great, and you bear it
       As answering to the weight. Would I might never
       O'ertake pursued success, but I do feel,
       By the rebound of yours, a grief that smites
       My very heart at root.
       CLEOPATRA   I thank you, sir.
105   Know you what Caesar means to do with me?
       DOLABELLA
       I am loath to tell you what I would you knew.
       CLEOPATRA   Nay, pray you, sir.
       DOLABELLA   Though he be honourable –
       CLEOPATRA   He'll lead me, then, in triumph.
       DOLABELLA   Madam, he will. I know't.

       Flourish. Enter PROCULEIUS, CAESAR, GALLUS,
       MAECENAS *and others of his train.*

110   ALL   Make way there! Caesar!
       CAESAR   Which is the Queen of Egypt?
       DOLABELLA   It is the Emperor, madam.
             [*Cleopatra kneels.*]
       CAESAR   Arise! You shall not kneel.
       I pray you rise. Rise, Egypt.
       CLEOPATRA   Sir, the gods
115   Will have it thus. My master and my lord
       I must obey.   [*She stands.*]
       CAESAR   Take to you no hard thoughts.
       The record of what injuries you did us,
       Though written in our flesh, we shall remember
       As things but done by chance.
       CLEOPATRA   Sole sir o'th' world,
120   I cannot project mine own cause so well
       To make it clear, but do confess I have
       Been laden with like frailties which before
       Have often shamed our sex.
       CAESAR   Cleopatra, know
       We will extenuate rather than enforce.
125   If you apply yourself to our intents,
       Which towards you are most gentle, you shall find
       A benefit in this change; but if you seek
       To lay on me a cruelty by taking
       Antony's course, you shall bereave yourself
130   Of my good purposes, and put your children
       To that destruction which I'll guard them from
       If thereon you rely. I'll take my leave.
       CLEOPATRA
       And may through all the world! 'Tis yours, and we,
       Your scutcheons and your signs of conquest, shall
135   Hang in what place you please. Here, my good lord.
             [*Hands him a paper.*]
       CAESAR   You shall advise me in all for Cleopatra.
       CLEOPATRA   This is the brief of money, plate and jewels

       I am possessed of. 'Tis exactly valued,
       Not petty things admitted. Where's Seleucus?

             Enter SELEUCUS.

       SELEUCUS   Here, madam.   140
       CLEOPATRA
       This is my treasurer. Let him speak, my lord,
       Upon his peril, that I have reserved
       To myself nothing. Speak the truth, Seleucus.
       SELEUCUS   Madam,
       I had rather seel my lips than to my peril   145
       Speak that which is not.
       CLEOPATRA   What have I kept back?
       SELEUCUS
       Enough to purchase what you have made known.
       CAESAR   Nay, blush not, Cleopatra. I approve
       Your wisdom in the deed.
       CLEOPATRA   See, Caesar! O behold
       How pomp is followed! Mine will now be yours   150
       And, should we shift estates, yours would be mine.
       The ingratitude of this Seleucus does
       Even make me wild. O slave, of no more trust
       Than love that's hired! What, go'st thou back?
          Thou shalt
       Go back, I warrant thee! But I'll catch thine eyes 155
       Though they had wings! Slave! Soulless villain! Dog!
       O rarely base!
       CAESAR   Good queen, let us entreat you.
       CLEOPATRA
       O Caesar, what a wounding shame is this,
       That – thou vouchsafing here to visit me,
       Doing the honour of thy lordliness   160
       To one so meek – that mine own servant should
       Parcel the sum of my disgraces by
       Addition of his envy! Say, good Caesar,
       That I some lady trifles have reserved,
       Immoment toys, things of such dignity   165
       As we greet modern friends withal; and say
       Some nobler token I have kept apart
       For Livia and Octavia, to induce
       Their mediation, must I be unfolded
       With one that I have bred? The gods! It smites me   170
       Beneath the fall I have. [*to Seleucus*] Prithee go hence,
       Or I shall show the cinders of my spirits
       Through th'ashes of my chance. Wert thou a man,
       Thou wouldst have mercy on me.
       CAESAR   Forbear, Seleucus.
                                   Exit Seleucus.
       CLEOPATRA
       Be it known that we, the greatest, are misthought   175
       For things that others do, and when we fall,
       We answer others' merits in our name,
       Are therefore to be pitied.
       CAESAR   Cleopatra,
       Not what you have reserved nor what acknowledged
       Put we i'th' roll of conquest. Still be't yours;   180
       Bestow it at your pleasure, and believe

Caesar's no merchant to make prize with you
Of things that merchants sold. Therefore be cheered;
Make not your thoughts your prisons. No, dear queen,
185 For we intend so to dispose you as
Yourself shall give us counsel. Feed and sleep.
Our care and pity is so much upon you
That we remain your friend; and so, adieu.

CLEOPATRA   My master and my lord!
CAESAR   Not so. Adieu.

Flourish. Exeunt Caesar and his train.

CLEOPATRA
190 He words me, girls, he words me, that I should not
Be noble to myself. But hark thee, Charmian.
    [*Whispers to Charmian.*]
IRAS   Finish, good lady. The bright day is done
And we are for the dark.
CLEOPATRA   Hie thee again.
I have spoke already and it is provided.
Go put it to the haste.
195 CHARMIAN   Madam, I will.

Enter DOLABELLA.

DOLABELLA   Where's the Queen?
CHARMIAN   Behold, sir.   *Exit.*
CLEOPATRA   Dolabella!
DOLABELLA
Madam, as thereto sworn by your command,
Which my love makes religion to obey,
I tell you this: Caesar through Syria
200 Intends his journey, and within three days
You with your children will he send before.
Make your best use of this. I have performed
Your pleasure and my promise.
CLEOPATRA   Dolabella,
I shall remain your debtor.
DOLABELLA   I, your servant.
205 Adieu, good queen. I must attend on Caesar.
CLEOPATRA   Farewell and thanks.   *Exit Dolabella.*
                        Now, Iras, what think'st thou?
Thou an Egyptian puppet shall be shown
In Rome as well as I. Mechanic slaves
With greasy aprons, rules and hammers shall
210 Uplift us to the view. In their thick breaths,
Rank of gross diet, shall we be enclouded
And forced to drink their vapour.
IRAS   The gods forbid!
CLEOPATRA   Nay, 'tis most certain, Iras. Saucy lictors
Will catch at us like strumpets, and scald rhymers
215 Ballad us out o'tune. The quick comedians
Extemporally will stage us and present
Our Alexandrian revels; Antony
Shall be brought drunken forth; and I shall see
Some squeaking Cleopatra boy my greatness
I'th' posture of a whore.
220 IRAS   O the good gods!
CLEOPATRA   Nay, that's certain.
IRAS   I'll never see't, for I am sure my nails

Are stronger than mine eyes!
CLEOPATRA   Why, that's the way
To fool their preparation and to conquer
Their most absurd intents.

Enter CHARMIAN.

                              Now, Charmian!   225
Show me, my women, like a queen. Go fetch
My best attires. I am again for Cydnus
To meet Mark Antony. Sirrah Iras, go.
Now, noble Charmian, we'll dispatch indeed,
And when thou hast done this chare, I'll give thee leave   230
To play till doomsday. Bring our crown and all.

Exit Iras.
[*A noise within*]

Wherefore's this noise?

Enter a Guardsman.

GUARDSMAN   Here is a rural fellow
That will not be denied your highness' presence.
He brings you figs.
CLEOPATRA   Let him come in.   *Exit Guardsman.*
                              What poor an instrument   235
May do a noble deed! He brings me liberty.
My resolution's placed, and I have nothing
Of woman in me. Now from head to foot
I am marble-constant. Now the fleeting moon
No planet is of mine.

Enter Guardsman and Clown with a basket.

GUARDSMAN   This is the man.   240
CLEOPATRA   Avoid, and leave him.   *Exit Guardsman.*
Hast thou the pretty worm of Nilus there
That kills and pains not?
CLOWN   Truly, I have him; but I would not be the party
that should desire you to touch him, for his biting is   245
immortal. Those that do die of it do seldom or never
recover.
CLEOPATRA   Remember'st thou any that have died on't?
CLOWN   Very many; men and women too. I heard of one
of them no longer than yesterday – a very honest   250
woman, but something given to lie, as a woman should
not do but in the way of honesty – how she died of the
biting of it, what pain she felt. Truly, she makes a very
good report o'th' worm; but he that will believe all
that they say shall never be saved by half that they do.   255
But this is most falliable, the worm's an odd worm.
CLEOPATRA   Get thee hence. Farewell.
CLOWN   I wish you all joy of the worm. [*Sets down his
basket.*]
CLEOPATRA   Farewell.
CLOWN   You must think this, look you, that the worm   260
will do his kind.
CLEOPATRA   Ay, ay. Farewell.
CLOWN   Look you, the worm is not to be trusted but in
the keeping of wise people; for, indeed, there is no
goodness in the worm.   265

CLEOPATRA   Take thou no care; it shall be heeded.

CLOWN   Very good. Give it nothing, I pray you, for it is
not worth the feeding.

CLEOPATRA   Will it eat me?

270   CLOWN   You must not think I am so simple but I know
the devil himself will not eat a woman. I know that a
woman is a dish for the gods if the devil dress her not.
But truly, these same whoreson devils do the gods
great harm in their women, for in every ten that they
275   make, the devils mar five.

CLEOPATRA   Well, get thee gone. Farewell.

CLOWN   Yes, forsooth. I wish you joy o'th' worm.   *Exit.*

Enter IRAS *with a robe, crown and other jewels.*

CLEOPATRA
Give me my robe. Put on my crown. I have
Immortal longings in me. Now no more
280   The juice of Egypt's grape shall moist this lip.
    [*The women dress her.*]
Yare, yare, good Iras! Quick! Methinks I hear
Antony call. I see him rouse himself
To praise my noble act. I hear him mock
The luck of Caesar, which the gods give men
285   To excuse their after wrath. Husband, I come!
Now to that name my courage prove my title!
I am fire and air; my other elements
I give to baser life. So, have you done?
Come, then, and take the last warmth of my lips.
290   Farewell, kind Charmian. Iras, long farewell.
    [*Kisses them. Iras falls and dies.*]
Have I the aspic in my lips? Dost fall?
If thou and nature can so gently part,
The stroke of death is as a lover's pinch
Which hurts and is desired. Dost thou lie still?
295   If thus thou vanishest, thou tell'st the world
It is not worth leave-taking.

CHARMIAN
Dissolve, thick cloud, and rain, that I may say
The gods themselves do weep!

CLEOPATRA   This proves me base.
If she first meet the curled Antony,
300   He'll make demand of her, and spend that kiss
Which is my heaven to have.
    [*to the asp; applying it to her breast*]
                            Come, thou mortal wretch,
With thy sharp teeth this knot intrinsicate
Of life at once untie. Poor venomous fool,
Be angry and dispatch. O, couldst thou speak,
305   That I might hear thee call great Caesar ass
Unpolicied!

CHARMIAN   O eastern star!

CLEOPATRA   Peace, peace!
Dost thou not see my baby at my breast
That sucks the nurse asleep?

CHARMIAN   O break! O break!

CLEOPATRA   As sweet as balm, as soft as air, as gentle –
310   O Antony! – Nay, I will take thee too.

[*Applies another asp to her arm.*]
What should I stay –   [*Dies.*]

CHARMIAN   In this vile world? So fare thee well.
Now boast thee, Death, in thy possession lies
A lass unparalleled. Downy windows, close,
And golden Phoebus, never be beheld   315
Of eyes again so royal! Your crown's awry;
I'll mend it, and then play.

Enter the Guard, *rustling in.*

1 GUARD   Where's the Queen?

CHARMIAN   Speak softly. Wake her not.

1 GUARD   Caesar hath sent –

CHARMIAN   Too slow a messenger.
    [*Applies an asp.*]
O come apace! Dispatch! I partly feel thee.   320

1 GUARD
Approach ho! All's not well. Caesar's beguiled.

2 GUARD
There's Dolabella sent from Caesar. Call him.
                            Exit a Guardsman.

1 GUARD
What work is here, Charmian? Is this well done?

CHARMIAN   It is well done, and fitting for a princess
Descended of so many royal kings.   325
Ah, soldier!   [*Charmian dies.*]

Enter DOLABELLA.

DOLABELLA   How goes it here?

2 GUARD   All dead.

DOLABELLA   Caesar, thy thoughts
Touch their effects in this. Thyself art coming
To see performed the dreaded act which thou
So sought'st to hinder.   330

Enter CAESAR *and all his train, marching.*

ALL BUT CAESAR   A way there! A way for Caesar!

DOLABELLA   O sir, you are too sure an augurer:
That you did fear is done.

CAESAR   Bravest at the last,
She levelled at our purposes and, being royal,
Took her own way. The manner of their deaths?   335
I do not see them bleed.

DOLABELLA   Who was last with them?

1 GUARD
A simple countryman that brought her figs.
This was his basket.

CAESAR   Poisoned, then.

1 GUARD   O Caesar,
This Charmian lived but now; she stood and spake.
I found her trimming up the diadem   340
On her dead mistress. Tremblingly she stood,
And on the sudden dropped.

CAESAR   O noble weakness!
If they had swallowed poison, 'twould appear
By external swelling; but she looks like sleep,
As she would catch another Antony   345

In her strong toil of grace.
DOLABELLA   Here on her breast
There is a vent of blood, and something blown;
The like is on her arm.
1 GUARD   This is an aspic's trail, and these fig leaves
350   Have slime upon them such as th'aspic leaves
Upon the caves of Nile.
CAESAR   Most probable
That so she died, for her physician tells me
She hath pursued conclusions infinite
Of easy ways to die. Take up her bed,
And bear her women from the monument.   355
She shall be buried by her Antony.
No grave upon the earth shall clip in it
A pair so famous. High events as these
Strike those that make them, and their story is
No less in pity than his glory which   360
Brought them to be lamented. Our army shall
In solemn show attend this funeral,
And then to Rome. Come, Dolabella, see
High order in this great solemnity.
          Exeunt omnes, the Soldiers bearing the dead bodies.

As You Like It

As You Like It seems to have been written about 1599, though it was first published in the Folio of 1623, where it is the tenth of the comedies. The list of Shakespeare's comedies in Francis Meres's *Palladis Tamia*, published in 1598, omits this play, but it was listed in the Stationers' Register on 4 August 1600 as one of four of 'My lord chamberlain's men's plays' that were ordered 'to be stayed' from publication. It is, therefore, roughly contemporaneous with *Much Ado About Nothing*.

The play is based on Thomas Lodge's popular prose romance, *Rosalynde: Euphues' Golden Legacy* (1590), and indeed Lodge's breezy presentation of his tale 'to the Gentleman readers' – 'if you like it, so' – may well have suggested the title of Shakespeare's play. Lodge's story of Rosader and Rosalynde, itself based on the fourteenth-century *Tale of Gamelyn*, provides virtually all the elements of the plot of Shakespeare's play.

Lodge's novel is one of many late Elizabethan examples of pastoral, a literary mode with classical precedents reaching back to the Greek writer Theocritus, but which in Elizabethan England became a fashionable form seemingly celebrating the virtues of simplicity but doing so in an extravagantly artificial manner. Lodge never criticizes the artificiality of his pastoral tale, but Shakespeare, in giving prominence to the love affair of Rosalind and Orlando (Lodge's Rosader), lessening the sensationalism of Lodge's plot and adding to his cast of characters, provides alternative views of Lodge's idealized story, exposing its artificiality to ironies and revealing the realities that conventions, both literary and social, obscure and, in some cases, ameliorate.

The most important of the play's counter-voices are Touchstone and Jaques, each similarly sceptical of the idealizing imagination. For the clown, Touchstone, the absurdities he encounters are occasions genially to expose the inconsistencies of the human heart, while for Jaques they become hard evidence for his own cynicism and melancholy. Touchstone indeed marries, joining, with Audrey, the parade of couples marching two by two at the end, but Jaques insistently remains outside the magic circle, going off to join the penitent Duke Frederick, though not before offering the couples his own surprisingly benevolent wishes.

The similarity of Jaques's blessings to Hymen's suggests the play's complex focus. Characters are redeemed and reunited in the Forest of Arden, but there is no magic in the forest. The natural is no more held up as an ideal than is the artificial, the country no more free from criticism than the Court. The happy end that the play provides is made possible not by qualities inhering in a locale but by an enduring quality of human goodness, most apparent perhaps in Rosalind's resilience and creativity, but also evident in Celia, Orlando, Old Adam, Duke Senior and all who come to recognize the natural bonds of humankind.

As You Like It may well have been an early play performed in the Globe in 1599. Jaques's 'All the world's a stage' (2.7.140) would have resonated wittily in the new theatre, which allegedly bore a motto from Petronius: '*totus mundus agit histrionem*'. Indeed, such self-consciousness is marked throughout; Jaques's fears that characters will speak in 'blank verse' (4.1.29–30) call attention to the theatre poetry, just as Rosalind's male disguise and subsequent female 'pretence' (to say nothing of her line in the epilogue, 'If I were a woman . . .') foreground the theatre's convention of boys acting female parts.

For all the play's awareness of itself as theatre, there is no record of an early performance (only a later tradition that it was performed by the King's Men at Wilton in December 1603), and it was not until the mid–eighteenth century that the play became popular on the stage, its attractive roles for women certainly part of its new appeal. On the modern stage it has been regularly played, its paradoxical combination of innocence and cynicism, of romanticism and realism, making it a popular comedy able to speak both to our knowledge and to our dreams.

The Arden text is based on the 1623 First Folio.

ROSALIND	*daughter of Duke Senior*
CELIA	*daughter of Duke Frederick*
DUKE SENIOR (Ferdinand)	*living in exile*
DUKE FREDERICK	*his usurping brother*
ORLANDO	*youngest son of Sir Rowland de Boys*
OLIVER	*his eldest brother*
ADAM	*servant in the de Boys household*
DENNIS	*Oliver's servant*
CHARLES	*Duke Frederick's wrestler*
LE BEAU	*a courtier*
TOUCHSTONE	*a clown*
AMIENS	*a lord, follower of Duke Senior*
JAQUES	*a melancholy gentleman*
CORIN	
SILVIUS	*shepherds*
PHOEBE	*a shepherdess*
AUDREY	*a country girl*
SIR OLIVER MAR–TEXT	*a country vicar*
WILLIAM	*a country youth*
HYMEN	
JAQUES DE BOYS	*second son of Sir Rowland de Boys*
LORDS	*attendant on Duke Frederick*
LORDS	*companions of Duke Senior*
FORESTERS	
Two PAGES	*attendant on Duke Senior*

Attendants

1.1   *Enter* ORLANDO *and* ADAM.

ORLANDO   As I remember, Adam, it was upon this fashion bequeathed me by will but poor a thousand crowns, and, as thou sayst, charged my brother on his blessing to breed me well; and there begins my sadness. My brother Jaques he keeps at school and report speaks goldenly of his profit. For my part, he keeps me rustically at home or, to speak more properly, stays me here at home unkept; for call you that keeping, for a gentleman of my birth, that differs not from the stalling of an ox? His horses are bred better, for besides that they are fair with their feeding, they are taught their manage and to that end riders dearly hired; but I, his brother, gain nothing under him but growth, for the which his animals on his dunghills are as much bound to him as I. Besides this nothing that he so plentifully gives me, the something that nature gave me his countenance seems to take from me. He lets me feed with his hinds, bars me the place of a brother and, as much as in him lies, mines my gentility with my education. This is it, Adam, that grieves me, and the spirit of my father, which I think is within me, begins to mutiny against this servitude. I will no longer endure it, though yet I know no wise remedy how to avoid it.

Enter OLIVER.

ADAM   Yonder comes my master, your brother.

ORLANDO   Go apart, Adam, and thou shalt hear how he will shake me up.

OLIVER   Now, sir, what make you here?

ORLANDO   Nothing. I am not taught to make anything.

OLIVER   What mar you then, sir?

ORLANDO   Marry, sir, I am helping you to mar that which God made, a poor unworthy brother of yours, with idleness.

OLIVER   Marry, sir, be better employed and be naught awhile.

ORLANDO   Shall I keep your hogs and eat husks with them? What prodigal portion have I spent that I should come to such penury?

OLIVER   Know you where you are, sir?

ORLANDO   O, sir, very well: here in your orchard.

OLIVER   Know you before whom, sir?

ORLANDO   Ay, better than him I am before knows me. I know you are my eldest brother, and in the gentle condition of blood you should so know me. The courtesy of nations allows you my better in that you are the first-born, but the same tradition takes not away my blood, were there twenty brothers betwixt us. I have as much of my father in me as you, albeit I confess your coming before me is nearer to his reverence.

OLIVER   What, boy!

ORLANDO   Come, come, elder brother, you are too young in this!

OLIVER   Wilt thou lay hands on me, villain?

ORLANDO   I am no villain. I am the youngest son of Sir Rowland de Boys; he was my father, and he is thrice a villain that says such a father begot villains. Wert thou not my brother I would not take this hand from thy throat till this other had pulled out thy tongue for saying so. Thou hast railed on thyself.

ADAM   Sweet masters, be patient. For your father's remembrance, be at accord.

OLIVER   Let me go, I say.

ORLANDO   I will not till I please. You shall hear me. My father charged you in his will to give me good education. You have trained me like a peasant, obscuring and hiding from me all gentleman-like qualities. The spirit of my father grows strong in me, and I will no longer endure it! Therefore allow me such exercises as may become a gentleman, or give me the poor allottery my father left me by testament; with that I will go buy my fortunes.

OLIVER   And what wilt thou do? Beg when that is spent? Well, sir, get you in. I will not long be troubled with you; you shall have some part of your will. I pray you leave me.

ORLANDO   I will no further offend you than becomes me for my good.

OLIVER   Get you with him, you old dog.

ADAM   Is 'old dog' my reward? Most true, I have lost my teeth in your service. God be with my old master, he would not have spoke such a word.

Exeunt Orlando and Adam.

OLIVER   Is it even so? Begin you to grow upon me? I will physic your rankness, and yet give no thousand crowns neither. Holla, Dennis!

Enter DENNIS.

DENNIS   Calls your worship?

OLIVER   Was not Charles, the Duke's wrestler, here to speak with me?

DENNIS   So please you, he is here at the door and importunes access to you.

OLIVER   Call him in.   *Exit Dennis.*
'Twill be a good way – and tomorrow the wrestling is.

Enter CHARLES.

CHARLES   Good morrow to your worship.

OLIVER   Good Monsieur Charles. What's the new news at the new court?

CHARLES   There's no news at the court, sir, but the old news: that is, the old Duke is banished by his younger brother the new Duke, and three or four loving lords have put themselves into voluntary exile with him, whose lands and revenues enrich the new Duke; therefore he gives them good leave to wander.

OLIVER   Can you tell if Rosalind, the Duke's daughter, be banished with her father?

CHARLES   O no; for the Duke's daughter, her cousin, so loves her, being ever from their cradles bred together, that she would have followed her exile or have died to stay behind her. She is at the court and no less beloved

of her uncle than his own daughter, and never two
ladies loved as they do.

OLIVER   Where will the old Duke live?

CHARLES   They say he is already in the Forest of Arden
110 and a many merry men with him, and there they live
like the old Robin Hood of England. They say many
young gentlemen flock to him every day and fleet the
time carelessly as they did in the golden world.

OLIVER   What, you wrestle tomorrow before the new
115 Duke?

CHARLES   Marry, do I, sir, and I came to acquaint you
with a matter. I am given, sir, secretly to understand
that your younger brother Orlando hath a disposition
to come in disguised against me to try a fall. Tomorrow,
120 sir, I wrestle for my credit, and he that escapes me
without some broken limb shall acquit him well. Your
brother is but young and tender, and for your love I
would be loath to foil him, as I must for my own
honour if he come in. Therefore out of my love to you
125 I came hither to acquaint you withal, that either you
might stay him from his intendment or brook such
disgrace well as he shall run into, in that it is a thing of
his own search and altogether against my will.

OLIVER   Charles, I thank thee for thy love to me, which
130 thou shalt find I will most kindly requite. I had myself
notice of my brother's purpose herein and have by
underhand means laboured to dissuade him from it,
but he is resolute. I'll tell thee, Charles, it is the
stubbornest young fellow of France, full of ambition,
135 an envious emulator of every man's good parts, a secret
and villainous contriver against me his natural brother.
Therefore use thy discretion; I had as lief thou didst
break his neck as his finger. And thou wert best look
to't; for if thou dost him any slight disgrace, or if he do
140 not mightily grace himself on thee, he will practise
against thee by poison, entrap thee by some treacherous
device, and never leave thee till he hath ta'en thy life by
some indirect means or other. For I assure thee (and
almost with tears I speak it) there is not one so young
145 and so villainous this day living. I speak but brotherly
of him, but should I anatomize him to thee as he is, I
must blush and weep, and thou must look pale and
wonder.

CHARLES   I am heartily glad I came hither to you. If he
150 come tomorrow I'll give him his payment. If ever he go
alone again I'll never wrestle for prize more. And so
God keep your worship.   *Exit.*

OLIVER   Farewell, good Charles. – Now will I stir this
gamester. I hope I shall see an end of him; for my soul
155 – yet I know not why – hates nothing more than he. Yet
he's gentle, never schooled and yet learned, full of
noble device, of all sorts enchantingly beloved, and
indeed so much in the heart of the world, and especially
of my own people, who best know him, that I am
160 altogether misprized. But it shall not be so long. This
wrestler shall clear all. Nothing remains but that I
kindle the boy thither, which now I'll go about.   *Exit.*

1.2   *Enter* ROSALIND *and* CELIA.

CELIA   I pray thee, Rosalind, sweet my coz, be merry.

ROSALIND   Dear Celia, I show more mirth than I am
mistress of.

CELIA   And would you yet were merrier.

ROSALIND   Unless you could teach me to forget a   5
banished father you must not learn me how to
remember any extraordinary pleasure.

CELIA   Herein I see thou lov'st me not with the full
weight that I love thee. If my uncle, thy banished
father, had banished thy uncle, the Duke my father, so   10
thou hadst been still with me I could have taught my
love to take thy father for mine. So wouldst thou, if the
truth of thy love to me were so righteously tempered as
mine is to thee.

ROSALIND   Well, I will forget the condition of my estate   15
to rejoice in yours.

CELIA   You know my father hath no child but I, nor
none is like to have, and truly when he dies thou shalt
be his heir, for what he hath taken away from thy father
perforce, I will render thee again in affection. By mine   20
honour I will! And when I break that oath let me turn
monster. Therefore, my sweet Rose, my dear Rose, be
merry.

ROSALIND   From henceforth I will, coz, and devise
sports. Let me see: what think you of falling in love?   25

CELIA   Marry, I prithee do, to make sport withal – but
love no man in good earnest, nor no further in sport
neither than with safety of a pure blush thou mayst in
honour come off again.

ROSALIND   What shall be our sport then?   30

CELIA   Let us sit and mock the good housewife Fortune
from her wheel, that her gifts may henceforth be
bestowed equally.

ROSALIND   I would we could do so, for her benefits are
mightily misplaced – and the bountiful blind woman   35
doth most mistake in her gifts to women.

CELIA   'Tis true, for those that she makes fair she scarce
makes honest, and those that she makes honest she
makes very ill-favouredly.

ROSALIND   Nay, now thou goest from Fortune's office   40
to Nature's; Fortune reigns in gifts of the world not in
the lineaments of Nature.

Enter TOUCHSTONE.

CELIA   No? When Nature hath made a fair creature may
she not by Fortune fall into the fire? Though Nature
hath given us wit to flout at Fortune, hath not Fortune   45
sent in this fool to cut off the argument?

ROSALIND   Indeed there is Fortune too hard for Nature,
when Fortune makes Nature's natural the cutter-off of
Nature's wit.

CELIA   Peradventure this is not Fortune's work neither,   50
but Nature's, who, perceiving our natural wits too dull
to reason of such goddesses, hath sent this natural for
our whetstone; for always the dullness of the fool is the

55 whetstone of the wits. – How now, wit, whither wander you?

TOUCHSTONE   Mistress, you must come away to your father.

CELIA   Were you made the messenger?

60 TOUCHSTONE   No, by mine honour, but I was bid to come for you.

ROSALIND   Where learned you that oath, fool?

TOUCHSTONE   Of a certain knight that swore by his honour they were good pancakes, and swore by his honour the mustard was naught. Now I'll stand to it:

65 the pancakes were naught and the mustard was good, and yet was not the knight forsworn.

CELIA   How prove you that in the great heap of your knowledge?

ROSALIND   Ay, marry, now unmuzzle your wisdom.

70 TOUCHSTONE   Stand you both forth now. Stroke your chins and swear by your beards that I am a knave.

CELIA   By our beards – if we had them – thou art.

TOUCHSTONE   By my knavery – if I had it – then I were. But if you swear by that that is not, you are not forsworn.

75 No more was this knight swearing by his honour, for he never had any; or if he had, he had sworn it away before ever he saw those pancakes or that mustard.

CELIA   Prithee, who is't that thou mean'st?

TOUCHSTONE   [*to Rosalind*]   One that old Ferdinand,

80 your father, loves.

ROSALIND   My father's love is enough to honour him. Enough! Speak no more of him. You'll be whipped for taxation one of these days.

TOUCHSTONE   The more pity that fools may not speak

85 wisely what wise men do foolishly.

CELIA   By my troth, thou sayst true. For since the little wit that fools have was silenced, the little foolery that wise men have makes a great show.

Enter LE BEAU.

Here comes Monsieur Le Beau.

90 ROSALIND   With his mouth full of news.

CELIA   Which he will put on us as pigeons feed their young.

ROSALIND   Then shall we be news-crammed.

CELIA   All the better; we shall be the more marketable.

95 *Bonjour*, Monsieur Le Beau, what's the news?

LE BEAU   Fair princess, you have lost much good sport.

CELIA   Sport? Of what colour?

LE BEAU   What colour, madam? How shall I answer you?

100 ROSALIND   As wit and Fortune will.

TOUCHSTONE   Or as the Destinies decrees.

CELIA   Well said – that was laid on with a trowel.

TOUCHSTONE   Nay, if I keep not my rank –

ROSALIND   Thou loosest thy old smell.

105 LE BEAU   You amaze me, ladies. I would have told you of good wrestling, which you have lost the sight of.

ROSALIND   Yet tell us the manner of the wrestling.

LE BEAU   I will tell you the beginning and, if it please

your ladyships, you may see the end, for the best is yet

110 to do; and here – where you are – they are coming to perform it.

CELIA   Well, the beginning that is dead and buried?

LE BEAU   There comes an old man and his three sons –

CELIA   I could match this beginning with an old tale.

115 LE BEAU   Three proper young men of excellent growth and presence –

ROSALIND   With bills on their necks: 'Be it known unto all men by these presents.'

LE BEAU   The eldest of the three wrestled with Charles,

120 the Duke's wrestler, which Charles in a moment threw him and broke three of his ribs, that there is little hope of life in him. So he served the second and so the third. Yonder they lie, the poor old man their father making such pitiful dole over them that all the beholders take

125 his part with weeping.

ROSALIND   Alas!

TOUCHSTONE   But what is the sport, Monsieur, that the ladies have lost?

LE BEAU   Why, this that I speak of.

130 TOUCHSTONE   Thus men may grow wiser every day. It is the first time that ever I heard breaking of ribs was sport for ladies.

CELIA   Or I, I promise thee.

ROSALIND   But is there any else longs to see this broken

135 music in his sides? Is there yet another dotes upon rib-breaking? Shall we see this wrestling, cousin?

LE BEAU   You must if you stay here, for here is the place appointed for the wrestling and they are ready to perform it.   [*Flourish*]

140 CELIA   Yonder sure they are coming. Let us now stay and see it.

Enter DUKE FREDERICK, *Lords,* ORLANDO, CHARLES *and Attendants.*

DUKE FREDERICK   Come on. Since the youth will not be entreated, his own peril on his forwardness.

ROSALIND   Is yonder the man?

145 LE BEAU   Even he, madam.

CELIA   Alas, he is too young. Yet he looks successfully.

DUKE FREDERICK   How now, daughter – and cousin. Are you crept hither to see the wrestling?

ROSALIND   Ay, my liege, so please you give us leave.

150 DUKE FREDERICK   You will take little delight in it, I can tell you; there is such odds in the man. In pity of the challenger's youth I would fain dissuade him, but he will not be entreated. Speak to him, ladies; see if you can move him.

155 CELIA   Call him hither, good Monsieur Le Beau.

DUKE FREDERICK   Do so; I'll not be by.

LE BEAU   Monsieur the challenger, the princess calls for you.

ORLANDO   I attend them with all respect and duty.

160 ROSALIND   Young man, have you challenged Charles the wrestler?

ORLANDO   No, fair princess. He is the general

challenger. I come but in as others do, to try with him
the strength of my youth.

165   CELIA   Young gentleman, your spirits are too bold for
your years. You have seen cruel proof of this man's
strength. If you saw yourself with your eyes or knew
yourself with your judgement, the fear of your
170   adventure would counsel you to a more equal
enterprise. We pray you for your own sake to embrace
your own safety and give over this attempt.

  ROSALIND   Do, young sir. Your reputation shall not
therefore be misprized. We will make it our suit to the
Duke that the wrestling might not go forward.

175   ORLANDO   I beseech you, punish me not with your hard
thoughts, wherein I confess me much guilty to deny so
fair and excellent ladies anything. But let your fair eyes
and gentle wishes go with me to my trial, wherein if I
be foiled there is but one shamed that was never
180   gracious, if killed, but one dead that is willing to be so.
I shall do my friends no wrong, for I have none to
lament me; the world no injury, for in it I have nothing.
Only in the world I fill up a place which may be better
supplied when I have made it empty.

185   ROSALIND   The little strength that I have, I would it
were with you.

  CELIA   And mine to eke out hers.

  ROSALIND   Fare you well. Pray heaven I be deceived in
you.

190   CELIA   Your heart's desires be with you.

  CHARLES   Come, where is this young gallant that is so
desirous to lie with his mother earth?

  ORLANDO   Ready, sir, but his will hath in it a more
modest working.

195   DUKE FREDERICK   You shall try but one fall.

  CHARLES   No, I warrant your grace you shall not entreat
him to a second that have so mightily persuaded him
from a first.

  ORLANDO   You mean to mock me after; you should not
200   have mocked me before. But come your ways.

  ROSALIND   Now Hercules be thy speed, young man!

  CELIA   I would I were invisible, to catch the strong
fellow by the leg. [*Orlando and Charles wrestle.*]

  ROSALIND   O excellent young man!

205   CELIA   If I had a thunderbolt in mine eye I can tell who
should down. [*Shout. Charles is thrown.*]

  DUKE FREDERICK   No more, no more.

  ORLANDO   Yes, I beseech your grace:
I am not yet well breathed.

  DUKE FREDERICK   How dost thou, Charles?

  LE BEAU   He cannot speak, my lord.

  DUKE FREDERICK   Bear him away.
        Exeunt Touchstone and Attendants with Charles.
210   What is thy name, young man?

  ORLANDO   Orlando, my liege, the youngest son of Sir
Rowland de Boys.

  DUKE FREDERICK
I would thou hadst been son to some man else.
The world esteemed thy father honourable,

But I did find him still mine enemy.   215
Thou shouldst have better pleased me with this deed
Hadst thou descended from another house.
But fare thee well, thou art a gallant youth.
I would thou hadst told me of another father.
      Exeunt Duke Frederick, Le Beau and Lords.

  CELIA   Were I my father, coz, would I do this?   220

  ORLANDO   I am more proud to be Sir Rowland's son,
His youngest son, and would not change that calling
To be adopted heir to Frederick.

  ROSALIND   My father loved Sir Rowland as his soul,
And all the world was of my father's mind.   225
Had I before known this young man his son
I should have given him tears unto entreaties
Ere he should thus have ventured.

  CELIA   Gentle cousin,
Let us go thank him and encourage him.
My father's rough and envious disposition   230
Sticks me at heart. – Sir, you have well deserved.
If you do keep your promises in love
But justly as you have exceeded all promise,
Your mistress shall be happy.

  ROSALIND   Gentleman,
[*giving him a chain from her neck*]
Wear this for me – one out of suits with fortune,   235
That could give more but that her hand lacks means.
Shall we go, coz?

  CELIA   Ay. – Fare you well, fair gentleman.

  ORLANDO   Can I not say, I thank you? My better parts
Are all thrown down, and that which here stands up
Is but a quintain, a mere lifeless block.   240

  ROSALIND
He calls us back. My pride fell with my fortunes.
I'll ask him what he would. – Did you call, sir?
Sir, you have wrestled well and overthrown
More than your enemies.

  CELIA   Will you go, coz?

  ROSALIND   Have with you. – Fare you well.   245
          Exeunt Rosalind and Celia.

  ORLANDO
What passion hangs these weights upon my tongue?
I cannot speak to her, yet she urged conference.

               Enter LE BEAU.

O poor Orlando, thou art overthrown!
Or Charles or something weaker masters thee.

  LE BEAU   Good sir, I do in friendship counsel you   250
To leave this place, albeit you have deserved
High commendation, true applause and love.
Yet such is now the Duke's condition
That he misconsters all that you have done.
The Duke is humorous; what he is indeed   255
More suits you to conceive than I to speak of.

  ORLANDO
I thank you, sir; and pray you, tell me this:
Which of the two was daughter of the Duke
That here was at the wrestling?

LE BEAU

260   Neither his daughter, if we judge by manners,
        But yet indeed the taller is his daughter.
        The other is daughter to the banished Duke,
        And here detained by her usurping uncle
        To keep his daughter company, whose loves
265   Are dearer than the natural bond of sisters.
        But I can tell you that of late this Duke
        Hath ta'en displeasure 'gainst his gentle niece,
        Grounded upon no other argument
        But that the people praise her for her virtues,
270   And pity her for her good father's sake;
        And on my life his malice 'gainst the lady
        Will suddenly break forth. Sir, fare you well.
        Hereafter in a better world than this
        I shall desire more love and knowledge of you.

275 ORLANDO   I rest much bounden to you; fare you well.

                                          Exit Le Beau.

        Thus must I from the smoke into the smother,
        From tyrant Duke unto a tyrant brother.
        But heavenly Rosalind!   *Exit.*

1.3   *Enter* CELIA *and* ROSALIND.

CELIA   Why, cousin, why, Rosalind! Cupid have mercy!
        Not a word?

ROSALIND   Not one to throw at a dog.

CELIA   No, thy words are too precious to be cast away
5   upon curs – throw some of them at me. Come, lame me
        with reasons.

ROSALIND   Then there were two cousins laid up, when
        the one should be lamed with reasons and the other
        mad without any.

10 CELIA   But is all this for your father?

ROSALIND   No, some of it is for my child's father. O,
        how full of briers is this working-day world!

CELIA   They are but burs, cousin, thrown upon thee in
        holiday foolery. If we walk not in the trodden paths our
15   very petticoats will catch them.

ROSALIND   I could shake them off my coat; these burs
        are in my heart.

CELIA   Hem them away.

ROSALIND   I would try, if I could cry 'hem' and have
20   him.

CELIA   Come, come, wrestle with thy affections.

ROSALIND   O, they take the part of a better wrestler
        than myself.

CELIA   O, a good wish upon you! You will try in time in
25   despite of a fall. But turning these jests out of service,
        let us talk in good earnest. Is it possible on such a
        sudden you should fall into so strong a liking with old
        Sir Rowland's youngest son?

ROSALIND   The Duke my father loved his father dearly.

30 CELIA   Doth it therefore ensue that you should love his
        son dearly? By this kind of chase I should hate him for
        my father hated his father dearly; yet I hate not
        Orlando.

ROSALIND   No, faith, hate him not, for my sake.

CELIA   Why should I not? Doth he not deserve well?   35

                Enter DUKE FREDERICK *with Lords.*

ROSALIND   Let me love him for that, and do you love
        him because I do. Look, here comes the Duke.

CELIA   With his eyes full of anger.

DUKE FREDERICK
        Mistress, dispatch you with your safest haste
        And get you from our court.

ROSALIND   Me, uncle?

DUKE FREDERICK   You, cousin.   40
        Within these ten days if that thou be'st found
        So near our public court as twenty miles,
        Thou diest for it.

ROSALIND   I do beseech your grace,
        Let me the knowledge of my fault bear with me.
        If with myself I hold intelligence,   45
        Or have acquaintance with mine own desires,
        If that I do not dream, or be not frantic –
        As I do trust I am not – then, dear uncle,
        Never so much as in a thought unborn
        Did I offend your highness.

DUKE FREDERICK   Thus do all traitors.   50
        If their purgation did consist in words,
        They are as innocent as grace itself.
        Let it suffice thee that I trust thee not.

ROSALIND   Yet your mistrust cannot make me a traitor.
        Tell me whereon the likelihoods depends?   55

DUKE FREDERICK
        Thou art thy father's daughter, there's enough.

ROSALIND
        So was I when your highness took his dukedom;
        So was I when your highness banished him.
        Treason is not inherited, my lord,
        Or if we did derive it from our friends,   60
        What's that to me? My father was no traitor.
        Then good my liege, mistake me not so much
        To think my poverty is treacherous.

CELIA   Dear sovereign, hear me speak.

DUKE FREDERICK
        Ay, Celia, we stayed her for your sake,   65
        Else had she with her father ranged along.

CELIA   I did not then entreat to have her stay;
        It was your pleasure and your own remorse.
        I was too young that time to value her,
        But now I know her. If she be a traitor,   70
        Why, so am I. We still have slept together,
        Rose at an instant, learned, played, ate together,
        And whereso'er we went, like Juno's swans,
        Still we went coupled and inseparable.

DUKE FREDERICK
        She is too subtle for thee, and her smoothness,   75
        Her very silence and her patience
        Speak to the people, and they pity her.
        Thou art a fool. She robs thee of thy name,
        And thou wilt show more bright and seem more
        virtuous

80   When she is gone. Then open not thy lips.
Firm and irrevocable is my doom
Which I have passed upon her. She is banished.

CELIA   Pronounce that sentence then on me, my liege;
I cannot live out of her company

DUKE FREDERICK

85   You are a fool. You, niece, provide yourself.
If you outstay the time, upon mine honour
And in the greatness of my word, you die.

Exeunt Duke Frederick and Lords.

CELIA   O my poor Rosalind, whither wilt thou go?
Wilt thou change fathers? I will give thee mine.

90   I charge thee, be not thou more grieved than I am.

ROSALIND   I have more cause.

CELIA   Thou hast not, cousin.
Prithee, be cheerful. Knowst thou not the Duke
Hath banished me, his daughter?

ROSALIND   That he hath not.

CELIA   No, hath not? Rosalind lacks then the love

95   Which teacheth thee that thou and I am one.
Shall we be sundered? Shall we part, sweet girl?
No, let my father seek another heir!
Therefore devise with me how we may fly,
Whither to go and what to bear with us,

100   And do not seek to take your change upon you
To bear your griefs yourself and leave me out.
For by this heaven, now at our sorrows pale,
Say what thou canst, I'll go along with thee.

ROSALIND   Why, whither shall we go?

105   CELIA   To seek my uncle in the Forest of Arden.

ROSALIND   Alas, what danger will it be to us,
Maids as we are, to travel forth so far!
Beauty provoketh thieves sooner than gold.

CELIA   I'll put myself in poor and mean attire,

110   And with a kind of umber smirch my face –
The like do you; so shall we pass along
And never stir assailants.

ROSALIND   Were it not better,
Because that I am more than common tall,
That I did suit me all points like a man?

115   A gallant curtal-axe upon my thigh,
A boar-spear in my hand, and in my heart,
Lie there what hidden woman's fear there will,
We'll have a swashing and a martial outside,
As many other mannish cowards have

120   That do outface it with their semblances.

CELIA   What shall I call thee when thou art a man?

ROSALIND
I'll have no worse a name than Jove's own page,
And therefore look you call me Ganymede.
But what will you be called?

125   CELIA   Something that hath a reference to my state:
No longer Celia, but Aliena.

ROSALIND   But cousin, what if we assayed to steal
The clownish fool out of your father's court?
Would he not be a comfort to our travail?

130   CELIA   He'll go along o'er the wide world with me.

Leave me alone to woo him. Let's away,
And get our jewels and our wealth together,
Devise the fittest time and safest way
To hide us from pursuit that will be made
After my flight. Now go we in content   135
To liberty and not to banishment.   *Exeunt.*

2.1   *Enter* DUKE SENIOR, AMIENS *and two or three*
Lords dressed as foresters.

DUKE SENIOR
Now, my co-mates and brothers in exile,
Hath not old custom made this life more sweet
Than that of painted pomp? Are not these woods
More free from peril than the envious court?
Here feel we not the penalty of Adam,   5
The seasons' difference – as the icy fang
And churlish chiding of the winter's wind,
Which when it bites and blows upon my body
Even till I shrink with cold, I smile and say:
'This is no flattery. These are counsellors   10
That feelingly persuade me what I am.'
Sweet are the uses of adversity,
Which, like the toad, ugly and venomous,
Wears yet a precious jewel in his head;
And this our life, exempt from public haunt,   15
Finds tongues in trees, books in the running brooks,
Sermons in stones, and good in everything.

AMIENS   I would not change it. Happy is your grace
That can translate the stubbornness of fortune
Into so quiet and so sweet a style.   20

DUKE SENIOR   Come, shall we go and kill us venison?
And yet it irks me the poor dappled fools,
Being native burghers of this desert city,
Should in their own confines with forked heads
Have their round haunches gored.

1 LORD   Indeed, my lord,   25
The melancholy Jaques grieves at that,
And in that kind swears you do more usurp
Than doth your brother that hath banished you.
Today my Lord of Amiens and myself
Did steal behind him as he lay along   30
Under an oak, whose antic root peeps out
Upon the brook that brawls along this wood;
To the which place a poor sequestered stag,
That from the hunter's aim had ta'en a hurt,
Did come to languish; and indeed, my lord,   35
The wretched animal heaved forth such groans
That their discharge did stretch his leathern coat
Almost to bursting, and the big round tears
Coursed one another down his innocent nose
In piteous chase. And thus the hairy fool,   40
Much marked of the melancholy Jaques,
Stood on th'extremest verge of the swift brook,
Augmenting it with tears.

DUKE SENIOR   But what said Jaques?
Did he not moralize this spectacle?

45 1 LORD   O yes, into a thousand similes.
First, for his weeping into the needless stream:
'Poor deer,' quoth he, 'thou mak'st a testament
As worldlings do, giving thy sum of more
To that which had too much.' Then being there alone,
50 Left and abandoned of his velvet friend:
''Tis right,' quoth he, 'thus misery doth part
The flux of company.' Anon a careless herd,
Full of the pasture, jumps along by him
And never stays to greet him. 'Ay,' quoth Jaques,
55 'Sweep on, you fat and greasy citizens!
'Tis just the fashion. Wherefore do you look
Upon that poor and broken bankrupt there?'
Thus most invectively he pierceth through
The body of country, city, court,
60 Yea, and of this our life, swearing that we
Are mere usurpers, tyrants and what's worse,
To fright the animals and to kill them up
In their assigned and native dwelling-place.
DUKE SENIOR
And did you leave him in this contemplation?
65 2 LORD   We did, my lord, weeping and commenting
Upon the sobbing deer.
DUKE SENIOR   Show me the place.
I love to cope him in these sullen fits,
For then he's full of matter.
1 LORD   I'll bring you to him straight.   *Exeunt.*

2.2   *Enter* DUKE FREDERICK *with* Lords.

DUKE FREDERICK
Can it be possible that no man saw them?
It cannot be! Some villains of my court
Are of consent and sufferance in this.
1 LORD   I cannot hear of any that did see her.
5 The ladies, her attendants of her chamber,
Saw her abed, and in the morning early
They found the bed untreasured of their mistress.
2 LORD   My lord, the roynish clown, at whom so oft
Your grace was wont to laugh, is also missing.
10 Hisperia, the princess' gentlewoman,
Confesses that she secretly o'erheard
Your daughter and her cousin much commend
The parts and graces of the wrestler
That did but lately foil the sinewy Charles;
15 And she believes wherever they are gone
That youth is surely in their company.
DUKE FREDERICK
Send to his brother; fetch that gallant hither.
If he be absent bring his brother to me.
I'll make him find him. Do this suddenly!
20 And let not search and inquisition quail
To bring again these foolish runaways.   *Exeunt.*

2.3   *Enter* ORLANDO *and* ADAM.

ORLANDO   Who's there?
ADAM   What, my young master? O my gentle master,

O my sweet master, O you memory
Of old Sir Rowland! Why, what make you here?
Why are you virtuous? Why do people love you?   5
And wherefore are you gentle, strong, and valiant?
Why would you be so fond to overcome
The bonny prizer of the humorous Duke?
Your praise is come too swiftly home before you.
Know you not, master, to some kind of men   10
Their graces serve them but as enemies?
No more do yours. Your virtues, gentle master,
Are sanctified and holy traitors to you.
O what a world is this, when what is comely
Envenoms him that bears it!   15
ORLANDO   Why, what's the matter?
ADAM   O unhappy youth,
Come not within these doors! Within this roof
The enemy of all your graces lives.
Your brother – no, no brother, yet the son –
Yet not the son; I will not call him son   20
Of him I was about to call his father –
Hath heard your praises, and this night he means
To burn the lodging where you use to lie,
And you within it. If he fail of that
He will have other means to cut you off;   25
I overheard him and his practices.
This is no place; this house is but a butchery.
Abhor it, fear it, do not enter it!
ORLANDO
Why whither, Adam, wouldst thou have me go?
ADAM   No matter whither so you come not here.   30
ORLANDO
What, wouldst thou have me go and beg my food,
Or with a base and boisterous sword enforce
A thievish living on the common road?
This I must do, or know not what to do.
Yet this I will not do, do how I can.   35
I rather will subject me to the malice
Of a diverted blood and bloody brother.
ADAM   But do not so. I have five hundred crowns,
The thrifty hire I saved under your father,
Which I did store to be my foster-nurse,   40
When service should in my old limbs lie lame
And unregarded age in corners thrown.
Take that, and He that doth the ravens feed,
Yea, providently caters for the sparrow,
Be comfort to my age. Here is the gold: 45
All this I give you. Let me be your servant.
Though I look old, yet I am strong and lusty,
For in my youth I never did apply
Hot and rebellious liquors in my blood,
Nor did not with unbashful forehead woo   50
The means of weakness and debility.
Therefore my age is as a lusty winter,
Frosty but kindly Let me go with you.
I'll do the service of a younger man
In all your business and necessities.   55
ORLANDO   O good old man, how well in thee appears

The constant service of the antique world,
Where servants sweat for duty not for meed.
Thou art not for the fashion of these times,
60 Where none will sweat but for promotion,
And, having that, do choke their service up
Even with the having. It is not so with thee.
But, poor old man, thou prun'st a rotten tree,
That cannot so much as a blossom yield
65 In lieu of all thy pains and husbandry.
But come thy ways, we'll go along together,
And ere we have thy youthful wages spent
We'll light upon some settled low content.
ADAM   Master, go on and I will follow thee
70 To the last gasp with truth and loyalty.
From seventeen years till now almost fourscore
Here lived I, but now live here no more.
At seventeen years many their fortunes seek,
But at fourscore it is too late a week.
75 Yet fortune cannot recompense me better
Than to die well and not my master's debtor. *Exeunt.*

2.4   *Enter* ROSALIND *as Ganymede,* CELIA
as Aliena and TOUCHSTONE.

ROSALIND   O Jupiter, how weary are my spirits!
TOUCHSTONE   I care not for my spirits if my legs were
not weary.
ROSALIND   I could find in my heart to disgrace my
5   man's apparel and to cry like a woman, but I must
comfort the weaker vessel, as doublet and hose ought
to show itself courageous to petticoat. Therefore
courage, good Aliena.
CELIA   I pray you bear with me, I cannot go no further.
10 TOUCHSTONE   For my part, I had rather bear with you
than bear you. Yet I should bear no cross if I did bear
you, for I think you have no money in your purse.
ROSALIND   Well, this is the Forest of Arden.
TOUCHSTONE   Ay, now am I in Arden, the more fool I!
15   When I was at home I was in a better place, but
travellers must be content.

Enter CORIN *and* SILVIUS.

ROSALIND   Ay, be so, good Touchstone. Look you, who
comes here? A young man and an old in solemn talk.
CORIN   That is the way to make her scorn you still.
20 SILVIUS   O Corin, that thou knewst how I do love her!
CORIN   I partly guess, for I have loved ere now.
SILVIUS   No, Corin, being old, thou canst not guess,
Though in thy youth thou wast as true a lover
As ever sighed upon a midnight pillow.
25   But if thy love were ever like to mine –
As sure I think did never man love so –
How many actions most ridiculous
Hast thou been drawn to by thy fantasy?
CORIN   Into a thousand that I have forgotten.
30 SILVIUS   O, thou didst then never love so heartily!
If thou rememb'rest not the slightest folly

That ever love did make thee run into,
Thou hast not loved.
Or if thou hast not sat as I do now,
35   Wearing thy hearer in thy mistress' praise,
Thou hast not loved.
Or if thou hast not broke from company
Abruptly as my passion now makes me,
Thou hast not loved.
40   O Phoebe, Phoebe, Phoebe!   *Exit.*
ROSALIND
Alas, poor shepherd, searching of thy wound
I have by hard adventure found mine own.
TOUCHSTONE   And I mine. I remember when I was in
love I broke my sword upon a stone and bid him
45   take that for coming a-night to Jane Smile; and I
remember the kissing of her batlet, and the cow's
dugs that her pretty chopped hands had milked; and
I remember the wooing of a peascod instead of her,
from whom I took two cods, and, giving her them
50   again, said with weeping tears: 'Wear these for my
sake.' We that are true lovers run into strange capers.
But as all is mortal in nature, so is all nature in love
mortal in folly.
ROSALIND   Thou speak'st wiser than thou art ware of.
55 TOUCHSTONE   Nay, I shall ne'er be ware of mine own
wit till I break my shins against it.
ROSALIND   Jove, Jove, this shepherd's passion
Is much upon my fashion!
TOUCHSTONE   And mine, but it grows something stale
60   with me.
CELIA   I pray you, one of you question yon man
If he for gold will give us any food.
I faint almost to death.
TOUCHSTONE   Holla, you clown!
65 ROSALIND   Peace, fool, he's not thy kinsman.
CORIN   Who calls?
TOUCHSTONE   Your betters, sir.
CORIN   Else are they very wretched.
ROSALIND [*to Touchstone*]
Peace, I say. – Good even to you, friend.
70 CORIN   And to you, gentle sir, and to you all.
ROSALIND   I prithee, shepherd, if that love or gold
Can in this desert place buy entertainment,
Bring us where we may rest ourselves and feed.
Here's a young maid with travel much oppressed
75   And faints for succour.
CORIN   Fair sir, I pity her
And wish, for her sake more than for mine own,
My fortunes were more able to relieve her.
But I am shepherd to another man
And do not shear the fleeces that I graze.
80   My master is of churlish disposition
And little recks to find the way to heaven
By doing deeds of hospitality.
Besides, his cote, his flocks and bounds of feed
Are now on sale, and at our sheepcote now,
85   By reason of his absence, there is nothing

That you will feed on. But what is, come see,
And in my voice most welcome shall you be.
ROSALIND
What is he that shall buy his flock and pasture?
CORIN
That young swain that you saw here but erewhile,
90 That little cares for buying anything.
ROSALIND   I pray thee, if it stand with honesty,
Buy thou the cottage, pasture and the flock,
And thou shalt have to pay for it of us.
CELIA   And we will mend thy wages. I like this place
95 And willingly could waste my time in it.
CORIN   Assuredly the thing is to be sold.
Go with me. If you like upon report
The soil, the profit and this kind of life,
I will your very faithful feeder be,
100 And buy it with your gold right suddenly.   *Exeunt.*

2.5   *Enter* AMIENS, JAQUES *and other* Lords
dressed as foresters.

AMIENS [*Sings.*]
Under the greenwood tree
Who loves to lie with me
And turn his merry note
Unto the sweet bird's throat,
5 Come hither, come hither, come hither!
ALL [*Sing.*]
Here shall he see no enemy
But winter and rough weather.
JAQUES   More, more, I prithee, more.
AMIENS   It will make you melancholy, Monsieur Jaques.
10 JAQUES   I thank it; more, I prithee, more. I can suck
melancholy out of a song as a weasel sucks eggs. More,
I prithee, more!
AMIENS   My voice is ragged: I know I cannot please
you.
15 JAQUES   I do not desire you to please me; I do desire you
to sing. Come, more, another *stanzo* – call you 'em
stanzos?
AMIENS   What you will, Monsieur Jaques.
JAQUES   Nay, I care not for their names: they owe me
20 nothing. Will you sing?
AMIENS   More at your request than to please myself.
JAQUES   Well then, if ever I thank any man I'll thank
you; but that they call compliment is like th'encounter
of two dog-apes. And when a man thanks me heartily,
25 methinks I have given him a penny and he renders me
the beggarly thanks. Come, sing; – and you that will
not, hold your tongues.
AMIENS   Well, I'll end the song. Sirs, cover the while.
The Duke will drink under this tree; he hath been all
30 this day to look you.
JAQUES   And I have been all this day to avoid him; he is
too disputable for my company. I think of as many
matters as he, but I give heaven thanks and make no
boast of them. Come, warble, come.

AMIENS [*Sings.*]
Who doth ambition shun   35
And loves to live i'th' sun,
Seeking the food he eats
And pleased with what he gets,
Come hither, come hither, come hither!
ALL [*Sing.*]
Here shall he see no enemy   40
But winter and rough weather.
JAQUES   I'll give you a verse to this note that I made
yesterday in despite of my invention.
AMIENS   And I'll sing it.
JAQUES   Thus it goes. [*Gives Amiens a paper.*]   45
AMIENS [*Sings.*]
If it do come to pass
That any man turn ass,
Leaving his wealth and ease
A stubborn will to please,
Ducdame, ducdame, ducdame!   50
ALL [*Sing.*]
Here shall he see gross fools as he
An if he will come to me.
AMIENS   What's that 'ducdame'?
JAQUES   'Tis a Greek invocation to call fools into a
circle. I'll go sleep if I can; if I cannot, I'll rail against   55
all the first-born of Egypt.
AMIENS   And I'll go seek the Duke; his banquet is
prepared.   *Exeunt.*

2.6   *Enter* ORLANDO *and* ADAM.

ADAM   Dear master,
I can go no further. O, I die for food!
Here lie I down and measure out my grave.
Farewell, kind master.
ORLANDO
Why, how now, Adam? No greater heart in thee?   5
Live a little, comfort a little, cheer thyself a little. If this
uncouth forest yield anything savage I will either be food
for it or bring it for food to thee. Thy conceit is nearer
death than thy powers. For my sake, be comfortable; hold
death awhile at the arm's end. I will here be with thee   10
presently, and if I bring thee not something to eat I will
give thee leave to die. But if thou diest before I come,
thou art a mocker of my labour. Well said, thou look'st
cheerly, and I'll be with thee quickly. Yet thou liest in the
bleak air. Come, I will bear thee to some shelter and thou 15
shalt not die for lack of a dinner if there live anything in
this desert. Cheerly, good Adam.   *Exeunt.*

2.7   *Enter* DUKE SENIOR, AMIENS *and* Lords
dressed as outlaws.

DUKE SENIOR   I think he be transformed into a beast,
For I can nowhere find him like a man.
1 LORD   My lord, he is but even now gone hence;
Here was he merry, hearing of a song.
DUKE SENIOR   If he, compact of jars, grow musical,   5

We shall have shortly discord in the spheres.
Go seek him, tell him I would speak with him.

Enter JAQUES.

1 LORD   He saves my labour by his own approach.
DUKE SENIOR
10   Why; how now, Monsieur! What a life is this
That your poor friends must woo your company!
What, you look merrily.
JAQUES   A fool, a fool! I met a fool i'th' forest,
A motley fool – a miserable world!
15   As I do live by food, I met a fool,
Who laid him down and basked him in the sun,
And railed on Lady Fortune in good terms,
In good set terms – and yet a motley fool!
'Good morrow, fool,' quoth I. 'No, sir,' quoth he,
'Call me not fool till heaven hath sent me fortune.'
20   And then he drew a dial from his poke,
And looking on it with lack-lustre eye
Says very wisely, 'It is ten o'clock.
Thus we may see', quoth he, 'how the world wags.
'Tis but an hour ago since it was nine,
25   And after one hour more 'twill be eleven.
And so from hour to hour we ripe and ripe,
And then from hour to hour we rot and rot,
And thereby hangs a tale.' When I did hear
The motley fool thus moral on the time,
30   My lungs began to crow like chanticleer,
That fools should be so deep-contemplative,
And I did laugh *sans* intermission
An hour by his dial. O noble fool,
A worthy fool! Motley's the only wear!
35   DUKE SENIOR   What fool is this?
JAQUES
O worthy fool! – One that hath been a courtier,
And says if ladies be but young and fair
They have the gift to know it. And in his brain,
Which is as dry as the remainder biscuit
40   After a voyage, he hath strange places crammed
With observation, the which he vents
In mangled forms. O that I were a fool!
I am ambitious for a motley coat.
DUKE SENIOR   Thou shalt have one.
JAQUES   It is my only suit,
45   Provided that you weed your better judgements
Of all opinion that grows rank in them
That I am wise. I must have liberty
Withal, as large a charter as the wind
To blow on whom I please, for so fools have,
50   And they that are most galled with my folly,
They most must laugh. And why, sir, must they so?
The why is plain as way to parish church.
He that a fool doth very wisely hit
Doth very foolishly, although he smart,
55   Not to seem senseless of the bob. If not,
The wise man's folly is anatomized
Even by the squandering glances of the fool.

Invest me in my motley. Give me leave
To speak my mind, and I will through and through
Cleanse the foul body of th'infected world,   60
If they will patiently receive my medicine.
DUKE SENIOR
Fie on thee! I can tell what thou wouldst do.
JAQUES   What, for a counter, would I do but good?
DUKE SENIOR
Most mischievous foul sin in chiding sin.
For thou thyself hast been a libertine,   65
As sensual as the brutish sting itself,
And all th'embossed sores and headed evils
That thou with licence of free foot hast caught
Wouldst thou disgorge into the general world.
JAQUES   Why, who cries out on pride   70
That can therein tax any private party?
Doth it not flow as hugely as the sea
Till that the weary very means do ebb?
What woman in the city do I name,
When that I say the city-woman bears   75
The cost of princes on unworthy shoulders?
Who can come in and say that I mean her,
When such a one as she, such is her neighbour?
Or what is he of basest function,
That says his bravery is not on my cost –   80
Thinking that I mean him – but therein suits
His folly to the mettle of my speech?
There then – how then, what then? Let me see wherein
My tongue hath wronged him. If it do him right,
Then he hath wronged himself If he be free,   85
Why then my taxing like a wild goose flies
Unclaimed of any man. But who comes here?

Enter ORLANDO *with sword drawn.*

ORLANDO   Forbear and eat no more!
JAQUES   Why, I have ate none yet.
ORLANDO   Nor shalt not till necessity be served.   90
JAQUES   Of what kind should this cock come of?
DUKE SENIOR
Art thou thus boldened, man, by thy distress?
Or else a rude despiser of good manners,
That in civility thou seem'st so empty?
ORLANDO
You touched my vein at first. The thorny point   95
Of bare distress hath ta'en from me the show
Of smooth civility; yet am I inland bred
And know some nurture. But forbear, I say!
He dies that touches any of this fruit
Till I and my affairs are answered.   100
JAQUES   An you will not be answered with reason, I
must die.
DUKE SENIOR
What would you have? Your gentleness shall force
More than your force move us to gentleness.
ORLANDO   I almost die for food – and let me have it.   105
DUKE SENIOR
Sit down and feed and welcome to our table.

ORLANDO
Speak you so gently? Pardon me, I pray you.
I thought that all things had been savage here
And therefore put I on the countenance
110 Of stern commandment. But whate'er you are,
That in this desert inaccessible,
Under the shade of melancholy boughs,
Lose and neglect the creeping hours of time –
If ever you have looked on better days,
115 If ever been where bells have knolled to church,
If ever sat at any good man's feast,
If ever from your eyelids wiped a tear,
And know what 'tis to pity and be pitied –
Let gentleness my strong enforcement be,
120 In the which hope, I blush and hide my sword.
DUKE SENIOR   True is it that we have seen better days,
And have with holy bell been knolled to church,
And sat at good men's feasts, and wiped our eyes
Of drops that sacred pity hath engendered;
125 And therefore sit you down in gentleness
And take upon command what help we have
That to your wanting may be ministered.
ORLANDO   Then but forbear your food a little while,
Whiles like a doe I go to find my fawn,
130 And give it food. There is an old poor man
Who after me hath many a weary step
Limped in pure love. Till he be first sufficed,
Oppressed with two weak evils, age and hunger,
I will not touch a bit.
DUKE SENIOR   Go find him out,
135 And we will nothing waste till you return.
ORLANDO
I thank ye, and be blest for your good comfort.   *Exit.*
DUKE SENIOR
Thou seest we are not all alone unhappy.
This wide and universal theatre
Presents more woeful pageants than the scene
Wherein we play in.
140 JAQUES   All the world's a stage,
And all the men and women merely players.
They have their exits and their entrances,
And one man in his time plays many parts,
His acts being seven ages. At first the infant,
145 Mewling and puking in the nurse's arms;
Then the whining schoolboy, with his satchel
And shining morning face, creeping like snail
Unwillingly to school; and then the lover,
Sighing like furnace, with a woeful ballad
150 Made to his mistress' eyebrow; then a soldier,
Full of strange oaths and bearded like the pard,
Jealous in honour, sudden and quick in quarrel,
Seeking the bubble reputation
Even in the cannon's mouth; and then the
justice,
155 In fair round belly with good capon lined,
With eyes severe and beard of formal cut,

Full of wise saws and modern instances;
And so he plays his part. The sixth age shifts
Into the lean and slippered pantaloon,
160 With spectacles on nose and pouch on side,
His youthful hose well saved, a world too wide
For his shrunk shank, and his big manly voice,
Turning again toward childish treble, pipes
And whistles in his sound. Last scene of all,
165 That ends this strange eventful history,
Is second childishness and mere oblivion,
Sans teeth, *sans* eyes, *sans* taste, *sans* everything.

Enter ORLANDO *bearing* ADAM.

DUKE SENIOR
Welcome. Set down your venerable burden
And let him feed.
ORLANDO   I thank you most for him.
ADAM   So had you need;
170 I scarce can speak to thank you for myself
DUKE SENIOR   Welcome, fall to. I will not trouble you
As yet to question you about your fortunes.
Give us some music, and good cousin, sing.
AMIENS [*Sings.*]
Blow, blow, thou winter wind,   175
Thou art not so unkind
As man's ingratitude.
Thy tooth is not so keen
Because thou art not seen,
Although thy breath be rude.   180
Hey-ho, sing hey-ho, unto the green holly.
Most friendship is feigning, most loving mere folly.
Then hey-ho, the holly!
This life is most jolly.

Freeze, freeze, thou bitter sky,   185
That dost not bite so nigh
As benefits forgot.
Though thou the waters warp,
Thy sting is not so sharp
As friend remembered not.   190
Hey-ho, sing hey-ho, unto the green holly.
Most friendship is feigning, most loving mere folly.
Then hey-ho, the holly!
This life is most jolly.
DUKE SENIOR
If that you be the good Sir Rowland's son,   195
As you have whispered faithfully you were,
And as mine eye doth his effigies witness,
Most truly limned and living in your face,
Be truly welcome hither. I am the Duke
That loved your father. The residue of your fortune   200
Go to my cave and tell me. – Good old man,
Thou art right welcome as thy master is.
[*to Lords*] Support him by the arm.
[*to Orlando*]   Give me your hand
And let me all your fortunes understand.   *Exeunt.*

3.1 *Enter* DUKE FREDERICK, *Lords and* OLIVER.

DUKE FREDERICK
Not see him since? Sir, sir, that cannot be.
But were I not the better part made mercy
I should not seek an absent argument
Of my revenge, thou present. But look to it!
5 Find out thy brother wheresoe'er he is;
Seek him with candle. Bring him dead or living
Within this twelvemonth, or turn thou no more
To seek a living in our territory.
Thy lands, and all things that thou dost call thine
10 Worth seizure, do we seize into our hands,
Till thou canst quit thee by thy brother's mouth
Of what we think against thee.

OLIVER
O that your highness knew my heart in this:
I never loved my brother in my life.

DUKE FREDERICK
15 More villain thou! Well, push him out of doors,
And let my officers of such a nature
Make an extent upon his house and lands.
Do this expediently, and turn him going.   *Exeunt.*

3.2   *Enter* ORLANDO *with a writing.*

ORLANDO
Hang there, my verse, in witness of my love.
And thou, thrice-crowned queen of night, survey
With thy chaste eye, from thy pale sphere above,
Thy huntress' name that my full life doth sway.
5 O Rosalind, these trees shall be my books,
And in their barks my thoughts I'll character,
That every eye which in this forest looks
Shall see thy virtue witnessed everywhere.
Run, run, Orlando, carve on every tree
10 The fair, the chaste and unexpressive she!   *Exit.*

Enter CORIN *and* TOUCHSTONE.

CORIN   And how like you this shepherd's life, Master
Touchstone?

TOUCHSTONE   Truly, shepherd, in respect of itself, it is
a good life; but in respect that it is a shepherd's life, it
15 is naught. In respect that it is solitary, I like it very well;
but in respect that it is private, it is a very vile life. Now
in respect it is in the fields, it pleaseth me well; but in
respect it is not in the court, it is tedious. As it is a
spare life, look you, it fits my humour well; but as there
20 is no more plenty in it, it goes much against my
stomach. Hast any philosophy in thee, shepherd?

CORIN   No more but that I know the more one sickens
the worse at ease he is; and that he that wants money,
means and content is without three good friends; that
25 the property of rain is to wet and fire to burn; that good
pasture makes fat sheep; and that a great cause of the
night is lack of the sun; that he that hath learned no wit
by nature nor art may complain of poor breeding or
comes of a very dull kindred.

TOUCHSTONE   Such a one is a natural philosopher. 30
Wast ever in court, shepherd?

CORIN   No, truly.

TOUCHSTONE   Then thou art damned.

CORIN   Nay, I hope.

TOUCHSTONE   Truly, thou art damned, like an ill- 35
roasted egg, all on one side.

CORIN   For not being at court? Your reason?

TOUCHSTONE   Why, if thou never wast at court thou
never sawst good manners; if thou never sawst good
manners then thy manners must be wicked, and 40
wickedness is sin and sin is damnation. Thou art in a
parlous state, shepherd.

CORIN   Not a whit, Touchstone. Those that are good
manners at the court are as ridiculous in the country as
the behaviour of the country is most mockable at the 45
court. You told me you salute not at the court but you
kiss your hands. That courtesy would be uncleanly if
courtiers were shepherds.

TOUCHSTONE   Instance, briefly. Come, instance.

CORIN   Why, we are still handling our ewes, and their 50
fells, you know, are greasy.

TOUCHSTONE   Why, do not your courtier's hands
sweat? And is not the grease of a mutton as wholesome
as the sweat of a man? Shallow, shallow. A better
instance, I say. Come. 55

CORIN   Besides, our hands are hard.

TOUCHSTONE   Your lips will feel them the sooner –
shallow again. A more sounder instance, come.

CORIN   And they are often tarred over with the surgery
of our sheep, and would you have us kiss tar? The 60
courtier's hands are perfumed with civet.

TOUCHSTONE   Most shallow man! Thou worm's meat
in respect of a good piece of flesh indeed! Learn of the
wise and perpend. Civet is of a baser birth than tar, the
very uncleanly flux of a cat. Mend the instance, 65
shepherd.

CORIN   You have too courtly a wit for me, I'll rest.

TOUCHSTONE   Wilt thou rest damned? God help
thee, shallow man! God make incision in thee, thou
art raw! 70

CORIN   Sir, I am a true labourer. I earn that I eat, get
that I wear; owe no man hate, envy no man's happiness;
glad of other men's good, content with my harm; and
the greatest of my pride is to see my ewes graze and my
lambs suck. 75

TOUCHSTONE   That is another simple sin in you: to
bring the ewes and the rams together and to offer to get
your living by the copulation of cattle; to be bawd to a
bell-wether and to betray a she-lamb of a twelvemonth
to a crooked-pated old cuckoldly ram, out of all 80
reasonable match. If thou be'st not damned for this,
the devil himself will have no shepherds. I cannot see
else how thou shouldst scape.

Enter ROSALIND *as Ganymede, with a writing.*

CORIN   Here comes young Master Ganymede, my new
mistress's brother. 85

ROSALIND [*Reads.*]
> From the east to western Inde
> No jewel is like Rosalind.
> Her worth being mounted on the wind
> Through all the world bears Rosalind.
> All the pictures fairest lined
> Are but black to Rosalind.
> Let no fair be kept in mind
> But the fair of Rosalind.

TOUCHSTONE I'll rhyme you so eight years together, dinners and suppers and sleeping-hours excepted. It is the right butter-women's rank to market.

ROSALIND Out, fool!

TOUCHSTONE For a taste –
> If a hart do lack a hind,
> Let him seek out Rosalind.
> If the cat will after kind,
> So be sure will Rosalind.
> Winter garments must be lined,
> So must slender Rosalind.
> They that reap must sheaf and bind,
> Then to cart with Rosalind.
> Sweetest nut hath sourest rind,
> Such a nut is Rosalind.
> He that sweetest rose will find
> Must find love's prick – and Rosalind.

This is the very false gallop of verses. Why do you infect yourself with them?

ROSALIND Peace, you dull fool, I found them on a tree.

TOUCHSTONE Truly, the tree yields bad fruit.

ROSALIND I'll graft it with you, and then I shall graft it with a medlar. Then it will be the earliest fruit i'th' country, for you'll be rotten ere you be half ripe, and that's the right virtue of the medlar.

TOUCHSTONE You have said. – But whether wisely or no, let the forest judge.

Enter CELIA *as Aliena with a writing.*

ROSALIND Peace, here comes my sister reading. Stand aside.

CELIA [*Reads.*]
> Why should this a desert be,
> For it is unpeopled? No!
> Tongues I'll hang on every tree
> That shall civil sayings show:
> Some, how brief the life of man
> Runs his erring pilgrimage,
> That the stretching of a span
> Buckles in his sum of age;
> Some, of violated vows
> 'Twixt the souls of friend and friend.
> But upon the fairest boughs,
> Or at every sentence' end,
> Will I 'Rosalinda' write,
> Teaching all that read to know
> The quintessence of every sprite
> Heaven would in little show.

> Therefore heaven Nature charged
> That one body should be filled
> With all graces wide-enlarged.
> Nature presently distilled
> Helen's cheek but not her heart,
> Cleopatra's majesty,
> Atalanta's better part,
> Sad Lucretia's modesty.
> Thus Rosalind of many parts
> By heavenly synod was devised,
> Of many faces, eyes and hearts
> To have the touches dearest prized.
> Heaven would that she these gifts should have,
> And I to live and die her slave.

ROSALIND O most gentle pulpiter, what tedious homily of love have you wearied your parishioners withal, and never cried: 'Have patience, good people!'

CELIA How now! Back, friends. – Shepherd, go off a little; go with him, sirrah.

TOUCHSTONE Come, shepherd, let us make an honourable retreat, though not with bag and baggage yet with scrip and scrippage.   *Exit with Corin.*

CELIA Didst thou hear these verses?

ROSALIND O yes, I heard them all, and more too, for some of them had in them more feet than the verses would bear.

CELIA That's no matter – the feet might bear the verses.

ROSALIND Ay, but the feet were lame and could not bear themselves without the verse, and therefore stood lamely in the verse.

CELIA But didst thou hear, without wondering, how thy name should be hanged and carved upon these trees?

ROSALIND I was seven of the nine days out of the wonder before you came; for look here what I found on a palm-tree. I was never so berhymed since Pythagoras' time that I was an Irish rat, which I can hardly remember.

CELIA Trow you who hath done this?

ROSALIND Is it a man?

CELIA And a chain that you once wore about his neck – change you colour?

ROSALIND I prithee, who?

CELIA O Lord, Lord, it is a hard matter for friends to meet; but mountains may be removed with earthquakes and so encounter.

ROSALIND Nay, but who is it?

CELIA Is it possible?

ROSALIND Nay, I prithee now, with most petitionary vehemence, tell me who it is.

CELIA O wonderful, wonderful, and most wonderful wonderful, and yet again wonderful, and after that out of all hooping!

ROSALIND Good my complexion! Dost thou think, though I am caparisoned like a man, I have a doublet and hose in my disposition? One inch of delay more is a South Sea of discovery. I prithee tell me who is it quickly and speak apace. I would thou couldst stammer, that thou mightst pour this concealed man out of thy mouth as wine comes out of a narrow-mouthed bottle – either too much at once or none at all. I prithee take the cork out of thy mouth that I may drink thy tidings.

200 CELIA   So you may put a man in your belly.

ROSALIND   Is he of God's making? What manner of man? Is his head worth a hat? Or his chin worth a beard?

CELIA   Nay, he hath but a little beard.

205 ROSALIND   Why, God will send more if the man will be thankful. Let me stay the growth of his beard, if thou delay me not the knowledge of his chin.

CELIA   It is young Orlando, that tripped up the wrestler's heels and your heart both in an instant.

210 ROSALIND   Nay, but the devil take mocking! Speak sad brow and true maid.

CELIA   I'faith, coz, 'tis he.

ROSALIND   Orlando?

CELIA   Orlando.

215 ROSALIND   Alas the day, what shall I do with my doublet and hose? What did he when thou sawst him? What said he? How looked he? Wherein went he? What makes he here? Did he ask for me? Where remains he? How parted he with thee? And when shalt thou see him

220 again? Answer me in one word.

CELIA   You must borrow me Gargantua's mouth first. 'Tis a word too great for any mouth of this age's size. To say ay and no to these particulars is more than to answer in a catechism.

225 ROSALIND   But doth he know that I am in this forest and in man's apparel? Looks he as freshly as he did the day he wrestled?

CELIA   It is as easy to count atomies as to resolve the propositions of a lover; but take a taste of my finding

230 him and relish it with good observance. I found him under a tree, like a dropped acorn –

ROSALIND   It may well be called Jove's tree when it drops forth such fruit.

CELIA   Give me audience, good madam.

235 ROSALIND   Proceed.

CELIA   There lay he stretched along like a wounded knight –

ROSALIND   Though it be pity to see such a sight, it well becomes the ground.

240 CELIA   Cry holla to thy tongue, I prithee: it curvets unseasonably. He was furnished like a hunter –

ROSALIND   O ominous, he comes to kill my heart!

CELIA   I would sing my song without a burden – thou bring'st me out of tune.

245 ROSALIND   Do you not know I am a woman? When I think, I must speak. Sweet, say on.

Enter ORLANDO *and* JAQUES.

CELIA   You bring me out. Soft, comes he not here?

ROSALIND   'Tis he! Slink by and note him.

JAQUES   I thank you for your company but, good faith, I

250 had as lief have been myself alone.

ORLANDO   And so had I, but yet for fashion' sake I thank you too for your society.

JAQUES   God b'wi' you, let's meet as little as we can.

ORLANDO   I do desire we may be better strangers.

255 JAQUES   I pray you, mar no more trees with writing love-songs in their barks.

ORLANDO   I pray you, mar no more of my verses with reading them ill-favouredly.

JAQUES   Rosalind is your love's name?

260 ORLANDO   Yes, just.

JAQUES   I do not like her name.

ORLANDO   There was no thought of pleasing you when she was christened.

JAQUES   What stature is she of?

265 ORLANDO   Just as high as my heart.

JAQUES   You are full of pretty answers. Have you not been acquainted with goldsmiths' wives, and conned them out of rings?

ORLANDO   Not so; but I answer you right painted cloth,

270 from whence you have studied your questions.

JAQUES   You have a nimble wit; I think 'twas made of Atalanta's heels. Will you sit down with me, and we two will rail against our mistress the world and all our misery?

275 ORLANDO   I will chide no breather in the world but myself, against whom I know most faults.

JAQUES   The worst fault you have is to be in love.

ORLANDO   'Tis a fault I will not change for your best virtue. I am weary of you.

280 JAQUES   By my troth, I was seeking for a fool when I found you.

ORLANDO   He is drowned in the brook. Look but in and you shall see him.

JAQUES   There I shall see mine own figure.

285 ORLANDO   Which I take to be either a fool or a cipher.

JAQUES   I'll tarry no longer with you. Farewell, good Signior Love.   *Exit Jaques.*

ORLANDO   I am glad of your departure. Adieu, good Monsieur Melancholy

290 ROSALIND   I will speak to him like a saucy lackey and under that habit play the knave with him. – Do you hear, forester?

ORLANDO   Very well; what would you?

ROSALIND   I pray you, what is't o'clock?

295 ORLANDO   You should ask me what time o'day. There's no clock in the forest.

ROSALIND   Then there is no true lover in the forest, else sighing every minute and groaning every hour would detect the lazy foot of time as well as a clock.

300 ORLANDO   And why not the swift foot of time? Had not that been as proper?

ROSALIND   By no means, sir. Time travels in divers paces with divers persons. I'll tell you who Time ambles withal, who Time trots withal, who Time

305 gallops withal and who he stands still withal.

ORLANDO   I prithee, who doth he trot withal?

ROSALIND   Marry, he trots hard with a young maid

between the contract of her marriage and the day it is
solemnized. If the interim be but a se'nnight, Time's
310 pace is so hard that it seems the length of seven year.

ORLANDO   Who ambles Time withal?

ROSALIND   With a priest that lacks Latin, and a rich
man that hath not the gout; for the one sleeps easily
because he cannot study, and the other lives merrily
315 because he feels no pain; the one lacking the burden of
lean and wasteful learning, the other knowing no
burden of heavy tedious penury. These Time ambles
withal.

ORLANDO   Who doth he gallop withal?

320 ROSALIND   With a thief to the gallows; for though he go
as softly as foot can fall, he thinks himself too soon
there.

ORLANDO   Who stays it still withal?

ROSALIND   With lawyers in the vacation; for they sleep
325 between term and term and then they perceive not
how time moves.

ORLANDO   Where dwell you, pretty youth?

ROSALIND   With this shepherdess, my sister, here in the
skirts of the forest, like fringe upon a petticoat.

330 ORLANDO   Are you native of this place?

ROSALIND   As the coney that you see dwell where she is
kindled.

ORLANDO   Your accent is something finer than you
could purchase in so removed a dwelling.

335 ROSALIND   I have been told so of many. But indeed, an
old religious uncle of mine taught me to speak, who was
in his youth an inland man – one that knew courtship
too well, for there he fell in love. I have heard him read
many lectures against it, and I thank God I am not a
340 woman, to be touched with so many giddy offences as
he hath generally taxed their whole sex withal.

ORLANDO   Can you remember any of the principal evils
that he laid to the charge of women?

ROSALIND   There were none principal – they were all like
345 one another as ha'pence are, every one fault seeming
monstrous till his fellow-fault came to match it.

ORLANDO   I prithee, recount some of them.

ROSALIND   No. I will not cast away my physic but on
those that are sick. There is a man haunts the forest
350 that abuses our young plants with carving 'Rosalind'
on their barks; hangs odes upon hawthorns and elegies
on brambles; all, forsooth, deifying the name of
Rosalind. If I could meet that fancy-monger I would
give him some good counsel, for he seems to have the
355 quotidian of love upon him.

ORLANDO   I am he that is so love-shaked. I pray you tell
me your remedy.

ROSALIND   There is none of my uncle's marks upon
you. He taught me how to know a man in love, in which
360 cage of rushes I am sure you are not prisoner.

ORLANDO   What were his marks?

ROSALIND   A lean cheek, which you have not; a blue eye
and sunken, which you have not; an unquestionable
spirit, which you have not; a beard neglected, which

you have not – but I pardon you for that, for simply   365
your having in beard is a younger brother's revenue.
Then your hose should be ungartered, your bonnet
unbanded, your sleeve unbuttoned, your shoe untied,
and everything about you demonstrating a careless
desolation. But you are no such man. You are rather   370
point-device in your accoutrements, as loving yourself
than seeming the lover of any other.

ORLANDO   Fair youth, I would I could make thee
believe I love.

ROSALIND   Me believe it? You may as soon make her   375
that you love believe it, which I warrant she is apter to
do than to confess she does. That is one of the points in
the which women still give the lie to their consciences.
But in good sooth, are you he that hangs the verses on
the trees, wherein Rosalind is so admired?   380

ORLANDO   I swear to thee, youth, by the white hand of
Rosalind, I am that he, that unfortunate he.

ROSALIND   But are you so much in love as your rhymes
speak?

ORLANDO   Neither rhyme nor reason can express how   385
much.

ROSALIND   Love is merely a madness, and I tell you
deserves as well a dark house and a whip as madmen
do; and the reason why they are not so punished and
cured is that the lunacy is so ordinary that the whippers   390
are in love too. Yet I profess curing it by counsel.

ORLANDO   Did you ever cure any so?

ROSALIND   Yes, one, and in this manner. He was to
imagine me his love, his mistress, and I set him every
day to woo me. At which time would I – being but a   395
moonish youth – grieve, be effeminate, changeable,
longing and liking, proud, fantastical, apish, shallow,
inconstant, full of tears, full of smiles; for every
passion something and for no passion truly anything,
as boys and women are for the most part cattle of this   400
colour; would now like him, now loath him; then
entertain him, then forswear him; now weep for him,
then spit at him; that I drave my suitor from his mad
humour of love to a living humour of madness, which
was to forswear the full stream of the world and to live   405
in a nook merely monastic. And thus I cured him, and
this way will I take upon me to wash your liver as clean
as a sound sheep's heart, that there shall not be one
spot of love in't.

ORLANDO   I would not be cured, youth.   410

ROSALIND   I would cure you, if you would but call me
Rosalind and come every day to my cote and woo me.

ORLANDO   Now by the faith of my love, I will. Tell me
where it is.

ROSALIND   Go with me to it and I'll show it you; and by   415
the way you shall tell me where in the forest you live.
Will you go?

ORLANDO   With all my heart, good youth.

ROSALIND   Nay, you must call me Rosalind. Come,
sister, will you go?   *Exeunt.*   420

3.3   *Enter* TOUCHSTONE, AUDREY *and*
         JAQUES *behind.*

TOUCHSTONE   Come apace, good Audrey – I will fetch
   up your goats, Audrey. And how, Audrey? Am I the
   man yet? Doth my simple feature content you?

AUDREY   Your features, Lord warrant us! What features?

5   TOUCHSTONE   I am here with thee and thy goats, as the
   most capricious poet, honest Ovid, was among the
   Goths.

JAQUES [*aside*]   O knowledge ill-inhabited, worse than
   Jove in a thatched house.

10   TOUCHSTONE   When a man's verses cannot be
   understood, nor a man's good wit seconded with the
   forward child, understanding, it strikes a man more
   dead than a great reckoning in a little room. Truly, I
   would the gods had made thee poetical.

15   AUDREY   I do not know what poetical is. Is it honest in
   deed and word? Is it a true thing?

TOUCHSTONE   No, truly; for the truest poetry is the
   most faining, and lovers are given to poetry, and what
   they swear in poetry may be said, as lovers, they do
20   feign.

AUDREY   Do you wish then that the gods had made me
   poetical?

TOUCHSTONE   I do truly, for thou swear'st to me thou
   art honest. Now if thou wert a poet I might have some
25   hope thou didst feign.

AUDREY   Would you not have me honest?

TOUCHSTONE   No, truly, unless thou wert hard-
   favoured; for honesty coupled to beauty is to have
   honey a sauce to sugar.

30   JAQUES [*aside*]   A material fool.

AUDREY   Well, I am not fair, and therefore I pray the
   gods make me honest.

TOUCHSTONE   Truly; and to cast away honesty upon a
   foul slut were to put good meat into an unclean dish.

35   AUDREY   I am not a slut, though I thank the gods I am
   foul.

TOUCHSTONE   Well, praised be the gods for thy
   foulness: sluttishness may come hereafter. But be it as
   it may be, I will marry thee. And to that end I have
40   been with Sir Oliver Mar-text, the vicar of the next
   village, who hath promised to meet me in this place of
   the forest and to couple us.

JAQUES [*aside*]   I would fain see this meeting.

AUDREY   Well, the gods give us joy!

45   TOUCHSTONE   Amen. – A man may, if he were of a
   fearful heart, stagger in this attempt, for here we have
   no temple but the wood, no assembly but horn-beasts.
   But what though? Courage! As horns are odious, they
   are necessary. It is said, many a man knows no end of
50   his goods; right. Many a man has good horns and
   knows no end of them. Well, that is the dowry of his
   wife – 'tis none of his own getting. Horns? Even so.
   Poor men alone? No, no, the noblest deer hath them as
   huge as the rascal. Is the single man therefore blessed?
55   No. As a walled town is more worthier than a village, so

is the forehead of a married man more honourable
than the bare brow of a bachelor. And by how much
defence is better than no skill, by so much is a horn
more precious than to want.

Enter SIR OLIVER MAR-TEXT.

Here comes Sir Oliver. Sir Oliver Mar-text, you are   60
well met. Will you dispatch us here under this tree or
shall we go with you to your chapel?

SIR OLIVER MAR-TEXT   Is there none here to give the
woman?

TOUCHSTONE   I will not take her on gift of any man.   65

SIR OLIVER MAR-TEXT   Truly she must be given or the
marriage is not lawful.

JAQUES [*Advances.*]   Proceed, proceed. I'll give her.

TOUCHSTONE   Good even, good Master What-ye-
call't, how do you, sir? You are very well met. God'ild   70
you for your last company. I am very glad to see you.
Even a toy in hand here, sir – nay, pray be covered.

JAQUES   Will you be married, motley?

TOUCHSTONE   As the ox hath his bow, sir, the horse his
curb and the falcon her bells, so man hath his desires;   75
and as pigeons bill, so wedlock would be nibbling.

JAQUES   And will you, being a man of your breeding, be
married under a bush like a beggar? Get you to church,
and have a good priest that can tell you what marriage
is. This fellow will but join you together as they join   80
wainscot; then one of you will prove a shrunk panel
and, like green timber, warp, warp.

TOUCHSTONE   I am not in the mind but I were better to
be married of him than of another, for he is not like to
marry me well, and not being well married it will be a   85
good excuse for me hereafter to leave my wife.

JAQUES   Go thou with me
   And let me counsel thee.

TOUCHSTONE   Come, sweet Audrey,
   We must be married, or we must live in bawdry.   90
   Farewell, good Master Oliver. Not
   [*singing and dancing*]
              O sweet Oliver,
              O brave Oliver,
            Leave me not behind thee.
   But   95
              Wind away,
              Be gone, I say,
            I will not to wedding with thee.
                  Exit Touchstone with Audrey and Jaques.

SIR OLIVER MAR-TEXT   'Tis no matter.
   Ne'er a fantastical knave of them all   100
   Shall flout me out of my calling.   *Exit.*

3.4   *Enter* ROSALIND *as Ganymede and* CELIA
         as Aliena.

ROSALIND   Never talk to me, I will weep.

CELIA   Do, I prithee, but yet have the grace to consider
that tears do not become a man.

ROSALIND   But have I not cause to weep?

5 CELIA   As good cause as one would desire; therefore
weep.

ROSALIND   His very hair is of the dissembling colour.

CELIA   Something browner then Judas's. Marry, his
kisses are Judas's own children.

10 ROSALIND   I'faith, his hair is of a good colour.

CELIA   An excellent colour – your chestnut was ever the
only colour.

ROSALIND   And his kissing is as full of sanctity as the
touch of holy bread.

15 CELIA   He hath bought a pair of cast lips of Diana – a
nun of winter's sisterhood kisses not more religiously;
the very ice of chastity is in them.

ROSALIND   But why did he swear he would come this
morning and comes not?

20 CELIA   Nay certainly there is no truth in him.

ROSALIND   Do you think so?

CELIA   Yes. I think he is not a pick-purse nor a horse-
stealer – but for his verity in love I do think him as
concave as a covered goblet or a worm-eaten nut.

25 ROSALIND   Not true in love?

CELIA   Yes, when he is in, but I think he is not in.

ROSALIND   You have heard him swear downright he was.

CELIA   'Was' is not 'is'. Besides, the oath of a lover is no
stronger than the word of a tapster: they are both the
30 confirmer of false reckonings. He attends here in the
forest on the Duke your father.

ROSALIND   I met the Duke yesterday and had much
question with him. He asked me of what parentage I
was. I told him of as good as he, so he laughed and let
35 me go. But what talk we of fathers when there is such a
man as Orlando?

CELIA   O, that's a brave man! He writes brave verses,
speaks brave words, swears brave oaths and breaks
them bravely quite traverse athwart the heart of his
40 lover, as a puny tilter, that spurs his horse but on one
side, breaks his staff like a noble goose. But all's brave
that youth mounts and folly guides.

Enter CORIN.

Who comes here?

CORIN   Mistress and master, you have oft enquired
45 After the shepherd that complained of love,
Who you saw sitting by me on the turf,
Praising the proud disdainful shepherdess
That was his mistress.

CELIA   Well, and what of him?

CORIN   If you will see a pageant truly played
50 Between the pale complexion of true love
And the red glow of scorn and proud disdain,
Go hence a little and I shall conduct you,
If you will mark it.

ROSALIND   O come, let us remove –
The sight of lovers feedeth those in love.
55 Bring us to this sight, and you shall say
I'll prove a busy actor in their play.   *Exeunt.*

3.5   *Enter SILVIUS and PHOEBE.*

SILVIUS
Sweet Phoebe, do not scorn me, do not, Phoebe.
Say that you love me not, but say not so
In bitterness. The common executioner,
Whose heart th'accustomed sight of death makes hard,
Falls not the axe upon the humbled neck   5
But first begs pardon. Will you sterner be
Than he that dies and lives by bloody drops?

*Enter ROSALIND as Ganymede, CELIA
as Aliena and CORIN. They stand aside.*

PHOEBE   I would not be thy executioner;
I fly thee for I would not injure thee.
Thou tell'st me there is murder in mine eye.   10
'Tis pretty, sure, and very probable
That eyes, that are the frail'st and softest things,
Who shut their coward gates on atomies,
Should be called tyrants, butchers, murderers.
Now I do frown on thee with all my heart,   15
And if mine eyes can wound, now let them kill thee.
Now counterfeit to swoon – why now fall down!
Or if thou canst not – O, for shame, for shame –
Lie not, to say mine eyes are murderers.
Now show the wound mine eye hath made in thee.   20
Scratch thee but with a pin, and there remains
Some scar of it; lean thou upon a rush,
The cicatrice and capable impressure
Thy palm some moment keeps. But now mine eyes,
Which I have darted at thee, hurt thee not,   25
Nor I am sure there is no force in eyes
That can do hurt.

SILVIUS   O dear Phoebe,
If ever – as that ever may be near –
You meet in some fresh cheek the power of fancy,   30
Then shall you know the wounds invisible
That love's keen arrows make.

PHOEBE   But till that time
Come not thou near me. And when that time comes,
Afflict me with thy mocks, pity me not,
As till that time I shall not pity thee.   35

ROSALIND *[Advances.]*
And why, I pray you? Who might be your mother,
That you insult, exult, and all at once
Over the wretched? What though you have no beauty –
As by my faith I see no more in you
Than without candle may go dark to bed –   40
Must you be therefore proud and pitiless?
Why, what means this? Why do you look on me?
I see no more in you than in the ordinary
Of Nature's sale-work. 'Od's my little life,
I think she means to tangle my eyes too!   45
No, faith, proud mistress, hope not after it.
'Tis not your inky brows, your black silk hair,
Your bugle eyeballs, nor your cheek of cream,
That can entame my spirits to your worship.

50 You foolish shepherd, wherefore do you follow her
Like foggy south, puffing with wind and rain?
You are a thousand times a properer man
Than she a woman. 'Tis such fools as you
That makes the world full of ill-favoured children.
55 'Tis not her glass but you that flatters her,
And out of you she sees herself more proper
Than any of her lineaments can show her.
But, mistress, know yourself; down on your knees,
And thank heaven fasting for a good man's love.
60 For I must tell you friendly in your ear:
Sell when you can, you are not for all markets.
Cry the man mercy, love him, take his offer;
Foul is most foul, being foul to be a scoffer.
So take her to thee, shepherd. Fare you well.
65 PHOEBE   Sweet youth, I pray you chide a year together!
I had rather hear you chide than this man woo.
ROSALIND   He's fallen in love with your foulness, [*to
Silvius*] and she'll fall in love with my anger. If it be so,
as fast as she answers thee with frowning looks, I'll
70 sauce her with bitter words.
– Why look you so upon me?
PHOEBE   For no ill will I bear you.
ROSALIND   I pray you do not fall in love with me,
For I am falser than vows made in wine.
Besides, I like you not.
75 [*to Silvius*]   If you will know my house,
'Tis at the tuft of olives here hard by.
Will you go, sister? Shepherd, ply her hard.
Come, sister. Shepherdess, look on him better,
And be not proud. Though all the world could see,
80 None could be so abused in sight as he.
Come, to our flock.   *Exeunt Rosalind, Celia and Corin.*
PHOEBE   Dead shepherd, now I find thy saw of might:
'Who ever loved, that loved not at first sight?'
SILVIUS   Sweet Phoebe –
PHOEBE   Ha? – What sayst thou, Silvius?
85 SILVIUS   Sweet Phoebe, pity me.
PHOEBE   Why, I am sorry for thee, gentle Silvius.
SILVIUS   Wherever sorrow is, relief would be.
If you do sorrow at my grief in love,
By giving love your sorrow and my grief
90 Were both extermined.
PHOEBE   Thou hast my love, is not that neighbourly?
SILVIUS   I would have you.
PHOEBE   Why, that were covetousness!
Silvius, the time was that I hated thee –
And yet it is not that I bear thee love –
95 But since that thou canst talk of love so well,
Thy company, which erst was irksome to me,
I will endure, and I'll employ thee too.
But do not look for further recompense
Than thine own gladness that thou art employed.
100 SILVIUS   So holy and so perfect is my love,
And I in such a poverty of grace,
That I shall think it a most plenteous crop
To glean the broken ears after the man

That the main harvest reaps. Loose now and then
A scattered smile, and that I'll live upon. 105
PHOEBE
Knowst thou the youth that spoke to me erewhile?
SILVIUS   Not very well, but I have met him oft,
And he hath bought the cottage and the bounds
That the old Carlot once was master of
PHOEBE   Think not I love him though I ask for him. 110
'Tis but a peevish boy – yet he talks well.
But what care I for words? Yet words do well
When he that speaks them pleases those that hear.
It is a pretty youth – not very pretty –
But sure he's proud, and yet his pride becomes him. 115
He'll make a proper man. The best thing in him
Is his complexion; and faster than his tongue
Did make offence, his eye did heal it up.
He is not very tall, yet for his years he's tall;
His leg is but so-so, and yet 'tis well. 120
There was a pretty redness in his lip,
A little riper and more lusty red
Than that mixed in his cheek. 'Twas just the difference
Betwixt the constant red and mingled damask.
There be some women, Silvius, had they marked him 125
In parcels as I did, would have gone near
To fall in love with him; but for my part
I love him not – nor hate him not. And yet
I have more cause to hate him than to love him,
For what had he to do to chide at me? 130
He said mine eyes were black and my hair black,
And now I am remembered, scorned at me.
I marvel why I answered not again.
But that's all one – omittance is no quittance.
I'll write to him a very taunting letter 135
And thou shalt bear it. Wilt thou, Silvius?
SILVIUS   Phoebe, with all my heart.
PHOEBE   I'll write it straight.
The matter's in my head and in my heart;
I will be bitter with him and passing short. 140
Go with me, Silvius.   *Exeunt.*

4.1   *Enter* ROSALIND *as Ganymede,* CELIA
as Aliena and JAQUES.

JAQUES   I prithee, pretty youth, let me be better
acquainted with thee.
ROSALIND   They say you are a melancholy fellow.
JAQUES   I am so; I do love it better than laughing.
ROSALIND   Those that are in extremity of either are 5
abominable fellows and betray themselves to every
modern censure worse than drunkards.
JAQUES   Why, 'tis good to be sad and say nothing.
ROSALIND   Why then, 'tis good to be a post.
JAQUES   I have neither the scholar's melancholy, which 10
is emulation; nor the musician's, which is fantastical;
nor the courtier's, which is proud; nor the soldier's,
which is ambitious; nor the lawyer's, which is politic;
nor the lady's, which is nice; nor the lover's, which
is all these; but it is a melancholy of mine own, 15

compounded of many simples, extracted from many objects, and indeed the sundry computation of my travels, in which my often rumination wraps me in a most humorous sadness.

ROSALIND A traveller! By my faith, you have great reason to be sad. I fear you have sold your own lands to see other men's. Then to have seen much and to have nothing is to have rich eyes and poor hands.

JAQUES Yes, I have gained my experience.

Enter ORLANDO.

ROSALIND And your experience makes you sad. I had rather have a fool to make me merry than experience to make me sad – and to travel for it too.

ORLANDO Good day and happiness, dear Rosalind.

JAQUES Nay then, God b'wi' you an you talk in blank verse. *Exit.*

ROSALIND Farewell, Monsieur Traveller. Look you lisp and wear strange suits; disable all the benefits of your own country; be out of love with your nativity and almost chide God for making you that countenance you are, or I will scarce think you have swam in a gondola. Why, how now, Orlando, where have you been all this while? You a lover? An you serve me such another trick, never come in my sight more!

ORLANDO My fair Rosalind, I come within an hour of my promise.

ROSALIND Break an hour's promise in love? He that will divide a minute into a thousand parts, and break but a part of the thousand part of a minute in the affairs of love, it may be said of him that Cupid hath clapped him o'th' shoulder, but I'll warrant him heart-whole.

ORLANDO Pardon me, dear Rosalind.

ROSALIND Nay, an you be so tardy, come no more in my sight. I had as lief be wooed of a snail.

ORLANDO Of a snail?

ROSALIND Ay, of a snail, for though he comes slowly he carries his house on his head – a better jointure, I think, than you make a woman. Besides, he brings his destiny with him.

ORLANDO What's that?

ROSALIND Why, horns – which such as you are fain to be beholding to your wives for; but he comes armed in his fortune and prevents the slander of his wife.

ORLANDO Virtue is no horn-maker and my Rosalind is virtuous.

ROSALIND And I am your Rosalind.

CELIA It pleases him to call you so, but he hath a Rosalind of a better leer than you.

ROSALIND Come, woo me, woo me – for now I am in a holiday humour and like enough to consent. What would you say to me now, an I were your very, very Rosalind?

ORLANDO I would kiss before I spoke.

ROSALIND Nay, you were better speak first, and when you were gravelled for lack of matter you might take occasion to kiss. Very good orators when they are out, they will spit, and for lovers lacking (God warrant us) matter, the cleanliest shift is to kiss.

ORLANDO How if the kiss be denied?

ROSALIND Then she puts you to entreaty and there begins new matter.

ORLANDO Who could be out, being before his beloved mistress?

ROSALIND Marry, that should you, if I were your mistress, or I should think my honesty ranker than my wit.

ORLANDO What, of my suit?

ROSALIND Not out of your apparel and yet out of your suit. Am not I your Rosalind?

ORLANDO I take some joy to say you are because I would be talking of her.

ROSALIND Well, in her person, I say I will not have you.

ORLANDO Then, in mine own person, I die.

ROSALIND No, faith, die by attorney. The poor world is almost six thousand years old, and in all this time there was not any man died in his own person (videlicet, in a love-cause). Troilus had his brains dashed out with a Grecian club, yet he did what he could to die before, and he is one of the patterns of love. Leander, he would have lived many a fair year though Hero had turned nun, if it had not been for a hot midsummer night; for, good youth, he went but forth to wash him in the Hellespont and, being taken with the cramp, was drowned, and the foolish chroniclers of that age found it was Hero of Sestos. But these are all lies. Men have died from time to time and worms have eaten them, but not for love.

ORLANDO I would not have my right Rosalind of this mind, for I protest her frown might kill me.

ROSALIND By this hand, it will not kill a fly. But come, now I will be your Rosalind in a more coming-on disposition, and ask me what you will, I will grant it.

ORLANDO Then love me, Rosalind.

ROSALIND Yes, faith, will I, Fridays and Saturdays and all.

ORLANDO And wilt thou have me?

ROSALIND Ay, and twenty such.

ORLANDO What sayst thou?

ROSALIND Are you not good?

ORLANDO I hope so.

ROSALIND Why then, can one desire too much of a good thing? Come, sister, you shall be the priest and marry us. Give me your hand, Orlando. What do you say, sister?

ORLANDO Pray thee, marry us.

CELIA I cannot say the words.

ROSALIND You must begin: 'Will you, Orlando –'

CELIA Go to. – Will you, Orlando, have to wife this Rosalind?

ORLANDO I will.

ROSALIND Ay, but when?

ORLANDO Why now, as fast as she can marry us.

ROSALIND   Then you must say: 'I take thee, Rosalind, for wife.'

ORLANDO   I take thee, Rosalind, for wife.

130 ROSALIND   I might ask you for your commission. But I do take thee, Orlando, for my husband. There's a girl goes before the priest, and certainly a woman's thought runs before her actions.

ORLANDO   So do all thoughts – they are winged.

135 ROSALIND   Now tell me how long you would have her after you have possessed her?

ORLANDO   For ever and a day.

ROSALIND   Say 'a day' without the 'ever'. No, no, Orlando, men are April when they woo, December

140 when they wed. Maids are May when they are maids, but the sky changes when they are wives. I will be more jealous of thee than a Barbary cock-pigeon over his hen, more clamorous than a parrot against rain, more new-fangled than an ape, more giddy in my desires

145 than a monkey. I will weep for nothing, like Diana in the fountain, and I will do that when you are disposed to be merry. I will laugh like a hyena, and that when thou art inclined to sleep.

ORLANDO   But will my Rosalind do so?

150 ROSALIND   By my life, she will do as I do.

ORLANDO   O, but she is wise.

ROSALIND   Or else she could not have the wit to do this – the wiser, the waywarder. Make the doors upon a woman's wit and it will out at the casement. Shut that

155 and 'twill out at the keyhole. Stop that, 'twill fly with the smoke out at the chimney:

ORLANDO   A man that had a wife with such a wit, he might say, 'Wit, whither wilt?'

ROSALIND   Nay, you might keep that check for it till you

160 met your wife's wit going to your neighbour's bed.

ORLANDO   And what wit could wit have to excuse that?

ROSALIND   Marry, to say she came to seek you there. You shall never take her without her answer unless you take her without her tongue. O, that woman that

165 cannot make her fault her husband's occasion, let her never nurse her child herself, for she will breed it like a fool!

ORLANDO   For these two hours, Rosalind, I will leave thee.

170 ROSALIND   Alas, dear love, I cannot lack thee two hours.

ORLANDO   I must attend the Duke at dinner. By two o'clock I will be with thee again.

ROSALIND   Ay, go your ways, go your ways. I knew what you would prove. My friends told me as much and I

175 thought no less. That flattering tongue of yours won me. 'Tis but one cast away, and so, come death! Two o'clock is your hour?

ORLANDO   Ay, sweet Rosalind.

ROSALIND   By my troth, and in good earnest, and so

180 God mend me, and by all pretty oaths that are not dangerous, if you break one jot of your promise or come one minute behind your hour, I will think you the most pathetical break-promise and the most hollow

lover and the most unworthy of her you call Rosalind
185 that may be chosen out of the gross band of the unfaithful. Therefore beware my censure and keep your promise.

ORLANDO   With no less religion than if thou wert indeed my Rosalind. So adieu.

190 ROSALIND   Well, Time is the old justice that examines all such offenders, and let Time try Adieu.

Exit Orlando.

CELIA   You have simply misused our sex in your love-prate! We must have your doublet and hose plucked over your head and show the world what the bird hath
195 done to her own nest.

ROSALIND   O coz, coz, coz, my pretty little coz, that thou didst know how many fathom deep I am in love! But it cannot be sounded – my affection hath an unknown bottom, like the Bay of Portugal.

200 CELIA   Or rather bottomless, that as fast as you pour affection in, it runs out.

ROSALIND   No, that same wicked bastard of Venus that was begot of thought, conceived of spleen and born of madness, that blind rascally boy that abuses everyone's
205 eyes because his own are out, let him be judge how deep I am in love. I tell thee, Aliena, I cannot be out of the sight of Orlando. I'll go find a shadow and sigh till he come.

CELIA   And I'll sleep.   *Exeunt.*

4.2   *Enter* JAQUES, Lords *and* Foresters.

JAQUES   Which is he that killed the deer?

1 LORD   Sir, it was I.

JAQUES   Let's present him to the Duke like a Roman conqueror, and it would do well to set the deer's horns upon his head for a branch of victory. Have you no
5 song, forester, for this purpose?

1 FORESTER   Yes, sir.

JAQUES   Sing it. 'Tis no matter how it be in tune so it make noise enough.   [*Music*]

1 FORESTER [*Sings.*]
10   What shall he have that killed the deer?
    His leather skin and horns to wear.

JAQUES   Then sing him home; the rest shall bear this burden.

ALL [*Sing.*]
    Take thou no scorn to wear the horn –
15   It was a crest ere thou wast born.
      Thy father's father wore it
      And thy father bore it.
    The horn, the horn, the lusty horn
    Is not a thing to laugh to scorn!   *Exeunt.*

4.3   *Enter* ROSALIND *as Ganymede and* CELIA
     as Aliena.

ROSALIND   How say you now, is it not past two o'clock? And here much Orlando.

CELIA   I warrant you, with pure love and troubled brain
he hath ta'en his bow and arrows and is gone forth to
sleep.   5

Enter SILVIUS *with a letter.*

Look who comes here.
SILVIUS   My errand is to you, fair youth.
My gentle Phoebe did bid me give you this.
I know not the contents, but as I guess   10
By the stern brow and waspish action
Which she did use as she was writing of it,
It bears an angry tenor. Pardon me,
I am but as a guiltless messenger.
ROSALIND   Patience herself would startle at this letter
And play the swaggerer. Bear this, bear all!   15
She says I am not fair, that I lack manners;
She calls me proud, and that she could not love me,
Were man as rare as phoenix. 'Od's my will,
Her love is not the hare that I do hunt.
Why writes she so to me? Well, shepherd, well,   20
This is a letter of your own device.
SILVIUS   No, I protest, I know not the contents.
Phoebe did write it.
ROSALIND   Come, come, you are a fool,
And turned into the extremity of love.
I saw her hand – she has a leathern hand,   25
A freestone-coloured hand – I verily did think
That her old gloves were on, but 'twas her hands.
She has a housewife's hand – but that's no matter.
I say she never did invent this letter;
This is a man's invention and his hand.   30
SILVIUS   Sure, it is hers.
ROSALIND   Why, 'tis a boisterous and a cruel style,
A style for challengers. Why, she defies me,
Like Turk to Christian. Women's gentle brain
Could not drop forth such giant-rude invention,   35
Such Ethiop words, blacker in their effect
Than in their countenance. Will you hear the letter?
SILVIUS   So please you, for I never heard it yet,
Yet heard too much of Phoebe's cruelty.
ROSALIND
She Phoebes me. Mark how the tyrant writes.   40
[*Reads.*]
    Art thou god to shepherd turned,
    That a maiden's heart hath burned?
Can a woman rail thus?
SILVIUS   Call you this railing?
ROSALIND [*Reads.*]
    Why, thy godhead laid apart,   45
    Warr'st thou with a woman's heart?
Did you ever hear such railing?
    Whiles the eye of man did woo me,
    That could do no vengeance to me.
– Meaning me a beast –   50
    If the scorn of your bright eyne
    Have power to raise such love in mine,

    Alack, in me what strange effect
    Would they work in mild aspect?
    Whiles you chid me, I did love,   55
    How then might your prayers move?
    He that brings these lines to thee
    Little knows this love in me;
    And by him seal up thy mind,
    Whether that thy youth and kind   60
    Will the faithful offer take
    Of me, and all that I can make,
    Or else by him my love deny,
    And then I'll study how to die.
SILVIUS   Call you this chiding?
CELIA   Alas, poor shepherd.   65
ROSALIND   Do you pity him? No, he deserves no pity.
– Wilt thou love such a woman? What, to make thee an
instrument and play false strains upon thee? Not to be
endured! Well, go your way to her, for I see love hath
made thee a tame snake, and say this to her: that if she   70
love me, I charge her to love thee. If she will not, I will
never have her unless thou entreat for her. If you be a
true lover, hence and not a word, for here comes more
company.   *Exit Silvius.*

Enter OLIVER.

OLIVER
Good morrow, fair ones. Pray you, if you know,   75
Where in the purlieus of this forest stands
A sheepcote fenced about with olive-trees?
CELIA
West of this place, down in the neighbour bottom;
The rank of osiers by the murmuring stream,
Left on your right hand, brings you to the place.   80
But at this hour the house doth keep itself –
There's none within.
OLIVER   If that an eye may profit by a tongue,
Then should I know you by description,
Such garments and such years: 'The boy is fair,   85
Of female favour, and bestows himself
Like a ripe sister; the woman low,
And browner than her brother.' [*to Rosalind*] Are not you
The owner of the house I did enquire for?
CELIA   It is no boast, being asked, to say we are.   90
OLIVER   Orlando doth commend him to you both,
And to that youth he calls his Rosalind
He sends this bloody napkin. – Are you he?
ROSALIND   I am. What must we understand by this?
OLIVER   Some of my shame, if you will know of me   95
What man I am, and how and why and where
This handkerchief was stained.
CELIA   I pray you tell it.
OLIVER
When last the young Orlando parted from you,
He left a promise to return again
Within an hour, and pacing through the forest,   100
Chewing the food of sweet and bitter fancy,
Lo, what befell. He threw his eye aside,

And mark what object did present itself.
Under an oak, whose boughs were mossed with age
105   And high top bald with dry antiquity,
A wretched ragged man, o'ergrown with hair,
Lay sleeping on his back; about his neck
A green and gilded snake had wreathed itself,
Who with her head, nimble in threats, approached
110   The opening of his mouth. But suddenly
Seeing Orlando, it unlinked itself
And with indented glides did slip away
Into a bush; under which bush's shade
A lioness, with udders all drawn dry,
115   Lay couching, head on ground, with catlike watch
When that the sleeping man should stir. For 'tis
The royal disposition of that beast
To prey on nothing that doth seem as dead.
This seen, Orlando did approach the man
120   And found it was his brother, his elder brother.
CELIA   O, I have heard him speak of that same brother,
And he did render him the most unnatural
That lived amongst men.
OLIVER   And well he might so do,
For well I know he was unnatural.
125   ROSALIND   But to Orlando: did he leave him there,
Food to the sucked and hungry lioness?
OLIVER   Twice did he turn his back and purposed so;
But kindness, nobler ever than revenge,
And nature, stronger than his just occasion,
130   Made him give battle to the lioness,
Who quickly fell before him, in which hurtling
From miserable slumber I awaked.
CELIA   Are you his brother?
ROSALIND   Was't you he rescued?
CELIA   Was't you that did so oft contrive to kill him?
135   OLIVER   'Twas I, but 'tis not I. I do not shame
To tell you what I was, since my conversion
So sweetly tastes, being the thing I am.
ROSALIND   But for the bloody napkin?
OLIVER   By and by
When from the first to last betwixt us two
140   Tears our recountments had most kindly bathed –
As how I came into that desert place –
I'brief, he led me to the gentle Duke
Who gave me fresh array and entertainment,
Committing me unto my brother's love,
145   Who led me instantly unto his cave;
There stripped himself and here, upon his arm,
The lioness had torn some flesh away;
Which all this while had bled. And now he fainted,
And cried in fainting upon Rosalind.
150   Brief, I recovered him, bound up his wound,
And after some small space, being strong at heart,
He sent me hither, stranger as I am,
To tell this story, that you might excuse
His broken promise; and to give this napkin,
155   Dyed in his blood, unto the shepherd youth

That he in sport doth call his Rosalind.
          [*Rosalind faints.*]
CELIA   Why, how now, Ganymede – sweet Ganymede!
OLIVER   Many will swoon when they do look on blood.
CELIA   There is more in it. Cousin – Ganymede!
OLIVER   Look, he recovers.   160
ROSALIND   I would I were at home.
CELIA   We'll lead you thither.
– I pray you, will you take him by the arm?
OLIVER   Be of good cheer, youth. You a man?
You lack a man's heart.
ROSALIND   I do so, I confess it.   165
Ah, sirrah, a body would think this was well
counterfeited. I pray you tell your brother how well I
counterfeited. Heigh-ho –
OLIVER   This was not counterfeit: there is too great
testimony in your complexion that it was a passion of   170
earnest.
ROSALIND   Counterfeit, I assure you.
OLIVER   Well then, take a good heart, and counterfeit to
be a man.
ROSALIND   So I do. But i'faith, I should have been a   175
woman by right.
CELIA   Come, you look paler and paler. Pray you, draw
homewards. Good sir, go with us.
OLIVER   That will I, for I must bear answer back
How you excuse my brother, Rosalind.   180
ROSALIND   I shall devise something; but I pray you
commend my counterfeiting to him. Will you go?
                                                              Exeunt.

5.1   *Enter* TOUCHSTONE *and* AUDREY.

TOUCHSTONE   We shall find a time, Audrey; patience,
gentle Audrey.
AUDREY   Faith, the priest was good enough, for all the
old gentleman's saying.
TOUCHSTONE   A most wicked Sir Oliver, Audrey, a   5
most vile Mar-text! But Audrey, there is a youth here
in the forest lays claim to you.
AUDREY   Ay, I know who 'tis. He hath no interest in me
in the world.

                    Enter WILLIAM.

Here comes the man you mean.   10
TOUCHSTONE   It is meat and drink to me to see a clown.
By my troth, we that have good wits have much to
answer for. We shall be flouting; we cannot hold.
WILLIAM   Good ev'n, Audrey.
AUDREY   God ye good ev'n, William.   15
WILLIAM   And good ev'n to you, sir.
TOUCHSTONE   Good ev'n, gentle friend. Cover thy
head, cover thy head. Nay, prithee be covered. How old
are you, friend?
WILLIAM   Five-and-twenty, sir.   20
TOUCHSTONE   A ripe age. Is thy name William?
WILLIAM   William, sir.

TOUCHSTONE A fair name. Wast born i'th' forest here?

WILLIAM Ay, sir, I thank God.

TOUCHSTONE 'Thank God' – a good answer. Art rich?

WILLIAM Faith, sir, so-so.

TOUCHSTONE 'So-so' is good, very good, very excellent good – and yet it is not, it is but so-so. Art thou wise?

WILLIAM Ay, sir, I have a pretty wit.

TOUCHSTONE Why, thou sayst well. I do now remember a saying: 'The fool doth think he is wise, but the wise man knows himself to be a fool.' The heathen philosopher, when he had a desire to eat a grape, would open his lips when he put it into his mouth, meaning thereby that grapes were made to eat and lips to open. You do love this maid?

WILLIAM I do, sir.

TOUCHSTONE Give me your hand. Art thou learned?

WILLIAM No, sir.

TOUCHSTONE Then learn this of me: to have is to have. For it is a figure in rhetoric that drink, being poured out of a cup into a glass, by filling the one doth empty the other. For all your writers do consent that *ipse* is 'he'. Now you are not *ipse*, for I am he.

WILLIAM Which he, sir?

TOUCHSTONE He, sir, that must marry this woman. Therefore, you clown, abandon (which is, in the vulgar, 'leave') the society (which in the boorish is 'company') of this female (which in the common is 'woman'); which together is: 'abandon the society of this female', or, clown, thou perishest! Or to thy better understanding, diest. Or (to wit) I kill thee, make thee away, translate thy life into death, thy liberty into bondage. I will deal in poison with thee, or in bastinado or in steel. I will bandy with thee in faction; I will o'errun thee with policy. I will kill thee a hundred and fifty ways! Therefore tremble and depart.

AUDREY Do, good William.

WILLIAM God rest you merry, sir.   *Exit.*

Enter CORIN.

CORIN Our master and mistress seeks you. Come away, away.

TOUCHSTONE Trip, Audrey, trip, Audrey! I attend, I attend.   *Exeunt.*

5.2   *Enter* ORLANDO *and* OLIVER.

ORLANDO Is't possible that on so little acquaintance you should like her? That but seeing, you should love her? And loving, woo? And wooing, she should grant? And will you persever to enjoy her?

OLIVER Neither call the giddiness of it in question, the poverty of her, the small acquaintance, my sudden wooing nor her sudden consenting. But say with me, I love Aliena. Say with her that she loves me. Consent with both that we may enjoy each other. It shall be to your good, for my father's house and all the revenue that was old Sir Rowland's will I estate upon you, and here live and die a shepherd.

Enter ROSALIND *as Ganymede.*

ORLANDO You have my consent. Let your wedding be tomorrow. Thither will I invite the Duke and all's contented followers. Go you and prepare Aliena; for look you, here comes my Rosalind.

ROSALIND God save you, brother.

OLIVER And you, fair sister.   *Exit.*

ROSALIND O my dear Orlando, how it grieves me to see thee wear thy heart in a scarf!

ORLANDO It is my arm.

ROSALIND I thought thy heart had been wounded with the claws of a lion.

ORLANDO Wounded it is, but with the eyes of a lady.

ROSALIND Did your brother tell you how I counterfeited to swoon when he showed me your handkerchief?

ORLANDO Ay, and greater wonders than that.

ROSALIND O, I know where you are. Nay, 'tis true. There was never anything so sudden but the fight of two rams, and Caesar's thrasonical brag of 'I came, saw and overcame.' For your brother and my sister no sooner met but they looked; no sooner looked but they loved; no sooner loved but they sighed; no sooner sighed but they asked one another the reason; no sooner knew the reason but they sought the remedy; and in these degrees have they made a pair of stairs to marriage, which they will climb incontinent or else be incontinent before marriage. They are in the very wrath of love and they will together. Clubs cannot part them.

ORLANDO They shall be married tomorrow, and I will bid the Duke to the nuptial. But O, how bitter a thing it is to look into happiness through another man's eyes! By so much the more shall I tomorrow be at the height of heart-heaviness, by how much I shall think my brother happy in having what he wishes for.

ROSALIND Why then, tomorrow I cannot serve your turn for Rosalind?

ORLANDO I can live no longer by thinking.

ROSALIND I will weary you then no longer with idle talking. Know of me, then – for now I speak to some purpose – that I know you are a gentleman of good conceit. I speak not this that you should bear a good opinion of my knowledge, insomuch I say I know you are. Neither do I labour for a greater esteem than may in some little measure draw a belief from you, to do yourself good and not to grace me. Believe then, if you please, that I can do strange things. I have since I was three year old conversed with a magician, most profound in his art and yet not damnable. If you do love Rosalind so near the heart as your gesture cries it out, when your brother marries Aliena shall you marry her. I know into what straits of fortune she is driven and it is not impossible to me, if it appear not inconvenient to you, to set her before your eyes tomorrow, human as she is, and without any danger.

ORLANDO Speak'st thou in sober meanings?

ROSALIND   By my life I do, which I tender dearly, though I say I am a magician. Therefore put you in your best array, bid your friends; for if you will be married tomorrow you shall, and to Rosalind if you will.

70

Enter SILVIUS *and* PHOEBE.

Look, here comes a lover of mine and a lover of hers.
PHOEBE   Youth, you have done me much ungentleness
75   To show the letter that I writ to you.
ROSALIND   I care not if I have; it is my study
To seem despiteful and ungentle to you.
You are there followed by a faithful shepherd.
Look upon him; love him; he worships you.
PHOEBE
80   Good shepherd, tell this youth what 'tis to love.
SILVIUS   It is to be all made of sighs and tears,
And so am I for Phoebe.
PHOEBE   And I for Ganymede.
ORLANDO   And I for Rosalind.
85   ROSALIND   And I for no woman.
SILVIUS   It is to be all made of faith and service,
And so am I for Phoebe.
PHOEBE   And I for Ganymede.
ORLANDO   And I for Rosalind.
90   ROSALIND   And I for no woman.
SILVIUS   It is to be all made of fantasy,
All made of passion, and all made of wishes,
All adoration, duty and observance,
All humbleness, all patience and impatience,
95   All purity, all trial, all obedience,
And so am I for Phoebe.
PHOEBE   And so am I for Ganymede.
ORLANDO   And so am I for Rosalind.
ROSALIND   And so am I for no woman.
PHOEBE [*to Rosalind*]
100   If this be so, why blame you me to love you?
SILVIUS [*to Phoebe*]
If this be so, why blame you me to love you?
ORLANDO   If this be so, why blame you me to love you?
ROSALIND   Who do you speak to, 'Why blame you me to love you?'
105   ORLANDO   To her that is not here nor doth not hear.
ROSALIND   Pray you no more of this, 'tis like the howling of Irish wolves against the moon. [*to Silvius*] I will help you if I can. [*to Phoebe*] I would love you if I could. – Tomorrow meet me all together. [*to Phoebe*]
110   I will marry you, if ever I marry woman, and I'll be married tomorrow. [*to Orlando*] I will satisfy you, if ever I satisfied man, and you shall be married tomorrow. [*to Silvius*] I will content you, if what pleases you contents you, and you shall be married tomorrow.
115   [*to Orlando*] As you love Rosalind, meet. [*to Silvius*] As you love Phoebe, meet. – And as I love no woman, I'll meet. So fare you well. I have left you commands.
SILVIUS   I'll not fail, if I live.

PHOEBE   Nor I.
ORLANDO   Nor I.   *Exeunt.*

5.3   *Enter* TOUCHSTONE *and* AUDREY.

TOUCHSTONE   Tomorrow is the joyful day, Audrey, tomorrow will we be married.
AUDREY   I do desire it with all my heart; and I hope it is no dishonest desire, to desire to be a woman of the world?   5

Enter two Pages.

Here come two of the banished Duke's pages.
1 PAGE   Well met, honest gentleman.
TOUCHSTONE   By my troth, well met. Come, sit, sit, and a song.
2 PAGE   We are for you, sit i'th' middle.   10
1 PAGE   Shall we clap into't roundly without hawking or spitting or saying we are hoarse, which are the only prologues to a bad voice?
2 PAGE   I'faith, I'faith, and both in a tune like two gipsies on a horse.   15
PAGES [*Sing.*]
        It was a lover and his lass,
            With a hey and a ho and a hey nonino,
        That o'er the green cornfield did pass,
            In spring-time, the only pretty ring-time,
        When birds do sing, hey ding a ding a ding,   20
            Sweet lovers love the spring.

        Between the acres of the rye,
            With a hey and a ho and a hey nonino,
        These pretty country folks would lie,
            In spring-time, the only pretty ring-time,   25
        When birds do sing, hey ding a ding a ding,
            Sweet lovers love the spring.

        This carol they began that hour,
            With a hey and a ho and a hey nonino,
        How that a life was but a flower,   30
            In spring-time, the only pretty ring-time,
        When birds do sing, hey ding a ding a ding,
            Sweet lovers love the spring.

        And therefore take the present time,
            With a hey and a ho and a hey nonino,   35
        For love is crowned with the prime,
            In spring-time, the only pretty ring-time,
        When birds do sing, hey ding a ding a ding,
            Sweet lovers love the spring.

TOUCHSTONE   Truly, young gentlemen, though there   40
was no great matter in the ditty, yet the note was very untunable.
1 PAGE   You are deceived, sir, we kept time, we lost not our time.
TOUCHSTONE   By my troth, yes. I count it but time lost   45
to hear such a foolish song. God b'wi' you, and God mend your voices. Come, Audrey.   *Exeunt.*

5.4   *Enter* DUKE SENIOR, AMIENS, JAQUES,
ORLANDO, OLIVER *and* CELIA *as Aliena.*

DUKE SENIOR
Dost thou believe, Orlando, that the boy
Can do all this that he hath promised?

ORLANDO
I sometimes do believe and sometimes do not,
As those that fear to hope, and know to fear.

Enter ROSALIND *as Ganymede,* SILVIUS *and* PHOEBE.

ROSALIND
5   Patience once more whiles our compact is urged.
[*to Duke Senior*] You say if I bring in your Rosalind
You will bestow her on Orlando here?

DUKE SENIOR
That would I, had I kingdoms to give with her.

ROSALIND [*to Orlando*]
And you say you will have her when I bring her?

10   ORLANDO   That would I, were I of all kingdoms king.

ROSALIND [*to Phoebe*]
You say you'll marry me if I be willing?

PHOEBE   That will I, should I die the hour after.

ROSALIND   But if you do refuse to marry me
You'll give yourself to this most faithful shepherd?

15   PHOEBE   So is the bargain.

ROSALIND [*to Silvius*]
You say that you'll have Phoebe if she will?

SILVIUS
Though to have her and death were both one thing.

ROSALIND
I have promised to make all this matter even.
Keep you your word, O Duke, to give your daughter,
20   You yours, Orlando, to receive his daughter.
Keep you your word, Phoebe, that you'll marry me,
Or else, refusing me, to wed this shepherd.
Keep your word, Silvius, that you'll marry her
If she refuse me; and from hence I go
25   To make these doubts all even.

Exeunt Rosalind and Celia.

DUKE SENIOR   I do remember in this shepherd boy
Some lively touches of my daughter's favour.

ORLANDO   My lord, the first time that I ever saw him
Methought he was a brother to your daughter.
30   But my good lord, this boy is forest-born
And hath been tutored in the rudiments
Of many desperate studies by his uncle,
Whom he reports to be a great magician,
Obscured in the circle of this forest.

Enter TOUCHSTONE *and* AUDREY.

35   JAQUES   There is sure another flood toward, and these
couples are coming to the ark. Here comes a pair of
very strange beasts, which in all tongues are called
fools.

TOUCHSTONE   Salutation and greeting to you all.

40   JAQUES   Good my lord, bid him welcome. This is the
motley-minded gentleman that I have so often met in
the forest. He hath been a courtier, he swears.

TOUCHSTONE   If any man doubt that, let him put me to
my purgation. I have trod a measure; I have flattered a
lady; I have been politic with my friend, smooth with   45
mine enemy; I have undone three tailors; I have had
four quarrels and like to have fought one.

JAQUES   And how was that ta'en up?

TOUCHSTONE   Faith, we met and found the quarrel was
upon the seventh cause.   50

JAQUES   How, seventh cause? – Good my lord, like this
fellow.

DUKE SENIOR   I like him very well.

TOUCHSTONE   God'ild you, sir, I desire you of the like.
I press in here, sir, amongst the rest of the country   55
copulatives, to swear and to forswear according as
marriage binds and blood breaks; – a poor virgin, sir,
an ill-favoured thing, sir, but mine own; a poor humour
of mine, sir, to take that that no man else will. Rich
honesty dwells like a miser, sir, in a poor house, as your   60
pearl in your foul oyster.

DUKE SENIOR   By my faith, he is very swift and
sententious.

TOUCHSTONE   According to the fool's bolt, sir, and
such dulcet diseases.   65

JAQUES   But for the seventh cause – how did you find
the quarrel on the seventh cause?

TOUCHSTONE   Upon a lie seven times removed – bear
your body more seeming, Audrey – as thus, sir. I did
dislike the cut of a certain courtier's beard. He sent me   70
word if I said his beard was not cut well, he was in the
mind it was. This is called the 'retort courteous'. If I
sent him word again it was not well cut, he would send
me word he cut it to please himself This is called the
'quip modest'. If again it was not well cut, he disabled   75
my judgement. This is called the 'reply churlish'. If
again it was not well cut, he would answer I spake not
true. This is called the 'reproof valiant'. If again it was
not well cut, he would say I lie. This is called the
'countercheck quarrelsome' – and so to the 'lie   80
circumstantial' and the 'lie direct'.

JAQUES   And how oft did you say his beard was not well
cut?

TOUCHSTONE   I durst go no further than the lie
circumstantial, nor he durst not give me the lie direct;   85
and so we measured swords and parted.

JAQUES   Can you nominate in order now the degrees of
the lie?

TOUCHSTONE   O sir, we quarrel in print, by the book,
as you have books for good manners. I will name you   90
the degrees: the first, the retort courteous; the second,
the quip modest; the third, the reply churlish; the
fourth, the reproof valiant; the fifth, the counter-check
quarrelsome; the sixth, the lie with circumstance; the
seventh, the lie direct. All these you may avoid but the   95
lie direct and you may avoid that too with an 'if'. I
knew when seven justices could not take up a quarrel,

but when the parties were met themselves, one of them
thought but of an 'if': as, 'if you said so, then I said so';
100 and they shook hands and swore brothers. Your 'if' is
the only peacemaker; much virtue in 'if'.

JAQUES   Is not this a rare fellow, my lord? He's as good
at anything, and yet a fool.

DUKE SENIOR   He uses his folly like a stalking-horse
105 and under the presentation of that he shoots his wit.

Enter HYMEN *with* ROSALIND *and* CELIA
both undisguised. Still music.

HYMEN   Then is there mirth in heaven
When earthly things made even
    Atone together.
Good Duke, receive thy daughter.
110 Hymen from heaven brought her,
    Yea, brought her hither,
That thou mightst join her hand with his,
Whose heart within his bosom is.

ROSALIND [*to Duke Senior*]
To you I give myself, for I am yours.
115 [*to Orlando*] To you I give myself, for I am yours.

DUKE SENIOR
If there be truth in sight, you are my daughter.

ORLANDO
If there be truth in sight, you are my Rosalind.

PHOEBE   If sight and shape be true,
Why then, my love adieu.

120 ROSALIND   I'll have no father, if you be not he.
I'll have no husband, if you be not he.
Nor ne'er wed woman, if you be not she.

HYMEN   Peace, ho. I bar confusion.
'Tis I must make conclusion
125   Of these most strange events.
Here's eight that must take hands
To join in Hymen's bands,
    If truth holds true contents.
[*to Celia and Oliver*]
You and you no cross shall part.
[*to Rosalind and Orlando*]
130 You and you are heart in heart.
[*to Phoebe*]
You to his love must accord
Or have a woman to your lord.
[*to Audrey and Touchstone*]
You and you are sure together
As the winter to foul weather.
135 Whiles a wedlock hymn we sing,
Feed yourselves with questioning,
That reason wonder may diminish
How thus we met, and these things finish.

SONG

Wedding is great Juno's crown,
140   O blessed bond of board and bed.
'Tis Hymen peoples every town,
    High wedlock then be honoured.

Honour, high honour and renown
To Hymen, god of every town.

DUKE SENIOR
O my dear niece, welcome thou art to me   145
Even daughter; welcome in no less degree.

PHOEBE
I will not eat my word, now thou art mine,
Thy faith my fancy to thee doth combine.

Enter JAQUES DE BOYS, *the second brother.*

JAQUES DE BOYS
Let me have audience for a word or two.
I am the second son of old Sir Rowland   150
That bring these tidings to this fair assembly.
Duke Frederick, hearing how that every day
Men of great worth resorted to this forest,
Addressed a mighty power, which were on foot
In his own conduct, purposely to take   155
His brother here and put him to the sword;
And to the skirts of this wild wood he came,
Where meeting with an old religious man,
After some question with him, was converted
Both from his enterprise and from the world,   160
His crown bequeathing to his banished brother,
And all their lands restored to them again
That were with him exiled. This to be true
I do engage my life.

DUKE SENIOR   Welcome, young man.
Thou offer'st fairly to thy brothers' wedding: 165
To one his lands withheld, and to the other
A land itself at large, a potent dukedom.
First, in this forest let us do those ends
That here were well begun and well begot;
And after, every of this happy number   170
That have endured shrewd days and nights with us
Shall share the good of our returned fortune,
According to the measure of their states.
Meantime, forget this new-fall'n dignity
And fall into our rustic revelry.   175
Play, music! And you brides and bridegrooms all,
With measure heaped in joy to th' measures fall.

JAQUES
Sir, by your patience.
[*to Jaques de Boys*]   If I heard you rightly,
The Duke hath put on a religious life
And thrown into neglect the pompous court.   180

JAQUES DE BOYS   He hath.

JAQUES   To him will I; out of these convertites
There is much matter to be heard and learned.
[*to Duke Senior*] You to your former honour I bequeath:
Your patience and your virtue well deserves it.   185
[*to Orlando*] You to a love that your true faith doth
    merit;
[*to Oliver*] You to your land and love and great allies;
[*to Silvius*] You to a long and well-deserved bed;
[*to Touchstone*] And you to wrangling, for thy loving
    voyage

190 Is but for two months victualled. – So to your pleasures,
I am for other than for dancing measures.

DUKE SENIOR Stay, Jaques, stay.

JAQUES To see no pastime, I. What you would have
I'll stay to know at your abandoned cave.   *Exit.*

DUKE SENIOR

195 Proceed, proceed! We'll begin these rites
As we do trust they'll end, in true delights.

Music and dance. Exeunt all but Rosalind.

EPILOGUE

ROSALIND It is not the fashion to see the lady the
Epilogue, but it is no more unhandsome than to see the
lord the Prologue. If it be true that good wine needs no
bush, 'tis true that a good play needs no epilogue. Yet
5 to good wine they do use good bushes, and good plays
prove the better by the help of good epilogues. What a
case am I in then, that am neither a good epilogue, nor
cannot insinuate with you in the behalf of a good play.
I am not furnished like a beggar, therefore to beg will
not become me. My way is to conjure you, and I'll   10
begin with the women. I charge you, O women, for the
love you bear to men, to like as much of this play as
please you. And I charge you, O men, for the love you
bear to women (as I perceive by your simpering none
of you hates them), that between you and the women   15
the play may please. If I were a woman I would kiss as
many of you as had beards that pleased me, complexions
that liked me and breaths that I defied not. And I am
sure as many as have good beards, or good faces, or
sweet breaths will for my kind offer, when I make   20
curtsy, bid me farewell.   *Exit.*

The Comedy of Errors

First published in the Folio of 1623 as the fifth of the comedies, *The Comedy of Errors* was nonetheless among Shakespeare's earliest plays, and seems, on grounds both of its style and of its topical references, to belong to the early 1590s (perhaps 1593–4). Its first recorded performance was on 28 December 1594, during the Christmas revels at Gray's Inn. The revels were occasions for satirical speeches, inversions of social hierarchy, and the festivities of music, dancing and entertainment. The particular revel in question seems to have been a confused and tumultuous affair (so much so that it was afterwards called 'The Night of Errors'), which came to a conclusion, very late in the evening, with the presentation of a play: after 'dancing and revelling with gentlewomen . . . a Comedy of Errors (like to Plautus his *Menechmus* was played by the players'.

The reference is almost certainly to Shakespeare's play, which is clearly based on Plautus' *Menaechmi*, a lively farce of twins separated in their youth. In *Menaechmi*, both twins, unknown to each other, find themselves in Epidamnus, where one has been raised by a merchant and the other has just arrived. They are constantly mistaken for one another, to the dismay of the citizens and the bewilderment of the brothers themselves. Only when they are seen together at the end is the cause of the confusions made clear; they are then reunited and propose to return together to Syracuse, home of the visiting brother, and start their lives anew. As the play closes, the twin from Epidamnus prepares to sell all his property – including his shrewish wife.

Shakespeare outdoes Plautus and multiplies the potential confusions by giving his twin brothers twin servants, likewise separated in infancy. He also borrows from another play by Plautus, *Amphitruo*, for 3.1, where Adriana excludes her husband from his own house while dining with his twin, whom she has mistaken for him. Shakespeare shifts his action from Epidamnus to Ephesus, famous for its Temple of Diana, but also well known to his audience from St Paul's journey to the city (Acts 19) and his Epistle to the Ephesians. This location imports Christian values into Plautus' action and contributes to the emotional and psychological gravity that finds its full voice in the family reunion at the end and in the cancelling of the death sentence on Egeon, both so different in spirit from the cynicism of the ending of the *Menaechmi*.

The Comedy of Errors is Shakespeare's shortest play,

only some 1700 lines long. In common only with *The Tempest*, it observes the neoclassical unities of time and place, pseudo-realistic conventions that help to give urgency to the action and to intensify the sudden, maddening topsy-turvydom of the Ephesian world. Once regarded as a set piece, a self-conscious experiment in writing Roman comedy, adolescent in some respects, *The Comedy of Errors* is now admired for establishing themes and techniques that Shakespeare would develop and deepen in the mature comedies and later romances. Its affinities with *Twelfth Night* and *Pericles* are particularly marked. With its dual set of twins, *Errors* is one of Shakespeare's early forays into the problematic area of human identity, while the play's themes of madness and magic give it a potentially dark edge. It also offers, in Adriana, an important study of a strong, if comical, female character, very different from the wife in Plautus.

In its own terms, then, *The Comedy of Errors* is a highly satisfying play and a reliable crowd-pleaser. The recognition of its theatrical effectiveness, a late nineteenth-century discovery, depended upon recovering the staging practices of the Elizabethan theatre. In the eighteenth and earlier nineteenth centuries the play was thought too indecorous and inconsequential to be played without adaptation, and Thomas Hull's version, called simply *The Twins*, with added songs and an intensified love interest, largely displaced it from the stage. In 1895 William Poel, with his Elizabethan Stage Society, returned the play once more to Gray's Inn, where he attempted to reproduce the fluid staging of its original performances. The important production by Theodore Komisarjevsky in 1938 in Stratford-upon-Avon abandoned realism for abstraction, inserted music and dance, mixed various styles and turned the play into a tour de force of theatrical entertainment. The production showed *Error*'s richness and gave it a home in the repertoire. Today it is a popular play, regularly revived and often inventively staged. Its comic ingenuity and energy make it accessible and attractive to audiences, who are often surprised to find behind the slapstick comedy of situation a more complex and sustaining story, as broken families are knit together in an action that can indeed seem, as it does for Antipholus of Syracuse, enchanted.

The Arden text is based on the 1623 First Folio.

EGEON, Merchant of Syracuse — *father to the Antipholuses and husband to the Abbess, though separated from all*

Solinus, DUKE of Ephesus

ANTIPHOLUS OF SYRACUSE
ANTIPHOLUS OF EPHESUS } — *twin brothers, sons to the Merchant of Syracuse and the Abbess but unknown to each other*

DROMIO OF SYRACUSE
DROMIO OF EPHESUS } — *twin brothers, slaves to the two Antipholuses*

ADRIANA — *wife to Antipholus of Ephesus*
LUCIANA — *sister to Adriana*
Emilia, an ABBESS at Ephesus — *wife to Egeon*

JAILER
FIRST MERCHANT — *friend to Antipholus of Syracuse*
ANGELO — *a goldsmith*
BALTHAZAR — *a merchant*
LUCE (or Nell) — *kitchen-maid in Adriana's household*
SECOND MERCHANT — *creditor to Angelo*
OFFICER
COURTESAN
Doctor PINCH — *a schoolmaster and conjuror*
MESSENGER

Attendant to the Duke, three or four Attendants to Doctor Pinch,
Headsman, other Officers

The Comedy of Errors

1.1   *Enter* Solinus, *the* DUKE *of Ephesus, with*
      EGEON, *the* Merchant of Syracuse, Jailer
      and other Attendants.

EGEON   Proceed, Solinus, to procure my fall,
    And by the doom of death end woes and all.

DUKE   Merchant of Syracusa, plead no more:
    I am not partial to infringe our laws.
5   The enmity and discord which of late
    Sprang from the rancorous outrage of your duke
    To merchants, our well-dealing countrymen,
    Who, wanting guilders to redeem their lives,
    Have sealed his rigorous statutes with their bloods,
10   Excludes all pity from our threatening looks;
    For, since the mortal and intestine jars
    'Twixt thy seditious countrymen and us,
    It hath in solemn synods been decreed,
    Both by the Syracusans and ourselves,
15   To admit no traffic to our adverse towns.
    Nay, more: if any born at Ephesus
    Be seen at Syracusan marts and fairs;
    Again, if any Syracusan born
    Come to the Bay of Ephesus, he dies,
20   His goods confiscate to the Duke's dispose,
    Unless a thousand marks be levied
    To quit the penalty and ransom him.
    Thy substance, valued at the highest rate,
    Cannot amount unto a hundred marks:
25   Therefore, by law thou art condemned to die.

EGEON
    Yet this my comfort: when your words are done,
    My woes end likewise with the evening sun.

DUKE   Well, Syracusan, say in brief the cause
    Why thou departed'st from thy native home,
30   And for what cause thou cam'st to Ephesus.

EGEON   A heavier task could not have been imposed
    Than I to speak my griefs unspeakable.
    Yet that the world may witness that my end
    Was wrought by nature, not by vile offence,
35   I'll utter what my sorrow gives me leave.
    In Syracusa was I born, and wed
    Unto a woman, happy but for me,
    And by me, had not our hap been bad.
    With her I lived in joy; our wealth increased
40   By prosperous voyages I often made
    To Epidamium, till my factor's death,
    And the great care of goods at random left,
    Drew me from kind embracements of my spouse;
    From whom my absence was not six months old
45   Before herself (almost at fainting under
    The pleasing punishment that women bear)
    Had made provision for her following me,
    And soon and safe arrived where I was.
    There had she not been long but she became
50   A joyful mother of two goodly sons,
    And, which was strange, the one so like the other
    As could not be distinguished but by names.

That very hour, and in the self-same inn,
A meaner woman was delivered
Of such a burden, male twins, both alike.   55
Those, for their parents were exceeding poor,
I bought, and brought up to attend my sons.
My wife, not meanly proud of two such boys,
Made daily motions for our home return.
Unwilling, I agreed. Alas! too soon   60
We came aboard.
A league from Epidamium had we sailed
Before the always wind-obeying deep
Gave any tragic instance of our harm.
But longer did we not retain much hope,   65
For what obscured light the heavens did grant
Did but convey unto our fearful minds
A doubtful warrant of immediate death;
Which, though myself would gladly have embraced,
Yet the incessant weepings of my wife,   70
Weeping before for what she saw must come,
And piteous plainings of the pretty babes,
That mourned for fashion, ignorant what to fear,
Forced me to seek delays for them and me.
And this it was, for other means was none: 75
The sailors sought for safety by our boat
And left the ship, then sinking-ripe, to us.
My wife, more careful for the latter-born,
Had fastened him unto a small spare mast
Such as seafaring men provide for storms;   80
To him one of the other twins was bound,
Whilst I had been like heedful of the other.
The children thus disposed, my wife and I,
Fixing our eyes on whom our care was fixed,
Fastened ourselves at either end the mast,   85
And floating straight, obedient to the stream,
Was carried towards Corinth, as we thought.
At length the sun, gazing upon the earth,
Dispersed those vapours that offended us,
And by the benefit of his wished light   90
The seas waxed calm, and we discovered
Two ships from far, making amain to us:
Of Corinth that, of Epidaurus this.
But ere they came – O, let me say no more!
Gather the sequel by that went before.   95

DUKE   Nay, forward, old man; do not break off so,
    For we may pity, though not pardon thee.

EGEON   O, had the gods done so, I had not now
    Worthily termed them merciless to us;
    For ere the ships could meet, by twice five leagues,   100
    We were encountered by a mighty rock,
    Which being violently borne upon,
    Our helpful ship was splitted in the midst;
    So that, in this unjust divorce of us,
    Fortune had left to both of us alike   105
    What to delight in, what to sorrow for.
    Her part, poor soul, seeming as burdened
    With lesser weight, but not with lesser woe,
    Was carried with more speed before the wind,

110 And in our sight they three were taken up
By fishermen of Corinth, as we thought.
At length another ship had seized on us,
And, knowing whom it was their hap to save,
Gave healthful welcome to their shipwrecked guests,
115 And would have reft the fishers of their prey
Had not their bark been very slow of sail;
And therefore homeward did they bend their course.
Thus have you heard me severed from my bliss,
That by misfortunes was my life prolonged
120 To tell sad stories of my own mishaps.

DUKE　And for the sake of them thou sorrow'st for,
Do me the favour to dilate at full
What have befall'n of them and thee till now.

EGEON　My youngest boy, and yet my eldest care,
125 At eighteen years became inquisitive
After his brother, and importuned me
That his attendant, so his case was like,
Reft of his brother, but retained his name,
Might bear him company in the quest of him;
130 Whom whilst I laboured of a love to see,
I hazarded the loss of whom I loved.
Five summers have I spent in farthest Greece,
Roaming clean through the bounds of Asia,
And coasting homeward came to Ephesus,
135 Hopeless to find, yet loath to leave unsought
Or that or any place that harbours men.
But here must end the story of my life;
And happy were I in my timely death,
Could all my travels warrant me they live.

140 DUKE　Hapless Egeon, whom the fates have marked
To bear the extremity of dire mishap:
Now, trust me, were it not against our laws,
Against my crown, my oath, my dignity,
Which princes, would they, may not disannul,
145 My soul should sue as advocate for thee.
But, though thou art adjudged to the death,
And passed sentence may not be recalled
But to our honour's great disparagement,
Yet will I favour thee in what I can.
150 Therefore, merchant, I'll limit thee this day
To seek thy hope by beneficial help.
Try all the friends thou hast in Ephesus;
Beg thou or borrow to make up the sum,
And live. If no, then thou art doomed to die.
155 Jailer, take him to thy custody.

JAILER　I will, my lord.

EGEON
Hopeless and helpless doth Egeon wend,
But to procrastinate his lifeless end. 　　*Exeunt.*

1.2　　*Enter* ANTIPHOLUS OF SYRACUSE,
First Merchant *and* DROMIO
OF SYRACUSE.

1 MERCHANT
Therefore, give out you are of Epidamium,

Lest that your goods too soon be confiscate.
This very day a Syracusan merchant
Is apprehended for arrival here,
And, not being able to buy out his life, 　　5
According to the statute of the town
Dies ere the weary sun set in the west.
　　[*Offers a purse to Antipholus.*]
There is your money that I had to keep.

ANTIPHOLUS OF SYRACUSE [*to Dromio, giving the purse*]
Go, bear it to the Centaur, where we host,
And stay there, Dromio, till I come to thee. 　　10
Within this hour it will be dinner-time;
Till that, I'll view the manners of the town,
Peruse the traders, gaze upon the buildings,
And then return and sleep within mine inn;
For with long travel I am stiff and weary. 　　15
Get thee away.

DROMIO OF SYRACUSE
Many a man would take you at your word
And go indeed, having so good a mean. 　　*Exit.*

ANTIPHOLUS OF SYRACUSE
A trusty villain, sir, that very oft,
When I am dull with care and melancholy, 　　20
Lightens my humour with his merry jests.
What, will you walk with me about the town
And then go to my inn and dine with me?

1 MERCHANT　I am invited, sir, to certain merchants,
Of whom I hope to make much benefit; 　　25
I crave your pardon. Soon at five o'clock,
Please you, I'll meet with you upon the mart,
And afterward consort you till bedtime;
My present business calls me from you now.

ANTIPHOLUS OF SYRACUSE
Farewell till then. I will go lose myself, 　　30
And wander up and down to view the city.

1 MERCHANT
Sir, I commend you to your own content. 　　*Exit.*

ANTIPHOLUS OF SYRACUSE
He that commends me to mine own content
Commends me to the thing I cannot get:
I to the world am like a drop of water 　　35
That in the ocean seeks another drop;
Who, falling there to find his fellow forth,
Unseen, inquisitive, confounds himself.
So I, to find a mother and a brother,
In quest of them, unhappy, lose myself. 　　40

　　　　Enter DROMIO OF EPHESUS.

Here comes the almanac of my true date.
– What now? How chance thou art returned so soon?

DROMIO OF EPHESUS
'Returned so soon'? Rather approached too late!
The capon burns, the pig falls from the spit;
The clock hath strucken twelve upon the bell; 　　45
My mistress made it one upon my cheek.
She is so hot because the meat is cold;
The meat is cold because you come not home;

You come not home because you have no stomach;
50   You have no stomach, having broke your fast.
But we that know what 'tis to fast and pray
Are penitent for your default today.

ANTIPHOLUS OF SYRACUSE
Stop in your wind, sir; tell me this, I pray:
Where have you left the money that I gave you?

DROMIO OF EPHESUS
55   O, sixpence that I had o'Wednesday last
To pay the saddler for my mistress' crupper?
The saddler had it, sir; I kept it not.

ANTIPHOLUS OF SYRACUSE
I am not in a sportive humour now;
Tell me, and dally not: where is the money?
60   We being strangers here, how dar'st thou trust
So great a charge from thine own custody?

DROMIO OF EPHESUS
I pray you, jest, sir, as you sit at dinner.
I from my mistress come to you in post;
If I return, I shall be post indeed,
65   For she will score your fault upon my pate.
Methinks your maw, like mine, should be your clock
And strike you home without a messenger.

ANTIPHOLUS OF SYRACUSE
Come, Dromio, come, these jests are out of season;
Reserve them till a merrier hour than this.
70   Where is the gold I gave in charge to thee?

DROMIO OF EPHESUS
To me, sir? Why, you gave no gold to me!

ANTIPHOLUS OF SYRACUSE
Come on, sir knave, have done your foolishness,
And tell me how thou hast disposed thy charge.

DROMIO OF EPHESUS
My charge was but to fetch you from the mart
75   Home to your house, the Phoenix, sir, to dinner;
My mistress and her sister stays for you.

ANTIPHOLUS OF SYRACUSE
Now as I am a Christian answer me
In what safe place you have bestowed my money,
Or I shall break that merry sconce of yours
80   That stands on tricks when I am undisposed.
Where is the thousand marks thou hadst of me?

DROMIO OF EPHESUS
I have some marks of yours upon my pate,
Some of my mistress' marks upon my shoulders,
But not a thousand marks between you both.
85   If I should pay your worship those again,
Perchance you will not bear them patiently.

ANTIPHOLUS OF SYRACUSE
Thy 'mistress' marks'? What 'mistress', slave, hast thou?

DROMIO OF EPHESUS
Your worship's wife, my mistress at the Phoenix;
She that doth fast till you come home to dinner,
90   And prays that you will hie you home to dinner.

ANTIPHOLUS OF SYRACUSE
What, wilt thou flout me thus unto my face,
Being forbid?   [*Strikes Dromio.*]
          There, take you that, sir knave.

DROMIO OF EPHESUS
What mean you, sir? For God's sake hold your hands!
Nay, an you will not, sir, I'll take my heels.   *Exit.*

ANTIPHOLUS OF SYRACUSE
Upon my life, by some device or other   95
The villain is o'er-raught of all my money.
They say this town is full of cozenage –
As, nimble jugglers that deceive the eye,
Dark-working sorcerers that change the mind,
Soul-killing witches that deform the body,   100
Disguised cheaters, prating mountebanks
And many such – like liberties of sin.
If it prove so, I will be gone the sooner.
I'll to the Centaur to go seek this slave;
I greatly fear my money is not safe.   *Exit.*   105

2.1   *Enter* ADRIANA, *wife to Antipholus*
             of Ephesus, with LUCIANA, *her sister.*

ADRIANA
Neither my husband nor the slave returned
That in such haste I sent to seek his master?
Sure, Luciana, it is two o'clock.

LUCIANA   Perhaps some merchant hath invited him,
And from the mart he's somewhere gone to dinner.   5
Good sister, let us dine, and never fret.
A man is master of his liberty;
Time is their master, and when they see time
They'll go or come: if so, be patient, sister.

ADRIANA   Why should their liberty than ours be more?   10

LUCIANA   Because their business still lies out o'door.

ADRIANA   Look when I serve him so, he takes it ill.

LUCIANA   O, know he is the bridle of your will.

ADRIANA   There's none but asses will be bridled so.

LUCIANA   Why, headstrong liberty is lashed with woe.   15
There's nothing situate under heaven's eye
But hath his bound in earth, in sea, in sky.
The beasts, the fishes and the winged fowls
Are their males' subjects and at their controls.
Man, more divine, the master of all these,   20
Lord of the wide world and wild watery seas,
Indued with intellectual sense and souls,
Of more pre-eminence than fish and fowls,
Are masters to their females, and their lords:
Then let your will attend on their accords.   25

ADRIANA   This servitude makes you to keep unwed.

LUCIANA   Not this, but troubles of the marriage bed.

ADRIANA
But were you wedded, you would bear some sway.

LUCIANA   Ere I learn love, I'll practise to obey.

ADRIANA   How if your husband start some otherwhere?   30

LUCIANA   Till he come home again, I would forbear.

ADRIANA
Patience unmoved! – No marvel though she pause:
They can be meek that have no other cause.
– A wretched soul bruised with adversity,
We bid be quiet when we hear it cry;   35
But were we burdened with like weight of pain,

As much or more we should ourselves complain.
So thou, that hast no unkind mate to grieve thee,
With urging helpless patience would relieve me;
40   But if thou live to see like right bereft,
This fool-begged patience in thee will be left.
LUCIANA   Well, I will marry one day but to try.

Enter DROMIO OF EPHESUS.

Here comes your man: now is your husband nigh.
ADRIANA   Say, is your tardy master now at hand?
45   DROMIO OF EPHESUS   Nay, he's at two hands with me,
and that my two ears can witness.
ADRIANA
Say, didst thou speak with him? Knowst thou his mind?
DROMIO OF EPHESUS
Ay, ay, he told his mind upon mine ear;
Beshrew his hand, I scarce could understand it.
LUCIANA
Spake he so doubtfully, thou couldst not feel his
50   meaning?
DROMIO OF EPHESUS   Nay, he struck so plainly, I could
too well feel his blows, and withal so doubtfully that I
could scarce understand them.
ADRIANA   But say, I prithee, is he coming home?
55   It seems he hath great care to please his wife.
DROMIO OF EPHESUS
Why, mistress, sure my master is horn-mad.
ADRIANA   'Horn-mad', thou villain?
DROMIO OF EPHESUS
I mean not cuckold-mad! But sure he is stark mad:
When I desired him to come home to dinner,
60   He asked me for a thousand marks in gold.
''Tis dinner-time', quoth I; 'My gold!', quoth he.
'Your meat doth burn', quoth I; 'My gold!', quoth he.
'Will you come home?', quoth I; 'My gold!', quoth he.
'Where is the thousand marks I gave thee, villain?'
65   'The pig', quoth I, 'is burned'; 'My gold!', quoth he.
'My mistress, sir –', quoth I; 'Hang up thy mistress!
I know not thy mistress, out on thy mistress!'
LUCIANA   Quoth who?
DROMIO OF EPHESUS   Quoth my master.
70   'I know', quoth he, 'no house, no wife, no mistress.'
So that my errand, due unto my tongue,
I thank him, I bore home upon my shoulders:
For, in conclusion, he did beat me there.
ADRIANA
Go back again, thou slave, and fetch him home.
DROMIO OF EPHESUS
75   'Go back again', and be new-beaten home?
For God's sake, send some other messenger!
ADRIANA   Back, slave, or I will break thy pate across.
DROMIO OF EPHESUS
And he will bless that cross with other beating;
Between you I shall have a holy head.
ADRIANA
Hence, prating peasant!   [*Beats him.*]
80   Fetch thy master home.

DROMIO OF EPHESUS
Am I so round with you as you with me
That like a football you do spurn me thus?
You spurn me hence, and he will spurn me hither;
If I last in this service, you must case me in leather.
                                        Exit.
LUCIANA   Fie, how impatience loureth in your face!   85
ADRIANA   His company must do his minions grace,
Whilst I at home starve for a merry look.
Hath homely age th'alluring beauty took
From my poor cheek? Then he hath wasted it.
Are my discourses dull? Barren my wit?   90
If voluble and sharp discourse be marred,
Unkindness blunts it more than marble hard.
Do their gay vestments his affections bait?
That's not my fault: he's master of my state.
What ruins are in me that can be found   95
By him not ruined? Then is he the ground
Of my defeatures. My decayed fair
A sunny look of his would soon repair.
But, too-unruly deer, he breaks the pale
And feeds from home; poor I am but his stale.   100
LUCIANA
Self-harming jealousy! Fie, beat it hence.
ADRIANA
Unfeeling fools can with such wrongs dispense.
I know his eye doth homage otherwhere,
Or else what lets it but he would be here?
Sister, you know he promised me a chain: 105
Would that alone, alone he would detain,
So he would keep fair quarter with his bed.
I see the jewel best enamelled
Will lose his beauty – and though gold bides still
That others touch, yet often-touching will   110
Wear gold – and any man that hath a name
By falsehood and corruption doth it shame.
Since that my beauty cannot please his eye,
I'll weep what's left away, and weeping die.
LUCIANA
How many fond fools serve mad jealousy!   *Exeunt.*   115

2.2   *Enter* ANTIPHOLUS OF SYRACUSE.

ANTIPHOLUS OF SYRACUSE
The gold I gave to Dromio is laid up
Safe at the Centaur, and the heedful slave
Is wandered forth in care to seek me out.
By computation and mine host's report,
I could not speak with Dromio since at first   5
I sent him from the mart.

Enter DROMIO OF SYRACUSE.

                            See, here he comes.
– How now, sir, is your merry humour altered?
As you love strokes, so jest with me again.
You know no Centaur? You received no gold?
Your mistress sent to have me 'home to dinner'?   10

My house was at the Phoenix? Wast thou mad,
That thus so madly thou didst answer me?

DROMIO OF SYRACUSE
What answer, sir? When spake I such a word?

ANTIPHOLUS OF SYRACUSE
Even now, even here, not half an hour since.

DROMIO OF SYRACUSE
15   I did not see you since you sent me hence,
Home to the Centaur with the gold you gave me.

ANTIPHOLUS OF SYRACUSE
Villain, thou didst deny the gold's receipt,
And told'st me of a mistress and a dinner,
For which I hope thou felt'st I was displeased.

DROMIO OF SYRACUSE
20   I am glad to see you in this merry vein;
What means this jest? I pray you, master, tell me.

ANTIPHOLUS OF SYRACUSE
Yea, dost thou jeer and flout me in the teeth?
Think'st thou I jest? Hold, take thou that
      [*beating Dromio*], and that!

DROMIO OF SYRACUSE
Hold sir, for God's sake! Now your jest is earnest:
25   Upon what bargain do you give it me?

ANTIPHOLUS OF SYRACUSE
Because that I familiarly sometimes
Do use you for my fool and chat with you,
Your sauciness will jest upon my love,
And make a common of my serious hours.
30   When the sun shines let foolish gnats make sport,
But creep in crannies when he hides his beams;
If you will jest with me, know my aspect,
And fashion your demeanour to my looks,
Or I will beat this method in your sconce.

35   DROMIO OF SYRACUSE   'Sconce', call you it? So you
would leave battering, I had rather have it a 'head'. An
you use these blows long, I must get a sconce for my
head, and ensconce it, too, or else I shall seek my wit in
my shoulders. But, I pray, sir, why am I beaten?

40   ANTIPHOLUS OF SYRACUSE   Dost thou not know?

DROMIO OF SYRACUSE   Nothing, sir, but that I am
beaten.

ANTIPHOLUS OF SYRACUSE   Shall I tell you why?

DROMIO OF SYRACUSE   Ay, sir, and wherefore; for, they
45   say, every why hath a wherefore.

ANTIPHOLUS OF SYRACUSE
'Why' first: for flouting me; and then 'wherefore':
For urging it the second time to me.

DROMIO OF SYRACUSE
Was there ever any man thus beaten out of season,
When in the why and the wherefore is neither rhyme
      nor reason?
50   Well, sir, I thank you.

ANTIPHOLUS OF SYRACUSE   Thank me, sir, for what?

DROMIO OF SYRACUSE   Marry, sir, for this something
that you gave me for nothing.

ANTIPHOLUS OF SYRACUSE   I'll make you amends
55   next, to give you nothing for something. But say, sir, is
it dinner-time?

DROMIO OF SYRACUSE   No, sir, I think the meat wants
that I have.

ANTIPHOLUS OF SYRACUSE   In good time, sir, what's that?

DROMIO OF SYRACUSE   Basting.   60

ANTIPHOLUS OF SYRACUSE   Well, sir, then 'twill be dry.

DROMIO OF SYRACUSE   If it be, sir, I pray you, eat none
of it.

ANTIPHOLUS OF SYRACUSE   Your reason?

DROMIO OF SYRACUSE   Lest it make you choleric, and   65
purchase me another dry basting.

ANTIPHOLUS OF SYRACUSE   Well, sir, learn to jest in
good time: there's a time for all things.

DROMIO OF SYRACUSE   I durst have denied that before
you were so choleric.   70

ANTIPHOLUS OF SYRACUSE   By what rule, sir?

DROMIO OF SYRACUSE   Marry, sir, by a rule as plain as
the plain bald pate of Father Time himself.

ANTIPHOLUS OF SYRACUSE   Let's hear it.

DROMIO OF SYRACUSE   There's no time for a man to   75
recover his hair that grows bald by nature.

ANTIPHOLUS OF SYRACUSE   May he not do it by fine
and recovery?

DROMIO OF SYRACUSE   Yes, to pay a fine for a periwig
and recover the lost hair of another man.   80

ANTIPHOLUS OF SYRACUSE   Why is Time such a
niggard of hair, being, as it is, so plentiful an excrement?

DROMIO OF SYRACUSE   Because it is a blessing that he
bestows on beasts; and what he hath scanted men in
hair he hath given them in wit.   85

ANTIPHOLUS OF SYRACUSE   Why, but there's many a
man hath more hair than wit.

DROMIO OF SYRACUSE   Not a man of those but he hath
the wit to lose his hair.

ANTIPHOLUS OF SYRACUSE   Why, thou didst conclude   90
hairy men plain dealers without wit.

DROMIO OF SYRACUSE   The plainer dealer, the sooner
lost; yet he loseth it in a kind of jollity.

ANTIPHOLUS OF SYRACUSE   For what reason?

DROMIO OF SYRACUSE   For two, and sound ones, too.   95

ANTIPHOLUS OF SYRACUSE   Nay, not sound, I pray
you.

DROMIO OF SYRACUSE   Sure ones, then.

ANTIPHOLUS OF SYRACUSE   Nay, not sure, in a thing
falsing.   100

DROMIO OF SYRACUSE   Certain ones, then.

ANTIPHOLUS OF SYRACUSE   Name them.

DROMIO OF SYRACUSE   The one, to save the money
that he spends in tiring; the other, that at dinner they
should not drop in his porridge.   105

ANTIPHOLUS OF SYRACUSE   You would all this time
have proved there is no time for all things.

DROMIO OF SYRACUSE   Marry, and did, sir: namely,
e'en no time to recover hair lost by nature.

ANTIPHOLUS OF SYRACUSE   But your reason was not   110
substantial, why there is no time to recover.

DROMIO OF SYRACUSE   Thus I mend it: Time himself
is bald, and, therefore, to the world's end will have bald
followers.

115 ANTIPHOLUS OF SYRACUSE   I knew 'twould be a bald
conclusion.

Enter ADRIANA, *beckoning to them, and* LUCIANA.

But soft! Who wafts us yonder?
ADRIANA   Ay, ay, Antipholus, look strange and frown:
Some other mistress hath thy sweet aspects;
120 I am not Adriana, nor thy wife.
The time was once when thou unurged wouldst vow
That never words were music to thine ear,
That never object pleasing in thine eye,
That never touch well welcome to thy hand,
125 That never meat sweet-savoured in thy taste,
Unless I spake, or looked, or touched, or carved to thee.
How comes it now, my husband, O, how comes it,
That thou art then estranged from thyself?
'Thyself' I call it, being strange to me
130 That, undividable, incorporate,
Am better than thy dear self's better part.
  [*Reaches for him.*]
Ah, do not tear away thyself from me!
For know, my love: as easy mayst thou fall
A drop of water in the breaking gulf,
135 And take unmingled thence that drop again
Without addition or diminishing,
As take from me thyself, and not me, too.
How dearly would it touch thee to the quick
Shouldst thou but hear I were licentious?
140 And that this body, consecrate to thee,
By ruffian lust should be contaminate?
Wouldst thou not spit at me, and spurn at me,
And hurl the name of 'husband' in my face,
And tear the stained skin off my harlot brow,
145 And from my false hand cut the wedding ring,
And break it with a deep-divorcing vow?
I know thou canst, and, therefore, see thou do it!
I am possessed with an adulterate blot;
My blood is mingled with the crime of lust:
150 For if we two be one, and thou play false,
I do digest the poison of thy flesh,
Being strumpeted by thy contagion.
Keep, then, fair league and truce with thy true bed:
I live dis-stained, thou undishonoured.
ANTIPHOLUS OF SYRACUSE
155 Plead you to me, fair dame? I know you not:
In Ephesus I am but two hours old,
As strange unto your town as to your talk,
Who, every word by all my wit being scanned,
Wants wit in all, one word to understand.
LUCIANA
160 Fie, brother! How the world is changed with you:
When were you wont to use my sister thus?
She sent for you by Dromio home to dinner.
ANTIPHOLUS OF SYRACUSE   By Dromio?
DROMIO OF SYRACUSE   By me?
ADRIANA
165 By thee, and this thou didst return from him:

That he did buffet thee, and, in his blows,
Denied my house for his, me for his wife.
ANTIPHOLUS OF SYRACUSE [*to Dromio*]
Did you converse, sir, with this gentlewoman?
What is the course and drift of your compact?
DROMIO OF SYRACUSE
I, sir? I never saw her till this time.   170
ANTIPHOLUS OF SYRACUSE
Villain, thou lie'st! For even her very words
Didst thou deliver to me on the mart.
DROMIO OF SYRACUSE
I never spake with her in all my life.
ANTIPHOLUS OF SYRACUSE
How can she thus, then, call us by our names? –
Unless it be by inspiration.   175
ADRIANA   How ill agrees it with your gravity
To counterfeit thus grossly with your slave,
Abetting him to thwart me in my mood.
Be it my wrong, you are from me exempt;
But wrong not that wrong with a more contempt.   180
Come, I will fasten [*taking his arm*] on this sleeve of thine:
Thou art an elm, my husband, I a vine,
Whose weakness, married to thy stronger state,
Makes me with thy strength to communicate.
If aught possess thee from me, it is dross,   185
Usurping ivy, briar or idle moss,
Who, all for want of pruning, with intrusion
Infect thy sap, and live on thy confusion.
ANTIPHOLUS OF SYRACUSE [*aside*]
To me she speaks; she moves me for her theme.
What, was I married to her in my dream?   190
Or sleep I now and think I hear all this?
What error drives our eyes and ears amiss?
Until I know this sure uncertainty,
I'll entertain the offered fallacy.
LUCIANA
Dromio, go bid the servants spread for dinner.   195
DROMIO OF SYRACUSE [*aside*]
O, for my beads! I cross me [*crossing himself*] for a sinner.
This is the fairy land; O, spite of spites,
We talk with goblins, owls and sprites!
If we obey them not, this will ensue:
They'll suck our breath or pinch us black and blue.   200
LUCIANA
Why prat'st thou to thyself and answer'st not?
Dromio, thou *Dromio*, thou snail, thou slug, thou sot.
DROMIO OF SYRACUSE [*to Antipholus*]
I am transformed, master, am I not?
ANTIPHOLUS OF SYRACUSE
I think thou art in mind, and so am I.
DROMIO OF SYRACUSE
Nay, master, both in mind and in my shape.   205
ANTIPHOLUS OF SYRACUSE
Thou hast thine own form.
DROMIO OF SYRACUSE   No, I am an ape.
LUCIANA
If thou art changed to aught, 'tis to an ass.

DROMIO OF SYRACUSE

    'Tis true: she rides me, and I long for grass.

    'Tis so, I am an ass, else it could never be

210   But I should know her as well as she knows me.

ADRIANA

    Come, come, no longer will I be a fool,

    To put the finger in the eye and weep,

    Whilst man and master laughs my woes to scorn.

    Come, sir, to dinner. – Dromio, keep the gate.

215   – Husband, I'll dine above with you today,

    And shrive you of a thousand idle pranks.

    – Sirrah, if any ask you for your master,

    Say he dines forth, and let no creature enter.

    – Come, sister. – Dromio, play the porter well.

ANTIPHOLUS OF SYRACUSE [*aside*]

220   Am I in earth, in heaven or in hell?

    Sleeping or waking? Mad or well advised?

    Known unto these, and to myself disguised?

    I'll say as they say, and persever so,

    And in this mist at all adventures go.

DROMIO OF SYRACUSE

225   Master, shall I be porter at the gate?

ADRIANA   Ay, and let none enter, lest I break your pate.

LUCIANA   Come, come, Antipholus, we dine too late.

Exeunt, with Dromio last.

3.1   *Enter* ANTIPHOLUS OF EPHESUS,
his man DROMIO, ANGELO *the goldsmith and*
BALTHAZAR *the merchant.*

ANTIPHOLUS OF EPHESUS

    Good Signor Angelo, you must excuse us all;

    My wife is shrewish when I keep not hours.

    Say that I lingered with you at your shop

    To see the making of her carcanet,

5   And that tomorrow you will bring it home.

    [*Indicates Dromio.*] But here's a villain that would face
      me down

    He met me on the mart, and that I beat him

    And charged him with a thousand marks in gold,

    And that I did deny my wife and house.

    [*to Dromio*] Thou drunkard, thou, what didst thou

10   mean by this?

DROMIO OF EPHESUS

    Say what you will, sir, but I know what I know;

    That you beat me at the mart I have your hand to show.

    If the skin were parchment and the blows you gave
      were ink,

    Your own handwriting would tell you what I think.

ANTIPHOLUS OF EPHESUS   I think thou art an ass.

15 DROMIO OF EPHESUS   Marry, so it doth appear

    By the wrongs I suffer and the blows I bear.

    I should kick, being kicked; and, being at that pass,

    You would keep from my heels and beware of an ass.

ANTIPHOLUS OF EPHESUS

    Y'are sad, Signor Balthazar. Pray God our cheer

20   May answer my good will and your good welcome here.

BALTHAZAR

    I hold your dainties cheap, sir, and your welcome dear.

ANTIPHOLUS OF EPHESUS

    O, Signor Balthazar, either at flesh or fish,

    A table full of welcome makes scarce one dainty dish.

BALTHAZAR

    Good meat, sir, is common; that every churl affords.

ANTIPHOLUS OF EPHESUS

    And welcome more common, for that's nothing but

      words.   25

BALTHAZAR

    Small cheer and great welcome makes a merry feast.

ANTIPHOLUS OF EPHESUS

    Ay, to a niggardly host and more sparing guest.

    But though my cates be mean, take them in good part:

    Better cheer may you have, but not with better heart.

    [*Attempts to open the door of his house.*]

    But soft, my door is locked. [*to Dromio*] Go bid them

      let us in.   30

DROMIO OF EPHESUS [*calling*]

    Maud, Bridget, Marian, Cic'ly, Gillian, Ginn!

DROMIO OF SYRACUSE [*within, on the other side of the door*]

    Mome, malt-horse, capon, coxcomb, idiot, patch!

    Either get thee from the door or sit down at the hatch.

    Dost thou conjure for wenches, that thou call'st for
      such store,

    When one is one too many? Go, get thee from the door.   35

DROMIO OF EPHESUS

    What patch is made our porter? – My master stays in
      the street.

DROMIO OF SYRACUSE [*within*]

    Let him walk from whence he came, lest he catch cold
      on's feet.

ANTIPHOLUS OF EPHESUS

    Who talks within there? Ho, open the door!

DROMIO OF SYRACUSE [*within*]

    Right, sir, I'll tell you when, an you'll tell me wherefore.

ANTIPHOLUS OF EPHESUS

    'Wherefore'? For my dinner: I have not dined today.   40

DROMIO OF SYRACUSE [*within*]

    Nor today here you must not; come again when you
      may.

ANTIPHOLUS OF EPHESUS

    What art thou that keep'st me out from the house I owe?

DROMIO OF SYRACUSE [*within*]

    The porter for this time, sir, and my name is Dromio.

DROMIO OF EPHESUS

    O villain, thou hast stolen both mine office and my
      name;

    The one ne'er got me credit, the other mickle blame;   45

    If thou hadst been Dromio today in my place,

    Thou wouldst have changed thy place for a name, and
      thy name for an ass.

Enter LUCE *within the house.*

LUCE [*within*]

    What a coil is there, Dromio! Who are those at the gate?

DROMIO OF EPHESUS   Let my master in, Luce.

LUCE [_within_]   Faith, no; he comes too late,
And so tell your master.

50   DROMIO OF EPHESUS   O Lord, I must laugh!
Have at you with a proverb: 'Shall I set in my staff?'

LUCE [_within_]
Have at you with another: that's 'When? Can you tell?'

DROMIO OF SYRACUSE [_within_]
If thy name be called 'Luce', Luce, thou hast
answered him well.

ANTIPHOLUS OF EPHESUS [_to Luce_]
Do you hear, you minion? You'll let us in, I hope?

LUCE [_within_]
I thought to have asked you.

55   DROMIO OF SYRACUSE [_within_]   And you said, no.

DROMIO OF EPHESUS
So, come – help.   [_They beat the door._]
                        Well struck! There was blow for blow.

ANTIPHOLUS OF EPHESUS
Thou baggage, let me in!

LUCE [_within_]   Can you tell for whose sake?

DROMIO OF EPHESUS   Master, knock the door hard.

LUCE [_within_]   Let him knock till it ache.

ANTIPHOLUS OF EPHESUS
You'll cry for this, minion, if I beat the door down.
    [_Beats on the door._]

LUCE [_within_]

60   What needs all that, and a pair of stocks in the town?
                                              Exit.

Enter ADRIANA, _above, within the house._

ADRIANA [_within_]
Who is that at the door that keeps all this noise?

DROMIO OF SYRACUSE [_within_]
By my troth, your town is troubled with unruly boys.

ANTIPHOLUS OF EPHESUS [_to Adriana_]
Are you there, wife? You might have come before.

ADRIANA [_within_]
Your wife, sir knave? Go, get you from the door.   _Exit._

DROMIO OF EPHESUS

65   If you went in pain, master, this 'knave' would go sore.

ANGELO [_to Antipholus_]
Here is neither cheer, sir, nor welcome; we would fain
have either.

BALTHAZAR
In debating which was best, we shall part with neither.

DROMIO OF EPHESUS
They stand at the door, master; bid them welcome
hither.

ANTIPHOLUS OF EPHESUS
There is something in the wind, that we cannot get in.

DROMIO OF EPHESUS
You would say so, master, if your garments were

70   thin.
Your cake is warm within; you stand here in the cold.
It would make a man mad as a buck to be so bought
and sold.

ANTIPHOLUS OF EPHESUS
Go fetch me something: I'll break ope the gate.

DROMIO OF SYRACUSE [_within_]
Break any breaking here, and I'll break your knave's
pate.

DROMIO OF EPHESUS
A man may break a word with you, sir, and words are
but wind;   75
Ay, and break it in your face, so he break it not behind.

DROMIO OF SYRACUSE [_within_]
It seems thou want'st breaking. Out upon thee, hind!

DROMIO OF EPHESUS
Here's too much 'Out upon thee!' I pray thee let me in.

DROMIO OF SYRACUSE [_within_]
Ay, when fowls have no feathers and fish have no fin.

ANTIPHOLUS OF EPHESUS
Well, I'll break in: go borrow me a crow.   80

DROMIO OF EPHESUS
A crow without feather? Master, mean you so?
For a fish without a fin, there's a fowl without a feather.
[_to Dromio of Syracuse_] If a crow help us in, sirrah,
we'll pluck a crow together.

ANTIPHOLUS OF EPHESUS
Go, get thee gone; fetch me an iron crow.

BALTHAZAR   Have patience, sir. O, let it not be so!   85
Herein you war against your reputation,
And draw within the compass of suspect
Th'unviolated honour of your wife.
Once, this: your long experience of her wisdom,
Her sober virtue, years and modesty   90
Plead on her part some cause to you unknown;
And doubt not, sir, but she will well excuse
Why at this time the doors are made against you.
Be ruled by me: depart in patience,
And let us to the Tiger all to dinner,   95
And about evening come yourself alone
To know the reason of this strange restraint.
If by strong hand you offer to break in
Now in the stirring passage of the day,
A vulgar comment will be made of it;   100
And that supposed by the common rout
Against your yet ungalled estimation,
That may with foul intrusion enter in
And dwell upon your grave when you are dead;
For slander lives upon succession,   105
Forever housed where it gets possession.

ANTIPHOLUS OF EPHESUS
You have prevailed. I will depart in quiet,
And in despite of wrath mean to be merry:
I know a wench of excellent discourse,
Pretty and witty, wild and yet, too, gentle.   110
There will we dine. This woman that I mean,
My wife – but I protest, without desert –
Hath oftentimes upbraided me withal.
To her will we to dinner. [_to Angelo_] Get you
home
And fetch the chain; by this, I know, 'tis made.   115

Bring it, I pray you, to the Porpentine,
For there's the house. That chain will I bestow –
Be it for nothing but to spite my wife –
Upon mine hostess there. Good sir, make haste.
120 Since mine own doors refuse to entertain me,
I'll knock elsewhere to see if they'll disdain me.

ANGELO
I'll meet you at that place some hour hence.

ANTIPHOLUS OF EPHESUS
Do so; this jest shall cost me some expense.

Exeunt Antipholus and Dromio of Ephesus,
Angelo and Balthazar. Exit separately
Dromio of Syracuse.

3.2   *Enter* LUCIANA *with* ANTIPHOLUS OF
SYRACUSE.

LUCIANA
And may it be that you have quite forgot
A husband's office? Shall, Antipholus,
Even in the spring of love, thy love-springs rot?
Shall love, in building, grow so ruinous?
5 If you did wed my sister for her wealth,
Then for her wealth's sake use her with more kindness.
Or if you like elsewhere, do it by stealth:
Muffle your false love with some show of blindness;
Let not my sister read it in your eye;
10 Be not thy tongue thy own shame's orator;
Look sweet, speak fair, become disloyalty;
Apparel vice like virtue's harbinger;
Bear a fair presence, though your heart be tainted;
Teach sin the carriage of a holy saint;
15 Be secret-false: what need she be acquainted?
What simple thief brags of his own attaint?
'Tis double wrong to truant with your bed
And let her read it in thy looks at board.
Shame hath a bastard fame, well managed;
20 Ill deeds is doubled with an evil word.
Alas, poor women! Make us but believe,
Being compact of credit, that you love us;
Though others have the arm, show us the sleeve:
We in your motion turn, and you may move us.
25 Then, gentle brother, get you in again;
Comfort my sister, cheer her, call her 'wife'.
'Tis holy sport to be a little vain
When the sweet breath of flattery conquers strife.

ANTIPHOLUS OF SYRACUSE
Sweet mistress – what your name is else, I know not,
30 Nor by what wonder you do hit of mine –
Less in your knowledge and your grace you show not
Than our earth's wonder, more than earth divine.
Teach me, dear creature, how to think and speak;
Lay open to my earthy, gross conceit –
35 Smothered in errors, feeble, shallow, weak –
The folded meaning of your words' deceit.
Against my soul's pure truth why labour you
To make it wander in an unknown field?

Are you a god? Would you create me new?
Transform me, then, and to your power I'll yield. 40
But if that I am I, then well I know,
Your weeping sister is no wife of mine,
Nor to her bed no homage do I owe.
Far more, far more, to you do I decline.
O, train me not, sweet mermaid, with thy note, 45
To drown me in thy sister's flood of tears:
Sing, siren, for thyself, and I will dote.
Spread o'er the silver waves thy golden hairs,
And as a bed I'll take thee, and there lie,
And in that glorious supposition think 50
He gains by death that hath such means to die.
Let love, being light, be drowned if she sink!

LUCIANA
What, are you mad, that you do reason so?

ANTIPHOLUS OF SYRACUSE
Not mad, but mated; how I do not know.

LUCIANA
It is a fault that springeth from your eye. 55

ANTIPHOLUS OF SYRACUSE
For gazing on your beams, fair sun, being by.

LUCIANA
Gaze where you should, and that will clear your
sight.

ANTIPHOLUS OF SYRACUSE
As good to wink, sweet love, as look on night.

LUCIANA   Why call you me 'love'? Call my sister so.

ANTIPHOLUS OF SYRACUSE
Thy sister's sister.

LUCIANA   That's my sister.

ANTIPHOLUS OF SYRACUSE   No; 60
It is thyself, mine own self's better part,
Mine eye's clear eye, my dear heart's dearer heart,
My food, my fortune and my sweet hope's aim,
My sole earth's heaven, and my heaven's claim.

LUCIANA   All this my sister is, or else should be. 65

ANTIPHOLUS OF SYRACUSE
Call thyself 'sister', sweet, for I am thee.
Thee will I love, and with thee lead my life;
Thou hast no husband yet, nor I no wife:
Give me thy hand.   [*Offers to take her hand.*]

LUCIANA   O, soft, sir, hold you still;
I'll fetch my sister to get her good will.   *Exit.* 70

Enter DROMIO OF SYRACUSE, *running.*

ANTIPHOLUS OF SYRACUSE
Why, how now, Dromio, where run'st thou so fast?

DROMIO OF SYRACUSE   Do you know me, sir? Am I
Dromio? Am I your man? Am I myself?

ANTIPHOLUS OF SYRACUSE
Thou art Dromio, thou art my man, thou art
thyself.

DROMIO OF SYRACUSE   I am an ass, I am a woman's 75
man, and besides myself.

ANTIPHOLUS OF SYRACUSE
What woman's man? And how besides thyself?

DROMIO OF SYRACUSE   Marry, sir, besides myself I am
due to a woman: one that claims me, one that haunts
me, one that will have me.

ANTIPHOLUS OF SYRACUSE   What claim lays she to thee?

DROMIO OF SYRACUSE   Marry, sir, such claim as you
would lay to your horse; and she would have me as a
beast – not that, I being a beast, she would have me, but
that she, being a very beastly creature, lays claim to me.

ANTIPHOLUS OF SYRACUSE   What is she?

DROMIO OF SYRACUSE   A very reverend body: ay, such
a one as a man may not speak of without he say, 'sir-
reverence'. I have but lean luck in the match, and yet is
she a wondrous fat marriage.

ANTIPHOLUS OF SYRACUSE   How dost thou mean, a
'fat marriage'?

DROMIO OF SYRACUSE   Marry, sir, she's the kitchen
wench, and all grease; and I know not what use to put
her to but to make a lamp of her, and run from her by
her own light. I warrant her rags and the tallow in them
will burn a Poland winter. If she lives till doomsday,
she'll burn a week longer than the whole world.

ANTIPHOLUS OF SYRACUSE   What complexion is she of?

DROMIO OF SYRACUSE   Swart like my shoe, but her
face nothing like so clean kept. For why? She sweats; a
man may go overshoes in the grime of it.

ANTIPHOLUS OF SYRACUSE   That's a fault that water
will mend.

DROMIO OF SYRACUSE   No, sir, 'tis in grain; Noah's
flood could not do it.

ANTIPHOLUS OF SYRACUSE   What's her name?

DROMIO OF SYRACUSE   Nell, sir; but her name and
three quarters – that's an ell and three quarters – will
not measure her from hip to hip.

ANTIPHOLUS OF SYRACUSE   Then she bears some
breadth?

DROMIO OF SYRACUSE   No longer from head to foot
than from hip to hip: she is spherical, like a globe. I
could find out countries in her.

ANTIPHOLUS OF SYRACUSE   In what part of her body
stands Ireland?

DROMIO OF SYRACUSE   Marry, sir, in her buttocks; I
found it out by the bogs.

ANTIPHOLUS OF SYRACUSE   Where Scotland?

DROMIO OF SYRACUSE   I found it by the barrenness,
hard in the palm of her hand.

ANTIPHOLUS OF SYRACUSE   Where France?

DROMIO OF SYRACUSE   In her forehead, armed and
reverted, making war against her hair.

ANTIPHOLUS OF SYRACUSE   Where England?

DROMIO OF SYRACUSE   I looked for the chalky cliffs,
but I could find no whiteness in them. But I guess it
stood in her chin, by the salt rheum that ran between
France and it.

ANTIPHOLUS OF SYRACUSE   Where Spain?

DROMIO OF SYRACUSE   Faith, I saw it not, but I felt it
hot in her breath.

ANTIPHOLUS OF SYRACUSE   Where America, the
Indies?

DROMIO OF SYRACUSE   O, sir, upon her nose, all o'er
embellished with rubies, carbuncles, sapphires, declining
their rich aspect to the hot breath of Spain, who sent
whole armadas of carracks to be ballast at her nose.

ANTIPHOLUS OF SYRACUSE   Where stood Belgia, the
Netherlands?

DROMIO OF SYRACUSE   O, sir, I did not look so low. To
conclude, this drudge or diviner laid claim to me,
called me 'Dromio', swore I was assured to her, told
me what privy marks I had about me – as the mark of
my shoulder, the mole in my neck, the great wart on
my left arm – that I, amazed, ran from her as a witch.
And I think if my breast had not been made of faith,
and my heart of steel,
She had transformed me to a curtal dog, and made
me turn i'th' wheel.

ANTIPHOLUS OF SYRACUSE
Go, hie thee presently, post to the road;
An if the wind blow any way from shore,
I will not harbour in this town tonight.
If any bark put forth, come to the mart,
Where I will walk till thou return to me.
If everyone knows us, and we know none,
'Tis time, I think, to trudge, pack and be gone.

DROMIO OF SYRACUSE
As from a bear a man would run for life,
So fly I from her that would be my wife.   *Exit.*

ANTIPHOLUS OF SYRACUSE
There's none but witches do inhabit here,
And therefore 'tis high time that I were hence.
She that doth call me 'husband', even my soul
Doth for a wife abhor. But her fair sister,
Possessed with such a gentle, sovereign grace,
Of such enchanting presence and discourse,
Hath almost made me traitor to myself.
But lest myself be guilty to self-wrong,
I'll stop mine ears against the mermaid's song.

Enter ANGELO *with the chain.*

ANGELO   Master Antipholus –

ANTIPHOLUS OF SYRACUSE   Ay, that's my name.

ANGELO   I know it well, sir. Lo, here's the chain.
I thought to have ta'en you at the Porpentine;
The chain, unfinished, made me stay thus long.
    [*Presents the chain.*]

ANTIPHOLUS OF SYRACUSE
What is your will that I shall do with this?

ANGELO
What please yourself, sir: I have made it for you.

ANTIPHOLUS OF SYRACUSE
Made it for me, sir? I bespoke it not.

ANGELO
Not once, nor twice, but twenty times you have.
Go home with it, and please your wife withal,
And soon at supper-time I'll visit you,
And then receive my money for the chain.

ANTIPHOLUS OF SYRACUSE
I pray you, sir, receive the money now,

180 For fear you ne'er see chain nor money more.

ANGELO
You are a merry man, sir; fare you well.   *Exit.*

ANTIPHOLUS OF SYRACUSE
What I should think of this I cannot tell;
But this I think: there's no man is so vain
That would refuse so fair an offered chain.
185 I see a man here needs not live by shifts,
When in the streets he meets such golden gifts.
I'll to the mart, and there for Dromio stay;
If any ship put out, then straight, away!   *Exit.*

4.1   *Enter* Second Merchant, ANGELO *the*
goldsmith and an Officer.

2 MERCHANT [*to Angelo*]
You know since Pentecost the sum is due,
And since I have not much importuned you;
Nor now I had not, but that I am bound
To Persia, and want guilders for my voyage.
5 Therefore make present satisfaction,
Or I'll attach you by this officer.

ANGELO   Even just the sum that I do owe to you
Is growing to me by Antipholus,
And in the instant that I met with you
10 He had of me a chain; at five o'clock
I shall receive the money for the same.
Pleaseth you walk with me down to his house,
I will discharge my bond, and thank you, too.

Enter ANTIPHOLUS OF EPHESUS, *wearing*
the Courtesan's ring, and DROMIO OF EPHESUS
from the Courtesan's.

OFFICER
That labour may you save: see where he comes.

ANTIPHOLUS OF EPHESUS [*to Dromio*]
15 While I go to the goldsmith's house, go thou
And buy a rope's end. That will I bestow
Among my wife and her confederates
For locking me out of my doors by day. –
But soft, I see the goldsmith. – Get thee gone,
20 Buy thou a rope and bring it home to me.

DROMIO OF EPHESUS
I buy a thousand pound a year, I buy a rope.   *Exit.*

ANTIPHOLUS OF EPHESUS [*to Angelo*]
A man is well holp up that trusts to you:
I promised your presence and the chain,
But neither chain nor goldsmith came to me.
25 Belike you thought our love would last too long
If it were chained together, and therefore came not.

ANGELO
Saving your merry humour, [*offering a paper*] here's
the note
How much your chain weighs to the utmost carat,
The fineness of the gold and chargeful fashion,
30 Which doth amount to three odd ducats more
Than I stand debted to this gentleman.

I pray you see him presently discharged,
For he is bound to sea, and stays but for it.

ANTIPHOLUS OF EPHESUS
I am not furnished with the present money;
Besides, I have some business in the town.   35
Good signor, take the stranger to my house,
And with you take the chain, and bid my wife
Disburse the sum on the receipt thereof.
Perchance I will be there as soon as you.

ANGELO   Then you will bring the chain to her yourself?   40

ANTIPHOLUS OF EPHESUS
No, bear it with you, lest I come not time enough.

ANGELO   Well, sir, I will. Have you the chain about you?

ANTIPHOLUS OF EPHESUS
An if I have not, sir, I hope you have,
Or else you may return without your money.

ANGELO   Nay, come, I pray you, sir, give me the chain;   45
Both wind and tide stays for this gentleman,
And I, to blame, have held him here too long.

ANTIPHOLUS OF EPHESUS
Good Lord! You use this dalliance to excuse
Your breach of promise to the Porpentine.
I should have chid you for not bringing it,   50
But, like a shrew, you first begin to brawl.

2 MERCHANT [*to Angelo*]
The hour steals on; I pray you, sir, dispatch.

ANGELO [*to Antipholus*]
You hear how he importunes me. – The chain!

ANTIPHOLUS OF EPHESUS
Why, give it to my wife, and fetch your money.

ANGELO
Come, come, you know I gave it you even now.   55
Either send the chain, or send me by some token.

ANTIPHOLUS OF EPHESUS
Fie! Now you run this humour out of breath.
Come, where's the chain? I pray you, let me see it.

2 MERCHANT   My business cannot brook this dalliance.
[*to Antipholus*] Good sir, say whe'er you'll answer me
or no.   60
If not, I'll leave him to the officer.

ANTIPHOLUS OF EPHESUS
I answer you? What should I answer you?

ANGELO   The money that you owe me for the chain.

ANTIPHOLUS OF EPHESUS
I owe you none till I receive the chain.

ANGELO   You know I gave it you half an hour since.   65

ANTIPHOLUS OF EPHESUS
You gave me none. You wrong me much to say so.

ANGELO   You wrong me more, sir, in denying it.
Consider how it stands upon my credit.

2 MERCHANT   Well, officer, arrest him at my suit.

OFFICER [*to Angelo*]   I do,
And charge you in the Duke's name to obey me.   70

ANGELO   This touches me in reputation.
[*to Antipholus*] Either consent to pay this sum for
me,
Or I attach you by this officer.

ANTIPHOLUS OF EPHESUS
  Consent to pay thee that I never had?
75 Arrest me, foolish fellow, if thou dar'st.
ANGELO [*Gives money to Officer.*]
  Here is thy fee: arrest him, officer.
  – I would not spare my brother in this case
  If he should scorn me so apparently.
OFFICER [*to Antipholus*]
  I do arrest you, sir; you hear the suit.
ANTIPHOLUS OF EPHESUS
80 I do obey thee till I give thee bail.
  [*to Angelo*] But, sirrah, you shall buy this sport as dear
  As all the metal in your shop will answer.
ANGELO   Sir, sir, I shall have law in Ephesus,
  To your notorious shame, I doubt it not.

        Enter DROMIO OF SYRACUSE *from the bay.*

DROMIO OF SYRACUSE
85 Master, there's a bark of Epidamium
  That stays but till her owner comes aboard;
  And then, sir, she bears away. Our fraughtage, sir,
  I have conveyed aboard, and I have bought
  The oil, the balsamum and *aqua-vitae.*
90 The ship is in her trim; the merry wind
  Blows fair from land: they stay for naught at all
  But for their owner, master, and yourself.
ANTIPHOLUS OF EPHESUS
  How now? A madman? Why, thou peevish sheep,
  What ship of Epidamium stays for me?
DROMIO OF SYRACUSE
95 A ship you sent me to, to hire waftage.
ANTIPHOLUS OF EPHESUS
  Thou drunken slave, I sent thee for a rope,
  And told thee to what purpose and what end.
DROMIO OF SYRACUSE
  You sent me for a rope's end as soon!
  You sent me to the bay, sir, for a bark.
ANTIPHOLUS OF EPHESUS
100 I will debate this matter at more leisure,
  And teach your ears to list me with more heed.
  To Adriana, villain, hie thee straight:
  [*offering Dromio a key*] Give her this key, and tell her,
    in the desk
  That's covered o'er with Turkish tapestry,
105 There is a purse of ducats: let her send it.
  Tell her I am arrested in the street
  And that shall bail me. Hie thee, slave. Be gone!
  – On, officer, to prison, till it come.
        Exeunt all but Dromio of Syracuse.
DROMIO OF SYRACUSE
  'To Adriana': that is where we dined,
110 Where Dowsabel did claim me for her husband;
  She is too big, I hope, for me to compass.
  Thither I must, although against my will,
  For servants must their masters' minds fulfil.
        Exit with the key.

4.2   *Enter* ADRIANA *and* LUCIANA.

ADRIANA
  Ah, Luciana, did he tempt thee so?
    Mightst thou perceive austerely in his eye
  That he did plead in earnest? Yea or no?
    Looked he or red or pale, or sad or merrily?
  What observation mad'st thou in this case   5
  Of his heart's meteors tilting in his face?
LUCIANA   First he denied you had in him no right.
ADRIANA
  He meant he did me none; the more my spite.
LUCIANA   Then swore he that he was a stranger here.
ADRIANA
  And true he swore, though yet forsworn he were.   10
LUCIANA   Then pleaded I for you.
ADRIANA   And what said he?
LUCIANA   That love I begged for you, he begged of me.
ADRIANA   With what persuasion did he tempt thy love?
LUCIANA
  With words that in an honest suit might move.
  First he did praise my beauty, then my speech.   15
ADRIANA   Didst speak him fair?
LUCIANA   Have patience, I beseech.
ADRIANA
  I cannot, nor I will not, hold me still;
  My tongue, though not my heart, shall have his will.
  He is deformed, crooked, old and sere,
  Ill-faced, worse bodied, shapeless everywhere;   20
  Vicious, ungentle, foolish, blunt, unkind,
  Stigmatical in making, worse in mind.
LUCIANA   Who would be jealous, then, of such a one?
  No evil lost is wailed when it is gone.
ADRIANA
  Ah, but I think him better than I say,   25
    And yet would herein others' eyes were worse.
  Far from her nest the lapwing cries away;
    My heart prays for him, though my tongue do curse.

        Enter DROMIO OF SYRACUSE, *running, with the key.*

DROMIO OF SYRACUSE [*Offers the key.*]
  Here, go – the desk, the purse! Sweet now, make haste!
LUCIANA   How hast thou lost thy breath?
DROMIO OF SYRACUSE   By running fast. 30
ADRIANA   Where is thy master, Dromio? Is he well?
DROMIO OF SYRACUSE
  No, he's in Tartar limbo, worse than hell:
  A devil in an everlasting garment hath him,
  One whose hard heart is buttoned up with steel;
  A fiend, a fairy, pitiless and rough;   35
  A wolf, nay, worse, a fellow all in buff;
  A backfriend, a shoulder-clapper, one that countermands
  The passages of alleys, creeks and narrow lands;
  A hound that runs counter, and yet draws dry-foot well,
  One that before the Judgement carries poor souls to hell. 40
ADRIANA   Why, man, what is the matter?

DROMIO OF SYRACUSE
  I do not know the matter; he is 'rested on the case.
ADRIANA What, is he arrested? Tell me at whose suit?
DROMIO OF SYRACUSE
  I know not at whose suit he is arrested well;
45 But is in a suit of buff which 'rested him, that can I tell.
  Will you send him, mistress, redemption – the money
    in his desk?
ADRIANA
  Go fetch it, sister.   *Exit Luciana with the key.*
                – This I wonder at,
  That he unknown to me should be in debt.
  Tell me, was he arrested on a band?
DROMIO OF SYRACUSE
50 Not on a band, but on a stronger thing:
  A chain, a chain – do you not hear it ring?
ADRIANA What, the chain?
DROMIO OF SYRACUSE   No, no, the bell; 'tis time
    that I were gone:
  It was two ere I left him, and now the clock strikes one.
ADRIANA
  The hours come back! That did I never hear.
DROMIO OF SYRACUSE
  O, yes, if any hour meet a sergeant, 'a turns back for
55   very fear.
ADRIANA
  As if time were in debt? How fondly dost thou reason!
DROMIO OF SYRACUSE
  Time is a very bankrupt, and owes more than he's
    worth to season.
  Nay, he's a thief, too: have you not heard men say
  That Time comes stealing on by night and day?
60 If 'a be in debt and theft, and a sergeant in the way,
  Hath he not reason to turn back an hour in a day?

Enter LUCIANA *with the purse.*

ADRIANA [*Offers the purse.*]
  Go, Dromio, there's the money. Bear it straight
  And bring thy master home immediately.
                Exit Dromio with the purse.
  Come, sister, I am pressed down with conceit:
65 Conceit, my comfort and my injury.   *Exeunt.*

4.3   *Enter* ANTIPHOLUS OF SYRACUSE, *with the chain.*

ANTIPHOLUS OF SYRACUSE
  There's not a man I meet but doth salute me
  As if I were their well-acquainted friend,
  And everyone doth call me by my name.
  Some tender money to me; some invite me;
5 Some other give me thanks for kindnesses;
  Some offer me commodities to buy.
  Even now a tailor called me in his shop,
  And showed me silks that he had bought for me,
  And therewithal took measure of my body.
10 Sure, these are but imaginary wiles,
  And Lapland sorcerers inhabit here.

Enter DROMIO OF SYRACUSE, *with the purse.*

DROMIO OF SYRACUSE Master, [*presenting the purse*]
  here's the gold you sent me for. – What, have you got
  the picture of old Adam new-apparelled?
ANTIPHOLUS OF SYRACUSE
  What gold is this? What Adam dost thou mean?   15
DROMIO OF SYRACUSE Not that Adam that kept the
  paradise, but that Adam that keeps the prison: he that
  goes in the calf's skin that was killed for the Prodigal;
  he that came behind you, sir, like an evil angel, and bid
  you forsake your liberty.   20
ANTIPHOLUS OF SYRACUSE I understand thee not.
DROMIO OF SYRACUSE No? Why, 'tis a plain case:
  he that went like a bass viol in a case of leather; the
  man, sir, that when gentlemen are tired gives them a
  sob and rests them; he, sir, that takes pity on decayed   25
  men and gives them suits of durance; he that sets up
  his rest to do more exploits with his mace than a
  morris-pike.
ANTIPHOLUS OF SYRACUSE What, thou mean'st an
  officer?   30
DROMIO OF SYRACUSE Ay, sir, the sergeant of the
  band: he that brings any man to answer it that breaks
  his band; one that thinks a man always going to bed
  and says, 'God give you good rest'.
ANTIPHOLUS OF SYRACUSE Well, sir, there rest in   35
  your foolery. Is there any ships puts forth tonight?
  May we be gone?
DROMIO OF SYRACUSE Why, sir, I brought you word
  an hour since that the bark *Expedition* put forth
  tonight, and then were you hindered by the sergeant to   40
  tarry for the hoy *Delay*. [*Offers the purse.*] Here are the
  angels that you sent for to deliver you.
ANTIPHOLUS OF SYRACUSE
  The fellow is distract, and so am I,
  And here we wander in illusions –
  Some blessed power deliver us from hence!   45

Enter a Courtesan.

COURTESAN Well met, well met, Master Antipholus.
  I see, sir, you have found the goldsmith now:
  Is that the chain you promised me today?
ANTIPHOLUS OF SYRACUSE
  Satan, avoid! I charge thee, tempt me not!
DROMIO OF SYRACUSE Master, is this Mistress Satan?   50
ANTIPHOLUS OF SYRACUSE It is the devil.
DROMIO OF SYRACUSE Nay, she is worse, she is the
  devil's dam, and here she comes in the habit of a
  light wench, and thereof comes that the wenches say,
  'God damn me' – that's as much to say, 'God make   55
  me a light wench'. It is written they appear to men
  like angels of light; light is an effect of fire, and fire
  will burn: *ergo*, light wenches will burn. Come not near
  her.
COURTESAN
  Your man and you are marvellous merry, sir.   60

Will you go with me? We'll mend our dinner here.

DROMIO OF SYRACUSE   Master, if you do, expect spoon-meat, or bespeak a long spoon.

ANTIPHOLUS OF SYRACUSE   Why, Dromio?

65 DROMIO OF SYRACUSE   Marry, he must have a long spoon that must eat with the devil.

ANTIPHOLUS OF SYRACUSE [*to Courtesan*]
Avoid then, fiend! What tell'st thou me of supping?
Thou art, as you are all, a sorceress;
I conjure thee to leave me and be gone.

COURTESAN

70 Give me the ring of mine you had at dinner,
Or for my diamond the chain you promised,
And I'll be gone, sir, and not trouble you.

DROMIO OF SYRACUSE   Some devils ask but the parings of one's nail, a rush, a hair, a drop of blood, a pin, a
75 nut, a cherry-stone; but she, more covetous, would have a chain. Master, be wise: an if you give it her, the devil will shake her chain and fright us with it.

COURTESAN   I pray you, sir, my ring, or else the chain;
I hope you do not mean to cheat me so.

ANTIPHOLUS OF SYRACUSE

80 Avaunt, thou witch! – Come, Dromio, let us go.

DROMIO OF SYRACUSE
'Fly pride', says the peacock; mistress, that you know.
           Exeunt Antipholus and Dromio of Syracuse.

COURTESAN   Now, out of doubt, Antipholus is mad,
Else would he never so demean himself.
A ring he hath of mine worth forty ducats,
85 And for the same he promised me a chain;
Both one and other he denies me now.
The reason that I gather he is mad,
Besides this present instance of his rage,
Is a mad tale he told today at dinner
90 Of his own doors being shut against his entrance.
Belike his wife, acquainted with his fits,
On purpose shut the doors against his way.
My way is now to hie home to his house
And tell his wife that, being lunatic,
95 He rushed into my house and took perforce
My ring away. This course I fittest choose,
For forty ducats is too much to lose.   *Exit.*

4.4   *Enter* ANTIPHOLUS OF EPHESUS,
        wearing the ring, with a jailer,
           the Officer.

ANTIPHOLUS OF EPHESUS
Fear me not, man, I will not break away;
I'll give thee, ere I leave thee, so much money
To warrant thee as I am 'rested for.
My wife is in a wayward mood today
5 And will not lightly trust the messenger;
That I should be attached in Ephesus,
I tell you 'twill sound harshly in her ears. –

Enter DROMIO OF EPHESUS
with a rope's end.

Here comes my man; I think he brings the money.
[*to Dromio*] How now, sir? Have you that I sent you for?

DROMIO OF EPHESUS [*Offers the rope.*]
Here's that, I warrant you, will pay them all.   10

ANTIPHOLUS OF EPHESUS
But where's the money?

DROMIO OF EPHESUS
Why, sir, I gave the money for the rope.

ANTIPHOLUS OF EPHESUS
Five hundred ducats, villain, for a rope?

DROMIO OF EPHESUS
I'll serve you, sir, five hundred at the rate.

ANTIPHOLUS OF EPHESUS
To what end did I bid thee hie thee home?   15

DROMIO OF EPHESUS
To a rope's end, sir, and to that end am I returned.

ANTIPHOLUS OF EPHESUS
And 'to that end', sir, I will welcome you.
      [*Beats Dromio with the rope's end.*]

OFFICER   Good sir, be patient.

DROMIO OF EPHESUS   Nay, 'tis for me to be patient: I am in adversity!   20

OFFICER   Good now, hold thy tongue.

DROMIO OF EPHESUS   Nay, rather persuade him to hold his hands.

ANTIPHOLUS OF EPHESUS   Thou whoreson, senseless villain! [*Beats him.*]   25

DROMIO OF EPHESUS   I would I were senseless, sir, that I might not feel your blows.

ANTIPHOLUS OF EPHESUS   Thou art sensible in nothing but blows, and so is an ass.

DROMIO OF EPHESUS   I am an ass, indeed: you may prove   30
it by my long ears. – I have served him from the hour of
my nativity to this instant and have nothing at his hands
for my service but blows. When I am cold, he heats me
with beating; when I am warm, he cools me with beating.
I am waked with it when I sleep, raised with it when I sit,   35
driven out of doors with it when I go from home,
welcomed home with it when I return. Nay, I bear it on
my shoulders as a beggar wont her brat, and I think when
he hath lamed me, I shall beg with it from door to door.

Enter ADRIANA, LUCIANA,
Courtesan *and a schoolmaster called*
PINCH.

ANTIPHOLUS OF EPHESUS
Come, go along; my wife is coming yonder.   40

DROMIO OF EPHESUS   Mistress, *respice finem*, 'respect
your end'; or rather, to prophesy like the parrot,
'beware the rope's end'.

ANTIPHOLUS OF EPHESUS   Wilt thou still talk?
     [*Beats Dromio.*]

COURTESAN [*to Adriana*]
  How say you now? Is not your husband mad?

45

ADRIANA   His incivility confirms no less.
  – Good Doctor Pinch, you are a conjuror:
  Establish him in his true sense again,
  And I will please you what you will demand.

LUCIANA   Alas, how fiery and how sharp he looks!

50

COURTESAN   Mark how he trembles in his ecstasy.

PINCH   Give me your hand, and let me feel your pulse.

ANTIPHOLUS OF EPHESUS
  There is my hand, and let it feel your ear.
    [*Offers to strike Pinch.*]

PINCH   I charge thee, Satan, housed within this man,
  To yield possession to my holy prayers,
  And to thy state of darkness hie thee straight;
  I conjure thee by all the saints in heaven.

55

ANTIPHOLUS OF EPHESUS
  Peace, doting wizard, peace; I am not mad.

ADRIANA   O, that thou wert not, poor distressed soul.

ANTIPHOLUS OF EPHESUS
  You minion, you, are these your customers?
  Did this companion with the saffron face
  Revel and feast it at my house today,
  Whilst upon me the guilty doors were shut,
  And I denied to enter in my house?

60

ADRIANA
  O husband, God doth know you dined at home,
  Where would you had remained until this time,
  Free from these slanders and this open shame.

65

ANTIPHOLUS OF EPHESUS
  'Dined at home'? [*to Dromio*] Thou, villain, what sayst
    thou?

DROMIO OF EPHESUS
  Sir, sooth to say, you did not dine at home.

ANTIPHOLUS OF EPHESUS
  Were not my doors locked up, and I shut out?

70

DROMIO OF EPHESUS
  Perdie, your doors were locked, and you shut out.

ANTIPHOLUS OF EPHESUS
  And did not she herself revile me there?

DROMIO OF EPHESUS
  Sans fable, she herself reviled you there.

ANTIPHOLUS OF EPHESUS
  Did not her kitchen-maid rail, taunt and scorn me?

DROMIO OF EPHESUS
  Certes she did; the kitchen vestal scorned you.

75

ANTIPHOLUS OF EPHESUS
  And did not I in rage depart from thence?

DROMIO OF EPHESUS
  In verity, you did; – my bones bears witness,
  That since have felt the vigour of his rage.

ADRIANA [*to Pinch*]
  Is't good to soothe him in these contraries?

80

PINCH   It is no shame: the fellow finds his vein
  And, yielding to him, humours well his frenzy.

ANTIPHOLUS OF EPHESUS [*to Adriana*]
  Thou hast suborned the goldsmith to arrest me.

ADRIANA   Alas, I sent you money to redeem you,
  By Dromio here, who came in haste for it.

DROMIO OF EPHESUS
  Money by me? – Heart and good will you might,
  But surely, master, not a rag of money.

85

ANTIPHOLUS OF EPHESUS
  Went'st not thou to her for a purse of ducats?

ADRIANA   He came to me, and I delivered it.

LUCIANA   And I am witness with her that she did.

DROMIO OF EPHESUS
  God and the rope-maker bear me witness
  That I was sent for nothing but a rope.

90

PINCH   Mistress, both man and master is possessed:
  I know it by their pale and deadly looks.
  They must be bound and laid in some dark room.

ANTIPHOLUS OF EPHESUS
  [*to Adriana*] Say wherefore didst thou lock me forth
    today?
  [*to Dromio*] And why dost thou deny the bag of gold?

95

ADRIANA   I did not, gentle husband, lock thee forth.

DROMIO OF EPHESUS
  And, gentle master, I received no gold,
  But I confess, sir, that we were locked out.

ADRIANA
  Dissembling villain, thou speak'st false in both.

100

ANTIPHOLUS OF EPHESUS
  Dissembling harlot, thou art false in all,
  And art confederate with a damned pack
  To make a loathsome, abject scorn of me;
  But with these nails I'll pluck out those false eyes
  That would behold in me this shameful sport.
    [*Threatens Adriana.*]

105

ADRIANA
  O, bind him, bind him! Let him not come near me!

PINCH   More company!

Enter three or four and offer to bind him. He strives.

                    The fiend is strong within him.

LUCIANA   Ay me, poor man, how pale and wan he looks.

ANTIPHOLUS OF EPHESUS
  What, will you murder me? – Thou, jailer, thou,
  I am thy prisoner: wilt thou suffer them
  To make a rescue?

110

OFFICER   Masters, let him go:
  He is my prisoner, and you shall not have him.

PINCH   Go bind this man, for he is frantic too.
    [*They offer to bind Dromio.*]

ADRIANA [*to Officer*]
  What wilt thou do, thou peevish officer?
  Hast thou delight to see a wretched man
  Do outrage and displeasure to himself?

115

OFFICER   He is my prisoner; if I let him go,
  The debt he owes will be required of me.

ADRIANA   I will discharge thee ere I go from thee;
  Bear me forthwith unto his creditor,
  And, knowing how the debt grows, I will pay it.
  – Good Master Doctor, see him safe conveyed

120

Home to my house. O, most unhappy day!

ANTIPHOLUS OF EPHESUS   O, most unhappy strumpet!

DROMIO OF EPHESUS

125   Master, I am here entered in bond for you.

ANTIPHOLUS OF EPHESUS

Out on thee, villain! Wherefore dost thou mad me?

DROMIO OF EPHESUS   Will you be bound for nothing?

Be mad, good master: cry 'The devil!'

LUCIANA   God help, poor souls! How idly do they talk.

ADRIANA

130   [*to Pinch*] Go bear him hence.

                       Exeunt Pinch and his men with
                       Antipholus and Dromio of Ephesus.

                   – Sister, go you with me.

[*to Officer*] Say now, whose suit is he arrested at?

OFFICER   One Angelo, a goldsmith; do you know him?

ADRIANA   I know the man. What is the sum he owes?

OFFICER   Two hundred ducats.

ADRIANA   Say, how grows it due?

135   OFFICER   Due for a chain your husband had of him.

ADRIANA

He did bespeak a chain for me, but had it not.

COURTESAN   Whenas your husband all in rage today

Came to my house and took away my ring –

The ring I saw upon his finger now –

140   Straight after did I meet him with a chain.

ADRIANA   It may be so, but I did never see it.

– Come, jailer, bring me where the goldsmith is;

I long to know the truth hereof at large.

         Enter ANTIPHOLUS OF SYRACUSE, *wearing*
        the chain, with his rapier drawn, and DROMIO
                   OF SYRACUSE.

LUCIANA   God, for thy mercy! They are loose again.

ADRIANA

145   And come with naked swords! Let's call more help

To have them bound again.

OFFICER   Away, they'll kill us!

            Exeunt all but Antipholus and Dromio of
              Syracuse, as fast as may be, frighted.

ANTIPHOLUS OF SYRACUSE

I see these witches are afraid of swords.

DROMIO OF SYRACUSE

She that would be your wife now ran from you.

ANTIPHOLUS OF SYRACUSE

Come to the Centaur; fetch our stuff from thence:

150   I long that we were safe and sound aboard.

DROMIO OF SYRACUSE   Faith, stay here this night; they

will surely do us no harm. You saw they speak us fair,

give us gold: methinks they are such a gentle nation

that, but for the mountain of mad flesh that claims

155   marriage of me, I could find in my heart to stay here

still and turn witch.

ANTIPHOLUS OF SYRACUSE

I will not stay tonight for all the town;

Therefore, away, to get our stuff aboard.   *Exeunt.*

         Enter the Second Merchant
            and ANGELO *the goldsmith.*

ANGELO   I am sorry, sir, that I have hindered you,

But I protest he had the chain of me,

Though most dishonestly he doth deny it.

2 MERCHANT

How is the man esteemed here in the city?

ANGELO   Of very reverend reputation, sir,   5

Of credit infinite, highly beloved,

Second to none that lives here in the city;

His word might bear my wealth at any time.

    Enter ANTIPHOLUS OF SYRACUSE, *wearing*
    the chain, and DROMIO OF SYRACUSE *again.*

2 MERCHANT   Speak softly; yonder, as I think, he walks.

ANGELO   'Tis so, and that self chain about his neck   10

Which he forswore most monstrously to have.

Good sir, draw near to me; I'll speak to him:

– Signor Antipholus, I wonder much

That you would put me to this shame and trouble,

And not without some scandal to yourself,   15

With circumstance and oaths so to deny

This chain which now you wear so openly.

Beside the charge, the shame, imprisonment,

You have done wrong to this my honest friend,

Who, but for staying on our controversy,   20

Had hoisted sail and put to sea today.

This chain you had of me; can you deny it?

ANTIPHOLUS OF SYRACUSE

I think I had; I never did deny it.

2 MERCHANT

Yes, that you did, sir, and forswore it, too.

ANTIPHOLUS OF SYRACUSE

Who heard me to deny it or forswear it?   25

2 MERCHANT

These ears of mine, thou knowst, did hear thee.

Fie on thee, wretch! 'Tis pity that thou liv'st

To walk where any honest men resort.

ANTIPHOLUS OF SYRACUSE

Thou art a villain to impeach me thus!

I'll prove mine honour and mine honesty   30

Against thee presently, if thou dar'st stand.

2 MERCHANT

I dare, and do defy thee for a villain!   [*They draw.*]

    Enter ADRIANA, LUCIANA, Courtesan
        and others with ropes.

ADRIANA

Hold, hurt him not, for God's sake; he is mad!

Some get within him, take his sword away.

Bind Dromio too, and bear them to my house.   35

DROMIO OF SYRACUSE

Run, master, run; for God's sake, take a house!

This is some priory; in, or we are spoiled!

    Exeunt Antipholus and Dromio of Syracuse to the priory.

Enter Emilia, *the* Lady ABBESS.

ABBESS　Be quiet, people. Wherefore throng you hither?
ADRIANA　To fetch my poor distracted husband hence;
40　　Let us come in, that we may bind him fast
　　And bear him home for his recovery.
ANGELO　I knew he was not in his perfect wits.
2 MERCHANT　I am sorry now that I did draw on him.
ABBESS　How long hath this possession held the man?
45　ADRIANA　This week he hath been heavy, sour, sad,
　　And much different from the man he was;
　　But till this afternoon his passion
　　Ne'er broke into extremity of rage.
ABBESS　Hath he not lost much wealth by wrack of sea?
50　　Buried some dear friend? Hath not else his eye
　　Strayed his affection in unlawful love? –
　　A sin prevailing much in youthful men,
　　Who give their eyes the liberty of gazing.
　　Which of these sorrows is he subject to?
55　ADRIANA　To none of these, except it be the last,
　　Namely, some love that drew him oft from home.
ABBESS　You should for that have reprehended him.
ADRIANA　Why, so I did.
ABBESS　　　　　　Ay, but not rough enough.
ADRIANA　As roughly as my modesty would let me.
ABBESS　Haply, in private.
60　ADRIANA　　　　　　　And in assemblies, too.
ABBESS　Ay, but not enough.
ADRIANA　It was the copy of our conference:
　　In bed he slept not for my urging it;
　　At board he fed not for my urging it;
65　　Alone, it was the subject of my theme;
　　In company I often glanced it;
　　Still did I tell him it was vile and bad.
ABBESS　And thereof came it that the man was mad:
　　The venom clamours of a jealous woman
70　　Poisons more deadly than a mad dog's tooth.
　　It seems his sleeps were hindered by thy railing,
　　And thereof comes it that his head is light.
　　Thou sayst his meat was sauced with thy upbraidings:
　　Unquiet meals make ill digestions;
75　　Thereof the raging fire of fever bred,
　　And what's a fever but a fit of madness?
　　Thou sayst his sports were hindered by thy brawls:
　　Sweet recreation barred, what doth ensue
　　But moody and dull melancholy,
80　　Kinsman to grim and comfortless despair,
　　And at her heels a huge infectious troop
　　Of pale distemperatures and foes to life?
　　In food, in sport and life-preserving rest
　　To be disturbed would mad or man or beast;
85　　The consequence is, then, thy jealous fits
　　Hath scared thy husband from the use of wits.
LUCIANA　She never reprehended him but mildly,
　　When he demeaned himself rough, rude and wildly.
　　[*to Adriana*] Why bear you these rebukes and answer
　　　not?

ADRIANA　She did betray me to my own reproof.　　90
　　– Good people, enter and lay hold on him.
ABBESS　No, not a creature enters in my house.
ADRIANA
　　Then let your servants bring my husband forth.
ABBESS　Neither. He took this place for sanctuary,
　　And it shall privilege him from your hands　　95
　　Till I have brought him to his wits again
　　Or lose my labour in assaying it.
ADRIANA　I will attend my husband, be his nurse,
　　Diet his sickness, for it is my office,
　　And will have no attorney but myself;　　100
　　And therefore let me have him home with me.
ABBESS　Be patient, for I will not let him stir
　　Till I have used the approved means I have,
　　With wholesome syrups, drugs and holy prayers,
　　To make of him a formal man again.　　105
　　It is a branch and parcel of mine oath,
　　A charitable duty of my order;
　　Therefore depart, and leave him here with me.
ADRIANA　I will not hence and leave my husband here;
　　And ill it doth beseem your holiness　　110
　　To separate the husband and the wife.
ABBESS
　　Be quiet and depart: thou shalt not have him.　*Exit.*
LUCIANA　[*to Adriana*]
　　Complain unto the Duke of this indignity.
ADRIANA　Come, go; I will fall prostrate at his feet,
　　And never rise until my tears and prayers　　115
　　Have won his grace to come in person hither
　　And take perforce my husband from the Abbess.
2 MERCHANT　By this, I think, the dial points at five;
　　Anon, I'm sure, the Duke himself in person
　　Comes this way to the melancholy vale,　　120
　　The place of death and sorry execution,
　　Behind the ditches of the abbey here.
ANGELO　Upon what cause?
2 MERCHANT　To see a reverend Syracusan merchant,
　　Who put unluckily into this bay　　125
　　Against the laws and statutes of this town,
　　Beheaded publicly for his offence.

Enter Solinus, *the* DUKE *of Ephesus, and*
EGEON, *the Merchant of Syracuse, bareheaded*
and bound, with the Headsman and other Officers.

ANGELO
　　See where they come; we will behold his death.
LUCIANA　Kneel to the Duke before he pass the abbey.
DUKE　Yet once again proclaim it publicly,　　130
　　If any friend will pay the sum for him,
　　He shall not die, so much we tender him.
ADRIANA　[*kneeling*]
　　Justice, most sacred Duke, against the Abbess!
DUKE　She is a virtuous and a reverend lady;
　　It cannot be that she hath done thee wrong.　　135
ADRIANA
　　May it please your grace, Antipholus, my husband,

Who I made lord of me and all I had
At your important letters – this ill day,
A most outrageous fit of madness took him,

140 That desp'rately he hurried through the street,
With him his bondman, all as mad as he,
Doing displeasure to the citizens
By rushing in their houses, bearing thence
Rings, jewels, anything his rage did like.

145 Once did I get him bound and sent him home,
Whilst to take order for the wrongs I went,
That here and there his fury had committed.
Anon, I wot not by what strong escape,
He broke from those that had the guard of him,

150 And with his mad attendant and himself,
Each one with ireful passion, with drawn swords,
Met us again and, madly bent on us,
Chased us away; till, raising of more aid,
We came again to bind them. Then they fled

155 Into this abbey, whither we pursued them,
And here the Abbess shuts the gates on us,
And will not suffer us to fetch him out,
Nor send him forth, that we may bear him hence.
Therefore, most gracious Duke, with thy
        command,
Let him be brought forth and borne hence for

160 help.

DUKE [*Raises Adriana.*]
Long since, thy husband served me in my wars,
And I to thee engaged a prince's word,
When thou didst make him master of thy bed,
To do him all the grace and good I could.

165 – Go, some of you, knock at the abbey gate
And bid the Lady Abbess come to me;
I will determine this before I stir.

Enter a Messenger.

MESSENGER
O, mistress, mistress, shift and save yourself!
My master and his man are both broke loose,

170 Beaten the maids a-row and bound the doctor,
Whose beard they have singed off with brands of fire,
And ever as it blazed, they threw on him
Great pails of puddled mire to quench the hair.
My master preaches patience to him, and the while

175 His man with scissors nicks him like a fool;
And sure, unless you send some present help,
Between them they will kill the conjuror.

ADRIANA   Peace, fool; thy master and his man are here,
And that is false thou dost report to us.

180 MESSENGER   Mistress, upon my life, I tell you true;
I have not breathed almost since I did see it.
He cries for you and vows, if he can take you,
To scorch your face and to disfigure you.   [*Cry within*]
Hark, hark! I hear him, mistress; fly, be gone!

DUKE
Come, stand by me. Fear nothing. – Guard with
185   halberds!

Enter ANTIPHOLUS OF EPHESUS, *wearing the ring,
and* DROMIO OF EPHESUS.

ADRIANA   Ay me, it is my husband! Witness you
That he is borne about invisible:
Even now we housed him in the abbey here,
And now he's there, past thought of human reason.

ANTIPHOLUS OF EPHESUS
Justice, most gracious Duke! O, grant me justice,   190
Even for the service that long since I did thee,
When I bestrid thee in the wars and took
Deep scars to save thy life; even for the blood
That then I lost for thee, now grant me justice!

EGEON [*aside*]
Unless the fear of death doth make me dote,   195
I see my son Antipholus and Dromio.

ANTIPHOLUS OF EPHESUS
Justice, sweet prince, against that woman there:
She whom thou gav'st to me to be my wife,
That hath abused and dishonoured me,
Even in the strength and height of injury;   200
Beyond imagination is the wrong
That she this day hath shameless thrown on me.

DUKE   Discover how, and thou shalt find me just.

ANTIPHOLUS OF EPHESUS
This day, great Duke, she shut the doors upon me
While she with harlots feasted in my house.   205

DUKE   A grievous fault. – Say, woman, didst thou so?

ADRIANA   No, my good lord. Myself, he and my sister
Today did dine together; so befall my soul
As this is false he burdens me withal.

LUCIANA   Ne'er may I look on day nor sleep on night   210
But she tells to your highness simple truth.

ANGELO   O perjured woman! They are both forsworn:
In this the madman justly chargeth them.

ANTIPHOLUS OF EPHESUS
My liege, I am advised what I say,
Neither disturbed with the effect of wine,   215
Nor heady-rash, provoked with raging ire,
Albeit my wrongs might make one wiser mad.
This woman locked me out this day from dinner;
That goldsmith there, were he not packed with her,
Could witness it, for he was with me then,   220
Who parted with me to go fetch a chain,
Promising to bring it to the Porpentine,
Where Balthazar and I did dine together.
Our dinner done, and he not coming thither,
I went to seek him. In the street I met him,   225
And in his company that gentleman.
[*Indicates Second Merchant.*]
There did this perjured goldsmith swear me down
That I this day of him received the chain,
Which, God he knows, I saw not. For the which
He did arrest me with an officer.   230
I did obey, and sent my peasant home
For certain ducats; he with none returned.
Then fairly I bespoke the officer

To go in person with me to my house.
235 By th' way, we met
My wife, her sister and a rabble more
Of vile confederates; along with them
They brought one Pinch, a hungry, lean-faced villain,
A mere anatomy, a mountebank,
240 A threadbare juggler and a fortune-teller,
A needy, hollow-eyed, sharp-looking wretch,
A living dead man. This pernicious slave,
Forsooth, took on him as a conjuror,
And gazing in mine eyes, feeling my pulse
245 And with no-face, as 'twere, out-facing me,
Cries out, I was 'possessed'. Then all together
They fell upon me, bound me, bore me thence,
And in a dark and dankish vault at home
There left me and my man, both bound together,
250 Till, gnawing with my teeth my bonds in sunder,
I gained my freedom, and immediately
Ran hither to your grace, whom I beseech
To give me ample satisfaction
For these deep shames and great indignities.
ANGELO
255 My lord, in truth, thus far I witness with him:
That he dined not at home, but was locked out.
DUKE   But had he such a chain of thee, or no?
ANGELO   He had, my lord, and when he ran in here
These people saw the chain about his neck.
2 MERCHANT [*to Antipholus*]
260 Besides, I will be sworn these ears of mine
Heard you confess you had the chain of him,
After you first forswore it on the mart,
And thereupon I drew my sword on you;
And then you fled into this abbey here,
265 From whence, I think, you are come by miracle.
ANTIPHOLUS OF EPHESUS
[*to Second Merchant*] I never came within these abbey
walls,
Nor ever didst thou draw thy sword on me;
[*to Angelo*] I never saw the chain, so help me heaven,
[*to Adriana*] And this is false you burden me withal.
270 DUKE   Why, what an intricate impeach is this!
I think you all have drunk of Circe's cup:
[*to Second Merchant*] If here you housed him, here he
would have been;
[*to Adriana*] If he were mad, he would not plead so
coldly;
[*to Luciana*] You say he dined at home; the goldsmith
here
275 Denies that saying. [*to Dromio*] Sirrah, what say you?
DROMIO OF EPHESUS [*Points to the Courtesan.*]
Sir, he dined with her there, at the Porpentine.
COURTESAN
He did, and from my finger snatched that ring.
ANTIPHOLUS OF EPHESUS
'Tis true, my liege, this ring I had of her.
DUKE [*to Courtesan*]
Saw'st thou him enter at the abbey here?

COURTESAN   As sure, my liege, as I do see your grace.   280
DUKE   Why, this is strange: – Go call the Abbess hither.
– I think you are all mated, or stark mad.
                              Exit one to the Abbess.
EGEON   Most mighty Duke, vouchsafe me speak a word;
Haply I see a friend will save my life
And pay the sum that may deliver me.   285
DUKE   Speak freely, Syracusan, what thou wilt.
EGEON [*to Antipholus*]
Is not your name, sir, called Antipholus?
And is not that your bondman Dromio?
DROMIO OF EPHESUS
Within this hour I was his bondman, sir,
But he, I thank him, gnawed in two my cords: 290
Now am I Dromio, and his man, unbound.
EGEON   I am sure you both of you remember me.
DROMIO OF EPHESUS
Ourselves we do remember, sir, by you,
For lately we were bound as you are now.
You are not Pinch's patient, are you, sir?   295
EGEON [*to Antipholus*]
Why look you strange on me? You know me well.
ANTIPHOLUS OF EPHESUS
I never saw you in my life till now.
EGEON
O, grief hath changed me since you saw me last,
And careful hours with Time's deformed hand
Have written strange defeatures in my face.   300
But tell me yet, dost thou not know my voice?
ANTIPHOLUS OF EPHESUS   Neither.
EGEON   Dromio, nor thou?
DROMIO OF EPHESUS   No, trust me, sir, nor I.
EGEON   I am sure thou dost!
DROMIO OF EPHESUS   Ay, sir, but I am sure I do not,
and whatsoever a man denies, you are now bound to   305
believe him.
EGEON   Not know my voice! – O Time's extremity,
Hast thou so cracked and splitted my poor tongue
In seven short years that here my only son
Knows not my feeble key of untuned cares?   310
Though now this grained face of mine be hid
In sap-consuming winter's drizzled snow,
And all the conduits of my blood froze up,
Yet hath my night of life some memory,
My wasting lamps some fading glimmer left,   315
My dull deaf ears a little use to hear;
All these old witnesses – I cannot err –
Tell me thou art my son Antipholus.
ANTIPHOLUS OF EPHESUS
I never saw my father in my life.
EGEON   But seven years since, in Syracusa, boy,   320
Thou knowst we parted. But perhaps, my son,
Thou sham'st to acknowledge me in misery.
ANTIPHOLUS OF EPHESUS
The Duke and all that know me in the city
Can witness with me that it is not so.
I ne'er saw Syracusa in my life.   325

DUKE   I tell thee, Syracusan, twenty years
Have I been patron to Antipholus,
During which time he ne'er saw Syracusa.
I see thy age and dangers make thee dote.

Enter Emilia, *the* ABBESS, *with* ANTIPHOLUS
OF SYRACUSE, *wearing the chain, and* DROMIO
OF SYRACUSE.

ABBESS
330   Most mighty Duke, behold a man much wronged.
[*All gather to see them.*]
ADRIANA   I see two husbands, or mine eyes deceive me.
DUKE   One of these men is genius to the other;
And so of these, which is the natural man
And which the spirit? Who deciphers them?
DROMIO OF SYRACUSE
335   I, sir, am Dromio; command him away.
DROMIO OF EPHESUS
I, sir, am Dromio; pray, let me stay.
ANTIPHOLUS OF SYRACUSE
Egeon, art thou not? Or else his ghost.
DROMIO OF SYRACUSE
O my old master! – Who hath bound him here?
ABBESS   Whoever bound him, I will loose his bonds,
340   And gain a husband by his liberty.
[*Unbinds him.*]
– Speak, old Egeon, if thou be'st the man
That hadst a wife once called Emilia
That bore thee at a burden two fair sons.
O, if thou be'st the same Egeon, speak,
345   And speak unto the same Emilia.
DUKE   Why, here begins his morning story right:
These two Antipholus', these two so like,
And these two Dromios, one in semblance –
Besides his urging of her wrack at sea –
350   These are the parents to these children,
Which accidentally are met together.
EGEON   If I dream not, thou art Emilia;
If thou art she, tell me, where is that son
That floated with thee on the fatal raft?
355   ABBESS   By men of Epidamium he and I
And the twin Dromio all were taken up;
But, by and by, rude fishermen of Corinth
By force took Dromio and my son from them,
And me they left with those of Epidamium.
360   What then became of them I cannot tell;
I, to this fortune that you see me in.
DUKE [*to Antipholus of Syracuse*]
Antipholus, thou cam'st from Corinth first.
ANTIPHOLUS OF SYRACUSE
No, sir, not I; I came from Syracuse.
DUKE   Stay, stand apart; I know not which is which.
ANTIPHOLUS OF EPHESUS
365   I came from Corinth, my most gracious lord –
DROMIO OF EPHESUS   And I with him.
ANTIPHOLUS OF EPHESUS
– Brought to this town by that most famous warrior,

Duke Menaphon, your most renowned uncle.
ADRIANA   Which of you two did dine with me today?
ANTIPHOLUS OF SYRACUSE
I, gentle mistress.
ADRIANA   And are not you my husband?   370
ANTIPHOLUS OF EPHESUS   No, I say nay to that.
ANTIPHOLUS OF SYRACUSE
And so do I, yet did she call me so;
And this fair gentlewoman, her sister here,
Did call me brother. [*to Luciana*] What I told you then
I hope I shall have leisure to make good,   375
If this be not a dream I see and hear.
ANGELO   That is the chain, sir, which you had of me.
ANTIPHOLUS OF SYRACUSE
I think it be, sir; I deny it not.
ANTIPHOLUS OF EPHESUS [*to Angelo*]
And you, sir, for this chain arrested me.
ANGELO   I think I did, sir; I deny it not.   380
ADRIANA [*to Antipholus of Ephesus*]
I sent you money, sir, to be your bail,
By Dromio, but I think he brought it not.
DROMIO OF EPHESUS   No, none by me.
ANTIPHOLUS OF SYRACUSE [*Shows the purse to Adriana.*]
This purse of ducats I received from you,
And Dromio my man did bring them me.   385
– I see we still did meet each other's man,
And I was ta'en for him, and he for me,
And thereupon these errors are arose.
ANTIPHOLUS OF EPHESUS [*to the Duke*]
These ducats pawn I for my father here.
DUKE   It shall not need: thy father hath his life.   390
COURTESAN [*to Antipholus of Ephesus*]
Sir, I must have that diamond from you.
ANTIPHOLUS OF EPHESUS [*Gives the ring.*]
There, take it, and much thanks for my good
cheer.
ABBESS   Renowned Duke, vouchsafe to take the pains
To go with us into the abbey here
And hear at large discoursed all our fortunes;   395
– And all that are assembled in this place,
That by this sympathized one-day's error
Have suffered wrong, go, keep us company,
And we shall make full satisfaction.
– Thirty-three years have I but gone in travail   400
Of you, my sons, and till this present hour
My heavy burden ne'er delivered.
– The Duke, my husband and my children both,
And you, the calendars of their nativity,
Go to a gossips' feast, and go with me;   405
After so long grief, such nativity!
DUKE   With all my heart I'll gossip at this feast.
*Exeunt omnes, except the two Dromios
and two Antipholus brothers.*
DROMIO OF SYRACUSE [*to Antipholus of Ephesus*]
Master, shall I fetch your stuff from shipboard?
ANTIPHOLUS OF EPHESUS
Dromio, what stuff of mine hast thou embarked?

DROMIO OF SYRACUSE

410   Your goods that lay at host, sir, in the Centaur.

ANTIPHOLUS OF SYRACUSE [*to Antipholus of Ephesus*]

    He speaks to me; – I am your master, Dromio.

    Come, go with us; we'll look to that anon.

    Embrace thy brother there; rejoice with him.

                Exeunt the Antipholus brothers.

DROMIO OF SYRACUSE

    There is a fat friend at your master's house,

415   That kitchened me for you today at dinner;

    She now shall be my sister, not my wife.

DROMIO OF EPHESUS

    Methinks you are my glass and not my brother:

    I see by you I am a sweet-faced youth.

    Will you walk in to see their gossiping?

DROMIO OF SYRACUSE   Not I, sir; you are my elder.   420

DROMIO OF EPHESUS   That's a question; how shall we

    try it?

DROMIO OF SYRACUSE   We'll draw cuts for the senior;

    till then, lead thou first.

DROMIO OF EPHESUS

    Nay then, thus: [*embracing him*] we came into the   425

        world like brother and brother;

    And now let's go hand in hand, not one before another.

                        Exeunt.

Coriolanus

Coriolanus was first published in the Folio of 1623 as the first of the tragedies. On stylistic grounds it is usually dated about 1608, and possible topical references seem to confirm that date. The citizens' anger over the shortage of corn may well refer to the corn riots of 1607 in the Midlands (which would have lent immediacy to the 'sedition at Rome' described by Plutarch as partly motivated 'by reason of famine'), and 'the coal of fire upon the ice' may allude to the great frost in the winter of 1607–8 when the Thames froze and, according to a contemporary pamphlet, entrepreneurial Londoners were 'ready with pans of coals to warm your fingers'.

The main source of the play is Plutarch's 'Life of Caius Martius Coriolanus' in his *Lives of the Noble Grecians and Romans* which Shakespeare read in the English translation by Thomas North (1579). Plutarch's 'Life' is a straightforward biography, beginning with Caius Martius' ancestry and ending with his death. Shakespeare found in Plutarch all the necessary details for his play, but he imposed, as always, a different shape and emphasis to suit his dramatic vision, and amplified the roles of Menenius, Aufidius and Volumnia to bear greater significance. By contrast with the astonishing variety and amplitude of its immediate predecessor, *Antony and Cleopatra*, also based on Plutarch, *Coriolanus* is sober and austere, its main character no 'mine of bounty' like Antony but arrogant and rigid, even in his virtue 'too noble for the world'.

Shakespeare exploits the conflict between Coriolanus and the people of Rome, but not as a simple opposition of the noble individual and the 'multiplying swarm'. Coriolanus is, indeed, a man of integrity, but if he is too honest to fawn before the populace for its support, he is also proud and contemptuous, caring little for Rome's citizens, 'the mutable, rank-scented meinie' (3.1.68), and finally willing to sacrifice the city itself to satisfy his honour. Conversely, the people, who rightly resent his aristocratic disdain and precociously declare that 'the people are the city', are themselves fickle and easily manipulated by the tribunes. Perhaps, as S.T. Coleridge suggested, the play 'illustrates the wonderful philosophic impartiality in Shakespeare's politics'; certainly its political sympathies are multiple and complex.

While *Coriolanus* marks a further stage in Shakespeare's exploration of Rome and *romanitas*, it focuses on an earlier moment in Roman history than either *Antony and Cleopatra* or its predecessor, *Julius Caesar*. Between them *Coriolanus* and *Julius Caesar* virtually define the historical limits of the Roman Republic. Caius Martius' victory at Corioli, from which he earned his surname, was won in 439 BCE, almost 400 years before the murder of Julius Caesar in the Forum (44 BCE), one of the events which led to the foundation of the Roman Empire under Augustus (Shakespeare's Octavius Caesar).

The early republic portrayed in *Coriolanus* would, however, certainly have been of interest to many in Shakespeare's audiences, who would have found in the struggle between an elected government, dependent for its authority upon the will of the people, and a polity still overseen by traditional aristocratic privilege, a powerful image of political strains just beginning to be articulated in the political discourses of Jacobean England.

But the play is also the play of a tragic individual, noble but flawed, his strengths and weaknesses inextricably entangled. Not only are his virtues more fit for war than for peace; his nobility too easily degenerates into an isolating pride and a withering contempt for others: 'You speak o'th' people as if you were a god / To punish, not a man of their infirmity' (3.1.83–4). But he is indeed a man of their infirmity, whose very drive to excel is born of a human need and vulnerability he fears to acknowledge. His self-chosen isolation, his wish that he could be, however improbably, 'author of himself' (5.3.36), is revealed to be a terrible compensation for the world of relatedness he would, but at last cannot, deny. In his last Roman play Shakespeare joins the personal and the political in a bleak vision of both the city and its greatest hero tragically self-divided.

The role of Coriolanus has been memorably played by leading actors from John Philip Kemble to Laurence Olivier, but in performance the part of his mother, Volumnia, whose victory over her son is the play's major climax, is of almost equal significance. The play's complex embodiment of its political debates has led to its propagandist use in support of all political positions from monarchist to communist: performances of it have been known to provoke civil unrest and even riots.

The Arden text is based on the 1623 First Folio.

ROMANS

Caius MARTIUS	*later* Caius Martius CORIOLANUS
VOLUMNIA	*his mother*
VIRGILIA	*his wife*
YOUNG MARTIUS	*his son*
COMINIUS	*consul and general*
MENENIUS Agrippa	
Titus LARTIUS	
SICINIUS Velutus	*tribune of the people*
Junius BRUTUS	*tribune of the people*
VALERIA	
NICANOR	

Roman PATRICIANS, *including* SENATORS, NOBLES, Gentry, young Nobility
Roman CITIZENS, *including* GENTLEWOMAN, Plebeians, Attendants, Usher
Roman officials, including MESSENGERS, Two OFFICERS of the Capitol, AEDILES, HERALD, Lictors
ROMAN *army, including* LIEUTENANT, SOLDIERS, Captains, Drummer, Trumpeter, Colour-bearer, Scout

VOLSCIANS

Tullus AUFIDIUS	*general*
ADRIAN	

VOLSCIAN *army, including* LIEUTENANT, WATCHMEN, SOLDIERS,
Attendants, Drummers, Colour-bearers
SENATORS of Corioles
LORDS
Three SERVINGMEN, *including* COTUS
CONSPIRATORS
CITIZENS, *including* Commoners

1.1   *Enter a company of mutinous* Citizens
with staves, clubs and other weapons.

1 CITIZEN   Before we proceed any further, hear me
speak.

ALL   Speak, speak.

1 CITIZEN   You are all resolved rather to die than to
5   famish?

ALL   Resolved, resolved.

1 CITIZEN   First, you know Caius Martius is chief
enemy to the people.

ALL   We know't, we know't.

10   1 CITIZEN   Let us kill him, and we'll have corn at our
own price. Is't a verdict?

ALL   No more talking on't. Let it be done. Away, away.

2 CITIZEN   One word, good citizens.

1 CITIZEN   We are accounted poor citizens, the
15   patricians good. What authority surfeits on would
relieve us. If they would yield us but the superfluity
while it were wholesome, we might guess they relieved
us humanely. But they think we are too dear. The
leanness that afflicts us, the object of our misery, is as
20   an inventory to particularize their abundance; our
sufferance is a gain to them. Let us revenge this with
our pikes ere we become rakes; for the gods know, I
speak this in hunger for bread, not in thirst for revenge.

2 CITIZEN   Would you proceed especially against Caius
25   Martius?

ALL   Against him first. He's a very dog to the
commonalty.

2 CITIZEN   Consider you what services he has done for
his country?

30   1 CITIZEN   Very well, and could be content to give him
good report for't, but that he pays himself with being
proud.

ALL   Nay, but speak not maliciously.

1 CITIZEN   I say unto you, what he hath done famously,
35   he did it to that end. Though soft-conscienced men
can be content to say it was for his country, he did it to
please his mother, and to be partly proud – which he is,
even to the altitude of his virtue.

2 CITIZEN   What he cannot help in his nature, you
40   account a vice in him. You must in no way say he is
covetous.

1 CITIZEN   If I must not, I need not be barren of
accusations. He hath faults, with surplus, to tire in
repetition. [*Shouts within*] What shouts are these? The
45   other side o'th' city is risen. Why stay we prating here?
To th' Capitol.

ALL   Come, come.

1 CITIZEN   Soft, who comes here?

Enter MENENIUS *Agrippa.*

2 CITIZEN   Worthy Menenius Agrippa, one that hath
50   always loved the people.

1 CITIZEN   He's one honest enough. Would all the rest
were so!

MENENIUS

What work's, my countrymen, in hand? Where go you
With bats and clubs? The matter? Speak, I pray you.

2 CITIZEN   Our business is not unknown to th' Senate;   55
they have had inkling this fortnight what we intend to
do, which now we'll show 'em in deeds. They say poor
suitors have strong breaths; they shall know we have
strong arms too.

MENENIUS

Why, masters, my good friends, mine honest
    neighbours,   60
Will you undo yourselves?

2 CITIZEN   We cannot, sir; we are undone already.

MENENIUS   I tell you, friends, most charitable care
Have the patricians of you. For your wants,
Your suffering in this dearth, you may as well   65
Strike at the heaven with your staves, as lift them
Against the Roman state, whose course will on
The way it takes, cracking ten thousand curbs
Of more strong link asunder than can ever
Appear in your impediment. For the dearth,   70
The gods, not the patricians, make it, and
Your knees to them, not arms, must help. Alack,
You are transported by calamity
Thither where more attends you, and you slander
The helms o'th' state, who care for you like fathers,   75
When you curse them as enemies.

2 CITIZEN   Care for us? True, indeed, they ne'er cared
for us yet. Suffer us to famish, and their store-houses
crammed with grain; make edicts for usury, to support
usurers; repeal daily any wholesome act established   80
against the rich, and provide more piercing statutes
daily to chain up and restrain the poor. If the wars eat
us not up, they will; and there's all the love they bear us.

MENENIUS   Either you must
Confess yourselves wondrous malicious   85
Or be accused of folly. I shall tell you
A pretty tale. It may be you have heard it,
But since it serves my purpose, I will venture
To stale't a little more.

2 CITIZEN   Well, I'll hear it, sir. Yet you must not think   90
to fob off our disgrace with a tale. But an't please you,
deliver.

MENENIUS

There was a time, when all the body's members
Rebelled against the belly, thus accused it:
That only like a gulf it did remain   95
I'th' midst o'th' body, idle and unactive,
Still cupboarding the viand, never bearing
Like labour with the rest, where th'other instruments
Did see and hear, devise, instruct, walk, feel
And, mutually participate, did minister   100
Unto the appetite and affection common
Of the whole body. The belly answered –

2 CITIZEN   Well, sir, what answer made the belly?

MENENIUS   Sir, I shall tell you. With a kind of smile,
Which ne'er came from the lungs, but even thus –   105

For, look you, I may make the belly smile
As well as speak – it tauntingly replied
To th' discontented members, the mutinous parts
That envied his receipt; even so most fitly,
110 As you malign our senators, for that
They are not such as you.

2 CITIZEN   Your belly's answer – what?
The kingly crowned head, the vigilant eye,
The counsellor heart, the arm our soldier,
Our steed the leg, the tongue our trumpeter,
115 With other muniments and petty helps
In this our fabric, if that they –

MENENIUS   What then?
Fore me, this fellow speaks! What then? What then?

2 CITIZEN
Should by the cormorant belly be restrained,
Who is the sink o'th' body.

MENENIUS   Well, what then?

120 2 CITIZEN   The former agents, if they did complain,
What could the belly answer?

MENENIUS   I will tell you,
If you'll bestow a small (of what you have little)
Patience awhile, you'st hear the belly's answer.

2 CITIZEN   You're long about it.

MENENIUS   Note me this, good friend;
125 Your most grave belly was deliberate,
Not rash like his accusers, and thus answered:
'True is it, my incorporate friends,' quoth he,
'That I receive the general food at first
Which you do live upon, and fit it is,
130 Because I am the store-house and the shop
Of the whole body. But, if you do remember,
I send it through the rivers of your blood
Even to the court, the heart, to th' seat o'th' brain,
And, through the cranks and offices of man,
135 The strongest nerves and small inferior veins
From me receive that natural competency
Whereby they live. And though that all at once' –
You, my good friends, this says the belly, mark me –

2 CITIZEN   Ay, sir, well, well.

MENENIUS   'Though all at once cannot
140 See what I do deliver out to each,
Yet I can make my audit up that all
From me do back receive the flour of all
And leave me but the bran.' What say you to't?

2 CITIZEN   It was an answer. How apply you this?

145 MENENIUS   The senators of Rome are this good belly,
And you the mutinous members. For examine
Their counsels and their cares, digest things rightly,
Touching the weal o'th' common, you shall find
No public benefit which you receive
150 But it proceeds or comes from them to you,
And no way from yourselves. What do you think?
You, the great toe of this assembly?

2 CITIZEN   I the great toe? Why the great toe?

MENENIUS
For that, being one o'th' lowest, basest, poorest

Of this most wise rebellion, thou goest foremost.   155
Thou rascal, that art worst in blood to run,
Lead'st first to win some vantage.
But make you ready your stiff bats and clubs:
Rome and her rats are at the point of battle;
The one side must have bale.

Enter Caius MARTIUS.

          Hail, noble Martius!   160

MARTIUS
Thanks. What's the matter, you dissentious rogues,
That, rubbing the poor itch of your opinion,
Make yourselves scabs?

2 CITIZEN   We have ever your good word.

MARTIUS
He that will give good words to thee will flatter
Beneath abhorring. What would you have, you curs,   165
That like nor peace nor war? The one affrights you,
The other makes you proud. He that trusts to you,
Where he should find you lions finds you hares,
Where foxes, geese you are – no surer, no,
Than is the coal of fire upon the ice,   170
Or hailstone in the sun. Your virtue is
To make him worthy whose offence subdues him
And curse that justice did it. Who deserves greatness
Deserves your hate, and your affections are
A sick man's appetite, who desires most that   175
Which would increase his evil. He that depends
Upon your favours swims with fins of lead
And hews down oaks with rushes. Hang ye! Trust ye?
With every minute you do change a mind,
And call him noble that was now your hate,   180
Him vile that was your garland. What's the matter,
That in these several places of the city
You cry against the noble senate, who,
Under the gods, keep you in awe, which else
Would feed on one another? [*to Menenius*] What's
     their seeking?   185

MENENIUS
For corn at their own rates, whereof they say
The city is well stored.

MARTIUS   Hang 'em! They say?
They'll sit by th' fire and presume to know
What's done i'th' Capitol: who's like to rise,
Who thrives and who declines; side factions, and give
     out   190
Conjectural marriages, making parties strong
And feebling such as stand not in their liking
Below their cobbled shoes. They say there's grain
     enough?
Would the nobility lay aside their ruth
And let me use my sword, I'd make a quarry   195
With thousands of these quartered slaves as high
As I could pitch my lance.

MENENIUS
Nay, these are almost thoroughly persuaded,
For, though abundantly they lack discretion,

200 Yet are they passing cowardly. But I beseech you,
What says the other troop?

MARTIUS   They are dissolved. Hang 'em!
They said they were an-hungry, sighed forth proverbs –
That hunger broke stone walls, that dogs must eat,
That meat was made for mouths, that the gods
        sent not
205 Corn for the rich men only. With these shreds
They vented their complainings, which being
        answered
And a petition granted them – a strange one,
To break the heart of generosity
And make bold power look pale – they threw their caps
210 As they would hang them on the horns o'th' moon,
Shouting their emulation.

MENENIUS   What is granted them?

MARTIUS
Five tribunes to defend their vulgar wisdoms,
Of their own choice. One's Junius Brutus,
Sicinius Velutus, and I know not. 'Sdeath,
215 The rabble should have first unroofed the city
Ere so prevailed with me! It will in time
Win upon power and throw forth greater themes
For insurrection's arguing.

MENENIUS   This is strange.

MARTIUS [*to the Citizens*]
Go get you home, you fragments.

Enter a Messenger *hastily.*

MESSENGER   Where's Caius Martius?
220 MARTIUS   Here. What's the matter?

MESSENGER   The news is, sir, the Volsces are in arms.

MARTIUS
I am glad on't. Then we shall ha' means to vent
Our musty superfluity. See, our best elders.

Enter SICINIUS Velutus, Junius BRUTUS,
COMINIUS, Titus LARTIUS, *with other* Senators.

1 SENATOR
Martius, 'tis true that you have lately told us,
The Volsces are in arms.
225 MARTIUS   They have a leader,
Tullus Aufidius, that will put you to't.
I sin in envying his nobility,
And were I any thing but what I am,
I would wish me only he.

COMINIUS   You have fought together!
230 MARTIUS   Were half to half the world by th'ears and he
Upon my party, I'd revolt to make
Only my wars with him. He is a lion
That I am proud to hunt.

1 SENATOR   Then, worthy Martius,
Attend upon Cominius to these wars.

COMINIUS   It is your former promise.
235 MARTIUS   Sir, it is,
And I am constant. Titus Lartius, thou
Shalt see me once more strike at Tullus' face.

What, art thou stiff? Stand'st out?

LARTIUS   No, Caius Martius,
I'll lean upon one crutch and fight with t'other
Ere stay behind this business.

MENENIUS   O, true-bred!   240

1 SENATOR   Your company to th' Capitol, where I know
Our greatest friends attend us.

LARTIUS [*to Cominius*]   Lead you on.
[*to Martius*] Follow Cominius. We must follow you,
Right worthy you priority.

COMINIUS   Noble Martius.

1 SENATOR [*to the Citizens*]
Hence to your homes, be gone.

MARTIUS   Nay, let them follow.   245
The Volsces have much corn. Take these rats thither
To gnaw their garners. [*to the Citizens*] Worshipful
        mutineers,
Your valour puts well forth. Pray follow.

Exeunt Martius, Patricians and Messenger.
Citizens steal away. Sicinius and Brutus remain.

SICINIUS   Was ever man so proud as is this Martius?

BRUTUS   He has no equal.   250

SICINIUS
When we were chosen tribunes for the people –

BRUTUS   Marked you his lip and eyes?

SICINIUS   Nay, but his taunts.

BRUTUS
Being moved, he will not spare to gird the gods.

SICINIUS   Bemock the modest moon.

BRUTUS   The present wars devour him! He is grown   255
Too proud to be so valiant.

SICINIUS   Such a nature,
Tickled with good success, disdains the shadow
Which he treads on at noon. But I do wonder
His insolence can brook to be commanded
Under Cominius.

BRUTUS   Fame, at the which he aims,   260
In whom already he's well graced, cannot
Better be held nor more attained than by
A place below the first; for what miscarries
Shall be the general's fault, though he perform
To th'utmost of a man, and giddy censure   265
Will then cry out of Martius, 'O, if he
Had borne the business!'

SICINIUS   Besides, if things go well,
Opinion that so sticks on Martius shall
Of his demerits rob Cominius.

BRUTUS   Come,
Half all Cominius' honours are to Martius,   270
Though Martius earned them not; and all his faults
To Martius shall be honours, though indeed
In aught he merit not.

SICINIUS   Let's hence and hear
How the dispatch is made, and in what fashion,
More than his singularity, he goes   275
Upon this present action.

BRUTUS   Let's along.   *Exeunt.*

1.2 *Enter* Tullus AUFIDIUS *with*
Senators of Corioles.

1 SENATOR   So, your opinion is, Aufidius,
That they of Rome are entered in our counsels
And know how we proceed.

AUFIDIUS   Is it not yours?
Whatever have been thought on in this state
5   That could be brought to bodily act, ere Rome
Had circumvention? 'Tis not four days gone
Since I heard thence; these are the words – I think
I have the letter here – yes, here it is.
[*Reads.*] *They have pressed a power, but it is not known*
10 *Whether for east or west. The dearth is great,*
The people mutinous, and it is rumoured
Cominius, Martius your old enemy
Who is of Rome worse hated than of you,
And Titus Lartius, a most valiant Roman,
15 *These three lead on this preparation*
Whither 'tis bent. Most likely 'tis for you.
Consider of it.

1 SENATOR   Our army's in the field.
We never yet made doubt but Rome was ready
To answer us.

AUFIDIUS   Nor did you think it folly
20 To keep your great pretences veiled till when
They needs must show themselves, which in the
      hatching
It seemed appeared to Rome. By the discovery
We shall be shortened in our aim, which was
To take in many towns, ere, almost, Rome
Should know we were a-foot.

25 2 SENATOR   Noble Aufidius,
Take your commission; hie you to your bands,
Let us alone to guard Corioles.
If they set down before's, for the remove
Bring up your army. But, I think, you'll find
They've not prepared for us.

30 AUFIDIUS   O, doubt not that.
I speak from certainties. Nay more,
Some parcels of their power are forth already,
And only hitherward. I leave your honours.
If we and Caius Martius chance to meet,
35 'Tis sworn between us we shall ever strike
Till one can do no more.

ALL   The gods assist you!

AUFIDIUS   And keep your honours safe.

1 SENATOR   Farewell.

2 SENATOR   Farewell.

ALL   Farewell.   *Exeunt.*

1.3   *Enter* VOLUMNIA *and* VIRGILIA,
mother and wife to Martius. They set
them down on two low stools and sew.

VOLUMNIA   I pray you, daughter, sing, or express
yourself in a more comfortable sort. If my son were my
husband, I should freelier rejoice in that absence

wherein he won honour than in the embracements of
his bed, where he would show most love. When yet he   5
was but tender-bodied and the only son of my womb,
when youth with comeliness plucked all gaze his way,
when for a day of kings' entreaties a mother should not
sell him an hour from her beholding, I, considering
how honour would become such a person – that it was   10
no better than picture-like to hang by th' wall, if
renown made it not stir – was pleased to let him seek
danger where he was like to find fame. To a cruel war I
sent him, from whence he returned, his brows bound
with oak. I tell thee, daughter, I sprang not more in joy   15
at first hearing he was a man-child than now in first
seeing he had proved himself a man.

VIRGILIA   But had he died in the business, madam, how
then?

VOLUMNIA   Then his good report should have been my   20
son; I therein would have found issue. Hear me profess
sincerely: had I a dozen sons, each in my love alike, and
none less dear than thine and my good Martius, I had
rather had eleven die nobly for their country than one
voluptuously surfeit out of action.   25

Enter a Gentlewoman.

GENTLEWOMAN [*to Volumnia*]   Madam, the lady Valeria
is come to visit you.

VIRGILIA [*to Volumnia*]   Beseech you give me leave to
retire myself.

VOLUMNIA   Indeed you shall not.   30
Methinks I hear hither your husband's drum,
See him pluck Aufidius down by th' hair,
As children from a bear the Volsces shunning him.
Methinks I see him stamp thus, and call thus:
'Come on, you cowards, you were got in fear   35
Though you were born in Rome!' His bloody brow
With his mailed hand then wiping, forth he goes
Like to a harvestman that's tasked to mow
Or all or lose his hire.

VIRGILIA   His bloody brow? O Jupiter, no blood!   40

VOLUMNIA   Away, you fool! It more becomes a man
Than gilt his trophy. The breasts of Hecuba
When she did suckle Hector looked not lovelier
Than Hector's forehead when it spit forth blood
At Grecian sword contemning.
[*to Gentlewoman*]   Tell Valeria   45
We are fit to bid her welcome.   *Exit Gentlewoman.*

VIRGILIA   Heavens bless my lord from fell Aufidius.

VOLUMNIA   He'll beat Aufidius' head below his knee
And tread upon his neck.

Enter VALERIA *with an Usher, and the* Gentlewoman.

VALERIA   My ladies both, good day to you.   50

VOLUMNIA   Sweet madam.

VIRGILIA   I am glad to see your ladyship.

VALERIA   How do you both? You are manifest house-
keepers. [*to Volumnia*] What are you sewing here? A fine
spot in good faith. [*to Virgilia*] How does your little son?   55

VIRGILIA   I thank your ladyship; well, good madam.

VOLUMNIA   He had rather see the swords and hear a
drum than look upon his schoolmaster.

VALERIA   O'my word, the father's son! I'll swear 'tis a
60   very pretty boy. O'my troth, I looked upon him
o'Wednesday half an hour together. 'Has such a
confirmed countenance. I saw him run after a gilded
butterfly, and when he caught it, he let it go again, and
after it again, and over and over he comes, and up
65   again, catched it again. Or whether his fall enraged
him, or how 'twas, he did so set his teeth and tear it. O,
I warrant, how he mammocked it.

VOLUMNIA   One on's father's moods.

VALERIA   Indeed, la, 'tis a noble child.

70   VIRGILIA   A crack, madam.

VALERIA   Come, lay aside your stitchery. I must have
you play the idle housewife with me this afternoon.

VIRGILIA   No, good madam. I will not out of doors.

VALERIA   Not out of doors?

75   VOLUMNIA   She shall, she shall.

VIRGILIA   Indeed no, by your patience. I'll not over the
threshold till my lord return from the wars.

VALERIA   Fie, you confine yourself most unreasonably.
Come, you must go visit the good lady that lies in.

80   VIRGILIA   I will wish her speedy strength and visit her
with my prayers, but I cannot go thither.

VOLUMNIA   Why, I pray you?

VIRGILIA   'Tis not to save labour, nor that I want love.

VALERIA   You would be another Penelope. Yet they say
85   all the yarn she spun in Ulysses' absence did but fill
Ithaca full of moths. Come, I would your cambric were
sensible as your finger, that you might leave pricking it
for pity. Come, you shall go with us.

VIRGILIA   No, good madam, pardon me, indeed I will
90   not forth.

VALERIA   In truth, la, go with me, and I'll tell you
excellent news of your husband.

VIRGILIA   O, good madam, there can be none yet.

VALERIA   Verily, I do not jest with you: there came news
95   from him last night.

VIRGILIA   Indeed, madam?

VALERIA   In earnest, it's true: I heard a senator speak it.
Thus it is: the Volsces have an army forth, against
whom Cominius the general is gone with one part of
100   our Roman power. Your lord and Titus Lartius are set
down before their city Corioles. They nothing doubt
prevailing and to make it brief wars. This is true on
mine honour, and so, I pray, go with us.

VIRGILIA   Give me excuse, good madam, I will obey you
105   in everything hereafter.

VOLUMNIA   [*to Valeria*]   Let her alone, lady, as she is
now. She will but disease our better mirth.

VALERIA   In truth, I think she would. [*to Virgilia*] Fare
you well then. [*to Volumnia*] Come, good sweet lady.
110   Prithee, Virgilia, turn thy solemness out o'door and go
along with us.

VIRGILIA   No, at a word, madam. Indeed I must not. I
wish you much mirth.

VALERIA   Well then, farewell.   *Exeunt.*

1.4   *Enter* MARTIUS, Titus LARTIUS, *with Drum,*
a Trumpeter and Colours, with Captains
and Soldiers, *as before the city Corioles; to*
them a Messenger.

MARTIUS   Yonder comes news. A wager they have met.

LARTIUS   My horse to yours, no.

MARTIUS   'Tis done.

LARTIUS   Agreed.

MARTIUS   [*to the Messenger*]
Say, has our general met the enemy?

MESSENGER
They lie in view but have not spoke as yet.

LARTIUS   So, the good horse is mine.

MARTIUS   I'll buy him of you.   5

LARTIUS
No, I'll nor sell nor give him. Lend you him I will
For half a hundred years.
[*to the Trumpeter*]   Summon the town.

MARTIUS
How far off lie these armies?

MESSENGER
Within this mile and half.

MARTIUS
Then shall we hear their 'larum, and they ours.   10
Now Mars, I prithee, make us quick in work,
That we with smoking swords may march from hence
To help our fielded friends.
[*to the Trumpeter*]   Come, blow thy blast.
                              [*They sound a parley.*]

Enter two Senators *with others on the walls of Corioles.*

[*to the Senators*] Tullus Aufidius, is he within your walls?

1 SENATOR
No, nor a man that fears you less than he,   15
That's lesser than a little.   [*Drum afar off*]
                              Hark, our drums
Are bringing forth our youth. We'll break our walls
Rather than they shall pound us up. Our gates,
Which yet seem shut, we have but pinned with
   rushes;
They'll open of themselves.   [*Alarum far off*]
                              Hark you, far off.   20
There is Aufidius. List what work he makes
Amongst your cloven army.
                    [*Exeunt Volscians from the walls.*]

MARTIUS   O, they are at it!

LARTIUS   Their noise be our instruction. Ladders ho!

Enter the army of the Volsces.

MARTIUS   They fear us not, but issue forth their city.
Now put your shields before your hearts and fight   25
With hearts more proof than shields. Advance, brave
   Titus.   *Exit Lartius.*
They do disdain us much beyond our thoughts,
Which makes me sweat with wrath. Come on, my
   fellows.
He that retires, I'll take him for a Volsce,

30	And he shall feel mine edge.
	[*Alarum. The Romans are beat back to their trenches.*]

Enter MARTIUS *cursing.*

MARTIUS   All the contagion of the south light on you,
You shames of Rome! You herd of – boils and
      plagues
Plaster you o'er, that you may be abhorred
Farther than seen, and one infect another

35   Against the wind a mile! You souls of geese
That bear the shapes of men, how have you run
From slaves that apes would beat! Pluto and hell!
All hurt behind, backs red, and faces pale
With flight and agued fear. Mend and charge home,

40   Or by the fires of heaven I'll leave the foe
And make my wars on you. Look to 't. Come on!
If you'll stand fast, we'll beat them to their wives,
As they us to our trenches. Follow 's!
      [*Another alarum and Martius follows the Volscian
            army to gates which are opened.*]
So, now the gates are ope. Now prove good seconds.

45   'Tis for the followers fortune widens them,
Not for the fliers. Mark me, and do the like.
      *The Volscian army retreats through the gates
            and Martius follows them.*

1 SOLDIER   Foolhardiness! not I.
2 SOLDIER   Nor I.
      [*Alarum continues. The gates are closed
            and Martius is shut in.*]

1 SOLDIER   See they have shut him in.
50   ALL   To th' pot, I warrant him.

Enter Titus LARTIUS.

LARTIUS   What is become of Martius?
ALL   Slain, sir, doubtless.
1 SOLDIER   Following the fliers at the very heels,
With them he enters, who upon the sudden
55   Clapped to their gates. He is himself alone
To answer all the city.
LARTIUS   O, noble fellow,
Who sensibly out-dares his senseless sword
And, when it bows, stand'st up! Thou art left,
      Martius.
A carbuncle entire, as big as thou art,
60   Were not so rich a jewel. Thou wast a soldier
Even to Cato's wish, not fierce and terrible
Only in strokes, but with thy grim looks and
The thunder-like percussion of thy sounds
Thou mad'st thine enemies shake, as if the world
Were feverous and did tremble.

Enter MARTIUS *bleeding, assaulted by the enemy.*

1 SOLDIER   Look, sir.
65   LARTIUS   O, 'tis Martius.
Let's fetch him off, or make remain alike.
      They fight, and all enter the city.

1.5		*Enter certain* Romans *with spoils.*
1 ROMAN	This will I carry to Rome.	
2 ROMAN	And I this.	
3 ROMAN	A murrain on 't, I took this for silver. *Exeunt.*	
	[*Alarum continues still afar off.*]	

Enter MARTIUS *and* Titus LARTIUS *with a Trumpet.*

MARTIUS
See here these movers that do prize their hours
At a cracked drachma! Cushions, leaden spoons,   5
Irons of a doit, doublets that hangmen would
Bury with those that wore them, these base slaves,
Ere yet the fight be done, pack up. Down with them!
And hark, what noise the general makes. To him!
There is the man of my soul's hate, Aufidius,   10
Piercing our Romans. Then, valiant Titus, take
Convenient numbers to make good the city,
Whilst I, with those that have the spirit, will haste
To help Cominius.
LARTIUS   Worthy sir, thou bleed'st.
Thy exercise hath been too violent   15
For a second course of fight.
MARTIUS   Sir, praise me not.
My work hath yet not warmed me. Fare you well.
The blood I drop is rather physical
Than dangerous to me. To Aufidius thus I will
Appear and fight.
LARTIUS   Now the fair goddess Fortune   20
Fall deep in love with thee and her great charms
Misguide thy opposers' swords, bold gentleman!
Prosperity be thy page.
MARTIUS   Thy friend no less
Than those she placeth highest. So farewell.
LARTIUS
Thou worthiest Martius.   *Exit Martius.*   25
[*to the Trumpeter*] Go sound thy trumpet in the
      market-place.
Call thither all the officers o'th' town,
Where they shall know our mind. Away.   *Exeunt.*

1.6	*Enter* COMINIUS, *as it were in
retire, with Soldiers.*

COMINIUS
Breathe you, my friends. Well fought. We are come off
Like Romans, neither foolish in our stands
Nor cowardly in retire. Believe me, sirs,
We shall be charged again. Whiles we have struck,
By interims and conveying gusts we have heard   5
The charges of our friends. The Roman gods
Lead their successes as we wish our own,
That both our powers, with smiling fronts encountering,
May give you thankful sacrifice!

Enter a Messenger.

                                    Thy news?

10 MESSENGER   The citizens of Corioles have issued
And given to Lartius and to Martius battle.
I saw our party to their trenches driven
And then I came away.
COMINIUS   Though thou speak'st truth,
Methinks thou speak'st not well. How long is't since?
15 MESSENGER   Above an hour, my lord.
COMINIUS
'Tis not a mile; briefly we heard their drums.
How couldst thou in a mile confound an hour
And bring thy news so late?
MESSENGER   Spies of the Volsces
Held me in chase, that I was forced to wheel
20 Three or four miles about; else had I, sir,
Half an hour since brought my report.

Enter MARTIUS.

COMINIUS   Who's yonder
That does appear as he were flayed? O gods,
He has the stamp of Martius, and I have
Beforetime seen him thus.
25 MARTIUS   Come I too late?
COMINIUS
The shepherd knows not thunder from a tabor
More than I know the sound of Martius' tongue
From every meaner man.
MARTIUS   Come I too late?
COMINIUS   Ay, if you come not in the blood of others,
But mantled in your own.
30 MARTIUS   O, let me clip ye
In arms as sound as when I wooed, in heart
As merry as when our nuptial day was done
And tapers burned to bedward.   [*They embrace.*]
COMINIUS
Flower of warriors, how is't with Titus Lartius?
35 MARTIUS   As with a man busied about decrees,
Condemning some to death and some to exile,
Ransoming him or pitying, threatening th'other;
Holding Corioles in the name of Rome,
Even like a fawning greyhound in the leash,
To let him slip at will.
40 COMINIUS   Where is that slave
Which told me they had beat you to your trenches?
Where is he? Call him hither.
MARTIUS   Let him alone;
He did inform the truth. But for our gentlemen,
The common file – a plague! tribunes for them! –
45 The mouse ne'er shunned the cat as they did budge
From rascals worse than they.
COMINIUS   But how prevailed you?
MARTIUS   Will the time serve to tell? I do not think.
Where is the enemy? Are you lords o'th' field?
If not, why cease you till you are so?
50 COMINIUS   Martius, we have at disadvantage fought
And did retire to win our purpose.
MARTIUS
How lies their battle? Know you on which side

They have placed their men of trust?
COMINIUS   As I guess, Martius,
Their bands i'th' vanguard are the Antiates
Of their best trust; o'er them Aufidius,   55
Their very heart of hope.
MARTIUS   I do beseech you,
By all the battles wherein we have fought,
By th' blood we have shed together, by th' vows we
have made
To endure friends, that you directly set me
Against Aufidius and his Antiates,   60
And that you not delay the present but,
Filling the air with swords advanced and darts,
We prove this very hour.
COMINIUS   Though I could wish,
You were conducted to a gentle bath
And balms applied to you, yet dare I never   65
Deny your asking. Take your choice of those
That best can aid your action.
MARTIUS   Those are they
That most are willing. [*to the Soldiers*] If any such be
here,
(As it were sin to doubt) that love this painting
Wherein you see me smeared, if any fear   70
Lesser his person than an ill report,
If any think brave death outweighs bad life
And that his country's dearer than himself,
Let him alone, or so many so minded,
Wave thus [*waving his sword*] to express his disposition,   75
And follow Martius.
   [*They all shout and wave their swords, take him up in
   their arms and cast up their caps.*]
O, me alone! Make you a sword of me?
If these shows be not outward, which of you
But is four Volsces? None of you but is
Able to bear against the great Aufidius   80
A shield as hard as his. A certain number –
Though thanks to all – must I select from all.
The rest shall bear the business in some other fight,
As cause will be obeyed. [*to Cominius*] Please you to
march
And I shall quickly draw out my command,   85
Which men are best inclined.
COMINIUS   March on, my fellows.
Make good this ostentation and you shall
Divide in all with us.   *Exeunt.*

1.7   Titus LARTIUS, *having set a guard upon*
         Corioles, going with Drum and Trumpet toward
         Cominius and Caius Martius, enters with
         a Lieutenant, *other Soldiers and a Scout.*

LARTIUS   So, let the ports be guarded. Keep your duties
As I have set them down. If I do send, dispatch
Those centuries to our aid; the rest will serve
For a short holding. If we lose the field
We cannot keep the town.

LIEUTENANT   Fear not our care, sir.
LARTIUS   Hence; and shut your gates upon's.
    [*to the Scout*] Our guider, come; to th' Roman camp
    conduct us.   *Exeunt.*

1.8   *Alarum, as in battle. Enter* MARTIUS *and*
         AUFIDIUS *at several doors.*

MARTIUS
I'll fight with none but thee, for I do hate thee
Worse than a promise-breaker.
AUFIDIUS   We hate alike:
Not Afric owns a serpent I abhor
More than thy fame and envy. Fix thy foot.
MARTIUS   Let the first budger die the other's slave,
And the gods doom him after.
AUFIDIUS   If I fly, Martius, hollo me like a hare.
MARTIUS   Within these three hours, Tullus,
Alone I fought in your Corioles' walls
And made what work I pleased. 'Tis not my blood
Wherein thou seest me masked. For thy revenge,
Wrench up thy power to th' highest.
AUFIDIUS   Wert thou the Hector
That was the whip of your bragged progeny
Thou shouldst not scape me here.

    Here they fight, and certain Volsces come in the
        aid of Aufidius.

Officious and not valiant, you have shamed me
In your condemned seconds.
    [*Martius fights till they be driven in breathless.*]
                          Exeunt.

1.9   *Alarum. A retreat is sounded. Flourish.*
    Enter at one door COMINIUS, *with the*
    Romans, at another door MARTIUS, *with his*
        left arm in a scarf.

COMINIUS   If I should tell thee o'er this thy day's work
Thou't not believe thy deeds. But I'll report it
Where senators shall mingle tears with smiles;
Where great patricians shall attend, and shrug,
I'th' end admire; where ladies shall be frighted
And, gladly quaked, hear more; where the dull
    tribunes,
That with the fusty plebeians hate thine honours,
Shall say against their hearts 'We thank the gods
Our Rome hath such a soldier.'
Yet cam'st thou to a morsel of this feast,
Having fully dined before.

    Enter Titus LARTIUS *with his power, from the pursuit.*

LARTIUS   O general,
Here is the steed, we the caparison.
Hadst thou beheld –
MARTIUS   Pray now, no more. My mother,
Who has a charter to extol her blood,

When she does praise me, grieves me.
I have done as you have done, that's what I can,
Induced as you have been, that's for my country.
He that has but effected his good will
Hath overta'en mine act.
COMINIUS   You shall not be
The grave of your deserving; Rome must know
The value of her own. 'Twere a concealment
Worse than a theft, no less than a traducement,
To hide your doings and to silence that
Which, to the spire and top of praises vouched,
Would seem but modest. Therefore, I beseech you –
In sign of what you are, not to reward
What you have done – before our army hear me.
MARTIUS
I have some wounds upon me, and they smart
To hear themselves remembered.
COMINIUS   Should they not,
Well might they fester 'gainst ingratitude,
And tent themselves with death. Of all the horses –
Whereof we have ta'en good, and good store – of all
The treasure in this field achieved and city,
We render you the tenth, to be ta'en forth,
Before the common distribution,
At your only choice.
MARTIUS   I thank you, general,
But cannot make my heart consent to take
A bribe to pay my sword. I do refuse it,
And stand upon my common part with those
That have beheld the doing.   [*A long flourish*]
    [*They all cry,* 'Martius, Martius', *cast up their caps*
      and lances. Cominius and Lartius stand bare.]
May these same instruments which you profane
Never sound more. When drums and trumpets shall
I'th' field prove flatterers, let courts and cities be
Made all of false-faced soothing. When steel grows soft
As the parasite's silk, let him be made
An ovator for th' wars. No more, I say!
For that I have not washed my nose that bled,
Or foiled some debile wretch, which without note
Here's many else have done, you shout me forth
In acclamations hyperbolical,
As if I loved my little should be dieted
In praises sauced with lies.
COMINIUS   Too modest are you,
More cruel to your good report than grateful
To us that give you truly. By your patience,
If 'gainst yourself you be incensed, we'll put you,
Like one that means his proper harm, in manacles,
Then reason safely with you. Therefore be it known,
As to us, to all the world, that Caius Martius
Wears this war's garland, in token of the which,
My noble steed, known to the camp, I give him,
With all his trim belonging; and from this time,
For what he did before Corioles, call him,
With all th'applause and clamour of the host,
Martius Caius Coriolanus!

65 Bear th'addition nobly ever!
                [Flourish. Trumpets sound, and drums.]
ALL   Martius Caius Coriolanus.
CORIOLANUS   I will go wash.
  And when my face is fair you shall perceive
  Whether I blush or no. Howbeit, I thank you.
  [to Cominius] I mean to stride your steed, and at all
    times
70   To under-crest your good addition
  To th' fairness of my power.
COMINIUS   So, to our tent,
  Where, ere we do repose us, we will write
  To Rome of our success. You, Titus Lartius,
  Must to Corioles back. Send us to Rome
75   The best, with whom we may articulate
  For their own good and ours.
LARTIUS   I shall, my Lord.
CORIOLANUS   The gods begin to mock me:
  I, that now refused most princely gifts,
  Am bound to beg of my lord general.
80 COMINIUS   Take't, 'tis yours. What is't?
CORIOLANUS   I sometime lay here in Corioles,
  At a poor man's house; he used me kindly.
  He cried to me; I saw him prisoner,
  But then Aufidius was within my view
85   And wrath o'erwhelmed my pity. I request you
  To give my poor host freedom.
COMINIUS   O, well begged!
  Were he the butcher of my son, he should
  Be free as is the wind. Deliver him, Titus.
LARTIUS   Martius, his name.
CORIOLANUS   By Jupiter, forgot!
90   I am weary; yea, my memory is tired.
  Have we no wine here?
COMINIUS   Go we to our tent.
  The blood upon your visage dries; 'tis time
  It should be looked to. Come.
                Exeunt. A flourish of cornets.

1.10   *Enter* Tullus AUFIDIUS, *bloody, with two*
            or three Soldiers.

AUFIDIUS   The town is ta'en.
1 SOLDIER   'Twill be delivered back on good condition.
AUFIDIUS   Condition?
  I would I were a Roman, for I cannot,
5   Being a Volsce, be that I am. Condition?
  What good condition can a treaty find
  I'th' part that is at mercy? Five times, Martius,
  I have fought with thee; so often hast thou beat me,
  And wouldst do so, I think, should we encounter
10   As often as we eat. By th'elements,
  If e'er again I meet him beard to beard,
  He's mine, or I am his. Mine emulation
  Hath not that honour in't it had, for where
  I thought to crush him in an equal force,
15   True sword to sword, I'll poach at him some way.

  Or wrath or craft may get him.
1 SOLDIER   He's the devil.
AUFIDIUS
  Bolder, though not so subtle. My valour's poisoned
  With only suffering stain by him, for him
  Shall fly out of itself. Nor sleep nor sanctuary,
  Being naked, sick, nor fane nor Capitol,   20
  The prayers of priests, nor times of sacrifice –
  Embargements all of fury – shall lift up
  Their rotten privilege and custom 'gainst
  My hate to Martius. Where I find him, were it
  At home upon my brother's guard, even there,   25
  Against the hospitable canon, would I
  Wash my fierce hand in's heart. Go you to th' city,
  Learn how 'tis held, and what they are that must
  Be hostages for Rome.
1 SOLDIER   Will not you go?
AUFIDIUS
  I am attended at the cypress grove. I pray you –   30
  'Tis south the city mills – bring me word thither
  How the world goes, that to the pace of it
  I may spur on my journey.
1 SOLDIER   I shall, sir.   *Exeunt.*

2.1   *Enter* MENENIUS *with the two Tribunes*
         of the people, SICINIUS *and* BRUTUS.

MENENIUS   The augurer tells me we shall have news
  tonight.
BRUTUS   Good or bad?
MENENIUS   Not according to the prayer of the people,
  for they love not Martius.   5
SICINIUS   Nature teaches beasts to know their friends.
MENENIUS   Pray you, who does the wolf love?
SICINIUS   The lamb.
MENENIUS   Ay, to devour him, as the hungry plebeians
  would the noble Martius.   10
BRUTUS   He's a lamb indeed that baas like a bear.
MENENIUS   He's a bear indeed that lives like a lamb.
  You two are old men; tell me one thing that I shall ask
  you.
SICINIUS, BRUTUS   Well, sir.   15
MENENIUS   In what enormity is Martius poor in that
  you two have not in abundance?
BRUTUS   He's poor in no one fault, but stored with all.
SICINIUS   Especially in pride.
BRUTUS   And topping all others in boasting.   20
MENENIUS   This is strange now. Do you two know how
  you are censured here in the city – I mean of us o'th'
  right-hand file? Do you?
SICINIUS, BRUTUS   Why? How are we censured?
MENENIUS   Because you talk of pride now – will you not   25
  be angry?
SICINIUS, BRUTUS   Well, well, sir, well.
MENENIUS   Why, 'tis no great matter, for a very little
  thief of occasion will rob you of a great deal of patience.
  Give your dispositions the reins and be angry at your   30

pleasures – at the least, if you take it as a pleasure to you in being so. You blame Martius for being proud.

BRUTUS   We do it not alone, sir.

MENENIUS   I know you can do very little alone, for your helps are many, or else your actions would grow wondrous single – your abilities are too infant-like for doing much alone. You talk of pride. O that you could turn your eyes toward the napes of your necks and make but an interior survey of your good selves! O that you could!

SICINIUS, BRUTUS   What then, sir?

MENENIUS   Why, then you should discover a brace of unmeriting, proud, violent, testy magistrates (alias fools) as any in Rome.

SICINIUS   Menenius, you are known well enough too.

MENENIUS   I am known to be a humorous patrician, and one that loves a cup of hot wine, with not a drop of allaying Tiber in't; said to be something imperfect in favouring the first complaint, hasty and tinder-like upon too trivial motion; one that converses more with the buttock of the night than with the forehead of the morning. What I think, I utter, and spend my malice in my breath. Meeting two such wealsmen as you are (I cannot call you Lycurguses), if the drink you give me touch my palate adversely, I make a crooked face at it. I cannot say your worships have delivered the matter well, when I find the ass in compound with the major part of your syllables. And though I must be content to bear with those that say you are reverend grave men, yet they lie deadly that tell you have good faces. If you see this in the map of my microcosm, follows it that I am known well enough too? What harm can your bisson conspectuities glean out of this character, if I be known well enough too?

BRUTUS   Come, sir, come, we know you well enough.

MENENIUS   You know neither me, yourselves, nor anything. You are ambitious for poor knaves' caps and legs. You wear out a good wholesome forenoon in hearing a cause between an orange-wife and a faucet-seller, and then rejourn the controversy of threepence to a second day of audience. When you are hearing a matter between party and party, if you chance to be pinched with the colic, you make faces like mummers, set up the bloody flag against all patience and, in roaring for a chamber-pot, dismiss the controversy bleeding, the more entangled by your hearing. All the peace you make in their cause is calling both the parties knaves. You are a pair of strange ones.

BRUTUS   Come, come, you are well understood to be a perfecter giber for the table than a necessary bencher in the Capitol.

MENENIUS   Our very priests must become mockers if they shall encounter such ridiculous subjects as you are. When you speak best unto the purpose it is not worth the wagging of your beards, and your beards deserve not so honourable a grave as to stuff a botcher's cushion, or to be entombed in an ass's packsaddle. Yet you must

be saying Martius is proud, who, in a cheap estimation, is worth all your predecessors since Deucalion, though peradventure some of the best of 'em were hereditary hangmen. Good e'en to your worships. More of your conversation would infect my brain, being the herdsmen of the beastly plebeians. I will be bold to take my leave of you. [*Brutus and Sicinius stand aside.*]

Enter VOLUMNIA, VIRGILIA *and* VALERIA.

How now, my as fair as noble ladies – and the moon, were she earthly, no nobler – whither do you follow your eyes so fast?

VOLUMNIA   Honourable Menenius, my boy Martius approaches. For the love of Juno, let's go.

MENENIUS   Ha? Martius coming home?

VOLUMNIA   Ay, worthy Menenius, and with most prosperous approbation.

MENENIUS [*throwing up his cap*]   Take my cap, Jupiter, and I thank thee. Ho! Martius coming home?

VIRGILIA, VALERIA   Nay, 'tis true.

VOLUMNIA   Look, here's a letter from him, the state hath another, his wife another, and, I think, there's one at home for you.

MENENIUS   I will make my very house reel tonight. A letter for me?

VIRGILIA   Yes, certain, there's a letter for you; I saw't.

MENENIUS   A letter for me? It gives me an estate of seven years' health, in which time I will make a lip at the physician. The most sovereign prescription in Galen is but empiricutic and, to this preservative, of no better report than a horse-drench. Is he not wounded? He was wont to come home wounded.

VIRGILIA   O, no, no, no!

VOLUMNIA   O, he is wounded, I thank the gods for't!

MENENIUS   So do I too, if it be not too much. Brings 'a victory in his pocket, the wounds become him.

VOLUMNIA   On's brows. Menenius, he comes the third time home with the oaken garland.

MENENIUS   Has he disciplined Aufidius soundly?

VOLUMNIA   Titus Lartius writes they fought together but Aufidius got off.

MENENIUS   And 'twas time for him too, I'll warrant him that. An he had stayed by him, I would not have been so 'fidiussed for all the chests in Corioles and the gold that's in them. Is the Senate possessed of this?

VOLUMNIA   Good ladies, let's go. Yes, yes, yes. The Senate has letters from the general, wherein he gives my son the whole name of the war. He hath in this action outdone his former deeds doubly.

VALERIA   In truth, there's wondrous things spoke of him.

MENENIUS   Wondrous! Ay, I warrant you, and not without his true purchasing.

VIRGILIA   The gods grant them true.

VOLUMNIA   True? Pooh-whoo!

MENENIUS   True? I'll be sworn they are true. Where is he wounded? [*to the Tribunes*] God save your good

worships. Martius is coming home. He has more cause
to be proud. [*to Volumnia*] Where is he wounded?

VOLUMNIA   I'th' shoulder and i'th' left arm. There will
be large cicatrices to show the people when he shall
stand for his place. He received in the repulse of
Tarquin seven hurts i'th' body.

MENENIUS   One i'th' neck and two i'th' thigh – there's
nine that I know.

VOLUMNIA   He had, before this last expedition, twenty-
five wounds upon him.

MENENIUS   Now it's twenty-seven; every gash was
an enemy's grave. [*A shout and flourish*] Hark, the
trumpets.

VOLUMNIA   These are the ushers of Martius. Before him
He carries noise, and behind him he leaves tears.
Death, that dark Spirit, in's nervy arm doth lie,
Which being advanced, declines, and then men die.

A sennet. Enter COMINIUS *the general and* Titus
LARTIUS; *between them* CORIOLANUS, *crowned with
an oaken garland, with Captains and Soldiers, and a*
Herald. *Trumpets sound.*

HERALD   Know, Rome, that all alone Martius did fight
Within Corioles' gates, where he hath won,
With fame, a name to 'Martius Caius'; these
In honour follows 'Coriolanus'.
Welcome to Rome, renowned Coriolanus.
                                        [*Sound flourish.*]

ALL   Welcome to Rome, renowned Coriolanus.

CORIOLANUS   No more of this, it does offend my heart.
Pray now no more.

COMINIUS   Look, sir, your mother.

CORIOLANUS [*to Volumnia*]   O,
You have, I know, petitioned all the gods
For my prosperity.   [*Kneels.*]

VOLUMNIA   Nay, my good soldier, up,
My gentle Martius, worthy Caius, and
By deed-achieving honour newly named –
What is it? – 'Coriolanus' must I call thee?   [*He rises.*]
But O, thy wife.

CORIOLANUS [*to Virgilia*]   My gracious silence, hail.
Wouldst thou have laughed had I come coffined home,
That weep'st to see me triumph? Ah, my dear,
Such eyes the widows in Corioles wear
And mothers that lack sons.

MENENIUS   Now the gods crown thee.

CORIOLANUS
And live you yet? [*to Valeria*] O, my sweet lady, pardon.

VOLUMNIA
I know not where to turn. O, welcome home!
And welcome, general, and you're welcome all.

MENENIUS
A hundred thousand welcomes! I could weep,
And I could laugh; I am light and heavy. Welcome!
A curse begin at very root on's heart,
That is not glad to see thee. Yon are three
That Rome should dote on. Yet, by the faith of men,

We have some old crab-trees here at home that will not
Be grafted to your relish. Yet welcome, warriors!
We call a nettle but a nettle,
And the faults of fools but folly.

COMINIUS   Ever right.

CORIOLANUS   Menenius, ever, ever.

HERALD   Give way there, and go on.

CORIOLANUS [*to Volumnia and Virgilia*]
                          Your hand, and yours?
Ere in our own house I do shade my head
The good patricians must be visited,
From whom I have received not only greetings
But with them change of honours.

VOLUMNIA   I have lived,
To see inherited my very wishes,
And the buildings of my fancy. Only
There's one thing wanting, which I doubt not but
Our Rome will cast upon thee.

CORIOLANUS   Know, good mother,
I had rather be their servant in my way,
Than sway with them in theirs.

COMINIUS   On, to the Capitol.
        *Flourish of cornets. Exeunt in state as before
        all but Brutus and Sicinius who come forward.*

BRUTUS
All tongues speak of him, and the bleared sights
Are spectacled to see him. Your prattling nurse
Into a rapture lets her baby cry,
While she chats him. The kitchen malkin pins
Her richest lockram 'bout her reechy neck,
Clamb'ring the walls to eye him. Stalls, bulks, windows
Are smothered up, leads filled and ridges horsed
With variable complexions, all agreeing
In earnestness to see him. Seld-shown flamens
Do press among the popular throngs, and puff
To win a vulgar station. Our veiled dames
Commit the war of white and damask in
Their nicely guarded cheeks to th' wanton spoil
Of Phoebus' burning kisses. Such a pother,
As if that whatsoever god who leads him
Were slyly crept into his human powers
And gave him graceful posture.

SICINIUS   On the sudden I warrant him consul.

BRUTUS   Then our office may, during his power, go sleep.

SICINIUS   He cannot temperately transport his honours,
From where he should begin and end, but will
Lose those he hath won.

BRUTUS   In that there's comfort.

SICINIUS   Doubt not
The commoners, for whom we stand, but they
Upon their ancient malice will forget,
With the least cause, these his new honours, which
That he will give them make I as little question
As he is proud to do't.

BRUTUS   I heard him swear,
Were he to stand for consul, never would he
Appear i'th' market-place nor on him put

The napless vesture of humility,
Nor, showing, as the manner is, his wounds
To th' people, beg their stinking breaths.

SICINIUS   'Tis right.

BRUTUS   It was his word. O, he would miss it rather
235   Than carry it but by the suit of the gentry to him
And the desire of the nobles.

SICINIUS   I wish no better
Than have him hold that purpose and to put it
In execution.

BRUTUS   'Tis most like he will.

SICINIUS   It shall be to him then as our good wills,
A sure destruction.

240   BRUTUS   So it must fall out
To him, or our authority's for an end.
We must suggest the people in what hatred
He still hath held them; that to's power he would
Have made them mules, silenced their pleaders and
245   Dispropertied their freedoms, holding them
In human action and capacity
Of no more soul nor fitness for the world
Than camels in their war, who have their provand
Only for bearing burdens and sore blows
For sinking under them.

250   SICINIUS   This, as you say, suggested
At some time when his soaring insolence
Shall teach the people – which time shall not want,
If he be put upon't, and that's as easy
As to set dogs on sheep – will be his fire
255   To kindle their dry stubble, and their blaze
Shall darken him for ever.

Enter a Messenger.

BRUTUS   What's the matter?

MESSENGER   You are sent for to the Capitol.
'Tis thought that Martius shall be consul.
I have seen the dumb men throng to see him, and
260   The blind to hear him speak. Matrons flung gloves,
Ladies and maids their scarves and handkerchiefs,
Upon him as he passed. The nobles bended
As to Jove's statue, and the commons made
A shower and thunder with their caps and shouts.
I never saw the like.

265   BRUTUS   Let's to the Capitol,
And carry with us ears and eyes for th' time
But hearts for the event.

SICINIUS   Have with you.   *Exeunt.*

2.2   *Enter two* Officers *to lay cushions,*
                    as it were in the Capitol.

1 OFFICER   Come, come, they are almost here. How
many stand for consulships?

2 OFFICER   Three, they say, but 'tis thought of everyone
Coriolanus will carry it.

5   1 OFFICER   That's a brave fellow, but he's vengeance
proud, and loves not the common people.

2 OFFICER   'Faith, there hath been many great men that
have flattered the people who ne'er loved them, and
there be many that they have loved, they know not
wherefore; so that if they love they know not why they   10
hate upon no better a ground. Therefore, for
Coriolanus neither to care whether they love or hate
him manifests the true knowledge he has in their
disposition and, out of his noble carelessness, lets
them plainly see't.   15

1 OFFICER   If he did not care whether he had their love
or no he waved indifferently 'twixt doing them neither
good nor harm. But he seeks their hate with greater
devotion than they can render it him, and leaves
nothing undone that may fully discover him their   20
opposite. Now to seem to affect the malice and
displeasure of the people is as bad as that which he
dislikes, to flatter them for their love.

2 OFFICER   He hath deserved worthily of his country,
and his ascent is not by such easy degrees as those who,   25
having been supple and courteous to the people,
bonneted, without any further deed to have them at all
into their estimation and report. But he hath so
planted his honours in their eyes and his actions in
their hearts that for their tongues to be silent and not   30
confess so much were a kind of ungrateful injury. To
report otherwise were a malice that, giving itself the
lie, would pluck reproof and rebuke from every ear
that heard it.

1 OFFICER   No more of him; he's a worthy man. Make   35
way, they are coming.

*A sennet. Enter the Patricians and the Tribunes of
the people, Lictors before them;* CORIOLANUS,
MENENIUS, COMINIUS *the Consul. The Patricians
take their places and sit.* SICINIUS *and* BRUTUS
take their places by themselves. CORIOLANUS *stands.*

MENENIUS   Having determined of the Volsces, and
To send for Titus Lartius, it remains,
As the main point of this our after-meeting,
To gratify his noble service that   40
Hath thus stood for his country. Therefore please you,
Most reverend and grave elders, to desire
The present consul, and last general
In our well-found successes, to report
A little of that worthy work performed   45
By Martius Caius Coriolanus, whom
We met here both to thank and to remember
With honours like himself.   [*Coriolanus sits.*]

1 SENATOR   Speak, good Cominius.
Leave nothing out for length, and make us think
Rather our state's defective for requital   50
Than we to stretch it out. [*to the Tribunes*] Masters
    o'th' people,
We do request your kindest ears and, after,
Your loving motion toward the common body
To yield what passes here.

SICINIUS   We are convented

Upon a pleasing treaty, and have hearts 55
Inclinable to honour and advance
The theme of our assembly.
BRUTUS   Which the rather
We shall be blessed to do if he remember
A kinder value of the people than
He hath hereto prized them at.
MENENIUS   That's off, that's off. 60
I would you rather had been silent. Please you
To hear Cominius speak?
BRUTUS   Most willingly,
But yet my caution was more pertinent
Than the rebuke you give it.
MENENIUS   He loves your people,
But tie him not to be their bedfellow. 65
Worthy Cominius, speak.
        [*Coriolanus rises and offers to go away.*]
                              Nay, keep your place.
1 SENATOR Sit, Coriolanus. Never shame to hear
What you have nobly done.
CORIOLANUS   Your honours' pardon,
I had rather have my wounds to heal again
Than hear say how I got them.
BRUTUS   Sir, I hope 70
My words disbenched you not?
CORIOLANUS   No, sir, yet oft
When blows have made me stay I fled from words.
You soothed not, therefore hurt not; but your people,
I love them as they weigh –
MENENIUS   Pray now, sit down.
CORIOLANUS
I had rather have one scratch my head i'th' sun 75
When the alarum were struck than idly sit
To hear my nothings monstered.   *Exit Coriolanus.*
MENENIUS   Masters of the people,
Your multiplying spawn how can he flatter –
That's thousand to one good one – when you now see
He had rather venture all his limbs for honour 80
Than one on's ears to hear it? Proceed, Cominius.
COMINIUS I shall lack voice: the deeds of Coriolanus
Should not be uttered feebly. It is held
That valour is the chiefest virtue and
Most dignifies the haver. If it be, 85
The man I speak of cannot in the world
Be singly counterpoised. At sixteen years,
When Tarquin made a head for Rome, he fought
Beyond the mark of others. Our then dictator,
Whom with all praise I point at, saw him fight 90
When with his Amazonian chin he drove
The bristled lips before him. He bestrid
An o'erpressed Roman and, i'th' consul's view,
Slew three opposers. Tarquin's self he met
And struck him on his knee. In that day's feats, 95
When he might act the woman in the scene
He proved best man i'th' field, and for his meed
Was brow-bound with the oak. His pupil age
Man-entered thus, he waxed like a sea

And in the brunt of seventeen battles since 100
He lurched all swords of the garland. For this last,
Before and in Corioles, let me say
I cannot speak him home. He stopped the fliers
And by his rare example made the coward
Turn terror into sport. As weeds before 105
A vessel under sail, so men obeyed
And fell below his stem. His sword, death's stamp,
Where it did mark, it took; from face to foot
He was a thing of blood, whose every motion
Was timed with dying cries. Alone he entered 110
The mortal gate of th' city, which he painted
With shunless destiny, aidless came off
And with a sudden reinforcement struck
Corioles like a planet. Now all's his,
When by and by the din of war gan pierce 115
His ready sense. Then straight his doubled spirit
Requickened what in flesh was fatigate
And to the battle came he, where he did
Run reeking o'er the lives of men, as if
'Twere a perpetual spoil; and till we called 120
Both field and city ours he never stood
To ease his breast with panting.
MENENIUS   Worthy man.
1 SENATOR He cannot but with measure fit the honours
Which we devise him.
COMINIUS   Our spoils he kicked at,
And looked upon things precious as they were 125
The common muck of the world. He covets less
Than misery itself would give, rewards
His deeds with doing them, and is content
To spend the time to end it.
MENENIUS He's right noble. Let him be called for. 130
1 SENATOR Call Coriolanus.
OFFICER   He doth appear.

                    Enter CORIOLANUS.

MENENIUS The senate, Coriolanus, are well pleased
To make thee consul.
CORIOLANUS I do owe them still my life and services.
MENENIUS
It then remains that you do speak to the people. 135
CORIOLANUS I do beseech you,
Let me o'erleap that custom, for I cannot
Put on the gown, stand naked and entreat them,
For my wounds' sake, to give their suffrage. Please you
That I may pass this doing.
SICINIUS   Sir, the people 140
Must have their voices, neither will they bate
One jot of ceremony.
MENENIUS   Put them not to't.
Pray you go fit you to the custom, and
Take to you, as your predecessors have,
Your honour with your form.
CORIOLANUS   It is a part 145
That I shall blush in acting, and might well
Be taken from the people.

BRUTUS   Mark you that.
CORIOLANUS   To brag unto them 'Thus I did, and thus',
      Show them th'unaching scars which I should hide,
150   As if I had received them for the hire
      Of their breath only.
MENENIUS   Do not stand upon't. –
      We recommend to you, tribunes of the people,
      Our purpose to them, and to our noble consul
      Wish we all joy and honour.
155   SENATORS   To Coriolanus come all joy and honour.
                  Flourish of cornets. Then exeunt all but
                                      Sicinius and Brutus.
BRUTUS   You see how he intends to use the people.
SICINIUS
      May they perceive's intent! He will require them
      As if he did contemn what he requested
      Should be in them to give.
BRUTUS   Come, we'll inform them
160   Of our proceedings here; on th' market-place
      I know they do attend us.   *Exeunt.*

2.3   *Enter seven or eight* Citizens.

1 CITIZEN   Once, if he do require our voices, we ought
      not to deny him.
2 CITIZEN   We may, sir, if we will.
3 CITIZEN   We have power in ourselves to do it, but it is
5   a power that we have no power to do. For, if he show us
      his wounds and tell us his deeds, we are to put our
      tongues into those wounds and speak for them. So, if
      he tell us his noble deeds, we must also tell him our
      noble acceptance of them. Ingratitude is monstrous,
10   and for the multitude to be ingrateful were to make a
      monster of the multitude, of the which we, being
      members, should bring ourselves to be monstrous
      members.
1 CITIZEN   And to make us no better thought of, a little
15   help will serve; for once we stood up about the corn, he
      himself stuck not to call us the many-headed multitude.
3 CITIZEN   We have been called so of many, not that our
      heads are some brown, some black, some abram, some
      bald, but that our wits are so diversely coloured; and
20   truly, I think if all our wits were to issue out of one
      skull, they would fly east, west, north, south, and their
      consent of one direct way should be at once to all the
      points o'th' compass.
2 CITIZEN   Think you so? Which way do you judge my
25   wit would fly?
3 CITIZEN   Nay, your wit will not so soon out as another
      man's will; 'tis strongly wedged up in a blockhead. But
      if it were at liberty, 'twould sure southward.
2 CITIZEN   Why that way?
30   3 CITIZEN   To lose itself in a fog where, being three parts
      melted away with rotten dews, the fourth would return
      for conscience' sake, to help to get thee a wife.
2 CITIZEN   You are never without your tricks; you may,
      you may.

3 CITIZEN   Are you all resolved to give your voices?   35
      But that's no matter; the greater part carries it, I say. If
      he would incline to the people there was never a
      worthier man.

            Enter CORIOLANUS *in a gown of humility*
                  and a hat, with MENENIUS.

      Here he comes, and in the gown of humility. Mark his
      behaviour. We are not to stay all together, but to come   40
      by him where he stands, by ones, by twos, and by threes.
      He's to make his requests by particulars, wherein every
      one of us has a single honour in giving him our own
      voices with our own tongues. Therefore follow me, and
      I'll direct you how you shall go by him.   45
ALL   Content, content.   *Exeunt.*
MENENIUS
      O sir, you are not right. Have you not known
      The worthiest men have done't?
CORIOLANUS   What must I say?
      'I pray, sir'? Plague upon't, I cannot bring
      My tongue to such a pace. 'Look, sir, my wounds!   50
      I got them in my country's service, when
      Some certain of your brethren roared and ran
      From th' noise of our own drums.'
MENENIUS
      O me, the gods! You must not speak of that.
      You must desire them to think upon you.   55
CORIOLANUS   Think upon me? Hang 'em!
      I would they would forget me, like the virtues
      Which our divines lose by 'em.
MENENIUS   You'll mar all.
      I'll leave you. Pray you speak to 'em, I pray you,
      In wholesome manner.   *Exit.*

            Enter three of the Citizens.

CORIOLANUS   Bid them wash their faces   60
      And keep their teeth clean. So, here comes a brace.
      You know the cause, sir, of my standing here.
3 CITIZEN   We do, sir. Tell us what hath brought you
      to't.
CORIOLANUS   Mine own desert.   65
2 CITIZEN   Your own desert.
CORIOLANUS   Ay, but not mine own desire.
3 CITIZEN   How not your own desire?
CORIOLANUS   No, sir, 'twas never my desire yet to
      trouble the poor with begging.   70
3 CITIZEN   You must think, if we give you anything, we
      hope to gain by you.
CORIOLANUS   Well then, I pray, your price o'th'
      consulship?
1 CITIZEN   The price is to ask it kindly.   75
CORIOLANUS   Kindly, sir, I pray let me ha't. I have
      wounds to show you which shall be yours in private. [*to
      2 Citizen*] Your good voice, sir. What say you?
2 CITIZEN   You shall ha't, worthy sir.
CORIOLANUS   A match, sir. There's in all two worthy   80
      voices begged. I have your alms. Adieu.

3 CITIZEN   But this is something odd.

2 CITIZEN   An 'twere to give again – but 'tis no matter.

Exeunt the three Citizens.

Enter two other Citizens.

CORIOLANUS   Pray you now, if it may stand with the
85 tune of your voices that I may be consul, I have here
the customary gown.

4 CITIZEN   You have deserved nobly of your country,
and you have not deserved nobly.

CORIOLANUS   Your enigma?

90 4 CITIZEN   You have been a scourge to her enemies, you
have been a rod to her friends; you have not indeed
loved the common people.

CORIOLANUS   You should account me the more virtuous
that I have not been common in my love. I will, sir,
95 flatter my sworn brother, the people, to earn a dearer
estimation of them. 'Tis a condition they account
gentle; and, since the wisdom of their choice is rather
to have my hat than my heart, I will practise the
insinuating nod and be off to them most counterfeitly;
100 that is, sir, I will counterfeit the bewitchment of some
popular man and give it bountiful to the desirers.
Therefore, beseech you I may be consul.

5 CITIZEN   We hope to find you our friend, and therefore
give you our voices heartily.

105 4 CITIZEN   You have received many wounds for your
country.

CORIOLANUS   I will not seal your knowledge with
showing them. I will make much of your voices, and so
trouble you no farther.

110 BOTH CITIZENS   The gods give you joy, sir, heartily.

Exeunt Citizens.

CORIOLANUS   Most sweet voices.
Better it is to die, better to starve,
Than crave the hire which first we do deserve.
Why in this wolvish toge should I stand here
115 To beg of Hob and Dick that does appear
Their needless vouches? Custom calls me to't.
What custom wills in all things, should we do't,
The dust on antique time would lie unswept,
And mountainous error be too highly heaped
120 For truth to o'erpeer. Rather than fool it so,
Let the high office and the honour go
To one that would do thus. I am half through;
The one part suffered, the other will I do.

Enter three Citizens *more.*

Here come more voices.
125 Your voices? For your voices I have fought;
Watched for your voices; for your voices bear
Of wounds two dozen odd; battles thrice six
I have seen and heard of; for your voices
Have done many things, some less, some more.
130 Your voices? Indeed I would be consul.

6 CITIZEN   He has done nobly, and cannot go without
any honest man's voice.

7 CITIZEN   Therefore let him be consul. The gods give
him joy and make him good friend to the people!

ALL   Amen, amen. God save thee, noble consul!   135

CORIOLANUS   Worthy voices.   *Exeunt Citizens.*

Enter MENENIUS, *with* BRUTUS *and* SICINIUS.

MENENIUS
You have stood your limitation, and the tribunes
Endue you with the people's voice. Remains
That, in th'official marks invested, you
Anon do meet the Senate.

CORIOLANUS   Is this done?   140

SICINIUS   The custom of request you have discharged.
The people do admit you, and are summoned
To meet anon upon your approbation.

CORIOLANUS   Where? At the Senate-house?

SICINIUS   There, Coriolanus.

CORIOLANUS   May I change these garments?

SICINIUS   You may, sir.   145

CORIOLANUS
That I'll straight do, and, knowing myself again,
Repair to th' Senate-house.

MENENIUS
I'll keep you company. [*to the Tribunes*] Will you along?

BRUTUS   We stay here for the people.

SICINIUS   Fare you well.

Exeunt Coriolanus and Menenius.

He has it now; and by his looks, methinks,   150
'Tis warm at's heart.

BRUTUS   With a proud heart he wore
His humble weeds. Will you dismiss the people?

Enter the Plebeians.

SICINIUS
How now, my masters, have you chose this man?

1 CITIZEN   He has our voices, sir.

BRUTUS   We pray the gods he may deserve your loves.   155

2 CITIZEN   Amen, sir. To my poor unworthy notice,
He mocked us when he begged our voices.

3 CITIZEN   Certainly, he flouted us downright.

1 CITIZEN
No, 'tis his kind of speech; he did not mock us.

2 CITIZEN   Not one amongst us, save yourself, but says   160
He used us scornfully. He should have showed us
His marks of merit, wounds received for's country.

SICINIUS   Why, so he did, I am sure.

ALL THE CITIZENS   No, no; no man saw 'em.

3 CITIZEN
He said he had wounds which he could show in private,
And with his hat, thus waving it in scorn,   165
'I would be consul,' says he. 'Aged custom,
But by your voices, will not so permit me.
Your voices therefore.' When we granted that,
Here was, 'I thank you for your voices, thank you,
Your most sweet voices. Now you have left your voices,   170
I have no further with you.' Was not this mockery?

SICINIUS   Why either were you ignorant to see't,

Or, seeing it, of such childish friendliness
To yield your voices?

BRUTUS   Could you not have told him,
As you were lessoned: when he had no power,
But was a petty servant to the state,
He was your enemy, ever spake against
Your liberties and the charters that you bear
I'th' body of the weal; and now arriving
A place of potency and sway o'th' state,
If he should still malignantly remain
Fast foe to th' plebeii, your voices might
Be curses to yourselves? You should have said
That, as his worthy deeds did claim no less
Than what he stood for, so his gracious nature
Would think upon you for your voices and
Translate his malice towards you into love,
Standing your friendly lord.

SICINIUS   Thus to have said,
As you were fore-advised, had touched his spirit
And tried his inclination, from him plucked
Either his gracious promise, which you might,
As cause had called you up, have held him to,
Or else it would have galled his surly nature
Which easily endures not article
Tying him to aught. So putting him to rage,
You should have ta'en th'advantage of his choler
And passed him unelected.

BRUTUS   Did you perceive
He did solicit you in free contempt
When he did need your loves, and do you think
That his contempt shall not be bruising to you
When he hath power to crush? Why, had your bodies
No heart among you? Or had you tongues to cry
Against the rectorship of judgement?

SICINIUS   Have you,
Ere now, denied the asker, and now again,
Of him that did not ask but mock, bestow
Your sued-for tongues?

3 CITIZEN   He's not confirmed; we may deny him yet.

2 CITIZEN   And will deny him!
I'll have five hundred voices of that sound.

1 CITIZEN
I twice five hundred, and their friends to piece 'em.

BRUTUS   Get you hence instantly, and tell those friends
They have chose a consul that will from them take
Their liberties, make them of no more voice
Than dogs that are as often beat for barking
As therefore kept to do so.

SICINIUS   Let them assemble,
And on a safer judgement all revoke
Your ignorant election. Enforce his pride
And his old hate unto you. Besides, forget not
With what contempt he wore the humble weed,
How in his suit he scorned you; but your loves,
Thinking upon his services, took from you
Th'apprehension of his present portance,
Which most gibingly, ungravely he did fashion

175

180

185

190

195

200

205

210

215

220

After the inveterate hate he bears you.

BRUTUS   Lay
A fault on us, your tribunes; that we laboured
No impediment between, but that you must
Cast your election on him.

SICINIUS   Say you chose him
More after our commandment than as guided
By your own true affections, and that your minds
Preoccupied with what you rather must do
Than what you should, made you against the grain
To voice him consul. Lay the fault on us.

BRUTUS   Ay, spare us not. Say we read lectures to you,
How youngly he began to serve his country,
How long continued, and what stock he springs of,
The noble house o'th' Martians, from whence came
That Ancus Martius, Numa's daughter's son,
Who after great Hostilius here was king,
Of the same house Publius and Quintus were,
That our best water brought by conduits hither;
And Censorinus that was so surnamed,
And nobly named so, twice being censor,
Was his great ancestor.

SICINIUS   One thus descended,
That hath beside well in his person wrought
To be set high in place, we did commend
To your remembrances. But you have found,
Scaling his present bearing with his past,
That he's your fixed enemy, and revoke
Your sudden approbation.

BRUTUS   Say you ne'er had done't –
Harp on that still – but by our putting on;
And presently, when you have drawn your number,
Repair to th' Capitol.

ALL CITIZENS   We will so. Almost all
Repent in their election.   *Exeunt Plebeians.*

BRUTUS   Let them go on.
This mutiny were better put in hazard
Than stay, past doubt, for greater.
If, as his nature is, he fall in rage
With their refusal, both observe and answer
The vantage of his anger.

SICINIUS   To th' Capitol, come.
We will be there before the stream o'th' people,
And this shall seem, as partly 'tis, their own,
Which we have goaded onward.   *Exeunt.*

225

230

235

240

245

250

255

260

3.1   *Cornets. Enter* CORIOLANUS, MENENIUS, *all
the gentry,* COMINIUS, Titus LARTIUS *and other*
Senators.

CORIOLANUS   Tullus Aufidius then had made new head?

LARTIUS
He had, my lord, and that it was which caused
Our swifter composition.

CORIOLANUS   So then the Volsces stand but as at first,
Ready, when time shall prompt them, to make road
Upon's again.

5

COMINIUS   They are worn, lord consul, so
　　That we shall hardly in our ages see
　　Their banners wave again.

CORIOLANUS [*to Lartius*]   Saw you Aufidius?

LARTIUS   On safeguard he came to me, and did curse
　　Against the Volsces for they had so vilely
　　Yielded the town. He is retired to Antium.

CORIOLANUS   Spoke he of me?

LARTIUS   He did, my lord.

CORIOLANUS   How? What?

LARTIUS   How often he had met you sword to sword;
　　That of all things upon the earth he hated
　　Your person most; that he would pawn his fortunes
　　To hopeless restitution, so he might
　　Be called your vanquisher.

CORIOLANUS   At Antium lives he?

LARTIUS   At Antium.

CORIOLANUS   I wish I had a cause to seek him there,
　　To oppose his hatred fully. Welcome home.

　　Enter SICINIUS *and* BRUTUS.

　　Behold, these are the tribunes of the people,
　　The tongues o'th' common mouth. I do despise them,
　　For they do prank them in authority
　　Against all noble sufferance.

SICINIUS   Pass no further.

CORIOLANUS   Ha? What is that?

BRUTUS   It will be dangerous to go on. No further.

CORIOLANUS   What makes this change?

MENENIUS   The matter?

COMINIUS
　　Hath he not passed the noble and the common?

BRUTUS   Cominius, no.

CORIOLANUS   Have I had children's voices?

1 SENATOR
　　Tribunes, give way: he shall to th' market-place.

BRUTUS   The people are incensed against him.

SICINIUS   Stop,
　　Or all will fall in broil.

CORIOLANUS   Are these your herd?
　　Must these have voices, that can yield them now
　　And straight disclaim their tongues? What are your
　　　offices?
　　You being their mouths, why rule you not their teeth?
　　Have you not set them on?

MENENIUS   Be calm, be calm.

CORIOLANUS   It is a purposed thing and grows by plot
　　To curb the will of the nobility.
　　Suffer't, and live with such as cannot rule
　　Nor ever will be ruled.

BRUTUS   Call't not a plot.
　　The people cry you mocked them, and of late,
　　When corn was given them gratis, you repined,
　　Scandalled the suppliants for the people, called them
　　Time-pleasers, flatterers, foes to nobleness.

CORIOLANUS   Why, this was known before.

BRUTUS   Not to them all.

CORIOLANUS   Have you informed them sithence?

BRUTUS   How? I inform them?

COMINIUS   You are like to do such business.

BRUTUS   Not unlike each way to better yours.

CORIOLANUS
　　Why then should I be consul? By yon clouds
　　Let me deserve so ill as you, and make me
　　Your fellow tribune.

SICINIUS   You show too much of that
　　For which the people stir. If you will pass
　　To where you are bound, you must enquire your way,
　　Which you are out of, with a gentler spirit,
　　Or never be so noble as a consul,
　　Nor yoke with him for tribune.

MENENIUS   Let's be calm.

COMINIUS
　　The people are abused. Set on! This paltering
　　Becomes not Rome, nor has Coriolanus
　　Deserved this so dishonoured rub, laid falsely
　　I'th' plain way of his merit.

CORIOLANUS   Tell me of corn!
　　This was my speech, and I will speak't again.

MENENIUS   Not now, not now.

1 SENATOR   Not in this heat, sir, now.

CORIOLANUS   Now as I live,
　　I will. My nobler friends, I crave their pardons.
　　For the mutable, rank-scented meinie, let them
　　Regard me, as I do not flatter, and
　　Therein behold themselves. I say again,
　　In soothing them we nourish 'gainst our Senate
　　The cockle of rebellion, insolence, sedition,
　　Which we ourselves have ploughed for, sowed and
　　　scattered,
　　By mingling them with us, the honoured number,
　　Who lack not virtue, no, nor power, but that
　　Which they have given to beggars.

MENENIUS   Well, no more.

1 SENATOR   No more words, we beseech you.

CORIOLANUS   How? No more?
　　As for my country I have shed my blood,
　　Not fearing outward force, so shall my lungs
　　Coin words till their decay against those measles
　　Which we disdain should tetter us, yet sought
　　The very way to catch them.

BRUTUS   You speak o'th' people as if you were a god
　　To punish, not a man of their infirmity.

SICINIUS   'Twere well we let the people know't.

MENENIUS   What, what? His choler?

CORIOLANUS
　　Choler? Were I as patient as the midnight sleep,
　　By Jove, 'twould be my mind.

SICINIUS   It is a mind that shall remain a poison
　　Where it is, not poison any further.

CORIOLANUS   'Shall remain'?
　　Hear you this Triton of the minnows? Mark you
　　His absolute 'shall'?

COMINIUS   'Twas from the canon.

CORIOLANUS   'Shall'?
O good but most unwise patricians, why,
You grave but reckless senators, have you thus
Given Hydra here to choose an officer
95   That with his peremptory 'shall', being but
The horn and noise o'th' monster's, wants not spirit
To say he'll turn your current in a ditch
And make your channel his? If he have power,
Then vail your ignorance; if none, awake
100 Your dangerous lenity. If you are learned,
Be not as common fools; if you are not,
Let them have cushions by you. You are plebeians,
If they be senators, and they are no less
When, both your voices blended, the great'st taste
105 Most palates theirs. They choose their magistrate,
And such a one as he, who puts his 'shall',
His popular 'shall', against a graver bench
Than ever frowned in Greece. By Jove himself,
It makes the consuls base; and my soul aches
110 To know, when two authorities are up,
Neither supreme, how soon confusion
May enter 'twixt the gap of both and take
The one by th'other.
COMINIUS   Well, on to th' market-place.
CORIOLANUS   Whoever gave that counsel to give forth
115 The corn o'th' storehouse gratis, as 'twas used
Sometime in Greece –
MENENIUS   Well, well, no more of that.
CORIOLANUS
Though there the people had more absolute power –
I say they nourished disobedience, fed
The ruin of the state.
BRUTUS   Why shall the people give
One that speaks thus their voice?
120 CORIOLANUS   I'll give my reasons,
More worthier than their voices. They know the corn
Was not our recompense, resting well assured
They ne'er did service for't. Being pressed to th' war,
Even when the navel of the state was touched,
125 They would not thread the gates. This kind of service
Did not deserve corn gratis. Being i'th' war,
Their mutinies and revolts, wherein they showed
Most valour, spoke not for them. Th'accusation
Which they have often made against the Senate,
130 All cause unborn, could never be the native
Of our so frank donation. Well, what then?
How shall this bosom multiplied digest
The Senate's courtesy? Let deeds express
What's like to be their words: 'We did request it,
135 We are the greater poll, and in true fear
They gave us our demands.' Thus we debase
The nature of our seats, and make the rabble
Call our cares fears, which will in time
Break ope the locks o'th' Senate and bring in
The crows to peck the eagles.
140 MENENIUS   Come, enough.
BRUTUS   Enough, with over-measure.

CORIOLANUS   No, take more.
What may be sworn by, both divine and human,
Seal what I end withal! This double worship,
Where one part does disdain with cause, the other
Insult without all reason, where gentry, title, wisdom   145
Cannot conclude but by the yea and no
Of general ignorance, it must omit
Real necessities, and give way the while
To unstable slightness. Purpose so barred, it follows
Nothing is done to purpose. Therefore beseech you –   150
You that will be less fearful than discreet,
That love the fundamental part of state
More than you doubt the change on't, that prefer
A noble life before a long, and wish
To jump a body with a dangerous physic   155
That's sure of death without it – at once pluck out
The multitudinous tongue; let them not lick
The sweet which is their poison. Your dishonour
Mangles true judgement, and bereaves the state
Of that integrity which should become't,   160
Not having the power to do the good it would
For th'ill which doth control't.
BRUTUS   He's said enough.
SICINIUS   He's spoken like a traitor, and shall answer
As traitors do.
CORIOLANUS   Thou wretch, despite o'erwhelm thee!
What should the people do with these bald tribunes,   165
On whom depending, their obedience fails
To th' greater bench? In a rebellion,
When what's not meet but what must be was law,
Then were they chosen. In a better hour
Let what is meet be said it must be meet,   170
And throw their power i'th' dust.
BRUTUS   Manifest treason.
SICINIUS   This a consul? No.
BRUTUS   The aediles, ho!

Enter an Aedile.

              Let him be apprehended.
SICINIUS   Go call the people –   *Exit Aedile.*
[*to Coriolanus*]   in whose name myself
Attach thee as a traitorous innovator,   175
A foe to th' public weal. Obey, I charge thee,
And follow to thine answer.
CORIOLANUS   Hence, old goat.
ALL THE PATRICIANS   We'll surety him.
COMINIUS [*to Sicinius*]   Aged sir, hands off.
CORIOLANUS [*to Sicinius*]
Hence, rotten thing, or I shall shake thy bones
Out of thy garments.
SICINIUS   Help ye, citizens!   180

Enter a rabble of Citizens *with the* Aediles.

MENENIUS   On both sides more respect.
SICINIUS
Here's he that would take from you all your power.
BRUTUS   Seize him, aediles.

ALL CITIZENS   Down with him! Down with him!
185 2 SENATOR   Weapons, weapons, weapons!
      [*They all bustle about Coriolanus.*]
ALL   Tribunes! Patricians! Citizens! What ho!
      Sicinius! Brutus! Coriolanus! Citizens!
      Peace! Peace! Peace! Stay! Hold! Peace!
MENENIUS   What is about to be? I am out of breath.
190 Confusion's near. I cannot speak. – You, tribunes,
      To th' people! Coriolanus, patience!
      Speak, good Sicinius.
SICINIUS   Hear me, people, peace!
ALL CITIZENS
      Let's hear our tribune! Peace! Speak, speak, speak.
SICINIUS   You are at point to lose your liberties.
195 Martius would have all from you, Martius
      Whom late you have named for consul.
MENENIUS   Fie, fie, fie!
      This is the way to kindle, not to quench.
1 SENATOR   To unbuild the city and to lay all flat.
SICINIUS   What is the city but the people?
200 ALL CITIZENS   True, the people are the city.
BRUTUS   By the consent of all, we were established
      The people's magistrates.
ALL CITIZENS   You so remain.
MENENIUS   And so are like to do.
205 COMINIUS   That is the way to lay the city flat,
      To bring the roof to the foundation,
      And bury all which yet distinctly ranges
      In heaps and piles of ruin.
SICINIUS   This deserves death.
BRUTUS   Or let us stand to our authority,
210 Or let us lose it. We do here pronounce,
      Upon the part o'th' people, in whose power
      We were elected theirs, Martius is worthy
      Of present death.
SICINIUS   Therefore lay hold of him,
      Bear him to th' rock Tarpeian, and from thence
      Into destruction cast him.
215 BRUTUS   Aediles, seize him.
ALL CITIZENS   Yield, Martius, yield.
MENENIUS   Hear me one word.
      Beseech you, tribunes, hear me but a word.
AEDILES   Peace, peace!
MENENIUS
      Be that you seem, truly your country's friend,
220 And temperately proceed to what you would
      Thus violently redress.
BRUTUS   Sir, those cold ways
      That seem like prudent helps are very poisonous
      Where the disease is violent. Lay hands upon him
      And bear him to the rock.
      [*Coriolanus draws his sword.*]
CORIOLANUS   No, I'll die here.
225 There's some among you have beheld me fighting.
      Come try upon yourselves what you have seen me.
MENENIUS
      Down with that sword! Tribunes, withdraw a while.

BRUTUS   Lay hands upon him.
MENENIUS   Help Martius, help,
      You that be noble, help him young and old!
ALL CITIZENS   Down with him, down with him!   230
      In this mutiny the Tribunes, the Aediles
            and the people are beat in and exeunt.
MENENIUS [*to Coriolanus*]
      Go, get you to your house. Be gone, away!
      All will be naught else.
2 SENATOR [*to Coriolanus*]   Get you gone.
CORIOLANUS   Stand fast.
      We have as many friends as enemies.
MENENIUS   Shall it be put to that?
1 SENATOR   The gods forbid!
      [*to Coriolanus*] I prithee, noble friend, home to thy
            house.   235
      Leave us to cure this cause.
MENENIUS   For 'tis a sore
      Upon us you cannot tent yourself.
      Be gone, beseech you.
COMINIUS   Come, sir, along with us.
CORIOLANUS
      I would they were barbarians, as they are,
      Though in Rome littered; not Romans, as they are
            not,   240
      Though calved i'th' porch o'th' Capitol.
MENENIUS   Be gone,
      Put not your worthy rage into your tongue.
      One time will owe another.
CORIOLANUS
      On fair ground I could beat forty of them.
MENENIUS   I could myself take up a brace o'th' best   245
      Of them, yea, the two tribunes!
COMINIUS   But now 'tis odds beyond arithmetic,
      And manhood is called foolery when it stands
      Against a falling fabric. [*to Coriolanus*] Will you hence,
      Before the tag return, whose rage doth rend   250
      Like interrupted waters, and o'erbear
      What they are used to bear?
MENENIUS [*to Coriolanus*]   Pray you, be gone.
      I'll try whether my old wit be in request
      With those that have but little. This must be patched
      With cloth of any colour.
COMINIUS   Nay, come away.   255
            Exeunt Coriolanus and Cominius.
PATRICIAN   This man has marred his fortune.
MENENIUS   His nature is too noble for the world.
      He would not flatter Neptune for his trident,
      Or Jove for's power to thunder. His heart's his mouth.
      What his breast forges that his tongue must vent,   260
      And, being angry, does forget that ever
      He heard the name of death.   [*A noise within*]
      Here's goodly work!
PATRICIAN   I would they were abed!
MENENIUS
      I would they were in Tiber! What the vengeance,
      Could he not speak 'em fair?

Enter BRUTUS *and* SICINIUS *with the rabble*
of Citizens *again.*

265 SICINIUS   Where is this viper,
     That would depopulate the city, and
     Be every man himself?
MENENIUS   You worthy tribunes –
SICINIUS   He shall be thrown down the Tarpeian rock
     With rigorous hands. He hath resisted law,
270   And therefore law shall scorn him further trial
     Than the severity of the public power,
     Which he so sets at naught.
1 CITIZEN   He shall well know
     The noble tribunes are the people's mouths
     And we their hands.
ALL CITIZENS   He shall, sure on't.
MENENIUS   Sir, sir!
275 SICINIUS   Peace!
MENENIUS
     Do not cry havoc where you should but hunt
     With modest warrant.
SICINIUS   Sir, how comes't that you
     Have holp to make this rescue?
MENENIUS   Hear me speak!
     As I do know the consul's worthiness,
     So can I name his faults.
280 SICINIUS   Consul? What consul?
MENENIUS   The consul Coriolanus.
BRUTUS   He consul!
ALL CITIZENS   No, no, no, no, no.
MENENIUS
     If by the tribunes' leave and yours, good people,
     I may be heard, I would crave a word or two,
285   The which shall turn you to no further harm
     Than so much loss of time.
SICINIUS   Speak briefly then,
     For we are peremptory to dispatch
     This viperous traitor. To eject him hence
     Were but one danger, and to keep him here
290   Our certain death. Therefore it is decreed
     He dies tonight.
MENENIUS   Now the good gods forbid
     That our renowned Rome, whose gratitude
     Towards her deserved children is enrolled
     In Jove's own book, like an unnatural dam
295   Should now eat up her own.
SICINIUS   He's a disease that must be cut away.
MENENIUS   O, he's a limb that has but a disease:
     Mortal to cut it off, to cure it easy.
     What has he done to Rome that's worthy death?
300   Killing our enemies, the blood he hath lost –
     Which I dare vouch is more than that he hath
     By many an ounce – he dropped it for his country;
     And what is left, to lose it by his country
     Were to us all that do't and suffer it
     A brand to th'end o'th' world.
305 SICINIUS   This is clean cam.

BRUTUS   Merely awry. When he did love his country
     It honoured him.
SICINIUS   The service of the foot,
     Being once gangrened, is not then respected
     For what before it was.
BRUTUS   We'll hear no more.
     [*to the Citizens*] Pursue him to his house and pluck
       him thence,   310
     Lest his infection, being of catching nature,
     Spread further.
MENENIUS   One word more, one word!
     This tiger-footed rage, when it shall find
     The harm of unscanned swiftness, will, too late,
     Tie leaden pounds to's heels. Proceed by process,   315
     Lest parties – as he is beloved – break out
     And sack great Rome with Romans.
BRUTUS   If it were so?
SICINIUS   What do ye talk?
     Have we not had a taste of his obedience?   320
     Our aediles smote, ourselves resisted? Come.
MENENIUS   Consider this: he has been bred i'th' wars
     Since 'a could draw a sword, and is ill-schooled
     In bolted language. Meal and bran together
     He throws without distinction. Give me leave,   325
     I'll go to him and undertake to bring him
     Where he shall answer by a lawful form –
     In peace – to his utmost peril.
1 SENATOR   Noble tribunes,
     It is the humane way. The other course
     Will prove too bloody, and the end of it   330
     Unknown to the beginning.
SICINIUS   Noble Menenius,
     Be you then as the people's officer.
     [*to the Citizens*] Masters, lay down your weapons.
BRUTUS   Go not home.
SICINIUS   Meet on the market-place.
     [*to Menenius*]   We'll attend you there,
     Where if you bring not Martius, we'll proceed   335
     In our first way.
MENENIUS   I'll bring him to you.
     [*to the Senators*] Let me desire your company. He
       must come,
     Or what is worst will follow.
1 SENATOR   Pray you, let's to him.   *Exeunt.*

3.2   *Enter* CORIOLANUS *with* Nobles.

CORIOLANUS
     Let them pull all about mine ears, present me
     Death on the wheel or at wild horses' heels,
     Or pile ten hills on the Tarpeian rock,
     That the precipitation might down stretch
     Below the beam of sight, yet will I still   5
     Be thus to them.

Enter VOLUMNIA.

NOBLE   You do the nobler.

CORIOLANUS   I muse my mother
    Does not approve me further, who was wont
10   To call them woollen vassals, things created
    To buy and sell with groats, to show bare heads
    In congregations, to yawn, be still and wonder
    When one but of my ordinance stood up
    To speak of peace or war. [*to Volumnia*] I talk of you.
15   Why did you wish me milder? Would you have me
    False to my nature? Rather say I play
    The man I am.
VOLUMNIA   O sir, sir, sir,
    I would have had you put your power well on
    Before you had worn it out.
CORIOLANUS   Let't go.
VOLUMNIA
20   You might have been enough the man you are
    With striving less to be so. Lesser had been
    The tryings of your dispositions, if
    You had not showed them how ye were disposed
    Ere they lacked power to cross you.
CORIOLANUS   Let them hang.
25 VOLUMNIA   Ay, and burn too.

Enter MENENIUS *with the* Senators.

MENENIUS
    Come, come, you have been too rough, something too
      rough.
    You must return and mend it.
1 SENATOR   There's no remedy,
    Unless by not so doing our good city
    Cleave in the midst and perish.
VOLUMNIA   Pray be counselled.
30   I have a heart as little apt as yours,
    But yet a brain that leads my use of anger
    To better vantage.
MENENIUS   Well said, noble woman.
    Before he should thus stoop to th' herd, but that
    The violent fit o'th' time craves it as physic
35   For the whole state, I would put mine armour on
    Which I can scarcely bear.
CORIOLANUS   What must I do?
MENENIUS   Return to th' tribunes.
CORIOLANUS   Well, what then? what then?
MENENIUS   Repent what you have spoke.
CORIOLANUS   Fore them? I cannot do it to the gods,
    Must I then do't to them?
40 VOLUMNIA   You are too absolute,
    Though therein you can never be too noble
    But when extremities speak. I have heard you say,
    Honour and policy, like unsevered friends,
    I'th' war do grow together. Grant that, and tell me
45   In peace what each of them by th'other lose
    That they combine not there.
CORIOLANUS   Tush, tush!
MENENIUS   A good demand.
VOLUMNIA   If it be honour in your wars to seem
    The same you are not, which for your best ends

You adopt your policy, how is it less or worse
That it shall hold companionship in peace   50
With honour as in war, since that to both
It stands in like request?
CORIOLANUS   Why force you this?
VOLUMNIA   Because that now it lies you on to speak
    To th' people, not by your own instruction,
    Nor by th' matter which your heart prompts you,   55
    But with such words that are but roted in
    Your tongue, though but bastards and syllables
    Of no allowance to your bosom's truth.
    Now, this no more dishonours you at all
    Than to take in a town with gentle words,   60
    Which else would put you to your fortune and
    The hazard of much blood.
    I would dissemble with my nature where
    My fortunes and my friends at stake required
    I should do so in honour. I am in this   65
    Your wife, your son, these senators, the nobles;
    And you will rather show our general louts
    How you can frown than spend a fawn upon 'em
    For the inheritance of their loves and safeguard
    Of what that want might ruin.
MENENIUS   Noble lady!   70
    [*to Coriolanus*] Come, go with us, speak fair. You may
      salve so
    Not what is dangerous present but the loss
    Of what is past.
VOLUMNIA   I prithee now, my son,
    Go to them, with this bonnet in thy hand,
    And thus far having stretched it – here be with them –   75
    Thy knee bussing the stones – for in such business
    Action is eloquence and the eyes of th'ignorant
    More learned than the ears – waving thy head,
    Which often thus correcting thy stout heart,
    Now humble as the ripest mulberry   80
    That will not hold the handling; or say to them
    Thou art their soldier and, being bred in broils,
    Hast not the soft way which, thou dost confess,
    Were fit for thee to use as they to claim
    In asking their good loves, but thou wilt frame   85
    Thyself, forsooth, hereafter theirs so far
    As thou hast power and person.
MENENIUS   This but done
    Even as she speaks, why, their hearts were yours,
    For they have pardons, being asked, as free
    As words to little purpose.
VOLUMNIA   Prithee now,   90
    Go and be ruled, although I know thou hadst rather
    Follow thine enemy in a fiery gulf
    Than flatter him in a bower.

Enter COMINIUS.

          Here is Cominius.
COMINIUS
    I have been i'th' market-place; and, sir, 'tis fit
    You make strong party or defend yourself   95

By calmness or by absence. All's in anger.

MENENIUS   Only fair speech.

COMINIUS   I think 'twill serve, if he
Can thereto frame his spirit.

VOLUMNIA   He must and will.
[*to Coriolanus*] Prithee now, say you will and go
    about it.

CORIOLANUS

100 Must I go show them my unbarbed sconce?
Must I with my base tongue give to my noble heart
A lie that it must bear? Well, I will do't.
Yet were there but this single plot to lose,
This mould of Martius, they to dust should grind it
105 And throw't against the wind. To th' market-place!
You have put me now to such a part which never
I shall discharge to th' life.

COMINIUS   Come, come, we'll prompt you.

VOLUMNIA   I prithee now, sweet son, as thou hast said
My praises made thee first a soldier, so,
110 To have my praise for this, perform a part
Thou hast not done before.

CORIOLANUS   Well, I must do't.
Away my disposition and possess me
Some harlot's spirit! My throat of war be turned,
Which choired with my drum, into a pipe
115 Small as an eunuch or the virgin voice
That babies lull asleep! The smiles of knaves
Tent in my cheeks, and schoolboys' tears take up
The glasses of my sight! A beggar's tongue
Make motion through my lips and my armed knees
120 Who bowed but in my stirrup bend like his
That hath received an alms! – I will not do't,
Lest I surcease to honour mine own truth
And by my body's action teach my mind
A most inherent baseness.

VOLUMNIA   At thy choice then!
125 To beg of thee it is my more dishonour
Than thou of them. Come all to ruin. Let
Thy mother rather feel thy pride than fear
Thy dangerous stoutness, for I mock at death
With as big heart as thou. Do as thou list.
130 Thy valiantness was mine, thou suck'st it from me,
But owe thy pride thyself.

CORIOLANUS   Pray be content.
Mother, I am going to the market-place.
Chide me no more. I'll mountebank their loves,
Cog their hearts from them and come home beloved
135 Of all the trades in Rome. Look, I am going.
Commend me to my wife. I'll return consul
Or never trust to what my tongue can do
I'th' way of flattery further.

VOLUMNIA   Do your will.   *Exit.*

COMINIUS

Away! The tribunes do attend you. Arm yourself
140 To answer mildly, for they are prepared
With accusations, as I hear, more strong
Than are upon you yet.

CORIOLANUS   The word is 'mildly'. Pray you, let us go.
Let them accuse me by invention, I
Will answer in mine honour.

MENENIUS   Ay, but mildly.   145

CORIOLANUS   Well, 'mildly' be it then, 'mildly'.
                                                Exeunt.

3.3   *Enter* SICINIUS *and* BRUTUS.

BRUTUS   In this point charge him home: that he affects
Tyrannical power. If he evade us there,
Enforce him with his envy to the people,
And that the spoil got on the Antiates
Was ne'er distributed.

                    Enter an Aedile.

                        What, will he come?   5

AEDILE   He's coming.

BRUTUS   How accompanied?

AEDILE   With old Menenius and those senators
That always favoured him.

SICINIUS   Have you a catalogue
Of all the voices that we have procured,
Set down by th' poll?

AEDILE   I have, 'tis ready.   10

SICINIUS   Have you collected them by tribes?

AEDILE   I have.

SICINIUS   Assemble presently the people hither,
And when they hear me say, 'It shall be so,
I'th' right and strength o'th' commons', be it either
For death, for fine or banishment, then let them,   15
If I say 'Fine', cry 'Fine', if 'Death', cry 'Death',
Insisting on the old prerogative
And power i'th' truth o'th' cause.

AEDILE   I shall inform them.

BRUTUS   And when such time they have begun to cry
Let them not cease but with a din confused   20
Enforce the present execution
Of what we chance to sentence.

AEDILE   Very well.

SICINIUS   Make them be strong and ready for this hint
When we shall hap to give't them.

BRUTUS   Go, about it.   *Exit Aedile.*
Put him to choler straight. He hath been used   25
Ever to conquer and to have his worth
Of contradiction. Being once chafed, he cannot
Be reined again to temperance; then he speaks
What's in his heart, and that is there which looks
With us to break his neck.   30

SICINIUS   Well, here he comes.

            Enter CORIOLANUS, MENENIUS *and* COMINIUS
                with other Senators *and Patricians.*

MENENIUS [*to Coriolanus*]   Calmly, I do beseech you.

CORIOLANUS [*to Menenius*]
Ay, as an hostler that for th' poorest piece
Will bear the knave by th' volume.

[*aloud*] Th' honoured gods
Keep Rome in safety and the chairs of justice
35 Supplied with worthy men, plant love among's,
Throng our large temples with the shows of peace
And not our streets with war.
1 SENATOR Amen, Amen.
MENENIUS A noble wish.

Enter the Aedile *with the* Citizens.

SICINIUS Draw near, ye people.
AEDILE List to your tribunes. Audience!
Peace, I say!
CORIOLANUS First hear me speak.
40 BOTH TRIBUNES Well, say. – Peace ho!
CORIOLANUS
Shall I be charged no further than this present?
Must all determine here?
SICINIUS I do demand
If you submit you to the people's voices,
Allow their officers and are content
45 To suffer lawful censure for such faults
As shall be proved upon you.
CORIOLANUS I am content.
MENENIUS Lo, citizens, he says he is content.
The warlike service he has done, consider. Think
Upon the wounds his body bears, which show
Like graves i'th' holy churchyard.
50 CORIOLANUS Scratches with briars,
Scars to move laughter only.
MENENIUS Consider further
That when he speaks not like a citizen,
You find him like a soldier. Do not take
His rougher accents for malicious sounds,
55 But, as I say, such as become a soldier
Rather than envy you.
COMINIUS Well, well, no more.
CORIOLANUS What is the matter
That, being passed for consul with full voice,
I am so dishonoured that the very hour
You take it off again?
60 SICINIUS Answer to us.
CORIOLANUS Say then! 'Tis true, I ought so.
SICINIUS
We charge you that you have contrived to take
From Rome all seasoned office and to wind
Yourself into a power tyrannical,
65 For which you are a traitor to the people.
CORIOLANUS How? 'Traitor'?
MENENIUS Nay, temperately – your promise!
CORIOLANUS
The fires i'th' lowest hell fold in the people!
Call me their traitor, thou injurious tribune!
Within thine eyes sat twenty thousand deaths,
70 In thy hands clutched as many millions, in
Thy lying tongue both numbers, I would say
'Thou liest' unto thee, with a voice as free,
As I do pray the gods.

SICINIUS Mark you this, people?
ALL CITIZENS To th' rock, to th' rock with him!
75 SICINIUS Peace!
We need not put new matter to his charge.
What you have seen him do and heard him speak,
Beating your officers, cursing yourselves,
Opposing laws with strokes, and here defying
80 Those whose great power must try him – even this
So criminal and in such capital kind
Deserves th'extremest death.
BRUTUS But since he hath
Served well for Rome –
CORIOLANUS What do you prate of service?
BRUTUS I talk of that that know it.
CORIOLANUS You?
MENENIUS
85 Is this the promise that you made your mother?
COMINIUS Know, I pray you –
CORIOLANUS I'll know no further.
Let them pronounce the steep Tarpeian death,
Vagabond exile, flaying, pent to linger
But with a grain a day, I would not buy
90 Their mercy at the price of one fair word,
Nor check my courage for what they can give,
To have't with saying 'Good morrow'.
SICINIUS For that he has,
As much as in him lies, from time to time
Inveighed against the people, seeking means
95 To pluck away their power – as now at last
Given hostile strokes and that not in the presence
Of dreaded justice but on the ministers
That doth distribute it – in the name o'th' people
And in the power of us the tribunes, we,
100 E'en from this instant, banish him our city
In peril of precipitation
From off the rock Tarpeian, never more
To enter our Rome gates. I'th' people's name
I say it shall be so.
ALL CITIZENS
105 It shall be so, it shall be so! Let him away!
He's banished and it shall be so!
COMINIUS
Hear me, my masters and my common friends.
SICINIUS He's sentenced. No more hearing.
COMINIUS Let me speak.
I have been consul and can show for Rome
110 Her enemies' marks upon me. I do love
My country's good with a respect more tender,
More holy and profound than mine own life,
My dear wife's estimate, her womb's increase
And treasure of my loins. Then if I would
Speak that –
115 SICINIUS We know your drift. Speak what?
BRUTUS There's no more to be said, but he is banished
As enemy to the people and his country.
It shall be so.
ALL CITIZENS It shall be so, it shall be so!

CORIOLANUS
You common cry of curs whose breath I hate
120   As reek o'th' rotten fens, whose loves I prize
As the dead carcasses of unburied men,
That do corrupt my air, I banish you.
And here remain with your uncertainty!
Let every feeble rumour shake your hearts;
125   Your enemies with nodding of their plumes
Fan you into despair! Have the power still
To banish your defenders till at length
Your ignorance – which finds not till it feels,
Making but reservation of yourselves,
130   Still your own foes – deliver you as most
Abated captives to some nation
That won you without blows! Despising
For you the city, thus I turn my back.
There is a world elsewhere.

Exeunt Coriolanus, Cominius, Menenius
with the other Senators and Patricians.
[*The citizens all shout and throw up their caps.*]

135   AEDILE   The people's enemy is gone, is gone!
ALL CITIZENS
Our enemy is banished, he is gone! Hoo! Hoo!
SICINIUS   Go see him out at gates and follow him,
As he hath followed you, with all despite.
Give him deserved vexation. Let a guard
140   Attend us through the city.
ALL CITIZENS
Come, come, let's see him out at gates, come.
The gods preserve our noble tribunes! Come. *Exeunt.*

4.1   *Enter* CORIOLANUS, VOLUMNIA,
VIRGILIA, MENENIUS, COMINIUS *with the*
young Nobility of Rome.

CORIOLANUS
Come, leave your tears. A brief farewell. The beast
With many heads butts me away. Nay, mother,
Where is your ancient courage? You were used
To say extremities was the trier of spirits;
5   That common chances common men could bear;
That when the sea was calm all boats alike
Showed mastership in floating; fortune's blows,
When most struck home, being gentle wounded craves
A noble cunning. You were used to load me
10   With precepts that would make invincible
The heart that conned them.
VIRGILIA   O heavens! O heavens!
CORIOLANUS   Nay, I prithee, woman.
VOLUMNIA
Now the red pestilence strike all trades in Rome
And occupations perish!
CORIOLANUS   What, what, what!
15   I shall be loved when I am lacked. Nay, mother,
Resume that spirit when you were wont to say,
If you had been the wife of Hercules,
Six of his labours you'd have done and saved

Your husband so much sweat. Cominius,
Droop not; adieu. Farewell, my wife, my mother.   20
I'll do well yet. Thou old and true Menenius,
Thy tears are salter than a younger man's
And venomous to thine eyes. My sometime general,
I have seen thee stern and thou hast oft beheld
Heart-hardening spectacles. Tell these sad women   25
'Tis fond to wail inevitable strokes
As 'tis to laugh at 'em. My mother, you wot well
My hazards still have been your solace and –
Believe't not lightly – though I go alone,
Like to a lonely dragon that his fen   30
Makes feared and talked of more than seen, your son
Will or exceed the common or be caught
With cautelous baits and practice.
VOLUMNIA   My first son,
Whither wilt thou go? Take good Cominius
With thee awhile. Determine on some course   35
More than a wild exposure to each chance
That starts i'th' way before thee.
CORIOLANUS   O the gods!
COMINIUS   I'll follow thee a month, devise with thee
Where thou shalt rest, that thou mayst hear of us
And we of thee. So, if the time thrust forth   40
A cause for thy repeal, we shall not send
O'er the vast world to seek a single man
And lose advantage which doth ever cool
I'th' absence of the needer.
CORIOLANUS   Fare ye well.
Thou hast years upon thee and thou art too full   45
Of the wars' surfeits to go rove with one
That's yet unbruised. Bring me but out at gate.
Come, my sweet wife, my dearest mother, and
My friends of noble touch. When I am forth
Bid me farewell and smile. I pray you, come.   50
While I remain above the ground you shall
Hear from me still and never of me aught
But what is like me formerly.
MENENIUS   That's worthily
As any ear can hear. Come, let's not weep.
If I could shake off but one seven years   55
From these old arms and legs, by the good gods
I'd with thee every foot.
CORIOLANUS   Give me thy hand.
Come.   *Exeunt.*

4.2   *Enter the two tribunes,* SICINIUS *and* BRUTUS,
with the Aedile.

SICINIUS [*to the Aedile*]
Bid them all home. He's gone, and we'll no further.
The nobility are vexed, whom we see have sided
In his behalf.
BRUTUS   Now we have shown our power,
Let us seem humbler after it is done
Than when it was a-doing.
SICINIUS [*to the Aedile*]   Bid them home.   5

Say their great enemy is gone, and they
Stand in their ancient strength.

BRUTUS   Dismiss them home.   *Exit Aedile.*
Here comes his mother.

     Enter VOLUMNIA, VIRGILIA *and* MENENIUS.

SICINIUS   Let's not meet her.
BRUTUS   Why?
SICINIUS   They say she's mad.
10   BRUTUS   They have ta'en note of us. Keep on your way.
VOLUMNIA
O, you're well met. Th' hoarded plague o'th' gods
Requite your love.
MENENIUS   Peace, peace, be not so loud.
VOLUMNIA
If that I could for weeping, you should hear –
Nay, and you shall hear some.
   [*to Sicinius*]   Will you be gone?
VIRGILIA [*to Brutus*]
15   You shall stay too! I would I had the power
To say so to my husband.
SICINIUS [*to Volumnia*]   Are you mankind?
VOLUMNIA   Ay, fool. Is that a shame? Note but this, fool:
Was not a man my father? Hadst thou foxship
To banish him that struck more blows for Rome
Than thou hast spoken words?
20   SICINIUS   O blessed heavens!
VOLUMNIA
More noble blows than ever thou wise words,
And for Rome's good. I'll tell thee what – yet go!
Nay, but thou shalt stay too. I would my son
Were in Arabia and thy tribe before him,
His good sword in his hand.
SICINIUS   What then?
25   VIRGILIA   What then?
He'd make an end of thy posterity.
VOLUMNIA   Bastards, and all.
Good man, the wounds that he does bear for Rome!
MENENIUS   Come, come, peace.
30   SICINIUS   I would he had continued to his country
As he began, and not unknit himself
The noble knot he made.
BRUTUS   I would he had.
VOLUMNIA
'I would he had'? 'Twas you incensed the rabble,
Cats, that can judge as fitly of his worth
35   As I can of those mysteries which heaven
Will not have earth to know.
BRUTUS [*to Sicinius*]   Pray, let's go.
VOLUMNIA   Now pray, sir, get you gone.
You have done a brave deed. Ere you go, hear this:
As far as doth the Capitol exceed
40   The meanest house in Rome, so far my son –
This lady's husband here, this, do you see? –
Whom you have banished does exceed you all.
BRUTUS   Well, well, we'll leave you.
SICINIUS   Why stay we to be baited

With one that wants her wits?   *Exeunt Tribunes.*
VOLUMNIA   Take my prayers with you.
I would the gods had nothing else to do   45
But to confirm my curses. Could I meet 'em
But once a day, it would unclog my heart
Of what lies heavy to't.
MENENIUS   You have told them home
And, by my troth, you have cause. You'll sup with me?
VOLUMNIA   Anger's my meat: I sup upon myself   50
And so shall starve with feeding.
   [*to Virgilia*]   Come, let's go.
Leave this faint puling and lament as I do,
In anger Juno-like. Come, come, come.
          Exeunt Volumnia and Virgilia.
MENENIUS   Fie, fie, fie.   *Exit.*

4.3   *Enter* NICANOR, *a Roman, and* ADRIAN,
          a Volsce.

NICANOR   I know you well, sir, and you know me. Your
name, I think, is Adrian.
ADRIAN   It is so, sir. Truly, I have forgot you.
NICANOR   I am a Roman, and my services are, as you
are, against 'em. Know you me yet?   5
ADRIAN   Nicanor, no?
NICANOR   The same, sir.
ADRIAN   You had more beard when I last saw you but
your favour is well appeared by your tongue. What's
the news in Rome? I have a note from the Volscian state   10
to find you out there. You have well saved me a day's
journey.
NICANOR   There hath been in Rome strange
insurrections, the people against the senators,
patricians and nobles.   15
ADRIAN   Hath been? Is it ended then? Our state thinks
not so. They are in a most warlike preparation, and
hope to come upon them in the heat of their division.
NICANOR   The main blaze of it is past but a small thing
would make it flame again, for the nobles receive so to   20
heart the banishment of that worthy Coriolanus that
they are in a ripe aptness to take all power from the
people and to pluck from them their tribunes for ever.
This lies glowing, I can tell you, and is almost mature
for the violent breaking out.   25
ADRIAN   Coriolanus banished?
NICANOR   Banished, sir.
ADRIAN   You will be welcome with this intelligence,
Nicanor.
NICANOR   The day serves well for them now. I have   30
heard it said the fittest time to corrupt a man's wife is
when she's fallen out with her husband. Your noble
Tullus Aufidius will appear well in these wars, his great
opposer Coriolanus being now in no request of his
country.   35
ADRIAN   He cannot choose. I am most fortunate thus
accidentally to encounter you. You have ended my
business, and I will merrily accompany you home.

NICANOR   I shall between this and supper tell you
most strange things from Rome, all tending to the
40
good of their adversaries. Have you an army ready,
say you?

ADRIAN   A most royal one: the centurions and their
charges distinctly billeted already in th'entertainment
45
and to be on foot at an hour's warning.

NICANOR   I am joyful to hear of their readiness and
am the man, I think, that shall set them in present
action. So, sir, heartily well met, and most glad of
your company.

ADRIAN   You take my part from me, sir. I have the most
50
cause to be glad of yours.

NICANOR   Well, let us go together.   *Exeunt.*

4.4   *Enter* CORIOLANUS *in mean apparel,*
disguised and muffled.

CORIOLANUS   A goodly city is this Antium. City,
'Tis I that made thy widows. Many an heir
Of these fair edifices fore my wars
Have I heard groan and drop. Then know me not,
5
Lest that thy wives with spits and boys with stones
In puny battle slay me.

Enter a Citizen.

Save you, sir.

CITIZEN
And you.

CORIOLANUS   Direct me, if it be your will,
Where great Aufidius lies. Is he in Antium?

CITIZEN
He is, and feasts the nobles of the state
At his house this night.

10
CORIOLANUS   Which is his house, beseech you?

CITIZEN   This here before you.

CORIOLANUS   Thank you, sir, farewell.   *Exit Citizen.*
O world, thy slippery turns! Friends now fast sworn,
Whose double bosoms seems to wear one heart,
15
Whose hours, whose bed, whose meal and exercise
Are still together, who twin, as 'twere, in love
Unseparable, shall within this hour,
On a dissension of a doit, break out
To bitterest enmity. So fellest foes,
20
Whose passions and whose plots have broke their sleep
To take the one the other, by some chance,
Some trick not worth an egg, shall grow dear friends
And interjoin their issues. So with me.
My birthplace hate I, and my love's upon
25
This enemy town. I'll enter. If he slay me
He does fair justice; if he give me way,
I'll do his country service.   *Exit.*

4.5   *Music plays. Enter first* Servingman.

1 SERVINGMAN   Wine, wine, wine! What service is
here? I think our fellows are asleep.   *Exit.*

Enter second Servingman.

2 SERVINGMAN   Where's Cotus? My master calls for
him. Cotus!   *Exit.*

Enter CORIOLANUS.

CORIOLANUS
A goodly house. The feast smells well, but I   5
Appear not like a guest.

Enter the first Servingman.

1 SERVINGMAN   What would you have, friend? Whence
are you? Here's no place for you. Pray go to the door!
Exit.

CORIOLANUS
I have deserved no better entertainment
In being Coriolanus.   10

Enter second Servingman.

2 SERVINGMAN   Whence are you, sir? Has the porter his
eyes in his head that he gives entrance to such
companions? Pray get you out.

CORIOLANUS   Away.

2 SERVINGMAN   Away? Get you away.   15

CORIOLANUS   Now thou'rt troublesome.

2 SERVINGMAN   Are you so brave? I'll have you talked
with anon.

Enter third Servingman.
The first meets him.

3 SERVINGMAN   What fellow's this?

1 SERVINGMAN   A strange one as ever I looked on. I   20
cannot get him out o'th' house. Prithee, call my master
to him.

3 SERVINGMAN   What have you to do here, fellow? Pray
you avoid the house.

CORIOLANUS
Let me but stand. I will not hurt your hearth.   25

3 SERVINGMAN   What are you?

CORIOLANUS   A gentleman.

3 SERVINGMAN   A marvellous poor one.

CORIOLANUS   True, so I am

3 SERVINGMAN   Pray you, poor gentleman, take up   30
some other station. Here's no place for you. Pray you,
avoid. Come.

CORIOLANUS   Follow your function. Go and batten on
cold bits. [*Pushes him away from him.*]

3 SERVINGMAN   What, you will not? – Prithee tell my   35
master what a strange guest he has here.

2 SERVINGMAN   And I shall.   *Exit.*

3 SERVINGMAN   Where dwell'st thou?

CORIOLANUS   Under the canopy.

3 SERVINGMAN   Under the canopy?   40

CORIOLANUS   Ay.

3 SERVINGMAN   Where's that?

CORIOLANUS   I'th' city of kites and crows.

3 SERVINGMAN I'th' city of kites and crows? What an
45 ass it is! Then thou dwell'st with daws too?
CORIOLANUS No, I serve not thy master.
3 SERVINGMAN How, sir? Do you meddle with my
master?
CORIOLANUS Ay, 'tis an honester service than to
50 meddle with thy mistress. Thou prat'st and prat'st.
Serve with thy trencher. Hence! [*Beats him away.*]
Exit third Servingman.

Enter AUFIDIUS *with the second* Servingman.

AUFIDIUS Where is this fellow?
2 SERVINGMAN Here, sir. I'd have beaten him like a dog
but for disturbing the lords within.
[*First and second Servingmen stand aside.*]
AUFIDIUS
55 Whence com'st thou? What wouldst thou? Thy name?
Why speak'st not? Speak, man. What's thy name?
CORIOLANUS [*unmuffling*] If, Tullus,
Not yet thou knowst me, and seeing me dost not
Think me for the man I am, necessity
Commands me name myself.
AUFIDIUS What is thy name?
60 CORIOLANUS A name unmusical to the Volscians' ears
And harsh in sound to thine.
AUFIDIUS Say, what's thy name?
Thou hast a grim appearance and thy face
Bears a command in't. Though thy tackle's torn,
Thou show'st a noble vessel. What's thy name?
CORIOLANUS
65 Prepare thy brow to frown. Knowst thou me yet?
AUFIDIUS I know thee not. Thy name?
CORIOLANUS
My name is Caius Martius who hath done
To thee particularly and to all the Volsces
Great hurt and mischief. Thereto witness may
70 My surname Coriolanus. The painful service,
The extreme dangers and the drops of blood
Shed for my thankless country are requited
But with that surname – a good memory
And witness of the malice and displeasure
75 Which thou shouldst bear me. Only that name remains.
The cruelty and envy of the people,
Permitted by our dastard nobles, who
Have all forsook me, hath devoured the rest,
And suffered me by th' voice of slaves to be
80 Whooped out of Rome. Now this extremity
Hath brought me to thy hearth, not out of hope –
Mistake me not – to save my life, for, if
I had feared death, of all the men i'th' world
I would have 'voided thee. But in mere spite
85 To be full quit of those my banishers
Stand I before thee here. Then if thou hast
A heart of wreak in thee that wilt revenge
Thine own particular wrongs and stop those maims
Of shame seen through thy country, speed thee
straight

And make my misery serve thy turn. So use it   90
That my revengeful services may prove
As benefits to thee, for I will fight
Against my cankered country with the spleen
Of all the under-fiends. But if so be
Thou dar'st not this, and that to prove more fortunes   95
Thou'rt tired, then, in a word, I also am
Longer to live most weary, and present
My throat to thee and to thy ancient malice,
Which not to cut would show thee but a fool,
Since I have ever followed thee with hate,   100
Drawn tuns of blood out of thy country's breast
And cannot live but to thy shame, unless
It be to do thee service.
AUFIDIUS O Martius, Martius!
Each word thou hast spoke hath weeded from my heart
A root of ancient envy. If Jupiter   105
Should from yon cloud speak divine things
And say ''Tis true', I'd not believe them more
Than thee, all-noble Martius. Let me twine
Mine arms about that body, where against
My grained ash an hundred times hath broke   110
And scarred the moon with splinters.
[*Embraces Coriolanus.*] Here I clip
The anvil of my sword and do contest
As hotly and as nobly with thy love
As ever in ambitious strength I did
Contend against thy valour. Know thou first,   115
I loved the maid I married; never man
Sighed truer breath. But that I see thee here,
Thou noble thing, more dances my rapt heart
Than when I first my wedded mistress saw
Bestride my threshold. Why, thou Mars, I tell thee   120
We have a power on foot, and I had purpose
Once more to hew thy target from thy brawn
Or lose mine arm for't. Thou hast beat me out
Twelve several times and I have nightly since
Dreamt of encounters 'twixt thyself and me –   125
We have been down together in my sleep,
Unbuckling helms, fisting each other's throat –
And waked half dead with nothing. Worthy Martius,
Had we no other quarrel else to Rome but that
Thou art thence banished, we would muster all   130
From twelve to seventy and, pouring war
Into the bowels of ungrateful Rome,
Like a bold flood o'erbear't. O, come, go in,
And take our friendly senators by th' hands
Who now are here taking their leaves of me   135
Who am prepared against your territories,
Though not for Rome itself.
CORIOLANUS You bless me, gods.
AUFIDIUS
Therefore, most absolute sir, if thou wilt have
The leading of thine own revenges, take
Th'one half of my commission and set down –   140
As best thou art experienced, since thou knowst
Thy country's strength and weakness – thine own ways:

Whether to knock against the gates of Rome
Or rudely visit them in parts remote
145 To fright them ere destroy. But come in.
Let me commend thee first to those that shall
Say yea to thy desires. A thousand welcomes!
And more a friend than ere an enemy;
Yet, Martius, that was much. Your hand. Most
welcome!   *Exeunt Coriolanus and Aufidius.*
[*First and second Servingmen come forward.*]

150 1 SERVINGMAN   Here's a strange alteration!

2 SERVINGMAN   By my hand, I had thought to have
strucken him with a cudgel and yet my mind gave me
his clothes made a false report of him.

1 SERVINGMAN   What an arm he has! He turned me
155 about with his finger and his thumb as one would set
up a top.

2 SERVINGMAN   Nay, I knew by his face that there was
something in him. He had, sir, a kind of face,
methought – I cannot tell how to term it.

160 1 SERVINGMAN   He had so, looking, as it were – would I
were hanged but I thought there was more in him than
I could think.

2 SERVINGMAN   So did I, I'll be sworn. He is simply the
rarest man i'th'world.

165 1 SERVINGMAN   I think he is; but a greater soldier than
he, you wot one.

2 SERVINGMAN   Who? My master?

1 SERVINGMAN   Nay, it's no matter for that.

2 SERVINGMAN   Worth six on him.

170 1 SERVINGMAN   Nay, not so neither; but I take him to
be the greater soldier.

2 SERVINGMAN   Faith, look you, one cannot tell how to
say that. For the defence of a town our general is
excellent.

175 1 SERVINGMAN   Ay, and for an assault too.

Enter the third Servingman.

3 SERVINGMAN   O slaves, I can tell you news, news, you
rascals.

1, 2 SERVINGMEN   What, what, what? Let's partake.

3 SERVINGMAN   I would not be a Roman of all nations.
180 I had as lief be a condemned man.

1, 2 SERVINGMEN   Wherefore? Wherefore?

3 SERVINGMAN   Why, here's he that was wont to thwack
our general, Caius Martius.

1 SERVINGMAN   Why do you say 'thwack our general'?

185 3 SERVINGMAN   I do not say 'thwack our general'; but
he was always good enough for him.

2 SERVINGMAN   Come, we are fellows and friends. He
was ever too hard for him. I have heard him say so
himself.

190 1 SERVINGMAN   He was too hard for him directly, to say
the truth on't. Before Corioles he scotched him and
notched him like a carbonado.

2 SERVINGMAN   An he had been cannibally given, he
might have boiled and eaten him too.

195 1 SERVINGMAN   But more of thy news.

3 SERVINGMAN   Why, he is so made on here within as if
he were son and heir to Mars, set at upper end o'th'
table, no question asked him by any of the senators but
they stand bald before him. Our general himself makes
a mistress of him, sanctifies himself with's hand and   200
turns up the white o'th' eye to his discourse. But the
bottom of the news is, our general is cut i'th' middle
and but one half of what he was yesterday, for the other
has half, by the entreaty and grant of the whole table.
He'll go, he says, and sowl the porter of Rome gates by   205
th'ears. He will mow all down before him, and leave his
passage polled.

2 SERVINGMAN   And he's as like to do't as any man I can
imagine.

3 SERVINGMAN   Do't? He will do't, for look you, sir, he   210
has as many friends as enemies, which friends, sir, as it
were, durst not, look you, sir, show themselves, as we
term it, his friends whilst he's in directitude.

1 SERVINGMAN   'Directitude'? What's that?

3 SERVINGMAN   But when they shall see, sir, his crest   215
up again and the man in blood, they will out of their
burrows like conies after rain and revel all with him.

1 SERVINGMAN   But when goes this forward?

3 SERVINGMAN   Tomorrow, today, presently. You shall
have the drum struck up this afternoon. 'Tis as it were   220
a parcel of their feast and to be executed ere they wipe
their lips.

2 SERVINGMAN   Why, then we shall have a stirring
world again. This peace is nothing, but to rust iron,
increase tailors and breed ballad-makers.   225

1 SERVINGMAN   Let me have war, say I. It exceeds peace
as far as day does night. It's sprightly walking, audible
and full of vent. Peace is a very apoplexy, lethargy,
mulled, deaf, sleepy, insensible, a getter of more
bastard children than war's a destroyer of men.   230

2 SERVINGMAN   'Tis so, and as wars in some sort may
be said to be a ravisher, so it cannot be denied but
peace is a great maker of cuckolds.

1 SERVINGMAN   Ay, and it makes men hate one another.

3 SERVINGMAN   Reason: because they then less need   235
one another. The wars for my money. I hope to see
Romans as cheap as Volscians. [*Sound within*] They are
rising, they are rising.

1, 2 SERVINGMEN   In, in, in, in.   *Exeunt.*

4.6   *Enter the two tribunes,* SICINIUS *and* BRUTUS.

SICINIUS
We hear not of him, neither need we fear him.
His remedies are tame, the present peace
And quietness of the people, which before
Were in wild hurry. Here do we make his friends
Blush that the world goes well, who rather had,   5
Though they themselves did suffer by't, behold
Dissentious numbers pestering streets than see
Our tradesmen singing in their shops and going
About their functions friendly.

BRUTUS   We stood to't in good time.

Enter MENENIUS.

10   Is this Menenius?

SICINIUS   'Tis he, 'tis he. O, he is grown most kind
  Of late. – Hail, sir!

MENENIUS   Hail to you both.

SICINIUS   Your Coriolanus is not much missed
  But with his friends. The commonwealth doth stand

15   And so would do were he more angry at it.

MENENIUS
  All's well and might have been much better if
  He could have temporized.

SICINIUS   Where is he, hear you?

MENENIUS   Nay, I hear nothing.
  His mother and his wife hear nothing from him.

Enter three or four Citizens.

ALL CITIZENS [*to the Tribunes*]
  The gods preserve you both.

20   SICINIUS   Good e'en, our neighbours.

BRUTUS   Good e'en to you all, good e'en to you all.

1 CITIZEN
  Ourselves, our wives and children, on our knees
  Are bound to pray for you both.

SICINIUS   Live and thrive.

BRUTUS   Farewell, kind neighbours.

25   We wished Coriolanus had loved you as we did.

ALL CITIZENS   Now the gods keep you!

BOTH TRIBUNES   Farewell, farewell. *Exeunt Citizens.*

SICINIUS   This is a happier and more comely time
  Than when these fellows ran about the streets
  Crying confusion.

BRUTUS   Caius Martius was

30   A worthy officer i'th' war, but insolent,
  O'ercome with pride, ambitious past all thinking,
  Self-loving.

SICINIUS   And affecting one sole throne
  Without assistance.

MENENIUS   I think not so.

SICINIUS   We should by this, to all our lamentation,

35   If he had gone forth consul found it so.

BRUTUS
  The gods have well prevented it and Rome
  Sits safe and still without him.

Enter an Aedile.

AEDILE   Worthy tribunes,
  There is a slave whom we have put in prison
  Reports the Volsces with two several powers

40   Are entered in the Roman territories
  And with the deepest malice of the war
  Destroy what lies before 'em.

MENENIUS   'Tis Aufidius,
  Who, hearing of our Martius' banishment,
  Thrusts forth his horns again into the world

45   Which were inshelled when Martius stood for Rome

And durst not once peep out.

SICINIUS   Come, what talk you of Martius?

BRUTUS [*to the Aedile*]
  Go see this rumourer whipped. It cannot be
  The Volsces dare break with us.

MENENIUS   Cannot be?
  We have record that very well it can,

50   And three examples of the like hath been
  Within my age. But reason with the fellow,
  Before you punish him, where he heard this,
  Lest you shall chance to whip your information
  And beat the messenger who bids beware
  Of what is to be dreaded.

SICINIUS   Tell not me.   55
  I know this cannot be.

BRUTUS   Not possible.

Enter a Messenger.

MESSENGER   The nobles in great earnestness are going
  All to the senate-house. Some news is coming
  That turns their countenances.

SICINIUS   'Tis this slave –
  [*to the Aedile*] Go whip him fore the people's eyes!
    – his raising,   60
  Nothing but his report.

MESSENGER   Yes, worthy sir,
  The slave's report is seconded, and more,
  More fearful, is delivered.

SICINIUS   What more fearful?

MESSENGER   It is spoke freely out of many mouths –
  How probable I do not know – that Martius,   65
  Joined with Aufidius, leads a power 'gainst Rome
  And vows revenge as spacious as between
  The young'st and oldest thing.

SICINIUS   This is most likely!

BRUTUS   Raised only that the weaker sort may wish
  Good Martius home again.   70

SICINIUS   The very trick on't.

MENENIUS   This is unlikely.
  He and Aufidius can no more atone
  Than violent'st contrariety.

Enter a second Messenger.

2 MESSENGER   You are sent for to the Senate.   75
  A fearful army, led by Caius Martius
  Associated with Aufidius, rages
  Upon our territories and have already
  O'erborne their way, consumed with fire and took
  What lay before them.   80

Enter COMINIUS.

COMINIUS [*to the Tribunes*]
  O, you have made good work.

MENENIUS   What news? What news?

COMINIUS
  You have holp to ravish your own daughters and
  To melt the city leads upon your pates,

To see your wives dishonoured to your noses –

85 MENENIUS   What's the news? What's the news?

COMINIUS   Your temples burned in their cement and
Your franchises, whereon you stood, confined
Into an auger's bore.

MENENIUS   Pray now, your news.
[*to the Tribunes*] You have made fair work, I fear me.
[*to Cominius*]   Pray, your news.
If Martius should be joined wi'th' Volscians –

90 COMINIUS   If?
He is their god. He leads them like a thing
Made by some other deity than nature
That shapes man better, and they follow him
Against us brats with no less confidence
95 Than boys pursuing summer butterflies
Or butchers killing flies.

MENENIUS [*to the Tribunes*]   You have made good work,
You and your apron-men, you that stood so much
Upon the voice of occupation and
The breath of garlic-eaters!

100 COMINIUS   He'll shake your Rome about your ears.

MENENIUS   As Hercules did shake down mellow fruit.
You have made fair work!

BRUTUS   But is this true, sir?

COMINIUS   Ay, and you'll look pale
105 Before you find it other. All the regions
Do smilingly revolt and who resists
Are mocked for valiant ignorance
And perish constant fools. Who is't can blame him?
Your enemies and his find something in him.

110 MENENIUS   We are all undone, unless
The noble man have mercy.

COMINIUS   Who shall ask it?
The tribunes cannot do't for shame; the people
Deserve such pity of him as the wolf
Does of the shepherds. For his best friends, if they
115 Should say 'Be good to Rome', they charged him even
As those should do that had deserved his hate
And therein showed like enemies.

MENENIUS   'Tis true,
If he were putting to my house the brand
That should consume it, I have not the face
To say, 'Beseech you, cease'.
120 [*to the Tribunes*]   You have made fair hands,
You and your crafts! You have crafted fair!

COMINIUS   You have brought
A trembling upon Rome such as was never
S'incapable of help.

BOTH TRIBUNES   Say not we brought it.

MENENIUS
How? Was't we? We loved him but, like beasts
125 And cowardly nobles, gave way unto your clusters
Who did hoot him out o'th' city.

COMINIUS   But I fear
They'll roar him in again. Tullus Aufidius,
The second name of men, obeys his points
As if he were his officer. Desperation

Is all the policy, strength and defence   130
That Rome can make against them.

Enter a troop of Citizens.

MENENIUS   Here come the clusters.
And is Aufidius with him? [*to the Citizens*] You are they
That made the air unwholesome when you cast
Your stinking greasy caps in hooting
At Coriolanus' exile. Now he's coming   135
And not a hair upon a soldier's head
Which will not prove a whip. As many coxcombs
As you threw caps up will he tumble down
And pay you for your voices. 'Tis no matter.
If he could burn us all into one coal,   140
We have deserved it.

ALL THE CITIZENS   Faith, we hear fearful news.

1 CITIZEN   For mine own part,
When I said banish him, I said 'twas pity.

2 CITIZEN   And so did I.

3 CITIZEN   And so did I and, to say the truth, so did very   145
many of us. That we did, we did for the best, and
though we willingly consented to his banishment, yet it
was against our will.

COMINIUS   You're goodly things, you voices.

MENENIUS   You have made good work,
You and your cry. [*to Cominius*] Shall's to the Capitol?   150

COMINIUS
O ay, what else?   *Exeunt Cominius and Menenius.*

SICINIUS   Go, masters, get you home. Be not dismayed.
These are a side that would be glad to have
This true which they so seem to fear. Go home
And show no sign of fear.   155

1 CITIZEN   The gods be good to us! Come, masters, let's
home. I ever said we were i'th' wrong when we
banished him.

2 CITIZEN   So did we all. But come, let's home.

Exeunt Citizens.

BRUTUS   I do not like this news.   160

SICINIUS   Nor I.

BRUTUS
Let's to the Capitol. Would half my wealth
Would buy this for a lie.

SICINIUS   Pray, let's go.   *Exeunt.*

4.7   *Enter* AUFIDIUS *with his* Lieutenant.

AUFIDIUS   Do they still fly to th' Roman?

LIEUTENANT
I do not know what witchcraft's in him, but
Your soldiers use him as the grace fore meat,
Their talk at table and their thanks at end
And you are darkened in this action, sir,   5
Even by your own.

AUFIDIUS   I cannot help it now,
Unless by using means I lame the foot
Of our design. He bears himself more proudlier,
Even to my person, than I thought he would

10 When first I did embrace him. Yet his nature
In that's no changeling and I must excuse
What cannot be amended.

LIEUTENANT   Yet I wish, sir –
I mean for your particular – you had not
Joined in commission with him but either
15 Have borne the action of yourself or else
To him had left it solely.

AUFIDIUS   I understand thee well and be thou sure,
When he shall come to his account, he knows not
What I can urge against him. Although it seems –
20 And so he thinks, and is no less apparent
To th' vulgar eye – that he bears all things fairly
And shows good husbandry for the Volscian state,
Fights dragon-like and does achieve as soon
As draw his sword, yet he hath left undone
25 That which shall break his neck or hazard mine
Whene'er we come to our account.

LIEUTENANT
Sir, I beseech you, think you he'll carry Rome?

AUFIDIUS   All places yields to him ere he sits down
And the nobility of Rome are his;
30 The senators and patricians love him too.
The tribunes are no soldiers and their people
Will be as rash in the repeal as hasty
To expel him thence. I think he'll be to Rome
As is the osprey to the fish, who takes it
35 By sovereignty of nature. First he was
A noble servant to them but he could not
Carry his honours even. Whether 'twas pride,
Which out of daily fortune ever taints
The happy man; whether defect of judgement,
40 To fail in the disposing of those chances
Which he was lord of; or whether nature,
Not to be other than one thing, not moving
From th' casque to th' cushion but commanding peace
Even with the same austerity and garb
45 As he controlled the war; but one of these –
As he hath spices of them all – not all,
For I dare so far free him – made him feared,
So hated and so banished. But he has a merit
To choke it in the utterance. So our virtues
50 Lie in th'interpretation of the time
And power, unto itself most commendable,
Hath not a tomb so evident as a chair
T'extol what it hath done.
One fire drives out one fire, one nail one nail,
55 Rights by rights falter, strengths by strengths do fail.
Come, let's away. When, Caius, Rome is thine,
Thou art poor'st of all; then shortly art thou mine.
Exeunt.

5.1   *Enter* MENENIUS, COMINIUS, SICINIUS
and BRUTUS, *the two Tribunes, with others.*

MENENIUS [*to the Tribunes*]
No, I'll not go. You hear what he hath said

Which was sometime his general, who loved him
In a most dear particular. He called me father –
But what o'that? Go you that banished him;
A mile before his tent fall down and knee   5
The way into his mercy. Nay, if he coyed
To hear Cominius speak, I'll keep at home.

COMINIUS   He would not seem to know me.

MENENIUS [*to the Tribunes*]   Do you hear?

COMINIUS   Yet one time he did call me by my name.
I urged our old acquaintance and the drops   10
That we have bled together. 'Coriolanus'
He would not answer to, forbade all names.
He was a kind of nothing, titleless,
Till he had forged himself a name o'th' fire
Of burning Rome.

MENENIUS [*to the Tribunes*]   Why, so; you have made
good work!   15
A pair of tribunes that have wracked for Rome,
To make coals cheap – a noble memory!

COMINIUS   I minded him how royal 'twas to pardon
When it was less expected. He replied
It was a bare petition of a state   20
To one whom they had punished.

MENENIUS   Very well.
Could he say less?

COMINIUS   I offered to awaken his regard
For's private friends. His answer to me was
He could not stay to pick them in a pile   25
Of noisome musty chaff. He said 'twas folly,
For one poor grain or two, to leave unburnt
And still to nose th'offence.

MENENIUS   For one poor grain or two?
I am one of those; his mother, wife, his child
And this brave fellow too: we are the grains,   30
[*to the Tribunes*] You are the musty chaff, and you are
smelt
Above the moon. We must be burnt for you.

SICINIUS   Nay, pray be patient. If you refuse your aid
In this so never-needed help, yet do not
Upbraid's with our distress. But sure, if you   35
Would be your country's pleader, your good tongue,
More than the instant army we can make,
Might stop our countryman.

MENENIUS   No, I'll not meddle.

SICINIUS   Pray you go to him.

MENENIUS   What should I do?

BRUTUS   Only make trial what your love can do   40
For Rome towards Martius.

MENENIUS   Well, and say that Martius return me,
As Cominius is returned, unheard – what then? –
But as a discontented friend, grief-shot
With his unkindness. Say't be so?

SICINIUS   Yet your good will   45
Must have that thanks from Rome after the measure
As you intended well.

MENENIUS   I'll undertake't.
I think he'll hear me. Yet to bite his lip

And hum at good Cominius much unhearts me.
50 He was not taken well: he had not dined.
The veins unfilled, our blood is cold and then
We pout upon the morning, are unapt
To give or to forgive; but when we have stuffed
These pipes and these conveyances of our blood
55 With wine and feeding, we have suppler souls
Than in our priest-like fasts. Therefore I'll watch him
Till he be dieted to my request
And then I'll set upon him.

BRUTUS You know the very road into his kindness
And cannot lose your way.

60 MENENIUS   Good faith, I'll prove him,
Speed how it will. I shall ere long have knowledge
Of my success.   *Exit.*

COMINIUS   He'll never hear him.

SICINIUS   Not?

COMINIUS   I tell you, he does sit in gold, his eye
65 Red as 'twould burn Rome, and his injury
The jailer to his pity. I kneeled before him;
'Twas very faintly he said 'Rise', dismissed me
Thus, with his speechless hand. What he would do
He sent in writing after me, what he would not,
Bound with an oath to hold to his conditions.
70 So that all hope is vain
Unless his noble mother and his wife,
Who, as I hear, mean to solicit him
For mercy to his country. Therefore let's hence
And with our fair entreaties haste them on. *Exeunt.*

5.2   *Enter* MENENIUS *to the two* Watchmen.

1 WATCHMAN   Stay. Whence are you?

2 WATCHMAN   Stand and go back.

MENENIUS
You guard like men; 'tis well. But by your leave,
I am an officer of state and come
To speak with Coriolanus.

5 1 WATCHMAN   From whence?

MENENIUS   From Rome.

1 WATCHMAN   You may not pass. You must return.
Our general will no more hear from thence.

2 WATCHMAN
You'll see your Rome embraced with fire before
You'll speak with Coriolanus.

MENENIUS   Good my friends,
10 If you have heard your general talk of Rome
And of his friends there, it is lots to blanks
My name hath touched your ears. It is Menenius.

1 WATCHMAN
Be it so, go back. The virtue of your name
Is not here passable.

MENENIUS   I tell thee, fellow,
15 Thy general is my lover. I have been
The book of his good acts whence men have read
His fame unparalleled, haply amplified,
For I have ever verified my friends,

Of whom he's chief, with all the size that verity
Would without lapsing suffer. Nay, sometimes, 20
Like to a bowl upon a subtle ground,
I have tumbled past the throw, and in his praise
Have, almost, stamped the leasing. Therefore, fellow,
I must have leave to pass.

1 WATCHMAN   Faith sir, if you had told as many lies in 25
his behalf as you have uttered words in your own, you
should not pass here, no, though it were as virtuous to
lie as to live chastely. Therefore go back.

MENENIUS Prithee, fellow, remember my name is
Menenius, always factionary on the party of your general. 30

2 WATCHMAN   Howsoever you have been his liar, as you
say you have, I am one that, telling true under him,
must say you cannot pass. Therefore go back.

MENENIUS Has he dined, canst thou tell? For I would
not speak with him till after dinner. 35

1 WATCHMAN   You are a Roman, are you?

MENENIUS   I am as thy general is.

1 WATCHMAN   Then you should hate Rome, as he does.
Can you, when you have pushed out your gates the
very defender of them and in a violent popular 40
ignorance given your enemy your shield, think to front
his revenges with the easy groans of old women, the
virginal palms of your daughters or with the palsied
intercession of such a decayed dotant as you seem to
be? Can you think to blow out the intended fire your 45
city is ready to flame in with such weak breath as this?
No, you are deceived. Therefore back to Rome and
prepare for your execution. You are condemned; our
general has sworn you out of reprieve and pardon.

MENENIUS   Sirrah, if thy captain knew I were here, he 50
would use me with estimation.

1 WATCHMAN   Come, my captain knows you not.

MENENIUS   I mean thy general.

1 WATCHMAN   My general cares not for you. Back I say,
go, lest I let forth your half-pint of blood. Back! That's 55
the utmost of your having. Back!

MENENIUS   Nay, but fellow, fellow –

Enter CORIOLANUS *with* AUFIDIUS.

CORIOLANUS   What's the matter?

MENENIUS [*to first Watchman*] Now, you companion,
I'll say an errand for you. You shall know now that I am 60
in estimation. You shall perceive that a jack guardant
cannot office me from my son Coriolanus. Guess but
my entertainment with him if thou stand'st not i'th'
state of hanging or of some death more long in
spectatorship and crueller in suffering. Behold now 65
presently and swoon for what's to come upon thee. [*to
Coriolanus*] The glorious gods sit in hourly synod
about thy particular prosperity and love thee no worse
than thy old father Menenius does. O my son, my son!
Thou art preparing fire for us. Look thee, here's water 70
to quench it. I was hardly moved to come to thee but,
being assured none but myself could move thee, I have
been blown out of our gates with sighs and conjure

thee to pardon Rome and thy petitionary countrymen.
75   The good gods assuage thy wrath and turn the dregs of
it upon this varlet here – this, who like a block hath
denied my access to thee.

CORIOLANUS   Away!

MENENIUS   How? Away?

CORIOLANUS
80   Wife, mother, child, I know not. My affairs
Are servanted to others. Though I owe
My revenge properly, my remission lies
In Volscian breasts. That we have been familiar,
Ingrate forgetfulness shall poison rather
85   Than pity note how much. Therefore be gone.
Mine ears against your suits are stronger than
Your gates against my force. Yet, for I loved thee,
Take this along;   [*Gives him a letter.*]
I writ it for thy sake
And would have sent it. Another word, Menenius,
90   I will not hear thee speak. – This man, Aufidius,
Was my beloved in Rome; yet thou behold'st.

AUFIDIUS   You keep a constant temper.

Exeunt Coriolanus and Aufidius.
The Guard and Menenius remain.

1 WATCHMAN   Now, sir, is your name Menenius?

2 WATCHMAN   'Tis a spell, you see, of much power. You
95   know the way home again.

1 WATCHMAN   Do you hear how we are shent for
keeping your greatness back?

2 WATCHMAN   What cause do you think I have to
swoon?

100   MENENIUS   I neither care for th' world nor your general.
For such things as you, I can scarce think there's any,
you're so slight. He that hath a will to die by himself
fears it not from another. Let your general do his
worst. For you, be that you are long and your misery
105   increase with your age. I say to you, as I was said to,
'Away!'   *Exit.*

1 WATCHMAN   A noble fellow, I warrant him.

2 WATCHMAN   The worthy fellow is our general. He's
the rock, the oak, not to be wind-shaken.   *Exeunt.*

5.3   *Enter* CORIOLANUS *and* AUFIDIUS *with Volscian*
soldiers. Coriolanus sits in a chair of state.

CORIOLANUS
We will before the walls of Rome tomorrow
Set down our host. My partner in this action,
You must report to th' Volscian lords how plainly
I have borne this business.

AUFIDIUS   Only their ends
5   You have respected, stopped your ears against
The general suit of Rome, never admitted
A private whisper, no, not with such friends
That thought them sure of you.

CORIOLANUS   This last old man,
Whom with a cracked heart I have sent to Rome,
10   Loved me above the measure of a father,

Nay, godded me indeed. Their latest refuge
Was to send him, for whose old love I have –
Though I showed sourly to him – once more offered
The first conditions which they did refuse
And cannot now accept, to grace him only   15
That thought he could do more. A very little
I have yielded to. Fresh embassies and suits,
Nor from the state nor private friends, hereafter
Will I lend ear to. [*Shout within*] Ha? What shout is this?
Shall I be tempted to infringe my vow   20
In the same time 'tis made? I will not.

Enter VIRGILIA, VOLUMNIA, YOUNG MARTIUS,
VALERIA, *with attendants.*

My wife comes foremost, then the honoured mould
Wherein this trunk was framed, and in her hand
The grandchild to her blood. But out, affection!
All bond and privilege of nature break!   25
Let it be virtuous to be obstinate.
[*Virgilia curtsies.*] What is that curtsy worth? Or those
doves' eyes,
Which can make gods forsworn? I melt, and am not
Of stronger earth than others.   [*Volumnia bows.*]
My mother bows,
As if Olympus to a molehill should   30
In supplication nod; and my young boy
Hath an aspect of intercession which
Great Nature cries 'Deny not'. Let the Volsces
Plough Rome and harrow Italy, I'll never
Be such a gosling to obey instinct, but stand   35
As if a man were author of himself
And knew no other kin.

VIRGILIA   My lord and husband.

CORIOLANUS
These eyes are not the same I wore in Rome.

VIRGILIA   The sorrow that delivers us thus changed
Makes you think so.

CORIOLANUS   Like a dull actor now,   40
I have forgot my part and I am out,
Even to a full disgrace. Best of my flesh,
Forgive my tyranny but do not say
For that 'Forgive our Romans'.   [*They kiss.*]
O, a kiss
Long as my exile, sweet as my revenge!   45
Now, by the jealous queen of heaven, that kiss
I carried from thee, dear, and my true lip
Hath virgined it e'er since. You gods, I prate
And the most noble mother of the world
Leave unsaluted. Sink, my knee, i'th' earth;   [*Kneels.*]   50
Of thy deep duty more impression show
Than that of common sons.

VOLUMNIA   O, stand up blessed,
Whilst with no softer cushion than the flint
I kneel before thee and unproperly
Show duty as mistaken all this while   55
Between the child and parent.   [*Kneels.*]

CORIOLANUS   What's this?

Your knees to me? To your corrected son?   [*Rises.*]
Then let the pebbles on the hungry beach
Fillip the stars; then let the mutinous winds
60   Strike the proud cedars 'gainst the fiery sun,
Murdering impossibility to make
What cannot be slight work.   [*Raises her.*]
VOLUMNIA   Thou art my warrior.
I holp to frame thee.   [*Gestures to Valeria.*]
                    Do you know this lady?
CORIOLANUS   The noble sister of Publicola,
65   The moon of Rome, chaste as the icicle
That's candied by the frost from purest snow
And hangs on Dian's temple – Dear Valeria!
VOLUMNIA [*showing Young Martius*]
This is a poor epitome of yours,
Which by th'interpretation of full time
May show like all yourself.
70   CORIOLANUS [*to Young Martius*]   The god of soldiers,
With the consent of supreme Jove, inform
Thy thoughts with nobleness, that thou mayst prove
To shame unvulnerable and stick i'th' wars
Like a great sea-mark, standing every flaw
And saving those that eye thee!
75   VOLUMNIA   Your knee, sirrah.
[*Young Martius kneels.*]
CORIOLANUS   That's my brave boy.
VOLUMNIA   Even he, your wife, this lady and myself
Are suitors to you.
CORIOLANUS   I beseech you, peace!
Or, if you'd ask, remember this before:
80   The thing I have forsworn to grant may never
Be held by you denials. Do not bid me
Dismiss my soldiers or capitulate
Again with Rome's mechanics. Tell me not
Wherein I seem unnatural. Desire not
85   T'allay my rages and revenges with
Your colder reasons.
VOLUMNIA   O, no more, no more!
You have said you will not grant us any thing,
For we have nothing else to ask but that
Which you deny already. Yet we will ask
90   That, if you fail in our request, the blame
May hang upon your hardness. Therefore hear us.
CORIOLANUS
Aufidius and you Volsces, mark, for we'll
Hear nought from Rome in private.   [*Sits.*]
                        Your request?
VOLUMNIA
Should we be silent and not speak, our raiment
95   And state of bodies would bewray what life
We have led since thy exile. Think with thyself
How more unfortunate than all living women
Are we come hither, since that thy sight, which should
Make our eyes flow with joy, hearts dance with comforts,
100   Constrains them weep and shake with fear and sorrow,
Making the mother, wife and child to see
The son, the husband and the father tearing

His country's bowels out; and to poor we
Thine enmity's most capital. Thou barr'st us
Our prayers to the gods, which is a comfort   105
That all but we enjoy, for how can we,
Alas, how can we for our country pray,
Whereto we are bound, together with thy victory,
Whereto we are bound? Alack, or we must lose
The country, our dear nurse, or else thy person,   110
Our comfort in the country. We must find
An evident calamity, though we had
Our wish, which side should win. For either thou
Must as a foreign recreant be led
With manacles through our streets or else   115
Triumphantly tread on thy country's ruin
And bear the palm for having bravely shed
Thy wife and children's blood. For myself, son,
I purpose not to wait on fortune till
These wars determine. If I cannot persuade thee   120
Rather to show a noble grace to both parts
Than seek the end of one, thou shalt no sooner
March to assault thy country than to tread –
Trust to't, thou shalt not – on thy mother's womb
That brought thee to this world.
VIRGILIA   Ay, and mine   125
That brought you forth this boy to keep your name
Living to time.
YOUNG MARTIUS   'A shall not tread on me.
I'll run away till I am bigger, but then I'll fight.
CORIOLANUS
Not of a woman's tenderness to be
Requires nor child nor woman's face to see.   130
I have sat too long.   [*Rises.*]
VOLUMNIA   Nay, go not from us thus.
If it were so that our request did tend
To save the Romans, thereby to destroy
The Volsces whom you serve, you might condemn us
As poisonous of your honour. No, our suit   135
Is that you reconcile them: while the Volsces
May say 'This mercy we have showed', the Romans
'This we received', and each in either side
Give the all-hail to thee and cry 'Be blest
For making up this peace!' Thou knowst, great son,   140
The end of war's uncertain; but this certain,
That if thou conquer Rome, the benefit
Which thou shalt thereby reap is such a name
Whose repetition will be dogged with curses,
Whose chronicle thus writ: 'The man was noble,   145
But with his last attempt he wiped it out,
Destroyed his country, and his name remains
To th'ensuing age abhorred.' Speak to me, son.
Thou hast affected the fine strains of honour,
To imitate the graces of the gods,   150
To tear with thunder the wide cheeks o'th' air
And yet to charge thy sulphur with a bolt
That should but rive an oak. Why dost not speak?
Think'st thou it honourable for a nobleman
Still to remember wrongs? Daughter, speak you;   155

He cares not for your weeping. Speak thou, boy;
Perhaps thy childishness will move him more
Than can our reasons. There's no man in the world
More bound to's mother, yet here he lets me prate
160 Like one i'th' stocks. Thou hast never in thy life
Showed thy dear mother any courtesy,
When she, poor hen, fond of no second brood,
Has clucked thee to the wars and safely home
Loaden with honour. Say my request's unjust
165 And spurn me back. But, if it be not so,
Thou art not honest and the gods will plague thee
That thou restrain'st from me the duty which
To a mother's part belongs. He turns away.
Down, ladies; let us shame him with our knees.
170 To his surname 'Coriolanus' 'longs more pride
Than pity to our prayers. Down! An end,
This is the last. [*The Ladies and Young Martius kneel.*]
        So, we will home to Rome
And die among our neighbours. – Nay, behold's.
This boy, that cannot tell what he would have
175 But kneels and holds up hands for fellowship,
Does reason our petition with more strength
Than thou hast to deny't. – Come, let us go. [*They rise.*]
This fellow had a Volscian to his mother,
His wife is in Corioles and his child
180 Like him by chance. – Yet give us our dispatch.
I am hushed until our city be afire
And then I'll speak a little.
    [*He holds her by the hand, silent.*]
CORIOLANUS   O, mother, mother!
What have you done? Behold, the heavens do ope,
The gods look down and this unnatural scene
185 They laugh at. O, my mother, mother! O!
You have won a happy victory to Rome
But for your son, believe it, O, believe it,
Most dangerously you have with him prevailed,
If not most mortal to him. But let it come. –
190 Aufidius, though I cannot make true wars,
I'll frame convenient peace. Now, good Aufidius,
Were you in my stead, would you have heard
A mother less? Or granted less, Aufidius?
AUFIDIUS   I was moved withal.
CORIOLANUS   I dare be sworn you were
195 And, sir, it is no little thing to make
Mine eyes to sweat compassion. But, good sir,
What peace you'll make, advise me. For my part,
I'll not to Rome; I'll back with you and pray you
Stand to me in this cause. – O mother! Wife!
AUFIDIUS [*aside*]
200 I am glad thou hast set thy mercy and thy honour
At difference in thee. Out of that I'll work
Myself a former fortune.
CORIOLANUS [*to Volumnia and Virgilia*] Ay, by and by.
But we will drink together and you shall bear
A better witness back than words, which we
205 On like conditions will have counter-sealed.
Come, enter with us. Ladies, you deserve

To have a temple built you; all the swords
In Italy and her confederate arms
Could not have made this peace.   *Exeunt.*

5.4   *Enter* MENENIUS *and* SICINIUS.

MENENIUS See you yon quoin o'th' Capitol, yon
cornerstone?
SICINIUS Why, what of that?
MENENIUS If it be possible for you to displace it with
your little finger, there is some hope the ladies of   5
Rome, especially his mother, may prevail with him.
But I say there is no hope in't. Our throats are
sentenced and stay upon execution.
SICINIUS Is't possible that so short a time can alter the
condition of a man?   10
MENENIUS There is difference between a grub and a
butterfly; yet your butterfly was a grub. This Martius is
grown from man to dragon. He has wings; he's more
than a creeping thing.
SICINIUS He loved his mother dearly.   15
MENENIUS So did he me and he no more remembers
his mother now than an eight-year-old horse. The
tartness of his face sours ripe grapes. When he walks,
he moves like an engine and the ground shrinks
before his treading. He is able to pierce a corslet with   20
his eye, talks like a knell and his hum is a battery.
He sits in his state as a thing made for Alexander.
What he bids be done is finished with his bidding. He
wants nothing of a god but eternity and a heaven to
throne in.   25
SICINIUS Yes, mercy, if you report him truly.
MENENIUS I paint him in the character. Mark what
mercy his mother shall bring from him. There is no
more mercy in him than there is milk in a male tiger.
That shall our poor city find – and all this is long of   30
you.
SICINIUS The gods be good unto us.
MENENIUS No, in such a case the gods will not be good
unto us. When we banished him we respected not
them and, he returning to break our necks, they   35
respect not us.

    Enter a Messenger.

MESSENGER [*to Sicinius*]
Sir, if you'd save your life, fly to your house.
The plebeians have got your fellow tribune
And hale him up and down, all swearing if
The Roman ladies bring not comfort home   40
They'll give him death by inches.

    Enter another Messenger.

SICINIUS   What's the news?
2 MESSENGER
Good news, good news. The ladies have prevailed,
The Volscians are dislodged and Martius gone.
A merrier day did never yet greet Rome,

No, not th'expulsion of the Tarquins.

45   SICINIUS   Friend,
Art thou certain this is true? Is't most certain?

2 MESSENGER   As certain as I know the sun is fire.
Where have you lurked that you make doubt of it?
Ne'er through an arch so hurried the blown tide
As the recomforted through th' gates.
[Trumpets, hautboys, drums beat, all together.]

50   Why, hark you,
The trumpets, sackbuts, psalteries and fifes,
Tabors and cymbals and the shouting Romans
Make the sun dance. *[A shout within]* Hark you!

MENENIUS   This is good news:
I will go meet the ladies. This Volumnia

55   Is worth of consuls, senators, patricians,
A city full; of tribunes such as you,
A sea and land full. You have prayed well today.
This morning for ten thousand of your throats
I'd not have given a doit.
[Sound still with the shouts]   Hark, how they joy!

SICINIUS *[to second Messenger]*

60   First, the gods bless you for your tidings; next,
Accept my thankfulness.

2 MESSENGER
Sir, we have all great cause to give great thanks.

SICINIUS   They are near the city?

2 MESSENGER   Almost at point to enter.

SICINIUS   We'll meet them, and help the joy.   *Exeunt.*

5.5   *Enter two* Senators *with ladies* VOLUMNIA,
            VIRGILIA, VALERIA *and* YOUNG MARTIUS,
            passing over the stage, with other Lords.

SENATOR
Behold our patroness, the life of Rome!
Call all your tribes together, praise the gods,
And make triumphant fires. Strew flowers before them.
Unshout the noise that banished Martius,

5   Repeal him with the welcome of his mother.
Cry 'Welcome, ladies, welcome!'

ALL   Welcome, ladies, welcome!
A flourish with drums and trumpets. Exeunt.

5.6   *Enter* Tullus AUFIDIUS *with Attendants.*

AUFIDIUS   Go tell the lords o'th' city I am here.
Deliver them this paper. *[Gives a paper.]* Having read it,
Bid them repair to th' market-place where I,
Even in theirs and in the commons' ears,

5   Will vouch the truth of it. Him I accuse
The city ports by this hath entered and
Intends t'appear before the people, hoping
To purge himself with words. Dispatch.
                              Exeunt attendants.

Enter three or four Conspirators *of Aufidius' faction.*

                              Most welcome!

1 CONSPIRATOR   How is it with our general?

AUFIDIUS   Even so
As with a man by his own alms impoisoned   10
And with his charity slain.

2 CONSPIRATOR   Most noble sir,
If you do hold the same intent wherein
You wished us parties, we'll deliver you
Of your great danger.

AUFIDIUS   Sir, I cannot tell.
We must proceed as we do find the people.   15

3 CONSPIRATOR
The people will remain uncertain whilst
'Twixt you there's difference, but the fall of either
Makes the survivor heir of all.

AUFIDIUS   I know it,
And my pretext to strike at him admits
A good construction. I raised him and I pawned   20
Mine honour for his truth; who being so heightened,
He watered his new plants with dews of flattery,
Seducing so my friends, and to this end
He bowed his nature, never known before
But to be rough, unswayable and free.   25

3 CONSPIRATOR   Sir, his stoutness
When he did stand for consul, which he lost
By lack of stooping –

AUFIDIUS   That I would have spoke of.
Being banished for't, he came unto my hearth,
Presented to my knife his throat. I took him,   30
Made him joint-servant with me, gave him way
In all his own desires; nay, let him choose
Out of my files, his projects to accomplish,
My best and freshest men; served his designments
In mine own person, holp to reap the fame   35
Which he did end all his and took some pride
To do myself this wrong, till at the last
I seemed his follower, not partner, and
He waged me with his countenance as if
I had been mercenary.

1 CONSPIRATOR   So he did, my lord.   40
The army marvelled at it and, in the last,
When he had carried Rome and that we looked
For no less spoil than glory –

AUFIDIUS   There was it,
For which my sinews shall be stretched upon him.
At a few drops of women's rheum, which are   45
As cheap as lies, he sold the blood and labour
Of our great action. Therefore shall he die
And I'll renew me in his fall.
                    *[Drums and trumpets sounds, with great
                              shouts of the people.]*
                              But hark.

1 CONSPIRATOR
Your native town you entered like a post
And had no welcomes home; but he returns   50
Splitting the air with noise.

2 CONSPIRATOR   And patient fools,
Whose children he hath slain, their base throats tear

With giving him glory.

3 CONSPIRATOR   Therefore at your vantage,
Ere he express himself or move the people
55   With what he would say, let him feel your sword,
Which we will second. When he lies along,
After your way his tale pronounced shall bury
His reasons with his body.

AUFIDIUS   Say no more.
Here come the lords.

          Enter the LORDS *of the city.*

60   ALL LORDS   You are most welcome home.
AUFIDIUS   I have not deserved it.
But, worthy lords, have you with heed perused
What I have written to you?
ALL LORDS   We have.
1 LORD   And grieve to hear't.
What faults he made before the last, I think
65   Might have found easy fines. But there to end
Where he was to begin and give away
The benefit of our levies, answering us
With our own charge, making a treaty where
There was a yielding – this admits no excuse.
70   AUFIDIUS   He approaches; you shall hear him.

          Enter CORIOLANUS *marching with Drum and*
          Colours, the Commoners *being with him.*

CORIOLANUS   Hail, lords! I am returned your soldier,
No more infected with my country's love
Than when I parted hence, but still subsisting
Under your great command. You are to know
75   That prosperously I have attempted and
With bloody passage led your wars even to
The gates of Rome. Our spoils we have brought home
Doth more than counterpoise a full third part
The charges of the action. We have made peace
80   With no less honour to the Antiates
Than shame to th' Romans. And we here deliver,
Subscribed by th' consuls and patricians,
Together with the seal o'th' Senate, what
We have compounded on.   [*Offers the Lords a paper.*]
85   AUFIDIUS   Read it not, noble lords,
But tell the traitor in the highest degree
He hath abused your powers.
CORIOLANUS   'Traitor'? How now?
AUFIDIUS   Ay, 'traitor', Martius.
CORIOLANUS   'Martius'?
90   AUFIDIUS   Ay, Martius, Caius Martius. Dost thou think
I'll grace thee with that robbery, thy stolen name
'Coriolanus', in Corioles?
You lords and heads o'th' state, perfidiously
He has betrayed your business and given up
95   For certain drops of salt, your city Rome –
I say 'your city' – to his wife and mother,
Breaking his oath and resolution like
A twist of rotten silk, never admitting
Counsel o'th' war. But at his nurse's tears

He whined and roared away your victory   100
That pages blushed at him and men of heart
Looked wondering each at others.
CORIOLANUS   Hear'st thou, Mars?
AUFIDIUS
Name not the god, thou boy of tears.
CORIOLANUS   Ha?
AUFIDIUS   No more.
CORIOLANUS
Measureless liar, thou hast made my heart
Too great for what contains it. 'Boy'? O slave! –   105
Pardon me, lords, 'tis the first time that ever
I was forced to scold. Your judgements, my grave lords,
Must give this cur the lie and his own notion –
Who wears my stripes impressed upon him, that
Must bear my beating to his grave – shall join   110
To thrust the lie unto him.
1 LORD   Peace both and hear me speak.
CORIOLANUS   Cut me to pieces, Volsces men and lads;
Stain all your edges on me. 'Boy', false hound!
If you have writ your annals true, 'tis there
That, like an eagle in a dovecote, I   115
Fluttered your Volscians in Corioles.
Alone I did it. 'Boy'!
AUFIDIUS   Why, noble lords,
Will you be put in mind of his blind fortune,
Which was your shame, by this unholy braggart,
Fore your own eyes and ears?
ALL CONSPIRATORS   Let him die for't!   120
ALL PEOPLE   Tear him to pieces! Do it presently! He
killed my son! My daughter! He killed my cousin
Marcus! He killed my father!
2 LORD   Peace, ho! No outrage! Peace!
The man is noble, and his fame folds in   125
This orb o'th' earth. His last offences to us
Shall have judicious hearing. Stand, Aufidius,
And trouble not the peace.
CORIOLANUS   O that I had him,
With six Aufidiuses, or more, his tribe,
To use my lawful sword!
AUFIDIUS   Insolent villain!   130
ALL CONSPIRATORS   Kill, kill, kill, kill, kill him!
          [*Two conspirators draw and kill Martius who falls.*
          Aufidius stands on him.]
LORDS   Hold, hold, hold, hold!
AUFIDIUS   My noble masters, hear me speak.
1 LORD   O Tullus!
2 LORD
Thou hast done a deed whereat valour will weep.
3 LORD   Tread not upon him. Masters all, be quiet.   135
Put up your swords.
AUFIDIUS
My lords, when you shall know – as in this rage
Provoked by him you cannot – the great danger
Which this man's life did owe you, you'll rejoice
That he is thus cut off. Please it your honours   140
To call me to your Senate, I'll deliver

Myself your loyal servant, or endure
Your heaviest censure.
1 LORD   Bear from hence his body
And mourn you for him. Let him be regarded
As the most noble corpse that ever herald   145
Did follow to his urn.
2 LORD   His own impatience
Takes from Aufidius a great part of blame.
Let's make the best of it.
AUFIDIUS   My rage is gone

And I am struck with sorrow. Take him up.
Help three o'th' chiefest soldiers; I'll be one.   150
Beat thou the drum that it speak mournfully.
Trail your steel pikes. Though in this city he
Hath widowed and unchilded many a one,
Which to this hour bewail the injury,
Yet he shall have a noble memory.   155
Assist.   *Exeunt bearing the body of Martius.*
                             A dead march sounded.

Cymbeline

One of Shakespeare's late romances, *Cymbeline* can also justly be termed a tragical-comical-historical-pastoral play. That generic compound may seem as risible as the character who utters it, but Polonius' concoction conveys Shakespeare's frequent mixing of genres throughout his career. This play fuses motifs and plot lines from Greek and medieval romance, comedy, folktale, tragedy, tragicomedy and history. It also recapitulates elements from many plays Shakespeare wrote before 1610, including an angry king, a wicked queen who manipulates her uxorious husband, a son excessively dependent on his mother, a jealous husband who wagers against a villainous Italian, and a slandered princess. The play's copious finale that reunites long-lost family members combines *anagnorisis* and *peripeteia* to produce twenty-four revelations and five confessions in a scene so wonderfully comic and simultaneously moving that it signals the playwright's virtuosity while masterfully resolving the plots' complexities.

Probably completed and performed in 1610, *Cymbeline* was first printed in the First Folio of 1623. The play was positioned last in the collection published after Shakespeare's death, which may be appropriate to its recapitulations of his previous works. Its location among the tragedies reflects ancient and neoclassical definitions of tragedy for plays with a double plot and a happy ending, but the designation has occasioned endless confusion about *Cymbeline*'s genre and its quality. It is now most often associated with the other late romances that Shakespeare wrote around the same time, *Pericles*, *The Winter's Tale* and *The Tempest*, each of which resolves the problems of fractured families and broken trust through forgiveness and providential interventions. Its heroine is here called 'Innogen', the standard spelling of that name in Shakespeare's sources and other works of that time. A minim error in reading 'nn' as 'm' probably produced the playtext's unusual spelling of 'Imogen', so major editions since 1986 have corrected it to 'Innogen'.

The play adapts the calumny plot in which a woman falsely accused of being unchaste is finally vindicated; that was a staple of medieval romance. Shakespeare used the plot for *The Merry Wives of Windsor*, *Much Ado About Nothing*, *Othello* and *The Winter's Tale* as well as for *Cymbeline*. The scepticism of Innogen's would-be seducer Iachimo that any woman can be faithful, and the outspoken misogyny of her husband Posthumus when he believes she has betrayed him, are basic tropes of that plot. What is distinctive about it here is that Posthumus eventually regrets ordering her death and forgives his wife for 'wrying but a little' (5.1.5) even *before* he learns she is innocent. To escape his order for her murder, Innogen travels to Wales in male disguise, where she meets but does not recognize as her brothers the king's two sons, who were abducted years before. The stagings of non-normative desire that ensue offer engaging alternatives to misogyny's rigid gender binaries.

This play also draws on the history of Britain as recounted in Raphael Holinshed's *Chronicles*, especially in the character of Cymbeline, who ruled ancient Britain in the first century CE. Around that time Britain experienced the predations of colonialism through the Roman occupation, yet King James I likened himself to the Roman emperor Augustus in his attempts to join England and Scotland in a united Britain and enlarge his country's territories in Ireland and the New World. The play stages invasions at personal and national levels when Innogen, Britain's heir to the throne, is at risk of being raped by an Italian and the Romans invade Britain to retain it as part of their empire. Its resolution restores the integrity of the royal body and manages an accommodation between Britain and Rome while reclaiming the nation's lands.

Cymbeline was 'well liked' by Charles I in its 1634 revival. During the Restoration the play was rewritten to be more patriotic, and in the second half of the eighteenth century its frequent performances placed it among the top ten of Shakespeare's plays. Innogen has the third largest female role in the canon after Rosalind and Cleopatra, and she was a particular favourite in the nineteenth century. Performances during the play's first 300 years were severely cut, excluding Posthumus' dream, the vision of his family, Jupiter's descent and his prophecy, but by the end of the twentieth century its full text was increasingly staged. Productions emphasizing its metatheatricality and compassionate reconciliations have particularly delighted audiences in the current century.

The Arden text is based on the 1623 First Folio.

THE BRITONS

CYMBELINE	*King of Britain*
INNOGEN	*his daughter by his first wife, later disguised as Fidele*
POSTHUMUS Leonatus	*a gentleman and her husband*
GUIDERIUS, known as Polydore	
ARVIRAGUS, known as Cadwal	*Cymbeline's sons, abducted by Belarius*
BELARIUS, known as Morgan	*Lord banished by Cymbeline*
QUEEN	*Cymbeline's second wife*
CLOTEN	*her son, Cymbeline's stepson*
PISANIO	*Posthumus' servant*
CORNELIUS	*a doctor*
Two GENTLEMEN	*of Cymbeline's court*
Two LORDS	*attending on Cloten*
LORDS	*attending on Cymbeline*
HELEN	*lady attending on Innogen*
DOROTHY	*lady attending on Innogen*
LADIES	*attending on the Queen*
Two BRITON CAPTAINS	
Two JAILERS	

THE ITALIANS

PHILARIO	*friend of Posthumus' father*
IACHIMO	
FRENCHMAN	*friends of Philario*
Spaniard	
Dutchman	

THE ROMANS

CAIUS LUCIUS	*ambassador to Britain, later general of the Roman forces*
SOOTHSAYER	*called Philharmonus*
Two ROMAN SENATORS	
ROMAN CAPTAINS	
TRIBUNES	

THE APPARITIONS

JUPITER	*king of the Roman gods*
SICILIUS Leonatus	*father to Posthumus*
MOTHER	*to Posthumus*
Two BROTHERS	*to Posthumus*

Attendants at Cymbeline's court, Musicians, Messengers, Briton and Roman Soldiers

Cymbeline

1.1   *Enter two* Gentlemen.

1 GENTLEMAN
You do not meet a man but frowns. Our bloods
No more obey the heavens than our courtiers
Still seem as does the King.
2 GENTLEMAN   But what's the matter?
1 GENTLEMAN
His daughter, and the heir of's kingdom, whom   5
He purposed to his wife's sole son – a widow
That late he married – hath referred herself
Unto a poor but worthy gentleman. She's wedded,
Her husband banished, she imprisoned. All
Is outward sorrow, though I think the King
Be touched at very heart.
2 GENTLEMAN   None but the King?   10
1 GENTLEMAN
He that hath lost her, too. So is the Queen,
That most desired the match. But not a courtier,
Although they wear their faces to the bent
Of the King's looks, hath a heart that is not
Glad at the thing they scowl at.
2 GENTLEMAN   And why so?   15
1 GENTLEMAN
He that hath missed the princess is a thing
Too bad for bad report; and he that hath her
(I mean that married her – alack, good man,
And therefore banished) is a creature such
As, to seek through the regions of the earth   20
For one his like, there would be something failing
In him that should compare. I do not think
So fair an outward and such stuff within
Endows a man but he.
2 GENTLEMAN   You speak him far.
1 GENTLEMAN   I do extend him, sir, within himself,   25
Crush him together rather than unfold
His measure duly.
2 GENTLEMAN   What's his name and birth?
1 GENTLEMAN   I cannot delve him to the root. His father
Was called Sicilius, who did join his honour
Against the Romans with Cassibelan   30
But had his titles by Tenantius, whom
He served with glory and admired success,
So gained the sur-addition 'Leonatus';
And had besides this gentleman in question
Two other sons who in the wars o'th' time   35
Died with their swords in hand. For which their father,
Then old and fond of issue, took such sorrow
That he quit being; and his gentle lady,
Big of this gentleman (our theme) deceased
As he was born. The King, he takes the babe   40
To his protection, calls him Posthumus Leonatus,
Breeds him and makes him of his bedchamber,
Puts to him all the learnings that his time
Could make him the receiver of, which he took
As we do air, fast as 'twas ministered,   45
And in's spring became a harvest; lived in court

(Which rare it is to do) most praised, most loved,
A sample to the youngest, to th' more mature
A glass that feated them, and to the graver
A child that guided dotards. To his mistress,   50
For whom he now is banished, her own price
Proclaims how she esteemed him; and his virtue
By her election may be truly read
What kind of man he is.
2 GENTLEMAN   I honour him
Even out of your report. But pray you tell me,   55
Is she sole child to th' King?
1 GENTLEMAN   His only child.
He had two sons – if this be worth your hearing,
Mark it – the eldest of them at three years old,
I'th' swathing clothes the other, from their nursery
Were stolen, and to this hour no guess in knowledge   60
Which way they went.
2 GENTLEMAN   How long is this ago?
1 GENTLEMAN   Some twenty years.
2 GENTLEMAN
That a king's children should be so conveyed,
So slackly guarded, and the search so slow   65
That could not trace them!
1 GENTLEMAN   Howsoe'er 'tis strange,
Or that the negligence may well be laughed at,
Yet is it true, sir.
2 GENTLEMAN   I do well believe you.

               Enter the QUEEN, POSTHUMUS *and* INNOGEN.

1 GENTLEMAN
We must forbear. Here comes the gentleman,
The Queen and Princess.   *Exeunt the two Gentlemen.*   70
QUEEN   No, be assured you shall not find me, daughter,
After the slander of most stepmothers,
Evil-eyed unto you. You're my prisoner, but
Your jailer shall deliver you the keys
That lock up your restraint. For you, Posthumus,   75
So soon as I can win th'offended King,
I will be known your advocate. Marry, yet
The fire of rage is in him, and 'twere good
You leaned unto his sentence with what patience
Your wisdom may inform you.
POSTHUMUS   Please your Highness,   80
I will from hence today.
QUEEN   You know the peril.
I'll fetch a turn about the garden, pitying
The pangs of barred affections, though the King
Hath charged you should not speak together.   *Exit.*
INNOGEN
O dissembling courtesy! How fine this tyrant   85
Can tickle where she wounds! My dearest husband,
I something fear my father's wrath, but nothing –
Always reserved my holy duty – what
His rage can do on me. You must be gone,
And I shall here abide the hourly shot   90
Of angry eyes, not comforted to live
But that there is this jewel in the world

That I may see again.

POSTHUMUS　　　　　　My queen, my mistress!
O lady, weep no more, lest I give cause
To be suspected of more tenderness
Than doth become a man. I will remain
The loyal'st husband that did e'er plight troth.
My residence in Rome, at one Philario's,
Who to my father was a friend, to me
Known but by letter; thither write, my queen,
And with mine eyes I'll drink the words you send,
Though ink be made of gall.

Enter QUEEN.

QUEEN　　　　　　　　Be brief, I pray you.
If the King come, I shall incur I know not
How much of his displeasure. [*aside*] Yet I'll move him
To walk this way. I never do him wrong
But he does buy my injuries to be friends,
Pays dear for my offences.　　　　　*Exit.*

POSTHUMUS　　　　　Should we be taking leave
As long a term as yet we have to live,
The loathness to depart would grow. Adieu.

INNOGEN　Nay, stay a little.
Were you but riding forth to air yourself,
Such parting were too petty. Look here, love:
This diamond was my mother's. Take it, heart,
　[*She gives him a ring.*]
But keep it till you woo another wife,
When Innogen is dead.

POSTHUMUS　　　　　How, how? Another?
You gentle gods, give me but this I have,
And cere up my embracements from a next
With bonds of death.　　[*He puts on the ring.*]
　　　　　　　Remain, remain thou here
While sense can keep it on. And sweetest, fairest,
As I my poor self did exchange for you
To your so infinite loss, so in our trifles
I still win of you. For my sake wear this:
It is a manacle of love. I'll place it
Upon this fairest prisoner.
　[*He puts the bracelet on her arm.*]

INNOGEN　　　　　　O the gods!
When shall we see again?

Enter CYMBELINE *and Lords.*

POSTHUMUS　　　　　Alack, the King.

CYMBELINE
Thou basest thing, avoid hence, from my sight!
If after this command thou fraught the court
With thy unworthiness, thou diest. Away!
Thou'rt poison to my blood.

POSTHUMUS　　　　　The gods protect you
And bless the good remainders of the court.
I am gone.　　　　　　　　　　*Exit.*

INNOGEN　There cannot be a pinch in death
More sharp than this is.

CYMBELINE　　　　　O disloyal thing,

That shouldst repair my youth, thou heap'st
A year's age on me.

INNOGEN　　　　　I beseech you, sir,
Harm not yourself with your vexation.
I am senseless of your wrath. A touch more rare
Subdues all pangs, all fears.

CYMBELINE　　　　　Past grace? Obedience?

INNOGEN
Past hope and in despair: that way past grace.

CYMBELINE
That mightst have had the sole son of my queen!

INNOGEN　O blessed that I might not! I chose an eagle
And did avoid a puttock.

CYMBELINE
Thou took'st a beggar, wouldst have made my throne
A seat for baseness.

INNOGEN　　　　　No, I rather added
A lustre to it.

CYMBELINE　O thou vile one!

INNOGEN　　　　　　Sir,
It is your fault that I have loved Posthumus:
You bred him as my playfellow, and he is
A man worth any woman; over-buys me
Almost the sum he pays.

CYMBELINE　　　　　What, art thou mad?

INNOGEN
Almost, sir. Heaven restore me! Would I were
A neatherd's daughter, and my Leonatus
Our neighbour shepherd's son.

Enter QUEEN.

CYMBELINE　　　　　Thou foolish thing!
[*to Queen*] They were again together! You have done
Not after our command. [*to Lords*] Away with her,
And pen her up.

QUEEN　　　　　Beseech your patience. – Peace,
Dear lady daughter, peace. – Sweet sovereign,
Leave us to ourselves, and make yourself some comfort
Out of your best advice.

CYMBELINE　　　　　Nay, let her languish
A drop of blood a day and, being aged,
Die of this folly.　　　　　*Exit with Lords.*

QUEEN　　　　　Fie, you must give way.

Enter PISANIO.

Here is your servant. – How now, sir? What news?

PISANIO　My lord your son drew on my master.

QUEEN　　　　　　　　　　Ha?
No harm, I trust, is done?

PISANIO　　　　　　There might have been,
But that my master rather played than fought
And had no help of anger. They were parted
By gentlemen at hand.

QUEEN　　　　　I am very glad on't.

INNOGEN
Your son's my father's friend; he takes his part
To draw upon an exile. O brave sir!

I would they were in Afric both together,
Myself by with a needle, that I might prick
170 The goer-back. – Why came you from your master?
PISANIO On his command: he would not suffer me
To bring him to the haven; left these notes
Of what commands I should be subject to
When't pleas'd you to employ me.
QUEEN   This hath been
175 Your faithful servant. I dare lay mine honour
He will remain so.
PISANIO   I humbly thank your highness.
QUEEN Pray walk awhile.
INNOGEN [*to Pisanio*]
About some half hour hence, pray you speak with me.
You shall at least go see my lord aboard.
180 For this time leave me.   *Exeunt.*

1.2   *Enter* CLOTEN *and two* Lords.

1 LORD Sir, I would advise you to shift a shirt. The
violence of action hath made you reek as a sacrifice.
Where air comes out, air comes in. There's none
abroad so wholesome as that you vent.
5 CLOTEN If my shirt were bloody, then to shift it. Have I
hurt him?
2 LORD [*aside*] No, faith, not so much as his patience.
1 LORD Hurt him? His body's a passable carcass if he be
not hurt. It is a thoroughfare for steel if it be not hurt.
10 2 LORD [*aside*] His steel was in debt; it went o'th'
backside the town.
CLOTEN The villain would not stand me.
2 LORD [*aside*] No, but he fled forward still, toward your
face.
15 1 LORD Stand you? You have land enough of your own,
but he added to your having, gave you some ground.
2 LORD [*aside*] As many inches as you have oceans.
Puppies!
CLOTEN I would they had not come between us.
20 2 LORD [*aside*] So would I, till you had measured how
long a fool you were upon the ground.
CLOTEN And that she should love this fellow and refuse
me!
2 LORD [*aside*] If it be a sin to make a true election, she
25 is damned.
1 LORD Sir, as I told you always, her beauty and her
brain go not together. She's a good sign, but I have
seen small reflection of her wit.
2 LORD [*aside*] She shines not upon fools, lest the
30 reflection should hurt her.
CLOTEN Come, I'll to my chamber. Would there had
been some hurt done.
2 LORD [*aside*] I wish not so, unless it had been the fall
of an ass, which is no great hurt.
35 CLOTEN [*to Second Lord*] You'll go with us?
1 LORD I'll attend your lordship.
CLOTEN Nay, come, let's go together.
2 LORD Well, my lord.   *Exeunt.*

1.3   *Enter* INNOGEN *and* PISANIO.

INNOGEN
I would thou grew'st unto the shores o'th' haven
And question'dst every sail. If he should write
And I not have it, 'twere a paper lost
As offered mercy is. What was the last
That he spake to thee?
PISANIO   It was his queen, his queen.   5
INNOGEN
Then waved his handkerchief?
PISANIO   And kissed it, madam.
INNOGEN Senseless linen, happier therein than I!
And that was all?
PISANIO   No, madam. For so long
As he could make me with this eye or ear
Distinguish him from others, he did keep   10
The deck, with glove or hat or handkerchief
Still waving, as the fits and stirs of's mind
Could best express how slow his soul sailed on,
How swift his ship.
INNOGEN   Thou shouldst have made him
As little as a crow, or less, ere left   15
To after-eye him.
PISANIO   Madam, so I did.
INNOGEN
I would have broke mine eye-strings, cracked them,
but
To look upon him till the diminution
Of space had pointed him sharp as my needle;
Nay, followed him till he had melted from   20
The smallness of a gnat to air, and then
Have turned mine eye and wept. But good Pisanio,
When shall we hear from him?
PISANIO   Be assured madam,
With his next vantage.
INNOGEN I did not take my leave of him, but had   25
Most pretty things to say. Ere I could tell him
How I would think on him at certain hours,
Such thoughts and such, or I could make him swear
The shes of Italy should not betray
Mine interest and his honour, or have charged him   30
At the sixth hour of morn, at noon, at midnight,
T'encounter me with orisons – for then
I am in heaven for him – or ere I could
Give him that parting kiss which I had set
Betwixt two charming words, comes in my father,   35
And, like the tyrannous breathing of the north,
Shakes all our buds from growing.

Enter a Lady.

LADY   The Queen, madam,
Desires your highness' company.
INNOGEN [*to Pisanio*]
Those things I bid you do, get them dispatched.
I will attend the Queen.
PISANIO   Madam, I shall.   *Exeunt.*   40

1.4 *Enter* PHILARIO, IACHIMO, *a* Frenchman,
a Dutchman and a Spaniard.

IACHIMO   Believe it, sir, I have seen him in Britain. He
was then of a crescent note, expected to prove so
worthy as since he hath been allowed the name of. But
I could then have looked on him without the help of
admiration, though the catalogue of his endowments
had been tabled by his side and I to peruse him by
items.

PHILARIO   You speak of him when he was less furnished
than now he is with that which makes him both without
and within.

FRENCHMAN   I have seen him in France. We had very
many there could behold the sun with as firm eyes as
he.

IACHIMO   This matter of marrying his king's daughter,
wherein he must be weighed rather by her value than
his own, words him, I doubt not, a great deal from the
matter.

FRENCHMAN   And then his banishment.

IACHIMO   Ay, and the approbation of those that weep
this lamentable divorce under her colours are
wonderfully to extend him, be it but to fortify her
judgement, which else an easy battery might lay flat for
taking a beggar without less quality. But how comes it
he is to sojourn with you? How creeps acquaintance?

PHILARIO   His father and I were soldiers together, to
whom I have been often bound for no less than my life.

Enter POSTHUMUS.

Here comes the Briton. Let him be so entertained
amongst you as suits with gentlemen of your knowing
to a stranger of his quality. – I beseech you all, be
better known to this gentleman, whom I commend to
you as a noble friend of mine. How worthy he is I will
leave to appear hereafter, rather than story him in his
own hearing.

FRENCHMAN   Sir, we have known together in Orleans.

POSTHUMUS   Since when I have been debtor to you for
courtesies which I will be ever to pay, and yet pay still.

FRENCHMAN   Sir, you o'er-rate my poor kindness. I was
glad I did atone my countryman and you. It had been
pity you should have been put together with so mortal
a purpose as then each bore, upon importance of so
slight and trivial a nature.

POSTHUMUS   By your pardon, sir, I was then a young
traveller, rather shunned to go even with what I heard
than in my every action to be guided by others'
experiences; but upon my mended judgement – if I
offend to say it is mended – my quarrel was not
altogether slight.

FRENCHMAN   Faith, yes, to be put to the arbitrement of
swords, and by such two that would by all likelihood
have confounded one the other, or have fallen both.

IACHIMO   Can we with manners ask what was the
difference?

FRENCHMAN   Safely, I think. 'Twas a contention in
public which may, without contradiction, suffer the
report. It was much like an argument that fell out last
night, where each of us fell in praise of our country
mistresses, this gentleman at that time vouching – and
upon warrant of bloody affirmation – his to be more
fair, virtuous, wise, chaste, constant, qualified and less
attemptable than any the rarest of our ladies in France.

IACHIMO   That lady is not now living, or this
gentleman's opinion, by this, worn out.

POSTHUMUS   She holds her virtue still, and I my mind.

IACHIMO   You must not so far prefer her 'fore ours of
Italy.

POSTHUMUS   Being so far provoked as I was in France,
I would abate her nothing, though I profess myself her
adorer, not her friend.

IACHIMO   As fair and as good – a kind of hand-in-hand
comparison – had been something too fair and too
good for any lady in Britain. If she went before others
I have seen as that diamond of yours outlustres many I
have beheld, I could not but believe she excelled many;
but I have not seen the most precious diamond that is,
nor you the lady.

POSTHUMUS   I praised her as I rated her: so do I my
stone.

IACHIMO   What do you esteem it at?

POSTHUMUS   More than the world enjoys.

IACHIMO   Either your unparagoned mistress is dead, or
she's outprized by a trifle.

POSTHUMUS   You are mistaken: the one may be sold or
given, or if there were wealth enough for the purchase
or merit for the gift; the other is not a thing for sale,
and only the gift of the gods.

IACHIMO   Which the gods have given you?

POSTHUMUS   Which by their graces I will keep.

IACHIMO   You may wear her in title yours, but you know
strange fowl light upon neighbouring ponds. Your ring
may be stolen too, so your brace of unprizable
estimations: the one is but frail and the other casual. A
cunning thief or a that-way-accomplished courtier
would hazard the winning both of first and last.

POSTHUMUS   Your Italy contains none so accomplished
a courtier to convince the honour of my mistress if, in
the holding or loss of that, you term her frail. I do
nothing doubt you have store of thieves;
notwithstanding, I fear not my ring.

PHILARIO   Let us leave here, gentlemen.

POSTHUMUS   Sir, with all my heart. This worthy signor,
I thank him, makes no stranger of me. We are familiar
at first.

IACHIMO   With five times so much conversation I
should get ground of your fair mistress, make her go
back even to the yielding, had I admittance and
opportunity to friend.

POSTHUMUS   No, no.

IACHIMO   I dare thereupon pawn the moiety of my
estate to your ring, which in my opinion o'ervalues it

something. But I make my wager rather against your
confidence than her reputation; and to bar your offence
herein too, I durst attempt it against any lady in the
world.

POSTHUMUS   You are a great deal abused in too bold a
persuasion, and I doubt not you sustain what you're
worthy of by your attempt.

IACHIMO   What's that?

POSTHUMUS   A repulse; though your attempt, as you
call it, deserve more – a punishment, too.

PHILARIO   Gentlemen, enough of this. It came in too
suddenly. Let it die as it was born, and I pray you be
better acquainted.

IACHIMO   Would I had put my estate and my
neighbour's on th'approbation of what I have spoke.

POSTHUMUS   What lady would you choose to assail?

IACHIMO   Yours, whom in constancy you think stands
so safe. I will lay you ten thousand ducats to your ring
that, commend me to the court where your lady is,
with no more advantage than the opportunity of a
second conference, and I will bring from thence that
honour of hers which you imagine so reserved.

POSTHUMUS   I will wage against your gold, gold to it.
My ring I hold dear as my finger: 'tis part of it.

IACHIMO   You are a friend, and therein the wiser. If you
buy ladies' flesh at a million a dram, you cannot
preserve it from tainting. But I see you have some
religion in you, that you fear.

POSTHUMUS   This is but a custom in your tongue. You
bear a graver purpose, I hope.

IACHIMO   I am the master of my speeches and would
undergo what's spoken, I swear.

POSTHUMUS   Will you? I shall but lend my diamond till
your return. Let there be covenants drawn between's.
My mistress exceeds in goodness the hugeness of your
unworthy thinking. I dare you to this match. Here's
my ring.

PHILARIO   I will have it no lay.

IACHIMO   By the gods, it is one. If I bring you no
sufficient testimony that I have enjoyed the dearest
bodily part of your mistress, my ten thousand ducats are
yours; so is your diamond, too. If I come off and leave
her in such honour as you have trust in, she your jewel,
this your jewel and my gold are yours, provided I have
your commendation for my more free entertainment.

POSTHUMUS   I embrace these conditions. Let us have
articles betwixt us. Only thus far you shall answer: if
you make your voyage upon her and give me directly to
understand you have prevailed, I am no further your
enemy; she is not worth our debate. If she remain
unseduced, you not making it appear otherwise, for
your ill opinion and th'assault you have made to her
chastity, you shall answer me with your sword.

IACHIMO   Your hand, a covenant. We will have these
things set down by lawful counsel, and straight away for
Britain, lest the bargain should catch cold and starve. I
will fetch my gold and have our two wagers recorded.

POSTHUMUS   Agreed.   *Exit with Iachimo.*

FRENCHMAN   Will this hold, think you?

PHILARIO   Signor Iachimo will not from it. Pray, let us
follow 'em.   *Exeunt.*

1.5   *Enter* QUEEN, *Ladies and* CORNELIUS.

QUEEN
Whiles yet the dew's on ground, gather those flowers.
Make haste. Who has the note of them?

LADY   I, madam.

QUEEN   Dispatch.   *Exeunt Ladies.*
Now, Master Doctor, have you brought those drugs?

CORNELIUS
Pleaseth your highness, ay. Here they are, madam.
   [*He gives her a box.*]
But I beseech your grace, without offence –
My conscience bids me ask – wherefore you have
Commanded of me these most poisonous compounds,
Which are the movers of a languishing death,
But though slow, deadly.

QUEEN   I wonder, doctor,
Thou ask'st me such a question. Have I not been
Thy pupil long? Hast thou not learned me how
To make perfumes? Distill? Preserve? Yea, so
That our great King himself doth woo me oft
For my confections? Having thus far proceeded,
Unless thou think'st me devilish, is't not meet
That I did amplify my judgement in
Other conclusions? I will try the forces
Of these thy compounds on such creatures as
We count not worth the hanging – but none human –
To try the vigour of them and apply
Allayments to their act, and by them gather
Their several virtues and effects.

CORNELIUS   Your highness
Shall from this practice but make hard your heart.
Besides, the seeing these effects will be
Both noisome and infectious.

QUEEN   O, content thee.

Enter PISANIO.

[*aside*] Here comes a flattering rascal; upon him
Will I first work. He's for his master,
And enemy to my son. – How now, Pisanio? –
Doctor, your service for this time is ended;
Take your own way.

CORNELIUS [*aside*]   I do suspect you, madam,
But you shall do no harm.

QUEEN [*to Pisanio, drawing him aside*]   Hark thee, a word.

CORNELIUS
I do not like her. She doth think she has
Strange lingering poisons. I do know her spirit,
And will not trust one of her malice with
A drug of such damned nature. Those she has
Will stupefy and dull the sense awhile,
Which first, perchance, she'll prove on cats and dogs,

Then afterward up higher; but there is
40 No danger in what show of death it makes
More than the locking up the spirits a time,
To be more fresh, reviving. She is fooled
With a most false effect; and I the truer
So to be false with her.

QUEEN   No further service, doctor,
Until I send for thee.

45 CORNELIUS   I humbly take my leave.   *Exit.*

QUEEN
Weeps she still, sayst thou? Dost thou think in time
She will not quench and let instructions enter
Where folly now possesses? Do thou work.
When thou shalt bring me word she loves my son,
50 I'll tell thee on the instant thou art then
As great as is thy master – greater, for
His fortunes all lie speechless, and his name
Is at last gasp. Return he cannot, nor
Continue where he is. To shift his being
55 Is to exchange one misery with another,
And every day that comes comes to decay
A day's work in him. What shalt thou expect
To be depender on a thing that leans,
Who cannot be new built, nor has no friends
So much as but to prop him?

[She drops the box. Pisanio picks it up.]
60   Thou tak'st up
Thou knowst not what; but take it for thy labour.
It is a thing I made which hath the King
Five times redeemed from death. I do not know
What is more cordial. Nay, I prithee, take it.
65 It is an earnest of a farther good
That I mean to thee. Tell thy mistress how
The case stands with her; do't as from thyself.
Think what a chance thou changest on, but think
Thou hast thy mistress still – to boot, my son,
70 Who shall take notice of thee. I'll move the King
To any shape of thy preferment such
As thou'lt desire; and then myself, I chiefly,
That set thee on to this desert, am bound
To load thy merit richly. Call my women.
Think on my words.   *Exit Pisanio.*
75   A sly and constant knave,
Not to be shaked; the agent for his master
And the remembrancer of her to hold
The handfast to her lord. I have given him that
Which, if he take, shall quite unpeople her
80 Of liegers for her sweet, and which she after,
Except she bend her humour, shall be assured
To taste of too.

Enter PISANIO, and Ladies with flowers.
                   So, so. Well done, well done.
The violets, cowslips, and the primroses
Bear to my closet. – Fare thee well, Pisanio.
Think on my words.   *Exeunt Queen and Ladies.*
85 PISANIO   And shall do.

But when to my good lord I prove untrue,
I'll choke myself. There's all I'll do for you.   *Exit.*

1.6   *Enter INNOGEN alone.*

INNOGEN   A father cruel and a stepdame false,
A foolish suitor to a wedded lady
That hath her husband banished. O, that husband,
My supreme crown of grief, and those repeated
Vexations of it! Had I been thief-stolen   5
As my two brothers, happy; but most miserable
Is the desire that's glorious. Blessed be those,
How mean soe'er, that have their honest wills,
Which seasons comfort.

Enter PISANIO and IACHIMO.

                        Who may this be? Fie!
PISANIO   Madam, a noble gentleman of Rome   10
Comes from my lord with letters.
IACHIMO   Change you, madam?
The worthy Leonatus is in safety
And greets your highness dearly.
                 [He gives her the letters.]
INNOGEN   Thanks, good sir.
You're kindly welcome.   *[She reads the letters.]*
IACHIMO *[aside]*
All of her that is out of door, most rich.   15
If she be furnished with a mind so rare,
She is alone th'Arabian bird, and I
Have lost the wager. Boldness be my friend.
Arm me audacity from head to foot,
Or, like the Parthian, I shall flying fight;   20
Rather, directly fly.
INNOGEN *[Reads.]* *He is one of the noblest note, to whose*
kindnesses I am most infinitely tied. Reflect upon him
accordingly, as you value your trust. Leonatus.
So far I read aloud,   25
But even the very middle of my heart
Is warmed by th' rest and take it thankfully.
You are as welcome, worthy sir, as I
Have words to bid you, and shall find it so
In all that I can do.
IACHIMO   Thanks, fairest lady.   30
What, are men mad? Hath nature given them eyes
To see this vaulted arch and the rich crop
Of sea and land, which can distinguish 'twixt
The fiery orbs above and the twinned stones
Upon th'unnumbered beach, and can we not   35
Partition make with spectacles so precious
'Twixt fair and foul?
INNOGEN   What makes your admiration?
IACHIMO   It cannot be i'th' eye, for apes and monkeys
'Twixt two such shes would chatter this way and
Contemn with mows the other; nor i'th' judgement, 40
For idiots in this case of favour would
Be wisely definite; nor i'th' appetite:
Sluttery, to such neat excellence opposed,

Should make desire vomit emptiness,
45 Not so allured to feed.
INNOGEN What is the matter, trow?
IACHIMO The cloyed will,
That satiate yet unsatisfied desire, that tub
Both filled and running, ravening first the lamb,
Longs after for the garbage.
INNOGEN What, dear sir,
50 Thus raps you? Are you well?
IACHIMO
Thanks, madam, well. [*to Pisanio*] Beseech you, sir,
Desire my man's abode where I did leave him.
He's strange and peevish.
PISANIO I was going, sir,
To give him welcome. *Exit.*
INNOGEN Continues well my lord?
His health, beseech you?
55 IACHIMO Well, madam.
INNOGEN Is he disposed to mirth? I hope he is.
IACHIMO Exceeding pleasant: none a stranger there
So merry and so gamesome. He is called
The Briton Reveller.
INNOGEN When he was here
60 He did incline to sadness, and oft-times
Not knowing why.
IACHIMO I never saw him sad.
There is a Frenchman his companion, one
An eminent monsieur that, it seems, much loves
A Gallian girl at home. He furnaces
65 The thick sighs from him, whiles the jolly Briton –
Your lord I mean – laughs from's free lungs, cries 'O,
Can my sides hold, to think that man who knows
By history, report, or his own proof
What woman is, yea, what she cannot choose
70 But must be, will's free hours languish
For assured bondage?'
INNOGEN Will my lord say so?
IACHIMO
Ay, madam, with his eyes in flood with laughter.
It is a recreation to be by
And hear him mock the Frenchman. But heavens know
Some men are much to blame.
75 INNOGEN Not he, I hope.
IACHIMO
Not he; but yet heaven's bounty towards him might
Be used more thankfully. In himself 'tis much;
In you, which I account his, beyond all talents.
Whilst I am bound to wonder, I am bound
To pity, too.
80 INNOGEN What do you pity, sir?
IACHIMO Two creatures heartily.
INNOGEN Am I one, sir?
You look on me. What wrack discern you in me
Deserves your pity?
IACHIMO Lamentable! What,
To hide me from the radiant sun and solace
I'th' dungeon by a snuff?

INNOGEN I pray you, sir, 85
Deliver with more openness your answers
To my demands. Why do you pity me?
IACHIMO That others do –
I was about to say, enjoy your – but
It is an office of the gods to venge it, 90
Not mine to speak on't.
INNOGEN You do seem to know
Something of me or what concerns me. Pray you,
Since doubting things go ill often hurts more
Than to be sure they do – for certainties
Either are past remedies or, timely knowing, 95
The remedy then born – discover to me
What both you spur and stop.
IACHIMO Had I this cheek
To bathe my lips upon; this hand whose touch,
Whose every touch, would force the feeler's soul
To th'oath of loyalty; this object, which 100
Takes prisoner the wild motion of mine eye,
Fixing it only here: should I, damned then,
Slaver with lips as common as the stairs
That mount the Capitol; join grips with hands
Made hard with hourly falsehood (falsehood, as 105
With labour); then by-peeping in an eye
Base and illustrous as the smoky light
That's fed with stinking tallow? It were fit
That all the plagues of hell should at one time
Encounter such revolt.
INNOGEN My Lord, I fear, 110
Has forgot Britain.
IACHIMO And himself. Not I,
Inclined to this intelligence, pronounce
The beggary of his change, but 'tis your graces
That from my mutest conscience to my tongue
Charms this report out.
INNOGEN Let me hear no more. 115
IACHIMO
O dearest soul, your cause doth strike my heart
With pity that doth make me sick. A lady
So fair, and fastened to an empery
Would make the great'st king double, to be partnered
With tomboys hired with that self exhibition 120
Which your own coffers yield; with diseased ventures
That play with all infirmities for gold
Which rottenness can lend nature; such boiled stuff
As well might poison poison. Be revenged,
Or she that bore you was no queen, and you 125
Recoil from your great stock.
INNOGEN Revenged?
How should I be revenged? If this be true –
As I have such a heart that both mine ears
Must not in haste abuse – if it be true,
How should I be revenged?
IACHIMO Should he make me 130
Live like Diana's priest betwixt cold sheets,
Whiles he is vaulting variable ramps
In your despite, upon your purse? Revenge it.

135 I dedicate myself to your sweet pleasure,
More noble than that runagate to your bed,
And will continue fast to your affection,
Still close as sure.

INNOGEN   What ho, Pisanio!

IACHIMO   Let me my service tender on your lips.

INNOGEN   Away, I do condemn mine ears that have
140 So long attended thee. If thou wert honourable
Thou wouldst have told this tale for virtue, not
For such an end thou seek'st, as base as strange.
Thou wrong'st a gentleman who is as far
From thy report as thou from honour, and
145 Solicits here a lady that disdains
Thee and the devil alike. – What ho, Pisanio! –
The King my father shall be made acquainted
Of thy assault. If he shall think it fit
A saucy stranger in his court to mart
150 As in a Romish stew and to expound
His beastly mind to us, he hath a court
He little cares for and a daughter who
He not respects at all. – What ho, Pisanio!

IACHIMO   O happy Leonatus! I may say
155 The credit that thy lady hath of thee
Deserves thy trust, and thy most perfect goodness
Her assured credit. – Blessed live you long,
A lady to the worthiest sir that ever
Country called his; and you his mistress, only
160 For the most worthiest fit. Give me your pardon.
I have spoke this to know if your affiance
Were deeply rooted, and shall make your lord
That which he is new o'er; and he is one
The truest mannered, such a holy witch
165 That he enchants societies into him.
Half all men's hearts are his.

INNOGEN   You make amends.

IACHIMO   He sits 'mongst men like a descended god.
He hath a kind of honour sets him off
More than a mortal seeming. Be not angry,
170 Most mighty Princess, that I have adventured
To try your taking of a false report, which hath
Honoured with confirmation your great judgement
In the election of a sir so rare,
Which you know cannot err. The love I bear him
175 Made me to fan you thus, but the gods made you,
Unlike all others, chaffless. Pray, your pardon.

INNOGEN
All's well, sir. Take my power i'th' court for yours.

IACHIMO   My humble thanks. I had almost forgot
T'entreat your grace but in a small request
180 And yet of moment too, for it concerns
Your lord; myself and other noble friends
Are partners in the business.

INNOGEN   Pray what is't?

IACHIMO   Some dozen Romans of us and your lord –
The best feather of our wing – have mingled sums
185 To buy a present for the Emperor,
Which I, the factor for the rest, have done

In France. 'Tis plate of rare device and jewels
Of rich and exquisite form, their values great,
And I am something curious, being strange,
190 To have them in safe stowage. May it please you
To take them in protection?

INNOGEN   Willingly,
And pawn mine honour for their safety. Since
My lord hath interest in them, I will keep them
In my bedchamber.

IACHIMO   They are in a trunk
195 Attended by my men. I will make bold
To send them to you only for this night:
I must aboard tomorrow.

INNOGEN   O no, no.

IACHIMO   Yes, I beseech, or I shall short my word
By length'ning my return. From Gallia
200 I crossed the seas on purpose and on promise
To see your grace.

INNOGEN   I thank you for your pains,
But not away tomorrow.

IACHIMO   O, I must, madam.
Therefore I shall beseech you, if you please
To greet your lord with writing, do't tonight.
205 I have outstood my time, which is material
To th' tender of our present.

INNOGEN   I will write.
Send your trunk to me: it shall safe be kept
And truly yielded you. You're very welcome. *Exeunt.*

2.1   *Enter* CLOTEN *and the two* Lords.

CLOTEN   Was there ever man had such luck? When I
kissed the jack, upon an upcast to be hit away! I had a
hundred pound on't, and then a whoreson jackanapes
must take me up for swearing, as if I borrowed mine
oaths of him and might not spend them at my pleasure.   5

1 LORD   What got he by that? You have broke his pate
with your bowl.

2 LORD [*aside*]   If his wit had been like him that broke it,
it would have run all out.

CLOTEN   When a gentleman is disposed to swear, it is   10
not for any standers-by to curtail his oaths, ha?

2 LORD [*aside*]   No my lord, nor crop the ears of them.

CLOTEN   Whoreson dog! I give him satisfaction? Would
he had been one of my rank.

2 LORD [*aside*]   To have smelled like a fool.   15

CLOTEN   I am not vexed more at anything in th'earth. A
pox on't! I had rather not be so noble as I am. They
dare not fight with me because of the Queen my
mother. Every jack-slave hath his bellyful of fighting,
and I must go up and down like a cock that nobody can   20
match.

2 LORD [*aside*]   You are cock and capon, too, and you
crow cock with your comb on.

CLOTEN   Sayst thou?

2 LORD   It is not fit your lordship should undertake   25
every companion that you give offence to.

CLOTEN   No, I know that, but it is fit I should commit
offence to my inferiors.

2 LORD   Aye, it is fit for your lordship only.

30 CLOTEN   Why, so I say.

1 LORD   Did you hear of a stranger that's come to court
tonight?

CLOTEN   A stranger, and I not know on't?

2 LORD   [*aside*]   He's a strange fellow himself and knows
35 it not.

1 LORD   There's an Italian come, and 'tis thought one of
Leonatus' friends.

CLOTEN   Leonatus? A banished rascal, and he's another,
whatsoever he be. Who told you of this stranger?

40 1 LORD   One of your lordship's pages.

CLOTEN   Is it fit I went to look upon him? Is there no
derogation in't?

2 LORD   You cannot derogate, my lord.

CLOTEN   Not easily, I think.

45 2 LORD   [*aside*]   You are a fool granted, therefore your
issues, being foolish, do not derogate.

CLOTEN   Come, I'll go see this Italian. What I have lost
today at bowls, I'll win tonight of him. Come, go.

2 LORD   I'll attend your lordship.

Exit Cloten and 1 Lord.

50 That such a crafty devil as is his mother
Should yield the world this ass! A woman that
Bears all down with her brain, and this her son
Cannot take two from twenty for his heart
And leave eighteen. Alas, poor princess,
55 Thou divine Innogen, what thou endur'st
Betwixt a father by thy stepdame governed,
A mother hourly coining plots, a wooer
More hateful than the foul expulsion is
Of thy dear husband, than that horrid act
60 Of the divorce he'd make. The heavens hold firm
The walls of thy dear honour, keep unshaked
That temple, thy fair mind, that thou mayst stand
T'enjoy thy banished lord and this great land.   *Exit.*

2.2   *Enter* INNOGEN *in her bed. A trunk is nearby.*
Enter to her HELEN, *a Lady.*

INNOGEN   Who's there? My woman Helen?

HELEN   Please you, madam.

INNOGEN   What hour is it?

HELEN   Almost midnight, madam.

INNOGEN
I have read three hours then; mine eyes are weak.
Fold down the leaf where I have left. To bed.
5 Take not away the taper, leave it burning,
And if thou canst awake by four o'th' clock,
I prithee, call me. Sleep hath seized me wholly.

Exit Helen.

To your protection I commend me, gods.
From fairies and the tempters of the night,
10 Guard me, beseech ye.   [*Sleeps.*]

IACHIMO *comes from the trunk.*

IACHIMO
The crickets sing, and man's o'er-laboured sense
Repairs itself by rest. Our Tarquin thus
Did softly press the rushes ere he wakened
The chastity he wounded. Cytherea,
How bravely thou becom'st thy bed! Fresh lily,   15
And whiter than the sheets! That I might touch,
But kiss, one kiss. Rubies unparagoned,
How dearly they do't. 'Tis her breathing that
Perfumes the chamber thus. The flame o'th' taper
Bows toward her and would under-peep her lids   20
To see th'enclosed lights, now canopied
Under these windows, white and azure laced
With blue of heaven's own tinct. But my design –
To note the chamber. I will write all down.

[*He begins to write.*]

Such and such pictures, there the window, such   25
Th'adornment of her bed, the arras, figures,
Why, such and such, and the contents o'th' story.
Ah, but some natural notes about her body,
Above ten thousand meaner moveables,
Would testify t'enrich mine inventory.   30
O sleep, thou ape of death, lie dull upon her,
And be her sense but as a monument
Thus in a chapel lying. Come off, come off –

[*He takes off her bracelet.*]

As slippery as the Gordian knot was hard.
'Tis mine, and this will witness outwardly,   35
As strongly as the conscience does within,
To th' madding of her lord. On her left breast
A mole, cinque-spotted, like the crimson drops
I'th' bottom of a cowslip. Here's a voucher
Stronger than ever law could make; this secret   40
Will force him think I have picked the lock and ta'en
The treasure of her honour. No more. To what end?
Why should I write this down that's riveted,
Screwed to my memory? She hath been reading late
The tale of Tereus: here the leaf's turned down   45
Where Philomel gave up. I have enough;
To th' trunk again, and shut the spring of it.
Swift, swift, you dragons of the night, that dawning
May bare the raven's eye. I lodge in fear;
Though this a heavenly angel, hell is here.   50

[*Clock strikes.*]

One, two, three: time, time.   *Exit.*

2.3   *Enter* CLOTEN *and the two* Lords.

1 LORD   Your lordship is the most patient man in loss,
the most coldest that ever turned up ace.

CLOTEN   It would make any man cold to lose.

1 LORD   But not every man patient after the noble
temper of your lordship. You are most hot and furious   5
when you win.

CLOTEN   Winning will put any man into courage. If I
could get this foolish Innogen, I should have gold
enough. It's almost morning, is't not?

10 1 LORD   Day, my Lord.

CLOTEN   I would this music would come. I am advised
to give her music o' mornings; they say it will penetrate.

Enter Musicians with stringed instruments.

Come on, tune. If you can penetrate her with your
fingering, so; we'll try with tongue, too. If none will do,
15 let her remain, but I'll never give o'er. First, a very
excellent good-conceited thing; after a wonderful
sweet air with admirable rich words to it; and then let
her consider.

SONG

MUSICIAN
Hark, hark, the lark at heaven's gate sings,
20   And Phoebus 'gins arise,
His steeds to water at those springs
    On chaliced flowers that lies,
And winking Mary-buds begin to ope their golden
    eyes.
With every thing that pretty is, my lady sweet, arise,
25   Arise, arise.

CLOTEN   So, get you gone. If this penetrate, I will
consider your music the better; if it do not, it is a voice
in her ears which horsehairs and calves' guts, nor the
voice of unpaved eunuch to boot, can never amend.

Exeunt Musicians.

Enter CYMBELINE and QUEEN.

30 2 LORD   Here comes the King.

CLOTEN   I am glad I was up so late, for that's the reason
I was up so early. He cannot choose but take this service
I have done fatherly. – Good morrow to your majesty
and to my gracious mother.

CYMBELINE
35 Attend you here the door of our stern daughter?
Will she not forth?

CLOTEN   I have assailed her with musics, but she
vouchsafes no notice.

CYMBELINE
The exile of her minion is too new.
40 She hath not yet forgot him. Some more time
Must wear the print of his remembrance out,
And then she's yours.

QUEEN   You are most bound to th' King,
Who lets go by no vantages that may
Prefer you to his daughter. Frame yourself
45 To orderly solicity, and be friended
With aptness of the season; make denials
Increase your services; so seem as if
You were inspired to do those duties which
You tender to her, that you in all obey her,
50 Save when command to your dismission tends,
And therein you are senseless.

CLOTEN   Senseless? Not so.

Enter a Messenger.

MESSENGER   So like you, sir, ambassadors from Rome:
The one is Caius Lucius.

CYMBELINE   A worthy fellow,
Albeit he comes on angry purpose now;
But that's no fault of his. We must receive him   55
According to the honour of his sender,
And towards himself, his goodness forespent on us,
We must extend our notice. – Our dear son,
When you have given good morning to your mistress,
Attend the Queen and us. We shall have need   60
T'employ you towards this Roman. – Come, our
    Queen.   *Exeunt all but Cloten.*

CLOTEN   If she be up, I'll speak with her; if not,
Let her lie still and dream. By your leave, ho!

                        [*Knocks.*]

– I know her women are about her: what
If I do line one of their hands? 'Tis gold   65
Which buys admittance – oft it doth – yea, and makes
Diana's rangers false themselves, yield up
Their deer to th' stand o' th' stealer, and 'tis gold
Which makes the true man killed and saves the thief,
Nay, sometime hangs both thief and true man. What   70
Can it not do and undo? I will make
One of her women lawyer to me, for
I yet not understand the case myself. –
By your leave!   [*Knocks.*]

Enter DOROTHY, a lady.

DOROTHY   Who's there that knocks?

CLOTEN   A gentleman.

DOROTHY   No more?   75

CLOTEN   Yes, and a gentlewoman's son.

DOROTHY   That's more
Than some whose tailors are as dear as yours
Can justly boast of. What's your lordship's pleasure?

CLOTEN   Your lady's person. Is she ready?

DOROTHY   Ay,
To keep her chamber.

CLOTEN   There is gold for you.   80
Sell me your good report.

DOROTHY   How, my good name? Or to report of you
What I shall think is good?

Enter INNOGEN.

                The Princess.   *Exit.*

CLOTEN
Good morrow, fairest sister. Your sweet hand.

INNOGEN
Good morrow, sir. You lay out too much pains   85
For purchasing but trouble. The thanks I give
Is telling you that I am poor of thanks
And scarce can spare them.

CLOTEN   Still I swear I love you.

INNOGEN   If you but said so, 'twere as deep with me;
If you swear still, your recompense is still   90
That I regard it not.

CLOTEN   This is no answer.

INNOGEN
But that you shall not say I yield being silent,
I would not speak. I pray you spare me. Faith,
I shall unfold equal discourtesy
95   To your best kindness. One of your great knowing
Should learn, being taught, forbearance.
CLOTEN   To leave you in your madness, 'twere my sin;
I will not.
INNOGEN   Fools cure not mad folks.
CLOTEN   Do you call me fool?
100 INNOGEN   As I am mad, I do.
If you'll be patient, I'll no more be mad;
That cures us both. I am much sorry, sir,
You put me to forget a lady's manners
By being so verbal, and learn now for all
105 That I which know my heart do here pronounce
By th' very truth of it: I care not for you,
And am so near the lack of charity
To accuse myself I hate you, which I had rather
You felt than make't my boast.
CLOTEN   You sin against
110 Obedience, which you owe your father. For
The contract you pretend with that base wretch,
One bred of alms and fostered with cold dishes,
With scraps o'th' court, it is no contract, none;
And though it be allowed in meaner parties
115 – Yet who than he more mean? – to knit their souls,
On whom there is no more dependency
But brats and beggary, in self-figured knot,
Yet you are curbed from that enlargement by
The consequence o'th' crown, and must not foil
120 The precious note of it with a base slave,
A hilding for a livery, a squire's cloth,
A pantler – not so eminent.
INNOGEN   Profane fellow,
Wert thou the son of Jupiter, and no more
But what thou art besides, thou wert too base
125 To be his groom. Thou wert dignified enough,
Even to the point of envy, if 'twere made
Comparative for your virtues to be styled
The under-hangman of his kingdom and hated
For being preferred so well.
CLOTEN   The south fog rot him!
INNOGEN
130 He never can meet more mischance than come
To be but named of thee. His meanest garment
That ever hath but clipped his body is dearer
In my respect than all the hairs above thee,
Were they all made such men. How now, Pisanio!

Enter PISANIO.

135 CLOTEN   His garment? Now the devil –
INNOGEN   To Dorothy my woman hie thee presently.
CLOTEN   His garment?
INNOGEN   I am sprited with a fool,
Frighted and angered worse. Go bid my woman
Search for a jewel that too casually

Hath left mine arm; it was thy master's. 'Shrew me   140
If I would lose it for a revenue
Of any king's in Europe. I do think
I saw't this morning. Confident I am
Last night 'twas on mine arm; I kissed it.
I hope it be not gone to tell my lord   145
That I kiss aught but he.
PISANIO   'Twill not be lost.
INNOGEN
I hope so. Go and search.   *Exit Pisanio.*
CLOTEN   You have abused me.
His meanest garment?
INNOGEN   Ay, I said so, sir.
If you will make't an action, call witness to't.
CLOTEN   I will inform your father.
INNOGEN   Your mother, too.   150
She's my good lady and will conceive, I hope,
But the worst of me. So I leave you, sir,
To th' worst of discontent.   *Exit.*
CLOTEN   I'll be revenged.
His meanest garment? Well.   *Exit.*

2.4   *Enter* POSTHUMUS *and* PHILARIO.

POSTHUMUS   Fear it not, sir. I would I were so sure
To win the King as I am bold her honour
Will remain hers.
PHILARIO   What means do you make to him?
POSTHUMUS   Not any, but abide the change of time,
Quake in the present winter's state, and wish   5
That warmer days would come. In these seared hopes
I barely gratify your love; they failing,
I must die much your debtor.
PHILARIO   Your very goodness and your company
O'erpays all I can do. By this, your King   10
Hath heard of great Augustus. Caius Lucius
Will do's commission throughly. And I think
He'll grant the tribute, send th'arrearages,
Or look upon our Romans, whose remembrance
Is yet fresh in their grief.
POSTHUMUS   I do believe –   15
Statist though I am none, nor like to be –
That this will prove a war; and you shall hear
The legions now in Gallia sooner landed
In our not-fearing Britain than have tidings
Of any penny tribute paid. Our countrymen   20
Are men more ordered than when Julius Caesar
Smiled at their lack of skill but found their courage
Worthy his frowning at. Their discipline,
Now wing-led with their courages, will make known
To their approvers they are people such   25
That mend upon the world.

Enter IACHIMO.

PHILARIO   See Iachimo.
POSTHUMUS
The swiftest harts have posted you by land,

And winds of all the corners kissed your sails
To make your vessel nimble.

PHILARIO　　　　　　　　　　　Welcome, sir.

POSTHUMUS

30 I hope the briefness of your answer made
The speediness of your return.

IACHIMO　　　　　　　　　　Your lady
Is one of the fairest that I have looked upon.

POSTHUMUS
And therewithal the best, or let her beauty
Look through a casement to allure false hearts
And be false with them.

35 IACHIMO　　　　　　　　Here are letters for you.

POSTHUMUS　Their tenor good, I trust.

IACHIMO　　　　　　　　　　'Tis very like.

PHILARIO　Was Caius Lucius in the Briton court
When you were there?

IACHIMO　　　　　　He was expected then,
But not approached.

POSTHUMUS　　　　　All is well yet.
40 Sparkles this stone as it was wont, or is't not
Too dull for your good wearing?

IACHIMO　　　　　　　　　　　If I have lost it,
I should have lost the worth of it in gold.
I'll make a journey twice as far t'enjoy
A second night of such sweet shortness which
45 Was mine in Britain, for the ring is won.

POSTHUMUS　The stone's too hard to come by.

IACHIMO　　　　　　　　　　Not a whit,
Your lady being so easy.

POSTHUMUS　　　　　　Make not, sir,
Your loss your sport. I hope you know that we
Must not continue friends.

IACHIMO　　　　　　　Good sir, we must
50 If you keep covenant. Had I not brought
The knowledge of your mistress home, I grant
We were to question farther; but I now
Profess myself the winner of her honour
Together with your ring, and not the wronger
55 Of her or you, having proceeded but
By both your wills.

POSTHUMUS　　　If you can make't apparent
That you have tasted her in bed, my hand
And ring is yours. If not, the foul opinion
You had of her pure honour gains or loses
60 Your sword or mine, or masterless leaves both
To who shall find them.

IACHIMO　　　　　　Sir, my circumstances,
Being so near the truth as I will make them,
Must first induce you to believe, whose strength
I will confirm with oath which I doubt not
65 You'll give me leave to spare when you shall find
You need it not.

POSTHUMUS　　　Proceed.

IACHIMO　　　　　　First, her bedchamber –
Where I confess I slept not, but profess
Had that was well worth watching – it was hanged

With tapestry of silk and silver, the story
Proud Cleopatra when she met her Roman, 70
And Cydnus swelled above the banks, or for
The press of boats or pride: a piece of work
So bravely done, so rich, that it did strive
In workmanship and value, which I wondered
Could be so rarely and exactly wrought, 75
Since the true life on't was –

POSTHUMUS　　　　　　　This is true,
And this you might have heard of here by me
Or by some other.

IACHIMO　　　　　　More particulars
Must justify my knowledge.

POSTHUMUS　　　　　So they must,
Or do your honour injury.

IACHIMO　　　　　　The chimney 80
Is south the chamber, and the chimney-piece
Chaste Dian bathing. Never saw I figures
So likely to report themselves. The cutter
Was as another nature, dumb; out-went her,
Motion and breath left out.

POSTHUMUS　　　　　This is a thing 85
Which you might from relation likewise reap,
Being, as it is, much spoke of.

IACHIMO　　　　　　The roof o'th' chamber,
With golden cherubins is fretted. Her andirons –
I had forgot them – were two winking cupids
Of silver, each on one foot standing, nicely 90
Depending on their brands.

POSTHUMUS　　　　　This is her honour!
Let it be granted you have seen all this – and praise
Be given to your remembrance – the description
Of what is in her chamber nothing saves
The wager you have laid.

IACHIMO　　　　　Then if you can 95
Be pale, I beg but leave to air this jewel. See!

　　[*He shows the bracelet.*]

And now 'tis up again. It must be married
To that your diamond. I'll keep them.

POSTHUMUS　　　　　　Jove!
Once more let me behold it. Is it that
Which I left with her?

IACHIMO　　　　　Sir, I thank her, that. 100
She stripped it from her arm. I see her yet.
Her pretty action did outsell her gift,
And yet enriched it, too. She gave it me,
And said she prized it once.

POSTHUMUS　　　　　Maybe she plucked it off
To send it me.

IACHIMO　　She writes so to you, doth she? 105

POSTHUMUS
O no, no, no, 'tis true. Here, take this too.

　　[*He gives Iachimo the ring.*]

It is a basilisk unto mine eye,
Kills me to look on't. Let there be no honour
Where there is beauty, truth where semblance, love
Where there's another man. The vows of women 110

268

Of no more bondage be to where they are made
Than they are to their virtues, which is nothing.
O, above measure false!

PHILARIO   Have patience, sir,
And take your ring again; 'tis not yet won.
115 It may be probable she lost it, or
Who knows if one her women, being corrupted,
Hath stolen it from her.

POSTHUMUS   Very true,
And so I hope he came by't. Back my ring.
    [*He takes back the ring.*]
120 Render to me some corporal sign about her
More evident than this, for this was stolen.

IACHIMO   By Jupiter, I had it from her arm.

POSTHUMUS
Hark you, he swears; by Jupiter he swears.
'Tis true, nay keep the ring; 'tis true. I am sure
125 She would not lose it. Her attendants are
All sworn and honourable. They induced to steal it?
And by a stranger? No, he hath enjoyed her.
The cognizance of her incontinency
Is this: she hath bought the name of whore thus dearly.
    [*He gives Iachimo the ring again.*]
There, take thy hire, and all the fiends of hell
Divide themselves between you!

130 PHILARIO   Sir, be patient.
This is not strong enough to be believed
Of one persuaded well of.

POSTHUMUS   Never talk on't.
She hath been colted by him.

IACHIMO   If you seek
For further satisfying, under her breast –
135 Worthy the pressing – lies a mole, right proud
Of that most delicate lodging. By my life
I kissed it, and it gave me present hunger
To feed again, though full. You do remember
This stain upon her?

POSTHUMUS   Ay, and it doth confirm
140 Another stain as big as hell can hold,
Were there no more but it.

IACHIMO   Will you hear more?

POSTHUMUS
Spare your arithmetic. Never count the turns.
Once, and a million.

IACHIMO   I'll be sworn.

POSTHUMUS   No swearing.
If you will swear you have not done't, you lie,
145 And I will kill thee if thou dost deny
Thou'st made me cuckold.

IACHIMO   I'll deny nothing.

POSTHUMUS
O that I had her here to tear her limb-meal!
I will go there and do't i'th' court, before
Her father. I'll do something –   *Exit.*

PHILARIO   Quite besides
150 The government of patience. You have won.
Let's follow him and pervert the present wrath

He hath against himself.

IACHIMO   With all my heart.   *Exeunt.*

2.5   *Enter* POSTHUMUS.

POSTHUMUS
Is there no way for men to be, but women
Must be half-workers? We are all bastards,
And that most venerable man which I
Did call my father was I know not where
When I was stamped. Some coiner with his tools   5
Made me a counterfeit; yet my mother seemed
The Dian of that time, so doth my wife
The non-pareil of this. O vengeance, vengeance!
Me of my lawful pleasure she restrained
And prayed me oft forbearance; did it with   10
A pudency so rosy, the sweet view on't
Might well have warmed old Saturn, that I thought her
As chaste as unsunned snow. O, all the devils!
This yellow Iachimo, in an hour, was't not?
Or less, at first? Perchance he spoke not, but   15
Like a full-acorned boar, a German one,
Cried 'O!' and mounted; found no opposition
But what he looked for should oppose, and she
Should from encounter guard. Could I find out
The woman's part in me – for there's no motion   20
That tends to vice in man but I affirm
It is the woman's part: be it lying, note it,
The woman's; flattering, hers; deceiving, hers;
Lust and rank thoughts, hers, hers; revenges, hers;
Ambitions, covetings, change of prides, disdain,   25
Nice-longing, slanders, mutability,
All faults that name – nay, that hell knows – why hers
In part or all, but rather all, for even to vice
They are not constant but are changing still,
One vice but of a minute old for one   30
Not half so old as that. I'll write against them,
Detest them, curse them. Yet 'tis greater skill
In a true hate to pray they have their will.
The very devils cannot plague them better.   *Exit.*

3.1   *Enter in state* CYMBELINE, QUEEN, CLOTEN
    and Lords at one door, and at another, CAIUS
    LUCIUS *and Attendants.*

CYMBELINE
Now say, what would Augustus Caesar with us?

LUCIUS   When Julius Caesar – whose remembrance yet
Lives in men's eyes, and will to ears and tongues
Be theme and hearing ever – was in this Britain
And conquered it, Cassibelan, thine uncle,   5
Famous in Caesar's praises no whit less
Than in his feats deserving it, for him
And his succession granted Rome a tribute,
Yearly three thousand pounds, which by thee lately
Is left untendered.

QUEEN   And to kill the marvel,   10

Shall be so ever.

CLOTEN   There be many Caesars,
Ere such another Julius. Britain's a world
By itself, and we will nothing pay
For wearing our own noses.

QUEEN   That opportunity
15 Which then they had to take from's, to resume
We have again. Remember sir, my liege,
The kings your ancestors, together with
The natural bravery of your isle, which stands
As Neptune's park, ribbed and paled in
20 With oaks unscalable and roaring waters,
With sands that will not bear your enemies' boats,
But suck them up to th' topmast. A kind of conquest
Caesar made here, but made not here his brag
Of 'came and saw and overcame'. With shame –
25 The first that ever touched him – he was carried
From off our coast, twice beaten, and his shipping,
Poor ignorant baubles, on our terrible seas
Like eggshells moved upon their surges, cracked
As easily 'gainst our rocks. For joy whereof,
30 The famed Cassibelan, who was once at point –
O giglot Fortune! – to master Caesar's sword,
Made Lud's town with rejoicing fires bright,
And Britons strut with courage.

CLOTEN   Come, there's no more tribute to be paid. Our
35 kingdom is stronger than it was at that time and, as I
said, there is no more such Caesars. Other of them may
have crooked noses, but to owe such straight arms, none.

CYMBELINE   Son, let your mother end.

CLOTEN   We have yet many among us can grip as hard
40 as Cassibelan. I do not say I am one, but I have a hand.
Why tribute? Why should we pay tribute? If Caesar
can hide the sun from us with a blanket, or put the
moon in his pocket, we will pay him tribute for light;
else, sir, no more tribute, pray you now.

45 CYMBELINE   You must know,
Till the injurious Romans did extort
This tribute from us, we were free. Caesar's ambition,
Which swelled so much that it did almost stretch
The sides o'th' world, against all colour here
50 Did put the yoke upon's, which to shake off
Becomes a warlike people, whom we reckon
Ourselves to be. We do say then to Caesar,
Our ancestor was that Mulmutius which
Ordained our laws, whose use the sword of Caesar
55 Hath too much mangled, whose repair and franchise
Shall, by the power we hold, be our good deed,
Though Rome be therefore angry. Mulmutius made
   our laws,
Who was the first of Britain which did put
His brows within a golden crown and called
Himself a king.

60 LUCIUS   I am sorry, Cymbeline,
That I am to pronounce Augustus Caesar –
Caesar that hath moe kings his servants than
Thyself domestic officers – thine enemy.

Receive it from me then: war and confusion
In Caesar's name pronounce I 'gainst thee. Look   65
For fury not to be resisted. Thus defied,
I thank thee for myself.

CYMBELINE   Thou art welcome, Caius.
Thy Caesar knighted me; my youth I spent
Much under him; of him I gathered honour,
Which he to seek of me again, perforce,   70
Behoves me keep at utterance. I am perfect
That the Pannonians and Dalmatians for
Their liberties are now in arms, a precedent
Which not to read would show the Britons cold;
So Caesar shall not find them.

LUCIUS   Let proof speak.   75

CLOTEN   His majesty bids you welcome. Make pastime
with us a day or two or longer. If you seek us afterwards in other terms, you shall find us in our salt-water
girdle. If you beat us out of it, it is yours; if you fall in
the adventure, our crows shall fare the better for you,   80
and there's an end.

LUCIUS   So, sir.

CYMBELINE
I know your master's pleasure, and he mine.
All the remain is 'Welcome'.   *Exeunt.*

3.2   *Enter* PISANIO *reading of a letter.*

PISANIO   How? Of adultery? Wherefore write you not
What monster's her accuser? Leonatus,
O master, what a strange infection
Is fall'n into thy ear? What false Italian,
As poisonous tongued as handed, hath prevailed   5
On thy too ready hearing? Disloyal? No.
She's punished for her truth and undergoes,
More goddess-like than wife-like, such assaults
As would take in some virtue. O my master,
Thy mind to her is now as low as were   10
Thy fortunes. How? That I should murder her
Upon the love and truth and vows which I
Have made to thy command? I, her? Her blood?
If it be so to do good service, never
Let me be counted serviceable. How look I,   15
That I should seem to lack humanity,
So much as this fact comes to?
[*Reads.*]   *Do't. The letter
That I have sent her, by her own command,
Shall give thee opportunity.* O damned paper,
Black as the ink that's on thee. Senseless bauble,   20
Art thou a fedary for this act, and look'st
So virgin-like without?

                Enter INNOGEN.

                        Lo, here she comes.
I am ignorant in what I am commanded.

INNOGEN   How now, Pisanio?

PISANIO   Madam, here is a letter from my lord.   25

INNOGEN   Who, thy lord? That is my lord, Leonatus?

O, learn'd indeed were that astronomer
That knew the stars as I his characters:
He'd lay the future open. You good gods,
30   Let what is here contained relish of love,
Of my lord's health, of his content – yet not
That we two are asunder, let that grieve him;
Some griefs are med'cinable, that is one of them,
For it doth physic love – of his content,
35   All but in that. Good wax, thy leave. Blest be
You bees that make these locks of counsel. Lovers
And men in dangerous bonds pray not alike:
Though forfeiters you cast in prison, yet
You clasp young Cupid's tables. Good news, gods.
40   [*Reads.*] *Justice and your father's wrath, should he take*
me in his dominion, could not be so cruel to me as you, O
the dearest of creatures, would even renew me with your
eyes. Take notice that I am in Cambria at Milford Haven.
What your own love will out of this advise you, follow. So
45   *he wishes you all happiness that remains loyal to his vow,*
and your increasing in love.   *Leonatus Posthumus.*
O for a horse with wings! Hear'st thou, Pisanio?
He is at Milford Haven! Read and tell me
How far 'tis thither. If one of mean affairs
50   May plod it in a week, why may not I
Glide thither in a day? Then, true Pisanio,
Who long'st like me to see thy lord, who long'st
(O let me bate) but not like me, yet long'st
But in a fainter kind – O, not like me,
55   For mine's beyond beyond – say and speak thick
(Love's counsellor should fill the bores of hearing
To th' smothering of the sense) how far it is
To this same blessed Milford. And by th' way
Tell me how Wales was made so happy as
60   T'inherit such a haven. But first of all,
How we may steal from hence, and for the gap
That we shall make in time, from our hence-going
And our return, to excuse. But first, how get hence?
Why should excuse be born or ere begot?
65   We'll talk of that hereafter. Prithee speak,
How many score of miles may we well ride
'Twixt hour and hour?

PISANIO   One score 'twixt sun and sun,
Madam, 's enough for you, and too much too.

INNOGEN   Why, one that rode to's execution, man,
70   Could never go so slow. I have heard of riding wagers,
Where horses have been nimbler than the sands
That run i'th' clock's behalf, but this is fool'ry.
Go, bid my woman feign a sickness, say
She'll home to her father, and provide me presently
75   A riding suit no costlier than would fit
A franklin's housewife.

PISANIO   Madam, you're best consider –

INNOGEN   I see before me, man. Nor here, nor here,
Nor what ensues but have a fog in them
That I cannot look through. Away, I prithee,
80   Do as I bid thee. There's no more to say.
Accessible is none but Milford way.   *Exeunt.*

3.3   *Enter* BELARIUS, GUIDERIUS *and* ARVIRAGUS
         from a cave.

BELARIUS   A goodly day not to keep house with such
Whose roof's as low as ours. Stoop, boys: this gate
Instructs you how t'adore the heavens and bows you
To a morning's holy office. The gates of monarchs
Are arched so high that giants may jet through   5
And keep their impious turbans on without
Good morrow to the sun. Hail, thou fair heaven!
We house i'th' rock, yet use thee not so hardly
As prouder livers do.

GUIDERIUS   Hail, heaven!

ARVIRAGUS   Hail, heaven!

BELARIUS
Now for our mountain sport. Up to yond hill,   10
Your legs are young; I'll tread these flats. Consider,
When you above perceive me like a crow,
That it is place which lessens and sets off,
And you may then revolve what tales I have told you
Of courts, of princes, of the tricks in war.   15
This service is not service, so being done,
But being so allowed. To apprehend thus
Draws us a profit from all things we see,
And often to our comfort shall we find
The sharded beetle in a safer hold   20
Than is the full-winged eagle. O, this life
Is nobler than attending for a check,
Richer than doing nothing for a babe,
Prouder than rustling in unpaid-for silk;
Such gain the cap of him that makes him fine   25
Yet keeps his book uncrossed. No life to ours.

GUIDERIUS
Out of your proof you speak: we poor unfledged
Have never winged from view o'th' nest, nor know
  not
What air's from home. Haply this life is best,
If quiet life be best, sweeter to you   30
That have a sharper known, well corresponding
With your stiff age. But unto us it is
A cell of ignorance, travelling abed,
A prison for a debtor that not dares
To stride a limit.

ARVIRAGUS   What should we speak of   35
When we are old as you? When we shall hear
The rain and wind beat dark December, how
In this our pinching cave shall we discourse
The freezing hours away? We have seen nothing.
We are beastly: subtle as the fox for prey,   40
Like warlike as the wolf for what we eat.
Our valour is to chase what flies; our cage
We make a choir, as doth the prisoned bird,
And sing our bondage freely.

BELARIUS   How you speak!
Did you but know the city's usuries   45
And felt them knowingly: the art o'th' court,
As hard to leave as keep, whose top to climb

Is certain falling, or so slipp'ry that
The fear's as bad as falling; the toil o'th' war,
50 A pain that only seems to seek out danger
I'th' name of fame and honour, which dies i'th' search
And hath as oft a sland'rous epitaph
As record of fair act; nay, many times
Doth ill deserve by doing well; what's worse,
55 Must curtsy at the censure. O boys, this story
The world may read in me: my body's marked
With Roman swords, and my report was once
First with the best of note. Cymbeline loved me,
And when a soldier was the theme, my name
60 Was not far off. Then was I as a tree
Whose boughs did bend with fruit; but in one night
A storm or robbery, call it what you will,
Shook down my mellow hangings, nay my leaves,
And left me bare to weather.

GUIDERIUS   Uncertain favour.
BELARIUS
65 My fault being nothing, as I have told you oft,
But that two villains, whose false oaths prevailed
Before my perfect honour, swore to Cymbeline
I was confederate with the Romans. So
Followed my banishment, and this twenty years
70 This rock and these demesnes have been my world,
Where I have lived at honest freedom, paid
More pious debts to heaven than in all
The fore-end of my time. But up to th' mountains!
This is not hunters' language. He that strikes
75 The venison first shall be the lord o'th' feast;
To him the other two shall minister,
And we will fear no poison which attends
In place of greater state. I'll meet you in the valleys.
          Exeunt Guiderius and Arviragus.
How hard it is to hide the sparks of nature.
80 These boys know little they are sons to th' King,
Nor Cymbeline dreams that they are alive.
They think they are mine, and though trained up
      thus meanly
I'th' cave wherein they bow, their thoughts do hit
The roofs of palaces, and nature prompts them
85 In simple and low things to prince it much
Beyond the trick of others. This Polydore,
The heir of Cymbeline and Britain, who
The King his father called Guiderius – Jove!
When on my three-foot stool I sit and tell
90 The warlike feats I have done, his spirits fly out
Into my story; say, 'Thus mine enemy fell,
And thus I set my foot on's neck', even then
The princely blood flows in his cheek, he sweats,
Strains his young nerves, and puts himself in posture
95 That acts my words. The younger brother, Cadwal,
Once Arviragus, in as like a figure
Strikes life into my speech, and shows much more
His own conceiving.   [*A hunting-horn sounds.*]
          Hark, the game is roused!
O Cymbeline, heaven and my conscience knows

Thou didst unjustly banish me, whereon   100
At three and two years old I stole these babes,
Thinking to bar thee of succession, as
Thou reft'st me of my lands. Euriphile,
Thou wast their nurse; they took thee for their mother,
And every day do honour to her grave.   105
Myself, Belarius, that am Morgan called,
They take for natural father.   [*A hunting-horn sounds.*]
           The game is up.   *Exit.*

3.4   *Enter* PISANIO *and* INNOGEN.

INNOGEN
Thou told'st me when we came from horse, the place
Was near at hand. Ne'er longed my mother so
To see me first as I have now. Pisanio, man,
Where is Posthumus? What is in thy mind
That makes thee stare thus? Wherefore breaks that
    sigh   5
From th'inward of thee? One but painted thus
Would be interpreted a thing perplexed
Beyond self-explication. Put thyself
Into a haviour of less fear ere wildness
Vanquish my staider senses. What's the matter?   10
    [*Pisanio gives her a letter.*]
Why tender'st thou that paper to me with
A look untender? If't be summer news,
Smile to't before; if winterly, thou need'st
But keep that count'nance still. My husband's hand?
That drug-damned Italy hath out-craftied him   15
And he's at some hard point. Speak, man: thy tongue
May take off some extremity, which to read
Would be even mortal to me.
PISANIO   Please you read,
And you shall find me, wretched man, a thing
The most disdained of fortune.   20
INNOGEN [*Reads.*]
Thy mistress, Pisanio, hath played the strumpet in my bed,
the testimonies whereof lies bleeding in me. I speak not out
of weak surmises, but from proof as strong as my grief, and
as certain as I expect my revenge. That part thou, Pisanio,
must act for me, if thy faith be not tainted with the breach   25
of hers. Let thine own hands take away her life. I shall
give thee opportunity at Milford Haven – she hath my
letter for the purpose – where, if thou fear to strike and to
make me certain it is done, thou art the pander to her
dishonour and equally to me disloyal.   30
PISANIO [*aside*]
What shall I need to draw my sword? The paper
Hath cut her throat already. No, 'tis slander,
Whose edge is sharper than the sword, whose tongue
Out-venoms all the worms of Nile, whose breath
Rides on the posting winds and doth belie   35
All corners of the world. Kings, queens and states,
Maids, matrons, nay the secrets of the grave
This viperous slander enters. – What cheer, madam?
INNOGEN   False to his bed? What is it to be false?

40   To lie in watch there and to think on him?
        To weep 'twixt clock and clock? If sleep charge nature,
        To break it with a fearful dream of him
        And cry myself awake? That's false to's bed, is it?

PISANIO   Alas, good lady.

45 INNOGEN   I false? Thy conscience witness, Iachimo,
        Thou didst accuse him of incontinency.
        Thou then look'dst like a villain; now, methinks,
        Thy favour's good enough. Some jay of Italy,
        Whose mother was her painting, hath betrayed him.
50   Poor I am stale, a garment out of fashion,
        And for I am richer than to hang by th' walls,
        I must be ripped. To pieces with me! O,
        Men's vows are women's traitors. All good seeming
        By thy revolt, O husband, shall be thought
55   Put on for villainy; not born where't grows,
        But worn a bait for ladies.

PISANIO   Good madam, hear me –

INNOGEN
        True honest men, being heard like false Aeneas,
        Were in his time thought false, and Sinon's weeping
        Did scandal many a holy tear, took pity
60   From most true wretchedness. So thou, Posthumus,
        Wilt lay the leaven on all proper men;
        Goodly and gallant shall be false and perjured
        From thy great fail. [*to Pisanio*] Come fellow, be thou
          honest,
        Do thou thy master's bidding. When thou seest him,
65   A little witness my obedience. Look,
        I draw the sword myself.
          [*She draws Pisanio's sword and offers it to him.*]
              Take it, and hit
        The innocent mansion of my love, my heart.
        Fear not, 'tis empty of all things but grief.
        Thy master is not there, who was indeed
70   The riches of it. Do his bidding, strike.
        Thou mayst be valiant in a better cause,
        But now thou seem'st a coward.

PISANIO   [*He throws away the sword.*]
              Hence, vile instrument.
        Thou shalt not damn my hand.

INNOGEN   Why, I must die,
        And if I do not by thy hand, thou art
75   No servant of thy master's. Against self-slaughter
        There is a prohibition so divine
        That cravens my weak hand. Come, here's my heart.
        Something's afore't. Soft, soft, we'll no defence,
        Obedient as the scabbard. What is here?
          [*She pulls letters from her bodice.*]
80   The scriptures of the loyal Leonatus,
        All turned to heresy? Away, away,
          [*She throws the letters away.*]
        Corrupters of my faith, you shall no more
        Be stomachers to my heart. Thus may poor fools
        Believe false teachers. Though those that are betrayed
85   Do feel the treason sharply, yet the traitor
        Stands in worse case of woe. And thou, Posthumus,

        That didst set up my disobedience 'gainst the King
        My father, and makes me put into contempt the suits
        Of princely fellows, shalt hereafter find
        It is no act of common passage but   90
        A strain of rareness; and I grieve myself
        To think, when thou shalt be disedged by her
        That now thou tirest on, how thy memory
        Will then be panged by me. Prithee dispatch,
        The lamb entreats the butcher. Where's thy knife?   95
        Thou art too slow to do thy master's bidding
        When I desire it too.

PISANIO   O gracious lady,
        Since I received command to do this business,
        I have not slept one wink.

INNOGEN   Do't, and to bed then.

PISANIO   I'll wake mine eyeballs out first.

INNOGEN   Wherefore then   100
        Didst undertake it? Why hast thou abused
        So many miles with a pretence? This place?
        Mine action, and thine own? Our horses' labour?
        The time inviting thee? The perturbed court
        For my being absent, whereunto I never   105
        Purpose return? Why hast thou gone so far
        To be unbent when thou hast ta'en thy stand,
        Th'elected deer before thee?

PISANIO   But to win time
        To lose so bad employment, in the which
        I have considered of a course. Good lady,   110
        Hear me with patience.

INNOGEN   Talk thy tongue weary. Speak.
        I have heard I am a strumpet, and mine ear,
        Therein false struck, can take no greater wound
        Nor tent to bottom that. But speak.

PISANIO   Then, madam,
        I thought you would not back again.

INNOGEN   Most like,   115
        Bringing me here to kill me.

PISANIO   Not so, neither.
        But if I were as wise as honest, then
        My purpose would prove well. It cannot be
        But that my master is abused. Some villain,
        Ay, and singular in his art, hath done you both   120
        This cursed injury.

INNOGEN   Some Roman courtesan.

PISANIO   No, on my life.
        I'll give but notice you are dead and send him
        Some bloody sign of it, for 'tis commanded
        I should do so. You shall be missed at court,   125
        And that will well confirm it.

INNOGEN   Why, good fellow,
        What shall I do the while? Where bide? How live?
        Or in my life what comfort when I am
        Dead to my husband?

PISANIO   If you'll back to'th' court –

INNOGEN   No court, no father, nor no more ado   130
        With that harsh, noble, simple nothing,
        That Cloten, whose love-suit hath been to me

As fearful as a siege.

PISANIO   If not at court,
Then not in Britain must you bide.

INNOGEN   Where then?
135 Hath Britain all the sun that shines? Day, night,
Are they not but in Britain? I'th' world's volume
Our Britain seems as of it but not in't,
In a great pool a swan's nest. Prithee, think
There's livers out of Britain.

PISANIO   I am most glad
140 You think of other place. Th'ambassador,
Lucius the Roman, comes to Milford Haven
Tomorrow. Now, if you could wear a mind
Dark as your fortune is, and but disguise
That which t'appear itself must not yet be
145 But by self-danger, you should tread a course
Pretty and full of view; yea, haply near
The residence of Posthumus; so nigh, at least,
That though his actions were not visible, yet
Report should render him hourly to your ear,
As truly as he moves.

INNOGEN   O, for such means,
150 Though peril to my modesty, not death on't,
I would adventure.

PISANIO   Well then, here's the point:
You must forget to be a woman: change
Command into obedience, fear and niceness
155 (The handmaids of all women, or more truly
Woman it pretty self) into a waggish courage,
Ready in gibes, quick-answered, saucy, and
As quarrelous as the weasel. Nay, you must
Forget that rarest treasure of your cheek,
160 Exposing it – but O, the harder heart!
Alack, no remedy – to the greedy touch
Of common-kissing Titan, and forget
Your laboursome and dainty trims wherein
You made great Juno angry.

INNOGEN   Nay, be brief.
165 I see into thy end and am almost
A man already.

PISANIO   First make yourself but like one.
Fore-thinking this, I have already fit –
'Tis in my cloakbag – doublet, hat, hose, all
That answer to them. Would you in their serving,
170 And with what imitation you can borrow
From youth of such a season, 'fore noble Lucius
Present yourself, desire his service, tell him
Wherein you're happy – which will make him know
If that his head have ear in music – doubtless
175 With joy he will embrace you, for he's honourable
And, doubling that, most holy. Your means abroad:
You have me, rich, and I will never fail
Beginning nor supplyment.

INNOGEN   Thou art all the comfort
The gods will diet me with. Prithee away.
180 There's more to be considered, but we'll even
All that good time will give us. This attempt

I am soldier to and will abide it with
A prince's courage. Away, I prithee.

PISANIO   Well, madam, we must take a short farewell,
Lest being missed, I be suspected of   185
Your carriage from the court. My noble mistress,
Here is a box – I had it from the Queen –
What's in't is precious. If you are sick at sea,
Or stomach-qualmed at land, a dram of this
Will drive away distemper. To some shade   190
And fit you to your manhood. May the gods
Direct you to the best.

INNOGEN   Amen. I thank thee.   *Exeunt.*

3.5   *Enter* CYMBELINE, QUEEN, CLOTEN,
        LUCIUS *and Lords and Attendants.*

CYMBELINE   Thus far, and so farewell.

LUCIUS   Thanks, royal sir.
My emperor hath wrote I must from hence,
And am right sorry that I must report ye
My master's enemy.

CYMBELINE   Our subjects, sir,
Will not endure his yoke, and for ourself   5
To show less sovereignty than they must needs
Appear unkinglike.

LUCIUS   So, sir. I desire of you
A conduct over land to Milford Haven.
Madam, all joy befall your grace, and you.

CYMBELINE
My lords, you are appointed for that office: 10
The due of honour in no point omit.
So farewell, noble Lucius.

LUCIUS   Your hand, my lord.

CLOTEN   Receive it friendly, but from this time forth
I wear it as your enemy.

LUCIUS   Sir, the event
Is yet to name the winner. Fare you well.   15

CYMBELINE
Leave not the worthy Lucius, good my lords,
Till he have crossed the Severn. Happiness.
                        Exeunt Lucius and Lords.

QUEEN   He goes hence frowning, but it honours us
That we have given him cause.

CLOTEN   'Tis all the better.
Your valiant Britons have their wishes in it.   20

CYMBELINE   Lucius hath wrote already to the Emperor
How it goes here. It fits us therefore ripely
Our chariots and our horsemen be in readiness.
The powers that he already hath in Gallia
Will soon be drawn to head, from whence he moves 25
His war for Britain.

QUEEN   'Tis not sleepy business,
But must be looked to speedily and strongly.

CYMBELINE   Our expectation that it would be thus
Hath made us forward. But my gentle queen,
Where is our daughter? She hath not appeared   30
Before the Roman, nor to us hath tendered

The duty of the day. She looks us like
A thing more made of malice than of duty;
We have noted it. Call her before us, for
We have been too slight in sufferance.

                 Exit a Messenger.

35 QUEEN   Royal sir,
Since the exile of Posthumus, most retired
Hath her life been, the cure whereof, my lord,
'Tis time must do. Beseech your majesty,
Forbear sharp speeches to her. She's a lady
40 So tender of rebukes that words are strokes,
And strokes death to her.

             Enter a Messenger.

CYMBELINE   Where is she, sir? How
Can her contempt be answered?
MESSENGER   Please you, sir,
Her chambers are all locked, and there's no answer
That will be given to th' loud'st of noise we make.
45 QUEEN   My Lord, when last I went to visit her,
She prayed me to excuse her keeping close,
Whereto constrained by her infirmity
She should that duty leave unpaid to you
Which daily she was bound to proffer. This
50 She wished me to make known, but our great court
Made me too blame in memory.
CYMBELINE   Her doors locked?
Not seen of late? Grant, heavens, that which I
Fear prove false.   *Exeunt Cymbeline and Attendants.*
QUEEN   Son, I say, follow the King.
CLOTEN   That man of hers, Pisanio, her old servant,
I have not seen these two days.
55 QUEEN   Go, look after.   *Exit Cloten.*
Pisanio, thou that stand'st so for Posthumus –
He hath a drug of mine. I pray his absence
Proceed by swallowing that, for he believes
It is a thing most precious. But for her,
60 Where is she gone? Haply despair hath seized her,
Or, winged with fervour of her love, she's flown
To her desired Posthumus. Gone she is
To death or to dishonour, and my end
Can make good use of either. She being down,
65 I have the placing of the British crown.

             Enter CLOTEN.

How now, my son?
CLOTEN   'Tis certain she is fled.
Go in and cheer the King. He rages, none
Dare come about him.
QUEEN [*aside*]   All the better. May
This night forestall him of the coming day.   *Exit.*
70 CLOTEN   I love and hate her, for she's fair and royal,
And that she hath all courtly parts more exquisite
Than lady, ladies, woman. From every one
The best she hath, and she of all compounded
Outsells them all. I love her, therefore, but
75 Disdaining me and throwing favours on

The low Posthumus slanders so her judgement
That what's else rare is choked, and in that point
I will conclude to hate her, nay, indeed,
To be revenged upon her. For when fools shall –

             Enter PISANIO.

Who is here? What, are you packing, sirrah?   80
Come hither. Ah, you precious pander! Villain,
Where is thy lady? In a word, or else
Thou art straightway with the fiends.
PISANIO   O good my lord!
CLOTEN   Where is thy lady? Or, by Jupiter,
I will not ask again. Close villain,   85
I'll have this secret from thy heart or rip
Thy heart to find it. Is she with Posthumus,
From whose so many weights of baseness cannot
A dram of worth be drawn?
PISANIO   Alas, my lord,
How can she be with him? When was she missed?   90
He is in Rome.
CLOTEN   Where is she, sir? Come nearer,
No farther halting. Satisfy me home,
What is become of her?
PISANIO   O my all-worthy lord!
CLOTEN   All-worthy villain,
Discover where thy mistress is at once,   95
At the next word. No more of 'worthy lord'.
Speak, or thy silence on the instant is
Thy condemnation and thy death.
PISANIO   Then, sir,
This paper is the history of my knowledge
Touching her flight.   [*He presents a letter.*]
CLOTEN   Let's see't. I will pursue her   100
Even to Augustus' throne.
PISANIO [*aside*]   Or this or perish.
She's far enough, and what he learns by this
May prove his travail, not her danger.
CLOTEN   Hum.
PISANIO [*aside*]
I'll write to my lord she's dead. O Innogen,
Safe mayst thou wander, safe return again.   105
CLOTEN   Sirrah, is this letter true?
PISANIO   Sir, as I think.
CLOTEN   It is Posthumus' hand, I know't. Sirrah, if
thou wouldst not be a villain but do me true service,
undergo those employments wherein I should have   110
cause to use thee with a serious industry – that is, what
villainy soe'er I bid thee do, to perform it directly and
truly – I would think thee an honest man. Thou
shouldst neither want my means for thy relief nor my
voice for thy preferment.   115
PISANIO   Well, my good lord.
CLOTEN   Wilt thou serve me? For since patiently and
constantly thou hast stuck to the bare fortune of that
beggar Posthumus, thou canst not in the course of
gratitude but be a diligent follower of mine. Wilt thou   120
serve me?

PISANIO Sir, I will.

CLOTEN Give me thy hand, here's my purse. Hast any
of thy late master's garments in thy possession?

125 PISANIO I have, my lord, at my lodging the same suit he
wore when he took leave of my lady and mistress.

CLOTEN The first service thou dost me, fetch that suit
hither. Let it be thy first service, go.

PISANIO I shall my lord.   *Exit.*

130 CLOTEN Meet thee at Milford Haven! – I forgot to ask
him one thing, I'll remember't anon. – Even there, thou
villain Posthumus, will I kill thee. I would these
garments were come. She said upon a time – the
bitterness of it I now belch from my heart – that she
135 held the very garment of Posthumus in more respect
than my noble and natural person, together with the
adornment of my qualities. With that suit upon my back
will I ravish her – first kill him, and in her eyes. There
shall she see my valour, which will then be a torment to
140 her contempt. He on the ground, my speech of
insultment ended on his dead body, and when my lust
hath dined – which, as I say, to vex her, I will execute in
the clothes that she so praised – to the court I'll knock
her back, foot her home again. She hath despised me
145 rejoicingly, and I'll be merry in my revenge.

Enter PISANIO with Posthumus' clothes.

Be those the garments?

PISANIO Ay, my noble lord.

CLOTEN How long is't since she went to Milford Haven?

PISANIO She can scarce be there yet.

150 CLOTEN Bring this apparel to my chamber. That is the
second thing that I have commanded thee. The third is
that thou wilt be a voluntary mute to my design. Be but
duteous and true, preferment shall tender itself to
thee. My revenge is now at Milford, would I had wings
155 to follow it. Come, and be true.   *Exit.*

PISANIO Thou bidst me to my loss, for true to thee
Were to prove false, which I will never be
To him that is most true. To Milford go,
And find not her whom thou pursuest. Flow, flow
160 You heavenly blessings on her. This fool's speed
Be crossed with slowness; labour be his meed.   *Exit.*

3.6 *Enter INNOGEN alone in boy's clothes,
before a cave.*

I see a man's life is a tedious one.
I have tired myself, and for two nights together
Have made the ground my bed. I should be sick
But that my resolution helps me. Milford,
5 When from the mountain top Pisanio showed thee,
Thou wast within a ken. O Jove, I think
Foundations fly the wretched – such, I mean,
Where they should be relieved. Two beggars told me
I could not miss my way. Will poor folks lie,
10 That have afflictions on them, knowing 'tis
A punishment or trial? Yes, no wonder,

When rich ones scarce tell true. To lapse in fullness
Is sorer than to lie for need, and falsehood
Is worse in kings than beggars. My dear lord,
Thou art one o'th' false ones. Now I think on thee   15
My hunger's gone, but even before I was
At point to sink for food. But what is this?
Here is a path to't. 'Tis some savage hold.
I were best not call; I dare not call; yet famine
Ere clean it o'erthrow nature, makes it valiant.   20
Plenty and peace breeds cowards, hardness ever
Of hardiness is mother. Ho! Who's here?
If any thing that's civil, speak; if savage,
Take or lend. Ho! No answer? Then I'll enter.
Best draw my sword, and if mine enemy   25
But fear the sword like me, he'll scarcely look on't.
Such a foe, good heavens.   *Exit into the cave.*

Enter BELARIUS, GUIDERIUS and ARVIRAGUS.

BELARIUS
You, Polydore, have proved best woodman and
Are master of the feast. Cadwal and I
Will play the cook and servant, 'tis our match.   30
The sweat of industry would dry and die
But for the end it works to. Come, our stomachs
Will make what's homely savoury. Weariness
Can snore upon the flint when resty sloth
Finds the down pillow hard. Now peace be here,   35
Poor house, that keep'st thyself.   *Exit into the cave.*

GUIDERIUS   I am throughly weary.

ARVIRAGUS I am weak with toil, yet strong in appetite.

GUIDERIUS
There is cold meat i'th' cave. We'll browse on that
Whilst what we have killed be cooked.

Enter BELARIUS.

BELARIUS   Stay, come not in.
But that it eats our victuals, I should think   40
Here were a fairy.

GUIDERIUS   What's the matter, sir?

BELARIUS By Jupiter, an angel – or if not,
An earthly paragon. Behold diviness
No elder than a boy.

Enter INNOGEN.

INNOGEN   Good masters, harm me not.
Before I entered here I called, and thought   45
To have begged or bought what I have took. Good troth,
I have stolen naught, nor would not, though I had found
Gold strewed i'th' floor. Here's money for my meat.
I would have left it on the board so soon
As I had made my meal, and parted   50
With prayers for the provider.

GUIDERIUS   Money, youth?

ARVIRAGUS All gold and silver rather turn to dirt,
As 'tis no better reckoned but of those
Who worship dirty gods.

INNOGEN   I see you're angry.

55 Know, if you kill me for my fault, I should
Have died had I not made it.

BELARIUS   Whither bound?

INNOGEN   To Milford Haven.

BELARIUS   What's your name?

INNOGEN   Fidele, sir. I have a kinsman who
Is bound for Italy. He embarked at Milford,
60 To whom being going, almost spent with hunger,
I am fallen in this offence.

BELARIUS   Prithee, faire youth,
Think us no churls, nor measure our good minds
By this rude place we live in. Well encountered.
'Tis almost night; you shall have better cheer
65 Ere you depart, and thanks to stay and eat it.
Boys, bid him welcome.

GUIDERIUS   Were you a woman, youth,
I should woo hard, but be your groom in honesty.
Ay, bid for you as I'd buy.

ARVIRAGUS   I'll make't my comfort
He is a man, I'll love him as my brother.
70 And such a welcome as I'd give to him
After long absence, such is yours. Most welcome!
Be spritely, for you fall 'mongst friends.

INNOGEN   'Mongst friends,
If brothers! [*aside*] Would it had been so, that they
Had been my father's sons. Then had my prize
75 Been less, and so more equal ballasting
To thee, Posthumus.

BELARIUS   He wrings at some distress.

GUIDERIUS   Would I could free't.

ARVIRAGUS   Or I, whate'er it be,
What pain it cost, what danger. Gods!

BELARIUS   Hark, boys.
[*They talk apart.*]

INNOGEN   Great men
80 That had a court no bigger than this cave,
That did attend themselves, and had the virtue
Which their own conscience sealed them, laying by
That nothing gift of differing multitudes,
Could not outpeer these twain. Pardon me, gods,
85 I'd change my sex to be companion with them,
Since Leonatus' false.

BELARIUS   It shall be so.
Boys, we'll go dress our hunt. Fair youth, come in.
Discourse is heavy, fasting. When we have supped,
We'll mannerly demand thee of thy story,
So far as thou wilt speak it.

90 GUIDERIUS   Pray, draw near.

ARVIRAGUS
The night to th'owl and morn to th' lark less welcome.

INNOGEN   Thanks, sir.

ARVIRAGUS   I pray, draw near.   *Exeunt into the cave.*

3.7   *Enter two* Roman Senators, *and* Tribunes.

1 SENATOR   This is the tenor of the Emperor's writ:
That since the common men are now in action

'Gainst the Pannonians and Dalmatians,
And that the legions now in Gallia are
Full weak to undertake our wars against   5
The fall'n-off Britons, that we do incite
The gentry to this business. He creates
Lucius proconsul, and to you the tribunes
For this immediate levy, he commands
His absolute commission. Long live Caesar.   10

TRIBUNE   Is Lucius general of the forces?

2 SENATOR   Ay.

TRIBUNE   Remaining now in Gallia?

1 SENATOR   With those legions
Which I have spoke of, whereunto your levy
Must be supplyant. The words of your commission
Will tie you to the numbers and the time   15
Of their dispatch.

TRIBUNE   We will discharge our duty.   *Exeunt.*

4.1   *Enter* CLOTEN *alone in Posthumus' clothes.*

CLOTEN   I am near to th' place where they should
meet, if Pisanio have mapped it truly. How fit his
garments serve me! Why should his mistress, who was
made by him that made the tailor, not be fit too? The
rather – saving reverence of the word – for 'tis said a   5
woman's fitness comes by fits. Therein I must play the
workman. I dare speak it to myself, for it is not
vainglory for a man and his glass to confer in his own
chamber. I mean, the lines of my body are as well
drawn as his: no less young, more strong, not beneath   10
him in fortunes, beyond him in the advantage of the
time, above him in birth, alike conversant in general
services, and more remarkable in single oppositions.
Yet this imperseverant thing loves him in my despite.
What mortality is! Posthumus, thy head, which now is   15
growing upon thy shoulders, shall within this hour be
off, thy mistress enforced, thy garments cut to pieces
before her face; and all this done, spurn her home to
her father, who may haply be a little angry for my so
rough usage; but my mother, having power of his   20
testiness, shall turn all into my commendations. My
horse is tied up safe. Out sword, and to a sore purpose!
Fortune put them into my hand. This is the very
description of their meeting place, and the fellow dares
not deceive me.   *Exit.*   25

4.2   *Enter* BELARIUS, GUIDERIUS, ARVIRAGUS *and*
INNOGEN *as Fidele from the cave.*

BELARIUS   You are not well. Remain here in the cave,
We'll come to you after hunting.

ARVIRAGUS   Brother, stay here.
Are we not brothers?

INNOGEN   So man and man should be,
But clay and clay differs in dignity,
Whose dust is both alike. I am very sick.   5

GUIDERIUS   Go you to hunting, I'll abide with him.

INNOGEN　So sick I am not, yet I am not well;
　　　But not so citizen a wanton as
　　　To seem to die ere sick. So please you, leave me,
10　　Stick to your journal course: the breach of custom
　　　Is breach of all. I am ill, but your being by me
　　　Cannot amend me. Society is no comfort
　　　To one not sociable. I am not very sick,
　　　Since I can reason of it. Pray you trust me here,
15　　I'll rob none but myself, and let me die
　　　Stealing so poorly.
GUIDERIUS　　　　　　I love thee: I have spoke it,
　　　How much the quantity, the weight as much,
　　　As I do love my father.
BELARIUS　　　　　　What? How, how?
ARVIRAGUS　If it be sin to say so, sir, I yoke me
20　　In my good brother's fault. I know not why
　　　I love this youth, and I have heard you say,
　　　Love's reason's without reason. The bier at door
　　　And a demand who is't shall die, I'd say
　　　My father, not this youth.
BELARIUS [aside]　　　　　O noble strain!
25　　O worthiness of nature, breed of greatness!
　　　Cowards father cowards, and base things sire base;
　　　Nature hath meal and bran, contempt and grace.
　　　I'm not their father, yet who this should be
　　　Doth miracle itself, loved before me. –
　　　'Tis the ninth hour o'th' morn.
30　ARVIRAGUS　　　　　　Brother, farewell.
INNOGEN　I wish ye sport.
ARVIRAGUS　　　　　You health. – So please you, sir.
INNOGEN [aside]
　　　These are kind creatures. Gods, what lies I have
　　　　heard.
　　　Our courtiers say all's savage but at court.
　　　Experience, O thou disprov'st report!
35　　Th'imperious seas breeds monsters; for the dish,
　　　Poor tributary rivers as sweet fish.
　　　I am sick still, heart-sick. Pisanio,
　　　I'll now taste of thy drug.
　　　　[She takes the drug. The men speak apart.]
GUIDERIUS　　　　　I could not stir him.
　　　He said he was gentle, but unfortunate;
40　　Dishonestly afflicted, but yet honest.
ARVIRAGUS　Thus did he answer me, yet said hereafter
　　　I might know more.
BELARIUS　　　　　To th' field, to th' field!
　　　We'll leave you for this time. Go in, and rest.
ARVIRAGUS　We'll not be long away.
BELARIUS　　　　　　Pray, be not sick,
　　　For you must be our housewife.
45　INNOGEN　　　　　Well or ill,
　　　I am bound to you.　　　　　*Exit into the cave.*
BELARIUS　　　　And shalt be ever.
　　　This youth, howe'er distressed, appears he hath had
　　　Good ancestors.
ARVIRAGUS　　　How angel-like he sings!

GUIDERIUS
　　　But his neat cookery! He cut our roots in characters,
　　　And sauced our broths as Juno had been sick　　50
　　　And he her dieter.
ARVIRAGUS　　　　　Nobly he yokes
　　　A smiling with a sigh, as if the sigh
　　　Was that it was for not being such a smile;
　　　The smile, mocking the sigh, that it would fly
　　　From so divine a temple to commix　　　55
　　　With winds that sailors rail at.
GUIDERIUS　　　　　　I do note
　　　That grief and patience, rooted in him both,
　　　Mingle their spurs together.
ARVIRAGUS　　　　　Grow patience,
　　　And let the stinking elder, grief, untwine
　　　His perishing root with the increasing vine.　　60
BELARIUS
　　　It is great morning. Come away. Who's there?

　　　　　　　Enter CLOTEN.

CLOTEN　I cannot find those runagates; that villain
　　　Hath mocked me. I am faint.
BELARIUS [to Guiderius and Arviragus]
　　　　　　　　　Those runagates?
　　　Means he not us? I partly know him: 'tis
　　　Cloten, the son o'th' Queen. I fear some ambush.　65
　　　I saw him not these many years and yet
　　　I know 'tis he. We are held as outlaws. Hence!
GUIDERIUS [to Belarius and Arviragus]
　　　He is but one. You and my brother search
　　　What companies are near. Pray you, away.
　　　Let me alone with him.　　*Exit Belarius and Arviragus.*
CLOTEN　　　　　　Soft, what are you　　70
　　　That fly me thus? Some villain mountaineers?
　　　I have heard of such. What slave art thou?
GUIDERIUS　　　　　　A thing
　　　More slavish did I ne'er than answering
　　　A slave without a knock.
CLOTEN　　　　　　Thou art a robber,
　　　A law-breaker, a villain. Yield thee, thief.　　75
GUIDERIUS　To who? To thee? What art thou? Have not I
　　　An arm as big as thine, a heart as big?
　　　Thy words I grant are bigger, for I wear not
　　　My dagger in my mouth. Say what thou art,
　　　Why I should yield to thee.
CLOTEN　　　　　　Thou villain base,　　80
　　　Know'st me not by my clothes?
GUIDERIUS　　　　　No, nor thy tailor, rascal.
　　　Who is thy grandfather? He made those clothes,
　　　Which, as it seems, make thee.
CLOTEN　　　　　　Thou precious varlet,
　　　My tailor made them not.
GUIDERIUS　　　　　Hence then, and thank
　　　The man that gave them thee. Thou art some fool.　85
　　　I am loath to beat thee.
CLOTEN　　　　　　Thou injurious thief,

Hear but my name and tremble.

GUIDERIUS   What's thy name?

CLOTEN   Cloten, thou villain.

GUIDERIUS   Cloten, thou double villain, be thy name,
90   I cannot tremble at it. Were it Toad, or Adder, Spider,
'Twould move me sooner.

CLOTEN   To thy further fear,
Nay, to thy mere confusion, thou shalt know
I am son to th' Queen.

GUIDERIUS   I am sorry for't, not seeming
So worthy as thy birth.

CLOTEN   Art not afeard?

GUIDERIUS
95   Those that I reverence, those I fear, the wise.
At fools I laugh, not fear them.

CLOTEN   Die the death.
When I have slain thee with my proper hand,
I'll follow those that even now fled hence,
And on the gates of Lud's town set your heads.
Yield, rustic mountaineer.   *Fight and exeunt.*

Enter BELARIUS *and* ARVIRAGUS.

100   BELARIUS   No company's abroad?

ARVIRAGUS
None in the world. You did mistake him, sure.

BELARIUS   I cannot tell. Long is it since I saw him,
But time hath nothing blurred those lines of favour
Which then he wore. The snatches in his voice
105   And burst of speaking were as his. I am absolute
'Twas very Cloten.

ARVIRAGUS   In this place we left them.
I wish my brother make good time with him,
You say he is so fell.

BELARIUS   Being scarce made up,
I mean to man, he had not apprehension
110   Of roaring terrors; for defect of judgement
Is oft the cause of fear.

Enter GUIDERIUS *with Cloten's head.*

But see, thy brother.

GUIDERIUS   This Cloten was a fool, an empty purse,
There was no money in't. Not Hercules
Could have knocked out his brains, for he had none.
115   Yet I not doing this, the fool had borne
My head as I do his.

BELARIUS   What hast thou done?

GUIDERIUS
I am perfect what: cut off one Cloten's head,
Son to the Queen, after his own report,
Who called me traitor, mountaineer, and swore
120   With his own single hand he'd take us in,
Displace our heads where, thank the gods, they grow
And set them on Lud's town.

BELARIUS   We are all undone.

GUIDERIUS   Why, worthy father, what have we to lose
But that he swore to take, our lives? The law

Protects not us, then why should we be tender   125
To let an arrogant piece of flesh threat us,
Play judge and executioner all himself,
For we do fear the law? What company
Discover you abroad?

BELARIUS   No single soul
Can we set eye on, but in all safe reason   130
He must have some attendants. Though his humour
Was nothing but mutation – ay, and that
From one bad thing to worse – not frenzy,
Not absolute madness could so far have raved
To bring him here alone. Although perhaps   135
It may be heard at court that such as we
Cave here, hunt here, are outlaws, and in time
May make some stronger head, the which he hearing –
As it is like him – might break out and swear
He'd fetch us in, yet is't not probable   140
To come alone, either he so undertaking
Or they so suffering. Then on good ground we fear,
If we do fear this body hath a tail
More perilous than the head.

ARVIRAGUS   Let ord'nance
Come as the gods foresay it; howsoe'er,   145
My brother hath done well.

BELARIUS   I had no mind
To hunt this day. The boy Fidele's sickness
Did make my way long forth.

GUIDERIUS   With his own sword,
Which he did wave against my throat, I have ta'en
His head from him. I'll throw't into the creek   150
Behind our rock, and let it to the sea
And tell the fishes he's the Queen's son, Cloten.
That's all I reck.   *Exit.*

BELARIUS   I fear 'twill be revenged.
Would, Polydore, thou hadst not done't, though valour
Becomes thee well enough.

ARVIRAGUS   Would I had done't,   155
So the revenge alone pursued me. Polydore,
I love thee brotherly, but envy much
Thou hast robbed me of this deed. I would revenges
That possible strength might meet would seek us
through
And put us to our answer.

BELARIUS   Well, 'tis done.   160
We'll hunt no more today, nor seek for danger
Where there's no profit. I prithee, to our rock.
You and Fidele play the cooks; I'll stay
Till hasty Polydore return, and bring him
To dinner presently.

ARVIRAGUS   Poor sick Fidele.   165
I'll willingly to him. To gain his colour,
I'd let a parish of such Clotens blood,
And praise myself for charity.   *Exit into the cave.*

BELARIUS   O thou goddess,
Thou divine Nature, thyself thou blazon'st
In these two princely boys! They are as gentle   170

As zephyrs blowing below the violet,
Not wagging his sweet head, and yet as rough,
Their royal blood enchafed, as the rud'st wind
That by the top doth take the mountain pine
175 And make him stoop to th' vale. 'Tis wonder
That an invisible instinct should frame them
To royalty unlearned, honour untaught,
Civility not seen from other, valour
That wildly grows in them but yields a crop
180 As if it had been sowed. Yet still it's strange
What Cloten's being here to us portends,
Or what his death will bring us.

Enter GUIDERIUS.

GUIDERIUS   Where's my brother?
I have sent Cloten's clotpoll down the stream
In embassy to his mother. His body's hostage
For his return.   *Solemn music*]
185 BELARIUS   My ingenious instrument!
Hark, Polydore, it sounds. But what occasion
Hath Cadwal now to give it motion? Hark!
GUIDERIUS Is he at home?
BELARIUS   He went hence even now.
GUIDERIUS
What does he mean? Since death of my dear'st mother
190 It did not speak before. All solemn things
Should answer solemn accidents. The matter?
Triumphs for nothing and lamenting toys
Is jollity for apes and grief for boys.
Is Cadwal mad?

Enter from the cave ARVIRAGUS, *with* INNOGEN *as dead,
bearing her in his arms.*

BELARIUS   Look, here he comes,
195 And brings the dire occasion in his arms
Of what we blame him for.
ARVIRAGUS   The bird is dead
That we have made so much on. I had rather
Have skipped from sixteen years of age to sixty,
To have turned my leaping time into a crutch,
Than have seen this.
200 GUIDERIUS   O sweetest, fairest lily.
My brother wears thee not the one half so well
As when thou grew'st thyself.
BELARIUS   O melancholy,
Who ever yet could sound thy bottom, find
The ooze, to show what coast thy sluggish crare
205 Might easiliest harbour in. Thou blessed thing,
Jove knows what man thou mightst have made, but I,
Thou diedst a most rare boy, of melancholy.
How found you him?
ARVIRAGUS   Stark, as you see,
Thus smiling, as some fly had tickled slumber,
210 Not as death's dart being laughed at; his right cheek
Reposing on a cushion.
GUIDERIUS   Where?
ARVIRAGUS   O'th' floor,

His arms thus leagued. I thought he slept, and put
My clouted brogues from off my feet, whose rudeness
Answered my steps too loud.
GUIDERIUS   Why, he but sleeps.
If he be gone, he'll make his grave a bed.   215
With female fairies will his tomb be haunted,
And worms will not come to thee.
ARVIRAGUS   With fairest flowers
Whilst summer lasts and I live here, Fidele,
I'll sweeten thy sad grave. Thou shalt not lack
The flower that's like thy face, pale primrose, nor   220
The azured harebell, like thy veins; no, nor
The leaf of eglantine, whom not to slander,
Outsweetened not thy breath. The ruddock would
With charitable bill – O bill sore shaming
Those rich-left heirs that let their fathers lie   225
Without a monument – bring thee all this,
Yea, and furred moss besides, when flowers are none,
To winter-ground thy corpse.
GUIDERIUS   Prithee have done,
And do not play in wench-like words with that
Which is so serious. Let us bury him   230
And not protract with admiration what
Is now due debt to th' grave.
ARVIRAGUS   Say, where shall's lay him?
GUIDERIUS By good Euriphile, our mother.
ARVIRAGUS   Be't so,
And let us, Polydore, though now our voices
Have got the mannish crack, sing him to th' ground   235
As once to our mother: use like note and words,
Save that Euriphile must be Fidele.
GUIDERIUS Cadwal,
I cannot sing. I'll weep, and word it with thee,
For notes of sorrow out of tune are worse   240
Than priests and fanes that lie.
ARVIRAGUS   We'll speak it then.
BELARIUS
Great griefs, I see, med'cine the less, for Cloten
Is quite forgot. He was a queen's son, boys,
And though he came our enemy, remember
He was paid for that. Though mean and mighty rotting   245
Together have one dust, yet reverence,
That angel of the world, doth make distinction
Of place 'tween high and low. Our foe was princely,
And though you took his life as being our foe,
Yet bury him as a prince.
GUIDERIUS   Pray you, fetch him hither.   250
Thersites' body is as good as Ajax'
When neither are alive.
ARVIRAGUS   If you'll go fetch him,
We'll say our song the whilst. Brother, begin.
                                        Exit Belarius.
GUIDERIUS Nay, Cadwal, we must lay his head to th'east.
My father hath a reason for't.
ARVIRAGUS   'Tis true.   255
GUIDERIUS Come on then, and remove him.
ARVIRAGUS   So, begin.

SONG

GUIDERIUS	Fear no more the heat o'th' sun,
	Nor the furious winter's rages,
	Thou thy worldly task hast done,
	Home art gone and ta'en thy wages.
	Golden lads and girls all must,
	As chimney-sweepers, come to dust.
ARVIRAGUS	Fear no more the frown o'th' great,
	Thou art past the tyrant's stroke.
	Care no more to clothe and eat,
	To thee the reed is as the oak.
	The sceptre, learning, physic must,
	All follow this and come to dust.
GUIDERIUS	Fear no more the lightning flash,
ARVIRAGUS	Nor th'all-dreaded thunder-stone.
GUIDERIUS	Fear not slander, censure rash,
ARVIRAGUS	Thou hast finished joy and moan.
BOTH	All lovers young, all lovers must
	Consign to thee and come to dust.
GUIDERIUS	No exorcizer harm thee,
ARVIRAGUS	Nor no witchcraft charm thee.
GUIDERIUS	Ghost unlaid forbear thee.
ARVIRAGUS	Nothing ill come near thee.
BOTH	Quiet consummation have,
	And renowned be thy grave.

Enter BELARIUS *with the body of* CLOTEN.

GUIDERIUS
We have done our obsequies. Come, lay him down.
BELARIUS
Here's a few flowers, but 'bout midnight more:
The herbs that have on them cold dew o'th' night
Are strewings fitt'st for graves. Upon their faces.
You were as flowers, now withered; even so
These herblets shall, which we upon you strew.
Come on, away; apart upon our knees.
The ground that gave them first has them again.
Their pleasures here are past, so is their pain.
Exeunt Belarius, Guiderius and Arviragus.
[*Innogen awakes.*]
INNOGEN   Yes sir, to Milford Haven, which is the way?
I thank you. By yond bush? Pray, how far thither?
'Od's pittikins: can it be six mile yet?
I have gone all night. 'Faith, I'll lie down and sleep.
[*She becomes aware of the body.*]
But soft, no bedfellow! O gods and goddesses!
These flowers are like the pleasures of the world,
This bloody man the care on't. I hope I dream,
For so I thought I was a cave-keeper
And cook to honest creatures. But 'tis not so.
'Twas but a bolt of nothing, shot at nothing,
Which the brain makes of fumes. Our very eyes
Are sometimes like our judgements, blind. Good faith,
I tremble still with fear, but if there be
Yet left in heaven as small a drop of pity

As a wren's eye, feared gods, a part of it.
The dream's here still. Even when I wake it is
Without me as within me, not imagined, felt.
A headless man? The garments of Posthumus?
I know the shape of 's leg; this is his hand,
His foot Mercurial, his Martial thigh,
The brawns of Hercules, but his Jovial face –
Murder in heaven? How? 'Tis gone. Pisanio,
All curses madded Hecuba gave the Greeks,
And mine to boot, be darted on thee! Thou,
Conspired with that irregulous devil, Cloten,
Hath here cut off my lord. To write and read
Be henceforth treacherous. Damned Pisanio
Hath with his forged letters – damned Pisanio –
From this most bravest vessel of the world
Struck the main-top! O Posthumus, alas,
Where is thy head? Where's that? Ay me, where's that?
Pisanio might have killed thee at the heart
And left thy head on. How should this be? Pisanio?
'Tis he and Cloten: malice and lucre in them
Have laid this woe here. O 'tis pregnant, pregnant!
The drug he gave me, which he said was precious
And cordial to me, have I not found it
Murd'rous to th' senses? That confirms it home.
This is Pisanio's deed, and Cloten. O,
Give colour to my pale cheek with thy blood,
That we the horrider may seem to those
Which chance to find us. O, my lord, my lord!
[*She smears her face with blood and lies on the body.*]

Enter LUCIUS, ROMAN CAPTAINS, *and to them a*
SOOTHSAYER.

CAPTAIN   The legions garrisoned in Gallia
After your will have crossed the sea, attending
You here at Milford Haven with your ships.
They are in readiness.
LUCIUS   But what from Rome?
CAPTAIN   The senate hath stirred up the confiners
And gentlemen of Italy, most willing spirits
That promise noble service, and they come
Under the conduct of bold Iachimo,
Siena's brother.
LUCIUS   When expect you them?
CAPTAIN
With the next benefit o'th' wind.
LUCIUS   This forwardness
Makes our hopes fair. Command our present numbers
Be mustered: bid the captains look to't.
Exit one or more.
[*to Soothsayer*]   Now sir,
What have you dreamed of late of this war's purpose?
SOOTHSAYER
Last night the very gods showed me a vision –
I fast, and prayed for their intelligence – thus:
I saw Jove's bird, the Roman eagle, winged
From the spongy south to this part of the west,
There vanished in the sunbeams, which portends,

350 Unless my sins abuse my divination,
Success to th' Roman host.
LUCIUS   Dream often so,
And never false.   [*He sees the body.*]
                          Soft, ho, what trunk is here
Without his top? The ruin speaks that sometime
It was a worthy building. How, a page?
355 Or dead or sleeping on him? But dead rather,
For Nature doth abhor to make his bed
With the defunct, or sleep upon the dead.
Let's see the boy's face.
CAPTAIN   He's alive, my lord.
LUCIUS   He'll then instruct us of this body. Young one,
360 Inform us of thy fortunes, for it seems
They crave to be demanded. Who is this
Thou mak'st thy bloody pillow? Or who was he
That, otherwise than noble nature did,
Hath altered that good picture? What's thy interest
365 In this sad wrack? How came't? Who is't?
What art thou?
INNOGEN   I am nothing; or if not,
Nothing to be were better. This was my master,
A very valiant Briton and a good,
That here by mountaineers lies slain. Alas,
370 There is no more such masters. I may wander
From east to occident, cry out for service,
Try many, all good; serve truly; never
Find such another master.
LUCIUS   'Lack, good youth,
Thou mov'st no less with thy complaining than
375 Thy master in bleeding. Say his name, good friend.
INNOGEN   Richard du Champ. [*aside*] If I do lie and do
No harm by it, though the gods hear, I hope
They'll pardon it. – Say you, sir?
LUCIUS   Thy name?
INNOGEN   Fidele, sir.
LUCIUS   Thou dost approve thyself the very same:
380 Thy name well fits thy faith, thy faith thy name.
Wilt take thy chance with me? I will not say
Thou shalt be so well mastered, but be sure
No less beloved. The Roman Emperor's letters
Sent by a consul to me should not sooner
385 Than thine own worth prefer thee. Go with me.
INNOGEN   I'll follow, sir. But first, an't please the gods,
I'll hide my master from the flies as deep
As these poor pickaxes can dig; and when
With wildwood leaves and weeds I ha' strewed his
      grave
390 And on it said a century of prayers,
Such as I can, twice o'er, I'll weep and sigh,
And leaving so his service, follow you,
So please you entertain me.
LUCIUS   Ay, good youth,
And rather father thee than master thee. My friends,
395 The boy hath taught us manly duties. Let us
Find out the prettiest daisied plot we can,
And make him with our pikes and partisans

A grave. Come, arm him. Boy, he is preferred
By thee to us, and he shall be interred
As soldiers can. Be cheerful, wipe thine eyes. 400
Some falls are means the happier to arise.
                          Exeunt with the body.

4.3   *Enter* CYMBELINE, Lords *and* PISANIO.

CYMBELINE
Again, and bring me word how 'tis with her.
                                    Exit a Lord.
A fever with the absence of her son,
A madness, of which her life's in danger. Heavens,
How deeply you at once do touch me. Innogen,
The great part of my comfort, gone; my Queen 5
Upon a desperate bed, and in a time
When fearful wars point at me; her son gone,
So needful for this present. It strikes me past
The hope of comfort. [*to Pisanio*] But for thee, fellow,
Who needs must know of her departure and 10
Dost seem so ignorant, we'll enforce it from thee
By a sharp torture.
PISANIO   Sir, my life is yours:
I humbly set it at your will. But for my mistress,
I nothing know where she remains, why gone,
Nor when she purposes return. Beseech your highness, 15
Hold me your loyal servant.
LORD   Good my liege,
The day that she was missing, he was here.
I dare be bound he's true and shall perform
All parts of his subjection loyally. For Cloten,
There wants no diligence in seeking him, 20
And will no doubt be found.
CYMBELINE   The time is troublesome.
[*to Pisanio*] We'll slip you for a season, but our jealousy
Does yet depend.
LORD   So please your majesty,
The Roman legions, all from Gallia drawn,
Are landed on your coast with a supply 25
Of Roman gentlemen by the Senate sent.
CYMBELINE
Now for the counsel of my son and Queen.
I am amazed with matter.
LORD   Good my liege,
Your preparation can affront no less
Than what you hear of. Come more, for more you're
      ready. 30
The want is but to put those powers in motion
That long to move.
CYMBELINE   I thank you. Let's withdraw
And meet the time as it seeks us. We fear not
What can from Italy annoy us, but
We grieve at chances here. Away. 35
                          Exeunt Cymbeline and Lords.
PISANIO   I heard no letter from my master since
I wrote him Innogen was slain. 'Tis strange.
Nor hear I from my mistress, who did promise

To yield me often tidings. Neither know I
40 What is betid to Cloten, but remain
Perplexed in all. The heavens still must work.
Wherein I am false, I am honest; not true, to be true.
These present wars shall find I love my country
Even to the note o'th' King, or I'll fall in them.
45 All other doubts by time let them be cleared:
Fortune brings in some boats that are not steered.   *Exit.*

4.4   *A confused noise of troops is heard. Enter*
BELARIUS, GUIDERIUS *and* ARVIRAGUS.

GUIDERIUS   The noise is round about us.
BELARIUS   Let us from it.
ARVIRAGUS   What pleasure, sir, find we in life, to lock it
From action and adventure?
GUIDERIUS   Nay, what hope
5   Have we in hiding us? This way the Romans
Must or for Britons slay us, or receive us
For barbarous and unnatural revolts
During their use, and slay us after.
BELARIUS   Sons,
We'll higher to the mountains, there secure us.
To the King's party there's no going. Newness
10   Of Cloten's death – we being not known, not mustered
Among the bands – may drive us to a render
Where we have lived, and so extort from's that
Which we have done, whose answer would be death
Drawn on with torture.
GUIDERIUS   This is, sir, a doubt
15   In such a time nothing becoming you,
Nor satisfying us.
ARVIRAGUS   It is not likely
That when they hear the Roman horses neigh,
Behold their quartered fires, have both their eyes
And ears so cloyed importantly as now,
20   That they will waste their time upon our note
To know from whence we are.
BELARIUS   O, I am known
Of many in the army. Many years,
Though Cloten then but young, you see, not wore him
From my remembrance. And besides, the King
25   Hath not deserved my service nor your loves,
Who find in my exile the want of breeding,
The certainty of this hard life; aye hopeless
To have the courtesy your cradle promised,
But to be still hot summer's tanlings and
The shrinking slaves of winter.
30 GUIDERIUS   Than be so,
Better to cease to be. Pray, sir, to th'army.
I and my brother are not known; yourself
So out of thought, and thereto so o'ergrown,
Cannot be questioned.
ARVIRAGUS   By this sun that shines
35   I'll thither. What thing is't that I never
Did see man die, scarce ever looked on blood
But that of coward hares, hot goats, and venison,

Never bestrid a horse save one that had
A rider like myself, who ne'er wore rowel
Nor iron on his heel? I am ashamed   40
To look upon the holy sun, to have
The benefit of his blest beams, remaining
So long a poor unknown.
GUIDERIUS   By heavens, I'll go.
If you will bless me, sir, and give me leave,
I'll take the better care; but if you will not,   45
The hazard therefore due fall on me by
The hands of Romans.
ARVIRAGUS   So say I, amen.
BELARIUS   No reason I, since of your lives you set
So slight a valuation, should reserve
My cracked one to more care. Have with you, boys.   50
If in your country wars you chance to die,
That is my bed too, lads, and there I'll lie.
Lead, lead. [*aside*] The time seems long, their blood
    thinks scorn,
Till it fly out and show them princes born.   *Exeunt.*

5.1   *Enter* POSTHUMUS *alone dressed as an*
Italian gentleman, carrying a bloody cloth.

POSTHUMUS
Yea, bloody cloth, I'll keep thee, for I wished
Thou shouldst be coloured thus. You married ones,
If each of you should take this course, how many
Must murder wives much better than themselves
For wrying but a little. O Pisanio,   5
Every good servant does not all commands;
No bond but to do just ones. Gods, if you
Should have ta'en vengeance on my faults, I never
Had lived to put on this; so had you saved
The noble Innogen to repent, and struck   10
Me, wretch, more worth your vengeance. But alack,
You snatch some hence for little faults; that's love
To have them fall no more. You some permit
To second ills with ills, each elder worse,
And make them dread it, to the doers' thrift.   15
But Innogen is your own: do your best wills,
And make me blest to obey. I am brought hither
Among th'Italian gentry and to fight
Against my lady's kingdom. 'Tis enough
That, Britain, I have killed thy mistress. Peace,   20
I'll give no wound to thee. Therefore, good heavens,
Hear patiently my purpose. I'll disrobe me
Of these Italian weeds and suit myself
As does a Briton peasant.   [*He changes clothes.*]
                        So I'll fight
Against the part I come with; so I'll die   25
For thee, O Innogen, even for whom my life
Is every breath a death; and thus unknown,
Pitied nor hated, to the face of peril
Myself I'll dedicate. Let me make men know
More valour in me than my habits show.   30
Gods, put the strength o'th' Leonati in me.

To shame the guise o'th' world, I will begin
The fashion: less without and more within.   *Exit.*

5.2 *Enter* LUCIUS, IACHIMO *and the Roman army at*
one door, and the Briton army at another, LEONATUS
POSTHUMUS *following like a poor soldier. They march*
over and go out. Then enter again in skirmish IACHIMO
and POSTHUMUS: *he vanquisheth and disarmeth*
IACHIMO, *and then leaves him.*

IACHIMO   The heaviness and guilt within my bosom
  Takes off my manhood. I have belied a lady,
  The princess of this country, and the air on't
  Revengingly enfeebles me; or could this carl,
5 A very drudge of nature's, have subdued me
  In my profession? Knighthoods and honours borne
  As I wear mine are titles but of scorn.
  If that thy gentry, Britain, go before
  This lout as he exceeds our lords, the odds
10 Is, that we scarce are men and you are gods.   *Exit.*

The battle continues, the Britons fly, CYMBELINE *is taken.*
Then enter to his rescue BELARIUS, GUIDERIUS
and ARVIRAGUS.

BELARIUS
  Stand, stand! We have th'advantage of the ground,
  The lane is guarded. Nothing routs us but
  The villainy of our fears.
GUIDERIUS *and* ARVIRAGUS   Stand, stand and fight!

Enter POSTHUMUS, *and seconds the Britons.*
They rescue CYMBELINE, *and exeunt.*
Then enter LUCIUS, IACHIMO *and* INNOGEN
as Fidele.

LUCIUS [*to Innogen*]
  Away, boy, from the troops, and save thyself,
15 For friends kill friends, and the disorder's such
  As war were hoodwinked.
IACHIMO   'Tis their fresh supplies.
LUCIUS   It is a day turned strangely. Or betimes
  Let's reinforce, or fly.   *Exeunt.*

5.3   *Enter* POSTHUMUS *and a Briton* Lord.

LORD
  Cam'st thou from where they made the stand?
POSTHUMUS   I did,
  Though you, it seems, come from the fliers?
LORD   Ay.
POSTHUMUS   No blame be to you, sir, for all was lost,
  But that the heavens fought. The King himself
5 Of his wings destitute, the army broken,
  And but the backs of Britons seen, all flying
  Through a strait lane; the enemy full-hearted,
  Lolling the tongue with slaught'ring, having work
  More plentiful than tools to do't, struck down
10 Some mortally, some slightly touched, some falling

Merely through fear, that the strait pass was dammed
With dead men, hurt behind, and cowards living
To die with lengthened shame.
LORD   Where was this lane?
POSTHUMUS
  Close by the battle, ditched, and walled with turf,
  Which gave advantage to an ancient soldier,   15
  An honest one, I warrant, who deserved
  So long a breeding as his white beard came to,
  In doing this for's country. Athwart the lane,
  He, with two striplings (lads more like to run
  The country base than to commit such slaughter,   20
  With faces fit for masks, or rather fairer
  Than those for preservation cased, or shame)
  Made good the passage, cried to those that fled,
  'Our Britons' harts die flying, not our men.
  To darkness fleet souls that fly backwards. Stand,   25
  Or we are Romans, and will give you that
  Like beasts which you shun beastly, and may save
  But to look back in frown. Stand, stand!' These three,
  Three thousand confident, in act as many –
  For three performers are the file, when all   30
  The rest do nothing – with this word '"Stand",
        stand',
  Accommodated by the place, more charming
  With their own nobleness, which could have turned
  A distaff to a lance, gilded pale looks;
  Part shame, part spirit renewed, that some turned
        coward   35
  But by example (O, a sin in war,
  Damned in the first beginners) 'gan to look
  The way that they did and to grin like lions
  Upon the pikes o'th' hunters. Then began
  A stop i'th' chaser, a retire; anon   40
  A rout, confusion thick; forthwith they fly
  Chickens, the way which they stooped eagles; slaves,
  The strides they victors made; and now our cowards,
  Like fragments in hard voyages, became
  The life o'th' need. Having found the back door open   45
  Of the unguarded hearts, heavens, how they wound!
  Some slain before, some dying, some their friends
  O'erborne i'th former wave, ten chased by one,
  Are now each one the slaughterman of twenty.
  Those that would die or ere resist are grown   50
  The mortal bugs o'th' field.
LORD   This was strange chance:
  A narrow lane, an old man, and two boys.
POSTHUMUS   Nay, do not wonder at it. You are made
  Rather to wonder at the things you hear
  Than to work any. Will you rhyme upon't,   55
  And vent it for a mock'ry? Here is one:
  'Two boys, an old man twice a boy, a lane,
  Preserved the Britons, was the Romans' bane.'
LORD   Nay, be not angry, sir.
POSTHUMUS   'Lack, to what end?
  Who dares not stand his foe, I'll be his friend,   60
  For if he'll do as he is made to do,

I know he'll quickly fly my friendship too.
You have put me into rhyme.
LORD   Farewell, you're angry. *Exit.*
POSTHUMUS
Still going? This is a lord! O noble misery
65 To be i'th' field and ask 'What news?' of me.
Today, how many would have given their honours
To have saved their carcasses, took heel to do't,
And yet died, too. I, in mine own woe charmed,
Could not find death where I did hear him groan,
70 Nor feel him where he struck. Being an ugly monster,
'Tis strange he hides him in fresh cups, soft beds,
Sweet words, or hath moe ministers than we
That draw his knives i'th' war. Well, I will find him;
  [*He changes back to his Italian clothing.*]
For being now a favourer to the Briton,
75 No more a Briton, I have resumed again
The part I came in. Fight I will no more,
But yield me to the veriest hind that shall
Once touch my shoulder. Great the slaughter is
Here made by th' Roman; great the answer be
80 Britons must take. For me, my ransom's death.
On either side I come to spend my breath,
Which neither here I'll keep nor bear again,
But end it by some means for Innogen.

   Enter two Briton CAPTAINS *and Soldiers.*

1 CAPTAIN Great Jupiter be praised, Lucius is taken.
85 'Tis thought the old man and his sons were angels.
2 CAPTAIN There was a fourth man, in a silly habit,
That gave th'affront with them.
1 CAPTAIN   So 'tis reported,
But none of 'em can be found. Stand, who's there?
POSTHUMUS A Roman,
90 Who had not now been drooping here if seconds
Had answered him.
2 CAPTAIN   Lay hands on him: a dog,
A leg of Rome shall not return to tell
What crows have pecked them here. He brags his service
As if he were of note. Bring him to th' King. *Exeunt.*

5.4 *Enter* CYMBELINE, BELARIUS, GUIDERIUS,
  ARVIRAGUS, PISANIO, *Roman Captives and two*
  JAILERS. *Enter two Briton* Captains *with*
  POSTHUMUS, *dressed as an Italian. The*
  Captains present POSTHUMUS *to* CYMBELINE,
  who delivers him over to a Jailer. Exeunt
  all except Posthumus and Jailers, who put
  manacles on him.

1 JAILER
You shall not now be stolen. You have locks upon you,
So graze as you find pasture.
2 JAILER   Ay, or a stomach.
       Exeunt Jailers.
POSTHUMUS
Most welcome, bondage, for thou art a way,

I think, to liberty. Yet am I better
Than one that's sick o'th' gout, since he had rather 5
Groan so in perpetuity than be cured
By th' sure physician, death, who is the key
T'unbar these locks. My conscience, thou art fettered
More than my shanks and wrists. You good gods,
 give me
The penitent instrument to pick that bolt, 10
Then free for ever. Is't enough I am sorry?
So children temporal fathers do appease;
Gods are more full of mercy. Must I repent,
I cannot do it better than in gyves,
Desired more than constrained. To satisfy, 15
If of my freedom 'tis the main part, take
No stricter render of me than my all.
I know you are more clement than vile men,
Who of their broken debtors take a third,
A sixth, a tenth, letting them thrive again 20
On their abatement; that's not my desire.
For Innogen's dear life, take mine, and though
'Tis not so dear, yet 'tis a life; you coined it.
'Tween man and man they weigh not every stamp;
Though light, take pieces for the figure's sake, 25
You rather, mine being yours; and so, great powers,
If you will make this audit, take this life,
And cancel these cold bonds. O Innogen,
I'll speak to thee in silence. [*He sleeps.*]

  Solemn music. Enter, as in an apparition, SICILIUS
Leonatus, *father to Posthumus, an old man, attired like a*
warrior, leading in his hand an ancient matron, his wife, and
  MOTHER *to Posthumus, with music before them. Then,*
  after other music, follows the two young Leonati,
BROTHERS *to Posthumus, with wounds as they died in the*
  wars. They circle Posthumus round as he lies sleeping.

SICILIUS
No more, thou thunder-master, show thy spite on
 mortal flies. 30
With Mars fall out, with Juno chide, that thy adulteries
Rates and revenges.
Hath my poor boy done aught but well, whose face I
 never saw?
I died whilst in the womb he stayed, attending
 nature's law,
Whose father then – as men report, thou orphans'
 father art – 35
Thou shouldst have been, and shielded him from this
 earth-vexing smart.
MOTHER
Lucina lent not me her aid, but took me in my throes,
That from me was Posthumus ripped, came crying
 'mongst his foes.
A thing of pity.
SICILIUS
Great nature, like his ancestry, moulded the stuff so fair 40
That he deserved the praise o'th' world as great
 Sicilius' heir.

1 BROTHER
When once he was mature for man, in Britain where
    was he
That could stand up his parallel, or fruitful object be
In eye of Innogen, that best could deem his dignity?

MOTHER
With marriage wherefore was he mocked, to be exiled,
45   and thrown
From Leonati seat, and cast from her, his dearest one,
Sweet Innogen?

SICILIUS
Why did you suffer Iachimo, slight thing of Italy,
To taint his nobler heart and brain with needless
    jealousy,
50 And to become the geck and scorn o'th' other's villainy?

2 BROTHER
For this, from stiller seats we came, our parents and
    us twain,
That, striking in our country's cause, fell bravely and
    were slain,
Our fealty and Tenantius' right with honour to maintain.

1 BROTHER
Like hardiment Posthumus hath to Cymbeline
    performed.
Then Jupiter, thou king of gods, why hast thou thus
55   adjourned
The graces for his merits due, being all to dolours
    turned?

SICILILUS
Thy crystal window ope, look out, no longer exercise
Upon a valiant race thy harsh and potent injuries.

MOTHER
Since, Jupiter, our son is good, take off his miseries.

SILICIUS
Peep through thy marble mansion, help, or we poor
60   ghosts will cry
To th' shining synod of the rest, against thy deity.

BROTHERS
Help, Jupiter, or we appeal, and from thy justice fly.

JUPITER descends in thunder and lightning, sitting
upon an eagle. He throws a thunder bolt. The ghosts
fall on their knees.

JUPITER   No more, you petty spirits of region low,
Offend our hearing. Hush! How dare you ghosts
65 Accuse the thunderer, whose bolt, you know,
Sky-planted, batters all rebelling coasts.
Poor shadows of Elysium, hence, and rest
Upon your never-withering banks of flowers.
Be not with mortal accidents oppressed:
70 No care of yours it is; you know 'tis ours.
Whom best I love, I cross, to make my gift,
The more delayed, delighted. Be content.
Your low-laid son our godhead will uplift;
His comforts thrive, his trials well are spent.
75 Our Jovial star reigned at his birth, and in
Our temple was he married. Rise, and fade.
He shall be lord of Lady Innogen,

And happier much by his affliction made.
    [*He gives a tablet to the ghosts.*]
This tablet lay upon his breast, wherein
Our pleasure his full fortune doth confine.   80
And so away. No farther with your din
Express impatience, lest you stir up mine.
Mount, eagle, to my palace crystalline.   *Ascends.*

SICILIUS   He came in thunder; his celestial breath
Was sulphurous to smell; the holy eagle   85
Stooped, as to foot us. His ascension is
More sweet than our blest fields. His royal bird
Prunes the immortal wing and claws his beak,
As when his god is pleased.

ALL   Thanks, Jupiter.

SICILIUS   The marble pavement closes, he is entered   90
His radiant roof. Away, and, to be blest,
Let us with care perform his great behest.
                                The ghosts vanish.

POSTHUMUS [*Awakes.*]
Sleep, thou hast been a grandsire and begot
A father to me, and thou hast created
A mother and two brothers. But, O scorn,   95
Gone! They went hence so soon as they were born,
And so I am awake. Poor wretches that depend
On greatness' favour dream as I have done,
Wake, and find nothing. But, alas, I swerve.
Many dream not to find, neither deserve,   100
And yet are steeped in favours; so am I
That have this golden chance and know not why.
What fairies haunt this ground? A book? O rare one,
Be not, as is our fangled world, a garment
Nobler than that it covers. Let thy effects   105
So follow to be most unlike our courtiers,
As good as promise.
[*Reads.*] *Whenas a lion's whelp shall to himself unknown,*
without seeking find, and be embraced by a piece of tender
air; and when from a stately cedar shall be lopped branches   110
which, being dead many years, shall after revive, be
jointed to the old stock, and freshly grow; then shall
Posthumus end his miseries, Britain be fortunate and
flourish in peace and plenty.
'Tis still a dream, or else such stuff as madmen   115
Tongue and brain not; either both, or nothing,
Or senseless speaking, or a speaking such
As sense cannot untie. Be what it is,
The action of my life is like it, which I'll keep,
If but for sympathy.   120

Enter JAILER.

JAILER   Come, sir, are you ready for death?
POSTHUMUS   Over-roasted rather; ready long ago.
JAILER   Hanging is the word, sir. If you be ready for
that, you are well cooked.
POSTHUMUS   So if I prove a good repast to the   125
spectators, the dish pays the shot.
JAILER   A heavy reckoning for you, sir. But the comfort
is, you shall be called to no more payments, fear no
more tavern bills, which are as often the sadness of

130 parting as the procuring of mirth. You come in faint
for want of meat, depart reeling with too much drink,
sorry that you have paid too much, and sorry that you
are paid too much, purse and brain both empty: the
brain the heavier for being too light, the purse too
135 light, being drawn of heaviness. O, of this contradiction
you shall now be quit. O the charity of a penny cord: it
sums up thousands in a trice. You have no true debitor
and creditor but it. Of what's past, is and to come, the
discharge. Your neck, sir, is pen, book and counters; so
140 the acquittance follows.

POSTHUMUS   I am merrier to die than thou art to live.

JAILER   Indeed, sir, he that sleeps feels not the
toothache, but a man that were to sleep your sleep, and
a hangman to help him to bed, I think he would change
145 places with his officer; for look you, sir, you know not
which way you shall go.

POSTHUMUS   Yes indeed do I, fellow.

JAILER   Your death has eyes in's head, then; I have not
seen him so pictured. You must either be directed by
150 some that take upon them to know, or take upon
yourself that which I am sure you do not know, or
jump the after-enquiry on your own peril; and how you
shall speed in your journey's end, I think you'll never
return to tell on.

155 POSTHUMUS   I tell thee, fellow, there are none want
eyes to direct them the way I am going but such as
wink and will not use them.

JAILER   What an infinite mock is this, that a man should
have the best use of eyes to see the way of blindness.
160 I am sure hanging's the way of winking.

Enter a Messenger.

MESSENGER   Knock off his manacles, bring your
prisoner to the King.

POSTHUMUS   Thou bring'st good news, I am called to
be made free.

165 JAILER   I'll be hanged then.

POSTHUMUS   Thou shalt be then freer than a jailer; no
bolts for the dead.

JAILER   Unless a man would marry a gallows and beget
young gibbets, I never saw one so prone. Yet, on my
170 conscience, there are verier knaves desire to live, for all
he be a Roman; and there be some of them too that die
against their wills; so should I, if I were one. I would
we were all of one mind, and one mind good. O, there
were desolation of jailers and gallowses! I speak against
175 my present profit, but my wish hath a preferment in't.

Exeunt.

5.5   *Enter* CYMBELINE, BELARIUS, GUIDERIUS, ARVIRAGUS, PISANIO *and* Lords.

CYMBELINE [*to Belarius, Guiderius and Arviragus*]
Stand by my side, you whom the gods have made
Preservers of my throne. Woe is my heart
That the poor soldier that so richly fought,
Whose rags shamed gilded arms, whose naked breast

Stepped before targes of proof, cannot be found.   5
He shall be happy that can find him, if
Our grace can make him so.

BELARIUS   I never saw
Such noble fury in so poor a thing,
Such precious deeds in one that promised naught
But beggary and poor looks.

CYMBELINE   No tidings of him?   10

PISANIO
He hath been searched among the dead and living,
But no trace of him.

CYMBELINE   To my grief I am
The heir of his reward, which I will add
[*to Belarius, Guiderius and Arviragus*]
To you, the liver, heart, and brain of Britain,
By whom, I grant, she lives. 'Tis now the time   15
To ask of whence you are. Report it.

BELARIUS   Sir,
In Cambria are we born, and gentlemen.
Further to boast were neither true nor modest,
Unless I add, we are honest.

CYMBELINE   Bow your knees.
[*They kneel and are knighted by Cymbeline.*]
Arise, my knights o'th' battle. I create you   20
Companions to our person, and will fit you
With dignities becoming your estates.

Enter CORNELIUS *and* Ladies.

There's business in these faces. Why so sadly
Greet you our victory? You look like Romans,
And not o'th' court of Britain.

CORNELIUS   Hail great King,   25
To sour your happiness, I must report
The Queen is dead.

CYMBELINE   Who worse than a physician
Would this report become? But I consider,
By medicine life may be prolonged, yet death
Will seize the doctor too. How ended she?   30

CORNELIUS   With horror, madly dying, like her life,
Which, being cruel to the world, concluded
Most cruel to her self. What she confessed
I will report, so please you. These her women
Can trip me if I err, who with wet cheeks   35
Were present when she finished.

CYMBELINE   Prithee, say.

CORNELIUS
First, she confessed she never loved you, only
Affected greatness got by you, not you;
Married your royalty, was wife to your place,
Abhorred your person.

CYMBELINE   She alone knew this,   40
And but she spoke it dying, I would not
Believe her lips in opening it. Proceed.

CORNELIUS
Your daughter, whom she bore in hand to love
With such integrity, she did confess
Was as a scorpion to her sight, whose life,   45
But that her flight prevented it, she had

Ta'en off by poison.

CYMBELINE   O most delicate fiend!
Who is't can read a woman? Is there more?

CORNELIUS
    More, sir, and worse. She did confess she had
50   For you a mortal mineral which, being took,
    Should by the minute feed on life, and ling'ring,
    By inches waste you. In which time she purposed
    By watching, weeping, tendance, kissing, to
    O'ercome you with her show; and in time,
55   When she had fitted you with her craft, to work
    Her son into th'adoption of the crown;
    But failing of her end by his strange absence,
    Grew shameless-desperate, opened in despite
    Of heaven and men her purposes, repented
60   The evils she hatched were not effected; so
    Despairing died.

CYMBELINE   Heard you all this, her women?

LADIES We did, so please your highness.

CYMBELINE   Mine eyes
    Were not in fault, for she was beautiful;
    Mine ears that heard her flattery, nor my heart,
65   That thought her like her seeming. It had been vicious
    To have mistrusted her; yet, O my daughter,
    That it was folly in me thou mayst say,
    And prove it in thy feeling. Heaven mend all.

Enter LUCIUS, IACHIMO, SOOTHSAYER *and other Roman*
prisoners, POSTHUMUS *Leonatus, dressed as an Italian,*
behind, and INNOGEN *as Fidele, all guarded*
by Briton Soldiers.

    Thou com'st not, Caius, now for tribute. That
70   The Britons have razed out, though with the loss
    Of many a bold one, whose kinsmen have made suit
    That their good souls may be appeased with slaughter
    Of you their captives, which ourself have granted.
    So think of your estate.

LUCIUS   Consider, sir, the chance of war: the day
75   Was yours by accident. Had it gone with us,
    We should not, when the blood was cool, have
      threatened
    Our prisoners with the sword. But since the gods
    Will have it thus, that nothing but our lives
80   May be called ransom, let it come. Sufficeth
    A Roman with a Roman's heart can suffer.
    Augustus lives to think on't; and so much
    For my peculiar care. This one thing only
    I will entreat: my boy, a Briton born,
85   Let him be ransomed. Never master had
    A page so kind, so duteous, diligent,
    So tender over his occasions, true,
    So feat, so nurse-like; let his virtue join
    With my request, which I'll make bold your highness
90   Cannot deny. He hath done no Briton harm,
    Though he have served a Roman. Save him, sir,
    And spare no blood beside.

CYMBELINE   I have surely seen him;

His favour is familiar to me. Boy,
Thou hast looked thyself into my grace,
And art mine own. I know not why, wherefore,   95
To say, 'Live, boy'. Ne'er thank thy master. Live,
And ask of Cymbeline what boon thou wilt
Fitting my bounty and thy state, I'll give it;
Yea, though thou do demand a prisoner
The noblest ta'en.

INNOGEN   I humbly thank your highness.   100

LUCIUS   I do not bid thee beg my life, good lad,
And yet I know thou wilt.

INNOGEN   No, no, alack,
There's other work in hand. I see a thing
Bitter to me as death. Your life, good master,
Must shuffle for itself.

LUCIUS   The boy disdains me,   105
He leaves me, scorns me. Briefly die their joys
That place them on the truth of girls and boys.
Why stands he so perplexed?

CYMBELINE   What wouldst thou, boy?
I love thee more and more; think more and more
What's best to ask. Knowst him thou look'st on? Speak,   110
Wilt have him live? Is he thy kin, thy friend?

INNOGEN
He is a Roman, no more kin to me
Than I to your highness, who, being born your vassal,
Am something nearer.

CYMBELINE   Wherefore ey'st him so?

INNOGEN   I'll tell you, sir, in private, if you please   115
To give me hearing.

CYMBELINE   Ay, with all my heart,
And lend my best attention. What's thy name?

INNOGEN   Fidele, sir.

CYMBELINE   Thou'rt my good youth, my page;
I'll be thy master. Walk with me, speak freely.   120
    [*They talk apart.*]

BELARIUS [*to Guiderius and Arviragus*]
Is not this boy revived from death?

ARVIRAGUS   One sand another
Not more resembles that sweet rosy lad
Who died and was Fidele. What think you?

GUIDERIUS   The same dead thing alive.

BELARIUS
Peace, peace, see further. He eyes us not, forbear.   125
Creatures may be alike. Were't he, I am sure
He would have spoke to us.

GUIDERIUS   But we see him dead.

BELARIUS   Be silent; let's see further.

PISANIO [*aside*]   It is my mistress.
Since she is living, let the time run on
To good or bad.

CYMBELINE [*to Innogen*] Come, stand thou by our side,   130
Make thy demand aloud. [*to Iachimo*] Sir, step you
    forth.
Give answer to this boy, and do it freely,
Or by our greatness and the grace of it,
Which is our honour, bitter torture shall

135   Winnow the truth from falsehood. [*to Innogen*] On,
               speak to him.

INNOGEN   My boon is that this gentleman may render
              Of whom he had this ring.

POSTHUMUS [*aside*]   What's that to him?

CYMBELINE [*to Iachimo*]
              That diamond upon your finger: say
              How came it yours?

140 IACHIMO   Thou'lt torture me to leave unspoken that
              Which, to be spoke, would torture thee.

CYMBELINE   How, me?

IACHIMO   I am glad to be constrained to utter that
              Which torments me to conceal. By villainy
              I got this ring. 'Twas Leonatus' jewel,
              Whom thou didst banish, and – which more may
145   grieve thee,
              As it doth me – a nobler sir ne'er lived
              'Twixt sky and ground. Wilt thou hear more, my lord?

CYMBELINE   All that belongs to this.

IACHIMO   That paragon, thy daughter,
              For whom my heart drops blood, and my false spirits
150   Quail to remember – give me leave, I faint.

CYMBELINE
              My daughter? What of her? Renew thy strength.
              I had rather thou shouldst live while nature will
              Than die ere I hear more. Strive, man, and speak.

IACHIMO   Upon a time – unhappy was the clock
155   That struck the hour; it was in Rome – accursed
              The mansion where; 'twas at a feast – O would
              Our viands had been poisoned (or at least
              Those which I heaved to head); the good Posthumus
              (What should I say? he was too good to be
160   Where ill men were, and was the best of all
              Amongst the rar'st of good ones) sitting sadly,
              Hearing us praise our loves of Italy
              For beauty that made barren the swelled boast
              Of him that best could speak; for feature laming
165   The shrine of Venus or straight-pight Minerva,
              Postures beyond brief nature; for condition,
              A shop of all the qualities that man
              Loves woman for; besides that hook of wiving,
              Fairness which strikes the eye –

CYMBELINE   I stand on fire.
              Come to the matter.

170 IACHIMO   All too soon I shall,
              Unless thou wouldst grieve quickly. This Posthumus,
              Most like a noble lord in love and one
              That had a royal lover, took his hint,
              And not dispraising whom we praised – therein
175   He was as calm as virtue – he began
              His mistress' picture, which, by his tongue being made,
              And then a mind put in't, either our brags
              Were cracked of kitchen trulls or his description
              Proved us unspeaking sots.

CYMBELINE   Nay, nay, to th' purpose.

180 IACHIMO   Your daughter's chastity: there it begins.
              He spake of her as Dian had hot dreams

              And she alone were cold, whereat I, wretch,
              Made scruple of his praise and wagered with him
              Pieces of gold 'gainst this which then he wore
              Upon his honoured finger, to attain   185
              In suit the place of's bed and win this ring
              By hers and mine adultery. He, true knight,
              No lesser of her honour confident
              Than I did truly find her, stakes this ring,
              And would so had it been a carbuncle   190
              Of Phoebus' wheel, and might so safely had it
              Been all the worth of's car. Away to Britain
              Post I in this design. Well may you, sir,
              Remember me at court, where I was taught
              Of your chaste daughter the wide difference   195
              'Twixt amorous and villainous. Being thus quenched
              Of hope, not longing, mine Italian brain
              'Gan in your duller Britain operate
              Most vilely; for my vantage, excellent.
              And to be brief, my practice so prevailed   200
              That I returned with simular proof enough
              To make the noble Leonatus mad
              By wounding his belief in her renown
              With tokens thus, and thus: averring notes
              Of chamber-hanging, pictures, this her bracelet –   205
              O cunning how I got it – nay some marks
              Of secret on her person, that he could not
              But think her bond of chastity quite cracked,
              I having ta'en the forfeit. Whereupon –
              Methinks I see him now –

POSTHUMUS   Ay, so thou dost,   210
              Italian fiend! Ay me, most credulous fool,
              Egregious murderer, thief, anything
              That's due to all the villains past, in being,
              To come. O give me cord, or knife, or poison,
              Some upright justicer. Thou, King, send out   215
              For torturers ingenious: it is I
              That all th'abhorred things o'th' earth amend
              By being worse than they. I am Posthumus,
              That killed thy daughter – villain-like, I lie –
              That caused a lesser villain than myself,   220
              A sacrilegious thief, to do't. The temple
              Of virtue was she; yea, and she herself.
              Spit and throw stones, cast mire upon me, set
              The dogs o'th' street to bay me. Every villain
              Be called Posthumus Leonatus, and   225
              Be villainy less than 'twas. O Innogen!
              My queen, my life, my wife. O Innogen,
              Innogen, Innogen.

INNOGEN   Peace, my lord. Hear, hear –

POSTHUMUS
              Shall's have a play of this? Thou scornful page,
              There lie thy part.   [*He strikes her and she falls.*]

PISANIO   O gentlemen, help!   230
              Mine and your mistress! O my lord Posthumus,
              You ne'er killed Innogen till now. Help, help!
              Mine honoured lady.

CYMBELINE   Does the world go round?

POSTHUMUS
  How comes these staggers on me?
PISANIO   Wake, my mistress.
CYMBELINE
235 If this be so, the gods do mean to strike me
  To death with mortal joy.
PISANIO   How fares my mistress?
INNOGEN O, get thee from my sight!
  Thou gav'st me poison. Dangerous fellow, hence.
  Breathe not where princes are.
CYMBELINE   The tune of Innogen.
240 PISANIO Lady, the gods throw stones of sulphur on me if
  That box I gave you was not thought by me
  A precious thing. I had it from the Queen.
CYMBELINE New matter still.
INNOGEN   It poisoned me.
CORNELIUS   O gods!
  I left out one thing which the Queen confessed,
245 Which must approve thee honest. 'If Pisanio
  Have', said she, 'given his mistress that confection
  Which I gave him for cordial, she is served
  As I would serve a rat.'
CYMBELINE   What's this, Cornelius?
CORNELIUS The Queen, sir, very oft importuned me
250 To temper poisons for her, still pretending
  The satisfaction of her knowledge only
  In killing creatures vile, as cats and dogs
  Of no esteem. I, dreading that her purpose
  Was of more danger, did compound for her
255 A certain stuff which, being ta'en, would cease
  The present power of life, but in short time
  All offices of nature should again
  Do their due functions. Have you ta'en of it?
INNOGEN Most like I did, for I was dead.
BELARIUS   My boys,
  There was our error.
260 GUIDERIUS   This is sure Fidele.
INNOGEN
  Why did you throw your wedded lady from you?
    [*She embraces him.*]
  Think that you are upon a rock, and now
  Throw me again.
POSTHUMUS   Hang there like fruit, my soul,
  Till the tree die.
CYMBELINE   How now, my flesh, my child?
265 What, mak'st thou me a dullard in this act?
  Wilt thou not speak to me?
INNOGEN [*Kneels.*]   Your blessing, sir.
BELARIUS [*to Guiderius and Arviragus*]
  Though you did love this youth, I blame ye not;
  You had a motive for't.
CYMBELINE   My tears that fall
  Prove holy water on thee. [*He raises her.*] Innogen,
  Thy mother's dead.
270 INNOGEN   I am sorry for't, my lord.
CYMBELINE
  Oh, she was naught, and 'long of her it was

  That we meet here so strangely. But her son
  Is gone, we know not how nor where.
PISANIO   My lord,
  Now fear is from me, I'll speak truth. Lord Cloten
275 Upon my lady's missing, came to me
  With his sword drawn, foamed at the mouth, and swore
  If I discovered not which way she was gone,
  It was my instant death. By accident
  I had a feigned letter of my master's
280 Then in my pocket, which directed him
  To seek her on the mountains near to Milford,
  Where in a frenzy, in my master's garments,
  Which he enforced from me, away he posts
  With unchaste purpose, and with oath to violate
285 My lady's honour. What became of him,
  I further know not.
GUIDERIUS   Let me end the story:
  I slew him there.
CYMBELINE   Marry, the gods forfend!
  I would not thy good deeds should from my lips
  Pluck a hard sentence. Prithee, valiant youth,
  Deny't again.
GUIDERIUS   I have spoke it, and I did it.
290
CYMBELINE He was a prince.
GUIDERIUS A most incivil one. The wrongs he did me
  Were nothing prince-like, for he did provoke me
  With language that would make me spurn the sea
  If it could so roar to me. I cut off's head,
295 And am right glad he is not standing here
  To tell this tale of mine.
CYMBELINE   I am sorrow for thee.
  By thine own tongue thou art condemned, and must
  Endure our law. Thou'rt dead.
INNOGEN   That headless man
  I thought had been my lord.
CYMBELINE [*to Soldiers*]   Bind the offender,
300 And take him from our presence.
BELARIUS   Stay, sir King.
  This man is better than the man he slew,
  As well descended as thyself, and hath
  More of thee merited than a band of Clotens
  Had ever scar for. [*to Soldiers*] Let his arms alone;
305 They were not born for bondage.
CYMBELINE   Why, old soldier,
  Wilt thou undo the worth thou art unpaid for
  By tasting of our wrath? How of descent
  As good as we?
ARVIRAGUS   In that he spake too far.
CYMBELINE
  And thou shalt die for't.
BELARIUS   We will die all three
310 But I will prove that two on's are as good
  As I have given out him. My sons, I must
  For mine own part unfold a dangerous speech,
  Though haply well for you.
ARVIRAGUS   Your danger's ours.
GUIDERIUS And our good his.

315 BELARIUS   Have at it then, by leave:
    Thou hadst, great King, a subject who
    Was called Belarius.
    CYMBELINE   What of him? He is
    A banished traitor.
    BELARIUS   He it is that hath
    Assumed this age; indeed a banished man,
    I know not how a traitor.
320 CYMBELINE   Take him hence.
    The whole world shall not save him.
    BELARIUS   Not too hot.
    First pay me for the nursing of thy sons,
    And let it be confiscate all so soon
    As I have received it.
    CYMBELINE   Nursing of my sons?
325 BELARIUS   I am too blunt and saucy. Here's my knee.
    [*Kneels.*] Ere I arise, I will prefer my sons;
    Then spare not the old father. Mighty sir,
    These two young gentlemen that call me father
    And think they are my sons are none of mine.
330   They are the issue of your loins, my liege,
    And blood of your begetting.
    CYMBELINE   How, my issue?
    BELARIUS   So sure as you your father's. I, old Morgan,
    Am that Belarius whom you sometime banished.
    Your pleasure was my mere offence, my punishment
335   Itself, and all my treason; that I suffered
    Was all the harm I did. These gentle princes,
    For such and so they are, these twenty years
    Have I trained up; those arts they have as I
    Could put into them. My breeding was, sir,
340   As your highness knows. Their nurse Euriphile,
    Whom for the theft I wedded, stole these children
    Upon my banishment. I moved her to't,
    Having received the punishment before
    For that which I did then. Beaten for loyalty
345   Excited me to treason. Their dear loss,
    The more of you 'twas felt, the more it shaped
    Unto my end of stealing them. But, gracious sir,
    Here are your sons again, and I must lose
    Two of the sweet'st companions in the world.
350   The benediction of these covering heavens
    Fall on their heads like dew, for they are worthy
    To inlay heaven with stars.
    CYMBELINE   Thou weep'st, and speak'st.
    The service that you three have done is more
    Unlike than this thou tell'st. I lost my children.
355   If these be they, I know not how to wish
    A pair of worthier sons.
    BELARIUS [*Rises.*]   Be pleased a while.
    This gentleman whom I call Polydore,
    Most worthy prince, as yours, is true Guiderius;
    This gentleman, my Cadwal, Arviragus,
360   Your younger princely son. He, sir, was lapped
    In a most curious mantle wrought by th' hand
    Of his queen mother, which for more probation
    I can with ease produce.

CYMBELINE   Guiderius had
    Upon his neck a mole, a sanguine star:
    It was a mark of wonder.
    BELARIUS   This is he, 365
    Who hath upon him still that natural stamp.
    It was wise nature's end in the donation
    To be his evidence now.
    CYMBELINE   O, what am I?
    A mother to the birth of three? Ne'er mother
    Rejoiced deliverance more. Blest pray you be, 370
    That after this strange starting from your orbs,
    You may reign in them now. O Innogen,
    Thou hast lost by this a kingdom.
    INNOGEN   No, my lord,
    I have got two worlds by't. O my gentle brothers,
    Have we thus met? O never say hereafter 375
    But I am truest speaker. You called me brother
    When I was but your sister; I you brothers,
    When ye were so indeed.
    CYMBELINE   Did you e'er meet?
    ARVIRAGUS   Ay, my good lord.
    GUIDERIUS   And at first meeting loved,
    Continued so, until we thought he died. 380
    CORNELIUS
    By the Queen's dram she swallowed.
    CYMBELINE   O rare instinct!
    When shall I hear all through? This fierce abridgement
    Hath to it circumstantial branches which
    Distinction should be rich in. Where, how lived you?
    And when came you to serve our Roman captive? 385
    How parted with your brothers? How first met them?
    Why fled you from the court? And whither? These
    And your three motives to the battle, with
    I know not how much more, should be demanded,
    And all the other by-dependences 390
    From chance to chance; but nor the time nor place
    Will serve our long inter'gatories. See,
    Posthumus anchors upon Innogen,
    And she, like harmless lightning, throws her eye
    On him, her brothers, me, her master, hitting 395
    Each object with a joy. The counterchange
    Is severally in all. Let's quit this ground,
    And smoke the temple with our sacrifices.
    [*to Belarius*] Thou art my brother: so we'll hold thee
    ever.
    INNOGEN [*to Belarius*]
    You are my father too, and did relieve me 400
    To see this gracious season.
    CYMBELINE   All o'erjoyed
    Save these in bonds. Let them be joyful too,
    For they shall taste our comfort.
    INNOGEN [*to Lucius*]   My good master,
    I will yet do you service.
    LUCIUS   Happy be you.
    CYMBELINE   The forlorn soldier that so nobly fought, 405
    He would have well becomed this place, and graced
    The thankings of a king.

Cymbeline

POSTHUMUS   I am, sir,
The soldier that did company these three
In poor beseeming. 'Twas a fitment for
410 The purpose I then followed. That I was he,
Speak, Iachimo: I had you down and might
Have made you finish.
IACHIMO [*Kneels.*]   I am down again,
But now my heavy conscience sinks my knee
As then your force did. Take that life, beseech you,
415 Which I so often owe; but your ring first,
And here the bracelet of the truest princess
That ever swore her faith.
        [*He gives Posthumus the ring and bracelet.*]
POSTHUMUS [*Raises him.*]   Kneel not to me.
The power that I have on you is to spare you,
The malice towards you to forgive you. Live,
And deal with others better.
420 CYMBELINE   Nobly doomed.
We'll learn our freeness of a son-in-law:
Pardon's the word to all.
ARVIRAGUS [*to Posthumus*]   You holp us, sir,
As you did mean indeed to be our brother.
Joyed are we that you are.
POSTHUMUS
425 Your servant, princes. Good my lord of Rome,
Call forth your soothsayer. As I slept, methought
Great Jupiter, upon his eagle backed,
Appeared to me with other spritely shows
Of mine own kindred. When I waked, I found
430 This label on my bosom, whose containing
Is so from sense in hardness that I can
Make no collection of it. Let him show
His skill in the construction.
LUCIUS   Philharmonus.
SOOTHSAYER
Here, my good lord.
LUCIUS   Read, and declare the meaning.
435 SOOTHSAYER [*Reads.*]   *Whenas a lion's whelp shall, to
himself unknown, without seeking find, and be embraced
by a piece of tender air; and when from a stately cedar
shall be lopped branches which, being dead many years,
shall after revive, be jointed to the old stock, and freshly
440 grow; then shall Posthumus end his miseries, Britain be
fortunate, and flourish in peace and plenty.*
Thou, Leonatus, art the lion's whelp,
The fit and apt construction of thy name,
Being *leo-natus*, doth import so much.

[*to Cymbeline*] The piece of tender air, thy virtuous
    daughter,   445
Which we call *mollis aer*, and *mollis aer*
We term it *mulier*; which *mulier* I divine
Is this most constant wife, who even now,
Answering the letter of the oracle,
[*to Posthumus*] Unknown to you, unsought, were
    clipped about   450
With this most tender air.
CYMBELINE   This hath some seeming.
SOOTHSAYER
The lofty cedar, royal Cymbeline,
Personates thee, and thy lopped branches point
Thy two sons forth, who, by Belarius stol'n,
For many years thought dead, are now revived,   455
To the majestic cedar joined, whose issue
Promises Britain peace and plenty.
CYMBELINE   Well,
My peace we will begin. And Caius Lucius,
Although the victor, we submit to Caesar,
And to the Roman empire, promising   460
To pay our wonted tribute, from the which
We were dissuaded by our wicked Queen,
Whom heavens in justice both on her and hers
Have laid most heavy hand.
SOOTHSAYER   The fingers of the powers above do tune 465
The harmony of this peace. The vision
Which I made known to Lucius ere the stroke
Of this yet scarce-cold battle, at this instant
Is full accomplished. For the Roman eagle
From south to west on wing soaring aloft,   470
Lessened herself, and in the beams o'th' sun
So vanished; which foreshowed our princely eagle,
Th'imperial Caesar, should again unite
His favour with the radiant Cymbeline,
Which shines here in the west.
CYMBELINE   Laud we the gods,   475
And let our crooked smokes climb to their nostrils
From our blest altars. Publish we this peace
To all our subjects. Set we forward. Let
A Roman and a British ensign wave
Friendly together. So through Lud's town march,   480
And in the temple of great Jupiter
Our peace we'll ratify, seal it with feasts.
Set on there. Never was a war did cease,
Ere bloody hands were washed, with such a peace.
                                        Exeunt.

Double Falsehood, or The Distressed Lovers

Why is a play premiered at Drury Lane on Wednesday 13 February 1727, with the un-Shakespearean title *Double Falsehood or, The Distressed Lovers*, included in the Arden *Complete Works*? Its editor/adaptor/impresario or, as some sceptics would say, author Lewis Theobald *claimed* that it was a rediscovered lost play by Shakespeare. The Arden edition has assessed the evidence in the case, helping to create a consensus, now widely accepted by mainstream Shakespearean scholars and publishers, that Theobald possessed, and further 'edited' a Restoration adaptation (possibly by William Davenant or Thomas Betterton) of a Shakespeare/Fletcher original. A brief resumé of the evidence is presented here.

In 1780, the Shakespearean scholar George Steevens called attention to the fact that the bookseller-publisher Humphrey Moseley had laid claim to copyright of a title called 'The History of Cardenio. By Mr Fletcher. & Shakespeare' in the Stationers' Register on 9 September 1653. He also observed that this play was acted in 1613. His fellow Shakespearean Isaac Reed further speculated that there might be a connection between such a missing Shakespeare/Fletcher play and a play entitled *Double Falsehood* performed in late 1727 and published early in 1728. Steevens's source for a Cardenio play being performed in 1613 was a manuscript now in the Bodleian Library: MS Rawlinson A.239 fol. 47^{r-v} records two entries in the accounts of the King's Treasurer of the Chamber making payment to the actor John Heminge(s) for performing a play variously called 'Cardenna' and 'Cardenno' on 20 May and 8 June 1613. Cardenna/Cardenno are variants of the name Cardenio, a character familiar from Cervantes' *Don Quixote* (Madrid, 1605), which had been translated into English by Thomas Shelton in 1612 as *The History of the Valorous and Witty Knight Errant, Don Quixote of the Mancha*.

The great Shakespearean scholar Lewis Theobald of course knew his Cervantes, and he could possibly have been familiar with the Moseley copyrights. Those, including 'The History of Cardenio', became the property of the publisher Jacob Tonson the Younger on 5 April 1718, and shortly after that, Theobald's acquaintance Charles Gildon wrote about the existence of a Shakespeare play that the Drury Lane managers were refusing to stage. In 1718–19, therefore, a 'lost play' was in the air. Although Theobald's play did not feature a character called Cardenio, or any other Cervantean name, it told what is recognizably the Cardenio story. The 1728

published play-text has a Preface defending it from scepticism about its authorship by claiming that Theobald possessed several manuscript copies, one of which is 'of above sixty years' standing, in the handwriting of Mr Downes, the famous old prompter'. He implied that others ('great judges') had seen the play in manuscript and dismissed Fletcher as a possible collaborator. By 1729, Alexander Pope explicitly ridiculed any Shakespearean involvement in his *Dunciad Variorum*.

One form taken by Pope's scepticism was self-defeating. He showed that Theobald printed as prose what were actually perfectly functioning iambic pentameters. How likely is it that Theobald would have planted verse 'fossils', only to cover them up? Would he, a lawyer by profession, procure a Royal licence that effectively makes the King a witness for the genuineness of the text? The play is briefer than all extant plays by Shakespeare and Fletcher, with lesions that suggest earlier revision and truncation – unless we think that Theobald put them there. Generically, the play is a romantic tragicomedy the plot of which describes an emotional parabola similar to those found in late Shakespeare and in late Shakespeare/Fletcher collaborations – and this some sixty years before Edmond Malone's *An Attempt to Ascertain the Order in which the Plays of Shakespeare Were Written* (1778) laid the groundwork for all subsequent attempts at Shakespearean chronology. Close scrutiny of the dramaturgy of *Double Falsehood* confirms that Shakespeare's (and Fletcher's) later plays, especially *The Two Noble Kinsmen*, *Pericles* and *Cymbeline*, are particularly relevant to its construction. *The Two Gentlemen of Verona*, *Hamlet* and *All's Well* are also prominent in the allusive tissue of the text.

Modern textual scholarship and stylometric analysis has rendered implausible the possibility that *Double Falsehood* is a whole-cloth forgery. Metrical and lexical analysis has established John Fletcher as part-author beyond reasonable doubt. Some of the play's phrasing can be traced back to Shelton's translation, the presumed source for the lost original. Shakespeare has been more difficult to detect, but every serious analyst has found that the play contains his 'DNA' replicated in character, plot and genre, as well as in particular lines and passages of text, his hand being especially prominent in the first act.

The Arden text is based on Lewis Theobald's edition of 1728, as staged in 1727 with painted sliding scenes.

DUKE Angelo	
RODERICK	*his elder son*
HENRIQUEZ	*his younger son*
DON BERNARD	*father to Leonora*
LEONORA	
CAMILLO	*father to Julio*
JULIO	*in love with Leonora*
VIOLANTE	*a maid, in love with Henriquez*
CITIZEN	
MASTER of the Flocks	
SHEPHERDS	
FABIAN	
LOPEZ	
GERALD	*servant to Henriquez*
MAIDS	
SERVANTS	
Churchman	
GENTLEMEN	

Attendants, Courtiers, Musicians

Scene: the province of Andalucia in Spain

Double Falsehood

PROLOGUE

Written by Philip Frowde, Esq. and spoken
by Mr Wilks

As in some region where indulgent skies
Enrich the soil, a thousand plants arise
Frequent and bold; a thousand landscapes meet
Our ravish'd view, irregularly sweet:
We gaze, divided, now on these, now those;   5
While all one beauteous wilderness compose.
Such Shakespeare's genius was. Let Britons boast
The glorious birth, and, eager, strive who most
Shall celebrate his verse; for while we raise
Trophies of fame to him, ourselves we praise: 10
Display the talents of a British mind,
Where all is great, free, open, unconfin'd.
Be it our pride to reach his daring flight,
And relish beauties he alone could write.
Most modern authors, fearful to aspire,   15
With imitation cramp their genial fire;
The well-schemed plan keep strict before their eyes,
Dwell on proportions, trifling decencies;
While noble nature all neglected lies.
Nature, that claims precedency of place,   20
Perfection's basis, and essential grace!
Nature so intimately Shakespeare knew,
From her first springs his sentiments he drew;
Most greatly wild they flow, and when most wild,
        yet true.
While these, secure in what the critics teach,   25
Of servile laws still dread the dangerous breach,
His vast, unbounded soul disdain'd their rule,
Above the precepts of the pedant school!
O, could the Bard, revisiting our light,
Receive these honours done his shade tonight,   30
How would he bless the scene this age displays,
Transcending his Eliza's golden days!
When great AUGUSTUS fills the British throne,
And his lov'd consort makes the muse her own,
How would he joy to see fair merit's claim   35
Thus answer'd in his own reviving fame!
How cry with pride – 'Oblivion I forgive;
This my last child to latest times shall live:
Lost to the world, well for the birth it stay'd;
To this auspicious era well delay'd.'   40

[*Curtain rises.*]

1.1   *A royal palace*

DUKE Angelo, RODERICK
and Courtiers discovered.

RODERICK   My gracious father, this unwonted strain
    Visits my heart with sadness.
DUKE   Why, my son?
    Making my death familiar to my tongue

Digs not my grave one jot before the date.
I've worn the garland of my honours long   5
And would not leave it wither'd to thy brow
But flourishing and green; worthy the man
Who with my dukedoms heirs my better glories.
RODERICK
This praise, which is my pride, spreads me with blushes.
DUKE   Think not that I can flatter thee, my Roderick,   10
    Or let the scale of love o'erpoize my judgement.
    Like a fair glass of retrospection, thou
    Reflect'st the virtues of my early youth,
    Making my old blood mend its pace with transport;
    While fond Henriquez, thy irregular brother,   15
    Sets the large credit of his name at stake,
    A truant to my wishes and his birth.
    His taints of wildness hurt our nicer honour
    And call for swift reclaim.
RODERICK   I trust my brother
    Will, by the vantage of his cooler wisdom,   20
    Erewhile redeem the hot escapes of youth
    And court opinion with a golden conduct.
DUKE   Be thou a prophet in that kind suggestion!
    But I, by fears weighing his unweigh'd course,
    Interpret for the future from the past;   25
    And strange misgivings why he hath of late
    By importunity and strain'd petition
    Wrested our leave of absence from the Court
    Awake suspicion. Thou art inward with him;
    And, haply, from the bosom'd trust canst shape   30
    Some formal cause to qualify my doubts.
RODERICK
    Why he hath press'd this absence, sir, I know not;
    But have his letters of a modern date,
    Wherein by Julio, good Camillo's son
    (Who, as he says, shall follow hard upon,   35
    And whom I with the growing hour expect),
    He doth solicit the return of gold
    To purchase certain horse that like him well.
    This Julio he encounter'd first in France,
    And lovingly commends him to my favour;   40
    Wishing, I would detain him some few days,
    To know the value of his well-plac'd trust.
DUKE   O, do it, Roderick; and assay to mould him
    An honest spy upon thy brother's riots.
    Make us acquainted when the youth arrives.   45
    We'll see this Julio, and he shall from us
    Receive the secret loan his friend requires.
    Bring him to court.   *Exeunt.*

1.2   *Prospect of a village at a distance*

Enter CAMILLO *with a letter.*

CAMILLO   How comes the Duke to take such notice
    of my son that he must needs have him in court and
    I must send him upon the view of his letter?
    Horsemanship! What horsemanship has Julio? I think

he can no more but gallop a hackney, unless he
practis'd riding in France. It may be he did so, for he
was there a good continuance. But I have not heard
him speak much of his horsemanship. That's no
matter. If he be not a good horseman, all's one in such
a case – he must bear. Princes are absolute; they
may do what they will in anything, save what they
cannot do.

Enter JULIO.

O come on, sir; read this paper. [*Gives him the letter.*]
No more ado, but read it. It must not be answer'd by
my hand, nor yours, but in gross, by your person, your
sole person. Read aloud.

JULIO   Please you to let me first o'erlook it, sir.

CAMILLO   I was this other day in a spleen against your
new suits. I do now think some fate was the tailor that
hath fitted them, for this hour they are for the palace of
the Duke. Your father's house is too dusty.

JULIO [*aside*]   Hem! To court? Which is the better, to
serve a mistress, or a duke? I am sued to be his slave,
and I sue to be Leonora's.

CAMILLO   You shall find your horsemanship much
prais'd there. Are you so good a horseman?

JULIO   I have been ere now commended for my seat, or
mock'd.

CAMILLO   Take one commendation with another, every
third's a mock. Affect not therefore to be prais'd.
Here's a deal of command and entreaty mix'd. There's
no denying – you must go; peremptorily he enforces
that.

JULIO [*aside*]   What fortune soever my going shall
encounter cannot be good fortune. What I part withal
unseasons any other goodness.

CAMILLO   You must needs go; he rather conjures than
importunes.

JULIO [*aside*]   No moving of my love suit to him now –

CAMILLO   Great fortunes have grown out of less
grounds.

JULIO [*aside*]   What may her father think of me, who
expects to be solicited this very night?

CAMILLO   Those scatter'd pieces of virtue which are in
him, the Court will solder together, varnish and rectify.

JULIO [*aside*]   He will surely think I deal too slightly, or
unmannerly, or foolishly, indeed – nay, dishonestly, to
bear him in hand with my father's consent, who yet
hath not been touch'd with so much as a request to it.

CAMILLO   Well, sir, have you read it over?

JULIO   Yes, sir.

CAMILLO   And consider'd it?

JULIO   As I can.

CAMILLO   If you are courted by good fortune, you
must go.

JULIO   So it please you, sir.

CAMILLO   By any means, and tomorrow. Is it not there
the limit of his request?

JULIO   It is, sir.

CAMILLO   I must bethink me of some necessaries
without which you might be unfurnish'd, and my
supplies shall at all convenience follow you. Come to
my closet by and by; I would there speak with you.

Exit. Julio remains alone.

JULIO   I do not see that fervour in the maid
Which youth and love should kindle. She consents,
As 'twere, to feed without an appetite;
Tells me she is content and plays the coy one,
Like those that subtly make their words their ward,
Keeping address at distance. This affection
Is such a feign'd one as will break untouch'd;
Die frosty ere it can be thaw'd; while mine,
Like to a clime beneath Hyperion's eye,
Burns with one constant heat. I'll straight go to her,
Pray her to regard my honour – but she greets me –

Enter LEONORA *and Maid.*

See how her beauty doth enrich the place!
O, add the music of thy charming tongue,
Sweet as the lark that wakens up the morn,
And make me think it paradise indeed.
I was about to seek thee, Leonora,
And chide thy coldness, love.

LEONORA   What says your father?

JULIO   I have not mov'd him yet.

LEONORA   Then do not, Julio.

JULIO   Not move him? Was it not your own command
That his consent should ratify our loves?

LEONORA
Perhaps it was: but now I've chang'd my mind.
You purchase at too dear a rate, that puts you
To woo me and your father too. Besides,
As he perchance may say you shall not have me,
You who are so obedient must discharge me
Out of your fancy. Then, you know, 'twill prove
My shame and sorrow, meeting such repulse,
To wear the willow in my prime of youth.

JULIO   O do not rack me with these ill-plac'd doubts,
Nor think though age has in my father's breast
Put out love's flame, he therefore has not eyes,
Or is in judgement blind. You wrong your beauties.
Venus will frown if you disprize her gifts,
That have a face would make a frozen hermit
Leap from his cell and burn his beads to kiss it;
Eyes, that are nothing but continual births
Of new desires in those that view their beams.
You cannot have a cause to doubt.

LEONORA   Why, Julio?
When you that dare not choose without your father
And where you love you dare not vouch it; must not,
Though you have eyes, see with 'em. Can I, think you,
Somewhat, perhaps, infected with your suit,
Sit down content to say you would but dare not?

JULIO   Urge not suspicions of what cannot be.
You deal unkindly – misbecomingly
I'm loath to say, for all that waits on you

110 Is grac'd and graces. No impediment
Shall bar my wishes but such grave delays
As reason presses patience with, which blunt not
But rather whet our loves. Be patient, sweet.

LEONORA
Patient! What else? My flames are in the flint.

115 Haply to lose a husband I may weep;
Never to get one. When I cry for bondage,
Let freedom quit me.

JULIO   From what a spirit comes this?
I now perceive too plain you care not for me.
Duke, I obey thy summons, be its tenor

120 Whate'er it will. If war, I come thy soldier;
Or if to waste my silken hours at court,
The slave of fashion, I with willing soul
Embrace the lazy banishment for life,
Since Leonora has pronounc'd my doom.

LEONORA
125 What do you mean? Why talk you of the Duke?
Wherefore of war, or court, or banishment?

JULIO   How this new note is grown of me, I know not,
But the Duke writes for me. Coming to move
My father in our bus'ness, I did find him
130 Reading this letter; whose contents require
My instant service and repair to court.

LEONORA   Now I perceive the birth of these delays,
Why Leonora was not worth your suit.
Repair to court? Ay, there you shall perhaps,
135 Rather past doubt, behold some choicer beauty,
Rich in her charms, train'd to the arts of soothing,
Shall prompt you to a spirit of hardiness,
To say, 'So please you, father, I have chosen
This mistress for my own.'

JULIO   Still you mistake me.
140 Ever your servant I profess myself;
And will not blot me with a change, for all
That sea and land inherit.

LEONORA   But when go you?

JULIO
Tomorrow, love – so runs the Duke's command,
Stinting our farewell kisses, cutting off
145 The forms of parting and the interchange
Of thousand precious vows with haste too rude.
Lovers have things of moment to debate
More than a prince, or dreaming statesman, know:
Such ceremonies wait on Cupid's throne.
Why heav'd that sigh?

150 LEONORA   O Julio, let me whisper
What but for parting I should blush to tell thee.
My heart beats thick with fears, lest the gay scene,
The splendours of a court, should from thy breast
Banish my image, kill my int'rest in thee,
155 And I be left, the scoff of maids, to drop
A widow's tear for thy departed faith.

JULIO   O let assurance, strong as words can bind,
Tell thy pleas'd soul I will be wondrous faithful;
True, as the sun is to his race of light,

As shade to darkness, as desire to beauty: 160
And when I swerve, let wretchedness o'ertake me
Great as e'er falsehood met, or change can merit.

LEONORA   Enough; I'm satisfied, and will remain
Yours, with a firm and untir'd constancy.
Make not your absence long; old men are wav'ring,   165
And sway'd by int'rest more than promise giv'n.
Should some fresh offer start when you're away,
I may be press'd to something which must put
My faith, or my obedience, to the rack.

JULIO   Fear not but I with swiftest wing of time   170
Will labour my return. And in my absence,
My noble friend, and now our honour'd guest,
The Lord Henriquez will in my behalf
Hang at your father's ear and with kind hints
Pour'd from a friendly tongue secure my claim   175
And play the lover for thy absent Julio.

LEONORA   Is there no instance of a friend turn'd false?
Take heed of that: no love by proxy, Julio.
My father –

Enter DON BERNARD.

DON BERNARD   What, Julio, in public? This wooing   180
is too urgent. Is your father yet mov'd in the suit, who
must be the prime unfolder of this business?

JULIO   I have not yet, indeed, at full possess'd
My father whom it is my service follows,
But only that I have a wife in chase.   185

DON BERNARD   Chase! Let chase alone. No matter for
that. You may halt after her whom you profess to
pursue, and catch her too. Marry, not unless your
father let you slip. Briefly, I desire you (for she tells me
my instructions shall be both eyes and feet to her) no   190
farther to insist in your requiring till, as I have formerly
said, Camillo make known to me that his good liking
goes along with us. Which but once breath'd, all is
done; till when, the business has no life, and cannot
find a beginning.   195

JULIO   Sir, I will know his mind, ere I taste sleep.
At morn you shall be learn'd in his desire.
I take my leave – O virtuous Leonora,
Repose, sweet – as thy beauties, seal thy eyes.
Once more, adieu. I have thy promise, love;   200
Remember, and be faithful.   *Exit.*

DON BERNARD   His father is as unsettled as he is
wayward in his disposition. If I thought young Julio's
temper were not mended by the metal of his mother, I
should be something crazy in giving my consent to this   205
match. And, to tell you true, if my eyes might be the
directors to your mind, I could in this town look upon
twenty men of more delicate choice. I speak not this
altogether to unbend your affections to him; but the
meaning of what I say is, that you set such price upon   210
yourself to him as many, and much his betters, would
buy you at (and reckon those virtues in you at the rate
of their scarcity), to which if he come not up, you
remain for a better mart.

LEONORA My obedience, sir, is chain'd to your
advice. 215

DON BERNARD 'Tis well said, and wisely. I fear your
lover is a little folly-tainted; which, shortly after it
proves so, you will repent.

LEONORA Sir, I confess I approve him of all the men I 220
know; but that approbation is nothing till season'd by
your consent.

DON BERNARD We shall hear soon what his father will
do, and so proceed accordingly. I have no great heart to
the business, neither will I with any violence oppose it, 225
but leave it to that power which rules in these
conjunctions, and there's an end. Come, haste we
homeward, girl. *Exeunt.*

1.3 *Enter* HENRIQUEZ *and* Servants *with lights.*

HENRIQUEZ
Bear the lights close. Where is the music, sirs?
SERVANT Coming, my lord.
HENRIQUEZ   Let 'em not come too near.
[*aside*] This maid,
For whom my sighs ride on the night's chill vapour, 5
Is born most humbly, though she be as fair
As nature's richest mould and skill can make her,
Mended with strong imagination.
But what of that? Th'obscureness of her birth
Cannot eclipse the lustre of her eyes,
Which make her all one light. 10
[*to Musicians*]   Strike up, my masters,
But touch the strings with a religious softness;
Teach sound to languish through the night's dull ear,
Till melancholy start from her lazy couch
And carelessness grow convert to attention.
                                              [*Music plays.*]
[*aside*] She drives me into wonder when I sometimes 15
Hear her discourse. The Court, whereof report
And guess alone inform her, she will rave at,
As if she there sev'n reigns had slander'd time.
Then, when she reasons on her country state,
Health, virtue, plainness and simplicity, 20
On beauties true in title, scorning art,
Freedom as well to do as think what's good;
My heart grows sick of birth and empty rank,
And I become a villager in wish.
[*to Musicians*] Play on – she sleeps too sound. Be still, 25
and vanish. *Exeunt Servants.*
A gleam of day breaks sudden from her window:
O taper, graced by that midnight hand!

VIOLANTE *appears above at her window.*

VIOLANTE
Who is't that woos at this late hour? What are you?
HENRIQUEZ
One who for your dear sake –
VIOLANTE   Watches the starless night!
My lord Henriquez, or my ear deceives me. 30

You've had my answer, and 'tis more than strange
You'll combat these repulses. Good my lord,
Be friend to your own health; and give me leave,
Securing my poor fame, nothing to pity
What pangs you swear you suffer. 'Tis impossible 35
To plant your choice affections in my shade,
At least for them to grow there.
HENRIQUEZ   Why, Violante?
VIOLANTE Alas sir, there are reasons numberless
To bar your aims. Be warn'd to hours more
wholesome;
For these you watch in vain. I have read stories 40
(I fear too true ones), how young lords like you
Have thus besung mean windows, rhym'd their
suff'rings
E'en to th'abuse of things divine, set up
Plain girls, like me, the idols of their worship,
Then left them to bewail their easy faith 45
And stand the world's contempt.
HENRIQUEZ   Your memory,
Too faithful to the wrongs of few lost maids,
Makes fear too general.
VIOLANTE   Let us be homely,
And let us too be chaste, doing you lords no wrong,
But crediting your oaths with such a spirit 50
As you profess them; so no party trusted
Shall make a losing bargain. Home, my lord!
What you can say is most unseasonable; what sing,
Most absonant and harsh. Nay, your perfume,
Which I smell hither, cheers not my sense 55
Like our field-violet's breath.
HENRIQUEZ   Why, this dismission
Does more invite my staying.
VIOLANTE   Men of your temper
Make ev'rything their bramble. But I wrong
That which I am preserving, my maid's name,
To hold so long discourse. Your virtues guide you 60
T'effect some nobler purpose. *Exit.*
HENRIQUEZ   Stay, bright maid!
Come back, and leave me with a fairer hope.
She's gone – who am I, that am thus contemn'd?
The second son to a prince? Yes. Well, what then?
Why, your great birth forbids you to descend 65
To a low alliance. Hers is the self-same stuff
Whereof we dukes are made, but clay more pure;
And take away my title, which is acquir'd
Not by myself, but thrown by fortune on me,
Or by the merit of some ancestor 70
Of singular quality – she doth inherit
Deserts t'outweigh me. I must stoop to gain her;
Throw all my gay comparisons aside
And turn my proud additions out of service,
Rather than keep them to become my masters. 75
The dignities we wear are gifts of pride,
And laugh'd at by the wise, as mere outside. *Exit.*

End of the first act

2.1 *The prospect of a village*

Enter FABIAN *and* LOPEZ; HENRIQUEZ
on the opposite side.

LOPEZ [*to Fabian*]   Soft, soft you, neighbour; who comes
here? Pray you, slink aside.   [*They withdraw.*]

HENRIQUEZ   Ha! Is it come to this? O the devil, the
devil, the devil!

FABIAN [*to Lopez*]   Lo you now, for want of the discreet 5
ladle of a cool understanding will this fellow's brains
boil over!

HENRIQUEZ

To have enjoy'd her, I would have given – what?
All that at present I could boast my own,
And the reversion of the world to boot 10
Had the inheritance been mine. And now –
Just doom of guilty joys! – I grieve as much
That I have rifled all the stores of beauty,
Those charms of innocence and artless love,
As just before I was devour'd with sorrow, 15
That she refus'd my vows and shut the door
Upon my ardent longings.

LOPEZ [*to Fabian*]   Love! Love! Downright love! I see by
the foolishness of it.

HENRIQUEZ   Now then to recollection – was't not so? A 20
promise first of marriage – not a promise only, for
'twas bound with surety of a thousand oaths – and
those not light ones neither.
Yet I remember too, those oaths could not prevail.
Th'unpractis'd maid trembled to meet my love. 25
By force alone I snatch'd th'imperfect joy,
Which now torments my memory. Not love,
But brutal violence prevail'd; to which
The time and place and opportunity
Were accessories most dishonourable. 30
Shame, shame upon it!

FABIAN [*to Lopez*]   What a heap of stuff's this? I fancy
this fellow's head would make a good pedlar's pack,
neighbour.

HENRIQUEZ   Hold, let me be severe to myself, but not 35
unjust. Was it a rape then? No. Her shrieks, her
exclamations then had drove me from her. True, she did
not consent: as true, she did resist; but still in silence all.
'Twas but the coyness of a modest bride,
Not the resentment of a ravish'd maid. 40
And is the man yet born, who would not risk
The guilt to meet the joy? The guilt! That's true.
But then the danger, the tears, the clamours of the
ruin'd maid, pursuing me to court. That, that, I fear
will (as it already does my conscience) something 45
shatter my honour. What's to be done? But now I have
no choice. Fair Leonora reigns confessed the tyrant
queen of my revolted heart and Violante seems a short
usurper there. Julio's already by my arts remov'd. O
friendship! 50
How wilt thou answer that? O, that a man
Could reason down this fever of the blood,

Or soothe with words the tumult in his heart!
Then, Julio, I might be indeed thy friend.
They, they only should condemn me, 55
Who, born devoid of passion, ne'er have prov'd
The fierce disputes 'twixt virtue and desire.
While they, who have, like me,
The loose escapes of youthful nature known,
Must wink at mine, indulgent to their own. 60

Exit Henriquez.

LOPEZ   This man is certainly mad, and may be
mischievous. Prithee, neighbour, let's follow him; but
at some distance, for fear of the worst.

Exeunt Fabian and Lopez after Henriquez.

2.2 *An apartment*

Enter VIOLANTE *alone.*

VIOLANTE   Whom shall I look upon without a blush?
There's not a maid whose eye with virgin gaze
Pierces not to my guilt. What will't avail me
To say I was not willing?
Nothing, but that I publish my dishonour, 5
And wound my fame anew. O misery,
To seem to all one's neighbours rich, yet know
One's self necessitous and wretched.

Enter Maid, *and afterwards* GERALD *with a letter.*

MAID   Madam, here's Gerald, Lord Henriquez' servant.
He brings a letter to you. 10

VIOLANTE
A letter to me? [*aside*] How I tremble now!
[*to Gerald*] Your lord's for court, good Gerald, is he not?

GERALD   Not so, lady.

VIOLANTE [*aside*]
O my presaging heart! [*to Gerald*] When goes he then?

GERALD
His business now steers him some other course. 15

VIOLANTE
Whither, I pray you? [*aside*] How my fears torment me!

GERALD   Some two months' progress.

VIOLANTE   Whither, whither, sir, I do beseech you?
Good heav'ns, I lose all patience. Did he deliberate this,
or was the business but then conceiv'd when it was 20
born?

GERALD   Lady, I know not that, nor is it in the command
I have to wait your answer. For the perusing the letter I
commend you to your leisure.

Exeunt Gerald and Maid.

VIOLANTE   To hearts like mine suspense is misery. 25
Wax, render up thy trust: be the contents
Prosp'rous or fatal, they are all my due.
[*Reads.*] *Our prudence should now teach us to forget
what our indiscretion has committed. I have already made
one step towards this wisdom, by prevailing on myself to* 30
bid you farewell.
O, wretched and betray'd! Lost Violante!

Heart-wounded with a thousand perjur'd vows,
Poison'd with studied language, and bequeath'd
35 To desperation. I am now become
The tomb of my own honour, a dark mansion
For death alone to dwell in. I invite thee,
Consuming desolation, to this temple,
Now fit to be thy spoil. The ruin'd fabric,
40 Which cannot be repair'd, at once o'erthrow.
What must I do – but that's not worth my thought.
I will commend to hazard all the time
That I shall spend hereafter. Farewell, my father,
Whom I'll no more offend; and men, adieu,
45 Whom I'll no more believe; and maids, adieu,
Whom I'll no longer shame. The way I go
As yet I know not – sorrow be my guide.   *Exit.*

2.3 *Prospect of a village, before Don Bernard's house*

Enter HENRIQUEZ.

HENRIQUEZ
Where were the eyes, the voice, the various charms,
Each beauteous particle, each nameless grace,
Parents of glowing love? All these in her
It seems were not, but a disease in me
5   That fancied graces in her. Who ne'er beheld
More than a hawthorn shall have cause to say
The cedar's a tall tree, and scorn the shade
The lov'd bush once had lent him. Soft! Mine
honour
Begins to sicken in this black reflection.
10 How can it be that with my honour safe
I should pursue Leonora for my wife?
That were accumulating injuries,
To Violante first, and now to Julio;
To her a perjur'd wretch, to him perfidious,
15 And to myself in strongest terms accus'd
Of murd'ring Honour wilfully, without which
My dog's the creature of the nobler kind.
But Pleasure is too strong for Reason's curb,
And Conscience sinks o'er-power'd with Beauty's
sweets.
20 Come, Leonora, auth'ress of my crime,
Appear and vindicate thy empire here;
Aid me to drive this ling'ring Honour hence,
And I am wholly thine.

Enter to him DON BERNARD *and* LEONORA.

DON BERNARD
Fie, my good lord, why would you wait without?
25 If you suspect your welcome, I have brought
My Leonora to assure you of it.
HENRIQUEZ [*Salutes Leonora.*]
O kiss, sweet as the odours of the spring,
But cold as dews that dwell on morning flow'rs!
Say, Leonora, has your father conquer'd?
30 Shall Duty then at last obtain the prize,

Which you refus'd to Love? And shall Henriquez
Owe all his happiness to good Bernardo?
Ah no! I read my ruin in your eyes;
That sorrow, louder than a thousand tongues,
Pronounces my despair.
DON BERNARD   Come, Leonora,   35
You are not now to learn this noble lord
(Whom but to name restores my failing age)
Has with a lover's eye beheld your beauty,
Through which his heart speaks more than language
can.
It offers joy and happiness to you,   40
And honour to our house. Imagine then
The birth and qualities of him that loves you,
Which when you know, you cannot rate too dear.
LEONORA   My father, on my knees I do beseech you
To pause one moment on your daughter's ruin.   45
I vow my heart e'en bleeds that I must thank you
For your past tenderness, and yet distrust
That which is yet behind. Consider, sir,
Whoe'er's th'occasion of another's fault,
Cannot himself be innocent. O, give not   50
The censuring world occasion to reproach
Your harsh commands, or to my charge lay that
Which most I fear, the fault of disobedience.
DON BERNARD   Prithee, fear neither the one, nor the
other. I tell thee, girl, there's more fear than danger.   55
For my own part, as soon as thou art married to this
noble lord, my fears will be over.
LEONORA   Sir, I should be the vainest of my sex
Not to esteem myself unworthy far
Of this high honour. Once there was a time   60
When to have heard my lord Henriquez' vows
Might have subdued my unexperienc'd heart,
And made me wholly his. But that's now past:
And my firm-plighted faith by your consent
Was long since given to the injur'd Julio.   65
DON BERNARD   Why then, by my consent e'en take it
back again. Thou, like a simple wench, hast given thy
affections to a fellow that does not care a farthing for
them; one that has left thee for a jaunt to court, as who
should say, 'I'll get a place now; 'tis time enough to   70
marry, when I'm turn'd out of it.'
HENRIQUEZ
So, surely, it should seem, most lovely maid.
Julio, alas, feels nothing of my passion:
His love is but th'amusement of an hour,
A short relief from business, or ambition,   75
The sport of youth and fashion of the age.
O, had he known the hopes, the doubts, the ardours,
Or half the fond varieties of passion
That play the tyrant with my tortur'd soul,
He had not left thee to pursue his fortune,   80
To practise cringes in a slavish circle
And barter real bliss for unsure honour.
LEONORA [*aside*]   O, the opposing wind,
Should'ring the tide, makes here a fearful billow.

85 I needs must perish in it. [*to Henriquez*] O my lord,
Is it then possible you can forget
What's due to your great name and princely birth,
To friendship's holy law, to faith repos'd,
To truth, to honour and poor injur'd Julio?

90 O think, my lord, how much this Julio loves you;
Recall his services, his well-tried faith;
Think too, this very hour, where'er he be,
Your favour is the envy of the Court
And secret triumph of his grateful heart.

95 Poor Julio, how securely thou depend'st
Upon the faith and honour of thy master.
Mistaken youth! This very hour he robs thee
Of all thy heart holds dear. 'Tis so Henriquez
Repays the merits of unhappy Julio. [*Weeps.*]

HENRIQUEZ [*aside*]
100 My slumb'ring honour catches the alarm.
I was to blame to parley with her thus:
She's shown me to myself. It troubles me.

DON BERNARD Mad, mad. Stark mad, by this light.

LEONORA
I but begin to be so. [*to Don Bernard*] I conjure you,
105 By all the tender interests of nature,
By the chaste love 'twixt you and my dear mother
(O holy heav'n, that she were living now!)
Forgive and pity me. O sir, remember,
I've heard my mother say a thousand times
110 Her father would have forc'd her virgin choice,
But when the conflict was 'twixt love and duty,
Which should be first obey'd, my mother quickly
Paid up her vows to love and married you.
You thought this well, and she was prais'd for this.
115 For this her name was honour'd. Disobedience
Was ne'er imputed to her; her firm love
Conquer'd whate'er oppos'd it, and she prosper'd
Long time your wife. My case is now the same:
You are the father which you then condemn'd;
120 I what my mother was, but not so happy.

DON BERNARD Go to, you're a fool. No doubt you have
old stories enough to undo you. What, you can't throw
yourself away but by precedent, ha? You will needs be
married to one that will none of you? You will be happy
125 nobody's way but your own, forsooth. But, d'ye mark
me, spare your tongue for the future – and that's using
you hardly too, to bid you spare what you have a great
deal too much of. Go, go your ways, and, d'ye hear, get
ready within these two days to be married to a husband
130 you don't deserve. Do it, or, by my dead father's soul,
you are no acquaintance of mine.

HENRIQUEZ
She weeps. Be gentler to her, good Bernardo.

LEONORA
Then woe the day! I'm circled round with fire;
No way for my escape but through the flames.
135 O, can I e'er resolve to live without
A father's blessing, or abandon Julio?
With other maids the choice were not so hard;

Int'rest, that rules the world, has made at last
A merchandise of hearts, and virgins now
140 Choose as they're bid and wed without esteem.
By nobler springs shall my affections move,
Nor own a master but the man I love. *Exit.*

DON BERNARD Go thy ways, contradiction. – Follow
her, my lord, follow her, in the very heat. This
145 obstinacy must be combated by importunity as
obstinate. *Exit Henriquez after her.*
The girl says right; her mother was just such another.
I remember two of us courted her at the same time.
She lov'd neither of us, but she chose me purely to
150 spite that surly old blockhead my father-in-law. Who
comes here? Camillo? Now the refusing part will lie on
my side.

Enter CAMILLO.

CAMILLO My worthy neighbour, I am much in
fortune's favour to find you thus alone. I have a suit to
155 you.

DON BERNARD Please to name it, sir.

CAMILLO Sir, I have long held you in singular esteem,
and what I shall now say will be a proof of it. You know,
sir, I have but one son.

DON BERNARD Ay, sir.
160
CAMILLO And the fortune I am blest withal, you pretty
well know what it is.

DON BERNARD 'Tis a fair one, sir.

CAMILLO Such as it is, the whole reversion is my son's.
165 He is now engag'd in his attendance on our master the
Duke. But ere he went, he left with me the secret of his
heart, his love for your fair daughter. For your consent,
he said, 'twas ready. I took a night, indeed, to think
upon it and now have brought you mine, and am come
170 to bind the contract with half my fortune in present,
the whole some time hence, and in the meanwhile my
hearty blessing. Ha? What say you to't, Don Bernard?

DON BERNARD Why, really, neighbour – I must own, I
have heard something of this matter.

CAMILLO Heard something of it? No doubt you have.
175
DON BERNARD Yes, now I recollect it well.

CAMILLO Was it so long ago, then?

DON BERNARD Very long ago, neighbour – on Tuesday
last.

CAMILLO What, am I mock'd in this business, Don
180 Bernard?

DON BERNARD Not mock'd, good Camillo, not mock'd.
But in love matters, you know, there are abundance of
changes in half an hour. Time, time, neighbour, plays
tricks with all of us.
185
CAMILLO Time, sir! What tell you me of time? Come, I
see how this goes. Can a little time take a man by the
shoulder and shake off his honour? Let me tell you,
neighbour, it must either be a strong wind, or a very
mellow honesty that drops so easily. Time, quoth'a?
190
DON BERNARD Look'e, Camillo, will you please to put
your indignation in your pocket for half a moment

while I tell you the whole truth of the matter. My
daughter, you must know, is such a tender soul she
195 cannot possibly see a duke's younger son without
falling desperately in love with him. Now you know,
neighbour, when greatness rides post after a man of my
years 'tis both prudence and good breeding to let one's
self be overtaken by it. And who can help all this? I
200 profess, it was not my seeking, neighbour.

CAMILLO   I profess, a fox might earth in the hollowness
of your heart, neighbour, and there's an end. If I were
to give a bad conscience its true likeness it should be
drawn after a very near neighbour to a certain poor
205 neighbour of yours. Neighbour – with a pox!

DON BERNARD   Nay, you are so nimble with me you will
hear nothing.

CAMILLO   Sir, if I must speak nothing, I will hear
nothing. As for what you have to say, if it comes from
210 your heart, 'tis a lie before you speak it. I'll to Leonora;
and if I find her in the same story, why, I shall believe
your wife was true to you and your daughter is your
own. Fare you well.

Exit, as into Don Bernard's house.

DON BERNARD   Ay, but two words must go to that
215 bargain. It happens that I am at present of opinion my
daughter shall receive no more company today – at
least no such visits as yours.

Exit Don Bernard, following him.

2.4   *Changes to another prospect of Don Bernard's house.*

Enter LEONORA, *above.*

LEONORA   How tediously I've waited at the window,
Yet know not one that passes. Should I trust
My letter to a stranger whom I think
To bear an honest face (in which sometimes
5 We fancy we are wondrous skilful), then
I might be much deceiv'd. This late example
Of base Henriquez, bleeding in me now,
From each good aspect takes away my trust,
For his face seem'd to promise truth and honour.
10 Since nature's gifts in noblest forms deceive,
Be happy you that want 'em! Here comes one.
I've seen him, though I know him not. He has
An honest face too – that's no matter – sir!

Enter Citizen.

CITIZEN   To me?

15 LEONORA   As you were of a virtuous matron born
(There is no doubt, you are), I do conjure you
Grant me one boon. Say, do you know me, sir?

CITIZEN   Ay, Leonora, and your worthy father.

LEONORA   I have not time to press the suit I've to you
20 With many words. Nay, I should want the words
Though I had leisure. But for love of justice,
And as you pity misery – but I wander
Wide from my subject. Know you Julio, sir?

CITIZEN   Yes, very well; and love him too as well.

LEONORA   O, there an angel spake! Then I conjure you, 25
Convey this paper to him: and believe me,
You do heav'n service in't, and shall have cause
Not to repent your pains. I know not what
Your fortune is – pardon me, gentle sir,
That I am bold to offer this.

[Throws down a purse with money.]

DON BERNARD *[within]*   Leonora – 30

LEONORA   I trust to you; heav'n put it in your heart
To work me some relief.

CITIZEN   Doubt it not, lady. You have mov'd me so,
That though a thousand dangers barr'd my way,
I'd dare 'em all to serve you.   *Exit.* 35

LEONORA
Thanks from a richer hand than mine requite you!

DON BERNARD *[within]*   Why, daughter –

LEONORA
I come. – O Julio, feel but half my grief,
And thou wilt outfly time to bring relief.

Exit Leonora from the window.

End of the second act

3.1   *The prospect of a village*

Enter JULIO *with a letter, and* Citizen.

CITIZEN   When from the window she did bow and call,
Her passions shook her voice, and from her eyes
Mistemper and distraction, with strange wildness,
Bespoke concern above a common sorrow.

JULIO   Poor Leonora! Treacherous, damn'd Henriquez! 5
She bids me fill my memory with her danger.
I do, my Leonora. Yes, I fill
The region of my thought with nothing else.
Lower she tells me here that this affair
Shall yield a testimony of her love 10
And prays her letter may come safe and sudden.
This pray'r the heav'ns have heard, and I beseech 'em
To hear all pray'rs she makes.

CITIZEN   Have patience, sir.

JULIO   O my good friend, methinks I am too patient.
Is there a treachery like this in baseness 15
Recorded anywhere? It is the deepest.
None but itself can be its parallel –
And from a friend profess'd! Friendship? Why, 'tis
A word forever maim'd. In human nature
It was a thing the noblest; and 'mong beasts 20
It stood not in mean place. Things of fierce nature
Hold amity and concordance. Such a villainy
A writer could not put down in his scene
Without taxation of his auditory
For fiction most enormous.

CITIZEN   These upbraidings 25
Cool time while they are vented.

JULIO   I am counsell'd.
For you, evermore thanks. You've done much for us

So gently press'd to't that I may persuade me
You'll do a little more.

CITIZEN   Put me t'employment

30   That's honest, though not safe, with my best spirits
I'll give't accomplishment.

JULIO   No more but this –
For I must see Leonora, and to appear
Like Julio, as I am, might haply spoil
Some good event ensuing. Let me crave

35   Th'exchange of habit with you: some disguise
May bear me to my love unmark'd and secret.

CITIZEN
You shall not want. Yonder's the house before us;
Make haste to reach it.   *Exit.*

JULIO   Still I thank you, sir.
O Leonora, stand but this rude shock,

40   Hold out thy faith against the dread assault
Of this base lord, the service of my life
Shall be devoted to repay thy constancy.   *Exit.*

3.2   *Don Bernard's house*

Enter LEONORA *in wedding attire.*

LEONORA   I've hop'd to th' latest minute hope can give.
He will not come. He's not receiv'd my letter.
Maybe some other view has from our home
Repeal'd his chang'd eye: for what business can

5   Excuse a tardiness thus wilful? None.
Well then, it is not business. O! That letter,
I say, is not deliver'd, or he's sick;
Or – O suggestion, wherefore wilt thou fright me? –
Julio does to Henriquez on mere purpose,

10   On plotted purpose, yield me up, and he
Hath chose another mistress. All presumptions
Make pow'rful to this point: his own protraction,
Henriquez left behind – that strain lack'd jealousy,
Therefore lack'd love. So sure as life shall empty

15   Itself in death, this new surmise of mine
Is a bold certainty. 'Tis plain and obvious,
Henriquez would not, durst not, thus infringe
The law of friendship, thus provoke a man
That bears a sword and wears his flag of youth

20   As fresh as he. He durst not. 'Tis contrivance,
Gross-daubing 'twixt them both. But I'm o'erheard.
    [*Going*]

Enter JULIO, *disguised.*

JULIO   Stay, Leonora. Has this outward veil
Quite lost me to thy knowledge?   [*Reveals himself.*]

LEONORA ·   O my Julio!
Thy presence ends the stern debate of doubt

25   And cures me of a thousand heartsick fears
Sprung from thy absence, yet awakes a train
Of other sleeping terrors. Do you weep?

JULIO   No, Leonora. When I weep, it must be
The substance of mine eye. Would I could weep;

30   For then mine eye would drop upon my heart

And 'suage the fire there.

LEONORA   You are full possess'd
How things go here. First, welcome heartily;
Welcome to th'ending of my last good hour.
Now summer bliss and gaudy days are gone,
My lease in 'em's expir'd.

JULIO   Not so, Leonora.   35

LEONORA   Yes, Julio, yes; an everlasting storm
Is come upon me, which I can't bear out.
I cannot stay much talk; we have lost leisure.
And thus it is: your absence hath giv'n breeding
To what my letter hath declar'd, and is   40
This instant on th'effecting.   [*Flourish within*]
                    Hark! The music
Is now on tuning which must celebrate
This bus'ness so discordant. Tell me then
What you will do.

JULIO   I know not what. Advise me.
I'll kill the traitor.

LEONORA   O, take heed: his death   45
Betters our cause no whit. No killing, Julio.

JULIO   My blood stands still and all my faculties
Are by enchantment dull'd. You gracious pow'rs,
The guardians of sworn faith and suff'ring virtue,
Inspire prevention of this dreaded mischief!   50
This moment is our own; let's use it, love,
And fly o'th' instant from this house of woe.

LEONORA   Alas, impossible! My steps are watch'd;
There's no escape for me. You must stay too.

JULIO   What, stay, and see thee ravish'd from my arms?   55
I'll force thy passage. Wear I not a sword?
Ne'er on man's thigh rode better. If I suffer
The traitor play his part – if I not do
Manhood and justice honour – let me be deem'd
A tame, pale coward, whom the night owl's hoot   60
May turn to aspen leaf; some man take this,
    [*indicating his sword*]
Give me a distaff for it.

LEONORA   Patience, Julio,
And trust to me. I have forethought the means
To disappoint these nuptials.   [*Music within*]
                    Hark! Again!
These are the bells knoll for us. See, the lights   65
Move this way, Julio. Quick, behind yon arras
And take thy secret stand. Dispute it not;
I have my reasons – you anon shall know them.
There you may mark the passages of the night.
Yet more: I charge you by the dearest ties,   70
Whate'er you see, or hear, whate'er shall hap,
In your concealment rest a silent statue.
Nay, hide thee straight, or [*Shows a dagger.*] see – I'm
    arm'd, and vow
To fall a bleeding sacrifice before thee.
    [*Thrusts him out to the arras.*]
I dare not tell thee of my purpose, Julio,   75
Lest it should wrap thee in such agonies
Which my love could not look on.

*Scene opens to a large hall. An altar
prepared with tapers.*

*Enter at one door Servants with lights,
HENRIQUEZ, DON BERNARD and Churchman.
At another, Attendants to Leonora. Henriquez runs to her.*

HENRIQUEZ   Why, Leonora, wilt thou with this gloom
Darken my triumph, suff'ring discontent
80 And wan displeasure to subdue that cheek
Where love should sit enthron'd? Behold your slave.
Nay, frown not, for each hour of growing time
Shall task me to thy service, till by merit
Of dearest love I blot the low-born Julio
From thy fair mind.

85 LEONORA   So I shall make it foul.
This counsel is corrupt.

HENRIQUEZ   Come, you will change –

LEONORA   Why would you make a wife of such a one,
That is so apt to change? This foul proceeding
Still speaks against itself and vilifies
90 The purest of your judgement. For your birth's sake
I will not dart my hoarded curses at you
Nor give my meanings language. For the love
Of all good things together, yet take heed
And spurn the tempter back.

DON BERNARD
95 I think you're mad. Perverse and foolish wretch!

LEONORA   How may I be obedient and wise too?
Of my obedience, sir, I cannot strip me,
Nor can I then be wise. Grace against grace!
Ungracious if I not obey a father,
100 Most perjur'd if I do. – Yet, lord, consider,
Or ere too late, or ere that knot be tied
Which may with violence damnable be broken,
No other way dissever'd – yet consider,
You wed my body, not my heart, my lord,
105 No part of my affection. Sounds it well
That Julio's love is Lord Henriquez' wife?
Have you an ear for this harsh sound?

HENRIQUEZ
No shot of reason can come near the place
Where my love's fortified. The day shall come
110 Wherein you'll chide this backwardness and bless
Our fervour in this course.

LEONORA   No, no, Henriquez,
When you shall find what prophet you are prov'd,
You'll prophesy no more.

DON BERNARD   Have done this talking.
If you will cleave to your obedience, do't;
115 If not, unbolt the portal and be gone:
My blessing stay behind you.

LEONORA   Sir, your pardon.
I will not swerve a hair's breadth from my duty;
It shall first cost me dear.

DON BERNARD   Well then, to th'point.
Give me your hand.   [*Leonora gives her hand.*]
                    My honour'd lord, receive

My daughter of me – nay, no dragging back,   120
But with my curses – whom I frankly give you,
And wish you joy and honour.
                    [*As Don Bernard goes to give Leonora to Henriquez,
                    Julio advances from the arras, and steps between.*]

JULIO   Hold, Don Bernard.
Mine is the elder claim.

DON BERNARD   What are you, sir?

JULIO
A wretch that's almost lost to his own knowledge,
Struck through with injuries.

HENRIQUEZ   Ha! Julio? – Hear you,   125
Were you not sent on our commands to court?
Order'd to wait your fair dismission thence?
And have you dar'd, knowing you are our vassal,
To steal away unprivileg'd and leave
My business and your duty unaccomplish'd?   130

JULIO
Ungen'rous lord! The circumstance of things
Should stop the tongue of question. You have
     wrong'd me;
Wrong'd me so basely, in so dear a point
As stains the cheek of honour with a blush,
Cancels the bonds of service, bids allegiance   135
Throw to the wind all high respects of birth,
Title, and eminence; and in their stead
Fills up the panting heart with just defiance.
If you have sense of shame or justice, lord,
Forego this bad intent, or with your sword   140
Answer me like a man and I shall thank you.
Julio once dead, Leonora may be thine;
But living, she's a prize too rich to part with.

HENRIQUEZ
Vain man! The present hour is fraught with business
Of richer moment. Love shall first be serv'd.   145
Then, if your courage hold to claim it of me,
I may have leisure to chastise this boldness.

JULIO
Nay, then I'll seize my right.

HENRIQUEZ   What, here, a brawl?
My servants – turn this boist'rous sworder forth,
And see he come not to disturb our joys.   150

JULIO   Hold, dogs! Leonora! Coward, base Henriquez!
                    Julio is seized, and dragged out by the Servants.
                    Leonora swoons.

HENRIQUEZ
She dies upon me. Help!

DON BERNARD   Throng not about her,
But give her air.
                    [*As they endeavour to recover her, a paper drops
                    from her.*]

HENRIQUEZ   What paper's that? Let's see it.
It is her own handwriting.

DON BERNARD   Bow her head!
'Tis but her fright; she will recover soon.   155
What learn you by that paper, good my lord?

HENRIQUEZ   That she would do the violence to herself

Which nature hath anticipated on her.
What dagger means she? Search her well, I pray you.
160 DON BERNARD   Here is the dagger. O, the stubborn sex,
Rash e'en to madness!
HENRIQUEZ   Bear her to her chamber.
Life flows in her again. Pray, bear her hence,
And tend her as you would the world's best treasure.
                              Women carry Leonora off.
Don Bernard, this wild tumult soon will cease,
165 The cause remov'd, and all return to calmness.
Passions in women are as short in working
As strong in their effect. Let the priest wait.
Come, go we in. My soul is all on fire
And burns impatient of this forc'd delay.
                              Exeunt, and the scene closes.

3.3   *Prospect of a village at a distance*

              Enter RODERICK.

RODERICK   Julio's departure thus in secret from me,
With the long doubtful absence of my brother
(Who cannot suffer, but my father feels it),
Have trusted me with strong suspicions
5 And dreams, that will not let me sleep, nor eat,
Nor taste those recreations health demands:
But, like a whirlwind, hither have they snatch'd me
Perforce, to be resolv'd. I know my brother
Had Julio's father for his host: from him
Enquiry may befriend me.

              Enter CAMILLO.

                              Old sir, I'm glad
10 To've met you thus. What ails the man? Camillo –
CAMILLO   Ha?
RODERICK   Is't possible you should forget your friends?
CAMILLO
Friends! What are those?
RODERICK   Why, those that love you, sir.
CAMILLO
15 You're none of those, sure, if you be Lord Roderick.
RODERICK   Yes, I am that Lord Roderick, and I lie not
If I protest, I love you passing well.
CAMILLO   You lov'd my son too passing well, I take it:
One that believ'd too suddenly his court-creed.
RODERICK [*aside*]   All is not well.
20   [*to Camillo*]   Good old man, do not rail.
CAMILLO
My lord, my lord, you've dealt dishonourably.
RODERICK
Good sir, I am so far from doing wrongs
Of that base strain, I understand you not.
CAMILLO
Indeed! You know not neither, o' my conscience,
25 How your most virtuous brother, noble Henriquez
(You look so like him, lord, you are the worse for't;
Rots upon such dissemblers!), under colour

Of buying coursers, and I know not what,
Bought my poor boy out of possession
E'en of his plighted faith. Was not this honour?   30
And this a constant friend?
RODERICK   I dare not say so.
CAMILLO
Now you have robb'd him of his love, take all;
Make up your malice and dispatch his life too.
RODERICK   If you would hear me, sir –
CAMILLO   Your brave old father
Would have been torn in pieces with wild horses   35
Ere he had done this treachery. On my conscience,
Had he but dreamt you two durst have committed
This base, unmanly crime –
RODERICK   Why, this is madness –
CAMILLO
I've done. I've eas'd my heart; now you may talk.
RODERICK   Then, as I am a gentleman, believe me   40
(For I will lie for no man), I'm so far
From being guilty of the least suspicion
Of sin that way that, fearing the long absence
Of Julio and my brother might beget
Something to start at, hither have I travell'd   45
To know the truth of you.

              Enter VIOLANTE *behind.*

VIOLANTE
My servant loiters. Sure, he means me well.
    [*Catches sight of Camillo.*]
Camillo, and a stranger? These may give me
Some comfort from their talk. I'll step aside
And hear what fame is stirring.   [*Violante retires.*]
RODERICK   Why this wond'ring?   50
CAMILLO   Can there be one so near in blood as you are
To that Henriquez, and an honest man?
RODERICK
While he was good, I do confess my nearness;
But since his fall from honour he's to me
As a strange face I saw but yesterday,   55
And as soon lost.
CAMILLO   I ask your pardon, lord.
I was too rash and bold.
RODERICK   No harm done, sir.
CAMILLO   But is it possible you should not hear
The passage 'twixt Leonora and your brother?
RODERICK   None of all this.

              Enter Citizen.

CAMILLO   How now?   60
CITIZEN   I bear you tidings, sir, which I could wish
Some other tongue deliver'd.
CAMILLO   Whence, I pray you?
CITIZEN   From your son, sir.
CAMILLO   Prithee, where is he?
CITIZEN   That's more than I know now, sir.
But this I can assure you; he has left   65
The city raging mad. Heav'n comfort him!

He came to that curs'd marriage – the fiends take it!
CAMILLO
    Prithee, be gone, and bid the bell knoll for me.
    I have had one foot in the grave some time.
70 Nay, go, good friend; thy news deserve no thanks.
                                        Exit Citizen.
    How does your lordship?
RODERICK   That's well said, old man.
    I hope all shall be well yet.
CAMILLO   It had need,
    For 'tis a crooked world. Farewell, poor boy!

            Enter DON BERNARD.

DON BERNARD
    This comes of forcing women where they hate.
75 It was my own sin; and I am rewarded.
    Now I am like an aged oak, alone,
    Left for all tempests. I would cry, but cannot.
    I'm dried to death almost with these vexations.
    Lord, what a heavy load I have within me!
    My heart – my heart – my heart!
80 CAMILLO   Has this ill weather
    Met with thee too?
DON BERNARD   O, wench, that I were with thee!
CAMILLO   You do not come to mock at me now?
DON BERNARD   Ha?
CAMILLO   Do not dissemble. Thou mayst find a knave
    As bad as thou art to undo thee too.
85 I hope to see that day before I die yet.
DON BERNARD   It needeth not, Camillo; I am knave
    Sufficient to myself. If thou wilt rail,
    Do it as bitterly as thou canst think of,
    For I deserve it. Draw thy sword and strike me
90 And I will thank thee for't. I've lost my daughter.
    She's stol'n away; and whither gone, I know not.
CAMILLO   She has a fair blessing in being from you, sir.
    I was too poor a brother for your greatness;
    You must be grafted into noble stocks
95 And have your titles rais'd. My state was laugh'd at
    And my alliance scorn'd. I've lost a son too,
    Which must not be put up so.   [*Offers to draw.*]
RODERICK   Hold; be counsell'd.
    You've equal losses; urge no farther anger.
    Heav'n, pleas'd now at your love, may bring again,
100 And no doubt will, your children to your comforts:
    In which adventure my foot shall be foremost.
    And one more will I add: my honour'd father,
    Who has a son to grieve for too, though tainted.
    Let your joint sorrow be as balm to heal
    These wounds of adverse fortune.
105 DON BERNARD   Come, Camillo,
    Do not deny your love; for charity
    I ask it of you. Let this noble lord
    Make brothers of us, whom our own cross fates
    Could never join. What I have been, forget;
110 What I intend to be, believe and nourish.
    I do confess my wrongs; give me your hand.

CAMILLO
    Heav'n make thee honest – there.   [*Gives his hand.*]
RODERICK   'Tis done like good men.
    Now there rests naught but that we part and each
    Take sev'ral ways in quest of our lost friends.
    Some of my train o'er the wild rocks shall wait you.   115
    Our best search ended, here we'll meet again
    And tell the fortunes of our separate travels.   *Exeunt.*
            [*Violante comes forward.*]
VIOLANTE
    I would your brother had but half your virtue!
    Yet there remains a little spark of hope
    That lights me to some comfort. The match is cross'd,   120
    The parties separate, and I again
    May come to see this man that has betray'd me
    And wound his conscience for it. Home again
    I will not go, whatever fortune guides me,
    Though ev'ry step I went I trod upon   125
    Dangers as fearful and as pale as death.
    No, no, Henriquez; I will follow thee
    Where there is day. Time may beget a wonder.

            Enter Servant.

    O, are you come? What news?
SERVANT   None but the worst. Your father   130
    Makes mighty offers yonder by a crier,
    To anyone can bring you home again.
VIOLANTE   Art thou corrupted?
SERVANT   No.
VIOLANTE   Wilt thou be honest?
SERVANT   I hope you do not fear me.
VIOLANTE   Indeed I do not. Thou hast an honest face;   135
    And such a face, when it deceives – take heed –
    Is curs'd of all heav'n's creatures.
SERVANT   I'll hang first.
VIOLANTE
    Heav'n bless thee from that end! I've heard a man
    Say more than this – and yet that man was false.
    Thou'lt not be so, I hope.
SERVANT   By my life, mistress –   140
VIOLANTE   Swear not; I credit thee. But prithee, though,
    Take heed thou dost not fail. I do not doubt thee;
    Yet I have trusted such a serious face
    And been abus'd too.
SERVANT   If I fail your trust –
VIOLANTE   I do thee wrong to hold thy honesty   145
    At distance thus. Thou shalt know all my fortunes.
    Get me a shepherd's habit.
SERVANT   Well. What else?
VIOLANTE
    And wait me in the evening where I told thee.
    There thou shalt know my farther ends. Take heed –
SERVANT   D'ye fear me still?
VIOLANTE   No; this is only counsel.   150
    My life and death I have put equally
    Into thy hand. Let not rewards nor hopes
    Be cast into the scale to turn thy faith.

155 Be honest but for virtue's sake, that's all;
He that has such a treasure cannot fall.   *Exeunt.*

End of the third act

4.1   *A wide plain, with a prospect of mountains*
at a distance

Enter MASTER *of the Flocks, three or four*
Shepherds *and* VIOLANTE *in boy's clothes.*

1 SHEPHERD   Well, he's as sweet a man, heav'n comfort
him, as ever these eyes look'd on.

2 SHEPHERD   If he have a mother, I believe, neighbours,
she's a woe-woman for him at this hour.

MASTER
5   Why should he haunt these wild unpeopled mountains
Where nothing dwells but hunger and sharp winds?

1 SHEPHERD   His melancholy, sir, that's the main devil
does it. Go to, I fear he has had too much foul play
offer'd him.

10 MASTER   How gets he meat?

2 SHEPHERD   Why, now and then he takes our victuals
from us, though we desire him to eat, and instead of a
short grace, beats us well and soundly and then falls to.

MASTER   Where lies he?

15 1 SHEPHERD   E'en where the night o'ertakes him.

2 SHEPHERD   Now will I be hang'd an some fair-snouted
skittish woman or other be not at the end of this
madness.

1 SHEPHERD   Well, if he lodg'd within the sound of us I
20 knew our music would allure him. How attentively he
stood and how he fix'd his eyes when your boy sung his
love ditty. O, here he comes again.

MASTER   Let him alone; he wonders strangely at us.

1 SHEPHERD   Not a word, sirs, to cross him, as you love
25 your shoulders.

2 SHEPHERD   He seems much disturb'd. I believe the
mad fit is upon him.

Enter JULIO.

JULIO   Horsemanship! Hell – riding shall be abolish'd.
Turn the barb'd steed loose to his native wildness;
30 It is a beast too noble to be made
The property of man's baseness. What a letter
Wrote he to's brother! What a man was I?
Why, Perseus did not know his seat like me;
The Parthian, that rides swift without the rein,
35 Match'd not my grace and firmness. Shall this lord
Die, when men pray for him? Think you 'tis meet?

1 SHEPHERD [*to Julio*]   I don't know what to say. [*to*
Master and Second Shepherd] Neither I, nor all the
confessors in Spain, can unriddle this wild stuff.

40 JULIO   I must to court; be usher'd into grace
By a large list of praises ready penn'd!
O devil! What a venomous world is this,
When commendations are the baits to ruin.
All these good words were gyves and fetters, sir,

To keep me bolted there, while the false sender   45
Play'd out the game of treach'ry.
[*to Second Shepherd*]   Hold; come hither.
You have an aspect, sir, of wondrous wisdom,
And, as it seems, are travell'd deep in knowledge.
Have you e'er seen the phoenix of the earth,
The bird of paradise?

2 SHEPHERD   In troth, not I, sir.   50

JULIO
I have, and known her haunts, and where she built
Her spicy nest; till, like a credulous fool,
I show'd the treasure to a friend in trust,
And he hath robb'd me of her. Trust no friend:
Keep thy heart's counsels close. Hast thou a mistress?   55
Give her not out in words, nor let thy pride
Be wanton to display her charms to view.
Love is contagious, and a breath of praise
Or a slight glance has kindled up its flame,
And turn'd a friend a traitor. 'Tis in proof,   60
And it has hurt my brain.

1 SHEPHERD   Marry, now there is some moral in his
madness, and we may profit by it.

MASTER   See, he grows cool, and pensive.
Go towards him, boy, but do not look that way.   65

VIOLANTE   Alas! I tremble –

JULIO   O, my pretty youth!
Come hither, child. Did not your song imply
Something of love?

1 SHEPHERD [*to Master and Second Shepherd*]   Ha, ha –
goes it there? Now if the boy be witty, we shall trace   70
something.

VIOLANTE   Yes, sir, it was the subject.

JULIO
Sit here then. Come, shake not, good pretty soul,
Nor do not fear me. I'll not do thee wrong.

VIOLANTE   Why do you look so on me?

JULIO   I have reasons.   75
It puzzles my philosophy to think
That the rude blast, hot sun and dashing rains
Have made no fiercer war upon thy youth,
Nor hurt the bloom of that vermilion cheek.
You weep too, do you not?

VIOLANTE   Sometimes I do.   80

JULIO   I weep sometimes too. You're extremely young.

VIOLANTE
Indeed, I've seen more sorrows far than years.

JULIO   Yet all these have not broken your complexion.
You have a strong heart, and you are the happier.
I warrant, you're a very loving woman.   85

VIOLANTE
A woman, sir? [*aside*] I fear he's found me out.

2 SHEPHERD [*to Master and First Shepherd*]   He takes
the boy for a woman. Mad again!

JULIO   You've met some disappointment, some foul play
Has cross'd your love. I read it in your face.   90

VIOLANTE   You read a truth then.

JULIO   Where can lie the fault?

Is't in the man, or some dissembling knave
He put in trust? Ho! Have I hit the cause?

VIOLANTE   You're not far off.

95 JULIO   This world is full of coz'ners, very full;
Young virgins must be wary in their ways.
I've known a duke's son do as great a knavery.
Will you be rul'd by me?

VIOLANTE   Yes.

JULIO   Kill yourself.
'Twill be a terror to the villain's conscience
The longest day he lives.

100 VIOLANTE   By no means. What?
Commit self-murder!

JULIO   Yes; I'll have it so.

1 SHEPHERD   I fear his fit is returning. Take heed of all
hands. [*to Julio*] Sir, do you want anything?

JULIO [*to Second Shepherd*]
Thou liest, thou canst not hurt me. I am proof
'Gainst farther wrongs. [*to Violante*] Steal close
105   behind me, lady.
I will avenge thee.

VIOLANTE   Thank the heav'ns, I'm free.

JULIO
O treach'rous, base Henriquez! Have I caught thee?
[*Julio seizes on Second Shepherd.*]
                                 Violante runs out.

2 SHEPHERD [*to First Shepherd and Master*]
Help! Help, good neighbours; he will kill me else.

JULIO
Here thou shalt pay thy heart-blood for the wrongs
110 Thou'st heap'd upon this head. Faith-breaker! Villain!
I'll suck thy life-blood.

1 SHEPHERD
Good sir, have patience; this is no Henriquez.
[*First Shepherd and Master rescue Second Shepherd.*]

JULIO   Well, let him slink to court and hide a coward.
Not all his father's guards shall shield him there;
115 Or if he prove too strong for mortal arm,
I will solicit ev'ry saint in heav'n
To lend me vengeance. I'll about it straight.
The wrathful elements shall wage this war;
Furies shall haunt him; vultures gnaw his heart
120 And nature pour forth all her stores of plagues
To join in punishment of trust betray'd.   *Exit.*

2 SHEPHERD   Go thy ways, and a vengeance go with
thee! Pray, feel my nose. Is it fast, neighbours?

1 SHEPHERD   'Tis as well as may be.

125 2 SHEPHERD   He pull'd at it as he would have dragg'd a
bullock backward by the tail. An't had been some
men's nose that I know, neighbours, who knows where
it had been now? He has given me such a devilish dash
o'er the mouth that I feel I shall never whistle to my
130 sheep again. Then they'll make holiday.

1 SHEPHERD   Come, shall we go, for I fear if the youth
return our second course will be much more against
our stomachs.

MASTER   Walk you afore; I will but give my boy

Some short instructions, and I'll follow straight.   135
We'll crash a cup together.

1 SHEPHERD   Pray, do not linger.

MASTER
I will not, sirs.   *Exeunt First and Second Shepherds.*
This must not be a boy.
His voice, mien, gesture, ev'rything he does,
Savour of soft and female delicacy.
He but puts on this seeming, and his garb   140
Speaks him of such a rank as well persuades me
He plays the swain rather to cloak some purpose
Than forc'd to't by a need. I've waited long
To mark the end he has in his disguise,
But am not perfect in't. The madman's coil   145
Has driv'n him shaking hence. These fears betray him.
If he prove right, I'm happy. O, he's here.

               Enter VIOLANTE.

Come hither, boy; where did you leave the flock, child?
[*Strokes her cheek.*]

VIOLANTE   Grazing below, sir. [*aside*] What does he
mean, to stroke one o'the cheek so? I hope I'm not   150
betray'd.

MASTER
Have you learnt the whistle yet, and when to fold?
And how to make the dog bring in the strayers?

VIOLANTE
Time, sir, will furnish me with all these rules.
My will is able, but my knowledge weak, sir.   155

MASTER
That's a good child. Why dost thou blush, my boy?
[*aside*] 'Tis certainly a woman. [*to Violante*] Speak,
my boy.

VIOLANTE [*aside*]
Heav'n, how I tremble. [*to Master*] 'Tis unusual to me
To find such kindness at a master's hand,
That am a poor boy, ev'ry way unable,   160
Unless it be in pray'rs, to merit it.
Besides, I've often heard old people say
Too much indulgence makes boys rude and saucy.

MASTER   Are you so cunning?

VIOLANTE [*aside*]   How his eyes shake fire,
And measure ev'ry piece of youth about me!   165
[*to Master*] The ewes want water, sir. Shall I go drive
'em
Down to the cisterns? Shall I make haste, sir?
[*aside*] Would I were five miles from him.
[*Master seizes her.*]   How he grips me!

MASTER   Come, come, all this is not sufficient, child,
To make a fool of me. This is a fine hand,   170
A delicate fine hand. Never change colour –
You understand me – and a woman's hand.

VIOLANTE   You're strangely out. Yet if I were a woman,
I know you are so honest and so good
That, though I wore disguises for some ends,   175
You would not wrong me –

MASTER   Come, you're made for love.

Will you comply? I'm madder with this talk.
There's nothing you can say can take my edge off.

VIOLANTE
O, do but quench these foul affections in you

180 That like base thieves have robb'd you of your reason,
And I will be a woman and begin
So sad a story that if there be aught
Of human in you, or a soul that's gentle,
You cannot choose but pity my lost youth.

185 MASTER   No stories now –

VIOLANTE   Kill me directly, sir.
As you have any goodness, take my life.

RODERICK [*within*]   Hoa! Shepherd, will you hear, sir?

MASTER   What bawling rogue is that, i'th' devil's name?

VIOLANTE
Blessings upon him, whatsoe'er he be!   *Runs out.*

Enter RODERICK.

190 RODERICK   Good even, my friend. I thought you all had
been asleep in this country.

MASTER   You had lied then, for you were waking when
you thought so.

RODERICK [*Takes off his hat.*]   I thank you, sir.

195 MASTER [*Indicates his hat.*]   I pray, be cover'd; 'tis not so
much worth, sir.

RODERICK   Was that thy boy ran crying?

MASTER   Yes; what then?

RODERICK   Why dost thou beat him so?

200 MASTER   To make him grow.

RODERICK   A pretty med'cine! Thou canst not tell me
the way to the next nunnery?

MASTER   How do you know that? Yes, I can tell you, but
the question is, whether I will or no. And, indeed, I will

205 not. Fare you well.   *Exit.*

RODERICK
What a brute fellow's this! Are they all thus?
My brother Henriquez tells me by his letters,
The mistress of his soul not far from hence
Hath taken sanctuary; from which he prays

210 My aid to bring her back. From what Camillo
Hinted, I wear some doubts. Here 'tis appointed
That we should meet. It must be here. 'Tis so.
He comes.

Enter HENRIQUEZ.

Now, brother, what's this post-haste business

215 You hurry me about? Some wenching matter –

HENRIQUEZ   My letter told you, sir.

RODERICK
'Tis true it tells me that you've lost a mistress
Whom your heart bleeds for, but the means to win her
From her close life, I take it, is not mention'd.
You're ever in these troubles.

220 HENRIQUEZ   Noble brother,
I own, I have too freely giv'n a scope
To youth's intemp'rate heat and rash desires.
But think not that I would engage your virtues

To any cause wherein my constant heart
Attended not my eye. Till now my passions   225
Reign'd in my blood, ne'er pierc'd into my mind;
But I'm a convert grown to purest thoughts
And must in anguish spend my days to come
If I possess not her. So much I love.

RODERICK   The means? She's in a cloister, is she not?   230
Within whose walls to enter as we are
Will never be. Few men but friars come there,
Which we shall never make.

HENRIQUEZ   If that would do it,
I would make anything.

RODERICK   Are you so hot?
[*aside*] I'll serve him, be it but to save his honour.   235
[*to Henriquez*] To feign a corpse – by th' mass, it shall
be so!
We must pretend we do transport a body
As 'twere to's funeral; and coming late by,
Crave a night's leave to rest the hearse i'th' convent.
That be our course, for to such charity   240
Strict zeal and custom of the house give way.

HENRIQUEZ   And, opportune, a vacant hearse pass'd by
From rites but new perform'd. This for a price
We'll hire, to put our scheme in act. Ho! Gerald.

Enter GERALD, *whom Henriquez whispers;*
then Gerald goes out.

RODERICK
When we're once lodg'd, the means of her conveyance   245
By safe and secret force with ease we'll compass.
But, brother, know my terms. If that your mistress
Will to the world come back, and she appear
An object worthy in our father's eye,
Woo her and win her; but if his consent   250
Keep not pace with your purpose –

HENRIQUEZ   Doubt it not.
I've look'd not with a common eye, but chose
A noble virgin, who to make her so
Has all the gifts of heav'n and earth upon her.
If ever woman yet could be an angel,   255
She is the nearest.

RODERICK   Well, a lover's praise
Feasts not a common ear. Now to our plot.
We shall bring night in with us.   *Exeunt.*

4.2   *Enter* JULIO *and two* Gentlemen.

1 GENTLEMAN   Good sir, compose yourself.

JULIO   O Leonora,
That heav'n had made thee stronger than a woman.
How happy had I been!

1 GENTLEMAN [*to Second Gentleman*]   He's calm again.
I'll take this interval to work upon him.
[*to Julio*] These wild and solitary places, sir,   5
But feed your pain. Let better reason guide you,
And quit this forlorn state that yields no comfort.

[*Lute sounds within.*]

JULIO
Ha! Hark, a sound from heav'n! Do you hear nothing?

1 GENTLEMAN
Yes sir, the touch of some sweet instrument.
Here's no inhabitant.

10 JULIO   No, no, the better.

1 GENTLEMAN
This is a strange place to hear music in.

JULIO   I'm often visited with these sweet airs.
The spirit of some hapless man that died
And left his love hid in a faithless woman
15 Sure haunts these mountains.

VIOLANTE [*Sings within.*]
          Fond Echo, forego thy light strain,
              And heedfully hear a lost maid;
          Go tell the false ear of the swain
              How deeply his vows have betray'd.
20   Go, tell him what sorrows I bear;
              See yet if his heart feel my woe;
          'Tis now he must heal my despair,
              Or death will make pity too slow.

1 GENTLEMAN
See, how his soul strives in him! This sad strain
Has search'd him to the heart.

25 JULIO   Excellent sorrow!
You never lov'd?

1 GENTLEMAN   No.

JULIO   Peace; and learn to grieve then.

VIOLANTE [*Sings within.*]
          Go, tell him what sorrows I bear,
              See yet if his heart feel my woe;
          'Tis now he must heal my despair,
30   Or death will make pity too slow.

JULIO   Is not this heav'nly?

1 GENTLEMAN   I never heard the like, sir.

JULIO
I'll tell you, my good friends – but pray, say nothing –
I'm strangely touch'd with this. The heav'nly sound
Diffuses a sweet peace through all my soul.
35 But yet I wonder what new, sad companion
Grief has brought hither to out-bid my sorrows.
Stand off, stand off, stand off – friends, it appears.
    [*Julio and Gentlemen withdraw.*]

        Enter VIOLANTE *with her hair loose.*

VIOLANTE
How much more grateful are these craggy mountains
And these wild trees than things of nobler natures;
40 For these receive my plaints and mourn again
In many echoes to me. All good people
Are fall'n asleep forever. None are left,
That have the sense and touch of tenderness
For virtue's sake – no, scarce their memory –
45 From whom I may expect counsel in fears,
Ease to complainings or redress of wrongs.

JULIO   This is a moving sorrow, but say nothing.

VIOLANTE   What dangers have I run and to what insults

Expos'd this ruin of myself ? O, mischief
On that soul-spotted hind, my vicious master!   50
Who would have thought that such poor worms as they –
Whose best feed is coarse bread, whose bev'rage,
    water –
Should have so much rank blood? I shake all over
And blush to think what had become of me
If that good man had not reliev'd me from him.   55

JULIO   Since she is not Leonora, she is heav'nly.
When she speaks next, listen as seriously
As women do that have their loves at sea
What wind blows ev'ry morning.

VIOLANTE   I cannot get this false man's memory   60
Out of my mind. You maidens that shall live
To hear my mournful tale when I am ashes,
Be wise; and to an oath no more give credit,
To tears, to vows – false both! – or anything
A man shall promise, than to clouds that now   65
Bear such a pleasing shape and now are nothing.
For they will cozen (if they may be cozen'd)
The very gods they worship. Valour, justice,
Discretion, honesty and all they covet
To make them seeming saints are but the wiles   70
By which these sirens lure us to destruction.

JULIO   Do not you weep now? I could drop myself
Into a fountain for her.

1 GENTLEMAN
She weeps extremely.

JULIO   Let her weep; 'tis well.
Her heart will break else. Great sorrows live in tears.   75

VIOLANTE   O false Henriquez!

JULIO   Ha!

VIOLANTE   And O, thou fool,
Forsaken Violante – whose belief
And childish love have made thee so – go, die!
For there is nothing left thee now to look for
That can bring comfort but a quiet grave.   80
There all the miseries I long have felt
And those to come shall sweetly sleep together.
Fortune may guide that false Henriquez hither
To weep repentance o'er my pale, dead corpse
And cheer my wand'ring spirit with those lov'd
    obsequies.   [*Going*]   85

JULIO [*Comes forward.*]
Stay, lady, stay. Can it be possible
That you are Violante?

VIOLANTE   That lost name
Spoken by one that needs must know my fortunes
Has taken much fear from me. Who are you, sir?
For, sure, I am that hopeless Violante.   90

JULIO   And I, as far from any earthly comfort
That I know yet, the much-wrong'd Julio.

VIOLANTE   Julio!

JULIO   I once was thought so. If the curst Henriquez
Had pow'r to change you to a boy, why, lady,
Should not that mischief make me anything,   95
That have an equal share in all the miseries

His crimes have flung upon us?

VIOLANTE   Well I know it.
And pardon me I could not know your virtues
Before your griefs. Methought when last we met
100 The accent of your voice struck on my ear
Like something I had known, but floods of sorrow
Drown'd the remembrance. If you'll please to sit
(Since I have found a suff'ring true companion)
And give me hearing, I will tell you something
105 Of Leonora that may comfort you.

JULIO   Blessing upon thee! Henceforth, I protest
Never to leave thee, if heav'n say 'Amen'.
But soft, let's shift our ground, guide our sad steps
To some remoter gloom, where undisturb'd
110 We may compare our woes; dwell on the tale
Of mutual injuries till our eyes run o'er
And we infect each other with fresh sorrows.
Talk'd you of comfort? 'Tis the food of fools,
And we will none on't but indulge despair.
115   So, worn with griefs, steal to the Cave of Death
And in a sigh give up our latest breath.   *Exeunt.*

End of the fourth act

5.1   *The prospect of the mountains continued*

Enter RODERICK, LEONORA *veil'd,* HENRIQUEZ, *and*
Attendants as mourners.

RODERICK   Rest certain, lady, nothing shall betide you
But fair and noble usage. Pardon me
That hitherto a course of violence
Has snatch'd you from that seat of contemplation
To which you gave your after-life.

5 LEONORA   Where am I?
RODERICK
Not in the nunnery. Never blush, nor tremble;
Your honour has as fair a guard as when
Within a cloister. Know then, what is done
(Which, I presume, you understand not truly)
10 Has this use, to preserve the life of one
Dying for love of you: my brother, and your friend.
Under which colour we desir'd to rest
Our hearse one night within your hallow'd walls,
Where we surpris'd you.

LEONORA   Are you that Lord Roderick,
15 So spoken of for virtue and fair life,
And dare you lose these to be advocate
For such a brother, such a sinful brother,
Such an unfaithful, treacherous, brutal brother?

RODERICK [*Looks at Henriquez.*]
This is a fearful charge.

LEONORA   If you would have me
20 Think you still bear respect for virtue's name,
As you would wish your daughters, thus distress'd,
Might find a guard, protect me from Henriquez
And I am happy.

RODERICK   Come, sir, make your answer,

For as I have a soul, I am asham'd on't.

HENRIQUEZ   O Leonora, see, thus self-condemn'd   25
I throw me at your feet and sue for mercy.
If I have err'd, impute it to my love:
The tyrant god that bows us to his sway,
Rebellious to the laws of reas'ning men,
That will not have his votaries' actions scann'd,   30
But calls it justice when we most obey him.
He but commanded what your eyes inspir'd,
Whose sacred beams, darted into my soul,
Have purg'd the mansion from impure desires
And kindled in my heart a vestal's flame.   35

LEONORA
Rise, rise, my lord, this well-dissembled passion
Has gain'd you nothing but a deeper hate.
Should I imagine he can truly love me
That, like a villain, murders my desires?
Or should I drink that wine, and think it cordial,   40
When I see poison in't?

RODERICK [*Leads Leonora aside.*]   Draw this way, lady.
I am not perfect in your story yet,
But see you've had some wrongs that want redress.
Only you must have patience to go with us
To yon small lodge, which meets the sight from hence,   45
Where your distress shall find the due respect.
Till when, your griefs shall govern me as much
As nearness and affection to my brother.
Call my attendants yours and use them freely,
For, as I am a gentleman, no pow'r   50
Above your own will shall come near your person.

As they are going out, VIOLANTE *enters in boy's clothes,*
and plucks Roderick by the sleeve; the rest go out.

VIOLANTE
Your ear a moment: scorn not my tender youth.

RODERICK [*Calls after them.*]
Look to the lady there. I follow straight.
– What ails this boy? Why dost thou single me?

VIOLANTE   The due observance of your noble virtue   55
Vow'd to this mourning virgin makes me bold
To give it more employment.

RODERICK   Art not thou
The surly shepherd's boy that, when I call'd
To know the way, ran crying by me?

VIOLANTE   Yes, sir.
And I thank heav'n and you for helping me.   60

RODERICK   How did I help thee, boy?

VIOLANTE   I do but seem so, sir, and am indeed
A woman – one your brother once has lov'd,
Or, heav'n forgive him else, he lied extremely.

RODERICK
Weep not, good maid. O, this licentious brother!   65
But how came you a wand'rer on these mountains?

VIOLANTE
That as we pass, an't please you, I'll discover.
I will assure you, sir, these barren mountains
Hold many wonders of your brother's making.

70   Here wanders hapless Julio, worthy man!
      Besides himself with wrongs.
RODERICK   That once again –
VIOLANTE
      Sir, I said, Julio. Sleep weigh'd down his eyelids,
      Oppress'd with watching, just as you approach'd us.
RODERICK
      O brother, we shall sound the depths of falsehood.
75   If this be true, no more but guide me to him,
      I hope a fair end will succeed all yet.
      If it be he, by your leave, gentle brother,
      I'll see him serv'd first. Maid, you have o'erjoy'd me.
      Thou shalt have right too. Make thy fair appeal
80   To the good Duke, and doubt not but thy tears
      Shall be repaid with interest from his justice.
      Lead me to Julio.   *Exeunt.*

5.2   *An apartment in the lodge*

        Enter DUKE, DON BERNARD *and* CAMILLO.

CAMILLO   Ay, then your grace had had a son more, he, a
      daughter; and I, an heir. But let it be as 'tis; I cannot
      mend it. One way or other, I shall rub it over with
      rubbing to my grave, and there's an end on't.
DUKE
5   Our sorrows cannot help us, gentlemen.
CAMILLO   Hang me, sir, if I shed one tear more. By
      Jove, I've wept so long I'm as blind as justice. When I
      come to see my hawks (which I held a toy next to my
      son), if they be but house-high I must stand aiming at
10   them like a gunner.
DUKE   Why, he mourns like a man. Don Bernard, you
      Are still like April, full of show'rs and dews;
      And yet I blame you not, for I myself
      Feel the self-same affections. – Let them go.
      They're disobedient children.
15   DON BERNARD   Ay, my lord.
      Yet they may turn again.
CAMILLO   Let them e'en have their swing. They're
      young and wanton; the next storm we shall have them
      gallop homeward, whining as pigs do in the wind.
20   DON BERNARD   Would I had my daughter any way.
CAMILLO   Wouldst thou have her with bairn, man, tell
      me that?
DON BERNARD   I care not, if an honest father got it.
CAMILLO   You might have had her so in this good time,
25   Had my son had her. Now you may go seek
      Your fool to stop a gap with.
DUKE
      You say that Rod'rick charg'd you here should wait him.
      He has o'erslipp'd the time at which his letters
      Of speed request that I should also meet him.
30   I fear some bad event is usher'd in
      By this delay. How now?

            Enter Gentleman.

GENTLEMAN   So please your grace,

Lord Rod'rick makes approach.
DUKE   I thank thee, fellow,
      For thy so timely news. Comes he alone?
GENTLEMAN   No sir, attended well, and in his train
      Follows a hearse with all due rites of mourning.   *Exit.*   35
DUKE   Heav'n send Henriquez live!
CAMILLO   'Tis my poor Julio.

            Enter RODERICK *hastily.*

DUKE   O welcome, welcome, welcome, good Rod'rick!
      Say, what news?
CAMILLO   Do you bring joy or grief, my lord? For me,
      Come what can come, I'll live a month or two   40
      If the gout please, curse my physician once more,
      And then –
                        Under this stone
                    Lies sev'nty-one.
RODERICK   Signior, you do express a manly patience.   45
      My noble father, something I have brought
      To ease your sorrows: my endeavours have not
      Been altogether barren in my journey.
DUKE   It comes at need, boy; but I hop'd it from thee.

            Enter LEONORA *veiled,* HENRIQUEZ
                    behind, and Attendants.

RODERICK   The company I bring will bear me witness   50
      The busiest of my time has been employ'd
      On this good task. Don Bernard finds beneath
      This veil his daughter; you, my royal father,
      Behind that lady find a wand'ring son.
      How I met with them and how brought them hither   55
      More leisure must unfold.
HENRIQUEZ [*aside*]   My father here!
      And Julio's! O confusion! [*to the Duke*] Low as earth
      I bow me for your pardon.
DON BERNARD   O my girl!
      [*Embraces Leonora.*] Thou bringst new life.
DUKE [*to Roderick*]   And you, my son, restore me
      One comfort here that has been missing long.   60
      [*to Henriquez*] I hope thy follies thou hast left abroad.
CAMILLO   Ay, ay; you've all comforts but I. You have
      ruin'd me, kill'd my poor boy – cheated and ruin'd
      him; and I have no comfort.
RODERICK   Be patient, signior. Time may guide my hand   65
      To work you comfort too.
CAMILLO   I thank your lordship.
      Would grandsire Time had been so kind to've done it,
      We might have joy'd together like good fellows;
      But he's so full of business, good old man,
      'Tis wonder he could do the good he has done.   70
DON BERNARD
      Nay, child, be comforted. These tears distract me.
DUKE   Hear your good father, lady.
LEONORA   Willingly.
DUKE   The voice of parents is the voice of gods:
      For to their children they are heav'n's lieutenants;
      Made fathers not for common uses merely   75

Of procreation (beasts and birds would be
As noble then as we are), but to steer
The wanton freight of youth through storms and
    dangers,
Which with full sails they bear upon, and straighten
80   The moral line of life they bend so often.
For these are we made fathers; and for these
May challenge duty on our children's part.
Obedience is the sacrifice of angels,
Whose form you carry.

DON BERNARD   Hear the Duke, good wench.

LEONORA
85   I do most heedfully. [*to the Duke*] My gracious lord,
Let me be so unmanner'd to request
He would not farther press me with persuasions
O'th' instant hour, but have the gentle patience
To bury this keen suit till I shake hands
With my old sorrows –

90 CAMILLO   Why dost look at me?
Alas! I cannot help thee.

LEONORA   And but weep
A farewell to my murder'd Julio –

CAMILLO
Blessing be with thy soul whene'er it leaves thee!

LEONORA
For such sad rites must be perform'd, my lord,
95   Ere I can love again. Maids that have lov'd,
If they be worth that noble testimony,
Wear their loves here, my lord – here, in their
    hearts –
Deep, deep within; not in their eyes, or accents.
Such may be slipp'd away, or with two tears
100 Wash'd out of all remembrance: mine, no physic
But time, or death, can cure.

HENRIQUEZ
You make your own conditions, and I seal them
Thus on your virtuous hand.

CAMILLO   Well, wench, thy equal
Shall not be found in haste, I give thee that.
105 Thou art a right one, ev'ry inch. Thy father
(For, without doubt, that snuff never begot thee)
Was some choice fellow, some true gentleman.
I give thy mother thanks for't – there's no harm done.
Would I were young again and had but thee,
110 A good horse under me and a good sword,
And thus much for inheritance.   [*Snaps his fingers.*]
    [*In the course of this speech Violante offers once or
    twice to show herself, but goes back.*]

DUKE   What boy's that,
Has offer'd twice or thrice to break upon us?
I've noted him, and still he falls back fearful.

RODERICK   A little boy, sir, like a shepherd?

DUKE   Yes.

RODERICK
115 'Tis your page, brother – one that was so, late.

HENRIQUEZ
My page! What page?

RODERICK   E'en so he says, your page;
And more, and worse, you stole him from his friends
And promis'd him preferment.

HENRIQUEZ   I, preferment!

RODERICK   And on some slight occasion let him slip
Here on these mountains, where he had been starv'd,   120
Had not my people found him as we travell'd.
This was not handsome, brother.

HENRIQUEZ   You are merry.

RODERICK You'll find it sober truth.

DUKE   If so, 'tis ill.

HENRIQUEZ
'Tis fiction all, sir. Brother, you must please
To look some other fool to put these tricks on;   125
They are too obvious. – Please your grace, give leave
T'admit the boy. If he know me and say
I stole him from his friends and cast him off,
Know me no more. Brother, pray do not wrong me.

Enter VIOLANTE *in boy's clothes.*

RODERICK Here is the boy. If he deny this to you,   130
Then I have wrong'd you.

DUKE   Hear me: what's thy name, boy?

VIOLANTE   Florio, an't like your grace.

DUKE   A pretty child.
Where wast thou born?

VIOLANTE   On t'other side the mountains.

DUKE What are thy friends?

VIOLANTE   A father, sir; but poor.

DUKE
How camest thou hither? How, to leave thy father?   135

VIOLANTE [*pointing to Henriquez*]
That noble gentleman pleas'd once to like me
And, not to lie, so much to dote upon me
That with his promises he won my youth
And duty from my father: him I follow'd.

RODERICK
How say you now, brother?

CAMILLO   Ay, my lord, how say you?   140

HENRIQUEZ   As I have life and soul, 'tis all a trick, sir.
I never saw the boy before.

VIOLANTE   O sir,
Call not your soul to witness in a wrong:
And 'tis not noble in you to despise
What you have made thus. If I lie, let justice   145
Turn all her rods upon me.

DUKE   Fie, Henriquez;
There is no trace of cunning in this boy.

CAMILLO
A good boy! [*to Violante*] Be not fearful; speak thy
    mind, child.
Nature, sure, meant thou shouldst have been a
    wench –
And then't had been no marvel he had bobb'd thee.   150

DUKE Why did he put thee from him?

VIOLANTE   That to me
Is yet unknown, sir. For my faith he could not;

I never did deceive him. For my service
He had no just cause; what my youth was able,
155   My will still put in act to please my master.
I cannot steal, therefore that can be nothing
To my undoing; no, nor lie. My breeding,
Though it be plain, is honest.

DUKE   Weep not, child.

CAMILLO   This lord has abused men, women and
160   children already. What farther plot he has, the devil
knows.

DUKE   If thou canst bring a witness of thy wrong
(Else it would be injustice to believe thee,
He having sworn against it), thou shalt have,
165   I bind it with my honour, satisfaction
To thine own wishes.

VIOLANTE   I desire no more, sir.
I have a witness, and a noble one,
For truth and honesty.

RODERICK   Go, bring him hither.
                                        Exit Violante.

HENRIQUEZ   This lying boy will take him to his heels,
And leave me slander'd.

170   RODERICK   No; I'll be his voucher.

HENRIQUEZ   Nay then 'tis plain: this is confederacy.

RODERICK   That he has been an agent in your service
Appears from this. Here is a letter, brother
(Produc'd, perforce, to give him credit with me),
175   The writing, yours; the matter, love; for so,
He says, he can explain it.

CAMILLO   Then, belike,
A young he-bawd.

HENRIQUEZ   This forgery confounds me!

DUKE   Read it, Roderick.

RODERICK [*Reads.*]   *Our prudence should now teach us to*
forget what our indiscretion has committed. I have already
made one step towards this wisdom –

HENRIQUEZ
Hold, sir. [*aside*] My very words to Violante!

180   DUKE   Go on.

HENRIQUEZ   My gracious father, give me pardon;
I do confess I some such letter wrote
(The purport all too trivial for your ear),
But how it reach'd this young dissembler's hands
185   Is what I cannot solve. For, on my soul
And by the honours of my birth and house,
The minion's face till now I never saw.

RODERICK
Run not too far in debt on protestation.
Why should you do a child this wrong?

HENRIQUEZ   Go to.

190   Your friendships past warrant not this abuse.
If you provoke me thus, I shall forget
What you are to me. This is a mere practice
And villainy to draw me into scandal.

RODERICK
No more; you are a boy. Here comes a witness,
Shall prove you so. No more.

Enter JULIO, *disguised;* VIOLANTE *as a woman.*

HENRIQUEZ   Another rascal!   195

DUKE   Hold!

HENRIQUEZ [*seeing Violante*]   Ha!

DUKE   What's here?

HENRIQUEZ [*aside*]
By all my sins, the injur'd Violante.

RODERICK
Now, sir, whose practice breaks?

CAMILLO [*to Henriquez*]   Is this a page?

RODERICK   One that has done him service,
And he has paid her for't, but broke his covenant.   200

VIOLANTE
My lord, I come not now to wound your spirit.
Your pure affection dead, which first betray'd me.
My claim die with it! Only let me not
Shrink to the grave with infamy upon me.
Protect my virtue, though it hurt your faith,   205
And my last breath shall speak Henriquez noble.

HENRIQUEZ [*aside*]
What a fierce conflict shame and wounded honour
Raise in my breast – but honour shall o'ercome.
She looks as beauteous and as innocent
As when I wrong'd her. [*to Violante*] Virtuous Violante –   210
Too good for me – dare you still love a man
So faithless as I am? I know you love me.
Thus, thus and thus [*kissing her*] I print my vow'd
       repentance:
Let all men read it here. My gracious father,
Forgive, and make me rich with your consent,   215
This is my wife; no other would I choose,
Were she a queen.

CAMILLO
Here's a new change. Bernard looks dull upon't.

HENRIQUEZ
And fair Leonora, from whose virgin arms
I forc'd my wrong'd friend Julio, O forgive me.   220
Take home your holy vows and let him have 'em
That has deserv'd them. O that he were here,
That I might own the baseness of my wrong
And purpos'd recompense. My Violante,
You must again be widow'd: for I vow   225
A ceaseless pilgrimage, ne'er to know joy,
Till I can give it to the injur'd Julio.

CAMILLO
This almost melts me. But my poor lost boy –

RODERICK   I'll stop that voyage, brother.
[*Presents Julio still in disguise.*]   Gentle lady,
What think you of this honest man?

LEONORA   Alas!   230
My thoughts, my lord, were all employ'd within!
He has a face makes me remember something
I have thought well of. How he looks upon me!
Poor man, he weeps. Ha! Stay, it cannot be –
He has his eye, his features, shape and gesture –   235
Would he would speak.

JULIO [*Throws off his disguise.*] Leonora!

LEONORA   Yes, 'tis he.

    O ecstasy of joy! [*They embrace.*]

CAMILLO   Now, what's the matter?

RODERICK

    Let 'em alone; they're almost starv'd for kisses.

CAMILLO   Stand forty foot off; no man trouble 'em.

240   Much good may't do your hearts! What is he, lord,

    What is he?

RODERICK   A certain son of yours.

CAMILLO   The devil he is!

RODERICK

    If he be the devil, that devil must call you father.

CAMILLO

    By your leave a little, ho. Are you my Julio?

JULIO [*Kneels.*]

245   My duty tells me so, sir,

    Still on my knees. But love engross'd me all.

    [*Rises and embraces Leonora.*] O Leonora, do I once

       more hold thee?

CAMILLO   Nay, to't again. I will not hinder you a kiss.

    [*Leaps.*] 'Tis he –

LEONORA

    The righteous pow'rs at length have crown'd our

250   loves.

    Think, Julio, from the storm that's now o'erblown,

    Though sour affliction combat hope awhile,

    When lovers swear true faith the list'ning angels

    Stand on the golden battlements of heav'n

255   And waft their vows to the eternal throne.

    Such were our vows, and so are they repaid.

DUKE   E'en as you are, we'll join your hands together.

    A providence above our pow'r rules all.

    [*to Henriquez*] Ask him forgiveness, boy.

JULIO   He has it, sir.

    The fault was love's, not his.

260 HENRIQUEZ   Brave, gen'rous Julio!

    I knew thy nobleness of old, and priz'd it

    Till passion made me blind. Once more, my friend,

    Share in a heart that ne'er shall wrong thee more.

    And brother –

RODERICK   This embrace cuts off excuses.

265 DUKE   I must, in part, repair my son's offence.

    At your best leisure, Julio, know our Court;

    And, Violante (for I know you now),

    I have a debt to pay. Your good old father

    Once when I chas'd the boar preserv'd my life.

270   For that good deed, and for your virtue's sake,

    Though your descent be low, call me your father.

    A match drawn out of honesty and goodness

    Is pedigree enough. Are you all pleas'd?

    Gives her to Henriquez.

CAMILLO   All.

HENRIQUEZ, DON BERNARD   All, sir.

JULIO   All.

DUKE   And I not least. We'll now return to court;   275

    And that short travel, and your loves completed,

    Shall, as I trust, for life restrain these wand'rings.

    There, the solemnity and grace I'll do

    Your sev'ral nuptials shall approve my joy,

    And make griev'd lovers that your story read   280

    Wish true love's wand'rings may like yours succeed.

Curtain falls.

EPILOGUE

Written by a friend

Spoken by MRS OLDFIELD

Well, heaven defend us from these ancient plays,

These moral bards of good Queen Bess's days!

They write from virtue's laws and think no further,

But draw a rape as dreadful as a murder.

You modern wits, more deeply vers'd in nature,   5

Can tip the wink, to tell us you know better;

As who should say, ''Tis no such killing matter –

We've heard old stories told, and yet ne'er

    wond'rd,

Of many a prude that has endur'd a hundred:

And Violante grieves, or we're mistaken,   10

Not because ravish'd, but because – forsaken.'

Had this been written to the modern stage

Her manners had been copied from the age.

Then, though she had been once a little wrong,

She still had had the grace to've held her tongue,   15

And after all with downcast looks been led

Like any virgin to the bridal bed.

There, if the good man question'd her misdoing,

She'd stop him short: 'Pray, who made you so knowing?

What, doubt my virtue! What's your base intention?   20

Sir, that's a point above your comprehension.'

Well, heav'n be prais'd, the virtue of our times

Secures us from our gothic grandsires' crimes.

Rapes, magic, new opinions, which before

Have fill'd our chronicles, are now no more: 25

And this reforming age may justly boast

That dreadful sin polygamy is lost.

So far from multiplying wives, 'tis known

Our husbands find they've work enough with one.

Then, as for rapes, those dangerous days are past: 30

Our dapper sparks are seldom in such haste.

In Shakespeare's age the English youth inspir'd,

Lov'd as they fought by him and beauty fir'd.

'Tis yours to crown the Bard, whose magic strain

Could charm the heroes of that glorious reign   35

Which humbled to the dust the pride of Spain.

Hamlet

A short play called *The Tragical History of Hamlet, Prince of Denmark* was printed in 1603. The title-page ascribed it to William Shakespeare, and claimed that it had been 'diverse times acted by his Highnesse servants in the Cittie of London: as also in the two Universities of Cambridge and Oxford, and else-where'; this text is known as the First Quarto (Q1). Another version soon appeared, variously dated 1604 or 1605, claiming on its title-page to be 'Newly imprinted and enlarged to almost as much againe as it was, according to the true and perfect Coppie'; this text is known as the Second Quarto (Q2). Its claim as to length is more or less accurate, and it is also a much more careful and coherent text than Q1, which has generally been dismissed as a 'bad' quarto, an unreliable version put together from the memories of actors or reporters. Finally, yet a third text (F) appeared in the First Folio in 1623, very like Q2 in many ways, but lacking around 230 lines that are in Q2 and adding around 70 lines of its own; it also has numerous minor verbal variants, some of which seem to be corrections but others of which are substitutions or errors.

Scholars have accepted both Q2 and F as authorial versions, with recent opinion inclining towards seeing F as Shakespeare's revision of Q2. The most significant of F's 'cuts' is the omission of the whole of 4.4 after the first eight lines, including Hamlet's last soliloquy, but there are other major omissions in 1.1, 1.4, 3.4, 4.7 and 5.2. Most editions of *Hamlet* virtually ignore Q1 but include all the lines from both Q2 and F, providing a composite or 'conflated' text. Some recent editions bracket the Q2-only lines, or even consign them to an appendix.

The play is usually dated around 1600, just after *Julius Caesar*, whose story is mentioned in 1.1, 3.2 and 5.1. Shakespeare's Brutus in some ways prefigures his Hamlet and presumably the same actor, Richard Burbage, played both roles. Shakespeare's previous tragedies at this point were *Titus Andronicus* and *Romeo and Juliet*, both of which share *Hamlet*'s revenge theme; he went on to write *Othello*, *King Lear* and *Macbeth* over the next six years. *Hamlet* was an immediate and enduring success. Its story derives ultimately from a twelfth-century history of Denmark written in Latin by Saxo Grammaticus, but Shakespeare also seems to have used a 1580 French version by François de Belleforest and a lost play on the topic, now referred to as the *Ur-Hamlet*, probably by Thomas Kyd, whose *Spanish Tragedy* has many features in common with *Hamlet*.

Hamlet has a relatively unbroken history of performance, not only in England but virtually throughout the world; there have been over fifty films based on it. It was heavily cut in the Restoration but, unlike most of the other plays, was not radically adapted or rewritten. Nevertheless it has inspired many spin-offs, sequels, prequels and parodies. The title-role has always attracted and challenged actors (including a large number of women). The play is endlessly quoted, and some key moments – the appearance of the Ghost on the battlements, the man in black holding a skull, the drowning of Ophelia – are instantly recognizable from countless illustrations. The character of the hero has been taken as representative of the spirit of entire countries, particularly Germany and Russia, while its political situation has been seen to parallel that in countries as different as Romania and South Africa.

Generally hailed until very recently as Shakespeare's 'greatest play', *Hamlet* is still performed and studied more often than its only rival, *King Lear*. The annual bibliographies published by *Shakespeare Quarterly* show that around 400 items (editions, translations, books and essays) appear on *Hamlet* every year, as compared with around 200 on *King Lear*. It remains to be seen whether a mid-twentieth-century shift in taste towards *King Lear* will be sustained or whether *Hamlet* will reassert its pre-eminence.

This volume, like the Arden Shakespeare Third Series, prints all three early texts. Why print three texts? Traditionally, editors and theatre directors have offered a 'conflated' text, usually a combination of Q2 and F. During the 1980s scholars became less satisfied with this method of, in effect, suppressing the differences between surviving early texts, and began to offer more than one text of plays such as *King Lear*. The text of *King Lear* in this volume highlights the different readings of the Quarto and Folio by the use of superscripts, and some texts in the Arden Third

Series (for example, *King Henry V* and *Romeo and Juliet*) include facsimiles of Quarto texts printed during Shakespeare's lifetime. *Hamlet* is the only play to appear in this volume in more than one text. Each text is treated as an independent entity, not because the texts are entirely independent of each other, but because none of the evidence of possible dependence is sufficiently overwhelming or widespread to oblige any particular act of conflation as a

result. The three texts are remarkably distinct entities, and each deserves to be offered to readers and theatre practitioners as a text in its own right with its own puzzles and challenges. Comparing the three texts opens up new questions: for example, is the earlier placing of 'To be or not to be' in Q1 more effective? And is the play improved by the omission of Hamlet's last soliloquy as in F?

The Tragical History of Hamlet, Prince of Denmark

The First Quarto
(1603)

Until 1823, when a copy was found in a private library, scholars were unaware of the existence of Q1. It is a crude version of the play, but it has much of the same plot and a rough gist of a great deal of the same dialogue that is found in Q2 and F. At first it was thought to be Shakespeare's first draft. However, the theory then developed that it was in fact a shortened bootleg version of the play, concocted probably from memory by disaffected actors looking to make money by selling it to a publishing house. This meant that, despite being dated '1603', its text did not predate the texts lying behind Q2 and F. Above all, it was not authentic Shakespeare, but a 'memorial reconstruction' by persons unknown. This theory came to determine most editions of the play throughout the twentieth century, and, indeed, is still widely held. In recent years some scholars have begun to revive the original idea that Q1 is by Shakespeare and to argue that it was composed early in his career, possibly in 1589. It is sometimes performed, and has been shown to work well on the stage.

HAMLET	*Prince of Denmark*
GHOST	*of Hamlet's father, the late King Hamlet of Denmark*
KING	*of Denmark, brother of the late King*
QUEEN Gertred	*Hamlet's mother and his father's widow, now married to the King*
CORAMBIS	*the King's councillor*
LEARTES	*Corambis' son*
OFELIA	*Corambis' daughter*
MONTANO	*Corambis' man*
HORATIO	*Hamlet's friend and fellow student*
ROSSENCRAFT GILDERSTONE	*other fellow students*
VOLTEMAR CORNELIA	*Danish ambassadors to Norway*
FIRST SENTINEL BARNARDO MARCELLUS	*sentinels*
BRAGGART GENTLEMAN	*a courtier*
PLAYERS	*playing* Prologue, Player Duke, Player Duchess *and* Lucianus
GRAVEDIGGER	*a clown*
SECOND MAN	*another clown*
PRIEST	
LORDS	
FORTENBRASSE	*Prince of Norway*
AMBASSADORS	*from England*

Attendants, Norwegian Drum, Norwegian Soldiers

Hamlet (Q1)

Sc. 1   *Enter* First Sentinel *and* BARNARDO.   [1.1]

1 SENTINEL   Stand, who is that?

BARNARDO   'Tis I.

1 SENTINEL

O you come most carefully upon your watch.

BARNARDO

An if you meet Marcellus and Horatio,

The partners of my watch, bid them make haste.

5   1 SENTINEL   I will. See, who goes there?

Enter HORATIO *and* MARCELLUS.

HORATIO   Friends to this ground.

MARCELLUS   And liegemen to the Dane.

[*to First Sentinel*] O farewell honest soldier. Who hath

relieved you?

1 SENTINEL

Barnardo hath my place. Give you goodnight.   *Exit.*

MARCELLUS   Holla, Barnardo!

BARNARDO   Say, is Horatio there?

10   HORATIO   A piece of him.

BARNARDO

Welcome, Horatio, welcome, good Marcellus.

MARCELLUS

What, hath this thing appeared again tonight?

BARNARDO   I have seen nothing.

MARCELLUS   Horatio says 'tis but our fantasy

15   And will not let belief take hold of him,

Touching this dreaded sight twice seen by us.

Therefore I have entreated him along

With us to watch the minutes of this night

That, if again this apparition come,

20   He may approve our eyes and speak to it.

HORATIO   Tut, 'twill not appear.

BARNARDO   Sit down, I pray, and let us once again

Assail your ears, that are so fortified,

What we have two nights seen.

HORATIO   Well, sit we down,

25   And let us hear Barnardo speak of this.

BARNARDO   Last night of all,

When yonder star that's westward from the pole

Had made his course to illumine that part of heaven

Where now it burns, the bell then tolling one –

Enter GHOST.

MARCELLUS

30   Break off your talk, see where it comes again!

BARNARDO

In the same figure like the King that's dead.

MARCELLUS   Thou art a scholar – speak to it, Horatio.

BARNARDO   Looks it not like the King?

HORATIO

Most like. It horrors me with fear and wonder.

BARNARDO   It would be spoke to.

35   MARCELLUS   Question it, Horatio.

HORATIO   What art thou that thus usurps the state

In which the majesty of buried Denmark

Did sometimes walk? By heaven, I charge thee speak.

MARCELLUS   It is offended.   *Exit Ghost.*

BARNARDO   See, it stalks away.

HORATIO

Stay, speak, speak, by heaven I charge thee, speak.   40

MARCELLUS   'Tis gone and makes no answer.

BARNARDO

How now, Horatio, you tremble and look pale.

Is not this something more than fantasy?

What think you on't?

HORATIO   Afore my God, I might not this believe   45

Without the sensible and true avouch

Of my own eyes.

MARCELLUS   Is it not like the King?

HORATIO   As thou art to thyself.

Such was the very armour he had on

When he the ambitious Norway combated.   50

So frowned he once, when in an angry parle

He smote the sledded Polacks on the ice.

'Tis strange.

MARCELLUS

Thus twice before, and jump at this dead hour,

With martial stalk he passed through our watch.   55

HORATIO   In what particular to work, I know not,

But in the thought and scope of my opinion

This bodes some strange eruption to the state.

MARCELLUS

Good, now sit down, and tell me he that knows,

Why this same strict and most observant watch   60

So nightly toils the subject of the land,

And why such daily cost of brazen cannon

And foreign mart for implements of war,

Why such impress of shipwrights, whose sore task

Does not divide the Sunday from the week.   65

What might be toward, that this sweaty march

Doth make the night joint labourer with the day,

Who is't that can inform me?

HORATIO   Marry, that can I.

At least the whisper goes so. Our late King,

Who as you know was by Fortenbrasse of Norway –   70

Thereto pricked on by a most emulous cause –

Dared to the combat in which our valiant Hamlet

(For so this side of our known world esteemed him)

Did slay this Fortenbrasse, who by a sealed compact

Well ratified by law and heraldry   75

Did forfeit with his life all those his lands

Which he stood seized of by the conqueror,

Against the which a moiety competent

Was gaged by our King. Now sir, young Fortenbrasse,

Of inapproved mettle hot and full,   80

Hath in the skirts of Norway here and there

Sharked up a sight of lawless resolutes

For food and diet to some enterprise

That hath a stomach in't. And this, I take it,

Is the chief head and ground of this our watch.   85

Enter the GHOST.

But lo, behold, see where it comes again.
I'll cross it, though it blast me. Stay, illusion.
If there be any good thing to be done,
That may do ease to thee and grace to me,
90   Speak to me.
If thou art privy to thy country's fate,
Which happily foreknowing may prevent,
O speak to me.
Or if thou hast extorted in thy life
95   Or hoarded treasure in the womb of earth,
For which, they say, you spirits oft walk in death,
Speak to me, stay and speak. Speak.   [*The cock crows.*]
Stop it, Marcellus!
BARNARDO   'Tis here.   *Exit Ghost.*
HORATIO   'Tis here.
MARCELLUS   'Tis gone.
O, we do it wrong, being so majestical,
100   To offer it the show of violence,
For it is as the air invulnerable,
And our vain blows malicious mockery.
BARNARDO   It was about to speak when the cock crew.
HORATIO   And then it faded like a guilty thing
105   Upon a fearful summons. I have heard
The cock, that is the trumpet to the morning,
Doth with his early and shrill-crowing throat
Awake the god of day and, at his sound,
Whether in earth or air, in sea or fire,
110   The stravagant and erring spirit hies
To his confines – and of the truth hereof
This present object made probation.
MARCELLUS   It faded on the crowing of the cock.
Some say, that ever 'gainst that season comes
115   Wherein our Saviour's birth is celebrated
The bird of dawning singeth all night long.
And then, they say, no spirit dare walk abroad,
The nights are wholesome, then no planet strikes,
No fairy takes, nor witch hath power to charm,
120   So gracious and so hallowed is that time.
HORATIO   So have I heard, and do in part believe it.
But see, the sun in russet mantle clad
Walks o'er the dew of yon high mountain top.
Break we our watch up and, by my advice,
125   Let us impart what we have seen tonight
Unto young Hamlet; for upon my life
This spirit, dumb to us, will speak to him.
Do you consent we shall acquaint him with it,
As needful in our love, fitting our duty?
130   MARCELLUS   Let's do't, I pray, and I this morning know
Where we shall find him most conveniently.   *Exeunt.*

Sc. 2   *Enter* KING, QUEEN (Gertred),   [1.2]
            HAMLET, LEARTES, CORAMBIS *and the two*
            ambassadors CORNELIA *and* VOLTEMAR,
                with Attendants.

KING   Lords, we here have writ to Fortenbrasse,
Nephew to old Norway who, impudent

And bedrid, scarcely hears of this his
Nephew's purpose. And we here dispatch
You, good Cornelia, and you, Voltemar,   5
For bearers of these greetings to old Norway,
Giving to you no further personal power
To business with the King
Than those related articles do show.
Farewell, and let your haste commend your duty.   10
CORNELIA, VOLTEMAR
In this and all things will we show our duty.
KING   We doubt nothing. Heartily farewell.
                Exeunt Cornelia and Voltemar.
And now, Leartes, what's the news with you?
You said you had a suit: what is't, Leartes?
LEARTES   My gracious lord, your favourable licence,   15
Now that the funeral rites are all performed,
I may have leave to go again to France.
For though the favour of your grace might stay me
Yet something is there whispers in my heart
Which makes my mind and spirits bend all for
    France.   20
KING   Have you your father's leave, Leartes?
CORAMBIS
He hath, my lord, wrung from me a forced grant
And I beseech you grant your highness' leave.
KING   With all our heart, Leartes, fare thee well.
LEARTES   I in all love and duty take my leave.   *Exit.*   25
KING   And now, princely son Hamlet,
What means these sad and melancholy moods?
For your intent going to Wittenberg
We hold it most unmeet and unconvenient,
Being the joy and half-heart of your mother.   30
Therefore let me entreat you stay in Court,
All Denmark's hope, our cousin and dearest son.
HAMLET   My lord, 'tis not the sable suit I wear,
No, nor the tears that still stand in my eyes,
Nor the distracted haviour in the visage,   35
Nor all together mixed with outward semblance,
Is equal to the sorrow of my heart.
Him have I lost I must of force forgo,
These but the ornaments and suits of woe.
KING   This shows a loving care in you, son Hamlet,   40
But you must think your father lost a father,
That father dead lost his, and so shall be
Until the general ending. Therefore
Cease laments, it is a fault 'gainst heaven,
Fault 'gainst the dead, a fault 'gainst nature,   45
And in reason's common course most certain
None lives on earth but he is born to die.
QUEEN   Let not thy mother lose her prayers, Hamlet,
Stay here with us, go not to Wittenberg.
HAMLET   I shall in all my best obey you, madam.   50
KING   Spoke like a kind and a most loving son.
And there's no health the King shall drink today
But the great cannon to the clouds shall tell
The rouse the King shall drink unto Prince Hamlet.
                Exeunt all but Hamlet.

55	HAMLET O that this too much grieved and sallied flesh
	Would melt to nothing, or that the universal
	Globe of heaven would turn all to a chaos!
	O God, within two months, no not two – married
	Mine uncle! O, let me not think of it,
60	My father's brother; but no more like

HAMLET   O that this too much grieved and sallied flesh
Would melt to nothing, or that the universal
Globe of heaven would turn all to a chaos!
O God, within two months, no not two – married
Mine uncle! O, let me not think of it,
My father's brother; but no more like
My father than I to Hercules.
Within two months, ere yet the salt of most
Unrighteous tears had left their flushing
In her galled eyes, she married. O God, a beast
Devoid of reason would not have made
Such speed! Frailty, thy name is Woman.
Why, she would hang on him, as if increase
Of appetite had grown by what it looked on.
O wicked, wicked speed, to make such
Dexterity to incestuous sheets
Ere yet the shoes were old
With which she followed my dead father's corpse
Like Niobe, all tears. Married! Well, it is not,
Nor it cannot come to good;
But break, my heart, for I must hold my tongue.

Enter HORATIO, MARCELLUS *and* BARNARDO.

HORATIO   Health to your lordship.
HAMLET   I am very glad to see you –
Horatio, or I much forget myself.
HORATIO
The same, my lord, and your poor servant ever.
HAMLET
O my good friend, I change that name with you.
But what make you from Wittenberg, Horatio?
Marcellus!
MARCELLUS   My good lord.
HAMLET   I am very glad to see you. Good even, sirs.
But what is your affair in Elsinore?
We'll teach you to drink deep ere you depart.
HORATIO   A truant disposition, my good lord.
HAMLET   Nor shall you make me truster
Of your own report against yourself.
Sir, I know you are no truant,
But what is your affair in Elsinore?
HORATIO
My good lord, I came to see your father's funeral.
HAMLET   O, I prithee do not mock me, fellow student,
I think it was to see my mother's wedding.
HORATIO   Indeed, my lord, it followed hard upon.
HAMLET
Thrift, thrift, Horatio, the funeral baked meats
Did coldly furnish forth the marriage tables,
Would I had met my dearest foe in heaven
Ere ever I had seen that day, Horatio.
O my father, my father, methinks I see my father.
HORATIO   Where, my lord?
HAMLET   Why, in my mind's eye, Horatio.
HORATIO   I saw him once – he was a gallant king.
HAMLET   He was a man, take him for all in all,
I shall not look upon his like again.

HORATIO   My lord, I think I saw him yesternight.
HAMLET   Saw, who?
HORATIO   My lord, the King your father.
HAMLET   Aha! The King my father, kee you?
HORATIO   Season your admiration for a while
With an attentive ear till I may deliver,
Upon the witness of these gentlemen,
This wonder to you.
HAMLET   For God's love let me hear it.
HORATIO   Two nights together had these gentlemen,
Marcellus and Barnardo, on their watch
In the dead vast and middle of the night,
Been thus encountered by a figure like your father,
Armed to point, exactly cap-à-pie,
Appears before them thrice: he walks
Before their weak and fear-oppressed eyes
Within his truncheon's length while they distilled
Almost to jelly with the act of fear
Stands dumb and speak not to him. This to me
In dreadful secrecy impart they did,
And I with them the third night kept the watch
Where, as they had delivered form of the thing,
Each part made true and good,
The apparition comes. I knew your father,
These hands are not more like.
HAMLET   'Tis very strange.
HORATIO
As I do live, my honoured lord, 'tis true
And we did think it right done in our duty
To let you know it.
HAMLET   Where was this?
MARCELLUS
My lord, upon the platform where we watched.
HAMLET   Did you not speak to it?
HORATIO   My lord, we did, but answer made it none.
Yet once methought it was about to speak
And lifted up his head to motion
Like as he would speak, but even then
The morning cock crew loud, and in all haste
It shrunk in haste away, and vanished our sight.
HAMLET   Indeed, indeed, sirs, but this troubles me.
Hold you the watch tonight?
HORATIO, MARCELLUS, BARNARDO
                                    We do, my lord.
HAMLET   Armed say ye?
HORATIO, MARCELLUS, BARNARDO
                                    Armed, my good lord.
HAMLET   From top to toe?
HORATIO, MARCELLUS, BARNARDO
                              My good lord, from head to foot.
HAMLET   Why, then saw you not his face?
HORATIO   O yes, my lord, he wore his beaver up.
HAMLET   How looked he – frowningly?
HORATIO
A countenance more in sorrow than in anger.
HAMLET   Pale, or red?
HORATIO   Nay, very pale.

Line numbers: 105, 110, 115, 120, 125, 130, 135, 140, 145
Left line numbers: 65, 70, 75, 80, 85, 90, 95, 100

HAMLET   And fixed his eyes upon you?

HORATIO   Most constantly.

HAMLET   I would I had been there.

HORATIO   It would ha' much amazed you.

HAMLET   Yea, very like, very like. Stayed it long?

HORATIO

150   While one with moderate pace might tell a hundred.

MARCELLUS   O longer, longer.

HAMLET   His beard was grizzled, no?

HORATIO   It was as I have seen it in his life,
         A sable silver.

HAMLET   I will watch tonight.
         Perchance 'twill walk again.

HORATIO   I warrant it will.

155 HAMLET   If it assume my noble father's person
         I'll speak to it, if hell itself should gape
         And bid me hold my peace. Gentlemen,
         If you have hitherto concealed this sight
         Let it be tenable in your silence still,

160   And whatsoever else shall chance tonight
         Give it an understanding, but no tongue.
         I will requite your loves. So fare you well.
         Upon the platform 'twixt eleven and twelve
         I'll visit you.

HORATIO, MARCELLUS, BARNARDO
                    Our duties to your honour.

HAMLET

165   O your loves, your loves, as mine to you. Farewell.
                    Exeunt all but Hamlet.
         My father's spirit in arms. Well, all's not well.
         I doubt some foul play. Would the night were come.
         Till then, sit still my soul – foul deeds will rise
         Though all the world o'erwhelm them, to men's eyes.
                    Exit.

Sc. 3   *Enter* LEARTES *and* OFELIA.   [1.3]

LEARTES   My necessaries are embarked. I must aboard,
         But, ere I part, mark what I say to thee:
         I see Prince Hamlet makes a show of love –
         Beware, Ofelia, do not trust his vows;

5   Perhaps he loves you now, and now his tongue
         Speaks from his heart. But yet take heed, my sister,
         The chariest maid is prodigal enough
         If she unmask her beauty to the moon.
         Virtue itself scapes not calumnious thoughts.

10   Believe't, Ofelia, therefore keep aloof
         Lest that he trip thy honour and thy fame.

OFELIA   Brother, to this I have lent attentive ear
         And doubt not but to keep my honour firm.
         But, my dear brother, do not you

15   Like to a cunning sophister
         Teach me the path and ready way to heaven
         While you, forgetting what is said to me,
         Yourself like to a careless libertine
         Doth give his heart his appetite at full

20   And little recks how that his honour dies.

LEARTES   No, fear it not, my dear Ofelia.
         Here comes my father:
         Occasion smiles upon a second leave.

                    Enter CORAMBIS.

CORAMBIS
         Yet here, Leartes? Aboard, aboard for shame!
         The wind sits in the shoulder of your sail   25
         And you are stayed for. There, my blessing with thee,
         And these few precepts in thy memory.
         Be thou familiar but by no means vulgar;
         Those friends thou hast, and their adoptions tried,
         Grapple them to thee with a hoop of steel,   30
         But do not dull the palm with entertain
         Of every new unfledged courage.
         Beware of entrance into a quarrel but, being in,
         Bear it that the opposed may beware of thee.
         Costly thy apparel as thy purse can buy   35
         But not expressed in fashion,
         For the apparel oft proclaims the man
         And they of France of the chief rank and station
         Are of a most select and general chief in that.
         This above all: to thy own self be true   40
         And it must follow as the night the day
         Thou canst not then be false to anyone.
         Farewell, my blessing with thee.

LEARTES   I humbly take my leave. Farewell, Ofelia,
         And remember well what I have said to you.   45

OFELIA   It is already locked within my heart
         And you yourself shall keep the key of it.

                    Exit Leartes.

CORAMBIS   What is't, Ofelia, he hath said to you?

OFELIA   Something touching the Prince Hamlet.

CORAMBIS
         Marry, well thought on: 'tis given me to understand   50
         That you have been too prodigal of your maiden
            presence
         Unto Prince Hamlet. If it be so –
         As so 'tis given to me, and that in way of caution –
         I must tell you, you do not understand yourself
         So well as befits my honour and your credit.   55

OFELIA
         My lord, he hath made many tenders of his love to
            me.

CORAMBIS   Tenders? Ay, ay, tenders you may call them.

OFELIA   And withal such earnest vows –

CORAMBIS   Springes to catch woodcocks.
         What, do not I know when the blood doth burn   60
         How prodigal the tongue lends the heart vows?
         In brief, be more scanter of your maiden presence
         Or, tendering thus, you'll tender me a fool.

OFELIA   I shall obey, my lord, in all I may.

CORAMBIS   Ofelia, receive none of his letters,   65
         For lovers' lines are snares to entrap the heart.
         Refuse his tokens: both of them are keys
         To unlock Chastity unto Desire.
         Come in, Ofelia. Such men often prove

70   Great in their words but little in their love.

OFELIA   I will, my lord.   *Exeunt.*

Sc. 4   *Enter* HAMLET, HORATIO   [1.4]
            and MARCELLUS.

HAMLET   The air bites shrewd;

It is an eager and a nipping wind.

What hour is't?

HORATIO   I think it lacks of twelve.

MARCELLUS   No, 'tis struck.

HORATIO   Indeed, I heard it not.

     [*Sound of kettledrum, trumpet and cannon*]

5   What doth this mean, my lord?

HAMLET

O, the King doth wake tonight and takes his rouse,

Keeps wassail and the swaggering upspring reels,

And as he dreams, his draughts of Rhenish down,

The kettledrum and trumpet thus bray out

The triumphs of his pledge.

10 HORATIO   Is it a custom here?

HAMLET   Ay, marry is't and, though I am

Native here and to the manner born,

It is a custom more honoured in the breach

Than in the observance.

         Enter the GHOST.

HORATIO   Look, my lord, it comes.

15 HAMLET   Angels and ministers of grace defend us!

Be thou a spirit of health or goblin damned,

Bring with thee airs from heaven or blasts from hell,

Be thy intents wicked or charitable,

Thou comest in such questionable shape

20 That I will speak to thee. I'll call thee Hamlet,

King, Father, royal Dane! O answer me,

Let me not burst in ignorance, but say why

Thy canonized bones hearsed in death

Have burst their ceremonies, why thy sepulchre

25 In which we saw thee quietly interred

Hath burst his ponderous and marble jaws

To cast thee up again. What may this mean

That thou, dead corpse, again in complete steel,

Revisits thus the glimpses of the moon,

30 Making night hideous, and we fools of nature

So horridly to shake our disposition

With thoughts beyond the reaches of our souls?

Say. Speak. Wherefore? What may this mean?

HORATIO   It beckons you, as though it had something

35 To impart to you alone.

MARCELLUS   Look with what courteous action

It waves you to a more removed ground –

But do not go with it!

HORATIO   No, by no means, my lord.

HAMLET   It will not speak: then will I follow it.

HORATIO

40 What if it tempt you toward the flood, my lord,

That beckles o'er his base into the sea

And there assume some other horrible shape

Which might deprive your sovereignty of reason

And drive you into madness? Think of it.

HAMLET   Still am I called. Go on, I'll follow thee.   45

HORATIO   My lord, you shall not go.

HAMLET   Why, what should be the fear?

I do not set my life at a pin's fee

And, for my soul, what can it do to that –

Being a thing immortal like itself?   50

Go on, I'll follow thee.

MARCELLUS

My lord, be ruled, you shall not go.

HAMLET

My fate cries out and makes each petty artery

As hardy as the Nemean lion's nerve.

Still am I called – unhand me, gentlemen –   55

By heaven I'll make a ghost of him that lets me!

Away, I say! – Go on, I'll follow thee.

         Exeunt Ghost and Hamlet.

HORATIO   He waxeth desperate with imagination.

MARCELLUS

Something is rotten in the state of Denmark.

HORATIO   Have after. To what issue will this sort?   60

MARCELLUS

Let's follow. 'Tis not fit thus to obey him.   *Exeunt.*

Sc. 5   *Enter* GHOST *and* HAMLET.   [1.5]

HAMLET   I'll go no further. Whither wilt thou lead me?

GHOST   Mark me.

HAMLET   I will.

GHOST   I am thy father's spirit,

Doomed for a time to walk the night,

And all the day confined in flaming fire

Till the foul crimes done in my days of nature   5

Are purged and burnt away.

HAMLET   Alas, poor ghost.

GHOST   Nay, pity me not, but to my unfolding

Lend thy listening ear. But that I am forbid

To tell the secrets of my prison-house

I would a tale unfold whose lightest word   10

Would harrow up thy soul, freeze thy young blood,

Make thy two eyes like stars start from their spheres,

Thy knotted and combined locks to part

And each particular hair to stand on end

Like quills upon the fretful porpentine.   15

But this same blazon must not be to ears

Of flesh and blood: Hamlet, if ever thou

Didst thy dear father love –

HAMLET   O God!

GHOST   Revenge his foul and most unnatural murder.   20

HAMLET   Murder!

GHOST   Yea, murder in the highest degree

As in the least 'tis bad, but mine most foul,

Beastly and unnatural.

HAMLET   Haste me to know it

That with wings as swift as meditation

Or the thought of it may sweep to my revenge.

GHOST   O, I find thee apt, and duller shouldst thou be
   Than the fat weed which roots itself in ease
   On Lethe wharf. Brief let me be:
   'Tis given out that, sleeping in my orchard,
30 A serpent stung me. So the whole ear of Denmark
   Is with a forged process of my death
   Rankly abused. But know, thou noble youth,
   He that did sting thy father's heart
   Now wears his crown.

HAMLET   O my prophetic soul!
   My uncle! My uncle!

35 GHOST   Yea, he,
   That incestuous wretch, won to his will with gifts
   – O wicked will and gifts that have the power
   So to seduce – my most seeming-virtuous Queen.
   But virtue, as it never will be moved
40 Though lewdness court it in a shape of heaven,
   So lust, though to a radiant angel linked,
   Would sate itself from a celestial bed
   And prey on garbage.
   But soft, methinks I scent the morning's air.
45 Brief let me be. Sleeping within my orchard –
   My custom always in the afternoon –
   Upon my secure hour thy uncle came
   With juice of hebona in a vial,
   And through the porches of my ears did pour
50 The leperous distilment, whose effect
   Holds such an enmity with blood of man
   That, swift as quicksilver, it posteth through
   The natural gates and alleys of the body
   And turns the thin and wholesome blood
55 Like eager droppings into milk,
   And all my smooth body barked and tettered over.
   Thus was I sleeping by a brother's hand
   Of crown, of queen, of life, of dignity
   At once deprived, no reckoning made of,
60 But sent unto my grave
   With all my accounts and sins upon my head.
   O horrible, most horrible!

HAMLET   O God!

GHOST   If thou hast nature in thee bear it not
   But, howsoever, let not thy heart conspire
65 Against thy mother aught; leave her to heaven
   And to the burden that her conscience bears.
   I must be gone.
   The glow-worm shows the matin to be near
   And 'gins to pale his uneffectual fire.
70 Hamlet, adieu, adieu, adieu. Remember me. *Exit.*

HAMLET   O all you host of heaven! O earth! What else?
   And shall I couple hell? Remember thee?
   Yes, thou poor ghost.
   From the tables of my memory, I'll wipe away
75 All saws of books, all trivial fond conceits
   That ever youth or else observance noted,
   And thy remembrance all alone shall sit.
   Yes, yes, by heaven, a damned, pernicious villain:

25 Murderous, bawdy, smiling, damned villain!
   My tables – meet it is I set it down   80
   That one may smile and smile and be a villain.
   At least I am sure it may be so in Denmark.
   So, uncle, there you are, there you are.
   Now to the words: it is 'Adieu, adieu. Remember me.'
   So 'tis enough. I have sworn.   85

    Enter HORATIO *and* MARCELLUS.

HORATIO   My lord, my lord!

MARCELLUS   Lord Hamlet!

HORATIO   Illo, lo, ho, ho!

MARCELLUS   Illo, lo, so, ho, so, come, boy, come!

HORATIO   Heavens secure him.

MARCELLUS   How is't, my noble lord?

HORATIO   What news, my lord?

HAMLET   O, wonderful, wonderful.

HORATIO   Good my lord, tell it.

HAMLET   No, not I. You'll reveal it. 90

HORATIO   Not I, my lord, by heaven.

MARCELLUS   Nor I, my lord.

HAMLET
   How say you then – would heart of man once think it? –
   But you'll be secret?

HORATIO, MARCELLUS   Ay, by heaven, my lord.

HAMLET
   There's never a villain dwelling in all Denmark
   But he's an arrant knave.   95

HORATIO   There need no ghost come from the grave
   To tell you this.

HAMLET   Right. You are in the right. And therefore
   I hold it meet, without more circumstance at all,
   We shake hands and part, you as your business 100
   And desires shall lead you (for, look you, every man
   Hath business and desires, such as it is)
   And, for my own poor part, I'll go pray.

HORATIO
   These are but wild and whirling words, my lord.

HAMLET   I am sorry they offend you. Heartily, 105
   Yes, faith, heartily.

HORATIO   There's no offence, my lord.

HAMLET   Yes, by Saint Patrick, but there is, Horatio.
   And much offence too. Touching this vision,
   It is an honest ghost – that let me tell you.
   For your desires to know what is between us, 110
   O'ermaster it as you may. And now, kind friends,
   As you are friends, scholars and gentlemen,
   Grant me one poor request.

HORATIO, MARCELLUS   What is't, my lord?

HAMLET
   Never make known what you have seen tonight.

HORATIO, MARCELLUS   My lord, we will not. 115

HAMLET   Nay, but swear.

HORATIO   In faith, my lord, not I.

MARCELLUS   Nor I, my lord, in faith.

HAMLET
   Nay, upon my sword. Indeed, upon my sword.

GHOST [*under the stage*] Swear.

HAMLET

120   Ha, ha! Come you here – this fellow in the cellarage! –
Here consent to swear.

HORATIO   Propose the oath, my lord.

HAMLET   Never to speak what you have seen tonight.
Swear by my sword.

125   GHOST   Swear.

HAMLET

Hic et ubique? Nay then, we'll shift our ground.
Come hither, gentlemen, and lay your hands
Again upon this sword. Never to speak
Of that which you have seen, swear by my sword.

130   GHOST   Swear.

HAMLET

Well said, old mole, canst work in the earth so fast?
A worthy pioner. Once more remove.

HORATIO   Day and night, but this is wondrous strange.

HAMLET   And therefore as a stranger give it welcome:

135   There are more things in heaven and earth, Horatio,
Than are dreamt of in your philosophy.
But come here, as before, you never shall –
How strange or odd soe'er I bear myself
(As I perchance hereafter shall think meet

140   To put an antic disposition on) –
That you at such times seeing me never shall
With arms encumbered thus, or this headshake,
Or by pronouncing some undoubtful phrase
As 'Well, well, we know', or 'We could an if we would',

145   Or 'There be an if they might', or such ambiguous
Giving out, to note that you know aught of me.
This not to do, so grace and mercy
At your most need help you, swear.

GHOST   Swear.

150   HAMLET   Rest, rest, perturbed spirit. So, gentlemen,
In all my love I do commend me to you,
And what so poor a man as Hamlet may
To pleasure you, God willing shall not want.
Nay come, let's go together.

155   But still your fingers on your lips, I pray.
The time is out of joint. O cursed spite,
That ever I was born to set it right.
Nay come, let's go together.   *Exeunt.*

Sc. 6   *Enter* CORAMBIS *and* MONTANO.   [2.1]

CORAMBIS   Montano, here, these letters to my son
And this same money with my blessing to him,
And bid him ply his learning, good Montano.

MONTANO   I will, my lord.

5   CORAMBIS   You shall do very well, Montano, to say
thus: 'I knew the gentleman' – or 'know his father'. To
inquire the manner of his life, as thus – being amongst
his acquaintance you may say you saw him 'at such a
time' – mark you me – 'at game, or drinking, swearing

10   or drabbing' – you may go so far.

MONTANO   My lord, that will impeach his reputation.

CORAMBIS   I'faith not a whit, no, not a whit. Now
happily he closeth with you in the consequence – as
you may bridle it, not disparage him a jot – What was
I about to say?   15

MONTANO   He closeth with him in the consequence.

CORAMBIS   Ay, you say right. He closeth with him thus
– this will he say – let me see what he will say – marry,
this: 'I saw him yesterday', or 't'other day', or 'then',
or 'at such a time', 'a-dicing', or 'at tennis', ay, or   20
'drinking drunk', or 'entering of a house of lightness'
(*viz.* brothel). Thus, sir, do we that know the world,
being men of reach, by indirections find directions
forth. And so shall you my son. You ha' me, ha' you
not?   25

MONTANO   I have, my lord.

CORAMBIS   Well, fare you well. Commend me to him.

MONTANO   I will, my lord.

CORAMBIS   And bid him ply his music.

MONTANO   My lord, I will.   30

CORAMBIS   Farewell.   *Exit Montano.*

Enter OFELIA.

How now, Ofelia, what's the news with you?

OFELIA   O my dear father, such a change in nature,
So great an alteration in a prince –
So pitiful to him, fearful to me –   35
A maiden's eye ne'er looked on.

CORAMBIS   Why, what's the matter, my Ofelia?

OFELIA

O, young Prince Hamlet, the only flower of Denmark,
He is bereft of all the wealth he had.
The jewel that adorned his feature most   40
Is filched and stol'n away: his wit's bereft him.
He found me walking in the gallery all alone.
There comes he to me with a distracted look,
His garters lagging down, his shoes untied,
And fixed his eyes so steadfast on my face   45
As if they had vowed this is their latest object.
Small while he stood, but grips me by the wrist,
And there he holds my pulse till, with a sigh,
He doth unclasp his hold and parts away
Silent, as is the mid-time of the night.   50
And, as he went, his eye was still on me,
For thus his head over his shoulder looked –
He seemed to find the way without his eyes,
For out of doors he went without their help.
And so did leave me.

CORAMBIS   Mad for thy love!   55
What, have you given him any cross words of late?

OFELIA   I did repel his letters, deny his gifts,
As you did charge me.

CORAMBIS   Why, that hath made him mad.
By heaven, 'tis as proper for our age to cast
Beyond ourselves as 'tis for the younger sort   60
To leave their wantonness. Well, I am sorry
That I was so rash. But what remedy?
Let's to the King. This madness may prove,

Though wild awhile, yet more true to thy love.

Exeunt.

Sc. 7   *Enter* KING, QUEEN,   [2.2]
            ROSSENCRAFT *and* GILDERSTONE.

KING

Right noble friends – that our dear cousin Hamlet
Hath lost the very heart of all his sense
It is most right, and we most sorry for him.
Therefore we do desire, even as you tender
5 Our care to him and our great love to you,
That you will labour but to wring from him
The cause and ground of his distemperance.
Do this, the King of Denmark shall be thankful.

ROSSENCRAFT

My lord, whatsoever lies within our power
10 Your majesty may more command in words
Than use persuasions to your liegemen, bound
By love, by duty and obedience.

GILDERSTONE

What we may do for both your majesties
To know the grief troubles the Prince your son,
15 We will endeavour all the best we may.
So, in all duty, do we take our leave.

KING   Thanks, Gilderstone, and gentle Rossencraft.
QUEEN   Thanks, Rossencraft, and gentle Gilderstone.

Exeunt Rossencraft and Gilderstone.

Enter CORAMBIS *and* OFELIA.

CORAMBIS   My lord, the ambassadors are joyfully
20 Returned from Norway.
KING   Thou still hast been the father of good news.
CORAMBIS   Have I, my lord? I assure your grace,
I hold my duty as I hold my life
Both to my God and to my sovereign King;
25 And I believe, or else this brain of mine
Hunts not the train of policy so well
As it had wont to do, but I have found
The very depth of Hamlet's lunacy.
QUEEN [*to King*]   God grant he hath.

Enter the ambassadors, VOLTEMAR *and* CORNELIA.

KING

30 Now, Voltemar, what from our brother Norway?
VOLTEMAR   Most fair returns of greetings and desires.
Upon our first he sent forth to suppress
His nephew's levies, which to him appeared
To be a preparation 'gainst the Polack.
35 But, better looked into, he truly found
It was against your highness; whereat, grieved
That so his sickness, age and impotence
Was falsely borne in hand, sends out arrests
On Fortenbrasse, which he in brief obeys,
40 Receives rebuke from Norway, and, in fine,
Makes vow before his uncle never more

To give the assay of arms against your majesty.
Whereon old Norway, overcome with joy,
Gives him three thousand crowns in annual fee
And his commission to employ those soldiers,   45
So levied as before, against the Polack,
With an entreaty herein further shown
That it would please you to give quiet pass
Through your dominions for that enterprise
On such regards of safety and allowances   50
As therein are set down.
KING   It likes us well, and at fit time and leisure
We'll read and answer these his articles.
Meantime, we thank you for your well-took labour.
Go to your rest; at night we'll feast together.   55
Right welcome home.

Exeunt Voltemar and Cornelia.

CORAMBIS   This business is very well dispatched.
Now, my lord,
Touching the young Prince Hamlet, certain it is
That he is mad: mad let us grant him, then.   60
Now, to know the cause of this effect –
Or else to say the cause of this defect
(For this effect defective comes by cause) –
QUEEN   Good my lord, be brief.
CORAMBIS   Madam, I will.
My lord, I have a daughter – have while she's mine   65
(For that we think is surest we often lose) –
Now, to the Prince. My lord, but note this letter,
The which my daughter in obedience
Delivered to my hands –
KING   Read it, my lord.
CORAMBIS   Mark, my lord: 70
[*Reads.*]   *Doubt that in earth is fire,*
              Doubt that the stars do move,
              Doubt truth to be a liar
              But do not doubt I love.
To the beautiful Ofelia, thine ever, the most unhappy   75
Prince Hamlet.
My lord, what do you think of me?
Ay, or what might you think when I saw this?
KING
As of a true friend and a most loving subject.
CORAMBIS   I would be glad to prove so.   80
Now, when I saw this letter, thus I bespake my maiden:
Lord Hamlet is a prince out of your star
And one that is unequal for your love.
Therefore I did command her refuse his letters,
Deny his tokens and to absent herself.   85
She as my child obediently obeyed me.
Now, since which time, seeing his love thus crossed
– Which I took to be idle and but sport –
He straightway grew into a melancholy,
From that unto a fast, then unto distraction,   90
Then into a sadness, from that unto a madness,
And so, by continuance and weakness of the brain,
Into this frenzy which now possesseth him.

An if this be not true, take this from this.

95 KING Think you 'tis so?

CORAMBIS How? So, my lord? I would very fain know
That thing that I have said 'tis so positively
And it hath fallen out otherwise.
Nay, if circumstances lead me on
100 I'll find it out if it were hid as deep
As the centre of the earth.

KING How should we try this same?

CORAMBIS Marry, my good lord, thus:
The Prince's walk is here in the gallery:
105 There let Ofelia walk until he comes.
Yourself and I will stand close in the study:
There shall you hear the effect of all his heart.
An if it prove any otherwise than love
Then let my censure fail another time.

110 KING See where he comes, poring upon a book.

Enter HAMLET.

CORAMBIS
Madam, will it please your grace to leave us here?

QUEEN With all my heart.   *Exit.*

CORAMBIS And here, Ofelia, read you on this book
And walk aloof. The King shall be unseen.
[*Corambis and King hide.*]

115 HAMLET To be, or not to be – ay, there's the point.
To die, to sleep – is that all? Ay, all.
No, to sleep, to dream – ay, marry, there it goes,
For in that dream of death, when we're awaked
And borne before an everlasting judge
120 From whence no passenger ever returned –
The undiscovered country, at whose sight
The happy smile and the accursed damned.
But for this, the joyful hope of this,
Who'd bear the scorns and flattery of the world –
125 Scorned by the right rich, the rich cursed of the poor,
The widow being oppressed, the orphan wronged,
The taste of hunger, or a tyrant's reign,
And thousand more calamities besides –
To grunt and sweat under this weary life
130 When that he may his full quietus make
With a bare bodkin? Who would this endure,
But for a hope of something after death,
Which puzzles the brain and doth confound the sense –
Which makes us rather bear those evils we have
135 Than fly to others that we know not of?
Ay, that – O, this conscience makes cowards of us all.
– Lady, in thy orisons be all my sins remembered.

OFELIA My lord, I have sought opportunity, which now
I have, to redeliver to your worthy hands a small
140 remembrance – such tokens which I have received of
you.

HAMLET Are you fair?

OFELIA My lord!

HAMLET Are you honest?

145 OFELIA What means my lord?

HAMLET That if you be fair and honest your beauty
should admit no discourse to your honesty.

OFELIA My lord, can beauty have better privilege than
with honesty?

HAMLET Yea, marry may it. For Beauty may sooner   150
transform Honesty from what she was into a bawd
than Honesty can transform Beauty. This was
sometimes a paradox, but now the time gives it scope.
I never gave you nothing.

OFELIA My lord, you know right well you did and, with   155
them, such earnest vows of love as would have moved
the stoniest breast alive.
But now, too true I find:
Rich gifts wax poor when givers grow unkind.

HAMLET I never loved you.   160

OFELIA You made me believe you did.

HAMLET O, thou shouldst not ha' believed me! Go to a
nunnery, go. Why shouldst thou be a breeder of sinners?
I am myself indifferent honest, but I could accuse myself
of such crimes it had been better my mother had ne'er   165
borne me. O, I am very proud, ambitious, disdainful,
with more sins at my beck than I have thoughts to put
them in. What should such fellows as I do, crawling
between heaven and earth? To a nunnery, go. We are
arrant knaves all. Believe none of us. To a nunnery, go! 170

OFELIA [*aside*] O heavens secure him!

HAMLET Where's thy father?

OFELIA At home, my lord.

HAMLET For God's sake, let the doors be shut on him!
He may play the fool nowhere but in his own house. To   175
a nunnery, go!

OFELIA [*aside*] Help him, good God!

HAMLET If thou dost marry, I'll give thee this plague to
thy dowry: be thou as chaste as ice, as pure as snow,
thou shalt not scape calumny. To a nunnery, go!   180

OFELIA Alas, what change is this!

HAMLET But if thou wilt needs marry, marry a fool. For
wise men know well enough what monsters you make
of them. To a nunnery, go!

OFELIA [*aside*] Pray God restore him!   185

HAMLET Nay, I have heard of your paintings too – God
hath given you one face and you make yourselves
another. You fig, and you amble, and you nickname
God's creatures, making your wantonness your
ignorance. A pox! 'Tis scurvy! I'll no more of it – it   190
hath made me mad. I'll no more marriages. All that are
married, but one, shall live. The rest shall keep as they
are. To a nunnery, go. To a nunnery, go!   *Exit.*

OFELIA
Great God of heaven, what a quick change is this!
The courtier, scholar, soldier, all in him,   195
All dashed and splintered thence! O, woe is me
To ha' seen what I have seen, see what I see!   *Exit.*

KING [*Comes forward with Corambis.*]
Love? No, no, that's not the cause –
Some deeper thing it is that troubles him.

CORAMBIS

200   Well, something it is. My lord, content you awhile:
I will myself go feel him. Let me work.
I'll try him every way.

Enter HAMLET.

    See where he comes!
Send you those gentlemen. Let me alone
To find the depth of this. Away, be gone!   *Exit King.*
205   Now, my good lord, do you know me?

HAMLET   Yea, very well: you're a fishmonger.

CORAMBIS   Not I, my lord!

HAMLET   Then, sir, I would you were so honest a man.
For to be honest as this age goes is one man to be
210   picked out of ten thousand.

CORAMBIS   What do you read, my lord?

HAMLET   Words, words.

CORAMBIS   What's the matter, my lord?

HAMLET   Between who?

215 CORAMBIS   I mean the matter you read, my lord.

HAMLET   Marry, most vile heresy. For here the satirical
satyr writes that old men have hollow eyes, weak backs,
grey beards, pitiful weak hams, gouty legs – all which,
sir, I most potently believe not. For, sir, yourself shall
220   be old as I am if, like a crab, you could go backward.

CORAMBIS [*aside*]   How pregnant his replies are – and
full of wit! Yet at first he took me for a fishmonger. All
this comes by love, the vehemency of love, and when I
was young I was very idle and suffered much ecstasy in
225   love, very near this. [*to Hamlet*] Will you walk out of
the air, my lord?

HAMLET   Into my grave.

CORAMBIS [*aside*]   By the mass, that's out of the air,
indeed! Very shrewd answers. [*to Hamlet*] My lord, I
230   will take my leave of you.

Enter GILDERSTONE *and* ROSSENCRAFT.

HAMLET   You can take nothing from me, sir, I will more
willingly part withal – old doting fool!

CORAMBIS   You seek Prince Hamlet? See, there he is.
                                          Exit.

GILDERSTONE   Health to your lordship!

235 HAMLET   What, Gilderstone and Rossencraft! Welcome,
kind schoolfellows, to Elsinore.

GILDERSTONE   We thank your grace, and would be very
glad you were as when we were at Wittenberg.

HAMLET   I thank you. But is this visitation free of
240   yourselves – or were you not sent for? Tell me true.
Come, I know the good King and Queen sent for you:
there is a kind of confession in your eye. Come, I know
you were sent for.

GILDERSTONE   What say you?

245 HAMLET   Nay then, I see how the wind sits. Come, you
were sent for.

ROSSENCRAFT   My lord, we were – and willingly – if we
might know the cause and ground of your discontent –

HAMLET   Why, I want preferment.

250 ROSSENCRAFT   I think not so, my lord.

HAMLET   Yes, faith. This great world, you see, contents
me not. No, nor the spangled heavens, nor earth, nor
sea. No, nor man that is so glorious a creature contents
not me. No, nor woman too – though you laugh.

255 GILDERSTONE   My lord, we laugh not at that.

HAMLET   Why did you laugh, then, when I said man did
not content me?

GILDERSTONE   My lord, we laughed, when you said
man did not content you, what entertainment the
260   players shall have! We boarded them o'the way; they
are coming to you.

HAMLET   Players – what players be they?

ROSSENCRAFT   My lord, the tragedians of the city –
those that you took delight to see so often.

265 HAMLET   How comes it that they travel? Do they grow
resty?

GILDERSTONE   No, my lord, their reputation holds as it
was wont.

HAMLET   How then?

270 GILDERSTONE   I'faith, my lord, novelty carries it away.
For the principal public audience that came to them
are turned to private plays, and to the humour of
children.

HAMLET   I do not greatly wonder of it, for those that
275   would make mops and mows at my uncle when my
father lived now give a hundred – two hundred –
pounds for his picture. But they shall be welcome. He
that plays the King shall have tribute of me, the
venturous Knight shall use his foil and target, the
280   Lover shall sigh gratis, the Clown shall make them
laugh that are tickled in the lungs, or the blank verse
shall halt for't, and the Lady shall have leave to speak
her mind freely.

The trumpets sound. Enter CORAMBIS.

Do you see yonder great baby? He is not yet out of his
285   swaddling-clouts.

GILDERSTONE   That may be, for they say an old man is
twice a child.

HAMLET   I'll prophesy to you he comes to tell me
o'the players. – You say true, o'Monday last, 'twas so
290   indeed.

CORAMBIS   My lord, I have news to tell you!

HAMLET   My lord, I have news to tell you. When
Roscius was an actor in Rome –

CORAMBIS   The actors are come hither, my lord!

295 HAMLET   Buzz, buzz!

CORAMBIS   The best actors in Christendom, either
for comedy, tragedy, history, pastoral, pastoral-
historical, historical-comical, comical-historical-pastoral,
tragedy-historical – Seneca cannot be too heavy nor
300   Plautus too light, for the law hath writ those are the
only men.

HAMLET   *O Jephthah, judge of Israel! What a treasure
hadst thou!*

CORAMBIS   Why, what a treasure had he, my lord?

305 HAMLET   Why,
          One fair daughter and no more –
          The which he loved passing well.
     CORAMBIS [*aside*]   Ah, still harping o' my daughter! [*to
          Hamlet*] Well, my lord, if you call me Jephthah, I have
310   a daughter that I love passing well.
     HAMLET   Nay, that follows not.
     CORAMBIS   What follows then, my lord?
     HAMLET   Why,
          By lot,
315   Or God wot,
          Or as it came to pass,
          And so it was –
     The first verse of the godly ballad will tell you all.

          Enter Players.

     For look you where my abridgement comes! Welcome,
320 masters, welcome all! What, my old friend, thy face is
     valanced since I saw thee last – com'st thou to beard
     me in Denmark? My young lady and mistress! By'r
     Lady, but your ladyship is grown by the altitude of a
     chopine higher than you were. Pray God, sir, your
325 voice, like a piece of uncurrent gold, be not cracked in
     the ring. Come on, masters, we'll even to't – like
     French falconers, fly at anything we see. Come, a taste
     of your quality – a speech, a passionate speech.
     PLAYERS   What speech, my good lord?
330 HAMLET   I heard thee speak a speech once, but it
     was never acted – or, if it were, never above twice. For,
     as I remember, it pleased not the vulgar. It was caviare
     to the million. But to me and others that received
     it in the like kind – cried in the top of their judgements
335 – an excellent play, set down with as great modesty as
     cunning. One said there was no sallets in the lines
     to make them savoury but called it an honest
     method, as wholesome as sweet. Come, a speech in
     it I chiefly remember was Aeneas' tale to Dido –
340 and then especially where he talks of princes'
     slaughter. If it live in thy memory begin at this line –
     let me see –
     The rugged Pyrrhus, like th' Hyrcanian beast –
     No, 'tis not so. It begins with Pyrrhus. O, I have it!
345 *The rugged Pyrrhus – he whose sable arms,*
     Black as his purpose, did the night resemble
     When he lay couched in the ominous horse,
     Hath now his black and grim complexion smeared
     With heraldry more dismal, head to foot.
350 *Now is he total guise, horridly tricked*
     With blood of fathers, mothers, daughters, sons,
     Baked and imparched in coagulate gore,
     Rifted in earth and fire – old grandsire Priam seeks –
     So, go on!
355 CORAMBIS   Afore God, my lord, well spoke – and with
          good accent!
     1 PLAYER
     Anon he finds him striking too short at Greeks.
     His antique sword, rebellious to his arm,

Lies where it falls, unable to resist.
Pyrrhus at Priam drives but, all in rage,   360
Strikes wide. But with the whiff and wind
Of his fell sword th'unnerved father falls.
CORAMBIS   Enough, my friend, 'tis too long.
HAMLET   It shall to the barber's with your beard. A pox!
     He's for a jig or a tale of bawdry or else he sleeps.   365
     Come on – to Hecuba, come.
1 PLAYER
But who, O who had seen the mobled queen . . .
CORAMBIS   'Mobled queen' is good. Faith, very good!
1 PLAYER
. . . All in the alarum and fear of death rose up,
And o'er her weak and all-o'erteeming loins   370
A blanket, and a kercher on that head
Where late the diadem stood – who this had seen,
With tongue-envenomed speech would treason have
*   pronounced.*
For if the gods themselves had seen her then,
When she saw Pyrrhus with malicious strokes   375
Mincing her husband's limbs,
It would have made milch the burning eyes of heaven,
And passion in the gods.
CORAMBIS   Look, my lord, if he hath not changed his
     colour and hath tears in his eyes. No more, good heart, 380
     no more!
HAMLET   'Tis well, 'tis very well. I pray, my lord, will
     you see the players well bestowed? I tell you they are
     the chronicles and brief abstracts of the time. After
     your death, I can tell you, you were better have a bad 385
     epithet than their ill report while you live.
CORAMBIS   My lord, I will use them according to their
     deserts.
HAMLET   O, far better, man – use every man after his
     deserts, then who should scape whipping? Use them   390
     after your own honour and dignity – the less they
     deserve the greater credit's yours.
CORAMBIS   Welcome, my good fellows!   *Exit.*
HAMLET   Come hither, masters. Can you not play *The*
     Murder of Gonzago?   395
PLAYERS   Yes, my lord.
HAMLET   And couldst not thou for a need study me
     some dozen or sixteen lines which I would set down
     and insert?
PLAYERS   Yes, very easily, my good lord.   400
HAMLET   'Tis well. I thank you. Follow that lord and –
     do you hear, sirs – take heed you mock him not. [*to
     Rossencraft and Gilderstone*] Gentlemen, for your
     kindness I thank you, and for a time I would desire you
     leave me.   405
GILDERSTONE   Our love and duty is at your command.
                              Exeunt all but Hamlet.
HAMLET   Why, what a dunghill idiot slave am I!
     Why, these players here draw water from eyes
     For Hecuba. Why, what is Hecuba to him,
     Or he to Hecuba?   410
     What would he do an if he had my loss –

His father murdered and a crown bereft him?
He would turn all his tears to drops of blood,
Amaze the standers-by with his laments,
415 Strike more than wonder in the judicial ears,
Confound the ignorant and make mute the wise.
Indeed, his passion would be general.
Yet I, like to an ass and John-a-Dreams,
Having my father murdered by a villain,
420 Stand still and let it pass! Why, sure I am a coward.
Who plucks me by the beard, or twits my nose,
Gives me the lie i'th' throat down to the lungs?
Sure, I should take it. Or else I have no gall,
Or, by this, I should ha' fatted all the region kites
425 With this slave's offal, this damned villain –
Treacherous, bawdy, murderous villain!
Why, this is brave, that I the son of my dear father
Should, like a scullion, like a very drab,
Thus rail in words. About my brain!
430 I have heard that guilty creatures sitting at a play
Hath, by the very cunning of the scene,
Confessed a murder committed long before.
This spirit that I have seen may be the devil
And, out of my weakness and my melancholy
435 (As he is very potent with such men),
Doth seek to damn me.
I will have sounder proofs – the play's the thing
Wherein I'll catch the conscience of the King. *Exit.*

Sc. 8 *Enter* KING, QUEEN, CORAMBIS, [3.1]
GILDERSTONE *and* ROSSENCRAFT.

KING Lords, can you by no means find
The cause of our son Hamlet's lunacy?
You, being so near in love even from his youth,
Methinks should gain more than a stranger should.
GILDERSTONE
5 My lord, we have done all the best we could
To wring from him the cause of all his grief,
But still he puts us off and by no means
Would make an answer to that we exposed.
ROSSENCRAFT
Yet was he something more inclined to mirth
10 Before we left him, and I take it
He hath given order for a play tonight,
At which he craves your highness' company.
KING With all our heart: it likes us very well.
Gentlemen, seek still to increase his mirth.
15 Spare for no cost, our coffers shall be open
And we unto yourselves will still be thankful.
GILDERSTONE, ROSSENCRAFT
In all we can, be sure you shall command.
QUEEN
Thanks, gentlemen, and what the Queen of Denmark
May pleasure you be sure you shall not want.
20 GILDERSTONE We'll once again unto the noble Prince.
KING Thanks to you both.
Exeunt Gilderstone and Rossencraft.

Gertred, you'll see this play?
QUEEN My lord, I will. And it joys me at the soul
He is inclined to any kind of mirth.
CORAMBIS Madam, I pray be ruled by me
And, my good sovereign, give me leave to speak: 25
We cannot yet find out the very ground
Of his distemperance. Therefore, I hold it meet,
If so it please you, else they shall not meet,
And thus it is –
KING What is't, Corambis?
CORAMBIS Marry, my good lord, this: 30
Soon, when the sports are done,
Madam, send you in haste to speak with him
And I myself will stand behind the arras.
There question you the cause of all his grief
And then in love and nature unto you 35
He'll tell you all. My lord, how think you on't?
KING It likes us well. Gertred, what say you?
QUEEN With all my heart. Soon will I send for him.
CORAMBIS Myself will be that happy messenger
Who hopes his grief will be revealed to her. *Exeunt.* 40

Sc. 9 *Enter* HAMLET *and* Players. [3.2]

HAMLET Pronounce me this speech trippingly o'the
tongue as I taught thee. Marry, an you mouth it, as a
many of your players do, I'd rather hear a town-bull
bellow than such a fellow speak my lines. Nor do not
saw the air thus with your hands but give everything 5
his action with temperance. O, it offends me to the soul
to hear a robustious periwig fellow to tear a passion in
tatters, into very rags, to split the ears of the ignorant
– who for the most part are capable of nothing but
dumb-shows and noises – I would have such a fellow 10
whipped for o'erdoing Termagant: it out-Herods
Herod!
1 PLAYER My lord, we have indifferently reformed that
among us.
HAMLET The better, the better! Mend it altogether! 15
There be fellows that I have seen play (and heard
others commend them – and that highly, too) that,
having neither the gait of Christian, pagan nor Turk,
have so strutted and bellowed that you would ha'
thought some of Nature's journeymen had made men 20
(and not made them well), they imitated humanity so
abhominable. Take heed, avoid it.
1 PLAYER I warrant you, my lord.
HAMLET And – do you hear? – let not your Clown
speak more than is set down. There be of them, I can 25
tell you, that will laugh themselves to set on some
quantity of barren spectators to laugh with them –
albeit there is some necessary point in the play then to
be observed. O, 'tis vile and shows a pitiful ambition in
the fool that useth it. And then you have some again 30
that keeps one suit of jests – as a man is known by one
suit of apparel – and gentlemen quotes his jests down
in their tables before they come to the play, as thus:

'Cannot you stay till I eat my porridge?' and 'You owe
35 me a quarter's wages!' and 'My coat wants a cullison!'
and 'Your beer is sour!' and, blabbering with his lips
and thus keeping in his cinquepace of jests when, God
knows, the warm Clown cannot make a jest unless by
chance – as the blind man catcheth a hare – masters,
40 tell him of it.

1 PLAYER We will, my lord.

HAMLET Well, go make you ready.   *Exeunt Players.*
Horatio!

Enter HORATIO.

HORATIO Here, my lord.

45 HAMLET Horatio, thou art even as just a man
As e'er my conversation coped withal.

HORATIO O my lord!

HAMLET   Nay, why should I flatter thee?
Why should the poor be flattered?
What gain should I receive by flattering thee
50 That nothing hath but thy good mind?
Let flattery sit on those time-pleasing tongues
To gloze with hem that loves to hear their praise,
And not with such as thou, Horatio.
There is a play tonight wherein one scene they have
55 Comes very near the murder of my father.
When thou shalt see that act afoot
Mark thou the King, do but observe his looks,
For I mine eyes will rivet to his face.
An if he do not bleach and change at that,
60 It is a damned ghost that we have seen.
Horatio, have a care: observe him well.

HORATIO My lord, mine eyes shall still be on his face
And not the smallest alteration
That shall appear in him but I shall note it.

65 HAMLET Hark, they come.

Enter KING, QUEEN, CORAMBIS, OFELIA,
ROSSENCRAFT *and* GILDERSTONE.

KING How now, son Hamlet, how fare you? Shall we
have a play?

HAMLET I'faith, the chameleon's dish, not capon-
crammed – feed o'the air. Ay, father! [*to Corambis*] My
70 lord, you played in the university.

CORAMBIS That I did, my lord, and I was counted a
good actor.

HAMLET What did you enact there?

CORAMBIS My lord, I did act Julius Caesar. I was killed
75 in the Capitol. Brutus killed me.

HAMLET It was a brute part of him to kill so capital a
calf! Come, be these players ready?

QUEEN Hamlet, come, sit down by me.

HAMLET No, by my faith, mother. Here's a metal more
80 attractive. [*to Ofelia*] Lady, will you give me leave (and
so forth) to lay my head in your lap?

OFELIA No, my lord.

HAMLET Upon your lap. What do you think I meant –
contrary matters?

Enter in a dumb-show Players *as a duke and a
duchess. He sits down in an arbour. She leaves him.
Then enters a* Player *as* Lucianus *with poison in a vial
and pours it in his ears and goes away. Then the
duchess cometh and finds him dead and goes away
with the other.*   *Exeunt.*

85 OFELIA What means this, my lord?

HAMLET This is miching mallico. That means
mischief.

Enter a Player *as the* Prologue.

OFELIA What doth this mean, my lord?

HAMLET You shall hear anon. This fellow will tell you
90 all.

OFELIA Will he tell us what this show means?

HAMLET Ay, or any show you'll show him. Be not
afeared to show – he'll not be afeared to tell. O, these
players cannot keep counsel, they'll tell all.

PROLOGUE
95 *For us and for our tragedy*
Here stooping to your clemency
We beg your hearing patiently.   *Exit.*

HAMLET Is't a prologue or a posy for a ring?

OFELIA 'Tis short, my lord.

100 HAMLET As women's love.

Enter the Player Duke *and* Player Duchess.

PLAYER DUKE
Full forty years are past – their date is gone –
Since happy time joined both our hearts as one.
And now the blood that filled my youthful veins
Runs weakly in their pipes, and all the strains
105 *Of music which whilom pleased mine ear*
Is now a burden that age cannot bear.
And therefore sweet Nature must pay his due:
To heaven must I – and leave the earth with you.

PLAYER DUCHESS
O say not so, lest that you kill my heart.
110 *When death takes you let life from me depart.*

PLAYER DUKE
Content thyself. When ended is my date
Thou mayst, perchance, have a more noble mate,
More wise, more youthful, and one –

PLAYER DUCHESS
O, speak no more, for then I am accursed:
115 *None weds the second but she kills the first.*
A second time I kill my lord that's dead
When second husband kisses me in bed.

HAMLET O, wormwood! Wormwood!

PLAYER DUKE
I do believe you, sweet, what now you speak.
120 *But what we do determine oft we break –*
For our demises still are overthrown:
Our thoughts are ours, their end's none of our own.
So, think you will no second husband wed,
But die thy thoughts when thy first lord is dead.

PLAYER DUCHESS

125   *Both here and there pursue me lasting strife*
If, once a widow, ever I be wife.

HAMLET   If she should break now!

PLAYER DUKE

'Tis deeply sworn. Sweet, leave me here awhile.
My spirits grow dull, and fain I would beguile
The tedious time with sleep.

130   PLAYER DUCHESS   *Sleep rock thy brain*
And never come mischance between us twain.   *Exit.*

HAMLET   Madam, how do you like this play?

QUEEN   The lady protests too much.

HAMLET   O, but she'll keep her word.

135   KING   Have you heard the argument? Is there no offence
in it?

HAMLET   No offence in the world; poison in jest, poison
in jest.

KING   What do you call the name of the play?

140   HAMLET   *Mousetrap.* Marry, how? Trapically. This play
is the image of a murder done in Guiana. Albertus was
the duke's name, his wife Baptista. Father, it is a
knavish piece o'work. But what o'that? It toucheth not
us – you and I that have free souls – let the galled jade

145   wince.

Enter Lucianus.

This is one Lucianus, nephew to the king.

OFELIA   You're as good as a chorus, my lord.

HAMLET   I could interpret the love you bear if I saw the
poopies dallying.

150   OFELIA   You're very pleasant, my lord.

HAMLET   Who, I? Your only jig-maker! Why, what
should a man do but be merry – for look how cheerfully
my mother looks: my father died within these two
hours.

155   OFELIA   Nay, 'tis twice two months, my lord.

HAMLET   Two months? Nay, then, let the devil wear
black, for I'll have a suit of sables! Jesus, two months
dead and not forgotten yet? Nay, then, there's some
likelihood a gentleman's death may outlive memory.

160   But, by my faith, he must build churches then, or else
he must follow the old epithet: 'With ho, with ho, the
hobbyhorse is forgot!'

OFELIA   Your jests are keen, my lord.

HAMLET   It would cost you a groaning to take them off.

165   OFELIA   Still better – and worse!

HAMLET   So you must take your husband. [*to Players*]
Begin! Murderer, begin! A pox! Leave thy damnable
faces and begin! Come!
'*The croaking raven doth bellow for revenge!*'

LUCIANUS

170   *Thoughts black, hands apt, drugs fit, and time agreeing –*
Confederate season, else no creature seeing.
Thou mixture rank, of midnight weeds collected,
With Hecate's bane thrice blasted, thrice infected.
Thy natural magic and dire property

175   *One wholesome life usurps immediately!*

[*Pours the poison in his ears.*]   *Exit.*

HAMLET   He poisons him for his estate.

KING   Lights! I will to bed.

CORAMBIS   The King rises. Lights, ho!
Exeunt all but Hamlet and Horatio.

HAMLET   What, frighted with false fires?
Then let the stricken deer go weep,   180
The hart ungalled play,
For some must laugh while some must weep –
Thus runs the world away!

HORATIO   The King is moved, my lord.

HAMLET   Ay, Horatio. I'll take the ghost's word for   185
more than all the coin in Denmark!

Enter ROSSENCRAFT *and* GILDERSTONE.

ROSSENCRAFT   Now, my lord, how is't with you?

HAMLET
An if the King likes not the tragedy,
Why, then – belike he likes it not, perdie!

ROSSENCRAFT   We are very glad to see your grace so   190
pleasant. My good lord, let us again entreat to know of
you the ground and cause of your distemperature.

GILDERSTONE   My lord, your mother craves to speak
with you.

HAMLET   We shall obey, were she ten times our mother.   195

ROSSENCRAFT   But, my good lord, shall I entreat thus
much?

HAMLET   I pray, will you play upon this pipe?

ROSSENCRAFT   Alas, my lord, I cannot.

HAMLET [*to Gilderstone*]   Pray, will my you?   200

GILDERSTONE   I have no skill, my lord.

HAMLET   Why look, it is a thing of nothing: 'tis but
stopping of these holes and, with a little breath from
your lips, it will give most delicate music.

GILDERSTONE   But this cannot we do, my lord.   205

HAMLET   Pray now, pray, heartily – I beseech you!

ROSSENCRAFT   My lord, we cannot.

HAMLET   Why, how unworthy a thing would you make
of me? You would seem to know my stops. You would
play upon me. You would search the very inward part   210
of my heart and dive into the secret of my soul.
Zounds! Do you think I am easier to be played on than
a pipe? Call me what instrument you will, though you
can fret me, yet you cannot play upon me. Besides – to
be demanded by a sponge!   215

ROSSENCRAFT   How! A sponge, my lord?

HAMLET   Ay, sir, a sponge that soaks up the King's
countenance, favours and rewards; that makes his
liberality your storehouse. But such as you do the King
in the end best service, for he doth keep you as an ape   220
doth nuts – in the corner of his jaw. First mouths you,
then swallows you. So, when he hath need of you, 'tis
but squeezing of you, and, sponge, you shall be dry
again, you shall!

ROSSENCRAFT   Well, my lord, we'll take our leave.   225

HAMLET   Farewell, farewell. God bless you!
Exeunt Rossencraft and Gilderstone.

Enter CORAMBIS.

CORAMBIS   My lord, the Queen would speak with you.

HAMLET   Do you see yonder cloud in the shape of a
camel?

230   CORAMBIS   'Tis like a camel indeed.

HAMLET   Now methinks it's like a weasel.

CORAMBIS   'Tis backed like a weasel.

HAMLET   Or like a whale.

CORAMBIS   Very like a whale.

235   HAMLET   Why, then, tell my mother I'll come by and by.
                                          Exit Corambis.
Goodnight, Horatio.

HORATIO   Goodnight unto your lordship.   *Exit.*

HAMLET   My mother she hath sent to speak with me!
O God, let ne'er

The heart of Nero enter this soft bosom.

240   Let me be cruel, not unnatural.
I will speak daggers. Those sharp words being spent,
To do her wrong my soul shall ne'er consent.   *Exit.*

Sc. 10   *Enter* KING.   [3.3]

KING   O that this wet that falls upon my face
Would wash the crime clear from my conscience!
When I look up to heaven I see my trespass,
The earth doth still cry out upon my fact.

5   Pay me the murder of a brother and a king
And the adulterous fault I have committed.
O, these are sins that are unpardonable!
Why, say thy sins were blacker than is jet —
Yet may contrition make them as white as snow.

10   Ay, but still to persever in a sin
It is an act 'gainst the universal power!
Most wretched man, stoop, bend thee to thy prayer;
Ask grace of heaven to keep thee from despair.
       [*He kneels.*]

Enter HAMLET.

HAMLET [*aside*]   Ay, so.
Come forth and work thy last [*Draws sword.*] – and

15   thus he dies,
And so am I revenged! No, not so.
He took my father sleeping, his sins brimful.
And how his soul stood to the state of heaven
Who knows, save the immortal powers?

20   And shall I kill him now,
When he is purging of his soul,
Making his way for heaven?
This is a benefit and not revenge!
No, get thee up again. [*Sheathes sword.*] When he's at
       game,

25   Swearing, taking his carouse, drinking drunk,
Or in the incestuous pleasure of his bed,
Or at some act
That hath no relish of salvation in't —
Then trip him that his heels may kick at heaven

And fall as low as hell! My mother stays.   30
This physic but prolongs thy weary days!   *Exit.*

KING   My words fly up, my sins remain below.
No king on earth is safe if God's his foe.   *Exit.*

Sc. 11   *Enter* QUEEN *and* CORAMBIS.   [3.4]

CORAMBIS   Madam, I hear young Hamlet coming. I'll
shroud myself behind the arras.

QUEEN   Do so, my lord. [*Corambis hides behind the
arras.*]

HAMLET [*offstage*]   Mother, mother!

Enter HAMLET.

O, are you here? How is't with you, mother?   5

QUEEN   How is't with you?

HAMLET   I'll tell you, but first we'll make all safe.

QUEEN   Hamlet, thou hast thy father much offended.

HAMLET   Mother, you have my father much offended.

QUEEN   How now, boy?

HAMLET   How now, mother?   10
Come here. Sit down. For you shall hear me speak.

QUEEN   What wilt thou do? Thou wilt not murder me?
Help, ho!

CORAMBIS [*behind the arras*]
               Help for the Queen!

HAMLET   Ay, a rat!
   [*Stabs Corambis through the arras.*]
Dead for a ducat! Rash intruding fool,
Farewell. I took thee for thy better.

QUEEN   Hamlet,   15
What hast thou done?

HAMLET   Not so much harm, good mother,
As to kill a king and marry with his brother.

QUEEN   How? Kill a king?

HAMLET
Ay, a king! Nay, sit you down and, ere you part,
If you be made of penetrable stuff,   20
I'll make your eyes look down into your heart
And see how horrid there and black it shows.

QUEEN
Hamlet, what mean'st thou by these killing words?

HAMLET
Why, this I mean. See here, behold this picture.
It is the portraiture of your deceased husband.   25
See here, a face to outface Mars himself;
An eye at which his foes did tremble at;
A front wherein all virtues are set down
For to adorn a king and gild his crown;
Whose heart went hand in hand even with that vow   30
He made to you in marriage. And he is dead:
Murdered, damnably murdered. This was your husband.
Look you now,
Here is your husband with a face like Vulcan,
A look fit for a murder and a rape,   35
A dull, dead, hanging look, and a hell-bred eye
To affright children and amaze the world.

And this same have you left to change with this!
What devil thus hath cozened you at hob-man
   blind?
40   Ah, have you eyes, and can you look on him
That slew my father and your dear husband –
To live in the incestuous pleasure of his bed?
QUEEN   O Hamlet, speak no more.
HAMLET   To leave him that bare a monarch's mind
45   For a king of clouts, of very shreds!
QUEEN   Sweet Hamlet, cease.
HAMLET   Nay, but still to persist and dwell in sin,
To sweat under the yoke of infamy,
To make increase of shame, to seal damnation –
50   QUEEN   Hamlet, no more.
HAMLET   Why, appetite with you is in the wane;
Your blood runs backward now from whence it
   came.
Who'll chide hot blood within a virgin's heart
When lust shall dwell within a matron's breast?
55   QUEEN   Hamlet, thou cleaves my heart in twain.
HAMLET   O, throw away the worser part of it,
And keep the better –

Enter the GHOST *in his night-gown.*

Save me, save me, you gracious powers above,
And hover over me with your celestial wings! –
60   Do you not come your tardy son to chide
That I thus long have let revenge slip by?
O do not glare with looks so pitiful,
Lest that my heart of stone yield to compassion
And every part that should assist revenge
65   Forgo their proper powers and fall to pity.
GHOST   Hamlet, I once again appear to thee
To put thee in remembrance of my death.
Do not neglect, nor long time put it off.
But I perceive by thy distracted looks
70   Thy mother's fearful, and she stands amazed:
Speak to her, Hamlet, for her sex is weak.
Comfort thy mother. Hamlet, think on me.
HAMLET   How is't with you, lady?
QUEEN   Nay, how is't with you
That thus you bend your eyes on vacancy
75   And hold discourse with nothing but with air?
HAMLET   Why, do you nothing hear?
QUEEN   Not I.
HAMLET   Nor do you nothing see?
QUEEN   No, neither.
HAMLET   No?
Why, see, the King my father,
My father in the habit as he lived!
80   Look you how pale he looks!
See how he steals away out of the portal!
Look, there he goes!   *Exit Ghost.*
QUEEN   Alas, it is the weakness of thy brain
Which makes thy tongue to blazon thy heart's grief.
85   But, as I have a soul, I swear by heaven
I never knew of this most horrid murder.

But, Hamlet, this is only fantasy
And, for my love, forget these idle fits.
HAMLET
Idle? No, mother: my pulse doth beat like yours.
It is not madness that possesseth Hamlet.   90
O, mother, if ever you did my dear father love,
Forbear the adulterous bed tonight
And win yourself by little, as you may.
In time it may be you will loath him quite.
And, mother, but assist me in revenge,   95
And in his death your infamy shall die.
QUEEN   Hamlet, I vow by that Majesty
That knows our thoughts and looks into our hearts
I will conceal, consent and do my best –
What stratagem soe'er thou shalt devise.   100
HAMLET   It is enough. Mother, goodnight!
Come, sir – I'll provide for you a grave,
Who was in life a foolish, prating knave.
          Exit Hamlet with the dead body.

Enter the KING *and lords* ROSSENCRAFT   [4.1]
     and GILDERSTONE.

KING   Now, Gertred,
What says our son? How do you find him?   105
QUEEN   Alas, my lord, as raging as the sea.
Whenas he came, I first bespake him fair,
But then he throws and tosses me about
As one forgetting that I was his mother –
At last I called for help and, as I cried   *110
Corambis called. Which Hamlet no sooner heard
But whips me out his rapier and cries
'A rat! A rat!'
And in his rage the good old man he kills.
KING   Why, this his madness will undo our state.   115
Lords, go to him: enquire the body out.
GILDERSTONE
We will, my lord.   *Exeunt Rossencraft and Gilderstone.*
KING   Gertred, your son shall presently to England.
His shipping is already furnished
And we have sent by Rossencraft and Gilderstone   120
Our letters to our dear brother of England
For Hamlet's welfare and his happiness.
Haply the air and climate of the country
May please him better than his native home.
See where he comes.   125

Enter HAMLET, ROSSENCRAFT,   [4.3]
   GILDERSTONE *and another Lord.*

GILDERSTONE
My lord, we can by no means know of him
   Where the body is.
KING   Now, son Hamlet, where is this dead body?
HAMLET   At supper. Not where he is eating but where
   he is eaten: a certain company of politic worms are   130
   even now at him. Father, your fat king and your lean
   beggar are but variable services – two dishes to one
   mess. Look you, a man may fish with that worm that

hath eaten of a king and a beggar eat that fish which
135   that worm hath caught –

KING   What of this?

HAMLET   Nothing, father, but to tell you how a king
may go a progress through the guts of a beggar.

KING   But, son Hamlet, where is this body?

140 HAMLET   In heaven. If you chance to miss him there,
Father, you had best look in the other parts below
For him, and if you cannot find him there
You may chance to nose him as you go up the lobby.

KING [*to Lord*]   Make haste and find him out.

          Exit Lord.

HAMLET

145   Nay, do you hear? Do not make too much haste:
I'll warrant you he'll stay till you come!

KING   Well, son Hamlet,
We in care of you – but specially
In tender preservation of your health,

150   The which we prize even as our proper self –
It is our mind you forthwith go for England.
The wind sits fair, you shall aboard tonight.
Lord Rossencraft and Gilderstone shall go
Along with you.

HAMLET   O, with all my heart.
Farewell, mother.

155 KING   Your loving father, Hamlet!

HAMLET   My mother, I say. You married my mother,
My mother is your wife, man and wife is one flesh
– And so, my mother! Farewell. For England, ho!

      Exeunt all but the King and Queen.

KING

Gertred, leave me, and take your leave of Hamlet.

      Exit Queen.

160 To England is he gone, ne'er to return.
Our letters are unto the King of England –
That on the sight of them, on his allegiance,
He presently without demanding why –
That Hamlet lose his head; for he must die.

165 There's more in him than shallow eyes can see;
He once being dead, why then our state is free.   *Exit.*

Sc. 12   *Enter* FORTENBRASSE,   **[4.4]**
        Drum and Soldiers.

FORTENBRASSE

Captain, from us go greet the King of Denmark.
Tell him that Fortenbrasse, nephew to old Norway,
Craves a free pass and conduct over his land,
According to the articles agreed on.

5 You know our rendezvous: go, march away!   *Exeunt.*

Sc. 13   *Enter* KING *and* QUEEN.   **[4.5]**

KING   Hamlet is shipped for England. Fare him well.
I hope to hear good news from thence ere long
If everything fall out to our content,
As I do make no doubt but so it shall.

QUEEN   God grant it may. Heavens keep my Hamlet safe!   5
But this mischance of old Corambis' death
Hath pierced so the young Ofelia's heart
That she, poor maid, is quite bereft her wits.

KING   Alas, dear heart! And on the other side
We understand her brother's come from France   10
And he hath half the heart of all our land.
And hardly he'll forget his father's death,
Unless by some means he be pacified.

QUEEN   O, see where the young Ofelia is!

    Enter OFELIA *playing on a lute,*
      and her hair down, singing.

OFELIA [*Sings.*]

    'How should I your true love know   15
    From another man?'
    'By his cockle hat, and his staff,
    And his sandal shoon.

    White his shroud as mountain snow,
    Larded with sweet flowers,   20
    That bewept to the grave did not go
    With true lovers' showers.'

    'He is dead and gone, lady,
    He is dead and gone.
    At his head a grass green turf,   25
    At his heels a stone.'

KING   How is't with you, sweet Ofelia?

OFELIA   Well, God yield you, it grieves me to see how
they laid him in the cold ground – I could not choose
but weep.   30

[*Sings.*]   'And will he not come again?
    And will he not come again?'
    'No, no, he's gone
    And we cast away moan,
    And he never will come again.   35

    His beard as white as snow,
    All flaxen was his poll.
    He is dead, he is gone
    And we cast away moan.
    God ha' mercy on his soul.'   40

And of all Christian souls, I pray God! God be with
you, ladies, God be with you!   *Exit.*

KING   A pretty wretch! This is a change indeed.
O Time, how swiftly runs our joys away!
Content on earth was never certain bred.   45
Today we laugh and live, tomorrow dead.

      [*A noise within*]

How now! What noise is that?

    Enter LEARTES.

LEARTES [*to his offstage followers*]   Stay there until I come.
– O thou vile King, give me my father! Speak, say
where's my father!   50

KING Dead.

LEARTES Who hath murdered him? Speak – I'll not be
juggled with – for he is murdered.

QUEEN True, but not by him.

55 LEARTES By whom? By heaven I'll be resolved.

KING Let him go, Gertred. Away! I fear him not:
There's such divinity doth wall a king
That treason dares not look on.
Let him go, Gertred. That your father is murdered
60 'Tis true, and we most sorry for it,
Being the chiefest pillar of our state.
Therefore will you, like a most desperate gamester
Swoopstake-like, draw at friend and foe and all?

LEARTES
To his good friends thus wide I'll ope mine arms
65 And lock them in my heart. But to his foes
I will no reconcilement but by blood.

KING Why, now you speak like a most loving son.
And that in soul we sorrow for his death
Yourself ere long shall be a witness.
70 Meanwhile, be patient and content yourself.

Enter OFELIA *as before.*

LEARTES Who's this? Ofelia? O, my dear sister!
Is't possible a young maid's life
Should be as mortal as an old man's saw?
O heavens themselves! How now, Ofelia?

75 OFELIA Well, God-a-mercy, I ha' been gathering of
flowers. Here, here is rue for you – you may call it herb-
a-grace o'Sundays. Here's some for me too. You must
wear your rue with a difference. There's a daisy. Here,
love, there's rosemary for you for remembrance – I
80 pray, love, remember. And there's pansy for thoughts.

LEARTES
A document in madness. Thoughts! Remembrance!
O God, O God!

OFELIA There is fennel for you. I would ha' given you
some violets, but they all withered when my father
85 died. Alas, they say the owl was a baker's daughter. We
see what we are but cannot tell what we shall be.
[*Sings.*]
For bonny sweet Robin is all my joy –

LEARTES
Thoughts and afflictions, torments worse than hell!

OFELIA Nay, love, I pray you make no words of this now,
90 I pray now you shall sing 'a-down' and you 'a-down-a'.
'Tis o'the king's daughter and the false steward, and if
anybody ask you of anything, say you this:
[*Sings.*]
Tomorrow is Saint Valentine's Day
All in the morning betime
95 And a maid at your window
To be your valentine.

The young man rose
And donned his clothes
And dupped the chamber door:

100 Let in the maid
That out a maid
Never departed more.
Nay, I pray mark, now:
[*Sings.*]
By Gis and by Saint Charity
105 Away and fie for shame!
Young men will do't
When they come to't –
By Cock they are to blame.

Quoth she, 'Before you tumbled me
110 You promised me to wed.'
'So would I ha' done,
By yonder sun,
If thou hadst not come to my bed.'
So God be with you all, God be with you, ladies, God
115 be with you, love. *Exit Ofelia and Queen.*

LEARTES Grief upon grief,
My father murdered, my sister thus distracted:
Cursed be his soul that wrought this wicked act.

KING Content you, good Leartes, for a time.
120 Although I know your grief is as a flood,
Brimful of sorrow, but forbear awhile
And think already the revenge is done
On him that makes you such a hapless son.

LEARTES
You have prevailed, my lord. Awhile I'll strive
125 To bury grief within a tomb of wrath,
Which once unhearsed, then the world shall hear
Leartes had a father he held dear!

KING No more of that. Ere many days be done
You shall hear that you do not dream upon. *Exeunt.*

Sc. 14 *Enter* HORATIO *and the* QUEEN.

HORATIO Madam, your son is safe arrived in Denmark:
This letter I even now received of him
Wherein he writes how he escaped the danger
And subtle treason that the King had plotted.
5 Being crossed by the contention of the winds,
He found the packet sent to the King of England,
Wherein he saw himself betrayed to death
As, at his next convers'ion with your grace,
He will relate the circumstance at full.

10 QUEEN Then I perceive there's treason in his looks
That seemed to sugar o'er his villainy.
But I will soothe and please him for a time
(For murderous minds are always jealous).
But know not you, Horatio, where he is?

15 HORATIO Yes, madam, and he hath appointed me
To meet him on the east side of the city
Tomorrow morning.

QUEEN O, fail not, good Horatio,
And withal commend me a mother's care to him –
Bid him awhile be wary of his presence
20 Lest that he fail in that he goes about.

HORATIO
　　Madam, never make doubt of that. I think by this
　　The news be come to Court he is arrived.
　　Observe the King and you shall quickly find,
　　Hamlet being here, things fell not to his mind.
QUEEN
25　But what became of Gilderstone and Rossencraft?
HORATIO　He being set ashore, they went for England.
　　And in the packet there writ down that doom
　　To be performed on them 'pointed for him.
　　And, by great chance, he had his father's seal –
30　So all was done without discovery.
QUEEN　Thanks be to heaven for blessing of the Prince!
　　Horatio, once again I take my leave,
　　With thousand mother's blessings to my son.
HORATIO　Madam, adieu.　　　　　　　　　*Exeunt.*

Sc. 15　　　*Enter* KING *and* LEARTES.　　　[4.7]

KING　Hamlet from England! Is it possible?
　　What chance is this? They are gone, and he come home!
LEARTES　O, he is welcome! By my soul he is –
5　At it my jocund heart doth leap for joy
　　That I shall live to tell him, thus he dies.
KING　Leartes, content yourself. Be ruled by me
　　And you shall have no let for your revenge.
LEARTES　My will, not all the world!
KING　Nay, but, Leartes, mark the plot I have laid:
10　I have heard him often, with a greedy wish,
　　Upon some praise that he hath heard of you
　　Touching your weapon, wish with all his heart
　　He might be once tasked for to try your cunning.
LEARTES　And how for this?
15　KING　Marry, Leartes, thus: I'll lay a wager
　　(Shall be on Hamlet's side and you shall give the
　　　　odds)
　　The which will draw him with a more desire
　　To try the mastery – that in twelve venies
　　You gain not three of him. Now, this being granted,
20　When you are hot in midst of all your play,
　　Among the foils shall a keen rapier lie,
　　Steeped in a mixture of deadly poison
　　That, if it draws but the least dram of blood
　　In any part of him, he cannot live.
25　This being done will free you from suspicion
　　And not the dearest friend that Hamlet loved
　　Will ever have Leartes in suspect.
LEARTES　My lord, I like it well.
　　But say Lord Hamlet should refuse this match?
30　KING　I'll warrant you. We'll put on you
　　Such a report of singularity
　　Will bring him on, although against his will
　　And, lest that all should miss,
　　I'll have a potion that shall ready stand
35　In all his heat when that he calls for drink,
　　Shall be his period and our happiness.
LEARTES　'Tis excellent. O would the time were come!

Enter the QUEEN.

　　Here comes the Queen.
KING　How now, Gertred? Why look you heavily?
QUEEN　O, my lord, the young Ofelia,　　　　40
　　Having made a garland of sundry sorts of flowers,
　　Sitting upon a willow by a brook,
　　The envious sprig broke. Into the brook she fell
　　And for a while her clothes, spread wide abroad,
　　Bore the young lady up and there she sat　　45
　　Smiling even mermaid-like 'twixt heaven and earth,
　　Chanting old sundry tunes uncapable,
　　As it were, of her distress. But long it could not be
　　Till that her clothes, being heavy with their drink,
　　Dragged the sweet wretch to death.
LEARTES　　　　　　　So – she is drowned?　50
　　Too much of water hast thou, Ofelia!
　　Therefore I will not drown thee in my tears.
　　Revenge it is must yield this heart relief.
　　For woe begets woe, and grief hangs on grief.　　*Exeunt.*

Sc. 16　　　　*Enter two Clowns,*　　　[5.1]
　　　　　　a Gravedigger *and a* Second Man.

GRAVEDIGGER　I say no, she ought not to be buried in
　　Christian burial.
2 MAN　Why, sir?
GRAVEDIGGER　Marry, because she's drowned.
2 MAN　But she did not drown herself.　　　　5
GRAVEDIGGER　No, that's certain, the water drowned
　　her.
2 MAN　Yea, but it was against her will.
GRAVEDIGGER　No, I deny that. For, look you, sir – I
　　stand here: if the water come to me I drown not myself　10
　　but, if I go to the water and am there drowned, ergo I
　　am guilty of my own death. You're gone, go, you're
　　gone, sir.
2 MAN　Ay, but see: she hath Christian burial because
　　she is a great woman.　　　　15
GRAVEDIGGER　Marry, more's the pity that great folk
　　should have more authority to hang or drown
　　themselves more than other people. Go fetch me a
　　stoup of drink. But, before thou goest, tell me one
　　thing: who builds strongest of a mason, a shipwright or　20
　　a carpenter?
2 MAN　Why, a mason. For he builds all of stone and will
　　endure long.
GRAVEDIGGER　That's pretty. To't again, to't again.
2 MAN　Why, then, a carpenter. For he builds the　　25
　　gallows, and that brings many a one to his long home.
GRAVEDIGGER　Pretty, again. The gallows doth well.
　　Marry, how does it well? The gallows does well
　　to them that do ill. Go, get thee gone. And if anyone
　　ask thee hereafter, say a grave-maker. For the houses　30
　　he builds last till doomsday. Fetch me a stoup of
　　beer. Go.　　　　　　　　　*Exit Second Man.*

Enter HAMLET *and* HORATIO.

[*Sings.*]

> A pickaxe and a spade, a spade
> For and a winding sheet,
35 Most fit it is for 'twill be made
> For such a guest most meet.

[*He throws up a skull.*]

HAMLET   Hath this fellow any feeling of himself that is
thus merry in making of a grave? See how the slave
jowls their heads against the earth!

40 HORATIO   My lord, custom hath made it in him seem
nothing.

GRAVEDIGGER [*Sings.*]

> A pickaxe and a spade, a spade,
> For and a winding sheet,
45 Most fit it is for to be made
> For such a guest most meet.

[*Throws up another skull.*]

HAMLET   Look you, there's another, Horatio! Why may't
not be the skull of some lawyer? Methinks he should
indict that fellow of an action of battery for knocking
him about the pate with's shovel. Now where is your
50 quirks and quillets now, your vouchers and double
vouchers, your leases and freehold and tenements?
Why, that same box there will scarce hold the conveyance
of his land, and must his honour lie there? O pitiful
transformance! I prithee tell me, Horatio, is parchment
55 made of sheepskins?

HORATIO   Ay, my lord. And of calves' skins too.

HAMLET   I'faith, they prove themselves sheep and
calves that deal with them or put their trust in them.
[*Gravedigger throws up another skull.*] There's another!
60 Why may not that be such a one's skull that praised my
lord such a one's horse when he meant to beg him?
Horatio, I prithee let's question yonder fellow. Now,
my friend, whose grave is this?

GRAVEDIGGER   Mine, sir.

65 HAMLET   But who must lie in it?

GRAVEDIGGER   If I should say I should, I should lie in
my throat, sir.

HAMLET   What man must be buried here?

GRAVEDIGGER   No man, sir.

70 HAMLET   What woman?

GRAVEDIGGER   No woman neither, sir. But, indeed, one
that was a woman.

HAMLET [*to Horatio*]   An excellent fellow, by the Lord,
Horatio. This seven years have I noted it: the toe of the
75 peasant comes so near the heel of the courtier that he
galls his kibe. [*to Gravedigger*] I prithee tell me one
thing: how long will a man lie in the ground before he
rots?

GRAVEDIGGER   I'faith, sir, if he be not rotten before he
80 be laid in (as we have many pocky corpses) he will last
you eight years – a tanner will last you eight years full
out, or nine.

HAMLET   And why a tanner?

GRAVEDIGGER   Why, his hide is so tanned with his trade
85 that it will hold out water – that's a parlous devourer of

your dead body, a great soaker. Look you, here's a skull
hath been here this dozen year – let me see, ay, ever
since our last King Hamlet slew Fortenbrasse in
combat – young Hamlet's father, he that's mad.

90 HAMLET   Ay, marry, how came he mad?

GRAVEDIGGER   I'faith, very strangely – by losing of his
wits.

HAMLET   Upon what ground?

GRAVEDIGGER   O'this ground, in Denmark.

95 HAMLET   Where is he now?

GRAVEDIGGER   Why, now they sent him to England.

HAMLET   To England! Wherefore?

GRAVEDIGGER   Why, they say he shall have his wits
there. Or if he have not 'tis no great matter there: it
100 will not be seen there.

HAMLET   Why not there?

GRAVEDIGGER   Why, there, they say, the men are as mad
as he.

HAMLET   Whose skull was this?

105 GRAVEDIGGER   This? A plague on him! A mad rogue's it
was. He poured once a whole flagon of Rhenish of my
head. Why, do not you know him? This was one
Yorick's skull.

HAMLET   Was this? I prithee let me see it! Alas, poor
110 Yorick! I knew him, Horatio. A fellow of infinite mirth.
He hath carried me twenty times upon his back. Here
hung those lips that I have kissed a hundred times. And
to see now! They abhor me! Where's your jests now,
Yorick – your flashes of merriment? Now go to my
115 lady's chamber and bid her paint herself an inch thick,
to this she must come. Yorick! Horatio, I prithee tell me
one thing. Dost thou think that Alexander looked thus?

HORATIO   Even so, my lord.

HAMLET   And smelt thus?

120 HORATIO   Ay, my lord, no otherwise.

HAMLET   No? Why might not imagination work as thus
of Alexander? Alexander died. Alexander was buried.
Alexander became earth. Of earth we make clay. And,
Alexander being but clay, why might not time bring to
125 pass that he might stop the bunghole of a beer-barrel?

> Imperious Caesar, dead and turned to clay,
> Might stop a hole to keep the wind away.

Enter KING, QUEEN, LEARTES *and
other Lords, with a* Priest *after
the coffin.*

What funeral's this, that all the Court laments?
It shows to be some noble parentage.
130 Stand by awhile.

LEARTES
What ceremony else? Say, what ceremony else?

PRIEST   My lord, we have done all that lies in us
And more than well the church can tolerate:
She hath had a dirge sung for her maiden soul
And, but for favour of the King and you,
135 She had been buried in the open fields,

Where now she is allowed Christian burial.

LEARTES   So? I tell thee, churlish priest,
A ministering angel shall my sister be
When thou liest howling!

140 HAMLET *[to Horatio]*   The fair Ofelia dead!

QUEEN   Sweets to the sweet. Farewell.
I had thought to adorn thy bridal bed, fair maid,
And not to follow thee unto thy grave.

LEARTES   Forbear the earth awhile. Sister, farewell.
     [Leartes leaps into the grave.]

145 Now pour your earth on, Olympus-high,
And make a hill to o'ertop old Pelion!
     [Hamlet leaps in after Leartes.]

HAMLET   What's he that conjures so?
Behold, 'tis I – Hamlet the Dane!

LEARTES   The devil take thy soul!

HAMLET   O, thou prayest not well.

150 I prithee take thy hand from off my throat,
For there is something in me dangerous
Which let thy wisdom fear. Hold off thy hand!
I loved Ofelia as dear
As twenty brothers could. Show me what thou

155 Wilt do for her. Wilt fight? Wilt fast? Wilt pray?
Wilt drink up vessels? Eat a crocodile?
I'll do't! Com'st thou here to whine?
And where thou talk'st of burying thee alive
Here let us stand and let them throw on us

160 Whole hills of earth, till with the height thereof
Make Ossa as a wart!

KING   Forbear, Leartes: now is he mad as is the sea,
Anon as mild and gentle as a dove.
Therefore, awhile give his wild humour scope.

HAMLET

165 What is the reason, sir, that you wrong me thus?
I never gave you cause. But stand away,
A cat will mew, a dog will have a day.
     Exeunt Hamlet and Horatio.

QUEEN   Alas, it is his madness makes him thus
And not his heart, Leartes.

KING

My lord, 'tis so. *[aside to Leartes]* But we'll no longer
170   trifle:
This very day shall Hamlet drink his last,
For presently we mean to send to him.
Therefore, Leartes, be in readiness.

LEARTES *[aside to King]*
My lord, till then my soul will not be quiet.

175 KING   Come, Gertred, we'll have Leartes and our son
Made friends and lovers, as befits them both,
Even as they tender us and love their country.

QUEEN   God grant they may.   *Exeunt.*

Sc. 17   *Enter* HAMLET *and* HORATIO.   **[5.2]**

HAMLET   Believe me, it grieves me much, Horatio,
That to Leartes I forgot myself
For by myself methinks I feel his grief

Though there's a difference in each other's wrong.

     Enter a braggart Gentleman.

Horatio – but mark yon water-fly –   5
The Court knows him but he knows not the Court.

GENTLEMAN   Now God save thee, sweet Prince
Hamlet.

HAMLET   And you, sir. *[aside to Horatio]* Foh! How the
musk-cod smells!   10

GENTLEMAN   I come with an embassage from his
majesty to you.

HAMLET   I shall, sir, give you attention. By my troth,
methinks 'tis very cold.

GENTLEMAN   It is, indeed, very rawish cold.   15

HAMLET   'Tis hot, methinks.

GENTLEMAN   Very swoltery hot. The King, sweet
Prince, hath laid a wager on your side: six Barbary
horse against six French rapiers, with all their
accoutrements, too, o'the carriages – in good faith,   20
they are very curiously wrought!

HAMLET   The carriages, sir? I do not know what you
mean.

GENTLEMAN   The girdles and hangers, sir – and
suchlike.   25

HAMLET   The word had been more cousin-german
to the phrase if he could have carried the cannon by
his side. And how's the wager? I understand you
now.

GENTLEMAN   Marry, sir, that young Leartes in twelve   30
venies at rapier and dagger do not get three odds of
you. And on your side the King hath laid and desires
you to be in readiness.

HAMLET   Very well. If the King dare venture his wager,
I dare venture my skill. When must this be?   35

GENTLEMAN   My lord, presently. The King and her
majesty, with the rest of the best judgement in the
Court, are coming down into the outward palace.

HAMLET   Go, tell his majesty I will attend him.

GENTLEMAN   I shall deliver your most sweet   40
answer.   *Exit.*

HAMLET   You may, sir, none better! For you're spiced:
else he had a bad nose could not smell a fool.

HORATIO   He will disclose himself without enquiry!

HAMLET   Believe me, Horatio, my heart is on the   45
sudden very sore all hereabout.

HORATIO   My lord, forbear the challenge then.

HAMLET   No, Horatio, not I. If danger be now, why then
it is not to come. There's a predestinate providence in
the fall of a sparrow. Here comes the King.   50

     Enter KING, QUEEN, LEARTES *and* Lords.

KING   Now, son Hamlet, we have laid upon your head,
And make no question but to have the best.

HAMLET   Your majesty hath laid o'the weaker side.

KING   We doubt it not. Deliver them the foils.

HAMLET   First, Leartes, here's my hand and love,   55
Protesting that I never wronged Leartes.

If Hamlet in his madness did amiss
That was not Hamlet but his madness did it.
And all the wrong I e'er did to Leartes
60   I here proclaim was madness.
Therefore let's be at peace and think I have shot
Mine arrow o'er the house and hurt my brother.

LEARTES
Sir, I am satisfied in nature but in terms of honour
I'll stand aloof and will no reconcilement
65   Till by some elder masters of our time
I may be satisfied.

KING   Give them the foils.

HAMLET   I'll be your foil, Leartes. These foils have all a
length. Come on, sir. [*Here they play.*] A hit!

LEARTES   No, none.

70   HAMLET   Judgement?

GENTLEMAN   A hit, a most palpable hit.

LEARTES   Well, come again. [*They play again.*]

HAMLET   Another! Judgement?

LEARTES   Ay, I grant – a touch, a touch.

75   KING   Here, Hamlet, the King doth drink a health to
thee!

QUEEN   Here, Hamlet, take my napkin, wipe thy face.

KING   Give him the wine.

HAMLET   Set it by, I'll have another bout first. I'll drink
80   anon.

QUEEN   Here, Hamlet, thy mother drinks to thee. [*She
drinks.*]

KING   Do not drink, Gertred. [*aside*] O, 'tis the poisoned
cup!

HAMLET   Leartes, come, you dally with me. I pray you
85   pass with your most cunning'st play.

LEARTES   Ay? Say you so? Have at you! I'll hit you now,
my lord. [*aside*] And yet it goes almost against my
conscience.

HAMLET   Come on, sir.
[*They catch one another's rapiers and both are
wounded. Leartes falls down. The Queen falls down.*]

90   KING   Look to the Queen.

QUEEN   O, the drink, the drink! Hamlet, the drink!
[*Dies.*]

HAMLET   Treason, ho! Keep the gates!

LORDS   How is't, my lord Leartes?

LEARTES   Even as a coxcomb should:
95   Foolishly slain with my own weapon. Hamlet,
Thou hast not in thee half an hour of life –
The fatal instrument is in thy hand,
Unbated and envenomed. Thy mother's poisoned.
That drink was made for thee.

HAMLET   The poisoned instrument within my hand?   100
Then venom to thy venom – die damned villain!
Come, drink – here lies thy union, here!
[*The King dies.*]

LEARTES   O, he is justly served.
Hamlet, before I die, here take my hand
And, withal, my love. I do forgive thee.   [*Leartes dies.*]   105

HAMLET   And I thee.
O, I am dead, Horatio, fare thee well.

HORATIO
No, I am more an antique Roman than a Dane.
Here is some poison left.

HAMLET   Upon my love I charge thee let it go.   110
O fie, Horatio. An if thou shouldst die
What a scandal wouldst thou leave behind?
What tongue should tell the story of our deaths
If not from thee? O my heart sinks, Horatio.
Mine eyes have lost their sight, my tongue his use.   115
Farewell, Horatio. Heaven receive my soul.   [*Dies.*]

Enter VOLTEMAR *and the* Ambassadors *from
England. Enter* FORTENBRASSE *with his train.*

FORTENBRASSE   Where is this bloody sight?

HORATIO   If aught of woe or wonder you'd behold
Then look upon this tragic spectacle.

FORTENBRASSE
O imperious Death! How many princes   120
Hast thou at one draught bloodily shot to death?

AMBASSADORS
Our embassy that we have brought from England –
Where be these princes that should hear us speak?
O most unlooked-for time! Unhappy country!

HORATIO
Content yourselves. I'll show to all the ground,   125
The first beginning of this tragedy.
Let there a scaffold be reared up in the market-place
And let the state of the world be there,
Where you shall hear such a sad story told
That never mortal man could more unfold.   130

FORTENBRASSE
I have some rights of memory to this kingdom
Which now to claim my leisure doth invite me.
Let four of our chiefest captains
Bear Hamlet like a soldier to his grave,
For he was likely, had he lived,   135
To ha' proved most royal.
Take up the body. Such a sight as this
Becomes the fields but here doth much amiss.

Exeunt.

The Tragical History of Hamlet, Prince of Denmark

The Second Quarto
(1604–5)

Q2 is the longest text of the play, and the tradition of adding the F-only lines makes it even longer. The conflation of Folio and Quarto texts of *Hamlet* began with one of the earliest editors, Nicholas Rowe, who in 1709 combined readings from the Sixth Quarto (Q6, 1676) and the Fourth Folio (F4, 1685); these later publications derived from Q2 and F respectively and were presumably the most recent texts Rowe had to hand. During the eighteenth and nineteenth centuries editors continued to combine Quarto and Folio readings, and by the 1860s a more or less stable conflated text had evolved, which was only seriously challenged in the 1960s. Editors and theatre practitioners have, however, rarely been content with this stable conflated text, any more than they have with a Q2 or F text alone, and every edition, like every production, tends to be eclectic, taking readings from both traditions according to individual taste as often as scholarly conviction.

HAMLET	*Prince of Denmark*
GHOST	*of Hamlet's father, the late King Hamlet of Denmark*
KING Claudius	*of Denmark, brother of the late King*
QUEEN Gertrude	*Hamlet's mother and his father's widow, now married to King Claudius*
POLONIUS	*King Claudius' councillor*
LAERTES	*Polonius' son*
OPHELIA	*Polonius' daughter*
REYNALDO	*Polonius' man*
FOLLOWERS	*of Laertes*
HORATIO	*Hamlet's friend and fellow student*

ROSENCRANTZ
GUILDENSTERN } *other fellow students*

VOLTEMAND
CORNELIUS } *Danish ambassadors to Norway*

BARNARDO
FRANCISCO } *sentinels*
MARCELLUS

OSRIC	*a courtier*
PLAYERS	*playing* Prologue, Player King, Player Queen *and* Lucianus
GRAVEDIGGER	*a clown*
SECOND MAN	*another clown*
PRIEST	
LORDS	
GENTLEMEN	
MESSENGERS	
SAILORS	

FORTINBRAS	*Prince of Norway*
CAPTAIN	*in Norwegian army*
AMBASSADORS	*from England*

Attendants, Courtiers, Trumpets, Kettledrums, Drums, Officers, Norwegian Soldiers

Hamlet (Q2)

1.1 *Enter* BARNARDO *and* FRANCISCO, *two sentinels.*

BARNARDO   Who's there?

FRANCISCO
    Nay, answer me. Stand and unfold yourself.

BARNARDO   Long live the King.

FRANCISCO   Barnardo?

BARNARDO   He.

FRANCISCO   You come most carefully upon your hour.

BARNARDO
5   'Tis now struck twelve. Get thee to bed, Francisco.

FRANCISCO   For this relief much thanks. 'Tis bitter cold
    And I am sick at heart.

BARNARDO   Have you had quiet guard?

FRANCISCO   Not a mouse stirring.

BARNARDO   Well, goodnight.
10   If you do meet Horatio and Marcellus,
    The rivals of my watch, bid them make haste.

Enter HORATIO *and* MARCELLUS.

FRANCISCO   I think I hear them. Stand ho, who is there?

HORATIO   Friends to this ground.

MARCELLUS   And liegemen to the Dane.

FRANCISCO   Give you goodnight.

MARCELLUS
15   O farewell, honest soldiers; who hath relieved you?

FRANCISCO
    Barnardo hath my place. Give you goodnight.   *Exit.*

MARCELLUS   Holla, Barnardo!

BARNARDO   Say, what, is Horatio there?

HORATIO   A piece of him.

BARNARDO   Welcome Horatio, welcome good Marcellus.

20 HORATIO   What, has this thing appeared again tonight?

BARNARDO   I have seen nothing.

MARCELLUS   Horatio says 'tis but our fantasy
    And will not let belief take hold of him
    Touching this dreaded sight twice seen of us.
25   Therefore I have entreated him along
    With us to watch the minutes of this night
    That, if again this apparition come,
    He may approve our eyes and speak to it.

HORATIO   Tush, tush, 'twill not appear.

BARNARDO   Sit down awhile,
30   And let us once again assail your ears
    That are so fortified against our story
    What we have two nights seen.

HORATIO   Well, sit we down,
    And let us hear Barnardo speak of this.

BARNARDO   Last night of all,
35   When yond same star that's westward from the pole
    Had made his course t'illume that part of heaven
    Where now it burns, Marcellus and myself,
    The bell then beating one –

Enter GHOST.

MARCELLUS
    Peace, break thee off, look where it comes again.

BARNARDO
    In the same figure like the King that's dead.   40

MARCELLUS   Thou art a scholar – speak to it, Horatio.

BARNARDO   Looks 'a not like the King? Mark it, Horatio.

HORATIO
    Most like. It harrows me with fear and wonder.

BARNARDO   It would be spoke to.

MARCELLUS   Speak to it, Horatio.

HORATIO
    What art thou that usurp'st this time of night   45
    Together with that fair and warlike form
    In which the majesty of buried Denmark
    Did sometimes march? By heaven, I charge thee speak.

MARCELLUS   It is offended.

BARNARDO   See, it stalks away.

HORATIO   Stay, speak, speak, I charge thee speak.   50

Exit Ghost.

MARCELLUS   'Tis gone and will not answer.

BARNARDO
    How now, Horatio, you tremble and look pale.
    Is not this something more than fantasy?
    What think you on't?

HORATIO   Before my God, I might not this believe   55
    Without the sensible and true avouch
    Of mine own eyes.

MARCELLUS   Is it not like the King?

HORATIO   As thou art to thyself.
    Such was the very armour he had on
    When he the ambitious Norway combated.   60
    So frowned he once, when in an angry parle
    He smote the sledded Polacks on the ice.
    'Tis strange.

MARCELLUS
    Thus twice before, and jump at this dead hour,
    With martial stalk hath he gone by our watch.   65

HORATIO
    In what particular thought to work, I know not,
    But in the gross and scope of mine opinion
    This bodes some strange eruption to our state.

MARCELLUS
    Good now, sit down, and tell me he that knows
    Why this same strict and most observant watch   70
    So nightly toils the subject of the land,
    And with such daily cost of brazen cannon
    And foreign mart for implements of war,
    Why such impress of shipwrights, whose sore task
    Does not divide the Sunday from the week.   75
    What might be toward that this sweaty haste
    Doth make the night joint labourer with the day?
    Who is't that can inform me?

HORATIO   That can I.
    At least the whisper goes so. Our last King,
    Whose image even but now appeared to us,   80
    Was as you know by Fortinbras of Norway –
    Thereto pricked on by a most emulate pride –
    Dared to the combat, in which our valiant Hamlet
    (For so this side of our known world esteemed him)

85　Did slay this Fortinbras, who by a sealed compact	Stop it, Marcellus!
Well ratified by law and heraldry	MARCELLUS　Shall I strike it with my partisan?
Did forfeit with his life all these his lands	HORATIO　Do, if it will not stand.
Which he stood seized of to the conqueror;	BARNARDO　　　'Tis here.
Against the which a moiety competent	HORATIO　　　　　　'Tis here.　*Exit Ghost.*　140
90　Was gaged by our King, which had return	MARCELLUS　'Tis gone.
To the inheritance of Fortinbras	We do it wrong being so majestical
Had he been vanquisher, as by the same co-mart	To offer it the show of violence,
And carriage of the article design	For it is as the air, invulnerable,
His fell to Hamlet. Now, sir, young Fortinbras,	And our vain blows malicious mockery.　145
95　Of unimproved mettle, hot and full,	BARNARDO　It was about to speak when the cock crew.
Hath in the skirts of Norway here and there	HORATIO　And then it started like a guilty thing
Sharked up a list of lawless resolutes	Upon a fearful summons. I have heard
For food and diet to some enterprise	The cock that is the trumpet to the morn
That hath a stomach in't, which is no other,	Doth with his lofty and shrill-sounding throat　150
100　As it doth well appear unto our state,	Awake the god of day and, at his warning,
But to recover of us by strong hand	Whether in sea or fire, in earth or air,
And terms compulsatory those foresaid lands	Th'extravagant and erring spirit hies
So by his father lost. And this, I take it,	To his confine – and of the truth herein
Is the main motive of our preparations,	This present object made probation.　155
105　The source of this our watch, and the chief head	MARCELLUS　It faded on the crowing of the cock.
Of this post-haste and rummage in the land.	Some say that ever 'gainst that season comes
BARNARDO　I think it be no other but e'en so.	Wherein our Saviour's birth is celebrated
Well may it sort that this portentous figure	This bird of dawning singeth all night long,
Comes armed through our watch so like the King	And then, they say, no spirit dare stir abroad,　160
110　That was and is the question of these wars.	The nights are wholesome, then no planets strike,
HORATIO　A mote it is to trouble the mind's eye.	No fairy takes, nor witch hath power to charm,
In the most high and palmy state of Rome	So hallowed and so gracious is that time.
A little ere the mightiest Julius fell	HORATIO　So have I heard and do in part believe it.
The graves stood tenantless and the sheeted dead	But look, the morn in russet mantle clad　165
115　Did squeak and gibber in the Roman streets;	Walks o'er the dew of yon high eastward hill.
At stars with trains of fire and dews of blood,	Break we our watch up and by my advice
Disasters in the sun; and the moist star	Let us impart what we have seen tonight
Upon whose influence Neptune's empire stands	Unto young Hamlet, for upon my life
Was sick almost to doomsday with eclipse.	This spirit dumb to us will speak to him.　170
120　And even the like precurse of feared events,	Do you consent we shall acquaint him with it
As harbingers preceding still the fates	As needful in our loves, fitting our duty?
And prologue to the omen coming on,	MARCELLUS
Have heaven and earth together demonstrated	Let's do't, I pray, and I this morning know
Unto our climatures and countrymen.	Where we shall find him most convenient.　*Exeunt.*
Enter GHOST.	1.2　*Flourish. Enter* Claudius, KING *of Denmark,*
	Gertrude *the* QUEEN, *Council – as* POLONIUS
125　But soft, behold, lo where it comes again;	*and his son* LAERTES *and* HAMLET, *with others*
I'll cross it though it blast me. Stay, illusion.	*including* VOLTEMAND *and* CORNELIUS.
[*It spreads his arms.*]	
If thou hast any sound or use of voice,	KING　Though yet of Hamlet our dear brother's death
Speak to me.	The memory be green, and that it us befitted
If there be any good thing to be done	To bear our hearts in grief, and our whole kingdom
130　That may to thee do ease and grace to me,	To be contracted in one brow of woe,
Speak to me.	Yet so far hath discretion fought with nature　5
If thou art privy to thy country's fate	That we with wisest sorrow think on him
Which happily foreknowing may avoid,	Together with remembrance of ourselves.
O, speak.	Therefore our sometime sister, now our Queen,
135　Or if thou hast uphoarded in thy life	Th'imperial jointress to this warlike state,
Extorted treasure in the womb of earth –	Have we, as 'twere with a defeated joy,　10
For which they say your spirits oft walk in death –	With an auspicious and a dropping eye,
Speak of it, stay and speak.　[*The cock crows.*]	

With mirth in funeral and with dirge in marriage,
In equal scale weighing delight and dole,
Taken to wife. Nor have we herein barred
Your better wisdoms, which have freely gone
With this affair along. For all, our thanks.
Now follows that you know: young Fortinbras,
Holding a weak supposal of our worth
Or thinking by our late dear brother's death
Our state to be disjoint and out of frame –
Co-leagued with this dream of his advantage –
He hath not failed to pester us with message
Importing the surrender of those lands
Lost by his father with all bands of law
To our most valiant brother. So much for him.
Now for ourself, and for this time of meeting,
Thus much the business is: we have here writ
To Norway, uncle of young Fortinbras –
Who impotent and bedrid scarcely hears
Of this his nephew's purpose – to suppress
His further gait herein, in that the levies,
The lists and full proportions are all made
Out of his subject; and we here dispatch
You, good Cornelius, and you, Voltemand,
For bearers of this greeting to old Norway,
Giving to you no further personal power
To business with the King more than the scope
Of these delated articles allow.
Farewell, and let your haste commend your duty.

CORNELIUS, VOLTEMAND
    In that and all things will we show our duty.
KING   We doubt it nothing. Heartily farewell.
                        Exeunt Voltemand and Cornelius.
    And now, Laertes, what's the news with you?
    You told us of some suit – what is't, Laertes?
    You cannot speak of reason to the Dane
    And lose your voice. What wouldst thou beg,
        Laertes,
    That shall not be my offer, not thy asking?
    The head is not more native to the heart,
    The hand more instrumental to the mouth,
    Than is the throne of Denmark to thy father.
    What wouldst thou have, Laertes?

LAERTES   My dread lord,
    Your leave and favour to return to France,
    From whence though willingly I came to Denmark
    To show my duty in your coronation,
    Yet now I must confess, that duty done,
    My thoughts and wishes bend again toward France
    And bow them to your gracious leave and pardon.
KING
    Have you your father's leave? What says Polonius?
POLONIUS
    He hath, my lord, wrung from me my slow leave
    By laboursome petition, and at last
    Upon his will I sealed my hard consent.
    I do beseech you give him leave to go.
KING   Take thy fair hour, Laertes, time be thine

And thy best graces spend it at thy will.
But now, my cousin Hamlet, and my son –
HAMLET   A little more than kin, and less than kind.   65
KING   How is it that the clouds still hang on you?
HAMLET
    Not so much, my lord, I am too much in the 'son'.
QUEEN   Good Hamlet, cast thy nighted colour off
    And let thine eye look like a friend on Denmark.
    Do not for ever with thy vailed lids   70
    Seek for thy noble father in the dust.
    Thou knowst 'tis common all that lives must die,
    Passing through nature to eternity.
HAMLET   Ay, madam, it is common.
QUEEN   If it be
    Why seems it so particular with thee?   75
HAMLET
    'Seems', madam – nay it is, I know not 'seems'.
    'Tis not alone my inky cloak, cold mother,
    Nor customary suits of solemn black,
    Nor windy suspiration of forced breath,
    No, nor the fruitful river in the eye,   80
    Nor the dejected haviour of the visage,
    Together with all forms, moods, shapes of grief,
    That can denote me truly. These indeed 'seem',
    For they are actions that a man might play,
    But I have that within which passes show,   85
    These but the trappings and the suits of woe.
KING
    'Tis sweet and commendable in your nature, Hamlet,
    To give these mourning duties to your father,
    But you must know your father lost a father,
    That father lost lost his, and the survivor bound   90
    In filial obligation for some term
    To do obsequious sorrow; but to persever
    In obstinate condolement is a course
    Of impious stubbornness, 'tis unmanly grief,
    It shows a will most incorrect to heaven,   95
    A heart unfortified, or mind impatient,
    An understanding simple and unschooled;
    For what we know must be, and is as common
    As any the most vulgar thing to sense –
    Why should we in our peevish opposition   100
    Take it to heart? Fie, 'tis a fault to heaven,
    A fault against the dead, a fault to nature,
    To reason most absurd, whose common theme
    Is death of fathers, and who still hath cried
    From the first corpse till he that died today   105
    'This must be so.' We pray you throw to earth
    This unprevailing woe, and think of us
    As of a father, for let the world take note
    You are the most immediate to our throne,
    And with no less nobility of love   110
    Than that which dearest father bears his son
    Do I impart toward you. For your intent
    In going back to school in Wittenberg
    It is most retrograde to our desire,
    And we beseech you bend you to remain   115

Here in the cheer and comfort of our eye,
Our chiefest courtier, cousin, and our son.
QUEEN   Let not thy mother lose her prayers, Hamlet.
I pray thee stay with us, go not to Wittenberg.
120   HAMLET   I shall in all my best obey you, madam.
KING   Why, 'tis a loving and a fair reply.
Be as ourself in Denmark. Madam, come –
This gentle and unforced accord of Hamlet
Sits smiling to my heart, in grace whereof
125   No jocund health that Denmark drinks today
But the great cannon to the clouds shall tell
And the King's rouse the heaven shall bruit again,
Re-speaking earthly thunder. Come away.
                    Flourish. Exeunt all but Hamlet.
HAMLET   O that this too too sallied flesh would melt,
130   Thaw and resolve itself into a dew,
Or that the Everlasting had not fixed
His canon 'gainst self-slaughter. O God, God,
How weary, stale, flat and unprofitable
Seem to me all the uses of this world!
135   Fie on't, ah, fie, 'tis an unweeded garden
That grows to seed, things rank and gross in nature
Possess it merely. That it should come thus:
But two months dead – nay not so much, not two –
So excellent a king, that was to this
140   Hyperion to a satyr, so loving to my mother
That he might not beteem the winds of heaven
Visit her face too roughly. Heaven and earth,
Must I remember? Why, she should hang on him
As if increase of appetite had grown
145   By what it fed on. And yet within a month
(Let me not think on't – Frailty, thy name is Woman),
A little month, or e'er those shoes were old
With which she followed my poor father's body,
Like Niobe, all tears. Why, she –
150   O God, a beast that wants discourse of reason
Would have mourned longer – married with my uncle,
My father's brother (but no more like my father
Than I to Hercules). Within a month,
Ere yet the salt of most unrighteous tears
155   Had left the flushing in her galled eyes,
She married. O most wicked speed! To post
With such dexterity to incestuous sheets,
It is not, nor it cannot come to good;
But break, my heart, for I must hold my tongue.

Enter HORATIO, MARCELLUS *and* BARNARDO.

HORATIO
Hail to your lordship.
160   HAMLET   I am glad to see you well –
Horatio, or I do forget myself.
HORATIO
The same, my lord, and your poor servant ever.
HAMLET
Sir, my good friend, I'll change that name with you.
And what make you from Wittenberg, Horatio?
Marcellus!

MARCELLUS   My good lord.   165
HAMLET
I am very glad to see you. [*to Barnardo*] Good even,
    sir. –
But what in faith make you from Wittenberg?
HORATIO   A truant disposition, good my lord.
HAMLET   I would not hear your enemy say so,
Nor shall you do my ear that violence   170
To make it truster of your own report
Against yourself. I know you are no truant;
But what is your affair in Elsinore?
We'll teach you for to drink ere you depart.
HORATIO   My lord, I came to see your father's funeral.   175
HAMLET   I prithee do not mock me, fellow student,
I think it was to see my mother's wedding.
HORATIO   Indeed, my lord, it followed hard upon.
HAMLET
Thrift, thrift, Horatio, the funeral baked meats
Did coldly furnish forth the marriage tables.   180
Would I had met my dearest foe in heaven
Or ever I had seen that day, Horatio.
My father, methinks I see my father.
HORATIO   Where, my lord?
HAMLET   In my mind's eye, Horatio.
HORATIO   I saw him once – 'a was a goodly king.   185
HAMLET   'A was a man, take him for all in all,
I shall not look upon his like again.
HORATIO   My lord, I think I saw him yesternight.
HAMLET   Saw, who?
HORATIO   My lord, the King your father.
HAMLET   The King my father?   190
HORATIO   Season your admiration for a while
With an attent ear till I may deliver
Upon the witness of these gentlemen
This marvel to you.
HAMLET   For God's love let me hear!
HORATIO   Two nights together had these gentlemen,   195
Marcellus and Barnardo, on their watch
In the dead waste and middle of the night
Been thus encountered: a figure like your father
Armed at point, exactly cap-à-pie,
Appears before them and with solemn march   200
Goes slow and stately by them; thrice he walked
By their oppressed and fear-surprised eyes
Within his truncheon's length whilst they, distilled
Almost to jelly with the act of fear,
Stand dumb and speak not to him. This to me   205
In dreadful secrecy impart they did,
And I with them the third night kept the watch
Where, as they had delivered, both in time,
Form of the thing, each word made true and good,
The apparition comes. I knew your father,   210
These hands are not more like.
HAMLET   But where was this?
MARCELLUS
My lord, upon the platform where we watch.
HAMLET   Did you not speak to it?

HORATIO   My lord, I did,
But answer made it none. Yet once methought
215   It lifted up it head and did address
Itself to motion like as it would speak.
But even then the morning cock crew loud
And at the sound it shrunk in haste away
And vanished from our sight.
HAMLET   'Tis very strange.
220   HORATIO   As I do live, my honoured lord, 'tis true,
And we did think it writ down in our duty
To let you know of it.
HAMLET   Indeed, sirs, but this troubles me.
Hold you the watch tonight?
HORATIO, MARCELLUS, BARNARDO   We do, my lord.
HAMLET   Armed, say you?
225   HORATIO, MARCELLUS, BARNARDO   Armed, my lord.
HAMLET   From top to toe?
HORATIO, MARCELLUS, BARNARDO
                                My lord, from head to foot.
HAMLET   Then saw you not his face.
HORATIO   O yes, my lord, he wore his beaver up.
HAMLET   What looked he – frowningly?
HORATIO
230   A countenance more in sorrow than in anger.
HAMLET   Pale, or red?
HORATIO   Nay, very pale.
HAMLET   And fixed his eyes upon you?
HORATIO   Most constantly.
HAMLET   I would I had been there.
HORATIO   It would have much amazed you.
HAMLET   Very like.
235   Stayed it long?
HORATIO
While one with moderate haste might tell a hundred.
MARCELLUS, BARNARDO   Longer, longer.
HORATIO   Not when I saw't.
HAMLET   His beard was grizzled, no?
HORATIO   It was as I have seen it in his life:
A sable silvered.
240   HAMLET   I will watch tonight.
Perchance 'twill walk again.
HORATIO   I warrant it will.
HAMLET   If it assume my noble father's person
I'll speak to it, though hell itself should gape
And bid me hold my peace. I pray you all,
245   If you have hitherto concealed this sight
Let it be tenable in your silence still
And whatsomever else shall hap tonight
Give it an understanding but no tongue,
I will requite your loves. So, fare you well.
250   Upon the platform 'twixt eleven and twelve
I'll visit you.
HORATIO, MARCELLUS, BARNARDO
                Our duty to your honour.
HAMLET   Your loves, as mine to you, farewell.
                                Exeunt all but Hamlet.
My father's spirit – in arms! All is not well;

I doubt some foul play. Would the night were come.
Till then sit still my soul – foul deeds will rise   255
Though all the earth o'erwhelm them to men's eyes.
                                                Exit.

1.3   *Enter* LAERTES *and* OPHELIA *his sister.*

LAERTES   My necessaries are embarked; farewell.
And sister, as the winds give benefit
And convey is assistant, do not sleep
But let me hear from you.
OPHELIA   Do you doubt that?
LAERTES   For Hamlet and the trifling of his favour,   5
Hold it a fashion and a toy in blood,
A violet in the youth of primy nature,
Forward, not permanent, sweet, not lasting,
The perfume and suppliance of a minute,
No more.
OPHELIA   No more but so.
LAERTES   Think it no more.   10
For nature crescent does not grow alone
In thews and bulks, but as this temple waxes
The inward service of the mind and soul
Grows wide withal. Perhaps he loves you now,
And now no soil nor cautel doth besmirch   15
The virtue of his will; but you must fear,
His greatness weighed, his will is not his own.
He may not, as unvalued persons do,
Carve for himself, for on his choice depends
The safety and health of this whole state,   20
And therefore must his choice be circumscribed
Unto the voice and yielding of that body
Whereof he is the head. Then if he says he loves you
It fits your wisdom so far to believe it
As he in his particular act and place   25
May give his saying deed, which is no further
Than the main voice of Denmark goes withal.
Then weigh what loss your honour may sustain
If with too credent ear you list his songs
Or lose your heart, or your chaste treasure open   30
To his unmastered importunity.
Fear it, Ophelia, fear it, my dear sister,
And keep you in the rear of your affection
Out of the shot and danger of desire.
The chariest maid is prodigal enough   35
If she unmask her beauty to the moon.
Virtue itself scapes not calumnious strokes.
The canker galls the infants of the spring
Too oft before their buttons be disclosed,
And in the morn and liquid dew of youth   40
Contagious blastments are most imminent.
Be wary then: best safety lies in fear,
Youth to itself rebels, though none else near.
OPHELIA   I shall the effect of this good lesson keep
As watchman to my heart. But, good my brother,   45
Do not as some ungracious pastors do
Show me the steep and thorny way to heaven

Whiles, a puffed and reckless libertine,
Himself the primrose path of dalliance treads
And recks not his own rede.

50 LAERTES   O fear me not.
I stay too long.

Enter POLONIUS.

But here my father comes.
A double blessing is a double grace:
Occasion smiles upon a second leave.

POLONIUS
Yet here, Laertes? Aboard, aboard for shame!
55 The wind sits in the shoulder of your sail
And you are stayed for. There, my blessing with thee,
And these few precepts in thy memory
Look thou character: give thy thoughts no tongue
Nor any unproportioned thought his act.
60 Be thou familiar but by no means vulgar;
Those friends thou hast, and their adoption tried,
Grapple them unto thy soul with hoops of steel,
But do not dull thy palm with entertainment
Of each new-hatched, unfledged courage. Beware
65 Of entrance to a quarrel but, being in,
Bear't that th'opposed may beware of thee.
Give every man thy ear but few thy voice;
Take each man's censure but reserve thy judgement.
Costly thy habit as thy purse can buy
70 But not expressed in fancy – rich, not gaudy;
For the apparel oft proclaims the man
And they in France of the best rank and station
Are of all most select and generous chief in that.
Neither a borrower nor a lender, boy,
75 For loan oft loses both itself and friend
And borrowing dulleth th'edge of husbandry.
This above all, to thine own self be true
And it must follow as the night the day
Thou canst not then be false to any man.
80 Farewell, my blessing season this in thee.
LAERTES   Most humbly do I take my leave, my lord.
POLONIUS
The time invests you. Go, your servants tend.
LAERTES   Farewell, Ophelia, and remember well
What I have said to you.
OPHELIA   'Tis in my memory locked
85 And you yourself shall keep the key of it.
LAERTES   Farewell.   *Exit.*
POLONIUS   What is't, Ophelia, he hath said to you?
OPHELIA
So please you, something touching the Lord Hamlet.
POLONIUS   Marry, well bethought:
90 'Tis told me he hath very oft of late
Given private time to you, and you yourself
Have of your audience been most free and bounteous.
If it be so – as so 'tis put on me,
And that in way of caution – I must tell you
95 You do not understand yourself so clearly
As it behoves my daughter and your honour.

What is between you? Give me up the truth.
OPHELIA   He hath, my lord, of late made many tenders
Of his affection to me.
POLONIUS   Affection? Pooh, you speak like a green girl   100
Unsifted in such perilous circumstance.
Do you believe his 'tenders', as you call them?
OPHELIA   I do not know, my lord, what I should think.
POLONIUS
Marry, I will teach you; think yourself a baby
That you have ta'en these tenders for true pay   105
Which are not sterling. Tender yourself more dearly
Or – not to crack the wind of the poor phrase,
Wronging it thus – you'll tender me a fool.
OPHELIA   My lord, he hath importuned me with love
In honourable fashion.   110
POLONIUS   Ay, 'fashion' you may call it. Go to, go to.
OPHELIA
And hath given countenance to his speech, my lord,
With almost all the holy vows of heaven.
POLONIUS
Ay, springes to catch woodcocks – I do know
When the blood burns how prodigal the soul   115
Lends the tongue vows. These blazes, daughter,
Giving more light than heat, extinct in both
Even in their promise as it is a-making,
You must not take for fire. From this time
Be something scanter of your maiden presence;   120
Set your entreatments at a higher rate
Than a command to parle. For Lord Hamlet,
Believe so much in him that he is young
And with a larger tether may he walk
Than may be given you. In few, Ophelia,   125
Do not believe his vows, for they are brokers
Not of that dye which their investments show
But mere implorators of unholy suits
Breathing like sanctified and pious bonds
The better to beguile. This is for all;   130
I would not in plain terms from this time forth
Have you so slander any moment leisure
As to give words or talk with the Lord Hamlet.
Look to't, I charge you. Come your ways.
OPHELIA   I shall obey, my lord.   *Exeunt.*   135

1.4   *Enter* HAMLET, HORATIO *and* MARCELLUS.

HAMLET   The air bites shrewdly; it is very cold.
HORATIO   It is nipping, and an eager air.
HAMLET   What hour now?
HORATIO   I think it lacks of twelve.
MARCELLUS   No, it is struck.
HORATIO   Indeed, I heard it not.
It then draws near the season   5
Wherein the spirit held his wont to walk.
            [*A flourish of trumpets and two pieces goes off.*]
What does this mean, my lord?
HAMLET
The King doth wake tonight and takes his rouse,

Keeps wassail and the swaggering upspring reels,
10 And as he drains his draughts of Rhenish down
The kettledrum and trumpet thus bray out
The triumph of his pledge.

HORATIO   Is it a custom?

HAMLET   Ay, marry is't,
But to my mind, though I am native here
15 And to the manner born, it is a custom
More honoured in the breach than the observance.
This heavy-headed revel east and west
Makes us traduced and taxed of other nations:
They clepe us drunkards and with swinish phrase
20 Soil our addition, and indeed it takes
From our achievements, though performed at height,
The pith and marrow of our attribute.
So oft it chances in particular men
That, for some vicious mole of nature in them,
25 As in their birth wherein they are not guilty
(Since nature cannot choose his origin),
By their o'ergrowth of some complexion
Oft breaking down the pales and forts of reason,
Or by some habit that too much o'erleavens
30 The form of plausive manners – that these men,
Carrying, I say, the stamp of one defect
(Being Nature's livery or Fortune's star),
His virtues else, be they as pure as grace,
As infinite as man may undergo,
35 Shall in the general censure take corruption
From that particular fault: the dram of eale
Doth all the noble substance of a doubt
To his own scandal –

Enter GHOST.

HORATIO   Look, my lord, it comes.

HAMLET   Angels and ministers of grace defend us!
40 Be thou a spirit of health or goblin damned,
Bring with thee airs from heaven or blasts from hell,
Be thy intents wicked or charitable,
Thou com'st in such a questionable shape
That I will speak to thee. I'll call thee Hamlet,
45 King, father, royal Dane. O answer me,
Let me not burst in ignorance but tell
Why thy canonized bones hearsed in death
Have burst their cerements, why the sepulchre
Wherein we saw thee quietly interred
50 Hath oped his ponderous and marble jaws
To cast thee up again. What may this mean
That thou, dead corpse, again in complete steel,
Revisits thus the glimpses of the moon,
Making night hideous, and we fools of nature
55 So horridly to shake our disposition
With thoughts beyond the reaches of our souls?
Say why is this? Wherefore? What should we do?
     [*Ghost beckons.*]

HORATIO   It beckons you to go away with it
As if it some impartment did desire
To you alone.

MARCELLUS   Look with what courteous action   60
It waves you to a more removed ground,
But do not go with it.

HORATIO   No, by no means.

HAMLET   It will not speak: then I will follow it.

HORATIO   Do not, my lord.

HAMLET   Why, what should be the fear?
I do not set my life at a pin's fee,   65
And for my soul – what can it do to that,
Being a thing immortal as itself?
It waves me forth again. I'll follow it.

HORATIO
What if it tempt you toward the flood, my lord,
Or to the dreadful summit of the cliff   70
That beetles o'er his base into the sea,
And there assume some other horrible form
Which might deprive your sovereignty of reason
And draw you into madness? Think of it:
The very place puts toys of desperation   75
Without more motive into every brain
That looks so many fathoms to the sea
And hears it roar beneath.

HAMLET   It waves me still.
Go on, I'll follow thee.

MARCELLUS   You shall not go, my lord.

HAMLET   Hold off your hands.   80

HORATIO   Be ruled, you shall not go.

HAMLET   My fate cries out
And makes each petty artery in this body
As hardy as the Nemean lion's nerve.
Still am I called – unhand me, gentlemen –
By heaven I'll make a ghost of him that lets me! 85
I say away! – Go on! I'll follow thee.

                       Exeunt Ghost and Hamlet.

HORATIO   He waxes desperate with imagination.

MARCELLUS   Let's follow. 'Tis not fit thus to obey him.

HORATIO   Have after. To what issue will this come?

MARCELLUS
Something is rotten in the state of Denmark.   90

HORATIO   Heaven will direct it.

MARCELLUS   Nay, let's follow him.   *Exeunt.*

1.5   *Enter* GHOST *and* HAMLET.

HAMLET
Whither wilt thou lead me? Speak! I'll go no further.

GHOST   Mark me.

HAMLET   I will.

GHOST   My hour is almost come
When I to sulphurous and tormenting flames
Must render up myself.

HAMLET   Alas, poor ghost.

GHOST   Pity me not, but lend thy serious hearing   5
To what I shall unfold.

HAMLET   Speak, I am bound to hear.

GHOST   So art thou to revenge when thou shalt hear.

HAMLET   What?

GHOST   I am thy father's spirit,

10   Doomed for a certain term to walk the night

And for the day confined to fast in fires

Till the foul crimes done in my days of nature

Are burnt and purged away. But that I am forbid

To tell the secrets of my prison-house

15   I could a tale unfold whose lightest word

Would harrow up thy soul, freeze thy young blood,

Make thy two eyes like stars start from their spheres,

Thy knotted and combined locks to part

And each particular hair to stand on end

20   Like quills upon the fearful porpentine –

But this eternal blazon must not be

To ears of flesh and blood. List, list, O list,

If thou didst ever thy dear father love –

HAMLET   O God!

GHOST

25   – Revenge his foul and most unnatural murder!

HAMLET   Murder!

GHOST   Murder most foul – as in the best it is –

But this most foul, strange and unnatural.

HAMLET   Haste me to know't that I with wings as swift

30   As meditation or the thoughts of love

May sweep to my revenge.

GHOST   I find thee apt.

And duller shouldst thou be than the fat weed

That roots itself in ease on Lethe wharf

Wouldst thou not stir in this. Now, Hamlet, hear:

35   'Tis given out that, sleeping in my orchard,

A serpent stung me. So the whole ear of Denmark

Is by a forged process of my death

Rankly abused. But know, thou noble youth,

The serpent that did sting thy father's life

Now wears his crown.

40   HAMLET   O my prophetic soul!

My uncle!

GHOST   Ay, that incestuous, that adulterate beast,

With witchcraft of his wits, with traitorous gifts –

O wicked wit and gifts that have the power

45   So to seduce – won to his shameful lust

The will of my most seeming-virtuous Queen.

O Hamlet, what falling off was there,

From me whose love was of that dignity

That it went hand in hand even with the vow

50   I made to her in marriage, and to decline

Upon a wretch whose natural gifts were poor

To those of mine.

But Virtue, as it never will be moved

Though Lewdness court it in a shape of heaven,

55   So Lust, though to a radiant angel linked,

Will sate itself in a celestial bed

And prey on garbage.

But soft, methinks I scent the morning air.

Brief let me be. Sleeping within my orchard –

60   My custom always of the afternoon –

Upon my secure hour thy uncle stole

With juice of cursed hebona in a vial

And in the porches of my ears did pour

The leperous distilment whose effect

65   Holds such an enmity with blood of man

That swift as quicksilver it courses through

The natural gates and alleys of the body

And with a sudden vigour it doth possess

And curd like eager droppings into milk

70   The thin and wholesome blood. So did it mine

And a most instant tetter barked about

Most lazar-like with vile and loathsome crust

All my smooth body.

Thus was I sleeping by a brother's hand

75   Of life, of crown, of queen at once dispatched,

Cut off even in the blossoms of my sin,

Unhouseled, disappointed, unaneled,

No reckoning made but sent to my account

With all my imperfections on my head.

80   O horrible, O horrible, most horrible!

If thou hast nature in thee bear it not,

Let not the royal bed of Denmark be

A couch for luxury and damned incest.

But howsomever thou pursues this act

85   Taint not thy mind nor let thy soul contrive

Against thy mother aught; leave her to heaven

And to those thorns that in her bosom lodge

To prick and sting her. Fare thee well at once:

The glow-worm shows the matin to be near

90   And 'gins to pale his uneffectual fire.

Adieu, adieu, adieu, remember me.   *Exit.*

HAMLET

O all you host of heaven, O earth – what else? –

And shall I couple hell? O fie! Hold, hold, my heart,

And you, my sinews, grow not instant old

95   But bear me swiftly up. Remember thee?

Ay, thou poor ghost, whiles memory holds a seat

In this distracted globe. Remember thee?

Yea, from the table of my memory

I'll wipe away all trivial fond records,

100   All saws of books, all forms, all pressures past

That youth and observation copied there

And thy commandment all alone shall live

Within the book and volume of my brain

Unmixed with baser matter. Yes, by heaven,

105   O most pernicious woman,

O villain, villain, smiling damned villain,

My tables! Meet it is I set it down

That one may smile and smile and be a villain –

At least I am sure it may be so in Denmark.

110   So, uncle, there you are. Now to my word.

It is 'Adieu, adieu, remember me.'

I have sworn't.

Enter HORATIO *and* MARCELLUS.

HORATIO   My lord, my lord!

MARCELLUS   Lord Hamlet!

HORATIO   Heavens secure him!

HAMLET   So be it.

MARCELLUS   Illo, ho, ho, my lord!

115 HAMLET   Hillo, ho, ho, boy, come and come!

MARCELLUS   How is't, my noble lord?

HORATIO   What news, my lord?

HAMLET   O, wonderful.

HORATIO   Good my lord, tell it.

HAMLET   No, you will reveal it.

HORATIO   Not I, my lord, by heaven.

MARCELLUS   Nor I, my lord.

HAMLET

120   How say you then – would heart of man once think it? –
    But you'll be secret?

HORATIO, MARCELLUS   Ay, by heaven.

HAMLET

    There's never a villain dwelling in all Denmark
    But he's an arrant knave.

HORATIO

    There needs no ghost, my lord, come from the grave
    To tell us this.

125 HAMLET   Why, right, you are in the right!
    And so without more circumstance at all
    I hold it fit that we shake hands and part –
    You as your business and desire shall point you
    (For every man hath business and desire
130   Such as it is) and for my own poor part
    I will go pray.

HORATIO

    These are but wild and whirling words, my lord.

HAMLET   I am sorry they offend you – heartily,
    Yes, faith, heartily.

HORATIO   There's no offence, my lord.

135 HAMLET   Yes, by Saint Patrick, but there is, Horatio,
    And much offence too. Touching this vision here
    It is an honest ghost – that let me tell you.
    For your desire to know what is between us
    O'ermaster it as you may. And now, good friends,
140   As you are friends, scholars and soldiers,
    Give me one poor request.

HORATIO   What is't, my lord? We will.

HAMLET

    Never make known what you have seen tonight.

HORATIO, MARCELLUS

    My lord, we will not.

HAMLET   Nay, but swear't.

145 HORATIO   In faith, my lord, not I.

MARCELLUS   Nor I, my lord, in faith.

HAMLET   Upon my sword.

MARCELLUS   We have sworn, my lord, already.

HAMLET   Indeed, upon my sword, indeed.

GHOST [*Cries under the stage.*]
    Swear.

HAMLET

150   Ha, ha, boy, sayst thou so? Art thou there, truepenny?
    Come on, you hear this fellow in the cellarage?
    Consent to swear.

HORATIO   Propose the oath, my lord.

HAMLET   Never to speak of this that you have seen,

Swear by my sword.

GHOST   Swear. 155

HAMLET   *Hic et ubique?* Then we'll shift our ground.
    Come hither, gentlemen, and lay your hands
    Again upon my sword. Swear by my sword
    Never to speak of this that you have heard.

GHOST   Swear by his sword. 160

HAMLET
    Well said, old mole, canst work i'th' earth so fast?
    A worthy pioner! Once more remove, good friends.

HORATIO   O day and night, but this is wondrous strange.

HAMLET   And therefore as a stranger give it welcome:
    There are more things in heaven and earth, Horatio, 165
    Than are dreamt of in your philosophy. But come,
    Here as before: never – so help you mercy,
    How strange or odd some'er I bear myself
    (As I perchance hereafter shall think meet
    To put an antic disposition on) – 170
    That you at such times seeing me never shall
    With arms encumbered thus, or this headshake,
    Or by pronouncing of some doubtful phrase
    As 'Well, well, we know', or 'We could an if we would',
    Or 'If we list to speak', or 'There be an if they might', 175
    Or such ambiguous giving out to note
    That you know aught of me. This do swear,
    So grace and mercy at your most need help you.

GHOST   Swear.

HAMLET   Rest, rest, perturbed spirit. So, gentlemen, 180
    With all my love I do commend me to you,
    And what so poor a man as Hamlet is
    May do t'express his love and friending to you
    God willing shall not lack. Let us go in together
    And still your fingers on your lips, I pray. 185
    The time is out of joint; O cursed spite
    That ever I was born to set it right!
    Nay, come, let's go together.   *Exeunt.*

2.1   *Enter old* POLONIUS *with his man*
    REYNALDO *or two.*

POLONIUS
    Give him this money and these notes, Reynaldo.

REYNALDO   I will, my lord.

POLONIUS
    You shall do marvellous wisely, good Reynaldo,
    Before you visit him to make inquire
    Of his behaviour.

REYNALDO   My lord, I did intend it. 5

POLONIUS
    Marry, well said, very well said. Look you, sir,
    Inquire me first what Danskers are in Paris,
    And how, and who, what means, and where they keep,
    What company, at what expense, and finding
    By this encompassment and drift of question 10
    That they do know my son, come you more nearer
    Than your particular demands will touch it;
    Take you as 'twere some distant knowledge of him,

As thus, 'I know his father and his friends

15 And in part him' – do you mark this, Reynaldo?

REYNALDO   Ay, very well, my lord.

POLONIUS

'And in part him, but', you may say, 'not well.

But if 't be he I mean he's very wild,

Addicted so and so', and there put on him

20 What forgeries you please. Marry, none so rank

As may dishonour him – take heed of that –

But, sir, such wanton, wild and usual slips

As are companions noted and most known

To youth and liberty.

REYNALDO   As gaming, my lord?

25 POLONIUS   Ay, or drinking, fencing, swearing,

Quarrelling, drabbing – you may go so far.

REYNALDO   My lord, that would dishonour him.

POLONIUS   Faith, as you may season it in the charge.

You must not put another scandal on him

30 That he is open to incontinency –

That's not my meaning – but breathe his faults so

quaintly

That they may seem the taints of liberty,

The flash and outbreak of a fiery mind,

A savageness in unreclaimed blood

Of general assault.

35 REYNALDO   But my good lord –

POLONIUS   Wherefore should you do this?

REYNALDO   Ay, my lord,

I would know that.

POLONIUS   Marry, sir, here's my drift –

And I believe it is a fetch of wit –

You laying these slight sallies on my son

40 As 'twere a thing a little soiled with working,

Mark you, your party in converse (him you would sound)

Having ever seen in the prenominate crimes

The youth you breathe of guilty, be assured

He closes with you in this consequence:

45 'Good sir' (or so), or 'friend' or 'gentleman',

According to the phrase or the addition

Of man and country.

REYNALDO   Very good, my lord.

POLONIUS   And then, sir, does 'a this, 'a does –

What was I about to say? By the mass, I was about to

50 say something! Where did I leave?

REYNALDO   At 'closes in the consequence'.

POLONIUS   At 'closes in the consequence', ay, marry.

He closes thus: 'I know the gentleman,

I saw him yesterday, or th'other day,

55 Or then, or then, with such or such, and as you say

There was 'a gaming, there o'ertook in's rouse,

There falling out at tennis', or perchance

'I saw him enter such a house of sale',

Videlicet a brothel, or so forth. See you now

60 Your bait of falsehood take this carp of truth,

And thus do we of wisdom and of reach,

With windlasses and with assays of bias,

By indirections find directions out:

So by my former lecture and advice

Shall you my son. You have me, have you not?   65

REYNALDO   My lord, I have.

POLONIUS   God buy ye, fare ye well.

REYNALDO   Good my lord.

POLONIUS   Observe his inclination in yourself.

REYNALDO   I shall, my lord.

POLONIUS   And let him ply his music.

REYNALDO   Well, my lord.   70

POLONIUS   Farewell.   *Exit Reynaldo.*

Enter OPHELIA.

                        How now, Ophelia, what's the matter?

OPHELIA

O my lord, my lord, I have been so affrighted.

POLONIUS   With what, i'th' name of God?

OPHELIA   My lord, as I was sewing in my closet

Lord Hamlet, with his doublet all unbraced,   75

No hat upon his head, his stockings fouled,

Ungartered and down-gyved to his ankle,

Pale as his shirt, his knees knocking each other,

And with a look so piteous in purport

As if he had been loosed out of hell   80

To speak of horrors, he comes before me.

POLONIUS   Mad for thy love?

OPHELIA   My lord, I do not know,

But truly I do fear it.

POLONIUS   What said he?

OPHELIA   He took me by the wrist and held me hard,

Then goes he to the length of all his arm   85

And with his other hand thus o'er his brow

He falls to such perusal of my face

As 'a would draw it. Long stayed he so;

At last, a little shaking of mine arm

And thrice his head thus waving up and down,   90

He raised a sigh so piteous and profound

As it did seem to shatter all his bulk

And end his being. That done, he lets me go

And with his head over his shoulder turned

He seemed to find his way without his eyes   95

(For out o'doors he went without their helps)

And to the last bended their light on me.

POLONIUS   Come, go with me: I will go seek the King.

This is the very ecstasy of love,

Whose violent property fordoes itself   100

And leads the will to desperate undertakings

As oft as any passions under heaven

That does afflict our natures. I am sorry –

What, have you given him any hard words of late?

OPHELIA   No, my good lord, but as you did command   105

I did repel his letters and denied

His access to me.

POLONIUS   That hath made him mad.

I am sorry that with better heed and judgement

I had not quoted him. I feared he did but trifle

And meant to wrack thee – but beshrew my jealousy –   110

By heaven it is as proper to our age

To cast beyond ourselves in our opinions
As it is common for the younger sort
To lack discretion. Come, go we to the King:
This must be known which, being kept close, might
115   move
More grief to hide than hate to utter love.
Come.   *Exeunt.*

2.2   *Flourish. Enter* KING *and* QUEEN,
        ROSENCRANTZ *and* GUILDENSTERN
          and other Courtiers.

KING   Welcome, dear Rosencrantz and Guildenstern.
  Moreover that we much did long to see you
  The need we have to use you did provoke
  Our hasty sending. Something have you heard
5   Of Hamlet's transformation – so call it
  Sith nor th'exterior nor the inward man
  Resembles that it was. What it should be
  More than his father's death, that thus hath put him
  So much from th'understanding of himself
10   I cannot dream of. I entreat you both
  That, being of so young days brought up with him
  And sith so neighboured to his youth and haviour,
  That you vouchsafe your rest here in our Court
  Some little time, so by your companies
15   To draw him on to pleasures and to gather
  So much as from occasion you may glean,
  Whether aught to us unknown afflicts him thus
  That opened lies within our remedy.
QUEEN   Good gentlemen, he hath much talked of you
20   And sure I am two men there is not living
  To whom he more adheres. If it will please you
  To show us so much gentry and good will
  As to expend your time with us awhile
  For the supply and profit of our hope,
25   Your visitation shall receive such thanks
  As fits a king's remembrance.
ROSENCRANTZ   Both your majesties
  Might by the sovereign power you have of us
  Put your dread pleasures more into command
  Than to entreaty.
GUILDENSTERN   But we both obey
30   And here give up ourselves in the full bent
  To lay our service freely at your feet
  To be commanded.
KING   Thanks, Rosencrantz, and gentle Guildenstern.
QUEEN   Thanks, Guildenstern, and gentle Rosencrantz.
35   And I beseech you instantly to visit
  My too much changed son. Go some of you
  And bring these gentlemen where Hamlet is.
GUILDENSTERN
  Heavens make our presence and our practices
  Pleasant and helpful to him.
QUEEN   Ay, amen.
        Exeunt Rosencrantz, Guildenstern and
                one or more Courtiers.

Enter POLONIUS.

POLONIUS
  Th'ambassadors from Norway, my good lord,   40
  Are joyfully returned.
KING   Thou still hast been the father of good news.
POLONIUS   Have I, my lord? I assure my good liege
  I hold my duty as I hold my soul,
  Both to my God and to my gracious King;   45
  And I do think, or else this brain of mine
  Hunts not the trail of policy so sure
  As it hath used to do, that I have found
  The very cause of Hamlet's lunacy.
KING   O, speak of that, that do I long to hear.   50
POLONIUS   Give first admittance to th'ambassadors.
  My news shall be the fruit to that great feast.
KING   Thyself do grace to them and bring them in.
  He tells me, my dear Gertrude, he hath found
  The head and source of all your son's distemper.   55
QUEEN   I doubt it is no other but the main –
  His father's death and our hasty marriage.
KING   Well, we shall sift him.

      Enter VOLTEMAND *and* CORNELIUS.

                Welcome, my good friends.
  Say, Voltemand, what from our brother Norway?
VOLTEMAND
  Most fair return of greetings and desires.   60
  Upon our first he sent out to suppress
  His nephew's levies, which to him appeared
  To be a preparation 'gainst the Polack;
  But, better looked into, he truly found
  It was against your highness; whereat, grieved   65
  That so his sickness, age and impotence
  Was falsely borne in hand, sends out arrests
  On Fortinbras, which he in brief obeys,
  Receives rebuke from Norway and, in fine,
  Makes vow before his uncle never more   70
  To give th'assay of arms against your majesty.
  Whereon old Norway, overcome with joy,
  Gives him threescore thousand crowns in annual fee
  And his commission to employ those soldiers
  So levied (as before) against the Polack,   75
  With an entreaty herein further shown
  That it might please you to give quiet pass
  Through your dominions for this enterprise
  On such regards of safety and allowance
  As therein are set down.
KING   It likes us well,   80
  And at our more considered time we'll read,
  Answer and think upon this business;
  Meantime, we thank you for your well-took labour.
  Go to your rest, at night we'll feast together.
  Most welcome home.
      Exeunt Voltemand, Cornelius and Courtiers.
POLONIUS   This business is well ended.   85
  My liege and madam, to expostulate

What majesty should be, what duty is,
Why day is day, night night, and time is time,
Were nothing but to waste night, day and time;
90 Therefore, brevity is the soul of wit
And tediousness the limbs and outward flourishes.
I will be brief: your noble son is mad.
Mad call I it, for to define true madness,
What is't but to be nothing else but mad?
But let that go.
95 QUEEN   More matter with less art.
POLONIUS Madam, I swear I use no art at all.
That he's mad, 'tis true, 'tis true 'tis pity,
And pity 'tis 'tis true: a foolish figure!
But farewell it, for I will use no art.
100 Mad let us grant him then, and now remains
That we find out the cause of this effect –
Or rather say the cause of this defect,
For this effect defective comes by cause.
Thus it remains, and the remainder thus. Perpend,
105 I have a daughter – have while she is mine –
Who in her duty and obedience, mark,
Hath given me this. Now gather and surmise.
[*Reads.*] *To the celestial and my soul's idol, the most*
beautified Ophelia – that's an ill phrase, a vile phrase,
110 'beautified' is a vile phrase, but you shall hear – *thus in*
her excellent white bosom, these, etc.
QUEEN Came this from Hamlet to her?
POLONIUS
Good madam, stay awhile: I will be faithful.
[*Reads.*]   *Doubt thou the stars are fire,*
115   *Doubt that the sun doth move,*
                         Doubt truth to be a liar,
                         But never doubt I love.
O dear Ophelia, I am ill at these numbers. I have not art
to reckon my groans, but that I love thee best, O most best,
120 *believe it. Adieu. Thine evermore, most dear lady, whilst*
this machine is to him. Hamlet.
This in obedience hath my daughter shown me;
And more about hath his solicitings
As they fell out, by time, by means and place,
All given to my ear.
125 KING   But how hath she
Received his love?
POLONIUS   What do you think of me?
KING   As of a man faithful and honourable.
POLONIUS
I would fain prove so. But what might you think
When I had seen this hot love on the wing –
130 As I perceived it (I must tell you that)
Before my daughter told me – what might you,
Or my dear majesty your Queen here, think
If I had played the desk or table-book,
Or given my heart a working mute and dumb,
135 Or looked upon this love with idle sight,
What might you think? No, I went round to work
And my young mistress thus I did bespeak:
'Lord Hamlet is a prince out of thy star.

This must not be.' And then I prescripts gave her
That she should lock herself from his resort,   140
Admit no messengers, receive no tokens;
Which done, she took the fruits of my advice,
And he, repelled, a short tale to make,
Fell into a sadness, then into a fast,
Thence to a watch, thence into a weakness,   145
Thence to lightness, and by this declension
Into the madness wherein now he raves,
And all we mourn for.
KING   Do you think this?
QUEEN   It may be, very like.
POLONIUS
Hath there been such a time – I would fain know that –   150
That I have positively said 'tis so
When it proved otherwise?
KING   Not that I know.
POLONIUS   Take this from this if this be otherwise.
If circumstances lead me I will find
Where truth is hid, though it were hid indeed   155
Within the centre.
KING   How may we try it further?
POLONIUS
You know sometimes he walks four hours together
Here in the lobby?
QUEEN   So he does, indeed.
POLONIUS
At such a time I'll loose my daughter to him.
Be you and I behind an arras then,   160
Mark the encounter: if he love her not
And be not from his reason fallen thereon
Let me be no assistant for a state
But keep a farm and carters.
KING   We will try it.

Enter HAMLET.

QUEEN
But look where sadly the poor wretch comes reading.   165
POLONIUS   Away, I do beseech you both, away.
I'll board him presently. O, give me leave.
                              Exeunt King and Queen.
How does my good lord Hamlet?
HAMLET   Well, God-a-mercy.
POLONIUS   Do you know me, my lord?   170
HAMLET   Excellent well, you are a fishmonger.
POLONIUS   Not I, my lord.
HAMLET   Then I would you were so honest a man.
POLONIUS   Honest, my lord?
HAMLET   Ay, sir, to be honest as this world goes is to be   175
one man picked out of ten thousand.
POLONIUS   That's very true, my lord.
HAMLET   For if the sun breed maggots in a dead dog,
being a good kissing carrion – have you a daughter?
POLONIUS   I have, my lord.   180
HAMLET   Let her not walk i'th' sun: conception is a
blessing but as your daughter may conceive, friend –
look to't.

POLONIUS [*aside*]   How say you by that? Still harping
185   on my daughter. Yet he knew me not at first, 'a said I
was a fishmonger! 'A is far gone; and truly, in my youth
I suffered much extremity for love, very near this. I'll
speak to him again. – What do you read, my lord?

HAMLET   Words, words, words.

190 POLONIUS   What is the matter, my lord?

HAMLET   Between who?

POLONIUS   I mean the matter that you read, my lord.

HAMLET   Slanders, sir. For the satirical rogue says here
that old men have grey beards, that their faces are
195   wrinkled, their eyes purging thick amber and plumtree
gum, and that they have a plentiful lack of wit together
with most weak hams – all which, sir, though I most
powerfully and potently believe, yet I hold it not
honesty to have it thus set down. For yourself, sir,
200   shall grow old as I am – if, like a crab, you could go
backward.

POLONIUS [*aside*]   Though this be madness yet there is
method in't. — Will you walk out of the air, my lord?

HAMLET   Into my grave.

205 POLONIUS [*aside*]   Indeed, that's out of the air. How
pregnant sometimes his replies are – a happiness that
often madness hits on, which reason and sanity could
not so prosperously be delivered of. I will leave him and
my daughter. – My lord, I will take my leave of you.

210 HAMLET   You cannot take from me anything that I will
not more willingly part withal – except my life, except
my life, except my life.

POLONIUS   Fare you well, my lord.

HAMLET   These tedious old fools.

Enter GUILDENSTERN *and* ROSENCRANTZ.

215 POLONIUS   You go to seek the Lord Hamlet? There he is.

ROSENCRANTZ [*to Polonius*]   God save you, sir.

                                    Exit Polonius.

GUILDENSTERN   My honoured lord.

ROSENCRANTZ   My most dear lord.

HAMLET   My excellent good friends. How dost thou,
220   Guildenstern? Ah, Rosencrantz! Good lads, how do
you both?

ROSENCRANTZ   As the indifferent children of the earth.

GUILDENSTERN   Happy, in that we are not ever happy.
On Fortune's cap we are not the very button.

225 HAMLET   Nor the soles of her shoe.

ROSENCRANTZ   Neither, my lord.

HAMLET   Then you live about her waist, or in the
middle of her favours.

GUILDENSTERN   Faith, her privates we.

230 HAMLET   In the secret parts of Fortune? O, most true –
she is a strumpet. What news?

ROSENCRANTZ   None, my lord, but the world's grown
honest.

HAMLET   Then is doomsday near – but your news is not
235   true. But, in the beaten way of friendship, what make
you at Elsinore?

ROSENCRANTZ   To visit you, my lord, no other occasion.

HAMLET   Beggar that I am, I am ever poor in thanks,
but I thank you, and sure, dear friends, my thanks are
too dear a halfpenny. Were you not sent for? Is it your   240
own inclining? Is it a free visitation? Come, come, deal
justly with me. Come, come, nay speak.

GUILDENSTERN   What should we say, my lord?

HAMLET   Anything but to th' purpose. You were sent
for, and there is a kind of confession in your looks,   245
which your modesties have not craft enough to colour.
I know the good King and Queen have sent for you.

ROSENCRANTZ   To what end, my lord?

HAMLET   That you must teach me. But let me conjure
you, by the rights of our fellowship, by the consonancy   250
of our youth, by the obligation of our ever-preserved
love, and by what more dear a better proposer can
charge you withal, be even and direct with me whether
you were sent for or no.

ROSENCRANTZ   What say you?   255

HAMLET   Nay then, I have an eye of you. If you love me,
hold not off.

GUILDENSTERN   My lord, we were sent for.

HAMLET   I will tell you why. So shall my anticipation
prevent your discovery and your secrecy to the King   260
and Queen moult no feather. I have of late, but
wherefore I know not, lost all my mirth, forgone all
custom of exercises and, indeed, it goes so heavily with
my disposition that this goodly frame the earth seems
to me a sterile promontory, this most excellent canopy   265
the air, look you, this brave o'erhanging firmament,
this majestical roof fretted with golden fire, why it
appeareth nothing to me but a foul and pestilent
congregation of vapours. What piece of work is a man
– how noble in reason; how infinite in faculties, in form   270
and moving; how express and admirable in action; how
like an angel in apprehension; how like a god; the
beauty of the world; the paragon of animals. And yet to
me what is this quintessence of dust? Man delights not
me – nor women neither, though by your smiling you   275
seem to say so.

ROSENCRANTZ   My lord, there was no such stuff in my
thoughts.

HAMLET   Why did ye laugh then, when I said man
delights not me?   280

ROSENCRANTZ   To think, my lord, if you delight not in
man what lenten entertainment the players shall
receive from you; we coted them on the way and hither
are they coming to offer you service.

HAMLET   He that plays the King shall be welcome – his   285
majesty shall have tribute on me – the Adventurous
Knight shall use his foil and target, the Lover shall not
sigh gratis, the Humorous Man shall end his part in
peace, and the Lady shall say her mind freely or the
blank verse shall halt for't. What players are they?   290

ROSENCRANTZ   Even those you were wont to take such
delight in, the tragedians of the city.

HAMLET   How chances it they travel? Their residence,
both in reputation and profit, was better both ways.

295 ROSENCRANTZ I think their inhibition comes by the
means of the late innovation.

HAMLET Do they hold the same estimation they did
when I was in the city? Are they so followed?

ROSENCRANTZ No, indeed are they not.

300 HAMLET It is not very strange, for my uncle is King of
Denmark, and those that would make mouths at him
while my father lived give twenty, forty, fifty, a hundred
ducats apiece for his picture in little. 'Sblood, there is
something in this more than natural if philosophy
305 could find it out.   [*A flourish*]

GUILDENSTERN There are the players!

HAMLET Gentlemen, you are welcome to Elsinore.
Your hands, come, then! Th'appurtenance of welcome
is fashion and ceremony. Let me comply with you in
310 this garb lest my extent to the players, which I tell you
must show fairly outwards, should more appear like
entertainment than yours. You are welcome. But my
uncle-father and aunt-mother are deceived.

GUILDENSTERN In what, my dear lord?

315 HAMLET I am but mad north-north-west. When the
wind is southerly I know a hawk from a handsaw.

Enter POLONIUS.

POLONIUS Well be with you, gentlemen.

HAMLET Hark you, Guildenstern, and you too – at
each ear a hearer. That great baby you see there is not
320 yet out of his swaddling clouts.

ROSENCRANTZ Happily he is the second time come to
them, for they say an old man is twice a child.

HAMLET I will prophesy he comes to tell me of the
players. Mark it. – You say right, sir, o'Monday
325 morning, 'twas then indeed.

POLONIUS My lord, I have news to tell you.

HAMLET My lord, I have news to tell you. When
Roscius was an actor in Rome –

POLONIUS The actors are come hither, my lord.

330 HAMLET Buzz, buzz.

POLONIUS Upon my honour.

HAMLET Then came each actor on his ass.

POLONIUS The best actors in the world, either for
tragedy, comedy, history, pastoral, pastoral-comical,
335 historical-pastoral, scene individable or poem
unlimited. Seneca cannot be too heavy nor Plautus too
light for the law of writ and the liberty. These are the
only men.

HAMLET *O Jephthah, judge of Israel, what a treasure*
340 *hadst thou?*

POLONIUS What a treasure had he, my lord?

HAMLET Why,
        One fair daughter and no more,
        The which he loved passing well.

345 POLONIUS [*aside*] Still on my daughter.

HAMLET Am I not i'th' right, old Jephthah?

POLONIUS If you call me Jephthah, my lord, I have a
daughter that I love passing well.

HAMLET Nay, that follows not.

POLONIUS What follows then, my lord?   350

HAMLET Why,
        As by lot,
            God wot,
        and then, you know,
                It came to pass,   355
                As most like it was.

The first row of the pious chanson will show you more,
for look where my abridgement comes.

Enter the Players.

You are welcome, masters, welcome all. I am glad to see
thee well. Welcome, good friends. O old friend, why,   360
thy face is valanced since I saw thee last! Com'st thou
to beard me in Denmark? What, my young lady and
mistress! By'r Lady, your ladyship is nearer to heaven
than when I saw you last by the altitude of a chopine.
Pray God your voice, like a piece of uncurrent gold, be   365
not cracked within the ring. Masters, you are all
welcome. We'll e'en to't like French falconers – fly at
anything we see. We'll have a speech straight. Come,
give us a taste of your quality. Come, a passionate
speech.   370

1 PLAYER What speech, my good lord?

HAMLET I heard thee speak me a speech once – but it
was never acted, or, if it was, not above once, for the
play I remember pleased not the million, 'twas caviare
to the general. But it was, as I received it, and others   375
whose judgements in such matters cried in the top of
mine, an excellent play, well digested in the scenes, set
down with as much modesty as cunning. I remember
one said there were no sallets in the lines to make the
matter savoury nor no matter in the phrase that might   380
indict the author of affection, but called it an honest
method, as wholesome as sweet, and by very much
more handsome than fine. One speech in't I chiefly
loved – 'twas Aeneas' talk to Dido, and thereabout of it
especially when he speaks of Priam's slaughter. If it   385
live in your memory begin at this line – let me see, let
me see –
The rugged Pyrrhus like th' Hyrcanian beast . . .
– 'Tis not so. It begins with Pyrrhus.
The rugged Pyrrhus, he whose sable arms,   390
Black as his purpose, did the night resemble
When he lay couched in th'ominous horse,
Hath now this dread and black complexion smeared
With heraldry more dismal, head to foot.
Now is he total gules, horridly tricked   395
With blood of fathers, mothers, daughters, sons,
Baked and impasted with the parching streets
That lend a tyrannous and a damned light
To their lord's murder; roasted in wrath and fire,
And thus o'ersized with coagulate gore,   400
With eyes like carbuncles, the hellish Pyrrhus
Old grandsire Priam seeks.

So proceed you.

POLONIUS 'Fore God, my lord, well spoken – with good accent and good discretion.

1 PLAYER   *Anon he finds him,*
Striking too short at Greeks. His antique sword,
Rebellious to his arm, lies where it falls,
Repugnant to command. Unequal matched,
Pyrrhus at Priam drives, in rage strikes wide,
But with the whiff and wind of his fell sword
Th'unnerved father falls. Then senseless Ilium
Seeming to feel this blow, with flaming top
Stoops to his base and with a hideous crash
Takes prisoner Pyrrhus' ear. For lo, his sword
Which was declining on the milky head
Of reverend Priam seemed i'th' air to stick.
So as a painted tyrant Pyrrhus stood
Like a neutral to his will and matter,
Did nothing.
But as we often see against some storm
A silence in the heavens, the rack stand still,
The bold winds speechless and the orb below
As hush as death, anon the dreadful thunder
Doth rend the region, so after Pyrrhus' pause
A roused vengeance sets him new a-work
And never did the Cyclops' hammers fall
On Mars's armour, forged for proof eterne,
With less remorse than Pyrrhus' bleeding sword
Now falls on Priam.
Out, out, thou strumpet Fortune! All you gods
In general synod take away her power,
Break all the spokes and fellies from her wheel
And bowl the round nave down the hill of heaven
As low as to the fiends.

POLONIUS   This is too long.

HAMLET   It shall to the barber's with your beard. Prithee say on – he's for a jig, or a tale of bawdry, or he sleeps. Say on, come to Hecuba.

1 PLAYER   *But who – ah woe – had seen the mobled queen –*

HAMLET   'The mobled queen'!

POLONIUS   That's good.

1 PLAYER
– Run barefoot up and down, threatening the flames
With bisson rheum, a clout upon that head
Where late the diadem stood and, for a robe,
About her lank and all-o'erteemed loins,
A blanket in the alarm of fear caught up.
Who this had seen, with tongue in venom steeped,
'Gainst Fortune's state would treason have pronounced.
But if the gods themselves did see her then,
When she saw Pyrrhus make malicious sport
In mincing with his sword her husband limbs,
The instant burst of clamour that she made
(Unless things mortal move them not at all)
Would have made milch the burning eyes of heaven
And passion in the gods.

POLONIUS   Look where he has not turned his colour and has tears in's eyes. – Prithee no more!

HAMLET   'Tis well. I'll have thee speak out the rest of this soon. [*to Polonius*] Good my lord, will you see the players well bestowed? Do you hear, let them be well used, for they are the abstract and brief chronicles of the time: after your death you were better have a bad epitaph than their ill report while you live.

POLONIUS   My lord, I will use them according to their desert.

HAMLET   God's bodkin, man, much better! Use every man after his desert and who shall scape whipping? Use them after your own honour and dignity – the less they deserve the more merit is in your bounty. Take them in.

POLONIUS   Come, sirs.

HAMLET   Follow him, friends. We'll hear a play tomorrow. [*aside to First Player*] Dost thou hear me, old friend? Can you play *The Murder of Gonzago*?

1 PLAYER   Ay, my lord.

HAMLET   We'll ha't tomorrow night. You could for need study a speech of some dozen lines, or sixteen lines, which I would set down and insert in't, could you not?

1 PLAYER   Ay, my lord.

HAMLET   Very well. Follow that lord – and look you mock him not. [*to other Players*] My good friends, I'll leave you till night. You are welcome to Elsinore.

ROSENCRANTZ   Good my lord.

HAMLET
Ay so, God buy to you.   *Exeunt all but Hamlet.*
    Now I am alone.
O, what a rogue and peasant slave am I!
Is it not monstrous that this player here,
But in a fiction, in a dream of passion,
Could force his soul so to his own conceit
That from her working all the visage wanned
– Tears in his eyes, distraction in his aspect,
A broken voice, and his whole function suiting
With forms to his conceit – and all for nothing –
For Hecuba.
What's Hecuba to him, or he to her,
That he should weep for her? What would he do
Had he the motive and that for passion
That I have? He would drown the stage with tears
And cleave the general ear with horrid speech,
Make mad the guilty and appal the free,
Confound the ignorant and amaze indeed
The very faculties of eyes and ears. Yet I,
A dull and muddy-mettled rascal, peak
Like John-a-dreams, unpregnant of my cause,
And can say nothing. No, not for a king
Upon whose property and most dear life
A damned defeat was made. Am I a coward?
Who calls me villain, breaks my pate across,
Plucks off my beard and blows it in my face,
Tweaks me by the nose, gives me the lie i'th' throat
As deep as to the lungs? Who does me this,

Ha? 'Swounds, I should take it. For it cannot be
But I am pigeon-livered and lack gall
To make oppression bitter, or ere this
I should ha' fatted all the region kites
515 With this slave's offal – bloody, bawdy villain,
Remorseless, treacherous, lecherous, kindless villain.
Why, what an ass am I: this is most brave,
That I, the son of a dear murdered,
Prompted to my revenge by heaven and hell,
520 Must like a whore unpack my heart with words
And fall a-cursing like a very drab,
A stallion! Fie upon't, foh! About, my brains!
Hum, I have heard
That guilty creatures sitting at a play
525 Have by the very cunning of the scene
Been struck so to the soul that presently
They have proclaimed their malefactions.
For murder, though it have no tongue, will speak
With most miraculous organ. I'll have these players
530 Play something like the murder of my father
Before mine uncle. I'll observe his looks,
I'll tent him to the quick. If 'a do blench
I know my course. The spirit that I have seen
May be a de'il, and the de'il hath power
535 T'assume a pleasing shape. Yea, and perhaps
Out of my weakness and my melancholy,
As he is very potent with such spirits,
Abuses me to damn me! I'll have grounds
More relative than this. The play's the thing
540 Wherein I'll catch the conscience of the King.   *Exit.*

3.1   *Enter* KING, QUEEN, POLONIUS, OPHELIA,
     ROSENCRANTZ, GUILDENSTERN *and Lords.*

KING   And can you by no drift of conference
Get from him why he puts on this confusion,
Grating so harshly all his days of quiet
With turbulent and dangerous lunacy?
ROSENCRANTZ
5   He does confess he feels himself distracted
But from what cause 'a will by no means speak.
GUILDENSTERN
Nor do we find him forward to be sounded
But with a crafty madness keeps aloof
When we would bring him on to some confession
Of his true state.
10 QUEEN   Did he receive you well?
ROSENCRANTZ   Most like a gentleman.
GUILDENSTERN
But with much forcing of his disposition.
ROSENCRANTZ
Niggard of question, but of our demands
Most free in his reply.
15 QUEEN   Did you assay him to any pastime?
ROSENCRANTZ   Madam, it so fell out that certain players
We o'erraught on the way. Of these we told him
And there did seem in him a kind of joy

To hear of it. They are here about the Court
And, as I think, they have already order   20
This night to play before him.
POLONIUS   'Tis most true,
And he beseeched me to entreat your majesties
To hear and see the matter.
KING   With all my heart, and it doth much content me
To hear him so inclined.   25
Good gentlemen, give him a further edge
And drive his purpose into these delights.
ROSENCRANTZ   We shall, my lord.
     Exeunt Rosencrantz and Guildenstern and Lords.
KING   Sweet Gertrude, leave us two.
For we have closely sent for Hamlet hither
That he, as 'twere by accident, may here   30
Affront Ophelia. Her father and myself –
We'll so bestow ourselves that, seeing unseen,
We may of their encounter frankly judge
And gather by him as he is behaved
If 't be th'affliction of his love or no   35
That thus he suffers for.
QUEEN   I shall obey you.
And for your part, Ophelia, I do wish
That your good beauties be the happy cause
Of Hamlet's wildness. So shall I hope your virtues
Will bring him to his wonted way again   40
To both your honours.
OPHELIA   Madam, I wish it may.
     Exit Queen.
POLONIUS
Ophelia, walk you here. (Gracious, so please you,
We will bestow ourselves.) Read on this book
That show of such an exercise may colour
Your loneliness. We are oft too blame in this –   45
'Tis too much proved that with devotion's visage
And pious action we do sugar o'er
The devil himself.
KING   O, 'tis too true.
[*aside*] How smart a lash that speech doth give my
    conscience!
The harlot's cheek beautied with plastering art   50
Is not more ugly to the thing that helps it
Than is my deed to my most painted word.
O heavy burden!
POLONIUS   I hear him coming – withdraw, my lord.
     [*King and Polonius hide behind an arras.*]

     Enter HAMLET.

HAMLET   To be, or not to be – that is the question;   55
Whether 'tis nobler in the mind to suffer
The slings and arrows of outrageous fortune
Or to take arms against a sea of troubles
And by opposing end them; to die: to sleep –
No more, and by a sleep to say we end   60
The heartache and the thousand natural shocks
That flesh is heir to: 'tis a consummation
Devoutly to be wished – to die: to sleep –

To sleep, perchance to dream – ay, there's the rub,
65 For in that sleep of death what dreams may come
When we have shuffled off this mortal coil
Must give us pause: there's the respect
That makes calamity of so long life.
For who would bear the whips and scorns of time,
70 Th'oppressor's wrong, the proud man's contumely,
The pangs of despised love, the law's delay,
The insolence of office and the spurns
That patient merit of th'unworthy takes,
When he himself might his quietus make
75 With a bare bodkin. Who would fardels bear
To grunt and sweat under a weary life
But that the dread of something after death
(The undiscovered country from whose bourn
No traveller returns) puzzles the will
80 And makes us rather bear those ills we have
Than fly to others that we know not of.
Thus conscience does make cowards –
And thus the native hue of resolution
Is sicklied o'er with the pale cast of thought,
85 And enterprises of great pitch and moment
With this regard their currents turn awry
And lose the name of action. Soft you now,
The fair Ophelia! Nymph, in thy orisons
Be all my sins remembered.

OPHELIA   Good my lord,
90 How does your honour for this many a day?

HAMLET   I humbly thank you, well.

OPHELIA   My lord, I have remembrances of yours
That I have longed long to redeliver.
I pray you now receive them.

95 HAMLET   No, not I. I never gave you aught.

OPHELIA
My honoured lord, you know right well you did,
And with them words of so sweet breath composed
As made these things more rich. Their perfume lost,
Take these again, for to the noble mind
100 Rich gifts wax poor when givers prove unkind.
There, my lord.

HAMLET   Ha! Ha! Are you honest?

OPHELIA   My lord?

HAMLET   Are you fair?

105 OPHELIA   What means your lordship?

HAMLET   That if you be honest and fair you should
admit no discourse to your beauty.

OPHELIA   Could Beauty, my lord, have better commerce
than with Honesty?

110 HAMLET   Ay, truly. For the power of Beauty will sooner
transform Honesty from what it is to a bawd than the
force of Honesty can translate Beauty into his likeness.
This was sometime a paradox, but now the time gives
it proof. I did love you once.

115 OPHELIA   Indeed, my lord, you made me believe so.

HAMLET   You should not have believed me. For virtue
cannot so inoculate our old stock but we shall relish of
it. I loved you not.

OPHELIA   I was the more deceived.

HAMLET   Get thee to a nunnery! Why wouldst thou be a 120
breeder of sinners? I am myself indifferent honest but
yet I could accuse me of such things that it were better
my mother had not borne me. I am very proud,
revengeful, ambitious, with more offences at my beck
than I have thoughts to put them in, imagination to 125
give them shape, or time to act them in. What should
such fellows as I do crawling between earth and
heaven? We are arrant knaves – believe none of us. Go
thy ways to a nunnery. Where's your father?

OPHELIA   At home, my lord. 130

HAMLET   Let the doors be shut upon him that he may
play the fool nowhere but in's own house. Farewell.

OPHELIA [*aside*]   O help him, you sweet heavens!

HAMLET   If thou dost marry, I'll give thee this plague
for thy dowry: be thou as chaste as ice, as pure as snow, 135
thou shalt not escape calumny. Get thee to a nunnery.
Farewell. Or, if thou wilt needs marry, marry a fool, for
wise men know well enough what monsters you make
of them. To a nunnery go, and quickly too. Farewell.

OPHELIA [*aside*]   Heavenly powers restore him. 140

HAMLET   I have heard of your paintings well enough.
God hath given you one face and you make yourselves
another. You jig and amble and you lisp, you nickname
God's creatures and make your wantonness ignorance.
Go to, I'll no more on't. It hath made me mad. I say we 145
will have no more marriage. Those that are married
already – all but one – shall live. The rest shall keep as
they are. To a nunnery, go!   *Exit.*

OPHELIA   O, what a noble mind is here o'erthrown!
The courtier's, soldier's, scholar's eye, tongue, sword, 150
Th'expectation and rose of the fair state,
The glass of fashion and the mould of form,
Th'observed of all observers, quite, quite down.
And I, of ladies most deject and wretched,
That sucked the honey of his musicked vows, 155
Now see what noble and most sovereign reason
Like sweet bells jangled out of time and harsh –
That unmatched form and stature of blown youth
Blasted with ecstasy. O woe is me
T'have seen what I have seen, see what I see. 160
[*King and Polonius step forward from behind the arras.*]

KING   Love! His affections do not that way tend.
Nor what he spake, though it lacked form a little,
Was not like madness. There's something in his soul
O'er which his melancholy sits on brood
And I do doubt the hatch and the disclose 165
Will be some danger – which for to prevent
I have in quick determination
Thus set it down. He shall with speed to England
For the demand of our neglected tribute.
Haply the seas and countries different 170
With variable objects shall expel
This something-settled matter in his heart
Whereon his brains still beating puts him thus
From fashion of himself. What think you on't?

POLONIUS   It shall do well. But yet do I believe 175
The origin and commencement of his grief
Sprung from neglected love. How now, Ophelia?
You need not tell us what Lord Hamlet said –
We heard it all. My lord, do as you please,
But if you hold it fit after the play 180
Let his Queen-mother all alone entreat him
To show his grief. Let her be round with him
And I'll be placed, so please you, in the ear
Of all their conference. If she find him not,
To England send him or confine him where 185
Your wisdom best shall think.

KING   It shall be so.
Madness in great ones must not unwatched go.
Exeunt.

3.2   *Enter* HAMLET *and three of the* Players.

HAMLET   Speak the speech, I pray you, as I pronounced
it to you – trippingly on the tongue. But if you mouth
it as many of our players do, I had as lief the town-crier
spoke my lines. Nor do not saw the air too much with
your hand, thus, but use all gently; for, in the very 5
torrent, tempest and, as I may say, whirlwind of your
passion, you must acquire and beget a temperance that
may give it smoothness. O, it offends me to the soul to
hear a robustious periwig-pated fellow tear a passion to
tatters, to very rags, to split the ears of the groundlings, 10
who for the most part are capable of nothing but
inexplicable dumb-shows and noise. I would have such
a fellow whipped for o'erdoing Termagant – it
out-Herods Herod. Pray you avoid it.

PLAYER   I warrant your honour. 15

HAMLET   Be not too tame neither, but let your own
discretion be your tutor. Suit the action to the word, the
word to the action, with this special observance – that
you o'erstep not the modesty of nature. For anything so
o'erdone is from the purpose of playing whose end, 20
both at the first and now, was and is to hold as 'twere the
mirror up to Nature to show Virtue her feature, Scorn
her own image, and the very age and body of the time
his form and pressure. Now this overdone, or come
tardy off, though it makes the unskilful laugh, cannot 25
but make the judicious grieve, the censure of which one
must in your allowance o'erweigh a whole theatre of
others. O, there be players that I have seen play and
heard others praised – and that highly – not to speak it
profanely, that neither having th'accent of Christians 30
nor the gait of Christian, pagan nor man have so
strutted and bellowed that I have thought some of
Nature's journeymen had made men, and not made
them well, they imitated humanity so abhominably.

PLAYER   I hope we have reformed that indifferently 35
with us.

HAMLET   O, reform it altogether, and let those that play
your clowns speak no more than is set down for them.
For there be of them that will themselves laugh to set

on some quantity of barren spectators to laugh too, 40
though in the meantime some necessary question of
the play be then to be considered. – That's villainous
and shows a most pitiful ambition in the fool that uses
it. Go, make you ready.   *Exeunt Players.*

Enter POLONIUS, GUILDENSTERN *and* ROSENCRANTZ.

How now, my lord, will the King hear this piece of 45
work?

POLONIUS   And the Queen too, and that presently.

HAMLET   Bid the players make haste.   *Exit Polonius.*
Will you two help to hasten them?

ROSENCRANTZ   Ay, my lord.
Exeunt Rosencrantz and Guildenstern.

HAMLET   What ho, Horatio!

Enter HORATIO.

HORATIO   Here, sweet lord, at your service. 50

HAMLET   Horatio, thou art e'en as just a man
As e'er my conversation coped withal.

HORATIO   O my dear lord –

HAMLET   Nay, do not think I flatter,
For what advancement may I hope from thee
That no revenue hast but thy good spirits 55
To feed and clothe thee? Why should the poor be
    flattered?
No, let the candied tongue lick absurd pomp
And crook the pregnant hinges of the knee
Where thrift may follow fawning. Dost thou hear?
Since my dear soul was mistress of her choice 60
And could of men distinguish her election
Sh'ath sealed thee for herself. For thou hast been
As one in suffering all that suffers nothing –
A man that Fortune's buffets and rewards
Hast ta'en with equal thanks. And blest are those 65
Whose blood and judgement are so well co-meddled
That they are not a pipe for Fortune's finger
To sound what stop she please. Give me that man
That is not passion's slave and I will wear him
In my heart's core – ay, in my heart of heart – 70
As I do thee. Something too much of this:
There is a play tonight before the King –
One scene of it comes near the circumstance
Which I have told thee of my father's death.
I prithee when thou seest that act afoot, 75
Even with the very comment of thy soul
Observe my uncle. If his occulted guilt
Do not itself unkennel in one speech
It is a damned ghost that we have seen
And my imaginations are as foul 80
As Vulcan's stithy. Give him heedful note,
For I mine eyes will rivet to his face
And after we will both our judgements join
In censure of his seeming.

HORATIO   Well, my lord
If 'a steal aught the whilst this play is playing 85
And scape detected I will pay the theft.

Enter Trumpets and Kettledrums, KING, QUEEN,
POLONIUS, OPHELIA, ROSENCRANTZ *and*
GUILDENSTERN.

HAMLET [*to Horatio*] They are coming to the play. I
must be idle. Get you a place.

KING How fares our cousin Hamlet?

90 HAMLET Excellent, i'faith! Of the chameleon's dish – I
eat the air, promise-crammed. You cannot feed capons
so.

KING I have nothing with this answer, Hamlet. These
words are not mine.

95 HAMLET No, nor mine now, my lord. [*to Polonius*] You
played once i'th' university, you say?

POLONIUS That did I, my lord, and was accounted a
good actor.

HAMLET What did you enact?

100 POLONIUS I did enact Julius Caesar. I was killed i'th'
Capitol. Brutus killed me.

HAMLET It was a brute part of him to kill so capital a
calf there. Be the players ready?

ROSENCRANTZ Ay, my lord, they stay upon your
105 patience.

QUEEN Come hither, my dear Hamlet, sit by me.

HAMLET No, good mother, here's metal more attractive.

POLONIUS [*to King*] O ho, do you mark that!

HAMLET Lady, shall I lie in your lap?

110 OPHELIA No, my lord.

HAMLET Do you think I meant country matters?

OPHELIA I think nothing, my lord.

HAMLET That's a fair thought to lie between maids' legs.

OPHELIA What is, my lord?

115 HAMLET Nothing.

OPHELIA You are merry, my lord.

HAMLET Who, I?

OPHELIA Ay, my lord.

HAMLET O God, your only jig-maker! What should a
120 man do but be merry, for look you how cheerfully my
mother looks, and my father died within's two hours!

OPHELIA Nay, 'tis twice two months, my lord.

HAMLET So long? Nay, then, let the devil wear black,
for I'll have a suit of sables! O heavens – die two
125 months ago and not forgotten yet? Then there's hope a
great man's memory may outlive his life half a year!
But, by'r Lady, 'a must build churches then, or else
shall 'a suffer not thinking on – with the hobby-horse
whose epitaph is 'For O! For O! The hobby-horse is
130 forgot!'   [*The trumpets sounds. Dumb-show follows.*]

Enter Players *as a king and a queen, the queen embracing him
and he her. He takes her up and declines his head upon her
neck. He lies him down upon a bank of flowers. She seeing
him asleep leaves him. Anon come in a* Player *as another
man, takes off his crown, kisses it, pours poison in the
sleeper's ears and leaves him. The queen returns, finds the
king dead, makes passionate action. The poisoner with some
three or four* Players *come in again, seem to condole with er.
The dead body is carried away. The poisoner woos the queen*

*with gifts. She seems harsh awhile but in the end accepts
love.*   *Exeunt.*

OPHELIA What means this, my lord?

HAMLET Marry, this munching mallico! It means
mischief.

OPHELIA Belike this show imports the argument of the
play.   135

Enter a Player *as the* Prologue.

HAMLET We shall know by this fellow. The players
cannot keep council – they'll tell all.

OPHELIA Will 'a tell us what this show meant?

HAMLET Ay, or any show that you will show him. Be not
you ashamed to show, he'll not shame to tell you what   140
it means.

OPHELIA You are naught, you are naught. I'll mark the
play.

PROLOGUE
*For us and for our tragedy,
Here stooping to your clemency,*   145
We beg your hearing patiently.   *Exit.*

HAMLET Is this a prologue or the posy of a ring?

OPHELIA 'Tis brief, my lord.

HAMLET As woman's love.

Enter PLAYER KING *and* PLAYER QUEEN.

PLAYER KING
Full thirty times hath Phoebus' cart gone round   150
*Neptune's salt wash and Tellus' orbed ground
And thirty dozen moons with borrowed sheen
About the world have times twelve thirties been
Since love our hearts and Hymen did our hands
Unite commutual in most sacred bands.*   155
PLAYER QUEEN
*So many journeys may the sun and moon
Make us again count o'er ere love be done.
But woe is me, you are so sick of late,
So far from cheer and from our former state,
That I distrust you. Yet, though I distrust,*   160
*Discomfort you, my lord, it nothing must.
For women fear too much, even as they love,
And women's fear and love hold quantity –
Either none, in neither aught, or in extremity.
Now what my love is proof hath made you know*   165
*And, as my love is sized, my fear is so.
Where love is great, the littlest doubts are fear,
Where little fears grow great, great love grows there.*
PLAYER KING
*Faith, I must leave thee, love, and shortly too,
My operant powers their functions leave to do,*   170
*And thou shalt live in this fair world behind
Honoured, beloved, and haply one as kind
For husband shalt thou –*
PLAYER QUEEN   *O, confound the rest!
Such love must needs be treason in my breast.
In second husband let me be accurst:*   175

None wed the second but who killed the first.
HAMLET   That's wormwood!
PLAYER QUEEN
   The instances that second marriage move
   Are base respects of thrift, but none of love.
180   *A second time I kill my husband dead*
   When second husband kisses me in bed.
PLAYER KING
   I do believe you think what now you speak.
   But what we do determine oft we break.
   Purpose is but the slave to memory,
185   *Of violent birth but poor validity,*
   Which now like fruit unripe sticks on the tree
   But fall unshaken when they mellow be.
   Most necessary 'tis that we forget
   To pay ourselves what to ourselves is debt.
190   *What to ourselves in passion we propose,*
   The passion ending doth the purpose lose.
   The violence of either grief or joy
   Their own enactures with themselves destroy.
   Where joy most revels grief doth most lament,
195   *Grief joys, joy grieves, on slender accident.*
   This world is not for aye, nor 'tis not strange
   That even our loves should with our fortunes change,
   For 'tis a question left us yet to prove
   Whether Love lead Fortune or else Fortune Love.
200   *The great man down, you mark his favourite flies,*
   The poor advanced makes friends of enemies,
   And hitherto doth Love on Fortune tend,
   For who not needs shall never lack a friend,
   And who in want a hollow friend doth try
205   *Directly seasons him his enemy.*
   But orderly to end where I begun,
   Our wills and fates do so contrary run
   That our devices still are overthrown.
   Our thoughts are ours, their ends none of our own:
210   *So think thou wilt no second husband wed*
   But die thy thoughts when thy first lord is dead.
PLAYER QUEEN
   Nor earth to me give food nor heaven light,
   Sport and repose lock from me day and night.
   To desperation turn my trust and hope
215   *And anchor's cheer in prison be my scope.*
   Each opposite that blanks the face of joy
   Meet what I would have well and it destroy.
   Both here and hence pursue me lasting strife
   If once I be a widow ever I be a wife.
220 HAMLET   If she should break it now!
PLAYER KING
   'Tis deeply sworn. Sweet, leave me here awhile.
   My spirits grow dull, and fain I would beguile
   The tedious day with sleep.
PLAYER QUEEN   *Sleep rock thy brain,*
   And never come mischance between us twain.
   [*He sleeps.*]   *Exit.*
225 HAMLET   Madam, how like you this play?
QUEEN   The lady doth protest too much, methinks.

HAMLET   O, but she'll keep her word.
KING   Have you heard the argument? Is there no offence
   in't?
HAMLET   No, no, they do but jest. Poison in jest. No   230
   offence i'th' world.
KING   What do you call the play?
HAMLET   *The Mousetrap.* Marry, how tropically! This
   play is the image of a murder done in Vienna. Gonzago
   is the duke's name, his wife Baptista. You shall see anon   235
   'tis a knavish piece of work, but what of that? Your
   majesty and we that have free souls – it touches us not.
   Let the galled jade wince, our withers are unwrung.

                Enter LUCIANUS.

   This is one Lucianus, nephew to the king.
OPHELIA   You are as good as a chorus, my lord.   240
HAMLET   I could interpret between you and your love if
   I could see the puppets dallying.
OPHELIA   You are keen, my lord, you are keen.
HAMLET   It would cost you a groaning to take off mine
   edge.   245
OPHELIA   Still better and worse.
HAMLET   So you mistake your husbands. Begin,
   murderer: leave thy damnable faces and begin. Come,
   'the croaking raven doth bellow for revenge.'
LUCIANUS
   Thoughts black, hands apt, drugs fit, and time agreeing,   250
   Considerate season else no creature seeing,
   Thou mixture rank, of midnight weeds collected,
   With Hecate's ban thrice blasted, thrice infected,
   Thy natural magic and dire property
   On wholesome life usurps immediately.   255
   [*Pours the poison in his ears.*]
HAMLET   'A poisons him i'th' garden for his estate. His
   name's Gonzago. The story is extant and written in
   very choice Italian. You shall see anon how the
   murderer gets the love of Gonzago's wife.
OPHELIA   The King rises.   260
QUEEN   How fares my lord?
POLONIUS   Give o'er the play.
KING   Give me some light, away.
POLONIUS   Lights! Lights! Lights!
            Exeunt all but Hamlet and Horatio.
HAMLET
   Why let the stricken deer go weep,   265
   The hart ungalled play,
   For some must watch while some must sleep.
   Thus runs the world away.
   Would not this, sir, and a forest of feathers, if the rest
   of my fortunes turn Turk with me, with provincial roses   270
   on my razed shoes, get me a fellowship in a cry of players?
HORATIO   Half a share.
HAMLET   A whole one, I.
   For thou dost know, O Damon dear,
   This realm dismantled was   275
   Of Jove himself, and now reigns here
   A very, very pajock.

HORATIO   You might have rhymed.

HAMLET   O good Horatio, I'll take the Ghost's word for
280   a thousand pound. Didst perceive?

HORATIO   Very well, my lord.

HAMLET   Upon the talk of the poisoning.

HORATIO   I did very well note him.

HAMLET   Ah ha! Come, some music! Come, the recorders!
285   For if the King like not the comedy
        Why then belike he likes it not, perdie.
    Come, some music!

Enter ROSENCRANTZ *and* GUILDENSTERN.

GUILDENSTERN   Good my lord, vouchsafe me a word
    with you.

290   HAMLET   Sir, a whole history.

GUILDENSTERN   The King, sir –

HAMLET   Ay, sir, what of him?

GUILDENSTERN   – is in his retirement marvellous
    distempered.

295   HAMLET   With drink, sir?

GUILDENSTERN   No, my lord, with choler.

HAMLET   Your wisdom should show itself more richer
    to signify this to the doctor, for for me to put him to
    his purgation would perhaps plunge him into more
300   choler.

GUILDENSTERN   Good my lord, put your discourse
    into some frame and start not so wildly from my affair.

HAMLET   I am tame, sir, pronounce.

GUILDENSTERN   The Queen your mother in most great
305   affliction of spirit hath sent me to you.

HAMLET   You are welcome.

GUILDENSTERN   Nay, good my lord, this courtesy is
    not of the right breed. If it shall please you to make me
    a wholesome answer, I will do your mother's
310   commandment. If not, your pardon and my return
    shall be the end of business.

HAMLET   Sir, I cannot.

ROSENCRANTZ   What, my lord?

HAMLET   Make you a wholesome answer. My wit's
315   diseased. But, sir, such answer as I can make you shall
    command. Or rather, as you say, my mother. Therefore
    no more. But to the matter – my mother, you say?

ROSENCRANTZ   Then thus she says. Your behaviour
    hath struck her into amazement and admiration.

320   HAMLET   O wonderful son that can so 'stonish a
    mother! But is there no sequel at the heels of this
    mother's admiration? Impart.

ROSENCRANTZ   She desires to speak with you in her
    closet ere you go to bed.

325   HAMLET   We shall obey, were she ten times our mother.
    Have you any further trade with us?

ROSENCRANTZ   My lord, you once did love me.

HAMLET   And do still, by these pickers and stealers.

ROSENCRANTZ   Good my lord, what is your cause of
330   distemper? You do surely bar the door upon your own
    liberty if you deny your griefs to your friend.

HAMLET   Sir, I lack advancement.

ROSENCRANTZ   How can that be, when you have the voice
    of the King himself for your succession in Denmark?

HAMLET   Ay, sir, but while the grass grows – the proverb   335
    is something musty.

Enter the Players *with recorders.*

O, the recorders! Let me see one. To withdraw with
you, why do you go about to recover the wind of me, as
if you would drive me into a toil?

GUILDENSTERN   O my lord, if my duty be too bold, my   340
    love is too unmannerly.

HAMLET   I do not well understand that. Will you play
    upon this pipe?

GUILDENSTERN   My lord, I cannot.

HAMLET   I pray you.   345

GUILDENSTERN   Believe me, I cannot.

HAMLET   I do beseech you.

GUILDENSTERN   I know no touch of it, my lord.

HAMLET   It is as easy as lying. Govern these ventages
    with your fingers and thumb, give it breath with your   350
    mouth, and it will discourse most eloquent music.
    Look you, these are the stops.

GUILDENSTERN   But these cannot I command to any
    utterance of harmony. I have not the skill.

HAMLET   Why, look you now how unworthy a thing you   355
    make of me: you would play upon me! You would seem
    to know my stops, you would pluck out the heart of my
    mystery, you would sound me from my lowest note to
    my compass. And there is much music, excellent voice,
    in this little organ. Yet cannot you make it speak.   360
    'Sblood! Do you think I am easier to be played on than
    a pipe? Call me what instrument you will, though you
    fret me you cannot play upon me.

Enter POLONIUS.

God bless you, sir.

POLONIUS   My lord, the Queen would speak with you,   365
    and presently.

HAMLET   Do you see yonder cloud that's almost in
    shape of a camel?

POLONIUS   By th' mass and 'tis like a camel indeed.

HAMLET   Methinks it is like a weasel.   370

POLONIUS   It is backed like a weasel.

HAMLET   Or like a whale?

POLONIUS   Very like a whale.

HAMLET   Then I will come to my mother, by and by.
    [*aside*] They fool me to the top of my bent. – I will   375
    come by and by. – Leave me, friends. – I will. Say so.
    'By and by' is easily said.   *Exeunt all but Hamlet.*
    'Tis now the very witching time of night
    When churchyards yawn and hell itself breaks out
    Contagion to this world. Now could I drink hot blood   380
    And do such business as the bitter day
    Would quake to look on. Soft, now to my mother.
    O heart, lose not thy nature. Let not ever
    The soul of Nero enter this firm bosom –
    Let me be cruel, not unnatural: 385

I will speak daggers to her but use none.
My tongue and soul in this be hypocrites.
How in my words somever she be shent
To give them seals never my soul consent. *Exit.*

3.3 *Enter* KING, ROSENCRANTZ *and*
GUILDENSTERN.

KING   I like him not, nor stands it safe with us
To let his madness range. Therefore prepare you.
I your commission will forthwith dispatch
And he to England shall along with you.
5   The terms of our estate may not endure
Hazard so near us as doth hourly grow
Out of his brows.
GUILDENSTERN   We will ourselves provide.
Most holy and religious fear it is
To keep those many many bodies safe
10   That live and feed upon your majesty.
ROSENCRANTZ   The single and peculiar life is bound
With all the strength and armour of the mind
To keep itself from noyance; but much more
That spirit upon whose weal depends and rests
15   The lives of many. The cess of majesty
Dies not alone, but like a gulf doth draw
What's near it with it; or it is a massy wheel
Fixed on the summit of the highest mount
To whose huge spokes ten thousand lesser things
20   Are mortised and adjoined, which when it falls
Each small annexment, petty consequence,
Attends the boisterous ruin. Never alone
Did the king sigh but with a general groan.
KING   Arm you, I pray you, to this speedy voyage
25   For we will fetters put about this fear
Which now goes too free-footed.
ROSENCRANTZ   We will haste us.
Exeunt Rosencrantz and Guildenstern.

Enter POLONIUS.

POLONIUS
My lord, he's going to his mother's closet.
Behind the arras I'll convey myself
To hear the process. I'll warrant she'll tax him home
30   And, as you said – and wisely was it said –
'Tis meet that some more audience than a mother
(Since nature makes them partial) should o'er-hear
The speech of vantage. Fare you well, my liege,
I'll call upon you ere you go to bed
And tell you what I know.
35   KING   Thanks, dear my lord.
Exit Polonius.
O, my offence is rank: it smells to heaven;
It hath the primal eldest curse upon't –
A brother's murder. Pray can I not:
Though inclination be as sharp as will,
40   My stronger guilt defeats my strong intent
And like a man to double business bound

I stand in pause where I shall first begin
And both neglect. What if this cursed hand
Were thicker than itself with brother's blood?
Is there not rain enough in the sweet heavens   45
To wash it white as snow? Whereto serves mercy
But to confront the visage of offence?
And what's in prayer but this twofold force
– To be forestalled ere we come to fall
Or pardoned, being down? Then I'll look up: 50
My fault is past. But O, what form of prayer
Can serve my turn: 'Forgive me my foul murder'?
That cannot be, since I am still possessed
Of those effects for which I did the murder,
My crown, mine own ambition and my Queen.   55
May one be pardoned and retain th'offence?
In the corrupted currents of this world
Offence's gilded hand may shove by justice,
And oft 'tis seen the wicked prize itself
Buys out the law; but 'tis not so above: 60
There is no shuffling, there the action lies
In his true nature, and we ourselves compelled
Even to the teeth and forehead of our faults
To give in evidence. What then? What rests?
Try what repentance can – what can it not? –   65
Yet what can it, when one cannot repent?
O wretched state, O bosom black as death,
O limed soul that struggling to be free
Art more engaged. Help, angels, make assay.
Bow, stubborn knees, and heart with strings of steel   70
Be soft as sinews of the new-born babe.
All may be well.

Enter HAMLET.

HAMLET   Now might I do it. But now 'a is a-praying.
And now I'll do it [*Draws sword.*] – and so 'a goes to
    heaven,
And so am I revenged! That would be scanned: 75
A villain kills my father, and for that
I, his sole son, do this same villain send
To heaven.
Why, this is base and silly, not revenge.
'A took my father grossly full of bread   80
With all his crimes broad blown, as flush as May,
And how his audit stands who knows, save heaven,
But in our circumstance and course of thought
'Tis heavy with him. And am I then revenged
To take him in the purging of his soul   85
When he is fit and seasoned for his passage?
No.   [*Sheathes sword.*]
Up sword, and know thou a more horrid hent
When he is drunk, asleep or in his rage,
Or in th'incestuous pleasure of his bed,   90
At game a-swearing, or about some act
That has no relish of salvation in't.
Then trip him that his heels may kick at heaven
And that his soul may be as damned and black
As hell whereto it goes. My mother stays;   95

This physic but prolongs thy sickly days. *Exit.*

KING　My words fly up, my thoughts remain below.

Words without thoughts never to heaven go. *Exit.*

3.4　　　*Enter* QUEEN *and* POLONIUS.

POLONIUS

'A will come straight. Look you lay home to him.

Tell him his pranks have been too broad to bear with,

And that your grace hath screened and stood between

Much heat and him. I'll silence me even here.

Pray you be round.

5　QUEEN　　　　　　I'll warrant you, fear me not.

Withdraw, I hear him coming.

　　[*Polonius hides behind the arras.*]

　　　　　Enter HAMLET.

HAMLET　Now, mother, what's the matter?

QUEEN　Hamlet, thou hast thy father much offended.

HAMLET　Mother, you have my father much offended.

10　QUEEN　Come, come, you answer with an idle tongue.

HAMLET　Go, go, you question with a wicked tongue.

QUEEN　Why, how now, Hamlet!

HAMLET　　　　　　　　　What's the matter now?

QUEEN　Have you forgot me?

HAMLET　　　　　　　No, by the rood, not so.

You are the Queen, your husband's brother's wife,

15　And, would it were not so, you are my mother.

QUEEN　Nay then, I'll set those to you that can speak.

HAMLET

Come, come, and sit you down. You shall not budge.

You go not till I set you up a glass

Where you may see the inmost part of you.

20　QUEEN　What wilt thou do? Thou wilt not murder me –

Help, ho!

POLONIUS [*behind the arras*]

　　　　　　What ho! Help!

HAMLET　How now! A rat! Dead for a ducat, dead!

　　[*Kills Polonius.*]

POLONIUS

O, I am slain!

QUEEN　　　　O me, what hast thou done?

HAMLET　Nay, I know not. Is it the King?

25　QUEEN　O, what a rash and bloody deed is this!

HAMLET

A bloody deed – almost as bad, good mother,

As kill a king and marry with his brother.

QUEEN　As kill a king?

HAMLET　　　　　Ay, lady, it was my word.

　　[*Uncovers the body of Polonius.*]

– Thou wretched, rash, intruding fool, farewell:

30　I took thee for thy better. Take thy fortune;

Thou find'st to be too busy is some danger.

– Leave wringing of your hands. Peace, sit you down

And let me wring your heart. For so I shall

If it be made of penetrable stuff,

35　If damned custom have not brazed it so

That it be proof and bulwark against sense.

QUEEN

What have I done that thou dar'st wag thy tongue

In noise so rude against me?

HAMLET　　　　　　　　Such an act

That blurs the grace and blush of modesty,

40　Calls virtue hypocrite, takes off the rose

From the fair forehead of an innocent love

And sets a blister there, makes marriage vows

As false as dicers' oaths – O, such a deed

As from the body of contraction plucks

45　The very soul, and sweet religion makes

A rhapsody of words. Heaven's face does glow

O'er this solidity and compound mass

With heated visage as against the doom,

Is thought-sick at the act.

QUEEN　　　　　　　Ay me, what act

50　That roars so loud and thunders in the index?

HAMLET　Look here upon this picture, and on this,

The counterfeit presentment of two brothers:

See what a grace was seated on this brow,

Hyperion's curls, the front of Jove himself,

55　An eye like Mars to threaten and command,

A station like the herald Mercury

New-lighted on a heaven-kissing hill,

A combination and a form indeed

Where every god did seem to set his seal

60　To give the world assurance of a man;

This was your husband. Look you now what follows:

Here is your husband like a mildewed ear

Blasting his wholesome brother. Have you eyes?

Could you on this fair mountain leave to feed

65　And batten on this moor? Ha, have you eyes?

You cannot call it love, for at your age

The heyday in the blood is tame, it's humble

And waits upon the judgement, and what judgement

Would step from this to this? Sense, sure, you have –

70　Else could you not have motion. But sure, that sense

Is apoplexed, for madness would not err

Nor sense to ecstasy was ne'er so thralled

But it reserved some quantity of choice

To serve in such a difference. What devil was't

75　That thus hath cozened you at hoodman-blind?

Eyes without feeling, feeling without sight,

Ears without hands or eyes, smelling sans all,

Or but a sickly part of one true sense

Could not so mope. O shame, where is thy blush?

80　Rebellious hell,

If thou canst mutine in a matron's bones,

To flaming youth let virtue be as wax

And melt in her own fire; proclaim no shame

When the compulsive ardour gives the charge,

85　Since frost itself as actively doth burn

And reason pardons will.

QUEEN　　　　　　O Hamlet, speak no more.

Thou turn'st my very eyes into my soul

And there I see such black and grieved spots

As will leave there their tinct.

HAMLET   Nay, but to live
90   In the rank sweat of an enseamed bed
Stewed in corruption, honeying and making love
Over the nasty sty –

QUEEN   O speak to me no more!
These words like daggers enter in my ears.
No more, sweet Hamlet.

HAMLET   A murderer and a villain,
95   A slave that is not twentieth part the kith
Of your precedent lord, a vice of kings,
A cutpurse of the empire and the rule,
That from a shelf the precious diadem stole
And put it in his pocket, –

QUEEN   No more!

HAMLET   – a king of shreds and patches –

Enter GHOST.

100   Save me and hover o'er me with your wings,
You heavenly guards! What would your gracious
    figure?

QUEEN   Alas, he's mad!

HAMLET   Do you not come your tardy son to chide
That, lapsed in time and passion, lets go by
105   Th'important acting of your dread command?
O say!

GHOST   Do not forget! This visitation
Is but to whet thy almost blunted purpose.
But look, amazement on thy mother sits!
O step between her and her fighting soul.
110   Conceit in weakest bodies strongest works.
Speak to her, Hamlet.

HAMLET
How is it with you, lady?

QUEEN   Alas, how is't with you,
That you do bend your eye on vacancy
And with th'incorporal air do hold discourse?
115   Forth at your eyes your spirits wildly peep,
And as the sleeping soldiers in th'alarm
Your bedded hair like life in excrements
Start up and stand on end. O gentle son,
Upon the heat and flame of thy distemper
120   Sprinkle cool patience. Whereon do you look?

HAMLET
On him, on him! Look you how pale he glares,
His form and cause conjoined preaching to stones
Would make them capable. [*to Ghost*] Do not look
    upon me
Lest with this piteous action you convert
125   My stern effects! Then what I have to do
Will want true colour, tears perchance for blood.

QUEEN   To whom do you speak this?

HAMLET   Do you see nothing there?

QUEEN   Nothing at all, yet all that is I see.

130 HAMLET   Nor did you nothing hear?

QUEEN   No, nothing but ourselves.

HAMLET   Why, look you there! Look how it steals away –

My father in his habit as he lived.
Look where he goes even now out at the portal!

                              Exit Ghost.

QUEEN   This is the very coinage of your brain. 135
This bodiless creation ecstasy
Is very cunning in.

HAMLET
My pulse as yours doth temperately keep time
And makes as healthful music. It is not madness
That I have uttered. Bring me to the test 140
And I the matter will reword, which madness
Would gambol from. Mother, for love of grace
Lay not that flattering unction to your soul
That not your trespass but my madness speaks.
It will but skin and film the ulcerous place 145
Whiles rank corruption mining all within
Infects unseen. Confess yourself to heaven,
Repent what's past, avoid what is to come,
And do not spread the compost on the weeds
To make them ranker. Forgive me this my virtue, 150
For in the fatness of these pursy times
Virtue itself of Vice must pardon beg.
Yea, curb and woo for leave to do him good.

QUEEN   O Hamlet, thou hast cleft my heart in twain.

HAMLET   O throw away the worser part of it 155
And live the purer with the other half.
Goodnight, but go not to my uncle's bed;
Assume a virtue if you have it not.
That monster Custom, who all sense doth eat
Of habits devil, is angel yet in this, 160
That to the use of actions fair and good
He likewise gives a frock or livery
That aptly is put on. Refrain tonight
And that shall lend a kind of easiness
To the next abstinence, the next more easy. 165
For use almost can change the stamp of nature
And either shame the devil or throw him out
With wondrous potency. Once more goodnight,
And when you are desirous to be blessed
I'll blessing beg of you. For this same lord 170
I do repent, but heaven hath pleased it so
To punish me with this, and this with me,
That I must be their scourge and minister.
I will bestow him and will answer well
The death I gave him. So again goodnight. 175
I must be cruel only to be kind.
This bad begins and worse remains behind.
One word more, good lady!

QUEEN   What shall I do?

HAMLET   Not this, by no means, that I bid you do –
Let the bloat King tempt you again to bed, 180
Pinch wanton on your cheek, call you his mouse
And let him for a pair of reechy kisses,
Or paddling in your neck with his damned fingers,
Make you to ravel all this matter out
That I essentially am not in madness 185
But mad in craft. 'Twere good you let him know,

For who that's but a queen – fair, sober, wise –
Would from a paddock, from a bat, a gib,
Such dear concernings hide? Who would do so?
190 No, in despite of sense and secrecy
Unpeg the basket on the house's top,
Let the birds fly and like the famous ape
To try conclusions in the basket creep
And break your own neck down.
195 QUEEN   Be thou assured, if words be made of breath
And breath of life, I have no life to breathe
What thou hast said to me.
HAMLET   I must to England – you know that.
QUEEN   Alack, I had forgot; 'tis so concluded on.
HAMLET
200 There's letters sealed and my two schoolfellows –
Whom I will trust as I will adders fanged –
They bear the mandate, they must sweep my way
And marshal me to knavery. Let it work.
For 'tis the sport to have the enginer
205 Hoist with his own petard, and't shall go hard
But I will delve one yard below their mines
And blow them at the moon. O, 'tis most sweet
When in one line two crafts directly meet.
This man shall set me packing;
210 I'll lug the guts into the neighbour room.
Mother, goodnight indeed. This councillor
Is now most still, most secret and most grave,
Who was in life a most foolish prating knave.
Come, sir, to draw toward an end with you.
215 Goodnight, mother.
Exit Hamlet tugging in Polonius.

4.1   *Enter* KING *with* ROSENCRANTZ *and*
GUILDENSTERN.

KING
There's matter in these sighs, these profound heaves.
You must translate; 'tis fit we understand them.
Where is your son?
QUEEN
Bestow this place on us a little while.
Exeunt Rosencrantz and Guildenstern.
5   Ah, mine own lord, what have I seen tonight!
KING   What, Gertrude? How does Hamlet?
QUEEN   Mad as the sea and wind when both contend
Which is the mightier. In his lawless fit,
Behind the arras hearing something stir,
10 Whips out his rapier, cries 'A rat, a rat!'
And in this brainish apprehension kills
The unseen good old man.
KING   O heavy deed!
It had been so with us had we been there.
His liberty is full of threats to all,
15 To you yourself, to us, to everyone.
Alas, how shall this bloody deed be answered?
It will be laid to us whose providence
Should have kept short, restrained and out of haunt

This mad young man. But so much was our love,
We would not understand what was most fit, 20
But like the owner of a foul disease,
To keep it from divulging, let it feed
Even on the pith of life. Where is he gone?
QUEEN   To draw apart the body he hath killed,
O'er whom – his very madness like some ore 25
Among a mineral of metals base
Shows itself pure – 'a weeps for what is done.
KING   O Gertrude, come away.
The sun no sooner shall the mountains touch
But we will ship him hence, and this vile deed 30
We must with all our majesty and skill
Both countenance and excuse. Ho, Guildenstern!

Enter ROSENCRANTZ *and* GUILDENSTERN.

Friends both, go join you with some further aid:
Hamlet in madness hath Polonius slain
And from his mother's closet hath he dragged him. 35
Go seek him out, speak fair and bring the body
Into the chapel. I pray you haste in this.
Exeunt Rosencrantz and Guildenstern.
Come, Gertrude, we'll call up our wisest friends
And let them know both what we mean to do
And what's untimely done. [   ] 40
Whose whisper o'er the world's diameter,
As level as the cannon to his blank,
Transports his poisoned shot, may miss our name
And hit the woundless air. O come away,
My soul is full of discord and dismay.   *Exeunt.* 45

4.2   *Enter* HAMLET.

HAMLET   Safely stowed! But soft, what noise? Who calls
on Hamlet? O, here they come!

Enter ROSENCRANTZ, GUILDENSTERN *and others.*

ROSENCRANTZ   What have you done, my lord, with the
dead body?
HAMLET   Compound it with dust, whereto 'tis kin. 5
ROSENCRANTZ   Tell us where 'tis, that we may take it
thence and bear it to the chapel.
HAMLET   Do not believe it.
ROSENCRANTZ   Believe what?
HAMLET   That I can keep your council and not mine 10
own. Besides, to be demanded of a sponge! What
replication should be made by the son of a king?
ROSENCRANTZ   Take you me for a sponge, my lord?
HAMLET   Ay, sir – that soaks up the King's countenance,
his rewards, his authorities. But such officers do the 15
King best service in the end: he keeps them like an ape
in the corner of his jaw, first mouthed to be last
swallowed. When he needs what you have gleaned, it is
but squeezing you and, sponge, you shall be dry again!
ROSENCRANTZ   I understand you not, my lord. 20
HAMLET   I am glad of it. A knavish speech sleeps in a
foolish ear.

ROSENCRANTZ My lord, you must tell us where the
 body is, and go with us to the King.

25 HAMLET The body is with the King, but the King is not
 with the body. The King is a thing.

GUILDENSTERN A thing, my lord?

HAMLET Of nothing. Bring me to him. *Exeunt.*

4.3 *Enter* KING *and two or three.*

KING I have sent to seek him and to find the body.
 How dangerous is it that this man goes loose!
 Yet must not we put the strong law on him:
 He's loved of the distracted multitude,
5 Who like not in their judgement but their eyes,
 And where 'tis so th'offender's scourge is weighed
 But never the offence. To bear all smooth and even
 This sudden sending him away must seem
 Deliberate pause; diseases desperate grown
10 By desperate appliance are relieved,
 Or not at all.

   Enter ROSENCRANTZ *and* GUILDENSTERN
    and all the rest.

   How now, what hath befallen?

ROSENCRANTZ
 Where the dead body is bestowed, my lord,
 We cannot get from him.

KING   But where is he?

ROSENCRANTZ
 Without, my lord, guarded, to know your pleasure.

KING Bring him before us.

15 ROSENCRANTZ   Ho! Bring in the lord!

   Enter HAMLET *and Attendants.*

KING Now, Hamlet, where's Polonius?

HAMLET At supper.

KING At supper! Where?

HAMLET Not where he eats but where 'a is eaten. A
20 certain convocation of politic worms are e'en at him.
 Your worm is your only emperor for diet. We fat all
 creatures else to fat us, and we fat ourselves for maggots.
 Your fat king and your lean beggar is but variable
 service, two dishes but to one table. That's the end.

25 KING Alas, alas.

HAMLET A man may fish with the worm that hath eat of
 a king and eat of the fish that hath fed of that worm.

KING What dost thou mean by this?

HAMLET Nothing but to show you how a king may go a
30 progress through the guts of a beggar.

KING Where is Polonius?

HAMLET In heaven. Send thither to see. If your
 messenger find him not there, seek him i'th' other
 place yourself. But if indeed you find him not within
35 this month you shall nose him as you go up the stairs
 into the lobby.

KING [*to some Attendants*] Go, seek him there!

HAMLET 'A will stay till you come.

    Exeunt Attendants.

KING Hamlet, this deed for thine especial safety –
 Which we do tender, as we dearly grieve 40
 For that which thou hast done – must send thee
  hence.
 Therefore prepare thyself:
 The bark is ready and the wind at help,
 Th'associates tend and everything is bent
 For England.

HAMLET   For England?

KING   Ay, Hamlet.

HAMLET   Good. 45

KING So is it if thou knewst our purposes.

HAMLET
 I see a cherub that sees them. But come, for
  England.
 Farewell, dear mother.

KING   Thy loving father, Hamlet.

HAMLET
 My mother. Father and mother is man and wife.
 Man and wife is one flesh. So – my mother. 50
 Come, for England!   *Exit.*

KING   Follow him at foot.
 Tempt him with speed aboard.
 Delay it not – I'll have him hence tonight.
 Away, for everything is sealed and done
 That else leans on th'affair. Pray you make haste. 55

    Exeunt all but the King.

 And England, if my love thou hold'st at aught
 As my great power thereof may give thee sense,
 Since yet thy cicatrice looks raw and red
 After the Danish sword, and thy free awe
 Pays homage to us, thou mayst not coldly set 60
 Our sovereign process, which imports at full
 By letters congruing to that effect
 The present death of Hamlet. Do it, England!
 For like the hectic in my blood he rages
 And thou must cure me. Till I know 'tis done, 65
 Howe'er my haps my joys will ne'er begin. *Exit.*

4.4 *Enter* FORTINBRAS *and a* Captain
   with his army over the stage.

FORTINBRAS
 Go, Captain, from me greet the Danish King:
 Tell him that by his licence Fortinbras
 Craves the conveyance of a promised march
 Over his kingdom. You know the rendezvous.
 If that his majesty would aught with us 5
 We shall express our duty in his eye,
 And let him know so.

CAPTAIN   I will do't, my lord.

FORTINBRAS Go softly on. *Exeunt all but Captain.*

   Enter HAMLET, ROSENCRANTZ,
    GUILDENSTERN *and others.*

HAMLET   Good sir, whose powers are these?

CAPTAIN	They are of Norway, sir.

10 **HAMLET**   How purposed, sir, I pray you?

CAPTAIN   Against some part of Poland.

HAMLET   Who commands them, sir?

CAPTAIN   The nephew to old Norway, Fortinbras.

HAMLET   Goes it against the main of Poland, sir,

15   Or for some frontier?

CAPTAIN   Truly to speak, and with no addition,
We go to gain a little patch of ground
That hath in it no profit but the name.
To pay five ducats – five – I would not farm it,

20   Nor will it yield to Norway or the Pole
A ranker rate should it be sold in fee.

HAMLET   Why then the Polack never will defend it.

CAPTAIN   Yes, it is already garrisoned.

HAMLET

Two thousand souls and twenty thousand ducats

25   Will not debate the question of this straw.
This is th'impostume of much wealth and peace
That inward breaks and shows no cause without
Why the man dies. I humbly thank you, sir.

CAPTAIN   God buy you, sir.   *Exit.*

ROSENCRANTZ   Will't please you go, my lord?

30 **HAMLET**   I'll be with you straight. Go a little before.
  [*Rosencrantz, Guildenstern and the others move away.*]
How all occasions do inform against me
And spur my dull revenge. What is a man
If his chief good and market of his time
Be but to sleep and feed? A beast – no more.

35   Sure he that made us with such large discourse,
Looking before and after, gave us not
That capability and godlike reason
To fust in us unused. Now whether it be
Bestial oblivion or some craven scruple

40   Of thinking too precisely on th'event
(A thought which quartered hath but one part wisdom
And ever three parts coward) I do not know
Why yet I live to say this thing's to do,
Sith I have cause and will and strength and means

45   To do't. Examples gross as earth exhort me –
Witness this army of such mass and charge,
Led by a delicate and tender prince
Whose spirit with divine ambition puffed
Makes mouths at the invisible event

50   Exposing what is mortal and unsure
To all that fortune, death and danger dare
Even for an eggshell. Rightly to be great
Is not to stir without great argument
But greatly to find quarrel in a straw

55   When honour's at the stake. How stand I then
That have a father killed, a mother stained,
Excitements of my reason and my blood,
And let all sleep; while to my shame I see
The imminent death of twenty thousand men

60   That for a fantasy and trick of fame
Go to their graves like beds, fight for a plot
Whereon the numbers cannot try the cause,

Which is not tomb enough and continent
To hide the slain? O, from this time forth
My thoughts be bloody or be nothing worth.   *Exeunt.*   65

4.5   *Enter* HORATIO, QUEEN *and a* Gentleman.

QUEEN   I will not speak with her.

GENTLEMAN   She is importunate – indeed, distract.
Her mood will needs be pitied.

QUEEN   What would she have?

GENTLEMAN
She speaks much of her father, says she hears
There's tricks i'th' world, and hems and beats her heart,   5
Spurns enviously at straws, speaks things in doubt
That carry but half sense. Her speech is nothing,
Yet the unshaped use of it doth move
The hearers to collection. They yawn at it
And botch the words up fit to their own thoughts   10
Which, as her winks and nods and gestures yield them,
Indeed would make one think there might be thought,
Though nothing sure, yet much unhappily.

HORATIO
'Twere good she were spoken with, for she may strew
Dangerous conjectures in ill-breeding minds.   15
Let her come in.   *Exit Gentleman.*

Enter OPHELIA.

QUEEN [*aside*]
To my sick soul, as sin's true nature is,
Each toy seems prologue to some great amiss,
So full of artless jealousy is guilt
It spills itself in fearing to be spilt.   20

OPHELIA
Where is the beauteous majesty of Denmark?

QUEEN   How now, Ophelia?

OPHELIA [*Sings.*]
How should I your true love know
From another one?
By his cockle hat and staff   25
And his sandal shoon.

QUEEN   Alas, sweet lady, what imports this song?

OPHELIA   Say you? Nay, pray you, mark.
  [*Sings.*]
He is dead and gone, lady,
He is dead and gone.   30
At his head a grass-green turf,
At his heels a stone.
O ho!

QUEEN   Nay, but Ophelia –

OPHELIA   Pray you mark.   35
  [*Sings.*]
White his shroud as the mountain snow –

Enter KING.

QUEEN   Alas, look here, my lord.

OPHELIA [*Sings.*]
Larded all with sweet flowers

40 Which bewept to the ground did not go
    With true-love showers.
KING How do you, pretty lady?
OPHELIA Well, good dild you. They say the owl was a
    baker's daughter. Lord, we know what we are but know
    not what we may be. God be at your table.
45 KING Conceit upon her father –
OPHELIA Pray, let's have no words of this, but when
    they ask you what it means, say you this:
    [*Sings.*]
        Tomorrow is Saint Valentine's Day
        All in the morning betime,
50   And I a maid at your window
        To be your valentine.

        Then up he rose and donned his clothes
        And dupped the chamber door –
        Let in the maid that out a maid
55   Never departed more.
KING Pretty Ophelia –
OPHELIA Indeed, without an oath I'll make an end on't.
    [*Sings.*]
        By Gis and by Saint Charity,
        Alack and fie for shame,
60   Young men will do't if they come to't:
        By Cock they are to blame.

        Quoth she, 'Before you tumbled me
        You promised me to wed.'
    He answers:
65   'So would I ha' done by yonder sun
        An thou hadst not come to my bed.'
KING How long hath she been thus?
OPHELIA I hope all will be well. We must be patient. But
    I cannot choose but weep to think they would lay him
70 i'th' cold ground. My brother shall know of it. And so
    I thank you for your good counsel. Come, my coach!
    Goodnight, ladies, goodnight. Sweet ladies, goodnight,
    goodnight.   *Exit.*
KING
    Follow her close. Give her good watch, I pray you.
                                          Exit Horatio.
75 O, this is the poison of deep grief. It springs
    All from her father's death, and now behold –
    O Gertrude, Gertrude,
    When sorrows come they come not single spies
    But in battalions: first, her father slain;
80 Next, your son gone, and he most violent author
    Of his own just remove; the people muddied,
    Thick and unwholesome in thoughts and whispers
    For good Polonius' death, and we have done but greenly
    In hugger-mugger to inter him; poor Ophelia
85 Divided from herself and her fair judgement,
    Without the which we are pictures or mere beasts;
    Last, and as much containing as all these,
    Her brother is in secret come from France,
    Feeds on this wonder, keeps himself in clouds

90 And wants not buzzers to infect his ear
    With pestilent speeches of his father's death –
    Wherein necessity, of matter beggared,
    Will nothing stick our person to arraign
    In ear and ear. O my dear Gertrude, this,
95 Like to a murdering-piece in many places
    Gives me superfluous death.   [*A noise within*]

            Enter a Messenger.

                              Attend!
    Where is my Switzers? Let them guard the door.
    What is the matter?
MESSENGER   Save yourself, my lord.
    The ocean overpeering of his list
100 Eats not the flats with more impiteous haste
    Than young Laertes in a riotous head
    O'erbears your officers. The rabble call him lord
    And, as the world were now but to begin,
    Antiquity forgot, custom not known,
105 The ratifiers and props of every word,
    They cry, 'Choose we: Laertes shall be king!' –
    Caps, hands and tongue, applaud it to the clouds –
    'Laertes shall be king! Laertes king!'
QUEEN How cheerfully on the false trail they cry.
                                      [*A noise within*]
110 O, this is counter, you false Danish dogs!
KING The doors are broke.

        Enter LAERTES *with* Followers.

LAERTES
    Where is this king? Sirs, stand you all without.
FOLLOWERS No, let's come in.
LAERTES   I pray you give me leave.
FOLLOWERS We will, we will.
LAERTES I thank you, keep the door.
                    Exeunt Followers and Messenger.
                              O thou vile King,
115 Give me my father.
QUEEN   Calmly, good Laertes.
LAERTES
    That drop of blood that's calm proclaims me bastard,
    Cries 'Cuckold!' to my father, brands the harlot
    Even here between the chaste unsmirched brow
    Of my true mother.
KING   What is the cause, Laertes,
120 That thy rebellion looks so giant-like?
    Let him go, Gertrude, do not fear our person.
    There's such divinity doth hedge a king
    That treason can but peep to what it would,
    Acts little of his will. Tell me, Laertes,
125 Why thou art thus incensed. Let him go, Gertrude.
    Speak, man.
LAERTES   Where is my father?
KING   Dead.
QUEEN But not by him.
KING   Let him demand his fill.

LAERTES   How came he dead? I'll not be juggled with.
130   To hell allegiance, vows to the blackest devil,
      Conscience and grace to the profoundest pit.
      I dare damnation. To this point I stand –
      That both the worlds I give to negligence.
      Let come what comes, only I'll be revenged
      Most throughly for my father.
135   KING   Who shall stay you?
      LAERTES   My will, not all the world's.
      And for my means I'll husband them so well
      They shall go far with little.
      KING   Good Laertes,
      If you desire to know the certainty
140   Of your dear father, is't writ in your revenge
      That swoopstake you will draw both friend and foe,
      Winner and loser?
      LAERTES   None but his enemies.
      KING   Will you know them, then?
      LAERTES
      To his good friends thus wide I'll ope my arms
145   And like the kind life-rendering pelican
      Repast them with my blood.
      KING   Why, now you speak
      Like a good child and a true gentleman.
      That I am guiltless of your father's death
      And am most sensibly in grief for it
150   It shall as level to your judgement 'pear
      As day does to your eye.   [*A noise within*]

                    Enter OPHELIA.

      LAERTES   Let her come in.
      How now, what noise is that?
      O heat, dry up my brains, tears seven times salt
155   Burn out the sense and virtue of mine eye.
      By heaven, thy madness shall be paid with weight
      Till our scale turn the beam. O rose of May,
      Dear maid, kind sister, sweet Ophelia,
      O heavens, is't possible a young maid's wits
      Should be as mortal as a poor man's life?
      OPHELIA [*Sings.*]
160   They bore him bare-faced on the bier
                  And in his grave rained many a tear.
      Fare you well, my dove.
      LAERTES
      Hadst thou thy wits and didst persuade revenge
      It could not move thus.
165   OPHELIA   You must sing 'a-down a-down', an you call
      him 'a-down-a'. O how the wheel becomes it. It is the
      false steward that stole his master's daughter.
      LAERTES   This nothing's more than matter.
      OPHELIA   There's rosemary: that's for remembrance.
170   Pray you, love, remember. And there is pansies: that's
      for thoughts.
      LAERTES
      A document in madness – thoughts and remembrance
         fitted!
      OPHELIA   There's fennel for you, and columbines.

There's rue for you, and here's some for me. We may
call it herb of grace o'Sundays. You may wear your rue   175
with a difference. There's a daisy. I would give you
some violets, but they withered all when my father
died. They say 'a made a good end.
[*Sings.*]   For bonny sweet Robin is all my joy.
LAERTES   Thought and afflictions, passion, hell itself   180
She turns to favour and to prettiness.
OPHELIA [*Sings.*]
            And will 'a not come again?
            And will 'a not come again?
            No, no, he is dead,
            Go to thy deathbed.   185
            He never will come again.

            His beard was as white as snow,
            Flaxen was his poll.
            He is gone, he is gone,
            And we cast away moan.   190
            God a' mercy on his soul.
And of all Christians' souls. God buy you.   *Exit.*
LAERTES   Do you see this, O God?
KING
Laertes, I must commune with your grief
Or you deny me right. Go but apart,   195
Make choice of whom your wisest friends you will,
And they shall hear and judge 'twixt you and me.
If by direct or by collateral hand
They find us touched, we will our kingdom give –
Our crown, our life, and all that we call ours –   200
To you in satisfaction. But, if not,
Be you content to lend your patience to us
And we shall jointly labour with your soul
To give it due content.
LAERTES   Let this be so.
His means of death, his obscure funeral –   205
No trophy, sword nor hatchment o'er his bones,
No noble rite, nor formal ostentation –
Cry to be heard as 'twere from heaven to earth
That I must call't in question.
KING   So you shall,
And where th'offence is let the great axe fall.   210
I pray you go with them.   *Exeunt.*

4.6   *Enter* HORATIO *and a* Gentleman.

HORATIO   What are they that would speak with me?
GENTLEMAN   Sea-faring men, sir. They say they have
letters for you.
HORATIO   Let them come in.   *Exit Gentleman.*
I do not know from what part of the world I should be   5
greeted if not from Lord Hamlet.

                    Enter Sailors.

SAILOR   God bless you, sir.
HORATIO   Let Him bless thee too.
SAILOR   'A shall, sir, an please Him. There's a letter for

10   you, sir – it came from th'ambassador that was bound
for England – if your name be Horatio, as I am let to
know it is.

HORATIO [*Reads.*] *Horatio, when thou shalt have*
overlooked this, give these fellows some means to the King:
15   *they have letters for him. Ere we were two days old at sea,*
a pirate of very warlike appointment gave us chase.
Finding ourselves too slow of sail, we put on a compelled
valour and in the grapple I boarded them. On the instant
they got clear of our ship, so I alone became their prisoner.
20   *They have dealt with me like thieves of mercy, but they*
knew what they did: I am to do a turn for them. Let the
King have the letters I have sent, and repair thou to me
with as much speed as thou wouldest fly death. I have
words to speak in thine ear will make thee dumb. Yet are
25   *they much too light for the bore of the matter. These good*
fellows will bring thee where I am. Rosencrantz and
Guildenstern hold their course for England. Of them I
have much to tell thee. Farewell. He that thou knowest
thine. Hamlet.

Come. I will give you way for these your letters.
30   And do't the speedier that you may direct me
To him from whom you brought them.   *Exeunt.*

4.7   *Enter* KING *and* LAERTES.

KING
Now must your conscience my acquittance seal
And you must put me in your heart for friend
Sith you have heard and with a knowing ear
That he which hath your noble father slain
5   Pursued my life.

LAERTES   It well appears. But tell me
Why you proceed not against these feats
So criminal and so capital in nature
As by your safety, greatness, wisdom, all things else,
You mainly were stirred up.

10   KING   O, for two special reasons
Which may to you perhaps seem much unsinewed
But yet to me they're strong. The Queen his mother
Lives almost by his looks and for myself,
My virtue or my plague, be it either which,
15   She is so conjunct to my life and soul
That as the star moves not but in his sphere
I could not but by her. The other motive
Why to a public count I might not go
Is the great love the general gender bear him,
20   Who, dipping all his faults in their affection,
Work like the spring that turneth wood to stone,
Convert his gyves to graces, so that my arrows,
Too slightly timbered for so loud a wind,
Would have reverted to my bow again
25   But not where I have aimed them.

LAERTES   And so have I a noble father lost,
A sister driven into desperate terms
Whose worth, if praises may go back again,
Stood challenger on mount of all the age

For her perfections. But my revenge will come.   30
KING
Break not your sleeps for that; you must not think
That we are made of stuff so flat and dull
That we can let our beard be shook with danger
And think it pastime. You shortly shall hear more.
I loved your father and we love ourself,   35
And that, I hope, will teach you to imagine –

          Enter a Messenger *with letters.*

MESSENGER   These to your majesty, this to the Queen.
KING   From Hamlet! Who brought them?
MESSENGER
Sailors, my lord, they say. I saw them not.
They were given me by Claudio. He received them   40
Of him that brought them.
KING   Laertes, you shall hear them.
Leave us.   *Exit Messenger.*
[*Reads.*] *High and mighty. You shall know I am set*
naked on your kingdom. Tomorrow shall I beg leave to see
your kingly eyes. When I shall (first asking you pardon)   45
thereunto recount the occasion of my sudden return.
What should this mean? Are all the rest come back,
Or is it some abuse, and no such thing?
LAERTES   Know you the hand?
KING   'Tis Hamlet's character. 'Naked',
And in a postscript here he says 'alone'.   50
Can you devise me?
LAERTES   I am lost in it, my lord, but let him come.
It warms the very sickness in my heart
That I live and tell him to his teeth
'Thus didst thou.'
KING   If it be so, Laertes –   55
As how should it be so, how otherwise? –
Will you be ruled by me?
LAERTES   Ay, my lord,
So you will not o'errule me to a peace.
KING   To thine own peace. If he be now returned
As checking at his voyage, and that he means   60
No more to undertake it, I will work him
To an exploit, now ripe in my device,
Under the which he shall not choose but fall.
And for his death no wind of blame shall breathe
But even his mother shall uncharge the practice   65
And call it accident.
LAERTES   My lord, I will be ruled
The rather if you could devise it so
That I might be the organ.
KING   It falls right.
You have been talked of since your travel much,
And that in Hamlet's hearing, for a quality   70
Wherein they say you shine. Your sum of parts
Did not together pluck such envy from him
As did that one, and that in my regard
Of the unworthiest siege.
LAERTES   What part is that, my lord?   75
KING   A very ribbon in the cap of youth.

Yet needful too, for youth no less becomes
The light and careless livery that it wears
Than settled age his sables and his weeds
80 Importing health and graveness. Two months since
Here was a gentleman of Normandy –
I have seen myself, and served against, the French
And they can well on horseback, but this gallant
Had witchcraft in't; he grew unto his seat
85 And to such wondrous doing brought his horse
As had he been incorpsed and demi-natured
With the brave beast. So far he topped my thought
That I in forgery of shapes and tricks
Come short of what he did.
LAERTES   A Norman was't?
KING   A Norman.
LAERTES   Upon my life, Lamord!
90 KING   The very same.
LAERTES   I know him well. He is the brooch, indeed,
And gem of all the nation.
KING   He made confession of you
And gave you such a masterly report
95 For art and exercise in your defence,
And for your rapier most especial,
That he cried out 'twould be a sight indeed
If one could match you. Th'escrimers of their nation
He swore had neither motion, guard nor eye
100 If you opposed them. Sir, this report of his
Did Hamlet so envenom with his envy
That he could nothing do but wish and beg
Your sudden coming o'er to play with you.
Now out of this –
LAERTES   What out of this, my lord?
105 KING   Laertes, was your father dear to you?
Or are you like the painting of a sorrow,
A face without a heart?
LAERTES   Why ask you this?
KING   Not that I think you did not love your father
But that I know love is begun by time
110 And that I see in passages of proof
Time qualifies the spark and fire of it.
There lives within the very flame of love
A kind of wick or snuff that will abate it,
And nothing is at a like goodness still,
115 For goodness growing to a pleurisy
Dies in his own too much. That we would do
We should do when we would, for this 'would' changes
And hath abatements and delays as many
As there are tongues, are hands, are accidents,
120 And then this 'should' is like a spendthrift's sigh
That hurts by easing. But to the quick of th'ulcer –
Hamlet comes back. What would you undertake
To show yourself in deed your father's son
More than in words?
LAERTES   To cut his throat i'th' church.
125 KING   No place indeed should murder sanctuarize.
Revenge should have no bounds. But, good Laertes,
Will you do this? Keep close within your chamber;

Hamlet returned shall know you are come home;
We'll put on those shall praise your excellence
And set a double varnish on the fame   130
The Frenchman gave you, bring you in fine together
And wager on your heads. He being remiss,
Most generous and free from all contriving,
Will not peruse the foils, so that with ease,
Or with a little shuffling, you may choose   135
A sword unbated and in a pass of practice
Requite him for your father.
LAERTES   I will do't.
And for that purpose I'll anoint my sword.
I bought an unction of a mountebank
So mortal that, but dip a knife in it,   140
Where it draws blood no cataplasm so rare,
Collected from all simples that have virtue
Under the moon, can save the thing from death
That is but scratched withal. I'll touch my point
With this contagion, that if I gall him slightly   145
It may be death.
KING   Let's further think of this,
Weigh what convenience both of time and means
May fit us to our shape. If this should fail
And that our drift look through our bad performance
'Twere better not essayed. Therefore this project   150
Should have a back or second that might hold
If this did blast in proof. Soft, let me see:
We'll make a solemn wager on your cunnings –
I ha't!
When in your motion you are hot and dry   155
(As make your bouts more violent to that end)
And that he calls for drink, I'll have preferred him
A chalice for the nonce, whereon but sipping,
If he by chance escape your venomed stuck,
Our purpose may hold there. But stay, what noise?   160

Enter QUEEN.

QUEEN   One woe doth tread upon another's heel,
So fast they follow. Your sister's drowned, Laertes.
LAERTES   Drowned! O, where?
QUEEN   There is a willow grows askant the brook
That shows his hoary leaves in the glassy stream.   165
Therewith fantastic garlands did she make
Of crowflowers, nettles, daisies and long purples,
That liberal shepherds give a grosser name
But our cold maids do dead men's fingers call them.
There on the pendent boughs her crownet weeds   170
Clambering to hang, an envious sliver broke,
When down her weedy trophies and herself
Fell in the weeping brook. Her clothes spread wide
And mermaid-like awhile they bore her up,
Which time she chanted snatches of old lauds   175
As one incapable of her own distress,
Or like a creature native and endued
Unto that element. But long it could not be
Till that her garments, heavy with their drink,
Pulled the poor wretch from her melodious lay   180

To muddy death.

LAERTES   Alas, then she is drowned.

QUEEN   Drowned, drowned.

LAERTES   Too much of water hast thou, poor Ophelia,
And therefore I forbid my tears. But yet
185   It is our trick – nature her custom holds
Let shame say what it will. [*Weeps.*] When these are
    gone
The woman will be out. Adieu, my lord,
I have a speech o'fire that fain would blaze
But that this folly drowns it.   *Exit.*

KING   Let's follow, Gertrude.
190   How much I had to do to calm his rage!
Now fear I this will give it start again.
Therefore let's follow.   *Exeunt.*

5.1   *Enter two Clowns, a* GRAVEDIGGER
              and a Second Man.

GRAVEDIGGER   Is she to be buried in Christian burial,
when she wilfully seeks her own salvation?

2 MAN   I tell thee she is. Therefore make her grave
straight. The crowner hath sat on her and finds it
5   Christian burial.

GRAVEDIGGER   How can that be unless she drowned
herself in her own defence?

2 MAN   Why, 'tis found so.

GRAVEDIGGER   It must be *se offendendo*. It cannot be else.
10   For here lies the point: if I drown myself wittingly, it
argues an act, and an act hath three branches – it is to
act, to do, to perform. Argal, she drowned herself
wittingly.

2 MAN   Nay, but hear you, goodman delver.

15   GRAVEDIGGER   Give me leave. Here lies the water – good.
Here stands the man – good. If the man go to this water
and drown himself, it is, willy-nilly, he goes. Mark you
that. But if the water come to him and drown him, he
drowns not himself. Argal, he that is not guilty of his
20   own death shortens not his own life.

2 MAN   But is this law?

GRAVEDIGGER   Ay, marry is't. Crowner's 'quest law.

2 MAN   Will you ha' the truth on't? If this had not been
a gentlewoman she should have been buried out
25   o'Christian burial.

GRAVEDIGGER   Why, there thou sayst, and the more
pity that great folk should have countenance in this
world to drown or hang themselves more than their
even-Christen. Come, my spade. There is no ancient
30   gentlemen but gardeners, ditchers and grave-makers.
They hold up Adam's profession.

2 MAN   Was he a gentleman?

GRAVEDIGGER   'A was the first that ever bore arms. I'll
put another question to thee. If thou answerest me not
35   to the purpose, confess thyself.

2 MAN   Go to.

GRAVEDIGGER   What is he that builds stronger than
either the mason, the shipwright or the carpenter?

2 MAN   The gallows-maker, for that outlives a thousand
tenants.   40

GRAVEDIGGER   I like thy wit well, in good faith. The
gallows does well. But how does it well? It does well to
those that do ill. Now, thou dost ill to say the gallows is
built stronger than the church. Argal, the gallows may
do well to thee. To't again, come.   45

2 MAN   Who builds stronger than a mason, a shipwright
or a carpenter?

GRAVEDIGGER   Ay, tell me that and unyoke.

2 MAN   Marry, now I can tell.

GRAVEDIGGER   To't!   50

2 MAN   Mass, I cannot tell.

GRAVEDIGGER   Cudgel thy brains no more about it, for
your dull ass will not mend his pace with beating. And
when you are asked this question next, say a grave-
maker. The houses he makes lasts till doomsday. Go get   55
thee in and fetch me a stoup of liquor.

                                        Exit Second Man.

[*Sings.*]
    In youth when I did love, did love,
    Methought it was very sweet
    To contract-a the time for-a my behove,
    O, methought there-a was nothing-a meet!   60

              Enter HAMLET *and* HORATIO.

HAMLET   Has this fellow no feeling of his business? 'A
sings in grave-making.

HORATIO   Custom hath made it in him a property of
easiness.

HAMLET   'Tis e'en so. The hand of little employment   65
hath the daintier sense.

GRAVEDIGGER [*Sings.*]
    But age with his stealing steps
    Hath clawed me in his clutch
    And hath shipped me into the land
    As if I had never been such.   70
    [*Throws up a skull.*]

HAMLET   That skull had a tongue in it and could sing
once. How the knave jowls it to the ground, as if 'twere
Cain's jawbone, that did the first murder. This might be
the pate of a politician which this ass now o'erreaches –
one that would circumvent God, might it not?   75

HORATIO   It might, my lord.

HAMLET   Or of a courtier which could say, 'Good
morrow, sweet lord, how dost thou, sweet lord?' This
might be my Lord Such-a-One, that praised my Lord
Such-a-One's horse when 'a went to beg it, might it   80
not?

HORATIO   Ay, my lord.

HAMLET   Why, e'en so. And now my Lady Worm's –
chapless and knocked about the mazard with a sexton's
spade. Here's fine revolution an we had the trick to see't. 85
Did these bones cost no more the breeding
but to play at loggets with them? Mine ache to think
on't.

GRAVEDIGGER [*Sings.*]

A pickaxe and a spade, a spade,
For and a shrouding-sheet,
O, a pit of clay for to be made
For such a guest is meet.

[*Throws up another skull.*]

HAMLET   There's another! Why, may not that be the
skull of a lawyer? Where be his quiddities now – his
quillets, his cases, his tenures and his tricks? Why does
he suffer this mad knave now to knock him about the
sconce with a dirty shovel and will not tell him of his
action of battery? Hum! This fellow might be in's time
a great buyer of land, with his statutes, his recognizances,
his fines, his double vouchers, his recoveries. To have
his fine pate full of fine dirt! Will vouchers vouch him
no more of his purchases and doubles than the length
and breadth of a pair of indentures? The very
conveyances of his lands will scarcely lie in this box, and
must th'inheritor himself have no more, ha?

HORATIO   Not a jot more, my lord.

HAMLET   Is not parchment made of sheepskins?

HORATIO   Ay, my lord, and of calves' skins too.

HAMLET   They are sheep and calves which seek out
assurance in that. I will speak to this fellow. Whose
grave's this, sirrah?

GRAVEDIGGER   Mine, sir,

[*Sings.*]
O, a pit of clay for to be made –

HAMLET   I think it be thine, indeed, for thou liest in't.

GRAVEDIGGER   You lie out on't, sir, and therefore 'tis
not yours. For my part I do not lie in't, yet it is mine.

HAMLET   Thou dost lie in't, to be in't and say it is thine.
'Tis for the dead, not for the quick. Therefore thou liest.

GRAVEDIGGER   'Tis a quick lie, sir, 'twill away again from
me to you.

HAMLET   What man dost thou dig it for?

GRAVEDIGGER   For no man, sir.

HAMLET   What woman, then?

GRAVEDIGGER   For none, neither.

HAMLET   Who is to be buried in't?

GRAVEDIGGER   One that was a woman, sir, but rest her
soul she's dead.

HAMLET [*to Horatio*]   How absolute the knave is! We must
speak by the card or equivocation will undo us. By the
Lord, Horatio, this three years I have took note of it,
the age is grown so picked that the toe of the peasant
comes so near the heel of the courtier he galls his kibe.
– How long hast thou been grave-maker?

GRAVEDIGGER   Of the days i'th' year I came to't that day
that our last King Hamlet overcame Fortinbras.

HAMLET   How long is that since?

GRAVEDIGGER   Cannot you tell that? Every fool can
tell that! It was that very day that young Hamlet was
born – he that is mad and sent into England.

HAMLET   Ay, marry. Why was he sent into England?

GRAVEDIGGER   Why, because 'a was mad. 'A shall
recover his wits there. Or if 'a do not, 'tis no great
matter there.

HAMLET   Why?

GRAVEDIGGER   'Twill not be seen in him there. There
the men are as mad as he.

HAMLET   How came he mad?

GRAVEDIGGER   Very strangely, they say.

HAMLET   How, strangely?

GRAVEDIGGER   Faith, e'en with losing his wits.

HAMLET   Upon what ground?

GRAVEDIGGER   Why, here in Denmark. I have been
sexton here, man and boy, thirty years.

HAMLET   How long will a man lie i'th' earth ere he
rot?

GRAVEDIGGER   Faith, if 'a be not rotten before 'a die (as
we have many pocky corpses that will scarce hold the
laying in) 'a will last you some eight year – or nine year
– a tanner will last you nine year.

HAMLET   Why he more than another?

GRAVEDIGGER   Why, sir, his hide is so tanned with his
trade that 'a will keep out water a great while. And your
water is a sore decayer of your whoreson dead body.
Here's a skull now hath lien you i'th' earth three and
twenty years.

HAMLET   Whose was it?

GRAVEDIGGER   A whoreson mad fellow's it was. Whose
do you think it was?

HAMLET   Nay, I know not.

GRAVEDIGGER   A pestilence on him for a mad rogue. 'A
poured a flagon of Rhenish on my head once! This
same skull, sir, was, sir, Yorick's skull, the King's jester.

HAMLET   This?

GRAVEDIGGER   E'en that.

HAMLET   Alas, poor Yorick. I knew him, Horatio. A
fellow of infinite jest, of most excellent fancy. He hath
bore me on his back a thousand times, and now how
abhorred in my imagination it is. My gorge rises at it.
Here hung those lips that I have kissed I know not how
oft. Where be your jibes now – your gambols, your
songs, your flashes of merriment, that were wont to set
the table on a roar? Not one now to mock your own
grinning, quite chapfallen. Now get you to my lady's
table and tell her, let her paint an inch thick, to this
favour she must come. Make her laugh at that. Prithee,
Horatio, tell me one thing.

HORATIO   What's that, my lord?

HAMLET   Dost thou think Alexander looked o'this
fashion i'th' earth?

HORATIO   E'en so.

HAMLET   And smelt so? Pah!

HORATIO   E'en so, my lord.

HAMLET   To what base uses we may return, Horatio!
Why may not imagination trace the noble dust of
Alexander till 'a find it stopping a bung-hole?

HORATIO   'Twere to consider too curiously to consider so.

HAMLET   No, faith, not a jot. But to follow him thither
with modesty enough and likelihood to lead it:
Alexander died, Alexander was buried, Alexander
returneth to dust, the dust is earth, of earth we make

loam, and why of that loam whereto he was converted
might they not stop a beer-barrel?

  Imperious Caesar, dead and turned to clay,
  Might stop a hole to keep the wind away.
205 O, that that earth which kept the world in awe
  Should patch a wall t'expel the water's flaw.

Enter KING, QUEEN, LAERTES *and other Lords,*
with a Priest *after the corpse.*

 But soft, but soft awhile, here comes the King,
 The Queen, the courtiers. Who is this they follow?
 And with such maimed rites? This doth betoken
210 The corpse they follow did with desperate hand
 Fordo it own life. 'Twas of some estate.
 Couch we awhile and mark.
  [*Hamlet and Horatio stand aside.*]
LAERTES What ceremony else?
HAMLET [*aside to Horatio*]
 That is Laertes – a very noble youth, mark.
215 LAERTES What ceremony else?
PRIEST Her obsequies have been as far enlarged
 As we have warranty. Her death was doubtful;
 And but that great command o'ersways the order
 She should in ground unsanctified been lodged
220 Till the last trumpet: for charitable prayers,
 Flints and pebbles should be thrown on her.
 Yet here she is allowed her virgin crants,
 Her maiden strewments, and the bringing home
 Of bell and burial.
LAERTES Must there no more be done?
225 PRIEST   No more be done.
 We should profane the service of the dead
 To sing a requiem and such rest to her
 As to peace-parted souls.
LAERTES   Lay her i'th' earth,
 And from her fair and unpolluted flesh
230 May violets spring. I tell thee, churlish priest,
 A ministering angel shall my sister be
 When thou liest howling.
HAMLET [*aside to Horatio*] What, the fair Ophelia?
QUEEN Sweets to the sweet. Farewell.
 I hoped thou shouldst have been my Hamlet's wife:
235 I thought thy bride-bed to have decked, sweet maid,
 And not have strewed thy grave.
LAERTES   O, treble woe
 Fall ten times double on that cursed head
 Whose wicked deed thy most ingenious sense
 Deprived thee of. Hold off the earth awhile,
240 Till I have caught her once more in mine arms.
  [*Leaps in the grave.*]
 Now pile your dust upon the quick and dead
 Till of this flat a mountain you have made
 T'o'ertop old Pelion or the skyish head
 Of blue Olympus.
HAMLET [*Comes forward.*] What is he whose grief
245 Bears such an emphasis, whose phrase of sorrow
 Conjures the wandering stars and makes them stand

Like wonder-wounded hearers? This is I,
Hamlet the Dane.
LAERTES [*Leaps out and grapples with him.*]
     The devil take thy soul!
HAMLET Thou pray'st not well.
 I prithee take thy fingers from my throat,   250
 For, though I am not splenative rash,
 Yet have I in me something dangerous
 Which let thy wisdom fear. Hold off thy hand.
KING Pluck them asunder.
QUEEN   Hamlet! Hamlet!
LORDS   Gentlemen!
HORATIO Good my lord, be quiet.   255
HAMLET Why, I will fight with him upon this theme
 Until my eyelids will no longer wag.
QUEEN O my son, what theme?
HAMLET I loved Ophelia – forty thousand brothers
 Could not with all their quantity of love   260
 Make up my sum. What wilt thou do for her?
KING O, he is mad, Laertes.
QUEEN For love of God, forbear him.
HAMLET 'Swounds, show me what thou'lt do.
 Woul't weep, woul't fight, woul't fast, woul't tear
  thyself,   265
 Woul't drink up eisel, eat a crocodile?
 I'll do't. Dost come here to whine,
 To outface me with leaping in her grave?
 Be buried quick with her, and so will I.
 And if thou prate of mountains let them throw 270
 Millions of acres on us till our ground,
 Singeing his pate against the burning zone,
 Make Ossa like a wart. Nay, an thou'lt mouth,
 I'll rant as well as thou.
QUEEN   This is mere madness,
 And thus awhile the fit will work on him.   275
 Anon, as patient as the female dove
 When that her golden couplets are disclosed,
 His silence will sit drooping.
HAMLET   Hear you, sir,
 What is the reason that you use me thus?
 I loved you ever – but it is no matter.   280
 Let Hercules himself do what he may,
 The cat will mew and dog will have his day. *Exit.*
KING I pray thee, good Horatio, wait upon him.
             Exit Horatio.
[*aside to Laertes*] Strengthen your patience in our last
 night's speech,
We'll put the matter to the present push.   285
– Good Gertrude, set some watch over your son.
This grave shall have a living monument.
An hour of quiet thereby shall we see;
Till then in patience our proceeding be. *Exeunt.*

5.2   *Enter* HAMLET *and* HORATIO.
HAMLET
 So much for this, sir. Now shall you see the other:

You do remember all the circumstance?

HORATIO   Remember it, my lord?

HAMLET   Sir, in my heart there was a kind of fighting
5 That would not let me sleep. Methought I lay
Worse than the mutines in the bilboes. Rashly –
And praised be rashness for it – let us know
Our indiscretion sometime serves us well
When our deep plots do fall – and that should learn us
10 There's a divinity that shapes our ends,
Rough-hew them how we will.

HORATIO   That is most certain.

HAMLET   Up from my cabin,
My sea-gown scarfed about me, in the dark
Groped I to find out them, had my desire,
15 Fingered their packet, and in fine withdrew
To mine own room again, making so bold,
My fears forgetting manners, to unfold
Their grand commission; where I found, Horatio,
A royal knavery, an exact command
20 (Larded with many several sorts of reasons
Importing Denmark's health, and England's too)
With – ho! – such bugs and goblins in my life,
That on the supervise, no leisure bated
– No, not to stay the grinding of the axe! –
My head should be struck off.

25 HORATIO   Is't possible?

HAMLET
Here's the commission; read it at more leisure.
But wilt thou hear now how I did proceed?

HORATIO   I beseech you.

HAMLET   Being thus benetted round with villains,
30 Or I could make a prologue to my brains
They had begun the play. I sat me down,
Devised a new commission, wrote it fair –
I once did hold it as our statists do
A baseness to write fair and laboured much
35 How to forget that learning, but, sir, now
It did me yeoman's service – wilt thou know
Th'effect of what I wrote?

HORATIO   Ay, good my lord.

HAMLET   An earnest conjuration from the King,
As England was his faithful tributary,
40 As love between them like the palm might flourish,
As peace should still her wheaten garland wear
And stand a comma 'tween their amities,
And many such like 'as', sir, of great charge,
That on the view and knowing of these contents,
45 Without debatement further more or less,
He should those bearers put to sudden death,
Not shriving time allowed.

HORATIO   How was this sealed?

HAMLET   Why even in that was heaven ordinant:
I had my father's signet in my purse –
50 Which was the model of that Danish seal –
Folded the writ up in the form of th'other,
Subscribed it, gave't th'impression, placed it safely,
The changeling never known. Now the next day

Was our sea-fight, and what to this was sequent
Thou knowest already.   55

HORATIO   So Guildenstern and Rosencrantz go to't.

HAMLET
They are not near my conscience. Their defeat
Does by their own insinuation grow.
'Tis dangerous when the baser nature comes
Between the pass and fell incensed points   60
Of mighty opposites.

HORATIO   Why, what a king is this!

HAMLET   Does it not, think thee, stand me now upon?
He that hath killed my King and whored my mother,
Popped in between th'election and my hopes,
Thrown out his angle for my proper life   65
And with such cozenage. Is't not perfect conscience?

Enter OSRIC, *a courtier.*

OSRIC   Your lordship is right welcome back to Denmark.

HAMLET   I humbly thank you, sir. [*aside to Horatio*]
Dost know this water-fly?

HORATIO [*aside*]   No, my good lord.   70

HAMLET [*aside*]   Thy state is the more gracious, for 'tis
a vice to know him. He hath much land, and fertile.
Let a beast be lord of beasts and his crib shall stand at
the king's mess. 'Tis a chough but, as I say, spacious in
the possession of dirt.   75

OSRIC   Sweet lord, if your lordship were at leisure I
should impart a thing to you from his majesty.

HAMLET   I will receive it, sir, with all diligence of spirit.
Your bonnet to his right use: 'tis for the head.

OSRIC   I thank your lordship, it is very hot.   80

HAMLET   No, believe me, 'tis very cold; the wind is
northerly.

OSRIC   It is indifferent cold, my lord, indeed.

HAMLET   But yet methinks it is very sultry and hot, or
my complexion –   85

OSRIC   Exceedingly, my lord, it is very sultry, as 'twere
– I cannot tell how. My lord, his majesty bade me
signify to you that 'a has laid a great wager on your
head. Sir, this is the matter –

HAMLET   I beseech you remember.   90

OSRIC   Nay, good my lord, for my ease, in good faith.
Sir, here is newly come to court Laertes – believe me,
an absolute gentleman, full of most excellent
differences, of very soft society and great showing.
Indeed, to speak sellingly of him, he is the card or   95
calendar of gentry, for you shall find in him the
continent of what part a gentleman would see.

HAMLET   Sir, his definement suffers no perdition in
you, though I know to divide him inventorially would
dazzle th'arithmetic of memory, and yet but yaw   100
neither, in respect of his quick sail; but in the verity of
extolment I take him to be a soul of great article and his
infusion of such dearth and rareness as, to make true
diction of him, his semblable is his mirror, and who
else would trace him, his umbrage, nothing more.   105

OSRIC   Your lordship speaks most infallibly of him.

HAMLET　The concernancy, sir – why do we wrap the gentleman in our more rawer breath?

OSRIC　Sir?

110　HORATIO　Is't not possible to understand in another tongue? You will do't, sir, really.

HAMLET　What imports the nomination of this gentleman?

OSRIC　Of Laertes.

115　HORATIO　His purse is empty already – all's golden words are spent.

HAMLET　Of him, sir.

OSRIC　I know you are not ignorant –

HAMLET　I would you did, sir. Yet, in faith, if you did, it

120　would not much approve me. Well, sir?

OSRIC　You are not ignorant of what excellence Laertes is.

HAMLET　I dare not confess that, lest I should compare with him in excellence. But to know a man well were to

125　know himself.

OSRIC　I mean, sir, for his weapon. But in the imputation laid on him by them in his meed he's unfellowed.

HAMLET　What's his weapon?

OSRIC　Rapier and dagger.

130　HAMLET　That's two of his weapons. But well.

OSRIC　The King, sir, hath wagered with him six Barbary horses, against the which he has impawned, as I take it, six French rapiers and poniards, with their assigns, as girdle, hanger and so. Three of the carriages,

135　in faith, are very dear to fancy, very responsive to the hilts, most delicate carriages and of very liberal conceit.

HAMLET　What call you the carriages?

HORATIO　I knew you must be edified by the margin ere

140　you had done.

OSRIC　The carriages, sir, are the hangers.

HAMLET　The phrase would be more germane to the matter if we could carry a cannon by our sides. I would it might be 'hangers' till then. But on. Six Barbary

145　horses against six French swords, their assigns and three liberal-conceited carriages – that's the French bet against the Danish. Why, is this all you call it?

OSRIC　The King, sir, hath laid, sir, that in a dozen passes between yourself and him he shall not exceed

150　you three hits. He hath laid on twelve for nine, and it would come to immediate trial if your lordship would vouchsafe the answer.

HAMLET　How if I answer no?

OSRIC　I mean, my lord, the opposition of your person

155　in trial.

HAMLET　Sir, I will walk here in the hall. If it please his majesty, it is the breathing time of day with me. Let the foils be brought, the gentleman willing and the King hold his purpose – I will win for him an I can; if not, I

160　will gain nothing but my shame and the odd hits.

OSRIC　Shall I deliver you so?

HAMLET　To this effect, sir, after what flourish your nature will.

OSRIC　I commend my duty to your lordship.

HAMLET　Yours. 'A does well to commend it himself.　165

Exit Osric.

There are no tongues else for's turn.

HORATIO　This lapwing runs away with the shell on his head.

HAMLET　'A did so, sir, with his dug before 'a sucked it.

Thus has he, and many more of the same breed that I　170

know the drossy age dotes on, only got the tune of the time and, out of an habit of encounter, a kind of yeasty collection, which carries them through and through the most profane and winnowed opinions; and do but blow them to their trial – the bubbles are out.　175

Enter a Lord.

LORD　My lord, his majesty commended him to you by young Osric, who brings back to him that you attend him in the hall. He sends to know if your pleasure hold to play with Laertes, or that you will take longer time.

HAMLET　I am constant to my purposes. They follow　180

the King's pleasure. If his fitness speaks, mine is ready. Now or whensoever, provided I be so able as now.

LORD　The King and Queen and all are coming down.

HAMLET　In happy time.

LORD　The Queen desires you to use some gentle　185

entertainment to Laertes before you fall to play.

HAMLET　She well instructs me.　　　*Exit Lord.*

HORATIO　You will lose, my lord.

HAMLET　I do not think so. Since he went into France I have been in continual practice. I shall win at the odds.　190

Thou wouldst not think how ill all's here about my heart – but it is no matter.

HORATIO　Nay, good my lord –

HAMLET　It is but foolery, but it is such a kind of gaingiving as would perhaps trouble a woman.　195

HORATIO　If your mind dislike anything, obey it. I will forestall their repair hither and say you are not fit.

HAMLET　Not a whit. We defy augury. There is special providence in the fall of a sparrow. If it be, 'tis not to come. If it be not to come, it will be now. If it be not　200

now, yet it will come. The readiness is all, since no man of aught he leaves knows what is't to leave betimes. Let be.

A table prepared. Trumpets, Drums and Officers with cushions, foils and daggers. Enter KING, QUEEN, LAERTES, OSRIC *and all the state.*

KING

Come, Hamlet, come and take this hand from me.

[*Puts Laertes' hand into Hamlet's.*]

HAMLET

Give me your pardon, sir. I have done you wrong,　205

But pardon't as you are a gentleman.

This presence knows, and you must needs have heard,

How I am punished with a sore distraction.

What I have done

That might your nature, honour and exception　210

Roughly awake, I here proclaim was madness.
Was't Hamlet wronged Laertes? Never Hamlet.
If Hamlet from himself be ta'en away
And when he's not himself does wrong Laertes,
215 Then Hamlet does it not; Hamlet denies it.
Who does it then? His madness. If 't be so,
Hamlet is of the faction that is wronged –
His madness is poor Hamlet's enemy.
Let my disclaiming from a purposed evil
220 Free me so far in your most generous thoughts
That I have shot my arrow o'er the house
And hurt my brother.

LAERTES   I am satisfied in nature,
Whose motive in this case should stir me most
To my revenge. But in my terms of honour
225 I stand aloof and will no reconcilement
Till by some elder masters of known honour
I have a voice and precedent of peace
To keep my name ungored. But all that time
I do receive your offered love like love
And will not wrong it.

230 HAMLET   I embrace it freely
And will this brothers' wager frankly play.
Give us the foils.

LAERTES   Come, one for me.

HAMLET   I'll be your foil, Laertes. In mine ignorance
Your skill shall like a star i'th' darkest night
Stick fiery off indeed.

235 LAERTES   You mock me, sir.

HAMLET   No, by this hand.

KING   Give them the foils, young Osric. Cousin Hamlet,
You know the wager.

HAMLET   Very well, my lord.
Your grace has laid the odds o'th' weaker side.

240 KING   I do not fear it. I have seen you both
But since he is better we have therefore odds.

LAERTES   This is too heavy, let me see another.

HAMLET
This likes me well. These foils have all a length?

OSRIC   Ay, my good lord.

245 KING   Set me the stoups of wine upon that table.
If Hamlet give the first or second hit
Or quit in answer of the third exchange
Let all the battlements their ordnance fire.
The King shall drink to Hamlet's better breath
250 And in the cup an union shall he throw
Richer than that which four successive kings
In Denmark's crown have worn. Give me the cups,
And let the kettle to the trumpet speak,
The trumpet to the cannoneer without,
255 The cannons to the heavens, the heaven to earth.
                              [*Trumpets the while*]
Now the King drinks to Hamlet. Come, begin.
And you, the judges, bear a wary eye.

HAMLET   Come on, sir.

LAERTES   Come, my lord. [*They play.*]

260 HAMLET   One!

LAERTES   No!

HAMLET   Judgement?

OSRIC   A hit, a very palpable hit.
                    [*Drum, trumpets and shot*]

LAERTES   Well, again.

KING   Stay, give me drink. Hamlet, this pearl is thine: 265
Here's to thy health. Give him the cup.

HAMLET   I'll play this bout first. Set it by awhile.
[*They play.*]
Come, another hit! – What say you?

LAERTES   I do confess't.

KING   Our son shall win.

QUEEN   He's fat and scant of breath. 270
Here, Hamlet, take my napkin, rub thy brows –
The Queen carouses to thy fortune, Hamlet.

HAMLET   Good madam.

KING   Gertrude, do not drink.

QUEEN   I will, my lord. I pray you pardon me. 275

KING [*aside*]
It is the poisoned cup! It is too late.

HAMLET   I dare not drink yet, madam. By and by.

QUEEN   Come, let me wipe thy face.

LAERTES [*aside to King*]
My lord, I'll hit him now.

KING [*aside to Laertes*]   I do not think't.

LAERTES [*aside*]
And yet it is almost against my conscience. 280

HAMLET   Come for the third, Laertes, you do but dally.
I pray you pass with your best violence.
I am sure you make a wanton of me.

LAERTES   Say you so? Come on. [*They play.*]

OSRIC   Nothing neither way. 285

LAERTES   Have at you now!
        [*In scuffling they change rapiers.*]

KING   Part them – they are incensed.

HAMLET   Nay, come again. [*Queen falls.*]

OSRIC   Look to the Queen there, ho!

HORATIO   They bleed on both sides. How is it, my lord? 290

OSRIC   How is't, Laertes?

LAERTES
Why, as a woodcock to mine own springe, Osric:
I am justly killed with mine own treachery.

HAMLET
How does the Queen?

KING   She swoons to see them bleed.

QUEEN
No, no, the drink, the drink, O my dear Hamlet, 295
The drink, the drink – I am poisoned. [*Dies.*]

HAMLET   O villainy, ho! Let the door be locked.
Treachery! Seek it out.   *Exit Osric.*

LAERTES   It is here, Hamlet, thou art slain.
No medicine in the world can do thee good: 300
In thee there is not half an hour's life;
The treacherous instrument is in thy hand
Unbated and envenomed. The foul practice
Hath turned itself on me. Lo, here I lie,
Never to rise again. Thy mother's poisoned – 305

I can no more – the King, the King's to blame.

HAMLET
The point envenomed too? Then venom to thy
      work!   [*Hurts the King.*]

LORDS   Treason, treason!

KING   O, yet defend me, friends, I am but hurt.

310 HAMLET   Here, thou incestuous, damned Dane!
      Drink of this potion. Is the union here?
      Follow my mother.   [*King dies.*]

LAERTES   He is justly served.
      It is a poison tempered by himself.
      Exchange forgiveness with me, noble Hamlet,
315   Mine and my father's death come not upon thee,
      Nor thine on me.   [*Dies.*]

HAMLET   Heaven make thee free of it. I follow thee.
      I am dead, Horatio. Wretched Queen, adieu.
      You that look pale and tremble at this chance,
320   That are but mutes or audience to this act,
      Had I but time (as this fell sergeant Death
      Is strict in his arrest) – O, I could tell you –
      But let it be. Horatio, I am dead.
      Thou livest: report me and my cause aright
      To the unsatisfied.

325 HORATIO   Never believe it.
      I am more an antique Roman than a Dane:
      Here's yet some liquor left.

HAMLET   As thou'rt a man
      Give me the cup. Let go! By heaven I'll ha't!
      O God, Horatio, what a wounded name,
      Things standing thus unknown, shall I leave behind
330   me!
      If thou didst ever hold me in thy heart
      Absent thee from felicity awhile
      And in this harsh world draw thy breath in pain
      To tell my story.
            [*A march afar off and a sound of shooting*]
      What warlike noise is this?

            Enter OSRIC.

OSRIC
335   Young Fortinbras with conquest come from Poland
      To th'ambassadors of England gives
      This warlike volley.

HAMLET   O, I die, Horatio.
      The potent poison quite o'ercrows my spirit,
      I cannot live to hear the news from England,
340   But I do prophesy th'election lights
      On Fortinbras: he has my dying voice.
      So tell him with th'occurrents more and less
      Which have solicited. – The rest is silence.   [*Dies.*]

HORATIO
      Now cracks a noble heart. Goodnight, sweet Prince,
345   And flights of angels sing thee to thy rest.

Why does the drum come hither?

Enter FORTINBRAS *with his train and the* Ambassadors.

FORTINBRAS   Where is this sight?

HORATIO   What is it you would see?
      If aught of woe or wonder, cease your search.

FORTINBRAS
      This quarry cries on havoc. O proud Death,
      What feast is toward in thine eternal cell   350
      That thou so many princes at a shot
      So bloodily hast struck?

AMBASSADOR   The sight is dismal
      And our affairs from England come too late.
      The ears are senseless that should give us hearing
      To tell him his commandment is fulfilled   355
      That Rosencrantz and Guildenstern are dead.
      Where should we have our thanks?

HORATIO   Not from his mouth,
      Had it th'ability of life to thank you;
      He never gave commandment for their death.
      But, since so jump upon this bloody question   360
      You from the Polack wars and you from England
      Are here arrived, give order that these bodies
      High on a stage be placed to the view,
      And let me speak to th' yet unknowing world
      How these things came about. So shall you hear   365
      Of carnal, bloody and unnatural acts,
      Of accidental judgements, casual slaughters,
      Of deaths put on by cunning, and for no cause,
      And in this upshot purposes mistook
      Fallen on th'inventors' heads. All this can I   370
      Truly deliver.

FORTINBRAS   Let us haste to hear it
      And call the noblest to the audience.
      For me, with sorrow I embrace my fortune.
      I have some rights of memory in this kingdom
      Which now to claim my vantage doth invite me.   375

HORATIO   Of that I shall have also cause to speak
      And from his mouth whose voice will draw no more.
      But let this same be presently performed
      Even while men's minds are wild, lest more
            mischance
      On plots and errors happen.

FORTINBRAS   Let four captains   380
      Bear Hamlet like a soldier to the stage,
      For he was likely, had he been put on,
      To have proved most royal. And for his passage
      The soldiers' music and the rite of war
      Speak loudly for him.   385
      Take up the bodies. Such a sight as this
      Becomes the field but here shows much amiss.
      Go, bid the soldiers shoot.   *Exeunt.*

The Tragedy of Hamlet, Prince of Denmark

The First Folio
(1623)

F's dialogue is closer to Q2's than either is to Q1's. Nevertheless, F and Q2 differ in numerous readings. The most discussed of these is the first line of Hamlet's first soliloquy in 1.2, where Q2 has the word 'sallied' (which most editors emend to 'sullied', i.e. contaminated) while F has 'solid'. Our choice of reading colours our understanding of Hamlet's mood and behaviour. F is 230 lines shorter than Q2, and the absence of Hamlet's long soliloquy beginning 'How all occasions do inform against me' (4.4.31 in Q2), in which he compares his own behaviour as an avowed revenger with that of Fortinbras, has prompted some directors to go on and cut the whole of Fortinbras' part (indeed this always happened between 1732 and 1897). This allows them to end the play with the emotional impact of Hamlet's sudden death, rather than the subsequent tonal shift to a picture of foreign invasion and coup, thereby encouraging a largely apolitical reading of the play. On the other hand, Q2 lacks F's line at 2.2.242, 'Denmark's a prison', which directors living under oppressive regimes such as the former Soviet Union have often seized on to promote the idea that under its current king Denmark is a kind of police state.

LIST OF ROLES

HAMLET	*Prince of Denmark*
GHOST	*of Hamlet's father, the late King Hamlet of Denmark*
KING Claudius	*of Denmark, brother of the late King*
QUEEN Gertrude	*Hamlet's mother and his father's widow, now married to King Claudius*
POLONIUS	*King Claudius' councillor*
LAERTES	*Polonius' son*
OPHELIA	*Polonius' daughter*
REYNOLDO	*Polonius' man*
FOLLOWERS	*of Laertes*
HORATIO	*Hamlet's friend and fellow student*
ROSINCRANCE GUILDENSTERNE	*other fellow students*
VOLTEMAND CORNELIUS	*Danish ambassadors to Norway*
BARNARDO FRANCISCO MARCELLUS	*sentinels*
OSRICKE	*a courtier*
PLAYERS	*playing* Prologue, Player King, Player Queen *and* Lucianus
GRAVEDIGGER	*a clown*
SECOND MAN	*another clown*
PRIEST	
LORDS	
GENTLEMEN	
SAILOR	
MESSENGERS	
ATTENDANTS	
FORTINBRAS	*Prince of Norway*
CAPTAIN	*in Norwegian army*
AMBASSADOR	*from England*

Courtiers, Guardsmen, Recorder Player, Norwegian Drum, Norwegian Colours, Norwegian Soldiers

1.1   *Enter* BARNARDO *and* FRANCISCO, *two sentinels.*

BARNARDO   Who's there?

FRANCISCO
Nay, answer me. Stand and unfold yourself.

BARNARDO   Long live the King.

FRANCISCO   Barnardo?

BARNARDO   He.

FRANCISCO   You come most carefully upon your hour.

BARNARDO
5 'Tis now struck twelve. Get thee to bed, Francisco.

FRANCISCO
For this relief much thanks. 'Tis bitter cold
And I am sick at heart.

BARNARDO   Have you had quiet guard?

FRANCISCO   Not a mouse stirring.

BARNARDO   Well, goodnight.
10 If you do meet Horatio and Marcellus,
The rivals of my watch, bid them make haste.

Enter HORATIO *and* MARCELLUS.

FRANCISCO   I think I hear them. Stand: who's there?

HORATIO   Friends to this ground.

MARCELLUS   And liegemen to the Dane.

FRANCISCO   Give you goodnight.

MARCELLUS
15 O farewell, honest soldier. Who hath relieved you?

FRANCISCO
Barnardo has my place. Give you goodnight.   *Exit.*

MARCELLUS   Holla, Barnardo!

BARNARDO   Say, what, is Horatio there?

HORATIO   A piece of him.

BARNARDO
Welcome, Horatio; welcome, good Marcellus.

MARCELLUS
20 What, has this thing appeared again tonight?

BARNARDO   I have seen nothing.

MARCELLUS   Horatio says 'tis but our fantasy
And will not let belief take hold of him
Touching this dreaded sight twice seen of us.
25 Therefore I have entreated him along
With us, to watch the minutes of this night
That, if again this apparition come,
He may approve our eyes and speak to it.

HORATIO   Tush, tush, 'twill not appear.

BARNARDO   Sit down awhile,
30 And let us once again assail your ears
That are so fortified against our story
What we two nights have seen.

HORATIO   Well, sit we down,
And let us hear Barnardo speak of this.

BARNARDO   Last night of all,
35 When yond same star that's westward from the pole
Had made his course t'illume that part of heaven
Where now it burns, Marcellus and myself,
The bell then beating one –

Enter the GHOST.

MARCELLUS
Peace, break thee off! Look where it comes again.

BARNARDO
40 In the same figure like the King that's dead.

MARCELLUS   Thou art a scholar – speak to it, Horatio.

BARNARDO
Looks it not like the King? Mark it, Horatio.

HORATIO
Most like. It harrows me with fear and wonder.

BARNARDO   It would be spoke to.

MARCELLUS   Question it, Horatio.

HORATIO
45 What art thou that usurp'st this time of night
Together with that fair and warlike form
In which the majesty of buried Denmark
Did sometimes march? By heaven, I charge thee speak.

MARCELLUS   It is offended.

BARNARDO   See, it stalks away.

HORATIO   Stay, speak. Speak. I charge thee speak.
50
Exit the Ghost.

MARCELLUS   'Tis gone, and will not answer.

BARNARDO
How now, Horatio? You tremble and look pale.
Is not this something more than fantasy?
What think you on't?

HORATIO   Before my God, I might not this believe
55 Without the sensible and true avouch
Of mine own eyes.

MARCELLUS   Is it not like the King?

HORATIO   As thou art to thyself.
Such was the very armour he had on
When th'ambitious Norway combated.
60 So frowned he once, when in an angry parle
He smote the sledded Polacks on the ice.
'Tis strange.

MARCELLUS
Thus twice before, and just at this dead hour,
With martial stalk hath he gone by our watch. 65

HORATIO
In what particular thought to work I know not,
But in the gross and scope of my opinion
This bodes some strange eruption to our state.

MARCELLUS
Good now, sit down, and tell me he that knows
70 Why this same strict and most observant watch
So nightly toils the subject of the land,
And why such daily cast of brazen cannon
And foreign mart for implements of war.
Why such impress of shipwrights, whose sore task
75 Does not divide the Sunday from the week.
What might be toward that this sweaty haste
Doth make the night joint labourer with the day?
Who is't that can inform me?

HORATIO   That can I.
At least the whisper goes so. Our last King,

80 Whose image even but now appeared to us,
    Was, as you know, by Fortinbras of Norway –
    Thereto pricked on by a most emulate pride –
    Dared to the combat, in which our valiant Hamlet
    (For so this side of our known world esteemed him)
85 Did slay this Fortinbras, who by a sealed compact
    Well ratified by law and heraldry
    Did forfeit with his life all those his lands
    Which he stood seized on to the conqueror;
    Against the which a moiety competent
90 Was gaged by our King, which had returned
    To the inheritance of Fortinbras
    Had he been vanquisher, as by the same covenant
    And carriage of the article design
    His fell to Hamlet. Now, sir, young Fortinbras,
95 Of unimproved mettle, hot and full,
    Hath in the skirts of Norway, here and there,
    Sharked up a list of landless resolutes
    For food and diet to some enterprise
    That hath a stomach in't, which is no other –
100 And it doth well appear unto our state –
    But to recover of us by strong hand
    And terms compulsative those foresaid lands
    So by his father lost. And this, I take it,
    Is the main motive of our preparations,
105 The source of this our watch, and the chief head
    Of this post-haste and rummage in the land.

                    Enter GHOST *again.*

    But soft, behold: lo, where it comes again.
    I'll cross it though it blast me. Stay, illusion!
    If thou hast any sound, or use of voice,
110 Speak to me.
    If there be any good thing to be done,
    That may to thee do ease and grace to me,
    Speak to me.
    If thou art privy to thy country's fate,
115 Which happily foreknowing may avoid,
    O speak.
    Or if thou hast uphoarded in thy life
    Extorted treasure in the womb of earth –
    For which they say you spirits oft walk in death –
    Speak of it. Stay and speak.   [*The cock crows.*]
120   Stop it, Marcellus!
    MARCELLUS   Shall I strike at it with my partisan?
    HORATIO   Do, if it will not stand.
    BARNARDO   'Tis here.
    HORATIO   'Tis here.
                                        Exit Ghost.
    MARCELLUS   'Tis gone.
    We do it wrong, being so majestical,
125 To offer it the show of violence,
    For it is as the air, invulnerable,
    And our vain blows malicious mockery.
    BARNARDO   It was about to speak when the cock crew.
    HORATIO   And then it started like a guilty thing
130 Upon a fearful summons. I have heard

    The cock that is the trumpet to the day
    Doth with his lofty and shrill-sounding throat
    Awake the god of day; and at his warning,
    Whether in sea, or fire, in earth, or air,
    Th'extravagant and erring spirit hies   135
    To his confine; and of the truth herein
    This present object made probation.
    MARCELLUS   It faded on the crowing of the cock.
    Some says that ever 'gainst that season comes
    Wherein our Saviour's birth is celebrated   140
    The bird of dawning singeth all night long,
    And then, they say, no spirit can walk abroad,
    The nights are wholesome, then no planets strike,
    No fairy talks, nor witch hath power to charm,
    So hallowed and so gracious is the time.   145
    HORATIO   So have I heard, and do in part believe it.
    But look, the morn in russet mantle clad
    Walks o'er the dew of yon high eastern hill.
    Break we our watch up, and by my advice
    Let us impart what we have seen tonight   150
    Unto young Hamlet. For, upon my life,
    This spirit dumb to us will speak to him.
    Do you consent we shall acquaint him with it,
    As needful in our loves, fitting our duty?
    MARCELLUS
    Let's do't, I pray, and I this morning know   155
    Where we shall find him most conveniently.   *Exeunt.*

1.2 *Enter* Claudius, KING *of Denmark,* Gertrude
     the QUEEN, HAMLET, POLONIUS, LAERTES
         and his sister OPHELIA, *Lords attendant.*

KING   Though yet of Hamlet our dear brother's death
    The memory be green, and that it us befitted
    To bear our hearts in grief, and our whole kingdom
    To be contracted in one brow of woe,
    Yet so far hath discretion fought with nature   5
    That we with wisest sorrow think on him,
    Together with remembrance of ourselves.
    Therefore our sometimes sister, now our Queen,
    Th'imperial jointress of this warlike state,
    Have we, as 'twere with a defeated joy,   10
    With one auspicious and one dropping eye,
    With mirth in funeral and with dirge in marriage,
    In equal scale weighing delight and dole,
    Taken to wife. Nor have we herein barred
    Your better wisdoms, which have freely gone   15
    With this affair along. For all, our thanks.
    Now follows that you know: young Fortinbras,
    Holding a weak supposal of our worth
    Or thinking by our late dear brother's death
    Our state to be disjoint and out of frame –   20
    Co-leagued with the dream of his advantage –
    He hath not failed to pester us with message
    Importing the surrender of those lands
    Lost by his father, with all bonds of law,
    To our most valiant brother. So much for him.   25

Enter VOLTEMAND *and Cornelius.*

Now for ourself, and for this time of meeting.
Thus much the business is: we have here writ
To Norway, uncle of young Fortinbras –
Who, impotent and bedrid, scarcely hears
Of this his nephew's purpose – to suppress   30
His further gait herein, in that the levies,
The lists and full proportions are all made
Out of his subject; and we here dispatch
You, good Cornelius, and you, Voltemand,
For bearing of this greeting to old Norway,   35
Giving to you no further personal power
To business with the King more than the scope
Of these dilated articles allow.
Farewell and let your haste commend your duty.

VOLTEMAND
In that, and all things, will we show our duty.   40

KING   We doubt it nothing. Heartily farewell.
                    Exeunt Voltemand and Cornelius.
And now, Laertes, what's the news with you?
You told us of some suit. What is't, Laertes?
You cannot speak of reason to the Dane
And lose your voice. What wouldst thou beg, Laertes,   45
That shall not be my offer, not thy asking?
The head is not more native to the heart,
The hand more instrumental to the mouth,
Than is the throne of Denmark to thy father.
What wouldst thou have, Laertes?

LAERTES   Dread my lord,   50
Your leave and favour to return to France,
From whence though willingly I came to Denmark
To show my duty in your coronation,
Yet now I must confess, that duty done,
My thoughts and wishes bend again towards France,   55
And bow them to your gracious leave and pardon.

KING
Have you your father's leave? What says Polonius?

POLONIUS   He hath, my lord.
I do beseech you give him leave to go.

KING   Take thy fair hour, Laertes, time be thine,   60
And thy best graces spend it at thy will.
But now, my cousin Hamlet, and my son!

HAMLET   A little more than kin, and less than kind.

KING   How is it that the clouds still hang on you?   65

HAMLET   Not so, my lord, I am too much i'th' sun.

QUEEN   Good Hamlet, cast thy nightly colour off
And let thine eye look like a friend on Denmark.
Do not for ever with thy veiled lids
Seek for thy noble father in the dust.   70
Thou knowst 'tis common – all that lives must die,
Passing through nature to eternity.

HAMLET   Ay, madam, it is common.

QUEEN   If it be,
Why seems it so particular with thee?

HAMLET
'Seems', madam? Nay, it is, I know not 'seems'.

'Tis not alone my inky cloak, good mother,   75
Nor customary suits of solemn black,
Nor windy suspiration of forced breath,
No, nor the fruitful river in the eye,
Nor the dejected haviour of the visage,
Together with all forms, moods, shows of grief,   80
That can denote me truly. These indeed 'seem',
For they are actions that a man might play;
But I have that within which passeth show,
These but the trappings, and the suits of woe.

KING
'Tis sweet and commendable in your nature, Hamlet,   85
To give these mourning duties to your father;
But you must know your father lost a father,
That father lost lost his, and the survivor bound
In filial obligation for some term
To do obsequious sorrow. But to persever   90
In obstinate condolement is a course
Of impious stubbornness; 'tis unmanly grief;
It shows a will most incorrect to heaven,
A heart unfortified, a mind impatient,
An understanding simple, and unschooled.   95
For what we know must be, and is as common
As any the most vulgar thing to sense –
Why should we in our peevish opposition
Take it to heart? Fie, 'tis a fault to heaven,
A fault against the dead, a fault to nature,   100
To reason most absurd, whose common theme
Is death of fathers, and who still hath cried,
From the first corpse till he that died today,
'This must be so.' We pray you throw to earth
This unprevailing woe, and think of us   105
As of a father. For let the world take note
You are the most immediate to our throne
And with no less nobility of love
Than that which dearest father bears his son
Do I impart towards you. For your intent   110
In going back to school in Wittenberg,
It is most retrograde to our desire;
And we beseech you bend you to remain
Here in the cheer and comfort of our eye,
Our chiefest courtier, cousin, and our son.   115

QUEEN   Let not thy mother lose her prayers, Hamlet.
I prithee stay with us, go not to Wittenberg.

HAMLET   I shall in all my best obey you, madam.

KING   Why, 'tis a loving and a fair reply.
Be as ourself in Denmark. Madam, come –   120
This gentle and unforced accord of Hamlet
Sits smiling to my heart; in grace whereof
No jocund health that Denmark drinks today
But the great cannon to the clouds shall tell
And the King's rouse the heavens shall bruit again,   125
Re-speaking earthly thunder. Come away.
                    Exeunt all but Hamlet.

HAMLET   O that this too too solid flesh would melt,
Thaw, and resolve itself into a dew,
Or that the Everlasting had not fixed

130	His canon 'gainst self-slaughter. O God, O God!
	How weary, stale, flat and unprofitable
	Seems to me all the uses of this world!
	Fie on't! O fie, fie, 'tis an unweeded garden
	That grows to seed: things rank and gross in nature
135	Possess it merely. That it should come to this!
	But two months dead – nay, not so much, not two –
	So excellent a king, that was to this
	Hyperion to a satyr, so loving to my mother
	That he might not beteem the winds of heaven
140	Visit her face too roughly. Heaven and earth,
	Must I remember? Why, she would hang on him
	As if increase of appetite had grown
	By what it fed on. And yet within a month!
	(Let me not think on't – Frailty, thy name is Woman.)
145	A little month, or e'er those shoes were old
	With which she followed my poor father's body,
	Like Niobe, all tears. Why, she, even she –
	O heaven, a beast that wants discourse of reason
	Would have mourned longer! – married with mine uncle,
150	My father's brother (but no more like my father
	Than I to Hercules). Within a month!
	Ere yet the salt of most unrighteous tears
	Had left the flushing of her galled eyes,
	She married. O most wicked speed, to post
155	With such dexterity to incestuous sheets!
	It is not, nor it cannot come to good.
	But break, my heart, for I must hold my tongue.

Enter HORATIO, BARNARDO *and* MARCELLUS.

HORATIO   Hail to your lordship.

HAMLET   I am glad to see you well –
Horatio, or I do forget myself.

HORATIO

160   The same, my lord, and your poor servant ever.

HAMLET

Sir, my good friend, I'll change that name with you.
And what make you from Wittenberg, Horatio?
Marcellus!

MARCELLUS   My good lord.

HAMLET

I am very glad to see you. [*to Barnardo*] Good even,
sir. –

165   But what in faith make you from Wittenberg?

HORATIO   A truant disposition, good my lord.

HAMLET   I would not have your enemy say so;
Nor shall you do mine ear that violence
To make it truster of your own report

170   Against yourself. I know you are no truant.
But what is your affair in Elsinore?
We'll teach you to drink deep ere you depart.

HORATIO   My lord, I came to see your father's funeral.

HAMLET   I pray thee do not mock me, fellow student,

175   I think it was to see my mother's wedding.

HORATIO   Indeed, my lord, it followed hard upon.

HAMLET

Thrift, thrift, Horatio, the funeral baked meats

	Did coldly furnish forth the marriage tables.
	Would I had met my dearest foe in heaven
180	Ere I had ever seen that day, Horatio.
	My father, methinks I see my father.

HORATIO   O where, my lord?

HAMLET   In my mind's eye, Horatio.

HORATIO   I saw him once; he was a goodly king.

HAMLET   He was a man, take him for all in all:
185   I shall not look upon his like again.

HORATIO   My lord, I think I saw him yesternight.

HAMLET   Saw? Who?

HORATIO   My lord, the King your father.

HAMLET   The King my father?

HORATIO   Season your admiration for a while,
190   With an attent ear, till I may deliver,
Upon the witness of these gentlemen
This marvel to you.

HAMLET   For heaven's love let me hear.

HORATIO

	Two nights together had these gentlemen,
	Marcellus and Barnardo, on their watch
195	In the dead waste and middle of the night
	Been thus encountered: a figure like your father
	Armed at all points exactly, cap-à-pie,
	Appears before them and with solemn march
	Goes slow and stately by them; thrice he walked
200	By their oppressed and fear-surprised eyes
	Within his truncheon's length, whilst they, bestilled
	Almost to jelly with the act of fear,
	Stand dumb and speak not to him. This to me
	In dreadful secrecy impart they did,
205	And I with them the third night kept the watch
	Where, as they had delivered, both in time,
	Form of the thing, each word made true and good,
	The apparition comes. I knew your father;
	These hands are not more like.

HAMLET   But where was this?

MARCELLUS

210   My lord, upon the platform where we watched.

HAMLET   Did you not speak to it?

HORATIO   My lord, I did;
But answer made it none. Yet once methought
It lifted up it head and did address
Itself to motion like as it would speak.
215   But even then the morning cock crew loud
And at the sound it shrunk in haste away,
And vanished from our sight.

HAMLET   'Tis very strange.

HORATIO   As I do live, my honoured lord, 'tis true;
And we did think it writ down in our duty
220   To let you know of it.

HAMLET   Indeed, indeed, sirs; but this troubles me.
Hold you the watch tonight?

MARCELLUS, BARNARDO   We do, my lord.

HAMLET   Armed, say you?

MARCELLUS, BARNARDO   Armed, my lord.

HAMLET   From top to toe?

MARCELLUS, BARNARDO
My lord, from head to foot.
225 HAMLET   Then saw you not his face?
HORATIO   O yes, my lord, he wore his beaver up.
HAMLET   What, looked he frowningly?
HORATIO
A countenance more in sorrow than in anger.
HAMLET   Pale, or red?
HORATIO   Nay, very pale.
230 HAMLET   And fixed his eyes upon you?
HORATIO   Most constantly.
HAMLET   I would I had been there.
HORATIO   It would have much amazed you.
HAMLET   Very like, very like. Stayed it long?
HORATIO
While one with moderate haste might tell a hundred.
235 MARCELLUS, BARNARDO   Longer, longer.
HORATIO   Not when I saw't.
HAMLET   His beard was grizzly? No?
HORATIO   It was, as I have seen it in his life,
A sable silvered.
HAMLET
I'll watch tonight. Perchance 'twill wake again.
240 HORATIO   I warrant you it will.
HAMLET   If it assume my noble father's person
I'll speak to it, though hell itself should gape
And bid me hold my peace. I pray you all,
If you have hitherto concealed this sight
245 Let it be treble in your silence still,
And, whatsoever else shall hap tonight,
Give it an understanding but no tongue.
I will requite your loves. So, fare ye well.
Upon the platform, 'twixt eleven and twelve,
I'll visit you.
HORATIO, MARCELLUS, BARNARDO
250 Our duty to your honour.
HAMLET   Your love, as mine to you. Farewell.
Exeunt all but Hamlet.
My father's spirit in arms! All is not well.
I doubt some foul play. Would the night were come.
Till then sit still my soul. Foul deeds will rise,
255 Though all the earth o'erwhelm them, to men's eyes.
Exit.

1.3   *Enter LAERTES and OPHELIA.*

LAERTES   My necessaries are embarked. Farewell.
And sister, as the winds give benefit
And convoy is assistant, do not sleep
But let me hear from you.
OPHELIA   Do you doubt that?
5 LAERTES   For Hamlet and the trifling of his favours,
Hold it a fashion and a toy in blood;
A violet in the youth of primy nature;
Forward, not permanent; sweet, not lasting;
The suppliance of a minute – no more.
OPHELIA   No more but so.

LAERTES   Think it no more.   10
For nature crescent does not grow alone
In thews and bulk, but as his temple waxes
The inward service of the mind and soul
Grows wide withal. Perhaps he loves you now,
And now no soil nor cautel doth besmirch   15
The virtue of his will; but you must fear,
His greatness weighed, his will is not his own.
For he himself is subject to his birth –
He may not, as unvalued persons do,
Carve for himself; for on his choice depends   20
The sanctity and health of the whole state.
And therefore must his choice be circumscribed
Unto the voice and yielding of that body
Whereof he is the head. Then, if he says he loves you,
It fits your wisdom so far to believe it   25
As he in his peculiar sect and force
May give his saying deed, which is no further
Than the main voice of Denmark goes withal.
Then weigh what loss your honour may sustain
If with too credent ear you list his songs,   30
Or lose your heart, or your chaste treasure open
To his unmastered importunity.
Fear it, Ophelia, fear it, my dear sister,
And keep within the rear of your affection,
Out of the shot and danger of desire.   35
The chariest maid is prodigal enough
If she unmask her beauty to the moon.
Virtue itself scapes not calumnious strokes.
The canker galls the infants of the spring
Too oft before the buttons be disclosed,   40
And in the morn and liquid dew of youth
Contagious blastments are most imminent.
Be wary then: best safety lies in fear;
Youth to itself rebels, though none else near.
OPHELIA   I shall th'effect of this good lesson keep   45
As watchman to my heart. But, good my brother,
Do not, as some ungracious pastors do,
Show me the steep and thorny way to heaven
Whilst, like a puffed and reckless libertine,
Himself the primrose path of dalliance treads   50
And recks not his own rede.
LAERTES   O, fear me not.
I stay too long.

Enter POLONIUS.

But here my father comes.
A double blessing is a double grace:
Occasion smiles upon a second leave.
POLONIUS
Yet here, Laertes? Aboard, aboard for shame!   55
The wind sits in the shoulder of your sail
And you are stayed for there. My blessing with
you;
And these few precepts in thy memory
See thou character: give thy thoughts no tongue
Nor any unproportioned thought his act.   60

Be thou familiar, but by no means vulgar.
The friends thou hast, and their adoption tried,
Grapple them to thy soul with hoops of steel;
But do not dull thy palm with entertainment
65 Of each unhatched, unfledged comrade. Beware
Of entrance to a quarrel but, being in,
Bear't that th'opposed may beware of thee.
Give every man thine ear, but few thy voice.
Take each man's censure, but reserve thy
    judgement.
70 Costly thy habit as thy purse can buy,
But not expressed in fancy – rich, not gaudy.
For the apparel oft proclaims the man,
And they in France of the best rank and station
Are of all most select and generous chief in that.
75 Neither a borrower nor a lender be,
For loan oft loses both itself and friend,
And borrowing dulls the edge of husbandry.
This above all, to thine own self be true
And it must follow, as the night the day,
80 Thou canst not then be false to any man.
Farewell – my blessing season this in thee.
LAERTES Most humbly do I take my leave, my lord.
POLONIUS
    The time invites you. Go, your servants tend.
LAERTES Farewell, Ophelia, and remember well
    What I have said to you.
85 OPHELIA   'Tis in my memory locked,
    And you yourself shall keep the key of it.
LAERTES   Farewell.   *Exit.*
POLONIUS   What is't, Ophelia, he hath said to you?
OPHELIA
    So please you, something touching the Lord Hamlet.
90 POLONIUS   Marry, well bethought.
    'Tis told me he hath very oft of late
    Given private time to you, and you yourself
    Have of your audience been most free and
        bounteous.
    If it be so – as so 'tis put on me,
95 And that in way of caution – I must tell you
    You do not understand yourself so clearly
    As it behoves my daughter and your honour.
    What is between you? Give me up the truth.
OPHELIA   He hath, my lord, of late made many tenders
100   Of his affection to me.
POLONIUS
    Affection? Pooh! You speak like a green girl,
    Unsifted in such perilous circumstance.
    Do you believe his 'tenders', as you call them?
OPHELIA   I do not know, my lord, what I should think.
POLONIUS
105   Marry, I'll teach you. Think yourself a baby
    That you have ta'en his tenders for true pay,
    Which are not sterling. Tender yourself more dearly,
    Or – not to crack the wind of the poor phrase,
    Roaming it thus – you'll tender me a fool.
110 OPHELIA   My lord, he hath importuned me with love

In honourable fashion.
POLONIUS Ay, 'fashion' you may call it. Go to, go to.
OPHELIA And hath given countenance to his speech,
    My lord, with all the vows of heaven.
115 POLONIUS Ay, springes to catch woodcocks! I do know,
    When the blood burns, how prodigal the soul
    Gives the tongue vows. These blazes, daughter,
    Giving more light than heat, extinct in both
    Even in their promise as it is a-making,
120   You must not take for fire. For this time, daughter,
    Be somewhat scanter of your maiden presence.
    Set your entreatments at a higher rate
    Than a command to parley. For Lord Hamlet,
    Believe so much in him, that he is young
125   And with a larger tether may he walk
    Than may be given you. In few, Ophelia,
    Do not believe his vows; for they are brokers,
    Not of the eye which their investments show,
    But mere implorators of unholy suits,
130   Breathing like sanctified and pious bonds
    The better to beguile. This is for all.
    I would not, in plain terms, from this time forth
    Have you so slander any moment leisure
    As to give words or talk with the Lord Hamlet.
135   Look to't, I charge you. Come your ways.
OPHELIA   I shall obey, my lord.   *Exeunt.*

1.4   *Enter* HAMLET, HORATIO
           and MARCELLUS.

HAMLET   The air bites shrewdly: is it very cold?
HORATIO   It is a nipping and an eager air.
HAMLET   What hour now?
HORATIO   I think it lacks of twelve.
MARCELLUS   No, it is struck.
HORATIO   Indeed I heard it not.
    Then it draws near the season   5
    Wherein the spirit held his wont to walk.
        [*Sounds of kettledrum, trumpet and cannon*]
    What does this mean, my lord?
HAMLET
    The King doth wake tonight and takes his rouse,
    Keeps wassails and the swaggering upspring reels,
    And as he drains his draughts of Rhenish down   10
    The kettledrum and trumpet thus bray out
    The triumph of his pledge.
HORATIO   Is it a custom?
HAMLET   Ay, marry is't
    And to my mind, though I am native here
    And to the manner born, it is a custom   15
    More honoured in the breach than the observance.

          Enter GHOST.

HORATIO   Look, my lord, it comes.
HAMLET   Angels and ministers of grace defend us!
    Be thou a spirit of health or goblin damned,
    Bring with thee airs from heaven or blasts from hell,   20

Be thy events wicked or charitable,
Thou com'st in such a questionable shape
That I will speak to thee. I'll call thee Hamlet,
King, father, royal Dane. O, O answer me,
25 Let me not burst in ignorance, but tell
Why thy canonized bones hearsed in death
Have burst their cerements, why the sepulchre
Wherein we saw thee quietly inurned
Hath oped his ponderous and marble jaws
30 To cast thee up again. What may this mean,
That thou, dead corpse, again in complete steel,
Revisits thus the glimpses of the moon,
Making night hideous, and we fools of nature
So horridly to shake our disposition
35 With thoughts beyond the reaches of our souls?
Say, why is this? Wherefore? What should we do?
　　　[*Ghost beckons Hamlet.*]
HORATIO　　It beckons you to go away with it,
As if it some impartment did desire
To you alone.
MARCELLUS　　Look with what courteous action
40 It wafts you to a more removed ground –
But do not go with it.
HORATIO　　　　No, by no means.
HAMLET　　It will not speak. Then will I follow it.
HORATIO　　Do not, my lord.
HAMLET　　　　　Why, what should be the fear?
I do not set my life at a pin's fee;
45 And for my soul – what can it do to that,
Being a thing immortal as itself?
It waves me forth again. I'll follow it.
HORATIO
What if it tempt you toward the flood, my lord?
Or to the dreadful summit of the cliff
50 That beetles o'er his base into the sea,
And there assumes some other horrible form
Which might deprive your sovereignty of reason
And draw you into madness? Think of it!
HAMLET　　It wafts me still. Go on, I'll follow thee.
MARCELLUS　　You shall not go, my lord.
55 HAMLET　　　　　Hold off your hand.
HORATIO　　Be ruled. You shall not go.
HAMLET　　　　　My fate cries out
And makes each petty artery in this body
As hardy as the Nemean lion's nerve.
Still am I called? – Unhand me, gentlemen. –
60 By heaven, I'll make a ghost of him that lets me!
I say away! – Go on! I'll follow thee.
　　　　　Exeunt Ghost and Hamlet.
HORATIO　　He waxes desperate with imagination.
MARCELLUS　　Let's follow. 'Tis not fit thus to obey him.
HORATIO　　Have after. To what issue will this come?
MARCELLUS
65 Something is rotten in the state of Denmark.
HORATIO　　Heaven will direct it.
MARCELLUS　　　　Nay, let's follow him.　*Exeunt.*

1.5　　　*Enter* GHOST *and* HAMLET.
HAMLET
Where wilt thou lead me? Speak! I'll go no further.
GHOST　　Mark me.
HAMLET　　　　I will.
GHOST　　　　　　My hour is almost come
When I to sulphurous and tormenting flames
Must render up myself.
HAMLET　　　　　Alas, poor ghost.
GHOST　　Pity me not, but lend thy serious hearing　5
To what I shall unfold.
HAMLET　　　　　Speak, I am bound to hear.
GHOST　　So art thou to revenge when thou shalt hear.
HAMLET　　What?
GHOST　　I am thy father's spirit,
Doomed for a certain term to walk the night,　10
And for the day confined to fast in fires
Till the foul crimes done in my days of nature
Are burnt and purged away! But that I am forbid
To tell the secrets of my prison-house,
I could a tale unfold whose lightest word　15
Would harrow up thy soul, freeze thy young blood,
Make thy two eyes like stars start from their spheres,
Thy knotty and combined locks to part
And each particular hair to stand on end
Like quills upon the fretful porpentine –　20
But this eternal blazon must not be
To ears of flesh and blood. List, Hamlet, O, list,
If thou didst ever thy dear father love –
HAMLET　　O heaven!
GHOST
– Revenge his foul and most unnatural murder!　25
HAMLET　　Murder?
GHOST　　Murder most foul – as in the best it is –
But this most foul, strange and unnatural.
HAMLET
Haste, haste me to know it, that with wings as swift
As meditation, or the thoughts of love,　30
May sweep to my revenge.
GHOST　　　　　I find thee apt.
And duller shouldst thou be than the fat weed
That rots itself in ease on Lethe wharf
Wouldst thou not stir in this. Now, Hamlet, hear:
It's given out that, sleeping in mine orchard,　35
A serpent stung me. So the whole ear of Denmark
Is by a forged process of my death
Rankly abused. But know, thou noble youth,
The serpent that did sting thy father's life
Now wears his crown.
HAMLET　　　　　O my prophetic soul!　40
Mine uncle!
GHOST
Ay, that incestuous, that adulterate beast,
With witchcraft of his wits, with traitorous gifts –
O wicked wit and gifts, that have the power
So to seduce! – won to this shameful lust　45

The will of my most seeming-virtuous Queen.
O Hamlet, what a falling off was there!
From me, whose love was of that dignity
That it went hand in hand even with the vow
50 I made to her in marriage – and to decline
Upon a wretch whose natural gifts were poor
To those of mine.
But Virtue, as it never will be moved,
Though Lewdness court it in a shape of heaven,
55 So Lust, though to a radiant angel linked,
Will sate itself in a celestial bed
And prey on garbage.
But soft, methinks I scent the morning's air.
Brief let me be. Sleeping within mine orchard –
60 My custom always in the afternoon –
Upon my secure hour thy uncle stole
With juice of cursed hebenon in a vial
And in the porches of mine ears did pour
The leperous distilment, whose effect
65 Holds such an enmity with blood of man
That, swift as quicksilver, it courses through
The natural gates and alleys of the body,
And with a sudden vigour it doth posset
And curd, like eager droppings into milk,
70 The thin and wholesome blood. So did it mine,
And a most instant tetter baked about
Most lazar-like with vile and loathsome crust
All my smooth body.
Thus was I, sleeping, by a brother's hand
75 Of life, of crown and queen at once dispatched,
Cut off even in the blossoms of my sin,
Unhouseled, disappointed, unaneled,
No reckoning made, but sent to my account
With all my imperfections on my head.
80 O horrible, O horrible, most horrible!
If thou hast nature in thee bear it not;
Let not the royal bed of Denmark be
A couch for luxury and damned incest.
But howsoever thou pursuest this act
85 Taint not thy mind, nor let thy soul contrive
Against thy mother aught. Leave her to heaven,
And to those thorns that in her bosom lodge,
To prick and sting her. Fare thee well at once.
The glow-worm shows the matin to be near
90 And 'gins to pale his uneffectual fire.
Adieu, adieu, Hamlet. Remember me.   *Exit.*

HAMLET
O all you host of heaven! O earth! – What else? –
And shall I couple hell? O fie! Hold, my heart,
And you, my sinews, grow not instant old,
95 But bear me stiffly up. Remember thee?
Ay, thou poor ghost, while memory holds a seat
In this distracted globe. Remember thee?
Yea, from the table of my memory
I'll wipe away all trivial fond records,
100 All saws of books, all forms, all pressures past,
That youth and observation copied there,

And thy commandment all alone shall live
Within the book and volume of my brain,
Unmixed with baser matter. Yes, yes, by heaven!
O most pernicious woman!   105
O villain, villain, smiling damned villain!
My tables, my tables! Meet it is I set it down,
That one may smile and smile and be a villain.
At least I'm sure it may be so in Denmark.
So, uncle, there you are. Now to my word.   110
It is 'Adieu, adieu. Remember me.'
I have sworn't.
HORATIO, MARCELLUS [*within*]
My lord, my lord!

Enter HORATIO *and* MARCELLUS.

MARCELLUS   Lord Hamlet!
HORATIO   Heaven secure him!
MARCELLUS   So be it.
HORATIO   Illo, ho, ho, my lord!
HAMLET   Hillo, ho, ho, boy, come bird, come!   115
MARCELLUS   How is't, my noble lord?
HORATIO   What news, my lord?
HAMLET   O, wonderful!
HORATIO   Good my lord, tell it.
HAMLET   No, you'll reveal it.
HORATIO   Not I, my lord, by heaven.
MARCELLUS   Nor I, my lord.
HAMLET
How say you then – would heart of man once think it? –   120
But you'll be secret?
HORATIO, MARCELLUS   Ay, by heaven, my lord.
HAMLET
There's ne'er a villain dwelling in all Denmark
But he's an arrant knave.
HORATIO
There needs no ghost, my lord, come from the grave
To tell us this.
HAMLET   Why, right, you are i'th' right!   125
And so, without more circumstance at all,
I hold it fit that we shake hands and part –
You, as your business and desires shall point you
(For every man has business and desire
Such as it is), and for mine own poor part,   130
Look you, I'll go pray.
HORATIO
These are but wild and hurling words, my lord.
HAMLET   I'm sorry they offend you – heartily;
Yes, faith, heartily.
HORATIO   There's no offence, my lord.
HAMLET   Yes, by Saint Patrick, but there is, my lord,   135
And much offence too. Touching this vision here,
It is an honest ghost – that let me tell you.
For your desire to know what is between us,
O'ermaster't as you may. And now, good friends,
As you are friends, scholars and soldiers,   140
Give me one poor request.
HORATIO   What is't, my lord? We will.

HAMLET
Never make known what you have seen tonight.

HORATIO, MARCELLUS
My lord, we will not.

HAMLET   Nay, but swear't.

145 HORATIO   In faith, my lord, not I.

MARCELLUS   Nor I, my lord, in faith.

HAMLET   Upon my sword.

MARCELLUS   We have sworn, my lord, already.

HAMLET   Indeed, upon my sword. Indeed.

GHOST [*Cries under the stage.*]
Swear.

HAMLET
150 Ah ha, boy, sayst thou so? Art thou there, truepenny?
Come on, you hear this fellow in the cellarage?
Consent to swear.

HORATIO   Propose the oath, my lord.

HAMLET   Never to speak of this that you have seen.
Swear by my sword.

155 GHOST   Swear.

HAMLET
Hic et ubique? Then we'll shift for ground.
Come hither, gentlemen,
And lay your hands again upon my sword.
Never to speak of this that you have heard.
160 Swear by my sword.

GHOST   Swear.

HAMLET
Well said, old mole, canst work i'th' ground so fast?
A worthy pioner! Once more remove, good friends.

HORATIO   O day and night, but this is wondrous strange.

165 HAMLET   And therefore as a stranger give it welcome.
There are more things in heaven and earth, Horatio,
Than are dreamt of in our philosophy. But come,
Here as before: never – so help you mercy,
How strange or odd soe'er I bear myself
170 (As I perchance hereafter shall think meet
To put an antic disposition on) –
That you at such time seeing me never shall
With arms encumbered thus, or thus, head shake,
Or by pronouncing of some doubtful phrase
175 As 'Well, we know', or 'We could an if we would',
Or 'If we list to speak', or 'There be an if they might',
Or such ambiguous giving out to note
That you know aught of me. This not to do,
So grace and mercy at your most need help you,
180 Swear.

GHOST   Swear.

HAMLET   Rest, rest, perturbed spirit! So, gentlemen,
With all my love I do commend me to you,
And what so poor a man as Hamlet is
185 May do t'express his love and friending to you,
God willing shall not lack. Let us go in together,
And still your fingers on your lips, I pray.
The time is out of joint. O cursed spite,
That ever I was born to set it right!
190 Nay, come let's go together.   *Exeunt.*

2.1   *Enter* POLONIUS *and* REYNOLDO.

POLONIUS
Give him his money and these notes, Reynoldo.

REYNOLDO   I will, my lord.

POLONIUS
You shall do marvellous wisely, good Reynoldo,
Before you visit him you make inquiry
Of his behaviour.

REYNOLDO   My lord, I did intend it.   5

POLONIUS
Marry, well said. Very well said. Look you, sir,
Inquire me first what Danskers are in Paris,
And how, and who, what means, and where they keep,
What company, at what expense; and finding
By this encompassment and drift of question   10
That they do know my son, come you more nearer
Than your particular demands will touch it;
Take you as 'twere some distant knowledge of him,
And thus, 'I know his father and his friends
And in part him' – do you mark this, Reynoldo?   15

REYNOLDO   Ay, very well, my lord.

POLONIUS
'And in part him, but', you may say, 'not well.
But if 't be he I mean he's very wild,
Addicted so and so'; and there put on him
What forgeries you please. Marry, none so rank   20
As may dishonour him – take heed of that –
But, sir, such wanton, wild and usual slips
As are companions noted and most known
To youth and liberty.

REYNOLDO   As gaming, my lord?

POLONIUS   Ay, or drinking, fencing, swearing,   25
Quarrelling, drabbing – you may go so far.

REYNOLDO   My lord, that would dishonour him.

POLONIUS
Faith no, as you may season it in the charge.
You must not put another scandal on him
That he is open to incontinency –   30
That's not my meaning – but breathe his faults so
   quaintly
That they may seem the taints of liberty,
The flash and outbreak of a fiery mind,
A savageness in unreclaimed blood
Of general assault.

REYNOLDO   But my good lord –   35

POLONIUS   Wherefore should you do this?

REYNOLDO   Ay, my lord,
I would know that.

POLONIUS   Marry, sir, here's my drift –
And I believe it is a fetch of warrant –
You laying these slight sullies on my son
As 'twere a thing a little soiled i'th' working.   40
Mark you, your party in converse (him you would
   sound)
Having ever seen in the prenominate crimes
The youth you breathe of guilty, be assured

He closes with you in this consequence:
45 'Good sir' (or so), or 'friend' or 'gentleman',
According to the phrase and the addition
Of man and country.
REYNOLDO   Very good, my lord.
POLONIUS   And then, sir, does he this, he does –
What was I about to say? I was about to say something.
50 Where did I leave?
REYNOLDO   At 'closes in the consequence',
At 'friend' (or so), and 'gentleman'.
POLONIUS   At 'closes in the consequence', ay, marry.
He closes with you thus: 'I know the gentleman,
55 I saw him yesterday, or t'other day,
Or then, or then, with such and such, and as you say
There was he gaming, there o'ertook in's rouse,
There falling out at tennis', or perchance
'I saw him enter such a house of sale',
60 *Videlicet* a brothel, or so forth. See you now,
Your bait of falsehood takes this carp of truth;
And thus do we of wisdom and of reach,
With windlasses and with assays of bias,
By indirections find directions out:
65 So by my former lecture and advice
Shall you my son. You have me, have you not?
REYNOLDO   My lord, I have.
POLONIUS   God buy you, fare you well.
REYNOLDO   Good my lord.
POLONIUS   Observe his inclination in yourself.
REYNOLDO   I shall, my lord.
70 POLONIUS   And let him ply his music.
REYNOLDO   Well, my lord.
POLONIUS   Farewell.   *Exit Reynoldo.*

Enter OPHELIA.

How now, Ophelia, what's the matter?

OPHELIA   Alas, my lord, I have been so affrighted.
POLONIUS   With what, in the name of heaven?
75 OPHELIA   My lord, as I was sewing in my chamber
Lord Hamlet, with his doublet all unbraced,
No hat upon his head, his stockings fouled,
Ungartered and down-gyved to his ankle,
Pale as his shirt, his knees knocking each other,
80 And with a look so piteous in purport
As if he had been loosed out of hell
To speak of horrors, he comes before me.
POLONIUS   Mad for thy love?
OPHELIA   My lord, I do not know,
But truly I do fear it.
POLONIUS   What said he?
85 OPHELIA   He took me by the wrist and held me hard.
Then goes he to the length of all his arm
And with his other hand thus o'er his brow
He falls to such perusal of my face
As he would draw it. Long stayed he so.
90 At last, a little shaking of mine arm,
And thrice his head thus waving up and down,

He raised a sigh so piteous and profound
That it did seem to shatter all his bulk
And end his being. That done, he lets me go,
95 And with his head over his shoulders turned
He seemed to find his way without his eyes
(For out o'doors he went without their help)
And to the last bended their light on me.
POLONIUS   Go with me: I will go seek the King.
100 This is the very ecstasy of love,
Whose violent property fordoes itself,
And leads the will to desperate undertakings
As oft as any passion under heaven
That does afflict our natures. I am sorry –
105 What, have you given him any hard words of late?
OPHELIA   No, my good lord, but, as you did command,
I did repel his letters and denied
His access to me.
POLONIUS   That hath made him mad.
I am sorry that with better speed and judgement
110 I had not quoted him. I feared he did but trifle
And meant to wrack thee. But beshrew my jealousy –
It seems it is as proper to our age
To cast beyond ourselves in our opinions
As it is common for the younger sort
115 To lack discretion. Come, go we to the King:
This must be known which, being kept close, might
move
More grief to hide than hate to utter love.   *Exeunt.*

2.2   *Enter* KING, QUEEN, ROSINCRANCE,
               GUILDENSTERNE *and others.*

KING   Welcome, dear Rosincrance and Guildensterne.
Moreover that we much did long to see you
The need we have to use you did provoke
Our hasty sending. Something have you heard
5 Of Hamlet's transformation – so I call it
Since not th'exterior nor the inward man
Resembles that it was. What it should be,
More than his father's death, that thus hath put him
So much from th'understanding of himself
10 I cannot deem of. I entreat you both
That, being of so young days brought up with him
And since so neighboured to his youth and humour,
That you vouchsafe your rest here in our Court
Some little time, so by your companies
15 To draw him on to pleasures and to gather
So much as from occasions you may glean,
That opened lies within our remedy.
QUEEN   Good gentlemen, he hath much talked of you,
And, sure I am, two men there are not living
20 To whom he more adheres. If it will please you
To show us so much gentry and good will
As to expend your time with us awhile
For the supply and profit of our hope,
Your visitation shall receive such thanks
As fits a king's remembrance.

ROSINCRANCE   Both your majesties
  Might by the sovereign power you have of us
  Put your dread pleasures more into command
  Than to entreaty.
GUILDENSTERNE   We both obey,
  And here give up ourselves, in the full bent,
  To lay our services freely at your feet,
  To be commanded.
KING
  Thanks, Rosincrance, and gentle Guildensterne.
QUEEN
  Thanks, Guildensterne, and gentle Rosincrance.
  And I beseech you instantly to visit
  My too much changed son. Go some of ye,
  And bring the gentlemen where Hamlet is.
GUILDENSTERNE
  Heavens make our presence and our practices
  Pleasant and helpful to him.
QUEEN   Amen.
    Exeunt Rosincrance, Guildensterne and
                    one or more Courtiers.

    Enter POLONIUS.

POLONIUS
  Th'ambassadors from Norway, my good lord,
  Are joyfully returned.
KING   Thou still hast been the father of good news.
POLONIUS
  Have I, my lord? Assure you, my good liege,
  I hold my duty, as I hold my soul,
  Both to my God, one to my gracious King.
  And I do think, or else this brain of mine
  Hunts not the trail of policy so sure
  As I have used to do, that I have found
  The very cause of Hamlet's lunacy.
KING   O, speak of that: that I do long to hear.
POLONIUS   Give first admittance to th'ambassadors.
  My news shall be the fruit to that great feast.
KING   Thyself do grace to them and bring them in.
                    Exit Polonius.
  He tells me, my sweet Queen, that he hath found
  The head and source of all your son's distemper.
QUEEN   I doubt it is no other but the main –
  His father's death and our o'er-hasty marriage.
KING   Well, we shall sift him.

    Enter POLONIUS, VOLTEMAND *and Cornelius.*

                    Welcome, good friends.
  Say, Voltemand, what from our brother Norway?
VOLTEMAND
  Most fair return of greetings and desires.
  Upon our first he sent out to suppress
  His nephew's levies, which to him appeared
  To be a preparation 'gainst the Polack.
  But, better looked into, he truly found
  It was against your highness; whereat, grieved
  That so his sickness, age and impotence

25
30
35
40
45
50
55
60
65

Was falsely borne in hand, sends out arrests
On Fortinbras, which he, in brief, obeys,
Receives rebuke from Norway, and, in fine,
Makes vow before his uncle never more
To give th'assay of arms against your majesty.
Whereon old Norway, overcome with joy,
Gives him three thousand crowns in annual fee
And his commission to employ those soldiers,
So levied, as before, against the Polack,
With an entreaty herein further shown
That it might please you to give quiet pass
Through your dominions for his enterprise,
On such regards of safety and allowance
As therein are set down.
KING   It likes us well;
  And at our more considered time we'll read,
  Answer, and think upon this business.
  Meantime, we thank you for your well-took labour.
  Go to your rest; at night we'll feast together.
  Most welcome home.
    Exeunt Voltemand, Cornelius and Courtiers.
POLONIUS   This business is very well ended.
  My liege, and madam, to expostulate
  What majesty should be, what duty is,
  Why day is day, night night, and time is time,
  Were nothing but to waste night, day and time.
  Therefore, since brevity is the soul of wit,
  And tediousness the limbs and outward flourishes,
  I will be brief. Your noble son is mad.
  Mad call I it, for to define true madness,
  What is't but to be nothing else but mad?
  But let that go.
QUEEN   More matter, with less art.
POLONIUS   Madam, I swear I use no art at all.
  That he is mad, 'tis true; 'tis true 'tis pity;
  And pity it is true: a foolish figure!
  But farewell it, for I will use no art.
  Mad let us grant him then, and now remains
  That we find out the cause of this effect –
  Or rather say the cause of this defect,
  For this effect defective comes by cause.
  Thus it remains, and the remainder thus. Perpend,
  I have a daughter – have whilst she is mine –
  Who in her duty and obedience, mark,
  Hath given me this. Now gather and surmise.
  [*Reads the letter.*] *To the celestial and my soul's idol, the*
  most beautified Ophelia – that's an ill phrase, a vile
  phrase, 'beautified' is a vile phrase, but you shall hear:
  these in her excellent white bosom, these –
QUEEN   Came this from Hamlet to her?
POLONIUS
  Good madam, stay awhile: I will be faithful.
  [*Reads.*]
            Doubt thou the stars are fire,
            Doubt that the sun doth move,
            Doubt truth to be a liar,
            But never doubt I love.

70
75
80
85
90
95
100
105
110
115

O dear Ophelia, I am ill at these numbers. I have not art
to reckon my groans, but that I love thee best, O most best,
120 *believe it. Adieu. Thine evermore, most dear lady, whilst*
this machine is to him. Hamlet.
This in obedience hath my daughter showed me;
And, more above, hath his soliciting
As they fell out, by time, by means and place,
All given to mine ear.

125 KING   But how hath she
Received his love?

POLONIUS   What do you think of me?

KING   As of a man, faithful and honourable.

POLONIUS
I would fain prove so. But what might you think,
When I had seen this hot love on the wing –
130 As I perceived it (I must tell you that)
Before my daughter told me – what might you,
Or my dear majesty your Queen here, think,
If I had played the desk or table-book,
Or given my heart a winking, mute and dumb,
135 Or looked upon this love with idle sight,
What might you think? No, I went round to work,
And my young mistress thus I did bespeak:
'Lord Hamlet is a prince out of thy star.
This must not be.' And then I precepts gave her
140 That she should lock herself from his resort,
Admit no messengers, receive no tokens.
Which done, she took the fruits of my advice,
And he, repulsed, a short tale to make,
Fell into a sadness, then into a fast,
145 Thence to a watch, thence into a weakness,
Thence to a lightness, and by this declension
Into the madness wherein now he raves,
And all we wail for.

KING   Do you think 'tis this?

QUEEN   It may be very likely.

POLONIUS
150 Hath there been such a time – I'd fain know that –
That I have positively said 'tis so
When it proved otherwise?

KING   Not that I know.

POLONIUS   Take this from this, if this be otherwise.
If circumstances lead me I will find
155 Where truth is hid, though it were hid indeed
Within the centre.

KING   How may we try it further?

POLONIUS
You know sometimes he walks four hours together
Here in the lobby?

QUEEN   So he has, indeed.

POLONIUS   At such a time I'll loose my daughter to him.
160 Be you and I behind an arras then,
Mark the encounter: if he love her not
And be not from his reason fallen thereon,
Let me be no assistant for a state
And keep a farm and carters.

KING   We will try it.

Enter HAMLET *reading on a book.*

QUEEN
But look where sadly the poor wretch comes
reading.   165

POLONIUS   Away, I do beseech you both, away.
I'll board him presently. O, give me leave.

Exeunt King and Queen.

How does my good lord Hamlet?

HAMLET   Well, God-a-mercy.

POLONIUS   Do you know me, my lord?   170

HAMLET   Excellent, excellent well: you're a fishmonger.

POLONIUS   Not I, my lord.

HAMLET   Then I would you were so honest a man.

POLONIUS   Honest, my lord?

HAMLET   Ay, sir: to be honest as this world goes is to be   175
one man picked out of two thousand.

POLONIUS   That's very true, my lord.

HAMLET   For if the sun breed maggots in a dead dog,
being a good kissing carrion – have you a daughter?

POLONIUS   I have, my lord.   180

HAMLET   Let her not walk i'th' sun. Conception is a
blessing, but not as your daughter may conceive –
friend, look to't.

POLONIUS [*aside*]   How say you by that? Still harping on
my daughter. Yet he knew me not at first, he said I was   185
a fishmonger! He is far gone, far gone. And truly, in my
youth I suffered much extremity for love, very near this.
I'll speak to him again. – What do you read, my lord?

HAMLET   Words, words, words.

POLONIUS   What is the matter, my lord?   190

HAMLET   Between who?

POLONIUS   I mean the matter you read, my lord.

HAMLET   Slanders, sir. For the satirical slave says here
that old men have grey beards, that their faces are
wrinkled, their eyes purging thick amber or plumtree   195
gum, and that they have a plentiful lack of wit, together
with weak hams. All which, sir, though I most
powerfully and potently believe, yet I hold it not
honesty to have it thus set down. For you yourself, sir,
should be old as I am if, like a crab, you could go   200
backward.

POLONIUS [*aside*]   Though this be madness yet there is
method in't. – Will you walk out of the air, my lord?

HAMLET   Into my grave?

POLONIUS [*aside*]   Indeed, that is out o'th' air. How   205
pregnant sometimes his replies are! A happiness that
often madness hits on, which reason and sanity could
not so prosperously be delivered of. I will leave him
and suddenly contrive the means of meeting between
him and my daughter. – My honourable lord, I will   210
most humbly take my leave of you.

HAMLET   You cannot, sir, take from me anything that
I will more willingly part withal – except my life, my
life.

POLONIUS   Fare you well, my lord.   215

HAMLET   These tedious old fools.

Enter ROSINCRANCE *and* GUILDENSTERNE.

POLONIUS You go to seek my Lord Hamlet? There
he is.

ROSINCRANCE [*to Polonius*] God save you, sir.
Exit Polonius.

220 GUILDENSTERNE Mine honoured lord!

ROSINCRANCE My most dear lord!

HAMLET My excellent good friends! How dost thou,
Guildensterne? O, Rosincrance! Good lads, how
do ye both?

225 ROSINCRANCE As the indifferent children of the earth.

GUILDENSTERNE Happy, in that we are not over-happy.
On Fortune's cap we are not the very button.

HAMLET Nor the soles of her shoe?

ROSINCRANCE Neither, my lord.

230 HAMLET Then you live about her waist, or in the
middle of her favour!

GUILDENSTERNE Faith, her privates we.

HAMLET In the secret parts of Fortune? O, most true
– she is a strumpet. What's the news?

235 ROSINCRANCE None, my lord, but that the world's
grown honest.

HAMLET Then is doomsday near! But your news is not
true. Let me question more in particular. What have
you, my good friends, deserved at the hands of Fortune

240 that she sends you to prison hither?

GUILDENSTERNE Prison, my lord?

HAMLET Denmark's a prison.

ROSINCRANCE Then is the world one.

HAMLET A goodly one, in which there are many

245 confines, wards and dungeons – Denmark being one
o'th' worst.

ROSINCRANCE We think not so, my lord.

HAMLET Why, then 'tis none to you; for there is nothing
either good or bad, but thinking makes it so. To me it is

250 a prison.

ROSINCRANCE Why, then your ambition makes it one:
'tis too narrow for your mind.

HAMLET O God, I could be bounded in a nutshell and
count myself a king of infinite space – were it not that

255 I have bad dreams.

GUILDENSTERNE Which dreams, indeed, are ambition;
for the very substance of the ambitious is merely the
shadow of a dream.

HAMLET A dream itself is but a shadow.

260 ROSINCRANCE Truly, and I hold ambition of so airy
and light a quality that it is but a shadow's shadow.

HAMLET Then are our beggars bodies, and our
monarchs and outstretched heroes the beggars'
shadows. Shall we to th' Court? For, by my fay, I

265 cannot reason.

ROSINCRANCE, GUILDENSTERNE We'll wait upon you.

HAMLET No such matter. I will not sort you with the
rest of my servants, for, to speak to you like an honest
man, I am most dreadfully attended. But, in the beaten

270 way of friendship, what make you at Elsinore?

ROSINCRANCE To visit you, my lord, no other occasion.

HAMLET Beggar that I am, I am even poor in thanks.
But I thank you, and sure, dear friends, my thanks are
too dear a halfpenny. Were you not sent for? Is it your
own inclining? Is it a free visitation? Come, deal justly   275
with me. Come, come, nay speak.

GUILDENSTERNE What should we say, my lord?

HAMLET Why, anything. But to the purpose – you were
sent for, and there is a kind of confession in your looks,
which your modesties have not craft enough to colour.   280
I know the good King and Queen have sent for you.

ROSINCRANCE To what end, my lord?

HAMLET That you must teach me. But let me conjure
you, by the rights of our fellowship, by the consonancy
of our youth, by the obligation of our ever-preserved   285
love, and by what more dear a better proposer could
charge you withal, be even and direct with me whether
you were sent for or no.

ROSINCRANCE What say you?

HAMLET Nay then, I have an eye of you. If you love me,   290
hold not off.

GUILDENSTERNE My lord, we were sent for.

HAMLET I will tell you why. So shall my anticipation
prevent your discovery and your secrecy to the King
and Queen moult no feather. I have of late, but   295
wherefore I know not, lost all my mirth, forgone all
custom of exercise; and, indeed, it goes so heavily with
my disposition that this goodly frame, the earth, seems
to me a sterile promontory. This most excellent canopy
the air, look you, this brave o'erhanging, this majestical   300
roof fretted with golden fire – why it appears no other
thing to me than a foul and pestilent congregation of
vapours. What a piece of work is a man! How noble in
reason! How infinite in faculty! In form and moving
how express and admirable! In action, how like an   305
angel! In apprehension, how like a god! The beauty of
the world, the paragon of animals – and yet to me what
is this quintessence of dust? Man delights not me – no,
nor woman neither, though by your smiling you seem
to say so.   310

ROSINCRANCE My lord, there was no such stuff in my
thoughts.

HAMLET Why did you laugh when I said man delights
not me?

ROSINCRANCE To think, my lord, if you delight not in   315
man, what lenten entertainment the players shall
receive from you. We coted them on the way and hither
are they coming to offer you service.

HAMLET He that plays the King shall be welcome – his
majesty shall have tribute of me – the Adventurous   320
Knight shall use his foil and target, the Lover shall not
sigh gratis, the Humorous Man shall end his part in
peace, the Clown shall make those laugh whose lungs are
tickled o'th' sear, and the Lady shall say her mind freely
or the blank verse shall halt for't. What players are they?   325

ROSINCRANCE Even those you were wont to take
delight in, the tragedians of the city.

HAMLET   How chances it they travel? Their residence, both in reputation and profit, was better both ways.

330 ROSINCRANCE   I think their inhibition comes by the means of the late innovation.

HAMLET   Do they hold the same estimation they did when I was in the city? Are they so followed?

ROSINCRANCE   No, indeed they are not.

335 HAMLET   How comes it? Do they grow rusty?

ROSINCRANCE   Nay, their endeavour keeps in the wonted pace. But there is, sir, an eyrie of children, little eyases that cry out on the top of question and are most tyrannically clapped for't. These are now the

340 fashion, and so berattle the common stages (so they call them) that many wearing rapiers are afraid of goose-quills and dare scarce come thither.

HAMLET   What, are they children? Who maintains 'em? How are they escotted? Will they pursue the quality no

345 longer than they can sing? Will they not say afterwards if they should grow themselves to common players – as it is most like if their means are no better – their writers do them wrong to make them exclaim against their own succession?

350 ROSINCRANCE   Faith, there has been much to-do on both sides, and the nation holds it no sin to tar them to controversy. There was for a while no money bid for argument unless the poet and the player went to cuffs in the question.

355 HAMLET   Is't possible?

GUILDENSTERNE   O, there has been much throwing about of brains.

HAMLET   Do the boys carry it away?

ROSINCRANCE   Ay, that they do, my lord – Hercules and

360 his load too.

HAMLET   It is not strange, for mine uncle is King of Denmark, and those that would make mows at him while my father lived give twenty, forty, an hundred ducats apiece for his picture in little. There is

365 something in this more than natural if philosophy could find it out.   [*Flourish for the Players*]

GUILDENSTERNE   There are the players!

HAMLET   Gentlemen, you are welcome to Elsinore. Your hands, come! The appurtenance of welcome is

370 fashion and ceremony. Let me comply with you in the garb lest my extent to the players, which I tell you must show fairly outward, should more appear like entertainment than yours. You are welcome. But my uncle-father and aunt-mother are deceived.

375 GUILDENSTERNE   In what, my dear lord?

HAMLET   I am but mad north-north-west. When the wind is southerly I know a hawk from a handsaw.

Enter POLONIUS.

POLONIUS   Well be with you, gentlemen.

HAMLET   Hark you, Guildensterne, and you too – at

380 each ear a hearer. That great baby you see there is not yet out of his swathing clouts.

ROSINCRANCE   Happily he's the second time come to

them, for they say an old man is twice a child.

HAMLET   I will prophesy. He comes to tell me of the players. Mark it. – You say right, sir, for o'Monday 385 morning 'twas so indeed.

POLONIUS   My lord, I have news to tell you.

HAMLET   My lord, I have news to tell you. When Roscius, an actor in Rome –

POLONIUS   The actors are come hither, my lord. 390

HAMLET   Buzz, buzz.

POLONIUS   Upon mine honour.

HAMLET
      Then can each actor on his ass –

POLONIUS   The best actors in the world, either for tragedy, comedy, history, pastoral, pastorical- 395 comical, historical-pastoral, tragical-historical, tragical-comical-historical-pastoral, scene individable or poem unlimited. Seneca cannot be too heavy nor Plautus too light for the law of writ and the liberty. These are the only men. 400

HAMLET
      O Jephthah, judge of Israel,
      What a treasure hadst thou?

POLONIUS   What a treasure had he, my lord?

HAMLET   Why,
      One fair daughter and no more, 405
      The which he loved passing well.

POLONIUS [*aside*]   Still on my daughter.

HAMLET   Am I not i'th' right, old Jephthah?

POLONIUS   If you call me Jephthah, my lord – I have a daughter that I love passing well. 410

HAMLET   Nay, that follows not.

POLONIUS   What follows then, my lord?

HAMLET   Why,
      As by lot,
      God wot, 415
and then, you know,
      It came to pass,
      As most like it was.
The first row of the pious chanson will show you more, for look where my abridgements come. 420

Enter four or five Players.

You're welcome, masters, welcome all. I am glad to see thee well. Welcome, good friends. O my old friend! Thy face is valiant since I saw thee last! Com'st thou to beard me in Denmark? What, my young lady and mistress! By'r Lady, your ladyship is nearer heaven 425 than when I saw you last by the altitude of a chopine. Pray God your voice, like a piece of uncurrent gold, be not cracked within the ring. Masters, you are all welcome. We'll e'en to't like French falconers – fly at anything we see. We'll have a speech straight. Come, 430 give us a taste of your quality. Come, a passionate speech.

1 PLAYER   What speech, my lord?

HAMLET   I heard thee speak me a speech once – but it was never acted. Or, if it was, not above once, for the 435

play I remember pleased not the million, 'twas caviare
to the general. But it was, as I received it, and others
whose judgement in such matters cried in the top of
mine, an excellent play, well digested in the scenes, set
down with as much modesty as cunning. I remember
one said there was no sallets in the lines to make
the matter savoury, nor no matter in the phrase that
might indict the author of affectation, but called it
an honest method. One chief speech in it I chiefly
loved – 'twas Aeneas' tale to Dido, and thereabout of it
especially where he speaks of Priam's slaughter. If it
live in your memory, begin at this line – let me see, let
me see –
The rugged Pyrrhus like th' Hyrcanian beast . . .
– It is not so. It begins with Pyrrhus.
The rugged Pyrrhus, he whose sable arms,
Black as his purpose, did the night resemble
When he lay couched in the ominous horse,
Hath now this dread and black complexion smeared
With heraldry more dismal. Head to foot
Now is he total gules, horridly tricked
With blood of fathers, mothers, daughters, sons,
Baked and impasted with the parching streets
That lend a tyrannous and damned light
To their vile murders; roasted in wrath and fire,
And thus o'ersized with coagulate gore,
With eyes like carbuncles, the hellish Pyrrhus
Old grandsire Priam seeks.

POLONIUS 'Fore God, my lord, well spoken – with
good accent and good discretion.

1 PLAYER   *Anon he finds him,*
Striking too short at Greeks. His antique sword,
Rebellious to his arm, lies where it falls,
Repugnant to command. Unequal match!
Pyrrhus at Priam drives, in rage strikes wide
But with the whiff and wind of his fell sword
Th'unnerved father falls. Then senseless Ilium,
Seeming to feel his blow, with flaming top
Stoops to his base and with a hideous crash
Takes prisoner Pyrrhus' ear. For lo, his sword
Which was declining on the milky head
Of reverend Priam seemed i'th' air to stick.
So as a painted tyrant Pyrrhus stood –
And, like a neutral to his will and matter,
Did nothing.
But as we often see, against some storm,
A silence in the heavens, the rack stand still,
The bold winds speechless, and the orb below
As hush as death, anon the dreadful thunder
Doth rend the region; so, after Pyrrhus' pause,
A roused vengeance sets him new a-work,
And never did the Cyclops' hammers fall
On Mars his armours, forged for proof eterne,
With less remorse than Pyrrhus' bleeding sword
Now falls on Priam.
Out, out, thou strumpet Fortune! All you gods
In general synod take away her power;

Break all the spokes and fellies from her wheel
And bowl the round nave down the hill of heaven
As low as to the fiends.

POLONIUS This is too long.

HAMLET It shall to th' barber's with your beard. Prithee
say on – he's for a jig, or a tale of bawdry, or he sleeps.
Say on, come to Hecuba.

1 PLAYER
But who, O who, had seen the inobled queen –

HAMLET 'The inobled queen'!

POLONIUS That's good – 'inobled queen' is good.

1 PLAYER
– Run barefoot up and down, threatening the flame
With bisson rheum, a clout about that head
Where late the diadem stood and, for a robe,
About her lank and all-o'erteemed loins,
A blanket in th'alarum of fear caught up.
Who this had seen, with tongue in venom steeped,
'Gainst Fortune's state would treason have pronounced.
But if the gods themselves did see her then,
When she saw Pyrrhus make malicious sport
In mincing with his sword her husband's limbs,
The instant burst of clamour that she made
(Unless things mortal move them not at all)
Would have made milch the burning eyes of heaven,
And passion in the gods.

POLONIUS Look where he has not turned his colour,
and has tears in's eyes. – Pray you no more!

HAMLET 'Tis well. I'll have thee speak out the rest
soon. [*to Polonius*] Good my lord, will you see the
players well bestowed? Do ye hear, let them be well
used, for they are the abstracts and brief chronicles of
the time. After your death you were better have a bad
epitaph than their ill report while you lived.

POLONIUS My lord, I will use them according to their
desert.

HAMLET God's bodikins, man, better! Use every man
after his desert and who should scape whipping? Use
them after your own honour and dignity – the less
they deserve, the more merit is in your bounty. Take
them in.

POLONIUS Come, sirs.   *Exit.*

HAMLET Follow him, friends. We'll hear a play
tomorrow. – [*aside to First Player*] Dost thou hear me,
old friend? Can you play *The Murder of Gonzago*?

1 PLAYER Ay, my lord.

HAMLET We'll ha't tomorrow night. You could for a
need study a speech of some dozen or sixteen lines,
which I would set down and insert in't, could ye not?

1 PLAYER Ay, my lord.

HAMLET Very well. Follow that lord – and look you
mock him not. [*to other Players*] My good friends, I'll
leave you till night. You are welcome to Elsinore.

ROSINCRANCE Good my lord.

HAMLET Ay so, god buy ye.   *Exeunt all but Hamlet.*
                          Now I am alone.
O, what a rogue and peasant slave am I!

Is it not monstrous that this player here,
But in a fiction, in a dream of passion,
Could force his soul so to his whole conceit
550   That, from her working, all his visage warmed
– Tears in his eyes, distraction in's aspect,
A broken voice, and his whole function suiting
With forms to his conceit? And all for nothing?
For Hecuba?
555   What's Hecuba to him, or he to Hecuba,
That he should weep for her? What would he do
Had he the motive and the cue for passion
That I have? He would drown the stage with tears
And cleave the general ear with horrid speech,
560   Make mad the guilty and appal the free,
Confound the ignorant and amaze indeed
The very faculty of eyes and ears. Yet I,
A dull and muddy-mettled rascal, peak
Like John-a-dreams unpregnant of my cause,
565   And can say nothing. No, not for a king,
Upon whose property and most dear life
A damned defeat was made. Am I a coward?
Who calls me villain? Breaks my pate across?
Plucks off my beard, and blows it in my face?
570   Tweaks me by th' nose? Gives me the lie i'th' throat,
As deep as to the lungs? Who does me this?
Ha? Why, I should take it. For it cannot be
But I am pigeon-livered, and lack gall
To make oppression bitter, or ere this
575   I should have fatted all the region kites
With this slave's offal, bloody – a bawdy villain,
Remorseless, treacherous, lecherous, kindless villain!
O vengeance!
Whoa! What an ass am I! Ay, sure, this is most
     brave,
580   That I, the son of the dear murdered,
Prompted to my revenge by heaven and hell,
Must, like a whore, unpack my heart with words
And fall a-cursing like a very drab,
A scullion! Fie upon't, foh! About, my brain!
585   I have heard
That guilty creatures sitting at a play
Have by the very cunning of the scene
Been struck so to the soul that presently
They have proclaimed their malefactions.
590   For murder, though it have no tongue, will speak
With most miraculous organ. I'll have these players
Play something like the murder of my father
Before mine uncle. I'll observe his looks.
I'll tent him to the quick. If he but blench
595   I know my course. The spirit that I have seen
May be the devil, and the devil hath power
T'assume a pleasing shape. Yea, and perhaps
Out of my weakness and my melancholy,
As he is very potent with such spirits,
600   Abuses me to damn me! I'll have grounds
More relative than this. The play's the thing
Wherein I'll catch the conscience of the King.   *Exit.*

3.1   *Enter* KING, QUEEN, POLONIUS, OPHELIA,
          ROSINCRANCE, GUILDENSTERNE *and Lords.*

KING
And can you by no drift of circumstance
Get from him why he puts on this confusion,
Grating so harshly all his days of quiet
With turbulent and dangerous lunacy?
ROSINCRANCE
He does confess he feels himself distracted   5
But from what cause he will by no means speak.
GUILDENSTERNE
Nor do we find him forward to be sounded,
But with a crafty madness keeps aloof
When we would bring him on to some confession
Of his true state.
QUEEN   Did he receive you well?   10
ROSINCRANCE   Most like a gentleman.
GUILDENSTERNE
But with much forcing of his disposition.
ROSINCRANCE
Niggard of question, but of our demands
Most free in his reply.
QUEEN   Did you assay him to any pastime?   15
ROSINCRANCE
Madam, it so fell out that certain players
We o'erraught on the way. Of these we told him,
And there did seem in him a kind of joy
To hear of it. They are about the Court
And, as I think, they have already order   20
This night to play before him.
POLONIUS   'Tis most true;
And he beseeched me to entreat your majesties
To hear and see the matter.
KING
With all my heart; and it doth much content me
To hear him so inclined. Good gentlemen,   25
Give him a further edge and drive his purpose on
To these delights.
ROSINCRANCE   We shall, my lord.
         Exeunt Rosincrance, Guildensterne and Lords.
KING   Sweet Gertrude, leave us too.
For we have closely sent for Hamlet hither
That he, as 'twere by accident, may here   30
Affront Ophelia.
Her father and myself – lawful espials –
Will so bestow ourselves that, seeing unseen,
We may of their encounter frankly judge
And gather by him as he is behaved   35
If't be th'affliction of his love or no
That thus he suffers for.
QUEEN   I shall obey you.
And for your part, Ophelia, I do wish
That your good beauties be the happy cause
Of Hamlet's wildness. So shall I hope your virtues   40
Will bring him to his wonted way again
To both your honours.

OPHELIA   Madam, I wish it may.
Exit Queen.
POLONIUS
Ophelia, walk you here. (Gracious, so please ye,
We will bestow ourselves.) Read on this book
45   That show of such an exercise may colour
Your loneliness. We are oft too blame in this –
'Tis too much proved that with devotion's visage
And pious action we do sugar o'er
The devil himself.
KING   O, 'tis true.
[*aside*] How smart a lash that speech doth give my
50   conscience!
The harlot's cheek beautied with plastering art
Is not more ugly to the thing that helps it
Than is my deed to my most painted word.
O heavy burden!
POLONIUS
55   I hear him coming – let's withdraw, my lord.
[*King and Polonius hide behind an arras.*]

Enter HAMLET.

HAMLET   To be, or not to be – that is the question.
Whether 'tis nobler in the mind to suffer
The slings and arrows of outrageous fortune
Or to take arms against a sea of troubles
60   And by opposing end them. To die: to sleep –
No more; and by a sleep to say we end
The heartache and the thousand natural shocks
That flesh is heir to? 'Tis a consummation
Devoutly to be wished. To die: to sleep –
65   To sleep: perchance to dream. Ay, there's the rub,
For in that sleep of death what dreams may come
When we have shuffled off this mortal coil
Must give us pause. There's the respect
That makes calamity of so long life.
70   For who would bear the whips and scorns of time,
The oppressor's wrong, the poor man's contumely,
The pangs of disprized love, the law's delay,
The insolence of office and the spurns
That patient merit of the unworthy takes,
75   When he himself might his quietus make
With a bare bodkin? Who would these fardels bear
To grunt and sweat under a weary life
But that the dread of something after death
(The undiscovered country from whose bourn
80   No traveller returns) puzzles the will
And makes us rather bear those ills we have
Than fly to others that we know not of.
Thus conscience does make cowards of us all
And thus the native hue of resolution
85   Is sicklied o'er with the pale cast of thought,
And enterprises of great pith and moment
With this regard their currents turn away
And lose the name of action. Soft you now,
The fair Ophelia! Nymph, in thy orisons
Be all my sins remembered.

OPHELIA   Good my lord,   90
How does your honour for this many a day?
HAMLET   I humbly thank you, well, well, well.
OPHELIA   My lord, I have remembrances of yours
That I have longed long to redeliver.
I pray you now receive them.   95
HAMLET   No, no. I never gave you aught.
OPHELIA
My honoured lord, I know right well you did,
And with them words of so sweet breath composed
As made the things more rich. Then, perfume lost,
Take these again, for to the noble mind   100
Rich gifts wax poor when givers prove unkind.
There, my lord.
HAMLET   Ha! Ha! Are you honest?
OPHELIA   My lord?
HAMLET   Are you fair?   105
OPHELIA   What means your lordship?
HAMLET   That if you be honest and fair your honesty
should admit no discourse to your beauty.
OPHELIA   Could Beauty, my lord, have better commerce
than your Honesty?   110
HAMLET   Ay, truly. For the power of Beauty will sooner
transform Honesty from what it is to a bawd than the
force of Honesty can translate Beauty into his likeness.
This was sometime a paradox, but now the time gives
it proof. I did love you once.   115
OPHELIA   Indeed, my lord, you made me believe so.
HAMLET   You should not have believed me. For virtue
cannot so inoculate our old stock but we shall relish of
it. I loved you not.
OPHELIA   I was the more deceived.   120
HAMLET   Get thee to a nunnery! Why wouldst thou
be a breeder of sinners? I am myself indifferent
honest but yet I could accuse me of such things that it
were better my mother had not borne me. I am very
proud, revengeful, ambitious, with more offences at   125
my beck than I have thoughts to put them in,
imagination to give them shape, or time to act them in.
What should such fellows as I do crawling between
heaven and earth? We are arrant knaves all – believe
none of us. Go thy ways to a nunnery. Where's your   130
father?
OPHELIA   At home, my lord.
HAMLET   Let the doors be shut upon him, that he may
play the fool no way but in's own house. Farewell.
OPHELIA [*aside*]   O help him, you sweet heavens!   135
HAMLET   If thou dost marry, I'll give thee this plague
for thy dowry: be thou as chaste as ice, as pure as snow,
thou shalt not escape calumny. Get thee to a nunnery.
Go. Farewell. Or, if thou wilt needs marry, marry a
fool, for wise men know well enough what monsters   140
you make of them. To a nunnery go, and quickly too.
Farewell.
OPHELIA [*aside*]   O heavenly powers, restore him.
HAMLET   I have heard of your prattlings too
well enough. God has given you one pace and you   145

make yourself another. You jig, you amble and you
lisp, and nickname God's creatures and make your
wantonness your ignorance. Go to, I'll no more on't. It
hath made me mad. I say we will have no more
150 marriages. Those that are married already – all but
one – shall live. The rest shall keep as they are. To a
nunnery, go! *Exit.*

OPHELIA   O, what a noble mind is here o'erthrown!
The courtier's, soldier's, scholar's eye, tongue, sword,
155 Th'expectancy and rose of the fair state,
The glass of fashion and the mould of form,
Th'observed of all observers, quite, quite down.
And I, of ladies most deject and wretched,
That sucked the honey of his music vows,
160 Now see that noble and most sovereign reason
Like sweet bells jangled out of tune and harsh –
That unmatched form and feature of blown youth
Blasted with ecstasy. O, woe is me
T'have seen what I have seen, see what I see.
[*King and Polonius step forward from behind the arras.*]

165 KING   Love! His affections do not that way tend.
Nor what he spake, though it lacked form a little,
Was not like madness. There's something in
his soul
O'er which his melancholy sits on brood
And I do doubt the hatch and the disclose
170 Will be some danger – which to prevent
I have in quick determination
Thus set it down. He shall with speed to England
For the demand of our neglected tribute.
Haply the seas and countries different
175 With variable objects shall expel
This something-settled matter in his heart
Whereon his brains still beating puts him thus
From fashion of himself. What think you on't?

POLONIUS   It shall do well. But yet do I believe
180 The origin and commencement of this grief
Sprung from neglected love. How now, Ophelia?
You need not tell us what Lord Hamlet said –
We heard it all. My lord, do as you please,
But if you hold it fit after the play
185 Let his Queen-mother all alone entreat him
To show his griefs. Let her be round with him
And I'll be placed, so please you, in the ear
Of all their conference. If she find him not,
To England send him or confine him where
Your wisdom best shall think.

190 KING   It shall be so.
Madness in great ones must not unwatched go.
Exeunt.

3.2   *Enter* HAMLET *and two or three of the* Players.

HAMLET   Speak the speech, I pray you, as I pronounced
it to you, trippingly on the tongue. But if you mouth it
as many of your players do, I had as lief the town-
crier had spoke my lines. Nor do not saw the air too
much – your hand, thus – but use all gently. For, in the   5
very torrent, tempest and, as I may say, the whirlwind
of passion, you must acquire and beget a temperance
that may give it smoothness. O, it offends me to the
soul to see a robustious periwig-pated fellow tear a
passion to tatters, to very rags, to split the ears of the   10
groundlings, who for the most part are capable of
nothing but inexplicable dumb-shows and noise. I
could have such a fellow whipped for o'erdoing
Termagant – it out-Herods Herod. Pray you avoid it.

PLAYER   I warrant your honour.   15

HAMLET   Be not too tame neither, but let your own
discretion be your tutor. Suit the action to the word, the
word to the action, with this special observance – that
you o'erstep not the modesty of nature. For anything so
overdone is from the purpose of playing whose end,   20
both at the first and now, was and is to hold as 'twere the
mirror up to Nature, to show Virtue her own feature,
Scorn her own image, and the very age and body of the
time his form and pressure. Now this overdone, or
come tardy off, though it make the unskilful laugh,   25
cannot but make the judicious grieve, the censure of the
which one must in your allowance o'erweigh a whole
theatre of others. O, there be players that I have seen
play and heard others praise – and that highly – not to
speak it profanely, that neither having the accent of   30
Christians nor the gait of Christian, pagan nor no man
have so strutted and bellowed that I have thought some
of Nature's journeymen had made men, and not made
them well, they imitated humanity so abhominably.

PLAYER   I hope we have reformed that indifferently   35
with us, sir.

HAMLET   O, reform it altogether – and let those that
play your clowns speak no more than is set down for
them. For there be of them that will themselves laugh
to set on some quantity of barren spectators to laugh   40
too, though in the meantime some necessary question
of the play be then to be considered. That's villainous
and shows a most pitiful ambition in the fool that uses
it. Go, make you ready. *Exeunt Players.*

Enter POLONIUS, ROSINCRANCE *and* GUILDENSTERNE.

How now, my lord, will the King hear this piece of work?   45

POLONIUS   And the Queen too, and that presently.

HAMLET   Bid the players make haste. *Exit Polonius.*
Will you two help to hasten them?

ROSINCRANCE, GUILDENSTERNE   We will, my lord.
Exeunt.

HAMLET   What ho, Horatio!

Enter HORATIO.

HORATIO   Here, sweet lord, at your service.

HAMLET   Horatio, thou art e'en as just a man   50
As e'er my conversation coped withal.

HORATIO   O my dear lord –

HAMLET   Nay, do not think I flatter,

For what advancement may I hope from thee
That no revenue hast but thy good spirits
To feed and clothe thee? Why should the poor be
        flattered?
No, let the candied tongue lick absurd pomp
And crook the pregnant hinges of the knee
Where thrift may follow feigning. Dost thou hear?
Since my dear soul was mistress of my choice
And could of men distinguish, her election
Hath sealed thee for herself. For thou hast been
As one in suffering all that suffers nothing –
A man that Fortune's buffets and rewards
Hath ta'en with equal thanks. And blest are those
Whose blood and judgement are so well co-mingled
That they are not a pipe for Fortune's finger
To sound what stop she please. Give me that man
That is not passion's slave, and I will wear him
In my heart's core – ay, in my heart of heart –
As I do thee. Something too much of this.
There is a play tonight before the King –
One scene of it comes near the circumstance,
Which I have told thee, of my father's death.
I prithee, when thou seest that act afoot,
Even with the very comment of thy soul
Observe mine uncle. If his occulted guilt
Do not itself unkennel in one speech
It is a damned ghost that we have seen
And my imaginations are as foul
As Vulcan's stithy. Give him needful note,
For I mine eyes will rivet to his face
And after we will both our judgements join
To censure of his seeming.

HORATIO   Well, my lord,
If he steal aught the whilst this play is playing
And scape detecting, I will pay the theft.

Enter KING, QUEEN, POLONIUS, OPHELIA,
and other Lords
attendant with his Guard carrying torches. Danish march.
Sound a flourish.

HAMLET [*to Horatio*]   They are coming to the play. I
must be idle. Get you a place.

KING   How fares our cousin Hamlet?

HAMLET   Excellent, i'faith! Of the chameleon's dish –
I eat the air, promise-crammed. You cannot feed
capons so.

KING   I have nothing with this answer, Hamlet. These
words are not mine.

HAMLET   No, nor mine. [*to Polonius*] Now, my lord, you
played once i'th' university, you say?

POLONIUS   That I did, my lord, and was accounted a
good actor.

HAMLET   And what did you enact?

POLONIUS   I did enact Julius Caesar. I was killed i'th'
Capitol. Brutus killed me.

HAMLET   It was a brute part of him to kill so capital a
calf there. Be the players ready?

ROSINCRANCE   Ay, my lord, they stay upon your
patience.

QUEEN   Come hither, my dear Hamlet, sit by me.   105

HAMLET   No, good mother, here's metal more attractive.

POLONIUS [*aside to King*]   O ho, do you mark that!

HAMLET   Lady, shall I lie in your lap?

OPHELIA   No, my lord.

HAMLET   I mean my head upon your lap.   110

OPHELIA   Ay, my lord.

HAMLET   Do you think I meant country matters?

OPHELIA   I think nothing, my lord.

HAMLET   That's a fair thought to lie between maids'
legs.   115

OPHELIA   What is, my lord?

HAMLET   Nothing.

OPHELIA   You are merry, my lord!

HAMLET   Who, I?

OPHELIA   Ay, my lord.   120

HAMLET   O God, your only jig-maker! What should
a man do but be merry, for look you how cheerfully
my mother looks, and my father died within's two
hours!

OPHELIA   Nay, 'tis twice two months, my lord.   125

HAMLET   So long? Nay, then, let the devil wear black, for
I'll have a suit of sables! O heavens – die two months
ago and not forgotten yet? Then there's hope a great
man's memory may outlive his life half a year! But, by'r
Lady, he must build churches then, or else shall he   130
suffer not thinking on – with the hobby-horse, whose
epitaph is 'For O! For O! The hobby-horse is forgot!'

Hautboys play. The dumb-show enters. Enter Players *as a*
king and queen very lovingly, the queen embracing him.
She kneels and makes show of protestation unto him. He
takes her up and declines his head upon her neck; lays him
down upon a bank of flowers. She seeing him asleep leaves
him. Anon comes in a Player *as a fellow, takes off his*
crown, kisses it and pours poison in the king's ears and
exits. The queen returns, finds the king dead and makes
passionate action. The poisoner with Players *as some two*
or three mutes comes in again, seeming to lament with her.
The dead body is carried away. The poisoner woos the
queen with gifts. She seems loath and unwilling awhile but
in the end accepts his love.   *Exeunt.*

OPHELIA   What means this, my lord?

HAMLET   Marry, this is miching mallico. That means
mischief.   135

OPHELIA   Belike this show imports the argument of the
play?

HAMLET   We shall know by these fellows. The players
cannot keep counsel – they'll tell all.

OPHELIA   Will they tell us what this show meant?   140

HAMLET   Ay, or any show that you'll show him. Be not
you ashamed to show, he'll not shame to tell you what
it means.

OPHELIA   You are naught, you are naught. I'll mark the
play.   145

Enter a Player *as* Prologue.

PROLOGUE

  For us and for our tragedy
  Here stooping to your clemency
  We beg your hearing patiently.   *Exit.*

HAMLET   Is this a prologue, or the posy of a ring?

150 OPHELIA   'Tis brief, my lord.

HAMLET   As woman's love.

Enter Player King *and* Player Queen.

PLAYER KING

  Full thirty times hath Phoebus' cart gone round
  Neptune's salt wash and Tellus' orbed ground,
  And thirty dozen moons with borrowed sheen
155 *About the world have times twelve thirties been*
  Since love our hearts and Hymen did our hands
  Unite commutual in most sacred bands.

PLAYER QUEEN

  So many journeys may the sun and moon
  Make us again count o'er ere love be done.
160 *But woe is me, you are so sick of late,*
  So far from cheer and from your former state,
  That I distrust you. Yet, though I distrust,
  Discomfort you, my lord, it nothing must.
  For women's fear and love holds quantity –
165 *In neither aught, or in extremity.*
  Now what my love is proof hath made you know,
  And, as my love is sized, my fear is so.

PLAYER KING

  Faith, I must leave thee, love, and shortly too,
  My operant powers my functions leave to do,
170 *And thou shalt live in this fair world behind*
  Honoured, beloved, and haply one as kind
  For husband shalt thou –

PLAYER QUEEN   *O, confound the rest!*
  Such love must needs be treason in my breast.
  In second husband let me be accurst:
175 *None wed the second but who killed the first.*

HAMLET   Wormwood! Wormwood!

PLAYER QUEEN

  The instances that second marriage move
  Are base respects of thrift, but none of love.
  A second time I kill my husband dead
180 *When second husband kisses me in bed.*

PLAYER KING

  I do believe you think what now you speak,
  But what we do determine oft we break.
  Purpose is but the slave to memory,
  Of violent birth but poor validity,
185 *Which now like fruit unripe sticks on the tree*
  But fall unshaken when they mellow be.
  Most necessary 'tis that we forget
  To pay ourselves what to ourselves is debt.
  What to ourselves in passion we propose,
190 *The passion ending doth the purpose lose.*
  The violence of either grief or joy

  Their own enactors with themselves destroy.
  Where joy most revels grief doth most lament,
  Grief joys, joy grieves, on slender accident.
  This world is not for aye, nor 'tis not strange   195
  That even our loves should with our fortunes change,
  For 'tis a question left us yet to prove
  Whether Love lead Fortune or else Fortune Love.
  The great man down, you mark his favourites flies,
  The poor advanced makes friends of enemies,   200
  And hitherto doth Love on Fortune tend,
  For who not needs shall never lack a friend;
  And who in want a hollow friend doth try
  Directly seasons him his enemy.
  But orderly to end where I begun,   205
  Our wills and fates do so contrary run
  That our devices still are overthrown.
  Our thoughts are ours, their ends none of our own:
  So think thou wilt no second husband wed,
  But die thy thoughts when thy first lord is dead.   210

PLAYER QUEEN

  Nor earth to give me food nor heaven light,
  Sport and repose lock from me day and night;
  Each opposite that blanks the face of joy
  Meet what I would have well and it destroy;
  Both here and hence pursue me lasting strife   215
  If once a widow ever I be wife.

HAMLET   If she should break it now!

PLAYER KING

  'Tis deeply sworn. Sweet, leave me here awhile.
  My spirits grow dull and fain I would beguile
  The tedious day with sleep.

PLAYER QUEEN   *Sleep rock thy brain*   220
  [*He sleeps.*]
  And never come mischance between us twain.   *Exit.*

HAMLET   Madam, how like you this play?

QUEEN   The lady protests too much, methinks.

HAMLET   O, but she'll keep her word.

KING   Have you heard the argument? Is there no offence   225
in't?

HAMLET   No, no, they do but jest. Poison in jest. No
offence i'th' world.

KING   What do you call the play?

HAMLET   *The Mousetrap.* Marry, how? Tropically. This   230
play is the image of a murder done in Vienna. Gonzago
is the duke's name, his wife Baptista. You shall see
anon 'tis a knavish piece of work, but what o'that? Your
majesty and we that have free souls – it touches us not.
Let the galled jade wince, our withers are unwrung.   235

Enter Lucianus.

This is one Lucianus, nephew to the king.

OPHELIA   You are a good chorus, my lord.

HAMLET   I could interpret between you and your love,
if I could see the puppets dallying.

OPHELIA   You are keen, my lord, you are keen.   240

HAMLET   It would cost you a groaning to take off my
edge.

OPHELIA   Still better and worse.

HAMLET   So you mistake husbands. Begin, murderer:
pox, leave thy damnable faces and begin. Come, 'the
croaking raven doth bellow for revenge.'

LUCIANUS
Thoughts black, hands apt, drugs fit, and time agreeing,
Confederate season else no creature seeing,
Thou mixture rank, of midnight weeds collected,
With Hecate's ban thrice blasted, thrice infected,
Thy natural magic and dire property
On wholesome life usurp immediately.
[*Pours the poison in his ears.*]

HAMLET   He poisons him i'th' garden for's estate. His
name's Gonzago. The story is extant and writ in choice
Italian. You shall see anon how the murderer gets the
love of Gonzago's wife.

OPHELIA   The King rises.

HAMLET   What, frighted with false fire?

QUEEN   How fares my lord?

POLONIUS   Give o'er the play.

KING   Give me some light, away!

LORDS   Lights! Lights! Lights!

Exeunt all but Hamlet and Horatio.

HAMLET
Why let the stricken deer go weep,
The hart ungalled play,
For some must watch while some must sleep;
So runs the world away.
Would not this, sir, and a forest of feathers, if the rest
of my fortunes turn Turk with me, with two provincial
roses on my razed shoes, get me a fellowship in a cry of
players, sir?

HORATIO   Half a share.

HAMLET   A whole one, I.
For thou dost know, O Damon dear,
This realm dismantled was
Of Jove himself, and now reigns here
A very, very pajock.

HORATIO   You might have rhymed.

HAMLET   O good Horatio, I'll take the Ghost's word for
a thousand pound. Didst perceive?

HORATIO   Very well, my lord.

HAMLET   Upon the talk of the poisoning?

HORATIO   I did very well note him.

Enter ROSINCRANCE *and* GUILDENSTERNE.

HAMLET   O, ha! Come, some music! Come, the
recorders!
For if the King like not the comedy
Why then belike he likes it not, perdie.
Come, some music!

GUILDENSTERNE   Good my lord, vouchsafe me a word
with you.

HAMLET   Sir, a whole history.

GUILDENSTERNE   The King, sir –

HAMLET   Ay, sir, what of him?

GUILDENSTERNE   – is in his retirement marvellous
distempered.

HAMLET   With drink, sir?

GUILDENSTERNE   No, my lord, rather with choler.

HAMLET   Your wisdom should show itself more richer
to signify this to his doctor; for, for me to put him to
his purgation would perhaps plunge him into far more
choler.

GUILDENSTERNE   Good my lord, put your discourse
into some frame and start not so wildly from my affair.

HAMLET   I am tame, sir. Pronounce.

GUILDENSTERNE   The Queen your mother in most
great affliction of spirit hath sent me to you.

HAMLET   You are welcome.

GUILDENSTERNE   Nay, good my lord, this courtesy is
not of the right breed. If it shall please you to make me
a wholesome answer, I will do your mother's
commandment. If not, your pardon and my return
shall be the end of my business.

HAMLET   Sir, I cannot.

GUILDENSTERNE   What, my lord?

HAMLET   Make you a wholesome answer. My wit's
diseased. But, sir, such answers as I can make you shall
command. Or rather, you say, my mother. Therefore
no more, but to the matter – my mother, you say?

ROSINCRANCE   Then thus she says. Your behaviour
hath struck her into amazement and admiration.

HAMLET   O wonderful son that can so astonish a
mother! But is there no sequel at the heels of this
mother's admiration?

ROSINCRANCE   She desires to speak with you in her
closet ere you go to bed.

HAMLET   We shall obey, were she ten times our mother.
Have you any further trade with us?

ROSINCRANCE   My lord, you once did love me.

HAMLET   So I do still, by these pickers and stealers.

ROSINCRANCE   Good my lord, what is your cause of
distemper? You do freely bar the door of your own
liberty if you deny your griefs to your friend.

HAMLET   Sir, I lack advancement.

ROSINCRANCE   How can that be, when you have the voice
of the King himself for your succession in Denmark?

HAMLET   Ay, but while the grass grows – the proverb is
something musty.

Enter one with a recorder.

O, the recorder! Let me see. To withdraw with you,
why do you go about to recover the wind of me, as if
you would drive me into a toil?

GUILDENSTERNE   O my lord, if my duty be too bold,
my love is too unmannerly.

HAMLET   I do not well understand that. Will you play
upon this pipe?

GUILDENSTERNE   My lord, I cannot.

HAMLET   I pray you.

GUILDENSTERNE   Believe me, I cannot.

HAMLET   I do beseech you.

GUILDENSTERNE   I know no touch of it, my lord.

HAMLET   'Tis as easy as lying. Govern these ventages
with your finger and thumb, give it breath with your

mouth, and it will discourse most excellent music.
Look you, these are the stops.

GUILDENSTERNE   But these cannot I command to any
utterance of harmony. I have not the skill.

355 HAMLET   Why, look you now how unworthy a thing
you make of me: you would play upon me! You would
seem to know my stops, you would pluck out the heart
of my mystery, you would sound me from my lowest
note to the top of my compass. And there is much
360 music, excellent voice, in this little organ. Yet cannot
you make it. Why, do you think that I am easier to be
played on than a pipe? Call me what instrument
you will, though you can fret me you cannot play
upon me.

Enter POLONIUS.

365 God bless you, sir.

POLONIUS   My lord, the Queen would speak with you,
and presently.

HAMLET   Do you see that cloud? That's almost in shape
like a camel.

370 POLONIUS   By th' mass and it's like a camel indeed.

HAMLET   Methinks it is like a weasel.

POLONIUS   It is backed like a weasel.

HAMLET   Or like a whale?

POLONIUS   Very like a whale.

375 HAMLET   Then will I come to my mother, by and by.
[*aside*] They fool me to the top of my bent. – I will
come by and by.

POLONIUS   I will say so.   *Exit.*

HAMLET [*aside*]   'By and by' is easily said. – Leave me,
380 friends.   *Exeunt all but Hamlet.*
'Tis now the very witching time of night
When churchyards yawn, and hell itself breathes out
Contagion to this world. Now could I drink hot blood
And do such bitter business as the day
385 Would quake to look on. Soft now, to my mother.
O heart, lose not thy nature. Let not ever
The soul of Nero enter this firm bosom –
Let me be cruel, not unnatural:
I will speak daggers to her but use none.
390 My tongue and soul in this be hypocrites.
How in my words somever she be shent
To give them seals never my soul consent.   *Exit.*

3.3   *Enter KING, ROSINCRANCE and*
              GUILDENSTERNE.

KING   I like him not, nor stands it safe with us
To let his madness range. Therefore prepare you.
I your commission will forthwith dispatch,
And he to England shall along with you.
5 The terms of our estate may not endure
Hazard so dangerous as doth hourly grow
Out of his lunacies.

GUILDENSTERNE   We will ourselves provide.
Most holy and religious fear it is

To keep those many many bodies safe
That live and feed upon your majesty.   10

ROSINCRANCE   The single and peculiar life is bound
With all the strength and armour of the mind
To keep itself from noyance; but much more
That spirit upon whose spirit depends and rests
The lives of many. The cease of majesty   15
Dies not alone, but like a gulf doth draw
What's near it with it. It is a massy wheel
Fixed on the summit of the highest mount
To whose huge spokes ten thousand lesser things
Are mortised and adjoined; which, when it falls,   20
Each small annexment, petty consequence,
Attends the boisterous ruin. Never alone
Did the King sigh but with a general groan.

KING   Arm you, I pray you, to this speedy voyage;
For we will fetters put upon this fear,   25
Which now goes too free-footed.

ROSINCRANCE, GUILDENSTERNE   We will haste us.
              Exeunt Rosincrance and Guildensterne.

Enter POLONIUS.

POLONIUS   My lord, he's going to his mother's closet.
Behind the arras I'll convey myself
To hear the process. I'll warrant she'll tax him home,
And, as you said – and wisely was it said –   30
'Tis meet that some more audience than a mother
(Since nature makes them partial) should o'erhear
The speech of vantage. Fare you well, my liege,
I'll call upon you ere you go to bed
And tell you what I know.

KING   Thanks, dear my lord.   35
                                   Exit Polonius.
O, my offence is rank! It smells to heaven.
It hath the primal eldest curse upon't:
A brother's murder. Pray can I not,
Though inclination be as sharp as will.
My stronger guilt defeats my strong intent   40
And like a man to double business bound
I stand in pause where I shall first begin
And both neglect. What if this cursed hand
Were thicker than itself with brother's blood?
Is there not rain enough in the sweet heavens   45
To wash it white as snow? Whereto serves mercy
But to confront the visage of offence?
And what's in prayer but this twofold force
– To be forestalled ere we come to fall,
Or pardoned, being down? Then I'll look up: 50
My fault is past. But O, what form of prayer
Can serve my turn? 'Forgive me my foul murder'?
That cannot be, since I am still possessed
Of those effects for which I did the murder,
My crown, mine own ambition and my Queen.   55
May one be pardoned and retain th'offence?
In the corrupted currents of this world
Offence's gilded hand may shove by justice,
And oft 'tis seen the wicked prize itself

60 Buys out the law. But 'tis not so above,
There is no shuffling, there the action lies
In his true nature, and we ourselves compelled
Even to the teeth and forehead of our faults
To give in evidence. What then? What rests?
65 Try what repentance can – what can it not? –
Yet what can it, when one cannot repent?
O wretched state, O bosom black as death,
O limed soul that, struggling to be free,
Art more engaged. Help, angels, make assay.
70 Bow, stubborn knees, and heart with strings of steel,
Be soft as sinews of the newborn babe.
All may be well.

Enter HAMLET.

HAMLET   Now might I do it pat, now he is praying.
And now I'll do't [*Draws sword.*] – and so he goes to
heaven,
75 And so am I revenged! That would be scanned,
A villain kills my father, and for that
I, his foul son, do this same villain send
To heaven.
O this is hire and salary, not revenge.
80 He took my father grossly full of bread
With all his crimes broad blown, as fresh as May,
And how his audit stands who knows, save heaven;
But in our circumstance and course of thought
'Tis heavy with him. And am I then revenged
85 To take him in the purging of his soul
When he is fit and seasoned for his passage?
No.   [*Sheathes sword.*]
Up, sword, and know thou a more horrid hent
When he is drunk asleep, or in his rage,
90 Or in th'incestuous pleasure of his bed,
At gaming, swearing, or about some act
That has no relish of salvation in't,
Then trip him that his heels may kick at heaven
And that his soul may be as damned and black
95 As hell whereto it goes. My mother stays,
This physic but prolongs thy sickly days.   *Exit.*
KING   My words fly up, my thoughts remain below.
Words without thoughts never to heaven go.   *Exit.*

3.4   *Enter* QUEEN *and* POLONIUS.

POLONIUS
He will come straight. Look you lay home to him.
Tell him his pranks have been too broad to bear with,
And that your grace hath screened and stood between
Much heat and him. I'll silence me e'en here.
5 Pray you be round with him.
HAMLET (*within*)
Mother, mother, mother.
QUEEN   I'll warrant you, fear me not.
Withdraw, I hear him coming.
[*Polonius hides behind the arras.*]

Enter HAMLET.

HAMLET   Now, mother, what's the matter?
QUEEN   Hamlet, thou hast thy father much offended.   10
HAMLET   Mother, you have my father much offended.
QUEEN   Come, come, you answer with an idle tongue.
HAMLET   Go, go, you question with an idle tongue.
QUEEN   Why, how now, Hamlet!
HAMLET   What's the matter now?
QUEEN   Have you forgot me?
HAMLET   No, by the rood, not so.   15
You are the Queen, your husband's brother's wife,
But would you were not so. You are my mother.
QUEEN   Nay, then, I'll set those to you that can speak.
HAMLET
Come, come, and sit you down. You shall not budge.
You go not till I set you up a glass   20
Where you may see the inmost part of you.
QUEEN   What wilt thou do? Thou wilt not murder me –
Help, help, ho!
POLONIUS [*behind the arras*]
                    What ho! Help, help, help!
HAMLET   How now! A rat! Dead for a ducat, dead!
[*Kills Polonius.*]
POLONIUS   O, I am slain!
QUEEN   O me, what hast thou done?   25
HAMLET   Nay, I know not. Is it the King?
QUEEN   O, what a rash and bloody deed is this!
HAMLET   A bloody deed – almost as bad, good mother,
As kill a king and marry with his brother.
QUEEN   As kill a king?
HAMLET   Ay, lady, 'twas my word.   30
[*Uncovers the body of Polonius.*]
– Thou wretched, rash, intruding fool, farewell:
I took thee for thy betters. Take thy fortune;
Thou find'st to be too busy is some danger. –
Leave wringing of your hands. Peace, sit you down
And let me wring your heart. For so I shall   35
If it be made of penetrable stuff,
If damned custom have not brazed it so
That it is proof and bulwark against sense.
QUEEN
What have I done that thou dar'st wag thy tongue
In noise so rude against me?
HAMLET   Such an act   40
That blurs the grace and blush of modesty,
Calls virtue hypocrite, takes off the rose
From the fair forehead of an innocent love
And makes a blister there, makes marriage vows
As false as dicers' oaths – O, such a deed   45
As from the body of contraction plucks
The very soul, and sweet religion makes
A rhapsody of words. Heaven's face doth glow,
Yea, this solidity and compound mass,
With tristful visage as against the doom,   50
Is thought-sick at the act.
QUEEN   Ay me, what act,
That roars so loud and thunders in the index?
HAMLET   Look here upon this picture, and on this,

The counterfeit presentment of two brothers:
55 See what a grace was seated on his brow,
Hyperion's curls, the front of Jove himself,
An eye like Mars to threaten or command,
A station like the herald Mercury
New-lighted on a heaven-kissing hill;
60 A combination and a form indeed
Where every god did seem to set his seal
To give the world assurance of a man.
This was your husband. Look you now what follows:
Here is your husband, like a mildewed ear
65 Blasting his wholesome brother. Have you eyes?
Could you on this fair mountain leave to feed
And batten on this moor? Ha? Have you eyes?
You cannot call it love, for at your age
The heyday in the blood is tame, it's humble
70 And waits upon the judgement, and what judgement
Would step from this to this? What devil was't
That thus hath cozened you at hoodman-blind?
O shame, where is thy blush? Rebellious hell,
If thou canst mutine in a matron's bones,
75 To flaming youth let virtue be as wax
And melt in her own fire. Proclaim no shame
When the compulsive ardour gives the charge,
Since frost itself as actively doth burn
As reason panders will.
QUEEN   O Hamlet, speak no more.
80 Thou turn'st mine eyes into my very soul,
And there I see such black and grained spots
As will not leave their tinct.
HAMLET   Nay, but to live
In the rank sweat of an enseamed bed
Stewed in corruption, honeying and making love
Over the nasty sty –
85 QUEEN   O speak to me no more!
These words like daggers enter in mine ears.
No more, sweet Hamlet.
HAMLET   A murderer and a villain,
A slave that is not twentieth part the tithe
Of your precedent lord, a vice of kings,
90 A cutpurse of the empire and the rule
That from a shelf the precious diadem stole
And put it in his pocket, –
QUEEN   No more!
HAMLET   – a king of shreds and patches –

Enter GHOST.

Save me and hover o'er me with your wings,
You heavenly guards! What would you, gracious figure?
QUEEN
95 Alas, he's mad!
HAMLET
Do you not come your tardy son to chide
That, lapsed in time and passion, lets go by
Th'important acting of your dread command?
O say!
GHOST   Do not forget! This visitation

Is but to whet thy almost blunted purpose. 100
But look, amazement on thy mother sits!
O, step between her and her fighting soul.
Conceit in weakest bodies strongest works.
Speak to her, Hamlet.
HAMLET   How is it with you, lady?
QUEEN   Alas, how is't with you, 105
That you bend your eye on vacancy
And with th'incorporal air do hold discourse?
Forth at your eyes your spirits wildly peep
And, as the sleeping soldiers in th'alarm,
Your bedded hair like life in excrements 110
Start up and stand on end. O gentle son,
Upon the heat and flame of thy distemper
Sprinkle cool patience. Whereon do you look?
HAMLET
On him, on him! Look you how pale he glares;
His form and cause conjoined, preaching to stones 115
Would make them capable. [*to Ghost*] Do not look
     upon me,
Lest with this piteous action you convert
My stern effects! Then what I have to do
Will want true colour, tears perchance for blood.
QUEEN   To who do you speak this? 120
HAMLET   Do you see nothing there?
QUEEN   Nothing at all, yet all that is I see.
HAMLET   Nor did you nothing hear?
QUEEN   No, nothing but ourselves.
HAMLET
Why, look you, there! Look how it steals away – 125
My father in his habit as he lived.
Look where he goes even now out at the portal!
                          Exit Ghost
QUEEN   This is the very coinage of your brain.
This bodiless creation ecstasy
Is very cunning in.
HAMLET   Ecstasy? 130
My pulse as yours doth temperately keep time
And makes as healthful music. It is not madness
That I have uttered. Bring me to the test
And I the matter will reword, which madness
Would gambol from. Mother, for love of grace, 135
Lay not a flattering unction to your soul
That not your trespass but my madness speaks.
It will but skin and film the ulcerous place,
Whilst rank corruption mining all within
Infects unseen. Confess yourself to heaven, 140
Repent what's past, avoid what is to come,
And do not spread the compost o'er the weeds
To make them rank. Forgive me this my virtue,
For in the fatness of these pursy times
Virtue itself of Vice must pardon beg. 145
Yea, curb and woo for leave to do him good.
QUEEN   O Hamlet, thou hast cleft my heart in twain.
HAMLET   O throw away the worser part of it
And live the purer with the other half.
Goodnight, but go not to mine uncle's bed, 150

Assume a virtue if you have it not.
Refrain tonight,
And that shall lend a kind of easiness
To the next abstinence. Once more goodnight,
155 And when you are desirous to be blessed
I'll blessing beg of you. For this same lord
I do repent, but heaven hath pleased it so
To punish me with this, and this with me,
That I must be their scourge and minister.
160 I will bestow him and will answer well
The death I gave him. So again, goodnight.
I must be cruel only to be kind.
Thus bad begins and worse remains behind.
QUEEN   What shall I do?
165 HAMLET   Not this, by no means, that I bid you do –
Let the blunt King tempt you again to bed,
Pinch wanton on your cheek, call you his mouse
And let him for a pair of reechy kisses,
Or paddling in your neck with his damned fingers,
170 Make you to ravel all this matter out
That I essentially am not in madness
But mad in craft. 'Twere good you let him know,
For who that's but a queen – fair, sober, wise –
Would from a paddock, from a bat, a gib,
175 Such dear concernings hide? Who would do so?
No, in despite of sense and secrecy
Unpeg the basket on the house's top,
Let the birds fly and like the famous ape
To try conclusions in the basket creep
180 And break your own neck down.
QUEEN   Be thou assured, if words be made of breath
And breath of life, I have no life to breathe
What thou hast said to me.
HAMLET   I must to England – you know that?
185 QUEEN   Alack, I had forgot; 'tis so concluded on.
HAMLET   This man shall set me packing;
I'll lug the guts into the neighbour room.
Mother, goodnight. Indeed this councillor
Is now most still, most secret and most grave
190 Who was in life a foolish prating knave.
Come, sir, to draw toward an end with you.
Goodnight, mother.   *Exit Hamlet tugging in Polonius.*

Enter KING.   [4.1]

KING   There's matters in these sighs.
These profound heaves you must translate:
'Tis fit we understand them. Where is your son?
195 QUEEN   Ah, my good lord, what have I seen tonight?
KING   What, Gertrude? How does Hamlet?
QUEEN   Mad as the seas and wind when both contend
Which is the mightier, in his lawless fit,
Behind the arras hearing something stir,
200 He whips his rapier out, and cries 'A rat, a rat!'
And in his brainish apprehension kills
The unseen good old man.
KING   O heavy deed!
It had been so with us had we been there.

His liberty is full of threats to all,
To you yourself, to us, to everyone.   205
Alas, how shall this bloody deed be answered?
It will be laid to us, whose providence
Should have kept short, restrained and out of haunt
This mad young man. But so much was our love
We would not understand what was most fit   210
But, like the owner of a foul disease
To keep it from divulging, lets it feed
Even on the pith of life. Where is he gone?
QUEEN   To draw apart the body he hath killed,
O'er whom his very madness like some ore   215
Among a mineral of metals base
Shows itself pure – he weeps for what is done.
KING   O Gertrude, come away.
The sun no sooner shall the mountains touch
But we will ship him hence, and this vile deed   220
We must with all our majesty and skill
Both countenance and excuse. Ho, Guildensterne!

Enter ROSINCRANCE *and* GUILDENSTERNE.

Friends both, go join you with some further aid:
Hamlet in madness hath Polonius slain
And from his mother's closet hath he dragged him.   225
Go seek him out, speak fair and bring the body
Into the chapel. I pray you haste in this.
            Exeunt Rosincrance and Guildensterne.
Come, Gertrude, we'll call up our wisest friends
To let them know both what we mean to do
And what's untimely done. O come away,   230
My soul is full of discord and dismay.   *Exeunt.*

3.5   *Enter* HAMLET.   [4.2]

HAMLET   Safely stowed!
ROSINCRANCE, GUILDENSTERNE [*offstage*]   Hamlet,
Lord Hamlet!
HAMLET   What noise? Who calls on Hamlet? O, here
they come!   5

Enter ROSINCRANCE *and* GUILDENSTERNE.

ROSINCRANCE   What have you done, my lord, with the
dead body?
HAMLET   Compounded it with dust, whereto 'tis
kin.
ROSINCRANCE   Tell us where 'tis, that we may take it   10
thence and bear it to the chapel.
HAMLET   Do not believe it.
ROSINCRANCE   Believe what?
HAMLET   That I can keep your council and not mine
own. Besides, to be demanded of a sponge! What   15
replication should be made by the son of a king?
ROSINCRANCE   Take you me for a sponge, my lord?
HAMLET   Ay, sir – that soaks up the King's countenance,
his rewards, his authorities. But such officers do the
King best service in the end: he keeps them like an ape   20
in the corner of his jaw, first mouthed to be last

swallowed. When he needs what you have gleaned, it is
but squeezing you and, sponge, you shall be dry
again!

25   ROSINCRANCE   I understand you not, my lord.

HAMLET   I am glad of it. A knavish speech sleeps in a
foolish ear.

ROSINCRANCE   My lord, you must tell us where the
body is, and go with us to the King.

30   HAMLET   The body is with the King, but the King is not
with the body. The King is a thing.

GUILDENSTERNE   A thing, my lord?

HAMLET   Of nothing. Bring me to him. Hide fox and all
after.   *Exeunt.*

3.6   *Enter* KING.   [4.3]

KING   I have sent to seek him and to find the body.
How dangerous is it that this man goes loose!
Yet must not we put the strong law on him:
He's loved of the distracted multitude,
5   Who like not in their judgement but their eyes,
And where 'tis so th'offender's scourge is weighed
But ne'er the offence. To bear all smooth and even
This sudden sending him away must seem
Deliberate pause; diseases desperate grown
10   By desperate appliance are relieved,
Or not at all.

             Enter ROSINCRANCE

             How now, what hath befallen?

ROSINCRANCE
Where the dead body is bestowed, my lord,
We cannot get from him.

KING   But where is he?

ROSINCRANCE
Without, my lord, guarded, to know your pleasure.

15   KING   Bring him before us.

ROSINCRANCE   Ho, Guildensterne! Bring in my lord!

       Enter HAMLET *and* GUILDENSTERNE
             and Attendants.

KING   Now, Hamlet, where's Polonius?

HAMLET   At supper.

KING   At supper! Where?

20   HAMLET   Not where he eats but where he is eaten.
A certain convocation of worms are e'en at him.
Your worm is your only emperor for diet. We fat
all creatures else to fat us, and we fat ourself for
maggots. Your fat king and your lean beggar is but
25   variable service, two dishes but to one table. That's
the end.

KING   What dost thou mean by this?

HAMLET   Nothing but to show you how a king may go a
progress through the guts of a beggar.

30   KING   Where is Polonius?

HAMLET   In heaven. Send thither to see. If your
messenger find him not there, seek him i'th' other

place yourself. But indeed if you find him not this
month you shall nose him as you go up the stairs into
the lobby.   35

KING [*to some Attendants*]   Go, seek him there!

HAMLET   He will stay till ye come.

                             Exeunt Attendants.

KING   Hamlet,
This deed of thine for thine especial safety –
Which we do tender, as we dearly grieve   40
For that which thou hast done – must send thee hence
With fiery quickness. Therefore prepare thyself:
The bark is ready and the wind at help,
Th'associates tend and everything at bent
For England.

HAMLET   For England?

KING   Ay, Hamlet.

HAMLET   Good.   45

KING   So is it, if thou knewst our purposes.

HAMLET
I see a cherub that sees him. But come, for England.
Farewell, dear mother.

KING   Thy loving father, Hamlet.

HAMLET
My mother. Father and mother is man and wife.
Man and wife is one flesh, and so – my mother.   50
Come, for England!   *Exit.*

KING   Follow him at foot.
Tempt him with speed aboard.
Delay it not – I'll have him hence tonight.
Away, for everything is sealed and done
That else leans on th'affair. Pray you make haste.   55

                     Exeunt all but King.

And England, if my love thou hold'st at aught,
As my great power thereof may give thee sense,
Since yet thy cicatrice looks raw and red
After the Danish sword, and thy free awe
Pays homage to us, thou mayst not coldly set   60
Our sovereign process, which imports at full
By letters conjuring to that effect
The present death of Hamlet. Do it, England!
For like the hectic in my blood he rages,
And thou must cure me. Till I know 'tis done,   65
Howe'er my haps my joys were ne'er begun.   *Exit.*

3.7   *Enter* FORTINBRAS *and a* Captain   [4.4]
                 with an army.

FORTINBRAS
Go, Captain, from me greet the Danish King:
Tell him that by his licence Fortinbras
Claims the conveyance of a promised march
Over his kingdom. You know the rendezvous.
If that his majesty would aught with us   5
We shall express our duty in his eye,
And let him know so.

CAPTAIN   I will do't, my lord.

FORTINBRAS   Go safely on.   *Exeunt.*

4.1   *Enter* QUEEN *and* HORATIO.   [**4.5**]

QUEEN   I will not speak with her.

HORATIO   She is importunate – indeed, distract.
Her mood will needs be pitied.

QUEEN   What would she have?

HORATIO
She speaks much of her father, says she hears
There's tricks i'th' world, and hems and beats her heart,
Spurns enviously at straws, speaks things in doubt
That carry but half sense. Her speech is nothing,
Yet the unshaped use of it doth move
The hearers to collection. They aim at it
And botch the words up fit to their own thoughts,
Which, as her winks and nods and gestures yield them,
Indeed would make one think there would be thought
Though nothing sure, yet much unhappily.

QUEEN
'Twere good she were spoken with, for she may strew
Dangerous conjectures in ill-breeding minds.
Let her come in.
[*aside*] To my sick soul, as sin's true nature is,
Each toy seems prologue to some great amiss,
So full of artless jealousy is guilt
It spills itself in fearing to be spilt.

Enter OPHELIA *distracted.*

OPHELIA   Where is the beauteous majesty of Denmark?

QUEEN   How now, Ophelia?

OPHELIA [*Sings.*]
How should I your true love know
From another one?
By his cockle hat and staff
And his sandal shoon.

QUEEN   Alas, sweet lady, what imports this song?

OPHELIA   Say you? Nay, pray you, mark.
[*Sings.*]
He is dead and gone, lady,
He is dead and gone.
At his head a grass-green turf,
At his heels a stone.

Enter KING.

QUEEN   Nay, but Ophelia –

OPHELIA   Pray you mark.
[*Sings.*]
White his shroud as the mountain snow –

QUEEN   Alas, look here, my lord.

OPHELIA [*Sings.*]
Larded with sweet flowers
Which bewept to the grave did not go
With true love showers.

KING   How do ye, pretty lady?

OPHELIA   Well, God dild you. They say the owl was a
baker's daughter. Lord, we know what we are, but
know not what we may be. God be at your table.

KING   Conceit upon her father –

OPHELIA   Pray you, let's have no words of this, but
when they ask you what it means, say you this:
[*Sings.*]
Tomorrow is Saint Valentine's Day
All in the morning betime,
And I a maid at your window
To be your valentine.

Then up he rose and donned his clothes
And dupped the chamber door –
Let in the maid that out a maid
Never departed more.

KING   Pretty Ophelia –

OPHELIA   Indeed, la! Without an oath I'll make an end
on't.
[*Sings.*]
By Gis and by Saint Charity,
Alack and fie for shame,
Young men will do't if they come to't:
By Cock they are to blame.

Quoth she, 'Before you tumbled me
You promised me to wed.'
'So would I ha' done by yonder sun
And thou hadst not come to my bed.'

KING   How long hath she been thus?

OPHELIA   I hope all will be well. We must be patient.
But I cannot choose but weep to think they should lay
him i'th' cold ground. My brother shall know of it.
And so I thank you for your good council. Come, my
coach! Goodnight, ladies. Goodnight, sweet ladies.
Goodnight, goodnight.   *Exit.*

KING
Follow her close. Give her good watch, I pray you.
Exit Horatio.
O, this is the poison of deep grief. It springs
All from her father's death. O Gertrude, Gertrude,
When sorrows comes they come not single spies
But in battalia. First, her father slain;
Next, your son gone, and he most violent author
Of his own just remove; the people muddied
Thick and unwholesome in their thoughts and
whispers
For good Polonius' death – and we have done but
greenly
In hugger-mugger to inter him. Poor Ophelia
Divided from herself and her fair judgement,
Without the which we are pictures or mere beasts;
Last, and as much containing as all these,
Her brother is in secret come from France,
Keeps on his wonder, keeps himself in clouds
And wants not buzzers to infect his ear
With pestilent speeches of his father's death;
Wherein necessity, of matter beggared,
Will nothing stick our persons to arraign
In ear and ear. O my dear Gertrude, this,
Like to a murdering piece in many places

Gives me superfluous death.   [*A noise within*]

Enter a Messenger.

95   QUEEN   Alack, what noise is this?
      KING
        Where are my Switzers? Let them guard the door.
        What is the matter?
      MESSENGER   Save yourself, my lord.
        The ocean overpeering of his list
        Eats not the flats with more impiteous haste
100   Than young Laertes in a riotous head
        O'erbears your officers. The rabble call him lord
        And, as the world were now but to begin,
        Antiquity forgot, custom not known,
        The ratifiers and props of every word,
105   They cry, 'Choose we! Laertes shall be king!' –
        Caps, hands and tongues applaud it to the clouds –
        'Laertes shall be king! Laertes king!'   *Exit.*
      QUEEN   How cheerfully on the false trail they cry.
        O, this is counter, you false Danish dogs! [*Noise within*]
110   KING   The doors are broke.

Enter LAERTES.

      LAERTES
        Where is the King? – Sirs, stand you all without.
      FOLLOWERS [*offstage*]
        No, let's come in.
      LAERTES   I pray you give me leave.
      FOLLOWERS [*offstage*]   We will, we will.
      LAERTES
        I thank you, keep the door. – O, thou vile King,
        Give me my father.
115   QUEEN   Calmly, good Laertes.
      LAERTES
        That drop of blood that calms proclaims me bastard,
        Cries 'Cuckold!' to my father, brands the harlot
        Even here between the chaste unsmirched brow
        Of my true mother.
      KING   What is the cause, Laertes,
120   That thy rebellion looks so giant-like?
        Let him go, Gertrude; do not fear our person.
        There's such divinity doth hedge a king
        That treason can but peep to what it would,
        Acts little of his will. Tell me, Laertes,
125   Why thou art thus incensed. Let him go, Gertrude.
        Speak, man.
      LAERTES   Where's my father?
      KING   Dead.
      QUEEN   But not by him.
      KING   Let him demand his fill.
      LAERTES   How came he dead? I'll not be juggled with.
        To hell allegiance, vows to the blackest devil,
130   Conscience and grace to the profoundest pit.
        I dare damnation. To this point I stand –
        That both the worlds I give to negligence.
        Let come what comes, only I'll be revenged
        Most throughly for my father.

      KING   Who shall stay you?
      LAERTES   My will, not all the world.   135
        And for my means, I'll husband them so well
        They shall go far with little.
      KING   Good Laertes,
        If you desire to know the certainty
        Of your dear father's death, is't writ in your
          revenge
        That swoopstake you will draw both friend and foe,   140
        Winner and loser?
      LAERTES   None but his enemies.
      KING   Will you know them, then?
      LAERTES
        To his good friends thus wide I'll ope my arms
        And like the kind life-rendering pelican
        Repast them with my blood.
      KING   Why, now you speak   145
        Like a good child and a true gentleman.
        That I am guiltless of your father's death
        And am most sensible in grief for it
        It shall as level to your judgement pierce
        As day does to your eye.
      FOLLOWERS [*offstage*]   Let her come in!   150

Enter OPHELIA.

      LAERTES   How now, what noise is that?
        O heat, dry up my brains, tears seven times salt
        Burn out the sense and virtue of mine eye.
        By heaven, thy madness shall be paid by weight
        Till our scale turns the beam. O rose of May,   155
        Dear maid, kind sister, sweet Ophelia,
        O heavens, is't possible a young maid's wits
        Should be as mortal as an old man's life?
        Nature is fine in love, and where 'tis fine
        It sends some precious instance of itself   160
        After the thing it loves.
      OPHELIA [*Sings.*]
                    They bore him bare-faced on the bier,
                    Hey non nonny, nonny, hey nonny,
                    And on his grave rains many a tear.
        Fare you well, my dove.   165
      LAERTES   Hadst thou thy wits and didst persuade revenge
        It could not move thus.
      OPHELIA   You must sing 'down a-down', an' you call
        him a 'down-a'. O, how the wheel becomes it! It is the
        false steward that stole his master's daughter.   170
      LAERTES   This nothing's more than matter.
      OPHELIA   There's rosemary: that's for remembrance.
        Pray, love, remember. And there is pansies: that's for
        thoughts.
      LAERTES
        A document in madness – thoughts and remembrance
          fitted!   175
      OPHELIA   There's fennel for you, and columbines.
        There's rue for you, and here's some for me. We may
        call it herb-grace o'Sundays. O, you must wear your
        rue with a difference. There's a daisy. I would give you

180 some violets, but they withered all when my father
died. They say he made a good end.
[*Sings.*]
　　　　　For bonny sweet Robin is all my joy.

LAERTES　Thought and affliction, passion, hell itself
She turns to favour and to prettiness.

OPHELIA [*Sings.*]
185　　　　　　And will he not come again?
　　　　　　And will he not come again?
　　　　　　No, no, he is dead,
　　　　　　Go to thy deathbed.
　　　　　　He never will come again.
190　　　　　　His beard as white as snow,
　　　　　　All flaxen was his poll.
　　　　　　He is gone, he is gone,
　　　　　　And we cast away moan.
　　　　　　Gramercy on his soul.
195　And of all Christian souls, I pray God. God buy ye.
　　　　　　　　　　　　　　　　　　　　Exit.

LAERTES　Do you see this, you gods?

KING　Laertes, I must commune with your grief
Or you deny me right. Go but apart,
Make choice of whom your wisest friends you will,
200 And they shall hear and judge 'twixt you and me.
If by direct or by collateral hand
They find us touched, we will our kingdom give –
Our crown, our life and all that we call ours –
To you in satisfaction. But, if not,
205 Be you content to lend your patience to us
And we shall jointly labour with your soul
To give it due content.

LAERTES　　　　　　　　Let this be so.
His means of death, his obscure burial –
No trophy, sword nor hatchment o'er his bones,
210 No noble rite, nor formal ostentation –
Cry to be heard as 'twere from heaven to earth –
That I must call in question.

KING　　　　　　　　So you shall,
And, where th'offence is, let the great axe fall.
I pray you go with me.　　　　　　　*Exeunt.*

4.2　　*Enter* HORATIO *with an* Attendant.　　[4.6]

HORATIO　What are they that would speak with me?

ATTENDANT　Sailors, sir. They say they have letters for
you.

HORATIO　Let them come in.　　　　*Exit Attendant.*
5 I do not know from what part of the world I should be
greeted if not from Lord Hamlet.

　　　　　　　　　Enter Sailor.

SAILOR　God bless you, sir.

HORATIO　Let Him bless thee too.

SAILOR　He shall, sir, an't please Him. There's a letter
10 for you, sir – it comes from th'ambassadors that was
bound for England – if your name be Horatio, as I am
let to know it is.

HORATIO [*Reads the letter.*]　*Horatio, when thou shalt
have overlooked this, give these fellows some means to the
King: they have letters for him. Ere we were two days old* 15
*at sea, a pirate of very warlike appointment gave us chase.
Finding ourselves too slow of sail we put on a compelled
valour. In the grapple I boarded them. On the instant they
got clear of our ship, so I alone became their prisoner. They
have dealt with me like thieves of mercy, but they knew* 20
*what they did: I am to do a good turn for them. Let the
King have the letters I have sent, and repair thou to me
with as much haste as thou wouldest fly death. I have
words to speak in your ear will make thee dumb. Yet are
they much too light for the bore of the matter. These good* 25
*fellows will bring thee where I am. Rosincrance and
Guildensterne hold their course for England. Of them I
have much to tell thee. Farewell. He that thou knowest
thine. Hamlet.*
Come. I will give you way for these your letters. 30
And do't the speedier that you may direct me
To him from whom you brought them.　　*Exeunt.*

4.3　　*Enter* KING *and* LAERTES.　　[4.7]

KING　Now must your conscience my acquittance seal
And you must put me in your heart for friend
Sith you have heard, and with a knowing ear,
That he which hath your noble father slain
Pursued my life.

LAERTES　　　　　It well appears. But tell me 5
Why you proceeded not against these feats,
So crimeful and so capital in nature,
As by your safety, wisdom, all things else,
You mainly were stirred up.

KING　O, for two special reasons, 10
Which may to you perhaps seem much unsinewed
And yet to me they are strong. The Queen his mother
Lives almost by his looks and for myself,
My virtue or my plague, be it either which,
She's so conjunctive to my life and soul 15
That as the star moves not but in his sphere
I could not but by her. The other motive
Why to a public count I might not go
Is the great love the general gender bear him,
Who, dipping all his faults in their affection, 20
Would, like the spring that turneth wood to stone,
Convert his gyves to graces. So that my arrows,
Too slightly timbered for so loud a wind,
Would have reverted to my bow again
But not where I had armed them. 25

LAERTES　And so have I a noble father lost,
A sister driven into desperate terms
Who has, if praises may go back again,
Stood challenger on mount of all the age
For her perfections. But my revenge will come. 30

KING
Break not your sleeps for that; you must not think
That we are made of stuff so flat and dull

That we can let our beard be shook with danger
And think it pastime. You shortly shall hear more.
35   I loved your father and we love ourself,
And that, I hope, will teach you to imagine –

                    Enter a Messenger.

How now, what news?
MESSENGER   Letters, my lord, from Hamlet.
This to your majesty, this to the Queen.
KING   From Hamlet! Who brought them?
MESSENGER
40   Sailors, my lord, they say. I saw them not;
They were given me by Claudio. He received them.
KING   Laertes, you shall hear them. – Leave us.
                                        Exit Messenger.
[*Reads.*] *High and mighty. You shall know I am set naked*
on your kingdom. Tomorrow shall I beg leave to see your
45   *kingly eyes. When I shall (first asking your pardon*
thereunto) recount th'occasions of my sudden, and more
strange, return. Hamlet.
What should this mean? Are all the rest come back?
Or is it some abuse? Or no such thing?
LAERTES   Know you the hand?
50   KING   'Tis Hamlet's character. 'Naked',
And in a postscript here he says 'alone'.
Can you advise me?
LAERTES   I'm lost in it, my lord; but let him come.
It warms the very sickness in my heart
55   That I shall live and tell him to his teeth
'Thus didest thou.'
KING   If it be so, Laertes – as how should it be so,
How otherwise? – will you be ruled by me?
LAERTES   If so you'll not o'errule me to a peace.
60   KING   To thine own peace. If he be now returned
As checking at his voyage, and that he means
No more to undertake it, I will work him
To an exploit, now ripe in my device,
Under the which he shall not choose but fall.
65   And for his death no wind of blame shall breathe
But even his mother shall uncharge the practice
And call it accident. Some two months hence
Here was a gentleman of Normandy –
I've seen myself and served against the French,
70   And they ran well on horseback, but this gallant
Had witchcraft in't; he grew into his seat
And to such wondrous doing brought his horse
As had he been incorpsed and demi-natured
With the brave beast. So far he passed my thought
75   That I in forgery of shapes and tricks
Come short of what he did.
LAERTES   A Norman was't?
KING   A Norman.
LAERTES   Upon my life, Lamound!
KING   The very same.
LAERTES   I know him well. He is the brooch, indeed,
And gem of all our nation.
80   KING   He made confession of you

And gave you such a masterly report
For art and exercise in your defence
And for your rapier most especially
That he cried out 'twould be a sight indeed
If one could match you, sir. This report of his   85
Did Hamlet so envenom with his envy
That he could nothing do but wish and beg
Your sudden coming o'er to play with him.
Now out of this –
LAERTES   What out of this, my lord?
KING   Laertes, was your father dear to you?   90
Or are you like the painting of a sorrow:
A face without a heart?
LAERTES   Why ask you this?
KING   Not that I think you did not love your father,
But that I know love is begun by time
And that I see in passages of proof   95
Time qualifies the spark and fire of it.
Hamlet comes back. What would you undertake
To show yourself your father's son indeed
More than in words?
LAERTES   To cut his throat i'th' church.
KING   No place indeed should murder sanctuarize.   100
Revenge should have no bounds. But, good Laertes,
Will you do this? Keep close within your chamber;
Hamlet returned shall know you are come home;
We'll put on those shall praise your excellence
And set a double varnish on the fame   105
The Frenchman gave you, bring you in fine together
And wager on your heads. He being remiss,
Most generous and free from all contriving,
Will not peruse the foils, so that with ease,
Or with a little shuffling, you may choose   110
A sword unbated and in a pass of practice
Requite him for your father.
LAERTES   I will do't.
And for that purpose I'll anoint my sword.
I bought an unction of a mountebank
So mortal I but dipped a knife in it,   115
Where it draws blood no cataplasm so rare,
Collected from all simples that have virtue
Under the moon, can save the thing from death
That is but scratched withal. I'll touch my point
With this contagion, that if I gall him slightly   120
It may be death.
KING   Let's further think of this,
Weigh what convenience both of time and means
May fit us to our shape. If this should fail
And that our drift look through our bad performance
'Twere better not assayed. Therefore this project   125
Should have a back or second that might hold
If this should blast in proof. Soft, let me see:
We'll make a solemn wager on your comings –
I ha't! When in your motion you are hot and dry
(As make your bouts more violent to the end)   130
And that he calls for drink, I'll have prepared him
A chalice for the nonce, whereon but sipping,

If he by chance escape your venomed stuck,
Our purpose may hold there.

Enter QUEEN.

How, sweet Queen?
135 QUEEN   One woe doth tread upon another's heel,
So fast they'll follow. Your sister's drowned, Laertes.
LAERTES   Drowned! O where?
QUEEN   There is a willow grows aslant a brook
That shows his hoar leaves in the glassy stream.
140 There with fantastic garlands did she come
Of crowflowers, nettles, daisies and long purples
That liberal shepherds give a grosser name
But our cold maids do dead men's fingers call them.
There on the pendent boughs her coronet weeds
145 Clambering to hang, an envious sliver broke,
When down the weedy trophies and herself
Fell in the weeping brook. Her clothes spread wide
And mermaid-like awhile they bore her up,
Which time she chanted snatches of old tunes
150 As one incapable of her own distress,
Or like a creature native and endued
Unto that element. But long it could not be
Till that her garments heavy with their drink
Pulled the poor wretch from her melodious lay
To muddy death.
155 LAERTES   Alas, then is she drowned?
QUEEN   Drowned, drowned.
LAERTES   Too much of water hast thou, poor Ophelia,
And therefore I forbid my tears. But yet
It is our trick – nature her custom holds
Let shame say what it will. [*Weeps.*] When these are
160   gone
The woman will be out. Adieu, my lord,
I have a speech of fire that fain would blaze
But that this folly douts it.   *Exit.*
KING   Let's follow, Gertrude.
How much I had to do to calm his rage!
165 Now fear I this will give it start again.
Therefore let's follow.   *Exeunt.*

5.1   *Enter two Clowns, a* Gravedigger
               and a Second Man.

GRAVEDIGGER   Is she to be buried in Christian burial,
that wilfully seeks her own salvation?
2 MAN   I tell thee she is – and therefore make her grave
straight. The crowner hath sat on her and finds it
5   Christian burial.
GRAVEDIGGER   How can that be unless she drowned
herself in her own defence?
2 MAN   Why, 'tis found so.
GRAVEDIGGER   It must be *se offendendo*. It cannot be
10   else. For here lies the point: if I drown myself wittingly,
it argues an act, and an act hath three branches – it is
to act, to do, and to perform. Argal, she drowned
herself wittingly.

2 MAN   Nay, but hear you, goodman delver.
GRAVEDIGGER   Give me leave. Here lies the water –   15
good. Here stands the man – good. If the man go to
this water and drown himself, it is, will he nill he, he
goes. Mark you that? But if the water come to him and
drown him, he drowns not himself. Argal, he that is
not guilty of his own death shortens not his own life.   20
2 MAN   But is this law?
GRAVEDIGGER   Ay, marry is't. Crowner's 'quest law.
2 MAN   Will you ha' the truth on't? If this had not been
a gentlewoman she should have been buried out of
Christian burial.   25
GRAVEDIGGER   Why, there thou sayst. And the more
pity that great folk should have countenance in this
world to drown or hang themselves more than their
even-Christian. Come, my spade. There is no ancient
gentlemen but gardeners, ditchers and grave-makers.   30
They hold up Adam's profession.
2 MAN   Was he a gentleman?
GRAVEDIGGER   He was the first that ever bore arms.
2 MAN   Why, he had none.
GRAVEDIGGER   What, art a heathen? How dost thou   35
understand the Scripture? The Scripture says Adam
digged. Could he dig without arms? I'll put another
question to thee. If thou answerest me not to the
purpose, confess thyself –
2 MAN   Go to.   40
GRAVEDIGGER   What is he that builds stronger than
either the mason, the shipwright or the carpenter?
2 MAN   The gallows-maker, for that frame outlives a
thousand tenants.
GRAVEDIGGER   I like thy wit well, in good faith. The   45
gallows does well. But how does it well? It does well to
those that do ill. Now, thou dost ill to say the gallows is
built stronger than the church. Argal, the gallows may
do well to thee. To't again, come.
2 MAN   Who builds stronger than a mason, a shipwright   50
or a carpenter?
GRAVEDIGGER   Ay, tell me that and unyoke.
2 MAN   Marry, now I can tell.
GRAVEDIGGER   To't!
2 MAN   Mass, I cannot tell.   55

Enter HAMLET *and* HORATIO *afar off.*

GRAVEDIGGER   Cudgel thy brains no more about it, for
your dull ass will not mend his pace with beating. And
when you are asked this question next, say a grave-
maker. The houses that he makes lasts till doomsday.
Go get thee to Johan, fetch me a stoup of liquor.   60
                              Exit Second Man.
[*Sings.*]
      In youth when I did love, did love,
         Methought it was very sweet
      To contract-a the time for-a my behove,
         O, methought there was nothing meet!
HAMLET   Has this fellow no feeling of his business that   65
he sings at grave-making?

HORATIO   Custom hath made it in him a property of
easiness.

HAMLET   'Tis e'en so. The hand of little employment
70   hath the daintier sense.

GRAVEDIGGER [*Sings.*]
   But age with his stealing steps
   Hath caught me in his clutch
   And hath shipped me intil the land
   As if I had never been such.
   [*Throws up a skull.*]

75   HAMLET   That skull had a tongue in it and could sing
once. How the knave jowls it to th' ground, as if it were
Cain's jawbone, that did the first murder. It might be
the pate of a politician which this ass o'er-offices – one
that could circumvent God, might it not?

80   HORATIO   It might, my lord.

HAMLET   Or of a courtier which could say, 'Good morrow,
sweet lord; how dost thou, good lord?' This might be my
Lord Such-a-One, that praised my Lord Such-a-One's
horse when he meant to beg it, might it not?

85   HORATIO   Ay, my lord.

HAMLET   Why e'en so. And now my Lady Worm's –
chapless and knocked about the mazard with a sexton's
spade. Here's fine revolution if we had the trick to
see't. Did these bones cost no more the breeding but to
90   play at loggets with 'em? Mine ache to think on't.

GRAVEDIGGER [*Sings.*]
   A pickaxe and a spade, a spade,
   For and a shrouding-sheet,
   O, a pit of clay for to be made
   For such a guest is meet.
   [*Throws up another skull.*]

95   HAMLET   There's another! Why, might not that be the
skull of a lawyer? Where be his quiddits now – his
quillets? His cases? His tenures and his tricks? Why
does he suffer this rude knave now to knock him about
the sconce with a dirty shovel and will not tell him of
100   his action of battery? Hum! This fellow might be in's
time a great buyer of land, with his statutes, his
recognizances, his fines, his double vouchers, his
recoveries. Is this the fine of his fines, and the recovery
of his recoveries – to have his fine pate full of fine dirt?
105   Will his vouchers vouch him no more of his purchases,
and double ones too, than the length and breadth of a
pair of indentures? The very conveyances of his lands
will hardly lie in this box, and must the inheritor
himself have no more? Ha?

110   HORATIO   Not a jot more, my lord.

HAMLET   Is not parchment made of sheepskins?

HORATIO   Ay, my lord, and of calfskins too.

HAMLET   They are sheep and calves that seek out
assurance in that. I will speak to this fellow. Whose
115   grave's this, sir?

GRAVEDIGGER   Mine, sir.
   [*Sings.*]
   O, a pit of clay for to be made
   For such a guest is meet.

HAMLET   I think it be thine, indeed: for thou liest in't.

GRAVEDIGGER   You lie out on't, sir, and therefore it is   120
not yours. For my part I do not lie in't; and yet it is
mine.

HAMLET   Thou dost lie in't, to be in't and say 'tis thine.
'Tis for the dead, not for the quick. Therefore thou
liest.   125

GRAVEDIGGER   'Tis a quick lie, sir, 'twill away again
from me to you.

HAMLET   What man dost thou dig it for?

GRAVEDIGGER   For no man, sir.

HAMLET   What woman, then?   130

GRAVEDIGGER   For none, neither.

HAMLET   Who is to be buried in't?

GRAVEDIGGER   One that was a woman, sir; but, rest her
soul, she's dead.

HAMLET   [*aside to Horatio*]   How absolute the knave   135
is! We must speak by the card or equivocation will
undo us. By the Lord, Horatio, these three years I have
taken note of it, the age is grown so picked that the toe
of the peasant comes so near the heels of our courtier
he galls his kibe. – How long hast thou been a   140
grave-maker?

GRAVEDIGGER   Of all the days i'th' year I came to't
that day that our last King Hamlet o'ercame
Fortinbras.

HAMLET   How long is that since?   145

GRAVEDIGGER   Cannot you tell that? Every fool can
tell that! It was the very day that young Hamlet was
born – he that was mad and sent into England.

HAMLET   Ay, marry. Why was he sent into England?

GRAVEDIGGER   Why, because he was mad. He shall   150
recover his wits there, or, if he do not, it's no great
matter there.

HAMLET   Why?

GRAVEDIGGER   'Twill not be seen in him. There the
men are as mad as he.   155

HAMLET   How came he mad?

GRAVEDIGGER   Very strangely, they say.

HAMLET   How, strangely?

GRAVEDIGGER   Faith, e'en with losing his wits.

HAMLET   Upon what ground?   160

GRAVEDIGGER   Why, here in Denmark. I have been
sexton here, man and boy, thirty years.

HAMLET   How long will a man lie i'th' earth ere he rot?

GRAVEDIGGER   I'faith, if he be not rotten before he die
(as we have many pocky corpses nowadays that will   165
scarce hold the laying in) he will last you some eight
year – or nine year – a tanner will last you nine year.

HAMLET   Why he more than another?

GRAVEDIGGER   Why, sir, his hide is so tanned with his
trade that he will keep out water a great while. And   170
your water is a sore decayer of your whoreson dead
body. Here's a skull now – this skull has lain in the
earth three and twenty years.

HAMLET   Whose was it?

GRAVEDIGGER   A whoreson mad fellow's it was. Whose   175
do you think it was?

HAMLET   Nay, I know not.

GRAVEDIGGER   A pestilence on him for a mad rogue. 'A
poured a flagon of Rhenish on my head once! This
180   same skull, sir – this same skull, sir, was Yorick's skull,
the King's jester.
HAMLET   This?
GRAVEDIGGER   E'en that.
HAMLET   Let me see. Alas, poor Yorick. I knew him,
185   Horatio. A fellow of infinite jest, of most excellent
fancy. He hath borne me on his back a thousand times,
and how abhorred my imagination is. My gorge rises at
it. Here hung those lips that I have kissed I know not
how oft. Where be your jibes now? Your gambols? Your
190   songs? Your flashes of merriment that were wont to set
the table on a roar? No one now to mock your own
jeering? Quite chopfallen. Now get you to my lady's
chamber and tell her, let her paint an inch thick, to this
favour she must come. Make her laugh at that. Prithee,
195   Horatio, tell me one thing.
HORATIO   What's that, my lord?
HAMLET   Dost thou think Alexander looked o' this
fashion i'th' earth?
HORATIO   E'en so.
200   HAMLET   And smelt so? Puh!
HORATIO   E'en so, my lord.
HAMLET   To what base uses we may return, Horatio!
Why may not imagination trace the noble dust of
Alexander till he find it stopping a bung-hole?
205   HORATIO   'Twere to consider too curiously to consider
so.
HAMLET   No, faith, not a jot. But to follow him thither
with modesty enough and likelihood to lead it: as thus,
Alexander died, Alexander was buried, Alexander
210   returneth into dust, the dust is earth, of earth we make
loam, and why of that loam whereto he was converted
might they not stop a beer-barrel?
Imperial Caesar, dead and turned to clay,
Might stop a hole to keep the wind away.
215   O, that that earth which kept the world in awe
Should patch a wall t'expel the winter's flaw!

Enter KING, QUEEN, LAERTES, *a* Priest, *and a coffin, with
Lords attendant and a* Gentleman.

But soft, but soft – aside – here comes the King,
The Queen, the courtiers. Who is that they follow,
And with such maimed rites? This doth betoken
220   The corpse they follow did with desperate hand
Fordo it own life. 'Twas some estate.
Couch we awhile and mark.
      [*Hamlet and Horatio stand aside.*]
LAERTES   What ceremony else?
HAMLET [*aside to Horatio*]
That is Laertes, a very noble youth – mark.
225   LAERTES   What ceremony else?
PRIEST   Her obsequies have been as far enlarged
As we have warrantise. Her death was doubtful;
And but that great command o'ersways the order
She should in ground unsanctified have lodged

Till the last trumpet: for charitable prayer,   230
Shards, flints and pebbles should be thrown on her.
Yet here she is allowed her virgin rites,
Her maiden strewments, and the bringing home
Of bell and burial.
LAERTES   Must there no more be done?
PRIEST   No more be done!   235
We should profane the service of the dead
To sing sage requiem and such rest to her
As to peace-parted souls.
LAERTES   Lay her i'th' earth,
And from her fair and unpolluted flesh
May violets spring. I tell thee, churlish priest,   240
A ministering angel shall my sister be
When thou liest howling.
HAMLET [*aside to Horatio*]   What, the fair Ophelia?
QUEEN   Sweets to the sweet. Farewell.
I hoped thou shouldst have been my Hamlet's wife:
I thought thy bride-bed to have decked, sweet maid,   245
And not t'have strewed thy grave.
LAERTES   O, terrible woe
Fall ten times treble on that cursed head
Whose wicked deed thy most ingenious sense
Deprived thee of. Hold off the earth awhile,
Till I have caught her once more in mine arms.   250
      [*Leaps in the grave.*]
Now pile your dust upon the quick and dead
Till of this flat a mountain you have made
To o'ertop old Pelion or the skyish head
Of blue Olympus.
HAMLET [*Comes forward.*]   What is he whose griefs
Bears such an emphasis, whose phrase of sorrow   255
Conjures the wandering stars and makes them
      stand
Like wonder-wounded hearers? This is I,
Hamlet the Dane.
LAERTES [*Leaps out and grapples with him.*]
                        The devil take thy soul!
HAMLET   Thou pray'st not well.
I prithee take thy fingers from my throat.   260
Sir, though I am not splenative and rash,
Yet have I something in me dangerous
Which let thy wiseness fear. Away thy hand.
KING   Pluck them asunder.
QUEEN   Hamlet! Hamlet!
GENTLEMAN   Good my lord, be quiet.
HAMLET   Why, I will fight with him upon this theme   265
Until my eyelids will no longer wag.
QUEEN   O my son, what theme?
HAMLET   I loved Ophelia. Forty thousand brothers
Could not with all their quantity of love
Make up my sum. What wilt thou do for her?   270
KING   O, he is mad, Laertes.
QUEEN   For love of God, forbear him.
HAMLET   Come, show me what thou'lt do.
Woul't weep? Woul't fight? Woul't tear thyself?
Woul't drink up eisel, eat a crocodile?   275

I'll do't! Dost thou come here to whine,
To outface me with leaping in her grave?
Be buried quick with her, and so will I.
And if thou prate of mountains, let them throw
280 Millions of acres on us till our ground,
Singeing his pate against the burning zone,
Make Ossa like a wart. Nay, an thou'lt mouth,
I'll rant as well as thou.
KING   This is mere madness,
And thus a while the fit will work on him.
285 Anon, as patient as the female dove
When that her golden couplet are disclosed,
His silence will sit drooping.
HAMLET   Hear you, sir,
What is the reason that you use me thus?
I loved you ever – but it is no matter.
290 Let Hercules himself do what he may,
The cat will mew and dog will have his day.   *Exit.*
KING   I pray you, good Horatio, wait upon him.
                                        Exit Horatio.
[*aside to Laertes*] Strengthen your patience in our last
        night's speech,
We'll put the matter to the present push.
295 – Good Gertrude, set some watch over your son.
This grave shall have a living monument.
An hour of quiet shortly shall we see;
Till then in patience our proceeding be.   *Exeunt.*

5.2   *Enter* HAMLET *and* HORATIO.

HAMLET
So much for this, sir. Now, let me see, the other:
You do remember all the circumstance?
HORATIO   Remember it, my lord?
HAMLET   Sir, in my heart there was a kind of fighting
5   That would not let me sleep. Methought I lay
Worse than the mutines in the bilboes. Rashly –
And praise be rashness for it – let us know
Our indiscretion sometimes serves us well
When our dear plots do pall – and that should
        teach us
10   There's a divinity that shapes our ends,
Rough-hew them how we will.
HORATIO   That is most certain.
HAMLET   Up from my cabin,
My sea-gown scarfed about me, in the dark
Groped I to find out them, had my desire,
15   Fingered their packet, and in fine withdrew
To mine own room again, making so bold
(My fears forgetting manners) to unseal
Their grand commission; where I found, Horatio,
O royal knavery, an exact command
20   (Larded with many several sorts of reason
Importing Denmark's health, and England's too)
With – ho! – such bugs and goblins in my life
That on the supervise, no leisure bated –
No, not to stay the grinding of the axe! –

My head should be struck off.
HORATIO   Is't possible?   25
HAMLET
Here's the commission; read it at more leisure.
But wilt thou hear me how I did proceed?
HORATIO   I beseech you.
HAMLET   Being thus benetted round with villains,
Ere I could make a prologue to my brains   30
They had begun the play. I sat me down,
Devised a new commission, wrote it fair –
I once did hold it as our statists do
A baseness to write fair and laboured much
How to forget that learning, but, sir, now   35
It did me yeoman's service – wilt thou know
The effects of what I wrote?
HORATIO   Ay, good my lord.
HAMLET   An earnest conjuration from the King,
As England was his faithful tributary,
As love between them as the palm should flourish,   40
As peace should still her wheaten garland wear
And stand a comma 'tween their amities,
And many suchlike 'as'es of great charge,
That on the view and know of these contents
Without debatement further more or less   45
He should the bearers put to sudden death,
Not shriving time allowed.
HORATIO   How was this sealed?
HAMLET   Why, even in that was heaven ordinate:
I had my father's signet in my purse –
Which was the model of that Danish seal –   50
Folded the writ up in form of the other,
Subscribed it, gave't th'impression, placed it safely,
The changeling never known. Now the next day
Was our sea-fight, and what to this was sequent
Thou knowst already.   55
HORATIO   So Guildensterne and Rosincrance go to't.
HAMLET
Why, man, they did make love to this employment,
They are not near my conscience. Their defeat
Doth by their own insinuation grow.
'Tis dangerous when the baser nature comes   60
Between the pass and fell incensed points
Of mighty opposites.
HORATIO   Why, what a king is this!
HAMLET
Does it not, think'st thee, stand me now upon?
He that hath killed my King and whored my mother,
Popped in between th'election and my hopes,   65
Thrown out his angle for my proper life
And with such cozenage. Is't not perfect conscience
To quit him with this arm? And is't not to be damned
To let this canker of our nature come
In further evil?   70
HORATIO
It must be shortly known to him from England
What is the issue of the business there.
HAMLET   It will be short. The interim's mine,

And a man's life's no more than to say one.
75 But I am very sorry, good Horatio,
That to Laertes I forgot myself,
For by the image of my cause I see
The portraiture of his. I'll count his favours;
But sure the bravery of his grief did put me
80 Into a towering passion.

Enter young OSRICKE.

HORATIO   Peace, who comes here?

OSRICKE   Your lordship is right welcome back to
Denmark.

HAMLET   I humbly thank you, sir. [*aside to Horatio*]
85 Dost know this waterfly?

HORATIO [*aside*]   No, my good lord.

HAMLET [*aside*]   Thy state is the more gracious, for 'tis
a vice to know him. He hath much land, and fertile.
Let a beast be lord of beasts, and his crib shall stand at
90 the king's mess. 'Tis a chough; but, as I say, spacious in
the possession of dirt.

OSRICKE   Sweet lord, if your friendship were at leisure I
should impart a thing to you from his majesty.

HAMLET   I will receive it with all diligence of spirit. Put
95 your bonnet to his right use: 'tis for the head.

OSRICKE   I thank your lordship, 'tis very hot.

HAMLET   No, believe me, 'tis very cold; the wind is
northerly.

OSRICKE   It is indifferent cold, my lord, indeed.

100 HAMLET   Methinks it is very sultry and hot for my
complexion.

OSRICKE   Exceedingly, my lord, it is very sultry, as
'twere – I cannot tell how. But, my lord, his majesty
bade me signify to you that he has laid a great wager on
105 your head. Sir, this is the matter –

HAMLET   I beseech you, remember.

OSRICKE   Nay, in good faith, for mine ease, in good
faith. Sir, you are not ignorant of what excellence
Laertes is at his weapon.

110 HAMLET   What's his weapon?

OSRICKE   Rapier and dagger.

HAMLET   That's two of his weapons. But well.

OSRICKE   The King, sir, has waged with him six Barbary
horses, against the which he imponed, as I take it, six
115 French rapiers and poniards, with their assigns, as
girdle, hangers, or so. Three of the carriages, in faith,
are very dear to fancy, very responsive to the hilts,
most delicate carriages and of very liberal conceit.

HAMLET   What call you the carriages?

120 OSRICKE   The carriages, sir, are the hangers.

HAMLET   The phrase would be more germane to the
matter if we could carry cannon by our sides. I would
it might be hangers till then. But on. Six Barbary
horses against six French swords, their assigns and
125 three liberal-conceited carriages – that's the French
bet against the Danish. Why is this 'imponed', as you
call it?

OSRICKE   The King, sir, hath laid that, in a dozen passes
between you and him, he shall not exceed you three
130 hits. He hath on't twelve for nine, and that would come
to immediate trial if your lordship would vouchsafe the
answer.

HAMLET   How if I answer no?

OSRICKE   I mean, my lord, the opposition of your
135 person in trial.

HAMLET   Sir, I will walk here in the hall. If it please
his majesty – 'tis the breathing time of day with
me – let the foils be brought. The gentleman willing
and the King hold his purpose, I will win for him if
140 I can. If not, I'll gain nothing but my shame and the
odd hits.

OSRICKE   Shall I redeliver you e'en so?

HAMLET   To this effect, sir, after what flourish your
nature will.

145 OSRICKE   I commend my duty to your lordship.

HAMLET   Yours, yours.   *Exit Osricke.*
He does well to commend it himself. There are no
tongues else for's turn.

HORATIO   This lapwing runs away with the shell on his
150 head.

HAMLET   He did comply with his dug before he sucked
it. Thus had he, and many more of the same bevy that
I know the drossy age dotes on, only got the tune of the
time and outward habit of encounter, a kind of yeasty
155 collection which carries them through and through the
most fanned and winnowed opinions; and do but blow
them to their trials – the bubbles are out.

HORATIO   You will lose this wager, my lord.

HAMLET   I do not think so. Since he went into France I
160 have been in continual practice. I shall win at the odds.
But thou wouldst not think how all here about my
heart – but it is no matter.

HORATIO   Nay, good my lord.

HAMLET   It is but foolery; but it is such a kind of
165 gaingiving as would perhaps trouble a woman.

HORATIO   If your mind dislike anything, obey. I will
forestall their repair hither and say you are not fit.

HAMLET   Not a whit. We defy augury. There's a special
providence in the fall of a sparrow. If it be now, 'tis not
170 to come. If it be not to come, it will be now. If it be not
now, yet it will come. The readiness is all. Since no man
has aught of what he leaves, what is't to leave betimes?

Enter KING, QUEEN, LAERTES, OSRICKE *and* Lords,
*with other Attendants with foils and gauntlets, a table and
flagons of wine on it.*

KING
Come, Hamlet, come and take this hand from me.
[*Puts Laertes' hand into Hamlet's.*]

HAMLET
Give me your pardon, sir. I've done you wrong,
175 But pardon't as you are a gentleman.
This presence knows, and you must needs have heard,
How I am punished with sore distraction.
What I have done

180	That might your nature, honour and exception Roughly awake, I here proclaim was madness. Was't Hamlet wronged Laertes? Never Hamlet. If Hamlet from himself be ta'en away And when he's not himself does wrong Laertes, Then Hamlet does it not; Hamlet denies it.

180 That might your nature, honour and exception
    Roughly awake, I here proclaim was madness.
    Was't Hamlet wronged Laertes? Never Hamlet.
    If Hamlet from himself be ta'en away
    And when he's not himself does wrong Laertes,
185 Then Hamlet does it not; Hamlet denies it.
    Who does it then? His madness? If 't be so
    Hamlet is of the faction that is wronged –
    His madness is poor Hamlet's enemy.
    Sir, in this audience,
    Let my disclaiming from a purposed evil
190 Free me so far in your most generous thoughts
    That I have shot mine arrow o'er the house
    And hurt my mother.
LAERTES   I am satisfied in nature,
    Whose motive in this case should stir me most
    To my revenge. But in my terms of honour
195 I stand aloof and will no reconcilement
    Till by some elder masters of known honour
    I have a voice and precedent of peace
    To keep my name ungorged. But till that time
    I do receive your offered love like love
    And will not wrong it.
200 HAMLET   I do embrace it freely
    And will this brothers' wager frankly play.
    Give us the foils. Come on.
LAERTES   Come, one for me.
HAMLET   I'll be your foil, Laertes. In mine ignorance
    Your skill shall like a star i'th' darkest night
    Stick fiery off indeed.
205 LAERTES   You mock me, sir.
HAMLET   No, by this hand.
KING
    Give them the foils, young Osricke. Cousin Hamlet,
    You know the wager.
HAMLET   Very well, my lord.
    Your grace hath laid the odds o'th' weaker side.
210 KING   I do not fear it. I have seen you both
    But since he is bettered we have therefore odds.
LAERTES   This is too heavy, let me see another.
HAMLET
    This likes me well. These foils have all a length?
        [*Prepare to play.*]
OSRICKE   Ay, my good lord.
215 KING   Set me the stoups of wine upon that table.
    If Hamlet give the first or second hit
    Or quit in answer of the third exchange
    Let all the battlements their ordnance fire.
    The King shall drink to Hamlet's better breath
220 And in the cup an union shall he throw
    Richer than that which four successive kings
    In Denmark's crown have worn. Give me the cups
    And let the kettle to the trumpets speak,
    The trumpet to the cannoneer without,
225 The cannons to the heavens, the heaven to earth.
    Now the King drinks to Hamlet. Come, begin.
    And you, the judges, bear a wary eye.

HAMLET   Come on, sir.
LAERTES   Come on, sir. [*They play.*]
HAMLET   One!
230 LAERTES   No!
HAMLET   Judgement?
OSRICKE   A hit, a very palpable hit.
LAERTES   Well, again.
235 KING   Stay, give me drink. Hamlet, this pearl is thine:
    Here's to thy health. Give him the cup.
                [*Trumpets sound and shot goes off.*]
HAMLET   I'll play this bout first. Set by awhile. Come,
    another hit! – What say you?
LAERTES   A touch, a touch, I do confess.
KING   Our son shall win.
240 QUEEN   He's fat and scant of breath.
    Here's a napkin, rub thy brows –
    The Queen carouses to thy fortune, Hamlet.
HAMLET   Good madam.
KING   Gertrude, do not drink.
245 QUEEN   I will, my lord. I pray you pardon me.
KING [*aside*]
    It is the poisoned cup! It is too late.
HAMLET   I dare not drink yet, madam. By and by.
QUEEN   Come, let me wipe thy face.
LAERTES [*aside to King*]
    My lord, I'll hit him now.
KING[*aside to Laertes*]   I do not think't.
LAERTES [*aside*]
250   And yet 'tis almost 'gainst my conscience.
HAMLET   Come for the third, Laertes, you but dally.
    I pray you pass with your best violence.
    I am afeared you make a wanton of me.
LAERTES   Say you so? Come on.   [*They play.*]
255 OSRICKE   Nothing neither way.
LAERTES   Have at you now!
    [*In scuffling they change rapiers.*]
KING   Part them – they are incensed.
HAMLET   Nay, come – again. [*Queen falls.*]
OSRICKE   Look to the Queen there, ho!
260 HORATIO   They bleed on both sides. How is't, my lord?
OSRICKE   How is't, Laertes?
LAERTES
    Why, as a woodcock to mine own springe, Osricke:
    I am justly killed with mine own treachery.
HAMLET   How does the Queen?
KING   She swoons to see them bleed.
QUEEN
265   No, no, the drink, the drink, O my dear Hamlet,
    The drink, the drink – I am poisoned.   [*Dies.*]
HAMLET   O villainy! Ho! Let the door be locked.
    Treachery! Seek it out.   *Exit Osricke.*
LAERTES   It is here, Hamlet – Hamlet, thou art slain.
270 No medicine in the world can do thee good:
    In thee there is not half an hour of life;
    The treacherous instrument is in thy hand
    Unbated and envenomed. The foul practice
    Hath turned itself on me. Lo, here I lie

275 Never to rise again. Thy mother's poisoned –
I can no more – the King, the King's to blame.
HAMLET
The point envenomed too? Then venom to thy work!
[*Hurts the King.*]
LORDS Treason, treason!
KING O yet defend me, friends. I am but hurt.
HAMLET
280 Here, thou incestuous, murderous, damned Dane!
Drink off this potion. Is thy union here?
Follow my mother. [*King dies.*]
LAERTES He is justly served.
It is a poison tempered by himself.
Exchange forgiveness with me, noble Hamlet,
285 Mine and my father's death come not upon thee,
Nor thine on me. [*Dies.*]
HAMLET Heaven make thee free of it. I follow thee.
I am dead, Horatio. Wretched Queen, adieu.
You that look pale and tremble at this chance,
290 That are but mutes or audience to this act,
Had I but time (as this fell sergeant Death
Is strict in his arrest) – O, I could tell you –
But let it be. Horatio, I am dead.
Thou liv'st: report me and my causes right
To the unsatisfied.
295 HORATIO Never believe it.
I am more an antique Roman than a Dane:
Here's yet some liquor left.
HAMLET As th'art a man
Give me the cup. Let go! By heaven I'll have't!
O good Horatio, what a wounded name,
300 Things standing thus unknown, shall live behind me!
If thou didst ever hold me in thy heart
Absent thee from felicity awhile
And in this harsh world draw thy breath in pain
To tell my story. [*March afar off and shout within*]
What warlike noise is this?

Enter OSRICKE.

OSRICKE
305 Young Fortinbras with conquest come from Poland
To th'ambassadors of England gives
This warlike volley.
HAMLET O, I die, Horatio.
The potent poison quite o'ercrows my spirit,
I cannot live to hear the news from England,
310 But I do prophesy th'election lights
On Fortinbras: he has my dying voice.
So tell him with the occurrence more and less
Which have solicited. The rest is silence.
O, O, O, O. [*Dies.*]
HORATIO
315 Now crack a noble heart. Goodnight, sweet Prince,
And flights of angels sing thee to thy rest.
Why does the drum come hither?

Enter FORTINBRAS *and English* Ambassador *with Drum,*
Colours and Attendants.

FORTINBRAS Where is this sight?
HORATIO What is it ye would see?
If aught of woe or wonder, cease your search.
FORTINBRAS
This quarry cries on havoc. O proud Death, 320
What feast is toward in thine eternal cell
That thou so many princes at a shoot
So bloodily hast struck?
AMBASSADOR The sight is dismal
And our affairs from England come too late.
The ears are senseless that should give us hearing 325
To tell him his commandment is fulfilled,
That Rosincrance and Guildensterne are dead.
Where should we have our thanks?
HORATIO Not from his mouth,
Had it th'ability of life to thank you;
He never gave commandment for their death. 330
But since so jump upon this bloody question
You from the Polack wars and you from England
Are here arrived, give order that these bodies
High on a stage be placed to the view
And let me speak to th' yet unknowing world 335
How these things came about. So shall you hear
Of carnal, bloody and unnatural acts,
Of accidental judgements, casual slaughters,
Of deaths put on by cunning, and forced cause,
And in this upshot purposes mistook 340
Fall'n on the inventors' heads. All this can I
Truly deliver.
FORTINBRAS Let us haste to hear it
And call the noblest to the audience.
For me, with sorrow I embrace my fortune.
I have some rights of memory in this kingdom 345
Which are to claim. My vantage doth invite me.
HORATIO Of that I shall have also cause to speak
And from his mouth whose voice will draw on more.
But let this same be presently performed
Even whiles men's minds are wild, lest more mischance 350
On plots and errors happen.
FORTINBRAS Let four captains
Bear Hamlet like a soldier to the stage,
For he was likely, had he been put on,
To have proved most royally. And for his passage
The soldier's music and the rites of war 355
Speak loudly for him.
Take up the body. Such a sight as this
Becomes the field but here shows much amiss.
Go, bid the soldiers shoot.
Exeunt marching, after the which a
peal of ordnance are shot off.

Julius Caesar

Julius Caesar seems to have been one of the first plays to be performed in the new Globe theatre in the summer or autumn of 1599: Thomas Platter, a Swiss doctor who was in London from 18 September to 20 October, recorded having seen a performance of 'the tragedy of the first Emperor Julius' on 21 September which was in all probability Shakespeare's play. It is unlikely to have been written earlier since it is not included in the list of plays given by Francis Meres in *Palladis Tamia* (1598), but allusions to it begin to appear in 1600, indicating that it was a popular and influential work. It was not published, however, until it was included in the First Folio in 1623, as the fifth of the tragedies, in an unusually accurate text based apparently on a very clear manuscript, formerly thought to be authorial but now assumed to be a good scribal copy.

While today *Julius Caesar* tends to be categorized as a 'classical tragedy' or a 'Roman play', and discussed in relation to later plays of this kind such as *Antony and Cleopatra* and *Coriolanus*, its immediate context in Shakespeare's career as a dramatist gives it equally strong links with *King Henry V* and *Hamlet*. By 1599 Shakespeare had written only two 'straight' tragedies, *Titus Andronicus* and *Romeo and Juliet*, though some of the English history plays had been printed with the word 'tragedy' on their title-pages. He seems to have been reading and thinking about Julius Caesar when he wrote *King Henry V* (also generally dated 1599) since in the Chorus to Act 5 he compares the triumphant return of Henry to England to the greeting of 'conquering Caesar' by the senators and plebeians of 'antique Rome' – the material of the opening scene of this play. A further link is provided by Fluellen's comparison of Henry and Alexander in 4.7 of *King Henry V*: Shakespeare read about Alexander in Thomas North's translation of Plutarch's *Lives of the Noble Grecians and Romans*, where Alexander is paired with Julius Caesar in Plutarch's system of providing parallel Greek and Roman

biographies. Shakespeare, who used Plutarch extensively in *Julius Caesar*, seems to suggest that Henry V could be added as a third, English example of a great military leader.

As *King Henry V* looks forward to *Julius Caesar*, the latter play looks forward to *Hamlet*. The difficulty Brutus faces in arriving at his decision to kill Caesar can be compared with Hamlet's dilemma over killing Claudius, and the way Brutus describes the 'interim' between 'the acting of a dreadful thing / And the first motion' at 2.1.63–4 is if anything more accurate about Hamlet's situation than it is about his own. The 'sheeted dead' squeaking and gibbering in the Roman streets 'A little ere the mightiest Julius fell' are remembered in the first scene of *Hamlet*, and Polonius recalls acting the part of Caesar in 3.2.

While *Hamlet* quickly became a personal tragedy, with many of its political passages cut in performance, the theatrical and critical history of *Julius Caesar* has seen debate centred on its main political issue: were the conspirators justified in killing Caesar? The question was familiar to educated people in Elizabethan England as a stock topic for debate or 'disputation' in schools and universities. In the theatre, where *Julius Caesar* has been one of the most frequently performed of Shakespeare's plays, there has been a long tradition of presenting Brutus as a sympathetic hero and endorsing his republican sympathies; critics, and especially editors of the play, have been more inclined to find fault with him and to view the murder of Caesar as a crime or even 'sacrilege'. Many twentieth-century productions since Orson Welles's sensational 1937 New York version (subtitled 'Death of a Dictator') have modernized and simplified the play's politics by presenting Caesar as a Fascist leader like Hitler or Mussolini.

The Arden text is based on the 1623 First Folio.

Julius CAESAR

Marcus BRUTUS

Caius CASSIUS

CASKA

DECIUS Brutus

CINNA *conspirators against Julius Caesar*

METELLUS Cimber

TREBONIUS

Caius LIGARIUS

OCTAVIUS Caesar

Mark ANTONY *triumvirs after the death of Caesar*

LEPIDUS

CALPHURNIA *wife of Caesar*

PORTIA *wife of Brutus*

LUCIUS *personal servant to Brutus*

CICERO

PUBLIUS *senators*

POPILIUS Lena

MURELLUS *tribunes of the people*

FLAVIUS

CINNA *a poet*

LUCILIUS

TITINIUS

MESSALA *supporters of Brutus and Cassius, and officers in their army*

Young CATO

STRATO

VARRUS

CLAUDIO

CLITUS *soldiers with Brutus and Cassius*

DARDANIUS

VOLUMNIUS

PINDARUS

ARTEMIDORUS

CARPENTER

COBBLER

POET

SOOTHSAYER

SERVANT to Caesar

SERVANT to Antony

SERVANT to Octavius

MESSENGER

Five PLEBEIANS

Three SOLDIERS *in the army of Brutus*

Two SOLDIERS *in the army of Antony*

GHOST of Caesar

Commoners, Soldiers and others

Julius Caesar

1.1 *Enter* FLAVIUS, MURELLUS *and certain*
          Commoners *over the stage.*

FLAVIUS
  Hence! home, you idle creatures, get you home!
  Is this a holiday? What, know you not
  (Being mechanical) you ought not walk
  Upon a labouring day, without the sign
5 Of your profession? Speak, what trade art thou?
CARPENTER   Why, sir, a carpenter.
MURELLUS   Where is thy leather apron, and thy rule?
  What dost thou with thy best apparel on?
  You, sir, what trade are you?
10 COBBLER   Truly, sir, in respect of a fine workman, I am
  but as you would say, a cobbler.
MURELLUS
  But what trade art thou? Answer me directly.
COBBLER   A trade, sir, that I hope I may use with a safe
  conscience, which is indeed, sir, a mender of bad soles.
FLAVIUS
  What trade, thou knave? Thou naughty knave, what
15   trade?
COBBLER   Nay I beseech you, sir, be not out with me:
  yet if you be out, sir, I can mend you.
MURELLUS   What mean'st thou by that? Mend me, thou
  saucy fellow?
20 COBBLER   Why, sir, cobble you.
FLAVIUS   Thou art a cobbler, art thou?
COBBLER   Truly, sir, all that I live by, is with the awl: I
  meddle with no tradesman's matters, nor women's
  matters; but withal I am indeed, sir, a surgeon to old
25 shoes; when they are in great danger, I recover them.
  As proper men as ever trod upon neat's leather have
  gone upon my handiwork.
FLAVIUS   But wherefore art not in thy shop today?
  Why dost thou lead these men about the streets?
30 COBBLER   Truly, sir, to wear out their shoes, to get
  myself into more work. But indeed, sir, we make
  holiday to see Caesar and to rejoice in his triumph.
MURELLUS
  Wherefore rejoice? What conquest brings he home?
  What tributaries follow him to Rome
35 To grace in captive bonds his chariot wheels?
  You blocks, you stones, you worse than senseless
     things!
  O you hard hearts, you cruel men of Rome,
  Knew you not Pompey? Many a time and oft
  Have you climbed up to walls and battlements,
40 To towers and windows, yea, to chimney-tops,
  Your infants in your arms, and there have sat
  The livelong day, with patient expectation,
  To see great Pompey pass the streets of Rome:
  And when you saw his chariot but appear,
45 Have you not made an universal shout,
  That Tiber trembled underneath her banks
  To hear the replication of your sounds
  Made in her concave shores?
  And do you now put on your best attire?

  And do you now cull out a holiday?   50
  And do you now strew flowers in his way,
  That comes in triumph over Pompey's blood?
  Be gone!
  Run to your houses, fall upon your knees,
  Pray to the gods to intermit the plague   55
  That needs must light on this ingratitude.
FLAVIUS   Go, go, good countrymen, and for this fault
  Assemble all the poor men of your sort;
  Draw them to Tiber banks, and weep your tears
  Into the channel, till the lowest stream   60
  Do kiss the most exalted shores of all.
                        Exeunt all the Commoners.
  See where their basest mettle be not moved.
  They vanish tongue-tied in their guiltiness.
  Go you down that way towards the Capitol.
  This way will I. Disrobe the images,   65
  If you do find them decked with ceremonies.
MURELLUS   May we do so?
  You know it is the feast of Lupercal.
FLAVIUS   It is no matter. Let no images
  Be hung with Caesar's trophies. I'll about,   70
  And drive away the vulgar from the streets.
  So do you too, where you perceive them thick.
  These growing feathers plucked from Caesar's wing
  Will make him fly an ordinary pitch,
  Who else would soar above the view of men,   75
  And keep us all in servile fearfulness.   *Exeunt.*

1.2 *Enter* CAESAR, ANTONY *for the course,*
          CALPHURNIA, PORTIA, DECIUS, CICERO,
          BRUTUS, CASSIUS, CASKA, *a* Soothsayer;
          after them MURELLUS *and* FLAVIUS.

CAESAR   Calphurnia.
CASKA   Peace, ho! Caesar speaks.
CAESAR   Calphurnia.
CALPHURNIA   Here, my lord.
CAESAR   Stand you directly in Antonio's way
  When he doth run his course. Antonio.
ANTONY   Caesar, my lord.   5
CAESAR   Forget not in your speed, Antonio,
  To touch Calphurnia; for our elders say,
  The barren touched in this holy chase
  Shake off their sterile curse.
ANTONY   I shall remember.
  When Caesar says 'Do this', it is performed.   10
CAESAR   Set on, and leave no ceremony out.   [*Music*]
SOOTHSAYER   Caesar!
CAESAR   Ha! Who calls?
CASKA   Bid every noise be still. Peace yet again!
CAESAR   Who is it in the press that calls on me?   15
  I hear a tongue shriller than all the music
  Cry 'Caesar!' Speak. Caesar is turned to hear.
SOOTHSAYER   Beware the Ides of March.
CAESAR   What man is that?
BRUTUS   A soothsayer bids you beware the Ides of March.
CAESAR   Set him before me. Let me see his face.   20

CASSIUS Fellow, come from the throng. Look upon
  Caesar.
CAESAR
  What sayst thou to me now? Speak once again.
SOOTHSAYER Beware the Ides of March.
CAESAR
25   He is a dreamer. Let us leave him. Pass.   [*Sennet*]
                  Exeunt all but Brutus and Cassius.
CASSIUS Will you go see the order of the course?
BRUTUS Not I.
CASSIUS I pray you, do.
BRUTUS I am not gamesome. I do lack some part
30   Of that quick spirit that is in Antony.
    Let me not hinder, Cassius, your desires;
    I'll leave you.
CASSIUS Brutus, I do observe you now of late.
    I have not from your eyes that gentleness
35   And show of love as I was wont to have.
    You bear too stubborn and too strange a hand
    Over your friend, that loves you.
BRUTUS   Cassius,
    Be not deceived. If I have veiled my look,
    I turn the trouble of my countenance
40   Merely upon myself. Vexed I am
    Of late with passions of some difference,
    Conceptions only proper to myself
    Which give some soil, perhaps, to my behaviours.
    But let not therefore my good friends be grieved
45   (Among which number, Cassius, be you one)
    Nor construe any further my neglect
    Than that poor Brutus, with himself at war,
    Forgets the shows of love to other men.
CASSIUS
    Then, Brutus, I have much mistook your passion,
50   By means whereof this breast of mine hath buried
    Thoughts of great value, worthy cogitations.
    Tell me, good Brutus, can you see your face?
BRUTUS No, Cassius; for the eye sees not itself
    But by reflection, by some other things.
55 CASSIUS 'Tis just,
    And it is very much lamented, Brutus,
    That you have no such mirrors as will turn
    Your hidden worthiness into your eye,
    That you might see your shadow: I have heard
60   Where many of the best respect in Rome
    (Except immortal Caesar) speaking of Brutus,
    And groaning underneath this age's yoke,
    Have wished that noble Brutus had his eyes.
BRUTUS
    Into what dangers would you lead me, Cassius,
65   That you would have me seek into myself
    For that which is not in me?
CASSIUS
    Therefore, good Brutus, be prepared to hear.
    And since you know you cannot see yourself
    So well as by reflection, I your glass
70   Will modestly discover to yourself

    That of yourself which you yet know not of.
    And be not jealous on me, gentle Brutus.
    Were I a common laughter, or did use
    To stale with ordinary oaths my love
    To every new protester; if you know   75
    That I do fawn on men, and hug them hard,
    And after scandal them; or if you know
    That I profess myself in banqueting
    To all the rout, then hold me dangerous.
                    [*Flourish, and shout*]
BRUTUS
    What means this shouting? I do fear the people   80
    Choose Caesar for their king.
CASSIUS   Ay, do you fear it?
    Then must I think you would not have it so.
BRUTUS I would not, Cassius, yet I love him well.
    But wherefore do you hold me here so long?
    What is it that you would impart to me?   85
    If it be aught toward the general good,
    Set honour in one eye, and death i'th' other,
    And I will look on both indifferently.
    For let the gods so speed me as I love
    The name of honour more than I fear death.   90
CASSIUS I know that virtue to be in you, Brutus,
    As well as I do know your outward favour.
    Well, honour is the subject of my story.
    I cannot tell what you and other men
    Think of this life; but for my single self   95
    I had as lief not be as live to be
    In awe of such a thing as I myself.
    I was born free as Caesar, so were you;
    We both have fed as well, and we can both
    Endure the winter's cold as well as he.   100
    For once, upon a raw and gusty day,
    The troubled Tiber chafing with her shores,
    Caesar said to me, 'Dar'st thou, Cassius, now
    Leap in with me into this angry flood
    And swim to yonder point?' Upon the word,   105
    Accoutred as I was, I plunged in
    And bade him follow; so indeed he did.
    The torrent roared, and we did buffet it
    With lusty sinews, throwing it aside,
    And stemming it with hearts of controversy.   110
    But ere we could arrive the point proposed
    Caesar cried, 'Help me, Cassius, or I sink!'
    I, as Aeneas, our great ancestor,
    Did from the flames of Troy upon his shoulder
    The old Anchises bear, so from the waves of Tiber   115
    Did I the tired Caesar: and this man
    Is now become a god, and Cassius is
    A wretched creature, and must bend his body
    If Caesar carelessly but nod on him.
    He had a fever when he was in Spain,   120
    And when the fit was on him I did mark
    How he did shake. 'Tis true, this god did shake:
    His coward lips did from their colour fly,
    And that same eye, whose bend doth awe the world,

125 Did lose his lustre: I did hear him groan:
Ay, and that tongue of his that bade the Romans
Mark him, and write his speeches in their books,
'Alas,' it cried, 'give me some drink, Titinius',
As a sick girl. Ye gods, it doth amaze me
130 A man of such a feeble temper should
So get the start of the majestic world
And bear the palm alone.   [*Shout. Flourish.*]
BRUTUS   Another general shout?
I do believe that these applauses are
For some new honours that are heaped on Caesar.
135 CASSIUS   Why, man, he doth bestride the narrow world
Like a colossus, and we petty men
Walk under his huge legs and peep about
To find ourselves dishonourable graves.
Men at some time are masters of their fates.
140 The fault, dear Brutus, is not in our stars
But in ourselves, that we are underlings.
'Brutus' and 'Caesar': what should be in that
   'Caesar'?
Why should that name be sounded more than yours?
Write them together: yours is as fair a name:
145 Sound them, it doth become the mouth as well.
Weigh them, it is as heavy: conjure with 'em,
'Brutus' will start a spirit as soon as 'Caesar'.
Now in the names of all the gods at once,
Upon what meat doth this our Caesar feed
150 That he is grown so great? Age, thou art shamed!
Rome, thou hast lost the breed of noble bloods!
When went there by an age, since the great flood,
But it was famed with more than with one man?
When could they say, till now, that talked of Rome,
155 That her wide walks encompassed but one man?
Now is it Rome indeed, and room enough,
When there is in it but one only man.
O, you and I have heard our fathers say
There was a Brutus once that would have brooked
160 Th'eternal devil to keep his state in Rome
As easily as a king.
BRUTUS   That you do love me, I am nothing jealous:
What you would work me to, I have some aim:
How I have thought of this and of these times
165 I shall recount hereafter. For this present,
I would not, so with love I might entreat you,
Be any further moved. What you have said
I will consider: what you have to say
I will with patience hear, and find a time
170 Both meet to hear and answer such high things.
Till then, my noble friend, chew upon this:
Brutus had rather be a villager
Than to repute himself a son of Rome
Under these hard conditions as this time
Is like to lay upon us.
175 CASSIUS   I am glad
That my weak words have struck but thus much
   show
Of fire from Brutus.

Enter CAESAR *and his train.*

BRUTUS   The games are done, and Caesar is returning.
CASSIUS   As they pass by, pluck Caska by the sleeve,
And he will, after his sour fashion, tell you   180
What hath proceeded worthy note today.
BRUTUS   I will do so: but look you, Cassius,
The angry spot doth glow on Caesar's brow,
And all the rest look like a chidden train:
Calphurnia's cheek is pale, and Cicero   185
Looks with such ferret and such fiery eyes
As we have seen him in the Capitol
Being crossed in conference by some senators.
CASSIUS   Caska will tell us what the matter is.
CAESAR   Antonio.   190
ANTONY   Caesar.
CAESAR   Let me have men about me that are fat,
Sleek-headed men, and such as sleep a-nights.
Yond Cassius has a lean and hungry look:
He thinks too much: such men are dangerous.   195
ANTONY   Fear him not, Caesar, he's not dangerous.
He is a noble Roman, and well given.
CAESAR   Would he were fatter! But I fear him not:
Yet if my name were liable to fear
I do not know the man I should avoid   200
So soon as that spare Cassius. He reads much,
He is a great observer, and he looks
Quite through the deeds of men. He loves no plays
As thou dost, Antony; he hears no music.
Seldom he smiles, and smiles in such a sort   205
As if he mocked himself and scorned his spirit
That could be moved to smile at anything.
Such men as he be never at heart's ease
Whiles they behold a greater than themselves,
And therefore are they very dangerous.   210
I rather tell thee what is to be feared
Than what I fear: for always I am Caesar.
Come on my right hand, for this ear is deaf,
And tell me truly what thou think'st of him.   [*Sennet*]
                              Exeunt Caesar and his train.
CASKA   You pulled me by the cloak. Would you speak   215
   with me?
BRUTUS   Ay, Caska, tell us what hath chanced today
That Caesar looks so sad.
CASKA   Why, you were with him, were you not?
BRUTUS
I should not then ask Caska what had chanced.   220
CASKA   Why, there was a crown offered him; and being
offered him, he put it by with the back of his hand,
thus, and then the people fell a-shouting.
BRUTUS   What was the second noise for?
CASKA   Why, for that too.   225
CASSIUS
They shouted thrice: what was the last cry for?
CASKA   Why, for that too.
BRUTUS   Was the crown offered him thrice?
CASKA   Ay, marry, was't, and he put it by thrice, every

230 time gentler than other; and at every putting-by, mine
honest neighbours shouted.

CASSIUS Who offered him the crown?

CASKA Why, Antony.

BRUTUS Tell us the manner of it, gentle Caska.

235 CASKA I can as well be hanged as tell the manner of it.
It was mere foolery: I did not mark it. I saw Mark
Antony offer him a crown – yet 'twas not a crown
neither, 'twas one of these coronets – and, as I told
you, he put it by once; but for all that, to my thinking,
240 he would fain have had it. Then he offered it to him
again; then he put it by again; but to my thinking, he
was very loth to lay his fingers off it. And then he
offered it the third time; he put it the third time by;
and still as he refused it the rabblement hooted, and
245 clapped their chopped hands, and threw up their
sweaty nightcaps, and uttered such a deal of stinking
breath because Caesar refused the crown that it had
almost choked Caesar; for he swooned and fell down at
it. And for mine own part, I durst not laugh, for fear of
250 opening my lips and receiving the bad air.

CASSIUS But soft, I pray you: what, did Caesar swoon?

CASKA He fell down in the market-place, and foamed at
mouth, and was speechless.

BRUTUS 'Tis very like. He hath the falling sickness.

255 CASSIUS No, Caesar hath it not: but you, and I,
And honest Caska, we have the falling sickness.

CASKA I know not what you mean by that, but I am sure
Caesar fell down. If the tag-rag people did not clap
him and hiss him according as he pleased and
260 displeased them, as they use to do the players in the
theatre, I am no true man.

BRUTUS What said he when he came unto himself?

CASKA Marry, before he fell down, when he perceived
the common herd was glad he refused the crown, he
265 plucked me ope his doublet and offered them his throat
to cut. An I had been a man of any occupation, if I
would not have taken him at a word, I would I might go
to hell among the rogues. And so he fell. When he came
to himself again, he said, if he had done or said anything
270 amiss, he desired their worships to think it was his
infirmity. Three or four wenches where I stood cried,
'Alas, good soul', and forgave him with all their hearts.
But there's no heed to be taken of them: if Caesar had
stabbed their mothers, they would have done no less.

275 BRUTUS And after that he came thus sad away.

CASKA Ay.

CASSIUS Did Cicero say anything?

CASKA Ay, he spoke Greek.

CASSIUS To what effect?

280 CASKA Nay, an I tell you that, I'll ne'er look you i'th'
face again. But those that understood him, smiled at
one another, and shook their heads; but for mine own
part, it was Greek to me. I could tell you more news
too: Murellus and Flavius, for pulling scarves off
285 Caesar's images, are put to silence. Fare you well.
There was more foolery yet, if I could remember it.

CASSIUS Will you sup with me tonight, Caska?

CASKA No, I am promised forth.

CASSIUS Will you dine with me tomorrow?

CASKA Ay, if I be alive, and your mind hold, and your 290
dinner worth the eating.

CASSIUS Good. I will expect you.

CASKA Do so. Farewell, both.   *Exit.*

BRUTUS What a blunt fellow is this grown to be!
He was quick mettle when he went to school. 295

CASSIUS So is he now, in execution
Of any bold or noble enterprise,
However he puts on this tardy form.
This rudeness is a sauce to his good wit,
Which gives men stomach to digest his words 300
With better appetite.

BRUTUS   And so it is.
For this time I will leave you.
Tomorrow if you please to speak with me
I will come home to you: or, if you will,
Come home to me, and I will wait for you. 305

CASSIUS
I will do so. Till then, think of the world. *Exit Brutus.*
Well, Brutus, thou art noble: yet I see
Thy honourable mettle may be wrought
From that it is disposed. Therefore it is meet
That noble minds keep ever with their likes; 310
For who so firm that cannot be seduced?
Caesar doth bear me hard, but he loves Brutus.
If I were Brutus now, and he were Cassius,
He should not humour me. I will this night
In several hands in at his windows throw, 315
As if they came from several citizens,
Writings all tending to the great opinion
That Rome holds of his name – wherein obscurely
Caesar's ambition shall be glanced at.
And after this, let Caesar seat him sure, 320
For we will shake him, or worse days endure. *Exit.*

1.3   *Thunder and lightning. Enter* CASKA
        and CICERO.

CICERO Good even, Caska. Brought you Caesar home?
Why are you breathless, and why stare you so?

CASKA Are you not moved, when all the sway of earth
Shakes like a thing unfirm? O Cicero,
I have seen tempests when the scolding winds 5
Have rived the knotty oaks, and I have seen
Th'ambitious ocean swell, and rage, and foam,
To be exalted with the threatening clouds:
But never till tonight, never till now,
Did I go through a tempest dropping fire. 10
Either there is a civil strife in heaven,
Or else the world, too saucy with the gods,
Incenses them to send destruction.

CICERO Why, saw you anything more wonderful?

CASKA A common slave – you know him well by sight – 15
Held up his left hand, which did flame and burn

Like twenty torches joined; and yet his hand,
Not sensible of fire, remained unscorched.
Besides – I ha'not since put up my sword –
20 Against the Capitol I met a lion
Who glazed upon me and went surly by
Without annoying me. And there were drawn
Upon a heap a hundred ghastly women
Transformed with their fear, who swore they saw
25 Men, all in fire, walk up and down the streets.
And yesterday the bird of night did sit
Even at noonday upon the market-place
Hooting and shrieking. When these prodigies
Do so conjointly meet, let not men say,
30 'These are their reasons, they are natural':
For I believe they are portentous things
Unto the climate that they point upon.
CICERO   Indeed it is a strange-disposed time.
But men may construe things after their fashion
35 Clean from the purpose of the things themselves.
Comes Caesar to the Capitol tomorrow?
CASKA   He doth, for he did bid Antonio
Send word to you he would be there tomorrow.
CICERO   Good night then, Caska: this disturbed sky
Is not to walk in.
40 CASKA   Farewell, Cicero.   *Exit Cicero.*

Enter CASSIUS.

CASSIUS   Who's there?
CASKA   A Roman.
CASSIUS   Caska, by your voice.
CASKA   Your ear is good. Cassius, what night is this?
CASSIUS   A very pleasing night to honest men.
CASKA   Whoever knew the heavens menace so?
CASSIUS
45 Those that have known the earth so full of faults.
For my part, I have walked about the streets,
Submitting me unto the perilous night,
And thus unbraced, Caska, as you see,
Have bared my bosom to the thunder-stone:
50 And when the cross blue lightning seemed to open
The breast of heaven, I did present myself
Even in the aim and very flash of it.
CASKA
But wherefore did you so much tempt the heavens?
It is the part of men to fear and tremble
55 When the most mighty gods by tokens send
Such dreadful heralds to astonish us.
CASSIUS   You are dull, Caska, and those sparks of life
That should be in a Roman you do want
Or else you use not. You look pale, and gaze,
60 And put on fear, and cast yourself in wonder
To see the strange impatience of the heavens.
But if you would consider the true cause
Why all these fires, why all these gliding ghosts,
Why birds and beasts, from quality and kind,
65 Why old men, fools, and children calculate,
Why all these things change from their ordinance

Their natures and preformed faculties
To monstrous quality, why, you shall find
That heaven hath infused them with these spirits
70 To make them instruments of fear and warning
Unto some monstrous state.
Now could I, Caska, name to thee a man
Most like this dreadful night
That thunders, lightens, opens graves and roars
75 As doth the lion in the Capitol:
A man no mightier than thyself, or me,
In personal action, yet prodigious grown
And fearful, as these strange eruptions are.
CASKA   'Tis Caesar that you mean. Is it not, Cassius?
CASSIUS   Let it be who it is: for Romans now
80 Have thews and limbs like to their ancestors:
But woe the while, our fathers' minds are dead,
And we are governed with our mothers' spirits:
Our yoke and sufferance show us womanish.
CASKA   Indeed, they say the senators tomorrow
85 Mean to establish Caesar as a king,
And he shall wear his crown by sea and land
In every place save here in Italy.
CASSIUS   I know where I will wear this dagger then:
Cassius from bondage will deliver Cassius.
90 Therein, ye gods, ye make the weak most strong;
Therein, ye gods, you tyrants do defeat.
Nor stony tower, nor walls of beaten brass,
Nor airless dungeon, nor strong links of iron,
Can be retentive to the strength of spirit:
95 But life being weary of these worldly bars
Never lacks power to dismiss itself.
If I know this, know all the world besides,
That part of tyranny that I do bear
I can shake off at pleasure.   [*Thunder still*]
100 CASKA   So can I.
So every bondman in his own hand bears
The power to cancel his captivity.
CASSIUS   And why should Caesar be a tyrant then?
Poor man, I know he would not be a wolf
105 But that he sees the Romans are but sheep.
He were no lion, were not Romans hinds.
Those that with haste will make a mighty fire
Begin it with weak straws. What trash is Rome?
What rubbish, and what offal? when it serves
110 For the base matter to illuminate
So vile a thing as Caesar? But, O grief,
Where hast thou led me? I perhaps speak this
Before a willing bondman: then I know
My answer must be made. But I am armed
115 And dangers are to me indifferent.
CASKA   You speak to Caska, and to such a man
That is no fleering tell-tale. Hold, my hand.
Be factious for redress of all these griefs
And I will set this foot of mine as far
As who goes farthest.
120 CASSIUS   There's a bargain made.
Now know you, Caska, I have moved already

Some certain of the noblest-minded Romans
To undergo with me an enterprise
Of honourable dangerous consequence;
125 And I do know by this, they stay for me
In Pompey's Porch. For now this fearful night
There is no stir or walking in the streets;
And the complexion of the element
In favour's like the work we have in hand,
130 Most bloody, fiery and most terrible.

Enter CINNA.

CASKA   Stand close awhile, for here comes one in haste.
CASSIUS   'Tis Cinna. I do know him by his gait.
   He is a friend. Cinna, where haste you so?
CINNA
   To find out you. Who's that? Metellus Cimber?
135 CASSIUS   No, it is Caska, one incorporate
   To our attempts. Am I not stayed for, Cinna?
CINNA   I am glad on't. What a fearful night is this?
   There's two or three of us have seen strange sights.
CASSIUS   Am I not stayed for? Tell me.
CINNA   Yes, you are.
140   O Cassius, if you could
   But win the noble Brutus to our party –
CASSIUS   Be you content. Good Cinna, take this paper
   And look you lay it in the praetor's chair
   Where Brutus may but find it. And throw this
145   In at his window. Set this up with wax
   Upon old Brutus' statue. All this done,
   Repair to Pompey's Porch, where you shall find us.
   Is Decius Brutus and Trebonius there?
CINNA   All but Metellus Cimber, and he's gone
150   To seek you at your house. Well, I will hie,
   And so bestow these papers as you bade me.
CASSIUS
   That done, repair to Pompey's Theatre.   *Exit Cinna.*
   Come, Caska, you and I will yet ere day
   See Brutus at his house. Three parts of him
155   Is ours already, and the man entire
   Upon the next encounter yields him ours.
CASKA   O he sits high in all the people's hearts:
   And that which would appear offence in us
   His countenance, like richest alchemy,
160   Will change to virtue and to worthiness.
CASSIUS
   Him, and his worth, and our great need of him
   You have right well conceited. Let us go,
   For it is after midnight, and ere day
   We will awake him and be sure of him.   *Exeunt.*

2.1   *Enter* BRUTUS *in his orchard.*

BRUTUS   What, Lucius, ho?
   I cannot by the progress of the stars
   Give guess how near to day – Lucius, I say?
   I would it were my fault to sleep so soundly.
5   When, Lucius, when? Awake, I say: what, Lucius!

Enter LUCIUS.

LUCIUS   Called you, my lord?
BRUTUS   Get me a taper in my study, Lucius.
   When it is lighted, come and call me here.
LUCIUS   I will, my lord.   *Exit.*
10 BRUTUS   It must be by his death: and for my part
   I know no personal cause to spurn at him
   But for the general. He would be crowned:
   How that might change his nature, there's the question.
   It is the bright day that brings forth the adder,
15   And that craves wary walking. Crown him that,
   And then I grant we put a sting in him
   That at his will he may do danger with.
   Th'abuse of greatness is when it disjoins
   Remorse from power; and to speak truth of Caesar
20   I have not known when his affections swayed
   More than his reason. But 'tis a common proof
   That lowliness is young ambition's ladder
   Whereto the climber upward turns his face;
   But when he once attains the upmost round
25   He then unto the ladder turns his back,
   Looks in the clouds, scorning the base degrees
   By which he did ascend. So Caesar may.
   Then, lest he may, prevent. And since the quarrel
   Will bear no colour for the thing he is,
30   Fashion it thus: that what he is, augmented,
   Would run to these and these extremities.
   And therefore think him as a serpent's egg
   Which hatched, would as his kind grow mischievous,
   And kill him in the shell.

Enter LUCIUS.

35 LUCIUS   The taper burneth in your closet, sir.
   Searching the window for a flint, I found
   This paper, thus sealed up, and I am sure
   It did not lie there when I went to bed.
   [*Gives him the letter.*]
BRUTUS   Get you to bed again, it is not day.
40   Is not tomorrow, boy, the first of March?
LUCIUS   I know not, sir.
BRUTUS   Look in the calendar and bring me word.
LUCIUS   I will, sir.   *Exit.*
BRUTUS   The exhalations whizzing in the air
45   Give so much light that I may read by them.
   [*Opens the letter and reads.*]
   'Brutus, thou sleep'st; awake and see thyself.
   Shall Rome, et cetera. Speak, strike, redress.'
   'Brutus, thou sleep'st; awake.'
   Such instigations have been often dropped
50   Where I have took them up.
   'Shall Rome, et cetera.' Thus must I piece it out:
   Shall Rome stand under one man's awe? What Rome?
   My ancestors did from the streets of Rome
   The Tarquin drive, when he was called a king.
55   'Speak, strike, redress.' Am I entreated
   To speak and strike? O Rome, I make thee promise,

If the redress will follow, thou receivest
Thy full petition at the hand of Brutus.

Enter LUCIUS.

LUCIUS
Sir, March is wasted fifteen days.   [*Knock within*]

60 BRUTUS   'Tis good. Go to the gate: somebody knocks.
Exit Lucius.

Since Cassius first did whet me against Caesar
I have not slept.
Between the acting of a dreadful thing
And the first motion, all the interim is
65 Like a phantasma or a hideous dream:
The genius and the mortal instruments
Are then in council, and the state of man,
Like to a little kingdom, suffers then
The nature of an insurrection.

Enter LUCIUS.

70 LUCIUS   Sir, 'tis your brother Cassius at the door,
Who doth desire to see you.
BRUTUS   Is he alone?
LUCIUS
No, sir, there are moe with him.
BRUTUS   Do you know them?
LUCIUS   No, sir, their hats are plucked about their ears
And half their faces buried in their cloaks,
75 That by no means I may discover them
By any mark of favour.
BRUTUS   Let 'em enter.   *Exit Lucius.*
They are the faction. O conspiracy,
Sham'st thou to show thy dangerous brow by night,
When evils are most free? O then by day
80 Where wilt thou find a cavern dark enough
To mask thy monstrous visage? Seek none, conspiracy:
Hide it in smiles and affability;
For if thou path, thy native semblance on,
Not Erebus itself were dim enough
85 To hide thee from prevention.

Enter the conspirators: CASSIUS, CASKA, DECIUS, CINNA,
METELLUS *and* TREBONIUS.

CASSIUS   I think we are too bold upon your rest.
Good morrow, Brutus. Do we trouble you?
BRUTUS   I have been up this hour, awake all night.
Know I these men that come along with you?
90 CASSIUS   Yes, every man of them; and no man here
But honours you, and every one doth wish
You had but that opinion of yourself
Which every noble Roman bears of you.
This is Trebonius.
BRUTUS   He is welcome hither.
CASSIUS   This, Decius Brutus.
95 BRUTUS   He is welcome too.
CASSIUS
This, Caska. This, Cinna. And this, Metellus Cimber.
BRUTUS   They are all welcome.

What watchful cares do interpose themselves
Betwixt your eyes and night?
CASSIUS   Shall I entreat a word?
[*They whisper.*]
DECIUS
Here lies the east. Doth not the day break here?   100
CASKA   No.
CINNA   O pardon, sir, it doth, and yon grey lines
That fret the clouds are messengers of day.
CASKA   You shall confess that you are both deceived.
Here, as I point my sword, the sun arises,   105
Which is a great way growing on the south,
Weighing the youthful season of the year.
Some two months hence, up higher toward the north
He first presents his fire, and the high east
Stands as the Capitol, directly here.   110
BRUTUS [*Comes forward with Cassius.*]
Give me your hands all over, one by one.
CASSIUS   And let us swear our resolution.
BRUTUS   No, not an oath. If not the face of men,
The sufferance of our souls, the time's abuse;
If these be motives weak, break off betimes,   115
And every man hence to his idle bed.
So let high-sighted tyranny range on
Till each man drop by lottery. But if these,
As I am sure they do, bear fire enough
To kindle cowards, and to steel with valour   120
The melting spirits of women: then, countrymen,
What need we any spur but our own cause
To prick us to redress? What other bond
Than secret Romans that have spoke the word
And will not palter? And what other oath,   125
Than honesty to honesty engaged,
That this shall be, or we will fall for it?
Swear priests and cowards, and men cautelous,
Old feeble carrions, and such suffering souls
That welcome wrongs: unto bad causes swear   130
Such creatures as men doubt. But do not stain
The even virtue of our enterprise,
Nor th'insuppressive mettle of our spirits,
To think that or our cause or our performance
Did need an oath, when every drop of blood   135
That every Roman bears, and nobly bears,
Is guilty of a several bastardy
If he do break the smallest particle
Of any promise that hath passed from him.
CASSIUS   But what of Cicero? Shall we sound him?   140
I think he will stand very strong with us.
CASKA   Let us not leave him out.
CINNA   No, by no means.
METELLUS   O let us have him, for his silver hairs
Will purchase us a good opinion,
And buy men's voices to commend our deeds.   145
It shall be said his judgement ruled our hands.
Our youths and wildness shall no whit appear,
But all be buried in his gravity.
BRUTUS   O name him not. Let us not break with him,

150 For he will never follow anything
That other men begin.
CASSIUS   Then leave him out.
CASKA   Indeed he is not fit.
DECIUS   Shall no man else be touched but only Caesar?
CASSIUS   Decius, well urged. I think it is not meet
155 Mark Antony, so well beloved of Caesar,
Should outlive Caesar. We shall find of him
A shrewd contriver. And you know his means
If he improve them may well stretch so far
As to annoy us all: which to prevent
160 Let Antony and Caesar fall together.
BRUTUS
Our course will seem too bloody, Caius Cassius,
To cut the head off and then hack the limbs –
Like wrath in death and envy afterwards –
For Antony is but a limb of Caesar.
165 Let's be sacrificers but not butchers, Caius.
We all stand up against the spirit of Caesar,
And in the spirit of men there is no blood.
O that we then could come by Caesar's spirit
And not dismember Caesar! But, alas,
170 Caesar must bleed for it. And, gentle friends,
Let's kill him boldly, but not wrathfully:
Let's carve him as a dish fit for the gods,
Not hew him as a carcass fit for hounds.
And let our hearts, as subtle masters do,
175 Stir up their servants to an act of rage
And after seem to chide 'em. This shall make
Our purpose necessary and not envious,
Which so appearing to the common eyes,
We shall be called purgers, not murderers.
180 And for Mark Antony, think not of him,
For he can do no more than Caesar's arm
When Caesar's head is off.
CASSIUS   Yet I fear him,
For in the ingrafted love he bears to Caesar –
BRUTUS   Alas, good Cassius, do not think of him.
185 If he love Caesar, all that he can do
Is to himself – take thought, and die for Caesar.
And that were much he should, for he is given
To sports, to wildness and much company.
TREBONIUS   There is no fear in him. Let him not die,
190 For he will live and laugh at this hereafter.
                                    [*Clock strikes.*]
BRUTUS   Peace! Count the clock.
CASSIUS   The clock hath stricken three.
TREBONIUS   'Tis time to part.
CASSIUS   But it is doubtful yet
Whether Caesar will come forth this day or no,
For he is superstitious grown of late,
195 Quite from the main opinion he held once
Of fantasy, of dreams and ceremonies.
It may be these apparent prodigies,
The unaccustomed terror of this night
And the persuasion of his augurers,
200 May hold him from the Capitol today.

DECIUS   Never fear that. If he be so resolved
I can o'ersway him: for he loves to hear
That unicorns may be betrayed with trees,
And bears with glasses, elephants with holes,
Lions with toils and men with flatterers.   205
But when I tell him he hates flatterers,
He says he does, being then most flattered.
Let me work.
For I can give his humour the true bent,
And I will bring him to the Capitol.   210
CASSIUS   Nay, we will all of us be there to fetch him.
BRUTUS   By the eighth hour. Is that the uttermost?
CINNA   Be that the uttermost, and fail not then.
METELLUS   Caius Ligarius doth bear Caesar hard,
Who rated him for speaking well of Pompey.   215
I wonder none of you have thought of him.
BRUTUS   Now, good Metellus, go along by him.
He loves me well, and I have given him reasons.
Send him but hither and I'll fashion him.
CASSIUS
The morning comes upon's. We'll leave you, Brutus.   220
And, friends, disperse yourselves – but all remember
What you have said, and show yourselves true Romans.
BRUTUS   Good gentlemen, look fresh and merrily.
Let not our looks put on our purposes,
But bear it as our Roman actors do,   225
With untired spirits and formal constancy.
And so good morrow to you every one.
                          Exeunt all but Brutus.
Boy! Lucius! Fast asleep? It is no matter.
Enjoy the honey-heavy dew of slumber.
Thou hast no figures, nor no fantasies   230
Which busy care draws in the brains of men.
Therefore thou sleep'st so sound.

                    Enter PORTIA.

PORTIA   Brutus, my lord.
BRUTUS
Portia, what mean you? Wherefore rise you now?
It is not for your health thus to commit
Your weak condition to the raw cold morning.   235
PORTIA
Nor for yours neither. Y'have ungently, Brutus,
Stole from my bed: and yesternight at supper
You suddenly arose, and walked about,
Musing, and sighing, with your arms across;
And when I asked you what the matter was   240
You stared upon me with ungentle looks.
I urged you further: then you scratched your head
And too impatiently stamped with your foot.
Yet I insisted, yet you answered not
But with an angry wafture of your hand   245
Gave sign for me to leave you. So I did,
Fearing to strengthen that impatience
Which seemed too much enkindled, and withal
Hoping it was but an effect of humour,
Which sometime hath his hour with every man.   250

It will not let you eat, nor talk, nor sleep;
And could it work so much upon your shape
As it hath much prevailed on your condition,
I should not know you Brutus. Dear my lord,
255   Make me acquainted with your cause of grief.
BRUTUS   I am not well in health, and that is all.
PORTIA   Brutus is wise, and were he not in health,
He would embrace the means to come by it.
BRUTUS   Why, so I do. Good Portia, go to bed.
260 PORTIA   Is Brutus sick, and is it physical
To walk unbraced and suck up the humours
Of the dank morning? What, is Brutus sick?
And will he steal out of his wholesome bed
To dare the vile contagion of the night?
265   And tempt the rheumy and unpurged air
To add unto his sickness? No, my Brutus,
You have some sick offence within your mind
Which by the right and virtue of my place
I ought to know of: and upon my knees
270   I charm you, by my once commended beauty,
By all your vows of love, and that great vow
Which did incorporate and make us one,
That you unfold to me, your self, your half,
Why you are heavy – and what men tonight
275   Have had resort to you: for here have been
Some six or seven who did hide their faces
Even from darkness.
BRUTUS   Kneel not, gentle Portia.
PORTIA   I should not need, if you were gentle Brutus.
Within the bond of marriage, tell me, Brutus,
280   Is it excepted I should know no secrets
That appertain to you? Am I your self
But as it were in sort or limitation,
To keep with you at meals, comfort your bed
And talk to you sometimes? Dwell I but in the suburbs
285   Of your good pleasure? If it be no more,
Portia is Brutus' harlot, not his wife.
BRUTUS   You are my true and honourable wife,
As dear to me as are the ruddy drops
That visit my sad heart.
PORTIA
290   If this were true, then I should know this secret.
I grant I am a woman: but withal
A woman that Lord Brutus took to wife.
I grant I am a woman: but withal
A woman well reputed, Cato's daughter.
295   Think you I am no stronger than my sex
Being so fathered and so husbanded?
Tell me your counsels. I will not disclose 'em.
I have made strong proof of my constancy,
Giving myself a voluntary wound,
300   Here in the thigh. Can I bear that with patience
And not my husband's secrets?
BRUTUS   O ye gods,
Render me worthy of this noble wife!   [*Knock*]
Hark, hark, one knocks. Portia, go in a while,
And by and by thy bosom shall partake

The secrets of my heart.   305
All my engagements I will construe to thee,
All the charactery of my sad brows.
Leave me with haste.   *Exit Portia.*

Enter LUCIUS *and* Caius LIGARIUS.

                  Lucius, who's that knocks?
LUCIUS   Here is a sick man that would speak with you.
BRUTUS   Caius Ligarius, that Metellus spake of.   310
Boy, stand aside. Caius Ligarius, how?
LIGARIUS
Vouchsafe good morrow from a feeble tongue.
BRUTUS
O, what a time have you chose out, brave Caius,
To wear a kerchief? Would you were not sick!
LIGARIUS   I am not sick if Brutus have in hand   315
Any exploit worthy the name of honour.
BRUTUS   Such an exploit have I in hand, Ligarius,
Had you a healthful ear to hear of it.
LIGARIUS   By all the gods that Romans bow before,
I here discard my sickness. Soul of Rome,   320
Brave son, derived from honourable loins,
Thou like an exorcist hast conjured up
My mortified spirit. Now bid me run
And I will strive with things impossible,
Yea, get the better of them. What's to do?   325
BRUTUS
A piece of work that will make sick men whole.
LIGARIUS
But are not some whole that we must make sick?
BRUTUS   That must we also. What it is, my Caius,
I shall unfold to thee as we are going
To whom it must be done.
LIGARIUS   Set on your foot,   330
And with a heart new-fired I follow you,
To do I know not what: but it sufficeth
That Brutus leads me on.   [*Thunder*]
BRUTUS   Follow me, then.   *Exeunt.*

2.2   *Thunder and lightning. Enter* Julius CAESAR
            in his nightgown.

CAESAR
Nor heaven nor earth have been at peace tonight.
Thrice hath Calphurnia in her sleep cried out,
'Help ho: they murder Caesar.' Who's within?

Enter a Servant.

SERVANT   My lord?
CAESAR   Go bid the priests do present sacrifice   5
And bring me their opinions of success.
SERVANT   I will, my lord.   *Exit.*

Enter CALPHURNIA.

CALPHURNIA
What mean you, Caesar? Think you to walk forth?
You shall not stir out of your house today.

CAESAR

    Caesar shall forth. The things that threatened me

    Ne'er looked but on my back: when they shall see

    The face of Caesar, they are vanished.

CALPHURNIA   Caesar, I never stood on ceremonies,

    Yet now they fright me. There is one within,

    Besides the things that we have heard and seen,

    Recounts most horrid sights seen by the watch.

    A lioness hath whelped in the streets,

    And graves have yawned and yielded up their dead.

    Fierce fiery warriors fight upon the clouds

    In ranks and squadrons and right form of war,

    Which drizzled blood upon the Capitol.

    The noise of battle hurtled in the air,

    Horses do neigh, and dying men did groan,

    And ghosts did shriek and squeal about the streets.

    O Caesar, these things are beyond all use,

    And I do fear them.

CAESAR   What can be avoided

    Whose end is purposed by the mighty gods?

    Yet Caesar shall go forth, for these predictions

    Are to the world in general as to Caesar.

CALPHURNIA

    When beggars die there are no comets seen;

    The heavens themselves blaze forth the death of princes.

CAESAR   Cowards die many times before their deaths;

    The valiant never taste of death but once.

    Of all the wonders that I yet have heard,

    It seems to me most strange that men should fear,

    Seeing that death, a necessary end,

    Will come when it will come.

Enter Servant.

    What say the augurers?

SERVANT   They would not have you to stir forth today.

    Plucking the entrails of an offering forth,

    They could not find a heart within the beast.

CAESAR   The gods do this in shame of cowardice.

    Caesar should be a beast without a heart

    If he should stay at home today for fear.

    No, Caesar shall not. Danger knows full well

    That Caesar is more dangerous than he.

    We are two lions littered in one day,

    And I the elder and more terrible,

    And Caesar shall go forth.

CALPHURNIA   Alas, my lord,

    Your wisdom is consumed in confidence.

    Do not go forth today. Call it my fear

    That keeps you in the house, and not your own.

    We'll send Mark Antony to the Senate House,

    And he shall say you are not well today.

    Let me upon my knee prevail in this.

CAESAR   Mark Antony shall say I am not well,

    And for thy humour I will stay at home.

Enter DECIUS.

    Here's Decius Brutus. He shall tell them so.

DECIUS   Caesar, all hail. Good morrow, worthy Caesar,

    I come to fetch you to the Senate House.

CAESAR   And you are come in very happy time

    To bear my greeting to the senators

    And tell them that I will not come today.

    Cannot is false; and that I dare not, falser.

    I will not come today. Tell them so, Decius.

CALPHURNIA   Say he is sick.

CAESAR   Shall Caesar send a lie?

    Have I in conquest stretched mine arm so far

    To be afeard to tell greybeards the truth?

    Decius, go tell them Caesar will not come.

DECIUS   Most mighty Caesar, let me know some cause,

    Lest I be laughed at when I tell them so.

CAESAR   The cause is in my will, I will not come,

    That is enough to satisfy the Senate.

    But for your private satisfaction,

    Because I love you, I will let you know.

    Calphurnia here, my wife, stays me at home.

    She dreamt tonight she saw my statue,

    Which, like a fountain with an hundred spouts,

    Did run pure blood; and many lusty Romans

    Came smiling and did bathe their hands in it.

    And these she does apply for warnings and portents

    And evils imminent, and on her knee

    Hath begged that I will stay at home today.

DECIUS   This dream is all amiss interpreted.

    It was a vision, fair and fortunate.

    Your statue spouting blood in many pipes

    In which so many smiling Romans bathed

    Signifies that from you great Rome shall suck

    Reviving blood, and that great men shall press

    For tinctures, stains, relics and cognizance.

    This by Calphurnia's dream is signified.

CAESAR   And this way have you well expounded it.

DECIUS   I have, when you have heard what I can say.

    And know it now: the Senate have concluded

    To give this day a crown to mighty Caesar.

    If you shall send them word you will not come,

    Their minds may change. Besides, it were a mock

    Apt to be rendered, for some one to say,

    'Break up the Senate till another time

    When Caesar's wife shall meet with better dreams.'

    If Caesar hide himself, shall they not whisper,

    'Lo, Caesar is afraid'?

    Pardon me, Caesar, for my dear, dear love

    To your proceeding bids me tell you this,

    And reason to my love is liable.

CAESAR

    How foolish do your fears seem now, Calphurnia!

    I am ashamed I did yield to them.

    Give me my robe, for I will go.

Enter BRUTUS, Caius LIGARIUS, METELLUS Cimber,
    CASKA, TREBONIUS, CINNA *and* PUBLIUS.

    And look where Publius is come to fetch me.

PUBLIUS   Good morrow, Caesar.

CAESAR   Welcome, Publius.
110 What, Brutus, are you stirred so early too?
Good morrow, Caska. Caius Ligarius,
Caesar was ne'er so much your enemy
As that same ague which hath made you lean.
What is't o'clock?
BRUTUS   Caesar, 'tis strucken eight.
115 CAESAR   I thank you for your pains and courtesy.

Enter ANTONY.

See, Antony, that revels long a-nights,
Is notwithstanding up. Good morrow, Antony.
ANTONY
So to most noble Caesar.
CAESAR   Bid them prepare within.
I am too blame to be thus waited for.
120 Now, Cinna. Now, Metellus. What, Trebonius,
I have an hour's talk in store for you.
Remember that you call on me today:
Be near me, that I may remember you.
TREBONIUS   Caesar, I will, [*aside*] And so near will I be
125 That your best friends shall wish I had been further.
CAESAR
Good friends, go in, and taste some wine with me,
And we, like friends, will straightway go together.
BRUTUS [*aside*]
That every like is not the same, O Caesar,
The heart of Brutus earns to think upon.   *Exeunt.*

2.3   *Enter* ARTEMIDORUS *reading a paper.*

ARTEMIDORUS   *Caesar, beware of Brutus. Take heed of
Cassius. Come not near Caska. Have an eye to Cinna.
Trust not Trebonius. Mark well Metellus Cimber. Decius
Brutus loves thee not. Thou hast wronged Caius Ligarius.
5 There is but one mind in all these men, and it is bent
against Caesar. If thou beest not immortal, look about
you. Security gives way to conspiracy. The mighty gods
defend thee.*
                                   Thy lover, Artemidorus.
10 Here will I stand till Caesar pass along
And as a suitor will I give him this.
My heart laments that virtue cannot live
Out of the teeth of emulation.
If thou read this, O Caesar, thou mayst live;
15 If not, the Fates with traitors do contrive.   *Exit.*

2.4   *Enter* PORTIA *and* LUCIUS.

PORTIA   I prithee, boy, run to the Senate House.
Stay not to answer me, but get thee gone.
Why dost thou stay?
LUCIUS   To know my errand, madam.
PORTIA   I would have had thee there and here again
5 Ere I can tell thee what thou shouldst do there.
[*aside*] O constancy, be strong upon my side:
Set a huge mountain 'tween my heart and tongue.
I have a man's mind, but a woman's might.

How hard it is for women to keep counsel.
[*to Lucius*] Art thou here yet?
LUCIUS   Madam, what should I do?   10
Run to the Capitol, and nothing else?
And so return to you, and nothing else?
PORTIA   Yes, bring me word, boy, if thy lord look well,
For he went sickly forth; and take good note
What Caesar doth, what suitors press to him.   15
Hark, boy, what noise is that?
LUCIUS   I hear none, madam.
PORTIA   Prithee listen well.
I heard a bustling rumour like a fray,
And the wind brings it from the Capitol.
LUCIUS   Sooth, madam, I hear nothing.   20

Enter the Soothsayer.

PORTIA
Come hither, fellow. Which way hast thou been?
SOOTHSAYER   At mine own house, good lady.
PORTIA   What is't o'clock?
SOOTHSAYER   About the ninth hour, lady.
PORTIA   Is Caesar yet gone to the Capitol?
SOOTHSAYER   Madam, not yet. I go to take my stand   25
To see him pass on to the Capitol.
PORTIA   Thou hast some suit to Caesar, hast thou not?
SOOTHSAYER   That I have, lady, if it will please Caesar
To be so good to Caesar as to hear me:
I shall beseech him to befriend himself.   30
PORTIA
Why, knowst thou any harm's intended towards him?
SOOTHSAYER   None that I know will be,
Much that I fear may chance.
Good morrow to you. Here the street is narrow.
The throng that follows Caesar at the heels,   35
Of senators, of praetors, common suitors,
Will crowd a feeble man almost to death.
I'll get me to a place more void, and there
Speak to great Caesar as he comes along.   *Exit.*
PORTIA   I must go in. Ay me, how weak a thing   40
The heart of woman is. O Brutus,
The heavens speed thee in thy enterprise.
Sure the boy heard me. Brutus hath a suit
That Caesar will not grant. O, I grow faint:
Run, Lucius, and commend me to my lord.   45
Say I am merry. Come to me again
And bring me word what he doth say to thee.
                        Exeunt at separate doors.

3.1   *Flourish. Enter* CAESAR, BRUTUS,
            CASSIUS, CASKA, DECIUS, METELLUS,
            TREBONIUS, CINNA, ANTONY, LEPIDUS,
            ARTEMIDORUS, PUBLIUS, POPILIUS Lena
                    and the Soothsayer.

CAESAR   The Ides of March are come.
SOOTHSAYER   Ay, Caesar, but not gone.
ARTEMIDORUS   Hail, Caesar. Read this schedule.

DECIUS   Trebonius doth desire you to o'er-read
5   At your best leisure this his humble suit.
ARTEMIDORUS
         O Caesar, read mine first, for mine's a suit
         That touches Caesar nearer. Read it, great Caesar.
CAESAR   What touches us ourself shall be last served.
ARTEMIDORUS   Delay not, Caesar, read it instantly!
CAESAR   What, is the fellow mad?
10 PUBLIUS   Sirrah, give place.
CASSIUS   What, urge you your petitions in the street?
         Come to the Capitol.
              [*Caesar and his followers move upstage.*]
POPILIUS   I wish your enterprise today may thrive.
CASSIUS   What enterprise, Popilius?
POPILIUS   Fare you well.
15 BRUTUS   What said Popilius Lena?
CASSIUS   He wished today our enterprise might thrive.
         I fear our purpose is discovered.
BRUTUS   Look how he makes to Caesar. Mark him.
CASSIUS   Caska, be sudden, for we fear prevention.
20   Brutus, what shall be done? If this be known,
         Cassius or Caesar never shall turn back,
         For I will slay myself.
BRUTUS   Cassius, be constant.
         Popilius Lena speaks not of our purposes,
         For look, he smiles, and Caesar doth not change.
CASSIUS
25   Trebonius knows his time: for look you, Brutus,
         He draws Mark Antony out of the way.
                        Exeunt Antony and Trebonius.
DECIUS   Where is Metellus Cimber? Let him go
         And presently prefer his suit to Caesar.
BRUTUS   He is addressed. Press near and second him.
30 CINNA   Caska, you are the first that rears your hand.
CAESAR   Are we all ready? What is now amiss
         That Caesar and his Senate must redress?
METELLUS
         Most high, most mighty and most puissant Caesar,
         Metellus Cimber throws before thy seat
         An humble heart –
35 CAESAR   I must prevent thee, Cimber:
         These couchings and these lowly courtesies
         Might fire the blood of ordinary men,
         And turn pre-ordinance and first decree
         Into the lane of children. Be not fond
40   To think that Caesar bears such rebel blood
         That will be thawed from the true quality
         With that which melteth fools – I mean sweet words,
         Low-crooked curtsies and base spaniel fawning.
         Thy brother by decree is banished.
45   If thou dost bend and pray and fawn for him
         I spurn thee like a cur out of my way.
         Know, Caesar doth not wrong, nor without cause
         Will he be satisfied.
METELLUS   Is there no voice more worthy than my own
50   To sound more sweetly in great Caesar's ear
         For the repealing of my banished brother?

BRUTUS   I kiss thy hand, but not in flattery, Caesar,
         Desiring thee that Publius Cimber may
         Have an immediate freedom of repeal.
CAESAR   What, Brutus?
CASSIUS   Pardon, Caesar: Caesar, pardon.   55
         As low as to thy foot doth Cassius fall
         To beg enfranchisement for Publius Cimber.
CAESAR   I could be well moved if I were as you:
         If I could pray to move, prayers would move me.
         But I am constant as the northern star,   60
         Of whose true-fixed and resting quality
         There is no fellow in the firmament.
         The skies are painted with unnumbered sparks:
         They are all fire, and every one doth shine;
         But there's but one in all doth hold his place. 65
         So in the world: 'tis furnished well with men,
         And men are flesh and blood, and apprehensive.
         Yet in the number I do know but one
         That unassailable holds on his rank
         Unshaked of motion. And that I am he   70
         Let me a little show it even in this,
         That I was constant Cimber should be banished
         And constant do remain to keep him so.
CINNA   O Caesar –
CAESAR   Hence! Wilt thou lift up Olympus?
DECIUS   Great Caesar –
CAESAR   Doth not Brutus bootless kneel?   75
CASKA   Speak hands for me!   [*They stab Caesar.*]
CAESAR   *Et tu, Brute?* – Then fall, Caesar.   [*Dies.*]
CINNA   Liberty! Freedom! Tyranny is dead!
         Run hence, proclaim, cry it about the streets.
CASSIUS   Some to the common pulpits and cry out   80
         Liberty, freedom and enfranchisement!
BRUTUS   People and senators, be not affrighted.
         Fly not. Stand still. Ambition's debt is paid.
CASKA   Go to the pulpit, Brutus.
DECIUS   And Cassius too.
BRUTUS   Where's Publius?   85
CINNA   Here, quite confounded with this mutiny.
METELLUS
         Stand fast together, lest some friend of Caesars
         Should chance –
BRUTUS   Talk not of standing. Publius, good cheer.
         There is no harm intended to your person,   90
         Nor to no Roman else. So tell them, Publius.
CASSIUS   And leave us, Publius, lest that the people
         Rushing on us, should do your age some mischief.
BRUTUS   Do so, and let no man abide this deed
         But we the doers.   95

                    Enter TREBONIUS.

CASSIUS   Where is Antony?
TREBONIUS   Fled to his house amazed.
         Men, wives and children stare, cry out and run,
         As it were doomsday.
BRUTUS   Fates, we will know your pleasures.
         That we shall die we know; 'tis but the time

100 And drawing days out, that men stand upon.

CASKA Why, he that cuts off twenty years of life

Cuts off so many years of fearing death.

BRUTUS Grant that, and then is death a benefit.

So are we Caesar's friends that have abridged

105 His time of fearing death. Stoop, Romans, stoop,

And let us bathe our hands in Caesar's blood

Up to the elbows and besmear our swords.

Then walk we forth even to the market-place,

And waving our red weapons o'er our heads

110 Let's all cry, 'Peace, Freedom and Liberty'.

CASSIUS Stoop, then, and wash. How many ages hence

Shall this our lofty scene be acted over

In states unborn and accents yet unknown?

BRUTUS How many times shall Caesar bleed in sport

115 That now on Pompey's basis lies along,

No worthier than the dust?

CASSIUS   So oft as that shall be,

So often shall the knot of us be called

The men who gave their country liberty.

DECIUS What, shall we forth?

CASSIUS   Ay, every man away.

120 Brutus shall lead, and we will grace his heels

With the most boldest and best hearts of Rome.

Enter a Servant.

BRUTUS Soft, who comes here? A friend of Antony's.

SERVANT Thus, Brutus, did my master bid me kneel.

Thus did Mark Antony bid me fall down,

125 And being prostrate thus he bade me say:

Brutus is noble, wise, valiant and honest.

Caesar was mighty, bold, royal and loving.

Say I love Brutus and I honour him.

Say I feared Caesar, honoured him and loved him.

130 If Brutus will vouchsafe that Antony

May safely come to him and be resolved

How Caesar hath deserved to lie in death,

Mark Antony shall not love Caesar dead

So well as Brutus living, but will follow

135 The fortunes and affairs of noble Brutus

Thorough the hazards of this untrod state

With all true faith. So says my master Antony.

BRUTUS Thy master is a wise and valiant Roman;

I never thought him worse.

140 Tell him, so please him come unto this place

He shall be satisfied; and by my honour

Depart untouched.

SERVANT   I'll fetch him presently.   *Exit.*

BRUTUS I know that we shall have him well to friend.

CASSIUS I wish we may; but yet I have a mind

145 That fears him much, and my misgiving still

Falls shrewdly to the purpose.

Enter ANTONY.

BRUTUS

But here comes Antony. Welcome, Mark Antony.

ANTONY O mighty Caesar! Dost thou lie so low?

Are all thy conquests, glories, triumphs, spoils,

Shrunk to this little measure? Fare thee well. 150

I know not, gentlemen, what you intend,

Who else must be let blood, who else is rank.

If I myself, there is no hour so fit

As Caesar's death's hour, nor no instrument

Of half that worth as those your swords, made rich 155

With the most noble blood of all this world.

I do beseech ye, if you bear me hard,

Now, whilst your purple hands do reek and smoke,

Fulfil your pleasure. Live a thousand years,

I shall not find myself so apt to die. 160

No place shall please me so, no mean of death,

As here by Caesar, and by you cut off,

The choice and master spirits of this age.

BRUTUS O Antony, beg not your death of us:

Though now we must appear bloody and cruel, 165

As by our hands and this our present act

You see we do, yet see you but our hands

And this the bleeding business they have done:

Our hearts you see not. They are pitiful,

And pity to the general wrong of Rome – 170

As fire drives out fire, so pity pity –

Hath done this deed on Caesar. For your part,

To you our swords have leaden points, Mark Antony.

Our arms in strength of malice, and our hearts

Of brothers' temper, do receive you in, 175

With all kind love, good thoughts and reverence.

CASSIUS Your voice shall be as strong as any man's

In the disposing of new dignities.

BRUTUS Only be patient till we have appeased

The multitude, beside themselves with fear, 180

And then we will deliver you the cause

Why I, that did love Caesar when I struck him,

Have thus proceeded.

ANTONY   I doubt not of your wisdom.

Let each man render me his bloody hand.

First, Marcus Brutus, will I shake with you. 185

Next, Caius Cassius, do I take your hand.

Now, Decius Brutus, yours. Now yours, Metellus.

Yours, Cinna; and my valiant Caska, yours.

Though last, not least in love, yours good Trebonius.

Gentlemen all: alas, what shall I say? 190

My credit now stands on such slippery ground

That one of two bad ways you must conceit me,

Either a coward or a flatterer.

That I did love thee, Caesar, O 'tis true:

If then thy spirit look upon us now, 195

Shall it not grieve thee dearer than thy death

To see thy Antony making his peace,

Shaking the bloody fingers of thy foes?

Most noble in the presence of thy corse,

Had I as many eyes as thou hast wounds, 200

Weeping as fast as they stream forth thy blood,

It would become me better than to close

In terms of friendship with thine enemies.

Pardon me, Julius! Here wast thou bayed, brave hart.

Here didst thou fall. And here thy hunters stand
Signed in thy spoil and crimsoned in thy lethe.
O world, thou wast the forest to this hart,
And this indeed, O world, the heart of thee.
How like a deer, Strucken by many princes,
Dost thou here lie?
CASSIUS   Mark Antony –
ANTONY   Pardon me, Caius Cassius.
The enemies of Caesar shall say this:
Then, in a friend, it is cold modesty.
CASSIUS   I blame you not for praising Caesar so,
But what compact mean you to have with us?
Will you be pricked in number of our friends,
Or shall we on, and not depend on you?
ANTONY   Therefore I took your hands, but was indeed
Swayed from the point by looking down on Caesar.
Friends am I with you all, and love you all,
Upon this hope, that you shall give me reasons
Why and wherein Caesar was dangerous.
BRUTUS   Or else were this a savage spectacle.
Our reasons are so full of good regard
That were you, Antony, the son of Caesar,
You should be satisfied.
ANTONY   That's all I seek,
And am moreover suitor that I may
Produce his body to the market-place,
And in the pulpit, as becomes a friend,
Speak in the order of his funeral.
BRUTUS   You shall, Mark Antony.
CASSIUS   Brutus, a word with you.
[*aside*] You know not what you do. Do not consent
That Antony speak in his funeral.
Know you how much the people may be moved
By that which he will utter.
BRUTUS   By your pardon:
I will myself into the pulpit first,
And show the reason of our Caesar's death.
What Antony shall speak, I will protest
He speaks by leave and by permission;
And that we are contented Caesar shall
Have all true rites and lawful ceremonies,
It shall advantage more than do us wrong.
CASSIUS   I know not what may fall. I like it not.
BRUTUS   Mark Antony, here, take you Caesar's body.
You shall not in your funeral speech blame us,
But speak all good you can devise of Caesar,
And say you do't by our permission:
Else shall you not have any hand at all
About his funeral. And you shall speak
In the same pulpit whereto I am going,
After my speech is ended.
ANTONY   Be it so.
I do desire no more.
BRUTUS   Prepare the body, then, and follow us.
                    Exeunt all but Antony.
ANTONY   O pardon me, thou bleeding piece of earth,
That I am meek and gentle with these butchers.

205
210
215
220
225
230
235
240
245
250
255

Thou art the ruins of the noblest man
That ever lived in the tide of times.
Woe to the hand that shed this costly blood.
Over thy wounds now I do prophesy
(Which like dumb mouths do ope their ruby lips
To beg the voice and utterance of my tongue)
A curse shall light upon the limbs of men:
Domestic fury and fierce civil strife
Shall cumber all the parts of Italy:
Blood and destruction shall be so in use,
And dreadful objects so familiar,
That mothers shall but smile when they behold
Their infants quartered with the hands of war:
All pity choked with custom of fell deeds,
And Caesar's spirit, ranging for revenge,
With Ate by his side come hot from hell,
Shall in these confines, with a monarch's voice,
Cry havoc and let slip the dogs of war,
That this foul deed shall smell above the earth
With carrion men, groaning for burial.

Enter Octavius' Servant.

You serve Octavius Caesar, do you not?
SERVANT   I do, Mark Antony.
ANTONY   Caesar did write for him to come to Rome.
SERVANT   He did receive his letters and is coming,
And bid me say to you by word of mouth –
O Caesar!
ANTONY   Thy heart is big: get thee apart and weep.
Passion, I see, is catching, for mine eyes,
Seeing those beads of sorrow stand in thine,
Begin to water. Is thy master coming?
SERVANT
He lies tonight within seven leagues of Rome.
ANTONY
Post back with speed and tell him what hath
    chanced.
Here is a mourning Rome, a dangerous Rome,
No Rome of safety for Octavius yet.
Hie hence, and tell him so. Yet stay awhile –
Thou shalt not back till I have borne this corpse
Into the market-place. There shall I try
In my oration how the people take
The cruel issue of these bloody men,
According to the which thou shalt discourse
To young Octavius of the state of things.
Lend me your hand.   *Exeunt.*

260
265
270
275
280
285
290
295

3.2   *Enter* BRUTUS *and* CASSIUS *with the* Plebeians.

PLEBEIANS   We will be satisfied: let us be satisfied.
BRUTUS
Then follow me, and give me audience, friends.
Cassius, go you into the other street
And part the numbers:
Those that will hear me speak, let 'em stay here.
Those that will follow Cassius, go with him

5

And public reasons shall be rendered
Of Caesar's death.   [*Goes into the pulpit.*]
1 PLEBEIAN   I will hear Brutus speak.
2 PLEBEIAN
I will hear Cassius, and compare their reasons
When severally we hear them rendered.   10
                    Exeunt Cassius and some of the Plebeians.
3 PLEBEIAN   The noble Brutus is ascended. Silence.
BRUTUS   Be patient till the last.
    Romans, countrymen and lovers, hear me for my cause
and be silent, that you may hear. Believe me for mine
honour and have respect to mine honour, that you may   15
believe. Censure me in your wisdom and awake your
senses, that you may the better judge. If there be any in
this assembly, any dear friend of Caesar's, to him I say,
that Brutus' love to Caesar was no less than his. If then
that friend demand why Brutus rose against Caesar,   20
this is my answer: not that I loved Caesar less, but that
I loved Rome more. Had you rather Caesar were living,
and die all slaves, than that Caesar were dead, to live
all freemen? As Caesar loved me, I weep for him; as
he was fortunate, I rejoice at it; as he was valiant, I   25
honour him: but as he was ambitious, I slew him.
There is tears, for his love; joy, for his fortune; honour,
for his valour; and death, for his ambition. Who is
here so base, that would be a bondman? If any, speak,
for him have I offended. Who is here so rude, that   30
would not be a Roman? If any, speak, for him have I
offended. Who is here so vile, that will not love his
country? If any, speak, for him have I offended. I pause
for a reply.
ALL   None, Brutus, none.   35
BRUTUS   Then none have I offended. I have done no
more to Caesar, than you shall do to Brutus. The
question of his death is enrolled in the Capitol: his
glory not extenuated, wherein he was worthy, nor his   40
offences enforced, for which he suffered death.

    Enter Mark ANTONY *with* CAESAR's *body.*

    Here comes his body, mourned by Mark Antony, who,
though he had no hand in his death, shall receive the
benefit of his dying, a place in the commonwealth, as
which of you shall not? With this I depart, that as I   45
slew my best lover for the good of Rome, I have the
same dagger for myself, when it shall please my
country to need my death. [*Comes down.*]
ALL   Live Brutus, live, live.
1 PLEBEIAN
Bring him with triumph home unto his house.
2 PLEBEIAN   Give him a statue with his ancestors.   50
3 PLEBEIAN   Let him be Caesar.
4 PLEBEIAN   Caesar's better parts
Shall be crowned in Brutus.
1 PLEBEIAN
We'll bring him to his house with shouts and clamours.
BRUTUS   My countrymen.
2 PLEBEIAN   Peace, silence, Brutus speaks.

1 PLEBEIAN   Peace ho.   55
BRUTUS   Good countrymen, let me depart alone,
And, for my sake, stay here with Antony:
Do grace to Caesar's corpse and grace his speech
Tending to Caesar's glories, which Mark Antony,
By our permission, is allowed to make.   60
I do intreat you, not a man depart
Save I alone, till Antony have spoke.   *Exit.*
1 PLEBEIAN   Stay ho, and let us hear Mark Antony.
3 PLEBEIAN   Let him go up into the public chair.
We'll hear him. Noble Antony, go up.   65
ANTONY   For Brutus' sake I am beholding to you.
    [*Goes into the pulpit.*]
4 PLEBEIAN
What does he say of Brutus?
3 PLEBEIAN   He says, for Brutus' sake
He finds himself beholding to us all.
4 PLEBEIAN
'Twere best he speak no harm of Brutus here.
1 PLEBEIAN   This Caesar was a tyrant.
3 PLEBEIAN   Nay, that's certain.   70
We are blest that Rome is rid of him.
2 PLEBEIAN   Peace, let us hear what Antony can say.
ANTONY   You gentle Romans.
ALL   Peace ho, let us hear him.
ANTONY
Friends, Romans, countrymen, lend me your ears:
I come to bury Caesar, not to praise him.   75
The evil that men do lives after them:
The good is oft interred with their bones.
So let it be with Caesar. The noble Brutus
Hath told you Caesar was ambitious:
If it were so, it was a grievous fault,   80
And grievously hath Caesar answered it.
Here, under leave of Brutus and the rest
(For Brutus is an honourable man;
So are they all, all honourable men)
Come I to speak in Caesar's funeral.   85
He was my friend, faithful and just to me;
But Brutus says, he was ambitious,
And Brutus is an honourable man.
He hath brought many captives home to Rome,
Whose ransoms did the general coffers fill.   90
Did this in Caesar seem ambitious?
When that the poor have cried, Caesar hath wept:
Ambition should be made of sterner stuff.
Yet Brutus says, he was ambitious,
And Brutus is an honourable man.   95
You all did see, that on the Lupercal,
I thrice presented him a kingly crown,
Which he did thrice refuse. Was this ambition?
Yet Brutus says, he was ambitious,
And sure he is an honourable man.   100
I speak not to disprove what Brutus spoke,
But here I am to speak what I do know.
You all did love him once, not without cause:
What cause withholds you then to mourn for him?

105 O judgement, thou art fled to brutish beasts
     And men have lost their reason. Bear with me.
     My heart is in the coffin there with Caesar,
     And I must pause till it come back to me.
       PLEBEIAN
       Methinks there is much reason in his sayings.
110   2 PLEBEIAN   If thou consider rightly of the matter,
       Caesar has had great wrong.
       3 PLEBEIAN   Has he, masters?
       I fear there will a worse come in his place.
       4 PLEBEIAN
       Mark ye his words? He would not take the crown;
       Therefore 'tis certain he was not ambitious.
115   1 PLEBEIAN   If it be found so, some will dear abide it.
       2 PLEBEIAN
       Poor soul, his eyes are red as fire with weeping.
       3 PLEBEIAN
       There's not a nobler man in Rome than Antony.
       4 PLEBEIAN   Now mark him; he begins again to speak.
     ANTONY   But yesterday the word of Caesar might
120 Have stood against the world. Now lies he there,
     And none so poor to do him reverence.
     O masters! If I were disposed to stir
     Your hearts and minds to mutiny and rage,
     I should do Brutus wrong, and Cassius wrong,
125 Who (you all know) are honourable men.
     I will not do them wrong. I rather choose
     To wrong the dead, to wrong myself and you,
     Than I will wrong such honourable men.
     But here's a parchment, with the seal of Caesar.
130 I found it in his closet. 'Tis his will.
     Let but the commons hear this testament –
     Which, pardon me, I do not mean to read –
     And they would go and kiss dead Caesar's wounds,
     And dip their napkins in his sacred blood,
135 Yea, beg a hair of him for memory,
     And, dying, mention it within their wills,
     Bequeathing it as a rich legacy
     Unto their issue.
       4 PLEBEIAN   We'll hear the will. Read it, Mark Antony.
140   ALL   The will, the will. We will hear Caesar's will.
     ANTONY
     Have patience, gentle friends. I must not read it.
     It is not meet you know how Caesar loved you.
     You are not wood, you are not stones, but men:
     And being men, hearing the will of Caesar,
145 It will inflame you, it will make you mad.
     'Tis good you know not that you are his heirs,
     For if you should, O what would come of it?
       4 PLEBEIAN   Read the will, we'll hear it, Antony.
       You shall read us the will, Caesar's will.
150 ANTONY   Will you be patient? Will you stay awhile?
     I have o'ershot myself to tell you of it.
     I fear I wrong the honourable men
     Whose daggers have stabbed Caesar: I do fear it.
       4 PLEBEIAN   They were traitors: honourable men?
155   ALL   The will, the testament.

       2 PLEBEIAN
       They were villains, murderers. The will, read the will.
     ANTONY   You will compel me then to read the will?
     Then make a ring about the corpse of Caesar,
     And let me show you him that made the will.
     Shall I descend? And will you give me leave?   160
       ALL   Come down.
       2 PLEBEIAN   Descend.
       [*Antony comes down from the pulpit.*]
       3 PLEBEIAN   You shall have leave.
       4 PLEBEIAN   A ring.
       Stand round.
       1 PLEBEIAN   Stand from the hearse, stand from the body.
       2 PLEBEIAN   Room for Antony, most noble Antony.
     ANTONY   Nay, press not so upon me. Stand far off.   165
       ALL   Stand back. Room, bear back.
     ANTONY   If you have tears, prepare to shed them now.
     You all do know this mantle. I remember
     The first time ever Caesar put it on.
     'Twas on a summer's evening in his tent,   170
     That day he overcame the Nervii.
     Look, in this place ran Cassius' dagger through:
     See what a rent the envious Caska made:
     Through this, the well-beloved Brutus stabbed,
     And as he plucked his cursed steel away,   175
     Mark how the blood of Caesar followed it,
     As rushing out of doors to be resolved
     If Brutus so unkindly knocked or no;
     For Brutus, as you know, was Caesar's angel.
     Judge, O you gods, how dearly Caesar loved him.   180
     This was the most unkindest cut of all:
     For when the noble Caesar saw him stab,
     Ingratitude, more strong than traitor's arms,
     Quite vanquished him: then burst his mighty heart;
     And in his mantle muffling up his face,   185
     Even at the base of Pompey's statue,
     Which all the while ran blood, great Caesar fell.
     O what a fall was there, my countrymen!
     Then I, and you, and all of us fell down,
     Whilst bloody treason flourished over us.   190
     O, now you weep, and I perceive you feel
     The dint of pity: these are gracious drops.
     Kind souls, what weep you when you but behold
     Our Caesar's vesture wounded? Look you here,
     Here is himself, marred as you see with traitors.   195
       1 PLEBEIAN   O piteous spectacle!
       2 PLEBEIAN   O noble Caesar!
       3 PLEBEIAN   O woeful day!
       4 PLEBEIAN   O traitors, villains!
       1 PLEBEIAN   O most bloody sight!
       2 PLEBEIAN   We will be revenged!
       ALL   Revenge! About! Seek! Burn! Fire! Kill! Slay!
       Let not a traitor live!
     ANTONY   Stay, countrymen.   200
       1 PLEBEIAN   Peace there, hear the noble Antony.
       ALL
       We'll hear him, we'll follow him, we'll die with him!

ANTONY
    Good friends, sweet friends, let me not stir you up
    To such a sudden flood of mutiny:
205   They that have done this deed are honourable.
    What private griefs they have, alas, I know not,
    That made them do it: they are wise and honourable
    And will no doubt with reasons answer you.
    I come not, friends, to steal away your hearts.
210   I am no orator, as Brutus is,
    But, as you know me all, a plain blunt man
    That love my friend, and that they know full well
    That gave me public leave to speak of him.
    For I have neither wit, nor words, nor worth,
215   Action, nor utterance, nor the power of speech
    To stir men's blood. I only speak right on:
    I tell you that which you yourselves do know,
    Show you sweet Caesar's wounds, poor poor dumb
      mouths,
    And bid them speak for me. But were I Brutus,
220   And Brutus Antony, there were an Antony
    Would ruffle up your spirits and put a tongue
    In every wound of Caesar that should move
    The stones of Rome to rise and mutiny.
ALL   We'll mutiny.
225 1 PLEBEIAN   We'll burn the house of Brutus.
3 PLEBEIAN   Away then, come, seek the conspirators.
ANTONY   Yet hear me, countrymen, yet hear me speak.
ALL   Peace ho, hear Antony, most noble Antony.
ANTONY
    Why, friends, you go to do you know not what.
230   Wherein hath Caesar thus deserved your loves?
    Alas, you know not. I must tell you then.
    You have forgot the will I told you of.
ALL   Most true. The will, let's stay and hear the will.
ANTONY   Here is the will, and under Caesar's seal.
    To every Roman citizen he gives,
235   To every several man, seventy-five drachmas.
2 PLEBEIAN
    Most noble Caesar, we'll revenge his death.
3 PLEBEIAN
    O royal Caesar!
ANTONY   Hear me with patience.
ALL   Peace ho.
ANTONY   Moreover, he hath left you all his walks,
    His private arbours and new-planted orchards,
240   On this side Tiber. He hath left them you
    And to your heirs for ever: common pleasures
    To walk abroad and recreate yourselves.
    Here was a Caesar: when comes such another?
1 PLEBEIAN   Never, never. Come, away, away.
245   We'll burn his body in the holy place,
    And with the brands fire all the traitors' houses.
    Take up the body.
2 PLEBEIAN   Go fetch fire.
3 PLEBEIAN   Pluck down benches.
250 4 PLEBEIAN   Pluck down forms, windows, anything.
               Exit Plebeians with the body.

ANTONY   Now let it work. Mischief, thou art afoot:
    Take thou what course thou wilt.

            Enter Servant.

                 How now, fellow?
SERVANT   Sir, Octavius is already come to Rome.
ANTONY
    Where is he?
SERVANT   He and Lepidus are at Caesar's house.
ANTONY   And thither will I straight to visit him.   255
    He comes upon a wish. Fortune is merry
    And in this mood will give us anything.
SERVANT   I heard him say Brutus and Cassius
    Are rid like madmen through the gates of Rome.
ANTONY   Belike they had some notice of the people   260
    How I had moved them. Bring me to Octavius.
                      Exeunt.

3.3   *Enter* CINNA *the poet, and after him the*
             Plebeians.

CINNA   I dreamt tonight that I did feast with Caesar,
    And things unluckily charge my fantasy.
    I have no will to wander forth of doors,
    Yet something leads me forth.
1 PLEBEIAN   What is your name?   5
2 PLEBEIAN   Whither are you going?
3 PLEBEIAN   Where do you dwell?
4 PLEBEIAN   Are you a married man or a bachelor?
2 PLEBEIAN   Answer every man directly.
1 PLEBEIAN   Ay, and briefly.   10
4 PLEBEIAN   Ay, and wisely.
3 PLEBEIAN   Ay, and truly, you were best.
CINNA   What is my name? Whither am I going? Where
    do I dwell? Am I a married man or a bachelor? Then to
    answer every man, directly and briefly, wisely and   15
    truly: wisely I say, I am a bachelor.
2 PLEBEIAN   That's as much as to say they are fools that
    marry. You'll bear me a bang for that, I fear. Proceed,
    directly.
CINNA   Directly, I am going to Caesar's funeral.   20
1 PLEBEIAN   As a friend or an enemy?
CINNA   As a friend.
2 PLEBEIAN   That matter is answered directly.
4 PLEBEIAN   For your dwelling, briefly.
CINNA   Briefly, I dwell by the Capitol.   25
3 PLEBEIAN   Your name, sir, truly.
CINNA   Truly, my name is Cinna.
1 PLEBEIAN   Tear him to pieces, he's a conspirator.
CINNA   I am Cinna the poet, I am Cinna the poet.
4 PLEBEIAN   Tear him for his bad verses, tear him for   30
    his bad verses.
CINNA   I am not Cinna the conspirator.
4 PLEBEIAN   It is no matter, his name's Cinna.
    Pluck but his name out of his heart and turn him
    going.   35
3 PLEBEIAN   Tear him, tear him! [*They set upon him.*]

ALL   Come, brands, ho! Firebrands! To Brutus', to
    Cassius', burn all! Some to Decius' house, and some to
    Casca's, some to Ligarius'! Away, go!
          Exeunt all the Plebeians dragging off Cinna.

4.1   *Enter* ANTONY, OCTAVIUS *and* LEPIDUS.

ANTONY
    These many, then, shall die; their names are pricked.
OCTAVIUS
    Your brother too must die; consent you, Lepidus?
LEPIDUS   I do consent.
OCTAVIUS   Prick him down, Antony.
LEPIDUS   Upon condition Publius shall not live,
5   Who is your sister's son, Mark Antony.
ANTONY
    He shall not live. Look, with a spot I damn him.
    But, Lepidus, go you to Caesar's house:
    Fetch the will hither, and we shall determine
    How to cut off some charge in legacies.
10 LEPIDUS   What, shall I find you here?
OCTAVIUS   Or here, or at the Capitol.   *Exit Lepidus.*
ANTONY   This is a slight unmeritable man,
    Meet to be sent on errands: is it fit,
    The threefold world divided, he should stand
    One of the three to share it?
15 OCTAVIUS   So you thought him,
    And took his voice who should be pricked to die
    In our black sentence and proscription.
ANTONY   Octavius, I have seen more days than you;
    And though we lay these honours on this man
20   To ease ourselves of diverse slanderous loads,
    He shall but bear them as the ass bears gold,
    To groan and sweat under the business,
    Either led or driven, as we point the way:
    And having brought our treasure where we will,
25   Then take we down his load and turn him off,
    Like to the empty ass, to shake his ears
    And graze in commons.
OCTAVIUS   You may do your will;
    But he's a tried and valiant soldier.
ANTONY   So is my horse, Octavius, and for that
30   I do appoint him store of provender.
    It is a creature that I teach to fight,
    To wind, to stop, to run directly on,
    His corporal motion governed by my spirit,
    And, in some taste, is Lepidus but so:
35   He must be taught, and trained, and bid go forth;
    A barren-spirited fellow; one that feeds
    On objects, arts and imitations
    Which, out of use and staled by other men,
    Begin his fashion. Do not talk of him
40   But as a property. And now, Octavius,
    Listen great things. Brutus and Cassius
    Are levying powers. We must straight make head.
    Therefore let our alliance be combined,
    Our best friends made, our means stretched,

And let us presently go sit in counsel,   45
How covert matters may be best disclosed,
And open perils surest answered.
OCTAVIUS   Let us do so: for we are at the stake
    And baved about with many enemies.
    And some that smile have in their hearts, I fear,   50
    Millions of mischiefs.   *Exeunt.*

4.2   *Drum. Enter* BRUTUS, LUCILIUS *and the*
          army. TITINIUS *and* PINDARUS *meet them.*

BRUTUS   Stand ho.
LUCILIUS   Give the word, ho, and stand.
BRUTUS   What now, Lucilius, is Cassius near?
LUCILIUS   He is at hand, and Pindarus is come
    To do you salutation from his master.   5
BRUTUS   He greets me well. Your master, Pindarus,
    In his own change, or by ill officers,
    Hath given me some worthy cause to wish
    Things done, undone: but if he be at hand
    I shall be satisfied.
PINDARUS   I do not doubt   10
    But that my noble master will appear
    Such as he is, full of regard and honour.
BRUTUS   He is not doubted. A word, Lucilius,
    How he received you: let me be resolved.
LUCILIUS   With courtesy and with respect enough,   15
    But not with such familiar instances
    Nor with such free and friendly conference
    As he hath used of old.
BRUTUS   Thou hast described
    A hot friend, cooling. Ever note, Lucilius,
    When love begins to sicken and decay   20
    It useth an enforced ceremony.
    There are no tricks in plain and simple faith:
    But hollow men, like horses hot at hand,
    Make gallant show and promise of their mettle:
                                [Low march within]
    But when they should endure the bloody spur,   25
    They fall their crests, and like deceitful jades
    Sink in the trial. Comes his army on?
LUCILIUS
    They mean this night in Sardis to be quartered.
    The greater part, the horse in general,
    Are come with Cassius.

          Enter CASSIUS *and his powers.*

BRUTUS   Hark, he is arrived.   30
    March gently on to meet him.
CASSIUS   Stand ho.
BRUTUS   Stand ho. Speak the word along.
1 SOLDIER   Stand.
2 SOLDIER   Stand.
3 SOLDIER   Stand.   35
CASSIUS
    Most noble brother, you have done me wrong.
BRUTUS   Judge me, you gods; wrong I mine enemies?

And if not so, how should I wrong a brother?

CASSIUS

40 Brutus, this sober form of yours hides wrongs,
And when you do them –

BRUTUS   Cassius, be content.
Speak your griefs softly. I do know you well.
Before the eyes of both our armies here,
Which should perceive nothing but love from us,
45 Let us not wrangle. Bid them move away:
Then in my tent, Cassius, enlarge your griefs
And I will give you audience.

CASSIUS   Pindarus,
Bid our commanders lead their charges off
A little from this ground.

50 BRUTUS   Lucilius, do you the like, and let no man
Come to our tent till we have done our conference.
Let Lucius and Titinius guard our door.

Exeunt all but Brutus and Cassius.

4.3

CASSIUS
That you have wronged me doth appear in this:
You have condemned and noted Lucius Pella
For taking bribes here of the Sardians;
Wherein my letters, praying on his side
5 Because I knew the man, was slighted off.

BRUTUS   You wronged yourself to write in such a case.

CASSIUS   In such a time as this it is not meet
That every nice offence should bear his comment.

BRUTUS   Let me tell you, Cassius, you yourself
10 Are much condemned to have an itching palm,
To sell and mart your offices for gold
To undeservers.

CASSIUS   I, an itching palm?
You know that you are Brutus that speaks this,
Or, by the gods, this speech were else your last.

BRUTUS
15 The name of Cassius honours this corruption,
And chastisement doth therefore hide his head.

CASSIUS   Chastisement?

BRUTUS
Remember March, the Ides of March remember:
Did not great Julius bleed for justice' sake?
20 What villain touched his body, that did stab
And not for justice? What, shall one of us,
That struck the foremost man of all this world
But for supporting robbers: shall we now
Contaminate our fingers with base bribes,
25 And sell the mighty space of our large honours
For so much trash as may be grasped thus?
I had rather be a dog and bay the moon
Than such a Roman.

CASSIUS   Brutus, bait not me.
I'll not endure it. You forget yourself
30 To hedge me in. I am a soldier, I,
Older in practice, abler than yourself

To make conditions.

BRUTUS   Go to, you are not, Cassius.

CASSIUS   I am.

BRUTUS   I say you are not.

CASSIUS   Urge me no more. I shall forget myself. 35
Have mind upon your health. Tempt me no farther.

BRUTUS   Away, slight man!

CASSIUS   Is't possible?

BRUTUS   Hear me, for I will speak.
Must I give way and room to your rash choler?
Shall I be frighted when a madman stares? 40

CASSIUS   O ye gods, ye gods, must I endure all this?

BRUTUS
All this? Ay, more: fret till your proud heart break.
Go show your slaves how choleric you are,
And make your bondmen tremble. Must I budge?
Must I observe you? Must I stand and crouch 45
Under your testy humour? By the gods,
You shall digest the venom of your spleen
Though it do split you; for, from this day forth,
I'll use you for my mirth, yea for my laughter,
When you are waspish.

CASSIUS   Is it come to this? 50

BRUTUS   You say you are a better soldier:
Let it appear so. Make your vaunting true
And it shall please me well. For mine own part,
I shall be glad to learn of noble men.

CASSIUS
You wrong me every way: you wrong me, Brutus. 55
I said an elder soldier, not a better.
Did I say better?

BRUTUS   If you did, I care not.

CASSIUS
When Caesar lived he durst not thus have moved me.

BRUTUS
Peace, peace, you durst not so have tempted him.

CASSIUS   I durst not? 60

BRUTUS   No.

CASSIUS   What, durst not tempt him?

BRUTUS   For your life you durst not.

CASSIUS   Do not presume too much upon my love:
I may do that I shall be sorry for.

BRUTUS   You have done that you should be sorry for. 65
There is no terror, Cassius, in your threats:
For I am armed so strong in honesty
That they pass by me as the idle wind,
Which I respect not. I did send to you
For certain sums of gold, which you denied me, 70
For I can raise no money by vile means:
By heaven, I had rather coin my heart
And drop my blood for drachmas, than to wring
From the hard hands of peasants their vile trash
By any indirection. I did send 75
To you for gold to pay my legions,
Which you denied me: was that done like Cassius?
Should I have answered Caius Cassius so?
When Marcus Brutus grows so covetous,

80   To lock such rascal counters from his friends,
           Be ready gods with all your thunderbolts,
           Dash him to pieces!
CASSIUS   I denied you not.
BRUTUS   You did.
CASSIUS   I did not. He was but a fool
           That brought my answer back. Brutus hath rived my
             heart.
85   A friend should bear his friend's infirmities,
           But Brutus makes mine greater than they are.
BRUTUS   I do not, till you practise them on me.
CASSIUS   You love me not.
BRUTUS   I do not like your faults.
CASSIUS   A friendly eye could never see such faults.
90 BRUTUS   A flatterer's would not, though they do appear
           As huge as high Olympus.
CASSIUS   Come, Antony, and young Octavius, come,
           Revenge yourselves alone on Cassius,
           For Cassius is a-weary of the world:
95   Hated by one he loves, braved by his brother,
           Checked like a bondman; all his faults observed,
           Set in a notebook, learned and conned by rote
           To cast into my teeth. O I could weep
           My spirit from mine eyes! There is my dagger,
100   And here my naked breast: within, a heart
           Dearer than Pluto's mine, richer than gold.
           If that thou beest a Roman, take it forth.
           I that denied thee gold will give my heart.
           Strike as thou didst at Caesar: for I know,
105   When thou didst hate him worst, thou lov'dst him better
           Than ever thou lov'dst Cassius.
BRUTUS   Sheathe your dagger:
           Be angry when you will, it shall have scope:
           Do what you will, dishonour shall be humour.
           O Cassius, you are yoked with a lamb
110   That carries anger as the flint bears fire,
           Who, much enforced, shows a hasty spark
           And straight is cold again.
CASSIUS   Hath Cassius lived
           To be but mirth and laughter to his Brutus,
           When grief and blood ill-tempered vexeth him?
115 BRUTUS   When I spoke that, I was ill-tempered too.
CASSIUS   Do you confess so much? Give me your hand.
BRUTUS   And my heart too.
CASSIUS   O Brutus!
BRUTUS   What's the matter?
CASSIUS   Have you not love enough to bear with me,
           When that rash humour which my mother gave me
           Makes me forgetful?
120 BRUTUS   Yes, Cassius, and from henceforth
           When you are over-earnest with your Brutus,
           He'll think your mother chides, and leave you so.

Enter a Poet, LUCILIUS *and* TITINIUS.

POET   Let me go in to see the generals.
           There is some grudge between 'em; 'tis not meet
           They be alone.

LUCILIUS   You shall not come to them.   125
POET   Nothing but death shall stay me.
CASSIUS   How now? What's the matter?
POET   For shame, you generals, what do you mean?
           Love and be friends, as two such men should be,
           For I have seen more years, I'm sure, than ye.   130
CASSIUS   Ha, ha, how vildly doth this cynic rhyme.
BRUTUS   Get you hence, sirrah; saucy fellow, hence.
CASSIUS   Bear with him, Brutus, 'tis his fashion.
BRUTUS   I'll know his humour when he knows his time.
           What should the wars do with these jigging fools?   135
           Companion, hence.
CASSIUS   Away, away, be gone.   *Exit Poet.*
BRUTUS   Lucilius and Titinius, bid the commanders
           Prepare to lodge their companies tonight.
CASSIUS
           And come yourselves, and bring Messala with you
           Immediately to us.   *Exeunt Lucilius and Titinius.*
BRUTUS [*Calls.*]   Lucius! A bowl of wine.   140
CASSIUS   I did not think you could have been so angry.
BRUTUS   O Cassius, I am sick of many griefs.
CASSIUS   Of your philosophy you make no use
           If you give place to accidental evils.
BRUTUS   No man bears sorrow better. Portia is dead.   145
CASSIUS   Ha? Portia?
BRUTUS   She is dead.
CASSIUS   How scaped I killing when I crossed you so?
           O insupportable and touching loss!
           Upon what sickness?
BRUTUS   Impatient of my absence,   150
           And grief that young Octavius with Mark Antony
           Have made themselves so strong – for with her death
           That tidings came – with this she fell distract,
           And, her attendants absent, swallowed fire.
CASSIUS   And died so?
BRUTUS   Even so.
CASSIUS   O ye immortal gods!   155

Enter LUCIUS *with wine and tapers.*

BRUTUS   Speak no more of her: give me a bowl of wine.
           In this I bury all unkindness, Cassius.   *Drinks.*
CASSIUS   My heart is thirsty for that noble pledge.
           Fill, Lucius, till the wine o'er-swell the cup.
           I cannot drink too much of Brutus' love.   160

                           Exit Lucius.

Enter TITINIUS *and* MESSALA.

BRUTUS   Come in, Titinius. Welcome, good Messala.
           Now sit we close about this taper here
           And call in question our necessities.
CASSIUS   Portia, art thou gone?
BRUTUS   No more, I pray you.
           Messala, I have here received letters   165
           That young Octavius and Mark Antony
           Come down upon us with a mighty power,
           Bending their expedition toward Philippi.
MESSALA   Myself have letters of the selfsame tenor.

170	BRUTUS With what addition?
	MESSALA That by proscription and bills of outlawry
	Octavius, Antony and Lepidus
	Have put to death an hundred senators.
	BRUTUS Therein our letters do not well agree.
175	Mine speak of seventy senators that died
	By their proscriptions, Cicero being one.
	CASSIUS Cicero one?
	MESSALA Cicero is dead,
	And by that order of proscription.
	Had you your letters from your wife, my lord?
180	BRUTUS No, Messala.
	MESSALA Nor nothing in your letters writ of her?
	BRUTUS Nothing, Messala.
	MESSALA That methinks is strange.
	BRUTUS Why ask you? Hear you aught of her in yours?
	MESSALA No, my lord.
185	BRUTUS Now, as you are a Roman, tell me true.
	MESSALA Then like a Roman bear the truth I tell,
	For certain she is dead, and by strange manner.
	BRUTUS Why, farewell, Portia: we must die, Messala:
	With meditating that she must die once
190	I have the patience to endure it now.
	MESSALA
	Even so great men great losses should endure.
	CASSIUS I have as much of this in art as you,
	But yet my nature could not bear it so.
	BRUTUS Well, to our work alive. What do you think
195	Of marching to Philippi presently?
	CASSIUS I do not think it good.
	BRUTUS Your reason?
	CASSIUS This it is:
	'Tis better that the enemy seek us,
	So shall he waste his means, weary his soldiers,
	Doing himself offence, whilst we, lying still,
200	Are full of rest, defence and nimbleness.
	BRUTUS
	Good reasons must of force give place to better:
	The people 'twixt Philippi and this ground
	Do stand but in a forced affection,
	For they have grudged us contribution.
205	The enemy, marching along by them,
	By them shall make a fuller number up,
	Come on refreshed, new-added and encouraged;
	From which advantage shall we cut him off
	If at Philippi we do face him there,
	These people at our back.
210	CASSIUS Hear me, good brother.
	BRUTUS Under your pardon. You must note beside
	That we have tried the utmost of our friends,
	Our legions are brimful, our cause is ripe.
	The enemy increaseth every day;
215	We, at the height, are ready to decline.
	There is a tide in the affairs of men
	Which, taken at the flood, leads on to fortune:
	Omitted, all the voyage of their life
	Is bound in shallows and in miseries.

220	On such a full sea are we now afloat,
	And we must take the current when it serves,
	Or lose our ventures.
	CASSIUS Then with your will go on.
	We'll along ourselves, and meet them at Philippi.
	BRUTUS The deep of night is crept upon our talk,
225	And nature must obey necessity,
	Which we will niggard with a little rest.
	There is no more to say.
	CASSIUS No more. Good night.
	Early tomorrow will we rise, and hence.
	Enter LUCIUS.
	BRUTUS Lucius. My gown. *Exit Lucius.*
	Farewell, good Messala.
230	Good night, Titinius. Noble, noble Cassius,
	Good night, and good repose.
	CASSIUS O my dear brother,
	This was an ill beginning of the night.
	Never come such division 'tween our souls.
	Let it not, Brutus.
	Enter LUCIUS *with the gown.*
	BRUTUS Everything is well.
	CASSIUS Good night, my lord.
235	BRUTUS Good night, good brother.
	TITINIUS, MESSALA
	Good night, Lord Brutus.
	BRUTUS Farewell, every one.
	Exeunt Cassius, Titinius and Messala.
	Give me the gown. Where is thy instrument?
	LUCIUS
	Here in the tent.
	BRUTUS What, thou speak'st drowsily?
	Poor knave, I blame thee not; thou art o'erwatched.
240	Call Claudio and some other of my men.
	I'll have them sleep on cushions in my tent.
	LUCIUS Varrus and Claudio!
	Enter VARRUS *and* CLAUDIO.
	VARRUS Calls my lord?
	BRUTUS I pray you, sirs, lie in my tent and sleep.
245	It may be I shall raise you by and by
	On business to my brother Cassius.
	VARRUS
	So please you, we will stand and watch your pleasure.
	BRUTUS I will not have it so: lie down, good sirs.
	It may be I shall otherwise bethink me.
250	Look, Lucius, here's the book I sought for so:
	I put it in the pocket of my gown.
	LUCIUS I was sure your lordship did not give it me.
	BRUTUS Bear with me, good boy, I am much forgetful.
	Canst thou hold up thy heavy eyes awhile
255	And touch thy instrument a strain or two?
	LUCIUS Ay, my lord, an't please you.
	BRUTUS It does, my boy.
	I trouble thee too much, but thou art willing.

LUCIUS   It is my duty, sir.

BRUTUS   I should not urge thy duty past thy might.

260   I know young bloods look for a time of rest.

LUCIUS   I have slept, my lord, already.

BRUTUS   It was well done, and thou shalt sleep again.
   I will not hold thee long. If I do live,
   I will be good to thee.   [*Music, and a song*]

265   This is a sleepy tune: O murderous slumber!
   Layest thou thy leaden mace upon my boy
   That plays thee music? Gentle knave, good night:
   I will not do thee so much wrong to wake thee.
   If thou dost nod, thou break'st thy instrument;

270   I'll take it from thee; and, good boy, good night.
   Let me see, let me see: is not the leaf turned down
   Where I left reading? Here it is, I think.

Enter the Ghost *of Caesar.*

   How ill this taper burns. Ha! Who comes here?
   I think it is the weakness of mine eyes

275   That shapes this monstrous apparition.
   It comes upon me: art thou any thing?
   Art thou some god, some angel, or some devil,
   That mak'st my blood cold, and my hair to stare?
   Speak to me what thou art.

GHOST   Thy evil spirit, Brutus.

280 BRUTUS   Why com'st thou?

GHOST   To tell thee thou shalt see me at Philippi.

BRUTUS   Well: then I shall see thee again?

GHOST   Ay, at Philippi.

BRUTUS

   Why, I will see thee at Philippi then: *Exit Ghost.*

285   Now I have taken heart thou vanishest.
   Ill spirit, I would hold more talk with thee.
   Boy, Lucius, Varrus, Claudio, sirs, awake!
   Claudio!

LUCIUS   The strings, my lord, are false.

290 BRUTUS   He thinks he still is at his instrument.
   Lucius, awake.

LUCIUS   My lord?

BRUTUS

   Didst thou dream, Lucius, that thou so cried'st out?

LUCIUS   My lord, I do not know that I did cry.

295 BRUTUS   Yes, that thou didst. Didst thou see anything?

LUCIUS   Nothing, my lord.

BRUTUS   Sleep again, Lucius. Sirrah Claudio,
   Fellow, thou, awake!

VARRUS   My lord?

CLAUDIO   My lord?

BRUTUS   Why did you so cry out, sirs, in your sleep?

BOTH   Did we, my lord?

300 BRUTUS   Ay. Saw you anything?

VARRUS   No, my lord, I saw nothing.

CLAUDIO   Nor I, my lord.

BRUTUS   Go and commend me to my brother Cassius.
   Bid him set on his powers betimes before
   And we will follow.

BOTH   It shall be done, my lord.   *Exeunt.*

5.1   *Enter* OCTAVIUS, ANTONY *and their army.*

OCTAVIUS   Now, Antony, our hopes are answered.
   You said the enemy would not come down,
   But keep the hills and upper regions.
   It proves not so: their battles are at hand.
   They mean to warn us at Philippi here,   5
   Answering before we do demand of them.

ANTONY   Tut, I am in their bosoms and I know
   Wherefore they do it: they could be content
   To visit other places, and come down
   With fearful bravery, thinking by this face   10
   To fasten in our thoughts that they have courage.
   But 'tis not so.

Enter a Messenger.

MESSENGER   Prepare you, generals:
   The enemy comes on in gallant show.
   Their bloody sign of battle is hung out,
   And something to be done immediately.   15

ANTONY   Octavius, lead your battle softly on,
   Upon the left hand of the even field.

OCTAVIUS   Upon the right hand I. Keep thou the left.

ANTONY   Why do you cross me in this exigent?

OCTAVIUS   I do not cross you: but I will do so.   [*March*]   20

Drum. Enter BRUTUS, CASSIUS *and their army:*
   LUCILIUS, TITINIUS, MESSALA *and others.*

BRUTUS   They stand, and would have parley.

CASSIUS   Stand fast, Titinius. We must out and talk.

OCTAVIUS   Mark Antony, shall we give sign of battle?

ANTONY   No, Caesar, we will answer on their charge.
   Make forth, the generals would have some words.   25

OCTAVIUS [*to a Commander*]   Stir not until the signal.

BRUTUS   Words before blows: is it so, countrymen?

OCTAVIUS   Not that we love words better, as you do.

BRUTUS

   Good words are better than bad strokes, Octavius.

ANTONY

   In your bad strokes, Brutus, you give good words.   30
   Witness the hole you made in Caesar's heart,
   Crying, 'Long live! Hail, Caesar!'

CASSIUS   Antony,
   The posture of your blows are yet unknown;
   But, for your words, they rob the Hybla bees
   And leave them honeyless.

ANTONY   Not stingless too?   35

BRUTUS   O yes, and soundless too.
   For you have stol'n their buzzing, Antony,
   And very wisely threat before you sting.

ANTONY

   Villains! You did not so, when your vile daggers
   Hacked one another in the sides of Caesar.   40
   You showed your teeth like apes, and fawned like
     hounds,
   And bowed like bondsmen, kissing Caesar's feet;
   Whilst damned Caska, like a cur, behind

Struck Caesar in the neck. O you flatterers!

45 CASSIUS   Flatterers? Now, Brutus, thank yourself.
This tongue had not offended so today
If Cassius might have ruled.

OCTAVIUS
Come, come, the cause. If arguing makes us sweat,
The proof of it will turn to redder drops:
50 Look, I draw a sword against conspirators.
When think you that the sword goes up again?
Never till Caesar's three and thirty wounds
Be well avenged, or till another Caesar
Have added slaughter to the sword of traitors.

55 BRUTUS   Caesar, thou canst not die by traitors' hands
Unless thou bring'st them with thee.

OCTAVIUS   So I hope.
I was not born to die on Brutus' sword.

BRUTUS   O, if thou wert the noblest of thy strain,
Young man, thou couldst not die more honourable.

CASSIUS
60 A peevish schoolboy, worthless of such honour,
Joined with a masquer and a reveller.

ANTONY   Old Cassius still.

OCTAVIUS   Come, Antony, away.
Defiance, traitors, hurl we in your teeth.
If you dare fight today, come to the field;
65 If not, when you have stomachs.
                                   Exeunt Octavius, Antony and army.

CASSIUS
Why now, blow wind, swell billow and swim bark.
The storm is up and all is on the hazard.

BRUTUS   Ho, Lucilius, hark, a word with you.

LUCILIUS   My lord.   [*Brutus speaks apart to Lucilius.*]

CASSIUS   Messala.

MESSALA   What says my general?

70 CASSIUS   Messala,
This is my birthday: as this very day
Was Cassius born. Give me thy hand, Messala:
Be thou my witness that against my will
(As Pompey was) am I compelled to set
75 Upon one battle all our liberties.
You know that I held Epicurus strong
And his opinion: now I change my mind
And partly credit things that do presage.
Coming from Sardis, on our former ensign
80 Two mighty eagles fell and there they perched,
Gorging and feeding from our soldiers' hands,
Who to Philippi here consorted us:
This morning are they fled away and gone,
And in their steads do ravens, crows and kites
85 Fly o'er our heads and downward look on us
As we were sickly prey: their shadows seem
A canopy most fatal, under which
Our army lies, ready to give up the ghost.

MESSALA   Believe not so.

CASSIUS   I but believe it partly,
90 For I am fresh of spirit and resolved
To meet all perils very constantly.

BRUTUS [*Comes forward.*]   Even so, Lucilius.

CASSIUS   Now, most noble Brutus,
The gods today stand friendly, that we may,
Lovers in peace, lead on our days to age.
But since the affairs of men rest still incertain,   95
Let's reason with the worst that may befall.
If we do lose this battle, then is this
The very last time we shall speak together.
What are you then determined to do?

BRUTUS   Even by the rule of that philosophy   100
By which I did blame Cato for the death
Which he did give himself – I know not how,
But I do find it cowardly and vile,
For fear of what might fall, so to prevent
The time of life – arming myself with patience   105
To stay the providence of some high powers
That govern us below.

CASSIUS   Then, if we lose this battle,
You are contented to be led in triumph
Thorough the streets of Rome?

BRUTUS
No, Cassius, no: think not, thou noble Roman,   110
That ever Brutus will go bound to Rome.
He bears too great a mind. But this same day
Must end that work the Ides of March begun;
And whether we shall meet again, I know not:
Therefore our everlasting farewell take: 115
For ever and for ever farewell, Cassius.
If we do meet again, why, we shall smile;
If not, why then this parting was well made.

CASSIUS   For ever and for ever farewell, Brutus:
If we do meet again, we'll smile indeed;   120
If not, 'tis true this parting was well made.

BRUTUS   Why then, lead on. O that a man might know
The end of this day's business ere it come:
But it sufficeth that the day will end,
And then the end is known. Come ho, away.   *Exeunt.*   125

5.2   *Alarum. Enter* BRUTUS *and* MESSALA.

BRUTUS   Ride, ride, Messala, ride, and give these bills
Unto the legions on the other side.   [*Loud alarum*]
Let them set on at once, for I perceive
But cold demeanour in Octavius' wing,
And sudden push gives them the overthrow.   5
Ride, ride, Messala. Let them all come down.   *Exeunt.*

5.3   *Alarums. Enter* CASSIUS *and* TITINIUS.

CASSIUS   O look, Titinius, look, the villains fly:
Myself have to mine own turned enemy:
This ensign here of mine was turning back;
I slew the coward and did take it from him.

TITINIUS   O Cassius, Brutus gave the word too early,   5
Who having some advantage on Octavius
Took it too eagerly: his soldiers fell to spoil,
Whilst we by Antony are all enclosed.

Enter PINDARUS.

PINDARUS Fly further off, my lord, fly further off,
10   Mark Antony is in your tents, my lord:
     Fly, therefore, noble Cassius, fly far off.
CASSIUS   This hill is far enough. Look, look, Titinius,
     Are those my tents where I perceive the fire?
TITINIUS They are, my lord.
CASSIUS   Titinius, if thou lovest me,
15   Mount thou my horse and hide thy spurs in him,
     Till he have brought thee up to yonder troops
     And here again, that I may rest assured
     Whether yond troops are friend or enemy.
TITINIUS
     I will be here again, even with a thought.   *Exit.*
20 CASSIUS   Go, Pindarus, get higher on that hill;
     My sight was ever thick: regard, Titinius,
     And tell me what thou not'st about the field.
                              Exit Pindarus.
     This day I breathed first. Time is come round;
     And where I did begin, there shall I end.
25   My life is run his compass. Sirrah, what news?
PINDARUS [*above*]   O my lord!
CASSIUS   What news?
PINDARUS   Titinius is enclosed round about
     With horsemen, that make to him on the spur,
30   Yet he spurs on. Now they are almost on him.
     Now, Titinius. Now some light: O, he lights too.
     He's ta'en. [*Shout.*] And hark, they shout for joy.
CASSIUS   Come down, behold no more:
     O, coward that I am, to live so long,
35   To see my best friend ta'en before my face.

Enter PINDARUS.

     Come hither, sirrah.
     In Parthia did I take thee prisoner,
     And then I swore thee, saving of thy life,
     That whatsoever I did bid thee do,
40   Thou shouldst attempt it. Come now, keep thine oath.
     Now be a free man, and with this good sword
     That ran through Caesar's bowels, search this bosom.
     Stand not to answer: here, take thou the hilts,
     And when my face is covered, as 'tis now,
45   Guide thou the sword – Caesar, thou art revenged
     Even with the sword that killed thee.
         [*Pindarus kills him.*]
PINDARUS   So, I am free; yet would not so have been
     Durst I have done my will. O Cassius!
     Far from this country Pindarus shall run,
50   Where never Roman shall take note of him.   *Exit.*

Enter TITINIUS *and* MESSALA.

MESSALA   It is but change, Titinius: for Octavius
     Is overthrown by noble Brutus' power,
     As Cassius' legions are by Antony.
TITINIUS   These tidings will well comfort Cassius.
MESSALA   Where did you leave him?

TITINIUS   All disconsolate,   55
     With Pindarus his bondman, on this hill.
MESSALA   Is not that he that lies upon the ground?
TITINIUS   He lies not like the living. O, my heart!
MESSALA   Is not that he?
TITINIUS   No, this was he, Messala,
     But Cassius is no more. O setting sun: 60
     As in thy red rays thou dost sink tonight,
     So in his red blood Cassius' day is set.
     The sun of Rome is set. Our day is gone;
     Clouds, dews and dangers come: our deeds are done.
     Mistrust of my success hath done this deed.   65
MESSALA
     Mistrust of good success hath done this deed.
     O hateful Error, Melancholy's child,
     Why dost thou show to the apt thoughts of men
     The things that are not? Error, soon conceived,
     Thou never com'st unto a happy birth   70
     But kill'st the mother that engendered thee.
TITINIUS   What, Pindarus? Where art thou, Pindarus?
MESSALA   Seek him, Titinius, whilst I go to meet
     The noble Brutus, thrusting this report
     Into his ears. I may say thrusting it: 75
     For piercing steel and darts envenomed
     Shall be as welcome to the ears of Brutus
     As tidings of this sight.
TITINIUS   Hie you, Messala,
     And I will seek for Pindarus the while.   *Exit Messala.*
     Why didst thou send me forth, brave Cassius?   80
     Did I not meet thy friends, and did not they
     Put on my brows this wreath of victory
     And bid me give it thee? Didst thou not hear their
         shouts?
     Alas, thou hast misconstrued everything.
     But hold thee, take this garland on thy brow;   85
     Thy Brutus bid me give it thee, and I
     Will do his bidding. Brutus, come apace,
     And see how I regarded Caius Cassius.
     By your leave, gods. This is a Roman's part.
     Come, Cassius' sword, and find Titinius' heart.   90
         [*Dies.*]

     Alarum. Enter BRUTUS, MESSALA, Young CATO,
         STRATO, VOLUMNIUS *and* LUCILIUS.

BRUTUS   Where, where, Messala, doth his body lie?
MESSALA   Lo yonder, and Titinius mourning it.
BRUTUS   Titinius' face is upward.
CATO   He is slain.
BRUTUS   O Julius Caesar, thou art mighty yet.
     Thy spirit walks abroad and turns our swords   95
     In our own proper entrails.   [*Low alarums*]
CATO   Brave Titinius.
     Look whe'er he have not crowned dead Cassius.
BRUTUS   Are yet two Romans living such as these?
     The last of all the Romans, fare thee well:
     It is impossible that ever Rome   100
     Should breed thy fellow. Friends, I owe more tears

To this dead man than you shall see me pay.
I shall find time, Cassius: I shall find time.
Come therefore, and to Thasos send his body.
His funerals shall not be in our camp, 105
Lest it discomfort us. Lucilius, come,
And come, young Cato: let us to the field.
Labio and Flavio set our battles on.
'Tis three o'clock; and, Romans, yet ere night,
We shall try fortune in a second fight. *Exeunt.* 110

5.4   *Alarum. Enter* BRUTUS, MESSALA,
       Young CATO, LUCILIUS *and* FLAVIUS.

BRUTUS   Yet, countrymen: O yet, hold up your heads!
       Exit fighting, followed by Messala and Flavius.
CATO   What bastard doth not? Who will go with me?
I will proclaim my name about the field.
I am the son of Marcus Cato, ho!
A foe to tyrants and my country's friend. 5
I am the son of Marcus Cato, ho!

       Enter Soldiers *and fight.*

LUCILIUS   And I am Brutus, Marcus Brutus, I!
Brutus, my country's friend: know me for Brutus!
    [*Young Cato is killed.*]
O young and noble Cato, art thou down?
Why, now thou diest as bravely as Titinius, 10
And mayst be honoured, being Cato's son.
1 SOLDIER   Yield, or thou diest.
LUCILIUS   Only I yield to die.
There is so much that thou wilt kill me straight:
Kill Brutus and be honoured in his death.
1 SOLDIER   We must not: a noble prisoner! 15

       Enter ANTONY.

2 SOLDIER   Room, ho! Tell Antony, Brutus is ta'en.
1 SOLDIER   I'll tell the news. Here comes the general.
Brutus is ta'en, Brutus is ta'en, my lord.
ANTONY   Where is he?
LUCILIUS   Safe, Antony; Brutus is safe enough. 20
I dare assure thee that no enemy
Shall ever take alive the noble Brutus.
The gods defend him from so great a shame!
When you do find him, or alive or dead,
He will be found like Brutus, like himself. 25
ANTONY   This is not Brutus, friend, but, I assure you,
A prize no less in worth. Keep this man safe;
Give him all kindness. I had rather have
Such men my friends than enemies. Go on,
And see whe'er Brutus be alive or dead, 30
And bring us word unto Octavius' tent
How everything is chanced. *Exeunt.*

5.5   *Enter* BRUTUS, DARDANIUS, CLITUS,
       STRATO *and* VOLUMNIUS.

BRUTUS
Come, poor remains of friends, rest on this rock.

CLITUS   Statilius showed the torchlight, but, my lord,
He came not back. He is or ta'en or slain.
BRUTUS   Sit thee down, Clitus. Slaying is the word.
It is a deed in fashion. Hark thee, Clitus.   [*Whispers.*] 5
CLITUS   What, I, my lord? No, not for all the world.
BRUTUS   Peace, then. No words.
CLITUS   I'll rather kill myself.
BRUTUS   Hark thee, Dardanius.   [*Whispers.*]
DARDANIUS   Shall I do such a deed?
CLITUS   O Dardanius!
DARDANIUS   O Clitus! 10
CLITUS   What ill request did Brutus make to thee?
DARDANIUS   To kill him, Clitus. Look, he meditates.
CLITUS   Now is that noble vessel full of grief,
That it runs over even at his eyes.
BRUTUS   Come hither, good Volumnius, list a word. 15
VOLUMNIUS   What says my lord?
BRUTUS   Why this, Volumnius:
The ghost of Caesar hath appeared to me
Two several times by night: at Sardis once,
And this last night, here in Philippi fields:
I know my hour is come.
VOLUMNIUS   Not so, my lord. 20
BRUTUS   Nay, I am sure it is, Volumnius.
Thou seest the world, Volumnius, how it goes.
Our enemies have beat us to the pit.   [*Low alarums*]
It is more worthy to leap in ourselves
Than tarry till they push us. Good Volumnius, 25
Thou knowst that we two went to school together:
Even for that our love of old, I prithee
Hold thou my sword-hilts while I run on it.
VOLUMNIUS   That's not an office for a friend, my lord.
                          [*Alarum still*]
CLITUS   Fly, fly, my lord, there is no tarrying here. 30
BRUTUS   Farewell to you; and you; and you, Volumnius.
Strato, thou hast been all this while asleep:
Farewell to thee too, Strato. Countrymen:
My heart doth joy that yet in all my life
I found no man but he was true to me. 35
I shall have glory by this losing day
More than Octavius and Mark Antony
By this vile conquest shall attain unto.
So fare you well at once, for Brutus' tongue
Hath almost ended his life's history: 40
Night hangs upon mine eyes: my bones would rest,
That have but laboured to attain this hour.
                          [*Alarum. Cry within, 'Fly, fly, fly.'*]
CLITUS   Fly, my lord, fly!
BRUTUS   Hence; I will follow.
       Exeunt Clitus, Dardanius and Volumnius.
I prithee, Strato, stay thou by thy lord.
Thou art a fellow of a good respect: 45
Thy life hath had some smatch of honour in it.
Hold then my sword, and turn away thy face,
While I do run upon it. Wilt thou, Strato?
STRATO
Give me your hand first. Fare you well, my lord.

BRUTUS   Farewell, good Strato – [*Runs on his sword.*]

50   Caesar, now be still.
  I killed not thee with half so good a will.   [*Dies.*]

Alarm. Retreat. Enter ANTONY, OCTAVIUS, MESSALA,
                 LUCILIUS *and the army.*

OCTAVIUS   What man is that?
MESSALA
  My master's man. Strato, where is thy master?
STRATO   Free from the bondage you are in, Messala,

55   The conquerors can but make a fire of him:
  For Brutus only overcame himself,
  And no man else hath honour by his death.
LUCILIUS
  So Brutus should be found. I thank thee, Brutus,
  That thou hast proved Lucilius' saying true.

60   OCTAVIUS   All that served Brutus, I will entertain them.
  Fellow, wilt thou bestow thy time with me?
STRATO   Ay, if Messala will prefer me to you.

OCTAVIUS   Do so, good Messala.
MESSALA   How died my master, Strato?
STRATO   I held the sword and he did run on it.   65
MESSALA   Octavius, then take him to follow thee,
  That did the latest service to my master.
ANTONY   This was the noblest Roman of them all:
  All the conspirators save only he
  Did that they did in envy of great Caesar.   70
  He only, in a general honest thought
  And common good to all, made one of them.
  His life was gentle, and the elements
  So mixed in him that nature might stand up
  And say to all the world, 'This was a man!'   75
OCTAVIUS   According to his virtue let us use him,
  With all respect and rites of burial.
  Within my tent his bones tonight shall lie,
  Most like a soldier, ordered honourably.
  So call the field to rest, and let's away,   80
  To part the glories of this happy day.   *Exeunt omnes.*

King Edward III

King Edward III was first entered in the Stationers' Register by Cuthbert Burby as 'A book Intitled Edward the Third and the blacke prince their warres wth kinge Iohn of Fraunce' in December 1595, and published the following year as 'The Raigne of K: Edward the third'. The title-page of the first Quarto notes performances 'about the city of London', but identifies neither author nor acting company. The unnamed printer was Thomas Scarlet. Despite its absence from the First Folio, the play has been associated with Shakespeare since Edward Capell's edition of it in his *Prolusions* (1760). It is a play of two parts: the pursuit of (illicit) love (Scenes 2 and 3) – often referred to as the 'Countess scenes' – and the pursuit of war. It is the former that has been most often associated with Shakespeare's writings, particularly his poetry (*The Rape of Lucrece*, *Venus and Adonis* and the sonnets) and the plays of the early 1590s (*The Two Gentlemen of Verona*, *King Richard III* and the three parts of *King Henry VI*).

King Edward III dramatizes events of the Hundred Years War: the English victories at Sluys, Crécy and Poitiers, and the mid-fourteenth-century taking of Calais, using as its main sources Lord Berners's English version of the *Chronicles* of Jean Froissart (translated between 1521 and 1525 on the orders of Henry VIII) and the 1587 second edition of the *Chronicles* of Raphael Holinshed. The play creates a simple narrative of a just war against an unreasonable aggressor, contrasting English honour and chivalry with French over-confidence and pride. Balancing this is King Edward's infatuation with the Countess of Salisbury, whom he is called on to rescue from the boorish hands of the Scottish King David II while she defends the border castle of her absent husband, the Earl of Salisbury. The Earl meanwhile is fighting in Brittany on King Edward's behalf. Froissart's *Chronicles* are supplemented by William Painter's *The Palace of Pleasure* (1566–7) in providing material for the love plot. The play was reprinted in 1599, but its mockery of the Scots may have contributed to its disappearance after the succession of the Scottish King James VI to the English throne in 1603. The earliest explicit reference to

performance of a play about Edward III is in Thomas Heywood's *An Apology for Actors* (where a Countess of Salisbury appears in a list of women extolled for their virtues). This was published in 1612 but written five or more years earlier and therefore does not imply a Jacobean revival. No clear evidence is known of a revival of the play between the 1590s and the late nineteenth century.

The religious civil war in France after 1589 provided the main context and motivation for the play: it served as a call-to-arms for Englishmen to join the troops in France in Elizabeth I's bid to support the Protestant cause under the French King Henry IV. While the play's jingoistic tone may be uncomfortable – particularly for modern directors – evidence for its popularity at the end of the sixteenth century includes the play's full representation in John Bodenham's *Bel-vedére* (1600), an anthology of quotations from current poetry and plays, and publication of a ballad of 'King Edward and the Countess of Salisbury' written by Thomas Deloney between 1596 and 1599. In the late nineteenth century the Countess scenes were the play's main source of interest, leading to William Poel's adaptation of them into a one-act play, *Love's Constancy* (performed from the 1890s and published *c.* 1906). Selective interest in the play continued in the twentieth century with John Barton's inclusion of the scene of King Edward and his confidant, Lodwick, in *The Hollow Crown, An Entertainment by and about the Kings and Queens of England* (1962). From the 1980s onwards, the number of full productions of the play increased, particularly as Shakespeare's name became more confidently attached, either as co-author or, perhaps more likely, reviser. Anthony Clark directed it for the Royal Shakespeare Company in 2002. *King Edward III* has now been performed worldwide (and translated into several languages), and the play's chivalric values, with its emphasis on the importance of oaths, honour and fidelity, have acquired fresh resonance.

The Arden text is based on the 1596 First Quarto. At 8.109–13, braces contain lines very likely to be misplaced.

THE ENGLISH AND THEIR SUPPORTERS

KING EDWARD	*the third, of England*
QUEEN Philippa	*his wife*
PRINCE EDWARD	*Prince of Wales, their son*
Earl of DERBY	
Earl of WARWICK	
COUNTESS of Salisbury	*his daughter*
Earl of SALISBURY	*her husband*
Sir William MONTAGUE	*his nephew*
Lord AUDLEY	
Lord PERCY	
LODWICK	*King Edward's secretary*
John COPELAND	*Northern squire*
Two SQUIRES	
HERALD	
Sir Robert of ARTOIS	*created Earl of Richmond*
Lord MONTFORT	*Duke of Brittany*
GOBIN de Grâce	*a French prisoner*

THE SCOTS

KING DAVID	*the second, of Scotland*
Sir William DOUGLAS	
Two MESSENGERS	

THE FRENCH AND THEIR SUPPORTERS

KING JOHN	*of France*
Prince CHARLES, Duke of Normandy	*his eldest son*
Prince PHILIP	*his youngest son*
Duke of LORRAINE	
VILLIERS	*a noble French prisoner*
MARINER	
Three FRENCHMEN	
CITIZEN	
WOMAN with two children	
CAPTAIN	
Six POOR FRENCHMEN	} *of Calais*
Six CITIZENS	
Three HERALDS	
CAPTAIN	*in King John's army*
King of BOHEMIA	
POLONIAN CAPTAIN	

Four English Heralds; Danish, Muscovite and Polish Soldiers; French and English Soldiers; Drummers, Trumpeters

King Edward III

Sc. 1   *Enter* KING EDWARD, DERBY,   [1.1]
         PRINCE EDWARD, AUDLEY,
         WARWICK *and* ARTOIS.

KING EDWARD
  Robert of Artois, banished though thou be
  From France, thy native country, yet with us
  Thou shalt retain as great a seigniory,
  For we create thee Earl of Richmond here.
  And now go forwards with our pedigree:
  Who next succeeded Philip le Beau?
ARTOIS   Three sons of his, which all successfully
  Did sit upon their father's regal throne,
  Yet died and left no issue of their loins.
KING EDWARD   But was my mother sister unto those?
ARTOIS   She was, my lord, and only Isabel
  Was all the daughters that this Philip had,
  Whom afterward your father took to wife;
  And from the fragrant garden of her womb
  Your gracious self, the flower of Europe's hope,
  Derived is inheritor to France.
  But note the rancour of rebellious minds:
  When thus the lineage of Beau was out,
  The French obscured your mother's privilege
  And, though she were the next of blood, proclaimed
  John of the house of Valois now their king.
  The reason was they say the realm of France,
  Replete with princes of great parentage,
  Ought not admit a governor to rule
  Except he be descended of the male:
  And that's the special ground of their contempt,
  Wherewith they study to exclude your grace.
KING EDWARD
  But they shall find that forged ground of theirs
  To be but dusty heaps of brittle sand.
ARTOIS   Perhaps it will be thought a heinous thing
  That I, a Frenchman, should discover this;
  But, heaven I call to record of my vows,
  It is not hate, nor any private wrong,
  But love unto my country and the right
  Provokes my tongue thus lavish in report.
  You are the lineal watchman of our peace,
  And John of Valois indirectly climbs.
  What then should subjects but embrace their king;
  And wherein may our duty more be seen
  Than striving to rebate a tyrant's pride
  And place the true shepherd of our commonwealth?
KING EDWARD
  This counsel, Artois, like to fruitful showers,
  Hath added growth unto my dignity;
  And by the fiery vigour of thy words
  Hot courage is engendered in my breast,
  Which heretofore was racked in ignorance
  But now doth mount with golden wings of fame,
  And will approve fair Isabel's descent
  Able to yoke their stubborn necks with steel

That spurn against my sovereignty in France.   50
                    [*Sound a horn.*]
  A messenger. Lord Audley, know from whence.

    Enter a messenger, LORRAINE.

AUDLEY
  The Duke of Lorraine, having crossed the seas,
  Entreats he may have conference with your highness.
KING EDWARD
  Admit him, lords, that we may hear the news.
  Say, Duke of Lorraine, wherefore art thou come?   55
LORRAINE
  The most renowned prince, King John of France,
  Doth greet thee, Edward, and by me commands
  That for so much as by his liberal gift
  The Guyenne dukedom is entailed to thee
  Thou do him lowly homage for the same.   60
  And for that purpose here I summon thee
  Repair to France within these forty days,
  That there, according as the custom is,
  Thou mayst be sworn true liegeman to our King;
  Or else thy title in that province dies,   65
  And he himself will repossess the place.
KING EDWARD   See how occasion laughs me in the face;
  No sooner minded to prepare for France
  But straight I am invited – nay, with threats,
  Upon a penalty enjoined to come.   70
  'Twere but a childish part to say him nay.
  Lorraine, return this answer to thy lord:
  I mean to visit him, as he requests.
  But how? Not servilely disposed to bend,
  But like a conqueror to make him bow.   75
  His lame unpolished shifts are come to light,
  And truth hath pulled the visor from his face
  That set a gloss upon his arrogance.
  Dare he command a fealty in me?
  Tell him the crown that he usurps is mine,   80
  And where he sets his foot he ought to kneel.
  'Tis not a petty dukedom that I claim
  But all the whole dominions of the realm,
  Which if with grudging he refuse to yield,
  I'll take away those borrowed plumes of his   85
  And send him naked to the wilderness.
LORRAINE
  Then, Edward, here, in spite of all thy lords,
  I do pronounce defiance to thy face.
PRINCE EDWARD
  Defiance, Frenchman? We rebound it back,
  Even to the bottom of thy master's throat.   90
  And, be it spoke with reverence of the King,
  My gracious father, and these other lords,
  I hold thy message but as scurrilous,
  And him that sent thee like the lazy drone
  Crept up by stealth unto the eagle's nest,   95
  From whence we'll shake him with so rough a storm
  As others shall be warned by his harm.

WARWICK   Bid him leave off the lion's case he wears,
    Lest meeting with the lion in the field
100   He chance to tear him piecemeal for his pride.

ARTOIS   The soundest counsel I can give his grace
    Is to surrender ere he be constrained.
    A voluntary mischief hath less scorn
    Than when reproach with violence is borne.

105 LORRAINE   Degenerate traitor! Viper to the place
    Where thou was fostered in thine infancy,
    Bear'st thou a part in this conspiracy?

KING EDWARD
    Lorraine, behold the sharpness of this steel.
    [*He draws his sword.*]
    Fervent desire that sits against my heart
110   Is far more thorny-pricking than this blade,
    That with the nightingale I shall be scarred
    As oft as I dispose myself to rest
    Until my colours be displayed in France.
    This is thy final answer; so, be gone.

115 LORRAINE   It is not that, nor any English brave,
    Afflicts me so as doth his poisoned view
    That is most false should most of all be true.   *Exit.*

KING EDWARD
    Now, lords, our fleeting bark is under sail,
    Our gage is thrown and war is soon begun,
120   But not so quickly brought unto an end.

        Enter MONTAGUE.

    But wherefore comes Sir William Montague?
    How stands the league between the Scot and us?

MONTAGUE
    Cracked and dissevered, my renowned lord.
    The treacherous King no sooner was informed
125   Of your withdrawing of your army back,
    But straight forgetting of his former oath
    He made invasion on the bordering towns.
    Berwick is won, Newcastle spoiled and lost,
    And now the tyrant hath begirt with siege
130   The castle of Roxborough, where enclosed
    The Countess Salisbury is like to perish.

KING EDWARD
    That is thy daughter, Warwick, is it not,
    Whose husband hath in Brittain served so long
    About the planting of Lord Montfort there?

135 WARWICK   It is, my lord.

KING EDWARD
    Ignoble David, hast thou none to grieve
    But silly ladies with thy threatening arms?
    But I will make you shrink your snaily horns.
    First therefore, Audley, this shall be thy charge:
140   Go levy footmen for our wars in France.
    And Ned, take muster of our men-at-arms,
    In every shire elect a several band;
    Let them be soldiers of a lusty spirit
    Such as dread nothing but dishonour's blot.
145   Be wary therefore, since we do commence
    A famous war, and with so mighty a nation.

    Derby, be thou ambassador for us
    Unto our father-in-law, the Earl of Hainault;
    Make him acquainted with our enterprise,
    And likewise will him, with our own allies   150
    That are in Flanders, to solicit too
    The Emperor of Almain in our name.
    Myself, whilst you are jointly thus employed,
    Will with these forces that I have at hand
    March, and once more repulse the traitorous Scot.   155
    But, sirs, be resolute; we shall have wars
    On every side – and Ned, thou must begin
    Now to forget thy study and thy books
    And ure thy shoulders to an armour's weight.

PRINCE EDWARD
    As cheerful sounding to my youthful spleen   160
    This tumult is of war's increasing broils
    As at the coronation of a king
    The joyful clamours of the people are,
    When '*Ave Caesar*' they pronounce aloud.
    Within this school of honour I shall learn   165
    Either to sacrifice my foes to death
    Or in a rightful quarrel spend my breath.

KING EDWARD
    Then cheerfully forward, each a several way;
    In great affairs 'tis naught to use delay.   *Exeunt.*

Sc. 2   *Enter the* COUNTESS *above.*   **[1.2]**

COUNTESS   Alas, how much in vain my poor eyes gaze
    For succour that my sovereign should send.
    Ah, cousin Montague, I fear thou wants
    The lively spirit sharply to solicit
    With vehement suit the King in my behalf: 5
    Thou dost not tell him what a grief it is
    To be the scornful captive to a Scot,
    Either to be wooed with broad untuned oaths
    Or forced by rough insulting barbarism;
    Thou dost not tell him if he here prevail   10
    How much they will deride us in the north,
    And in their vile, uncivil, skipping jigs
    Bray forth their conquest and our overthrow,
    Even in the barren, bleak and fruitless air.

        Enter KING DAVID, DOUGLAS *and* LORRAINE.

    I must withdraw: the everlasting foe   15
    Comes to the wall. I'll closely step aside
    And list their babble, blunt and full of pride.
    [*Withdraws.*]

KING DAVID
    My lord of Lorraine, to our brother of France
    Commend us, as the man in Christendom
    That we most reverence and entirely love.   20
    Touching your embassage, return and say
    That we with England will not enter parley,
    Nor never make fair weather or take truce,
    But burn their neighbour towns and so persist
    With eager roads beyond their city York.   25

And never shall our bonny riders rest –
Nor rusting canker have the time to eat
Their light-borne snaffles nor their nimble spurs –
Nor lay aside their jacks of gimmaled mail,
30 Nor hang their staves of grained Scottish ash
In peaceful wise upon their city walls,
Nor from their buttoned tawny leathern belts
Dismiss their biting whinyards, till your King
Cry out, 'Enough! Spare England now for pity.'
35 Farewell, and tell him that you leave us here,
Before this castle. Say you came from us
Even when we had it yielded to our hands.

LORRAINE   I take my leave, and fairly will return
Your acceptable greeting to my King.   *Exit.*

40 KING DAVID   Now, Douglas, to our former task again,
For the division of this certain spoil.

DOUGLAS   My liege, I crave the lady and no more.

KING DAVID
Nay, soft ye, sir, first I must make my choice,
And first I do bespeak her for myself.

45 DOUGLAS   Why then, my liege, let me enjoy her jewels.

KING DAVID
Those are her own, still liable to her,
And who inherits her hath those withal.

Enter a Scots Messenger, *in haste.*

1 MESSENGER
My liege, as we were pricking on the hills
To fetch in booty, marching hitherward
50 We might descry a mighty host of men.
The sun reflecting on the armour showed
A field of plate, a wood of picks advanced.
Bethink your highness speedily herein:
An easy march within four hours will bring
55 The hindmost rank unto this place, my liege.

KING DAVID
Dislodge, dislodge, it is the King of England.

DOUGLAS [*Calls.*]
Jemmy, my man, saddle my bonny black.

KING DAVID
Mean'st thou to fight, Douglas? We are too weak.

DOUGLAS   I know it well, my liege, and therefore fly.

COUNTESS [*Comes forward.*]
60 My lords of Scotland, will ye stay and drink?

KING DAVID
She mocks at us, Douglas. I cannot endure it.

COUNTESS
Say, good my lord, which is he must have the lady,
And which her jewels? I am sure, my lords,
Ye will not hence till you have shared the spoils.

KING DAVID
65 She heard the messenger, and heard our talk,
And now that comfort makes her scorn at us.

Enter another Messenger.

2 MESSENGER
Arm, my good lord! O, we are all surprised!

COUNTESS   After the French ambassador, my liege,
And tell him that you dare not ride to York.
Excuse it that your bonny horse is lame.   70

KING DAVID   She heard that too. Intolerable grief!
Woman, farewell, although I do not stay.   *Exeunt Scots.*

COUNTESS   'Tis not for fear, and yet you run away.
O happy comfort, welcome to our house.
The confident and boisterous-boasting Scot,   75
That swore before my walls they would not back
For all the armed power of this land,
With faceless fear, that ever turns his back,
Turned hence again the blasting north-east wind
Upon the bare report and name of arms.   80

Enter MONTAGUE.

O summer's day, see where my cousin comes.

MONTAGUE   How fares my aunt? We are not Scots.
Why do you shut your gates against your friends?

COUNTESS   Well may I give a welcome, cousin, to thee,
For thou com'st well to chase my foes from hence.   85

MONTAGUE
The King himself is come in person hither.
Dear aunt, descend and gratulate his highness.

COUNTESS   How may I entertain his majesty
To show my duty and his dignity?   *Exit.*

Enter KING EDWARD, WARWICK, ARTOIS *with*
LODWICK *and others.*

KING EDWARD
What, are the stealing foxes fled and gone   90
Before we could uncouple at their heels?

WARWICK   They are, my liege, but with a cheerful cry,
Hot hounds and hardy chase them at the heels.

Enter COUNTESS, *below.*

KING EDWARD
This is the Countess, Warwick, is it not?

WARWICK
Even she, my liege, whose beauty tyrants' fear,   95
As a May blossom with pernicious winds,
Hath sullied, withered, overcast and done.

KING EDWARD
Hath she been fairer, Warwick, than she is?

WARWICK   My gracious King, fair is she not at all
If that herself were by to stain herself   100
As I have seen her when she was herself.

KING EDWARD [*aside*]
What strange enchantment lurked in those her eyes
When they excelled this excellence they have,
That now her dim decline hath power to draw
My subject eyes from piercing majesty   105
To gaze on her with doting admiration?

COUNTESS [*Kneels.*]
In duty lower than the ground I kneel,
And for my dull knees bow my feeling heart
To witness my obedience to your highness
With many millions of a subject's thanks   110

For this your royal presence, whose approach
Hath driven war and danger from my gate.
KING EDWARD   Lady, stand up.   [*She rises.*]
                      I come to bring thee peace,
However thereby I have purchased war.
115 COUNTESS   No war to you, my liege – the Scots are gone,
And gallop home toward Scotland with their hate.
KING EDWARD [*aside*]
    Lest yielding here I pine in shameful love –
    Come, we'll pursue the Scots. Artois, away.
COUNTESS   A little while, my gracious sovereign, stay,
120   And let the power of a mighty king
    Honour our roof. My husband in the wars,
    When he shall hear it, will triumph for joy.
    Then, dear my liege, now niggard not thy state;
    Being at the wall, enter our homely gate.
KING EDWARD
125   Pardon me, Countess, I will come no near;
    I dreamed tonight of treason, and I fear.
COUNTESS   Far from this place let ugly treason lie.
KING EDWARD [*aside*]
    No farther off than her conspiring eye,
    Which shoots infected poison in my heart
130   Beyond repulse of wit or cure of art.
    Now in the sun alone it doth not lie
    With light to take light from a mortal eye,
    For here two day-stars that mine eyes would see
    More than the sun steals mine own light from me.
135   Contemplative desire, desire to be
    In contemplation that may master thee. –
    Warwick, Artois, to horse and let's away.
COUNTESS
    What might I speak to make my sovereign stay?
KING EDWARD [*aside*]
    What needs a tongue to such a speaking eye,
140   That more persuades than winning oratory?
COUNTESS   Let not thy presence, like the April sun,
    Flatter our earth and suddenly be done;
    More happy do not make our outward wall
    Than thou wilt grace our inner house withal.
145   Our house, my liege, is like a country swain,
    Whose habit rude and manners blunt and plain
    Presageth naught, yet inly beautified
    With bounty's riches and fair, hidden pride;
    For where the golden ore doth buried lie,
150   The ground, undecked with nature's tapestry,
    Seems barren, sere, unfertile, fruitless, dry,
    And where the upper turf of earth doth boast
    His pride, perfumes and parti-coloured coast,
    Delve there, and find this issue and their pride
155   To spring from ordure and corruption's side.
    But to make up my all-too-long compare,
    These ragged walls no testimony are
    What is within, but like a cloak doth hide
    From weather's waste the under garnished pride.
160   More gracious than my terms can let thee be,
    Entreat thyself to stay awhile with me.

KING EDWARD [*aside*]
    As wise as fair. What fond fit can be heard
    When wisdom keeps the gate as beauty's guard? –
    Countess, albeit my business urgeth me,
    It shall attend while I attend on thee.   165
    Come on, my lords, here will I host tonight.
                     Exeunt all but Lodwick.
LODWICK   [2.1]
    I might perceive his eye in her eye lost,
    His ear to drink her sweet tongue's utterance,
    And changing passions, like inconstant clouds
    That rack upon the carriage of the winds,   170
    Increase and die in his disturbed cheeks.
    Lo, when she blushed, even then did he look pale,
    As if her cheeks by some enchanted power
    Attracted had the cherry blood from his;
    Anon, with reverent fear when she grew pale,   175
    His cheeks put on their scarlet ornaments,
    But no more like her oriental red
    Than brick to coral or live things to dead.
    Why did he then thus counterfeit her looks?
    If she did blush, 'twas tender modest shame,   180
    Being in the sacred presence of a king;
    If he did blush, 'twas red immodest shame,
    To vail his eyes amiss, being a king;
    If she looked pale, 'twas silly woman's fear,
    To bear herself in presence of a king;   185
    If he looked pale, it was with guilty fear,
    To dote amiss being a mighty king.
    Then Scottish wars, farewell. I fear 'twill prove
    A lingering English siege of peevish love.

              Enter KING EDWARD.

    Here comes his highness, walking all alone.   190
KING EDWARD
    She is grown more fairer far since I came hither,
    Her voice more silver every word than other,
    Her wit more fluent. What a strange discourse
    Unfolded she of David and his Scots:
    'Even thus', quoth she, 'he spake', and then spoke
        broad,   195
    With epithets and accents of the Scot,
    But somewhat better than the Scot could speak,
    'And thus', quoth she, and answered then herself –
    For who could speak like her? But she herself
    Breathes from the wall an angel's note from heaven   200
    Of sweet defiance to her barbarous foes.
    When she would talk of peace, methinks her tongue
    Commanded war to prison; when of war,
    It wakened Caesar from his Roman grave
    To hear war beautified by her discourse.   205
    Wisdom is foolishness but in her tongue,
    Beauty a slander but in her fair face,
    There is no summer but in her cheerful looks
    Nor frosty winter but in her disdain.
    I cannot blame the Scots that did besiege her,   210
    For she is all the treasure of our land;

But call them cowards that they ran away
Having so rich and fair a cause to stay.
Art thou there, Lodwick? Give me ink and paper.

215 LODWICK   I will, my liege.
KING EDWARD
And bid the lords hold on their play at chess,
For we will walk and meditate alone.

LODWICK   I will, my sovereign.   *Exit.*

KING EDWARD   This fellow is well read in poetry
220 And hath a lusty and persuasive spirit.
I will acquaint him with my passion,
Which he shall shadow with a veil of lawn
Through which the queen of beauty's queen shall see
Herself the ground of my infirmity.

Enter LODWICK.

225 Hast thou pen, ink and paper ready, Lodwick?
LODWICK   Ready, my liege.
KING EDWARD   Then in the summer arbour sit by me,
Make it our council house or cabinet.
Since green our thoughts, green be the conventicle
230 Where we will ease us by disburdening them.
Now, Lodwick, invocate some golden muse
To bring thee hither an enchanted pen,
That may for sighs set down true sighs indeed
Talking of grief to make thee ready groan;
235 And, when thou writ'st of tears, encouch the word
Before and after with such sweet laments
That it may raise drops in a Tartar's eye,
And make a flint-heart Scythian pitiful –
For so much moving hath a poet's pen.
240 Then if thou be a poet, move thou so,
And be enriched by thy sovereign's love;
For if the touch of sweet concordant strings
Could force attendance in the ears of hell,
How much more shall the strains of poets' wit
245 Beguile and ravish soft and human minds?
LODWICK   To whom, my lord, shall I direct my style?
KING EDWARD
To one that shames the fair and sots the wise,
Whose body is an abstract or a brief
Contains each general virtue in the world.
250 Better than 'beautiful' thou must begin,
Devise for fair a fairer word than 'fair',
And every ornament that thou wouldst praise,
Fly it a pitch above the soar of praise.
For flattery fear thou not to be convicted,
255 For were thy admiration ten times more,
Ten times ten thousand more the worth exceeds
Of that thou art to praise thy praise's worth.
Begin. I will to contemplate the while.
Forget not to set down how passionate,
260 How heart-sick and how full of languishment
Her beauty makes me.
LODWICK   Write I to a woman?
KING EDWARD
What beauty else could triumph over me,

Or who but women do our love-lays greet?
What, think'st thou I did bid thee praise a horse?
265 LODWICK   Of what condition or estate she is
'Twere requisite that I should know, my lord.
KING EDWARD   Of such estate that hers is as a throne
And my estate the footstool where she treads.
Then mayst thou judge what her condition is
270 By the proportion of her mightiness.
Write on, while I peruse her in my thoughts.
Her voice to music, or the nightingale –
To music every summer-leaping swain
Compares his sunburnt lover when she speaks.
275 And why should I speak of the nightingale?
The nightingale sings of adulterate wrong,
And that compared is too satirical;
For sin, though sin, would not be so esteemed,
But rather virtue sin, sin virtue deemed.
280 'Her hair, far softer than the silkworm's twist,
Like to a flattering glass doth make more fair
The yellow amber' – 'Like a flattering glass'
Comes in too soon, for writing of her eyes
I'll say that like a glass they catch the sun,
285 And thence the hot reflection doth rebound
Against my breast and burns my heart within.
Ah, what a world of descant makes my soul
Upon this voluntary ground of love!
Come, Lodwick, hast thou turned thy ink to gold?
290 If not, write but in letters capital
My mistress' name, and it will gild thy paper.
Read, Lodwick, read.
Fill thou the empty hollows of mine ears
With the sweet hearing of thy poetry.
295 LODWICK   I have not to a period brought her praise.
KING EDWARD   Her praise is as my love, both infinite,
Which apprehend such violent extremes
That they disdain an ending period.
Her beauty hath no match but my affection,
Hers more than most, mine most, and more than
        more –   300
Hers more to praise than tell the sea by drops,
Nay, more than drop the massy earth by sands
And sand by sand print them in memory.
Then wherefore talk'st thou of a period
To that which craves unended admiration?   305
Read, let us hear.
LODWICK
More fair and chaste than is the queen of shades, –
KING EDWARD
That line hath two faults, gross and palpable.
Compar'st thou her to the pale queen of night,
Who being set in dark seems therefore light?   310
What is she when the sun lifts up his head
But like a fading taper, dim and dead?
My love shall brave the eye of heaven at noon
And, being unmasked, outshine the golden sun!
LODWICK   What is the other fault, my sovereign lord?   315
KING EDWARD   Read o'er the line again.

LODWICK   *More fair and chaste –*

KING EDWARD   I did not bid thee talk of chastity,
    To ransack so the treasure of her mind,
    For I had rather have her chased than chaste.
320   Out with the moon line, I will none of it –
    And let me have her likened to the sun:
    Say she hath thrice more splendour than the sun,
    That her perfections emulates the sun,
    That she breeds sweets as plenteous as the sun,
325   That she doth thaw cold winter like the sun,
    That she doth cheer fresh summer like the sun,
    That she doth dazzle gazers like the sun,
    And in this application to the sun
    Bid her be free and general as the sun,
330   Who smiles upon the basest weed that grows
    As lovingly as on the fragrant rose.
    Let's see what follows that same moonlight line.

LODWICK
    More fair and chaste than is the queen of shades,
    More bold in constancy –

KING EDWARD   'In constancy'? Than who?
335 LODWICK   *– than Judith was.*

KING EDWARD
    O monstrous line! Put in the next a sword
    And I shall woo her to cut off my head.
    Blot, blot, good Lodwick. Let us hear the next.

LODWICK   There's all that yet is done.

KING EDWARD
340   I thank thee then thou hast done little ill,
    But what is done is passing, passing ill.
    No, let the captain talk of boisterous war,
    The prisoner of immured dark constraint,
    The sick man best sets down the pangs of death,
345   The man that starves the sweetness of a feast,
    The frozen soul the benefit of fire,
    And every grief his happy opposite.
    Love cannot sound well but in lovers' tongues.
    Give me the pen and paper, I will write.

Enter COUNTESS.

350   But soft, here comes the treasurer of my spirit.
    Lodwick, thou knowst not how to draw a battle;
    These wings, these flankers and these squadrons
    Argue in thee defective discipline.
    Thou shouldst have placed this here, this other here.

COUNTESS
355   Pardon my boldness, my thrice-gracious lord.
    Let my intrusion here be called my duty,
    That comes to see my sovereign how he fares.

KING EDWARD [*to Lodwick*]
    Go, draw the same; I tell thee in what form.

LODWICK   I go.   *Exit.*
360 COUNTESS   Sorry I am to see my liege so sad.
    What may thy subject do to drive from thee
    Thy gloomy consort, sullen melancholy?

KING EDWARD   Ah, lady, I am blunt and cannot strew
    The flowers of solace in a ground of shame.

    Since I came hither, Countess, I am wronged.   365

COUNTESS   Now God forbid that any in my house
    Should think my sovereign wrong. Thrice-gentle King,
    Acquaint me with thy cause of discontent.

KING EDWARD   How near then shall I be to remedy?

COUNTESS   As near, my liege, as all my woman's power   370
    Can pawn itself to buy thy remedy.

KING EDWARD
    If thou speak'st true, then have I my redress.
    Engage thy power to redeem my joys
    And I am joyful, Countess; else I die.

COUNTESS   I will, my liege.

KING EDWARD   Swear, Countess, that thou wilt.   375

COUNTESS   By heaven, I will.

KING EDWARD   Then take thyself a little way aside
    And tell thyself a king doth dote on thee.
    Say that within thy power it doth lie
    To make him happy, and that thou hast sworn   380
    To give him all the joy within thy power.
    Do this, and tell me when I shall be happy.

COUNTESS   All this is done, my thrice-dread sovereign.
    That power of love that I have power to give
    Thou hast, with all devout obedience.   385
    Employ me how thou wilt in proof thereof.

KING EDWARD
    Thou hear'st me say that I do dote on thee.

COUNTESS   If on my beauty, take it if thou canst –
    Though little, I do prize it ten times less;
    If on my virtue, take it if thou canst,   390
    For virtue's store by giving doth augment;
    Be it on what it will that I can give
    And thou canst take away, inherit it.

KING EDWARD   It is thy beauty that I would enjoy.

COUNTESS   O, were it painted I would wipe it off   395
    And dispossess myself to give it thee;
    But, sovereign, it is soldered to my life,
    Take one, and both, for like an humble shadow
    It haunts the sunshine of my summer's life.

KING EDWARD
    But thou mayst lend it me to sport withal.   400

COUNTESS   As easy may my intellectual soul
    Be lent away, and yet my body live,
    As lend my body, palace to my soul,
    Away from her and yet retain my soul.
    My body is her bower, her court, her abbey,   405
    And she an angel, pure, divine, unspotted.
    If I should lend her house, my lord, to thee,
    I kill my poor soul and my poor soul me.

KING EDWARD
    Didst thou not swear to give me what I would?

COUNTESS   I did, my liege, so what you would I could.   410

KING EDWARD
    I wish no more of thee than thou mayst give,
    Nor beg I do not but I rather buy –
    That is thy love – and for that love of thine,
    In rich exchange I tender to thee mine.

COUNTESS But that your lips were sacred, my lord,   415
You would profane the holy name of love.
That love you offer me you cannot give,
For Caesar owes that tribute to his queen;
That love you beg of me I cannot give,
For Sara owes that duty to her lord.   420
He that doth clip or counterfeit your stamp
Shall die, my lord; and will your sacred self
Commit high treason against the King of heaven
To stamp His image in forbidden metal,
Forgetting your allegiance and your oath?   425
In violating marriage' sacred law
You break a greater honour than yourself:
To be a king is of a younger house
Than to be married; your progenitor,
Sole-reigning Adam on the universe,   430
By God was honoured for a married man,
But not by Him anointed for a king.
It is a penalty to break your statutes,
Though not enacted with your highness' hand;
How much more to infringe the holy act   435
Made by the mouth of God, sealed with His hand.
I know my sovereign, in my husband's love
Who now doth loyal service in his wars,
Doth but to try the wife of Salisbury
Whether she will hear a wanton's tale or no.   440
Lest being therein guilty by my stay,
From that, not from my liege, I turn away.   *Exit.*

KING EDWARD
Whether is her beauty by her words divine,
Or are her words sweet chaplains to her beauty?
Like as the wind doth beautify a sail   445
And as a sail becomes the unseen wind,
So do her words her beauty, beauty words.
O, that I were a honey-gathering bee,
To bear the comb of virtue from this flower,
And not a poison-sucking, envious spider,   450
To turn the juice I take to deadly venom.
Religion is austere, and beauty gentle,
Too strict a guardian for so fair a ward.
O, that she were as is the air to me!
Why, so she is, for when I would embrace her,   455
This do I, and catch nothing but myself.
I must enjoy her, for I cannot beat
With reason and reproof fond love away.

Enter WARWICK.

Here comes her father. I will work with him
To bear my colours in this field of love.   460

WARWICK How is it that my sovereign is so sad?
May I, with pardon, know your highness' grief,
And that my old endeavour will remove it,
It shall not cumber long your majesty.

KING EDWARD
A kind and voluntary gift thou proffer'st   465
That I was forward to have begged of thee.
But O, thou world, great nurse of flattery,
Why dost thou tip men's tongues with golden words
And peise their deeds with weight of heavy lead
That fair performance cannot follow promise?   470
O, that a man might hold the heart's close book
And choke the lavish tongue when it doth utter
The breath of falsehood not charactered there.

WARWICK Far be it from the honour of my age
That I should owe bright gold and render lead;   475
Age is a cynic, not a flatterer.
I say again that if I knew your grief,
And that by me it may be lessened,
My proper harm should buy your highness' good.

KING EDWARD
These are the vulgar tenders of false men   480
That never pay the duty of their words.
Thou wilt not stick to swear what thou hast said,
But when thou knowst my grief's condition,
This rash-disgorged vomit of thy word
Thou wilt eat up again and leave me helpless.   485

WARWICK By heaven, I will not, though your majesty
Did bid me run upon your sword and die.

KING EDWARD
Say that my grief is no way medicinable
But by the loss and bruising of thine honour?

WARWICK If nothing but that loss may vantage you,   490
I would account that loss my vantage too.

KING EDWARD
Think'st that thou canst unswear thy oath again?

WARWICK I cannot, nor I would not if I could.

KING EDWARD
But if thou dost, what shall I say to thee?

WARWICK What may be said to any perjured villain   495
That breaks the sacred warrant of an oath.

KING EDWARD
What wilt thou say to one that breaks an oath?

WARWICK
That he hath broke his faith with God and man,
And from them both stands excommunicate.

KING EDWARD What office were it to suggest a man   500
To break a lawful and religious vow?

WARWICK An office for the devil, not for man.

KING EDWARD That devil's office must thou do for me,
Or break thy oath, or cancel all the bonds
Of love and duty 'twixt thyself and me.   505
And therefore, Warwick, if thou art thyself,
The lord and master of thy word and oath,
Go to thy daughter and in my behalf
Command her, woo her, win her anyways
To be my mistress and my secret love.   510
I will not stand to hear thee make reply;
Thy oath break hers, or let thy sovereign die.   *Exit.*

WARWICK O doting King! O detestable office!
Well may I tempt myself to wrong myself
When he hath sworn me by the name of God   515
To break a vow made by the name of God.
What if I swear by this right hand of mine
To cut this right hand off? The better way

Were to profane the idol than confound it.
520 But neither will I do: I'll keep mine oath,
And to my daughter make a recantation
Of all the virtue I have preached to her.
I'll say she must forget her husband Salisbury,
If she remember to embrace the King;
525 I'll say an oath may easily be broken,
But not so easily pardoned being broken;
I'll say it is true charity to love,
But not true love to be so charitable;
I'll say his greatness may bear out the shame,
530 But not his kingdom can buy out the sin;
I'll say it is my duty to persuade,
But not her honesty to give consent.

Enter COUNTESS.

See where she comes. Was never father had
Against his child an embassage so bad.
535 COUNTESS My lord and father, I have sought for you.
My mother and the peers importune you
To keep in presence of his majesty
And do your best to make his highness merry.
WARWICK [*aside*]
How shall I enter in this graceless errand?
540 I must not call her child, for where's the father
That will in such a suit seduce his child?
Then 'Wife of Salisbury' shall I so begin?
No, he's my friend, and where is found the friend
That will do friendship such endamagement? –
545 Neither my daughter nor my dear friend's wife,
I am not Warwick as thou think'st I am,
But an attorney from the court of hell
That thus have housed my spirit in his form
To do a message to thee from the King.
550 The mighty King of England dotes on thee.
He that hath power to take away thy life
Hath power to take thy honour; then consent
To pawn thine honour rather than thy life:
Honour is often lost and got again,
555 But life, once gone, hath no recovery.
The sun that withers hay doth nourish grass;
The King that would distain thee will advance thee.
The poets write that great Achilles' spear
Could heal the wound it made; the moral is,
560 What mighty men misdo, they can amend.
The lion doth become his bloody jaws
And grace his foragement by being mild
When vassal fear lies trembling at his feet;
The King will in his glory hide thy shame,
565 And those that gaze on him to find out thee
Will lose their eyesight looking in the sun.
What can one drop of poison harm the sea,
Whose hugy vastures can digest the ill
And make it lose his operation?
570 The King's great name will temper thy misdeeds
And give the bitter potion of reproach

A sugared, sweet and most delicious taste;
Besides, it is no harm to do the thing
Which without shame could not be left undone.
Thus have I in his majesty's behalf   575
Apparelled sin in virtuous sentences,
And dwell upon thy answer in his suit.
COUNTESS Unnatural besiege! Woe me, unhappy,
To have escaped the danger of my foes
And to be ten times worse envired by friends!   580
Hath he no means to stain my honest blood
But to corrupt the author of my blood
To be his scandalous and vile solicitor?
No marvel though the branch be then infected
When poison hath encompassed the root;   585
No marvel though the leprous infant die
When the stern dame envenometh the dug.
Why then, give sin a passport to offend
And youth the dangerous rein of liberty.
Blot out the strict forbidding of the law,   590
And cancel every canon that prescribes
A shame for shame, or penance for offence.
No, let me die, if his too boisterous will
Will have it so, before I will consent
To be an actor in his graceless lust.   595
WARWICK
Why, now thou speak'st as I would have thee speak,
And mark how I unsay my words again:
An honourable grave is more esteemed
Than the polluted closet of a king;
The greater man, the greater is the thing,   600
Be it good or bad, that he shall undertake;
An unreputed mote flying in the sun
Presents a greater substance than it is;
The freshest summer's day doth soonest taint
The loathed carrion that it seems to kiss;   605
Deep are the blows made with a mighty axe;
That sin doth ten times aggravate itself
That is committed in a holy place;
An evil deed done by authority
Is sin and subornation; deck an ape   610
In tissue, and the beauty of the robe
Adds but the greater scorn unto the beast.
A spacious field of reasons could I urge
Between his glory, daughter, and thy shame:
That poison shows worst in a golden cup;   615
Dark night seems darker by the lightning flash;
Lilies that fester smell far worse than weeds;
And every glory that inclines to sin,
The shame is treble by the opposite.
So leave I with my blessing in thy bosom,   620
Which then convert to a most heavy curse
When thou convert'st from honour's golden name
To the black faction of bed-blotting shame.
COUNTESS
I'll follow thee, and when my mind turns so,
My body sink my soul in endless woe.   *Exeunt.*   625

Sc. 3 *Enter at one door* DERBY [2.2]
from France, at another door
AUDLEY *with a Drum.*

DERBY Thrice-noble Audley, well encountered here.
How is it with our sovereign and his peers?

AUDLEY 'Tis full a fortnight since I saw his highness,
What time he sent me forth to muster men,
5 Which I accordingly have done, and bring them hither
In fair array before his majesty.
What news, my lord of Derby, from the Emperor?

DERBY As good as we desire: the Emperor
Hath yielded to his highness friendly aid,
10 And makes our King lieutenant-general
In all his lands and large dominions.
Then *via* for the spacious bounds of France!

AUDLEY
What, doth his highness leap to hear these news?

DERBY I have not yet found time to open them;
15 The King is in his closet, malcontent,
For what I know not, but he gave in charge
Till after dinner none should interrupt him.
The Countess Salisbury and her father Warwick,
Artois and all look underneath the brows.

AUDLEY
20 Undoubtedly then something is amiss. [*Flourish*]

DERBY The trumpets sound; the King is now abroad.

Enter KING EDWARD.

AUDLEY Here comes his highness.

DERBY Befall my sovereign all my sovereign's wish.

KING EDWARD [*aside*]
Ah, that thou wert a witch to make it so.

DERBY The Emperor greeteth you –

25 KING EDWARD [*aside*] Would it were the Countess.

DERBY And hath accorded to your highness' suit.

KING EDWARD [*aside*]
Thou liest. She hath not, but I would she had.

AUDLEY All love and duty to my lord the King.

KING EDWARD [*aside*]
Well, all but one is none. [*to Audley*] What news with
you?

30 AUDLEY I have, my liege, levied those horse and foot
According to your charge, and brought them hither.

KING EDWARD
Then let those foot trudge hence upon those horse
According to our discharge, and be gone.
Derby, I'll look upon the Countess' mind anon.

35 DERBY The Countess' mind, my liege?

KING EDWARD I mean the Emperor. Leave me alone.

AUDLEY [*aside to Derby*] What is his mind?

DERBY Let's leave him to his humour.
Exeunt all but the King.

KING EDWARD
Thus from the heart's abundance speaks the tongue:
Countess for Emperor – and indeed why not?
40 She is as imperator over me, and I to her

Am as a kneeling vassal that observes
The pleasure or displeasure of her eye.

Enter LODWICK.

What says the more than Cleopatra's match
To Caesar now?

LODWICK That yet, my liege, ere night
45 She will resolve your majesty. [*Drum within*]

KING EDWARD
What drum is this that thunders forth this march
To start the tender Cupid in my bosom?
Poor sheepskin, how it brawls with him that beateth it!
Go, break the thundering parchment bottom out,
50 And I will teach it to conduct sweet lines
Unto the bosom of a heavenly nymph,
For I will use it as my writing paper,
And so reduce him from a scolding drum
To be the herald and dear counsel bearer
55 Betwixt a goddess and a mighty king.
Go, bid the drummer learn to touch the lute,
Or hang him in the braces of his drum,
For now we think it an uncivil thing
To trouble heaven with such harsh resounds. Away.
Exit Lodwick.
60 The quarrel that I have requires no arms
But these of mine, and these shall meet my foe
In a deep march of penetrable groans.
My eyes shall be my arrows, and my sighs
Shall serve me as the vantage of the wind
65 To whirl away my sweet'st artillery.
Ah but, alas, she wins the sun of me,
For that is she herself, and thence it comes
That poets term the wanton warrior blind;
But love hath eyes as judgement to his steps,
70 Till too much loved glory dazzles them.

Enter LODWICK.

How now?

LODWICK
My liege, the drum that struck the lusty march
Stands with Prince Edward, your thrice-valiant son.
Exit.

Enter PRINCE EDWARD.

KING EDWARD [*aside*]
I see the boy. O, how his mother's face
75 Modelled in his corrects my strayed desire
And rates my heart and chides my thievish eye,
Who being rich enough in seeing her
Yet seeks elsewhere, and basest theft is that
Which cannot cloak itself on poverty. –
80 Now, boy, what news?

PRINCE EDWARD
I have assembled, my dear lord and father,
The choicest buds of all our English blood
For our affairs to France; and here we come
To take direction from your majesty.

85 KING EDWARD [*aside*]   Still do I see in him delineate
        His mother's visage: those his eyes are hers,
        Who looking wistly on me make me blush,
        For faults against themselves give evidence.
        Lust is a fire, and men like lanterns show
        Light lust within themselves even through
90   themselves.
        Away, loose silks of wavering vanity!
        Shall the large limit of fair Brittany
        By me be overthrown, and shall I not
        Master this little mansion of myself?
95   Give me an armour of eternal steel,
        I go to conquer kings, and shall I not then
        Subdue myself, and be my enemies' friend?
        It must not be. – Come, boy, forward, advance;
        Let's with our colours sweet the air of France.

                Enter LODWICK.

    LODWICK
100   My liege, the Countess, with a smiling cheer,
        Desires access unto your majesty.
    KING EDWARD [*aside*]
        Why, there it goes: that very smile of hers
        Hath ransomed captive France, and set the King,
        The Dauphin and the peers at liberty. –
105   Go, leave me, Ned, and revel with thy friends.
                                Exit Prince Edward.
        [*aside*] Thy mother is but black and thou, like her,
        Dost put it in my mind how foul she is. –
        Go, fetch the Countess hither in thy hand,
                                Exit Lodwick.
        And let her chase away these winter clouds,
110   For she gives beauty both to heaven and earth.
        The sin is more to hack and hew poor men
        Than to embrace in an unlawful bed
        The register of all rarieties
        Since leathern Adam till this youngest hour.

            Enter LODWICK, *with the* COUNTESS.

115   Go, Lodwick, put thy hand into thy purse;
        Play, spend, give, riot, waste, do what thou wilt,
        So thou wilt hence awhile and leave me here.
                                Exit Lodwick.
        Now, my soul's playfellow, art thou come
        To speak the more than heavenly word of 'yea'
120   To my objection in thy beauteous love?
    COUNTESS
        My father, on his blessing, hath commanded –
    KING EDWARD
        That thou shalt yield to me?
    COUNTESS   Ay, dear my liege, your due.
    KING EDWARD
        And that, my dearest love, can be no less
        Than right for right, and render love for love.
    COUNTESS
125   Than wrong for wrong, and endless hate for hate.
        But sith I see your majesty so bent

        That my unwillingness, my husband's love,
        Your high estate nor no respect respected
        Can be my help, but that your mightiness
        Will overbear and awe these dear regards,   130
        I bind my discontent to my content,
        And what I would not, I'll compel I will,
        Provided that yourself remove those lets
        That stand between your highness' love and mine.
    KING EDWARD
        Name them, fair Countess, and by heaven I will.   135
    COUNTESS   It is their lives that stand between our love
        That I would have choked up, my sovereign.
    KING EDWARD   Whose lives, my lady?
    COUNTESS   My thrice-loving liege,
        Your Queen, and Salisbury, my wedded husband,
        Who living have that title in our love   140
        That we cannot bestow but by their death.
    KING EDWARD   Thy opposition is beyond our law.
    COUNTESS   So is your desire. If the law
        Can hinder you to execute the one,
        Let it forbid you to attempt the other.   145
        I cannot think you love me as you say
        Unless you do make good what you have sworn.
    KING EDWARD
        No more; thy husband and the Queen shall die.
        Fairer thou art by far than Hero was,
        Beardless Leander not so strong as I: 150
        He swam an easy current for his love,
        But I will through a Hellespont of blood
        To arrive at Sestos, where my Hero lies.
    COUNTESS
        Nay, you'll do more, you'll make the river too
        With their heart-bloods that keep our love asunder, 155
        Of which my husband and your wife are twain.
    KING EDWARD
        Thy beauty makes them guilty of their death
        And gives in evidence that they shall die;
        Upon which verdict I, their judge, condemn them.
    COUNTESS [*aside*]
        O perjured beauty, more corrupted judge!   160
        When to the great Star-chamber o'er our heads
        The universal sessions calls to count
        This packing evil, we both shall tremble for it.
    KING EDWARD   What says my fair love, is she resolute?
    COUNTESS
        Resolute to be dissolved, and therefore this: 165
        Keep but thy word, great King, and I am thine.
        Stand where thou dost; I'll part a little from thee –
        And see how I will yield me to thy hands.
        Here by my side doth hang my wedding-knives:
        Take thou the one, and with it kill thy Queen,   170
        And learn by me to find her where she lies;
        And with this other I'll dispatch my love,
        Which now lies fast asleep within my heart.
        When they are gone, then I'll consent to love.
        Stir not, lascivious King, to hinder me;   175
        My resolution is more nimbler far

Than thy prevention can be in my rescue,
And if thou stir, I strike. Therefore stand still,
And hear the choice that I will put thee to:
180 Either swear to leave thy most unholy suit
And never henceforth to solicit me,
Or else, by heaven, this sharp-pointed knife
Shall stain thy earth with that which thou would stain –
My poor chaste blood. [*Kneels.*]
            Swear, Edward, swear,
185 Or I will strike, and die before thee here.
KING EDWARD
Even by that Power I swear that gives me now
The power to be ashamed of myself,
I never mean to part my lips again
In any words that tends to such a suit.
190 Arise, true English lady, whom our isle
May better boast of than ever Roman might
Of her whose ransacked treasury hath tasked
The vain endeavour of so many pens.
Arise, and be my fault thy honour's fame,
195 Which after ages shall enrich thee with.
    [*He raises her.*]
I am awaked from this idle dream.
[*Calls.*] Warwick, my son, Derby, Artois and Audley,
Brave warriors all, where are you all this while?

Enter all: PRINCE EDWARD, WARWICK, AUDLEY,
         DERBY *and* ARTOIS.

Warwick, I make thee Warden of the North.
200 Thou, Prince of Wales, and Audley, straight to sea,
Scour to Newhaven; some there stay for me.
Myself, Artois and Derby will through Flanders
To greet our friends there and to crave their aid.
This night will scarce suffice me to discover
205 My folly's siege against a faithful lover,
For ere the sun shall gild the eastern sky,
We'll wake him with our martial harmony. *Exeunt.*

Sc. 4   *Enter* KING JOHN *of France, his two sons,*   [3.1]
        CHARLES, *Duke of Normandy,*
       and PHILIP, *and the* Duke of LORRAINE.

KING JOHN   Here, till our navy of a thousand sail
Have made a breakfast to our foe by sea,
Let us encamp, to wait their happy speed.
Lorraine, what readiness is Edward in?
5 How hast thou heard that he provided is
Of martial furniture for this exploit?
LORRAINE   To lay aside unnecessary soothing
And not to spend the time in circumstance,
'Tis bruited for a certainty, my lord,
10 That he's exceeding strongly fortified.
His subjects flock as willingly to war
As if unto a triumph they were led.
CHARLES   England was wont to harbour malcontents,
Bloodthirsty and seditious Catilines,
15 Spendthrifts and such as gape for nothing else

But changing and alteration of the state;
And is it possible
That they are now so loyal in themselves?
LORRAINE   All but the Scot, who solemnly protests,
As heretofore I have informed his grace,   20
Never to sheathe his sword or take a truce.
KING JOHN
Ah, that's the anchorage of some better hope.
But on the other side, to think what friends
King Edward hath retained in Netherland
Among those ever-bibbing epicures –   25
Those frothy Dutchmen, puffed with double beer,
That drink and swill in every place they come –
Doth not a little aggravate mine ire;
Besides we hear the Emperor conjoins
And stalls him in his own authority.   30
But all the mightier that their number is,
The greater glory reaps the victory.
Some friends have we beside domestic power:
The stern Polonian and the warlike Dane,
The King of Boheme, and of Sicily,   35
Are all become confederates with us,
And as I think are marching hither apace.
                 [*Drums within*]
But soft, I hear the music of their drums,
By which I guess that their approach is near.

Enter the King of BOHEMIA *with Danes, and a* Polonian
     Captain *with other Soldiers another way.*

BOHEMIA
King John of France, as league and neighbourhood   40
Requires when friends are any way distressed,
I come to aid thee with my country's force.
POLONIAN CAPTAIN
And from great Moscow, fearful to the Turk,
And lofty Poland, nurse of hardy men,
I bring these servitors to fight for thee,   45
Who willingly will venture in thy cause.
KING JOHN
Welcome, Bohemian King, and welcome all;
This your great kindness I will not forget.
Besides your plentiful rewards in crowns
That from our treasury ye shall receive,   50
There comes a hare-brained nation decked in pride,
The spoil of whom will be a treble game.
And now my hope is full, my joy complete.
At sea we are as puissant as the force
Of Agamemnon in the haven of Troy;   55
By land with Xerxes we compare of strength,
Whose soldiers drank up rivers in their thirst.
Then Bayard-like, blind, overweening Ned,
To reach at our imperial diadem
Is either to be swallowed of the waves   60
Or hacked a'pieces when thou com'st ashore.

Enter a MARINER.

MARINER   Near to the coast I have described, my lord,

As I was busy in my watchful charge,
The proud armado of King Edward's ships,
65 Which at the first far off when I did ken
Seemed as it were a grove of withered pines;
But drawing near, their glorious bright aspect,
Their streaming ensigns wrought of coloured silk,
Like to a meadow full of sundry flowers
70 Adorns the naked bosom of the earth.
Majestical the order of their course,
Figuring the horned circle of the moon,
And on the top-gallant of the admiral,
And likewise all the handmaids of his train,
75 The arms of England and of France unite
Are quartered equally by heralds' art.
Thus titely carried with a merry gale
They plough the ocean hitherward amain.
KING JOHN   Dare he already crop the fleur-de-lys?
80 I hope, the honey being gathered thence,
He with the spider, afterward approached,
Shall suck forth deadly venom from the leaves.
But where's our navy? How are they prepared
To wing themselves against this flight of ravens?
MARINER
85 They, having knowledge brought them by the scouts,
Did break from anchor straight, and puffed with rage,
No otherwise than were their sails with wind,
Made forth, as when the empty eagle flies
To satisfy his hungry, griping maw.
KING JOHN
90 There's for thy news; return unto thy bark,
And if thou scape the bloody stroke of war
And do survive the conflict, come again
And let us hear the manner of the fight.
                                        Exit Mariner.
Mean space, my lords, 'tis best we be dispersed
95 To several places lest they chance to land:
First you, my lord, with your Bohemian troops,
Shall pitch your battles on the lower hand;
My eldest son, the Duke of Normandy,
Together with this aid of Muscovites,
100 Shall climb the higher ground another way;
Here in the middle coast, betwixt you both,
Philip, my youngest boy, and I will lodge.
So, lords, be gone and look unto your charge:
You stand for France, an empire fair and large.
                    Exeunt all but King John and Philip.
105 Now tell me, Philip, what is thy conceit
Touching the challenge that the English make?
PHILIP   I say, my lord, claim Edward what he can,
And bring he ne'er so plain a pedigree,
'Tis you are in possession of the crown,
110 And that's the surest point of all the law;
But were it not, yet ere he should prevail
I'll make a conduit of my dearest blood
Or chase those straggling upstarts home again.
KING JOHN
Well said, young Philip. Call for bread and wine,

That we may cheer our stomachs with repast   115
To look our foes more sternly in the face.
        [*Bread and wine brought in.*]
                            [*The battle heard afar off.*]
Now is begun the heavy day at sea.
Fight, Frenchmen, fight; be like the field of bears
When they defend their younglings in their caves.
Steer, angry Nemesis, the happy helm,   120
That with the sulphur battles of your rage
The English fleet may be dispersed and sunk.   [*Shot*]
PHILIP   O father, how this echoing cannon shot,
Like sweetest harmony, digests my cates.
KING JOHN
Now, boy, thou hear'st what thundering terror 'tis   125
To buckle for a kingdom's sovereignty.
The earth with giddy trembling when it shakes,
Or when the exhalations of the air
Breaks in extremity of lightning flash,
Affrights not more than kings when they dispose   130
To show the rancour of their high-swoll'n hearts.
                                            [*Retreat*]
Retreat is sounded; one side hath the worse.
O, if it be the French, sweet Fortune, turn,
And in thy turning change the froward winds,
That with advantage of a favouring sky   135
Our men may vanquish and the other fly.

                Enter MARINER.

My heart misgives. – Say, mirror of pale death,
To whom belongs the honour of this day.
Relate, I pray thee, if thy breath will serve,
The sad discourse of this discomfiture.   140
MARINER   I will, my lord.
My gracious sovereign, France hath ta'en the foil,
And boasting Edward triumphs with success.
These iron-hearted navies,
When last I was reporter to your grace,   145
Both full of angry spleen, of hope and fear,
Hasting to meet each other in the face,
At last conjoined, and by their admiral
Our admiral encountered many shot.
By this the other, that beheld these twain   150
Give earnest-penny of a further wrack,
Like fiery dragons took their haughty flight
And, likewise meeting, from their smoky wombs
Sent many grim ambassadors of death.
Then 'gan the day to turn to gloomy night,   155
And darkness did as well enclose the quick
As those that were but newly reft of life.
No leisure served for friends to bid farewell,
And if it had, the hideous noise was such
As each to other seemed deaf and dumb.   160
Purple the sea, whose channel filled as fast
With streaming gore that from the maimed fell
As did her gushing moisture break into
The cranny cleftures of the through-shot planks.
Here flew a head dissevered from the trunk,   165

There mangled arms and legs were tossed aloft
As when a whirlwind takes the summer dust
And scatters it in middle of the air.
Then might ye see the reeling vessels split
170 And tottering sink into the ruthless flood
Until their lofty tops were seen no more.
All shifts were tried both for defence and hurt;
And now the effect of valour and of force,
Of resolution and of cowardice,
175 Were lively pictured; how the one for fame,
The other by compulsion laid about.
Much did the *Nonpareille*, that brave ship,
So did the black snake of Boulogne, than which
A bonnier vessel never yet spread sail.
180 But all in vain; both sun, the wind and tide
Revolted all unto our foemen's side,
That we perforce were fain to give them way,
And they are landed. Thus my tale is done;
We have untimely lost, and they have won.
KING JOHN
185 Then rests there nothing but with present speed
To join our several forces all in one
And bid them battle ere they range too far.
Come, gentle Philip, let us hence depart;
This soldier's words have pierced thy father's heart.

Exeunt.

Sc. 5   *Enter two* Frenchmen, *a* Woman,   [3.2]
and two little Children, with baggage;
meet them another Citizen.

CITIZEN
Well met, my masters. How now, what's the news,
And wherefore are ye laden thus with stuff?
What, is it quarter day that you remove
And carry bag and baggage too?
1 FRENCHMAN
5 Quarter day? Ay, and quartering day, I fear.
Have ye not heard the news that flies abroad?
CITIZEN   What news?
2 FRENCHMAN
How the French navy is destroyed at sea,
And that the English army is arrived.
10 CITIZEN   What then?
1 FRENCHMAN
'What then', quoth you? Why, is't not time to fly
When envy and destruction is so nigh?
CITIZEN
Content thee, man, they are far enough from hence
And will be met, I warrant ye, to their cost
15 Before they break so far into the realm.
1 FRENCHMAN
Ay, so the grasshopper doth spend the time
In mirthful jollity till winter come,
And then too late he would redeem his time
When frozen cold hath nipped his careless head.
20 He that no sooner will provide a cloak

Than when he sees it doth begin to rain
May peradventure for his negligence
Be throughly washed when he suspects it not.
We that have charge, and such a train as this,
Must look in time to look for them and us,   25
Lest when we would we cannot be relieved.
CITIZEN   Belike you then despair of ill success
And think your country will be subjugate.
2 FRENCHMAN
We cannot tell; 'tis good to fear the worst.
CITIZEN   Yet rather fight than like unnatural sons   30
Forsake your loving parents in distress.
1 FRENCHMAN
Tush, they that have already taken arms
Are many fearful millions in respect
Of that small handful of our enemies.
But 'tis a rightful quarrel must prevail: 35
Edward is son unto our late King's sister,
Where John Valois is three degrees removed.
WOMAN   Besides, there goes a prophecy abroad,
Published by one that was a friar once,
Whose oracles have many times proved true;   40
And now he says the time will shortly come
Whenas a lion roused in the west
Shall carry hence the fleur-de-lys of France.
These, I can tell ye, and suchlike surmises
Strike many Frenchmen cold unto the heart.   45

Enter another Frenchman.

3 FRENCHMAN
Fly, countrymen and citizens of France!
Sweet-flowering peace, the root of happy life,
Is quite abandoned and expulsed the land,
Instead of whom ransacked, constraining war
Sits like to ravens upon your houses' tops.   50
Slaughter and mischief walk within your streets
And unrestrained make havoc as they pass,
The form whereof even now myself beheld
Upon this fair mountain whence I came;
For so far off as I directed mine eyes   55
I might perceive five cities all on fire,
Cornfields and vineyards burning like an oven,
And as the leaking vapour in the wind
Turned but aside, I likewise might discern
The poor inhabitants, escaped the flame,   60
Fall numberless upon the soldiers' pikes.
Three ways these dreadful ministers of wrath
Do tread the measures of their tragic march:
Upon the right hand comes the conquering King,
Upon the left his hot, unbridled son,   65
And in the midst their nation's glittering host,
All which though distant yet conspire in one
To leave a desolation where they come.
Fly, therefore, citizens, if you be wise,
Seek out some habitation further off.   70
Here if you stay your wives will be abused,
Your treasure shared before your weeping eyes.

Shelter you yourselves, for now the storm doth rise.
                    [*Drum afar off*]
Away, away! Methinks I hear their drums!
75   Ah, wretched France, I greatly fear thy fall,
Thy glory shaketh like a tottering wall.   *Exeunt.*

Sc. 6   *Enter* KING EDWARD *and the* Earl of   [3.3]
          DERBY *with Soldiers, and*
                GOBIN de Grâce.

KING EDWARD
Where is the Frenchman by whose cunning guide
We found the shallow of this river Somme
And had direction how to pass the sea?
GOBIN   Here, my good lord.
KING EDWARD
5   How art thou called? Tell me thy name.
GOBIN   Gobin de Grâce, if please your excellence.
KING EDWARD
Then, Gobin, for the service thou hast done
We here enlarge and give thee liberty,
And for recompense beside this good
10   Thou shalt receive five hundred marks in gold.
                    Exit Gobin.
I know not how we should have met our son,
Whom now in heart I wish I might behold.

          Enter ARTOIS.

ARTOIS
Good news, my lord, the Prince is hard at hand,
And with him comes Lord Audley and the rest,
15   Whom since our landing we could never meet.

Enter PRINCE EDWARD, Lord AUDLEY *and Soldiers.*

KING EDWARD
Welcome, fair Prince. How hast thou sped, my son,
Since thy arrival on the coast of France?
PRINCE EDWARD
Successfully, I thank the gracious heavens:
Some of their strongest cities we have won,
20   As Harfleur, Lô, Crotoy and Carentan,
And others wasted, leaving at our heels
A wide apparent field and beaten path
For solitariness to progress in;
For who in scorn refused our proffered peace
25   Endured the penalty of sharp revenge.
Yet those that would submit we kindly pardoned.
KING EDWARD
Ah, France, why shouldst thou be this obstinate
Against the kind embracement of thy friends?
How gently had we thought to touch thy breast
30   And set our foot upon thy tender mould,
But that in froward and disdainful pride
Thou, like a skittish and untamed colt,
Dost start aside and strike us with thy heels.
But tell me, Ned, in all thy warlike course
35   Hast thou not seen the usurping King of France?

PRINCE EDWARD
Yes, my good lord; and not two hours ago,
With full a hundred thousand fighting men,
Upon the one side with the river's bank
And on the other both his multitudes.
I feared he would have cropped our smaller power,   40
But happily perceiving your approach
He hath withdrawn himself to Crécy plains,
Whereas it seemeth by his good array
He means to bid us battle presently.
KING EDWARD
He shall be welcome; that's the thing we crave.   45

          Enter KING JOHN, CHARLES, Duke of
                Normandy, *and* LORRAINE, King of
                BOHEMIA, *young* PHILIP *and Soldiers.*

KING JOHN
Edward, know that John, the true King of France,
Musing thou shouldst encroach upon his land
And, in thy tyrannous proceeding, slay
His faithful subjects and subvert his towns,
Spits in thy face, and in this manner following   50
Upbraids thee with thine arrogant intrusion.
First, I condemn thee for a fugitive,
A thievish pirate and a needy mate,
One that hath either no abiding place
Or else, inhabiting some barren soil   55
Where neither herb or fruitful grain is had,
Dost altogether live by pilfering;
Next, insomuch thou hast infringed thy faith,
Broke league and solemn covenant made with me,
I hold thee for a false pernicious wretch;   60
And last of all, although I scorn to cope
With one so much inferior to myself,
Yet in respect thy thirst is all for gold,
Thy labour rather to be feared than loved,
To satisfy thy lust in either part   65
Here am I come, and with me have I brought
Exceeding store of treasure, pearl and coin.
Leave therefore now to persecute the weak,
And armed entering conflict with the armed
Let it be seen, 'mongst other petty thefts,   70
How thou canst win this pillage manfully.
KING EDWARD   If gall or wormwood have a pleasant taste
Then is thy salutation honey-sweet;
But as the one hath no such property,
So is the other most satirical.   75
Yet wot how I regard thy worthless taunts:
If thou have uttered them to foil my fame
Or dim the reputation of my birth,
Know that thy wolvish barking cannot hurt;
If slyly to insinuate with the world   80
And with a strumpet's artificial line
To paint thy vicious and deformed cause,
Be well assured the counterfeit will fade
And in the end thy foul defects be seen;
But if thou didst it to provoke me on –   85

As who should say I were but timorous
Or, coldly negligent, did need a spur –
Bethink thyself how slack I was at sea,
How since my landing I have won no towns,
Entered no further but upon the coast
And there have ever since securely slept.
But if I have been otherwise employed,
Imagine, Valois, whether I intend
To skirmish not for pillage but for the crown
Which thou dost wear, and that I vow to have,
Or one of us shall fall into his grave.

PRINCE EDWARD
Look not for cross invectives at our hands
Or railing execrations of despite.
Let creeping serpents hide in hollow banks
Sting with their tongues, we have remorseless swords,
And they shall plead for us and our affairs.
Yet thus much briefly, by my father's leave:
As all the immodest poison of thy throat
Is scandalous and most notorious lies,
And our pretended quarrel is truly just,
So end the battle when we meet today;
May either of us prosper and prevail
Or luckless-cursed receive eternal shame.

KING EDWARD
That needs no further question, and I know
His conscience witnesseth it is my right.
Therefore, Valois, say, wilt thou yet resign
Before the sickle's thrust into the corn
Or that enkindled fury turn to flame?

KING JOHN
Edward, I know what right thou hast in France,
And ere I basely will resign my crown
This champion field shall be a pool of blood
And all our prospect as a slaughter-house.

PRINCE EDWARD
Ay, that approves thee, tyrant, what thou art,
No father, king or shepherd of thy realm,
But one that tears her entrails with thy hands
And like a thirsty tiger suck'st her blood.

AUDLEY   You peers of France, why do you follow him
That is so prodigal to spend your lives?

CHARLES   Whom should they follow, aged impotent,
But he that is their true-born sovereign?

KING EDWARD
Upbraid'st thou him because within his face
Time hath engraved deep characters of age?
Know that these grave scholars of experience,
Like stiff-grown oaks, will stand immovable
When whirlwind quickly turns up younger trees.

DERBY   Was ever any of thy father's house
King but thyself before this present time?
Edward's great lineage by the mother's side
Five hundred years hath held the sceptre up.
Judge then, conspirators, by this descent,
Which is the true-born sovereign, this or that.

PHILIP   Father, range your battles, prate no more.

These English fain would spend the time in words,
That, night approaching, they might escape unfought.

KING JOHN
Lords, and my loving subjects, now's the time
That your intended force must bide the touch.
Therefore, my friends, consider this in brief:
He that you fight for is your natural king,
He against whom you fight a foreigner;
He that you fight for rules in clemency
And reins you with a mild and gentle bit,
He against whom you fight, if he prevail,
Will straight enthrone himself in tyranny,
Make slaves of you and with a heavy hand
Curtail and curb your sweetest liberty.
Then to protect your country and your king
Let but the haughty courage of your hearts
Answer the number of your able hands
And we shall quickly chase these fugitives.
For what's this Edward but a belly-god,
A tender and lascivious wantonness
That th'other day was almost dead for love?
And what, I pray you, is his goodly guard?
Such as but scant them of their chines of beef
And take away their downy featherbeds
And presently they are as resty-stiff
As 'twere a many over-ridden jades.
Then, Frenchmen, scorn that such should be your lords
And rather bind ye them in captive bands.

ALL FRENCHMEN
Vive le Roi! God save King John of France!

KING JOHN
Now on this plain of Crécy spread yourselves,
And, Edward, when thou dar'st, begin the fight.

KING EDWARD
We presently will meet thee, John of France.
                    Exeunt all French.
And, English lords, let us resolve the day
Either to clear us of that scandalous crime
Or be entombed in our innocence.
And, Ned, because this battle is the first
That ever yet thou fought'st in pitched field,
As ancient custom is of martialists,
To dub thee with the type of chivalry
In solemn manner we will give thee arms.
Come, therefore, heralds, orderly bring forth
A strong attirement for the Prince my son.

Enter four Heralds, bringing in a coat-armour,
a helmet, a lance and a shield.

[*Gives him coat-armour.*]
Edward Plantagenet, in the name of God,
As with this armour I impale thy breast,
So be thy noble, unrelenting heart
Walled in with flint of matchless fortitude,
That never base affections enter there.
Fight and be valiant, conquer where thou com'st.
Now follow, lords, and do him honour too.

DERBY [*Gives him helmet.*]
　Edward Plantagenet, Prince of Wales,
　As I do set this helmet on thy head,
　Wherewith the chamber of thy brain is fenced,
　So may thy temples with Bellona's hand
190　Be still adorned with laurel victory.
　Fight and be valiant, conquer where thou com'st.
AUDLEY [*Gives him lance.*]
　Edward Plantagenet, Prince of Wales,
　Receive this lance into thy manly hand;
　Use it in fashion of a brazen pen
195　To draw forth bloody stratagems in France
　And print thy valiant deeds in honour's book.
　Fight and be valiant, conquer where thou com'st.
ARTOIS [*Gives him shield.*]
　Edward Plantagenet, Prince of Wales,
　Hold, take this target, wear it on thy arm;
200　And may the view thereof, like Perseus' shield,
　Astonish and transform thy gazing foes
　To senseless images of meagre death.
　Fight and be valiant, conquer where thou com'st.
KING EDWARD
　Now wants there naught but knighthood, which
　　deferred
205　We leave till thou hast won it in the field.
PRINCE EDWARD
　My gracious father, and ye forward peers,
　This honour you have done me animates
　And cheers my green, yet-scarce-appearing strength
　With comfortable good-presaging signs,
210　No otherwise than did old Jacob's words
　Whenas he breathed his blessings on his sons.
　These hallowed gifts of yours when I profane,
　Or use them not to glory of my God,
　To patronage the fatherless and poor,
215　Or for the benefit of England's peace,
　Be numb my joints, wax feeble both mine arms,
　Wither my heart that like a sapless tree
　I may remain the map of infamy.
KING EDWARD
　Then thus our steeled battles shall be ranged:
220　The leading of the vaward, Ned, is thine,
　To dignify whose lusty spirit the more
　We temper it with Audley's gravity,
　That, courage and experience joined in one,
　Your manage may be second unto none;
225　For the main battles I will guide myself;
　And, Derby, in the rearward march behind.
　That orderly disposed and set in 'rray,
　Let us to horse, and God grant us the day.　　*Exeunt.*

Sc. 7　　*Alarum. Enter a many* Frenchmen *flying;*　[3.4]
　　after them PRINCE EDWARD *running; and exeunt.*
　　Then enter KING JOHN *and* Duke of LORRAINE.

KING JOHN
　O, Lorraine, say, what mean our men to fly?
　Our number is far greater than our foe's.

LORRAINE　The garrison of Genoese, my lord,
　That came from Paris, weary with their march,
　Grudging to be so suddenly employed,　　　　5
　No sooner in the forefront took their place
　But straight retiring so dismayed the rest
　As likewise they betook themselves to flight;
　In which, for haste to make a safe escape,
　More in the clustering throng are pressed to death　　10
　Than by the enemy a thousandfold.
KING JOHN　O hapless fortune! Let us yet assay
　If we can counsel some of them to stay.　　*Exeunt.*

Sc. 8　　*Enter* KING EDWARD *and* AUDLEY.　　[3.5]

KING EDWARD
　Lord Audley, whiles our son is in the chase,
　Withdraw our powers unto this little hill
　And here a season let us breathe ourselves.
AUDLEY　I will, my lord.　　　　*Exit. Sound retreat.*
KING EDWARD
　Just-dooming Heaven, whose secret providence　　5
　To our gross judgement is inscrutable,
　How are we bound to praise Thy wondrous works
　That hast this day given way unto the right,
　And made the wicked stumble at themselves.

Enter ARTOIS.

ARTOIS　Rescue, King Edward, rescue for thy son!　　10
KING EDWARD　Rescue, Artois? What, is he prisoner,
　Or by violence felled beside his horse?
ARTOIS　Neither, my lord, but narrowly beset
　With turning Frenchmen whom he did pursue,
　As 'tis impossible that he should scape,　　　　15
　Except your highness presently descend.
KING EDWARD
　Tut, let him fight. We gave him arms today,
　And he is labouring for a knighthood, man.

Enter DERBY.

DERBY
　The Prince, my lord, the Prince! O, succour him!
　He's close encompassed with a world of odds.　　20
KING EDWARD　Then will he win a world of honour too
　If he by valour can redeem him thence;
　If not, what remedy? We have more sons
　Than one to comfort our declining age.

Enter AUDLEY.

AUDLEY　Renowned Edward, give me leave, I pray,　　25
　To lead my soldiers where I may relieve
　Your grace's son, in danger to be slain.
　The snares of French like emmets on a bank
　Muster about him, whilst he, lion-like,
　Entangled in the net of their assaults,　　　　30
　Franticly rends and bites the woven toil;
　But all in vain, he cannot free himself.
KING EDWARD　Audley, content. I will not have a man,
　On pain of death, sent forth to succour him.

35 This is the day – ordained by destiny
To season his courage with those grievous thoughts –
That, if he breaketh out, Nestor's years on earth
Will make him savour still of this exploit.

DERBY   Ah, but he shall not live to see those days.

40 KING EDWARD   Why then, his epitaph is lasting praise.

AUDLEY   Yet, good my lord, 'tis too much wilfulness
To let his blood be spilt that may be saved.

KING EDWARD
Exclaim no more, for none of you can tell
Whether a borrowed aid will serve or no.

45 Perhaps he is already slain, or ta'en,
And dare a falcon when she's in her flight
And ever after she'll be haggard-like.
Let Edward be delivered by our hands
And still in danger he'll expect the like,

50 But if himself himself redeem from thence
He will have vanquished, cheerful, death and fear,
And ever after dread their force no more
Than if they were but babes or captive slaves.

AUDLEY   O, cruel father! Farewell Edward, then.

55 DERBY   Farewell, sweet Prince, the hope of chivalry.

ARTOIS   O, would my life might ransom him from death!
[Trumpets sound retreat.]

KING EDWARD   But soft, methinks I hear
The dismal charge of trumpets' loud retreat.
All are not slain, I hope, that went with him;

60 Some will return with tidings, good or bad.

Enter PRINCE EDWARD *in triumph, bearing in his
hand his shivered lance, his sword borne by a Soldier,
and the* King *of* BOHEMIA *borne before, wrapped in
the colours. They run and embrace him.*

AUDLEY   O joyful sight, victorious Edward lives!

DERBY   Welcome, brave Prince.

KING EDWARD   Welcome, Plantagenet.

PRINCE EDWARD
[Kneels and kisses his father's hand, then rises.]
First having done my duty as beseemed,
Lords, I regreet you all with hearty thanks.

65 And now behold, after my winter's toil,
My painful voyage on the boisterous sea
Of war's devouring gulfs and steely rocks,
I bring my freight unto the wished port,
My summer's hope, my travel's sweet reward;

70 And here with humble duty I present
This sacrifice, this first-fruit of my sword,
Cropped and cut down even at the gate of death:
The King of Boheme, father, whom I slew,
When thousands had entrenched me round about

75 And lay as thick upon my battered crest
As on an anvil with their ponderous glaives.
Yet marble courage still did underprop,
And when my weary arms with often blows –
Like the continual-labouring woodman's axe

80 That is enjoined to fell a load of oaks –
Began to falter, straight I would recover
My gifts you gave me, and my zealous vow,

And then new courage made me fresh again,
That in despite I carved my passage forth
And put the multitude to speedy flight. 85
Lo, thus hath Edward's hand filled your request
And done, I hope, the duty of a knight.

KING EDWARD
Ay, well thou hast deserved a knighthood, Ned;
*[Prince Edward kneels; King Edward takes the
Prince's sword from the Soldier.]*
And therefore with thy sword, yet reeking warm
With blood of those that sought to be thy bane, 90
Arise, Prince Edward, trusty knight-at-arms.
This day thou hast confounded me with joy
And proved thyself fit heir unto a king.

PRINCE EDWARD
Here is a note, my gracious lord, of those
That in this conflict of our foes were slain: 95
[Reads.] Eleven princes of esteem, fourscore barons, a
hundred and twenty knights and thirty thousand
common soldiers; and of our men, a thousand.

KING EDWARD
Our God be praised. Now, John of France, I hope
Thou knowst King Edward for no wantonness, 100
No lovesick cockney, nor his soldiers jades.
But which way is the fearful King escaped?

PRINCE EDWARD
Towards Poitiers, noble father, and his sons.

KING EDWARD
Ned, thou and Audley shall pursue them still.
Myself and Derby will to Calais straight 105
And there begirt that haven town with siege.
Now lies it on an upshot, therefore strike
And wistly follow whiles the game's on foot.
{What picture's this?

PRINCE EDWARD   A pelican, my lord,
Wounding her bosom with her crooked beak, 110
That so her nest of young ones might be fed
With drops of blood that issue from her heart:
The motto '*Sic et vos*, and so should you'.}   *Exeunt.*

Sc. 9   *Enter* Lord MONTFORT *with a coronet*   [4.1]
       in his hand, with him the Earl *of* SALISBURY.

MONTFORT   My lord of Salisbury, since by your aid
Mine enemy, Sir Charles of Blois, is slain,
And I again am quietly possessed
In Brittain's dukedom, know that I resolve,
For this kind furtherance of your King and you, 5
To swear allegiance to his majesty;
In sign whereof, receive this coronet.
Bear it unto him, and withal mine oath
Never to be but Edward's faithful friend.

SALISBURY   I take it, Montfort. Thus I hope ere long 10
The whole dominions of the realm of France
Will be surrendered to his conquering hand.
                   Exit Montfort.
Now if I knew but safely how to pass,
I would to Calais gladly meet his grace,

15   Whither I am by letters certified
    That he intends to have his host removed.
    It shall be so; this policy will serve.
    [*Calls*.] Ho, who's within? Bring Villiers to me.

Enter VILLIERS.

    Villiers, thou knowst thou art my prisoner,
20   And that I might for ransom if I would
    Require of thee a hundred thousand francs,
    Or else retain and keep thee captive still.
    But so it is that for a smaller charge
    Thou mayst be quit, an if thou wilt thyself,
25   And this it is: procure me but a passport
    Of Charles, the Duke of Normandy, that I
    Without restraint may have recourse to Calais
    Through all the countries where he hath to do –
    Which thou mayst easily obtain, I think,
30   By reason I have often heard thee say
    He and thou were students once together –
    And then thou shalt be set at liberty.
    How sayst thou, wilt thou undertake to do it?
VILLIERS   I will, my lord, but I must speak with him.
SALISBURY
35   Why so thou shalt. Take horse and post from hence.
    Only before thou goest, swear by thy faith
    That if thou canst not compass my desire
    Thou wilt return my prisoner back again,
    And that shall be sufficient warrant for me.
40 VILLIERS   To that condition I agree, my lord,
    And will unfeignedly perform the same.
SALISBURY   Farewell, Villiers.   *Exit Villiers.*
    Thus once I mean to try a Frenchman's faith.   *Exit.*

Sc. 10   *Enter* KING EDWARD *and* DERBY,   [4.2]
              with Soldiers.

KING EDWARD
    Since they refuse our proffered league, my lord,
    And will not ope their gates and let us in,
    We will entrench ourselves on every side,
    That neither victuals nor supply of men
5   May come to succour this accursed town.
    Famine shall combat where our swords are stopped.
DERBY   The promised aid that made them stand aloof
    Is now retired and gone another way;
    It will repent them of their stubborn will.

Enter six poor Frenchmen.

10   But what are these poor ragged slaves, my lord?
KING EDWARD
    Ask what they are; it seems they come from Calais.
DERBY   You wretched patterns of despair and woe,
    What, are you living men, or gliding ghosts
    Crept from your graves to walk upon the earth?
POOR FRENCHMAN
15   No ghosts, my lord, but men that breathe a life
    Far worse than is the quiet sleep of death.

    We are distressed poor inhabitants
    That long have been diseased, sick and lame;
    And now, because we are not fit to serve,
    The captain of the town hath thrust us forth,   20
    That so expense of victuals may be saved.
KING EDWARD
    A charitable deed no doubt, and worthy praise.
    But how do you imagine then to speed?
    We are your enemies. In such a case,
    We can no less but put ye to the sword,   25
    Since when we proffered truce it was refused.
POOR FRENCHMAN
    An if your grace no otherwise vouchsafe,
    As welcome death is unto us as life.
KING EDWARD
    Poor silly men, much wronged and more distressed.
    Go, Derby, go, and see they be relieved;   30
    Command that victuals be appointed them
    And give to every one five crowns apiece.
                  Exit Derby with poor men.
    The lion scorns to touch the yielding prey,
    And Edward's sword must flesh itself in such
    As wilful stubbornness hath made perverse.   35

Enter Lord PERCY.

    Lord Percy, welcome. What's the news in England?
PERCY
    The Queen, my lord, commends her to your grace,
    And from her highness and the lord vicegerent
    I bring this happy tidings of success:
    David of Scotland, lately up in arms,   40
    Thinking belike he soonest should prevail,
    Your highness being absent from the realm,
    Is by the fruitful service of your peers
    And painful travail of the Queen herself –
    That, big with child, was every day in arms –   45
    Vanquished, subdued and taken prisoner.
KING EDWARD
    Thanks, Percy, for thy news, with all my heart.
    What was he took him prisoner in the field?
PERCY   A squire, my lord, John Copeland is his name,
    Who since entreated by her majesty   50
    Denies to make surrender of his prize
    To any but unto your grace alone,
    Whereat the Queen is grievously displeased.
KING EDWARD
    Well then, we'll have a pursuivant dispatch
    To summon Copeland hither out of hand,   55
    And with him he shall bring his prisoner king.
PERCY   The Queen, my lord, herself by this' at sea
    And purposeth, as soon as wind will serve,
    To land at Calais and to visit you.
KING EDWARD
    She shall be welcome, and to wait her coming   60
    I'll pitch my tent near to the sandy shore.

Enter a French Captain.

CAPTAIN   The burgesses of Calais, mighty King,
   Have by a council willingly decreed
   To yield the town and castle to your hands,
65   Upon condition it will please your grace
   To grant them benefit of life and goods.
KING EDWARD
   They will so! Then belike they may command,
   Dispose, elect and govern as they list.
   No, sirrah, tell them since they did refuse
70   Our princely clemency at first proclaimed,
   They shall not have it now, although they would.
   I will accept of naught but fire and sword,
   Except within these two days six of them
   That are the wealthiest merchants in the town
75   Come naked all but for their linen shirts,
   With each a halter hanged about his neck,
   And prostrate yield themselves upon their knees
   To be afflicted, hanged or what I please;
   And so you may inform their masterships.
                 Exeunt all but Captain.
80 CAPTAIN   Why, this it is to trust a broken staff.
   Had we not been persuaded John our King
   Would with his army have relieved the town,
   We had not stood upon defiance so;
   But now 'tis past that no man can recall,
85   And better some do go to wrack than all.   *Exit.*

Sc. 11 *Enter* CHARLES, Duke of Normandy,   **[4.3]**
              and VILLIERS.

CHARLES
   I wonder, Villiers, thou shouldst importune me
   For one that is our deadly enemy.
VILLIERS   Not for his sake, my gracious lord, so much
   Am I become an earnest advocate
5   As that thereby my ransom will be quit.
CHARLES
   Thy ransom, man? Why need'st thou talk of that?
   Art thou not free? And are not all occasions
   That happen for advantage of our foes
   To be accepted of and stood upon?
10 VILLIERS   No, good my lord, except the same be just;
   For profit must with honour be commixed,
   Or else our actions are but scandalous.
   But, letting pass these intricate objections,
   Will't please your highness to subscribe or no?
15 CHARLES   Villiers, I will not nor I cannot do it.
   Salisbury shall not have his will so much
   To claim a passport how it please himself.
VILLIERS   Why, then I know the extremity, my lord:
   I must return to prison whence I came.
20 CHARLES   Return? I hope thou wilt not.
   What bird that hath escaped the fowler's gin
   Will not beware how she's ensnared again?
   Or what is he so senseless and secure
   That having hardly passed a dangerous gulf
25   Will put himself in peril there again?

VILLIERS   Ah, but it is mine oath, my gracious lord,
   Which I in conscience may not violate,
   Or else a kingdom should not draw me hence.
CHARLES   Thine oath? Why, that doth bind thee to abide.
   Hast thou not sworn obedience to thy prince?   30
VILLIERS   In all things that uprightly he commands:
   But either to persuade or threaten me
   Not to perform the covenant of my word
   Is lawless, and I need not to obey.
CHARLES   Why is it lawful for a man to kill   35
   And not to break a promise with his foe?
VILLIERS
   To kill, my lord, when war is once proclaimed,
   So that our quarrel be for wrongs received,
   No doubt is lawfully permitted us;
   But in an oath we must be well advised   40
   How we do swear, and when we once have sworn
   Not to infringe it, though we die therefore.
   Therefore, my lord, as willing I return
   As if I were to fly to paradise.   [*Offers to leave.*]
CHARLES   Stay, my Villiers. Thine honourable mind   45
   Deserves to be eternally admired.
   Thy suit shall be no longer thus deferred.
   Give me the paper, I'll subscribe to it:
     [*Signs the passport.*]
   And where tofore I loved thee as Villiers,
   Hereafter I'll embrace thee as myself.   50
   Stay, and be still in favour with thy lord.
VILLIERS   I humbly thank your grace. I must dispatch
   And send this passport first unto the Earl,
   And then I will attend your highness' pleasure.
CHARLES
   Do so, Villiers: *Exit Villiers.*
          and Charles, when he hath need,   55
   Be such his soldiers, howsoever he speed.

          Enter KING JOHN.

KING JOHN
   Come, Charles, and arm thee. Edward is entrapped,
   The Prince of Wales is fallen into our hands
   And we have compassed him; he cannot scape.
CHARLES   But will your highness fight today?   60
KING JOHN
   What else, my son, he's scarce eight thousand strong,
   And we are threescore thousand at the least.
CHARLES   I have a prophecy, my gracious lord,
   Wherein is written what success is like
   To happen us in this outrageous war;   65
   It was delivered me at Crécy's field,
   By one that is an aged hermit there.
   'When feathered fowl shall make thine army tremble,
   And flint-stones rise and break the battle 'rray,
   Then think on him that doth not now dissemble,   70
   For that shall be the hapless, dreadful day.
   Yet, in the end, thy foot thou shalt advance
   As far in England as thy foe in France.'
KING JOHN   By this it seems we shall be fortunate:

75 For as it is impossible that stones
    Should ever rise and break the battle 'rray
    Or airy fowl make men-in-arms to quake,
    So is it like we shall not be subdued.
    Or say this might be true, yet in the end,
80 Since he doth promise we shall drive him hence
    And forage their country as they have done ours,
    By this revenge that loss will seem the less.
    But all are frivolous fancies, toys and dreams.
    Once we are sure we have ensnared the son,
85 Catch we the father after how we can.   *Exeunt.*

Sc. 12   *Enter* PRINCE EDWARD,   [4.4]
                    AUDLEY *and others.*

PRINCE EDWARD
    Audley, the arms of death embrace us round,
    And comfort have we none, save that to die
    We pay sour earnest for a sweeter life.
    At Crécy field our clouds of warlike smoke
5   Choked up those French mouths and dissevered them;
    But now their multitudes of millions hide –
    Masking, as 'twere – the beauteous burning sun,
    Leaving no hope to us but sullen dark
    And eyeless terror of all-ending night.
10 AUDLEY   This sudden, mighty and expedient head
    That they have made, fair Prince, is wonderful.
    Before us in the valley lies the King,
    Vantaged with all that heaven and earth can yield,
    His party stronger battled than our whole;
15 His son, the braving Duke of Normandy,
    Hath trimmed the mountain on our right hand up
    In shining plate, that now the aspiring hill
    Shows like a silver quarry, or an orb,
    Aloft the which the banners, bannerets
20 And new-replenished pendants cuff the air
    And beat the winds that for their gaudiness
    Struggles to kiss them; on our left hand lies
    Philip, the younger issue of the King,
    Coating the other hill in such array
25 That all his gilded upright pikes do seem
    Straight trees of gold, the pendants pendent leaves,
    And their device of antique heraldry,
    Quartered in colours seeming sundry fruits,
    Makes it the orchard of the Hesperides;
30 Behind us too the hill doth bear his height,
    For like a half moon, opening but one way,
    It rounds us in – there at our backs are lodged
    The fatal crossbows, and the battle there
    Is governed by the rough Chatillion.
35 Then thus it stands: the valley for our flight
    The King binds in; the hills on either hand
    Are proudly royalized by his sons;
    And on the hill behind stands certain death
    In pay and service with Chatillion.
PRINCE EDWARD
40 Death's name is much more mighty than his deeds.

    Thy parcelling this power hath made it more
    Than all the world and, call it but a power,
    These quarters, squadrons and these regiments,
    Before, behind us and on either hand,
    Are but a power. When we name a man,   45
    His hand, his foot, his head hath several strengths,
    And being all but one self instant strength,
    Why, all this many, Audley, is but one,
    And we can call it all but one man's strength.
    He that hath far to go tells it by miles;   50
    If he should tell the steps, it kills his heart.
    The drops are infinite that make a flood,
    And yet thou knowst we call it but a rain.
    As many sands as these my hands can hold
    Are but my handful of so many sands,   55
    Easily ta'en up and quickly thrown away:
    But if I stand to count them, sand by sand,
    The number would confound my memory
    And make a thousand millions of a task
    Which briefly is no more indeed than one.   60
    There is but one France, one King of France;
    That France hath no more kings, and that same King
    Hath but the puissant legion of one king –
    And we have one. Then apprehend no odds,
    For one to one is fair equality.   65

          Enter an Herald *from King John.*

    What tidings messenger? Be plain and brief.
1 HERALD
    The King of France, my sovereign lord and master,
    Greets by me his foe, the Prince of Wales.
    If thou call forth a hundred men of name,
    Of lords, knights, squires and English gentlemen,   70
    And with thyself and those kneel at his feet,
    He straight will fold his bloody colours up
    And ransom shall redeem lives forfeited.
    If not, this day shall drink more English blood
    Than e'er was buried in our Brittish earth.   75
    What is thy answer to his proffered mercy?
PRINCE EDWARD
    This heaven that covers France contains the mercy
    That draws from me submissive orisons.
    That such base breath should vanish from my lips
    To urge the plea of mercy to a man,   80
    The Lord forbid. Return, and tell the King
    My tongue is made of steel and it shall beg
    My mercy on his coward burgonet.
    Tell him my colours are as red as his,
    My men as bold, our English arms as strong.   85
    Return him my defiance in his face.
1 HERALD   I go.   *Exit.*

          Enter another Herald, *from Charles.*

PRINCE EDWARD   What news with thee?
2 HERALD
    The Duke of Normandy, my lord and master,
    Pitying thy youth is so engirt with peril,   90

472

By me hath sent a nimble-jointed jennet,
As swift as ever yet thou didst bestride,
And therewithal he counsels thee to fly,
Else Death himself hath sworn that thou shalt die.

PRINCE EDWARD
95 Back with the beast unto the beast that sent him:
Tell him I cannot sit a coward's horse.
Bid him today bestride the jade himself,
For I will stain my horse quite o'er with blood
And double-gild my spurs but I will catch him.
100 So tell the capering boy, and get thee gone.
                                    Exit 2 Herald.

        Enter another Herald, *from Philip.*

3 HERALD   Edward of Wales, Philip, the second son
To the most mighty Christian King of France,
Seeing thy body's living date expired,
All full of charity and Christian love,
105 Commends this book, full-fraught with prayers,
To thy fair hand, and for thy hour of life
Entreats thee that thou meditate therein
And arm thy soul for her long journey towards.
        [*Gives book to Prince Edward.*]
Thus have I done his bidding and return.
        [*Offers to go.*]

PRINCE EDWARD
110 Herald of Philip, greet thy lord from me:
All good that he can send I can receive.
But think'st thou not the unadvised boy
Hath wronged himself in thus far tendering me?
Haply he cannot pray without the book –
115 I think him no divine extemporal.
Then render back this commonplace of prayer
        [*Returns book to Herald.*]
To do himself good in adversity.
Besides, he knows not my sins' quality
And therefore knows no prayers for my avail.
120 Ere night his prayer may be to pray to God
To put it in my heart to hear his prayer.
So tell the courtly wanton, and be gone.

3 HERALD   I go.   *Exit.*

PRINCE EDWARD
How confident their strength and number makes
        them.
125 Now, Audley, sound those silver wings of thine
And let those milk-white messengers of Time
Show thy time's learning in this dangerous time.
Thyself art bruised and bit with many broils,
And stratagems forepast with iron pens
130 Are texted in thine honourable face;
Thou art a married man in this distress,
But danger woos me as a blushing maid.
Teach me an answer to this perilous time.

AUDLEY   To die is all as common as to live,
135 The one in choice the other holds in chase;
For from the instant we begin to live
We do pursue and hunt the time to die.

First bud we, then we blow and after seed,
Then presently we fall, and, as a shade
Follows the body, so we follow death.   140
If, then, we hunt for death, why do we fear it?
If we fear it, why do we follow it?
If we do follow it, how can we shun it?
If we do fear, with fear we do but aid
The thing we fear to seize on us the sooner;   145
If we fear not, yet no resolved proffer
Can overthrow the limit of our fate,
For, whether ripe or rotten, drop we shall
As we do draw the lottery of our doom.

PRINCE EDWARD
Ah, good old man, a thousand thousand armours   150
These words of thine have buckled on my back.
Ah, what an idiot hast thou made of life,
To seek the thing it fears, and how disgraced
The imperial victory of murdering Death,
Since all the lives his conquering arrows strike   155
Seek him, and he not them, to shame his glory.
I will not give a penny for a life,
Nor half a halfpenny to shun grim death.
Since for to live is but to seek to die
And dying but beginning of new life,   160
Let come the hour when He that rules it will;
To live or die I hold indifferent.   *Exeunt.*

Sc. 13   *Enter* KING JOHN *and* CHARLES.   [4.5]

KING JOHN   A sudden darkness hath defaced the sky,
The winds are crept into their caves for fear,
The leaves move not, the world is hushed and still,
The birds cease singing and the wandering brooks
Murmur no wonted greeting to their shores.   5
Silence attends some wonder and expecteth
That heaven should pronounce some prophecy.
Whence, or from whom, proceeds this silence, Charles?

CHARLES   Our men with open mouths and staring eyes
Look on each other as they did attend   10
Each other's words, and yet no creature speaks:
A tongue-tied fear hath made a midnight hour
And speeches sleep through all the waking regions.

KING JOHN   But now the pompous sun in all his pride
Looked through his golden coach upon the world,   15
And on a sudden hath he hid himself,
That now the under-earth is as a grave,
Dark, deadly, silent and uncomfortable.
                        [*A clamour of ravens*]
Hark, what a deadly outcry do I hear!

        Enter PHILIP.

CHARLES   Here comes my brother Philip.
KING JOHN   All dismayed. –   20
What fearful words are those thy looks presage?

PHILIP   A flight, a flight –
KING JOHN
Coward, what flight? Thou liest, there needs no flight.

PHILIP   A flight –

25   KING JOHN   Awake thy craven powers, and tell on
        The substance of that very fear indeed
        Which is so ghastly printed in thy face.
        What is the matter?

PHILIP   A flight of ugly ravens
        Do croak and hover o'er our soldiers' heads

30   And keep in triangles and cornered squares
        Right as our forces are embattled.
        With their approach there came this sudden fog
        Which now hath hid the airy flower of heaven
        And made at noon a night unnatural

35   Upon the quaking and dismayed world.
        In brief, our soldiers have let fall their arms
        And stand like metamorphosed images,
        Bloodless and pale, one gazing on another.

KING JOHN [*aside*]
        Ay, now I call to mind the prophecy,

40   But I must give no entrance to a fear. –
        Return and hearten up these yielding souls.
        Tell them the ravens, seeing them in arms,
        So many fair against a famished few,
        Come but to dine upon their handiwork

45   And prey upon the carrion that they kill,
        For when we see a horse laid down to die,
        Although not dead, the ravenous birds
        Sit watching the departure of his life;
        Even so these ravens for the carcasses

50   Of those poor English that are marked to die
        Hover about, and if they cry to us,
        'Tis but for meat that we must kill for them.
        Away, and comfort up my soldiers,
        And sound the trumpets and at once dispatch

55   This little business of a silly fraud.   *Exit Philip.*

            Another noise. SALISBURY *brought in by*
                    a French Captain.

CAPTAIN   Behold, my liege, this knight and forty moe,
        Of whom the better part are slain and fled,
        With all endeavour sought to break our ranks
        And make their way to the encompassed Prince.

60   Dispose of him as please your majesty.

KING JOHN
        Go, and the next bough, soldier, that thou seest,
        Disgrace it with his body presently;
        For I do hold a tree in France too good

65   To be the gallows of an English thief.

SALISBURY   My lord of Normandy, I have your pass
        And warrant for my safety through this land.

CHARLES   Villiers procured it for thee, did he not?

SALISBURY   He did.

CHARLES   And it is current; thou shalt freely pass.

70   KING JOHN   Ay, freely to the gallows to be hanged,
        Without denial or impediment!
        Away with him.

CHARLES   I hope your highness will not so disgrace me
        And dash the virtue of my seal-at-arms.

He hath my never-broken name to show,   75
Charactered with this princely hand of mine;
And rather let me leave to be a prince
Than break the stable verdict of a prince.
I do beseech you, let him pass in quiet.

KING JOHN
Thou and thy word lie both in my command;   80
What canst thou promise that I cannot break?
Which of these twain is greater infamy,
To disobey thy father, or thyself?
Thy word nor no man's may exceed his power,
Nor that same man doth never break his word   85
That keeps it to the utmost of his power.
The breach of faith dwells in the soul's consent,
Which if thyself without consent do break
Thou art not charged with the breach of faith.
Go, hang him, for thy licence lies in me,   90
And my constraint stands the excuse for thee.

CHARLES   What, am I not a soldier in my word?
Then arms, adieu, and let them fight that list!
Shall I not give my girdle from my waist
But with a guardian I shall be controlled   95
To say I may not give my things away?
Upon my soul, had Edward, Prince of Wales,
Engaged his word, writ down his noble hand
For all your knights to pass his father's land,
The royal King to grace his warlike son   100
Would not alone safe-conduct give to them,
But with all bounty feasted them and theirs.

KING JOHN
Dwell'st thou on precedents? Then be it so.
Say, Englishman, of what degree thou art.

SALISBURY   An earl in England though a prisoner here,   105
And those that know me call me Salisbury.

KING JOHN
Then, Salisbury, say whither thou art bound.

SALISBURY
To Calais, where my liege, King Edward, is.

KING JOHN   To Calais, Salisbury? Then to Calais pack
And bid the King prepare a noble grave   110
To put his princely son, black Edward, in.
And as thou travell'st westward from this place,
Some two leagues hence there is a lofty hill –
Whose top seems topless, for the embracing sky
Doth hide his high head in her azure bosom –   115
Upon whose tall top when thy foot attains,
Look back upon the humble vale beneath,
Humble of late, but now made proud with arms,
And thence behold the wretched Prince of Wales,
Hooped with a bond of iron round about.   120
After which sight, to Calais spur amain,
And say the Prince was smothered and not slain.
And tell the King this is not all his ill,
For I will greet him ere he thinks I will.
Away, be gone. The smoke but of our shot   125
Will choke our foes, though bullets hit them not.
                                            Exeunt.

Sc. 14   *Alarum. Enter* PRINCE EDWARD   [4.6]
             and ARTOIS.

ARTOIS
How fares your grace? Are you not shot, my lord?
PRINCE EDWARD
No, dear Artois, but choked with dust and smoke
And stepped aside for breath and fresher air.
ARTOIS
Breathe, then, and to it again. The amazed French
Are quite distract with gazing on the crows,
And were our quivers full of shafts again
Your grace should see a glorious day of this.
O, for more arrows, Lord! That is our want.
PRINCE EDWARD
Courage, Artois, a fig for feathered shafts
When feathered fowls do bandy on our side;
What need we fight and sweat and keep a coil
When railing crows outscold our adversaries?
Up, up, Artois, the ground itself is armed.
Fire-containing flint! Command our bows
To hurl away their parti-coloured yew
And to it with stones. Away, Artois, away!
My soul doth prophesy we win the day.   *Exeunt.*

Sc. 15   *Alarum. Enter* KING JOHN.   [4.7]

KING JOHN
Our multitudes are in themselves confounded,
Dismayed and distraught; swift-starting fear
Hath buzzed a cold dismay through all our army
And every petty disadvantage prompts
The fear-possessed, abject soul to fly.
Myself, whose spirit is steel to their dull lead –
What with recalling of the prophecy,
And that our native stones from English arms
Rebel against us – find myself attainted
With strong surprise of weak and yielding fear.

Enter CHARLES.

CHARLES
Fly, father, fly; the French do kill the French!
Some that would stand let drive at some that fly;
Our drums strike nothing but discouragement;
Our trumpets sound dishonour and retire;
The spirit of fear, that feareth naught but death,
Cowardly works confusion on itself.

Enter PHILIP.

PHILIP
Pluck out your eyes and see not this day's shame!
An arm hath beat an army; one poor David
Hath with a stone foiled twenty stout Goliaths.
Some twenty naked starvelings with small flints
Hath driven back a puissant host of men,
Arrayed and fenced in all accomplements.

KING JOHN
Mort Dieu, they quoit at us and kill us up!
No less than forty thousand wicked elders
Have forty lean slaves this day stoned to death.   25
CHARLES   O, that I were some other countryman!
This day hath set derision on the French,
And all the world will blurt and scorn at us.
KING JOHN   What, is there no hope left?
PHILIP   No hope but death to bury up our shame.   30
KING JOHN
Make up once more with me. The twentieth part
Of those that live are men enow to quail
The feeble handful on the adverse part.
CHARLES
Then charge again; if heaven be not opposed,
We cannot lose the day.   35
KING JOHN   On, away.   *Exeunt.*

Sc. 16   *Enter* AUDLEY *wounded,*   [4.8]
             and rescued by two Squires.

1 SQUIRE   How fares my lord?
AUDLEY   Even as a man may do
That dines at such a bloody feast as this.
1 SQUIRE   I hope, my lord, that is no mortal scar.
AUDLEY   No matter if it be; the count is cast,
And in the worst ends but a mortal man.   5
Good friends, convey me to the princely Edward,
That in the crimson bravery of my blood
I may become him with saluting him.
I'll smile and tell him that this open scar
Doth end the harvest of his Audley's war.   *Exeunt.*   10

Sc. 17   *Enter* PRINCE EDWARD, KING JOHN,   [4.9]
             CHARLES *and all, with ensigns spread.*
             Retreat sounded.

PRINCE EDWARD
Now, John in France, and lately John of France,
Thy bloody ensigns are my captive colours;
And you, high-vaunting Charles of Normandy,
That once today sent me a horse to fly,
Are now the subjects of my clemency.   5
Fie, lords, is it not a shame that English boys
Whose early days are yet not worth a beard
Should in the bosom of your kingdom thus,
One against twenty, beat you up together?
KING JOHN
Thy fortune not thy force hath conquered us.   10
PRINCE EDWARD
An argument that heaven aids the right.

Enter ARTOIS, *with* PHILIP.

See, see, Artois doth bring with him along
The late good-counsel giver to my soul.
Welcome, Artois, and welcome, Philip, too.

15 Who now of you or I have need to pray?
Now is the proverb verified in you:
'Too bright a morning breeds a louring day.'

Sound trumpets. Enter AUDLEY, *supported
by the two* Squires.

But say, what grim discouragement comes here?
Alas, what thousand armed men of France
20 Have writ that note of death in Audley's face?
Speak, thou that woo'st death with thy careless smile
And look'st so merrily upon thy grave
As if thou wert enamoured on thine end,
What hungry sword hath so bereaved thy face
25 And lopped a true friend from my loving soul?
AUDLEY   O Prince, thy sweet bemoaning speech to me
Is as a mournful knell to one dead sick.
PRINCE EDWARD
Dear Audley, if my tongue ring out thy end,
My arms shall be thy grave. What may I do
30 To win thy life, or to revenge thy death?
If thou wilt drink the blood of captive kings,
Or that it were restorative, command
A health of kings' blood and I'll drink to thee.
If honour may dispense for thee with death,
35 The never-dying honour of this day
Share wholly, Audley, to thyself and live.
AUDLEY   Victorious Prince – that thou art so, behold
A Caesar's fame in kings' captivity –
If I could hold dim death but at a bay
40 Till I did see my liege thy royal father,
My soul should yield this castle of my flesh,
This mangled tribute, with all willingness,
To darkness, consummation, dust and worms.
PRINCE EDWARD
Cheerly, bold man, thy soul is all too proud
45 To yield her city, for one little breach,
Should be divorced from her earthly spouse
By the soft temper of a Frenchman's sword.
Lo, to repair thy life I give to thee
Three thousand marks a year in English land.
50 AUDLEY   I take thy gift to pay the debts I owe.
These two poor squires redeemed me from the
French
With lusty and dear hazard of their lives.
What thou hast given me I give to them;
And, as thou lov'st me, Prince, lay thy consent
55 To this bequeath in my last testament.
PRINCE EDWARD
Renowned Audley, live and have from me
This gift twice doubled to these squires and thee.
But live or die, what thou hast given away
To these and theirs shall lasting freedom stay.
60 Come, gentlemen, I will see my friend bestowed
Within an easy litter, then we'll march
Proudly toward Calais with triumphant pace,
Unto my royal father, and there bring
The tribute of my wars, fair France his king.   *Exeunt.*

Sc. 18   *Enter six* CITIZENS *in their shirts,*   [5.1]
barefoot, with halters about their necks.
Enter at another door KING EDWARD, QUEEN
Philippa, DERBY, *Soldiers.*

KING EDWARD
No more, Queen Philippe, pacify yourself;
Copeland, except he can excuse his fault,
Shall find displeasure written in our looks.
And now unto this proud resisting town:
Soldiers, assault, I will no longer stay   5
To be deluded by their false delays.
Put all to sword and make the spoil your own.
CITIZENS   Mercy, King Edward! Mercy, gracious lord!
KING EDWARD
Contemptuous villains, call ye now for truce?
Mine ears are stopped against your bootless cries.   10
Sound drums alarum. Draw threatening swords!
1 CITIZEN   Ah, noble prince, take pity on this town
And hear us, mighty King.
We claim the promise that your highness made:
The two days' respite is not yet expired,   15
And we are come with willingness to bear
What torturing death or punishment you please,
So that the trembling multitude be saved.
KING EDWARD
My promise? Well, I do confess as much;
But I require the chiefest citizens   20
And men of most account that should submit.
You peradventure are but servile grooms,
Or some felonious robbers on the sea
Whom, apprehended, law would execute
Albeit severity lay dead in us.   25
No, no, ye cannot overreach us thus.
2 CITIZEN   The sun, dread lord, that in the western fall
Beholds us now low-brought through misery,
Did in the orient purple of the morn
Salute our coming forth when we were known,   30
Or may our portion be with damned fiends.
KING EDWARD   If it be so, then let our covenant stand;
We take possession of the town in peace.
But for yourselves, look you for no remorse
But, as imperial justice hath decreed,   35
Your bodies shall be dragged about these walls
And after feel the stroke of quartering steel.
This is your doom. Go, soldiers, see it done.
QUEEN   Ah, be more mild unto these yielding men.
It is a glorious thing to stablish peace,   40
And kings approach the nearest unto God
By giving life and safety unto men.
As thou intendest to be King of France
So let her people live to call thee king;
For what the sword cuts down or fire hath spoiled   45
Is held in reputation none of ours.
KING EDWARD
Although experience teach us this is true –
That peaceful quietness brings most delight

When most of all abuses are controlled –
Yet, insomuch it shall be known that we
As well can master our affections
As conquer other by the dint of sword,
Philippe, prevail, we yield to thy request.
These men shall live to boast of clemency,
And, Tyranny, strike terror to thyself.

2 CITIZEN
Long live your highness! Happy be your reign!

KING EDWARD
Go, get you hence, return unto the town,
And if this kindness hath deserved your love,
Learn then to reverence Edward as your king.

Exeunt Citizens.

Now might we hear of our affairs abroad
We would till gloomy winter were o'erspent
Dispose our men in garrison awhile.

Enter COPELAND *and* KING DAVID.

But who comes here?

DERBY Copeland, my lord, and David, King of Scots.

KING EDWARD
Is this the proud, presumptuous squire of the north
That would not yield his prisoner to my Queen?

COPELAND I am, my liege, a northern squire indeed,
But neither proud nor insolent, I trust.

KING EDWARD
What moved thee, then, to be so obstinate
To contradict our royal Queen's desire?

COPELAND No wilful disobedience, mighty lord,
But my desert, and public law at arms.
I took the King myself in single fight
And, like a soldier, would be loth to lose
The least pre-eminence that I had won.
And Copeland straight upon your highness' charge
Is come to France and with a lowly mind
Doth vail the bonnet of his victory.
Receive, dread lord, the custom of my freight,
The wealthy tribute of my labouring hands,
Which should long since have been surrendered up
Had but your gracious self been there in place.

QUEEN
But, Copeland, thou didst scorn the King's command
Neglecting our commission in his name.

COPELAND
His name I reverence, but his person more:
His name shall keep me in allegiance still,
But to his person I will bend my knee.

KING EDWARD
I pray thee, Philippe, let displeasure pass.
This man doth please me and I like his words,
For what is he that will attempt great deeds
And lose the glory that ensues the same?
All rivers have recourse unto the sea,
And Copeland's faith relation to his king.
[*to Copeland*] Kneel, therefore, down. Now rise, King
    Edward's knight;

And to maintain thy state I freely give   95
Five hundred marks a year to thee and thine.

Enter SALISBURY.

Welcome, Lord Salisbury. What news from Brittain?

SALISBURY
This, mighty King: the country we have won,
And John de Montfort, regent of that place,
Presents your highness with this coronet,   100
Protesting true allegiance to your grace.

KING EDWARD
We thank thee for thy service, valiant Earl;
Challenge our favour, for we owe it thee.

SALISBURY But now, my lord, as this is joyful news,
So must my voice be tragical again   105
And I must sing of doleful accidents.

KING EDWARD
What, have our men the overthrow at Poitiers,
Or is our son beset with too much odds?

SALISBURY He was, my lord, and as my worthless self
With forty other serviceable knights,   110
Under safe-conduct of the Dauphin's seal,
Did travel that way, finding him distressed,
A troop of lances met us on the way,
Surprised and brought us prisoners to the King;
Who, proud of this and eager of revenge,   115
Commanded straight to cut off all our heads.
And surely we had died but that the Duke,
More full of honour than his angry sire,
Procured our quick deliverance from thence.
But ere we went, 'Salute your King,' quoth he,   120
'Bid him provide a funeral for his son,
Today our sword shall cut his thread of life,
And sooner than he thinks we'll be with him
To quittance those displeasures he hath done.'
This said, we passed, not daring to reply;   125
Our hearts were dead, our looks diffused and wan.
Wandering, at last we climbed unto a hill
From whence, although our grief were much before,
Yet now to see the occasion with our eyes
Did thrice so much increase our heaviness,   130
For there, my lord, O there we did descry
Down in a valley how both armies lay.
The French had cast their trenches like a ring,
And every barricado's open front
Was thick embossed with brazen ordinance.   135
Here stood a battle of ten thousand horse;
There twice as many pikes in quadrant wise;
Here crossbows, there deadly-wounding darts;
And in the midst, like to a slender point
Within the compass of the horizon,   140
As 'twere a rising bubble in the sea,
A hazel wand amidst a wood of pines,
Or as a bear fast chained unto a stake,
Stood famous Edward, still expecting when
Those dogs of France would fasten on his flesh.   145
Anon the death-procuring knell begins:

Off go the cannons, that with trembling noise
Did shake the very mountain where they stood;
Then sound the trumpets clangour in the air;
150 The battles join, and when we could no more
Discern the difference 'twixt the friend and foe,
So intricate the dark confusion was,
Away we turned our watery eyes with sighs
As black as powder fuming into smoke.
155 And thus, I fear, unhappy have I told
The most untimely tale of Edward's fall.

QUEEN Ah me, is this my welcome into France?
Is this the comfort that I looked to have
When I should meet with my beloved son?
160 Sweet Ned, I would thy mother in the sea
Had been prevented of this mortal grief.

KING EDWARD
Content thee, Philippe, 'tis not tears will serve
To call him back if he be taken hence.
Comfort thyself as I do, gentle Queen,
165 With hope of sharp, unheard-of-dire revenge!
He bids me to provide his funeral:
And so I will, but all the peers in France
Shall mourners be and weep out bloody tears
Until their empty veins be dry and sere;
170 The pillars of his hearse shall be their bones;
The mould that covers him, their city ashes;
His knell the groaning cries of dying men;
And in the stead of tapers on his tomb,
An hundred fifty towers shall burning blaze,
175 While we bewail our valiant son's decease.

After a flourish sounded within, enter an Herald.

HERALD Rejoice, my lord; ascend the imperial throne!
The mighty and redoubted Prince of Wales,
Great servitor to bloody Mars in arms,
The Frenchman's terror and his country's fame,
180 Triumphant rideth, like a Roman peer;
And lowly at his stirrup comes afoot
King John of France together with his son
In captive bonds; whose diadem he brings
To crown thee with and to proclaim thee king.

KING EDWARD
185 Away with mourning, Philippe, wipe thine eyes!
Sound trumpets, welcome in Plantagenet.

Flourish. Enter PRINCE EDWARD, KING JOHN,
PHILIP, AUDLEY, ARTOIS.

As things long lost when they are found again,
So doth my son rejoice his father's heart,
For whom even now my soul was much perplexed.
190 QUEEN Be this a token to express my joy,
For inward passions will not let me speak.
[*Kisses him.*]

PRINCE EDWARD
My gracious father, here receive the gift,
This wreath of conquest and reward of war,
Got with as mickle peril of our lives

As e'er was thing of price before this day. 195
[*Gives him crown of France.*]
Install your highness in your proper right;
And herewithal I render to your hands
These prisoners, chief occasion of our strife.

KING EDWARD
So, John of France, I see you keep your word.
You promised to be sooner with ourself 200
Than we did think for, and 'tis so indeed.
But had you done at first as now you do,
How many civil towns had stood untouched
That now are turned to ragged heaps of stones.
How many people's lives mightst thou have saved 205
That are untimely sunk into their graves.

KING JOHN Edward, recount not things irrevocable.
Tell me what ransom thou requir'st to have.

KING EDWARD
Thy ransom, John, hereafter shall be known.
But first to England thou must cross the seas 210
To see what entertainment it affords;
Howe'er it falls, it cannot be so bad
As ours hath been since we arrived in France.

KING JOHN [*aside*]
Accursed man, of this I was foretold,
But did misconstrue what the prophet told. 215

PRINCE EDWARD [*Kneels.*]
Now, Father, this petition Edward makes
To Thee, whose grace hath been his strongest
    shield:
That as Thy pleasure chose me for the man
To be the instrument to show Thy power,
So Thou wilt grant that many princes more 220
Bred and brought up within that little isle
May still be famous for like victories. [*Rises.*]
And, for my part, the bloody scars I bear,
The weary nights that I have watched in field,
The dangerous conflicts I have often had, 225
The fearful menaces were proffered me,
The heat and cold, and what else might displease,
I wish were now redoubled twenty-fold,
So that hereafter ages, when they read
The painful traffic of my tender youth, 230
Might thereby be inflamed with such resolve
As not the territories of France alone,
But likewise Spain, Turkey and what countries else
That justly would provoke fair England's ire
Might at their presence tremble and retire. 235

KING EDWARD
Here, English lords, we do proclaim a rest,
An intercession of our painful arms.
Sheathe up your swords, refresh your weary limbs,
Peruse your spoils, and after we have breathed
A day or two within this haven town, 240
God willing, then for England we'll be shipped,
Where in a happy hour I trust we shall
Arrive: three Kings, two Princes and a Queen.
Exeunt.

King Henry IV, Part 1

King Henry IV, Part 1 was from the first both a theatrical and a literary success, as popular in the bookstalls as on the stage. Entered in the Stationers' Register on 25 February 1598, as 'The historye of Henry the iiijth' (it was not until the 1623 Folio that the play was published as *The First Part of King Henry the Fourth*), the play quickly became a best-seller. Two editions appeared in 1598 (the first surviving only in a single sheet, now in the Folger Shakespeare Library), and seven more editions were published before 1640, making it not only Shakespeare's most frequently reprinted play before the Interregnum but also one of the most popular of all printed plays in the period. In the theatre also it continuously thrived, though early references to specific performances are few.

Probably first performed in 1597, it held the stage throughout the seventeenth century. In a commendatory poem to Shakespeare's *Poems* (1640), Leonard Digges noted that, while Ben Jonson's plays no longer drew an audience large enough to cover the costs of production, 'let but Falstaff come, / Hal, Poins, the rest, you scarce shall have a room, / All is so pestered'.

Much of the play's popularity is no doubt due to the appeal of Falstaff. Indeed, in the seventeenth century there are more references to the fat knight than to any other dramatic character, though he first appeared on the stage with the name 'Sir John Oldcastle'. A well-known fifteenth-century Lollard who had been burned as a heretic, Oldcastle emerged a century later as a celebrated precursor of the Protestant martyrs. Shakespeare's irreverent treatment of the historical figure seems to have offended William Brooke, Lord Cobham, who held his title in descent from Oldcastle's wife. Brooke was Queen Elizabeth's Lord Chamberlain from August 1596 to his death on 5 March 1597, and he seems to have insisted on the change of name. It has even been suggested that publication of the play was required to prove that Shakespeare and his acting company had complied with the Lord Chamberlain's demand.

By whatever name, however, the irrepressible knight has long delighted readers and audiences, offering a vital alternative to the sober world of political consideration over which Henry IV rules. The two men stand as opposing father figures for Prince Henry, one fat and full of life, the other 'portly' only in his power, each in turn drawing the commitment of the Prince who must, as history dictates, finally reject revel for responsibility and accept his destiny to rule. There is a third vector in the play, however, that further complicates his choice: the chivalric energies of the rebel Hotspur that lead Henry IV to wish this son of Northumberland his child instead of Hal. But on the battlefield at Shrewsbury the Prince displays both heroism and magnanimity, proving himself a worthy successor and putting to rest fears either that the irresponsible tavern world has claimed him or that he is only the self-regarding son of a calculating father.

The play, of course, is a 'history' and appears as the third of ten such in the catalogue of the 1623 Folio, but though it concerns the reign of a historical English king and is largely based upon Holinshed's *Chronicles*, it is hardly faithful to the historical record. Not only does it select, restructure and change that history (for example, Hotspur was in fact three years older than the King rather than the Prince's contemporary), but it mixes in completely invented material, that very tavern world that threatens to keep the Prince from his fate. It is precisely this that has made the play so continuously popular: that it is more than its historical plot. It mingles kings and clowns, history and comedy, challenging the exclusive logic of the aristocratic, political action with its rich variety and demotic energy.

The Arden text is based on the two Quartos of 1598.

KING Henry the Fourth
PRINCE Henry of Wales (Hal *or* Harry)
Lord John of LANCASTER   }   *sons of King Henry*
Earl of WESTMORLAND
Sir Walter BLOUNT
Thomas Percy, Earl of WORCESTER
Henry Percy, Earl of NORTHUMBERLAND   *his older brother*
Henry Percy, *known as* HOTSPUR   *Northumberland's son*
LADY PERCY (Kate)   *Hotspur's wife*
Lord Edmund MORTIMER   *Lady Percy's brother*
LADY MORTIMER   *his wife*
Owen GLENDOWER   *Lady Mortimer's father*
Earl of DOUGLAS
Sir Richard VERNON
Richard Scrope, ARCHBISHOP of York
SIR MICHAEL   *a member of the Archbishop's household*
Sir John FALSTAFF
Edward (Ned) POINS
BARDOLL
PETO
HOSTESS (Mistress Quickly)
FRANCIS   *a drawer*
VINTNER
GADSHILL
1 CARRIER (Mugs)
2 CARRIER (Tom)
CHAMBERLAIN
OSTLER
SHERIFF
Two TRAVELLERS
MESSENGERS
SERVANT

Lords, Soldiers, Attendants, Travellers

1.1   *Enter the* KING, Lord John of LANCASTER,
       Earl of WESTMORLAND, *with others.*

KING   So shaken as we are, so wan with care,
        Find we a time for frighted peace to pant
        And breathe short-winded accents of new broils
        To be commenced in strands afar remote.
5   No more the thirsty entrance of this soil
        Shall daub her lips with her own children's blood;
        No more shall trenching war channel her fields,
        Nor bruise her flowerets with the armed hoofs
        Of hostile paces. Those opposed eyes,
10   Which, like the meteors of a troubled heaven,
        All of one nature, of one substance bred,
        Did lately meet in the intestine shock
        And furious close of civil butchery,
        Shall now in mutual well-beseeming ranks
15   March all one way and be no more opposed
        Against acquaintance, kindred and allies.
        The edge of war, like an ill-sheathed knife,
        No more shall cut his master. Therefore, friends,
        As far as to the sepulchre of Christ
20   (Whose soldier now, under whose blessed cross
        We are impressed and engaged to fight)
        Forthwith a power of English shall we levy,
        Whose arms were moulded in their mothers' womb
        To chase these pagans in those holy fields
25   Over whose acres walked those blessed feet,
        Which fourteen hundred years ago were nailed
        For our advantage on the bitter cross.
        But this our purpose now is twelve month old,
        And bootless 'tis to tell you we will go.
30   Therefor we meet not now. – Then let me hear
        Of you, my gentle cousin Westmorland,
        What yesternight our Council did decree
        In forwarding this dear expedience.
WESTMORLAND
        My liege, this haste was hot in question,
35   And many limits of the charge set down
        But yesternight, when all athwart there came
        A post from Wales, loaden with heavy news,
        Whose worst was that the noble Mortimer,
        Leading the men of Herefordshire to fight
40   Against the irregular and wild Glendower,
        Was by the rude hands of that Welshman taken,
        A thousand of his people butchered,
        Upon whose dead corpse there was such misuse,
        Such beastly shameless transformation,
45   By those Welshwomen done, as may not be
        Without much shame retold or spoken of.
KING   It seems then that the tidings of this broil
        Brake off our business for the Holy Land.
WESTMORLAND
        This matched with other did, my gracious lord,
50   For more uneven and unwelcome news
        Came from the north, and thus it did import:
        On Holy Rood Day the gallant Hotspur there

(Young Harry Percy) and brave Archibald,
That ever-valiant and approved Scot,
At Humbleton met, where they did spend   55
A sad and bloody hour,
As by discharge of their artillery
And shape of likelihood the news was told;
For he that brought them, in the very heat
And pride of their contention, did take horse,   60
Uncertain of the issue any way.
KING   Here is a dear, a true industrious friend,
        Sir Walter Blount, new lighted from his horse,
        Stained with the variation of each soil
        Betwixt that Humbleton and this seat of ours; 65
        And he hath brought us smooth and welcome news.
        The Earl of Douglas is discomfited.
        Ten thousand bold Scots, two-and-twenty knights,
        Balked in their own blood, did Sir Walter see
        On Humbleton's plains. Of prisoners Hotspur took 70
        Murdoch, Earl of Fife and eldest son
        To beaten Douglas, and the Earl of Atholl,
        Of Moray, Angus, and Menteith;
        And is not this an honourable spoil,
        A gallant prize? Ha, cousin, is it not?   75
WESTMORLAND
        In faith, it is: a conquest for a prince to boast of.
KING   Yea, there thou mak'st me sad and mak'st me sin
        In envy that my lord Northumberland
        Should be the father to so blest a son,
        A son who is the theme of honour's tongue,   80
        Amongst a grove the very straightest plant,
        Who is sweet Fortune's minion and her pride;
        Whilst I, by looking on the praise of him,
        See riot and dishonour stain the brow
        Of my young Harry. O, that it could be proved 85
        That some night-tripping fairy had exchanged
        In cradle clothes our children where they lay,
        And called mine 'Percy', his 'Plantagenet';
        Then would I have his Harry, and he mine.
        But let him from my thoughts. What think you, coz, 90
        Of this young Percy's pride? The prisoners
        Which he in this adventure hath surprised
        To his own use he keeps, and sends me word
        I shall have none but Murdoch, Earl of Fife.
WESTMORLAND
        This is his uncle's teaching; this is Worcester, 95
        Malevolent to you in all aspects,
        Which makes him prune himself and bristle up
        The crest of youth against your dignity.
KING   But I have sent for him to answer this,
        And for this cause awhile we must neglect   100
        Our holy purpose to Jerusalem.
        Cousin, on Wednesday next our Council we
        Will hold at Windsor. So inform the lords,
        But come yourself with speed to us again,
        For more is to be said and to be done   105
        Than out of anger can be uttered.
WESTMORLAND   I will, my liege.   *Exeunt.*

1.2   *Enter* PRINCE of Wales *and* Sir John FALSTAFF.

FALSTAFF   Now, Hal, what time of day is it, lad?

PRINCE   Thou art so fat-witted with drinking of old sack, and unbuttoning thee after supper, and sleeping upon benches after noon, that thou hast forgotten to demand that truly which thou wouldst truly know. What a devil hast thou to do with the time of the day? Unless hours were cups of sack, and minutes capons, and clocks the tongues of bawds, and dials the signs of leaping-houses, and the blessed sun himself a fair hot wench in flame-coloured taffeta, I see no reason why thou shouldst be so superfluous to demand the time of the day.

FALSTAFF   Indeed you come near me now, Hal, for we that take purses go by the moon and the seven stars, and not by Phoebus, he, 'that wand'ring knight so fair'. And I prithee, sweet wag, when thou art a king, as God save thy grace – 'majesty', I should say, for grace thou wilt have none –

PRINCE   What, none?

FALSTAFF   No, by my troth, not so much as will serve to be prologue to an egg and butter.

PRINCE   Well, how then? Come roundly, roundly.

FALSTAFF   Marry then, sweet wag, when thou art king, let not us that are squires of the night's body be called thieves of the day's beauty. Let us be Diana's foresters, gentlemen of the shade, minions of the moon, and let men say we be men of good government, being governed, as the sea is, by our noble and chaste mistress the moon, under whose countenance we steal.

PRINCE   Thou sayst well, and it holds well too, for the fortune of us that are the moon's men doth ebb and flow like the sea, being governed, as the sea is, by the moon. As for proof now: a purse of gold most resolutely snatched on Monday night and most dissolutely spent on Tuesday morning, got with swearing 'Lay by!', and spent with crying 'Bring in!', now in as low an ebb as the foot of the ladder, and by and by in as high a flow as the ridge of the gallows.

FALSTAFF   By the Lord, thou sayst true, lad – and is not my hostess of the tavern a most sweet wench?

PRINCE   As the honey of Hybla, my old lad of the castle – and is not a buff jerkin a most sweet robe of durance?

FALSTAFF   How now, how now, mad wag? What, in thy quips and thy quiddities? What a plague have I to do with a buff jerkin?

PRINCE   Why, what a pox have I to do with my hostess of the tavern?

FALSTAFF   Well, thou hast called her to a reckoning many a time and oft.

PRINCE   Did I ever call for thee to pay thy part?

FALSTAFF   No, I'll give thee thy due; thou hast paid all there.

PRINCE   Yea, and elsewhere, so far as my coin would stretch, and where it would not I have used my credit.

FALSTAFF   Yea, and so used it that were it not here apparent that thou art heir apparent – but I prithee, sweet wag, shall there be gallows standing in England when thou art king? And resolution thus fubbed as it is with the rusty curb of old Father Antic the law? Do not thou, when thou art king, hang a thief.

PRINCE   No, thou shalt.

FALSTAFF   Shall I? O, rare! By the Lord, I'll be a brave judge!

PRINCE   Thou judgest false already. I mean thou shalt have the hanging of the thieves and so become a rare hangman.

FALSTAFF   Well, Hal, well, and in some sort it jumps with my humour as well as waiting in the court, I can tell you.

PRINCE   For obtaining of suits?

FALSTAFF   Yea, for obtaining of suits, whereof the hangman hath no lean wardrobe. 'Sblood, I am as melancholy as a gib cat or a lugged bear.

PRINCE   Or an old lion or a lover's lute.

FALSTAFF   Yea, or the drone of a Lincolnshire bagpipe.

PRINCE   What sayst thou to a hare, or the melancholy of Moorditch?

FALSTAFF   Thou hast the most unsavoury similes and art indeed the most comparative, rascalliest, sweet young prince. But Hal, I prithee trouble me no more with vanity. I would to God thou and I knew where a commodity of good names were to be bought. An old lord of the Council rated me the other day in the street about you, sir, but I marked him not; and yet he talked very wisely, but I regarded him not; and yet he talked wisely and in the street too.

PRINCE   Thou didst well, for wisdom cries out in the streets and no man regards it.

FALSTAFF   O, thou hast damnable iteration and art indeed able to corrupt a saint. Thou hast done much harm upon me, Hal; God forgive thee for it. Before I knew thee, Hal, I knew nothing, and now am I, if a man should speak truly, little better than one of the wicked. I must give over this life, and I will give it over. By the Lord, an I do not, I am a villain. I'll be damned for never a king's son in Christendom.

PRINCE   Where shall we take a purse tomorrow, Jack?

FALSTAFF   Zounds, where thou wilt, lad. I'll make one; an I do not, call me villain and baffle me.

PRINCE   I see a good amendment of life in thee, from praying to purse-taking.

FALSTAFF   Why, Hal, 'tis my vocation, Hal; 'tis no sin for a man to labour in his vocation.

Enter POINS.

Poins! Now shall we know if Gadshill have set a match. O, if men were to be saved by merit, what hole in hell were hot enough for him? This is the most omnipotent villain that ever cried 'Stand!' to a true man.

PRINCE   Good morrow, Ned.

POINS   Good morrow, sweet Hal. – What says Monsieur 110
Remorse? What says Sir John Sack and Sugar, Jack?
How agrees the devil and thee about thy soul, that thou
soldest him on Good Friday last for a cup of madeira
and a cold capon's leg?

PRINCE   Sir John stands to his word. The devil shall 115
have his bargain, for he was never yet a breaker of
proverbs; he will give the devil his due.

POINS [*to Falstaff*]   Then art thou damned for keeping
thy word with the devil.

PRINCE   Else he had been damned for cozening the devil. 120

POINS   But my lads, my lads, tomorrow morning by
four o'clock early, at Gad's Hill, there are pilgrims
going to Canterbury with rich offerings and traders
riding to London with fat purses. I have vizards for
you all; you have horses for yourselves. Gadshill lies 125
tonight in Rochester. I have bespoke supper tomorrow
night in Eastcheap. We may do it as secure as sleep. If
you will go, I will stuff your purses full of crowns; if
you will not, tarry at home and be hanged.

FALSTAFF   Hear ye, Yedward, if I tarry at home and go 130
not, I'll hang you for going.

POINS   You will, chops?

FALSTAFF   Hal, wilt thou make one?

PRINCE   Who? I rob? I a thief? Not I, by my faith.

FALSTAFF   There's neither honesty, manhood nor good 135
fellowship in thee, nor thou cam'st not of the blood
royal, if thou darest not stand for ten shillings.

PRINCE   Well then, once in my days I'll be a madcap.

FALSTAFF   Why, that's well said.

PRINCE   Well, come what will, I'll tarry at home. 140

FALSTAFF   By the Lord, I'll be a traitor then, when thou
art king.

PRINCE   I care not.

POINS   Sir John, I prithee leave the Prince and me
alone. I will lay him down such reasons for this 145
adventure that he shall go.

FALSTAFF   Well, God give thee the spirit of persuasion
and him the ears of profiting, that what thou speakest
may move and what he hears may be believed, that the
true prince may, for recreation sake, prove a false thief, 150
for the poor abuses of the time want countenance.
Farewell. You shall find me in Eastcheap.

PRINCE   Farewell, the latter spring; farewell, All-hallown
summer.   *Exit Falstaff.*

POINS   Now, my good sweet honey lord, ride with us 155
tomorrow. I have a jest to execute that I cannot manage
alone. Falstaff, Peto, Bardoll and Gadshill shall rob those
men that we have already waylaid – yourself and I will
not be there – and when they have the booty, if you and
I do not rob them, cut this head off from my shoulders. 160

PRINCE   How shall we part with them in setting forth?

POINS   Why, we will set forth before or after them and
appoint them a place of meeting, wherein it is at our
pleasure to fail. And then will they adventure upon the
exploit themselves, which they shall have no sooner 165
achieved but we'll set upon them.

PRINCE   Yea, but 'tis like that they will know us by our
horses, by our habits and by every other appointment
to be ourselves.

POINS   Tut, our horses they shall not see. I'll tie them in 170
the wood. Our vizards we will change after we leave
them, and, sirrah, I have cases of buckram for the
nonce, to immask our noted outward garments.

PRINCE   Yea, but I doubt they will be too hard for us.

POINS   Well, for two of them, I know them to be as true- 175
bred cowards as ever turned back, and for the third, if
he fight longer than he sees reason, I'll forswear arms.
The virtue of this jest will be the incomprehensible lies
that this same fat rogue will tell us when we meet at
supper: how thirty at least he fought with, what wards, 180
what blows, what extremities he endured; and in the
reproof of this lives the jest.

PRINCE   Well, I'll go with thee. Provide us all things
necessary and meet me tomorrow night in Eastcheap.
There I'll sup. Farewell. 185

POINS   Farewell, my lord.   *Exit Poins.*

PRINCE   I know you all, and will awhile uphold
The unyoked humour of your idleness.
Yet herein will I imitate the sun,
Who doth permit the base contagious clouds 190
To smother up his beauty from the world,
That, when he please again to be himself,
Being wanted, he may be more wondered at
By breaking through the foul and ugly mists
Of vapours that did seem to strangle him. 195
If all the year were playing holidays,
To sport would be as tedious as to work;
But when they seldom come, they wished-for come,
And nothing pleaseth but rare accidents.
So when this loose behaviour I throw off 200
And pay the debt I never promised,
By how much better than my word I am,
By so much shall I falsify men's hopes;
And, like bright metal on a sullen ground,
My reformation, glittering o'er my fault, 205
Shall show more goodly and attract more eyes
Than that which hath no foil to set it off.
I'll so offend to make offence a skill,
Redeeming time when men think least I will.   *Exit.*

1.3   *Enter the* KING, NORTHUMBERLAND,
WORCESTER, HOTSPUR, *Sir Walter* BLOUNT,
with others.

KING   My blood hath been too cold and temperate,
Unapt to stir at these indignities,
And you have found me, for accordingly
You tread upon my patience; but be sure
I will from henceforth rather be myself, 5
Mighty and to be feared, than my condition,
Which hath been smooth as oil, soft as young down,
And therefore lost that title of respect
Which the proud soul ne'er pays but to the proud.

WORCESTER

10   Our house, my sovereign liege, little deserves
     The scourge of greatness to be used on it,
     And that same greatness, too, which our own hands
     Have holp to make so portly.

NORTHUMBERLAND [*to the King*]

     My lord –

15   KING   Worcester, get thee gone, for I do see
     Danger and disobedience in thine eye.
     O sir, your presence is too bold and peremptory,
     And majesty might never yet endure
     The moody frontier of a servant brow.

20   You have good leave to leave us. When we need
     Your use and counsel we shall send for you.

                                             Exit Worcester.
     [*to Northumberland*] You were about to speak.

NORTHUMBERLAND   Yea, my good lord.
     Those prisoners in your highness' name demanded,
     Which Harry Percy here at Humbleton took,

25   Were, as he says, not with such strength denied
     As is delivered to your majesty.
     Either envy, therefore, or misprision
     Is guilty of this fault and not my son.

HOTSPUR   My liege, I did deny no prisoners.

30   But I remember, when the fight was done,
     When I was dry with rage and extreme toil,
     Breathless and faint, leaning upon my sword,
     Came there a certain lord, neat and trimly dressed,
     Fresh as a bridegroom, and his chin, new reaped,

35   Showed like a stubble-land at harvest-home.
     He was perfumed like a milliner,
     And 'twixt his finger and his thumb he held
     A pouncet-box, which ever and anon
     He gave his nose and took't away again

40   (Who therewith angry, when it next came there,
     Took it in snuff) and still he smiled and talked;
     And, as the soldiers bore dead bodies by,
     He called them 'untaught knaves', 'unmannerly'
     To bring a slovenly unhandsome corpse

45   Betwixt the wind and his nobility.
     With many holiday and lady terms
     He questioned me, amongst the rest demanded
     My prisoners in your majesty's behalf.
     I then, all smarting with my wounds being cold,

50   To be so pestered with a popinjay,
     Out of my grief and my impatience
     Answered neglectingly, I know not what –
     He should or he should not – for he made me mad
     To see him shine so brisk, and smell so sweet

55   And talk so like a waiting gentlewoman
     Of guns, and drums, and wounds, God save the mark!
     And telling me 'the sovereign'st thing on earth'
     Was 'parmaceti' for an inward bruise,
     And that it was great pity, so it was,

60   This 'villainous saltpetre' should be digged
     Out of the bowels of the harmless earth,
     Which many a good tall fellow had destroyed

     So cowardly, and but for these 'vile guns'
     He would himself have been a soldier.
     This bald, unjointed chat of his, my lord,   65
     I answered indirectly, as I said,
     And I beseech you, let not his report
     Come current for an accusation
     Betwixt my love and your high majesty.

BLOUNT [*to the King*]

     The circumstance considered, good my lord,   70
     Whate'er Lord Harry Percy then had said
     To such a person, and in such a place,
     At such a time, with all the rest retold,
     May reasonably die and never rise
     To do him wrong or any way impeach   75
     What then he said, so he unsay it now.

KING   Why, yet he doth deny his prisoners,
     But with proviso and exception:
     That we at our own charge shall ransom straight
     His brother-in-law, the foolish Mortimer,   80
     Who, on my soul, hath wilfully betrayed
     The lives of those that he did lead to fight
     Against that great magician, damned Glendower,
     Whose daughter, as we hear, that Earl of March
     Hath lately married. Shall our coffers then   85
     Be emptied to redeem a traitor home?
     Shall we buy treason and indent with fears
     When they have lost and forfeited themselves?
     No, on the barren mountains let him starve;
     For I shall never hold that man my friend   90
     Whose tongue shall ask me for one penny cost
     To ransom home revolted Mortimer.

HOTSPUR   'Revolted Mortimer'!
     He never did fall off, my sovereign liege,
     But by the chance of war. To prove that true   95
     Needs no more but one tongue for all those wounds,
     Those mouthed wounds, which valiantly he took
     When on the gentle Severn's sedgy bank,
     In single opposition, hand to hand,
     He did confound the best part of an hour   100
     In changing hardiment with great Glendower.
     Three times they breathed, and three times did they
        drink,
     Upon agreement, of swift Severn's flood,
     Who, then affrighted with their bloody looks,
     Ran fearfully among the trembling reeds   105
     And hid his crisp head in the hollow bank
     Bloodstained with these valiant combatants.
     Never did bare and rotten policy
     Colour her working with such deadly wounds,
     Nor never could the noble Mortimer   110
     Receive so many, and all willingly.
     Then let not him be slandered with revolt.

KING   Thou dost belie him, Percy; thou dost belie him.
     He never did encounter with Glendower.
     I tell thee, he durst as well have met the devil alone   115
     As Owen Glendower for an enemy.
     Art thou not ashamed? But, sirrah, henceforth

Let me not hear you speak of Mortimer.
Send me your prisoners with the speediest means,
120 Or you shall hear in such a kind from me
As will displease you. – My lord Northumberland,
We license your departure with your son.
[*to Hotspur*] Send us your prisoners, or you will hear
of it.
    Exit King [*with all but Hotspur and Northumberland*].
HOTSPUR   An if the devil come and roar for them
125 I will not send them. I will after straight
And tell him so, for I will ease my heart,
Albeit I make a hazard of my head.
NORTHUMBERLAND
  What, drunk with choler? Stay and pause awhile.

       Enter WORCESTER.

Here comes your uncle.
HOTSPUR   'Speak of Mortimer'?
130 Zounds, I will speak of him, and let my soul
Want mercy if I do not join with him.
Yea, on his part I'll empty all these veins
And shed my dear blood drop by drop in the dust,
But I will lift the down-trod Mortimer
135 As high in the air as this unthankful King,
As this ingrate and cankered Bolingbroke.
NORTHUMBERLAND [*to Worcester*]
  Brother, the King hath made your nephew mad.
WORCESTER   Who struck this heat up after I was gone?
HOTSPUR   He will forsooth have all my prisoners;
140 And when I urged the ransom once again
Of my wife's brother, then his cheek looked pale
And on my face he turned an eye of death,
Trembling even at the name of 'Mortimer'.
WORCESTER
  I cannot blame him: was not he proclaimed
145 By Richard, that dead is, the next of blood?
NORTHUMBERLAND
  He was; I heard the proclamation.
And then it was when the unhappy King
(Whose wrongs in us God pardon!) did set forth
Upon his Irish expedition,
150 From whence he, intercepted, did return
To be deposed and shortly murdered.
WORCESTER
  And for whose death we in the world's wide mouth
Live scandalized and foully spoken of.
HOTSPUR   But soft, I pray you; did King Richard then
155 Proclaim my brother, Edmund Mortimer,
Heir to the crown?
NORTHUMBERLAND   He did; myself did hear it.
HOTSPUR   Nay, then I cannot blame his cousin King
That wished him on the barren mountains starve.
But shall it be that you that set the crown
160 Upon the head of this forgetful man
And for his sake wear the detested blot
Of murderous subornation – shall it be
That you a world of curses undergo,

Being the agents or base second means,
The cords, the ladder, or the hangman rather?   165
O, pardon me that I descend so low
To show the line and the predicament
Wherein you range under this subtle King!
Shall it for shame be spoken in these days,
Or fill up chronicles in time to come,   170
That men of your nobility and power
Did gage them both in an unjust behalf
(As both of you, God pardon it, have done)
To put down Richard, that sweet lovely rose,
And plant this thorn, this canker, Bolingbroke?   175
And shall it in more shame be further spoken
That you are fooled, discarded and shook off
By him for whom these shames ye underwent?
No! Yet time serves wherein you may redeem
Your banished honours and restore yourselves   180
Into the good thoughts of the world again,
Revenge the jeering and disdained contempt
Of this proud King, who studies day and night
To answer all the debt he owes to you
Even with the bloody payment of your deaths.   185
Therefore, I say –
WORCESTER   Peace, cousin, say no more.
And now I will unclasp a secret book,
And to your quick-conceiving discontents
I'll read you matter deep and dangerous,
As full of peril and adventurous spirit   190
As to o'erwalk a current roaring loud
On the unsteadfast footing of a spear.
HOTSPUR   If he fall in, good night. Or sink or swim,
Send danger from the east unto the west,
So honour cross it from the north to south –   195
And let them grapple. O, the blood more stirs
To rouse a lion than to start a hare!
NORTHUMBERLAND [*to Worcester*]
  Imagination of some great exploit
Drives him beyond the bounds of patience.
HOTSPUR   By heaven, methinks it were an easy leap   200
To pluck bright honour from the pale-faced moon,
Or dive into the bottom of the deep,
Where fathom-line could never touch the ground,
And pluck up drowned honour by the locks,
So he that doth redeem her thence might wear,   205
Without corrival, all her dignities.
But out upon this half-faced fellowship!
WORCESTER [*to Northumberland*]
  He apprehends a world of figures here
But not the form of what he should attend.
[*to Hotspur*] Good cousin, give me audience for a while.   210
HOTSPUR   I cry you mercy.
WORCESTER   Those same noble Scots
That are your prisoners –
HOTSPUR   I'll keep them all.
By God, he shall not have a scot of them;
No, if a scot would save his soul he shall not.
I'll keep them, by this hand.

215 WORCESTER   You start away
And lend no ear unto my purposes.
Those prisoners you shall keep.
HOTSPUR   Nay, I will; that's flat.
He said he would not ransom Mortimer,
Forbade my tongue to speak of Mortimer;
220 But I will find him when he lies asleep,
And in his ear I'll holler 'Mortimer!'
Nay, I'll have a starling shall be taught to speak
Nothing but 'Mortimer' and give it him
To keep his anger still in motion.
225 WORCESTER   Hear you, cousin, a word.
HOTSPUR   All studies here I solemnly defy,
Save how to gall and pinch this Bolingbroke
And that same sword-and-buckler Prince of Wales
(But that I think his father loves him not
230 And would be glad he met with some mischance,
I would have him poisoned with a pot of ale).
WORCESTER   Farewell, kinsman. I'll talk to you
When you are better tempered to attend.
NORTHUMBERLAND [*to Hotspur*]
Why, what a wasp-stung and impatient fool
235 Art thou to break into this woman's mood,
Tying thine ear to no tongue but thine own!
HOTSPUR
Why, look you, I am whipped and scourged with rods,
Nettled and stung with pismires, when I hear
Of this vile politician Bolingbroke.
240 In Richard's time – what do you call the place?
A plague upon it. It is in Gloucestershire.
'Twas where the madcap duke his uncle kept,
His uncle York, where I first bowed my knee
Unto this king of smiles, this Bolingbroke.
245 'Sblood, when you and he came back from Ravenspur.
NORTHUMBERLAND   At Berkeley castle?
HOTSPUR   You say true.
Why, what a candy deal of courtesy
This fawning greyhound then did proffer me!
250 'Look when his infant fortune came to age',
And 'gentle Harry Percy', and 'kind cousin'.
O, the devil take such cozeners!
– God forgive me. Good uncle, tell your tale;
I have done.
WORCESTER   Nay, if you have not, to it again;
We will stay your leisure.
255 HOTSPUR   I have done, i'faith.
WORCESTER
Then once more to your Scottish prisoners.
Deliver them up without their ransom straight,
And make the Douglas' son your only mean
For powers in Scotland, which, for divers reasons
260 Which I shall send you written, be assured
Will easily be granted. [*to Northumberland*] You, my
     lord,
Your son in Scotland being thus employed,
Shall secretly into the bosom creep
Of that same noble prelate well beloved,

The Archbishop.
HOTSPUR   Of York, is it not?
WORCESTER   True, who bears hard   265
His brother's death at Bristol, the Lord Scrope.
I speak not this in estimation
As what I think might be, but what I know
Is ruminated, plotted and set down,
And only stays but to behold the face   270
Of that occasion that shall bring it on.
HOTSPUR   I smell it. Upon my life, it will do well.
NORTHUMBERLAND
Before the game is afoot thou still let'st slip.
HOTSPUR   Why, it cannot choose but be a noble plot –
And then the power of Scotland and of York   275
To join with Mortimer, ha?
WORCESTER   And so they shall.
HOTSPUR   In faith, it is exceedingly well aimed.
WORCESTER   And 'tis no little reason bids us speed
To save our heads by raising of a head;
For, bear ourselves as even as we can,   280
The King will always think him in our debt,
And think we think ourselves unsatisfied,
Till he hath found a time to pay us home.
And see already how he doth begin
To make us strangers to his looks of love.   285
HOTSPUR   He does; he does. We'll be revenged on him.
WORCESTER   Cousin, farewell. No further go in this
Than I by letters shall direct your course.
When time is ripe, which will be suddenly,
I'll steal to Glendower and Lord Mortimer,   290
Where you and Douglas and our powers at once,
As I will fashion it, shall happily meet
To bear our fortunes in our own strong arms,
Which now we hold at much uncertainty.
NORTHUMBERLAND
Farewell, good brother. We shall thrive, I trust. 295
HOTSPUR [*to Worcester*]
Uncle, adieu. O, let the hours be short
Till fields and blows and groans applaud our sport!
                                        Exeunt.

2.1   *Enter a* Carrier *with a lantern in his hand.*

1 CARRIER   Hey-ho! An it be not four by the day, I'll be
hanged. Charles's Wain is over the new chimney, and
yet our horse not packed. – What, ostler!
OSTLER [*within*]   Anon, anon!
1 CARRIER   I prithee, Tom, beat Cut's saddle; put a few   5
flocks in the point. Poor jade is wrung in the withers,
out of all cess.

                Enter another Carrier.

2 CARRIER   Peas and beans are as dank here as a dog, and
that is the next way to give poor jades the bots. This
house is turned upside down since Robin Ostler died.   10
1 CARRIER   Poor fellow never joyed since the price of
oats rose; it was the death of him.

2 CARRIER   I think this be the most villainous house in all London road for fleas. I am stung like a tench.

15 1 CARRIER   Like a tench? By the mass, there is ne'er a king christen could be better bit than I have been since the first cock.

2 CARRIER   Why, they will allow us ne'er a jordan, and then we leak in your chimney, and your chamber lye
20 breeds fleas like a loach.

1 CARRIER   What, ostler! Come away, and be hanged! Come away!

2 CARRIER   I have a gammon of bacon and two races of ginger to be delivered as far as Charing Cross.

25 1 CARRIER   God's body, the turkeys in my pannier are quite starved! What, ostler! A plague on thee, hast thou never an eye in thy head? Canst not hear? An 'twere not as good deed as drink to break the pate on thee, I am a very villain. Come, and be hanged! Hast no faith in
30 thee?

Enter GADSHILL.

GADSHILL   Good morrow, carriers. What's o'clock?

1 CARRIER   I think it be two o'clock.

GADSHILL   I prithee, lend me thy lantern to see my gelding in the stable.

35 1 CARRIER   Nay, by God, soft. I know a trick worth two of that, i'faith.

GADSHILL   [*to Second Carrier*]   I pray thee, lend me thine.

2 CARRIER   Ay, when, canst tell? 'Lend me thy lantern,'
40 quoth he. Marry, I'll see thee hanged first.

GADSHILL   Sirrah carrier, what time do you mean to come to London?

2 CARRIER   Time enough to go to bed with a candle, I warrant thee. – Come, neighbour Mugs, we'll call up
45 the gentlemen. They will along with company, for they have great charge.   *Exeunt Carriers.*

Enter Chamberlain.

GADSHILL   What ho, chamberlain!

CHAMBERLAIN   'At hand', quoth Pickpurse.

GADSHILL   That's even as fair as ' "At hand", quoth the
50 chamberlain,' for thou variest no more from picking of purses than giving direction doth from labouring: thou layest the plot how.

CHAMBERLAIN   Good morrow, Master Gadshill. It holds current that I told you yesternight. There's a
55 franklin in the Weald of Kent hath brought three hundred marks with him in gold. I heard him tell it to one of his company last night at supper – a kind of auditor, one that hath abundance of charge too, God knows what. They are up already, and call for eggs and
60 butter. They will away presently.

GADSHILL   Sirrah, if they meet not with Saint Nicholas's clerks, I'll give thee this neck.

CHAMBERLAIN   No, I'll none of it; I pray thee keep that for the hangman, for I know thou worshippest Saint
65 Nicholas as truly as a man of falsehood may.

GADSHILL   What talkest thou to me of the hangman? If I hang, I'll make a fat pair of gallows; for, if I hang, old Sir John hangs with me, and thou knowest he is no starveling. Tut, there are other Trojans that thou dreamest not of,
70 the which for sport sake are content to do the profession some grace, that would, if matters should be looked into, for their own credit sake make all whole. I am joined with no foot-landrakers, no long-staff sixpenny strikers, none of these mad mustachio purple-hued maltworms, but
75 with nobility and tranquillity, burgomasters and great oneyers, such as can hold in, such as will strike sooner than speak, and speak sooner than drink, and drink sooner than pray – and yet, zounds, I lie, for they pray continually to their saint the commonwealth, or, rather,
80 not pray to her but prey on her, for they ride up and down on her and make her their boots.

CHAMBERLAIN   What, the commonwealth their boots? Will she hold out water in foul way?

GADSHILL   She will, she will; justice hath liquored her.
85 We steal as in a castle, cocksure. We have the receipt of fern-seed; we walk invisible.

CHAMBERLAIN   Nay, by my faith, I think you are more beholden to the night than to fern-seed for your walking invisible.

90 GADSHILL   Give me thy hand; thou shalt have a share in our purchase, as I am a true man.

CHAMBERLAIN   Nay, rather let me have it as you are a false thief.

GADSHILL   Go to. *Homo* is a common name to all men.
95 Bid the ostler bring my gelding out of the stable. Farewell, you muddy knave.   *Exeunt.*

2.2   *Enter* PRINCE, POINS, PETO *and* BARDOLL.

POINS   Come, shelter, shelter! I have removed Falstaff's horse, and he frets like a gummed velvet.

PRINCE   Stand close! [*Poins, Peto and Bardoll hide.*]

Enter FALSTAFF.

FALSTAFF   Poins! Poins, and be hanged! Poins!

5 PRINCE   Peace, ye fat-kidneyed rascal! What a brawling dost thou keep!

FALSTAFF   Where's Poins, Hal?

PRINCE   He is walked up to the top of the hill. I'll go seek him. [*Hides with the others.*]

10 FALSTAFF   I am accursed to rob in that thief's company. The rascal hath removed my horse and tied him I know not where. If I travel but four foot by the square further afoot, I shall break my wind. Well, I doubt not but to die a fair death for all this, if I scape hanging for killing that
15 rogue. I have forsworn his company hourly any time this two-and-twenty years, and yet I am bewitched with the rogue's company. If the rascal have not given me medicines to make me love him, I'll be hanged. It could not be else: I have drunk medicines. Poins! Hal! A
20 plague upon you both! Bardoll! Peto! I'll starve ere I'll

rob a foot further. An 'twere not as good a deed as drink to turn true man and to leave these rogues, I am the veriest varlet that ever chewed with a tooth. Eight yards of uneven ground is threescore and ten miles afoot with me, and the stony-hearted villains know it well enough. A plague upon it when thieves cannot be true one to another! [*They whistle.*] Whew! [*Prince, Poins, Bardoll and Peto come forward.*] A plague upon you all! Give me my horse, you rogues; give me my horse and be hanged!

PRINCE Peace, ye fat-guts. Lie down, lay thine ear close to the ground and list if thou canst hear the tread of travellers.

FALSTAFF Have you any levers to lift me up again being down? 'Sblood, I'll not bear my own flesh so far afoot again for all the coin in thy father's exchequer. What a plague mean ye to colt me thus?

PRINCE Thou liest: thou art not colted; thou art uncolted.

FALSTAFF I prithee, good Prince Hal, help me to my horse, good king's son.

PRINCE Out, ye rogue; shall I be your ostler?

FALSTAFF Hang thyself in thine own heir-apparent garters! If I be ta'en, I'll peach for this. An I have not ballads made on you all and sung to filthy tunes, let a cup of sack be my poison. When a jest is so forward, and afoot too! I hate it.

Enter GADSHILL.

GADSHILL Stand!

FALSTAFF So I do, against my will.

POINS O, 'tis our setter; I know his voice, Bardoll. – What news?

GADSHILL Case ye, case ye; on with your vizards! There's money of the King's coming down the hill; 'tis going to the King's exchequer.

FALSTAFF You lie, ye rogue; 'tis going to the King's tavern.

GADSHILL There's enough to make us all –

FALSTAFF To be hanged.

PRINCE Sirs, you four shall front them in the narrow lane; Ned Poins and I will walk lower. If they scape from your encounter, then they light on us.

PETO How many be there of them?

GADSHILL Some eight or ten.

FALSTAFF Zounds, will they not rob us?

PRINCE What, a coward, Sir John Paunch?

FALSTAFF Indeed I am not John of Gaunt, your grandfather, but yet no coward, Hal.

PRINCE Well, we leave that to the proof.

POINS Sirrah Jack, thy horse stands behind the hedge. When thou needest him, there thou shalt find him. Farewell, and stand fast.

FALSTAFF Now cannot I strike him, if I should be hanged.

PRINCE [*aside to Poins*] Ned, where are our disguises?

POINS [*aside to the Prince*] Here, hard by. Stand close.

Exeunt Prince and Poins.

FALSTAFF Now, my masters, happy man be his dole, say I. Every man to his business.

Enter the Travellers.

1 TRAVELLER Come, neighbour, the boy shall lead our horses down the hill. We'll walk afoot awhile and ease our legs.

THIEVES Stand!

2 TRAVELLER Jesus bless us!

FALSTAFF Strike! Down with them! Cut the villains' throats! Ah, whoreson caterpillars, bacon-fed knaves! They hate us youth. Down with them! Fleece them!

1 TRAVELLER O, we are undone, both we and ours for ever!

FALSTAFF Hang ye, gorbellied knaves, are ye undone? No, ye fat chuffs; I would your store were here. On, bacons, on! What, ye knaves? Young men must live. You are grand-jurors, are ye? We'll jure ye, faith. [*Here they rob them and bind them.*] *Exeunt.*

Enter the PRINCE *and* POINS.

PRINCE The thieves have bound the true men; now could thou and I rob the thieves, and go merrily to London, it would be argument for a week, laughter for a month, and a good jest for ever.

POINS Stand close. I hear them coming. [*They conceal themselves.*]

Enter the Thieves *again.*

FALSTAFF Come, my masters, let us share, and then to horse before day. An the Prince and Poins be not two arrant cowards, there's no equity stirring. There's no more valour in that Poins than in a wild duck. [*As they are sharing, the Prince and Poins set upon them.*]

PRINCE Your money!

POINS Villains!

They all run away, and Falstaff, after a blow or two, runs away too, leaving the booty behind them.

PRINCE
Got with much ease. Now merrily to horse.
The thieves are all scattered and possessed with fear
So strongly that they dare not meet each other.
Each takes his fellow for an officer.
Away, good Ned. Falstaff sweats to death
And lards the lean earth as he walks along.
Were't not for laughing, I should pity him.

POINS How the fat rogue roared! *Exeunt.*

2.3 *Enter* HOTSPUR *alone, reading a letter.*

HOTSPUR *But for mine own part, my lord, I could be well contented to be there, in respect of the love I bear your house.* He could be contented; why is he not then? In the respect of the love he bears our house! He shows in this he loves his own barn better than he loves our house. Let me see some more. *The purpose you*

undertake is dangerous – Why, that's certain: 'tis
dangerous to take a cold, to sleep, to drink; but I tell
you, my lord fool, out of this nettle, danger, we pluck
this flower, safety. *The purpose you undertake is*
dangerous, the friends you have named uncertain, the time
itself unsorted, and your whole plot too light for the
counterpoise of so great an opposition. Say you so; say
you so? I say unto you again you are a shallow, cowardly
hind, and you lie. What a lack-brain is this! By the
Lord, our plot is a good plot as ever was laid, our
friends true and constant; a good plot, good friends,
and full of expectation; an excellent plot, very good
friends. What a frosty-spirited rogue is this! Why, my
lord of York commends the plot and the general course
of the action. Zounds, an I were now by this rascal, I
could brain him with his lady's fan. Is there not my
father, my uncle and myself, Lord Edmund Mortimer,
my lord of York and Owen Glendower? Is there not,
besides, the Douglas? Have I not all their letters to
meet me in arms by the ninth of the next month, and
are they not some of them set forward already? What a
pagan rascal is this! An infidel! Ha, you shall see now,
in very sincerity of fear and cold heart will he to the
King and lay open all our proceedings! O, I could
divide myself and go to buffets for moving such a dish
of skim-milk with so honourable an action! Hang him!
Let him tell the King. We are prepared; I will set
forward tonight.

Enter his LADY.

How now, Kate? I must leave you within these two
hours.

LADY PERCY   O my good lord, why are you thus alone?
For what offence have I this fortnight been
A banished woman from my Harry's bed?
Tell me, sweet lord, what is't that takes from thee
Thy stomach, pleasure and thy golden sleep?
Why dost thou bend thine eyes upon the earth
And start so often when thou sitt'st alone?
Why hast thou lost the fresh blood in thy cheeks
And given my treasures and my rights of thee
To thick-eyed musing and curst melancholy?
In thy faint slumbers I by thee have watched
And heard thee murmur tales of iron wars,
Speak terms of manage to thy bounding steed,
Cry 'Courage! To the field!' And thou hast talked
Of sallies and retires, of trenches, tents,
Of palisadoes, frontiers, parapets,
Of basilisks, of cannon, culverin,
Of prisoners' ransom, and of soldiers slain,
And all the currents of a heady fight.
Thy spirit within thee hath been so at war,
And thus hath so bestirred thee in thy sleep,
That beads of sweat have stood upon thy brow
Like bubbles in a late-disturbed stream,
And in thy face strange motions have appeared
Such as we see when men restrain their breath

On some great sudden hest. O, what portents are
  these?
Some heavy business hath my lord in hand,
And I must know it, else he loves me not.
HOTSPUR
What ho!

Enter Servant.

      Is Gilliams with the packet gone?
SERVANT   He is, my lord, an hour ago.
HOTSPUR
Hath Butler brought those horses from the sheriff?
SERVANT   One horse, my lord, he brought even now.
HOTSPUR   What horse? Roan? A crop-ear, is it not?
SERVANT   It is, my lord.
HOTSPUR   That Roan shall be my throne.
Well, I will back him straight. O, Esperance!
Bid Butler lead him forth into the park.

                        Exit Servant.
LADY PERCY   But hear you, my lord.
HOTSPUR   What sayst thou, my lady?
LADY PERCY   What is it carries you away?
HOTSPUR   Why, my horse,
My love, my horse.
LADY PERCY   Out, you mad-headed ape!
A weasel hath not such a deal of spleen
As you are tossed with. In faith,
I'll know your business, Harry, that I will.
I fear my brother Mortimer doth stir
About his title and hath sent for you
To line his enterprise; but if you go –
HOTSPUR   So far afoot? I shall be weary, love.
LADY PERCY   Come, come, you paraquito, answer me
Directly unto this question that I ask.
In faith, I'll break thy little finger, Harry,
An if thou wilt not tell me all things true.
HOTSPUR
Away, away, you trifler! Love? I love thee not;
I care not for thee, Kate. This is no world
To play with mammets and to tilt with lips.
We must have bloody noses and cracked crowns,
And pass them current, too – God s' me, my horse! –
What sayst thou, Kate? What wouldst thou have with
  me?
LADY PERCY   Do you not love me? Do you not indeed?
Well, do not, then, for since you love me not
I will not love myself. Do you not love me?
Nay, tell me if you speak in jest or no.
HOTSPUR   Come, wilt thou see me ride?
And when I am a-horseback, I will swear
I love thee infinitely. But hark you, Kate.
I must not have you henceforth question me
Whither I go, nor reason whereabout.
Whither I must, I must, and, to conclude,
This evening must I leave you, gentle Kate.
I know you wise but yet no farther wise
Than Harry Percy's wife. Constant you are

105　But yet a woman; and for secrecy
　　No lady closer, for I well believe
　　Thou wilt not utter what thou dost not know.
　　And so far will I trust thee, gentle Kate.
　　LADY PERCY　How! So far?
110　HOTSPUR　Not an inch further. But hark you, Kate,
　　Whither I go, thither shall you go too.
　　Today will I set forth, tomorrow you.
　　Will this content you, Kate?
　　LADY PERCY　　　　　　It must, of force.　*Exeunt.*

2.4　　　　　　*Enter* PRINCE.

PRINCE　Ned, prithee come out of that fat room and
　　lend me thy hand to laugh a little.

Enter POINS.

POINS　Where hast been, Hal?
PRINCE　With three or four loggerheads, amongst three
5　　or fourscore hogsheads. I have sounded the very bass
　　string of humility. Sirrah, I am sworn brother to a
　　leash of drawers and can call them all by their Christian
　　names, as Tom, Dick and Francis. They take it already,
　　upon their salvation, that, though I be but Prince of
10　　Wales, yet I am the king of courtesy, and tell me flatly I
　　am no proud jack, like Falstaff, but a Corinthian, a lad
　　of mettle, a good boy – by the Lord, so they call me –
　　and when I am King of England I shall command all
　　the good lads in Eastcheap. They call drinking deep
15　　'dyeing scarlet', and, when you breathe in your
　　watering, they cry 'Hem!' and bid you 'Play it off!' To
　　conclude, I am so good a proficient in one quarter of an
　　hour that I can drink with any tinker in his own
　　language during my life. I tell thee, Ned, thou hast lost
20　　much honour that thou wert not with me in this action.
　　But, sweet Ned – to sweeten which name of Ned I give
　　thee this pennyworth of sugar, clapped even now into
　　my hand by an underskinker, one that never spake
　　other English in his life than 'Eight shillings and
25　　sixpence', and 'You are welcome', with this shrill
　　addition, 'Anon, anon, sir! Score a pint of bastard in
　　the Half-moon!' or so. But, Ned, to drive away the
　　time till Falstaff come, I prithee, do thou stand in some
　　by-room, while I question my puny drawer to what end
30　　he gave me the sugar, and do thou never leave calling
　　'Francis!', that his tale to me may be nothing but
　　'Anon'. Step aside, and I'll show thee a precedent.
　　　　　　　　　　　　　　　　Exit Poins.
POINS　[*within*]　Francis!
PRINCE　Thou art perfect.
35　POINS　[*within*]　Francis!

Enter Drawer [FRANCIS].

FRANCIS　Anon, anon, sir! – Look down into the
　　Pomegranate, Ralph!
PRINCE　Come hither, Francis.
FRANCIS　My lord?

PRINCE　How long hast thou to serve, Francis?　　40
FRANCIS　Forsooth, five years, and as much as to –
POINS　[*within*]　Francis!
FRANCIS　Anon, anon, sir!
PRINCE　Five year! By'r Lady, a long lease for the
　　clinking of pewter. But, Francis, darest thou be so　45
　　valiant as to play the coward with thy indenture, and
　　show it a fair pair of heels, and run from it?
FRANCIS　O Lord, sir, I'll be sworn upon all the books in
　　England, I could find in my heart –
POINS　[*within*]　Francis!　　50
FRANCIS　Anon, sir!
PRINCE　How old art thou, Francis?
FRANCIS　Let me see; about Michaelmas next I shall be –
POINS　[*within*]　Francis!
FRANCIS　Anon, sir! [*to the Prince*] Pray, stay a little, my　55
　　lord.
PRINCE　Nay, but hark you, Francis. For the sugar thou
　　gavest me, 'twas a pennyworth, was't not?
FRANCIS　O Lord, I would it had been two!
PRINCE　I will give thee for it a thousand pound. Ask me　60
　　when thou wilt, and thou shalt have it.
POINS　[*within*]　Francis!
FRANCIS　Anon, anon.
PRINCE　'Anon', Francis? No, Francis. But tomorrow,
　　Francis; or, Francis, o'Thursday; or, indeed, Francis,　65
　　when thou wilt. But Francis –
FRANCIS　My lord?
PRINCE　Wilt thou rob this leathern-jerkin, crystal-
　　button, not-pated, agate-ring, puke-stocking, caddis-
　　garter, smooth-tongue, Spanish-pouch?　　70
FRANCIS　O Lord, sir, who do you mean?
PRINCE　Why, then, your brown bastard is your only
　　drink! For look you, Francis, your white canvas doublet
　　will sully. In Barbary, sir, it cannot come to so much.
FRANCIS　What, sir?　　75
POINS　[*within*]　Francis!
PRINCE　Away, you rogue! Dost thou not hear them call?
　　[*Here they both call him. The Drawer stands amazed,
　　not knowing which way to go.*]

Enter Vintner.

VINTNER　What, standest thou still and hear'st such a
　　calling? Look to the guests within.　　*Exit Francis.*
　　My lord, old Sir John with half a dozen more are at the　80
　　door. Shall I let them in?
PRINCE　Let them alone awhile and then open the door.
　　　　　　　　　　　　　　　　Exit Vintner.
　　Poins!

Enter POINS.

POINS　Anon, anon, sir!
PRINCE　Sirrah, Falstaff and the rest of the thieves are at　85
　　the door. Shall we be merry?
POINS　As merry as crickets, my lad. But hark ye, what
　　cunning match have you made with this jest of the
　　drawer? Come, what's the issue?

PRINCE   I am now of all humours that have showed
themselves humours since the old days of Goodman
Adam to the pupil age of this present twelve o'clock at
midnight.

Enter FRANCIS.

What's o'clock, Francis?

FRANCIS   Anon, anon, sir.   *Exit.*

PRINCE   That ever this fellow should have fewer words
than a parrot, and yet the son of a woman! His industry
is upstairs and downstairs, his eloquence the parcel of
a reckoning. I am not yet of Percy's mind, the Hotspur
of the North, he that kills me some six or seven dozen
of Scots at a breakfast, washes his hands, and says to
his wife, 'Fie upon this quiet life! I want work.' 'O my
sweet Harry', says she, 'how many hast thou killed
today?' 'Give my roan horse a drench', says he, and
answers, 'Some fourteen', an hour after, 'a trifle, a
trifle'. I prithee, call in Falstaff. I'll play Percy, and that
damned brawn shall play Dame Mortimer his wife.
'Rivo!' says the drunkard. Call in Ribs; call in Tallow.

Enter FALSTAFF, BARDOLL, PETO *and* GADSHILL,
followed by FRANCIS *carrying wine.*

POINS   Welcome, Jack. Where hast thou been?

FALSTAFF   A plague of all cowards, I say, and a vengeance
too. Marry and amen! – Give me a cup of sack, boy. –
Ere I lead this life long, I'll sew netherstocks and mend
them, and foot them too. A plague of all cowards. –
Give me a cup of sack, rogue. – Is there no virtue
extant? [*Francis hands Falstaff a cup and he drinketh.*]

PRINCE   Didst thou never see Titan kiss a dish of butter
(pitiful-hearted Titan) that melted at the sweet tale of
the sun? If thou didst, then behold that compound.

FALSTAFF [*to Francis*]   You rogue, here's lime in this
sack too. – There is nothing but roguery to be found in
villainous man, yet a coward is worse than a cup of sack
with lime in it. A villainous coward! Go thy ways, old
Jack; die when thou wilt. If manhood, good manhood,
be not forgot upon the face of the earth, then am I a
shotten herring. There lives not three good men
unhanged in England and one of them is fat and grows
old, God help the while. A bad world, I say. I would I
were a weaver; I could sing psalms or anything. A
plague of all cowards, I say still.

PRINCE   How now, woolsack, what mutter you?

FALSTAFF   A king's son! If I do not beat thee out of thy
kingdom with a dagger of lath and drive all thy subjects
afore thee like a flock of wild geese, I'll never wear hair
on my face more. You, Prince of Wales!

PRINCE   Why, you whoreson round man, what's the
matter?

FALSTAFF   Are not you a coward? Answer me to that.
And Poins there?

POINS   Zounds, ye fat paunch, an ye call me coward, by
the Lord, I'll stab thee.

FALSTAFF   I call thee coward? I'll see thee damned ere I
call thee coward, but I would give a thousand pound I
could run as fast as thou canst. You are straight enough
in the shoulders; you care not who sees your back. Call
you that backing of your friends? A plague upon such
backing! Give me them that will face me. – Give me a
cup of sack; I am a rogue if I drunk today.

PRINCE   O villain, thy lips are scarce wiped since thou
drunkest last.

FALSTAFF   All is one for that. [*He drinketh.*] A plague of
all cowards, still say I.

PRINCE   What's the matter?

FALSTAFF   What's the matter? There be four of us here
have ta'en a thousand pound this day morning.

PRINCE   Where is it, Jack? Where is it?

FALSTAFF   Where is it? Taken from us it is. A hundred
upon poor four of us.

PRINCE   What, a hundred, man?

FALSTAFF   I am a rogue if I were not at half-sword with
a dozen of them, two hours together. I have scaped by
miracle. I am eight times thrust through the doublet,
four through the hose, my buckler cut through and
through, my sword hacked like a handsaw. *Ecce signum!*
I never dealt better since I was a man. All would not do.
A plague of all cowards! [*Indicates Gadshill, Peto and
Bardoll.*] Let them speak. If they speak more or less
than truth, they are villains and the sons of darkness.

PRINCE   Speak, sirs, how was it?

BARDOLL   We four set upon some dozen –

FALSTAFF [*to the Prince*]   Sixteen at least, my lord.

BARDOLL   And bound them.

PETO   No, no, they were not bound.

FALSTAFF   You rogue, they were bound, every man of
them, or I am a Jew else, an 'Ebrew Jew.

BARDOLL   As we were sharing, some six or seven fresh
men set upon us.

FALSTAFF   And unbound the rest, and then come in the
other.

PRINCE   What, fought you with them all?

FALSTAFF   All? I know not what you call all, but if I
fought not with fifty of them, I am a bunch of radish.
If there were not two- or three-and-fifty upon poor old
Jack, then am I no two-legged creature.

PRINCE   Pray God you have not murdered some of
them.

FALSTAFF   Nay, that's past praying for. I have peppered
two of them. Two I am sure I have paid, two rogues in
buckram suits. I tell thee what, Hal, if I tell thee a lie,
spit in my face, call me horse. Thou knowest my old
ward. Here I lay, and thus I bore my point. Four rogues
in buckram let drive at me.

PRINCE   What, four? Thou saidst but two even now.

FALSTAFF   Four, Hal; I told thee four.

POINS   Ay, ay, he said four.

FALSTAFF   These four came all afront and mainly thrust
at me. I made me no more ado, but took all their seven
points in my target, thus.

PRINCE   Seven? Why, there were but four even now.

FALSTAFF   In buckram?

200 POINS   Ay, four in buckram suits.

FALSTAFF   Seven, by these hilts, or I am a villain else.

PRINCE [*to Poins*]   Prithee, let him alone. We shall have more anon.

FALSTAFF   Dost thou hear me, Hal?

205 PRINCE   Ay, and mark thee too, Jack.

FALSTAFF   Do so, for it is worth the listening to. These nine in buckram that I told thee of –

PRINCE   So, two more already.

FALSTAFF   Their points being broken –

210 POINS   Down fell their hose.

FALSTAFF   Began to give me ground, but I followed me close, came in foot and hand, and, with a thought, seven of the eleven I paid.

PRINCE   O monstrous! Eleven buckram men grown out
215 of two!

FALSTAFF   But, as the devil would have it, three misbegotten knaves in Kendal green came at my back and let drive at me, for it was so dark, Hal, that thou couldst not see thy hand.

220 PRINCE   These lies are like their father that begets them, gross as a mountain, open, palpable. Why, thou claybrained guts, thou knotty-pated fool, thou whoreson obscene greasy tallow-catch.

FALSTAFF   What, art thou mad? Art thou mad? Is not
225 the truth the truth?

PRINCE   Why, how couldst thou know these men in Kendal green when it was so dark thou couldst not see thy hand? Come, tell us your reason. What sayst thou to this?

230 POINS   Come, your reason, Jack, your reason.

FALSTAFF   What, upon compulsion? Zounds, an I were at the strappado, or all the racks in the world, I would not tell you on compulsion. Give you a reason on compulsion? If reasons were as plentiful as
235 blackberries, I would give no man a reason upon compulsion, I.

PRINCE   I'll be no longer guilty of this sin. This sanguine coward, this bed-presser, this horse-back-breaker, this huge hill of flesh –

240 FALSTAFF   'Sblood, you starveling, you eel-skin, you dried neat's tongue, you bull's pizzle, you stock-fish! O, for breath to utter what is like thee! You tailor's yard, you sheath, you bow-case, you vile standing tuck –

PRINCE   Well, breathe awhile and then to it again, and
245 when thou hast tired thyself in base comparisons, hear me speak but this.

POINS   Mark, Jack.

PRINCE   We two saw you four set on four, and bound them, and were masters of their wealth. Mark now how
250 a plain tale shall put you down. Then did we two set on you four, and, with a word, outfaced you from your prize, and have it, yea, and can show it you here in the house. And, Falstaff, you carried your guts away as

nimbly, with as quick dexterity, and roared for mercy, and still run and roared, as ever I heard bull-calf. What
255 a slave art thou to hack thy sword as thou hast done and then say it was in fight! What trick, what device, what starting-hole canst thou now find out to hide thee from this open and apparent shame?

POINS   Come, let's hear, Jack. What trick hast thou now?   260

FALSTAFF   By the Lord, I knew ye as well as he that made ye. Why, hear you, my masters: was it for me to kill the heir apparent? Should I turn upon the true prince? Why, thou knowest I am as valiant as Hercules, but beware instinct. The lion will not touch the true
265 prince; instinct is a great matter. I was now a coward on instinct. I shall think the better of myself, and thee, during my life – I for a valiant lion and thou for a true prince. But, by the Lord, lads, I am glad you have the money. [*Calls.*] Hostess, clap to the doors. Watch
270 tonight; pray tomorrow. – Gallants, lads, boys, hearts of gold, all the titles of good fellowship come to you! What, shall we be merry? Shall we have a play extempore?

PRINCE   Content, and the argument shall be thy
275 running away.

FALSTAFF   Ah, no more of that, Hal, an thou lovest me.

Enter HOSTESS.

HOSTESS   O Jesu, my lord the Prince!

PRINCE   How now, my lady the hostess; what sayst thou to me?   280

HOSTESS   Marry, my lord, there is a nobleman of the court at door would speak with you. He says he comes from your father.

PRINCE   Give him as much as will make him a royal man and send him back again to my mother.   285

FALSTAFF   What manner of man is he?

HOSTESS   An old man.

FALSTAFF   What doth Gravity out of his bed at midnight? Shall I give him his answer?

PRINCE   Prithee do, Jack.   290

FALSTAFF   Faith, and I'll send him packing.   *Exit.*

PRINCE   Now, sirs: [*to Gadshill*] by'r Lady, you fought fair; so did you, Peto; so did you, Bardoll. You are lions too; you ran away upon instinct. You will not touch the true prince, no, fie!   295

BARDOLL   Faith, I ran when I saw others run.

PRINCE   Faith, tell me now in earnest, how came Falstaff's sword so hacked?

PETO   Why, he hacked it with his dagger, and said he would swear truth out of England but he would make
300 you believe it was done in fight, and persuaded us to do the like.

BARDOLL   Yea, and to tickle our noses with speargrass to make them bleed, and then to beslubber our garments with it and swear it was the blood of true
305 men. I did that I did not this seven year before: I blushed to hear his monstrous devices.

PRINCE   O villain, thou stolest a cup of sack eighteen
years ago, and wert taken with the manner, and ever
310   since thou hast blushed extempore. Thou hadst fire
and sword on thy side, and yet thou ran'st away. What
instinct hadst thou for it?

BARDOLL   My lord, do you see these meteors? Do you
behold these exhalations?

315   PRINCE   I do.

BARDOLL   What think you they portend?

PRINCE   Hot livers and cold purses.

BARDOLL   Choler, my lord, if rightly taken.

PRINCE   No, if rightly taken, halter.

Enter FALSTAFF.

320   Here comes lean Jack; here comes bare-bone. How
now, my sweet creature of bombast? How long is't ago,
Jack, since thou sawest thine own knee?

FALSTAFF   My own knee? When I was about thy years,
Hal, I was not an eagle's talon in the waist; I could have
325   crept into any alderman's thumb-ring. A plague of
sighing and grief, it blows a man up like a bladder.
There's villainous news abroad. Here was Sir John
Bracy from your father; you must to the court in the
morning. That same mad fellow of the north, Percy,
330   and he of Wales that gave Amaimon the bastinado and
made Lucifer cuckold, and swore the devil his true
liegeman upon the cross of a Welsh hook – what a
plague call you him?

POINS   Owen Glendower.

335   FALSTAFF   Owen, Owen, the same; and his son-in-law
Mortimer, and old Northumberland, and that
sprightly Scot of Scots Douglas, that runs a-horseback
up a hill perpendicular –

PRINCE   He that rides at high speed and with his pistol
340   kills a sparrow flying.

FALSTAFF   You have hit it.

PRINCE   So did he never the sparrow.

FALSTAFF   Well, that rascal hath good mettle in him; he
will not run.

345   PRINCE   Why, what a rascal art thou, then, to praise him
so for running!

FALSTAFF   A-horseback, ye cuckoo, but afoot he will not
budge a foot.

PRINCE   Yes, Jack, upon instinct.

350   FALSTAFF   I grant ye, upon instinct. Well, he is there
too, and one Murdoch, and a thousand blue-caps
more. Worcester is stolen away tonight. Thy father's
beard is turned white with the news. You may buy land
now as cheap as stinking mackerel.

355   PRINCE   Why then, it is like if there come a hot June and
this civil buffeting hold, we shall buy maidenheads as
they buy hobnails: by the hundreds.

FALSTAFF   By the mass, lad, thou sayst true; it is like we
shall have good trading that way. But tell me, Hal, art
360   not thou horrible afeard? Thou being heir apparent,
could the world pick thee out three such enemies again
as that fiend Douglas, that spirit Percy and that devil

Glendower? Art thou not horribly afraid? Doth not thy
blood thrill at it?

365   PRINCE   Not a whit, i'faith. I lack some of thy 'instinct'.

FALSTAFF   Well, thou wilt be horribly chid tomorrow
when thou comest to thy father. If thou love me,
practise an answer.

PRINCE   Do thou stand for my father and examine me
370   upon the particulars of my life.

FALSTAFF   Shall I? Content. This chair shall be my
state, this dagger my sceptre and this cushion my
crown.

PRINCE   Thy state is taken for a joint-stool, thy golden
375   sceptre for a leaden dagger and thy precious rich
crown for a pitiful bald crown.

FALSTAFF   Well, an the fire of grace be not quite out of
thee, now shalt thou be moved. Give me a cup of sack
to make my eyes look red, that it may be thought I have
380   wept, for I must speak in passion, and I will do it in
King Cambyses' vein.

PRINCE   Well, here is my leg.

FALSTAFF   And here is my speech. Stand aside, nobility.

HOSTESS   O Jesu, this is excellent sport, i'faith.

FALSTAFF

385   Weep not, sweet Queen, for trickling tears are vain.

HOSTESS   O the father, how he holds his countenance!

FALSTAFF

For God's sake, lords, convey my tristful Queen,
For tears do stop the floodgates of her eyes.

HOSTESS   O Jesu, he doth it as like one of these harlotry
390   players as ever I see!

FALSTAFF   Peace, good pint-pot; peace, good tickle-
brain. – Harry, I do not only marvel where thou
spendest thy time but also how thou art accompanied.
For though the camomile, the more it is trodden on the
395   faster it grows, so youth, the more it is wasted the
sooner it wears. That thou art my son I have partly thy
mother's word, partly my own opinion, but chiefly a
villainous trick of thine eye and a foolish hanging of
thy nether lip that doth warrant me. If then thou be
400   son to me – here lies the point – why, being son to me,
art thou so pointed at? Shall the blessed sun of heaven
prove a micher and eat blackberries? A question not to
be asked. Shall the son of England prove a thief and
take purses? A question to be asked. There is a thing,
405   Harry, which thou hast often heard of, and it is known
to many in our land by the name of pitch. This pitch,
as ancient writers do report, doth defile; so doth the
company thou keepest. For, Harry, now I do not speak
to thee in drink but in tears, not in pleasure but in
410   passion, not in words only but in woes also. And yet
there is a virtuous man whom I have often noted in thy
company, but I know not his name.

PRINCE   What manner of man, an it like your majesty?

FALSTAFF   A goodly, portly man, i'faith, and a corpulent;
415   of a cheerful look, a pleasing eye and a most noble
carriage; and, as I think, his age some fifty, or, by'r
Lady, inclining to threescore. And now I remember

me: his name is Falstaff. If that man should be lewdly
given, he deceiveth me, for, Harry, I see virtue in his
420 looks. If, then, the tree may be known by the fruit, as
the fruit by the tree, then peremptorily I speak it: there
is virtue in that Falstaff. Him keep with; the rest
banish. And tell me now, thou naughty varlet, tell me,
where hast thou been this month?

425 PRINCE   Dost thou speak like a king? Do thou stand for
me, and I'll play my father.

FALSTAFF   Depose me? If thou dost it half so gravely, so
majestically both in word and matter, hang me up by
the heels for a rabbit sucker or a poulter's hare.

430 PRINCE   Well, here I am set.

FALSTAFF   And here I stand. – Judge, my masters.

PRINCE   Now, Harry, whence come you?

FALSTAFF   My noble lord, from Eastcheap.

PRINCE   The complaints I hear of thee are grievous.

435 FALSTAFF   'Sblood, my lord, they are false. – Nay, I'll
tickle ye for a young prince, i'faith.

PRINCE   Swearest thou, ungracious boy? Henceforth
ne'er look on me. Thou art violently carried away from
grace. There is a devil haunts thee in the likeness of an
440 old fat man; a tun of man is thy companion. Why dost
thou converse with that trunk of humours, that
bolting-hutch of beastliness, that swollen parcel of
dropsies, that huge bombard of sack, that stuffed
cloak-bag of guts, that roasted Manningtree ox with
445 the pudding in his belly, that reverend Vice, that grey
Iniquity, that father Ruffian, that Vanity in years?
Wherein is he good, but to taste sack and drink it?
Wherein neat and cleanly, but to carve a capon and eat
it? Wherein cunning, but in craft? Wherein crafty, but
450 in villainy? Wherein villainous, but in all things?
Wherein worthy, but in nothing?

FALSTAFF   I would your grace would take me with you.
Whom means your grace?

PRINCE   That villainous, abominable misleader of
455 youth, Falstaff, that old white-bearded Satan.

FALSTAFF   My lord, the man I know.

PRINCE   I know thou dost.

FALSTAFF   But to say I know more harm in him than in
myself were to say more than I know. That he is old,
460 the more the pity; his white hairs do witness it. But
that he is, saving your reverence, a whoremaster, that I
utterly deny. If sack and sugar be a fault, God help the
wicked. If to be old and merry be a sin, then many an
old host that I know is damned. If to be fat be to be
465 hated, then Pharaoh's lean kine are to be loved. No,
my good lord, banish Peto, banish Bardoll, banish
Poins, but for sweet Jack Falstaff, kind Jack Falstaff,
true Jack Falstaff, valiant Jack Falstaff, and therefore
more valiant being as he is old Jack Falstaff, banish
470 not him thy Harry's company, banish not him thy
Harry's company. Banish plump Jack and banish all
the world.

Loud knocking within. Exeunt Bardoll and Hostess.

PRINCE   I do; I will.

Enter BARDOLL *running.*

BARDOLL   O my lord, my lord, the sheriff with a most
monstrous watch is at the door.   475

FALSTAFF   Out, ye rogue! Play out the play. I have much
to say in the behalf of that Falstaff.

Enter the HOSTESS.

HOSTESS   O Jesu, my lord, my lord!

PRINCE   Hey, hey! The devil rides upon a fiddlestick.
What's the matter.   480

HOSTESS   The sheriff and all the watch are at the door.
They are come to search the house. Shall I let them in?

FALSTAFF   Dost thou hear, Hal? Never call a true piece
of gold a counterfeit. Thou art essentially made
without seeming so.   485

PRINCE   And thou a natural coward without instinct.

FALSTAFF   I deny your major. If you will deny the
sheriff, so; if not, let him enter. If I become not a cart
as well as another man, a plague on my bringing up. I
hope I shall as soon be strangled with a halter as   490
another.

PRINCE   Go hide thee behind the arras. – The rest walk
up above. Now, my masters, for a true face and good
conscience.

FALSTAFF   Both which I have had, but their date is out;   495
and therefore I'll hide me. [*Hides behind the arras.*]

Exeunt all but the Prince and Peto.

PRINCE   Call in the sheriff.

Enter Sheriff *and the* Carrier.

Now, master sheriff, what is your will with me?

SHERIFF
First, pardon me, my lord. A hue and cry
Hath followed certain men unto this house.   500

PRINCE   What men?

SHERIFF   One of them is well known, my gracious lord,
A gross, fat man.

CARRIER   As fat as butter.

PRINCE   The man, I do assure you, is not here,   505
For I myself at this time have employed him.
And, sheriff, I will engage my word to thee
That I will by tomorrow dinner-time
Send him to answer thee or any man
For anything he shall be charged withal.   510
And so let me entreat you leave the house.

SHERIFF   I will, my lord. There are two gentlemen
Have in this robbery lost three hundred marks.

PRINCE   It may be so. If he have robbed these men,
He shall be answerable. And so, farewell.   515

SHERIFF   Good night, my noble lord.

PRINCE   I think it is good morrow, is it not?

SHERIFF   Indeed, my lord, I think it be two o'clock.

Exit with Carrier.

PRINCE   This oily rascal is known as well as Paul's. Go
call him forth.   520

PETO [*Pulls back the arras.*] Falstaff! Fast asleep
  behind the arras and snorting like a horse.

PRINCE   Hark how hard he fetches breath. Search his
  pockets. [*Peto searcheth his pocket and findeth certain*
525 *papers.*] What hast thou found?

PETO   Nothing but papers, my lord.

PRINCE   Let's see what they be. Read them.

PETO [*Reads.*]

    Item: a capon   *2s. 2d.*
    Item: sauce   *4d.*
530   *Item: sack, two gallons*   *5s. 8d.*
    Item: anchovies and sack after supper *2s. 6d.*
    Item: bread   *ob.*

PRINCE   O monstrous! But one halfpennyworth of
  bread to this intolerable deal of sack! What there is else
535 keep close; we'll read it at more advantage. There let
  him sleep till day. I'll to the court in the morning. We
  must all to the wars, and thy place shall be honourable.
  I'll procure this fat rogue a charge of foot, and I know
  his death will be a march of twelvescore. The money
540 shall be paid back again with advantage. Be with me
  betimes in the morning, and so good morrow, Peto.

PETO   Good morrow, good my lord.

                The Prince closes the arras, and exeunt.

3.1   *Enter* HOTSPUR, WORCESTER,
      Lord MORTIMER *and* Owen GLENDOWER.

MORTIMER   These promises are fair, the parties sure,
  And our induction full of prosperous hope.

HOTSPUR   Lord Mortimer and cousin Glendower, will
  you sit down? And uncle Worcester – A plague upon it,
5 I have forgot the map!

GLENDOWER   No, here it is. Sit, cousin Percy.
  Sit, good cousin Hotspur, for by that name,
  As oft as Lancaster doth speak of you,
  His cheek looks pale, and with a rising sigh
  He wisheth you in heaven.

10 HOTSPUR   And you in hell
  As oft as he hears Owen Glendower spoke of.

GLENDOWER   I cannot blame him. At my nativity
  The front of heaven was full of fiery shapes,
  Of burning cressets; and at my birth
15 The frame and huge foundation of the earth
  Shaked like a coward.

HOTSPUR   Why, so it would have done at the same
  season if your mother's cat had but kittened, though
  yourself had never been born.

GLENDOWER
20 I say the earth did shake when I was born.

HOTSPUR   And I say the earth was not of my mind,
  If you suppose as fearing you it shook.

GLENDOWER
  The heavens were all on fire; the earth did tremble.

HOTSPUR
  O, then the earth shook to see the heavens on fire
25 And not in fear of your nativity.

  Diseased nature oftentimes breaks forth
  In strange eruptions. Oft the teeming earth
  Is with a kind of colic pinched and vexed
  By the imprisoning of unruly wind
30 Within her womb, which for enlargement striving
  Shakes the old beldam earth and topples down
  Steeples and moss-grown towers. At your birth
  Our grandam earth, having this distemperature,
  In passion shook.

GLENDOWER   Cousin, of many men
  I do not bear these crossings. Give me leave   35
  To tell you once again that at my birth
  The front of heaven was full of fiery shapes,
  The goats ran from the mountains, and the herds
  Were strangely clamorous to the frighted fields.
  These signs have marked me extraordinary,   40
  And all the courses of my life do show
  I am not in the roll of common men.
  Where is he living, clipped in with the sea
  That chides the banks of England, Scotland, Wales,
  Which calls me pupil or hath read to me?   45
  And bring him out that is but woman's son
  Can trace me in the tedious ways of art
  And hold me pace in deep experiments.

HOTSPUR   I think there's no man speaks better Welsh.
  I'll to dinner.   50

MORTIMER
  Peace, cousin Percy; you will make him mad.

GLENDOWER   I can call spirits from the vasty deep.

HOTSPUR   Why, so can I, or so can any man,
  But will they come when you do call for them?

GLENDOWER
  Why, I can teach you, cousin, to command the devil.   55

HOTSPUR
  And I can teach thee, coz, to shame the devil:
  By telling truth. 'Tell truth, and shame the devil.'
  If thou have power to raise him, bring him hither,
  And I'll be sworn I have power to shame him hence.
  O, while you live, 'tell truth and shame the devil'.   60

MORTIMER
  Come, come, no more of this unprofitable chat.

GLENDOWER
  Three times hath Henry Bolingbroke made head
  Against my power; thrice from the banks of Wye
  And sandy-bottomed Severn have I sent him
  Bootless home and weather-beaten back.   65

HOTSPUR
  Home without boots, and in foul weather too!
  How scapes he agues, in the devil's name?

GLENDOWER
  Come, here is the map. Shall we divide our right
  According to our threefold order ta'en?

MORTIMER   The Archdeacon hath divided it   70
  Into three limits very equally:
  England, from Trent and Severn hitherto,
  By south and east is to my part assigned;
  All westward, Wales beyond the Severn shore

75 And all the fertile land within that bound,
    To Owen Glendower; – and, dear coz, to you
    The remnant northward lying off from Trent.
    And our indentures tripartite are drawn,
    Which, being sealed interchangeably –
80 A business that this night may execute –
    Tomorrow, cousin Percy, you and I
    And my good lord of Worcester will set forth
    To meet your father and the Scottish power,
    As is appointed us, at Shrewsbury.
85 My father Glendower is not ready yet,
    Nor shall we need his help these fourteen days.
    [*to Glendower*] Within that space you may have drawn
        together
    Your tenants, friends and neighbouring gentlemen.
    GLENDOWER
    A shorter time shall send me to you, lords;
90 And in my conduct shall your ladies come,
    From whom you now must steal and take no leave,
    For there will be a world of water shed
    Upon the parting of your wives and you.
    HOTSPUR
    Methinks my moiety, north from Burton here,
95 In quantity equals not one of yours.
    See how this river comes me cranking in
    And cuts me from the best of all my land
    A huge half-moon, a monstrous scantle, out.
    I'll have the current in this place dammed up,
100 And here the smug and silver Trent shall run
    In a new channel fair and evenly.
    It shall not wind with such a deep indent
    To rob me of so rich a bottom here.
    GLENDOWER
    Not wind? It shall; it must. You see it doth.
    MORTIMER
    Yea, but mark how he bears his course and runs me
105   up
    With like advantage on the other side,
    Gelding the opposed continent as much
    As on the other side it takes from you.
    WORCESTER
    Yea, but a little charge will trench him here,
110 And on this north side win this cape of land,
    And then he runs straight and even.
    HOTSPUR   I'll have it so; a little charge will do it.
    GLENDOWER   I'll not have it altered.
    HOTSPUR   Will not you?
    GLENDOWER   No, nor you shall not.
    HOTSPUR   Who shall say me nay?
115 GLENDOWER   Why, that will I.
    HOTSPUR   Let me not understand you, then: speak it in
    Welsh.
    GLENDOWER
    I can speak English, lord, as well as you,
    For I was trained up in the English court,
120 Where, being but young, I framed to the harp
    Many an English ditty lovely well

    And gave the tongue a helpful ornament –
    A virtue that was never seen in you.
    HOTSPUR
    Marry, and I am glad of it, with all my heart.
    I had rather be a kitten and cry 'mew'   125
    Than one of these same metre ballad-mongers.
    I had rather hear a brazen can'stick turned
    Or a dry wheel grate on the axle-tree,
    And that would set my teeth nothing on edge,
    Nothing so much as mincing poetry.   130
    'Tis like the forced gait of a shuffling nag.
    GLENDOWER   Come, you shall have Trent turned.
    HOTSPUR   I do not care. I'll give thrice so much land
    To any well-deserving friend;
    But, in the way of bargain, mark ye me,   135
    I'll cavil on the ninth part of a hair.
    Are the indentures drawn? Shall we be gone?
    GLENDOWER
    The moon shines fair. You may away by night.
    I'll haste the writer, and withal
    Break with your wives of your departure hence.   140
    I am afraid my daughter will run mad,
    So much she doteth on her Mortimer.   *Exit*.
    MORTIMER
    Fie, cousin Percy, how you cross my father!
    HOTSPUR   I cannot choose. Sometime he angers me
    With telling me of the moldwarp and the ant,   145
    Of the dreamer Merlin and his prophecies,
    And of a dragon and a finless fish,
    A clip-winged griffin and a moulten raven,
    A couching lion and a ramping cat,
    And such a deal of skimble-skamble stuff   150
    As puts me from my faith. I tell you what:
    He held me last night at least nine hours
    In reckoning up the several devils' names
    That were his lackeys. I cried, 'Hum!' and 'Well,
        go to',
    But marked him not a word. O, he is as tedious   155
    As a tired horse, a railing wife,
    Worse than a smoky house. I had rather live
    With cheese and garlic in a windmill, far,
    Than feed on cates and have him talk to me
    In any summer-house in Christendom.   160
    MORTIMER   In faith, he is a worthy gentleman,
    Exceedingly well read and profited
    In strange concealments, valiant as a lion,
    And wondrous affable, and as bountiful
    As mines of India. Shall I tell you, cousin?   165
    He holds your temper in a high respect
    And curbs himself even of his natural scope
    When you come cross his humour; faith, he does.
    I warrant you, that man is not alive
    Might so have tempted him as you have done   170
    Without the taste of danger and reproof.
    But do not use it oft, let me entreat you.
    WORCESTER [*to Hotspur*]
    In faith, my lord, you are too wilful-blame

And, since your coming hither, have done enough
175 To put him quite besides his patience.
You must needs learn, lord, to amend this fault.
Though sometimes it show greatness, courage, blood
(And that's the dearest grace it renders you),
Yet oftentimes it doth present harsh rage,
180 Defect of manners, want of government,
Pride, haughtiness, opinion and disdain,
The least of which haunting a nobleman
Loseth men's hearts and leaves behind a stain
Upon the beauty of all parts besides,
185 Beguiling them of commendation.
HOTSPUR
Well I am schooled. Good manners be your speed.

Enter GLENDOWER *with the* LADIES PERCY
and MORTIMER.

Here come our wives, and let us take our leave.
[*Lady Mortimer speaks to Mortimer in Welsh.*]
MORTIMER
This is the deadly spite that angers me:
My wife can speak no English, I no Welsh.
GLENDOWER
190 My daughter weeps; she'll not part with you.
She'll be a soldier, too; she'll to the wars.
MORTIMER
Good father, tell her that she and my aunt Percy
Shall follow in your conduct speedily.
[*Glendower speaks to her in Welsh, and she answers*
him in the same.]
GLENDOWER
She is desperate here – a peevish, self-willed harlotry,
195 One that no persuasion can do good upon.
[*The Lady speaks in Welsh.*]
MORTIMER
I understand thy looks. That pretty Welsh,
Which thou pourest down from these swelling
heavens,
I am too perfect in, and but for shame
In such a parley should I answer thee.
[*The Lady speaks again in Welsh.*]
200 MORTIMER I understand thy kisses, and thou mine,
And that's a feeling disputation;
But I will never be a truant, love,
Till I have learnt thy language, for thy tongue
Makes Welsh as sweet as ditties highly penned,
205 Sung by a fair queen in a summer's bower
With ravishing division to her lute.
GLENDOWER Nay, if you melt, then will she run mad.
[*The Lady speaks again in Welsh.*]
MORTIMER O, I am ignorance itself in this!
GLENDOWER
She bids you on the wanton rushes lay you down
210 And rest your gentle head upon her lap,
And she will sing the song that pleaseth you,
And on your eyelids crown the god of sleep,

Charming your blood with pleasing heaviness,
Making such difference 'twixt wake and sleep
As is the difference betwixt day and night   215
The hour before the heavenly harnessed team
Begins his golden progress in the east.
MORTIMER
With all my heart, I'll sit and hear her sing.
By that time will our book, I think, be drawn.
GLENDOWER
Do so, and those musicians that shall play to you   220
Hang in the air a thousand leagues from hence,
And straight they shall be here. Sit and attend.
HOTSPUR   Come, Kate; thou art perfect in lying down.
Come, quick, quick, that I may lay my head in thy lap.
LADY PERCY   Go, ye giddy goose!   [*The music plays.*] 225
HOTSPUR
Now I perceive the devil understands Welsh,
And 'tis no marvel he is so humorous.
By'r Lady, he is a good musician.
LADY PERCY
Then should you be nothing but musical,
For you are altogether governed by humours.   230
Lie still, ye thief, and hear the lady sing in Welsh.
HOTSPUR   I had rather hear Lady, my brach, howl in Irish.
LADY PERCY   Wouldst thou have thy head broken?
HOTSPUR   No.
LADY PERCY   Then be still.   235
HOTSPUR   Neither; 'tis a woman's fault.
LADY PERCY   Now God help thee!
HOTSPUR   To the Welsh lady's bed.
LADY PERCY   What's that?
HOTSPUR   Peace; she sings. [*Here the Lady sings a Welsh* 240
song.] Come, Kate, I'll have your song too.
LADY PERCY   Not mine, in good sooth.
HOTSPUR   Not yours, in good sooth!
Heart, you swear like a comfit-maker's wife:
'Not you, in good sooth,' and 'As true as I live!'   245
And 'As God shall mend me!' and 'As sure as day!'
And givest such sarcenet surety for thy oaths
As if thou never walk'st further than Finsbury.
Swear me, Kate, like a lady as thou art,
A good mouth-filling oath, and leave 'in sooth'   250
And such protest of pepper gingerbread
To velvet-guards and Sunday citizens.
Come, sing.
LADY PERCY   I will not sing.
HOTSPUR   'Tis the next way to turn tailor or be   255
redbreast teacher. An the indentures be drawn, I'll
away within these two hours; and so come in when ye
will.   *Exit.*
GLENDOWER
Come, come, Lord Mortimer. You are as slow
As hot Lord Percy is on fire to go.   260
By this our book is drawn. We'll but seal
And then to horse immediately.
MORTIMER   With all my heart. *Exeunt.*

3.2 *Enter* KING, PRINCE *of Wales and others.*

KING

Lords, give us leave; the Prince of Wales and I must
  have
Some private conference. But be near at hand,
For we shall presently have need of you.   *Exeunt Lords.*
– I know not whether God will have it so
5 For some displeasing service I have done,
That, in His secret doom, out of my blood
He'll breed revengement and a scourge for me;
But thou dost in thy passages of life
Make me believe that thou art only marked
10 For the hot vengeance and the rod of heaven
To punish my mistreadings. Tell me else,
Could such inordinate and low desires,
Such poor, such bare, such lewd, such mean attempts,
Such barren pleasures, rude society
15 As thou art matched withal and grafted to,
Accompany the greatness of thy blood
And hold their level with thy princely heart?

PRINCE   So please your majesty, I would I could
Quit all offences with as clear excuse
20 As well as I am doubtless I can purge
Myself of many I am charged withal.
Yet such extenuation let me beg
As, in reproof of many tales devised
(Which oft the ear of greatness needs must hear),
25 By smiling pickthanks and base newsmongers,
I may for some things true, wherein my youth
Hath faulty wandered and irregular,
Find pardon on my true submission.

KING   God pardon thee! Yet let me wonder, Harry,
30 At thy affections, which do hold a wing
Quite from the flight of all thy ancestors.
Thy place in Council thou hast rudely lost,
Which by thy younger brother is supplied,
And art almost an alien to the hearts
35 Of all the court and princes of my blood.
The hope and expectation of thy time
Is ruined, and the soul of every man
Prophetically do forethink thy fall.
Had I so lavish of my presence been,
40 So common-hackneyed in the eyes of men,
So stale and cheap to vulgar company,
Opinion, that did help me to the crown,
Had still kept loyal to possession
And left me in reputeless banishment,
45 A fellow of no mark nor likelihood.
By being seldom seen, I could not stir
But, like a comet, I was wondered at,
That men would tell their children 'This is he!'
Others would say, 'Where? Which is Bolingbroke?'
50 And then I stole all courtesy from heaven
And dressed myself in such humility
That I did pluck allegiance from men's hearts,
Loud shouts and salutations from their mouths,

Even in the presence of the crowned King.
Thus did I keep my person fresh and new,   55
My presence like a robe pontifical,
Ne'er seen but wondered at; and so my state,
Seldom but sumptuous, showed like a feast
And won by rareness such solemnity.
The skipping King, he ambled up and down   60
With shallow jesters and rash bavin wits,
Soon kindled and soon burnt; carded his state,
Mingled his royalty with cap'ring fools,
Had his great name profaned with their scorns,
And gave his countenance against his name   65
To laugh at gibing boys and stand the push
Of every beardless vain comparative;
Grew a companion to the common streets,
Enfeoffed himself to popularity,
That, being daily swallowed by men's eyes,   70
They surfeited with honey and began
To loathe the taste of sweetness, whereof a little
More than a little is by much too much.
So, when he had occasion to be seen,
He was but as the cuckoo is in June,   75
Heard, not regarded; seen, but with such eyes
As, sick and blunted with community,
Afford no extraordinary gaze
Such as is bent on sun-like majesty
When it shines seldom in admiring eyes,   80
But rather drowsed and hung their eyelids down,
Slept in his face, and rendered such aspect
As cloudy men use to their adversaries,
Being with his presence glutted, gorged and full.
And in that very line, Harry, standest thou,   85
For thou hast lost thy princely privilege
With vile participation. Not an eye
But is a-weary of thy common sight,
Save mine, which hath desired to see thee more,
Which now doth that I would not have it do,   90
Make blind itself with foolish tenderness.

PRINCE   I shall hereafter, my thrice-gracious lord,
Be more myself.

KING   For all the world,
As thou art to this hour was Richard then,
When I from France set foot at Ravenspur,   95
And even as I was then is Percy now.
Now by my sceptre, and my soul to boot,
He hath more worthy interest to the state
Than thou, the shadow of succession;
For, of no right, nor colour like to right,   100
He doth fill fields with harness in the realm,
Turns head against the lion's armed jaws,
And, being no more in debt to years than thou,
Leads ancient lords and reverend bishops on
To bloody battles and to bruising arms.   105
What never-dying honour hath he got
Against renowned Douglas, whose high deeds,
Whose hot incursions and great name in arms,
Holds from all soldiers chief majority

110 And military title capital
Through all the kingdoms that acknowledge Christ.
Thrice hath this Hotspur, Mars in swaddling-clothes,
This infant warrior, in his enterprises
Discomfited great Douglas; ta'en him once,
115 Enlarged him, and made a friend of him,
To fill the mouth of deep defiance up
And shake the peace and safety of our throne.
And what say you to this? Percy, Northumberland,
The Archbishop's grace of York, Douglas, Mortimer,
120 Capitulate against us and are up.
But wherefore do I tell these news to thee?
Why, Harry, do I tell thee of my foes,
Which art my nearest and dearest enemy?
Thou that art like enough, through vassal fear,
125 Base inclination and the start of spleen,
To fight against me under Percy's pay,
To dog his heels and curtsy at his frowns,
To show how much thou art degenerate.
PRINCE   Do not think so. You shall not find it so;
130 And God forgive them that so much have swayed
Your majesty's good thoughts away from me.
I will redeem all this on Percy's head
And in the closing of some glorious day
Be bold to tell you that I am your son,
135 When I will wear a garment all of blood
And stain my favours in a bloody mask,
Which washed away shall scour my shame with it.
And that shall be the day, whene'er it lights,
That this same child of honour and renown,
140 This gallant Hotspur, this all-praised knight,
And your unthought-of Harry chance to meet.
For every honour sitting on his helm,
Would they were multitudes, and on my head
My shames redoubled, for the time will come
145 That I shall make this northern youth exchange
His glorious deeds for my indignities.
Percy is but my factor, good my lord,
To engross up glorious deeds on my behalf;
And I will call him to so strict account
150 That he shall render every glory up,
Yea, even the slightest worship of his time,
Or I will tear the reckoning from his heart.
This, in the name of God, I promise here,
The which, if He be pleased I shall perform,
155 I do beseech your majesty may salve
The long-grown wounds of my intemperance.
If not, the end of life cancels all bonds,
And I will die a hundred thousand deaths
Ere break the smallest parcel of this vow.
160 KING   A hundred thousand rebels die in this.
Thou shalt have charge and sovereign trust herein.

Enter BLOUNT.

How now, good Blount? Thy looks are full of speed.
BLOUNT   So hath the business that I come to speak of.
Lord Mortimer of Scotland hath sent word

That Douglas and the English rebels met   165
The eleventh of this month at Shrewsbury.
A mighty and a fearful head they are,
If promises be kept on every hand,
As ever offered foul play in a state.
KING   The Earl of Westmorland set forth today,   170
With him my son, Lord John of Lancaster,
For this advertisement is five days old.
On Wednesday next, Harry, you shall set forward.
On Thursday we ourselves will march.
Our meeting is Bridgnorth, and, Harry, you   175
Shall march through Gloucestershire, by which account,
Our business valued, some twelve days hence
Our general forces at Bridgnorth shall meet.
Our hands are full of business. Let's away.
Advantage feeds him fat while men delay.   *Exeunt.*   180

3.3   *Enter* FALSTAFF *and* BARDOLL.

FALSTAFF   Bardoll, am I not fallen away vilely since this
last action? Do I not bate? Do I not dwindle? Why, my
skin hangs about me like an old lady's loose gown. I am
withered like an old apple-john. Well, I'll repent, and
that suddenly, while I am in some liking. I shall be out   5
of heart shortly, and then I shall have no strength to
repent. An I have not forgotten what the inside of a
church is made of, I am a peppercorn, a brewer's
horse. The inside of a church! Company, villainous
company, hath been the spoil of me.   10
BARDOLL   Sir John, you are so fretful you cannot live
long.
FALSTAFF   Why, there is it. Come, sing me a bawdy
song; make me merry. I was as virtuously given as a
gentleman need to be. Virtuous enough: swore little;   15
diced not above seven times – a week; went to a bawdy-
house not above once in a quarter – of an hour; paid
money that I borrowed – three or four times; lived well
and in good compass. And now I live out of all order,
out of all compass.   20
BARDOLL   Why, you are so fat, Sir John, that you must
needs be out of all compass, out of all reasonable
compass, Sir John.
FALSTAFF   Do thou amend thy face, and I'll amend my
life. Thou art our admiral, thou bearest the lantern in   25
the poop, but 'tis in the nose of thee. Thou art the
Knight of the Burning Lamp.
BARDOLL   Why, Sir John, my face does you no harm.
FALSTAFF   No, I'll be sworn, I make as good use of it as
many a man doth of a death's head, or a *memento mori*.   30
I never see thy face but I think upon hell-fire and
Dives that lived in purple: for there he is in his robes,
burning, burning. If thou wert any way given to
virtue, I would swear by thy face; my oath should be 'By
this fire that is God's angel.' But thou art altogether   35
given over and wert indeed, but for the light in thy face,
the son of utter darkness. When thou rann'st up
Gad's Hill in the night to catch my horse, if I did not

think thou hadst been an *ignis fatuus*, or a ball of
40   wildfire, there's no purchase in money. O, thou art a
perpetual triumph, an everlasting bonfire-light! Thou
hast saved me a thousand marks in links and torches
walking with thee in the night betwixt tavern and
tavern, but the sack that thou hast drunk me would
45   have bought me lights as good cheap at the dearest
chandler's in Europe. I have maintained that salamander
of yours with fire any time this two-and-thirty years,
God reward me for it.

BARDOLL   'Sblood, I would my face were in your belly!
50   FALSTAFF   God-a-mercy! So should I be sure to be
heartburned.

Enter HOSTESS.

How now, Dame Partlet the hen, have you enquired yet
who picked my pocket?

HOSTESS   Why, Sir John, what do you think, Sir John?
55   Do you think I keep thieves in my house? I have
searched, I have enquired, so has my husband, man by
man, boy by boy, servant by servant. The tithe of a hair
was never lost in my house before.

FALSTAFF   Ye lie, hostess: Bardoll was shaved and lost
60   many a hair, and I'll be sworn my pocket was picked.
Go to, you are a woman, go.

HOSTESS   Who, I? No, I defy thee. God's light, I was
never called so in mine own house before.

FALSTAFF   Go to, I know you well enough.
65   HOSTESS   No, Sir John, you do not know me, Sir John;
I know you, Sir John. You owe me money, Sir John,
and now you pick a quarrel to beguile me of it. I bought
you a dozen of shirts to your back.

FALSTAFF   Dowlas, filthy dowlas. I have given them
70   away to bakers' wives; they have made bolters of them.

HOSTESS   Now, as I am a true woman, holland of eight
shillings an ell. You owe money here besides, Sir John,
for your diet, and by-drinkings, and money lent you:
four-and-twenty pound.

75   FALSTAFF   [*Points to Bardoll.*]   He had his part of it. Let
him pay.

HOSTESS   He? Alas, he is poor; he hath nothing.

FALSTAFF   How? Poor? Look upon his face. What call
you rich? Let them coin his nose; let them coin his
80   cheeks. I'll not pay a denier. What, will you make a
younker of me? Shall I not take mine ease in mine inn,
but I shall have my pocket picked? I have lost a seal
ring of my grandfather's worth forty mark.

HOSTESS   [*to Bardoll*]   O Jesu, I have heard the Prince
85   tell him, I know not how oft, that that ring was copper!

FALSTAFF   How? The Prince is a jack, a sneak-up.
'Sblood, an he were here I would cudgel him like a dog
if he would say so.

Enter the PRINCE *with* PETO *marching, and* FALSTAFF
meets him, playing upon his truncheon like a fife.

How now, lad? Is the wind in that door, i'faith? Must
90   we all march?

BARDOLL   Yea, two and two, Newgate fashion.

HOSTESS   My lord, I pray you hear me.

PRINCE   What sayst thou, Mistress Quickly? How
doth thy husband? I love him well; he is an honest
man.   95

HOSTESS   Good my lord, hear me.

FALSTAFF   Prithee, let her alone and list to me.

PRINCE   What sayst thou, Jack?

FALSTAFF   The other night I fell asleep here, behind the
arras, and had my pocket picked. This house is turned   100
bawdy-house: they pick pockets.

PRINCE   What didst thou lose, Jack?

FALSTAFF   Wilt thou believe me, Hal? Three or four
bonds of forty pound apiece and a seal ring of my
grandfather's.   105

PRINCE   A trifle, some eightpenny matter.

HOSTESS   So I told him, my lord, and I said I heard your
grace say so. And, my lord, he speaks most vilely of
you, like a foul-mouthed man as he is, and said he
would cudgel you.   110

PRINCE   What? He did not.

HOSTESS   There's neither faith, truth nor womanhood
in me else.

FALSTAFF   There's no more faith in thee than in a
stewed prune, nor no more truth in thee than in a   115
drawn fox, and, for womanhood, Maid Marian may be
the deputy's wife of the ward to thee. Go, you thing,
go!

HOSTESS   Say, what thing, what thing?

FALSTAFF   What thing? Why, a thing to thank God on.   120

HOSTESS   I am no thing to thank God on. I would thou
shouldst know it. I am an honest man's wife, and,
setting thy knighthood aside, thou art a knave to call
me so.

FALSTAFF   Setting thy womanhood aside, thou art a   125
beast to say otherwise.

HOSTESS   Say, what beast, thou knave thou.

FALSTAFF   What beast? Why, an otter.

PRINCE   An otter, Sir John? Why an otter?

FALSTAFF   Why? She's neither fish nor flesh; a man   130
knows not where to have her.

HOSTESS   Thou art an unjust man in saying so. Thou or
any man knows where to have me, thou knave thou.

PRINCE   Thou sayst true, hostess, and he slanders thee
most grossly.   135

HOSTESS   So he doth you, my lord, and said this other
day you owed him a thousand pound.

PRINCE   Sirrah, do I owe you a thousand pound?

FALSTAFF   A thousand pound, Hal? A million. Thy love
is worth a million. Thou owest me thy love.   140

HOSTESS   Nay, my lord, he called you 'jack' and said he
would cudgel you.

FALSTAFF   Did I, Bardoll?

BARDOLL   Indeed, Sir John, you said so.

FALSTAFF   Yea, if he said my ring was copper.   145

PRINCE   I say 'tis copper. Darest thou be as good as thy
word now?

FALSTAFF   Why, Hal, thou knowest as thou art but man
I dare, but, as thou art prince, I fear thee as I fear the
150   roaring of the lion's whelp.
PRINCE   And why not as the lion?
FALSTAFF   The King himself is to be feared as the lion.
Dost thou think I'll fear thee as I fear thy father? Nay,
an I do, I pray God my girdle break.
155   PRINCE   O, if it should, how would thy guts fall about
thy knees! But, sirrah, there's no room for faith, truth
nor honesty in this bosom of thine; it is all filled up
with guts and midriff. Charge an honest woman with
picking thy pocket? Why, thou whoreson, impudent,
160   embossed rascal, if there were anything in thy pocket
but tavern reckonings, memorandums of bawdy-
houses and one poor pennyworth of sugar-candy to
make thee long-winded, if thy pocket were enriched
with any other injuries but these, I am a villain. And yet
165   you will stand to it; you will not pocket up wrong. Art
thou not ashamed?
FALSTAFF   Dost thou hear, Hal? Thou knowest in the
state of innocency Adam fell, and what should poor
Jack Falstaff do in the days of villainy? Thou seest I
170   have more flesh than another man and therefore more
frailty. You confess, then, you picked my pocket?
PRINCE   It appears so by the story.
FALSTAFF   Hostess, I forgive thee. Go make ready
breakfast, love thy husband, look to thy servants,
175   cherish thy guests. Thou shalt find me tractable to any
honest reason; thou seest I am pacified still. Nay,
prithee, be gone.   *Exit Hostess.*
Now, Hal, to the news at court: for the robbery, lad,
how is that answered?
180   PRINCE   O, my sweet beef, I must still be good angel to
thee. The money is paid back again.
FALSTAFF   O, I do not like that paying back; 'tis a double
labour.
PRINCE   I am good friends with my father and may do
185   anything.
FALSTAFF   Rob me the exchequer the first thing thou
dost, and do it with unwashed hands too.
BARDOLL   Do, my lord.
PRINCE   I have procured thee, Jack, a charge of foot.
190   FALSTAFF   I would it had been of horse. Where shall I
find one that can steal well? O, for a fine thief of the age
of two-and-twenty or thereabouts. I am heinously
unprovided. Well, God be thanked for these rebels;
they offend none but the virtuous. I laud them; I praise
195   them.
PRINCE   Bardoll.
BARDOLL   My lord?
PRINCE   Go bear this letter to Lord John of Lancaster –
To my brother John; this to my lord of Westmorland.
                                                Exit Bardoll.
200   Go, Peto, to horse, to horse, for thou and I
Have thirty miles to ride yet ere dinner time.
                                                Exit Peto.

Jack, meet me tomorrow in the Temple hall
At two o'clock in the afternoon.
There shalt thou know thy charge and there receive
Money and order for their furniture.   205
The land is burning, Percy stands on high,
And either we or they must lower lie.
FALSTAFF   Rare words! Brave world!   [*Calls.*]
                         Hostess, my breakfast, come!
O, I could wish this tavern were my drum!   *Exeunt.*

4.1   *Enter* HOTSPUR, WORCESTER *and* DOUGLAS.

HOTSPUR   Well said, my noble Scot. If speaking truth
In this fine age were not thought flattery,
Such attribution should the Douglas have
As not a soldier of this season's stamp
Should go so general current through the world.   5
By God, I cannot flatter. I do defy
The tongues of soothers, but a braver place
In my heart's love hath no man than yourself.
Nay, task me to my word; approve me, lord.
DOUGLAS   Thou art the king of honour.   10
No man so potent breathes upon the ground
But I will beard him.
HOTSPUR   Do so, and 'tis well.

                Enter Messenger *with letters.*

What letters hast thou there? [*to Douglas*] I can but
thank you.
MESSENGER   These letters come from your father.
HOTSPUR
Letters from him? Why comes he not himself?   15
MESSENGER
He cannot come, my lord. He is grievous sick.
HOTSPUR   Zounds, how has he the leisure to be sick
In such a jostling time? Who leads his power?
Under whose government come they along?
MESSENGER   His letters bears his mind, not I, my lord. 20
WORCESTER   I prithee, tell me: doth he keep his bed?
MESSENGER   He did, my lord, four days ere I set forth;
And at the time of my departure thence
He was much feared by his physicians.
WORCESTER
I would the state of time had first been whole   25
Ere he by sickness had been visited.
His health was never better worth than now.
HOTSPUR
Sick now? Droop now? This sickness doth infect
The very life-blood of our enterprise.
'Tis catching hither, even to our camp.   30
He writes me here that inward sickness –
And that his friends by deputation could not
So soon be drawn; nor did he think it meet
To lay so dangerous and dear a trust
On any soul removed but on his own.   35
Yet doth he give us bold advertisement

That with our small conjunction we should on
To see how fortune is disposed to us,
For, as he writes, 'there is no quailing now,
40 Because the King is certainly possessed
Of all our purposes'. What say you to it?
WORCESTER   Your father's sickness is a maim to us.
HOTSPUR   A perilous gash, a very limb lopped off.
And yet, in faith, it is not. His present want
45 Seems more than we shall find it. Were it good
To set the exact wealth of all our states
All at one cast, to set so rich a main
On the nice hazard of one doubtful hour?
It were not good, for therein should we read
50 The very bottom and the soul of hope,
The very list, the very utmost bound
Of all our fortunes.
DOUGLAS   Faith, and so we should,
Where now remains a sweet reversion:
We may boldly spend upon the hope of what is to
come in.
55 A comfort of retirement lives in this.
HOTSPUR   A rendezvous, a home to fly unto,
If that the devil and mischance look big
Upon the maidenhead of our affairs.
WORCESTER   But yet I would your father had been here.
60 The quality and hair of our attempt
Brooks no division. It will be thought
By some that know not why he is away
That wisdom, loyalty and mere dislike
Of our proceedings kept the Earl from hence;
65 And think how such an apprehension
May turn the tide of fearful faction
And breed a kind of question in our cause.
For, well you know, we of the off'ring side
Must keep aloof from strict arbitrement
70 And stop all sight-holes, every loop from whence
The eye of reason may pry in upon us.
This absence of your father's draws a curtain
That shows the ignorant a kind of fear
Before not dreamt of.
HOTSPUR   You strain too far.
75 I rather of his absence make this use:
It lends a lustre and more great opinion,
A larger dare to our great enterprise,
Than if the Earl were here; for men must think
If we without his help can make a head
80 To push against a kingdom, with his help
We shall o'erturn it topsy-turvy down.
Yet all goes well; yet all our joints are whole.
DOUGLAS   As heart can think. There is not such a word
Spoke of in Scotland as this term of fear.

Enter Sir Richard VERNON.

85 HOTSPUR   My cousin Vernon! Welcome, by my soul.
VERNON
Pray God my news be worth a welcome, lord.

The Earl of Westmorland, seven thousand strong,
Is marching hitherwards; with him Prince John.
HOTSPUR   No harm. What more?
VERNON   And, further, I have learned
The King himself in person is set forth,   90
Or hitherwards intended speedily,
With strong and mighty preparation.
HOTSPUR   He shall be welcome too. Where is his son,
The nimble-footed madcap Prince of Wales,
And his comrades that daffed the world aside   95
And bid it pass?
VERNON   All furnished, all in arms,
All plumed like ostriches, that with the wind
Bated like eagles having lately bathed,
Glittering in golden coats like images,
As full of spirit as the month of May   100
And gorgeous as the sun at midsummer,
Wanton as youthful goats, wild as young bulls.
I saw young Harry with his beaver on,
His cuisses on his thighs, gallantly armed,
Rise from the ground like feathered Mercury,   105
And vaulted with such ease into his seat
As if an angel dropped down from the clouds
To turn and wind a fiery Pegasus
And witch the world with noble horsemanship.
HOTSPUR
No more, no more. Worse than the sun in March   110
This praise doth nourish agues. Let them come!
They come like sacrifices in their trim,
And to the fire-eyed maid of smoky war
All hot and bleeding will we offer them.
The mailed Mars shall on his altar sit   115
Up to the ears in blood. I am on fire
To hear this rich reprisal is so nigh,
And yet not ours! Come, let me taste my horse,
Who is to bear me like a thunderbolt
Against the bosom of the Prince of Wales.   120
Harry to Harry shall, hot horse to horse,
Meet and ne'er part till one drop down a corpse.
O, that Glendower were come.
VERNON   There is more news.
I learned in Worcester, as I rode along,
He cannot draw his power this fourteen days.   125
DOUGLAS   That's the worst tidings that I hear of yet.
WORCESTER   Ay, by my faith, that bears a frosty sound.
HOTSPUR
What may the King's whole battle reach unto?
VERNON   To thirty thousand.
HOTSPUR   Forty let it be.
My father and Glendower being both away,   130
The powers of us may serve so great a day.
Come, let us take a muster speedily.
Doomsday is near. Die all; die merrily.
DOUGLAS   Talk not of dying; I am out of fear
Of death or death's hand for this one half year.   135
                                                            Exeunt.

4.2 *Enter* FALSTAFF *and* BARDOLL.

FALSTAFF Bardoll, get thee before to Coventry. Fill me
a bottle of sack. Our soldiers shall march through.
We'll to Sutton Coldfield tonight.

BARDOLL Will you give me money, captain?

FALSTAFF Lay out, lay out.

BARDOLL This bottle makes an angel.

FALSTAFF An if it do, take it for thy labour; an if it make
twenty, take them all. I'll answer the coinage. Bid my
lieutenant Peto meet me at town's end.

BARDOLL I will, captain. Farewell.   *Exit.*

FALSTAFF If I be not ashamed of my soldiers, I am a
soused gurnet. I have misused the King's press
damnably. I have got, in exchange of a hundred and
fifty soldiers, three hundred and odd pounds. I press
me none but good householders, yeomen's sons;
inquire me out contracted bachelors, such as had been
asked twice on the banns, such a commodity of warm
slaves as had as lief hear the devil as a drum, such as
fear the report of a caliver worse than a struck fowl or
a hurt wild duck. I pressed me none but such toasts-
and-butter, with hearts in their bellies no bigger than
pins' heads, and they have bought out their services;
and now my whole charge consists of ensigns,
corporals, lieutenants, gentlemen of companies –
slaves as ragged as Lazarus in the painted cloth where
the glutton's dogs licked his sores – and such as indeed
were never soldiers, but discarded unjust servingmen,
younger sons to younger brothers, revolted tapsters
and ostlers trade-fallen – the cankers of a calm world
and a long peace, ten times more dishonourable-
ragged than an old feazed ensign. And such have I
to fill up the rooms of them as have bought out
their services that you would think that I had a
hundred and fifty tattered prodigals lately come from
swine-keeping, from eating draff and husks. A mad
fellow met me on the way and told me I had unloaded
all the gibbets and pressed the dead bodies. No eye
hath seen such scarecrows. I'll not march through
Coventry with them, that's flat. Nay, and the villains
march wide betwixt the legs as if they had gyves on,
for indeed I had the most of them out of prison.
There's not a shirt and a half in all my company, and
the half-shirt is two napkins tacked together and
thrown over the shoulders like a herald's coat without
sleeves; and the shirt, to say the truth, stolen from my
host at Saint Albans or the red-nose innkeeper of
Daventry. But that's all one; they'll find linen enough
on every hedge.

Enter the PRINCE *and the* Lord of WESTMORLAND.

PRINCE How now, blown Jack? How now, quilt?

FALSTAFF What, Hal? How now, mad wag? What a
devil dost thou in Warwickshire? – My good lord of
Westmorland, I cry you mercy. I thought your honour
had already been at Shrewsbury.

WESTMORLAND Faith, Sir John, 'tis more than time
that I were there – and you too – but my powers are
there already. The King, I can tell you, looks for us all.
We must away all night.

FALSTAFF Tut, never fear me. I am as vigilant as a cat to
steal cream.

PRINCE I think to steal cream indeed, for thy theft hath
already made thee butter. But tell me, Jack, whose
fellows are these that come after?

FALSTAFF Mine, Hal, mine.

PRINCE I did never see such pitiful rascals.

FALSTAFF Tut, tut, good enough to toss; food for
powder, food for powder. They'll fill a pit as well as
better. Tush, man, mortal men, mortal men.

WESTMORLAND Ay, but Sir John, methinks they are
exceeding poor and bare, too beggarly.

FALSTAFF Faith, for their poverty, I know not where
they had that, and for their bareness I am sure they
never learned that of me.

PRINCE No, I'll be sworn, unless you call three fingers
in the ribs bare. But, sirrah, make haste. Percy is
already in the field.   *Exit.*

FALSTAFF What, is the King encamped?

WESTMORLAND He is, Sir John. I fear we shall stay too
long.

FALSTAFF

Well, to the latter end of a fray and the beginning of a
    feast

Fits a dull fighter and a keen guest.   *Exeunt.*

4.3 *Enter* HOTSPUR, WORCESTER, DOUGLAS
and VERNON.

HOTSPUR We'll fight with him tonight.

WORCESTER   It may not be.

DOUGLAS You give him then advantage.

VERNON   Not a whit.

HOTSPUR Why say you so? Looks he not for supply?

VERNON So do we.

HOTSPUR   His is certain; ours is doubtful.

WORCESTER

Good cousin, be advised. Stir not tonight.

VERNON [*to Hotspur*] Do not, my lord.

DOUGLAS   You do not counsel well.
You speak it out of fear and cold heart.

VERNON Do me no slander, Douglas. By my life
(And I dare well maintain it with my life),
If well-respected honour bid me on,
I hold as little counsel with weak fear
As you, my lord, or any Scot that this day lives.
Let it be seen tomorrow in the battle
Which of us fears.

DOUGLAS   Yea, or tonight.

VERNON   Content.

HOTSPUR Tonight, say I.

VERNON Come, come, it may not be. I wonder much,
Being men of such great leading as you are,

That you foresee not what impediments
Drag back our expedition. Certain horse

20 Of my cousin Vernon's are not yet come up.
Your uncle Worcester's horse came but today,
And now their pride and mettle is asleep,
Their courage with hard labour tame and dull,
That not a horse is half the half of himself.

25 HOTSPUR   So are the horses of the enemy
In general journey-bated and brought low.
The better part of ours are full of rest.

WORCESTER   The number of the King exceedeth ours.
For God's sake, cousin, stay till all come in.

[*The trumpet sounds a parley.*]

Enter Sir Walter BLOUNT.

30 BLOUNT   I come with gracious offers from the King,
If you vouchsafe me hearing and respect.

HOTSPUR
Welcome, Sir Walter Blount; and would to God
You were of our determination.
Some of us love you well, and even those some

35 Envy your great deservings and good name
Because you are not of our quality
But stand against us like an enemy.

BLOUNT   And God defend but still I should stand so,
So long as out of limit and true rule

40 You stand against anointed majesty.
But to my charge: the King hath sent to know
The nature of your griefs and whereupon
You conjure from the breast of civil peace
Such bold hostility, teaching his duteous land

45 Audacious cruelty. If that the King
Have any way your good deserts forgot,
Which he confesseth to be manifold,
He bids you name your griefs, and with all speed
You shall have your desires with interest

50 And pardon absolute for yourself and these
Herein misled by your suggestion.

HOTSPUR
The King is kind, and well we know the King
Knows at what time to promise, when to pay.
My father and my uncle and myself

55 Did give him that same royalty he wears;
And when he was not six-and-twenty strong,
Sick in the world's regard, wretched and low,
A poor unminded outlaw sneaking home,
My father gave him welcome to the shore;

60 And when he heard him swear and vow to God
He came but to be Duke of Lancaster,
To sue his livery and beg his peace
With tears of innocency and terms of zeal,
My father, in kind heart and pity moved,

65 Swore him assistance and performed it too.
Now when the lords and barons of the realm
Perceived Northumberland did lean to him,
The more and less came in with cap and knee,
Met him in boroughs, cities, villages,

Attended him on bridges, stood in lanes,   70
Laid gifts before him, proffered him their oaths,
Gave him their heirs as pages, followed him
Even at the heels in golden multitudes.
He presently, as greatness knows itself,
Steps me a little higher than his vow   75
Made to my father while his blood was poor
Upon the naked shore at Ravenspur,
And now forsooth takes on him to reform
Some certain edicts and some strait decrees
That lie too heavy on the commonwealth,   80
Cries out upon abuses, seems to weep
Over his country's wrongs; and, by this face,
This seeming brow of justice, did he win
The hearts of all that he did angle for;
Proceeded further: cut me off the heads   85
Of all the favourites that the absent King
In deputation left behind him here
When he was personal in the Irish war.

BLOUNT   Tut, I came not to hear this.

HOTSPUR   Then to the point.
In short time after, he deposed the King,   90
Soon after that deprived him of his life,
And in the neck of that tasked the whole state;
To make that worse, suffered his kinsman March
(Who is, if every owner were well placed,
Indeed his king) to be engaged in Wales,   95
There without ransom to lie forfeited;
Disgraced me in my happy victories,
Sought to entrap me by intelligence,
Rated mine uncle from the Council board,
In rage dismissed my father from the court,   100
Broke oath on oath, committed wrong on wrong,
And, in conclusion, drove us to seek out
This head of safety and withal to pry
Into his title, the which we find
Too indirect for long continuance.   105

BLOUNT   Shall I return this answer to the King?

HOTSPUR   Not so, Sir Walter. We'll withdraw awhile.
Go to the King, and let there be impawned
Some surety for a safe return again,
And in the morning early shall mine uncle   110
Bring him our purposes. And so farewell.

BLOUNT   I would you would accept of grace and love.

HOTSPUR   And maybe so we shall.

BLOUNT   Pray God you do.   *Exeunt.*

4.4   *Enter the* ARCHBISHOP *of York and*
                SIR MICHAEL.

ARCHBISHOP
Hie, good Sir Michael, bear this sealed brief
With winged haste to the Lord Marshal,
This to my cousin Scrope, and all the rest
To whom they are directed. If you knew
How much they do import, you would make haste.   5

SIR MICHAEL   My good lord, I guess their tenor.

ARCHBISHOP   Like enough you do.
Tomorrow, good Sir Michael, is a day
Wherein the fortune of ten thousand men
Must bide the touch; for, sir, at Shrewsbury,
As I am truly given to understand,
The King with mighty and quick-raised power
Meets with Lord Harry. And I fear, Sir Michael,
What with the sickness of Northumberland,
Whose power was in the first proportion,
And what with Owen Glendower's absence thence,
Who with them was a rated sinew too,
And comes not in, o'erruled by prophecies,
I fear the power of Percy is too weak
To wage an instant trial with the King.

SIR MICHAEL   Why, my good lord, you need not fear;
There is Douglas and Lord Mortimer –

ARCHBISHOP   No, Mortimer is not there.

SIR MICHAEL
But there is Murdoch, Vernon, Lord Harry Percy,
And there is my lord of Worcester, and a head
Of gallant warriors, noble gentlemen.

ARCHBISHOP
And so there is; but yet the King hath drawn
The special head of all the land together:
The Prince of Wales, Lord John of Lancaster,
The noble Westmorland and warlike Blount,
And many more corrivals and dear men
Of estimation and command in arms.

SIR MICHAEL
Doubt not, my lord, they shall be well opposed.

ARCHBISHOP   I hope no less, yet needful 'tis to fear;
And to prevent the worst, Sir Michael, speed.
For if Lord Percy thrive not, ere the King
Dismiss his power he means to visit us,
For he hath heard of our confederacy,
And 'tis but wisdom to make strong against him.
Therefore make haste. I must go write again
To other friends. And so farewell, Sir Michael.
                                        Exeunt.

5.1   *Enter the* KING, PRINCE *of Wales,*
          Lord John of LANCASTER, *Sir Walter*
               BLOUNT *and* FALSTAFF.

KING   How bloodily the sun begins to peer
Above yon bulky hill. The day looks pale
At his distemperature.

PRINCE   The southern wind
Doth play the trumpet to his purposes,
And by his hollow whistling in the leaves
Foretells a tempest and a blustering day.

KING   Then with the losers let it sympathize,
For nothing can seem foul to those that win.
                          [*The trumpet sounds.*]

          Enter WORCESTER *and* VERNON.

How now, my lord of Worcester? 'Tis not well

That you and I should meet upon such terms   10
As now we meet. You have deceived our trust
And made us doff our easy robes of peace
To crush our old limbs in ungentle steel.
This is not well, my lord; this is not well.
What say you to it? Will you again unknit   15
This churlish knot of all-abhorred war
And move in that obedient orb again
Where you did give a fair and natural light,
And be no more an exhaled meteor,
A prodigy of fear and a portent   20
Of broached mischief to the unborn times?

WORCESTER   Hear me, my liege:
For mine own part I could be well content
To entertain the lag-end of my life
With quiet hours, for I protest   25
I have not sought the day of this dislike.

KING   You have not sought it? How comes it, then?

FALSTAFF   Rebellion lay in his way, and he found it.

PRINCE [*to Falstaff*]   Peace, chewet, peace.

WORCESTER [*to the King*]
It pleased your majesty to turn your looks   30
Of favour from myself and all our house;
And yet I must remember you, my lord,
We were the first and dearest of your friends.
For you my staff of office did I break
In Richard's time, and posted day and night   35
To meet you on the way and kiss your hand
When yet you were in place and in account
Nothing so strong and fortunate as I.
It was myself, my brother and his son
That brought you home and boldly did outdare   40
The dangers of the time. You swore to us –
And you did swear that oath at Doncaster –
That you did nothing purpose 'gainst the state,
Nor claim no further than your new-fall'n right,
The seat of Gaunt, dukedom of Lancaster.   45
To this we swore our aid, but in short space
It rained down fortune show'ring on your head,
And such a flood of greatness fell on you –
What with our help, what with the absent King,
What with the injuries of a wanton time,   50
The seeming sufferances that you had borne,
And the contrarious winds that held the King
So long in his unlucky Irish wars
That all in England did repute him dead –
And from this swarm of fair advantages   55
You took occasion to be quickly wooed
To grip the general sway into your hand,
Forgot your oath to us at Doncaster
And, being fed by us, you used us so
As that ungentle gull, the cuckoo's bird,   60
Useth the sparrow: did oppress our nest,
Grew by our feeding to so great a bulk
That even our love durst not come near your sight
For fear of swallowing. But with nimble wing
We were enforced for safety sake to fly   65

Out of your sight and raise this present head
Whereby we stand opposed by such means
As you yourself have forged against yourself
By unkind usage, dangerous countenance
70 And violation of all faith and troth
Sworn to us in your younger enterprise.
KING   These things indeed you have articulate,
Proclaimed at market crosses, read in churches,
To face the garment of rebellion
75 With some fine colour that may please the eye
Of fickle changelings and poor discontents,
Which gape and rub the elbow at the news
Of hurly-burly innovation;
And never yet did insurrection want
80 Such water colours to impaint his cause,
Nor moody beggars starving for a time
Of pell-mell havoc and confusion.
PRINCE   In both your armies there is many a soul
Shall pay full dearly for this encounter
85 If once they join in trial. Tell your nephew
The Prince of Wales doth join with all the world
In praise of Henry Percy. By my hopes,
This present enterprise set off his head,
I do not think a braver gentleman,
90 More active-valiant or more valiant-young,
More daring or more bold, is now alive
To grace this latter age with noble deeds.
For my part, I may speak it to my shame,
I have a truant been to chivalry,
95 And so I hear he doth account me too.
Yet this before my father's majesty:
I am content that he shall take the odds
Of his great name and estimation,
And will, to save the blood on either side,
100 Try fortune with him in a single fight.
KING
And, Prince of Wales, so dare we venture thee,
Albeit considerations infinite
Do make against it. – No, good Worcester, no.
We love our people well, even those we love
105 That are misled upon your cousin's part;
And will they take the offer of our grace,
Both he and they and you, yea, every man
Shall be my friend again, and I'll be his.
So tell your cousin, and bring me word
110 What he will do. But, if he will not yield,
Rebuke and dread correction wait on us,
And they shall do their office. So be gone.
We will not now be troubled with reply.
We offer fair; take it advisedly.
                              Exeunt Worcester and Vernon.
115 PRINCE   It will not be accepted, on my life.
The Douglas and the Hotspur both together
Are confident against the world in arms.
KING   Hence, therefore, every leader to his charge,
For on their answer will we set on them;

And God befriend us as our cause is just!   120
                    Exeunt all but the Prince and Falstaff.
FALSTAFF   Hal, if thou see me down in the battle and
bestride me, so; 'tis a point of friendship.
PRINCE   Nothing but a colossus can do thee that
friendship. Say thy prayers, and farewell.
FALSTAFF   I would 'twere bedtime, Hal, and all well.   125
PRINCE   Why, thou owest God a death.   *Exit.*
FALSTAFF   'Tis not due yet. I would be loath to pay him
before his day. What need I be so forward with him
that calls not on me? Well, 'tis no matter; honour
pricks me on. Yea, but how if honour prick me off   130
when I come on? How then? Can honour set to a leg?
No. Or an arm? No. Or take away the grief of a
wound? No. Honour hath no skill in surgery, then? No.
What is honour? A word. What is in that word
'honour'? What is that 'honour'? Air. A trim reckoning. 135
Who hath it? He that died o'Wednesday. Doth he feel
it? No. Doth he hear it? No. 'Tis insensible then? Yea,
to the dead. But will it not live with the living? No.
Why? Detraction will not suffer it. Therefore I'll none
of it. Honour is a mere scutcheon. And so ends my   140
catechism.   *Exit.*

5.2   *Enter* WORCESTER *and* Sir Richard VERNON.

WORCESTER
O no, my nephew must not know, Sir Richard,
The liberal and kind offer of the King.
VERNON   'Twere best he did.
WORCESTER   Then are we all undone.
It is not possible, it cannot be
The King should keep his word in loving us.   5
He will suspect us still and find a time
To punish this offence in other faults.
Supposition all our lives shall be stuck full of eyes,
For treason is but trusted like the fox,
Who, never so tame, so cherished and locked up,   10
Will have a wild trick of his ancestors.
Look how we can, or sad or merrily,
Interpretation will misquote our looks,
And we shall feed like oxen at a stall,
The better cherished still the nearer death.   15
My nephew's trespass may be well forgot;
It hath the excuse of youth and heat of blood,
And an adopted name of privilege:
A hare-brained hotspur governed by a spleen.
All his offences live upon my head   20
And on his father's. We did train him on,
And, his corruption being ta'en from us,
We as the spring of all shall pay for all.
Therefore, good cousin, let not Harry know
In any case the offer of the King.   25
VERNON   Deliver what you will; I'll say 'tis so.

                    Enter HOTSPUR *and* DOUGLAS.

Here comes your cousin.
HOTSPUR   My uncle is returned.
  Deliver up my lord of Westmorland.
  – Uncle, what news?
WORCESTER   The King will bid you battle presently.
DOUGLAS   Defy him by the lord of Westmorland.
HOTSPUR   Lord Douglas, go you and tell him so.
DOUGLAS
  Marry, and shall, and very willingly.   *Exit Douglas.*
WORCESTER   There is no seeming mercy in the King.
HOTSPUR   Did you beg any? God forbid!
WORCESTER   I told him gently of our grievances,
  Of his oath-breaking, which he mended thus:
  By now forswearing that he is forsworn.
  He calls us 'rebels', 'traitors', and will scourge
  With haughty arms this hateful name in us.

         Enter DOUGLAS.

DOUGLAS   Arm, gentlemen, to arms; for I have thrown
  A brave defiance in King Henry's teeth,
  And Westmorland, that was engaged, did bear it,
  Which cannot choose but bring him quickly on.
WORCESTER
  The Prince of Wales stepped forth before the King
  And, nephew, challenged you to single fight.
HOTSPUR   O, would the quarrel lay upon our heads
  And that no man might draw short breath today
  But I and Harry Monmouth! Tell me, tell me,
  How showed his tasking? Seemed it in contempt?
VERNON   No, by my soul. I never in my life
  Did hear a challenge urged more modestly,
  Unless a brother should a brother dare
  To gentle exercise and proof of arms,
  He gave you all the duties of a man,
  Trimmed up your praises with a princely tongue,
  Spoke your deservings like a chronicle,
  Making you ever better than his praise
  By still dispraising praise valued with you;
  And, which became him like a prince indeed,
  He made a blushing cital of himself
  And chid his truant youth with such a grace
  As if he mastered there a double spirit
  Of teaching and of learning instantly.
  There did he pause. But let me tell the world,
  If he outlive the envy of this day,
  England did never owe so sweet a hope
  So much misconstrued in his wantonness.
HOTSPUR   Cousin, I think thou art enamoured
  On his follies. Never did I hear
  Of any prince so wild a liberty.
  But, be he as he will, yet once ere night
  I will embrace him with a soldier's arm
  That he shall shrink under my courtesy.
  – Arm, arm with speed! And fellows, soldiers, friends,
  Better consider what you have to do
  Than I, that have not well the gift of tongue,
  Can lift your blood up with persuasion.

         Enter a Messenger.

1 MESSENGER   My lord, here are letters for you.
HOTSPUR   I cannot read them now.   80
  – O gentlemen, the time of life is short;
  To spend that shortness basely were too long
  If life did ride upon a dial's point,
  Still ending at the arrival of an hour.
  An if we live, we live to tread on kings;   85
  If die, brave death when princes die with us.
  Now, for our consciences, the arms are fair
  When the intent of bearing them is just.

       Enter another Messenger.

2 MESSENGER
  My lord, prepare; the King comes on apace.
HOTSPUR   I thank him that he cuts me from my tale,   90
  For I profess not talking; only this:
  Let each man do his best. And here draw I
  A sword whose temper I intend to stain
  With the best blood that I can meet withal
  In the adventure of this perilous day.   95
  Now Esperance! Percy! And set on!
  Sound all the lofty instruments of war,
  And by that music let us all embrace,
  For, heaven to earth, some of us never shall
  A second time do such a courtesy.   100
      [*Here they embrace. The trumpets sound.*]
                   Exeunt.

5.3   *The* KING *enters with his power and they*
     pass over the stage. Alarum to the battle.
   Then enter DOUGLAS *and* Sir Walter BLOUNT
        wearing the King's colours.

BLOUNT
  What is thy name that in battle thus thou crossest me?
  What honour dost thou seek upon my head?
DOUGLAS   Know then my name is Douglas,
  And I do haunt thee in the battle thus
  Because some tell me that thou art a king.   5
BLOUNT   They tell thee true.
DOUGLAS
  The Lord of Stafford dear today hath bought
  Thy likeness, for instead of thee, King Harry,
  This sword hath ended him. So shall it thee
  Unless thou yield thee as my prisoner.   10
BLOUNT   I was not born a yielder, thou proud Scot,
  And thou shalt find a king that will revenge
  Lord Stafford's death.   [*They fight. Douglas kills Blount.*]

         Then enter HOTSPUR.

HOTSPUR
  O Douglas, hadst thou fought at Humbleton thus,
  I never had triumphed upon a Scot.   15
DOUGLAS
  All's done; all's won. Here breathless lies the King.

HOTSPUR   Where?

DOUGLAS   Here.

HOTSPUR

This, Douglas? No. I know this face full well.

20   A gallant knight he was; his name was Blount,
Semblably furnished like the King himself.

DOUGLAS [*to the fallen Blount*]

A fool go with thy soul, whither it goes!
A borrowed title hast thou bought too dear.
Why didst thou tell me that thou wert a king?

25   HOTSPUR   The King hath many marching in his coats.

DOUGLAS   Now, by my sword, I will kill all his coats.
I'll murder all his wardrobe, piece by piece,
Until I meet the King.

HOTSPUR   Up and away!
Our soldiers stand full fairly for the day.   *Exeunt.*

Alarum. Enter FALSTAFF *alone.*

30   FALSTAFF   Though I could scape shot-free at London, I
fear the shot here. Here's no scoring but upon the pate.
Soft, who are you? Sir Walter Blount. There's honour
for you. Here's no vanity. I am as hot as molten lead
and as heavy too. God keep lead out of me; I need no

35   more weight than mine own bowels. I have led my
ragamuffins where they are peppered; there's not three
of my hundred and fifty left alive, and they are for the
town's end to beg during life.

Enter the PRINCE.

But who comes here?

PRINCE

40   What, stands thou idle here? Lend me thy sword.
Many a noble man lies stark and stiff
Under the hoofs of vaunting enemies,
Whose deaths are yet unrevenged. I prithee,
Lend me thy sword.

45   FALSTAFF   O Hal, I prithee, give me leave to breathe
awhile. Turk Gregory never did such deeds in arms as
I have done this day. I have paid Percy; I have made
him sure.

PRINCE   He is indeed – and living to kill thee.

50   I prithee, lend me thy sword.

FALSTAFF   Nay, before God, Hal, if Percy be alive thou
gets not my sword. But take my pistol if thou wilt.

PRINCE   Give it me. What, is it in the case?

FALSTAFF   Ay, Hal. 'Tis hot; 'tis hot. There's that will

55   sack a city. [*The Prince draws it out, and finds it to be a
bottle of sack.*]

PRINCE   What, is it a time to jest and dally now?
[*He throws the bottle at him.*]   *Exit.*

FALSTAFF   Well, if Percy be alive, I'll pierce him. If he
do come in my way, so; if he do not, if I come in his
willingly, let him make a carbonado of me. I like not

60   such grinning honour as Sir Walter hath. Give me life,
which if I can save, so. If not, honour comes unlooked
for, and there's an end.   *Exit with Blount's body.*

5.4   *Alarum. Excursions. Enter the* KING, *the*
PRINCE, Lord John of LANCASTER *and the*
Earl of WESTMORLAND.

KING

I prithee, Harry, withdraw thyself; thou bleed'st too
much.
Lord John of Lancaster, go you with him.

LANCASTER   Not I, my lord, unless I did bleed too.

PRINCE   I beseech your majesty, make up,
Lest your retirement do amaze your friends.   5

KING   I will do so.
My lord of Westmorland, lead him to his tent.

WESTMORLAND

Come, my lord, I'll lead you to your tent.

PRINCE   Lead me, my lord? I do not need your help,
And God forbid a shallow scratch should drive   10
The Prince of Wales from such a field as this,
Where stained nobility lies trodden on
And rebels' arms triumph in massacres!

LANCASTER

We breathe too long. Come, cousin Westmorland;
Our duty this way lies. For God's sake, come.   15
Exeunt Lancaster and Westmorland.

PRINCE   By God, thou hast deceived me, Lancaster;
I did not think thee lord of such a spirit.
Before I loved thee as a brother, John,
But now I do respect thee as my soul.

KING   I saw him hold Lord Percy at the point   20
With lustier maintenance than I did look for
Of such an ungrown warrior.

PRINCE   O, this boy lends mettle to us all!   *Exit.*

Enter DOUGLAS.

DOUGLAS   Another king! They grow like Hydra's heads.
I am the Douglas, fatal to all those   25
That wear those colours on them. What art thou
That counterfeit'st the person of a king?

KING

The King himself, who, Douglas, grieves at heart
So many of his shadows thou hast met
And not the very King. I have two boys   30
Seek Percy and thyself about the field,
But seeing thou fall'st on me so luckily
I will assay thee; and defend thyself.

DOUGLAS   I fear thou art another counterfeit,
And yet, in faith, thou bearest thee like a king.   35
But mine I am sure thou art, whoe'er thou be,
And thus I win thee.   [*They fight.*]

The King being in danger, enter PRINCE *of Wales.*

PRINCE   Hold up thy head, vile Scot, or thou art like
Never to hold it up again. The spirits
Of valiant Shirley, Stafford, Blount are in my arms.   40
It is the Prince of Wales that threatens thee,
Who never promiseth but he means to pay.
They fight. Douglas flieth.

Cheerly, my lord. How fares your grace?
Sir Nicholas Gawsey hath for succour sent,
45 And so hath Clifton. I'll to Clifton straight.
KING   Stay and breathe awhile.
Thou hast redeemed thy lost opinion
And showed thou mak'st some tender of my life
In this fair rescue thou hast brought to me.
50 PRINCE   O God, they did me too much injury
That ever said I hearkened for your death.
If it were so, I might have let alone
The insulting hand of Douglas over you,
Which would have been as speedy in your end
55 As all the poisonous potions in the world,
And saved the treacherous labour of your son.
KING
Make up to Clifton; I'll to Sir Nicholas Gawsey.   *Exit.*

Enter HOTSPUR.

HOTSPUR   If I mistake not, thou art Harry Monmouth.
PRINCE   Thou speak'st as if I would deny my name.
HOTSPUR   My name is Harry Percy.
60 PRINCE   Why then, I see
A very valiant rebel of the name.
I am the Prince of Wales, and think not, Percy,
To share with me in glory any more.
Two stars keep not their motion in one sphere,
65 Nor can one England brook a double reign
Of Harry Percy and the Prince of Wales.
HOTSPUR   Nor shall it, Harry, for the hour is come
To end the one of us, and would to God
Thy name in arms were now as great as mine.
70 PRINCE   I'll make it greater ere I part from thee,
And all the budding honours on thy crest
I'll crop to make a garland for my head.
HOTSPUR
I can no longer brook thy vanities.   [*They fight.*]

Enter FALSTAFF.

FALSTAFF   Well said, Hal! To it, Hal! Nay, you shall find
75 no boy's play here, I can tell you.

Enter DOUGLAS. *He fighteth with Falstaff,*
who falls down as if he were dead.

Exit Douglas.
[*The Prince killeth Hotspur.*]
HOTSPUR   O Harry, thou hast robbed me of my youth.
I better brook the loss of brittle life
Than those proud titles thou hast won of me.
They wound my thoughts worse than thy sword my
flesh.
80 But thoughts, the slaves of life, and life, time's fool,
And time, that takes survey of all the world,
Must have a stop. O, I could prophesy,
But that the earthy and cold hand of death
Lies on my tongue. No, Percy, thou art dust
85 And food for —   [*He dies.*]

PRINCE
For worms, brave Percy. Fare thee well, great heart.
Ill-weaved ambition, how much art thou shrunk!
When that this body did contain a spirit
A kingdom for it was too small a bound,
90 But now two paces of the vilest earth
Is room enough. This earth that bears thee dead
Bears not alive so stout a gentleman.
If thou wert sensible of courtesy
I should not make so dear a show of zeal.
95 But let my favours hide thy mangled face,
And even in thy behalf I'll thank myself
For doing these fair rites of tenderness.
Adieu, and take thy praise with thee to heaven.
Thy ignominy sleep with thee in the grave
100 But not remembered in thy epitaph.
[*He spieth Falstaff on the ground.*]
What, old acquaintance! Could not all this flesh
Keep in a little life? Poor Jack, farewell.
I could have better spared a better man.
O, I should have a heavy miss of thee
105 If I were much in love with vanity.
Death hath not struck so fat a deer today,
Though many dearer in this bloody fray.
Embowelled will I see thee by and by;
Till then, in blood by noble Percy lie.   *Exit.*
[*Falstaff riseth up.*]
110 FALSTAFF   Embowelled? If thou embowel me today, I'll
give you leave to powder me, and eat me too, tomorrow.
'Sblood, 'twas time to counterfeit, or that hot
termagant Scot had paid me, scot and lot too.
Counterfeit? I lie; I am no counterfeit. To die is to be a
115 counterfeit, for he is but the counterfeit of a man who
hath not the life of a man. But to counterfeit dying
when a man thereby liveth is to be no counterfeit but
the true and perfect image of life indeed. The better
part of valour is discretion, in the which better part I
120 have saved my life. Zounds, I am afraid of this
gunpowder Percy, though he be dead. How if he
should counterfeit too and rise? By my faith, I am
afraid he would prove the better counterfeit. Therefore
I'll make him sure, yea, and I'll swear I killed him.
125 Why may not he rise as well as I? Nothing confutes me
but eyes, and nobody sees me. [*Stabs the body.*]
Therefore, sirrah, with a new wound in your thigh,
come you along with me. [*He takes up Hotspur on his
back.*]

Enter PRINCE *and* John of LANCASTER.

PRINCE
Come, brother John. Full bravely hast thou fleshed
Thy maiden sword.
130 LANCASTER   But soft; whom have we here?
Did you not tell me this fat man was dead?
PRINCE   I did; I saw him dead,
Breathless and bleeding on the ground.

135 [*to Falstaff*] Art thou alive, or is it fantasy
That plays upon our eyesight? I prithee speak;
We will not trust our eyes without our ears.
Thou art not what thou seem'st.

FALSTAFF   No, that's certain: I am not a double man.
[*He drops Hotspur's body.*] But, if I be not Jack Falstaff,
140 then am I a jack. There is Percy. If your father will do
me any honour, so; if not, let him kill the next Percy
himself. I look to be either earl or duke, I can assure
you.

PRINCE
Why, Percy I killed myself, and saw thee dead.

145 FALSTAFF   Didst thou? Lord, Lord, how this world is
given to lying! I grant you I was down and out of
breath, and so was he; but we rose both at an instant
and fought a long hour by Shrewsbury clock. If I may
be believed, so; if not, let them that should reward
150 valour bear the sin upon their own heads. I'll take it
upon my death I gave him this wound in the thigh. If
the man were alive and would deny it, zounds, I would
make him eat a piece of my sword.

LANCASTER   This is the strangest tale that ever I heard.

155 PRINCE   This is the strangest fellow, brother John.
[*to Falstaff*] Come, bring your luggage nobly on your
back.
For my part, if a lie may do thee grace
I'll gild it with the happiest terms I have.
                              [*A retreat is sounded.*]
The trumpet sounds retreat; the day is ours.
160 Come, brother, let us to the highest of the field
To see what friends are living, who are dead.   *Exeunt.*

FALSTAFF   I'll follow, as they say, for reward. He that
rewards me, God reward him. If I do grow great,
I'll grow less, for I'll purge and leave sack and live
165 cleanly, as a nobleman should do.
                              Exit carrying the body.

5.5   *The trumpets sound. Enter the* KING,
            PRINCE *of Wales, Lord John of* LANCASTER,
            Earl of WESTMORLAND, *with* WORCESTER
                     and VERNON *prisoners.*

KING   Thus ever did rebellion find rebuke.
Ill-spirited Worcester, did not we send grace,

Pardon and terms of love to all of you?
And wouldst thou turn our offers contrary,
Misuse the tenor of thy kinsman's trust?   5
Three knights upon our party slain today,
A noble earl and many a creature else
Had been alive this hour
If like a Christian thou hadst truly borne
Betwixt our armies true intelligence.   10

WORCESTER   What I have done my safety urged me to;
And I embrace this fortune patiently,
Since not to be avoided it falls on me.

KING   Bear Worcester to the death and Vernon too.
Other offenders we will pause upon.   15
            Exeunt Worcester and Vernon under guard.
How goes the field?

PRINCE   The noble Scot, Lord Douglas, when he saw
The fortune of the day quite turned from him,
The noble Percy slain and all his men
Upon the foot of fear, fled with the rest;   20
And, falling from a hill, he was so bruised
That the pursuers took him. At my tent
The Douglas is, and I beseech your grace
I may dispose of him.

KING   With all my heart.

PRINCE   Then, brother John of Lancaster, to you   25
This honourable bounty shall belong.
Go to the Douglas and deliver him
Up to his pleasure, ransomless and free.
His valours shown upon our crests today
Have taught us how to cherish such high deeds   30
Even in the bosom of our adversaries.

LANCASTER   I thank your grace for this high courtesy,
Which I shall give away immediately.

KING   Then this remains, that we divide our power.
You, son John, and my cousin Westmorland,   35
Towards York shall bend you with your dearest speed
To meet Northumberland and the prelate Scrope,
Who, as we hear, are busily in arms.
Myself and you, son Harry, will towards Wales
To fight with Glendower and the Earl of March.   40
Rebellion in this land shall lose his sway
Meeting the check of such another day;
And, since this business so fair is done,
Let us not leave till all our own be won.   *Exeunt.*

King Henry IV, Part 2

'The second parte of the history of kinge HENRY the iiijth with the humours of Sir JOHN FFALLSTAFF' was entered in the Stationers' Register on 23 August 1600, and a Quarto was published that year, printed by Valentine Simmes. One scene, 3.1, in which King Henry makes his belated first appearance, was accidentally omitted. To insert it Simmes set four new leaves, which not only include the missing scene but reprint the surrounding lines from the end of 2.4 and the beginning of 3.2. The two states of the 1600 Quarto, with or without 3.1, mark the only appearance of the play in print before the 1623 Folio, a surprising fact given the extraordinary popularity of *King Henry IV, Part 1*.

The Quarto text serves as the primary authority for most modern editions. The Folio, however, includes eight substantial passages absent from the Quarto, and seems in other places authoritatively to correct and add to the earlier text, so it too must be taken into account by editors. In other particulars, however, the Folio seems further from Shakespeare's own hand than the Quarto, regularizing its colloquialisms and purging the text of most of its oaths and profanities.

The play was written soon after *King Henry IV, Part 1*, probably early in 1598, but more as a sequel than as the second half of a single ten-act dramatic entity. Had two plays been clearly in his mind from the outset, Shakespeare would no doubt have parcelled out the historical material more evenly. Though *Part 2* brings the action forward to King Henry's death and Hal's accession to the throne, the play does more than merely complete the history of the reign. Shakespeare echoes the structure of the earlier play, transposing it into a darker key. *Part 2* also ignores various aspects of the plot of *Part 1*, even neglecting the reconciliation of father and son that ends the earlier play.

Yet if the trajectory of the action is the same in each play, dividing interest between the King and Prince, the rebels and Falstaff, the history in *Part 2* is more troubled and troubling. The climactic battles of each play, while structurally analogous, starkly establish the plays' different tones. *Part 1*'s glorious victory at Shrewsbury, where Hal magnificently proves himself a worthy successor, is paralleled by the betrayal at Gaultree Forest, where Prince John of Lancaster displays not the chivalric magnanimity of Hal but a prudential cynicism all too appropriate to the dispiriting world of this play.

Hal does not even appear on stage until 2.2, and his first line is telling: 'Before God, I am exceeding weary.' Even Falstaff is here more tired and cynical than in *Part 1*, his actions meaner, his wit less agile. Though his presence is still engaging, he shows the marks of the disease that infects the play world. He first enters worrying about the doctor's report about his urine sample, and his own diagnosis is that he suffers from 'consumption of the purse'.

Falstaff in this play is no longer a father figure for Hal; indeed the two are rarely together onstage, and the play's most notorious moment is the fat knight's public rejection. Falstaff eagerly anticipates the crowning of his erstwhile tavern friend as King, but the 'Hal' he knew is no more. The once wayward Prince is now King of England, and coldly tells Falstaff: 'Presume not that I am the thing I was' (5.5.55). The newly crowned Henry V has no choice but to repudiate the dissolute knight, but audiences inevitably feel that the new King gives up some of his humanity in so fully taking on his necessary public role. It is here, in the way in which Henry performs the rejection, in the degree of evident regret, in the extent to which he realizes what he has lost and what he has become, that productions of this complex and unsettling play reveal their moral focus.

Though never as popular on stage as its predecessor, *Part 2* has a distinguished performance history. It was one of the plays performed at Court in the winter of 1612–13 to celebrate the wedding of Princess Elizabeth and Frederick, the Elector Palatine. After the Restoration it continued to be played, but often in adaptations that emphasized the role of Falstaff, or in conflations of the two parts. Such conflations go back at least as far as 1622–3, when Sir Edward Dering prepared one for his own private theatricals, but the tradition survives into the twentieth century, as in Orson Welles's film *Chimes at Midnight* (1966) and an extraordinary production of *Enrico IV* by the Colletivo di Parma, first staged in Italy in 1982 and brought to London the following year.

The Arden text is based on the 1600 Quarto, supplemented by the 1623 First Folio. Seven extended passages unique to the Folio are marked with superscript F.

RUMOUR *the presenter*
KING Henry the Fourth
PRINCE Henry (Harry) *afterwards crowned* KING *Henry the Fifth*
Prince JOHN of Lancaster ⎫
Humphrey, Duke of GLOUCESTER ⎬ *sons to Henry the Fourth, and brethren to Henry the Fifth*
Thomas, Duke of CLARENCE ⎭

Henry Percy, Earl of NORTHUMBERLAND ⎫
ARCHBISHOP of York ⎪
Lord MOWBRAY, Earl Marshal ⎪
Lord HASTINGS ⎪
LORD BARDOLPH ⎬ *opposites against King Henry the Fourth*
TRAVERS ⎪
MORTON ⎪
Sir John COLLEVILE ⎭

Earl of WARWICK ⎫
Earl of WESTMORLAND ⎪
Earl of Surrey ⎪
Sir John Blunt ⎪
GOWER ⎬ *of the King's party*
HARCOURT ⎪
Lord Chief JUSTICE ⎪
SERVANT *to the Lord Chief Justice* ⎭

Ned POINS ⎫
Sir John FALSTAFF ⎪
BARDOLPH ⎪
Ancient PISTOL ⎬ *irregular humorists*
PETO ⎪
PAGE *to Falstaff* ⎭

Robert SHALLOW ⎫
SILENCE ⎬ *both country justices*

DAVY *servant to Shallow*

FANG ⎫
SNARE ⎬ *two sergeants*

Ralph MOULDY ⎫
Simon SHADOW ⎪
Thomas WART ⎬ *country soldiers*
Francis FEEBLE ⎪
Peter BULLCALF ⎭

LADY NORTHUMBERLAND *Northumberland's wife*
LADY PERCY *Percy's widow*
HOSTESS, Mistress Quickly
DOLL Tearsheet
Speaker of the EPILOGUE

FRANCIS, *a drawer*
DRAWER
Two BEADLES
Three STREWERS *of rushes*
PORTER
MESSENGER
Page to the King

Soldiers, Captain, Musicians, Servants, Attendants

INDUCTION

Enter RUMOUR *painted full of tongues.*

RUMOUR   Open your ears; for which of you will stop
  The vent of hearing when loud Rumour speaks?
  I from the orient to the drooping west,
  Making the wind my post-horse, still unfold
5   The acts commenced on this ball of earth.
  Upon my tongues continual slanders ride,
  The which in every language I pronounce,
  Stuffing the ears of men with false reports.
  I speak of peace while covert enmity,
10   Under the smile of safety, wounds the world;
  And who but Rumour, who but only I,
  Make fearful musters and prepared defence
  Whiles the big year, swoll'n with some other grief,
  Is thought with child by the stern tyrant War?
15   And no such matter. Rumour is a pipe
  Blown by surmises, Jealousy's conjectures,
  And of so easy and so plain a stop
  That the blunt monster with uncounted heads,
  The still discordant wav'ring multitude,
20   Can play upon it. But what need I thus
  My well-known body to anatomize
  Among my household? Why is Rumour here?
  I run before King Harry's victory,
  Who in a bloody field by Shrewsbury
25   Hath beaten down young Hotspur and his troops,
  Quenching the flame of bold rebellion
  Even with the rebels' blood. But what mean I
  To speak so true at first? My office is
  To noise abroad that Harry Monmouth fell
30   Under the wrath of noble Hotspur's sword,
  And that the King before the Douglas' rage
  Stooped his anointed head as low as death.
  This have I rumoured through the peasant towns
  Between that royal field of Shrewsbury
35   And this worm-eaten hole of ragged stone
  Where Hotspur's father, old Northumberland,
  Lies crafty-sick. The posts come tiring on,
  And not a man of them brings other news
  Than they have learnt of me. From Rumour's tongues
  They bring smooth comforts false, worse than
40   true wrongs.   *Exit.*

1.1   *Enter the* LORD BARDOLPH *at one door.*

LORD BARDOLPH   Who keeps the gate here, ho?

Enter the Porter *at another door.*

                         Where is the Earl?
PORTER   What shall I say you are?
LORD BARDOLPH   Tell thou the Earl
  That the Lord Bardolph doth attend him here.
PORTER   His lordship is walked forth into the orchard.
5   Please it your honour knock but at the gate,
  And he himself will answer.

Enter the Earl of NORTHUMBERLAND
carrying a crutch and wearing a coif.

LORD BARDOLPH   Here comes the Earl.
                          Exit Porter.
NORTHUMBERLAND
  What news, Lord Bardolph? Every minute now
  Should be the father of some stratagem.
  The times are wild; contention, like a horse
  Full of high feeding, madly hath broke loose   10
  And bears down all before him.
LORD BARDOLPH   Noble Earl,
  I bring you certain news from Shrewsbury.
NORTHUMBERLAND   Good, an God will.
LORD BARDOLPH   As good as heart can wish.
  The King is almost wounded to the death,
  And, in the fortune of my lord your son,   15
  Prince Harry slain outright, and both the Blunts
  Killed by the hand of Douglas. Young Prince John
  And Westmorland and Stafford fled the field,
  And Harry Monmouth's brawn, the hulk Sir John,
  Is prisoner to your son. O, such a day!   20
  So fought, so followed, and so fairly won,
  Came not till now to dignify the times
  Since Caesar's fortunes.
NORTHUMBERLAND   How is this derived?
  Saw you the field? Came you from Shrewsbury?
LORD BARDOLPH
  I spake with one, my lord, that came from thence,   25
  A gentleman well bred and of good name,
  That freely rendered me these news for true.

Enter TRAVERS.

NORTHUMBERLAND
  Here comes my servant Travers, who I sent
  On Tuesday last to listen after news.
LORD BARDOLPH   My lord, I overrode him on the way,   30
  And he is furnished with no certainties
  More than he haply may retail from me.
NORTHUMBERLAND
  Now, Travers, what good tidings comes with you?
TRAVERS
  My lord, Sir John Umfreville turned me back
  With joyful tidings, and, being better horsed,   35
  Out-rode me. After him came spurring hard
  A gentleman almost forspent with speed,
  That stopped by me to breathe his bloodied horse.
  He asked the way to Chester, and of him
  I did demand what news from Shrewsbury.   40
  He told me that rebellion had bad luck,
  And that young Harry Percy's spur was cold.
  With that he gave his able horse the head,
  And bending forward struck his armed heels
  Against the panting sides of his poor jade   45
  Up to the rowel head; and starting so
  He seemed in running to devour the way,
  Staying no longer question.

NORTHUMBERLAND   Ha? Again:
Said he young Harry Percy's spur was cold?
50 Of Hotspur, Coldspur? That rebellion
Had met ill luck?

LORD BARDOLPH   My lord, I'll tell you what:
If my young lord your son have not the day,
Upon mine honour, for a silken point
I'll give my barony. Never talk of it.

NORTHUMBERLAND
55 Why should that gentleman that rode by Travers
Give then such instances of loss?

LORD BARDOLPH   Who, he?
He was some hilding fellow that had stol'n
The horse he rode on, and, upon my life,
Spoke at a venture.

                    Enter MORTON.

                    Look, here comes more news.

NORTHUMBERLAND
60 Yea, this man's brow, like to a title-leaf,
Foretells the nature of a tragic volume:
So looks the strand whereon the imperious flood
Hath left a witnessed usurpation.
Say, Morton, didst thou come from Shrewsbury?

65 MORTON   I ran from Shrewsbury, my noble lord,
Where hateful death put on his ugliest mask
To fright our party.

NORTHUMBERLAND   How doth my son and brother?
Thou tremblest, and the whiteness in thy cheek
Is apter than thy tongue to tell thy errand.
70 Even such a man, so faint, so spiritless,
So dull, so dead in look, so woebegone,
Drew Priam's curtain in the dead of night
And would have told him half his Troy was burnt;
But Priam found the fire ere he his tongue,
75 And I my Percy's death ere thou report'st it.
This thou wouldst say: 'Your son did thus and thus;
Your brother thus; so fought the noble Douglas',
Stopping my greedy ear with their bold deeds.
But in the end, to stop my ear indeed,
80 Thou hast a sigh to blow away this praise,
Ending with 'Brother, son, and all are dead.'

MORTON   Douglas is living, and your brother yet;
But for my lord your son –

NORTHUMBERLAND   Why, he is dead?
See what a ready tongue suspicion hath!
85 He that but fears the thing he would not know
Hath by instinct knowledge from others' eyes
That what he feared is chanced. Yet speak, Morton;
Tell thou an earl his divination lies,
And I will take it as a sweet disgrace
90 And make thee rich for doing me such wrong.

MORTON   You are too great to be by me gainsaid;
Your spirit is too true, your fears too certain.

NORTHUMBERLAND
Yet, for all this, say not that Percy's dead.
I see a strange confession in thine eye;

Thou shak'st thy head and hold'st it fear or sin   95
To speak a truth. If he be slain,
The tongue offends not that reports his death;
And he doth sin that doth belie the dead,
Not he which says the dead is not alive.
Yet the first bringer of unwelcome news   100
Hath but a losing office, and his tongue
Sounds ever after as a sullen bell,
Remembered tolling a departing friend.

LORD BARDOLPH
I cannot think, my lord, your son is dead.

MORTON   I am sorry I should force you to believe   105
That which I would to God I had not seen;
But these mine eyes saw him in bloody state,
Rend'ring faint quittance, wearied and out-breathed,
To Harry Monmouth, whose swift wrath beat down
The never-daunted Percy to the earth,   110
From whence with life he never more sprung up.
In few, his death, whose spirit lent a fire
Even to the dullest peasant in his camp,
Being bruited once, took fire and heat away
From the best-tempered courage in his troops;   115
For from his metal was his party steeled,
Which once in him abated, all the rest
Turned on themselves, like dull and heavy lead.
And as the thing that's heavy in itself
Upon enforcement flies with greatest speed,   120
So did our men, heavy in Hotspur's loss,
Lend to this weight such lightness with their fear
That arrows fled not swifter toward their aim
Than did our soldiers, aiming at their safety,
Fly from the field. Then was that noble Worcester 125
So soon ta'en prisoner; and that furious Scot,
The bloody Douglas, whose well-labouring sword
Had three times slain th'appearance of the King,
'Gan vail his stomach and did grace the shame
Of those that turned their backs, and in his flight, 130
Stumbling in fear, was took. The sum of all
Is that the King hath won, and hath sent out
A speedy power to encounter you, my lord,
Under the conduct of young Lancaster
And Westmorland. This is the news at full.   135

NORTHUMBERLAND
For this I shall have time enough to mourn.
In poison there is physic; and these news,
Having been well, that would have made me sick,
Being sick, have in some measure made me well.
And as the wretch whose fever-weakened joints   140
Like strengthless hinges buckle under life,
Impatient of his fit, breaks like a fire
Out of his keeper's arms, even so my limbs,
Weakened with grief, being now enraged with grief,
Are thrice themselves. Hence, therefore, thou nice
        crutch!   145
[*Tosses crutch aside.*]
A scaly gauntlet now with joints of steel
Must glove this hand. And hence, thou sickly coif!

[Snatches off coif.]
Thou art a guard too wanton for the head
Which princes, fleshed with conquest, aim to hit.
150 Now bind my brows with iron, and approach
The ragged'st hour that time and spite dare bring
To frown upon th'enraged Northumberland!
Let heaven kiss earth! Now let not nature's hand
Keep the wild flood confined! Let order die!
155 And let this world no longer be a stage
To feed contention in a ling'ring act;
But let one spirit of the first-born Cain
Reign in all bosoms, that, each heart being set
On bloody courses, the rude scene may end
160 And darkness be the burier of the dead.

LORD BARDOLPH
This strained passion doth you wrong, my lord.

MORTON
Sweet earl, divorce not wisdom from your honour;
The lives of all your loving complices
Lean on your health, the which, if you give o'er
165 To stormy passion, must perforce decay.
ᶠYou cast th'event of war, my noble lord,
And summed the account of chance before you said
'Let us make head.' It was your presurmise
That in the dole of blows your son might drop.
170 You knew he walked o'er perils, on an edge,
More likely to fall in than to get o'er.
You were advised his flesh was capable
Of wounds and scars, and that his forward spirit
Would lift him where most trade of danger ranged.
175 Yet did you say 'Go forth'; and none of this,
Though strongly apprehended, could restrain
The stiff-borne action. What hath then befall'n,
Or what hath this bold enterprise brought forth,
More than that being which was like to be?ᶠ

180 LORD BARDOLPH   We all that are engaged to this loss
Knew that we ventured on such dangerous seas
That if we wrought out life 'twas ten to one;
And yet we ventured for the gain proposed,
Choked the respect of likely peril feared,
185 And since we are o'erset, venture again.
Come, we will all put forth body and goods.

MORTON
'Tis more than time. *[to Northumberland]* And, my
    most noble lord,
I hear for certain, and dare speak the truth,
ᶠThe gentle Archbishop of York is up
190 With well-appointed powers: he is a man
Who with a double surety binds his followers.
My lord your son had only but the corpse,
But shadows and the shows of men, to fight;
For that same word 'rebellion' did divide
195 The action of their bodies from their souls,
And they did fight with queasiness, constrained
As men drink potions, that their weapons only
Seemed on our side; but for their spirits and souls,
This word, 'rebellion', it had froze them up

As fish are in a pond. But now the Bishop   200
Turns insurrection to religion,
Supposed sincere and holy in his thoughts.
He's followed both with body and with mind,
And doth enlarge his rising with the blood
Of fair King Richard scraped from Pomfret stones;   205
Derives from heaven his quarrel and his cause;
Tells them he doth bestride a bleeding land
Gasping for life under great Bolingbroke;
And more and less do flock to follow him.ᶠ

NORTHUMBERLAND
I knew of this before, but, to speak truth,   210
This present grief had wiped it from my mind.
Go in with me, and counsel every man
The aptest way for safety and revenge.
Get posts and letters, and make friends with speed;
Never so few, and never yet more need.   *Exeunt.*   215

1.2   *Enter* Sir John FALSTAFF *alone,*
    with his PAGE *bearing his sword and buckler.*

FALSTAFF   Sirrah, you giant, what says the doctor to my
water?
PAGE   He said, sir, the water itself was a good healthy
water, but for the party that owed it, he might have
more diseases than he knew for.   5
FALSTAFF   Men of all sorts take a pride to gird at me.
The brain of this foolish compounded clay-man is not
able to invent anything that intends to laughter more
than I invent or is invented on me; I am not only witty
in myself, but the cause that wit is in other men. I do   10
here walk before thee like a sow that hath overwhelmed
all her litter but one. If the Prince put thee into my
service for any other reason than to set me off, why
then I have no judgement. Thou whoreson mandrake,
thou art fitter to be worn in my cap than to wait at my   15
heels. I was never manned with an agate till now, but I
will inset you neither in gold nor silver, but in vile
apparel, and send you back again to your master for a
jewel – the juvenal, the Prince your master, whose chin
is not yet fledge. I will sooner have a beard grow in the   20
palm of my hand than he shall get one off his cheek,
and yet he will not stick to say his face is a face royal.
God may finish it when He will, 'tis not a hair amiss
yet. He may keep it still at a face royal, for a barber
shall never earn sixpence out of it; and yet he'll be   25
crowing as if he had writ man ever since his father was
a bachelor. He may keep his own grace, but he's almost
out of mine, I can assure him. – What said Master
Dommelton about the satin for my short cloak and my
slops?   30
PAGE   He said, sir, you should procure him better
assurance than Bardolph. He would not take his bond
and yours; he liked not the security.
FALSTAFF   Let him be damned like the glutton! Pray
God his tongue be hotter! A whoreson Achitophel, a   35
rascal – yea forsooth knave – to bear a gentleman in

hand and then stand upon 'security'. The whoreson
smoothy-pates do now wear nothing but high shoes
and bunches of keys at their girdles; and if a man is
through with them in honest taking up, then they must
stand upon security. I had as lief they would put
ratsbane in my mouth as offer to stop it with security. I
looked 'a should have sent me two and twenty yards of
satin, as I am a true knight, and he sends me 'security'!
Well he may sleep in security, for he hath the horn of
abundance, and the lightness of his wife shines through
it – where's Bardolph? – and yet cannot he see, though
he have his own lanthorn to light him.

PAGE   He's gone in Smithfield to buy your worship a
horse.

FALSTAFF   I bought him in Paul's, and he'll buy me a
horse in Smithfield. An I could get me but a wife in the
stews, I were manned, horsed and wived.

Enter Lord Chief JUSTICE *and* Servant.

PAGE   Sir, here comes the nobleman that committed the
Prince for striking him about Bardolph.

FALSTAFF   Wait close, I will not see him.

JUSTICE   What's he that goes there?

SERVANT   Falstaff, an't please your lordship.

JUSTICE   He that was in question for the robbery?

SERVANT   He, my lord; but he hath since done good
service at Shrewsbury and, as I hear, is now going with
some charge to the Lord John of Lancaster.

JUSTICE   What, to York? Call him back again.

SERVANT   Sir John Falstaff!

FALSTAFF   Boy, tell him I am deaf.

PAGE   You must speak louder; my master is deaf.

JUSTICE   I am sure he is, to the hearing of anything
good. [*to Servant*] Go pluck him by the elbow; I must
speak with him.

SERVANT   Sir John?

FALSTAFF   What, a young knave and begging? Is there
not wars? Is there not employment? Doth not the King
lack subjects? Do not the rebels need soldiers? Though
it be a shame to be on any side but one, it is worse
shame to beg than to be on the worst side, were it worse
than the name of rebellion can tell how to make it.

SERVANT   You mistake me, sir.

FALSTAFF   Why, sir, did I say you were an honest man?
Setting my knighthood and my soldiership aside, I had
lied in my throat if I had said so.

SERVANT   I pray you, sir, then set your knighthood and
your soldiership aside and give me leave to tell you,
you lie in your throat if you say I am any other than an
honest man.

FALSTAFF   I give thee leave to tell me so? I lay aside that
which grows to me? If thou get'st any leave of me, hang
me; if thou tak'st leave, thou wert better be hanged.
You hunt counter. Hence! Avaunt!

SERVANT   Sir, my lord would speak with you.

JUSTICE   Sir John Falstaff, a word with you.

FALSTAFF   My good lord, God give your lordship good
time of day. I am glad to see your lordship abroad. I
heard say your lordship was sick: I hope your lordship
goes abroad by advice. Your lordship, though not clean
past your youth, have yet some smack of an ague in
you, some relish of the saltness of time in you, and I
most humbly beseech your lordship to have a reverend
care of your health.

JUSTICE   Sir John, I sent for you before your expedition
to Shrewsbury.

FALSTAFF   An't please your lordship, I hear his majesty
is returned with some discomfort from Wales.

JUSTICE   I talk not of his majesty. You would not come
when I sent for you.

FALSTAFF   And I hear moreover his highness is fallen
into this same whoreson apoplexy.

JUSTICE   Well, God mend him. I pray you let me speak
with you.

FALSTAFF   This apoplexy, as I take it, is a kind of
lethargy, an't please your lordship, a kind of sleeping in
the blood, a whoreson tingling.

JUSTICE   What tell you me of it? Be it as it is.

FALSTAFF   It hath it original from much grief, from
study, and perturbation of the brain. I have read the
cause of his effects in Galen: it is a kind of deafness.

JUSTICE   I think you are fallen into the disease, for you
hear not what I say to you.

FALSTAFF   Very well, my lord, very well; rather, an't
please you, it is the disease of not listening, the malady
of not marking, that I am troubled withal.

JUSTICE   To punish you by the heels would amend the
attention of your ears, and I care not if I do become
your physician.

FALSTAFF   I am as poor as Job, my lord, but not so
patient. Your lordship may minister the potion of
imprisonment to me in respect of poverty; but how I
should be your patient to follow your prescriptions, the
wise may make some dram of a scruple or indeed a
scruple itself.

JUSTICE   I sent for you, when there were matters against
you for your life, to come speak with me.

FALSTAFF   As I was then advised by my learned counsel
in the laws of this land-service, I did not come.

JUSTICE   Well, the truth is, Sir John, you live in great
infamy.

FALSTAFF   He that buckles himself in my belt cannot
live in less.

JUSTICE   Your means are very slender, and your waste is
great.

FALSTAFF   I would it were otherwise; I would my means
were greater and my waist slender.

JUSTICE   You have misled the youthful Prince.

FALSTAFF   The young Prince hath misled me. I am the
fellow with the great belly, and he my dog.

JUSTICE   Well, I am loath to gall a new-healed wound.
Your day's service at Shrewsbury hath a little gilded
over your night's exploit on Gad's Hill. You may thank
th'unquiet time for your quiet o'erposting that action.

FALSTAFF   My lord –

50 JUSTICE   But since all is well, keep it so: wake not a
sleeping wolf.

FALSTAFF   To wake a wolf is as bad as smell a fox.

JUSTICE   What? You are as a candle, the better part
burnt out.

55 FALSTAFF   A wassail candle, my lord, all tallow: if I did
say of wax, my growth would approve the truth.

JUSTICE   There is not a white hair in your face but
should have his effect of gravity.

FALSTAFF   His effect of gravy, gravy, gravy.

60 JUSTICE   You follow the young Prince up and down like
his ill angel.

FALSTAFF   Not so, my lord. Your ill angel is light, but I
hope he that looks upon me will take me without
weighing; and yet in some respects I grant I cannot go.
65 I cannot tell. Virtue is of so little regard in these coster-
mongers' times that true valour is turned bearherd,
pregnancy is made a tapster, and his quick wit wasted
in giving reckonings. All the other gifts appertinent to
man, as the malice of his age shapes them, are not
70 worth a gooseberry. You that are old consider not the
capacities of us that are young. You do measure the
heat of our livers with the bitterness of your galls; and
we that are in the vaward of our youth, I must confess,
are wags too.

75 JUSTICE   Do you set down your name in the scroll of
youth, that are written down old with all the characters
of age? Have you not a moist eye, a dry hand, a yellow
cheek, a white beard, a decreasing leg, an increasing
belly? Is not your voice broken, your wind short, your
80 chin double, your wit single, and every part about you
blasted with antiquity? And will you yet call yourself
young? Fie, fie, fie, Sir John!

FALSTAFF   My lord, I was born about three of the clock
in the afternoon, with a white head and something a
85 round belly. For my voice, I have lost it with hallowing
and singing of anthems. To approve my youth further,
I will not. The truth is, I am only old in judgement and
understanding; and he that will caper with me for a
thousand marks, let him lend me the money, and have
90 at him! For the box of the ear that the Prince gave you,
he gave it like a rude prince, and you took it like a
sensible lord: I have checked him for it, and the young
lion repents – marry, not in ashes and sackcloth, but in
new silk and old sack.

95 JUSTICE   Well, God send the Prince a better companion.

FALSTAFF   God send the companion a better prince; I
cannot rid my hands of him.

JUSTICE   Well, the King hath severed you: I hear you
are going with Lord John of Lancaster against the
200 Archbishop and the Earl of Northumberland.

FALSTAFF   Yea, I thank your pretty sweet wit for it. But
look you pray, all you that kiss my lady Peace at home,
that our armies join not in a hot day; for, by the Lord,
I take but two shirts out with me, and I mean not to
205 sweat extraordinarily. If it be a hot day, and I brandish

anything but a bottle, I would I might never spit white
again. There is not a dangerous action can peep out his
head but I am thrust upon it. Well, I cannot last ever;
but it was alway yet the trick of our English nation, if
they have a good thing, to make it too common. If ye 210
will needs say I am an old man, you should give me
rest. I would to God my name were not so terrible to
the enemy as it is. I were better to be eaten to death
with a rust than to be scoured to nothing with perpetual
motion. 215

JUSTICE   Well, be honest, be honest, and God bless your
expedition.

FALSTAFF   Will your lordship lend me a thousand
pound to furnish me forth?

JUSTICE   Not a penny, not a penny. You are too impatient 220
to bear crosses. Fare you well; commend me to my
cousin Westmorland.

Exeunt Lord Chief Justice and Servant.

FALSTAFF   If I do, fillip me with a three-man beetle. A
man can no more separate age and covetousness than 'a
can part young limbs and lechery; but the gout galls 225
the one and the pox pinches the other, and so both the
degrees prevent my curses. – Boy?

PAGE   Sir?

FALSTAFF   What money is in my purse?

PAGE   Seven groats and two pence. 230

FALSTAFF   I can get no remedy against this consumption
of the purse. Borrowing only lingers and lingers it out,
but the disease is incurable. [*Hands letters to Page.*] Go
bear this letter to my Lord of Lancaster, this to the
Prince, this to the Earl of Westmorland, and this to old 235
mistress Ursula, whom I have weekly sworn to marry
since I perceived the first white hair of my chin. About
it; you know where to find me. *Exit Page.*
A pox of this gout, or a gout of this pox, for the one or
the other plays the rogue with my great toe. 'Tis no 240
matter if I do halt: I have the wars for my colour, and
my pension shall seem the more reasonable. A good
wit will make use of anything. I will turn diseases to
commodity. *Exit.*

1.3   *Enter the* ARCHBISHOP *of York,*
Thomas MOWBRAY, *Earl Marshal,*
the Lord HASTINGS *and* LORD BARDOLPH.

ARCHBISHOP
Thus have you heard our cause and known our
means;
And, my most noble friends, I pray you all
Speak plainly your opinions of our hopes.
And first, Lord Marshal, what say you to it?

MOWBRAY
I well allow the occasion of our arms 5
But gladly would be better satisfied
How in our means we should advance ourselves
To look with forehead bold and big enough
Upon the power and puissance of the King.

HASTINGS
10   Our present musters grow upon the file
     To five and twenty thousand men of choice,
     And our supplies live largely in the hope
     Of great Northumberland, whose bosom burns
     With an incensed fire of injuries.
LORD BARDOLPH
15   The question then, Lord Hastings, standeth thus:
     Whether our present five and twenty thousand
     May hold up head without Northumberland.
HASTINGS   With him we may.
LORD BARDOLPH   Yea, marry, there's the point.
     But if without him we be thought too feeble,
20   My judgement is we should not step too far
     Till we had his assistance by the hand;
     For in a theme so bloody-faced as this,
     Conjecture, expectation and surmise
     Of aids incertain should not be admitted.
ARCHBISHOP
25   'Tis very true, Lord Bardolph, for indeed
     It was young Hotspur's cause at Shrewsbury.
LORD BARDOLPH
     It was, my lord, who lined himself with hope,
     Eating the air and promise of supply,
     Flatt'ring himself in project of a power
30   Much smaller than the smallest of his thoughts;
     And so with great imagination,
     Proper to madmen, led his powers to death
     And, winking, leapt into destruction.
HASTINGS   But by your leave, it never yet did hurt
35   To lay down likelihoods and forms of hope.
LORD BARDOLPH   ᶠYes, if this present quality of war –
     Indeed, the instant action, a cause on foot –
     Lives so in hope as in an early spring
     We see th'appearing buds, which to prove fruit
40   Hope gives not so much warrant as despair
     That frosts will bite them. When we mean to build,
     We first survey the plot, then draw the model;
     And when we see the figure of the house,
     Then must we rate the cost of the erection
45   Which, if we find outweighs ability,
     What do we then but draw anew the model
     In fewer offices, or at least desist
     To build at all? Much more in this great work,
     Which is almost to pluck a kingdom down
50   And set another up, should we survey
     The plot of situation and the model,
     Consent upon a sure foundation,
     Question surveyors, know our own estate,
     How able such a work to undergo,
55   To weigh against his opposite; or elseᶠ
     We fortify in paper and in figures,
     Using the names of men instead of men,
     Like one that draws the model of an house
     Beyond his power to build it, who, half through,
60   Gives o'er and leaves his part-created cost
     A naked subject to the weeping clouds

     And waste for churlish winter's tyranny.
HASTINGS
     Grant that our hopes, yet likely of fair birth,
     Should be stillborn, and that we now possessed
     The utmost man of expectation,   65
     I think we are a body strong enough,
     Even as we are, to equal with the King.
LORD BARDOLPH
     What, is the King but five and twenty thousand?
HASTINGS
     To us no more; nay, not so much, Lord Bardolph;
     For his divisions, as the times do brawl,   70
     Are in three heads: one power against the French,
     And one against Glendower, perforce a third
     Must take up us. So is the unfirm King
     In three divided, and his coffers sound
     With hollow poverty and emptiness.   75
ARCHBISHOP
     That he should draw his several strengths together
     And come against us in full puissance
     Need not to be dreaded.
HASTINGS   If he should do so,
     He leaves his back unarmed, the French and Welsh
     Baying him at the heels: never fear that.   80
LORD BARDOLPH
     Who is it like should lead his forces hither?
HASTINGS
     The Duke of Lancaster and Westmorland;
     Against the Welsh, himself and Harry Monmouth.
     But who is substituted against the French
     I have no certain notice.
ARCHBISHOP   ᶠLet us on,   85
     And publish the occasion of our arms.
     The commonwealth is sick of their own choice;
     Their over-greedy love hath surfeited.
     An habitation giddy and unsure
     Hath he that buildeth on the vulgar heart.   90
     O thou fond many, with what loud applause
     Didst thou beat heaven with blessing Bolingbroke
     Before he was what thou wouldst have him be?
     And being now trimmed in thine own desires,
     Thou, beastly feeder, art so full of him   95
     That thou provok'st thyself to cast him up.
     So, so, thou common dog, didst thou disgorge
     Thy glutton bosom of the royal Richard,
     And now thou wouldst eat thy dead vomit up
     And howl'st to find it. What trust is in these times?   100
     They that when Richard lived would have him die
     Are now become enamoured on his grave.
     Thou, that threw'st dust upon his goodly head
     When through proud London he came sighing on
     After th'admired heels of Bolingbroke,   105
     Cry'st now, 'O earth, yield us that king again
     And take thou this!' O thoughts of men accursed!
     Past and to come seems best; things present, worst.ᶠ
ᶠMOWBRAYᶠ
     Shall we go draw our numbers, and set on?

HASTINGS

110   We are time's subjects, and time bids be gone.   *Exeunt.*

2.1   *Enter* HOSTESS *of the tavern, and an*
                              Officer, FANG.

HOSTESS   Master Fang, have you entered the action?

FANG   It is entered.

HOSTESS   Where's your yeoman? Is't a lusty yeoman?
              Will 'a stand to't?

5   FANG   Sirrah – Where's Snare?

HOSTESS   O Lord, ay, good Master Snare.

                         Enter SNARE.

SNARE   Here, here.

FANG   Snare, we must arrest Sir John Falstaff.

HOSTESS   Yea, good Master Snare, I have entered him
10   and all.

SNARE   It may chance cost some of us our lives, for he
              will stab.

HOSTESS   Alas the day, take heed of him. He stabbed me
              in mine own house, most beastly in good faith. 'A cares
15   not what mischief he does; if his weapon be out, he will
              foin like any devil. He will spare neither man, woman
              nor child.

FANG   If I can close with him, I care not for his thrust.

HOSTESS   No, nor I neither. I'll be at your elbow.

20   FANG   An I but fist him once, an 'a come but within my
              vice –

HOSTESS   I am undone by his going, I warrant you: he's
              an infinitive thing upon my score. Good Master
              Fang, hold him sure! Good Master Snare, let him not
25   scape! 'A comes continuantly to Pie Corner, saving
              your manhoods, to buy a saddle, and he is indited to
              dinner to the Lubber's Head in Lumbert Street to
              Master Smooths the silkman. I pray you, since my
              exion is entered and my case so openly known to the
30   world, let him be brought in to his answer. A hundred
              mark is a long one for a poor lone woman to bear; and
              I have borne, and borne, and borne, and have been
              fubbed off, and fubbed off, and fubbed off, from this
              day to that day, that it is a shame to be thought on.
35   There is no honesty in such dealing, unless a woman
              should be made an ass and a beast to bear every knave's
              wrong.

                  Enter Sir John FALSTAFF, BARDOLPH
                        and the Boy [PAGE].

         Yonder he comes, and that arrant malmsey-nose knave
         Bardolph with him. Do your offices, do your offices,
40   Master Fang and Master Snare! Do me, do me, do me
         your offices!

FALSTAFF   How now, whose mare's dead? What's the
              matter?

FANG   I arrest you at the suit of Mistress Quickly.

45   FALSTAFF   Away, varlets! – Draw, Bardolph! Cut me off
              the villain's head! Throw the quean in the channel!

[*Fang and Snare attempt to apprehend Falstaff.*
A brawl ensues.]

HOSTESS   Throw me in the channel? I'll throw thee in
              the channel! Wilt thou, wilt thou, thou bastardly
              rogue? – Murder! Murder! – Ah, thou honeysuckle
              villain, wilt thou kill God's officers and the King's? Ah,   50
              thou honeyseed rogue! Thou art a honeyseed, a man
              queller, and a woman queller!

FALSTAFF   Keep them off, Bardolph.

OFFICERS   A rescue, a rescue!

HOSTESS   Good people, bring a rescue or two! – Thou   55
              wot, wot thou? Thou wot, wot ta? – Do, do, thou rogue!
              Do, thou hempseed!

PAGE [*to Hostess*]   Away, you scullion, you rampallian,
              you fustilarian! I'll tickle your catastrophe.

                  Enter Lord Chief JUSTICE *and his Men.*

JUSTICE   What is the matter? Keep the peace here, ho!   60

HOSTESS   Good my lord, be good to me. I beseech you
              stand to me.

JUSTICE
         How now, Sir John? What are you brawling here?
         Doth this become your place, your time and business?
         You should have been well on your way to York.   65
         [*to Fang*] Stand from him, fellow! Wherefore hang'st
              thou upon him?

HOSTESS   O my most worshipful lord, an't please your
              grace, I am a poor widow of Eastcheap, and he is
              arrested at my suit.

JUSTICE   For what sum?   70

HOSTESS   It is more than for some, my lord; it is for all I
              have! He hath eaten me out of house and home. He
              hath put all my substance into that fat belly of his; [*to
              Falstaff*] but I will have some of it out again, or I will
              ride thee a'nights like the mare.   75

FALSTAFF   I think I am as like to ride the mare if I have
              any vantage of ground to get up.

JUSTICE   How comes this, Sir John? What man of good
              temper would endure this tempest of exclamation? Are
              you not ashamed to enforce a poor widow to so rough a   80
              course to come by her own?

FALSTAFF [*to Hostess*]   What is the gross sum that I owe
              thee?

HOSTESS   Marry, if thou wert an honest man, thyself
              and the money too. Thou didst swear to me upon a   85
              parcel-gilt goblet, sitting in my Dolphin chamber at
              the round table by a seacoal fire upon Wednesday in
              Wheeson week, when the Prince broke thy head for
              liking his father to a singing man of Windsor – thou
              didst swear to me then, as I was washing thy wound, to   90
              marry me and make me 'my lady', thy wife. Canst thou
              deny it? Did not goodwife Keech the butcher's wife
              come in then and call me gossip Quickly, coming in to
              borrow a mess of vinegar, telling us she had a good
              dish of prawns, whereby thou didst desire to eat some,   95
              whereby I told thee they were ill for a green wound?
              And didst thou not, when she was gone downstairs,

desire me to be no more so familiarity with such poor
people, saying that ere long they should call me
madam? And didst thou not kiss me, and bid me fetch
thee thirty shillings? I put thee now to thy book-oath;
deny it if thou canst.

FALSTAFF My lord, this is a poor mad soul, and she
says up and down the town that her eldest son is like
you. She hath been in good case; and the truth is,
poverty hath distracted her. But for these foolish
officers, I beseech you I may have redress against
them.

JUSTICE Sir John, Sir John, I am well acquainted with
your manner of wrenching the true cause the false way.
It is not a confident brow, nor the throng of words that
come with such more-than-impudent sauciness from
you, can thrust me from a level consideration. You
have, as it appears to me, practised upon the easy-
yielding spirit of this woman, and made her serve your
uses both in purse and in person.

HOSTESS Yea, in truth, my lord.

JUSTICE Pray thee, peace. [*to Falstaff*] Pay her the debt
you owe her, and unpay the villainy you have done with
her: the one you may do with sterling money, and the
other with current repentance.

FALSTAFF My lord, I will not undergo this sneap
without reply. You call honorable boldness 'impudent
sauciness'. If a man will make curtsy and say nothing,
he is virtuous. No, my lord, my humble duty
remembered, I will not be your suitor. I say to you I do
desire deliverance from these officers, being upon
hasty employment in the King's affairs.

JUSTICE You speak as having power to do wrong; but
answer in th'effect of your reputation, and satisfy the
poor woman.

FALSTAFF Come hither, hostess. [*Takes her aside.*]

Enter a Messenger [GOWER].

JUSTICE Now, Master Gower, what news?

GOWER
The King, my lord, and Harry, Prince of Wales,
Are near at hand; the rest the paper tells.
[*Hands a paper to the Lord Chief Justice, who reads it.*]

FALSTAFF As I am a gentleman!

HOSTESS Faith, you said so before.

FALSTAFF As I am a gentleman; come, no more words
of it.

HOSTESS By this heavenly ground I tread on, I must be
fain to pawn both my plate and the tapestry of my
dining chambers.

FALSTAFF Glasses, glasses is the only drinking. And for
thy walls, a pretty slight drollery, or the story of the
prodigal, or the German hunting in waterwork is
worth a thousand of these bed-hangers and these fly-
bitten tapestries. Let it be ten pounds, if thou canst.
Come, an 'twere not for thy humours, there's not a
better wench in England. Go wash thy face and draw
the action. Come, thou must not be in this humour

with me. Dost not know me? Come, come; I know thou
wast set on to this.

HOSTESS Pray thee, Sir John, let it be but twenty
nobles; i'faith, I am loath to pawn my plate, so God
save me, la!

FALSTAFF Let it alone; I'll make other shift. You'll be a
fool still.

HOSTESS Well, you shall have it, though I pawn my
gown. I hope you'll come to supper. You'll pay me all
together?

FALSTAFF Will I live? [*to Bardolph*] Go with her. With
her! Hook on, hook on.

HOSTESS Will you have Doll Tearsheet meet you at
supper?

FALSTAFF No more words; let's have her.
Exeunt Hostess and Sergeant Fang
with Snare, Bardolph and Page.

JUSTICE [*to Gower*] I have heard better news.

FALSTAFF What's the news, my lord?

JUSTICE [*to Gower*] Where lay the King tonight?

GOWER At Basingstoke, my lord.

FALSTAFF I hope, my lord, all's well. What is the news,
my lord?

JUSTICE [*to Gower*] Come all his forces back?

GOWER No; fifteen hundred foot, five hundred horse
Are marched up to my lord of Lancaster
Against Northumberland and the Archbishop.

FALSTAFF
Comes the King back from Wales, my noble lord?

JUSTICE [*to Gower*]
You shall have letters of me presently.
Come, go along with me, good Master Gower.

FALSTAFF My lord!

JUSTICE What's the matter?

FALSTAFF Master Gower, shall I entreat you with me to
dinner?

GOWER I must wait upon my good lord here. I thank
you, good Sir John.

JUSTICE Sir John, you loiter here too long, being you
are to take soldiers up in counties as you go.

FALSTAFF Will you sup with me, Master Gower?

JUSTICE What foolish master taught you these manners,
Sir John?

FALSTAFF Master Gower, if they become me not, he
was a fool that taught them me. – This is the right
fencing grace, my lord: tap for tap, and so part fair.

JUSTICE Now the Lord lighten thee, thou art a great
fool.   *Exeunt at separate doors.*

2.2   *Enter* PRINCE *Henry and* POINS.

PRINCE Before God, I am exceeding weary.

POINS Is't come to that? I had thought weariness durst
not have attached one of so high blood.

PRINCE Faith, it does me, though it discolours the
complexion of my greatness to acknowledge it. Doth it
not show vilely in me to desire small beer?

POINS   Why, a prince should not be so loosely studied as to remember so weak a composition.

PRINCE   Belike, then, my appetite was not princely got, for, by my troth, I do now remember the poor creature small beer. But indeed, these humble considerations make me out of love with my greatness. What a disgrace is it to me to remember thy name, or to know thy face tomorrow! Or to take note how many pair of silk stockings thou hast, with these and those that were thy peach-coloured once; or to bear the inventory of thy shirts, as: one for superfluity and another for use. But that the tennis-court keeper knows better than I; for it is a low ebb of linen with thee when thou keepest not racket there, as thou hast not done a great while, because the rest of the low countries have made a shift to eat up thy holland. And God knows whether those that bawl out the ruins of thy linen shall inherit His kingdom, but the midwives say the children are not in the fault whereupon the world increases and kindreds are mightily strengthened.

POINS   How ill it follows, after you have laboured so hard, you should talk so idly! Tell me, how many good young princes would do so, their fathers being so sick as yours at this time is?

PRINCE   Shall I tell thee one thing, Poins?

POINS   Yes, faith, and let it be an excellent good thing.

PRINCE   It shall serve among wits of no higher breeding than thine.

POINS   Go to, I stand the push of your one thing that you will tell.

PRINCE   Marry, I tell thee it is not meet that I should be sad now my father is sick, albeit I could tell to thee, as to one it pleases me for fault of a better to call my friend, I could be sad, and sad indeed, too.

POINS   Very hardly, upon such a subject.

PRINCE   By this hand, thou thinkest me as far in the devil's book as thou and Falstaff for obduracy and persistency. Let the end try the man. But I tell thee, my heart bleeds inwardly that my father is so sick; and keeping such vile company as thou art hath in reason taken from me all ostentation of sorrow.

POINS   The reason?

PRINCE   What wouldst thou think of me if I should weep?

POINS   I would think thee a most princely hypocrite.

PRINCE   It would be every man's thought, and thou art a blessed fellow to think as every man thinks. Never a man's thought in the world keeps the roadway better than thine. Every man would think me an hypocrite indeed. And what accites your most worshipful thought to think so?

POINS   Why, because you have been so lewd and so much engraffed to Falstaff.

PRINCE   And to thee.

POINS   By this light, I am well spoke on: I can hear it with mine own ears. The worst that they can say of me is that I am a second brother and that I am a proper fellow of my hands, and those two things I confess I cannot help. By the mass, here comes Bardolph.

Enter BARDOLPH *and* Boy [PAGE].

PRINCE   And the boy that I gave Falstaff. 'A had him from me Christian, and look if the fat villain have not transformed him ape.

BARDOLPH   God save your grace.

PRINCE   And yours, most noble Bardolph.

POINS [*to Bardolph*]   Come, you virtuous ass, you bashful fool, must you be blushing? Wherefore blush you now? What a maidenly man at arms are you become! Is't such a matter to get a pottle-pot's maidenhead?

PAGE   'A calls me e'en now, my lord, through a red lattice, and I could discern no part of his face from the window. At last I spied his eyes, and methought he had made two holes in the ale-wife's petticoat and so peeped through.

PRINCE [*to Poins*]   Has not the boy profited?

BARDOLPH [*to Page*]   Away, you whoreson upright rabbit! Away!

PAGE [*to Bardolph*]   Away, you rascally Althaea's dream! Away!

PRINCE   Instruct us, boy: what dream, boy?

PAGE   Marry, my lord, Althaea dreamt she was delivered of a firebrand, and therefore I call him her dream.

PRINCE   A crown's worth of good interpretation; there 'tis, boy. [*Gives him a coin.*]

POINS   O, that this blossom could be kept from cankers! Well, there is sixpence to preserve thee. [*Gives him a coin.*]

BARDOLPH   An you do not make him hanged among you, the gallows shall have wrong.

PRINCE   And how doth thy master, Bardolph?

BARDOLPH   Well, my lord. He heard of your grace's coming to town. There's a letter for you. [*Hands letter to Prince.*]

POINS   Delivered with good respect. And how doth the Martlemas your master?

BARDOLPH   In bodily health, sir.

POINS   Marry, the immortal part needs a physician, but that moves not him: though that be sick, it dies not.

PRINCE   I do allow this wen to be as familiar with me as my dog; and he holds his place, for look you how he writes. [*Shows Poins the letter.*]

POINS [*Reads.*]   *John Falstaff, Knight.* – Every man must know that, as oft as he has occasion to name himself, even like those that are kin to the King; for they never prick their finger but they say, 'There's some of the King's blood spilt!' 'How comes that?' says he that takes upon him not to conceive. The answer is as ready as a borrower's cap: 'I am the King's poor cousin, sir!'

PRINCE   Nay, they will be kin to us, or they will fetch it from Japheth. But the letter: [*Reads.*] *Sir John Falstaff, Knight, to the son of the King nearest his father, Harry, Prince of Wales, greeting.*

POINS   Why, this is a certificate.

PRINCE   Peace! [*Reads.*] *I will imitate the honourable Romans in brevity.*

120   POINS   He sure means brevity in breath: short-winded.

PRINCE [*Reads.*]   *I commend me to thee, I commend thee, and I leave thee. Be not too familiar with Poins, for he misuses thy favours so much that he swears thou art to marry his sister Nell. Repent at idle times as thou mayst,*

125   *and so farewell.*

Thine by yea and no – which is as much as to say, as thou usest him – Jack Falstaff with my family, John with my brothers and sisters, and Sir John with all Europe.

POINS   My lord, I'll steep this letter in sack and make

130   him eat it!

PRINCE   That's to make him eat twenty of his words. But do you use me thus, Ned? Must I marry your sister?

POINS   God send the wench no worse fortune, but I

135   never said so.

PRINCE   Well, thus we play the fools with time, and the spirits of the wise sit in the clouds and mock us. – Is your master here in London?

BARDOLPH   Yea, my lord.

140   PRINCE   Where sups he? Doth the old boar feed in the old frank?

BARDOLPH   At the old place, my lord, in Eastcheap.

PRINCE   What company?

PAGE   Ephesians, my lord, of the old church.

145   PRINCE   Sup any women with him?

PAGE   None, my lord, but old Mistress Quickly and Mistress Doll Tearsheet.

PRINCE   What pagan may that be?

PAGE   A proper gentlewoman, sir, and a kinswoman of

150   my master's.

PRINCE   Even such kin as the parish heifers are to the town bull. – Shall we steal upon them, Ned, at supper?

POINS   I am your shadow, my lord; I'll follow you.

PRINCE   Sirrah – you boy, and Bardolph – no word to

155   your master that I am yet come to town. There's for your silence. [*Gives them coins.*]

BARDOLPH   I have no tongue, sir.

PAGE   And for mine, sir, I will govern it.

PRINCE   Fare you well. Go.

Exeunt Bardolph and Page.

160   This Doll Tearsheet should be some road.

POINS   I warrant you, as common as the way between Saint Albans and London.

PRINCE   How might we see Falstaff bestow himself tonight in his true colours and not ourselves be seen?

165   POINS   Put on two leathern jerkins and aprons, and wait upon him at his table as drawers.

PRINCE   From a god to a bull? A heavy descension: it was Jove's case. From a prince to a prentice? A low transformation: that shall be mine, for in everything

170 ·   the purpose must weigh with the folly. Follow me, Ned.   *Exeunt.*

2.3   *Enter the* Earl of NORTHUMBERLAND,
       his wife, LADY NORTHUMBERLAND,
       and the wife to Harry Percy, LADY PERCY.

NORTHUMBERLAND
I pray thee, loving wife and gentle daughter,
Give even way unto my rough affairs.
Put not you on the visage of the times
And be like them, to Percy, troublesome.

LADY NORTHUMBERLAND
I have given over. I will speak no more.   5
Do what you will; your wisdom be your guide.

NORTHUMBERLAND
Alas, sweet wife, my honour is at pawn,
And but my going, nothing can redeem it.

LADY PERCY
O yet, for God's sake, go not to these wars.
The time was, father, that you broke your word,   10
When you were more endeared to it than now –
When your own Percy, when my heart's dear Harry,
Threw many a northward look to see his father
Bring up his powers; but he did long in vain.
Who then persuaded you to stay at home?   15
There were two honours lost: yours and your son's.
For yours, the God of heaven brighten it!
For his, it stuck upon him as the sun
In the grey vault of heaven, and by his light
Did all the chivalry of England move   20
To do brave acts. He was indeed the glass
Wherein the noble youth did dress themselves.
ᶠHe had no legs that practised not his gait;
And speaking thick, which nature made his blemish,
Became the accents of the valiant,   25
For those that could speak low and tardily
Would turn their own perfection to abuse
To seem like him – so that in speech, in gait,
In diet, in affections of delight,
In military rules, humours of blood,   30
He was the mark and glass, copy and book,
That fashioned others. And him – O wondrous him!
O miracle of men! – him did you leave,
Second to none, unseconded by you,
To look upon the hideous god of war   35
In disadvantage, to abide a field
Where nothing but the sound of Hotspur's name
Did seem defensible: so you left him.
Never, O never do his ghost the wrong
To hold your honour more precise and nice   40
With others than with him. Let them alone!
The Marshal and the Archbishop are strong.
Had my sweet Harry had but half their numbers,
Today might I, hanging on Hotspur's neck,
Have talked of Monmouth's grave.ᶠ

NORTHUMBERLAND   Beshrew your heart,   45
Fair daughter; you do draw my spirits from me
With new lamenting ancient oversights.
But I must go and meet with danger there,

Or it will seek me in another place
And find me worse provided.

LADY NORTHUMBERLAND   O, fly to Scotland
50 Till that the nobles and the armed commons
Have of their puissance made a little taste!

LADY PERCY
If they get ground and vantage of the King,
Then join you with them like a rib of steel
55 To make strength stronger. But, for all our loves,
First let them try themselves. So did your son:
He was so suffered. So came I a widow;
And never shall have length of life enough
To rain upon remembrance with mine eyes,
60 That it may grow and sprout as high as heaven
For recordation to my noble husband.

NORTHUMBERLAND
Come, come, go in with me. 'Tis with my mind
As with the tide swelled up unto his height
That makes a still stand, running neither way.
65 Fain would I go to meet the Archbishop,
But many thousand reasons hold me back.
I will resolve for Scotland: there am I
Till time and vantage crave my company.   *Exeunt.*

2.4   *Enter two* Drawers, FRANCIS *and*
Drawer, *who carries a dish of apple-johns.*

FRANCIS   What the devil hast thou brought there?
Apple-johns? Thou knowest Sir John cannot endure
an apple-john.

DRAWER   Mass, thou sayst true. The Prince once set a
5   dish of apple-johns before him and told him there were
five more Sir Johns and, putting off his hat, said, 'I will
now take my leave of these six dry, round, old, withered
knights!' It angered him to the heart, but he hath
forgot that.

10 FRANCIS   Why then, cover and set them down, and see
if thou canst find out Sneak's noise. Mistress Tearsheet
would fain hear some music.

DRAWER   Dispatch! The room where they supped is too
hot; they'll come in straight.

15 FRANCIS   Sirrah, here will be the Prince and Master
Poins anon, and they will put on two of our jerkins and
aprons, and Sir John must not know of it. Bardolph
hath brought word.

DRAWER   By the mass, here will be old utas! It will be an
20   excellent stratagem.

FRANCIS   I'll see if I can find out Sneak.   *Exit.*

Enter the HOSTESS *Mistress Quickly and* DOLL
Tearsheet.

HOSTESS   I'faith, sweetheart, methinks now you are in
an excellent good temporality. Your pulsidge beats as
extraordinarily as heart would desire, and your colour,
I warrant you, is as red as any rose, in good truth, la!
25 But, i'faith, you have drunk too much canaries, and
that's a marvellous searching wine, and it perfumes the

blood ere one can say, 'What's this?' How do you now?

DOLL   Better than I was. Hem!

30 HOSTESS   Why, that's well said. A good heart's worth
gold. Lo, here comes Sir John.

Enter Sir John FALSTAFF.

FALSTAFF [*Sings.*]   'When Arthur first in court' –
Empty the jordan!   *Exit Drawer.*
– 'and was a worthy king' – How now, Mistress Doll?

35 HOSTESS   Sick of a calm, yea, good faith.

FALSTAFF   So is all her sect. An they be once in a calm,
they are sick.

DOLL   A pox damn you, you muddy rascal! Is that all the
comfort you give me?

40 FALSTAFF   You make fat rascals, Mistress Doll.

DOLL   I make them? Gluttony and diseases make; I
make them not.

FALSTAFF   If the cook help to make the gluttony, you
help to make the diseases, Doll. We catch of you, Doll,
45   we catch of you. Grant that, my poor virtue, grant
that.

DOLL   Yea, Jesu, our chains and our jewels.

FALSTAFF [*Sings.*]   'Your brooches, pearls and ouches!'
– For to serve bravely is to come halting off, you know;
50   to come off the breach with his pike bent bravely, and
to surgery bravely, to venture upon the charged
chambers bravely –

DOLL   Hang yourself, you muddy conger, hang
yourself!

55 HOSTESS   By my troth, this is the old fashion. You two
never meet but you fall to some discord! You are both,
i'good truth, as rheumatic as two dry toasts; you
cannot one bear with another's confirmities. What the
goodyear! One must bear, [*to Doll*] and that must be
60   you: you are the weaker vessel, as they say, the emptier
vessel.

DOLL   Can a weak empty vessel bear such a huge full
hogshead? There's a whole merchant's venture of
Bordeaux stuff in him! You have not seen a hulk better
65   stuffed in the hold. Come, I'll be friends with thee,
Jack: thou art going to the wars, and whether I shall
ever see thee again or no there is nobody cares.

Enter Drawer.

DRAWER   Sir, Ancient Pistol's below and would speak
with you.

70 DOLL   Hang him, swaggering rascal! Let him not come
hither. It is the foul-mouth'dst rogue in England!

HOSTESS   If he swagger, let him not come here! No, by
my faith, I must live among my neighbours; I'll no
swaggerers. I am in good name and fame with the very
75   best. – Shut the door! – There comes no swaggerers
here. I have not lived all this while to have swaggering
now. – Shut the door, I pray you!

FALSTAFF   Dost thou hear, hostess?

HOSTESS   Pray ye pacify yourself, Sir John; there comes
80   no swaggerers here.

FALSTAFF   Dost thou hear? It is mine ancient.

HOSTESS   Tilly-fally, Sir John, ne'er tell me. An your
ancient swagger, 'a comes not in my doors! I was before
Master Tisick the debuty t'other day, and as he said to
85   me – 'twas no longer ago than Wed'sday last, i'good
faith – 'Neighbour Quickly,' says he – Master Dumbe
our minister was by then – 'Neighbour Quickly,' says
he, 'receive those that are civil, for', said he, 'you are in
an ill name.' Now 'a said so; I can tell whereupon.
90   'For', says he, 'you are an honest woman, and well
thought on; therefore take heed what guests you
receive. Receive', says he, 'no swaggering companions.'
There comes none here! You would bless you to hear
what he said. No, I'll no swaggerers.

95   FALSTAFF   He's no swaggerer, hostess. A tame cheater,
i'faith: you may stroke him as gently as a puppy
greyhound. He'll not swagger with a barbary hen if her
feathers turn back in any show of resistance. – Call him
up, drawer!   *Exit Drawer.*

100   HOSTESS   Cheater, call you him? I will bar no honest
man my house, nor no cheater; but I do not love
swaggering, by my troth. I am the worse when one says
'swagger'! Feel, masters, how I shake. Look you, I
warrant you!

105   DOLL   So you do, hostess.

HOSTESS   Do I? Yea, in very truth do I, an 'twere an
aspen leaf. I cannot abide swaggerers.

Enter Ancient PISTOL, BARDOLPH *and* Boy [PAGE].

PISTOL   God save you, Sir John.

FALSTAFF   Welcome, Ancient Pistol. Here, Pistol, I
110   charge you with a cup of sack; do you discharge upon
mine hostess.

PISTOL   I will discharge upon her, Sir John, with two
bullets.

FALSTAFF   She is pistol-proof; sir, you shall not hardly
115   offend her.

HOSTESS   Come, I'll drink no proofs, nor no bullets; I'll
drink no more than will do me good. For no man's
pleasure, I.

PISTOL   Then to you, Mistress Dorothy! I will charge
120   you.

DOLL   Charge me? I scorn you, scurvy companion.
What, you poor, base, rascally, cheating, lack-linen
mate? Away, you mouldy rogue, away! I am meat for
your master.

125   PISTOL   I know you, Mistress Dorothy.

DOLL   Away, you cutpurse rascal! You filthy bung, away!
By this wine, I'll thrust my knife in your mouldy chaps
an you play the saucy cuttle with me. Away, you bottle-
ale rascal, you basket-hilt stale juggler, you! Since
130   when, I pray you, sir? God's light, with two points on
your shoulder? Much!

PISTOL   God let me not live, but I will murder your ruff
for this!

FALSTAFF   No more, Pistol; I would not have you go off
135   here. Discharge yourself of our company, Pistol.

HOSTESS   No, good Captain Pistol; not here, sweet
captain!

DOLL   Captain! Thou abominable damned cheater, art
thou not ashamed to be called captain? An captains
were of my mind, they would truncheon you out for   140
taking their names upon you before you have earned
them! You a captain? You slave, for what? For tearing a
poor whore's ruff in a bawdy house? – He a captain?
Hang him, rogue! He lives upon mouldy stewed
prunes and dried cakes. A captain? God's light, these   145
villains will make the word as odious as the word
'occupy', which was an excellent good word before it
was ill-sorted; therefore captains had need look to't.

BARDOLPH   Pray thee go down, good ancient.

FALSTAFF   Hark thee hither, Mistress Doll.   150

PISTOL   Not I! I tell thee what, Corporal Bardolph, I
could tear her! I'll be revenged of her!

PAGE   Pray thee go down.

PISTOL   I'll see her damned first! To Pluto's damned
lake – by this hand – to th'infernal deep, with Erebus   155
and tortures vile also! Hold hook and line, say I! Down!
Down, dogs! Down, faitours! Have we not Hiren here?
[*Draws his sword.*]

HOSTESS   Good Captain Peesel, be quiet; 'tis very late,
i'faith. I beseek you now, aggravate your choler.

PISTOL   These be good humours indeed! Shall pack-   160
horses, and hollow pampered jades of Asia, which
cannot go but thirty mile a day, compare with Caesars
and with Cannibals and Troyant Greeks? Nay, rather
damn them with King Cerberus, and let the welkin
roar! Shall we fall foul for toys?   165

HOSTESS   By my troth, captain, these are very bitter
words.

BARDOLPH   Be gone, good ancient! This will grow to a
brawl anon.

PISTOL   Die men like dogs, give crowns like pins!   170
Have we not Hiren here?

HOSTESS   A'my word, Captain, there's none such here.
What the goodyear, do you think I would deny her? For
God's sake, be quiet.

PISTOL   Then feed and be fat, my fair Calipolis! Come,   175
give's some sack. *Si fortune me tormente sperato me
contento*. Fear we broadsides? No, let the fiend give fire!
Give me some sack; – and sweetheart [*to his sword*], lie
thou there. – Come we to full points here? And are
etceteras no things?   180

FALSTAFF   Pistol, I would be quiet.

PISTOL   Sweet knight, I kiss thy neaf. What! We have
seen the seven stars.

DOLL   For God's sake, thrust him downstairs! I cannot
endure such a fustian rascal.   185

PISTOL   Thrust him downstairs? Know we not Galloway
nags?

FALSTAFF   Quoit him down, Bardolph, like a shove-
groat shilling. Nay, an 'a do nothing but speak nothing,
'a shall be nothing here.   190

BARDOLPH   Come, get you downstairs.

PISTOL [*Snatches up his sword.*] What, shall we have
incision? Shall we imbrue? Then death rock me asleep,
abridge my doleful days! Why then, let grievous,
195 ghastly, gaping wounds untwine the sisters three!
Come, Atropos, I say!

HOSTESS Here's goodly stuff toward.

FALSTAFF Give me my rapier, boy!

DOLL I pray thee, Jack, I pray thee, do not draw!

200 FALSTAFF Get you downstairs!
> [*Falstaff draws his sword and exchanges thrusts with
> Pistol.*]

HOSTESS Here's a goodly tumult! I'll forswear keeping
house afore I'll be in these tirrits and frights. So!
Murder, I warrant now! Alas, alas, put up your naked
weapons! Put up your naked weapons!
> *Exit Pistol, pursued by Bardolph.*

205 DOLL I pray thee, Jack, be quiet. The rascal's gone. Ah,
you whoreson little valiant villain, you!

HOSTESS Are you not hurt i'th' groin? Methought 'a
made a shrewd thrust at your belly.

Enter BARDOLPH.

FALSTAFF Have you turned him out a'doors?

210 BARDOLPH Yea, sir; the rascal's drunk. You have hurt
him, sir, i'th' shoulder.

FALSTAFF A rascal, to brave me!

DOLL Ah, you sweet little rogue, you! Alas, poor ape,
how thou sweat'st! Come, let me wipe thy face. Come
215 on, you whoreson chops! Ah, rogue, i'faith, I love thee.
Thou art as valorous as Hector of Troy, worth five of
Agamemnon, and ten times better than the Nine
Worthies! Ah, villain!

FALSTAFF A rascally slave! I will toss the rogue in a
220 blanket.

DOLL Do, an thou dar'st for thy heart. An thou dost, I'll
canvas thee between a pair of sheets.

Enter FRANCIS *with Music, Sneak's band.
Bardolph and Hostess talk aside.*

PAGE The music is come, sir.

FALSTAFF Let them play. – Play, sirs!   [*Music*]
225 Sit on my knee, Doll. A rascal, bragging slave! The
rogue fled from me like quicksilver.

DOLL I'faith, and thou follow'dst him like a church.
Thou whoreson little tidy Bartholomew boar-pig,
when wilt thou leave fighting a'days and foining
230 a'nights and begin to patch up thine old body for
heaven?

Enter PRINCE *Henry and* POINS *dressed as drawers, and
standing apart.*

FALSTAFF Peace, good Doll. Do not speak like a
death's-head: do not bid me remember mine end.

DOLL Sirrah, what humour's the Prince of?

235 FALSTAFF A good shallow young fellow. 'A would have
made a good pantler; 'a would a' chipped bread well.

DOLL They say Poins has a good wit.

FALSTAFF He a good wit? Hang him, baboon! His wit's
as thick as Tewkesbury mustard! There's no more
conceit in him than is in a mallet.   240

DOLL Why does the Prince love him so, then?

FALSTAFF Because their legs are both of a bigness, and
'a plays at quoits well, and eats conger and fennel, and
drinks off candles' ends for flap-dragons, and rides the
wild mare with the boys, and jumps upon joint-stools,   245
and swears with a good grace, and wears his boots very
smooth like unto the sign of the Leg, and breeds no
bate with telling of discreet stories; and such other
gambol faculties 'a has that show a weak mind and an
able body, for the which the Prince admits him. For the   250
Prince himself is such another. The weight of a hair
will turn the scales between their *haber de poiz*.

PRINCE Would not this nave of a wheel have his ears
cut off?

POINS Let's beat him before his whore.   255

PRINCE Look whe'er the withered elder hath not his
poll clawed like a parrot.

POINS Is it not strange that desire should so many years
outlive performance?

FALSTAFF Kiss me, Doll. [*She kisses him.*]   260

PRINCE Saturn and Venus this year in conjunction?
What says th'almanac to that?

POINS And look whether the fiery trigon his man be not
lisping to his master's old tables, his notebook, his
counsel-keeper.   265

FALSTAFF Thou dost give me flattering busses.

DOLL By my troth, I kiss thee with a most constant
heart.

FALSTAFF I am old, I am old.

DOLL I love thee better than I love e'er a scurvy young   270
boy of them all.

FALSTAFF What stuff wilt have a kirtle of? I shall
receive money a'Thursday: shalt have a cap tomorrow.
– A merry song! – Come, it grows late; we'll to bed.
Thou't forget me when I am gone.   275

DOLL By my troth, thou't set me a-weeping an thou
sayst so. Prove that ever I dress myself handsome till
thy return! Well, hearken a'th' end.

FALSTAFF Some sack, Francis!

PRINCE, POINS [*coming forward*] Anon, anon, sir!   280

FALSTAFF Ha? A bastard son of the King's? – And art
not thou Poins his brother?

PRINCE Why, thou globe of sinful continents, what a
life dost thou lead?

FALSTAFF A better than thou: I am a gentleman, thou   285
art a drawer.

PRINCE Very true, sir, and I come to draw you out by
the ears.

HOSTESS O, the Lord preserve thy grace! By my troth,
welcome to London. Now the Lord bless that sweet   290
face of thine! O Jesu, are you come from Wales?

FALSTAFF Thou whoreson mad compound of majesty,
by this light flesh and corrupt blood [*Indicates Doll.*],
thou art welcome!

295   DOLL   How? You fat fool, I scorn you!

POINS [*to Prince*]   My lord, he will drive you out of your revenge and turn all to a merriment if you take not the heat.

300   PRINCE [*to Falstaff*]   You whoreson candle-mine, you! How vilely did you speak of me now before this honest, virtuous, civil gentlewoman!

HOSTESS   God's blessing of your good heart, and so she is, by my troth.

FALSTAFF [*to Prince*]   Didst thou hear me?

305   PRINCE   Yea, and you knew me as you did when you ran away by Gad's Hill. You knew I was at your back and spoke it on purpose to try my patience.

FALSTAFF   No, no, no, not so; I did not think thou wast within hearing.

310   PRINCE   I shall drive you then to confess the wilful abuse, and then I know how to handle you.

FALSTAFF   No abuse, Hal, a'mine honour; no abuse.

PRINCE   Not to dispraise me, and call me pantler and bread-chipper and I know not what?

315   FALSTAFF   No abuse, Hal.

POINS   No abuse?

FALSTAFF   No abuse, Ned, i'th' world! Honest Ned, none. I dispraised him before the wicked, [*to Prince*] that the wicked might not fall in love with thee – in
320   which doing I have done the part of a careful friend and a true subject, and thy father is to give me thanks for it. No abuse, Hal; none, Ned, none. No, faith, boys, none.

PRINCE   See now whether pure fear and entire cowardice
325   doth not make thee wrong this virtuous gentlewoman to close with us. Is she of the wicked? Is thine hostess here of the wicked? Or is thy boy of the wicked? Or honest Bardolph, whose zeal burns in his nose, of the wicked?

330   POINS   Answer, thou dead elm, answer!

FALSTAFF   The fiend hath pricked down Bardolph irrecoverable, and his face is Lucifer's privy kitchen, where he doth nothing but roast malt-worms. For the boy, there is a good angel about him, but the devil
335   blinds him too.

PRINCE   For the women?

FALSTAFF   For one of them, she's in hell already and burns poor souls. For th'other, I owe her money, and whether she be damned for that I know not.

340   HOSTESS   No, I warrant you.

FALSTAFF   No, I think thou art not. I think thou art quit for that. Marry, there is another indictment upon thee, for suffering flesh to be eaten in thy house contrary to the law, for the which I think thou wilt howl.

345   HOSTESS   All vict'lers do so. What's a joint of mutton or two in a whole Lent?

PRINCE   You, gentlewoman.

DOLL   What says your grace?

FALSTAFF   His grace says that which his flesh rebels
350   against.

[*Peto knocks at door.*]

HOSTESS   Who knocks so loud at door? Look to th' door there, Francis.   *Exit Francis.*

Enter PETO.

PRINCE   Peto, how now, what news?

PETO   The King your father is at Westminster,
And there are twenty weak and wearied posts   355
Come from the north; and as I came along
I met and overtook a dozen captains,
Bare-headed, sweating, knocking at the taverns,
And asking every one for Sir John Falstaff.

PRINCE   By heaven, Poins, I feel me much to blame   360
So idly to profane the precious time
When tempest of commotion, like the south,
Borne with black vapour, doth begin to melt
And drop upon our bare unarmed heads.
Give me my sword and cloak. – Falstaff, good night.   365
Exeunt Prince and Poins with Peto.

FALSTAFF   Now comes in the sweetest morsel of the night, and we must hence and leave it unpicked.
Knocking within. Exit Bardolph.
More knocking at the door?

Enter BARDOLPH.

How now, what's the matter?

BARDOLPH   You must away to court, sir, presently.   370
A dozen captains stay at door for you.

FALSTAFF [*to Page*]   Pay the musicians, sirrah.
Exit Page, with Sneak's band.
Farewell, hostess; farewell, Doll. You see, my good
wenches, how men of merit are sought after. The
undeserver may sleep when the man of action is called   375
on. Farewell, good wenches! If I be not sent away post,
I will see you again ere I go.

DOLL   I cannot speak! If my heart be not ready to burst
. . . Well, sweet Jack, have a care of thyself.

FALSTAFF   Farewell, farewell.   *Exit with Bardolph.*   380

HOSTESS   Well, fare thee well. I have known thee these
twenty-nine years, come peascod time; but an honester
and truer-hearted man . . .Well, fare thee well.

Enter BARDOLPH.

BARDOLPH   Mistress Tearsheet!

HOSTESS   What's the matter?   385

BARDOLPH   Bid Mistress Tearsheet come to my master.

HOSTESS   O, run, Doll! Run, run, good Doll! Come. –
She comes blubbered! – Yea, will you come, Doll?
Exeunt.

3.1   *Enter the* KING *in his nightgown with a Page.*

KING   Go, call the Earls of Surrey and of Warwick;
But ere they come, bid them o'er-read these letters
And well consider of them.   [*Gives letters to Page.*]
Make good speed. *Exit Page.*
How many thousand of my poorest subjects
Are at this hour asleep? O sleep! O gentle sleep!   5

Nature's soft nurse, how have I frighted thee,
That thou no more wilt weigh my eyelids down
And steep my senses in forgetfulness?
Why rather, sleep, liest thou in smoky cribs,
10   Upon uneasy pallets stretching thee
And hushed with buzzing night-flies to thy slumber,
Than in the perfumed chambers of the great,
Under the canopies of costly state
And lulled with sound of sweetest melody?
15   O thou dull god, why li'st thou with the vile
In loathsome beds and leav'st the kingly couch
A watch-case or a common 'larum bell?
Wilt thou upon the high and giddy mast
Seal up the ship-boy's eyes and rock his brains
20   In cradle of the rude, imperious surge
And in the visitation of the winds,
Who take the ruffian billows by the top,
Curling their monstrous heads and hanging them
With deafing clamour in the slippery clouds,
25   That, with the hurly, death itself awakes?
Canst thou, O partial sleep, give then repose
To the wet sea-son in an hour so rude,
And in the calmest and most stillest night,
With all appliances and means to boot,
30   Deny it to a king? Then happy low, lie down!
Uneasy lies the head that wears a crown.

          Enter WARWICK, *Surrey and Sir John Blunt.*

WARWICK   Many good morrows to your majesty.
KING   Is it good morrow, lords?
WARWICK   'Tis one a'clock, and past.
35   KING   Why then, good morrow to you all, my lords.
          Have you read o'er the letter that I sent you?
WARWICK   We have, my liege.
KING   Then you perceive the body of our kingdom,
          How foul it is, what rank diseases grow,
40   And with what danger, near the heart of it.
WARWICK   It is but as a body yet distempered
          Which to his former strength may be restored
          With good advice and little medicine.
          My Lord Northumberland will soon be cooled.
45   KING   O God, that one might read the book of fate
          And see the revolution of the times
          Make mountains level, and the continent,
          Weary of solid firmness, melt itself
          Into the sea; and other times to see
50   The beachy girdle of the ocean
          Too wide for Neptune's hips. How chances, mocks
          And changes fill the cup of alteration
          With divers liquors! O, if this were seen,
          The happiest youth, viewing his progress through –
55   What perils past, what crosses to ensue –
          Would shut the book and sit him down and die!
          'Tis not ten years gone
          Since Richard and Northumberland, great friends,
          Did feast together, and in two year after
60   Were they at wars. It is but eight years since

This Percy was the man nearest my soul,
Who like a brother toiled in my affairs
And laid his love and life under my foot;
Yea, for my sake, even to the eyes of Richard
65   Gave him defiance. But which of you was by –
[*to Warwick*] You, cousin Neville, as I may remember –
When Richard, with his eye brimful of tears,
Then checked and rated by Northumberland,
Did speak these words, now proved a prophecy?
70   'Northumberland, thou ladder by the which
My cousin Bolingbroke ascends my throne' –
Though then, God knows, I had no such intent,
But that necessity so bowed the state
That I and greatness were compelled to kiss –
75   'The time shall come', thus did he follow it,
'The time will come that foul sin, gathering head,
Shall break into corruption' – so went on,
Foretelling this same time's condition
And the division of our amity.
80   WARWICK   There is a history in all men's lives
Figuring the natures of the times deceased,
The which observed, a man may prophesy
With a near aim of the main chance of things
As yet not come to life, who in their seeds
85   And weak beginning lie intreasured.
Such things become the hatch and brood of time;
And by the necessary form of this
King Richard might create a perfect guess
That great Northumberland, then false to him,
90   Would of that seed grow to greater falseness,
Which should not find a ground to root upon
Unless on you.
KING   Are these things then necessities?
Then let us meet them like necessities,
And that same word even now cries out on us.
95   They say the Bishop and Northumberland
Are fifty thousand strong.
WARWICK   It cannot be, my lord.
Rumour doth double, like the voice and echo,
The numbers of the feared. Please it your grace
To go to bed. Upon my soul, my lord,
100   The powers that you already have sent forth
Shall bring this prize in very easily.
To comfort you the more, I have received
A certain instance that Glendower is dead.
Your majesty hath been this fortnight ill,
105   And these unseasoned hours perforce must add
Unto your sickness.
KING   I will take your counsel;
And were these inward wars once out of hand,
We would, dear lords, unto the Holy Land.   *Exeunt.*

3.2   *Enter* Justice SHALLOW *and* Justice SILENCE.

SHALLOW   Come on, come on, come on; give me your
hand, sir, give me your hand, sir. An early stirrer, by
the rood! And how doth my good cousin Silence?

SILENCE   Good morrow, good cousin Shallow.

SHALLOW   And how doth my cousin your bedfellow?
And your fairest daughter and mine, my god-daughter
Ellen?

SILENCE   Alas, a black woosel, cousin Shallow.

SHALLOW   By yea and no, sir. I dare say my cousin
William is become a good scholar. He is at Oxford still,
is he not?

SILENCE   Indeed, sir, to my cost.

SHALLOW   'A must then to the Inns a'Court shortly. I
was once of Clement's Inn, where I think they will talk
of mad Shallow yet.

SILENCE   You were called lusty Shallow then, cousin.

SHALLOW   By the mass, I was called anything; and I
would have done anything indeed, too – and roundly,
too. There was I, and little John Doyt of Staffordshire,
and black George Barnes, and Francis Pickbone, and
Will Squele, a Cotsole man: you had not four such
swinge-bucklers in all the Inns a'Court again! And I
may say to you, we knew where the bona robas were
and had the best of them at commandment. Then was
Jack Falstaff – now Sir John – a boy, and page to
Thomas Mowbray, Duke of Norfolk.

SILENCE   This Sir John, cousin, that comes hither anon
about soldiers?

SHALLOW   The same Sir John, the very same. I see him
break Scoggin's head at the court gate when 'a was a
crack not thus high; and the very same day did I fight
with one Samson Stockfish, a fruiterer, behind Gray's
Inn. Jesu, Jesu, the mad days that I have spent! And to
see how many of my old acquaintance are dead.

SILENCE   We shall all follow, cousin.

SHALLOW   Certain, 'tis certain; very sure, very sure.
Death, as the psalmist saith, is certain to all; all shall
die. How a good yoke of bullocks at Stamford fair?

SILENCE   By my troth, I was not there.

SHALLOW   Death is certain. Is old Dooble of your town
living yet?

SILENCE   Dead, sir.

SHALLOW   Jesu, Jesu, dead! 'A drew a good bow, and
dead? 'A shot a fine shoot. John a'Gaunt loved him
well and betted much money on his head. Dead! 'A
would have clapped i'th' clout at twelve score and
carried you a forehand shaft at fourteen and fourteen
and a half, that it would have done a man's heart good
to see. How a score of ewes now?

SILENCE   Thereafter as they be; a score of good ewes
may be worth ten pounds.

SHALLOW   And is old Dooble dead?

SILENCE   Here come two of Sir John Falstaff's men, as I
think.

Enter BARDOLPH *and one with him.*

Good morrow, honest gentlemen.

BARDOLPH   I beseech you, which is Justice Shallow?

SHALLOW   I am Robert Shallow, sir, a poor esquire of
this county and one of the King's justices of the peace.
What is your good pleasure with me?

BARDOLPH   My captain, sir, commends him to you: my
captain Sir John Falstaff – a tall gentleman, by heaven,
and a most gallant leader.

SHALLOW   He greets me well, sir. I knew him a good
backsword man. How doth the good knight? May I ask
how my lady his wife doth?

BARDOLPH   Sir, pardon; a soldier is better
accommodated than with a wife.

SHALLOW   It is well said, in faith, sir, and it is well said
indeed, too: 'better accommodated' – it is good; yea,
indeed is it. Good phrases are surely, and ever were,
very commendable. 'Accommodated': it comes of
accommodo. Very good, a good phrase.

BARDOLPH   Pardon, sir, I have heard the word. Phrase,
you call it? By this day, I know not the phrase; but I will
maintain the word with my sword to be a soldier-like
word and a word of exceeding good command, by
heaven! 'Accommodated': that is, when a man is, as
they say, accommodated, or when a man is being
whereby 'a may be thought to be accommodated,
which is an excellent thing.

Enter FALSTAFF.

SHALLOW   It is very just. Look, here comes good Sir
John! – Give me your good hand, give me your
worship's good hand! By my troth, you like well and
bear your years very well. Welcome, good Sir John!

FALSTAFF   I am glad to see you well, good Master
Robert Shallow. [*to Silence*] Master Soccard, as I think?

SHALLOW   No, Sir John, it is my cousin Silence, in
commission with me.

FALSTAFF   Good Master Silence, it well befits you
should be of the peace.

SILENCE   Your good worship is welcome.

FALSTAFF   Fie, this is hot weather, gentlemen! Have you
provided me here half a dozen sufficient men?

SHALLOW   Marry, we have, sir. Will you sit?

FALSTAFF [*Sits.*]   Let me see them, I beseech you.

SHALLOW   Where's the roll? Where's the roll? Where's
the roll? Let me see, let me see, let me see: so, so, so, so,
so, so, so. Yea, marry, sir. Rafe Mouldy! Let them
appear as I call; let them do so, let them do so. Let me
see. Where is Mouldy?

Enter MOULDY.

MOULDY   Here, an't please you.

SHALLOW   What think you, Sir John? A good-limbed
fellow, young, strong and of good friends.

FALSTAFF   Is thy name Mouldy?

MOULDY   Yea, an't please you.

FALSTAFF   'Tis the more time thou wert used.

SHALLOW   Ha, ha, ha! Most excellent, i'faith: things
that are mouldy lack use! Very singular good; in faith,
well said, Sir John, very well said.

FALSTAFF   Prick him.

MOULDY   I was pricked well enough before, and you

could have let me alone. My old dame will be undone
now for one to do her husbandry and her drudgery.
You need not to have pricked me. There are other men
115　fitter to go out than I.

FALSTAFF　Go to! Peace, Mouldy. You shall go, Mouldy.
It is time you were spent.

MOULDY　Spent?

SHALLOW　Peace, fellow, peace! Stand aside. Know you
120　where you are? – For th'other, Sir John, let me see
Simon Shadow.

FALSTAFF　Yea, marry, let me have him to sit under.
He's like to be a cold soldier.

SHALLOW　Where's Shadow?

Enter SHADOW.

125　SHADOW　Here, sir.

FALSTAFF　Shadow, whose son art thou?

SHADOW　My mother's son, sir.

FALSTAFF　Thy mother's son! Like enough, and thy
father's shadow; so the son of the female is the shadow
130　of the male. It is often so indeed, but much of the
father's substance.

SHALLOW　Do you like him, Sir John?

FALSTAFF　Shadow will serve for summer. Prick him,
for we have a number of shadows fill up the muster
135　book.

SHALLOW　Thomas Wart!

FALSTAFF　Where's he?

Enter WART.

WART　Here, sir.

FALSTAFF　Is thy name Wart?

140　WART　Yea, sir.

FALSTAFF　Thou art a very ragged wart.

SHALLOW　Shall I prick him, Sir John?

FALSTAFF　It were superfluous, for his apparel is built
upon his back, and the whole frame stands upon pins.
145　Prick him no more.

SHALLOW　Ha, ha, ha! You can do it, sir, you can do it! I
commend you well. – Francis Feeble!

Enter FEEBLE.

FEEBLE　Here, sir.

SHALLOW　What trade art thou, Feeble?

150　FEEBLE　A woman's tailor, sir.

SHALLOW　Shall I prick him, sir?

FALSTAFF　You may; but if he had been a man's tailor,
he'd a' pricked you. [*to Feeble*] Wilt thou make as many
holes in an enemy's battle as thou hast done in a
155　woman's petticoat?

FEEBLE　I will do my good will, sir; you can have no
more.

FALSTAFF　Well said, good woman's tailor! Well said,
courageous Feeble! Thou wilt be as valiant as the
160　wrathful dove or most magnanimous mouse. – Prick
the woman's tailor well, Master Shallow, deep Master
Shallow.

FEEBLE　I would Wart might have gone, sir.

FALSTAFF　I would thou wert a man's tailor, that thou
mightst mend him and make him fit to go. I cannot put
165　him to a private soldier, that is the leader of so many
thousands. Let that suffice, most forcible Feeble.

FEEBLE　It shall suffice, sir.

FALSTAFF　I am bound to thee, reverend Feeble. – Who
is next?

170　SHALLOW　Peter Bullcalf o'th' green.

FALSTAFF　Yea, marry, let's see Bullcalf.

Enter BULLCALF.

BULLCALF　Here, sir.

FALSTAFF　'Fore God, a likely fellow! Come, prick
Bullcalf till he roar again.

175　BULLCALF　O Lord, good my lord captain –

FALSTAFF　What, dost thou roar before thou art pricked?

BULLCALF　O Lord, sir, I am a diseased man!

FALSTAFF　What disease hast thou?

BULLCALF　A whoreson cold, sir; a cough, sir, which I
180　caught with ringing in the King's affairs upon his
coronation day, sir.

FALSTAFF　Come, thou shalt go to the wars in a gown.
We will have away thy cold, and I will take such order
that thy friends shall ring for thee. – Is here all?

185　SHALLOW　Here is two more called than your number.
You must have but four here, sir; and so I pray you go
in with me to dinner.

FALSTAFF　Come, I will go drink with you, but I cannot
tarry dinner. I am glad to see you, by my troth, Master
190　Shallow.

SHALLOW　O Sir John, do you remember since we lay
all night in the Windmill in Saint George's Field?

FALSTAFF　No more of that, Master Shallow.

SHALLOW　Ha, 'twas a merry night! And is Jane
195　Nightwork alive?

FALSTAFF　She lives, Master Shallow.

SHALLOW　She never could away with me.

FALSTAFF　Never, never. She would always say she
could not abide Master Shallow.

200　SHALLOW　By the mass, I could anger her to th' heart.
She was then a bona roba. Doth she hold her own well?

FALSTAFF　Old, old, Master Shallow.

SHALLOW　Nay, she must be old. She cannot choose but
be old. Certain she's old, and had Robin Nightwork by
205　old Nightwork before I came to Clement's Inn.

SILENCE　That's fifty-five year ago.

SHALLOW　Ha, cousin Silence, that thou hadst seen that
that this knight and I have seen! – Ha, Sir John? Said I
well?

210　FALSTAFF　We have heard the chimes at midnight,
Master Shallow.

SHALLOW　That we have, that we have, that we have; in
faith, Sir John, we have. Our watchword was 'Hem,
boys!' Come, let's to dinner; come, let's to dinner.
215　Jesus, the days that we have seen! Come, come.

Exeunt Falstaff, Shallow and Silence.

BULLCALF   Good Master Corporate Bardolph, stand
my friend and here's four Harry ten shillings in French
crowns for you. [*Offers coins.*] In very truth, sir, I had as
220   lief be hanged, sir, as go; and yet for mine own part,
sir, I do not care, but rather because I am unwilling,
and for mine own part have a desire to stay with my
friends; else, sir, I did not care for mine own part so
much.

225   BARDOLPH [*Takes coins.*]   Go to, stand aside.

MOULDY   And good Master Corporal Captain, for my
old dame's sake, stand my friend. She has nobody to do
anything about her when I am gone, and she is old and
cannot help herself. [*Offers coins.*] You shall have forty,
230   sir.

BARDOLPH [*Takes coins.*]   Go to, stand aside.

FEEBLE   By my troth, I care not. A man can die but
once. We owe God a death. I'll ne'er bear a base mind.
An't be my destiny, so; an't be not, so. No man's too
235   good to serve 's prince; and let it go which way it will,
he that dies this year is quit for the next.

BARDOLPH   Well said. Th'art a good fellow.

FEEBLE   Faith, I'll bear no base mind.

Enter FALSTAFF *and the* Justices.

FALSTAFF   Come, sir, which men shall I have?

240   SHALLOW   Four of which you please.

BARDOLPH [*apart to Falstaff*]   Sir, a word with you. I
have three pound to free Mouldy and Bullcalf.

FALSTAFF [*apart*]   Go to, well.

SHALLOW   Come, Sir John, which four will you have?

245   FALSTAFF   Do you choose for me.

SHALLOW   Marry, then: Mouldy, Bullcalf, Feeble and
Shadow.

FALSTAFF   Mouldy and Bullcalf! For you, Mouldy, stay
at home till you are past service; and for your part,
250   Bullcalf, grow till you come unto it. I will none of you.

Exeunt Mouldy and Bullcalf.

SHALLOW   Sir John, Sir John, do not yourself wrong!
They are your likeliest men, and I would have you
served with the best.

FALSTAFF   Will you tell me, Master Shallow, how to
255   choose a man? Care I for the limb, the thews, the stature,
bulk and big assemblance of a man? Give me the spirit,
Master Shallow! Here's Wart: you see what a ragged
appearance it is. 'A shall charge you and discharge you
with the motion of a pewterer's hammer, come off and
260   on swifter than he that gibbets on the brewer's bucket.
And this same half-faced fellow Shadow? Give me this
man! He presents no mark to the enemy: the foeman
may with as great aim level at the edge of a penknife.
And for a retreat, how swiftly will this Feeble, the
265   woman's tailor, run off! O, give me the spare men, and
spare me the great ones! – Put me a caliver into Wart's
hand, Bardolph. [*Bardolph hands Wart a caliver.*]

BARDOLPH   Hold, Wart! Traverse! Thas, thas, thas!

FALSTAFF   Come, manage me your caliver. So. Very
270   well. Go to, very good, exceeding good. – O, give me

always a little, lean, old, chopped, bald shot. – Well
said, i'faith, Wart! Th'art a good scab. Hold, there's a
tester for thee. [*Gives Wart a coin.*]

SHALLOW   He is not his craft's master; he doth not do it
275   right. I remember at Mile End Green, when I lay at
Clement's Inn – I was then Sir Dagonet in Arthur's
Show – there was a little quiver fellow, and 'a would
manage you his piece thus; and 'a would about and
about, and come you in, and come you in. 'Rah, tah,
280   tah!' would 'a say; 'Bounce!' would 'a say; and away
again would 'a go, and again would 'a come. I shall
ne'er see such a fellow.

FALSTAFF   These fellows will do well, Master Shallow.
God keep you, Master Silence; I will not use many
285   words with you. Fare you well, gentlemen both; I thank
you. I must a dozen mile tonight. – Bardolph, give the
soldiers coats.

SHALLOW   Sir John, the Lord bless you; God prosper
your affairs; God send us peace. At your return, visit
290   our house; let our old acquaintance be renewed.
Peradventure I will with ye to the court.

FALSTAFF   'Fore God, would you would.

SHALLOW   Go to, I have spoke at a word. God keep you.

FALSTAFF   Fare you well, gentle gentlemen.

Exit Shallow with Silence.

On, Bardolph, lead the men away.   295

Exit Bardolph with Shadow, Wart and Feeble.

As I return I will fetch off these justices. I do see the
bottom of Justice Shallow. Lord, Lord, how subject
we old men are to this vice of lying! This same
starved justice hath done nothing but prate to me of
the wildness of his youth and the feats he hath done   300
about Turnbull Street, and every third word a lie,
duer paid to the hearer than the Turk's tribute. I
do remember him at Clement's Inn like a man made
after supper of a cheese paring. When 'a was naked
he was for all the world like a forked radish with a   305
head fantastically carved upon it with a knife. 'A
was so forlorn that his dimensions to any thick sight
were invincible. 'A was the very genius of famine,
yet lecherous as a monkey, and the whores called
him mandrake. 'A came ever in the rearward of the   310
fashion, and sung those tunes to the overscutched
housewives that he heard the car-men whistle, and
sware they were his fancies or his goodnights. And
now is this Vice's dagger become a squire and talks
as familiarly of John a'Gaunt as if he had been   315
sworn brother to him; and I'll be sworn 'a ne'er
saw him but once in the tilt-yard, and then he burst
his head for crowding among the marshal's men. I
saw it and told John a'Gaunt he beat his own name,
for you might have thrust him and all his apparel   320
into an eel-skin. The case of a treble hautboy was
a mansion for him, a court; and now has he land
and beefs. Well, I'll be acquainted with him if I
return, and 't shall go hard, but I'll make him a
philosopher's two stones to me. If the young dace be   325

a bait for the old pike, I see no reason in the law of
nature but I may snap at him. Let time shape, and
there an end.   *Exit.*

4.1   *Enter the* ARCHBISHOP *of York,* MOWBRAY,
           HASTINGS *and a Captain within the*
           Forest of Gaultree.

ARCHBISHOP   What is this forest called?
HASTINGS
  'Tis Gaultree Forest, an't shall please your grace.
ARCHBISHOP
  Here stand, my lords, and send discoverers forth
  To know the numbers of our enemies.
HASTINGS   We have sent forth already.
5 ARCHBISHOP   'Tis well done.
  My friends and brethren in these great affairs,
  I must acquaint you that I have received
  New-dated letters from Northumberland,
  Their cold intent, tenor and substance thus:
10 Here doth he wish his person with such powers
  As might hold sortance with his quality,
  The which he could not levy; whereupon
  He is retired, to ripe his growing fortunes,
  To Scotland, and concludes in hearty prayers
15 That your attempts may overlive the hazard
  And fearful meeting of their opposite.
MOWBRAY
  Thus do the hopes we have in him touch ground
  And dash themselves to pieces.

              Enter Messenger.

HASTINGS   Now, what news?
MESSENGER   West of this forest, scarcely off a mile,
20 In goodly form comes on the enemy,
  And, by the ground they hide, I judge their number
  Upon or near the rate of thirty thousand.
MOWBRAY   The just proportion that we gave them out.
  Let us sway on and face them in the field.

              Enter WESTMORLAND.

ARCHBISHOP
25 What well-appointed leader fronts us here?
MOWBRAY   I think it is my Lord of Westmorland.
WESTMORLAND
  Health and fair greeting from our general:
  The prince Lord John and Duke of Lancaster.
ARCHBISHOP
  Say on, my Lord of Westmorland, in peace,
  What doth concern your coming.
30 WESTMORLAND   Then, my lord,
  Unto your grace do I in chief address
  The substance of my speech. If that rebellion
  Came like itself, in base and abject routs
  Led on by bloody youth, guarded with rage
35 And countenanced by boys and beggary –
  I say, if damned commotion so appear

In his true, native and most proper shape,
You, reverend father, and these noble lords
Had not been here to dress the ugly form
Of base and bloody insurrection   40
With your fair honours. You, Lord Archbishop,
Whose see is by a civil peace maintained,
Whose beard the silver hand of peace hath touched,
Whose learning and good letters peace hath tutored,
Whose white investments figure innocence,   45
The dove and very blessed spirit of peace:
Wherefore do you so ill translate yourself
Out of the speech of peace that bears such grace
Into the harsh and boist'rous tongue of war,
Turning your books to graves, your ink to blood,   50
Your pens to lances, and your tongue divine
To a loud trumpet and a point of war?
ARCHBISHOP
  Wherefore do I this? So the question stands.
  Briefly, to this end: we are all diseased,
  ᶠAnd with our surfeiting and wanton hours   55
  Have brought ourselves into a burning fever,
  And we must bleed for it; of which disease
  Our late King Richard, being infected, died.
  But, my most noble Lord of Westmorland,
  I take not on me here as a physician,   60
  Nor do I as an enemy to peace
  Troop in the throngs of military men,
  But rather show a while like fearful war
  To diet rank minds sick of happiness
  And purge th'obstructions which begin to stop   65
  Our very veins of life. Hear me more plainly.
  I have in equal balance justly weighed
  What wrongs our arms may do, what wrongs we suffer,
  And find our griefs heavier than our offences.
  We see which way the stream of time doth run   70
  And are enforced from our most quiet there
  By the rough torrent of occasion,
  And have the summary of all our griefs,
  When time shall serve, to show in articles,
  Which long ere this we offered to the King   75
  And might by no suit gain our audience.
  When we are wronged and would unfold our griefs,
  We are denied access unto his person
  Even by those men that most have done us wrong.ᶠ
  The dangers of the days but newly gone,   80
  Whose memory is written on the earth
  With yet-appearing blood, and the examples
  Of every minute's instance, present now,
  Hath put us in these ill-beseeming arms
  Not to break peace, or any branch of it,   85
  But to establish here a peace indeed,
  Concurring both in name and quality.
WESTMORLAND   Whenever yet was your appeal denied?
  Wherein have you been galled by the King?
  What peer hath been suborned to grate on you,   90
  That you should seal this lawless, bloody book
  Of forged rebellion with a seal divine

And consecrate commotion's bitter edge?

ARCHBISHOP   My brother general, the commonwealth.
95   To brother born, an household cruelty,
     I make my quarrel in particular.

WESTMORLAND   There is no need of any such redress;
     Or if there were, it not belongs to you.

MOWBRAY   Why not to him in part, and to us all
100   That feel the bruises of the days before
     And suffer the condition of these times
     To lay a heavy and unequal hand
     Upon our honours?

WESTMORLAND   O my good Lord Mowbray,
     Construe the times to their necessities
105   And you shall say indeed it is the time,
     And not the King, that doth you injuries.
     Yet for your part, it not appears to me
     Either from the King or in the present time
     That you should have an inch of any ground
110   To build a grief on. Were you not restored
     To all the Duke of Norfolk's signories,
     Your noble and right well-remembered father's?

MOWBRAY   What thing, in honour, had my father lost
     That need to be revived and breathed in me?
115   The king that loved him, as the state stood then,
     Was force perforce compelled to banish him;
     And then that Henry Bolingbroke and he,
     Being mounted and both roused in their seats,
     Their neighing coursers daring of the spur,
120   Their armed staves in charge, their beavers down,
     Their eyes of fire sparkling through sights of steel,
     And the loud trumpet blowing them together –
     Then, then, when there was nothing could have
        stayed
     My father from the breast of Bolingbroke –
125   O, when the King did throw his warder down,
     His own life hung upon the staff he threw;
     Then threw he down himself and all their lives
     That by indictment and by dint of sword
     Have since miscarried under Bolingbroke.

WESTMORLAND
130   You speak, Lord Mowbray, now you know not what.
     The Earl of Hereford was reputed then
     In England the most valiant gentleman.
     Who knows on whom Fortune would then have
        smiled?
     But if your father had been victor there,
135   He ne'er had borne it out of Coventry;
     For all the country in a general voice
     Cried hate upon him, and all their prayers and love
     Were set on Hereford, whom they doted on,
     And blessed and graced indeed more than the King.
140   But this is mere digression from my purpose.
     Here come I from our princely general
     To know your griefs, to tell you from his grace
     That he will give you audience; and wherein
     It shall appear that your demands are just,
145   You shall enjoy them, everything set off

That might so much as think you enemies.

MOWBRAY   But he hath forced us to compel this offer,
     And it proceeds from policy, not love.

WESTMORLAND   Mowbray, you overween to take it so.
     This offer comes from mercy, not from fear;   150
     For lo, within a ken our army lies,
     Upon mine honour, all too confident
     To give admittance to a thought of fear.
     Our battle is more full of names than yours,
     Our men more perfect in the use of arms,   155
     Our armour all as strong, our cause the best;
     Then reason will our hearts should be as good.
     Say you not, then, our offer is compelled.

MOWBRAY   Well, by my will, we shall admit no parley.

WESTMORLAND
     That argues but the shame of your offence: 160
     A rotten case abides no handling.

HASTINGS   Hath the Prince John a full commission,
     In very ample virtue of his father,
     To hear and absolutely to determine
     Of what conditions we shall stand upon?   165

WESTMORLAND
     That is intended in the general's name.
     I muse you make so slight a question.

ARCHBISHOP [*Offers a paper.*]
     Then take, my Lord of Westmorland, this schedule,
     For this contains our general grievances.
     Each several article herein redressed,   170
     All members of our cause both here and hence
     That are ensinewed to this action,
     Acquitted by a true substantial form
     And present execution of our wills,
     To us and our purposes confined   175
     We come within our awful banks again
     And knit our powers to the arm of peace.

WESTMORLAND [*Takes the paper.*]
     This will I show the general. Please you, lords,
     In sight of both our battles we may meet
     And either end in peace – which God so frame! –   180
     Or to the place of diff'rence call the swords
     Which must decide it.

ARCHBISHOP   My lord, we will do so.
                               Exit Westmorland.

MOWBRAY   There is a thing within my bosom tells me
     That no conditions of our peace can stand.

HASTINGS   Fear you not that: if we can make our peace   185
     Upon such large terms and so absolute
     As our conditions shall consist upon,
     Our peace shall stand as firm as rocky mountains.

MOWBRAY   Yea, but our valuation shall be such
     That every slight and false-derived cause –   190
     Yea, every idle, nice and wanton reason –
     Shall to the King taste of this action,
     That, were our royal faiths martyrs in love,
     We shall be winnowed with so rough a wind
     That even our corn shall seem as light as chaff   195
     And good from bad find no partition.

ARCHBISHOP
No, no, my lord, note this: the King is weary
Of dainty and such picking grievances,
For he hath found to end one doubt by death
200 Revives two greater in the heirs of life;
And therefore will he wipe his tables clean
And keep no tell-tale to his memory
That may repeat and history his loss
To new remembrance. For full well he knows
205 He cannot so precisely weed this land
As his misdoubts present occasion.
His foes are so enrooted with his friends
That, plucking to unfix an enemy,
He doth unfasten so and shake a friend,
210 So that this land, like an offensive wife
That hath enraged him on to offer strokes,
As he is striking, holds his infant up
And hangs resolved correction in the arm
That was upreared to execution.
215 HASTINGS Besides, the King hath wasted all his rods
On late offenders, that he now doth lack
The very instruments of chastisement,
So that his power, like to a fangless lion,
May offer but not hold.
220 ARCHBISHOP   'Tis very true;
And therefore be assured, my good Lord Marshal,
If we do now make our atonement well,
Our peace will, like a broken limb united,
Grow stronger for the breaking.

Enter WESTMORLAND.

MOWBRAY   Be it so.
Here is returned my Lord of Westmorland.
WESTMORLAND
225 The Prince is here at hand. Pleaseth your lordship
To meet his grace just distance 'tween our armies?

Enter Prince JOHN *and his Army.*

MOWBRAY
Your Grace of York, in God's name, then, set forward.
ARCHBISHOP [*to Mowbray*]
Before, and greet his grace.
[*to Westmorland*]   My lord, we come.
[*Led by Mowbray, they cross to meet Prince John.*]
JOHN
You are well encountered here, my cousin Mowbray.
230 Good day to you, gentle Lord Archbishop,
And so to you, Lord Hastings, and to all.
My Lord of York, it better showed with you
When that your flock, assembled by the bell,
Encircled you to hear with reverence
235 Your exposition on the holy text
Than now to see you here, an iron man,
Cheering a rout of rebels with your drum,
Turning the word to sword and life to death.
That man that sits within a monarch's heart
240 And ripens in the sunshine of his favour,

Would he abuse the countenance of the king,
Alack, what mischiefs might he set abroach
In shadow of such greatness? With you, Lord Bishop,
Is it even so. Who hath not heard it spoken
245 How deep you were within the books of God –
To us, the speaker in His parliament;
To us, th'imagined voice of God Himself,
The very opener and intelligencer
Between the grace, the sanctities of heaven,
250 And our dull workings? O, who shall believe
But you misuse the reverence of your place,
Imply the countenance and grace of heaven,
As a false favourite doth his prince's name,
In deeds dishonourable? You have ta'en up,
255 Under the counterfeited zeal of God,
The subjects of His substitute, my father,
And both against the peace of heaven and him
Have here upswarmed them.
ARCHBISHOP   Good my Lord of Lancaster,
I am not here against your father's peace;
260 But, as I told my Lord of Westmorland,
The time misordered doth, in common sense,
Crowd us and crush us to this monstrous form
To hold our safety up. I sent your grace
The parcels and particulars of our grief,
The which hath been with scorn shoved from the
      court,
265
Whereon this Hydra, son of war, is born,
Whose dangerous eyes may well be charmed asleep
With grant of our most just and right desires,
And true obedience, of this madness cured,
270 Stoop tamely to the foot of majesty.
MOWBRAY If not, we ready are to try our fortunes
To the last man.
HASTINGS   And though we here fall down,
We have supplies to second our attempt;
If they miscarry, theirs shall second them,
275 And so success of mischief shall be born,
And heir from heir shall hold his quarrel up
Whiles England shall have generation.
JOHN You are too shallow, Hastings, much too shallow,
To sound the bottom of the after-times.
WESTMORLAND
280 Pleaseth your grace to answer them directly
How far forth you do like their articles.
JOHN I like them all and do allow them well,
And swear here, by the honour of my blood,
My father's purposes have been mistook,
285 And some about him have too lavishly
Wrested his meaning and authority.
[*to Archbishop*] My lord, these griefs shall be with
      speed redressed;
Upon my soul, they shall. If this may please you,
Discharge your powers unto their several counties,
290 As we will ours; and here, between the armies,
Let's drink together friendly and embrace,
That all their eyes may bear these tokens home

Of our restored love and amity.
[*Attendant passes cups.*]

ARCHBISHOP
I take your princely word for these redresses.

295 JOHN   I give it you and will maintain my word,
And thereupon I drink unto your grace.   [*Drinks.*]

HASTINGS   Go, captain, and deliver to the army
This news of peace. Let them have pay, and part.
I know it will well please them. Hie thee, captain!
Exit Captain.

ARCHBISHOP
300   To you, my noble Lord of Westmorland.   [*Drinks.*]

WESTMORLAND
I pledge your grace;   [*Drinks.*]
and if you knew what pains
I have bestowed to breed this present peace,
You would drink freely. But my love to ye
Shall show itself more openly hereafter.

ARCHBISHOP   I do not doubt you.

305 WESTMORLAND   I am glad of it.
Health to my lord and gentle cousin Mowbray!
[*Drinks.*]

MOWBRAY   You wish me health in very happy season,
For I am on the sudden something ill.

ARCHBISHOP   Against ill chances men are ever merry,
310   But heaviness foreruns the good event.

WESTMORLAND
Therefore be merry, coz, since sudden sorrow
Serves to say thus: some good thing comes tomorrow.

ARCHBISHOP   Believe me, I am passing light in spirit.

MOWBRAY
So much the worse, if your own rule be true.
[*Shout within*]

JOHN
315   The word of peace is rendered. Hark how they shout!

MOWBRAY   This had been cheerful after victory.

ARCHBISHOP   A peace is of the nature of a conquest,
For then both parties nobly are subdued
And neither party loser.

JOHN [*to Westmorland*]   Go, my lord,
320   And let our army be discharged too.
Exit Westmorland.
[*to Archbishop*] And, good my lord, so please you, let
our trains
March by us, that we may peruse the men
We should have coped withal.

ARCHBISHOP   Go, good Lord Hastings,
And ere they be dismissed, let them march by.
Exit Hastings.

325 JOHN   I trust, lords, we shall lie tonight together.

Enter WESTMORLAND.

Now, cousin, wherefore stands our army still?

WESTMORLAND
The leaders, having charge from you to stand,
Will not go off until they hear you speak.

JOHN   They know their duties.

Enter HASTINGS.

HASTINGS [*to Archbishop*]
My lord, our army is dispersed already.   330
Like youthful steers unyoked they take their courses
East, west, north, south; or like a school broke up,
Each hurries toward his home and sporting place.

WESTMORLAND
Good tidings, my Lord Hastings, for the which
I do arrest thee, traitor, of high treason.   335
And you, Lord Archbishop, and you, Lord
Mowbray,
Of capital treason I attach you both.

MOWBRAY   Is this proceeding just and honourable?

WESTMORLAND   Is your assembly so?

ARCHBISHOP   Will you thus break your faith?

JOHN   I pawned thee none.   340
I promised you redress of these same grievances
Whereof you did complain, which, by mine honour,
I will perform with a most Christian care.
But for you rebels, look to taste the due
Meet for rebellion.   345
Most shallowly did you these arms commence,
Fondly brought here and foolishly sent hence.
Strike up our drums! Pursue the scattered stray!
God, and not we, hath safely fought today.
Some guard these traitors to the block of death –   350
[*Soldiers arrest the Archbishop, Hastings and
Mowbray.*]
Treason's true bed and yielder-up of breath.
Exeunt.

4.2   *Alarum. Excursions. Enter*
FALSTAFF and COLLEVILE.

FALSTAFF   What's your name, sir? Of what condition
are you, and of what place?

COLLEVILE   I am a knight, sir, and my name is Collevile
of the Dale.

FALSTAFF   Well, then: Collevile is your name, a knight   5
is your degree, and your place the dale. Collevile shall
be still your name, a traitor your degree, and the
dungeon your place – a place deep enough so shall you
be still Collevile of the Dale.

COLLEVILE   Are not you Sir John Falstaff?   10

FALSTAFF   As good a man as he, sir, whoe'er I am. Do ye
yield, sir, or shall I sweat for you? If I do sweat, they are
the drops of thy lovers and they weep for thy death.
Therefore rouse up fear and trembling, and do
observance to my mercy.   15

COLLEVILE   I think you are Sir John Falstaff, and in that
thought yield me.

FALSTAFF   I have a whole school of tongues in this belly
of mine, and not a tongue of them all speaks any other
word but my name. An I had but a belly of any   20
indifferency, I were simply the most active fellow in
Europe. My womb, my womb, my womb undoes me.
Here comes our general.

Enter Prince JOHN, WESTMORLAND,
Sir John Blunt and the rest.

JOHN   The heat is past; follow no further now.
Call in the powers, good cousin Westmorland.
                                                 Exit Westmorland. Sound retreat.
25
Now, Falstaff, where have you been all this while?
When everything is ended, then you come.
These tardy tricks of yours will, on my life,
One time or other break some gallows' back.

30
FALSTAFF   I would be sorry, my lord, but it should
be thus. I never knew yet but rebuke and check was
the reward of valour. Do you think me a swallow, an
arrow or a bullet? Have I, in my poor and old motion,
35
the expedition of thought? I have speeded hither with
the very extremest inch of possibility; I have foundered
nine score and odd posts; and here, travel-tainted as I
am, have in my pure and immaculate valour taken Sir
John Collevile of the Dale, a most furious knight and
40
valorous enemy. But what of that? He saw me and
yielded, that I may justly say with the hook-nosed
fellow of Rome, 'There, cousin: I came, saw and
overcame.'
JOHN   It was more of his courtesy than your deserving.
45
FALSTAFF   I know not. Here he is, and here I yield him.
And I beseech your grace let it be booked with the rest
of this day's deeds, or, by the Lord, I will have it in a
particular ballad else with mine own picture on the top
on't, Collevile kissing my foot. To the which course if I
50
be enforced, if you do not all show like gilt twopences
to me and I, in the clear sky of fame, o'ershine you as
much as the full moon doth the cinders of the element
which show like pins' heads to her, believe not the
word of the noble. Therefore let me have right, and let
desert mount.
55
JOHN   Thine's too heavy to mount.
FALSTAFF   Let it shine, then.
JOHN   Thine's too thick to shine.
FALSTAFF   Let it do something, my good lord, that may
do me good, and call it what you will.
JOHN   Is thy name Collevile?
60
COLLEVILE   It is, my lord.
JOHN   A famous rebel art thou, Collevile.
FALSTAFF   And a famous true subject took him.
COLLEVILE   I am, my lord, but as my betters are
That led me hither. Had they been ruled by me,
65
You should have won them dearer than you have.
FALSTAFF   I know not how they sold themselves, but
thou, like a kind fellow, gavest thyself away gratis, and
I thank thee for thee.

Enter WESTMORLAND.

JOHN   Now, have you left pursuit?
70
WESTMORLAND   Retreat is made and execution stayed.
JOHN   Send Collevile with his confederates
To York, to present execution.
Blunt, lead him hence and see you guard him sure.
                                                 Exit Blunt with Collevile.

And now dispatch we toward the court, my lords;
I hear the King my father is sore sick.
75
Our news shall go before us to his majesty,
[*to Westmorland*] Which, cousin, you shall bear to
     comfort him,
And we with sober speed will follow you.
FALSTAFF   My lord, I beseech you give me leave to go
through Gloucestershire and, when you come to court,
80
stand my good lord in your good report.
JOHN   Fare you well, Falstaff. I, in my condition,
Shall better speak of you than you deserve.
                                                 Exeunt all but Falstaff.
FALSTAFF   I would you had the wit; 'twere better than
your dukedom. Good faith, this same young sober-
85
blooded boy doth not love me, nor a man cannot make
him laugh. But that's no marvel: he drinks no wine.
There's never none of these demure boys come to any
proof, for thin drink doth so over-cool their blood, and
making many fish meals, that they fall into a kind of
90
male green-sickness; and then, when they marry, they
get wenches. They are generally fools and cowards –
which some of us should be, too, but for inflammation.
A good sherris sack hath a twofold operation in it. It
ascends me into the brain, dries me there all the foolish
95
and dull and crudy vapours which environ it, makes it
apprehensive, quick, forgetive, full of nimble, fiery and
delectable shapes, which, delivered o'er to the voice,
the tongue, which is the birth, becomes excellent wit.
The second property of your excellent sherris is the
100
warming of the blood, which before, cold and settled,
left the liver white and pale, which is the badge of
pusillanimity and cowardice. But the sherris warms it
and makes it course from the inwards to the parts'
extremes. It illumineth the face, which as a beacon gives
105
warning to all the rest of this little kingdom, man, to
arm; and then the vital commoners and inland petty
spirits muster me all to their captain, the heart, who,
great and puffed up with this retinue, doth any deed of
courage. And this valour comes of sherris, so that skill
110
in the weapon is nothing without sack, for that sets it
a-work; and learning, a mere hoard of gold kept by a
devil till sack commences it and sets it in act and use.
Hereof comes it that Prince Harry is valiant; for the
cold blood he did naturally inherit of his father he hath
115
like lean, sterile and bare land manured, husbanded and
tilled with excellent endeavour of drinking good and
good store of fertile sherris, that he is become very hot
and valiant. If I had a thousand sons, the first human
principle I would teach them should be to forswear thin
120
potations and to addict themselves to sack.

Enter BARDOLPH.

How now, Bardolph?
BARDOLPH   The army is discharged all and gone.
FALSTAFF   Let them go. I'll through Gloucestershire,
and there will I visit Master Robert Shallow, Esquire.
125
I have him already temp'ring between my finger

and my thumb, and shortly will I seal with him. Come
away.   *Exeunt.*

4.3   *Enter the* KING, WARWICK, Thomas,
            Duke of CLARENCE, Humphrey, Duke
            of GLOUCESTER, *and Attendants.*

KING   Now, lords, if God doth give successful end
     To this debate that bleedeth at our doors,
     We will our youth lead on to higher fields
     And draw no swords but what are sanctified.
5   Our navy is addressed, our power collected,
     Our substitutes in absence well invested,
     And everything lies level to our wish;
     Only we want a little personal strength,
     And pause us till these rebels now afoot
10   Come underneath the yoke of government.
WARWICK
     Both which we doubt not but your majesty
     Shall soon enjoy.
KING   Humphrey, my son of Gloucester,
     Where is the Prince your brother?
GLOUCESTER
     I think he's gone to hunt, my lord, at Windsor.
KING   And how accompanied?
15 GLOUCESTER   I do not know, my lord.
KING
     Is not his brother Thomas of Clarence with him?
GLOUCESTER
     No, my good lord; he is in presence here.
CLARENCE [*Steps forward.*]
     What would my lord and father?
KING   Nothing but well to thee, Thomas of Clarence.
20   How chance thou art not with the Prince thy brother?
     He loves thee, and thou dost neglect him, Thomas.
     Thou hast a better place in his affection
     Than all thy brothers. Cherish it, my boy,
     And noble offices thou mayst effect
25   Of mediation, after I am dead,
     Between his greatness and thy other brethren.
     Therefore omit him not, blunt not his love,
     Nor lose the good advantage of his grace
     By seeming cold or careless of his will;
30   For he is gracious, if he be observed:
     He hath a tear for pity and a hand
     Open as day for meting charity.
     Yet notwithstanding, being incensed, he is flint,
     As humourous as winter, and as sudden
35   As flaws congealed in the spring of day.
     His temper therefore must be well observed.
     Chide him for faults, and do it reverently,
     When you perceive his blood inclined to mirth;
     But being moody, give him time and scope
40   Till that his passions, like a whale on ground,
     Confound themselves with working. Learn this,
        Thomas,
     And thou shalt prove a shelter to thy friends,
     A hoop of gold to bind thy brothers in,

     That the united vessel of their blood,
     Mingled with venom of suggestion –   45
     As force perforce the age will pour it in –
     Shall never leak, though it do work as strong
     As aconitum or rash gunpowder.
CLARENCE   I shall observe him with all care and love.
KING   Why art thou not at Windsor with him, Thomas?   50
CLARENCE   He is not there today. He dines in London.
KING   And how accompanied?
CLARENCE
     With Poins and other his continual followers.
KING
     Most subject is the fattest soil to weeds,
     And he, the noble image of my youth,   55
     Is overspread with them; therefore, my grief
     Stretches itself beyond the hour of death.
     The blood weeps from my heart when I do shape
     In forms imaginary th'unguided days
     And rotten times that you shall look upon   60
     When I am sleeping with my ancestors;
     For when his headstrong riot hath no curb,
     When rage and hot blood are his counsellors,
     When means and lavish manners meet together,
     O, with what wings shall his affections fly   65
     Towards fronting peril and opposed decay!
WARWICK
     My gracious lord, you look beyond him quite.
     The Prince but studies his companions
     Like a strange tongue, wherein, to gain the language,
     'Tis needful that the most immodest word   70
     Be looked upon and learnt, which, once attained,
     Your highness knows, comes to no further use
     But to be known and hated. So, like gross terms,
     The Prince will in the perfectness of time
     Cast off his followers, and their memory   75
     Shall as a pattern or a measure live
     By which his grace must mete the lives of other,
     Turning past evils to advantages.
KING   'Tis seldom when the bee doth leave her comb
     In the dead carrion.

                 Enter WESTMORLAND.

                      Who's here? Westmorland?   80
WESTMORLAND
     Health to my sovereign, and new happiness
     Added to that that I am to deliver.
     Prince John your son doth kiss your grace's hand:
     Mowbray, the Bishop Scroop, Hastings and all
     Are brought to the correction of your law.   85
     There is not now a rebel's sword unsheathed,
     But Peace puts forth her olive everywhere.
     The manner how this action hath been borne
     Here at more leisure may your highness read,
     With every course in his particular.   [*Offers a paper.*]   90
KING   O Westmorland, thou art a summer bird
     Which ever in the haunch of winter sings
     The lifting up of day!

Enter HARCOURT.

Look, here's more news.

HARCOURT   From enemies heavens keep your majesty,
5   And when they stand against you, may they fall
As those that I am come to tell you of.
The Earl Northumberland and the Lord Bardolph,
With a great power of English and of Scots,
Are by the Shrieve of Yorkshire overthrown.
00   The manner and true order of the fight
This packet, please it you, contains at large.
    [*Offers packet.*]

KING
And wherefore should these good news make me sick?
Will Fortune never come with both hands full,
But wet her fair words still in foulest terms?
05   She either gives a stomach and no food –
Such are the poor, in health; or else a feast
And takes away the stomach – such are the rich,
That have abundance and enjoy it not.
I should rejoice now at this happy news,
10   And now my sight fails and my brain is giddy.
O me, come near me, now I am much ill.   [*Swoons.*]

GLOUCESTER   Comfort, your majesty.

CLARENCE   O, my royal father!

WESTMORLAND
My sovereign lord, cheer up yourself. Look up!

WARWICK   Be patient, princes. You do know these fits
15   Are with his highness very ordinary.
Stand from him; give him air. He'll straight be well.

CLARENCE
No, no, he cannot long hold out these pangs.
Th'incessant care and labour of his mind
Hath wrought the mure that should confine it in
20   So thin that life looks through.

GLOUCESTER   The people fear me, for they do observe
Unfathered heirs and loathly births of nature.
The seasons change their manners, as the year
Had found some months asleep and leapt them over.

CLARENCE
25   The river hath thrice flowed, no ebb between,
And the old folk, Time's doting chronicles,
Say it did so a little time before
That our great-grandsire Edward sicked and died.

WARWICK   Speak lower, princes, for the King recovers.
30   GLOUCESTER   This apoplexy will certain be his end.

KING   I pray you, take me up and bear me hence
Into some other chamber.
    [*A bed is thrust forth; the King is moved to it.*]
Let there be no noise made, my gentle friends,
Unless some dull and favourable hand
35   Will whisper music to my weary spirit.

WARWICK   Call for the music in the other room.
                    Exit Attendant. Music within.

KING   Set me the crown upon my pillow here.

CLARENCE   His eye is hollow, and he changes much.

WARWICK   Less noise, less noise.

Enter PRINCE Henry.

PRINCE   Who saw the Duke of Clarence?

CLARENCE   I am here, brother, full of heaviness.   140

PRINCE   How now, rain within doors and none abroad?
How doth the King?

GLOUCESTER   Exceeding ill.

PRINCE   Heard he the good news yet? Tell it him.

WARWICK   He altered much upon the hearing it.   145

PRINCE   If he be sick with joy, he'll recover without
physic.

WARWICK
Not so much noise, my lords. Sweet prince, speak low;
The King your father is disposed to sleep.

CLARENCE   Let us withdraw into the other room.   150

WARWICK   Will't please your grace to go along with us?

PRINCE   No, I will sit and watch here by the King.
                Exeunt all but the King and Prince.
Why doth the crown lie there upon his pillow,
Being so troublesome a bedfellow?
O polished perturbation, golden care,   155
That keep'st the ports of slumber open wide
To many a watchful night, sleep with it now –
Yet not so sound and half so deeply sweet
As he whose brow with homely biggen bound
Snores out the watch of night. O majesty!   160
When thou dost pinch thy bearer, thou dost sit
Like a rich armour worn in heat of day
That scald'st with safety. By his gates of breath
There lies a downy feather which stirs not;
Did he suspire, that light and weightless down   165
Perforce must move. My gracious lord? My father?
This sleep is sound indeed. This is a sleep
That from this golden rigol hath divorced
So many English kings. Thy due from me
Is tears and heavy sorrows of the blood,   170
Which nature, love and filial tenderness
Shall, O dear father, pay thee plenteously.
My due from thee is this imperial crown,
Which, as immediate from thy place and blood,
Derives itself to me.   [*Puts crown on his head.*]
                Lo where it sits,   175
Which God shall guard; and put the world's whole
    strength
Into one giant arm, it shall not force
This lineal honour from me. This from thee
Will I to mine leave, as 'tis left to me.   *Exit.*
    [*The King awakes.*]

KING   Warwick! Gloucester! Clarence!   180

Enter WARWICK, GLOUCESTER *and* CLARENCE.

CLARENCE   Doth the King call?

WARWICK   What would your majesty?

KING   Why did you leave me here alone, my lords?

CLARENCE
We left the Prince my brother here, my liege,
Who undertook to sit and watch by you.

KING
185   The Prince of Wales? Where is he? Let me see him.
         He is not here.
WARWICK   This door is open; he is gone this way.
GLOUCESTER
         He came not through the chamber where we stayed.
KING
         Where is the crown? Who took it from my pillow?
190 WARWICK   When we withdrew, my liege, we left it here.
KING
         The Prince hath ta'en it hence. Go, seek him out.
         Is he so hasty that he doth suppose
         My sleep my death?
         Find him, my Lord of Warwick; chide him hither.
                                          Exit Warwick.
195   This part of his conjoins with my disease
         And helps to end me. See, sons, what things you are,
         How quickly Nature falls into revolt
         When gold becomes her object?
         For this the foolish, over-careful fathers
200   Have broke their sleep with thoughts,
         Their brains with care, their bones with industry.
         For this they have engrossed and pill'd up
         The cankered heaps of strange-achieved gold.
         For this they have been thoughtful to invest
205   Their sons with arts and martial exercises,
         When, like the bee tolling from every flower,
         Our thighs packed with wax, our mouths with
             honey,
         We bring it to the hive and, like the bees,
         Are murdered for our pains. This bitter taste
210   Yields his engrossments to the ending father.

                      Enter WARWICK.

         Now, where is he that will not stay so long
         Till his friend Sickness have determined me?
WARWICK
         My lord, I found the Prince in the next room
         Washing with kindly tears his gentle cheeks,
215   With such a deep demeanour in great sorrow
         That tyranny, which never quaffed but blood,
         Would, by beholding him, have washed his knife
         With gentle eye-drops. He is coming hither.
KING   But wherefore did he take away the crown?

                 Enter PRINCE *Henry*
                   carrying the crown.

220   Lo where he comes. Come hither to me, Harry.
         – Depart the chamber; leave us here alone.
                 Exeunt Gloucester, Clarence and Warwick.
PRINCE   I never thought to hear you speak again.
KING   Thy wish was father, Harry, to that thought.
         I stay too long by thee; I weary thee.
225   Dost thou so hunger for mine empty chair
         That thou wilt needs invest thee with my honours
         Before thy hour be ripe? O foolish youth,
         Thou seek'st the greatness that will overwhelm thee!

         Stay but a little, for my cloud of dignity
         Is held from falling with so weak a wind   230
         That it will quickly drop. My day is dim.
         Thou hast stol'n that which after some few hours
         Were thine without offence, and at my death
         Thou hast sealed up my expectation.
         Thy life did manifest thou lov'dst me not,   235
         And thou wilt have me die assured of it.
         Thou hid'st a thousand daggers in thy thoughts,
         Whom thou hast whetted on thy stony heart
         To stab at half an hour of my life.
         What, canst thou not forbear me half an hour?   240
         Then get thee gone and dig my grave thyself,
         And bid the merry bells ring to thine ear
         That thou art crowned, not that I am dead.
         Let all the tears that should bedew my hearse
         Be drops of balm to sanctify thy head: 245
         Only compound me with forgotten dust;
         Give that which gave thee life unto the worms.
         Pluck down my officers, break my decrees;
         For now a time is come to mock at form.
         Harry the Fifth is crowned! Up, vanity!   250
         Down, royal state! All you sage counsellors, hence,
         And to the English court assemble now
         From every region apes of idleness!
         Now, neighbour confines, purge you of your scum.
         Have you a ruffian that will swear, drink, dance,   255
         Revel the night, rob, murder, and commit
         The oldest sins the newest kind of ways?
         Be happy! He will trouble you no more.
         England shall double gild his treble guilt;
         England shall give him office, honour, might;   260
         For the fifth Harry from curbed licence plucks
         The muzzle of restraint, and the wild dog
         Shall flesh his tooth on every innocent.
         O my poor kingdom, sick with civil blows!
         When that my care could not withhold thy riots,   265
         What wilt thou do when riot is thy care?
         O, thou wilt be a wilderness again,
         Peopled with wolves, thy old inhabitants.
PRINCE [*Kneels.*]
         O pardon me, my liege. But for my tears,
         The moist impediments unto my speech,   270
         I had forestalled this dear and deep rebuke
         Ere you with grief had spoke and I had heard
         The course of it so far. There is your crown,
         And He that wears the crown immortally
         Long guard it yours! If I affect it more   275
         Than as your honour and as your renown,
         Let me no more from this obedience rise,
         Which my most inward, true and duteous spirit
         Teacheth this prostrate and exterior bending.
         God witness with me, when I here came in   280
         And found no course of breath within your majesty,
         How cold it struck my heart. If I do feign,
         O let me in my present wildness die
         And never live to show th'incredulous world

85   The noble change that I have purposed.
      Coming to look on you, thinking you dead,
      And dead almost, my liege, to think you were,
      I spake unto this crown as having sense
      And thus upbraided it: 'The care on thee depending
90   Hath fed upon the body of my father;
      Therefore thou best of gold art worse than gold:
      Other, less fine in carat, more precious,
      Preserving life in med'cine potable;
      But thou, most fine, most honoured, most renowned,
95   Hath eat thy bearer up.' Thus, my most royal liege,
      Accusing it, I put it on my head
      To try with it, as with an enemy
      That had before my face murdered my father,
      The quarrel of a true inheritor.
00   But if it did infect my blood with joy
      Or swell my thoughts to any strain of pride,
      If any rebel or vain spirit of mine
      Did with the least affection of a welcome
      Give entertainment to the might of it,
05   Let God forever keep it from my head
      And make me as the poorest vassal is
      That doth with awe and terror kneel to it.
      KING   God put in thy mind to take it hence,
      That thou mightst win the more thy father's love,
10   Pleading so wisely in excuse of it.
      Come hither, Harry; sit thou by my bed
      And hear, I think, the very latest counsel
      That ever I shall breathe. God knows, my son,
      By what bypaths and indirect, crook'd ways
15   I met this crown; and I myself know well
      How troublesome it sat upon my head.
      To thee it shall descend with better quiet,
      Better opinion, better confirmation,
      For all the soil of the achievement goes
20   With me into into the earth. It seemed in me
      But as an honour snatched with boist'rous hand,
      And I had many living to upbraid
      My gain of it by their assistances,
      Which daily grew to quarrel and to bloodshed,
25   Wounding supposed peace. All these bold fears
      Thou see'st with peril I have answered,
      For all my reign hath been but as a scene
      Acting that argument. And now my death
      Changes the mood, for what in me was purchased
30   Falls upon thee in a more fairer sort.
      So thou the garland wear'st successively;
      Yet, though thou stand'st more sure than I could do,
      Thou art not firm enough, since griefs are green,
      And all my friends, which thou must make thy friends,
35   Have but their stings and teeth newly ta'en out,
      By whose fell working I was first advanced
      And by whose power I well might lodge a fear
      To be again displaced; which to avoid,
      I cut them off, and had a purpose now
40   To lead out many to the Holy Land,
      Lest rest and lying still might make them look

      Too near unto my state. Therefore, my Harry,
      Be it thy course to busy giddy minds
      With foreign quarrels, that action hence borne out
      May waste the memory of the former days.   345
      More would I, but my lungs are wasted so
      That strength of speech is utterly denied me.
      How I came by the crown, O God forgive,
      And grant it may with thee in true peace live.
      PRINCE   You won it, wore it, kept it, gave it me;   350
      Then plain and right must my possession be,
      Which I with more than with a common pain
      'Gainst all the world will rightfully maintain.

                    Enter Prince JOHN *of Lancaster.*

      KING   Look, look! Here comes my John of Lancaster.
      JOHN   Health, peace and happiness to my royal father.   355
      KING   Thou bringst me happiness and peace, son John;
      But health, alack, with youthful wings is flown
      From this bare, withered trunk. Upon thy sight
      My worldly business makes a period.
      Where is my Lord of Warwick?
      PRINCE   My Lord of Warwick!   360

                          Enter WARWICK.

      KING   Doth any name particular belong
      Unto the lodging where I first did swoon?
      WARWICK   'Tis called Jerusalem, my noble lord.
      KING   Laud be to God, even there my life must end.
      It hath been prophesied to me many years   365
      I should not die but in Jerusalem,
      Which vainly I supposed the Holy Land.
      But bear me to that chamber: there I'll lie.
      In that Jerusalem shall Harry die.   *Exeunt.*

      5.1   *Enter* SHALLOW, FALSTAFF, BARDOLPH
                     and PAGE.

      SHALLOW   By cock and pie, sir, you shall not away
      tonight. – What, Davy, I say!
      FALSTAFF   You must excuse me, Master Robert Shallow.
      SHALLOW   I will not excuse you. You shall not be
      excused. Excuses shall not be admitted. There is no   5
      excuse shall serve. You shall not be excused. – Why,
      Davy!

                  Enter DAVY, *with papers in hand.*

      DAVY   Here, sir.
      SHALLOW   Davy, Davy, Davy, Davy, let me see, Davy,
      let me see, Davy, let me see. Yea, marry, William Cook: 10
      bid him come hither. – Sir John, you shall not be
      excused.
      DAVY   Marry, sir, thus: those precepts cannot be served.
      And again, sir, shall we sow the hade land with wheat?
      SHALLOW   With red wheat, Davy. But for William Cook   15
      – are there no young pigeons?
      DAVY   Yes, sir. Here is now the smith's note for shoeing
      and plough-irons.

SHALLOW   Let it be cast and paid. – Sir John, you shall
20   not be excused.
DAVY   Now, sir, a new link to the bucket must needs be
had. And, sir, do you mean to stop any of William's
wages about the sack he lost at Hinckley Fair?
SHALLOW   'A shall answer it. Some pigeons, Davy, a
25   couple of short-legged hens, a joint of mutton and any
pretty little tiny kickshaws, tell William Cook.
DAVY   Doth the man of war stay all night, sir?
SHALLOW   Yea, Davy, I will use him well. A friend i'th'
court is better than a penny in purse. Use his men well,
30   Davy, for they are arrant knaves and will backbite.
DAVY   No worse than they are back-bitten, sir, for they
have marvellous foul linen.
SHALLOW   Well conceited, Davy. About thy business,
Davy.
35   DAVY   I beseech you, sir, to countenance William Visor
of Woncote against Clement Perkes a'th' hill.
SHALLOW   There is many complaints, Davy, against
that Visor. That Visor is an arrant knave, on my
knowledge.
40   DAVY   I grant your worship that he is a knave, sir; but
yet God forbid, sir, but a knave should have some
countenance at his friend's request. An honest man,
sir, is able to speak for himself when a knave is not. I
have served your worship truly, sir, this eight years. An
45   I cannot once or twice in a quarter bear out a knave
against an honest man, I have little credit with your
worship. The knave is mine honest friend, sir;
therefore I beseech you let him be countenanced.
SHALLOW   Go to, I say; he shall have no wrong. Look
50   about, Davy.   *Exit Davy.*
Where are you, Sir John? Come, come; off with
your boots! – Give me your hand, Master Bardolph.
BARDOLPH   I am glad to see your worship.
SHALLOW   I thank thee with my heart, kind Master
55   Bardolph. [*to Page*] And welcome, my tall fellow!
Come, Sir John.
FALSTAFF   I'll follow you, good Master Robert Shallow.
Exit Shallow.
Bardolph, look to our horses.
Exeunt Bardolph and Page.
If I were sawed into quantities I should make four dozen
60   of such bearded hermits' staves as Master Shallow. It is
a wonderful thing to see the semblable coherence of his
men's spirits and his. They, by observing him, do bear
themselves like foolish justices; he, by conversing with
them, is turned into a justice-like servingman. Their
65   spirits are so married in conjunction with the
participation of society that they flock together in
consent like so many wild geese. If I had a suit to Master
Shallow, I would humour his men with the imputation
of being near their master; if to his men, I would curry
70   with Master Shallow that no man could better
command his servants. It is certain that either wise
bearing or ignorant carriage is caught, as men take
diseases one of another; therefore, let men take heed of

their company. I will devise matter enough out of this
Shallow to keep Prince Harry in continual laughter the   75
wearing out of six fashions, which is four terms, or two
actions; and 'a shall laugh without intervallums. O, it is
much that a lie with a slight oath and a jest with a sad
brow will do with a fellow that never had the ache in his
shoulders! O, you shall see him laugh till his face be like   80
a wet cloak ill laid up!
SHALLOW [*within*]   Sir John!
FALSTAFF   I come, Master Shallow. I come, Master
Shallow.   *Exit.*

5.2   *Enter* WARWICK *at one door, and the*
           Lord Chief JUSTICE *at another door.*

WARWICK
How now, my Lord Chief Justice, whither away?
JUSTICE   How doth the King?
WARWICK
Exceeding well. His cares are now all ended.
JUSTICE   I hope not dead.
WARWICK   He's walked the way of nature,
And to our purposes he lives no more.   5
JUSTICE
I would his majesty had called me with him.
The service that I truly did his life
Hath left me open to all injuries.
WARWICK
Indeed, I think the young King loves you not.
JUSTICE   I know he doth not, and do arm myself   10
To welcome the condition of the time,
Which cannot look more hideously upon me
Than I have drawn it in my fantasy.

Enter Prince JOHN, Thomas, Duke of CLARENCE, *and*
        Humphrey, Duke of GLOUCESTER.

WARWICK   Here come the heavy issue of dead Harry.
O, that the living Harry had the temper   15
Of he, the worst of these three gentlemen!
How many nobles then should hold their places
That must strike sail to spirits of vile sort?
JUSTICE   O God, I fear all will be overturned.
JOHN
Good morrow, cousin Warwick; [*to Justice*] good
morrow.   20
CLARENCE, GLOUCESTER
Good morrow, cousin.
JOHN   We meet like men that had forgot to speak.
WARWICK   We do remember, but our argument
Is all too heavy to admit much talk.
JOHN
Well, peace be with him that hath made us heavy.   25
JUSTICE   Peace be with us, lest we be heavier.
GLOUCESTER [*to Justice*]
O good my lord, you have lost a friend indeed,
And I dare swear you borrow not that face
Of seeming sorrow. It is sure your own.

JOHN [*to Justice*]

    Though no man be assured what grace to find,

    You stand in coldest expectation.

    I am the sorrier. Would 'twere otherwise.

CLARENCE [*to Justice*]

    Well, you must now speak Sir John Falstaff fair,

    Which swims against your stream of quality.

JUSTICE   Sweet princes, what I did I did in honour,

    Led by th'impartial conduct of my soul;

    And never shall you see that I will beg

    A ragged and forestalled remission.

    If truth and upright innocency fail me,

    I'll to the King my master that is dead

    And tell him who hath sent me after him.

Enter Prince Henry *as* KING *and Blunt.*

WARWICK   Here comes the Prince.

JUSTICE   Good morrow, and God save your majesty.

KING   This new and gorgeous garment, majesty,

    Sits not so easy on me as you think.

    Brothers, you mix your sadness with some fear.

    This is the English, not the Turkish, court:

    Not Amurath an Amurath succeeds,

    But Harry, Harry. Yet be sad, good brothers,

    For, by my faith, it very well becomes you.

    Sorrow so royally in you appears

    That I will deeply put the fashion on

    And wear it in my heart. Why then, be sad;

    But entertain no more of it, good brothers,

    Than a joint burden laid upon us all.

    For me, by heaven, I bid you be assured,

    I'll be your father and your brother too:

    Let me but bear your love, I'll bear your cares.

    Yet weep that Harry's dead, and so will I;

    But Harry lives that will convert those tears

    By number into hours of happiness.

BROTHERS   We hope no otherwise from your majesty.

KING

    You all look strangely on me, [*to Justice*] and you most.

    You are, I think, assured I love you not.

JUSTICE   I am assured, if I be measured rightly,

    Your majesty hath no just cause to hate me.

KING

    No? How might a prince of my great hopes forget

    So great indignities you laid upon me?

    What – rate, rebuke and roughly send to prison

    Th'immediate heir of England? Was this easy?

    May this be washed in Lethe and forgotten?

JUSTICE   I then did use the person of your father.

    The image of his power lay then in me;

    And in th'administration of his law,

    Whiles I was busy for the commonwealth,

    Your highness pleased to forget my place,

    The majesty and power of law and justice,

    The image of the king whom I presented,

    And struck me in my very seat of judgement,

    Whereon, as an offender to your father,

    I gave bold way to my authority

    And did commit you. If the deed were ill,

    Be you contented, wearing now the garland,

    To have a son set your decrees at naught?

    To pluck down justice from our awful bench?

    To trip the course of law and blunt the sword

    That guards the peace and safety of your person?

    Nay, more: to spurn at your most royal image

    And mock your workings in a second body?

    Question your royal thoughts, make the case yours,

    Be now the father and propose a son,

    Hear your own dignity so much profaned,

    See your most dreadful laws so loosely slighted,

    Behold yourself so by a son disdained;

    And then imagine me taking your part

    And in your power soft silencing your son.

    After this cold consideration, sentence me;

    And as you are a king, speak in your state

    What I have done that misbecame my place,

    My person, or my liege's sovereignty.

KING   You are right, Justice, and you weigh this well;

    Therefore still bear the balance and the sword.

    And I do wish your honours may increase

    Till you do live to see a son of mine

    Offend you and obey you as I did;

    So shall I live to speak my father's words:

    'Happy am I that have a man so bold

    That dares do justice on my proper son,

    And not less happy having such a son

    That would deliver up his greatness so.'

    Into the hands of justice you did commit me,

    For which I do commit into your hand

    Th'unstained sword that you have used to bear,

    With this remembrance: that you use the same

    With the like bold, just and impartial spirit

    As you have done 'gainst me. There is my hand.

    You shall be as a father to my youth;

    My voice shall sound as you do prompt mine ear,

    And I will stoop and humble my intents

    To your well-practised, wise directions.

    – And, princes all, believe me, I beseech you,

    My father is gone wild into his grave,

    For in his tomb lie my affections;

    And with his spirits sadly I survive

    To mock the expectation of the world,

    To frustrate prophecies and to raze out

    Rotten opinion, who hath writ me down

    After my seeming. The tide of blood in me

    Hath proudly flowed in vanity till now:

    Now doth it turn and ebb back to the sea,

    Where it shall mingle with the state of floods

    And flow henceforth in formal majesty.

    Now call we our high court of parliament,

    And let us choose such limbs of noble counsel

    That the great body of our state may go

    In equal rank with the best-governed nation,

    That war or peace or both at once may be

As things acquainted and familiar to us,
In which you, father, shall have foremost hand.
140   Our coronation done, we will accite,
As I before remembered, all our state;
And, God consigning to my good intents,
No prince nor peer shall have just cause to say,
'God shorten Harry's happy life one day!'   *Exeunt.*

5.3   *Enter Sir John* FALSTAFF, SHALLOW,
    SILENCE, DAVY, BARDOLPH *and* PAGE.

SHALLOW   Nay, you shall see my orchard, where, in an
arbour, we will eat a last year's pippin of mine own
graffing with a dish of caraways and so forth. Come,
cousin Silence, and then to bed.
5 FALSTAFF   'Fore God, you have here goodly dwelling,
and rich.
SHALLOW   Barren, barren, barren; beggars all, beggars
all, Sir John. Marry, good air. – Spread, Davy; spread,
Davy. [*Davy spreads a tablecloth.*] Well said, Davy.
10 FALSTAFF   This Davy serves you for good uses. He is
your serving-man and your husband.
SHALLOW   A good varlet, a good varlet, a very good
varlet, Sir John. By the mass, I have drunk too much
sack at supper! A good varlet. Now sit down, now sit
15 down. [*to Silence*] Come, cousin.
SILENCE   Ah, sirrah, quoth 'a, we shall
  [*Sings.*]   Do nothing but eat and make good cheer,
    And praise God for the merry year,
    When flesh is cheap and females dear,
20   And lusty lads roam here and there
    So merrily,
    And ever among so merrily.
FALSTAFF   There's a merry heart, good Master Silence!
I'll give you a health for that anon.
25 SHALLOW   Give Master Bardolph some wine, Davy.
DAVY   Sweet sir, sit; I'll be with you anon. – Most sweet
sir, sit. – Master Page, good Master Page, sit. – Proface!
What you want in meat we'll have in drink, but you
must bear. The heart's all.   *Exit.*
30 SHALLOW   Be merry, Master Bardolph; [*to Page*] and
my little soldier there, be merry.
SILENCE [*Sings.*]
    Be merry, be merry, my wife has all,
    For women are shrews, both short and tall.
    'Tis merry in hall when beards wags all;
35   And welcome merry Shrovetide!
    Be merry, be merry.
FALSTAFF   I did not think Master Silence had been a
man of this mettle.
SILENCE   Who, I? I have been merry twice and once ere
40 now.

       Enter DAVY.

DAVY   There's a dish of leather-coats for you.
SHALLOW   Davy!
DAVY   Your worship, I'll be with you straight. – A cup of
wine, sir?

SILENCE [*Sings.*]
    A cup of wine, that's brisk and fine,   45
    And drink unto thee, leman mine;
    And a merry heart lives long-a.
FALSTAFF   Well said, Master Silence.
SILENCE   And we shall be merry, now comes in the
sweet a'th' night.   50
FALSTAFF [*Drinks.*]   Health and long life to you, Master
Silence!
SILENCE [*Sings.*]
    Fill the cup and let it come!
    I'll pledge you a mile to th' bottom.
SHALLOW   Honest Bardolph, welcome! If thou want'st   55
anything and wilt not call, beshrew thy heart. [*to Page*]
Welcome, my little tiny thief; and welcome indeed, too.
I'll drink to Master Bardolph and to all the cabileros
about London. [*Drinks.*]
DAVY   I hope to see London once ere I die.   60
BARDOLPH   An I might see you there, Davy!
SHALLOW   By the mass, you'll crack a quart together,
ha? Will you not, Master Bardolph?
BARDOLPH   Yea, sir, in a pottle-pot.
SHALLOW   By God's liggens, I thank thee. The knave   65
will stick by thee. I can assure thee that 'a will not out,
'a; 'tis true bred!
BARDOLPH   And I'll stick by him, sir.
SHALLOW   Why, there spoke a king! Lack nothing; be
merry!   70
  [*One knocks at door.*]
  Look who's at door there, ho! Who knocks?
       Exit Davy.
FALSTAFF   Why, now you have done me right.
SILENCE [*Sings.*]
    Do me right
    And dub me knight,
    Samingo.   75
    Is't not so?
FALSTAFF   'Tis so.
SILENCE   Is't so? Why then, say an old man can do
somewhat.

       Enter DAVY.

DAVY   An 't please your worship, there's one Pistol come   80
from the court with news.
FALSTAFF   From the court? Let him come in.

       Enter PISTOL.

How now, Pistol?
PISTOL   Sir John, God save you.
FALSTAFF   What wind blew you hither, Pistol?   85
PISTOL   Not the ill wind which blows no man to good.
Sweet knight, thou art now one of the greatest men in
this realm.
SILENCE   By'r Lady, I think 'a be, but goodman Puff of
Bar'son.   90
PISTOL   Puff?
  Puff i'thy teeth, most recreant coward base!

Sir John, I am thy Pistol and thy friend,
And helter skelter have I rode to thee;
5 And tidings do I bring, and lucky joys
And golden times and happy news of price.

FALSTAFF   I pray thee now, deliver them like a man of
this world.

PISTOL   A foutre for the world and worldlings base!
00   I speak of Africa and golden joys.

FALSTAFF   O base Assyrian knight, what is thy news?
Let King Cophetua know the truth thereof.

SILENCE [*Sings.*]
And Robin Hood, Scarlet and John.

PISTOL   Shall dunghill curs confront the Helicons?
05   And shall good news be baffled?
Then, Pistol, lay thy head in Fury's lap!

SHALLOW   Honest gentleman, I know not your
breeding.

PISTOL   Why then, lament therefor.

10 SHALLOW   Give me pardon, sir. If, sir, you come with
news from the court, I take it there's but two ways:
either to utter them or conceal them. I am, sir, under
the King in some authority.

PISTOL   Under which king, besonian? Speak or die!

SHALLOW   Under King Harry.

15 PISTOL   Harry the Fourth or Fifth?

SHALLOW   Harry the Fourth.

PISTOL   A foutre for thine office!
Sir John, thy tender lambkin now is King.
Harry the Fifth's the man! I speak the truth.
When Pistol lies, do this   [*Makes the fig.*]
and fig me like
The bragging Spaniard.

20 FALSTAFF   What, is the old King dead?

PISTOL   As nail in door. The things I speak are just.

FALSTAFF   Away, Bardolph! Saddle my horse! Master
Robert Shallow, choose what office thou wilt in the
land; 'tis thine! Pistol, I will double charge thee with
25   dignities.

BARDOLPH   O joyful day! I would not take a knighthood
for my fortune!

PISTOL   What? I do bring good news.

FALSTAFF [*to Davy*]   Carry Master Silence to bed.
                              Exeunt Davy and Silence.
30   Master Shallow – my Lord Shallow – be what thou
wilt: I am Fortune's steward. Get on thy boots; we'll
ride all night. O sweet Pistol! Away, Bardolph!
                              Exit Bardolph.
Come, Pistol, utter more to me, and withal devise
something to do thyself good. Boot, boot, Master
35   Shallow!   *Exit Shallow.*
I know the young King is sick for me. Let us take any
man's horses: the laws of England are at my
commandment. Blessed are they that have been my
friends, and woe to my Lord Chief Justice!
                              Exit with Page.

40 PISTOL   Let vultures vile seize on his lungs also!
'Where is the life that late I led,' say they?

Why, here it is! Welcome these pleasant days!   *Exit.*

5.4   *Enter* Beadles *dragging in* HOSTESS
Quickly *and* DOLL Tearsheet.

HOSTESS   No, thou arrant knave, I would to God that I
might die that I might have thee hanged! Thou hast
drawn my shoulder out of joint.

BEADLE   The constables have delivered her over to me,
and she shall have whipping-cheer, I warrant her.   5
There hath been a man or two killed about her.

DOLL   Nut-hook, nut-hook, you lie! Come on. I'll tell
thee what, thou damned tripe-visaged rascal: an the
child I go with do miscarry, thou wert better thou
hadst struck thy mother, thou paper-faced villain!   10

HOSTESS   O the Lord, that Sir John were come! I would
make this a bloody day to somebody. But I pray God
the fruit of her womb miscarry.

BEADLE   If it do, you shall have a dozen of cushions
again. You have but eleven now. Come, I charge you   15
both go with me, for the man is dead that you and
Pistol beat amongst you.

DOLL   I'll tell you what, you thin man in a censer, I will
have you as soundly swinged for this – you bluebottle
rogue, you filthy famished correctioner! If you be not   20
swinged, I'll forswear half-kirtles.

BEADLE   Come, come, you she-knight-errant, come!

HOSTESS   O God, that right should thus overcome
might! Well, of sufferance comes ease.

DOLL   Come, you rogue, come; bring me to a justice.   25

HOSTESS   Ay, come, you starved bloodhound.

DOLL   Goodman death! Goodman bones!

HOSTESS   Thou atomy, thou!

DOLL   Come, you thin thing. Come, you rascal.

BEADLE   Very well.   *Exeunt.*   30

5.5   *Enter three* Strewers *of rushes.*

1 STREWER   More rushes, more rushes!

2 STREWER   The trumpets have sounded twice.

3 STREWER   'Twill be two a'clock ere they come from
the coronation. Dispatch, dispatch!   *Exeunt.*

Trumpets sound, and the KING *and his train pass over the
stage. After them enter* FALSTAFF, SHALLOW, PISTOL,
BARDOLPH *and the* Boy [PAGE].

FALSTAFF   Stand here by me, Master Shallow! I will   5
make the King do you grace. I will leer upon him as 'a
comes by, and do but mark the countenance that he
will give me.

PISTOL   God bless thy lungs, good knight!

FALSTAFF   Come here, Pistol; stand behind me. [*to*   10
Shallow] O, if I had had time to have made new liveries,
I would have bestowed the thousand pound I borrowed
of you! But 'tis no matter. This poor show doth better;
this doth infer the zeal I had to see him.

PISTOL   It doth so.   15

FALSTAFF   It shows my earnestness of affection –

PISTOL   It doth so.

FALSTAFF   My devotion –

PISTOL   It doth, it doth, it doth.

20 FALSTAFF   As it were to ride day and night and not to deliberate, not to remember, not to have patience to shift me –

SHALLOW   It is best, certain.

FALSTAFF   – but to stand stained with travel and sweat-
25 ing with desire to see him, thinking of nothing else, putting all affairs else in oblivion, as if there were nothing else to be done but to see him.

PISTOL   'Tis *semper idem*, for *absque hoc nihil est*; 'tis in every part.

30 SHALLOW   'Tis so indeed.

PISTOL   My knight, I will inflame thy noble liver and make thee rage! Thy Doll and Helen of thy noble thoughts is in base durance and contagious prison, haled thither by most mechanical and dirty hand.
35 Rouse up Revenge from ebon den with fell Alecto's snake, for Doll is in. Pistol speaks nought but truth.

FALSTAFF   I will deliver her.

[*Shouts within. Trumpets sound.*]

PISTOL

There roared the sea, and trumpet clangour sounds.

Enter the KING *and his train, his* Brothers, *the* Lord Chief
JUSTICE *and others.*

FALSTAFF

God save thy grace, King Hal, my royal Hal!

40 PISTOL   The heavens thee guard and keep, most royal imp of fame!

FALSTAFF   God save thee, my sweet boy!

KING

My Lord Chief Justice, speak to that vain man.

JUSTICE [*to Falstaff*]

Have you your wits? Know you what 'tis you speak?

FALSTAFF

45 My King, my Jove, I speak to thee, my heart!

KING   I know thee not, old man. Fall to thy prayers.
How ill white hairs becomes a fool and jester!
I have long dreamt of such a kind of man,
So surfeit-swelled, so old and so profane;
50 But being awaked, I do despise my dream.
Make less thy body hence, and more thy grace.
Leave gormandizing: know the grave doth gape
For thee thrice wider than for other men.
Reply not to me with a fool-born jest.
55 Presume not that I am the thing I was,
For God doth know, so shall the world perceive,
That I have turned away my former self;
So will I those that kept me company.
When thou dost hear I am as I have been,
60 Approach me, and thou shalt be as thou wast,
The tutor and the feeder of my riots.
Till then, I banish thee on pain of death,

As I have done the rest of my misleaders,
Not to come near our person by ten mile.

[*also addressing Falstaff's companions*]

For competence of life I will allow you, 65
That lack of means enforce you not to evils;
And as we hear you do reform yourselves,
We will, according to your strengths and qualities,
Give you advancement. [*to Justice*] Be it your charge,
my lord,
To see performed the tenor of my word. 70
Set on.   *Exit King with his train.*

FALSTAFF   Master Shallow, I owe you a thousand pound.

SHALLOW   Yea, marry, Sir John, which I beseech you to let me have home with me. 75

FALSTAFF   That can hardly be, Master Shallow. Do not you grieve at this: I shall be sent for in private to him. Look you, he must seem thus to the world. Fear not your advancements. I will be the man yet that shall make you great. 80

SHALLOW   I cannot perceive how, unless you give me your doublet and stuff me out with straw. I beseech you, good Sir John, let me have five hundred of my thousand.

FALSTAFF   Sir, I will be as good as my word. This that 85
you heard was but a colour.

SHALLOW   A colour that I fear you will die in, Sir John.

FALSTAFF   Fear no colours. Go with me to dinner. Come, Lieutenant Pistol; come Bardolph. I shall be sent for soon at night. 90

Enter the Lord Chief JUSTICE *and* Prince JOHN
with Officers.

JUSTICE [*to Officers*]

Go, carry Sir John Falstaff to the Fleet.
Take all his company along with him.

FALSTAFF   My lord, my lord!

JUSTICE   I cannot now speak. I will hear you soon.
Take them away. 95

PISTOL   *Si fortuna me tormenta, spero contenta.*

*Exeunt Officers with Falstaff, Pistol,
Shallow, Bardolph and Page.*

JOHN   I like this fair proceeding of the King's.
He hath intent his wonted followers
Shall all be very well provided for,
But all are banished till their conversations
Appear more wise and modest to the world. 100

JUSTICE   And so they are.

JOHN   The King hath called his parliament, my lord.

JUSTICE   He hath.

JOHN   I will lay odds that, ere this year expire,
We bear our civil swords and native fire 105
As far as France. I heard a bird so sing,
Whose music, to my thinking, pleased the King.
Come, will you hence?   *Exeunt.*

EPILOGUE 1

Enter the Speaker of the EPILOGUE.

First my fear, then my curtsy, last my speech.
My fear is your displeasure; my curtsy, my duty; and
my speech, to beg your pardons. If you look for a
good speech now, you undo me; for what I have to
say is of mine own making, and what indeed I should
say will, I doubt, prove mine own marring. But to the
purpose, and so to the venture. Be it known to you, as
it is very well, I was lately here in the end of a
displeasing play to pray your patience for it and to
promise you a better. I meant indeed to pay you with
this, which, if like an ill venture it come unluckily
home, I break, and you, my gentle creditors, lose. Here
I promised you I would be, and here I commit my body
to your mercies. Bate me some, and I will pay you some
and, as most debtors do, promise you infinitely. And so
I kneel down before you [*Kneels.*] – but, indeed, to
pray for the Queen.

EPILOGUE 2

If my tongue cannot entreat you to acquit me, will you
command me to use my legs? And yet that were but
light payment, to dance out of your debt. But a good
conscience will make any possible satisfaction, and so
would I. All the gentlewomen here have forgiven me.
If the gentlemen will not, then the gentlemen do not
agree with the gentlewomen, which was never seen in
such an assembly.

One word more, I beseech you. If you be not too
much cloyed with fat meat, our humble author will
continue the story with Sir John in it and make you
merry with fair Katherine of France, where, for
anything I know, Falstaff shall die of a sweat unless
already 'a be killed with your hard opinions; for
Oldcastle died martyr, and this is not the man. My
tongue is weary. When my legs are too, I will bid you
good night.   *Dances a jig, then exits.*

King Henry V

King Henry V was first published in 1600 as *The Cronicle History of Henry the fift*. The printed play is about half the length of the one that would appear as the fifth of the histories in the Folio in 1623, lacking the choruses and omitting many passages and three entire scenes (1.1, 3.1 and 4.2). Possibly it is a 'reported' text, compiled by some process of recollection, probably by actors in a production; perhaps one based on a script abridged for performance on tour. The Folio text derives not from this early Quarto but from a manuscript, just possibly one in Shakespeare's own hand. Thus it serves as the basis of all modern editions, though the Quarto may well reflect an early staging of the play.

Apparently written about 1599, *King Henry V* could have been the first play performed at the Globe. The Chorus's apology for the limited resources of the 'wooden O' in which the action must be performed is perhaps an ironic reference to the fine new playhouse that had opened that year. The play contains Shakespeare's only un-questionable reference to a current event, which allows us to date it with some precision. Speaking of King Henry's triumphant re-entry into London after Agincourt, the Chorus compares the excitement that greets Henry to the enthusiastic response that would occur 'Were now the General of our gracious Empress, / As in good time he may, from Ireland coming, / Bringing rebellion broached on his sword' (5.0.30–2). These lines probably refer to the Earl of Essex, who had been sent by Elizabeth to Ireland in late March of 1599 to put down the rebellion led by Hugh O'Neill. Essex, however, failed in his charge and returned to London in late September. He was put under house arrest for leaving his command and was tried and sentenced in June of 1600. If the Chorus's lines are indeed a reference to Essex, the play must have been acted between March and September of 1599, between his optimistic departure and the ignominy of his return.

Essex's adventure could not have provided the impetus for the play itself, which is the foreseen conclusion of Hal's *Bildungsspiel* in the two parts of *King Henry IV*, though Henry V is the charismatic national hero that Essex aspired to be. Shakespeare's play can indeed be seen as an examination of the claims of heroic achievement, imparting a mythic shape and significance to the history of Henry's reign by organizing the historical material he found in Raphael Holinshed's *Chronicles* (1587) along the lines mapped out earlier by Edward Hall in his chronicle with the heading 'The Victorious Reign of King Henry V'. Henry leads a band of brave and loyal soldiers against a much larger force of arrogant Frenchmen, and the astounding victory at Agincourt confirms England's military and moral superiority. If this does not exactly conform to the facts of history, it does conform to the poetic logic of giant killing.

But if the play allows us to see and enjoy the great military and political achievements of Henry, it enables us also to see their costs. Shakespeare allows alternative angles of vision to the heroic. While the Chorus speaks the language of heroic idealization, the comic plot that parallels and comments on the historical action shows us a world of baser motive. The very structure of the play depends upon such ironic contrasts; the promises of the Chorus introducing each act are inevitably frustrated by the action that follows, as when at the beginning we are told that we shall see the confrontation of 'two mighty monarchies' (1.0.20) but see instead the political manoeuvrings of worldly churchmen urging the French war to avoid a confiscatory bill.

The lustre of the celebrated war will certainly be tarnished if it is seen to be motivated not by a principled desire to regain lost rights but by the self-interest of a Church desperate to retain its wealth. Indeed, it is precisely by allowing an audience to see the uncertain genesis of the famous victories that Shakespeare begins his exploration of the necessarily imperfect man who must play the King. Performances on stage and screen have not always wished to see this qualification of Henry's heroic achievements; Laurence Olivier's film version, completed during World War II, understandably ignored all the play's darker tones. But Shakespeare's play, though not cynical about heroic action, is always aware of the matrix of human fallibility in which it is grounded. 'The King is a good king', as Nym says (2.1.123), 'but it must be as it may'.

The Arden text is based on the 1623 First Folio.

CHORUS

KING Henry the Fifth

Duke of CLARENCE
Duke of BEDFORD } *his brothers*
Duke of GLOUCESTER

Duke of EXETER   *his uncle*

Duke of YORK

Earl of HUNTINGDON

Earl of SALISBURY

Earl of WARWICK

Earl of WESTMORLAND

Richard, Earl of CAMBRIDGE
Henry, Lord SCROOP of Masham } *conspirators against the King*
Sir Thomas GREY

Archbishop of CANTERBURY

Bishop of ELY

Sir Thomas ERPINGHAM
Captain FLUELLEN
Captain GOWER } *officers in the King's army*
Captain JAMY
Captain MACMORRIS

John BATES
Alexander COURT } *soldiers in the King's army*
Michael WILLIAMS

An English Herald

BARDOLPH
NYM } *associates of Sir John Falstaff*
PISTOL

A BOY   *Falstaff's page*

Nell, HOSTESS   *of an Eastcheap tavern; formerly Mistress Quickly,*
now married to Pistol

Charles the Sixth, the FRENCH KING

QUEEN ISABEL   *the French Queen*

Louis the DAUPHIN   *their son*

Princess KATHERINE   *their daughter*

ALICE   *a lady attending on Princess Katherine*

Duke of BERRY

Duke of BOURBON

Duke of BRITAIN

Duke of BURGUNDY

Duke of ORLEANS

Charles Delabreth, the CONSTABLE   *of France*

Earl of GRANDPRÉ

Lord RAMBURES

GOVERNOR   *of Harfleur*

MONTJOY   *the French herald*

Two French Ambassadors to the King of England
Monsieur Le Fer, a FRENCH SOLDIER
A French Messenger

Attendants; Lords; Soldiers; Citizens of Harfleur

PROLOGUE

Enter CHORUS.

CHORUS O for a muse of fire, that would ascend
    The brightest heaven of invention,
    A kingdom for a stage, princes to act,
    And monarchs to behold the swelling scene!
    Then should the warlike Harry, like himself,   5
    Assume the port of Mars, and at his heels,
    Leashed in like hounds, should famine, sword and fire
    Crouch for employment. But pardon, gentles all,
    The flat unraisèd spirits that hath dared
    On this unworthy scaffold to bring forth   10
    So great an object. Can this cockpit hold
    The vasty fields of France? Or may we cram
    Within this wooden O the very casques
    That did affright the air at Agincourt?
    O pardon, since a crooked figure may   15
    Attest in little place a million,
    And let us, ciphers to this great account,
    On your imaginary forces work.
    Suppose within the girdle of these walls
    Are now confined two mighty monarchies,   20
    Whose high uprearèd and abutting fronts
    The perilous narrow ocean parts asunder.
    Piece out our imperfections with your thoughts.
    Into a thousand parts divide one man
    And make imaginary puissance.   25
    Think, when we talk of horses, that you see them
    Printing their proud hoofs i'th' receiving earth.
    For 'tis your thoughts that now must deck our kings,
    Carry them here and there, jumping o'er times,
    Turning th'accomplishment of many years   30
    Into an hour-glass: for the which supply,
    Admit me Chorus to this history,
    Who prologue-like your humble patience pray,
    Gently to hear, kindly to judge our play.   *Exit.*

1.1   *Enter the* Archbishop of CANTERBURY
        and the Bishop of ELY.

CANTERBURY
    My lord, I'll tell you, that self bill is urged
    Which in th'eleventh year of the last king's reign
    Was like and had indeed against us passed
    But that the scambling and unquiet time
    Did push it out of farther question.   5
ELY   But how, my lord, shall we resist it now?
CANTERBURY
    It must be thought on. If it pass against us
    We lose the better half of our possession:
    For all the temporal lands which men devout
    By testament have given to the Church   10
    Would they strip from us, being valued thus:
    As much as would maintain, to the King's honour,
    Full fifteen earls and fifteen hundred knights,
    Six thousand and two hundred good esquires,

    And to relief of lazars and weak age,   15
    Of indigent faint souls past corporal toil,
    A hundred almshouses right well supplied,
    And to the coffers of the King beside,
    A thousand pounds by th' year. Thus runs the bill.
ELY   This would drink deep.
CANTERBURY   'Twould drink the cup and all.   20
ELY   But what prevention?
CANTERBURY
    The King is full of grace and fair regard.
ELY   And a true lover of the holy Church.
CANTERBURY
    The courses of his youth promised it not.
    The breath no sooner left his father's body   25
    But that his wildness, mortified in him,
    Seemed to die too; yea, at that very moment,
    Consideration like an angel came
    And whipped th'offending Adam out of him,
    Leaving his body as a paradise   30
    T'envelop and contain celestial spirits.
    Never was such a sudden scholar made,
    Never came reformation in a flood
    With such a heady currence scouring faults,
    Nor never Hydra-headed wilfulness   35
    So soon did lose his seat, and all at once,
    As in this king.
ELY   We are blessed in the change.
CANTERBURY   Hear him but reason in divinity
    And, all-admiring, with an inward wish
    You would desire the King were made a prelate.   40
    Hear him debate of commonwealth affairs,
    You would say it hath been all in all his study.
    List his discourse of war, and you shall hear
    A fearful battle rendered you in music.
    Turn him to any cause of policy,   45
    The Gordian knot of it he will unloose,
    Familiar as his garter, that when he speaks,
    The air, a chartered libertine, is still,
    And the mute wonder lurketh in men's ears
    To steal his sweet and honeyed sentences.   50
    So that the art and practic part of life
    Must be the mistress to this theoric:
    Which is a wonder how his grace should glean it,
    Since his addiction was to courses vain,
    His companies unlettered, rude, and shallow,   55
    His hours filled up with riots, banquets, sports,
    And never noted in him any study,
    Any retirement, any sequestration
    From open haunts and popularity.
ELY   The strawberry grows underneath the nettle,   60
    And wholesome berries thrive and ripen best
    Neighboured by fruit of baser quality.
    And so the Prince obscured his contemplation
    Under the veil of wildness, which, no doubt,
    Grew like the summer grass, fastest by night,   65
    Unseen, yet crescive in his faculty.
CANTERBURY   It must be so, for miracles are ceased,

And therefore we must needs admit the means
How things are perfected.

ELY   But my good lord,
70   How now for mitigation of this bill
Urged by the Commons? Doth his majesty
Incline to it, or no?

CANTERBURY   He seems indifferent,
Or rather swaying more upon our part
Than cherishing th'exhibitors against us.
75   For I have made an offer to his majesty,
Upon our spiritual convocation,
And in regard of causes now in hand
Which I have opened to his grace at large,
As touching France, to give a greater sum
80   Than ever at one time the clergy yet
Did to his predecessors part withal.

ELY   How did this offer seem received, my lord?

CANTERBURY   With good acceptance of his majesty,
Save that there was not time enough to hear,
85   As I perceived his grace would fain have done,
The severals and unhidden passages
Of his true titles to some certain dukedoms,
And generally to the crown and seat of France,
Derived from Edward, his great-grandfather.
90 ELY   What was th'impediment that broke this off?

CANTERBURY
The French ambassador upon that instant
Craved audience, and the hour I think is come
To give him hearing. Is it four o'clock?

ELY   It is.
95 CANTERBURY   Then go we in, to know his embassy,
Which I could with a ready guess declare
Before the Frenchman speak a word of it.

ELY   I'll wait upon you, and I long to hear it.   *Exeunt.*

1.2   *Enter the* KING, GLOUCESTER, BEDFORD,
        CLARENCE, WARWICK, WESTMORLAND
        and EXETER *and Attendants.*

KING   Where is my gracious lord of Canterbury?

EXETER   Not here in presence.

KING   Send for him, good uncle.
                        Exit an Attendant.

WESTMORLAND
Shall we call in th'ambassador, my liege?

KING   Not yet, my cousin: we would be resolved,
5   Before we hear him, of some things of weight
That task our thoughts concerning us and France.

      Enter the Archbishop of CANTERBURY
          and the Bishop of ELY.

CANTERBURY
God and his angels guard your sacred throne
And make you long become it!

KING   Sure, we thank you.
My learned lord, we pray you to proceed
10   And justly and religiously unfold

Why the law Salic that they have in France
Or should or should not bar us in our claim.
And God forbid, my dear and faithful lord,
That you should fashion, wrest or bow your reading
Or nicely charge your understanding soul   15
With opening titles miscreate, whose right
Suits not in native colours with the truth.
For God doth know how many now in health
Shall drop their blood in approbation
Of what your reverence shall incite us to.   20
Therefore take heed how you impawn our person,
How you awake our sleeping sword of war:
We charge you in the name of God take heed.
For never two such kingdoms did contend
Without much fall of blood, whose guiltless drops   25
Are every one a woe, a sore complaint
'Gainst him whose wrongs gives edge unto the swords
That makes such waste in brief mortality.
Under this conjuration speak, my lord,
For we will hear, note, and believe in heart   30
That what you speak is in your conscience washed
As pure as sin with baptism.

CANTERBURY
Then hear me, gracious sovereign, and you peers
That owe your selves, your lives and services
To this imperial throne. There is no bar   35
To make against your highness' claim to France
But this which they produce from Pharamond:
In terram Salicam mulieres ne succedant,
'No woman shall succeed in Salic land':
Which Salic land the French unjustly gloze   40
To be the realm of France, and Pharamond
The founder of this law and female bar.
Yet their own authors faithfully affirm
That the land Salic is in Germany,
Between the floods of Sala and of Elbe,   45
Where Charles the Great, having subdued the
     Saxons,
There left behind and settled certain French,
Who, holding in disdain the German women
For some dishonest manners of their life,
Established then this law, to wit, no female   50
Should be inheritrix in Salic land;
Which Salic (as I said, 'twixt Elbe and Sala)
Is at this day in Germany called Meissen.
Then doth it well appear the Salic law
Was not devised for the realm of France.   55
Nor did the French possess the Salic land
Until four hundred one-and-twenty years
After defunction of King Pharamond,
Idly supposed the founder of this law,
Who died within the year of our redemption   60
Four hundred twenty-six, and Charles the Great
Subdued the Saxons and did seat the French
Beyond the river Sala in the year
Eight hundred five. Besides, their writers say,
King Pepin, which deposed Childeric,   65

Did as heir general, being descended
Of Blithild, which was daughter to King Clothair,
Make claim and title to the crown of France.
Hugh Capet also, who usurped the crown
70 Of Charles the Duke of Lorraine, sole heir male
Of the true line and stock of Charles the Great,
To fine his title with some shows of truth,
Though in pure truth it was corrupt and naught,
Conveyed himself as heir to th' Lady Lingard,
75 Daughter to Charlemagne, who was the son
To Louis the Emperor, and Louis the son
Of Charles the Great. Also King Louis the Ninth,
Who was sole heir to the usurper Capet,
Could not keep quiet in his conscience,
80 Wearing the crown of France, till satisfied
That fair Queen Isabel, his grandmother,
Was lineal of the Lady Ermengard,
Daughter to Charles the foresaid Duke of Lorraine,
By the which marriage the line of Charles the Great
85 Was reunited to the crown of France.
So that, as clear as is the summer's sun,
King Pepin's title, and Hugh Capet's claim,
King Louis his satisfaction, all appear
To hold in right and title of the female.
90 So do the kings of France unto this day,
Howbeit they would hold up this Salic law
To bar your highness claiming from the female,
And rather choose to hide them in a net
Than amply to embare their crooked titles
95 Usurped from you and your progenitors.
KING
May I with right and conscience make this claim?
CANTERBURY   The sin upon my head, dread sovereign:
For in the Book of Numbers is it writ,
'When the man dies, let the inheritance
100 Descend unto the daughter.' Gracious lord,
Stand for your own, unwind your bloody flag,
Look back into your mighty ancestors.
Go, my dread lord, to your great-grandsire's tomb,
From whom you claim; invoke his warlike spirit,
105 And your great-uncle's, Edward the Black Prince,
Who on the French ground played a tragedy,
Making defeat on the full power of France,
Whiles his most mighty father on a hill
Stood smiling to behold his lion's whelp
110 Forage in blood of French nobility.
O noble English, that could entertain
With half their forces the full pride of France
And let another half stand laughing by,
All out of work and cold for action!
115 ELY   Awake remembrance of these valiant dead,
And with your puissant arm renew their feats.
You are their heir, you sit upon their throne,
The blood and courage that renowned them
Runs in your veins, and my thrice-puissant liege
120 Is in the very May-morn of his youth,
Ripe for exploits and mighty enterprises.

EXETER   Your brother kings and monarchs of the earth
Do all expect that you should rouse yourself
As did the former lions of your blood.
WESTMORLAND
They know your grace hath cause, and means, and
    might;   125
So doth your highness. Never king of England
Had nobles richer and more loyal subjects,
Whose hearts have left their bodies here in England
And lie pavilioned in the fields of France.
CANTERBURY   O let their bodies follow, my dear liege,   130
With blood and sword and fire to win your right;
In aid whereof we of the spirituality
Will raise your highness such a mighty sum
As never did the clergy at one time
Bring in to any of your ancestors.   135
KING   We must not only arm t'invade the French,
But lay down our proportions to defend
Against the Scot, who will make road upon us
With all advantages.
CANTERBURY
They of those marches, gracious sovereign,   140
Shall be a wall sufficient to defend
Our inland from the pilfering borderers.
KING   We do not mean the coursing snatchers only,
But fear the main intendment of the Scot,
Who hath been still a giddy neighbour to us.   145
For you shall read that my great-grandfather
Never went with his forces into France
But that the Scot on his unfurnished kingdom
Came pouring like the tide into a breach,
With ample and brim fullness of his force,   150
Galling the gleaned land with hot assays,
Girding with grievous siege castles and towns,
That England, being empty of defence,
Hath shook and trembled at th'ill neighbourhood.
CANTERBURY
She hath been then more feared than harmed, my
    liege.   155
For hear her but exampled by herself:
When all her chivalry hath been in France
And she a mourning widow of her nobles,
She hath herself not only well defended
But taken and impounded as a stray   160
The King of Scots, whom she did send to France,
To fill King Edward's fame with prisoner kings
And make her chronicle as rich with praise
As is the ooze and bottom of the sea
With sunken wrack and sumless treasuries.   165
WESTMORLAND
But there's a saying very old and true,
        If that you will France win,
        Then with Scotland first begin.
For once the eagle England being in prey,
To her unguarded nest the weasel Scot   170
Comes sneaking and so sucks her princely eggs,
Playing the mouse in absence of the cat,

To 'tame and havoc more than she can eat.
EXETER
  It follows then the cat must stay at home;
175 Yet that is but a crushed necessity,
  Since we have locks to safeguard necessaries
  And pretty traps to catch the petty thieves.
  While that the armed hand doth fight abroad
  Th'advised head defends itself at home.
180 For government, though high and low and lower
  Put into parts, doth keep in one concent,
  Congreeing in a full and natural close
  Like music.
CANTERBURY   True. Therefore doth heaven divide
  The state of man in diverse functions,
185 Setting endeavour in continual motion,
  To which is fixed, as an aim or butt,
  Obedience. For so work the honey-bees,
  Creatures that by a rule in nature teach
  The act of order to a peopled kingdom.
190 They have a king and officers of sorts,
  Where some like magistrates correct at home,
  Others like merchants venture trade abroad,
  Others like soldiers, armed in their stings,
  Make boot upon the summer's velvet buds,
195 Which pillage they with merry march bring home
  To the tent-royal of their emperor,
  Who busied in his majesty surveys
  The singing masons building roofs of gold,
  The civil citizens kneading up the honey,
200 The poor mechanic porters crowding in
  Their heavy burdens at his narrow gate,
  The sad-eyed justice, with his surly hum,
  Delivering o'er to executors pale
  The lazy yawning drone. I this infer,
205 That many things having full reference
  To one consent may work contrariously,
  As many arrows loosed several ways
  Come to one mark,
  As many several ways meet in one town,
210 As many fresh streams meet in one salt sea,
  As many lines close in the dial's centre.
  So may a thousand actions once afoot
  End in one purpose and be all well borne
  Without defeat. Therefore to France, my liege.
215 Divide your happy England into four,
  Whereof take you one quarter into France
  And you withal shall make all Gallia shake.
  If we with thrice such powers left at home
  Cannot defend our own doors from the dog,
220 Let us be worried and our nation lose
  The name of hardiness and policy.
KING
  Call in the messengers sent from the Dauphin.
              Exeunt some Attendants.
  Now are we well resolved; and by God's help
  And yours, the noble sinews of our power,
225 France being ours, we'll bend it to our awe

Or break it all to pieces. Or there we'll sit,
Ruling in large and ample empery
O'er France and all her almost kingly dukedoms,
Or lay these bones in an unworthy urn,
Tombless, with no remembrance over them.   230
Either our history shall with full mouth
Speak freely of our acts, or else our grave
Like Turkish mute shall have a tongueless mouth,
Not worshipped with a waxen epitaph.

        Enter Ambassadors of France
        with Attendants carrying a tun.

Now are we well prepared to know the pleasure   235
Of our fair cousin Dauphin; for we hear
Your greeting is from him, not from the King.
AMBASSADOR
May't please your majesty to give us leave
Freely to render what we have in charge,
Or shall we sparingly show you far off   240
The Dauphin's meaning and our embassy?
KING   We are no tyrant but a Christian king,
Unto whose grace our passion is as subject
As are our wretches fettered in our prisons:
Therefore with frank and with uncurbed plainness   245
Tell us the Dauphin's mind.
AMBASSADOR   Thus then, in few.
Your highness lately sending into France
Did claim some certain dukedoms in the right
Of your great predecessor King Edward the Third.
In answer of which claim the Prince our master   250
Says that you savour too much of your youth
And bids you be advised. There's naught in France
That can be with a nimble galliard won;
You cannot revel into dukedoms there.
He therefore sends you, meeter for your spirit,   255
This tun of treasure, and in lieu of this
Desires you let the dukedoms that you claim
Hear no more of you. This the Dauphin speaks.
KING
What treasure, uncle?
EXETER   Tennis-balls, my liege.
KING   We are glad the Dauphin is so pleasant with us.   260
His present and your pains we thank you for.
When we have matched our rackets to these balls
We will in France, by God's grace, play a set
Shall strike his father's crown into the hazard.
Tell him he hath made a match with such a wrangler   265
That all the courts of France shall be disturbed
With chases. And we understand him well,
How he comes o'er us with our wilder days,
Not measuring what use we made of them.
We never valued this poor seat of England,   270
And therefore living hence did give ourself
To barbarous licence, as 'tis ever common
That men are merriest when they are from home.
But tell the Dauphin I will keep my state,
Be like a king and show my sail of greatness,   275

When I do rouse me in my throne of France.
For that have I laid by my majesty
And plodded like a man for working-days,
But I will rise there with so full a glory
280 That I will dazzle all the eyes of France,
Yea, strike the Dauphin blind to look on us.
And tell the pleasant Prince this mock of his
Hath turned his balls to gun-stones, and his soul
Shall stand sore charged for the wasteful vengeance
285 That shall fly with them; for many a thousand widows
Shall this his mock mock out of their dear husbands,
Mock mothers from their sons, mock castles down,
And some are yet ungotten and unborn
That shall have cause to curse the Dauphin's scorn.
290 But this lies all within the will of God,
To whom I do appeal, and in whose name
Tell you the Dauphin I am coming on
To venge me as I may, and to put forth
My rightful hand in a well-hallowed cause.
295 So get you hence in peace. And tell the Dauphin
His jest will savour but of shallow wit
When thousands weep more than did laugh at it. –
Convey them with safe conduct. – Fare you well.
Exeunt Ambassadors and Attendants.
EXETER   This was a merry message.
300 KING   We hope to make the sender blush at it.
Therefore, my lords, omit no happy hour
That may give furtherance to our expedition,
For we have now no thought in us but France,
Save those to God that run before our business.
305 Therefore let our proportions for these wars
Be soon collected and all things thought upon
That may with reasonable swiftness add
More feathers to our wings, for, God before,
We'll chide this Dauphin at his father's door.
310 Therefore let every man now task his thought,
That this fair action may on foot be brought.
Flourish. Exeunt.

2.0   *Enter* CHORUS.

CHORUS   Now all the youth of England are on fire,
And silken dalliance in the wardrobe lies.
Now thrive the armourers, and honour's thought
Reigns solely in the breast of every man.
5 They sell the pasture now to buy the horse,
Following the mirror of all Christian kings
With winged heels, as English Mercuries.
For now sits expectation in the air
And hides a sword from hilts unto the point
10 With crowns imperial, crowns and coronets,
Promised to Harry and his followers.
The French, advised by good intelligence
Of this most dreadful preparation,
Shake in their fear, and with pale policy
15 Seek to divert the English purposes.

O England, model to thy inward greatness,
Like little body with a mighty heart,
What mightst thou do, that honour would thee do,
Were all thy children kind and natural!
20 But see, thy fault France hath in thee found out,
A nest of hollow bosoms, which he fills
With treacherous crowns; and three corrupted men,
One, Richard Earl of Cambridge, and the second,
Henry Lord Scroop of Masham, and the third,
25 Sir Thomas Grey, knight, of Northumberland,
Have, for the gilt of France, – O guilt indeed! –
Confirmed conspiracy with fearful France,
And by their hands this grace of kings must die,
If hell and treason hold their promises,
30 Ere he take ship for France, and in Southampton.
Linger your patience on and well digest
Th'abuse of distance, and we'll force our play.
The sum is paid, the traitors are agreed,
The King is set from London, and the scene
35 Is now transported, gentles, to Southampton.
There is the playhouse now, there must you sit,
And thence to France shall we convey you safe
And bring you back, charming the narrow seas
To give you gentle pass; for if we may,
40 We'll not offend one stomach with our play.
But till the King come forth and not till then
Unto Southampton do we shift our scene.   *Exit.*

2.1   *Enter* Corporal NYM *and* Lieutenant
BARDOLPH, *meeting.*

BARDOLPH   Well met, Corporal Nym.
NYM   Good morrow, Lieutenant Bardolph.
BARDOLPH   What, are Ancient Pistol and you friends
yet?
5 NYM   For my part I care not. I say little; but when time
shall serve there shall be smiles; but that shall be as it
may. I dare not fight, but I will wink and hold out mine
iron. It is a simple one, but what though? It will toast
cheese, and it will endure cold as another man's sword
10 will, and there's an end.
BARDOLPH   I will bestow a breakfast to make you
friends, and we'll be all three sworn brothers to France.
Let't be so, good Corporal Nym.
NYM   Faith, I will live so long as I may, that's the
15 certain of it, and when I cannot live any longer, I
will do as I may. That is my rest, that is the rendezvous
of it.
BARDOLPH   It is certain, Corporal, that he is married to
Nell Quickly, and certainly she did you wrong, for you
20 were troth-plight to her.
NYM   I cannot tell. Things must be as they may. Men
may sleep, and they may have their throats about them
at that time, and some say knives have edges. It must be
as it may. Though patience be a tired mare, yet she will
25 plod. There must be conclusions. Well, I cannot tell.

Enter PISTOL *and* HOSTESS.

BARDOLPH   Here comes Ancient Pistol and his wife.
Good Corporal, be patient here.

NYM   How now, mine host Pistol?

PISTOL   Base tyke, call'st thou me host?
30 Now by this hand I swear I scorn the term;
Nor shall my Nell keep lodgers.

HOSTESS   No, by my troth, not long. For we cannot
lodge and board a dozen or fourteen gentlewomen that
live honestly by the prick of their needles but it will be
35 thought we keep a bawdy-house straight.
[*Nym draws his sword.*]
O well-a-day, Lady, if he be not drawn! Now we shall
see wilful adultery and murder committed.
[*Pistol draws his sword.*]

BARDOLPH   Good Lieutenant, good Corporal, offer
nothing here.

40 NYM   Pish!

PISTOL
Pish for thee, Iceland dog, thou prick-eared cur of
Iceland!

HOSTESS   Good Corporal Nym, show thy valour and
put up your sword. [*Nym and Pistol sheathe their
swords.*]

NYM   [*to Pistol*]   Will you shog off? I would have you
45 solus.

PISTOL   *Solus*, egregious dog? O viper vile!
The *solus* in thy most marvailous face,
The *solus* in thy teeth, and in thy throat,
And in thy hateful lungs, yea, in thy maw, perdy,
50 And, which is worse, within thy nasty mouth!
I do retort the *solus* in thy bowels,
For I can take, and Pistol's cock is up,
And flashing fire will follow.

NYM   I am not Barbason, you cannot conjure me. I have
55 an humour to knock you indifferently well. If you grow
foul with me, Pistol, I will scour you with my rapier, as
I may, in fair terms. If you would walk off, I would
prick your guts a little, in good terms, as I may, and
that's the humour of it.

60 PISTOL   O braggart vile and damned furious wight,
The grave doth gape, and doting death is near;
Therefore exhale.   [*Pistol and Nym draw their swords.*]

BARDOLPH [*Draws his sword.*]   Hear me, hear me what I
say. He that strikes the first stroke, I'll run him up to
65 the hilts, as I am a soldier.

PISTOL   An oath of mickle might, and fury shall abate.
[*All sheathe their swords.*]
Give me thy fist, thy fore-foot to me give.
Thy spirits are most tall.

NYM   I will cut thy throat one time or other, in fair
70 terms, that is the humour of it.

PISTOL   'Couple a gorge'!
That is the word. I thee defy again.
O hound of Crete, think'st thou my spouse to get?
No, to the spital go,

And from the powdering-tub of infamy   75
Fetch forth the lazar kite of Cressid's kind,
Doll Tearsheet she by name, and her espouse.
I have and I will hold the quondam Quickly
For the only she; and *pauca*, there's enough.
Go to.   80

Enter the BOY.

BOY   Mine host Pistol, you must come to my master,
and you, hostess. He is very sick and would to bed.
Good Bardolph, put thy face between his sheets and
do the office of a warming-pan. Faith, he's very ill.

BARDOLPH   Away, you rogue!   85

HOSTESS   By my troth, he'll yield the crow a pudding
one of these days. The King has killed his heart. Good
husband, come home presently.
Exeunt Hostess and Boy.

BARDOLPH   Come, shall I make you two friends? We
must to France together. Why the devil should we keep 90
knives to cut one another's throats?

PISTOL
Let floods o'erswell and fiends for food howl on!

NYM   You'll pay me the eight shillings I won of you at
betting?

PISTOL   Base is the slave that pays.   95

NYM   That now I will have; that's the humour of it.

PISTOL   As manhood shall compound: push home!
[*Pistol and Nym draw their swords.*]

BARDOLPH [*Draws his sword.*]   By this sword, he that
makes the first thrust, I'll kill him. By this sword, I will.

PISTOL
Sword is an oath, and oaths must have their course.   100
[*He sheathes his sword.*]

BARDOLPH   Corporal Nym, an thou wilt be friends, be
friends. An thou wilt not, why then, be enemies with
me too. Prithee, put up.

NYM   I shall have my eight shillings?

PISTOL   A noble shalt thou have, and present pay,   105
And liquor likewise will I give to thee,
And friendship shall combine and brotherhood.
I'll live by Nym and Nym shall live by me.
Is not this just? For I shall sutler be
Unto the camp, and profits will accrue.   110
Give me thy hand.

NYM   I shall have my noble?

PISTOL   In cash, most justly paid.

NYM   Well, then, that's the humour of't. [*Nym and
Bardolph sheathe their swords. Pistol and Nym shake
hands.*]

Enter HOSTESS.

HOSTESS   As ever you come of women, come in quickly 115
to Sir John. Ah, poor heart, he is so shaked of a burning
quotidian tertian that it is most lamentable to behold.
Sweet men, come to him.   *Exit.*

NYM   The King hath run bad humours on the knight,
that's the even of it.   120

PISTOL   Nym, thou hast spoke the right;
  His heart is fracted and corroborate.
NYM   The King is a good king, but it must be as it may.
  He passes some humours and careers.
125 PISTOL   Let us condole the knight, for, lambkins, we
  will live.   *Exeunt.*

2.2   *Enter* EXETER, BEDFORD *and*
                          WESTMORLAND.

BEDFORD
  'Fore God, his grace is bold to trust these traitors.
EXETER   They shall be apprehended by and by.
WESTMORLAND
  How smooth and even they do bear themselves,
  As if allegiance in their bosoms sat,
5   Crowned with faith and constant loyalty!
BEDFORD   The King hath note of all that they intend,
  By interception, which they dream not of.
EXETER   Nay, but the man that was his bedfellow,
  Whom he hath dulled and cloyed with gracious
      favours,
10   That he should for a foreign purse so sell
  His sovereign's life to death and treachery!

        Sound trumpets. Enter the KING, SCROOP,
        CAMBRIDGE *and* GREY, *Lords and Soldiers.*

KING   Now sits the wind fair, and we will aboard. –
  My lord of Cambridge, and my kind lord of Masham,
  And you, my gentle knight, give me your thoughts:
15   Think you not that the powers we bear with us
  Will cut their passage through the force of France,
  Doing the execution and the act
  For which we have in head assembled them?
SCROOP   No doubt, my liege, if each man do his best.
20 KING   I doubt not that, since we are well persuaded
  We carry not a heart with us from hence
  That grows not in a fair consent with ours,
  Nor leave not one behind that doth not wish
  Success and conquest to attend on us.
25 CAMBRIDGE
  Never was monarch better feared and loved
  Than is your majesty; there's not, I think, a subject
  That sits in heart-grief and uneasiness
  Under the sweet shade of your government.
GREY   True: those that were your father's enemies
30   Have steeped their galls in honey and do serve you
  With hearts create of duty and of zeal.
KING   We therefore have great cause of thankfulness,
  And shall forget the office of our hand
  Sooner than quittance of desert and merit
35   According to their weight and worthiness.
SCROOP   So service shall with steeled sinews toil,
  And labour shall refresh itself with hope
  To do your grace incessant services.
KING   We judge no less. – Uncle of Exeter,
40   Enlarge the man committed yesterday

That railed against our person. We consider
  It was excess of wine that set him on,
  And on his more advice we pardon him.
SCROOP   That's mercy, but too much security.
  Let him be punished, sovereign, lest example   45
  Breed, by his sufferance, more of such a kind.
KING   O let us yet be merciful.
CAMBRIDGE
  So may your highness, and yet punish too.
GREY   Sir,
  You show great mercy if you give him life,   50
  After the taste of much correction.
KING   Alas, your too much love and care of me
  Are heavy orisons 'gainst this poor wretch.
  If little faults proceeding on distemper
  Shall not be winked at, how shall we stretch our eye 55
  When capital crimes, chewed, swallowed, and digested,
  Appear before us? – We'll yet enlarge that man,
  Though Cambridge, Scroop and Grey, in their dear
      care
  And tender preservation of our person,
  Would have him punished. And now to our French
      causes.   60
  Who are the late commissioners?
CAMBRIDGE   I one, my lord;
  Your highness bade me ask for it today.
SCROOP   So did you me, my liege.
GREY   And me, my royal sovereign.   65
KING [*Gives papers.*]
  Then, Richard Earl of Cambridge, there is yours;
  There yours, Lord Scroop of Masham; and, sir knight,
  Grey of Northumberland, this same is yours:
  Read them, and know I know your worthiness. –
  My lord of Westmorland and uncle Exeter,   70
  We will aboard tonight. – Why, how now, gentlemen!
  What see you in those papers, that you lose
  So much complexion? – Look ye how they change!
  Their cheeks are paper. – Why, what read you there,
  That hath so cowarded and chased your blood   75
  Out of appearance?
      [*Cambridge, Scroop and Grey fall upon their knees.*]
CAMBRIDGE   I do confess my fault
  And do submit me to your highness' mercy.
GREY, SCROOP   To which we all appeal.
KING   The mercy that was quick in us but late
  By your own counsel is suppressed and killed: 80
  You must not dare, for shame, to talk of mercy,
  For your own reasons turn into your bosoms
  As dogs upon their masters, worrying you. –
  See you, my princes and my noble peers,
  These English monsters! My lord of Cambridge
      here,   85
  You know how apt our love was to accord
  To furnish him with all appertinents
  Belonging to his honour; and this man
  Hath for a few light crowns lightly conspired
  And sworn unto the practices of France   90

To kill us here in Hampton. To the which
This knight, no less for bounty bound to us
Than Cambridge is, hath likewise sworn. – But oh,
What shall I say to thee, Lord Scroop, thou cruel,
95 Ingrateful, savage and inhuman creature,
Thou that didst bear the key of all my counsels,
That knewst the very bottom of my soul,
That almost mightst have coined me into gold
Wouldst thou have practised on me for thy use?
100 May it be possible that foreign hire
Could out of thee extract one spark of evil
That might annoy my finger? 'Tis so strange
That though the truth of it stands off as gross
As black on white, my eye will scarcely see it.
105 Treason and murder ever kept together,
As two yoke-devils sworn to either's purpose,
Working so grossly in a natural cause
That admiration did not whoop at them.
But thou, 'gainst all proportion, didst bring in
110 Wonder to wait on treason and on murder;
And whatsoever cunning fiend it was
That wrought upon thee so preposterously
Hath got the voice in hell for excellence.
All other devils that suggest by treasons
115 Do botch and bungle up damnation
With patches, colours and with forms being fetched
From glistering semblances of piety;
But he that tempered thee, bade thee stand up,
Gave thee no instance why thou shouldst do treason
120 Unless to dub thee with the name of traitor.
If that same demon that hath gulled thee thus
Should with his lion-gait walk the whole world,
He might return to vasty Tartar back
And tell the legions 'I can never win
125 A soul so easy as that Englishman's.'
O how hast thou with jealousy infected
The sweetness of affiance! Show men dutiful?
Why, so didst thou. Seem they grave and learned?
Why, so didst thou. Come they of noble family?
130 Why, so didst thou. Seem they religious?
Why, so didst thou. Or are they spare in diet,
Free from gross passion or of mirth or anger,
Constant in spirit, not swerving with the blood,
Garnished and decked in modest complement,
135 Not working with the eye without the ear,
And but in purged judgement trusting neither?
Such and so finely boulted didst thou seem:
And thus thy fall hath left a kind of blot
To mark the full-fraught man and best endued
140 With some suspicion. I will weep for thee,
For this revolt of thine, methinks, is like
Another fall of man. – Their faults are open.
Arrest them to the answer of the law,
And God acquit them of their practices!
            [*Cambridge, Scroop and Grey rise.*]
145 EXETER   I arrest thee of high treason, by the name of
Richard Earl of Cambridge.

I arrest thee of high treason, by the name of Henry
Lord Scroop of Masham.
I arrest thee of high treason, by the name of Thomas
Grey, knight, of Northumberland.   150
SCROOP   Our purposes God justly hath discovered,
And I repent my fault more than my death,
Which I beseech your highness to forgive,
Although my body pay the price of it.
CAMBRIDGE
For me, the gold of France did not seduce,   155
Although I did admit it as a motive
The sooner to effect what I intended.
But God be thanked for prevention,
Which I in sufferance heartily will rejoice,
Beseeching God and you to pardon me.   160
GREY   Never did faithful subject more rejoice
At the discovery of most dangerous treason
Than I do at this hour joy o'er myself,
Prevented from a damned enterprise.
My fault, but not my body, pardon, sovereign.   165
KING   God quit you in his mercy! Hear your sentence.
You have conspired against our royal person,
Joined with an enemy proclaimed and fixed,
And from his coffers
Received the golden earnest of our death;   170
Wherein you would have sold your king to slaughter,
His princes and his peers to servitude,
His subjects to oppression and contempt,
And his whole kingdom into desolation.
Touching our person seek we no revenge,   175
But we our kingdom's safety must so tender,
Whose ruin you have sought, that to her laws
We do deliver you. Get ye therefore hence,
Poor miserable wretches, to your death,
The taste whereof God of his mercy give   180
You patience to endure, and true repentance
Of all your dear offences! – Bear them hence.
            Exeunt Cambridge, Scroop and Grey, guarded.
Now, lords, for France; the enterprise whereof
Shall be to you as us, like glorious.
We doubt not of a fair and lucky war,   185
Since God so graciously hath brought to light
This dangerous treason lurking in our way
To hinder our beginnings. We doubt not now
But every rub is smoothed on our way.
Then forth, dear countrymen. Let us deliver   190
Our puissance into the hand of God,
Putting it straight in expedition.
Cheerly to sea; the signs of war advance.
No king of England, if not king of France!
            Flourish. Exeunt.

2.3   *Enter* PISTOL, NYM, BARDOLPH,
            BOY *and* HOSTESS.

HOSTESS   Prithee, honey-sweet husband, let me bring
thee to Staines.

PISTOL No; for my manly heart doth earn.
    Bardolph, be blithe. Nym, rouse thy vaunting veins.
5   Boy, bristle thy courage up;
    For Falstaff he is dead, and we must earn therefore.
BARDOLPH Would I were with him, wheresome'er he
    is, either in heaven or in hell!
HOSTESS Nay, sure, he's not in hell; he's in Arthur's
10   bosom, if ever man went to Arthur's bosom. 'A made a
    finer end, and went away an it had been any christom
    child. 'A parted even just between twelve and one,
    even at the turning o'th' tide. For after I saw him
    fumble with the sheets and play wi'th' flowers, and
15   smile upon his fingers' ends, I knew there was but one
    way; for his nose was as sharp as a pen, and 'a babbled
    of green fields. 'How now, Sir John?' quoth I, 'what,
    man! be o' good cheer.' So 'a cried out 'God, God,
    God!' three or four times. Now I, to comfort him, bid
20   him 'a should not think of God; I hoped there was no
    need to trouble himself with any such thoughts yet. So
    'a bade me lay more clothes on his feet. I put my hand
    into the bed and felt them, and they were as cold as any
    stone. Then I felt to his knees, and so up'ard and
25   up'ard, and all was as cold as any stone.
NYM They say he cried out of sack.
HOSTESS Ay, that 'a did.
BARDOLPH And of women.
HOSTESS Nay, that 'a did not.
30 BOY Yes, that 'a did, and said they were devils incarnate.
HOSTESS 'A could never abide carnation, 'twas a colour
    he never liked.
BOY 'A said once the devil would have him about women.
HOSTESS 'A did in some sort, indeed, handle women;
35   but then he was rheumatic and talked of the Whore of
    Babylon.
BOY Do you not remember 'a saw a flea stick upon
    Bardolph's nose and 'a said it was a black soul burning
    in hell-fire?
40 BARDOLPH Well, the fuel is gone that maintained that
    fire; that's all the riches I got in his service.
NYM Shall we shog? The King will be gone from
    Southampton.
PISTOL
    Come, let's away. – My love, give me thy lips.
      [*Kisses her.*]
45   Look to my chattels and my moveables.
    Let senses rule. The word is 'Pitch and pay'.
    Trust none;
    For oaths are straws, men's faiths are wafer-cakes,
    And Holdfast is the only dog, my duck;
50   Therefore *Caveto* be thy counsellor.
    Go, clear thy crystals. – Yoke-fellows in arms,
    Let us to France, like horse-leeches, my boys,
    To suck, to suck, the very blood to suck!
BOY And that's but unwholesome food, they say.
55 PISTOL Touch her soft mouth, and march.
BARDOLPH Farewell, hostess. [*Kisses her.*]
NYM I cannot kiss, that is the humour of it; but adieu.

PISTOL
    Let housewifery appear; keep close, I thee command.
HOSTESS Farewell. Adieu.   *Exeunt.*

2.4   *Flourish. Enter the* FRENCH KING, *the*
        DAUPHIN, *the* CONSTABLE *and the*
        Dukes of BERRY *and* BRITAIN.

FRENCH KING
    Thus comes the English with full power upon us,
    And more than carefully it us concerns
    To answer royally in our defences.
    Therefore the Dukes of Berry and of Britain,
    Of Brabant and of Orleans, shall make forth,   5
    And you, Prince Dauphin, with all swift dispatch,
    To line and new repair our towns of war
    With men of courage and with means defendant,
    For England his approaches makes as fierce
    As waters to the sucking of a gulf.   10
    It fits us then to be as provident
    As fear may teach us, out of late examples
    Left by the fatal and neglected English
    Upon our fields.
DAUPHIN   My most redoubted father,
    It is most meet we arm us 'gainst the foe,   15
    For peace itself should not so dull a kingdom,
    Though war nor no known quarrel were in question,
    But that defences, musters, preparations,
    Should be maintained, assembled, and collected,
    As were a war in expectation.   20
    Therefore, I say, 'tis meet we all go forth
    To view the sick and feeble parts of France.
    And let us do it with no show of fear,
    No, with no more than if we heard that England
    Were busied with a Whitsun morris-dance.   25
    For, my good liege, she is so idly kinged,
    Her sceptre so fantastically borne
    By a vain, giddy, shallow, humorous youth,
    That fear attends her not.
CONSTABLE   O peace, Prince Dauphin!
    You are too much mistaken in this king.   30
    Question your grace the late ambassadors,
    With what great state he heard their embassy,
    How well supplied with noble counsellors,
    How modest in exception, and withal
    How terrible in constant resolution,   35
    And you shall find his vanities forespent
    Were but the outside of the Roman Brutus,
    Covering discretion with a coat of folly,
    As gardeners do with ordure hide those roots
    That shall first spring and be most delicate.   40
DAUPHIN Well, 'tis not so, my lord High Constable;
    But though we think it so, it is no matter.
    In cases of defence 'tis best to weigh
    The enemy more mighty than he seems.
    So the proportions of defence are filled,   45
    Which, of a weak and niggardly projection,

Doth like a miser spoil his coat with scanting
A little cloth.
FRENCH KING   Think we King Harry strong;
And, princes, look you strongly arm to meet him.
50 The kindred of him hath been fleshed upon us,
And he is bred out of that bloody strain
That haunted us in our familiar paths.
Witness our too much memorable shame
When Cressy battle fatally was struck,
55 And all our princes captived, by the hand
Of that black name, Edward, Black Prince of Wales;
Whiles that his mountain sire, on mountain
standing
Up in the air, crowned with the golden sun,
Saw his heroical seed, and smiled to see him,
60 Mangle the work of nature and deface
The patterns that by God and by French fathers
Had twenty years been made. This is a stem
Of that victorious stock, and let us fear
The native mightiness and fate of him.

Enter a Messenger.

MESSENGER
65 Ambassadors from Harry, King of England,
Do crave admittance to your majesty.
FRENCH KING
We'll give them present audience. Go and bring them.
                                    Exit Messenger.
You see this chase is hotly followed, friends.
DAUPHIN
Turn head and stop pursuit, for coward dogs
70 Most spend their mouths when what they seem to
threaten
Runs far before them. Good my sovereign,
Take up the English short and let them know
Of what a monarchy you are the head.
Self-love, my liege, is not so vile a sin
As self-neglecting.

Enter EXETER, *with Attendants.*

75 FRENCH KING   From our brother England?
EXETER   From him, and thus he greets your majesty:
He wills you, in the name of God Almighty,
That you divest yourself and lay apart
The borrowed glories that by gift of heaven,
80 By law of nature and of nations, longs
To him and to his heirs, namely the crown
And all wide-stretched honours that pertain
By custom and the ordinance of times
Unto the crown of France. That you may know
85 'Tis no sinister nor no awkward claim,
Picked from the worm-holes of long-vanished days,
Nor from the dust of old oblivion raked,
He sends you this most memorable line,
In every branch truly demonstrative,
90 Willing you overlook this pedigree.
And when you find him evenly derived

From his most famed of famous ancestors,
Edward the Third, he bids you then resign
Your crown and kingdom indirectly held
From him the native and true challenger. 95
[Gives the French King a paper.]
FRENCH KING   Or else what follows?
EXETER   Bloody constraint; for if you hide the crown
Even in your heart, there will he rake for it.
Therefore in fierce tempest is he coming,
In thunder and in earthquake, like a Jove, 100
That if requiring fail, he will compel.
And bids you, in the bowels of the Lord,
Deliver up the crown and to take mercy
On the poor souls for whom this hungry war
Opens his vasty jaws; and on your head 105
Turning the widows' tears, the orphans' cries,
The dead men's blood, the pining maidens' groans,
For husbands, fathers and betrothed lovers
That shall be swallowed in this controversy.
This is his claim, his threatening, and my message – 110
Unless the Dauphin be in presence here,
To whom expressly I bring greeting too.
FRENCH KING
For us, we will consider of this further.
Tomorrow shall you bear our full intent
Back to our brother England.
DAUPHIN   For the Dauphin, 115
I stand here for him. What to him from England?
EXETER   Scorn and defiance, slight regard, contempt,
And anything that may not misbecome
The mighty sender, doth he prize you at.
Thus says my king: an if your father's highness 120
Do not, in grant of all demands at large,
Sweeten the bitter mock you sent his majesty,
He'll call you to so hot an answer for it
That caves and womby vaultages of France
Shall chide your trespass and return your mock 125
In second accent of his ordinance.
DAUPHIN   Say if my father render fair return
It is against my will, for I desire
Nothing but odds with England. To that end,
As matching to his youth and vanity, 130
I did present him with the Paris-balls.
EXETER   He'll make your Paris Louvre shake for it,
Were it the mistress-court of mighty Europe.
And be assured you'll find a difference,
As we his subjects have in wonder found, 135
Between the promise of his greener days
And these he masters now. Now he weighs time
Even to the utmost grain. That you shall read
In your own losses, if he stay in France.
FRENCH KING
Tomorrow shall you know our mind at full. 140
[Flourish]
EXETER   Dispatch us with all speed, lest that our king
Come here himself to question our delay,
For he is footed in this land already.

FRENCH KING
    You shall be soon dispatched with fair conditions.
145   A night is but small breath and little pause
    To answer matters of this consequence.
                                        Flourish. Exeunt.

3.0   *Enter* CHORUS.

CHORUS   Thus with imagined wing our swift scene flies
    In motion of no less celerity
    Than that of thought. Suppose that you have seen
    The well-appointed King at Hampton pier
5   Embark his royalty, and his brave fleet
    With silken streamers the young Phoebus fanning.
    Play with your fancies, and in them behold
    Upon the hempen tackle ship-boys climbing;
    Hear the shrill whistle which doth order give
10   To sounds confused; behold the threaden sails,
    Borne with th'invisible and creeping wind,
    Draw the huge bottoms through the furrowed sea,
    Breasting the lofty surge. O do but think
    You stand upon the rivage and behold
15   A city on th'inconstant billows dancing,
    For so appears this fleet majestical,
    Holding due course to Harfleur. Follow, follow!
    Grapple your minds to sternage of this navy,
    And leave your England as dead midnight still,
20   Guarded with grandsires, babies and old women,
    Either past or not arrived to pith and puissance.
    For who is he, whose chin is but enriched
    With one appearing hair, that will not follow
    These culled and choice-drawn cavaliers to France?
25   Work, work your thoughts, and therein see a siege;
    Behold the ordnance on their carriages,
    With fatal mouths gaping on girded Harfleur.
    Suppose th'ambassador from the French comes back,
    Tells Harry that the King doth offer him
30   Katherine his daughter and with her, to dowry,
    Some petty and unprofitable dukedoms.
    The offer likes not; and the nimble gunner
    With linstock now the devilish cannon touches,
                    [*Alarum, and chambers go off.*]
    And down goes all before them. Still be kind,
35   And eke out our performance with your mind.   *Exit.*

3.1   *Alarum. Enter Soldiers with scaling-*
        ladders at Harfleur. Enter the KING, EXETER,
            BEDFORD *and* GLOUCESTER.

KING
    Once more unto the breach, dear friends, once more,
    Or close the wall up with our English dead.
    In peace there's nothing so becomes a man
    As modest stillness and humility;
5   But when the blast of war blows in our ears,
    Then imitate the action of the tiger:
    Stiffen the sinews, conjure up the blood,

    Disguise fair nature with hard-favoured rage.
    Then lend the eye a terrible aspect;
    Let it pry through the portage of the head   10
    Like the brass cannon; let the brow o'erwhelm it
    As fearfully as doth a galled rock
    O'erhang and jutty his confounded base,
    Swilled with the wild and wasteful ocean.
    Now set the teeth and stretch the nostril wide,   15
    Hold hard the breath and bend up every spirit
    To his full height. On, on, you noble English,
    Whose blood is fet from fathers of war-proof,
    Fathers that like so many Alexanders
    Have in these parts from morn till even fought,   20
    And sheathed their swords for lack of argument.
    Dishonour not your mothers; now attest
    That those whom you called fathers did beget you.
    Be copy now to men of grosser blood
    And teach them how to war. And you, good yeomen,   25
    Whose limbs were made in England, show us here
    The mettle of your pasture; let us swear
    That you are worth your breeding – which I doubt
        not,
    For there is none of you so mean and base
    That hath not noble lustre in your eyes.   30
    I see you stand like greyhounds in the slips,
    Straining upon the start. The game's afoot.
    Follow your spirit, and upon this charge
    Cry 'God for Harry! England and Saint George!'
                    Exeunt. Alarum, and chambers go off.

3.2   *Enter* NYM, BARDOLPH, PISTOL *and* BOY.

BARDOLPH   On, on, on, on, on, to the breach, to the
    breach!
NYM   Pray thee, Corporal, stay; the knocks are too hot,
    and for mine own part I have not a case of lives. The
    humour of it is too hot that is the very plain-song of it.   5
PISTOL
    The plain-song is most just, for humours do abound.
    Knocks go and come, God's vassals drop and die,
            And sword and shield
            In bloody field
            Doth win immortal fame.   10
BOY   Would I were in an alehouse in London! I would
    give all my fame for a pot of ale and safety.
PISTOL   And I.
            If wishes would prevail with me
            My purpose should not fail with me,   15
            But thither would I hie.
BOY   As duly –
            But not as truly –
            As bird doth sing on bough.

                    Enter FLUELLEN.

FLUELLEN [*Beats them.*]
    Up to the breach, you dogs! Avaunt, you cullions!   20
PISTOL   Be merciful, great duke, to men of mould!

Abate thy rage, abate thy manly rage,
Abate thy rage, great duke!
Good bawcock, bate thy rage! Use lenity, sweet
    chuck!

25 NYM   These be good humours! Your honour runs bad
    humours!   *Exeunt all but Boy.*

BOY   As young as I am, I have observed these three
swashers. I am boy to them all three, but all they three,
though they would serve me, could not be man to me,
30 for indeed three such antics do not amount to a man.
For Bardolph, he is white-livered and red-faced, by the
means whereof 'a faces it out but fights not. For Pistol,
he hath a killing tongue and a quiet sword, by the
means whereof 'a breaks words and keeps whole
35 weapons. For Nym, he hath heard that men of few
words are the best men, and therefore he scorns to say
his prayers lest 'a should be thought a coward: but his
few bad words are matched with as few good deeds,
for 'a never broke any man's head but his own, and that
40 was against a post when he was drunk. They will steal
anything, and call it purchase. Bardolph stole a lute-
case, bore it twelve leagues, and sold it for three-
halfpence. Nym and Bardolph are sworn brothers in
filching, and in Calais they stole a fire-shovel. I knew
45 by that piece of service the men would carry coals.
They would have me as familiar with men's pockets as
their gloves or their handkerchiefs, which makes much
against my manhood if I should take from another's
pocket to put into mine, for it is plain pocketing up of
50 wrongs. I must leave them and seek some better
service; their villainy goes against my weak stomach,
and therefore I must cast it up.   *Exit.*

Enter GOWER *and* FLUELLEN, *meeting.*

GOWER   Captain Fluellen, you must come presently to
the mines; the Duke of Gloucester would speak with
55 you.
FLUELLEN   To the mines? Tell you the Duke it is not so
good to come to the mines; for, look you, the mines is not
according to the disciplines of the wars; the concavities
of it is not sufficient; for, look you, th'athversary, you
60 may discuss unto the Duke, look you, is digt himself
four yard under the countermines. By Cheshu, I think 'a
will plow up all, if there is not better directions.
GOWER   The Duke of Gloucester, to whom the order
of the siege is given, is altogether directed by an Irish-
65 man, a very valiant gentleman, i'faith.
FLUELLEN   It is Captain Macmorris, is it not?
GOWER   I think it be.
FLUELLEN   By Cheshu, he is an ass, as any is in the
world. I will verify as much in his beard. He has no
70 more directions in the true disciplines of the wars, look
you, of the Roman disciplines, than is a puppy-dog.

Enter MACMORRIS *and* JAMY.

GOWER   Here 'a comes, and the Scots captain, Captain
Jamy, with him.

FLUELLEN   Captain Jamy is a marvellous falorous
gentleman, that is certain, and of great expedition and
knowledge in th'anchient wars, upon my particular
knowledge of his directions. By Cheshu, he will maintain
his argument as well as any military man in the world, in
the disciplines of the pristine wars of the Romans.
80 JAMY   I say guid day, Captain Fluellen.
FLUELLEN   God-den to your worship, good Captain
James.
GOWER   How now, Captain Macmorris, have you quit
the mines? Have the pioneers given o'er?
85 MACMORRIS   By Chrish, la, 'tish ill done; the work ish
give over, the trompet sound the retreat. By my hand I
swear, and my father's soul, the work ish ill done; it ish
give over. I would have blowed up the town, so Chrish
save me, la, in an hour. Oh, 'tish ill done, 'tish ill done;
90 by my hand, 'tish ill done!
FLUELLEN   Captain Macmorris, I beseech you now, will
you vouchsafe me, look you, a few disputations with
you as partly touching or concerning the disciplines of
the wars, the Roman wars, in the way of argument,
95 look you, and friendly communication? Partly to
satisfy my opinion, and partly for the satisfaction, look
you, of my mind, as touching the direction of the
military discipline, that is the point.
JAMY   It sall be vara guid, guid feith, guid captains
100 baith, and I sall quit you, with guid leave, as I may pick
occasion; that sall I, marry.
MACMORRIS   It is no time to discourse, so Chrish save
me. The day is hot, and the weather, and the wars, and
the King, and the Dukes. It is no time to discourse, the
105 town is besieched, and the trumpet call us to the
breach, and we talk, and, be Chrish, do nothing. 'Tis
shame for us all, so God sa' me, 'tis shame to stand
still, it is shame, by my hand; and there is throats to be
cut, and works to be done, and there ish nothing done,
110 so Chrish sa' me, la!
JAMY   By the mess, ere these eyes of mine take
themselves to slumber I'll dae guid service, or I'll lig
i'th' grund for it. I owe God a death, and I'll pay't as
valorously as I may, that sall I surely do, that is the breff
115 and the long. Marry, I wad full fain heard some
question 'tween you twa.
FLUELLEN   Captain Macmorris, I think, look you,
under your correction, there is not many of your
nation –
120 MACMORRIS   Of my nation? What ish my nation? Ish a
villain, and a bastard, and a knave, and a rascal? What
ish my nation? Who talks of my nation?
FLUELLEN   Look you, if you take the matter otherwise
than is meant, Captain Macmorris, peradventure I
125 shall think you do not use me with that affability as in
discretion you ought to use me, look you, being as good
a man as yourself, both in the disciplines of war, and in
the derivation of my birth, and in other particularities.
MACMORRIS   I do not know you so good a man as
130 myself. So Chrish save me, I will cut off your head.

GOWER   Gentlemen both, you will mistake each other.

JAMY   Ah, that's a foul fault.   [*A parley is sounded.*]

GOWER   The town sounds a parley.

FLUELLEN   Captain Macmorris, when there is more
135   better opportunity to be required, look you, I will be so
bold as to tell you I know the disciplines of war, and
there is an end.   *Exeunt.*

3.3   *The* GOVERNOR *and others upon the walls.*
Enter the KING *and all his train before the gates.*

KING   How yet resolves the Governor of the town?
This is the latest parle we will admit.
Therefore to our best mercy give yourselves,
Or like to men proud of destruction
5   Defy us to our worst; for, as I am a soldier,
A name that in my thoughts becomes me best,
If I begin the battery once again,
I will not leave the half-achieved Harfleur
Till in her ashes she lie buried.
10   The gates of mercy shall be all shut up,
And the fleshed soldier, rough and hard of heart,
In liberty of bloody hand shall range
With conscience wide as hell, mowing like grass
Your fresh fair virgins and your flowering infants.
15   What is it then to me if impious war,
Arrayed in flames like to the prince of fiends,
Do with his smirched complexion all fell feats
Enlinked to waste and desolation?
What is't to me, when you yourselves are cause,
20   If your pure maidens fall into the hand
Of hot and forcing violation?
What rein can hold licentious wickedness
When down the hill he holds his fierce career?
We may as bootless spend our vain command
25   Upon th'enraged soldiers in their spoil
As send precepts to the leviathan
To come ashore. Therefore, you men of Harfleur,
Take pity of your town and of your people
Whiles yet my soldiers are in my command,
30   Whiles yet the cool and temperate wind of grace
O'erblows the filthy and contagious clouds
Of heady murder, spoil and villainy.
If not, why, in a moment look to see
The blind and bloody soldier with foul hand
35   Defile the locks of your shrill-shrieking daughters,
Your fathers taken by the silver beards,
And their most reverend heads dashed to the walls,
Your naked infants spitted upon pikes,
Whiles the mad mothers with their howls confused
40   Do break the clouds, as did the wives of Jewry
At Herod's bloody-hunting slaughtermen.
What say you? Will you yield and this avoid?
Or, guilty in defence, be thus destroyed?

GOVERNOR   Our expectation hath this day an end.
45   The Dauphin, whom of succours we entreated,
Returns us that his powers are yet not ready

To raise so great a siege. Therefore, dread King,
We yield our town and lives to thy soft mercy.
Enter our gates, dispose of us and ours,
50   For we no longer are defensible.

KING
Open your gates.   *Exit Governor.*
          Come, uncle Exeter,
Go you and enter Harfleur; there remain
And fortify it strongly 'gainst the French.
Use mercy to them all. For us, dear uncle,
55   The winter coming on and sickness growing
Upon our soldiers, we will retire to Calais.
Tonight in Harfleur will we be your guest;
Tomorrow for the march are we addressed.
                    Flourish, and enter the town.

3.4   *Enter* KATHERINE *and* ALICE,
an old Gentlewoman.

KATHERINE   *Alice, tu as été en Angleterre, et tu bien parles
le langage.*

ALICE   *Un peu, madame.*

KATHERINE   *Je te prie m'enseigner; il faut que j'apprenne
à parler. Comment appelez-vous la main en anglais?*   5

ALICE   *La main, elle est appelée* de hand.

KATHERINE   *De* hand. *Et les doigts?*

ALICE   *Les doigts? Ma foi, j'oublie les doigts, mais je me
souviendrai. Les doigts, je pense qu'ils sont appelés* de
fingres; *oui*, de fingres.   10

KATHERINE   *La main*, de hand; *les doigts*, de fingres. *Je
pense que je suis le bon écolier. J'ai gagné deux mots
d'anglais vitement. Comment appelez-vous les ongles?*

ALICE   *Les ongles, nous les appelons* de nails.

KATHERINE   *De* nails. *Écoutez; dites-moi si je parle bien:*   15
de hand, de fingres, *et* de nails.

ALICE   *C'est bien dit, madame; il est fort bon anglais.*

KATHERINE   *Dites-moi l'anglais pour le bras.*

ALICE   *De* arm, *madame.*

KATHERINE   *Et le coude?*   20

ALICE   *D'*elbow.

KATHERINE   *D'*elbow. *Je m'en fais la répétition de tous les
mots que vous m'avez appris dès à présent.*

ALICE   *Il est trop difficile, madame, comme je pense.*

KATHERINE   *Excusez-moi, Alice. Écoutez:* d'hand, de   25
fingres, de nails, de arm, de bilbow.

ALICE   *D'*elbow, *madame.*

KATHERINE   *O Seigneur Dieu, je m'en oublie! D'*elbow.
Comment appelez-vous le col?

ALICE   *De* nick, *madame.*   30

KATHERINE   *De* nick. *Et le menton?*

ALICE   *De* chin.

KATHERINE   *De* sin. *Le col*, de nick; *le menton*, de sin.

ALICE   *Oui. Sauf votre honneur, en vérité, vous prononcez
les mots aussi droit que les natifs d'Angleterre.*   35

KATHERINE   *Je ne doute point d'apprendre, par la grâce de
Dieu, et en peu de temps.*

ALICE   *N'avez-vous déjà oublié ce que je vous ai enseigné?*

KATHERINE   *Non, je le réciterai à vous promptement:*
40   *d'hand, de fingres, de mails, –*
ALICE   De nails, *madame.*
KATHERINE   *De nails, de arm, de ilbow –*
ALICE   *Sauf votre honneur,* d'elbow.
KATHERINE   *Ainsi dis-je,* d'elbow *– de nick, et de sin.*
45   *Comment appelez-vous le pied et la robe?*
ALICE   De foot, *madame, et de* coun.
KATHERINE   De foot, *et de* coun? *O Seigneur Dieu, ils*
       sont les mots de son mauvais, corruptible, gros, et
       impudique, et non pour les dames d'honneur d'user. Je ne
50   *voudrais prononcer ces mots devant les seigneurs de France*
       pour tout le monde. Foh! De foot *et de* coun! *Néanmoins,*
       je réciterai une autre fois ma leçon ensemble: d'hand, de
       fingres, de nails, *d'*arm, *d'*elbow, de nick, de sin, de
       foot, de coun.
55   ALICE   *Excellent, madame!*
KATHERINE   *C'est assez pour une fois. Allons-nous à dîner.*
                                                        Exeunt.

3.5   *Enter the* KING *of France, the* DAUPHIN,
            the Duke of BRITAIN, *the* CONSTABLE
            of France *and others.*

FRENCH KING
       'Tis certain he hath passed the river Somme.
CONSTABLE   An if he be not fought withal, my lord,
       Let us not live in France; let us quit all
       And give our vineyards to a barbarous people.
5   DAUPHIN   *O Dieu vivant*! Shall a few sprays of us,
       The emptying of our fathers' luxury,
       Our scions, put in wild and savage stock,
       Spirt up so suddenly into the clouds
       And overlook their grafters?
BRITAIN
10   Normans, but bastard Normans, Norman bastards!
       Mort de ma vie, if they march along
       Unfought withal, but I will sell my dukedom
       To buy a slobbery and a dirty farm
       In that nook-shotten isle of Albion.
CONSTABLE
15   *Dieu de batailles,* where have they this mettle?
       Is not their climate foggy, raw and dull,
       On whom, as in despite, the sun looks pale,
       Killing their fruit with frowns? Can sodden water,
       A drench for sur-reined jades, their barley-broth,
20   Decoct their cold blood to such valiant heat?
       And shall our quick blood, spirited with wine,
       Seem frosty? O, for honour of our land,
       Let us not hang like roping icicles
       Upon our houses' thatch, whiles a more frosty
          people
25   Sweat drops of gallant youth in our rich fields!
       Poor we may call them in their native lords.
DAUPHIN   By faith and honour,
       Our madams mock at us and plainly say
       Our mettle is bred out, and they will give

Their bodies to the lust of English youth,   30
To new-store France with bastard warriors.
BRITAIN   They bid us to the English dancing-schools
       And teach lavoltas high and swift corantos,
       Saying our grace is only in our heels,
       And that we are most lofty runaways.   35
FRENCH KING
       Where is Montjoy the herald? Speed him hence:
       Let him greet England with our sharp defiance.
       Up, princes, and with spirit of honour edged
       More sharper than your swords hie to the field.
       Charles Delabreth, High Constable of France,   40
       You Dukes of Orleans, Bourbon and of Berry,
       Alençon, Brabant, Bar and Burgundy,
       Jaques Chatillon, Rambures, Vaudemont,
       Beaumont, Grandpré, Roussi and Fauconbridge,
       Foix, Lestrelles, Boucicault and Charolais,   45
       High dukes, great princes, barons, lords and knights,
       For your great seats now quit you of great shames.
       Bar Harry England, that sweeps through our land
       With pennons painted in the blood of Harfleur.
       Rush on his host as doth the melted snow   50
       Upon the valleys, whose low vassal seat
       The Alps doth spit and void his rheum upon.
       Go down upon him, you have power enough,
       And in a captive chariot into Rouen
       Bring him our prisoner.
CONSTABLE   This becomes the great.   55
       Sorry am I his numbers are so few,
       His soldiers sick and famished in their march,
       For I am sure when he shall see our army
       He'll drop his heart into the sink of fear
       And for achievement offer us his ransom.   60
FRENCH KING
       Therefore, Lord Constable, haste on Montjoy,
       And let him say to England that we send
       To know what willing ransom he will give. –
       Prince Dauphin, you shall stay with us in Rouen.
DAUPHIN   Not so, I do beseech your majesty.   65
FRENCH KING
       Be patient, for you shall remain with us. –
       Now forth, Lord Constable and princes all,
       And quickly bring us word of England's fall.   *Exeunt.*

3.6   *Enter the English and Welsh Captains*
            GOWER *and* FLUELLEN, *meeting.*

GOWER   How now, Captain Fluellen, come you from the
       bridge?
FLUELLEN   I assure you there is very excellent services
       committed at the bridge.
GOWER   Is the Duke of Exeter safe?   5
FLUELLEN   The Duke of Exeter is as magnanimous as
       Agamemnon, and a man that I love and honour with
       my soul, and my heart, and my duty, and my life, and
       my living, and my uttermost power. He is not, God be
       praised and blessed, any hurt in the world, but keeps   10

the bridge most valiantly, with excellent discipline.
There is an anchient lieutenant there at the pridge, I
think in my very conscience he is as valiant a man as
Mark Antony, and he is a man of no estimation in the
world, but I did see him do as gallant service –

GOWER   What do you call him?

FLUELLEN   He is called Anchient Pistol.

GOWER   I know him not.

Enter PISTOL.

FLUELLEN   Here is the man.

PISTOL   Captain, I thee beseech to do me favours.
The Duke of Exeter doth love thee well.

FLUELLEN   Ay, I praise God, and I have merited some
love at his hands.

PISTOL   Bardolph, a soldier firm and sound of heart,
Of buxom valour, hath, by cruel fate
And giddy Fortune's furious fickle wheel,
That goddess blind
That stands upon the rolling restless stone –

FLUELLEN   By your patience, Anchient Pistol. Fortune
is painted blind, with a muffler afore her eyes, to signify
to you that Fortune is blind; and she is painted also
with a wheel, to signify to you, which is the moral of it,
that she is turning, and inconstant, and mutability, and
variation; and her foot, look you, is fixed upon a
spherical stone, which rolls, and rolls, and rolls. In
good truth, the poet makes a most excellent description
of it: Fortune is an excellent moral.

PISTOL   Fortune is Bardolph's foe, and frowns on him,
For he hath stolen a pax,
And hanged must 'a be, a damned death!
Let gallows gape for dog, let man go free,
And let not hemp his windpipe suffocate!
But Exeter hath given the doom of death
For pax of little price.
Therefore go speak – the Duke will hear thy
   voice –
And let not Bardolph's vital thread be cut
With edge of penny cord and vile reproach.
Speak, Captain, for his life, and I will thee requite.

FLUELLEN   Anchient Pistol, I do partly understand your
meaning.

PISTOL   Why then, rejoice therefor.

FLUELLEN   Certainly, Anchient, it is not a thing to
rejoice at; for if, look you, he were my brother, I would
desire the Duke to use his good pleasure and put him
to execution; for discipline ought to be used.

PISTOL
Die and be damned, and *fico* for thy friendship!

FLUELLEN   It is well.

PISTOL   The fig of Spain!   *Exit.*

FLUELLEN   Very good.

GOWER   Why, this is an arrant counterfeit rascal, I
remember him now – a bawd, a cutpurse.

FLUELLEN   I'll assure you 'a uttered as prave words at

the pridge as you shall see in a summer's day. But it is
very well; what he has spoke to me, that is well, I
warrant you, when time is serve.

GOWER   Why, 'tis a gull, a fool, a rogue, that now and
then goes to the wars to grace himself at his return into
London under the form of a soldier. And such fellows
are perfect in the great commanders' names, and they
will learn you by rote where services were done, at such
and such a sconce, at such a breach, at such a convoy;
who came off bravely, who was shot, who disgraced,
what terms the enemy stood on. And this they con
perfectly in the phrase of war, which they trick up with
new-tuned oaths; and what a beard of the General's
cut and a horrid suit of the camp will do among
foaming bottles and ale-washed wits is wonderful to be
thought on. But you must learn to know such slanders
of the age, or else you may be marvellously mistook.

FLUELLEN   I tell you what, Captain Gower: I do
perceive he is not the man that he would gladly make
show to the world he is. If I find a hole in his coat, I will
tell him my mind.   [*Drum within.*]
Hark you, the King is coming, and I must speak with
him from the pridge.

Drum and Colours. Enter the KING *and* GLOUCESTER
and his poor Soldiers.

God pless your majesty!

KING
How now, Fluellen, cam'st thou from the bridge?

FLUELLEN   Ay, so please your majesty. The Duke of
Exeter has very gallantly maintained the pridge; the
French is gone off, look you, and there is gallant and
most prave passages. Marry, th'athversary was have
possession of the pridge, but he is enforced to retire,
and the Duke of Exeter is master of the pridge. I can
tell your majesty, the Duke is a prave man.

KING   What men have you lost, Fluellen?

FLUELLEN   The perdition of th'athversary hath been
very great, reasonable great. Marry, for my part, I
think the Duke hath lost never a man, but one that is
like to be executed for robbing a church, one Bardolph,
if your majesty know the man. His face is all bubuncles,
and whelks, and knobs, and flames o' fire, and his lips
blows at his nose, and it is like a coal of fire, sometimes
plue and sometimes red; but his nose is executed, and
his fire's out.

KING   We would have all such offenders so cut off; and
we give express charge that in our marches through the
country there be nothing compelled from the villages,
nothing taken but paid for, none of the French
upbraided or abused in disdainful language; for when
lenity and cruelty play for a kingdom, the gentler
gamester is the soonest winner.

Tucket. Enter MONTJOY.

MONTJOY   You know me by my habit.

KING
Well then, I know thee: what shall I know of thee?

MONTJOY My master's mind.

115 KING Unfold it.

MONTJOY Thus says my king: 'Say thou to Harry of England, though we seemed dead, we did but sleep. Advantage is a better soldier than rashness. Tell him we could have rebuked him at Harfleur, but that we
120 thought not good to bruise an injury till it were full ripe. Now we speak upon our cue, and our voice is imperial. England shall repent his folly, see his weakness, and admire our sufferance. Bid him therefore consider of his ransom, which must proportion the
125 losses we have borne, the subjects we have lost, the disgrace we have digested, which in weight to re-answer, his pettiness would bow under. For our losses, his exchequer is too poor; for th'effusion of our blood, the muster of his kingdom too faint a number;
130 and for our disgrace, his own person kneeling at our feet but a weak and worthless satisfaction. To this add defiance, and tell him, for conclusion, he hath betrayed his followers, whose condemnation is pronounced.' So far my king and master, so much my office.

135 KING What is thy name? I know thy quality.

MONTJOY Montjoy.

KING Thou dost thy office fairly. Turn thee back, And tell thy king I do not seek him now, But could be willing to march on to Calais
140 Without impeachment; for, to say the sooth, Though 'tis no wisdom to confess so much Unto an enemy of craft and vantage, My people are with sickness much enfeebled, My numbers lessened, and those few I have
145 Almost no better than so many French; Who when they were in health, I tell thee, herald, I thought upon one pair of English legs Did march three Frenchmen. Yet forgive me, God, That I do brag thus! This your air of France
150 Hath blown that vice in me. I must repent. Go therefore, tell thy master here I am. My ransom is this frail and worthless trunk, My army but a weak and sickly guard. Yet, God before, tell him we will come on,
155 Though France himself and such another neighbour Stand in our way. [*Gives a purse.*]
There's for thy labour, Montjoy. Go, bid thy master well advise himself. If we may pass, we will; if we be hindered, We shall your tawny ground with your red blood
160 Discolour. And so, Montjoy, fare you well. The sum of all our answer is but this: We would not seek a battle as we are, Nor as we are, we say, we will not shun it: So tell your master.

MONTJOY
165 I shall deliver so. Thanks to your highness. *Exit.*

GLOUCESTER I hope they will not come upon us now.

KING
We are in God's hand, brother, not in theirs. – March to the bridge. – It now draws toward night. Beyond the river we'll encamp ourselves, And on tomorrow bid them march away. *Exeunt.* 170

3.7 *Enter the* CONSTABLE *of France,*
the Lord RAMBURES, ORLEANS *and the*
DAUPHIN, *with others.*

CONSTABLE Tut, I have the best armour of the world. Would it were day!

ORLEANS You have an excellent armour; but let my horse have his due.

CONSTABLE It is the best horse of Europe. 5

ORLEANS Will it never be morning?

DAUPHIN My lord of Orleans and my lord High Constable, you talk of horse and armour?

ORLEANS You are as well provided of both as any prince in the world. 10

DAUPHIN What a long night is this! I will not change my horse with any that treads but on four pasterns. Ch'ha! He bounds from the earth as if his entrails were hairs – *le cheval volant*, the Pegasus, *qui a les narines de feu!* When I bestride him, I soar, I am a hawk. He trots 15 the air. The earth sings when he touches it; the basest horn of his hoof is more musical than the pipe of Hermes.

ORLEANS He's of the colour of the nutmeg.

DAUPHIN And of the heat of the ginger. It is a beast for 20 Perseus; he is pure air and fire, and the dull elements of earth and water never appear in him but only in patient stillness while his rider mounts him. He is indeed a horse, and all other jades you may call beasts.

CONSTABLE Indeed, my lord, it is a most absolute and 25 excellent horse.

DAUPHIN It is the prince of palfreys; his neigh is like the bidding of a monarch, and his countenance enforces homage.

ORLEANS No more, cousin. 30

DAUPHIN Nay, the man hath no wit that cannot, from the rising of the lark to the lodging of the lamb, vary deserved praise on my palfrey. It is a theme as fluent as the sea. Turn the sands into eloquent tongues and my horse is argument for them all. 'Tis a subject for a 35 sovereign to reason on, and for a sovereign's sovereign to ride on, and for the world, familiar to us and unknown, to lay apart their particular functions and wonder at him. I once writ a sonnet in his praise and began thus: 'Wonder of nature!' 40

ORLEANS I have heard a sonnet begin so to one's mistress.

DAUPHIN Then did they imitate that which I composed to my courser, for my horse is my mistress.

ORLEANS Your mistress bears well. 45

DAUPHIN Me well, which is the prescript praise and perfection of a good and particular mistress.

CONSTABLE   Nay, for methought yesterday your mistress shrewdly shook your back.

DAUPHIN   So perhaps did yours.

CONSTABLE   Mine was not bridled.

DAUPHIN   O then belike she was old and gentle, and you rode like a kern of Ireland, your French hose off and in your strait strossers.

CONSTABLE   You have good judgement in horsemanship.

DAUPHIN   Be warned by me then: they that ride so, and ride not warily, fall into foul bogs. I had rather have my horse to my mistress.

CONSTABLE   I had as lief have my mistress a jade.

DAUPHIN   I tell thee, Constable, my mistress wears his own hair.

CONSTABLE   I could make as true a boast as that if I had a sow to my mistress.

DAUPHIN   '*Le chien est retourné à son propre vomissement, et la truie lavée au bourbier.*' Thou mak'st use of anything.

CONSTABLE   Yet do I not use my horse for my mistress, or any such proverb so little kin to the purpose.

RAMBURES   My Lord Constable, the armour that I saw in your tent tonight, are those stars or suns upon it?

CONSTABLE   Stars, my lord.

DAUPHIN   Some of them will fall tomorrow, I hope.

CONSTABLE   And yet my sky shall not want.

DAUPHIN   That may be, for you bear a many superfluously, and 'twere more honour some were away.

CONSTABLE   Even as your horse bears your praises, who would trot as well were some of your brags dismounted.

DAUPHIN   Would I were able to load him with his desert! Will it never be day? I will trot tomorrow a mile, and my way shall be paved with English faces.

CONSTABLE   I will not say so, for fear I should be faced out of my way. But I would it were morning, for I would fain be about the ears of the English.

RAMBURES   Who will go to hazard with me for twenty prisoners?

CONSTABLE   You must first go yourself to hazard ere you have them.

DAUPHIN   'Tis midnight; I'll go arm myself.   *Exit.*

ORLEANS   The Dauphin longs for morning.

RAMBURES   He longs to eat the English.

CONSTABLE   I think he will eat all he kills.

ORLEANS   By the white hand of my lady, he's a gallant prince.

CONSTABLE   Swear by her foot, that she may tread out the oath.

ORLEANS   He is simply the most active gentleman of France.

CONSTABLE   Doing is activity, and he will still be doing.

ORLEANS   He never did harm that I heard of.

CONSTABLE   Nor will do none tomorrow; he will keep that good name still.

ORLEANS   I know him to be valiant.

CONSTABLE   I was told that by one that knows him better than you.

ORLEANS   What's he?

CONSTABLE   Marry, he told me so himself, and he said he cared not who knew it.

ORLEANS   He needs not, it is no hidden virtue in him.

CONSTABLE   By my faith, sir, but it is: never anybody saw it but his lackey. 'Tis a hooded valour, and when it appears it will bate.

ORLEANS   'Ill will never said well.'

CONSTABLE   I will cap that proverb with 'There is flattery in friendship.'

ORLEANS   And I will take up that with 'Give the devil his due.'

CONSTABLE   Well placed: there stands your friend for the devil. Have at the very eye of that proverb with 'A pox of the devil.'

ORLEANS   You are the better at proverbs by how much 'A fool's bolt is soon shot.'

CONSTABLE   You have shot over.

ORLEANS   'Tis not the first time you were overshot.

Enter a Messenger.

MESSENGER   My lord High Constable, the English lie within fifteen hundred paces of your tents.

CONSTABLE   Who hath measured the ground?

MESSENGER   The Lord Grandpré.

CONSTABLE   A valiant and most expert gentleman.

Exit Messenger.

Would it were day! Alas, poor Harry of England! He longs not for the dawning as we do.

ORLEANS   What a wretched and peevish fellow is this King of England, to mope with his fat-brained followers so far out of his knowledge!

CONSTABLE   If the English had any apprehension they would run away.

ORLEANS   That they lack, for if their heads had any intellectual armour they could never wear such heavy headpieces.

RAMBURES   That island of England breeds very valiant creatures: their mastiffs are of unmatchable courage.

ORLEANS   Foolish curs, that run winking into the mouth of a Russian bear and have their heads crushed like rotten apples. You may as well say that's a valiant flea that dare eat his breakfast on the lip of a lion.

CONSTABLE   Just, just; and the men do sympathize with the mastiffs in robustious and rough coming on, leaving their wits with their wives. And then give them great meals of beef and iron and steel, they will eat like wolves and fight like devils.

ORLEANS   Ay, but these English are shrewdly out of beef.

CONSTABLE   Then shall we find tomorrow they have only stomachs to eat and none to fight. Now is it time to arm; come, shall we about it?

ORLEANS   It is now two o'clock; but, let me see, by ten We shall have each a hundred Englishmen.   *Exeunt.*

4.0   *Enter* CHORUS.

CHORUS Now entertain conjecture of a time
        When creeping murmur and the poring dark
        Fills the wide vessel of the universe.
        From camp to camp through the foul womb of night
5   The hum of either army stilly sounds,
        That the fixed sentinels almost receive
        The secret whispers of each other's watch.
        Fire answers fire, and through their paly flames
        Each battle sees the other's umbered face.
10   Steed threatens steed, in high and boastful neighs
        Piercing the night's dull ear; and from the tents
        The armourers accomplishing the knights,
        With busy hammers closing rivets up,
        Give dreadful note of preparation.
15   The country cocks do crow, the clocks do toll,
        And the third hour of drowsy morning name.
        Proud of their numbers and secure in soul,
        The confident and over-lusty French
        Do the low-rated English play at dice,
20   And chide the cripple tardy-gaited night
        Who like a foul and ugly witch doth limp
        So tediously away. The poor condemned English,
        Like sacrifices, by their watchful fires
        Sit patiently and inly ruminate
25   The morning's danger; and their gesture sad,
        Investing lank-lean cheeks and war-worn coats,
        Presenteth them unto the gazing moon
        So many horrid ghosts. O now, who will behold
        The royal captain of this ruined band
30   Walking from watch to watch, from tent to tent,
        Let him cry 'Praise and glory on his head!'
        For forth he goes and visits all his host,
        Bids them good morrow with a modest smile,
        And calls them brothers, friends and countrymen.
35   Upon his royal face there is no note
        How dread an army hath enrounded him,
        Nor doth he dedicate one jot of colour
        Unto the weary and all-watched night,
        But freshly looks and overbears attaint
40   With cheerful semblance and sweet majesty,
        That every wretch, pining and pale before,
        Beholding him plucks comfort from his looks.
        A largess universal, like the sun,
        His liberal eye doth give to every one,
45   Thawing cold fear, that mean and gentle all
        Behold, as may unworthiness define,
        A little touch of Harry in the night.
        And so our scene must to the battle fly,
        Where – oh for pity! – we shall much disgrace
50   With four or five most vile and ragged foils
        Right ill-disposed in brawl ridiculous
        The name of Agincourt. Yet sit and see,
        Minding true things by what their mockeries be. *Exit.*

4.1   *Enter the* KING *and* GLOUCESTER,
                 meeting BEDFORD.

KING Gloucester, 'tis true that we are in great danger;
      The greater therefore should our courage be. –
      Good morrow, brother Bedford. God Almighty!
      There is some soul of goodness in things evil,
      Would men observingly distil it out: 5
      For our bad neighbour makes us early stirrers,
      Which is both healthful and good husbandry.
      Besides, they are our outward consciences
      And preachers to us all, admonishing
      That we should dress us fairly for our end.   10
      Thus may we gather honey from the weed
      And make a moral of the devil himself.

                Enter ERPINGHAM.

      Good morrow, old Sir Thomas Erpingham.
      A good soft pillow for that good white head
      Were better than a churlish turf of France.   15
ERPINGHAM
      Not so, my liege, this lodging likes me better,
      Since I may say 'Now lie I like a king.'
KING 'Tis good for men to love their present pains
      Upon example: so the spirit is eased,
      And when the mind is quickened, out of doubt   20
      The organs, though defunct and dead before,
      Break up their drowsy grave and newly move
      With casted slough and fresh legerity.
      Lend me thy cloak, Sir Thomas. – Brothers both,
      Commend me to the princes in our camp;   25
      Do my good morrow to them, and anon
      Desire them all to my pavilion.
GLOUCESTER   We shall, my liege.
ERPINGHAM   Shall I attend your grace?
KING   No, my good knight;
      Go with my brothers to my lords of England.   30
      I and my bosom must debate awhile,
      And then I would no other company.
ERPINGHAM
      The Lord in heaven bless thee, noble Harry!
                          Exeunt all but the King.
KING God-a-mercy, old heart, thou speak'st cheerfully.

                Enter PISTOL.

PISTOL   Che vous là?   35
KING   A friend.
PISTOL   Discuss unto me, art thou officer,
      Or art thou base, common and popular?
KING   I am a gentleman of a company.
PISTOL   Trail'st thou the puissant pike?   40
KING   Even so. What are you?
PISTOL   As good a gentleman as the Emperor.
KING   Then you are a better than the King.
PISTOL   The King's a bawcock and a heart of gold,
      A lad of life, an imp of Fame,   45

Of parents good, of fist most valiant.
I kiss his dirty shoe, and from heart-string
I love the lovely bully. What is thy name?

KING Harry le Roy.

PISTOL Le Roy?
A Cornish name: art thou of Cornish crew?

KING No, I am a Welshman.

PISTOL Know'st thou Fluellen?

KING Yes.

PISTOL Tell him I'll knock his leek about his pate
Upon Saint Davy's day.

KING Do not you wear your dagger in your cap that day,
lest he knock that about yours.

PISTOL Art thou his friend?

KING And his kinsman too.

PISTOL The *fico* for thee then!

KING I thank you. God be with you!

PISTOL My name is Pistol called.   *Exit.*

KING It sorts well with your fierceness.

Enter FLUELLEN *and* GOWER, *separately.*

GOWER Captain Fluellen!

FLUELLEN 'So! In the name of Jesu Christ, speak
fewer. It is the greatest admiration in the universal
world when the true and anchient prerogatifs and laws
of the wars is not kept. If you would take the pains but
to examine the wars of Pompey the Great you shall
find, I warrant you, that there is no tiddle-taddle nor
pibble-pabble in Pompey's camp. I warrant you, you
shall find the ceremonies of the wars, and the cares of
it, and the forms of it, and the sobriety of it, and the
modesty of it, to be otherwise.

GOWER Why, the enemy is loud; you hear him all night.

FLUELLEN If the enemy is an ass and a fool and a
prating coxcomb, is it meet, think you, that we should
also, look you, be an ass and a fool and a prating
coxcomb, in your own conscience now?

GOWER I will speak lower.

FLUELLEN I pray you and beseech you that you will.

Exeunt Gower and Fluellen.

KING Though it appear a little out of fashion,
There is much care and valour in this Welshman.

Enter three Soldiers, JOHN BATES,
ALEXANDER COURT *and*
MICHAEL WILLIAMS.

COURT Brother John Bates, is not that the morning
which breaks yonder?

BATES I think it be; but we have no great cause to desire
the approach of day.

WILLIAMS We see yonder the beginning of the day, but I
think we shall never see the end of it. – Who goes there?

KING A friend.

WILLIAMS Under what captain serve you?

KING Under Sir Thomas Erpingham.

WILLIAMS A good old commander and a most kind
gentleman. I pray you, what thinks he of our estate?

KING Even as men wrecked upon a sand, that look to be
washed off the next tide.

BATES He hath not told his thought to the King?

KING No, nor it is not meet he should. For though I
speak it to you, I think the King is but a man, as I am:
the violet smells to him as it doth to me; the element
shows to him as it doth to me; all his senses have but
human conditions; his ceremonies laid by, in his
nakedness he appears but a man; and though his
affections are higher mounted than ours, yet when they
stoop they stoop with the like wing. Therefore when he
sees reason of fears as we do, his fears, out of doubt, be
of the same relish as ours are. Yet, in reason, no man
should possess him with any appearance of fear, lest
he, by showing it, should dishearten his army.

BATES He may show what outward courage he will, but
I believe, as cold a night as 'tis, he could wish himself
in Thames up to the neck; and so I would he were, and
I by him, at all adventures, so we were quit here.

KING By my troth, I will speak my conscience of the
King. I think he would not wish himself anywhere but
where he is.

BATES Then I would he were here alone; so should he be
sure to be ransomed, and a many poor men's lives saved.

KING I dare say you love him not so ill to wish him here
alone, howsoever you speak this to feel other men's
minds. Methinks I could not die anywhere so contented
as in the King's company, his cause being just and his
quarrel honourable.

WILLIAMS That's more than we know.

BATES Ay, or more than we should seek after, for we
know enough if we know we are the King's subjects. If
his cause be wrong, our obedience to the King wipes
the crime of it out of us.

WILLIAMS But if the cause be not good, the King
himself hath a heavy reckoning to make when all those
legs and arms and heads chopped off in a battle shall
join together at the latter day and cry all 'We died at
such a place', some swearing, some crying for a
surgeon, some upon their wives left poor behind them,
some upon the debts they owe, some upon their
children rawly left. I am afeard there are few die well
that die in a battle, for how can they charitably dispose
of anything when blood is their argument? Now if
these men do not die well it will be a black matter for
the King, that led them to it, who to disobey were
against all proportion of subjection.

KING So if a son that is by his father sent about
merchandise do sinfully miscarry upon the sea, the
imputation of his wickedness, by your rule, should be
imposed upon his father that sent him; or if a servant,
under his master's command transporting a sum of
money, be assailed by robbers and die in many
irreconciled iniquities, you may call the business of the
master the author of the servant's damnation. But this
is not so: the King is not bound to answer the particular
endings of his soldiers, the father of his son, nor the

master of his servant; for they purpose not their death
when they purpose their services. Besides, there is no
155 king, be his cause never so spotless, if it come to the
arbitrement of swords, can try it out with all unspotted
soldiers. Some, peradventure, have on them the guilt of
premeditated and contrived murder, some of beguiling
virgins with the broken seals of perjury, some, making
160 the wars their bulwark, that have before gored the
gentle bosom of peace with pillage and robbery. Now if
these men have defeated the law and outrun native
punishment, though they can outstrip men, they have
no wings to fly from God. War is his beadle, war is his
165 vengeance; so that here men are punished for before
breach of the King's laws in now the King's quarrel.
Where they feared the death they have borne life away,
and where they would be safe they perish. Then if they
die unprovided, no more is the King guilty of their
170 damnation than he was before guilty of those impieties
for the which they are now visited. Every subject's duty
is the King's, but every subject's soul is his own.
Therefore should every soldier in the wars do as every
sick man in his bed, wash every mote out of his
175 conscience; and dying so, death is to him advantage; or
not dying, the time was blessedly lost wherein such
preparation was gained; and in him that escapes, it
were not sin to think that, making God so free an offer,
he let him outlive that day to see his greatness and to
180 teach others how they should prepare.

WILLIAMS 'Tis certain, every man that dies ill, the ill
upon his own head; the King is not to answer it.

BATES   I do not desire he should answer for me, and yet
I determine to fight lustily for him.

185 KING   I myself heard the King say he would not be
ransomed.

WILLIAMS   Ay, he said so to make us fight cheerfully;
but when our throats are cut he may be ransomed and
we ne'er the wiser.

190 KING   If I live to see it, I will never trust his word after.

WILLIAMS   You pay him then! That's a perilous shot out
of an elder-gun that a poor and a private displeasure
can do against a monarch. You may as well go about to
turn the sun to ice with fanning in his face with a
195 peacock's feather. You'll never trust his word after!
Come, 'tis a foolish saying.

KING   Your reproof is something too round; I should be
angry with you if the time were convenient.

WILLIAMS   Let it be a quarrel between us, if you live.

200 KING   I embrace it.

WILLIAMS   How shall I know thee again?

KING   Give me any gage of thine and I will wear it in my
bonnet. Then if ever thou dar'st acknowledge it I will
make it my quarrel.

205 WILLIAMS   Here's my glove. Give me another of thine.

KING   There. [*They exchange gloves.*]

WILLIAMS   This will I also wear in my cap. If ever thou
come to me and say after tomorrow 'This is my glove',
by this hand I will take thee a box on the ear.

210 KING   If ever I live to see it I will challenge it.

WILLIAMS   Thou dar'st as well be hanged.

KING   Well, I will do it, though I take thee in the King's
company.

WILLIAMS   Keep thy word. Fare thee well.

215 BATES   Be friends, you English fools, be friends! We have
French quarrels enough, if you could tell how to reckon.

KING   Indeed, the French may lay twenty French
crowns to one they will beat us, for they bear them on
their shoulders, but it is no English treason to cut
220 French crowns, and tomorrow the King himself will be
a clipper.   *Exeunt Soldiers.*

Upon the King! 'Let us our lives, our souls,
Our debts, our careful wives,
Our children and our sins lay on the King!'
225 We must bear all. O hard condition,
Twin-born with greatness, subject to the breath
Of every fool whose sense no more can feel
But his own wringing! What infinite heart's ease
Must kings neglect that private men enjoy!
230 And what have kings that privates have not too,
Save ceremony, save general ceremony?
And what art thou, thou idol ceremony?
What kind of god art thou, that suffer'st more
Of mortal griefs than do thy worshippers?
235 What are thy rents, what are thy comings-in?
O ceremony, show me but thy worth!
What is thy soul, O adoration?
Art thou aught else but place, degree and form,
Creating awe and fear in other men,
240 Wherein thou art less happy, being feared,
Than they in fearing?
What drink'st thou oft, instead of homage sweet,
But poisoned flattery? O be sick, great greatness,
And bid thy ceremony give thee cure!
245 Think'st thou the fiery fever will go out
With titles blown from adulation?
Will it give place to flexure and low bending?
Canst thou, when thou command'st the beggar's knee,
Command the health of it? No, thou proud dream
250 That play'st so subtly with a king's repose,
I am a king that find thee, and I know
'Tis not the balm, the sceptre and the ball,
The sword, the mace, the crown imperial,
The intertissued robe of gold and pearl,
255 The farced title running 'fore the king,
The throne he sits on, nor the tide of pomp
That beats upon the high shore of this world,
No, not all these, thrice-gorgeous ceremony,
Not all these, laid in bed majestical,
260 Can sleep so soundly as the wretched slave,
Who with a body filled and vacant mind
Gets him to rest, crammed with distressful bread:
Never sees horrid night, the child of hell,
But like a lackey from the rise to set
265 Sweats in the eye of Phoebus, and all night
Sleeps in Elysium; next day after dawn

Doth rise and help Hyperion to his horse,
And follows so the ever-running year
With profitable labour to his grave.
70 And but for ceremony such a wretch,
Winding up days with toil and nights with sleep,
Had the fore-hand and vantage of a king.
The slave, a member of the country's peace,
Enjoys it, but in gross brain little wots
75 What watch the King keeps to maintain the peace,
Whose hours the peasant best advantages.

Enter ERPINGHAM.

ERPINGHAM
My lord, your nobles, jealous of your absence,
Seek through your camp to find you.
KING   Good old knight,
Collect them all together at my tent.
I'll be before thee.
80 ERPINGHAM   I shall do't, my lord.   *Exit.*
KING [*Kneels.*]
O God of battles, steel my soldiers' hearts;
Possess them not with fear. Take from them now
The sense of reckoning, if th'opposed numbers
Pluck their hearts from them. Not today, O Lord,
85 O not today, think not upon the fault
My father made in compassing the crown.
I Richard's body have interred new,
And on it have bestowed more contrite tears
Than from it issued forced drops of blood.
90 Five hundred poor I have in yearly pay,
Who twice a day their withered hands hold up
Toward heaven to pardon blood; and I have built
Two chantries, where the sad and solemn priests
Sing still for Richard's soul. More will I do,
95 Though all that I can do is nothing worth,
Since that my penitence comes after all,
Imploring pardon.
GLOUCESTER [*within*] My liege!
KING [*Rises.*]   My brother Gloucester's voice?

Enter GLOUCESTER.

I know thy errand, I will go with thee.
The day, my friends and all things stay for me. *Exeunt.*

4.2   *Enter the* DAUPHIN, ORLEANS
              and RAMBURES.

ORLEANS
The sun doth gild our armour; up, my lords!
DAUPHIN *Monte à cheval!* My horse, *varlet laquais*, ha!
ORLEANS O brave spirit!
DAUPHIN *Via, les eaux et terre!*
ORLEANS *Rien puis? L'air et feu?*
DAUPHIN *Cieux*, cousin Orleans!

Enter CONSTABLE.

              Now, my lord Constable!

CONSTABLE
Hark, how our steeds for present service neigh!
DAUPHIN
Mount them and make incision in their hides,
That their hot blood may spin in English eyes
And dout them with superfluous courage, ha!   10
RAMBURES
What, will you have them weep our horses' blood?
How shall we then behold their natural tears?

Enter Messenger.

MESSENGER
The English are embattled, you French peers.
                                                  Exit.
CONSTABLE
To horse, you gallant princes, straight to horse!
Do but behold yon poor and starved band,   15
And your fair show shall suck away their souls,
Leaving them but the shales and husks of men.
There is not work enough for all our hands,
Scarce blood enough in all their sickly veins
To give each naked curtle-axe a stain   20
That our French gallants shall today draw out
And sheathe for lack of sport. Let us but blow on them,
The vapour of our valour will o'erturn them.
'Tis positive 'gainst all exceptions, lords,
That our superfluous lackeys and our peasants   25
Who in unnecessary action swarm
About our squares of battle were enough
To purge this field of such a hilding foe,
Though we upon this mountain's basis by
Took stand for idle speculation: 30
But that our honours must not. What's to say?
A very little little let us do,
And all is done. Then let the trumpets sound
The tucket sonance and the note to mount,
For our approach shall so much dare the field   35
That England shall couch down in fear and yield.

Enter GRANDPRÉ.

GRANDPRÉ
Why do you stay so long, my lords of France?
Yon island carrions, desperate of their bones,
Ill-favouredly become the morning field.
Their ragged curtains poorly are let loose,   40
And our air shakes them passing scornfully.
Big Mars seems bankrupt in their beggared host
And faintly through a rusty beaver peeps.
The horsemen sit like fixed candlesticks
With torch-staves in their hand, and their poor jades   45
Lob down their heads, drooping the hides and hips,
The gum down-roping from their pale-dead eyes,
And in their palled dull mouths the gimmaled bit
Lies foul with chewed grass, still and motionless.
And their executors, the knavish crows,   50
Fly o'er them all, impatient for their hour.
Description cannot suit itself in words

To demonstrate the life of such a battle
In life so lifeless as it shows itself.

CONSTABLE

55   They have said their prayers, and they stay for death.

DAUPHIN

Shall we go send them dinners and fresh suits
And give their fasting horses provender,
And after fight with them?

CONSTABLE   I stay but for my guidon. To the field!

60   I will the banner from a trumpet take
And use it for my haste. Come, come away!
The sun is high and we outwear the day.   *Exeunt.*

4.3   *Enter* GLOUCESTER, BEDFORD, EXETER,
        ERPINGHAM *with all his host*, SALISBURY *and*
                   WESTMORLAND.

GLOUCESTER   Where is the King?

BEDFORD

The King himself is rode to view their battle.

WESTMORLAND

Of fighting men they have full threescore thousand.

EXETER

There's five to one; besides, they all are fresh.

SALISBURY

5   God's arm strike with us! 'Tis a fearful odds.
God bye you, princes all; I'll to my charge.
If we no more meet till we meet in heaven,
Then joyfully, my noble lord of Bedford,
My dear lord Gloucester, and my good lord Exeter,
10   And my kind kinsman, warriors all, adieu.

BEDFORD

Farewell, good Salisbury, and good luck go with thee.

EXETER   Farewell, kind lord. Fight valiantly today.
And yet I do thee wrong to mind thee of it,
For thou art framed of the firm truth of valour.
                              Exit Salisbury.

15 BEDFORD   He is as full of valour as of kindness,
Princely in both.

                 Enter the KING.

WESTMORLAND   O that we now had here
But one ten thousand of those men in England
That do no work today!

KING   What's he that wishes so?
My cousin Westmorland? No, my fair cousin:
20   If we are marked to die, we are enough
To do our country loss, and if to live,
The fewer men, the greater share of honour.
God's will, I pray thee wish not one man more.
By Jove, I am not covetous for gold,
25   Nor care I who doth feed upon my cost;
It earns me not if men my garments wear:
Such outward things dwell not in my desires.
But if it be a sin to covet honour

I am the most offending soul alive.
No, faith, my coz, wish not a man from England.   30
God's peace, I would not lose so great an honour
As one man more, methinks, would share from me,
For the best hope I have. O do not wish one more!
Rather proclaim it, Westmorland, through my host,
That he which hath no stomach to this fight,   35
Let him depart; his passport shall be made
And crowns for convoy put into his purse.
We would not die in that man's company
That fears his fellowship to die with us.
This day is called the feast of Crispian.   40
He that outlives this day and comes safe home
Will stand a-tiptoe when this day is named
And rouse him at the name of Crispian.
He that shall see this day and live old age
Will yearly on the vigil feast his neighbours,   45
And say 'Tomorrow is Saint Crispian.'
Then will he strip his sleeve and show his scars,
And say 'These wounds I had on Crispin's day.'
Old men forget; yet all shall be forgot
But he'll remember, with advantages,   50
What feats he did that day. Then shall our names,
Familiar in his mouth as household words,
Harry the King, Bedford and Exeter,
Warwick and Talbot, Salisbury and Gloucester,
Be in their flowing cups freshly remembered.   55
This story shall the good man teach his son,
And Crispin Crispian shall ne'er go by
From this day to the ending of the world
But we in it shall be remembered,
We few, we happy few, we band of brothers.   60
For he today that sheds his blood with me
Shall be my brother; be he ne'er so vile,
This day shall gentle his condition.
And gentlemen in England now abed
Shall think themselves accursed they were not here,   65
And hold their manhoods cheap whiles any speaks
That fought with us upon Saint Crispin's day.

                 Enter SALISBURY.

SALISBURY

My sovereign lord, bestow yourself with speed.
The French are bravely in their battles set
And will with all expedience charge on us.   70

KING   All things are ready, if our minds be so.

WESTMORLAND

Perish the man whose mind is backward now!

KING

Thou dost not wish more help from England, coz?

WESTMORLAND

God's will, my liege, would you and I alone,
Without more help, could fight this royal battle!   75

KING

Why, now thou hast unwished five thousand men,

Which likes me better than to wish us one.
You know your places. God be with you all!

Tucket. Enter MONTJOY.

MONTJOY
    Once more I come to know of thee, King Harry,   80
    If for thy ransom thou wilt now compound,
    Before thy most assured overthrow:
    For certainly thou art so near the gulf
    Thou needs must be englutted. Besides, in mercy,
    The Constable desires thee thou wilt mind   85
    Thy followers of repentance, that their souls
    May make a peaceful and a sweet retire
    From off these fields where, wretches, their poor
       bodies
    Must lie and fester.
KING   Who hath sent thee now?
MONTJOY   The Constable of France.
KING   I pray thee bear my former answer back: 90
    Bid them achieve me and then sell my bones.
    Good God, why should they mock poor fellows thus?
    The man that once did sell the lion's skin
    While the beast lived, was killed with hunting him.
    A many of our bodies shall no doubt   95
    Find native graves, upon the which, I trust,
    Shall witness live in brass of this day's work.
    And those that leave their valiant bones in France,
    Dying like men, though buried in your dunghills,
    They shall be famed, for there the sun shall greet them,   100
    And draw their honours reeking up to heaven,
    Leaving their earthly parts to choke your clime,
    The smell whereof shall breed a plague in France.
    Mark then abounding valour in our English,
    That being dead, like to the bullets crazing,   105
    Break out into a second course of mischief,
    Killing in relapse of mortality.
    Let me speak proudly. Tell the Constable
    We are but warriors for the working-day;
    Our gayness and our gilt are all besmirched   110
    With rainy marching in the painful field.
    There's not a piece of feather in our host
    (Good argument, I hope, we will not fly),
    And time hath worn us into slovenry.
    But by the mass, our hearts are in the trim,   115
    And my poor soldiers tell me yet ere night
    They'll be in fresher robes, or they will pluck
    The gay new coats o'er the French soldiers' heads
    And turn them out of service. If they do this,
    As, if God please, they shall, my ransom then   120
    Will soon be levied. Herald, save thou thy labour:
    Come thou no more for ransom, gentle herald.
    They shall have none, I swear, but these my joints,
    Which if they have as I will leave 'em them
    Shall yield them little, tell the Constable.   125
MONTJOY   I shall, King Harry. And so fare thee well:
    Thou never shalt hear herald any more.   *Exit.*

KING
    I fear thou wilt once more come again for a ransom.

Enter YORK.

YORK   My lord, most humbly on my knee I beg
    The leading of the vaward.   130
KING
    Take it, brave York. – Now, soldiers, march away,
    And how thou pleasest, God, dispose the day!   *Exeunt.*

4.4   *Alarum. Excursions. Enter* PISTOL,
                FRENCH SOLDIER *and* BOY.

PISTOL   Yield, cur!
FRENCH SOLDIER   *Je pense que vous êtes le gentilhomme*
    de bonne qualité.
PISTOL   *Qualité? 'Caleno custore me'!*
    Art thou a gentleman? What is thy name? Discuss.   5
FRENCH SOLDIER   *O Seigneur Dieu!*
PISTOL
    O Signieur Dew should be a gentleman. –
    Perpend my words, O Signieur Dew, and mark:
    O Signieur Dew, thou diest on point of fox,
    Except, O Signieur, thou do give to me   10
    Egregious ransom.
FRENCH SOLDIER   *O prenez miséricorde! Ayez pitié de*
    moi!
PISTOL   Moy shall not serve, I will have forty moys,
    Or I will fetch thy rim out at thy throat   15
    In drops of crimson blood.
FRENCH SOLDIER   *Est-il impossible d'échapper la force de*
    ton bras?
PISTOL   Brass, cur?
    Thou damned and luxurious mountain goat,   20
    Offer'st me brass?
FRENCH SOLDIER   *O pardonnez-moi!*
PISTOL   Say'st thou me so? Is that a ton of moys?
    Come hither, boy;
    Ask me this slave in French what is his name.   25
BOY   *Écoutez. Comment êtes-vous appelé?*
FRENCH SOLDIER   *Monsieur le Fer.*
BOY   He says his name is Master Fer.
PISTOL   Master Fer? I'll fer him, and firk him, and
    ferret him. Discuss the same in French unto him.   30
BOY   I do not know the French for fer, and ferret and firk.
PISTOL   Bid him prepare, for I will cut his throat.
FRENCH SOLDIER   *Que dit-il, monsieur?*
BOY   *Il me commande à vous dire que vous faites vous prêt,*
    car ce soldat ici est disposé tout à cette heure de couper   35
    votre gorge.
PISTOL   Owy, cuppele gorge, permafoy,
    Peasant, unless thou give me crowns, brave crowns;
    Or mangled shalt thou be by this my sword.
FRENCH SOLDIER   *O je vous supplie pour l'amour de Dieu*   40
    me pardonner! Je suis le gentilhomme de bonne maison:
    gardez ma vie, et je vous donnerai deux cents écus.
PISTOL   What are his words?

BOY   He prays you to save his life: he is a gentleman of
45   a good house, and for his ransom he will give you two
        hundred crowns.
PISTOL   Tell him
        My fury shall abate, and I the crowns will take.
FRENCH SOLDIER   *Petit monsieur, que dit-il?*
50 BOY   *Encore qu'il est contre son jurement de pardonner aucun*
        prisonnier, néanmoins, pour les écus que vous lui ici promettez,
        il est content à vous donner la liberté, le franchisement.
FRENCH SOLDIER   [*to Pistol*]   *Sur mes genoux je vous*
        donne mille remerciements, et je m'estime heureux que j'ai
55   *tombé entre les mains d'un chevalier, comme je pense, le*
        plus brave, vaillant et très distingué seigneur d'Angleterre.
PISTOL   Expound unto me, boy.
BOY   He gives you upon his knees a thousand thanks,
        and he esteems himself happy that he hath fallen into
60   the hands of one, as he thinks, the most brave, valorous
        and thrice-worthy *seigneur* of England.
PISTOL   As I suck blood, I will some mercy show.
        Follow me.
BOY   *Suivez-vous le grand capitaine.*
                        Exeunt Pistol and French Soldier.
65   I did never know so full a voice issue from so empty a
        heart; but the saying is true, 'The empty vessel makes
        the greatest sound.' Bardolph and Nym had ten times
        more valour than this roaring devil i'th' old play, that
        every vice may pare his nails with a wooden dagger,
70   and they are both hanged, and so would this be if he
        durst steal anything adventurously. I must stay with
        the lackeys with the luggage of our camp; the French
        might have a good prey of us if he knew of it, for there
        is none to guard it but boys.   *Exit.*

4.5   *Enter* CONSTABLE, ORLEANS, BOURBON,
        the DAUPHIN *and* RAMBURES.

CONSTABLE   *O diable!*
ORLEANS   *O Seigneur! Le jour est perdu, tout est perdu!*
DAUPHIN   *Mort de ma vie*, all is confounded, all!
        Mortal reproach and everlasting shame
5   Sits mocking in our plumes. *O méchante Fortune!*
                                    [*A short alarum*]
        Do not run away.
CONSTABLE   Why, all our ranks are broke.
DAUPHIN   O perdurable shame! Let's stab ourselves.
        Be these the wretches that we played at dice for?
ORLEANS   Is this the king we sent to for his ransom?
BOURBON
        Shame, and eternal shame, nothing but
10   shame!
        Let us die instant. Once more back again,
        And he that will not follow Bourbon now,
        Let him go home and with his cap in hand
        Like a base pandar hold the chamber-door
15   Whilst by a slave no gentler than my dog
        His fairest daughter is contaminated.

CONSTABLE
        Disorder, that hath spoiled us, friend us now!
        Let us on heaps go offer up our lives.
ORLEANS   We are enough yet living in the field
        To smother up the English in our throngs   20
        If any order might be thought upon.
BOURBON   The devil take order now! I'll to the throng.
        Let life be short, else shame will be too long.   *Exeunt.*

4.6   *Alarum. Enter the* KING *and his train,*
                        with Prisoners.

KING
        Well have we done, thrice-valiant countrymen,
        But all's not done: yet keep the French the field.
                        Exeunt Soldiers and Prisoners.

                Enter EXETER.

EXETER
        The Duke of York commends him to your majesty.
KING   Lives he, good uncle? Thrice within this hour
        I saw him down, thrice up again and fighting;   5
        From helmet to the spur all blood he was.
EXETER   In which array, brave soldier, doth he lie,
        Larding the plain; and by his bloody side,
        Yoke-fellow to his honour-owing wounds,
        The noble Earl of Suffolk also lies.   10
        Suffolk first died, and York, all haggled over,
        Comes to him, where in gore he lay insteeped,
        And takes him by the beard, kisses the gashes
        That bloodily did yawn upon his face.
        He cries aloud 'Tarry, my cousin Suffolk!   15
        My soul shall thine keep company to heaven.
        Tarry, sweet soul, for mine, then fly abreast,
        As in this glorious and well-foughten field
        We kept together in our chivalry.'
        Upon these words I came and cheered him up;   20
        He smiled me in the face, raught me his hand,
        And with a feeble gripe says 'Dear my lord,
        Commend my service to my sovereign.'
        So did he turn, and over Suffolk's neck
        He threw his wounded arm and kissed his lips,   25
        And so, espoused to death, with blood he sealed
        A testament of noble-ending love.
        The pretty and sweet manner of it forced
        Those waters from me which I would have stopped,
        But I had not so much of man in me,   30
        And all my mother came into mine eyes
        And gave me up to tears.
KING   I blame you not,
        For hearing this I must perforce compound
        With my full eyes, or they will issue too.   [*Alarum*]
        But hark, what new alarum is this same?   35
        The French have reinforced their scattered men.
        Then every soldier kill his prisoners!
        Give the word through.   *Exeunt.*

4.7   *Enter* FLUELLEN *and* GOWER.

FLUELLEN   Kill the poys and the luggage! 'Tis expressly against the law of arms. 'Tis as arrant a piece of knavery, mark you now, as can be offert, in your conscience now, is it not?

GOWER   'Tis certain there's not a boy left alive, and the cowardly rascals that ran from the battle ha' done this slaughter. Besides, they have burned and carried away all that was in the King's tent, wherefore the King most worthily hath caused every soldier to cut his prisoner's throat. O, 'tis a gallant king!

FLUELLEN   Ay, he was porn at Monmouth, Captain Gower. What call you the town's name where Alexander the Pig was born?

GOWER   Alexander the Great.

FLUELLEN   Why, I pray you, is not pig great? The pig, or the great, or the mighty, or the huge, or the magnanimous, are all one reckonings, save the phrase is a little variations.

GOWER   I think Alexander the Great was born in Macedon: his father was called Philip of Macedon, as I take it.

FLUELLEN   I think it is in Macedon where Alexander is porn. I tell you, Captain, if you look in the maps of the world, I warrant you shall find, in the comparisons between Macedon and Monmouth, that the situations, look you, is both alike. There is a river in Macedon, and there is also moreover a river at Monmouth. It is called Wye at Monmouth, but it is out of my prains what is the name of the other river; but 'tis all one, 'tis alike as my fingers is to my fingers, and there is salmons in both. If you mark Alexander's life well, Harry of Monmouth's life is come after it indifferent well, for there is figures in all things. Alexander, God knows, and you know, in his rages, and his furies, and his wraths, and his cholers, and his moods, and his displeasures, and his indignations, and also being a little intoxicate in his prains, did in his ales and his angers, look you, kill his best friend Clytus.

GOWER   Our king is not like him in that: he never killed any of his friends.

FLUELLEN   It is not well done, mark you now, to take the tales out of my mouth ere it is made an end and finished. I speak but in the figures and comparisons of it. As Alexander killed his friend Clytus, being in his ales and his cups, so also Harry Monmouth, being in his right wits and his good judgements, turned away the fat knight with the great-belly doublet: he was full of jests, and gipes, and knaveries, and mocks; I have forgot his name.

GOWER   Sir John Falstaff.

FLUELLEN   That is he. I'll tell you, there is good men porn at Monmouth.

GOWER   Here comes his majesty.

Alarum. Enter KING HARRY *with* BOURBON *as his prisoner,* WARWICK, GLOUCESTER, EXETER, *a Herald and others, with Prisoners. Flourish.*

KING   I was not angry since I came to France   55
Until this instant. Take a trumpet, herald;
Ride thou unto the horsemen on yon hill.
If they will fight with us bid them come down,
Or void the field: they do offend our sight.
If they'll do neither, we will come to them   60
And make them skirr away as swift as stones
Enforced from the old Assyrian slings.
Besides, we'll cut the throats of those we have,
And not a man of them that we shall take
Shall taste our mercy. Go and tell them so.   65

Enter MONTJOY.

EXETER
Here comes the herald of the French, my liege.
GLOUCESTER
His eyes are humbler than they used to be.
KING
How now, what means this, herald? Know'st thou not
That I have fined these bones of mine for ransom?
Com'st thou again for ransom?
MONTJOY   No, great King: 70
I come to thee for charitable licence
That we may wander o'er this bloody field
To look our dead and then to bury them;
To sort our nobles from our common men.
For many of our princes – woe the while! –   75
Lie drowned and soaked in mercenary blood;
So do our vulgar drench their peasant limbs
In blood of princes; and their wounded steeds
Fret fetlock-deep in gore and with wild rage
Yerk out their armed heels at their dead masters,   80
Killing them twice. O give us leave, great King,
To view the field in safety and dispose
Of their dead bodies.
KING   I tell thee truly, herald,
I know not if the day be ours or no,
For yet a many of your horsemen peer   85
And gallop o'er the field.
MONTJOY   The day is yours.
KING   Praised be God, and not our strength, for it!
What is this castle called that stands hard by?
MONTJOY   They call it Agincourt.
KING   Then call we this the field of Agincourt,   90
Fought on the day of Crispin Crispian.
FLUELLEN   Your grandfather of famous memory, an't please your majesty, and your great-uncle Edward the Plack Prince of Wales, as I have read in the chronicles, fought a most prave pattle here in France.   95
KING   They did, Fluellen.
FLUELLEN   Your majesty says very true. If your majesty is remembered of it, the Welshmen did good service in

100 a garden where leeks did grow, wearing leeks in their
Monmouth caps, which your majesty know to this
hour is an honourable badge of the service; and I do
believe your majesty takes no scorn to wear the leek
upon Saint Tavy's day.

KING   I wear it for a memorable honour,

105   For I am Welsh, you know, good countryman.

FLUELLEN   All the water in Wye cannot wash your
majesty's Welsh plood out of your pody, I can tell you
that. God pless it and preserve it, as long as it pleases
his grace, and his majesty too!

110 KING   Thanks, good my countryman.

FLUELLEN   By Jeshu, I am your majesty's countryman,
I care not who know it. I will confess it to all the world:
I need not to be ashamed of your majesty, praised be
God, so long as your majesty is an honest man.

KING
God keep me so!

Enter WILLIAMS.

115   Our herald go with him:
Bring me just notice of the numbers dead
On both our parts.
Exeunt Montjoy, Gower and the English Herald.
Call yonder fellow hither.

EXETER   Soldier, you must come to the King.

KING   Soldier, why wear'st thou that glove in thy cap?

120 WILLIAMS   An't please your majesty, 'tis the gage of one
that I should fight withal, if he be alive.

KING   An Englishman?

WILLIAMS   An't please your majesty, a rascal that
swaggered with me last night, who if 'a live and ever

125   dare to challenge this glove, I have sworn to take him a
box o'th' ear; or if I can see my glove in his cap, which
he swore as he was a soldier he would wear if 'a lived, I
will strike it out soundly.

KING   What think you, Captain Fluellen, is it fit this

130   soldier keep his oath?

FLUELLEN   He is a craven and a villain else, an't please
your majesty, in my conscience.

KING   It may be his enemy is a gentleman of great sort,
quite from the answer of his degree.

135 FLUELLEN   Though he be as good a gentleman as the
devil is, as Lucifer and Belzebub himself, it is necessary,
look your grace, that he keep his vow and his oath. If he
be perjured, see you now, his reputation is as arrant a
villain and a jack-sauce as ever his black shoe trod upon

140   God's ground and his earth, in my conscience, la!

KING   Then keep thy vow, sirrah, when thou meet'st the
fellow.

WILLIAMS   So I will, my liege, as I live.

KING   Who serv'st thou under?

145 WILLIAMS   Under Captain Gower, my liege.

FLUELLEN   Gower is a good captain, and is good
knowledge and literature in the wars.

KING   Call him hither to me, soldier.

WILLIAMS   I will, my liege.   *Exit.*

150 KING   Here, Fluellen, wear thou this favour for me and
stick it in thy cap. When Alençon and myself were
down together I plucked this glove from his helm. If
any man challenge this he is a friend to Alençon and an
enemy to our person. If thou encounter any such,
155   apprehend him, an thou dost me love.

FLUELLEN   Your grace does me as great honours as can
be desired in the hearts of his subjects. I would fain see
the man that has but two legs that shall find himself
aggriefed at this glove, that is all; I would fain but see it
160   once, an't please God of his grace that I might.

KING   Know'st thou Gower?

FLUELLEN   He is my dear friend, an't please you.

KING   Pray thee go seek him and bring him to my tent.

FLUELLEN   I will fetch him.   *Exit.*

165 KING   My lord of Warwick and my brother Gloucester,
Follow Fluellen closely at the heels.
The glove which I have given him for a favour
May haply purchase him a box o'th' ear;
It is the soldier's. I by bargain should

170   Wear it myself. Follow, good cousin Warwick.
If that the soldier strike him – as I judge
By his blunt bearing he will keep his word –
Some sudden mischief may arise of it,
For I do know Fluellen valiant

175   And, touched with choler, hot as gunpowder,
And quickly will return an injury.
Follow, and see there be no harm between them. –
Go you with me, uncle of Exeter.   *Exeunt.*

4.8   *Enter* GOWER *and* WILLIAMS.

WILLIAMS   I warrant it is to knight you, Captain.

Enter FLUELLEN.

FLUELLEN   God's will and his pleasure, Captain, I
beseech you now, come apace to the King: there is
more good toward you, peradventure, than is in your
5   knowledge to dream of.

WILLIAMS   Sir, know you this glove?

FLUELLEN   Know the glove? I know the glove is a glove.

WILLIAMS   I know this, and thus I challenge it. [*Strikes
him.*]

FLUELLEN   'Sblood, an arrant traitor as any's in the
10   universal world, or in France, or in England!

GOWER   How now, sir, you villain!

WILLIAMS   Do you think I'll be forsworn?

FLUELLEN   Stand away, Captain Gower: I will give
treason his payment into plows, I warrant you.

15 WILLIAMS   I am no traitor.

FLUELLEN   That's a lie in thy throat.

Enter Soldiers.

I charge you in his majesty's name apprehend him,
he's a friend of the Duke Alençon's.

Enter WARWICK *and* GLOUCESTER.

WARWICK   How now, how now, what's the matter?

FLUELLEN My lord of Warwick, here is, praised be
God for it, a most contagious treason come to light,
look you, as you shall desire in a summer's day.

Enter the KING *and* EXETER.

Here is his majesty.

KING How now, what's the matter?

FLUELLEN My liege, here is a villain and a traitor that,
look your grace, has struck the glove which your
majesty is take out of the helmet of Alençon.

WILLIAMS My liege, this was my glove, here is the
fellow of it; and he that I gave it to in change promised
to wear it in his cap; I promised to strike him if he did.
I met this man with my glove in his cap, and I have
been as good as my word.

FLUELLEN Your majesty hear now, saving your
majesty's manhood, what an arrant, rascally, beggarly,
lousy knave it is. I hope your majesty is pear me
testimony, and witness, and avouchment that this is the
glove of Alençon that your majesty is give me, in your
conscience now.

KING Give me thy glove, soldier. Look, here is the
fellow of it.
'Twas I indeed thou promised'st to strike,
And thou hast given me most bitter terms.

FLUELLEN An't please your majesty, let his neck answer
for it, if there is any martial law in the world.

KING
How canst thou make me satisfaction?

WILLIAMS All offences, my lord, come from the heart:
never came any from mine that might offend your
majesty.

KING It was our self thou didst abuse.

WILLIAMS Your majesty came not like your self: you
appeared to me but as a common man – witness the
night, your garments, your lowliness; and what your
highness suffered under that shape, I beseech you take
it for your own fault and not mine, for had you been as
I took you for, I made no offence; therefore I beseech
your highness pardon me. [*Kneels.*]

KING [*Raises him.*]
Here, uncle Exeter, fill this glove with crowns
And give it to this fellow. – Keep it, fellow,
And wear it for an honour in thy cap
Till I do challenge it. – Give him the crowns. –
And Captain, you must needs be friends with him.

FLUELLEN By this day and this light, the fellow has
mettle enough in his belly. – Hold, there is twelve
pence for you, and I pray you to serve God, and keep
you out of prawls and prabbles, and quarrels and
dissensions, and I warrant you it is the better for you.

WILLIAMS I will none of your money.

FLUELLEN It is with a good will. I can tell you, it will
serve you to mend your shoes. Come, wherefore should
you be so pashful? Your shoes is not so good. 'Tis a
good shilling, I warrant you, or I will change it.

Enter Herald.

KING Now, herald, are the dead numbered?

HERALD
Here is the number of the slaughtered French.
[*Gives the King a paper.*]

KING What prisoners of good sort are taken, uncle?

EXETER Charles, Duke of Orleans, nephew to the King; 75
John, Duke of Bourbon, and Lord Boucicault.
Of other lords and barons, knights and squires,
Full fifteen hundred, besides common men.

KING
This note doth tell me of ten thousand French
That in the field lie slain. Of princes in this number 80
And nobles bearing banners, there lie dead
One hundred twenty-six. Added to these,
Of knights, esquires and gallant gentlemen,
Eight thousand and four hundred, of the which
Five hundred were but yesterday dubbed knights. 85
So that in these ten thousand they have lost
There are but sixteen hundred mercenaries;
The rest are princes, barons, lords, knights, squires
And gentlemen of blood and quality.
The names of those their nobles that lie dead: 90
Charles Delabreth, High Constable of France;
Jaques of Chatillon, Admiral of France;
The Master of the Crossbows, Lord Rambures;
Great Master of France, the brave Sir Guichard
    Dauphin;
John, Duke of Alençon; Anthony, Duke of Brabant, 95
The brother to the Duke of Burgundy;
And Edward, Duke of Bar: of lusty earls,
Grandpré and Roussi, Fauconbridge and Foix,
Beaumont and Marie, Vaudemont and Lestrelles.
Here was a royal fellowship of death. 100
Where is the number of our English dead?
[*Herald gives him another paper.*]
Edward the Duke of York; the Earl of Suffolk;
Sir Richard Keighley; Davy Gam, esquire;
None else of name, and of all other men
But five-and-twenty. O God, thy arm was here; 105
And not to us but to thy arm alone
Ascribe we all. When, without stratagem,
But in plain shock and even play of battle,
Was ever known so great and little loss
On one part and on th'other? Take it, God, 110
For it is none but thine.

EXETER   'Tis wonderful.

KING Come, go we in procession to the village,
And be it death proclaimed through our host
To boast of this, or take that praise from God
Which is his only. 115

FLUELLEN Is it not lawful, an't please your majesty, to
tell how many is killed?

KING Yes, Captain, but with this acknowledgement,
That God fought for us.

FLUELLEN Yes, in my conscience, he did us great good. 120

KING   Do we all holy rites.
Let there be sung *Non nobis* and *Te Deum*,
The dead with charity enclosed in clay,
And then to Calais, and to England then,
125   Where ne'er from France arrived more happy men.

Exeunt.

5.0   *Enter CHORUS.*

CHORUS
Vouchsafe to those that have not read the story
That I may prompt them; and of such as have,
I humbly pray them to admit th'excuse
Of time, of numbers and due course of things
5   Which cannot in their huge and proper life
Be here presented. Now we bear the King
Toward Calais: grant him there; there seen,
Heave him away upon your winged thoughts
Athwart the sea. Behold, the English beach
10   Pales in the flood with men, with wives and boys,
Whose shouts and claps outvoice the deep-mouthed sea,
Which like a mighty whiffler 'fore the King
Seems to prepare his way. So let him land,
And solemnly see him set on to London.
15   So swift a pace hath thought that even now
You may imagine him upon Blackheath,
Where that his lords desire him to have borne
His bruised helmet and his bended sword
Before him through the city. He forbids it,
20   Being free from vainness and self-glorious pride,
Giving full trophy, signal and ostent
Quite from himself to God. But now behold,
In the quick forge and working-house of thought,
How London doth pour out her citizens.
25   The Mayor and all his brethren in best sort,
Like to the senators of th'antique Rome
With the plebeians swarming at their heels,
Go forth and fetch their conquering Caesar in;
As, by a lower but as loving likelihood,
30   Were now the General of our gracious Empress,
As in good time he may, from Ireland coming,
Bringing rebellion broached on his sword,
How many would the peaceful city quit
To welcome him! Much more, and much more cause,
35   Did they this Harry. Now in London place him.
As yet the lamentation of the French
Invites the King of England's stay at home.
The Emperor's coming in behalf of France,
To order peace between them [
40   ] and omit
All the occurrences, whatever chanced,
Till Harry's back return again to France.
There must we bring him; and myself have played
The interim, by remembering you 'tis past.
45   Then brook abridgement and your eyes advance
After your thoughts straight back again to France.

Exit.

GOWER   Nay, that's right. But why wear you your leek
today? Saint Davy's day is past.
FLUELLEN   There is occasions and causes why and
wherefore in all things. I will tell you ass my friend,
Captain Gower. The rascally, scald, beggarly, lousy,   5
pragging knave Pistol, which you and yourself and all
the world know to be no petter than a fellow, look you
now, of no merits, he is come to me and prings me
pread and salt yesterday, look you, and bid me eat my
leek. It was in a place where I could not breed no   10
contention with him, but I will be so bold as to wear it
in my cap till I see him once again, and then I will tell
him a little piece of my desires.

Enter PISTOL.

GOWER   Why, here he comes, swelling like a turkey-cock.
FLUELLEN   'Tis no matter for his swellings nor his   15
turkey-cocks. – God pless you, Anchient Pistol, you
scurvy, lousy knave, God pless you!
PISTOL
Ha, art thou bedlam? Dost thou thirst, base Trojan,
To have me fold up Parca's fatal web?
Hence! I am qualmish at the smell of leek.   20
FLUELLEN   I peseech you heartily, scurvy, lousy knave,
at my desires, and my requests, and my petitions, to
eat, look you, this leek. Because, look you, you do not
love it, nor your affections and your appetites and your
digestions does not agree with it, I would desire you to   25
eat it.
PISTOL   Not for Cadwallader and all his goats.
FLUELLEN [*Strikes him with a cudgel.*]   There is one goat
for you. Will you be so good, scald knave, as eat it?
PISTOL   Base Trojan, thou shalt die.   30
FLUELLEN   You say very true, scald knave, when God's
will is. I will desire you to live in the meantime and eat
your victuals. [*Strikes him.*] Come, there is sauce for it.
You called me yesterday mountain-squire, but I will
make you today a squire of low degree. I pray you, fall   35
to; if you can mock a leek you can eat a leek.
GOWER   Enough, Captain, you have astonished him.
FLUELLEN   I say I will make him eat some part of my leek,
or I will peat his pate four days. – Bite, I pray you; it is
good for your green wound and your ploody coxcomb.   40
PISTOL   Must I bite?
FLUELLEN   Yes, certainly, and out of doubt and out of
question too, and ambiguities.
PISTOL   By this leek, I will most horribly revenge –
[*Fluellen threatens him.*] I eat and eat – I swear –   45
FLUELLEN   Eat, I pray you. Will you have some more
sauce to your leek? There is not enough leek to swear by.
PISTOL   Quiet thy cudgel, thou dost see I eat.
FLUELLEN   Much good do you, scald knave, heartily.
Nay, pray you, throw none away; the skin is good for   50
your broken coxcomb. When you take occasions to see
leeks hereafter, I pray you mock at 'em, that is all.

PISTOL   Good.

FLUELLEN   Ay, leeks is good. Hold you, there is a groat
to heal your pate.

PISTOL   Me a groat?

FLUELLEN   Yes, verily and in truth, you shall take it, or
I have another leek in my pocket which you shall eat.

PISTOL   I take thy groat in earnest of revenge.

FLUELLEN   If I owe you anything, I will pay you in
cudgels: you shall be a woodmonger, and buy nothing
of me but cudgels. God bye you, and keep you, and
heal your pate.   *Exit.*

PISTOL   All hell shall stir for this.

GOWER   Go, go, you are a counterfeit cowardly knave.
Will you mock at an ancient tradition, begun upon an
honourable respect and worn as a memorable trophy of
predeceased valour, and dare not avouch in your deeds
any of your words? I have seen you gleeking and galling
at this gentleman twice or thrice. You thought because
he could not speak English in the native garb he could
not therefore handle an English cudgel. You find it
otherwise, and henceforth let a Welsh correction teach
you a good English condition. Fare ye well.   *Exit.*

PISTOL
Doth Fortune play the huswife with me now?
News have I that my Nell is dead i'th' spital
Of malady of France,
And there my rendezvous is quite cut off.
Old I do wax, and from my weary limbs
Honour is cudgelled. Well, bawd I'll turn,
And something lean to cutpurse of quick hand.
To England will I steal, and there I'll steal;
And patches will I get unto these cudgelled scars,
And swear I got them in the Gallia wars.   *Exit.*

5.2   *Enter at one door* KING HENRY, EXETER,
BEDFORD, WARWICK *and other Lords*
(GLOUCESTER, WESTMORLAND, CLARENCE
and HUNTINGDON). *At another,* QUEEN
ISABEL, *the* FRENCH KING, KATHERINE,
ALICE, *the* Duke of BURGUNDY, *and
other French.*

KING
Peace to this meeting, wherefore we are met.
Unto our brother France and to our sister
Health and fair time of day; joy and good wishes
To our most fair and princely cousin Katherine;
And, as a branch and member of this royalty,
By whom this great assembly is contrived,
We do salute you, Duke of Burgundy;
And, princes French and peers, health to you all.

FRENCH KING
Right joyous are we to behold your face,
Most worthy brother England; fairly met.
So are you, princes English, every one.

QUEEN
So happy be the issue, brother England,

Of this good day and of this gracious meeting,
As we are now glad to behold your eyes,
Your eyes which hitherto have borne in them   15
Against the French that met them in their bent
The fatal balls of murdering basilisks.
The venom of such looks we fairly hope
Have lost their quality, and that this day
Shall change all griefs and quarrels into love.   20

KING   To cry amen to that, thus we appear.

QUEEN   You English princes all, I do salute you.

BURGUNDY
My duty to you both, on equal love,
Great Kings of France and England. That I have
    laboured
With all my wits, my pains and strong endeavours,   25
To bring your most imperial majesties
Unto this bar and royal interview
Your mightiness on both parts best can witness.
Since then my office hath so far prevailed
That face to face and royal eye to eye   30
You have congreeted, let it not disgrace me
If I demand before this royal view
What rub or what impediment there is
Why that the naked, poor and mangled peace,
Dear nurse of arts, plenties and joyful births,   35
Should not in this best garden of the world,
Our fertile France, put up her lovely visage?
Alas, she hath from France too long been chased,
And all her husbandry doth lie on heaps,
Corrupting in it own fertility.   40
Her vine, the merry cheerer of the heart,
Unpruned dies; her hedges even-pleached,
Like prisoners wildly overgrown with hair,
Put forth disordered twigs; her fallow leas
The darnel, hemlock and rank fumitory   45
Doth root upon, while that the coulter rusts
That should deracinate such savagery.
The even mead, that erst brought sweetly forth
The freckled cowslip, burnet and green clover,
Wanting the scythe, all uncorrected, rank,   50
Conceives by idleness, and nothing teems
But hateful docks, rough thistles, kecksies, burrs,
Losing both beauty and utility.
And as our vineyards, fallows, meads and hedges,
Defective in their natures, grow to wildness,   55
Even so our houses and our selves and children
Have lost, or do not learn for want of time,
The sciences that should become our country,
But grow like savages, as soldiers will
That nothing do but meditate on blood,   60
To swearing and stern looks, diffused attire,
And everything that seems unnatural.
Which to reduce into our former favour
You are assembled; and my speech entreats
That I may know the let why gentle peace   65
Should not expel these inconveniences
And bless us with her former qualities.

KING   If, Duke of Burgundy, you would the peace
Whose want gives growth to th'imperfections
70   Which you have cited, you must buy that peace
With full accord to all our just demands,
Whose tenors and particular effects
You have, enscheduled briefly, in your hands.
BURGUNDY
The King hath heard them, to the which as yet
There is no answer made.
75   KING   Well then, the peace
Which you before so urged lies in his answer.
FRENCH KING   I have but with a cursitory eye
O'er-glanced the articles. Pleaseth your grace
To appoint some of your council presently
80   To sit with us once more, with better heed
To re-survey them, we will suddenly
Pass our accept and peremptory answer.
KING   Brother, we shall. – Go, uncle Exeter,
And brother Clarence, and you, brother Gloucester,
85   Warwick and Huntingdon, go with the King,
And take with you free power to ratify,
Augment or alter, as your wisdoms best
Shall see advantageable for our dignity,
Anything in or out of our demands,
90   And we'll consign thereto. – Will you, fair sister,
Go with the princes, or stay here with us?
QUEEN   Our gracious brother, I will go with them.
Haply a woman's voice may do some good
When articles too nicely urged be stood on.
95   KING   Yet leave our cousin Katherine here with us:
She is our capital demand, comprised
Within the fore-rank of our articles.
QUEEN   She hath good leave.
                Exeunt all but King and Katherine and Alice.
KING   Fair Katherine, and most fair,
Will you vouchsafe to teach a soldier terms
100   Such as will enter at a lady's ear
And plead his love-suit to her gentle heart?
KATHERINE   Your majesty shall mock at me; I cannot
speak your England.
KING   O fair Katherine, if you will love me soundly with
105   your French heart I will be glad to hear you confess it
brokenly with your English tongue. Do you like me,
Kate?
KATHERINE   *Pardonnez-moi*, I cannot tell vat is 'like me'.
KING   An angel is like you, Kate, and you are like an
110   angel.
KATHERINE   *Que dit-il, que je suis semblable à les anges?*
ALICE   *Oui, vraiment, sauf votre grâce, ainsi dit-il.*
KING   I said so, dear Katherine, and I must not blush to
affirm it.
115   KATHERINE   *O bon Dieu, les langues des hommes sont
pleines de tromperies!*
KING   What says she, fair one? That the tongues of men
are full of deceits?
ALICE   *Oui*, dat de tongues of de mans is be full of
120   deceits: dat is de Princess.

KING   The Princess is the better Englishwoman. I'faith,
Kate, my wooing is fit for thy understanding. I am glad
thou canst speak no better English, for if thou couldst
thou wouldst find me such a plain king that thou
wouldst think I had sold my farm to buy my crown. I   125
know no ways to mince it in love but directly to say 'I
love you.' Then if you urge me farther than to say 'Do
you in faith?', I wear out my suit. Give me your answer,
i'faith do, and so clap hands and a bargain. How say
you, lady?   130
KATHERINE   *Sauf votre honneur*, me understand veil.
KING   Marry, if you would put me to verses or to dance
for your sake, Kate, why, you undid me: for the one I
have neither words nor measure, and for the other I
have no strength in measure, yet a reasonable measure   135
in strength. If I could win a lady at leapfrog, or by
vaulting into my saddle with my armour on my back,
under the correction of bragging be it spoken, I should
quickly leap into a wife. Or if I might buffet for my love
or bound my horse for her favours, I could lay on like a   140
butcher and sit like a jackanapes, never off. But before
God, Kate, I cannot look greenly nor gasp out my
eloquence, nor I have no cunning in protestation, only
downright oaths, which I never use till urged, nor never
break for urging. If thou canst love a fellow of this   145
temper, Kate, whose face is not worth sunburning, that
never looks in his glass for love of anything he sees
there, let thine eye be thy cook. I speak to thee plain
soldier. If thou canst love me for this, take me; if not, to
say to thee that I shall die is true; but for thy love, by the   150
Lord, no; yet I love thee too. And while thou liv'st, dear
Kate, take a fellow of plain and uncoined constancy, for
he perforce must do right, because he hath not the gift
to woo in other places; for these fellows of infinite
tongue, that can rhyme themselves into ladies' favours,   155
they do always reason themselves out again. What, a
speaker is but a prater, a rhyme is but a ballad. A good
leg will fall, a straight back will stoop, a black beard will
turn white, a curled pate will grow bald, a fair face will
wither, a full eye will wax hollow; but a good heart,   160
Kate, is the sun and the moon, or rather the sun and
not the moon, for it shines bright and never changes,
but keeps his course truly. If thou would have such a
one, take me; and take me, take a soldier; take a soldier,
take a king. And what sayst thou then to my love?   165
Speak, my fair, and fairly, I pray thee.
KATHERINE   Is it possible dat I sould love de enemy of
France?
KING   No, it is not possible you should love the enemy
of France, Kate: but in loving me you should love the   170
friend of France; for I love France so well that I will not
part with a village of it; I will have it all mine: and
Kate, when France is mine, and I am yours, then yours
is France, and you are mine.
KATHERINE   I cannot tell vat is dat.   175
KING   No, Kate? I will tell thee in French, which I am
sure will hang upon my tongue like a new-married wife

about her husband's neck, hardly to be shook off. *Je,*
quand j'ai le possession de France, et quand vous avez le
possession de moi – let me see, what then? Saint Denis be
my speed! – *donc votre est France, et vous êtes mienne.* It
is as easy for me, Kate, to conquer the kingdom as to
speak so much more French. I shall never move thee in
French, unless it be to laugh at me.

KATHERINE *Sauf votre honneur, le français que vous*
parlez, il est meilleur que l'anglais lequel je parle.

KING No, faith, is't not, Kate; but thy speaking of my
tongue, and I thine, most truly-falsely, must needs be
granted to be much at one. But Kate, dost thou
understand thus much English? 'Canst thou love me?'

KATHERINE I cannot tell.

KING Can any of your neighbours tell, Kate? I'll ask
them. Come, I know thou lovest me, and at night,
when you come into your closet, you'll question this
gentlewoman about me; and I know, Kate, you will to
her dispraise those parts in me that you love with your
heart: but, good Kate, mock me mercifully, the rather,
gentle Princess, because I love thee cruelly. If ever thou
be'st mine, Kate, as I have a saving faith within me tells
me thou shalt, I get thee with scambling, and thou
must therefore needs prove a good soldier-breeder.
Shall not thou and I, between Saint Denis and Saint
George, compound a boy, half French, half English,
that shall go to Constantinople and take the Turk by
the beard? Shall we not? What sayst thou, my fair
flower-de-luce?

KATHERINE I do not know dat.

KING No, 'tis hereafter to know, but now to promise: do
but now promise, Kate, you will endeavour for your
French part of such a boy, and for my English moiety
take the word of a king and a bachelor. How answer
you, *la plus belle Katherine du monde, mon très cher et*
divin déesse?

KATHERINE Your majesty 'ave *fausse* French enough to
deceive de most *sage demoiselle* dat is *en France.*

KING Now fie upon my false French! By mine honour,
in true English, I love thee, Kate: by which honour I
dare not swear thou lovest me, yet my blood begins to
flatter me that thou dost, notwithstanding the poor
and untempering effect of my visage. Now beshrew my
father's ambition! He was thinking of civil wars when
he got me: therefore was I created with a stubborn
outside, with an aspect of iron, that when I come to
woo ladies I fright them. But in faith, Kate, the elder I
wax the better I shall appear. My comfort is that old
age, that ill layer-up of beauty, can do no more spoil
upon my face. Thou hast me, if thou hast me, at the
worst; and thou shalt wear me, if thou wear me, better
and better. And therefore tell me, most fair Katherine,
will you have me? Put off your maiden blushes, avouch
the thoughts of your heart with the looks of an empress,
take me by the hand, and say 'Harry of England, I am
thine': which word thou shalt no sooner bless mine ear
withal but I will tell thee aloud 'England is thine,

Ireland is thine, France is thine, and Henry Plantagenet
is thine', who, though I speak it before his face, if he be
not fellow with the best king, thou shalt find the best
king of good fellows. Come, your answer in broken
music, for thy voice is music and thy English broken.
Therefore, queen of all, Katherine, break thy mind to
me in broken English: wilt thou have me?

KATHERINE Dat is as it sall please *le roi mon père.*

KING Nay, it will please him well, Kate; it shall please
him, Kate.

KATHERINE Den it sall also content me.

KING Upon that I kiss your hand, and I call you my
Queen.

KATHERINE *Laissez, mon seigneur, laissez, laissez! Ma*
foi, je ne veux point que vous abaissiez votre grandeur en
baisant la main d'une de votre seigneurie indigne serviteur.
Excusez-moi, je vous supplie, mon très-puissant seigneur.

KING Then I will kiss your lips, Kate.

KATHERINE *Les dames et demoiselles pour être baisées*
devant leurs noces, il n'est pas la coutume de France.

KING Madam my interpreter, what says she?

ALICE Dat it is not be de fashion *pour les* ladies of
France – I cannot tell vat is *baiser en* Anglish.

KING To kiss.

ALICE Your majesty *entend* bettre *que moi.*

KING It is not a fashion for the maids in France to kiss
before they are married, would she say?

ALICE *Oui, vraiment.*

KING O Kate, nice customs curtsy to great kings. Dear
Kate, you and I cannot be confined within the weak list
of a country's fashion. We are the makers of manners,
Kate, and the liberty that follows our places stops the
mouth of all find-faults, as I will do yours for upholding
the nice fashion of your country in denying me a kiss:
therefore patiently, and yielding – [*Kisses her.*] You
have witchcraft in your lips, Kate: there is more
eloquence in a sugar touch of them than in the tongues
of the French Council, and they should sooner
persuade Harry of England than a general petition of
monarchs. Here comes your father.

Enter the French Power *and the* English Lords.

BURGUNDY God save your majesty! My royal cousin,
Teach you our Princess English?

KING I would have her learn, my fair cousin, how
perfectly I love her, and that is good English.

BURGUNDY Is she not apt?

KING Our tongue is rough, coz, and my condition is
not smooth, so that having neither the voice nor the
heart of flattery about me I cannot so conjure up the
spirit of love in her that he will appear in his true
likeness.

BURGUNDY Pardon the frankness of my mirth if I
answer you for that. If you would conjure in her, you
must make a circle; if conjure up love in her in his true
likeness, he must appear naked and blind. Can you
blame her then, being a maid yet rosed over with the

290   virgin crimson of modesty, if she deny the appearance
of a naked blind boy in her naked seeing self? It were,
my lord, a hard condition for a maid to consign to.
KING   Yet they do wink and yield, as love is blind and
enforces.
295   BURGUNDY   They are then excused, my lord, when they
see not what they do.
KING   Then good my lord, teach your cousin to consent
winking.
BURGUNDY   I will wink on her to consent, my lord, if
300   you will teach her to know my meaning. For maids well
summered and warm kept are like flies at Bartholomew-
tide, blind, though they have their eyes; and then they
will endure handling, which before would not abide
looking on.
305   KING   This moral ties me over to time and a hot
summer; and so I shall catch the fly, your cousin, in the
latter end, and she must be blind too.
BURGUNDY   As love is, my lord, before that it loves.
KING   It is so: and you may some of you thank love for
310   my blindness, who cannot see many a fair French city
for one fair French maid that stands in my way.
FRENCH KING   Yes, my lord, you see them perspectively,
the cities turned into a maid; for they are all girdled
with maiden walls that no war hath entered.
315   KING   Shall Kate be my wife?
FRENCH KING   So please you.
KING   I am content, so the maiden cities you talk of may
wait on her: so the maid that stood in the way for my
wish shall show me the way to my will.
FRENCH KING
320   We have consented to all terms of reason.
KING   Is't so, my lords of England?
WESTMORLAND   The King hath granted every article:
His daughter first, and in the sequel all,
According to their firm proposed natures.
325   EXETER   Only he hath not yet subscribed this, where
your majesty demands that the King of France, having
any occasion to write for matter of grant, shall name
your highness in this form and with this addition:
[*Reads.*] in French, *Notre très cher fils Henri, roi*
330   *d'Angleterre, héritier de France*; and thus in Latin,
Praeclarissimus filius noster Henricus, rex Angliae et
haeres Franciae.
FRENCH KING
Nor this I have not, brother, so denied
But your request shall make me let it pass.
335   KING   I pray you then, in love and dear alliance,
Let that one article rank with the rest,

And thereupon give me your daughter.
FRENCH KING
Take her, fair son, and from her blood raise up
Issue to me, that the contending kingdoms
Of France and England, whose very shores look pale   340
With envy of each other's happiness,
May cease their hatred, and this dear conjunction
Plant neighbourhood and Christian-like accord
In their sweet bosoms, that never war advance
His bleeding sword 'twixt England and fair France.   345
LORDS   Amen.
KING   Now welcome, Kate, and bear me witness all
That here I kiss her as my sovereign queen.
     [*Kisses her.*]   [*Flourish*]
QUEEN   God, the best maker of all marriages,
Combine your hearts in one, your realms in one!   350
As man and wife, being two, are one in love,
So be there 'twixt your kingdoms such a spousal
That never may ill office or fell jealousy,
Which troubles oft the bed of blessed marriage,
Thrust in between the paction of these kingdoms   355
To make divorce of their incorporate league;
That English may as French, French Englishmen,
Receive each other. God speak this amen.
ALL   Amen.
KING   Prepare we for our marriage; on which day,   360
My lord of Burgundy, we'll take your oath,
And all the peers', for surety of our leagues.
Then shall I swear to Kate, and you to me,
And may our oaths well kept and prosperous be!
                         Sennet. Exeunt.

EPILOGUE

Enter CHORUS.

CHORUS   Thus far, with rough and all-unable pen,   365
Our bending author hath pursued the story,
In little room confining mighty men,
Mangling by starts the full course of their glory.
   Small time, but in that small most greatly lived
This star of England. Fortune made his sword   370
By which the world's best garden he achieved,
And of it left his son imperial lord.
   Henry the Sixth, in infant bands crowned King
Of France and England, did this king succeed,
Whose state so many had the managing   375
That they lost France and made his England bleed,
   Which oft our stage hath shown; and for their sake
   In your fair minds let this acceptance take.   *Exit.*

King Henry VI, Part 1

First published as the sixth of the histories in the Folio of 1623, *King Henry VI, Part 1* may have been written as early as 1589: more certainly it was ready for the stage by 1592. A play entitled 'harey the vj' was performed at the Rose on 3 March 1592 by Lord Strange's Men, and it is usually assumed that it was this play. Later that year, Thomas Nashe remarked upon the play's extraordinary appeal, writing of how 'the brave *Talbot* (the terror of the French)' triumphed in the theatre, where 'ten thousand spectators at least (at several times) . . . imagine they behold him fresh bleeding'.

For all its early success, since 1734, when Lewis Theobald asserted that it was not 'entirely of his writing', scholars have wondered if the play was solely the product of Shakespeare's pen. Like the present Arden editor, Edward Burns, many have come to believe that it was a collaboration – as were so many Elizabethan plays – written by Shakespeare with Nashe and two other dramatists, perhaps Robert Greene and George Peele, in spite of the fact that Heminges and Condell, who included it in the Folio, seem to have regarded it as Shakespeare's alone. In any case, the question of authorship can make little difference to our sense of the work.

The three plays on Henry VI are the first of the history plays which, along with *King Richard III*, treat the end of the Plantagenet dynasty. The political and military achievements of Henry V are undone by the civil dissension that follows his death, as his son, who succeeded as a nine-month-old infant, proves unable to unify the country. *King Henry VI, Part 1* moves from the funeral of Henry V in 1422 to the impending marriage of Henry VI to Margaret of Anjou, covering some twenty-three years (actually the play covers more than thirty, as the death of Talbot took place only in 1453, eight years after the last event in the play), proceeding episodically across time and space to tell its tale of England weakened by disunity and faction at home.

As Nashe's comment reveals, the play's most powerful source of appeal was the character of Talbot, the 'terror of the French' (1.4.41), an exemplary hero, who stands as an ideal of physical and moral excellence. His very name inspires his men. '"A Talbot, a Talbot!"', they cry, rushing 'into the bowels of the battle' (1.1.128–9). His rigid commitment to chivalric values, however, prevents him from fleeing the battlefield in a lost cause, prematurely depriving England of its greatest hero and also of Talbot's only son (another of Shakespeare's changes of history; in fact Talbot was succeeded as Earl of Shrewsbury by a surviving son, also named John). Thus, though the play ends with an English triumph, the nation is weakened and made vulnerable, not only by Talbot's death but by the political faction that was its direct cause.

The play's other memorable character is Joan of Arc. She is Talbot's chief rival, heroine of the French, though in English eyes she is no holy maid but something monstrous, at once erotic and demonic. That she is French, but also that she is an assertive and powerful woman, marks her as unnatural; her presence is thoroughly discredited, identified entirely with its challenge to English virtue – though the history plays' readiness to demonize all women of action perhaps suggests that it is as much an insecure masculinity that is at risk.

Henry VI himself is of strangely little dramatic consequence in the play. He does not appear onstage until 3.1 – no doubt this is, in part, because he was less than one year old when the action begins – but the virtual absence from this play of the king whose name it bears is arguably its most telling dramatic point, unmistakable evidence of the power vacuum that each of the squabbling factions seeks to fill.

The play was an early success on stage, performed at least fifteen times in 1592 alone, but it has been seldom staged since. A performance at Stratford in 1889 advertised itself as the first since Shakespeare's time, and modern audiences rarely have an opportunity to see it whole. If seen at all, it is often as a much reduced element in adaptations and conflations of the three parts of *King Henry VI*, as in John Barton's two-part *Wars of the Roses* (1963), or in the two-part adaptation by Charles Wood for the Royal Shakespeare Company's trilogy of *The Plantagenets* in 1988. In 1977, however, Terry Hands directed all three plays in sequence at Stratford-upon-Avon, and in 2000–1 the Royal Shakespeare Company staged them as part of its ambitious series 'This England, the Histories', comprising all the histories from *Richard II* to *Richard III* in chronological order.

The Arden text is based on the 1623 First Folio.

LONDON AND THE ENGLISH COURT

Duke of GLOUCESTER	*Protector of the realm, in the minority of the King*
Duke of EXETER	
Earl of WARWICK	
Bishop of WINCHESTER	*Henry Beaufort, great-uncle to the King, and later Cardinal*
Duke of SOMERSET	
WOODVILLE	*Lieutenant of the Tower of London*
RICHARD Plantagenet	*Later Duke of YORK, and Regent of France*
Duke of SUFFOLK	*(William de la Pole)*
VERNON	*a gentleman of the Inns of Court, who joins the party of Richard Plantagenet*
Edmund MORTIMER	
KING Henry the Sixth	
BASSET	*a follower of the Duke of Somerset*
Three MESSENGERS	*to the funeral of Henry V*
Two WARDERS	*of the Tower of London*
SERVINGMEN	*of Winchester and Gloucester*
MAYOR	*of London*
His OFFICERS	
LAWYER	*of the Temple*
GAOLERS	*of Edmund Mortimer*
LEGATE	*from the Pope to Winchester*

Ambassadors to the English court

THE ENGLISH ARMY IN FRANCE

Duke of BEDFORD	*Regent of France*
Earl of SALISBURY	
Sir John TALBOT	*later Earl of Shrewsbury*
Sir Thomas GARGRAVE	
Sir William GLANSDALE	
Sir John FASTOLFE	
Sir William LUCY	
JOHN	*Talbot's son*
SOLDIER	*at the siege of Orleans*
MESSENGER	*to Sir John Talbot*
Talbot's CAPTAIN	
MESSENGER	*to York*
SERVANT	*to Sir John Talbot*

Soldiers, two Attendants on Bedford, Guards

THE FRENCH

CHARLES, the Dolphin (Dauphin) of France	*crowned by the French as King Charles VII, a title unrecognised by the English*
Duke of ALENÇON	
REIGNIER	*Duke of Anjou and Maine, King of Naples and Jerusalem*
BASTARD of Orleans	
JOAN Puzel (Pucelle)	*a peasant*
Duke of BURGUNDY	
COUNTESS of Auvergne	
MARGARET	*daughter of King Reignier*
Master GUNNER of Orleans	
Master Gunner's BOY	*his son*
SERGEANT	*of a band*
Two SENTINELS	*before Orleans*
MESSENGER	*to Talbot from the Countess of Auvergne*
PORTER	*to the Countess of Auvergne*
Four SOLDIERS	*at Rouen*
WATCH	*of the City of Rouen*
Governor of Paris	
CAPTAIN	*of the French forces in Bordeaux*
SCOUT	
SHEPHERD	*who claims to be Joan Puzel's father*

Soldiers, Fiends, Herald

1.1 *Dead march. Enter the funeral of King Henry the*
Fifth, attended on by the Duke of BEDFORD, *Regent*
of France; the Duke of GLOUCESTER, *Protector; the*
Duke of EXETER; *the* Earl of WARWICK; *the* Bishop
of WINCHESTER; *and the* Duke of SOMERSET.

BEDFORD
Hung be the heavens with black. Yield day to night.
Comets, importing change of times and states,
Brandish your crystal tresses in the sky
And with them scourge the bad revolting stars
That have consented unto Henry's death –   5
King Henry the Fifth, too famous to live long.
England ne'er lost a king of so much worth.
GLOUCESTER   England ne'er had a king until his time.
Virtue he had, deserving to command,
His brandished sword did blind men with his beams,   10
His arms spread wider than a dragon's wings,
His sparkling eyes, replete with wrathful fire,
More dazzled and drove back his enemies
Than midday sun fierce bent against their faces.
What should I say? His deeds exceed all speech;   15
He ne'er lift up his hand but conquered.
EXETER
We mourn in black, why mourn we not in blood?
Henry is dead, and never shall revive:
Upon a wooden coffin we attend,
And death's dishonourable victory   20
We with our stately presence glorify,
Like captives bound to a triumphant car.
What? Shall we curse the planets of mishap
That plotted thus our glory's overthrow?
Or shall we think the subtle-witted French   25
Conjurers and sorcerers, that, afraid of him,
By magic verses have contrived his end?
WINCHESTER   He was a king, blest of the King of kings.
Unto the French the dreadful Judgement Day
So dreadful will not be as was his sight.   30
The battles of the Lord of Hosts he fought;
The Church's prayers made him so prosperous.
GLOUCESTER
The Church? Where is it? Had not churchmen prayed,
His thread of life had not so soon decayed.
None do you like but an effeminate prince,   35
Whom like a schoolboy you may overawe.
WINCHESTER
Gloucester, whate'er we like, thou art Protector,
And lookest to command the prince and realm.
Thy wife is proud, she holdeth thee in awe,
More than God or religious churchmen may.   40
GLOUCESTER
Name not religion, for thou lov'st the flesh,
And ne'er throughout the year to church thou goest –
Except it be to pray against thy foes.
BEDFORD
Cease, cease these jars and rest your minds in peace.
Let's to the altar. Heralds wait on us.   45

Instead of gold we'll offer up our arms –
Since arms avail not now that Henry's dead.
Posterity, await for wretched years,
When at their mothers' moistened eyes babes shall
    suck,
Our isle be made a nourish of salt tears,   50
And none but women left to wail the dead.
Henry the Fifth, thy ghost I invocate:
Prosper this realm, keep it from civil broils,
Combat with adverse planets in the heavens;
A far more glorious star thy soul will make   55
Than Julius Caesar, or bright –

Enter a Messenger.

MESSENGER   My honourable lords, health to you all.
Sad tidings bring I to you out of France,
Of loss, of slaughter and discomfiture.
Guyenne, Champagne, Reims, Rouen, Orleans,   60
Paris, Gisors, Poitiers are all quite lost.
BEDFORD
What sayest thou, man, before dead Henry's corse?
Speak softly, or the loss of those great towns
Will make him burst his lead and rise from death.
GLOUCESTER   Is Paris lost? Is Rouen yielded up?   65
If Henry were recalled to life again
These news would cause him once more yield the
    ghost.
EXETER
How were they lost? What treachery was used?
MESSENGER
No treachery, but want of men and money.
Amongst the soldiers this is muttered: 70
That here you maintain several factions,
And whilst a field should be dispatched and fought
You are disputing of your generals.
One would have lingering wars, with little cost.
Another would fly swift, but wanteth wings.   75
A third thinks, without expense at all,
By guileful fair words peace may be obtained.
Awake, awake, English nobility,
Let not sloth dim your honours new begot;
Cropped are the flower-de-luces in your arms;   80
Of England's coat one half is cut away.   *Exit.*
EXETER   Were our tears wanting to this funeral
These tidings would call forth her flowing tides.
BEDFORD   Me they concern; regent I am of France.
Give me my steeled coat. I'll fight for France.   85
Away with these disgraceful wailing robes;
Wounds will I lend the French, instead of eyes,
To weep their intermissive miseries.

Enter to them another Messenger.

2 MESSENGER
Lords, view these letters, full of bad mischance.
France is revolted from the English quite,   90
Except some petty towns of no import.

The Dolphin Charles is crowned king in Reims.
The Bastard of Orleans with him is joined.
Reignier, Duke of Anjou, doth take his part.
95 The Duke of Alençon flieth to his side.   *Exit.*
EXETER   The Dolphin crowned king? All fly to him?
O whither shall we fly from this reproach?
GLOUCESTER
We will not fly, but to our enemies' throats.
Bedford, if thou be slack, I'll fight it out.
BEDFORD
100 Gloucester, why doubt'st thou of my forwardness?
An army have I mustered in my thoughts,
Wherewith already France is overrun.

Enter another Messenger.

3 MESSENGER
My gracious lords – to add to your laments,
Wherewith you now bedew King Henry's hearse,
105 I must inform you of a dismal fight
Betwixt the stout Lord Talbot and the French.
WINCHESTER   What? Wherein Talbot overcame, is't so?
3 MESSENGER
O no: wherein Lord Talbot was o'erthrown.
The circumstance I'll tell you at more large.
110 The tenth of August last, this dreadful lord
Retiring from the siege of Orleans,
Having full scarce six thousand in his troop,
By three and twenty thousand of the French
Was round encompassed and set upon.
115 No leisure had he to enrank his men.
He wanted pikes to set before his archers,
Instead whereof sharp stakes plucked out of hedges
They pitched in the ground confusedly,
To keep the horsemen off from breaking in.
120 More than three hours the fight continued,
Where valiant Talbot, above human thought,
Enacted wonders with his sword and lance.
Hundreds he sent to hell, and none durst stand him.
Here, there and everywhere enraged he slew.
125 The French exclaimed the devil was in arms,
All the whole army stood agazed on him.
His soldiers, spying his undaunted spirit,
'A Talbot, a Talbot' cried out amain,
And rushed into the bowels of the battle.
130 Here had the conquest fully been sealed up,
If Sir John Fastolfe had not played the coward.
He being in the vanguard, placed behind
With purpose to relieve and follow them,
Cowardly fled, not having struck one stroke.
135 Hence grew the general wrack and massacre.
Enclosed were they with their enemies.
A base villain, to win the Dolphin's grace,
Thrust Talbot with a spear into the back –
Whom all France, with their chief assembled strength,
140 Durst not presume to look once in the face.
BEDFORD   Is Talbot slain? Then I will slay myself,
For living idly here in pomp and ease

Whilst such a worthy leader, wanting aid,
Unto his dastard foemen is betrayed.
3 MESSENGER   O no, he lives, but is took prisoner,   145
And Lord Scales with him, and Lord Hungerford:
Most of the rest slaughtered, or took likewise.
BEDFORD   His ransom there is none but I shall pay.
I'll hale the Dolphin headlong from his throne;
His crown shall be the ransom of my friend.   150
Four of their lords I'll change for one of ours.
Farewell, my masters. To my task will I.
Bonfires in France forthwith I am to make,
To keep our great Saint George's feast withal.
Ten thousand soldiers with me I will take,   155
Whose bloody deeds shall make all Europe quake.
3 MESSENGER
So you had need, for Orleans is besieged.
The English army is grown weak and faint:
The Earl of Salisbury craveth supply
And hardly keeps his men from mutiny,   160
Since they, so few, watch such a multitude.   *Exit.*
EXETER   Remember, lords, your oaths to Henry sworn:
Either to quell the Dolphin utterly,
Or bring him in obedience to your yoke.
BEDFORD   I do remember it, and here take my leave,   165
To go about my preparation.   *Exit.*
GLOUCESTER   I'll to the Tower with all the haste I can,
To view th'artillery and munition,
And then I will proclaim young Henry king.   *Exit.*
EXETER   To Eltham will I, where the young King is,   170
Being ordained his special governor,
And for his safety there I'll best devise.   *Exit.*
WINCHESTER
Each hath his place and function to attend.
I am left out; for me nothing remains.
But long I will not be Jack out of office.   175
The King from Eltham I intend to steal,
And sit at chiefest stern of public weal.
                          Exit Winchester one way. Exit the funeral
                          another way, with Warwick and Somerset.

1.2   *Sound a flourish. Enter* CHARLES *the*
            Dolphin, ALENÇON *and* REIGNIER, *marching*
                      with Drum and Soldiers.

CHARLES   Mars his true moving, even as in the heavens
So in the earth, to this day is not known.
Late did he shine upon the English side:
Now we are victors – upon us he smiles.
What towns of any moment but we have?   5
At pleasure here we lie near Orleans:
Otherwhiles, the famished English, like pale ghosts,
Faintly besiege us one hour in a month.
ALENÇON
They want their porridge and their fat bull-beeves:
Either they must be dieted like mules   10
And have their provender tied to their mouths,
Or piteous they will look, like drowned mice.

REIGNIER   Let's raise the siege: why live we idly here?
    Talbot is taken, whom we wont to fear.
15   Remaineth none but mad-brained Salisbury,
    And he may well in fretting spend his gall;
    Nor men nor money hath he to make war.
CHARLES   Sound, sound alarum, we will rush on them.
    Now for the honour of the forlorn French:
20   Him I forgive my death that killeth me
    When he sees me go back one foot, or fly.   *Exeunt.*

Here alarum. They are beaten back by the English, with
great loss. Enter CHARLES, ALENÇON *and* REIGNIER.

CHARLES   Who ever saw the like? What men have I?
    Dogs, cowards, dastards! I would ne'er have fled,
    But that they left me midst my enemies.
25 REIGNIER   Salisbury is a desperate homicide;
    He fighteth as one weary of his life.
    The other lords, like lions wanting food,
    Do rush upon us as their hungry prey.
ALENÇON   Froissart, a countryman of ours, records
30   England all Olivers and Rolands bred
    During the time Edward the Third did reign.
    More truly now may this be verified,
    For none but Samsons and Goliases
    It sendeth forth to skirmish. One to ten?
35   Lean raw-boned rascals – who would e'er suppose
    They had such courage and audacity?
CHARLES
    Let's leave this town, for they are hare-brained slaves,
    And hunger will enforce them to be more eager.
    Of old I know them; rather with their teeth
40   The walls they'll tear down than forsake the siege.
REIGNIER   I think by some odd gimmers or device
    Their arms are set, like clocks, still to strike on;
    Else ne'er could they hold out so as they do.
    By my consent, we'll even let them alone.
45 ALENÇON   Be it so.

Enter the BASTARD *of Orleans.*

BASTARD
    Where's the Prince Dolphin? I have news for him.
CHARLES   Bastard of Orleans, thrice welcome to us.
BASTARD
    Methinks your looks are sad, your cheer appalled.
    Hath the late overthrow wrought this offence?
50   Be not dismayed, for succour is at hand:
    A holy maid hither with me I bring,
    Which by a vision sent to her from heaven
    Ordained is to raise this tedious siege
    And drive the English forth the bounds of France.
55   The spirit of deep prophecy she hath,
    Exceeding the nine sibyls of old Rome:
    What's past and what's to come she can descry.
    Speak, shall I call her in? Believe my words,
    For they are certain and unfallible.
60 CHARLES   Go call her in: but first – to try her skill –
    Reignier, stand thou as Dolphin in my place.

    Question her proudly, let thy looks be stern.
    By this means shall we sound what skill she hath.

Enter JOAN Puzel.

REIGNIER
    Fair maid, is't thou wilt do these wondrous feats?
JOAN   Reignier, is't thou that thinkest to beguile me?   65
    Where is the Dolphin? Come, come from behind.
    I know thee well, though never seen before.
    Be not amazed, there's nothing hid from me.
    In private will I talk with thee apart.
    Stand back, you lords, and give us leave awhile.   70
REIGNIER   She takes upon her bravely at first dash.
JOAN   Dolphin, I am by birth a shepherd's daughter,
    My wit untrained in any kind of art;
    Heaven and Our Lady gracious hath it pleased
    To shine on my contemptible estate.   75
    Lo, whilst I waited on my tender lambs
    And to sun's parching heat displayed my cheeks,
    God's mother deigned to appear to me
    And, in a vision full of majesty,
    Willed me to leave my base vocation   80
    And free my country from calamity:
    Her aid she promised and assured success.
    In complete glory she revealed herself.
    And, whereas I was black and swart before,
    With those clear rays which she infused on me,   85
    That beauty am I blest with, which you may see.
    Ask me what question thou canst possible
    And I will answer unpremeditated;
    My courage try by combat, if thou dar'st,
    And thou shalt find that I exceed my sex.   90
    Resolve on this: thou shalt be fortunate,
    If thou receive me for thy warlike mate.
CHARLES
    Thou hast astonished me with thy high terms.
    Only this proof I'll of thy valour make –
    In single combat thou shalt buckle with me,   95
    And, if thou vanquishest, thy words are true;
    Otherwise I renounce all confidence.
JOAN   I am prepared. Here is my keen-edged sword,
    Decked with five flower-de-luces on each side,
    The which at Touraine, in Saint Katherine's
        churchyard,   100
    Out of a great deal of old iron, I chose forth.
CHARLES
    Then come, o' God's name. I fear no woman.
JOAN   And while I live I'll ne'er fly from a man.
    [*Here they fight and Joan Puzel overcomes.*]
CHARLES   Stay, stay thy hands. Thou art an Amazon
    And fightest with the sword of Deborah.   105
JOAN   Christ's mother helps me, else I were too weak
CHARLES
    Whoe'er helps thee, 'tis thou that must help me.
    Impatiently I burn with thy desire,
    My heart and hands thou hast at once subdued.
    Excellent Puzel, if thy name be so,   110

Let me thy servant and not sovereign be.
'Tis the French Dolphin sueth to thee thus.
JOAN   I must not yield to any rights of love,
For my profession's sacred from above:
115 When I have chased all thy foes from hence,
Then will I think upon a recompense.
CHARLES
Meantime look gracious on thy prostrate thrall.
REIGNIER   My lord, methinks, is very long in talk.
ALENÇON
Doubtless he shrives this woman to her smock –
120 Else ne'er could he so long protract his speech.
REIGNIER
Shall we disturb him, since he keeps no mean?
ALENÇON
He may mean more than we poor men do know:
These women are shrewd tempters with their tongues.
REIGNIER
My lord, where are you? What devise you on?
125 Shall we give o'er Orleans, or no?
JOAN   Why no, I say. Distrustful recreants!
Fight till the last gasp. I'll be your guard.
CHARLES   What she says I'll confirm. We'll fight it out.
JOAN   Assigned am I to be the English scourge.
130 This night the siege assuredly I'll raise.
Expect Saint Martin's summer, halcyons' days,
Since I have entered into these wars.
Glory is like a circle in the water,
Which never ceaseth to enlarge itself
135 Till by broad spreading it disperse to nought.
With Henry's death the English circle ends:
Dispersed are the glories it included.
Now am I like that proud insulting ship
Which Caesar and his fortune bare at once.
140 CHARLES   Was Mahomet inspired with a dove?
Thou with an eagle art inspired then.
Helen, the mother of great Constantine,
Nor yet Saint Philip's daughters were like thee.
Bright star of Venus, fallen down on the earth,
145 How may I reverently worship thee enough?
ALENÇON   Leave off delays, and let us raise the siege.
REIGNIER
Woman, do what thou canst to save our honours,
Drive them from Orleans and be immortalized.
CHARLES   Presently we'll try. Come, let's away about it.
150 No prophet will I trust, if she prove false.   *Exeunt.*

1.3   *Enter* GLOUCESTER, *with his* Servingmen
in blue coats.

GLOUCESTER   I am come to survey the Tower this day:
Since Henry's death I fear there is conveyance.
Where be these warders that they wait not here?
Open the gates, 'tis Gloucester that calls.

Enter two Warders *on the walls.*

5 1 WARDER   Who's there, that knocks so imperiously?

1 SERVINGMAN   It is the noble Duke of Gloucester.
2 WARDER   Whoe'er he be, you may not be let in.
1 SERVINGMAN
Villains, answer you so the Lord Protector?
1 WARDER   The Lord protect him – so we answer him.
10 We do no otherwise than we are willed.
GLOUCESTER
Who willed you? Or whose will stands but mine?
There's none Protector of the realm, but I.
Break up the gates, I'll be your warrantise;
Shall I be flouted thus by dunghill grooms?
    [*Gloucester's Men rush at the Tower gates, and
    Woodville, the Lieutenant, speaks within.*]
WOODVILLE
What noise is this? What traitors have we here?   15
GLOUCESTER   Lieutenant, is it you whose voice I hear?
Open the gates, here's Gloucester that would enter.
WOODVILLE
Have patience, noble duke, I may not open;
The Cardinal of Winchester forbids.
From him I have express commandment   20
That thou nor none of thine shall be let in.
GLOUCESTER
Faint-hearted Woodville, prizest him 'fore me?
Arrogant Winchester, that haughty prelate
Whom Henry, our late sovereign, ne'er could brook?
Thou art no friend to God, or to the King: 25
Open the gates, or I'll shut thee out shortly.
SERVINGMEN   Open the gates unto the Lord Protector,
Or we'll burst them open, if that you come not quickly.

Enter, to the Protector at the Tower gates,
WINCHESTER, *and his Men in tawny coats.*

WINCHESTER
How now, ambitious Humphrey, what means this?
GLOUCESTER
Peeled priest, dost thou command me to be shut out?   30
WINCHESTER   I do, thou most usurping proditor –
And not Protector – of the King, or realm.
GLOUCESTER   Stand back, thou manifest conspirator,
Thou that contrived'st to murder our dead lord,
Thou that giv'st whores indulgences to sin;   35
I'll canvas thee in thy broad cardinal's hat
If thou proceed in this thy insolence.
WINCHESTER
Nay, stand thou back – I will not budge a foot.
This be Damascus, be thou cursed Cain,
To slay thy brother Abel, if thou wilt.   40
GLOUCESTER
I will not slay thee, but I'll drive thee back:
Thy scarlet robes as a child's bearing cloth
I'll use to carry thee out of this place.
WINCHESTER
Do what thou dar'st, I beard thee to thy face.
GLOUCESTER
What? Am I dared, and bearded to my face?   45
Draw, men, for all this privileged place.

Blue coats to tawny coats. Priest, beware your beard;
I mean to tug it and to cuff you soundly.
Under my feet I stamp thy cardinal's hat.
50 In spite of Pope or dignities of Church,
Here by the cheeks I'll drag thee up and down.

WINCHESTER
Gloucester, thou wilt answer this before the Pope.

GLOUCESTER   Winchester goose, I cry, a rope, a rope.
Now beat them hence – why do you let them stay?
55 Thee I'll chase hence, thou wolf in sheep's array.
Out, tawny coats – out, scarlet hypocrite.

Here Gloucester's Men beat out the Cardinal's Men, and
enter in the hurly-burly the Mayor of London *and*
his Officers.

MAYOR
Fie, lords, that you, being supreme magistrates,
Thus contumeliously should break the peace.

GLOUCESTER
Peace, mayor, thou knowst little of my wrongs.
60 Here's Beaufort, that regards nor God nor king,
Hath here distrained the Tower to his use.

WINCHESTER   Here's Gloucester, a foe to citizens,
One that still motions war and never peace,
O'ercharging your free purses with large fines –
65 That seeks to overthrow religion,
Because he is Protector of the realm,
And would have armour here out of the Tower,
To crown himself king and suppress the Prince.

GLOUCESTER
I will not answer thee with words, but blows.
[*Here they skirmish again.*]

70 MAYOR   Naught rests for me, in this tumultuous strife,
But to make open proclamation.
Come, officer, as loud as e'er thou canst.
[*The Officer gives the cry.*]

OFFICER   *All manner of men, assembled here in arms this*
day against God's peace and the King's, we charge and
75 *command you, in his Highness's name, to repair to your*
several dwelling places, and not to wear, handle or use any
sword, weapon or dagger henceforward, upon pain of death.

GLOUCESTER   Cardinal, I'll be no breaker of the law:
But we shall meet and break our minds at large.

WINCHESTER
80 Gloucester, we'll meet to thy cost, be sure.
Thy heart-blood I will have for this day's work.

MAYOR   I'll call for clubs, if you will not away:
[*to the audience*] This Cardinal's more haughty than
the devil.

GLOUCESTER
Mayor, farewell: thou dost but what thou mayst.

85 WINCHESTER   Abominable Gloucester, guard thy head,
For I intend to have it ere long.
Exeunt Winchester, Gloucester and their Men.

MAYOR   See the coast cleared, and then we will depart.
Good God, these nobles should such stomachs bear!
I myself fight not once in forty year.   *Exeunt.*

1.4   *Enter the* Master Gunner of Orleans *and his* Boy.

GUNNER   Sirrah, thou knowst how Orleans is besieged,
And how the English have the suburbs won.

BOY   Father, I know, and oft have shot at them –
Howe'er, unfortunate, I missed my aim.

GUNNER   But now thou shalt not: be thou ruled by me.   5
Chief master gunner am I of this town –
Something I must do to procure me grace.
The Prince's espials have informed me
How the English, in the suburbs close entrenched,
Went through a secret grate of iron bars   10
In yonder tower, to overpeer the city
And thence discover how with most advantage
They may vex us with shot or with assault.
To intercept this inconvenience,
A piece of ordnance 'gainst it I have placed,   15
And even these three days have I watched if I could
see them.
Now do thou watch, for I can stay no longer.
If thou spiest any, run and bring me word,
And thou shalt find me at the Governor's.

BOY   Father, I warrant you, take you no care.   20
Exit Gunner.
I'll never trouble you, if I may spy them.   *Exit.*

Enter SALISBURY *and* TALBOT *on the turrets,*
with others, Sir Thomas GARGRAVE *and*
Sir William GLANSDALE.

SALISBURY   Talbot, my life, my joy, again returned?
How wert thou handled, being prisoner?
Or by what means got'st thou to be released?
Discourse, I prithee, on this turret's top.   25

TALBOT   The Earl of Bedford had a prisoner
Called the brave Lord Ponton de Saintrailles:
For him was I exchanged and ransomed.
But with a baser man of arms by far,
Once, in contempt, they would have bartered me: 30
Which I, disdaining, scorned and craved death,
Rather than I would be so peeled esteemed.
In fine, redeemed I was as I desired.
But O, the treacherous Fastolfe wounds my heart,
Whom with my bare fists I would execute,   35
If I now had him brought into my power.

SALISBURY
Yet tellest thou not how thou wert entertained.

TALBOT
With scoffs and scorns and contumelious taunts.
In open market-place produced they me
To be a public spectacle to all.   40
'Here', said they, 'is the terror of the French,
The scarecrow that affrights our children so.'
Then broke I from the officers that led me
And with my nails digged stones out of the ground
To hurl at the beholders of my shame.   45
My grisly countenance made others fly;
None durst come near for fear of sudden death.

In iron walls they deemed me not secure:
So great fear of my name 'mongst them were spread
50 That they supposed I could rend bars of steel
And spurn in pieces posts of adamant.
Wherefore a guard of chosen shot I had,
That walked about me every minute while,
And if I did but stir out of my bed
55 Ready they were to shoot me to the heart.

Enter the Boy *with a linstock lit and burning, and passes
over the stage.*

SALISBURY
I grieve to hear what torments you endured;
But we will be revenged sufficiently.
Now it is supper-time in Orleans.
Here, through this grate, I count each one
60 And view the Frenchmen how they fortify.
Let us look in: the sight will much delight thee.
Sir Thomas Gargrave and Sir William Glansdale,
Let me have your express opinions –
Where is best place to make our battery next?
GARGRAVE
65 I think at the north gate, for there stands lords.
GLANSDALE And I, here, at the bulwark of the bridge.
TALBOT For aught I see, this city must be famished,
Or with light skirmishes enfeebled.
*[Here they shoot from offstage, and Salisbury and
Gargrave fall down.]*
SALISBURY
O Lord, have mercy on us, wretched sinners.
70 GARGRAVE O Lord, have mercy on me, woeful man.
TALBOT
What chance is this that suddenly hath crossed us?
Speak, Salisbury; at least, if thou canst, speak.
How far'st thou, mirror of all martial men?
One of thy eyes and thy cheek's side struck off?
75 Accursed tower, accursed fatal hand,
That hath contrived this woeful tragedy.
In thirteen battles Salisbury o'ercame:
Henry the Fifth he first trained to the wars.
Whilst any trump did sound or drum struck up,
80 His sword did ne'er leave striking in the field.
Yet liv'st thou, Salisbury? Though thy speech doth
  fail,
One eye thou hast to look to heaven for grace.
The sun with one eye vieweth all the world.
Heaven, be thou gracious to none alive,
85 If Salisbury wants mercy at thy hands.
Bear hence his body – I will help to bury it.
Sir Thomas Gargrave, hast thou any life?
Speak unto Talbot, nay, look up to him.
Salisbury, cheer thy spirit with this comfort;
90 Thou shalt not die whiles –
He beckons with his hand and smiles on me
As who should say, 'When I am dead and gone,
Remember to avenge me on the French'.

Plantagenet, I will; and like thee, Nero,
Play on the lute, beholding the towns burn: 95
Wretched shall France be only in my name.
[Here an alarum, and it thunders and lightens.]
What stir is this? What tumult's in the heavens?
Whence cometh this alarum and the noise?

Enter a Messenger.

MESSENGER
My lord, my lord, the French have gathered head.
The Dolphin, with one Joan de Puzel joined – 100
A holy prophetess, new risen up –
Is come with a great power to raise the siege.
[Here Salisbury lifteth himself up, and groans.]
TALBOT Hear, hear, how dying Salisbury doth groan:
It irks his heart he cannot be revenged.
Frenchmen, I'll be a Salisbury to you. 105
Puzel or Pucelle, Dolphin or dogfish,
Your hearts I'll stamp out with my horse's heels
And make a quagmire of your mingled brains.
Convey me Salisbury into his tent –
And then we'll try what these dastard Frenchmen
  dare. *Alarum. Exeunt.* 110

1.5 *Here an alarum again, and* TALBOT *pursueth*
CHARLES *the Dolphin, and driveth him;*
then enter JOAN *Puzel driving Englishmen before her.*
Then enter TALBOT.

TALBOT
Where is my strength, my valour and my force?
Our English troops retire, I cannot stay them;
A woman clad in armour chaseth them.
[Puzel approaches him.]
Here, here she comes. I'll have a bout with thee –
Devil, or devil's dam, I'll conjure thee. 5
Blood will I draw on thee – thou art a witch –
And straightway give thy soul to him thou serv'st.
JOAN Come, come, 'tis only I that must disgrace thee.
[Here they fight.]
TALBOT Heavens, can you suffer hell so to prevail?
My breast I'll burst with straining of my courage 10
And from my shoulders crack my arms asunder,
But I will chastise this high-minded strumpet.
[They fight again.]
JOAN Talbot, farewell. Thy hour is not yet come.
I must go victual Orleans forthwith.
*[A short alarum: then Charles passes over the stage
and enters the town with Soldiers.]*
O'ertake me if thou canst – I scorn thy strength. 15
Go, go – cheer up thy hungry, starved men,
Help Salisbury to make his testament.
This day is ours, as many more shall be. *Exit.*
TALBOT My thoughts are whirled like a potter's wheel,
I know not where I am nor what I do. 20
A witch by fear, not force, like Hannibal,

Drives back our troops and conquers as she lists:
So bees with smoke and doves with noisome stench
Are from their hives and houses driven away.
They called us, for our fierceness, English dogs;   25
Now like to whelps we crying run away.
                                    [*A short alarum*]
Hark, countrymen – either renew the fight
Or tear the lions out of England's coat.
Renounce your soil, give sheep in lions' stead;
Sheep run not half so treacherous from the wolf,   30
Or horse or oxen from the leopard,
As you fly from your oft-subdued slaves.
   [*Alarum. Here another skirmish in which the English
   attempt to enter Orleans.*]
It will not be, retire into your trenches.
You all consented unto Salisbury's death,
For none would strike a stroke in his revenge.   35
Puzel is entered into Orleans
In spite of us or aught that we could do.
O would I were to die with Salisbury:
The shame hereof will make me hide my head.
   *Exit Talbot. Alarum. The English sound a retreat and
         exeunt. The French sound a flourish.*

Enter on the walls JOAN Puzel, CHARLES *the Dolphin,*
   REIGNIER, ALENÇON *and Soldiers.*

JOAN   Advance our waving colours on the walls.   40
   Rescued is Orleans from the English.
   Thus Joan de Puzel hath performed her word.
CHARLES   Divinest creature, Astraea's daughter,
   How shall I honour thee for this success?
   Thy promises are like Adonis' garden,   45
   That one day bloomed and fruitful were the next.
   France, triumph in thy glorious prophetess.
   Recovered is the town of Orleans;
   More blessed hap did ne'er befall our state.
REIGNIER
   Why ring not out the bells aloud throughout the town? 50
   Dolphin, command the citizens make bonfires
   And feast and banquet in the open streets,
   To celebrate the joy that God hath given us.
ALENÇON
   All France will be replete with mirth and joy,
   When they shall hear how we have played the men.   55
CHARLES   'Tis Joan, not we, by whom the day is won:
   For which I will divide my crown with her,
   And all the priests and friars in my realm
   Shall in procession sing her endless praise.
   A statelier pyramis to her I'll rear   60
   Than Rhodope's or Memphis' ever was.
   In memory of her, when she is dead,
   Her ashes, in an urn more precious
   Than the rich-jewelled coffer of Darius,
   Transported shall be at high festivals   65
   Before the kings and queens of France.
   No longer on Saint Denis will we cry,

But Joan de Puzel shall be France's saint.
Come in, and let us banquet royally,
After this golden day of victory.   *Flourish. Exeunt.*   70

2.1   *Enter on the walls a French* Sergeant
                of a band, with two Sentinels.

SERGEANT   Sirs, take your places and be vigilant.
   If any noise or soldier you perceive
   Near to the walls, by some apparent sign
   Let us have knowledge at the court of guard.
1 SENTINEL   Sergeant, you shall.   *Exit Sergeant.*
                              Thus are poor servitors,   5
   When others sleep upon their quiet beds,
   Constrained to watch in darkness, rain and cold.

Enter TALBOT, BEDFORD *and* BURGUNDY, *with three
                scaling ladders.*

TALBOT   Lord Regent, and redoubted Burgundy –
   By whose approach the regions of Artois,
   Wallon and Picardy are friends to us –   10
   This happy night the Frenchmen are secure,
   Having all day caroused and banqueted.
   Embrace we then this opportunity
   As fitting best to quittance their deceit,
   Contrived by art and baleful sorcery.   15
BEDFORD
   Coward of France! How much he wrongs his fame,
   Despairing of his own arms' fortitude,
   To join with witches and the help of hell.
BURGUNDY   Traitors have never other company.
   But what's that Puzel, whom they term so pure?   20
TALBOT   A maid, they say.
BEDFORD   A maid? And be so martial?
BURGUNDY
   Pray God she prove not masculine ere long –
   If underneath the standard of the French
   She carry armour, as she hath begun.
TALBOT
   Well, let them practise and converse with spirits.   25
   God is our fortress, in whose conquering name
   Let us resolve to scale their flinty bulwarks.
BEDFORD   Ascend, brave Talbot. We will follow thee.
TALBOT   Not altogether. Better far, I guess,
   That we do make our entrance several ways: 30
   That if it chance that one of us do fail
   The other yet may rise against their force.
BEDFORD   Agreed; I'll to yond corner.
BURGUNDY   And I to this.
TALBOT
   And here will Talbot mount, or make his grave.
   Now, Salisbury, for thee and for the right   35
   Of English Henry, shall this night appear
   How much in duty I am bound to both.
         [*The English cry,* 'Saint George, a Talbot'
                     as they enter Orleans.]

1 SENTINEL
  Arm, arm, the enemy doth make assault.
                                        Exeunt French Sentinels.

  The French leap over the walls in their shirts.
  Enter several ways the BASTARD, ALENÇON, REIGNIER,
        half ready and half unready.

ALENÇON   How now, my lords? What, all unready so?
40   BASTARD   Unready? Ay, and glad we scaped so well.
REIGNIER
  'Twas time, I trow, to wake and leave our beds,
  Hearing alarums at our chamber doors.
ALENÇON   Of all exploits since first I followed arms,
  Ne'er heard I of a warlike enterprise
45   More venturous or desperate than this.
BASTARD   I think this Talbot be a fiend of hell.
REIGNIER   If not of hell, the heavens sure favour him.
ALENÇON   Here cometh Charles. I marvel how he sped.

          Enter CHARLES *and* JOAN.

BASTARD   Tut, holy Joan was his defensive guard.
50   CHARLES   Is this thy cunning, thou deceitful dame?
  Didst thou at first, to flatter us withal,
  Make us partakers of a little gain,
  That now our loss might be ten times so much?
JOAN   Wherefore is Charles impatient with his friend?
55   At all times will you have my power alike?
  Sleeping or waking, must I still prevail,
  Or will you blame and lay the fault on me?
  Improvident soldiers, had your watch been good,
  This sudden mischief never could have fallen.
60   CHARLES   Duke of Alençon, this was your default,
  That, being captain of the watch tonight,
  Did look no better to that weighty charge.
ALENÇON   Had all your quarters been as safely kept
  As that whereof I had the government,
65   We had not been thus shamefully surprised.
BASTARD   Mine was secure.
REIGNIER   And so was mine, my lord.
CHARLES   And for myself, most part of all this night
  Within her quarter and mine own precinct
  I was employed in passing to and fro
70   About relieving of the sentinels;
  Then how, or which way, should they first break in?
JOAN   Question, my lords, no further of the case
  'How, or which way?'; 'tis sure they found some place
  But weakly guarded, where the breach was made.
75   And now there rests no other shift but this –
  To gather our soldiers, scattered and dispersed,
  And lay new platforms to endamage them.

  Alarum. Enter an English Soldier, *crying,* 'A Talbot, a
  Talbot'; *they fly, leaving their clothes behind.*

SOLDIER   I'll be so bold to take what they have left.
  The cry of 'Talbot' serves me for a sword –
80   For I have loaden me with many spoils,
  Using no other weapon but his name.   *Exit.*

2.2   *Enter* TALBOT, BEDFORD, BURGUNDY
         with a Captain, *and Soldiers carrying the body*
         of Salisbury, their drums beating a dead march.

BEDFORD   The day begins to break, and night is fled,
  Whose pitchy mantle overveiled the earth.
  Here sound retreat and cease our hot pursuit.
                              [*They sound retreat.*]
TALBOT   Bring forth the body of old Salisbury,
  And here advance it in the market-place,   5
  The middle centre of this cursed town.
  Now have I paid my vow unto his soul.
  For every drop of blood was drawn from him
  There hath at least five Frenchmen died tonight.
  And that hereafter ages may behold   10
  What ruin happened in revenge of him,
  Within their chiefest temple I'll erect
  A tomb wherein his corpse shall be interred,
  Upon the which, that everyone may read,
  Shall be engraved the sack of Orleans,   15
  The treacherous manner of his mournful death,
  And what a terror he had been to France.
  But, lords, in all our bloody massacre
  I muse we met not with the Dolphin's grace,
  His new-come champion, virtuous Joan of Aire,   20
  Nor any of his false confederates.
BEDFORD
  'Tis thought, Lord Talbot, when the fight began,
  Roused on the sudden from their drowsy beds,
  They did, amongst the troops of armed men,
  Leap o'er the walls for refuge in the field.   25
BURGUNDY   Myself, as far as I could well discern
  For smoke and dusky vapours of the night,
  Am sure I scared the Dolphin and his trull,
  When arm in arm they both came swiftly running,
  Like to a pair of loving turtle-doves   30
  That could not live asunder day or night.
  After that things are set in order here
  We'll follow them with all the power we have.

          Enter a Messenger.

MESSENGER
  All hail, my lords. Which of this princely train
  Call ye the warlike Talbot, for his acts   35
  So much applauded through the realm of France?
TALBOT
  Here is the Talbot. Who would speak with him?
MESSENGER   The virtuous lady, Countess of Auvergne,
  With modesty admiring thy renown,
  By me entreats, great lord, thou wouldst vouchsafe   40
  To visit her poor castle where she lies,
  That she may boast she hath beheld the man
  Whose glory fills the world with loud report.
BURGUNDY   Is it even so? Nay, then I see our wars
  Will turn unto a peaceful comic sport,   45
  When ladies crave to be encountered with.
  You may not, my lord, despise her gentle suit.

TALBOT   Ne'er trust me then; for when a world of men
Could not prevail with all their oratory,
50 Yet hath a woman's kindness overruled.
And therefore tell her I return great thanks
And in submission will attend on her.
Will not your honours bear me company?
BEDFORD   No, truly, 'tis more than manners will:
55 And I have heard it said unbidden guests
Are often welcomest when they are gone.
TALBOT   Why then, alone (since there's no remedy)
I mean to prove this lady's courtesy.
Come hither, captain, you perceive my mind.
    [*The Captain comes forward; Talbot whispers to him.*]
60 CAPTAIN   I do, my lord, and mean accordingly. *Exeunt.*

2.3   *Enter* COUNTESS *of Auvergne, and her* Porter.

COUNTESS   Porter, remember what I gave in charge;
And when you have done so, bring the keys to me.
PORTER   Madam, I will.   *Exit.*
COUNTESS   The plot is laid. If all things fall out right
5 I shall as famous be by this exploit
As Scythian Tomyris by Cyrus' death.
Great is the rumour of this dreadful knight,
And his achievements of no less account:
Fain would mine eyes be witness with mine ears,
10 To give their censure of these rare reports.

    Enter Messenger *and* TALBOT.

MESSENGER
Madam, according as your ladyship desired,
By message craved, so is Lord Talbot come.
COUNTESS   And he is welcome. What? Is this the man?
MESSENGER   Madam, it is.
COUNTESS   Is this the scourge of France?
15 Is this the Talbot, so much feared abroad
That with his name the mothers still their babes?
I see report is fabulous and false.
I thought I should have seen some Hercules,
A second Hector for his grim aspect
20 And large proportion of his strong-knit limbs.
Alas, this is a child, a silly dwarf:
It cannot be this weak and writhled shrimp
Should strike such terror to his enemies.
TALBOT   Madam, I have been bold to trouble you;
25 But, since your ladyship is not at leisure,
I'll sort some other time to visit you.
COUNTESS
What means he now? Go ask him whither he goes.
MESSENGER   Stay, my Lord Talbot, for my lady craves
To know the cause of your abrupt departure.
30 TALBOT   Marry, for that she's in a wrong belief,
I go to certify her Talbot's here.

    Enter Porter *with keys.*

COUNTESS   If thou be he, then art thou prisoner.
TALBOT   Prisoner? To whom?

COUNTESS   To me, bloodthirsty lord;
And for that cause I trained thee to my house.
35 Long time thy shadow hath been thrall to me,
For in my gallery thy picture hangs.
But now the substance shall endure the like,
And I will chain these legs and arms of thine,
That hast by tyranny these many years
40 Wasted our country, slain our citizens
And sent our sons and husbands captivate.
TALBOT   Ha, ha, ha.
COUNTESS
Laughest thou, wretch? Thy mirth shall turn to
    moan.
TALBOT   I laugh to see your ladyship so fond
45 To think that you have aught but Talbot's shadow
Whereon to practise your severity.
COUNTESS   Why? Art not thou the man?
TALBOT   I am indeed.
COUNTESS   Then have I substance too.
TALBOT   No, no, I am but shadow of myself:
You are deceived, my substance is not here;
50 For what you see is but the smallest part
And least proportion of humanity.
I tell you, madam, were the whole frame here,
It is of such a spacious lofty pitch
Your roof were not sufficient to contain't.
55 COUNTESS   This is a riddling merchant, for the nonce.
He will be here, and yet he is not here:
How can these contrarieties agree?
TALBOT   That will I show you presently.
    [*Winds his horn. Drums strike up. A peal
                                of ordnance.*]

    Enter Soldiers.

How say you, madam? Are you now persuaded
60 That Talbot is but shadow of himself?
These are his substance, sinews, arms and strength,
With which he yoketh your rebellious necks,
Razeth your cities and subverts your towns,
And in a moment makes them desolate.
65 COUNTESS   Victorious Talbot, pardon my abuse.
I find thou art no less than fame hath bruited,
And more than may be gathered by thy shape.
Let my presumption not provoke thy wrath,
For I am sorry that with reverence
70 I did not entertain thee as thou art.
TALBOT   Be not dismayed, fair lady, nor misconster
The mind of Talbot as you did mistake
The outward composition of his body.
What you have done hath not offended me;
75 Nor other satisfaction do I crave,
But only, with your patience, that we may
Taste of your wine and see what cates you have,
For soldiers' stomachs always serve them well.
COUNTESS
With all my heart – and think me honoured
80 To feast so great a warrior in my house.   *Exeunt.*

2.4   *Enter* RICHARD Plantagenet, WARWICK,
     SOMERSET, SUFFOLK, VERNON *and a* Lawyer.

RICHARD
   Great lords, and gentlemen, what means this silence?
   Dare no man answer in a case of truth?

SUFFOLK   Within the Temple Hall we were too loud;
   The garden here is more convenient.

5   RICHARD   Then say at once if I maintained the truth;
   Or else was wrangling Somerset in th'error?

SUFFOLK   Faith, I have been a truant in the law
   And never yet could frame my will to it,
   And therefore frame the law unto my will.

SOMERSET
10   Judge you, my lord of Warwick, then, between us.

WARWICK
   Between two hawks, which flies the higher pitch,
   Between two dogs, which hath the deeper mouth,
   Between two blades, which bears the better temper,
   Between two horses, which doth bear him best,
15   Between two girls, which hath the merriest eye,
   I have perhaps some shallow spirit of judgement:
   But in these nice sharp quillets of the law,
   Good faith, I am no wiser than a daw.

RICHARD   Tut, tut, here is a mannerly forbearance:
20   The truth appears so naked on my side
   That any purblind eye may find it out.

SOMERSET   And on my side it is so well apparelled,
   So clear, so shining and so evident,
   That it will glimmer through a blind man's eye.

RICHARD
25   Since you are tongue-tied and so loath to speak,
   In dumb significants proclaim your thoughts.
   Let him that is a true-born gentleman
   And stands upon the honour of his birth,
   If he suppose that I have pleaded truth,
30   From off this briar pluck a white rose with me.

SOMERSET   Let him that is no coward nor no flatterer,
   But dare maintain the party of the truth,
   Pluck a red rose from off this thorn with me.

WARWICK   I love no colours: and, without all colour
35   Of base insinuating flattery,
   I pluck this white rose with Plantagenet.

SUFFOLK   I pluck this red rose with young Somerset,
   And say withal I think he held the right.

VERNON   Stay, lords and gentlemen, and pluck no more
40   Till you conclude that he upon whose side
   The fewest roses are cropped from the tree
   Shall yield the other in the right opinion.

SOMERSET   Good Master Vernon, it is well objected:
   If I have fewest I subscribe in silence.

45   RICHARD   And I.

VERNON   Then, for the truth and plainness of the case,
   I pluck this pale and maiden blossom here,
   Giving my verdict on the white rose side.

SOMERSET   Prick not your finger as you pluck it off,
50   Lest, bleeding, you do paint the white rose red

   And fall on my side so, against your will.

VERNON   If I, my lord, for my opinion bleed,
   Opinion shall be surgeon to my hurt
   And keep me on the side where still I am.

SOMERSET   Well, well, come on, who else?   55

LAWYER   Unless my study and my books be false,
   The argument you held was wrong in you;
   In sign whereof I pluck a white rose too.

RICHARD   Now, Somerset, where is your argument?

SOMERSET   Here in my scabbard, meditating that   60
   Shall dye your white rose in a bloody red.

RICHARD
   Meantime your cheeks do counterfeit our roses;
   For pale they look with fear, as witnessing
   The truth on our side.

SOMERSET   No, Plantagenet:
   'Tis not for fear, but anger, that thy cheeks   65
   Blush for pure shame, to counterfeit our roses –
   And yet thy tongue will not confess thy error.

RICHARD   Hath not thy rose a canker, Somerset?

SOMERSET   Hath not thy rose a thorn, Plantagenet?

RICHARD   Ay, sharp and piercing to maintain his truth,   70
   Whiles thy consuming canker eats his falsehood.

SOMERSET
   Well, I'll find friends to wear my bleeding roses
   That shall maintain what I have said is true,
   Where false Plantagenet dare not be seen.

RICHARD   Now, by this maiden blossom in my hand,   75
   I scorn thee and thy fashion, peevish boy.

SUFFOLK   Turn not thy scorns this way, Plantagenet.

RICHARD
   Proud Poole, I will, and scorn both him and thee.

SUFFOLK   I'll turn my part thereof into thy throat.

SOMERSET   Away, away, good William de la Pole –   80
   We grace the yeoman by conversing with him.

WARWICK
   Now, by God's will, thou wrong'st him, Somerset:
   His grandfather was Lionel, Duke of Clarence,
   Third son to the third Edward, King of England.
   Spring crestless yeomen from so deep a root?   85

RICHARD   He bears him on the place's privilege,
   Or durst not, for his craven heart, say thus.

SOMERSET
   By him that made me, I'll maintain my words
   On any plot of ground in Christendom.
   Was not thy father Richard, Earl of Cambridge,   90
   For treason executed in our late king's days?
   And by his treason stand'st not thou attainted,
   Corrupted, and exempt from ancient gentry?
   His trespass yet lives guilty in thy blood,
   And till thou be restored thou art a yeoman.   95

RICHARD   My father was attached, not attainted,
   Condemned to die for treason, but no traitor;
   And that I'll prove on better men than Somerset,
   Were growing time once ripened to my will.
   For your partaker Poole, and you yourself,   100
   I'll note you in my book of memory,

To scourge you for this apprehension;
Look to it well, and say you are well warned.

SOMERSET   Ah, thou shalt find us ready for thee still,
105   And know us by these colours for thy foes,
For these my friends in spite of thee shall wear.

RICHARD   And, by my soul, this pale and angry rose,
As cognizance of my blood-drinking hate,
Will I for ever, and my faction, wear
110   Until it wither with me to my grave
Or flourish to the height of my degree.

SUFFOLK
Go forward, and be choked with thy ambition:
And so farewell, until I meet thee next.   *Exit.*

SOMERSET
Have with thee, Pole. Farewell, ambitious Richard.
                                                 Exit.
RICHARD
115   How I am braved, and must perforce endure it.

WARWICK   This blot that they object against your house
Shall be whipped out in the next parliament,
Called for the truce of Winchester and Gloucester:
And if thou be not then created York,
120   I will not live to be accounted Warwick.
Meantime, in signal of my love to thee,
Against proud Somerset and William Poole
Will I upon thy party wear this rose.
And here I prophesy: this brawl today,
125   Grown to this faction in the Temple Garden,
Shall send between the red rose and the white
A thousand souls to death and deadly night.

RICHARD   Good Master Vernon, I am bound to you,
That you on my behalf would pluck a flower.

130   VERNON   In your behalf, still will I wear the same.

LAWYER   And so will I.

RICHARD   Thanks, gentle.
Come, let us four to dinner: I dare say
This quarrel will drink blood another day.   *Exeunt.*

2.5   *Enter* MORTIMER, *brought in a chair, and* Gaolers.

MORTIMER   Kind keepers of my weak decaying age,
Let dying Mortimer here rest himself.
Even like a man new haled from the rack,
So fare my limbs with long imprisonment;
5   And these grey locks, the pursuivants of death,
Nestor-like aged, in an age of care,
Argue the end of Edmund Mortimer.
These eyes, like lamps whose wasting oil is spent,
Wax dim, as drawing to their exigent;
10   Weak shoulders, overborne with burdening grief,
And pithless arms, like to a withered vine
That droops his sapless branches to the ground.
Yet are these feet, whose strengthless stay is numb,
Unable to support this lump of clay,
15   Swift-winged with desire to get a grave,
As witting I no other comfort have.
But tell me, keeper, will my nephew come?

GAOLER   Richard Plantagenet, my lord, will come:
We sent unto the Temple, unto his chamber,
And answer was returned that he will come.   20

MORTIMER   Enough; my soul shall then be satisfied.
Poor gentleman, his wrong doth equal mine.
Since Henry Monmouth first began to reign –
Before whose glory I was great in arms –
This loathsome sequestration have I had;   25
And even since then hath Richard been obscured,
Deprived of honour and inheritance.
But now the arbitrator of despairs,
Just death, kind umpire of men's miseries,
With sweet enlargement doth dismiss me hence: 30
I would his troubles likewise were expired,
That so he might recover what was lost.

Enter RICHARD.

GAOLER   My lord, your loving nephew now is come.

MORTIMER
Richard Plantagenet, my friend, is he come?

RICHARD   Ay, noble uncle, thus ignobly used,   35
Your nephew, late despised Richard, comes.

MORTIMER
Direct mine arms – I may embrace his neck,
And in his bosom spend my latter gasp.
O tell me when my lips do touch his cheeks,
That I may kindly give one fainting kiss.   40
And now declare, sweet stem from York's great stock,
Why didst thou say of late thou wert despised?

RICHARD   First, lean thine aged back against mine arm,
And in that ease I'll tell thee my disease.
This day, in argument upon a case,   45
Some words there grew 'twixt Somerset and me,
Among which terms he used his lavish tongue
And did upbraid me with my father's death;
Which obloquy set bars before my tongue,
Else with the like I had requited him.   50
Therefore, good uncle, for my father's sake –
In honour of a true Plantagenet –
And for alliance' sake, declare the cause
My father, Earl of Cambridge, lost his head.

MORTIMER
That cause, fair nephew, that imprisoned me,   55
And hath detained me all my flowering youth
Within a loathsome dungeon, there to pine,
Was cursed instrument of his decease.

RICHARD   Discover more at large what cause that was,
For I am ignorant and cannot guess.   60

MORTIMER   I will, if that my fading breath permit,
And death approach not ere my tale be done.
Henry the Fourth, grandfather to this King,
Deposed his nephew Richard, Edward's son,
The first begotten and the lawful heir   65
Of Edward, king, the third of that descent,
During whose reign the Percies of the north,
Finding his usurpation most unjust,
Endeavoured my advancement to the throne.

70 The reason moved these warlike lords to this
Was for that – young Richard thus removed,
Leaving no heir begotten of his body –
I was the next by birth and parentage:
For by my mother I derived am
75 From Lionel, Duke of Clarence, third son
To King Edward the Third, whereas he
From John of Gaunt doth bring his pedigree,
Being but fourth of that heroic line.
But mark: as in this haughty great attempt
80 They laboured to plant the rightful heir,
I lost my liberty and they their lives.
Long after this, when Henry the Fifth,
Succeeding his father Bolingbroke, did reign,
Thy father, Earl of Cambridge then – derived
85 From famous Edmund Langley, Duke of York –
Marrying my sister, that thy mother was,
Again, in pity of my hard distress,
Levied an army, weening to redeem
And have installed me in the diadem;
90 But as the rest, so fell that noble earl,
And was beheaded. Thus the Mortimers,
In whom the title rested, were suppressed.
RICHARD   Of which, my lord, your honour is the last.
MORTIMER   True; and thou seest that I no issue have,
95 And that my fainting words do warrant death.
Thou art my heir. The rest, I wish thee gather.
But yet be wary in thy studious care.
RICHARD   Thy grave admonishments prevail with me.
But yet, methinks, my father's execution
100 Was nothing less than bloody tyranny.
MORTIMER   With silence, nephew, be thou politic.
Strong fixed is the house of Lancaster,
And, like a mountain, not to be removed.
But now thy uncle is removing hence,
105 As princes do their courts, when they are cloyed
With long continuance in a settled place.
RICHARD   O uncle, would some part of my young years
Might but redeem the passage of your age.
MORTIMER
Thou dost then wrong me, as that slaughterer doth
110 Which giveth many wounds when one will kill.
Mourn not, except thou sorrow for my good;
Only give order for my funeral.
And so farewell, and fair be all thy hopes,
And prosperous be thy life in peace and war.   [*Dies.*]
115 RICHARD   And peace, no war, befall thy parting soul.
In prison hast thou spent a pilgrimage
And like a hermit overpassed thy days.
Well, I will lock his counsel in my breast,
And what I do imagine – let that rest.
120 Keepers, convey him hence, and I myself
Will see his burial better than his life.
        Exeunt Gaolers, bearing out the body of Mortimer.
Here dies the dusky torch of Mortimer,
Choked with ambition of the meaner sort.

And for those wrongs, those bitter injuries
Which Somerset hath offered to my house, 125
I doubt not but with honour to redress.
And therefore haste I to the parliament –
Either to be restored to my blood,
Or make my will th'advantage of my good.   *Exit.*

3.1   *Flourish. Enter* KING, EXETER, GLOUCESTER,
WINCHESTER, WARWICK, SOMERSET, SUFFOLK,
RICHARD Plantagenet. *Gloucester offers to put up
a bill; Winchester snatches it, tears it.*

WINCHESTER
Com'st thou with deep premeditated lines?
With written pamphlets, studiously devised?
Humphrey of Gloucester, if thou canst accuse,
Or aught intend'st to lay unto my charge,
Do it without invention, suddenly, 5
As I with sudden and extemporal speech
Purpose to answer what thou canst object.
GLOUCESTER
Presumptuous priest, this place commands my
    patience,
Or thou shouldst find thou hast dishonoured me.
Think not, although in writing I preferred 10
The manner of thy vile outrageous crimes,
That therefore I have forged or am not able
Verbatim to rehearse the method of my pen.
No, prelate, such is thy audacious wickedness,
Thy lewd, pestiferous and dissentious pranks, 15
As very infants prattle of thy pride.
Thou art a most pernicious usurer,
Froward by nature, enemy to peace,
Lascivious, wanton – more than well beseems
A man of thy profession and degree. 20
And for thy treachery, what's more manifest,
In that thou laid'st a trap to take my life,
As well at London Bridge as at the Tower?
Beside, I fear me, if thy thoughts were sifted,
The King, thy sovereign, is not quite exempt 25
From envious malice of thy swelling heart.
WINCHESTER
Gloucester, I do defy thee. Lords, vouchsafe
To give me hearing what I shall reply.
If I were covetous, ambitious, or perverse –
As he will have me – how am I so poor? 30
Or how haps it I seek not to advance
Or raise myself, but keep my wonted calling?
And for dissension, who preferreth peace
More than I do? – except I be provoked.
No, my good lords, it is not that offends, 35
It is not that that hath incensed the Duke.
It is because no one should sway but he,
No one but he should be about the King;
And that engenders thunder in his breast
And makes him roar these accusations forth. 40

But he shall know I am as good –
GLOUCESTER   As good?
Thou bastard of my grandfather!
WINCHESTER   Ay, lordly sir; for what are you, I pray,
But one imperious in another's throne?
45 GLOUCESTER   Am I not Protector, saucy priest?
WINCHESTER   And am not I a prelate of the Church?
GLOUCESTER   Yes, as an outlaw in a castle keeps
And useth it to patronage his theft.
WINCHESTER   Unreverent Gloucester!
GLOUCESTER   Thou art reverend
50 Touching thy spiritual function, not thy life.
WINCHESTER   Rome shall remedy this.
GLOUCESTER   Roam thither, then.
WARWICK [*to Winchester*]
My lord, it were your duty to forbear.
SOMERSET   Ay, see the Bishop be not overborne.
Methinks my lord should be religious
55 And know the office that belongs to such.
WARWICK   Methinks his lordship should be humbler:
It fitteth not a prelate so to plead.
SOMERSET   Yes, when his holy state is touched so near.
WARWICK   State – holy or unhallowed – what of that?
60 Is not his grace Protector to the King?
RICHARD [*to the audience*]
Plantagenet, I see, must hold his tongue,
Lest it be said, 'Speak, sirrah, when you should.
Must your bold verdict enter talk with lords?'
Else would I have a fling at Winchester.
65 KING   Uncles of Gloucester and of Winchester,
The special watchmen of our English weal,
I would prevail – if prayers might prevail –
To join your hearts in love and amity.
O what a scandal is it to our crown
70 That two such noble peers as ye should jar?
Believe me, lords – my tender years can tell –
Civil dissension is a viperous worm,
That gnaws the bowels of the commonwealth.
    [*A noise within. Gloucester's men shout:* 'Down with
                                  the tawny coats'.]
What tumult's this?
WARWICK   An uproar, I dare warrant,
75 Begun through malice of the Bishop's men.
    [*A noise again. Gloucester's and Winchester's men shout:*
                                  'Stones, stones'.]

Enter Mayor.

MAYOR   O my good lords, and virtuous Henry,
Pity the city of London, pity us:
The Bishop and the Duke of Gloucester's men,
Forbidden late to carry any weapon,
80 Have filled their pockets full of pebble stones
And, banding themselves in contrary parts,
Do pelt so fast at one another's pate
That many have their giddy brains knocked out.
Our windows are broke down in every street,

And we, for fear, compelled to shut our shops.   85

Enter Servingmen *of Gloucester and Winchester in
skirmish, with bloody pates.*

KING   We charge you, on allegiance to ourself,
To hold your slaughtering hands and keep the peace.
Pray, uncle Gloucester, mitigate this strife.
1 SERVINGMAN   Nay, if we be forbidden stones, we'll
fall to it with our teeth.   90
2 SERVINGMAN   Do what ye dare, we are as resolute.
    [*Skirmish again.*]
GLOUCESTER
You of my household, leave this peevish broil
And set this unaccustomed fight aside.
3 SERVINGMAN
My lord, we know your grace to be a man
Just and upright, and for your royal birth   95
Inferior to none but to his majesty;
And ere that we will suffer such a prince,
So kind a father of the commonweal,
To be disgraced by an ink-horn mate,
We and our wives and children all will fight,   100
And have our bodies slaughtered by thy foes.
1 SERVINGMAN   Ay, and the very parings of our nails
Shall pitch a field when we are dead. [*They begin again.*]
GLOUCESTER   Stay, stay, I say:
And if you love me, as you say you do,   105
Let me persuade you to forbear awhile.
KING   O, how this discord doth afflict my soul.
Can you, my lord of Winchester, behold
My sighs and tears, and will not once relent?
Who should be pitiful, if you be not?   110
Or who should study to prefer a peace
If holy churchmen take delight in broils?
WARWICK
Yield, my lord Protector, yield, Winchester –
Except you mean with obstinate repulse
To slay your sovereign and destroy the realm.   115
You see what mischief, and what murder too,
Hath been enacted through your enmity:
Then be at peace – except ye thirst for blood.
WINCHESTER   He shall submit, or I will never yield.
GLOUCESTER
Compassion on the King commands me stoop,   120
Or I would see his heart out ere the priest
Should ever get that privilege of me.
WARWICK   Behold, my lord of Winchester – the Duke
Hath banished moody discontented fury,
As by his smoothed brows it doth appear.   125
Why look you still so stern and tragical?
GLOUCESTER   Here, Winchester, I offer thee my hand.
    [*Winchester ignores Gloucester's offered hand.*]
KING   Fie, uncle Beaufort, I have heard you preach
That malice was a great and grievous sin:
And will not you maintain the thing you teach,   130
But prove a chief offender in the same?

WARWICK   Sweet King! The Bishop hath a kindly gird.
For shame, my lord of Winchester, relent;
What, shall a child instruct you what to do?
WINCHESTER
135   Well, Duke of Gloucester, I will yield to thee.
Love for thy love and hand for hand I give.
      [*He takes Gloucester's hand.*]
GLOUCESTER   Ay, but I fear me with a hollow heart.
See here, my friends and loving countrymen,
This token serveth for a flag of truce
140   Betwixt ourselves, and all our followers:
So help me God, as I dissemble not.
WINCHESTER   So help me God, as I intend it not.
KING   O loving uncle, kind Duke of Gloucester,
How joyful am I made by this contract.
145   Away, my masters, trouble us no more,
But join in friendship, as your lords have done.
1 SERVINGMAN   Content. I'll to the surgeon's.
2 SERVINGMAN   And so will I.
3 SERVINGMAN   And I will see what physic the tavern
150   affords.   *Exeunt Servingmen and Mayor.*
WARWICK   Accept this scroll, most gracious sovereign,
Which in the right of Richard Plantagenet
We do exhibit to your majesty.
GLOUCESTER
Well urged, my lord of Warwick – for, sweet prince,
155   An if your grace mark every circumstance,
You have great reason to do Richard right,
Especially for those occasions
At Eltham Place I told your majesty.
KING   And those occasions, uncle, were of force.
160   Therefore, my loving lords, our pleasure is
That Richard be restored to his blood.
WARWICK   Let Richard be restored to his blood:
So shall his father's wrongs be recompensed.
WINCHESTER   As will the rest, so willeth Winchester.
165   KING   If Richard will be true, not that alone
But all the whole inheritance I give
That doth belong unto the house of York,
From whence you spring by lineal descent.
RICHARD   Thy humble servant vows obedience
170   And humble service till the point of death.
KING   Stoop then and set your knee against my foot:
And, in reguerdon of that duty done,
I girt thee with the valiant sword of York.
Rise, Richard, like a true Plantagenet,
175   And rise created princely Duke of York.
RICHARD   And so thrive Richard, as thy foes may fall:
And, as my duty springs, so perish they
That grudge one thought against your majesty.
ALL   Welcome, high prince, the mighty Duke of York.
SOMERSET [*to the audience*]
180   Perish, base prince, ignoble Duke of York.
GLOUCESTER   Now will it best avail your majesty
To cross the seas and to be crowned in France:
The presence of a king engenders love
Amongst his subjects and his loyal friends,

As it disanimates his enemies.   185
KING
When Gloucester says the word, King Henry goes –
For friendly counsel cuts off many foes.
GLOUCESTER   Your ships already are in readiness.
            Sennet. Flourish. Exeunt all but Exeter.
EXETER   Ay, we may march in England or in France,
Not seeing what is likely to ensue.   190
This late dissension grown betwixt the peers
Burns under feigned ashes of forged love
And will at last break out into a flame:
As festered members rot but by degree,
Till bones and flesh and sinews fall away,   195
So will this base and envious discord breed.
And now I fear that fatal prophecy,
Which in the time of Henry, named the Fifth,
Was in the mouth of every sucking babe –
That Henry born at Monmouth should win all,   200
And Henry born at Windsor lose all:
Which is so plain that Exeter doth wish
His days may finish ere that hapless time.   *Exit.*

3.2   *Enter* JOAN *Puzel, disguised as a poor*
      peasant, with four Soldiers *with sacks*
            upon their backs.

JOAN   These are the city gates, the gates of Rouen,
Through which our policy must make a breach.
Take heed – be wary how you place your words;
Talk like the vulgar sort of market men
That come to gather money for their corn.   5
If we have entrance, as I hope we shall,
And that we find the slothful watch but weak,
I'll by a sign give notice to our friends
That Charles the Dolphin may encounter them.
SOLDIER   Our sacks shall be a mean to sack the city,   10
And we be lords and rulers over Rouen.
Therefore we'll knock.   [*They knock.*]
WATCH [*within*]   Qui est là?
JOAN   Paysans, les pauvres gens de France,
Poor market folks that come to sell their corn.
WATCH [*within*]   Enter, go in – the market bell is rung.   15
      [*Opens the gate.*]
JOAN   Now, Rouen, I'll shake thy bulwarks to the ground.
                  Exeunt into the town.

      Enter CHARLES, *the* BASTARD, ALENÇON
            and REIGNIER.

CHARLES   Saint Denis bless this happy stratagem,
And once again we'll sleep secure in Rouen.
BASTARD   Here entered Puzel and her practisants.
Now she is there, how will she specify   20
'Here is the best and safest passage in'?
REIGNIER
By thrusting out a torch from yonder tower;
Which, once discerned, shows that her meaning is,
No way to that – for weakness – which she entered.

Enter JOAN Puzel, *on the top, thrusting*
out a torch, burning.

JOAN   Behold, this is the happy wedding torch 25
That joineth Rouen unto her countrymen –
But burning fatal to the Talbonites.
BASTARD   See, noble Charles, the beacon of our friend;
The burning torch in yonder turret stands.
CHARLES   Now shine it like a comet of revenge, 30
A prophet to the fall of all our foes.
REIGNIER   Defer no time, delays have dangerous ends.
Enter and cry 'The Dolphin' presently,
And then do execution on the watch.
Alarum and exeunt into the town.

An alarum. Enter TALBOT *in an excursion.*

TALBOT
France, thou shalt rue this treason with thy tears, 35
If Talbot but survive thy treachery.
Puzel, that witch, that damned sorceress,
Hath wrought this hellish mischief unawares,
That hardly we escaped the pride of France.
Exit. An alarum, excursions.

Enter BEDFORD, *brought in sick in a chair by two*
Attendants. Enter TALBOT *and* BURGUNDY *without;*
within, JOAN Puzel, CHARLES, *the* BASTARD *and*
REIGNIER *on the walls.*

JOAN   Good morrow, gallants; want ye corn for bread? 40
I think the Duke of Burgundy will fast
Before he'll buy again at such a rate.
'Twas full of darnel: do you like the taste?
BURGUNDY   Scoff on, vile fiend and shameless courtesan.
I trust ere long to choke thee with thine own, 45
And make thee curse the harvest of that corn.
CHARLES
Your grace may starve perhaps before that time.
BEDFORD
O let no words, but deeds, revenge this treason.
JOAN   What will you do, good greybeard? Break a lance
And run a-tilt at death within a chair? 50
TALBOT   Foul fiend of France and hag of all despite,
Encompassed with thy lustful paramours,
Becomes it thee to taunt his valiant age
And twit with cowardice a man half dead?
Damsel, I'll have a bout with you again, 55
Or else let Talbot perish with this shame.
JOAN   Are ye so hot, sir? Yet, Puzel, hold thy peace;
If Talbot do but thunder, rain will follow.
[*The English whisper together in counsel.*]
God speed the parliament: who shall be the speaker?
TALBOT   Dare ye come forth and meet us in the field? 60
JOAN   Belike your lordship takes us then for fools,
To try if that our own be ours or no.
TALBOT   I speak not to that railing Hecate,
But unto thee, Alençon, and the rest.
Will ye, like soldiers, come and fight it out? 65

ALENÇON   *Seigneur*, no.
TALBOT   *Seigneur*, hang: base muleteers of France –
Like peasant footboys do they keep the walls
And dare not take up arms like gentlemen.
JOAN   Away, captains; let's get us from the walls, 70
For Talbot means no goodness by his looks.
Goodbye, my lord. We came but to tell you that we are
here. *Exeunt from the walls.*
TALBOT   And there will we be too, ere it be long,
Or else reproach be Talbot's greatest fame.
Vow, Burgundy, by honour of thy house, 75
Pricked on by public wrongs sustained in France,
Either to get the town again, or die.
And I, as sure as English Henry lives,
And as his father here was conqueror,
As sure as in this late betrayed town 80
Great *Coeur de Lion*'s heart was buried,
So sure I swear to get the town or die.
BURGUNDY   My vows are equal partners with thy vows.
TALBOT   But ere we go regard this dying prince,
The valiant Duke of Bedford. Come, my lord, 85
We will bestow you in some better place,
Fitter for sickness and for crazy age.
BEDFORD   Lord Talbot, do not so dishonour me.
Here will I sit, before the walls of Rouen,
And will be partner of your weal or woe. 90
BURGUNDY
Courageous Bedford, let us now persuade you.
BEDFORD   Not to be gone from hence; for once I read
That stout Pendragon, in his litter sick,
Came to the field, and vanquished his foes.
Methinks I should revive the soldiers' hearts, 95
Because I ever found them as myself.
TALBOT   Undaunted spirit in a dying breast!
Then be it so: heavens keep old Bedford safe.
And now no more ado, brave Burgundy,
But gather we our forces out of hand 100
And set upon our boasting enemy.
Exeunt all but Bedford and two Attendants.

An alarum; excursions. Enter Sir John
FASTOLFE *and a* Captain.

CAPTAIN
Whither away, Sir John Fastolfe, in such haste?
FASTOLFE   Whither away? To save myself by flight –
We are like to have the overthrow again.
CAPTAIN   What? Will you fly, and leave Lord Talbot? 105
FASTOLFE
Ay, all the Talbots in the world, to save my life. *Exit.*
CAPTAIN
Cowardly knight, ill fortune follow thee. *Exit.*

Retreat. Excursions. JOAN Puzel, ALENÇON *and*
CHARLES *enter and fly.*

BEDFORD   Now, quiet soul, depart when heaven please,
For I have seen our enemies' overthrow.
What is the trust or strength of foolish man? 110

They that of late were daring with their scoffs
Are glad and fain by flight to save themselves.
  Bedford dies, and is carried in, by two, in his chair.

An alarum. Enter TALBOT, BURGUNDY *and the rest.*

TALBOT Lost – and recovered in a day again!
This is a double honour, Burgundy;
115 Yet heavens have glory for this victory.
BURGUNDY Warlike and martial Talbot, Burgundy
Enshrines thee in his heart, and there erects
Thy noble deeds as valour's monuments.
TALBOT Thanks, gentle duke. But where is Puzel now?
120 I think her old familiar is asleep.
Now where's the Bastard's braves and Charles his
  gleeks?
What, all amort? Rouen hangs her head for grief
That such a valiant company are fled.
Now will we take some order in the town,
125 Placing therein some expert officers,
And then depart to Paris to the King,
For there young Henry with his nobles lie.
BURGUNDY
What wills Lord Talbot pleaseth Burgundy.
TALBOT But yet before we go let's not forget
130 The noble Duke of Bedford, late deceased,
But see his exequies fulfilled in Rouen.
A braver soldier never couched lance,
A gentler heart did never sway in court.
But kings and mightiest potentates must die,
135 For that's the end of human misery. *Exeunt.*

3.3 *Enter* CHARLES, *the* BASTARD, ALENÇON
   and JOAN Puzel.

JOAN Dismay not, princes, at this accident,
Nor grieve that Rouen is so recovered:
Care is no cure, but rather corrosive,
For things that are not to be remedied.
5 Let frantic Talbot triumph for a while,
And like a peacock sweep along his tail;
We'll pull his plumes and take away his train,
If Dolphin and the rest will be but ruled.
CHARLES We have been guided by thee hitherto
10 And of thy cunning had no diffidence.
One sudden foil shall never breed distrust.
BASTARD Search out thy wit for secret policies
And we will make thee famous through the world.
ALENÇON We'll set thy statue in some holy place
15 And have thee reverenced like a blessed saint.
Employ thee then, sweet virgin, for our good.
JOAN Then thus it must be – this doth Joan devise:
By fair persuasions mixed with sugared words
We will entice the Duke of Burgundy
20 To leave the Talbot and to follow us.
CHARLES Ay marry, sweeting, if we could do that,
France were no place for Henry's warriors,

Nor should that nation boast it so with us,
But be extirped from our provinces.
ALENÇON
For ever should they be expulsed from France, 25
And not have title of an earldom here.
JOAN Your honours shall perceive how I will work
To bring this matter to the wished end.
   [*Drum sounds afar off.*]
Hark – by the sound of drum you may perceive
Their powers are marching unto Paris-ward. 30
  [*Here sound an English march offstage.*]
There goes the Talbot with his colours spread,
And all the troops of English after him.
   [*French march sounds offstage.*]
Now in the rearward comes the Duke and his:
Fortune, in favour, makes him lag behind.
Summon a parley. We will talk with him. 35
   [*Trumpets sound a parley.*]
CHARLES A parley with the Duke of Burgundy.

Enter BURGUNDY.

BURGUNDY Who craves a parley with the Burgundy?
JOAN
The princely Charles of France, thy countryman.
BURGUNDY
What sayst thou, Charles? For I am marching hence.
CHARLES
Speak, Puzel, and enchant him with thy words. 40
JOAN Brave Burgundy, undoubted hope of France,
Stay, let thy humble handmaid speak to thee.
BURGUNDY Speak on, but be not over-tedious.
JOAN Look on thy country, look on fertile France,
And see the cities and the towns defaced 45
By wasting ruin of the cruel foe,
As looks the mother on her lowly babe
When death doth close his tender-dying eyes.
See, see the pining malady of France,
Behold the wounds, the most unnatural wounds, 50
Which thou thyself hast given her woeful breast.
O turn thy edged sword another way,
Strike those that hurt, and hurt not those that help:
One drop of blood drawn from thy country's bosom
Should grieve thee more than streams of foreign gore. 55
Return thee therefore with a flood of tears
And wash away thy country's stained spots.
BURGUNDY [*aside*]
Either she hath bewitched me with her words,
Or nature makes me suddenly relent.
JOAN
Besides, all French and France exclaims on thee, 60
Doubting thy birth and lawful progeny.
Who join'st thou with but with a lordly nation,
That will not trust thee but for profit's sake?
When Talbot hath set footing once in France
And fashioned thee that instrument of ill, 65
Who then but English Henry will be lord,

And thou be thrust out, like a fugitive?
Call we to mind – and mark but this for proof –
Was not the Duke of Orleans thy foe?
70 And was he not in England prisoner?
But when they heard he was thine enemy
They set him free without his ransom paid,
In spite of Burgundy and all his friends.
See then, thou fight'st against thy countrymen
75 And join'st with them will be thy slaughter-men.
Come, come, return; return, thou wandering lord.
Charles and the rest will take thee in their arms.

BURGUNDY [*aside*]
I am vanquished: these haughty words of hers
Have battered me like roaring cannon-shot
80 And made me almost yield upon my knees. –
Forgive me, country, and sweet countrymen;
And, lords, accept this hearty kind embrace.
My forces and my power of men are yours.
So farewell, Talbot. I'll no longer trust thee.
85 JOAN   Done like a Frenchman: turn and turn again.
CHARLES
Welcome, brave Duke. Thy friendship makes us fresh.
BASTARD   And doth beget new courage in our breasts.
ALENÇON   Puzel hath bravely played her part in this
And doth deserve a coronet of gold.
CHARLES
90 Now let us on, my lords, and join our powers,
And seek how we may prejudice the foe.   *Exeunt.*

3.4   *Enter the* KING, GLOUCESTER, WINCHESTER,
Richard Plantagenet, *now* Duke of YORK, SUFFOLK,
SOMERSET, WARWICK, VERNON *and* BASSET,
EXETER; *to them, with his Soldiers,* TALBOT.

TALBOT   My gracious Prince and honourable peers,
Hearing of your arrival in this realm
I have awhile given truce unto my wars
To do my duty to my sovereign.
5 In sign whereof, this arm – that hath reclaimed
To your obedience fifty fortresses,
Twelve cities and seven walled towns of strength,
Beside five hundred prisoners of esteem –
Lets fall his sword before your highness' feet,
[*Kneels.*]
10 And with submissive loyalty of heart
Ascribes the glory of his conquest got
First to my God, and next unto your grace.
KING   Is this the Lord Talbot, uncle Gloucester,
That hath so long been resident in France?
15 GLOUCESTER   Yes, if it please your majesty, my liege.
KING   Welcome, brave captain and victorious lord.
When I was young – as yet I am not old –
I do remember how my father said
A stouter champion never handled sword.
20 Long since we were resolved of your truth,
Your faithful service and your toil in war;

Yet never have you tasted our reward,
Or been reguerdoned with so much as thanks,
Because till now we never saw your face.
Therefore stand up, and for these good deserts   25
We here create you Earl of Shrewsbury,
And in our coronation take your place.
Sennet. Flourish. Exeunt all but Vernon and Basset.
VERNON   Now, sir, to you, that were so hot at sea,
Disgracing of these colours that I wear
In honour of my noble lord of York –   30
Dar'st thou maintain the former words thou spak'st?
BASSET   Yes, sir, as well as you dare patronage
The envious barking of your saucy tongue
Against my lord the Duke of Somerset.
VERNON   Sirrah, thy lord I honour as he is.   35
BASSET   Why, what is he? As good a man as York.
VERNON   Hark ye, not so; in witness, take ye that.
[*Strikes him.*]
BASSET   Villain, thou knowest the law of arms is such
That whoso draws a sword, 'tis present death –
Or else this blow should broach thy dearest blood. 40
But I'll unto his majesty, and crave
I may have liberty to venge this wrong –
When, thou shalt see, I'll meet thee to thy cost.
VERNON   Well, miscreant, I'll be there as soon as you
And after meet you sooner than you would.   *Exeunt.*   45

4.1   *Enter* KING, GLOUCESTER, WINCHESTER,
YORK, SUFFOLK, SOMERSET, WARWICK,
TALBOT, *Governor of Paris and* EXETER.

GLOUCESTER
Lord Bishop, set the crown upon his head.
WINCHESTER
God save King Henry, of that name the Sixth.
GLOUCESTER   Now, Governor of Paris, take your oath:
That you elect no other king but him,
Esteem none friends but such as are his friends,   5
And none your foes but such as shall pretend
Malicious practices against his state.
This shall ye do, so help you righteous God.
Exit Governor.

Enter FASTOLFE.

FASTOLFE
My gracious sovereign, as I rode from Calais
To haste unto your coronation,   10
A letter was delivered to my hands,
Writ to your grace from the Duke of Burgundy.
TALBOT   Shame to the Duke of Burgundy, and thee.
[*Tears the emblem of the Garter from Fastolfe's leg.*]
I vowed, base knight, when I did meet thee next
To tear the Garter from thy craven's leg,   15
Which I have done, because unworthily
Thou wast installed in that high degree.
Pardon me, princely Henry, and the rest:

This dastard, at the battle of Patay, –
20 When but in all I was six thousand strong,
And that the French were almost ten to one –
Before we met, or that a stroke was given,
Like to a trusty squire, did run away;
In which assault we lost twelve hundred men.
25 Myself and divers gentlemen beside
Were there surprised and taken prisoners.
Then judge, great lords, if I have done amiss;
Or whether that such cowards ought to wear
This ornament of knighthood, yea or no?
30 GLOUCESTER   To say the truth, this fact was infamous
And ill beseeming any common man,
Much more a knight, a captain and a leader.
TALBOT   When first this order was ordained, my lords,
Knights of the Garter were of noble birth,
35 Valiant and virtuous, full of haughty courage,
Such as were grown to credit by the wars;
Not fearing death nor shrinking for distress
But always resolute in most extremes.
He then that is not furnished in this sort
40 Doth but usurp the sacred name of knight,
Profaning this most honourable order,
And should (if I were worthy to be judge)
Be quite degraded, like a hedge-born swain
That doth presume to boast of gentle blood.
45 KING   Stain to thy countrymen, thou hear'st thy doom:
Be packing, therefore, thou that wast a knight,
Henceforth we banish thee on pain of death.
                                  Exit Fastolfe.
And now, my lord Protector, view the letter
Sent from our uncle, Duke of Burgundy.
GLOUCESTER
50 What means his grace, that he hath changed his style?
No more but, plain and bluntly, 'To the King'.
Hath he forgot he is his sovereign?
Or doth this churlish superscription
Pretend some alteration in good will?
55 What's here? *I have upon especial cause,*
Moved with compassion of my country's wrack,
Together with the pitiful complaints
Of such as your oppression feeds upon,
Forsaken your pernicious faction
60 *And joined with Charles, the rightful King of France.*
O monstrous treachery: can this be so,
That in alliance, amity and oaths
There should be found such false dissembling
    guile?
KING   What? Doth my uncle Burgundy revolt?
GLOUCESTER
65 He doth, my lord, and is become your foe.
KING   Is that the worst this letter doth contain?
GLOUCESTER
It is the worst – and all, my lord, he writes.
KING   Why then, Lord Talbot there shall talk with him
And give him chastisement for this abuse.
70 How say you, my lord, are you not content?

TALBOT
Content, my liege? Yes: but that I am prevented,
I should have begged I might have been employed.
KING
Then gather strength and march unto him straight.
Let him perceive how ill we brook his treason
And what offence it is to flout his friends.   75
TALBOT   I go, my lord, in heart desiring still
You may behold confusion of your foes.   *Exit.*

Enter VERNON *and* BASSET.

VERNON   Grant me the combat, gracious sovereign.
BASSET   And me, my lord, grant me the combat too.
YORK   This is my servant: hear him, noble prince.   80
SOMERSET   And this is mine: sweet Henry, favour him.
KING   Be patient, lords, and give them leave to speak.
Say, gentlemen, what makes you thus exclaim,
And wherefore crave you combat? Or with whom?
VERNON   With him, my lord, for he hath done me wrong.   85
BASSET   And I with him, for he hath done me wrong.
KING   What is that wrong whereof you both complain?
First let me know and then I'll answer you.
BASSET   Crossing the sea from England into France,
This fellow here with envious carping tongue   90
Upbraided me about the rose I wear,
Saying the sanguine colour of the leaves
Did represent my master's blushing cheeks
When stubbornly he did repugn the truth
About a certain question in the law   95
Argued betwixt the Duke of York and him –
With other vile and ignominious terms.
In confutation of which rude reproach
And in defence of my lord's worthiness
I crave the benefit of law of arms.   100
VERNON   And that is my petition, noble lord:
For though he seem with forged quaint conceit
To set a gloss upon his bold intent,
Yet know, my lord, I was provoked by him,
And he first took exceptions at this badge,   105
Pronouncing that the paleness of this flower
Bewrayed the faintness of my master's heart.
YORK   Will not this malice, Somerset, be left?
SOMERSET
Your private grudge, my lord of York, will out,
Though ne'er so cunningly you smother it.   110
KING
Good Lord, what madness rules in brainsick men,
When for so slight and frivolous a cause
Such factious emulations shall arise?
Good cousins both, of York and Somerset,
Quiet yourselves, I pray, and be at peace.   115
YORK   Let this dissension first be tried by fight,
And then your highness shall command a peace.
SOMERSET   The quarrel toucheth none but us alone;
Betwixt ourselves let us decide it then.
YORK   There is my pledge; accept it, Somerset.   120
    [*York throws down his gauntlet.*]

VERNON   Nay, let it rest where it began at first.

BASSET   Confirm it so, mine honourable lord.

GLOUCESTER   Confirm it so? Confounded be your strife
And perish ye with your audacious prate.
Presumptuous vassals, are you not ashamed
With this immodest clamorous outrage
To trouble and disturb the King and us?
And you, my lords, methinks you do not well
To bear with their perverse objections –
Much less to take occasion from their mouths
To raise a mutiny betwixt yourselves.
Let me persuade you take a better course.

EXETER
It grieves his highness. Good my lords, be friends.

KING   Come hither, you that would be combatants.
Henceforth I charge you, as you love our favour,
Quite to forget this quarrel and the cause.
And you, my lords, remember where we are –
In France, amongst a fickle wavering nation.
If they perceive dissension in our looks,
And that within ourselves we disagree,
How will their grudging stomachs be provoked
To wilful disobedience and rebel!
Beside, what infamy will there arise
When foreign princes shall be certified
That for a toy, a thing of no regard,
King Henry's peers and chief nobility
Destroyed themselves and lost the realm of France!
O think upon the conquest of my father,
My tender years, and let us not forgo
That for a trifle that was bought with blood.
Let me be umpire in this doubtful strife.
   [*Takes the red rose from Basset.*]
I see no reason, if I wear this rose,
That anyone should therefore be suspicious
I more incline to Somerset than York:
Both are my kinsmen, and I love them both.
As well they may upbraid me with my crown
Because, forsooth, the King of Scots is crowned.
But your discretions better can persuade
Than I am able to instruct or teach;
And therefore, as we hither came in peace,
So let us still continue peace and love.
Cousin of York, we institute your grace
To be our regent in these parts of France:
And, good my lord of Somerset, unite
Your troops of horsemen with his bands of foot,
And like true subjects, sons of your progenitors,
Go cheerfully together and digest
Your angry choler on your enemies.
Ourself, my lord Protector and the rest
After some respite will return to Calais,
From thence to England – where I hope ere long
To be presented, by your victories,
With Charles, Alençon and that traitorous rout.
   Flourish. Exeunt all but York, Warwick,
   Exeter and Vernon.

WARWICK   My lord of York, I promise you the King
Prettily, methought, did play the orator.

YORK   And so he did, but yet I like it not,
In that he wears the badge of Somerset.

WARWICK
Tush, that was but his fancy. Blame him not.
I dare presume, sweet prince, he thought no harm.

YORK   An if I wist he did – but let it rest;
Other affairs must now be managed.
   Exeunt all but Exeter.

EXETER
Well didst thou, Richard, to suppress thy voice;
For had the passions of thy heart burst out
I fear we should have seen deciphered there
More rancorous spite, more furious raging broils,
Than yet can be imagined or supposed:
But howsoe'er, no simple man that sees
This jarring discord of nobility,
This shouldering of each other in the court,
This factious bandying of their favourites,
But that it doth presage some ill event.
'Tis much when sceptres are in children's hands,
But more when envy breeds unkind division –
There comes the ruin, there begins confusion.   *Exit.*

4.2   *Enter* TALBOT *with Trumpet and Drum,*
   before Bordeaux.

TALBOT   Go to the gates of Bordeaux, trumpeter;
Summon their general unto the wall.
   [*Trumpet sounds for parley.*]

   Enter Captain *aloft.*

English John Talbot, captain, calls you forth,
Servant in arms to Harry, King of England.
And thus he would: open your city gates,
Be humble to us, call my sovereign yours
And do him homage as obedient subjects,
And I'll withdraw me and my bloody power.
But if you frown upon this proffered peace
You tempt the fury of my three attendants,
Lean famine, quartering steel and climbing fire,
Who, in a moment, even with the earth
Shall lay your stately and air-braving towers,
If you forsake the offer of their love.

CAPTAIN   Thou ominous and fearful owl of death,
Our nation's terror and their bloody scourge,
The period of thy tyranny approacheth.
On us thou canst not enter but by death:
For I protest we are well fortified
And strong enough to issue out and fight.
If thou retire, the Dolphin well appointed
Stands with the snares of war to tangle thee.
On either hand thee there are squadrons pitched
To wall thee from the liberty of flight;
And no way canst thou turn thee for redress
But death doth front thee with apparent spoil

And pale destruction meets thee in the face.
Ten thousand French have ta'en the sacrament
To rive their dangerous artillery
30 Upon no Christian soul but English Talbot.
Lo, there thou stand'st a breathing valiant man
Of an invincible unconquered spirit:
This is the latest glory of thy praise
That I, thy enemy, due thee withal;
35 For ere the glass that now begins to run
Finish the process of his sandy hour,
These eyes that see thee now well coloured
Shall see thee withered, bloody, pale and dead.

                              [*Drum afar off*]

Hark, hark; the Dolphin's drum, a warning bell,
40 Sings heavy music to thy timorous soul,
And mine shall ring thy dire departure out.   *Exit.*
TALBOT   He fables not. I hear the enemy.
Out, some light horsemen, and peruse their wings.
O negligent and heedless discipline –
45 How are we parked and bounded in a pale –
A little herd of England's timorous deer
Mazed with a yelping kennel of French curs.
If we be English deer, be then in blood:
Not rascal-like to fall down with a pinch,
50 But rather, moody-mad and desperate stags,
Turn on the bloody hounds with heads of steel
And make the cowards stand aloof at bay.
Sell every man his life as dear as mine
And they shall find dear deer of us, my friends.
55 God and Saint George, Talbot and England's right,
Prosper our colours in this dangerous fight.   *Exit.*

4.3   *Enter a* Messenger *that meets* YORK.
         Enter YORK *with Trumpet and many Soldiers.*

YORK   Are not the speedy scouts returned again,
That dogged the mighty army of the Dolphin?
MESSENGER
They are returned, my lord, and give it out
That he is marched to Bordeaux with his power
5 To fight with Talbot; as he marched along,
By your espials were discovered
Two mightier troops than that the Dolphin led,
Which joined with him and made their march for
    Bordeaux.
YORK   A plague upon that villain Somerset,
10 That thus delays my promised supply
Of horsemen, that were levied for this siege.
Renowned Talbot doth expect my aid,
And I am louted by a traitor villain,
And cannot help the noble chevalier.
15 God comfort him in this necessity.
If he miscarry, farewell wars in France.

         Enter another messenger, Sir William LUCY.

LUCY   Thou princely leader of our English strength –
Never so needful on the earth of France –

Spur to the rescue of the noble Talbot,
Who now is girdled with a waste of iron   20
And hemmed about with grim destruction.
To Bordeaux, warlike Duke, to Bordeaux, York,
Else farewell Talbot, France and England's honour.
YORK   O God, that Somerset, who in proud heart
Doth stop my cornets, were in Talbot's place;   25
So should we save a valiant gentleman
By forfeiting a traitor and a coward.
Mad ire and wrathful fury makes me weep,
That thus we die while remiss traitors sleep.
LUCY   O send some succour to the distressed lord.   30
YORK   He dies, we lose, I break my warlike word.
We mourn, France smiles; we lose, they daily get,
All long of this vile traitor Somerset.
LUCY   Then God take mercy on brave Talbot's soul,
And on his son, young John, who two hours since   35
I met in travail toward his warlike father.
This seven years did not Talbot see his son,
And now they meet where both their lives are done.
YORK   Alas, what joy shall noble Talbot have,
To bid his young son welcome to his grave.   40
Away, vexation almost stops my breath,
That sundered friends greet in the hour of death.
Lucy, farewell; no more my fortune can
But curse the cause I cannot aid the man.
Maine, Blois, Poitiers and Tours are won away,   45
Long all of Somerset and his delay.

                              Exeunt all but Lucy.

LUCY   Thus, while the vulture of sedition
Feeds in the bosom of such great commanders,
Sleeping neglection doth betray to loss
The conquest of our scarce-cold conqueror,   50
That ever-living man of memory,
Henry the Fifth. Whiles they each other cross,
Lives, honours, lands and all hurry to loss.

         Enter SOMERSET *with his army and*
              a Captain *of Talbot's.*

SOMERSET   It is too late, I cannot send them now.
This expedition was by York and Talbot   55
Too rashly plotted. All our general force
Might with a sally of the very town
Be buckled with: the over-daring Talbot
Hath sullied all his gloss of former honour
By this unheedful, desperate, wild adventure.   60
York set him on to fight and die in shame,
That, Talbot dead, great York might bear the name.
CAPTAIN [*to Somerset*]
Here is Sir William Lucy, who, with me,
Set from our o'ermatched forces forth for aid.
SOMERSET
How now, Sir William, whither were you sent?   65
LUCY
Whither, my lord? From bought and sold Lord Talbot
Who – ringed about with bold adversity –
Cries out for noble York and Somerset

To beat assailing death from his weak regions;
And whiles the honourable captain there
Drops bloody sweat from his war-wearied limbs
And, in advantage lingering, looks for rescue,
You, his false hopes, the trust of England's honour,
Keep off aloof with worthless emulation.
Let not your private discord keep away
The levied succours that should lend him aid,
While he, renowned noble gentleman,
Yield up his life unto a world of odds.
Orleans the Bastard, Charles, Burgundy,
Alençon, Reignier, compass him about,
And Talbot perisheth by your default.

SOMERSET
York set him on, York should have sent him aid.

LUCY   And York as fast upon your grace exclaims,
Swearing that you withhold his levied host,
Collected for this expedition.

SOMERSET
York lies. He might have sent, and had the horse.
I owe him little duty and less love,
And take foul scorn to fawn on him by sending.

LUCY   The fraud of England, not the force of France,
Hath now entrapped the noble-minded Talbot.
Never to England shall he bear his life,
But dies betrayed to fortune by your strife.

SOMERSET
Come – go – I will dispatch the horsemen straight:
Within six hours they will be at his aid.

LUCY   Too late comes rescue: he is ta'en or slain,
For fly he could not, if he would have fled;
And fly would Talbot never, though he might.

SOMERSET   If he be dead – brave Talbot, then, adieu.

LUCY
His fame lives in the world, his shame in you.   *Exeunt.*

4.4   *Enter* TALBOT *and his son* JOHN.

TALBOT   O young John Talbot, I did send for thee
To tutor thee in stratagems of war,
That Talbot's name might be in thee revived
When sapless age and weak unable limbs
Should bring thy father to his drooping chair.
But – O malignant and ill-boding stars –
Now thou art come unto a feast of death,
A terrible and unavoided danger.
Therefore, dear boy, mount on my swiftest horse,
And I'll direct thee how thou shalt escape
By sudden flight. Come – dally not, be gone.

JOHN   Is my name Talbot? And am I your son?
And shall I fly? O, if you love my mother,
Dishonour not her honourable name
To make a bastard and a slave of me.
The world will say, 'He is not Talbot's blood,
That basely fled when noble Talbot stood'.

TALBOT   Fly, to revenge my death if I be slain.

JOHN   He that flies so will ne'er return again.

TALBOT   If we both stay we both are sure to die.   20

JOHN   Then let me stay and, father, do you fly.
Your loss is great – so your regard should be;
My worth unknown – no loss is known in me.
Upon my death the French can little boast;
In yours they will, in you all hopes are lost.   25
Flight cannot stain the honour you have won;
But mine it will, that no exploit have done.
You fled for vantage, everyone will swear;
But if I bow they'll say it was for fear.
There is no hope that ever I will stay   30
If the first hour I shrink and run away.
Here on my knee I beg mortality,
Rather than life preserved with infamy.   [*Kneels.*]

TALBOT   Shall all thy mother's hopes lie in one tomb?

JOHN   Ay, rather than I'll shame my mother's womb.   35

TALBOT   Upon my blessing I command thee go.
[*John rises.*]

JOHN   To fight I will, but not to fly the foe.

TALBOT   Part of thy father may be saved in thee.

JOHN   No part of him but will be shame in me.

TALBOT
Thou never hadst renown, nor canst not lose it.   40

JOHN   Yes, your renowned name: shall flight abuse it?

TALBOT
Thy father's charge shall clear thee from that stain.

JOHN   You cannot witness for me, being slain.
If death be so apparent, then both fly.

TALBOT   And leave my followers here to fight and die?   45
My age was never tainted with such shame.

JOHN   And shall my youth be guilty of such blame?
No more can I be severed from your side
Than can yourself yourself in twain divide.
Stay, go, do what you will, the like do I;   50
For live I will not, if my father die.

TALBOT   Then here I take my leave of thee, fair son,
Born to eclipse thy life this afternoon.
Come, side by side together live and die,
And soul with soul from France to heaven fly.   55

Alarum. Exit Talbot.

Enter ALENÇON, BASTARD *and* BURGUNDY *in*
excursions, wherein Talbot's son is hemmed about by the
three Frenchmen, as he goes after his father, and TALBOT
re-enters and rescues him.

TALBOT
Saint George and victory! Fight, soldiers, fight.
The regent hath with Talbot broke his word
And left us to the rage of France his sword.
Where is John Talbot? Pause, and take thy breath.
I gave thee life, and rescued thee from death.   60

JOHN   O twice my father, twice am I thy son:
The life thou gav'st me first was lost and done,
Till with thy warlike sword, despite of fate,
To my determined time thou gav'st new date.

TALBOT
When from the Dolphin's crest thy sword struck fire   65

It warmed thy father's heart with proud desire
Of bold-faced victory. Then leaden age,
Quickened with youthful spleen and warlike rage,
Beat down Alençon, Orleans, Burgundy,
70 And from the pride of Gallia rescued thee.
The ireful bastard Orleans, that drew blood
From thee, my boy, and had the maidenhood
Of thy first fight, I soon encountered,
And, interchanging blows, I quickly shed
75 Some of his bastard blood, and in disgrace
Bespoke him thus: 'Contaminated, base
And misbegotten blood I spill of thine,
Mean and right poor, for that pure blood of mine
Which thou didst force from Talbot, my brave boy'.
80 Here, purposing the Bastard to destroy,
Came in strong rescue. Speak, thy father's care:
Art thou not weary, John? How dost thou fare?
Wilt thou yet leave the battle, boy, and fly,
Now thou art sealed the son of chivalry?
85 Fly, to revenge my death when I am dead;
The help of one stands me in little stead.
O, too much folly is it, well I wot,
To hazard all our lives in one small boat.
If I today die not with Frenchmen's rage,
90 Tomorrow I shall die with mickle age.
By me they nothing gain, an if I stay,
'Tis but the shortening of my life one day;
In thee thy mother dies, our household's name,
My death's revenge, thy youth and England's fame.
95 All these, and more, we hazard by thy stay;
All these are saved, if thou wilt fly away.
JOHN   The sword of Orleans hath not made me smart:
These words of yours draw life-blood from my heart.
On that advantage, bought with such a shame,
100 To save a paltry life and slay bright fame?
Before young Talbot from old Talbot fly,
The coward horse that bears me fall and die!
And like me to the peasant boys of France,
To be shame's scorn, and subject of mischance.
105 Surely, by all the glory you have won,
An if I fly I am not Talbot's son.
Then talk no more of flight, it is no boot:
If son to Talbot, die at Talbot's foot.
TALBOT   Then follow thou thy desperate sire of Crete,
110 Thou Icarus; thy life to me is sweet.
If thou wilt fight, fight by thy father's side,
And, commendable proved, let's die in pride.   *Exeunt.*

Alarum. Excursions. Enter old TALBOT *led by a* Servant.

TALBOT   Where is my other life? Mine own is gone.
O where's young Talbot? Where is valiant John?
115 Triumphant death, smeared with captivity,
Young Talbot's valour makes me smile at thee.
When he perceived me shrink and on my knee,
His bloody sword he brandished over me
And like a hungry lion did commence
120 Rough deeds of rage and stern impatience.

But when my angry guardant stood alone,
Tendering my ruin and assailed of none,
Dizzy-eyed fury and great rage of heart
Suddenly made him from my side to start
Into the clustering battle of the French, 125
And in that sea of blood my boy did drench
His over-mounting spirit, and there died
My Icarus, my blossom, in his pride.

Enter Soldiers with JOHN Talbot, *borne.*

SERVANT   O my dear lord, lo where your son is borne.
TALBOT
Thou antic death, which laugh'st us here to scorn, 130
Anon from thy insulting tyranny,
Coupled in bonds of perpetuity,
Two Talbots, winged, through the lither sky
In thy despite shall scape mortality.
O thou, whose wounds become hard-favoured death, 135
Speak to thy father ere thou yield thy breath:
Brave death by speaking, whether he will or no;
Imagine him a Frenchman, and thy foe.
Poor boy, he smiles, methinks, as who should say,
'Had death been French, then death had died today'. 140
Come, come, and lay him in his father's arms;
My spirit can no longer bear these harms.
Soldiers, adieu. I have what I would have,
Now my old arms are young John Talbot's grave.   *Dies.*

Enter CHARLES, ALENÇON, BURGUNDY, *the* BASTARD
and JOAN Puzel.

CHARLES   Had York and Somerset brought rescue in, 145
We should have found a bloody day of this.
BASTARD
How the young whelp of Talbot's, raging wood,
Did flesh his puny sword in Frenchmen's blood.
JOAN   Once I encountered him, and thus I said:
'Thou maiden youth, be vanquished by a maid'. 150
But with a proud majestical high scorn
He answered thus: 'Young Talbot was not born
To be the pillage of a giglot wench'.
So, rushing in the bowels of the French,
He left me proudly, as unworthy fight. 155
BURGUNDY
Doubtless he would have made a noble knight.
See where he lies inhearsed in the arms
Of the most bloody nurser of his harms.
BASTARD
Hew them to pieces. Hack their bones asunder,
Whose life was England's glory, Gallia's wonder. 160
CHARLES   O no, forbear. For that which we have fled
During the life, let us not wrong it dead.

Enter Sir William LUCY *with a French Herald.*

LUCY   Herald, conduct me to the Dolphin's tent,
To know who hath obtained the glory of the day.
CHARLES   On what submissive message art thou sent? 165
LUCY   Submission, Dolphin? 'Tis a mere French word:

We English warriors wot not what it means.
I come to know what prisoners thou hast ta'en,
And to survey the bodies of the dead.
70 CHARLES   For prisoners ask'st thou? Hell our prison is.
But tell me whom thou seek'st.
LUCY   But where's the great Alcides of the field? –
Valiant Lord Talbot, Earl of Shrewsbury,
Created for his rare success in arms
75 Great Earl of Washford, Waterford and Valence,
Lord Talbot of Goodrig and Urchinfield,
Lord Strange of Blackmere, Lord Verdon of Alton,
Lord Cromwell of Wingfield, Lord Furnival of
Sheffield,
The thrice victorious Lord of Falconbridge,
80 Knight of the noble order of Saint George,
Worthy Saint Michael and the Golden Fleece,
Great marshal to Henry the Sixth
Of all his wars within the realm of France.
JOAN   Here's a silly stately style indeed:
85 The Turk, that two and fifty kingdoms hath,
Writes not so tedious a style as this.
Him that thou magnifiest with all these titles
Stinking and fly-blown lies here at our feet.
LUCY   Is Talbot slain, the Frenchmen's only scourge,
90 Your kingdom's terror and black Nemesis?
O, were mine eyeballs into bullets turned,
That I in rage might shoot them at your faces.
O, that I could but call these dead to life,
It were enough to fright the realm of France.
95 Were but his picture left amongst you here
It would amaze the proudest of you all.
Give me their bodies that I may bear them hence
And give them burial as beseems their worth.
JOAN   I think this upstart is old Talbot's ghost,
00 He speaks with such a proud commanding spirit.
For God's sake let him have him: to keep them here,
They would but stink, and putrefy the air.
CHARLES   Go, take their bodies hence.
LUCY   I'll bear them hence;
But from their ashes shall be reared
05 A phoenix that shall make all France afeared.
CHARLES
So we be rid of them, do with him what thou wilt.
And now to Paris, in this conquering vein.
All will be ours, now bloody Talbot's slain.   *Exeunt.*

5.1 *Sennet. Enter* KING, GLOUCESTER *and* EXETER.

KING   Have you perused the letters from the Pope,
The Emperor and the Earl of Armagnac?
GLOUCESTER   I have, my lord, and their intent is this:
They humbly sue unto your excellence
To have a godly peace concluded of
Between the realms of England and of France.
KING   How doth your grace affect their motion?
GLOUCESTER
Well, my good lord, and as the only means

To stop effusion of our Christian blood
And 'stablish quietness on every side.   10
KING   Ay marry, uncle, for I always thought
It was both impious and unnatural
That such immanity and bloody strife
Should reign among professors of one faith.
GLOUCESTER   Beside, my lord, the sooner to effect   15
And surer bind this knot of amity,
The Earl of Armagnac – near knit to Charles,
A man of great authority in France –
Proffers his only daughter to your grace
In marriage, with a large and sumptuous dowry.   20
KING   Marriage, uncle? Alas, my years are young,
And fitter is my study and my books
Than wanton dalliance with a paramour.
Yet call th'ambassadors and, as you please,
So let them have their answers every one.   25
I shall be well content with any choice
Tends to God's glory and my country's weal.

Enter WINCHESTER *and three Ambassadors,*
among them the papal Legate *and an Ambassador*
from the Earl of Armagnac.

EXETER   What, is my lord of Winchester installed
And called unto a cardinal's degree?
Then, I perceive, that will be verified   30
Henry the Fifth did sometime prophesy:
'If once he come to be a cardinal
He'll make his cap co-equal with the crown'.
KING   My lords ambassadors, your several suits
Have been considered and debated on.   35
Your purpose is both good and reasonable,
And therefore are we certainly resolved
To draw conditions of a friendly peace,
Which by my lord of Winchester we mean
Shall be transported presently to France.   40
GLOUCESTER [*to the Ambassador of the Earl of Armagnac*]
And for the proffer of my lord your master,
I have informed his highness so at large
As, liking of the lady's virtuous gifts,
Her beauty and the value of her dower,
He doth intend she shall be England's queen.   45
KING   In argument and proof of which contract,
Bear her this jewel, pledge of my affection.
[*Gives the Ambassador a ring.*]
And so, my lord Protector, see them guarded,
And safely brought to Dover, wherein shipped,
Commit them to the fortune of the sea.   50
Exeunt all but Winchester, who keeps back the papal Legate.
WINCHESTER
Stay, my lord legate. You shall first receive
The sum of money which I promised
Should be delivered to his holiness
For clothing me in these grave ornaments.
LEGATE   I will attend upon your lordship's leisure.   55
WINCHESTER   Now Winchester will not submit, I trow,
Or be inferior to the proudest peer;

Humphrey of Gloucester, thou shalt well perceive
That neither in birth or for authority
60 The Bishop will be overborne by thee.
I'll either make thee stoop and bend thy knee,
Or sack this country with a mutiny.   *Exeunt.*

5.2   *Enter* CHARLES, BURGUNDY, ALENÇON,
        the BASTARD, REIGNIER *and* JOAN.

CHARLES
These news, my lords, may cheer our drooping
        spirits:
'Tis said the stout Parisians do revolt
And turn again unto the warlike French.
ALENÇON
Then march to Paris, royal Charles of France,
5   And keep not back your powers in dalliance.
JOAN   Peace be amongst them if they turn to us;
Else ruin combat with their palaces.

Enter Scout.

SCOUT   Success unto our valiant general
And happiness to his accomplices.
CHARLES
10   What tidings send our scouts? I prithee, speak.
SCOUT   The English army, that divided was
Into two parties, is now conjoined in one
And means to give you battle presently.
CHARLES   Somewhat too sudden, sirs, the warning is;
15   But we will presently provide for them.
BURGUNDY   I trust the ghost of Talbot is not there.
Now he is gone, my lord, you need not fear.
JOAN   Of all base passions, fear is most accursed.
Command the conquest, Charles, it shall be thine:
20   Let Henry fret, and all the world repine.
CHARLES
Then on, my lords, and France be fortunate.   *Exeunt.*

Alarum. Excursions. Enter JOAN *Puzel.*

JOAN   The regent conquers and the Frenchmen fly.
Now help, ye charming spells and periapts,
And ye, choice spirits that admonish me
25   And give me signs of future accidents.   [*Thunder*]
You speedy helpers, that are substitutes
Under the lordly monarch of the north,
Appear, and aid me in this enterprise.

Enter Fiends.

This speedy and quick appearance argues proof
30   Of your accustomed diligence to me.
Now, ye familiar spirits, that are culled
Out of the powerful regions under earth,
Help me this once, that France may get the field.
[*They walk, and speak not.*]
O hold me not with silence over-long:
35   Where I was wont to feed you with my blood,
I'll lop a member off and give it you

In earnest of a further benefit
So you do condescend to help me now.
[*They hang their heads.*]
No hope to have redress? My body shall
40   Pay recompense if you will grant my suit.
[*They shake their heads.*]
Cannot my body nor blood sacrifice
Entreat you to your wonted furtherance?
Then take my soul – my body, soul, and all –
Before that England give the French the foil.
They depart.
45   See, they forsake me. Now the time is come
That France must vail her lofty-plumed crest,
And let her head fall into England's lap.
My ancient incantations are too weak,
And hell too strong for me to buckle with.
50   Now, France, thy glory droopeth to the dust.   *Exit.*

Excursions: BURGUNDY *and* YORK *enter and fight
hand to hand. French enter with* JOAN *and fly.
York captures Joan Puzel.*

YORK   Damsel of France, I think I have you fast.
Unchain your spirits now with spelling charms
And try if they can gain your liberty.
A goodly prize, fit for the devil's grace.
55   See how the ugly witch doth bend her brows
As if, with Circe, she would change my shape.
JOAN   Changed to a worser shape thou canst not be.
YORK   O, Charles the Dolphin is a proper man;
No shape but his can please your dainty eye.
JOAN   A plaguing mischief light on Charles and thee,
60   And may ye both be suddenly surprised
By bloody hands, in sleeping on your beds.
YORK   Fell banning hag, enchantress, hold thy tongue.
JOAN   I prithee, give me leave to curse awhile.
YORK   Curse, miscreant, when thou com'st to the stake.
65   *Exeunt.*

Alarum. Enter SUFFOLK *with* MARGARET *in his hand.*

SUFFOLK   Be what thou wilt, thou art my prisoner.
[*Gazes on her.*]
O fairest beauty, do not fear nor fly,
For I will touch thee but with reverent hands;
I kiss these fingers for eternal peace
70   And lay them gently on thy tender side.
Who art thou? Say, that I may honour thee.
MARGARET
Margaret my name, and daughter to a king,
The King of Naples – whosoe'er thou art.
SUFFOLK   An earl I am, and Suffolk am I called.
75   Be not offended, Nature's miracle;
Thou art allotted to be ta'en by me.
So doth the swan her downy cygnets save,
Keeping them prisoner underneath his wings.
Yet, if this servile usage once offend,
80   Go, and be free again as Suffolk's friend.
[*She is going.*]

O stay: [*to himself*] I have no power to let her pass.
My hand would free her, but my heart says no.
As plays the sun upon the glassy streams,
Twinkling another counterfeited beam,
So seems this gorgeous beauty to mine eyes.
Fain would I woo her, yet I dare not speak.
I'll call for pen and ink and write my mind.
Fie, de la Pole, disable not thyself:
Hast not a tongue? Is she not here?
Wilt thou be daunted at a woman's sight?
Ay. Beauty's princely majesty is such
Confounds the tongue, and makes the senses rough.
MARGARET　Say, Earl of Suffolk – if thy name be so –
What ransom must I pay before I pass?
For I perceive I am thy prisoner.
SUFFOLK [*to himself*]
How canst thou tell she will deny thy suit
Before thou make a trial of her love?
MARGARET
Why speak'st thou not? What ransom must I pay?
SUFFOLK [*to himself*]
She's beautiful, and therefore to be wooed:
She is a woman, therefore to be won.
MARGARET [*to herself*]
Wilt thou accept of ransom, yea or no?
SUFFOLK [*to himself*]
Fond man, remember that thou hast a wife.
Then how can Margaret be thy paramour?
MARGARET [*to herself*]
I were best to leave him, for he will not hear.
SUFFOLK [*to himself*]
There all is marred; there lies a cooling card.
MARGARET [*to herself*]
He talks at random: sure the man is mad.
SUFFOLK [*to himself*]
And yet a dispensation may be had.
MARGARET
And yet I would that you would answer me.
SUFFOLK [*to himself*]
I'll win this Lady Margaret. For whom?
Why, for my king. Tush, that's a wooden thing.
MARGARET　He talks of wood: it is some carpenter.
SUFFOLK [*to himself*]
Yet so my fancy may be satisfied,
And peace established between these realms.
But there remains a scruple in that too:
For though her father be the King of Naples,
Duke of Anjou and Maine, yet is he poor,
And our nobility will scorn the match.
MARGARET　Hear ye, captain? Are you not at leisure?
SUFFOLK [*to himself*]
It shall be so, disdain they ne'er so much.
Henry is youthful, and will quickly yield.
[*to Margaret*] Madam, I have a secret to reveal.
MARGARET [*to herself*]
What though I be enthralled? He seems a knight,
And will not any way dishonour me.

SUFFOLK　Lady, vouchsafe to listen what I say.
MARGARET [*to herself*]
Perhaps I shall be rescued by the French,　125
And then I need not crave his courtesy.
SUFFOLK　Sweet madam, give me hearing in a cause.
MARGARET [*to herself*]
Tush, women have been captivate ere now.
SUFFOLK　Lady, wherefore talk you so?
MARGARET　I cry you mercy, 'tis but *quid* for *quo*.　130
SUFFOLK　Say, gentle princess, would you not suppose
Your bondage happy, to be made a queen?
MARGARET　To be a queen in bondage is more vile
Than is a slave in base servility;
For princes should be free.
SUFFOLK　　　　　　　　　And so shall you,　135
If happy England's royal king be free.
MARGARET　Why, what concerns his freedom unto me?
SUFFOLK　I'll undertake to make thee Henry's queen,
To put a golden sceptre in thy hand
And set a precious crown upon thy head,　140
If thou wilt condescend to be my –
MARGARET　　　　　　　　　　　　What?
SUFFOLK　His love.
MARGARET　I am unworthy to be Henry's wife.
SUFFOLK　No, gentle madam; I unworthy am
To woo so fair a dame to be his wife –　145
And have no portion in the choice myself.
How say you, madam, are ye so content?
MARGARET　An if my father please, I am content.
SUFFOLK　Then call our captains and our colours forth,
And, madam, at your father's castle walls　150
We'll crave a parley to confer with him.
　　　　　　[*Sound trumpets, at Suffolk's command.*]

Enter REIGNIER *on the walls.*

See, Reignier, see, thy daughter prisoner.
REIGNIER　To whom?
SUFFOLK　　　　　　　To me.
REIGNIER　　　　　　　　　　Suffolk, what remedy?
I am a soldier, and unapt to weep,
Or to exclaim on fortune's fickleness.　155
SUFFOLK　Yes, there is remedy enough, my lord.
Consent – and for thy honour give consent –
Thy daughter shall be wedded to my king,
Whom I with pain have wooed and won thereto,
And this, her easy-held imprisonment,　160
Hath gained thy daughter princely liberty.
REIGNIER　Speaks Suffolk as he thinks?
SUFFOLK　　　　　　　　　　　Fair Margaret knows
That Suffolk doth not flatter, face or feign.
REIGNIER　Upon thy princely warrant I descend
To give thee answer of thy just demand.　165
　　　　　　　　　　Exit Reignier from the walls.
SUFFOLK　And here I will expect thy coming.
　　　　　　　　　　　　　[*Trumpets sound.*]

Enter REIGNIER.

REIGNIER   Welcome, brave earl, into our territories.
Command in Anjou what your honour pleases.
SUFFOLK
Thanks, Reignier, happy for so sweet a child,
170   Fit to be made companion with a king.
What answer makes your grace unto my suit?
REIGNIER
Since thou dost deign to woo her little worth
To be the princely bride of such a lord –
Upon condition I may quietly
175   Enjoy mine own, the country Maine and Anjou,
Free from oppression or the stroke of war –
My daughter shall be Henry's, if he please.
SUFFOLK   That is her ransom. I deliver her,
And those two counties I will undertake
180   Your grace shall well and quietly enjoy.
REIGNIER   And I – again in Henry's royal name,
As deputy unto that gracious king –
Give thee her hand for sign of plighted faith.
SUFFOLK   Reignier of France, I give thee kingly thanks,
185   Because this is in traffic of a king.
And yet methinks I could be well content
To be mine own attorney in this case.
I'll over then to England with this news,
And make this marriage to be solemnized.
190   So farewell, Reignier; set this diamond safe
In golden palaces, as it becomes.
REIGNIER   I do embrace thee, as I would embrace
The Christian prince King Henry were he here.
MARGARET
Farewell, my lord. Good wishes, praise and prayers
195   Shall Suffolk ever have of Margaret.
Exit Reignier. She is going after him,
when Suffolk stops her.
SUFFOLK
Farewell, sweet madam; but hark you, Margaret –
No princely commendations to my king?
MARGARET   Such commendations as becomes a maid,
A virgin and his servant, say to him.
200   SUFFOLK   Words sweetly placed, and modesty directed.
But, madam, I must trouble you again –
No loving token to his majesty?
MARGARET   Yes, my good lord: a pure unspotted heart,
Never yet taint with love, I send the King.
205   SUFFOLK   And this withal.   [*Kisses her.*]
MARGARET   That for thyself. I will not so presume
To send such peevish tokens to a king.   *Exit.*
SUFFOLK   O wert thou for myself! But Suffolk, stay,
Thou mayst not wander in that labyrinth:
210   There Minotaurs and ugly treasons lurk.
Solicit Henry with her wondrous praise,
Bethink thee on her virtues that surmount,
Mad natural graces that extinguish art;
Repeat their semblance often on the seas,
215   That when thou com'st to kneel at Henry's feet
Thou mayst bereave him of his wits with wonder.
Exit.

5.3   *Enter* YORK, WARWICK, Shepherd *and*
JOAN Puzel, *guarded.*

YORK   Bring forth that sorceress condemned to burn.
SHEPHERD
Ah, Joan, this kills thy father's heart outright.
Have I sought every country far and near
And – now it is my chance to find thee out –
Must I behold thy timeless cruel death?   5
Ah, Joan, sweet daughter Joan, I'll die with thee.
JOAN   Decrepit miser, base ignoble wretch,
I am descended of a gentler blood.
Thou art no father, nor no friend of mine.
SHEPHERD
Out, out! My lords, an please you, 'tis not so.   10
I did beget her, all the parish knows.
Her mother liveth yet, can testify
She was the first fruit of my bachelorship.
WARWICK   Graceless, wilt thou deny thy parentage?
YORK   This argues what her kind of life hath been,   15
Wicked and vile, and so her death concludes.
SHEPHERD   Fie, Joan, that thou wilt be so obstacle.
God knows, thou art a collop of my flesh,
And for thy sake have I shed many a tear.
Deny me not, I prithee, gentle Joan.   20
JOAN
Peasant, avaunt! [*to York*] You have suborned this man
Of purpose to obscure my noble birth.
SHEPHERD   'Tis true, I gave a noble to the priest
The morn that I was wedded to her mother.
Kneel down and take my blessing, good my girl.   25
Wilt thou not stoop? Now cursed be the time
Of thy nativity. I would the milk
Thy mother gave thee when thou suck'st her breast
Had been a little ratsbane for thy sake –
Or else, when thou didst keep my lambs a-field,   30
I wish some ravenous wolf had eaten thee.
Dost thou deny thy father, cursed drab?
O burn her, burn her, hanging is too good.   *Exit.*
YORK   Take her away, for she hath lived too long,
To fill the world with vicious qualities.   35
JOAN   First let me tell you whom you have condemned:
Not me begotten of a shepherd swain,
But issued from the progeny of kings;
Virtuous and holy, chosen from above
By inspiration of celestial grace   40
To work exceeding miracles on earth.
I never had to do with wicked spirits;
But you, that are polluted with your lusts,
Stained with the guiltless blood of innocents,
Corrupt and tainted with a thousand vices,   45
Because you want the grace that others have,
You judge it straight a thing impossible
To compass wonders but by help of devils.
No – misconceived, Joan of Aire hath been
A virgin from her tender infancy,   50
Chaste and immaculate in very thought,

Whose maiden-blood, thus rigorously effused,
Will cry for vengeance at the gates of heaven.

YORK   Ay, ay: away with her to execution.

WARWICK   And hark ye, sirs: because she is a maid,
Spare for no faggots, let there be enough.
Place barrels of pitch upon the fatal stake
That so her torture may be shortened.

JOAN   Will nothing turn your unrelenting hearts?
Then, Joan, discover thine infirmity,
That warranteth by law to be thy privilege.
I am with child, ye bloody homicides:
Murder not then the fruit within my womb,
Although ye hale me to a violent death.

YORK   Now heaven forfend, the holy maid with child?

WARWICK   The greatest miracle that e'er ye wrought.
Is all your strict preciseness come to this?

YORK   She and the Dolphin have been ingling.
I did imagine what would be her refuge.

WARWICK   Well, go to, we'll have no bastards live;
Especially since Charles must father it.

JOAN   You are deceived, my child is none of his.
It was Alençon that enjoyed my love.

YORK   Alençon, that notorious Machiavel?
It dies, an if it had a thousand lives.

JOAN   O give me leave, I have deluded you.
'Twas neither Charles, nor yet the Duke I named,
But Reignier, King of Naples, that prevailed.

WARWICK   A married man, that's most intolerable.

YORK   Why, here's a girl! I think she knows not well –
There were so many – whom she may accuse.

WARWICK   It's sign she hath been liberal and free.

YORK   And yet, forsooth, she is a virgin pure.
Strumpet, thy words condemn thy brat and thee.
Use no entreaty, for it is in vain.

JOAN
Then lead me hence – with whom I leave my curse.
May never glorious sun reflex his beams
Upon the country where you make abode,
But darkness and the gloomy shade of death
Environ you, till mischief and despair
Drive you to break your necks, or hang yourselves.

Exit, guarded.

Enter the Cardinal of WINCHESTER.

YORK   Break thou in pieces, and consume to ashes,
Thou foul accursed minister of hell.

WINCHESTER   Lord Regent, I do greet your excellence
With letters of commission from the King.
For know, my lords, the states of Christendom,
Moved with remorse of these outrageous broils,
Have earnestly implored a general peace
Betwixt our nation and the aspiring French;
And here at hand the Dolphin and his train
Approacheth, to confer about some matter.

YORK   Is all our travail turned to this effect?
After the slaughter of so many peers,
So many captains, gentlemen and soldiers

That in this quarrel have been overthrown   105
And sold their bodies for their country's benefit,
Shall we at last conclude effeminate peace?
Have we not lost most part of all the towns,
By treason, falsehood and by treachery,
Our great progenitors had conquered?   110
O Warwick, Warwick, I foresee with grief
The utter loss of all the realm of France.

WARWICK   Be patient, York. If we conclude a peace
It shall be with such strict and severe covenants
As little shall the Frenchmen gain thereby.   115

Enter CHARLES, ALENÇON, *the* BASTARD *and* REIGNIER.

CHARLES   Since, lords of England, it is thus agreed
That peaceful truce shall be proclaimed in France,
We come to be informed, by yourselves,
What the conditions of that league must be.

YORK   Speak, Winchester, for boiling choler chokes   120
The hollow passage of my poisoned voice
By sight of these, our baleful enemies.

WINCHESTER   Charles, and the rest, it is enacted thus:
That, in regard King Henry gives consent,
Of mere compassion and of lenity,   125
To ease your country of distressful war
And suffer you to breathe in fruitful peace,
You shall become true liegemen to his crown.
And Charles, upon condition thou wilt swear
To pay him tribute and submit thyself,   130
Thou shalt be placed as viceroy under him
And still enjoy thy regal dignity.

ALENÇON   Must he be then as shadow of himself –
Adorn his temples with a coronet,
And yet in substance and authority   135
Retain but privilege of a private man?
This proffer is absurd and reasonless.

CHARLES   'Tis known already that I am possessed
With more than half the Gallian territories,
And therein reverenced for their lawful king.   140
Shall I, for lucre of the rest unvanquished,
Detract so much from that prerogative
As to be called but viceroy of the whole?
No, lord ambassador; I'll rather keep
That which I have, than, coveting for more,   145
Be cast from possibility of all.

YORK   Insulting Charles, hast thou by secret means
Used intercession to obtain a league
And, now the matter grows to compromise,
Stand'st thou aloof upon comparison?   150
Either accept the title thou usurp'st –
Of benefit proceeding from our king,
And not of any challenge of desert –
Or we will plague thee with incessant wars.

[*The French turn to talk among themselves.*]

REIGNIER   My lord, you do not well in obstinacy   155
To cavil in the course of this contract.
If once it be neglected, ten to one
We shall not find like opportunity.

ALENÇON   To say the truth, it is your policy
160   To save your subjects from such massacre
And ruthless slaughters as are daily seen
By our proceeding in hostility:
And therefore take this compact of a truce –
Although you break it when your pleasure serves.
WARWICK
165   How sayest thou, Charles? Shall our condition stand?
CHARLES   It shall:
Only reserved you claim no interest
In any of our towns of garrison.
YORK   Then swear allegiance to his majesty:
170   As thou art knight, never to disobey
Nor be rebellious to the crown of England –
Thou nor thy nobles to the crown of England.
So, now dismiss your army when ye please.
Hang up your ensigns, let your drums be still,
175   For here we entertain a solemn peace.   *Exeunt.*

5.4   *Enter* SUFFOLK *in conference with the* KING,
GLOUCESTER *and* EXETER.

KING   Your wondrous rare description, noble earl,
Of beauteous Margaret hath astonished me.
Her virtues, graced with external gifts,
Do breed love's settled passions in my heart;
5   And like as rigour of tempestuous gusts
Provokes the mightiest hulk against the tide,
So am I driven, by breath of her renown,
Either to suffer shipwreck or arrive
Where I may have fruition of her love.
10   SUFFOLK   Tush, my good lord, this superficial tale
Is but a preface of her worthy praise:
The chief perfections of that lovely dame –
Had I sufficient skill to utter them –
Would make a volume of enticing lines
15   Able to ravish any dull conceit.
And, which is more, she is not so divine,
So full replete with choice of all delights,
But with as humble lowliness of mind
She is content to be at your command –
20   Command, I mean, of virtuous chaste intents –
To love and honour Henry as her lord.
KING   And otherwise will Henry ne'er presume.
Therefore, my lord Protector, give consent
That Margaret may be England's royal queen.
25   GLOUCESTER   So should I give consent to flatter sin.
You know, my lord, your highness is betrothed
Unto another lady of esteem;
How shall we then dispense with that contract,
And not deface your honour with reproach?
30   SUFFOLK   As doth a ruler with unlawful oaths,
Or one that, at a triumph having vowed
To try his strength, forsaketh yet the lists
By reason of his adversary's odds.
A poor earl's daughter is unequal odds
35   And therefore may be broke without offence.

GLOUCESTER
Why, what, I pray, is Margaret more than that?
Her father is no better than an earl,
Although in glorious titles he excel.
SUFFOLK   Yes, my lord, her father is a king,
The King of Naples and Jerusalem,   40
And of such great authority in France
As his alliance will confirm our peace,
And keep the Frenchmen in allegiance.
GLOUCESTER   And so the Earl of Armagnac may do,
Because he is near kinsman unto Charles.   45
EXETER
Beside, his wealth doth warrant a liberal dower,
Where Reignier sooner will receive than give.
SUFFOLK
A dower, my lords? Disgrace not so your king
That he should be so abject, base and poor
To choose for wealth, and not for perfect love.   50
Henry is able to enrich his queen,
And not to seek a queen to make him rich;
So worthless peasants bargain for their wives,
As market-men for oxen, sheep or horse.
Marriage is a matter of more worth   55
Than to be dealt in by attorneyship:
Not whom we will, but whom his grace affects,
Must be companion of his nuptial bed.
And therefore, lords, since he affects her most,
Most of all these reasons bindeth us: 60
In our opinions she should be preferred.
For what is wedlock forced but a hell,
An age of discord and continual strife?
Whereas the contrary bringeth bliss,
And is a pattern of celestial peace.   65
Whom should we match with Henry, being a
king,
But Margaret, that is daughter to a king?
Her peerless feature, joined with her birth,
Approves her fit for none but for a king.
Her valiant courage and undaunted spirit   70
(More than in women commonly is seen)
Will answer our hope in issue of a king.
For Henry, son unto a conqueror,
Is likely to beget more conquerors,
If with a lady of so high resolve   75
As is fair Margaret he be linked in love.
Then yield, my lords, and here conclude with me
That Margaret shall be queen, and none but she.
KING   Whether it be through force of your report,
My noble lord of Suffolk, or for that   80
My tender youth was never yet attaint
With any passion of inflaming love,
I cannot tell; but this I am assured –
I feel such sharp dissension in my breast,
Such fierce alarums both of hope and fear,   85
As I am sick with working of my thoughts.
Take therefore shipping post, my lord, to France.
Agree to any covenants, and procure

That lady Margaret do vouchsafe to come,
To cross the seas to England and be crowned
King Henry's faithful and anointed queen.
For your expenses and sufficient charge,
Among the people gather up a tenth.
Begone, I say, for till you do return
I rest perplexed with a thousand cares.
And you, good uncle, banish all offence:
If you do censure me by what you were,
Not what you are, I know it will excuse
This sudden execution of my will.

And so conduct me where, from company,   100
I may revolve and ruminate my grief.   *Exit.*
GLOUCESTER   Ay, grief, I fear me, both at first and last.
                    Exeunt Gloucester and Exeter.
SUFFOLK
Thus Suffolk hath prevailed, and thus he goes,
As did the youthful Paris once to Greece,
With hope to find the like event in love –   105
But prosper better than the Trojan did.
Margaret shall now be queen, and rule the King:
But I will rule both her, the King and realm.   *Exit.*

King Henry VI, Part 2

Before its appearance as the seventh of the histories in the Folio of 1623, a version of *King Henry VI, Part 2* was published in 1594 as *The First Part of the Contention betwixt the two famous Houses of York and Lancaster*. The 1594 Quarto was reprinted in 1600, and in 1619 this play and *King Henry VI, Part 3* (published in 1595 as *The true Tragedy of Richard Duke of York*) were combined and published as *The Whole Contention between the two Famous Houses, Lancaster and York*. These earliest printings of *Part 2* differ from the Folio text: they are shorter by about a third and seem to represent a reported version, put together probably by actors who had performed the play. Thus, in general, they have less authority than the fuller and better text available in the 1623 Folio, but they do provide, by virtue of their provenance, important evidence of early theatrical practice.

King Henry VI, Part 2, continues the history soon after it breaks off in *Part 1*, but with its own formal and thematic integrity. The play covers ten years of Henry's tumultuous reign, beginning with Margaret's coronation (which took place in May 1445, two years after the disgrace of Duke Humphrey's wife Eleanor, also included within the action), and continues to the Battle of St Albans (1455). France has now effectively been lost. The factionalism evident in *Part 1* finally bursts here into full-fledged civil war, and the aristocratic struggles for the throne have a demotic echo in the emergence of the popular unrest that explodes into Jack Cade's rebellion. Through it all, we can see the ominous emergence of one man able to impose his will on history, Richard Plantagenet, Duke of York.

Part 1 plays off England against France, Talbot against Joan, mighty opposites that work to define a model of English greatness, however vulnerable it is finally shown to be; *Part 2* confronts the stresses and tensions tearing at the fabric of the nation itself. This is a new world, no longer based on aristocratic honour and feudal obligation, but a world of appetite and ambition, a world in which neither Henry's piety nor Gloucester's virtue offers protection or relief.

Jack Cade's rebellion is perhaps a mere inset into the dismal story of aristocratic wrangles, but it is a telling episode. It can be seen as evidence of the dangerous unruliness of the rabble, a degrading comedy of misrule, but the rebels voice legitimate social concerns and aspirations. If the uprising seems finally a travesty of the desire for social justice, it is because their leader, Cade, is revealed as a pawn of York's ambitions and his pathetic mimic, rather than because the issues are themselves laughable.

Thirteen people die in *King Henry VI, Part 2*, none in easeful sleep. The language is of snakes, spiders and scorpions; bleeding heifers, slaughtered calves, innocent lambs threatened by wolves; butchers with axes and headless bodies on piles of dung. Not far beneath the veneer of courtly sophistication is a fierce and violent world that can no longer be ordered by the institutions and ceremonies designed to control the flux of reality. The fall of the good and innocent Humphrey, Duke of Gloucester, is at once symptom and at least partial cause of the lawlessness that reigns. His absence leaves the state without any effective force of social coherence. The idea of kingship itself is endlessly appealed to, but it is never a unifying centre for the country or the play; for the ambitious York it is only the object of his brazen will to power, and for the inept Henry it is a condition to be escaped: 'never subject longed to be a king / As I do long and wish to be a subject' (4.9.5–6).

Of the three parts of *King Henry VI*, Dr Johnson thought 'the second the best'. Certainly it is a powerful play, though one that modern audiences have had little chance to see. When played at all, it has usually been cut and adapted, as in John Barton's two-part *The Wars of the Roses* (1963), tailored from the three parts of *King Henry VI*, or in 1986 by the English Shakespeare Company and in 1988 by the Royal Shakespeare Company, both of which also condensed the three plays into two. In 1977, however, Terry Hands directed all three plays in sequence at Stratford-upon-Avon, and in 2000–1 the Royal Shakespeare Company staged them as part of its ambitious series 'This England, the Histories', comprising all histories from *Richard II* to *Richard III* in chronological order.

The Arden text is based on the 1623 First Folio.

LANCASTRIANS

KING Henry the Sixth
QUEEN Margaret
Humphrey, Duke of GLOUCESTER   *uncle of the King*
ELEANOR, Duchess of Gloucester
CARDINAL Beaufort, Bishop of Winchester   *great-uncle of the King*
Marquess of SUFFOLK
Duke of SOMERSET
Duke of BUCKINGHAM
OLD CLIFFORD
YOUNG CLIFFORD   *his son*
VAUX

YORKISTS

Richard, Duke of YORK
EDWARD
RICHARD   } *his sons*
Earl of SALISBURY
Earl of WARWICK   *his son*

PETITION AND COMBAT 1.3, 2.3

Thomas HORNER   *armourer*
PETER Thump   *his apprentice*
PETITIONERS, PRENTICES, NEIGHBOURS

CONJURATION 1.4

John HUME
John SOUTHWELL
Margery JOURDAIN   *a witch*
Roger BOLINBROKE   *a conjuror*
SPIRIT

THE FALSE MIRACLE 2.1

Simon SIMPCOX
Simpcox's WIFE
MAYOR of St Albans
BEADLE
TOWNSMEN

ELEANOR'S PENANCE 2.4

Sir John STANLEY
SHERIFF of London
HERALD, GUARDS
SERVANTS, OFFICERS, COMMONERS

GLOUCESTER'S MURDER 3.2

Two MURDERERS
COMMONS

SUFFOLK'S MURDER 4.1

LIEUTENANT
MASTER
Master's MATE
Walter WHITMORE
Two GENTLEMEN

CADE'S REBELLION 4.2–10

GEORGE

NICK

Jack CADE

Dick the BUTCHER

Smith the WEAVER

SAWYER

Rebels

Emmanuel the CLERK of Chartham

MICHAEL

Sir Humphrey STAFFORD

Stafford's BROTHER

Lord SAYE

Lord SCALES

Matthew GOUGH

Alexander IDEN

Drummers, Soldiers, Trumpeter, Citizens

OTHERS

Attendants, Falconers, Post, Messengers

1.1   *Flourish of trumpets; then hautboys. Enter the*
KING, GLOUCESTER, SALISBURY, WARWICK
and CARDINAL Beaufort, *on the one side;*
the QUEEN, SUFFOLK, YORK, SOMERSET
and BUCKINGHAM, *on the other;*
with Attendants.

SUFFOLK   As by your high imperial majesty
I had in charge at my depart for France,
As procurator to your excellence,
To marry Princess Margaret for your grace;
So, in the famous ancient city Tours,   5
In presence of the Kings of France and Sicil,
The Dukes of Orleans, Calaber, Bretagne and Alençon,
Seven earls, twelve barons and twenty reverend
   bishops,
I have performed my task and was espoused,
And humbly now upon my bended knee,   [*Kneels.*]   10
In sight of England and her lordly peers,
Deliver up my title in the Queen
To your most gracious hands, that are the substance
Of that great shadow I did represent;
The happiest gift that ever marquess gave,   15
The fairest queen that ever king received.
KING   Suffolk arise.   [*Suffolk rises.*]
                    – Welcome, Queen Margaret:
I can express no kinder sign of love
Than this kind kiss.   [*Kisses her.*]
                    – O Lord, that lends me life,
Lend me a heart replete with thankfulness!   20
For thou hast given me in this beauteous face
A world of earthly blessings to my soul,
If sympathy of love unite our thoughts.
QUEEN   Great King of England, and my gracious lord,
The mutual conference that my mind hath had   25
By day, by night, waking and in my dreams,
In courtly company, or at my beads,
With you mine alderliefest sovereign,
Makes me the bolder to salute my King
With ruder terms, such as my wit affords   30
And overjoy of heart doth minister.
KING   Her sight did ravish, but her grace in speech,
Her words y-clad with wisdom's majesty,
Makes me from wondering fall to weeping joys,
Such is the fulness of my heart's content.   35
Lords, with one cheerful voice welcome my love.
ALL [*Kneel.*]
Long live Queen Margaret, England's happiness!
QUEEN   We thank you all.   [*Flourish*]
SUFFOLK   My Lord Protector, so it please your grace,
Here are the articles of contracted peace   40
Between our sovereign and the French King Charles,
For eighteen months concluded by consent.
GLOUCESTER [*Reads.*]   Imprimis, *it is agreed between the*
French King Charles and William de la Pole, Marquess of
Suffolk, ambassador for Henry, King of England, that the   45
said Henry shall espouse the Lady Margaret, daughter

unto Reignier, King of Naples, Sicilia and Jerusalem,
and crown her Queen of England, ere the thirtieth of May
next ensuing. Item, *that the duchy of Anjou and the*
county of Maine shall be released and delivered to the   50
King her father – [*Lets the paper fall.*]
KING   Uncle, how now?
GLOUCESTER   Pardon me, gracious lord.
Some sudden qualm hath struck me at the heart
And dimmed mine eyes, that I can read no further.
KING   Uncle of Winchester, I pray read on.   55
CARDINAL [*Reads.*]   Item, *it is further agreed between*
them that the duchy of Anjou and the county of Maine
shall be released and delivered to the King her father, and
she sent over of the King of England's own proper cost and
charges, without having any dowry.   60
KING
They please us well. – Lord Marquess, kneel down.
   [*Suffolk kneels.*]
We here create thee the first Duke of Suffolk,
   [*Suffolk rises.*]
And girt thee with the sword. – Cousin of York,
We here discharge your grace from being regent
I'th' parts of France, till term of eighteen months   65
Be full expired. – Thanks, uncle Winchester,
Gloucester, York, Buckingham, Somerset,
Salisbury and Warwick.
We thank you all for this great favour done,
In entertainment to my princely Queen.   70
Come, let us in, and with all speed provide
To see her coronation be performed.
                    Exeunt King, Queen and Suffolk with
                    Attendants. Gloucester stays with all the rest.
GLOUCESTER
Brave peers of England, pillars of the state,
To you Duke Humphrey must unload his grief,
Your grief, the common grief of all the land.   75
What! Did my brother Henry spend his youth,
His valour, coin and people, in the wars?
Did he so often lodge in open field,
In winter's cold and summer's parching heat,
To conquer France, his true inheritance?   80
And did my brother Bedford toil his wits
To keep by policy what Henry got?
Have you yourselves, Somerset, Buckingham,
Brave York, Salisbury and victorious Warwick,
Received deep scars in France and Normandy?   85
Or hath mine uncle Beaufort and myself,
With all the learned council of the realm,
Studied so long, sat in the council house
Early and late, debating to and fro
How France and Frenchmen might be kept in awe,   90
And had his highness in his infancy
Crowned in Paris in despite of foes?
And shall these labours and these honours die?
Shall Henry's conquest, Bedford's vigilance,
Your deeds of war and all our counsel die?   95
O peers of England, shameful is this league;

Fatal this marriage, cancelling your fame,
Blotting your names from books of memory,
Razing the characters of your renown,
100　Defacing monuments of conquered France,
Undoing all, as all had never been!
CARDINAL
Nephew, what means this passionate discourse,
This peroration with such circumstance?
For France 'tis ours; and we will keep it still.
105　GLOUCESTER　Ay, uncle, we will keep it if we can,
But now it is impossible we should.
Suffolk, the new-made duke that rules the roast,
Hath given the duchy of Anjou and Maine
Unto the poor King Reignier, whose large style
110　Agrees not with the leanness of his purse.
SALISBURY　Now by the death of Him that died for all,
These counties were the keys of Normandy.
But wherefore weeps Warwick, my valiant son?
WARWICK　For grief that they are past recovery.
115　For were there hope to conquer them again
My sword should shed hot blood, mine eyes no tears.
Anjou and Maine! Myself did win them both;
Those provinces these arms of mine did conquer;
And are the cities that I got with wounds
120　Delivered up again with peaceful words?
Mort Dieu!
YORK　For Suffolk's Duke, may he be suffocate,
That dims the honour of this warlike isle!
France should have torn and rent my very heart
125　Before I would have yielded to this league.
I never read but England's kings have had
Large sums of gold and dowries with their wives;
And our King Henry gives away his own,
To match with her that brings no vantages.
130　GLOUCESTER　A proper jest, and never heard before,
That Suffolk should demand a whole fifteenth
For costs and charges in transporting her!
She should have stayed in France, and starved in France
Before –
135　CARDINAL　My Lord of Gloucester, now ye grow too hot:
It was the pleasure of my lord the King.
GLOUCESTER
My Lord of Winchester, I know your mind.
'Tis not my speeches that you do mislike,
But 'tis my presence that doth trouble ye.
140　Rancour will out: proud prelate, in thy face
I see thy fury. If I longer stay
We shall begin our ancient bickerings. –
Lordings, farewell; and say when I am gone,
I prophesied France will be lost ere long. 　　*Exit.*
145　CARDINAL　So, there goes our Protector in a rage.
'Tis known to you he is mine enemy,
Nay more, an enemy unto you all,
And no great friend, I fear me, to the King.
Consider, lords, he is the next of blood
150　And heir apparent to the English crown.
Had Henry got an empire by his marriage

And all the wealthy kingdoms of the west,
There's reason he should be displeased at it.
Look to it, lords; let not his smoothing words
Bewitch your hearts; be wise and circumspect.　155
What though the common people favour him,
Calling him 'Humphrey, the good Duke of Gloucester',
Clapping their hands and crying with loud voice,
'Jesu maintain your royal excellence!',
With 'God preserve the good Duke Humphrey!',　160
I fear me, lords, for all this flattering gloss,
He will be found a dangerous Protector.
BUCKINGHAM
Why should he then protect our sovereign,
He being of age to govern of himself?
Cousin of Somerset, join you with me,　　　165
And all together, with the Duke of Suffolk,
We'll quickly hoist Duke Humphrey from his seat.
CARDINAL　This weighty business will not brook delay;
I'll to the Duke of Suffolk presently. 　　*Exit.*
SOMERSET
Cousin of Buckingham, though Humphrey's pride　170
And greatness of his place be grief to us,
Yet let us watch the haughty Cardinal;
His insolence is more intolerable
Than all the princes' in the land beside.
If Gloucester be displaced, he'll be Protector.　175
BUCKINGHAM
Or thou or I, Somerset, will be Protectors,
Despite Duke Humphrey, or the Cardinal.
　　　　　　　　Exeunt Buckingham and Somerset.
SALISBURY　Pride went before; Ambition follows him.
While these do labour for their own preferment,
Behoves it us to labour for the realm.　　　180
I never saw but Humphrey, Duke of Gloucester,
Did bear him like a noble gentleman.
Oft have I seen the haughty Cardinal,
More like a soldier than a man o'th' church,
As stout and proud as he were lord of all,　　185
Swear like a ruffian, and demean himself
Unlike the ruler of a commonweal. –
Warwick, my son, the comfort of my age,
Thy deeds, thy plainness and thy housekeeping
Hath won thee greatest favour of the commons,　190
Excepting none but good Duke Humphrey. –
And, brother York, thy acts in Ireland
In bringing them to civil discipline;
Thy late exploits done in the heart of France
When thou wert regent for our sovereign,　　195
Have made thee feared and honoured of the people. –
Join we together for the public good,
In what we can to bridle and suppress
The pride of Suffolk and the Cardinal,
With Somerset's and Buckingham's ambition;　200
And, as we may, cherish Duke Humphrey's deeds,
While they do tend the profit of the land.
WARWICK　So God help Warwick, as he loves the land
And common profit of his country!

YORK

205   And so says York, [*aside*] for he hath greatest cause.

SALISBURY

    Then let's make haste and look unto the main.

WARWICK   Unto the main! O father, Maine is lost,

    That Maine which by main force Warwick did win,

    And would have kept so long as breath did last!

210   Main chance, father, you meant, but I meant Maine,

    Which I will win from France, or else be slain.

                   Exeunt Warwick and Salisbury.

YORK   Anjou and Maine are given to the French;

    Paris is lost; the state of Normandy

    Stands on a tickle point now they are gone.

215   Suffolk concluded on the articles,

    The peers agreed, and Henry was well pleased

    To change two dukedoms for a duke's fair daughter.

    I cannot blame them all – what is't to them?

    'Tis thine they give away, and not their own.

220   Pirates may make cheap pennyworths of their pillage

    And purchase friends, and give to courtesans,

    Still revelling like lords till all be gone;

    While as the silly owner of the goods

    Weeps over them, and wrings his hapless hands,

225   And shakes his head, and trembling stands aloof,

    While all is shared and all is borne away

    Ready to starve and dare not touch his own.

    So York must sit and fret and bite his tongue,

    While his own lands are bargained for and sold.

230   Methinks the realms of England, France and Ireland

    Bear that proportion to my flesh and blood

    As did the fatal brand Althaea burnt

    Unto the prince's heart of Calydon.

    Anjou and Maine both given unto the French!

235   Cold news for me, for I had hope of France

    Even as I have of fertile England's soil.

    A day will come when York shall claim his own;

    And therefore I will take the Nevilles' parts

    And make a show of love to proud Duke Humphrey,

240   And when I spy advantage, claim the crown,

    For that's the golden mark I seek to hit.

    Nor shall proud Lancaster usurp my right,

    Nor hold the sceptre in his childish fist,

    Nor wear the diadem upon his head,

245   Whose church-like humours fits not for a crown.

    Then, York, be still awhile, till time do serve.

    Watch thou and wake, when others be asleep,

    To pry into the secrets of the state;

    Till Henry, surfeiting in joys of love

250   With his new bride and England's dear-bought Queen,

    And Humphrey with the peers be fallen at jars.

    Then will I raise aloft the milk-white rose,

    With whose sweet smell the air shall be perfumed,

    And in my standard bear the arms of York,

255   To grapple with the house of Lancaster;

    And force perforce I'll make him yield the crown,

    Whose bookish rule hath pulled fair England down.

                             Exit.

1.2   *Enter* GLOUCESTER *and his wife* ELEANOR.

ELEANOR   Why droops my lord, like over-ripened corn

    Hanging the head at Ceres' plenteous load?

    Why doth the great Duke Humphrey knit his brows,

    As frowning at the favours of the world?

    Why are thine eyes fixed to the sullen earth,   5

    Gazing on that which seems to dim thy sight?

    What seest thou there? King Henry's diadem

    Enchased with all the honours of the world?

    If so, gaze on, and grovel on thy face,

    Until thy head be circled with the same.   10

    Put forth thy hand, reach at the glorious gold.

    What, is't too short? I'll lengthen it with mine;

    And having both together heaved it up,

    We'll both together lift our heads to heaven,

    And never more abase our sight so low   15

    As to vouchsafe one glance unto the ground.

GLOUCESTER

    O Nell, sweet Nell, if thou dost love thy lord,

    Banish the canker of ambitious thoughts.

    And may that hour, when I imagine ill

    Against my King and nephew, virtuous Henry,   20

    Be my last breathing in this mortal world!

    My troublous dreams this night doth make me sad.

ELEANOR

    What dreamed my lord? Tell me, and I'll requite it

    With sweet rehearsal of my morning's dream.

GLOUCESTER

    Methought this staff, mine office-badge in court,   25

    Was broke in twain; by whom I have forgot

    But, as I think, it was by th' Cardinal;

    And on the pieces of the broken wand

    Were placed the heads of Edmund, Duke of

       Somerset,

    And William de la Pole, first Duke of Suffolk.   30

    This was my dream; what it doth bode, God knows.

ELEANOR   Tut! This was nothing but an argument

    That he that breaks a stick of Gloucester's grove

    Shall lose his head for his presumption.

    But list to me, my Humphrey, my sweet Duke: 35

    Methought I sat in seat of majesty

    In the cathedral church of Westminster,

    And in that chair where kings and queens are crowned,

    Where Henry and Dame Margaret kneeled to me,

    And on my head did set the diadem.   40

GLOUCESTER   Nay, Eleanor, then must I chide outright:

    Presumptuous dame, ill-nurtured Eleanor!

    Art thou not second woman in the realm,

    And the Protector's wife, beloved of him?

    Hast thou not worldly pleasure at command,   45

    Above the reach or compass of thy thought?

    And wilt thou still be hammering treachery

    To tumble down thy husband and thyself

    From top of honour to disgrace's feet?

    Away from me and let me hear no more!   50

ELEANOR   What, what, my lord! Are you so choleric

With Eleanor, for telling but her dream?
Next time I'll keep my dreams unto myself,
And not be checked.

55 GLOUCESTER   Nay, be not angry, I am pleased again.

Enter Messenger.

MESSENGER
My Lord Protector, 'tis his highness' pleasure
You do prepare to ride unto Saint Albans,
Whereas the King and Queen do mean to hawk.
GLOUCESTER   I go. Come, Nell, thou wilt ride with us?
60 ELEANOR   Yes, my good lord, I'll follow presently.

Exeunt Gloucester and Messenger.

Follow I must; I cannot go before
While Gloucester bears this base and humble mind.
Were I a man, a duke and next of blood,
I would remove these tedious stumbling-blocks
65 And smooth my way upon their headless necks.
And, being a woman, I will not be slack
To play my part in Fortune's pageant. –
Where are you there? Sir John!

Enter HUME.

Nay, fear not, man,
We are alone; here's none but thee and I.
70 HUME   Jesus preserve your royal majesty!
ELEANOR   What sayst thou? Majesty! I am but grace.
HUME   But by the grace of God, and Hume's advice,
Your grace's title shall be multiplied.
ELEANOR
What sayst thou, man? Hast thou as yet conferred
75 With Margery Jourdain, the cunning witch,
With Roger Bolingbroke, the conjuror?
And will they undertake to do me good?
HUME   This they have promised, to show your highness
A spirit, raised from depth of underground,
80 That shall make answer to such questions
As by your grace shall be propounded him.
ELEANOR   It is enough, I'll think upon the questions.
When from Saint Albans we do make return
We'll see these things effected to the full.
85 Here, Hume, take this reward; make merry, man,
With thy confederates in this weighty cause.   *Exit.*
HUME   Hume must make merry with the Duchess' gold;
Marry, and shall. But how now, Sir John Hume!
Seal up your lips and give no words but mum;
90 The business asketh silent secrecy.
Dame Eleanor gives gold to bring the witch:
Gold cannot come amiss, were she a devil.
Yet have I gold flies from another coast:
I dare not say from the rich Cardinal
95 And from the great and new-made Duke of Suffolk,
Yet I do find it so. For, to be plain,
They, knowing Dame Eleanor's aspiring humour,
Have hired me to undermine the Duchess
And buzz these conjurations in her brain.
100 They say 'A crafty knave does need no broker,'

Yet am I Suffolk and the Cardinal's broker.
Hume, if you take not heed, you shall go near
To call them both a pair of crafty knaves.
Well, so it stands; and thus, I fear, at last
Hume's knavery will be the Duchess' wrack,   105
And her attainture will be Humphrey's fall.
Sort how it will, I shall have gold for all.   *Exit.*

1.3   *Enter three or four* Petitioners, PETER
the armourer's man being one.

1 PETITIONER   My masters, let's stand close. My Lord
Protector will come this way by and by, and then we
may deliver our supplications in the quill.
2 PETITIONER   Marry, the Lord protect him, for he's a
good man, Jesu bless him.   5

Enter SUFFOLK *and* QUEEN.

1 PETITIONER   Here 'a comes, methinks, and the Queen
with him. I'll be the first, sure.
2 PETITIONER   Come back, fool! This is the Duke of
Suffolk, and not my Lord Protector.
SUFFOLK   How now, fellow; wouldst anything with me?   10
1 PETITIONER   I pray, my lord, pardon me, I took ye for
my Lord Protector.
QUEEN   'For my Lord Protector'? Are your supplications
to his lordship? Let me see them. [*Takes First Petitioner's
supplication.*] What is thine?   15
1 PETITIONER   Mine is, an't please your grace, against
John Goodman, my Lord Cardinal's man, for keeping
my house and lands and wife and all from me.
SUFFOLK   Thy wife too! That's some wrong indeed. –
What's yours? What's here! [*Reads.*] *Against the Duke*   20
of Suffolk, for enclosing the commons of Melford. How
now, sir knave!
2 PETITIONER   Alas, sir, I am but a poor petitioner of
our whole township.
PETER [*Offers his petition.*]   Against my master Thomas   25
Horner, for saying that the Duke of York was rightful
heir to the crown.
QUEEN   What sayst thou? Did the Duke of York say he
was rightful heir to the crown?
PETER   That my master was? No, forsooth, my master   30
said that he was, and that the King was an usurer.
QUEEN   An usurper thou wouldst say.
PETER   Ay, forsooth, an usurper.
SUFFOLK   Who is there? [*Snatches Peter's supplication.*]

Enter Servant.

Take this fellow in, and send for his master with a   35
pursuivant presently. – We'll hear more of your matter
before the King.   *Exit Servant with Peter.*
QUEEN   And as for you, that love to be protected
Under the wings of our Protector's grace,
Begin your suits anew, and sue to him.   40
[*Tears the supplication.*]
Away, base cullions! Suffolk, let them go.

ALL PETITIONERS Come, let's be gone.   *Exeunt.*

QUEEN   My Lord of Suffolk, say, is this the guise,
            Is this the fashions in the court of England?
45   Is this the government of Britain's isle,
            And this the royalty of Albion's king?
            What, shall King Henry be a pupil still
            Under the surly Gloucester's governance?
            Am I a queen in title and in style
50   And must be made a subject to a duke?
            I tell thee, Pole, when in the city Tours
            Thou ran'st a-tilt in honour of my love
            And stol'st away the ladies' hearts of France,
            I thought King Henry had resembled thee
55   In courage, courtship and proportion.
            But all his mind is bent to holiness,
            To number Ave-Maries on his beads.
            His champions are the prophets and apostles,
            His weapons, holy saws of sacred writ;
60   His study is his tilt-yard, and his loves
            Are brazen images of canonized saints.
            I would the college of the cardinals
            Would choose him Pope, and carry him to Rome
            And set the triple crown upon his head:
65   That were a state fit for his Holiness.

SUFFOLK   Madam, be patient. As I was cause
            Your highness came to England, so will I
            In England work your grace's full content.

QUEEN   Beside the haughty Protector have we Beaufort,
70   The imperious churchman, Somerset, Buckingham
            And grumbling York; and not the least of these
            But can do more in England than the King.

SUFFOLK   And he of these that can do most of all
            Cannot do more in England than the Nevilles:
75   Salisbury and Warwick are no simple peers.

QUEEN   Not all these lords do vex me half so much
            As that proud dame, the Lord Protector's wife.
            She sweeps it through the court with troops of ladies,
            More like an empress than Duke Humphrey's wife.
80   Strangers in court do take her for the Queen.
            She bears a duke's revenues on her back,
            And in her heart she scorns our poverty.
            Shall I not live to be avenged on her?
            Contemptuous base-born callet as she is,
85   She vaunted 'mongst her minions t'other day
            The very train of her worst wearing gown
            Was better worth than all my father's lands,
            Till Suffolk gave two dukedoms for his daughter.

SUFFOLK   Madam, myself have limed a bush for her
90   And placed a choir of such enticing birds
            That she will light to listen to the lays
            And never mount to trouble you again.
            So let her rest; and, madam, list to me –
            For I am bold to counsel you in this –
95   Although we fancy not the Cardinal,
            Yet must we join with him and with the lords
            Till we have brought Duke Humphrey in disgrace.
            As for the Duke of York, this late complaint

            Will make but little for his benefit.
            So one by one we'll weed them all at last,   100
            And you yourself shall steer the happy helm.

            Sound a sennet. Enter the KING, GLOUCESTER,
            CARDINAL *Beaufort,* BUCKINGHAM, YORK,
            SALISBURY, WARWICK *and* ELEANOR.

KING   For my part, noble lords, I care not which;
            Or Somerset, or York, all's one to me.

YORK   If York have ill demeaned himself in France,
            Then let him be denied the regentship.   105

SOMERSET   If Somerset be unworthy of the place,
            Let York be regent; I will yield to him.

WARWICK   Whether your Grace be worthy, yea or no,
            Dispute not that; York is the worthier.

CARDINAL   Ambitious Warwick, let thy betters speak.   110

WARWICK   The Cardinal's not my better in the field.

BUCKINGHAM
            All in this presence are thy betters, Warwick.

WARWICK   Warwick may live to be the best of all.

SALISBURY
            Peace, son! – And show some reason, Buckingham,
            Why Somerset should be preferred in this.   115

QUEEN   Because the King, forsooth, will have it so.

GLOUCESTER   Madam, the King is old enough himself
            To give his censure. These are no women's matters.

QUEEN   If he be old enough, what needs your grace
            To be Protector of his excellence?   120

GLOUCESTER   Madam, I am Protector of the realm,
            And at his pleasure will resign my place.

SUFFOLK   Resign it then, and leave thine insolence.
            Since thou wert king – as who is king but thou? –
            The commonwealth hath daily run to wrack,   125
            The Dauphin hath prevailed beyond the seas,
            And all the peers and nobles of the realm
            Have been as bondmen to thy sovereignty.

CARDINAL
            The commons hast thou racked; the clergy's bags
            Are lank and lean with thy extortions.   130

SOMERSET
            Thy sumptuous buildings and thy wife's attire
            Have cost a mass of public treasury.

BUCKINGHAM   Thy cruelty in execution
            Upon offenders hath exceeded law,
            And left thee to the mercy of the law.   135

QUEEN   Thy sale of offices and towns in France,
            If they were known, as the suspect is great,
            Would make thee quickly hop without thy head.
                                                    Exit Gloucester.
            [*The Queen drops her fan.*]
            Give me my fan. What, minion! Can ye not?
            [*She gives Eleanor a box on the ear.*]
            I cry you mercy, madam; was it you?   140

ELEANOR   Was't I! Yea, I it was, proud Frenchwoman.
            Could I come near your beauty with my nails
            I'd set my ten commandments in your face.

KING   Sweet aunt, be quiet; 'twas against her will.

ELEANOR

145   Against her will? Good King, look to't in time;
    She'll pamper thee, and dandle thee like a baby.
    Though in this place most master wear no breeches,
    She shall not strike Dame Eleanor unrevenged. *Exit.*

BUCKINGHAM   Lord Cardinal, I will follow Eleanor,
150   And listen after Humphrey, how he proceeds.
    She's tickled now, her fury needs no spurs,
    She'll gallop far enough to her destruction.   *Exit.*

Enter GLOUCESTER.

GLOUCESTER   Now, lords, my choler being overblown
    With walking once about the quadrangle,
155   I come to talk of commonwealth affairs.
    As for your spiteful false objections,
    Prove them, and I lie open to the law.
    But God in mercy so deal with my soul
    As I in duty love my king and country.
160   But to the matter that we have in hand. –
    I say, my sovereign, York is meetest man
    To be your regent in the realm of France.

SUFFOLK   Before we make election, give me leave
    To show some reason, of no little force,
165   That York is most unmeet of any man.

YORK   I'll tell thee, Suffolk, why I am unmeet:
    First, for I cannot flatter thee in pride;
    Next, if I be appointed for the place,
    My Lord of Somerset will keep me here
170   Without discharge, money or furniture,
    Till France be won into the Dauphin's hands.
    Last time I danced attendance on his will
    Till Paris was besieged, famished and lost.

WARWICK   That can I witness, and a fouler fact
175   Did never traitor in the land commit.

SUFFOLK   Peace, headstrong Warwick!

WARWICK   Image of pride, why should I hold my peace?

Enter HORNER *the armourer and his man*
PETER, *guarded.*

SUFFOLK   Because here is a man accused of treason:
    Pray God the Duke of York excuse himself!

180 YORK   Doth anyone accuse York for a traitor?

KING
    What mean'st thou, Suffolk? Tell me, what are these?

SUFFOLK   Please it your majesty, this is the man
    That doth accuse his master of high treason.
    His words were these: that Richard, Duke of York,
185   Was rightful heir unto the English crown,
    And that your majesty was an usurper.

KING   Say, man, were these thy words?

HORNER   An't shall please your majesty, I never said
    nor thought any such matter. God is my witness, I am
190   falsely accused by the villain.

PETER   By these ten bones, my lords, he did speak them
    to me in the garret one night as we were scouring my
    Lord of York's armour.

YORK   Base dunghill villain and mechanical,

195   I'll have thy head for this thy traitor's speech! –
    I do beseech your royal majesty,
    Let him have all the rigour of the law.

HORNER   Alas, my lord, hang me if ever I spake the
    words. My accuser is my prentice, and when I did
200   correct him for his fault the other day, he did vow upon
    his knees he would be even with me. I have good
    witness of this, therefore I beseech your majesty, do
    not cast away an honest man for a villain's accusation.

KING   Uncle, what shall we say to this in law?

GLOUCESTER
205   This doom, my lord, if I may judge by case:
    Let Somerset be regent o'er the French,
    Because in York this breeds suspicion;
    And let these have a day appointed them
    For single combat in convenient place,
210   For he hath witness of his servant's malice.
    This is the law, and this Duke Humphrey's doom.

SOMERSET   I humbly thank your royal majesty.

HORNER   And I accept the combat willingly.

PETER   Alas, my lord, I cannot fight. For God's sake pity
215   my case! The spite of man prevaileth against me.
    O Lord, have mercy upon me! I shall never be able to
    fight a blow. O Lord, my heart!

GLOUCESTER
    Sirrah, or you must fight, or else be hanged.

KING   Away with them to prison, and the day
220   Of combat shall be the last of the next month.
    Come, Somerset, we'll see thee sent away.

Flourish. Exeunt.

1.4 *Enter* Margery JOURDAIN *(a witch), the two priests*
*(*HUME *and* SOUTHWELL *) and* BOLINGBROKE.

HUME   Come, my masters! The Duchess, I tell you,
    expects performance of your promises.

BOLINGBROKE   Master Hume, we are therefor provided.
    Will her ladyship behold and hear our exorcisms?

HUME   Ay, what else? Fear you not her courage.   5

BOLINGBROKE   I have heard her reported to be a
    woman of an invincible spirit; but it shall be convenient,
    Master Hume, that you be by her aloft, while we be
    busy below; and so, I pray you, go in God's name, and
    leave us.   *Exit Hume.*   10
    Mother Jourdain, be you prostrate and grovel on the
    earth; John Southwell, read you; and let us to our work.

Enter ELEANOR *aloft,* HUME *following.*

ELEANOR   Well said, my masters, and welcome all. To
    this gear, the sooner the better.

BOLINGBROKE
    Patience, good lady; wizards know their times.   15
    Deep night, dark night, the silent of the night,
    The time of night when Troy was set on fire,
    The time when screech-owls cry and ban-dogs howl,
    And spirits walk, and ghosts break up their graves;
    That time best fits the work we have in hand.   20

Madam, sit you, and fear not. Whom we raise
We will make fast within a hallowed verge.

Here do the ceremonies belonging, and make the circle;
Bolingbroke or Southwell reads, 'Conjuro te', etc. It
thunders and lightens terribly; then the Spirit *riseth.*

SPIRIT   *Adsum.*
JOURDAIN   Asnath,
25   By the eternal God whose name and power
Thou tremblest at, answer that I shall ask;
For till thou speak thou shalt not pass from hence.
SPIRIT   Ask what thou wilt – that I had said and done!
BOLINGBROKE [*Reads.*]
First of the King: what shall of him become?
30   SPIRIT   The duke yet lives that Henry shall depose,
But him outlive, and die a violent death.
        [*As the Spirit speaks, Southwell writes the answer.*]
BOLINGBROKE
Tell me, what fates awaits the Duke of Suffolk?
SPIRIT   By water shall he die and take his end.
BOLINGBROKE   *What shall betide the Duke of Somerset?*
35   SPIRIT   Let him shun castles:
Safer shall he be upon the sandy plains
Than where castles mounted stand.
Have done, for more I hardly can endure.
BOLINGBROKE
Descend to darkness and the burning lake!
40   False fiend, avoid!   *Thunder and lightning. Exit Spirit.*

Enter the Duke of YORK *and the* Duke of BUCKINGHAM
with their guard, Sir Humphrey STAFFORD,
and break in. Guards rush in above.

YORK   Lay hands upon these traitors and their trash!
Beldam, I think we watched you at an inch. –
What, madam, are you there? The King and
        commonweal
Are deeply indebted for this piece of pains.
45   My Lord Protector will, I doubt it not,
See you well guerdoned for these good deserts.
ELEANOR   Not half so bad as thine to England's king,
Injurious duke, that threatest where's no cause.
BUCKINGHAM   True, madam, none at all. [*Shows papers.*]
                                        What call you this? –
50   Away with them, let them be clapped up close
And kept asunder. – You, madam, shall with us. –
Stafford, take her to thee.   *Exit Stafford.*
                Exeunt Eleanor, Hume and Guard, above.
We'll see your trinkets here all forthcoming.
All away!
        Exeunt Jourdain, Southwell, Bolingbroke and Guard.
YORK
55   Lord Buckingham, methinks you watched her well. –
A pretty plot, well chosen to build upon. –
Now, pray, my lord, let's see the devil's writ.
What have we here?
[*Reads.*] *The duke yet lives that Henry shall depose,*
60   *But him outlive, and die a violent death.*

Why, this is just
Aio te, Aeacida, Romanos vincere posse.
Well, to the rest:
'*Tell me, what fate awaits the Duke of Suffolk?*'
By water shall he die, and take his end.   65
'*What shall betide the Duke of Somerset?*'
Let him shun castles.
Safer shall he be upon the sandy plains
Than where castles mounted stand.
Come, come, my lords, these oracles   70
Are hardly attained, and hardly understood.
The King is now in progress towards Saint Albans,
With him the husband of this lovely lady.
Thither goes these news as fast as horse can carry them:
A sorry breakfast for my Lord Protector.   75
BUCKINGHAM
Your grace shall give me leave, my Lord of York,
To be the post, in hope of his reward.
YORK   At your pleasure, my good lord.
                        Exit Buckingham.
                Who's within there, ho?

                Enter a Servingman.

Invite my Lords of Salisbury and Warwick
To sup with me tomorrow night. Away!   *Exeunt.*   80

2.1   *Enter the* KING, QUEEN, GLOUCESTER, CARDINAL
        and SUFFOLK, *with Falconers hallooing.*

QUEEN   Believe me, lords, for flying at the brook
I saw not better sport these seven years' day;
Yet, by your leave, the wind was very high
And, ten to one, old Joan had not gone out.
KING [*to Gloucester*]
But what a point, my lord, your falcon made   5
And what a pitch she flew above the rest!
To see how God in all his creatures works!
Yea, man and birds are fain of climbing high.
SUFFOLK   No marvel, an it like your majesty,
My Lord Protector's hawks do tower so well,   10
They know their master loves to be aloft,
And bears his thoughts above his falcon's pitch.
GLOUCESTER   My lord, 'tis but a base ignoble mind
That mounts no higher than a bird can soar.
CARDINAL
I thought as much: he would be above the clouds.   15
GLOUCESTER
Ay, my Lord Cardinal, how think you by that?
Were it not good your grace could fly to heaven?
KING   The treasury of everlasting joy.
CARDINAL
Thy heaven is on earth, thine eyes and thoughts
Beat on a crown, the treasure of thy heart,   20
Pernicious Protector, dangerous peer
That smooth'st it so with king and commonweal!
GLOUCESTER
What, Cardinal? Is your priesthood grown peremptory?

Tantaene animis coelestibus irae?
25   Churchmen so hot? Good uncle, hide such malice:
    With such holiness can you do it?
SUFFOLK   No malice, sir; no more than well becomes
    So good a quarrel and so bad a peer.
GLOUCESTER   As who, my lord?
SUFFOLK   Why, as you, my lord.
30   An't like your lordly Lord Protectorship.
GLOUCESTER
    Why, Suffolk, England knows thine insolence.
QUEEN   And thy ambition, Gloucester.
KING   I prithee, peace,
    Good Queen, and whet not on these furious peers;
    For blessed are the peacemakers on earth.
CARDINAL [*aside to Suffolk*]
35   Let me be blessed for the peace I make
    Against this proud Protector with my sword!
GLOUCESTER [*aside to Cardinal*]
    Faith, holy uncle, would 'twere come to that!
CARDINAL [*aside to Gloucester*]   Marry, when thou dar'st.
GLOUCESTER [*aside to Cardinal*]
    Make up no factious numbers for the matter,
40   In thine own person answer thy abuse.
CARDINAL [*aside to Gloucester*]
    Ay, where thou dar'st not peep; and if thou dar'st,
    This evening on the east side of the grove.
KING   How now, my lords?
CARDINAL   Believe me, cousin Gloucester,
    Had not your man put up the fowl so suddenly,
    We had had more sport.
45   [*aside to Gloucester*]   Come with thy two-hand sword.
GLOUCESTER   True uncle.
    [*aside to Cardinal*] Are ye advised? The east side of
    the grove.
CARDINAL [*aside to Gloucester*]   I am with you.
KING   Why, how now, uncle Gloucester?
GLOUCESTER   Talking of hawking, nothing else, my lord.
    [*aside to Cardinal*] Now, by God's mother, priest, I'll
50   shave your crown for this,
    Or all my fence shall fail.
CARDINAL [*aside to Gloucester*]   *Medice teipsum.* –
    Protector, see to't well, protect yourself.
KING   The winds grow high; so do your stomachs, lords.
55   How irksome is this music to my heart!
    When such strings jar what hope of harmony?
    I pray, my lords, let me compound this strife.

        Enter Townsman *crying,* 'A miracle!'

GLOUCESTER   What means this noise?
    Fellow, what miracle dost thou proclaim?
60 TOWNSMAN   A miracle! A miracle!
SUFFOLK
    Come to the King and tell him what miracle.
TOWNSMAN
    Forsooth, a blind man at Saint Alban's shrine
    Within this half-hour hath received his sight –
    A man that ne'er saw in his life before.

KING   Now God be praised, that to believing souls   65
    Gives light in darkness, comfort in despair!

    Enter the Mayor of Saint Albans *and his brethren,*
    with music, bearing the man SIMPCOX *between two*
    in a chair, his Wife *and Townsmen following.*

CARDINAL   Here comes the townsmen, on procession,
    To present your highness with the man.
KING   Great is his comfort in this earthly vale,
    Although by sight his sin be multiplied.   70
GLOUCESTER
    Stand by, my masters, bring him near the King.
    His highness' pleasure is to talk with him.
KING   Good fellow, tell us here the circumstance,
    That we for thee may glorify the Lord.
    What, hast thou been long blind and now restored?   75
SIMPCOX   Born blind, an't please your grace.
WIFE   Ay, indeed, was he.
SUFFOLK   What woman is this?
WIFE   His wife, an't like your worship.
GLOUCESTER
    Hadst thou been his mother, thou couldst have better
      told.
KING   Where wert thou born?
SIMPCOX   At Berwick in the north, an't like your grace.   80
KING
    Poor soul, God's goodness hath been great to thee.
    Let never day nor night unhallowed pass,
    But still remember what the Lord hath done.
QUEEN
    Tell me, good fellow, cam'st thou here by chance,
    Or of devotion to this holy shrine?   85
SIMPCOX   God knows, of pure devotion; being called
    A hundred times and oft'ner, in my sleep,
    By good Saint Alban, who said, 'Simon, come;
    Come offer at my shrine, and I will help thee.'
WIFE   Most true, forsooth; and many time and oft   90
    Myself have heard a voice to call him so.
CARDINAL   What, art thou lame?
SIMPCOX   Ay, God Almighty help me!
SUFFOLK   How cam'st thou so?
SIMPCOX   A fall off of a tree.
WIFE   A plum-tree, master.
GLOUCESTER   How long hast thou been blind?
SIMPCOX   O, born so, master.
GLOUCESTER   What, and wouldst climb a tree?   95
SIMPCOX   But that in all my life, when I was a youth.
WIFE   Too true, and bought his climbing very dear.
GLOUCESTER
    'Mass, thou lov'dst plums well, that wouldst venture so.
SIMPCOX
    Alas, good master, my wife desired some damsons,
    And made me climb, with danger of my life.   100
GLOUCESTER
    A subtle knave! But yet it shall not serve. –
    Let me see thine eyes; wink now – now open them.
    In my opinion yet thou seest not well.

SIMPCOX
    Yes, master, clear as day, I thank God and Saint Alban.
GLOUCESTER
105   Sayst thou me so? What colour is this cloak of?
SIMPCOX   Red, master, red as blood.
GLOUCESTER
    Why, that's well said. What colour is my gown of?
SIMPCOX   Black, forsooth, coal-black as jet.
KING   Why then, thou knowst what colour jet is of?
110 **SUFFOLK**   And yet, I think, jet did he never see.
GLOUCESTER
    But cloaks and gowns before this day a many.
WIFE   Never before this day, in all his life.
GLOUCESTER   Tell me, sirrah, what's my name?
SIMPCOX   Alas, master, I know not.
115 **GLOUCESTER**   What's his name?
SIMPCOX   I know not.
GLOUCESTER   Nor his?
SIMPCOX   No, indeed, master.
GLOUCESTER   What's thine own name?
120 **SIMPCOX**   Simon Simpcox, an if it please you, master.
GLOUCESTER   Then, Simon, sit there the lying'st knave
    In Christendom. If thou hadst been born blind
    Thou mightst as well have known all our names as
      thus
    To name the several colours we do wear.
125   Sight may distinguish of colours, but suddenly
    To nominate them all, it is impossible.
    My lords, Saint Alban here hath done a miracle.
    And would ye not think that cunning to be great
    That could restore this cripple to his legs again?
130 **SIMPCOX**   O master, that you could!
GLOUCESTER   My masters of Saint Albans, have you not
    Beadles in your town, and things called whips?
MAYOR   Yes, my lord, if it please your grace.
GLOUCESTER   Then send for one presently.
135 **MAYOR**   Sirrah, go fetch the beadle hither straight.
                    Exit a Townsman.
GLOUCESTER   Now fetch me a stool hither by and by. –
    Now, sirrah, if you mean to save yourself from
      whipping,
    Leap me over this stool, and run away.
SIMPCOX   Alas, master, I am not able to stand alone.
140   You go about to torture me in vain.

          Enter a Beadle *with whips.*

GLOUCESTER   Well, sir, we must have you find your legs.
    Sirrah beadle, whip him till he leap over that same stool.
BEADLE   I will, my lord. –
    Come on, sirrah, off with your doublet quickly.
SIMPCOX
145   Alas, master, what shall I do? I am not able to stand.
    [*After the Beadle hath hit him once, he leaps over the*
    stool and runs away; and they follow and cry, 'A
    miracle!']
KING   O God, seest thou this, and bearest so long?

QUEEN   It made me laugh to see the villain run.
GLOUCESTER   Follow the knave, and take this drab away.
WIFE   Alas, sir, we did it for pure need.
GLOUCESTER
    Let them be whipped through every market town   150
    Till they come to Berwick, from whence they came.
          Exeunt Wife, Beadle, Mayor and others.
CARDINAL   Duke Humphrey has done a miracle today.
SUFFOLK   True, made the lame to leap and fly away.
GLOUCESTER   But you have done more miracles than I
    You made in a day, my lord, whole towns to fly.   155

          Enter BUCKINGHAM.

KING   What tidings with our cousin Buckingham?
BUCKINGHAM   Such as my heart doth tremble to unfold.
    A sort of naughty persons, lewdly bent,
    Under the countenance and confederacy
    Of Lady Eleanor, the Protector's wife,   160
    The ringleader and head of all this rout,
    Have practised dangerously against your state,
    Dealing with witches and with conjurors,
    Whom we have apprehended in the fact,
    Raising up wicked spirits from under ground,   165
    Demanding of King Henry's life and death,
    And other of your highness' Privy Council,
    As more at large your grace shall understand.
CARDINAL   And so, my Lord Protector, by this means
    Your lady is forthcoming yet at London.   170
    This news, I think, hath turned your weapon's edge.
    'Tis like, my lord, you will not keep your hour.
GLOUCESTER
    Ambitious churchman, leave to afflict my heart.
    Sorrow and grief have vanquished all my powers,
    And, vanquished as I am, I yield to thee   175
    Or to the meanest groom.
KING   O God, what mischiefs work the wicked ones,
    Heaping confusion on their own heads thereby!
QUEEN   Gloucester, see here the tainture of thy nest,
    And look thyself be faultless, thou wert best.   180
GLOUCESTER   Madam, for myself, to heaven I do appeal
    How I have loved my king and commonweal;
    And for my wife I know not how it stands.
    Sorry I am to hear what I have heard.
    Noble she is, but if she have forgot   185
    Honour and virtue, and conversed with such
    As, like to pitch, defile nobility,
    I banish her my bed and company
    And give her as a prey to law and shame
    That hath dishonoured Gloucester's honest name.   190
KING   Well, for this night we will repose us here;
    Tomorrow toward London back again,
    To look into this business thoroughly
    And call these foul offenders to their answers,
    And poise the cause in Justice' equal scales,   195
    Whose beam stands sure, whose rightful cause
      prevails.   *Flourish. Exeunt.*

2.2 *Enter* YORK, SALISBURY *and* WARWICK.

YORK Now, my good Lords of Salisbury and Warwick,
Our simple supper ended, give me leave
In this close walk to satisfy myself
In craving your opinion of my title,
5   Which is infallible, to England's crown.

SALISBURY My lord, I long to hear it out at full.

WARWICK Sweet York, begin; an if thy claim be good,
The Nevilles are thy subjects to command.

YORK Then thus:
10 Edward the Third, my lords, had seven sons:
The first, Edward the Black Prince, Prince of Wales;
The second, William of Hatfield; and the third,
Lionel, Duke of Clarence; next to whom
Was John of Gaunt, the Duke of Lancaster;
15 The fifth was Edmund Langley, Duke of York;
The sixth was Thomas of Woodstock, Duke of
    Gloucester;
William of Windsor was the seventh and last.
Edward the Black Prince died before his father,
And left behind him Richard, his only son,
20 Who after Edward the Third's death reigned as king,
Till Henry Bolingbroke, Duke of Lancaster,
The eldest son and heir of John of Gaunt,
Crowned by the name of Henry the Fourth,
Seized on the realm, deposed the rightful king,
25 Sent his poor queen to France, from whence she came,
And him to Pomfret; where, as all you know,
Harmless Richard was murdered traitorously.

WARWICK Father, the Duke of York hath told the truth;
Thus got the house of Lancaster the crown.

YORK Which now they hold by force and not by right;
30 For Richard, the first son's heir being dead,
The issue of the next son should have reigned.

SALISBURY
But William of Hatfield died without an heir.

YORK
The third son, Duke of Clarence, from whose line
35 I claim the crown, had issue Philippe, a daughter,
Who married Edmund Mortimer, Earl of March;
Edmund had issue, Roger, Earl of March;
Roger had issue, Edmund, Anne and Eleanor.

SALISBURY This Edmund in the reign of Bolingbroke,
40 As I have read, laid claim unto the crown
And, but for Owen Glendower, had been king,
Who kept him in captivity till he died.
But to the rest.

YORK   His eldest sister, Anne,
My mother, being heir unto the crown,
45 Married Richard, Earl of Cambridge, who was son
To Edmund Langley, Edward the Third's fifth son.
By her I claim the kingdom; she was heir
To Roger, Earl of March, who was the son
Of Edmund Mortimer, who married Philippe,
50 Sole daughter unto Lionel, Duke of Clarence.
So, if the issue of the elder son

Succeed before the younger, I am king.

WARWICK
What plain proceeding is more plain than this?
Henry doth claim the crown from John of Gaunt,
The fourth son; York claims it from the third.   55
Till Lionel's issue fails, Gaunt's should not reign;
It fails not yet, but flourishes in thee
And in thy sons, fair slips of such a stock.
Then, father Salisbury, kneel we together,
    [*They kneel.*]
And, in this private plot, be we the first   60
That shall salute our rightful sovereign
With honour of his birthright to the crown.

BOTH
Long live our sovereign, Richard, England's king!

YORK We thank you, lords. [*They rise.*]
                But I am not your king
Till I be crowned and that my sword be stained   65
With heart-blood of the house of Lancaster;
And that's not suddenly to be performed
But with advice and silent secrecy.
Do you as I do in these dangerous days —
Wink at the Duke of Suffolk's insolence,   70
At Beaufort's pride, at Somerset's ambition,
At Buckingham, and all the crew of them,
Till they have snared the shepherd of the flock,
That virtuous prince, the good Duke Humphrey.
'Tis that they seek; and they, in seeking that,   75
Shall find their deaths, if York can prophesy.

SALISBURY
My lord, break we off; we know your mind at full.

WARWICK My heart assures me that the Earl of Warwick
Shall one day make the Duke of York a king.

YORK And, Neville, this I do assure myself: 80
Richard shall live to make the Earl of Warwick
The greatest man in England but the king.   *Exeunt.*

2.3 *Sound trumpets. Enter the* KING, *the* QUEEN,
    GLOUCESTER, YORK, SUFFOLK, SALISBURY;
    and ELEANOR, *Margery* JOURDAIN, SOUTHWELL,
    HUME *and* BOLINGBROKE, *under guard.*

KING
Stand forth, Dame Eleanor Cobham, Gloucester's
    wife.
In sight of God and us, your guilt is great;
Receive the sentence of the law for sin
Such as by God's book are adjudged to death.
You four, from hence to prison back again;   5
From thence unto the place of execution.
The witch in Smithfield shall be burnt to ashes,
And you three shall be strangled on the gallows.
You, madam, for you are more nobly born,
Despoiled of your honour in your life,   10
Shall, after three days' open penance done,
Live in your country here, in banishment
With Sir John Stanley in the Isle of Man.

ELEANOR
  Welcome is banishment; welcome were my death.
GLOUCESTER
15 Eleanor, the law, thou seest, hath judged thee:
  I cannot justify whom the law condemns.
  Mine eyes are full of tears, my heart of grief.
            Exeunt Eleanor and other prisoners, guarded.
  Ah, Humphrey, this dishonour in thine age
  Will bring thy head with sorrow to the ground! –
20 I beseech your majesty, give me leave to go;
  Sorrow would solace, and mine age would ease.
KING
  Stay, Humphrey, Duke of Gloucester. Ere thou go,
  Give up thy staff. Henry will to himself
  Protector be; and God shall be my hope,
25 My stay, my guide and lantern to my feet.
  And go in peace, Humphrey, no less beloved
  Than when thou wert Protector to thy king.
QUEEN I see no reason why a king of years
  Should be to be protected like a child.
30 God and King Henry govern England's realm!
  Give up your staff, sir, and the King his realm.
GLOUCESTER My staff? Here, noble Henry, is my staff:
  As willingly do I the same resign
  As e'er thy father Henry made it mine;
35 And even as willing at thy feet I leave it
  As others would ambitiously receive it.
        [*Lays down staff.*]
  Farewell, good King. When I am dead and gone
  May honourable peace attend thy throne.   *Exit.*
QUEEN Why, now is Henry King and Margaret Queen,
40 And Humphrey Duke of Gloucester scarce himself,
  That bears so shrewd a maim: two pulls at once;
  His lady banished, and a limb lopped off.
  This staff of honour raught,   [*Picks up staff.*]
                there let it stand
  Where it best fits to be, in Henry's hand.
SUFFOLK
45 Thus droops this lofty pine and hangs his sprays;
  Thus Eleanor's pride dies in her youngest days.
YORK Lords, let him go. Please it your majesty,
  This is the day appointed for the combat,
  And ready are the appellant and defendant,
50 The armourer and his man, to enter the lists,
  So please your highness to behold the fight.
QUEEN Ay, good my lord; for purposely therefore
  Left I the court to see this quarrel tried.
KING I'God's name, see the lists and all things fit;
55 Here let them end it, and God defend the right!
YORK I never saw a fellow worse bested,
  Or more afraid to fight, than is the appellant,
  The servant of this armourer, my lords.

      Enter at one door HORNER *the armourer and his*
      Neighbours, *drinking to him so much that he is*
      drunk; and he enters with a drum before him,
      and his staff with a sandbag fastened to it;

and at the other door PETER, *his man, with*
    a drum and sandbag, and Prentices
          drinking to him.

1 NEIGHBOUR Here, neighbour Horner, I drink to you
  in a cup of sack; and fear not, neighbour, you shall do   60
  well enough.
2 NEIGHBOUR And here, neighbour, here's a cup of
  charneco.
3 NEIGHBOUR And here's a pot of good double beer,
  neighbour: drink, and fear not your man.   65
HORNER Let it come, i'faith, and I'll pledge you all;
  and a fig for Peter!
1 PRENTICE Here, Peter, I drink to thee, and be not
  afraid.
2 PRENTICE Here, Peter, here's a pint of claret wine   70
  for thee.
3 PRENTICE And here's a quart for me; and be merry,
  Peter, and fear not thy master. Fight for credit of the
  prentices.
PETER I thank you all. Drink and pray for me, I pray   75
  you, for I think I have taken my last draught in this
  world. Here, Robin, an if I die, I give thee my apron;
  and Will, thou shalt have my hammer; and here, Tom,
  take all the money that I have. O Lord bless me, I pray
  God, for I am never able to deal with my master, he   80
  hath learnt so much fence already.
SALISBURY Come, leave your drinking, and fall to blows.
  Sirrah, what's thy name?
PETER Peter, forsooth.
SALISBURY Peter! What more?   85
PETER Thump.
SALISBURY Thump! Then see thou thump thy master
  well.
HORNER Masters, I am come hither, as it were, upon
  my man's instigation, to prove him a knave and myself   90
  an honest man; and touching the Duke of York, I will
  take my death I never meant him any ill, nor the King,
  nor the Queen; and therefore, Peter, have at thee with
  a downright blow!
YORK Dispatch! This knave's tongue begins to double.   95
  Sound trumpets!   [*Alarum to the combatants*]
  [*They fight, and Peter strikes Horner down.*]
HORNER Hold, Peter, hold! I confess, I confess treason.
  [*Dies.*]
YORK Take away his weapon. – Fellow, thank God and
  the good wine in thy master's way.
PETER [*Kneels.*] O God! Have I overcome mine enemies   100
  in this presence? O Peter, thou hast prevailed in right!
KING Go, take hence that traitor from our sight,
  For by his death we do perceive his guilt.
  And God in justice hath revealed to us
  The truth and innocence of this poor fellow,   105
  Which he had thought to have murdered wrongfully.
  Come, fellow,   [*Peter rises.*]
          follow us for thy reward.
              Sound a flourish. Exeunt.

2.4 *Enter* GLOUCESTER *and his* Servants *in mourning cloaks.*

GLOUCESTER
Thus sometimes hath the brightest day a cloud;
And after summer evermore succeeds
Barren winter, with his wrathful nipping cold;
So cares and joys abound, as seasons fleet.
Sirs, what's o'clock?

SERVANT   Ten, my lord.

GLOUCESTER   Ten is the hour that was appointed me
To watch the coming of my punished duchess;
Uneath may she endure the flinty streets,
To tread them with her tender-feeling feet.
Sweet Nell, ill can thy noble mind abrook
The abject people gazing on thy face
With envious looks, laughing at thy shame,
That erst did follow thy proud chariot wheels
When thou didst ride in triumph through the streets.
But soft, I think she comes; and I'll prepare
My tear-stained eyes, to see her miseries.

Enter ELEANOR *barefoot, and a white sheet about her, with*
a wax candle in her hand, and verses written on her back
and pinned on, and accompanied with the Sheriff *of*
London, *and Sir John* STANLEY *and Officers with bills*
and halberds and Commoners.

SERVANT
So please your grace, we'll take her from the sheriff.

GLOUCESTER   No, stir not for your lives; let her pass by.

ELEANOR   Come you, my lord, to see my open shame?
Now thou dost penance too. Look how they gaze!
See how the giddy multitude do point
And nod their heads and throw their eyes on thee.
Ah, Gloucester, hide thee from their hateful looks
And, in thy closet pent up, rue my shame
And ban thine enemies, both mine and thine.

GLOUCESTER   Be patient, gentle Nell, forget this grief.

ELEANOR   Ah, Gloucester, teach me to forget myself;
For whilst I think I am thy married wife
And thou a prince, Protector of this land,
Methinks I should not thus be led along,
Mailed up in shame, with papers on my back,
And followed with a rabble that rejoice
To see my tears and hear my deep-fet groans.
The ruthless flint doth cut my tender feet,
And when I start, the envious people laugh
And bid me be advised how I tread.
Ah, Humphrey, can I bear this shameful yoke?
Trowest thou that e'er I'll look upon the world,
Or count them happy that enjoys the sun?
No: dark shall be my light and night my day;
To think upon my pomp shall be my hell.
Sometime I'll say, 'I am Duke Humphrey's wife,
And he a prince and ruler of the land;
Yet so he ruled, and such a prince he was,
As he stood by whilst I, his forlorn duchess,

Was made a wonder and a pointing-stock
To every idle rascal follower.'
But be thou mild and blush not at my shame,
Nor stir at nothing, till the axe of death
Hang over thee, as sure it shortly will.   50
For Suffolk, he that can do all in all
With her that hateth thee and hates us all,
And York and impious Beaufort, that false priest,
Have all limed bushes to betray thy wings;
And fly thou how thou canst, they'll tangle thee.   55
But fear not thou until thy foot be snared,
Nor never seek prevention of thy foes.

GLOUCESTER   Ah, Nell, forbear! Thou aimest all awry.
I must offend before I be attainted;
And had I twenty times so many foes,   60
And each of them had twenty times their power,
All these could not procure me any scathe
So long as I am loyal, true and crimeless.
Wouldst have me rescue thee from this reproach?
Why yet thy scandal were not wiped away,   65
But I in danger for the breach of law.
Thy greatest help is quiet, gentle Nell:
I pray thee, sort thy heart to patience;
These few days' wonder will be quickly worn.

Enter a Herald.

HERALD
I summon your grace to his majesty's parliament,   70
Holden at Bury the first of this next month.

GLOUCESTER
And my consent ne'er asked herein before?
This is close dealing. Well, I will be there.   *Exit Herald.*
My Nell, I take my leave; and, master sheriff,
Let not her penance exceed the King's commission.   75

SHERIFF
An't please your grace, here my commission stays,
And Sir John Stanley is appointed now
To take her with him to the Isle of Man.

GLOUCESTER   Must you, Sir John, protect my lady here?

STANLEY
So am I given in charge, may't please your grace.   80

GLOUCESTER   Entreat her not the worse, in that I pray
You use her well. The world may laugh again,
And I may live to do you kindness if
You do it her. And so, Sir John, farewell.
     [*Gloucester begins to leave.*]

ELEANOR   What, gone, my lord, and bid me not farewell?   85

GLOUCESTER   Witness my tears, I cannot stay to speak.
                          Exeunt Gloucester and Servants.

ELEANOR   Art thou gone too? All comfort go with thee,
For none abides with me; my joy is death;
Death, at whose name I oft have been afeared,
Because I wished this world's eternity.   90
Stanley, I prithee go, and take me hence,
I care not whither, for I beg no favour;
Only convey me where thou art commanded.

STANLEY   Why, madam, that is to the Isle of Man,

95   There to be used according to your state.
      ELEANOR   That's bad enough, for I am but reproach;
      And shall I then be used reproachfully?
      STANLEY
      Like to a duchess, and Duke Humphrey's lady,
      According to that state you shall be used.
100   ELEANOR   Sheriff, farewell, and better than I fare,
      Although thou hast been conduct of my shame.
      SHERIFF   It is my office, and, madam, pardon me.
      ELEANOR   Ay, ay, farewell; thy office is discharged.
            Exit Sheriff with Officers and Commoners.
      Come, Stanley, shall we go?
      STANLEY
105   Madam, your penance done, throw off this sheet,
      And go we to attire you for our journey.
      ELEANOR   My shame will not be shifted with my sheet:
      No, it will hang upon my richest robes
      And show itself, attire me how I can.
110   Go, lead the way, I long to see my prison.   *Exeunt.*

3.1   *Sound a sennet. Enter two Heralds before, the*
           KING, QUEEN, CARDINAL, SUFFOLK, YORK,
           BUCKINGHAM, SALISBURY *and* WARWICK
           to the parliament, with Attendants.

      KING   I muse my Lord of Gloucester is not come.
      'Tis not his wont to be the hindmost man,
      Whate'er occasion keeps him from us now.
      QUEEN   Can you not see, or will ye not observe
5   The strangeness of his altered countenance?
      With what a majesty he bears himself,
      How insolent of late he is become, how proud,
      How peremptory, and unlike himself.
      We know the time since he was mild and affable;
10   An if we did but glance a far-off look,
      Immediately he was upon his knee,
      That all the court admired him for submission.
      But meet him now, and be it in the morn,
      When everyone will give the time of day,
15   He knits his brow and shows an angry eye
      And passeth by with stiff unbowed knee,
      Disdaining duty that to us belongs.
      Small curs are not regarded when they grin,
      But great men tremble when the lion roars;
20   And Humphrey is no little man in England.
      First note that he is near you in descent,
      And should you fall, he is the next will mount.
      Meseemeth then it is no policy,
      Respecting what a rancorous mind he bears
25   And his advantage following your decease,
      That he should come about your royal person
      Or be admitted to your highness' Council.
      By flattery hath he won the commons' hearts;
      And when he please to make commotion,
30   'Tis to be feared they all will follow him.
      Now 'tis the spring, and weeds are shallow-rooted;
      Suffer them now and they'll o'ergrow the garden

And choke the herbs for want of husbandry.
The reverent care I bear unto my lord
Made me collect these dangers in the Duke.   35
If it be fond, call it a woman's fear;
Which fear if better reasons can supplant,
I will subscribe and say I wronged the Duke.
My Lord of Suffolk, Buckingham and York,
Reprove my allegation if you can,   40
Or else conclude my words effectual.
SUFFOLK   Well hath your highness seen into this Duke;
And had I first been put to speak my mind,
I think I should have told your grace's tale.
The Duchess by his subornation,   45
Upon my life, began her devilish practices;
Or if he were not privy to those faults,
Yet by reputing of his high descent,
As next the King he was successive heir –
And such high vaunts of his nobility –   50
Did instigate the bedlam brainsick Duchess
By wicked means to frame our sovereign's fall.
Smooth runs the water where the brook is deep,
And in his simple show he harbours treason.
The fox barks not when he would steal the lamb.   55
No, no, my sovereign, Gloucester is a man
Unsounded yet and full of deep deceit.
CARDINAL   Did he not, contrary to form of law,
Devise strange deaths for small offences done?
YORK   And did he not, in his Protectorship,   60
Levy great sums of money through the realm
For soldiers' pay in France, and never sent it?
By means whereof the towns each day revolted.
BUCKINGHAM
Tut, these are petty faults to faults unknown
Which time will bring to light in smooth Duke
      Humphrey.   65
KING   My lords, at once: the care you have of us
To mow down thorns that would annoy our foot
Is worthy praise; but, shall I speak my conscience,
Our kinsman Gloucester is as innocent
From meaning treason to our royal person   70
As is the sucking lamb or harmless dove.
The Duke is virtuous, mild and too well given
To dream on evil or to work my downfall.
QUEEN
Ah, what's more dangerous than this fond affiance?
Seems he a dove? His feathers are but borrowed,   75
For he's disposed as the hateful raven.
Is he a lamb? His skin is surely lent him,
For he's inclined as is the ravenous wolves.
Who cannot steal a shape, that means deceit?
Take heed, my lord; the welfare of us all   80
Hangs on the cutting short that fraudful man.

            Enter SOMERSET.

SOMERSET   All health unto my gracious sovereign!
KING
Welcome, Lord Somerset. What news from France?

SOMERSET   That all your interest in those territories
85   Is utterly bereft you; all is lost.
KING
        Cold news, Lord Somerset; but God's will be done.
YORK [*aside*]   Cold news for me; for I had hope of France
        As firmly as I hope for fertile England.
        Thus are my blossoms blasted in the bud,
90   And caterpillars eat my leaves away;
        But I will remedy this gear ere long,
        Or sell my title for a glorious grave.

                Enter GLOUCESTER.

GLOUCESTER   All happiness unto my lord the King!
        Pardon, my liege, that I have stayed so long.
SUFFOLK
95   Nay, Gloucester, know that thou art come too soon,
        Unless thou wert more loyal than thou art.
        I do arrest thee of high treason here.
GLOUCESTER
        Well, Suffolk's Duke, thou shalt not see me blush,
        Nor change my countenance for this arrest.
100   A heart unspotted is not easily daunted.
        The purest spring is not so free from mud
        As I am clear from treason to my sovereign.
        Who can accuse me? Wherein am I guilty?
YORK
        'Tis thought, my lord, that you took bribes of France,
105   And, being Protector, stayed the soldiers' pay,
        By means whereof his highness hath lost France.
GLOUCESTER
        Is it but thought so? What are they that think it?
        I never robbed the soldiers of their pay,
        Nor ever had one penny bribe from France.
110   So help me God, as I have watched the night,
        Ay, night by night, in studying good for England!
        That doit that e'er I wrested from the King,
        Or any groat I hoarded to my use,
        Be brought against me at my trial day!
115   No: many a pound of mine own proper store,
        Because I would not tax the needy commons,
        Have I dispursed to the garrisons
        And never asked for restitution.
CARDINAL   It serves you well, my lord, to say so much.
GLOUCESTER
120   I say no more than truth, so help me God!
YORK   In your Protectorship you did devise
        Strange tortures for offenders, never heard of,
        That England was defamed by tyranny.
GLOUCESTER
        Why, 'tis well known that whiles I was Protector
125   Pity was all the fault that was in me,
        For I should melt at an offender's tears,
        And lowly words were ransom for their fault.
        Unless it were a bloody murderer,
        Or foul felonious thief that fleeced poor passengers,
130   I never gave them condign punishment.
        Murder indeed, that bloody sin, I tortured

        Above the felon or what trespass else.
SUFFOLK
        My lord, these faults are easy, quickly answered,
        But mightier crimes are laid unto your charge
        Whereof you cannot easily purge yourself.   135
        I do arrest you in his highness' name
        And here commit you to my Lord Cardinal
        To keep until your further time of trial.
KING   My Lord of Gloucester, 'tis my special hope
        That you will clear yourself from all suspense. 140
        My conscience tells me you are innocent.
GLOUCESTER
        Ah, gracious lord, these days are dangerous.
        Virtue is choked with foul ambition,
        And charity chased hence by rancour's hand;
        Foul subornation is predominant,   145
        And equity exiled your highness' land.
        I know their complot is to have my life;
        And if my death might make this island happy
        And prove the period of their tyranny,
        I would expend it with all willingness.   150
        But mine is made the prologue to their play;
        For thousands more that yet suspect no peril
        Will not conclude their plotted tragedy.
        Beaufort's red sparkling eyes blab his heart's malice,
        And Suffolk's cloudy brow his stormy hate;   155
        Sharp Buckingham unburdens with his tongue
        The envious load that lies upon his heart;
        And dogged York, that reaches at the moon,
        Whose overweening arm I have plucked back,
        By false accuse doth level at my life.   160
        And you, my sovereign lady, with the rest,
        Causeless have laid disgraces on my head
        And with your best endeavour have stirred up
        My liefest liege to be mine enemy.
        Ay, all of you have laid your heads together –   165
        Myself had notice of your conventicles –
        And all to make away my guiltless life.
        I shall not want false witness to condemn me,
        Nor store of treasons to augment my guilt.
        The ancient proverb will be well effected: 170
        A staff is quickly found to beat a dog.
CARDINAL   My liege, his railing is intolerable.
        If those that care to keep your royal person
        From treason's secret knife and traitor's rage
        Be thus upbraided, chid and rated at,   175
        And the offender granted scope of speech,
        'Twill make them cool in zeal unto your grace.
SUFFOLK   Hath he not twit our sovereign lady here
        With ignominious words, though clerkly couched,
        As if she had suborned some to swear   180
        False allegations to o'erthrow his state?
QUEEN   But I can give the loser leave to chide.
GLOUCESTER
        Far truer spoke than meant: I lose indeed –
        Beshrew the winners, for they played me false!
        And well such losers may have leave to speak.   185

BUCKINGHAM
    He'll wrest the sense and hold us here all day.
    Lord Cardinal, he is your prisoner.
CARDINAL   Sirs, take away the Duke and guard him sure.
GLOUCESTER
    Ah, thus King Henry throws away his crutch
190   Before his legs be firm to bear his body.
    Thus is the shepherd beaten from thy side,
    And wolves are gnarling who shall gnaw thee first.
    Ah, that my fear were false; ah, that it were!
    For, good King Henry, thy decay I fear.
            Exit Gloucester with Attendants.
195 KING   My lords, what to your wisdoms seemeth best
    Do, or undo, as if ourself were here.
   QUEEN   What, will your highness leave the parliament?
   KING   Ay, Margaret; my heart is drowned with grief,
    Whose flood begins to flow within mine eyes,
200   My body round engirt with misery;
    For what's more miserable than discontent?
    Ah, uncle Humphrey, in thy face I see
    The map of honour, truth and loyalty;
    And yet, good Humphrey, is the hour to come
205   That e'er I proved thee false or feared thy faith.
    What louring star now envies thy estate
    That these great lords and Margaret our Queen
    Do seek subversion of thy harmless life?
    Thou never didst them wrong, nor no man wrong.
210   And as the butcher takes away the calf
    And binds the wretch and beats it when it strains,
    Bearing it to the bloody slaughterhouse,
    Even so remorseless have they borne him hence;
    And as the dam runs lowing up and down,
215   Looking the way her harmless young one went,
    And can do naught but wail her darling's loss,
    Even so myself bewails good Gloucester's case
    With sad unhelpful tears, and with dimmed eyes
    Look after him, and cannot do him good,
220   So mighty are his vowed enemies.
    His fortunes I will weep, and 'twixt each groan
    Say, 'Who's a traitor, Gloucester he is none.'
         Exit with Buckingham, Salisbury and Warwick.
   QUEEN
    Free lords, cold snow melts with the sun's hot beams.
    Henry my lord is cold in great affairs,
225   Too full of foolish pity; and Gloucester's show
    Beguiles him, as the mournful crocodile
    With sorrow snares relenting passengers,
    Or as the snake, rolled in a flowering bank,
    With shining checkered slough doth sting a child
230   That for the beauty thinks it excellent.
    Believe me, lords, were none more wise than I –
    And yet herein I judge mine own wit good –
    This Gloucester should be quickly rid the world,
    To rid us from the fear we have of him.
235 CARDINAL   That he should die is worthy policy;
    But yet we want a colour for his death.
    'Tis meet he be condemned by course of law.

SUFFOLK   But in my mind that were no policy.
    The King will labour still to save his life,
    The commons haply rise to save his life;   240
    And yet we have but trivial argument,
    More than mistrust, that shows him worthy death.
YORK   So that, by this, you would not have him die?
SUFFOLK   Ah, York, no man alive so fain as I.
YORK [*aside*]
    'Tis York that hath more reason for his death. –   245
    But, my Lord Cardinal, and you, my Lord of Suffolk,
    Say as you think, and speak it from your souls:
    Were't not all one an empty eagle were set
    To guard the chicken from a hungry kite,
    As place Duke Humphrey for the King's Protector?   250
QUEEN   So the poor chicken should be sure of death.
SUFFOLK
    Madam, 'tis true; and were't not madness then
    To make the fox surveyor of the fold,
    Who being accused a crafty murderer,
    His guilt should be but idly posted over   255
    Because his purpose is not executed?
    No – let him die in that he is a fox,
    By nature proved an enemy to the flock,
    Before his chaps be stained with crimson blood,
    As Humphrey proved, by reasons, to my liege.   260
    And do not stand on quillets how to slay him;
    Be it by gins, by snares, by subtlety,
    Sleeping or waking, 'tis no matter how,
    So he be dead; for that is good deceit
    Which mates him first that first intends deceit.   265
QUEEN   Thrice-noble Suffolk, 'tis resolutely spoke.
SUFFOLK   Not resolute, except so much were done;
    For things are often spoke and seldom meant.
    But that my heart accordeth with my tongue –
    Seeing the deed is meritorious,   270
    And to preserve my sovereign from his foe –
    Say but the word, and I will be his priest.
CARDINAL
    But I would have him dead, my Lord of Suffolk,
    Ere you can take due orders for a priest.
    Say you consent and censure well the deed,   275
    And I'll provide his executioner;
    I tender so the safety of my liege.
SUFFOLK   Here is my hand; the deed is worthy doing.
QUEEN   And so say I.
YORK   And I: and now we three have spoke it,
    It skills not greatly who impugns our doom.   280
              Enter a Post.
POST   Great lords, from Ireland am I come amain
    To signify that rebels there are up
    And put the Englishmen unto the sword.
    Send succours, lords, and stop the rage betime,
    Before the wound do grow uncurable;   285
    For, being green, there is great hope of help.
CARDINAL
    A breach that craves a quick expedient stop!

What counsel give you in this weighty cause?
YORK   That Somerset be sent as regent thither.
290   'Tis meet that lucky ruler be employed;
Witness the fortune he hath had in France.
SOMERSET   If York, with all his far-fet policy,
Had been the regent there instead of me,
He never would have stayed in France so long.
295   YORK   No, not to lose it all, as thou hast done.
I rather would have lost my life betimes
Than bring a burden of dishonour home
By staying there so long till all were lost.
Show me one scar charactered on thy skin;
300   Men's flesh preserved so whole do seldom win.
QUEEN   Nay, then, this spark will prove a raging fire
If wind and fuel be brought to feed it with.
No more, good York. Sweet Somerset, be still.
Thy fortune, York, hadst thou been regent there,
305   Might happily have proved far worse than his.
YORK
What, worse than naught? Nay, then a shame take all!
SOMERSET   And in the number thee, that wishest shame.
CARDINAL   My Lord of York, try what your fortune is.
Th'uncivil kerns of Ireland are in arms
310   And temper clay with blood of Englishmen.
To Ireland will you lead a band of men
Collected choicely, from each county some,
And try your hap against the Irishmen?
315   YORK   I will, my lord, so please his majesty.
SUFFOLK   Why, our authority is his consent,
And what we do establish he confirms.
Then, noble York, take thou this task in hand.
YORK   I am content. Provide me soldiers, lords,
Whiles I take order for mine own affairs.
SUFFOLK
320   A charge, Lord York, that I will see performed.
But now return we to the false Duke Humphrey.
CARDINAL   No more of him; for I will deal with him
That henceforth he shall trouble us no more.
And so break off, the day is almost spent.
325   [*aside*] Lord Suffolk, you and I must talk of that event.
YORK   My Lord of Suffolk, within fourteen days
At Bristol I expect my soldiers;
For there I'll ship them all for Ireland.
SUFFOLK   I'll see it truly done, my Lord of York.
Exeunt all but York.
330   YORK   Now, York, or never, steel thy fearful thoughts,
And change misdoubt to resolution.
Be that thou hop'st to be, or what thou art
Resign to death; it is not worth th'enjoying.
Let pale-faced fear keep with the mean-born man
335   And find no harbour in a royal heart.
Faster than springtime showers comes thought on
thought,
And not a thought but thinks on dignity.
My brain, more busy than the labouring spider,
Weaves tedious snares to trap mine enemies.
340   Well, nobles, well; 'tis politicly done,

To send me packing with an host of men;
I fear me you but warm the starved snake
Who, cherished in your breasts, will sting your hearts.
'Twas men I lacked, and you will give them me;
I take it kindly, yet be well assured   345
You put sharp weapons in a madman's hands.
Whiles I in Ireland nurse a mighty band
I will stir up in England some black storm
Shall blow ten thousand souls to heaven or hell;
And this fell tempest shall not cease to rage   350
Until the golden circuit on my head,
Like to the glorious sun's transparent beams,
Do calm the fury of this mad-bred flaw.
And for a minister of my intent
I have seduced a headstrong Kentishman,   355
John Cade of Ashford,
To make commotion, as full well he can,
Under the title of John Mortimer.
In Ireland have I seen this stubborn Cade
Oppose himself against a troop of kerns,   360
And fought so long till that his thighs with darts
Were almost like a sharp-quilled porpentine;
And in the end, being rescued, I have seen
Him caper upright like a wild Morisco,
Shaking the bloody darts as he his bells.   365
Full often, like a shag-haired crafty kern,
Hath he conversed with the enemy
And, undiscovered, come to me again
And given me notice of their villainies.
This devil here shall be my substitute;   370
For that John Mortimer, which now is dead,
In face, in gait, in speech, he doth resemble.
By this I shall perceive the commons' mind,
How they affect the house and claim of York.
Say he be taken, racked and tortured,   375
I know no pain they can inflict upon him
Will make him say I moved him to those arms.
Say that he thrive, as 'tis great like he will,
Why then from Ireland come I with my strength
And reap the harvest which that rascal sowed.   380
For Humphrey being dead, as he shall be,
And Henry put apart, the next for me.   *Exit.*

3.2   *Enter two or three* Murderers *running over the*
stage, from the murder of Duke Humphrey.

1 MURDERER   Run to my Lord of Suffolk; let him know
We have dispatched the Duke as he commanded.
2 MURDERER   O that it were to do! What have we done?
Didst ever hear a man so penitent?

Enter SUFFOLK.

1 MURDERER   Here comes my lord.   5
SUFFOLK   Now, sirs, have you dispatched this thing?
1 MURDERER   Ay, my good lord, he's dead.
SUFFOLK   Why, that's well said. Go, get you to my house,
I will reward you for this venturous deed.

The King and all the peers are here at hand.
Have you laid fair the bed? Is all things well,
According as I gave directions?

1 MURDERER   'Tis, my good lord.

SUFFOLK   Away, be gone!   *Exeunt Murderers.*

Sound trumpets. Enter the KING, *the* QUEEN, CARDINAL,
    SOMERSET, *with Attendants.*

KING   Go, call our uncle to our presence straight;
Say we intend to try his grace today
If he be guilty, as 'tis published.

SUFFOLK   I'll call him presently, my noble lord.   *Exit.*

KING   Lords, take your places; and, I pray you all,
Proceed no straiter 'gainst our uncle Gloucester
Than from true evidence, of good esteem,
He be approved in practice culpable.

QUEEN   God forbid any malice should prevail
That faultless may condemn a noble man!
Pray God he may acquit him of suspicion!

KING
I thank thee, Meg; these words content me much.

Enter SUFFOLK.

How now? Why look'st thou pale? Why tremblest thou?
Where is our uncle? What's the matter, Suffolk?

SUFFOLK   Dead in his bed, my lord; Gloucester is dead.

QUEEN   Marry, God forfend!

CARDINAL   God's secret judgement. I did dream tonight
The Duke was dumb and could not speak a word.
    [*The King swoons.*]

QUEEN
How fares my lord? Help, lords, the King is dead!

SOMERSET   Rear up his body; wring him by the nose.

QUEEN   Run, go, help, help! O, Henry, ope thine eyes!

SUFFOLK   He doth revive again; madam, be patient.

KING   O heavenly God!

QUEEN   How fares my gracious lord?

SUFFOLK
Comfort, my sovereign! Gracious Henry, comfort!

KING   What, doth my Lord of Suffolk comfort me?
Came he right now to sing a raven's note,
Whose dismal tune bereft my vital powers;
And thinks he that the chirping of a wren,
By crying comfort from a hollow breast,
Can chase away the first-conceived sound?
Hide not thy poison with such sugared words;
Lay not thy hands on me – forbear, I say!
Their touch affrights me as a serpent's sting.
Thou baleful messenger, out of my sight!
Upon thy eyeballs murderous tyranny
Sits in grim majesty to fright the world.
Look not upon me, for thine eyes are wounding.
Yet do not go away; come, basilisk,
And kill the innocent gazer with thy sight.
For in the shade of death I shall find joy,
In life but double death, now Gloucester's dead.

QUEEN   Why do you rate my Lord of Suffolk thus?

Although the Duke was enemy to him,
Yet he most Christian-like laments his death.
And for myself, foe as he was to me,
Might liquid tears, or heart-offending groans,
Or blood-consuming sighs recall his life,
I would be blind with weeping, sick with groans,
Look pale as primrose with blood-drinking sighs,
And all to have the noble Duke alive.
What know I how the world may deem of me?
For it is known we were but hollow friends.
It may be judged I made the Duke away.
So shall my name with slander's tongue be wounded,
And princes' courts be filled with my reproach.
This get I by his death. Ay me, unhappy!
To be a queen, and crowned with infamy.

KING   Ah, woe is me for Gloucester, wretched man!

QUEEN   Be woe for me, more wretched than he is.
What, dost thou turn away and hide thy face?
I am no loathsome leper – look on me!
What? Art thou, like the adder, waxen deaf?
Be poisonous too and kill thy forlorn Queen.
Is all thy comfort shut in Gloucester's tomb?
Why then Queen Margaret was ne'er thy joy.
Erect his statue and worship it,
And make my image but an alehouse sign.
Was I for this nigh wrecked upon the sea
And twice by awkward wind from England's bank
Drove back again unto my native clime?
What boded this, but well-forewarning wind
Did seem to say, 'Seek not a scorpion's nest,
Nor set no footing on this unkind shore'?
What did I then, but cursed the gentle gusts
And he that loosed them forth their brazen caves
And bid them blow towards England's blessed shore
Or turn our stern upon a dreadful rock.
Yet Aeolus would not be a murderer,
But left that hateful office unto thee.
The pretty vaulting sea refused to drown me,
Knowing that thou wouldst have me drowned on shore
With tears as salt as sea through thy unkindness.
The splitting rocks cowered in the sinking sands
And would not dash me with their ragged sides,
Because thy flinty heart, more hard than they,
Might in thy palace perish Margaret.
As far as I could ken thy chalky cliffs,
When from thy shore the tempest beat us back,
I stood upon the hatches in the storm,
And when the dusky sky began to rob
My earnest-gaping sight of thy land's view,
I took a costly jewel from my neck –
A heart it was, bound in with diamonds –
And threw it towards thy land. The sea received it,
And so I wished thy body might my heart;
And even with this I lost fair England's view,
And bid mine eyes be packing with my heart,
And called them blind and dusky spectacles
For losing ken of Albion's wished coast.

How often have I tempted Suffolk's tongue –
15 The agent of thy foul inconstancy –
To sit and witch me, as Ascanius did
When he to madding Dido would unfold
His father's acts, commenced in burning Troy!
Am I not witched like her? Or thou not false like him?
20 Ay me, I can no more! Die, Margaret,
For Henry weeps that thou dost live so long!

Noise within. Enter WARWICK, SALISBURY
and many Commons.

WARWICK It is reported, mighty sovereign,
That good Duke Humphrey traitorously is murdered
By Suffolk and the Cardinal Beaufort's means.
25 The commons, like an angry hive of bees
That want their leader, scatter up and down
And care not who they sting in his revenge.
Myself have calmed their spleenful mutiny,
Until they hear the order of his death.
30 KING That he is dead, good Warwick, 'tis too true;
But how he died, God knows, not Henry.
Enter his chamber, view his breathless corpse,
And comment then upon his sudden death.
WARWICK That shall I do, my liege. Stay, Salisbury,
35 With the rude multitude till I return.
Exeunt severally Warwick, and Salisbury with the Commons.
KING O thou that judgest all things, stay my thoughts:
My thoughts that labour to persuade my soul
Some violent hands were laid on Humphrey's life.
If my suspect be false, forgive me, God,
40 For judgement only doth belong to thee.
Fain would I go to chafe his paly lips
With twenty thousand kisses, and to drain
Upon his face an ocean of salt tears,
To tell my love unto his dumb deaf trunk,
45 And with my fingers feel his hand unfeeling;
But all in vain are these mean obsequies.
And to survey his dead and earthy image,
What were it but to make my sorrow greater?

Bed put forth. Enter WARWICK.

WARWICK
Come hither, gracious sovereign, view this body.
[*Draws the curtains, and shows Gloucester in his bed.*]
50 KING That is to see how deep my grave is made,
For with his soul fled all my worldly solace;
For, seeing him, I see my life in death.
WARWICK As surely as my soul intends to live
With that dread King that took our state upon Him
55 To free us from his Father's wrathful curse,
I do believe that violent hands were laid
Upon the life of this thrice-famed duke.
SUFFOLK A dreadful oath, sworn with a solemn tongue!
What instance gives Lord Warwick for his vow?
60 WARWICK See how the blood is settled in his face.
Oft have I seen a timely-parted ghost
Of ashy semblance, meagre, pale and bloodless,

Being all descended to the labouring heart
Who, in the conflict that it holds with death,
165 Attracts the same for aidance 'gainst the enemy,
Which with the heart there cools and ne'er returneth
To blush and beautify the cheek again.
But see, his face is black and full of blood,
His eyeballs further out than when he lived,
170 Staring full ghastly like a strangled man;
His hair upreared, his nostrils stretched with
struggling;
His hands abroad displayed, as one that grasped
And tugged for life and was by strength subdued.
Look, on the sheets his hair, you see, is sticking;
175 His well-proportioned beard made rough and rugged,
Like to the summer's corn by tempest lodged.
It cannot be but he was murdered here;
The least of all these signs were probable.
[*Closes the curtains.*]
SUFFOLK
Why, Warwick, who should do the Duke to death?
180 Myself and Beaufort had him in protection,
And we, I hope, sir, are no murderers.
WARWICK
But both of you were vowed Duke Humphrey's foes,
And you, forsooth, had the good Duke to keep.
'Tis like you would not feast him like a friend,
185 And 'tis well seen he found an enemy.
QUEEN Then you, belike, suspect these noblemen
As guilty of Duke Humphrey's timeless death?
WARWICK Who finds the heifer dead and bleeding fresh
And sees fast by a butcher with an axe,
190 But will suspect 'twas he that made the slaughter?
Who finds the partridge in the puttock's nest
But may imagine how the bird was dead,
Although the kite soar with unbloodied beak?
Even so suspicious is this tragedy.
QUEEN
195 Are you the butcher, Suffolk? Where's your knife?
Is Beaufort termed a kite? Where are his talons?
[*The bed is withdrawn.*]
Exeunt Cardinal, Somerset and others.
SUFFOLK I wear no knife to slaughter sleeping men,
But here's a vengeful sword, rusted with ease,
That shall be scoured in his rancorous heart
200 That slanders me with murder's crimson badge.
Say, if thou dar'st, proud Lord of Warwickshire,
That I am faulty in Duke Humphrey's death.
WARWICK
What dares not Warwick, if false Suffolk dare him?
QUEEN He dares not calm his contumelious spirit,
205 Nor cease to be an arrogant controller,
Though Suffolk dare him twenty thousand times.
WARWICK Madam, be still, with reverence may I say;
For every word you speak in his behalf
Is slander to your royal dignity.
SUFFOLK Blunt-witted lord, ignoble in demeanour! 210
If ever lady wronged her lord so much,

Thy mother took into her blameful bed
Some stern untutored churl, and noble stock
Was graft with crab-tree slip, whose fruit thou art,
215 And never of the Nevilles' noble race.
WARWICK   But that the guilt of murder bucklers thee,
And I should rob the deathsman of his fee,
Quitting thee thereby of ten thousand shames,
And that my sovereign's presence makes me mild,
220 I would, false murderous coward, on thy knee
Make thee beg pardon for thy passed speech,
And say it was thy mother that thou meant'st,
That thou thyself wast born in bastardy;
And after all this fearful homage done,
225 Give thee thy hire and send thy soul to hell,
Pernicious blood-sucker of sleeping men!
SUFFOLK   Thou shalt be waking while I shed thy blood,
If from this presence thou dar'st go with me.
WARWICK   Away even now, or I will drag thee hence.
230 Unworthy though thou art, I'll cope with thee
And do some service to Duke Humphrey's ghost.
                              Exeunt Suffolk and Warwick.
KING   What stronger breastplate than a heart untainted?
Thrice is he armed that hath his quarrel just,
And he but naked, though locked up in steel,
235 Whose conscience with injustice is corrupted.
    [*A noise within. The commons cry*, 'Down with Suffolk!']
QUEEN   What noise is this?

Enter SUFFOLK *and* WARWICK *with their weapons drawn.*

KING
Why, how now, lords? Your wrathful weapons drawn
Here in our presence? Dare you be so bold?
Why, what tumultuous clamour have we here?
240 SUFFOLK   The traitorous Warwick with the men of Bury
Set all upon me, mighty sovereign.

    Enter SALISBURY *from the Commons, again crying,*
    'Down with Suffolk! Down with Suffolk!'

SALISBURY [*to the Commons, who try to enter*]
Sirs, stand apart; the King shall know your mind. –
Dread lord, the commons send you word by me,
Unless Lord Suffolk straight be done to death,
245 Or banished fair England's territories,
They will by violence tear him from your palace
And torture him with grievous lingering death.
They say, by him the good Duke Humphrey died;
They say, in him they fear your highness' death;
250 And mere instinct of love and loyalty,
Free from a stubborn opposite intent,
As being thought to contradict your liking,
Makes them thus forward in his banishment.
They say, in care of your most royal person,
255 That if your highness should intend to sleep
And charge that no man should disturb your rest,
In pain of your dislike, or pain of death,
Yet notwithstanding such a strait edict,
Were there a serpent seen, with forked tongue,

That slyly glided towards your majesty,   260
It were but necessary you were waked,
Lest, being suffered in that harmful slumber,
The mortal worm might make the sleep eternal.
And therefore do they cry, though you forbid,
That they will guard you, whe'er you will or no, 265
From such fell serpents as false Suffolk is,
With whose envenomed and fatal sting
Your loving uncle, twenty times his worth,
They say is shamefully bereft of life.
COMMONS [*within*]
An answer from the King, my Lord of Salisbury!   270
SUFFOLK
'Tis like the commons, rude unpolished hinds,
Could send such message to their sovereign.
But you, my lord, were glad to be employed
To show how quaint an orator you are.
But all the honour Salisbury hath won   275
Is that he was the lord ambassador
Sent from a sort of tinkers to the King.
COMMONS [*within*]
An answer from the King or we will all break in!
KING   Go, Salisbury, and tell them all from me
I thank them for their tender loving care;   280
And had I not been 'cited so by them,
Yet did I purpose as they do entreat.
For sure, my thoughts do hourly prophesy
Mischance unto my state by Suffolk's means.
And therefore by His majesty I swear,   285
Whose far unworthy deputy I am,
He shall not breathe infection in this air
But three days longer, on the pain of death.
                              Exit Salisbury.
QUEEN   O Henry, let me plead for gentle Suffolk!
KING   Ungentle Queen, to call him gentle Suffolk! 290
No more, I say; if thou dost plead for him
Thou wilt but add increase unto my wrath.
Had I but said, I would have kept my word;
But when I swear, it is irrevocable.
If after three days' space thou here be'st found 295
On any ground that I am ruler of,
The world shall not be ransom for thy life.
Come, Warwick, come; good Warwick, go with me;
I have great matters to impart to thee.
                    Exeunt all but Queen and Suffolk.
QUEEN   Mischance and sorrow go along with you! 300
Heart's discontent and sour affliction
Be playfellows to keep you company!
There's two of you, the devil make a third,
And threefold vengeance tend upon your steps.
SUFFOLK   Cease, gentle Queen, these execrations, 305
And let thy Suffolk take his heavy leave.
QUEEN   Fie, coward woman and soft-hearted wretch!
Hast thou not spirit to curse thine enemies?
SUFFOLK
A plague upon them! Wherefore should I curse them?
Could curses kill, as doth the mandrake's groan, 310

I would invent as bitter searching terms,
As curst, as harsh and horrible to hear,
Delivered strongly through my fixed teeth,
With full as many signs of deadly hate,
15 As lean-faced Envy in her loathsome cave.
My tongue should stumble in mine earnest words,
Mine eyes should sparkle like the beaten flint,
My hair be fixed on end, as one distract;
Ay, every joint should seem to curse and ban.
20 And even now my burdened heart would break
Should I not curse them. Poison be their drink!
Gall, worse than gall, the daintiest that they taste!
Their sweetest shade a grove of cypress trees;
Their chiefest prospect murdering basilisks;
25 Their softest touch as smart as lizards' stings;
Their music frightful as the serpent's hiss,
And boding screech-owls make the consort full!
All the foul terrors in dark-seated hell –
QUEEN   Enough, sweet Suffolk; thou torment'st thyself,
30 And these dread curses, like the sun 'gainst glass,
Or like an overcharged gun, recoil
And turns the force of them upon thyself.
SUFFOLK   You bade me ban, and will you bid me leave?
Now, by the ground that I am banished from,
35 Well could I curse away a winter's night
Though standing naked on a mountain top,
Where biting cold would never let grass grow,
And think it but a minute spent in sport.
QUEEN   O, let me entreat thee cease. Give me thy hand,
40 That I may dew it with my mournful tears;
[*Kisses his hand.*]
Nor let the rain of heaven wet this place
To wash away my woeful monuments.
O, could this kiss be printed in thy hand,
That thou mightst think upon these by the seal,
45 Through whom a thousand sighs are breathed for thee.
So, get thee gone that I may know my grief;
'Tis but surmised whiles thou art standing by,
As one that surfeits thinking on a want.
I will repeal thee or, be well assured,
50 Adventure to be banished myself.
And banished I am, if but from thee.
Go; speak not to me; even now be gone!
O, go not yet. Even thus, two friends condemned
Embrace, and kiss, and take ten thousand leaves,
55 Loather a hundred times to part than die.
Yet now farewell, and farewell life with thee.
SUFFOLK   Thus is poor Suffolk ten times banished,
Once by the King, and three times thrice by thee.
'Tis not the land I care for, wert thou thence:
60 A wilderness is populous enough,
So Suffolk had thy heavenly company.
For where thou art, there is the world itself,
With every several pleasure in the world;
And where thou art not, desolation.
65 I can no more. Live thou to joy thy life,
Myself no joy in naught but that thou liv'st.

Enter VAUX.

QUEEN   Whither goes Vaux so fast? What news, I prithee?
VAUX   To signify unto his majesty
That Cardinal Beaufort is at point of death;
For suddenly a grievous sickness took him,   370
That makes him gasp, and stare, and catch the air,
Blaspheming God and cursing men on earth.
Sometime he talks as if Duke Humphrey's ghost
Were by his side; sometime he calls the King
And whispers to his pillow, as to him,   375
The secrets of his overcharged soul.
And I am sent to tell his majesty
That even now he cries aloud for him.
QUEEN   Go, tell this heavy message to the King. –
Exit Vaux.
Ay me! What is this world? What news are these?   380
But wherefore grieve I at an hour's poor loss,
Omitting Suffolk's exile, my soul's treasure?
Why only, Suffolk, mourn I not for thee
And with the southern clouds contend in tears,
Theirs for the earth's increase, mine for my sorrow's? 385
Now get thee hence; the King, thou knowst, is coming.
If thou be found by me thou art but dead.
SUFFOLK   If I depart from thee I cannot live,
And in thy sight to die, what were it else
But like a pleasant slumber in thy lap?   390
Here could I breathe my soul into the air,
As mild and gentle as the cradle-babe
Dying with mother's dug between its lips;
Where, from thy sight, I should be raging mad
And cry out for thee to close up mine eyes,   395
To have thee with thy lips to stop my mouth;
So shouldst thou either turn my flying soul,
Or I should breathe it so into thy body,
And then it lived in sweet Elysium.
To die by thee were but to die in jest;   400
From thee to die were torture more than death.
O let me stay, befall what may befall!
QUEEN   Though parting be a fretful corrosive,
It is applied to a deathful wound.
To France, sweet Suffolk! Let me hear from thee;   405
For wheresoe'er thou art in this world's globe,
I'll have an Iris that shall find thee out.
Away!
SUFFOLK   I go.
QUEEN   And take my heart with thee. [*Kisses him.*]
SUFFOLK   A jewel locked into the woefullest cask
That ever did contain a thing of worth.   410
Even as a splitted bark, so sunder we:
This way fall I to death.   *Exit by one door.*
QUEEN   This way for me.   *Exit by another.*

3.3 *Enter the* KING, SALISBURY *and* WARWICK, *to the*
CARDINAL *in bed, raving and staring as if he were mad.*

KING
How fares my lord? Speak, Beaufort, to thy sovereign.

CARDINAL
  If thou be'st Death I'll give thee England's treasure,
  Enough to purchase such another island,
  So thou wilt let me live and feel no pain.
5 KING Ah, what a sign it is of evil life
  Where death's approach is seen so terrible!
WARWICK Beaufort, it is thy sovereign speaks to thee.
CARDINAL Bring me unto my trial when you will.
  Died he not in his bed? Where should he die?
10   Can I make men live whe'er they will or no?
  O, torture me no more! I will confess.
  Alive again? Then show me where he is.
  I'll give a thousand pound to look upon him.
  He hath no eyes, the dust hath blinded them.
15   Comb down his hair; look, look, it stands upright
  Like lime twigs set to catch my winged soul!
  Give me some drink, and bid the apothecary
  Bring the strong poison that I bought of him.
KING [*Kneels.*] O Thou eternal mover of the heavens,
20   Look with a gentle eye upon this wretch.
  O beat away the busy meddling fiend
  That lays strong siege unto this wretch's soul,
  And from his bosom purge this black despair.
WARWICK See how the pangs of death do make him grin.
25 SALISBURY Disturb him not; let him pass peaceably.
KING Peace to his soul, if God's good pleasure be.
  Lord Cardinal, if thou thinkst on heaven's bliss,
  Hold up thy hand, make signal of thy hope.
  [*Cardinal dies.*]
  He dies and makes no sign. O God, forgive him!
30 WARWICK So bad a death argues a monstrous life.
KING [*Rises.*] Forbear to judge, for we are sinners all.
  Close up his eyes, and draw the curtain close,
  And let us all to meditation.   *Exeunt.*

4.1   *Alarum. Fight at sea. Ordnance goes off.*
  Enter Lieutenant, SUFFOLK *disguised, a prisoner, the*
  Master *and Master's* Mate, *and* Walter WHITMORE,
  with two Gentlemen *as prisoners and others.*

LIEUTENANT The gaudy, blabbing and remorseful day
  Is crept into the bosom of the sea;
  And now loud-howling wolves arouse the jades
  That drag the tragic melancholy night,
5   Who with their drowsy, slow and flagging wings
  Clip dead men's graves and from their misty jaws
  Breathe foul contagious darkness in the air.
  Therefore bring forth the soldiers of our prize,
  For whilst our pinnace anchors in the Downs,
10   Here shall they make their ransom on the sand,
  Or with their blood stain this discoloured shore.
  Master, this prisoner   [*Indicates First Gentleman.*]
         freely give I thee,
  And thou that art his mate, make boot of this;
   [*Indicates Second Gentleman.*]
  The other,   [*Indicates Suffolk.*]
      Walter Whitmore, is thy share.

1 GENTLEMAN
  What is my ransom, master? Let me know.   15
MASTER
  A thousand crowns, or else lay down your head.
MATE And so much shall you give, or off goes yours.
LIEUTENANT
  What, think you much to pay two thousand crowns,
  And bear the name and port of gentlemen?
WHITMORE
  Cut both the villains' throats! [*to Suffolk*] For die
    you shall.   20
LIEUTENANT
  The lives of those which we have lost in fight
  Be counterpoised with such a petty sum.
1 GENTLEMAN
  I'll give it, sir, and therefore spare my life.
2 GENTLEMAN
  And so will I, and write home for it straight.
WHITMORE [*to Suffolk*]
  I lost mine eye in laying the prize aboard,   25
  And therefore to revenge it shalt thou die,
  And so should these, if I might have my will.
LIEUTENANT
  Be not so rash; take ransom, let him live.
SUFFOLK Look on my George; I am a gentleman.
  [*Reveals his badge.*]
  Rate me at what thou wilt, thou shalt be paid.   30
WHITMORE And so am I; my name is Walter Whitmore.
  How now! Why starts thou? What, doth death affright?
SUFFOLK
  Thy name affrights me, in whose sound is death.
  A cunning man did calculate my birth
  And told me that by water I should die.   35
  Yet let not this make thee be bloody-minded;
  Thy name is Gualtier, being rightly sounded.
WHITMORE Gualtier or Walter, which it is I care not.
  Never yet did base dishonour blur our name
  But with our sword we wiped away the blot.   40
  Therefore, when merchant-like I sell revenge,
  Broke be my sword, my arms torn and defaced
  And I proclaimed a coward through the world.
SUFFOLK Stay, Whitmore, for thy prisoner is a prince,
  The Duke of Suffolk, William de la Pole.   45
  [*Removes his cloak.*]
WHITMORE The Duke of Suffolk, muffled up in rags?
SUFFOLK Ay, but these rags are no part of the Duke.
  Jove sometime went disguised, and why not I?
LIEUTENANT But Jove was never slain as thou shalt be.
SUFFOLK
  Obscure and lousy swain, King Henry's blood,   50
  The honourable blood of Lancaster,
  Must not be shed by such a jaded groom.
  Hast thou not kissed thy hand and held my stirrup?
  And bare-head plodded by my foot-cloth mule,
  And thought thee happy when I shook my head?   55
  How often hast thou waited at my cup,
  Fed from my trencher, kneeled down at the board

When I have feasted with Queen Margaret?
Remember it, and let it make thee crestfallen,
Ay, and allay this thy abortive pride.
How in our voiding lobby hast thou stood
And duly waited for my coming forth?
This hand of mine hath writ in thy behalf
And therefore shall it charm thy riotous tongue.

WHITMORE
Speak, captain, shall I stab the forlorn swain?

LIEUTENANT
First let my words stab him, as he hath me.

SUFFOLK
Base slave, thy words are blunt, and so art thou.

LIEUTENANT
Convey him hence, and on our longboat's side
Strike off his head.

SUFFOLK   Thou dar'st not for thy own.

LIEUTENANT   Yes, poll!

SUFFOLK   Pole!

LIEUTENANT   Pool! Sir Pool! Lord!
Ay, kennel, puddle, sink, whose filth and dirt
Troubles the silver spring where England drinks;
Now will I dam up this thy yawning mouth
For swallowing the treasure of the realm.
Thy lips that kissed the Queen shall sweep the ground;
And thou that smil'dst at good Duke Humphrey's death
Against the senseless winds shall grin in vain
Who in contempt shall hiss at thee again.
And wedded be thou to the hags of hell
For daring to affy a mighty lord
Unto the daughter of a worthless king,
Having neither subject, wealth nor diadem.
By devilish policy art thou grown great
And, like ambitious Sulla, overgorged
With gobbets of thy mother's bleeding heart.
By thee Anjou and Maine were sold to France,
The false revolting Normans thorough thee
Disdain to call us lord, and Picardy
Hath slain their governors, surprised our forts
And sent the ragged soldiers wounded home.
The princely Warwick, and the Nevilles all,
Whose dreadful swords were never drawn in vain,
As hating thee, are rising up in arms.
And now the house of York, thrust from the crown
By shameful murder of a guiltless king
And lofty, proud, encroaching tyranny,
Burns with revenging fire, whose hopeful colours
Advance our half-faced sun, striving to shine,
Under which is writ '*Invitis nubibus*'.
The commons here in Kent are up in arms;
And, to conclude, reproach and beggary
Is crept into the palace of our King,
And all by thee. Away! Convey him hence.

SUFFOLK   O, that I were a god, to shoot forth thunder
Upon these paltry, servile, abject drudges!
Small things make base men proud: this villain here,
Being captain of a pinnace, threatens more

Than Bargulus, the strong Illyrian pirate.
Drones suck not eagles' blood, but rob beehives.
It is impossible that I should die   110
By such a lowly vassal as thyself.
Thy words move rage and not remorse in me.

LIEUTENANT   Ay, but my deeds shall stay thy fury soon.

SUFFOLK   I go of message from the Queen to France;
I charge thee waft me safely 'cross the Channel.   115

LIEUTENANT   Walter!

WHITMORE
Come, Suffolk, I must waft thee to thy death.

SUFFOLK   *Pene gelidus timor occupat artus;*
It is thee I fear.

WHITMORE
Thou shalt have cause to fear before I leave thee.   120
What, are ye daunted now? Now will ye stoop?

1 GENTLEMAN
My gracious lord, entreat him, speak him fair.

SUFFOLK   Suffolk's imperial tongue is stern and rough,
Used to command, untaught to plead for favour.
Far be it we should honour such as these   125
With humble suit: no, rather let my head
Stoop to the block than these knees bow to any
Save to the God of heaven and to my King;
And sooner dance upon a bloody pole
Than stand uncovered to the vulgar groom.   130
True nobility is exempt from fear;
More can I bear than you dare execute.

LIEUTENANT   Hale him away, and let him talk no more.

SUFFOLK   Come, soldiers, show what cruelty ye can,
That this my death may never be forgot.   135
Great men oft die by vile bezonians.
A Roman sworder and banditto slave
Murdered sweet Tully; Brutus' bastard hand
Stabbed Julius Caesar; savage islanders
Pompey the Great; and Suffolk dies by pirates.   140

                    Exit Whitmore with Suffolk and others.

LIEUTENANT
And as for these whose ransom we have set,
It is our pleasure one of them depart:
Therefore come you with us, and let him go.

                    Exeunt all but First Gentleman.

Enter WHITMORE *with Suffolk's body and head.*

WHITMORE   There let his head and lifeless body lie,
Until the Queen his mistress bury it.   *Exit.*   145

1 GENTLEMAN   O barbarous and bloody spectacle!
His body will I bear unto the King.
If he revenge it not, yet will his friends;
So will the Queen, that living held him dear.

                    Exit with the body and head.

4.2   *Enter two of the rebels,* GEORGE *and* NICK,
                    with long staves.

GEORGE   Come and get thee a sword, though made of a
lath; they have been up these two days.

NICK   They have the more need to sleep now, then.

GEORGE   I tell thee, Jack Cade the clothier means to
5   dress the commonwealth, and turn it, and set a new
nap upon it.

NICK   So he had need, for 'tis threadbare. Well, I say it
was never merry world in England since gentlemen
came up.

10 GEORGE   O miserable age! Virtue is not regarded in
handicraftsmen.

NICK   The nobility think scorn to go in leather aprons.

GEORGE   Nay, more, the King's Council are no good
workmen.

15 NICK   True; and yet it is said, 'Labour in thy vocation';
which is as much to say as, 'Let the magistrates be
labouring men'; and therefore should we be magistrates.

GEORGE   Thou hast hit it; for there's no better sign of a
brave mind than a hard hand.

20 NICK   I see them! I see them! There's Best's son, the
tanner of Wingham.

GEORGE   He shall have the skins of our enemies to make
dog's leather of.

NICK   And Dick the butcher.

25 GEORGE   Then is sin struck down like an ox, and
iniquity's throat cut like a calf.

NICK   And Smith the weaver.

GEORGE   Argo, their thread of life is spun.

NICK   Come, come, let's fall in with them.

Drum. Enter CADE, *Dick the Butcher, Smith the
Weaver, and a Sawyer, with infinite numbers carrying
long staves.*

30 CADE   We, John Cade, so termed of our supposed father –

BUTCHER [*aside*]   Or rather of stealing a cade of herrings.

CADE   For our enemies shall fall before us, inspired with
the spirit of putting down kings and princes. Command
silence.

35 BUTCHER   Silence!

CADE   My father was a Mortimer –

BUTCHER [*aside*]   He was an honest man, and a good
bricklayer.

CADE   My mother a Plantagenet –

40 BUTCHER [*aside*]   I knew her well, she was a midwife.

CADE   My wife descended of the Lacies –

BUTCHER [*aside*]   She was indeed a pedlar's daughter
and sold many laces.

WEAVER [*aside*]   But now of late, not able to travel with
45   her furred pack, she washes bucks here at home.

CADE   Therefore am I of an honourable house.

BUTCHER [*aside*]   Ay, by my faith, the field is honourable,
and there was he born, under a hedge; for his father
had never a house but the cage.

50 CADE   Valiant I am.

WEAVER [*aside*]   'A must needs, for beggary is valiant.

CADE   I am able to endure much.

BUTCHER [*aside*]   No question of that, for I have seen
him whipped three market days together.

55 CADE   I fear neither sword nor fire.

WEAVER [*aside*]   He need not fear the sword, for his coat
is of proof.

BUTCHER [*aside*]   But methinks he should stand in fear
of fire, being burnt i'th' hand for stealing of sheep.

CADE   Be brave, then, for your captain is brave, and   60
vows reformation. There shall be in England seven
half-penny loaves sold for a penny; the three-hooped
pot shall have ten hoops, and I will make it felony to
drink small beer. All the realm shall be in common,
and in Cheapside shall my palfrey go to grass. And   65
when I am king, as king I will be –

ALL   God save your majesty!

CADE   I thank you, good people. – There shall be no
money, all shall eat and drink on my score, and I will
apparel them all in one livery, that they may agree like   70
brothers and worship me their lord.

BUTCHER   The first thing we do, let's kill all the lawyers.

CADE   Nay, that I mean to do. Is not this a lamentable
thing, that of the skin of an innocent lamb should be
made parchment; that parchment, being scribbled o'er,   75
should undo a man? Some say the bee stings, but I say
'tis the bee's wax; for I did but seal once to a thing and
I was never mine own man since. How now? Who's
there?

Enter some, bringing forward the Clerk of Chartham.

WEAVER   The clerk of Chartham: he can write and read   80
and cast account.

CADE   O, monstrous!

WEAVER   We took him setting of boys' copies.

CADE   Here's a villain!

WEAVER   H'as a book in his pocket with red letters in't.   85

CADE   Nay, then, he is a conjuror.

BUTCHER   Nay, he can make obligations and write
court-hand.

CADE   I am sorry for't. The man is a proper man, of mine
honour; unless I find him guilty, he shall not die. Come   90
hither, sirrah, I must examine thee. What is thy name?

CLERK   Emmanuel.

BUTCHER   They use to write that on the top of letters.
'Twill go hard with you.

CADE   Let me alone. Dost thou use to write thy name?   95
Or hast thou a mark to thyself, like an honest plain-
dealing man?

CLERK   Sir, I thank God I have been so well brought up
that I can write my name.

ALL   He hath confessed: away with him! He's a villain   100
and a traitor.

CADE   Away with him, I say! Hang him with his pen and
inkhorn about his neck.   *Exit one with the Clerk.*

Enter MICHAEL.

MICHAEL   Where's our general?

CADE   Here I am, thou particular fellow.   105

MICHAEL   Fly, fly, fly! Sir Humphrey Stafford and his
brother are hard by, with the King's forces.

CADE   Stand, villain, stand, or I'll fell thee down. He

shall be encountered with a man as good as himself.
He is but a knight, is 'a?

MICHAEL No.

CADE To equal him I will make myself a knight
presently. [*Kneels.*] Rise up, Sir John Mortimer. [*Rises.*]
Now have at him!

Enter Sir Humphrey STAFFORD *and his* Brother
with Drum and Soldiers.

STAFFORD Rebellious hinds, the filth and scum of Kent,
Marked for the gallows, lay your weapons down;
Home to your cottages, forsake this groom.
The King is merciful, if you revolt.

BROTHER But angry, wrathful and inclined to blood,
If you go forward: therefore yield, or die.

CADE As for these silken-coated slaves, I pass not.
It is to you, good people, that I speak,
Over whom, in time to come, I hope to reign,
For I am rightful heir unto the crown.

STAFFORD Villain, thy father was a plasterer,
And thou thyself a shearman, art thou not?

CADE And Adam was a gardener.

BROTHER What of that?

CADE Marry, this: Edmund Mortimer, Earl of March,
Married the Duke of Clarence' daughter, did he not?

STAFFORD Ay, sir.

CADE By her he had two children at one birth.

BROTHER That's false.

CADE Ay, there's the question; but I say 'tis true.
The elder of them, being put to nurse,
Was by a beggar-woman stolen away;
And, ignorant of his birth and parentage,
Became a bricklayer when he came to age.
His son am I; deny it if you can.

BUTCHER Nay, 'tis too true, therefore he shall be King.

WEAVER Sir, he made a chimney in my father's house,
and the bricks are alive at this day to testify it; therefore
deny it not.

STAFFORD
And will you credit this base drudge's words,
That speaks he knows not what?

ALL Ay, marry, will we; therefore get ye gone.

BROTHER
Jack Cade, the Duke of York hath taught you this.

CADE [*aside*] He lies, for I invented it myself. – Go to,
sirrah, tell the King from me, that for his father's
sake, Henry the Fifth, in whose time boys went to
span-counter for French crowns, I am content he shall
reign, but I'll be Protector over him.

BUTCHER And furthermore, we'll have the Lord Saye's
head for selling the dukedom of Maine.

CADE And good reason, for thereby is England mained
and fain to go with a staff, but that my puissance holds
it up. Fellow kings, I tell you that that Lord Saye hath
gelded the commonwealth and made it an eunuch; and
more than that, he can speak French, and therefore he
is a traitor.

STAFFORD O gross and miserable ignorance!

CADE Nay, answer if you can: the Frenchmen are our
enemies; go to then, I ask but this – can he that speaks
with the tongue of an enemy be a good counsellor
or no?

ALL No, no, and therefore we'll have his head.

BROTHER Well, seeing gentle words will not prevail,
Assail them with the army of the King.

STAFFORD Herald, away, and throughout every town
Proclaim them traitors that are up with Cade;
That those which fly before the battle ends
May, even in their wives' and children's sight,
Be hanged up for example at their doors.
And you that be the King's friends, follow me.

Exeunt the two Staffords and Soldiers.

CADE And you that love the commons, follow me.
Now show yourselves men; 'tis for liberty.
We will not leave one lord, one gentleman:
Spare none but such as go in clouted shoon,
For they are thrifty honest men, and such
As would, but that they dare not, take our parts.

BUTCHER They are all in order and march toward us.

CADE But then are we in order when we are most out of
order. Come, march forward. *Exeunt.*

4.3 *Alarums to the fight, wherein both the Staffords
are slain. Enter* CADE *and the rest.*

CADE Where's Dick, the butcher of Ashford?

BUTCHER Here, sir.

CADE They fell before thee like sheep and oxen, and
thou behaved'st thyself as if thou hadst been in thine
own slaughterhouse. Therefore, thus will I reward
thee: the Lent shall be as long again as it is, and
thou shalt have a licence to kill for a hundred lacking
one.

BUTCHER I desire no more.

CADE And, to speak truth, thou deserv'st no less.
[*Takes up Stafford's sword.*] This monument of the
victory will I bear, and the bodies shall be dragged at
my horse heels till I do come to London, where we will
have the Mayor's sword borne before us.

BUTCHER If we mean to thrive and do good, break open
the gaols and let out the prisoners.

CADE Fear not that, I warrant thee. Come, let's march
towards London. *Exeunt dragging off the bodies.*

4.4 *Enter the* KING *with a supplication, and the* QUEEN
with Suffolk's head, *the Duke of* BUCKINGHAM
and the Lord SAYE.

QUEEN [*aside*]
Oft have I heard that grief softens the mind
And makes it fearful and degenerate;
Think therefore on revenge and cease to weep.
But who can cease to weep and look on this?
Here may his head lie on my throbbing breast;
But where's the body that I should embrace?

BUCKINGHAM
What answer makes your grace to the rebels'
   supplication?
KING   I'll send some holy bishop to entreat,
For God forbid so many simple souls
10   Should perish by the sword. And I myself,
Rather than bloody war shall cut them short,
Will parley with Jack Cade their general.
But stay, I'll read it over once again.
QUEEN [*aside*]
Ah, barbarous villains! Hath this lovely face
15   Ruled like a wandering planet over me
And could it not enforce them to relent,
That were unworthy to behold the same?
KING
Lord Saye, Jack Cade hath sworn to have thy head.
SAYE   Ay, but I hope your highness shall have his.
20 **KING**   How now, madam?
Still lamenting and mourning for Suffolk's death?
I fear me, love, if that I had been dead
Thou wouldest not have mourned so much for me.
QUEEN
No, my love, I should not mourn but die for thee.

Enter a Messenger.

KING
25   How now? What news? Why com'st thou in such haste?
MESSENGER   The rebels are in Southwark; fly, my lord!
Jack Cade proclaims himself Lord Mortimer,
Descended from the Duke of Clarence' house,
And calls your grace usurper, openly,
30   And vows to crown himself in Westminster.
His army is a ragged multitude
Of hinds and peasants, rude and merciless.
Sir Humphrey Stafford and his brother's death
Hath given them heart and courage to proceed.
35   All scholars, lawyers, courtiers, gentlemen,
They call false caterpillars and intend their death.
KING   O, graceless men! They know not what they do.
BUCKINGHAM   My gracious lord, retire to Killingworth
Until a power be raised to put them down.
40 **QUEEN**   Ah, were the Duke of Suffolk now alive,
These Kentish rebels would be soon appeased.
KING   Lord Saye, the traitors hateth thee,
Therefore away with us to Killingworth.
SAYE   So might your grace's person be in danger.
45   The sight of me is odious in their eyes;
And therefore in this city will I stay
And live alone, as secret as I may.

Enter another Messenger.

2 MESSENGER
Jack Cade hath almost gotten London Bridge;
The citizens fly and forsake their houses;
50   The rascal people, thirsting after prey,
Join with the traitor; and they jointly swear
To spoil the city and your royal court.

BUCKINGHAM
Then linger not, my lord: away, take horse!
KING   Come, Margaret. God, our hope, will succour us.
QUEEN [*aside*]
My hope is gone, now Suffolk is deceased.   55
KING   Farewell, my lord. Trust not the Kentish rebels.
BUCKINGHAM   Trust nobody, for fear you be betrayed.
SAYE   The trust I have is in mine innocence,
And therefore am I bold and resolute.   *Exeunt.*

4.5   *Enter Lord* SCALES *aloft upon the Tower walking.*
     Then enters two or three Citizens *below.*

SCALES   How now? Is Jack Cade slain?
1 CITIZEN   No, my lord, nor likely to be slain; for they
have won the bridge, killing all those that withstand
them. The Lord Mayor craves aid of your honour
from the Tower to defend the city from the rebels.   5
SCALES   Such aid as I can spare you shall command,
But I am troubled here with them myself;
The rebels have assayed to win the Tower.
But get you to Smithfield and gather head,
And thither I will send you Matthew Gough.   10
Fight for your king, your country and your lives!
And so farewell, for I must hence again.
                         Exeunt severally.

4.6   *Enter Jack* CADE *and the rest,*
     and strikes his staff on London Stone.

CADE   Now is Mortimer lord of this city. And here,
sitting upon London Stone, I charge and command
that, at the city's cost, the Pissing Conduit run nothing
but claret wine this first year of our reign. And now
henceforward it shall be treason for any that calls me   5
other than Lord Mortimer.

Enter a Soldier *running.*

SOLDIER   Jack Cade! Jack Cade!
CADE   Knock him down there. [*They kill him.*]
BUTCHER   If this fellow be wise, he'll never call ye Jack
Cade more. I think he hath a very fair warning. [*Reads*   10
Soldier's message.] My lord, there's an army gathered
together in Smithfield.
CADE   Come, then, let's go fight with them. But first go
and set London Bridge on fire; and, if you can, burn
down the Tower too. Come, let's away.   15
                        Exeunt with the body.

4.7   *Alarums. Matthew Gough is slain and all the rest.*
     Then enter Jack CADE *with his company.*

CADE   So, sirs: now go some and pull down the Savoy.
Others to th'Inns of Court; down with them all!
BUTCHER   I have a suit unto your lordship.
CADE   Be it a lordship, thou shalt have it for that word.
BUTCHER   Only that the laws of England may come out   5
of your mouth.

NICK [*aside*]   'Mass, 'twill be sore law then, for he was
    thrust in the mouth with a spear and 'tis not whole yet.
WEAVER [*aside*]   Nay, Nick, it will be stinking law, for
    his breath stinks with eating toasted cheese.
CADE   I have thought upon it, it shall be so. Away, burn
    all the records of the realm; my mouth shall be the
    parliament of England.
NICK [*aside*]   Then we are like to have biting statutes,
    unless his teeth be pulled out.
CADE   And henceforward all things shall be in common.

> *Enter a* Messenger.

MESSENGER   My lord, a prize, a prize! Here's the Lord
    Saye which sold the towns in France; he that made us
    pay one-and-twenty fifteens, and one shilling to the
    pound, the last subsidy.

> *Enter* GEORGE *with the* Lord SAYE.

CADE   Well, he shall be beheaded for it ten times. Ah,
    thou say, thou serge – nay, thou buckram lord! Now
    art thou within point-blank of our jurisdiction regal.
    What canst thou answer to my majesty for giving up of
    Normandy unto Mounsieur Basimecu, the Dolphin of
    France? Be it known unto thee by these presence, even
    the presence of Lord Mortimer, that I am the besom
    that must sweep the court clean of such filth as thou
    art. Thou hast most traitorously corrupted the youth
    of the realm in erecting a grammar school; and,
    whereas before our forefathers had no other books but
    the score and the tally, thou hast caused printing to be
    used and, contrary to the King his crown and dignity,
    thou hast built a paper-mill. It will be proved to thy
    face that thou hast men about thee that usually talk of
    a noun and a verb, and such abominable words as no
    Christian ear can endure to hear. Thou hast appointed
    justices of peace, to call poor men before them, about
    matters they were not able to answer. Moreover, thou
    hast put them in prison, and because they could not
    read thou hast hanged them, when indeed only for that
    cause they have been most worthy to live. Thou dost
    ride on a foot-cloth, dost thou not?
SAYE   What of that?
CADE   Marry, thou ought'st not to let thy horse wear a
    cloak when honester men than thou go in their hose
    and doublets.
BUTCHER   And work in their shirts too; as myself, for
    example, that am a butcher.
SAYE   You men of Kent –
BUTCHER   What say you of Kent?
SAYE   Nothing but this: 'tis *bona terra, mala gens*.
CADE   Away with him, away with him! He speaks Latin.
SAYE   Hear me but speak, and bear me where you will.
    Kent, in the *Commentaries* Caesar writ,
    Is termed the civil'st place of all this isle;
    Sweet is the country, because full of riches,
    The people liberal, valiant, active, wealthy;
    Which makes me hope you are not void of pity.

I sold not Maine, I lost not Normandy,   60
Yet to recover them would lose my life.
Justice with favour have I always done;
Prayers and tears have moved me, gifts could never.
When have I aught exacted at your hands,
Kent to maintain, the King, the realm and you?   65
Large gifts have I bestowed on learned clerks
Because my book preferred me to the King:
And seeing ignorance is the curse of God,
Knowledge the wing wherewith we fly to heaven,
Unless you be possessed with devilish spirits,   70
You cannot but forbear to murder me.
This tongue hath parleyed unto foreign kings
For your behoof –
CADE   Tut, when struck'st thou one blow in the field?
SAYE   Great men have reaching hands; oft have I struck   75
    Those that I never saw, and struck them dead.
GEORGE   O monstrous coward! What, to come behind
    folks?
SAYE
    These cheeks are pale with watching for your good.
CADE   Give him a box o'th' ear, and that will make 'em   80
    red again.
SAYE   Long sitting to determine poor men's causes
    Hath made me full of sickness and diseases.
CADE   Ye shall have a hempen caudle then and the help
    of hatchet.   85
BUTCHER   Why dost thou quiver, man?
SAYE   The palsy and not fear provokes me.
CADE   Nay, he nods at us, as who should say, 'I'll be even
    with you.' I'll see if his head will stand steadier on a
    pole, or no. Take him away and behead him.   90
SAYE   Tell me, wherein have I offended most?
    Have I affected wealth or honour? Speak.
    Are my chests filled up with extorted gold?
    Is my apparel sumptuous to behold?
    Whom have I injured, that ye seek my death?   95
    These hands are free from guiltless bloodshedding,
    This breast from harbouring foul deceitful thoughts.
    O, let me live!
CADE [*aside*]   I feel remorse in myself with his words,
    but I'll bridle it. He shall die, an it be but for pleading   100
    so well for his life. – Away with him! He has a familiar
    under his tongue; he speaks not i'God's name. Go, take
    him away, I say, and strike off his head presently; and
    then break into his son-in-law's house, Sir James
    Crowmer, and strike off his head, and bring them both   105
    upon two poles hither.
ALL   It shall be done.
SAYE   Ah, countrymen, if when you make your prayers
    God should be so obdurate as yourselves,
    How would it fare with your departed souls?   110
    And therefore yet relent and save my life!
CADE   Away with him! And do as I command ye.

> *Exeunt one or two with the Lord Saye.*

The proudest peer in the realm shall not wear a head
on his shoulders, unless he pay me tribute; there shall

115   not a maid be married, but she shall pay to me her
maidenhead ere they have it; men shall hold of me *in
capite*; and we charge and command that their wives be
as free as heart can wish or tongue can tell.

BUTCHER   My lord, when shall we go to Cheapside and
120   take up commodities upon our bills?

CADE   Marry, presently.

ALL   O brave!

           Enter one with the heads upon poles.

CADE   But is not this braver? Let them kiss one another,
for they loved well when they were alive. Now part
125   them again, lest they consult about the giving up of
some more towns in France. Soldiers, defer the spoil of
the city until night; for with these borne before us
instead of maces will we ride through the streets, and
at every corner have them kiss. Away!   *Exeunt.*

4.8   *Alarum and retreat. Enter again* CADE
           and all his rabblement.

CADE   Up Fish Street! Down Saint Magnus' Corner!
Kill and knock down! Throw them into Thames!
           [*Sound a parley.*]
What noise is this I hear?

     Enter BUCKINGHAM *and* OLD CLIFFORD, *attended.*

     Dare any be so bold to sound retreat or parley when I
5   command them kill?

BUCKINGHAM
     Ay, here they be that dare and will disturb thee!
     Know, Cade, we come ambassadors from the King
     Unto the commons, whom thou hast misled,
     And here pronounce free pardon to them all
10   That will forsake thee and go home in peace.

OLD CLIFFORD
     What say ye, countrymen? Will ye relent,
     And yield to mercy whilst 'tis offered you?
     Or let a rebel lead you to your deaths?
     Who loves the King and will embrace his pardon,
15   Fling up his cap and say, 'God save his majesty!'
     Who hateth him and honours not his father,
     Henry the Fifth, that made all France to quake,
     Shake he his weapon at us, and pass by.
           [*They forsake Cade.*]

ALL   God save the King! God save the King!
20 CADE   What, Buckingham and Clifford, are ye so brave?
And you, base peasants, do ye believe him? Will you
needs be hanged with your pardons about your necks?
Hath my sword therefore broke through London
gates, that you should leave me at the White Hart in
25   Southwark? I thought ye would never have given o'er
these arms till you had recovered your ancient freedom;
but you are all recreants and dastards and delight to
live in slavery to the nobility. Let them break your
backs with burdens, take your houses over your heads,
30   ravish your wives and daughters before your faces. For

me, I will make shift for one, and so God's curse light
upon you all!

ALL   We'll follow Cade! We'll follow Cade! [*They run to
Cade again.*]

OLD CLIFFORD   Is Cade the son of Henry the Fifth
That thus you do exclaim you'll go with him?   35
Will he conduct you through the heart of France
And make the meanest of you earls and dukes?
Alas, he hath no home, no place to fly to,
Nor knows he how to live but by the spoil,
Unless by robbing of your friends and us.   40
Were't not a shame that whilst you live at jar
The fearful French, whom you late vanquished,
Should make a start o'er seas and vanquish you?
Methinks already in this civil broil
I see them lording it in London streets,   45
Crying '*Villiago!*' unto all they meet.
Better ten thousand base-born Cades miscarry
Than you should stoop unto a Frenchman's mercy.
To France! To France! And get what you have lost!
Spare England, for it is your native coast.   50
Henry hath money, you are strong and manly;
God on our side, doubt not of victory.

ALL   A Clifford! A Clifford! We'll follow the King and
Clifford. [*They forsake Cade.*]

CADE [*aside*]   Was ever feather so lightly blown to and   55
fro as this multitude? The name of Henry the Fifth
hales them to an hundred mischiefs and makes them
leave me desolate. I see them lay their heads together
to surprise me. My sword make way for me, for here is
no staying. – In despite of the devils and hell, have   60
through the very midst of you! And heavens and
honour be witness that no want of resolution in me,
but only my followers' base and ignominious treasons,
makes me betake me to my heels.   *Exit.*

BUCKINGHAM
What, is he fled? Go some and follow him.   65
And he that brings his head unto the King
Shall have a thousand crowns for his reward.
           Exeunt some of them.
Follow me, soldiers; we'll devise a mean
To reconcile you all unto the King.   *Exeunt.*

4.9   *Sound trumpets. Enter* KING, QUEEN *and*
           SOMERSET *on the terrace aloft.*

KING   Was ever king that joyed an earthly throne
And could command no more content than I?
No sooner was I crept out of my cradle
But I was made a king at nine months old.
Was never subject longed to be a king   5
As I do long and wish to be a subject.

     Enter BUCKINGHAM *and* OLD CLIFFORD.

BUCKINGHAM   Health and glad tidings to your majesty.
KING   Why, Buckingham, is the traitor Cade surprised,
Or is he but retired to make him strong?

Enter multitudes with halters about their necks.

OLD CLIFFORD
He is fled, my lord, and all his powers do yield,
And humbly thus with halters on their necks
Expect your highness' doom of life or death.

KING   Then, heaven, set ope thy everlasting gates
To entertain my vows of thanks and praise.
Soldiers, this day have you redeemed your lives
And showed how well you love your prince and country.
Continue still in this so good a mind,
And Henry, though he be unfortunate,
Assure yourselves will never be unkind.
And so, with thanks and pardon to you all,
I do dismiss you to your several countries.

ALL   God save the King! God save the King!

Exeunt Rebels.

Enter a Messenger.

MESSENGER   Please it your grace to be advertised
The Duke of York is newly come from Ireland,
And with a puissant and a mighty power
Of gallowglasses and stout kerns
Is marching hitherward in proud array,
And still proclaimeth, as he comes along,
His arms are only to remove from thee
The Duke of Somerset, whom he terms a traitor.

KING
Thus stands my state, 'twixt Cade and York distressed,
Like to a ship that having scaped a tempest
Is straightway calmed and boarded with a pirate.
But now is Cade driven back, his men dispersed,
And now is York in arms to second him.
I pray thee, Buckingham, go and meet him,
And ask him what's the reason of these arms.
Tell him I'll send Duke Edmund to the Tower –
And, Somerset, we will commit thee thither,
Until his army be dismissed from him.

SOMERSET   My lord, I'll yield myself to prison willingly,
Or unto death, to do my country good.

KING   In any case, be not too rough in terms,
For he is fierce and cannot brook hard language.

BUCKINGHAM   I will, my lord, and doubt not so to deal
As all things shall redound unto your good.

KING   Come, wife, let's in, and learn to govern better;
For yet may England curse my wretched reign.

Flourish. Exeunt.

4.10   *Enter* CADE.

CADE   Fie on ambitions! Fie on myself that have a
sword and yet am ready to famish! These five days have
I hid me in these woods and durst not peep out, for all
the country is laid for me; but now am I so hungry that
if I might have a lease of my life for a thousand years, I
could stay no longer. Wherefore, o'er a brick wall have
I climbed into this garden, to see if I can eat grass, or
pick a sallet another while, which is not amiss to cool a

man's stomach this hot weather. And I think this word
'sallet' was born to do me good: for many a time, but   10
for a sallet, my brain-pan had been cleft with a brown
bill; and many a time, when I have been dry and
bravely marching, it hath served me instead of a quart
pot to drink in; and now the word 'sallet' must serve
me to feed on. [*Lies down picking of herbs and eating*   15
them.]

Enter IDEN *and his Men.*

IDEN   Lord, who would live turmoiled in the court
And may enjoy such quiet walks as these?
This small inheritance my father left me
Contenteth me, and worth a monarchy.
I seek not to wax great by others' waning   20
Or gather wealth I care not with what envy;
Sufficeth that I have maintains my state,
And sends the poor well pleased from my gate.

CADE [*aside*]   Here's the lord of the soil come to seize me
for a stray for entering his fee-simple without leave. –   25
Ah, villain, thou wilt betray me and get a thousand
crowns of the King by carrying my head to him; but
I'll make thee eat iron like an ostrich, and swallow my
sword like a great pin, ere thou and I part. [*Draws his*
sword.]

IDEN   Why, rude companion, whatsoe'er thou be,   30
I know thee not; why then should I betray thee?
Is't not enough to break into my garden
And like a thief to come to rob my grounds,
Climbing my walls in spite of me the owner,
But thou wilt brave me with these saucy terms?   35

CADE   Brave thee? Ay, by the best blood that ever was
broached, and beard thee too. Look on me well: I have
eat no meat these five days, yet come thou and thy five
men, an if I do not leave you all as dead as a doornail, I
pray God I may never eat grass more.   40

IDEN   Nay, it shall ne'er be said, while England stands,
That Alexander Iden, a squire of Kent,
Took odds to combat a poor famished man.
Oppose thy steadfast-gazing eyes to mine,
See if thou canst outface me with thy looks.   45
Set limb to limb, and thou art far the lesser;
Thy hand is but a finger to my fist,
Thy leg a stick compared with this truncheon.
My foot shall fight with all the strength thou hast;
An if mine arm be heaved in the air   50
Thy grave is digged already in the earth.
As for words, whose greatness answers words,
Let this my sword report what speech forbears.
[*Draws his sword.*]

CADE   By my valour, the most complete champion that
ever I heard! Steel, if thou turn the edge or cut not out   55
the burly-boned clown in chines of beef ere thou sleep
in thy sheath, I beseech God on my knees thou mayst
be turned to hobnails. [*They fight and Cade falls down.*]
O, I am slain! Famine and no other hath slain me. Let
ten thousand devils come against me, and give me but   60

the ten meals I have lost, and I'd defy them all. Wither,
garden, and be henceforth a burying place to all that
do dwell in this house, because the unconquered soul
of Cade is fled.

65   IDEN   Is't Cade that I have slain, that monstrous traitor?
Sword, I will hallow thee for this thy deed,
And hang thee o'er my tomb when I am dead.
Ne'er shall this blood be wiped from thy point,
But thou shalt wear it as a herald's coat
70   To emblaze the honour that thy master got.

CADE   Iden, farewell, and be proud of thy victory. Tell
Kent from me she hath lost her best man, and exhort
all the world to be cowards. For I, that never feared any,
am vanquished by famine, not by valour. [*Dies.*]

IDEN
75   How much thou wrong'st me, heaven be my judge.
Die, damned wretch, the curse of her that bore thee!
And as I thrust thy body in with my sword,
So wish I I might thrust thy soul to hell.
Hence will I drag thee headlong by the heels
80   Unto a dunghill, which shall be thy grave,
And there cut off thy most ungracious head,
Which I will bear in triumph to the King,
Leaving thy trunk for crows to feed upon.

Exeunt Iden and his Men with the body.

5.1   *Enter* YORK *and his army of Irish, with*
Drum and Colours.

YORK   From Ireland thus comes York to claim his right
And pluck the crown from feeble Henry's head.
Ring, bells, aloud; burn, bonfires, clear and bright,
To entertain great England's lawful king.
5   Ah, *sancta majestas*, who would not buy thee dear?
Let them obey that knows not how to rule.
This hand was made to handle nought but gold.
I cannot give due action to my words,
Except a sword or sceptre balance it;
10   A sceptre shall it have, have I a soul,
On which I'll toss the fleur-de-lis of France.

Enter BUCKINGHAM.

Whom have we here? Buckingham, to disturb me?
The King hath sent him, sure. I must dissemble.

BUCKINGHAM
York, if thou meanest well, I greet thee well.

15   YORK   Humphrey of Buckingham, I accept thy greeting.
Art thou a messenger, or come of pleasure?

BUCKINGHAM
A messenger from Henry, our dread liege,
To know the reason of these arms in peace;
Or why thou, being a subject as I am,
20   Against thy oath and true allegiance sworn,
Should raise so great a power without his leave
Or dare to bring thy force so near the court?

YORK [*aside*]   Scarce can I speak, my choler is so great.
O, I could hew up rocks and fight with flint,

I am so angry at these abject terms;   25
And now like Ajax Telamonius,
On sheep or oxen could I spend my fury.
I am far better born than is the King,
More like a king, more kingly in my thoughts.
But I must make fair weather yet awhile   30
Till Henry be more weak and I more strong. –
Buckingham, I prithee pardon me
That I have given no answer all this while;
My mind was troubled with deep melancholy.
The cause why I have brought this army hither   35
Is to remove proud Somerset from the King,
Seditious to his grace and to the state.

BUCKINGHAM
That is too much presumption on thy part;
But if thy arms be to no other end,
The King hath yielded unto thy demand: 40
The Duke of Somerset is in the Tower.

YORK   Upon thine honour, is he prisoner?

BUCKINGHAM   Upon mine honour, he is prisoner.

YORK   Then, Buckingham, I do dismiss my powers.
Soldiers, I thank you all; disperse yourselves;   45
Meet me tomorrow in Saint George's Field,
You shall have pay and everything you wish.

Exeunt Soldiers.

And let my sovereign, virtuous Henry,
Command my eldest son, nay, all my sons,
As pledges of my fealty and love;   50
I'll send them all, as willing as I live.
Lands, goods, horse, armour, anything I have
Is his to use, so Somerset may die.

BUCKINGHAM   York, I commend this kind submission.
We twain will go into his highness' tent.   55

Enter KING *and Attendants.*

KING   Buckingham, doth York intend no harm to us
That thus he marcheth with thee arm in arm?

YORK   In all submission and humility
York doth present himself unto your highness.

KING   Then what intends these forces thou dost bring?   60

YORK   To heave the traitor Somerset from hence
And fight against that monstrous rebel Cade,
Who since I heard to be discomfited.

Enter IDEN *with Cade's head.*

IDEN   If one so rude and of so mean condition
May pass into the presence of a king,   65
Lo, I present your grace a traitor's head,
The head of Cade, whom I in combat slew.

KING
The head of Cade! Great God, how just art Thou!
O let me view his visage, being dead,
That living wrought me such exceeding trouble.   70
Tell me, my friend, art thou the man that slew him?

IDEN   I was, an't like your majesty.

KING   How art thou called? And what is thy degree?

IDEN   Alexander Iden, that's my name;

'5   A poor esquire of Kent, that loves his King.

BUCKINGHAM
    So please it you, my lord, 'twere not amiss
    He were created knight for his good service.

KING   Iden, kneel down.   [*Iden kneels.*]
               Rise up a knight.   [*Iden rises.*]

30   We give thee for reward a thousand marks
    And will that thou henceforth attend on us.

IDEN   May Iden live to merit such a bounty,
    And never live but true unto his liege.   *Exit.*

Enter QUEEN *and* SOMERSET.

KING [*aside to Buckingham*]
    See, Buckingham, Somerset comes with the Queen.
    Go bid her hide him quickly from the Duke.

85 QUEEN   For thousand Yorks he shall not hide his head,
    But boldly stand and front him to his face.

YORK   How now! Is Somerset at liberty?
    Then, York, unloose thy long-imprisoned thoughts
    And let thy tongue be equal with thy heart.

90   Shall I endure the sight of Somerset?
    False king, why hast thou broken faith with me,
    Knowing how hardly I can brook abuse?
    'King' did I call thee? No, thou art not king,
    Not fit to govern and rule multitudes,

95   Which dar'st not, no, nor canst not rule a traitor.
    That head of thine doth not become a crown;
    Thy hand is made to grasp a palmer's staff
    And not to grace an awful princely sceptre.
    That gold must round engirt these brows of mine,

00   Whose smile and frown, like to Achilles' spear,
    Is able with the change to kill and cure.
    Here is a hand to hold a sceptre up
    And with the same to act controlling laws.
    Give place! By heaven, thou shalt rule no more

05   O'er him whom heaven created for thy ruler.

SOMERSET   O monstrous traitor! I arrest thee, York,
    Of capital treason 'gainst the King and crown.
    Obey, audacious traitor, kneel for grace.

YORK   Wouldst have me kneel? First let me ask of these

10   If they can brook I bow a knee to man.
    Sirrah, call in my sons to be my bail.   *Exit Attendant.*
    I know, ere they will have me go to ward
    They'll pawn their swords for my enfranchisement.

QUEEN   Call hither Clifford; bid him come amain,

15   To say if that the bastard boys of York
    Shall be the surety for their traitor father.
                            Exit Buckingham.

YORK   O blood-bespotted Neapolitan,
    Outcast of Naples, England's bloody scourge!
    The sons of York, thy betters in their birth,

20   Shall be their father's bail; and bane to those
    That for my surety will refuse the boys!

Enter EDWARD *and* RICHARD.

    See where they come. I'll warrant they'll make it
      good.

Enter OLD CLIFFORD *and* YOUNG CLIFFORD.

QUEEN   And here comes Clifford to deny their bail.

OLD CLIFFORD [*Kneels to Henry.*]
    Health and all happiness to my lord the King. [*Rises.*]

YORK   I thank thee, Clifford. Say, what news with thee?   125
    Nay, do not fright us with an angry look.
    We are thy sovereign, Clifford; kneel again.
    For thy mistaking so, we pardon thee.

OLD CLIFFORD   This is my king, York, I do not mistake;
    But thou mistakes me much to think I do.   130
    To Bedlam with him! Is the man grown mad?

KING   Ay, Clifford; a bedlam and ambitious humour
    Makes him oppose himself against his king.

OLD CLIFFORD   He is a traitor; let him to the Tower,
    And chop away that factious pate of his.   135

QUEEN   He is arrested, but will not obey;
    His sons, he says, shall give their words for him.

YORK   Will you not, sons?

EDWARD   Ay, noble father, if our words will serve.

RICHARD   And if words will not, then our weapons shall.   140

OLD CLIFFORD
    Why, what a brood of traitors have we here!

YORK   Look in a glass, and call thy image so.
    I am thy king, and thou a false-heart traitor.
    Call hither to the stake my two brave bears,
    That with the very shaking of their chains   145
    They may astonish these fell-lurking curs.
    Bid Salisbury and Warwick come to me.

Enter the Earls of WARWICK *and* SALISBURY.

OLD CLIFFORD
    Are these thy bears? We'll bait thy bears to death
    And manacle the bearherd in their chains,
    If thou dar'st bring them to the baiting-place.   150

RICHARD   Oft have I seen a hot o'erweening cur
    Run back and bite, because he was withheld;
    Who, being suffered, with the bear's fell paw
    Hath clapped his tail between his legs and cried;
    And such a piece of service will you do,   155
    If you oppose yourselves to match Lord Warwick.

OLD CLIFFORD
    Hence, heap of wrath, foul indigested lump,
    As crooked in thy manners as thy shape.

YORK   Nay, we shall heat you thoroughly anon.

OLD CLIFFORD
    Take heed, lest by your heat you burn yourselves.   160

KING   Why, Warwick, hath thy knee forgot to bow?
    Old Salisbury, shame to thy silver hair,
    Thou mad misleader of thy brainsick son!
    What, wilt thou on thy deathbed play the ruffian,
    And seek for sorrow with thy spectacles?   165
    O, where is faith? O, where is loyalty?
    If it be banished from the frosty head,
    Where shall it find a harbour in the earth?
    Wilt thou go dig a grave to find out war,
    And shame thine honourable age with blood?   170

Why art thou old, and want'st experience?
Or wherefore dost abuse it, if thou hast it?
For shame, in duty bend thy knee to me,
That bows unto the grave with mickle age.

175 SALISBURY   My lord, I have considered with myself
The title of this most renowned duke,
And in my conscience do repute his grace
The rightful heir to England's royal seat.

KING   Hast thou not sworn allegiance unto me?

180 SALISBURY   I have.

KING
Canst thou dispense with heaven for such an oath?

SALISBURY   It is great sin to swear unto a sin,
But greater sin to keep a sinful oath.
Who can be bound by any solemn vow

185 To do a murderous deed, to rob a man,
To force a spotless virgin's chastity,
To reave the orphan of his patrimony,
To wring the widow from her customed right,
And have no other reason for this wrong

190 But that he was bound by a solemn oath?

QUEEN   A subtle traitor needs no sophister.

KING   Call Buckingham, and bid him arm himself.

YORK   Call Buckingham, and all the friends thou hast.
I am resolved for death or dignity.

OLD CLIFFORD

195 The first, I warrant thee, if dreams prove true.

WARWICK   You were best to go to bed and dream again,
To keep thee from the tempest of the field.

OLD CLIFFORD   I am resolved to bear a greater storm
Than any thou canst conjure up today;

200 And that I'll write upon thy burgonet,
Might I but know thee by thy household badge.

WARWICK   Now by my father's badge, old Neville's crest,
The rampant bear chained to the ragged staff,
This day I'll wear aloft my burgonet,

205 As on a mountain top the cedar shows
That keeps his leaves in spite of any storm,
Even to affright thee with the view thereof.

OLD CLIFFORD
And from thy burgonet I'll rend thy bear
And tread it underfoot with all contempt,

210 Despite the bearherd that protects the bear.

YOUNG CLIFFORD   And so to arms, victorious father,
To quell the rebels and their complices.

RICHARD   Fie! Charity, for shame! Speak not in spite,
For you shall sup with Jesu Christ tonight.

YOUNG CLIFFORD

215 Foul stigmatic, that's more than thou canst tell.

RICHARD   If not in heaven, you'll surely sup in hell.
                               Exeunt severally.

5.2   *An inn-sign of the Castle is displayed.*
          Alarums to the battle. Enter WARWICK.

WARWICK   Clifford of Cumberland, 'tis Warwick calls;
An if thou dost not hide thee from the bear,

Now, when the angry trumpet sounds alarum,
And dead men's cries do fill the empty air,
Clifford, I say, come forth and fight with me!   5
Proud northern lord, Clifford of Cumberland,
Warwick is hoarse with calling thee to arms.

               Enter YORK.

How now, my noble lord! What, all afoot?

YORK   The deadly-handed Clifford slew my steed;
But match to match I have encountered him   10
And made a prey for carrion kites and crows
Even of the bonny beast he loved so well.

           Enter OLD CLIFFORD.

WARWICK   Of one or both of us the time is come.

YORK   Hold, Warwick, seek thee out some other chase,
For I myself must hunt this deer to death.   15

WARWICK
Then nobly, York; 'tis for a crown thou fight'st.
As I intend, Clifford, to thrive today,
It grieves my soul to leave thee unassailed.   *Exit.*

OLD CLIFFORD
What seest thou in me, York? Why dost thou pause?

YORK   With thy brave bearing should I be in love,   20
But that thou art so fast mine enemy.

OLD CLIFFORD
Nor should thy prowess want praise and esteem,
But that 'tis shown ignobly and in treason.

YORK   So let it help me now against thy sword
As I in justice and true right express it.   25

OLD CLIFFORD   My soul and body on the action both!

YORK   A dreadful lay! Address thee instantly.
       [*They fight, and Old Clifford falls.*]

OLD CLIFFORD   *La fin couronne les oeuvres.*   [*Dies.*]

YORK
Thus war hath given thee peace, for thou art still.
Peace with his soul, heaven, if it be thy will!   *Exit.*   30

          Enter YOUNG CLIFFORD.

YOUNG CLIFFORD
Shame and confusion! All is on the rout,
Fear frames disorder, and disorder wounds
Where it should guard. O war, thou son of hell,
Whom angry heavens do make their minister,
Throw in the frozen bosoms of our part   35
Hot coals of vengeance! Let no soldier fly.
He that is truly dedicate to war
Hath no self-love; nor he that loves himself
Hath not essentially, but by circumstance,
The name of valour.   [*Sees his dead father.*]
                    O, let the vile world end,   40
And the premised flames of the last day
Knit earth and heaven together!
Now let the general trumpet blow his blast,
Particularities and petty sounds
To cease! Wast thou ordained, dear father,   45
To lose thy youth in peace and to achieve

The silver livery of advised age,
And, in thy reverence and thy chair-days, thus
To die in ruffian battle? Even at this sight
50 My heart is turned to stone, and while 'tis mine
It shall be stony. York not our old men spares;
No more will I their babes; tears virginal
Shall be to me even as the dew to fire,
And beauty, that the tyrant oft reclaims,
55 Shall to my flaming wrath be oil and flax.
Henceforth I will not have to do with pity.
Meet I an infant of the house of York,
Into as many gobbets will I cut it
As wild Medea young Absyrtus did.
60 In cruelty will I seek out my fame.
Come, thou new ruin of old Clifford's house;
[*Takes him up on his back.*]
As did Aeneas old Anchises bear,
So bear I thee upon my manly shoulders;
But then Aeneas bare a living load,
65 Nothing so heavy as these woes of mine.
                                    Exit with the body.

Enter the Duke of SOMERSET *and*
RICHARD *fighting. Somerset is killed.*

RICHARD   So, lie thou there;
For underneath an alehouse' paltry sign,
The Castle in Saint Albans, Somerset
Hath made the wizard famous in his death.
70 Sword, hold thy temper; heart, be wrathful still:
Priests pray for enemies, but princes kill.
                                    Exit with the body.

Fight. Excursions. Enter KING, QUEEN *and others.*

QUEEN   Away, my lord! You are slow. For shame, away!
KING   Can we outrun the heavens? Good Margaret, stay.
QUEEN   What are you made of? You'll nor fight nor fly.
75 Now is it manhood, wisdom and defence
To give the enemy way and to secure us
By what we can, which can no more but fly.
                                [*Alarum afar off*]
If you be ta'en we then should see the bottom
Of all our fortunes; but if we haply scape –
80 As well we may, if not through your neglect –
We shall to London get, where you are loved
And where this breach now in our fortunes made
May readily be stopped.

Enter YOUNG CLIFFORD.

YOUNG CLIFFORD
But that my heart's on future mischief set,

I would speak blasphemy ere bid you fly;   85
But fly you must; uncurable discomfit
Reigns in the hearts of all our present part.
Away for your relief! And we will live
To see their day and them our fortune give.
Away, my lord, away!   *Exeunt*   90

5.3   *Alarum. Retreat. Enter* YORK, RICHARD,
Edward, WARWICK *and Soldiers*
with Drum and Colours.

YORK   Old Salisbury, who can report of him,
That winter lion, who in rage forgets
Aged contusions and all brush of time,
And, like a gallant in the brow of youth,
Repairs him with occasion? This happy day   5
Is not itself, nor have we won one foot
If Salisbury be lost.
RICHARD   My noble father,
Three times today I holp him to his horse,
Three times bestrid him; thrice I led him off,
Persuaded him from any further act;   10
But still where danger was, still there I met him,
And like rich hangings in a homely house,
So was his will in his old feeble body.
But, noble as he is, look where he comes.

Enter SALISBURY.

Now, by my sword, well hast thou fought today.   15
SALISBURY
By th' mass, so did we all. I thank you, Richard.
God knows how long it is I have to live,
And it hath pleased him that three times today
You have defended me from imminent death.
Well, lords, we have not got that which we have: 20
'Tis not enough our foes are this time fled,
Being opposites of such repairing nature.
YORK   I know our safety is to follow them,
For, as I hear, the King is fled to London
To call a present court of parliament.   25
Let us pursue him ere the writs go forth.
What says Lord Warwick? Shall we after them?
WARWICK   After them? Nay, before them if we can!
Now by my faith, lords, 'twas a glorious day.
Saint Albans' battle won by famous York   30
Shall be eternized in all age to come.
Sound drum and trumpets, and to London all,
And more such days as these to us befall!   *Exeunt.*

King Henry VI, Part 3

The textual history of *King Henry VI, Part 3*, is much like that of *Part 2*, and indeed is intertwined with it. *Part 3* also exists in two versions: it was published as the eighth of the histories in the Folio of 1623, though in 1595 a shorter version had appeared in an octavo printing, entitled *The true Tragedy of Richard Duke of York, and the death of good King Henry the Sixth, with the whole contention between the two houses Lancaster and York*. This was reprinted in 1600, and in 1619 *Parts 2* and *3* were published together as *The Whole Contention between the two Famous Houses, Lancaster and York*. These early printings of *Part 3* appear to be based on a memorial text, one reconstructed by actors, possibly those playing Warwick and Clifford. The Folio text is verbally superior and about a third as long again as the earlier printings.

The play must have been written about 1590. In a pamphlet published in September 1592, the dying Robert Greene parodied a line from it (1.4.137) in an attack on Shakespeare as an 'up-start Crow, beautified with our feathers, that with his Tygers hart wrapt in a Players hyde, supposes he is as well able to bombast out a blanke verse as the best of you'. Seemingly Greene objects that a mere actor and non-graduate like Shakespeare, who may well have performed in plays by Greene, would presume to compete with the dramatists, and he is bitter that Shakespeare has done so with such success. Whatever Greene's intent, his allusion provides a later limit for dating the play of the summer of 1592, when *A Groatsworth of Wit Purchased with a Million of Repentance* was written.

The play seems to have succeeded on the stage, though its early theatrical history is obscure. The 1595 octavo tells us on the title-page that the play 'was sundry times acted by the Right Honourable the Earl of Pembroke his servants', and the Folio has 'Sinklo' and 'Humphrey' as the speech prefixes for the two keepers in 3.1. Almost certainly these are the names of the actors who played the roles, John Sincler and Humphrey Jeffes, both members of Pembroke's Men in the 1590s. Little is known of this company or of Shakespeare's relation to it beyond the fact that it was active in London in 1592, was disbanded on tour in the provinces in the late summer of 1593 and apparently had a few of Shakespeare's plays in its

repertoire. Perhaps the shortened text of *King Henry VI, Part 3* was even prepared for its tour in 1593.

The play itself continues the history of Henry's reign from the very point where *Part 2* ends, though like *Parts 1* and *2* it stands as an independent play, with its own structure and thematic concerns. It picks up the action in the aftermath of the Lancastrian defeat at St Albans (1455) and continues the history to the death of Henry and the confirmation of Edward IV as King in 1471. As the seventeen-year scope demands, history is condensed, with events omitted, rearranged or fused together. Still, the broad outline follows the pattern Shakespeare found in the historical accounts of Edward Hall's *Union of the Two Noble and Illustre Families of Lancaster and York* (1548).

If in one sense *King Henry VI, Part 3* can be seen as a continuation of Shakespeare's dramatic meditation on the horrors of unchecked human appetite visible in the Wars of the Roses, in another it reveals a unique understanding of the tragedy that has befallen England. The object that has motivated the action is the crown, but here it is stripped of all dignity, a bone fought over by hungry dogs. The word 'crown' itself appears more often than in any other play, but rather than establishing its value, the repetition gradually erodes its meaning. The oscillations of rule, as power shifts back and forth from Henry to Edward, further evacuate what sacred authority might once have inhered in the crown. In this world, the pious Henry is clearly unsuited to rule, as he himself knows: the crown he seeks 'is called content' (3.1.64). This world demands harder men, and by the end the sinister figure of Richard of Gloucester emerges, the nightmare fulfilment of the play's deepest logic.

On the modern stage, the play has usually been seen in two-part conflations of the three plays, as in that by the Royal Shakespeare Company in 1988. In 1977, however, Terry Hands directed all three parts of *King Henry VI* in sequence at Stratford-upon-Avon, where in 1994 Katie Mitchell directed *Part 3* independently at The Other Place, and in 2000–1 the RSC staged all three plays as part of its chronological series 'This England, the Histories'.

The Arden text is based on the 1623 First Folio.

YORKISTS

Richard Plantagenet, Duke of YORK	*leader of the Yorkist faction*
EDWARD, Earl of March	*eldest son of the Duke of York, later inheritor of the title and* KING EDWARD *the Fourth*
GEORGE, *later* Duke of CLARENCE	*second son of the Duke of York*
RICHARD, *later* Duke of GLOUCESTER	*third son of the Duke of York*
Earl of RUTLAND	*youngest son of the Duke of York*
SIR JOHN MORTIMER	*uncle of the Duke of York*
Sir Hugh Mortimer	*brother of Sir John*
LADY GREY (*also* WIDOW)	*later* QUEEN ELIZABETH, *wife of King Edward the Fourth*
Prince Edward of York	*the future King Edward the Fifth*
Earl of WARWICK	*adherent of York, later of Lancaster*
Marquess of MONTAGUE	*brother of Warwick, adherent of York, later of Lancaster*
Duke of NORFOLK	
Lord HASTINGS	
Earl of Pembroke	
Lord Stafford	
Sir William Stanley	
Lord RIVERS	*brother of Lady Grey, adherent first of Lancaster, then of York*
LIEUTENANT	*of the Tower of London*
MAYOR of York	
Sir John MONTGOMERY	
TUTOR	*of Rutland*
Nurse	*of Prince Edward of York*
SON	*who has killed his father while fighting for York*
NOBLEMAN	
Three WATCHMEN	

LANCASTRIANS

KING HENRY the Sixth	*leader of the Lancastrian faction*
QUEEN MARGARET	*wife of King Henry*
PRINCE EDWARD	*son of King Henry*
Henry Tudor, Earl of Richmond	*the future King Henry the Seventh*
THIRD DUKE of Somerset	*adherent of both Lancaster and York*
Fourth Duke of SOMERSET	
Duke of EXETER	
Lord CLIFFORD	
Earl of NORTHUMBERLAND	
Earl of WESTMORLAND	
Earl of OXFORD	
Mayor of Coventry	
SOMERVILLE	
FATHER	*who has killed his son while fighting for Lancaster*
HUNTSMAN	

THE FRENCH

KING LEWIS the Eleventh	*of France*
LADY BONA	*sister-in-law of King Lewis*
Lord Bourbon	*French admiral*

OTHERS
Two KEEPERS
MESSENGERS
POSTS

Soldiers, Aldermen of York, Citizens of Coventry, Drummers, Trumpeters, Attendants

1.1 *Alarum. Enter* Richard Plantagenet,
the Duke of YORK, EDWARD, RICHARD,
NORFOLK, MONTAGUE, WARWICK, *with white
roses in their hats, and Soldiers.*

WARWICK   I wonder how the King escaped our hands.
YORK   While we pursued the horsemen of the north,
He slyly stole away, and left his men;
Whereat the great Lord of Northumberland,
Whose warlike ears could never brook retreat,   5
Cheered up the drooping army; and himself,
Lord Clifford and Lord Stafford, all abreast,
Charged our main battle's front, and breaking in,
Were by the swords of common soldiers slain.
EDWARD   Lord Stafford's father, Duke of Buckingham,   10
Is either slain or wounded dangerous.
I cleft his beaver with a downright blow.
That this is true, father, behold his blood.
MONTAGUE
And, brother, here's the Earl of Wiltshire's blood,
Whom I encountered as the battles joined.   15
RICHARD [*Shows the head of Somerset.*]
Speak thou for me, and tell them what I did.
YORK   Richard hath best deserved of all my sons.
But is your grace dead, my Lord of Somerset?
NORFOLK
Such hope have all the line of John of Gaunt.
RICHARD   Thus do I hope to shake King Henry's head.   20
WARWICK   And so do I. Victorious Prince of York,
Before I see thee seated in that throne
Which now the house of Lancaster usurps,
I vow by heaven these eyes shall never close.
This is the palace of the fearful King,   25
And this the regal seat. Possess it, York,
For this is thine and not King Henry's heirs'.
YORK   Assist me then, sweet Warwick, and I will,
For hither we have broken in by force.
NORFOLK   We'll all assist you; he that flies shall die.   30
YORK   Thanks, gentle Norfolk. Stay by me, my lords,
And soldiers, stay and lodge by me this night.
[*They go up to the chair of state.*]
WARWICK
And when the King comes, offer him no violence,
Unless he seek to thrust you out perforce.
YORK   The Queen this day here holds her parliament,   35
But little thinks we shall be of her council.
By words or blows here let us win our right.
RICHARD   Armed as we are, let's stay within this house.
WARWICK
The 'Bloody Parliament' shall this be called,
Unless Plantagenet, Duke of York, be king,   40
And bashful Henry deposed, whose cowardice
Hath made us bywords to our enemies.
YORK   Then leave me not; my lords, be resolute.
I mean to take possession of my right.
WARWICK   Neither the King, nor he that loves him best,   45
The proudest bird that holds up Lancaster,

Dares stir a wing if Warwick shake his bells.
I'll plant Plantagenet; root him up who dares.
Resolve thee, Richard; claim the English crown.

Flourish. Enter KING HENRY, CLIFFORD,
NORTHUMBERLAND, WESTMORLAND, EXETER,
with red roses in their hats, and the rest.

KING HENRY
My lords, look where the sturdy rebel sits   50
Even in the chair of state. Belike he means,
Backed by the power of Warwick, that false peer,
To aspire unto the crown and reign as king.
Earl of Northumberland, he slew thy father,
And thine, Lord Clifford, and you both have vowed
revenge   55
On him, his sons, his favourites and his friends.
NORTHUMBERLAND
If I be not, heavens be revenged on me.
CLIFFORD
The hope thereof makes Clifford mourn in steel.
WESTMORLAND
What, shall we suffer this? Let's pluck him down.
My heart for anger burns; I cannot brook it.   60
KING HENRY   Be patient, gentle Earl of Westmorland.
CLIFFORD   Patience is for poltroons, such as he.
He durst not sit there had your father lived.
My gracious lord, here in the Parliament
Let us assail the family of York.   65
NORTHUMBERLAND
Well hast thou spoken, cousin. Be it so.
KING HENRY   Ah, know you not the city favours them,
And they have troops of soldiers at their beck?
EXETER   But when the Duke is slain, they'll quickly fly.
KING HENRY
Far be the thought of this from Henry's heart,   70
To make a shambles of the Parliament House.
Cousin of Exeter, frowns, words and threats
Shall be the war that Henry means to use. —
Thou, factious Duke of York, descend my throne
And kneel for grace and mercy at my feet.   75
I am thy sovereign.
YORK   I am thine.
EXETER
For shame, come down. He made thee Duke of York.
YORK   It was my inheritance, as the earldom was.
EXETER   Thy father was a traitor to the crown.
WARWICK   Exeter, thou art a traitor to the crown,   80
In following this usurping Henry.
CLIFFORD
Whom should he follow but his natural king?
WARWICK
True, Clifford, and that's Richard, Duke of York.
KING HENRY
And shall I stand, and thou sit in my throne?
YORK   It must and shall be so. Content thyself.   85
WARWICK [*to Henry*]
Be Duke of Lancaster. Let him be King.

WESTMORLAND
He is both King and Duke of Lancaster,
And that the Lord of Westmorland shall maintain.
WARWICK And Warwick shall disprove it. You forget
90 That we are those which chased you from the field
And slew your fathers, and with colours spread
Marched through the city to the palace gates.
NORTHUMBERLAND
Yes, Warwick, I remember it to my grief;
And by his soul, thou and thy house shall rue it.
WESTMORLAND
95 Plantagenet, of thee and these thy sons,
Thy kinsmen and thy friends, I'll have more lives
Than drops of blood were in my father's veins.
CLIFFORD Urge it no more, lest that instead of words
I send thee, Warwick, such a messenger
100 As shall revenge his death before I stir.
WARWICK
Poor Clifford, how I scorn his worthless threats!
YORK Will you we show our title to the crown?
If not, our swords shall plead it in the field.
KING HENRY What title hast thou, traitor, to the crown?
105 Thy father was, as thou art, Duke of York,
Thy grandfather, Roger Mortimer, Earl of March.
I am the son of Henry the Fifth,
Who made the Dauphin and the French to stoop
And seized upon their towns and provinces.
110 WARWICK Talk not of France, sith thou hast lost it all.
KING HENRY The Lord Protector lost it and not I.
When I was crowned, I was but nine months old.
RICHARD
You are old enough now and yet methinks you lose.
Father, tear the crown from the usurper's head.
115 EDWARD Sweet father, do so; set it on your head.
MONTAGUE
Good brother, as thou lov'st and honourest arms,
Let's fight it out and not stand cavilling thus.
RICHARD
Sound drums and trumpets and the King will fly.
YORK Sons, peace.
KING HENRY
120 Peace thou, and give King Henry leave to speak.
WARWICK
Plantagenet shall speak first; hear him, lords,
And be you silent and attentive too,
For he that interrupts him shall not live.
KING HENRY
Think'st thou that I will leave my kingly throne,
125 Wherein my grandsire and my father sat?
No, first shall war unpeople this my realm.
Ay, and their colours, often borne in France,
And now in England to our heart's great sorrow,
Shall be my winding-sheet. Why faint you, lords?
130 My title's good, and better far than his.
WARWICK Prove it, Henry, and thou shalt be king.
KING HENRY
Henry the Fourth by conquest got the crown.

YORK 'Twas by rebellion against his King.
KING HENRY [aside]
I know not what to say. My title's weak. –
Tell me, may not a king adopt an heir?   135
YORK What then?
KING HENRY An if he may, then am I lawful king:
For Richard, in the view of many lords,
Resigned the crown to Henry the Fourth,
Whose heir my father was, and I am his.   140
YORK He rose against him, being his sovereign,
And made him to resign his crown perforce.
WARWICK Suppose, my lords, he did it unconstrained,
Think you 'twere prejudicial to his crown?
EXETER No, for he could not so resign his crown,   145
But that the next heir should succeed and reign.
KING HENRY Art thou against us, Duke of Exeter?
EXETER His is the right, and therefore pardon me.
YORK Why whisper you, my lords, and answer not?
EXETER My conscience tells me he is lawful king.   150
KING HENRY All will revolt from me and turn to him.
NORTHUMBERLAND [to York]
Plantagenet, for all the claim thou lay'st,
Think not that Henry shall be so deposed.
WARWICK Deposed he shall be, in despite of all.
NORTHUMBERLAND
Thou art deceived. 'Tis not thy southern power   155
Of Essex, Norfolk, Suffolk nor of Kent,
Which makes thee thus presumptuous and proud,
Can set the Duke up in despite of me.
CLIFFORD King Henry, be thy title right or wrong,
Lord Clifford vows to fight in thy defence.   160
May that ground gape and swallow me alive
Where I shall kneel to him that slew my father.
KING HENRY
O Clifford, how thy words revive my heart!
YORK Henry of Lancaster, resign thy crown.
What mutter you, or what conspire you, lords?   165
WARWICK Do right unto this princely Duke of York,
Or I will fill the house with armed men
And over the chair of state where now he sits
Write up his title with usurping blood.
[*He stamps with his foot, and the Soldiers show
themselves.*]
KING HENRY
My Lord of Warwick, hear me but one word: 170
Let me for this my lifetime reign as king.
YORK Confirm the crown to me and to mine heirs,
And thou shalt reign in quiet while thou liv'st.
KING HENRY I am content. Richard Plantagenet,
Enjoy the kingdom after my decease.   175
CLIFFORD
What wrong is this unto the Prince, your son!
WARWICK What good is this to England, and himself!
WESTMORLAND Base, fearful and despairing Henry!
CLIFFORD How hast thou injured both thyself and us.
WESTMORLAND I cannot stay to hear these articles.   180
NORTHUMBERLAND Nor I.

CLIFFORD [*to Northumberland*]
  Come, cousin, let us tell the Queen these news.
WESTMORLAND
  Farewell, faint-hearted and degenerate King,
  In whose cold blood no spark of honour bides.
NORTHUMBERLAND
185 Be thou a prey unto the house of York
  And die in bands for this unmanly deed.
CLIFFORD In dreadful war mayst thou be overcome,
  Or live in peace abandoned and despised.
        Exeunt Westmorland, Northumberland and
                Clifford, with their Soldiers.
WARWICK Turn this way, Henry, and regard them not.
EXETER
190 They seek revenge and therefore will not yield.
KING HENRY Ah, Exeter.
WARWICK   Why should you sigh, my lord?
KING HENRY
  Not for myself, Lord Warwick, but my son,
  Whom I unnaturally shall disinherit.
  But be it as it may. [*to York*] I here entail
195 The crown to thee and to thine heirs forever,
  Conditionally, that here thou take an oath
  To cease this civil war and, whilst I live,
  To honour me as thy King and sovereign,
  And neither by treason nor hostility
200 To seek to put me down and reign thyself.
YORK This oath I willingly take, and will perform.
WARWICK
  Long live King Henry! Plantagenet, embrace him.
KING HENRY
  And long live thou, and these thy forward sons.
YORK Now York and Lancaster are reconciled.
205 EXETER Accursed be he that seeks to make them foes.
           [*Sennet. Here they come down.*]
YORK Farewell my gracious lord, I'll to my castle.
      Exeunt York, his sons and their Soldiers.
WARWICK
  And I'll keep London with my soldiers.   *Exit.*
NORFOLK
  And I to Norfolk with my followers.   *Exit.*
MONTAGUE
  And I unto the sea, from whence I came.   *Exit.*
210 KING HENRY And I with grief and sorrow to the court.

    Enter QUEEN MARGARET *and* PRINCE EDWARD.

EXETER
  Here comes the Queen, whose looks bewray her
    anger.
  I'll steal away. [*Offers to leave.*]
KING HENRY Exeter, so will I.
QUEEN MARGARET
  Nay, go not from me; I will follow thee.
KING HENRY Be patient, gentle Queen, and I will stay.
QUEEN MARGARET
215 Who can be patient in such extremes?
  Ah, wretched man, would I had died a maid

And never seen thee, never borne thee son,
Seeing thou hast proved so unnatural a father.
Hath he deserved to lose his birthright thus?
Hadst thou but loved him half so well as I,   220
Or felt that pain which I did for him once,
Or nourished him, as I did with my blood,
Thou wouldst have left thy dearest heart-blood
  there,
Rather than have made that savage Duke thine heir
And disinherited thine only son.   225
PRINCE EDWARD Father, you cannot disinherit me.
  If you be king, why should not I succeed?
KING HENRY
  Pardon me, Margaret; pardon me, sweet son;
  The Earl of Warwick and the Duke enforced me.
QUEEN MARGARET
  Enforced thee? Art thou king, and wilt be forced? 230
  I shame to hear thee speak. Ah, timorous wretch,
  Thou hast undone thyself, thy son and me,
  And given unto the house of York such head
  As thou shalt reign but by their sufferance.
  To entail him and his heirs unto the crown, 235
  What is it, but to make thy sepulchre
  And creep into it far before thy time?
  Warwick is Chancellor and the lord of Calais;
  Stern Falconbridge commands the narrow seas;
  The Duke is made Protector of the realm; 240
  And yet shalt thou be safe? Such safety finds
  The trembling lamb environed with wolves.
  Had I been there, which am a silly woman,
  The soldiers should have tossed me on their pikes
  Before I would have granted to that act. 245
  But thou preferr'st thy life before thine honour.
  And seeing thou dost, I here divorce myself
  Both from thy table, Henry, and thy bed,
  Until that act of Parliament be repealed
  Whereby my son is disinherited. 250
  The northern lords, that have forsworn thy colours,
  Will follow mine if once they see them spread:
  And spread they shall be, to thy foul disgrace,
  And utter ruin of the house of York.
  Thus do I leave thee. Come, son, let's away. 255
  Our army is ready; come, we'll after them.
KING HENRY
  Stay, gentle Margaret, and hear me speak.
QUEEN MARGARET
  Thou hast spoke too much already. Get thee gone.
KING HENRY
  Gentle son Edward, thou wilt stay with me?
QUEEN MARGARET
  Ay, to be murdered by his enemies. 260
PRINCE EDWARD
  When I return with victory from the field
  I'll see your grace; till then, I'll follow her.
QUEEN MARGARET
  Come, son, away. We may not linger thus.
            Exit with Prince Edward.

KING HENRY

Poor Queen, how love to me and to her son

265 Hath made her break out into terms of rage.

Revenged may she be on that hateful Duke,

Whose haughty spirit, winged with desire,

Will coast my crown and, like an empty eagle,

Tire on the flesh of me and of my son.

270 The loss of those three lords torments my heart.

I'll write unto them and entreat them fair.

Come, cousin, you shall be the messenger.

EXETER   And I, I hope, shall reconcile them all.

Flourish. Exeunt.

1.2   *Enter* RICHARD, EDWARD *and* MONTAGUE.

RICHARD   Brother, though I be youngest, give me leave.

EDWARD   No, I can better play the orator.

MONTAGUE   But I have reasons strong and forcible.

Enter the Duke of YORK.

YORK   Why, how now, sons and brother, at a strife?

5   What is your quarrel? How began it first?

EDWARD   No quarrel, but a slight contention.

YORK   About what?

RICHARD

About that which concerns your grace and us:

The crown of England, father, which is yours.

YORK   Mine, boy? Not till King Henry be dead.

10 RICHARD   Your right depends not on his life or death.

EDWARD   Now you are heir; therefore enjoy it now.

By giving the house of Lancaster leave to breathe,

It will outrun you, father, in the end.

YORK   I took an oath that he should quietly reign.

15 EDWARD   But for a kingdom any oath may be broken.

I would break a thousand oaths to reign one year.

RICHARD

No. God forbid your grace should be forsworn.

YORK   I shall be, if I claim by open war.

RICHARD

I'll prove the contrary, if you'll hear me speak.

20 YORK   Thou canst not, son; it is impossible.

RICHARD   An oath is of no moment, being not took

Before a true and lawful magistrate

That hath authority over him that swears.

Henry had none, but did usurp the place.

25 Then, seeing 'twas he that made you to depose,

Your oath, my lord, is vain and frivolous.

Therefore, to arms. And, father, do but think

How sweet a thing it is to wear a crown,

Within whose circuit is Elysium

30 And all that poets feign of bliss and joy.

Why do we linger thus? I cannot rest

Until the white rose that I wear be dyed

Even in the lukewarm blood of Henry's heart.

YORK   Richard, enough. I will be king or die.

35 Brother, thou shalt to London presently

And whet on Warwick to this enterprise.

Thou, Richard, shalt to the Duke of Norfolk

And tell him privily of our intent.

You, Edward, shall unto my Lord Cobham,

With whom the Kentishmen will willingly rise.   40

In them I trust, for they are soldiers

Witty, courteous, liberal, full of spirit.

While you are thus employed, what resteth more,

But that I seek occasion how to rise,

And yet the King not privy to my drift,   45

Nor any of the house of Lancaster.

Enter a Messenger.

But stay, what news? Why com'st thou in such post?

MESSENGER

The Queen with all the northern earls and lords

Intend here to besiege you in your castle.

She is hard by with twenty thousand men,   50

And therefore fortify your hold, my lord   *Exit.*

YORK

Ay, with my sword. What, think'st thou that we fear

them?

Edward and Richard, you shall stay with me.

My brother Montague shall post to London.

Let noble Warwick, Cobham and the rest,   55

Whom we have left protectors of the King,

With powerful policy strengthen themselves

And trust not simple Henry nor his oaths.

MONTAGUE   Brother, I go; I'll win them, fear it not.

And thus most humbly I do take my leave.   *Exit.*   60

Enter SIR JOHN MORTIMER *and his brother*

Sir Hugh Mortimer.

YORK   Sir John and Sir Hugh Mortimer, mine uncles,

You are come to Sandal in a happy hour.

The army of the Queen mean to besiege us.

SIR JOHN MORTIMER

She shall not need; we'll meet her in the field.

YORK   What, with five thousand men?   65

RICHARD   Ay, with five hundred, father, for a need.

A woman's general. What should we fear?

[A march afar off]

EDWARD

I hear their drums. Let's set our men in order,

And issue forth and bid them battle straight.

YORK   Five men to twenty: though the odds be great,   70

I doubt not, uncle, of our victory.

Many a battle have I won in France,

When as the enemy hath been ten to one.

Why should I not now have the like success?

Alarum. Exeunt.

1.3   *Enter* RUTLAND *and his* Tutor.

RUTLAND   Ah, whither shall I fly to scape their hands?

Enter CLIFFORD *with Soldiers.*

Ah, tutor, look where bloody Clifford comes!

CLIFFORD
    Chaplain, away, thy priesthood saves thy life.
    As for the brat of the accursed Duke,
5   Whose father slew my father, he shall die.
TUTOR   And I, my lord, will bear him company.
CLIFFORD   Soldiers, away with him.
TUTOR   Ah, Clifford, murder not this innocent child,
    Lest thou be hated both of God and man.
                        Exit guarded.
10 CLIFFORD   How now, is he dead already? Or is it fear
    That makes him close his eyes? I'll open them.
RUTLAND   So looks the pent-up lion o'er the wretch
    That trembles under his devouring paws;
    And so he walks, insulting o'er his prey,
15   And so he comes to rend his limbs asunder.
    Ah, gentle Clifford, kill me with thy sword
    And not with such a cruel threat'ning look.
    Sweet Clifford, hear me speak before I die:
    I am too mean a subject for thy wrath;
20   Be thou revenged on men and let me live.
CLIFFORD
    In vain thou speak'st, poor boy; my father's blood
    Hath stopped the passage where thy words should enter.
RUTLAND   Then let my father's blood open it again.
    He is a man and, Clifford, cope with him.
CLIFFORD
25   Had I thy brethren here, their lives and thine
    Were not revenge sufficient for me.
    No, if I digged up thy forefathers' graves
    And hung their rotten coffins up in chains,
    It could not slake mine ire nor ease my heart.
30   The sight of any of the house of York
    Is as a Fury to torment my soul:
    And till I root out their accursed line
    And leave not one alive, I live in hell.
    Therefore —
35 RUTLAND   O, let me pray before I take my death;
    To thee I pray: sweet Clifford, pity me!
CLIFFORD   Such pity as my rapier's point affords.
RUTLAND
    I never did thee harm; why wilt thou slay me?
CLIFFORD   Thy father hath.
RUTLAND   But 'twas ere I was born.
40   Thou hast one son, for his sake pity me,
    Lest in revenge thereof, sith God is just,
    He be as miserably slain as I.
    Ah, let me live in prison all my days,
    And when I give occasion of offence
45   Then let me die, for now thou hast no cause.
CLIFFORD   No cause?
    Thy father slew my father; therefore die.   [*Stabs him.*]
RUTLAND   *Di faciant laudis summa sit ista tuae.*   [*Dies.*]
CLIFFORD   Plantagenet, I come, Plantagenet!
50   And this thy son's blood, cleaving to my blade,
    Shall rust upon my weapon till thy blood
    Congealed with this do make me wipe off both.
                   Exit with Rutland's body.

1.4   *Alarum. Enter* Richard, Duke of YORK.

YORK   The army of the Queen hath got the field.
    My uncles both are slain in rescuing me,
    And all my followers to the eager foe
    Turn back and fly like ships before the wind,
    Or lambs pursued by hunger-starved wolves.   5
    My sons, God knows what hath bechanced them;
    But this I know, they have demeaned themselves
    Like men born to renown, by life or death.
    Three times did Richard make a lane to me
    And thrice cried, 'Courage, father, fight it out!'   10
    And full as oft came Edward to my side,
    With purple falchion painted to the hilt
    In blood of those that had encountered him;
    And when the hardiest warriors did retire,
    Richard cried, 'Charge, and give no foot of ground!'   15
    And cried, 'A crown, or else a glorious tomb,
    A sceptre, or an earthly sepulchre!'
    With this we charged again, but, out, alas,
    We budged again, as I have seen a swan
    With bootless labour swim against the tide   20
    And spend her strength with overmatching waves.
                 [*A short alarum within*]
    Ah, hark, the fatal followers do pursue,
    And I am faint and cannot fly their fury;
    And were I strong, I would not shun their fury.
    The sands are numbered that makes up my life: 25
    Here must I stay, and here my life must end.

    Enter QUEEN MARGARET, CLIFFORD,
  NORTHUMBERLAND, *young* PRINCE EDWARD
             and Soldiers.

    Come bloody Clifford, rough Northumberland,
    I dare your quenchless fury to more rage;
    I am your butt and I abide your shot.
NORTHUMBERLAND
    Yield to our mercy, proud Plantagenet!   30
CLIFFORD   Ay, to such mercy as his ruthless arm
    With downright payment showed unto my father.
    Now Phaëton hath tumbled from his car
    And made an evening at the noontide prick.
YORK   My ashes, as the phoenix, may bring forth   35
    A bird that will revenge upon you all,
    And in that hope I throw mine eyes to heaven,
    Scorning whate'er you can afflict me with.
    Why come you not? What, multitudes, and fear?
CLIFFORD
    So cowards fight when they can fly no further,   40
    So doves do peck the falcon's piercing talons,
    So desperate thieves, all hopeless of their lives,
    Breathe out invectives 'gainst the officers.
YORK   O Clifford, but bethink thee once again,
    And in thy thought o'errun my former time: 45
    And, if thou canst for blushing, view this face
    And bite thy tongue that slanders him with cowardice
    Whose frown hath made thee faint and fly ere this.

CLIFFORD   I will not bandy with thee word for word,
But buckler with thee blows twice two for one.

QUEEN MARGARET
Hold, valiant Clifford, for a thousand causes
I would prolong awhile the traitor's life. –
Wrath makes him deaf: speak thou, Northumberland.

NORTHUMBERLAND
Hold, Clifford, do not honour him so much
To prick thy finger, though to wound his heart.
What valour were it when a cur doth grin
For one to thrust his hand between his teeth,
When he might spurn him with his foot away?
It is war's prize to take all vantages,
And ten to one is no impeach of valour.
[*They fight and take York.*]

CLIFFORD   Ay, ay, so strives the woodcock with the gin.

NORTHUMBERLAND
So doth the cony struggle in the net.

YORK   So triumph thieves upon their conquered booty;
So true men yield, with robbers so o'ermatched.

NORTHUMBERLAND
What would your grace have done unto him now?

QUEEN MARGARET
Brave warriors, Clifford and Northumberland,
Come, make him stand upon this molehill here
That raught at mountains with outstretched arms,
Yet parted but the shadow with his hand.
What, was it you that would be England's king?
Was't you that revelled in our Parliament
And made a preachment of your high descent?
Where are your mess of sons to back you now?
The wanton Edward and the lusty George?
And where's that valiant crookback prodigy,
Dickie, your boy, that with his grumbling voice
Was wont to cheer his dad in mutinies?
Or with the rest, where is your darling, Rutland?
Look, York, I stained this napkin with the blood
That valiant Clifford with his rapier's point
Made issue from the bosom of the boy;
And if thine eyes can water for his death,
I give thee this to dry thy cheeks withal.
Alas, poor York, but that I hate thee deadly
I should lament thy miserable state.
I prithee grieve to make me merry, York.
What, hath thy fiery heart so parched thine entrails
That not a tear can fall for Rutland's death?
Why art thou patient, man? Thou shouldst be mad;
And I to make thee mad do mock thee thus.
Stamp, rave and fret, that I may sing and dance.
Thou wouldst be fee'd, I see, to make me sport:
York cannot speak unless he wear a crown.
A crown for York, and, lords, bow low to him.
Hold you his hands whilst I do set it on.
Ay, marry, sir, now looks he like a king;
Ay, this is he that took King Henry's chair,
And this is he was his adopted heir.
But how is it that great Plantagenet

Is crowned so soon and broke his solemn oath?   100
As I bethink me, you should not be king
Till our King Henry had shook hands with death.
And will you pale your head in Henry's glory
And rob his temples of the diadem
Now, in his life, against your holy oath?   105
O, 'tis a fault too too unpardonable.
Off with the crown, and with the crown, his head,
And whilst we breathe take time to do him dead!

CLIFFORD   That is my office, for my father's sake.

QUEEN MARGARET
Nay, stay, let's hear the orisons he makes.   110

YORK
She-wolf of France, but worse than wolves of France,
Whose tongue more poisons than the adder's tooth!
How ill-beseeming is it in thy sex
To triumph like an Amazonian trull
Upon their woes whom Fortune captivates.   115
But that thy face is vizard-like, unchanging,
Made impudent with use of evil deeds,
I would assay, proud Queen, to make thee blush.
To tell thee whence thou cam'st, of whom derived,
Were shame enough to shame thee, were thou not
shameless.   120
Thy father bears the type of King of Naples,
Of both the Sicils and Jerusalem,
Yet not so wealthy as an English yeoman.
Hath that poor monarch taught thee to insult?
It needs not, nor it boots thee not, proud Queen,   125
Unless the adage must be verified
That beggars mounted run their horse to death.
'Tis beauty that doth oft make women proud,
But God he knows thy share thereof is small.
'Tis virtue that doth make them most admired;   130
The contrary doth make thee wondered at.
'Tis government that makes them seem divine;
The want thereof makes thee abominable.
Thou art as opposite to every good
As the Antipodes are unto us,   135
Or as the south to the Septentrion.
O, tiger's heart wrapped in a woman's hide,
How couldst thou drain the lifeblood of the child
To bid the father wipe his eyes withal,
And yet be seen to bear a woman's face?   140
Women are soft, mild, pitiful and flexible;
Thou stern, obdurate, flinty, rough, remorseless.
Bidd'st thou me rage? Why, now thou hast thy wish.
Wouldst have me weep? Why, now thou hast thy will.
For raging wind blows up incessant showers,   145
And when the rage allays, the rain begins:
These tears are my sweet Rutland's obsequies,
And every drop cries vengeance for his death
'Gainst thee, fell Clifford, and thee, false
Frenchwoman!

NORTHUMBERLAND
Beshrew me, but his passions moves me so   150
That hardly can I check my eyes from tears.

YORK   That face of his the hungry cannibals
Would not have touched, would not have stained with
      blood;
But you are more inhuman, more inexorable,
155   O, ten times more than tigers of Hyrcania.
See, ruthless Queen, a hapless father's tears.
This cloth thou dipp'd'st in blood of my sweet boy,
And I with tears do wash the blood away.
Keep thou the napkin and go boast of this,
160   And if thou tell'st the heavy story right,
Upon my soul the hearers will shed tears.
Yea, even my foes will shed fast-falling tears
And say, 'Alas, it was a piteous deed!'
There, take the crown, and with the crown my curse,
165   And in thy need such comfort come to thee
As now I reap at thy too cruel hand.
Hard-hearted Clifford, take me from the world,
My soul to heaven, my blood upon your heads!

NORTHUMBERLAND
Had he been slaughter-man to all my kin,
170   I should not for my life but weep with him
To see how inly sorrow gripes his soul.

QUEEN MARGARET
What, weeping-ripe, my Lord Northumberland?
Think but upon the wrong he did us all,
And that will quickly dry thy melting tears.

CLIFFORD [*Stabs York twice.*]
175   Here's for my oath; here's for my father's death!

QUEEN MARGARET [*Stabs York.*]
And here's to right our gentle-hearted King!

YORK   Open thy gate of mercy, gracious God,
My soul flies through these wounds to seek out
      thee!   [*Dies.*]

QUEEN MARGARET
Off with his head and set it on York gates,
180   So York may overlook the town of York.

            Flourish. Exeunt with the body.

2.1   *A march. Enter* EDWARD, RICHARD
            and their power.

EDWARD   I wonder how our princely father scaped,
Or whether he be scaped away or no
From Clifford's and Northumberland's pursuit.
Had he been ta'en, we should have heard the news;
5   Had he been slain, we should have heard the news;
Or had he scaped, methinks we should have heard
The happy tidings of his good escape.
How fares my brother? Why is he so sad?

RICHARD   I cannot joy until I be resolved
10   Where our right valiant father is become.
I saw him in the battle range about
And watched him how he singled Clifford forth.
Methought he bore him in the thickest troop
As doth a lion in a herd of neat,
15   Or as a bear encompassed round with dogs,
Who having pinched a few and made them cry,

The rest stand all aloof and bark at him.
So fared our father with his enemies;
So fled his enemies my warlike father;
Methinks 'tis prize enough to be his son.   20

      [*Three suns appear in the air.*]
See how the morning opes her golden gates
And takes her farewell of the glorious sun.
How well resembles it the prime of youth,
Trimmed like a younker prancing to his love.

EDWARD   Dazzle mine eyes, or do I see three suns?   25

RICHARD   Three glorious suns, each one a perfect sun,
Not separated with the racking clouds
But severed in a pale clear-shining sky.
See, see, they join, embrace and seem to kiss,
As if they vowed some league inviolable.   30
Now are they but one lamp, one light, one sun:
In this, the heaven figures some event.

EDWARD
'Tis wondrous strange, the like yet never heard of.
I think it cites us, brother, to the field,
That we, the sons of brave Plantagenet,   35
Each one already blazing by our meeds,
Should, notwithstanding, join our lights together
And over-shine the earth, as this the world.
Whate'er it bodes, henceforward will I bear
Upon my target three fair-shining suns.   40

RICHARD
Nay, bear three daughters: by your leave, I speak it,
You love the breeder better than the male.

            Enter a Messenger *blowing.*

But what art thou whose heavy looks foretell
Some dreadful story hanging on thy tongue?

MESSENGER   Ah, one that was a woeful looker-on   45
When as the noble Duke of York was slain,
Your princely father and my loving lord!

EDWARD   O, speak no more, for I have heard too much.

RICHARD   Say how he died, for I will hear it all.

MESSENGER   Environed he was with many foes   50
And stood against them, as the hope of Troy
Against the Greeks that would have entered Troy.
But Hercules himself must yield to odds:
And many strokes, though with a little axe,
Hews down and fells the hardest-timbered oak.   55
By many hands your father was subdued,
But only slaughtered by the ireful arm
Of unrelenting Clifford and the Queen,
Who crowned the gracious Duke in high despite,
Laughed in his face, and when with grief he wept,   60
The ruthless Queen gave him to dry his cheeks
A napkin steeped in the harmless blood
Of sweet young Rutland, by rough Clifford slain.
And after many scorns, many foul taunts,
They took his head and on the gates of York   65
They set the same, and there it doth remain,
The saddest spectacle that e'er I viewed.   *Exit.*

EDWARD   Sweet Duke of York, our prop to lean upon,

Now thou art gone we have no staff, no stay.
70 O Clifford, boist'rous Clifford, thou hast slain
The flower of Europe for his chivalry;
And treacherously hast thou vanquished him,
For hand to hand he would have vanquished thee.
Now my soul's palace is become a prison;
75 Ah, would she break from hence, that this my body
Might in the ground be closed up in rest,
For never henceforth shall I joy again.
Never, O never, shall I see more joy!

RICHARD   I cannot weep, for all my body's moisture
80 Scarce serves to quench my furnace-burning heart;
Nor can my tongue unload my heart's great burden,
For selfsame wind that I should speak withal
Is kindling coals that fires all my breast
And burns me up with flames that tears would quench.
85 To weep is to make less the depth of grief:
Tears then for babes; blows and revenge for me.
Richard, I bear thy name, I'll venge thy death
Or die renowned by attempting it.

EDWARD
His name that valiant Duke hath left with thee;
90 His dukedom and his chair with me is left.

RICHARD   Nay, if thou be that princely eagle's bird,
Show thy descent by gazing 'gainst the sun;
For chair and dukedom, throne and kingdom 'ssay,
Either that is thine or else thou wert not his.

March. Enter WARWICK, *Marquess of*
MONTAGUE *and their army.*

WARWICK
95 How now, fair lords? What fare, what news abroad?

RICHARD   Great lord of Warwick, if we should recount
Our baleful news, and at each word's deliverance
Stab poniards in our flesh till all were told,
The words would add more anguish than the wounds.
100 O valiant lord, the Duke of York is slain!

EDWARD   O Warwick, Warwick, that Planagenet
Which held thee dearly as his soul's redemption
Is by the stern Lord Clifford done to death!

WARWICK   Ten days ago I drowned these news in tears,
105 And now to add more measure to your woes,
I come to tell you things sith then befall'n.
After the bloody fray at Wakefield fought,
Where your brave father breathed his latest gasp,
Tidings, as swiftly as the posts could run,
110 Were brought me of your loss and his depart.
I, then in London, keeper of the King,
Mustered my soldiers, gathered flocks of friends,
Marched toward Saint Albans to intercept the Queen,
Bearing the King in my behalf along;
115 For by my scouts I was advertised
That she was coming with a full intent
To dash our late decree in Parliament
Touching King Henry's oath and your succession.
Short tale to make, we at Saint Albans met,
120 Our battles joined, and both sides fiercely fought.

But whether 'twas the coldness of the King,
Who looked full gently on his warlike Queen,
That robbed my soldiers of their heated spleen,
Or whether 'twas report of her success,
Or more than common fear of Clifford's rigour, 125
Who thunders to his captives blood and death,
I cannot judge; but to conclude with truth,
Their weapons like to lightning came and went;
Our soldiers', like the night-owl's lazy flight,
Or like an idle thresher with a flail, 130
Fell gently down as if they struck their friends.
I cheered them up with justice of our cause,
With promise of high pay and great rewards;
But all in vain, they had no heart to fight,
And we, in them, no hope to win the day, 135
So that we fled, the King unto the Queen;
Lord George your brother, Norfolk and myself,
In haste, post-haste, are come to join with you,
For in the marches here we heard you were,
Making another head to fight again. 140

EDWARD
Where is the Duke of Norfolk, gentle Warwick?
And when came George from Burgundy to England?

WARWICK
Some six miles off the Duke is with the soldiers;
And for your brother, he was lately sent
From your kind aunt, Duchess of Burgundy, 145
With aid of soldiers to this needful war.

RICHARD
'Twas odds, belike, when valiant Warwick fled.
Oft have I heard his praises in pursuit,
But ne'er till now his scandal of retire.

WARWICK
Nor now my scandal, Richard, dost thou hear; 150
For thou shalt know this strong right hand of mine
Can pluck the diadem from faint Henry's head
And wring the awful sceptre from his fist,
Were he as famous and as bold in war
As he is famed for mildness, peace and prayer. 155

RICHARD   I know it well, Lord Warwick; blame me not.
'Tis love I bear thy glories makes me speak.
But in this troublous time, what's to be done?
Shall we go throw away our coats of steel
And wrap our bodies in black mourning gowns, 160
Numb'ring our Ave-Maries with our beads?
Or shall we on the helmets of our foes
Tell our devotion with revengeful arms?
If for the last, say 'Ay', and to it, lords.

WARWICK
Why, therefore Warwick came to seek you out, 165
And therefore comes my brother Montague.
Attend me, lords. The proud insulting Queen,
With Clifford and the haught Northumberland,
And of their feather many moe proud birds,
Have wrought the easy-melting King like wax. 170
He swore consent to your succession,
His oath enrolled in the Parliament;

And now to London all the crew are gone
To frustrate both his oath and what beside
175 May make against the house of Lancaster.
Their power, I think, is thirty thousand strong.
Now, if the help of Norfolk and myself,
With all the friends that thou, brave Earl of March,
Amongst the loving Welshmen canst procure,
180 Will but amount to five and twenty thousand,
Why, *via*, to London will we march,
And once again bestride our foaming steeds,
And once again cry 'Charge!' upon our foes,
But never once again turn back and fly.

RICHARD
185 Ay, now methinks I hear great Warwick speak.
Ne'er may he live to see a sunshine day
That cries 'Retire!' if Warwick bid him stay.

EDWARD   Lord Warwick, on thy shoulder will I lean;
And when thou fail'st, as God forbid the hour,
190 Must Edward fall, which peril heaven forfend!

WARWICK
No longer Earl of March, but Duke of York;
The next degree is England's royal throne.
For King of England shalt thou be proclaimed
In every borough as we pass along;
195 And he that throws not up his cap for joy
Shall for the fault make forfeit of his head.
King Edward, valiant Richard, Montague,
Stay we no longer dreaming of renown,
But sound the trumpets and about our task.

RICHARD
200 Then, Clifford, were thy heart as hard as steel,
As thou hast shown it flinty by thy deeds,
I come to pierce it or to give thee mine.

EDWARD
Then strike up drums! God and Saint George for us!

Enter a Messenger.

WARWICK   How now, what news?

MESSENGER
205 The Duke of Norfolk sends you word by me,
The Queen is coming with a puissant host
And craves your company for speedy counsel.

WARWICK
Why, then, it sorts. Brave warriors, let's away.

Exeunt omnes.

2.2   *Flourish. Enter* KING HENRY,
QUEEN MARGARET, CLIFFORD,
NORTHUMBERLAND *and young*
PRINCE EDWARD, *with Drum and Trumpets.*
York's head is set above the gates.

QUEEN MARGARET
Welcome, my lord, to this brave town of York.
Yonder's the head of that arch-enemy
That sought to be encompassed with your crown.
Doth not the object cheer your heart, my lord?

KING HENRY
Ay, as the rocks cheer them that fear their wrack,   5
To see this sight it irks my very soul.
Withhold revenge, dear God. 'Tis not my fault,
Nor wittingly have I infringed my vow.

CLIFFORD   My gracious liege, this too much lenity
And harmful pity must be laid aside.   10
To whom do lions cast their gentle looks?
Not to the beast that would usurp their den.
Whose hand is that the forest bear doth lick?
Not his that spoils her young before her face.
Who scapes the lurking serpent's mortal sting?   15
Not he that sets his foot upon her back.
The smallest worm will turn, being trodden on,
And doves will peck in safeguard of their brood.
Ambitious York did level at thy crown,
Thou smiling while he knit his angry brows;   20
He, but a duke, would have his son a king
And raise his issue like a loving sire;
Thou, being a king, blest with a goodly son,
Didst yield consent to disinherit him,
Which argued thee a most unloving father.   25
Unreasonable creatures feed their young;
And though man's face be fearful to their eyes,
Yet in protection of their tender ones,
Who hath not seen them, even with those wings
Which sometime they have used with fearful flight,   30
Make war with him that climbed unto their nest,
Offering their own lives in their young's defence?
For shame, my liege, make them your precedent.
Were it not pity that this goodly boy
Should lose his birthright by his father's fault?   35
And long hereafter say unto his child,
'What my great-grandfather and grandsire got,
My careless father fondly gave away'?
Ah, what a shame were this. Look on the boy,
And let his manly face, which promiseth   40
Successful fortune, steel thy melting heart
To hold thine own and leave thine own with him.

KING HENRY
Full well hath Clifford played the orator,
Inferring arguments of mighty force.
But, Clifford, tell me, didst thou never hear   45
That things ill got had ever bad success?
And happy always was it for that son
Whose father for his hoarding went to hell?
I'll leave my son my virtuous deeds behind,
And would my father had left me no more.   50
For all the rest is held at such a rate
As brings a thousandfold more care to keep
Than in possession any jot of pleasure.
Ah, cousin York, would thy best friends did know
How it doth grieve me that thy head is here.   55

QUEEN MARGARET
My lord, cheer up your spirits: our foes are nigh,
And this soft courage makes your followers faint.
You promised knighthood to our forward son.

Unsheathe your sword and dub him presently.
Edward, kneel down.
KING HENRY   Edward Plantagenet, arise a knight,
And learn this lesson: draw thy sword in right.

PRINCE EDWARD
My gracious father, by your kingly leave,
I'll draw it as apparent to the crown
And in that quarrel use it to the death.

CLIFFORD   Why, that is spoken like a toward prince.

Enter a Messenger.

MESSENGER   Royal commanders, be in readiness,
For with a band of thirty thousand men
Comes Warwick, backing of the Duke of York,
And in the towns as they do march along,
Proclaims him king, and many fly to him.
Deraign your battle, for they are at hand.   *Exit.*

CLIFFORD
I would your highness would depart the field.
The Queen hath best success when you are absent.

QUEEN MARGARET
Ay, good my lord, and leave us to our fortune.

KING HENRY
Why that's my fortune too; therefore, I'll stay.

NORTHUMBERLAND
Be it with resolution, then, to fight.

PRINCE EDWARD
My royal father, cheer these noble lords
And hearten those that fight in your defence.
Unsheathe your sword, good father, cry 'Saint George!'

March. Enter EDWARD, WARWICK, RICHARD, GEORGE,
NORFOLK, MONTAGUE *and Soldiers.*

EDWARD
Now, perjured Henry, wilt thou kneel for grace
And set thy diadem upon my head,
Or bide the mortal fortune of the field?

QUEEN MARGARET
Go rate thy minions, proud insulting boy.
Becomes it thee to be thus bold in terms
Before thy sovereign and thy lawful King?

EDWARD   I am his king, and he should bow his knee.
I was adopted heir by his consent.
Since when his oath is broke; for as I hear,
You that are king, though he do wear the crown,
Have caused him, by new act of Parliament,
To blot out me and put his own son in.

CLIFFORD   And reason too;
Who should succeed the father but the son?

RICHARD   Are you there, butcher? O, I cannot speak!

CLIFFORD   Ay, crookback, here I stand to answer thee,
Or any he, the proudest of thy sort.

RICHARD
'Twas you that killed young Rutland, was it not?

CLIFFORD   Ay, and old York, and yet not satisfied.

RICHARD
For God's sake, lords, give signal to the fight.

WARWICK
What sayst thou, Henry, wilt thou yield the crown?

QUEEN MARGARET
Why, how now, long-tongued Warwick, dare you
    speak?
When you and I met at Saint Albans last,
Your legs did better service than your hands.

WARWICK
Then 'twas my turn to fly, and now 'tis thine.   105

CLIFFORD   You said so much before and yet you fled.

WARWICK
'Twas not your valour, Clifford, drove me thence.

NORTHUMBERLAND
No, nor your manhood that durst make you stay.

RICHARD   Northumberland, I hold thee reverently.
Break off the parley, for scarce I can refrain   110
The execution of my big-swoll'n heart
Upon that Clifford, that cruel child-killer.

CLIFFORD   I slew thy father: call'st thou him a child?

RICHARD   Ay, like a dastard and a treacherous coward,
As thou didst kill our tender brother Rutland.   115
But ere sunset I'll make thee curse the deed.

KING HENRY
Have done with words, my lords, and hear me speak.

QUEEN MARGARET
Defy them, then, or else hold close thy lips.

KING HENRY   I prithee, give no limits to my tongue:
I am a king and privileged to speak.   120

CLIFFORD
My liege, the wound that bred this meeting here
Cannot be cured by words; therefore, be still.

RICHARD   Then, executioner, unsheathe thy sword.
By him that made us all, I am resolved
That Clifford's manhood lies upon his tongue.   125

EDWARD   Say, Henry, shall I have my right or no?
A thousand men have broke their fasts today
That ne'er shall dine unless thou yield the crown.

WARWICK   If thou deny, their blood upon thy head,
For York in justice puts his armour on.   130

PRINCE EDWARD
If that be right which Warwick says is right,
There is no wrong, but everything is right.

RICHARD   Whoever got thee, there thy mother stands,
For well I wot thou hast thy mother's tongue.

QUEEN MARGARET
But thou art neither like thy sire nor dam,   135
But like a foul misshapen stigmatic,
Marked by the Destinies to be avoided,
As venom toads or lizards' dreadful stings.

RICHARD   Iron of Naples hid with English gilt,
Whose father bears the title of a king,   140
As if a channel should be called the sea,
Sham'st thou not, knowing whence thou art
    extraught,
To let thy tongue detect thy baseborn heart?

EDWARD
A wisp of straw were worth a thousand crowns

145 To make this shameless callet know herself.
Helen of Greece was fairer far than thou,
Although thy husband may be Menelaus;
And ne'er was Agamemnon's brother wronged
By that false woman, as this king by thee.
150 His father revelled in the heart of France,
And tamed the King and made the Dauphin stoop;
And had he matched according to his state,
He might have kept that glory to this day.
But when he took a beggar to his bed
155 And graced thy poor sire with his bridal day,
Even then that sunshine brewed a shower for him
That washed his father's fortunes forth of France
And heaped sedition on his crown at home.
For what hath broached this tumult but thy pride?
160 Hadst thou been meek, our title still had slept,
And we, in pity of the gentle King,
Had slipped our claim until another age.

GEORGE
But when we saw our sunshine made thy spring,
And that thy summer bred us no increase,
165 We set the axe to thy usurping root;
And though the edge hath something hit ourselves,
Yet know thou, since we have begun to strike,
We'll never leave till we have hewn thee down
Or bathed thy growing with our heated bloods.
170 EDWARD   And in this resolution, I defy thee,
Not willing any longer conference,
Since thou denied'st the gentle King to speak.
Sound trumpets! Let our bloody colours wave;
And either victory or else a grave!
175 QUEEN MARGARET   Stay Edward.
EDWARD   No, wrangling woman, we'll no longer stay.
These words will cost ten thousand lives this day.
Exeunt omnes.

2.3   *Alarum. Excursions. Enter* WARWICK.

WARWICK   Forspent with toil, as runners with a race,
I lay me down a little while to breathe;
For strokes received and many blows repaid
Have robbed my strong-knit sinews of their strength,
5 And, spite of spite, needs must I rest awhile.

Enter EDWARD *running.*

EDWARD
Smile, gentle heaven, or strike, ungentle death!
For this world frowns, and Edward's sun is clouded.

Enter GEORGE.

WARWICK
How now, my lord, what hap? What hope of good?
GEORGE   Our hap is loss, our hope but sad despair,
10 Our ranks are broke, and ruin follows us.
What counsel give you? Whither shall we fly?
EDWARD   Bootless is flight: they follow us with wings,
And weak we are and cannot shun pursuit.

Enter RICHARD.

RICHARD
Ah, Warwick, why hast thou withdrawn thyself?
Thy brother's blood the thirsty earth hath drunk,   15
Broached with the steely point of Clifford's lance;
And in the very pangs of death he cried,
Like to a dismal clangour heard from far,
'Warwick, revenge! Brother, revenge my death!'
So underneath the belly of their steeds,   20
That stained their fetlocks in his smoking blood,
The noble gentleman gave up the ghost.
WARWICK
Then let the earth be drunken with our blood.
I'll kill my horse, because I will not fly.
Why stand we like soft-hearted women here,   25
Wailing our losses whiles the foe doth rage,
And look upon, as if the tragedy
Were played in jest by counterfeiting actors?
Here on my knee I vow to God above:
I'll never pause again, never stand still,   30
Till either death hath closed these eyes of mine
Or Fortune given me measure of revenge.
EDWARD   O Warwick, I do bend my knee with thine,
And in this vow do chain my soul to thine.
And, ere my knee rise from the earth's cold face,   35
I throw my hands, mine eyes, my heart to Thee,
Thou setter-up and plucker-down of kings,
Beseeching Thee, if with Thy will it stands
That to my foes this body must be prey,
Yet that Thy brazen gates of heaven may ope   40
And give sweet passage to my sinful soul.
Now, lords, take leave until we meet again,
Where'er it be, in heaven or in earth.
RICHARD
Brother, give me thy hand; and, gentle Warwick,
Let me embrace thee in my weary arms.   45
I, that did never weep, now melt with woe
That winter should cut off our springtime so.
WARWICK
Away, away! Once more, sweet lords, farewell.
GEORGE   Yet let us all together to our troops
And give them leave to fly that will not stay,   50
And call them pillars that will stand to us;
And, if we thrive, promise them such rewards
As victors wear at the Olympian games.
This may plant courage in their quailing breasts,
For yet is hope of life and victory.   55
Forslow no longer; make we hence amain.   *Exeunt.*

2.4   *Excursions. Enter* RICHARD *at one
door and* CLIFFORD *at the other.*

RICHARD   Now, Clifford, I have singled thee alone.
Suppose this arm is for the Duke of York,
And this for Rutland, both bound to revenge,
Wert thou environed with a brazen wall.

CLIFFORD   Now, Richard, I am with thee here alone.
    This is the hand that stabbed thy father York,
    And this the hand that slew thy brother Rutland,
    And here's the heart that triumphs in their death
    And cheers these hands that slew thy sire and brother
    To execute the like upon thyself.
    And so, have at thee!

Alarums. They fight. WARWICK *comes*
and rescues Richard. Clifford flies.

RICHARD   Nay, Warwick, single out some other chase,
    For I myself will hunt this wolf to death.   *Exeunt.*

2.5   *Alarum. Enter* KING HENRY *alone.*

KING HENRY
    This battle fares like to the morning's war,
    When dying clouds contend with growing light,
    What time the shepherd, blowing of his nails,
    Can neither call it perfect day nor night.
    Now sways it this way, like a mighty sea
    Forced by the tide to combat with the wind.
    Now sways it that way, like the selfsame sea
    Forced to retire by fury of the wind.
    Sometime the flood prevails, and then the wind;
    Now one the better, then another best,
    Both tugging to be victors, breast to breast,
    Yet neither conqueror nor conquered:
    So is the equal poise of this fell war:
    Here on this molehill will I sit me down.
    To whom God will, there be the victory.
    For Margaret, my Queen, and Clifford too,
    Have chid me from the battle, swearing both
    They prosper best of all when I am thence.
    Would I were dead, if God's good will were so.
    For what is in this world but grief and woe?
    O God! Methinks it were a happy life
    To be no better than a homely swain,
    To sit upon a hill, as I do now,
    To carve out dials quaintly, point by point,
    Thereby to see the minutes how they run:
    How many makes the hour full complete,
    How many hours brings about the day,
    How many days will finish up the year,
    How many years a mortal man may live.
    When this is known, then to divide the times:
    So many hours must I tend my flock,
    So many hours must I take my rest,
    So many hours must I contemplate,
    So many hours must I sport myself,
    So many days my ewes have been with young,
    So many weeks ere the poor fools will ean,
    So many years ere I shall shear the fleece.
    So minutes, hours, days, weeks, months and years,
    Passed over to the end they were created,
    Would bring white hairs unto a quiet grave.

    Ah! What a life were this, how sweet, how lovely!
    Gives not the hawthorn bush a sweeter shade
    To shepherds looking on their silly sheep
    Than doth a rich embroidered canopy
    To kings that fear their subjects' treachery?   45
    O yes, it doth, a thousandfold it doth.
    And to conclude, the shepherd's homely curds,
    His cold thin drink out of his leather bottle,
    His wonted sleep under a fresh tree's shade,
    All which secure and sweetly he enjoys,   50
    Is far beyond a prince's delicates;
    His viands sparkling in a golden cup,
    His body couched in a curious bed,
    When care, mistrust and treason waits on him.

Alarum. Enter a Son *that hath killed his father at*
one door, and a Father *that hath killed his son at*
another door with their bodies.

SON   Ill blows the wind that profits nobody.   55
    This man, whom hand to hand I slew in fight,
    May be possessed with some store of crowns,
    And I, that haply take them from him now,
    May yet ere night yield both my life and them
    To some man else, as this dead man doth me.   60
    Who's this? God! It is my father's face,
    Whom in this conflict I unwares have killed.
    O heavy times, begetting such events!
    From London by the King was I pressed forth,
    My father, being the Earl of Warwick's man,   65
    Came on the part of York, pressed by his master.
    And I, who at his hands received my life,
    Have by my hands of life bereaved him.
    Pardon me, God, I knew not what I did;
    And pardon, father, for I knew not thee.   70
    My tears shall wipe away these bloody marks,
    And no more words, till they have flowed their fill.

KING HENRY   O piteous spectacle!? bloody times!
    While lions war and battle for their dens,
    Poor harmless lambs abide their enmity.   75
    Weep, wretched man; I'll aid thee tear for tear,
    And let our hearts and eyes, like civil war,
    Be blind with tears and break o'ercharged with grief.

[The Father comes forward, bearing of his son.]

FATHER   Thou that so stoutly hath resisted me,
    Give me thy gold, if thou hast any gold,   80
    For I have bought it with an hundred blows.
    But let me see: is this our foeman's face?
    Ah, no, no, no, it is mine only son!
    Ah, boy, if any life be left in thee,
    Throw up thine eye! See, see what showers arise,   85
    Blown with the windy tempest of my heart,
    Upon thy wounds, that kills mine eye and heart!
    O pity, God, this miserable age!
    What stratagems, how fell, how butcherly,
    Erroneous, mutinous and unnatural,   90
    This deadly quarrel daily doth beget!

O boy, thy father gave thee life too soon,
And hath bereft thee of thy life too late!
KING HENRY
Woe above woe! Grief more than common grief!
95   O that my death would stay these ruthful deeds!
O pity, pity, gentle heaven, pity!
The red rose and the white are on his face,
The fatal colours of our striving houses:
The one his purple blood right well resembles,
100   The other his pale cheeks methinks presenteth.
Wither one rose, and let the other flourish;
If you contend, a thousand lives must wither.
SON   How will my mother for a father's death
Take on with me, and ne'er be satisfied!
105 FATHER   How will my wife for slaughter of my son
Shed seas of tears, and ne'er be satisfied!
KING HENRY
How will the country for these woeful chances
Misthink the King, and not be satisfied!
SON   Was ever son so rued a father's death?
110 FATHER   Was ever father so bemoaned his son?
KING HENRY
Was ever king so grieved for subjects' woe?
Much is your sorrow; mine, ten times so much.
SON   I'll bear thee hence, where I may weep my fill.
Exit bearing his father.
FATHER
These arms of mine shall be thy winding-sheet;
115   My heart, sweet boy, shall be thy sepulchre,
For from my heart thine image ne'er shall go;
My sighing breast shall be thy funeral bell;
And so obsequious will thy father be
E'en for the loss of thee, having no more,
120   As Priam was for all his valiant sons.
I'll bear thee hence, and let them fight that will,
For I have murdered where I should not kill.
Exit bearing his son.
KING HENRY
Sad-hearted men, much overgone with care,
Here sits a king more woeful than you are.

Alarums. Excursions. Enter QUEEN MARGARET,
PRINCE EDWARD *and* EXETER.

PRINCE EDWARD
125   Fly, father, fly! For all your friends are fled,
And Warwick rages like a chafed bull:
Away, for Death doth hold us in pursuit.
QUEEN MARGARET
Mount you, my lord; towards Berwick post amain.
Edward and Richard, like a brace of greyhounds
130   Having the fearful flying hare in sight,
With fiery eyes sparkling for very wrath,
And bloody steel grasped in their ireful hands,
Are at our backs, and therefore hence amain.
EXETER   Away, for Vengeance comes along with them.
135   Nay, stay not to expostulate, make speed;
Or else come after. I'll away before.

KING HENRY
Nay, take me with thee, good sweet Exeter:
Not that I fear to stay, but love to go
Whither the Queen intends. Forward, away!   *Exeunt.*

2.6   *A loud alarum. Enter* CLIFFORD
wounded, with an arrow in his neck.

CLIFFORD   Here burns my candle out; ay, here it dies,
Which whiles it lasted gave King Henry light.
O Lancaster, I fear thy overthrow
More than my body's parting with my soul!
My love and fear glued many friends to thee,   5
And now I fall. Thy tough commixtures melts,
Impairing Henry, strength'ning misproud York.
The common people swarm like summer flies,
And whither fly the gnats but to the sun?
And who shines now but Henry's enemies?   10
O Phoebus, hadst thou never given consent
That Phaëton should check thy fiery steeds,
Thy burning car never had scorched the earth!
And Henry, hadst thou swayed as kings should do,
Or as thy father and his father did,   15
Giving no ground unto the house of York,
They never then had sprung like summer flies;
I and ten thousand in this luckless realm
Had left no mourning widows for our death,
And thou this day hadst kept thy chair in peace.   20
For what doth cherish weeds but gentle air?
And what makes robbers bold but too much lenity?
Bootless are plaints, and cureless are my wounds:
No way to fly, nor strength to hold out fight.
The foe is merciless and will not pity,   25
For at their hands I have deserved no pity.
The air hath got into my deadly wounds,
And much effuse of blood doth make me faint.
Come, York and Richard, Warwick and the rest:
I stabbed your fathers' bosoms; split my breast.   30

Alarum and retreat. Enter EDWARD, WARWICK,
RICHARD *and Soldiers,* MONTAGUE *and* GEORGE.

EDWARD
Now breathe we, lords; good fortune bids us pause
And smooth the frowns of war with peaceful looks.
Some troops pursue the bloody-minded Queen,
That led calm Henry, though he were a king,
As doth a sail filled with a fretting gust   35
Command an argosy to stem the waves.
But think you, lords, that Clifford fled with them?
WARWICK   No, 'tis impossible he should escape,
For, though before his face I speak the words,
Your brother Richard marked him for the grave,   40
And wheresoe'er he is, he's surely dead.
[Clifford groans.]
RICHARD
Whose soul is that which takes her heavy leave?
A deadly groan, like life and death's departing.

EDWARD   See who it is; and now the battle's ended,
45   If friend or foe, let him be gently used.

RICHARD   Revoke that doom of mercy, for 'tis Clifford,
            Who not contented that he lopped the branch
            In hewing Rutland when his leaves put forth,
            But set his murd'ring knife unto the root
50   From whence that tender spray did sweetly spring,
            I mean our princely father, Duke of York.

WARWICK
            From off the gates of York fetch down the head,
            Your father's head, which Clifford placed there;
            Instead whereof let this supply the room:
55   Measure for measure must be answered.

EDWARD
            Bring forth that fatal screech-owl to our house
            That nothing sung but death to us and ours:
            Now death shall stop his dismal threat'ning sound,
            And his ill-boding tongue no more shall speak.

60 WARWICK   I think his understanding is bereft.
            Speak, Clifford, dost thou know who speaks to thee?
            Dark cloudy death o'ershades his beams of life,
            And he nor sees, nor hears us what we say.

RICHARD   O would he did, and so perhaps he doth.
65   'Tis but his policy to counterfeit,
            Because he would avoid such bitter taunts
            Which in the time of death he gave our father.

GEORGE   If so thou think'st, vex him with eager words.

RICHARD   Clifford, ask mercy and obtain no grace.

70 EDWARD   Clifford, repent in bootless penitence.

WARWICK   Clifford, devise excuses for thy faults.

GEORGE   While we devise fell tortures for thy faults.

RICHARD   Thou didst love York, and I am son to York.

EDWARD   Thou pitied'st Rutland; I will pity thee.

75 GEORGE   Where's Captain Margaret to fence you now?

WARWICK
            They mock thee, Clifford: swear as thou wast wont.

RICHARD
            What, not an oath? Nay, then the world goes hard
            When Clifford cannot spare his friends an oath.
            I know by that he's dead, and, by my soul,
80   If this right hand would buy two hours' life,
            That I in all despite might rail at him,
            This hand should chop it off, and with the issuing
                blood
            Stifle the villain whose unstaunched thirst
            York and young Rutland could not satisfy.

WARWICK
85   Ay, but he's dead. Off with the traitor's head,
            And rear it in the place your father's stands.
            And now to London with triumphant march,
            There to be crowned England's royal king:
            From whence shall Warwick cut the sea to France
90   And ask the Lady Bona for thy queen.
            So shalt thou sinew both these lands together;
            And having France thy friend thou shalt not dread
            The scattered foe that hopes to rise again,
            For though they cannot greatly sting to hurt,

            Yet look to have them buzz to offend thine ears.   95
            First will I see the coronation;
            And then to Brittany I'll cross the sea
            To effect this marriage, so it please my lord.

EDWARD   Even as thou wilt, sweet Warwick, let it be;
            For in thy shoulder do I build my seat,   100
            And never will I undertake the thing
            Wherein thy counsel and consent is wanting.
            Richard, I will create thee Duke of Gloucester,
            And George, of Clarence. Warwick as ourself
            Shall do and undo as him pleaseth best.   105

RICHARD
            Let me be Duke of Clarence, George of Gloucester;
            For Gloucester's dukedom is too ominous.

WARWICK   Tut, that's a foolish observation.
            Richard, be Duke of Gloucester. Now to London,
            To see these honours in possession.   *Exeunt.*   110

3.1   *Enter two Keepers with crossbows
                in their hands.*

1 KEEPER
            Under this thick-grown brake we'll shroud ourselves,
            For through this laund anon the deer will come;
            And in this covert will we make our stand,
            Culling the principal of all the deer.

2 KEEPER   I'll stay above the hill, so both may shoot.   5

1 KEEPER   That cannot be; the noise of thy crossbow
            Will scare the herd, and so my shoot is lost.
            Here stand we both, and aim we at the best,
            And, for the time shall not seem tedious,
            I'll tell thee what befell me on a day   10
            In this self place where now we mean to stand.

2 KEEPER   Here comes a man; let's stay till he be past.

            Enter KING HENRY, *disguised, with a prayer book.*

KING HENRY
            From Scotland am I stol'n, even of pure love,
            To greet mine own land with my wishful sight.
            No, Harry, Harry, 'tis no land of thine;   15
            Thy place is filled, thy sceptre wrung from thee,
            Thy balm washed off wherewith thou wast anointed.
            No bending knee will call thee Caesar now,
            No humble suitors press to speak for right,
            No, not a man comes for redress of thee.   20
            For how can I help them, an not myself?

1 KEEPER   Ay, here's a deer whose skin's a keeper's fee!
            This is the quondam king; let's seize upon him.

KING HENRY   Let me embrace the sour adversaries,
            For wise men say it is the wisest course.   25

2 KEEPER   Why linger we? Let us lay hands upon him.

1 KEEPER   Forbear awhile; we'll hear a little more.

KING HENRY
            My Queen and son are gone to France for aid;
            And, as I hear, the great commanding Warwick
            Is thither gone, to crave the French King's sister   30
            To wife for Edward. If this news be true,

Poor Queen and son, your labour is but lost,
For Warwick is a subtle orator,
And Lewis a prince soon won with moving words.
35 By this account, then, Margaret may win him,
For she's a woman to be pitied much:
Her sighs will make a batt'ry in his breast;
Her tears will pierce into a marble heart;
The tiger will be mild whiles she doth mourn;
40 And Nero will be tainted with remorse
To hear and see her plaints, her brinish tears.
Ay, but she's come to beg, Warwick to give:
She on his left side, craving aid for Henry;
He on his right, asking a wife for Edward.
45 She weeps, and says her Henry is deposed;
He smiles, and says his Edward is installed:
That she, poor wretch, for grief can speak no more,
Whiles Warwick tells his title, smooths the wrong,
Inferreth arguments of mighty strength,
50 And in conclusion wins the King from her
With promise of his sister, and what else,
To strengthen and support King Edward's place.
O Margaret, thus 'twill be; and thou, poor soul,
Art then forsaken, as thou went'st forlorn.

2 KEEPER
55 Say, what art thou that talk'st of kings and queens?

KING HENRY
More than I seem, and less than I was born to:
A man at least, for less I should not be;
And men may talk of kings, and why not I?

2 KEEPER Ay, but thou talk'st as if thou wert a king.

KING HENRY
60 Why so I am, in mind, and that's enough.

2 KEEPER But if thou be a king where is thy crown?

KING HENRY
My crown is in my heart, not on my head:
Not decked with diamonds and Indian stones,
Nor to be seen. My crown is called content,
65 A crown it is that seldom kings enjoy.

2 KEEPER
Well, if you be a king crowned with content,
Your crown content and you must be contented
To go along with us, for, as we think,
You are the king King Edward hath deposed;
70 And we his subjects sworn in all allegiance
Will apprehend you as his enemy.

KING HENRY
But did you never swear and break an oath?

2 KEEPER No, never such an oath, nor will not now.

KING HENRY
Where did you dwell when I was King of England?

75 2 KEEPER Here in this country, where we now remain.

KING HENRY I was anointed king at nine months old.
My father and my grandfather were kings,
And you were sworn true subjects unto me:
And tell me, then, have you not broke your oaths?

1 KEEPER
80 No, for we were subjects but while you were king.

KING HENRY
Why, am I dead? Do I not breathe a man?
Ah, simple men, you know not what you sware.
Look, as I blow this feather from my face,
And as the air blows it to me again,
85 Obeying with my wind when I do blow,
And yielding to another when it blows,
Commanded always by the greater gust,
Such is the lightness of you common men.
But do not break your oaths: for of that sin
90 My mild entreaty shall not make you guilty.
Go where you will, the King shall be commanded;
And be you kings: command, and I'll obey.

1 KEEPER
We are true subjects to the King, King Edward.

KING HENRY So would you be again to Henry,
95 If he were seated as King Edward is.

1 KEEPER
We charge you, in God's name and the King's,
To go with us unto the officers.

KING HENRY
In God's name lead; your King's name be obeyed,
And what God will, that let your King perform;
100 And what he will, I humbly yield unto. *Exeunt.*

3.2 *Enter* KING EDWARD, RICHARD, Duke OF
GLOUCESTER, GEORGE, Duke OF CLARENCE,
and the WIDOW, Lady Grey.

KING EDWARD
Brother of Gloucester, at Saint Albans field
This lady's husband, Sir Richard Grey, was slain,
His lands then seized on by the conqueror.
Her suit is now to repossess those lands,
5 Which we in justice cannot well deny,
Because in quarrel of the house of York
The worthy gentleman did lose his life.

RICHARD OF GLOUCESTER
Your highness shall do well to grant her suit:
It were dishonour to deny it her.

KING EDWARD
10 It were no less, but yet I'll make a pause.

RICHARD OF GLOUCESTER [*aside to George*]
Yea, is it so?
I see the lady hath a thing to grant,
Before the King will grant her humble suit.

GEORGE OF CLARENCE [*aside to Richard*]
He knows the game: how true he keeps the wind!

RICHARD OF GLOUCESTER [*aside to George*]
15 Silence!

KING EDWARD Widow, we will consider of your suit;
And come some other time to know our mind.

WIDOW Right gracious lord, I cannot brook delay.
May it please your highness to resolve me now,
20 And what your pleasure is shall satisfy me.

RICHARD OF GLOUCESTER [*aside to George*]
Ay, widow? Then I'll warrant you all your lands,

An if what pleases him shall pleasure you.
Fight closer, or good faith, you'll catch a blow.
GEORGE OF CLARENCE [*aside to Richard*]
I fear her not, unless she chance to fall.
RICHARD OF GLOUCESTER [*aside to George*]
God forbid that, for he'll take vantages.
KING EDWARD
How many children hast thou, widow, tell me?
GEORGE OF CLARENCE [*aside to Richard*]
I think he means to beg a child of her.
RICHARD OF GLOUCESTER [*aside to George*]
Nay, then whip me: he'll rather give her two.
WIDOW   Three, my most gracious lord.
RICHARD OF GLOUCESTER [*aside to George*]
You shall have four, if you'll be ruled by him.
KING EDWARD
'Twere pity they should lose their father's lands.
WIDOW   Be pitiful, dread lord, and grant it then.
KING EDWARD
Lords, give us leave; I'll try this widow's wit.
    [*George and Richard stand aside.*]
RICHARD OF GLOUCESTER [*aside to George*]
Ay, good leave have you, for you will have leave,
Till youth take leave and leave you to the crutch.
KING EDWARD
Now tell me, madam, do you love your children?
WIDOW   Ay, full as dearly as I love myself.
KING EDWARD
And would you not do much to do them good?
WIDOW   To do them good, I would sustain some harm.
KING EDWARD
Then get your husband's lands, to do them good.
WIDOW   Therefore I came unto your majesty.
KING EDWARD
I'll tell you how these lands are to be got.
WIDOW
So shall you bind me to your highness' service.
KING EDWARD
What service wilt thou do me, if I give them?
WIDOW   What you command, that rests in me to do.
KING EDWARD
But you will take exceptions to my boon.
WIDOW   No, gracious lord, except I cannot do it.
KING EDWARD
Ay, but thou canst do what I mean to ask.
WIDOW
Why, then I will do what your grace commands.
RICHARD OF GLOUCESTER [*aside to George*]
He plies her hard, and much rain wears the marble.
GEORGE OF CLARENCE [*aside to Richard*]
As red as fire! Nay, then her wax must melt.
WIDOW   Why stops my lord? Shall I not hear my task?
KING EDWARD   An easy task: 'tis but to love a king.
WIDOW
That's soon performed, because I am a subject.
KING EDWARD
Why then, thy husband's lands I freely give thee.

WIDOW
I take my leave with many thousand thanks.
RICHARD OF GLOUCESTER [*aside to George*]
The match is made; she seals it with a curtsy.
KING EDWARD
But stay thee, 'tis the fruits of love I mean.
WIDOW   The fruits of love I mean, my loving liege.
KING EDWARD   Ay, but I fear me, in another sense.   60
What love, think'st thou, I sue so much to get?
WIDOW
My love till death, my humble thanks, my prayers:
That love which virtue begs and virtue grants.
KING EDWARD
No, by my troth, I did not mean such love.
WIDOW
Why then, you mean not as I thought you did.   65
KING EDWARD
But now you partly may perceive my mind.
WIDOW   My mind will never grant what I perceive
Your highness aims at, if I aim aright.
KING EDWARD   To tell thee plain, I aim to lie with thee.
WIDOW   To tell you plain, I had rather lie in prison.   70
KING EDWARD
Why then, thou shalt not have thy husband's lands.
WIDOW   Why then, mine honesty shall be my dower,
For by that loss I will not purchase them.
KING EDWARD
Therein thou wrong'st thy children mightily.
WIDOW
Herein your highness wrongs both them and me.   75
But, mighty lord, this merry inclination
Accords not with the sadness of my suit.
Please you dismiss me either with ay or no.
KING EDWARD   Ay, if thou wilt say 'ay' to my request;
No, if thou dost say 'no' to my demand.   80
WIDOW   Then 'no', my lord; my suit is at an end.
RICHARD OF GLOUCESTER [*aside to George*]
The widow likes him not: she knits her brows.
GEORGE OF CLARENCE [*aside to Richard*]
He is the bluntest wooer in Christendom.
KING EDWARD [*aside*]
Her looks doth argue her replete with modesty,
Her words doth show her wit incomparable;   85
All her perfections challenge sovereignty:
One way or other, she is for a king,
And she shall be my love, or else my queen. –
Say that King Edward take thee for his queen?
WIDOW   'Tis better said than done, my gracious lord: 90
I am a subject fit to jest withal,
But far unfit to be a sovereign.
KING EDWARD
Sweet widow, by my state I swear to thee,
I speak no more than what my soul intends,
And that is to enjoy thee for my love.   95
WIDOW   And that is more than I will yield unto.
I know I am too mean to be your queen
And yet too good to be your concubine.

KING EDWARD
  You cavil, widow: I did mean my queen.

WIDOW
100   'Twill grieve your grace my sons should call you father.

KING EDWARD
  No more than when my daughters call thee mother.
  Thou art a widow and thou hast some children,
  And, by God's mother, I, being but a bachelor,
  Have other some. Why, 'tis a happy thing
105   To be the father unto many sons.
  Answer no more, for thou shalt be my queen.

RICHARD OF GLOUCESTER [*aside to George*]
  The ghostly father now hath done his shrift.

GEORGE OF CLARENCE [*aside to Richard*]
  When he was made a shriver, 'twas for shift.

KING EDWARD
  Brothers, you muse what chat we two have had.

RICHARD OF GLOUCESTER
110   The widow likes it not, for she looks very sad.

KING EDWARD
  You'd think it strange if I should marry her.

GEORGE OF CLARENCE   To who, my lord?

KING EDWARD   Why, Clarence, to myself.

RICHARD OF GLOUCESTER
  That would be ten days' wonder at the least.

GEORGE OF CLARENCE
  That's a day longer than a wonder lasts.

RICHARD OF GLOUCESTER
115   By so much is the wonder in extremes.

KING EDWARD
  Well, jest on, brothers; I can tell you both,
  Her suit is granted for her husband's lands.

Enter a Nobleman.

NOBLEMAN
  My gracious lord, Henry, your foe, is taken
  And brought your prisoner to your palace gate.

KING EDWARD
120   See that he be conveyed unto the Tower,
  And go we, brothers, to the man that took him
  To question of his apprehension.
  Widow, go you along; lords, use her honourably.
                     Exeunt all but Richard.

RICHARD OF GLOUCESTER
  Ay, Edward will use women honourably.
125   Would he were wasted, marrow, bones and all,
  That from his loins no hopeful branch may spring
  To cross me from the golden time I look for.
  And yet, between my soul's desire and me,
  The lustful Edward's title buried,
130   Is Clarence, Henry and his son, young Edward,
  And all the unlooked-for issue of their bodies
  To take their rooms, ere I can place myself.
  A cold premeditation for my purpose.
  Why then, I do but dream on sovereignty
135   Like one that stands upon a promontory
  And spies a far-off shore where he would tread,

Wishing his foot were equal with his eye,
And chides the sea that sunders him from thence,
Saying he'll lade it dry to have his way:
So do I wish the crown, being so far off,   140
And so I chide the means that keeps me from it,
And so, I say, I'll cut the causes off,
Flattering me with impossibilities.
My eye's too quick, my heart o'erweens too much,
Unless my hand and strength could equal them.   145
Well, say there is no kingdom then for Richard:
What other pleasure can the world afford?
I'll make my heaven in a lady's lap,
And deck my body in gay ornaments
And witch sweet ladies with my words and looks.   150
O miserable thought, and more unlikely
Than to accomplish twenty golden crowns!
Why, Love forswore me in my mother's womb,
And, for I should not deal in her soft laws,
She did corrupt frail Nature with some bribe   155
To shrink mine arm up like a withered shrub;
To make an envious mountain on my back,
Where sits deformity to mock my body;
To shape my legs of an unequal size;
To disproportion me in every part,   160
Like to a chaos or an unlicked bear whelp,
That carries no impression like the dam.
And am I then a man to be beloved?
O monstrous fault to harbour such a thought!
Then, since this earth affords no joy to me   165
But to command, to check, to o'erbear such
As are of better person than myself,
I'll make my heaven to dream upon the crown
And, whiles I live, t'account this world but hell
Until my misshaped trunk that bears this head   170
Be round impaled with a glorious crown.
And yet I know not how to get the crown,
For many lives stand between me and home,
And I, like one lost in a thorny wood,
That rents the thorns and is rent with the thorns,   175
Seeking a way and straying from the way,
Not knowing how to find the open air,
But toiling desperately to find it out,
Torment myself to catch the English crown:
And from that torment I will free myself,   180
Or hew my way out with a bloody axe.
Why, I can smile, and murder whiles I smile,
And cry 'Content!' to that which grieves my heart,
And wet my cheeks with artificial tears,
And frame my face to all occasions.   185
I'll drown more sailors than the mermaid shall,
I'll slay more gazers than the basilisk,
I'll play the orator as well as Nestor,
Deceive more slyly than Ulysses could,
And, like a Sinon, take another Troy.   190
I can add colours to the chameleon,
Change shapes with Proteus for advantages,
And set the murderous Machiavel to school.

Can I do this, and cannot get a crown?
5 Tut, were it farther off, I'll pluck it down.   *Exit.*

3.3   *Flourish. Enter* LEWIS, *the French King;*
his sister, the LADY BONA; *and his Admiral,*
called Bourbon; PRINCE EDWARD,
QUEEN MARGARET *and the* Earl of OXFORD.
Lewis sits and riseth up again.

KING LEWIS
Fair Queen of England, worthy Margaret,
Sit down with us. It ill befits thy state
And birth that thou shouldst stand while Lewis doth
    sit.
QUEEN MARGARET
No, mighty King of France: now Margaret
Must strike her sail and learn awhile to serve
Where kings command. I was, I must confess,
Great Albion's Queen in former golden days,
But now mischance hath trod my title down
And with dishonour laid me on the ground,
Where I must take like seat unto my fortune
And to my humble seat conform myself.
KING LEWIS
Why say, fair Queen, whence springs this deep
    despair?
QUEEN MARGARET
From such a cause as fills mine eyes with tears
And stops my tongue, while heart is drowned in cares.
KING LEWIS   Whate'er it be, be thou still like thyself
And sit thee by our side.   [*Seats her by him.*]
                Yield not thy neck
To Fortune's yoke, but let thy dauntless mind
Still ride in triumph over all mischance.
Be plain, Queen Margaret, and tell thy grief:
It shall be eased, if France can yield relief.
QUEEN MARGARET
Those gracious words revive my drooping thoughts
And give my tongue-tied sorrows leave to speak.
Now therefore be it known to noble Lewis
That Henry, sole possessor of my love,
Is, of a king, become a banished man
And forced to live in Scotland a forlorn;
While proud ambitious Edward, Duke of York,
Usurps the regal title and the seat
Of England's true-anointed lawful King.
This is the cause that I, poor Margaret,
With this my son, Prince Edward, Henry's heir,
Am come to crave thy just and lawful aid.
An if thou fail us, all our hope is done.
Scotland hath will to help, but cannot help;
Our people and our peers are both misled,
Our treasure seized, our soldiers put to flight,
And, as thou seest, ourselves in heavy plight.
KING LEWIS
Renowned Queen, with patience calm the storm
While we bethink a means to break it off.

QUEEN MARGARET
The more we stay, the stronger grows our foe.   40
KING LEWIS
The more I stay, the more I'll succour thee.
QUEEN MARGARET
O, but impatience waiteth on true sorrow.

          Enter WARWICK.

And see where comes the breeder of my sorrow.
KING LEWIS
What's he approacheth boldly to our presence?
QUEEN MARGARET
Our Earl of Warwick, Edward's greatest friend.   45
KING LEWIS
Welcome, brave Warwick. What brings thee to
    France?
    [*He descends. She ariseth.*]
QUEEN MARGARET
Ay, now begins a second storm to rise,
For this is he that moves both wind and tide.
WARWICK   From worthy Edward, King of Albion,
My lord and sovereign and thy vowed friend,   50
I come in kindness and unfeigned love,
First, to do greetings to thy royal person,
And then to crave a league of amity,
And, lastly to confirm that amity
With nuptial knot, if thou vouchsafe to grant   55
That virtuous Lady Bona, thy fair sister,
To England's King in lawful marriage.
QUEEN MARGARET
If that go forward, Henry's hope is done.
WARWICK [*speaking to Lady Bona*]
And, gracious madam, in our King's behalf,
I am commanded, with your leave and favour,   60
Humbly to kiss your hand, and with my tongue
To tell the passion of my sovereign's heart,
Where Fame, late ent'ring at his heedful ears,
Hath placed thy beauty's image and thy virtue.
QUEEN MARGARET
King Lewis and Lady Bona, hear me speak   65
Before you answer Warwick. His demand
Springs not from Edward's well-meant honest love
But from deceit, bred by necessity:
For how can tyrants safely govern home
Unless abroad they purchase great alliance?   70
To prove him tyrant, this reason may suffice:
That Henry liveth still; but were he dead,
Yet here Prince Edward stands, King Henry's son.
Look, therefore, Lewis, that by this league and
    marriage
Thou draw not on thy danger and dishonour,   75
For though usurpers sway the rule awhile,
Yet heavens are just, and Time suppresseth wrongs.
WARWICK   Injurious Margaret.
PRINCE EDWARD   And why not 'Queen'?
WARWICK   Because thy father Henry did usurp,
And thou no more art prince than she is queen.   80

OXFORD

    Then Warwick disannuls great John of Gaunt,

    Which did subdue the greatest part of Spain;

    And after John of Gaunt, Henry the Fourth,

    Whose wisdom was a mirror to the wisest;

85   And after that wise prince, Henry the Fifth,

    Who by his prowess conquered all France:

    From these, our Henry lineally descends.

WARWICK

    Oxford, how haps it in this smooth discourse

    You told not how Henry the Sixth hath lost

90   All that which Henry the Fifth had gotten?

    Methinks these peers of France should smile at that.

    But, for the rest: you tell a pedigree

    Of threescore and two years, a silly time

    To make prescription for a kingdom's worth.

OXFORD

95   Why, Warwick, canst thou speak against thy liege

    Whom thou obeyed'st six and thirty years

    And not bewray thy treason with a blush?

WARWICK   Can Oxford, that did ever fence the right,

    Now buckler falsehood with a pedigree?

100   For shame, leave Henry and call Edward king.

OXFORD   Call him my king by whose injurious doom

    My elder brother, the lord Aubrey Vere,

    Was done to death? And more than so, my father,

    Even in the downfall of his mellowed years

105   When nature brought him to the door of death?

    No, Warwick, no: while life upholds this arm,

    This arm upholds the house of Lancaster.

WARWICK   And I the house of York.

KING LEWIS

    Queen Margaret, Prince Edward and Oxford,

110   Vouchsafe at our request to stand aside

    While I use further conference with Warwick.

        [*They stand aloof.*]

QUEEN MARGARET

    Heavens grant that Warwick's words bewitch him not.

KING LEWIS

    Now, Warwick, tell me, even upon thy conscience,

    Is Edward your true king? For I were loath

115   To link with him that were not lawful chosen.

WARWICK

    Thereon I pawn my credit and mine honour.

KING LEWIS   But is he gracious in the people's eye?

WARWICK   The more that Henry was unfortunate.

KING LEWIS   Then further: all dissembling set aside,

120   Tell me for truth the measure of his love

    Unto our sister Bona.

WARWICK   Such it seems

    As may beseem a monarch like himself.

    Myself have often heard him say and swear

    That this his love was an eternal plant

125   Whereof the root was fixed in virtue's ground,

    The leaves and fruit maintained with beauty's sun,

    Exempt from envy, but not from disdain,

    Unless the Lady Bona quit his pain.

KING LEWIS   Now, sister, let us hear your firm resolve.

LADY BONA   Your grant or your denial shall be mine.   130

    [*Speaks to Warwick.*] Yet I confess that often ere this

        day,

    When I have heard your King's desert recounted,

    Mine ear hath tempted judgement to desire.

KING LEWIS

    Then, Warwick, thus: our sister shall be Edward's.

    And now forthwith shall articles be drawn   135

    Touching the jointure that your King must make,

    Which with her dowry shall be counterpoised. –

    Draw near, Queen Margaret, and be a witness

    That Bona shall be wife to the English King.

PRINCE EDWARD

    To Edward, but not to the English King.   140

QUEEN MARGARET

    Deceitful Warwick, it was thy device

    By this alliance to make void my suit.

    Before thy coming, Lewis was Henry's friend.

KING LEWIS   And still is friend to him and Margaret.

    But if your title to the crown be weak,   145

    As may appear by Edward's good success,

    Then 'tis but reason that I be released

    From giving aid, which late I promised.

    Yet shall you have all kindness at my hand

    That your estate requires and mine can yield.   150

WARWICK   Henry now lives in Scotland at his ease,

    Where, having nothing, nothing can he lose.

    And as for you yourself, our quondam Queen,

    You have a father able to maintain you,

    And better 'twere you troubled him than France.   155

QUEEN MARGARET

    Peace, impudent and shameless Warwick,

    Proud setter-up and puller-down of kings!

    I will not hence till with my talk and tears,

    Both full of truth, I make King Lewis behold

    Thy sly conveyance and thy lord's false love,   160

    For both of you are birds of selfsame feather.

        [*Post blowing a horn within*]

KING LEWIS   Warwick, this is some post to us or thee.

Enter the Post.

POST [*Speaks to Warwick.*]

    My lord ambassador, these letters are for you,

    Sent from your brother, Marquess Montague.

    [*to Lewis*] These from our King unto your majesty.   165

    [*to Margaret*] And, madam, these for you; from whom,

        I know not.   [*They all read their letters.*]

OXFORD   I like it well that our fair Queen and mistress

    Smiles at her news, while Warwick frowns at his.

PRINCE EDWARD

    Nay, mark how Lewis stamps as he were nettled.

    I hope all's for the best.   170

KING LEWIS

    Warwick, what are thy news? And yours, fair Queen?

QUEEN MARGARET

    Mine, such as fill my heart with unhoped joys.

WARWICK   Mine, full of sorrow and heart's discontent.

KING LEWIS

What? Has your King married the Lady Grey,

175   And now, to soothe your forgery and his,
Sends me a paper to persuade me patience?
Is this th'alliance that he seeks with France?
Dare he presume to scorn us in this manner?

QUEEN MARGARET

I told your majesty as much before:

180   This proveth Edward's love and Warwick's honesty.

WARWICK

King Lewis, I here protest, in sight of heaven
And by the hope I have of heavenly bliss,
That I am clear from this misdeed of Edward's –
No more my King, for he dishonours me;

185   But most himself, if he could see his shame.
Did I forget that by the house of York
My father came untimely to his death?
Did I let pass th'abuse done to my niece?
Did I impale him with the regal crown?

190   Did I put Henry from his native right?
And am I guerdoned at the last with shame?
Shame on himself, for my desert is honour!
And, to repair my honour lost for him,
I here renounce him and return to Henry.

195   My noble Queen, let former grudges pass
And henceforth I am thy true servitor.
I will revenge his wrong to Lady Bona
And replant Henry in his former state.

QUEEN MARGARET

Warwick, these words have turned my hate to love,

200   And I forgive and quite forget old faults,
And joy that thou becom'st King Henry's friend.

WARWICK

So much his friend, ay, his unfeigned friend,
That if King Lewis vouchsafe to furnish us
With some few bands of chosen soldiers,

205   I'll undertake to land them on our coast
And force the tyrant from his seat by war.
'Tis not his new-made bride shall succour him;
And as for Clarence, as my letters tell me,
He's very likely now to fall from him

210   For matching more for wanton lust than honour,
Or than for strength and safety of our country.

LADY BONA   Dear brother, how shall Bona be revenged
But by thy help to this distressed Queen?

QUEEN MARGARET

Renowned prince, how shall poor Henry live

215   Unless thou rescue him from foul despair?

LADY BONA

My quarrel and this English Queen's are one.

WARWICK   And mine, fair Lady Bona, joins with yours.

KING LEWIS

And mine with hers, and thine, and Margaret's.
Therefore, at last, I firmly am resolved

220   You shall have aid.

QUEEN MARGARET

Let me give humble thanks for all at once.

KING LEWIS

Then, England's messenger, return in post
And tell false Edward, thy supposed king,
That Lewis of France is sending over masquers

225   To revel it with him and his new bride.
Thou seest what's passed; go fear thy King withal.

LADY BONA

Tell him in hope he'll prove a widower shortly
I wear the willow garland for his sake.

QUEEN MARGARET

Tell him my mourning weeds are laid aside,

230   And I am ready to put armour on.

WARWICK

Tell him from me that he hath done me wrong,
And therefore I'll uncrown him ere't be long.
There's thy reward; be gone.   *Exit Post.*

KING LEWIS   But, Warwick,
Thou and Oxford with five thousand men

235   Shall cross the seas and bid false Edward battle;
And, as occasion serves, this noble Queen
And Prince shall follow with a fresh supply.
Yet, ere thou go, but answer me one doubt:
What pledge have we of thy firm loyalty?

WARWICK   This shall assure my constant loyalty: 240
That, if our Queen and this young Prince agree,
I'll join mine eldest daughter and my joy
To him forthwith in holy wedlock bands.

QUEEN MARGARET

Yes, I agree, and thank you for your motion.

245   Son Edward, she is fair and virtuous;
Therefore, delay not: give thy hand to Warwick,
And, with thy hand, thy faith irrevocable
That only Warwick's daughter shall be thine.

PRINCE EDWARD

Yes, I accept her, for she well deserves it;

250   And here, to pledge my vow, I give my hand.
     [*Gives his hand to Warwick.*]

KING LEWIS

Why stay we now? These soldiers shall be levied,
And thou, Lord Bourbon, our High Admiral,
Shall waft them over with our royal fleet.
I long till Edward fall by war's mischance

255   For mocking marriage with a dame of France.
                    Exeunt all but Warwick.

WARWICK   I came from Edward as ambassador,
But I return his sworn and mortal foe:
Matter of marriage was the charge he gave me,
But dreadful war shall answer his demand.

260   Had he none else to make a stale but me?
Then none but I shall turn his jest to sorrow.
I was the chief that raised him to the crown,
And I'll be chief to bring him down again;
Not that I pity Henry's misery,

265   But seek revenge on Edward's mockery   *Exit.*

4.1 *Enter* RICHARD OF GLOUCESTER,
GEORGE OF CLARENCE, THIRD DUKE of
Somerset *and* MONTAGUE.

RICHARD OF GLOUCESTER
Now tell me, brother Clarence, what think you
Of this new marriage with the Lady Grey?
Hath not our brother made a worthy choice?
GEORGE OF CLARENCE
Alas, you know, 'tis far from hence to France;
5 How could he stay till Warwick made return?
THIRD DUKE   My lords, forbear this talk;
Here comes the King.

Flourish. Enter KING EDWARD, LADY GREY, *now*
Queen Elizabeth, *Pembroke, Stafford,* HASTINGS:
four stand on one side and four on the other.

RICHARD OF GLOUCESTER
                    And his well-chosen bride.
GEORGE OF CLARENCE
I mind to tell him plainly what I think.
KING EDWARD
Now, brother of Clarence, how like you our choice,
10 That you stand pensive, as half malcontent?
GEORGE OF CLARENCE
As well as Lewis of France, or the Earl of Warwick,
Which are so weak of courage and in judgement
That they'll take no offence at our abuse.
KING EDWARD
Suppose they take offence without a cause:
15 They are but Lewis and Warwick; I am Edward,
Your King and Warwick's, and must have my will.
RICHARD OF GLOUCESTER
And shall have your will, because our King;
Yet hasty marriage seldom proveth well.
KING EDWARD
Yea, brother Richard, are you offended too?
20 RICHARD OF GLOUCESTER   Not I, no!
God forbid that I should wish them severed,
Whom God hath joined together! Ay, and 'twere pity
To sunder them that yoke so well together.
KING EDWARD
Setting your scorns and your mislike aside,
25 Tell me some reason why the Lady Grey
Should not become my wife and England's queen?
And you too, Somerset and Montague,
Speak freely what you think.
GEORGE OF CLARENCE
Then this is mine opinion: that King Lewis
30 Becomes your enemy for mocking him
About the marriage of the Lady Bona.
RICHARD OF GLOUCESTER
And Warwick, doing what you gave in charge,
Is now dishonoured by this new marriage.
KING EDWARD
What if both Lewis and Warwick be appeased
35 By such invention as I can devise?

MONTAGUE
Yet to have joined with France in such alliance
Would more have strengthened this our
                    commonwealth
'Gainst foreign storms than any home-bred marriage.
HASTINGS   Why, knows not Montague that of itself
England is safe, if true within itself?   40
MONTAGUE
But the safer when 'tis backed with France.
HASTINGS
'Tis better using France than trusting France:
Let us be backed with God and with the seas,
Which he hath given for fence impregnable,
And with their helps only defend ourselves.   45
In them, and in ourselves, our safety lies.
GEORGE OF CLARENCE
For this one speech, Lord Hastings well deserves
To have the heir of the Lord Hungerford.
KING EDWARD
Ay, what of that? It was my will and grant,
And for this once my will shall stand for law.   50
RICHARD OF GLOUCESTER
And yet methinks your grace hath not done well
To give the heir and daughter of Lord Scales
Unto the brother of your loving bride.
She better would have fitted me, or Clarence;
But in your bride you bury brotherhood.   55
GEORGE OF CLARENCE
Or else you would not have bestowed the heir
Of the Lord Bonville on your new wife's son,
And leave your brothers to go speed elsewhere.
KING EDWARD   Alas, poor Clarence, is it for a wife
That thou art malcontent? I will provide thee.   60
GEORGE OF CLARENCE
In choosing for yourself, you showed your
                    judgement,
Which being shallow, you shall give me leave
To play the broker in mine own behalf.
And, to that end, I shortly mind to leave you.
KING EDWARD
Leave me, or tarry, Edward will be king   65
And not be tied unto his brother's will.
LADY GREY   My lords, before it pleased his majesty
To raise my state to title of a queen,
Do me but right, and you must all confess
That I was not ignoble of descent,   70
And meaner than myself have had like fortune.
But as this title honours me and mine,
So your dislikes, to whom I would be pleasing,
Doth cloud my joys with danger and with sorrow.
KING EDWARD
My love, forbear to fawn upon their frowns.   75
What danger or what sorrow can befall thee
So long as Edward is thy constant friend
And their true sovereign, whom they must obey?
Nay, whom they shall obey, and love thee too,
Unless they seek for hatred at my hands;   80

672

Which if they do, yet will I keep thee safe,
And they shall feel the vengeance of my wrath.
RICHARD OF GLOUCESTER [*aside*]
  I hear, yet say not much, but think the more.

Enter a Post.

KING EDWARD
  Now, messenger, what letters, or what news
  From France?
POST   My sovereign liege, no letters, and few words,
  But such as I without your special pardon
  Dare not relate.
KING EDWARD
  Go to, we pardon thee. Therefore, in brief,
  Tell me their words as near as thou canst guess
    them.
  What answer makes King Lewis unto our letters?
POST   At my depart, these were his very words:
  'Go tell false Edward, thy supposed king,
  That Lewis of France is sending over masquers,
  To revel it with him and his new bride.'
KING EDWARD
  Is Lewis so brave? Belike he thinks me Henry.
  But what said Lady Bona to my marriage?
POST
  These were her words, uttered with mild disdain:
  'Tell him, in hope he'll prove a widower shortly,
  I'll wear the willow garland for his sake.'
KING EDWARD
  I blame not her; she could say little less;
  She had the wrong. But what said Henry's Queen?
  For I have heard that she was there in place.
POST
  'Tell him', quoth she, 'my mourning weeds are done,
  And I am ready to put armour on.'
KING EDWARD   Belike she minds to play the Amazon.
  But what said Warwick to these injuries?
POST   He, more incensed against your majesty
  Than all the rest, discharged me with these words:
  'Tell him from me that he hath done me wrong,
  And therefore I'll uncrown him ere't be long.'
KING EDWARD
  Ha! Durst the traitor breathe out so proud words?
  Well, I will arm me, being thus forewarned.
  They shall have wars and pay for their presumption.
  But say, is Warwick friends with Margaret?
POST
  Ay, gracious sovereign, they are so linked in
    friendship
  That young Prince Edward marries Warwick's
    daughter.
GEORGE OF CLARENCE [*aside*]
  Belike, the elder; Clarence will have the younger. –
  Now, brother king, farewell, and sit you fast,
  For I will hence to Warwick's other daughter,
  That, though I want a kingdom, yet in marriage
  I may not prove inferior to yourself.

You that love me and Warwick, follow me.
          Exit Clarence, and Somerset follows.
RICHARD OF GLOUCESTER [*aside*]
  Not I. My thoughts aim at a further matter:
  I stay not for the love of Edward, but the crown.   125
KING EDWARD
  Clarence and Somerset both gone to Warwick?
  Yet am I armed against the worst can happen,
  And haste is needful in this desp'rate case.
  Pembroke and Stafford, you in our behalf
  Go levy men and make prepare for war.   130
  They are already, or quickly will be, landed.
  Myself in person will straight follow you.
              Exeunt Pembroke and Stafford.
  But ere I go, Hastings and Montague,
  Resolve my doubt. You twain, of all the rest,
  Are near to Warwick, by blood and by alliance.   135
  Tell me if you love Warwick more than me.
  If it be so, then both depart to him;
  I rather wish you foes than hollow friends.
  But if you mind to hold your true obedience,
  Give me assurance with some friendly vow,   140
  That I may never have you in suspect.
MONTAGUE
  So God help Montague, as he proves true.
HASTINGS
  And Hastings, as he favours Edward's cause.
KING EDWARD
  Now, brother Richard, will you stand by us?
RICHARD OF GLOUCESTER
  Ay, in despite of all that shall withstand you.   145
KING EDWARD   Why so. Then am I sure of victory.
  Now therefore let us hence, and lose no hour
  Till we meet Warwick, with his foreign power.
                                      Exeunt.

4.2   *Enter* WARWICK *and* OXFORD *in England,*
          with French Soldiers.

WARWICK   Trust me, my lord, all hitherto goes well.
  The common people by numbers swarm to us.

Enter GEORGE OF CLARENCE *and* SOMERSET.

  But see where Somerset and Clarence comes.
  Speak suddenly, my lords, are we all friends?
GEORGE OF CLARENCE   Fear not that, my lord.   5
WARWICK
  Then, gentle Clarence, welcome unto Warwick.
  And welcome, Somerset. I hold it cowardice
  To rest mistrustful where a noble heart
  Hath pawned an open hand in sign of love;
  Else might I think that Clarence, Edward's brother, 10
  Were but a feigned friend to our proceedings.
  But welcome, sweet Clarence, my daughter shall be
    thine.
  And now what rests but in night's coverture,
  Thy brother being carelessly encamped,

His soldiers lurking in the towns about,
And but attended by a simple guard,
We may surprise and take him at our pleasure?
Our scouts have found the adventure very easy;
That as Ulysses and stout Diomed
With sleight and manhood stole to Rhesus' tents
And brought from thence the Thracian fatal steeds,
So we, well covered with the night's black mantle,
At unawares may beat down Edward's guard
And seize himself. I say not 'slaughter him',
For I intend but only to surprise him.
You that will follow me to this attempt,
Applaud the name of Henry with your leader.
                              [*They all cry* 'Henry!']
Why then, let's on our way in silent sort,
For Warwick and his friends, God and Saint George!
                              Exeunt.

4.3 *Enter three* Watchmen *to guard the King's tent.*

1 WATCHMAN
Come on, my masters, each man take his stand.
The King by this is set him down to sleep.
2 WATCHMAN   What, will he not to bed?
1 WATCHMAN
Why, no, for he hath made a solemn vow
Never to lie and take his natural rest
Till Warwick or himself be quite suppressed.
2 WATCHMAN   Tomorrow, then, belike shall be the day,
If Warwick be so near as men report.
3 WATCHMAN   But say, I pray, what nobleman is that,
That with the King here resteth in his tent?
1 WATCHMAN
'Tis the Lord Hastings, the King's chiefest friend.
3 WATCHMAN
O, is it so? But why commands the King
That his chief followers lodge in towns about him,
While he himself keeps in the cold field?
2 WATCHMAN
'Tis the more honour, because more dangerous.
3 WATCHMAN   Ay but give me worship and quietness;
I like it better than a dangerous honour.
If Warwick knew in what estate he stands,
'Tis to be doubted he would waken him.
1 WATCHMAN
Unless our halberds did shut up his passage.
2 WATCHMAN
Ay, wherefore else guard we his royal tent
But to defend his person from night-foes?

Enter WARWICK, GEORGE OF CLARENCE, OXFORD,
    SOMERSET *and French Soldiers, silent all.*

WARWICK
This is his tent, and see where stand his guard.
Courage, my masters; honour now or never.
But follow me, and Edward shall be ours.
1 WATCHMAN   Who goes there?

2 WATCHMAN   Stay or thou diest!
Warwick and the rest cry all 'A Warwick! A Warwick!'
and set upon the guard, who fly, crying 'Arm! Arm!',
                    Warwick and the rest following them.

The drum playing and trumpet sounding, enter
    WARWICK, SOMERSET *and the rest, bringing*
    KING EDWARD *out in his gown, sitting in a chair.*
    RICHARD OF GLOUCESTER *and* HASTINGS
                    fly over the stage.

SOMERSET   What are they that fly there?
WARWICK   Richard and Hastings. Let them go. Here is
The Duke.
KING EDWARD
                    The Duke? Why, Warwick, when we parted,
Thou called'st me King.
WARWICK   Ay, but the case is altered.
When you disgraced me in my embassade,
Then I degraded you from being King
And come now to create you Duke of York.
Alas, how should you govern any kingdom,
That know not how to use ambassadors,
Nor how to be contented with one wife,
Nor how to use your brothers brotherly,
Nor how to study for the people's welfare,
Nor how to shroud yourself from enemies?
KING EDWARD
Yea, brother of Clarence, art thou here too?
Nay, then I see that Edward needs must down.
Yet, Warwick, in despite of all mischance,
Of thee thyself and all thy complices,
Edward will always bear himself as King.
Though Fortune's malice overthrow my state,
My mind exceeds the compass of her wheel.
WARWICK
Then, for his mind, be Edward England's King,
    [*Takes off his crown.*]
But Henry now shall wear the English crown,
And be true king indeed, thou but the shadow.
My Lord of Somerset, at my request,
See that, forthwith, Duke Edward be conveyed
Unto my brother, Archbishop of York.
When I have fought with Pembroke and his fellows,
I'll follow you, and tell what answer
Lewis and the Lady Bona send to him.
Now for a while farewell, good Duke of York.
    [*They lead him out forcibly.*]
KING EDWARD
What fates impose, that men must needs abide;
It boots not to resist both wind and tide.
                    Exeunt King Edward, Somerset and Soldiers.
OXFORD   What now remains, my lords, for us to do,
But march to London with our soldiers?
WARWICK   Ay, that's the first thing that we have to do,
To free King Henry from imprisonment
And see him seated in the regal throne.   *Exeunt.*

4.4   *Enter* RIVERS *and* LADY GREY, *now*
Queen Elizabeth.

RIVERS
    Madam, what makes in you this sudden change?
LADY GREY   Why, brother Rivers, are you yet to learn
    What late misfortune is befallen King Edward?
RIVERS
    What? Loss of some pitched battle against Warwick?
LADY GREY   No, but the loss of his own royal person.
RIVERS   Then is my sovereign slain?
LADY GREY   Ay, almost slain, for he is taken prisoner,
    Either betrayed by falsehood of his guard,
    Or by his foe surprised at unawares.
    And, as I further have to understand,   10
    Is new committed to the Bishop of York,
    Fell Warwick's brother and by that our foe.
RIVERS   These news I must confess are full of grief,
    Yet, gracious madam, bear it as you may;
    Warwick may lose, that now hath won the day.   15
LADY GREY
    Till then fair hope must hinder life's decay,
    And I the rather wean me from despair
    For love of Edward's offspring in my womb.
    This is it that makes me bridle passion
    And bear with mildness my misfortune's cross.   20
    Ay, ay, for this I draw in many a tear
    And stop the rising of blood-sucking sighs,
    Lest with my sighs or tears I blast or drown
    King Edward's fruit, true heir to th'English crown.
RIVERS   But madam, where is Warwick then become?   25
LADY GREY
    I am informed that he comes towards London
    To set the crown once more on Henry's head.
    Guess thou the rest: King Edward's friends must down.
    But to prevent the tyrant's violence –
    For trust not him that hath once broken faith –   30
    I'll hence forthwith unto the sanctuary,
    To save at least the heir of Edward's right.
    There shall I rest secure from force and fraud.
    Come, therefore, let us fly, while we may fly;
    If Warwick take us, we are sure to die.   *Exeunt.*   35

4.5   *Enter* RICHARD OF GLOUCESTER,
Lord HASTINGS *and Sir William Stanley,*
with Soldiers.

RICHARD OF GLOUCESTER
    Now, my Lord Hastings and Sir William Stanley,
    Leave off to wonder why I drew you hither,
    Into this chiefest thicket of the park.
    Thus stands the case: you know our King, my brother,
    Is prisoner to the bishop here, at whose hands   5
    He hath good usage and great liberty,
    And, often but attended with weak guard,
    Comes hunting this way to disport himself.
    I have advertised him by secret means,

    That, if about this hour he make this way   10
    Under the colour of his usual game,
    He shall here find his friends, with horse and men,
    To set him free from his captivity.

        Enter KING EDWARD *and a* Huntsman *with him.*

HUNTSMAN
    This way, my lord, for this way lies the game.
KING EDWARD
    Nay, this way, man. See where the huntsmen stand.   15
    Now, brother of Gloucester, Lord Hastings and the
        rest,
    Stand you thus close to steal the bishop's deer?
RICHARD OF GLOUCESTER
    Brother, the time and case requireth haste.
    Your horse stands ready at the park corner.
KING EDWARD   But whither shall we then?   20
HASTINGS
    To Lynn, my lord, and shipped from thence to
        Flanders.
RICHARD OF GLOUCESTER
    Well guessed, believe me, for that was my meaning.
KING EDWARD   Stanley, I will requite thy forwardness.
RICHARD OF GLOUCESTER
    But wherefore stay we? 'Tis no time to talk.
KING EDWARD
    Huntsman, what sayst thou? Wilt thou go along?   25
HUNTSMAN   Better do so than tarry and be hanged.
RICHARD OF GLOUCESTER
    Come then, away; let's ha' no more ado.
KING EDWARD
    Bishop, farewell; shield thee from Warwick's frown,
    And pray that I may repossess the crown.   *Exeunt.*

4.6   *Flourish. Enter* KING HENRY *the Sixth,*
GEORGE OF CLARENCE, WARWICK,
SOMERSET, *young Henry of Richmond,*
OXFORD, MONTAGUE *and* Lieutenant.

KING HENRY
    Master Lieutenant, now that God and friends
    Have shaken Edward from the regal seat
    And turned my captive state to liberty,
    My fear to hope, my sorrows unto joys
    At our enlargement, what are thy due fees?   5
LIEUTENANT
    Subjects may challenge nothing of their sov'reigns,
    But if an humble prayer may prevail,
    I then crave pardon of your majesty.
KING HENRY   For what, lieutenant, for well using me?
    Nay, be thou sure, I'll well requite thy kindness,   10
    For that it made my imprisonment a pleasure.
    Ay, such a pleasure as encaged birds
    Conceive, when after many moody thoughts,
    At last, by notes of household harmony,
    They quite forget their loss of liberty.   15
    But Warwick, after God thou set'st me free,

And chiefly, therefore, I thank God and thee.
He was the author, thou the instrument.
Therefore, that I may conquer Fortune's spite

20 By living low where Fortune cannot hurt me,
And that the people of this blessed land
May not be punished with my thwarting stars,
Warwick, although my head still wear the crown,
I here resign my government to thee,

25 For thou art fortunate in all thy deeds.

WARWICK
Your grace hath still been famed for virtuous
And now may seem as wise as virtuous
By spying and avoiding Fortune's malice,
For few men rightly temper with the stars.

30 Yet, in this one thing let me blame your grace,
For choosing me when Clarence is in place.

GEORGE OF CLARENCE
No, Warwick, thou art worthy of the sway,
To whom the heavens in thy nativity
Adjudged an olive branch and laurel crown

35 As likely to be blest in peace and war.
And therefore I yield thee my free consent.

WARWICK   And I choose Clarence only for Protector.

KING HENRY
Warwick and Clarence, give me both your hands.
Now join your hands, and with your hands your
      hearts,

40 That no dissension hinder government.
I make you both Protectors of this land,
While I myself will lead a private life
And in devotion spend my latter days,
To sin's rebuke and my Creator's praise.

WARWICK

45 What answers Clarence to his sovereign's will?

GEORGE OF CLARENCE
That he consents, if Warwick yield consent;
For on thy fortune I repose myself.

WARWICK
Why then, though loath, yet must I be content.
We'll yoke together, like a double shadow

50 To Henry's body, and supply his place,
I mean, in bearing weight of government,
While he enjoys the honour and his ease.
And Clarence, now then it is more than needful
Forthwith that Edward be pronounced a traitor

55 And all his lands and goods be confiscate.

GEORGE OF CLARENCE
What else? And that succession be determined.

WARWICK   Ay, therein Clarence shall not want his part.

KING HENRY   But with the first of all your chief affairs
Let me entreat, for I command no more,

60 That Margaret your Queen and my son Edward
Be sent for, to return from France with speed.
For till I see them here, by doubtful fear
My joy of liberty is half eclipsed.

GEORGE OF CLARENCE
It shall be done, my sovereign, with all speed.

KING HENRY   My Lord of Somerset, what youth is that   65
Of whom you seem to have so tender care?

SOMERSET
My liege, it is young Henry, Earl of Richmond.

KING HENRY
Come hither, England's hope.
      [*Lays his hand on Richmond's head.*]
                              If secret powers
Suggest but truth to my divining thoughts,
This pretty lad will prove our country's bliss.   70
His looks are full of peaceful majesty,
His head by nature framed to wear a crown,
His hand to wield a sceptre, and himself
Likely in time to bless a regal throne.
Make much of him, my lords, for this is he   75
Must help you more than you are hurt by me.

                  Enter a Post.

WARWICK   What news, my friend?

POST   That Edward is escaped from your brother
And fled, as he hears since, to Burgundy.

WARWICK   Unsavoury news! But how made he escape?   80

POST
He was conveyed by Richard, Duke of Gloucester,
And the Lord Hastings, who attended him
In secret ambush on the forest side
And from the bishop's huntsmen rescued him,
For hunting was his daily exercise.   85

WARWICK   My brother was too careless of his charge.
But let us hence, my sovereign, to provide
A salve for any sore that may betide.
            Exeunt all but Somerset, Richmond and Oxford.

SOMERSET
My lord, I like not of this flight of Edward's,
For doubtless Burgundy will yield him help,   90
And we shall have more wars before't be long.
As Henry's late presaging prophecy
Did glad my heart with hope of this young Richmond,
So doth my heart misgive me, in these conflicts,
What may befall him to his harm and ours.   95
Therefore, Lord Oxford, to prevent the worst,
Forthwith we'll send him hence to Brittany,
Till storms be past of civil enmity.

OXFORD   Ay, for if Edward repossess the crown,
'Tis like that Richmond, with the rest, shall down.   100

SOMERSET   It shall be so: he shall to Brittany.
Come, therefore, let's about it speedily.   *Exeunt.*

4.7   *Flourish. Enter* KING EDWARD, RICHARD
      OF GLOUCESTER, HASTINGS *and Soldiers.*

KING EDWARD
Now, brother Richard, Lord Hastings, and the rest:
Yet thus far Fortune maketh us amends,
And says that once more I shall interchange
My waned state for Henry's regal crown.
Well have we passed, and now repassed, the seas,   5

And brought desired help from Burgundy.
What then remains, we being thus arrived
From Ravenspurgh Haven before the gates of York,
But that we enter as into our dukedom?
[*Hastings knocks.*]

RICHARD OF GLOUCESTER
The gates made fast? Brother, I like not this.
For many men that stumble at the threshold
Are well foretold that danger lurks within.

KING EDWARD
Tush, man, abodements must not now affright us.
By fair or foul means we must enter in,
For hither will our friends repair to us.

HASTINGS
My liege, I'll knock once more to summon them.
[*Knocks.*]

Enter on the walls the Mayor of York *and his brethren.*

MAYOR   My lords, we were forewarned of your coming,
And shut the gates for safety of ourselves,
For now we owe allegiance unto Henry.

KING EDWARD
But, master mayor, if Henry be your king,
Yet Edward, at the least, is Duke of York.

MAYOR   True, my good lord, I know you for no less.

KING EDWARD
Why, and I challenge nothing but my dukedom,
As being well content with that alone.

RICHARD OF GLOUCESTER [*aside*]
But when the fox hath once got in his nose,
He'll soon find means to make the body follow.

HASTINGS
Why, master mayor, why stand you in a doubt?
Open the gates, we are King Henry's friends.

MAYOR   Ay, say you so? The gates shall then be opened.
[*He descends with his brethren.*]

RICHARD OF GLOUCESTER
A wise stout captain, and soon persuaded.

HASTINGS
The good old man would fain that all were well,
So 'twere not long of him. But being entered,
I doubt not, I, but we shall soon persuade
Both him and all his brothers unto reason.

Enter the Mayor *and two Aldermen.*

KING EDWARD
So, master mayor, these gates must not be shut
But in the night or in the time of war.
What, fear not, man, but yield me up the keys.
[*Takes his keys.*]
For Edward will defend the town and thee,
And all those friends that deign to follow me.

March. Enter MONTGOMERY *with Drum and Soldiers.*

RICHARD OF GLOUCESTER
Brother, this is Sir John Montgomery,
Our trusty friend, unless I be deceived.

KING EDWARD
Welcome, Sir John; but why come you in arms?

MONTGOMERY
To help King Edward in his time of storm,
As every loyal subject ought to do.

KING EDWARD
Thanks, good Montgomery, but we now forget   45
Our title to the crown, and only claim
Our dukedom, till God please to send the rest.

MONTGOMERY
Then fare you well, for I will hence again.
I came to serve a king and not a duke.
Drummer, strike up, and let us march away.   50
[*The Drum begins to march.*]

KING EDWARD
Nay, stay, Sir John, awhile, and we'll debate
By what safe means the crown may be recovered.

MONTGOMERY
What talk you of debating? In few words,
If you'll not here proclaim yourself our king,
I'll leave you to your fortune and be gone   55
To keep them back that come to succour you.
Why shall we fight, if you pretend no title?

RICHARD OF GLOUCESTER
Why brother, wherefore stand you on nice points?

KING EDWARD
When we grow stronger, then we'll make our claim.
Till then 'tis wisdom to conceal our meaning.   60

HASTINGS
Away with scrupulous wit, now arms must rule.

RICHARD OF GLOUCESTER
And fearless minds climb soonest unto crowns.
Brother, we will proclaim you out of hand.
The bruit thereof will bring you many friends.

KING EDWARD   Then be it as you will, for 'tis my right,   65
And Henry but usurps the diadem.

MONTGOMERY
Ay, now my sovereign speaketh like himself,
And now will I be Edward's champion.

HASTINGS
Sound trumpet, Edward shall be here proclaimed.
Come, fellow soldier, make thou proclamation.   70
[*Flourish. Sound.*]

SOLDIER [*Reads.*]
Edward the Fourth, by the Grace of God,
King of England and France, and Lord of Ireland, etc.

MONTGOMERY
And whosoe'er gainsays King Edward's right,
By this I challenge him to single fight.
[*Throws down his gauntlet.*]

ALL   Long live Edward the Fourth!   75

KING EDWARD
Thanks, brave Montgomery, and thanks unto you all.
If fortune serve me, I'll requite this kindness.
Now, for this night, let's harbour here in York,
And when the morning sun shall raise his car
Above the border of this horizon,   80

We'll forward towards Warwick and his mates;
For well I wot that Henry is no soldier.
Ah, froward Clarence, how evil it beseems thee
To flatter Henry and forsake thy brother!
85   Yet, as we may, we'll meet both thee and Warwick.
Come on, brave soldiers, doubt not of the day,
And that once gotten, doubt not of large pay.   *Exeunt.*

4.8   *Flourish. Enter* KING HENRY, WARWICK,
       MONTAGUE, GEORGE OF CLARENCE,
       OXFORD *and* EXETER.

WARWICK   What counsel, lords? Edward from Belgia,
With hasty Germans and blunt Hollanders,
Hath passed in safety through the narrow seas
And with his troops doth march amain to London,
5   And many giddy people flock to him.
KING HENRY   Let's levy men and beat him back again.
GEORGE OF CLARENCE
A little fire is quickly trodden out,
Which, being suffered, rivers cannot quench.
WARWICK   In Warwickshire I have true-hearted friends,
10   Not mutinous in peace, yet bold in war.
Those will I muster up, and thou, son Clarence,
Shalt stir up in Suffolk, Norfolk and in Kent,
The knights and gentlemen to come with thee.
Thou, brother Montague, in Buckingham,
15   Northampton and in Leicestershire shalt find
Men well inclined to hear what thou command'st.
And thou, brave Oxford, wondrous well beloved
In Oxfordshire, shalt muster up thy friends.
My sovereign, with the loving citizens,
20   Like to his island girt in with the ocean
Or modest Dian circled with her nymphs,
Shall rest in London till we come to him.
Fair lords, take leave, and stand not to reply.
Farewell, my sovereign.
KING HENRY
25   Farewell, my Hector, and my Troy's true hope.
GEORGE OF CLARENCE
In sign of truth, I kiss your highness' hand.
KING HENRY   Well-minded Clarence, be thou fortunate.
MONTAGUE   Comfort, my lord; and so I take my leave.
OXFORD   And thus I seal my truth and bid adieu.
30 KING HENRY   Sweet Oxford, and my loving Montague,
And all at once, once more a happy farewell.
WARWICK   Farewell, sweet lords, let's meet at Coventry.
       Exeunt all but King Henry and Exeter.
KING HENRY   Here at the palace will I rest awhile.
Cousin of Exeter, what thinks your lordship?
35   Methinks the power that Edward hath in field
Should not be able to encounter mine.
EXETER   The doubt is that he will seduce the rest.
KING HENRY
That's not my fear. My meed hath got me fame.
I have not stopped mine ears to their demands,
40   Nor posted off their suits with slow delays.

My pity hath been balm to heal their wounds.
My mildness hath allayed their swelling griefs.
My mercy dried their water-flowing tears.
I have not been desirous of their wealth,
45   Nor much oppressed them with great subsidies,
Nor forward of revenge, though they much erred.
Then why should they love Edward more than me?
No, Exeter, these graces challenge grace,
And when the lion fawns upon the lamb,
50   The lamb will never cease to follow him.
       [*Shout within,* 'A Lancaster! A Lancaster!']
EXETER   Hark, hark, my lord. What shouts are these?

       Enter KING EDWARD *with* RICHARD OF
       GLOUCESTER *and his Soldiers.*

KING EDWARD
Seize on the shamefaced Henry. Bear him hence,
And once again proclaim us King of England.
You are the fount that makes small brooks to flow:
55   Now stops thy spring, my sea shall suck them dry
And swell so much the higher by their ebb.
Hence with him to the Tower. Let him not speak.
       Some Soldiers exeunt with King Henry.
And lords, towards Coventry bend we our course,
Where peremptory Warwick now remains.
60   The sun shines hot, and if we use delay,
Cold biting winter mars our hoped-for hay.
RICHARD OF GLOUCESTER
Away betimes, before his forces join,
And take the great-grown traitor unawares.
Brave warriors, march amain towards Coventry.
       Exeunt.

5.1   *Enter* WARWICK, *the Mayor of Coventry,*
       two Messengers *and others upon the walls.*

WARWICK
Where is the post that came from valiant Oxford?
How far hence is thy lord, mine honest fellow?
1 MESSENGER
By this at Dunsmore, marching hitherward.   *Exit.*
WARWICK   How far off is our brother Montague?
5   Where is the post that came from Montague?
2 MESSENGER
By this at Daintry, with a puissant troop.   *Exit.*

       Enter SOMERVILLE.

WARWICK   Say, Somerville, what says my loving son?
And by thy guess how nigh is Clarence now?
SOMERVILLE
At Southam I did leave him with his forces
10   And do expect him here some two hours hence.
       [*A march afar off*]
WARWICK   Then Clarence is at hand, I hear his drum.
SOMERVILLE   It is not his, my lord, here Southam lies.
The drum your honour hears marcheth from
       Warwick.

WARWICK
Who should that be? Belike unlooked-for friends.
SOMERVILLE
15 They are at hand, and you shall quickly know.
Exit into the city.

March. Flourish. Enter KING EDWARD,
RICHARD OF GLOUCESTER *and Soldiers.*

KING EDWARD
Go, trumpet, to the walls and sound a parle.
RICHARD OF GLOUCESTER
See how the surly Warwick mans the wall.
WARWICK   O, unbid spite, is sportful Edward come?
Where slept our scouts, or how are they seduced,
20 That we could hear no news of his repair?
KING EDWARD
Now Warwick, wilt thou ope the city gates,
Speak gentle words, and humbly bend thy knee?
Call Edward king and at his hands beg mercy,
And he shall pardon thee these outrages.
25 WARWICK   Nay, rather wilt thou draw thy forces hence,
Confess who set thee up and plucked thee down?
Call Warwick patron and be penitent,
And thou shalt still remain the Duke of York.
RICHARD OF GLOUCESTER
I thought at least he would have said 'the King'.
30 Or did he make the jest against his will?
WARWICK   Is not a dukedom, sir, a goodly gift?
RICHARD OF GLOUCESTER
Ay, by my faith, for a poor earl to give.
I'll do thee service for so good a gift.
WARWICK
'Twas I that gave the kingdom to thy brother.
KING EDWARD
35 Why then, 'tis mine, if but by Warwick's gift.
WARWICK   Thou art no Atlas for so great a weight;
And, weakling, Warwick takes his gift again,
And Henry is my King, Warwick his subject.
KING EDWARD
But Warwick's King is Edward's prisoner.
40 And, gallant Warwick, do but answer this:
What is the body when the head is off?
RICHARD OF GLOUCESTER
Alas, that Warwick had no more forecast,
But whiles he thought to steal the single ten,
The King was slyly fingered from the deck.
45 You left poor Henry at the bishop's palace
And ten to one you'll meet him in the Tower.
KING EDWARD   'Tis even so, yet you are Warwick still.
RICHARD OF GLOUCESTER
Come, Warwick, take the time, kneel down, kneel down.
Nay, when? Strike now, or else the iron cools.
50 WARWICK   I had rather chop this hand off at a blow
And with the other fling it at thy face
Than bear so low a sail to strike to thee.
KING EDWARD
Sail how thou canst, have wind and tide thy friend,

This hand, fast wound about thy coal-black hair,
Shall, whiles thy head is warm and new cut off,   55
Write in the dust this sentence with thy blood,
'Wind-changing Warwick now can change no more.'

Enter OXFORD *with Drum and Colours.*

WARWICK
O cheerful colours, see where Oxford comes!
OXFORD   Oxford, Oxford for Lancaster!
[*Oxford and his forces enter the city.*]
RICHARD OF GLOUCESTER
The gates are open; let us enter, too.   60
KING EDWARD   So other foes may set upon our backs.
Stand we in good array, for they no doubt
Will issue out again and bid us battle.
If not, the city being but of small defence,
We'll quickly rouse the traitors in the same.   65
[*Enter Oxford on the walls.*]
WARWICK   O welcome, Oxford, for we want thy help.

Enter MONTAGUE *with Drum and Colours.*

MONTAGUE   Montague, Montague, for Lancaster!
[*Montague and his forces enter the city.*]
RICHARD OF GLOUCESTER
Thou and thy brother both shall buy this treason
Even with the dearest blood your bodies bear.
KING EDWARD
The harder matched, the greater victory.   70
My mind presageth happy gain and conquest.

Enter SOMERSET *with Drum and Colours.*

SOMERSET   Somerset, Somerset, for Lancaster!
[*Somerset and his forces enter the city.*]
RICHARD OF GLOUCESTER
Two of thy name, both Dukes of Somerset,
Have sold their lives unto the House of York,
And thou shalt be the third, if this sword hold.   75

Enter GEORGE OF CLARENCE *with Drum and Colours.*

WARWICK
And lo, where George of Clarence sweeps along,
Of force enough to bid his brother battle;
With whom an upright zeal to right prevails
More than the nature of a brother's love.
Come, Clarence, come. Thou wilt, if Warwick call.   80
GEORGE OF CLARENCE
Father of Warwick, know you what this means?
[*Takes the red rose out of his hat.*]
Look here, I throw my infamy at thee!
[*Throws it at Warwick.*]
I will not ruinate my father's house,
Who gave his blood to lime the stones together,
And set up Lancaster. Why, trowest thou, Warwick,   85
That Clarence is so harsh, so blunt, unnatural,
To bend the fatal instruments of war
Against his brother and his lawful King?
Perhaps thou wilt object my holy oath.

90 To keep that oath were more impiety
Than Jephthah, when he sacrificed his daughter.
I am so sorry for my trespass made
That, to deserve well at my brother's hands,
I here proclaim myself thy mortal foe.
95 With resolution, wheresoe'er I meet thee –
As I will meet thee, if thou stir abroad –
To plague thee, for thy foul misleading me.
And so, proud-hearted Warwick, I defy thee
And to my brothers turn my blushing cheeks.
100 Pardon me, Edward, I will make amends.
And Richard, do not frown upon my faults,
For I will henceforth be no more unconstant.
KING EDWARD
Now, welcome, more, and ten times more, beloved
Than if thou never hadst deserved our hate.
RICHARD OF GLOUCESTER
105 Welcome, good Clarence, this is brother-like.
WARWICK   O passing traitor, perjured and unjust.
KING EDWARD
What, Warwick, wilt thou leave the town and fight?
Or shall we beat the stones about thine ears?
WARWICK   Alas, I am not cooped here for defence.
110 I will away towards Barnet presently
And bid thee battle, Edward, if thou dar'st.
KING EDWARD
Yes, Warwick, Edward dares, and leads the way.
Lords, to the field. Saint George, and victory!
Exeunt. March. Warwick and his company follows.

5.2   *Alarum and excursions. Enter* KING EDWARD
      bringing forth WARWICK *wounded.*

KING EDWARD
So lie thou there. Die thou and die our fear,
For Warwick was a bug that feared us all.
Now, Montague, sit fast: I seek for thee,
That Warwick's bones may keep thine company.   *Exit.*
5 WARWICK   Ah, who is nigh? Come to me, friend or foe,
And tell me who is victor, York or Warwick?
Why ask I that? My mangled body shows –
My blood, my want of strength, my sick heart shows –
That I must yield my body to the earth
10 And, by my fall, the conquest to my foe.
Thus yields the cedar to the axe's edge
Whose arms gave shelter to the princely eagle,
Under whose shade the ramping lion slept,
Whose top branch overpeered Jove's spreading tree
15 And kept low shrubs from winter's powerful wind.
These eyes, that now are dimmed with death's black
      veil,
Have been as piercing as the midday sun
To search the secret treasons of the world.
The wrinkles in my brows, now filled with blood,
20 Were likened oft to kingly sepulchres,
For who lived king but I could dig his grave?
And who durst smile when Warwick bent his brow?

Lo, now my glory smeared in dust and blood.
My parks, my walks, my manors that I had
Even now forsake me, and of all my lands   25
Is nothing left me but my body's length.
Why, what is pomp, rule, reign but earth and dust?
And live we how we can, yet die we must.

Enter OXFORD *and* SOMERSET.

SOMERSET   Ah, Warwick, Warwick, wert thou as we are
We might recover all our loss again.   30
The Queen from France hath brought a puissant
      power;
Even now we heard the news. Ah, couldst thou fly.
WARWICK   Why, then, I would not fly. Ah, Montague,
If thou be there, sweet brother, take my hand
And with thy lips keep in my soul awhile.   35
Thou lov'st me not, for, brother, if thou didst,
Thy tears would wash this cold congealed blood
That glues my lips and will not let me speak.
Come quickly, Montague, or I am dead.
SOMERSET
Ah, Warwick, Montague hath breathed his last;   40
And to the latest gasp cried out for Warwick
And said, 'Commend me to my valiant brother.'
And more he would have said, and more he spoke,
Which sounded like a cannon in a vault,
That mought not be distinguished, but at last   45
I well might hear, delivered with a groan,
'O, farewell, Warwick.'
WARWICK
Sweet rest his soul. Fly, lords, and save yourselves,
For Warwick bids you all farewell to meet in
      heaven!   [*Dies.*]
OXFORD   Away, away, to meet the Queen's great power!   50
      Here they bear away his body. Exeunt.

5.3   *Flourish. Enter* KING EDWARD *in triumph,*
      with RICHARD OF GLOUCESTER, GEORGE OF
            CLARENCE *and the rest.*

KING EDWARD
Thus far our fortune keeps an upward course
And we are graced with wreaths of victory.
But in the midst of this bright-shining day,
I spy a black, suspicious, threat'ning cloud
That will encounter with our glorious sun   5
Ere he attain his easeful western bed.
I mean, my lords, those powers that the Queen
Hath raised in Gallia have arrived our coast
And, as we hear, march on to fight with us.
GEORGE OF CLARENCE
A little gale will soon disperse that cloud   10
And blow it to the source from whence it came.
Thy very beams will dry those vapours up,
For every cloud engenders not a storm.
RICHARD OF GLOUCESTER
The Queen is valued thirty thousand strong,

And Somerset with Oxford fled to her: 15
If she have time to breathe, be well assured
Her faction will be full as strong as ours.
KING EDWARD   We are advertised by our loving friends
That they do hold their course toward Tewkesbury.
We, having now the best at Barnet Field, 20
Will thither straight, for willingness rids way,
And as we march our strength will be augmented
In every county as we go along.
Strike up the drum. Cry 'Courage!' and away!

Exeunt.

5.4   *Flourish. March. Enter* QUEEN
          MARGARET, *young* PRINCE EDWARD,
          SOMERSET, OXFORD *and Soldiers.*

QUEEN MARGARET
Great lords, wise men ne'er sit and wail their loss
But cheerly seek how to redress their harms.
What though the mast be now blown overboard,
The cable broke, the holding-anchor lost
And half our sailors swallowed in the flood? 5
Yet lives our pilot still. Is't meet that he
Should leave the helm and, like a fearful lad,
With tearful eyes add water to the sea
And give more strength to that which hath too much,
Whiles in his moan the ship splits on the rock, 10
Which industry and courage might have saved?
Ah, what a shame; ah, what a fault were this.
Say Warwick was our anchor, what of that?
And Montague our topmast, what of him?
Our slaughtered friends the tackles, what of these? 15
Why, is not Oxford here another anchor?
And Somerset another goodly mast?
The friends of France our shrouds and tacklings?
And, though unskilful, why not Ned and I
For once allowed the skilful pilot's charge? 20
We will not from the helm to sit and weep,
But keep our course, though the rough wind say no,
From shelves and rocks that threaten us with wrack.
As good to chide the waves as speak them fair.
And what is Edward but a ruthless sea? 25
What Clarence but a quicksand of deceit?
And Richard but a ragged fatal rock?
All these the enemies to our poor bark.
Say you can swim: alas, 'tis but awhile;
Tread on the sand: why, there you quickly sink; 30
Bestride the rock: the tide will wash you off
Or else you famish; that's a threefold death.
This speak I, lords, to let you understand,
If case some one of you would fly from us,
That there's no hoped-for mercy with the brothers 35
More than with ruthless waves, with sands and rocks.
Why, courage, then! What cannot be avoided
'Twere childish weakness to lament or fear.
PRINCE EDWARD
Methinks a woman of this valiant spirit

Should, if a coward heard her speak these words, 40
Infuse his breast with magnanimity
And make him, naked, foil a man at arms.
I speak not this as doubting any here,
For did I but suspect a fearful man,
He should have leave to go away betimes, 45
Lest in our need he might infect another
And make him of like spirit to himself.
If any such be here, as God forbid,
Let him depart before we need his help.
OXFORD   Women and children of so high a courage, 50
And warriors faint? Why, 'twere perpetual shame!
O brave young Prince, thy famous grandfather
Doth live again in thee. Long mayst thou live
To bear his image and renew his glories.
SOMERSET   And he that will not fight for such a hope, 55
Go home to bed and, like the owl by day,
If he arise, be mocked and wondered at.
QUEEN MARGARET
Thanks, gentle Somerset; sweet Oxford, thanks.
PRINCE EDWARD
And take his thanks that yet hath nothing else.

Enter a Messenger.

MESSENGER
Prepare you, lords, for Edward is at hand, 60
Ready to fight; therefore be resolute.   *Exit.*
OXFORD   I thought no less; it is his policy
To haste thus fast to find us unprovided.
SOMERSET   But he's deceived; we are in readiness.
QUEEN MARGARET
This cheers my heart, to see your forwardness. 65
OXFORD
Here pitch our battle; hence we will not budge.

Flourish and march. Enter KING EDWARD,
RICHARD OF GLOUCESTER, GEORGE OF
CLARENCE *and Soldiers.*

KING EDWARD
Brave followers, yonder stands the thorny wood
Which by the heaven's assistance and your strength
Must by the roots be hewn up yet ere night.
I need not add more fuel to your fire, 70
For well I wot ye blaze to burn them out.
Give signal to the fight, and to it, lords!
QUEEN MARGARET
Lords, knights, and gentlemen, what I should say
My tears gainsay, for every word I speak
Ye see I drink the water of my eye. 75
Therefore, no more but this: Henry, your sovereign,
Is prisoner to the foe, his state usurped,
His realm a slaughterhouse, his subjects slain,
His statutes cancelled and his treasure spent,
And yonder is the wolf that makes this spoil. 80
You fight in justice. Then in God's name, lords,
Be valiant and give signal to the fight!

Alarum, retreat, excursions. Exeunt.

5.5   *Flourish. Enter* KING EDWARD, RICHARD
OF GLOUCESTER *and* GEORGE OF CLARENCE,
with QUEEN MARGARET, OXFORD *and*
SOMERSET, *prisoners.*

KING EDWARD
　　Now here a period of tumultuous broils.
　　Away with Oxford to Hammes Castle straight;
　　For Somerset, off with his guilty head.
　　Go bear them hence; I will not hear them speak.
OXFORD
5　　For my part, I'll not trouble thee with words.
　　　　　　　　　Exit Oxford, under guard.
SOMERSET
　　Nor I, but stoop with patience to my fortune.
　　　　　　　　　Exit Somerset, under guard.
QUEEN MARGARET
　　So part we sadly in this troublous world
　　To meet with joy in sweet Jerusalem.
KING EDWARD
　　Is proclamation made that who finds Edward
10　　Shall have a high reward, and he his life?
RICHARD OF GLOUCESTER
　　It is, and lo where youthful Edward comes.

Enter the PRINCE *under guard.*

KING EDWARD
　　Bring forth the gallant; let us hear him speak.
　　What? Can so young a thorn begin to prick?
　　Edward, what satisfaction canst thou make
15　　For bearing arms, for stirring up my subjects
　　And all the trouble thou hast turned me to?
PRINCE EDWARD
　　Speak like a subject, proud ambitious York.
　　Suppose that I am now my father's mouth:
　　Resign thy chair, and where I stand, kneel thou,
20　　Whilst I propose the selfsame words to thee
　　Which, traitor, thou wouldst have me answer to.
QUEEN MARGARET
　　Ah, that thy father had been so resolved!
RICHARD OF GLOUCESTER
　　That you might still have worn the petticoat
　　And ne'er have stol'n the breech from Lancaster.
25 PRINCE EDWARD   Let Aesop fable in a winter's night;
　　His currish riddles sorts not with this place.
RICHARD OF GLOUCESTER
　　By heaven, brat, I'll plague ye for that word!
QUEEN MARGARET
　　Ay, thou wast born to be a plague to men.
RICHARD OF GLOUCESTER
　　For God's sake, take away this captive scold!
PRINCE EDWARD
30　　Nay, take away this scolding crookback, rather!
KING EDWARD
　　Peace, wilful boy, or I will charm your tongue.
GEORGE OF CLARENCE
　　Untutored lad, thou art too malapert.

PRINCE EDWARD
　　I know my duty: you are all undutiful.
　　Lascivious Edward, and thou perjured George,
　　And thou misshapen Dick, I tell ye all   35
　　I am your better, traitors as ye are,
　　And thou usurp'st my father's right and mine.
KING EDWARD
　　Take that, the likeness of this railer here!   [*Stabs him.*]
RICHARD OF GLOUCESTER
　　Sprawl'st thou? Take that to end thy agony!
　　　　[*Richard stabs him.*]
GEORGE OF CLARENCE
　　And there's for twitting me with perjury!   40
　　　　[*Clarence stabs him.*]
QUEEN MARGARET   O, kill me too!
RICHARD OF GLOUCESTER   Marry, and shall.
　　　　[*Offers to kill her.*]
KING EDWARD
　　Hold, Richard, hold, for we have done too much.
RICHARD OF GLOUCESTER
　　Why should she live to fill the world with words?
KING EDWARD
　　What, doth she swoon? Use means for her recovery.   45
RICHARD OF GLOUCESTER
　　Clarence, excuse me to the King my brother;
　　I'll hence to London on a serious matter.
　　Ere ye come there, be sure to hear some news.
GEORGE OF CLARENCE   What? What?
RICHARD OF GLOUCESTER   The Tower. The Tower!   50
　　　　　　　　　　　　　　　　　Exit.
QUEEN MARGARET
　　O Ned, sweet Ned, speak to thy mother, boy.
　　Canst thou not speak? O traitors, murderers!
　　They that stabbed Caesar shed no blood at all,
　　Did not offend, nor were not worthy blame,
　　If this foul deed were by to equal it.   55
　　He was a man; this, in respect, a child,
　　And men ne'er spend their fury on a child.
　　What's worse than murderer, that I may name it?
　　No, no, my heart will burst an if I speak –
　　And I will speak, that so my heart may burst.   60
　　Butchers and villains! Bloody cannibals!
　　How sweet a plant have you untimely cropped!
　　You have no children, butchers; if you had,
　　The thought of them would have stirred up remorse.
　　But if you ever chance to have a child,   65
　　Look in his youth to have him so cut off
　　As, deathsmen, you have rid this sweet young
　　　　Prince!
KING EDWARD
　　Away with her. Go, bear her hence perforce.
QUEEN MARGARET
　　Nay, never bear me hence; dispatch me here.
　　Here sheath thy sword; I'll pardon thee my death.   70
　　What, wilt thou not? Then, Clarence, do it thou.
GEORGE OF CLARENCE
　　By heaven, I will not do thee so much ease.

QUEEN MARGARET

  Good Clarence, do; sweet Clarence, do thou do it.

GEORGE OF CLARENCE

  Didst thou not hear me swear I would not do it?

QUEEN MARGARET

75   Ay, but thou usest to forswear thyself.

  'Twas sin before, but now 'tis charity.

  What, wilt thou not? Where is that devil's butcher,
    Richard?

  Hard-favoured Richard? Richard, where art thou?

  Thou art not here. Murder is thy alms-deed;

80   Petitioners for blood thou ne'er put'st back.

KING EDWARD   Away, I say! I charge ye bear her hence.

QUEEN MARGARET

  So come to you and yours as to this Prince!

      Exit Queen guarded, with one bearing her son.

KING EDWARD   Where's Richard gone?

GEORGE OF CLARENCE

  To London all in post and, as I guess,

85   To make a bloody supper in the Tower.

KING EDWARD

  He's sudden if a thing comes in his head.

  Now march we hence. Discharge the common sort

  With pay and thanks, and let's away to London

  And see our gentle Queen how well she fares.

90   By this I hope she hath a son for me.   *Exeunt.*

5.6   *Enter* KING HENRY *the Sixth and*
        RICHARD OF GLOUCESTER, *with the*
        Lieutenant *on the Tower walls.*

RICHARD OF GLOUCESTER

  Good day my lord. What, at your book so hard?

KING HENRY

  Ay, my good lord. 'My lord' I should say, rather.

  'Tis sin to flatter; 'good' was little better.

  'Good Gloucester' and 'good devil' were alike,

5   And both preposterous. Therefore, not 'good lord'.

RICHARD OF GLOUCESTER

  Sirrah, leave us to ourselves. We must confer.

               Exit Lieutenant.

KING HENRY

  So flies the reckless shepherd from the wolf;

  So first the harmless sheep doth yield his fleece

  And next his throat unto the butcher's knife.

10   What scene of death hath Roscius now to act?

RICHARD OF GLOUCESTER

  Suspicion always haunts the guilty mind;

  The thief doth fear each bush an officer.

KING HENRY   The bird that hath been limed in a bush

  With trembling wings misdoubteth every bush.

15   And I, the hapless male to one sweet bird,

  Have now the fatal object in my eye

  Where my poor young was limed, was caught and
    killed.

RICHARD OF GLOUCESTER

  Why, what a peevish fool was that of Crete

  That taught his son the office of a fowl!

  And yet for all his wings the fool was drowned.   20

KING HENRY   I, Daedalus; my poor boy, Icarus;

  Thy father, Minos, that denied our course;

  The sun that seared the wings of my sweet boy,

  Thy brother Edward; and thyself, the sea,

  Whose envious gulf did swallow up his life.   25

  Ah, kill me with thy weapon, not with words!

  My breast can better brook thy dagger's point

  Than can my ears that tragic history.

  But wherefore dost thou come? Is't for my life?

RICHARD OF GLOUCESTER

  Think'st thou I am an executioner?   30

KING HENRY   A persecutor I am sure thou art;

  If murdering innocents be executing,

  Why then, thou art an executioner.

RICHARD OF GLOUCESTER

  Thy son I killed for his presumption.

KING HENRY

  Hadst thou been killed when first thou didst presume   35

  Thou hadst not lived to kill a son of mine.

  And thus I prophesy – that many a thousand

  Which now mistrust no parcel of my fear,

  And many an old man's sigh, and many a widow's,

  And many an orphan's water-standing eye,   40

  Men for their sons, wives for their husbands,

  Orphans for their parents' timeless death,

  Shall rue the hour that ever thou wast born.

  The owl shrieked at thy birth, an evil sign;

  The night-crow cried, aboding luckless time;   45

  Dogs howled; and hideous tempests shook down trees;

  The raven rooked her on the chimney's top;

  And chatt'ring pies in dismal discords sung.

  Thy mother felt more than a mother's pain,

  And yet brought forth less than a mother's hope: 50

  To wit, an undigested and deformed lump,

  Not like the fruit of such a goodly tree.

  Teeth hadst thou in thy head when thou wast born

  To signify thou cam'st to bite the world.

  And if the rest be true, which I have heard,   55

  Thou cam'st –

RICHARD OF GLOUCESTER

  I'll hear no more! Die, prophet, in thy speech,

    [*Stabs him.*]

  For this amongst the rest was I ordained.

KING HENRY

  Ay, and for much more slaughter after this.

  O God, forgive my sins and pardon thee.   [*Dies.*]   60

RICHARD OF GLOUCESTER

  What? Will the aspiring blood of Lancaster

  Sink in the ground? I thought it would have mounted.

  See how my sword weeps for the poor King's death.

  O may such purple tears be alway shed

  From those that wish the downfall of our house.   65

  If any spark of life be yet remaining,

  Down, down to hell, and say I sent thee thither!

    [*Stabs him again.*]

I that have neither pity, love nor fear.
Indeed, 'tis true that Henry told me of,
70 For I have often heard my mother say
I came into the world with my legs forward.
Had I not reason, think ye, to make haste,
And seek their ruin that usurped our right?
The midwife wondered and the women cried,
75 'O, Jesus bless us, he is born with teeth!'
And so I was, which plainly signified
That I should snarl, and bite and play the dog.
Then, since the heavens have shaped my body so,
Let hell make crook'd my mind to answer it.
80 I have no brother; I am like no brother.
And this word 'love', which greybeards call divine,
Be resident in men like one another
And not in me: I am myself alone.
Clarence, beware: thou keep'st me from the light,
85 But I will sort a pitchy day for thee;
For I will buzz abroad such prophecies
That Edward shall be fearful of his life;
And then to purge his fear, I'll be thy death.
King Henry and the Prince his son are gone;
90 Clarence, thy turn is next, and then the rest,
Counting myself but bad till I be best.
I'll throw thy body in another room,
And triumph, Henry, in thy day of doom!

Exit with the body.

5.7   *Flourish. Enter* KING EDWARD,
QUEEN ELIZABETH, GEORGE OF CLARENCE,
RICHARD OF GLOUCESTER, HASTINGS,
Nurse with infant Prince Edward, and Attendants.

KING EDWARD
Once more we sit in England's royal throne,
Repurchased with the blood of enemies.
What valiant foemen like to autumn's corn
Have we mowed down in tops of all their pride!
5 Three Dukes of Somerset, threefold renowned
For hardy and undoubted champions;
Two Cliffords, as the father and the son;
And two Northumberlands, two braver men
Ne'er spurred their coursers at the trumpet's sound.
With them the two brave bears, Warwick and
10   Montague,

That in their chains fettered the kingly lion
And made the forest tremble when they roared.
Thus have we swept suspicion from our seat
And made our footstool of security.
Come hither, Bess, and let me kiss my boy. 15
Young Ned, for thee, thine uncles and myself
Have in our armours watched the winter's night,
Went all afoot in summer's scalding heat,
That thou mightst repossess the crown in peace,
And of our labours thou shalt reap the gain. 20
RICHARD OF GLOUCESTER [*aside*]
I'll blast his harvest, if your head were laid;
For yet I am not looked on in the world.
This shoulder was ordained so thick to heave,
And heave it shall some weight or break my back.
Work thou the way and that shalt execute. 25
KING EDWARD
Clarence and Gloucester, love my lovely queen,
And kiss your princely nephew, brothers both.
GEORGE OF CLARENCE
The duty that I owe unto your majesty
I seal upon the lips of this sweet babe.
QUEEN ELIZABETH
Thanks, noble Clarence; worthy brother, thanks. 30
RICHARD OF GLOUCESTER
And that I love the tree from whence thou
    sprang'st,
Witness the loving kiss I give the fruit. –
[*aside*] To say the truth, so Judas kissed his master
And cried, 'All hail!', when as he meant all harm.
KING EDWARD   Now am I seated as my soul delights, 35
Having my country's peace and brothers' loves.
GEORGE OF CLARENCE
What will your grace have done with Margaret?
Reynard, her father, to the King of France
Hath pawned the Sicils and Jerusalem,
And hither have they sent it for her ransom. 40
KING EDWARD
Away with her and waft her hence to France.
And now what rests but that we spend the time
With stately triumphs, mirthful comic shows,
Such as befits the pleasure of the court.
Sound drums and trumpets! Farewell, sour annoy, 45
For here I hope begins our lasting joy.

Drums and trumpets. Exeunt omnes.

King Henry VIII

King Henry VIII, also known as *All Is True*, can be dated with unusual precision because it was being performed at the Globe on 29 June 1613 when the firing of cannon set light to the thatched roof and the theatre was burnt to the ground – fortunately without loss of life or injury. Several contemporary accounts of the fire refer to *King Henry VIII* as a new play at the time, so scholars agree in dating it to 1613, though some would put it back to the beginning of that year, arguing that it would have been appropriate for performance at Court during the wedding celebrations of King James I's daughter Elizabeth and Frederick, the Elector Palatine. Shakespeare's company, the King's Men, did perform six of his plays as contributions to the festivities but there is no definite proof that *King Henry VIII* was one of them.

It was printed as the last of Shakespeare's English history plays in the First Folio in 1623, and its historical material derives in part from the chronicles of Raphael Holinshed and Edward Hall – sources Shakespeare had used for his earlier histories – but it was composed some fourteen years after *Henry V*, the latest in the sequence of nine history plays Shakespeare had written between 1590 and 1599, and in some ways it is a different kind of play, having as many affinities with the late tragicomedies or 'romances' such as *The Winter's Tale* and *The Tempest* as it has with the histories. It comes no nearer to a battlefield than a description of the ceremonial 'Field of the Cloth of Gold', where Henry VIII met Francis I to inaugurate a peace treaty between England and France; and it presents its main political events, which provide an implicit history of the Reformation, as a series of set-pieces on the fall from greatness of some characters (the Duke of Buckingham, Katherine of Aragon, Cardinal Wolsey) and the rise of others (Anne Bullen, Thomas Cranmer). It ends with a celebration of the birth of the future Queen Elizabeth I and a tribute – which, in context, can be read as backhanded

– to her supposedly even more glorious successor, James I. It imbues its historical events with a degree of myth or symbolism and presents Henry as an intemperate monarch, repeatedly upstaged by his subjects, notably the prelates, Wolsey and Cranmer.

Most editors and scholars believe that this play, like *Cardenio* (now lost, but revised by Lewis Theobald as *Double Falsehood, or The Distressed Lovers* in 1728, and included in the Arden 3 series) and *The Two Noble Kinsmen*, was a collaboration between Shakespeare and John Fletcher. All three plays date from the period 1612–13 when Shakespeare was scaling down his level of participation in the King's Men's activities; Fletcher succeeded him as the chief dramatist of the company, and seems to have preferred to work collaboratively, writing plays with Francis Beaumont and Philip Massinger as well as with Shakespeare. The scenes in the play generally attributed to Shakespeare are 1.1, 1.2, 2.3, 2.4, 3.2 to line 203 and 5.1, although to separate out the work of one participant in a collaboration is, in a sense, to miss the point.

The play was revived during the Restoration and remained popular in the eighteenth and nineteenth centuries, partly because of the opportunities it afforded for lavish spectacle and pageantry; it tends to be performed at times of coronation. The roles of Wolsey and Katherine came to dominate productions and were performed by leading actors from John Philip Kemble and his sister Sarah Siddons in 1806 to Henry Irving and Ellen Terry in 1892; much of the play used to be cut in order to focus attention on these roles. Twentieth-century productions restored Henry to a central position and aimed for a more thoughtful and serious reading of the play, finding ironies and contradictions in it as well as theatrical display.

The Arden text is based on the 1623 First Folio.

LIST OF ROLES

IN ORDER OF APPEARANCE

PROLOGUE

Duke of NORFOLK	
Duke of BUCKINGHAM	
Lord ABERGAVENNY	*son-in-law to the Duke of Buckingham*
Cardinal WOLSEY	*Archbishop of York and Lord Chancellor*
SECRETARY	*to Cardinal Wolsey*
BRANDON	
SERGEANT-at-Arms	
KING Henry the Eighth	*of England*
Sir Thomas LOVELL	
KATHERINE	*of Aragon, Queen of England, later divorced*
Duke of SUFFOLK	
SURVEYOR	*to the Duke of Buckingham*
Lord CHAMBERLAIN	
Lord SANDYS	
ANNE Bullen	*maid of honour to Katherine, later Queen of England*
Sir Henry GUILDFORD	
SERVANT	*at Wolsey's party*
First GENTLEMAN	
Second GENTLEMAN	
Sir Nicholas VAUX	
Cardinal CAMPEIUS	*papal legate*
GARDINER	*the King's secretary, later Bishop of Winchester*
OLD LADY	*friend to Anne Bullen*
Bishop of LINCOLN	
GRIFFITH	*Gentleman Usher to Katherine*
SCRIBE	*to the court*
CRIER	*to the court*
Earl of SURREY	*son-in-law to the Duke of Buckingham*
Thomas CROMWELL	*Wolsey's secretary, later secretary to the Privy Council*
Lord CHANCELLOR	*(Sir Thomas More)*
GARTER	*King-of-Arms*
Third GENTLEMAN	
PATIENCE	*attendant on Katherine*
MESSENGER	*at Kimbolton*
Lord CAPUTIUS	*ambassador from the Holy Roman Emperor*
Gardiner's PAGE	
Sir Anthony DENNY	
Thomas CRANMER	*Archbishop of Canterbury*
Door KEEPER	*of the Council Chamber*
Doctor BUTTS	*the King's physician*
PORTER	
Porter's MAN	

EPILOGUE

Musicians, Guards, Secretaries, Noblemen, Ladies, Gentlemen,
Masquers, Tipstaves, Halberdiers, Attendants, Common People,
Vergers, Scribes, Archbishop of Canterbury, Bishops of Ely, Rochester
and St Asaph, Priests, Gentleman Usher, Women attendant on Katherine,
Judges, Choristers, Lord Mayor of London, Marquess of Dorset,
four Barons of the Cinque Ports, Bishop of London, Duchess of Norfolk,
six Dancers (spirits) in Katherine's vision, Marchioness of Dorset,
Aldermen, Servants, Grooms

Enter PROLOGUE.

PROLOGUE
I come no more to make you laugh: things now
That bear a weighty and a serious brow,
Sad, high and working, full of state and woe,
Such noble scenes as draw the eye to flow,
We now present. Those that can pity here 5
May, if they think it well, let fall a tear:
The subject will deserve it. Such as give
Their money out of hope they may believe
May here find truth, too. Those that come to see
Only a show or two and so agree 10
The play may pass, if they be still and willing
I'll undertake may see away their shilling
Richly in two short hours. Only they
That come to hear a merry, bawdy play,
A noise of targets, or to see a fellow 15
In a long motley coat guarded with yellow,
Will be deceived. For, gentle hearers, know
To rank our chosen truth with such a show
As fool and fight is, beside forfeiting
Our own brains and the opinion that we bring 20
To make that only true we now intend,
Will leave us never an understanding friend.
Therefore, for goodness' sake, and as you are known
The first and happiest hearers of the town,
Be sad, as we would make ye. Think ye see 25
The very persons of our noble story
As they were living; think you see them great,
And followed with the general throng and sweat
Of thousand friends; then, in a moment, see
How soon this mightiness meets misery; 30
And if you can be merry then, I'll say
A man may weep upon his wedding day. *Exit.*

1.1 *Enter the* Duke of NORFOLK *at one door.*
At the other, the Duke of BUCKINGHAM
and the Lord ABERGAVENNY.

BUCKINGHAM
Good morrow and well met. How have ye done
Since last we saw in France?
NORFOLK   I thank your grace,
Healthful, and ever since a fresh admirer
Of what I saw there.
BUCKINGHAM   An untimely ague
Stayed me a prisoner in my chamber when 5
Those suns of glory, those two lights of men,
Met in the vale of Andres.
NORFOLK   'Twixt Guînes and Ardres
I was then present, saw them salute on horseback,
Beheld them when they lighted, how they clung
In their embracement as they grew together – 10
Which had they, what four throned ones could have
   weighed
Such a compounded one?

BUCKINGHAM   All the whole time
I was my chamber's prisoner.
NORFOLK   Then you lost
The view of earthly glory. Men might say
Till this time pomp was single, but now married 15
To one above itself. Each following day
Became the next day's master, till the last
Made former wonders its. Today the French,
All clinquant, all in gold like heathen gods,
Shone down the English; and tomorrow they 20
Made Britain India. Every man that stood
Showed like a mine. Their dwarfish pages were
As cherubims, all gilt. The madams too,
Not used to toil, did almost sweat to bear
The pride upon them, that their very labour 25
Was to them as a painting. Now this masque
Was cried incomparable; and th'ensuing night
Made it a fool and beggar. The two kings,
Equal in lustre, were now best, now worst,
As presence did present them: him in eye, 30
Still him in praise, and being present both,
'Twas said they saw but one, and no discerner
Durst wag his tongue in censure. When these suns –
For so they phrase 'em – by their heralds challenged
The noble spirits to arms, they did perform 35
Beyond thought's compass – that former fabulous
   story
Being now seen possible enough, got credit
That Bevis was believed.
BUCKINGHAM   O, you go far.
NORFOLK As I belong to worship and affect
In honour honesty, the tract of everything 40
Would by a good discourser lose some life
Which action's self was tongue to. All was royal;
To the disposing of it naught rebelled;
Order gave each thing view; the office did
Distinctly his full function.
BUCKINGHAM   Who did guide – 45
I mean, who set the body and the limbs
Of this great sport together, as you guess?
NORFOLK One, certes, that promises no element
In such a business.
BUCKINGHAM   I pray you who, my lord?
NORFOLK All this was ordered by the good discretion 50
Of the right reverend Cardinal of York.
BUCKINGHAM
The devil speed him! No man's pie is freed
From his ambitious finger. What had he
To do in these fierce vanities? I wonder
That such a keech can with his very bulk 55
Take up the rays o'th' beneficial sun
And keep it from the earth.
NORFOLK   Surely, sir,
There's in him stuff that puts him to these ends;
For being not propped by ancestry, whose grace
Chalks successors their way, nor called upon 60
For high feats done to th' crown, neither allied

To eminent assistants, but spider-like,
Out of his self-drawing web, 'a gives us note
The force of his own merit makes his way
65 A gift that heaven gives for him, which buys
A place next to the King.
ABERGAVENNY   I cannot tell
What heaven hath given him – let some graver eye
Pierce into that – but I can see his pride
Peep through each part of him. Whence has he that?
70 If not from hell, the devil is a niggard
Or has given all before, and he begins
A new hell in himself.
BUCKINGHAM   Why the devil,
Upon this French going-out, took he upon him,
Without the privity o'th' King, t'appoint
75 Who should attend on him? He makes up the file
Of all the gentry, for the most part such
To whom as great a charge, as little honour
He meant to lay upon; and his own letter –
The honourable board of Council out –
Must fetch him in he papers.
80 ABERGAVENNY   I do know
Kinsmen of mine – three at the least – that have
By this so sickened their estates that never
They shall abound as formerly.
BUCKINGHAMQ   O, many
Have broke their backs with laying manors on 'em
85 For this great journey. What did this vanity
But minister communication of
A most poor issue?
NORFOLK   Grievingly, I think
The peace between the French and us not values
The cost that did conclude it.
BUCKINGHAM   Every man,
90 After the hideous storm that followed, was
A thing inspired and, not consulting, broke
Into a general prophecy, that this tempest,
Dashing the garment of this peace, aboded
The sudden breach on't.
NORFOLK   Which is budded out,
95 For France hath flawed the league, and hath attached
Our merchants' goods at Bordeaux.
ABERGAVENNY   Is it therefore
Th'ambassador is silenced?
NORFOLK   Marry, is't.
ABERGAVENNY   A proper title of a peace, and purchased
At a superfluous rate.
BUCKINGHAM   Why, all this business
Our reverend Cardinal carried.
100 NORFOLK   Like it your grace,
The state takes notice of the private difference
Betwixt you and the Cardinal. I advise you –
And take it from a heart that wishes towards you
Honour and plenteous safety – that you read
105 The Cardinal's malice and his potency
Together; to consider further that
What his high hatred would effect wants not

A minister in his power. You know his nature,
That he's revengeful, and I know his sword
Hath a sharp edge: it's long, and't may be said   110
It reaches far, and where 'twill not extend,
Thither he darts it. Bosom up my counsel;
You'll find it wholesome. Lo, where comes that rock
That I advise your shunning.

Enter Cardinal WOLSEY, *the purse borne before him,*
certain of the guard and two Secretaries *with papers. The*
Cardinal, in his passage, fixeth his eye on Buckingham, and
Buckingham on him, both full of disdain.

WOLSEY   The Duke of Buckingham's surveyor, ha?   115
Where's his examination?
SECRETARY   Here, so please you.
WOLSEY   Is he in person ready?
SECRETARY   Ay, please your grace.
WOLSEY
Well, we shall then know more, and Buckingham
Shall lessen this big look.
                    Exeunt Cardinal and his train.
BUCKINGHAM
This butcher's cur is venom-mouthed, and I   120
Have not the power to muzzle him: therefore best
Not wake him in his slumber. A beggar's book
Outworths a noble's blood.
NORFOLK   What, are you chafed?
Ask God for temperance: that's th'appliance only
Which your disease requires.
BUCKINGHAM   I read in's looks   125
Matter against me, and his eye reviled
Me as his abject object. At this instant
He bores me with some trick. He's gone to th' King:
I'll follow and out-stare him.
NORFOLK   Stay, my lord,
And let your reason with your choler question   130
What 'tis you go about. To climb steep hills
Requires slow pace at first. Anger is like
A full hot horse, who being allowed his way
Self-mettle tires him. Not a man in England
Can advise me like you: be to yourself   135
As you would to your friend.
BUCKINGHAM   I'll to the King,
And from a mouth of honour quite cry down
This Ipswich fellow's insolence, or proclaim
There's difference in no persons.
NORFOLK   Be advised:
Heat not a furnace for your foe so hot   140
That it do singe yourself. We may outrun
By violent swiftness that which we run at,
And lose by over-running. Know you not
The fire that mounts the liquor till't run o'er,
In seeming to augment it, wastes it? Be advised: 145
I say again there is no English soul
More stronger to direct you than yourself,
If with the sap of reason you would quench
Or but allay the fire of passion.

BUCKINGHAM   Sir,
50 I am thankful to you, and I'll go along
By your prescription; but this top-proud fellow –
Whom from the flow of gall I name not, but
From sincere motions – by intelligence
And proofs as clear as founts in July when
55 We see each grain of gravel, I do know
To be corrupt and treasonous.
NORFOLK   Say not 'treasonous'.
BUCKINGHAM
To th' King I'll say't, and make my vouch as strong
As shore of rock. Attend. This holy fox,
Or wolf, or both – for he is equal ravenous
60 As he is subtle, and as prone to mischief
As able to perform't – his mind and place
Infecting one another – yea, reciprocally –
Only to show his pomp as well in France
As here at home, suggests the King our master
65 To this last costly treaty, th'interview
That swallowed so much treasure and like a glass
Did break i'th' rinsing.
NORFOLK   Faith, and so it did.
BUCKINGHAM
Pray give me favour, sir. This cunning Cardinal
The articles o'th' combination drew
70 As himself pleased; and they were ratified
As he cried, 'Thus let be', to as much end
As give a crutch to th' dead. But our Count–Cardinal
Has done this, and 'tis well: for worthy Wolsey,
Who cannot err, he did it. Now this follows –
75 Which, as I take it, is a kind of puppy
To th'old dam treason – Charles the Emperor,
Under pretence to see the Queen his aunt –
For 'twas indeed his colour, but he came
To whisper Wolsey – here makes visitation.
80 His fears were that the interview betwixt
England and France might through their amity
Breed him some prejudice, for from this league
Peeped harms that menaced him. He privily
Deals with our Cardinal, and as I trow –
85 Which I do well, for I am sure the Emperor
Paid ere he promised, whereby his suit was granted
Ere it was asked – but when the way was made
And paved with gold, the Emperor thus desired
That he would please to alter the King's course
90 And break the foresaid peace. Let the King know,
As soon he shall by me, that thus the Cardinal
Does buy and sell his honour as he pleases,
And for his own advantage.
NORFOLK   I am sorry
To hear this of him, and could wish he were
Something mistaken in't.
95 **BUCKINGHAM**   No, not a syllable.
I do pronounce him in that very shape
He shall appear in proof.

Enter BRANDON, *a* Sergeant-at-Arms *before him,*
and two or three of the guard.

BRANDON   Your office, sergeant: execute it.
SERGEANT   Sir,
My lord the Duke of Buckingham, and Earl
Of Hereford, Stafford and Northampton, I   200
Arrest thee of high treason in the name
Of our most sovereign King.
BUCKINGHAM   Lo you, my lord,
The net has fallen upon me: I shall perish
Under device and practice.
BRANDON   I am sorry
To see you ta'en from liberty, to look on   205
The business present. 'Tis his highness' pleasure
You shall to th' Tower.
BUCKINGHAM   It will help me nothing
To plead mine innocence, for that dye is on me
Which makes my whitest part black. The will of
  heaven
Be done in this and all things: I obey.   210
O my lord Aberga'ny, fare you well.
BRANDON   Nay, he must bear you company.
[to Abergavenny]   The King
Is pleased you shall to th' Tower, till you know
How he determines further.
ABERGAVENNY   As the Duke said,
The will of heaven be done, and the King's pleasure   215
By me obeyed.
BRANDON   Here is a warrant from
The King t'attach Lord Montague and the bodies
Of the Duke's confessor, John de la Court,
One Gilbert Park, his chancellor –
BUCKINGHAM   So, so;
These are the limbs o'th' plot. No more, I hope?   220
BRANDON   A monk o'th' Chartreux.
BUCKINGHAM   O, Nicholas Hopkins?
BRANDON   He.
BUCKINGHAM
My surveyor is false: the o'er-great Cardinal
Hath showed him gold. My life is spanned already.
I am the shadow of poor Buckingham,
Whose figure even this instant cloud puts on   225
By darkening my clear sun. My lord, farewell.
                                                            Exeunt.

1.2   *Cornetts. Enter* KING *Henry, leaning on the*
        Cardinal's shoulder, the nobles, and
        Sir Thomas LOVELL; *the Cardinal places*
        himself under the King's feet on his right side.
        A Secretary attends the Cardinal.

KING   My life itself, and the best heart of it,
Thanks you for this great care. I stood i'th' level
Of a full-charged confederacy, and give thanks
To you that choked it. Let be called before us
That gentleman of Buckingham's: in person   5
I'll hear him his confessions justify,
And point by point the treasons of his master
He shall again relate.

A noise within crying 'Room for the Queen!' *who, as she*
enters is ushered by the Duke of NORFOLK. *Enter* Queen
KATHERINE, NORFOLK *and the* Duke of SUFFOLK.
Katherine kneels. King riseth from his state, takes her up,
and kisses her.

KATHERINE   Nay, we must longer kneel. I am a suitor.
KING   Arise, and take place by us.
    [*The King placeth her by him.*]
10   Half your suit
  Never name to us. You have half our power;
  The other moiety ere you ask is given.
  Repeat your will and take it.
KATHERINE   Thank your majesty.
  That you would love yourself, and in that love
15   Not unconsidered leave your honour nor
  The dignity of your office, is the point
  Of my petition.
KING   Lady mine, proceed.
KATHERINE   I am solicited – not by a few,
  And those of true condition – that your subjects
20   Are in great grievance. There have been commissions
  Sent down among 'em which hath flawed the heart
  Of all their loyalties; wherein although,
  My good lord Cardinal, they vent reproaches
  Most bitterly on you as putter-on
25   Of these exactions, yet the King our master –
  Whose honour heaven shield from soil – even he
    escapes not
  Language unmannerly, yea, such which breaks
  The sides of loyalty and almost appears
  In loud rebellion.
NORFOLK   Not almost appears,
30   It doth appear; for, upon these taxations,
  The clothiers all, not able to maintain
  The many to them longing, have put off
  The spinsters, carders, fullers, weavers, who,
  Unfit for other life, compelled by hunger
35   And lack of other means, in desperate manner,
  Daring th'event to th' teeth, are all in uproar,
  And danger serves among them.
KING   Taxation?
  Wherein, and what taxation? My lord Cardinal,
  You that are blamed for it alike with us,
  Know you of this taxation?
40 WOLSEY   Please you, sir,
  I know but of a single part in aught
  Pertains to th' state, and front but in that file
  Where others tell steps with me.
KATHERINE   No, my lord,
  You know no more than others, but you frame
45   Things that are known alike, which are not wholesome
  To those which would not know them and yet must
  Perforce be their acquaintance. These exactions
  Whereof my sovereign would have note, they are
  Most pestilent to th' hearing, and to bear 'em
50   The back is sacrifice to th' load. They say

  They are devised by you, or else you suffer
  Too hard an exclamation.
KING   Still 'exaction'!
  The nature of it? In what kind, let's know,
  Is this exaction?
KATHERINE   I am much too venturous
  In tempting of your patience, but am boldened   55
  Under your promised pardon. The subjects' grief
  Comes through commissions which compels from each
  The sixth part of his substance, to be levied
  Without delay; and the pretence for this
  Is named your wars in France. This makes bold mouths: 60
  Tongues spit their duties out, and cold hearts freeze
  Allegiance in them. Their curses now
  Live where their prayers did, and it's come to pass
  This tractable obedience is a slave
  To each incensed will. I would your highness   65
  Would give it quick consideration, for
  There is no primer baseness.
KING   By my life,
  This is against our pleasure.
WOLSEY   And for me,
  I have no further gone in this than by
  A single voice, and that not passed me but   70
  By learned approbation of the judges. If I am
  Traduced by ignorant tongues, which neither know
  My faculties nor person yet will be
  The chronicles of my doing, let me say
  'Tis but the fate of place and the rough brake   75
  That virtue must go through. We must not stint
  Our necessary actions in the fear
  To cope malicious censurers, which ever,
  As ravenous fishes do a vessel follow
  That is new-trimmed, but benefit no further   80
  Than vainly longing. What we oft do best,
  By sick interpreters, or weak ones, is
  Not ours or not allowed; what worst, as oft,
  Hitting a grosser quality, is cried up
  For our best act. If we shall stand still   85
  In fear our motion will be mocked or carped at,
  We should take root here where we sit,
  Or sit state-statues only.
KING   Things done well,
  And with a care, exempt themselves from fear;
  Things done without example in their issue   90
  Are to be feared. Have you a precedent
  Of this commission? I believe not any.
  We must not rend our subjects from our laws
  And stick them in our will. Sixth part of each?
  A trembling contribution! Why, we take   95
  From every tree lop, bark and part o'th' timber,
  And though we leave it with a root, thus hacked
  The air will drink the sap. To every county
  Where this is questioned send our letters with
  Free pardon to each man that has denied   100
  The force of this commission. Pray look to't:
  I put it to your care.

WOLSEY [*apart to his Secretary*]   A word with you.
    Let there be letters writ to every shire
    Of the King's grace and pardon. The grieved commons
105   Hardly conceive of me: let it be noised
    That through our intercession this revokement
    And pardon comes. I shall anon advise you
    Further in the proceeding.   *Exit Secretary.*

        Enter Surveyor.

KATHERINE   I am sorry that the Duke of Buckingham
    Is run in your displeasure.
110 KING   It grieves many.
    The gentleman is learned and a most rare speaker,
    To nature none more bound, his training such
    That he may furnish and instruct great teachers
    And never seek for aid out of himself. Yet see,
115   When these so noble benefits shall prove
    Not well disposed, the mind growing once corrupt,
    They turn to vicious forms, ten times more ugly
    Than ever they were fair. This man so complete,
    Who was enrolled 'mongst wonders – and when we,
120   Almost with ravished listening, could not find
    His hour of speech a minute – he, my lady,
    Hath into monstrous habits put the graces
    That once were his and is become as black
    As if besmeared in hell. Sit by us. You shall hear –
125   This was his gentleman in trust – of him
    Things to strike honour sad. Bid him recount
    The fore-recited practices, whereof
    We cannot feel too little, hear too much.
WOLSEY
    Stand forth, and with bold spirit relate what you,
130   Most like a careful subject, have collected
    Out of the Duke of Buckingham.
KING   Speak freely.
SURVEYOR   First, it was usual with him – every day
    It would infect his speech – that if the King
    Should without issue die, he'll carry it so
135   To make the sceptre his. These very words
    I've heard him utter to his son-in-law,
    Lord Abergavenny, to whom by oath he menaced
    Revenge upon the Cardinal.
WOLSEY   Please your highness note
    His dangerous conception in this point,
140   Not friended by his wish to your high person;
    His will is most malignant, and it stretches
    Beyond you to your friends.
KATHERINE   My learned lord Cardinal,
    Deliver all with charity.
KING   Speak on.
    How grounded he his title to the crown
145   Upon our fail? To this point hast thou heard him
    At any time speak aught?
SURVEYOR   He was brought to this
    By a vain prophecy of Nicholas Hopkins.
KING   What was that Hopkins?

SURVEYOR   Sir, a Chartreux friar,
    His confessor, who fed him every minute
    With words of sovereignty.
KING   How knowst thou this?   150
SURVEYOR
    Not long before your highness sped to France,
    The Duke being at the Rose, within the parish
    Saint Laurence Pountney, did of me demand
    What was the speech among the Londoners
    Concerning the French journey. I replied   155
    Men feared the French would prove perfidious,
    To the King's danger. Presently, the Duke
    Said 'twas the fear indeed, and that he doubted
    'Twould prove the verity of certain words
    Spoke by a holy monk, 'that oft', says he,   160
    'Hath sent to me, wishing me to permit
    John de la Court, my chaplain, a choice hour
    To hear from him a matter of some moment;
    Whom after, under the confession's seal,
    He solemnly had sworn that what he spoke   165
    My chaplain to no creature living but
    To me should utter, with demure confidence
    This pausingly ensued: "Neither the King, nor's heirs –
    Tell you the Duke – shall prosper. Bid him strive
    To purchase the love o'th' commonalty. The Duke   170
    Shall govern England."'
KATHERINE   If I know you well,
    You were the Duke's surveyor, and lost your office
    On the complaint o'th' tenants. Take good heed
    You charge not in your spleen a noble person
    And spoil your nobler soul. I say, take heed –   175
    Yes, heartily beseech you.
KING   Let him on:
[*to the Surveyor*] Go forward.
SURVEYOR   On my soul, I'll speak but truth.
    I told my lord the Duke, by th' devil's illusions
    The monk might be deceived, and that 'twas dangerous
    For him to ruminate on this so far until   180
    It forged him some design – which, being believed,
    It was much like to do. He answered, 'Tush,
    It can do me no damage,' adding further
    That had the King in his last sickness failed,
    The Cardinal's and Sir Thomas Lovell's heads   185
    Should have gone off.
KING   Ha? What, so rank? Ah, ha!
    There's mischief in this man. Canst thou say further?
SURVEYOR   I can, my liege.
KING   Proceed.
SURVEYOR   Being at Greenwich,
    After your highness had reproved the Duke
    About Sir William Bulmer –
KING   I remember   190
    Of such a time: being my sworn servant,
    The Duke retained him his. But on: what hence?
SURVEYOR
    'If', quoth he, 'I for this had been committed' –

As to the Tower, I thought – 'I would have played
195   The part my father meant to act upon
Th'usurper Richard, who being at Salisbury,
Made suit to come in's presence; which if granted,
As he made semblance of his duty would
Have put his knife into him.'

KING   A giant traitor.

WOLSEY
200   Now, madam, may his highness live in freedom
And this man out of prison?

KATHERINE   God mend all.

KING
There's something more would out of thee: what sayst?

SURVEYOR   After 'the Duke his father', with 'the knife',
He stretched him, and with one hand on his dagger,
205   Another spread on's breast, mounting his eyes,
He did discharge a horrible oath, whose tenor
Was, were he evil used, he would outgo
His father by as much as a performance
Does an irresolute purpose.

KING   There's his period:
210   To sheathe his knife in us. He is attached;
Call him to present trial. If he may
Find mercy in the law, 'tis his; if none,
Let him not seek't of us. By day and night,
He's traitor to th' height!   *Exeunt.*

1.3   *Enter* Lord CHAMBERLAIN *and* Lord SANDYS.

CHAMBERLAIN
Is't possible the spells of France should juggle
Men into such strange mysteries?

SANDYS   New customs,
Though they be never so ridiculous –
Nay, let 'em be unmanly – yet are followed.

CHAMBERLAIN
5   As far as I see, all the good our English
Have got by the late voyage is but merely
A fit or two o'th' face – but they are shrewd ones,
For when they hold 'em you would swear directly
Their very noses had been counsellors
10   To Pepin or Clotharius, they keep state so.

SANDYS
They have all new legs, and lame ones. One would
    take it,
That never see 'em pace before, the spavin
Or springhalt reigned among 'em.

CHAMBERLAIN   Death, my lord,
Their clothes are after such a pagan cut to't,
That sure they've worn out Christendom.

Enter Sir Thomas LOVELL.

15   How now?
What news, Sir Thomas Lovell?

LOVELL   Faith, my lord,
I hear of none but the new proclamation
That's clapped upon the Court Gate.

CHAMBERLAIN   What is't for?

LOVELL   The reformation of our travelled gallants
That fill the court with quarrels, talk and tailors.   20

CHAMBERLAIN
I'm glad 'tis there. Now I would pray our monsieurs
To think an English courtier may be wise
And never see the Louvre.

LOVELL   They must either,
For so run the conditions, leave those remnants
Of fool and feather that they got in France,   25
With all their honourable points of ignorance
Pertaining thereunto – as fights and fireworks;
Abusing better men than they can be
Out of a foreign wisdom – renouncing clean
The faith they have in tennis and tall stockings,   30
Short blistered breeches, and those types of travel,
And understand again like honest men,
Or pack to their old playfellows. There, I take it,
They may, *cum privilegio, oui*–away
The lag end of their lewdness and be laughed at.   35

SANDYS   'Tis time to give 'em physic, their diseases
Are grown so catching.

CHAMBERLAIN   What a loss our ladies
Will have of these trim vanities!

LOVELL   Ay, marry,
There will be woe indeed, lords. The sly whoresons
Have got a speeding trick to lay down ladies: 40
A French song and a fiddle has no fellow.

SANDYS   The devil fiddle 'em! I am glad they are going,
For sure there's no converting of 'em. Now
An honest country lord, as I am, beaten
A long time out of play, may bring his plainsong   45
And have an hour of hearing, and, by'r Lady,
Held current music too.

CHAMBERLAIN   Well said, Lord Sandys.
Your colt's tooth is not cast yet?

SANDYS   No, my lord,
Nor shall not while I have a stump.

CHAMBERLAIN   Sir Thomas,
Whither were you a-going?

LOVELL   To the Cardinal's.   50
Your lordship is a guest too.

CHAMBERLAIN   O, 'tis true.
This night he makes a supper, and a great one,
To many lords and ladies. There will be
The beauty of this kingdom, I'll assure you.

LOVELL
That churchman bears a bounteous mind indeed,   55
A hand as fruitful as the land that feeds us:
His dews fall everywhere.

CHAMBERLAIN   No doubt he's noble –
He had a black mouth that said other of him.

SANDYS   He may, my lord; 'has wherewithal. In him
Sparing would show a worse sin than ill doctrine.   60
Men of his way should be most liberal:
They are set here for examples.

CHAMBERLAIN   True, they are so,

But few now give so great ones. My barge stays.
Your lordship shall along. Come, good Sir Thomas,
We shall be late else, which I would not be,
For I was spoke to, with Sir Henry Guildford,
This night to be comptrollers.

SANDYS   I am your lordship's.   *Exeunt.*

1.4   *Hautboys. A small table under a state for the*
Cardinal; a longer table for the guests. Then enter
ANNE *Bullen and diverse other Ladies and*
Gentlemen, as guests, at one door. At another
door enter Sir Henry GUILDFORD.

GUILDFORD   Ladies, a general welcome from his grace
Salutes ye all. This night he dedicates
To fair content and you. None here, he hopes,
In all this noble bevy has brought with her
One care abroad: he would have all as merry
As, first, good company, good wine, good welcome
Can make good people.

          Enter Lord CHAMBERLAIN, Lord SANDYS *and*
                      Sir Thomas LOVELL.

                    O my lord, you're tardy.
The very thought of this fair company
Clapped wings to me.

CHAMBERLAIN   You are young, Sir Harry Guildford.
SANDYS   Sir Thomas Lovell, had the Cardinal
But half my lay thoughts in him, some of these
Should find a running banquet ere they rested
I think would better please 'em. By my life,
They are a sweet society of fair ones.

LOVELL   O, that your lordship were but now confessor
To one or two of these.

SANDYS   I would I were:
They should find easy penance.

LOVELL   Faith, how easy?
SANDYS   As easy as a down bed would afford it.
CHAMBERLAIN
Sweet ladies, will it please you sit? Sir Harry,
Place you that side; I'll take the charge of this.
His grace is entering. Nay, you must not freeze:
Two women placed together makes cold weather.
My lord Sandys, you are one will keep 'em waking:
Pray sit between these ladies.

SANDYS   By my faith,
And thank your lordship. By your leave, sweet ladies.
If I chance to talk a little wild, forgive me:
I had it from my father.

ANNE   Was he mad, sir?
SANDYS   O, very mad – exceeding mad in love, too –
But he would bite none. Just as I do now,
He would kiss you twenty with a breath.

CHAMBERLAIN   Well said, my lord.
So, now you're fairly seated, gentlemen,
The penance lies on you if these fair ladies
Pass away frowning.

SANDYS   For my little cure
Let me alone.

    Hautboys. Enter Cardinal WOLSEY *and takes his state.*

WOLSEY
You're welcome, my fair guests. That noble lady
Or gentleman that is not freely merry
Is not my friend. This, to confirm my welcome;
And to you all, good health!

SANDYS   Your grace is noble:
Let me have such a bowl may hold my thanks
And save me so much talking.

WOLSEY   My lord Sandys,
I am beholding to you. Cheer your neighbours.
Ladies, you are not merry. Gentlemen,
Whose fault is this?

SANDYS   The red wine first must rise
In their fair cheeks, my lord; then we shall have 'em
Talk us to silence.

ANNE   You are a merry gamester,
My lord Sandys.

SANDYS   Yes, if I make my play.
Here's to your ladyship; and pledge it, madam,
For 'tis to such a thing –

ANNE   You cannot show me.
SANDYS   I told your grace they would talk anon.
         [*Drum and trumpet. Chambers discharged.*]
WOLSEY   What's that?
CHAMBERLAIN   Look out there, some of ye.
WOLSEY   What warlike voice,
And to what end, is this? Nay, ladies, fear not:
By all the laws of war you're privileged.

               Enter a Servant.

CHAMBERLAIN   How now, what is't?
SERVANT   A noble troop of strangers,
For so they seem. They've left their barge and landed,
And hither make, as great ambassadors
From foreign princes.

WOLSEY   Good Lord Chamberlain,
Go, give 'em welcome – you can speak the French
tongue –
And pray receive 'em nobly, and conduct 'em
Into our presence, where this heaven of beauty
Shall shine at full upon them. Some attend him.
          Exit Lord Chamberlain, attended.
   [*All rise, and tables removed.*]
You have now a broken banquet, but we'll mend it.
A good digestion to you all, and once more
I shower a welcome on ye. Welcome all!

Hautboys. Enter KING *and others as masquers, habited like*
shepherds, ushered by the Lord CHAMBERLAIN. *They pass*
directly before the Cardinal and gracefully salute him.

A noble company. What are their pleasures?
CHAMBERLAIN
Because they speak no English, thus they prayed

To tell your grace: that having heard by fame
Of this so noble and so fair assembly
This night to meet here, they could do no less,
Out of the great respect they bear to beauty,
70 But leave their flocks and, under your fair conduct,
Crave leave to view these ladies and entreat
An hour of revels with 'em.

WOLSEY   Say, Lord Chamberlain,
They have done my poor house grace; for which I
    pay 'em
A thousand thanks and pray 'em take their pleasures.
    [*The masquers choose ladies. The King chooses Anne*
    Bullen.]

75 KING   The fairest hand I ever touched. O Beauty,
Till now I never knew thee.   [*Music. Dance.*]

WOLSEY   My lord.

CHAMBERLAIN   Your grace?

WOLSEY   Pray tell 'em thus much from me:
There should be one amongst 'em by his person
More worthy this place than myself, to whom,
80 If I but knew him, with my love and duty
I would surrender it.

CHAMBERLAIN   I will, my lord.
    [*Chamberlain talks in a whisper with the masquers*].

WOLSEY   What say they?

CHAMBERLAIN   Such a one they all confess
There is indeed, which they would have your grace
Find out, and he will take it.

WOLSEY   Let me see, then.
85 By all your good leaves, gentlemen, here I'll make
My royal choice.

KING   Ye have found him, Cardinal.
    [*Unmasks.*]
You hold a fair assembly. You do well, lord:
You are a churchman, or I'll tell you, Cardinal,
I should judge now unhappily.

WOLSEY   I am glad
Your grace is grown so pleasant.

90 KING   My lord Chamberlain,
Prithee come hither. What fair lady's that?

CHAMBERLAIN
An't please your grace, Sir Thomas Bullen's daughter,
The Viscount Rochford, one of her highness' women.

KING
By heaven, she is a dainty one. [*to Anne*] Sweetheart,
95 I were unmannerly to take you out
And not to kiss you. A health, gentlemen!
Let it go round.

WOLSEY   Sir Thomas Lovell, is the banquet ready
I'th' privy chamber?

LOVELL   Yes, my lord.

WOLSEY   Your grace,
100 I fear, with dancing is a little heated.

KING   I fear too much.

WOLSEY   There's fresher air, my lord,
In the next chamber.

KING   Lead in your ladies, everyone. Sweet partner,

I must not yet forsake you. Let's be merry,
Good my lord Cardinal. I have half a dozen healths   105
To drink to these fair ladies, and a measure
To lead 'em once again, and then let's dream
Who's best in favour. Let the music knock it.
    Exeunt with trumpets.

2.1   *Enter two* Gentlemen *at several doors.*

1 GENTLEMAN   Whither away so fast?

2 GENTLEMAN   O, God save ye.
Even to the Hall to hear what shall become
Of the great Duke of Buckingham.

1 GENTLEMAN   I'll save you
That labour, sir. All's now done but the ceremony
Of bringing back the prisoner.

2 GENTLEMAN   Were you there?   5

1 GENTLEMAN   Yes, indeed was I.

2 GENTLEMAN   Pray speak what has happened.

1 GENTLEMAN
You may guess quickly what.

2 GENTLEMAN   Is he found guilty?

1 GENTLEMAN   Yes, truly is he, and condemned upon't.

2 GENTLEMAN   I am sorry for't.

1 GENTLEMAN   So are a number more.

2 GENTLEMAN   But pray, how passed it?   10

1 GENTLEMAN   I'll tell you in a little. The great Duke
Came to the bar, where to his accusations
He pleaded still not guilty and alleged
Many sharp reasons to defeat the law.
The King's attorney, on the contrary,   15
Urged on the examinations, proofs, confessions,
Of diverse witnesses, which the Duke desired
To have brought *viva voce* to his face;
At which appeared against him his surveyor,
Sir Gilbert Park his chancellor, and John Court,   20
Confessor to him, with that devil monk,
Hopkins, that made this mischief.

2 GENTLEMAN   That was he
That fed him with his prophecies.

1 GENTLEMAN   The same.
All these accused him strongly, which he fain
Would have flung from him, but indeed he could not.   25
And so his peers, upon this evidence,
Have found him guilty of high treason. Much
He spoke, and learnedly, for life, but all
Was either pitied in him or forgotten.

2 GENTLEMAN   After all this, how did he bear himself?   30

1 GENTLEMAN
When he was brought again to th' bar to hear
His knell rung out, his judgement, he was stirred
With such an agony he sweat extremely
And something spoke in choler, ill and hasty;
But he fell to himself again, and sweetly   35
In all the rest showed a most noble patience.

2 GENTLEMAN   I do not think he fears death.

1 GENTLEMAN   Sure he does not;

He never was so womanish. The cause
He may a little grieve at.
2 GENTLEMAN   Certainly
The Cardinal is the end of this.
1 GENTLEMAN   'Tis likely,
By all conjectures: first, Kildare's attainder,
Then Deputy of Ireland, who removed,
Earl Surrey was sent thither, and in haste too,
Lest he should help his father.
2 GENTLEMAN   That trick of state
Was a deep envious one.
1 GENTLEMAN   At his return
No doubt he will requite it. This is noted,
And generally: whoever the King favours,
The Cardinal instantly will find employment –
And far enough from court, too.
2 GENTLEMAN   All the commons
Hate him perniciously and, o'my conscience,
Wish him ten fathom deep. This Duke as much
They love and dote on, call him 'bounteous
     Buckingham,
The mirror of all courtesy' –

Enter BUCKINGHAM *from his arraignment, Tipstaves before*
him, the axe with the edge towards him, Halberds on each
side, accompanied with Sir Thomas LOVELL, *Sir Nicholas*
VAUX, *Lord* SANDYS, *Attendants and Common People.*

1 GENTLEMAN   Stay there, sir,
And see the noble ruined man you speak of.
2 GENTLEMAN   Let's stand close and behold him.
BUCKINGHAM   All good people,
You that thus far have come to pity me,
Hear what I say, and then go home and lose me.
I have this day received a traitor's judgement,
And by that name must die; yet heaven bear witness,
And if I have a conscience, let it sink me,
Even as the axe falls, if I be not faithful.
The law I bear no malice for my death –
'T has done upon the premises but justice –
But those that sought it I could wish more Christians.
Be what they will, I heartily forgive 'em.
Yet let 'em look they glory not in mischief
Nor build their evils on the graves of great men,
For then my guiltless blood must cry against 'em.
For further life in this world I ne'er hope,
Nor will I sue, although the King have mercies
More than I dare make faults. You few that loved me
And dare be bold to weep for Buckingham,
His noble friends and fellows, whom to leave
Is only bitter to him, only dying,
Go with me like good angels to my end,
And as the long divorce of steel falls on me,
Make of your prayers one sweet sacrifice,
And lift my soul to heaven. Lead on, i'God's name.
LOVELL   I do beseech your grace, for charity,
If ever any malice in your heart
Were hid against me, now to forgive me frankly.

BUCKINGHAM   Sir Thomas Lovell, I as free forgive you
As I would be forgiven. I forgive all.
There cannot be those numberless offences
'Gainst me that I cannot take peace with. No black envy   85
Shall make my grave. Commend me to his grace,
And if he speak of Buckingham, pray tell him
You met him half in heaven. My vows and prayers
Yet are the King's and, till my soul forsake,
Shall cry for blessings on him. May he live   90
Longer than I have time to tell his years;
Ever beloved and loving may his rule be;
And when old Time shall lead him to his end,
Goodness and he fill up one monument.
LOVELL   To th' waterside I must conduct your grace,   95
Then give my charge up to Sir Nicholas Vaux,
Who undertakes you to your end.
VAUX [*to Attendants*]   Prepare there:
The Duke is coming. See the barge be ready,
And fit it with such furniture as suits
The greatness of his person.
BUCKINGHAM   Nay, Sir Nicholas,   100
Let it alone. My state now will but mock me.
When I came hither, I was Lord High Constable
And Duke of Buckingham; now, poor Edward Bohun.
Yet I am richer than my base accusers,
That never knew what truth meant. I now seal it,   105
And with that blood will make 'em one day groan for't.
My noble father, Henry of Buckingham,
Who first raised head against usurping Richard,
Flying for succour to his servant Banister,
Being distressed, was by that wretch betrayed,   110
And, without trial, fell. God's peace be with him.
Henry the Seventh succeeding, truly pitying
My father's loss, like a most royal prince,
Restored me to my honours and out of ruins
Made my name once more noble. Now his son,   115
Henry the Eighth, life, honour, name, and all
That made me happy at one stroke has taken
For ever from the world. I had my trial,
And must needs say a noble one, which makes me
A little happier than my wretched father.   120
Yet thus far we are one in fortunes: both
Fell by our servants, by those men we loved most –
A most unnatural and faithless service.
Heaven has an end in all. Yet, you that hear me,
This from a dying man receive as certain: 125
Where you are liberal of your loves and counsels,
Be sure you be not loose; for those you make friends
And give your hearts to, when they once perceive
The least rub in your fortunes, fall away
Like water from ye, never found again   130
But where they mean to sink ye. All good people,
Pray for me. I must now forsake ye. The last hour
Of my long weary life is come upon me.
Farewell, and when you would say something that is sad,
Speak how I fell. I have done, and God forgive me.   135
                    Exeunt Duke and train.

1 GENTLEMAN   O, this is full of pity. Sir, it calls,
   I fear, too many curses on their heads
   That were the authors.
2 GENTLEMAN   If the Duke be guiltless,
   'Tis full of woe. Yet I can give you inkling
140   Of an ensuing evil, if it fall,
   Greater than this.
1 GENTLEMAN   Good angels keep it from us.
   What may it be? You do not doubt my faith, sir?
2 GENTLEMAN
   This secret is so weighty 'twill require
   A strong faith to conceal it.
1 GENTLEMAN   Let me have it;
   I do not talk much.
145 2 GENTLEMAN   I am confident;
   You shall, sir. Did you not of late days hear
   A buzzing of a separation
   Between the King and Katherine?
1 GENTLEMAN   Yes, but it held not,
   For when the King once heard it, out of anger
150   He sent command to the Lord Mayor straight
   To stop the rumour and allay those tongues
   That durst disperse it.
2 GENTLEMAN   But that slander, sir,
   Is found a truth now, for it grows again
   Fresher then e'er it was, and held for certain
155   The King will venture at it. Either the Cardinal
   Or some about him near have, out of malice
   To the good Queen, possessed him with a scruple
   That will undo her. To confirm this, too,
   Cardinal Campeius is arrived, and lately,
   As all think, for this business.
160 1 GENTLEMAN   'Tis the Cardinal;
   And merely to revenge him on the Emperor
   For not bestowing on him at his asking
   The archbishopric of Toledo this is purposed.
2 GENTLEMAN
   I think you have hit the mark. But is't not cruel
   That she should feel the smart of this? The
165   Cardinal
   Will have his will, and she must fall.
1 GENTLEMAN   'Tis woeful.
   We are too open here to argue this.
   Let's think in private more.   *Exeunt.*

2.2 *Enter* Lord CHAMBERLAIN, *reading this letter.*

CHAMBERLAIN *My lord, the horses your lordship sent for,*
   with all the care I had I saw well chosen, ridden and
   furnished. They were young and handsome and of the best
   breed in the north. When they were ready to set out for
5   *London, a man of my lord Cardinal's, by commission and*
   main power, took 'em from me with this reason: his master
   would be served before a subject, if not before the King,
   which stopped our mouths, sir.
   I fear he will indeed. Well, let him have them;
10   He will have all, I think.

Enter to the Lord Chamberlain the Dukes of
NORFOLK *and* SUFFOLK.

NORFOLK   Well met, my lord Chamberlain.
CHAMBERLAIN   Good day to both your graces.
SUFFOLK   How is the King employed?
CHAMBERLAIN   I left him private,
   Full of sad thoughts and troubles.
NORFOLK   What's the cause?
CHAMBERLAIN
   It seems the marriage with his brother's wife   15
   Has crept too near his conscience.
SUFFOLK   No, his conscience
   Has crept too near another lady.
NORFOLK   'Tis so;
   This is the Cardinal's doing. The King–Cardinal,
   That blind priest, like the eldest son of Fortune,
   Turns what he list. The King will know him one day. 20
SUFFOLK
   Pray God he do. He'll never know himself else.
NORFOLK   How holily he works in all his business,
   And with what zeal! For now he has cracked the
      league
   Between us and the Emperor, the Queen's great
      nephew,
   He dives into the King's soul and there scatters   25
   Dangers, doubts, wringing of the conscience,
   Fears and despairs – and all these for his marriage.
   And out of all these, to restore the King,
   He counsels a divorce, a loss of her
   That like a jewel has hung twenty years   30
   About his neck yet never lost her lustre;
   Of her that loves him with that excellence
   That angels love good men with; even of her
   That, when the greatest stroke of Fortune falls,
   Will bless the King – and is not this course pious? 35
CHAMBERLAIN
   Heaven keep me from such counsel! 'Tis most true:
   These news are everywhere – every tongue speaks 'em,
   And every true heart weeps for't. All that dare
   Look into these affairs see this main end:
   The French king's sister. Heaven will one day open 40
   The King's eyes, that so long have slept upon
   This bold bad man.
SUFFOLK   And free us from his slavery.
NORFOLK   We had need pray,
   And heartily, for our deliverance,
   Or this imperious man will work us all   45
   From princes into pages. All men's honours
   Lie like one lump before him, to be fashioned
   Into what pitch he please.
SUFFOLK   For me, my lords,
   I love him not nor fear him: there's my creed.
   As I am made without him, so I'll stand,   50
   If the King please. His curses and his blessings
   Touch me alike: they're breath I not believe in.
   I knew him and I know him; so I leave him

To him that made him proud, the Pope.
NORFOLK   Let's in,
And with some other business put the King
From these sad thoughts that work too much upon
    him.
My lord, you'll bear us company?
CHAMBERLAIN   Excuse me;
The King has sent me otherwise. Besides,
You'll find a most unfit time to disturb him.
Health to your lordships.
NORFOLK   Thanks, my good lord Chamberlain.
       Exit Lord Chamberlain, and the King draws
                  the curtain and sits reading pensively.
SUFFOLK   How sad he looks. Sure he is much afflicted.
KING   Who's there? Ha?
NORFOLK   Pray God he be not angry.
KING
Who's there, I say? How dare you thrust yourselves
Into my private meditations?
Who am I? Ha?
NORFOLK   A gracious king that pardons all offences
Malice ne'er meant. Our breach of duty this way
Is business of estate, in which we come
To know your royal pleasure.
KING   Ye are too bold.
Go to. I'll make ye know your times of business.
Is this an hour for temporal affairs? Ha?

       Enter WOLSEY *and* CAMPEIUS *with a commission.*

Who's there? My good lord Cardinal? O my Wolsey,
The quiet of my wounded conscience,
Thou art a cure fit for a king. [*to Campeius*] You're
    welcome,
Most learned reverend sir, into our kingdom;
Use us and it. [*to Wolsey*] My good lord, have great
    care
I be not found a talker.
WOLSEY   Sir, you cannot.
I would your grace would give us but an hour
Of private conference.
KING [*to Norfolk and Suffolk*]   We are busy. Go.
NORFOLK [*aside to Suffolk*]
This priest has no pride in him!
SUFFOLK [*aside to Norfolk*]   Not to speak of.
I would not be so sick, though, for his place.
But this cannot continue.
NORFOLK [*aside to Suffolk*]   If it do,
I'll venture one have-at-him.
SUFFOLK [*aside to Norfolk*]   I another.
                       Exeunt Norfolk and Suffolk.
WOLSEY   Your grace has given a precedent of wisdom
Above all princes in committing freely
Your scruple to the voice of Christendom.
Who can be angry now? What envy reach you?
The Spaniard, tied by blood and favour to her,
Must now confess, if they have any goodness,
The trial just and noble. All the clerks –

I mean the learned ones in Christian kingdoms –
Have their free voices. Rome, the nurse of judgement,
Invited by your noble self, hath sent
One general tongue unto us: this good man,
This just and learned priest, Cardinal Campeius,   95
Whom once more I present unto your highness.
KING
And once more in mine arms I bid him welcome,
And thank the holy conclave for their loves:
They have sent me such a man I would have wished for.
CAMPEIUS
Your grace must needs deserve all strangers' loves,   100
You are so noble. To your highness' hand
I tender my commission, by whose virtue,
The court of Rome commanding, you, my lord
Cardinal of York, are joined with me their servant
In the unpartial judging of this business.   105
KING   Two equal men. The Queen shall be acquainted
Forthwith for what you come. Where's Gardiner?
WOLSEY   I know your majesty has always loved her
So dear in heart not to deny her that
A woman of less place might ask by law: 110
Scholars allowed freely to argue for her.
KING   Ay, and the best she shall have – and my favour
To him that does best: God forbid else. Cardinal,
Prithee call Gardiner to me, my new secretary:
I find him a fit fellow.   115

                       Enter GARDINER.

WOLSEY [*aside to Gardiner*]
Give me your hand. Much joy and favour to you;
You are the King's now.
GARDINER [*aside to Wolsey*]   But to be commanded
For ever by your grace, whose hand has raised me.
KING   Come hither, Gardiner.
            [*The King walks and whispers with Gardiner.*]
CAMPEIUS   My lord of York, was not one Doctor Pace   120
In this man's place before him?
WOLSEY   Yes, he was.
CAMPEIUS   Was he not held a learned man?
WOLSEY   Yes, surely.
CAMPEIUS
Believe me, there's an ill opinion spread, then,
Even of yourself, lord Cardinal.
WOLSEY   How? Of me?
CAMPEIUS   They will not stick to say you envied him,   125
And fearing he would rise – he was so virtuous –
Kept him a foreign man still, which so grieved him
That he ran mad and died.
WOLSEY   Heaven's peace be with him:
That's Christian care enough. For living murmurers
There's places of rebuke. He was a fool,   130
For he would needs be virtuous.
[*Gestures towards Gardiner.*]   That good fellow,
If I command him, follows my appointment.
I will have none so near else. Learn this, brother:
We live not to be griped by meaner persons.

135   KING   Deliver this with modesty to th' Queen.

                                          Exit Gardiner.

        The most convenient place that I can think of

        For such receipt of learning is Blackfriars:

        There ye shall meet about this weighty business.

        My Wolsey, see it furnished. O my lord,

140   Would it not grieve an able man to leave

        So sweet a bedfellow? But conscience, conscience –

        O, 'tis a tender place, and I must leave her.   *Exeunt.*

2.3   *Enter* ANNE Bullen *and an* Old Lady.

    ANNE

        Not for that neither. Here's the pang that pinches:

        His highness having lived so long with her and she

        So good a lady that no tongue could ever

        Pronounce dishonour of her – by my life,

5   She never knew harm-doing – O, now, after

        So many courses of the sun enthroned,

        Still growing in a majesty and pomp the which

        To leave a thousandfold more bitter than

        'Tis sweet at first t'acquire – after this process,

10   To give her the avaunt, it is a pity

        Would move a monster.

    OLD LADY   Hearts of most hard temper

        Melt and lament for her.

    ANNE   O, God's will! Much better

        She ne'er had known pomp: though't be temporal,

        Yet if that quarrel and Fortune do divorce

15   It from the bearer, 'tis a sufferance panging

        As soul and body's severing.

    OLD LADY   Alas, poor lady,

        She's a stranger now again.

    ANNE   So much the more

        Must pity drop upon her. Verily,

        I swear, 'tis better to be lowly born

20   And range with humble livers in content

        Than to be perked up in a glistering grief

        And wear a golden sorrow.

    OLD LADY   Our content

        Is our best having.

    ANNE   By my troth and maidenhead,

        I would not be a queen.

    OLD LADY   Beshrew me, I would,

25   And venture maidenhead for't; and so would you,

        For all this spice of your hypocrisy.

        You, that have so fair parts of woman on you,

        Have, too, a woman's heart which ever yet

        Affected eminence, wealth, sovereignty;

30   Which, to say sooth, are blessings; and which gifts –

        Saving your mincing – the capacity

        Of your soft cheveril conscience would receive,

        If you might please to stretch it.

    ANNE   Nay, good troth.

    OLD LADY

        Yes, troth and troth. You would not be a queen?

35   ANNE   No, not for all the riches under heaven.

    OLD LADY

        'Tis strange: a threepence bowed would hire me,

        Old as I am, to queen it. But I pray you,

        What think you of a duchess? Have you limbs

        To bear that load of title?

    ANNE   No, in truth.

    OLD LADY   Then you are weakly made. Pluck off a little: 40

        I would not be a young count in your way

        For more than blushing comes to. If your back

        Cannot vouchsafe this burden, 'tis too weak

        Ever to get a boy.

    ANNE   How you do talk!

        I swear again, I would not be a queen   45

        For all the world.

    OLD LADY   In faith, for little England

        You'd venture an emballing. I myself

        Would for Caernarfonshire, although there longed

        No more to th' crown but that. Lo, who comes here?

                 Enter Lord CHAMBERLAIN.

    CHAMBERLAIN

        Good morrow, ladies. What were't worth to know   50

        The secret of your conference?

    ANNE   My good lord,

        Not your demand: it values not your asking.

        Our mistress' sorrows we were pitying.

    CHAMBERLAIN   It was a gentle business, and becoming

        The action of good women. There is hope   55

        All will be well.

    ANNE   Now I pray God, amen.

    CHAMBERLAIN

        You bear a gentle mind, and heavenly blessings

        Follow such creatures. That you may, fair lady,

        Perceive I speak sincerely, and high note's

        Ta'en of your many virtues, the King's majesty   60

        Commends his good opinion of you, and

        Does purpose honour to you no less flowing

        Than Marchioness of Pembroke, to which title

        A thousand pound a year annual support

        Out of his grace he adds.

    ANNE   I do not know   65

        What kind of my obedience I should tender.

        More than my all is nothing; nor my prayers

        Are not words duly hallowed, nor my wishes

        More worth than empty vanities; yet prayers and wishes

        Are all I can return. Beseech your lordship,   70

        Vouchsafe to speak my thanks and my obedience,

        As from a blushing handmaid, to his highness,

        Whose health and royalty I pray for.

    CHAMBERLAIN   Lady,

        I shall not fail t'approve the fair conceit

        The King hath of you. [*aside*] I have perused her well.   75

        Beauty and honour in her are so mingled

        That they have caught the King, and who knows yet

        But from this lady may proceed a gem

        To lighten all this isle. [*to Anne*] I'll to the King

        And say I spoke with you.

ANNE   My honoured lord.   80

Exit Lord Chamberlain.

OLD LADY   Why, this it is: see, see!

I have been begging sixteen years in court –

Am yet a courtier beggarly, nor could

Come pat betwixt too early and too late

For any suit of pounds – and you (O, fate!),   85

A very fresh fish here – fie, fie, fie upon

This compelled fortune! – have your mouth filled up

Before you open it.

ANNE   This is strange to me.

OLD LADY   How tastes it? Is it bitter? Forty pence, no.

There was a lady once – 'tis an old story –   90

That would not be a queen, that would she not,

For all the mud in Egypt. Have you heard it?

ANNE   Come, you are pleasant.

OLD LADY   With your theme I could

O'ermount the lark. The Marchioness of Pembroke?

A thousand pounds a year, for pure respect?   95

No other obligation? By my life,

That promises more thousands: honour's train

Is longer than his foreskirt. By this time,

I know your back will bear a duchess. Say,

Are you not stronger than you were?

ANNE   Good lady,   100

Make yourself mirth with your particular fancy

And leave me out on't. Would I had no being

If this salute my blood a jot. It faints me

To think what follows.

The Queen is comfortless, and we forgetful   105

In our long absence. Pray do not deliver

What here you've heard to her.

OLD LADY   What do you think me?

Exeunt.

2.4   *Trumpets, sennet and cornetts. Enter two Vergers*
with short silver wands; next them two Scribes *in*
the habit of doctors; after them, the Archbishop
of Canterbury alone; after him, the Bishops of
LINCOLN, *Ely, Rochester and St Asaph; next them,*
with some small distance, follows a Gentleman, bearing
the purse with the great seal and a cardinal's hat; then
two Priests, bearing each a silver cross; then a Gentleman
Usher, bare-headed, accompanied with a Sergeant-at-arms,
bearing a silver mace; then two Gentlemen, bearing two
great silver pillars; after them, side by side, the two
Cardinals; *two Noblemen with the sword and mace.*
The KING *takes place under the cloth of state. The two*
Cardinals sit under him as judges. Queen KATHERINE,
attended by GRIFFITH, *takes place some distance from*
the King. The Bishops place themselves on each side the
court in manner of a consistory; below them the Scribes
and a Crier. *The Lords sit next the Bishops. The rest of*
the attendants stand in convenient order about the stage.

WOLSEY   Whilst our commission from Rome is read,

Let silence be commanded.

KING   What's the need?

It hath already publicly been read,

And on all sides th'authority allowed;

You may then spare that time.

WOLSEY   Be't so. Proceed.   5

SCRIBE

Say, 'Henry, King of England, come into the court.'

CRIER   Henry, King of England, come into the court.

KING   Here.

SCRIBE

Say, 'Katherine, Queen of England, come into the

court.'

CRIER

Katherine, Queen of England, come into the court.   10

[*The Queen makes no answer, rises out of her chair,*
goes about the court, comes to the King, and kneels at
his feet; then speaks.]

KATHERINE   Sir, I desire you do me right and justice,

And to bestow your pity on me, for

I am a most poor woman and a stranger,

Born out of your dominions, having here

No judge indifferent nor no more assurance   15

Of equal friendship and proceeding. Alas, sir,

In what have I offended you? What cause

Hath my behaviour given to your displeasure

That thus you should proceed to put me off

And take your good grace from me? Heaven witness   20

I have been to you a true and humble wife,

At all times to your will conformable,

Ever in fear to kindle your dislike,

Yea, subject to your countenance, glad or sorry

As I saw it inclined. When was the hour   25

I ever contradicted your desire,

Or made it not mine too? Or which of your friends

Have I not strove to love, although I knew

He were mine enemy? What friend of mine

That had to him derived your anger did I   30

Continue in my liking? Nay, gave notice

He was from thence discharged? Sir, call to mind

That I have been your wife in this obedience

Upward of twenty years, and have been blessed

With many children by you. If, in the course   35

And process of this time, you can report,

And prove it too, against mine honour aught,

My bond to wedlock, or my love and duty

Against your sacred person, in God's name

Turn me away and let the foulest contempt   40

Shut door upon me, and so give me up

To the sharpest kind of justice. Please you, sir,

The King your father was reputed for

A prince most prudent, of an excellent

And unmatched wit and judgement. Ferdinand,   45

My father, King of Spain, was reckoned one

The wisest prince that there had reigned by many

A year before. It is not to be questioned

That they had gathered a wise council to them

Of every realm, that did debate this business,   50

Who deemed our marriage lawful. Wherefore I
   humbly
Beseech you, sir, to spare me till I may
Be by my friends in Spain advised, whose counsel
I will implore. If not, i'th' name of God,
Your pleasure be fulfilled.

55 WOLSEY   You have here, lady,
And of your choice, these reverend fathers, men
Of singular integrity and learning,
Yea, the elect o'th' land, who are assembled
To plead your cause. It shall be therefore bootless
60 That longer you desire the court, as well
For your own quiet as to rectify
What is unsettled in the King.

CAMPEIUS   His grace
Hath spoken well and justly. Therefore, madam,
It's fit this royal session do proceed
65 And that without delay their arguments
Be now produced and heard.

KATHERINE   Lord Cardinal,
To you I speak.

WOLSEY   Your pleasure, madam.

KATHERINE   Sir,
I am about to weep; but, thinking that
We are a queen, or long have dreamed so, certain
70 The daughter of a king, my drops of tears
I'll turn to sparks of fire.

WOLSEY   Be patient yet.

KATHERINE   I will, when you are humble – nay, before,
Or God will punish me. I do believe,
Induced by potent circumstances, that
75 You are mine enemy, and make my challenge
You shall not be my judge. For it is you
Have blown this coal betwixt my lord and me,
Which God's dew quench. Therefore, I say again,
I utterly abhor, yea, from my soul
80 Refuse you for my judge, whom yet once more
I hold my most malicious foe and think not
At all a friend to truth.

WOLSEY   I do profess
You speak not like yourself, who ever yet
Have stood to charity and displayed th'effects
85 Of disposition gentle and of wisdom
O'er-topping woman's power. Madam, you do me
   wrong.
I have no spleen against you, nor injustice
For you or any. How far I have proceeded,
Or how far further shall, is warranted
90 By a commission from the Consistory,
Yea, the whole Consistory of Rome. You charge me
That I have 'blown this coal': I do deny it.
The King is present. If it be known to him
That I gainsay my deed, how may he wound,
95 And worthily, my falsehood – yea, as much
As you have done my truth. If he know
That I am free of your report, he knows
I am not of your wrong. Therefore in him

It lies to cure me, and the cure is to
Remove these thoughts from you, the which before   100
His highness shall speak in, I do beseech
You, gracious madam, to unthink your speaking,
And to say so no more.

KATHERINE   My lord, my lord,
I am a simple woman, much too weak
T'oppose your cunning. You're meek and
   humble-mouthed;   105
You sign your place and calling, in full seeming,
With meekness and humility; but your heart
Is crammed with arrogancy, spleen and pride.
You have, by fortune and his highness' favours,
Gone slightly o'er low steps, and now are mounted   110
Where powers are your retainers, and your words,
Domestics to you, serve your will as't please
Yourself pronounce their office. I must tell you,
You tender more your person's honour than
Your high profession spiritual; that again   115
I do refuse you for my judge; and here
Before you all, appeal unto the Pope,
To bring my whole cause 'fore His Holiness,
And to be judged by him.

         [*She curtsies to the King and offers to depart.*]

CAMPEIUS   The Queen is obstinate,
Stubborn to justice, apt to accuse it, and   120
Disdainful to be tried by't. 'Tis not well.
She's going away.

KING   Call her again.

CRIER
Katherine, Queen of England, come into the court!

GRIFFITH   Madam, you are called back.

KATHERINE
What need you note it? Pray you keep your way.   125
When you are called, return. Now the Lord help:
They vex me past my patience. Pray you, pass on.
I will not tarry: no, nor ever more
Upon this business my appearance make
In any of their courts.

         Exeunt Queen and her Attendants.

KING   Go thy ways, Kate.   130
That man i'th' world who shall report he has
A better wife, let him in naught be trusted
For speaking false in that. Thou art alone –
If thy rare qualities, sweet gentleness,
Thy meekness saint-like, wife-like government,   135
Obeying in commanding, and thy parts
Sovereign and pious else, could speak thee out –
The queen of earthly queens. She's noble born,
And like her true nobility she has
Carried herself towards me.

WOLSEY   Most gracious sir,   140
In humblest manner I require your highness
That it shall please you to declare in hearing
Of all these ears – for where I am robbed and bound,
There must I be unloosed, although not there
At once and fully satisfied – whether ever I   145

Did broach this business to your highness, or
Laid any scruple in your way which might
Induce you to the question on't, or ever
Have to you, but with thanks to God for such
150 A royal lady, spake one the least word that might
Be to the prejudice of her present state
Or touch of her good person?

KING   My lord Cardinal,
I do excuse you – yea, upon mine honour,
I free you from't. You are not to be taught
155 That you have many enemies that know not
Why they are so but, like to village curs,
Bark when their fellows do. By some of these
The Queen is put in anger. You're excused.
But will you be more justified? You ever
160 Have wished the sleeping of this business, never desired
It to be stirred, but oft have hindered, oft,
The passages made toward it. On my honour,
I speak my good lord Cardinal to this point
And thus far clear him. Now, what moved me to't,
165 I will be bold with time and your attention:
Then mark th'inducement. Thus it came: give heed
         to't.
My conscience first received a tenderness,
Scruple and prick on certain speeches uttered
By th' Bishop of Bayonne, then French ambassador,
170 Who had been hither sent on the debating
A marriage 'twixt the Duke of Orléans and
Our daughter Mary. I'th' progress of this business,
Ere a determinate resolution, he –
I mean the Bishop – did require a respite,
175 Wherein he might the King his lord advertise
Whether our daughter were legitimate
Respecting this our marriage with the dowager,
Sometimes our brother's wife. This respite shook
The bosom of my conscience, entered me,
180 Yea, with a spitting power, and made to tremble
The region of my breast; which forced such way
That many mazed considerings did throng
And pressed in with this caution. First, methought
I stood not in the smile of heaven, who had
185 Commanded nature that my lady's womb,
If it conceived a male child by me, should
Do no more offices of life to't than
The grave does to th' dead: for her male issue
Or died where they were made, or shortly after
190 This world had aired them. Hence I took a thought
This was a judgement on me, that my kingdom –
Well worthy the best heir o'th' world – should not
Be gladded in't by me. Then follows that
I weighed the danger which my realms stood in
195 By this my issue's fail, and that gave to me
Many a groaning throe. Thus hulling in
The wild sea of my conscience, I did steer
Toward this remedy whereupon we are
Now present here together: that's to say,
200 I meant to rectify my conscience – which

I then did feel full sick, and yet not well –
By all the reverend fathers of the land
And doctors learned. First, I began in private
With you, my lord of Lincoln. You remember
How under my oppression I did reek   205
When I first moved you?

LINCOLN   Very well, my liege.

KING   I have spoke long. Be pleased yourself to say
How far you satisfied me.

LINCOLN   So please your highness,
The question did at first so stagger me,
Bearing a state of mighty moment in't   210
And consequence of dread, that I committed
The daringest counsel which I had to doubt
And did entreat your highness to this course
Which you are running here.

KING   I then moved you,
My lord of Canterbury, and got your leave   215
To make this present summons. Unsolicited
I left no reverend person in this court,
But by particular consent proceeded
Under your hands and seals. Therefore go on,
For no dislike i'th' world against the person   220
Of the good Queen, but the sharp thorny points
Of my alleged reasons, drives this forward.
Prove but our marriage lawful, by my life
And kingly dignity, we are contented
To wear our mortal state to come with her,   225
Katherine, our Queen, before the primest creature
That's paragoned o'th' world.

CAMPEIUS   So please your highness,
The Queen being absent, 'tis a needful fitness
That we adjourn this court till further day.
Meanwhile must be an earnest motion   230
Made to the Queen to call back her appeal
She intends unto His Holiness.

KING [*aside*]   I may perceive
These cardinals trifle with me. I abhor
This dilatory sloth and tricks of Rome.
My learned and well-beloved servant, Cranmer,   235
Prithee return. With thy approach I know
My comfort comes along. – Break up the court!
I say, set on.   *Exeunt in manner as they entered.*

3.1   *Enter* Queen KATHERINE *and her*
                  Women, *as at work.*

KATHERINE
Take thy lute, wench. My soul grows sad with troubles.
Sing, and disperse 'em if thou canst. Leave working.

WOMAN [*Sings.*]
              Orpheus, with his lute, made trees
              And the mountain tops that freeze
              Bow themselves, when he did sing.   5
              To his music, plants and flowers
              Ever sprung, as sun and showers
              There had made a lasting spring.

Everything that heard him play,
10   Even the billows of the sea,
Hung their heads and then lay by.
In sweet music is such art,
Killing care and grief of heart
Fall asleep or, hearing, die.

Enter GRIFFITH.

15   KATHERINE   How now?
GRIFFITH
An't please your grace, the two great Cardinals
Wait in the presence.
KATHERINE   Would they speak with me?
GRIFFITH   They willed me say so, madam.
KATHERINE   Pray their graces
To come near.   *Exit Griffith.*
What can be their business
20   With me, a poor weak woman, fallen from favour?
I do not like their coming. Now I think on't,
They should be good men, their affairs as righteous –
But all hoods make not monks.

Enter the two Cardinals, WOLSEY *and* CAMPEIUS.

WOLSEY   Peace to your highness.
KATHERINE
Your graces find me here part of a housewife:
25   I would be all, against the worst may happen.
What are your pleasures with me, reverend lords?
WOLSEY
May it please you, noble madam, to withdraw
Into your private chamber? We shall give you
The full cause of our coming.
KATHERINE   Speak it here.
30   There's nothing I have done yet, o'my conscience,
Deserves a corner. Would all other women
Could speak this with as free a soul as I do.
My lords, I care not – so much I am happy
Above a number – if my actions
35   Were tried by every tongue, every eye saw 'em,
Envy and base opinion set against 'em,
I know my life so even. If your business
Seek me out, and that way I am wife in,
Out with it boldly. Truth loves open dealing.
40   WOLSEY   *Tanta est erga te mentis integritas, Regina*
serenissima –
KATHERINE   O, good my lord, no Latin.
I am not such a truant since my coming
As not to know the language I have lived in.
A strange tongue makes my cause more strange,
45   suspicious.
Pray speak in English. Here are some will thank you,
If you speak truth, for their poor mistress' sake.
Believe me, she has had much wrong. Lord Cardinal,
The willingest sin I ever yet committed
May be absolved in English.
50   WOLSEY   Noble lady,
I am sorry my integrity should breed –

And service to his majesty and you –
So deep suspicion where all faith was meant.
We come not by the way of accusation,
To taint that honour every good tongue blesses,   55
Nor to betray you any way to sorrow –
You have too much, good lady – but to know
How you stand minded in the weighty difference
Between the King and you, and to deliver,
Like free and honest men, our just opinions   60
And comforts to your cause.
CAMPEIUS   Most honoured madam,
My lord of York, out of his noble nature,
Zeal, and obedience he still bore your grace,
Forgetting, like a good man, your late censure
Both of his truth and him – which was too far –   65
Offers, as I do, in a sign of peace,
His service and his counsel.
KATHERINE [*aside*]   To betray me.
[*to them*] My lords, I thank you both for your good
wills.
Ye speak like honest men – pray God ye prove so.
But how to make ye suddenly an answer   70
In such a point of weight, so near mine honour –
More near my life, I fear – with my weak wit,
And to such men of gravity and learning,
In truth I know not. I was set at work
Among my maids, full little, God knows, looking   75
Either for such men or such business.
For her sake that I have been – for I feel
The last fit of my greatness – good your graces,
Let me have time and counsel for my cause.
Alas, I am a woman friendless, hopeless.   80
WOLSEY
Madam, you wrong the King's love with these fears:
Your hopes and friends are infinite.
KATHERINE   In England
But little for my profit. Can you think, lords,
That any Englishman dare give me counsel?
Or be a known friend 'gainst his highness' pleasure –   85
Though he be grown so desperate to be honest –
And live a subject? Nay, forsooth, my friends,
They that must weigh out my afflictions,
They that my trust must grow to, live not here:
They are, as all my other comforts, far hence   90
In mine own country, lords.
CAMPEIUS   I would your grace
Would leave your griefs and take my counsel.
KATHERINE   How, sir?
CAMPEIUS
Put your main cause into the King's protection.
He's loving and most gracious. 'Twill be much
Both for your honour better and your cause,   95
For if the trial of the law o'ertake ye,
You'll part away disgraced.
WOLSEY   He tells you rightly.
KATHERINE
Ye tell me what ye wish for both – my ruin.

Is this your Christian counsel? Out upon ye!
Heaven is above all yet: there sits a judge
That no king can corrupt.

CAMPEIUS   Your rage mistakes us.

KATHERINE
The more shame for ye. Holy men I thought ye,
Upon my soul, two reverend cardinal virtues –
But cardinal sins and hollow hearts I fear ye.
Mend 'em for shame, my lords. Is this your comfort?
The cordial that ye bring a wretched lady,
A woman lost among ye, laughed at, scorned?
I will not wish ye half my miseries:
I have more charity. But say I warned ye.
Take heed, for heaven's sake take heed, lest at once
The burden of my sorrows fall upon ye.

WOLSEY   Madam, this is a mere distraction.
You turn the good we offer into envy.

KATHERINE   Ye turn me into nothing. Woe upon ye,
And all such false professors! Would you have me –
If you have any justice, any pity,
If ye be anything but churchmen's habits –
Put my sick cause into his hands that hates me?
Alas, 'has banished me his bed already;
His love, too, long ago. I am old, my lords,
And all the fellowship I hold now with him
Is only my obedience. What can happen
To me above this wretchedness? All your studies
Make me a curse, like this.

CAMPEIUS   Your fears are worse.

KATHERINE
Have I lived thus long – let me speak myself,
Since virtue finds no friends – a wife, a true one,
A woman, I dare say without vainglory,
Never yet branded with suspicion –
Have I with all my full affections
Still met the King, loved him next heaven, obeyed him,
Been, out of fondness, superstitious to him,
Almost forgot my prayers to content him,
And am I thus rewarded? 'Tis not well, lords.
Bring me a constant woman to her husband,
One that ne'er dreamed a joy beyond his pleasure,
And to that woman, when she has done most,
Yet will I add an honour: a great patience.

WOLSEY
Madam, you wander from the good we aim at.

KATHERINE
My lord, I dare not make myself so guilty
To give up willingly that noble title
Your master wed me to. Nothing but death
Shall e'er divorce my dignities.

WOLSEY   Pray hear me.

KATHERINE
Would I had never trod this English earth
Or felt the flatteries that grow upon it.
Ye have angels' faces, but heaven knows your hearts.
What will become of me now, wretched lady?
I am the most unhappy woman living.

[*to her Women*] Alas, poor wenches, where are now
    your fortunes?
Shipwrecked upon a kingdom where no pity,
No friends, no hope, no kindred weep for me,
Almost no grave allowed me, like the lily
That once was mistress of the field and flourished,
I'll hang my head and perish.

WOLSEY   If your grace
Could but be brought to know our ends are honest,
You'd feel more comfort. Why should we, good lady,
Upon what cause, wrong you? Alas, our places,
The way of our profession, is against it.
We are to cure such sorrows, not to sow 'em.
For goodness' sake, consider what you do,
How you may hurt yourself, ay, utterly
Grow from the King's acquaintance, by this carriage.
The hearts of princes kiss obedience,
So much they love it, but to stubborn spirits
They swell and grow as terrible as storms.
I know you have a gentle, noble temper,
A soul as even as a calm. Pray think us
Those we profess: peacemakers, friends and servants.

CAMPEIUS
Madam, you'll find it so. You wrong your virtues
With these weak women's fears. A noble spirit,
As yours was put into you, ever casts
Such doubts as false coin from it. The King loves you:
Beware you lose it not. For us, if you please
To trust us in your business, we are ready
To use our utmost studies in your service.

KATHERINE
Do what ye will, my lords, and pray forgive me
If I have used myself unmannerly.
You know I am a woman, lacking wit
To make a seemly answer to such persons.
Pray do my service to his majesty:
He has my heart yet, and shall have my prayers
While I shall have my life. Come, reverend fathers,
Bestow your counsels on me. She now begs
That little thought when she set footing here
She should have bought her dignities so dear.

                                    Exeunt.

3.2   *Enter the* Duke *of* NORFOLK, Duke
            of SUFFOLK, Lord SURREY *and*
                Lord CHAMBERLAIN.

NORFOLK   If you will now unite in your complaints
And force them with a constancy, the Cardinal
Cannot stand under them. If you omit
The offer of this time, I cannot promise
But that you shall sustain more new disgraces
With these you bear already.

SURREY   I am joyful
To meet the least occasion that may give me
Remembrance of my father-in-law the Duke,
To be revenged on him.

SUFFOLK   Which of the peers

10   Have uncontemned gone by him, or at least
Strangely neglected? When did he regard
The stamp of nobleness in any person
Out of himself?

CHAMBERLAIN   My lords, you speak your pleasures.
What he deserves of you and me, I know;

15   What we can do to him – though now the time
Gives way to us – I much fear. If you cannot
Bar his access to th' King, never attempt
Anything on him, for he hath a witchcraft
Over the King in's tongue.

NORFOLK   O, fear him not:

20   His spell in that is out. The King hath found
Matter against him that for ever mars
The honey of his language. No, he's settled,
Not to come off, in his displeasure.

SURREY   Sir,
I should be glad to hear such news as this

25   Once every hour.

NORFOLK   Believe it, this is true.
In the divorce his contrary proceedings
Are all unfolded, wherein he appears
As I would wish mine enemy.

SURREY   How came
His practices to light?

SUFFOLK   Most strangely.

SURREY   O, how, how?

SUFFOLK

30   The Cardinal's letters to the Pope miscarried
And came to th'eye o'th' King, wherein was read
How that the Cardinal did entreat his holiness
To stay the judgement o'th' divorce; for if
It did take place, 'I do', quoth he, 'perceive

35   My King is tangled in affection to
A creature of the Queen's, Lady Anne Bullen.'

SURREY   Has the King this?

SUFFOLK   Believe it.

SURREY   Will this work?

CHAMBERLAIN
The King in this perceives him how he coasts
And hedges his own way. But in this point

40   All his tricks founder, and he brings his physic
After his patient's death. The King already
Hath married the fair lady.

SURREY   Would he had!

SUFFOLK   May you be happy in your wish, my lord,
For I profess you have it.

SURREY   Now all my joy
Trace the conjunction.

SUFFOLK   My amen to't.

45 NORFOLK   All men's.

SUFFOLK   There's order given for her coronation.
Marry, this is yet but young, and may be left
To some ears unrecounted. But, my lords,
She is a gallant creature, and complete

50   In mind and feature. I persuade me from her

Will fall some blessing to this land which shall
In it be memorized.

SURREY   But will the King
Digest this letter of the Cardinal's?
The Lord forbid.

NORFOLK   Marry, amen.

SUFFOLK   No, no:
There be more wasps that buzz about his nose   55
Will make this sting the sooner. Cardinal Campeius
Is stolen away to Rome; hath ta'en no leave;
Has left the cause o'th' King unhandled; and
Is posted as the agent of our Cardinal
To second all his plot. I do assure you   60
The King cried 'Ha!' at this.

CHAMBERLAIN   Now God incense him,
And let him cry 'Ha!' louder.

NORFOLK   But, my lord,
When returns Cranmer?

SUFFOLK   He is returned in his opinions, which
Have satisfied the King for his divorce,   65
Together with all famous colleges,
Almost, in Christendom. Shortly, I believe,
His second marriage shall be published, and
Her coronation. Katherine no more
Shall be called 'Queen', but 'Princess Dowager',   70
And 'widow to Prince Arthur'.

NORFOLK   This same Cranmer's
A worthy fellow, and hath ta'en much pain
In the King's business.

SUFFOLK   He has, and we shall see him
For it an archbishop.

NORFOLK   So I hear.

SUFFOLK   'Tis so.

Enter WOLSEY *and* CROMWELL.

The Cardinal.

NORFOLK   Observe, observe: he's moody.   75
[They stand apart.]

WOLSEY   The packet, Cromwell: gave't you the King?

CROMWELL   To his own hand, in's bedchamber.

WOLSEY   Looked he
O'th' inside of the paper?

CROMWELL   Presently
He did unseal them, and the first he viewed,
He did it with a serious mind; a heed   80
Was in his countenance. You he bade
Attend him here this morning.

WOLSEY   Is he ready
To come abroad?

CROMWELL   I think by this he is.

WOLSEY   Leave me a while.   *Exit Cromwell.*
It shall be to the Duchess of Alençon,   85
The French King's sister: he shall marry her.
Anne Bullen? No, I'll no Anne Bullens for him:
There's more in't than fair visage. Bullen?
No, we'll no Bullens. Speedily I wish
To hear from Rome. The Marchioness of Pembroke?   90

NORFOLK   He's discontented.

SUFFOLK   Maybe he hears the King
Does whet his anger to him.

SURREY   Sharp enough,
Lord, for thy justice.

WOLSEY
The late Queen's gentlewoman? A knight's daughter
To be her mistress' mistress? The Queen's Queen?   95
This candle burns not clear. 'Tis I must snuff it;
Then out it goes. What though I know her virtuous
And well-deserving? Yet I know her for
A spleeny Lutheran, and not wholesome to
Our cause, that she should lie i'th' bosom of   100
Our hard-ruled King. Again, there is sprung up
An heretic, an arch-one, Cranmer, one
Hath crawled into the favour of the King
And is his oracle.

NORFOLK   He is vexed at something.

Enter KING, *reading of a schedule, and* LOVELL.

SURREY   105
I would 'twere something that would fret the string,
The master-cord on's heart.

SUFFOLK   The King, the King.

KING   What piles of wealth hath he accumulated
To his own portion! And what expense by th'hour
Seems to flow from him! How i'th' name of thrift
Does he rake this together? – Now, my lords,   110
Saw you the Cardinal?

NORFOLK   My lord, we have
Stood here observing him. Some strange commotion
Is in his brain. He bites his lip, and starts,
Stops on a sudden, looks upon the ground,
Then lays his finger on his temple; straight   115
Springs out into fast gait; then stops again,
Strikes his breast hard, and anon he casts
His eye against the moon. In most strange postures
We have seen him set himself.

KING   It may well be   120
There is a mutiny in's mind. This morning,
Papers of state he sent me to peruse
As I required; and wot you what I found
There – on my conscience, put unwittingly?
Forsooth, an inventory, thus importing
The several parcels of his plate, his treasure,   125
Rich stuffs and ornaments of household, which
I find at such proud rate that it outspeaks
Possession of a subject.

NORFOLK   It's heaven's will;
Some spirit put this paper in the packet
To bless your eye withal.

KING   If we did think   130
His contemplation were above the earth
And fixed on spiritual object, he should still
Dwell in his musings. But I am afraid
His thinkings are below the moon, not worth
His serious considering.

[*King takes his seat; and whispers Lovell, who goes to
the Cardinal.*]

WOLSEY   Heaven forgive me.   135
[*to the King*] Ever God bless your highness.

KING   Good my lord,
You are full of heavenly stuff, and bear the inventory
Of your best graces in your mind, the which
You were now running o'er. You have scarce time
To steal from spiritual leisure a brief span   140
To keep your earthly audit. Sure, in that
I deem you an ill husband, and am glad
To have you therein my companion.

WOLSEY   Sir,
For holy offices I have a time; a time
To think upon the part of business which   145
I bear i'th' state; and nature does require
Her times of preservation which, perforce,
I, her frail son, amongst my brethren mortal,
Must give my tendance to.

KING   You have said well.

WOLSEY   And ever may your highness yoke together,   150
As I will lend you cause, my doing well
With my well saying.

KING   'Tis well said again,
And 'tis a kind of good deed to say well –
And yet words are no deeds. My father loved you:
He said he did, and with his deed did crown   155
His word upon you. Since I had my office,
I have kept you next my heart, have not alone
Employed you where high profits might come home,
But pared my present havings to bestow
My bounties upon you.

WOLSEY [*aside*]   What should this mean?   160

SURREY [*aside*]   The Lord increase this business!

KING   Have I not made you
The prime man of the state? I pray you tell me
If what I now pronounce you have found true,
And, if you may confess it, say withal
If you are bound to us or no. What say you?   165

WOLSEY   My sovereign, I confess your royal graces,
Showered on me daily, have been more than could
My studied purposes requite, which went
Beyond all man's endeavours. My endeavours
Have ever come too short of my desires,   170
Yet filed with my abilities. Mine own ends
Have been mine so that evermore they pointed
To th' good of your most sacred person and
The profit of the state. For your great graces
Heaped upon me – poor undeserver – I   175
Can nothing render but allegiant thanks;
My prayers to heaven for you; my loyalty,
Which ever has and ever shall be growing,
Till death, that winter, kill it.

KING   Fairly answered:
A loyal and obedient subject is   180
Therein illustrated. The honour of it
Does pay the act of it, as i'th' contrary

The foulness is the punishment. I presume
That as my hand has opened bounty to you,
My heart dropped love, my power rained honour,
more
185 On you than any, so your hand and heart,
Your brain, and every function of your power,
Should, notwithstanding that your bond of duty,
As 'twere in love's particular, be more
To me, your friend, than any.

190 WOLSEY   I do profess
That for your highness' good I ever laboured
More than mine own that am, have and will be.
Though all the world should crack their duty to you
And throw it from their soul – though perils did
195 Abound as thick as thought could make 'em, and
Appear in forms more horrid – yet my duty,
As doth a rock against the chiding flood,
Should the approach of this wild river break
And stand unshaken yours.

KING   'Tis nobly spoken.
200 Take notice, lords: he has a loyal breast,
For you have seen him open't.
[*Gives him papers.*]   Read o'er this,
And after, this, and then to breakfast with
What appetite you have.

Exit King, frowning upon the Cardinal; the nobles
throng after him, smiling and whispering.

WOLSEY   What should this mean?
What sudden anger's this? How have I reaped it?
205 He parted frowning from me, as if ruin
Leaped from his eyes. So looks the chafed lion
Upon the daring huntsman that has galled him,
Then makes him nothing. I must read this paper –
I fear, the story of his anger. 'Tis so:
210 This paper has undone me. 'Tis th'account
Of all that world of wealth I have drawn together
For mine own ends – indeed to gain the popedom
And fee my friends in Rome. O, negligence,
Fit for a fool to fall by! What cross devil
215 Made me put this main secret in the packet
I sent the King? Is there no way to cure this?
No new device to beat this from his brains?
I know 'twill stir him strongly. Yet I know
A way, if it take right, in spite of fortune
220 Will bring me off again. What's this? 'To th' Pope'?
The letter, as I live, with all the business
I writ to's Holiness. Nay then, farewell.
I have touched the highest point of all my greatness,
And from that full meridian of my glory
225 I haste now to my setting. I shall fall
Like a bright exhalation in the evening,
And no man see me more.

Enter to Wolsey the Dukes *of* NORFOLK *and* SUFFOLK,
the Earl *of* SURREY *and the* Lord CHAMBERLAIN.

NORFOLK
Hear the King's pleasure, Cardinal, who commands you

To render up the great seal presently
Into our hands, and to confine yourself   230
To Esher House, my lord of Winchester's,
Till you hear further from his highness.
WOLSEY   Stay.
Where's your commission, lords? Words cannot
carry
Authority so weighty.
SUFFOLK   Who dare cross 'em,
Bearing the King's will from his mouth expressly?   235
WOLSEY Till I find more than will or words to do it –
I mean your malice – know, officious lords,
I dare, and must, deny it. Now I feel
Of what coarse metal ye are moulded – envy!
How eagerly ye follow my disgraces   240
As if it fed ye, and how sleek and wanton
Ye appear in everything may bring my ruin!
Follow your envious courses, men of malice:
You have Christian warrant for 'em, and no doubt
In time will find their fit rewards. That seal   245
You ask with such a violence, the King –
Mine and your master – with his own hand gave
me;
Bade me enjoy it, with the place and honours,
During my life; and to confirm his goodness,
Tied it by letters patents. Now, who'll take it?   250
SURREY The King that gave it.
WOLSEY   It must be himself, then.
SURREY Thou art a proud traitor, priest.
WOLSEY   Proud lord, thou liest.
Within these forty hours Surrey durst better
Have burnt that tongue than said so.
SURREY   Thy ambition,
Thou scarlet sin, robbed this bewailing land   255
Of noble Buckingham, my father-in-law.
The heads of all thy brother cardinals,
With thee and all thy best parts bound together,
Weighed not a hair of his. Plague of your policy!
You sent me Deputy for Ireland,   260
Far from his succour, from the King, from all
That might have mercy on the fault thou gavest
him,
Whilst your great goodness, out of holy pity,
Absolved him with an axe.
WOLSEY   This, and all else
This talking lord can lay upon my credit,   265
I answer, is most false. The Duke by law
Found his deserts. How innocent I was
From any private malice in his end,
His noble jury and foul cause can witness.
If I loved many words, lord, I should tell you   270
You have as little honesty as honour,
That in the way of loyalty and truth
Toward the King, my ever royal master,
Dare mate a sounder man than Surrey can be,
And all that love his follies.
SURREY   By my soul,   275

Your long coat, priest, protects you; thou shouldst
  feel
My sword i'th' lifeblood of thee else. My lords,
Can ye endure to hear this arrogance?
And from this fellow? If we live thus tamely,
To be thus jaded by a piece of scarlet,
Farewell, nobility: let his grace go forward
And dare us with his cap, like larks.

WOLSEY   All goodness
Is poison to thy stomach.

SURREY   Yes, that 'goodness'
Of gleaning all the land's wealth into one,
Into your own hands, Cardinal, by extortion;
The 'goodness' of your intercepted packets
You writ to th' Pope against the King – your
  'goodness',
Since you provoke me, shall be most notorious.
My lord of Norfolk, as you are truly noble,
As you respect the common good, the state
Of our despised nobility, our issues –
Who, if he live, will scarce be gentlemen –
Produce the grand sum of his sins, the articles
Collected from his life. I'll startle you
Worse than the sacring-bell when the brown wench
Lay kissing in your arms, lord Cardinal.

WOLSEY
How much, methinks, I could despise this man,
But that I am bound in charity against it.

NORFOLK
Those articles, my lord, are in the King's hand;
But thus much: they are foul ones.

WOLSEY   So much fairer,
And spotless, shall mine innocence arise
When the King knows my truth.

SURREY   This cannot save you.
I thank my memory I yet remember
Some of these articles, and out they shall.
Now, if you can blush and cry 'Guilty', Cardinal,
You'll show a little honesty.

WOLSEY   Speak on, sir;
I dare your worst objections. If I blush,
It is to see a nobleman want manners.

SURREY
I had rather want those than my head. Have at you!
First, that without the King's assent or knowledge,
You wrought to be a legate, by which power
You maimed the jurisdiction of all bishops.

NORFOLK   Then, that in all you writ to Rome, or else
To foreign princes, '*ego et rex meus*'
Was still inscribed, in which you brought the King
To be your servant.

SUFFOLK   Then, that without the knowledge
Either of King or Council, when you went
Ambassador to the Emperor, you made bold
To carry into Flanders the great seal.

SURREY   *Item*, you sent a large commission
To Gregory de Cassado, to conclude,

Without the King's will or the state's allowance,
A league between his highness and Ferrara.

SUFFOLK   That out of mere ambition you have caused
Your holy hat to be stamped on the King's coin.

SURREY
Then, that you have sent innumerable substance –
By what means got, I leave to your own conscience –
To furnish Rome and to prepare the ways
You have for dignities, to the mere undoing
Of all the kingdom. Many more there are,
Which since they are of you, and odious,
I will not taint my mouth with.

CHAMBERLAIN   O my lord,
Press not a falling man too far. 'Tis virtue.
His faults lie open to the laws: let them,
Not you, correct him. My heart weeps to see him
So little of his great self.

SURREY   I forgive him.

SUFFOLK
Lord Cardinal, the King's further pleasure is,
Because all those things you have done of late
By your power legative within this kingdom
Fall into th' compass of a *praemunire*,
That therefore such a writ be sued against you
To forfeit all your goods, lands, tenements,
Chattels and whatsoever, and to be
Out of the King's protection. This is my charge.

NORFOLK   And so we'll leave you to your meditations
How to live better. For your stubborn answer
About the giving back the great seal to us,
The King shall know it and, no doubt, shall thank
  you.
So fare you well, my little good lord Cardinal.

                              Exeunt all but Wolsey.

WOLSEY   So, farewell to the little good you bear me.
Farewell? A long farewell to all my greatness.
This is the state of man. Today he puts forth
The tender leaves of hopes; tomorrow blossoms,
And bears his blushing honours thick upon him;
The third day comes a frost, a killing frost,
And when he thinks, good easy man, full surely
His greatness is a-ripening, nips his root,
And then he falls, as I do. I have ventured,
Like little wanton boys that swim on bladders,
This many summers in a sea of glory,
But far beyond my depth. My high-blown pride
At length broke under me and now has left me,
Weary and old with service, to the mercy
Of a rude stream that must for ever hide me.
Vain pomp and glory of this world, I hate ye!
I feel my heart new opened. O, how wretched
Is that poor man that hangs on princes' favours!
There is betwixt that smile we would aspire to,
That sweet aspect of princes, and their ruin
More pangs and fears than wars or women have;
And when he falls, he falls like Lucifer,
Never to hope again.

Enter CROMWELL, *standing amazed.*

                Why, how now, Cromwell?
CROMWELL   I have no power to speak, sir.
WOLSEY   What, amazed
  At my misfortunes? Can thy spirit wonder
375 A great man should decline? Nay, an you weep
  I am fallen indeed.
CROMWELL   How does your grace?
WOLSEY   Why, well.
  Never so truly happy, my good Cromwell.
  I know myself now, and I feel within me
  A peace above all earthly dignities,
380 A still and quiet conscience. The King has cured me,
  I humbly thank his grace, and from these shoulders,
  These ruined pillars, out of pity, taken
  A load would sink a navy – too much honour.
  O, 'tis a burden, Cromwell, 'tis a burden
385 Too heavy for a man that hopes for heaven.
CROMWELL
  I am glad your grace has made that right use of it.
WOLSEY   I hope I have. I am able now, methinks,
  Out of a fortitude of soul I feel,
  To endure more miseries and greater far
390 Than my weak-hearted enemies dare offer.
  What news abroad?
CROMWELL   The heaviest and the worst
  Is your displeasure with the King.
WOLSEY   God bless him.
CROMWELL
  The next is that Sir Thomas More is chosen
  Lord Chancellor in your place.
WOLSEY   That's somewhat sudden.
395 But he's a learned man. May he continue
  Long in his highness' favour, and do justice
  For truth's sake and his conscience, that his bones,
  When he has run his course and sleeps in blessings,
  May have a tomb of orphans' tears wept on him.
  What more?
400 CROMWELL   That Cranmer is returned with welcome,
  Installed lord Archbishop of Canterbury.
WOLSEY   That's news indeed.
CROMWELL   Last, that the Lady Anne,
  Whom the King hath in secrecy long married,
  This day was viewed in open as his Queen,
405 Going to chapel, and the voice is now
  Only about her coronation.
WOLSEY
  There was the weight that pulled me down. O
    Cromwell,
  The King has gone beyond me. All my glories
  In that one woman I have lost for ever.
410 No sun shall ever usher forth mine honours,
  Or gild again the noble troops that waited
  Upon my smiles. Go get thee from me, Cromwell:
  I am a poor fallen man, unworthy now
  To be thy lord and master. Seek the King –

  That sun I pray may never set. I have told him   415
  What, and how true, thou art. He will advance thee:
  Some little memory of me will stir him –
  I know his noble nature – not to let
  Thy hopeful service perish too. Good Cromwell,
  Neglect him not. Make use now, and provide   420
  For thine own future safety.
CROMWELL   O my lord,
  Must I then leave you? Must I needs forgo
  So good, so noble and so true a master?
  Bear witness, all that have not hearts of iron,
  With what a sorrow Cromwell leaves his lord.   425
  The King shall have my service, but my prayers
  For ever and for ever shall be yours.
WOLSEY   Cromwell, I did not think to shed a tear
  In all my miseries, but thou hast forced me,
  Out of thy honest truth, to play the woman.   430
  Let's dry our eyes, and thus far hear me, Cromwell,
  And when I am forgotten, as I shall be,
  And sleep in dull cold marble, where no mention
  Of me more must be heard of, say I taught thee.
  Say Wolsey, that once trod the ways of glory   435
  And sounded all the depths and shoals of honour,
  Found thee a way, out of his wreck, to rise in,
  A sure and safe one, though thy master missed it.
  Mark but my fall and that that ruined me.
  Cromwell, I charge thee, fling away ambition.   440
  By that sin fell the angels. How can man then,
  The image of his maker, hope to win by it?
  Love thyself last; cherish those hearts that hate thee.
  Corruption wins not more than honesty.
  Still in thy right hand carry gentle peace   445
  To silence envious tongues. Be just, and fear not.
  Let all the ends thou aimest at be thy country's,
  Thy God's, and truth's. Then if thou fallest, O
    Cromwell,
  Thou fallest a blessed martyr.
  Serve the King. And prithee lead me in: 450
  There take an inventory of all I have.
  To the last penny, 'tis the King's. My robe
  And my integrity to heaven is all
  I dare now call mine own. O Cromwell, Cromwell,
  Had I but served my God with half the zeal   455
  I served my King, he would not in mine age
  Have left me naked to mine enemies.
CROMWELL   Good sir, have patience.
WOLSEY   So I have. Farewell,
  The hopes of court: my hopes in heaven do dwell.
                              Exeunt.

4.1   *Enter two* Gentlemen, *meeting one another.*

1 GENTLEMAN   You're well met once again.
2 GENTLEMAN   So are you.
1 GENTLEMAN
  You come to take your stand here and behold
  The Lady Anne pass from her coronation?

2 GENTLEMAN
'Tis all my business. At our last encounter,
The Duke of Buckingham came from his trial.
1 GENTLEMAN
'Tis very true. But that time offered sorrow,
This, general joy.
2 GENTLEMAN   'Tis well. The citizens,
I am sure, have shown at full their royal minds –
As, let 'em have their rights, they are ever forward –
In celebration of this day with shows,
Pageants, and sights of honour.
1 GENTLEMAN   Never greater,
Nor, I'll assure you, better taken, sir.
2 GENTLEMAN
May I be bold to ask what that contains,
That paper in your hand?
1 GENTLEMAN   Yes, 'tis the list
Of those that claim their offices this day
By custom of the coronation.
The Duke of Suffolk is the first, and claims
To be High Steward; next, the Duke of Norfolk,
He to be Earl Marshal. You may read the rest.
2 GENTLEMAN
I thank you, sir. Had I not known those customs,
I should have been beholding to your paper.
But I beseech you, what's become of Katherine,
The Princess Dowager? How goes her business?
1 GENTLEMAN
That I can tell you too. The Archbishop
Of Canterbury, accompanied with other
Learned and reverend fathers of his order,
Held a late court at Dunstable, six miles off
From Ampthill, where the Princess lay; to which
She was often cited by them, but appeared not;
And, to be short, for not appearance and
The King's late scruple, by the main assent
Of all these learned men, she was divorced,
And the late marriage made of none effect;
Since which she was removed to Kimbolton,
Where she remains now sick.
2 GENTLEMAN   Alas, good lady.
                              [*Trumpets*]
The trumpets sound. Stand close. The Queen is
coming.

The order of the coronation

1 *A lively flourish of trumpets.*
2 *Then, two Judges.*
3 Lord CHANCELLOR, *with purse and mace before him.*
4 *Choristers singing. Music.*
5 *Mayor of London, bearing the mace. Then* GARTER, *in
   his coat of arms, and on his head he wears a gilt copper
   crown.*
6 *Marquess Dorset, bearing a sceptre of gold, on his head a
   demi-coronal of gold. With him the* Earl of SURREY,
   *bearing the rod of silver with the dove, crowned with an
   earl's coronet. Collars of esses.*

7 Duke of SUFFOLK, *in his robe of estate, his coronet on
   his head, bearing a long white wand, as High Steward.
   With him, the* Duke of NORFOLK, *with the rod of
   marshalship, a coronet on his head. Collars of esses.*
8 *A canopy, borne by four of the Cinque Ports; under it, the
   Queen* [ANNE] *in her robe, in her hair, richly adorned
   with pearl; crowned. On each side her, the* Bishops of
   London and Winchester.
9 *The old Duchess of Norfolk, in a coronal of gold wrought
   with flowers, bearing the Queen's train.*
10 *Certain Ladies or Countesses, with plain circlets of gold
   without flowers.*
            *Exeunt, first passing over the stage in order and
                state, and then a great flourish of trumpets.*
2 GENTLEMAN   A royal train, believe me. These I know.
Who's that that bears the sceptre?
1 GENTLEMAN   Marquess Dorset,
And that the Earl of Surrey with the rod.
2 GENTLEMAN
A bold brave gentleman. That should be   40
The Duke of Suffolk.
1 GENTLEMAN   'Tis the same: High Steward.
2 GENTLEMAN   And that my lord of Norfolk?
1 GENTLEMAN   Yes.
2 GENTLEMAN [*Sees Anne.*]   Heaven bless thee!
Thou hast the sweetest face I ever looked on.
Sir, as I have a soul, she is an angel.
Our King has all the Indies in his arms,   45
And more, and richer, when he strains that lady.
I cannot blame his conscience.
1 GENTLEMAN   They that bear
The cloth of honour over her are four barons
Of the Cinque Ports.
2 GENTLEMAN
Those men are happy, and so are all are near her. 50
I take it she that carries up the train
Is that old noble lady, Duchess of Norfolk?
1 GENTLEMAN   It is, and the rest are countesses.
2 GENTLEMAN
Their coronets say so. These are stars indeed –
1 GENTLEMAN   And sometimes falling ones.
2 GENTLEMAN   No more of that. 55

Enter a Third Gentleman.

1 GENTLEMAN
God save you, sir. Where have you been broiling?
3 GENTLEMAN
Among the crowd i'th' Abbey, where a finger
Could not be wedged in more. I am stifled
With the mere rankness of their joy.
2 GENTLEMAN   You saw
The ceremony?
3 GENTLEMAN   That I did.
1 GENTLEMAN   How was it?   60
3 GENTLEMAN   Well worth the seeing.
2 GENTLEMAN   Good sir, speak it to us.
3 GENTLEMAN   As well as I am able. The rich stream

Of lords and ladies, having brought the Queen
To a prepared place in the choir, fell off
65 A distance from her, while her grace sat down
To rest a while – some half an hour or so –
In a rich chair of state, opposing freely
The beauty of her person to the people –
Believe me, sir, she is the goodliest woman
70 That ever lay by man – which when the people
Had the full view of, such a noise arose
As the shrouds make at sea in a stiff tempest,
As loud and to as many tunes. Hats, cloaks –
Doublets, I think – flew up, and had their faces
75 Been loose, this day they had been lost. Such joy
I never saw before. Great-bellied women
That had not half a week to go, like rams
In the old time of war, would shake the press
And make 'em reel before 'em. No man living
80 Could say 'This is my wife' there, all were woven
So strangely in one piece.
2 GENTLEMAN　　　　　But what followed?
3 GENTLEMAN
At length her grace rose, and with modest paces
Came to the altar, where she kneeled and, saint-like,
Cast her fair eyes to heaven and prayed devoutly;
85 Then rose again and bowed her to the people,
When by the Archbishop of Canterbury
She had all the royal makings of a queen,
As holy oil, Edward Confessor's crown,
The rod, and bird of peace, and all such emblems
90 Laid nobly on her; which performed, the choir,
With all the choicest music of the kingdom,
Together sung *Te Deum*. So she parted,
And with the same full state paced back again
To York Place, where the feast is held.
1 GENTLEMAN　　　　　　　Sir,
95 You must no more call it 'York Place' – that's past;
For since the Cardinal fell, that title's lost.
'Tis now the King's, and called 'Whitehall'.
3 GENTLEMAN　　　　　　　　　　I know it,
But 'tis so lately altered that the old name
Is fresh about me.
2 GENTLEMAN　　　What two reverend bishops
100 Were those that went on each side of the Queen?
3 GENTLEMAN
Stokesley and Gardiner, the one of Winchester,
Newly preferred from the King's secretary;
The other, London.
2 GENTLEMAN　　　He of Winchester
Is held no great good lover of the Archbishop's,
The virtuous Cranmer.
105 3 GENTLEMAN　　　　　All the land knows that.
However, yet there is no great breach. When it comes,
Cranmer will find a friend will not shrink from him.
2 GENTLEMAN　　What may that be, I pray you?
3 GENTLEMAN　　　　　　　　Thomas Cromwell,
A man in much esteem wi'th' King, and truly
110 A worthy friend. The King has made him

Master o'th' Jewel House,
And one already of the Privy Council.
2 GENTLEMAN　He will deserve more.
3 GENTLEMAN　　　　　　Yes, without all doubt.
Come, gentlemen, ye shall go my way,
Which is to th' court, and there ye shall be my guests:　115
Something I can command. As I walk thither
I'll tell ye more.
1 & 2 GENTLEMEN　You may command us, sir. *Exeunt.*

4.2 　　*Enter* KATHERINE *Dowager, sick, led*
　　between GRIFFITH, *her gentleman usher,*
　　and PATIENCE, *her woman.*

GRIFFITH　How does your grace?
KATHERINE　　　　　　O Griffith, sick to death.
My legs like loaden branches bow to th'earth,
Willing to leave their burden. Reach a chair.　[*Sits.*]
So. Now, methinks, I feel a little ease.
Didst thou not tell me, Griffith, as thou leddest me,　5
That the great child of honour, Cardinal Wolsey,
Was dead?
GRIFFITH　Yes, madam, but I think your grace,
Out of the pain you suffered, gave no ear to't.
KATHERINE
Prithee, good Griffith, tell me how he died.
If well, he stepped before me happily　　　10
For my example.
GRIFFITH　　　Well, the voice goes, madam.
For after the stout Earl Northumberland
Arrested him at York and brought him forward,
As a man sorely tainted, to his answer,
He fell sick suddenly and grew so ill　　　15
He could not sit his mule.
KATHERINE　　　　Alas, poor man.
GRIFFITH
At last, with easy roads, he came to Leicester;
Lodged in the abbey, where the reverend abbot,
With all his convent, honourably received him;
To whom he gave these words: 'O father abbot,　20
An old man, broken with the storms of state,
Is come to lay his weary bones among ye.
Give him a little earth, for charity.'
So went to bed, where eagerly his sickness
Pursued him still, and three nights after this,　25
About the hour of eight, which he himself
Foretold should be his last, full of repentance,
Continual meditations, tears and sorrows,
He gave his honours to the world again,
His blessed part to heaven, and slept in peace.　30
KATHERINE
So may he rest: his faults lie gently on him.
Yet thus far, Griffith, give me leave to speak him,
And yet with charity. He was a man
Of an unbounded stomach, ever ranking
Himself with princes; one that by suggestion　35
Tied all the kingdom. Simony was fair play.

His own opinion was his law. I'th' presence
He would say untruths, and be ever double
Both in his words and meaning. He was never,
But where he meant to ruin, pitiful.   40
His promises were as he then was, mighty;
But his performance, as he is now, nothing.
Of his own body he was ill, and gave
The clergy ill example.
GRIFFITH   Noble madam,
Men's evil manners live in brass, their virtues   45
We write in water. May it please your highness
To hear me speak his good now?
KATHERINE   Yes, good Griffith;
I were malicious else.
GRIFFITH   This Cardinal,
Though from an humble stock, undoubtedly
Was fashioned to much honour. From his cradle   50
He was a scholar, and a ripe and good one,
Exceeding wise, fair-spoken and persuading;
Lofty and sour to them that loved him not,
But to those men that sought him, sweet as summer.
And though he were unsatisfied in getting –   55
Which was a sin – yet in bestowing, madam,
He was most princely: ever witness for him
Those twins of learning that he raised in you,
Ipswich and Oxford – one of which fell with him,
Unwilling to outlive the good that did it;   60
The other, though unfinished, yet so famous,
So excellent in art, and still so rising,
That Christendom shall ever speak his virtue.
His overthrow heaped happiness upon him,
For then, and not till then, he felt himself,   65
And found the blessedness of being little.
And, to add greater honours to his age
Than man could give him, he died fearing God.
KATHERINE After my death I wish no other herald,
No other speaker of my living actions,   70
To keep mine honour from corruption
But such an honest chronicler as Griffith.
Whom I most hated living, thou hast made me,
With thy religious truth and modesty,
Now in his ashes honour. Peace be with him.   75
Patience, be near me still, and set me lower.
I have not long to trouble thee. Good Griffith,
Cause the musicians play me that sad note
I named my knell, whilst I sit meditating
On that celestial harmony I go to.   80
                          [*Sad and solemn music*]
GRIFFITH
She is asleep. Good wench, let's sit down quiet,
For fear we wake her. Softly, gentle Patience.

The vision

Enter, solemnly tripping one after another, six
Personages, clad in white robes, wearing on their heads
garlands of bays, and golden vizards on their faces,
branches of bays or palm in their hands. They first

congé unto her, then dance; and at certain changes, the
first two hold a spare garland over her head, at which
the other four make reverend curtsies. Then the two
that held the garland deliver the same to the other next
two, who observe the same order in their changes and
holding the garland over her head. Which done, they
deliver the same garland to the last two, who likewise
observe the same order. At which (as it were by
inspiration) she makes in her sleep signs of rejoicing and
holdeth up her hands to heaven. And so, in their
dancing, vanish, carrying the garland with them.
                    The music continues.

KATHERINE
Spirits of peace, where are ye? Are ye all gone,
And leave me here in wretchedness behind ye?
GRIFFITH Madam, we are here.
KATHERINE   It is not you I call for.   85
Saw ye none enter since I slept?
GRIFFITH   None, madam.
KATHERINE No? Saw you not even now a blessed troop
Invite me to a banquet, whose bright faces
Cast thousand beams upon me, like the sun?
They promised me eternal happiness   90
And brought me garlands, Griffith, which I feel
I am not worthy yet to wear. I shall, assuredly.
GRIFFITH I am most joyful, madam, such good dreams
Possess your fancy.
KATHERINE   Bid the music leave.
They are harsh and heavy to me.   [*Music ceases.*]
PATIENCE   Do you note   95
How much her grace is altered on the sudden?
How long her face is drawn? How pale she looks,
And of an earthy cold? Mark her eyes.
GRIFFITH She is going, wench. Pray, pray.
PATIENCE   Heaven comfort her.

Enter a Messenger.

MESSENGER An't like your grace –
KATHERINE   You are a saucy fellow.   100
Deserve we no more reverence?
GRIFFITH [*to the Messenger*]   You are to blame,
Knowing she will not lose her wonted greatness,
To use so rude behaviour. Go to, kneel.
MESSENGER
I humbly do entreat your highness' pardon.
My haste made me unmannerly. There is staying   105
A gentleman sent from the King to see you.
KATHERINE
Admit him entrance, Griffith. But this fellow
Let me ne'er see again.   *Exit Messenger.*

Enter Lord CAPUTIUS.

                          If my sight fail not,
You should be lord ambassador from the Emperor,
My royal nephew, and your name Caputius.   110
CAPUTIUS Madam, the same. Your servant.

KATHERINE   O my lord,
The times and titles now are altered strangely
With me since first you knew me. But I pray you,
What is your pleasure with me?
CAPUTIUS   Noble lady,
115   First, mine own service to your grace; the next,
The King's request that I would visit you,
Who grieves much for your weakness and by me
Sends you his princely commendations
And heartily entreats you take good comfort.
KATHERINE
120   O my good lord, that comfort comes too late;
'Tis like a pardon after execution.
That gentle physic given in time had cured me,
But now I am past all comforts here but prayers.
How does his highness?
CAPUTIUS   Madam, in good health.
125   KATHERINE   So may he ever do, and ever flourish
When I shall dwell with worms and my poor name
Banished the kingdom. Patience, is that letter
I caused you write yet sent away?
PATIENCE   No, madam.
KATHERINE   Sir, I most humbly pray you to deliver
This to my lord the King.
130   CAPUTIUS   Most willing, madam.
KATHERINE
In which I have commended to his goodness
The model of our chaste loves, his young daughter –
The dews of heaven fall thick in blessings on her! –
Beseeching him to give her virtuous breeding –
135   She is young and of a noble, modest nature;
I hope she will deserve well – and a little
To love her for her mother's sake that loved him,
Heaven knows how dearly. My next poor petition
Is that his noble grace would have some pity
140   Upon my wretched women, that so long
Have followed both my fortunes faithfully;
Of which there is not one, I dare avow –
And now I should not lie – but will deserve,
For virtue and true beauty of the soul,
145   For honesty and decent carriage,
A right good husband – let him be a noble –
And sure those men are happy that shall have 'em.
The last is for my men – they are the poorest,
But poverty could never draw 'em from me –
150   That they may have their wages duly paid 'em,
And something over to remember me by.
If heaven had pleased to have given me longer life
And able means, we had not parted thus.
These are the whole contents, and, good my lord,
155   By that you love the dearest in this world,
As you wish Christian peace to souls departed,
Stand these poor people's friend, and urge the King
To do me this last right.
CAPUTIUS   By heaven, I will,
Or let me lose the fashion of a man.
160   KATHERINE   I thank you, honest lord. Remember me

In all humility unto his highness.
Say his long trouble now is passing
Out of this world. Tell him in death I blessed him,
For so I will. Mine eyes grow dim. Farewell,
My lord. Griffith, farewell. Nay, Patience,   165
You must not leave me yet: I must to bed.
Call in more women. When I am dead, good wench,
Let me be used with honour. Strew me over
With maiden flowers, that all the world may know
I was a chaste wife to my grave. Embalm me,   170
Then lay me forth. Although unqueened, yet like
A queen and daughter to a king inter me.
I can no more.   *Exeunt leading Katherine.*

5.1   *Enter* GARDINER, Bishop of Winchester,
       a Page *with a torch before him, met by*
                Sir Thomas LOVELL.

GARDINER   It's one o'clock, boy, is't not?
PAGE   It hath struck.
GARDINER   These should be hours for necessities,
Not for delights; times to repair our nature
With comforting repose, and not for us
To waste these times. Good hour of the night, Sir
     Thomas.   5
Whither so late?
LOVELL   Came you from the King, my lord?
GARDINER
I did, Sir Thomas, and left him at primero
With the Duke of Suffolk.
LOVELL   I must to him, too,
Before he go to bed. I'll take my leave.
GARDINER
Not yet, Sir Thomas Lovell. What's the matter?   10
It seems you are in haste. And if there be
No great offence belongs to't, give your friend
Some touch of your late business. Affairs that walk,
As they say spirits do, at midnight have
In them a wilder nature than the business   15
That seeks dispatch by day.
LOVELL   My lord, I love you,
And durst commend a secret to your ear
Much weightier than this work. The Queen's in
     labour –
They say in great extremity, and feared
She'll with the labour end.
GARDINER   The fruit she goes with   20
I pray for heartily, that it may find
Good time, and live. But, for the stock, Sir Thomas,
I wish it grubbed up now.
LOVELL   Methinks I could
Cry the amen, and yet my conscience says
She's a good creature and, sweet lady, does   25
Deserve our better wishes.
GARDINER   But sir, sir –
Hear me, Sir Thomas. You're a gentleman
Of mine own way. I know you wise, religious,

And let me tell you, it will ne'er be well –
30 'Twill not, Sir Thomas Lovell, take't of me –
Till Cranmer, Cromwell (her two hands) and she
Sleep in their graves.

LOVELL   Now, sir, you speak of two
The most remarked i'th' kingdom. As for Cromwell,
Beside that of the Jewel House, is made Master
35 O'th' Rolls and the King's secretary; further, sir,
Stands in the gap and trade of more preferments,
With which the time will load him. Th'Archbishop
Is the King's hand and tongue, and who dare speak
One syllable against him?

GARDINER   Yes, yes, Sir Thomas,
40 There are that dare, and I myself have ventured
To speak my mind of him; and indeed this day,
Sir – I may tell it you, I think – I have
Incensed the lords o'th' Council that he is –
For so I know he is, they know he is –
45 A most arch heretic, a pestilence
That does infect the land; with which they, moved,
Have broken with the King, who hath so far
Given ear to our complaint, of his great grace
And princely care foreseeing those fell mischiefs
50 Our reasons laid before him, hath commanded
Tomorrow morning to the Council board
He be convented. He's a rank weed, Sir Thomas,
And we must root him out. From your affairs
I hinder you too long. Good night, Sir Thomas.

LOVELL
55 Many good nights, my lord. I rest your servant.

Exeunt Gardiner and Page.

Enter KING *and* SUFFOLK.

KING   Charles, I will play no more tonight:
My mind's not on't. You are too hard for me.

SUFFOLK   Sir, I did never win of you before.

KING   But little, Charles,
60 Nor shall not, when my fancy's on my play.
Now, Lovell, from the Queen what is the news?

LOVELL   I could not personally deliver to her
What you commanded me, but by her woman
I sent your message, who returned her thanks
65 In the greatest humbleness and desired your highness
Most heartily to pray for her.

KING   What sayest thou? Ha?
To pray for her? What, is she crying out?

LOVELL
So said her woman, and that her sufferance made
Almost each pang a death.

KING   Alas, good lady.
70 SUFFOLK   God safely quit her of her burden, and
With gentle travail, to the gladding of
Your highness with an heir.

KING   'Tis midnight, Charles.
Prithee to bed, and in thy prayers remember
Th'estate of my poor Queen. Leave me alone,
75 For I must think of that which company

Would not be friendly to.

SUFFOLK   I wish your highness
A quiet night, and my good mistress will
Remember in my prayers.

KING   Charles, good night.

Exit Suffolk.

Enter Sir Anthony DENNY.

Well, sir, what follows?

DENNY   Sir, I have brought my lord the Archbishop,   80
As you commanded me.

KING   Ha? Canterbury?

DENNY   Ay, my good lord.

KING   'Tis true. Where is he, Denny?

DENNY   He attends your highness' pleasure.

KING   Bring him to us.

Exit Denny.

LOVELL [*aside*]
This is about that which the Bishop spake.
I am happily come hither.   85

Enter CRANMER *and* DENNY.

KING   Avoid the gallery! [*Lovell seems to stay.*]
                    Ha? I have said. Be gone.
What?   *Exeunt Lovell and Denny.*

CRANMER [*aside*]   I am fearful. Wherefore frowns he thus?
'Tis his aspect of terror. All's not well.

KING   How now, my lord? You do desire to know
Wherefore I sent for you.

CRANMER [*Kneels.*]   It is my duty   90
T'attend your highness' pleasure.

KING   Pray you, arise,
My good and gracious lord of Canterbury.
Come, you and I must walk a turn together:
I have news to tell you. Come, come: give me your
hand.
Ah, my good lord, I grieve at what I speak,   95
And am right sorry to repeat what follows.
I have, and most unwillingly, of late
Heard many grievous – I do say, my lord,
Grievous – complaints of you, which, being
considered,
Have moved us and our Council that you shall   100
This morning come before us, where I know
You cannot with such freedom purge yourself
But that, till further trial in those charges
Which will require your answer, you must take
Your patience to you and be well contented   105
To make your house our Tower. You a brother of us,
It fits we thus proceed, or else no witness
Would come against you.

CRANMER [*Kneels.*]   I humbly thank your highness,
And am right glad to catch this good occasion
Most throughly to be winnowed, where my chaff   110
And corn shall fly asunder. For I know
There's none stands under more calumnious tongues
Than I myself, poor man.

KING   Stand up, good Canterbury.
Thy truth and thy integrity is rooted
115   In us, thy friend. Give me thy hand. Stand up.
Prithee, let's walk. Now, by my halidom,
What manner of man are you? My lord, I looked
You would have given me your petition that
I should have ta'en some pains to bring together
120   Yourself and your accusers and to have heard you
Without endurance further.
CRANMER   Most dread liege,
The good I stand on is my truth and honesty.
If they shall fail, I with mine enemies
Will triumph o'er my person, which I weigh not
125   Being of those virtues vacant. I fear nothing
What can be said against me.
KING   Know you not
How your state stands i'th' world, with the whole
        world?
Your enemies are many and not small: their practices
Must bear the same proportion, and not ever
130   The justice and the truth o'th' question carries
The due o'th' verdict with it. At what ease
Might corrupt minds procure knaves as corrupt
To swear against you? Such things have been done.
You are potently opposed, and with a malice
135   Of as great size. Ween you of better luck –
I mean in perjured witness – than your master,
Whose minister you are, whiles here he lived
Upon this naughty earth? Go to, go to:
You take a precipice for no leap of danger,
And woo your own destruction.
140   CRANMER   God and your majesty
Protect mine innocence, or I fall into
The trap is laid for me.
KING   Be of good cheer.
They shall no more prevail than we give way to.
Keep comfort to you, and this morning see
145   You do appear before them. If they shall chance,
In charging you with matters, to commit you,
The best persuasions to the contrary
Fail not to use, and with what vehemency
Th'occasion shall instruct you. If entreaties
150   Will render you no remedy, this ring
Deliver them, and your appeal to us
There make before them. – Look, the good man weeps.
He's honest, on mine honour. God's blest mother,
I swear he is true-hearted, and a soul
155   None better in my kingdom. – Get you gone,
And do as I have bid you.   *Exit Cranmer.*
                                He has strangled
His language in his tears.

                Enter Old Lady; LOVELL follows.

LOVELL [*within*]   Come back! What mean you?
OLD LADY   I'll not come back. The tidings that I bring
Will make my boldness manners. [*to the King*] Now
        good angels

Fly o'er thy royal head and shade thy person   160
Under their blessed wings.
KING   Now by thy looks
I guess thy message. Is the Queen delivered?
Say 'Ay, and of a boy'.
OLD LADY   Ay, ay, my liege,
And of a lovely boy. The God of heaven
Both now and ever bless her: 'tis a girl   165
Promises boys hereafter. Sir, your Queen
Desires your visitation and to be
Acquainted with this stranger. 'Tis as like you
As cherry is to cherry.
KING   Lovell.
LOVELL   Sir?
KING   Give her an hundred marks. I'll to the Queen.   170
                                Exeunt King and Lovell.
OLD LADY
An hundred marks? By this light, I'll ha' more.
An ordinary groom is for such payment.
I will have more or scold it out of him.
Said I for this the girl was like to him? I'll
Have more, or else unsay't; and now, while 'tis hot,   175
I'll put it to the issue.   *Exit Old Lady.*

5.2   *Enter* CRANMER, *Archbishop of Canterbury.*

CRANMER
I hope I am not too late, and yet the gentleman
That was sent to me from the Council prayed me
To make great haste. All fast? What means this? Ho!
Who waits there?

                Enter [Door] *Keeper.*

                Sure you know me?
KEEPER   Yes, my lord,
But yet I cannot help you.
CRANMER   Why?
KEEPER   Your grace   5
Must wait till you be called for.

                Enter Doctor BUTTS.

CRANMER   So.
BUTTS [*aside*]   This is a piece of malice. I am glad
I came this way so happily. The King
Shall understand it presently.   *Exit Butts.*
CRANMER [*aside*]   'Tis Butts,
The King's physician. As he passed along,   10
How earnestly he cast his eyes upon me.
Pray heaven he sound not my disgrace. For certain,
This is of purpose laid by some that hate me –
God turn their hearts: I never sought their malice –
To quench mine honour. They would shame to
        make me   15
Wait else at door, a fellow Councillor
'Mong boys, grooms and lackeys. But their
        pleasures
Must be fulfilled, and I attend with patience.

Enter the KING *and* BUTTS *at a window above.*

BUTTS   I'll show your grace the strangest sight –
KING   What's that, Butts?
BUTTS
20   – I think your highness saw this many a day.
KING   Body o' me, where is it?
BUTTS   There, my lord:
     The high promotion of his grace of Canterbury,
     Who holds his state at door 'mongst pursuivants,
     Pages and footboys.
KING   Ha? 'Tis he indeed.
25   Is this the honour they do one another?
     'Tis well there's one above 'em yet. I had thought
     They had parted so much honesty among 'em –
     At least good manners – as not thus to suffer
     A man of his place, and so near our favour,
30   To dance attendance on their lordships' pleasures –
     And at the door, too, like a post with packets.
     By holy Mary, Butts, there's knavery!
     Let 'em alone, and draw the curtain close:
     We shall hear more anon.

A council table brought in with chairs and stools and
placed under the state. Enter Lord CHANCELLOR,
places himself at the upper end of the table, on the left
hand; a seat being left void above him, as for Canterbury's
seat. Duke of SUFFOLK, Duke of NORFOLK, SURREY,
     Lord CHAMBERLAIN, GARDINER *seat themselves in*
order on each side; CROMWELL *at lower end, as secretary.*

35   CHANCELLOR   Speak to the business, master secretary.
     Why are we met in Council?
CROMWELL   Please your honours,
     The chief cause concerns his grace of Canterbury.
GARDINER   Has he had knowledge of it?
CROMWELL   Yes.
NORFOLK   Who waits there?
KEEPER   Without, my noble lords?
GARDINER   Yes.
KEEPER   My lord Archbishop,
40   And has done half an hour to know your pleasures.
CHANCELLOR   Let him come in.
KEEPER   Your grace may enter now.
     [*Cranmer approaches the council table.*]
CHANCELLOR
     My good lord Archbishop, I'm very sorry
     To sit here at this present and behold
     That chair stand empty. But we all are men,
45   In our own natures frail, and capable
     Of our flesh – few are angels – out of which frailty
     And want of wisdom, you that best should teach us
     Have misdemeaned yourself, and not a little,
     Toward the King first, then his laws, in filling
50   The whole realm, by your teaching and your chaplains' –
     For so we are informed – with new opinions,
     Diverse and dangerous, which are heresies
     And, not reformed, may prove pernicious.

GARDINER   Which reformation must be sudden too,
55   My noble lords, for those that tame wild horses
     Pace 'em not in their hands to make 'em gentle,
     But stop their mouths with stubborn bits and spur 'em
     Till they obey the manage. If we suffer,
     Out of our easiness and childish pity
     To one man's honour, this contagious sickness,   60
     Farewell, all physic. And what follows then?
     Commotions, uproars, with a general taint
     Of the whole state, as of late days our neighbours,
     The upper Germany, can dearly witness,
     Yet freshly pitied in our memories.   65
CRANMER   My good lords, hitherto, in all the progress
     Both of my life and office, I have laboured,
     And with no little study, that my teaching
     And the strong course of my authority
     Might go one way, and safely; and the end   70
     Was ever to do well. Nor is there living –
     I speak it with a single heart, my lords –
     A man that more detests, more stirs against,
     Both in his private conscience and his place,
     Defacers of a public peace than I do.   75
     Pray heaven the King may never find a heart
     With less allegiance in it. Men that make
     Envy and crooked malice nourishment
     Dare bite the best. I do beseech your lordships
     That in this case, of justice, my accusers,   80
     Be what they will, may stand forth face to face
     And freely urge against me.
SUFFOLK   Nay, my lord,
     That cannot be. You are a Councillor,
     And by that virtue no man dare accuse you.
GARDINER
     My lord, because we have business of more moment,   85
     We will be short with you. 'Tis his highness' pleasure
     And our consent, for better trial of you,
     From hence you be committed to the Tower,
     Where, being but a private man again,
     You shall know many dare accuse you boldly –   90
     More than, I fear, you are provided for.
CRANMER
     Ah, my good lord of Winchester, I thank you;
     You are always my good friend. If your will pass,
     I shall both find your lordship judge and juror,
     You are so merciful. I see your end: 95
     'Tis my undoing. Love and meekness, lord,
     Become a churchman better than ambition.
     Win straying souls with modesty again;
     Cast none away. That I shall clear myself,
     Lay all the weight ye can upon my patience,   100
     I make as little doubt as you do conscience
     In doing daily wrongs. I could say more,
     But reverence to your calling makes me modest.
GARDINER   My lord, my lord, you are a sectary.
     That's the plain truth. Your painted gloss discovers,   105
     To men that understand you, words and weakness.
CROMWELL   My lord of Winchester, you're a little,

By your good favour, too sharp. Men so noble,
However faulty, yet should find respect
110 For what they have been. 'Tis a cruelty
To load a falling man.

GARDINER   Good master secretary,
I cry your honour mercy: you may worst
Of all this table say so.

CROMWELL   Why, my lord?

GARDINER   Do not I know you for a favourer
Of this new sect? Ye are not sound.

115 CROMWELL   Not sound?

GARDINER   Not sound, I say.

CROMWELL   Would you were half so honest!
Men's prayers then would seek you, not their fears.

GARDINER   I shall remember this bold language.

CROMWELL   Do.
Remember your bold life, too.

CHANCELLOR   This is too much.
Forbear, for shame, my lords.

GARDINER   I have done.

120 CROMWELL   And I.

CHANCELLOR [*to Cranmer*]
Then thus for you, my lord. It stands agreed,
I take it, by all voices, that forthwith
You be conveyed to th' Tower a prisoner,
There to remain till the King's further pleasure
125 Be known unto us. Are you all agreed, lords?

ALL   We are.

CRANMER   Is there no other way of mercy
But I must needs to th' Tower, my lords?

GARDINER   What other
Would you expect? You are strangely troublesome.
Let some o'th' guard be ready there.

Enter the Guard.

CRANMER   For me?
Must I go like a traitor thither?

130 GARDINER   Receive him,
And see him safe i'th' Tower.

CRANMER   Stay, good my lords,
I have a little yet to say. Look there, my lords.
By virtue of that ring, I take my cause
Out of the gripes of cruel men and give it
135 To a most noble judge, the King my master.

CHANCELLOR   This is the King's ring.

SURREY   'Tis no counterfeit.

SUFFOLK   'Tis the right ring, by heaven. I told ye all,
When we first put this dangerous stone a-rolling,
'Twould fall upon ourselves.

NORFOLK   Do you think, my lords,
140 The King will suffer but the little finger
Of this man to be vexed?

CHAMBERLAIN   'Tis now too certain.
How much more is his life in value with him?
Would I were fairly out on't.

CROMWELL   My mind gave me,
In seeking tales and informations

Against this man, whose honesty the devil   145
And his disciples only envy at,
Ye blew the fire that burns ye. Now have at ye!

Enter KING, *frowning on them. He takes his seat.*

GARDINER
Dread sovereign, how much are we bound to heaven
In daily thanks, that gave us such a prince,
Not only good and wise but most religious;   150
One that, in all obedience, makes the Church
The chief aim of his honour and, to strengthen
That holy duty out of dear respect,
His royal self in judgement comes to hear
The cause betwixt her and this great offender.   155

KING   You were ever good at sudden commendations,
Bishop of Winchester, but know I come not
To hear such flattery now, and in my presence
They are too thin and bare to hide offences.
To me you cannot reach, you play the spaniel   160
And think with wagging of your tongue to win me.
But whatsoe'er thou takest me for, I'm sure
Thou hast a cruel nature and a bloody.
[*to Cranmer*] Good man, sit down. Now let me see the
          proudest –
He that dares most – but wag his finger at thee.   165
By all that's holy, he had better starve
Than but once think his place becomes thee not.

SURREY   May it please your grace –

KING   No, sir, it does not please me.
I had thought I had had men of some understanding
And wisdom of my Council, but I find none.   170
Was it discretion, lords, to let this man,
This good man – few of you deserve that title –
This honest man, wait like a lousy footboy
At chamber door? And one as great as you are?
Why, what a shame was this! Did my commission   175
Bid ye so far forget yourselves? I gave ye
Power as he was a Councillor to try him,
Not as a groom. There's some of ye, I see,
More out of malice than integrity,
Would try him to the utmost, had ye mean,   180
Which ye shall never have while I live.

CHANCELLOR   Thus far,
My most dread sovereign, may it like your grace
To let my tongue excuse all. What was purposed
Concerning his imprisonment was rather –
If there be faith in men – meant for his trial   185
And fair purgation to the world than malice,
I'm sure, in me.

KING   Well, well, my lords, respect him.
Take him, and use him well: he's worthy of it.
I will say thus much for him: if a prince
May be beholding to a subject, I   190
Am, for his love and service, so to him.
Make me no more ado, but all embrace him.
Be friends, for shame, my lords! My lord of
          Canterbury,

I have a suit which you must not deny me:
195　That is, a fair young maid that yet wants baptism.
You must be godfather and answer for her.
CRANMER　The greatest monarch now alive may glory
In such an honour. How may I deserve it,
That am a poor and humble subject to you?
200　KING　Come, come, my lord, you'd spare your spoons!
You shall have two noble partners with you: the old
Duchess of Norfolk and Lady Marquess Dorset. Will
these please you?
Once more, my lord of Winchester, I charge you
Embrace and love this man.
205　GARDINER　　　　　　　　With a true heart
And brother's love I do it.
CRANMER　　　　　　　　And let heaven
Witness how dear I hold this confirmation.
KING
Good man, those joyful tears show thy true heart.
The common voice, I see, is verified
210　Of thee, which says thus: 'Do my lord of Canterbury
A shrewd turn, and he's your friend forever.'
Come, lords, we trifle time away. I long
To have this young one made a Christian.
As I have made ye one, lords, one remain:
215　So I grow stronger, you more honour gain.　*Exeunt.*

5.3　*Noise and tumult within. Enter* Porter *and his* Man.

PORTER　You'll leave your noise anon, ye rascals. Do you
take the court for Parish Garden? Ye rude slaves, leave
your gaping.
ONE [*within*]　Good master porter, I belong to th' larder.
5　PORTER　Belong to th' gallows, and be hanged, ye rogue!
Is this a place to roar in? Fetch me a dozen crab-tree
staves, and strong ones: these are but switches to 'em.
I'll scratch your heads. You must be seeing christenings?
Do you look for ale and cakes here, you rude rascals?
10　MAN　Pray, sir, be patient. 'Tis as much impossible,
Unless we sweep 'em from the door with cannons,
To scatter 'em as 'tis to make 'em sleep
On May-day morning – which will never be.
We may as well push against Paul's as stir 'em.
15　PORTER　How got they in, and be hanged?
MAN　Alas, I know not. How gets the tide in?
As much as one sound cudgel of four foot –
You see the poor remainder – could distribute,
I made no spare, sir.
PORTER　　　　　　　You did nothing, sir.
20　MAN　I am not Samson, nor Sir Guy, nor Colbrand,
To mow 'em down before me; but if I spared any
That had a head to hit, either young or old,
He or she, cuckold or cuckold-maker,
Let me ne'er hope to see a chine again –
25　And that I would not for a cow, God save her!
ONE [*within*]　Do you hear, master porter?
PORTER
I shall be with you presently, good master puppy.

[*to his Man*] Keep the door close, sirrah.
MAN　What would you have me do?
PORTER　What should you do, but knock 'em down by　30
th' dozens? Is this Moorfields to muster in? Or have we
some strange Indian with the great tool come to court,
the women so besiege us? Bless me, what a fry of
fornication is at door! On my Christian conscience,
this one christening will beget a thousand: here will be　35
father, godfather, and all together.
MAN　The spoons will be the bigger, sir. There is a fellow
somewhat near the door – he should be a brazier by his
face, for, o'my conscience, twenty of the dog-days now
reign in's nose. All that stand about him are under the　40
line: they need no other penance. That fire-drake did I
hit three times on the head, and three times was his
nose discharged against me. He stands there like a
mortar-piece, to blow us. There was a haberdasher's
wife of small wit near him that railed upon me till her　45
pinked porringer fell off her head for kindling such a
combustion in the state. I missed the meteor once and
hit that woman, who cried out 'Clubs!', when I might
see from far some forty truncheoners draw to her
succour, which were the hope o'th' Strand, where she　50
was quartered. They fell on; I made good my place; at
length they came to th' broomstaff to me; I defied 'em
still, when suddenly a file of boys behind 'em, loose
shot, delivered such a shower of pebbles that I was fain
to draw mine honour in and let 'em win the work. The　55
devil was amongst 'em, I think, surely.
PORTER　These are the youths that thunder at a
playhouse and fight for bitten apples, that no audience
but the 'Tribulation' of Tower Hill or the 'Limbs' of
Limehouse, their dear brothers, are able to endure. I　60
have some of 'em in *Limbo Patrum* – and there they are
like to dance these three days – besides the running
banquet of two beadles that is to come.

Enter Lord CHAMBERLAIN.

CHAMBERLAIN　Mercy o'me, what a multitude are here!
They grow still, too. From all parts they are coming,　65
As if we kept a fair here! Where are these porters,
These lazy knaves? You've made a fine hand, fellows!
There's a trim rabble let in! Are all these
Your faithful friends o'th' suburbs? We shall have
Great store of room, no doubt, left for the ladies,　70
When they pass back from the christening.
PORTER　　　　　　　　　An't please your honour,
We are but men, and what so many may do,
Not being torn a-pieces, we have done:
An army cannot rule 'em.
CHAMBERLAIN　　　　　　As I live,
If the King blame me for't, I'll lay ye all　75
By th' heels, and suddenly, and on your heads
Clap round fines for neglect. You're lazy knaves,
And here ye lie, baiting of bombards, when
Ye should do service. Hark, the trumpets sound:
They're come already from the christening.　80

Go break among the press and find a way out
To let the troop pass fairly, or I'll find
A Marshalsea shall hold ye play these two months.
PORTER   Make way there for the Princess!
MAN   You, great fellow,
85   Stand close up, or I'll make your head ache!
PORTER   You i'th' chamblet, get up o'th' rail –
I'll peck you o'er the pales else.   *Exeunt.*

5.4   *Enter Trumpets sounding; then two Aldermen,
Lord Mayor,* GARTER, CRANMER, *Duke of*
NORFOLK *with his marshal's staff, Duke of*
SUFFOLK, *two Noblemen bearing great standing
bowls for the christening gifts; then four Noblemen
bearing a canopy, under which the Duchess of
Norfolk, godmother, bearing the child richly habited
in a mantle, etc., train borne by a Lady; then follows
the Marchioness Dorset, the other godmother, and
Ladies. The troop pass once about the stage,
and Garter speaks.*

GARTER   Heaven, from thy endless goodness, send
prosperous life, long and ever happy, to the high and
mighty Princess of England, Elizabeth.

Flourish. Enter KING *and Guard.*

CRANMER [*Kneels.*]
And to your royal grace and the good Queen,
5   My noble partners and myself thus pray
All comfort, joy, in this most gracious lady
Heaven ever laid up to make parents happy
May hourly fall upon ye.
KING   Thank you, good lord Archbishop.
What is her name?
CRANMER   Elizabeth.
KING   Stand up, lord.
[*to the child*] With this kiss, take my blessing. God
10   protect thee,
Into whose hand I give thy life.
CRANMER   Amen.
KING   My noble gossips, you've been too prodigal.
I thank ye heartily: so shall this lady,
When she has so much English.
CRANMER   Let me speak, sir,
15   For heaven now bids me; and the words I utter
Let none think flattery, for they'll find 'em truth.
This royal infant – heaven still move about her –
Though in her cradle, yet now promises
Upon this land a thousand thousand blessings,
20   Which time shall bring to ripeness. She shall be –
But few now living can behold that goodness –
A pattern to all princes living with her
And all that shall succeed. Saba was never
More covetous of wisdom and fair virtue
25   Than this pure soul shall be. All princely graces
That mould up such a mighty piece as this is,
With all the virtues that attend the good,

Shall still be doubled on her. Truth shall nurse her;
Holy and heavenly thoughts still counsel her.
She shall be loved and feared. Her own shall bless
her;   30
Her foes shake like a field of beaten corn,
And hang their heads with sorrow. Good grows with
her.
In her days, every man shall eat in safety
Under his own vine what he plants, and sing
The merry songs of peace to all his neighbours.   35
God shall be truly known, and those about her
From her shall read the perfect ways of honour
And by those claim their greatness, not by blood.
Nor shall this peace sleep with her, but as when
The bird of wonder dies, the maiden phoenix,   40
Her ashes new create another heir
As great in admiration as herself,
So shall she leave her blessedness to one,
When heaven shall call her from this cloud of
darkness,
Who from the sacred ashes of her honour   45
Shall star-like rise as great in fame as she was,
And so stand fixed. Peace, plenty, love, truth, terror,
That were the servants to this chosen infant,
Shall then be his, and like a vine grow to him.
Wherever the bright sun of heaven shall shine,   50
His honour and the greatness of his name
Shall be, and make new nations. He shall flourish,
And, like a mountain cedar, reach his branches
To all the plains about him. Our children's children
Shall see this and bless heaven.
KING   Thou speakest wonders.   55
CRANMER   She shall be to the happiness of England
An aged princess. Many days shall see her,
And yet no day without a deed to crown it.
Would I had known no more. But she must die:
She must, the saints must have her. Yet a virgin,   60
A most unspotted lily, shall she pass to th' ground,
And all the world shall mourn her.
KING   O lord Archbishop,
Thou hast made me now a man. Never before
This happy child did I get anything.
This oracle of comfort has so pleased me   65
That when I am in heaven I shall desire
To see what this child does and praise my maker.
I thank ye all. To you, my good Lord Mayor,
And your good brethren, I am much beholding:
I have received much honour by your presence,   70
And ye shall find me thankful. Lead the way, lords:
Ye must all see the Queen, and she must thank ye –
She will be sick else. This day, no man think
'Has business at his house, for all shall stay:
This little one shall make it holiday.   *Exeunt.*   75

Enter EPILOGUE.

EPILOGUE   'Tis ten to one this play can never please
All that are here. Some come to take their ease,

And sleep an act or two (but those, we fear,
We've frighted with our trumpets, so 'tis clear
They'll say 'tis naught), others to hear the city
Abused extremely and to cry 'That's witty!'
(Which we have not done neither), that I fear
All the expected good we're like to hear

5

For this play at this time is only in
The merciful construction of good women,
For such a one we showed 'em. If they smile
And say 'twill do, I know within a while
All the best men are ours – for 'tis ill hap
If they hold when their ladies bid 'em clap.   *Exit.*

10

King John

King John is often undervalued among Shakespeare's histories. It stands separate from the history traced by the eight plays from *King Richard II* to *King Richard III*, which can be seen as England moving from its medieval past into its Tudor present, from 1398 to 1485. *King John* is set in a much earlier period; its action begins in 1199 with John recently crowned and ends with his death in 1216 and the succession of the young Prince Henry. Interestingly, what a later age would find most important in John's reign, the signing of Magna Carta in 1215, is never mentioned.

By 1598, however, Francis Meres could refer to *King John* along with six other plays as evidence of Shakespeare's excellence in writing 'tragedy', showing, among other things that the generic distinction between histories and tragedies was not yet clear and may well depend more on the tri-partite arrangement of the 1623 Folio than any fully developed contemporary generic theory for its currency. Its date of composition is, however, hard to pin down. It was certainly written after 1587, as it depends upon material Shakespeare found in the edition of Holinshed's *Chronicles* published that year.

Complicating the dating is the existence of a play called *The Troublesome Reign of King John* that was published anonymously in 1591, and then in 1611 with a title-page attribution to 'W. Sh.' and again in 1622, this time as by 'W. Shakespeare', though the attributions are presumably merely opportunistic or mistaken. The two plays, while paralleling one another in plot and structure, differ almost entirely in language, making it hard to think that they were written by the same person. One seems likely to be the source of the other, with a growing consensus that *The Troublesome Reign* is the earlier play.

Whenever *King John* was written, and whatever its relationship is to *The Troublesome Reign*, Shakespeare's play is remarkable. John's reign had interested Tudor historians mainly for the King's defiance of the Pope: although finally John was forced bow to Papal power, he was often seen as a proto-Protestant hero, whose unsuccessful resistance would ultimately be fulfilled with Henry VIII's break with Rome.

But Shakespeare play is no simple Protestant polemic. His John is a usurper and an opportunist. He has only a 'borrowed majesty' (1.1.4), and he is willing to suborn murder to preserve it. On the other hand, the Catholic Church is presented as a scheming and predatory enemy, eager to undermine England's national sovereignty and willing to murder its King. If the play has a moral centre at all, it is found in the puzzling figure of the Bastard, Philip Faulconbridge. The madcap Bastard understands the limitations of the conventional vocabularies of legitimacy and right, which so often are used to rationalize self-interest. He sees himself as 'a bastard to the time' (1.1.207), out of step with an age that is dishonest and self-seeking. Presented with the opportunity to take 'the ordering of this present time' (5.1.77), the Bastard refuses to take personal advantage, powerfully standing up and in for the King, and, after John dies, bowing in allegiance to the young King Henry.

There are no surviving records of any early performances, but the play was mentioned in 1669 as one of a group of plays 'formerly acted at Blackfriars' (the indoor theatre the King's Men had played at between 1608 and 1642) and assigned to 'his Majesties Servants at the New Theatre'. The first dated performance is one played at Covent Garden in 1737. Throughout the eighteenth and the first half of the nineteenth centuries, *King John* was popular on stage, in large part thanks to its historical spectacle and in particular to the star turn offered by the role of Constance, which was played by every major actress from Sarah Siddons to Sybil Thorndike. Surprisingly, *King John* became the first Shakespeare film to appear on film, when the British Mutoscope & Biograph Company in 1899 made four short films of scenes from a production of the play directed by and starring Herbert Beerbohm Tree. Stills from each of these have survived, and an incomplete version of John's death scene exists in Amsterdam at the EYE Film Institute Netherlands. Throughout the twentieth century and into the twenty-first, the play was infrequently produced, though in recent years, productions have again found in its realistic politics a play that speaks powerfully to both the difficulty of and the need for moral action when it is so easy to lose one's way 'Among the thorns and dangers of this world' (4.3.141).

The Arden text is based on the 1623 First Folio.

THE ENGLISH

KING JOHN	*of England*
Queen ELEANOR	*Queen Mother of England, mother to King John*
PRINCE HENRY	*son to King John, afterwards successor to his father as Henry III*
BLANCHE of Castile	*niece to King John*
Earl of SALISBURY	
Earl of PEMBROKE	*English nobles, both supporters*
Earl of ESSEX	*and opponents of John*
BIGOT, Earl of Norfolk	
Robert FAULCONBRIDGE	*son to the late Sir Robert Faulconbridge*
PHILIP the BASTARD	*(also known as Sir Richard Plantagenet) half-brother to Robert Faulconbridge*
HUBERT	*imperfectly obedient intimate of King John*
LADY FAULCONBRIDGE	*widow to the late Sir Robert Faulconbridge, mother to Philip and Robert*
James GURNEY	*servant to Lady Faulconbridge*
PETER of Pomfret	*a prophet*
Two EXECUTIONERS	*agents of John*
SHERIFF	
ENGLISH HERALD	
English MESSENGER	

THE FRENCH

KING PHILIP	*of France*
Lewis the DAUPHIN	*son to King Philip*
CHATILLON	*ambassador from France to King John*
MELUN	*a French lord, with some English blood*
FRENCH HERALD	
French MESSENGER	

THIRD PARTIES

ARTHUR	*Duke of Brittany, nephew to King John and rival to the English throne*
CONSTANCE	*mother to Arthur*
Limoges, Duke of AUSTRIA	*an ally of France*
Cardinal PANDULPH	*a papal legate*
CITIZENS of Angiers	

Lords, Officers, Soldiers, Trumpeters, Attendants

King John

1.1   *Flourish. Enter* KING JOHN, *Queen*
ELEANOR, *the* Earls of PEMBROKE, ESSEX
and SALISBURY, *attended, with* CHATILLON,
Ambassador of France, attended.

KING JOHN
Now say, Chatillon, what would France with us?
CHATILLON
Thus, after greeting, speaks the King of France
In my behaviour, to the majesty,
The borrowed majesty of England here.
ELEANOR   A strange beginning: borrowed majesty?
KING JOHN   Silence, good mother, hear the embassy.
CHATILLON
Philip of France, in right and true behalf
Of thy deceased brother, Geoffrey's son,
Arthur Plantagenet, lays most lawful claim
To this fair island, and the territories –
To Ireland, Poitiers, Anjou, Touraine, Maine –
Desiring thee to lay aside the sword
Which sways usurpingly these several titles,
And put the same into young Arthur's hand,
Thy nephew, and right royal sovereign.
KING JOHN   What follows if we disallow of this?
CHATILLON
The proud control of fierce and bloody war
To enforce these rights, so forcibly withheld.
KING JOHN
Here have we war for war, and blood for blood,
Controlment for controlment: so answer France.
CHATILLON
Then take my king's defiance from my mouth,
The farthest limit of my embassy.
KING JOHN   Bear mine to him, and so depart in peace.
Be thou as lightning in the eyes of France,
For ere thou canst report I will be there,
The thunder of my cannon shall be heard.
So hence: be thou the trumpet of our wrath
And sullen presage of your own decay.
An honourable conduct let him have:
Pembroke, look to't. Farewell, Chatillon.
    Exeunt Chatillon and Pembroke, attended.
ELEANOR   What now, my son? Have I not ever said
How that ambitious Constance would not cease
Till she had kindled France and all the world
Upon the right and party of her son?
This might have been prevented, and made whole
With very easy arguments of love,
Which now the manage of two kingdoms must
With fearful bloody issue arbitrate.
KING JOHN
Our strong possession, and our right for us.
ELEANOR
Your strong possession much more than your right,
Or else it must go wrong with you and me;
So much my conscience whispers in your ear,
Which none but God, and you, and I, shall hear.

Enter a Sheriff and whispers to Essex.

ESSEX   My liege, here is the strangest controversy
Come from the country to be judged by you   45
That e'er I heard: shall I produce the men?
KING JOHN   Let them approach.   *Exit Sheriff.*
Our abbeys and our priories shall pay
This expedition's charge.

    Enter ROBERT FAULCONBRIDGE *and*
    PHILIP *the* BASTARD.

               What men are you?
PHILIP   Your faithful subject, I, a gentleman   50
Born in Northamptonshire, and eldest son,
As I suppose, to Robert Faulconbridge,
A soldier by the honour-giving hand
Of Cordelion, knighted in the field.
KING JOHN   What art thou?   55
ROBERT   The son and heir to that same Faulconbridge.
KING JOHN   Is that the elder, and art thou the heir?
You came not of one mother then it seems.
PHILIP   Most certain of one mother, mighty king:
That is well known; and, as I think, one father.   60
But for the certain knowledge of that truth
I put you o'er to God and to my mother;
Of that I doubt, as all men's children may.
ELEANOR
Out on thee, rude man, thou dost shame thy mother,
And wound her honour with this diffidence.   65
PHILIP   I, madam? No, I have no reason for it,
That is my brother's plea, and none of mine,
The which if he can prove, 'a pops me out
At least from fair five hundred pound a year.
God guard my mother's honour, and my land.   70
KING JOHN
A good blunt fellow. Why, being younger born,
Doth he lay claim to thine inheritance?
PHILIP   I know not why, except to get the land;
But once he slandered me with bastardy.
But whe'er I be as true begot or no,   75
That still I lay upon my mother's head,
But that I am as well begot, my liege –
Fair fall the bones that took the pains for me –
Compare our faces, and be judge yourself
If old Sir Robert did beget us both   80
And were our father, and this son like him –
O, old Sir Robert, father, on my knee [*kneeling*]
I give God thanks I was not like to thee.
KING JOHN
Why what a madcap hath heaven lent us here?
ELEANOR   He hath a trick of Cordelion's face,   85
The accent of his tongue affecteth him.
Do you not read some tokens of my son
In the large composition of this man?
KING JOHN   Mine eye hath well examined his parts,
And finds them perfect Richard. Sirrah, speak: 90
What doth move you to claim your brother's land?

PHILIP　Because he hath a half-face like my father!
With half that face would he have all my land,
A half-faced groat, five hundred pound a year?

95 ROBERT　My gracious liege, when that my father lived,
Your brother did employ my father much –

PHILIP　Well sir, by this you cannot get my land.
Your tale must be how he employed my mother.

ROBERT　And once dispatched him in an embassy
100 To Germany, there with the Emperor
To treat of high affairs touching that time.
Th'advantage of his absence took the King,
And in the mean time sojourned at my father's,
Where how he did prevail I shame to speak.
105 But truth is truth, large lengths of seas and shores
Between my father and my mother lay,
As I have heard my father speak himself,
When this same lusty gentleman was got.
Upon his deathbed he by will bequeathed
110 His lands to me, and took it on his death
That this my mother's son was none of his;
And if he were, he came into the world
Full fourteen weeks before the course of time.
Then, good my liege, let me have what is mine,
115 My father's land, as was my father's will.

KING JOHN　Sirrah, your brother is legitimate:
Your father's wife did after wedlock bear him,
And if she did play false, the fault was hers –
Which fault lies on the hazards of all husbands
120 That marry wives. Tell me, how if my brother –
Who, as you say, took pains to get this son –
Had of your father claimed this son for his?
In sooth, good friend, your father might have kept
This calf, bred from his cow, from all the world,
125 In sooth he might. Then if he were my brother's,
My brother might not claim him, nor your father,
Being none of his, refuse him. This concludes:
My mother's son did get your father's heir,
Your father's heir must have your father's land.

130 ROBERT　Shall then my father's will be of no force
To dispossess that child which is not his?

PHILIP　Of no more force to dispossess me, sir,
Than was his will to get me, as I think.

ELEANOR
Whether hadst thou rather be: a Faulconbridge,
135 And like thy brother to enjoy thy land,
Or the reputed son of Cordelion,
Lord of thy presence, and no land beside?

PHILIP　Madam, an if my brother had my shape
And I had his, Sir Robert's his like him,
140 And if my legs were two such riding-rods,
My arms, such eel-skins stuffed, my face so thin,
That in mine ear I durst not stick a rose
Lest men should say, 'Look where three farthings goes',
And to his shape were heir to all this land,
145 Would I might never stir from off this place.
I would give it, every foot, to have this face:
I would not be Sir Nob in any case.

ELEANOR
I like thee well. Wilt thou forsake thy fortune,
Bequeath thy land to him and follow me?
I am a soldier, and now bound to France. 150

PHILIP　Brother, take you my land, I'll take my chance.
Your face hath got five hundred pound a year,
Yet sell your face for fivepence and 'tis dear.
Madam, I'll follow you unto the death.

ELEANOR　Nay, I would have you go before me thither. 155

PHILIP　Our country manners give our betters way.

KING JOHN　What is thy name?

PHILIP　Philip, my liege, so is my name begun,
Philip, good old Sir Robert's wife's eldest son.

KING JOHN
From henceforth bear his name whose form thou
　bearest: 160
Kneel thou down Philip, but rise more great.
　[*Knights him.*]
Arise Sir Richard, and Plantagenet.

BASTARD
Brother by th' mother's side, give me your hand:
My father gave me honour, yours gave land.
Now blessed be the hour by night or day 165
When I was got, Sir Robert was away.

ELEANOR　The very spirit of Plantagenet!
I am thy grandam, Richard; call me so.

BASTARD
Madam, by chance but not by truth, what though;
Something about a little from the right, 170
In at the window, or else o'er the hatch:
Who dares not stir by day must walk by night,
And have is have, how ever men do catch:
Near or far off, well won is still well shot,
And I am I, howe'er I was begot. 175

KING JOHN
Go, Faulconbridge, now hast thou thy desire:
A landless knight makes thee a landed squire.
Come, madam, and come, Richard, we must speed
For France, for France, for it is more than need.

BASTARD　Brother adieu, good fortune come to thee, 180
For thou wast got i'th' way of honesty.
　　　　　　　　　　　　Exeunt all but Bastard.
A foot of honour better than I was,
But many a many foot of land the worse.
Well, now can I make any Joan a lady.
'Good-den Sir Richard', 'Godamercy fellow' – 185
And if his name be George I'll call him Peter,
For new-made honour doth forget men's names:
'Tis too respective and too sociable
For your conversion. Now, your traveller,
He and his toothpick at my worship's mess, 190
And when my knightly stomach is sufficed,
Why then I suck my teeth and catechize
My picked man of countries. 'My dear sir' –
Thus leaning on mine elbow I begin –
'I shall beseech you' – that is Question now, 195
And then comes Answer like an Absey book.

'O sir,' says Answer, 'at your best command,
At your employment, at your service sir.'
'No sir,' says Question; 'Ay, sweet sir, at yours.'
And so ere Answer knows what Question would,
Saving in dialogue of compliment
And talking of the Alps and Apennines,
The Pyrenean and the River Po,
It draws toward supper in conclusion so.
But this is worshipful society,
And fits the mounting spirit like myself;
For he is but a bastard to the time
That doth not smack of observation,
And so am I whether I smack or no;
And not alone in habit and device,
Exterior form, outward accoutrement,
But from the inward motion to deliver
Sweet, sweet, sweet poison for the age's tooth,
Which though I will not practise to deceive,
Yet to avoid deceit I mean to learn,
For it shall strew the footsteps of my rising.
But who comes in such haste in riding robes?
What woman-post is this? Hath she no husband
That will take pains to blow a horn before her?

Enter LADY FAULCONBRIDGE *and* James GURNEY.

O me, 'tis my mother. How now, good lady,
What brings you here to court so hastily?

LADY FAULCONBRIDGE
Where is that slave thy brother? Where is he
That holds in chase mine honour up and down?

BASTARD   My brother Robert, old Sir Robert's son,
Colbrand the Giant, that same mighty man,
Is it Sir Robert's son that you seek so?

LADY FAULCONBRIDGE
Sir Robert's son? Ay, thou unreverend boy,
Sir Robert's son! Why scorn'st thou at Sir Robert?
He is Sir Robert's son, and so art thou.

BASTARD
James Gurney, wilt thou give us leave a while?

GURNEY
Good leave, good Philip.

BASTARD   Philip? Sparrow! James,
There's toys abroad, anon I'll tell thee more.
                                    Exit Gurney.
Madam, I was not old Sir Robert's son.
Sir Robert might have eat his part in me
Upon Good Friday, and ne'er broke his fast.
Sir Robert could do well – marry, to confess –
Could he get me? Sir Robert could not do it,
We know his handiwork. Therefore, good mother,
To whom am I beholding for these limbs?
Sir Robert never holp to make this leg.

LADY FAULCONBRIDGE
Hast thou conspired with thy brother too,
That for thine own gain shouldst defend mine honour?
What means this scorn, thou most untoward knave?

BASTARD   Knight, knight good mother, Basilisco-like:

What, I am dubbed, I have it on my shoulder.   245
But mother, I am not Sir Robert's son;
I have disclaimed Sir Robert and my land,
Legitimation, name, and all is gone.
Then, good my mother, let me know my father:
Some proper man I hope. Who was it, mother?   250

LADY FAULCONBRIDGE
Hast thou denied thyself a Faulconbridge?

BASTARD   As faithfully as I deny the devil.

LADY FAULCONBRIDGE
King Richard Cordelion was thy father.
By long and vehement suit I was seduced
To make room for him in my husband's bed –   255
God, lay not my transgression to thy charge!
Thou art the issue of my dear offence
Which was so strongly urged past my defence.

BASTARD   Now by this light, were I to get again,
Madam, I would not wish a better father.   260
Some sins do bear their privilege on earth,
And so doth yours. Your fault was not your folly;
Needs must you lay your heart at his dispose,
Subjected tribute to commanding love,
Against whose fury and unmatched force   265
The aweless lion could not wage the fight,
Nor keep his princely heart from Richard's hand.
He that perforce robs lions of their hearts
May easily win a woman's: ay, my mother,
With all my heart I thank thee for my father.   270
Who lives and dares but say thou didst not well
When I was got, I'll send his soul to hell.
Come, lady, I will show thee to my kin,
And they shall say, when Richard me begot,
If thou hadst said him nay it had been sin –   275
Who says it was, he lies, I say 'twas not.   *Exeunt.*

2.1   *Flourish. Enter before Angiers,* KING
           PHILIP *of France, Lewis the* DAUPHIN, *the*
           Duke of AUSTRIA, CONSTANCE, ARTHUR
           and the armies of France and Austria.

KING PHILIP   Before Angiers well met, brave Austria.
– Arthur, that great forerunner of thy blood,
Richard, that robbed the lion of his heart
And fought the holy wars in Palestine,
By this brave duke came early to his grave;   5
And for amends to his posterity
At our importance hither is he come
To spread his colours, boy, in thy behalf,
And to rebuke the usurpation
Of thy unnatural uncle, English John.   10
Embrace him, love him, give him welcome hither.

ARTHUR   God shall forgive you Cordelion's death
The rather that you give his offspring life,
Shadowing their right under your wings of war.
I give you welcome with a powerless hand,   15
But with a heart full of unstained love:
Welcome before the gates of Angiers, Duke.

[*Arthur and Austria embrace.*]

KING PHILIP
A noble boy, who would not do thee right?

AUSTRIA   Upon thy cheek lay I this zealous kiss,
20 As seal to this indenture of my love:
That to my home I will no more return
Till Angiers, and the right thou hast in France,
Together with that pale, that white-faced shore,
Whose foot spurns back the ocean's roaring tides,
25 And coops from other lands her islanders,
Even till that England hedged in with the main,
That water-walled bulwark, still secure
And confident from foreign purposes,
Even till that utmost corner of the west
30 Salute thee for her king. Till then, fair boy,
Will I not think of home, but follow arms.

CONSTANCE
O, take his mother's thanks, a widow's thanks,
Till your strong hand shall help to give him strength
To make a more requital to your love.

AUSTRIA
35 The peace of God is theirs that lift their swords
In such a just and charitable war.

KING PHILIP
Well then, to work. Our cannon shall be bent
Against the brows of this resisting town.
Call for our chiefest men of discipline
40 To cull the plots of best advantages.
We'll lay before this town our royal bones,
Wade to the market-place in Frenchmen's blood,
But we will make it subject to this boy.

CONSTANCE   Stay for an answer to your embassy
45 Lest unadvised you stain your swords with blood;
My Lord Chatillon may from England bring
That right in peace which here we urge in war,
And then we shall repent each drop of blood
That hot rash haste so indirectly shed.

Enter CHATILLON.

50 KING PHILIP   A wonder, lady: lo, upon thy wish
Our messenger Chatillon is arrived.
What England says, say briefly, gentle lord;
We coldly pause for thee. Chatillon, speak.

CHATILLON
Then turn your forces from this paltry siege
55 And stir them up against a mightier task.
England, impatient of your just demands
Hath put himself in arms; the adverse winds
Whose leisure I have stayed have given him time
To land his legions all as soon as I;
60 His marches are expedient to this town,
His forces strong, his soldiers confident.
With him along is come the mother queen,
An Ate stirring him to blood and strife;
With her, her niece, the Lady Blanche of Spain;
65 With them a bastard of the king-deceased;
And all th'unsettled humours of the land,

Rash, inconsiderate, fiery voluntaries
With ladies' faces and fierce dragons' spleens,
Have sold their fortunes at their native homes,
Bearing their birthrights proudly on their backs,   70
To make a hazard of new fortunes here.
In brief, a braver choice of dauntless spirits
Than now the English bottoms have waft o'er
Did never float upon the swelling tide
To do offence and scathe in Christendom.   75
[*Drums beat.*]
The interruption of their churlish drums
Cuts off more circumstance: they are at hand
To parley or to fight, therefore prepare.

KING PHILIP
How much unlooked for is this expedition.

AUSTRIA   By how much unexpected, by so much   80
We must awake endeavour for defence,
For courage mounteth with occasion.
Let them be welcome then, we are prepared.

Flourish. Enter KING JOHN, BASTARD, Queen
ELEANOR, BLANCHE, PEMBROKE, SALISBURY
and the English army.

KING JOHN
Peace be to France, if France in peace permit
Our just and lineal entrance to our own;   85
If not, bleed France, and peace ascend to heaven
Whiles we, God's wrathful agent, do correct
Their proud contempt that beats his peace to heaven.

KING PHILIP   Peace be to England, if that war return
From France to England, there to live in peace;   90
England we love, and for that England's sake,
With burden of our armour here we sweat.
This toil of ours should be a work of thine;
But thou from loving England art so far
That thou hast underwrought his lawful king,   95
Cut off the sequence of posterity,
Outfaced infant state, and done a rape
Upon the maiden virtue of the crown.
Look here upon thy brother Geoffrey's face:
These eyes, these brows, were moulded out of his.   100
This little abstract doth contain that large
Which died in Geoffrey, and the hand of time
Shall draw this brief into as huge a volume.
That Geoffrey was thy elder brother born,
And this his son; England was Geoffrey's right,   105
And this is Geoffrey's; in the name of God
How comes it then that thou art called a king,
When living blood doth in these temples beat
Which owe the crown that thou o'er-masterest?

KING JOHN
From whom hast thou this great commission, France,   110
To draw my answer from thy articles?

KING PHILIP
From that supernal Judge that stirs good thoughts
In any breast of strong authority
To look into the blots and stains of right:

115	That Judge hath made me guardian to this boy,
	Under whose warrant I impeach thy wrong
	And by whose help I mean to chastise it.
	KING JOHN Alack, thou dost usurp authority.
	KING PHILIP Excuse it is to beat usurping down.
120	ELEANOR Who is it thou dost call usurper, France?
	CONSTANCE Let me make answer: thy usurping son.
	ELEANOR Out, insolent! Thy bastard shall be king,
	That thou mayst be a queen, and check the world?
	CONSTANCE My bed was ever to thy son as true
125	As thine was to thy husband; and this boy
	Liker in feature to his father Geoffrey
	Than thou and John, in manners being as like
	As rain to water, or devil to his dam.
	My boy a bastard? By my soul, I think
130	His father never was so true begot.
	It cannot be an if thou wert his mother.
	ELEANOR
	There's a good mother boy, that blots thy father.
	CONSTANCE
	There's a good grandam boy, that would blot thee.
	AUSTRIA Peace!
	BASTARD Hear the crier.
	AUSTRIA What the devil art thou?
135	BASTARD One that will play the devil, sir, with you,
	An 'a may catch your hide and you alone.
	You are the hare of whom the proverb goes,
	Whose valour plucks dead lions by the beard.
	I'll smoke your skin-coat an I catch you right.
140	Sirrah, look to't, i'faith I will, i'faith.
	BLANCHE O, well did he become that lion's robe
	That did disrobe the lion of that robe.
	BASTARD It lies as sightly on the back of him
	As great Alcides' shoes upon an ass.
145	But, ass, I'll take that burden from your back,
	Or lay on that shall make your shoulders crack.
	AUSTRIA What cracker is this same that deafs our ears
	With this abundance of superfluous breath?
	King Philip, determine what we shall do straight.
	KING PHILIP
150	Women and fools, break off your conference.
	King John, this is the very sum of all:
	England and Ireland, Anjou, Touraine, Maine,
	In right of Arthur do I claim of thee.
	Wilt thou resign them and lay down thy arms?
155	KING JOHN My life as soon. I do defy thee, France.
	Arthur of Britain, yield thee to my hand,
	And out of my dear love I'll give thee more
	Than e'er the coward hand of France can win.
	Submit thee, boy.
	ELEANOR Come to thy grandam, child.
160	CONSTANCE Do child, go to it grandam child,
	Give grandam kingdom, and it grandam will
	Give it a plum, a cherry and a fig,
	There's a good grandam.
	ARTHUR Good my mother, peace.
	I would that I were low laid in my grave.

165	I am not worth this coil that's made for me.
	ELEANOR
	His mother shames him so, poor boy, he weeps.
	CONSTANCE
	Now shame upon you whe'er she does or no.
	His grandam's wrongs, and not his mother's shames
170	Draws those heaven-moving pearls from his poor eyes,
	Which heaven shall take in nature of a fee.
	Ay, with these crystal beads heaven shall be bribed
	To do him justice, and revenge on you.
	ELEANOR
	Thou monstrous slanderer of heaven and earth.
	CONSTANCE
175	Thou monstrous injurer of heaven and earth,
	Call not me slanderer! Thou and thine usurp
	The dominations, royalties and rights
	Of this oppressed boy. This is thy eldest son's son,
	Infortunate in nothing but in thee:
180	Thy sins are visited in this poor child,
	The canon of the law is laid on him,
	Being but the second generation
	Removed from thy sin-conceiving womb.
	KING JOHN Bedlam, have done.
	CONSTANCE I have but this to say,
185	That he is not only plagued for her sin,
	But God hath made her sin and her the plague
	On this removed issue, plagued for her,
	And with her plague, her sin; his injury
	Her injury, the beadle to her sin,
190	All punished in the person of this child,
	And all for her. A plague upon her!
	ELEANOR Thou unadvised scold, I can produce
	A will that bars the title of thy son.
	CONSTANCE
	Ay, who doubts that? A will – a wicked will,
	A woman's will, a cankered grandam's will.
	KING PHILIP
195	Peace, lady; pause, or be more temperate.
	It ill beseems this presence to cry aim
	To these ill-tuned repetitions.
	Some trumpet summon hither to the walls
	These men of Angiers: let us hear them speak
200	Whose title they admit, Arthur's or John's.
	Trumpet sounds. Enter Citizens *upon the walls.*
	CITIZEN Who is it that hath warned us to the walls?
	KING PHILIP
	'Tis France, for England –
	KING JOHN England for itself.
	You men of Angiers, and my loving subjects –
	KING PHILIP
	You loving men of Angiers, Arthur's subjects,
205	Our trumpet called you to this gentle parle –
	KING JOHN For our advantage; therefore hear us first.
	These flags of France that are advanced here
	Before the eye and prospect of your town
	Have hither marched to your endamagement.

210 The cannons have their bowels full of wrath,
And ready mounted are they to spit forth
Their iron indignation 'gainst your walls:
All preparation for a bloody siege
And merciless proceeding by these French
215 Confronts your city's eyes, your winking gates,
And, but for our approach, those sleeping stones
That as a waist doth girdle you about,
By the compulsion of their ordinance,
By this time from their fixed beds of lime
220 Had been dishabited, and wide havoc made
For bloody power to rush upon your peace.
But on the sight of us, your lawful king,
Who painfully with much expedient march
Have brought a counter-check before your gates
225 To save unscratched your city's threatened cheeks,
Behold the French amazed vouchsafe a parle.
And now, instead of bullets wrapped in fire
To make a shaking fever in your walls,
They shoot but calm words, folded up in smoke,
230 To make a faithless error in your ears,
Which trust accordingly, kind citizens,
And let us in. Your king, whose laboured spirits
Fore-wearied in this action of swift speed,
Craves harbourage within your city walls.
  KING PHILIP
235 When I have said, make answer to us both.
Lo, in this right hand, whose protection
      [*Takes Arthur's hand.*]
Is most divinely vowed upon the right
Of him it holds, stands young Plantagenet,
Son to the elder brother of this man,
240 And king o'er him, and all that he enjoys.
For this downtrodden equity we tread
In warlike march these greens before your town,
Being no further enemy to you
Than the constraint of hospitable zeal
245 In the relief of this oppressed child
Religiously provokes. Be pleased then
To pay that duty which you truly owe
To him that owes it, namely this young prince;
And then our arms, like to a muzzled bear
250 Save in aspect, hath all offence sealed up.
Our cannons' malice vainly shall be spent
Against th'invulnerable clouds of heaven,
And with a blessed and unvexed retire,
With unhacked swords, and helmets all unbruised,
255 We will bear home that lusty blood again
Which here we came to spout against your town,
And leave your children, wives and you in peace.
But if you fondly pass our proffered offer,
'Tis not the roundure of your old-faced walls
260 Can hide you from our messengers of war,
Though all these English and their discipline
Were harboured in their rude circumference.
Then tell us, shall your city call us lord,
In that behalf which we have challenged it?

265 Or shall we give the signal to our rage,
And stalk in blood to our possession?
CITIZEN
In brief, we are the King of England's subjects:
For him, and in his right, we hold this town.
KING JOHN   Acknowledge then the king, and let me in.
270 CITIZEN   That can we not: but he that proves the king,
To him will we prove loyal; till that time
Have we rammed up our gates against the world.
KING JOHN
Doth not the crown of England prove the king?
And if not that, I bring you witnesses:
275 Twice fifteen thousand hearts of England's breed –
BASTARD   Bastards and else.
KING JOHN   To verify our title with their lives.
KING PHILIP
As many and as well-born bloods as those –
BASTARD   Some bastards too.
280 KING PHILIP   Stand in his face to contradict his claim.
CITIZEN   Till you compound whose right is worthiest,
We for the worthiest hold the right from both.
KING JOHN
Then God forgive the sin of all those souls
That to their everlasting residence,
285 Before the dew of evening fall, shall fleet
In dreadful trial of our kingdom's king.
KING PHILIP
Amen, amen! Mount, chevaliers! To arms!
BASTARD   Saint George that swinged the dragon,
And e'er since sits on's horseback at mine hostess' door,
290 Teach us some fence! [*to Austria*] Sirrah, were I at home
At your den, sirrah, with your lioness,
I would set an ox-head to your lion's hide
And make a monster of you.
AUSTRIA   Peace, no more.
BASTARD   O, tremble, for you hear the lion roar.
KING JOHN
295 Up higher to the plain, where we'll set forth
In best appointment all our regiments.
BASTARD   Speed then to take advantage of the field.
KING PHILIP   It shall be so, and at the other hill
Command the rest to stand. God and our right!
        Exeunt on opposite sides, the English and French
            Kings with their forces; Citizens remain above.

Here after excursions, enter the Herald of France *with*
            Trumpeters to the gates.

FRENCH HERALD
You men of Angiers, open wide your gates   300
And let young Arthur, Duke of Britain, in;
Who, by the hand of France, this day hath made
Much work for tears in many an English mother,
Whose sons lie scattered on the bleeding ground.
Many a widow's husband grovelling lies,   305
Coldly embracing the discoloured earth,
And victory with little loss doth play
Upon the dancing banners of the French,

Who are at hand, triumphantly displayed,
10 To enter conquerors, and to proclaim
Arthur of Britain England's king, and yours.

Enter English Herald *with Trumpeter.*

ENGLISH HERALD
Rejoice, you men of Angiers, ring your bells:
King John, your king and England's, doth approach,
Commander of this hot malicious day.
15 Their armours that marched hence so silver bright
Hither return all gilt with Frenchmen's blood.
There stuck no plume in any English crest
That is removed by a staff of France;
Our colours do return in those same hands
20 That did display them when we first marched forth,
And like a jolly troop of huntsmen come
Our lusty English, all with purpled hands
Dyed in the dying slaughter of their foes.
Open your gates, and give the victors way.
25 CITIZEN   Heralds, from off our towers we might behold
From first to last the onset and retire
Of both your armies, whose equality
By our best eyes cannot be censured:
Blood hath bought blood, and blows have answered
blows,
Strength matched with strength, and power
30 confronted power.
Both are alike, and both alike we like –
One must prove greatest. While they weigh so even,
We hold our town for neither, yet for both.

Enter the two KINGS *with their powers, at several doors.*

KING JOHN
France, hast thou yet more blood to cast away?
35 Say, shall the current of our right run on,
Whose passage, vexed with thy impediment,
Shall leave his native channel and o'er-swell
With course disturbed e'en thy confining shores,
Unless thou let his silver water keep
40 A peaceful progress to the ocean.
KING PHILIP
England, thou hast not saved one drop of blood
In this hot trial more than we of France,
Rather lost more. And by this hand I swear
That sways the earth this climate overlooks,
45 Before we will lay down our just-borne arms
We'll put thee down, 'gainst whom these arms we bear,
Or add a royal number to the dead,
Gracing the scroll that tells of this war's loss
With slaughter coupled to the name of kings.
50 BASTARD   Ha, majesty! How high thy glory towers
When the rich blood of kings is set on fire.
O, now doth death line his dread chaps with steel:
The swords of soldiers are his teeth, his fangs,
And now he feasts, mousing the flesh of men
55 In undetermined differences of kings.
Why stand these royal fronts amazed thus?

Cry havoc, kings! Back to the stained field
You equal-potents, fiery-kindled spirits!
Then let confusion of one part confirm
The other's peace: till then, blows, blood, and death! 360
KING JOHN   Whose party do the townsmen yet admit?
KING PHILIP
Speak, citizens for England: who's your king?
CITIZEN
The King of England, when we know the king.
KING PHILIP
Know him in us, that here hold up his right –
KING JOHN   In us, that are our own great deputy, 365
And bear possession of our person here,
Lord of our presence, Angiers, and of you.
CITIZEN   A greater power than we denies all this,
And till it be undoubted, we do lock
Our former scruple in our strong barred gates, 370
Kings of our fear, until our fears resolved
Be by some certain king, purged and deposed.
BASTARD
By God, these scroyles of Angiers flout you, kings,
And stand securely on their battlements
As in a theatre, whence they gape and point 375
At your industrious scenes and acts of death.
Your royal presences be ruled by me:
Do like the mutines of Jerusalem,
Be friends awhile, and both conjointly bend
Your sharpest deeds of malice on this town. 380
By east and west let France and England mount
Their battering cannon, charged to the mouths,
Till their soul-fearing clamours have brawled down
The flinty ribs of this contemptuous city.
I'd play incessantly upon these jades, 385
Even till unfenced desolation
Leave them as naked as the vulgar air;
That done, dissever your united strengths
And part your mingled colours once again,
Turn face to face and bloody point to point, 390
Then in a moment Fortune shall cull forth
Out of one side her happy minion,
To whom in favour she shall give the day
And kiss him with a glorious victory.
How like you this wild counsel, mighty states? 395
Smacks it not something of the policy?
KING JOHN
Now by the sky that hangs above our heads
I like it well. France, shall we knit our powers
And lay this Angiers even with the ground,
Then after, fight who shall be king of it? 400
BASTARD [*to King Philip*]
And if thou hast the mettle of a king,
Being wronged as we are by this peevish town,
Turn thou the mouth of thy artillery,
As we will ours, against these saucy walls;
And when that we have dashed them to the ground, 405
Why then defy each other, and pell-mell
Make work upon ourselves, for heaven or hell.

KING PHILIP   Let it be so. Say, where will you assault?

KING JOHN   We from the west will send destruction
410   Into this city's bosom.

AUSTRIA   I from the north.

KING PHILIP   Our thunder from the south
    Shall rain their drift of bullets on this town.

BASTARD [*aside*]
    O prudent discipline! From north to south!
    Austria and France shoot in each other's mouth –
415   I'll stir them to it. Come, away, away!

CITIZEN   Hear us, great kings! Vouchsafe awhile to stay
    And I shall show you peace and fair-faced league;
    Win you this city without stroke or wound,
    Rescue those breathing lives to die in beds
420   That here come sacrifices for the field.
    Persever not, but hear me, mighty kings.

KING JOHN   Speak on with favour, we are bent to hear.

CITIZEN
    That daughter there of Spain, the Lady Blanche
    Is niece to England: look upon the years
425   Of Lewis the Dauphin, and that lovely maid.
    If lusty love should go in quest of beauty,
    Where should he find it fairer than in Blanche?
    If zealous love should go in search of virtue,
    Where should he find it purer than in Blanche?
430   If love ambitious sought a match of birth,
    Whose veins bound richer blood than Lady Blanche?
    Such as she is, in beauty, virtue, birth,
    Is the young Dauphin every way complete.
    If not complete of, say he is not she,
435   And she again wants nothing to name want,
    If want it be not, that she is not he.
    He is the half part of a blessed man
    Left to be finished by such as she,
    And she a fair divided excellence
440   Whose fullness of perfection lies in him.
    O, two such silver currents, when they join
    Do glorify the banks that bound them in;
    And two such shores, to two such streams made one,
    Two such controlling bounds shall you be, kings,
445   To these two princes, if you marry them.
    This union shall do more than battery can
    To our fast-closed gates: for at this match,
    With swifter spleen than powder can enforce,
    The mouth of passage shall we fling wide ope
450   And give you entrance; but without this match,
    The sea enraged is not half so deaf,
    Lions more confident, mountains and rocks
    More free from motion, no, not Death himself
    In mortal fury half so peremptory
    As we to keep this city.

    [*King Philip and Lewis the Dauphin, father and son,
    talk privately.*]

455 BASTARD   Here's a stay
    That shakes the rotten carcass of old Death
    Out of his rags. Here's a large mouth indeed,
    That spits forth death, and mountains, rocks and seas,
    Talks as familiarly of roaring lions
    As maids of thirteen do of puppy-dogs.   460
    What cannoneer begot this lusty blood?
    He speaks plain cannon fire, and smoke, and bounce;
    He gives the bastinado with his tongue;
    Our ears are cudgelled: not a word of his
    But buffets better than a fist of France.   465
    Zounds, I was never so bethumped with words
    Since I first called my brother's father Dad.

ELEANOR
    Son, list to this conjunction, make this match.
    Give with our niece a dowry large enough,
    For by this knot thou shalt so surely tie   470
    Thy now unsured assurance to the crown
    That yon green boy shall have no sun to ripe
    The bloom that promiseth a mighty fruit.
    I see a yielding in the looks of France:
    Mark how they whisper; urge them while their souls   475
    Are capable of this ambition,
    Lest zeal, now melted by the windy breath
    Of soft petitions, pity and remorse,
    Cool and congeal again to what it was.

CITIZEN   Why answer not the double majesties   480
    This friendly treaty of our threatened town?

KING PHILIP
    Speak, England, first, that hath been forward first
    To speak unto this city: what say you?

KING JOHN
    If that the Dauphin there, thy princely son,
    Can in this book of beauty read 'I love',   485
    Her dowry shall weigh equal with a queen:
    For Anjou, and fair Touraine, Maine, Poitiers,
    And all that we upon this side the sea –
    Except this city now by us besieged –
    Find liable to our crown and dignity,   490
    Shall gild her bridal bed and make her rich
    In titles, honours and promotions,
    As she in beauty, education, blood,
    Holds hand with any princess of the world.

KING PHILIP
    What sayst thou, boy? Look in the lady's face.   495

DAUPHIN   I do, my lord, and in her eye I find
    A wonder, or a wondrous miracle:
    The shadow of myself formed in her eye,
    Which, being but the shadow of your son,
    Becomes a sun and makes your son a shadow.   500
    I do protest I never loved myself,
    Till now infixed I beheld myself,
    Drawn in the flattering table of her eye.
    [*Whispers with Blanche*].

BASTARD [*aside*]
    'Drawn in the flattering table of her eye!'
    Hanged in the frowning wrinkle of her brow,   505
    And quartered in her heart, he doth espy
    Himself love's traitor. This is pity now,
    That hanged, and drawn, and quartered, there
    should be

In such a love so vile a lout as he.

BLANCHE [*to Dauphin*]

10   My uncle's will in this respect is mine.
If he see aught in you that makes him like,
That anything he sees which moves his liking
I can with ease translate it to my will;
Or if you will, to speak more properly,
15   I will enforce it easily to my love.
Further I will not flatter you, my lord,
That all I see in you is worthy love
Than this: that nothing do I see in you,
Though churlish thoughts themselves should be your
    judge,
20   That I can find should merit any hate.

KING JOHN

    What say these young ones? What say you my niece?

BLANCHE   That she is bound in honour still to do
What you in wisdom still vouchsafe to say.

KING JOHN

    Speak then, Prince Dauphin, can you love this lady?

25 DAUPHIN   Nay, ask me if I can refrain from love,
For I do love her most unfeignedly.

KING JOHN

    Then I do give Volquessen, Touraine, Maine,
Poitiers and Anjou, these five provinces
30   With her to thee, and this addition more,
Full thirty thousand marks of English coin.
Philip of France, if thou be pleased withal,
Command thy son and daughter to join hands.

KING PHILIP

    It likes us well, young princes: close your hands.
    [*Dauphin and Blanche clasp hands.*]

AUSTRIA   And your lips too, for I am well assured,
35   That I did so when I was first assured.

KING PHILIP   Now, citizens of Angiers, ope your gates:
Let in that amity which you have made,
For at Saint Mary's Chapel presently
The rites of marriage shall be solemnized.
40   Is not the Lady Constance in this troop?
I know she is not, for this match made up
Her presence would have interrupted much.
Where is she and her son, tell me, who knows?

DAUPHIN

    She is sad and passionate at your highness' tent.

KING PHILIP

45   And by my faith, this league that we have made
Will give her sadness very little cure.
Brother of England, how may we content
This widow lady? In her right we came,
Which we, God knows, have turned another way
50   To our own vantage.

KING JOHN   We will heal up all,
For we'll create young Arthur Duke of Britain
And Earl of Richmond, and this rich fair town
We make him lord of. Call the Lady Constance.
Some speedy messenger bid her repair
55   To our solemnity. I trust we shall,   *Exit Salisbury.*

If not fill up the measure of her will,
Yet in some measure satisfy her so
That we shall stop her exclamation.
Go we, as well as haste will suffer us,
To this unlooked-for, unprepared pomp.   560
    Exeunt all but Bastard.

BASTARD   Mad world, mad kings, mad composition!
John, to stop Arthur's title in the whole,
Hath willingly departed with a part,
And France, whose armour conscience buckled on,
Whom zeal and charity brought to the field   565
As God's own soldier, rounded in the ear
With that same purpose-changer, that sly devil,
That broker that still breaks the pate of faith,
That daily break-vow, he that wins of all,
Of kings, of beggars, old men, young men, maids –   570
Who having no external thing to lose
But the word maid, cheats the poor maid of that –
That smooth-faced gentleman, tickling Commodity.
Commodity, the bias of the world;
The world, who of itself is peised well,   575
Made to run even, upon even ground,
Till this advantage, this vile-drawing bias,
This sway of motion, this Commodity,
Makes it take head from all indifferency,
From all direction, purpose, course, intent.   580
And this same bias, this Commodity,
This bawd, this broker, this all-changing word,
Clapped on the outward eye of fickle France,
Hath drawn him from his own determined aid,
From a resolved and honourable war   585
To a most base and vile-concluded peace.
And why rail I on this Commodity?
But for because he hath not wooed me yet.
Not that I have the power to clutch my hand
When his fair angels would salute my palm,   590
But for my hand, as unattempted yet,
Like a poor beggar, raileth on the rich.
Well, whiles I am a beggar I will rail,
And say there is no sin but to be rich;
And being rich, my virtue then shall be   595
To say there is no vice but beggary.
Since kings break faith upon Commodity,
Gain be my lord, for I will worship thee.   *Exit.*

3.1   *Enter* CONSTANCE, ARTHUR *and* SALISBURY.

CONSTANCE

Gone to be married? Gone to swear a peace?
False blood to false blood joined! Gone to be friends?
Shall Lewis have Blanche, and Blanche those provinces?
It is not so, thou hast misspoke, misheard.
Be well advised, tell o'er thy tale again;   5
It cannot be, thou dost but say 'tis so.
I trust I may not trust thee, for thy word
Is but the vain breath of a common man:
Believe me, I do not believe thee, man;

10 I have a king's oath to the contrary.
Thou shalt be punished for thus frighting me,
For I am sick, and capable of fears,
Oppressed with wrongs, and therefore full of fears;
A widow, husbandless, subject to fears,
15 A woman naturally born to fears;
And though thou now confess thou didst but jest,
With my vexed spirits I cannot take a truce,
But they will quake and tremble all this day.
What dost thou mean by shaking of thy head?
20 Why dost thou look so sadly on my son?
What means that hand upon that breast of thine?
Why holds thine eye that lamentable rheum,
Like a proud river peering o'er his bounds?
Be these sad signs confirmers of thy words?
25 Then speak again, not all thy former tale,
But this one word, whether thy tale be true.
SALISBURY   As true as I believe you think them false,
That give you cause to prove my saying true.
CONSTANCE   O, if thou teach me to believe this sorrow,
30 Teach thou this sorrow how to make me die,
And let belief and life encounter so,
As doth the fury of two desperate men
Which in the very meeting fall and die.
Lewis marry Blanche? O, boy, then where art thou?
35 France friend with England? What becomes of me?
Fellow, be gone. I cannot brook thy sight,
This news hath made thee a most ugly man.
SALISBURY   What other harm have I, good lady, done
But spoke the harm that is by others done?
40 CONSTANCE   Which harm within itself so heinous is
As it makes harmful all that speak of it.
ARTHUR   I do beseech you, madam, be content.
CONSTANCE
If thou that bid'st me be content wert grim,
Ugly, and slanderous to thy mother's womb,
45 Full of unpleasing blots and sightless stains,
Lame, foolish, crooked, swart, prodigious,
Patched with foul moles and eye-offending marks,
I would not care, I then would be content;
For then I should not love thee, no, nor thou
50 Become thy great birth, nor deserve a crown.
But thou art fair, and at thy birth, dear boy,
Nature and Fortune joined to make thee great.
Of nature's gifts thou mayst with lilies boast
And with the half-blown rose. But Fortune, O,
55 She is corrupted, changed, and won from thee.
Sh'adulterates hourly with thine uncle John,
And with her golden hand hath plucked on France
To tread down fair respect of sovereignty
And made his majesty the bawd to theirs.
60 France is a bawd to Fortune and King John:
That strumpet Fortune, that usurping John.
Tell me, thou fellow, is not France forsworn?
Envenom him with words, or get thee gone
And leave those woes alone which I alone
Am bound to underbear.

SALISBURY   Pardon me madam,   65
I may not go without you to the kings.
CONSTANCE
Thou mayst, thou shalt, I will not go with thee.
I will instruct my sorrows to be proud,
For grief is proud and makes his owner stoop:
To me and to the state of my great grief   70
Let kings assemble, for my grief's so great
That no supporter but the huge firm earth
Can hold it up. Here I and sorrows sit;
[*Throws herself to the ground.*]
Here is my throne, bid kings come bow to it.
Exit Salisbury with Arthur.

Flourish. Enter KING JOHN, KING PHILIP *of France,*
Lewis the DAUPHIN, BLANCHE, ELEANOR, *the*
BASTARD, AUSTRIA.

KING PHILIP [*to Blanche*]
'Tis true, fair daughter, and this blessed day   75
Ever in France shall be kept festival.
To solemnize this day the glorious sun
Stays in his course and plays the alchemist,
Turning with splendour of his precious eye
The meagre cloddy earth to glittering gold.   80
The yearly course that brings this day about
Shall never see it but a holy day.
CONSTANCE [*Rises.*]   A wicked day, and not a holy day!
What hath this day deserved? What hath it done,
That it in golden letters should be set   85
Among the high tides in the calendar?
Nay, rather turn this day out of the week,
This day of shame, oppression, perjury.
Or, if it must stand still, let wives with child
Pray that their burdens may not fall this day,   90
Lest that their hopes prodigiously be crossed;
But on this day let seamen fear no wrack,
No bargains break that are not this day made;
This day all things begun come to ill end,
Yea, faith itself to hollow falsehood change.   95
KING PHILIP   By heaven, lady, you shall have no cause
To curse the fair proceedings of this day.
Have I not pawned to you my majesty?
CONSTANCE   You have beguiled me with a counterfeit
Resembling majesty, which, being touched and tried,   100
Proves valueless. You are forsworn, forsworn!
You came in arms to spill mine enemies' blood,
But now in arms you strengthen it with yours.
The grappling vigour and rough frown of war
Is cold in amity and painted peace,   105
And our oppression hath made up this league.
Arm, arm, you heavens, against these perjured kings!
A widow cries; be husband to me, Lord,
Let not the hours of this ungodly day
Wear out the day in peace, but ere sunset,   110
Set armed discord 'twixt these perjured kings.
Hear me, O, hear me!
AUSTRIA   Lady Constance, peace.

CONSTANCE   War, war, no peace! Peace is to me a war.
    O Limoges, O Austria, thou dost shame
    That bloody spoil. Thou slave, thou wretch, thou
15   coward,
    Thou little valiant, great in villainy,
    Thou ever strong upon the stronger side,
    Thou Fortune's champion that dost never fight
    But when her humorous ladyship is by
20 To teach thee safety: thou art perjured too,
    And sooth'st up greatness. What a fool art thou,
    A ramping fool, to brag and stamp and swear
    Upon my party. Thou cold-blooded slave,
    Hast thou not spoke like thunder on my side?
25 Been sworn my soldier, bidding me depend
    Upon thy stars, thy fortune and thy strength,
    And dost thou now fall over to my foes?
    Thou wear a lion's hide? Doff it for shame,
    And hang a calf's skin on those recreant limbs.
AUSTRIA
30 O, that a man should speak those words to me.
BASTARD
    And hang a calf's skin on those recreant limbs.
AUSTRIA   Thou dar'st not say so, villain, for thy life.
BASTARD   And hang a calf's skin on those recreant limbs.
KING JOHN [*to Bastard*]
    We like not this, thou dost forget thyself.

        Enter PANDULPH.

35 KING PHILIP   Here comes the holy legate of the Pope.
        [*Takes hand of King John.*]
    PANDULPH   Hail, you anointed deputies of God.
    To thee, King John, my holy errand is:
    I, Pandulph, of fair Milan cardinal,
    And from Pope Innocent the legate here,
40 Do in his name religiously demand
    Why thou against the Church, our holy mother,
    So wilfully dost spurn, and force perforce
    Keep Stephen Langton, chosen Archbishop
    Of Canterbury, from that holy see?
45 This, in our foresaid Holy Father's name,
    Pope Innocent, I do demand of thee.
    KING JOHN   What earthy name to interrogatories
    Can test the free breath of a sacred king?
    Thou canst not, Cardinal, devise a name
50 So slight, unworthy and ridiculous
    To charge me to an answer as the Pope.
    Tell him this tale, and from the mouth of England
    Add thus much more: that no Italian priest
    Shall tithe or toll in our dominions;
55 But as we, under God, are supreme head,
    So, under Him, that great supremacy
    Where we do reign we will alone uphold
    Without th'assistance of a mortal hand.
    So tell the Pope, all reverence set apart
60 To him and his usurped authority.
KING PHILIP
    Brother of England, you blaspheme in this.

KING JOHN
    Though you and all the kings of Christendom
    Are led so grossly by this meddling priest,
    Dreading the curse that money may buy out,
    And by the merit of vile gold, dross, dust,   165
    Purchase corrupted pardon of a man
    Who in that sale sells pardon from himself;
    Though you and all the rest so grossly led
    This juggling witchcraft with revenue cherish,
    Yet I alone, alone do me oppose   170
    Against the Pope, and count his friends my foes.
PANDULPH   Then by the lawful power that I have,
    Thou shalt stand cursed and excommunicate,
    And blessed shall he be that doth revolt
    From his allegiance to an heretic,   175
    And meritorious shall that hand be called,
    Canonized and worshipped as a saint,
    That takes away by any secret course
    Thy hateful life.
CONSTANCE   O, lawful let it be
    That I have room with Rome to curse awhile.   180
    Good Father Cardinal, cry thou 'Amen'
    To my keen curses, for without my wrong
    There is no tongue hath power to curse him right.
PANDULPH
    There's law and warrant, lady, for my curse.
CONSTANCE
    And for mine too; when law can do no right,   185
    Let it be lawful that law bar no wrong.
    Law cannot give my child his kingdom here,
    For he that holds his kingdom, holds the law;
    Therefore since law itself is perfect wrong,
    How can the law forbid my tongue to curse?   190
        [*Philip takes John's hand.*]
PANDULPH   Philip of France, on peril of a curse,
    Let go the hand of that arch-heretic,
    And raise the power of France upon his head,
    Unless he do submit himself to Rome.
ELEANOR
    Look'st thou pale, France? Do not let go thy hand.   195
CONSTANCE
    Look to that, devil, lest that France repent,
    And by disjoining hands, hell lose a soul.
AUSTRIA   King Philip, listen to the Cardinal.
BASTARD   And hang a calf's skin on his recreant limbs.
AUSTRIA   Well ruffian, I must pocket up these wrongs,   200
    Because –
BASTARD   Your breeches best may carry them.
KING JOHN   Philip, what sayst thou to the Cardinal?
CONSTANCE   What should he say, but as the Cardinal?
DAUPHIN   Bethink you, father, for the difference
    Is purchase of a heavy curse from Rome   205
    Or the light loss of England for a friend:
    Forgo the easier.
BLANCHE   That's the curse of Rome.
CONSTANCE
    O Lewis, stand fast, the devil tempts thee here

In likeness of a new untrimmed bride.

BLANCHE
210 The Lady Constance speaks not from her faith,
But from her need.

CONSTANCE   O, if thou grant my need,
Which only lives but by the death of faith,
That need must needs infer this principle:
That faith would live again by death of need.
215 O then tread down my need, and faith mounts up;
Keep my need up, and faith is trodden down.

KING JOHN
The King is moved, and answers not to this.

CONSTANCE [*to King Philip*]
O, be removed from him and answer well.

AUSTRIA   Do so, King Philip, hang no more in doubt.

BASTARD
220 Hang nothing but a calf's skin, most sweet lout.

KING PHILIP
I am perplexed, and know not what to say.

PANDULPH
What canst thou say but will perplex thee more
If thou stand excommunicate and curst?

KING PHILIP
Good reverend father, make my person yours
225 And tell me how you would bestow yourself?
This royal hand and mine are newly knit,
And the conjunction of our inward souls
Married in league, coupled and linked together
With all religious strength of sacred vows.
230 The latest breath that gave the sound of words
Was deep-sworn faith, peace, amity, true love
Between our kingdoms and our royal selves;
And e'en before this truce, but new before,
No longer than we well could wash our hands
235 To clap this royal bargain up of peace –
God knows they were besmeared and over-stained
With slaughter's pencil, where revenge did paint
The fearful difference of incensed kings –
And shall these hands so lately purged of blood,
240 So newly joined in love, so strong in both,
Unyoke this seizure and this kind regreet?
Play fast and loose with faith? So jest with God?
Make such unconstant children of ourselves,
As now again to snatch our palm from palm,
245 Unswear faith sworn, and on the marriage bed
Of smiling peace to march a bloody host,
And make a riot on the gentle brow
Of true sincerity? O holy sir,
My reverend father, let it not be so.
250 Out of your grace, devise, ordain, impose
Some gentle order, and then we shall be blest
To do your pleasure, and continue friends.

PANDULPH   All form is formless, order orderless,
Save what is opposite to England's love.
255 Therefore to arms! Be champion of our Church,
Or let the Church our mother breathe her curse,
A mother's curse, on her revolting son.

France, thou mayst hold a serpent by the tongue,
A cased lion by the mortal paw,
A fasting tiger safer by the tooth,   260
Than keep in peace that hand which thou dost hold.

KING PHILIP   I may disjoin my hand, but not my faith.

PANDULPH   So mak'st thou faith an enemy to faith,
And like a civil war set'st oath to oath,
Thy tongue against thy tongue. O, let thy vow   265
First made to God, first be to God performed:
That is to be the champion of our Church;
What since thou swor'st is sworn against thyself,
And may not be performed by thyself.
For that which thou hast sworn to do amiss   270
Is not amiss when it is truly done;
And being not done, where doing tends to ill,
The truth is then most done not doing it.
The better act of purposes mistook
Is to mistake again; though indirect,   275
Yet indirection thereby grows direct,
And falsehood falsehood cures, as fire cools fire
Within the scorched veins of one new burned.
It is religion that doth make vows kept,
But thou hast sworn against religion   280
By what thou swear'st against the thing thou swear'st,
And mak'st an oath the surety for thy truth
Against an oath; the truth thou art unsure
To swear, swears only not to be forsworn,
Else what a mockery should it be to swear?   285
But thou dost swear, only to be forsworn,
And most forsworn, to keep what thou dost swear.
Therefore thy later vows, against thy first,
Is in thyself rebellion to thyself;
And better conquest never canst thou make   290
Than arm thy constant and thy nobler parts
Against these giddy loose suggestions –
Upon which better part, our prayers come in,
If thou vouchsafe them. But if not, then know
The peril of our curses light on thee   295
So heavy as thou shalt not shake them off,
But in despair die under their black weight.

AUSTRIA   Rebellion, flat rebellion.

BASTARD   Will't not be?
Will not a calf's skin stop that mouth of thine?

DAUPHIN   Father, to arms.

BLANCHE   Upon thy wedding day?   300
Against the blood that thou hast married?
What, shall our feast be kept with slaughtered men?
Shall braying trumpets and loud churlish drums,
Clamours of hell, be measures to our pomp?
O husband, hear me! Ay, alack, how new   305
Is husband in my mouth? [*Kneels.*] E'en for that name,
Which till this time my tongue did ne'er pronounce,
Upon my knee I beg go not to arms
Against mine uncle.

CONSTANCE [*Kneels.*]
O, upon my knee made hard with kneeling,   310
I do pray to thee, thou virtuous Dauphin,

Alter not the doom forethought by God.

BLANCHE   Now shall I see thy love. What motive may
Be stronger with thee than the name of wife?

CONSTANCE

315   That which upholdeth him that thee upholds:
His honour. O, thine honour, Lewis, thine honour!

DAUPHIN   I muse your majesty doth seem so cold,
When such profound respects do pull you on?

PANDULPH   I will denounce a curse upon his head.

KING PHILIP

320   Thou shalt not need. England, I will fall from thee.
     [Drops John's hand.]

CONSTANCE   O fair return of banished majesty.

ELEANOR   O foul revolt of French inconstancy.

KING JOHN

France, thou shalt rue this hour within this hour.

BASTARD

Old Time the clock-setter, that bald sexton Time:

325   Is it as he will? Well then, France shall rue.

BLANCHE

The sun's o'ercast with blood: fair day, adieu.
Which is the side that I must go withal?
I am with both. Each army hath a hand,
And in their rage, I having hold of both,

330   They whirl asunder, and dismember me.
Husband, I cannot pray that thou mayst win;
Uncle, I needs must pray that thou mayst lose;
Father, I may not wish the fortune thine;
Grandam, I will not wish thy wishes thrive.

335   Whoever wins, on that side shall I lose:
Assured loss, before the match be played.

DAUPHIN   Lady, with me, with me thy fortune lies.

BLANCHE

There where my fortune lives, there my life dies.

KING JOHN

Cousin, go draw our puissance together.   *Exit Bastard.*

340   France, I am burned up with inflaming wrath,
A rage whose heat hath this condition
That nothing can allay, nothing but blood,
The blood and dearest valued blood of France.

KING PHILIP

Thy rage shall burn thee up, and thou shalt turn

345   To ashes ere our blood shall quench that fire.
Look to thyself, thou art in jeopardy.

KING JOHN

No more than he that threats. To arms let's hie! *Exeunt.*

3.2   *Alarums, excursions. Enter* BASTARD
         with Austria's head.

BASTARD   Now by my life this day grows wondrous hot.
Some airy devil hovers in the sky
And pours down mischief. Austria's head lie there,
While Philip breathes.   *[Throws down head.]*

      Enter KING JOHN, ARTHUR *and* HUBERT.

5   KING JOHN   Hubert, keep this boy. Philip, make up!

My mother is assailed in our tent
And ta'en, I fear.

BASTARD   My lord, I rescued her;
Her highness is in safety, fear you not.
But on, my liege! For very little pains

10   Will bring this labour to an happy end.
     *Exeunt King John and the Bastard (carrying Austria's
       head) at one door, Hubert and Arthur at another.*

3.3   *Alarms, excursions, retreat. Enter*
        KING JOHN, ELEANOR, ARTHUR,
          BASTARD, HUBERT, *Lords.*

KING JOHN *[to Eleanor]*
So shall it be. Your grace shall stay behind
So strongly guarded – *[to Arthur]* Cousin, look not sad,
Thy grandam loves thee, and thy uncle will
As dear be to thee as thy father was.

5   ARTHUR   O, this will make my mother die with grief.

KING JOHN *[to Bastard]*
Cousin, away for England. Haste before,
And ere our coming see thou shake the bags
Of hoarding abbots; the fat ribs of peace
Must by the hungry now be fed upon:

10   Imprisoned angels set at liberty.
Use our commission in his utmost force.

BASTARD

Bell, book and candle shall not drive me back
When gold and silver becks me to come on.
I leave your highness; grandam, I will pray,

15   If ever I remember to be holy,
For your fair safety: so I kiss your hand.

ELEANOR   Farewell, gentle cousin.

KING JOHN   Coz, farewell.   *Exit Bastard.*

ELEANOR *[Takes Arthur aside.]*
Come hither, little kinsman; hark, a word.

KING JOHN

Come hither, Hubert. O my gentle Hubert,

20   We owe thee much. Within this wall of flesh
There is a soul counts thee her creditor
And with advantage means to pay thy love.
And, my good friend, thy voluntary oath
Lives in this bosom, dearly cherished.

25   Give me thy hand. I had a thing to say,
But I will fit it with some better tune.
By God, Hubert, I am almost ashamed
To say what good respect I have of thee.

HUBERT   I am much bounden to your majesty.

KING JOHN

30   Good friend, thou hast no cause to say so yet,
But thou shalt have; and creep time ne'er so slow,
Yet it shall come for me to do thee good.
I had a thing to say, but let it go.
The sun is in the heaven, and the proud day,

35   Attended with the pleasures of the world,
Is all too wanton and too full of gauds
To give me audience. If the midnight bell

Did with his iron tongue and brazen mouth
Sound on into the drowsy race of night;
40   If this same were a churchyard where we stand,
And thou possessed with a thousand wrongs;
Or if that surly spirit, melancholy,
Had baked thy blood and made it heavy, thick,
Which else runs tickling up and down the veins,
45   Making that idiot laughter keep men's eyes
And strain their cheeks to idle merriment –
A passion hateful to my purposes –
Or if that thou couldst see me without eyes,
Hear me without thine ears, and make reply
50   Without a tongue, using conceit alone,
Without eyes, ears and harmful sound of words;
Then, in despite of brooded watchful day,
I would into thy bosom pour my thoughts.
But, ah, I will not, yet I love thee well,
55   And by my troth I think thou lov'st me well.

HUBERT   So well that what you bid me undertake,
Though that my death were adjunct to my act,
By God I would do it.

KING JOHN   Do not I know thou wouldst,
Good Hubert? Hubert – Hubert, throw thine eye
60   On yon young boy. I'll tell thee what, my friend,
He is a very serpent in my way,
And whereso'er this foot of mine doth tread
He lies before me: dost thou understand me?
Thou art his keeper.

HUBERT   And I'll keep him so
65   That he shall not offend your majesty.

KING JOHN   Death.

HUBERT   My lord.

KING JOHN   A grave.

HUBERT   He shall not live.

KING JOHN   Enough.
I could be merry now. Hubert, I love thee.
Well, I'll not say what I intend for thee –
Remember. Madam, fare you well,
70   I'll send those powers o'er to your majesty.

ELEANOR   My blessing go with thee.

KING JOHN [*to Arthur*]   For England, cousin, go.
Hubert shall be your man, attend on you
With all true duty. On toward Calais, ho!   *Exeunt.*

3.4   *Enter* KING PHILIP *of France,*
Lewis the DAUPHIN, PANDULPH, *Attendants.*

KING PHILIP   So by a roaring tempest on the flood
A whole armada of convected sail
Is scattered and disjoined from fellowship?

PANDULPH
Courage and comfort, all shall yet go well.

KING PHILIP
5   What can go well, when we have run so ill?
Are we not beaten? Is not Angiers lost?
Arthur ta'en prisoner? Divers dear friends slain?
And bloody England into England gone,

O'er-bearing interruption spite of France?

DAUPHIN   What he hath won, that hath he fortified: 10
So hot a speed, with such advice disposed,
Such temperate order in so fierce a cause,
Doth want example. Who hath read or heard
Of any kindred action like to this?

KING PHILIP
Well could I bear that England had this praise,   15
So we could find some pattern of our shame.

Enter CONSTANCE, *her hair dishevelled.*

Look who comes here! A grave unto a soul,
Holding th'eternal spirit 'gainst her will,
In the vile prison of afflicted breath.
I prithee, lady, go away with me.   20

CONSTANCE   Lo, now! Now see the issue of your peace.

KING PHILIP
Patience, good lady; comfort, gentle Constance.

CONSTANCE   No, I defy all counsel, all redress,
But that which ends all counsel, true redress:
Death! Death, O amiable, lovely death,   25
Thou odoriferous stench, sound rottenness,
Arise forth from the couch of lasting night,
Thou hate and terror to prosperity,
And I will kiss thy detestable bones,
And put my eyeballs in thy vaulty brows,   30
And ring these fingers with thy household worms,
And stop this gap of breath with fulsome dust,
And be a carrion monster like thyself.
Come, grin on me, and I will think thou smil'st,
And buss thee as thy wife: Misery's love,   35
O come to me!

KING PHILIP   O fair affliction, peace.

CONSTANCE   No, no, I will not, having breath to cry.
O, that my tongue were in the thunder's mouth!
Then with a passion would I shake the world
And rouse from sleep that fell anatomy   40
Which cannot hear a lady's feeble voice,
Which scorns a modern invocation.

PANDULPH   Lady, you utter madness, and not sorrow.

CONSTANCE   Thou art not holy to belie me so!
I am not mad: this hair I tear is mine,   45
My name is Constance, I was Geoffrey's wife,
Young Arthur is my son, and he is lost.
I am not mad; I would to God I were,
For then 'tis like I should forget myself.
O, if I could, what grief should I forget!   50
Preach some philosophy to make me mad,
And thou shalt be canonized, Cardinal:
For, being not mad, but sensible of grief,
My reasonable part produces reason
How I may be delivered of these woes   55
And teaches me to kill or hang myself.
If I were mad, I should forget my son,
Or madly think a babe of clouts were he.
I am not mad; too well, too well I feel
The different plague of each calamity.   60

KING PHILIP
Bind up those tresses. [*aside*] O, what love I note
In the fair multitude of those her hairs,
Where but by chance a silver drop hath fall'n:
Even to that drop ten thousand wiry friends
Do glue themselves in sociable grief
Like true, inseparable, faithful loves,
Sticking together in calamity.
CONSTANCE   To England, if you will.
KING PHILIP   Bind up your hairs.
CONSTANCE   Yes, that I will; and wherefore will I do it?
I tore them from their bonds, and cried aloud,
'O, that these hands could so redeem my son,
As they have given these hairs their liberty!'
But now I envy at their liberty,
And will again commit them to their bonds
Because my poor child is a prisoner.
[*Binds up her hair.*] And Father Cardinal, I have heard
    you say
That we shall see and know our friends in heaven:
If that be true, I shall see my boy again;
For since the birth of Cain, the first male child,
To him that did but yesterday suspire,
There was not such a gracious creature born.
But now will canker-sorrow eat my bud
And chase the native beauty from his cheek,
And he will look as hollow as a ghost,
As dim and meagre as an ague's fit,
And so he'll die; and, rising so again,
When I shall meet him in the court of heaven
I shall not know him; therefore never, never
Must I behold my pretty Arthur more.
PANDULPH   You hold too heinous a respect of grief.
CONSTANCE   He talks to me that never had a son.
KING PHILIP   You are as fond of grief as of your child.
CONSTANCE
Grief fills the room up of my absent child,
Lies in his bed, walks up and down with me,
Puts on his pretty looks, repeats his words,
Remembers me of all his gracious parts,
Stuffs out his vacant garments with his form;
Then, have I reason to be fond of grief?
Fare you well: had you such a loss as I,
I could give better comfort than you do.
[*Dishevels her hair.*] I will not keep this form upon my
    head
When there is such disorder in my wit.
O Lord! My boy, my Arthur, my fair son,
My life, my joy, my food, my all the world,
My widow-comfort, and my sorrows' cure!   *Exit.*
KING PHILIP
I fear some outrage, and I'll follow her.   *Exit.*
DAUPHIN
There's nothing in this world can make me joy.
Life is as tedious as a twice-told tale
Vexing the dull ear of a drowsy man;
And bitter shame hath spoiled the sweet word's taste,

That it yields nought but shame and bitterness.
PANDULPH   Before the curing of a strong disease,
Even in the instant of repair and health,
The fit is strongest; evils that take leave,
On their departure most of all show evil.   115
What have you lost by losing of this day?
DAUPHIN   All days of glory, joy and happiness.
PANDULPH   If you had won it, certainly you had.
No, no: when Fortune means to men most good,
She looks upon them with a threatening eye;   120
'Tis strange to think how much King John hath lost
In this which he accounts so clearly won.
Are not you grieved that Arthur is his prisoner?
DAUPHIN   As heartily as he is glad he hath him.
PANDULPH   Your mind is all as youthful as your blood.   125
Now hear me speak with a prophetic spirit:
For even the breath of what I mean to speak
Shall blow each dust, each straw, each little rub
Out of the path which shall directly lead
Thy foot to England's throne. And therefore mark: 130
John hath seized Arthur, and it cannot be
That whiles warm life plays in that infant's veins
The misplaced John should entertain an hour,
One minute, nay one quiet breath of rest.
A sceptre snatched with an unruly hand   135
Must be as boist'rously maintained as gained;
And he that stands upon a slippery place
Makes nice of no vile hold to stay him up:
That John may stand, then Arthur needs must fall.
So be it, for it cannot be but so.   140
DAUPHIN   But what shall I gain by young Arthur's fall?
PANDULPH
You, in the right of Lady Blanche your wife,
May then make all the claim that Arthur did.
DAUPHIN   And lose it, life and all, as Arthur did.
PANDULPH
How green you are, and fresh in this old world!   145
John lays you plots: the times conspire with you,
For he that steeps his safety in true blood
Shall find but bloody safety and untrue.
This act so evilly borne shall cool the hearts
Of all his people and freeze up their zeal   150
That none so small advantage shall step forth
To check his reign, but they will cherish it.
No natural exhalation in the sky,
No scope of nature, no distempered day,
No common wind, no customed event,   155
But they will pluck away his natural cause
And call them meteors, prodigies and signs,
Abortives, presages and tongues of heaven,
Plainly denouncing vengeance upon John.
DAUPHIN   Maybe he will not touch young Arthur's life,   160
But hold himself safe in his prisonment.
PANDULPH   O sir, when he shall hear of your approach,
If that young Arthur be not gone already,
Even at that news he dies; and then the hearts
Of all his people shall revolt from him   165

And kiss the lips of unacquainted change,
And pick strong matter of revolt and wrath
Out of the bloody fingers' ends of John.
Methinks I see this hurly all on foot;
170 And O, what better matter breeds for you,
Than I have named. The bastard Faulconbridge
Is now in England ransacking the Church,
Offending charity. If but a dozen French
Were there in arms, they would be as a call
175 To train ten thousand English to their side –
Or as a little snow, tumbled about,
Anon becomes a mountain. O noble Dauphin,
Go with me to the King. 'Tis wonderful
What may be wrought out of their discontent
180 Now that their souls are top-full of offence.
For England, go. I will whet on the King.
DAUPHIN
Strong reasons makes strange actions. Let us go:
If you say ay, the King will not say no.   *Exeunt.*

4.1   *Enter* HUBERT *and* Executioners
               with a rope and irons.

HUBERT   Heat me these irons hot, and look thou stand
Within the arras. When I strike my foot
Upon the bosom of the ground, rush forth
And bind the boy which you shall find with me
5 Fast to the chair. Be heedful: hence, and watch.
EXECUTIONER
I hope your warrant will bear out the deed.
HUBERT   Uncleanly scruples! Fear not you: look to't.
               Executioners withdraw behind the arras.
Young lad, come forth; I have to say with you.

               Enter ARTHUR.

ARTHUR   Good morrow, Hubert.
HUBERT   Good morrow, little prince.
10 ARTHUR   As little prince, having so great a title
To be more prince, as may be. You are sad.
HUBERT   Indeed, I have been merrier.
ARTHUR   'Mercy on me!
Methinks nobody should be sad but I.
Yet I remember, when I was in France
15 Young gentlemen would be as sad as night
Only for wantonness. By my Christendom,
So I were out of prison and kept sheep
I should be as merry as the day is long;
And so I would be here but that I doubt
20 My uncle practises more harm to me.
He is afraid of me, and I of him.
Is it my fault that I was Geoffrey's son?
No indeed is't not, and I would to God
I were your son, so you would love me, Hubert.
25 HUBERT [*aside*]   If I talk to him, with his innocent prate
He will awake my mercy, which lies dead:
Therefore I will be sudden, and dispatch.
ARTHUR   Are you sick, Hubert? You look pale today.

In sooth, I would you were a little sick,
That I might sit all night and watch with you.   30
I warrant I love you more than you do me.
HUBERT [*aside*]
His words do take possession of my bosom –
[*Shows warrant.*] Read here, young Arthur.
[*aside*]   How now, foolish rheum
Turning dispiteous torture out of door?
I must be brief, lest resolution drop   35
Out at mine eyes in tender womanish tears –
Can you not read it? Is it not fair writ?
ARTHUR   Too fairly Hubert, for so foul effect.
Must you with hot irons burn out both mine eyes?
HUBERT   Young boy, I must.
ARTHUR   And will you?
HUBERT   And I will.   40
ARTHUR
Have you the heart? When your head did but ache
I knit my handkerchief about your brows
(The best I had, a princess wrought it me)
And I did never ask it you again,
And with my hand at midnight held your head,   45
And like the watchful minutes to the hour
Still and anon cheered up the heavy time,
Saying 'What lack you?', and 'Where lies your grief?'
Or 'What good love may I perform for you?'
Many a poor man's son would have lain still   50
And ne're have spoke a loving word to you,
But you at your sick service had a prince.
Nay, you may think my love was crafty love,
And call it cunning. Do an if you will:
If God be pleased that you must use me ill,   55
Why then you must. Will you put out mine eyes –
These eyes, that never did nor never shall
So much as frown on you.
HUBERT   I have sworn to do it,
And with hot irons must I burn them out.
ARTHUR   Ah, none but in this iron age would do it! 60
The iron of itself, though heat red hot,
Approaching near these eyes, would drink my tears
And quench his fiery indignation
Even in the matter of mine innocence;
Nay, after that consume away in rust   65
But for containing fire to harm mine eye.
Are you more stubborn-hard than hammered iron?
An if an angel should have come to me
And told me Hubert should put out mine eyes
I would not have believed him: no tongue   70
But Hubert's.
HUBERT [*Stamps his foot.*]   Come forth!

               Enter Executioners *with rope and heated irons.*

                              Do as I bid you do.
ARTHUR   O, save me, Hubert, save me! My eyes are out
Even with the fierce looks of these bloody men.
HUBERT   Give me the iron, I say, and bind him here.
               [*Takes the iron; Executioners seize Arthur.*]

ARTHUR Alas, what need you be so boist'rous-rough?
I will not struggle, I will stand stone-still.
For God's sake, Hubert, let me not be bound!
Nay, hear me, Hubert! Drive these men away
And I will sit as quiet as a lamb;
I will not stir, nor wince, nor speak a word,
Nor look upon the iron angrily.
Thrust but these men away and I'll forgive you
Whatever torment you do put me to.

HUBERT [*to Executioners*]
Go stand within, let me alone with him.

EXECUTIONER
I am best pleased to be from such a deed.
                              Exeunt Executioners.

ARTHUR Alas, I then have chid away my friend!
He hath a stern look, but a gentle heart.
Let him come back, that his compassion may
Give life to yours.

HUBERT   Come, boy, prepare yourself.

ARTHUR Is there no remedy?

HUBERT   None, but to lose your eyes.

ARTHUR O God, that there were but a mote in yours,
A grain, a dust, a gnat, a wandering hair,
Any annoyance in that precious sense;
Then, feeling what small things are boist'rous there,
Your vile intent must needs seem horrible.

HUBERT
Is this your promise? Go to, hold your tongue.

ARTHUR Hubert, the utterance of a brace of tongues
Must needs want pleading for a pair of eyes.
Let me not hold my tongue! Let me not, Hubert!
Or, Hubert, if you will, cut out my tongue
So I may keep mine eyes. O, spare mine eyes,
Though to no use but still to look on you.
Lo, by my troth, the instrument is cold
And would not harm me.

HUBERT   I can heat it, boy.

ARTHUR No, in good sooth. The fire is dead with grief,
Being create for comfort, to be used
In undeserved extremes. See else yourself:
There is no malice in this burning coal;
The breath of heaven hath blown his spirit out
And strewed repentant ashes on his head.

HUBERT But with my breath I can revive it, boy.

ARTHUR An if you do, you will but make it blush
And glow with shame of your proceedings, Hubert.
Nay, it perchance will sparkle in your eyes,
And, like a dog that is compelled to fight,
Snatch at his master that doth tar him on.
All things that you should use to do me wrong
Deny their office: only you do lack
That mercy which fierce fire and iron extends,
Creatures of note for mercy-lacking uses.

HUBERT Well, see to live. I will not touch thine eye
For all the treasure that thine uncle owns.
Yet am I sworn, and I did purpose, boy,
With this same very iron to burn them out.

ARTHUR O, now you look like Hubert. All this while
You were disguised.

HUBERT   Peace: no more. Adieu,
Your uncle must not know but you are dead.
I'll fill these dogged spies with false reports,
And, pretty child, sleep doubtless, and secure
That Hubert for the wealth of all the world
Will not offend thee.

ARTHUR   O God! I thank you, Hubert.

HUBERT Silence, no more. Go closely in with me.
Much danger do I undergo for thee.   *Exeunt.*

4.2   *Flourish. Enter* KING JOHN, *crowned,*
          PEMBROKE, SALISBURY *and other Lords,*
                      and Attendants.

KING JOHN [*Seats himself on the throne.*]
Here once again we sit, once again crowned,
And looked upon, I hope, with cheerful eyes.

PEMBROKE
This 'once again', but that your highness pleased,
Was once superfluous. You were crowned before,
And that high royalty was ne'er plucked off,
The faiths of men ne'er stained with revolt,
Fresh expectation troubled not the land
With any longed-for change or better state.

SALISBURY
Therefore, to be possessed with double pomp,
To guard a title that was rich before,
To gild refined gold, to paint the lily,
To throw a perfume on the violet,
To smooth the ice, or add another hue
Unto the rainbow, or with taper-light
To seek the beauteous eye of heaven to garnish,
Is wasteful and ridiculous excess.

PEMBROKE But that your royal pleasure must be done,
This act is as an ancient tale new told,
And in the last repeating, troublesome
Being urged at a time unseasonable.

SALISBURY In this the antique and well-noted face
Of plain old form is much disfigured,
And, like a shifted wind unto a sail,
It makes the course of thoughts to fetch about,
Startles, and frights consideration,
Makes sound opinion sick, and truth suspected
For putting on so new a fashioned robe.

PEMBROKE
When workmen strive to do better than well
They do confound their skill in covetousness,
And oftentimes excusing of a fault
Doth make the fault the worser by th'excuse:
As patches set upon a little breach
Discredit more in hiding of the fault
Than did the fault before it was so patched.

SALISBURY
To this effect before you were new crowned
We breathed our counsel, but it pleased your highness

739

To overbear it; and we are all well pleased,
Since all, and every part of what we would
Doth make a stand at what your highness will.

40 KING JOHN   Some reasons of this double coronation
I have possessed you with, and think them strong.
And more, more strong, when lesser is my fear,
I shall endue you with. Meantime, but ask
What you would have reformed that is not well,
45 And well shall you perceive how willingly
I will both hear and grant you your requests.

PEMBROKE   Then I, as one that am the tongue of these
To sound the purposes of all their hearts
Both for myself and them, but chief of all
50 Your safety, for the which myself and them
Bend their best studies, heartily request
Th'enfranchisement of Arthur, whose restraint
Doth move the murmuring lips of discontent
To break into this dangerous argument:
55 If what in rest you have, in right you hold,
Why then your fears, which (as they say) attend
The steps of wrong, should move you to mew up
Your tender kinsman, and to choke his days
With barbarous ignorance, and deny his youth
60 The rich advantage of good exercise.
That the time's enemies may not have this
To grace occasions, let it be our suit
That you have bid us ask his liberty,
Which for our goods we do no further ask
65 Than, whereupon our weal on you depending
Counts it your weal, he have his liberty.

KING JOHN   Let it be so. I do commit his youth
To your direction.

Enter HUBERT.

Hubert, what news with you?
[_Hubert goes to the throne and speaks with King John
aside._]

PEMBROKE [_to Salisbury and Lords_]
This is the man should do the bloody deed;
70 He showed his warrant to a friend of mine.
The image of a wicked heinous fault
Lives in his eye, that close aspect of his
Doth show the mood of a much-troubled breast,
And I do fearfully believe 'tis done,
75 What we so feared he had a charge to do.

SALISBURY   The colour of the King doth come and go
Between his purpose and his conscience,
Like heralds 'twixt two dreadful battles set.
His passion is so ripe, it needs must break.

80 PEMBROKE   And when it breaks, I fear will issue thence
The foul corruption of a sweet child's death.

KING JOHN [_aloud to Lords_]
We cannot hold mortality's strong hand.
Good lords, although my will to give is living,
The suit which you demand is gone and dead:
85 He tells us Arthur is deceased tonight.

SALISBURY   Indeed we feared his sickness was past cure.

PEMBROKE
Indeed we heard how near his death he was
Before the child himself felt he was sick.
This must be answered, either here or hence.

KING JOHN
Why do you bend such solemn brows on me?   90
Think you I bear the shears of destiny?
Have I commandment on the pulse of life?

SALISBURY   It is apparent foul play, and 'tis shame
That greatness should so grossly offer it:
So thrive it in your game, and so farewell.   95

PEMBROKE   Stay yet, Lord Salisbury, I'll go with thee
And find th'inheritance of this poor child,
His little kingdom of a forced grave.
That blood which owned the breadth of all this isle,
Three foot of it doth hold. Bad world the while –   100
This must not be thus borne; this will break out
To all our sorrows, and ere long I doubt.
Exeunt Pembroke, Salisbury and other Lords.

KING JOHN   They burn in indignation. I repent:
There is no sure foundation set on blood,
No certain life achieved by others' death.   105

Enter Messenger.

A fearful eye thou hast. Where is that blood
That I have seen inhabit in those cheeks?
So foul a sky clears not without a storm:
Pour down thy weather. How goes all in France?

MESSENGER
From France to England: never such a power   110
For any foreign preparation
Was levied in the body of a land.
The copy of your speed is learned by them,
For when you should be told they do prepare,
The tidings comes that they are all arrived.   115

KING JOHN   O, where hath our intelligence been drunk?
Where hath it slept? Where is my mother's care,
That such an army could be drawn in France,
And she not hear of it?

MESSENGER   My liege, her ear
Is stopped with dust: the first of April died   120
Your noble mother, and, as I hear, my lord,
The Lady Constance in a frenzy died
Three days before – but this from rumour's tongue
I idly heard; if true or false I know not.

KING JOHN   Withhold thy speed, dreadful Occasion!   125
O, make a league with me till I have pleased
My discontented peers. What? Mother dead?
How wildly then walks my estate in France!
Under whose conduct came those powers of France
That thou for truth giv'st out are landed here?   130

MESSENGER   Under the Dauphin.

KING JOHN   Thou hast made me giddy
With these ill tidings.

Enter BASTARD _and_ PETER _of Pomfret._

Now! What says the world

To your proceedings? Do not seek to stuff
My head with more ill news, for it is full.

135 BASTARD   But if you be afeared to hear the worst,
Then let the worst, unheard, fall on your head.

KING JOHN   Bear with me, cousin, for I was amazed
Under the tide, but now I breathe again
Aloft the flood, and can give audience
140 To any tongue, speak it of what it will.

BASTARD   How I have sped among the clergymen
The sums I have collected shall express;
But as I travelled hither through the land
I find the people strangely fantasied,
145 Possessed with rumours, full of idle dreams,
Not knowing what they fear, but full of fear.
And here's a prophet that I brought with me
From forth the streets of Pomfret, whom I found
With many hundreds treading on his heels,
150 To whom he sung in rude harsh-sounding rhymes,
That ere the next Ascension Day at noon
Your highness should deliver up your crown.

KING JOHN   Thou idle dreamer, wherefore didst thou so?

PETER   Foreknowing that the truth will fall out so.

155 KING JOHN   Hubert, away with him, imprison him;
And on that day at noon whereon he says
I shall yield up my crown, let him be hanged.
Deliver him to safety and return,
For I must use thee.   *Exit Hubert with Peter of Pomfret.*
O my gentle cousin,
160 Hear'st thou the news abroad who are arrived?

BASTARD
The French, my lord; men's mouths are full of it.
Besides I met Lord Bigot and Lord Salisbury,
With eyes as red as new-enkindled fire,
And others more, going to seek the grave
165 Of Arthur, whom they say is killed tonight
On your suggestion.

KING JOHN   Gentle kinsman, go
And thrust thyself into their companies.
I have a way to win their loves again;
Bring them before me.

BASTARD   I will seek them out.

KING JOHN
170 Nay, but make haste, the better foot before.
O, let me have no subject enemies
When adverse foreigners affright my towns
With dreadful pomp of stout invasion.
Be Mercury, set feathers to thy heels
175 And fly like thought from them to me again.

BASTARD
The spirit of the time shall teach me speed.   *Exit.*

KING JOHN
Spoke like a sprightful noble gentleman.
[*to Messenger*] Go after him, for he perhaps shall need
Some messenger betwixt me and the peers,
And be thou he.

MESSENGER   With all my heart, my liege.   *Exit.*

180 KING JOHN   My mother dead!

Enter HUBERT.

HUBERT
My lord, they say five moons were seen tonight,
Four fixed, and the fifth did whirl about
The other four in wondrous motion.

KING JOHN   Five moons?

HUBERT   Old men and beldams in the streets   185
Do prophesy upon it dangerously.
Young Arthur's death is common in their mouths,
And when they talk of him they shake their heads,
And whisper one another in the ear;
And he that speaks doth grip the hearer's wrist,   190
Whilst he that hears makes fearful action
With wrinkled brows, with nods, with rolling eyes.
I saw a smith stand with his hammer, thus,
The whilst his iron did on the anvil cool,
With open mouth swallowing a tailor's news,   195
Who with his shears and measure in his hand,
Standing on slippers, which his nimble haste
Had falsely thrust upon contrary feet,
Told of a many thousand warlike French
That were embattled and ranked in Kent.   200
Another lean unwashed artificer
Cuts off his tale and talks of Arthur's death.

KING JOHN
Why seek'st thou to possess me with these fears?
Why urgest thou so oft young Arthur's death?
Thy hand hath murdered him. I had a mighty cause   205
To wish him dead, but thou hadst none to kill him.

HUBERT
No had, my lord! Why, did you not provoke me?

KING JOHN   It is the curse of kings to be attended
By slaves that take their humours for a warrant
To break within the bloody house of life,   210
And on the winking of authority
To understand a law, to know the meaning
Of dangerous majesty, when perchance it frowns
More upon humour than advised respect.

HUBERT [*Shows warrant.*]
Here is your hand and seal for what I did.   215

KING JOHN [*aside*]
O, when the last account 'twixt heaven and earth
Is to be made, then shall this hand and seal
Witness against us to damnation!
[*to Hubert*] How oft the sight of means to do ill deeds
Makes deeds ill done! Hadst not thou been by,   220
A fellow by the hand of nature marked,
Quoted and signed to do a deed of shame,
This murder had not come into my mind.
But taking note of thy abhorred aspect,
Finding thee fit for bloody villainy,   225
Apt, liable to be employed in danger,
I faintly broke with thee of Arthur's death;
And thou, to be endeared to a king,
Made it no conscience to destroy a prince.

HUBERT   My lord –   230

KING JOHN
Hadst thou but shook thy head or made a pause
When I spake darkly what I purposed,
Or turned an eye of doubt upon my face
As bid me tell my tale in express words,
235 Deep shame had struck me dumb, made me break off;
And those thy fears might have wrought fears in me.
But thou didst understand me by my signs
And didst in signs again parley with sin,
Yea, without stop, didst let thy heart consent,
240 And consequently, thy rude hand to act
The deed which both our tongues held vile to name.
Out of my sight, and never see me more!
My nobles leave me, and my state is braved
Even at my gates with ranks of foreign powers;
245 Nay, in the body of this fleshly land,
This kingdom, this confine of blood and breath,
Hostility and civil tumult reigns
Between my conscience and my cousin's death.
HUBERT   Arm you against your other enemies;
250 I'll make a peace between your soul and you.
Young Arthur is alive: this hand of mine
Is yet a maiden and an innocent hand,
Not painted with the crimson spots of blood.
Within this bosom never entered yet
255 The dreadful motion of a murderous thought,
And you have slandered nature in my form,
Which howsoever rude exteriorly,
Is yet the cover of a fairer mind
Than to be butcher of an innocent child.
260 KING JOHN   Doth Arthur live? O, haste thee to the peers,
Throw this report on their incensed rage,
And make them tame to their obedience.
Forgive the comment that my passion made
Upon thy feature, for my rage was blind,
265 And foul imaginary eyes of blood
Presented thee more hideous than thou art.
O, answer not, but to my closet bring
The angry lords with all expedient haste.
I conjure thee but slowly; run more fast!   *Exeunt.*

4.3   *Enter* ARTHUR *on the walls.*

ARTHUR   The wall is high, and yet will I leap down.
Good ground be pitiful and hurt me not!
There's few or none do know me; if they did,
This ship-boy's semblance hath disguised me quite.
5 I am afraid, and yet I'll venture it.
If I get down and do not break my limbs,
I'll find a thousand shifts to get away.
As good to die and go, as die and stay.   [*Leaps down.*]
O me, my uncle's spirit is in these stones.
10 Heaven take my soul, and England keep my bones.[*Dies.*]

Enter PEMBROKE, SALISBURY *and* BIGOT.

SALISBURY
Lords, I will meet him at Saint Edmundsbury.

It is our safety, and we must embrace
This gentle offer of the perilous time.
PEMBROKE
Who brought that letter from the cardinal?
SALISBURY   The Count Melun, a noble lord of France,   15
Whose private with me of the Dauphin's love
Is much more general than these lines import.
BIGOT   Tomorrow morning let us meet him then.
SALISBURY   Or rather then set forward, for 'twill be
Two long days' journey, lords, or ere we meet.   20

Enter BASTARD.

BASTARD
Once more today well met, distempered lords.
The King by me requests your presence straight.
SALISBURY   The King hath dispossessed himself of us.
We will not line his thin-bestained cloak
With our pure honours, nor attend the foot   25
That leaves the print of blood where'er it walks.
Return and tell him so; we know the worst.
BASTARD
Whate'er you think, good words I think were best.
SALISBURY
Our griefs and not our manners reason now.
BASTARD   But there is little reason in your grief.   30
Therefore 'twere reason you had manners now.
PEMBROKE   Sir, sir, impatience hath his privilege.
BASTARD   'Tis true: to hurt his master, no man else.
SALISBURY   This is the prison.
    [*Sees Arthur's body.*]   What is he lies here?
PEMBROKE
O death, made proud with pure and princely beauty!   35
The earth had not a hole to hide this deed.
SALISBURY
Murder, as hating what himself hath done,
Doth lay it open to urge on revenge.
BIGOT   Or when he doomed this beauty to a grave,
Found it too precious-princely for a grave.   40
SALISBURY [*to Bastard*]
Sir Richard, what think you? Have you beheld.
Or have you read, or heard, or could you think,
Or do you almost think, although you see,
That you do see? Could thought, without this object,
Form such another? This is the very top,   45
The height, the crest, or crest unto the crest,
Of murder's arms. This is the bloodiest shame,
The wildest savagery, the vilest stroke
That ever wall-eyed wrath or staring rage
Presented to the tears of soft remorse.   50
PEMBROKE
All murders past do stand excused in this,
And this so sole, and so unmatchable,
Shall give a holiness, a purity,
To the yet unbegotten sin of times,
And prove a deadly bloodshed but a jest,   55
Exampled by this heinous spectacle.
BASTARD   It is a damned and a bloody work,

The graceless action of a heavy hand,
If that it be the work of any hand.

SALISBURY If that it be the work of any hand? 60
We had a kind of light what would ensue.
It is the shameful work of Hubert's hand;
The practice and the purpose of the King –
From whose obedience I forbid my soul, 65
Kneeling before this ruin of sweet life,
And breathing to his breathless excellence
The incense of a vow, a holy vow,
Never to taste the pleasures of the world,
Never to be infected with delight, 70
Nor conversant with ease and idleness,
Till I have set a glory to this hand
By giving it the worship of revenge.

PEMBROKE, BIGOT [*Kneel.*]
Our souls religiously confirm thy words.

Enter HUBERT.

HUBERT Lords, I am hot with haste in seeking you. 75
Arthur doth live, the King hath sent for you.
[*The Lords rise.*]

SALISBURY O, he is bold, and blushes not at death.
Avaunt, thou hateful villain, get thee gone!

HUBERT I am no villain.

SALISBURY [*Draws his sword.*] Must I rob the law?

BASTARD Your sword is bright, sir, put it up again.

SALISBURY Not till I sheathe it in a murderer's skin. 80

HUBERT [*Draws his sword.*]
Stand back, Lord Salisbury, stand back I say!
By God, I think my sword's as sharp as yours.
I would not have you, lord, forget yourself,
Nor tempt the danger of my true defence
Lest I, by marking of your rage, forget 85
Your worth, your greatness and nobility.

BIGOT Out, dunghill! Dar'st thou brave a nobleman?

HUBERT Not for my life, but yet I dare defend
My innocent life against an emperor.

SALISBURY Thou art a murderer.

HUBERT Do not prove me so! 90
Yet I am none. Whose tongue soe'er speaks false,
Not truly speaks; who speaks not truly, lies.

PEMBROKE Cut him to pieces.

BASTARD [*Draws.*] Keep the peace, I say.

SALISBURY Stand by, or I shall gall you, Faulconbridge.

BASTARD Thou wert better gall the devil, Salisbury. 95
If thou but frown on me, or stir thy foot,
Or teach thy hasty spleen to do me shame,
I'll strike thee dead. Put up thy sword betime,
Or I'll so maul you and your toasting-iron
That you shall think the devil is come from hell. 100

BIGOT What wilt thou do, renownèd Faulconbridge?
Second a villain and a murderer?

HUBERT Lord Bigot, I am none.

BIGOT Who killed this prince?

HUBERT [*Puts up his sword.*]
'Tis not an hour since I left him well.

[*Weeps.*] I honoured him, I loved him, and will weep 105
My date of life out for his sweet life's loss.
[*The Lords and the Bastard put up their swords.*]

SALISBURY Trust not those cunning waters of his eyes,
For villainy is not without such rheum,
And he, long traded in it, makes it seem
Like rivers of remorse and innocency. 110
Away with me, all you whose souls abhor
Th'uncleanly savours of a slaughterhouse,
For I am stifled with this smell of sin.

BIGOT Away toward Bury, to the Dauphin there.

PEMBROKE [*to Bastard*]
There, tell the King, he may inquire us out. 115

Exeunt Lords.

BASTARD
Here's a good world! Knew you of this fair work?
Beyond the infinite and boundless reach
Of mercy, if thou didst this deed of death,
Art thou damned, Hubert.

HUBERT Do but hear me, sir.

BASTARD Ha! I'll tell thee what – 120
Thou'rt damned as black – nay nothing is so black!
Thou art more deep damned than Prince Lucifer.
There is not yet so ugly a fiend of hell
As thou shalt be, if thou didst kill this child.

HUBERT Upon my soul –

BASTARD If thou didst but consent 125
To this most cruel act, do but despair –
And if thou want'st a cord, the smallest thread
That ever spider twisted from her womb
Will serve to strangle thee; a rush will be a beam
To hang thee on. Or wouldst thou drown thyself, 130
Put but a little water in a spoon
And it shall be as all the ocean,
Enough to stifle such a villain up.
I do suspect thee very grievously.

HUBERT If I in act, consent or sin of thought, 135
Be guilty of the stealing that sweet breath
Which was embounded in this beauteous clay,
Let hell want pains enough to torture me.
I left him well!

BASTARD Go, bear him in thine arms.
[*Hubert takes up Arthur's body.*]
I am amazed, methinks, and lose my way 140
Among the thorns and dangers of this world.
How easy dost thou take all England up!
From forth this morsel of dead royalty,
The life, the right and truth of all this realm
Is fled to heaven, and England now is left 145
To tug and scamble, and to part by th' teeth
The unowed interest of proud-swelling state.
Now for the bare-picked bone of majesty
Doth doggèd war bristle his angry crest
And snarleth in the gentle eyes of peace. 150
Now powers from home and discontents at home
Meet in one line, and vast confusion waits,
As doth a raven on a sick-fallen beast,

The imminent decay of wrested pomp.
155 Now happy he, whose cloak and ceinture can
Hold out this tempest. Bear away that child,
And follow me with speed; I'll to the King.
A thousand businesses are brief in hand,
And heaven itself doth frown upon the land.

Exeunt, Hubert carrying Arthur's body.

5.1 *Flourish. Enter* KING JOHN *and*
PANDULPH *with the crown, Attendants.*

KING JOHN [*Gives the crown to Pandulph.*]
Thus have I yielded up into your hand
The circle of my glory.

PANDULPH [*Gives back the crown.*] Take again
From this my hand, as holding of the Pope,
Your sovereign greatness and authority.

KING JOHN
5 Now keep your holy word, go meet the French,
And from his Holiness use all your power
To stop their marches 'fore we are inflamed.
Our discontented counties do revolt;
Our people quarrel with obedience,
10 Swearing allegiance and the love of soul
To stranger blood, to foreign royalty.
This inundation of mistempered humour
Rests by you only to be qualified.
Then pause not, for the present time's so sick
15 That present medicine must be ministered,
Or overthrow incurably ensues.

PANDULPH It was my breath that blew this tempest up
Upon your stubborn usage of the Pope;
But since you are a gentle convertite,
20 My tongue shall hush again this storm of war
And make fair weather in your blustering land.
On this Ascension Day, remember well,
Upon your oath of service to the Pope,
Go I to make the French lay down their arms.

Exit with Attendants.

25 KING JOHN Is this Ascension Day? Did not the prophet
Say that before Ascension Day at noon
My crown I should give off? Even so I have –
I did suppose it should be on constraint,
But, God be thanked, it is but voluntary.

Enter BASTARD.

BASTARD
30 All Kent hath yielded: nothing there holds out
But Dover Castle. London hath received,
Like a kind host, the Dauphin and his powers.
Your nobles will not hear you, but are gone
To offer service to your enemy.
35 And wild amazement hurries up and down
The little number of your doubtful friends.

KING JOHN Would not my lords return to me again
After they heard young Arthur was alive?

BASTARD They found him dead, and cast into the streets,

An empty casket, where the jewel of life 40
By some damned hand was robbed and ta'en away.

KING JOHN That villain Hubert told me he did live.

BASTARD So on my soul he did for aught he knew.
But wherefore do you droop? Why look you sad?
Be great in act, as you have been in thought! 45
Let not the world see fear and sad distrust
Govern the motion of a kingly eye.
Be stirring as the time, be fire with fire,
Threaten the threatener, and outface the brow
Of bragging horror: so shall inferior eyes 50
That borrow their behaviours from the great,
Grow great by your example, and put on
The dauntless spirit of resolution.
Away, and glister like the god of war
When he intendeth to become the field; 55
Show boldness and aspiring confidence!
What, shall they seek the lion in his den,
And fright him there, and make him tremble there?
O, let it not be said! Forage, and run
To meet displeasure farther from the doors, 60
And grapple with him ere he come so nigh.

KING JOHN The legate of the Pope hath been with me,
And I have made a happy peace with him,
And he hath promised to dismiss the powers
Led by the Dauphin.

BASTARD O, inglorious league! 65
Shall we, upon the footing of our land,
Send fair-play orders, and make compromise,
Insinuation, parley and base truce
To arms invasive? Shall a beardless boy,
A cockered-silken wanton, brave our fields 70
And flesh his spirit in a warlike soil,
Mocking the air with colours idly spread,
And find no check? Let us, my liege, to arms!
Perchance the cardinal cannot make your peace,
Or if he do, let it at least be said 75
They saw we had a purpose of defence.

KING JOHN Have thou the ordering of this present time.

BASTARD
Away then with good courage! [*aside*] Yet I know
Our party may well meet a prouder foe. *Exeunt.*

5.2 *Enter (in arms)* Lewis the DAUPHIN,
with a document, SALISBURY, MELUN,
PEMBROKE, BIGOT, *Soldiers.*

DAUPHIN [*Gives document to Melun.*]
My Lord Melun, let this be copied out,
And keep it safe for our remembrance.
Return the precedent to these lords again,
That having our fair order written down,
Both they and we, perusing o'er these notes, 5
May know wherefore we took the sacrament
And keep our faiths firm and inviolable.

SALISBURY Upon our sides it never shall be broken.
And, noble Dauphin, albeit we swear

10 A voluntary zeal and unurged faith
To your proceedings, yet believe me, prince,
I am not glad that such a sore of time
Should seek a plaster by contemned revolt
And heal the inveterate canker of one wound
15 By making many. O, it grieves my soul
That I must draw this metal from my side
To be a widow-maker – O, and there
Where honourable rescue and defence
Cries out upon the name of Salisbury.
20 But such is the infection of the time
That for the health and physic of our right
We cannot deal but with the very hand
Of stern injustice and confused wrong.
And is't not pity, O my grieved friends,
25 That we, the sons and children of this isle,
Were born to see so sad an hour as this,
Wherein we step after a stranger, march
Upon her gentle bosom, and fill up
Her enemy's ranks – I must withdraw and weep
30 Upon the spot of this enforced cause –
To grace the gentry of a land remote,
And follow unacquainted colours here.
[*Weeps.*] What, here? O nation, that thou couldst
    remove:
That Neptune's arms who clippeth thee about
35 Would bear thee from the knowledge of thyself,
And grapple thee unto a pagan shore,
Where these two Christian armies might combine
The blood of malice in a vein of league,
And not to spend it so unneighbourly.
40 DAUPHIN   A noble temper dost thou show in this,
And great affections wrestling in thy bosom
Doth make an earthquake of nobility.
O, what a noble combat hast thou fought
Between compulsion and a brave respect!
45 Let me wipe off this honourable dew
That silverly doth progress on thy cheeks.
[*Wipes Salisbury's eyes.*] My heart hath melted at a
    lady's tears,
Being an ordinary inundation;
But this effusion of such manly drops,
50 This shower, blown up by tempest of the soul,
Startles mine eyes and makes me more amazed
Than had I seen the vaulty top of heaven
Figured quite o'er with burning meteors.
Lift up thy brow, renowned Salisbury,
55 And with a great heart heave away this storm.
Commend these waters to those baby eyes
That never saw the giant world enraged,
Nor met with fortune other than at feasts,
Full warm of blood, of mirth, of gossiping.
60 Come, come; for thou shalt thrust thy hand as deep
Into the purse of rich prosperity
As Lewis himself: so, nobles, shall you all
That knit your sinews to the strength of mine,
    [*Trumpet sounds.*]

And even there, methinks an angel spake.

Enter PANDULPH, *attended.*

Look where the holy legate comes apace   65
To give us warrant from the hand of God,
And on our actions set the name of right
With holy breath.
PANDULPH   Hail, noble prince of France.
The next is this: King John hath reconciled
Himself to Rome; his spirit is come in   70
That so stood out against the holy Church,
The great metropolis and see of Rome.
Therefore thy threatening colours now wind up,
And tame the savage spirit of wild war
That, like a lion fostered up at hand,   75
It may lie gently at the foot of peace
And be no further harmful than in show.
DAUPHIN   Your grace shall pardon me, I will not back.
I am too high-born to be propertied,
To be a secondary at control,   80
Or useful serving-man and instrument
To any sovereign state throughout the world.
Your breath first kindled the dead coals of war
Between this chastised kingdom and myself
And brought in matter that should feed this fire,   85
And now 'tis far too huge to be blown out
With that same weak wind which enkindled it.
You taught me how to know the face of right,
Acquainted me with interest to this land,
Yea, thrust this enterprise into my heart;   90
And come ye now to tell me John hath made
His peace with Rome? What is that peace to me?
I, by the honour of my marriage-bed,
After young Arthur, claim this land for mine;
And now it is half-conquered, must I back   95
Because that John hath made his peace with Rome?
Am I Rome's slave? What penny hath Rome borne?
What men provided? What munition sent
To underprop this action? Is't not I
That undergo this charge? Who else but I,   100
And such as to my claim are liable,
Sweat in this business and maintain this war?
Have I not heard these islanders shout out
'Vive le roi!' as I have banked their towns?
Have I not here the best cards for the game   105
To win this easy match played for a crown?
And shall I now give o'er the yielded set?
No! No, on my soul, it never shall be said.
PANDULPH   You look but on the outside of this work.
DAUPHIN   Outside or inside, I will not return   110
Till my attempt so much be glorified
As to my ample hope was promised
Before I drew this gallant head of war
And culled these fiery spirits from the world
To outlook conquest and to win renown   115
Even in the jaws of danger and of death.
    [*Trumpet sounds.*]

What lusty trumpet thus doth summon us?

Enter BASTARD.

BASTARD   According to the fair play of the world,
　　　Let me have audience: I am sent to speak.
120　　My holy lord of Milan, from the King
　　　I come to learn how you have dealt for him,
　　　And, as you answer, I do know the scope
　　　And warrant limited unto my tongue.
PANDULPH   The Dauphin is too wilful-opposite,
125　　And will not temporize with my entreaties:
　　　He flatly says he'll not lay down his arms.
BASTARD   By all the blood that ever fury breathed,
　　　The youth says well! Now hear our English king,
　　　For thus his royalty doth speak in me:
130　　He is prepared, and reason too he should.
　　　This apish and unmannerly approach,
　　　This harnessed mask and unadvised revel,
　　　This unhaired sauciness and boyish troops,
　　　The King doth smile at; and is well prepared
135　　To whip this dwarfish war, these pygmy arms,
　　　From out the circle of his territories.
　　　That hand which had the strength, even at your door,
　　　To cudgel you and make you take the hatch,
　　　To dive like buckets in concealed wells,
140　　To crouch in litter of your stable planks,
　　　To lie like pawns locked up in chests and trunks,
　　　To hug with swine, to seek sweet safety out
　　　In vaults and prisons, and to thrill and shake
　　　Even at the crying of your nation's crow,
145　　Thinking this voice an armed Englishman –
　　　Shall that victorious hand be feebled here
　　　That in your chambers gave you chastisement?
　　　No! Know the gallant monarch is in arms,
　　　And like an eagle o'er his eyrie towers,
150　　To souse annoyance that comes near his nest.
　　　And you degenerate, you ingrate revolts,
　　　You bloody Neroes, ripping up the womb
　　　Of your dear mother England, blush for shame!
　　　For your own ladies and pale-visaged maids
155　　Like Amazons come tripping after drums,
　　　Their thimbles into armed gauntlets change,
　　　Their needles to lances, and their gentle hearts
　　　To fierce and bloody inclination.
DAUPHIN
　　　There end thy brave, and turn thy face in peace.
160　　We grant thou canst out-scold us. Fare thee well,
　　　We hold our time too precious to be spent
　　　With such a brabbler.
PANDULPH　　　　　　　　Give me leave to speak.
BASTARD   No, I will speak.
DAUPHIN　　　　　　　We will attend to neither.
　　　Strike up the drums, and let the tongue of war
165　　Plead for our interest and our being here.
BASTARD
　　　Indeed, your drums, being beaten, will cry out;
　　　And so shall you, being beaten. Do but start

An echo with the clamour of thy drum,
And even at hand a drum is ready braced
That shall reverberate all as loud as thine.　　170
Sound but another, and another shall
As loud as thine rattle the welkin's ear,
And mock the deep-mouthed thunder, for at hand –
Not trusting to this halting legate here,
Whom he hath used rather for sport than need –　　175
Is warlike John, and in his forehead sits
A bare-ribbed death, whose office is this day
To feast upon whole thousands of the French.
DAUPHIN   Strike up our drums to find this danger out.
　　　　　　　　　　　　　　　　[*Drums sound.*]
BASTARD
　　　And thou shalt find it, Dauphin, do not doubt.   *Exeunt.*　　180

5.3　　*Alarums. Enter* KING JOHN *and* HUBERT.

KING JOHN
　　　How goes the day with us? O, tell me, Hubert.
HUBERT   Badly I fear; how fares your majesty?
KING JOHN   This fever that hath troubled me so long
　　　Lies heavy on me. O, my heart is sick.

Enter a Messenger.

MESSENGER
　　　My lord, your valiant kinsman Faulconbridge　　5
　　　Desires your majesty to leave the field
　　　And send him word by me which way you go.
KING JOHN
　　　Tell him toward Swinstead, to the abbey there.
MESSENGER   Be of good comfort, for the great supply
　　　That was expected by the Dauphin here　　10
　　　Are wrecked three nights ago on Goodwin Sands.
　　　This news was brought to Richard but even now;
　　　The French fight coldly and retire themselves.
KING JOHN   Ay me, this tyrant fever burns me up
　　　And will not let me welcome this good news.　　15
　　　Set on toward Swinstead. To my litter straight;
　　　Weakness possesseth me, and I am faint.　　*Exeunt.*

5.4　　*Enter* SALISBURY, PEMBROKE *and* BIGOT.

SALISBURY
　　　I did not think the King so stored with friends.
PEMBROKE   Up once again; put spirit in the French;
　　　If they miscarry, we miscarry too.
SALISBURY   That misbegotten devil Faulconbridge,
　　　In spite of spite, alone upholds the day.　　5
PEMBROKE
　　　They say King John, sore sick, hath left the field.

Enter MELUN *wounded, led.*

MELUN   Lead me to the revolts of England here.
SALISBURY   When we were happy we had other names.
PEMBROKE   It is the Count Melun.
SALISBURY　　　　　　　　Wounded to death.
MELUN   Fly, noble English, you are bought and sold.　　10

Unthread the rude eye of rebellion,
And welcome home again discarded faith.
Seek out King John and fall before his feet.
For if the French be lords of this loud day
15 He means to recompense the pains you take
By cutting off your heads: thus hath he sworn,
And I with him, and many more with me
Upon the altar at Saint Edmundsbury,
Even on that altar where we swore to you
20 Dear amity and everlasting love.

SALISBURY   May this be possible? May this be true?
MELUN   Have I not hideous death within my view,
Retaining but a quantity of life
Which bleeds away, even as a form of wax
25 Resolveth from his figure 'gainst the fire?
What in the world should make me now deceive,
Since I must lose the use of all deceit?
Why should I then be false, since it is true
That I must die here, and live hence by truth?
30 I say again, if Lewis do win the day
He is forsworn if e'er those eyes of yours
Behold another day break in the east.
But even this night, whose black contagious breath
Already smokes about the burning crest
35 Of the old, feeble and day-wearied sun,
Even this ill night, your breathing shall expire,
Paying the fine of rated treachery
Even with a treacherous fine of all your lives,
If Lewis by your assistance win the day.
40 Commend me to one Hubert, with your king.
The love of him, and this respect besides,
For that my grandsire was an Englishman,
Awakes my conscience to confess all this.
In lieu whereof, I pray you bear me hence
45 From forth the noise and rumour of the field,
Where I may think the remnant of my thoughts
In peace, and part this body and my soul
With contemplation and devout desires.
SALISBURY   We do believe thee, and beshrew my soul
50 But I do love the favour and the form
Of this most fair occasion, by the which
We will untread the steps of damned flight,
And like a bated and retired flood,
Leaving our rankness and irregular course,
55 Stoop low within those bounds we have o'erlooked
And calmly run on in obedience
Even to our ocean, to our great King John.
My arm shall give thee help to bear thee hence,
For I do see the cruel pangs of death
60 Right in thine eye. Away, my friends; new flight,
And happy newness, that intends old right.
Exeunt, assisting Melun.

5.5   *Enter* Lewis the DAUPHIN, *and his Train.*

DAUPHIN
The sun of heaven methought was loath to set,

But stayed and made the western welkin blush,
When English measured backward their own ground
In faint retire. O, bravely came we off,
When with a volley of our needless shot,   5
After such bloody toil, we bid goodnight
And wound our tottering colours clearly up,
Last in the field, and almost lords of it.

Enter a Messenger.

MESSENGER
Where is my prince, the Dauphin?
DAUPHIN   Here, what news?
MESSENGER
The Count Melun is slain. The English lords   10
By his persuasion are again fallen off;
And your supply, which you have wished so long,
Are cast away and sunk on Goodwin Sands.
DAUPHIN
Ah, foul, shrewd news! Beshrew thy very heart:
I did not think to be so sad tonight   15
As this hath made me. Who was he that said
King John did fly an hour or two before
The stumbling night did part our weary powers?
MESSENGER   Who ever spoke it, it is true, my lord.
DAUPHIN
Well, keep good quarter and good care tonight.   20
The day shall not be up so soon as I
To try the fair adventure of tomorrow.   *Exeunt.*

5.6   *Enter* BASTARD *and* HUBERT, *severally.*

HUBERT
Who's there? Speak, ho! Speak quickly, or I shoot.
BASTARD   A friend. What art thou?
HUBERT   Of the part of England.
BASTARD   Whither dost thou go?
HUBERT   What's that to thee?
BASTARD   Why may not I demand of thine affairs
As well as thou of mine? Hubert, I think.   5
HUBERT   Thou hast a perfect thought.
I will upon all hazards well believe
Thou art my friend that know'st my tongue so well.
Who art thou?
BASTARD   Who thou wilt. An if thou please,
Thou mayst befriend me so much as to think   10
I come one way of the Plantagenets.
HUBERT   Unkind remembrance! Thou and endless night
Have done me shame. Brave soldier, pardon me
That any accent breaking from thy tongue
Should scape the true acquaintance of mine ear.   15
BASTARD
Come, come, sans compliment, what news abroad?
HUBERT   Why, here walk I in the black brow of night
To find you out.
BASTARD   Brief then, and what's the news?
HUBERT   O my sweet sir, news fitting to the night,
Black, fearful, comfortless and horrible.   20

BASTARD   Show me the very wound of this ill news:
    I am no woman, I'll not swoon at it.
HUBERT   The King, I fear, is poisoned by a monk;
    I left him almost speechless, and broke out
25   To acquaint you with this evil, that you might
    The better arm you to the sudden time
    Than if you had at leisure known of this.
BASTARD   How did he take it? Who did taste to him?
HUBERT   A monk, I tell you, a resolved villain,
30   Whose bowels suddenly burst out. The King
    Yet speaks, and peradventure may recover.
BASTARD   Who didst thou leave to tend his majesty?
HUBERT
    Why, know you not? The lords are all come back
    And brought Prince Henry in their company,
35   At whose request the King hath pardoned them,
    And they are all about his majesty.
BASTARD   Withhold thine indignation, mighty God,
    And tempt us not to bear above our power.
    I'll tell thee, Hubert, half my power this night,
40   Passing these flats, are taken by the tide –
    These Lincoln Washes have devoured them;
    Myself, well mounted, hardly have escaped.
    Away before; conduct me to the King.
    I doubt he will be dead or e'er I come.   *Exeunt.*

5.7   *Enter* Prince HENRY, SALISBURY *and* BIGOT.

HENRY   It is too late. The life of all his blood
    Is touched corruptibly, and his pure brain,
    Which some suppose the soul's frail dwelling house,
    Doth by the idle comments that it makes
5   Foretell the ending of mortality.

Enter PEMBROKE.

PEMBROKE
    His highness yet doth speak, and holds belief
    That, being brought into the open air,
    It would allay the burning quality
    Of that fell poison which assaileth him.
HENRY
10   Let him be brought into the orchard here.   *Exit Bigot.*
    Doth he still rage?
PEMBROKE   He is more patient
    Than when you left him: even now, he sung.
HENRY   O vanity of sickness! Fierce extremes
    In their continuance will not feel themselves.
15   Death, having preyed upon the outward parts,
    Leaves them invisible, and his siege is now
    Against the mind, the which he pricks and wounds
    With many legions of strange fantasies,
    Which, in their throng and press to that last hold,
    Confound themselves. 'Tis strange that death should
20   sing.
    I am the cygnet to this pale faint swan,
    Who chants a doleful hymn to his own death,
    And from the organ-pipe of frailty, sings

    His soul and body to their lasting rest.
SALISBURY
    Be of good comfort, Prince, for you are born   25
    To set a form upon that indigest
    Which he hath left so shapeless and so rude.

KING JOHN *is brought in.*

KING JOHN   Ay, marry, now my soul hath elbow room:
    It would not out at windows nor at doors.
    There is so hot a summer in my bosom   30
    That all my bowels crumble up to dust.
    I am a scribbled form, drawn with a pen
    Upon a parchment, and against this fire
    Do I shrink up.
HENRY   How fares your majesty?
KING JOHN   Poisoned, ill fare; dead, forsook, cast off,   35
    And none of you will bid the winter come
    To thrust his icy fingers in my maw,
    Nor let my kingdom's rivers take their course
    Through my burned bosom, nor entreat the north
    To make his bleak winds kiss my parched lips   40
    And comfort me with cold. I do not ask you much.
    I beg cold comfort, and you are so strait
    And so ungrateful, you deny me that.
HENRY   O, that there were some virtue in my tears
    That might relieve you.
KING JOHN   The salt in them is hot.   45
    Within me is a hell, and there the poison
    Is, as a fiend, confined to tyrannize
    On unreprievable, condemned blood.

Enter BASTARD.

BASTARD   O, I am scalded with my violent motion
    And spleen of speed to see your majesty!   50
KING JOHN   O cousin, thou art come to set mine eye.
    The tackle of my heart is cracked and burnt,
    And all the shrouds wherewith my life should sail
    Are turned to one thread, one little hair.
    My heart hath one poor string to stay it by,   55
    Which holds but till thy news be uttered,
    And then all this thou seest is but a clod
    And module of confounded royalty.
BASTARD   The Dauphin is preparing hitherward,
    Where God he knows how we shall answer him.   60
    For in a night the best part of my power,
    As I upon advantage did remove,
    Were in the Washes all unwarily
    Devoured by the unexpected flood.   [*King John dies.*]
SALISBURY [*Sees that King John is dead.*]
    You breathe these dead news in as dead an ear.   65
    My liege, my lord! – but now a king, now thus.
HENRY   E'en so must I run on and e'en so stop.
    What surety of the world, what hope, what stay,
    When this was now a king, and now is clay?
BASTARD   Art thou gone so? I do but stay behind   70
    To do the office for thee of revenge,
    And then my soul shall wait on thee to heaven,

As it on earth hath been thy servant still.
[*to the Lords*] Now, now, you stars that move in your
    right spheres,
Where be your powers? Show now your mended
    faiths, 75
And instantly return with me again
To push destruction and perpetual shame
Out of the weak door of our fainting land.
Straight let us seek, or straight we shall be sought:
The Dauphin rages at our very heels. 80

SALISBURY   It seems you know not then so much as we.
The Cardinal Pandulph is within at rest,
Who half an hour since came from the Dauphin,
And brings from him such offers of our peace
As we with honour and respect may take 85
With purpose presently to leave this war.

BASTARD   He will the rather do it when he sees
Ourselves well sinewed to our defence.

SALISBURY   Nay, 'tis in a manner done already.
For many carriages he hath dispatched 90
To the seaside, and put his cause and quarrel
To the disposing of the cardinal,
With whom yourself, myself and other lords,
If you think meet, this afternoon will post
To consummate this business happily. 95

BASTARD   Let it be so; and you, my noble prince,
With other princes that may best be spared,
Shall wait upon your father's funeral.

HENRY   At Worcester must his body be interred,
For so he willed it.

BASTARD   Thither shall it then; 100
And happily may your sweet self put on
The lineal state and glory of the land –
To whom with all submission, on my knee,
I do bequeath my faithful services
And true subjection everlastingly.   [*Kneels.*] 105

SALISBURY   And the like tender of our love we make
To rest without a spot for evermore.
    [*The Lords kneel.*]

HENRY   I have a kind of soul that would give thanks,
And knows not how to do it but with tears.

BASTARD   O, let us pay the time but needful woe, 110
Since it hath been beforehand with our griefs.
This England never did, nor never shall
Lie at the proud foot of a conqueror
But when it first did help to wound itself.
Now these her princes are come home again, 115
Come the three corners of the world in arms
And we shall shock them. Naught shall make us rue,
If England to itself do rest but true.   *Exeunt.*

King Lear

King Lear was first printed in 1608 in quarto format as Shakespeare's *True Chronicle Historie of the Life and Death of King Lear and his three Daughters*. In 1623 another version of the play appeared in the First Folio as the eighth play among the tragedies. There are about 300 lines in the Quarto that are not in the Folio, and about 100 in the Folio that are not in the Quarto. There are also about 850 verbal variants between the two texts, some speeches are assigned differently, and there are some significant differences in characterization, particularly that of Edgar. Most editions of the play until the 1980s were 'conflated' versions, for which editors chose what they considered the best readings from the two texts to produce their own versions of *King Lear*. Many scholars, however, have now come to think that the Quarto *King Lear* represents Shakespeare's original version of the play, while the Folio text is his revision; and that the differences between the two texts are substantial enough that editorial conflation misrepresents the integrity of each. Some editions of the Complete Works now print both texts of the play. This Arden edition, however, is less confident that the two texts are as distinct as has been sometimes asserted; rather, it thinks of *King Lear* as a single work existing in two versions, neither of which can be thought superior to the other.

King Lear is usually dated 1604–5, putting it after *Hamlet* and *Othello* but before *Macbeth*. The 1608 Quarto title-page refers to a performance before King James I at Whitehall on 24 December 1606 (see Fig. 8, p. 8). Shakespeare knew the Lear story from Raphael Holinshed's *Chronicles* (1587) and from the *Mirror for Magistrates* (1574) as well as from a brief version in Edmund Spenser's *Faerie Queene* (1590: book 2, canto 10). He also knew, and may have acted in, an anonymous play called *The True Chronicle History of King Leir and his three daughters* (usually referred to as *King Leir*), which was published in 1605 but probably written and first performed around 1590. He complicated the Lear story by inventing Lear's madness and by adding the parallel plot of Gloucester and his sons, which derives from Philip Sidney's *Arcadia* (1590). He used Samuel Harsnett's *A Declaration of*

Egregious Popish Impostures (1603) for building up the characterization of Edgar as Poor Tom.

Nahum Tate's Restoration adaptation of Shakespeare's play (1681) is notorious for providing a happy ending, with Lear and Gloucester still alive and Cordelia betrothed to Edgar, who has earlier saved her from being raped by Edmund. This version, which also omitted the Fool, was thought to be more acceptable by readers and audiences until the mid-nineteenth century, but since then admiration for Shakespeare's bleak play has increased to the point that many people would now see *King Lear* as his greatest tragedy, surpassing even *Hamlet*. Its social and political vision of 'the promised end . . . Or image of that horror' (5.3.261–2) has appealed to a world threatened by genocide and environmental or nuclear catastrophe, while at the personal and familial level the play's presentation of conflict between the generations ('age is unnecessary') speaks to societies where people are living longer and the elderly make up an increasing proportion of the population. Modern productions and films frequently evoke Samuel Beckett's *Endgame* (1957), turning it into a kind of prophecy of the disintegration of modern as well as Renaissance civilization.

King Lear has been interpreted more positively as a tragedy of Christian suffering and redemption, or as one that embraces radical socialism ('So distribution should undo excess, / And each man have enough' (4.1.73–4)). However, despite the fact that a number of major characters are still alive at the end of the play and gestures are made towards 'sustain[ing]' 'the gored state' (5.3.319, the final impression is one of apocalyptic finality where an escape from suffering is all that can be hoped for.

The Arden text is based on the 1623 First Folio, but includes the material unique to the 1608 Quarto. Passages and words unique to the Quarto are marked at the beginning and end with superscript Q, while passages and words unique to the Folio are similarly marked with superscript F.

LEAR	*King of Britain*
GONERIL	*his eldest daughter*
REGAN	*his second daughter*
CORDELIA	*his youngest daughter*
Duke of ALBANY	*married to Goneril*
Duke of CORNWALL	*married to Regan*
King of FRANCE	
Duke of BURGUNDY	
Earl of GLOUCESTER	
EDGAR	*his elder son*
EDMUND	*his younger bastard son*
Earl of KENT	
FOOL	*attendant on Lear*
OSWALD	*Goneril's steward*
CURAN	*a follower of Gloucester*
OLD MAN	*Gloucester's tenant*

A Herald, a Captain, an Officer, a Doctor, Knights,
Gentlemen, Attendants, Servants and Messengers

1.1 *Enter* KENT, GLOUCESTER *and* EDMUND.

KENT   I thought the King had more affected the Duke
of Albany than Cornwall.

GLOUCESTER   It did always seem so to us: but now, in
the division of the kingdom, it appears not which of the
dukes he values most, for qualities are so weighed that
curiosity in neither can make choice of either's moiety.

KENT   Is not this your son, my lord?

GLOUCESTER   His breeding, sir, hath been at my charge.
I have so often blushed to acknowledge him that now
I am brazed to't.

KENT   I cannot conceive you.

GLOUCESTER   Sir, this young fellow's mother could;
whereupon she grew round-wombed, and had, indeed,
sir, a son for her cradle ere she had a husband for her
bed. Do you smell a fault?

KENT   I cannot wish the fault undone, the issue of it
being so proper.

GLOUCESTER   But I have a son, sir, by order of law,
some year elder than this, who yet is no dearer in my
account. Though this knave came something saucily to
the world before he was sent for, yet was his mother
fair, there was good sport at his making, and the
whoreson must be acknowledged. Do you know this
noble gentleman, Edmund?

EDMUND   No, my lord.

GLOUCESTER [*to Edmund*]   My lord of Kent: remember
him hereafter, as my honourable friend.

EDMUND   My services to your lordship.

KENT   I must love you, and sue to know you better.

EDMUND [*to Kent*]   Sir, I shall study deserving.

GLOUCESTER   He hath been out nine years, and away he
shall again. The King is coming.

Sennet. Enter ^Q*one bearing a coronet, then*^Q LEAR,
CORNWALL, ALBANY, GONERIL, REGAN, CORDELIA
and Attendants.

LEAR
   Attend the lords of France and Burgundy, Gloucester.

GLOUCESTER   I shall, my lord.   ^F*Exit.*^F

LEAR   Meantime we shall express our darker purpose.
   ^FGive me^F the map there. Know ^Fthat^F we have divided
   In three our kingdom; and 'tis our fast intent
   To shake all cares and business from our age,
   Conferring them on younger strengths, ^Fwhile we
   Unburdened crawl toward death. Our son of Cornwall,
   And you, our no less loving son of Albany,
   We have this hour a constant will to publish
   Our daughters' several dowers, that future strife
   May be prevented now.^F
   The ^Qtwo great^Q princes, France and Burgundy,
   Great rivals in our youngest daughter's love,
   Long in our court have made their amorous sojourn,
   And here are to be answered. Tell me, my daughters –
   ^FSince now we will divest us both of rule,
   Interest of territory, cares of state –^F

Which of you shall we say doth love us most,
That we our largest bounty may extend
Where nature doth with merit challenge. – Goneril,
Our eldest born, speak first.

GONERIL
   Sir, I ^Qdo^Q love you more than word can wield the
      matter,
   Dearer than eyesight, space and liberty,
   Beyond what can be valued, rich or rare,
   No less than life, with grace, health, beauty, honour.
   As much as child e'er loved, or father found,
   A love that makes breath poor and speech unable,
   Beyond all manner of so much I love you.

CORDELIA [*aside*]
   What shall Cordelia speak? Love, and be silent.

LEAR   Of all these bounds, even from this line to this,
   With shadowy forests ^Fand with champaigns riched,
   With plenteous rivers^F and wide-skirted meads,
   We make thee lady. To thine and Albany's issues
   Be this perpetual. – What says our second daughter,
   Our dearest Regan, wife of Cornwall? ^QSpeak.^Q

REGAN   ^QSir ^Q I am made of that self mettle as my sister,
   And prize me at her worth. In my true heart
   I find she names my very deed of love:
   Only she comes ^Ftoo^F short, that I profess
   Myself an enemy to all other joys
   Which the most precious square of sense possesses,
   And find I am alone felicitate
   In your dear highness' love.

CORDELIA [*aside*]   Then poor Cordelia,
   And yet not so, since I am sure my love's
   More ponderous than my tongue.

LEAR   To thee and thine hereditary ever
   Remain this ample third of our fair kingdom,
   No less in space, validity and pleasure
   Than that conferred on Goneril. – ^QBut^Q now our joy,
   Although our last and least, to whose young love
   ^FThe vines of France and milk of Burgundy
   Strive to be interessed,^F what can you say to draw
   A third more opulent than your sisters? ^FSpeak.^F

CORDELIA   Nothing, my lord.

^FLEAR   Nothing?

CORDELIA   Nothing.^F

LEAR
   ^QHow,^Q nothing will come of nothing. Speak again.

CORDELIA   Unhappy that I am, I cannot heave
   My heart into my mouth. I love your majesty
   According to my bond, no more nor less.

LEAR   How, how, ^FCordelia?^F Mend your speech a little,
   Lest you may mar your fortunes.

CORDELIA   Good my lord,
   You have begot me, bred me, loved me. I
   Return those duties back as are right fit,
   Obey you, love you and most honour you.
   Why have my sisters husbands, if they say
   They love you all? Haply when I shall wed,
   That lord whose hand must take my plight shall carry

Half my love with him, half my care and duty.
Sure I shall never marry like my sisters
ᵠTo love my father all.ᵠ

105 LEAR But goes thy heart with this?
CORDELIA Ay, my good lord.
LEAR So young and so untender?
CORDELIA So young, my lord, and true.
LEAR ᵠWellᵠ, let it be so. Thy truth then be thy dower,
110 For by the sacred radiance of the sun,
The mysteries of Hecate and the night,
By all the operation of the orbs
From whom we do exist and cease to be,
Here I disclaim all my paternal care,
115 Propinquity and property of blood,
And as a stranger to my heart and me
Hold thee from this for ever. The barbarous Scythian,
Or he that makes his generation messes
To gorge his appetite, shall ᶠto my bosomᶠ
120 Be as well neighboured, pitied and relieved,
As thou my sometime daughter.
KENT   Good my liege –
LEAR Peace, Kent,
Come not between the dragon and his wrath!
I loved her most, and thought to set my rest
On her kind nursery.
125 [*to Cordelia*]   Hence and avoid my sight.
So be my grave my peace, as here I give
Her father's heart from her. Call France. Who stirs?
Call Burgundy.   *Attendants rush off.*
              Cornwall and Albany,
With my two daughters' dowers, digest this third.
130 Let pride, which she calls plainness, marry her.
I do invest you jointly with my power,
Pre-eminence and all the large effects
That troop with majesty. Ourself by monthly course,
With reservation of an hundred knights
135 By you to be sustained, shall our abode
Make with you by due turn; only we shall retain
The name, and all th'addition to a king: the sway,
Revenue, execution of the rest,
Beloved sons, be yours; which to confirm,
This coronet part between you.
140 KENT   Royal Lear,
Whom I have ever honoured as my king,
Loved as my father, as my master followed,
As my great patron thought on in my prayers –
LEAR
The bow is bent and drawn; make from the shaft.
145 KENT Let it fall rather, though the fork invade
The region of my heart: be Kent unmannerly
When Lear is mad. What wouldst thou do, old man?
Think'st thou that duty shall have dread to speak,
When power to flattery bows? To plainness honour's
    bound
150 When majesty falls to folly. Reserve thy state,
And in thy best consideration check
This hideous rashness. Answer my life my judgement,

Thy youngest daughter does not love thee least,
Nor are those empty-hearted, whose low sounds
Reverb no hollowness.
155 LEAR   Kent, on thy life, no more.
KENT My life I never held but as ᵠaᵠ pawn
To wage against thine enemies, ne'er fear to lose it,
Thy safety being ᵠtheᵠ motive.
LEAR   Out of my sight!
KENT See better, Lear, and let me still remain
160 The true blank of thine eye.
LEAR Now by Apollo –
KENT   Now by Apollo, King,
Thou swear'st thy gods in vain.
LEAR   ᶠOᶠ vassal! Miscreant!
ᶠALBANY, CORNWALL Dear sir, forbear!ᶠ
KENT ᵠDo,ᵠ kill thy physician, and thy fee bestow
165 Upon the foul disease. Revoke thy gift,
Or whilst I can vent clamour from my throat
I'll tell thee thou dost evil.
LEAR Hear me, ᶠrecreant,ᶠ on thine allegiance, hear me:
That thou hast sought to make us break our vows,
170 Which we durst never yet, and with strained pride
To come betwixt our sentences and our power,
Which nor our nature, nor our place can bear,
Our potency made good, take thy reward.
Five days we do allot thee for provision,
175 To shield thee from disasters of the world,
And on the sixth to turn thy hated back
Upon our kingdom. If on the next day following
Thy banished trunk be found in our dominions,
The moment is thy death. Away! By Jupiter,
180 This shall not be revoked.
KENT
ᵠWhyᵠ, fare thee well, King; since thus thou wilt
    appear,
Freedom lives hence and banishment is here.
[*to Cordelia*] The gods to their dear shelter take thee,
    maid,
That justly think'st and hast most rightly said;
[*to Goneril and Regan*] And your large speeches may
    your deeds approve,
185 That good effects may spring from words of love.
Thus Kent, O princes, bids you all adieu;
He'll shape his old course in a country new. ᶠ*Exit.*ᶠ

ᶠ*Flourish.*ᶠ *Enter* GLOUCESTER *with* FRANCE,
and BURGUNDY *and* ᶠ*Attendants.*ᶠ

CORNWALL
Here's France and Burgundy, my noble lord.
LEAR My lord of Burgundy, 190
We first address toward you, who with this king
Hath rivalled for our daughter. What in the least
Will you require in present dower with her,
Or cease your quest of love?
BURGUNDY   ᶠMostᶠ royal majesty,
I crave no more than hath your highness offered – 195
Nor will you tender less?

LEAR   Right noble Burgundy,
When she was dear to us, we did hold her so,
But now her price is fallen. Sir, there she stands:
If aught within that little-seeming substance,
200   Or all of it, with our displeasure pieced,
And nothing more, may fitly like your grace,
She's there, and she is yours.
BURGUNDY   I know no answer.
LEAR   �QSirQ, will you, with those infirmities she owes,
Unfriended, new adopted to our hate,
205   Dowered with our curse and strangered with our oath,
Take her or leave her?
BURGUNDY   Pardon me, royal sir;
Election makes not up in such conditions.
LEAR
Then leave her, sir, for, by the power that made me,
I tell you all her wealth. [*to France*] For you, great king,
210   I would not from your love make such a stray
To match you where I hate, therefore beseech you
T'avert your liking a more worthier way
Than on a wretch whom nature is ashamed
Almost t'acknowledge hers.
FRANCE   This is most strange,
215   That she who even but now was your ᵠbestᵠ object,
The argument of your praise, balm of your age,
The best, the dearest, should in this trice of time
Commit a thing so monstrous, to dismantle
So many folds of favour. Sure her offence
220   Must be of such unnatural degree
That monsters it, or your fore-vouched affection
Fall into taint, which to believe of her
Must be a faith that reason without miracle
Should never plant in me.
225   CORDELIA   I yet beseech your majesty,
If for I want that glib and oily art
To speak and purpose not – since what I well intend,
I'll do't before I speak – that you make known
It is no vicious blot, murder, or foulness,
30   No unchaste action or dishonoured step,
That hath deprived me of your grace and favour,
But even for want of that for which I am richer,
A still soliciting eye and such a tongue
That I am glad I have not – though not to have it
Hath lost me in your liking.
35   LEAR   ᵠ Go to, go to,ᵠ better thou
Hadst not been born than not to have pleased me better.
FRANCE   Is it ᵠno moreᵠ but this? – a tardiness in nature,
Which often leaves the history unspoke
That it intends to do? My lord of Burgundy,
40   What say you to the lady? Love's not love
When it is mingled with regards that stands
Aloof from th'entire point. Will you have her?
She is herself a dowry.
BURGUNDY   Royal King,
Give but that portion which yourself proposed,
And here I take Cordelia by the hand,
45   Duchess of Burgundy.

LEAR   Nothing. I have sworn, ꟳI am firm.ꟳ
BURGUNDY [*to Cordelia*]
I am sorry then you have so lost a father
That you must lose a husband.
CORDELIA   Peace be with Burgundy.
250   Since that respect and fortunes are his love,
I shall not be his wife.
FRANCE   Fairest Cordelia, that art most rich being poor,
Most choice forsaken and most loved despised,
Thee and thy virtues here I seize upon,
255   Be it lawful I take up what's cast away.
Gods, gods! 'Tis strange that from their cold'st neglect
My love should kindle to inflamed respect.
Thy dowerless daughter, King, thrown to my chance,
Is queen of us, of ours and our fair France.
260   Not all the dukes of waterish Burgundy
Can buy this unprized, precious maid of me.
Bid them farewell, Cordelia, though unkind;
Thou losest here a better where to find.
LEAR   Thou hast her, France; let her be thine, for we
265   Have no such daughter, nor shall ever see
That face of hers again. Therefore, be gone,
Without our grace, our love, our benison.
Come, noble Burgundy.
        ꟳFlourish.ꟳ Exeunt ᵠLear and Burgundyᵠ, Cornwall,
            Albany, Gloucester, Edmund and Attendants.
FRANCE   Bid farewell to your sisters.
270   CORDELIA   The jewels of our father, with washed eyes
Cordelia leaves you. I know you what you are,
And like a sister am most loath to call
Your faults as they are named. Love well our father.
To your professed bosoms I commit him,
275   But yet, alas, stood I within his grace
I would prefer him to a better place.
So farewell to you both.
REGAN   Prescribe not us our duty.
GONERIL   Let your study
Be to content your lord, who hath received you
280   At fortune's alms. You have obedience scanted,
And well are worth the want that you have wanted.
CORDELIA
Time shall unfold what plighted cunning hides,
Who covert faults at last with shame derides.
Well may you prosper.
FRANCE   Come, ꟳmyꟳ fair Cordelia.
                        Exeunt France and Cordelia.
285   GONERIL   Sister, it is not ᵠaᵠ little I have to say of what
most nearly appertains to us both. I think our father
will hence tonight.
REGAN   That's most certain, and with you. Next month
with us.
290   GONERIL   You see how full of changes his age is. The
observation we have made of it hath ᵠ not ᵠ been little.
He always loved our sister most, and with what poor
judgement he hath now cast her off appears too grossly.
REGAN   'Tis the infirmity of his age, yet he hath ever
295   but slenderly known himself.

GONERIL   The best and soundest of his time hath been
     but rash; then must we look from his age to receive not
     alone the imperfections of long-engrafted condition,
     but therewithal ᶠtheᶠ unruly waywardness that infirm
300 and choleric years bring with them.
REGAN   Such unconstant starts are we like to have from
     him as this of Kent's banishment.
GONERIL   There is further compliment of leave-taking
     between France and him. Pray ᶠyouᶠ let us hit together.
305 If our father carry authority with such disposition as
     he bears, this last surrender of his will but offend us.
REGAN   We shall further think of it.
GONERIL   We must do something, and i'the heat.

                                              Exeunt.

1.2   *Enter* EDMUND, *the Bastard, holding a letter.*

EDMUND   Thou, Nature, art my goddess; to thy law
     My services are bound. Wherefore should I
     Stand in the plague of custom, and permit
     The curiosity of nations to deprive me?
5   For that I am some twelve or fourteen moonshines
     Lag of a brother? Why bastard? Wherefore base?
     When my dimensions are as well compact,
     My mind as generous and my shape as true
     As honest madam's issue? Why brand they us
10   With base? With baseness, bastardy? ᶠBase, base?ᶠ
     Who in the lusty stealth of nature take
     More composition and fierce quality
     Than doth within a dull stale tired bed
     Go to the creating ᵠof ᵠ a whole tribe of fops
15   Got 'tween a sleep and wake. Well, then,
     Legitimate Edgar, I must have your land.
     Our father's love is to the bastard Edmund
     As to the legitimate. ᶠFine word, 'legitimate'!ᶠ
     Well, my legitimate, if this letter speed
20   And my invention thrive, Edmund the base
     Shall top the legitimate. I grow, I prosper:
     Now gods, stand up for bastards!

                     Enter GLOUCESTER.

GLOUCESTER
     Kent banished thus? and France in choler parted?
     And the King gone tonight? Prescribed his power,
25   Confined to exhibition? All this done
     Upon the gad? – Edmund, how now, what news?
EDMUND [*Pockets the letter.*]   So please your lordship,
     none.
GLOUCESTER   Why so earnestly seek you to put up that
30   letter?
EDMUND   I know no news, my lord.
GLOUCESTER   What paper were you reading?
EDMUND   Nothing, my lord.
GLOUCESTER   No? What needed then that terrible
35   dispatch of it into your pocket? The quality of nothing
     hath not such need to hide itself. Let's see. – Come, if
     it be nothing, I shall not need spectacles.

EDMUND   I beseech you, sir, pardon me. It is a letter
     from my brother that I have not all o'er-read; ᶠandᶠ for
     so much as I have perused, I find it not fit for your   40
     o'er-looking.
GLOUCESTER   Give me the letter, sir.
EDMUND   I shall offend, either to detain or give it. The
     contents, as in part I understand them, are too blame.
GLOUCESTER   Let's see, let's see.   45
EDMUND   I hope, for my brother's justification, he
     wrote this but as an essay, or taste of my virtue.
GLOUCESTER [ᶠ*Reads*ᶠ.] *This policy,* ᵛ*and reverence*ᵛ *of age,*
     makes the world bitter to the best of our times, keeps our
     fortunes from us till our oldness cannot relish them. I begin   50
     to find an idle and fond bondage in the oppression of aged
     tyranny, who sways not as it hath power, but as it is
     suffered. Come to me, that of this I may speak more. If our
     father would sleep till I waked him, you should enjoy half
     his revenue for ever and live the beloved of your brother.   55
     Edgar. Hum! Conspiracy! Sleep till I wake him, you
     should enjoy half his revenue – My son Edgar, had he a
     hand to write this? A heart and brain to breed it in?
     When came this to you? Who brought it?
EDMUND   It was not brought me, my lord, there's the   60
     cunning of it. I found it thrown in at the casement of
     my closet.
GLOUCESTER   You know the character to be your
     brother's?
EDMUND   If the matter were good, my lord, I durst   65
     swear it were his; but, in respect of that, I would fain
     think it were not.
GLOUCESTER   It is his?
EDMUND   It is his hand, my lord; but I hope his heart is
     not in the contents.   70
GLOUCESTER   Has he never before sounded you in this
     business?
EDMUND   Never, my lord. But I have heard him oft
     maintain it to be fit that, sons at perfect age and fathers
     declined, the father should be as ward to the son and   75
     the son manage his revenue.
GLOUCESTER   O villain, villain! His very opinion in the
     letter. Abhorred villain! Unnatural, detested, brutish
     villain – worse than brutish! Go, sirrah, seek him. I'll
     apprehend him. Abominable villain, where is he?   80
EDMUND   I do not well know, my lord. If it shall please
     you to suspend your indignation against my brother
     till you can derive from him better testimony of his
     intent, you should run a certain course; where, if you
     violently proceed against him, mistaking his purpose, it   85
     would make a great gap in your own honour and shake in
     pieces the heart of his obedience. I dare pawn down my
     life for him, ᶠthatᶠ he hath writ this to feel my affection to
     your honour and to no other pretence of danger.
GLOUCESTER   Think you so?   90
EDMUND   If your honour judge it meet, I will place you
     where you shall hear us confer of this and by an
     auricular assurance have your satisfaction, and that
     without any further delay than this very evening.

GLOUCESTER He cannot be such a monster. 95

ᵠEDMUND Nor is not, sure.

GLOUCESTER To his father, that so tenderly and entirely loves him. Heaven and earth!ᵠ Edmund, seek him out. Wind me into him, I pray you: frame the business after your own wisdom. I would unstate 100 myself to be in a due resolution.

EDMUND I will seek him, sir, presently, convey the business as I shall find means and acquaint you withal.

GLOUCESTER These late eclipses in the sun and moon portend no good to us. Though the wisdom of Nature 105 can reason ꜰitꜰ thus and thus, yet nature finds itself scourged by the sequent effects. Love cools, friendship falls off, brothers divide: in cities, mutinies; in countries, discord; ꜰinꜰ palaces, treason; ꜰandꜰ the bond cracked 'twixt son and father. ꜰThis villain of 110 mine comes under the prediction – there's son against father. The King falls from bias of nature – there's father against child. We have seen the best of our time. Machinations, hollowness, treachery and all ruinous disorders follow us disquietly to our graves.ꜰ Find out 115 this villain, Edmund; it shall lose thee nothing. Do it carefully. – And the noble and true-hearted Kent banished, his offence honesty! ꜰ'Tisꜰ strange, ᵠstrange!ᵠ ꜰExit.ꜰ

EDMUND This is the excellent foppery of the world, 120 that when we are sick in fortune, often the surfeits of our own behaviour, we make guilty of our disasters the sun, the moon and ᵠthe ᵠ stars, as if we were villains on necessity, fools by heavenly compulsion, knaves, thieves and treachers by spherical predominance; 125 drunkards, liars and adulterers by an enforced obedience of planetary influence; and all that we are evil in by a divine thrusting on. An admirable evasion of whoremaster man, to lay his goatish disposition on the charge of a star. My father compounded with my 130 mother under the dragon's tail and my nativity was under Ursa Major, so that it follows I am rough and lecherous. ᵠFut!ᵠ I should have been that I am had the maidenliest star in the firmament twinkled on my bastardizing. 135

Enter EDGAR.

Pat he comes, like the catastrophe of the old comedy. My cue is villainous melancholy, with a sigh like Tom o'Bedlam. – O, these eclipses do portend these divisions. ꜰFa, sol, la, mi.ꜰ

EDGAR How now, brother Edmund, what serious 40 contemplation are you in?

EDMUND I am thinking, brother, of a prediction I read this other day, what should follow these eclipses.

EDGAR Do you busy yourself with that?

EDMUND I promise you, the effects he writes of succeed 45 unhappily, ᵠ as of unnaturalness between the child and the parent, death, dearth, dissolutions of ancient amities, divisions in state, menaces and maledictions against King and nobles, needless diffidences,

banishment of friends, dissipation of cohorts, nuptial 150 breaches and I know not what.

EDGAR How long have you been a sectary astronomical?

EDMUND Come, come,ᵠ when saw you my father last?

EDGAR ᵠWhy,ᵠ the night gone by.

EDMUND Spake you with him? 155

EDGAR ꜰAy,ꜰ two hours together.

EDMUND Parted you in good terms? Found you no displeasure in him, by word nor countenance?

EDGAR None at all.

EDMUND Bethink yourself wherein you may have 160 offended him, and at my entreaty forbear his presence until some little time hath qualified the heat of his displeasure, which at this instant so rageth in him that with the mischief of your person it would scarcely allay. 165

EDGAR Some villain hath done me wrong.

EDMUND That's my fear. ꜰI pray you have a continent forbearance till the speed of his rage goes slower; and, as I say, retire with me to my lodging, from whence I will fitly bring you to hear my lord speak. Pray ye, go: 170 there's my key. If you do stir abroad, go armed.

EDGAR Armed, brother?ꜰ

EDMUND Brother, I advise you to the best, ᵠ go armed.ᵠ I am no honest man if there be any good meaning toward you. I have told you what I have seen and 175 heard – but faintly; nothing like the image and horror of it. Pray you, away!

EDGAR Shall I hear from you anon?

EDMUND I do serve you in this business. *Exit Edgar.*
A credulous father and a brother noble, 180
Whose nature is so far from doing harms
That he suspects none – on whose foolish honesty
My practices ride easy. I see the business.
Let me, if not by birth, have lands by wit;
All with me's meet that I can fashion fit. *Exit.* 185

1.3 *Enter* GONERIL *and* OSWALD, *her steward.*

GONERIL Did my father strike my gentleman for chiding of his fool?

OSWALD Ay, madam.

GONERIL By day and night he wrongs me. Every hour
He flashes into one gross crime or other 5
That sets us all at odds. I'll not endure it.
His knights grow riotous and himself upbraids us
On every trifle. When he returns from hunting,
I will not speak with him; say I am sick.
If you come slack of former services 10
You shall do well; the fault of it I'll answer.

[*Horns within*]

OSWALD He's coming, madam, I hear him.

GONERIL Put on what weary negligence you please,
You and your fellows; I'd have it come to question.
If he distaste it, let him to my sister, 15
Whose mind and mine I know in that are one,
ᵠNot to be overruled. Idle old man,

That still would manage those authorities
That he hath given away. Now, by my life,
20 Old fools are babes again and must be used
With checks as flatteries, when they are seen abused.^Q
Remember what I have said.

OSWALD   ^QVery ^Q well, madam.

GONERIL
And let his knights have colder looks among you.
What grows of it no matter; advise your fellows so.
25 ^QI would breed from hence occasions, and I shall,
That I may speak.^Q I'll write straight to my sister
To hold my ^Qvery^Q course. ^QGo,^Q prepare for dinner.
Exeunt.

1.4   *Enter* KENT, *disguised* .

KENT   If but as well I other accents borrow
That can my speech diffuse, my good intent
May carry through itself to that full issue
For which I razed my likeness. Now, banished Kent,
5 If thou canst serve where thou dost stand condemned,
^FSo may it come^F thy master whom thou lov'st
Shall find thee full of labours.

^FHorns within.^F Enter *Lear ^Fand^F*
four or more Knights as *^FAttendants.^F*

LEAR   Let me not stay a jot for dinner; go, get it ready.
Exit First Knight.
[*to Kent*] How now, what art thou?
10 KENT   A man, sir.
LEAR   What dost thou profess? What wouldst thou with
us?
KENT   I do profess to be no less than I seem; to serve
him truly that will put me in trust, to love him that is
15 honest, to converse with him that is wise and says little,
to fear judgement, to fight when I cannot choose – and
to eat no fish.
LEAR   What art thou?
KENT   A very honest-hearted fellow, and as poor as the
20 King.
LEAR   If thou be'st as poor for a subject as he's for a
king, thou art poor enough. What wouldst thou?
KENT   Service.
LEAR   Who wouldst thou serve?
25 KENT   You.
LEAR   Dost thou know me, fellow?
KENT   No, sir; but you have that in your countenance
which I would fain call master.
LEAR   What's that?
30 KENT   Authority.
LEAR   What services canst ^Fthou^F do?
KENT   I can keep honest counsel, ride, run, mar a
curious tale in telling it and deliver a plain message
bluntly. That which ordinary men are fit for I am
35 qualified in, and the best of me is diligence.
LEAR   How old art thou?

KENT   Not so young, ^Fsir^F, to love a woman for singing,
nor so old to dote on her for anything. I have years on
my back forty-eight.
LEAR   Follow me, thou shalt serve me; if I like thee no   40
worse after dinner, I will not part from thee yet.
Dinner, ho, dinner! Where's my knave, my fool? Go
you and call my fool hither.   *Exit Second Knight.*

Enter OSWALD.

You, ^Fyou^F, sirrah, where's my daughter?
OSWALD   So please you –   ^F*Exit.*^F   45
LEAR   What says the fellow there? Call the clotpoll back.
Exit Third Knight.
Where's my fool? Ho, I think the world's asleep.

Enter Third Knight.

How now, where's that mongrel?
3 KNIGHT   He says, my lord, your daughter is not well.
LEAR   Why came not the slave back to me when I called   50
him?
3 KNIGHT   Sir, he answered me in the roundest manner,
he would not.
LEAR   He would not?
3 KNIGHT   My lord, I know not what the matter is, but   55
to my judgement your highness is not entertained with
that ceremonious affection as you were wont. There's a
great abatement ^Fof kindness^F appears as well in the
general dependants as in the Duke himself also, and
your daughter.   60
LEAR   Ha? Sayst thou so?
3 KNIGHT   I beseech you pardon me, my lord, if I be
mistaken, for my duty cannot be silent when I think
your highness wronged.
LEAR   Thou but rememberest me of mine own   65
conception. I have perceived a most faint neglect of
late, which I have rather blamed as mine own jealous
curiosity than as a very pretence and purpose of
unkindness. I will look further into't. But where's my
fool? I have not seen him this two days.   70
3 KNIGHT   Since my young lady's going into France, sir,
the fool hath much pined away.
LEAR   No more of that, I have noted it ^Fwell^F. Go you
and tell my daughter I would speak with her.
Exit Third Knight.
Go you; call hither my fool.   *Exit Fourth Knight.*   75

^FEnter OSWALD.^F

O you, sir, you, come you hither, sir: who am I, sir?
OSWALD   My lady's father.
LEAR   My lady's father? My lord's knave, you whoreson
dog, you slave, you cur!
OSWALD   I am none of these, my lord, I beseech your   80
pardon.
LEAR   Do you bandy looks with me, you rascal?
[*Strikes him.*]
OSWALD   I'll not be strucken, my lord.

KENT [*Trips him.*]   Nor tripped neither, you base football
85   player.
LEAR   I thank thee, fellow. Thou serv'st me and I'll love
    thee.
KENT   Come, sir, ⌜arise, away,⌝ I'll teach you differences.
90   Away, away; if you will measure your lubber's length
    again, tarry; but away, ⌜go to,⌝ have you wisdom? ⌜So!⌝
    [*Pushes him out.*]
LEAR   Now, ⌜my⌝ friendly knave, I thank thee. There's
    earnest of thy service. [*Gives him money.*]

Enter Fool.

FOOL   Let me hire him too; [*to Kent, holding out his cap*]
95   here's my coxcomb.
LEAR   How now, my pretty knave, how dost thou?
FOOL [*to Kent*]   Sirrah, you were best take my coxcomb.
KENT   Why, fool?
FOOL   Why? For taking one's part that's out of favour.
100   Nay, an thou canst not smile as the wind sits, thou'lt
    catch cold shortly. There, take my coxcomb. Why, this
    fellow has banished two on's daughters and did the
    third a blessing against his will – if thou follow him,
    thou must needs wear my coxcomb. [*to Lear*] How now,
    nuncle? Would I had two coxcombs and two daughters.
105 LEAR   Why, my boy?
FOOL   If I gave them all my living, I'd keep my coxcombs
    myself. There's mine; beg another of thy daughters.
LEAR   Take heed, sirrah, the whip.
FOOL   Truth's a dog ᵒ that ᵒ must to kennel; he must be
110   whipped out, when the Lady Brach may stand by the
    fire and stink.
LEAR   A pestilent gall to me.
FOOL   Sirrah, I'll teach thee a speech.
LEAR   Do.
115 FOOL   Mark it, nuncle:
        Have more than thou showest,
        Speak less than thou knowest,
        Lend less than thou owest,
        Ride more than thou goest,
120   Learn more than thou trowest,
        Set less than thou throwest,
        Leave thy drink and thy whore
        And keep in-a-door,
        And thou shalt have more
125   Than two tens to a score.
KENT   This is nothing, fool.
FOOL   Then ⌜'tis⌝ like the breath of an unfee'd lawyer,
    you gave me nothing for't. [*to Lear*] Can you make no
    use of nothing, nuncle?
130 LEAR   Why no, boy; nothing can be made out of nothing.
FOOL [*to Kent*]   Prithee tell him, so much the rent of his
    land comes to; he will not believe a fool.
LEAR   A bitter fool.
FOOL   Dost ⌜thou⌝ know the difference, my boy, between
135   a bitter fool and a sweet one?
LEAR   No, lad, teach me.

ᵒFOOL
    That lord that counselled thee to give away thy land,
    Come place him here by me; do thou for him stand.
    The sweet and bitter fool will presently appear,
    The one in motley here, the other found out there.   140
LEAR   Dost thou call me fool, boy?
FOOL   All thy other titles thou hast given away; that
    thou wast born with.
KENT   This is not altogether fool, my lord.
FOOL   No, faith, lords and great men will not let me; if   145
    I had a monopoly out, they would have part on't; and
    ladies too, they will not let me have all the fool to
    myself, they'll be snatching.ᵒ Nuncle, give me an egg
    and I'll give thee two crowns.
LEAR   What two crowns shall they be?   150
FOOL   Why, after I have cut the egg i'the middle and eat
    up the meat, the two crowns of the egg. When thou
    clovest thy crown i'the middle and gav'st away both
    parts, thou bor'st thine ass on thy back o'er the dirt.
    Thou hadst little wit in thy bald crown when thou   155
    gav'st thy golden one away. If I speak like myself in
    this, let him be whipped that first finds it so.
    [*Sings.*]   Fools had ne'er less grace in a year,
        For wise men are grown foppish,
        And know not how their wits to wear,   160
        Their manners are so apish.
LEAR   When were you wont to be so full of songs, sirrah?
FOOL   I have used it, nuncle, e'er since thou mad'st thy
    daughters thy mothers; for when thou gav'st them the
    rod and putt'st down thine own breeches,   165
    [*Sings.*]   Then they for sudden joy did weep
        And I for sorrow sung,
        That such a king should play bo-peep,
        And go the fools among.
    Prithee, nuncle, keep a schoolmaster that can teach thy   170
    fool to lie; I would fain learn to lie.
LEAR   An you lie, ⌜sirrah,⌝ we'll have you whipped.
FOOL   I marvel what kin thou and thy daughters are.
    They'll have me whipped for speaking true, thou'lt
    have me whipped for lying, and sometimes I am   175
    whipped for holding my peace. I had rather be any
    kind o'thing than a fool, and yet I would not be
    thee, nuncle. Thou hast pared thy wit o'both sides
    and left nothing i'the middle. Here comes one o'the
    parings.   180

Enter GONERIL.

LEAR
    How now, daughter? What makes that frontlet on?
    ᵒMethinksᵒ you are too much of late i'the frown.
FOOL   Thou wast a pretty fellow when thou hadst no
    need to care for her frowning. Now thou art an O
    without a figure; I am better than thou art now. I am a   185
    fool, thou art nothing. [*to Goneril*] Yes, forsooth, I will
    hold my tongue; so your face bids me, though you say
    nothing. Mum, mum!

He that keeps nor crust nor crumb,
190   Weary of all, shall want some.
[Points to Lear.] That's a shelled peascod.
GONERIL   Not only, sir, this your all-licensed fool,
But other of your insolent retinue
Do hourly carp and quarrel, breaking forth
195   In rank and not to be endured riots. Sir,
I had thought by making this well known unto you
To have found a safe redress, but now grow fearful
By what yourself too late have spoke and done,
That you protect this course and put ᶠitᶠ on
200   By your allowance; which if you should, the fault
Would not scape censure, nor the redresses sleep,
Which in the tender of a wholesome weal
Might in their working do you that offence
Which else were shame, that then necessity
205   Will call discreet proceeding.
FOOL   For you know, nuncle,
      The hedge-sparrow fed the cuckoo so long
      That it's had it head bit off by it young.
So out went the candle and we were left darkling.
210   LEAR   Are you our daughter?
GONERIL   ᵠCome, sir,ᵠ
I would you would make use of your good wisdom,
Whereof I know you are fraught, and put away
These dispositions, which of late transport you
215   From what you rightly are.
FOOL   May not an ass know when the cart draws the
horse? Whoop, Jug, I love thee.
LEAR
Does any here know me? ᵠWhyᵠ, this is not Lear.
Does Lear walk thus, speak thus? Where are his eyes?
220   Either his notion weakens, ᵠorᵠ his discernings are
lethargied – Ha! ᵠsleeping orᵠ waking? ᵠSureᵠ 'tis not
so. Who is it that can tell me who I am?
ᶠFOOLᶠ Lear's shadow.
ᵠLEAR   I would learn that, for by the marks of
225   sovereignty, knowledge and reason, I should be false
persuaded I had daughters.
FOOL   Which they will make an obedient father.ᵠ
LEAR   Your name, fair gentlewoman?
GONERIL   This admiration, sir, is much o'the savour
230   Of other your new pranks. I do beseech you
ᶠToᶠ understand my purposes aright:
As you are old and reverend, should be wise.
Here do you keep a hundred knights and squires,
Men so disordered, so debauched and bold,
235   That this our court, infected with their manners,
Shows like a riotous inn. Epicurism and lust
Makes ᶠitᶠ more like a tavern or a brothel
Than a graced palace. The shame itself doth speak
For instant remedy. Be then desired,
240   By her that else will take the thing she begs,
A little to disquantity your train,
And the remainders that shall still depend
To be such men as may besort your age,
Which know themselves, and you.

LEAR   Darkness and devils!
Saddle my horses; call my train together.   245
Degenerate bastard, I'll not trouble thee:
Yet have I left a daughter.
GONERIL
You strike my people, and your disordered rabble
Make servants of their betters.

           Enter ALBANY.

LEAR
Woe that too late repents! – ᵠ O sir, are you come?ᵠ   250
Is it your will? Speak, sir. – Prepare my horses.
                Exit a Knight.
Ingratitude, thou marble-hearted fiend,
More hideous when thou show'st thee in a child
Than the sea-monster.
ᶠALBANY   Pray, sir, be patient.
LEARᶠ *[to Goneril]*   Detested kite, thou liest.   255
My train are men of choice and rarest parts
That all particulars of duty know,
And in the most exact regard support
The worships of their name. O most small fault,
How ugly didst thou in Cordelia show,   260
Which like an engine wrenched my frame of nature
From the fixed place, drew from my heart all love
And added to the gall. O Lear, Learᶠ, Learᶠ!
[striking his head] Beat at this gate that let thy folly in
And thy dear judgement out. Go, go, my people.   265
       Exeunt Kent, Knights and Attendants.
ALBANY   My lord, I am guiltless as I am ignorant
ᶠOf what hath moved you.ᶠ
LEAR   It may be so, my lord.
Hear, Nature, hear, dear goddess, ᶠhear ᶠ:
Suspend thy purpose if thou didst intend
To make this creature fruitful.   270
Into her womb convey sterility,
Dry up in her the organs of increase,
And from her derogate body never spring
A babe to honour her. If she must teem,
Create her child of spleen, that it may live   275
And be a thwart disnatured torment to her.
Let it stamp wrinkles in her brow of youth,
With cadent tears fret channels in her cheeks,
Turn all her mother's pains and benefits
To laughter and contempt, that she may feel   280
How sharper than a serpent's tooth it is
To have a thankless child. Away, away!
           ᶠExeuntᶠ *Lear and Fool.*
ALBANY   Now gods that we adore, whereof comes this?
GONERIL   Never afflict yourself to know more of it,
But let his disposition have that scope   285
As dotage gives it.

       ᶠ*Enter* LEARᶠ, *followed by the* Fool.

LEAR   What, fifty of my followers at a clap?
Within a fortnight?
ALBANY   What's the matter, sir?

LEAR
I'll tell thee. [*to Goneril*] Life and death, I am
ashamed

290 That thou hast power to shake my manhood thus,
That these hot tears, which break from me perforce,
Should make thee worth them. Blasts and fogs upon
ᶠthee ᶠ!
Th'untented woundings of a father's curse

295 Pierce every sense about thee. Old fond eyes,
Beweep this cause again, I'll pluck ye out,
And cast you with the waters that you loose
To temper clay. �QYea, is't come to this?ᵠ
ᶠHa? Let it be so.ᶠ I have another daughter,

300 Who I am sure is kind and comfortable:
When she shall hear this of thee, with her nails
She'll flay thy wolvish visage. Thou shalt find
That I'll resume the shape which thou dost think
I have cast off for ever. ᵠ Thou shalt, I warrant thee.ᵠ
                              ᶠ*Exit* ᶠ.

305 GONERIL   Do you mark that, ᵠmy lordᵠ ?
ALBANY   I cannot be so partial, Goneril,
To the great love I bear you –
GONERIL   ᶠPray you, content.ᶠ
ᵠCome, sir, no more.ᵠ ᶠWhat, Oswald, ho?ᶠ
[*to the Fool*] You, ᶠsir, ᶠ more knave than fool, after
your master.

310 FOOL   Nuncle Lear, nuncle Lear, tarry, ᵠandᵠ take the
fool with ᶠthee:ᶠ
                    A fox when one has caught her,
                    And such a daughter,
                    Should sure to the slaughter,
                    If my cap would buy a halter;

315   So the fool follows after.   ᶠ*Exit* ᶠ.
GONERIL
ᶠThis man hath had good counsel – a hundred
knights!
'Tis politic, and safe, to let him keep
At point a hundred knights! Yes, that on every dream,
Each buzz, each fancy, each complaint, dislike,

320 He may enguard his dotage with their powers
And hold our lives in mercy. Oswald, I say!ᶠ
ALBANY   Well, you may fear too far.
GONERIL   Safer than trust too far.
Let me still take away the harms I fear,
Not fear still to be taken. I know his heart;

325 What he hath uttered I have writ my sister.
If she sustain him and his hundred knights
When I have showed th'unfitness –ᶠ

                  ᶠ*Enter* OSWALD.ᶠ

ᵠOSWALD   Here, madam.ᵠ

330 GONERIL   ᶠHow now, Oswald?ᶠ What, have you writ
that letter to my sister?
OSWALD   Ay, madam.
GONERIL   Take you some company and away to horse.
Inform her full of my particular fear,

335 And thereto add such reasons of your own

As may compact it more. Get you gone,
And hasten your return.   *Exit Oswald.*
                    No, no, my lord,
This milky gentleness and course of yours,
Though I condemn not, yet, under pardon,
You are much more attasked for want of wisdom   340
Than praised for harmful mildness.
ALBANY
How far your eyes may pierce I cannot tell;
Striving to better, oft we mar what's well.
GONERIL   Nay then –
ALBANY   Well, well, th'event.   *Exeunt.*   345

1.5   *Enter* LEAR, ᶠKENT, *disguised, and* Fool.ᶠ

LEAR [*to Kent*]   Go you before to Gloucester with these
letters. Acquaint my daughter no further with anything
you know than comes from her demand out of the
letter. If your diligence be not speedy, I shall be there
afore you.   5
KENT   I will not sleep, my lord, till I have delivered your
letter.   *Exit.*
FOOL   If a man's brains were in's heels, were't not in
danger of kibes?
LEAR   Ay, boy.   10
FOOL   Then I prithee be merry; thy wit shall not go
slipshod.
LEAR   Ha, ha, ha.
FOOL   Shalt see thy other daughter will use thee kindly,
for though she's as like this as a crab's like an apple, yet   15
I can tell what I can tell.
LEAR   ᵠWhy,ᵠ what canst ᵠthouᵠ tell, ᵠmyᵠ boy?
FOOL   She will taste as like this as a crab does to a crab.
Thou canst ᵠnotᵠ tell why one's nose stands i'the
middle on's face?   20
LEAR   No.
FOOL   Why, to keep one's eyes of either side's nose, that
what a man cannot smell out he may spy into.
LEAR   I did her wrong.
FOOL   Canst tell how an oyster makes his shell?   25
LEAR   No.
FOOL   Nor I neither; but I can tell why a snail has a
house.
LEAR   Why?
FOOL   Why, to put's head in, not to give it away to his   30
daughters and leave his horns without a case.
LEAR   I will forget my nature: so kind a father! Be my
horses ready?
FOOL   Thy asses are gone about 'em. The reason why
the seven stars are no more than seven is a pretty   35
reason.
LEAR   Because they are not eight.
FOOL   Yes ᶠindeed,ᶠ thou wouldst make a good fool.
LEAR   To take't again perforce – monster ingratitude!
FOOL   If thou wert my fool, nuncle, I'd have thee beaten   40
for being old before thy time.
LEAR   How's that?

FOOL   Thou shouldst not have been old till thou hadst
been wise.

45 LEAR   O let me not be mad, ꟙnot madꟙ, sweet heaven! ꟚI
would not be mad.Ꟛ
Keep me in temper, I would not be mad.

Enter a Gentleman.

ꟙHow now,ꟙ are the horses ready?

GENTLEMAN   Ready, my lord.

50 LEAR   Come, boy.   Ꟛ *Exeunt* Ꟛ *Lear and Gentleman.*

FOOL
She that's a maid now, and laughs at my departure,
Shall not be a maid long, unless things be cut shorter.
                                                            Exit.

2.1   *Enter* EDMUND *and* CURAN, *severally.*

EDMUND   Save thee, Curan.

CURAN   And you, sir. I have been with your father and
given him notice that the Duke of Cornwall and
ꟙReganꟙ his Duchess will be here with him this
5   night.

EDMUND   How comes that?

CURAN   Nay, I know not. You have heard of the news
abroad? – I mean the whispered ones, for they are yet
but ear-bussing arguments.

10 EDMUND   Not I; pray you, what are they?

CURAN   Have you heard of no likely wars toward 'twixt
the ꟚtwoꟚ dukes of Cornwall and Albany?

EDMUND   Not a word.

CURAN   You may ꟙdoꟙ then in time. Fare you well, sir.
                                                            ꟙ*Exit.*ꟙ

EDMUND
15   The Duke be here tonight? The better – best!
This weaves itself perforce into my business.
My father hath set guard to take my brother,
And I have one thing of a queasy question
Which I must act. Briefness and fortune work!
20   Brother, a word; descend, brother, I say.

Enter EDGAR.

My father watches; O ꟙsirꟙ, fly this place!
Intelligence is given where you are hid:
You have now the good advantage of the night.
Have you not spoken 'gainst the Duke of Cornwall
        ꟚaughtꟚ? –
25   He's coming hither, now, i'the night, i'the haste,
And Regan with him. Have you nothing said
Upon his party 'gainst the Duke of Albany?
Advise yourself.

EDGAR   I am sure on't, not a word.

EDMUND   I hear my father coming – pardon me;
30   In cunning I must draw my sword upon you.
ꟙDraw,ꟙ seem to defend yourself; now quit you well.
[*loudly*] Yield, come before my father! Light, ho, here!
[*to Edgar*] Fly, brother, ꟚflyꟚ! [*loudly*] Torches,
torches! – [*to Edgar*] So farewell.   ꟙ*Exit Edgar.*ꟙ

Some blood drawn on me would beget opinion
Of my more fierce endeavour.   [*Cuts his arm.*]
                        I have seen drunkards   35
Do more than this in sport. Father, father!
Stop, stop, no help?

Enter GLOUCESTER ꟙ*and Servants, with torches.*ꟙ

GLOUCESTER   Now, Edmund, where's the villain?

EDMUND
Here stood he in the dark, his sharp sword out,
Mumbling of wicked charms, conjuring the moon
To standꟚ'sꟚ auspicious mistress.

GLOUCESTER   But where is he?   40

EDMUND   Look, sir, I bleed.

GLOUCESTER   Where is the villain, Edmund?

EDMUND
Fled this way, sir, when by no means he could –

GLOUCESTER [*to Servants*]
Pursue him, ꟙho!ꟙ Go after!   *Servants rush off.*
                    – 'By no means' what?

EDMUND   Persuade me to the murder of your lordship,
But that I told him the revenging gods   45
'Gainst parricides did all their thunders bend,
Spoke with how manifold and strong a bond
The child was bound to the father. Sir, in fine,
Seeing how loathly opposite I stood
To his unnatural purpose, in fell motion,   50
With his prepared sword, he charges home
My unprovided body, latched mine arm;
But when he saw my best alarumed spirits,
Bold in the quarrel's right, roused to th'encounter,
Or whether ghasted by the noise I made,   55
Full suddenly he fled.

GLOUCESTER   Let him fly far:
Not in this land shall he remain uncaught,
And found – dispatch! The noble Duke, my master,
My worthy arch and patron, comes tonight;
By his authority I will proclaim it,   60
That he which finds him shall deserve our thanks,
Bringing the murderous coward to the stake:
He that conceals him, death!

EDMUND   When I dissuaded him from his intent,
And found him pight to do it, with curst speech   65
I threatened to discover him. He replied,
'Thou unpossessing bastard, dost thou think,
If I would stand against thee, would the reposal
Of any trust, virtue or worth in thee
Make thy words faithed? No, what I should deny,   70
As this I would, Ꟛay,Ꟛ though thou didst produce
My very character, I'd turn it all
To thy suggestion, plot and damned practice;
And thou must make a dullard of the world
If they not thought the profits of my death   75
Were very pregnant and potential spurs
To make thee seek it.'   [ꟙ*Tucket within*ꟙ]

GLOUCESTER   ꟙOꟙ strange and fastened villain,
Would he deny his letter, ꟙsaid he?ꟙ ꟚI never got him.Ꟛ

Hark, the Duke's trumpets; I know not why he comes.
All ports I'll bar, the villain shall not scape;
The Duke must grant me that. Besides, his picture
I will send far and near, that all the kingdom
May have ᶠdueᶠ note of him; and of my land,
Loyal and natural boy, I'll work the means
To make thee capable.

Enter CORNWALL, ᶠREGAN *and Attendants.*ᶠ

CORNWALL
How now, my noble friend? Since I came hither,
Which I can call but now, I have heard strange news.
REGAN   If it be true, all vengeance comes too short
Which can pursue th'offender. How dost, my lord?
GLOUCESTER
ᶠOᶠ madam, my old heart is cracked, it's cracked.
REGAN   What, did my father's godson seek your life?
He whom my father named, your Edgar?
GLOUCESTER   O lady, lady, shame would have it hid.
REGAN
Was he not companion with the riotous knights
That tended upon my father?
GLOUCESTER   I know not, madam; 'tis too bad, too bad.
EDMUND   Yes, madam, he was ᶠof that consortᶠ.
REGAN   No marvel, then, though he were ill affected.
'Tis they have put him on the old man's death,
To have th'expense and waste of his revenues.
I have this present evening from my sister
Been well informed of them, and with such cautions
That if they come to sojourn at my house
I'll not be there.
CORNWALL   Nor I, assure thee, Regan.
Edmund, I hear that you have shown your father
A child-like office.
EDMUND   It was my duty, sir.
GLOUCESTER [*to Cornwall*]
He did bewray his practice, and received
This hurt you see, striving to apprehend him.
CORNWALL   Is he pursued?
GLOUCESTER   Ay, my good lord.
CORNWALL   If he be taken, he shall never more
Be feared of doing harm. Make your own purpose
How in my strength you please. For you, Edmund,
Whose virtue and obedience doth this instant
So much commend itself, you shall be ours.
Natures of such deep trust we shall much need;
You we first seize on.
EDMUND   I shall serve you, ᶠsirᶠ, truly, however else.
GLOUCESTER   For him I thank your grace.
CORNWALL   You know not why we came to visit you?
REGAN   Thus out of season, threading dark-eyed night?
Occasions, noble Gloucester, of some poise
Wherein we must have use of your advice.
Our father he hath writ, so hath our sister,
Of differences, which I best thought it fit
To answer from our home. The several messengers
From hence attend dispatch. Our good old friend,

Lay comforts to your bosom, and bestow
Your needful counsel to our business,
Which craves the instant use.
GLOUCESTER   I serve you, madam.
Your graces are right welcome.   *Exeunt.* ᶠ*Flourish.*ᶠ

2.2   *Enter* KENT, *disguised, and*
                              OSWALD, ᶠ*severally.*ᶠ

OSWALD   Good dawning to thee, friend. Art of this
house?
KENT   Ay.
OSWALD   Where may we set our horses?
KENT   I'the mire.
OSWALD   Prithee, if thou lov'st me, tell me.
KENT   I love thee not.
OSWALD   Why then, I care not for thee.
KENT   If I had thee in Lipsbury pinfold, I would make
thee care for me.
OSWALD   Why dost thou use me thus? I know thee not.
KENT   Fellow, I know thee.
OSWALD   What dost thou know me for?
KENT   A knave, a rascal, an eater of broken meats; a base,
proud,   shallow,   beggarly,   three-suited-hundred-
pound,   filthy,   worsted-stocking knave; a lily-livered,
action-taking ᑫknave, aᑫ whoreson, glass-gazing, super-
serviceable, finical rogue; one trunk-inheriting slave,
one that wouldst be a bawd in way of good service and
art nothing but the composition of a knave, beggar,
coward, pander and the son and heir of a mongrel
bitch; ᶠoneᶠ whom I will beat into clamorous whining if
thou deniest the least syllable of thy addition.
OSWALD   ᶠWhy,ᶠ what a monstrous fellow art thou, thus
to rail on one that is neither known of thee, nor knows
thee!
KENT   What a brazen-faced varlet art thou to deny thou
knowest me? Is it two days ᑫ agoᑫ since I tripped up thy
heels and beat thee before the King? Draw, you rogue,
for though it be night, ᶠyetᶠ the moon shines. [*Draws his
sword.*] I'll make a sop o'the moonshine of you. ᑫDraw,ᑫ
you whoreson cullionly barber-monger! Draw!
OSWALD   Away, I have nothing to do with thee.
KENT   Draw, you rascal! You come with letters against
the King, and take Vanity the puppet's part against the
royalty of her father. Draw, you rogue, or I'll so
carbonado your shanks! – draw, you rascal, come your
ways!
OSWALD   Help, ho! Murder, help!
KENT   Strike, you slave. Stand, rogue, stand you neat
slave, strike! [*Beats him.*]
OSWALD   Help, ho! Murder, murder!

Enter EDMUND, ᑫ*with his rapier drawn,*ᑫ CORNWALL,
REGAN, GLOUCESTER *and* ᶠ*Servants.*ᶠ

EDMUND   How now, what's the matter? ᶠPart!ᶠ
KENT [*to Edmund*]   With you, goodman boy, if you
please. Come, I'll flesh ye; come on, young master.

GLOUCESTER Weapons? Arms? What's the matter here?

CORNWALL Keep peace upon your lives: he dies that strikes again. What is the matter?

50 REGAN The messengers from our sister and the King.

CORNWALL [*to Kent*] What is your difference? Speak.

OSWALD I am scarce in breath, my lord.

KENT No marvel, you have so bestirred your valour, you cowardly rascal; nature disclaims in thee – a tailor
55 made thee.

CORNWALL Thou art a strange fellow – a tailor make a man?

KENT ^QAy,^Q a tailor, sir; a stone-cutter or a painter could not have made him so ill, though they had been but
60 two years o'the trade.

CORNWALL [*to Oswald*] Speak yet: how grew your quarrel?

OSWALD This ancient ruffian, sir, whose life I have spared at suit of his grey beard –

65 KENT Thou whoreson zed, thou unnecessary letter! – My lord, if you will give me leave, I will tread this unbolted villain into mortar and daub the wall of a jakes with him. [*to Oswald*] Spare my grey beard, you wagtail?

70 CORNWALL Peace, sirrah. You beastly knave, know you no reverence?

KENT Yes, sir, but anger hath a privilege.

CORNWALL Why art thou angry?

KENT That such a slave as this should wear a sword,
75 Who wears no honesty. Such smiling rogues as these
Like rats oft bite the ⌐holy⌐ cords atwain
Which are too intrince t'unloose; smooth every
   passion
That in the natures of their lords rebel,
Bring oil to fire, snow to their colder moods,
80 Renege, affirm and turn their halcyon beaks
With every gale and vary of their masters,
Knowing naught, like dogs, but following.
[*to Oswald*] A plague upon your epileptic visage.
Smile you my speeches as I were a fool?
85 Goose, if I had you upon Sarum plain,
I'd drive ye cackling home to Camelot.

CORNWALL What, art thou mad, old fellow?

GLOUCESTER How fell you out, say that.

KENT No contraries hold more antipathy
90 Than I and such a knave.

CORNWALL
Why dost thou call him knave? What is his fault?

KENT His countenance likes me not.

CORNWALL
No more perchance does mine, nor his, nor hers.

KENT Sir, 'tis my occupation to be plain:
95 I have seen better faces in my time
Than stands on any shoulder that I see
Before me at this instant.

CORNWALL   This is some fellow
Who, having been praised for bluntness, doth affect

A saucy roughness and constrains the garb
Quite from his nature. He cannot flatter, he; 100
An honest mind and plain, he must speak truth;
An they will take it, so; if not, he's plain.
These kind of knaves I know, which in this plainness
Harbour more craft and more corrupter ends
Than twenty silly-ducking observants 105
That stretch their duties nicely.

KENT Sir, in good faith, ^Qor^Q in sincere verity,
Under th'allowance of your great aspect,
Whose influence, like the wreath of radiant fire
On flickering Phoebus' front –

CORNWALL   What mean'st ^Qthou^Q by this? 110

KENT To go out of my dialect, which you discommend
so much. I know, sir, I am no flatterer. He that beguiled
you in a plain accent was a plain knave, which for my
part I will not be, though I should win your displeasure
to entreat me to't. 115

CORNWALL [*to Oswald*] What was th'offence you gave
him?

OSWALD I never gave him any.
It pleased the King his master very late
To strike at me upon his misconstruction, 120
When he, compact and flattering his displeasure,
Tripped me behind; being down, insulted, railed
And put upon him such a deal of man
That worthied him, got praises of the King
For him attempting who was self-subdued; 125
And in the fleshment of this dread exploit
Drew on me here again.

KENT   None of these rogues and cowards
But Ajax is their fool.

CORNWALL   Fetch forth the stocks, ^Qho^Q!
                         Exeunt one or two Servants.
You stubborn, ancient knave, you reverend braggart,
We'll teach you.

KENT   ⌐Sir,⌐ I am too old to learn. 130
Call not your stocks for me; I serve the King,
On whose employment I was sent to you.
You shall do small respect, show too bold malice
Against the grace and person of my master,
Stocking his messenger.

CORNWALL   Fetch forth the stocks! 135
As I have life and honour, there shall he sit till noon.

REGAN
Till noon? Till night, my lord, and all night too.

KENT Why, madam, if I were your father's dog
You should not use me so.

REGAN   Sir, being his knave, I will.
[⌐*Stocks brought out.*⌐]

CORNWALL This is a fellow of the selfsame colour 140
Our sister speaks of. – Come, bring away the stocks.

GLOUCESTER Let me beseech your grace not to do so.
^QHis fault is much, and the good King, his master,
Will check him for't. Your purposed low correction
Is such as basest and contemnedst wretches 145
For pilferings and most common trespasses

Are punished with.ᵠ

The King, ᶠhis master, needs ᶠ must take it ill

That he, so slightly valued in his messenger,

Should have him thus restrained.

150 CORNWALL   I'll answer that.

REGAN   My sister may receive it much more worse

To have her gentleman abused, assaulted,

ᵠFor following her affairs. Put in his legs.ᵠ

     [*Kent is put in the stocks.*]

ᶠCORNWALLᶠ   Come, my ᵠgoodᵠ lord, away.

           ᶠ*Exeunt*ᶠ *all but Gloucester and Kent.*

GLOUCESTER

155 I am sorry for thee, friend; 'tis the Duke's pleasure,

Whose disposition all the world well knows

Will not be rubbed nor stopped. I'll entreat for thee.

KENT

Pray ᵠ youᵠ do not, sir. I have watched and travelled

    hard.

Some time I shall sleep out, the rest I'll whistle.

160 A good man's fortune may grow out at heels.

Give you good morrow.

GLOUCESTER

The Duke's too blame in this; 'twill be ill taken.

                        ᶠ*Exit.*ᶠ

KENT   Good King, that must approve the common saw,

Thou out of heaven's benediction com'st

165 To the warm sun.

Approach, thou beacon to this under-globe,

That by thy comfortable beams I may

Peruse this letter. Nothing almost sees miracles

But misery. I know 'tis from Cordelia,

170 Who hath most fortunately been informed

Of my obscured course, [*reading the letter*] *and shall*

    find time

From this enormous state, seeking to give

Losses their remedies. All weary and o'erwatched,

Take vantage, heavy eyes, not to behold

175 This shameful lodging.

Fortune, good night: smile once more; turn thy wheel.

     [ᵠ*Sleeps.*ᵠ]

          Enter EDGAR.   [2.3]

EDGAR   I heard myself proclaimed,

And by the happy hollow of a tree

180 Escaped the hunt. No port is free, no place

That guard and most unusual vigilance

Does not attend my taking. While I may scape

I will preserve myself, and am bethought

To take the basest and most poorest shape

185 That ever penury in contempt of man

Brought near to beast. My face I'll grime with filth,

Blanket my loins, elf all my hair in knots

And with presented nakedness outface

The winds and persecutions of the sky.

The country gives me proof and precedent

190 Of Bedlam beggars, who, with roaring voices,

Strike in their numbed ᶠandᶠ mortified ᵠbareᵠ arms

Pins, wooden pricks, nails, sprigs of rosemary;

And with this horrible object, from low farms,

Poor pelting villages, sheepcotes and mills,

Sometime with lunatic bans, sometime with prayers,   195

Enforce their charity. Poor Turlygod, poor Tom,

That's something yet: Edgar I nothing am.   *Exit.*

    Enter LEAR, ᶠ*Fool and a* Knight.ᶠ   [2.4]

LEAR

'Tis strange that they should so depart from home

And not send back my messenger.

KNIGHT   As I learned,

The night before there was no purpose ᶠin themᶠ   200

Of this remove.

KENT [*Wakes.*]   Hail to thee, noble master.

LEAR   Ha? Mak'st thou this shame thy pastime?

ᶠKENT   No, my lord.ᶠ

FOOL   Ha, ha, ᵠlookᵠ, he wears cruel garters. Horses are

tied by the heads, dogs and bears by the neck, monkeys

by the loins and men by the legs. When a man's   205

overlusty at legs, then he wears wooden nether-stocks.

LEAR [*to Kent*]

What's he that hath so much thy place mistook

To set thee here?

KENT   It is both he and she,

Your son and daughter.

LEAR   No.   210

KENT   Yes.

LEAR   No, I say.

KENT   I say, yea.

ᵠLEAR   No, no, they would not.

KENT   Yes, they have.ᵠ   215

LEAR   By Jupiter, I swear no.

ᶠKENT   By Juno, I swear ay.

LEARᶠ   They durst not do't:

They could not, would not do't – 'tis worse than murder

To do upon respect such violent outrage.

Resolve me with all modest haste which way   220

Thou mightst deserve or they impose this usage,

Coming from us.

KENT   My lord, when at their home

I did commend your highness' letters to them,

Ere I was risen from the place that showed

My duty kneeling, came there a reeking post,   225

Stewed in his haste, half breathless, panting forth

From Goneril, his mistress, salutations;

Delivered letters, spite of intermission,

Which presently they read; on those contents

They summoned up their meiny, straight took horse,   230

Commanded me to follow and attend

The leisure of their answer, gave me cold looks;

And meeting here the other messenger,

Whose welcome I perceived had poisoned mine,

Being the very fellow which of late   235

Displayed so saucily against your highness,

Having more man than wit about me, drew.

He raised the house with loud and coward cries.

240 Your son and daughter found this trespass worth
The shame which here it suffers.

ᶠFOOL Winter's not gone yet, if the wild geese fly that
way.

Fathers that wear rags
Do make their children blind,
245 But fathers that bear bags
Shall see their children kind:
Fortune, that arrant whore,
Ne'er turns the key to the poor.
But for all this thou shalt have as many dolours for thy
250 daughters as thou canst tell in a year.ᶠ

LEAR O, how this mother swells up toward my heart!
Hysterica passio, down, thou climbing sorrow,
Thy element's below. Where is this daughter?

KENT With the Earl, sir, ᶠhereᶠ within.

255 LEAR Follow me not; stay here. ᶠ*Exit.*ᶠ

KNIGHT Made you no more offence but what you speak
of?

KENT None. How chance the King comes with so small
a number?

260 FOOL An thou hadst been set i'the stocks for that
question, thou hadst well deserved it.

KENT Why, fool?

FOOL We'll set thee to school to an ant, to teach thee
there's no labouring i'the winter. All that follow their
265 noses are led by their eyes but blind men, and there's
not a nose among twenty but can smell him that's
stinking. Let go thy hold when a great wheel runs
down a hill lest it break thy neck with following ᵠitᵠ;
but the great one that goes upward, let him draw thee
270 after. When a wise man gives thee better counsel give
me mine again; I would have none but knaves follow it,
since a fool gives it.

That sir which serves ᶠand seeksᶠ for gain,
And follows but for form,
275 Will pack when it begins to rain,
And leave thee in the storm;
But I will tarry; the fool will stay,
And let the wise man fly:
The knave turns fool that runs away,
280 The fool no knave perdy.

KENT Where learned you this, fool?

FOOL Not i'the stocks, ᶠfool.ᶠ

Enter LEAR *and* GLOUCESTER.

LEAR
Deny to speak with me? They are sick, they are weary,
They ᶠhaveᶠ travelled all the night? – mere fetches ᵠayᵠ,
285 The images of revolt and flying off.
Fetch me a better answer.

GLOUCESTER My dear lord,
You know the fiery quality of the Duke,
How unremovable and fixed he is
In his own course.

290 LEAR Vengeance, plague, death, confusion!
Fiery? What quality? Why, Gloucester, Gloucester,

I'd speak with the Duke of Cornwall and his wife.

ᶠGLOUCESTER
Well, my good lord, I have informed them so.

LEAR
'Informed them'? Dost thou understand me, man?ᶠ

GLOUCESTER Ay, my good lord. 295

LEAR
The King would speak with Cornwall, the dear father
Would with his daughter speak, commands – tends
– service.
ᶠAre they 'informed' of this? My breath and blood!
'Fiery'?ᶠ The fiery Duke, tell the hot Duke that ᵠLearᵠ –
No, but not yet, maybe he is not well; 300
Infirmity doth still neglect all office
Whereto our health is bound. We are not ourselves
When nature, being oppressed, commands the mind
To suffer with the body. I'll forbear,
And am fallen out with my more headier will 305
To take the indisposed and sickly fit
For the sound man. [*Notices Kent.*]
Death on my state! Wherefore
Should he sit here? This act persuades me
That this remotion of the Duke and her
Is practice only. Give me my servant forth. 310
ᶠGoᶠ tell the Duke and's wife I'd speak with them,
Now, presently: bid them come forth and hear me,
Or at their chamber door I'll beat the drum
Till it cry sleep to death.

GLOUCESTER I would have all well betwixt you. 315
ᶠ*Exit.*ᶠ

LEAR O ᶠme,ᶠ my heart! My ᶠrisingᶠ heart! ᶠBut down!

FOOL Cry to it, nuncle, as the cockney did to the eels
when she put 'em i'the paste alive: she knapped 'em
o'the coxcombs with a stick, and cried 'Down, wantons,
down!' 'Twas her brother that in pure kindness to his 320
horse buttered his hay.

Enter CORNWALL, REGAN, ᶠGLOUCESTER
*and Servants.*ᶠ

LEAR Good morrow to you both.

CORNWALL Hail to your grace.
[ᶠ*Kent here set at liberty.*ᶠ]

REGAN I am glad to see your highness.

LEAR Regan, I think you are. I know what reason
I have to think so. If thou shouldst not be glad, 325
I would divorce me from thy mother's tomb,
Sepulchring an adultress. [*to Kent*] O, are you free?
Some other time for that. – Beloved Regan,
Thy sister's naught. O, Regan, she hath tied
Sharp-toothed unkindness, like a vulture, here. 330
[*Lays his hand on his heart.*]
I can scarce speak to thee; thou'lt not believe
With how depraved a quality – O, Regan!

REGAN I pray ᶠyou,ᶠ sir, take patience. I have hope
You less know how to value her desert
Than she to scant her duty.

ᶠLEAR Say? how is that? 335

REGAN   I cannot think my sister in the least
   Would fail her obligation. If, sir, perchance
   She have restrained the riots of your followers,
   'Tis on such ground and to such wholesome end
340   As clears her from all blame.ᶠ
   LEAR   My curses on her.
   REGAN   O, sir, you are old:
   Nature in you stands on the very verge
   Of her confine. You should be ruled and led
   By some discretion that discerns your state
345   Better than you yourself. Therefore I pray ᶠyouᶠ
   That to our sister you do make return;
   Say you have wronged her, ᵠsir.ᵠ
   LEAR   Ask her forgiveness?
   Do you ᶠbut ᶠ mark how this becomes the house?
   [*Kneels.*] Dear daughter, I confess that I am old;
350   Age is unnecessary. On my knees I beg
   That you'll vouchsafe me raiment, bed and food.
   REGAN   Good sir, no more. These are unsightly tricks.
   Return you to my sister.
   LEAR [*Rises.*]   Never, Regan:
   She hath abated me of half my train,
355   Looked black upon me, struck me with her tongue
   Most serpent-like, upon the very heart.
   All the stored vengeances of heaven fall
   On her ingrateful top! Strike her young bones,
   You taking airs, with lameness!
   CORNWALL   Fie, sir, fie!
   ᶠLEARᶠ
360   You nimble lightnings, dart your blinding flames
   Into her scornful eyes! Infect her beauty,
   You fen-sucked fogs, drawn by the powerful sun
   To fall and blister!
   REGAN   O, the blest gods!
   So will you wish on me when the rash mood ᶠis on.ᶠ
365   LEAR   No, Regan, thou shalt never have my curse.
   Thy tender-hafted nature shall not give
   Thee o'er to harshness. Her eyes are fierce, but thine
   Do comfort and not burn. 'Tis not in thee
   To grudge my pleasures, to cut off my train,
370   To bandy hasty words, to scant my sizes
   And, in conclusion, to oppose the bolt
   Against my coming in. Thou better knowst
   The offices of nature, bond of childhood,
   Effects of courtesy, dues of gratitude.
375   Thy half o'the kingdom hast thou not forgot,
   Wherein I thee endowed.
   REGAN   Good sir, to the purpose
              [ᶠ*Tucket within*ᶠ]
   LEAR   Who put my man i'the stocks?

Enter OSWALD.

   CORNWALL   What trumpet's that?
   REGAN   I know't, my sister's. This approves her letter
   That she would soon be here.
   [*to Oswald*]   Is your lady come?
380   LEAR   This is a slave whose easy borrowed pride

   Dwells in the fickle grace of her he follows.
   Out, varlet, from my sight!
   CORNWALL   What means your grace?

Enter GONERIL.

   LEAR
   Who stocked my servant? Regan, I have good hope
   Thou didst not know on't. Who comes here? O
      heavens!
   If you do love old men, if your sweet sway   385
   Allow obedience, if ᶠyouᶠ yourselves are old,
   Make it your cause. Send down, and take my part!
   [*to Goneril*] Art not ashamed to look upon this beard?
   O, Regan, will you take her by the hand?
   GONERIL
   Why not by the hand, sir? How have I offended?   390
   All's not offence that indiscretion finds
   And dotage terms so.
   LEAR   O sides, you are too tough!
   Will you yet hold? How came my man i'the stocks?
   CORNWALL   I set him there, sir; but his own disorders
   Deserved much less advancement.
   LEAR   You? Did you?   395
   REGAN   I pray you, father, being weak, seem so.
   If till the expiration of your month
   You will return and sojourn with my sister,
   Dismissing half your train, come then to me.
   I am now from home and out of that provision   400
   Which shall be needful for your entertainment.
   LEAR   Return to her? And fifty men dismissed?
   No! Rather I abjure all roofs and choose
   To wage against the enmity o'th' air –
   To be a comrade with the wolf and owl –   405
   Necessity's sharp pinch! Return with her?
   Why, the hot-blooded France, that dowerless took
   Our youngest born, I could as well be brought
   To knee his throne and squire-like pension beg,
   To keep base life afoot. Return with her?   410
   Persuade me rather to be slave and sumpter
   To this detested groom.   [*Points at Oswald.*]
   GONERIL   At your choice, sir.
   LEAR
   ᵠNowᵠ I prithee, daughter, do not make me mad:
   I will not trouble thee, my child. Farewell:
   We'll no more meet, no more see one another.   415
   But yet thou art my flesh, my blood, my daughter,
   Or rather a disease that's in my flesh,
   Which I must needs call mine. Thou art a boil,
   A plague sore, or embossed carbuncle
   In my corrupted blood. But I'll not chide thee: 420
   Let shame come when it will; I do not call it,
   I do not bid the thunder-bearer shoot,
   Nor tell tales of thee to high-judging Jove.
   Mend when thou canst, be better at thy leisure:
   I can be patient, I can stay with Regan,   425
   I and my hundred knights.
   REGAN   Not altogether so, ᵠsirᵠ.

I looked not for you yet, nor am provided
For your fit welcome. Give ear, sir, to my sister;
For those that mingle reason with your passion
430 Must be content to think you ᵒareᵒ old, and so –
But she knows what she does.
LEAR   Is this well spoken ᵒnowᵒ?
REGAN   I dare avouch it, sir. What, fifty followers?
Is it not well? What should you need of more?
Yea, or so many, sith that both charge and danger
435 Speak 'gainst so great a number? How in one house
Should many people, under two commands,
Hold amity? 'Tis hard, almost impossible.
GONERIL
Why might not you, my lord, receive attendance
From those that she calls servants or from mine?
REGAN
440 Why not, my lord? If then they chanced to slack ye
We could control them. If you will come to me –
For now I spy a danger – I entreat you
To bring but five and twenty: to no more
Will I give place or notice.
LEAR   I gave you all –
445 REGAN   And in good time you gave it.
LEAR   – Made you my guardians, my depositaries,
But kept a reservation to be followed
With such a number. What, must I come to you
With five and twenty? Regan, said you so?
450 REGAN   And speak't again, my lord: no more with me.
LEAR
Those wicked creatures yet do look well favoured
When others are more wicked; not being the worst
Stands in some rank of praise.
[*to Goneril*]   I'll go with thee;
Thy fifty yet doth double five and twenty,
And thou art twice her love.
455 GONERIL   Hear me, my lord:
What need you five and twenty? Ten? Or five?
To follow in a house where twice so many
Have a command to tend you?
REGAN   What need one?
LEAR   O, reason not the need! Our basest beggars
460 Are in the poorest thing superfluous;
Allow not nature more than nature needs,
Man's life is cheap as beast's. Thou art a lady;
If only to go warm were gorgeous,
Why, nature needs not what thou gorgeous wear'st,
465 Which scarcely keeps thee warm. But for true need –
You heavens, give me that patience, patience I need!
You see me here, you gods, a poor old man,
As full of grief as age, wretched in both:
If it be you that stirs these daughters' hearts
470 Against their father, fool me not so much
To bear it tamely; touch me with noble anger,
And let not women's weapons, water-drops,
Stain my man's cheeks. No, you unnatural hags,
I will have such revenges on you both
475 That all the world shall – I will do such things –

What they are yet I know not, but they shall be
The terrors of the earth! You think I'll weep,
No, I'll not weep.   [ᶠ*Storm and tempest*ᶠ]
I have full cause of weeping, but this heart
Shall break into a hundred thousand flaws   480
Or e'er I'll weep. O fool, I shall go mad.
        Exeunt ᵒ*Lear, Gloucester, Kent, Fool* ᵒ *and Knight.*
CORNWALL   Let us withdraw; 'twill be a storm.
REGAN   This house is little; the old man and's people
Cannot be well bestowed.
GONERIL   'Tis his own blame; hath put himself from rest   485
And must needs taste his folly.
REGAN   For his particular, I'll receive him gladly,
But not one follower.
GONERIL   So am I purposed.
Where is my lord of Gloucester?

                Enter GLOUCESTER.
CORNWALL
Followed the old man forth – he is returned.   490
GLOUCESTER   The King is in high rage.
ᶠCORNWALL   Whither is he going?
GLOUCESTER
He calls to horse,ᶠ but will I know not whither.
CORNWALL   'Tis best to give him way; he leads himself.
GONERIL [*to Gloucester*]
My lord, entreat him by no means to stay.   495
GLOUCESTER
Alack, the night comes on, and the high winds
Do sorely ruffle; for many miles about
There's scarce a bush.
REGAN   O sir, to wilful men
The injuries that they themselves procure
Must be their schoolmasters. Shut up your doors.   500
He is attended with a desperate train,
And what they may incense him to, being apt
To have his ear abused, wisdom bids fear.
CORNWALL
Shut up your doors, my lord; 'tis a wild night.
My Regan counsels well; come out o'the storm.   505
                                    Exeunt.

3.1   ᶠ*Storm still.*ᶠ *Enter* KENT, *disguised,*
                and a Knight, *severally.*

KENT   Who's there, besides foul weather?
KNIGHT   One minded like the weather, most unquietly.
KENT   I know you. Where's the King?
KNIGHT   Contending with the fretful elements;
Bids the wind blow the earth into the sea,   5
Or swell the curled waters 'bove the main,
That things might change, or cease; ᵒtears his white
    hair,
Which the impetuous blasts with eyeless rage
Catch in their fury and make nothing of,
Strives in his little world of man to outscorn   10
The to and fro conflicting wind and rain.

This night wherein the cub-drawn bear would couch,
The lion and the belly-pinched wolf
Keep their fur dry, unbonneted he runs,
And bids what will take all.^Q

KENT   But who is with him?

KNIGHT   None but the fool, who labours to outjest
His heart-struck injuries.

KENT   Sir, I do know you
And dare upon the warrant of my note
Commend a dear thing to you. There is division,
Although as yet the face of it is covered
With mutual cunning, 'twixt Albany and Cornwall,
^FWho have, as who have not that their great stars
Throned and set high, servants, who seem no less,
Which are to France the spies and speculations
Intelligent of our state – what hath been seen,
Either in snuffs and packings of the dukes,
Or the hard rein which both of them hath borne
Against the old kind King, or something deeper,
Whereof, perchance, these are but furnishings.^F
^QNow to you:
If on my credit you dare build so far
To make your speed to Dover, you shall find
Some that will thank you, making just report
Of how unnatural and bemadding sorrow
The King hath cause to plain.
I am a gentleman of blood and breeding,
And from some knowledge and assurance
Offer this office to you.^Q

KNIGHT   I will talk further with you.

KENT   No, do not.
For confirmation that I ^Fam^F much more
Than my out-wall, open this purse and take
What it contains. If you shall see Cordelia,
As fear not but you shall, show her this ring,
And she will tell you who your fellow is
That yet you do not know. Fie on this storm.
I will go seek the King.

KNIGHT   Give me your hand.
Have you no more to say?

KENT   Few words, but to effect
More than all yet: that when we have found the King,
^FIn which your pain^F that way, I'll this,
He that first lights on him holla the other.   *Exeunt.*

3.2   ^F*Storm still.*^F *Enter* LEAR *and* Fool.

LEAR   Blow winds and crack your cheeks! Rage, blow!
You cataracts and hurricanoes, spout
Till you have drenched our steeples, drowned the
    cocks!
You sulphurous and thought-executing fires,
Vaunt-couriers of oak-cleaving thunderbolts,
Singe my white head! And thou, all-shaking thunder,
Strike flat the thick rotundity o'the world,
Crack nature's moulds, all germens spill at once
That make ingrateful man!

FOOL   O, nuncle, court holy-water in a dry house is
better than this rain-water out o'door. Good nuncle,
in, ^Qand ^Q ask thy daughters blessing. Here's a night
pities neither wise men nor fools.

LEAR   Rumble thy bellyful! Spit fire, spout rain!
Nor rain, wind, thunder, fire are my daughters;
I tax not you, you elements, with unkindness.
I never gave you kingdom, called you children;
You owe me no subscription. ^QWhy^Q then, let fall
Your horrible pleasure. Here I stand your slave,
A poor, infirm, weak and despised old man.
But yet I call you servile ministers
That will with two pernicious daughters join
Your high-engendered battles 'gainst a head
So old and white as this. O ^Fho,^F 'tis foul.

FOOL   He that has a house to put's head in has a good
headpiece:
        The codpiece that will house
        Before the head has any,
        The head and he shall louse:
            So beggars marry many.
        The man that makes his toe
            What he his heart should make,
        Shall of a corn cry woe
            And turn his sleep to wake.
For there was never yet fair woman but she made
mouths in a glass.

Enter KENT, *disguised.*

LEAR   No, I will be the pattern of all patience;
I will say nothing.

KENT   Who's there?

FOOL   Marry, here's grace and a codpiece – that's a wise
man and a fool.

KENT [*to Lear*]
Alas, sir, are you here? Things that love night
Love not such nights as these. The wrathful skies
Gallow the very wanderers of the dark,
And make them keep their caves. Since I was man
Such sheets of fire, such bursts of horrid thunder,
Such groans of roaring wind and rain I never
Remember to have heard. Man's nature cannot carry
Th'affliction, nor the fear.

LEAR   Let the great gods
That keep this dreadful pudder o'er our heads
Find out their enemies now. Tremble, thou wretch,
That hast within thee undivulged crimes,
Unwhipped of justice. Hide thee, thou bloody hand,
Thou perjured, and thou simular of virtue
That art incestuous. Caitiff, to pieces shake,
That under covert and convenient seeming
Has practised on man's life. Close pent-up guilts
Rive your concealing continents and cry
These dreadful summoners grace. I am a man
More sinned against than sinning.

KENT   Alack, bareheaded?
Gracious my lord, hard by here is a hovel:

Some friendship will it lend you 'gainst the tempest.
Repose you there, while I to this hard house –
More harder than the stones whereof 'tis raised,
65 Which even but now, demanding after you,
Denied me to come in – return and force
Their scanted courtesy.

LEAR   My wits begin to turn.
[*to the Fool*] Come on, my boy. How dost my boy? Art
cold?
I am cold myself.
[*to Kent*]   Where is this straw, my fellow?
70 The art of our necessities is strange,
And can make vile things precious. Come; your hovel.
[*to the Fool*] Poor fool and knave, I have one part in
my heart
That's sorry yet for thee.

FOOL   He that has ᶠandᶠ a little tiny wit,
75   With heigh-ho, the wind and the rain,
           Must make content with his fortunes fit,
           Though the rain it raineth every day.

LEAR   True, ᵟmy goodᵟ boy.
[*to Kent*]   Come, bring us to this hovel.
                              Exeunt Lear and Kent.

ᶠFOOL   This is a brave night to cool a courtesan. I'll
80   speak a prophecy ere I go:
           When priests are more in word than matter,
           When brewers mar their malt with water,
           When nobles are their tailors' tutors,
           No heretics burned but wenches' suitors;
85   When every case in law is right,
           No squire in debt, nor no poor knight;
           When slanders do not live in tongues,
           Nor cut-purses come not to throngs,
           When usurers tell their gold i'the field,
90   And bawds and whores do churches build,
           Then shall the realm of Albion
           Come to great confusion:
           Then comes the time, who lives to see't,
           That going shall be used with feet.
95   This prophecy Merlin shall make, for I live before his
      time.   *Exit.*ᶠ

3.3   *Enter* GLOUCESTER *and* EDMUND,
                ᵟ*with lights*ᵟ.

GLOUCESTER   Alack, alack, Edmund, I like not this
   unnatural dealing. When I desired their leave that I
   might pity him, they took from me the use of mine
   own house; charged me on pain of perpetual
5 displeasure neither to speak of him, entreat for him, or
   any way sustain him.
EDMUND   Most savage and unnatural.
GLOUCESTER   Go to, say you nothing. There is division
   between the dukes, and a worse matter than that: I
10 have received a letter this night – 'tis dangerous to be
   spoken – I have locked the letter in my closet. These
   injuries the King now bears will be revenged home.

There is part of a power already footed; we must
incline to the King. I will look him and privily relieve
him. Go you and maintain talk with the Duke, that my   15
charity be not of him perceived. If he ask for me, I am
ill and gone to bed. If I die for it – as no less is
threatened me – the King my old master must be
relieved. There is strange things toward, Edmund;
pray you, be careful.   *Exit.*   20
EDMUND   This courtesy, forbid thee, shall the Duke
Instantly know and of that letter too.
This seems a fair deserving and must draw me
That which my father loses, no less than all.
The younger rises when the old doth fall.   *Exit.*   25

3.4   *Enter* LEAR, KENT, *disguised, and* Fool.

KENT   Here is the place, my lord: good my lord, enter;
The tyranny of the open night's too rough
For nature to endure.   [ᶠ*Storm still*ᶠ]
LEAR   Let me alone.
KENT   Good my lord, enter ᶠhereᶠ.
LEAR   Wilt break my heart?
KENT
I had rather break mine own. Good my lord, enter.   5
LEAR
Thou think'st 'tis much that this contentious storm
Invades us to the skin: so 'tis to thee.
But where the greater malady is fixed,
The lesser is scarce felt. Thou'dst shun a bear,
But if thy flight lay toward the roaring sea,   10
Thou'dst meet the bear i'the mouth. When the
   mind's free,
The body's delicate: this tempest in my mind
Doth from my senses take all feeling else,
Save what beats there, filial ingratitude.
Is it not as this mouth should tear this hand   15
For lifting food to't? But I will punish home;
No, I will weep no more. ᶠIn such a night
To shut me out? Pour on, I will endure.ᶠ
In such a night as this? O, Regan, Goneril,
Your old, kind father, whose frank heart gave ᵟyouᵟ all –   20
O, that way madness lies, let me shun that;
No more of that.
KENT   Good my lord, enter ᶠhereᶠ.
LEAR   Prithee go in thyself, seek thine own ease.
This tempest will not give me leave to ponder
On things would hurt me more. But I'll go in;   25
[*to the Fool*] ᶠIn boy, go first. You houseless poverty –
Nay, get thee in. I'll pray, and then I'll sleep.
                              *Exit*ᶠ *Fool.*
[*Kneels.*] Poor naked wretches, wheresoe'er you are,
That bide the pelting of this pitiless storm,
How shall your houseless heads and unfed sides,   30
Your looped and windowed raggedness, defend you
From seasons such as these? O, I have ta'en
Too little care of this. Take physic, pomp,
Expose thyself to feel what wretches feel,

35 That thou mayst shake the superflux to them
And show the heavens more just.

Enter Fool, *as from the hovel.*

ᶠEDGAR [*within*]   Fathom and half, fathom and half.
Poor Tom!ᶠ

FOOL   Come not in here, nuncle, here's a spirit. Help
40 me, help me!

KENT   Give me thy hand. Who's there?

FOOL   A spirit, ᶠa spirit.ᶠ He says his name's Poor Tom.

KENT   What art thou that dost grumble there i'the
straw? Come forth.

Enter EDGAR, *disguised as Poor Tom.*

45 EDGAR   Away, the foul fiend follows me. Through the
sharp hawthorn blows the ᵩ cold ᵩ wind. ᶠHumh,ᶠ go to
thy ᵩcoldᵩ bed and warm thee.

LEAR   Didst thou give all to thy ᵩtwoᵩ daughters? And
art thou come to this?

50 EDGAR   Who gives anything to Poor Tom, whom the
foul fiend hath led through fire and ᶠthrough flame,ᶠ
through ford and whirlpool, o'er bog and quagmire;
that hath laid knives under his pillow and halters in
his pew; set ratsbane by his porridge, made him
55 proud of heart, to ride on a bay trotting horse
over four-inched bridges, to course his own shadow
for a traitor? Bless thy five wits, Tom's a-cold. ᶠO
do, de, do, de, do, de:ᶠ bless thee from whirlwinds,
star-blasting and taking. Do Poor Tom some charity,
60 whom the foul fiend vexes. There could I have him
now, and there, and there again, ᶠand there.ᶠ

[ᶠ*Storm still*ᶠ]

LEAR   Have his daughters brought him to this pass?
Couldst thou save nothing? Wouldst thou give 'em
all?

65 FOOL   Nay, he reserved a blanket, else we had been all
shamed.

LEAR [*to Edgar*]
Now all the plagues that in the pendulous air
Hang fated o'er men's faults light on thy daughters.

KENT   He hath no daughters, sir.

LEAR
70 Death, traitor! Nothing could have subdued nature
To such a lowness but his unkind daughters.
Is it the fashion that discarded fathers
Should have thus little mercy on their flesh?
Judicious punishment: 'twas this flesh begot
75 Those pelican daughters.

EDGAR   Pillicock sat on Pillicock hill,
Alow, alow, loo, loo!

FOOL   This cold night will turn us all to fools and
madmen.

80 EDGAR   Take heed o'the foul fiend; obey thy parents,
keep thy word justly, swear not, commit not with man's
sworn spouse, set not thy sweet-heart on proud array.
Tom's a-cold.

LEAR   What hast thou been?

EDGAR   A serving-man, proud in heart and mind, that
85 curled my hair, wore gloves in my cap, served the lust
of my mistress' heart and did the act of darkness with
her; swore as many oaths as I spake words and broke
them in the sweet face of heaven. One that slept in the
contriving of lust and waked to do it. Wine loved I
90 deeply, dice dearly; and, in woman, out-paramoured
the Turk: false of heart, light of ear, bloody of hand;
hog in sloth, fox in stealth, wolf in greediness, dog in
madness, lion in prey. Let not the creaking of shoes,
nor the rustling of silks, betray thy poor heart to
95 woman. Keep thy foot out of brothels, thy hand out of
plackets, thy pen from lenders' books, and defy the
foul fiend. Still through the hawthorn blows the cold
wind, says suum, mun, nonny, Dauphin my boy, ᵩmyᵩ
boy, *cessez!* Let him trot by.   [ᶠ*Storm still*ᶠ]

100 LEAR   ᵩWhyᵩ, thou wert better in a grave than to
answer with thy uncovered body this extremity of the
skies. Is man no more than this? Consider him well.
Thou ow'st the worm no silk, the beast no hide, the
sheep no wool, the cat no perfume. ᶠHa?ᶠ Here's
105 three on's us are sophisticated; thou art the thing itself.
Unaccommodated man is no more but such a poor,
bare, forked animal as thou art. Off, off, you lendings:
come, unbutton ᶠhereᶠ. [*Tearing at his clothes, he is
restrained by Kent and the Fool.*]

ᶠ*Enter* GLOUCESTER, *with a torch .*ᶠ

110 FOOL   Prithee, nuncle, be contented; 'tis a naughty
night to swim in. Now a little fire in a wild field were
like an old lecher's heart, a small spark, all the rest on's
body cold. Look, here comes a walking fire.

EDGAR   This is the foul ᵩfiendᵩ Flibbertigibbet: he
115 begins at curfew and walks till the first cock; he gives
the web and the pin, squinies the eye and makes the
harelip; mildews the white wheat and hurts the poor
creature of earth.

Swithold footed thrice the wold;
120 He met the nightmare and her nine foal,
Bid her alight and her troth plight,
And aroint thee, witch, aroint thee.

KENT   How fares your grace?

LEAR   What's he?

125 KENT [*to Gloucester*]   Who's there? What is't you seek?

GLOUCESTER   What are you there? Your names?

EDGAR   Poor Tom, that eats the swimming frog, the
toad, the tadpole, the wall-newt and the water- ; that in
the fury of his heart, when the foul fiend rages, eats
130 cow-dung for salads; swallows the old rat and the
ditch-dog; drinks the green mantle of the standing
pool; who is whipped from tithing to tithing and
stocked, punished and imprisoned – who hath ᵩhadᵩ
three suits to his back, six shirts to his body,

135 Horse to ride and weapon to wear.
But mice and rats and such small deer
Have been Tom's food for seven long year.
Beware my follower. Peace Smulkin, peace, thou fiend.

GLOUCESTER
    What, hath your grace no better company?

140 EDGAR   The prince of darkness is a gentleman. Modo
    he's called, and Mahu.

GLOUCESTER
    Our flesh and blood, my lord, is grown so vile
    That it doth hate what gets it.

EDGAR   Poor Tom's a-cold.

GLOUCESTER [*to Lear*]

145   Go in with me. My duty cannot suffer
    T'obey in all your daughters' hard commands.
    Though their injunction be to bar my doors
    And let this tyrannous night take hold upon you,
    Yet have I ventured to come seek you out,

150   And bring you where both fire and food is ready.

LEAR   First let me talk with this philosopher:
    [*to Edgar*] What is the cause of thunder?

KENT   Good my lord,
    Take his offer, go into the house.

LEAR   I'll talk a word with this same learned Theban:

155   What is your study?

EDGAR   How to prevent the fiend and to kill vermin.

LEAR   Let me ask you one word in private.

KENT [*to Gloucester*]
    Importune him ᶠonce moreᶠ to go, my lord;
    His wits begin t'unsettle.

GLOUCESTER   Canst thou blame him?
                            [ᶠ*Storm still*ᶠ]

160   His daughters seek his death. Ah, that good Kent,
    He said it would be thus, poor banished man.
    Thou sayest the King grows mad; I'll tell thee, friend,
    I am almost mad myself. I had a son,
    Now outlawed from my blood; he sought my life,

165   But lately, very late. I loved him, friend,
    No father his son dearer. True to tell thee,
    The grief hath crazed my wits. What a night's this?
    [*to Lear*] I do beseech your grace.

LEAR   O, cry you mercy, ᶠsir.ᶠ
    [*to Edgar*] Noble philosopher, your company.

170 EDGAR   Tom's a-cold.

GLOUCESTER
    In, fellow, there, into the hovel; keep thee warm.

LEAR   Come, let's in all.

KENT   This way, my lord.

LEAR   With him;
    I will keep still with my philosopher.

KENT
    Good my lord, soothe him; let him take the fellow.

175 GLOUCESTER   Take you him on.

KENT   Sirrah, come on; go along with us.

LEAR   Come, good Athenian.

GLOUCESTER   No words, no words; hush.

EDGAR
    Childe Rowland to the dark tower came,

180   His word was still 'Fie, foh and fum,
    I smell the blood of a British man.'   ᶠ*Exeunt.*ᶠ

3.5   *Enter* CORNWALL *and* EDMUND.

CORNWALL   I will have my revenge, ere I depart his
house.

EDMUND   How, my lord, I may be censured that nature
thus gives way to loyalty something fears me to think
of.   5

CORNWALL   I now perceive it was not altogether your
brother's evil disposition made him seek his death, but
a provoking merit set a-work by a reprovable badness
in himself.

EDMUND   How malicious is my fortune, that I must   10
repent to be just? This is the letter ᶠwhichᶠ he spoke of,
which approves him an intelligent party to the
advantages of France. O heavens! That this treason
were ᶠnotᶠ, or not I the detector.

CORNWALL   Go with me to the Duchess.   15

EDMUND   If the matter of this paper be certain, you
have mighty business in hand.

CORNWALL   True or false, it hath made thee Earl of
Gloucester. Seek out where thy father is, that he may
be ready for our apprehension.   20

EDMUND [*aside*]   If I find him comforting the King, it
will stuff his suspicion more fully. [*to Cornwall*] I will
persever in my course of loyalty, though the conflict be
sore between that and my blood.

CORNWALL   I will lay trust upon thee and thou shalt   25
find a dear father in my love.   *Exeunt.*

3.6   *Enter* KENT, *disguised, and* GLOUCESTER.

GLOUCESTER   Here is better than the open air; take it
thankfully. I will piece out the comfort with what
addition I can. I will not be long from you.

KENT   All the power of his wits have given way to ᶠhisᶠ
impatience. The gods reward your kindness.   5
                                  Exit Gloucester.

Enter LEAR, EDGAR, *disguised as Poor Tom, and* Fool.

EDGAR   Frateretto calls me, and tells me Nero is an
angler in the lake of darkness. Pray, innocent, ᶠandᶠ
beware the foul fiend.

FOOL   Prithee, nuncle, tell me whether a madman be a
gentleman or a yeoman?   10

LEAR   A king, a king.

ᶠFOOL   No, he's a yeoman that has a gentleman to his
son; for he's a mad yeoman that sees his son a
gentleman before him.

LEARᶠ   To have a thousand with red burning spits   15
Come hizzing in upon 'em!

ᵠEDGAR   The foul fiend bites my back.

FOOL   He's mad that trusts in the tameness of a wolf, a
horse's health, a boy's love or a whore's oath.

LEAR   It shall be done, I will arraign them straight.   20
    [*to Edgar*] Come, sit thou here, most learned justicer.
    [*to the Fool*] Thou sapient sir, sit here. No, you she-
    foxes –

EDGAR Look where she stands and glares! Want'st thou
eyes at trial, madam?
     Come o'er the bourn, Bessy, to me.
FOOL   Her boat hath a leak,
          And she must not speak
          Why she dares not come over to thee.
EDGAR The foul fiend haunts Poor Tom in the voice of
a nightingale. Hoppedance cries in Tom's belly for two
white herring. Croak not, black angel, I have no food
for thee.
KENT How do you, sir? Stand you not so amazed.
Will you lie down and rest upon the cushions?
LEAR I'll see their trial first. Bring in their evidence.
[*to Edgar*] Thou robed man of justice, take thy place.
[*to the Fool*] And thou, his yoke-fellow of equity,
Bench by his side. [*to Kent*] You are o'the commission;
Sit you too.
EDGAR Let us deal justly.
     Sleepest or wakest thou, jolly shepherd?
          Thy sheep be in the corn;
          And for one blast of thy minikin mouth
          Thy sheep shall take no harm.
Purr, the cat is grey.
LEAR Arraign her first, 'tis Goneril – I here take my
oath before this honourable assembly – kicked the poor
King her father.
FOOL Come hither, mistress: is your name Goneril?
LEAR She cannot deny it.
FOOL Cry you mercy, I took you for a joint-stool.
LEAR
And here's another whose warped looks proclaim
What store her heart is made on. Stop her there!
Arms, arms, sword, fire, corruption in the place!
False justicer, why hast thou let her 'scape?ᵠ
EDGAR Bless thy five wits.
KENT O pity! Sir, where is the patience now
That you so oft have boasted to retain?
EDGAR [*aside*]
My tears begin to take his part so much
They mar my counterfeiting.
LEAR   The little dogs and all,
Trey, Blanch and Sweetheart, see, they bark at me.
EDGAR Tom will throw his head at them: avaunt, you curs!
          Be thy mouth or black or white,
          Tooth that poisons if it bite;
          Mastiff, greyhound, mongrel grim,
          Hound or spaniel, brach or him,
          ᶠOrᶠ bobtail tyke or trundle-tail,
          Tom will make him weep and wail;
          For with throwing thus my head,
          Dogs leap the hatch and all are fled.
Do, de, de, de. ᶠ*Cessez!*ᶠ Come, march to wakes and
fairs and market towns. Poor Tom, thy horn is dry.
LEAR Then let them anatomize Regan; see what breeds
about her heart. Is there any cause in nature that make
these hard hearts? [*to Edgar*] You, sir, I entertain ᵠyouᵠ
for one of my hundred; only I do not like the fashion of

your garments. You will say they are Persian ᵠ attireᵠ,
but let them be changed.
KENT Now, good my lord, lie here ᶠand restᶠ awhile.
LEAR Make no noise, make no noise, draw the curtains.
So, so, ᵠsoᵠ; we'll g'o to supper i'the morning ᵠso, so,
so.ᵠ [*He sleeps.*]
ᶠFOOL And I'll go to bed at noon.ᶠ

Enter GLOUCESTER.

GLOUCESTER
Come hither, friend; where is the King my master?
KENT
Here, sir, but trouble him not; his wits are gone.
GLOUCESTER
Good friend, I prithee take him in thy arms.
I have o'erheard a plot of death upon him.
There is a litter ready; lay him in't
And drive toward Dover, friend, where thou shalt
          meet
Both welcome and protection. Take up thy master:
If thou shouldst dally half an hour his life,
With thine and all that offer to defend him,
Stand in assured loss. Take up, take up,
And follow me, that will to some provision
Give thee quick conduct.
ᵠKENT   Oppressed nature sleeps.
This rest might yet have balmed thy broken sinews,
Which if convenience will not allow
Stand in hard cure. [*to the Fool*] Come, help to bear
          thy master;
Thou must not stay behind.ᵠ
GLOUCESTER   Come, come away!
          Exeunt all but Edgar;
          Kent and the Fool supporting Lear.
ᵠEDGAR When we our betters see bearing our woes,
We scarcely think our miseries our foes.
Who alone suffers, suffers most i'the mind,
Leaving free things and happy shows behind.
But then the mind much sufferance doth o'erskip,
When grief hath mates and bearing fellowship.
How light and portable my pain seems now,
When that which makes me bend makes the King
          bow,
He childed as I fathered. Tom, away;
Mark the high noises, and thyself bewray
When false opinion, whose wrong thoughts defile
          thee,
In thy just proof repeals and reconciles thee.
What will hap more tonight, safe 'scape the King.
Lurk, lurk!ᵠ   *Exit.*

3.7   *Enter* CORNWALL, REGAN, GONERIL,
          EDMUND ᶠ*and Servants.*ᶠ

CORNWALL [*to Goneril*] Post speedily to my lord your
husband. Show him this letter: the army of France is
landed. [*to Servants*] Seek out the traitor, Gloucester.

REGAN   Hang him instantly! [*Some Servants rush off.*]
5   GONERIL   Pluck out his eyes!
CORNWALL   Leave him to my displeasure. Edmund,
     keep you our sister company; the revenges we are
     bound to take upon your traitorous father are not fit
     for your beholding. Advise the Duke where you are
10   going to a most festinate preparation; we are bound
     to the like. Our posts shall be swift and intelligent
     betwixt us. Farewell, dear sister; farewell, my lord of
     Gloucester.

Enter OSWALD.

How now, where's the King?
OSWALD
15   My lord of Gloucester hath conveyed him hence.
     Some five- or six-and-thirty of his knights,
     Hot questrists after him, met him at gate,
     Who with some other of the lord's dependants
     Are gone with him toward Dover, where they boast
20   To have well-armed friends.
CORNWALL   Get horses for your mistress.

Exit Oswald.

GONERIL   Farewell, sweet lord and sister.
CORNWALL
     Edmund, farewell.   *Exeunt* ᵠ*Goneril and Edmund* ᵠ.
     [*to Servants*]   Go, seek the traitor Gloucester;
     Pinion him like a thief, bring him before us.

Servants leave.

25   Though ᶠwellᶠ we may not pass upon his life
     Without the form of justice, yet our power
     Shall do a courtesy to our wrath, which men
     May blame but not control. Who's there? The traitor?

Enter GLOUCESTER, ᵠ*brought in*
*by two or three*ᵠ ᶠ*Servants.*ᶠ

REGAN   Ingrateful fox, 'tis he.
CORNWALL   Bind fast his corky arms.
30   GLOUCESTER   What means your graces?
     Good my friends, consider; you are my guests.
     Do me no foul play, friends.
CORNWALL   Bind him, I say –
     [*Servants bind his arms.*]
REGAN   Hard, hard. O, filthy traitor!
GLOUCESTER   Unmerciful lady as you are, I'm none.
CORNWALL
     To this chair bind him. [*to Gloucester*] Villain, thou
35   shalt find –   [*Regan plucks his beard.*]
GLOUCESTER   By the kind gods, 'tis most ignobly done
     To pluck me by the beard.
REGAN   So white, and such a traitor?
GLOUCESTER   Naughty lady,
     These hairs which thou dost ravish from my chin
40   Will quicken and accuse thee. I am your host;
     With robber's hands my hospitable favours
     You should not ruffle thus. What will you do?
CORNWALL
     Come, sir, what letters had you late from France?

REGAN   Be simple answered, for we know the truth.
CORNWALL
     And what confederacy have you with the traitors,   45
     Late footed in the kingdom?
REGAN   To whose hands
     You have sent the lunatic King. Speak.
GLOUCESTER   I have a letter guessingly set down
     Which came from one that's of a neutral heart,
     And not from one opposed.
CORNWALL   Cunning.
REGAN   And false.   50
CORNWALL   Where hast thou sent the King?
GLOUCESTER   To Dover.
REGAN
     Wherefore to Dover? Wast thou not charged at peril –
CORNWALL
     Wherefore to Dover? Let him ᵠfirstᵠ answer that.
GLOUCESTER
     I am tied to the stake and I must stand the course.
REGAN   Wherefore to Dover, ᵠsirᵠ?   55
GLOUCESTER
     Because I would not see thy cruel nails
     Pluck out his poor old eyes; nor thy fierce sister
     In his anointed flesh stick boarish fangs.
     The sea, with such a storm as his bare head
     In hell-black night endured, would have buoyed up   60
     And quenched the stelled fires.
     Yet, poor old heart, he holp the heavens to rain.
     If wolves had at thy gate howled that stern time,
     Thou shouldst have said, 'Good porter, turn the key,
     All cruels else subscribed'; but I shall see   65
     The winged vengeance overtake such children.
CORNWALL
     See't shalt thou never. Fellows, hold the chair;
     Upon these eyes of thine I'll set my foot.
GLOUCESTER   He that will think to live till he be old,
     Give me some help! – O cruel! O you gods!   70
REGAN   One side will mock another – th'other too.
CORNWALL   If you see vengeance –
1 SERVANT   Hold your hand, my lord.
     I have served ᶠyouᶠ ever since I was a child,
     But better service have I never done you
     Than now to bid you hold.
REGAN   How now, you dog?   75
1 SERVANT   If you did wear a beard upon your chin,
     I'd shake it on this quarrel. What do you mean?
CORNWALL   My villein? [*They* ᵠ*draw and fight.*ᵠ]
1 SERVANT
     Nay then, come on, and take the chance of anger.
     [*He wounds Cornwall.*]
REGAN [*to another Servant*]
     Give me thy sword. A peasant stand up thus?   80
     [ᵠ *She takes a sword and runs at him behind.*ᵠ ᶠ*Kills*
     *him.*ᶠ]
1 SERVANT
     O, I am slain. My lord, you have one eye left
     To see some mischief on him. O!   [*He dies.*]

CORNWALL   Lest it see more, prevent it. Out, vile jelly,
Where is thy lustre now?
GLOUCESTER
85 All dark and comfortless? Where's my son Edmund?
Edmund, enkindle all the sparks of nature
To quit this horrid act.
REGAN   Out, ᶠtreacherousᶠ villain,
Thou call'st on him that hates thee. It was he
That made the overture of thy treasons to us,
90 Who is too good to pity thee.
GLOUCESTER   O my follies! Then Edgar was abused?
Kind gods, forgive me that and prosper him.
REGAN [*to a Servant*]
Go, thrust him out at gates and let him smell
His way to Dover. How is't, my lord? How look you?
95 CORNWALL   I have received a hurt. Follow me, lady.
[*to Servants*] Turn out that eyeless villain. Throw this
    slave
Upon the dunghill.
            Exeunt Servants ᶠwith Gloucesterᶠ *and the body.*
                    Regan, I bleed apace;
Untimely comes this hurt. Give me your arm.
                    Exeunt Cornwall and Regan.
ᵠ2 SERVANT   I'll never care what wickedness I do
If this man come to good.
100 3 SERVANT   If she live long
And in the end meet the old course of death,
Women will all turn monsters.
2 SERVANT   Let's follow the old Earl and get the bedlam
To lead him where he would. His roguish madness
105 Allows itself to anything.ᶠ
3 SERVANT
Go thou: I'll fetch some flax and whites of eggs
To apply to his bleeding face. Now heaven help him!
                                    *Exeunt.*ᵠ

4.1   *Enter* EDGAR, *disguised as Poor Tom.*

EDGAR   Yet better thus, and known to be contemned
Than still contemned and flattered. To be worst,
The lowest and most dejected thing of fortune,
Stands still in esperance, lives not in fear.
5 The lamentable change is from the best,
The worst returns to laughter. ᶠWelcome then,
Thou unsubstantial air that I embrace;
The wretch that thou hast blown unto the worst
Owes nothing to thy blasts.ᶠ

        Enter GLOUCESTER, *led by an* Old Man.

10 ᶠButᶠ who comes here? My father, poorly led?
World, world, O world!
But that thy strange mutations make us hate thee,
Life would not yield to age.
OLD MAN   O my good lord, I have been your tenant and
15 your father's tenant these fourscore ᶠyearsᶠ –
GLOUCESTER
Away, get thee away; good friend, be gone.

Thy comforts can do me no good at all;
Thee they may hurt.
OLD MAN   ᵠAlack, sir,ᵠ you cannot see your way.
GLOUCESTER   I have no way, and therefore want no eyes: 20
I stumbled when I saw. Full oft 'tis seen
Our means secure us and our mere defects
Prove our commodities. O dear son Edgar,
The food of thy abused father's wrath,
Might I but live to see thee in my touch,   25
I'd say I had eyes again.
OLD MAN   How now? Who's there?
EDGAR [*aside*]
O gods! Who is't can say 'I am at the worst'?
I am worse than e'er I was.
OLD MAN [*to Gloucester*]   'Tis poor mad Tom.
EDGAR [*aside*] And worse I may be yet; the worst is not
So long as we can say 'This is the worst.'   30
OLD MAN [*to Edgar*]   Fellow, where goest?
GLOUCESTER   Is it a beggar-man?
OLD MAN   Madman, and beggar too.
GLOUCESTER
He has some reason, else he could not beg.
I'the last night's storm I such a fellow saw,
Which made me think a man a worm. My son   35
Came then into my mind, and yet my mind
Was then scarce friends with him. I have heard more
    since:
As flies to wanton boys are we to the gods,
They kill us for their sport.
EDGAR [*aside*]   How should this be?
Bad is the trade that must play fool to sorrow,   40
Angering itself and others. [*to Gloucester*] Bless thee,
    master.
GLOUCESTER   Is that the naked fellow?
OLD MAN   Ay, my lord.
GLOUCESTER
ᵠ Then pritheeᵠ get thee away. If for my sake
Thou wilt o'ertake us hence a mile or twain
I'the way toward Dover, do it for ancient love,   45
And bring some covering for this naked soul,
Which I'll entreat to lead me.
OLD MAN   Alack, sir, he is mad.
GLOUCESTER
'Tis the time's plague when madmen lead the
    blind.
Do as I bid thee, or rather do thy pleasure;   50
Above the rest, be gone.
OLD MAN   I'll bring him the best 'pparel that I have,
Come on't what will.   ᶠExit.ᶠ
GLOUCESTER   Sirrah, naked fellow.
EDGAR
Poor Tom's a-cold. [*aside*] I cannot daub it further –   55
GLOUCESTER   Come hither, fellow.
EDGAR [*aside*]
ᶠAnd yet I must.ᶠ [*to Gloucester*] Bless thy sweet eyes,
    they bleed.
GLOUCESTER   Knowst thou the way to Dover?

EDGAR Both stile and gate, horseway and footpath.
60 Poor Tom hath been scared out of his good wits. Bless
thee, goodman's son, from the foul fiend. ᵠas Obidicut;
have been in Poor Tom at once, of lust, as Obidicut;
Hobbididence, prince of darkness; Mahu, of stealing;
Modo, of murder; Flibbertigibbet, of mopping and
65 mowing, who since possesses chambermaids and
waiting-women. So, bless thee, master.ᵠ

GLOUCESTER
Here, take this purse, thou whom the heaven's plagues
Have humbled to all strokes. That I am wretched
Makes thee the happier. Heavens deal so still!
70 Let the superfluous and lust-dieted man
That slaves your ordinance, that will not see
Because he does not feel, feel your power quickly:
So distribution should undo excess
And each man have enough. Dost thou know Dover?
75 EDGAR Ay, master.

GLOUCESTER
There is a cliff whose high and bending head
Looks fearfully in the confined deep:
Bring me but to the very brim of it,
And I'll repair the misery thou dost bear
80 With something rich about me. From that place
I shall no leading need.

EDGAR   Give me thy arm,
Poor Tom shall lead thee.   ᶠ*Exeunt.*ᶠ

4.2   *Enter* GONERIL, EDMUND,
                          followed by OSWALD.

GONERIL
Welcome, my lord. I marvel our mild husband
Not met us on the way. [*to Oswald*] Now, where's your
   master?
OSWALD Madam, within; but never man so changed.
I told him of the army that was landed;
5 He smiled at it. I told him you were coming;
His answer was 'The worse.' Of Gloucester's treachery
And of the loyal service of his son,
When I informed him, then he called me sot,
And told me I had turned the wrong side out.
10 What most he should dislike seems pleasant to him;
What like, offensive.
GONERIL [*to Edmund*] Then shall you go no further.
It is the cowish terror of his spirit,
That dares not undertake. He'll not feel wrongs
Which tie him to an answer. Our wishes on the way
15 May prove effects. Back, Edmund, to my brother;
Hasten his musters and conduct his powers.
I must change names at home and give the distaff
Into my husband's hands. This trusty servant
Shall pass between us. Ere long you are like to hear –
20 If you dare venture in your own behalf –
A mistress's command. Wear this.
[*She places a chain about his neck.*] Spare speech,
Decline your head. This kiss, if it durst speak,

Would stretch thy spirits up into the air.
Conceive, and fare thee well –
EDMUND Yours in the ranks of death.   ᶠ*Exit.*ᶠ
GONERIL   – my most dear Gloucester.   25
ᶠO, the difference of man and man!ᶠ
To thee a woman's services are due;
A fool usurps my bed.
OSWALD Madam, here comes my lord.   ᵠ*Exit.*ᵠ

                    ᶠ*Enter* ALBANY.ᶠ

GONERIL I have been worth the whistling.
ALBANY   O Goneril,   30
You are not worth the dust which the rude wind
Blows in your face. ᵠI fear your disposition;
That nature which contemns its origin
Cannot be bordered certain in itself.
She that herself will sliver and disbranch   35
From her material sap perforce must wither,
And come to deadly use.
GONERIL No more, the text is foolish.
ALBANY Wisdom and goodness to the vile seem vile;
Filths savour but themselves. What have you done?   40
Tigers, not daughters, what have you performed?
A father, and a gracious aged man
Whose reverence even the head-lugged bear would lick,
Most barbarous, most degenerate, have you madded.
Could my good brother suffer you to do it?   45
A man, a prince, by him so benefitted?
If that the heavens do not their visible spirits
Send quickly down to tame these vile offences,
It will come:
Humanity must perforce prey on itself,   50
Like monsters of the deep.ᵠ
GONERIL   Milk-livered man,
That bear'st a cheek for blows, a head for wrongs,
Who hast not in thy brows an eye discerning
Thine honour from thy suffering; ᵠthat not knowst
Fools do those villains pity who are punished   55
Ere they have done their mischief. Where's thy drum?
France spreads his banners in our noiseless land;
With plumed helm thy state begins to threat,
Whilst thou, a moral fool, sits still and cries,
'Alack, why does he so?'ᵠ
ALBANY   See thyself, devil: 60
Proper deformity shows not in the fiend
So horrid as in woman.
GONERIL   O vain fool!
ᵠALBANY
Thou changed and self-covered thing, for shame
Be-monster not thy feature. Were't my fitness
To let these hands obey my blood,   65
They are apt enough to dislocate and tear
Thy flesh and bones. Howe'er thou art a fiend,
A woman's shape doth shield thee.
GONERIL Marry, your manhood, mew! –ᵠ

                    Enter a Messenger.

70 ᵠALBANY   What news?ᵠ

MESSENGER
 O my good lord, the Duke of Cornwall's dead,
 Slain by his servant, going to put out
 The other eye of Gloucester.

ALBANY   Gloucester's eyes?

MESSENGER
75 A servant that he bred, thrilled with remorse,
 Opposed against the act, bending his sword
 To his great master, who, thereat enraged,
 Flew on him and amongst them felled him dead;
 But not without that harmful stroke which since
 Hath plucked him after.

ALBANY   This shows you are above,
80 You justicers, that these our nether crimes
 So speedily can venge. But, O, poor Gloucester,
 Lost he his other eye?

MESSENGER   Both, both, my lord.
 [*to Goneril*] This letter, madam, craves a speedy answer;
 'Tis from your sister.

GONERIL [*aside*]   One way I like this well;
85 But being widow, and my Gloucester with her,
 May all the building in my fancy pluck
 Upon my hateful life. Another way
 The news is not so tart. [*to the Messenger*] I'll read and
  answer.   ᵠ*Exit.*ᵠ

ALBANY
 Where was his son when they did take his eyes?

MESSENGER   Come with my lady hither.

90 ALBANY   He is not here.

MESSENGER   No, my good lord; I met him back again.

ALBANY   Knows he the wickedness?

MESSENGER
 Ay, my good lord, 'twas he informed against him
 And quit the house on purpose that their punishment
95 Might have the freer course.

ALBANY   Gloucester, I live
 To thank thee for the love thou showd'st the King
 And to revenge thine eyes. – Come hither, friend,
 Tell me what more thou knowst.   *Exeunt.*

4.3   ᵠ*Enter* KENT, *disguised, and a* Gentleman.

KENT   Why the King of France is so suddenly gone
 back, know you no reason?

GENTLEMAN   Something he left imperfect in the state
 which since his coming forth is thought of, which
5 imports to the kingdom so much fear and danger that
 his personal return was most required and necessary.

KENT   Who hath he left behind him General?

GENTLEMAN   The Marshal of France, Monsieur la Far.

KENT   Did your letters pierce the Queen to any
10 demonstration of grief?

GENTLEMAN
 Ay, sir. She took them, read them in my presence,
 And now and then an ample tear trilled down
 Her delicate cheek. It seemed she was a queen

 Over her passion, who, most rebel-like,
 Sought to be king o'er her.

KENT   O, then, it moved her?   15

GENTLEMAN   Not to a rage; patience and sorrow strove
 Who should express her goodliest. You have seen
 Sunshine and rain at once, her smiles and tears
 Were like a better way. Those happy smilets
 That played on her ripe lip seemed not to know   20
 What guests were in her eyes, which parted thence
 As pearls from diamonds dropped. In brief,
 Sorrow would be a rarity most beloved
 If all could so become it.

KENT   Made she no verbal question?   25

GENTLEMAN
 Faith, once or twice she heaved the name of father
 Pantingly forth as if it pressed her heart;
 Cried 'Sisters, sisters, shame of ladies, sisters!
 Kent, father, sisters! What, i'the storm, i'the night?
 Let pity not be believed!' There she shook   30
 The holy water from her heavenly eyes,
 And clamour mastered her; then away she started,
 To deal with grief alone.

KENT   It is the stars,
 The stars above us govern our conditions,
 Else one self mate and make could not beget   35
 Such different issues. You spoke not with her since?

GENTLEMAN   No.

KENT   Was this before the King returned?

GENTLEMAN   No, since.

KENT   Well, sir, the poor distressed Lear's i'the town,
 Who sometime in his better tune remembers   40
 What we are come about, and by no means
 Will yield to see his daughter.

GENTLEMAN   Why, good sir?

KENT
 A sovereign shame so elbows him. His own unkindness
 That stripped her from his benediction, turned her
 To foreign casualties, gave her dear rights   45
 To his dog-hearted daughters, these things sting
 His mind so venomously that burning shame
 Detains him from Cordelia.

GENTLEMAN   Alack, poor gentleman.

KENT
 Of Albany's and Cornwall's powers you heard not?

GENTLEMAN   'Tis so; they are afoot.   50

KENT   Well, sir, I'll bring you to our master, Lear,
 And leave you to attend him. Some dear cause
 Will in concealment wrap me up awhile.
 When I am known aright, you shall not grieve,
 Lending me this acquaintance.   55
 I pray you, go along with me.   *Exeunt.*ᵠ

4.4   *Enter* ᶠ*with Drum and Colours*ᶠ CORDELIA
   Gentleman, *Officer* ᶠ*and Soldiers.*ᶠ

CORDELIA   Alack, 'tis he. Why, he was met even now
 As mad as the vexed sea, singing aloud,

Crowned with rank fumiter and furrow-weeds,
With burdocks, hemlock, nettles, cuckoo-flowers,
5   Darnel and all the idle weeds that grow
In our sustaining corn. [*to Officer*] A century send
    forth;
Search every acre in the high-grown field
And bring him to our eye. What can man's wisdom
In the restoring his bereaved sense,
10   He that helps him take all my outward worth.
                              Exit Officer, with Soldiers.
GENTLEMAN   There is means, madam.
    Our foster nurse of nature is repose,
    The which he lacks: that to provoke in him
    Are many simples operative, whose power
    Will close the eye of anguish.
15 CORDELIA   All blest secrets,
    All you unpublished virtues of the earth,
    Spring with my tears. Be aidant and remediate
    In the good man's distress. Seek, seek for him,
    Lest his ungoverned rage dissolve the life
    That wants the means to lead it.

                    Enter Messenger.

20 MESSENGER   News, madam:
    The British powers are marching hitherward.
CORDELIA   'Tis known before. Our preparation stands
    In expectation of them. O dear father,
    It is thy business that I go about;
25   Therefore great France
    My mourning and important tears hath pitied.
    No blown ambition doth our arms incite,
    But love, dear love, and our aged father's right:
    Soon may I hear and see him.   *Exeunt.*

4.5   *Enter* REGAN *and* OSWALD.

REGAN   But are my brother's powers set forth?
OSWALD   Ay, madam.
REGAN   Himself in person ᶠthereᶠ?
OSWALD   Madam, with much ado; your sister is the
5   better soldier.
REGAN   Lord Edmund spake not with your lord at home?
OSWALD   No, madam.
REGAN   What might import my sister's letter to him?
OSWALD   I know not, lady.
10 REGAN   Faith, he is posted hence on serious matter.
    It was great ignorance, Gloucester's eyes being out,
    To let him live. Where he arrives he moves
    All hearts against us. Edmund, I think, is gone
    In pity of his misery to dispatch
15   His nighted life; moreover to descry
    The strength o'th' enemy.
OSWALD   I must needs after him, ᶠmadam,ᶠ with my letter.
REGAN   Our troops set forth tomorrow; stay with us.
    The ways are dangerous.
OSWALD   I may not, madam;
20   My lady charged my duty in this business.

REGAN
    Why should she write to Edmund? Might not you
    Transport her purposes by word? Belike –
    Some things, I know not what – I'll love thee much;
    Let me unseal the letter.
OSWALD   Madam, I had rather –
REGAN   I know your lady does not love her husband,   25
    I am sure of that; and at her late being here
    She gave strange oeillades and most speaking looks
    To noble Edmund. I know you are of her bosom.
OSWALD   I, madam?
REGAN   I speak in understanding; y'are, I know't.   30
    Therefore I do advise you take this note.
    My lord is dead; Edmund and I have talked,
    And more convenient is he for my hand
    Than for your lady's. You may gather more.
    If you do find him, pray you give him this;   35
    And when your mistress hears thus much from you,
    I pray desire her call her wisdom to her.
    So fare ᶠyouᶠ well.
    If you do chance to hear of that blind traitor,
    Preferment falls on him that cuts him off.   40
OSWALD
    Would I could meet ᵒhimᵒ, madam, I should show
    What party I do follow.
REGAN   Fare thee well.   *Exeunt.*

4.6   *Enter* GLOUCESTER *and* EDGAR, *in peasant's
                clothing and with a staff.*

GLOUCESTER
    When shall I come to the top of that same hill?
EDGAR   You do climb up it now. Look how we labour.
GLOUCESTER   Methinks the ground is even.
EDGAR   Horrible steep.
    Hark, do you hear the sea?
GLOUCESTER   No, truly.
EDGAR   Why then, your other senses grow imperfect   5
    By your eyes' anguish.
GLOUCESTER   So may it be indeed.
    Methinks thy voice is altered and thou speak'st
    In better phrase and matter than thou didst.
EDGAR   You're much deceived; in nothing am I changed
    But in my garments.
GLOUCESTER   Methinks you're better spoken.   10
EDGAR
    Come on, sir, here's the place. Stand still: how fearful
    And dizzy 'tis to cast one's eyes so low.
    The crows and choughs that wing the midway air
    Show scarce so gross as beetles. Half-way down
    Hangs one that gathers samphire, dreadful trade;   15
    Methinks he seems no bigger than his head.
    The fishermen that walk upon the beach
    Appear like mice, and yon tall anchoring barque
    Diminished to her cock, her cock a buoy
    Almost too small for sight. The murmuring surge   20
    That on th'unnumbered idle pebble chafes,

Cannot be heard so high. I'll look no more,
Lest my brain turn and the deficient sight
Topple down headlong.

GLOUCESTER   Set me where you stand.

25 EDGAR   Give me your hand: you are now within a foot
Of th'extreme verge. For all beneath the moon
Would I not leap upright.

GLOUCESTER   Let go my hand.
Here, friend, 's another purse, in it a jewel
Well worth a poor man's taking. Fairies and gods
30 Prosper it with thee. Go thou further off;
Bid me farewell and let me hear thee going.

EDGAR   Now fare ye well, good sir.

GLOUCESTER   With all my heart.

EDGAR [*aside*]   Why I do trifle thus with his despair
Is done to cure it.

GLOUCESTER [ᵒ*He kneels.*ᵒ]   O you mighty gods,
35 This world I do renounce and in your sights
Shake patiently my great affliction off.
If I could bear it longer and not fall
To quarrel with your great opposeless wills,
My snuff and loathed part of nature should
40 Burn itself out. If Edgar live, O, bless ꜰhimꜰ!
Now, fellow, fare thee well.   [ᵒ*He falls.*ᵒ]

EDGAR   Gone, sir; farewell.
[*aside*] And yet I know not how conceit may rob
The treasury of life when life itself
Yields to the theft. Had he been where he thought,
By this had thought been past.
45 [*to Gloucester*]   Alive or dead?
Ho, you, sir! ꜰFriend,ꜰ hear you, sir? Speak! –
[*aside*] Thus might he pass indeed. Yet he revives. –
What are you, sir?

GLOUCESTER   Away and let me die.

EDGAR
Hadst thou been aught but gossamer, feathers, air,
50 So many fathom down precipitating,
Thou'dst shivered like an egg; but thou dost breathe,
Hast heavy substance, bleed'st not, speak'st, art
    sound.
Ten masts at each make not the altitude
Which thou hast perpendicularly fell.
Thy life's a miracle. Speak yet again.

55 GLOUCESTER   But have I fallen, or no?

EDGAR   From the dread summit of this chalky bourn.
Look up a-height: the shrill-gorged lark so far
Cannot be seen or heard. Do but look up.

60 GLOUCESTER   Alack, I have no eyes.
Is wretchedness deprived that benefit
To end itself by death? 'Twas yet some comfort
When misery could beguile the tyrant's rage
And frustrate his proud will.

EDGAR   Give me your arm.
65 Up, so. How ꜰis'tꜰ? Feel you your legs? You stand.

GLOUCESTER   Too well, too well.

EDGAR   This is above all strangeness.
Upon the crown o'the cliff what thing was that

Which parted from you?

GLOUCESTER   A poor unfortunate beggar.

EDGAR   As I stood here below methought his eyes
70 Were two full moons. He had a thousand noses,
Horns whelked and waved like the enraged sea.
It was some fiend. Therefore, thou happy father,
Think that the clearest gods, who make them
    honours
Of men's impossibilities, have preserved thee.

75 GLOUCESTER   I do remember now. Henceforth I'll bear
Affliction till it do cry out itself
'Enough, enough' and die. That thing you speak of,
I took it for a man. Often 'twould say
'The fiend, the fiend'; he led me to that place.

EDGAR   Bear free and patient thoughts.

Enter LEAR ᵒ*mad* ᵒ, *crowned with wild flowers.*

                              But who comes here?   80
The safer sense will ne'er accommodate
His master thus.

LEAR   No, they cannot touch me for coining. I am the
King himself.

85 EDGAR   O thou side-piercing sight!

LEAR   Nature's above art in that respect. There's your
press-money. That fellow handles his bow like a crow-
keeper: draw me a clothier's yard. Look, look, a mouse:
peace, peace, this ꜰpiece ofꜰ toasted cheese will do't.
There's my gauntlet, I'll prove it on a giant. Bring up   90
the brown bills. O well flown, bird, i'the clout, i'the
clout! Hewgh! Give the word.

EDGAR   Sweet marjoram.

LEAR   Pass.

95 GLOUCESTER   I know that voice.

LEAR   Ha! Goneril ꜰwith a white beard?ꜰ They flattered
me like a dog and told me I had ꜰtheꜰ white hairs in my
beard ere the black ones were there. To say 'ay' and 'no'
to everything ꜰthatꜰ I said 'ay' and 'no' to was no good
divinity. When the rain came to wet me once and the   100
wind to make me chatter; when the thunder would not
peace at my bidding, there I found 'em, there I smelt
'em out. Go to, they are not men o'their words: they told
me I was everything; 'tis a lie, I am not ague-proof.

GLOUCESTER
The trick of that voice I do well remember: 105
Is't not the King?

LEAR   Ay, every inch a king.
When I do stare, see how the subject quakes.
I pardon that man's life. What was thy cause?
Adultery?
Thou shalt not die – die for adultery? No!   110
The wren goes to't and the small gilded fly
Does lecher in my sight. Let copulation thrive,
For Gloucester's bastard son was kinder to his father
Than were my daughters got 'tween the lawful sheets.
To't, luxury, pell-mell, for I lack soldiers.   115
Behold yon simp'ring dame,
Whose face between her forks presages snow,

That minces virtue and does shake the head
ᶠToᶠ hear of pleasure's name –
The fitchew, nor the soiled horse, goes to't with a more
riotous appetite. Down from the waist they are
centaurs, though women all above. But to the girdle do
the gods inherit, beneath is all the fiend's: there's hell,
there's darkness, there is the sulphurous pit, burning,
scalding, stench, consumption! Fie, fie, fie! Pah, pah!
Give me an ounce of civet, good apothecary, ᵠtoᵠ
sweeten my imagination. There's money for thee.

GLOUCESTER   O, let me kiss that hand!

LEAR   Let me wipe it first, it smells of mortality.

GLOUCESTER
O ruined piece of nature, this great world
Shall so wear out to naught. Dost thou know me?

LEAR   I remember thine eyes well enough. Dost thou
squiny at me?
No, do thy worst, blind Cupid, I'll not love.
Read thou this challenge, mark ᶠbutᶠ the penning of it.

GLOUCESTER
Were all thy letters suns, I could not see ᵠoneᵠ.

EDGAR [*aside*]   I would not take this from report: it is,
And my heart breaks at it.

LEAR   Read.

GLOUCESTER   What? With the case of eyes?

LEAR   Oh ho, are you there with me? No eyes in your
head, nor no money in your purse? Your eyes are in a
heavy case, your purse in a light, yet you see how this
world goes.

GLOUCESTER   I see it feelingly.

LEAR   What, art mad? A man may see how this world goes
with no eyes. Look with thine ears. See how yon justice
rails upon yon simple thief. Hark in thine ear: ᶠchange
places andᶠ handy-dandy, which is the justice, which is
the thief? Thou hast seen a farmer's dog bark at a
beggar?

GLOUCESTER   Ay, sir.

LEAR   And the creature run from the cur – there thou
mightst behold the great image of authority: a dog's
obeyed in office.
Thou, rascal beadle, hold thy bloody hand;
Why dost thou lash that whore? Strip thine own back;
Thou hotly lusts to use her in that kind
For which thou whipp'st her. The usurer hangs the
cozener.
Through tattered clothes great vices do appear;
Robes and furred gowns hide all. ᶠPlate sin with gold,
And the strong lance of justice hurtless breaks;
Arm it in rags, a pigmy's straw does pierce it.
None does offend, none, I say none. I'll able 'em;
Take that of me, my friend, who have the power
To seal th'accuser's lips.ᶠ Get thee glass eyes,
And like a scurvy politician seem
To see the things thou dost not. Now, ᶠnow, now, now,ᶠ
pull off my boots; harder, harder – so.

EDGAR [*aside*]   O matter and impertinency mixed,
Reason in madness.

LEAR   If thou wilt weep my fortunes, take my eyes.

I know thee well enough, thy name is Gloucester.
Thou must be patient. We came crying hither:
Thou knowst the first time that we smell the air
We wawl and cry. I will preach to thee: mark ᵠmeᵠ.

GLOUCESTER   Alack, alack the day!

LEAR   When we are born we cry that we are come
To this great stage of fools. This a good block:
It were a delicate stratagem to shoe
A troop of horse with felt. ᶠI'll put it in proofᶠ
And when I have stolen upon these son-in-laws,
Then kill, kill, kill, kill, kill, kill!

Enter a Gentleman, *and two Attendants.*

GENTLEMAN   O, here he is: lay hand upon him. Sir,
Your most dear ᶠdaughter –ᶠ

LEAR   No rescue? What, a prisoner? I am even
The natural fool of fortune. Use me well,
You shall have ransom. Let me have surgeons,
I am cut to the brains.

GENTLEMAN   You shall have anything.

LEAR   No seconds? All myself?
Why, this would make a man ᶠa manᶠ of salt,
To use his eyes for garden water-pots.
ᵠAy, and laying autumn's dust.ᵠ

ᵠ²GENTLEMAN   Good sir.ᵠ²

ᵠLEARᵠ   I will die bravely, like a ᶠsmugᶠ bridegroom.
What? I will be jovial. Come, come,
I am a king, ᵠmyᵠ masters, know you that?

GENTLEMAN   You are a royal one and we obey you.

LEAR   Then there's life in't. Come, an you get it,
You shall get it by running. ᶠSa, sa, sa, sa.ᶠ

Exit ᵠrunningᵠ, *followed by Attendants.*

GENTLEMAN
A sight most pitiful in the meanest wretch,
Past speaking of in a king. Thou hast one daughter
Who redeems nature from the general curse
Which twain have brought her to.

EDGAR   Hail, gentle sir.

GENTLEMAN   Sir, speed you. What's your will?

EDGAR   Do you hear aught,
ᶠSir,ᶠ of a battle toward?

GENTLEMAN   Most sure and vulgar.
Everyone hears that, which can distinguish sound.

EDGAR
But, by your favour, how near's the other army?

GENTLEMAN
Near, and on speedy foot. The main descry
Stands on the hourly thought.

EDGAR   I thank you, sir.
That's all.

GENTLEMAN
Though that the Queen on special cause is here,
Her army is moved on.

EDGAR   I thank you, sir

Exit Gentleman.

GLOUCESTER
You ever gentle gods, take my breath from me;
Let not my worser spirit tempt me again

To die before you please.

215 EDGAR   Well pray you, father.

GLOUCESTER   Now, good sir, what are you?

EDGAR

A most poor man, made tame to fortune's blows,
Who, by the art of known and feeling sorrows,
Am pregnant to good pity. Give me your hand;
I'll lead you to some biding.

220 GLOUCESTER   Hearty thanks.
The bounty and the benison of heaven
To boot, to boot.

Enter OSWALD.

OSWALD   A proclaimed prize; most happy!
That eyeless head of thine was first framed flesh
To raise my fortunes! Thou old, unhappy traitor,
225 Briefly thyself remember. The sword is out
That must destroy thee.

GLOUCESTER   Now let thy friendly hand
Put strength enough to't.   [*Edgar intervenes.*]

OSWALD   Wherefore, bold peasant,
Dar'st thou support a published traitor? Hence,
Lest ᶠthatᶠ th' infection of his fortune take
230 Like hold on thee. Let go his arm.

EDGAR   Ch'ill not let go, zir, without ᶠvurtherᶠ 'cagion.

OSWALD   Let go, slave, or thou diest.

EDGAR   Good gentleman, go your gait ᶠandᶠ let poor
volk pass. And 'ch'ud ha' been zwaggered out of my
235 life, 'twould not ha' been zo long ᶠas 'tisᶠ by a vortnight.
Nay, come not near th'old man; keep out, che vor ye, or
I'se try whether your costard or my baton be the
harder. Ch'ill be plain with you.

OSWALD   Out, dunghill. [*Draws his sword.* ᵠ*They fight.*ᵠ]

240 EDGAR   Ch'ill pick your teeth, zir. Come, no matter vor
your foins. [*Oswald falls.*]

OSWALD

Slave, thou hast slain me. Villain, take my purse.
If ever thou wilt thrive, bury my body,
And give the letters which thou find'st about me
245 To Edmund, Earl of Gloucester. Seek him out
Upon the English party. O untimely death, death!
[ᵠ*He dies.*ᵠ]

EDGAR   I know thee well; a serviceable villain,
As duteous to the vices of thy mistress
As badness would desire.

GLOUCESTER   What, is he dead?

250 EDGAR   Sit you down, father; rest you. –
Let's see these pockets: the letters that he speaks of
May be my friends. He's dead; I am only sorry
He had no other deathsman. Let us see:
Leave, gentle wax; and manners, blame us not.
255 To know our enemies' minds we rip their hearts,
Their papers is more lawful.
[ᶠ*Reads the letter.*ᶠ] *Let our reciprocal vows be remembered.*
You have many opportunities to cut him off. If your will
want not, time and place will be fruitfully offered. There is
260 *nothing done if he return the conqueror; then am I the*

prisoner, and his bed my gaol, from the loathed warmth
whereof, deliver me and supply the place for your labour.
Your (wife, so I would say) affectionate servant ᵠ*and for*
*you her own for venture.*ᵠ *Goneril.*

O indistinguished space of woman's will!   265
A plot upon her virtuous husband's life
And the exchange my brother. – Here in the sands
Thee I'll rake up, the post unsanctified
Of murderous lechers; and in the mature time,
With this ungracious paper strike the sight   270
Of the death-practised duke. For him 'tis well
That of thy death and business I can tell.
                              Exit, dragging the body.

GLOUCESTER
The King is mad: how stiff is my vile sense,
That I stand up and have ingenious feeling
Of my huge sorrows? Better I were distract;   275
So should my thoughts be severed from my griefs,
And woes by wrong imaginations lose
The knowledge of themselves.   [*Drum afar off*]

Enter EDGAR.

EDGAR   Give me your hand.
Far off methinks I hear the beaten drum.
Come, father, I'll bestow you with a friend.   *Exeunt.*   280

4.7   *Enter* CORDELIA, KENT, *disguised, and*
                              Gentleman.

CORDELIA   O thou good Kent, how shall I live and work
To match thy goodness? My life will be too short,
And every measure fail me.

KENT   To be acknowledged, madam, is o'erpaid.
All my reports go with the modest truth,   5
Nor more, nor clipped, but so.

CORDELIA   Be better suited;
These weeds are memories of those worser hours.
I prithee put them off.

KENT   Pardon, dear madam;
Yet to be known shortens my made intent.
My boon I make it that you know me not   10
Till time and I think meet.

CORDELIA
Then be't so, my good lord.
[*to the Gentleman*]   How does the King?

GENTLEMAN   Madam, sleeps still.

CORDELIA   O you kind gods!
Cure this great breach in his abused nature;   15
Th'untuned and jarring senses, O, wind up
Of this child-changed father.

GENTLEMAN   So please your majesty,
That we may wake the King? He hath slept long.

CORDELIA   Be governed by your knowledge and proceed
I'the sway of your own will. Is he arrayed?   20

ᶠ*Enter* LEAR *in a chair carried by Servants.*ᶠ

GENTLEMAN   Ay, madam. In the heaviness of sleep

We put fresh garments on him.
Be by, good madam, when we do awake him.
I doubt ᵩnotᵩ of his temperance.
ᵩCORDELIA   Very well.
GENTLEMAN
25   Please you draw near; louder the music there.ᵩ
CORDELIA   O my dear father, restoration hang
    Thy medicine on my lips, and let this kiss
    Repair those violent harms that my two sisters
    Have in thy reverence made.
KENT   Kind and dear princess!
CORDELIA
30   Had you not been their father, these white flakes
    Did challenge pity of them. Was this a face
    To be opposed against the warring winds?
    ᵩTo stand against the deep dread-bolted thunder,
    In the most terrible and nimble stroke
35   Of quick cross-lightning? To watch, poor perdu,
    With this thin helm?ᵩ Mine enemy's dog
    Though he had bit me should have stood that night
    Against my fire; and wast thou fain, poor father,
    To hovel thee with swine and rogues forlorn
40   In short and musty straw? Alack, alack!
    'Tis wonder that thy life and wits at once
    Had not concluded all. He wakes; speak to him.
GENTLEMAN   Madam, do you; 'tis fittest.
CORDELIA
    How does my royal lord? How fares your majesty?
45 LEAR   You do me wrong to take me out o'the grave.
    Thou art a soul in bliss, but I am bound
    Upon a wheel of fire that mine own tears
    Do scald like molten lead.
CORDELIA   Sir, ᶠdo youᶠ know me?
LEAR   You are a spirit, I know; where did you die?
50 CORDELIA   Still, still far wide.
GENTLEMAN   He's scarce awake; let him alone awhile.
LEAR
    Where have I been? Where am I? Fair daylight?
    I am mightily abused. I should ev'n die with pity
    To see another thus. I know not what to say.
55   I will not swear these are my hands: let's see –
    I feel this pinprick. Would I were assured
    Of my condition.
CORDELIA [Kneels.]   O look upon me, sir,
    And hold your hands in benediction o'er me!
    [She restrains him as he tries to kneel.]
    ᵩNo, sir,ᵩ you must not kneel.
LEAR   Pray do not mock ᶠmeᶠ.
60   I am a very foolish, fond old man,
    Fourscore and upward, ᶠnot an hour more nor less;ᶠ
    And to deal plainly,
    I fear I am not in my perfect mind.
    Methinks I should know you and know this man,
65   Yet I am doubtful; for I am mainly ignorant
    What place this is and all the skill I have
    Remembers not these garments; nor I know not
    Where I did lodge last night. Do not laugh at me,

For, as I am a man, I think this lady
    To be my child Cordelia.
CORDELIA   And so I am, ᶠI amᶠ.   70
LEAR   Be your tears wet? Yes, faith; I pray weep not.
    If you have poison for me, I will drink it.
    I know you do not love me, for your sisters
    Have, as I do remember, done me wrong.
    You have some cause, they have not.
CORDELIA   No cause, no cause.   75
LEAR   Am I in France?
KENT   In your own kingdom, sir.
LEAR   Do not abuse me.
GENTLEMAN
    Be comforted, good madam, the great rage
    You see is killed in him, ᵩand yet it is danger
    To make him even o'er the time he has lost.ᵩ   80
    Desire him to go in. Trouble him no more
    Till further settling.
CORDELIA   Will't please your highness walk?
LEAR   You must bear with me. Pray ᶠyouᶠ now, forget
    and forgive; I am old and foolish.
                        Exeunt. ᵩKent and the Gentleman remain.ᵩ
ᵩGENTLEMAN   Holds it true, sir, that the Duke of   85
    Cornwall was so slain?
KENT   Most certain, sir.
GENTLEMAN   Who is conductor of his people?
KENT   As 'tis said, the bastard son of Gloucester.
GENTLEMAN   They say Edgar his banished son is with   90
    the Earl of Kent in Germany.
KENT   Report is changeable; 'tis time to look about. The
    powers of the kingdom approach apace.
GENTLEMAN   The arbitrement is like to be bloody. Fare
    you well, sir.   Exit.   95
KENT   My point and period will be throughly wrought,
    Or well or ill as this day's battle's fought.   Exit.ᵩ

5.1   Enter ᶠwith Drum and Coloursᶠ EDMUND,
            REGAN, Gentlemen and Soldiers.

EDMUND [to a Gentleman]
    Know of the Duke if his last purpose hold,
    Or whether since he is advised by aught
    To change the course. He's full of alteration
    And self-reproving. Bring his constant pleasure.
                                    Exit Gentleman.
REGAN   Our sister's man is certainly miscarried.   5
EDMUND   'Tis to be doubted, madam.
REGAN   Now, sweet lord,
    You know the goodness I intend upon you:
    Tell me but truly, but then speak the truth,
    Do you not love my sister?
EDMUND   In honoured love.
REGAN   But have you never found my brother's way   10
    To the forfended place?
ᵩEDMUND   That thought abuses you.
REGAN   I am doubtful that you have been conjunct
    And bosomed with her, as far as we call hers.ᵩ

EDMUND   No, by mine honour, madam.

REGAN   I never shall endure her. Dear my lord,
Be not familiar with her.

EDMUND   Fear ᵠmeᵠ not –

Enter ᶠwith Drum and Coloursᶠ ALBANY,
GONERIL *and Soldiers.*

She and the Duke her husband.

ᵠGONERIL [*aside*]
I had rather lose the battle than that sister
Should loosen him and me.ᵠ

ALBANY   Our very loving sister, well be-met.
Sir, this I heard: the King is come to his daughter,
With others whom the rigour of our state
Forced to cry out. ᵠWhere I could not be honest
I never yet was valiant. For this business,
It touches us as France invades our land,
Not bolds the King, with others whom I fear
Most just and heavy causes make oppose.

EDMUND   Sir, you speak nobly.ᵠ

REGAN   Why is this reasoned?

GONERIL   Combine together 'gainst the enemy,
For these domestic and particular broils
Are not the question here.

ALBANY   Let's then determine with the ancient of war
on our proceeding.

ᵠEDMUND   I shall attend you presently at your tent.ᵠ
                                                        Exit.

REGAN   Sister, you'll go with us?

GONERIL   No.

REGAN   'Tis most convenient; pray ᵠyouᵠ go with us.

GONERIL   O ho, I know the riddle. I will go.

Exeunt Edmund, Regan, Goneril and ᶠboth the armies.ᶠ

As Albany is leaving, enter EDGAR, *in
peasant's clothing.*

EDGAR   If e'er your grace had speech with man so poor,
Hear me one word.

ALBANY [*to his Soldiers*]   I'll overtake you.
[*to Edgar*]   Speak.

EDGAR   Before you fight the battle, ope this letter.
If you have victory, let the trumpet sound
For him that brought it. Wretched though I seem,
I can produce a champion that will prove
What is avouched there. If you miscarry,
Your business of the world hath so an end
ᶠAnd machination ceases.ᶠ Fortune love you.

ALBANY   Stay till I have read the letter.

EDGAR   I was forbid it.
When time shall serve, let but the herald cry
And I'll appear again.   *Exit.*

ALBANY   Why, fare thee well. I will o'erlook thy paper.

Enter EDMUND.

EDMUND   The enemy's in view; draw up your powers.
[*Hands him a note.*] Here is the guess of their true
      strength and forces,

By diligent discovery; but your haste
Is now urged on you.

ALBANY   We will greet the time.   *Exit.*

EDMUND   To both these sisters have I sworn my love,
Each jealous of the other as the stung
Are of the adder. Which of them shall I take?
Both? One? Or neither? Neither can be enjoyed
If both remain alive. To take the widow
Exasperates, makes mad her sister Goneril,
And hardly shall I carry out my side,
Her husband being alive. Now then, we'll use
His countenance for the battle, which being done,
Let her who would be rid of him devise
His speedy taking off. As for the mercy
Which he intends to Lear and to Cordelia,
The battle done, and they within our power,
Shall never see his pardon; for my state
Stands on me to defend, not to debate.   *Exit.*

5.2   *Alarum ᶠwithinᶠ. Enter ᶠwith Drum and
Coloursᶠ* LEAR, CORDELIA *and Soldiers.
They pass over the stage ᶠand exeunt.ᶠ*

Enter EDGAR, *in peasant's clothing, and* GLOUCESTER.

EDGAR   Here, father, take the shadow of this tree
For your good host. Pray that the right may thrive.
If ever I return to you again
I'll bring you comfort.

GLOUCESTER   Grace go with you, sir.
                                                        Exit Edgar.

Alarum and retreat ᶠwithin. Enter EDGAR.ᶠ

EDGAR   Away, old man, give me thy hand, away!
King Lear hath lost, he and his daughter ta'en.
Give me thy hand; come on!

GLOUCESTER   No further, sir; a man may rot even here.

EDGAR   What, in ill thoughts again? Men must endure
Their going hence even as their coming hither.
Ripeness is all. Come on.

ᶠGLOUCESTER   And that's true too.
                                                        Exeunt.ᶠ

5.3   *Enter ᶠin conquest with Drum and Coloursᶠ*
EDMUND, *with* LEAR *and* CORDELIA
as prisoners, ᶠSoldiers and a Captain.ᶠ

EDMUND   Some officers take them away – good guard,
Until their greater pleasures first be known
That are to censure them.

CORDELIA   We are not the first
Who with best meaning have incurred the worst.
For thee, oppressed King, I am cast down;
Myself could else outfrown false fortune's frown.
Shall we not see these daughters and these sisters?

LEAR   No, no, ᶠno, noᶠ. Come, let's away to prison;
We two alone will sing like birds i'the cage.
When thou dost ask me blessing I'll kneel down

And ask of thee forgiveness. So we'll live
And pray, and sing, and tell old tales, and laugh
At gilded butterflies, and hear poor rogues
Talk of court news; and we'll talk with them too –
15 Who loses and who wins, who's in, who's out –
And take upon's the mystery of things
As if we were God's spies. And we'll wear out
In a walled prison packs and sects of great ones
That ebb and flow by the moon.
EDMUND [*to Soldiers*]   Take them away.
20 LEAR   Upon such sacrifices, my Cordelia,
The gods themselves throw incense. Have I caught
    thee?   [*Embraces her.*]
He that parts us shall bring a brand from heaven,
And fire us hence like foxes. Wipe thine eyes;
The good ꟼyearsꟼ shall devour them, flesh and fell,
25 Ere they shall make us weep!
We'll see 'em starved first: come.
                    ꟼ*Exeunt* ꟼ *Lear and Cordelia, guarded.*
EDMUND   Come hither, captain, hark:
Take thou this note. Go, follow them to prison.
One step I have advanced thee. If thou dost
30 As this instructs thee, thou dost make thy way
To noble fortunes. Know thou this, that men
Are as the time is; to be tender-minded
Does not become a sword. Thy great employment
Will not bear question: either say thou'lt do't,
Or thrive by other means.
35 CAPTAIN   I'll do't, my lord.
EDMUND
About it and write 'happy' when thou'st done't.
Mark, I say, instantly; and carry it so
As I have set it down.
ᵠCAPTAIN   I cannot draw a cart, nor eat dried oats.
40 If it be man's work, I'll do't.ᵠ   ꟼ*Exit.*ꟼ

                    ꟼ*Flourish.*ꟼ *Enter* ALBANY, GONERIL,
                    REGAN *and Soldiers with a Trumpeter.*

ALBANY   Sir, you have showed today your valiant strain
And fortune led you well. You have the captives
Who were the opposites of this day's strife:
I do require them of you, so to use them
45 As we shall find their merits and our safety
May equally determine.
EDMUND   Sir, I thought it fit
To send the old and miserable King
To some retention ᵠand appointed guard,ᵠ
Whose age had charms in it, whose title more,
50 To pluck the common bosom on his side,
And turn our impressed lances in our eyes
Which do command them. With him I sent the Queen,
My reason all the same; and they are ready
Tomorrow, or at further space, t'appear
55 Where you shall hold your session. ᵠAt this time
We sweat and bleed; the friend hath lost his friend,
And the best quarrels in the heat are cursed
By those that feel their sharpness.

The question of Cordelia and her father
Requires a fitter place.ᵠ
ALBANY   Sir, by your patience,   60
I hold you but a subject of this war,
Not as a brother.
REGAN   That's as we list to grace him.
Methinks our pleasure might have been demanded
Ere you had spoke so far. He led our powers,
Bore the commission of my place and person,   65
The which immediacy may well stand up
And call itself your brother.
GONERIL   Not so hot!
In his own grace he doth exalt himself
More than in your addition.
REGAN   In my rights,
By me invested, he compeers the best.   70
ALBANY
That were the most, if he should husband you.
REGAN   Jesters do oft prove prophets.
GONERIL   Holla, holla!
That eye that told you so looked but asquint.
REGAN   Lady, I am not well, else I should answer
From a full-flowing stomach. [*to Edmund*] General,   75
Take thou my soldiers, prisoners, patrimony;
ꟼDispose of them, of me, the walls is thine.ꟼ
Witness the world, that I create thee here
My lord and master.
GONERIL   Mean you to enjoy him ᵠthenᵠ?
ALBANY   The let-alone lies not in your good will.   80
EDMUND   Nor in thine, lord.
ALBANY   Half-blooded fellow, yes.
REGAN [*to Edmund*]
Let the drum strike and prove my title thine.
ALBANY   Stay yet, hear reason: Edmund, I arrest thee
On capital treason, and in thine attaint
This gilded serpent.   [*Points to Goneril.*]
[*to Regan*]   For your claim, fair sister,   85
I bar it in the interest of my wife:
'Tis she is sub-contracted to this lord,
And I, her husband, contradict your banns:
If you will marry, make your love to me;
My lady is bespoke.
ꟼGONERIL   An interlude!   90
ALBANYꟼ
Thou art armed, Gloucester. ꟼLet the trumpet
    sound.ꟼ
If none appear to prove upon thy person
Thy heinous, manifest and many treasons,
There is my pledge.   [*Throws down his gauntlet.*]
                    I'll make it on thy heart,
Ere I taste bread, thou art in nothing less   95
Than I have here proclaimed thee.
REGAN   Sick, O, sick!
GONERIL [*aside*]   If not, I'll ne'er trust medicine.
EDMUND
There's my exchange.   [*Throws down his gauntlet.*]
                    What in the world he is

That names me traitor, villain-like he lies.
100 Call by the trumpet: he that dares approach,
On him, on you – who not? – I will maintain
My truth and honour firmly.
ALBANY   A herald, ho!

          ᶠ*Enter a* Herald.ᶠ

[*to Edmund*] Trust to thy single virtue, for thy soldiers,
All levied in my name, have in my name
Took their discharge.
105 REGAN   My sickness grows upon me.
ALBANY   She is not well; convey her to my tent.
                    Exit Regan, supported.
Come hither, herald; let the trumpet sound
And read out this.   [ᶠ*A trumpet sounds.*ᶠ]
HERALD [ᶠ*Reads.*ᶠ]   *If any man of quality or degree within*
110   *the lists of the army will maintain upon Edmund, supposed*
Earl of Gloucester, that he is a manifold traitor, let him
appear by the third sound of the trumpet. He is bold in his
defence.   [ᶠ*First trumpet*ᶠ]
Again!   [ᶠ*Second trumpet*ᶠ]
115 Again!   [ᶠ*Third trumpet*ᶠ]
               [ᶠ*Trumpet answers within.*ᶠ]

          Enter EDGAR ᶠ*armed.*ᶠ

ALBANY   Ask him his purposes, why he appears
Upon this call o' the trumpet.
HERALD   What are you?
Your name, your quality, and why you answer
This present summons?
EDGAR   ᵠOᵠ know my name is lost,
120 By treason's tooth bare-gnawn and canker-bit;
Yet am I noble as the adversary
I come to cope ᵠwithalᵠ.
ALBANY   Which is that adversary?
EDGAR
What's he that speaks for Edmund, Earl of
          Gloucester?
EDMUND   Himself. What sayst thou to him?
EDGAR   Draw thy sword,
125 That if my speech offend a noble heart,
Thy arm may do thee justice. Here is mine.
     [*Draws his sword.*]
Behold: it is the privilege of mine honours,
My oath and my profession. I protest,
Maugre thy strength, youth, place and eminence,
130 Despite thy victor sword and fire-new fortune,
Thy valour and thy heart, thou art a traitor:
False to thy gods, thy brother and thy father,
Conspirant 'gainst this high illustrious prince,
And from th'extremest upward of thy head
135 To the descent and dust below thy foot
A most toad-spotted traitor. Say thou no,
This sword, this arm and my best spirits are bent
To prove upon thy heart, whereto I speak,
Thou liest.
EDMUND   In wisdom I should ask thy name,

But since thy outside looks so fair and warlike,   140
And that thy tongue some say of breeding breathes,
ᶠWhat safe and nicely I might well delayᶠ
By rule of knighthood, I disdain and spurn.
Back do I toss these treasons to thy head,
With the hell-hated lie o'erwhelm thy heart,   145
Which for they yet glance by and scarcely bruise,
This sword of mine shall give them instant way,
Where they shall rest for ever. Trumpets, speak.
     [ᶠ*Alarums. Fight.*ᶠ *Edmund falls.*]
ALBANY [*to Edgar*]   Save him, save him!
GONERIL   This is ᵠmereᵠ practice, Gloucester.
By the law of war thou wast not bound to answer   150
An unknown oppposite. Thou art not vanquished,
But cozened and beguiled.
ALBANY   Shut your mouth, dame,
Or with this paper shall I stop it.
[*to Edmund*]   ᶠHold, sir,ᶠ
Thou worse than any name, read thine own evil.
[*to Goneril*] ᵠNayᵠ, no tearing, lady; I perceive you
     know it.   155
GONERIL   Say if I do, the laws are mine, not thine.
Who can arraign me for't?   *Exit.*
ALBANY   Most monstrous! ᶠO!ᶠ
[*to Edmund*] Knowst thou this paper?
EDMUND   Ask me not what I know.
ALBANY [*to an Officer, who follows Goneril*]
Go after her; she's desperate, govern her.
EDMUND
What you have charged me with, that have I done,   160
And more, much more; the time will bring it out.
'Tis past and so am I. [*to Edgar*] But what art thou
That hast this fortune on me? If thou'rt noble,
I do forgive thee.
EDGAR   Let's exchange charity:
I am no less in blood than thou art, Edmund;   165
If more, the more thou'st wronged me.
My name is Edgar and thy father's son.
The gods are just and of our pleasant vices
Make instruments to plague us:
The dark and vicious place where thee he got   170
Cost him his eyes.
EDMUND   Thou'st spoken ᶠright, 'tisᶠ true;
The wheel is come full circle, I am here.
ALBANY [*to Edgar*]
Methought thy very gait did prophesy
A royal nobleness. I must embrace thee.
Let sorrow split my heart if ever I   175
Did hate thee or thy father.
EDGAR   Worthy prince, I know't.
ALBANY   Where have you hid yourself?
How have you known the miseries of your father?
EDGAR   By nursing them, my lord. List a brief tale,   180
And when 'tis told, O, that my heart would burst!
The bloody proclamation to escape
That followed me so near – O, our lives' sweetness,
That we the pain of death would hourly die

185	Rather than die at once! – taught me to shift
	Into a madman's rags, t'assume a semblance
	That very dogs disdained; and in this habit
	Met I my father with his bleeding rings,
	Their precious stones new lost; became his guide,
190	Led him, begged for him, saved him from despair,
	Never – O fault! – revealed myself unto him
	Until some half-hour past, when I was armed,
	Not sure, though hoping of this good success.
	I asked his blessing and from first to last
195	Told him our pilgrimage. But his flawed heart,
	Alack, too weak the conflict to support,
	'Twixt two extremes of passion, joy and grief,
	Burst smilingly.
	EDMUND This speech of yours hath moved me,
	And shall perchance do good; but speak you on,
200	You look as you had something more to say.
	ALBANY If there be more, more woeful, hold it in,
	For I am almost ready to dissolve
	Hearing of this.
	ᵠEDGAR This would have seemed a period
	To such as love not sorrow, but another
205	To amplify too much would make much more
	And top extremity.
	Whilst I was big in clamour, came there in a man
	Who, having seen me in my worst estate,
	Shunned my abhorred society, but then finding
210	Who 'twas that so endured, with his strong arms,
	He fastened on my neck and bellowed out
	As he'd burst heaven, threw him on my father,
	Told the most piteous tale of Lear and him
	That ever ear received, which in recounting
215	His grief grew puissant and the strings of life
	Began to crack. Twice then the trumpets sounded
	And there I left him tranced.
	ALBANY But who was this?
	EDGAR Kent, sir, the banished Kent, who in disguise
	Followed his enemy king and did him service
220	Improper for a slave.ᵠ

Enter a Gentleman ᵠ*with a bloody knife.*ᵠ

	GENTLEMAN Help, help, ᶠO, help!ᶠ
	EDGAR What kind of help?
	ᶠALBANY Speak, man.
	EDGARᶠ What means this bloody knife?
	GENTLEMAN 'Tis hot, it smokes,
	It came even from the heart of – ᶠO, she's dead!ᶠ
	ALBANY Who ᶠdeadᶠ? Speak, man.
225	GENTLEMAN Your lady, sir, your lady; and her sister
	By her is poisoned; she confesses it.
	EDMUND I was contracted to them both; all three
	Now marry in an instant.
	EDGAR Here comes Kent.

Enter KENT.

	ALBANY Produce the bodies, be they alive or dead.
	[*Goneril's and Regan's bodies brought out.*]

This judgement of the heavens that makes us tremble	230
Touches us not with pity – O, is this he?	
The time will not allow the compliment	
Which very manners urges.	
KENT I am come	
To bid my King and master aye good night.	
Is he not here?	
ALBANY Great thing of us forgot!	235
Speak, Edmund, where's the King? And where's	
Cordelia?	
Seest thou this object, Kent?	
KENT Alack, why thus?	
EDMUND Yet Edmund was beloved:	
The one the other poisoned for my sake,	
And after slew herself.	
ALBANY Even so; cover their faces.	240
EDMUND I pant for life. Some good I mean to do,	
Despite of mine own nature. Quickly send –	
Be brief in it – to the castle, for my writ	
Is on the life of Lear and on Cordelia;	
Nay, send in time.	
ALBANY Run, run, O run.	245
EDGAR To who, my lord? Who has the office?	
[*to Edmund*] Send	
Thy token of reprieve.	
EDMUND	
Well thought on: take my sword; ᵠthe captain,ᵠ	
Give it the captain.	
EDGAR [*to Gentleman*] Haste thee for thy life.	
Exit Gentleman.	
EDMUND He hath commission from thy wife and me	250
To hang Cordelia in the prison and	
To lay the blame upon her own despair,	
That she fordid herself.	
ALBANY The gods defend her. Bear him hence awhile.	
Edmund is carried off.	

Enter LEAR *with* CORDELIA *in his arms*
followed by the Gentleman.

LEAR	
Howl, howl, howl, ᵠhowlᵠ! O, you are men of stones!	255
Had I your tongues and eyes, I'd use them so	
That heaven's vault should crack: she's gone for ever.	
I know when one is dead and when one lives;	
She's dead as earth. [*He lays her down.*]	
Lend me a looking-glass;	
If that her breath will mist or stain the stone,	260
Why then she lives.	
KENT Is this the promised end?	
EDGAR Or image of that horror?	
ALBANY Fall, and cease.	
LEAR This feather stirs, she lives: if it be so,	
It is a chance which does redeem all sorrows	
That ever I have felt.	
KENT O, my good master!	265
LEAR Prithee, away!	
EDGAR 'Tis noble Kent, your friend.	

LEAR   A plague upon you murderers, traitors all;
   I might have saved her; now she's gone for ever.
   Cordelia, Cordelia, stay a little. Ha?
270   What is't thou sayst? Her voice was ever soft,
   Gentle and low, an excellent thing in woman.
   I killed the slave that was a-hanging thee.
GENTLEMAN   'Tis true, my lords, he did.
LEAR   Did I not, fellow?
   I have seen the day, with my good biting falchion
275   I would have made him skip. I am old now
   And these same crosses spoil me.
   [*to Kent*]   Who are you?
   Mine eyes are not o'the best, I'll tell you straight.
KENT   If Fortune brag of two she loved and hated,
   One of them we behold.
LEAR   ᶠ This is a dull sight:ᶠ are you not Kent?
280   KENT   The same;
   Your servant Kent; where is your servant Caius?
LEAR   He's a good fellow, I can tell ᶠyouᶠ that;
   He'll strike and quickly too. He's dead and rotten.
KENT   No, my good lord, I am the very man –
285   LEAR   I'll see that straight.
KENT   That from your first of difference and decay
   Have followed your sad steps –
LEAR   You're welcome hither.
KENT
   Nor no man else. All's cheerless, dark and deadly;
   Your eldest daughters have fordone themselves
   And desperately are dead.
290   LEAR   Ay, so I think.
ALBANY   He knows not what he says, and vain is it
   That we present us to him.

Enter a Messenger.

EDGAR   Very bootless.
MESSENGER [*to Albany*]   Edmund is dead, my lord.
ALBANY   That's but a trifle here.
295   You lords and noble friends, know our intent:
   What comfort to this ᶠgreatᶠ decay may come

Shall be applied. For us, we will resign
   During the life of this old majesty
   To him our absolute power;
   [*to Edgar and Kent*]   you to your rights,
   With boot and such addition as your honours   300
   Have more than merited. All friends shall taste
   The wages of their virtue and all foes
   The cup of their deservings. O, see, see!
LEAR   And my poor fool is hanged. No, no, ᶠnoᶠ life!
   Why should a dog, a horse, a rat have life   305
   And thou no breath at all? ᵟOᵟ thou'lt come no
      more,
   Never, never, never, ᶠnever, never.ᶠ
   [*to Edgar?*] Pray you undo this button. Thank you, sir.
      ᵟO, o, o, o.ᵟ
   ᶠDo you see this? Look on her: look, her lips,
   Look there, look there! [*He dies.*ᶠ]
EDGAR   He faints: my lord, my lord!   310
KENT   Break, heart, I prithee break.
EDGAR   Look up, my lord.
KENT
   Vex not his ghost; O, let him pass. He hates him
   That would upon the rack of this tough world
   Stretch him out longer.
EDGAR   ᵟOᵟ he is gone indeed.
KENT   The wonder is he hath endured so long;   315
   He but usurped his life.
ALBANY   Bear them from hence. Our present business
   Is ᵟtoᵟ general woe. [*to Edgar and Kent*] Friends of
      my soul, you twain,
   Rule in this realm and the gored state sustain.
KENT   I have a journey, sir, shortly to go;   320
   My master calls me, I must not say no.
EDGAR   The weight of this sad time we must obey,
   Speak what we feel, not what we ought to say.
   The oldest hath borne most; we that are young
   Shall never see so much, nor live so long.   325
      ᶠ*Exeunt with a dead march.*ᶠ

King Richard II

When this play first appeared in print in 1597 under the title *The Tragedy of King Richard the Second*, the episode showing Richard relinquishing his crown to Bolingbroke in 4.1 was omitted, as it was in subsequent editions until 1608. Scholars assume that this was because the deposition of a king was an inflammatory topic in Elizabethan England, and that the printed texts of the play (though not, apparently, the performances) were subject to political censorship. Such an assumption is supported by an anecdote recorded by William Lambarde in which Queen Elizabeth compared herself to Richard II, and by the incident in 1601 when the Earl of Essex paid for a special performance of a Richard II play, most likely Shakespeare's, on the eve of his abortive rebellion, presumably hoping it would incite people to assist him in deposing the Queen.

Despite the fact that one of the Globe shareholders described *King Richard II* in 1601 as 'so old and so long out of use that they should have small or no company at it', the play is usually dated around 1595, partly because it makes use of Samuel Daniel's *The Civil Wars*, of which the first four books were published that year. It must also have preceded the *King Henry IV* plays, which are dated 1596–7 on circumstantial evidence. The main source is Raphael Holinshed's account of the last two years of Richard's reign in his *Chronicles*, of which Shakespeare used the 1587 edition. He seems also to have consulted the translation of Jean Froissart's Chronicles by John Bouchier, Lord Berners, and possibly the anonymous play *Woodstock* (*c.* 1592–3) which focuses on the murder of the Duke of Gloucester (called 'Woodstock' by John of Gaunt in *King Richard II* at 1.2.1).

While *King Richard II* is the first play in Shakespeare's so-called second tetralogy on English history, it goes back in time to the beginning of the events that led to the Wars of the Roses. In the first tetralogy, consisting of the three *King Henry VI* plays and *King Richard III*, Shakespeare had dramatized history from the death of Henry V in 1422 through the long period of contention between the Houses of York and Lancaster to the death of Richard III and the establishment of the Tudor dynasty with the accession of Henry VII after the battle of Bosworth in 1485. The second tetralogy, consisting of *King Richard II*, the *King Henry IV* plays and *King Henry V*, forms a kind of extended prequel to the first by showing the deposition of Richard II and the usurpation of the throne by Henry Bolingbroke (who became Henry IV in 1399), Henry IV's problems with incipient rebellion, and his son Henry V's solution to the problem of unrest at home by taking his father's advice to 'busy giddy minds / With foreign quarrels' (*2 Henry IV* 4.3.343–4). As the final Chorus of *King Henry V* reminds us, this solution turns out to be a temporary one.

King Richard II seems to have been a popular play before the Civil War, but it ran into censorship problems during the Restoration and was little performed in the eighteenth century. In 1815 Edmund Kean reintroduced the play to the London stage, presenting Richard as a tragic hero rather than as an incompetent king, and interpretations of this kind, sometimes ending with the death of Richard, dominated the nineteenth century. As in the case of *Hamlet*, the twentieth century broadly continued this focus on the psychology of the individual hero at the expense of the play's political issues. In the last decades of the twentieth century, however, and into the twenty-first, productions have returned to the politics of the play, focusing on its presentation of troubling questions about power, authority and legitimacy.

The Arden text is based on the 1597 First Quarto, but includes a few readings derived from the 1623 First Folio. The adopted Folio readings are marked at the beginning and end by superscript F. Most notably they include the Folio's clearly superior version of the 'deposition scene' in Act 4, which did not appear in any of the first three Quarto editions and is first found in print in apparently contaminated form in the Fourth Quarto of 1608.

KING RICHARD the Second
QUEEN Isabel — *wife to King Richard*

John of GAUNT, Duke of Lancaster
Edmund of Langley, Duke of YORK — *uncles to King Richard*
DUCHESS OF YORK — *wife to Edmund of Langley*

Henry BOLINGBROKE, Earl of Derby,
Duke of Hereford; *afterwards*
KING HENRY the Fourth — *son to John of Gaunt*

Duke of AUMERLE, Earl of Rutland — *son to Duke of York*
DUCHESS OF GLOUCESTER — *widow of Thomas of Woodstock, Duke of Gloucester (uncle to King Richard)*

Thomas MOWBRAY, Duke of Norfolk

BAGOT
BUSHY — *favourites of King Richard*
GREEN

Henry Percy, Earl of NORTHUMBERLAND
HARRY PERCY (his son, *later surnamed* Hotspur) — *followers of Bolingbroke*
Lord ROSS
Lord WILLOUGHBY

Earl of SALISBURY
Bishop of CARLISLE
Sir Stephen SCROOP — *friends of King Richard*
ABBOT of Westminster
Duke of SURREY
Lord BERKELEY
Lord FITZWATER
Another LORD
LORD MARSHAL
Two HERALDS
Sir Piers of EXTON

CAPTAIN — *of the Welsh army*
Two LADIES — *attending upon Queen Isabel*
Two SERVANTS — *to Exton*
SERVINGMAN — *to York*
GARDENER
Two Gardener's MEN
KEEPER — *of the prison at Pomfret Castle*
GROOM — *of the Stable to King Richard*

Lords, Officers, Soldiers, Servants and other Attendants

1.1   *Enter* KING RICHARD, *John of*
      GAUNT, *Lord Marshal, with other Nobles*
      and Attendants.

KING RICHARD
  Old John of Gaunt, time-honoured Lancaster,
  Hast thou according to thy oath and band
  Brought hither Henry Hereford, thy bold son,
  Here to make good the boist'rous late appeal –
  Which then our leisure would not let us hear –
  Against the Duke of Norfolk, Thomas Mowbray?
GAUNT   I have, my liege.
KING RICHARD
  Tell me, moreover, hast thou sounded him
  If he appeal the Duke on ancient malice,
  Or worthily, as a good subject should,
  On some known ground of treachery in him?
GAUNT   As near as I could sift him on that argument,
  On some apparent danger seen in him
  Aimed at your highness; no inveterate malice.
KING RICHARD
  Then call them to our presence.   *Exeunt Attendants.*
                         Face to face,
  And frowning brow to brow, ourselves will hear
  The accuser and the accused freely speak.
  High-stomached are they both and full of ire,
  In rage, deaf as the sea, hasty as fire.

Enter BOLINGBROKE *and* MOWBRAY *with Attendants.*

BOLINGBROKE   Many years of happy days befall
  My gracious sovereign, my most loving liege!
MOWBRAY   Each day still better other's happiness
  Until the heavens, envying earth's good hap,
  Add an immortal title to your crown!
KING RICHARD
  We thank you both. Yet one but flatters us,
  As well appeareth by the cause you come,
  Namely, to appeal each other of high treason.
  Cousin of Hereford, what dost thou object
  Against the Duke of Norfolk, Thomas Mowbray?
BOLINGBROKE
  First – heaven be the record to my speech! –
  In the devotion of a subject's love,
  Tend'ring the precious safety of my prince,
  And free from other misbegotten hate,
  Come I appellant to this princely presence.
  Now, Thomas Mowbray, do I turn to thee,
  And mark my greeting well; for what I speak
  My body shall make good upon this earth,
  Or my divine soul answer it in heaven.
  Thou art a traitor and a miscreant,
  Too good to be so, and too bad to live,
  Since the more fair and crystal is the sky,
  The uglier seem the clouds that in it fly.
  Once more, the more to aggravate the note,
  With a foul traitor's name stuff I thy throat,
  And wish – so please my sovereign – ere I move,

What my tongue speaks my right-drawn sword may
  prove.
MOWBRAY   Let not my cold words here accuse my zeal.
  'Tis not the trial of a woman's war,
  The bitter clamour of two eager tongues,
  Can arbitrate this cause betwixt us twain;   50
  The blood is hot that must be cooled for this.
  Yet can I not of such tame patience boast
  As to be hushed and naught at all to say.
  First, the fair reverence of your highness curbs me
  From giving reins and spurs to my free speech,   55
  Which else would post until it had returned
  These terms of treason doubled down his throat.
  Setting aside his high blood's royalty,
  And let him be no kinsman to my liege,
  I do defy him, and I spit at him,   60
  Call him a slanderous coward and a villain;
  Which to maintain, I would allow him odds
  And meet him, were I tied to run afoot
  Even to the frozen ridges of the Alps,
  Or any other ground inhabitable   65
  Wherever Englishman durst set his foot.
  Meantime let this defend my loyalty:
  By all my hopes most falsely doth he lie.
BOLINGBROKE
  Pale trembling coward, there I throw my gage,
    [*Throws down his gage.*]
  Disclaiming here the kindred of the King,   70
  And lay aside my high blood's royalty,
  Which fear, not reverence, makes thee to except.
  If guilty dread have left thee so much strength
  As to take up mine honour's pawn, then stoop.
  By that and all the rites of knighthood else,   75
  Will I make good against thee, arm to arm,
  What I have spoke or thou canst worse devise.
MOWBRAY   I take it up;   [*Takes up gage.*]
                       and by that sword I swear
  Which gently laid my knighthood on my shoulder,
  I'll answer thee in any fair degree   80
  Or chivalrous design of knightly trial.
  And when I mount, alive may I not light
  If I be traitor or unjustly fight!
KING RICHARD [*to Bolingbroke*]
  What doth our cousin lay to Mowbray's charge?
  It must be great that can inherit us   85
  So much as of a thought of ill in him.
BOLINGBROKE
  Look what I speak, my life shall prove it true:
  That Mowbray hath received eight thousand nobles
  In name of lendings for your highness' soldiers,
  The which he hath detained for lewd employments,   90
  Like a false traitor and injurious villain.
  Besides I say, and will in battle prove,
  Or here or elsewhere to the furthest verge
  That ever was surveyed by English eye,
  That all the treasons for these eighteen years   95
  Complotted and contrived in this land

Fetch from false Mowbray their first head and spring.
Further I say, and further will maintain
Upon his bad life to make all this good,
100 That he did plot the Duke of Gloucester's death,
Suggest his soon-believing adversaries,
And consequently, like a traitor coward,
Sluiced out his innocent soul through streams of
    blood –
Which blood, like sacrificing Abel's, cries
105 Even from the tongueless caverns of the earth
To me for justice and rough chastisement.
And by the glorious worth of my descent,
This arm shall do it, or this life be spent!
KING RICHARD   How high a pitch his resolution soars!
110 Thomas of Norfolk, what sayst thou to this?
MOWBRAY   O, let my sovereign turn away his face
And bid his ears a little while be deaf
Till I have told this slander of his blood
How God and good men hate so foul a liar!
KING RICHARD
115 Mowbray, impartial are our eyes and ears.
Were he my brother, nay, my kingdom's heir,
As he is but my father's brother's son,
Now, by ᶠmyᶠ sceptre's awe, I make a vow
Such neighbour nearness to our sacred blood
120 Should nothing privilege him nor partialize
The unstooping firmness of my upright soul.
He is our subject, Mowbray; so art thou.
Free speech and fearless I to thee allow.
MOWBRAY   Then, Bolingbroke, as low as to thy heart
125 Through the false passage of thy throat, thou liest.
Three parts of that receipt I had for Calais
Disbursed I duly to his highness' soldiers;
The other part reserved I by consent,
For that my sovereign liege was in my debt
130 Upon remainder of a dear account
Since last I went to France to fetch his queen.
Now swallow down that lie. For Gloucester's death,
I slew him not, but to my own disgrace
Neglected my sworn duty in that case.
135 For you, my noble Lord of Lancaster,
The honourable father to my foe,
Once did I lay an ambush for your life –
A trespass that doth vex my grieved soul;
But ere I last received the sacrament
140 I did confess it and exactly begged
Your grace's pardon, and I hope I had it.
This is my fault. As for the rest appealed,
It issues from the rancour of a villain,
A recreant and most degenerate traitor,
145 Which in myself I boldly will defend,
And interchangeably hurl down my gage
Upon this overweening traitor's foot,
To prove myself a loyal gentleman
Even in the best blood chambered in his bosom. –
    [*Throws down his gage. Bolingbroke takes it up.*]
150 In haste whereof most heartily I pray

Your highness to assign our trial day.
KING RICHARD
Wrath-kindled gentlemen, be ruled by me:
Let's purge this choler without letting blood.
This we prescribe, though no physician;
155 Deep malice makes too deep incision.
Forget, forgive, conclude and be agreed;
Our doctors say this is no month to bleed.
Good uncle, let this end where it begun;
We'll calm the Duke of Norfolk, you your son.
160 GAUNT   To be a make-peace shall become my age. –
Throw down, my son, the Duke of Norfolk's gage.
KING RICHARD   And Norfolk, throw down his.
GAUNT   When, Harry, when?
Obedience bids I should not bid again.
KING RICHARD
Norfolk, throw down, we bid; there is no boot.
MOWBRAY
165 Myself I throw, dread sovereign, at thy foot.   [*Kneels.*]
My life thou shalt command, but not my shame.
The one my duty owes; but my fair name,
Despite of death that lives upon my grave,
To dark dishonour's use thou shalt not have.
170 I am disgraced, impeached and baffled here,
Pierced to the soul with Slander's venomed spear,
The which no balm can cure but his heart-blood
Which breathed this poison.
KING RICHARD   Rage must be withstood.
Give me his gage. Lions make leopards tame.
MOWBRAY
175 Yea, but not change his spots. Take but my shame,
And I resign my gage. My dear dear lord,
The purest treasure mortal times afford
Is spotless reputation; that away,
Men are but gilded loam or painted clay.
180 A jewel in a ten-times-barred-up chest
Is a bold spirit in a loyal breast.
Mine honour is my life; both grow in one.
Take honour from me, and my life is done.
Then, dear my liege, mine honour let me try;
185 In that I live, and for that will I die.
KING RICHARD [*to Bolingbroke*]
Cousin, throw up your gage; do you begin.
BOLINGBROKE
O, God defend my soul from such deep sin!
Shall I seem crest-fallen in my father's sight?
Or with pale beggar-fear impeach my height
190 Before this outdared dastard? Ere my tongue
Shall wound my honour with such feeble wrong
Or sound so base a parle, my teeth shall tear
The slavish motive of recanting fear
And spit it bleeding, in his high disgrace,
195 Where Shame doth harbour, even in Mowbray's face.
                    ᶠ*Exit Gaunt.*ᶠ
KING RICHARD
We were not born to sue but to command;
Which since we cannot do to make you friends,

Be ready as your lives shall answer it
At Coventry upon Saint Lambert's Day.
There shall your swords and lances arbitrate
The swelling difference of your settled hate.
Since we cannot atone you, we shall see
Justice design the victor's chivalry.
Lord Marshal, command our officers at arms
Be ready to direct these home alarms.   *Exeunt.*

1.2   *Enter* John of GAUNT *with the* DUCHESS
OF GLOUCESTER.

GAUNT   Alas, the part I had in Woodstock's blood
Doth more solicit me than your exclaims
To stir against the butchers of his life.
But since correction lieth in those hands
Which made the fault that we cannot correct,
Put we our quarrel to the will of heaven,
Who, when they see the hours ripe on earth,
Will rain hot vengeance on offenders' heads.
DUCHESS OF GLOUCESTER
Finds brotherhood in thee no sharper spur?
Hath love in thy old blood no living fire?
Edward's seven sons, whereof thyself art one,
Were as seven vials of his sacred blood,
Or seven fair branches springing from one root.
Some of those seven are dried by nature's course,
Some of those branches by the Destinies cut;
But Thomas, my dear lord, my life, my Gloucester,
One vial full of Edward's sacred blood,
One flourishing branch of his most royal root,
Is cracked, and all the precious liquor spilt,
Is hacked down, and his summer leaves all faded
By Envy's hand and Murder's bloody axe.
Ah, Gaunt, his blood was thine! That bed, that womb,
That mettle, that self mould that fashioned thee
Made him a man; and though thou livest and
          breathest,
Yet art thou slain in him. Thou dost consent
In some large measure to thy father's death,
In that thou seest thy wretched brother die,
Who was the model of thy father's life.
Call it not patience, Gaunt; it is despair.
In suff'ring thus thy brother to be slaughtered,
Thou show'st the naked pathway to thy life,
Teaching stern Murder how to butcher thee.
That which in mean men we entitle patience
Is pale cold cowardice in noble breasts.
What shall I say? To safeguard thine own life,
The best way is to venge my Gloucester's death.
GAUNT   God's is the quarrel, for God's substitute,
His deputy anointed in His sight,
Hath caused his death, the which if wrongfully,
Let heaven revenge, for I may never lift
An angry arm against His minister.
DUCHESS OF GLOUCESTER
Where then, alas, may I complain myself?

GAUNT   To God, the widow's champion and defence.
DUCHESS OF GLOUCESTER
Why then, I will. Farewell, old Gaunt.
Thou goest to Coventry, there to behold   45
Our cousin Hereford and fell Mowbray fight.
O, sit my husband's wrongs on Hereford's spear,
That it may enter butcher Mowbray's breast!
Or if misfortune miss the first career,
Be Mowbray's sins so heavy in his bosom   50
That they may break his foaming courser's back
And throw the rider headlong in the lists,
A caitiff recreant to my cousin Hereford!
Farewell, old Gaunt. Thy sometimes brother's wife,
With her companion, Grief, must end her life.   55
          [*Starts to leave.*]
GAUNT   Sister, farewell; I must to Coventry.
As much good stay with thee as go with me!
          [*Starts to leave.*]
DUCHESS OF GLOUCESTER
Yet one word more. Grief boundeth where it falls,
Not with the empty hollowness, but weight.
I take my leave before I have begun,   60
For sorrow ends not when it seemeth done.
Commend me to thy brother, Edmund York.
Lo, this is all. Nay, yet depart not so!
Though this be all, do not so quickly go;
I shall remember more. Bid him – ah, what? –   65
With all good speed at Pleshy visit me.
Alack, and what shall good old York there see
But empty lodgings and unfurnished walls,
Unpeopled offices, untrodden stones?
And what hear there for welcome but my groans?   70
Therefore commend me; let him not come there
To seek out sorrow that dwells everywhere.
Desolate, desolate, will I hence and die!
The last leave of thee takes my weeping eye.   *Exeunt.*

1.3   *Enter* Lord Marshal *and the* Duke
of AUMERLE.

LORD MARSHAL
My Lord Aumerle, is Harry Hereford armed?
AUMERLE   Yea, at all points, and longs to enter in.
LORD MARSHAL
The Duke of Norfolk, sprightfully and bold,
Stays but the summons of the appellant's trumpet.
AUMERLE
Why then, the champions are prepared and stay   5
For nothing but his majesty's approach.

The trumpets sound and KING RICHARD *enters with
his nobles,* ⌐GAUNT, BUSHY, BAGOT, GREEN *and
others*⌐ *with Attendants. When they are set, the
trumpets sound, and enter* ⌐MOWBRAY,⌐ *Duke of
Norfolk, in arms, defendant,* ⌐*with* 1 Herald⌐.

KING RICHARD   Marshal, demand of yonder champion
The cause of his arrival here in arms.

10   Ask him his name, and orderly proceed
To swear him in the justice of his cause.

LORD MARSHAL [*to Mowbray*]
In God's name and the King's, say who thou art
And why thou com'st thus knightly clad in arms,
Against what man thou com'st, and what thy quarrel.
Speak truly, on thy knighthood and thy oath,
15   As so defend thee heaven and thy valour.

MOWBRAY
My name is Thomas Mowbray, Duke of Norfolk,
Who hither come engaged by my oath –
Which God defend a knight should violate –
Both to defend my loyalty and truth
20   To God, my king and my succeeding issue
Against the Duke of Hereford that appeals me,
And, by the grace of God and this mine arm,
To prove him, in defending of myself,
A traitor to my God, my king and me;
25   And as I truly fight, defend me heaven.

The trumpets sound. Enter BOLINGBROKE, *Duke of*
Hereford, appellant, in armour, ⸢*with* 2 Herald⸣.

KING RICHARD   Marshal, ask of yonder knight in arms
Both who he is and why he cometh hither
Thus plated in habiliments of war,
And formally, according to our law,
30   Depose him in the justice of his cause.

LORD MARSHAL [*to Bolingbroke*]
What is thy name? And wherefore com'st thou hither
Before King Richard in his royal lists?
Against whom comest thou? And what's thy quarrel?
Speak like a true knight, so defend thee heaven.

BOLINGBROKE
35   Harry of Hereford, Lancaster and Derby
Am I, who ready here do stand in arms
To prove, by God's grace and my body's valour,
In lists, on Thomas Mowbray, Duke of Norfolk,
That he is a traitor, foul and dangerous,
40   To God of heaven, King Richard and to me;
And as I truly fight, defend me heaven.

LORD MARSHAL
On pain of death, no person be so bold
Or daring-hardy as to touch the lists
Except the Marshal and such officers
45   Appointed to direct these fair designs.

BOLINGBROKE
Lord Marshal, let me kiss my sovereign's hand
And bow my knee before his majesty.
For Mowbray and myself are like two men
That vow a long and weary pilgrimage;
50   Then let us take a ceremonious leave
And loving farewell of our several friends.

LORD MARSHAL
The appellant in all duty greets your highness
And craves to kiss your hand and take his leave.

KING RICHARD
We will descend and fold him in our arms.

Cousin of Hereford, as thy cause is right,   55
So be thy fortune in this royal fight.
Farewell, my blood, which if today thou shed,
Lament we may, but not revenge thee dead.

BOLINGBROKE   O, let no noble eye profane a tear
For me, if I be gored with Mowbray's spear.   60
As confident as is the falcon's flight
Against a bird do I with Mowbray fight.
[*to Lord Marshal*] My loving lord, I take my leave of
    you.
[*to Aumerle*] Of you, my noble cousin, Lord
    Aumerle;
Not sick, although I have to do with death,   65
But lusty, young and cheerly drawing breath. –
Lo, as at English feasts, so I regreet
The daintiest last, to make the end most sweet.
[*to Gaunt*] O thou, the earthly author of my
    blood,
Whose youthful spirit, in me regenerate,   70
Doth with a twofold vigour lift me up
To reach at victory above my head,
Add proof unto mine armour with thy prayers
And with thy blessings steel my lance's point,
That it may enter Mowbray's waxen coat   75
And furbish new the name of John o'Gaunt
Even in the lusty haviour of his son.

GAUNT   God in thy good cause make thee prosperous.
Be swift like lightning in the execution,
And let thy blows, doubly redoubled,   80
Fall like amazing thunder on the casque
Of thy adverse pernicious enemy.
Rouse up thy youthful blood, be valiant and live.

BOLINGBROKE
Mine innocence and Saint George to thrive!

MOWBRAY·   However God or Fortune cast my lot,   85
There lives or dies, true to King Richard's throne,
A loyal, just and upright gentleman.
Never did captive with a freer heart
Cast off his chains of bondage and embrace
His golden uncontrolled enfranchisement   90
More than my dancing soul doth celebrate
This feast of battle with mine adversary.
Most mighty liege, and my companion peers,
Take from my mouth the wish of happy years.
As gentle and as jocund as to jest   95
Go I to fight. Truth hath a quiet breast.

KING RICHARD   Farewell, my lord. Securely I espy
Virtue with Valour couched in thine eye.
Order the trial, Marshal, and begin.

LORD MARSHAL
Harry of Hereford, Lancaster and Derby,   100
Receive thy lance; and God defend the right.
    [*Attendant gives lance to Bolingbroke.*]

BOLINGBROKE
Strong as a tower in hope, I cry 'Amen'!

LORD MARSHAL [*to Attendant*]
Go bear this lance to Thomas, Duke of Norfolk.

[*Attendant gives lance to Mowbray.*]

2 HERALD   Harry of Hereford, Lancaster and Derby

05   Stands here for God, his sovereign and himself

On pain to be found false and recreant,

To prove the Duke of Norfolk, Thomas Mowbray,

A traitor to his God, his king and him,

And dares him to set forward to the fight.

1 HERALD

10   Here standeth Thomas Mowbray, Duke of Norfolk,

On pain to be found false and recreant,

Both to defend himself and to approve

Henry of Hereford, Lancaster and Derby

To God, his sovereign and to him disloyal,

15   Courageously, and with a free desire,

Attending but the signal to begin.

LORD MARSHAL

Sound trumpets, and set forward, combatants.

[*A charge is sounded;* King Richard throws down his
    warder.*]

Stay! The King hath thrown his warder down.

KING RICHARD

Let them lay by their helmets and their spears

20   And both return back to their chairs again.

Withdraw with us, and let the trumpets sound

While we return these Dukes what we decree.

[*A long flourish.* King Richard confers apart with
    Gaunt and other Nobles, then addresses Combatants.*]

Draw near,

And list what with our council we have done.

25   For that our kingdom's earth should not be soiled

With that dear blood which it hath fostered;

And for our eyes do hate the dire aspect

Of civil wounds ploughed up with neighbours' sword;

And for we think the eagle-winged pride

30   Of sky-aspiring and ambitious thoughts,

With rival-hating envy, set on you

To wake our peace, which in our country's cradle

Draws the sweet infant breath of gentle sleep,

Which so roused up with boist'rous untuned drums,

35   With harsh-resounding trumpets' dreadful bray

And grating shock of wrathful iron arms,

Might from our quiet confines fright fair peace,

And make us wade even in our kindred's blood:

Therefore, we banish you our territories.

40   You, cousin Hereford, upon pain of life,

Till twice five summers have enriched our fields,

Shall not regreet our fair dominions,

But tread the stranger paths of banishment.

BOLINGBROKE

Your will be done. This must my comfort be:

45   That sun that warms you here shall shine on me,

And those his golden beams to you here lent

Shall point on me and gild my banishment.

KING RICHARD

Norfolk, for thee remains a heavier doom,

Which I with some unwillingness pronounce:

50   The sly slow hours shall not determinate

The dateless limit of thy dear exile.

The hopeless word of 'never to return'

Breathe I against thee, upon pain of life.

MOWBRAY   A heavy sentence, my most sovereign liege,

And all unlooked for from your highness' mouth.   155

A dearer merit, not so deep a maim

As to be cast forth in the common air,

Have I deserved at your highness' hands.

The language I have learnt these forty years,

My native English, now I must forgo,   160

And now my tongue's use is to me no more

Than an unstringed viol or a harp,

Or like a cunning instrument cased up –

Or, being open, put into his hands

That knows no touch to tune the harmony.   165

Within my mouth you have engaoled my tongue,

Doubly portcullised with my teeth and lips,

And dull unfeeling barren Ignorance

Is made my gaoler to attend on me.

I am too old to fawn upon a nurse,   170

Too far in years to be a pupil now.

What is thy sentence then but speechless death,

Which robs my tongue from breathing native breath?

KING RICHARD   It boots thee not to be compassionate.

After our sentence, plaining comes too late.   175

MOWBRAY

Then thus I turn me from my country's light

To dwell in solemn shades of endless night.

[*Starts to leave.*]

KING RICHARD [*to Mowbray*]

Return again, and take an oath with thee.

[*to Bolingbroke and Mowbray*] Lay on our royal sword
    your banished hands.

[*They place their hands on King Richard's sword.*]

Swear by the duty that you owe to God –   180

Our part therein we banish with yourselves –

To keep the oath that we administer:

You never shall, so help you truth and God,

Embrace each other's love in banishment;

Nor never look upon each other's face;   185

Nor never write, regreet, nor reconcile

This louring tempest of your home-bred hate;

Nor never by advised purpose meet

To plot, contrive or complot any ill

'Gainst us, our state, our subjects or our land.   190

BOLINGBROKE   I swear.

MOWBRAY   And I, to keep all this.

BOLINGBROKE   Norfolk, so far as to mine enemy:

By this time, had the King permitted us,

One of our souls had wandered in the air,   195

Banished this frail sepulchre of our flesh,

As now our flesh is banished from this land.

Confess thy treasons ere thou fly the realm.

Since thou hast far to go, bear not along

The clogging burden of a guilty soul.   200

MOWBRAY   No, Bolingbroke. If ever I were traitor,

My name be blotted from the book of life,

And I from heaven banished as from hence!
But what thou art, God, thou and I do know;
205 And all too soon, I fear, the King shall rue.
Farewell, my liege. Now no way can I stray;
Save back to England, all the world's my way.   *Exit.*
KING RICHARD [*to Gaunt*]
Uncle, even in the glasses of thine eyes
I see thy grievèd heart. Thy sad aspect
210 Hath from the number of his banished years
Plucked four away. [*to Bolingbroke*] Six frozen winters
     spent,
Return with welcome home from banishment.
BOLINGBROKE How long a time lies in one little word!
Four lagging winters and four wanton springs
215 End in a word; such is the breath of kings.
GAUNT I thank my liege that in regard of me
He shortens four years of my son's exile.
But little vantage shall I reap thereby,
For ere the six years that he hath to spend
220 Can change their moons and bring their times about,
My oil-dried lamp and time-bewasted light
Shall be extinct with age and endless night.
My inch of taper will be burnt and done,
And blindfold Death not let me see my son.
KING RICHARD
225 Why uncle, thou hast many years to live.
GAUNT But not a minute, King, that thou canst give.
Shorten my days thou canst with sullen sorrow,
And pluck nights from me, but not lend a morrow.
Thou canst help Time to furrow me with age,
230 But stop no wrinkle in his pilgrimage;
Thy word is current with him for my death,
But dead, thy kingdom cannot buy my breath.
KING RICHARD
Thy son is banished upon good advice,
Whereto thy tongue a party-verdict gave.
235 Why at our justice seem'st thou then to lour?
GAUNT Things sweet to taste prove in digestion sour.
You urged me as a judge, but I had rather
You would have bid me argue like a father.
O, had it been a stranger, not my child,
240 To smooth his fault I should have been more mild.
A partial slander sought I to avoid,
And in the sentence my own life destroyed.
Alas, I looked when some of you should say
I was too strict to make mine own away;
245 But you gave leave to my unwilling tongue,
Against my will, to do myself this wrong.
KING RICHARD
Cousin, farewell, and uncle, bid him so.
Six years we banish him, and he shall go.
            ⌐*Flourish.*⌐ *Exit King Richard with his train.*
            Aumerle, Lord Marshal, Gaunt and Bolingbroke remain.
AUMERLE [*to Bolingbroke*]
Cousin, farewell. What presence must not know,
250 From where you do remain let paper show.   *Exit.*
LORD MARSHAL [*to Bolingbroke*]

My lord, no leave take I, for I will ride
As far as land will let me by your side.
            [*Bolingbroke fails to respond. Lord Marshal stands
            apart.*]
GAUNT O, to what purpose dost thou hoard thy words
That thou return'st no greeting to thy friends?
BOLINGBROKE I have too few to take my leave of you,   255
When the tongue's office should be prodigal
To breathe the abundant dolour of the heart.
GAUNT Thy grief is but thy absence for a time.
BOLINGBROKE
Joy absent, grief is present for that time.
GAUNT What is six winters? They are quickly gone.   260
BOLINGBROKE
To men in joy; but grief makes one hour ten.
GAUNT Call it a travel that thou tak'st for pleasure.
BOLINGBROKE My heart will sigh when I miscall it so,
Which finds it an enforced pilgrimage.
GAUNT The sullen passage of thy weary steps   265
Esteem as foil wherein thou art to set
The precious jewel of thy home return.
BOLINGBROKE
Nay, rather, every tedious stride I make
Will but remember me what a deal of world
I wander from the jewels that I love.   270
Must I not serve a long apprenticehood
To foreign passages, and in the end,
Having my freedom, boast of nothing else
But that I was a journeyman to Grief?
GAUNT All places that the eye of heaven visits   275
Are to a wise man ports and happy havens.
Teach thy necessity to reason thus:
There is no virtue like necessity.
Think not the King did banish thee,
But thou the King. Woe doth the heavier sit   280
Where it perceives it is but faintly borne.
Go, say I sent thee forth to purchase honour,
And not the King exiled thee; or suppose
Devouring pestilence hangs in our air,
And thou art flying to a fresher clime.   285
Look what thy soul holds dear, imagine it
To lie that way thou goest, not whence thou com'st.
Suppose the singing birds musicians,
The grass whereon thou tread'st the presence strewed,
The flowers fair ladies, and thy steps no more   290
Than a delightful measure or a dance;
For gnarling Sorrow hath less power to bite
The man that mocks at it and sets it light.
BOLINGBROKE O, who can hold a fire in his hand
By thinking on the frosty Caucasus?   295
Or cloy the hungry edge of appetite
By bare imagination of a feast?
Or wallow naked in December snow
By thinking on fantastic summer's heat?
O no, the apprehension of the good   300
Gives but the greater feeling to the worse.
Fell Sorrow's tooth doth never rankle more

Than when he bites but lanceth not the sore.
GAUNT
    Come, come, my son, I'll bring thee on thy way.
    Had I thy youth and cause, I would not stay.
BOLINGBROKE
    Then England's ground, farewell! Sweet soil, adieu –
    My mother and my nurse that bears me yet!
    Where'er I wander, boast of this I can,
    Though banished, yet a true-born Englishman.
                Exeunt Gaunt and Bolingbroke, followed
                          by Lord Marshal.

1.4   *Enter* KING RICHARD, *with* GREEN *and*
      BAGOT *at one door, and the* Lord AUMERLE
                at another.

KING RICHARD   We did observe. – Cousin Aumerle,
    How far brought you high Hereford on his way?
AUMERLE   I brought high Hereford, if you call him so,
    But to the next highway, and there I left him.
KING RICHARD
    And say, what store of parting tears were shed?
AUMERLE
    Faith, none for me, except the northeast wind,
    Which then blew bitterly against our faces,
    Awaked the sleeping rheum and so by chance
    Did grace our hollow parting with a tear.
KING RICHARD
    What said our cousin when you parted with him?
AUMERLE   'Farewell' –
    And, for my heart disdained that my tongue
    Should so profane the word, that taught me craft
    To counterfeit oppression of such grief
    That words seemed buried in my sorrow's grave.
    Marry, would the word 'farewell' have lengthened
      hours
    And added years to his short banishment
    He should have had a volume of farewells,
    But since it would not, he had none of me.
KING RICHARD
    He is our cousin, cousin, but 'tis doubt,
    When time shall call him home from banishment,
    Whether our kinsman come to see his friends.
    Ourself and Bushy, Bagot here and Green
    Observed his courtship to the common people –
    How he did seem to dive into their hearts
    With humble and familiar courtesy,
    What reverence he did throw away on slaves,
    Wooing poor craftsmen with the craft of smiles
    And patient underbearing of his fortune,
    As 'twere to banish their affects with him.
    Off goes his bonnet to an oyster-wench.
    A brace of draymen bid God speed him well,
    And had the tribute of his supple knee
    With 'Thanks, my countrymen, my loving friends',
    As were our England in reversion his,
    And he our subjects' next degree in hope.

GREEN
    Well, he is gone, and with him go these thoughts.
    Now for the rebels which stand out in Ireland,
    Expedient manage must be made, my liege,
    Ere further leisure yield them further means   40
    For their advantage and your highness' loss.
KING RICHARD   We will ourself in person to this war,
    And, for our coffers with too great a court
    And liberal largesse are grown somewhat light,
    We are enforced to farm our royal realm,   45
    The revenue whereof shall furnish us
    For our affairs in hand. If that come short,
    Our substitutes at home shall have blank charters
    Whereto, when they shall know what men are rich,
    They shall subscribe them for large sums of gold,   50
    And send them after to supply our wants;
    For we will make for Ireland presently.

                Enter BUSHY.

    ᶠBushy,ᶠ what news?
BUSHY   Old John of Gaunt is grievous sick, my lord,
    Suddenly taken, and hath sent post-haste   55
    To entreat your majesty to visit him.
KING RICHARD   Where lies he?
BUSHY   At Ely House.
KING RICHARD
    Now put it, God, in the physician's mind
    To help him to his grave immediately!   60
    The lining of his coffers shall make coats
    To deck our soldiers for these Irish wars.
    Come, gentlemen, let's all go visit him.
    Pray God we may make haste and come too late!
ALL   Amen!   *Exeunt.*   65

2.1   *Enter* John of GAUNT *sick, carried in a*
      chair, with the Duke of YORK, *and Servants.*

GAUNT   Will the King come that I may breathe my last
    In wholesome counsel to his unstaid youth?
YORK   Vex not yourself, nor strive not with your breath,
    For all in vain comes counsel to his ear.
GAUNT   O, but they say the tongues of dying men   5
    Enforce attention like deep harmony.
    Where words are scarce, they are seldom spent in vain,
    For they breathe truth that breathe their words in pain.
    He that no more must say is listened more
    Than they whom youth and ease have taught to glose.   10
    More are men's ends marked than their lives before.
    The setting sun and music at the close,
    As the last taste of sweets, is sweetest last,
    Writ in remembrance more than things long past.
    Though Richard my life's counsel would not hear,   15
    My death's sad tale may yet undeaf his ear.
YORK   No, it is stopped with other, flatt'ring sounds,
    As praises, of whose taste the wise are fond;
    Lascivious metres, to whose venom sound
    The open ear of youth doth always listen;   20

Report of fashions in proud Italy,
Whose manners still our tardy-apish nation
Limps after in base imitation.
Where doth the world thrust forth a vanity –
25   So it be new, there's no respect how vile –
That is not quickly buzzed into his ears?
Then all too late comes Counsel to be heard,
Where Will doth mutiny with Wit's regard.
Direct not him whose way himself will choose.
30   'Tis breath thou lack'st, and that breath wilt thou lose.
GAUNT   Methinks I am a prophet new inspired,
And thus, expiring, do foretell of him.
His rash fierce blaze of riot cannot last,
For violent fires soon burn out themselves;
35   Small showers last long but sudden storms are short;
He tires betimes that spurs too fast betimes;
With eager feeding food doth choke the feeder.
Light vanity, insatiate cormorant,
Consuming means, soon preys upon itself.
40   This royal throne of kings, this sceptred isle,
This earth of majesty, this seat of Mars,
This other Eden, demi-paradise,
This fortress built by Nature for herself
Against infection and the hand of war,
45   This happy breed of men, this little world,
This precious stone set in the silver sea,
Which serves it in the office of a wall
Or as a moat defensive to a house
Against the envy of less happier lands,
50   This blessed plot, this earth, this realm, this England,
This nurse, this teeming womb of royal kings,
Feared by their breed and famous by their birth,
Renowned for their deeds as far from home,
For Christian service and true chivalry,
55   As is the sepulchre in stubborn Jewry
Of the world's ransom, blessed Mary's son,
This land of such dear souls, this dear dear land,
Dear for her reputation through the world,
Is now leased out – I die pronouncing it –
60   Like to a tenement or pelting farm.
England, bound in with the triumphant sea,
Whose rocky shore beats back the envious siege
Of wat'ry Neptune, is now bound in with shame,
With inky blots and rotten parchment bonds.
65   That England that was wont to conquer others
Hath made a shameful conquest of itself.
Ah, would the scandal vanish with my life,
How happy then were my ensuing death!

Flourish. Enter KING RICHARD *and* QUEEN,
ᶠAUMERLE, BUSHY, GREEN, BAGOT, ROSS *and*
WILLOUGHBYᶠ, *with Attendants.*

YORK   The King is come. Deal mildly with his youth,
70   For young hot colts, being raged, do rage the more.
QUEEN   How fares our noble uncle Lancaster?
KING RICHARD
What comfort, man? How is't with aged Gaunt?

GAUNT   O, how that name befits my composition!
Old Gaunt indeed, and gaunt in being old.
Within me Grief hath kept a tedious fast,   75
And who abstains from meat that is not gaunt?
For sleeping England long time have I watched;
Watching breeds leanness, leanness is all gaunt.
The pleasure that some fathers feed upon
Is my strict fast – I mean my children's looks,   80
And therein fasting hast thou made me gaunt.
Gaunt am I for the grave, gaunt as a grave,
Whose hollow womb inherits naught but bones.
KING RICHARD
Can sick men play so nicely with their names?
GAUNT   No, misery makes sport to mock itself.   85
Since thou dost seek to kill my name in me,
I mock my name, great King, to flatter thee.
KING RICHARD
Should dying men flatter with those that live?
GAUNT   No, no, men living flatter those that die.
KING RICHARD
Thou, now a-dying, sayest thou flatterest me.   90
GAUNT   O no, thou diest, though I the sicker be.
KING RICHARD
I am in health, I breathe, and see thee ill.
GAUNT   Now He that made me knows I see thee ill –
Ill in myself to see, and in thee seeing ill.
Thy death-bed is no lesser than thy land,   95
Wherein thou liest in reputation sick;
And thou, too careless patient as thou art,
Committ'st thy anointed body to the cure
Of those physicians that first wounded thee.
A thousand flatterers sit within thy crown,   100
Whose compass is no bigger than thy head;
And yet, encaged in so small a verge,
The waste is no whit lesser than thy land.
O, had thy grandsire with a prophet's eye
Seen how his son's son should destroy his sons,   105
From forth thy reach he would have laid thy shame,
Deposing thee before thou wert possessed,
Which art possessed now to depose thyself.
Why, cousin, wert thou regent of the world,
It were a shame to let this land by lease;   110
But for thy world enjoying but this land,
Is it not more than shame to shame it so?
Landlord of England art thou now, not king.
Thy state of law is bondslave to the law,
And thou –
KING RICHARD   A lunatic lean-witted fool,   115
Presuming on an ague's privilege!
Darest with thy frozen admonition
Make pale our cheek, chasing the royal blood
With fury from his native residence?
Now, by my seat's right royal majesty,   120
Wert thou not brother to great Edward's son,
This tongue that runs so roundly in thy head
Should run thy head from thy unreverent shoulders!
GAUNT   O, spare me not, my brother Edward's son,

25 For that I was his father Edward's son.
That blood already, like the pelican,
Hast thou tapped out and drunkenly caroused.
My brother Gloucester, plain well-meaning soul –
Whom fair befall in heaven 'mongst happy souls! –
30 May be a precedent and witness good
That thou respect'st not spilling Edward's blood.
Join with the present sickness that I have,
And thy unkindness be like crooked Age
To crop at once a too long withered flower.
35 Live in thy shame, but die not shame with thee!
These words hereafter thy tormentors be.
Convey me to my bed, then to my grave.
Love they to live that love and honour have.
Exit borne off by Servants.
KING RICHARD
And let them die that age and sullens have,
40 For both hast thou, and both become the grave.
YORK   I do beseech your majesty, impute his words
To wayward sickliness and age in him.
He loves you, on my life, and holds you dear
As Harry, Duke of Hereford, were he here.
KING RICHARD
45 Right, you say true. As Hereford's love, so his;
As theirs, so mine; and all be as it is.

ᶠ*Enter* NORTHUMBERLAND.ᶠ

NORTHUMBERLAND
My liege, old Gaunt commends him to your majesty.
KING RICHARD   What says he?
NORTHUMBERLAND   Nay, nothing; all is said.
His tongue is now a stringless instrument;
50 Words, life and all old Lancaster hath spent.
YORK   Be York the next that must be bankrupt so!
Though death be poor, it ends a mortal woe.
KING RICHARD
The ripest fruit first falls, and so doth he.
His time is spent; our pilgrimage must be.
55 So much for that. Now for our Irish wars:
We must supplant those rough rug-headed kerns,
Which live like venom where no venom else
But only they have privilege to live.
And, for these great affairs do ask some charge,
60 Towards our assistance we do seize to us
The plate, coin, revenues and moveables
Whereof our uncle Gaunt did stand possessed.
YORK   How long shall I be patient? Ah, how long
Shall tender duty make me suffer wrong?
65 Not Gloucester's death, nor Hereford's banishment,
Nor Gaunt's rebukes, nor England's private wrongs,
Nor the prevention of poor Bolingbroke
About his marriage, nor my own disgrace
Have ever made me sour my patient cheek,
70 Or bend one wrinkle on my sovereign's face.
I am the last of noble Edward's sons,
Of whom thy father, Prince of Wales, was first.
In war was never lion raged more fierce,

In peace was never gentle lamb more mild
Than was that young and princely gentleman.   175
His face thou hast, for even so looked he,
Accomplished with the number of thy hours;
But when he frowned, it was against the French
And not against his friends. His noble hand
Did win what he did spend, and spent not that   180
Which his triumphant father's hand had won.
His hands were guilty of no kindred blood,
But bloody with the enemies of his kin.
O Richard! York is too far gone with grief,
Or else he never would compare between –   185
KING RICHARD   Why, uncle, what's the matter?
YORK   O my liege,
Pardon me, if you please; if not, I, pleased
Not to be pardoned, am content withal.
Seek you to seize and gripe into your hands
The royalties and rights of banished Hereford?   190
Is not Gaunt dead? And doth not Hereford live?
Was not Gaunt just? And is not Harry true?
Did not the one deserve to have an heir?
Is not his heir a well-deserving son?
Take Hereford's rights away, and take from Time   195
His charters and his customary rights;
Let not tomorrow then ensue today;
Be not thyself, for how art thou a king
But by fair sequence and succession?
Now, afore God – God forbid I say true –   200
If you do wrongfully seize Hereford's rights,
Call in the letters patents that he hath
By his attorneys-general to sue
His livery and deny his offered homage,
You pluck a thousand dangers on your head,   205
You lose a thousand well-disposed hearts
And prick my tender patience to those thoughts
Which honour and allegiance cannot think.
KING RICHARD
Think what you will, we seize into our hands
His plate, his goods, his money and his lands.   210
YORK   I'll not be by the while. My liege, farewell.
What will ensue hereof there's none can tell;
But by bad courses may be understood
That their events can never fall out good.   *Exit.*
KING RICHARD
Go, Bushy, to the Earl of Wiltshire straight.   215
Bid him repair to us to Ely House
To see this business. – Tomorrow next
We will for Ireland, and 'tis time, I trow.
And we create, in absence of ourself,
Our uncle York Lord Governor of England,   220
For he is just and always loved us well.
Come on, our queen. Tomorrow must we part.
Be merry, for our time of stay is short.
ᶠ*Flourish.*ᶠ *Exeunt all but Northumberland,*
ᶠ*Willoughby and Ross.*ᶠ

NORTHUMBERLAND
Well, lords, the Duke of Lancaster is dead.

225	ROSS And living, too, for now his son is duke.
	WILLOUGHBY Barely in title, not in revenues.
	NORTHUMBERLAND
	Richly in both, if Justice had her right.
	ROSS My heart is great, but it must break with silence

225 ROSS   And living, too, for now his son is duke.
    WILLOUGHBY   Barely in title, not in revenues.
    NORTHUMBERLAND
      Richly in both, if Justice had her right.
    ROSS   My heart is great, but it must break with silence
      Ere't be disburdened with a liberal tongue.
230 NORTHUMBERLAND
      Nay, speak thy mind, and let him ne'er speak more
      That speaks thy words again to do thee harm.
    WILLOUGHBY
      Tends that thou wouldst speak to the Duke of
        Hereford?
      If it be so, out with it boldly, man.
      Quick is mine ear to hear of good towards him.
235 ROSS   No good at all that I can do for him,
      Unless you call it good to pity him,
      Bereft and gelded of his patrimony.
    NORTHUMBERLAND
      Now, afore God, 'tis shame such wrongs are borne
      In him, a royal prince, and many moe
240   Of noble blood in this declining land.
      The King is not himself, but basely led
      By flatterers; and what they will inform
      Merely in hate 'gainst any of us all,
      That will the King severely prosecute
245   'Gainst us, our lives, our children and our heirs.
    ROSS   The commons hath he pilled with grievous taxes,
      And quite lost their hearts. The nobles hath he fined
      For ancient quarrels, and quite lost their hearts.
    WILLOUGHBY   And daily new exactions are devised,
250   As blanks, benevolences, and I wot not what.
      But what, i'God's name, doth become of this?
    NORTHUMBERLAND
      Wars hath not wasted it, for warred he hath not,
      But basely yielded upon compromise
      That which his ancestors achieved with blows.
255   More hath he spent in peace than they in wars.
    ROSS   The Earl of Wiltshire hath the realm in farm.
    WILLOUGHBY
      The King's grown bankrupt like a broken man.
    NORTHUMBERLAND
      Reproach and dissolution hangeth over him.
    ROSS   He hath not money for these Irish wars,
260   His burdenous taxations notwithstanding,
      But by the robbing of the banished Duke.
    NORTHUMBERLAND
      His noble kinsman! Most degenerate King!
      But, lords, we hear this fearful tempest sing,
      Yet seek no shelter to avoid the storm.
265   We see the wind sit sore upon our sails,
      And yet we strike not, but securely perish.
    ROSS   We see the very wrack that we must suffer,
      And unavoided is the danger now
      For suffering so the causes of our wrack.
    NORTHUMBERLAND
270   Not so. Even through the hollow eyes of Death
      I spy life peering, but I dare not say

      How near the tidings of our comfort is.
    WILLOUGHBY
      Nay, let us share thy thoughts as thou dost ours.
    ROSS   Be confident to speak, Northumberland.
275   We three are but thyself, and, speaking so,
      Thy words are but as thoughts. Therefore, be bold.
    NORTHUMBERLAND
      Then thus: I have from Le Port Blanc, a bay
      In Brittany, received intelligence
      That Harry, Duke of Hereford, Rainold Lord Cobham,
280   Thomas, son and heir to th'Earl of Arundel,
      That late broke from the Duke of Exeter,
      His brother, Archbishop late of Canterbury,
      Sir Thomas Erpingham, Sir Thomas Ramston,
      Sir John Norberry, Sir Robert Waterton and Francis
        Coint,
285   All these well furnished by the Duke of Brittany
      With eight tall ships, three thousand men of war,
      Are making hither with all due expedience,
      And shortly mean to touch our northern shore.
      Perhaps they had ere this, but that they stay
290   The first departing of the King for Ireland.
      If, then, we shall shake off our slavish yoke,
      Imp out our drooping country's broken wing,
      Redeem from broking pawn the blemished crown,
      Wipe off the dust that hides our sceptre's gilt
295   And make high majesty look like itself,
      Away with me in post to Ravenspurgh.
      But if you faint, as fearing to do so,
      Stay and be secret, and myself will go.
    ROSS   To horse, to horse! Urge doubts to them that fear.
    WILLOUGHBY
300   Hold out my horse and I will first be there.   *Exeunt.*

2.2   *Enter the* QUEEN, BUSHY *ᵛand*ᵛ BAGOT.

    BUSHY   Madam, your majesty is too much sad.
      You promised, when you parted with the King,
      To lay aside life-harming heaviness
      And entertain a cheerful disposition.
5   QUEEN   To please the King I did; to please myself
      I cannot do it. Yet I know no cause
      Why I should welcome such a guest as Grief,
      Save bidding farewell to so sweet a guest
      As my sweet Richard. Yet again, methinks,
10   Some unborn sorrow, ripe in Fortune's womb,
      Is coming towards me, and my inward soul
      With nothing trembles. At something it grieves
      More than with parting from my lord the King.
    BUSHY   Each substance of a grief hath twenty shadows,
15   Which shows like grief itself, but is not so;
      For Sorrow's eyes, glazed with blinding tears,
      Divides one thing entire to many objects,
      Like perspectives, which, rightly gazed upon,
      Show nothing but confusion; eyed awry,
20   Distinguish form. So your sweet majesty,
      Looking awry upon your lord's departure,

Find shapes of grief more than himself to wail,
Which, looked on as it is, is naught but shadows
Of what it is not. Then, thrice-gracious Queen,
More than your lord's departure weep not. More is
   not seen,
Or if it be, 'tis with false Sorrow's eye,
Which for things true weeps things imaginary.

QUEEN   It may be so; but yet my inward soul
Persuades me it is otherwise. Howe'er it be,
I cannot but be sad – so heavy sad
As thought, on thinking on no thought I think,
Makes me with heavy nothing faint and shrink.

BUSHY   'Tis nothing but conceit, my gracious lady.

QUEEN   'Tis nothing less. Conceit is still derived
From some forefather grief. Mine is not so,
For nothing hath begot my something grief,
Or something hath the nothing that I grieve.
'Tis in reversion that I do possess –
But what it is, that is not yet known what,
I cannot name. 'Tis nameless woe, I wot.

            ᶠ*Enter* GREEN.ᶠ

GREEN
God save your majesty! And well met, gentlemen.
I hope the King is not yet shipped for Ireland.

QUEEN   Why hop'st thou so? 'Tis better hope he is,
For his designs crave haste, his haste good hope.
Then wherefore dost thou hope he is not shipped?

GREEN
That he, our hope, might have retired his power
And driven into despair an enemy's hope,
Who strongly hath set footing in this land.
The banished Bolingbroke repeals himself,
And with uplifted arms is safe arrived
At Ravenspurgh.

QUEEN   Now God in heaven forbid!

GREEN   Ah, madam, 'tis too true; and, that is worse,
The lord Northumberland, his son, young Harry Percy,
The lords of Ross, Beaumont and Willoughby,
With all their powerful friends are fled to him.

BUSHY
Why have you not proclaimed Northumberland
And all the rest revolted faction, traitors?

GREEN   We have, whereupon the Earl of Worcester
Hath broken his staff, resigned his stewardship,
And all the household servants fled with him
To Bolingbroke.

QUEEN   So, Green, thou art the midwife to my woe,
And Bolingbroke my sorrow's dismal heir.
Now hath my soul brought forth her prodigy,
And I, a gasping new-delivered mother,
Have woe to woe, sorrow to sorrow joined.

BUSHY   Despair not, madam.

QUEEN   Who shall hinder me?
I will despair and be at enmity
With cozening Hope. He is a flatterer,
A parasite, a keeper-back of Death

Who gently would dissolve the bands of life,
Which false Hope lingers in extremity.

            ᶠ*Enter* YORK.ᶠ

GREEN   Here comes the Duke of York.

QUEEN   With signs of war about his aged neck.
O, full of careful business are his looks!
Uncle, for God's sake, speak comfortable words.

YORK   Should I do so, I should belie my thoughts.
Comfort's in heaven, and we are on the earth,
Where nothing lives but crosses, cares and grief.
Your husband, he is gone to save far off,
Whilst others come to make him lose at home.
Here am I left to underprop his land,
Who, weak with age, cannot support myself.
Now comes the sick hour that his surfeit made;
Now shall he try his friends that flattered him.

           ᶠ*Enter a* Servingman.ᶠ

SERVINGMAN [*to York*]
My lord, your son was gone before I came.

YORK   He was? Why, so! Go all which way it will!
The nobles they are fled, the commons they are cold
And will, I fear, revolt on Hereford's side.
Sirrah, get thee to Pleshy to my sister Gloucester;
Bid her send me presently a thousand pound.
Hold, take my ring.

SERVINGMAN
My lord, I had forgot to tell your lordship:
Today, as I came by, I called there –
But I shall grieve you to report the rest.

YORK   What is't, knave?

SERVINGMAN   An hour before I came, the Duchess died.

YORK   God for His mercy, what a tide of woes
Comes rushing on this woeful land at once!
I know not what to do. I would to God –
So my untruth had not provoked him to it –
The King had cut off my head with my brother's.
What, are there no posts dispatched for Ireland?
How shall we do for money for these wars?
[*to Queen*] Come, sister – cousin, I would say – pray
   pardon me.
[*to Servingman*] Go, fellow, get thee home; provide
   some carts
And bring away the armour that is there.
                        Exit Servingman.
[*to Bushy, Bagot and Green*] Gentlemen, will you go
   muster men?
If I know how or which way to order these affairs
Thus disorderly thrust into my hands,
Never believe me. Both are my kinsmen.
Th'one is my sovereign, whom both my oath
And duty bids defend; th'other again
Is my kinsman, whom the King hath wronged,
Whom conscience and my kindred bids to right.
Well, somewhat we must do. [*to Queen*] Come,
   cousin, I'll

Dispose of you. –
Gentlemen, go muster up your men,
And meet me presently at Berkeley ᶠCastleᶠ.
120 I should to Pleshy too,
But time will not permit. All is uneven,
And everything is left at six and seven.
                              Exeunt Duke of York and Queen.
BUSHY   The wind sits fair for news to go for Ireland,
But none returns. For us to levy power
125 Proportionable to the enemy is all unpossible.
GREEN   Besides, our nearness to the King in love
Is near the hate of those love not the King.
BAGOT
And that's the wavering commons, for their love
Lies in their purses; and whoso empties them,
130 By so much fills their hearts with deadly hate.
BUSHY
Wherein the King stands generally condemned.
BAGOT   If judgement lie in them, then so do we,
Because we ever have been near the King.
GREEN   Well, I will for refuge straight to Bristol Castle.
135 The Earl of Wiltshire is already there.
BUSHY   Thither will I with you, for little office
Will the hateful commons perform for us
Except like curs to tear us all to pieces.
[*to Bagot*] Will you go along with us?
140 BAGOT   No, I will to Ireland to his majesty.
Farewell. If heart's presages be not vain,
We three here part that ne'er shall meet again.
BUSHY
That's as York thrives to beat back Bolingbroke.
GREEN   Alas, poor Duke! The task he undertakes
145 Is numbering sands and drinking oceans dry.
Where one on his side fights, thousands will fly.
BAGOT   Farewell at once – for once, for all and ever.
BUSHY   Well, we may meet again.
BAGOT   I fear me, never.   ᶠ*Exeunt.*ᶠ

2.3   *Enter* BOLINGBROKE (ᶠDuke ofᶠ
           Hereford) ᶠ*and*ᶠ NORTHUMBERLAND
                 with Soldiers.

BOLINGBROKE   How far is it, my lord, to Berkeley now?
NORTHUMBERLAND   Believe me, noble lord,
I am a stranger here in Gloucestershire.
These high wild hills and rough uneven ways
5 Draws out our miles and makes them wearisome.
And yet your fair discourse hath been as sugar,
Making the hard way sweet and delectable.
But I bethink me what a weary way
From Ravenspurgh to Cotshall will be found
10 In Ross and Willoughby, wanting your company,
Which I protest hath very much beguiled
The tediousness and process of my travel.
But theirs is sweetened with the hope to have
The present benefit which I possess;
15 And hope to joy is little less in joy

Than hope enjoyed. By this the weary lords
Shall make their way seem short as mine hath done
By sight of what I have, your noble company.
BOLINGBROKE   Of much less value is my company
Than your good words.

                    Enter HARRY PERCY.

                              But who comes here?   20
NORTHUMBERLAND
It is my son, young Harry Percy,
Sent from my brother Worcester whencesoever.
Harry, how fares your uncle?
HARRY PERCY
I had thought, my lord, to have learned his health of
you.
NORTHUMBERLAND   Why, is he not with the Queen?   25
HARRY PERCY
No, my good lord. He hath forsook the court,
Broken his staff of office, and dispersed
The household of the King.
NORTHUMBERLAND   What was his reason?
He was not so resolved when last we spake together.
HARRY PERCY
Because your lordship was proclaimed traitor.   30
But he, my lord, is gone to Ravenspurgh
To offer service to the Duke of Hereford,
And sent me over by Berkeley to discover
What power the Duke of York had levied there,
Then with directions to repair to Ravenspurgh.   35
NORTHUMBERLAND
Have you forgot the Duke of Hereford, boy?
HARRY PERCY   No, my good lord; for that is not forgot
Which ne'er I did remember. To my knowledge
I never in my life did look on him.
NORTHUMBERLAND
Then learn to know him now. This is the Duke.   40
HARRY PERCY [*to Bolingbroke*]
My gracious lord, I tender you my service,
Such as it is, being tender, raw and young,
Which elder days shall ripen and confirm
To more approved service and desert.
BOLINGBROKE   I thank thee, gentle Percy; and be sure,   45
I count myself in nothing else so happy
As in a soul rememb'ring my good friends;
And as my fortune ripens with thy love,
It shall be still thy true love's recompense.
My heart this covenant makes; my hand thus seals it.   50
   [*Clasps Harry Percy's hand.*]
NORTHUMBERLAND [*to Harry Percy*]
How far is it to Berkeley, and what stir
Keeps good old York there with his men of war?
HARRY PERCY
There stands the castle by yon tuft of trees,
Manned with three hundred men, as I have heard.
And in it are the lords of York, Berkeley and
   Seymour –   55
None else of name and noble estimate.

Enter ROSS *and* WILLOUGHBY.

NORTHUMBERLAND
Here come the lords of Ross and Willoughby,
Bloody with spurring, fiery-red with haste.

BOLINGBROKE
Welcome, my lords. I wot your love pursues
A banished traitor. All my treasury
Is yet but unfelt thanks, which, more enriched,
Shall be your love and labour's recompense.

ROSS   Your presence makes us rich, most noble lord.

WILLOUGHBY
And far surmounts our labour to attain it.

BOLINGBROKE
Evermore thanks – the exchequer of the poor,
Which, till my infant fortune comes to years,
Stands for my bounty.

Enter BERKELEY.

                        But who comes here?

NORTHUMBERLAND
It is my lord of Berkeley, as I guess.

BERKELEY   My lord of Hereford, my message is to you –

BOLINGBROKE   My lord, my answer is – to 'Lancaster',
And I am come to seek that name in England;
And I must find that title in your tongue
Before I make reply to aught you say.

BERKELEY
Mistake me not, my lord, 'tis not my meaning
To rase one title of your honour out.
To you, my lord, I come, what lord you will,
From the most gracious regent of this land,
The Duke of York, to know what pricks you on
To take advantage of the absent time
And fright our native peace with self-borne arms.

Enter YORK *with Attendants.*

BOLINGBROKE
I shall not need transport my words by you.
Here comes his grace in person. My noble uncle!
[*Kneels.*]

YORK   Show me thy humble heart, and not thy knee,
Whose duty is deceivable and false.

BOLINGBROKE   My gracious uncle –

YORK   Tut, tut!
Grace me no grace, nor uncle me no uncle.
I am no traitor's uncle, and that word 'grace'
In an ungracious mouth is but profane.
Why have those banished and forbidden legs
Dared once to touch a dust of England's ground?
But then, more why – why have they dared to march
So many miles upon her peaceful bosom,
Frighting her pale-faced villages with war
And ostentation of despised arms?
Com'st thou because the anointed King is hence?
Why, foolish boy, the King is left behind,
And in my loyal bosom lies his power.
Were I but now *the* lord of such hot youth

As when brave Gaunt, thy father, and myself   100
Rescued the Black Prince, that young Mars of men,
From forth the ranks of many thousand French,
O, then how quickly should this arm of mine,
Now prisoner to the palsy, chastise thee
And minister correction to thy fault!   105

BOLINGBROKE
My gracious uncle, let me know my fault.
On what condition stands it and wherein?

YORK   Even in condition of the worst degree,
In gross rebellion and detested treason.
Thou art a banished man, and here art come,   110
Before the expiration of thy time,
In braving arms against thy sovereign.

BOLINGBROKE
As I was banished, I was banished Hereford;
But as I come, I come for Lancaster.
And noble uncle, I beseech your grace,   115
Look on my wrongs with an indifferent eye.
You are my father, for methinks in you
I see old Gaunt alive. O then, my father,
Will you permit that I shall stand condemned
A wandering vagabond, my rights and royalties   120
Plucked from my arms perforce and given away
To upstart unthrifts? Wherefore was I born?
If that my cousin king be King in England,
It must be granted I am Duke of Lancaster.
You have a son, Aumerle, my noble cousin.   125
Had you first died and he been thus trod down,
He should have found his uncle Gaunt a father
To rouse his wrongs and chase them to the bay.
I am denied to sue my livery here,
And yet my letters patents give me leave.   130
My father's goods are all distrained and sold,
And these, and all, are all amiss employed.
What would you have me do? I am a subject,
And I challenge law. Attorneys are denied me,
And therefore personally I lay my claim   135
To my inheritance of free descent.

NORTHUMBERLAND
The noble Duke hath been too much abused.

ROSS   It stands your grace upon to do him right.

WILLOUGHBY
Base men by his endowments are made great.

YORK   My lords of England, let me tell you this: 140
I have had feeling of my cousin's wrongs
And laboured all I could to do him right.
But in this kind to come – in braving arms
Be his own carver, and cut out his way
To find out right with wrong – it may not be.   145
And you that do abet him in this kind
Cherish rebellion and are rebels all.

NORTHUMBERLAND
The noble Duke hath sworn his coming is
But for his own; and for the right of that
We all have strongly sworn to give him aid.   150
And let him never see joy that breaks that oath!

YORK   Well, well, I see the issue of these arms.
        I cannot mend it, I must needs confess,
        Because my power is weak and all ill-left;
155   But if I could, by Him that gave me life,
        I would attach you all and make you stoop
        Unto the sovereign mercy of the King.
        But since I cannot, be it known unto you
        I do remain as neuter. So fare you well –
160   Unless you please to enter in the castle
        And there repose you for this night.
BOLINGBROKE   An offer, uncle, that we will accept;
        But we must win your grace to go with us
        To Bristol Castle, which, they say, is held
165   By Bushy, Bagot and their complices,
        The caterpillars of the commonwealth,
        Which I have sworn to weed and pluck away.
YORK   It may be I will go with you; but yet I'll pause,
        For I am loath to break our country's laws.
170   Nor friends nor foes, to me welcome you are.
        Things past redress are now with me past care.
                                        Exeunt.

2.4   *Enter* Earl of SALISBURY *and a*
                    Welsh Captain.

CAPTAIN   My lord of Salisbury, we have stayed ten days
        And hardly kept our countrymen together,
        And yet we hear no tidings from the King.
        Therefore we will disperse ourselves. Farewell.
5   SALISBURY   Stay yet another day, thou trusty Welshman.
        The King reposeth all his confidence in thee.
CAPTAIN
        'Tis thought the King is dead. We will not stay.
        The bay trees in our country are all withered,
        And meteors fright the fixed stars of heaven;
10   The pale-faced moon looks bloody on the earth,
        And lean-looked prophets whisper fearful change;
        Rich men look sad, and ruffians dance and leap,
        The one in fear to lose what they enjoy,
        The other to enjoy by rage and war.
15   These signs forerun the death or fall of kings.
        Farewell. Our countrymen are gone and fled,
        As well assured Richard their king is dead.   ᶠ*Exit.*ᶠ
SALISBURY   Ah, Richard, with the eyes of heavy mind
        I see thy glory like a shooting star
20   Fall to the base earth from the firmament.
        Thy sun sets weeping in the lowly west,
        Witnessing storms to come, woe and unrest.
        Thy friends are fled to wait upon thy foes,
        And crossly to thy good all fortune goes.   ᶠ*Exit.*ᶠ

3.1   *Enter* ᶠBOLINGBROKEᶠ (Duke of
        Hereford), YORK, NORTHUMBERLAND, ᶠROSS,
        HARRY PERCY, WILLOUGHBY, *with*ᶠ BUSHY
            and GREEN *as prisoners, and Soldiers.*

BOLINGBROKE   Bring forth these men.
        [*Bushy and Green stand forth.*]

Bushy and Green, I will not vex your souls –
Since presently your souls must part your bodies –
With too much urging your pernicious lives,
For 'twere no charity; yet to wash your blood   5
From off my hands, here in the view of men
I will unfold some causes of your deaths:
You have misled a prince, a royal king,
A happy gentleman in blood and lineaments,
By you unhappied and disfigured clean.   10
You have in manner with your sinful hours
Made a divorce betwixt his queen and him,
Broke the possession of a royal bed
And stained the beauty of a fair queen's cheeks
With tears drawn from her eyes by your foul wrongs.   15
Myself, a prince by fortune of my birth,
Near to the King in blood, and near in love
Till you did make him misinterpret me,
Have stooped my neck under your injuries
And sighed my English breath in foreign clouds,   20
Eating the bitter bread of banishment,
Whilst you have fed upon my signories,
Disparked my parks and felled my forest woods,
From my own windows torn my household coat,
Rased out my imprese, leaving me no sign   25
Save men's opinions and my living blood
To show the world I am a gentleman.
This and much more, much more than twice all this,
Condemns you to the death. See them delivered
    over
To execution and the hand of death.   30
BUSHY   More welcome is the stroke of death to me
        Than Bolingbroke to England. Lords, farewell.
GREEN   My comfort is that heaven will take our souls
        And plague injustice with the pains of hell.
BOLINGBROKE
        My Lord Northumberland, see them dispatched.   35
                    Exeunt Northumberland and Soldiers
                                with Bushy and Green.
        [*to York*] Uncle, you say the Queen is at your house.
        For God's sake, fairly let her be entreated.
        Tell her I send to her my kind commends;
        Take special care my greetings be delivered.
YORK   A gentleman of mine I have dispatched   40
        With letters of your love to her at large.
BOLINGBROKE
        Thanks, gentle uncle. Come, lords, away,
        To fight with Glendower and his complices.
        A while to work, and after holiday.   *Exeunt.*

3.2   ᶠ*Drums. Flourish and Colours.*ᶠ *Enter*
        KING ᶠRICHARD,ᶠ AUMERLE, Bishop of
                CARLISLE *and Soldiers.*

KING RICHARD
        Barkloughly Castle call they this at hand?
AUMERLE   Yea, my lord. How brooks your grace the air
        After your late tossing on the breaking seas?

KING RICHARD
    Needs must I like it well. I weep for joy
    To stand upon my kingdom once again.
    Dear earth, I do salute thee with my hand,
    Though rebels wound thee with their horses' hoofs.
    As a long-parted mother with her child
    Plays fondly with her tears and smiles in meeting,
10   So weeping, smiling, greet I thee, my earth,
    And do thee favours with my royal hands.
    Feed not thy sovereign's foe, my gentle earth,
    Nor with thy sweets comfort his ravenous sense,
    But let thy spiders that suck up thy venom
15   And heavy-gaited toads lie in their way,
    Doing annoyance to the treacherous feet
    Which with usurping steps do trample thee.
    Yield stinging nettles to mine enemies;
    And when they from thy bosom pluck a flower,
20   Guard it, I pray thee, with a lurking adder
    Whose double tongue may with a mortal touch
    Throw death upon thy sovereign's enemies.
    Mock not my senseless conjuration, lords.
    This earth shall have a feeling, and these stones
25   Prove armed soldiers, ere her native king
    Shall falter under foul rebellion's arms.
CARLISLE
    Fear not, my lord. That Power that made you king
    Hath power to keep you king in spite of all.
    The means that heavens yield must be embraced
30   And not neglected; else heaven would,
    And we will not. Heaven's offer we refuse –
    The proffered means of succour and redress.
AUMERLE   He means, my lord, that we are too remiss,
    Whilst Bolingbroke, through our security,
35   Grows strong and great in substance and in power.
KING RICHARD   Discomfortable cousin, knowst thou not
    That when the searching eye of heaven is hid
    Behind the globe and lights the lower world,
    Then thieves and robbers range abroad unseen
40   In murders and in outrage boldly here;
    But when from under this terrestrial ball
    He fires the proud tops of the eastern pines
    And darts his light through every guilty hole,
    Then murders, treasons and detested sins,
45   The cloak of night being plucked from off their backs,
    Stand bare and naked, trembling at themselves?
    So, when this thief, this traitor, Bolingbroke,
    Who all this while hath revelled in the night
    Whilst we were wand'ring with the Antipodes,
50   Shall see us rising in our throne, the east,
    His treasons will sit blushing in his face,
    Not able to endure the sight of day,
    But, self-affrighted, tremble at his sin.
    Not all the water in the rough rude sea
55   Can wash the balm off from an anointed king;
    The breath of worldly men cannot depose
    The deputy elected by the Lord.
    For every man that Bolingbroke hath pressed

    To lift shrewd steel against our golden crown,
    God for His Richard hath in heavenly pay   60
    A glorious angel. Then, if angels fight,
    Weak men must fall, for heaven still guards the right.

Enter SALISBURY.

    Welcome, my lord. How far off lies your power?
SALISBURY   Nor near nor farther off, my gracious lord,
    Than this weak arm. Discomfort guides my tongue   65
    And bids me speak of nothing but despair.
    One day too late, I fear me, noble lord,
    Hath clouded all thy happy days on earth.
    O, call back yesterday, bid time return,
    And thou shalt have twelve thousand fighting men!   70
    Today, today, unhappy day too late,
    O'erthrows thy joys, friends, fortune and thy state;
    For all the Welshmen, hearing thou wert dead,
    Are gone to Bolingbroke, dispersed and fled.
AUMERLE
    Comfort, my liege. Why looks your grace so pale?   75
KING RICHARD
    But now the blood of twenty thousand men
    Did triumph in my face, and they are fled;
    And till so much blood thither come again,
    Have I not reason to look pale and dead?
    All souls that will be safe, fly from my side,   80
    For Time hath set a blot upon my pride.
AUMERLE
    Comfort, my liege. Remember who you are.
KING RICHARD   I had forgot myself. Am I not king?
    Awake, thou coward Majesty, thou sleepest!
    Is not the King's name twenty thousand names?   85
    Arm, arm, my name! A puny subject strikes
    At thy great glory. Look not to the ground,
    Ye favourites of a king. Are we not high?
    High be our thoughts! I know my uncle York
    Hath power enough to serve our turn.

Enter SCROOP.

                           But who comes here?   90
SCROOP   More health and happiness betide my liege
    Than can my care-tuned tongue deliver him.
KING RICHARD
    Mine ear is open and my heart prepared.
    The worst is worldly loss thou canst unfold.
    Say, is my kingdom lost? Why, 'twas my care;   95
    And what loss is it to be rid of care?
    Strives Bolingbroke to be as great as we?
    Greater he shall not be. If he serve God,
    We'll serve Him too, and be his fellow so.
    Revolt our subjects? That we cannot mend.   100
    They break their faith to God as well as us.
    Cry woe, destruction, ruin and decay.
    The worst is death, and Death will have his day.
SCROOP   Glad am I that your highness is so armed
    To bear the tidings of calamity.   105
    Like an unseasonable stormy day,

Which makes the silver rivers drown their shores
As if the world were all dissolved to tears,
So high above his limits swells the rage
110 Of Bolingbroke, covering your fearful land
With hard bright steel and hearts harder than steel.
Whitebeards have armed their thin and hairless scalps
Against thy majesty; boys with women's voices
Strive to speak big and clap their female joints
115 In stiff unwieldy arms against thy crown;
Thy very beadsmen learn to bend their bows
Of double-fatal yew against thy state;
Yea, distaff-women manage rusty bills
Against thy seat. Both young and old rebel,
120 And all goes worse than I have power to tell.
KING RICHARD
    Too well, too well, thou tell'st a tale so ill.
    Where is the Earl of Wiltshire? Where is Bagot?
    What is become of Bushy? Where is Green? –
    That they have let the dangerous enemy
125 Measure our confines with such peaceful steps?
    If we prevail, their heads shall pay for it!
    I warrant they have made peace with Bolingbroke.
SCROOP
    Peace have they made with him indeed, my lord.
KING RICHARD
    O, villains, vipers damned without redemption!
130 Dogs easily won to fawn on any man!
    Snakes, in my heart-blood warmed, that sting my
        heart!
    Three Judases, each one thrice worse than Judas!
    Would they make peace? Terrible hell
    Make war upon their spotted souls for this!
135 SCROOP   Sweet love, I see, changing his property,
    Turns to the sourest and most deadly hate.
    Again uncurse their souls. Their peace is made
    With heads, and not with hands. Those whom you
        curse
    Have felt the worst of death's destroying wound
140 And lie full low, graved in the hollow ground.
AUMERLE
    Is Bushy, Green and the Earl of Wiltshire dead?
SCROOP   Ay, all of them at Bristol lost their heads.
AUMERLE   Where is the Duke my father with his power?
KING RICHARD
    No matter where. Of comfort no man speak!
145 Let's talk of graves, of worms and epitaphs,
    Make dust our paper and with rainy eyes
    Write sorrow on the bosom of the earth.
    Let's choose executors and talk of wills.
    And yet not so, for what can we bequeath
150 Save our deposed bodies to the ground?
    Our lands, our lives and all are Bolingbroke's,
    And nothing can we call our own but death
    And that small model of the barren earth
    Which serves as paste and cover to our bones.
155 For God's sake let us sit upon the ground
    And tell sad stories of the death of kings –

How some have been deposed, some slain in war,
Some haunted by the ghosts they have deposed,
Some poisoned by their wives, some sleeping killed –
All murdered. For within the hollow crown   160
That rounds the mortal temples of a king
Keeps Death his court; and there the antic sits,
Scoffing his state and grinning at his pomp,
Allowing him a breath, a little scene,
To monarchize, be feared and kill with looks,   165
Infusing him with self and vain conceit,
As if this flesh which walls about our life
Were brass impregnable; and humoured thus,
Comes at the last and with a little pin
Bores through his castle wall, and farewell, king!   170
Cover your heads, and mock not flesh and blood
With solemn reverence. Throw away respect,
Tradition, form and ceremonious duty,
For you have but mistook me all this while.
I live with bread like you, feel want,   175
Taste grief, need friends. Subjected thus,
How can you say to me I am a king?
CARLISLE
    My lord, wise men ne'er sit and wail their woes,
    But presently prevent the ways to wail.
    To fear the foe, since fear oppresseth strength,   180
    Gives in your weakness strength unto your foe,
    And so your follies fight against yourself.
    Fear and be slain – no worse can come to fight;
    And fight and die is death destroying Death,
    While fearing dying pays Death servile breath.   185
AUMERLE   My father hath a power. Enquire of him,
    And learn to make a body of a limb.
KING RICHARD
    Thou chid'st me well. Proud Bolingbroke, I come
    To change blows with thee for our day of doom.
    This ague fit of fear is overblown.   190
    An easy task it is to win our own.
    Say, Scroop, where lies our uncle with his power?
    Speak sweetly, man, although thy looks be sour.
SCROOP   Men judge by the complexion of the sky
    The state and inclination of the day;   195
    So may you by my dull and heavy eye.
    My tongue hath but a heavier tale to say.
    I play the torturer by small and small
    To lengthen out the worst that must be spoken:
    Your uncle York is joined with Bolingbroke,   200
    And all your northern castles yielded up,
    And all your southern gentlemen in arms
    Upon his party.
KING RICHARD   Thou hast said enough.
    [*to Aumerle*] Beshrew thee, cousin, which didst lead
        me forth
    Of that sweet way I was in to despair.   205
    What say you now? What comfort have we now?
    By heaven, I'll hate him everlastingly
    That bids me be of comfort any more.
    Go to Flint Castle. There I'll pine away.

A king, woe's slave, shall kingly woe obey. 210
That power I have, discharge, and let them go
To ear the land that hath some hope to grow,
For I have none. Let no man speak again
To alter this, for counsel is but vain.

AUMERLE   My liege, one word.

KING RICHARD   He does me double wrong 215
That wounds me with the flatteries of his tongue.
Discharge my followers. Let them hence away,
From Richard's night to Bolingbroke's fair day.

          ᶠ*Exeunt.*ᶠ

3.3   *Enter* ᶠ*with Trumpet, Drum and Colours*ᶠ
    BOLINGBROKE, YORK, NORTHUMBERLAND,
    ᶠ*Attendants*ᶠ *and Soldiers.*

BOLINGBROKE   So that by this intelligence we learn
The Welshmen are dispersed, and Salisbury
Is gone to meet the King, who lately landed
With some few private friends upon this coast.

NORTHUMBERLAND
The news is very fair and good, my lord: 5
Richard not far from hence hath hid his head.

YORK   It would beseem the Lord Northumberland
To say 'King Richard'. Alack the heavy day
When such a sacred king should hide his head.

NORTHUMBERLAND
Your grace mistakes; only to be brief 10
Left I his title out.

YORK   The time hath been,
Would you have been so brief with him, he would
Have been so brief ᶠwith youᶠ to shorten you,
For taking so the head, your whole head's length.

BOLINGBROKE
Mistake not, uncle, further than you should. 15

YORK   Take not, good cousin, further than you should,
Lest you mis-take: the heavens are o'er our heads.

BOLINGBROKE   I know it, uncle, and oppose not myself
Against their will.

    Enter HARRY PERCY.

          But who comes here?
Welcome, Harry. What, will not this castle yield? 20

HARRY PERCY   The castle royally is manned, my lord,
Against thy entrance.

BOLINGBROKE   Royally?
Why? It contains no king.

HARRY PERCY   Yes, my good lord,
It doth contain a king. King Richard lies 25
Within the limits of yon lime and stone,
And with him are the Lord Aumerle, Lord Salisbury,
Sir Stephen Scroop, besides a clergyman
Of holy reverence – who, I cannot learn.

NORTHUMBERLAND
O, belike it is the Bishop of Carlisle. 30

BOLINGBROKE [*to Northumberland*]   Noble lord,
Go to the rude ribs of that ancient castle;

Through brazen trumpet send the breath of parley
Into his ruined ears, and thus deliver:
Henry Bolingbroke 35
On both his knees doth kiss King Richard's hand
And sends allegiance and true faith of heart
To his most royal person, hither come
Even at his feet to lay my arms and power
Provided that my banishment repealed 40
And lands restored again be freely granted.
If not, I'll use the advantage of my power
And lay the summer's dust with showers of blood
Rained from the wounds of slaughtered Englishmen –
The which how far off from the mind of Bolingbroke 45
It is such crimson tempest should bedrench
The fresh green lap of fair King Richard's land
My stooping duty tenderly shall show.
Go signify as much, while here we march
Upon the grassy carpet of this plain. 50

    [*Northumberland with Trumpet goes to the walls.*]
Let's march without the noise of threat'ning drum,
That from this castle's tattered battlements
Our fair appointments may be well perused.
Methinks King Richard and myself should meet
With no less terror than the elements 55
Of fire and water, when their thund'ring shock
At meeting tears the cloudy cheeks of heaven.
Be he the fire, I'll be the yielding water;
The rage be his, whilst on the earth I rain
My waters – on the earth and not on him. 60
March on, and mark King Richard how he looks.

    The trumpets sound a ᶠ*parley without and answer*
*within; then a flourish.*ᶠ KING RICHARD *appeareth above*
on the walls with Bishop of ᶠCARLISLE, AUMERLE,
    SCROOP *and* SALISBURYᶠ.

See, see, King Richard doth himself appear,
As doth the blushing discontented sun
From out the fiery portal of the east,
When he perceives the envious clouds are bent 65
To dim his glory and to stain the track
Of his bright passage to the Occident.

YORK   Yet looks he like a king. Behold, his eye,
As bright as is the eagle's, lightens forth
Controlling majesty. Alack, alack for woe 70
That any harm should stain so fair a show!

KING RICHARD [*to Northumberland*]
We are amazed, and thus long have we stood
To watch the fearful bending of thy knee
Because we thought ourself thy lawful king.
And if we be, how dare thy joints forget 75
To pay their awful duty to our presence?
If we be not, show us the hand of God
That hath dismissed us from our stewardship;
For well we know no hand of blood and bone
Can gripe the sacred handle of our sceptre, 80
Unless he do profane, steal or usurp.
And though you think that all, as you have done,

Have torn their souls by turning them from us,
And we are barren and bereft of friends,
85 Yet know: my Master, God omnipotent,
Is mustering in His clouds on our behalf
Armies of pestilence, and they shall strike
Your children, yet unborn and unbegot,
That lift your vassal hands against my head
90 And threat the glory of my precious crown.
Tell Bolingbroke – for yon methinks he stands –
That every stride he makes upon my land
Is dangerous treason. He is come to open
The purple testament of bleeding war;
95 But ere the crown he looks for live in peace,
Ten thousand bloody crowns of mothers' sons
Shall ill become the flower of England's face,
Change the complexion of her maid-pale peace
To scarlet indignation, and bedew
100 Her pastor's grass with faithful English blood.

NORTHUMBERLAND
The King of Heaven forbid our lord the King
Should so with civil and uncivil arms
Be rushed upon! Thy thrice-noble cousin,
Harry Bolingbroke, doth humbly kiss thy hand;
105 And by the honourable tomb he swears
That stands upon your royal grandsire's bones,
And by the royalties of both your bloods –
Currents that spring from one most gracious head –
And by the buried hand of warlike Gaunt,
110 And by the worth and honour of himself,
Comprising all that may be sworn or said,
His coming hither hath no further scope
Than for his lineal royalties, and to beg
Enfranchisement immediate on his knees;
115 Which on thy royal party granted once,
His glittering arms he will commend to rust,
His barbed steeds to stables and his heart
To faithful service of your majesty.
This swears he, as he is a prince and just;
120 And, as I am a gentleman, I credit him.

KING RICHARD
Northumberland, say thus the King returns:
His noble cousin is right welcome hither,
And all the number of his fair demands
Shall be accomplished without contradiction.
125 With all the gracious utterance thou hast,
Speak to his gentle hearing kind commends.
    [*Northumberland with Trumpet returns to Bolingbroke.*]
[*to Aumerle*] We do debase ourselves, cousin, do we not,
To look so poorly and to speak so fair?
Shall we call back Northumberland and send
130 Defiance to the traitor, and so die?

AUMERLE
No, good my lord. Let's fight with gentle words
Till time lend friends, and friends their helpful swords.

KING RICHARD
O God, O God, that e'er this tongue of mine
That laid the sentence of dread banishment

On yon proud man should take it off again   135
With words of sooth! O, that I were as great
As is my grief, or lesser than my name!
Or that I could forget what I have been,
Or not remember what I must be now!
Swell'st thou, proud heart? I'll give thee scope to
    beat,   140
Since foes have scope to beat both thee and me.
    [*Northumberland returns to the walls.*]

AUMERLE
Northumberland comes back from Bolingbroke.

KING RICHARD
What must the King do now? Must he submit?
The King shall do it. Must he be deposed?
The King shall be contented. Must he lose   145
The name of King? I'God's name, let it go.
I'll give my jewels for a set of beads,
My gorgeous palace for a hermitage,
My gay apparel for an almsman's gown,
My figured goblets for a dish of wood,   150
My sceptre for a palmer's walking staff,
My subjects for a pair of carved saints
And my large kingdom for a little grave,
A little, little grave, an obscure grave;
Or I'll be buried in the King's highway,   155
Some way of common trade, where subjects' feet
May hourly trample on their sovereign's head;
For on my heart they tread now whilst I live,
And, buried once, why not upon my head?
Aumerle, thou weep'st, my tender-hearted cousin! 160
We'll make foul weather with despised tears;
Our sighs and they shall lodge the summer corn
And make a dearth in this revolting land.
Or shall we play the wantons with our woes
And make some pretty match with shedding tears, 165
As thus, to drop them still upon one place
Till they have fretted us a pair of graves
Within the earth; and, therein laid, there lies
Two kinsmen digged their graves with weeping
    eyes?
Would not this ill do well? Well, well, I see   170
I talk but idly, and you laugh at me.
    [*to Northumberland*] Most mighty prince, my Lord
    Northumberland,
What says King Bolingbroke? Will his majesty
Give Richard leave to live till Richard die?
You make a leg, and Bolingbroke says 'ay'.   175

NORTHUMBERLAND
My lord, in the base court he doth attend
To speak with you. May it please you to come down?

KING RICHARD
Down, down I come, like glist'ring Phaëton,
Wanting the manage of unruly jades.
In the base court? Base court where kings grow base 180
To come at traitors' calls and do them grace.
In the base court? Come down? Down court, down
    king!

For night-owls shriek where mounting larks should sing.
    Exeunt King Richard and his Followers from above.
    [*Northumberland returns to Bolingbroke.*]
BOLINGBROKE   What says his majesty?
NORTHUMBERLAND   Sorrow and grief of heart
  Makes him speak fondly like a frantic man. 185

   Flourish. Enter below KING RICHARD *and his Followers.*

  Yet he is come.
BOLINGBROKE   Stand all apart,
  And show fair duty to his majesty.   [*Kneels down.*]
  My gracious lord.
KING RICHARD
  Fair cousin, you debase your princely knee 190
  To make the base earth proud with kissing it.
  Me rather had my heart might feel your love
  Than my unpleased eye see your courtesy.
  Up cousin, up. Your heart is up, I know,
    [*Raises Bolingbroke.*]
  Thus high at least,   [*Indicates crown.*]
            although your knee be low. 195
BOLINGBROKE
  My gracious lord, I come but for mine own.
KING RICHARD
  Your own is yours, and I am yours and all.
BOLINGBROKE
  So far be mine, my most redoubted lord,
  As my true service shall deserve your love.
KING RICHARD
  Well you deserve. They well deserve to have 200
  That know the strong'st and surest way to get!
  [*to York*] Uncle, give me your hands. Nay, dry your
    eyes.
  Tears show their love, but want their remedies.
  [*to Bolingbroke*] Cousin, I am too young to be your
    father,
  Though you are old enough to be my heir. 205
  What you will have, I'll give, and willing too;
  For do we must what force will have us do.
  Set on towards London, cousin, is it so?
BOLINGBROKE   Yea, my good lord.
KING RICHARD   Then I must not say no.
    ᶠ*Flourish. Exeunt.*ᶠ

3.4   *Enter the* QUEEN *with two* Ladies.

QUEEN   What sport shall we devise here in this garden
  To drive away the heavy thought of care?
1 LADY   Madam, we'll play at bowls.
QUEEN   'Twill make me think the world is full of rubs,
  And that my fortune runs against the bias.
2 LADY   Madam, we'll dance. 5
QUEEN   My legs can keep no measure in delight
  When my poor heart no measure keeps in grief.
  Therefore, no dancing, girl; some other sport.
1 LADY   Madam, we'll tell tales. 10
QUEEN   Of sorrow or of joy?

1 LADY   Of either, madam.
QUEEN   Of neither, girl.
  For if of joy, being altogether wanting,
  It doth remember me the more of sorrow.
  Or if of grief, being altogether had, 15
  It adds more sorrow to my want of joy.
  For what I have I need not to repeat,
  And what I want it boots not to complain.
2 LADY   Madam, I'll sing.
QUEEN   'Tis well that thou hast cause;
  But thou shouldst please me better, wouldst thou weep. 20
2 LADY   I could weep, madam, would it do you good.
QUEEN   And I could sing, would weeping do me good,
  And never borrow any tear of thee.

    Enter GARDENER ᶠ*and his two* Menᶠ.

  But stay, here come the gardeners.
  Let's step into the shadow of these trees. 25
  My wretchedness unto a row of pins
  They will talk of state, for everyone doth so
  Against a change; woe is forerun with woe.
    [*Queen and Ladies stand apart.*]
GARDENER [*to one Man*]
  Go bind thou up young dangling apricocks,
  Which, like unruly children, make their sire 30
  Stoop with oppression of their prodigal weight.
  Give some supportance to the bending twigs.
  [*to the other Man*]
  Go thou, and, like an executioner,
  Cut off the heads of too fast-growing sprays
  That look too lofty in our commonwealth. 35
  All must be even in our government.
  You thus employed, I will go root away
  The noisome weeds, which without profit suck
  The soil's fertility from wholesome flowers.
1 MAN   Why should we in the compass of a pale 40
  Keep law and form and due proportion,
  Showing, as in a model, our firm estate,
  When our sea-walled garden, the whole land,
  Is full of weeds, her fairest flowers choked up,
  Her fruit trees all unpruned, her hedges ruined, 45
  Her knots disordered and her wholesome herbs
  Swarming with caterpillars?
GARDENER   Hold thy peace.
  He that hath suffered this disordered spring
  Hath now himself met with the fall of leaf.
  The weeds which his broad-spreading leaves did
    shelter, 50
  That seemed in eating him to hold him up,
  Are plucked up, root and all, by Bolingbroke –
  I mean the Earl of Wiltshire, Bushy, Green.
2 MAN   What, are they dead?
GARDENER   They are. And Bolingbroke
  Hath seized the wasteful King. O, what pity is it 55
  That he had not so trimmed and dressed his land
  As we this garden! We at time of year
  Do wound the bark, the skin of our fruit trees,

Lest, being over-proud in sap and blood,
With too much riches it confound itself.
Had he done so to great and growing men,
They might have lived to bear and he to taste
Their fruits of duty. Superfluous branches
We lop away that bearing boughs may live.
Had he done so, himself had borne the crown,
Which waste of idle hours hath quite thrown down.

1 MAN
What, think you then the King shall be deposed?
GARDENER   Depressed he is already, and deposed
'Tis doubt he will be. Letters came last night
To a dear friend of the good Duke of York's
That tell black tidings.
QUEEN   O, I am pressed to death
Through want of speaking!
[*Queen and Ladies come forward.*]
                              Thou, old Adam's likeness,
Set to dress this garden, how dares
Thy harsh rude tongue sound this unpleasing
      news?
What Eve, what serpent hath suggested thee
To make a second fall of cursed man?
Why dost thou say King Richard is deposed?
Dar'st thou, thou little better thing than earth,
Divine his downfall? Say where, when and how
Cam'st thou by this ill tidings? Speak, thou
      wretch!
GARDENER   Pardon me, madam. Little joy have I
To breathe this news; yet what I say is true.
King Richard he is in the mighty hold
Of Bolingbroke. Their fortunes both are weighed:
In your lord's scale is nothing but himself
And some few vanities that make him light;
But in the balance of great Bolingbroke,
Besides himself, are all the English peers,
And with that odds he weighs King Richard down.
Post you to London and you will find it so.
I speak no more than everyone doth know.
QUEEN   Nimble Mischance, that art so light of foot,
Doth not thy embassage belong to me,
And am I last that knows it? O, thou think'st
To serve me last that I may longest keep
Thy sorrow in my breast. Come, ladies, go
To meet at London London's king in woe.
What, was I born to this, that my sad look
Should grace the triumph of great Bolingbroke?
Gard'ner, for telling me these news of woe,
Pray God the plants thou graft'st may never grow!
                                        Exit with Ladies.
GARDENER
Poor Queen, so that thy state might be no worse,
I would my skill were subject to thy curse.
Here did she fall a tear. Here in this place
I'll set a bank of rue, sour herb of grace.
Rue e'en for ruth here shortly shall be seen
In the remembrance of a weeping queen.   *Exeunt.*

4.1   *Enter* BOLINGBROKE *with the lords,*
      ᶠAUMERLE, NORTHUMBERLAND, HARRY
      PERCY, FITZWATER, SURREY, Bishop of
      CARLISLE, ABBOT *of Westminster, another*
      Lord, *Herald*ᶠ *and Attendants to Parliament.*

BOLINGBROKE   Call forth Bagot.

      Enter ᶠ*Officers with*ᶠ BAGOT.

Now, Bagot, freely speak thy mind,
What thou dost know of noble Gloucester's death,
Who wrought it with the King, and who performed
The bloody office of his timeless end.
BAGOT   Then set before my face the Lord Aumerle.
BOLINGBROKE
Cousin, stand forth, and look upon that man.
      [*Aumerle comes forward.*]
BAGOT   My Lord Aumerle, I know your daring tongue
Scorns to unsay what once it hath delivered.
In that dead time when Gloucester's death was plotted,
I heard you say, 'Is not my arm of length,
That reacheth from the restful English court
As far as Calais to mine uncle's head?'
Amongst much other talk, that very time,
I heard you say that you had rather refuse
The offer of an hundred thousand crowns
Than Bolingbroke's return to England –
Adding withal how blest this land would be
In this your cousin's death.
AUMERLE   Princes and noble lords,
What answer shall I make to this base man?
Shall I so much dishonour my fair stars
On equal terms to give him chastisement?
Either I must, or have mine honour soiled
With the attainder of his sland'rous lips.
      [*Throws down his gage.*]
There is my gage, the manual seal of death
That marks thee out for hell. I say thou liest,
And will maintain what thou hast said is false
In thy heart-blood, though being all too base
To stain the temper of my knightly sword.
BOLINGBROKE   Bagot, forbear. Thou shalt not take it up.
AUMERLE   Excepting one, I would he were the best
In all this presence that hath moved me so.
FITZWATER [*to Aumerle*]
If that thy valour stand on sympathy,
There is my gage, Aumerle, in gage to thine.
      [*Throws down his gage.*]
By that fair sun which shows me where thou stand'st,
I heard thee say – and vauntingly thou spak'st it –
That thou wert cause of noble Gloucester's death.
If thou deniest it twenty times, thou liest!
And I will turn thy falsehood to thy heart,
Where it was forged, with my rapier's point.
AUMERLE   Thou dar'st not, coward, live to see that day.
      [*Takes up gage.*]
FITZWATER   Now, by my soul, I would it were this hour!

810

AUMERLE   Fitzwater, thou art damned to hell for this.

HARRY PERCY
45   Aumerle, thou liest. His honour is as true
     In this appeal as thou art all unjust.
     And that thou art so, there I throw my gage
     To prove it on thee to the extremest point
     Of mortal breathing.   [*Throws down his gage.*]
                           Seize it if thou dar'st.

50 AUMERLE   And if I do not, may my hands rot off
     And never brandish more revengeful steel
     Over the glittering helmet of my foe!
     [*Takes up gage.*]

ANOTHER LORD
     I task the earth to the like, forsworn Aumerle,
     And spur thee on with full as many lies
55   As may be halloed in thy treacherous ear
     From sun to sun.   [*Throws down his gage.*]
                       There is my honour's pawn.
     Engage it to the trial if thou dar'st.

AUMERLE   Who sets me else? By heaven, I'll throw at all.
     [*Throws down his gage and takes up the Lord's.*]
     I have a thousand spirits in one breast
60   To answer twenty thousand such as you.

SURREY   My Lord Fitzwater, I do remember well
     The very time Aumerle and you did talk.

FITZWATER   'Tis very true. You were in presence then,
     And you can witness with me this is true.

65 SURREY   As false, by heaven, as heaven itself is true!

FITZWATER   Surrey, thou liest.

SURREY   Dishonourable boy!
     That lie shall lie so heavy on my sword
     That it shall render vengeance and revenge
70   Till thou the lie-giver and that lie do lie
     In earth as quiet as thy father's skull,
     In proof whereof there is my honour's pawn.
     [*Throws down his gage.*]
     Engage it to the trial if thou dar'st.

FITZWATER
     How fondly dost thou spur a forward horse!
     [*Takes up gage.*]
75   If I dare eat, or drink, or breathe, or live,
     I dare meet Surrey in a wilderness
     And spit upon him, whilst I say he lies,
     And lies, and lies. There is ⌐my⌐ bond of faith
     To tie thee to my strong correction.
     [*Throws down his second gage.*]
     As I intend to thrive in this new world,
80   Aumerle is guilty of my true appeal.
     Besides, I heard the banished Norfolk say
     That thou, Aumerle, didst send two of thy men
     To execute the noble Duke at Calais.

AUMERLE   Some honest Christian trust me with a gage –
85   That Norfolk lies, here do I throw down this,
     If he may be repealed to try his honour.
     [*Borrowing a gage, throws it down.*]

BOLINGBROKE
     These differences shall all rest under gage

Till Norfolk be repealed. Repealed he shall be,
     And, though mine enemy, restored again
     To all his lands and signories. When he is returned,   90
     Against Aumerle we will enforce his trial.

CARLISLE   That honourable day shall ne'er be seen.
     Many a time hath banished Norfolk fought
     For Jesu Christ in glorious Christian field,
     Streaming the ensign of the Christian cross,   95
     Against black pagans, Turks and Saracens,
     And, toiled with works of war, retired himself
     To Italy, and there at Venice gave
     His body to that pleasant country's earth
     And his pure soul unto his captain Christ,   100
     Under whose colours he had fought so long.

BOLINGBROKE   Why, Bishop, is Norfolk dead?

CARLISLE   As surely as I live, my lord.

BOLINGBROKE
     Sweet Peace conduct his sweet soul to the bosom
     Of good old Abraham! Lords appellants,   105
     Your differences shall all rest under gage
     Till we assign you to your days of trial.

                    Enter YORK.

YORK   Great Duke of Lancaster, I come to thee
     From plume-plucked Richard, who with willing soul
     Adopts thee heir, and his high sceptre yields   110
     To the possession of thy royal hand.
     Ascend his throne, descending now from him,
     And long live Henry, of that name the fourth!

BOLINGBROKE
     In God's name I'll ascend the regal throne.

CARLISLE   Marry, God forbid!   115
     Worst in this royal presence may I speak,
     Yet best beseeming me to speak the truth.
     Would God that any in this noble presence
     Were enough noble to be upright judge
     Of noble Richard! Then true noblesse would   120
     Learn him forbearance from so foul a wrong.
     What subject can give sentence on his king?
     And who sits here that is not Richard's subject?
     Thieves are not judged but they are by to hear,
     Although apparent guilt be seen in them;   125
     And shall the figure of God's majesty,
     His captain, steward, deputy elect,
     Anointed, crowned, planted many years,
     Be judged by subject and inferior breath,
     And he himself not present? O, forfend it, God,   130
     That in a Christian climate souls refined
     Should show so heinous, black, obscene a deed.
     I speak to subjects, and a subject speaks,
     Stirred up by God, thus boldly for his king.
     My Lord of Hereford here, whom you call king,   135
     Is a foul traitor to proud Hereford's king.
     And if you crown him, let me prophesy
     The blood of English shall manure the ground,
     And future ages groan for this foul act.
     Peace shall go sleep with Turks and infidels,   140

And in this seat of peace tumultuous wars
Shall kin with kin and kind with kind confound.
Disorder, horror, fear and mutiny
Shall here inhabit, and this land be called
145 The field of Golgotha and dead men's skulls.
O, if you raise this house against this house,
It will the woefullest division prove
That ever fell upon this cursed earth.
Prevent it, resist it, let it not be so,
150 Lest child, child's children, cry against you, 'Woe!'.

NORTHUMBERLAND
Well have you argued, sir; and for your pains,
Of capital treason we arrest you here.
My Lord of Westminster, be it your charge
To keep him safely till his day of trial.
        [*Bishop of Carlisle is taken into custody.*]
155 ᶠMay it please you, lords, to grant the commons' suit?

BOLINGBROKE
Fetch hither Richard, that in common view
He may surrender. So we shall proceed
Without suspicion.

YORK   I will be his conduct.   *Exit with Officers.*

BOLINGBROKE
Lords, you that here are under our arrest,
160 Procure your sureties for your days of answer.
Little are we beholding to your love,
And little looked for at your helping hands.

        Enter KING RICHARD *and* YORK *with*
        Officers bearing the crown and sceptre.

KING RICHARD   Alack, why am I sent for to a king
Before I have shook off the regal thoughts
165 Wherewith I reigned? I hardly yet have learned
To insinuate, flatter, bow and bend my knee.
Give Sorrow leave awhile to tutor me
To this submission. Yet I well remember
The favours of these men. Were they not mine?
170 Did they not sometime cry 'All hail' to me?
So Judas did to Christ, but He in twelve
Found truth in all but one; I, in twelve thousand, none.
God save the King! Will no man say 'Amen'?
Am I both priest and clerk? Well then, Amen.
175 God save the King, although I be not he,
And yet Amen, if heaven do think him me.
To do what service am I sent for hither?

YORK   To do that office of thine own good will
Which tired majesty did make thee offer –
180 The resignation of thy state and crown
To Henry Bolingbroke.

KING RICHARD [*to York*] Give me the crown.
        [*Takes crown.*]
        [*to Bolingbroke*] Here, cousin, seize the crown. Here,
        cousin,
On this side my hand, and on that side thine.
Now is this golden crown like a deep well
185 That owes two buckets, filling one another,
The emptier ever dancing in the air,

The other down, unseen and full of water.
That bucket down and full of tears am I,
Drinking my griefs whilst you mount up on high.

BOLINGBROKE
I thought you had been willing to resign.   190

KING RICHARD
My crown I am, but still my griefs are mine.
You may my glories and my state depose,
But not my griefs; still am I king of those.

BOLINGBROKE
Part of your cares you give me with your crown.

KING RICHARD
Your cares set up do not pluck my cares down.   195
My care is loss of care, by old care done;
Your care is gain of care, by new care won.
The cares I give, I have, though given away;
They 'tend the crown, yet still with me they stay.

BOLINGBROKE   Are you contented to resign the crown? 200

KING RICHARD
Ay, no. No, ay; for I must nothing be.
Therefore, no 'no', for I resign to thee.
Now mark me how I will undo myself:
I give this heavy weight from off my head,
        [*Gives crown to Bolingbroke.*]
And this unwieldy sceptre from my hand,   205
        [*Takes up sceptre and gives it to Bolingbroke.*]
The pride of kingly sway from out my heart;
With mine own tears I wash away my balm,
With mine own hands I give away my crown,
With mine own tongue deny my sacred state,
With mine own breath release all duteous oaths.   210
All pomp and majesty I do forswear;
My manors, rents, revenues I forgo;
My acts, decrees and statutes I deny.
God pardon all oaths that are broke to me;
God keep all vows unbroke are made to thee.   215
Make me, that nothing have, with nothing grieved,
And thou with all pleased that hast all achieved.
Long mayst thou live in Richard's seat to sit,
And soon lie Richard in an earthy pit!
'God save King Henry', unkinged Richard says,   220
'And send him many years of sunshine days!' –
What more remains?
        [*Northumberland presents a paper to King Richard.*]

NORTHUMBERLAND   No more, but that you read
These accusations, and these grievous crimes
Committed by your person and your followers
Against the state and profit of this land,   225
That, by confessing them, the souls of men
May deem that you are worthily deposed.

KING RICHARD   Must I do so? And must I ravel out
My weaved-up follies? Gentle Northumberland,
If thy offences were upon record,   230
Would it not shame thee in so fair a troop
To read a lecture of them? If thou wouldst,
There shouldst thou find one heinous article
Containing the deposing of a king

And cracking the strong warrant of an oath,
Marked with a blot, damned in the book of heaven.
Nay, all of you that stand and look upon me,
Whilst that my wretchedness doth bait myself,
Though some of you, with Pilate, wash your hands,
Showing an outward pity, yet you Pilates
Have here delivered me to my sour cross,
And water cannot wash away your sin.

NORTHUMBERLAND
My lord, dispatch. Read o'er these articles.
    [*Presents the paper again.*]

KING RICHARD   Mine eyes are full of tears; I cannot see.
And yet salt water blinds them not so much
But they can see a sort of traitors here.
Nay, if I turn mine eyes upon myself,
I find myself a traitor with the rest;
For I have given here my soul's consent
T'undeck the pompous body of a king,
Made Glory base and Sovereignty a slave,
Proud Majesty a subject, State a peasant.

NORTHUMBERLAND   My lord –
KING RICHARD
No lord of thine, thou haught insulting man,
Nor no man's lord! I have no name, no title –
No, not that name was given me at the font –
But 'tis usurped. Alack the heavy day,
That I have worn so many winters out
And know not now what name to call myself.
O, that I were a mockery king of snow,
Standing before the sun of Bolingbroke,
To melt myself away in water-drops!
Good King; great King – and yet not greatly good –
An if my word be sterling yet in England,
Let it command a mirror hither straight,
That it may show me what a face I have,
Since it is bankrupt of his majesty.

BOLINGBROKE
Go, some of you, and fetch a looking-glass.
                              Exit Attendant.

NORTHUMBERLAND [*to King Richard*]
Read o'er this paper while the glass doth come.
    [*Presents the paper again.*]

KING RICHARD
Fiend, thou torments me ere I come to hell!

BOLINGBROKE
Urge it no more, my Lord Northumberland.

NORTHUMBERLAND
The commons will not then be satisfied.

KING RICHARD   They shall be satisfied. I'll read enough
When I do see the very book indeed
Where all my sins are writ, and that's myself.

            Enter one with a glass.

Give me that glass, and therein will I read.
    [*Takes looking-glass.*]
No deeper wrinkles yet? Hath Sorrow struck
So many blows upon this face of mine

And made no deeper wounds? O, flatt'ring glass,
Like to my followers in prosperity,
Thou dost beguile me. Was this face the face
That every day under his household roof
Did keep ten thousand men? Was this the face
That like the sun did make beholders wink?
Is this the face which faced so many follies,
That was at last outfaced by Bolingbroke?
A brittle glory shineth in this face –
As brittle as the glory is the face!   [*Shatters glass.*]
For there it is, cracked in an hundred shivers.
Mark, silent King, the moral of this sport,
How soon my sorrow hath destroyed my face.

BOLINGBROKE
The shadow of your sorrow hath destroyed
The shadow of your face.

KING RICHARD   Say that again.
The shadow of my sorrow? Ha, let's see.
'Tis very true, my grief lies all within;
And these external manners of laments
Are merely shadows to the unseen grief
That swells with silence in the tortured soul.
There lies the substance. And I thank thee, King,
For thy great bounty that not only giv'st
Me cause to wail, but teachest me the way
How to lament the cause. I'll beg one boon,
And then be gone and trouble you no more.
Shall I obtain it?

BOLINGBROKE   Name it, fair cousin.
KING RICHARD   'Fair cousin'? I am greater than a king;
For when I was a king, my flatterers
Were then but subjects. Being now a subject,
I have a king here to my flatterer.
Being so great, I have no need to beg.

BOLINGBROKE   Yet ask.
KING RICHARD   And shall I have?
BOLINGBROKE   You shall.
KING RICHARD   Then give me leave to go.
BOLINGBROKE   Whither?
KING RICHARD
Whither you will, so I were from your sights.

BOLINGBROKE
Go, some of you, convey him to the Tower.

KING RICHARD
O, good – 'Convey'! Conveyers are you all
That rise thus nimbly by a true king's fall.ᶠ
                    Exit King Richard under guard.

BOLINGBROKE
On Wednesday next we solemnly set down
Our coronation. Lords, prepare yourselves.
        Exeunt all but Abbot of Westminster, Bishop of
                              Carlisle and Aumerle.

ABBOT   A woeful pageant have we here beheld.
CARLISLE   The woe's to come. The children yet unborn
Shall feel this day as sharp to them as thorn.
AUMERLE   You holy clergymen, is there no plot
To rid the realm of this pernicious blot?

813

ABBOT   My lord,
    Before I freely speak my mind herein,
    You shall not only take the sacrament
    To bury mine intents, but also to effect
330   Whatever I shall happen to devise.
    I see your brows are full of discontent,
    Your hearts of sorrow and your eyes of tears.
    Come home with me to supper. I'll lay
    A plot shall show us all a merry day.   *Exeunt.*

5.1   *Enter the* QUEEN *with* Ladies.

QUEEN   This way the King will come. This is the way
    To Julius Caesar's ill-erected tower,
    To whose flint bosom my condemned lord
    Is doomed a prisoner by proud Bolingbroke.
5   Here let us rest, if this rebellious earth
    Have any resting for her true king's queen.

    Enter KING RICHARD ⌜*and Guard*⌝.

    But soft, but see, or rather do not see
    My fair rose wither. Yet look up, behold,
    That you in pity may dissolve to dew
10   And wash him fresh again with true-love tears.
    Ah, thou, the model where old Troy did stand,
    Thou map of honour, thou King Richard's tomb,
    And not King Richard! Thou most beauteous inn,
    Why should hard-favoured Grief be lodged in thee,
15   When Triumph is become an alehouse guest?
KING RICHARD
    Join not with grief, fair woman, do not so,
    To make my end too sudden. Learn, good soul,
    To think our former state a happy dream,
    From which awaked, the truth of what we are
20   Shows us but this. I am sworn brother, sweet,
    To grim Necessity, and he and I
    Will keep a league till death. Hie thee to France,
    And cloister thee in some religious house.
    Our holy lives must win a new world's crown,
25   Which our profane hours here have thrown down.
QUEEN   What, is my Richard both in shape and mind
    Transformed and weakened? Hath Bolingbroke
    Deposed thine intellect? Hath he been in thy heart?
    The lion, dying, thrusteth forth his paw
30   And wounds the earth, if nothing else, with rage
    To be o'erpowered; and wilt thou, pupil-like,
    Take the correction mildly, kiss the rod
    And fawn on rage with base humility,
    Which art a lion and the king of beasts?
KING RICHARD
35   A king of beasts, indeed! If aught but beasts,
    I had been still a happy king of men.
    Good sometimes queen, prepare thee hence for France.
    Think I am dead, and that even here thou tak'st,
    As from my death-bed, thy last living leave.
40   In winter's tedious nights sit by the fire
    With good old folks, and let them tell thee tales

    Of woeful ages long ago betid.
    And ere thou bid good night, to quite their griefs,
    Tell thou the lamentable tale of me
    And send the hearers weeping to their beds.   45
    For why the senseless brands will sympathize
    The heavy accent of thy moving tongue
    And in compassion weep the fire out;
    And some will mourn in ashes, some coal-black,
    For the deposing of a rightful king.   50

    Enter NORTHUMBERLAND *with Attendants.*

NORTHUMBERLAND
    My lord, the mind of Bolingbroke is changed.
    You must to Pomfret, not unto the Tower.
    And, madam, there is order ta'en for you:
    With all swift speed you must away to France.
KING RICHARD
    Northumberland, thou ladder wherewithal   55
    The mounting Bolingbroke ascends my throne,
    The time shall not be many hours of age
    More than it is ere foul sin, gathering head,
    Shall break into corruption. Thou shalt think
    Though he divide the realm and give thee half   60
    It is too little, helping him to all.
    He shall think that thou, which knowst the way
    To plant unrightful kings, wilt know again,
    Being ne'er so little urged, another way
    To pluck him headlong from the usurped throne.   65
    The love of wicked men converts to fear,
    That fear to hate, and hate turns one or both
    To worthy danger and deserved death.
NORTHUMBERLAND
    My guilt be on my head, and there an end.
    Take leave and part, for you must part forthwith.   70
KING RICHARD
    Doubly divorced! Bad men, you violate
    A twofold marriage, 'twixt my crown and me
    And then betwixt me and my married wife.
    [*to Queen*] Let me unkiss the oath 'twixt thee and
      me –
    And yet not so, for with a kiss 'twas made.   75
    [*to Northumberland*] Part us, Northumberland: I
      towards the north,
    Where shivering cold and sickness pines the clime;
    My wife to France, from whence, set forth in pomp,
    She came adorned hither like sweet May,
    Sent back like Hallowmas or short'st of day.   80
QUEEN   And must we be divided? Must we part?
KING RICHARD
    Ay, hand from hand, my love, and heart from heart.
QUEEN [*to Northumberland*]
    Banish us both, and send the King with me.
NORTHUMBERLAND
    That were some love, but little policy.
QUEEN   Then whither he goes, thither let me go.   85
KING RICHARD [*to Queen*]
    So two together, weeping, make one woe.

Weep thou for me in France, I for thee here;
Better far off than, near, be ne'er the near.
Go count thy way with sighs, I mine with groans.
QUEEN   So longest way shall have the longest moans.
KING RICHARD
Twice for one step I'll groan, the way being short,
And piece the way out with a heavy heart.
Come, come, in wooing Sorrow let's be brief,
Since, wedding it, there is such length in grief.
One kiss shall stop our mouths, and dumbly part;
Thus give I mine, and thus take I thy heart.
   [*They kiss.*]
QUEEN   Give me mine own again; 'twere no good part
To take on me to keep and kill thy heart.
   [*They kiss again.*]
So now I have mine own again, be gone,
That I may strive to kill it with a groan.
KING RICHARD
We make woe wanton with this fond delay.
Once more, adieu. The rest let Sorrow say.   *Exeunt.*

5.2   *Enter* Duke of YORK *and the* DUCHESS
OF YORK.

DUCHESS OF YORK
My lord, you told me you would tell the rest,
When weeping made you break the story off
Of our two cousins' coming into London.
YORK   Where did I leave?
DUCHESS OF YORK   At that sad stop, my lord,
Where rude misgoverned hands from windows'
   tops
Threw dust and rubbish on King Richard's head.
YORK   Then, as I said, the Duke, great Bolingbroke,
Mounted upon a hot and fiery steed,
Which his aspiring rider seemed to know,
With slow but stately pace kept on his course,
Whilst all tongues cried, 'God save thee, Bolingbroke!'.
You would have thought the very windows spake,
So many greedy looks of young and old
Through casements darted their desiring eyes
Upon his visage, and that all the walls
With painted imagery had said at once,
'Jesu preserve thee! Welcome, Bolingbroke!',
Whilst he, from the one side to the other turning,
Bare-headed, lower than his proud steed's neck,
Bespake them thus: 'I thank you, countrymen';
And thus still doing, thus he passed along.
DUCHESS OF YORK
Alack, poor Richard! Where rode he the whilst?
YORK   As in a theatre the eyes of men,
After a well-graced actor leaves the stage,
Are idly bent on him that enters next,
Thinking his prattle to be tedious,
Even so, or with much more contempt, men's eyes
Did scowl on gentle Richard. No man cried God save
   him!

No joyful tongue gave him his welcome home,
But dust was thrown upon his sacred head,   30
Which with such gentle sorrow he shook off,
His face still combating with tears and smiles,
The badges of his grief and patience,
That had not God for some strong purpose
   steeled
The hearts of men, they must perforce have melted   35
And barbarism itself have pitied him.
But heaven hath a hand in these events,
To whose high will we bound our calm contents.
To Bolingbroke are we sworn subjects now,
Whose state and honour I for aye allow.   40

        ˹*Enter* AUMERLE.˺

DUCHESS OF YORK   Here comes my son, Aumerle.
YORK   Aumerle that was,
But that is lost for being Richard's friend;
And, madam, you must call him Rutland now.
I am in Parliament pledge for his truth
And lasting fealty to the new-made king.   45
DUCHESS OF YORK
Welcome, my son. Who are the violets now
That strew the green lap of the new-come spring?
AUMERLE   Madam, I know not, nor I greatly care not.
God knows I had as lief be none as one.
YORK   Well, bear you well in this new spring of time, 50
Lest you be cropped before you come to prime.
What news from Oxford? Do these jousts and
   triumphs hold?
AUMERLE   For aught I know, my lord, they do.
YORK   You will be there, I know.
AUMERLE   If God prevent it not, I purpose so.   55
YORK   What seal is that that hangs without thy bosom?
Yea, look'st thou pale? Let me see the writing.
AUMERLE   My lord, 'tis nothing.
YORK   No matter, then, who see it.
I will be satisfied. Let me see the writing.
AUMERLE   I do beseech your grace to pardon me.   60
It is a matter of small consequence,
Which for some reasons I would not have seen.
YORK   Which for some reasons, sir, I mean to see.
I fear, I fear –
DUCHESS OF YORK   What should you fear?
'Tis nothing but some bond that he is entered into 65
For gay apparel 'gainst the triumph day.
YORK   Bound to himself? What doth he with a bond
That he is bound to? Wife, thou art a fool.
Boy, let me see the writing.
AUMERLE
I do beseech you, pardon me. I may not show it.   70
YORK   I will be satisfied. Let me see it, I say.
   [*He plucks it out of his bosom and reads it.*]
Treason, foul treason! Villain, traitor, slave!
DUCHESS OF YORK   What is the matter, my lord?
YORK [*Calls offstage.*]
Ho! Who's within there?

Enter Servingman.

Saddle my horse.

75 God for His mercy, what treachery is here!

DUCHESS OF YORK   Why, what is't, my lord?

YORK   Give me my boots, I say. Saddle my horse.

Exit Servingman.

Now, by mine honour, by my life, by my troth,

I will appeach the villain!

80 DUCHESS OF YORK   What is the matter?

YORK   Peace, foolish woman!

DUCHESS OF YORK

I will not peace. What is the matter, Aumerle?

AUMERLE   Good mother, be content. It is no more

Than my poor life must answer.

DUCHESS OF YORK   Thy life answer?

YORK *[to Servingman offstage]*

Bring me my boots! I will unto the King.

His Servingman *enters with his boots.*

DUCHESS OF YORK

85 Strike him, Aumerle! Poor boy, thou art amazed.

[to Servingman] Hence, villain! Never more come in

my sight!

YORK   Give me my boots, I say.

Servingman helps York put on his boots, then exit.

DUCHESS OF YORK   Why, York, what wilt thou do?

Wilt thou not hide the trespass of thine own?

90 Have we more sons? Or are we like to have?

Is not my teeming date drunk up with time?

And wilt thou pluck my fair son from mine age

And rob me of a happy mother's name?

Is he not like thee? Is he not thine own?

95 YORK   Thou fond madwoman,

Wilt thou conceal this dark conspiracy?

A dozen of them here have ta'en the sacrament

And interchangeably set down their hands

To kill the King at Oxford.

DUCHESS OF YORK   He shall be none;

100 We'll keep him here. Then what is that to him?

YORK   Away, fond woman! Were he twenty times my son,

I would appeach him.

DUCHESS OF YORK   Hadst thou groaned for him

As I have done, thou wouldest be more pitiful.

But now I know thy mind. Thou dost suspect

105 That I have been disloyal to thy bed,

And that he is a bastard, not thy son.

Sweet York, sweet husband, be not of that mind.

He is as like thee as a man may be,

Not like to me, or any of my kin,

And yet I love him.

110 YORK   Make way, unruly woman.   *Exit.*

DUCHESS OF YORK

After, Aumerle! Mount thee upon his horse!

Spur, post, and get before him to the King

And beg thy pardon ere he do accuse thee.

I'll not be long behind. Though I be old,

I doubt not but to ride as fast as York. 115

And never will I rise up from the ground

Till Bolingbroke have pardoned thee. Away, be gone!

ᶠ*Exeunt.*ᶠ

5.3   *Enter* ᶠBolingbroke,ᶠ *as* KING HENRY,
with HARRY ᶠPERCY *and other Lords*ᶠ.

KING HENRY   Can no man tell me of my unthrifty son?

'Tis full three months since I did see him last.

If any plague hang over us, 'tis he.

I would to God, my lords, he might be found.

Enquire at London, 'mongst the taverns there, 5

For there, they say, he daily doth frequent,

With unrestrained loose companions,

Even such, they say, as stand in narrow lanes

And beat our watch and rob our passengers,

While he, young wanton and effeminate boy, 10

Takes on the point of honour to support

So dissolute a crew.

HARRY PERCY

My lord, some two days since I saw the Prince,

And told him of those triumphs held at Oxford.

KING HENRY   And what said the gallant? 15

HARRY PERCY   His answer was he would unto the stews,

And from the common'st creature pluck a glove

And wear it as a favour, and with that

He would unhorse the lustiest challenger.

KING HENRY

As dissolute as desp'rate! Yet through both 20

I see some sparks of better hope, which elder years

May happily bring forth.

Enter AUMERLE, *amazed.*

But who comes here?

AUMERLE   Where is the King?

KING HENRY

What means our cousin that he stares and looks so

wildly?

AUMERLE

God save your grace! I do beseech your majesty 25

To have some conference with your grace alone.

KING HENRY *[to Lords]*

Withdraw yourselves, and leave us here alone.

Exeunt all but King Henry and Aumerle.

What is the matter with our cousin now?

AUMERLE

For ever may my knees grow to the earth,   *[Kneels.]*

My tongue cleave to the roof within my mouth, 30

Unless a pardon ere I rise or speak.

KING HENRY   Intended or committed was this fault?

If on the first, how heinous e'er it be,

To win thy after-love I pardon thee.   *[Aumerle rises.]*

AUMERLE   Then give me leave that I may turn the key, 35

That no man enter till my tale be done.

KING HENRY   Have thy desire. *[Aumerle locks the door.]*

[The Duke of York knocks at the door and crieth.]

YORK ᶠ[*within*]ᶠ   My liege, beware! Look to thyself!
  Thou hast a traitor in thy presence there.
KING HENRY [*to Aumerle*]
  Villain, I'll make thee safe.   [*Draws his sword.*]
AUMERLE
  Stay thy revengeful hand. Thou hast no cause to fear.
YORK [*within*]   Open the door, secure, foolhardy King!
  Shall I for love speak treason to thy face?
  Open the door, or I will break it open.
    [*King Henry unlocks the door.*]

ᶠ*Enter* YORK.ᶠ

KING HENRY   What is the matter, uncle? Speak!
  Recover breath. Tell us how near is danger,
  That we may arm us to encounter it.
YORK   Peruse this writing here, and thou shalt know
  The treason that my haste forbids me show.
    [*Presents the paper.*]
AUMERLE [*to King Henry*]
  Remember, as thou read'st, thy promise passed.
  I do repent me. Read not my name there;
  My heart is not confederate with my hand.
YORK [*to Aumerle*]
  It was, villain, ere thy hand did set it down.
  I tore it from the traitor's bosom, King.
  Fear, and not love, begets his penitence.
  Forget to pity him, lest pity prove
  A serpent that will sting thee to the heart.
KING HENRY   O heinous, strong and bold conspiracy!
  O loyal father of a treacherous son!
  Thou sheer, immaculate and silver fountain
  From whence this stream through muddy passages
  Hath held his current and defiled himself!
  Thy overflow of good converts to bad,
  And thy abundant goodness shall excuse
  This deadly blot in thy digressing son.
YORK   So shall my virtue be his vice's bawd,
  And he shall spend mine honour with his shame,
  As thriftless sons their scraping fathers' gold.
  Mine honour lives when his dishonour dies,
  Or my shamed life in his dishonour lies.
  Thou kill'st me in his life: giving him breath,
  The traitor lives, the true man's put to death.
DUCHESS OF YORK ᶠ[*within*]ᶠ
  What ho, my liege! For God's sake, let me in!
KING HENRY
  What shrill-voiced suppliant makes this eager cry?
DUCHESS OF YORK [*within*]
  A woman, and thy aunt. Great King, 'tis I.
  Speak with me, pity me, open the door!
  A beggar begs that never begged before.
KING HENRY   Our scene is altered from a serious thing,
  And now changed to 'The Beggar and the King'. –
  My dangerous cousin, let your mother in.
  I know she's come to pray for your foul sin.
    [*Aumerle opens the door.*]

ᶠ*Enter* DUCHESS OF YORK.ᶠ

YORK [*to King Henry*]
  If thou do pardon whosoever pray,
  More sins for this forgiveness prosper may.
  This festered joint cut off, the rest rest sound;
  This let alone will all the rest confound.   85
DUCHESS OF YORK
  O King, believe not this hard-hearted man.
  Love loving not itself none other can.
YORK   Thou frantic woman, what dost thou make here?
  Shall thy old dugs once more a traitor rear?
DUCHESS OF YORK
  Sweet York, be patient.   [*Kneels.*]
             Hear me, gentle liege.   90
KING HENRY   Rise up, good aunt!
DUCHESS OF YORK   Not yet, I thee beseech.
  For ever will I walk upon my knees
  And never see day that the happy sees
  Till thou give joy, until thou bid me joy,
  By pardoning Rutland, my transgressing boy.   95
AUMERLE
  Unto my mother's prayers I bend my knee.   [*Kneels.*]
YORK
  Against them both my true joints bended be.   [*Kneels.*]
  Ill mayst thou thrive if thou grant any grace.
DUCHESS OF YORK
  Pleads he in earnest? Look upon his face.
  His eyes do drop no tears; his prayers are in jest;   100
  His words come from his mouth, ours from our breast.
  He prays but faintly and would be denied;
  We pray with heart and soul and all beside.
  His weary joints would gladly rise, I know;
  Our knees still kneel till to the ground they grow.   105
  His prayers are full of false hypocrisy;
  Ours of true zeal and deep integrity.
  Our prayers do outpray his; then let them have
  That mercy which true prayer ought to have.
KING HENRY   Good aunt, stand up.
DUCHESS OF YORK   Nay, do not say 'Stand up'.   110
  Say 'Pardon' first, and afterwards 'Stand up'.
  An if I were thy nurse, thy tongue to teach,
  'Pardon' should be the first word of thy speech.
  I never longed to hear a word till now.
  Say 'Pardon', King; let pity teach thee how.   115
  The word is short, but not so short as sweet;
  No word like 'Pardon' for kings' mouths so meet.
YORK   Speak it in French, King; say 'Pardonne-moi'.
DUCHESS OF YORK [*to York*]
  Dost thou teach Pardon pardon to destroy?
  Ah, my sour husband, my hard-hearted lord,   120
  That sets the word itself against the word!
  [*to King Henry*] Speak 'Pardon' as 'tis current in our
    land;
  The chopping French we do not understand.
  Thine eye begins to speak, set thy tongue there;
  Or in thy piteous heart plant thou thine ear,   125

That, hearing how our plaints and prayers do pierce,
Pity may move thee 'Pardon' to rehearse.
KING HENRY   Good aunt, stand up.
DUCHESS OF YORK   I do not sue to stand.
Pardon is all the suit I have in hand.
130   KING HENRY   I pardon him, as God shall pardon me.
DUCHESS OF YORK
    O, happy vantage of a kneeling knee!
    Yet am I sick for fear. Speak it again,
    Twice saying 'Pardon' doth not pardon twain,
    But makes one pardon strong.
KING HENRY   With all my heart
    I pardon him.
135   DUCHESS OF YORK   A god on earth thou art!
        [*York, Duchess of York and Aumerle rise.*]
KING HENRY
    But for our trusty brother-in-law and the Abbot,
    With all the rest of that consorted crew,
    Destruction straight shall dog them at the heels.
    Good uncle, help to order several powers
140   To Oxford, or where'er these traitors are;
    They shall not live within this world, I swear,
    But I will have them if I once know where.
    Uncle, farewell, and so, cousin, adieu.
    Your mother well hath prayed, and prove you true.
DUCHESS OF YORK
145   Come, my old son. I pray God make thee new.   *Exeunt.*

5.4   *Enter* Sir Piers of EXTON *and*
                    two Servants.

EXTON
    Didst thou not mark the King, what words he spake:
    'Have I no friend will rid me of this living fear?'
    Was it not so?
1 SERVANT   These were his very words.
EXTON   'Have I no friend?' quoth he. He spake it twice,
5   And urged it twice together, did he not?
2 SERVANT   He did.
EXTON
    And speaking it, he wishtly looked on me,
    As who should say, 'I would thou wert the man
    That would divorce this terror from my heart',
10   Meaning the King at Pomfret. Come, let's go.
    I am the King's friend, and will rid his foe.   *ᵛExeunt.ᵛ*

5.5   *Enter* KING RICHARD *alone.*

KING RICHARD
    I have been studying how I may compare
    This prison where I live unto the world;
    And, for because the world is populous
    And here is not a creature but myself,
5   I cannot do it. Yet I'll hammer't out.
    My brain I'll prove the female to my soul,
    My soul the father, and these two beget
    A generation of still-breeding thoughts;

And these same thoughts people this little world,
In humours like the people of this world,   10
For no thought is contented. The better sort,
As thoughts of things divine, are intermixed
With scruples and do set the word itself
Against the word, as thus: 'Come, little ones';
And then again: 15
'It is as hard to come as for a camel
To thread the postern of a small needle's eye.'
Thoughts tending to ambition, they do plot
Unlikely wonders – how these vain weak nails
May tear a passage through the flinty ribs   20
Of this hard world, my ragged prison walls,
And, for they cannot, die in their own pride.
Thoughts tending to content flatter themselves
That they are not the first of Fortune's slaves,
Nor shall not be the last, like silly beggars   25
Who sitting in the stocks refuge their shame
That many have and others must sit there;
And in this thought they find a kind of ease,
Bearing their own misfortunes on the back
Of such as have before endured the like.   30
Thus play I in one person many people,
And none contented. Sometimes am I king;
Then treasons make me wish myself a beggar,
And so I am. Then crushing penury
Persuades me I was better when a king;   35
Then am I kinged again, and by and by
Think that I am unkinged by Bolingbroke,
And straight am nothing. But whate'er I be,
Nor I nor any man that but man is
With nothing shall be pleased till he be eased   40
With being nothing.   [*The music plays.*]
                    Music do I hear?
Ha, ha, keep time! How sour sweet music is
When time is broke and no proportion kept!
So is it in the music of men's lives.
And here have I the daintiness of ear   45
To check time broke in a disordered string,
But for the concord of my state and time
Had not an ear to hear my true time broke.
I wasted time, and now doth Time waste me;
For now hath Time made me his numb'ring clock.   50
My thoughts are minutes, and with sighs they jar
Their watches on unto mine eyes, the outward watch,
Whereto my finger, like a dial's point,
Is pointing still, in cleansing them from tears.
Now, sir, the sound that tells what hour it is   55
Are clamorous groans which strike upon my heart,
Which is the bell. So sighs, and tears, and groans
Show minutes, times, and hours. But my time
Runs posting on in Bolingbroke's proud joy,
While I stand fooling here, his jack o'the clock. 60
This music mads me! Let it sound no more;
                    [*Music ceases.*]
For though it have holp madmen to their wits,
In me it seems it will make wise men mad.

Yet blessing on his heart that gives it me,
For 'tis a sign of love; and love to Richard
Is a strange brooch in this all-hating world.

Enter a Groom *of the Stable.*

GROOM   Hail, royal Prince!
KING RICHARD   Thanks, noble peer.
The cheapest of us is ten groats too dear.
What art thou, and how comest thou hither
Where no man never comes but that sad dog
That brings me food to make misfortune live?
GROOM   I was a poor groom of thy stable, King,
When thou wert king, who, travelling towards York,
With much ado, at length have gotten leave
To look upon my sometimes royal master's face.
O, how it erned my heart when I beheld
In London streets, that coronation day,
When Bolingbroke rode on roan Barbary,
That horse that thou so often hast bestrid,
That horse that I so carefully have dressed!
KING RICHARD
Rode he on Barbary? Tell me, gentle friend,
How went he under him?
GROOM   So proudly as if he disdained the ground.
KING RICHARD
So proud that Bolingbroke was on his back?
That jade hath eat bread from my royal hand;
This hand hath made him proud with clapping
  him.
Would he not stumble? Would he not fall down,
Since pride must have a fall, and break the neck
Of that proud man that did usurp his back?
Forgiveness, horse. Why do I rail on thee,
Since thou, created to be awed by man,
Wast born to bear? I was not made a horse,
And yet I bear a burden like an ass,
Spurred, galled and tired by jauncing Bolingbroke.

Enter Keeper *to King Richard with* ᴵa dishᴵ *of meat.*

KEEPER *[to Groom]*
Fellow, give place. Here is no longer stay.
KING RICHARD *[to Groom]*
If thou love me, 'tis time thou wert away.
GROOM
What my tongue dares not, that my heart shall say.
                                                        Exit.
KEEPER   My lord, will't please you to fall to?
KING RICHARD   Taste of it first, as thou art wont to do.
KEEPER
My lord, I dare not. Sir Piers of Exton, who lately
Came from the King, commands the contrary.
KING RICHARD
The devil take Henry of Lancaster and thee!
Patience is stale, and I am weary of it.   *[Attacks Keeper.]*
KEEPER   Help, help, help!

The murderers, ᴵEXTON *and four of his
Servants,* ᴵ *rush in.*

KING RICHARD
How, now! What means Death in this rude assault?   105
Villain, thy own hand yields thy death's instrument.
  [Seizes a Servant's weapon and kills him with it.]
Go thou, and fill another room in hell!
  [Kills another Servant. Here Exton strikes him down.]
That hand shall burn in never-quenching fire
That staggers thus my person. Exton, thy fierce
  hand
Hath with the King's blood stained the King's own
  land.   110
Mount, mount, my soul! Thy seat is up on high,
Whilst my gross flesh sinks downward here to die.
  [Dies.]
EXTON   As full of valour as of royal blood!
Both have I spilled. O, would the deed were good!
For now the devil that told me I did well   115
Says that this deed is chronicled in hell.
This dead King to the living King I'll bear.
[to Keeper and remaining Servants]
Take hence the rest, and give them burial here.
                              ᴵ*Exeunt with the bodies.*ᴵ

5.6   ᴵ*Flourish.*ᴵ *Enter* Bolingbroke *as*
KING HENRY *with the* Duke of YORK, ᴵ*other
Lords, and Attendants*ᴵ.

KING HENRY   Kind uncle York, the latest news we hear
Is that the rebels have consumed with fire
Our town of Ci'cester in Gloucestershire,
But whether they be ta'en or slain we hear not.

Enter NORTHUMBERLAND.

Welcome, my lord. What is the news?   5
NORTHUMBERLAND
First, to thy sacred state wish I all happiness.
The next news is, I have to London sent
The heads of Salisbury, Spencer, Blunt and Kent.
The manner of their taking may appear
At large discoursed in this paper here.   10
  [Presents a paper.]
KING HENRY
We thank thee, gentle Percy, for thy pains,
And to thy worth will add right worthy gains.

Enter Lord FITZWATER.

FITZWATER
My lord, I have from Oxford sent to London
The heads of Brocas and Sir Bennet Seely,
Two of the dangerous consorted traitors   15
That sought at Oxford thy dire overthrow.
KING HENRY   Thy pains, Fitzwater, shall not be forgot.
Right noble is thy merit, well I wot.

Enter HARRY PERCY ᶠ*with* Bishop of
CARLISLEᶠ, *as prisoner.*

HARRY PERCY

20   The grand conspirator, Abbot of Westminster,
    With clog of conscience and sour melancholy,
    Hath yielded up his body to the grave.
    But here is Carlisle living, to abide
    Thy kingly doom and sentence of his pride.

KING HENRY   Carlisle this is your doom:

25   Choose out some secret place, some reverend room,
    More than thou hast, and with it joy thy life.
    So as thou liv'st in peace, die free from strife;
    For though mine enemy thou hast ever been,
    High sparks of honour in thee have I seen.

Enter EXTON *and Servants bearing the coffin.*

30   **EXTON**   Great King, within this coffin I present
    Thy buried fear. Herein all breathless lies
    The mightiest of thy greatest enemies,
    Richard of Bordeaux, by me hither brought.

KING HENRY

    Exton, I thank thee not, for thou hast wrought

A deed of slander with thy fatal hand   35
Upon my head and all this famous land.

EXTON

From your own mouth, my lord, did I this deed.

KING HENRY

They love not poison that do poison need,
Nor do I thee. Though I did wish him dead,
I hate the murderer, love him murdered.   40
The guilt of conscience take thou for thy labour,
But neither my good word nor princely favour.
With Cain go wander thorough shades of night,
And never show thy head by day nor light.

Exit Exton.

Lords, I protest, my soul is full of woe   45
That blood should sprinkle me to make me grow.
Come, mourn with me for what I do lament
And put on sullen black incontinent.
I'll make a voyage to the Holy Land
To wash this blood off from my guilty hand.   50
March sadly after; grace my mournings here
In weeping after this untimely bier.   ᶠ*Exeunt.*ᶠ

King Richard III

King Richard III was an early bestseller, and the play has enjoyed continuous popularity on the stage for over four centuries. Published first in 1597 in quarto form as *The Tragedy of King Richard the Third* without the name of a playwright, it was reprinted in 1598 with '*By* William Shake-speare' added to its title-page; four more quarto reprints followed before the play appeared among the histories in the impressive and expensive First Folio of 1623. The Folio text differs from the quartos, including close to 200 lines absent from them and omitting around 40 that they do print. The relation between the Quarto and Folio texts is complex: the Folio made use of an independent high-quality manuscript but also reproduced the Third Quarto (1602) for roughly one sixth of the play, while also consulting the Sixth Quarto (1622). Modern editions, whether based on Folio or Quarto texts, typically contain elements from both.

Richard III is the earliest English play to enjoy continuous success on the stage from its first performances to the present. Frequent references indicate its popularity in Shakespeare's time, with Richard Burbage in the title-role. It was performed at Court, probably not for the only time, in November 1633. Following the Restoration it retained its popularity, after 1700 in an adaptation by Colley Cibber which held the stage until Henry Irving restored a heavily cut version of Shakespeare's text for his 1877 production. The greatest actors of the eighteenth and nineteenth centuries performed versions of Cibber's text. Some of Cibber's 'improvements' – borrowing lines from *King Henry VI, Part 3*, omitting Margaret, Hastings, Clarence and Edward IV – have endured: some appear in the films of Laurence Olivier (1955) and Ian McKellen (1995). Its length, second only to that of *Hamlet*, has meant that the play is invariably cut in modern performances, as it probably was in Shakespeare's day.

The play's continuing popularity derives from the outrageously stagey wickedness of its title character. Richard is a star role: aware of his own impressive theatricality, he delights himself as much as the audience with his virtuosity and range. In the first three acts, he plays the concerned brother, the good-natured uncle, the jovial comrade, the humble Christian, the passionate lover. This last role is perhaps the most audacious, with Richard winning over Lady Anne in the very moment she mourns her husband and father-in-law while cursing Richard as their murderer.

After this astonishing success, he invites the audience's amazement: 'Was ever woman in this humour wooed? / Was ever woman in this humour won?' (1.2.230–1).

Shakespeare did not wholly invent the villainous Richard. Sir Thomas More's *History of Richard III* (*c.* 1516) was incorporated into subsequent accounts of Richard's reign in Edward Hall's *Union of the Two Noble and Illustre Families of Lancaster and York* (1548) and in Raphael Holinshed's *Chronicles* (1577, second edition 1587). Shakespeare dramatizes More's 'croke backed' murderer driven by 'ambicion' and capable of 'kiss[ing] whome hee thoughte to kyll'. More also provides Shakespeare with much of the ironic action and commentary concerning Edward IV, Buckingham and Hastings. However, there is nothing funny about More's Richard – or any Richard before Shakespeare – and the roles of Queen Margaret (dead before Richard became king) and Lady Anne (Richard's wife of many years) are Shakespeare's invention. These female figures may initially appear as Richard's victims, as he wittily turns Margaret's angry curses into a joke against herself and coerces Anne's consent; but by Act 4 Margaret and Anne contribute to an outspoken female resistance that also enlists Richard's mother and Queen Elizabeth. The Duchess of York's curses strike a vein with her son and return to haunt his terrified dreams, while Queen Elizabeth's cunning manoeuvres make a mockery of Richard's smug misogyny. In a sequence that ironically replays the wooing of Lady Anne, Elizabeth not only gets Richard to curse himself but tricks him into mistakenly believing that he has, yet again, bested a 'shallow, changing woman' (4.4.431).

The play ends at Bosworth in 1485 with Richmond victorious over 'the bloody dog' and crowned as King Henry VII. He concludes the play by asking God's blessing upon the Tudor dynasty that he inaugurates and praying that 'this fair land's peace' may 'long live here' (5.4.39–41), a prayer that must have resonated with audiences in the final years of the sixteenth century.

The Arden text is based on the First Folio, with some readings from the First Quarto, the latter marked at the beginning and end by superscript Q. In two extended passages F is a straight reprint of Q3 (1602), without the pervasive variants introduced elsewhere, except for some added stage directions: these passages are at 3.1.1–166 and from 5.3.49 to the end of the play.

KING EDWARD IV

DUCHESS of York — *mother of King Edward IV*

PRINCE Edward, *later King Edward V*
Richard, Duke of YORK } *sons of King Edward IV*

George, Duke of CLARENCE
RICHARD, Duke of Gloucester } *brothers of King Edward IV*
later KING RICHARD III

QUEEN ELIZABETH — *wife of King Edward IV*
Anthony Woodeville, Lord RIVERS — *brother of Queen Elizabeth*

Marquess of DORSET
Lord GREY } *sons of Queen Elizabeth*

Sir Thomas VAUGHAN

GHOST OF KING HENRY VI

QUEEN MARGARET — *widow of King Henry VI*
GHOST of PRINCE EDWARD — *son of King Henry VI*
Lady ANNE — *widow of Prince Edward, son of King Henry VI, and later wife of Richard, Duke of Gloucester*

William, Lord HASTINGS — *Lord Chamberlain*
Lord STANLEY, Earl of Derby
Henry, Earl of RICHMOND — *stepson of Stanley, later King Henry VII*

Earl of OXFORD
Sir James BLUNT
Sir Walter HERBERT } *Richmond's followers*
Sir William Brandon

Duke of BUCKINGHAM
Duke of NORFOLK
Sir Richard RATCLIFFE
Sir William CATESBY
Sir James TYRREL } *Richard, Duke of Gloucester's followers*
Sir Francis LOVELL
Thomas, Earl of SURREY
Two MURDERERS
PAGE

CARDINAL Bourchier — *Archbishop of Canterbury*
ARCHBISHOP of York
Bishop of ELY
Sir CHRISTOPHER Urswick — *a priest*
John, a PRIEST
Sir Robert BRAKENBURY — *Lieutenant of the Tower of London*
KEEPER of the Tower
Lord MAYOR of London
SCRIVENER
PURSUIVANT
SHERIFF

TRESSEL
BERKELEY } *gentlemen attending Lady Anne*
Three CITIZENS

BOY
DAUGHTER } *children of George, Duke of Clarence*

Lords, Bishops, Gentlemen, Aldermen, Citizens, Halberdiers, Soldiers, Attendants, Messengers

1.1 *Enter* RICHARD, *Duke of Gloucester, alone.*

RICHARD   Now is the winter of our discontent
Made glorious summer by this son of York,
And all the clouds that loured upon our house
In the deep bosom of the ocean buried.
Now are our brows bound with victorious wreaths,   5
Our bruised arms hung up for monuments,
Our stern alarums changed to merry meetings,
Our dreadful marches to delightful measures.
Grim-visaged War hath smoothed his wrinkled front;
And now, instead of mounting barbed steeds   10
To fright the souls of fearful adversaries,
He capers nimbly in a lady's chamber
To the lascivious pleasing of a lute.
But I, that am not shaped for sportive tricks,
Nor made to court an amorous looking-glass;   15
I, that am rudely stamped, and want love's majesty
To strut before a wanton ambling nymph;
I, that am curtailed of this fair proportion,
Cheated of feature by dissembling Nature,
Deformed, unfinished, sent before my time   20
Into this breathing world, scarce half made up,
And that so lamely and unfashionable
That dogs bark at me as I halt by them –
Why, I, in this weak piping time of peace,
Have no delight to pass away the time,   25
Unless to see my shadow in the sun
And descant on mine own deformity.
And therefore, since I cannot prove a lover
To entertain these fair well-spoken days,
I am determined to prove a villain   30
And hate the idle pleasures of these days.
Plots have I laid, inductions dangerous,
By drunken prophecies, libels and dreams,
To set my brother Clarence and the King
In deadly hate, the one against the other;   35
And if King Edward be as true and just
As I am subtle, false and treacherous,
This day should Clarence closely be mewed up
About a prophecy, which says that 'G'
Of Edward's heirs the murderer shall be.   40
Dive, thoughts, down to my soul; here Clarence
     comes.

Enter CLARENCE, *guarded, and* BRAKENBURY

Brother, good day. What means this armed guard
That waits upon your grace?
CLARENCE   His majesty,
Tendering my person's safety, hath appointed
This conduct to convey me to the Tower.   45
RICHARD   Upon what cause?
CLARENCE   Because my name is George.
RICHARD   Alack, my lord, that fault is none of yours;
He should for that commit your godfathers.
O, belike his majesty hath some intent
That you should be new christened in the Tower.   50

But what's the matter, Clarence, may I know?
CLARENCE   Yea, Richard, when I know; but I protest
As yet I do not. But, as I can learn,
He hearkens after prophecies and dreams,
And from the crossrow plucks the letter G;   55
And says a wizard told him that by 'G'
His issue disinherited should be.
And for my name of George begins with G,
It follows in his thought that I am he.
These, as I learn, and such like toys as these,   60
Hath moved his highness to commit me now.
RICHARD
Why, this it is, when men are ruled by women:
'Tis not the King that sends you to the Tower;
My Lady Grey his wife, Clarence, 'tis she
That tempers him to this extremity.   65
Was it not she and that good man of worship,
Anthony Woodeville, her brother there,
That made him send Lord Hastings to the Tower,
From whence this present day he is delivered?
We are not safe, Clarence; we are not safe.   70
CLARENCE   By heaven, I think there is no man secure
But the Queen's kindred and night-walking heralds
That trudge betwixt the King and Mistress Shore.
Heard you not what an humble suppliant
Lord Hastings was °to her° for his delivery?   75
RICHARD   Humbly complaining to her deity
Got my Lord Chamberlain his liberty.
I'll tell you what: I think it is our way,
If we will keep in favour with the King,
To be her men and wear her livery.   80
The jealous o'erworn widow and herself,
Since that our brother dubbed them gentlewomen,
Are mighty gossips in our monarchy.
BRAKENBURY
I beseech your graces both to pardon me.
His majesty hath straitly given in charge   85
That no man shall have private conference,
Of what degree soever, with your brother.
RICHARD
Even so; an't please your worship, Brakenbury,
You may partake of any thing we say.
We speak no treason, man; we say the King   90
Is wise and virtuous, and his noble Queen
Well struck in years, fair and not jealous.
We say that Shore's wife hath a pretty foot,
A cherry lip, a bonny eye, a passing pleasing tongue,
And that the Queen's kindred are made gentlefolks.   95
How say you, sir? Can you deny all this?
BRAKENBURY
With this, my lord, myself have nought to do.
RICHARD
Naught to do with Mistress Shore? I tell thee,
     fellow,
He that doth naught with her, excepting one,
Were best to do it secretly, alone.   100
BRAKENBURY   What one, my lord?

RICHARD
  Her husband, knave. Wouldst thou betray me?
BRAKENBURY
  I do beseech your grace to pardon me, and withal
  Forbear your conference with the noble Duke.
CLARENCE
105 We know thy charge, Brakenbury, and will obey.
RICHARD We are the Queen's abjects, and must obey.
  Brother, farewell. I will unto the King,
  And whatsoe'er you will employ me in,
  Were it to call King Edward's widow 'sister',
110 I will perform it to enfranchise you.
  Meantime, this deep disgrace in brotherhood
  Touches me deeper than you can imagine.
CLARENCE I know it pleaseth neither of us well.
RICHARD Well, your imprisonment shall not be long;
115 I will deliver you, or else lie for you.
  Meantime, have patience.
CLARENCE   I must perforce. Farewell.
        Exeunt Clarence, Brakenbury and guard.
RICHARD
  Go, tread the path that thou shalt ne'er return;
  Simple, plain Clarence, I do love thee so
  That I will shortly send thy soul to heaven,
120 If heaven will take the present at our hands.
  But who comes here? The new-delivered Hastings?

        Enter Lord HASTINGS.

HASTINGS Good time of day unto my gracious lord.
RICHARD As much unto my good Lord Chamberlain.
  Well are you welcome to this open air.
125 How hath your lordship brooked imprisonment?
HASTINGS
  With patience, noble lord, as prisoners must;
  But I shall live, my lord, to give them thanks
  That were the cause of my imprisonment.
RICHARD
  No doubt, no doubt; and so shall Clarence too,
130 For they that were your enemies are his
  And have prevailed as much on him as you.
HASTINGS More pity that the eagles should be mewed,
  Whiles kites and buzzards play at liberty.
RICHARD What news abroad?
135 HASTINGS No news so bad abroad as this at home:
  The King is sickly, weak and melancholy,
  And his physicians fear him mightily.
RICHARD
  Now by Saint John, that news is bad indeed.
  O, he hath kept an evil diet long,
140 And over-much consumed his royal person.
  'Tis very grievous to be thought upon.
  Where is he, in his bed?
HASTINGS He is.
RICHARD
  Go you before, and I will follow you.   *Exit Hastings.*
145 He cannot live, I hope, and must not die
  Till George be packed with post-horse up to heaven.

I'll in to urge his hatred more to Clarence
With lies well steeled with weighty arguments,
And if I fail not in my deep intent,
Clarence hath not another day to live;   150
Which done, God take King Edward to His mercy,
And leave the world for me to bustle in.
For then, I'll marry Warwick's youngest daughter.
What though I killed her husband and her father?
The readiest way to make the wench amends   155
Is to become her husband and her father;
The which will I, not all so much for love
As for another secret close intent
By marrying her which I must reach unto.
But yet I run before my horse to market: 160
Clarence still breathes; Edward still lives and reigns.
When they are gone, then must I count my gains.   *Exit.*

1.2 *Enter the corse of Henry the Sixth with Halberds to*
    guard it, Lady ANNE *being the mourner, attended by*
    TRESSEL, BERKELEY *and other* Gentlemen.

ANNE Set down, set down your honourable load,
  If honour may be shrouded in a hearse,
  Whilst I awhile obsequiously lament
  Th'untimely fall of virtuous Lancaster.
  Poor key-cold figure of a holy king,   5
  Pale ashes of the house of Lancaster,
  Thou bloodless remnant of that royal blood,
  Be it lawful that I invocate thy ghost
  To hear the lamentations of poor Anne,
  Wife to thy Edward, to thy slaughtered son,   10
  Stabbed by the selfsame hand that made these wounds.
  Lo, in these windows that let forth thy life
  I pour the helpless balm of my poor eyes.
  O, cursed be the hand that made these holes;
  Cursed the heart that had the heart to do it;   15
  Cursed the blood that let this blood from hence.
  More direful hap betide that hated wretch
  That makes us wretched by the death of thee
  Than I can wish to wolves, to spiders, toads
  Or any creeping venomed thing that lives.   20
  If ever he have child, abortive be it,
  Prodigious, and untimely brought to light,
  Whose ugly and unnatural aspect
  May fright the hopeful mother at the view,
  And that be heir to his unhappiness.   25
  If ever he have wife, let her be made
  More miserable by the death of him
  Than I am made by my young lord and thee.
  – Come now towards Chertsey with your holy load,
  Taken from Paul's to be interred there;   30
  And still, as you are weary of this weight,
  Rest you, whiles I lament King Henry's corse.

        Enter RICHARD, Duke of Gloucester.

RICHARD
  Stay, you that bear the corse, and set it down.

ANNE   What black magician conjures up this fiend
    To stop devoted charitable deeds?
RICHARD   Villains, set down the corse, or by Saint Paul,
    I'll make a corse of him that disobeys.
GENTLEMAN
    My lord, stand back and let the coffin pass.
RICHARD
    Unmannered dog, stand thou when I command!
    Advance thy halberd higher than my breast,
    Or by Saint Paul, I'll strike thee to my foot
    And spurn upon thee, beggar, for thy boldness.
ANNE   What, do you tremble? Are you all afraid?
    Alas, I blame you not, for you are mortal,
    And mortal eyes cannot endure the devil.
    – Avaunt, thou dreadful minister of hell!
    Thou hadst but power over his mortal body;
    His soul thou canst not have. Therefore begone.
RICHARD   Sweet saint, for charity, be not so curst.
ANNE
    Foul devil, for God's sake hence, and trouble us not,
    For thou hast made the happy earth thy hell,
    Filled it with cursing cries and deep exclaims.
    If thou delight to view thy heinous deeds,
    Behold this pattern of thy butcheries.
    – O gentlemen, see, see dead Henry's wounds
    Open their congealed mouths, and bleed afresh.
    – Blush, blush, thou lump of foul deformity,
    For 'tis thy presence that exhales this blood
    From cold and empty veins where no blood dwells.
    Thy deeds, inhuman and unnatural,
    Provokes this deluge most unnatural.
    – O God! which this blood mad'st, revenge his death.
    O earth! which this blood drink'st, revenge his death.
    Either heaven with lightning strike the murderer dead,
    Or earth gape open wide and eat him quick,
    As thou dost swallow up this good king's blood,
    Which his hell-governed arm hath butchered.
RICHARD   Lady, you know no rules of charity,
    Which renders good for bad, blessings for curses.
ANNE   Villain, thou knowst nor law of God nor man.
    No beast so fierce but knows some touch of pity.
RICHARD   But I know none, and therefore am no beast.
ANNE   O wonderful, when devils tell the truth!
RICHARD   More wonderful, when angels are so angry.
    Vouchsafe, divine perfection of a woman,
    Of these supposed crimes, to give me leave
    By circumstance, but to acquit myself.
ANNE   Vouchsafe, diffused infection of °a° man,
    Of these known evils, but to give me leave
    By circumstance, to curse thy cursed self.
RICHARD
    Fairer than tongue can name thee, let me have
    Some patient leisure to excuse myself.
ANNE
    Fouler than heart can think thee, thou canst make
    No excuse current but to hang thyself.
RICHARD   By such despair I should accuse myself.

ANNE   And by despairing shalt thou stand excused
    For doing worthy vengeance on thyself
    That didst unworthy slaughter upon others.
RICHARD   Say that I slew them not.
ANNE   Then say they were not slain.   90
    But dead they are, and, devilish slave, by thee.
RICHARD   I did not kill your husband.
ANNE   Why then he is alive.
RICHARD
    Nay, he is dead, and slain by Edward's hands.
ANNE
    In thy foul throat thou liest; Queen Margaret saw   95
    Thy murderous falchion smoking in his blood,
    The which thou once didst bend against her breast,
    But that thy brothers beat aside the point.
RICHARD   I was provoked by her slanderous tongue,
    That laid their guilt upon my guiltless shoulders.   100
ANNE   Thou wast provoked by thy bloody mind,
    That never dream'st on aught but butcheries.
    Didst thou not kill this king?
RICHARD   I grant ye.
ANNE
    Dost grant me, hedgehog? Then God grant me too
    Thou mayst be damned for that wicked deed.   105
    O, he was gentle, mild and virtuous.
RICHARD
    The better for the King of Heaven that hath him.
ANNE   He is in heaven, where thou shalt never come.
RICHARD
    Let him thank me that holp to send him thither,
    For he was fitter for that place than earth.   110
ANNE   And thou unfit for any place but hell.
RICHARD
    Yes, one place else, if you will hear me name it.
ANNE   Some dungeon.
RICHARD   Your bedchamber.
ANNE   Ill rest betide the chamber where thou liest.   115
RICHARD   So will it, madam, till I lie with you.
ANNE   I hope so.
RICHARD   I know so. But, gentle Lady Anne,
    To leave this keen encounter of our wits
    And fall something into a slower method:
    Is not the causer of the timeless deaths   120
    Of these Plantagenets, Henry and Edward,
    As blameful as the executioner?
ANNE   Thou wast the cause, and most accurst effect.
RICHARD   Your beauty was the cause of that effect:
    Your beauty, that did haunt me in my sleep   125
    To undertake the death of all the world,
    So I might live one hour in your sweet bosom.
ANNE   If I thought that, I tell thee, homicide,
    These nails should rend that beauty from my cheeks.
RICHARD
    These eyes could not endure that beauty's wrack;   130
    You should not blemish it, if I stood by.
    As all the world is cheered by the sun,
    So I by that. It is my day, my life.

ANNE

Black night o'ershade thy day, and death thy life.

RICHARD

135   Curse not thyself, fair creature; thou art both.

ANNE   I would I were, to be revenged on thee.

RICHARD   It is a quarrel most unnatural,

To be revenged on him that loveth thee.

ANNE   It is a quarrel just and reasonable,

140   To be revenged on him that killed my husband.

RICHARD   He that bereft thee, lady, of thy husband,

Did it to help thee to a better husband.

ANNE   His better doth not breathe upon the earth.

RICHARD   He lives that loves thee better than he could.

ANNE   Name him.

RICHARD   Plantagenet.

145   ANNE   Why, that was he.

RICHARD   The selfsame name, but one of better nature.

ANNE   Where is he?

RICHARD   Here. [*^QShe^Q spits at him.*]

Why dost thou spit at me?

ANNE   Would it were mortal poison, for thy sake.

RICHARD   Never came poison from so sweet a place.

150   ANNE   Never hung poison on a fouler toad.

Out of my sight! Thou dost infect mine eyes.

RICHARD   Thine eyes, sweet lady, have infected mine.

ANNE   Would they were basilisks, to strike thee dead.

RICHARD   I would they were, that I might die at once;

155   For now they kill me with a living death.

Those eyes of thine from mine have drawn salt tears,

Shamed their aspects with store of childish drops;

These eyes, which never shed remorseful tear –

No, when my father York and Edward wept

160   To hear the piteous moan that Rutland made

When black-faced Clifford shook his sword at him;

Nor when thy warlike father, like a child,

Told the sad story of my father's death

And twenty times made pause to sob and weep,

165   That all the standers-by had wet their cheeks

Like trees bedashed with rain – in that sad time

My manly eyes did scorn an humble tear;

And what these sorrows could not thence exhale,

Thy beauty hath, and made them blind with weeping.

170   I never sued to friend, nor enemy;

My tongue could never learn sweet smoothing word.

But now thy beauty is proposed my fee,

My proud heart sues, and prompts my tongue to speak.

[*She looks scornfully at him.*]

Teach not thy lip such scorn, for it was made

175   For kissing, lady, not for such contempt.

If thy revengeful heart cannot forgive,

Lo, here I lend thee this sharp-pointed sword,

Which if thou please to hide in this true breast

And let the soul forth that adoreth thee,

180   I lay it naked to the deadly stroke

And humbly beg the death upon my knee.

[*He kneels and lays his breast open, she offers at it
with his sword.*]

Nay, do not pause; for I did kill King Henry,

But 'twas thy beauty that provoked me.

Nay, now dispatch; 'twas I that stabbed young Edward,

But 'twas thy heavenly face that set me on.   185

[*She falls the sword.*]

Take up the sword again, or take up me.

ANNE   Arise, dissembler; though I wish thy death,

I will not be thy executioner.

RICHARD   Then bid me kill myself, and I will do it.

ANNE   I have already.

RICHARD   That was in thy rage.   190

Speak it again and, even with the word,

This hand, which for thy love did kill thy love,

Shall for thy love kill a far truer love;

To both their deaths shalt thou be accessary.

ANNE   I would I knew thy heart.   195

RICHARD   'Tis figured in my tongue.

ANNE   I fear me both are false.

RICHARD   Then never man was true.

ANNE   Well, well, put up your sword.

RICHARD   Say then my peace is made.   200

ANNE   That shalt thou know hereafter.

RICHARD   But shall I live in hope?

ANNE   All men I hope live so.

^QRICHARD^Q   Vouchsafe to wear this ring.

^QANNE   To take is not to give.^Q   205

RICHARD   Look how my ring encompasseth thy finger;

Even so thy breast encloseth my poor heart.

Wear both of them, for both of them are thine.

And if thy poor devoted servant may

But beg one favour at thy gracious hand,   210

Thou dost confirm his happiness forever.

ANNE   What is it?

RICHARD

That it may please you leave these sad designs

To him that hath most cause to be a mourner,

And presently repair to Crosby House,   215

Where, after I have solemnly interred

At Chertsey Monastery this noble king

And wet his grave with my repentant tears,

I will with all expedient duty see you.

For diverse unknown reasons, I beseech you,   220

Grant me this boon.

ANNE   With all my heart, and much it joys me too

To see you are become so penitent.

– Tressel and Berkeley, go along with me.

RICHARD   Bid me farewell.

ANNE   'Tis more than you deserve;   225

But since you teach me how to flatter you,

Imagine I have said farewell already.

Exeunt two with Anne.

GENTLEMAN   Towards Chertsey, noble lord?

RICHARD   No, to Whitefriars; there attend my coming.

Exeunt the rest with the corse.

Was ever woman in this humour wooed?   230

Was ever woman in this humour won?

I'll have her, but I will not keep her long.

What? I that killed her husband and his father,
To take her in her heart's extremest hate,
235 With curses in her mouth, tears in her eyes,
The bleeding witness of my hatred by,
Having God, her conscience and these bars against me,
And I, no friends to back my suit withal
But the plain devil and dissembling looks?
240 And yet to win her? All the world to nothing!
Ha!
Hath she forgot already that brave prince,
Edward, her lord, whom I, some three months since,
Stabbed in my angry mood at Tewkesbury?
245 A sweeter and a lovelier gentleman,
Framed in the prodigality of Nature,
Young, valiant, wise and, no doubt, right royal,
The spacious world cannot again afford;
And will she yet abase her eyes on me,
250 That cropped the golden prime of this sweet prince
And made her widow to a woeful bed?
On me, whose all not equals Edward's moiety?
On me, that halts and am misshapen thus?
My dukedom to a beggarly denier,
255 I do mistake my person all this while!
Upon my life, she finds, although I cannot,
Myself to be a marvellous proper man.
I'll be at charges for a looking-glass
And entertain a score or two of tailors
260 To study fashions to adorn my body;
Since I am crept in favour with myself,
I will maintain it with some little cost.
But first I'll turn yon fellow in his grave
And then return lamenting to my love.
265 Shine out, fair sun, till I have bought a glass,
That I may see my shadow as I pass.   *Exit.*

1.3   *Enter* QUEEN ELIZABETH, *Lord* RIVERS,
    the Marquess *of* DORSET *and Lord* GREY.

RIVERS
  Have patience, madam. There's no doubt his majesty
  Will soon recover his accustomed health.
GREY   In that you brook it ill, it makes him worse;
  Therefore for God's sake entertain good comfort
  And cheer his grace with quick and merry eyes.
QUEEN ELIZABETH
  If he were dead, what would betide on me?
GREY   No other harm but loss of such a lord.
QUEEN ELIZABETH
  The loss of such a lord includes all harms.
GREY   The heavens have blessed you with a goodly son
10 To be your comforter when he is gone.
QUEEN ELIZABETH   Ah, he is young, and his minority
  Is put unto the trust of Richard Gloucester,
  A man that loves not me, nor none of you.
RIVERS   Is it concluded he shall be Protector?
QUEEN ELIZABETH
15 It is determined, not concluded yet;

But so it must be, if the King miscarry.

Enter BUCKINGHAM *and* STANLEY, Earl of Derby.

GREY   Here come the lords of Buckingham and Derby.
BUCKINGHAM
  Good time of day unto your royal grace.
STANLEY
  God make your majesty joyful, as you have been.
QUEEN ELIZABETH
  The Countess Richmond, good my lord of Derby,   20
  To your good prayer will scarcely say amen.
  Yet Derby, notwithstanding she's your wife
  And loves not me, be you, good lord, assured
  I hate not you for her proud arrogance.
STANLEY   I do beseech you, either not believe   25
  The envious slanders of her false accusers,
  Or, if she be accused on true report,
  Bear with her weakness, which I think proceeds
  From wayward sickness, and no grounded malice.
QUEEN ELIZABETH
  Saw you the King today, my lord of Derby?   30
STANLEY   But now the Duke of Buckingham and I
  Are come from visiting his majesty.
QUEEN ELIZABETH
  What likelihood of his amendment, lords?
BUCKINGHAM
  Madam, good hope. His grace speaks cheerfully.
QUEEN ELIZABETH
  God grant him health. Did you confer with him?   35
BUCKINGHAM
  Ay, madam; he desires to make atonement
  Between the Duke of Gloucester and your brothers,
  And between them and my Lord Chamberlain,
  And sent to warn them to his royal presence.
QUEEN ELIZABETH
  Would all were well, but that will never be;   40
  I fear our happiness is at the height.

Enter RICHARD *and* HASTINGS.

RICHARD   They do me wrong, and I will not endure it!
  Who is it that complains unto the King
  That I, forsooth, am stern and love them not?
  By holy Paul, they love his grace but lightly   45
  That fill his ears with such dissentious rumours.
  Because I cannot flatter, and look fair,
  Smile in men's faces, smooth, deceive and cog,
  Duck with French nods and apish courtesy,
  I must be held a rancorous enemy.   50
  Cannot a plain man live and think no harm
  But thus his simple truth must be abused
  With silken, sly, insinuating jacks?
GREY   To who in all this presence speaks your grace?
RICHARD   To thee, that hast nor honesty nor grace.   55
  When have I injured thee? When done thee wrong?
  – Or thee? – Or thee? – Or any of your faction?
  A plague upon you all! His royal grace,

Whom God preserve better than you would wish,
60 Cannot be quiet scarce a breathing while
But you must trouble him with lewd complaints.

QUEEN ELIZABETH
Brother of Gloucester, you mistake the matter:
The King, on his own royal disposition
And not provoked by any suitor else,
65 Aiming, belike, at your interior hatred,
That in your outward action shows itself
Against my children, brothers and myself,
Makes him to send, that he may learn the ground.

RICHARD   I cannot tell; the world is grown so bad
70 That wrens make prey where eagles dare not perch.
Since every Jack became a gentleman,
There's many a gentle person made a jack.

QUEEN ELIZABETH
Come, come, we know your meaning, brother
     Gloucester.
You envy my advancement, and my friends'.
75 God grant we never may have need of you.

RICHARD
Meantime, God grants that I have need of you.
Our brother is imprisoned by your means,
Myself disgraced, and the nobility
Held in contempt, while great promotions
80 Are daily given to ennoble those
That scarce some two days since were worth a noble.

QUEEN ELIZABETH
By Him that raised me to this careful height
From that contented hap which I enjoyed,
I never did incense his majesty
85 Against the Duke of Clarence, but have been
An earnest advocate to plead for him.
My lord, you do me shameful injury
Falsely to draw me in these vile suspects.

RICHARD   You may deny that you were not the mean
90 Of my Lord Hastings' late imprisonment.

RIVERS   She may, my lord, for –

RICHARD
She may, Lord Rivers; why, who knows not so?
She may do more, sir, than denying that:
She may help you to many fair preferments,
95 And then deny her aiding hand therein
And lay those honours on your high desert.
What may she not? She may, ay, marry, may she.

RIVERS   What, marry, may she?

RICHARD   What, marry, may she? Marry with a king,
100 A bachelor, and a handsome stripling too;
Iwis your grandam had a worser match.

QUEEN ELIZABETH
My lord of Gloucester, I have too long borne
Your blunt upbraidings and your bitter scoffs.
By heaven, I will acquaint his majesty
105 Of those gross taunts that oft I have endured.
I had rather be a country servant maid
Than a great queen with this condition,
To be so baited, scorned and stormed at.

Enter old QUEEN MARGARET.

Small joy have I in being England's queen.

QUEEN MARGARET [*aside*]
And lessened be that small, God I beseech Him.   110
Thy honour, state and seat is due to me.

RICHARD
What? Threat you me with telling of the King?
ᵠTell him and spare not. Look what I have saidᵠ
I will avouch't in presence of the King.
I dare adventure to be sent to th' Tower.   115
'Tis time to speak; my pains are quite forgot.

QUEEN MARGARET [*aside*]
Out, devil! I do remember them too well:
Thou killed'st my husband Henry in the Tower,
And Edward, my poor son, at Tewkesbury.

RICHARD
Ere you were queen, ay, or your husband king,   120
I was a packhorse in his great affairs,
A weeder-out of his proud adversaries,
A liberal rewarder of his friends.
To royalize his blood, I spent mine own.

QUEEN MARGARET [*aside*]
Ay, and much better blood than his, or thine.   125

RICHARD
In all which time, you and your husband Grey
Were factious for the house of Lancaster.
– And Rivers, so were you. – Was not your husband
In Margaret's battle at Saint Albans slain?
– Let me put in your minds, if you forget,   130
What you have been ere this, and what you are;
Withal, what I have been, and what I am.

QUEEN MARGARET [*aside*]
A murderous villain, and so still thou art.

RICHARD
Poor Clarence did forsake his father Warwick,
Ay, and forswore himself – which Jesu pardon –   135

QUEEN MARGARET [*aside*]   Which God revenge.

RICHARD   To fight on Edward's party for the crown,
And for his meed, poor lord, he is mewed up.
I would to God my heart were flint, like Edward's,
Or Edward's soft and pitiful, like mine.   140
I am too childish-foolish for this world.

QUEEN MARGARET [*aside*]
Hie thee to hell for shame, and leave this world,
Thou cacodemon. There thy kingdom is.

RIVERS   My lord of Gloucester, in those busy days
Which here you urge to prove us enemies,   145
We followed then our lord, our sovereign king.
So should we you, if you should be our king.

RICHARD   If I should be? I had rather be a pedlar.
Far be it from my heart, the thought thereof.

QUEEN ELIZABETH
As little joy, my lord, as you suppose   150
You should enjoy, were you this country's king,
As little joy you may suppose in me
That I enjoy, being the queen thereof.

QUEEN MARGARET [*aside*]
    As little joy enjoys the queen thereof,
155   For I am she, and altogether joyless.
    I can no longer hold me patient. [*Comes forward.*]
    Hear me, you wrangling pirates, that fall out
    In sharing that which you have pilled from me:
    Which of you trembles not, that looks on me?
160   If not, that I am queen, you bow like subjects,
    Yet that, by you deposed, you quake like rebels.
    – Ah, gentle villain, do not turn away.

RICHARD
    Foul wrinkled witch, what mak'st thou in my sight?

QUEEN MARGARET
    But repetition of what thou hast marred;
165   That will I make before I let thee go.

RICHARD   Wert thou not banished on pain of death?

QUEEN MARGARET
    I was, but I do find more pain in banishment
    Than death can yield me here by my abode.
    A husband and a son thou ow'st to me;
170   – And thou a kingdom; – all of you, allegiance.
    This sorrow that I have, by right is yours,
    And all the pleasures you usurp are mine.

RICHARD   The curse my noble father laid on thee
    When thou didst crown his warlike brows with paper,
175   And with thy scorns drew'st rivers from his eyes,
    And then to dry them, gav'st the Duke a clout
    Steeped in the faultless blood of pretty Rutland –
    His curses then, from bitterness of soul
    Denounced against thee, are all fall'n upon thee;
180   And God, not we, hath plagued thy bloody deed.

QUEEN ELIZABETH
    So just is God, to right the innocent.

HASTINGS   O, 'twas the foulest deed to slay that babe,
    And the most merciless, that e'er was heard of.

RIVERS
    Tyrants themselves wept when it was reported.

185 DORSET   No man but prophesied revenge for it.

BUCKINGHAM
    Northumberland, then present, wept to see it.

QUEEN MARGARET
    What? Were you snarling all before I came,
    Ready to catch each other by the throat,
    And turn you all your hatred now on me?
190   Did York's dread curse prevail so much with heaven
    That Henry's death, my lovely Edward's death,
    Their kingdom's loss, my woeful banishment,
    Should all but answer for that peevish brat?
    Can curses pierce the clouds and enter heaven?
195   Why then give way, dull clouds, to my quick curses.
    Though not by war, by surfeit die your king,
    As ours by murder, to make him a king.
    – Edward thy son, that now is Prince of Wales,
    For Edward our son, that was Prince of Wales,
200   Die in his youth, by like untimely violence.
    Thyself a queen, for me that was a queen,
    Outlive thy glory, like my wretched self.

    Long mayst thou live to wail thy children's death
    And see another, as I see thee now,
205   Decked in thy rights, as thou art stalled in mine.
    Long die thy happy days before thy death,
    And, after many lengthened hours of grief,
    Die neither mother, wife, nor England's queen.
    – Rivers and Dorset, you were standers-by,
210   And so wast thou, Lord Hastings, when my son
    Was stabbed with bloody daggers. God, I pray Him,
    That none of you may live his natural age,
    But by some unlooked accident cut off.

RICHARD
    Have done thy charm, thou hateful withered hag.

QUEEN MARGARET
215   And leave out thee? Stay, dog, for thou shalt hear me.
    If heaven have any grievous plague in store
    Exceeding those that I can wish upon thee,
    O, let them keep it till thy sins be ripe,
    And then hurl down their indignation
220   On thee, the troubler of the poor world's peace.
    The worm of conscience still begnaw thy soul;
    Thy friends suspect for traitors while thou liv'st,
    And take deep traitors for thy dearest friends;
    No sleep close up that deadly eye of thine,
225   Unless it be while some tormenting dream
    Affrights thee with a hell of ugly devils.
    Thou elvish-marked, abortive, rooting hog,
    Thou that wast sealed in thy nativity
    The slave of nature and the son of hell;
230   Thou slander of thy heavy mother's womb,
    Thou loathed issue of thy father's loins,
    Thou rag of honour, thou detested –

RICHARD   Margaret.

QUEEN MARGARET   Richard!

RICHARD   Ha?

QUEEN MARGARET   I call thee not.

RICHARD   I cry thee mercy then, for I did think
235   That thou hadst called me all these bitter names.

QUEEN MARGARET
    Why, so I did, but looked for no reply.
    O, let me make the period to my curse.

RICHARD   'Tis done by me and ends in 'Margaret'.

QUEEN ELIZABETH [*to Queen Margaret*]
    Thus have you breathed your curse against yourself.

QUEEN MARGARET
240   Poor painted queen, vain flourish of my fortune,
    Why strew'st thou sugar on that bottled spider,
    Whose deadly web ensnareth thee about?
    Fool, fool, thou whet'st a knife to kill thyself.
    The day will come that thou shalt wish for me
245   To help thee curse this poisonous bunch-backed toad.

HASTINGS   False-boding woman, end thy frantic curse,
    Lest to thy harm thou move our patience.

QUEEN MARGARET
    Foul shame upon you, you have all moved mine.

RIVERS
    Were you well served, you would be taught your duty.

QUEEN MARGARET

250 To serve me well, you all should do me duty:
Teach me to be your queen, and you my subjects.
O, serve me well, and teach yourselves that duty.

DORSET Dispute not with her; she is lunatic.

QUEEN MARGARET
Peace, master Marquess, you are malapert.

255 Your fire-new stamp of honour is scarce current.
O, that your young nobility could judge
What 'twere to lose it and be miserable.
They that stand high have many blasts to shake them,
And if they fall, they dash themselves to pieces.

RICHARD

260 Good counsel, marry. Learn it, learn it, Marquess.

DORSET It touches you, my lord, as much as me.

RICHARD Ay, and much more; but I was born so high.
Our aerie buildeth in the cedar's top,
And dallies with the wind, and scorns the sun.

QUEEN MARGARET

265 And turns the sun to shade. Alas, alas,
Witness my son, now in the shade of death,
Whose bright out-shining beams thy cloudy wrath
Hath in eternal darkness folded up.
Your aerie buildeth in our aerie's nest.

270 O God, that seest it, do not suffer it;
As it is won with blood, lost be it so.

BUCKINGHAM
Peace, peace, for shame, if not for charity.

QUEEN MARGARET
Urge neither charity nor shame to me.
[*to the others*] Uncharitably with me have you dealt,

275 And shamefully my hopes by you are butchered.
My charity is outrage, life my shame,
And in that shame, still live my sorrow's rage.

BUCKINGHAM Have done, have done.

QUEEN MARGARET
O princely Buckingham, I'll kiss thy hand

280 In sign of league and amity with thee.
Now fair befall thee and thy noble house.
Thy garments are not spotted with our blood,
Nor thou within the compass of my curse.

BUCKINGHAM Nor no one here, for curses never pass

285 The lips of those that breathe them in the air.

QUEEN MARGARET
I will not think but they ascend the sky,
And there awake God's gentle sleeping peace.
O Buckingham, take heed of yonder dog.
Look when he fawns, he bites; and when he bites,

290 His venom tooth will rankle to the death.
Have not to do with him, beware of him;
Sin, death and hell have set their marks on him,
And all their ministers attend on him.

RICHARD What doth she say, my lord of Buckingham?

BUCKINGHAM

295 Nothing that I respect, my gracious lord.

QUEEN MARGARET
What, dost thou scorn me for my gentle counsel,

And soothe the devil that I warn thee from?
O, but remember this another day,
When he shall split thy very heart with sorrow,
And say poor Margaret was a prophetess. 300
– Live each of you, the subjects to his hate,
And he to yours, and all of you to God's. *Exit.*

BUCKINGHAM
My hair doth stand on end to hear her curses.

RIVERS And so doth mine. I muse why she's at liberty.

RICHARD I cannot blame her; by God's Holy Mother, 305
She hath had too much wrong, and I repent
My part thereof that I have done to her.

QUEEN ELIZABETH
I never did her any to my knowledge.

RICHARD Yet you have all the vantage of her wrong.
I was too hot to do somebody good 310
That is too cold in thinking of it now.
Marry, as for Clarence, he is well repaid:
He is franked up to fatting for his pains.
God pardon them that are the cause thereof.

RIVERS A virtuous and a Christian-like conclusion, 315
To pray for them that have done scathe to us.

RICHARD
So do I ever – [*Speaks to himself.*] being well advised,
For had I cursed now, I had cursed myself.

Enter CATESBY.

CATESBY Madam, his majesty doth call for you,
– And for your grace, – and yours, my gracious lord. 320

QUEEN ELIZABETH
Catesby, I come. – Lords, will you go with me?

RIVERS We wait upon your grace.
Exeunt all but ᵒRichardᵒ, *Duke of Gloucester.*

RICHARD I do the wrong, and first begin to brawl.
The secret mischiefs that I set abroach
I lay unto the grievous charge of others. 325
Clarence, who I indeed have cast in darkness,
I do beweep to many simple gulls,
Namely to Derby, Hastings, Buckingham,
And tell them 'tis the Queen and her allies
That stir the King against the Duke my brother. 330
Now they believe it, and withal whet me
To be revenged on Rivers, Dorset, Grey.
But then I sigh, and, with a piece of scripture,
Tell them that God bids us do good for evil;
And thus I clothe my naked villainy 335
With odd old ends, stol'n forth of Holy Writ,
And seem a saint when most I play the devil.

Enter two Murderers.

But soft, here come my executioners.
– How now, my hardy, stout, resolved mates;
Are you now going to dispatch this thing? 340

1 MURDERER
We are, my lord, and come to have the warrant,
That we may be admitted where he is.

RICHARD Well thought upon. I have it here about me.

When you have done, repair to Crosby Place;
But sirs, be sudden in the execution,
Withal obdurate; do not hear him plead,
For Clarence is well-spoken and perhaps
May move your hearts to pity, if you mark him.
1 MURDERER
  Tut, tut, my lord, we will not stand to prate.
  Talkers are no good doers; be assured
  We go to use our hands and not our tongues.
RICHARD
  Your eyes drop millstones when fools' eyes fall tears.
  I like you lads. About your business straight.
  Go, go, dispatch.
1 MURDERER   We will, my noble lord.   ᵠ*Exeunt.*ᵠ

1.4   *Enter* CLARENCE *and* Keeper.

KEEPER   Why looks your grace so heavily today?
CLARENCE   O, I have passed a miserable night,
  So full of fearful dreams, of ugly sights,
  That, as I am a Christian faithful man,
  I would not spend another such a night
  Though 'twere to buy a world of happy days,
  So full of dismal terror was the time.
KEEPER
  What was your dream, my lord? I pray you tell me.
CLARENCE
  Methoughts that I had broken from the Tower,
  And was embarked to cross to Burgundy;
  And in my company my brother Gloucester,
  Who from my cabin tempted me to walk
  Upon the hatches. There we looked toward England,
  And cited up a thousand heavy times,
  During the wars of York and Lancaster,
  That had befall'n us. As we paced along
  Upon the giddy footing of the hatches,
  Methought that Gloucester stumbled, and in falling
  Struck me (that thought to stay him) overboard
  Into the tumbling billows of the main.
  O Lord, methought what pain it was to drown,
  What dreadful noise of water in mine ears,
  What sights of ugly death within mine eyes.
  Methoughts I saw a thousand fearful wracks,
  A thousand men that fishes gnawed upon,
  Wedges of gold, great anchors, heaps of pearl,
  Inestimable stones, unvalued jewels,
  All scattered in the bottom of the sea.
  Some lay in dead men's skulls, and in the holes
  Where eyes did once inhabit, there were crept –
  As 'twere in scorn of eyes – reflecting gems,
  That wooed the slimy bottom of the deep
  And mocked the dead bones that lay scattered by.
KEEPER   Had you such leisure in the time of death
  To gaze upon these secrets of the deep?
CLARENCE   Methought I had, and often did I strive
  To yield the ghost, but still the envious flood
  Stopped in my soul and would not let it forth

To find the empty, vast and wandering air,
But smothered it within my panting bulk,
Who almost burst to belch it in the sea.
KEEPER   Awaked you not in this sore agony?
CLARENCE
  No, no, my dream was lengthened after life.
  O, then began the tempest to my soul.
  I passed, methought, the melancholy flood,
  With that sour ferryman which poets write of,
  Unto the kingdom of perpetual night.
  The first that there did greet my stranger-soul
  Was my great father-in-law, renowned Warwick,
  Who spake aloud: 'What scourge for perjury
  Can this dark monarchy afford false Clarence?'
  And so he vanished. Then came wandering by
  A shadow like an angel, with bright hair
  Dabbled in blood, and he shrieked out aloud:
  'Clarence is come, false, fleeting, perjured Clarence,
  That stabbed me in the field by Tewkesbury.
  Seize on him, furies! Take him unto torment!'
  With that, methought, a legion of foul fiends
  Environed me, and howled in mine ears
  Such hideous cries, that with the very noise
  I, trembling, waked, and for a season after
  Could not believe but that I was in hell,
  Such terrible impression made my dream.
KEEPER   No marvel, lord, though it affrighted you;
  I am afraid, methinks, to hear you tell it.
CLARENCE   Ah keeper, keeper, I have done these things,
  That now give evidence against my soul,
  For Edward's sake; and see how he requites me.
  – O God! If my deep prayers cannot appease Thee,
  But Thou wilt be avenged on my misdeeds,
  Yet execute Thy wrath in me alone;
  O, spare my guiltless wife and my poor children.
  – Keeper, I prithee sit by me awhile;
  My soul is heavy, and I fain would sleep.
KEEPER   I will, my lord. God give your grace good rest.

Enter BRAKENBURY, *the Lieutenant.*

BRAKENBURY
  Sorrow breaks seasons and reposing hours,
  Makes the night morning, and the noontide night.
  Princes have but their titles for their glories,
  An outward honour for an inward toil;
  And for unfelt imaginations
  They often feel a world of restless cares,
  So that between their titles and low name
  There's nothing differs but the outward fame.

Enter two Murderers.

1 MURDERER   Ho, who's here?
BRAKENBURY
  What wouldst thou, fellow? And how cam'st thou
    hither?
2 MURDERER   I would speak with Clarence, and I came
  hither on my legs.

BRAKENBURY   What, so brief?

1 MURDERER   'Tis better, sir, than to be tedious. – Let
him see our commission, and talk no more.

    [*Brakenbury reads.*]

BRAKENBURY   I am in this commanded to deliver
The noble Duke of Clarence to your hands.
I will not reason what is meant hereby
Because I will be guiltless from the meaning.
There lies the Duke asleep, and there the keys.
I'll to the King, and signify to him
That thus I have resigned to you my charge.

1 MURDERER   You may, sir; 'tis a point of wisdom. Fare
you well.   *Exeunt Brakenbury and Keeper.*

2 MURDERER   What, shall we stab him as he sleeps?

1 MURDERER   No. He'll say 'twas done cowardly, when
he wakes.

2 MURDERER   Why, he shall never wake until the great
Judgement Day.

1 MURDERER   Why, then he'll say we stabbed him
sleeping.

2 MURDERER   The urging of that word 'Judgement'
hath bred a kind of remorse in me.

1 MURDERER   What? Art thou afraid?

2 MURDERER   Not to kill him, having a warrant, but to
be damned for killing him, from the which no warrant
can defend me.

1 MURDERER   I thought thou hadst been resolute.

2 MURDERER   So I am, to let him live.

1 MURDERER   I'll back to the Duke of Gloucester and
tell him so.

2 MURDERER   Nay, I prithee stay a little. I hope this
passionate humour of mine will change. It was wont to
hold me but while one tells twenty.

1 MURDERER   How dost thou feel thyself now?

2 MURDERER   ᵠFaith,ᵠ some certain dregs of conscience
are yet within me.

1 MURDERER   Remember our reward when the deed's
done.

2 MURDERER   Zounds, he dies! I had forgot the reward.

1 MURDERER   Where's thy conscience now?

2 MURDERER   O, in the Duke of Gloucester's purse.

1 MURDERER   When he opens his purse to give us our
reward, thy conscience flies out.

2 MURDERER   'Tis no matter; let it go. There's few or
none will entertain it.

1 MURDERER   What if it come to thee again?

2 MURDERER   I'll not meddle with it; it makes a man a
coward: a man cannot steal but it accuseth him; a man
cannot swear but it checks him; a man cannot lie with
his neighbour's wife but it detects him. 'Tis a
blushing, shamefaced spirit that mutinies in a man's
bosom. It fills a man full of obstacles. It made me
once restore a purse of gold that by chance I found. It
beggars any man that keeps it. It is turned out of
towns and cities for a dangerous thing, and every
man that means to live well endeavours to trust to
himself, and live without it.

1 MURDERER   ᵠZounds,ᵠ 'tis even now at my elbow,
persuading me not to kill the Duke.

2 MURDERER   Take the devil in thy mind, and believe
him not. He would insinuate with thee but to make
thee sigh.

1 MURDERER   I am strong-framed; he cannot prevail
with me.

2 MURDERER   Spoke like a tall man that respects thy
reputation. Come, shall we fall to work?

1 MURDERER   Take him on the costard with the hilts of
thy sword, and then throw him into the malmsey butt
in the next room.

2 MURDERER   O excellent device! And make a sop of
him.

1 MURDERER   Soft, he wakes.

2 MURDERER   Strike!

1 MURDERER   No, we'll reason with him.

CLARENCE
Where art thou, keeper? Give me a cup of wine.

2 MURDERER
You shall have wine enough, my lord, anon.

CLARENCE   In God's name, what art thou?

1 MURDERER   A man, as you are.

CLARENCE   But not as I am, royal.

1 MURDERER   Nor you as we are, loyal.

CLARENCE
Thy voice is thunder, but thy looks are humble.

1 MURDERER
My voice is now the King's, my looks mine own.

CLARENCE
How darkly, and how deadly dost thou speak!
Your eyes do menace me. Why look you pale?
Who sent you hither? Wherefore do you come?

2 MURDERER   To, to, to –

CLARENCE   To murder me?

BOTH   Ay, ay.

CLARENCE   You scarcely have the hearts to tell me so,
And therefore cannot have the hearts to do it.
Wherein, my friends, have I offended you?

1 MURDERER
Offended us you have not, but the King.

CLARENCE   I shall be reconciled to him again.

2 MURDERER   Never, my lord; therefore prepare to die.

CLARENCE
Are you drawn forth among a world of men
To slay the innocent? What is my offence?
Where is the evidence that doth accuse me?
What lawful quest have given their verdict up
Unto the frowning judge? Or who pronounced
The bitter sentence of poor Clarence' death?
Before I be convict by course of law,
To threaten me with death is most unlawful.
I charge you, as you hope to have redemption,
ᵠBy Christ's dear blood, shed for our grievous sins,ᵠ
That you depart and lay no hands on me.
The deed you undertake is damnable.

1 MURDERER   What we will do, we do upon command.

2 MURDERER
And he that hath commanded is our king.

CLARENCE

95   Erroneous vassals, the great King of kings
     Hath in the table of His law commanded
     That thou shalt do no murder. Will you then
     Spurn at His edict, and fulfil a man's?
200 Take heed, for He holds vengeance in His hand,
     To hurl upon their heads that break His law.

2 MURDERER
And that same vengeance doth He hurl on thee
For false forswearing and for murder too.
Thou didst receive the sacrament to fight
In quarrel of the house of Lancaster.

205 1 MURDERER   And like a traitor to the name of God
     Didst break that vow, and with thy treacherous blade
     Unripp'st the bowels of thy sovereign's son.

2 MURDERER
Whom thou wast sworn to cherish and defend.

1 MURDERER
How canst thou urge God's dreadful law to us
210 When thou hast broke it in such dear degree?

CLARENCE   Alas! For whose sake did I that ill deed?
For Edward, for my brother, for his sake.
He sends you not to murder me for this,
For in that sin he is as deep as I.
215 If God will be avenged for the deed,
O, know you yet, He doth it publicly;
Take not the quarrel from His powerful arm.
He needs no indirect or lawless course
To cut off those that have offended Him.

220 1 MURDERER   Who made thee then a bloody minister,
When gallant-springing, brave Plantagenet,
That princely novice, was struck dead by thee?

CLARENCE   My brother's love, the devil and my rage.

1 MURDERER
Thy brother's love, our duty and thy faults
225 Provoke us hither now to slaughter thee.

CLARENCE   If you do love my brother, hate not me.
I am his brother, and I love him well.
If you are hired for meed, go back again,
And I will send you to my brother Gloucester,
230 Who shall reward you better for my life
Than Edward will for tidings of my death.

2 MURDERER
You are deceived; your brother Gloucester hates you.

CLARENCE   O no, he loves me, and he holds me dear.
Go you to him from me.

1 MURDERER   Ay, so we will.

CLARENCE
235 Tell him, when that our princely father York
Blessed his three sons with his victorious arm,
�QAnd charged us from his soul to love each other,ᵠ
He little thought of this divided friendship.
Bid Gloucester think on this, and he will weep.

1 MURDERER
240 Ay, millstones, as he lessoned us to weep.

CLARENCE   O, do not slander him, for he is kind.

1 MURDERER
Right, as snow in harvest. Come, you deceive yourself.
'Tis he that sends us to destroy you here.

CLARENCE   It cannot be, for he bewept my fortune,
And hugged me in his arms, and swore with sobs   245
That he would labour my delivery.

1 MURDERER   Why so he doth, when he delivers you
From this earth's thraldom to the joys of heaven.

2 MURDERER
Make peace with God, for you must die, my lord.

CLARENCE   Have you that holy feeling in your souls   250
To counsel me to make my peace with God,
And are you yet to your own souls so blind
That you will war with God by murdering me?
O sirs, consider: they that set you on
To do this deed will hate you for the deed.   255

2 MURDERER   What shall we do?

CLARENCE   Relent, and save your souls.
Which of you, if you were a prince's son,
Being pent from liberty, as I am now,
If two such murderers as yourselves came to you,
Would not entreat for life? Ay, you would beg,   260
Were you in my distress.

1 MURDERER
Relent? No. 'Tis cowardly and womanish.

CLARENCE   Not to relent is beastly, savage, devilish.
[*to 2 Murderer*] My friend, I spy some pity in thy
     looks.
O, if thine eye be not a flatterer,   265
Come thou on my side, and entreat for me;
A begging prince, what beggar pities not.

2 MURDERER   Look behind you, my lord.

1 MURDERER   Take that, and that!   [*Stabs him.*]
                                    If all this will not do,
I'll drown you in the malmsey butt within.   270
                              Exit with body.

2 MURDERER
A bloody deed, and desperately dispatched.
How fain, like Pilate, would I wash my hands
Of this most grievous murder.

                    Enter First Murderer.

1 MURDERER
How now? What mean'st thou that thou help'st me
     not?
By heaven, the Duke shall know how slack you have
     been.   275

2 MURDERER
I would he knew that I had saved his brother.
Take thou the fee, and tell him what I say,
For I repent me that the Duke is slain.   *Exit.*

1 MURDERER   So do not I. Go, coward as thou art.
Well, I'll go hide the body in some hole   280
Till that the Duke give order for his burial.
And when I have my meed, I will away,
For this will out, and then I must not stay.   *Exit.*

2.1 *Flourish. Enter* KING EDWARD *sick,*
QUEEN ELIZABETH, Lord Marquess
DORSET, RIVERS, HASTINGS, CATESBY,
BUCKINGHAM.

KING EDWARD
Why, so. Now have I done a good day's work.
You peers, continue this united league.
I every day expect an embassage
From my Redeemer to redeem me hence,
5 And more in peace my soul shall part to heaven,
Since I have made my friends at peace on earth.
– Hastings and Rivers, take each other's hand;
Dissemble not your hatred. Swear your love.

RIVERS
By heaven, my soul is purged from grudging hate,
10 And with my hand I seal my true heart's love.

HASTINGS   So thrive I, as I truly swear the like.

KING EDWARD
Take heed you dally not before your king,
Lest He that is the supreme King of kings
Confound your hidden falsehood, and award
15 Either of you to be the other's end.

HASTINGS   So prosper I, as I swear perfect love.

RIVERS   And I, as I love Hastings with my heart.

KING EDWARD
Madam, yourself is not exempt from this;
– Nor you, son Dorset; – Buckingham, nor you.
20 You have been factious one against the other.
– Wife, love Lord Hastings. Let him kiss your hand,
And what you do, do it unfeignedly.

QUEEN ELIZABETH
There, Hastings, I will never more remember
Our former hatred, so thrive I and mine.
[Hastings kisses her hand.]

KING EDWARD
25 Dorset, embrace him. – Hastings, love Lord Marquess.

DORSET   This interchange of love, I here protest,
Upon my part shall be inviolable.

HASTINGS   And so swear I.   *[They embrace.]*

KING EDWARD
Now, princely Buckingham, seal thou this league
30 With thy embracements to my wife's allies,
And make me happy in your unity.

BUCKINGHAM
Whenever Buckingham doth turn his hate
Upon your grace, but with all duteous love
Doth cherish you and yours, God punish me
35 With hate in those where I expect most love.
When I have most need to employ a friend,
And most assured that he is a friend,
Deep, hollow, treacherous and full of guile
Be he unto me. This do I beg of God,
40 When I am cold in love to you or yours.
[They embrace.]

KING EDWARD
A pleasing cordial, princely Buckingham,

Is this thy vow unto my sickly heart.
There wanteth now our brother Gloucester here
To make the blessed period of this peace.

Enter RATCLIFFE *and* RICHARD, Duke of
Gloucester.

BUCKINGHAM   And in good time,   45
Here comes Sir Richard Ratcliffe and the Duke.

RICHARD
Good morrow to my sovereign King and Queen,
And princely peers, a happy time of day.

KING EDWARD
Happy indeed, as we have spent the day.
Gloucester, we have done deeds of charity,   50
Made peace of enmity, fair love of hate,
Between these swelling, wrong-incensed peers.

RICHARD   A blessed labour, my most sovereign lord.
Among this princely heap, if any here
By false intelligence or wrong surmise   55
Hold me a foe;
If I unwittingly, or in my rage,
Have aught committed that is hardly borne,
By any in this presence, I desire
To reconcile me to his friendly peace.   60
'Tis death to me to be at enmity;
I hate it, and desire all good men's love.
– First, madam, I entreat true peace of you,
Which I will purchase with my duteous service;
– Of you, my noble cousin Buckingham,   65
If ever any grudge were lodged between us;
– Of you and you, Lord Rivers and of Dorset,
That all without desert have frowned on me;
– Dukes, earls, lords, gentlemen; indeed, of all.
I do not know that Englishman alive   70
With whom my soul is any jot at odds
More than the infant that is born tonight.
I thank my God for my humility.

QUEEN ELIZABETH
A holy day shall this be kept hereafter.
I would to God all strifes were well compounded.   75
My sovereign lord, I do beseech your highness
To take our brother Clarence to your grace.

RICHARD   Why, madam, have I offered love for this,
To be so flouted in this royal presence?
Who knows not that the gentle Duke is dead?   80
[They all start.]
You do him injury to scorn his corse.

KING EDWARD
Who knows not he is dead? Who knows he is?

QUEEN ELIZABETH
All-seeing heaven, what a world is this?

BUCKINGHAM
Look I so pale, Lord Dorset, as the rest?

DORSET   Ay, my good lord, and no man in the presence   85
But his red colour hath forsook his cheeks.

KING EDWARD
Is Clarence dead? The order was reversed.

RICHARD

But he, poor man, by your first order died,
And that a winged Mercury did bear;
90 Some tardy cripple bare the countermand,
That came too lag to see him buried.
God grant that some, less noble and less loyal,
Nearer in bloody thoughts, and not in blood,
Deserve not worse than wretched Clarence did,
95 And yet go current from suspicion.

Enter STANLEY, *Earl of Derby.*

STANLEY

[*Kneels.*] A boon, my sovereign, for my service done.

KING EDWARD

I prithee, peace. My soul is full of sorrow.

STANLEY   I will not rise, unless your highness hear me.

KING EDWARD

Then say at once what is it thou requests.

100 STANLEY   The forfeit, sovereign, of my servant's life,
Who slew today a riotous gentleman
Lately attendant on the Duke of Norfolk.

KING EDWARD

Have I a tongue to doom my brother's death,
And shall that tongue give pardon to a slave?
105 My brother killed no man; his fault was thought,
And yet his punishment was bitter death.
Who sued to me for him? Who, in my wrath,
Kneeled at my feet and bid me be advised?
Who spoke of brotherhood? Who spoke of love?
110 Who told me how the poor soul did forsake
The mighty Warwick and did fight for me?
Who told me in the field at Tewkesbury,
When Oxford had me down, he rescued me
And said, 'Dear brother, live, and be a king'?
115 Who told me, when we both lay in the field,
Frozen almost to death, how he did lap me
Even in his garments, and did give himself,
All thin and naked, to the numb-cold night?
All this from my remembrance brutish wrath
120 Sinfully plucked, and not a man of you
Had so much grace to put it in my mind.
But when your carters or your waiting vassals
Have done a drunken slaughter and defaced
The precious image of our dear Redeemer,
125 You straight are on your knees for pardon, pardon;
And I, unjustly too, must grant it you.
[*Stanley rises.*]
But for my brother, not a man would speak,
Nor I, ungracious, speak unto myself
For him, poor soul. The proudest of you all
130 Have been beholding to him in his life,
Yet none of you would once beg for his life.
O God! I fear Thy justice will take hold
On me, and you, and mine and yours for this.
– Come, Hastings, help me to my closet. – Ah, poor
Clarence.
*Exeunt some with King and Queen. Richard,
Buckingham, Stanley and Ratcliffe remain.*

RICHARD

This is the fruits of rashness: marked you not   135
How that the guilty kindred of the Queen
Looked pale when they did hear of Clarence' death?
O! They did urge it still unto the King.
God will revenge it. Come, lords, will you go
To comfort Edward with our company?   140

BUCKINGHAM   We wait upon your grace.   *Exeunt.*

2.2   *Enter the old* DUCHESS *of York,
with the two* Children *of Clarence.*

BOY   Good grandam, tell us, is our father dead?

DUCHESS   No, boy.

DAUGHTER

Why do °you° weep so oft, and beat your breast?
And cry, 'O Clarence, my unhappy son'?

BOY   Why do you look on us, and shake your head,   5
And call us orphans, wretches, castaways,
If that our noble father were alive?

DUCHESS   My pretty cousins, you mistake me both;
I do lament the sickness of the King,
As loath to lose him, not your father's death.   10
It were lost sorrow to wail one that's lost.

BOY   Then you conclude, my grandam, he is dead.
The King mine uncle is to blame for it.
God will revenge it, whom I will importune
With earnest prayers, all to that effect.   15

DAUGHTER   And so will I.

DUCHESS

Peace, children, peace. The King doth love you well.
Incapable and shallow innocents,
You cannot guess who caused your father's death.

BOY   Grandam, we can, for my good uncle Gloucester   20
Told me the King, provoked to it by the Queen,
Devised impeachments to imprison him;
And when my uncle told me so, he wept,
And pitied me, and kindly kissed my cheek,
Bade me rely on him as on my father,   25
And he would love me dearly as a child.

DUCHESS

Ah! That deceit should steal such gentle shape,
And with a virtuous visor hide deep vice.
He is my son, ay, and therein my shame,
Yet from my dugs he drew not this deceit.   30

BOY   Think you my uncle did dissemble, grandam?

DUCHESS   Ay, boy.

BOY   I cannot think it. Hark, what noise is this?

Enter QUEEN ELIZABETH *with her hair about her ears,*
RIVERS *and* DORSET *after her.*

QUEEN ELIZABETH

Ah! Who shall hinder me to wail and weep,
To chide my fortune, and torment myself?   35
I'll join with black despair against my soul
And to myself become an enemy.

DUCHESS   What means this scene of rude impatience?

QUEEN ELIZABETH   To make an act of tragic violence.

40 Edward, my lord, thy son, our king, is dead.
Why grow the branches, when the root is gone?
Why wither not the leaves that want their sap?
If you will live, lament; if die, be brief,
That our swift-winged souls may catch the King's,
45 Or like obedient subjects follow him
To his new kingdom of ne'er-changing night.
DUCHESS   Ah, so much interest have ᵠIᵠ in thy sorrow
As I had title in thy noble husband.
I have bewept a worthy husband's death
50 And lived with looking on his images;
But now two mirrors of his princely semblance
Are cracked in pieces by malignant death,
And I, for comfort, have but one false glass
That grieves me when I see my shame in him.
55 Thou art a widow, yet thou art a mother,
And hast the comfort of thy children left;
But death hath snatched my husband from mine arms
And plucked two crutches from my feeble hands,
Clarence and Edward. O, what cause have I,
60 Thine being but a moiety of my moan,
To overgo thy woes and drown thy cries!
BOY   Ah, aunt! You wept not for our father's death.
How can we aid you with our kindred tears?
DAUGHTER   Our fatherless distress was left unmoaned;
65 Your widow-dolour likewise be unwept.
QUEEN ELIZABETH   Give me no help in lamentation,
I am not barren to bring forth complaints:
All springs reduce their currents to mine eyes,
That I, being governed by the watery moon,
70 May send forth plenteous tears to drown the world.
Ah, for my husband, for my dear lord Edward!
CHILDREN
Ah, for our father, for our dear lord Clarence!
DUCHESS
Alas for both, both mine, Edward and Clarence!
QUEEN ELIZABETH
What stay had I but Edward? And he's gone.
CHILDREN
75 What stay had we but Clarence? And he's gone.
DUCHESS
What stays had I but they? And they are gone.
QUEEN ELIZABETH
Was never widow had so dear a loss.
CHILDREN   Were never orphans had so dear a loss.
DUCHESS   Was never mother had so dear a loss.
80 Alas! I am the mother of these griefs.
Their woes are parcelled; mine is general.
She for an Edward weeps, and so do I.
I for a Clarence weep, so doth not she.
These babes for Clarence weep, ᵠand so do I;ᵠ
85 I for an Edward weep,ᵠ so do not they.
Alas! You three, on me, threefold distressed,
Pour all your tears. I am your sorrow's nurse,
And I will pamper it with lamentation.
DORSET [*to Queen Elizabeth*]
Comfort, dear mother. God is much displeased

That you take with unthankfulness His doing. 90
In common worldly things, 'tis called ungrateful
With dull unwillingness to repay a debt
Which with a bounteous hand was kindly lent;
Much more to be thus opposite with heaven,
For it requires the royal debt it lent you. 95
RIVERS   Madam, bethink you, like a careful mother,
Of the young prince your son: send straight for him;
Let him be crowned. In him your comfort lives.
Drown desperate sorrow in dead Edward's grave
And plant your joys in living Edward's throne. 100

Enter RICHARD, BUCKINGHAM, STANLEY, Earl of
     Derby, HASTINGS *and* RATCLIFFE.

RICHARD   Sister, have comfort. All of us have cause
To wail the dimming of our shining star,
But none can help our harms by wailing them.
– Madam my mother, I do cry you mercy;
I did not see your grace. Humbly on my knee 105
I crave your blessing.   [*Kneels.*]
DUCHESS
God bless thee and put meekness in thy breast,
Love, charity, obedience and true duty.
RICHARD
Amen, [*rising; aside*] and make me die a good old
     man.
That is the butt-end of a mother's blessing; 110
I marvel that her grace did leave it out.
BUCKINGHAM
You cloudy princes and heart-sorrowing peers
That bear this heavy mutual load of moan,
Now cheer each other in each other's love.
Though we have spent our harvest of this king, 115
We are to reap the harvest of his son.
The broken rancour of your high-swoll'n hates,
But lately splintered, knit and joined together,
Must gently be preserved, cherished and kept.
Meseemeth good that with some little train 120
Forthwith from Ludlow the young Prince be fet
Hither to London, to be crowned our king.
RIVERS
Why with some little train, my lord of Buckingham?
BUCKINGHAM   Marry, my lord, lest by a multitude
The new-healed wound of malice should break out, 125
Which would be so much the more dangerous
By how much the estate is green and yet ungoverned.
Where every horse bears his commanding rein
And may direct his course as please himself,
As well the fear of harm as harm apparent, 130
In my opinion, ought to be prevented.
RICHARD   I hope the King made peace with all of us,
And the compact is firm and true in me.
RIVERS   And so in me, and so, I think, in all.
Yet since it is but green, it should be put 135
To no apparent likelihood of breach,
Which haply by much company might be urged;
Therefore I say with noble Buckingham

That it is meet so few should fetch the Prince.

140 HASTINGS   And so say I.

RICHARD   Then be it so, and go we to determine
Who they shall be that straight shall post to Ludlow.
– Madam, and you my sister, will you go
To give your censures in this business?

145 ᵠQUEEN ELIZABETH, DUCHESS
With all our hearts.ᵠ

          Exeunt all but Buckingham and Richard.

BUCKINGHAM
My lord, whoever journeys to the Prince,
For God's sake let not us two stay at home;
For by the way I'll sort occasion,
As index to the story we late talked of,
150 To part the Queen's proud kindred from the Prince.

RICHARD   My other self, my counsel's consistory,
My oracle, my prophet, my dear cousin,
I, as a child, will go by thy direction:
Toward Ludlow then, for we'll not stay behind.

          Exeunt.

2.3   *Enter one* Citizen *at one door, and*
       Another *at the other.*

1 CITIZEN
Good morrow, neighbour; whither away so fast?

2 CITIZEN   I promise you, I scarcely know myself.
Hear you the news abroad?

1 CITIZEN   Yes, that the King is dead.

2 CITIZEN
Ill news, by'r Lady. Seldom comes the better.
I fear, I fear, 'twill prove a giddy world.

         Enter another Citizen.

3 CITIZEN   Neighbours, God speed.

1 CITIZEN   Give you good morrow, sir.

3 CITIZEN
Doth the news hold of good King Edward's death?

2 CITIZEN   Ay sir, it is too true, God help the while.

3 CITIZEN
Then, masters, look to see a troublous world.

1 CITIZEN
No, no, by God's good grace, his son shall reign.

3 CITIZEN   Woe to that land that's governed by a child.

2 CITIZEN   In him there is a hope of government,
Which in his nonage, council under him,
And in his full and ripened years, himself,
No doubt shall then, and till then, govern well.

1 CITIZEN   So stood the state when Henry the Sixth
Was crowned in Paris but at nine months old.

3 CITIZEN
Stood the state so? No, no, good friends, God wot,
For then this land was famously enriched
With politic grave counsel; then the King
Had virtuous uncles to protect his grace.

1 CITIZEN
Why, so hath this, both by his father and mother.

3 CITIZEN   Better it were they all came by his father,
Or by his father there were none at all,
25 For emulation who shall now be nearest
Will touch us all too near, if God prevent not.
O, full of danger is the Duke of Gloucester,
And the Queen's sons and brothers haught and
    proud;
And were they to be ruled, and not to rule,
30 This sickly land might solace as before.

1 CITIZEN
Come, come, we fear the worst; all will be well.

3 CITIZEN
When clouds are seen, wise men put on their cloaks;
When great leaves fall, then winter is at hand;
When the sun sets, who doth not look for night?
35 Untimely storms makes men expect a dearth.
All may be well; but if God sort it so,
'Tis more than we deserve, or I expect.

2 CITIZEN   Truly, the hearts of men are full of fear.
You cannot reason almost with a man
40 That looks not heavily and full of dread.

3 CITIZEN   Before the days of change, still is it so.
By a divine instinct, men's minds mistrust
Ensuing danger, as by proof we see
The water swell before a boisterous storm.
45 But leave it all to God. Whither away?

2 CITIZEN   Marry, we were sent for to the justices.

3 CITIZEN   And so was I. I'll bear you company.

          Exeunt.

2.4   *Enter* ARCHBISHOP *of York,* *young* Duke of
       YORK, QUEEN ELIZABETH *and the*
         DUCHESS ᵠ*of York*ᵠ.

ARCHBISHOP
Last night, I hear, they lay at Stony Stratford,
And at Northampton they do rest tonight.
Tomorrow, or next day, they will be here.

DUCHESS   I long with all my heart to see the Prince.
5 I hope he is much grown since last I saw him.

QUEEN ELIZABETH
But I hear no. They say my son of York
Has almost overta'en him in his growth.

YORK   Ay, mother, but I would not have it so.

DUCHESS   Why, my good cousin, it is good to grow.

YORK   Grandam, one night as we did sit at supper, 10
My uncle Rivers talked how I did grow
More than my brother. 'Ay,' quoth my uncle Gloucester,
'Small herbs have grace; great weeds do grow apace.'
And since, methinks I would not grow so fast
Because sweet flowers are slow and weeds make haste. 15

DUCHESS
Good faith, good faith, the saying did not hold
In him that did object the same to thee.
He was the wretched'st thing when he was young,
So long a-growing, and so leisurely,
That if his rule were true, he should be gracious. 20

ARCHBISHOP

And so no doubt he is, my gracious madam.

DUCHESS I hope he is, but yet let mothers doubt.

YORK Now by my troth, if I had been remembered,

I could have given my uncle's grace a flout

25   To touch his growth nearer than he touched mine.

DUCHESS How, my young York? I prithee let me hear it.

YORK Marry, they say my uncle grew so fast

That he could gnaw a crust at two hours old;

'Twas full two years ere I could get a tooth.

30   Grandam, this would have been a biting jest.

DUCHESS I prithee, pretty York, who told thee this?

YORK Grandam, his nurse.

DUCHESS

His nurse? Why, she was dead ere thou wast born.

YORK If 'twere not she, I cannot tell who told me.

QUEEN ELIZABETH

35   A parlous boy; go to, you are too shrewd.

DUCHESS Good madam, be not angry with the child.

QUEEN ELIZABETH Pitchers have ears.

Enter a Messenger.

ARCHBISHOP Here comes a messenger. – What news?

MESSENGER

Such news, my lord, as grieves me to report.

40 QUEEN ELIZABETH How doth the Prince?

MESSENGER Well, madam, and in health.

DUCHESS What is thy news?

MESSENGER

Lord Rivers and Lord Grey are sent to Pomfret,

And with them Sir Thomas Vaughan, prisoners.

DUCHESS Who hath committed them?

45 MESSENGER   The mighty Dukes,

Gloucester and Buckingham.

ARCHBISHOP   For what offence?

MESSENGER The sum of all I can, I have disclosed.

Why, or for what, the nobles were committed

Is all unknown to me, my gracious lord.

50 QUEEN ELIZABETH Ay me! I see the ruin of my house:

The tiger now hath seized the gentle hind;

Insulting tyranny begins to jut

Upon the innocent and aweless throne.

Welcome destruction, blood and massacre.

55   I see, as in a map, the end of all.

DUCHESS Accursed and unquiet wrangling days,

How many of you have mine eyes beheld?

My husband lost his life to get the crown,

And often up and down my sons were tossed

60   For me to joy and weep their gain and loss.

And being seated, and domestic broils

Clean overblown, themselves the conquerors

Make war upon themselves, brother to brother,

Blood to blood, self against self. O preposterous

65   And frantic outrage, end thy damned spleen,

Or let me die, to look on earth no more.

QUEEN ELIZABETH

Come, come my boy, we will to sanctuary.

Madam, farewell.

DUCHESS   Stay, I will go with you.

QUEEN ELIZABETH You have no cause.

ARCHBISHOP [*to Queen Elizabeth*] My gracious lady,

go,

70   And thither bear your treasure and your goods.

For my part, I'll resign unto your grace

The seal I keep; and so betide to me

As well I tender you and all of yours.

Go, I'll conduct you to the sanctuary.   *Exeunt*.

3.1   *The Trumpets sound. Enter young* PRINCE

Edward, *the* Dukes of Gloucester *and* BUCKINGHAM,

ꟶLordꟶ CARDINAL, CATESBY, *with others.*

BUCKINGHAM

Welcome, sweet Prince, to London, to your chamber.

RICHARD

Welcome, dear cousin, my thoughts' sovereign.

The weary way hath made you melancholy.

PRINCE No, uncle, but our crosses on the way

Have made it tedious, wearisome and heavy.   5

I want more uncles here to welcome me.

RICHARD

Sweet Prince, the untainted virtue of your years

Hath not yet dived into the world's deceit,

Nor more can you distinguish of a man

Than of his outward show, which, God He knows,   10

Seldom or never jumpeth with the heart.

Those uncles which you want were dangerous;

Your grace attended to their sugared words

But looked not on the poison of their hearts.

God keep you from them, and from such false friends.   15

PRINCE

God keep me from false friends, but they were none.

RICHARD

My lord, the Mayor of London comes to greet you.

Enter Lord MAYOR *with others.*

MAYOR

God bless your grace with health and happy days.

PRINCE I thank you, good my lord, and thank you all.

I thought my mother and my brother York   20

Would long ere this have met us on the way.

Fie, what a slug is Hastings, that he comes not

To tell us whether they will come or no.

Enter Lord HASTINGS.

BUCKINGHAM

And in good time, here comes the sweating lord.

PRINCE

Welcome, my lord. What, will our mother come?   25

HASTINGS On what occasion God He knows, not I,

The Queen your mother and your brother York

Have taken sanctuary. The tender Prince

Would fain have come with me to meet your grace,

But by his mother was perforce withheld.   30

BUCKINGHAM
 Fie, what an indirect and peevish course
 Is this of hers! – Lord Cardinal, will your grace
 Persuade the Queen to send the Duke of York
 Unto his princely brother presently?
 – If she deny, Lord Hastings, go with him,
 And from her jealous arms pluck him perforce.

CARDINAL
 My lord of Buckingham, if my weak oratory
 Can from his mother win the Duke of York,
 Anon expect him here; but if she be obdurate
 To mild entreaties, God in heaven forbid
 We should infringe the holy privilege
 Of blessed sanctuary. Not for all this land,
 Would I be guilty of so deep a sin.

BUCKINGHAM
 You are too senseless-obstinate, my lord,
 Too ceremonious and traditional.
 Weigh it but with the grossness of this age,
 You break not sanctuary in seizing him.
 The benefit thereof is always granted
 To those whose dealings have deserved the place
 And those who have the wit to claim the place.
 This prince hath neither claimed it nor deserved it
 And therefore, in mine opinion, cannot have it.
 Then taking him from thence that is not there
 You break no privilege nor charter there.
 Oft have I heard of sanctuary men,
 But sanctuary children, never till now.

CARDINAL
 My lord, you shall o'errule my mind for once.
 – Come on, Lord Hastings, will you go with me?

HASTINGS   I go, my lord.

PRINCE
 Good lords, make all the speedy haste you may.
                    Exeunt Cardinal and Hastings.
 Say, uncle Gloucester, if our brother come,
 Where shall we sojourn till our coronation?

RICHARD   Where it seems best unto your royal self.
 If I may counsel you, some day or two
 Your highness shall repose you at the Tower;
 Then where you please and shall be thought most fit
 For your best health and recreation.

PRINCE   I do not like the Tower, of any place.
 – Did Julius Caesar build that place, my lord?

BUCKINGHAM
 He did, my gracious lord, begin that place,
 Which since succeeding ages have re-edified.

PRINCE   Is it upon record, or else reported
 Successively from age to age, he built it?

BUCKINGHAM   Upon record, my gracious lord.

PRINCE   But say, my lord, it were not registered,
 Methinks the truth should live from age to age,
 As 'twere retailed to all posterity,
 Even to the general all-ending day.

RICHARD [*aside*]
 So wise so young, they say, do never live long.

PRINCE   What say you, uncle?   80

RICHARD   I say, without characters fame lives long.
 [*aside*] Thus, like the formal Vice, Iniquity,
 I moralize two meanings in one word.

PRINCE   That Julius Caesar was a famous man,
 With what his valour did enrich his wit,   85
 His wit set down to make his valure live.
 Death makes no conquest of this conqueror,
 For now he lives in fame, though not in life.
 I'll tell you what, my cousin Buckingham.

BUCKINGHAM   What, my gracious lord?   90

PRINCE   An if I live until I be a man,
 I'll win our ancient right in France again
 Or die a soldier as I lived a king.

RICHARD [*aside*]
 Short summers lightly have a forward spring.

Enter young Duke of YORK, HASTINGS
 ᶠ*and*ᶠ CARDINAL.

BUCKINGHAM
 Now in good time here comes the Duke of York.   95

PRINCE
 Richard of York, how fares our loving brother?

YORK   Well, my dread lord – so must I call you now.

PRINCE   Ay, brother, to our grief, as it is yours.
 Too late he died that might have kept that title,
 Which by his death hath lost much majesty.   100

RICHARD   How fares our cousin, noble lord of York?

YORK   I thank you, gentle uncle. O my lord,
 You said that idle weeds are fast in growth.
 The Prince my brother hath outgrown me far.

RICHARD   He hath, my lord.

YORK   And therefore is he idle?   105

RICHARD   O my fair cousin, I must not say so.

YORK   Then he is more beholding to you than I.

RICHARD   He may command me as my sovereign,
 But you have power in me as in a kinsman.

YORK   I pray you, uncle, give me this dagger.   110

RICHARD   My dagger, little cousin? With all my heart.

PRINCE   A beggar, brother?

YORK   Of my kind uncle, that I know will give,
 And being but a toy, which is no grief to give.

RICHARD   A greater gift than that I'll give my cousin. 115

YORK   A greater gift? O, that's the sword to it.

RICHARD   Ay, gentle cousin, were it light enough.

YORK   O, then I see you will part but with light gifts;
 In weightier things you'll say a beggar nay.

RICHARD   It is too heavy for your grace to wear.   120

YORK   I weigh it lightly, were it heavier.

RICHARD
 What, would you have my weapon, little lord?

YORK   I would, that I might thank you as you call me.

RICHARD   How?

YORK   Little.   125

PRINCE   My lord of York will still be cross in talk.
 Uncle, your grace knows how to bear with him.

YORK   You mean to bear me, not to bear with me.

– Uncle, my brother mocks both you and me.
130 Because that I am little, like an ape,
He thinks that you should bear me on your shoulders.
BUCKINGHAM [*aside*]
With what a sharp-provided wit he reasons:
To mitigate the scorn he gives his uncle,
He prettily and aptly taunts himself.
135 So cunning and so young is wonderful.
RICHARD [*to the Prince*]
My lord, will't please you pass along?
Myself and my good cousin Buckingham
Will to your mother to entreat of her
To meet you at the Tower and welcome you.
YORK [*to the Prince*]
140 What, will you go unto the Tower, my lord?
PRINCE   My Lord Protector needs will have it so.
YORK   I shall not sleep in quiet at the Tower.
RICHARD   Why, what should you fear?
YORK   Marry, my uncle Clarence' angry ghost.
145 My grandam told me he was murdered there.
PRINCE   I fear no uncles dead.
RICHARD   Nor none that live, I hope.
PRINCE   An if they live, I hope I need not fear.
But come, my lord. With a heavy heart,
150 Thinking on them, go I unto the Tower.   [*^FA sennet^F*]
        Exeunt all but Richard,
        Buckingham ^Fand Catesby^F.
BUCKINGHAM
Think you, my lord, this little prating York
Was not incensed by his subtle mother
To taunt and scorn you thus opprobriously?
RICHARD   No doubt, no doubt. O, 'tis a perilous boy,
155 Bold, quick, ingenious, forward, capable.
He is all the mother's, from the top to toe.
BUCKINGHAM
Well, let them rest. – Come hither, Catesby.
Thou art sworn as deeply to effect what we intend
As closely to conceal what we impart.
160 Thou knowst our reasons, urged upon the way.
What think'st thou? Is it not an easy matter
To make William, Lord Hastings, of our mind
For the instalment of this noble Duke
In the seat royal of this famous isle?
165 CATESBY   He for his father's sake so loves the Prince
That he will not be won to aught against him.
BUCKINGHAM
What think'st thou then of Stanley? Will not he?
CATESBY   He will do all in all as Hastings doth.
BUCKINGHAM
Well then, no more but this: go, gentle Catesby,
170 And as it were far off, sound thou Lord Hastings
How he doth stand affected to our purpose
And summon him tomorrow to the Tower
To sit about the coronation.
If thou dost find him tractable to us,
175 Encourage him, and tell him all our reasons.
If he be leaden, icy, cold, unwilling,

Be thou so too, and so break off the talk,
And give us notice of his inclination;
For we tomorrow hold divided councils,
Wherein thyself shalt highly be employed.   180
RICHARD
Commend me to Lord William. Tell him, Catesby,
His ancient knot of dangerous adversaries
Tomorrow are let blood at Pomfret Castle,
And bid my lord, for joy of this good news,
Give Mistress Shore one gentle kiss the more.   185
BUCKINGHAM
Good Catesby, go effect this business soundly.
CATESBY   My good lords both, with all the heed I can.
RICHARD
Shall we hear from you, Catesby, ere we sleep?
CATESBY   You shall, my lord.
RICHARD
At Crosby House, there shall you find us both.   190
        Exit Catesby.
BUCKINGHAM
Now, my lord, what shall we do if we perceive
Lord Hastings will not yield to our complots?
RICHARD
Chop off his head; something we will determine.
And look when I am king, claim thou of me
The earldom of Hereford and all the moveables   195
Whereof the King my brother was possessed.
BUCKINGHAM
I'll claim that promise at your grace's hand.
RICHARD
And look to have it yielded with all kindness.
Come, let us sup betimes, that afterwards
We may digest our complots in some form.   *Exeunt.*   200

3.2   *Enter a Messenger to the door of Hastings.*

MESSENGER   My lord, my lord. [*Knocks.*]
HASTINGS [*within*]   Who knocks?
MESSENGER   One from the Lord Stanley.
HASTINGS [*within*]   What is't o'clock?
MESSENGER   Upon the stroke of four.

        Enter Lord HASTINGS.

HASTINGS
Cannot my Lord Stanley sleep these tedious nights?   5
MESSENGER   So it appears by that I have to say.
First, he commends him to your noble self.
HASTINGS   What then?
MESSENGER
Then certifies your lordship that this night
He dreamt the boar had razed off his helm.   10
Besides, he says there are two councils kept,
And that may be determined at the one
Which may make you and him to rue at th'other.
Therefore he sends to know your lordship's pleasure,
If you will presently take horse with him   15
And with all speed post with him toward the north,

To shun the danger that his soul divines.

HASTINGS   Go, fellow, go. Return unto thy lord.
Bid him not fear the separated council:
20 His honour and myself are at the one,
And at the other is my good friend Catesby,
Where nothing can proceed that toucheth us
Whereof I shall not have intelligence.
Tell him his fears are shallow, without instance;
25 And for his dreams, I wonder he's so simple
To trust the mockery of unquiet slumbers.
To fly the boar before the boar pursues
Were to incense the boar to follow us
And make pursuit where he did mean no chase.
30 Go, bid thy master rise and come to me,
And we will both together to the Tower,
Where he shall see the boar will use us kindly.

MESSENGER
I'll go, my lord, and tell him what you say.   *Exit.*

Enter CATESBY.

CATESBY   Many good morrows to my noble lord.

HASTINGS
35 Good morrow, Catesby. You are early stirring.
What news, what news, in this our tottering state?

CATESBY   It is a reeling world indeed, my lord,
And I believe will never stand upright
Till Richard wear the garland of the realm.

HASTINGS
40 How? Wear the garland? Dost thou mean the crown?

CATESBY   Ay, my good lord.

HASTINGS
I'll have this crown of mine cut from my shoulders
Before I'll see the crown so foul misplaced.
But canst thou guess that he doth aim at it?

CATESBY
45 Ay, on my life, and hopes to find you forward
Upon his party for the gain thereof;
And thereupon he sends you this good news,
That this same very day your enemies,
The kindred of the Queen, must die at Pomfret.

50 HASTINGS   Indeed, I am no mourner for that news,
Because they have been still my adversaries.
But that I'll give my voice on Richard's side
To bar my master's heirs in true descent,
God knows I will not do it, to the death.

CATESBY
55 God keep your lordship in that gracious mind.

HASTINGS
But I shall laugh at this a twelve-month hence,
That they which brought me in my master's hate,
I live to look upon their tragedy.
Well, Catesby, ere a fortnight make me older,
60 I'll send some packing that yet think not on't.

CATESBY   'Tis a vile thing to die, my gracious lord,
When men are unprepared and look not for it.

HASTINGS
O monstrous, monstrous! And so falls it out

With Rivers, Vaughan, Grey; and so 'twill do
With some men else that think themselves as safe 65
As thou and I, who, as thou knowst, are dear
To princely Richard and to Buckingham.

CATESBY   The princes both make high account of you –
[*aside*] For they account his head upon the Bridge.

HASTINGS
I know they do, and I have well deserved it. 70

Enter Lord STANLEY.

Come on, come on. Where is your boar-spear, man?
Fear you the boar and go so unprovided?

STANLEY
My lord, good morrow. – Good morrow, Catesby.
– You may jest on, but, by the Holy Rood,
I do not like these several councils, I. 75

HASTINGS
My lord, I hold my life as dear as ᵍyou doᵍ yours,
And never in my days, I do protest,
Was it so precious to me as 'tis now.
Think you, but that I know our state secure,
I would be so triumphant as I am? 80

STANLEY
The lords at Pomfret, when they rode from London,
Were jocund, and supposed their states were sure,
And they indeed had no cause to mistrust;
But yet you see how soon the day o'ercast.
This sudden stab of rancour I misdoubt. 85
Pray God, I say, I prove a needless coward.
What, shall we toward the Tower? The day is spent.

HASTINGS
Come, come, have with you. Wot you what, my lord?
Today the lords you talked of are beheaded.

STANLEY
They, for their truth, might better wear their heads 90
Than some that have accused them wear their hats.
But come, my lord, let's away.

Enter a Pursuivant.

HASTINGS
Go on before. I'll talk with this good fellow.
            Exeunt Lord Stanley and Catesby.
How now, sirrah? How goes the world with thee?

PURSUIVANT
The better that your lordship please to ask. 95

HASTINGS   I tell thee, man, 'tis better with me now
Than when thou met'st me last where now we meet.
Then was I going prisoner to the Tower
By the suggestion of the Queen's allies;
But now I tell thee – keep it to thyself – 100
This day those enemies are put to death,
And I in better state than e'er I was.

PURSUIVANT
God hold it to your honour's good content.

HASTINGS   Gramercy, fellow. There, drink that for me.
   [*Throws him his purse.*]

PURSUIVANT   I thank your honour.   *Exit.* 105

Enter a Priest.

PRIEST
  Well met, my lord. I am glad to see your honour.
HASTINGS
  I thank thee, good Sir John, with all my heart.
  I am in your debt for your last exercise.
  Come the next sabbath, and I will content you.
    [*He whispers in his ear.*]
110   PRIEST   I'll wait upon your lordship.

Enter BUCKINGHAM.

BUCKINGHAM
  What, talking with a priest, Lord Chamberlain?
  Your friends at Pomfret, they do need the priest;
  Your honour hath no shriving work in hand.
HASTINGS   Good faith, and when I met this holy man
115   The men you talk of came into my mind.
  What, go you toward the Tower?
BUCKINGHAM
  I do, my lord, but long I cannot stay there.
  I shall return before your lordship thence.
HASTINGS   Nay, like enough, for I stay dinner there.
BUCKINGHAM [*aside*]
120   And supper too, although thou knowst it not.
  – Come, will you go?
HASTINGS   I'll wait upon your lordship.   *Exeunt.*

3.3   *Enter* Sir Richard RATCLIFFE, *with Halberds,*
      carrying the nobles °RIVERS, GREY
      and VAUGHAN° *to death at Pomfret.*

RIVERS   Sir Richard Ratcliffe, let me tell thee this:
  Today shalt thou behold a subject die
  For truth, for duty and for loyalty.
GREY   God bless the Prince from all the pack of you.
5   A knot you are of damned bloodsuckers.
VAUGHAN
  You live, that shall cry woe for this hereafter.
RATCLIFFE   Dispatch. The limit of your lives is out.
RIVERS   O Pomfret, Pomfret! O thou bloody prison,
  Fatal and ominous to noble peers!
10   Within the guilty closure of thy walls,
  Richard the Second here was hacked to death;
  And for more slander to thy dismal seat,
  We give to thee our guiltless blood to drink.
GREY   Now Margaret's curse is fall'n upon our heads,
15   When she exclaimed on Hastings, you and I,
  For standing by when Richard stabbed her son.
RIVERS
  Then cursed she Richard; then cursed she
    Buckingham;
  Then cursed she Hastings. O, remember, God,
  To hear her prayer for them, as now for us.
20   And for my sister and her princely sons,
  Be satisfied, dear God, with our true blood,
  Which, as thou knowst, unjustly must be spilt.
RATCLIFFE   Make haste. The hour of death is expiate.

RIVERS
  Come, Grey, come, Vaughan. Let us here embrace.
  Farewell, until we meet again in heaven.   *Exeunt.*   25

3.4   *Enter* BUCKINGHAM, STANLEY, Earl of
      Derby, HASTINGS, Bishop of ELY, NORFOLK,
      RATCLIFFE, LOVELL, *with others, at a table.*

HASTINGS   Now, noble peers, the cause why we are met
  Is to determine of the coronation.
  In God's name speak: when is the royal day?
BUCKINGHAM   Is all things ready for the royal time?
STANLEY   It is, and wants but nomination.   5
ELY   Tomorrow, then, I judge a happy day.
BUCKINGHAM
  Who knows the Lord Protector's mind herein?
  Who is most inward with the noble Duke?
ELY
  Your grace, we think, should soonest know his mind.
BUCKINGHAM
  We know each other's faces; for our hearts,   10
  He knows no more of mine than I of yours,
  Or I of his, my lord, than you of mine.
  – Lord Hastings, you and he are near in love.
HASTINGS   I thank his grace, I know he loves me well;
  But for his purpose in the coronation,   15
  I have not sounded him, nor he delivered
  His gracious pleasure any way therein.
  But you, my honourable lords, may name the time,
  And in the Duke's behalf I'll give my voice,
  Which I presume he'll take in gentle part.   20

Enter RICHARD, Duke of Gloucester.

ELY   In happy time, here comes the Duke himself.
RICHARD
  My noble lords and cousins all, good morrow.
  I have been long a sleeper, but I trust
  My absence doth neglect no great design
  Which by my presence might have been concluded.   25
BUCKINGHAM
  Had you not come upon your cue, my lord,
  William, Lord Hastings, had pronounced your part –
  I mean your voice for crowning of the King.
RICHARD
  Than my Lord Hastings, no man might be bolder;
  His lordship knows me well, and loves me well.   30
  – My Lord of Ely, when I was last in Holborn
  I saw good strawberries in your garden there;
  I do beseech you, send for some of them.
ELY   Marry and will, my lord, with all my heart.
    Exit Bishop of Ely.
RICHARD   Cousin of Buckingham, a word with you.   35
  [*They talk apart.*] Catesby hath sounded Hastings in
    our business,
  And finds the testy gentleman so hot
  That he will lose his head ere give consent
  His master's child, as worshipfully he terms it,

40 Shall lose the royalty of England's throne.
BUCKINGHAM
Withdraw yourself awhile. I'll go with you.
                    Exeunt Richard and Buckingham.
STANLEY
We have not yet set down this day of triumph.
Tomorrow, in my judgement, is too sudden,
For I myself am not so well provided
45 As else I would be, were the day prolonged.

              Enter the Bishop of ELY.

ELY   Where is my lord the Duke of Gloucester?
I have sent for these strawberries.
HASTINGS
His grace looks cheerfully and smooth this morning.
There's some conceit or other likes him well
50 When that he bids good morrow with such spirit.
I think there's never a man in Christendom
Can lesser hide his love or hate than he,
For by his face straight shall you know his heart.
STANLEY   What of his heart perceive you in his face
55 By any livelihood he showed today?
HASTINGS
Marry, that with no man here he is offended,
For were he, he had shown it in his looks.

          Enter RICHARD *and* BUCKINGHAM.

RICHARD   I pray you all, tell me what they deserve
That do conspire my death with devilish plots
60 Of damned witchcraft, and that have prevailed
Upon my body with their hellish charms?
HASTINGS   The tender love I bear your grace, my lord,
Makes me most forward in this princely presence
To doom th'offenders, whosoe'er they be.
65 I say, my lord, they have deserved death.
RICHARD   Then be your eyes the witness of their evil.
Look how I am bewitched! Behold, mine arm
Is like a blasted sapling withered up;
And this is Edward's wife, that monstrous witch,
70 Consorted with that harlot, strumpet Shore,
That by their witchcraft thus have marked me.
HASTINGS   If they have done this deed, my noble lord –
RICHARD
If? Thou protector of this damned strumpet,
Talk'st thou to me of ifs? Thou art a traitor.
75 – Off with his head! Now by Saint Paul I swear
I will not dine until I see the same.
– Lovell and Ratcliffe, look that it be done.
– The rest that love me, rise and follow me.
            Exeunt. Lovell and Ratcliffe remain with
                              the Lord Hastings.
HASTINGS   Woe, woe for England, not a whit for me,
80 For I, too fond, might have prevented this.
Stanley did dream the boar did raze his helm,
And I did scorn it and disdain to fly.
Three times today my foot-cloth horse did stumble,
And started when he looked upon the Tower,

As loath to bear me to the slaughterhouse.   85
O, now I need the priest that spake to me.
I now repent I told the pursuivant,
As too triumphing, how mine enemies
Today at Pomfret bloodily were butchered,
And I myself secure in grace and favour.   90
O Margaret, Margaret, now thy heavy curse
Is lighted on poor Hastings' wretched head.
RATCLIFFE
Come, come, dispatch. The Duke would be at dinner.
Make a short shrift. He longs to see your head.
HASTINGS   O momentary grace of mortal men,   95
Which we more hunt for than the grace of God!
Who builds his hope in air of your good looks
Lives like a drunken sailor on a mast,
Ready with every nod to tumble down
Into the fatal bowels of the deep.   100
LOVELL
Come, come, dispatch. 'Tis bootless to exclaim.
HASTINGS   O bloody Richard! Miserable England,
I prophesy the fearfull'st time to thee
That ever wretched age hath looked upon.
– Come, lead me to the block; bear him my head. 105
They smile at me who shortly shall be dead.
                                    Exeunt.

3.5   *Enter* RICHARD *and* BUCKINGHAM
           in rotten armour, marvellous ill-favoured.

RICHARD
Come, cousin, canst thou quake and change thy colour,
Murder thy breath in middle of a word,
And then again begin, and stop again,
As if thou were distraught and mad with terror?
BUCKINGHAM   Tut, I can counterfeit the deep tragedian, 5
Speak, and look back, and pry on every side,
Tremble and start at wagging of a straw,
Intending deep suspicion. Ghastly looks
Are at my service, like enforced smiles,
And both are ready in their offices,   10
At any time to grace my stratagems.
But what, is Catesby gone?
RICHARD   He is, and see, he brings the Mayor along.

          Enter the Lord MAYOR *and* CATESBY.

BUCKINGHAM   Lord Mayor –
RICHARD   Look to the draw-bridge there!   15
BUCKINGHAM   Hark, a drum!
RICHARD   Catesby, o'erlook the walls!   *Exit Catesby.*
BUCKINGHAM   Lord Mayor, the reason we have sent –
RICHARD   Look back! Defend thee! Here are enemies.
BUCKINGHAM
God and our innocency defend and guard us.   20

       Enter LOVELL *and* RATCLIFFE, *with Hastings's head.*

RICHARD
Be patient. They are friends: Ratcliffe and Lovell.

LOVELL   Here is the head of that ignoble traitor,
The dangerous and unsuspected Hastings.

RICHARD   So dear I loved the man that I must weep.
25   I took him for the plainest harmless creature
That breathed upon the earth a Christian;
Made him my book, wherein my soul recorded
The history of all her secret thoughts.
So smooth he daubed his vice with show of virtue
30   That, his apparent open guilt omitted –
I mean his conversation with Shore's wife –
He lived from all attainder of suspects.

BUCKINGHAM
Well, well, he was the covert'st sheltered traitor
That ever lived.
35   Would you imagine, or almost believe,
Were't not that by great preservation
We live to tell it, that the subtle traitor
This day had plotted in the council house
To murder me and my good lord of Gloucester?

40   MAYOR   Had he done so?

RICHARD   What? Think you we are Turks or infidels?
Or that we would, against the form of law,
Proceed thus rashly in the villain's death,
But that the extreme peril of the case,
45   The peace of England, and our persons' safety,
Enforced us to this execution?

MAYOR   Now fair befall you! He deserved his death,
And your good graces both have well proceeded
To warn false traitors from the like attempts.

50   BUCKINGHAM   I never looked for better at his hands
After he once fell in with Mistress Shore.
Yet had we not determined he should die
Until your lordship came to see his end –
Which now the loving haste of these our friends,
55   Something against our meanings, have prevented –
Because, my lord, I would have had you heard
The traitor speak and timorously confess
The manner and the purpose of his treasons,
That you might well have signified the same
60   Unto the citizens, who haply may
Misconster us in him and wail his death.

MAYOR
But, my good lord, your graces' words shall serve
As well as I had seen and heard him speak;
And do not doubt, right noble princes both,
65   But I'll acquaint our duteous citizens
With all your just proceedings in this case.

RICHARD
And to that end we wished your lordship here,
T'avoid the censures of the carping world.

BUCKINGHAM
Which, since you come too late of our intent,
70   Yet witness what you hear we did intend.
And so, my good Lord Mayor, we bid farewell.

Exit Lord Mayor.

RICHARD   Go after, after, cousin Buckingham.
The Mayor towards Guildhall hies him in all post.

There, at your meetest vantage of the time,
Infer the bastardy of Edward's children.   75
Tell them how Edward put to death a citizen
Only for saying he would make his son
Heir to the crown, meaning indeed his house,
Which, by the sign thereof, was termed so.
Moreover, urge his hateful luxury   80
And bestial appetite in change of lust,
Which stretched unto their servants, daughters, wives,
Even where his raging eye or savage heart,
Without control, lusted to make a prey.
Nay, for a need, thus far come near my person: 85
Tell them, when that my mother went with child
Of that insatiate Edward, noble York
My princely father then had wars in France,
And by true computation of the time
Found that the issue was not his begot,   90
Which well appeared in his lineaments,
Being nothing like the noble duke, my father.
Yet touch this sparingly, as 'twere far off,
Because, my lord, you know my mother lives.

BUCKINGHAM   Doubt not, my lord; I'll play the orator   95
As if the golden fee for which I plead
Were for myself. And so, my lord, adieu.

RICHARD
If you thrive well, bring them to Baynard's Castle,
Where you shall find me well accompanied
With reverend fathers and well-learned bishops.   100

BUCKINGHAM   I go, and towards three or four o'clock
Look for the news that the Guildhall affords.

Exit Buckingham.

RICHARD   Go, Lovell, with all speed to Doctor Shaw.
[*to Ratcliffe*] Go thou to Friar Penker. Bid them both
Meet me within this hour at Baynard's Castle.   105

Exeunt Ratcliffe and Lovell.

Now will I go to take some privy order
To draw the brats of Clarence out of sight,
And to give order that no manner person
Have any time recourse unto the princes.   *Exit.*

3.6   *Enter a* Scrivener ᵠ*with a paper in his hand*ᵠ.

SCRIVENER
Here is the indictment of the good Lord Hastings,
Which in a set hand fairly is engrossed,
That it may be today read o'er in Paul's.
And mark how well the sequel hangs together:
Eleven hours I have spent to write it over,   5
For yesternight by Catesby was it sent me;
The precedent was full as long a-doing,
And yet within these five hours Hastings lived,
Untainted, unexamined, free, at liberty.
Here's a good world the while. Who is so gross   10
That cannot see this palpable device?
Yet who so bold but says he sees it not?
Bad is the world, and all will come to nought
When such ill dealing must be seen in thought.   *Exit.*

3.7   *Enter* RICHARD *and* BUCKINGHAM
at several doors.

RICHARD   How now, how now, what say the citizens?

BUCKINGHAM   Now by the Holy Mother of our Lord,
The citizens are mum, say not a word.

RICHARD
Touched you the bastardy of Edward's children?

BUCKINGHAM
5 I did, with his contract with Lady Lucy
And his contract by deputy in France;
Th'unsatiate greediness of his desire
And his enforcement of the city wives;
His tyranny for trifles; his own bastardy,
10 As being got your father then in France,
And his resemblance being not like the Duke.
Withal, I did infer your lineaments,
Being the right idea of your father,
Both in your form and nobleness of mind;
15 Laid open all your victories in Scotland,
Your discipline in war, wisdom in peace,
Your bounty, virtue, fair humility;
Indeed, left nothing fitting for your purpose
Untouched or slightly handled in discourse.
20 And when mine oratory drew toward end,
I bid them that did love their country's good
Cry, 'God save Richard, England's royal King!'

RICHARD   And did they so?

BUCKINGHAM
No, so God help me, they spake not a word,
25 But like dumb statues or breathing stones
Stared each on other and looked deadly pale;
Which when I saw, I reprehended them
And asked the Mayor what meant this wilful silence?
His answer was, the people were not used
30 To be spoke to but by the Recorder.
Then he was urged to tell my tale again:
'Thus saith the Duke; thus hath the Duke inferred' –
But nothing spoke in warrant from himself.
When he had done, some followers of mine own
35 At lower end of the hall hurled up their caps,
And some ten voices cried, 'God save King Richard!'
And thus I took the vantage of those few:
'Thanks, gentle citizens and friends,' quoth I;
'This general applause and cheerful shout
40 Argues your wisdom and your love to Richard:'
And even here brake off and came away.

RICHARD
What tongueless blocks were they! Would they not
    speak?
Will not the Mayor then, and his brethren, come?

BUCKINGHAM
The Mayor is here at hand. Intend some fear.
45 Be not you spoke with but by mighty suit;
And look you get a prayer book in your hand,
And stand between two churchmen, good my lord,
For on that ground I'll make a holy descant.

And be not easily won to our requests;
50 Play the maid's part: still answer nay, and take it.

RICHARD   I go, and if you plead as well for them
As I can say nay to thee for myself,
No doubt we bring it to a happy issue.

BUCKINGHAM
Go, go up to the leads, the Lord Mayor knocks.
ᵠ*Exit*ᵠ *Richard.*

Enter the Lord MAYOR *and* Citizens.

55 Welcome, my lord; I dance attendance here.
I think the Duke will not be spoke withal.

Enter CATESBY.

BUCKINGHAM
Now, Catesby, what says your lord to my request?

CATESBY   He doth entreat your grace, my noble lord,
To visit him tomorrow, or next day.
60 He is within, with two right reverend fathers,
Divinely bent to meditation;
And in no worldly suits would he be moved
To draw him from his holy exercise.

BUCKINGHAM
Return, good Catesby, to the gracious Duke;
65 Tell him myself, the Mayor and aldermen,
In deep designs, in matter of great moment,
No less importing than our general good,
Are come to have some conference with his grace.

CATESBY   I'll signify so much unto him straight. *Exit.*

BUCKINGHAM
70 Ah ha, my lord, this prince is not an Edward.
He is not lulling on a lewd love-bed,
But on his knees at meditation;
Not dallying with a brace of courtesans,
But meditating with two deep divines;
75 Not sleeping, to engross his idle body,
But praying, to enrich his watchful soul.
Happy were England, would this virtuous prince
Take on his grace the sovereignty thereof.
But sure I fear we shall not win him to it.

MAYOR
80 Marry, God defend his grace should say us nay.

BUCKINGHAM
I fear he will. Here Catesby comes again.

Enter CATESBY.

Now, Catesby, what says his grace?

CATESBY   He wonders to what end you have assembled
Such troops of citizens to come to him,
85 His grace not being warned thereof before.
He fears, my lord, you mean no good to him.

BUCKINGHAM   Sorry I am my noble cousin should
Suspect me that I mean no good to him.
By heaven, we come to him in perfect love;
90 And so once more return and tell his grace.
Exit ᵠ*Catesby*ᵠ.

When holy and devout religious men

Are at their beads, 'tis much to draw them thence,
So sweet is zealous contemplation.

Enter RICHARD *aloft, between two Bishops.*
Enter CATESBY.

MAYOR
See where his grace stands, 'tween two clergymen.
BUCKINGHAM
95   Two props of virtue for a Christian prince,
To stay him from the fall of vanity;
And see a book of prayer in his hand,
True ornaments to know a holy man.
– Famous Plantagenet, most gracious prince,
100   Lend favourable ear to our requests,
And pardon us the interruption
Of thy devotion and right Christian zeal.
RICHARD   My lord, there needs no such apology.
I do beseech your grace to pardon me,
105   Who, earnest in the service of my God,
Deferred the visitation of my friends.
But leaving this, what is your grace's pleasure?
BUCKINGHAM
Even that, I hope, which pleaseth God above
And all good men of this ungoverned isle.
110   RICHARD   I do suspect I have done some offence
That seems disgracious in the City's eye,
And that you come to reprehend my ignorance.
BUCKINGHAM
You have, my lord. Would it might please your grace,
On our entreaties, to amend your fault.
115   RICHARD   Else wherefore breathe I in a Christian land?
BUCKINGHAM
Know then, it is your fault that you resign
The supreme seat, the throne majestical,
The sceptered office of your ancestors,
Your state of fortune, and your due of birth,
120   The lineal glory of your royal house,
To the corruption of a blemished stock;
Whiles in the mildness of your sleepy thoughts,
Which here we waken to our country's good,
The noble isle doth want her proper limbs;
125   Her face defaced with scars of infamy,
Her royal stock graft with ignoble plants,
And almost shouldered in the swallowing gulf
Of dark forgetfulness and deep oblivion;
Which to recure, we heartily solicit
130   Your gracious self to take on you the charge
And kingly government of this your land,
Not as protector, steward, substitute,
Or lowly factor for another's gain,
But as successively from blood to blood,
135   Your right of birth, your empery, your own.
For this, consorted with the citizens,
Your very worshipful and loving friends,
And by their vehement instigation,
In this just cause come I to move your grace.
140   RICHARD   I cannot tell if to depart in silence

Or bitterly to speak in your reproof
Best fitteth my degree or your condition.
If not to answer, you might haply think
Tongue-tied ambition, not replying, yielded
To bear the golden yoke of sovereignty,   145
Which fondly you would here impose on me.
If to reprove you for this suit of yours,
So seasoned with your faithful love to me,
Then on the other side I checked my friends.
Therefore, to speak, and to avoid the first,   150
And then, in speaking, not to incur the last,
Definitively thus I answer you:
Your love deserves my thanks, but my desert
Unmeritable shuns your high request.
First, if all obstacles were cut away,   155
And that my path were even to the crown
As the ripe revenue and due of birth,
Yet so much is my poverty of spirit,
So mighty and so many my defects,
That I would rather hide me from my greatness,   160
Being a bark to brook no mighty sea,
Than in my greatness covet to be hid
And in the vapour of my glory smothered.
But, God be thanked, there is no need of me,
And much I need to help you, were there need.   165
The royal tree hath left us royal fruit,
Which, mellowed by the stealing hours of time,
Will well become the seat of majesty,
And make, no doubt, us happy by his reign.
On him I lay that you would lay on me: 170
The right and fortune of his happy stars,
Which God defend that I should wring from him.
BUCKINGHAM
My lord, this argues conscience in your grace,
But the respects thereof are nice and trivial,
All circumstances well considered.   175
You say that Edward is your brother's son;
So say we too, but not by Edward's wife.
For first was he contract to Lady Lucy –
Your mother lives a witness to his vow –
And afterward by substitute betrothed   180
To Bona, sister to the King of France.
These both put off, a poor petitioner,
A care-crazed mother to a many sons,
A beauty-waning and distressed widow,
Even in the afternoon of her best days,   185
Made prize and purchase of his wanton eye,
Seduced the pitch and height of his degree
To base declension and loathed bigamy.
By her, in his unlawful bed, he got
This Edward, whom our manners call the Prince.   190
More bitterly could I expostulate,
Save that, for reverence to some alive,
I give a sparing limit to my tongue.
Then, good my lord, take to your royal self
This proffered benefit of dignity,   195
If not to bless us and the land withal,

Yet to draw forth your noble ancestry
From the corruption of abusing times
Unto a lineal, true-derived course.

MAYOR   Do, good my lord. Your citizens entreat you.   200

BUCKINGHAM
Refuse not, mighty lord, this proffered love.

CATESBY   O, make them joyful. Grant their lawful suit.

RICHARD   Alas, why would you heap this care on me?
I am unfit for state and majesty.

I do beseech you, take it not amiss;   205
I cannot, nor I will not, yield to you.

BUCKINGHAM   If you refuse it, as in love and zeal
Loath to depose the child, your brother's son –
As well we know your tenderness of heart
And gentle, kind, effeminate remorse,   210
Which we have noted in you to your kindred,
And equally indeed to all estates –
Yet know, whe'er you accept our suit or no,
Your brother's son shall never reign our king,
But we will plant some other in the throne   215
To the disgrace and downfall of your house.
And in this resolution here we leave you.
– Come, citizens. Zounds, I'll entreat no more.

ᵠRICHARD   O, do not swear, my lord of Buckingham!ᵠ

Exeunt Buckingham and some others.

CATESBY
Call him again, sweet prince; accept their suit.   220
If you deny them, all the land will rue it.

RICHARD   Will you enforce me to a world of cares?
Call them again.   *Exit Catesby.*
I am not made of stones,
But penetrable to your kind entreaties,
Albeit against my conscience and my soul.   225

Enter BUCKINGHAM and the rest.

Cousin of Buckingham, and sage, grave men,
Since you will buckle fortune on my back,
To bear her burden, whe'er I will or no,
I must have patience to endure the load;
But if black scandal or foul-faced reproach   230
Attend the sequel of your imposition,
Your mere enforcement shall acquittance me
From all the impure blots and stains thereof,
For God doth know, and you may partly see,
How far I am from the desire of this.   235

MAYOR   God bless your grace; we see it and will say it.

RICHARD   In saying so, you shall but say the truth.

BUCKINGHAM   Then I salute you with this royal title:
Long live King Richard, England's worthy king!

ALL   Amen.   240

BUCKINGHAM
Tomorrow may it please you to be crowned?

RICHARD
Even when you please, for you will have it so.

BUCKINGHAM
Tomorrow, then, we will attend your grace,
And so most joyfully we take our leave.

RICHARD   Come, let us to our holy work again.   245
– Farewell, my cousin, farewell gentle friends.

Exeunt.

4.1   *Enter* QUEEN ELIZABETH, *the* DUCHESS *of*
York *and Marquess of* DORSET ᵠ*at one door*ᵠ;
ANNE, *Duchess of Gloucester, with*
Clarence's Daughter, ᵠ*at another door*ᵠ.

DUCHESS   Who meets us here? My niece Plantagenet,
Led in the hand of her kind aunt of Gloucester?
Now, for my life, she's wandering to the Tower,
On pure heart's love, to greet the tender Prince.
– Daughter, well met.

ANNE   God give your graces both   5
A happy and a joyful time of day.

QUEEN ELIZABETH
As much to you, good sister. Whither away?

ANNE   No farther than the Tower, and, as I guess,
Upon the like devotion as yourselves,
To gratulate the gentle Princes there.   10

QUEEN ELIZABETH
Kind sister, thanks. We'll enter all together.

Enter BRAKENBURY, *the Lieutenant.*

And in good time, here the Lieutenant comes.
Master Lieutenant, pray you, by your leave,
How doth the Prince and my young son of York?

BRAKENBURY
Right well, dear madam. By your patience,   15
I may not suffer you to visit them.
The King hath strictly charged the contrary.

QUEEN ELIZABETH
The King? Who's that?

BRAKENBURY   I mean the Lord Protector.

QUEEN ELIZABETH
The Lord protect him from that kingly title.
Hath he set bounds between their love and me?   20
I am their mother. Who shall bar me from them?

DUCHESS   I am their father's mother. I will see them.

ANNE
Their aunt I am in law, in love their mother.
Then bring me to their sights. I'll bear thy blame
And take thy office from thee, on my peril.   25

BRAKENBURY   No, madam, no. I may not leave it so.
I am bound by oath, and therefore pardon me.   *Exit.*

Enter STANLEY.

STANLEY   Let me but meet you ladies one hour hence,
And I'll salute your grace of York as mother
And reverend looker-on of two fair queens.   30
[*to Anne*] Come, madam, you must straight to
          Westminster,
There to be crowned Richard's royal queen.

QUEEN ELIZABETH   Ah, cut my lace asunder
That my pent heart may have some scope to beat,
Or else I swoon with this dead-killing news.   35

ANNE   Despiteful tidings. O, unpleasing news.
DORSET
  Be of good cheer, mother. How fares your grace?
QUEEN ELIZABETH
  O Dorset, speak not to me. Get thee gone.
  Death and destruction dogs thee at thy heels.
40   Thy mother's name is ominous to children.
  If thou wilt outstrip death, go, cross the seas
  And live with Richmond, from the reach of hell.
  Go hie thee, hie thee from this slaughterhouse,
  Lest thou increase the number of the dead
45   And make me die the thrall of Margaret's curse,
  Nor mother, wife, nor England's counted queen.
STANLEY
  Full of wise care is this your counsel, madam.
  [*to Dorset*] Take all the swift advantage of the hours.
  You shall have letters from me to my son
50   In your behalf, to meet you on the way.
  Be not ta'en tardy by unwise delay.
DUCHESS   O ill-dispersing wind of misery.
  O my accursed womb, the bed of death.
  A cockatrice hast thou hatched to the world,
55   Whose unavoided eye is murderous.
STANLEY   Come, madam, come. I in all haste was sent.
ANNE   And I with all unwillingness will go.
  O, would to God that the inclusive verge
  Of golden metal that must round my brow
60   Were red-hot steel to sear me to the brains.
  Anointed let me be with deadly venom,
  And die ere men can say 'God save the Queen'.
QUEEN ELIZABETH
  Go, go, poor soul; I envy not thy glory.
  To feed my humour wish thyself no harm.
65 ANNE   No? Why? When he that is my husband now
  Came to me as I followed Henry's corse,
  When scarce the blood was well washed from his hands
  Which issued from my other angel husband
  And that dear saint which then I weeping followed;
70   O when, I say, I looked on Richard's face,
  This was my wish: 'Be thou', quoth I, 'accursed
  For making me, so young, so old a widow;
  And when thou wed'st, let sorrow haunt thy bed;
  And be thy wife, if any be so mad,
75   More miserable by the life of thee
  Than thou hast made me by my dear lord's death.'
  Lo, ere I can repeat this curse again,
  Within so small a time, my woman's heart
  Grossly grew captive to his honey words
80   And proved the subject of mine own soul's curse,
  Which hitherto hath held mine eyes from rest;
  For never yet one hour in his bed
  Did I enjoy the golden dew of sleep,
  But with his timorous dreams was still awaked.
85   Besides, he hates me for my father Warwick,
  And will, no doubt, shortly be rid of me.
QUEEN ELIZABETH
  Poor heart, adieu. I pity thy complaining.

ANNE   No more than with my soul I mourn for yours.
DORSET   Farewell, thou woeful welcomer of glory.
ANNE   Adieu, poor soul, that tak'st thy leave of it.   90
DUCHESS [*to Dorset*]
  Go thou to Richmond, and good fortune guide thee,
  [*to Anne*] Go thou to Richard, and good angels tend
    thee.
  [*to Queen Elizabeth*] Go thou to sanctuary, and good
    thoughts possess thee.
  I to my grave, where peace and rest lie with me.
  Eighty-odd years of sorrow have I seen,   95
  And each hour's joy wracked with a week of teen.
QUEEN ELIZABETH
  Stay, yet look back with me unto the Tower.
  – Pity, you ancient stones, those tender babes
  Whom envy hath immured within your walls,
  Rough cradle for such little pretty ones;   100
  Rude ragged nurse, old sullen playfellow
  For tender princes, use my babies well.
  So foolish sorrows bids your stones farewell.   *Exeunt.*

4.2   ᵒ*The trumpets*ᵒ *sound a sennet. Enter* RICHARD
    in pomp, BUCKINGHAM, CATESBY, RATCLIFFE,
    LOVELL ᵒ*with other Nobles*ᵒ *and a* Page.

KING RICHARD
  Stand all apart. – Cousin of Buckingham.
BUCKINGHAM   My gracious sovereign.
KING RICHARD   Give me thy hand.
  [ᵒ*Here he ascendeth the throne.*ᵒ *Sound trumpets.*]
                Thus high, by thy advice
  And thy assistance is King Richard seated.
  But shall we wear these glories for a day?   5
  Or shall they last, and we rejoice in them?
BUCKINGHAM   Still live they, and forever let them last.
KING RICHARD
  Ah, Buckingham, now do I play the touch
  To try if thou be current gold indeed:
  Young Edward lives; think now what I would speak.   10
BUCKINGHAM   Say on, my loving lord.
KING RICHARD
  Why, Buckingham, I say I would be king.
BUCKINGHAM
  Why so you are, my thrice-renowned lord.
KING RICHARD
  Ha! Am I king? 'Tis so – but Edward lives.
BUCKINGHAM   True, noble prince.
KING RICHARD   O bitter consequence   15
  That Edward still should live 'true noble prince'!
  Cousin, thou wast not wont to be so dull.
  Shall I be plain? I wish the bastards dead,
  And I would have it suddenly performed.
  What sayst thou now? Speak suddenly. Be brief.   20
BUCKINGHAM   Your grace may do your pleasure.
KING RICHARD
  Tut, tut, thou art all ice; thy kindness freezes.
  Say, have I thy consent that they shall die?

BUCKINGHAM
  Give me some little breath, some pause, dear lord,
25 Before I positively speak in this.
  I will resolve you herein presently. *Exit.*
CATESBY [*aside to others*]
  The King is angry. See, he gnaws his lip.
KING RICHARD [*aside*]
  I will converse with iron-witted fools
  And unrespective boys. None are for me
30 That look into me with considerate eyes.
  High-reaching Buckingham grows circumspect.
  – Boy!
PAGE   My lord?
KING RICHARD
  Knowst thou not any whom corrupting gold
35 Will tempt unto a close exploit of death?
PAGE   I know a discontented gentleman
  Whose humble means match not his haughty spirit.
  Gold were as good as twenty orators,
  And will, no doubt, tempt him to anything.
KING RICHARD   What is his name?
40 PAGE   His name, my lord, is Tyrrel.
KING RICHARD
  I partly know the man. Go, call him hither, boy.
                              Exit Page.
  [*aside*] The deep-revolving, witty Buckingham
  No more shall be the neighbour to my counsels.
  Hath he so long held out with me, untired,
45 And stops he now for breath? Well, be it so.

  Enter STANLEY.

  How now, Lord Stanley, what's the news?
STANLEY   Know my loving lord,
  The Marquess Dorset, as I hear, is fled
  To Richmond, in the parts where he abides.
KING RICHARD
50 Come hither, Catesby. Rumour it abroad
  That Anne my wife is very grievous sick.
  I will take order for her keeping close.
  Inquire me out some mean poor gentleman,
  Whom I will marry straight to Clarence' daughter.
55 The boy is foolish, and I fear not him.
  Look how thou dream'st! I say again, give out
  That Anne my queen is sick and like to die.
  About it, for it stands me much upon
  To stop all hopes whose growth may damage me.
                              Exit Catesby.
60 I must be married to my brother's daughter,
  Or else my kingdom stands on brittle glass.
  Murder her brothers, and then marry her –
  Uncertain way of gain. But I am in
  So far in blood that sin will pluck on sin.
65 Tear-falling pity dwells not in this eye.

  Enter TYRREL.

  Is thy name Tyrrel?
TYRREL   James Tyrrel, and your most obedient subject.

KING RICHARD   Art thou indeed?
TYRREL   Prove me, my gracious lord.
KING RICHARD
  Dar'st thou resolve to kill a friend of mine?
TYRREL   Please you. But I had rather kill two enemies.   70
KING RICHARD
  Why then thou hast it. Two deep enemies,
  Foes to my rest, and my sweet sleep's disturbers,
  Are they that I would have thee deal upon.
  Tyrrel, I mean those bastards in the Tower.
TYRREL   Let me have open means to come to them,   75
  And soon I'll rid you from the fear of them.
KING RICHARD
  Thou sing'st sweet music. Hark, come hither, Tyrrel.
  Go by this token. Rise, and lend thine ear,
    [ᵠ*He*ᵠ *whispers* ᵠ*in his ear*ᵠ.]
  There is no more but so. Say it is done,
  And I will love thee and prefer thee for it.   80
TYRREL   I will dispatch it straight. *Exit.*

  Enter BUCKINGHAM.

BUCKINGHAM   My lord, I have considered in my mind
  The late request that you did sound me in.
KING RICHARD
  Well, let that rest. Dorset is fled to Richmond.
BUCKINGHAM   I hear the news, my lord.   85
KING RICHARD
  Stanley, he is your wife's son. Well, look unto it.
BUCKINGHAM
  My lord, I claim the gift, my due by promise,
  For which your honour and your faith is pawned:
  Th'earldom of Hereford and the moveables
  Which you have promised I shall possess.   90
KING RICHARD
  Stanley, look to your wife; if she convey
  Letters to Richmond, you shall answer it.
BUCKINGHAM
  What says your highness to my just request?
KING RICHARD   I do remember me, Henry the Sixth
  Did prophesy that Richmond should be king,   95
  When Richmond was a little peevish boy.
  A king perhaps –
ᵠBUCKINGHAM   My lord.
KING RICHARD
  How chance the prophet could not at that time
  Have told me, I being by, that I should kill him?
BUCKINGHAM   My lord, your promise for the earldom –   100
KING RICHARD   Richmond! When last I was at Exeter,
  The Mayor in courtesy showed me the castle
  And called it Rougemont, at which name I started,
  Because a bard of Ireland told me once
  I should not live long after I saw Richmond.   105
BUCKINGHAM   My lord –
KING RICHARD   Ay, what's o'clock?
BUCKINGHAM
  I am thus bold to put your grace in mind
  Of what you promised me.

KING RICHARD   Well, but what's o'clock?
110 BUCKINGHAM   Upon the stroke of ten.
KING RICHARD   Well, let it strike.
BUCKINGHAM   Why let it strike?
KING RICHARD
     Because that, like a jack, thou keep'st the stroke
     Betwixt thy begging and my meditation.
     I am not in the giving vein today.ᵛ
BUCKINGHAM
115   May it please you to resolve me in my suit?
KING RICHARD
     Thou troublest me; I am not in the vein.
                Exit followed by all but Buckingham.
BUCKINGHAM
     And is it thus? Repays he my deep service
     With such contempt? Made I him king for this?
     O, let me think on Hastings and be gone
120   To Brecknock while my fearful head is on.   *Exit.*

4.3   *Enter* TYRREL.

TYRREL   The tyrannous and bloody act is done,
     The most arch deed of piteous massacre
     That ever yet this land was guilty of.
     Dighton and Forrest, who I did suborn
5   To do this piece of ruthful butchery,
     Albeit they were fleshed villains, bloody dogs,
     Melted with tenderness and mild compassion,
     Wept like to children in their deaths' sad story.
     'O thus', quoth Dighton, 'lay the gentle babes'.
10   'Thus, thus', quoth Forrest, 'girdling one another
     Within their alabaster innocent arms.
     Their lips were four red roses on a stalk,
     And in their summer beauty kissed each other.
     A book of prayers on their pillow lay,
15   Which once', quoth Forrest, 'almost changed my mind.
     But, O, the Devil – ' There the villain stopped;
     When Dighton thus told on: 'We smothered
     The most replenished sweet work of nature,
     That from the prime creation e'er she framed.'
20   Hence both are gone with conscience and remorse;
     They could not speak, and so I left them both
     To bear this tidings to the bloody King.

         Enter ᵛKINGᵛ RICHARD.

     And here he comes. All health, my sovereign lord.
KING RICHARD   Kind Tyrrel, am I happy in thy news?
25 TYRREL   If to have done the thing you gave in charge
     Beget your happiness, be happy then,
     For it is done.
KING RICHARD   But didst thou see them dead?
TYRREL   I did, my lord.
KING RICHARD   And buried, gentle Tyrrel?
TYRREL   The chaplain of the Tower hath buried them,
30   But where, to say the truth, I do not know.
KING RICHARD
     Come to me, Tyrrel, soon at after-supper,

     When thou shalt tell the process of their death.
     Meantime, but think how I may do thee good,
     And be inheritor of thy desire.
     Farewell till then.
TYRREL   I humbly take my leave.   ᵛ*Exit.*ᵛ   35
KING RICHARD
     The son of Clarence have I pent up close,
     His daughter meanly have I matched in marriage,
     The sons of Edward sleep in Abraham's bosom,
     And Anne my wife hath bid this world good night.
     Now, for I know the Breton Richmond aims   40
     At young Elizabeth, my brother's daughter,
     And by that knot looks proudly on the crown,
     To her go I, a jolly thriving wooer.

         Enter RATCLIFFE.

RATCLIFFE   My lord.
KING RICHARD
     Good or bad news, that thou com'st in so bluntly?   45
RATCLIFFE
     Bad news, my lord. Morton is fled to Richmond,
     And Buckingham, backed with the hardy Welshmen,
     Is in the field, and still his power increaseth.
KING RICHARD
     Ely with Richmond troubles me more near
     Than Buckingham and his rash-levied strength.   50
     Come, I have learned that fearful commenting
     Is leaden servitor to dull delay.
     Delay leads impotent and snail-paced beggary;
     Then fiery expedition be my wing,
     Jove's Mercury, and herald for a king.   55
     Go muster men. My counsel is my shield.
     We must be brief when traitors brave the field.
                          Exeunt.

4.4   *Enter old* QUEEN MARGARET.

QUEEN MARGARET
     So now prosperity begins to mellow
     And drop into the rotten mouth of death.
     Here in these confines slyly have I lurked
     To watch the waning of mine enemies.
     A dire induction am I witness to,   5
     And will to France, hoping the consequence
     Will prove as bitter, black and tragical.
     Withdraw thee, wretched Margaret. Who comes
       here?   [*Stands aside.*]

       Enter DUCHESS ᵛof Yorkᵛ *and*
             QUEEN ELIZABETH.

QUEEN ELIZABETH
     Ah, my poor princes! Ah, my tender babes,
     My unblowed flowers, new-appearing sweets!   10
     If yet your gentle souls fly in the air
     And be not fixed in doom perpetual,
     Hover about me with your airy wings
     And hear your mother's lamentation.

QUEEN MARGARET [*aside*]
  Hover about her; say that right for right
  Hath dimmed your infant morn to aged night.

DUCHESS   So many miseries have crazed my voice
  That my woe-wearied tongue is still and mute.
  Edward Plantagenet, why art thou dead?

QUEEN MARGARET [*aside*]
  Plantagenet doth quit Plantagenet;
  Edward for Edward pays a dying debt.

QUEEN ELIZABETH
  Wilt thou, O God, fly from such gentle lambs
  And throw them in the entrails of the wolf?
  When didst thou sleep when such a deed was done?

QUEEN MARGARET [*aside*]
  When holy Harry died, and my sweet son.

DUCHESS
  Dead life, blind sight, poor mortal living ghost,
  Woe's scene, world's shame, grave's due by life
        usurped,
  Brief abstract and record of tedious days,
  Rest thy unrest on England's lawful earth,   [*Sits.*]
  Unlawfully made drunk with innocent blood.

QUEEN ELIZABETH
  Ah, that thou wouldst as soon afford a grave,
  As thou canst yield a melancholy seat,
  Then would I hide my bones, not rest them here.
  Ah, who hath any cause to mourn but we?   [*Sits.*]

QUEEN MARGARET [*Comes forward.*]
  If ancient sorrow be most reverend,
  Give mine the benefit of seniory,
  And let my griefs frown on the upper hand.
  If sorrow can admit society,
  ᵠTell over your woes again by viewing mine.ᵠ
  I had an Edward, till a Richard killed him;
  I had a husband, till a Richard killed him.
  Thou hadst an Edward, till a Richard killed him.
  Thou hadst a Richard, till a Richard killed him.

DUCHESS   I had a Richard too, and thou didst kill him;
  I had a Rutland too; thou holp'st to kill him.

QUEEN MARGARET
  Thou hadst a Clarence too, and Richard killed him.
  From forth the kennel of thy womb hath crept
  A hell-hound that doth hunt us all to death:
  That dog, that had his teeth before his eyes,
  To worry lambs and lap their gentle blood;
  That excellent grand tyrant of the earth,
  That reigns in galled eyes of weeping souls;
  That foul defacer of God's handiwork
  Thy womb let loose to chase us to our graves.
  O upright, just, and true-disposing God,
  How do I thank thee that this carnal cur
  Preys on the issue of his mother's body
  And makes her pew-fellow with others' moan.

DUCHESS   O Harry's wife, triumph not in my woes!
  God witness with me, I have wept for thine.

QUEEN MARGARET
  Bear with me. I am hungry for revenge,

And now I cloy me with beholding it.
Thy Edward he is dead, that killed my Edward,
Thy other Edward dead, to quit my Edward.
Young York, he is but boot, because both they
Matched not the high perfection of my loss.
Thy Clarence he is dead that stabbed my Edward,
And the beholders of this frantic play,
Th'adulterate Hastings, Rivers, Vaughan, Grey,
Untimely smothered in their dusky graves.
Richard yet lives, hell's black intelligencer,
Only reserved their factor to buy souls
And send them thither. But at hand, at hand
Ensues his piteous and unpitied end.
Earth gapes, hell burns, fiends roar, saints pray,
To have him suddenly conveyed from hence.
Cancel his bond of life, dear God I pray,
That I may live and say, 'The dog is dead.'

QUEEN ELIZABETH
  O, thou didst prophesy the time would come
  That I should wish for thee to help me curse
  That bottled spider, that foul bunch-backed toad.

QUEEN MARGARET
  I called thee then vain flourish of my fortune;
  I called thee then, poor shadow, painted queen,
  The presentation of but what I was,
  The flattering index of a direful pageant,
  One heaved a-high, to be hurled down below,
  A mother only mocked with two fair babes,
  A dream of what thou wast, a garish flag
  To be the aim of every dangerous shot,
  A sign of dignity, a breath, a bubble,
  A queen in jest, only to fill the scene.
  Where is thy husband now? Where be thy brothers?
  Where be thy two sons? Wherein dost thou joy?
  Who sues, and kneels, and says, 'God save the
        Queen'?
  Where be the bending peers that flattered thee?
  Where be the thronging troops that followed thee?
  Decline all this, and see what now thou art:
  For happy wife, a most distressed widow;
  For joyful mother, one that wails the name;
  For one being sued to, one that humbly sues;
  For queen, a very caitiff crowned with care;
  For she that scorned at me, now scorned of me;
  For she being feared of all, now fearing one;
  For she commanding all, obeyed of none.
  Thus hath the course of justice whirled about
  And left thee but a very prey to time,
  Having no more but thought of what thou wast,
  To torture thee the more, being what thou art.
  Thou didst usurp my place, and dost thou not
  Usurp the just proportion of my sorrow?
  Now thy proud neck bears half my burdened yoke,
  From which, even here I slip my wearied head
  And leave the burden of it all on thee.
  Farewell, York's wife, and queen of sad mischance.
  These English woes shall make me smile in France.

QUEEN ELIZABETH
O thou, well skilled in curses, stay awhile
And teach me how to curse mine enemies.
QUEEN MARGARET
Forbear to sleep the night, and fast the day;
Compare dead happiness with living woe;
120 Think that thy babes were sweeter than they were,
And he that slew them fouler than he is.
Bettering thy loss makes the bad causer worse.
Revolving this will teach thee how to curse.
QUEEN ELIZABETH
My words are dull. O, quicken them with thine.
QUEEN MARGARET
125 Thy woes will make them sharp and pierce like mine.
Exit.
DUCHESS Why should calamity be full of words?
QUEEN ELIZABETH
Windy attorneys to their clients' woes,
Airy succeeders of intestate joys,
Poor breathing orators of miseries,
130 Let them have scope, though what they will impart
Help nothing else, yet do they ease the heart.
DUCHESS
If so, then be not tongue-tied. Go with me,
And in the breath of bitter words let's smother
My damnèd son, that thy two sweet sons smothered.
[*Trumpet sounds.*]
135 The trumpet sounds. Be copious in exclaims.

Enter KING RICHARD *and his Train,*
including CATESBY, ᵠ*marching with Drums*
*and Trumpets*ᵠ.

KING RICHARD Who intercepts me in my expedition?
DUCHESS O, she that might have intercepted thee,
By strangling thee in her accursèd womb,
From all the slaughters, wretch, that thou hast done.
QUEEN ELIZABETH
140 Hid'st thou that forehead with a golden crown
Where should be branded, if that right were right,
The slaughter of the prince that owed that crown
And the dire death of my poor sons and brothers?
Tell me, thou villain-slave, where are my children?
DUCHESS Thou toad, thou toad, where is thy brother
145   Clarence,
And little Ned Plantagenet his son?
QUEEN ELIZABETH
Where is the gentle Rivers, Vaughan, Grey?
DUCHESS Where is kind Hastings?
KING RICHARD
A flourish, trumpets! Strike alarum, drums!
150 Let not the heavens hear these tell-tale women
Rail on the Lord's anointed. Strike, I say!
[*Flourish. Alarums.*]
Either be patient and entreat me fair,
Or with the clamorous report of war
Thus will I drown your exclamations.
155 DUCHESS Art thou my son?

KING RICHARD
Ay, I thank God, my father and yourself.
DUCHESS Then patiently hear my impatience.
KING RICHARD
Madam, I have a touch of your condition,
That cannot brook the accent of reproof.
DUCHESS O, let me speak.
KING RICHARD   Do then, but I'll not hear. 160
DUCHESS I will be mild and gentle in my words.
KING RICHARD
And brief, good mother, for I am in haste.
DUCHESS Art thou so hasty? I have stayed for thee,
God knows, in torment and in agony.
KING RICHARD And came I not at last to comfort you? 165
DUCHESS No, by the Holy Rood, thou knowst it well:
Thou cam'st on earth to make the earth my hell.
A grievous burden was thy birth to me;
Tetchy and wayward was thy infancy.
Thy school days frightful, desperate, wild and furious; 170
Thy prime of manhood daring, bold and venturous;
Thy age confirmed proud, subtle, sly and bloody,
More mild, but yet more harmful, kind in hatred.
What comfortable hour canst thou name
That ever graced me with thy company? 175
KING RICHARD
Faith, none but Humfrey Hower, that called your grace
To breakfast once, forth of my company.
If I be so disgracious in your eye,
Let me march on and not offend you, madam.
Strike up the drum.
DUCHESS   I prithee, hear me speak. 180
KING RICHARD You speak too bitterly.
DUCHESS   Hear me a word,
For I shall never speak to thee again.
KING RICHARD So.
DUCHESS Either thou wilt die by God's just ordinance
Ere from this war thou turn a conqueror, 185
Or I with grief and extreme age shall perish
And nevermore behold thy face again.
Therefore take with thee my most grievous curse,
Which in the day of battle tire thee more
Than all the complete armour that thou wear'st. 190
My prayers on the adverse party fight,
And there the little souls of Edward's children
Whisper the spirits of thine enemies
And promise them success and victory.
Bloody thou art; bloody will be thy end. 195
Shame serves thy life and doth thy death attend.
Exit.
QUEEN ELIZABETH
Though far more cause, yet much less spirit to curse
Abides in me. I say amen to her.
KING RICHARD
Stay, madam, I must talk a word with you.
QUEEN ELIZABETH
I have no more sons of the royal blood 200
For thee to slaughter. For my daughters, Richard,

They shall be praying nuns, not weeping queens,
And therefore level not to hit their lives.

KING RICHARD
You have a daughter called Elizabeth,
05   Virtuous and fair, royal and gracious.

QUEEN ELIZABETH
And must she die for this? O, let her live,
And I'll corrupt her manners, stain her beauty,
Slander myself as false to Edward's bed,
Throw over her the veil of infamy.
10 So she may live unscarred of bleeding slaughter,
I will confess she was not Edward's daughter.

KING RICHARD
Wrong not her birth. She is a royal princess.

QUEEN ELIZABETH
To save her life, I'll say she is not so.

KING RICHARD   Her life is safest only in her birth.

QUEEN ELIZABETH
15 And only in that safety died her brothers.

KING RICHARD
Lo, at their birth good stars were opposite.

QUEEN ELIZABETH
No, to their lives ill friends were contrary.

KING RICHARD   All unavoided is the doom of destiny.

QUEEN ELIZABETH
True, when avoided grace makes destiny.
20 My babes were destined to a fairer death,
If grace had blessed thee with a fairer life.

KING RICHARD
You speak as if that I had slain my cousins.

QUEEN ELIZABETH
Cousins indeed, and by their uncle cozened
Of comfort, kingdom, kindred, freedom, life.
25 Whose hand soever lanched their tender hearts,
Thy head, all indirectly, gave direction.
No doubt the murderous knife was dull and blunt
Till it was whetted on thy stone-hard heart,
To revel in the entrails of my lambs.
30 But that still use of grief makes wild grief tame,
My tongue should to thy ears not name my boys
Till that my nails were anchored in thine eyes,
And I in such a desperate bay of death,
Like a poor bark of sails and tackling reft,
35 Rush all to pieces on thy rocky bosom.

KING RICHARD   Madam, so thrive I in my enterprise
And dangerous success of bloody wars,
As I intend more good to you and yours
Than ever you and yours by me were harmed.

QUEEN ELIZABETH
40 What good is covered with the face of heaven,
To be discovered, that can do me good?

KING RICHARD
Th'advancement of your children, gentle lady.

QUEEN ELIZABETH
Up to some scaffold, there to lose their heads.

KING RICHARD
Unto the dignity and height of fortune,

The high imperial type of this earth's glory.   245

QUEEN ELIZABETH
Flatter my sorrow with report of it:
Tell me what state, what dignity, what honour,
Canst thou demise to any child of mine?

KING RICHARD
Even all I have – ay, and myself and all –
Will I withal endow a child of thine;   250
So in the Lethe of thy angry soul
Thou drown the sad remembrance of those wrongs
Which thou supposest I have done to thee.

QUEEN ELIZABETH
Be brief, lest that the process of thy kindness
Last longer telling than thy kindness' date.   255

KING RICHARD
Then know that from my soul I love thy daughter.

QUEEN ELIZABETH
My daughter's mother thinks it with her soul.

KING RICHARD   What do you think?

QUEEN ELIZABETH
That thou dost love my daughter from thy soul;
So from thy soul's love didst thou love her brothers,   260
And from my heart's love I do thank thee for it.

KING RICHARD
Be not so hasty to confound my meaning:
I mean that with my soul I love thy daughter
And do intend to make her queen of England.

QUEEN ELIZABETH
Well then, who dost thou mean shall be her king?   265

KING RICHARD
Even he that makes her queen. Who else should be?

QUEEN ELIZABETH   What, thou?

KING RICHARD   Even so. How think you of it?

QUEEN ELIZABETH   How canst thou woo her?

KING RICHARD   That would I learn of you,
As one being best acquainted with her humour.

QUEEN ELIZABETH   And wilt thou learn of me?

KING RICHARD   Madam, with all my heart.   270

QUEEN ELIZABETH
Send to her, by the man that slew her brothers,
A pair of bleeding hearts; thereon engrave
'Edward' and 'York'. Then haply will she weep.
Therefore present to her – as sometime Margaret
Did to thy father, steeped in Rutland's blood –   275
A handkerchief, which say to her did drain
The purple sap from her sweet brother's body,
And bid her wipe her weeping eyes withal.
If this inducement move her not to love,
Send her a letter of thy noble deeds: 280
Tell her thou mad'st away her uncle Clarence,
Her uncle Rivers, ay, and for her sake
Mad'st quick conveyance with her good aunt Anne.

KING RICHARD
You mock me, madam. This °is° not the way
To win your daughter.

QUEEN ELIZABETH   There is no other way,   285
Unless thou couldst put on some other shape

And not be Richard, that hath done all this.

KING RICHARD   Say that I did all this for love of her.

QUEEN ELIZABETH
Nay, then indeed she cannot choose but hate thee,
290 Having bought love with such a bloody spoil.

KING RICHARD
Look what is done cannot be now amended.
Men shall deal unadvisedly sometimes,
Which after-hours gives leisure to repent.
If I did take the kingdom from your sons,
295 To make amends, I'll give it to your daughter.
If I have killed the issue of your womb,
To quicken your increase I will beget
Mine issue of your blood upon your daughter.
A grandam's name is little less in love
300 Than is the doting title of a mother.
They are as children but one step below,
Even of your metal, of your very blood,
Of all one pain, save for a night of groans
Endured of her for whom you bid like sorrow.
305 Your children were vexation to your youth,
But mine shall be a comfort to your age.
The loss you have is but a son being king,
And by that loss your daughter is made queen.
I cannot make you what amends I would;
310 Therefore accept such kindness as I can.
Dorset your son, that with a fearful soul
Leads discontented steps in foreign soil,
This fair alliance quickly shall call home
To high promotions and great dignity.
315 The king that calls your beauteous daughter wife
Familiarly shall call thy Dorset brother.
Again shall you be mother to a king,
And all the ruins of distressful times
Repaired with double riches of content.
320 What! We have many goodly days to see.
The liquid drops of tears that you have shed
Shall come again, transformed to orient pearl,
Advantaging their love with interest
Of ten times double gain of happiness.
325 Go then, my mother; to thy daughter go.
Make bold her bashful years with your experience;
Prepare her ears to hear a wooer's tale;
Put in her tender heart th'aspiring flame
Of golden sovereignty; acquaint the princess
330 With the sweet silent hours of marriage joys;
And when this arm of mine hath chastised
The petty rebel, dull-brained Buckingham,
Bound with triumphant garlands will I come
And lead thy daughter to a conqueror's bed;
335 To whom I will retail my conquest won,
And she shall be sole victoress, Caesar's Caesar.

QUEEN ELIZABETH
What were I best to say? Her father's brother
Would be her lord? Or shall I say her uncle?
Or he that slew her brothers and her uncles?
340 Under what title shall I woo for thee,

That God, the law, my honour and her love
Can make seem pleasing to her tender years?

KING RICHARD
Infer fair England's peace by this alliance.

QUEEN ELIZABETH
Which she shall purchase with still lasting war.

KING RICHARD
Tell her the King, that may command, entreats. 345

QUEEN ELIZABETH
That at her hands, which the King's King forbids.

KING RICHARD
Say she shall be a high and mighty queen.

QUEEN ELIZABETH
To vail the title, as her mother doth.

KING RICHARD   Say I will love her everlastingly.

QUEEN ELIZABETH
But how long shall that title 'ever' last? 350

KING RICHARD
Sweetly in force, unto her fair life's end.

QUEEN ELIZABETH
But how long fairly shall her sweet life last?

KING RICHARD
As long as heaven and nature lengthens it.

QUEEN ELIZABETH
As long as hell and Richard likes of it.

KING RICHARD
Say I, her sovereign, am her subject low. 355

QUEEN ELIZABETH
But she, your subject, loathes such sovereignty.

KING RICHARD   Be eloquent in my behalf to her.

QUEEN ELIZABETH
An honest tale speeds best being plainly told.

KING RICHARD   Then plainly to her tell my loving tale.

QUEEN ELIZABETH
Plain and not honest is too harsh a style. 360

KING RICHARD
Your reasons are too shallow and too quick.

QUEEN ELIZABETH
O no, my reasons are too deep and dead,
Too deep and dead, poor infants, in their graves.

KING RICHARD
Harp not on that string, madam; that is past.

QUEEN ELIZABETH
Harp on it still shall I, till heart-strings break. 365

KING RICHARD
Now by my George, my Garter and my crown –

QUEEN ELIZABETH
Profaned, dishonoured and the third usurped.

KING RICHARD   I swear –

QUEEN ELIZABETH   By nothing, for this is no oath:
Thy George, profaned, hath lost his lordly honour;
Thy Garter, blemished, pawned his knightly virtue; 370
Thy crown, usurped, disgraced his kingly glory.
If something thou wouldst swear to be believed,
Swear then by something that thou hast not wronged.

KING RICHARD   Then by myself –

QUEEN ELIZABETH   Thyself is self-misused.

KING RICHARD　　Now by the world –

QUEEN ELIZABETH　　　　'Tis full of thy foul wrongs.

KING RICHARD　　My father's death –

QUEEN ELIZABETH　　　　Thy life hath it dishonoured.

KING RICHARD　　Why then, by God.

QUEEN ELIZABETH　　　　God's wrong is most of all.

If thou didst fear to break an oath with Him,

The unity the King my husband made

Thou hadst not broken, nor my brothers died.

If thou hadst feared to break an oath by Him,

Th'imperial metal circling now thy head

Had graced the tender temples of my child,

And both the princes had been breathing here,

Which now, too tender bed-fellows for dust,

Thy broken faith hath made the prey for worms.

What canst thou swear by now?

KING RICHARD　　　　　　The time to come.

QUEEN ELIZABETH

That thou hast wronged in the time o'erpast;

For I myself have many tears to wash

Hereafter time, for time past wronged by thee.

The children live whose fathers thou hast slaughtered,

Ungoverned youth, to wail it in their age;

The parents live whose children thou hast butchered,

Old barren plants, to wail it with their age.

Swear not by time to come, for that thou hast

Misused ere used, by times ill-used o'erpast.

KING RICHARD　　As I intend to prosper and repent,

So thrive I in my dangerous affairs

Of hostile arms. Myself myself confound!

Heaven and fortune bar me happy hours.

Day, yield me not thy light; nor, night, thy rest.

Be opposite all planets of good luck

To my proceeding, if with dear heart's love,

Immaculate devotion, holy thoughts,

I tender not thy beauteous, princely daughter.

In her consists my happiness and thine;

Without her follows to myself and thee,

Herself, the land and many a Christian soul,

Death, desolation, ruin and decay.

It cannot be avoided but by this;

It will not be avoided but by this.

Therefore, dear mother – I must call you so –

Be the attorney of my love to her:

Plead what I will be, not what I have been;

Not my deserts, but what I will deserve.

Urge the necessity and state of times,

And be not peevish found in great designs.

QUEEN ELIZABETH

Shall I be tempted of the devil thus?

KING RICHARD　　Ay, if the devil tempt you to do good.

QUEEN ELIZABETH　　Shall I forget myself to be myself?

KING RICHARD

Ay, if your self's remembrance wrong yourself.

QUEEN ELIZABETH　　Yet thou didst kill my children.

KING RICHARD

But in your daughter's womb I bury them,

Where, in that nest of spicery, they will breed

Selves of themselves, to your recomforture.

QUEEN ELIZABETH

Shall I go win my daughter to thy will?

KING RICHARD　　And be a happy mother by the deed.

QUEEN ELIZABETH　　I go, write to me very shortly,

And you shall understand from me her mind.

KING RICHARD

Bear her my true love's kiss; and so farewell.

　　　　　　　　　　Exit Queen Elizabeth.

Relenting fool, and shallow, changing woman.

　　　　　　　Enter RATCLIFFE.

How now, what news?

RATCLIFFE

Most mighty sovereign, on the western coast

Rideth a puissant navy. To our shores

Throng many doubtful hollow-hearted friends,

Unarmed and unresolved to beat them back.

'Tis thought that Richmond is their admiral,

And there they hull, expecting but the aid

Of Buckingham to welcome them ashore.

KING RICHARD

Some light-foot friend post to the Duke of Norfolk:

Ratcliffe, thyself – or Catesby. Where is he?

CATESBY　　Here, my good lord.

KING RICHARD　　　　　　Catesby, fly to the Duke.

CATESBY

I will, my lord, with all convenient haste.

KING RICHARD

Ratcliffe, come hither. Post to Salisbury.

When thou com'st thither –

[*to Catesby*]　　　　　　Dull unmindful villain,

Why stay'st thou here, and go'st not to the Duke?

CATESBY

First, mighty liege, tell me your highness' pleasure,

What from your grace I shall deliver to him.

KING RICHARD

O true, good Catesby. Bid him levy straight

The greatest strength and power that he can make

And meet me suddenly at Salisbury.

CATESBY　　I go.　　　　　　　　　　*Exit.*

RATCLIFFE

What, may it please you, shall I do at Salisbury?

KING RICHARD

Why, what wouldst thou do there before I go?

RATCLIFFE

Your highness told me I should post before.

KING RICHARD　　My mind is changed.

　　　　　Enter Lord STANLEY.

　　　　　　　　Stanley, what news with you?

STANLEY

None good, my liege, to please you with the hearing,

Nor none so bad but well may be reported.

KING RICHARD

Hoyday, a riddle! Neither good nor bad.

Line numbers: 375, 380, 385, 390, 395, 400, 405, 410, 415, 420, 425, 430, 435, 440, 445, 450, 455

<table>
<tr><td>460</td><td>

What need'st thou run so many miles about
When thou mayst tell thy tale the nearest way?
Once more, what news?

STANLEY   Richmond is on the seas.

KING RICHARD
    There let him sink, and be the seas on him,
    White-livered runagate. What doth he there?

</td></tr>
</table>

460

What need'st thou run so many miles about
When thou mayst tell thy tale the nearest way?
Once more, what news?
STANLEY   Richmond is on the seas.
KING RICHARD
  There let him sink, and be the seas on him,
  White-livered runagate. What doth he there?

465 STANLEY   I know not, mighty sovereign, but by guess.
KING RICHARD   Well, as you guess?
STANLEY
  Stirred up by Dorset, Buckingham and Morton,
  He makes for England, here to claim the crown.
KING RICHARD

470
  Is the chair empty? Is the sword unswayed?
  Is the King dead? The empire unpossessed?
  What heir of York is there alive but we?
  And who is England's king but great York's heir?
  Then tell me, what makes he upon the seas?
STANLEY   Unless for that, my liege, I cannot guess.
KING RICHARD

475
  Unless for that he comes to be your liege,
  You cannot guess wherefore the Welshman comes.
  Thou wilt revolt and fly to him, I fear.
STANLEY
  No, my good lord; therefore mistrust me not.
KING RICHARD
  Where is thy power, then, to beat him back?

480
  Where be thy tenants and thy followers?
  Are they not now upon the western shore,
  Safe-conducting the rebels from their ships?
STANLEY
  No, my good lord, my friends are in the north.
KING RICHARD
  Cold friends to me. What do they in the north

485
  When they should serve their sovereign in the west?
STANLEY
  They have not been commanded, mighty King.
  Pleaseth your majesty to give me leave,
  I'll muster up my friends and meet your grace
  Where and what time your majesty shall please.
KING RICHARD

490
  Ay, thou wouldst be gone to join with Richmond,
  But I'll not trust thee.
STANLEY   Most mighty sovereign,
  You have no cause to hold my friendship doubtful;
  I never was, nor never will be, false.
KING RICHARD
  Go then, and muster men, but leave behind

495
  Your son George Stanley. Look your heart be firm,
  Or else his head's assurance is but frail.
STANLEY   So deal with him as I prove true to you.

                                Exit Stanley.

Enter a Messenger.

MESSENGER
  My gracious sovereign, now in Devonshire,
  As I by friends am well advertised

  Sir Edward Courtney and the haughty prelate,   **500**
  Bishop of Exeter, his elder brother,
  With many more confederates are in arms.

Enter another Messenger.

2 MESSENGER
  In Kent, my liege, the Guilfords are in arms,
  And every hour more competitors
  Flock to the rebels, and their power grows strong.   **505**

Enter another Messenger.

3 MESSENGER   My lord, the army of great Buckingham –
KING RICHARD
  Out on you, owls! Nothing but songs of death.
  [*He striketh him.*]
  There, take thou that, till thou bring better news.
3 MESSENGER   The news I have to tell your majesty
  Is that by sudden floods and fall of waters   **510**
  Buckingham's army is dispersed and scattered,
  And he himself wandered away alone,
  No man knows whither.
KING RICHARD   I cry thee mercy.
  There is my purse to cure that blow of thine.
  Hath any well-advised friend proclaimed   **515**
  Reward to him that brings the traitor in?
3 MESSENGER
  Such proclamation hath been made, my lord.

Enter another Messenger.

4 MESSENGER
  Sir Thomas Lovell and Lord Marquess Dorset,
  'Tis said, my liege, in Yorkshire are in arms;
  But this good comfort bring I to your highness: **520**
  The Breton navy is dispersed by tempest.
  Richmond in Dorsetshire sent out a boat
  Unto the shore to ask those on the banks
  If they were his assistants, yea or no?
  Who answered him they came from Buckingham,   **525**
  Upon his party. He, mistrusting them,
  Hoised sail and made his course again for Brittany.
KING RICHARD
  March on, march on, since we are up in arms,
  If not to fight with foreign enemies,
  Yet to beat down these rebels here at home.   **530**

Enter CATESBY.

CATESBY   My liege, the Duke of Buckingham is taken.
  That is the best news. That the Earl of Richmond
  Is with a mighty power landed at Milford
  Is colder tidings, yet they must be told.
KING RICHARD
  Away towards Salisbury! While we reason here   **535**
  A royal battle might be won and lost.
  Someone take order Buckingham be brought
  To Salisbury. The rest march on with me.

                                Flourish. Exeunt.

4.5　　　*Enter* STANLEY, Earl of Derby *and*
　　　　　Sir CHRISTOPHER Urswick.

STANLEY

Sir Christopher, tell Richmond this from me:
That in the sty of the most deadly boar
My son George Stanley is franked up in hold;
If I revolt, off goes young George's head.
The fear of that holds off my present aid.
So get thee gone. Commend me to thy lord.
Withal, say that the Queen hath heartily consented
He should espouse Elizabeth her daughter.
But tell me, where is princely Richmond now?

CHRISTOPHER

At Pembroke or at Ha'rfordwest in Wales.

STANLEY　What men of name resort to him?

CHRISTOPHER

Sir Walter Herbert, a renowned soldier,
Sir Gilbert Talbot, Sir William Stanley,
Oxford, redoubted Pembroke, Sir James Blunt,
And Rice ap Thomas, with a valiant crew,
And many other of great name and worth;
And towards London do they bend their power,
If by the way they be not fought withal.

STANLEY　Well, hie thee to thy lord. I kiss his hand.
My letter will resolve him of my mind.
Farewell.　　　　　　　　　　　　*Exeunt.*

5.1　　　*Enter* BUCKINGHAM *with* Sheriff *and*
　　　　　Halberds, led to execution.

BUCKINGHAM

Will not King Richard let me speak with him?

SHERIFF　No, my good lord; therefore be patient.

BUCKINGHAM

Hastings, and Edward's children, Grey and Rivers,
Holy King Henry, and thy fair son Edward,
Vaughan and all that have miscarried
By underhand, corrupted, foul injustice,
If that your moody, discontented souls
Do through the clouds behold this present hour,
Even for revenge mock my destruction.
– This is All Souls' Day, fellow, is it not?

SHERIFF　It is.

BUCKINGHAM

Why then, All Souls' Day is my body's doomsday.
This is the day which, in King Edward's time,
I wished might fall on me when I was found
False to his children and his wife's allies.
This is the day wherein I wished to fall
By the false faith of him whom most I trusted.
This, this All Souls' Day to my fearful soul
Is the determined respite of my wrongs:
That high All-seer which I dallied with
Hath turned my feigned prayer on my head
And given in earnest what I begged in jest.
Thus doth he force the swords of wicked men
To turn their own points in their masters' bosoms.

Thus Margaret's curse falls heavy on my neck:　25
'When he', quoth she, 'shall split thy heart with
　　sorrow,
Remember Margaret was a prophetess.'
– Come, lead me, officers, to the block of shame.
Wrong hath but wrong, and blame the due of blame.
　　　　　Exeunt Buckingham with Officers.

5.2　　　*Enter* RICHMOND, OXFORD, BLUNT,
　　　　　HERBERT *and others, with*
　　　　　Drum and Colours.

RICHMOND

Fellows in arms, and my most loving friends,
Bruised underneath the yoke of tyranny,
Thus far into the bowels of the land
Have we marched on without impediment;
And here receive we from our father Stanley　　5
Lines of fair comfort and encouragement.
The wretched, bloody and usurping boar,
That spoiled your summer fields and fruitful vines,
Swills your warm blood like wash, and makes his
　　trough
In your embowelled bosoms, this foul swine　　10
Is now even in the centre of this isle,
Near to the town of Leicester, as we learn.
From Tamworth thither is but one day's march.
In God's name, cheerly on, courageous friends,
To reap the harvest of perpetual peace　　15
By this one bloody trial of sharp war.

OXFORD　Every man's conscience is a thousand men
To fight against this guilty homicide.

HERBERT　I doubt not but his friends will turn to us.

BLUNT

He hath no friends but what are friends for fear,　20
Which in his dearest need will fly from him.

RICHMOND

All for our vantage. Then in God's name, march.
True hope is swift and flies with swallow's wings;
Kings it makes gods, and meaner creatures kings.
　　　　　　　　　　　　Exeunt all.

5.3　　　*Enter* KING RICHARD *in arms, with*
　　　　　NORFOLK, RATCLIFFE *and the* Earl of
　　　　　SURREY, ⁰*with others*⁰.

KING RICHARD

Here pitch our tent, even here in Bosworth field.
– My lord of Surrey, why look you so sad?

SURREY　My heart is ten times lighter than my looks.

KING RICHARD　My lord of Norfolk.

NORFOLK　　　　　　　　Here, most gracious liege.

KING RICHARD

Norfolk, we must have knocks, ha, must we not?　5

NORFOLK　We must both give and take, my loving lord.

KING RICHARD

Up with my tent. Here will I lie tonight,

[Soldiers begin to set up Richard's tent.]
But where tomorrow? Well, all's one for that.
Who hath descried the number of the traitors?

NORFOLK
10   Six or seven thousand is their utmost power.

KING RICHARD
Why, our battalia trebles that account.
Besides, the King's name is a tower of strength
Which they upon the adverse faction want.
– Up with the tent! – Come, noble gentlemen,
15   Let us survey the vantage of the ground.
Call for some men of sound direction.
Let's lack no discipline, make no delay,
For lords, tomorrow is a busy day.
         [Richard's tent is ready].   *Exeunt.*

         Enter RICHMOND, *Sir William Brandon,*
         OXFORD *and* DORSET, *with* BLUNT,
         HERBERT *and others who set up*
                 Richmond's tent.

RICHMOND   The weary sun hath made a golden set,
20   And by the bright track of his fiery car
Gives token of a goodly day tomorrow.
– Sir William Brandon, you shall bear my standard.
– Give me some ink and paper in my tent;
I'll draw the form and model of our battle,
25   Limit each leader to his several charge,
And part in just proportion our small power.
– My lord of Oxford, you, Sir William Brandon,
And you, Sir Walter Herbert, stay with me.
The Earl of Pembroke keeps his regiment;
30   – Good Captain Blunt, bear my goodnight to him,
And by the second hour in the morning
Desire the Earl to see me in my tent.
Yet one thing more, good captain, do for me:
Where is Lord Stanley quartered, do you know?

BLUNT   Unless I have mista'en his colours much,
35   Which well I am assured I have not done,
His regiment lies half a mile at least
South from the mighty power of the King.

RICHMOND   If without peril it be possible,
40   Sweet Blunt, make some good means to speak with him,
And give him from me this most needful note.

BLUNT   Upon my life, my lord, I'll undertake it,
And so God give you quiet rest tonight.

RICHMOND
Good night, good Captain Blunt.   *Exit Blunt.*
                                    Come, gentlemen,
45   Let us consult upon tomorrow's business.
Into my tent; the dew is raw and cold.
         Richmond, Brandon, Dorset, Herbert and Oxford
              withdraw into the tent. The others exeunt.

         Enter to his tent ᵠKINGᵠ RICHARD,
         RATCLIFFE, NORFOLK, CATESBY
                 ᵠand othersᵠ.

KING RICHARD   What is't o'clock?

CATESBY   It's supper time, my lord; it's nine o'clock.

KING RICHARD
I will not sup tonight. Give me some ink and paper.
What, is my beaver easier than it was,   50
And all my armour laid into my tent?

CATESBY   It is, my liege, and all things are in readiness.

KING RICHARD   Good Norfolk, hie thee to thy charge,
Use careful watch, choose trusty sentinels.

NORFOLK   I go, my lord.   55

KING RICHARD
Stir with the lark tomorrow, gentle Norfolk.

NORFOLK   I warrant you, my lord.   ᶠ*Exit.*ᶠ

KING RICHARD   Catesby.

CATESBY   My lord.

KING RICHARD   Send out a pursuivant-at-arms
To Stanley's regiment. Bid him bring his power   60
Before sun-rising, lest his son George fall
Into the blind cave of eternal night.   *Exit Catesby.*
Fill me a bowl of wine. Give me a watch.
Saddle white Surrey for the field tomorrow.
Look that my staves be sound and not too heavy.   65
– Ratcliffe.

RATCLIFFE   My lord.

KING RICHARD
Sawst thou the melancholy Lord Northumberland?

RATCLIFFE   Thomas the Earl of Surrey and himself,
Much about cock-shut time, from troop to troop   70
Went through the army, cheering up the soldiers.

KING RICHARD
So, I am satisfied. Give me a bowl of wine.
I have not that alacrity of spirit
Nor cheer of mind that I was wont to have.
         [Wine is brought.]
Set it down. Is ink and paper ready?   75

RATCLIFFE   It is, my lord.

KING RICHARD   Bid my guard watch. Leave me.
Ratcliffe, about the mid of night come to my tent
And help to arm me. Leave me, I say.
                        Exit Ratcliffe with others.
         [Richard goes into his tent to sleep.]

         Enter STANLEY, *Earl of Derby to Richmond*
                 and Lords in his tent.

STANLEY   Fortune and Victory sit on thy helm.   80

RICHMOND   All comfort that the dark night can afford
Be to thy person, noble father-in-law.
Tell me, how fares our loving mother?

STANLEY   I, by attorney, bless thee from thy mother,
Who prays continually for Richmond's good.   85
So much for that. The silent hours steal on,
And flaky darkness breaks within the east.
In brief, for so the season bids us be,
Prepare thy battle early in the morning
And put thy fortune to the arbitrament   90
Of bloody strokes and mortal-staring war.
I, as I may – that which I would, I cannot –
With best advantage will deceive the time

And aid thee in this doubtful shock of arms.
But on thy side I may not be too forward,
95 Lest, being seen, thy brother, tender George,
Be executed in his father's sight.
Farewell. The leisure and the fearful time
Cuts off the ceremonious vows of love
100 And ample interchange of sweet discourse,
Which so-long-sundered friends should dwell upon.
God give us leisure for these rites of love.
Once more, adieu; be valiant and speed well.
RICHMOND   Good lords, conduct him to his regiment.
105 I'll strive with troubled thoughts to take a nap,
Lest leaden slumber peise me down tomorrow
When I should mount with wings of victory.
Once more, good night, kind lords and gentlemen.
                    Exeunt ᶠ*all but Richmond*ᶠ.
O Thou, whose captain I account myself,
110 Look on my forces with a gracious eye;
Put in their hands Thy bruising irons of wrath,
That they may crush down with a heavy fall
The usurping helmets of our adversaries;
Make us Thy ministers of chastisement,
115 That we may praise Thee in the victory.
To Thee I do commend my watchful soul,
Ere I let fall the windows of mine eyes:
Sleeping and waking, O, defend me still!   [ᶠ*Sleeps.*ᶠ]

Enter the GHOST *of young* PRINCE EDWARD,
    son ᶠ*to*ᶠ *Harry the Sixth.*

GHOST of PRINCE EDWARD [*to Richard*]
Let me sit heavy on thy soul tomorrow.
120 Think how thou stabb'st me in my prime of youth
At Tewkesbury. Despair therefore, and die.
[*to Richmond*] Be cheerful, Richmond, for the
    wronged souls
Of butchered princes fight in thy behalf.
King Henry's issue, Richmond, comforts thee.
                                        Exit.

Enter the GHOST *of* HENRY THE SIXTH.

GHOST of HENRY VI [*to Richard*]
125 When I was mortal, my anointed body
By thee was punched full of deadly holes.
Think on the Tower and me. Despair and die.
Harry the Sixth bids thee despair and die.
[*to Richmond*] Virtuous and holy, be thou conqueror.
130 Harry, that prophesied thou shouldst be king,
Doth comfort thee in thy sleep. Live and flourish.
                                        Exit.

Enter the GHOST *of* CLARENCE.

GHOST of CLARENCE [*to Richard*]
Let me sit heavy in thy soul tomorrow,
I, that was washed to death with fulsome wine,
Poor Clarence, by thy guile betrayed to death.
135 Tomorrow in the battle think on me,
And fall thy edgeless sword. Despair and die.

[*to Richmond*] Thou offspring of the house of
    Lancaster,
The wronged heirs of York do pray for thee.
Good angels guard thy battle. Live and flourish.
                                        Exit.

Enter the GHOSTS *of* RIVERS, GREY ᶠ*and*ᶠ VAUGHAN.

GHOST of RIVERS [*to Richard*]
Let me sit heavy in thy soul tomorrow,   140
Rivers that died at Pomfret. Despair and die.
GHOST of GREY [*to Richard*]
Think upon Grey, and let thy soul despair.
GHOST of VAUGHAN [*to Richard*]
Think upon Vaughan, and with guilty fear
Let fall thy lance. Despair and die.
ALL [*to Richmond*]
Awake, and think our wrongs in Richard's bosom   145
Will conquer him. Awake, and win the day.   *Exeunt.*

Enter the GHOSTS *of the two young* PRINCES.

GHOSTS of PRINCES [*to Richard*]
Dream on thy cousins smothered in the Tower.
Let us be lead within thy bosom, Richard,
And weigh thee down to ruin, shame and death.
Thy nephews' souls bid thee despair and die.   150
[*to Richmond*] Sleep, Richmond, sleep in peace and
    wake in joy;
Good angels guard thee from the boar's annoy.
Live, and beget a happy race of kings;
Edward's unhappy sons do bid thee flourish.
                                        Exeunt.

Enter the GHOST *of* HASTINGS.

GHOST of HASTINGS [*to Richard*]
Bloody and guilty, guiltily awake,   155
And in a bloody battle end thy days.
Think on Lord Hastings. Despair and die.
[*to Richmond*] Quiet, untroubled soul, awake, awake.
Arm, fight and conquer for fair England's sake.   *Exit.*

Enter the GHOST *of* Lady ANNE, *his wife.*

ᶠGHOST of ANNE [*to Richard*]ᶠ
Richard, thy wife, that wretched Anne, thy wife,   160
That never slept a quiet hour with thee,
Now fills thy sleep with perturbations.
Tomorrow in the battle think on me,
And fall thy edgeless sword. Despair and die.
[*to Richmond*] Thou quiet soul, sleep thou a quiet sleep. 165
Dream of success and happy victory.
Thy adversary's wife doth pray for thee.   *Exit.*

Enter the GHOST *of* BUCKINGHAM.

ᶠGHOST of BUCKINGHAM [*to Richard*]ᶠ
The first was I that helped thee to the crown;
The last was I that felt thy tyranny.
O, in the battle think on Buckingham,   170
And die in terror of thy guiltiness.

Dream on, dream on, of bloody deeds and death.
Fainting, despair; despairing, yield thy breath.
[*to Richmond*] I died for hope ere I could lend thee aid;
175 But cheer thy heart, and be thou not dismayed.
God and good angels fight on Richmond's side,
And Richard fall in height of all his pride.   *Exit.*
     [*Richard starteth up out of a dream.*]
KING RICHARD
     Give me another horse! Bind up my wounds!
     Have mercy, Jesu. – Soft, I did but dream.
180 O coward conscience, how dost thou afflict me!
     The lights burn blue. It is now dead midnight.
     Cold fearful drops stand on my trembling flesh.
     What do I fear? Myself? There's none else by.
     Richard loves Richard, that is, I am I.
185 Is there a murderer here? No. Yes, I am.
     Then fly! What, from myself? Great reason why?
     Lest I revenge. What, myself upon myself?
     Alack, I love myself. Wherefore? For any good
     That I myself have done unto myself?
190 O, no. Alas, I rather hate myself,
     For hateful deeds committed by myself.
     I am a villain. Yet I lie; I am not.
     Fool, of thyself speak well. Fool, do not flatter.
     My conscience hath a thousand several tongues,
195 And every tongue brings in a several tale,
     And every tale condemns me for a villain.
     Perjury, perjury, in the highest degree;
     Murder, stern murder, in the direst degree;
     All several sins, all used in each degree,
200 Throng to the bar, crying all, 'Guilty, guilty!'
     I shall despair. There is no creature loves me,
     And if I die, no soul will pity me.
     And wherefore should they, since that I myself
     Find in myself no pity to myself?
205 Methought the souls of all that I had murdered
     Came to my tent, and every one did threat
     Tomorrow's vengeance on the head of Richard.

               Enter RATCLIFFE.

RATCLIFFE   My lord.
KING RICHARD   Zounds, who is there?
RATCLIFFE
210 Ratcliffe, my lord, 'tis I. The early village cock
     Hath twice done salutation to the morn;
     Your friends are up and buckle on their armour.
KING RICHARD
     O Ratcliffe, I have dreamed a fearful dream!
     What think'st thou, will our friends prove all true?
RATCLIFFE   No doubt, my lord.
215 KING RICHARD   O Ratcliffe, I fear, I fear.
RATCLIFFE
     Nay, good my lord, be not afraid of shadows.
KING RICHARD
     By the Apostle Paul, shadows tonight
     Have struck more terror to the soul of Richard
     Than can the substance of ten thousand soldiers

Armed in proof, and led by shallow Richmond.   220
'Tis not yet near day. Come, go with me.
Under our tents I'll play the eavesdropper,
To see if any mean to shrink from me.
               Exeunt ᵛ*Richard and Ratcliffe*ᵛ.

Enter the Lords *to Richmond* ᵛ*sitting in his tent*ᵛ.

LORDS   Good morrow, Richmond.
RICHMOND   Cry mercy, lords and watchful gentlemen,   225
     That you have ta'en a tardy sluggard here.
LORD   How have you slept, my lord?
RICHMOND
     The sweetest sleep and fairest-boding dreams
     That ever entered in a drowsy head
     Have I since your departure had, my lords.   230
     Methought their souls whose bodies Richard murdered
     Came to my tent and cried on victory.
     I promise you my soul is very jocund
     In the remembrance of so fair a dream.
     How far into the morning is it, lords?   235
LORD   Upon the stroke of four.
RICHMOND
     Why, then 'tis time to arm and give direction.

               His oration to his soldiers.

     More than I have said, loving countrymen,
     The leisure and enforcement of the time
     Forbids to dwell upon. Yet remember this: 240
     God, and our good cause, fight upon our side.
     The prayers of holy saints and wronged souls,
     Like high-reared bulwarks, stand before our faces.
     Richard except, those whom we fight against
     Had rather have us win than him they follow.   245
     For, what is he they follow? Truly, gentlemen,
     A bloody tyrant and a homicide;
     One raised in blood, and one in blood established;
     One that made means to come by what he hath,
     And slaughtered those that were the means to help him; 250
     A base foul stone, made precious by the foil
     Of England's chair, where he is falsely set;
     One that hath ever been God's enemy.
     Then if you fight against God's enemy,
     God will, in justice, ward you as His soldiers;   255
     If you do sweat to put a tyrant down,
     You sleep in peace, the tyrant being slain;
     If you do fight against your country's foes,
     Your country's fat shall pay your pains the hire.
     If you do fight in safeguard of your wives,   260
     Your wives shall welcome home the conquerors.
     If you do free your children from the sword,
     Your children's children quits it in your age.
     Then in the name of God and all these rights,
     Advance your standards, draw your willing swords.   265
     For me, the ransom of my bold attempt
     Shall be this cold corpse on the earth's cold face;
     But if I thrive, the gain of my attempt
     The least of you shall share his part thereof.

270 Sound drums and trumpets boldly and cheerfully.
God, and Saint George, Richmond, and victory!
Exeunt.

Enter KING RICHARD, RATCLIFFE *and Soldiers.*

KING RICHARD
What said Northumberland, as touching Richmond?
RATCLIFFE   That he was never trained up in arms.
KING RICHARD
He said the truth. And what said Surrey then?
RATCLIFFE
275 He smiled and said, 'The better for our purpose.'
KING RICHARD   He was in the right, and so indeed it is.
[The clock striketh.]
Tell the clock there. Give me a calendar.
Who saw the sun today?
RATCLIFFE   Not I, my lord.
KING RICHARD
Then he disdains to shine, for by the book
280 He should have braved the east an hour ago.
A black day will it be to somebody.
Ratcliffe!
RATCLIFFE   My lord.
KING RICHARD   The sun will not be seen today.
The sky doth frown and lour upon our army.
285 I would these dewy tears were from the ground.
Not shine today? Why, what is that to me
More than to Richmond? For the selfsame heaven
That frowns on me looks sadly upon him.

Enter NORFOLK.

NORFOLK
Arm, arm, my lord! The foe vaunts in the field.
KING RICHARD
290 Come, bustle, bustle. Caparison my horse.
– Call up Lord Stanley; bid him bring his power.
– I will lead forth my soldiers to the plain,
And thus my battle shall be ordered:
My foreward shall be drawn out all in length,
295 Consisting equally of horse and foot;
Our archers shall be placed in the midst.
John, Duke of Norfolk, Thomas, Earl of Surrey,
Shall have the leading of this foot and horse.
They thus directed, we will follow
300 In the main battle, whose puissance on either side
Shall be well winged with our chiefest horse.
This, and Saint George to boot. What think'st thou,
Norfolk?
NORFOLK   A good direction, warlike sovereign.
[He sheweth him a paper.]
This found I on my tent this morning:
305 'Jockey of Norfolk, be not so bold,
For Dickon thy master is bought and sold.'
KING RICHARD   A thing devised by the enemy.
– Go, gentlemen, every man unto his charge.
Let not our babbling dreams affright our souls.
310 Conscience is but a word that cowards use,

Devised at first to keep the strong in awe.
Our strong arms be our conscience, swords our law.
March on, join bravely, let us to it pell-mell,
If not to heaven, then hand in hand to hell.

His oration to his army.

What shall I say more than I have inferred?   315
Remember whom you are to cope withal,
A sort of vagabonds, rascals and runaways,
A scum of Bretons and base lackey peasants,
Whom their o'ercloyed country vomits forth
To desperate adventures and assured destruction.   320
You sleeping safe, they bring to you unrest;
You having lands and blessed with beauteous wives,
They would restrain the one, distain the other.
And who doth lead them but a paltry fellow?
Long kept in Bretagne at our mother's cost,   325
A milksop, one that never in his life
Felt so much cold as over shoes in snow.
Let's whip these stragglers o'er the seas again,
Lash hence these overweening rags of France,
These famished beggars, weary of their lives,   330
Who, but for dreaming on this fond exploit,
For want of means, poor rats, had hanged themselves.
If we be conquered, let men conquer us,
And not these bastard Bretons, whom our fathers
Have in their own land beaten, bobbed and thumped,   335
And in record left them the heirs of shame.
Shall these enjoy our lands? Lie with our wives?
Ravish our daughters?   [ᶠ*Drum afar off*ᶠ]
                        Hark, I hear their drum.
Fight, gentlemen of England! – Fight, bold yeomen!
– Draw, archers, draw your arrows to the head!   340
– Spur your proud horses hard and ride in blood.
Amaze the welkin with your broken staves.

ᶠ*Enter a* Messenger.ᶠ

– What says Lord Stanley? Will he bring his power?
MESSENGER   My lord, he doth deny to come.
KING RICHARD   Off with his son George's head!   345
NORFOLK   My lord, the enemy is past the marsh:
After the battle let George Stanley die.
KING RICHARD
A thousand hearts are great within my bosom.
Advance our standards! Set upon our foes!
Our ancient word of courage, fair Saint George,   350
Inspire us with the spleen of fiery dragons.
Upon them! Victory sits on our helms.   *Exeunt.*

5.4   *Alarum, excursions. Enter* NORFOLK
              with Soldiers, and CATESBY.

CATESBY   Rescue, my lord of Norfolk. Rescue, rescue!
The King enacts more wonders than a man,
Daring an opposite to every danger.
His horse is slain, and all on foot he fights,
Seeking for Richmond in the throat of death.   5

Rescue, fair lord, or else the day is lost.

Exeunt Norfolk and Soldiers.

ᶠ*Alarums.*ᶠ *Enter* KING RICHARD.

KING RICHARD
    A horse, a horse, my kingdom for a horse!
CATESBY   Withdraw, my lord. I'll help you to a horse.
KING RICHARD   Slave, I have set my life upon a cast,
10   And I will stand the hazard of the die.
    I think there be six Richmonds in the field;
    Five have I slain today instead of him.
    A horse, a horse, my kingdom for a horse!   *Exeunt.*

5.5   *Alarum, Enter* KING RICHARD *and*
        RICHMOND; *they fight. Richard is slain. Then*
        retreat being sounded, exit Richmond, and
        Richard's body is removed. ᶠ*Flourish.*ᶠ *Enter*
        Richmond, STANLEY, *Earl of Derby, bearing*
        the crown, with other Lords and Soldiers.

RICHMOND
    God and your arms be praised, victorious friends:
    The day is ours; the bloody dog is dead.
STANLEY
    Courageous Richmond, well hast thou acquit thee.
        [*Presents the crown.*]
    Lo, here this long-usurped royalty
5   From the dead temples of this bloody wretch
    Have I plucked off to grace thy brows withal.
    Wear it, enjoy it and make much of it.
RICHMOND   Great God of heaven, say amen to all.
    But tell me, is young George Stanley living?
10   STANLEY   He is, my lord, and safe in Leicester town,
    Whither, if it please you, we may now withdraw us.

RICHMOND
    What men of name are slain on either side?
ᶠSTANLEYᶠ
    John, Duke of Norfolk, Walter, Lord Ferrers,
    Sir Robert Brakenbury and Sir William Brandon.
RICHMOND   Inter their bodies as become their births.   15
    Proclaim a pardon to the soldiers fled
    That in submission will return to us;
    And then, as we have ta'en the sacrament,
    We will unite the white rose and the red.
    Smile heaven upon this fair conjunction,   20
    That long have frowned upon their enmity.
    What traitor hears me and says not amen?
    England hath long been mad and scarred herself:
    The brother blindly shed the brother's blood;
    The father rashly slaughtered his own son;   25
    The son, compelled, been butcher to the sire.
    All this divided York and Lancaster,
    Divided in their dire division.
    O, now let Richmond and Elizabeth,
    The true succeeders of each royal house,   30
    By God's fair ordinance conjoin together;
    And let their heirs, God, if Thy will be so,
    Enrich the time to come with smooth-faced peace,
    With smiling plenty and fair prosperous days.
    Abate the edge of traitors, gracious Lord,   35
    That would reduce these bloody days again
    And make poor England weep in streams of blood.
    Let them not live to taste this land's increase
    That would with treason wound this fair land's peace.
    Now civil wounds are stopped; peace lives again.   40
    That she may long live here, God say amen.
        ᶠ*Exeunt.*ᶠ

Love's Labour's Lost

Love's Labour's Lost is generally labelled an 'early comedy' along with *The Two Gentlemen of Verona*, *The Taming of the Shrew* and *The Comedy of Errors*. The four plays show Shakespeare at the beginning of his career experimenting with a range of materials and moods including romantic intrigue, classical farce and traditional folktale. Unlike the other three plays in this category, *Love's Labour's Lost* does not have a readily identifiable narrative or dramatic source, though affinities have been discerned with both literary and real-life accounts of courtly activities. Its presentation of Rosaline as a 'dark' heroine has encouraged some readers to speculate on possible connections with the narrative recounted in Shakespeare's *Sonnets*. Somewhat blighted by its reputation as a 'topical' play, it is perhaps more often performed than studied today.

The 1598 First Quarto of the play is the earliest dramatic text to have 'by W. Shakespeare' on its title-page. *Love's Labour's Lost* is described as 'A pleasant conceited comedy' and we are informed that it was 'presented before her Highness this last Christmas'. The title-page further claims that the text is 'Newly corrected and augmented', implying that it was written and performed somewhat earlier than 1598, and perhaps that a previous edition, now lost, had been published. It is listed by Francis Meres (along with the mysterious *Love's Labour's Won*) as one of Shakespeare's comedies in his *Palladis Tamia* (also 1598), but it is usually dated 1594–5, mainly on internal evidence. It was revived in 1605 for performance at Court before Queen Anne. Some inconsistencies in the narrative, confusion over characters' names and repetition of dialogue in this text indicate that it was printed from Shakespeare's working manuscript.

The phrase 'conceited comedy' is in this case an appropriate designation of a play whose verbal wit and ingenuity must have dazzled its original audiences and can occasionally baffle modern ones. Not only the supposedly sophisticated courtiers but the lower-class characters play endlessly with language, achieving effects which can be brilliant, pedantic or bathetic, but are very frequently connected with obscenity. This has been one cause of the play's relative unpopularity, though recent productions have shown that it can work well on stage as a lively and quite acerbic courtship comedy. Some of the wordplay does seem to be topical – the play is self-conscious about what Moth refers to as 'a great feast of languages' (5.1.35–6) – but broader attempts to find historical models for the characters and situations are now widely discounted.

The play's title reflects its unconventional ending: in the short term at least the male lovers (with the surprising exception of Armado) have lost their labour in so far as they have not won the women. The closing songs are enigmatic, particularly in raising the threat of infidelity even before marriage is assured. A modern emphasis on the darker aspects of the play has taken more seriously such things as the breaking of vows, the cruelty of the courtiers to the amateur actors and the intrusion of death at the end. At the same time Berowne and Rosaline as sparring partners have appealed to actors and audiences as prototypes of Benedick and Beatrice in *Much Ado About Nothing*, and talented performers have proved that the comedy of Don Armado and Holofernes is still not past its sell-by date.

The Arden text is based on the 1598 First Quarto, with reference in some places to the 1623 First Folio.

KING Ferdinand of Navarre
BEROWNE
LONGAVILLE } lords attending the King
DUMAINE
PRINCESS of France
ROSALINE
MARIA } ladies attending the Princess
KATHERINE
BOYET *a lord attending the Princess*
Monsieur MARCADÉ *a messenger*
Don Adriano de ARMADO *a Spanish knight and braggart*
MOTH *his page, a boy*
HOLOFERNES *a schoolmaster*
NATHANIEL *a curate*
Anthony DULL *a constable*
COSTARD *a clown*
JAQUENETTA *a dairymaid*
FORESTER
LORDS *attending the Princess*

Blackamoors and others attending the King

864

Love's Labour's Lost

1.1   *Enter* Ferdinand, KING of Navarre,
BEROWNE, LONGAVILLE *and* DUMAINE.

KING   Let fame, that all hunt after in their lives,
Live registered upon our brazen tombs,
And then grace us in the disgrace of death;
When, spite of cormorant devouring time,
Th'endeavour of this present breath may buy
That honour which shall bate his scythe's keen edge,
And make us heirs of all eternity.
Therefore, brave conquerors – for so you are,
That war against your own affections
And the huge army of the world's desires –
Our late edict shall strongly stand in force.
Navarre shall be the wonder of the world,
Our court shall be a little academe,
Still and contemplative in living art.
You three, Berowne, Dumaine and Longaville,
Have sworn for three years' term to live with me,
My fellow-scholars, and to keep those statutes
That are recorded in this schedule here.
Your oaths are passed, and now subscribe your
      names,
That his own hand may strike his honour down
That violates the smallest branch herein.
If you are armed to do as sworn to do,
Subscribe to your deep oaths, and keep it too.
LONGAVILLE   I am resolved: 'tis but a three years' fast.
The mind shall banquet though the body pine.
Fat paunches have lean pates, and dainty bits
Make rich the ribs, but bankrupt quite the wits.
      [*Signs.*]
DUMAINE   My loving lord, Dumaine is mortified.
The grosser manner of these world's delights
He throws upon the gross world's baser slaves.
To love, to wealth, to pomp, I pine and die,
With all these living in philosophy.   [*Signs.*]
BEROWNE   I can but say their protestation over.
So much, dear liege, I have already sworn,
That is, to live and study here three years.
But there are other strict observances:
As not to see a woman in that term,
Which I hope well is not enrolled there;
And one day in a week to touch no food,
And but one meal on every day beside,
The which I hope is not enrolled there;
And then to sleep but three hours in the night,
And not be seen to wink of all the day,
When I was wont to think no harm all night
And make a dark night too of half the day,
Which I hope well is not enrolled there.
O, these are barren tasks, too hard to keep:
Not to see ladies, study, fast, not sleep.
KING   Your oath is passed to pass away from these.
BEROWNE   Let me say no, my liege, an if you please.
I only swore to study with your grace
And stay here in your court for three years' space.

LONGAVILLE
You swore to that, Berowne, and to the rest.
BEROWNE   By yea and nay, sir, then I swore in jest.
What is the end of study, let me know?   55
KING
Why, that to know which else we should not know.
BEROWNE
Things hid and barred, you mean, from common
      sense?
KING   Ay, that is study's god-like recompense.
BEROWNE   Come on then, I will swear to study so,
To know the thing I am forbid to know: 60
As thus, to study where I well may dine,
      When I to feast expressly am forbid;
Or study where to meet some mistress fine,
      When mistresses from common sense are hid.
Or, having sworn too hard-a-keeping oath,   65
Study to break it, and not break my troth.
If study's gain be thus, and this be so,
Study knows that which yet it doth not know.
Swear me to this, and I will ne'er say no.
KING   These be the stops that hinder study quite   70
And train our intellects to vain delight.
BEROWNE   Why, all delights are vain, but that most vain
Which, with pain purchased, doth inherit pain:
As painfully to pore upon a book
      To seek the light of truth, while truth the while   75
Doth falsely blind the eyesight of his look.
      Light seeking light doth light of light beguile;
So, ere you find where light in darkness lies,
Your light grows dark by losing of your eyes.
Study me how to please the eye indeed   80
      By fixing it upon a fairer eye,
Who dazzling so, that eye shall be his heed,
      And give him light that it was blinded by.
Study is like the heaven's glorious sun,
      That will not be deep-searched with saucy looks;   85
Small have continual plodders ever won,
      Save base authority from others' books.
These earthly godfathers of heaven's lights,
      That give a name to every fixed star,
Have no more profit of their shining nights   90
      Than those that walk and wot not what they are.
Too much to know is to know naught but fame,
And every godfather can give a name.
KING   How well he's read, to reason against reading.
DUMAINE   Proceeded well, to stop all good proceeding.   95
LONGAVILLE
He weeds the corn, and still lets grow the weeding.
BEROWNE
The spring is near when green geese are a-breeding.
DUMAINE   How follows that?
BEROWNE   Fit in his place and time.
DUMAINE   In reason nothing.
BEROWNE   Something then in rhyme.
KING   Berowne is like an envious sneaping frost,   100
      That bites the first-born infants of the spring.

BEROWNE

Well, say I am. Why should proud summer boast
Before the birds have any cause to sing?
Why should I joy in any abortive birth?
105 At Christmas I no more desire a rose
Than wish a snow in May's newfangled shows,
But like of each thing that in season grows.
So you, to study now it is too late,
Climb o'er the house to unlock the little gate.

110 KING   Well, sit you out. Go home, Berowne: adieu.

BEROWNE

No, my good lord, I have sworn to stay with you,
And though I have for barbarism spoke more
Than for that angel knowledge you can say,
Yet confident I'll keep what I have sworn
115 And bide the penance of each three years' day.
Give me the paper, let me read the same,
And to the strictest decrees I'll write my name.

KING   How well this yielding rescues thee from shame.

BEROWNE [*Reads.*]   *Item, That no woman shall come*
120 *within a mile of my court* – Hath this been proclaimed?

LONGAVILLE   Four days ago.

BEROWNE   Let's see the penalty – *On pain of losing her*
tongue. Who devised this penalty?

LONGAVILLE   Marry, that did I.

125 BEROWNE   Sweet lord, and why?

LONGAVILLE

To fright them hence with that dread penalty.

BEROWNE   A dangerous law against gentility.
Item, If any man be seen to talk with a woman within
the term of three years, he shall endure such public shame
130 *as the rest of the court can possible devise.*
This article, my liege, yourself must break,
For well you know here comes in embassy
The French King's daughter with yourself to speak –
A maid of grace and complete majesty –
135 About surrender up of Aquitaine
To her decrepit, sick and bedrid father.
Therefore this article is made in vain,
Or vainly comes th'admired Princess hither.

KING   What say you, lords? Why, this was quite forgot.

140 BEROWNE   So study evermore is overshot.
While it doth study to have what it would,
It doth forget to do the thing it should;
And when it hath the thing it hunteth most,
'Tis won as towns with fire: so won, so lost.

145 KING   We must of force dispense with this decree.
She must lie here on mere necessity.

BEROWNE   Necessity will make us all forsworn
Three thousand times within this three years' space;
For every man with his affects is born,
150 Not by might mastered, but by special grace.
If I break faith, this word shall speak for me:
I am forsworn 'on mere necessity'.
So to the laws at large I write my name,
And he that breaks them in the least degree
155 Stands in attainder of eternal shame.

Suggestions are to other as to me;
But I believe, although I seem so loath,
I am the last that will last keep his oath.   [*Signs.*]
But is there no quick recreation granted?

KING

Ay, that there is. Our court, you know, is haunted   160
With a refined traveller of Spain,
A man in all the world's new fashion planted,
That hath a mint of phrases in his brain,
One who the music of his own vain tongue
Doth ravish like enchanting harmony,   165
A man of compliments, whom right and wrong
Have chose as umpire of their mutiny.
This child of fancy, that Armado hight,
For interim to our studies shall relate
In high-born words the worth of many a knight   170
From tawny Spain, lost in the world's debate.
How you delight, my lords, I know not, I,
But I protest I love to hear him lie,
And I will use him for my minstrelsy.

BEROWNE   Armado is a most illustrious wight,   175
A man of fire-new words, fashion's own knight.

LONGAVILLE

Costard the swain and he shall be our sport,
And so to study three years is but short.

Enter DULL, *a Constable, with a letter, and* COSTARD.

DULL   Which is the Duke's own person?

BEROWNE   This, fellow. What wouldst?   180

DULL   I myself reprehend his own person, for I am his
grace's farborough. But I would see his own person in
flesh and blood.

BEROWNE   This is he.

DULL   Señor Arm . . . Arm . . . commends you. There's   185
villainy abroad. This letter will tell you more.

COSTARD   Sir, the contempts thereof are as touching me.

KING   A letter from the magnificent Armado.

BEROWNE   How low soever the matter, I hope in God
for high words.   190

LONGAVILLE   A high hope for a low heaven. God grant
us patience!

BEROWNE   To hear, or forbear hearing?

LONGAVILLE   To hear meekly, sir, and to laugh
moderately, or to forbear both.   195

BEROWNE   Well, sir, be it as the style shall give us cause
to climb in the merriness.

COSTARD   The matter is to me, sir, as concerning
Jaquenetta. The manner of it is, I was taken with the
manner.   200

BEROWNE   In what manner?

COSTARD   In manner and form following, sir, all those
three. I was seen with her in the manor-house, sitting
with her upon the form, and taken following her into
the park, which, put together, is 'in manner and form   205
following'. Now, sir, for the manner: it is the manner of
a man to speak to a woman; for the form: in some form.

BEROWNE   For the 'following', sir?

COSTARD   As it shall follow in my correction, and God
210   defend the right!

KING   Will you hear this letter with attention?

BEROWNE   As we would hear an oracle.

COSTARD   Such is the simplicity of man to hearken after
         the flesh.

215 KING [*Reads.*]   *Great deputy, the welkin's vicegerent, and*
         sole dominator of Navarre, my soul's earth's god and
         body's fostering patron –

COSTARD   Not a word of Costard yet.

KING   *So it is –*

220 COSTARD   It may be so; but if he say it is so, he is, in
         telling true, but so.

KING   Peace!

COSTARD   Be to me and every man that dares not fight.

KING   No words!

225 COSTARD   Of other men's secrets, I beseech you.

KING   *So it is, besieged with sable-coloured melancholy, I*
         did commend the black oppressing humour to the most
         wholesome physic of thy health-giving air; and, as I am a
         gentleman, betook myself to walk. The time, when? About
230   *the sixth hour, when beasts most graze, birds best peck*
         and men sit down to that nourishment which is called
         supper. So much for the time when. Now for the ground,
         which? Which, I mean, I walked upon. It is ycleped
         thy park. Then for the place, where? Where, I mean, I did
235   *encounter that obscene and most preposterous event that*
         draweth from my snow-white pen the ebon-coloured ink,
         which here thou viewest, beholdest, surveyest or seest. But
         to the place, where? It standeth north-north-east and by
         east from the west corner of thy curious-knotted garden.
240   *There did I see that low-spirited swain, that base minnow*
         of thy mirth –

COSTARD   Me?

KING   *That unlettered small-knowing soul –*

COSTARD   Me?

245 KING   *That shallow vassal –*

COSTARD   Still me?

KING   *Which, as I remember, hight Costard –*

COSTARD   O, me!

KING   *Sorted and consorted, contrary to thy established*
250   *proclaimed edict and continent canon, which with, O,*
         with – but with this I passion to say wherewith –

COSTARD   With a wench.

KING   *With a child of our grandmother Eve, a female, or,*
         for thy more sweet understanding, a woman. Him I, as my
255   *ever-esteemed duty pricks me on, have sent to thee, to*
         receive the meed of punishment, by thy sweet grace's
         officer, Anthony Dull, a man of good repute, carriage,
         bearing and estimation.

DULL   Me, an't shall please you. I am Anthony Dull.

260 KING   *For Jaquenetta, so is the weaker vessel called*
         which I apprehended with the aforesaid swain, I keep
         her as a vessel of thy law's fury, and shall, at the least
         of thy sweet notice, bring her to trial. Thine in all
         compliments of devoted and heartburning heat of duty,
265   *Don Adriano de Armado.*

BEROWNE   This is not so well as I looked for, but the
         best that ever I heard.

KING   Ay, the best for the worst. But, sirrah, what say
         you to this?

COSTARD   Sir, I confess the wench.   270

KING   Did you hear the proclamation?

COSTARD   I do confess much of the hearing it, but little
         of the marking of it.

KING   It was proclaimed a year's imprisonment to be
         taken with a wench.   275

COSTARD   I was taken with none, sir; I was taken with a
         damsel.

KING   Well, it was proclaimed damsel.

COSTARD   This was no damsel neither, sir; she was a
         virgin.   280

KING   It is so varied too, for it was proclaimed virgin.

COSTARD   If it were, I deny her virginity: I was taken
         with a maid.

KING   This maid will not serve your turn, sir.

COSTARD   This maid will serve my turn, sir.   285

KING   Sir, I will pronounce your sentence: you shall fast
         a week with bran and water.

COSTARD   I had rather pray a month with mutton and
         porridge.

KING   And Don Armado shall be your keeper.   290
         My lord Berowne, see him delivered o'er;
         And go we, lords, to put in practice that
              Which each to other hath so strongly sworn.
                   Exeunt the King, Longaville and Dumaine.

BEROWNE   I'll lay my head to any goodman's hat
              These oaths and laws will prove an idle scorn.   295
         Sirrah, come on.

COSTARD   I suffer for the truth, sir, for true it is, I was
         taken with Jaquenetta, and Jaquenetta is a true girl.
         And therefore welcome the sour cup of prosperity!
         Affliction may one day smile again, and, till then, sit 300
         thee down, sorrow.   *Exeunt.*

1.2   *Enter* ARMADO *and* MOTH, *his page.*

ARMADO   Boy, what sign is it when a man of great spirit
         grows melancholy?

MOTH   A great sign, sir, that he will look sad.

ARMADO   Why, sadness is one and the selfsame thing,
         dear imp.   5

MOTH   No, no, O Lord, sir, no.

ARMADO   How canst thou part sadness and melancholy,
         my tender juvenal?

MOTH   By a familiar demonstration of the working, my
         tough señor.   10

ARMADO   Why tough señor? Why tough señor?

MOTH   Why tender juvenal? Why tender juvenal?

ARMADO   I spoke it, tender juvenal, as a congruent
         epitheton appertaining to thy young days, which we
         may nominate tender.   15

MOTH   And I, tough señor, as an appertinent title to
         your old time, which we may name tough.

ARMADO   Pretty and apt.

MOTH   How mean you, sir? I pretty and my saying apt,
20   or I apt and my saying pretty?

ARMADO   Thou pretty, because little.

MOTH   Little pretty, because little. Wherefore apt?

ARMADO   And therefore apt, because quick.

MOTH   Speak you this in my praise, master?

25   ARMADO   In thy condign praise.

MOTH   I will praise an eel with the same praise.

ARMADO   What, that an eel is ingenious?

MOTH   That an eel is quick.

ARMADO   I do say thou art quick in answers. Thou
30   heatest my blood.

MOTH   I am answered sir.

ARMADO   I love not to be crossed.

MOTH [*aside*]   He speaks the mere contrary: crosses love
not him.

35   ARMADO   I have promised to study three years with the
Duke.

MOTH   You may do it in an hour, sir.

ARMADO   Impossible.

MOTH   How many is one thrice told?

40   ARMADO   I am ill at reckoning. It fitteth the spirit of a
tapster.

MOTH   You are a gentleman and a gamester, sir.

ARMADO   I confess both. They are both the varnish of a
complete man.

45   MOTH   Then I am sure you know how much the gross
sum of deuce-ace amounts to.

ARMADO   It doth amount to one more than two.

MOTH   Which the base vulgar do call three.

ARMADO   True.

50   MOTH   Why, sir, is this such a piece of study? Now
here is three studied ere ye'll thrice wink. And how
easy it is to put 'years' to the word 'three', and study
three years in two words, the dancing horse will
tell you.

55   ARMADO   A most fine figure!

MOTH [*aside*]   To prove you a cipher.

ARMADO   I will hereupon confess I am in love. And
as it is base for a soldier to love, so am I in love with
a base wench. If drawing my sword against the
60   humour of affection would deliver me from the
reprobate thought of it, I would take desire prisoner
and ransom him to any French courtier for a new-
devised curtsy. I think scorn to sigh; methinks I should
outswear Cupid. Comfort me, boy. What great men
65   have been in love?

MOTH   Hercules, master.

ARMADO   Most sweet Hercules! More authority, dear
boy, name more. And, sweet my child, let them be men
of good repute and carriage.

70   MOTH   Samson, master. He was a man of good carriage,
great carriage, for he carried the town-gates on his
back like a porter, and he was in love.

ARMADO   O well-knit Samson, strong-jointed Samson!
I do excel thee in my rapier as much as thou didst me

in carrying gates. I am in love too. Who was Samson's   75
love, my dear Moth?

MOTH   A woman, master.

ARMADO   Of what complexion?

MOTH   Of all the four, or the three, or the two, or one of
the four.   80

ARMADO   Tell me precisely of what complexion?

MOTH   Of the sea-water green, sir.

ARMADO   Is that one of the four complexions?

MOTH   As I have read, sir; and the best of them too.

ARMADO   Green indeed is the colour of lovers. But to   85
have a love of that colour, methinks Samson had small
reason for it. He surely affected her for her wit.

MOTH   It was so, sir, for she had a green wit.

ARMADO   My love is most immaculate white and red.

MOTH   Most maculate thoughts, master, are masked   90
under such colours.

ARMADO   Define, define, well-educated infant.

MOTH   My father's wit and my mother's tongue assist
me!

ARMADO   Sweet invocation of a child, most pretty and   95
pathetical!

MOTH   If she be made of white and red,
         Her faults will ne'er be known,
      For blushing cheeks by faults are bred,
         And fears by pale white shown.   100
      Then if she fear or be to blame,
         By this you shall not know,
      For still her cheeks possess the same
         Which native she doth owe.

A dangerous rhyme, master, against the reason of   105
white and red.

ARMADO   Is there not a ballad, boy, of the King and the
Beggar?

MOTH   The world was very guilty of such a ballad some
three ages since, but I think now 'tis not to be found,   110
or, if it were, it would neither serve for the writing nor
the tune.

ARMADO   I will have that subject newly writ o'er, that
I may example my digression by some mighty
precedent. Boy, I do love that country girl that I took   115
in the park with the rational hind Costard. She
deserves well.

MOTH [*aside*]   To be whipped: and yet a better love than
my master.

ARMADO   Sing, boy. My spirit grows heavy in love.   120

MOTH [*aside*]   And that's great marvel, loving a light
wench.

ARMADO   I say sing.

MOTH   Forbear till this company be passed.

Enter COSTARD, *the Clown,* DULL, *a Constable, and*
JAQUENETTA, *a wench.*

DULL   Sir, the Duke's pleasure is that you keep Costard   125
safe; and you must suffer him to take no delight, nor no
penance, but 'a must fast three days a week. For this

damsel, I must keep her at the park: she is allowed for
the dey-woman. Fare you well.

130 ARMADO [*aside*] I do betray myself with blushing. –
Maid –

JAQUENETTA Man.

ARMADO I will visit thee at the lodge.

JAQUENETTA That's hereby.

135 ARMADO I know where it is situate.

JAQUENETTA Lord, how wise you are!

ARMADO I will tell thee wonders.

JAQUENETTA With that face?

ARMADO I love thee.

140 JAQUENETTA So I heard you say.

ARMADO And so farewell.

JAQUENETTA Fair weather after you.

DULL Come, Jaquenetta, away.

Exeunt Dull and Jaquenetta.

ARMADO Villain, thou shalt fast for thy offences ere
145 thou be pardoned.

COSTARD Well, sir, I hope when I do it I shall do it on a
full stomach.

ARMADO Thou shalt be heavily punished.

COSTARD I am more bound to you than your fellows,
150 for they are but lightly rewarded.

ARMADO Take away this villain. Shut him up.

MOTH Come, you transgressing slave, away!

COSTARD Let me not be pent up, sir, I will fast being
loose.

155 MOTH No, sir, that were fast and loose. Thou shalt to
prison.

COSTARD Well, if ever I do see the merry days of
desolation that I have seen, some shall see –

MOTH What shall some see?

160 COSTARD Nay, nothing, Master Moth, but what they
look upon. It is not for prisoners to be too silent in
their words and therefore I will say nothing. I thank
God I have as little patience as another man and
therefore I can be quiet.   *Exeunt Moth and Costard.*

165 ARMADO I do affect the very ground, which is base,
where her shoe, which is baser, guided by her foot,
which is basest, doth tread. I shall be forsworn, which
is a great argument of falsehood, if I love. And how can
that be true love which is falsely attempted? Love is a
170 familiar; Love is a devil. There is no evil angel but
Love. Yet was Samson so tempted, and he had an
excellent strength. Yet was Solomon so seduced, and
he had a very good wit. Cupid's butt-shaft is too hard
for Hercules' club, and therefore too much odds for a
175 Spaniard's rapier. The first and second cause will not
serve my turn. The *passado* he respects not; the *duello*
he regards not. His disgrace is to be called boy, but his
glory is to subdue men. Adieu, valour; rust, rapier; be
still, drum, for your manager is in love. Yea, he loveth.
180 Assist me, some extemporal god of rhyme, for I am
sure I shall turn sonnet. Devise, wit; write, pen; for I
am for whole volumes in folio.   *Exit.*

2.1 *Enter the* PRINCESS *of France, with three
attending ladies,* ROSALINE, MARIA *and* KATHERINE,
and three lords, BOYET *and two others.*

BOYET Now, madam, summon up your dearest spirits.
Consider who the King your father sends,
To whom he sends and what's his embassy:
Yourself, held precious in the world's esteem,
To parley with the sole inheritor   5
Of all perfections that a man may owe,
Matchless Navarre; the plea of no less weight
Than Aquitaine, a dowry for a queen.
Be now as prodigal of all dear grace
As Nature was in making graces dear   10
When she did starve the general world beside
And prodigally gave them all to you.

PRINCESS
Good Lord Boyet, my beauty, though but mean,
Needs not the painted flourish of your praise.
Beauty is bought by judgement of the eye,   15
Not uttered by base sale of chapmen's tongues.
I am less proud to hear you tell my worth
Than you much willing to be counted wise
In spending your wit in the praise of mine.
But now to task the tasker. Good Boyet,   20
You are not ignorant all-telling fame
Doth noise abroad Navarre hath made a vow,
Till painful study shall outwear three years,
No woman may approach his silent court.
Therefore to's seemeth it a needful course,   25
Before we enter his forbidden gates,
To know his pleasure; and in that behalf,
Bold of your worthiness, we single you
As our best-moving fair solicitor.
Tell him the daughter of the King of France,   30
On serious business craving quick dispatch,
Importunes personal conference with his grace.
Haste, signify so much, while we attend,
Like humble-visaged suitors, his high will.

BOYET Proud of employment, willingly I go.   35

PRINCESS All pride is willing pride, and yours is so.

Exit Boyet.

Who are the votaries, my loving lords,
That are vow-fellows with this virtuous Duke?

LORD Longaville is one.

PRINCESS   Know you the man?

MARIA I know him, madam. At a marriage feast   40
Between Lord Perigort and the beauteous heir
Of Jaques Falconbridge, solemnized
In Normandy, saw I this Longaville.
A man of sovereign parts, he is esteemed,
Well fitted in arts, glorious in arms.   45
Nothing becomes him ill that he would well.
The only soil of his fair virtue's gloss –
If virtue's gloss will stain with any soil –
Is a sharp wit matched with too blunt a will,
Whose edge hath power to cut, whose will still wills   50

It should none spare that come within his power.
PRINCESS   Some merry mocking lord belike: is't so?
MARIA   They say so most that most his humours know.
PRINCESS
    Such short-lived wits do wither as they grow.
55   Who are the rest?
KATHERINE
    The young Dumaine, a well-accomplished youth,
    Of all that virtue love for virtue loved;
    Most power to do most harm, least knowing ill,
    For he hath wit to make an ill shape good,
60   And shape to win grace, though he had no wit.
    I saw him at the Duke Alençon's once;
    And much too little of that good I saw
    Is my report to his great worthiness.
ROSALINE   Another of these students at that time
65   Was there with him, if I have heard a truth.
    Berowne they call him, but a merrier man,
    Within the limit of becoming mirth,
    I never spent an hour's talk withal.
    His eye begets occasion for his wit,
70   For every object that the one doth catch
    The other turns to a mirth-moving jest,
    Which his fair tongue, conceit's expositor,
    Delivers in such apt and gracious words
    That aged ears play truant at his tales
75   And younger hearings are quite ravished,
    So sweet and voluble is his discourse.
PRINCESS   God bless my ladies! Are they all in love,
    That every one her own hath garnished
    With such bedecking ornaments of praise?
LORD   Here comes Boyet.

    Enter BOYET.

80 PRINCESS   Now, what admittance, lord?
BOYET   Navarre had notice of your fair approach,
    And he and his competitors in oath
    Were all addressed to meet you, gentle lady,
    Before I came. Marry, thus much I have learned:
85   He rather means to lodge you in the field,
    Like one that comes here to besiege his court,
    Than seek a dispensation for his oath,
    To let you enter his unpeopled house.

    Enter the KING *of Navarre,* BEROWNE, LONGAVILLE
       and DUMAINE *and Attendants.*

    Here comes Navarre.
90 KING   Fair Princess, welcome to the court of Navarre.
PRINCESS   'Fair' I give you back again, and 'welcome' I
    have not yet. The roof of this court is too high to be
    yours, and welcome to the wide fields too base to be
    mine.
95 KING   You shall be welcome, madam, to my court.
PRINCESS   I will be welcome then. Conduct me thither.
KING   Hear me, dear lady: I have sworn an oath.
PRINCESS   Our Lady help my lord! He'll be forsworn.
KING   Not for the world, fair madam, by my will.

PRINCESS
    Why, will shall break it; will, and nothing else.   100
KING   Your ladyship is ignorant what it is.
PRINCESS   Were my lord so, his ignorance were wise,
    Where now his knowledge must prove ignorance.
    I hear your grace hath sworn out housekeeping.
    'Tis deadly sin to keep that oath, my lord,   105
    And sin to break it.
    But pardon me, I am too sudden bold;
    To teach a teacher ill beseemeth me.
    Vouchsafe to read the purpose of my coming
    And suddenly resolve me in my suit.   110
    [Gives the King a paper.]
KING   Madam, I will, if suddenly I may.
PRINCESS   You will the sooner that I were away,
    For you'll prove perjured if you make me stay.
    [The King reads.]
BEROWNE *[to Rosaline]*
    Did not I dance with you in Brabant once?
ROSALINE   Did not I dance with you in Brabant once?   115
BEROWNE   I know you did.
ROSALINE   How needless was it then
    To ask the question!
BEROWNE   You must not be so quick.
ROSALINE
    'Tis long of you that spur me with such questions.
BEROWNE
    Your wit's too hot, it speeds too fast, 'twill tire.
ROSALINE   Not till it leave the rider in the mire.   120
BEROWNE   What time o'day?
ROSALINE   The hour that fools should ask.
BEROWNE   Now fair befall your mask.
ROSALINE   Fair fall the face it covers.
BEROWNE   And send you many lovers.   125
ROSALINE   Amen, so you be none.
BEROWNE   Nay, then will I be gone.   *[Leaves her.]*
KING   Madam, your father here doth intimate
    The payment of a hundred thousand crowns,
    Being but the one half of an entire sum   130
    Disbursed by my father in his wars.
    But say that he or we – as neither have –
    Received that sum, yet there remains unpaid
    A hundred thousand more, in surety of the which
    One part of Aquitaine is bound to us,   135
    Although not valued to the money's worth.
    If then the King your father will restore
    But that one half which is unsatisfied,
    We will give up our right in Aquitaine
    And hold fair friendship with his majesty.   140
    But that, it seems, he little purposeth:
    For here he doth demand to have repaid
    A hundred thousand crowns, and not demands,
    On payment of a hundred thousand crowns,
    To have his title live in Aquitaine,   145
    Which we much rather had depart withal,
    And have the money by our father lent,
    Than Aquitaine, so gelded as it is.

Dear Princess, were not his requests so far
From reason's yielding, your fair self should make
A yielding 'gainst some reason in my breast
And go well satisfied to France again.

PRINCESS   You do the King my father too much wrong
And wrong the reputation of your name,
In so unseeming to confess receipt
Of that which hath so faithfully been paid.

KING   I do protest I never heard of it.
And, if you prove it, I'll repay it back
Or yield up Aquitaine.

PRINCESS   We arrest your word.
Boyet, you can produce acquittances
For such a sum from special officers
Of Charles, his father.

KING   Satisfy me so.

BOYET   So please your grace, the packet is not come
Where that and other specialties are bound.
Tomorrow you shall have a sight of them.

KING   It shall suffice me; at which interview
All liberal reason I will yield unto.
Meantime, receive such welcome at my hand
As honour, without breach of honour, may
Make tender of to thy true worthiness.
You may not come, fair Princess, within my gates,
But here without you shall be so received
As you shall deem yourself lodged in my heart,
Though so denied fair harbour in my house.
Your own good thoughts excuse me, and farewell.
Tomorrow shall we visit you again.

PRINCESS
Sweet health and fair desires consort your grace.

KING   Thy own wish wish I thee in every place.

Exeunt the King, Longaville
and Dumaine.

BEROWNE   Lady, I will commend you to mine own
heart.

ROSALINE   Pray you, do my commendations; I would
be glad to see it.

BEROWNE   I would you heard it groan.

ROSALINE   Is the fool sick?

BEROWNE   Sick at the heart.

ROSALINE   Alack, let it blood.

BEROWNE   Would that do it good?

ROSALINE   My physic says ay.

BEROWNE   Will you prick't with your eye?

ROSALINE   *Non point*, with my knife.

BEROWNE   Now God save thy life.

ROSALINE   And yours from long living.

BEROWNE   I cannot stay thanksgiving.   *Exit.*

Enter DUMAINE.

DUMAINE
Sir, I pray you a word. What lady is that same?

BOYET   The heir of Alençon, Katherine her name.

DUMAINE   A gallant lady. Monsieur, fare you well.   *Exit.*

Enter LONGAVILLE.

LONGAVILLE
I beseech you a word. What is she in the white?

BOYET
A woman sometimes, an you saw her in the light.

LONGAVILLE
Perchance light in the light. I desire her name.

BOYET
She hath but one for herself; to desire that were a shame.   200

LONGAVILLE   Pray you, sir, whose daughter?

BOYET   Her mother's, I have heard.

LONGAVILLE   God's blessing on your beard!

BOYET   Good sir, be not offended.
She is an heir of Falconbridge.   205

LONGAVILLE   Nay, my choler is ended.
She is a most sweet lady.

BOYET   Not unlike, sir, that may be.   *Exit Longaville.*

Enter BEROWNE.

BEROWNE   What's her name in the cap?

BOYET   Rosaline, by good hap.   210

BEROWNE   Is she wedded or no?

BOYET   To her will sir, or so.

BEROWNE   You are welcome, sir. Adieu.

BOYET   Farewell to me, sir, and welcome to you.

Exit Berowne.

MARIA   That last is Berowne, the merry madcap lord.   215
Not a word with him but a jest.

BOYET   And every jest but a word.

PRINCESS
It was well done of you to take him at his word.

BOYET   I was as willing to grapple as he was to board.

KATHERINE   Two hot sheeps, marry!

BOYET   And wherefore not 'ships'?
No sheep, sweet lamb, unless we feed on your lips.   220

KATHERINE
You sheep, and I pasture. Shall that finish the jest?

BOYET   So you grant pasture for me.   [*Tries to kiss her.*]

KATHERINE   Not so, gentle beast.
My lips are no common, though several they be.

BOYET   Belonging to whom?

KATHERINE   To my fortunes and me.

PRINCESS
Good wits will be jangling; but, gentles, agree.   225
This civil war of wits were much better used
On Navarre and his bookmen, for here 'tis abused.

BOYET   If my observation, which very seldom lies
By the heart's still rhetoric disclosed with eyes,
Deceive me not now, Navarre is infected.   230

PRINCESS   With what?

BOYET   With that which we lovers entitle 'affected'.

PRINCESS   Your reason?

BOYET   Why, all his behaviours did make their retire
To the court of his eye, peeping thorough desire.   235
His heart, like an agate with your print impressed,
Proud with his form, in his eye pride expressed.

His tongue, all impatient to speak and not see,
Did stumble with haste in his eyesight to be.
240 All senses to that sense did make their repair,
To feel only looking on fairest of fair.
Methought all his senses were locked in his eye,
As jewels in crystal for some prince to buy;
Who, tendering their own worth from where they
    were glassed,
245 Did point you to buy them along as you passed.
His face's own margin did quote such amazes
That all eyes saw his eyes enchanted with gazes.
I'll give you Aquitaine, and all that is his,
An you give him for my sake but one loving kiss.

250 PRINCESS   Come, to our pavilion. Boyet is disposed.
BOYET
But to speak that in words which his eye hath disclosed.
I only have made a mouth of his eye
By adding a tongue which I know will not lie.
MARIA
Thou art an old love-monger, and speakest skilfully.
KATHERINE
255 He is Cupid's grandfather, and learns news of him.
ROSALINE
Then was Venus like her mother, for her father is but
    grim.
BOYET   Do you hear, my mad wenches?
MARIA   No.
BOYET   What then, do you see?
MARIA   Ay, our way to be gone.
BOYET   You are too hard for me.
                                    Exeunt omnes.

3.1   *Enter* ARMADO, *the Braggart, and* MOTH,
                    his Boy.

ARMADO   Warble, child, make passionate my sense of
    hearing.
MOTH [*Sings.*]   Concolinel.
ARMADO   Sweet air! Go, tenderness of years, take
5   this key, give enlargement to the swain, bring him
    festinately hither. I must employ him in a letter to my
    love.
MOTH   Master, will you win your love with a French
    brawl?
10 ARMADO   How meanest thou? Brawling in French?
MOTH   No, my complete master; but to jig off a tune at
    the tongue's end, canary to it with your feet, humour it
    with turning up your eyelids, sigh a note and sing a
    note, sometime through the throat as if you swallowed
15   love with singing love, sometime through the nose as if
    you snuffed up love by smelling love, with your hat
    penthouse-like o'er the shop of your eyes, with your
    arms crossed on your thin-belly doublet like a rabbit
    on a spit, or your hands in your pocket like a man after
20   the old painting; and keep not too long in one tune, but
    a snip and away. These are compliments, these are
    humours, these betray nice wenches that would be

betrayed without these; and make them men of note –
do you note me? – that most are affected to these.
ARMADO   How hast thou purchased this experience?   25
MOTH   By my penny of observation.
ARMADO   But O – But O –
MOTH   'The hobby-horse is forgot.'
ARMADO   Call'st thou my love 'hobby-horse'?
MOTH   No, master. The hobby-horse is but a colt, and   30
    your love perhaps a hackney. But have you forgot your
    love?
ARMADO   Almost I had.
MOTH   Negligent student! Learn her by heart.
ARMADO   By heart and in heart, boy.   35
MOTH   And out of heart, master. All those three I will
    prove.
ARMADO   What wilt thou prove?
MOTH   A man, if I live; and this 'by', 'in' and 'without'
    upon the instant. 'By' heart you love her, because your   40
    heart cannot come by her; 'in' heart you love her, because
    your heart is in love with her; and 'out' of heart you love
    her, being out of heart that you cannot enjoy her.
ARMADO   I am all these three.
MOTH   And three times as much more, and yet nothing   45
    at all.
ARMADO   Fetch hither the swain. He must carry me a
    letter.
MOTH   A message well sympathized: a horse to be
    ambassador for an ass.   50
ARMADO   Ha, ha, what sayest thou?
MOTH   Marry, sir, you must send the ass upon the
    horse, for he is very slow-gaited. But I go.
ARMADO   The way is but short. Away!
MOTH   As swift as lead, sir.   55
ARMADO   The meaning, pretty ingenious?
Is not lead a metal heavy, dull and slow?
MOTH   *Minime*, honest master; or rather, master, no.
ARMADO   I say lead is slow.
MOTH   You are too swift, sir, to say so.
Is that lead slow which is fired from a gun?   60
ARMADO   Sweet smoke of rhetoric!
He reputes me a cannon; and the bullet, that's he.
I shoot thee at the swain.
MOTH   Thump then, and I flee.   *Exit.*
ARMADO
A most acute juvenal, voluble and free of grace!
By thy favour, sweet welkin, I must sigh in thy face.   65
Most rude melancholy, valour gives thee place.
My herald is returned.

Enter MOTH, *the Page, and* COSTARD, *the Clown.*

MOTH
A wonder, master! Here's a costard broken in a shin.
ARMADO
Some enigma, some riddle. Come, thy l'envoy – begin.
COSTARD   No egma, no riddle, no l'envoy, no salve in   70
    the mail, sir! O, sir, plantain, a plain plantain! No
    l'envoy, no l'envoy, no salve, sir, but a plantain!

ARMADO   By virtue, thou enforcest laughter; thy silly
thought, my spleen; the heaving of my lungs provokes
me to ridiculous smiling. O, pardon me, my stars!
Doth the inconsiderate take *salve* for l'envoy, and the
word 'l'envoy' for a salve?

MOTH   Do the wise think them other? Is not l'envoy a
salve?

ARMADO

No, page; it is an epilogue or discourse to make plain
Some obscure precedence that hath tofore been sain.
I will example it:
            The fox, the ape and the humble-bee
            Were still at odds, being but three.
There's the moral. Now the l'envoy.

MOTH   I will add the l'envoy. Say the moral again.

ARMADO   The fox, the ape and the humble-bee
            Were still at odds, being but three.

MOTH   Until the goose came out of door,
            And stayed the odds by adding four.
Now will I begin your moral, and do you follow with
my l'envoy.
            The fox, the ape and the humble-bee
            Were still at odds, being but three.

ARMADO   Until the goose came out of door,
            Staying the odds by adding four.

MOTH   A good l'envoy, ending in the goose. Would you
desire more?

COSTARD
The boy hath sold him a bargain, a goose, that's flat.
Sir, your pennyworth is good, an your goose be fat.
To sell a bargain well is as cunning as fast and loose.
Let me see: a fat l'envoy – ay, that's a fat goose.

ARMADO
Come hither, come hither. How did this argument
begin?

MOTH   By saying that a costard was broken in a shin.
Then called you for the l'envoy.

COSTARD   True, and I for a plantain: thus came your
argument in. Then the boy's fat l'envoy, the goose that
you bought; and he ended the market.

ARMADO   But tell me, how was there a costard broken in
a shin?

MOTH   I will tell you sensibly.

COSTARD   Thou hast no feeling of it, Moth. I will speak
that l'envoy.
I, Costard, running out, that was safely within,
Fell over the threshold, and broke my shin.

ARMADO   We will talk no more of this matter.

COSTARD   Till there be more matter in the shin.

ARMADO   Sirrah Costard, I will enfranchise thee.

COSTARD   O, marry me to one Frances! I smell some
l'envoy, some goose in this.

ARMADO   By my sweet soul, I mean setting thee at
liberty, enfreedoming thy person. Thou wert immured,
restrained, captivated, bound.

COSTARD   True, true, and now you will be my purgation,
and let me loose.

ARMADO   I give thee thy liberty, set thee from durance,
and in lieu thereof impose on thee nothing but this:
[*Gives Costard a letter.*] bear this significant to the
country maid Jaquenetta. There is remuneration, [*Gives
Costard a coin.*] for the best ward of mine honour is
rewarding my dependants. Moth, follow.   *Exit.*

MOTH   Like the sequel, I. Signor Costard, adieu.   *Exit.*

COSTARD
My sweet ounce of man's flesh, my incony jew!
Now will I look to his remuneration. 'Remuneration'!
O, that's the Latin word for three farthings. Three
farthings – remuneration. 'What's the price of this
inkle?' 'One penny.' 'No, I'll give you a remuneration.'
Why, it carries it! 'Remuneration'! Why, it is a fairer
name than French crown. I will never buy and sell out
of this word.

Enter BEROWNE.

BEROWNE   My good knave Costard, exceedingly well
met.

COSTARD   Pray you, sir, how much carnation ribbon
may a man buy for a remuneration?

BEROWNE   What is a remuneration?

COSTARD   Marry, sir, halfpenny-farthing.

BEROWNE   Why then, three-farthing-worth of silk.

COSTARD   I thank your worship. God be wi'you.

BEROWNE   Stay, slave. I must employ thee.
As thou wilt win my favour, good my knave,
Do one thing for me that I shall entreat.

COSTARD   When would you have it done, sir?

BEROWNE   This afternoon.

COSTARD   Well, I will do it, sir. Fare you well.

BEROWNE   Thou knowest not what it is.

COSTARD   I shall know, sir, when I have done it.

BEROWNE   Why, villain, thou must know first.

COSTARD   I will come to your worship tomorrow
morning.

BEROWNE   It must be done this afternoon. Hark, slave,
it is but this:
The Princess comes to hunt here in the park,
And in her train there is a gentle lady;
When tongues speak sweetly, then they name her
name,
And Rosaline they call her. Ask for her
And to her white hand see thou do commend
This sealed-up counsel.   [*Gives Costard a letter.*]
            There's thy guerdon: go.
[*Gives Costard money.*]

COSTARD   Guerdon, O sweet guerdon! Better than
remuneration, elevenpence-farthing better. Most
sweet guerdon! I will do it, sir, in print. Guerdon!
Remuneration!   *Exit.*

BEROWNE
And I, forsooth, in love! I, that have been love's whip,
A very beadle to a humorous sigh,
A critic, nay, a night-watch constable,
A domineering pedant o'er the boy,

75

80

85

90

95

100

105

110

115

120

125

130

135

140

145

150

155

160

165

170

175

Than whom no mortal so magnificent!
This wimpled, whining, purblind, wayward boy,
This Signor Junior, giant dwarf, Dan Cupid,
Regent of love-rhymes, lord of folded arms,
180 Th'anointed sovereign of sighs and groans,
Liege of all loiterers and malcontents,
Dread prince of plackets, king of codpieces,
Sole imperator and great general
Of trotting paritors – O my little heart!
185 And I to be a corporal of his field
And wear his colours like a tumbler's hoop!
What? I love, I sue, I seek a wife?
A woman that is like a German clock,
Still a-repairing, ever out of frame
190 And never going aright, being a watch,
But being watched that it may still go right!
Nay, to be perjured, which is worst of all;
And among three to love the worst of all,
A whitely wanton with a velvet brow,
195 With two pitch-balls stuck in her face for eyes;
Ay, and by heaven, one that will do the deed
Though Argus were her eunuch and her guard.
And I to sigh for her, to watch for her,
To pray for her! Go to, it is a plague
200 That Cupid will impose for my neglect
Of his almighty dreadful little might.
Well, I will love, write, sigh, pray, sue and groan.
Some men must love my lady, and some Joan.   *Exit.*

4.1   *Enter the* PRINCESS, *a* Forester, *her ladies,*
      ROSALINE, MARIA *and* KATHERINE, *and her lords,*
         BOYET *and others.*

PRINCESS
    Was that the King that spurred his horse so hard
    Against the steep-up rising of the hill?
BOYET   I know not, but I think it was not he.
PRINCESS   Whoe'er 'a was, 'a showed a mounting mind.
5   Well, lords, today we shall have our dispatch;
    On Saturday we will return to France.
    Then, forester, my friend, where is the bush
    That we must stand and play the murderer in?
FORESTER   Hereby, upon the edge of yonder coppice,
10   A stand where you may make the fairest shoot.
PRINCESS   I thank my beauty, I am fair that shoot,
    And thereupon thou speak'st 'the fairest shoot'.
FORESTER   Pardon me, madam, for I meant not so.
PRINCESS
    What, what? First praise me, and again say no?
15   O, short-lived pride! Not fair? Alack for woe!
FORESTER   Yes, madam, fair.
PRINCESS   Nay, never paint me now.
    Where fair is not, praise cannot mend the brow.
    Here, good my glass, take this for telling true:
       [*Gives him money.*]
    Fair payment for foul words is more than due.
20   FORESTER   Nothing but fair is that which you inherit.

PRINCESS   See, see, my beauty will be saved by merit!
    O heresy in fair, fit for these days!
    A giving hand, though foul, shall have fair praise.
    But come, the bow. Now mercy goes to kill,
25   And shooting well is then accounted ill.
    Thus will I save my credit in the shoot:
    Not wounding, pity would not let me do't;
    If wounding, then it was to show my skill,
    That more for praise than purpose meant to kill.
30   And out of question so it is sometimes,
    Glory grows guilty of detested crimes,
    When for fame's sake, for praise, an outward part,
    We bend to that the working of the heart;
    As I for praise alone now seek to spill
35   The poor deer's blood, that my heart means no ill.
BOYET   Do not curst wives hold that self-sovereignty
    Only for praise' sake when they strive to be
    Lords o'er their lords?
PRINCESS   Only for praise, and praise we may afford
40   To any lady that subdues a lord.

       Enter COSTARD, *the Clown, with a letter.*

BOYET   Here comes a member of the commonwealth.
COSTARD   God dig-you-den all! Pray you which is the
    head lady?
PRINCESS   Thou shalt know her, fellow, by the rest that
45   have no heads.
COSTARD   Which is the greatest lady, the highest?
PRINCESS   The thickest and the tallest.
COSTARD   The thickest and the tallest. It is so, truth is
    truth.
50   An your waist, mistress, were as slender as my wit,
    One o'these maids' girdles for your waist should be fit.
    Are not you the chief woman? You are the thickest
    here.
PRINCESS   What's your will, sir? What's your will?
COSTARD
    I have a letter from Monsieur Berowne to one Lady
55   Rosaline.
PRINCESS
    O, thy letter, thy letter! He's a good friend of mine.
       [*Takes the letter.*]
    Stand aside, good bearer. Boyet, you can carve:
    Break up this capon.
BOYET   I am bound to serve.
       [*Examines the letter.*]
    This letter is mistook; it importeth none here.
    It is writ to Jaquenetta.
PRINCESS   We will read it, I swear.
60   Break the neck of the wax, and everyone give ear.
BOYET   [*Reads.*]   *By heaven, that thou art fair is most*
    infallible; true that thou art beauteous; truth itself that
    thou art lovely. More fairer than fair, beautiful than
    beauteous, truer than truth itself, have commiseration
65   *on thy heroical vassal. The magnanimous and most*
    illustrate King Cophetua set eye upon the pernicious
    and indubitate beggar Zenelophon, and he it was that

might rightly say, Veni, vidi, vici, *which to annothanize in the vulgar – O base and obscure vulgar! – videlicet, he came, see and overcame. He came, one; see, two; overcame, three. Who came? The King. Why did he come? To see. Why did he see? To overcome. To whom came he? To the beggar. What saw he? The beggar. Who overcame he? The beggar. The conclusion is victory. On whose side? The King's. The captive is enriched. On whose side? The beggar's. The catastrophe is a nuptial. On whose side? The King's? No, on both in one, or one in both. I am the King, for so stands the comparison, thou the beggar, for so witnesseth thy lowliness. Shall I command thy love? I may. Shall I enforce thy love? I could. Shall I entreat thy love? I will. What shalt thou exchange for rags? Robes. For tittles? Titles. For thyself? Me. Thus expecting thy reply, I profane my lips on thy foot, my eyes on thy picture and my heart on thy every part.*

> Thine in the dearest design of industry,
> Don Adriano de Armado.

Thus dost thou hear the Nemean lion roar
'Gainst thee, thou lamb, that standest as his prey.
Submissive fall his princely feet before,
And he from forage will incline to play.
But if thou strive, poor soul, what art thou then?
Food for his rage, repasture for his den.

PRINCESS
What plume of feathers is he that indited this letter?
What vane? What weathercock? Did you ever hear
better?

BOYET I am much deceived but I remember the style.

PRINCESS
Else your memory is bad, going o'er it erewhile.

BOYET
This Armado is a Spaniard that keeps here in court,
A phantasime, a Monarcho, and one that makes sport
To the Prince and his book-mates.

PRINCESS   Thou, fellow, a word.
Who gave thee this letter?

COSTARD   I told you: my lord.

PRINCESS
To whom shouldst thou give it?

COSTARD   From my lord to my lady.

PRINCESS From which lord to which lady?

COSTARD
From my lord Berowne, a good master of mine,
To a lady of France that he called Rosaline.

PRINCESS
Thou hast mistaken his letter. Come, lords, away.
[*to Rosaline*] Here, sweet, put up this; 'twill be thine
another day.

Exeunt all but Boyet, Rosaline, Maria and Costard.

BOYET Who is the shooter? Who is the shooter?

ROSALINE   Shall I teach you to know?

BOYET Ay, my continent of beauty.

ROSALINE   Why, she that bears the bow.
Finely put off!

BOYET My lady goes to kill horns, but if thou marry,
Hang me by the neck if horns that year miscarry.
Finely put on!

ROSALINE Well, then, I am the shooter.

BOYET   And who is your deer?   115

ROSALINE
If we choose by the horns, yourself come not near.
Finely put on indeed!

MARIA
You still wrangle with her, Boyet, and she strikes at
the brow.

BOYET But she herself is hit lower. Have I hit her now?

ROSALINE Shall I come upon thee with an old saying   120
that was a man when King Pepin of France was a little
boy, as touching the hit-it?

BOYET So I may answer thee with one as old, that was a
woman when Queen Guinevere of Britain was a little
wench, as touching the hit-it?   125

ROSALINE Thou canst not hit it, hit it, hit it,
        Thou canst not hit it, my good man.

BOYET   An I cannot, cannot, cannot,
        An I cannot, another can.   *Exit Rosaline.*

COSTARD
By my troth, most pleasant! How both did fit it!   130

MARIA
A mark marvellous well shot, for they both did hit it.

BOYET
A mark! O, mark but that mark! A mark, says my lady.
Let the mark have a prick in't, to mete at, if it may be.

MARIA Wide o'the bow hand! I'faith your hand is out.

COSTARD
Indeed, 'a must shoot nearer, or he'll ne'er hit the
clout.   135

BOYET
An if my hand be out, then belike your hand is in.

COSTARD
Then will she get the upshoot by cleaving the pin.

MARIA
Come, come, you talk greasily, your lips grow foul.

COSTARD
She's too hard for you at pricks, sir. Challenge her to
bowl.

BOYET
I fear too much rubbing. Good night, my good owl.   140

Exeunt Boyet and Maria.

COSTARD By my soul, a swain, a most simple clown!
Lord, lord, how the ladies and I have put him down!
O'my troth, most sweet jests, most incony vulgar wit,
When it comes so smoothly off, so obscenely, as it
were, so fit.
Armado o'th' t'other side – O, a most dainty man!   145
To see him walk before a lady and to bear her fan!
To see him kiss his hand and how most sweetly 'a will
swear!
And his page o' t'other side, that handful of wit!
Ah, heavens, it is a most pathetical nit!   [*Shout within*]
Sola, sola!   *Exit.*   150

4.2   *Enter* DULL, HOLOFERNES, *the Pedant,*
                          and NATHANIEL.

NATHANIEL   Very reverend sport, truly, and done in the
      testimony of a good conscience.
HOLOFERNES   The deer was, as you know, *sanguis*, in
      blood, ripe as the pomewater, who now hangeth like a
5   jewel in the ear of *caelo*, the sky, the welkin, the heaven,
      and anon falleth like a crab on the face of *terra*, the soil,
      the land, the earth.
NATHANIEL   Truly, Master Holofernes, the epithets
      are sweetly varied, like a scholar at the least: but, sir, I
10   assure ye it was a buck of the first head.
HOLOFERNES   Sir Nathaniel, *haud credo*.
DULL   'Twas not a 'auld grey doe', 'twas a pricket.
HOLOFERNES   Most barbarous intimation! Yet a kind of
      insinuation, as it were, *in via*, in way, of explication,
15   *facere*, as it were, replication, or rather *ostentare*, to
      show, as it were, his inclination, after his undressed,
      unpolished, uneducated, unpruned, untrained, or
      rather unlettered, or ratherest unconfirmed fashion, to
      insert again my *haud credo* for a deer.
20   DULL   I said the deer was not a 'auld grey doe', 'twas a
      pricket.
HOLOFERNES   Twice-sod simplicity, *bis coctus*!
      O, thou monster Ignorance, how deformed dost thou
            look!
NATHANIEL
      Sir, he hath never fed of the dainties that are bred in a
            book.
25   He hath not eat paper, as it were; he hath not drunk
      ink. His intellect is not replenished; he is only an
      animal, only sensible in the duller parts.
      And such barren plants are set before us that we
            thankful should be –
      Which we of taste and feeling are – for those parts
            that do fructify in us more than he.
      For as it would ill become me to be vain, indiscreet, or
30   a fool,
      So were there a patch set on learning, to see him in a
            school.
      But *omne bene*, say I, being of an old father's mind;
      Many can brook the weather, that love not the wind.
DULL
      You two are bookmen: can you tell me by your wit
      What was a month old at Cain's birth, that's not five
35   weeks old as yet?
HOLOFERNES   Dictynna, goodman Dull. Dictynna,
      goodman Dull.
DULL   What is Dictynna?
NATHANIEL   A title to Phoebe, to Luna, to the moon.
HOLOFERNES
40   The moon was a month old, when Adam was no more,
      And raught not to five weeks when he came to five
            score.
      Th'allusion holds in the exchange.
DULL   'Tis true indeed: the collusion holds in the
      exchange.

HOLOFERNES   God comfort thy capacity! I say   45
      th'allusion holds in the exchange.
DULL   And I say the pollution holds in the exchange, for
      the moon is never but a month old; and I say beside
      that 'twas a pricket that the Princess killed.
HOLOFERNES   Sir Nathaniel, will you hear an extemporal   50
      epitaph on the death of the deer? And, to humour the
      ignorant, call I the deer the Princess killed a pricket.
NATHANIEL   *Perge*, good Master Holofernes, *perge*, so it
      shall please you to abrogate scurrility.
HOLOFERNES   I will something affect the letter, for it   55
      argues facility.
      The preyful Princess pierced and pricked a pretty
            pleasing pricket;
            Some say a sore, but not a sore till now made
                  sore with shooting.
      The dogs did yell, put 'l' to sore, then sorrel jumps
            from thicket;
            Or pricket, sore, or else sorrel, the people fall
                  a-hooting.   60
      If sore be sore, then 'l' to sore makes fifty sores
            o'sorrel:
            Of one sore I an hundred make by adding but
                  one more 'l'.
NATHANIEL   A rare talent!
DULL   If a talent be a claw, look how he claws him with
      a talent.   65
HOLOFERNES   This is a gift that I have – simple, simple;
      a foolish extravagant spirit, full of forms, figures, shapes,
      objects, ideas, apprehensions, motions, revolutions.
      These are begot in the ventricle of memory, nourished
      in the womb of *pia mater* and delivered upon the   70
      mellowing of occasion. But the gift is good in those in
      whom it is acute, and I am thankful for it.
NATHANIEL   Sir, I praise the Lord for you, and so may
      my parishioners, for their sons are well tutored by you,
      and their daughters profit very greatly under you. You 75
      are a good member of the commonwealth.
HOLOFERNES   *Mehercle!* If their sons be ingenious,
      they shall want no instruction. If their daughters be
      capable, I will put it to them. But *vir sapit qui pauca
      loquitur*. A soul feminine saluteth us.   80

            Enter JAQUENETTA *with a letter and* COSTARD,
                          the Clown.

JAQUENETTA   God give you good morrow, Master
      Person.
HOLOFERNES   Master Person, quasi pierce-one? And if
      one should be pierced, which is the one?
COSTARD   Marry, Master Schoolmaster, he that is likest   85
      to a hogshead.
HOLOFERNES   'Of piercing a hogshead' – a good lustre
      of conceit in a turf of earth, fire enough for a flint,
      pearl enough for a swine: 'tis pretty, it is well.
JAQUENETTA   Good Master Parson, be so good as read   90
      me this letter. It was given me by Costard and sent me
      from Don Armado. I beseech you read it.

HOLOFERNES

Fauste precor, gelida quando pecus omne sub umbra
Ruminat –

and so forth. Ah, good old Mantuan, I may speak of
thee as the traveller doth of Venice:

Venetia, Venetia,

Chi non ti vede, non ti pretia.

Old Mantuan, old Mantuan, who understandeth thee
not, loves thee not.

[*Sings.*]　　　　　　Ut, re, sol, la, mi, fa.

Under pardon, sir, what are the contents? Or rather as
Horace says in his – What, my soul, verses?

NATHANIEL　　Ay, sir, and very learned.

HOLOFERNES　　Let me hear a staff, a stanza, a verse.
Lege, domine.

NATHANIEL [*Reads.*]

'If love make me forsworn, how shall I swear to love?
　　Ah, never faith could hold, if not to beauty vowed.
Though to myself forsworn, to thee I'll faithful
　　　　prove.
　　　　Those thoughts to me were oaks, to thee like osiers
　　　　　　bowed.
Study his bias leaves, and makes his book thine eyes,
　　Where all those pleasures live, that art would
　　　　comprehend.
If knowledge be the mark, to know thee shall suffice:
　　Well learned is that tongue, that well can thee
　　　　commend,
All ignorant that soul, that sees thee without wonder;
　　Which is to me some praise, that I thy parts
　　　　admire.
Thy eye Jove's lightning bears, thy voice his dreadful
　　　　thunder,
　　Which, not to anger bent, is music and sweet fire.
Celestial as thou art, O, pardon love this wrong,
　　That sings heaven's praise, with such an earthly
　　　　tongue.'

HOLOFERNES　　You find not the apostrophus and so miss
the accent. Let me supervise the canzonet. [*Takes the
letter.*] Here are only numbers ratified, but for the
elegancy, facility and golden cadence of poesy, *caret.*
Ovidius Naso was the man; and why indeed 'Naso', but
for smelling out the odoriferous flowers of fancy, the
jerks of invention? *Imitari* is nothing. So doth the
hound his master, the ape his keeper, the tired horse his
rider. But, damosella virgin, was this directed to you?

JAQUENETTA　　Ay, sir, from one Monsieur Berowne, one
of the strange queen's lords.

HOLOFERNES　　I will overglance the superscript. *To the
snow-white hand of the most beauteous Lady Rosaline.* I
will look again on the intellect of the letter, for the
nomination of the party writing to the person written
unto: *Your Ladyship's in all desired employment,
Berowne.* Sir Nathaniel, this Berowne is one of the
votaries with the King, and here he hath framed a letter
to a sequent of the stranger queen's, which accidentally,
or by the way of progression, hath miscarried. Trip and

go, my sweet, deliver this paper into the royal hand of the
King; it may concern much. Stay not thy compliment: I
forgive thy duty, adieu.

JAQUENETTA　　Good Costard, go with me. Sir, God save
your life.

COSTARD　　Have with thee, my girl.

Exeunt Costard and Jaquenetta.

NATHANIEL　　Sir, you have done this in the fear of God,
very religiously; and as a certain father saith –

HOLOFERNES　　Sir, tell not me of the father, I do fear
colourable colours. But to return to the verses: did
they please you, Sir Nathaniel?

NATHANIEL　　Marvellous well for the pen.

HOLOFERNES　　I do dine today at the father's of a certain
pupil of mine, where if, before repast, it shall please
you to gratify the table with a grace, I will, on my
privilege I have with the parents of the foresaid child
or pupil, undertake your *ben venuto*; where I will prove
those verses to be very unlearned, neither savouring of
poetry, wit, nor invention. I beseech your society.

NATHANIEL　　And thank you too, for society, saith the
text, is the happiness of life.

HOLOFERNES　　And certes, the text most infallibly
concludes it. [*to Dull*] Sir, I do invite you too: you shall
not say me nay. *Pauca verba.* Away, the gentles are at
their game and we will to our recreation.　　　*Exeunt.*

4.3　*Enter* BEROWNE *with a paper in his hand, alone.*

BEROWNE　　The King, he is hunting the deer; I am
coursing myself. They have pitched a toil; I am toiling
in a pitch, pitch that defiles. Defile, a foul word. Well,
set thee down, sorrow, for so they say the fool said, and
so say I, and I the fool. Well proved, wit! By the Lord,
this love is as mad as Ajax. It kills sheep, it kills me – I
a sheep. Well proved again, o'my side! I will not love; if
I do, hang me! I'faith, I will not. O, but her eye! By this
light, but for her eye, I would not love her – yes, for her
two eyes. Well, I do nothing in the world but lie, and lie
in my throat. By heaven, I do love, and it hath taught
me to rhyme, and to be melancholy. And here is part of
my rhyme, and here my melancholy. Well, she hath one
o'my sonnets already. The clown bore it, the fool sent
it, and the lady hath it. Sweet clown, sweeter fool,
sweetest lady! By the world, I would not care a pin if
the other three were in. Here comes one, with a paper.
God give him grace to groan! [*Stands aside.*]

Enter the KING *with a paper.*

KING　　Ay me!

BEROWNE　　Shot, by heaven! Proceed, sweet Cupid,
thou hast thumped him with thy birdbolt under the
left pap. In faith, secrets!

KING [*Reads.*]

'So sweet a kiss the golden sun gives not
　　To those fresh morning drops upon the rose,
As thy eye-beams when their fresh rays have smote

The night of dew that on my cheeks down flows.
Nor shines the silver moon one half so bright
　Through the transparent bosom of the deep
As doth thy face, through tears of mine, give light.
30　Thou shin'st in every tear that I do weep,
No drop but as a coach doth carry thee:
　So ridest thou triumphing in my woe.
Do but behold the tears that swell in me,
　And they thy glory through my grief will show.
35 But do not love thyself: then thou will keep
My tears for glasses, and still make me weep.
O Queen of queens, how far dost thou excel,
No thought can think, nor tongue of mortal tell.'
How shall she know my griefs? I'll drop the paper.
40 Sweet leaves shade folly. Who is he comes here?
　　　[*Steps aside.*]

　　　Enter LONGAVILLE *with a paper.*

　What, Longaville, and reading? Listen, ear!
BEROWNE　Now, in thy likeness, one more fool appear!
LONGAVILLE　Ay me, I am forsworn!
BEROWNE　Why, he comes in like a perjure, wearing
45　papers.
KING　In love, I hope. Sweet fellowship in shame.
BEROWNE　One drunkard loves another of the name.
LONGAVILLE　Am I the first that have been perjured so?
BEROWNE
　I could put thee in comfort: not by two that I know.
50　Thou makest the triumviry, the corner-cap of society,
　The shape of Love's Tyburn, that hangs up simplicity.
LONGAVILLE
　I fear these stubborn lines lack power to move.
　O sweet Maria, empress of my love,
　These numbers will I tear and write in prose.
BEROWNE
55　O, rhymes are guards on wanton Cupid's hose:
　Disfigure not his shop.
LONGAVILLE　　　　This same shall go.
　[*Reads the sonnet.*]
　'Did not the heavenly rhetoric of thine eye,
　　'Gainst whom the world cannot hold argument,
　Persuade my heart to this false perjury?
60　Vows for thee broke deserve not punishment.
　A woman I forswore, but I will prove,
　　Thou being a goddess, I forswore not thee.
　My vow was earthly, thou a heavenly love;
　　Thy grace being gained, cures all disgrace in me.
65　Vows are but breath, and breath a vapour is:
　　Then thou, fair sun, which on my earth dost shine,
　Exhal'st this vapour-vow; in thee it is.
　　If broken then, it is no fault of mine;
　If by me broke, what fool is not so wise
70　To lose an oath to win a paradise?'
BEROWNE
　This is the liver vein, which makes flesh a deity,
　A green goose a goddess. Pure, pure idolatry.
　God amend us, God amend! We are much out o'th' way.

　　　Enter DUMAINE *with a paper.*

LONGAVILLE
　By whom shall I send this? Company? Stay.
　　[*Stands aside.*]
BEROWNE　All hid, all hid, an old infant play.　　75
　Like a demi-god here sit I in the sky,
　And wretched fools' secrets heedfully o'er-eye.
　More sacks to the mill. O heavens, I have my wish!
　Dumaine transformed! Four woodcocks in a dish!
DUMAINE　O most divine Kate!　　80
BEROWNE　O most profane coxcomb!
DUMAINE　By heaven, the wonder in a mortal eye!
BEROWNE　By earth, she is not, corporal: there you lie.
DUMAINE　Her amber hairs for foul hath amber quoted.
BEROWNE　An amber-coloured raven was well noted.　　85
DUMAINE　As upright as the cedar.
BEROWNE　　　　　　　Stoop, I say.
　Her shoulder is with child.
DUMAINE　　　　　　As fair as day.
BEROWNE
　Ay, as some days, but then no sun must shine.
DUMAINE　O that I had my wish!
LONGAVILLE　　　　　And I had mine!
KING　And I mine too, good Lord!　　90
BEROWNE
　Amen, so I had mine! Is not that a good word?
DUMAINE　I would forget her, but a fever she
　Reigns in my blood and will remembered be.
BEROWNE　A fever in your blood? Why then incision
　Would let her out in saucers. Sweet misprision!　　95
DUMAINE　Once more I'll read the ode that I have writ.
BEROWNE　Once more I'll mark how love can vary wit.
DUMAINE [*Reads his sonnet.*]
　'On a day – alack the day! –
　Love, whose month is ever May,
　Spied a blossom passing fair　　100
　Playing in the wanton air.
　Through the velvet leaves the wind,
　All unseen, can passage find;
　That the lover, sick to death,
　Wished himself the heaven's breath.　　105
　"Air," quoth he, "thy cheeks may blow;
　Air, would I might triumph so!
　But, alack, my hand is sworn
　Ne'er to pluck thee from thy thorn.
　Vow, alack, for youth unmeet,　　110
　Youth so apt to pluck a sweet.
　Do not call it sin in me,
　That I am forsworn for thee;
　Thou for whom Jove would swear
　Juno but an Ethiop were,　　115
　And deny himself for Jove,
　Turning mortal for thy love."'
　This will I send, and something else more plain,
　That shall express my true love's fasting pain.
　O, would the King, Berowne and Longaville　　120

Were lovers too! Ill, to example ill,
Would from my forehead wipe a perjured note,
For none offend where all alike do dote.

LONGAVILLE [*Comes forward.*]
Dumaine, thy love is far from charity,
125   That in love's grief desirest society.
You may look pale, but I should blush, I know,
To be o'erheard and taken napping so.

KING [*Comes forward.*]
Come, sir, you blush. As his your case is such.
You chide at him, offending twice as much.
130   You do not love Maria? Longaville
Did never sonnet for her sake compile,
Nor never lay his wreathed arms athwart
His loving bosom to keep down his heart.
I have been closely shrouded in this bush,
135   And marked you both, and for you both did blush.
I heard your guilty rhymes, observed your fashion,
Saw sighs reek from you, noted well your passion.
'Ay me!' says one, 'O Jove!' the other cries.
One, her hairs were gold; crystal the other's eyes.
[*to Longaville*] You would for paradise break faith and
140   troth;
[*to Dumaine*] And Jove for your love would infringe an
oath.
What will Berowne say when that he shall hear
Faith infringed which such zeal did swear?
How will he scorn, how will he spend his wit!
145   How will he triumph, leap and laugh at it!
For all the wealth that ever I did see,
I would not have him know so much by me.

BEROWNE [*Comes forward.*]
Now step I forth to whip hypocrisy.
Ah, good my liege, I pray thee pardon me.
150   Good heart, what grace hast thou thus to reprove
These worms for loving, that art most in love?
Your eyes do make no coaches; in your tears
There is no certain princess that appears;
You'll not be perjured, 'tis a hateful thing;
155   Tush, none but minstrels like of sonneting!
But are you not ashamed? Nay, are you not,
All three of you, to be thus much o'ershot?
You found his mote, the King your mote did see;
But I a beam do find in each of three.
160   O, what a scene of foolery have I seen,
Of sighs, of groans, of sorrow and of teen!
O me, with what strict patience have I sat,
To see a king transformed to a gnat!
To see great Hercules whipping a gig,
165   And profound Solomon to tune a jig,
And Nestor play at push-pin with the boys,
And critic Timon laugh at idle toys.
Where lies thy grief? O, tell me, good Dumaine.
And, gentle Longaville, where lies thy pain?
170   And where my liege's? All about the breast?
A caudle, ho!

KING   Too bitter is thy jest.

Are we betrayed thus to thy over-view?

BEROWNE   Not you to me, but I betrayed by you;
I that am honest, I that hold it sin
To break the vow I am engaged in –   175
I am betrayed by keeping company
With men like you, men of inconstancy.
When shall you see me write a thing in rhyme?
Or groan for Joan? Or spend a minute's time
In pruning me? When shall you hear that I   180
Will praise a hand, a foot, a face, an eye,
A gait, a state, a brow, a breast, a waist,
A leg, a limb –

KING   Soft! Whither away so fast?
A true man, or a thief, that gallops so?

BEROWNE   I post from love. Good lover, let me go.   185

Enter JAQUENETTA *with a letter and* COSTARD,
the Clown.

JAQUENETTA   God bless the King!

KING   What present hast thou there?

COSTARD   Some certain treason.

KING   What makes treason here?

COSTARD   Nay, it makes nothing, sir.

KING   If it mar nothing neither,
The treason and you go in peace away together.

JAQUENETTA
I beseech your grace let this letter be read.   190
Our person misdoubts it; 'twas treason, he said.

KING
Berowne, read it over.   [*Berowne reads the letter.*]
               Where hadst thou it?

JAQUENETTA   Of Costard.

KING   Where hadst thou it?

COSTARD   Of Dun Adramadio, Dun Adramadio.   195
    [*Berowne tears the letter up.*]

KING   How now, what is in you? Why dost thou tear it?

BEROWNE
A toy, my liege, a toy. Your grace needs not fear it.

LONGAVILLE
It did move him to passion and therefore let's hear it.

DUMAINE [*Picks up the pieces.*]
It is Berowne's writing and here is his name.

BEROWNE [*to Costard*]
Ah, you whoreson loggerhead, you were born to do
  me shame.   200
Guilty, my lord, guilty: I confess, I confess.

KING   What?

BEROWNE
That you three fools lacked me fool to make up the
  mess.
He, he and you – and you, my liege – and I
Are pick-purses in love and we deserve to die.   205
O, dismiss this audience and I shall tell you more.

DUMAINE   Now the number is even.

BEROWNE   True, true, we are four.
Will these turtles be gone?

KING   Hence, sirs, away!

COSTARD
   Walk aside the true folk and let the traitors stay.
               Exeunt Costard and Jaquenetta.

210 BEROWNE   Sweet lords, sweet lovers, O, let us embrace!
   As true we are as flesh and blood can be,
   The sea will ebb and flow, heaven show his face;
   Young blood doth not obey an old decree.
   We cannot cross the cause why we were born;
215   Therefore of all hands must we be forsworn.
  KING
   What, did these rent lines show some love of thine?
  BEROWNE
   'Did they?' quoth you! Who sees the heavenly
     Rosaline
   That, like a rude and savage man of Ind,
   At the first opening of the gorgeous east,
220   Bows not his vassal head and, strucken blind,
   Kisses the base ground with obedient breast?
   What peremptory eagle-sighted eye
   Dares look upon the heaven of her brow
   That is not blinded by her majesty?
225 KING   What zeal, what fury hath inspired thee now?
   My love, her mistress, is a gracious moon;
   She, an attending star, scarce seen a light.
  BEROWNE   My eyes are then no eyes, nor I Berowne.
   O, but for my love, day would turn to night!
230   Of all complexions the culled sovereignty
   Do meet as at a fair in her fair cheek,
   Where several worthies make one dignity,
   Where nothing wants, that want itself doth seek.
   Lend me the flourish of all gentle tongues –
235   Fie, painted rhetoric! O, she needs it not.
   To things of sale, a seller's praise belongs:
   She passes praise; then praise too short doth blot.
   A withered hermit, five-score winters worn,
   Might shake off fifty, looking in her eye.
240   Beauty doth varnish age, as if new born,
   And gives the crutch the cradle's infancy.
   O, 'tis the sun that maketh all things shine.
  KING   By heaven, thy love is black as ebony!
  BEROWNE   Is ebony like her? O word divine!
245   A wife of such wood were felicity.
   O, who can give an oath? Where is a book?
   That I may swear beauty doth beauty lack
   If that she learn not of her eye to look.
   No face is fair that is not full so black.
250 KING   O paradox! Black is the badge of hell,
   The hue of dungeons and the school of night;
   And beauty's crest becomes the heavens well.
  BEROWNE
   Devils soonest tempt, resembling spirits of light.
   O, if in black my lady's brows be decked,
255   It mourns that painting and usurping hair
   Should ravish doters with a false aspect;
   And therefore is she born to make black fair.
   Her favour turns the fashion of the days,
   For native blood is counted painting now;

   And therefore red, that would avoid dispraise,   260
   Paints itself black, to imitate her brow.
  DUMAINE
   To look like her are chimney-sweepers black.
  LONGAVILLE
   And since her time are colliers counted bright.
  KING   And Ethiops of their sweet complexion crack.
  DUMAINE   Dark needs no candles now, for dark is light.   265
  BEROWNE   Your mistresses dare never come in rain,
   For fear their colours should be washed away.
  KING   'Twere good yours did; for, sir, to tell you plain,
   I'll find a fairer face not washed today.
  BEROWNE   I'll prove her fair, or talk till doomsday here.   270
  KING   No devil will fright thee then so much as she.
  DUMAINE   I never knew man hold vile stuff so dear.
  LONGAVILLE [*Shows his shoe.*]
   Look, here's thy love, my foot and her face see.
  BEROWNE   O, if the streets were paved with thine eyes,
   Her feet were much too dainty for such tread.   275
  DUMAINE   O, vile! Then, as she goes, what upward lies
   The street should see as she walked overhead.
  KING   But what of this? Are we not all in love?
  BEROWNE   O, nothing so sure, and thereby all forsworn.
  KING
   Then leave this chat and, good Berowne, now prove   280
   Our loving lawful and our faith not torn.
  DUMAINE   Ay, marry, there; some flattery for this evil.
  LONGAVILLE   O, some authority how to proceed.
   Some tricks, some quillets how to cheat the devil.
  DUMAINE   Some salve for perjury.
  BEROWNE   O, 'tis more than need.   285
   Have at you then, affection's men-at-arms.
   Consider what you first did swear unto:
   To fast, to study and to see no woman –
   Flat treason 'gainst the kingly state of youth.
   Say, can you fast? Your stomachs are too young,   290
   And abstinence engenders maladies.
   O, we have made a vow to study, lords,
   And in that vow we have forsworn our books;
   For when would you, my liege, or you, or you,
   In leaden contemplation have found out   295
   Such fiery numbers as the prompting eyes
   Of beauty's tutors have enriched you with?
   Other slow arts entirely keep the brain,
   And therefore, finding barren practisers,
   Scarce show a harvest of their heavy toil;   300
   But love, first learned in a lady's eyes,
   Lives not alone immured in the brain
   But with the motion of all elements
   Courses as swift as thought in every power
   And gives to every power a double power,   305
   Above their functions and their offices.
   It adds a precious seeing to the eye:
   A lover's eyes will gaze an eagle blind.
   A lover's ear will hear the lowest sound
   When the suspicious head of theft is stopped.   310
   Love's feeling is more soft and sensible

Than are the tender horns of cockled snails.
Love's tongue proves dainty Bacchus gross in
    taste,
For valour, is not Love a Hercules,
315 Still climbing trees in the Hesperides?
Subtle as Sphinx, as sweet and musical
As bright Apollo's lute, strung with his hair.
And when Love speaks, the voice of all the gods
Make heaven drowsy with the harmony.
320 Never durst poet touch a pen to write
Until his ink were tempered with Love's sighs.
O, then his lines would ravish savage ears
And plant in tyrants mild humility.
From women's eyes this doctrine I derive:
325 They sparkle still the right Promethean fire;
They are the books, the arts, the academes,
That show, contain and nourish all the world;
Else none at all in aught proves excellent.
Then fools you were these women to forswear,
330 Or, keeping what is sworn, you will prove fools.
For wisdom's sake, a word that all men love,
Or, for love's sake, a word that loves all men,
Or, for men's sake, the authors of these women,
Or women's sake, by whom we men are men,
335 Let us once lose our oaths to find ourselves,
Or else we lose ourselves to keep our oaths.
It is religion to be thus forsworn,
For charity itself fulfils the law,
And who can sever love from charity?
340 KING   Saint Cupid, then! And, soldiers, to the field!
BEROWNE
Advance your standards and upon them, lords!
Pell-mell, down with them! But be first advised
In conflict that you get the sun of them.
LONGAVILLE
Now to plain dealing. Lay these glozes by.
345 Shall we resolve to woo these girls of France?
KING   And win them too! Therefore let us devise
Some entertainment for them in their tents.
BEROWNE
First, from the park let us conduct them thither.
Then homeward every man attach the hand
350 Of his fair mistress. In the afternoon
We will with some strange pastime solace them,
Such as the shortness of the time can shape;
For revels, dances, masques and merry hours
Forerun fair Love, strewing her way with flowers.
355 KING   Away, away! No time shall be omitted
That will betime and may by us be fitted.
BEROWNE
Allons, allons!   *Exeunt the King, Longaville*
                                                 and Dumaine.
          Sowed cockle reaped no corn:
     And justice always whirls in equal measure.
     Light wenches may prove plagues to men forsworn;
60   If so, our copper buys no better treasure.   *Exit.*

5.1   *Enter* HOLOFERNES, *the Pedant,*
         NATHANIEL, *the Curate, and* DULL,
                 the Constable.

HOLOFERNES   *Satis quod sufficit.*
NATHANIEL   I praise God for you, sir. Your reasons at
dinner have been sharp and sententious, pleasant
without scurrility, witty without affection, audacious
without impudency, learned without opinion and   5
strange without heresy. I did converse this *quondam*
day with a companion of the King's, who is intituled,
nominated, or called, Don Adriano de Armado.
HOLOFERNES   *Novi hominem tanquam te.* His humour is
lofty, his discourse peremptory, his tongue filed, his   10
eye ambitious, his gait majestical and his general
behaviour vain, ridiculous and thrasonical. He is too
picked, too spruce, too affected, too odd, as it were, too
peregrinate, as I may call it.
NATHANIEL   A most singular and choice epithet.   15
          [*Draws out his table-book.*]
HOLOFERNES   He draweth out the thread of his
verbosity finer than the staple of his argument. I abhor
such fanatical phantasimes, such insociable and point-
device companions, such rackers of orthography, as to
speak 'dout' *sine* 'b', when he should say 'doubt', 'det'   20
when he should pronounce 'debt': d, e, b, t, not d, e, t.
He clepeth a calf 'cauf', half 'hauf'; neighbour *vocatur*
'nebour', neigh abbreviated 'ne'. This is abhominable,
which he would call 'abominable'. It insinuateth me of
insanie. *Ne intelligis, domine?* To make frantic, lunatic.   25
NATHANIEL   *Laus Deo, bone intelligo.*
HOLOFERNES   *Bone?* '*Bone*' for '*bene*'! Priscian a little
scratched; 'twill serve.

          Enter ARMADO, *the Braggart,* MOTH,
                 his Boy, and COSTARD.

NATHANIEL   *Videsne quis venit?*
HOLOFERNES   *Video et gaudeo.*   30
ARMADO   Chirrah!
HOLOFERNES   *Quare* 'chirrah', not 'sirrah'?
ARMADO   Men of peace, well encountered.
HOLOFERNES   Most military sir, salutation.
MOTH [*to Costard*]   They have been at a great feast of   35
languages and stolen the scraps.
COSTARD [*to Moth*]   O, they have lived long on the
alms-basket of words! I marvel thy master hath not
eaten thee for a word, for thou art not so long by the
head as *honorificabilitudinitatibus.* Thou art easier   40
swallowed than a flap-dragon.
MOTH   Peace! The peal begins.
ARMADO [*to Holofernes*]   Monsieur, are you not lettered?
MOTH   Yes, yes! He teaches boys the hornbook. What is
a, b, spelt backward with the horn on his head?   45
HOLOFERNES   Ba, *pueritia*, with a horn added.
MOTH   Ba, most silly sheep with a horn. You hear his
learning.
HOLOFERNES   *Quis, quis*, thou consonant?

MOTH   The last of the five vowels, if you repeat them; or
50   the fifth, if I.

HOLOFERNES   I will repeat them: a, e, i –

MOTH   The sheep. The other two concludes it: o, u.

ARMADO   Now, by the salt wave of the *Mediterraneum*, a
55   sweet touch, a quick venue of wit! Snip-snap, quick
and home! It rejoiceth my intellect. True wit!

MOTH   Offered by a child to an old man – which is
wit-old.

HOLOFERNES   What is the figure? What is the figure?

60   MOTH   Horns.

HOLOFERNES   Thou disputes like an infant. Go, whip
thy gig.

MOTH   Lend me your horn to make one and I will whip
about your infamy *manu cita*. A gig of a cuckold's horn!

65   COSTARD   An I had but one penny in the world, thou
shouldst have it to buy gingerbread. Hold, there is the
very remuneration I had of thy master, thou halfpenny
purse of wit, thou pigeon-egg of discretion. O, an the
heavens were so pleased that thou wert but my bastard,
70   what a joyful father wouldst thou make me! Go to, thou
hast it *ad dunghill*, at the fingers' ends, as they say.

HOLOFERNES   O, I smell false Latin: 'dunghill' for
unguem.

ARMADO   Arts-man, preambulate. We will be singuled
75   from the barbarous. Do you not educate youth at the
charge-house on the top of the mountain?

HOLOFERNES   Or *mons*, the hill.

ARMADO   At your sweet pleasure, for the mountain.

HOLOFERNES   I do, *sans question*.

80   ARMADO   Sir, it is the King's most sweet pleasure and
affection to congratulate the Princess at her pavilion in
the posteriors of this day, which the rude multitude
call the afternoon.

HOLOFERNES   The posterior of the day, most generous
85   sir, is liable, congruent and measurable for the
afternoon. The word is well culled, choice, sweet and
apt, I do assure you, sir, I do assure.

ARMADO   Sir, the King is a noble gentleman, and my
familiar, I do assure ye, very good friend. For what is
90   inward between us, let it pass. I do beseech thee,
remember thy courtesy: I beseech thee, apparel thy
head. And among other importunate and most serious
designs, and of great import indeed too – but let that
pass. For I must tell thee it will please his grace, by the
95   world, sometime to lean upon my poor shoulder and
with his royal finger thus dally with my excrement,
with my mustachio. But, sweet heart, let that pass. By
the world, I recount no fable! Some certain special
honours it pleaseth his greatness to impart to Armado,
100   a soldier, a man of travel, that hath seen the world. But
let that pass. The very all of all is – but, sweet heart, I
do implore secrecy – that the King would have me
present the Princess – sweet chuck – with some
delightful ostentation, or show, or pageant, or antic, or
105   firework. Now, understanding that the curate and your
sweet self are good at such eruptions and sudden

breaking-out of mirth, as it were, I have acquainted
you withal, to the end to crave your assistance.

HOLOFERNES   Sir, you shall present before her the
Nine Worthies. Sir Nathaniel, as concerning some   110
entertainment of time, some show in the posterior of
this day, to be rendered by our assistance, the King's
command and this most gallant, illustrate and learned
gentleman, before the Princess – I say, none so fit as to
present the Nine Worthies.   115

NATHANIEL   Where will you find men worthy enough
to present them?

HOLOFERNES   Joshua, yourself; this gallant gentleman,
Judas Maccabaeus; this swain, because of his great
limb or joint, shall pass Pompey the Great; the page,   120
Hercules.

ARMADO   Pardon, sir, error! He is not quantity enough
for that Worthy's thumb. He is not so big as the end of
his club.

HOLOFERNES   Shall I have audience? He shall present   125
Hercules in minority. His enter and exit shall be
strangling a snake; and I will have an apology for that
purpose.

MOTH   An excellent device! So if any of the audience
hiss, you may cry, 'Well done, Hercules! Now thou   130
crushest the snake!' That is the way to make an offence
gracious, though few have the grace to do it.

ARMADO   For the rest of the Worthies?

HOLOFERNES   I will play three myself.

MOTH   Thrice-worthy gentleman.   135

ARMADO   Shall I tell you a thing?

HOLOFERNES   We attend.

ARMADO   We will have, if this fadge not, an antic. I
beseech you, follow.

HOLOFERNES   *Via*, goodman Dull! Thou hast spoken   140
no word all this while.

DULL   Nor understood none neither, sir.

HOLOFERNES   *Allons!* We will employ thee.

DULL   I'll make one in a dance, or so; or I will play on
the tabor to the Worthies, and let them dance the hay.   145

HOLOFERNES   Most Dull, honest Dull! To our sport,
away!   *Exeunt.*

5.2   *Enter the ladies, the* PRINCESS, ROSALINE,
MARIA and KATHERINE.

PRINCESS   Sweet hearts, we shall be rich ere we depart
If fairings come thus plentifully in.
A lady walled about with diamonds!
Look you what I have from the loving King.

ROSALINE   Madam, came nothing else along with that?   5

PRINCESS
Nothing but this? Yes, as much love in rhyme
As would be crammed up in a sheet of paper
Writ o'both sides the leaf, margin and all,
That he was fain to seal on Cupid's name.

ROSALINE   That was the way to make his godhead wax,   10
For he hath been five thousand year a boy.

KATHERINE   Ay, and a shrewd unhappy gallows too.
ROSALINE
You'll ne'er be friends with him: 'a killed your sister.
KATHERINE   He made her melancholy, sad and heavy;
And so she died. Had she been light, like you,
Of such a merry, nimble, stirring spirit,
She might ha' been a grandam ere she died.
And so may you, for a light heart lives long.
ROSALINE
What's your dark meaning, mouse, of this light word?
KATHERINE   A light condition in a beauty dark.
ROSALINE
We need more light to find your meaning out.
KATHERINE   You'll mar the light by taking it in snuff;
Therefore I'll darkly end the argument.
ROSALINE   Look what you do, you do it still i'th' dark.
KATHERINE   So do not you, for you are a light wench.
ROSALINE   Indeed I weigh not you, and therefore light.
KATHERINE
You weigh me not? O, that's you care not for me!
ROSALINE   Great reason, for past cure is still past care.
PRINCESS   Well bandied both! A set of wit well played.
But, Rosaline, you have a favour too:
Who sent it? And what is it?
ROSALINE   I would you knew.
An if my face were but as fair as yours,
My favour were as great. Be witness this:
Nay, I have verses too, I thank Berowne;
The numbers true, and, were the numbering too,
I were the fairest goddess on the ground.
I am compared to twenty thousand fairs.
O, he hath drawn my picture in his letter!
PRINCESS   Anything like?
ROSALINE   Much in the letters, nothing in the praise.
PRINCESS   Beauteous as ink: a good conclusion.
KATHERINE   Fair as a text B in a copy-book.
ROSALINE
'Ware pencils, ho! Let me not die your debtor,
My red dominical, my golden letter.
O, that your face were not so full of O's!
PRINCESS   A pox of that jest and I beshrew all shrews.
But, Katherine, what was sent to you from fair
    Dumaine?
KATHERINE   Madam, this glove.
PRINCESS   Did he not send you twain?
KATHERINE   Yes, madam, and moreover
Some thousand verses of a faithful lover.
A huge translation of hypocrisy,
Vilely compiled, profound simplicity.
MARIA   This and these pearls to me sent Longaville.
The letter is too long by half a mile.
PRINCESS   I think no less. Dost thou not wish in heart
The chain were longer and the letter short?
MARIA   Ay, or I would these hands might never part.
PRINCESS   We are wise girls to mock our lovers so.
ROSALINE
They are worse fools to purchase mocking so.

That same Berowne I'll torture ere I go.   60
O that I knew he were but in by th' week!
How I would make him fawn, and beg, and seek,
And wait the season, and observe the times,
And spend his prodigal wits in bootless rhymes,
And shape his service wholly to my hests,   65
And make him proud to make me proud that jests!
So pair-taunt-like would I o'ersway his state,
That he should be my fool, and I his fate.
PRINCESS
None are so surely caught, when they are catched,
As wit turned fool. Folly, in wisdom hatched,   70
Hath wisdom's warrant and the help of school
And wit's own grace to grace a learned fool.
ROSALINE
The blood of youth burns not with such excess
As gravity's revolt to wantonness.
MARIA   Folly in fools bears not so strong a note   75
As foolery in the wise when wit doth dote,
Since all the power thereof it doth apply
To prove, by wit, worth in simplicity.

Enter BOYET.

PRINCESS   Here comes Boyet, and mirth is in his face.
BOYET
O, I am stabbed with laughter! Where's her grace?   80
PRINCESS   Thy news, Boyet?
BOYET   Prepare, madam, prepare!
Arm, wenches, arm! Encounters mounted are
Against your peace. Love doth approach disguised,
Armed in arguments: you'll be surprised.
Muster your wits, stand in your own defence,   85
Or hide your heads like cowards and fly hence.
PRINCESS   Saint Denis to Saint Cupid! What are they
That charge their breath against us? Say, scout, say.
BOYET   Under the cool shade of a sycamore
I thought to close mine eyes some half an hour,   90
When, lo, to interrupt my purposed rest,
Toward that shade I might behold addressed
The King and his companions. Warily
I stole into a neighbour thicket by
And overheard what you shall overhear: 95
That, by and by, disguised they will be here.
Their herald is a pretty knavish page
That well by heart hath conned his embassage.
Action and accent did they teach him there:
'Thus must thou speak and thus thy body bear.'   100
And ever and anon they made a doubt
Presence majestical would put him out;
'For', quoth the King, 'an angel shalt thou see;
Yet fear not thou, but speak audaciously.'
The boy replied, 'An angel is not evil;   105
I should have feared her had she been a devil.'
With that all laughed and clapped him on the shoulder,
Making the bold wag by their praises bolder.
One rubbed his elbow thus, and fleered, and swore
A better speech was never spoke before.   110

Another with his finger and his thumb
Cried, '*Via*, we will do't, come what will come!'
The third he capered and cried, 'All goes well!'
The fourth turned on the toe, and down he fell.
115   With that they all did tumble on the ground,
With such a zealous laughter, so profound,
That in this spleen ridiculous appears,
To check their folly, passion's solemn tears.
PRINCESS   But what, but what, come they to visit us?
120   BOYET   They do, they do, and are apparelled thus,
Like Muscovites, or Russians, as I guess.
Their purpose is to parley, court and dance,
And every one his love-suit will advance
Unto his several mistress, which they'll know
125   By favours several which they did bestow.
PRINCESS
And will they so? The gallants shall be tasked;
For, ladies, we will every one be masked,
And not a man of them shall have the grace,
Despite of suit, to see a lady's face.
130   Hold, Rosaline, this favour thou shalt wear,
And then the King will court thee for his dear.
Hold, take thou this, my sweet, and give me thine,
So shall Berowne take me for Rosaline.
And change you favours too; so shall your loves
135   Woo contrary, deceived by these removes.
ROSALINE
Come on, then, wear the favours most in sight.
KATHERINE   But in this changing what is your intent?
PRINCESS   The effect of my intent is to cross theirs.
They do it but in mockery merriment,
140   And mock for mock is only my intent.
Their several counsels they unbosom shall
To loves mistook, and so be mocked withal
Upon the next occasion that we meet,
With visages displayed to talk and greet.
145   ROSALINE   But shall we dance if they desire us to't?
PRINCESS   No, to the death we will not move a foot;
Nor to their penned speech render we no grace,
But while 'tis spoke each turn away her face.
BOYET   Why, that contempt will kill the speaker's heart
150   And quite divorce his memory from his part.
PRINCESS   Therefore I do it, and I make no doubt
The rest will e'er come in, if he be out.
There's no such sport as sport by sport o'erthrown,
To make theirs ours and ours none but our own.
155   So shall we stay, mocking intended game,
And they, well mocked, depart away with shame.
                                   [*Sound trumpet.*]
BOYET
The trumpet sounds. Be masked. The maskers come.

Enter Blackamoors with music, MOTH, *the Boy, with a
speech, and the rest of the Lords disguised.*

MOTH   *All hail the richest beauties on the earth!*
BOYET   Beauties no richer than rich taffeta.
160   MOTH   *A holy parcel of the fairest dames*

[*The ladies turn their backs to him.*]
That ever turned their – backs – to mortal views.
BEROWNE   *Their eyes,* villain, *their eyes.*
MOTH   *That ever turned their eyes to mortal views.*
Out –
BOYET   True! Out indeed!   165
MOTH   *Out of your favours, heavenly spirits, vouchsafe*
Not to behold –
BEROWNE   *Once to behold,* rogue!
MOTH   *Once to behold with your sun-beamed eyes –*
With your sun-beamed eyes –   170
BOYET   They will not answer to that epithet.
You were best call it 'daughter-beamed eyes'.
MOTH   They do not mark me and that brings me out.
BEROWNE
Is this your perfectness? Be gone, you rogue!
                                   Exit Moth.
ROSALINE
What would these strangers? Know their minds, Boyet.   175
If they do speak our language, 'tis our will
That some plain man recount their purposes.
Know what they would.
BOYET   What would you with the Princess?
BEROWNE   Nothing but peace and gentle visitation.
ROSALINE   What would they, say they?   180
BOYET   Nothing but peace and gentle visitation.
ROSALINE
Why, that they have, and bid them so be gone.
BOYET   She says you have it and you may be gone.
KING   Say to her, we have measured many miles
To tread a measure with her on this grass.   185
BOYET   They say that they have measured many a mile
To tread a measure with you on this grass.
ROSALINE   It is not so. Ask them how many inches
Is in one mile? If they have measured many,
The measure then of one is easily told.   190
BOYET   If to come hither you have measured miles,
And many miles, the Princess bids you tell
How many inches doth fill up one mile.
BEROWNE   Tell her we measure them by weary steps.
BOYET   She hears herself.
ROSALINE   How many weary steps,   195
Of many weary miles you have o'ergone,
Are numbered in the travel of one mile?
BEROWNE   We number nothing that we spend for you.
Our duty is so rich, so infinite,
That we may do it still without account.   200
Vouchsafe to show the sunshine of your face,
That we like savages may worship it.
ROSALINE   My face is but a moon and clouded too.
KING   Blessed are clouds, to do as such clouds do.
Vouchsafe, bright moon, and these thy stars, to shine – 205
Those clouds removed – upon our watery eyne.
ROSALINE   O vain petitioner! Beg a greater matter:
Thou now requests but moonshine in the water.
KING
Then, in our measure, do but vouchsafe one change.

210   Thou biddest me beg: this begging is not strange.

ROSALINE
Play music then! Nay, you must do it soon.
                              [Music plays.]
Not yet? No dance! Thus change I like the moon.

KING
Will you not dance? How come you thus estranged?

ROSALINE
You took the moon at full, but now she's changed.

215 KING   Yet still she is the moon and I the man.
The music plays, vouchsafe some motion to it.

ROSALINE   Our ears vouchsafe it.

KING   But your legs should do it.

ROSALINE
Since you are strangers and come here by chance,
We'll not be nice. Take hands. We will not dance.

220 KING   Why take we hands then?

ROSALINE   Only to part friends.
Curtsy, sweet hearts, and so the measure ends.
                               [Music stops.]

KING   More measure of this measure! Be not nice.

ROSALINE   We can afford no more at such a price.

KING   Price you yourselves. What buys your company?

ROSALINE   Your absence only.

225 KING   That can never be.

ROSALINE   Then cannot we be bought. And so adieu –
Twice to your visor and half once to you!

KING   If you deny to dance, let's hold more chat.

ROSALINE   In private then.

KING   I am best pleased with that.
    [They converse apart.]

BEROWNE
230 White-handed mistress, one sweet word with thee.

PRINCESS   Honey, and milk, and sugar: there is three.

BEROWNE   Nay then, two treys, an if you grow so nice,
Metheglin, wort and malmsey. Well run, dice!
There's half-a-dozen sweets.

PRINCESS   Seventh sweet, adieu.

235 Since you can cog, I'll play no more with you.

BEROWNE   One word in secret.

PRINCESS   Let it not be sweet.

BEROWNE   Thou griev'st my gall.

PRINCESS   Gall? Bitter.

BEROWNE   Therefore meet.
    [They converse apart.]

DUMAINE
Will you vouchsafe with me to change a word?

MARIA   Name it.

DUMAINE   Fair lady –

MARIA   Say you so? Fair lord!
Take that for your 'fair lady'.

240 DUMAINE   Please it you,
As much in private and I'll bid adieu.
    [They converse apart.]

KATHERINE
What, was your visor made without a tongue?

LONGAVILLE   I know the reason, lady, why you ask.

KATHERINE   O, for your reason! Quickly, sir, I long.

LONGAVILLE
You have a double tongue within your mask   245
And would afford my speechless visor half.

KATHERINE
'Veal', quoth the Dutchman. Is not veal a calf?

LONGAVILLE   A calf, fair lady.

KATHERINE   No, a fair lord calf.

LONGAVILLE   Let's part the word.

KATHERINE   No, I'll not be your half.
Take all and wean it; it may prove an ox.   250

LONGAVILLE
Look how you butt yourself in these sharp mocks.
Will you give horns, chaste lady? Do not so.

KATHERINE   Then die a calf before your horns do grow.

LONGAVILLE   One word in private with you ere I die.

KATHERINE
Bleat softly then; the butcher hears you cry.   255
    [They converse apart.]

BOYET   The tongues of mocking wenches are as keen
As is the razor's edge invisible,
Cutting a smaller hair than may be seen;
Above the sense of sense, so sensible
Seemeth their conference. Their conceits have wings   260
Fleeter than arrows, bullets, wind, thought, swifter
   things.

ROSALINE
Not one word more, my maids; break off, break off.

BEROWNE   By heaven, all dry-beaten with pure scoff!

KING   Farewell, mad wenches. You have simple wits.
            Exeunt the King, Lords and Blackamoors.

PRINCESS   Twenty adieus, my frozen Muscovites.   265
Are these the breed of wits so wondered at?

BOYET
Tapers they are, with your sweet breaths puffed out.

ROSALINE
Well-liking wits they have; gross, gross, fat, fat.

PRINCESS   O poverty in wit, kingly-poor flout!
Will they not, think you, hang themselves tonight?   270
   Or ever but in visors show their faces?
This pert Berowne was out of countenance quite.

ROSALINE   They were all in lamentable cases.
The King was weeping-ripe for a good word.

PRINCESS   Berowne did swear himself out of all suit.   275

MARIA   Dumaine was at my service, and his sword.
   'Non point,' quoth I; my servant straight was mute.

KATHERINE   Lord Longaville said I came o'er his heart;
   And trow you what he called me?

PRINCESS   Qualm perhaps?

KATHERINE   Yes, in good faith.

PRINCESS   Go, sickness as thou art!   280

ROSALINE
Well, better wits have worn plain statute-caps.
But will you hear? The King is my love sworn.

PRINCESS
And quick Berowne hath plighted faith to me.

KATHERINE   And Longaville was for my service born.

885

285   MARIA   Dumaine is mine as sure as bark on tree.

BOYET   Madam, and pretty mistresses, give ear:
Immediately they will again be here
In their own shapes, for it can never be
They will digest this harsh indignity.

PRINCESS   Will they return?

290   BOYET   They will, they will, God knows;
And leap for joy, though they are lame with blows.
Therefore change favours and, when they repair,
Blow like sweet roses in this summer air.

PRINCESS
How 'blow'? How 'blow'? Speak to be understood.

295   BOYET   Fair ladies masked are roses in their bud;
Dismasked, their damask sweet commixture shown,
Are angels vailing clouds, or roses blown.

PRINCESS   Avaunt, perplexity! What shall we do
If they return in their own shapes to woo?

300   ROSALINE   Good madam, if by me you'll be advised
Let's mock them still, as well known as disguised.
Let us complain to them what fools were here,
Disguised like Muscovites in shapeless gear;
And wonder what they were, and to what end

305   Their shallow shows and prologue vilely penned,
And their rough carriage so ridiculous,
Should be presented at our tent to us.

BOYET   Ladies, withdraw. The gallants are at hand.

PRINCESS   Whip to our tents, as roes runs o'er the land.

Exeunt the Princess and ladies.

Enter the KING *and the rest,* BEROWNE, LONGAVILLE
and DUMAINE, *as themselves.*

310   KING   Fair sir, God save you. Where's the Princess?

BOYET   Gone to her tent. Please it your majesty
Command me any service to her thither?

KING   That she vouchsafe me audience for one word.

BOYET   I will; and so will she, I know, my lord.   *Exit.*

315   BEROWNE   This fellow pecks up wit as pigeons peas
And utters it again when God doth please.
He is wit's pedlar and retails his wares
At wakes and wassails, meetings, markets, fairs;
And we that sell by gross, the Lord doth know,

320   Have not the grace to grace it with such show.
This gallant pins the wenches on his sleeve.
Had he been Adam, he had tempted Eve.
'A can carve too, and lisp. Why, this is he
That kissed his hand away in courtesy.

325   This is the ape of form, Monsieur the Nice,
That when he plays at tables chides the dice
In honourable terms. Nay, he can sing
A mean most meanly; and in ushering
Mend him who can. The ladies call him sweet.

330   The stairs, as he treads on them, kiss his feet.
This is the flower that smiles on everyone,
To show his teeth as white as whale's bone;
And consciences that will not die in debt
Pay him the due of 'honey-tongued Boyet'.

335   KING   A blister on his sweet tongue, with my heart,

That put Armado's page out of his part!

Enter the ladies, the PRINCESS, ROSALINE, MARIA *and*
KATHERINE, *with* BOYET.

BEROWNE
See where it comes! Behaviour, what wert thou
Till this man showed thee, and what art thou now?

KING   All hail, sweet madam, and fair time of day.

PRINCESS   'Fair' in 'all hail' is foul, as I conceive.   340

KING   Construe my speeches better, if you may.

PRINCESS   Then wish me better; I will give you leave.

KING   We came to visit you and purpose now
To lead you to our court. Vouchsafe it then.

PRINCESS
This field shall hold me, and so hold your vow.   345
Nor God nor I delights in perjured men.

KING   Rebuke me not for that which you provoke.
The virtue of your eye must break my oath.

PRINCESS
You nickname virtue: 'vice' you should have spoke;
For virtue's office never breaks men's troth.   350
Now, by my maiden honour, yet as pure
As the unsullied lily, I protest,
A world of torments though I should endure,
I would not yield to be your house's guest,
So much I hate a breaking cause to be   355
Of heavenly oaths, vowed with integrity.

KING   O, you have lived in desolation here,
Unseen, unvisited, much to our shame.

PRINCESS   Not so, my lord. It is not so, I swear.
We have had pastimes here and pleasant game: 360
A mess of Russians left us but of late.

KING   How, madam? Russians?

PRINCESS   Ay, in truth, my lord.
Trim gallants, full of courtship and of state.

ROSALINE   Madam, speak true! It is not so, my lord.
My lady, to the manner of the days,   365
In courtesy gives undeserving praise.
We four indeed confronted were with four
In Russian habit. Here they stayed an hour
And talked apace; and in that hour, my lord,
They did not bless us with one happy word.   370
I dare not call them fools, but this I think,
When they are thirsty, fools would fain have drink.

BEROWNE   This jest is dry to me. My gentle sweet,
Your wits makes wise things foolish. When we greet,
With eyes' best seeing, heaven's fiery eye,   375
By light we lose light. Your capacity
Is of that nature that to your huge store
Wise things seem foolish and rich things but poor.

ROSALINE
This proves you wise and rich, for in my eye –

BEROWNE   I am a fool and full of poverty.   380

ROSALINE   But that you take what doth to you belong,
It were a fault to snatch words from my tongue.

BEROWNE   O, I am yours, and all that I possess.

ROSALINE   All the fool mine?

BEROWNE   I cannot give you less.

385 ROSALINE   Which of the visors was it that you wore?

BEROWNE
Where, when, what visor? Why demand you this?

ROSALINE
There, then, that visor: that superfluous case
That hid the worse and showed the better face.

KING
We were descried. They'll mock us now downright.

390 DUMAINE   Let us confess and turn it to a jest.

PRINCESS
Amazed, my lord? Why looks your highness sad?

ROSALINE
Help! Hold his brows! He'll swoon. Why look you
     pale?
Seasick, I think, coming from Muscovy!

BEROWNE
Thus pour the stars down plagues for perjury.

395   Can any face of brass hold longer out?
Here stand I, lady; dart thy skill at me.
     Bruise me with scorn, confound me with a flout,
Thrust thy sharp wit quite through my ignorance,
     Cut me to pieces with thy keen conceit,

400 And I will wish thee never more to dance,
     Nor never more in Russian habit wait.
O, never will I trust to speeches penned,
     Nor to the motion of a schoolboy's tongue,
Nor never come in visor to my friend,

405   Nor woo in rhyme like a blind harper's song.
Taffeta phrases, silken terms precise,
     Three-piled hyperboles, spruce affectation,
Figures pedantical: these summer flies
     Have blown me full of maggot ostentation.

410 I do forswear them, and I here protest,
     By this white glove – how white the hand, God
          knows! –
Henceforth my wooing mind shall be expressed
     In russet yeas and honest kersey noes.
And, to begin: wench, so God help me, law!

415 My love to thee is sound, *sans* crack or flaw.

ROSALINE   *Sans* '*sans*', I pray you.

BEROWNE   Yet I have a trick
Of the old rage. Bear with me, I am sick;
I'll leave it by degrees. Soft, let us see:
Write 'Lord have mercy on us' on those three.

420 They are infected; in their hearts it lies;
They have the plague and caught it of your eyes.
These lords are visited: you are not free,
For the Lord's tokens on you do I see.

PRINCESS
No, they are free that gave these tokens to us.

425 BEROWNE   Our states are forfeit. Seek not to undo us.

ROSALINE
It is not so; for how can this be true,
That you stand forfeit, being those that sue?

BEROWNE   Peace! for I will not have to do with you.

ROSALINE   Nor shall not if I do as I intend.

BEROWNE [*to the other lords*]
Speak for yourselves. My wit is at an end.   430

KING
Teach us, sweet madam, for our rude transgression
Some fair excuse.

PRINCESS   The fairest is confession.
Were not you here but even now, disguised?

KING   Madam, I was.

PRINCESS   And were you well advised?

KING   I was, fair madam.

PRINCESS   When you then were here,   435
What did you whisper in your lady's ear?

KING   That more than all the world I did respect her.

PRINCESS
When she shall challenge this, you will reject her.

KING   Upon mine honour, no.

PRINCESS   Peace, peace, forbear!
Your oath once broke, you force not to forswear.   440

KING   Despise me when I break this oath of mine.

PRINCESS   I will; and therefore keep it. Rosaline,
What did the Russian whisper in your ear?

ROSALINE   Madam, he swore that he did hold me dear
As precious eyesight and did value me   445
Above this world; adding thereto, moreover,
That he would wed me, or else die my lover.

PRINCESS   God give thee joy of him. The noble lord
Most honourably doth uphold his word.

KING
What mean you, madam? By my life, my troth,   450
I never swore this lady such an oath.

ROSALINE   By heaven you did! And to confirm it plain,
You gave me this; but take it, sir, again.

KING   My faith and this the Princess I did give.
I knew her by this jewel on her sleeve.   455

PRINCESS   Pardon me, sir, this jewel did she wear,
And Lord Berowne, I thank him, is my dear.
What! Will you have me or your pearl again?

BEROWNE   Neither of either; I remit both twain.
I see the trick on't. Here was a consent,   460
Knowing aforehand of our merriment,
To dash it like a Christmas comedy.
Some carry-tale, some please-man, some slight zany,
Some mumble-news, some trencher-knight, some Dick
That smiles his cheek in years and knows the trick   465
To make my lady laugh when she's disposed,
Told our intents before; which, once disclosed,
The ladies did change favours and then we,
Following the signs, wooed but the sign of she.
Now, to our perjury to add more terror,   470
We are again forsworn in will and error.
Much upon this 'tis. [*to Boyet*] And might not you
Forestall our sport, to make us thus untrue?
Do not you know my lady's foot by th' squier,
     And laugh upon the apple of her eye?   475
And stand between her back, sir, and the fire,
     Holding a trencher, jesting merrily?
You put our page out – Go, you are allowed;

Die when you will, a smock shall be your shroud.
480   You leer upon me, do you? There's an eye
Wounds like a leaden sword.

BOYET   Full merrily
Hath this brave manage, this career, been run.

BEROWNE   Lo, he is tilting straight. Peace! I have done.

Enter COSTARD, the Clown.

Welcome, pure wit! Thou partest a fair fray.

485 COSTARD   O Lord, sir, they would know
Whether the three Worthies shall come in or no.

BEROWNE   What, are there but three?

COSTARD   No, sir, but it is vara fine,
For every one pursents three.

BEROWNE   And three times thrice is nine.

COSTARD

Not so, sir – under correction, sir – I hope it is not so.
You cannot beg us, sir, I can assure you, sir; we know
490   what we know.
I hope, sir, three times thrice, sir –

BEROWNE   Is not nine?

COSTARD   Under correction, sir, we know whereuntil it
doth amount.

BEROWNE   By Jove, I always took three threes for nine.

495 COSTARD   O Lord, sir, it were pity you should get your
living by reckoning, sir.

BEROWNE   How much is it?

COSTARD   O Lord, sir, the parties themselves, the
actors, sir, will show whereuntil it doth amount. For
500   mine own part, I am, as they say, but to parfect one
man in one poor man – Pompion the Great, sir.

BEROWNE   Art thou one of the Worthies?

COSTARD   It pleased them to think me worthy of
Pompey the Great. For mine own part, I know not the
505   degree of the Worthy, but I am to stand for him.

BEROWNE   Go bid them prepare.

COSTARD   We will turn it finely off, sir; we will take
some care.   *Exit.*

KING

Berowne, they will shame us. Let them not approach.

BEROWNE

510   We are shame-proof, my lord; and 'tis some policy
To have one show worse than the King's and his
    company.

KING   I say they shall not come.

PRINCESS   Nay, my good lord, let me o'errule you now.
That sport best pleases that doth least know how –
515   Where zeal strives to content and the contents
Dies in the zeal of that which it presents;
Their form confounded makes most form in mirth,
When great things labouring perish in their birth.

BEROWNE   A right description of our sport, my lord.

Enter ARMADO, the Braggart.

520 ARMADO   Anointed, I implore so much expense of thy
royal sweet breath as will utter a brace of words.
    [Armado and the King talk apart.]

PRINCESS   Doth this man serve God?

BEROWNE   Why ask you?

PRINCESS   'A speaks not like a man of God his making.

ARMADO   That is all one, my fair, sweet, honey monarch; 525
for, I protest, the schoolmaster is exceeding fantastical;
too, too vain; too, too vain; but we will put it, as they say,
to *fortuna de la guerra.* [*Gives the King a paper.*] I wish
you the peace of mind, most royal couplement.   *Exit.*

KING   Here is like to be a good presence of Worthies. He 530
presents Hector of Troy; the swain, Pompey the Great;
the parish curate, Alexander; Armado's page, Hercules;
the pedant, Judas Maccabaeus.
And if these four Worthies in their first show thrive,
These four will change habits and present the other five. 535

BEROWNE   There is five in the first show.

KING   You are deceived: 'tis not so.

BEROWNE   The pedant, the braggart, the hedge-priest,
the fool and the boy.
Abate throw at novum, and the whole world again 540
Cannot pick out five such, take each one in his vein.

KING

The ship is under sail and here she comes amain.

Enter COSTARD as Pompey.

COSTARD   *I Pompey am –*

BEROWNE   You lie, you are not he.

COSTARD   *I Pompey am –*

BOYET   With leopard's head on knee.

BEROWNE

Well said, old mocker. I must needs be friends with
  thee. 545

COSTARD   *I Pompey am, Pompey surnamed the Big.*

DUMAINE   The 'Great'.

COSTARD   It is 'Great', sir: *Pompey surnamed the Great,*
That oft in field, with targe and shield, did make my foe
  to sweat;
And travelling along this coast, I here am come by
  chance, 550
And lay my arms before the legs of this sweet lass of
  France.
If your ladyship would say, 'Thanks, Pompey', I had
  done.

PRINCESS   Great thanks, great Pompey.

COSTARD   'Tis not so much worth, but I hope I was
perfect. I made a little fault in 'Great'. 555

BEROWNE   My hat to a halfpenny, Pompey proves the
best Worthy.

Enter NATHANIEL, the Curate, for Alexander.

NATHANIEL

When in the world I lived, I was the world's
  commander;
By east, west, north and south, I spread my conquering
  might;
My scutcheon plain declares that I am Alisander. 560

BOYET

Your nose says no, you are not; for it stands too right.

BEROWNE
  Your nose smells 'no' in this, most tender-smelling
    knight.
PRINCESS
  The conqueror is dismayed. Proceed, good Alexander.
NATHANIEL
  When in the world I lived, I was the world's commander –
BOYET   Most true, 'tis right: you were so, Alisander.
BEROWNE   Pompey the Great –
COSTARD   Your servant, and Costard.
BEROWNE   Take away the conqueror; take away Alisander.
COSTARD   [*to Nathaniel*]   O sir, you have overthrown
  Alisander the conqueror. You will be scraped out of the
  painted cloth for this. Your lion, that holds his pole-axe
  sitting on a close-stool, will be given to Ajax. He will be
  the ninth Worthy. A conqueror, and afeard to speak?
  Run away for shame, Alisander.   *Nathaniel retires.*
  There, an't shall please you, a foolish mild man; an
  honest man, look you, and soon dashed. He is a
  marvellous good neighbour, faith, and a very good
  bowler; but for Alisander, alas you see how 'tis – a little
  o'erparted. But there are Worthies a-coming will speak
  their mind in some other sort.
PRINCESS   Stand aside, good Pompey.

  Enter HOLOFERNES, *the Pedant, as Judas,*
      and MOTH, *the Boy, as Hercules.*

HOLOFERNES   *Great Hercules is presented by this imp,*
    Whose club killed Cerberus, that three-headed canus,
    And when he was a babe, a child, a shrimp,
      Thus did he strangle serpents in his manus.
    Quoniam he seemeth in minority,
    Ergo I come with this apology.
  Keep some state in thy exit, and vanish.

                         Moth retires.

  Judas I am –
DUMAINE   A Judas!
HOLOFERNES   Not Iscariot, sir.
  Judas I am, ycleped Maccabaeus.
DUMAINE   Judas Maccabaeus clipped is plain Judas.
BEROWNE   A kissing traitor. How, art thou proved Judas?
HOLOFERNES   *Judas I am –*
DUMAINE   The more shame for you, Judas.
HOLOFERNES   What mean you, sir?
BOYET   To make Judas hang himself.
HOLOFERNES   Begin, sir; you are my elder.
BEROWNE   Well followed: Judas was hanged on an elder.
HOLOFERNES   I will not be put out of countenance.
BEROWNE   Because thou hast no face.
HOLOFERNES   What is this?
BOYET   A cittern-head.
DUMAINE   The head of a bodkin.
BEROWNE   A death's face in a ring.
LONGAVILLE   The face of an old Roman coin, scarce
  seen.
BOYET   The pommel of Caesar's falchion.
DUMAINE   The carved-bone face on a flask.

BEROWNE   Saint George's half-cheek in a brooch.
DUMAINE   Ay, and in a brooch of lead.
BEROWNE   Ay, and worn in the cap of a tooth-drawer.
  And now forward, for we have put thee in countenance.
HOLOFERNES   You have put me out of countenance.   615
BEROWNE   False! We have given thee faces.
HOLOFERNES   But you have outfaced them all.
BEROWNE   An thou wert a lion, we would do so.
BOYET   Therefore, as he is an ass, let him go.
  And so adieu, sweet Jude. Nay, why dost thou stay?   620
DUMAINE   For the latter end of his name.
BEROWNE
  For the ass to the Jude? Give it him. Jud-as, away!
HOLOFERNES
  This is not generous, not gentle, not humble.
BOYET
  A light for Monsieur Judas! It grows dark; he may
    stumble.   *Holofernes retires.*
PRINCESS   Alas, poor Maccabaeus, how hath he been   625
  baited!

      Enter ARMADO, *the Braggart, as Hector.*

BEROWNE   Hide thy head, Achilles! Here comes Hector
  in arms.
DUMAINE   Though my mocks come home by me, I will
  now be merry.   630
KING   Hector was but a Trojan in respect of this.
BOYET   But is this Hector?
KING   I think Hector was not so clean-timbered.
LONGAVILLE   His leg is too big for Hector's.
DUMAINE   More calf, certain.   635
BOYET   No, he is best endued in the small.
BEROWNE   This cannot be Hector.
DUMAINE   He's a god or a painter, for he makes faces.
ARMADO   *The armipotent Mars, of lances the almighty,*
    Gave Hector a gift –   640
DUMAINE   A gilt nutmeg.
BEROWNE   A lemon.
LONGAVILLE   Stuck with cloves.
DUMAINE   No, cloven.
ARMADO   Peace!   645
  The armipotent Mars, of lances the almighty,
    Gave Hector a gift, the heir of Ilion;
  A man so breathed that certain he would fight, yea,
    From morn till night, out of his pavilion.
  I am that flower –   650
DUMAINE   That mint!
LONGAVILLE   That columbine!
ARMADO   Sweet Lord Longaville, rein thy tongue.
LONGAVILLE   I must rather give it the rein, for it runs
  against Hector.   655
DUMAINE   Ay, and Hector's a greyhound.
ARMADO   The sweet war-man is dead and rotten. Sweet
  chucks beat not the bones of the buried. When he
  breathed, he was a man. But I will forward with my
  device. Sweet royalty, bestow on me the sense of   660
  hearing. [*Berowne steps forth.*]

PRINCESS   Speak, brave Hector; we are much delighted.

ARMADO   I do adore thy sweet grace's slipper.

BOYET   Loves her by the foot.

665 DUMAINE   He may not by the yard.

ARMADO   *This Hector far surmounted Hannibal;*
    The party is gone –

COSTARD   Fellow Hector, she is gone! She is two
months on her way.

670 ARMADO   What meanest thou?

COSTARD   Faith, unless you play the honest Trojan, the
poor wench is cast away: she's quick, the child brags in
her belly already. 'Tis yours.

ARMADO   Dost thou infamonize me among potentates?
675   Thou shalt die!

COSTARD   Then shall Hector be whipped for Jaquenetta
that is quick by him and hanged for Pompey that is
dead by him.

DUMAINE   Most rare Pompey!

680 BOYET   Renowned Pompey!

BEROWNE   Greater than 'Great'. Great, great, great
Pompey! Pompey the huge!

DUMAINE   Hector trembles.

BEROWNE   Pompey is moved. More Ates, more Ates!
685   Stir them on, stir them on!

DUMAINE   Hector will challenge him.

BEROWNE   Ay, if 'a have no more man's blood in his
belly than will sup a flea.

ARMADO   By the north pole, I do challenge thee.

690 COSTARD   I will not fight with a pole like a northern
man. I'll slash, I'll do it by the sword. I bepray you, let
me borrow my arms again.

DUMAINE   Room for the incensed Worthies.

COSTARD   I'll do it in my shirt.

695 DUMAINE   Most resolute Pompey!

MOTH   Master, let me take you a buttonhole lower. Do
you not see, Pompey is uncasing for the combat. What
mean you? You will lose your reputation.

ARMADO   Gentlemen and soldiers, pardon me. I will
700   not combat in my shirt.

DUMAINE   You may not deny it. Pompey hath made the
challenge.

ARMADO   Sweet bloods, I both may and will.

BEROWNE   What reason have you for't?

705 ARMADO   The naked truth of it is, I have no shirt. I go
woolward for penance.

MOTH   True, and it was enjoined him in Rome for want
of linen. Since when, I'll be sworn he wore none but a
dishclout of Jaquenetta's, and that 'a wears next his
710   heart for a favour.

    Enter a messenger, Monsieur MARCADÉ.

MARCADÉ   God save you, madam.

PRINCESS   Welcome, Marcadé,
But that thou interruptest our merriment.

MARCADÉ   I am sorry, madam, for the news I bring
Is heavy in my tongue. The King, your father –

PRINCESS   Dead, for my life!

MARCADÉ   Even so; my tale is told. 715

BEROWNE
Worthies, away! The scene begins to cloud.

ARMADO   For mine own part, I breathe free breath. I
have seen the day of wrong through the little hole of
discretion and I will right myself like a soldier.

    Exeunt Worthies.

KING   How fares your majesty? 720

PRINCESS   Boyet, prepare. I will away tonight.

KING   Madam, not so. I do beseech you, stay.

PRINCESS   Prepare, I say. I thank you, gracious lords,
For all your fair endeavours, and entreat,
Out of a new-sad soul, that you vouchsafe 725
In your rich wisdom to excuse or hide
The liberal opposition of our spirits,
If over-boldly we have borne ourselves
In the converse of breath. Your gentleness
Was guilty of it. Farewell, worthy lord! 730
A heavy heart bears not a nimble tongue.
Excuse me so, coming too short of thanks
For my great suit so easily obtained.

KING   The extreme parts of time extremely forms
All causes to the purpose of his speed 735
And often at his very loose decides
That which long process could not arbitrate.
And though the mourning brow of progeny
Forbid the smiling courtesy of love
The holy suit which fain it would convince, 740
Yet, since love's argument was first on foot,
Let not the cloud of sorrow jostle it
From what it purposed; since to wail friends lost
Is not by much so wholesome-profitable
As to rejoice at friends but newly found. 745

PRINCESS
I understand you not. My griefs are double.

BEROWNE
Honest plain words best pierce the ear of grief;
And by these badges understand the King.
For your fair sakes have we neglected time,
Played foul play with our oaths. Your beauty, ladies, 750
Hath much deformed us, fashioning our humours
Even to the opposed end of our intents;
And what in us hath seemed ridiculous –
As love is full of unbefitting strains,
All wanton as a child, skipping and vain, 755
Formed by the eye and therefore, like the eye,
Full of strange shapes, of habits and of forms,
Varying in subjects as the eye doth roll
To every varied object in his glance;
Which parti-coated presence of loose love 760
Put on by us, if, in your heavenly eyes,
Have misbecomed our oaths and gravities,
Those heavenly eyes that look into these faults,
Suggested us to make. Therefore, ladies,
Our love being yours, the error that love makes 765
Is likewise yours. We to ourselves prove false
By being once false, for ever to be true

To those that make us both – fair ladies, you.
And even that falsehood, in itself a sin,
Thus purifies itself and turns to grace.

PRINCESS   We have received your letters full of love,
Your favours, the ambassadors of love,
And in our maiden counsel rated them
At courtship, pleasant jest and courtesy,
As bombast and as lining to the time.
But more devout than this in our respects
Have we not been; and therefore met your loves
In their own fashion, like a merriment.

DUMAINE
Our letters, madam, showed much more than jest.

LONGAVILLE   So did our looks.

ROSALINE   We did not quote them so.

KING   Now, at the latest minute of the hour,
Grant us your loves.

PRINCESS   A time, methinks, too short
To make a world-without-end bargain in.
No, no, my lord, your grace is perjured much,
Full of dear guiltiness; and therefore this:
If for my love – as there is no such cause –
You will do aught, this shall you do for me:
Your oath I will not trust, but go with speed
To some forlorn and naked hermitage,
Remote from all the pleasures of the world,
There stay until the twelve celestial signs
Have brought about the annual reckoning.
If this austere insociable life
Change not your offer made in heat of blood;
If frosts and fasts, hard lodging and thin weeds,
Nip not the gaudy blossoms of your love,
But that it bear this trial and last love;
Then, at the expiration of the year,
Come challenge me, challenge me by these deserts,
And, by this virgin palm now kissing thine,
I will be thine. And, till that instance, shut
My woeful self up in a mourning house,
Raining the tears of lamentation
For the remembrance of my father's death.
If this thou do deny, let our hands part,
Neither entitled in the other's heart.

KING   If this, or more than this, I would deny,
To flatter up these powers of mine with rest,
The sudden hand of death close up mine eye!
Hence, hermit then – my heart is in thy breast.
   [*They converse apart.*]

DUMAINE   But what to me, my love? But what to me?
A wife?

KATHERINE   A beard, fair health and honesty;
With threefold love, I wish you all these three.

DUMAINE   O, shall I say, 'I thank you, gentle wife'?

KATHERINE   Not so, my lord. A twelvemonth and a day
I'll mark no words that smooth-faced wooers say.
Come when the King doth to my lady come;
Then, if I have much love, I'll give you some.

DUMAINE   I'll serve thee true and faithfully till then.

KATHERINE   Yet swear not, lest ye be forsworn again.
   [*They converse apart.*]

LONGAVILLE   What says Maria?

MARIA   At the twelvemonth's end
I'll change my black gown for a faithful friend.

LONGAVILLE
I'll stay with patience, but the time is long.

MARIA   The liker you; few taller are so young.
   [*They converse apart.*]

BEROWNE   Studies, my lady? Mistress, look on me.
Behold the window of my heart, mine eye,
What humble suit attends thy answer there.
Impose some service on me for thy love.

ROSALINE   Oft have I heard of you, my lord Berowne,
Before I saw you, and the world's large tongue
Proclaims you for a man replete with mocks,
Full of comparisons and wounding flouts,
Which you on all estates will execute
That lie within the mercy of your wit.
To weed this wormwood from your fruitful brain
And therewithal to win me, if you please –
Without the which I am not to be won –
You shall this twelvemonth term from day to day
Visit the speechless sick and still converse
With groaning wretches; and your task shall be
With all the fierce endeavour of your wit
To enforce the pained impotent to smile.

BEROWNE
To move wild laughter in the throat of death?
It cannot be, it is impossible.
Mirth cannot move a soul in agony.

ROSALINE   Why, that's the way to choke a gibing spirit,
Whose influence is begot of that loose grace
Which shallow laughing hearers give to fools.
A jest's prosperity lies in the ear
Of him that hears it, never in the tongue
Of him that makes it. Then, if sickly ears,
Deafed with the clamours of their own dear groans,
Will hear your idle scorns, continue then,
And I will have you and that fault withal;
But, if they will not, throw away that spirit,
And I shall find you empty of that fault,
Right joyful of your reformation.

BEROWNE
A twelvemonth? Well, befall what will befall,
I'll jest a twelvemonth in an hospital.

PRINCESS [*to the King*]
Ay, sweet my lord, and so I take my leave.

KING   No, madam, we will bring you on your way.

BEROWNE   Our wooing doth not end like an old play:
Jack hath not Jill. These ladies' courtesy
Might well have made our sport a comedy.

KING   Come, sir, it wants a twelvemonth and a day,
And then 'twill end.

BEROWNE   That's too long for a play.

Enter ARMADO, *the Braggart.*

ARMADO   Sweet majesty, vouchsafe me –
PRINCESS   Was not that Hector?
DUMAINE   The worthy knight of Troy.
870   ARMADO   I will kiss thy royal finger and take leave. I am
a votary; I have vowed to Jaquenetta to hold the plough
for her sweet love three year. But, most esteemed
greatness, will you hear the dialogue that the two
learned men have compiled, in praise of the owl and the
875   cuckoo? It should have followed in the end of our show.
KING   Call them forth quickly; we will do so.
ARMADO   Holla! Approach.

Enter all.

This side is Hiems, winter; this Ver, the spring: the one
maintained by the owl, th'other by the cuckoo. Ver, begin.

The Song.

880   VER   When daisies pied and violets blue
                And lady-smocks all silver-white
            And cuckoo-buds of yellow hue
                Do paint the meadows with delight,
            The cuckoo then on every tree
885   Mocks married men; for thus sings he:
                'Cuckoo!
            Cuckoo, cuckoo!' O, word of fear,
            Unpleasing to a married ear.

            When shepherds pipe on oaten straws
890   And merry larks are ploughmen's clocks,

When turtles tread and rooks and daws,
    And maidens bleach their summer smocks,
The cuckoo then, on every tree,
Mocks married men; for thus sings he:
    'Cuckoo!   895
Cuckoo, cuckoo!' O, word of fear,
Unpleasing to a married ear.

HIEMS   When icicles hang by the wall
            And Dick the shepherd blows his nail
        And Tom bears logs into the hall   900
            And milk comes frozen home in pail,
        When blood is nipped and ways be foul,
        Then nightly sings the staring owl:
            'Tu-whit, Tu-whoo!'
        A merry note,   905
        While greasy Joan doth keel the pot.

        When all aloud the wind doth blow
            And coughing drowns the parson's saw
        And birds sit brooding in the snow
            And Marian's nose looks red and raw,   910
        When roasted crabs hiss in the bowl,
        Then nightly sings the staring owl:
            'Tu-whit, Tu-whoo!'
        A merry note,
        While greasy Joan doth keel the pot.   915

ARMADO   The words of Mercury are harsh after the
songs of Apollo. You that way, we this way.   *Exeunt.*

Macbeth

Macbeth was not published until it appeared in the First Folio in 1623, but was almost certainly written in 1606, three years after the accession of James VI of Scotland to the throne of England as James I, and some months after the discovery of the Gunpowder Plot of November 1605, to which it may allude, especially in the Porter's jocular speeches. 'The Scottish play', as theatrical superstition dubs it, has been thought to have been written as a compliment to the king, who believed himself descended from Banquo and had written a work on witchcraft, *Daemonology* (1597, reprinted 1606). It has often been assumed that the first performance took place in July or August of 1606, during the state visit of James's brother-in-law, King Christian of Denmark, but there is no direct evidence for this. The only record of a contemporary performance is an account by Simon Forman, who saw the play in 1611. The play's attitude towards witchcraft is ambiguous, and while it deals in other matters topical in the new regime, it does not necessarily endorse James's unionist policies or offer support to any royalist orthodoxies.

The text that was printed in the Folio is short, less than two-thirds the average length of the other tragedies. It is also problematic in that some short passages in two scenes, 3.5 and 4.1, involving Hecate, Queen of the Witches and including two songs (referred to only by their opening phrases ('Come away, come away, *etc.*', 'Black spirits, *etc.*'), appear to be interpolations, probably written for Thomas Middleton's play *The Witch* (not then in print). While this position is now generally accepted, there remains uncertainty about several issues, such as the date when the interpolations may have been made and the reasons for their insertion. The extent of Middleton's involvement with the text of *Macbeth* is still debated, but it may not have extended beyond these passages.

Shakespeare's principal source was the Scottish section of Raphael Holinshed's *Chronicles*, possibly the 1577 edition; he had drawn on Holinshed for his English history plays and also for *King Lear*, written not long before *Macbeth*. He followed Holinshed's account of Macbeth's career in considerable detail but supplemented it with material drawn from the reigns of other Scottish kings. Changes of emphasis included the idealisation of Duncan, an inept ruler in Holinshed, and the suppression of Banquo's role in Duncan's assassination. Shakespeare may have consulted other works on Scottish history such as George Buchanan's *Rerum Scoticarum Historia* (1582) and perhaps John Leslie's *De Origine, Moribus, et Rebus Gestis Scotorum* (1578), although both existed only in Latin. Seneca's *Medea* may well have supplied suggestions for Lady Macbeth.

The play has always been popular on the stage, and since the 1660s has been continuously in production. Until the middle of the eighteenth century the text used was mostly that of William Davenant's adaptation (1664), which omitted the Porter and other scenes considered indecorous but introduced new scenes and gave particular prominence to the witches. Attempts to restore Shakespeare's text were made by David Garrick, but not until Samuel Phelps's production of 1847 did the singing witches disappear, and then not permanently. The nineteenth century saw the growth of interest in textual authenticity, and in the early twentieth the first attempt to return to early modern staging was made by William Poel in 1909. Although it has been said that no actor ever made his name in the part of Macbeth, almost all male actors of any stature have tried. Many female actors, however, have triumphed as his Lady. There have been numerous film versions of the play, and it has inspired works in a variety of media, including paintings, operas, poetry and novels.

The Arden text is based on the 1623 First Folio.

Duncan, KING of Scotland
MALCOLM   *his elder son*
DONALBAIN   *his younger son*

MACBETH, Thane of Glamis
LADY   *Macbeth's wife*
BANQUO
FLEANCE   *Banquo's son*
MACDUFF, Thane of Fife
WIFE   *Macduff's wife*
SON   *Macduff's son*

LENNOX
ROSS
ANGUS   *Thanes of Scotland*
MENTEITH
CAITHNESS

SIWARD, Earl of Northumberland
YOUNG SIWARD   *his son*

FIRST WITCH
SECOND WITCH   *three weird sisters*
THIRD WITCH
HECATE
Three other WITCHES
APPARITIONS

CAPTAIN
SEYTON   *retainer in Macbeth's household*
PORTER   *in Macbeth's household*
OLD MAN

Three MURDERERS
Other MURDERERS

DOCTOR   *at the English court*
DOCTOR   *in Macbeth's household*
Waiting GENTLEWOMAN   *in Macbeth's household*
LORDS, THANES
SERVANTS
MESSENGERS
SOLDIER

Attendants, Soldiers

Macbeth

1.1 *Thunder and lightning. Enter three* WITCHES.

1 WITCH   When shall we three meet again?
  In thunder, lightning, or in rain?
2 WITCH   When the hurly-burly's done,
  When the battle's lost, and won.
3 WITCH   That will be ere the set of sun.
1 WITCH   Where the place?
2 WITCH   Upon the heath.
3 WITCH   There to meet with Macbeth.
1 WITCH   I come, Gray-Malkin.
2 WITCH   Paddock calls.
3 WITCH   Anon.
ALL   Fair is foul, and foul is fair,
  Hover through the fog and filthy air.   *Exeunt.*

1.2   *Alarum within. Enter* KING Duncan,
     MALCOLM, DONALBAIN, LENNOX,
     with Attendants, meeting a bleeding Captain.

KING   What bloody man is that? He can report,
  As seemeth by his plight, of the revolt
  The newest state.
MALCOLM   This is the sergeant,
  Who like a good and hardy soldier fought
  'Gainst my captivity. Hail, brave friend.
  Say to the King the knowledge of the broil,
  As thou didst leave it.
CAPTAIN   Doubtful it stood,
  As two spent swimmers, that do cling together,
  And choke their art. The merciless Macdonald
  (Worthy to be a rebel, for to that
  The multiplying villainies of nature
  Do swarm upon him) from the Western Isles
  Of kerns and galloglasses is supplied,
  And Fortune, on his damned quarry smiling,
  Showed like a rebel's whore. But all's too weak:
  For brave Macbeth (well he deserves that name),
  Disdaining Fortune, with his brandished steel,
  Which smoked with bloody execution,
  Like Valour's minion, carved out his passage,
  Till he faced the slave,
  Which ne'er shook hands, nor bade farewell to him,
  Till he unseamed him from the nave to th' chops,
  And fixed his head upon our battlements.
KING   O valiant cousin, worthy gentleman.
CAPTAIN   As whence the sun 'gins his reflection,
  Shipwrecking storms and direful thunders,
  So from that spring, whence comfort seemed to come,
  Discomfort swells: mark, King of Scotland, mark,
  No sooner justice had, with valour armed,
  Compelled these skipping kerns to trust their heels,
  But the Norwegian lord, surveying vantage,
  With furbished arms, and new supplies of men,
  Began a fresh assault.
KING
  Dismayed not this our captains, Macbeth and
    Banquo?

CAPTAIN   Yes, as sparrows, eagles, or the hare, the lion.   35
  If I say sooth, I must report they were
  As cannons over-charged with double cracks,
  So they doubly redoubled strokes upon the foe.
  Except they meant to bathe in reeking wounds,
  Or memorize another Golgotha,   40
  I cannot tell. But I am faint;
  My gashes cry for help.
KING   So well thy words become thee as thy wounds,
  They smack of honour both. Go get him surgeons.
            Exit Captain with Attendants.

            Enter ROSS *and* ANGUS.

  Who comes here?
MALCOLM   The worthy Thane of Ross.   45
LENNOX   What a haste looks through his eyes.
  So should he look, that seems to speak things
    strange.
ROSS   God save the King.
KING   Whence cam'st thou, worthy thane?
ROSS   From Fife, great King,
  Where the Norwegian banners flout the sky,   50
  And fan our people cold.
  Norway himself, with terrible numbers,
  Assisted by that most disloyal traitor,
  The Thane of Cawdor, began a dismal conflict,
  Till that Bellona's bridegroom, lapped in proof,   55
  Confronted him with self-comparisons,
  Point against point, rebellious arm 'gainst arm,
  Curbing his lavish spirit; and to conclude,
  The victory fell on us.
KING   Great happiness.
ROSS
  That now Sweno, the Norways' king, craves
    composition.   60
  Nor would we deign him burial of his men,
  Till he disbursed, at Saint Colme's Inch,
  Ten thousand dollars, to our general use.
KING   No more that Thane of Cawdor shall deceive
  Our bosom interest. Go pronounce his present death,   65
  And with his former title greet Macbeth.
ROSS   I'll see it done.
KING
  What he hath lost, noble Macbeth hath won.   *Exeunt.*

1.3   *Thunder. Enter the three* WITCHES.

1 WITCH   Where hast thou been, sister?
2 WITCH   Killing swine.
3 WITCH   Sister, where thou?
1 WITCH   A sailor's wife had chestnuts in her lap
  And munched, and munched, and munched.
  'Give me,' quoth I.   5
  'Aroynt thee, witch,' the rump-fed ronyon cries.
  Her husband's to Aleppo gone, Master o'th' Tiger:
  But in a sieve I'll thither sail,
  And like a rat without a tail,

10 I'll do, I'll do, and I'll do.

2 WITCH   I'll give thee a wind.

1 WITCH   Th'art kind.

3 WITCH   And I another.

1 WITCH   I myself have all the other,

15 And the very ports they blow,
All the quarters that they know,
I'th' shipman's card.
I'll drain him dry as hay:
Sleep shall neither night nor day

20 Hang upon his penthouse lid:
He shall live a man forbid.
Weary sev'nights nine times nine
Shall he dwindle, peak, and pine:
Though his bark cannot be lost,

25 Yet it shall be tempest-tossed.
Look what I have.

2 WITCH   Show me, show me.

1 WITCH   Here I have a pilot's thumb,
Wrecked as homeward he did come.   [*Drum within*]

30 3 WITCH   A drum, a drum:
Macbeth doth come.

ALL   The weïrd sisters, hand in hand,
Posters of the sea and land,
Thus do go, about, about,

35 Thrice to thine, and thrice to mine,
And thrice again, to make up nine.
Peace, the charm's wound up.

Enter MACBETH *and* BANQUO.

MACBETH   So foul and fair a day I have not seen.

BANQUO   How far is't called to Forres? What are these,

40 So withered and so wild in their attire,
That look not like th'inhabitants o'th' earth,
And yet are on't? Live you, or are you aught
That man may question? You seem to
    understand me,
By each at once her choppy finger laying

45 Upon her skinny lips. You should be women,
And yet your beards forbid me to interpret
That you are so.

MACBETH   Speak if you can: what are you?

1 WITCH
All hail Macbeth, hail to thee, Thane of Glamis.

2 WITCH
All hail Macbeth, hail to thee, Thane of Cawdor.

3 WITCH

50 All hail Macbeth, that shalt be king hereafter.

BANQUO   Good sir, why do you start, and seem to fear
Things that do sound so fair? – I'th' name of truth,
Are ye fantastical, or that indeed
Which outwardly ye show? My noble partner

55 You greet with present grace, and great prediction
Of noble having and of royal hope,
That he seems rapt withal. To me you speak not.
If you can look into the seeds of time,
And say which grain will grow, and which will not,

Speak then to me, who neither beg nor fear   60
Your favours, nor your hate.

1 WITCH   Hail.

2 WITCH   Hail.

3 WITCH   Hail.

1 WITCH   Lesser than Macbeth, and greater.   65

2 WITCH   Not so happy, yet much happier.

3 WITCH   Thou shalt get kings, though thou be none:
So all hail Macbeth, and Banquo.

1 WITCH   Banquo, and Macbeth, all hail.

MACBETH   Stay, you imperfect speakers, tell me more.   70
By Finel's death, I know I am Thane of Glamis,
But how of Cawdor? The Thane of Cawdor lives
A prosperous gentleman: and to be king
Stands not within the prospect of belief,
No more than to be Cawdor. Say from whence   75
You owe this strange intelligence, or why
Upon this blasted heath you stop our way
With such prophetic greeting? Speak, I charge you.
                                Witches vanish.

BANQUO   The earth hath bubbles, as the water has,
And these are of them. Whither are they vanished?   80

MACBETH   Into the air; and what seemed corporal,
Melted, as breath into the wind.
Would they had stayed.

BANQUO   Were such things here as we do speak about?
Or have we eaten on the insane root,   85
That takes the reason prisoner?

MACBETH   Your children shall be kings.

BANQUO   You shall be king.

MACBETH   And Thane of Cawdor too: went it not so?

BANQUO
To th' self-same tune and words. Who's here?

Enter ROSS *and* ANGUS.

ROSS   The King hath happily received, Macbeth,   90
The news of thy success; and when he reads
Thy personal venture in the rebels' fight,
His wonders and his praises do contend
Which should be thine, or his. Silenced with
    that,
In viewing o'er the rest o'th' self-same day,   95
He finds thee in the stout Norwegian ranks,
Nothing afeared of what thyself didst make,
Strange images of death. As thick as tale
Came post with post, and every one did bear
Thy praises in his kingdom's great defence   100
And poured them down before him.

ANGUS   We are sent
To give thee from our royal master thanks,
Only to herald thee into his sight
•Not pay thee.

ROSS   And for an earnest of a greater honour,   105
He bade me, from him, call thee Thane of Cawdor:
In which addition, hail most worthy thane,
For it is thine.

BANQUO   What, can the devil speak true?

MACBETH
　The Thane of Cawdor lives. Why do you dress me
　In borrowed robes?
10 ANGUS　　　　　　　Who was the Thane lives yet,
　But under heavy judgement bears that life
　Which he deserves to lose.
　Whether he was combined with those of Norway,
　Or did line the rebel with hidden help
15 And vantage, or that with both he laboured
　In his country's wrack, I know not,
　But treasons capital, confessed and proved
　Have overthrown him.
MACBETH [*aside*]　　　Glamis and Thane of Cawdor:
　The greatest is behind. – Thanks for your pains.
　[*to Banquo*] Do you not hope your children shall be
20　　kings
　When those that gave the Thane of Cawdor to me
　Promised no less to them?
BANQUO　　　　　　　That, trusted home,
　Might yet enkindle you unto the crown,
　Besides the Thane of Cawdor. But 'tis strange:
25 And oftentimes, to win us to our harm,
　The instruments of darkness tell us truths,
　Win us with honest trifles, to betray's
　In deepest consequence.
　Cousins, a word, I pray you.
MACBETH [*aside*]　　　　　Two truths are told
30 As happy prologues to the swelling act
　Of the imperial theme. – I thank you, gentlemen. –
　This supernatural soliciting
　Cannot be ill; cannot be good. If ill,
　Why hath it given me earnest of success,
35 Commencing in a truth? I am Thane of Cawdor.
　If good, why do I yield to that suggestion
　Whose horrid image doth unfix my hair,
　And make my seated heart knock at my ribs,
　Against the use of nature? Present fears
40 Are less than horrible imaginings.
　My thought, whose murder yet is but fantastical,
　Shakes so my single state of man
　That function is smothered in surmise,
　And nothing is, but what is not.
45 BANQUO　Look how our partner's rapt.
MACBETH [*aside*]
　If chance will have me king, why chance may crown
　　me,
　Without my stir.
BANQUO　　　　　New honours come upon him,
　Like our strange garments, cleave not to their
　　mould,
　But with the aid of use.
MACBETH [*aside*]　　　Come what come may,
50 Time, and the hour, runs through the roughest day.
BANQUO　Worthy Macbeth, we stay upon your leisure.
MACBETH
　Give me your favour. My dull brain was wrought
　With things forgotten. Kind gentlemen, your pains

Are registered, where every day I turn
　The leaf to read them. Let us toward the King. 155
　Think upon what hath chanced; and at more time,
　The interim having weighed it, let us speak
　Our free hearts each to other.
BANQUO　　　　　　　Very gladly.
MACBETH　Till then, enough: come, friends.　*Exeunt.*

1.4　*Flourish. Enter* KING Duncan, LENNOX,
　　　MALCOLM, DONALBAIN *and Attendants.*

KING　Is execution done on Cawdor? Or not
　Those in commission yet returned?
MALCOLM　　　　　　　My liege,
　They are not yet come back. But I have spoke
　With one that saw him die, who did report,
　That very frankly he confessed his treasons, 5
　Implored your highness' pardon, and set forth
　A deep repentance. Nothing in his life
　Became him like the leaving it. He died
　As one that had been studied in his death,
　To throw away the dearest thing he owed, 10
　As 'twere a careless trifle.
KING　　　　　　　There's no art
　To find the mind's construction in the face:
　He was a gentleman on whom I built
　An absolute trust.

　　Enter MACBETH, BANQUO, ROSS *and* ANGUS.

　　　　　　　O worthiest cousin,
　The sin of my ingratitude even now 15
　Was heavy on me. Thou art so far before,
　That swiftest wing of recompense is slow
　To overtake thee. Would thou hadst less deserved,
　That the proportion both of thanks, and payment,
　Might have been mine. Only I have left to say, 20
　More is thy due, than more than all can pay.
MACBETH　The service and the loyalty I owe,
　In doing it, pays itself. Your highness' part
　Is to receive our duties; and our duties
　Are to your throne and state, children and servants, 25
　Which do but what they should, by doing everything
　Safe toward your love and honour.
KING　　　　　　　Welcome hither.
　I have begun to plant thee, and will labour
　To make thee full of growing. Noble Banquo,
　That hast no less deserved, nor must be known 30
　No less to have done so. Let me enfold thee
　And hold thee to my heart.
BANQUO　　　　　　　There if I grow
　The harvest is your own.
KING　　　　　　　My plenteous joys,
　Wanton in fullness, seek to hide themselves
　In drops of sorrow. Sons, kinsmen, thanes, 35
　And you whose places are the nearest, know:
　We will establish our estate upon
　Our eldest, Malcolm, whom we name hereafter,

The Prince of Cumberland, which honour must, 40
Not unaccompanied, invest him only.
But signs of nobleness, like stars, shall shine
On all deservers. From hence to Inverness,
And bind us further to you.

MACBETH   The rest is labour which is not used for you; 45
I'll be myself the harbinger, and make joyful
The hearing of my wife with your approach.
So, humbly take my leave.

KING   My worthy Cawdor.

MACBETH [*aside*]
The Prince of Cumberland: that is a step
On which I must fall down, or else o'er-leap,
For in my way it lies. Stars, hide your fires, 50
Let not light see my black and deep desires.
The eye wink at the hand; yet let that be
Which the eye fears, when it is done, to see.   *Exit.*

KING   True, worthy Banquo, he is full so valiant,
And in his commendations, I am fed: 55
It is a banquet to me. Let's after him,
Whose care is gone before to bid us welcome.
It is a peerless kinsman.   *Flourish. Exeunt.*

1.5   *Enter Macbeth's wife* [LADY] *alone with a letter.*

LADY   *They met me in the day of success, and I have learned*
by the perfectest report, they have more in them than mortal
knowledge. When I burned in desire to question them
further, they made themselves air, into which they vanished.
Whiles I stood rapt in the wonder of it, came missives from 5
the King, who all-hailed me 'Thane of Cawdor', by which
title before these weird sisters saluted me, and referred me to
the coming on of time, with 'Hail King that shalt be'. This
have I thought good to deliver thee, my dearest partner of
greatness, that thou mightst not lose the dues of rejoicing by 10
being ignorant of what greatness is promised thee. Lay it to
thy heart, and farewell.
Glamis thou art, and Cawdor, and shalt be
What thou art promised. Yet do I fear thy nature,
It is too full o'th' milk of human kindness 15
To catch the nearest way. Thou wouldst be great,
Art not without ambition, but without
The illness should attend it. What thou wouldst highly,
That wouldst thou holily; wouldst not play false,
And yet wouldst wrongly win. Thou'dst have, great
    Glamis, 20
That which cries, 'Thus thou must do', if thou have it;
And that which rather thou dost fear to do,
Than wishest should be undone. Hie thee hither,
That I may pour my spirits in thine ear,
And chastise with the valour of my tongue 25
All that impedes thee from the golden round,
Which fate and metaphysical aid doth seem
To have thee crowned withal.

Enter Messenger.

What is your tidings?

MESSENGER   The King comes here tonight.

LADY   Thou'rt mad to say it.
Is not thy master with him? Who, were't so, 30
Would have informed for preparation.

MESSENGER
So please you, it is true: our thane is coming.
One of my fellows had the speed of him,
Who, almost dead for breath, had scarcely more
Than would make up his message.

LADY   Give him tending, 35
He brings great news.   *Exit Messenger.*
                The raven himself is hoarse
That croaks the fatal entrance of Duncan
Under my battlements. Come you spirits
That tend on mortal thoughts, unsex me here,
And fill me from the crown to the toe, top-full 40
Of direst cruelty. Make thick my blood,
Stop up th'access and passage to remorse,
That no compunctious visitings of nature
Shake my fell purpose, nor keep peace between
Th'effect and it. Come to my woman's breasts, 45
And take my milk for gall, you murdering
    ministers,
Wherever, in your sightless substances,
You wait on nature's mischief. Come thick night,
And pall thee in the dunnest smoke of hell,
That my keen knife see not the wound it makes, 50
Nor heaven peep through the blanket of the dark
To cry, 'Hold, hold'.

Enter MACBETH.

                Great Glamis, worthy Cawdor,
Greater than both, by the all-hail hereafter,
Thy letters have transported me beyond
This ignorant present, and I feel now 55
The future in the instant.

MACBETH   My dearest love,
Duncan comes here tonight.

LADY   And when goes hence?

MACBETH   Tomorrow, as he purposes.

LADY   O never
Shall sun that morrow see.
Your face, my thane, is as a book, where men 60
May read strange matters; to beguile the time,
Look like the time, bear welcome in your eye,
Your hand, your tongue; look like the innocent
    flower,
But be the serpent under't. He that's coming
Must be provided for; and you shall put 65
This night's great business into my dispatch,
Which shall to all our nights and days to come,
Give solely sovereign sway and masterdom.

MACBETH   We will speak further.

LADY   Only look up clear;
To alter favour ever is to fear. 70
Leave all the rest to me.   *Exeunt.*

1.6 *Hautboys and Torches. Enter* KING
Duncan, MALCOLM, DONALBAIN,
BANQUO, LENNOX, MACDUFF, ROSS,
ANGUS *and Attendants.*

KING   This castle hath a pleasant seat, the air
Nimbly and sweetly recommends itself
Unto our gentle senses.

BANQUO   This guest of summer,
The temple-haunting martlet, does approve,
5   By his loved mansionry, that the heaven's breath
Smells wooingly here. No jutty frieze,
Buttress, nor coin of vantage, but this bird
Hath made his pendent bed, and procreant cradle:
Where they must breed and haunt, I have observed
The air is delicate.

Enter LADY.

10 KING   See, see, our honoured hostess.
The love that follows us, sometime is our trouble,
Which still we thank as love. Herein I teach you
How you shall bid God yield us for your pains,
And thank us for your trouble.

LADY   All our service,
15 In every point twice done, and then done double,
Were poor and single business, to contend
Against those honours deep and broad wherewith
Your majesty loads our house. For those of old,
And the late dignities heaped up to them,
We rest your hermits.

20 KING   Where's the Thane of Cawdor?
We coursed him at the heels, and had a purpose
To be his purveyor. But he rides well,
And his great love, sharp as his spur, hath holp him
To his home before us. Fair and noble hostess,
We are your guest tonight.

25 LADY   Your servants ever,
Have theirs, themselves, and what is theirs in count,
To make their audit at your highness' pleasure,
Still to return your own.

KING   Give me your hand.
Conduct me to mine host: we love him highly,
30 And shall continue our graces towards him.
By your leave, hostess.   *Exeunt.*

1.7 *Hautboys. Torches. Enter a Sewer and
divers Servants with dishes and service
over the stage. Then enter* MACBETH.

MACBETH
If it were done, when 'tis done, then 'twere well
It were done quickly. If th'assassination
Could trammel up the consequence, and catch
With his surcease, success: that but this blow
5   Might be the be-all and the end-all, here,
But here, upon this bank and shoal of time,
We'd jump the life to come. But in these cases,
We still have judgement here, that we but teach

Bloody instructions, which being taught, return
To plague th'inventor. This even-handed justice   10
Commends th'ingredience of our poisoned chalice
To our own lips. He's here in double trust:
First, as I am his kinsman, and his subject,
Strong both against the deed. Then, as his host,
Who should against his murderer shut the door,   15
Not bear the knife myself. Besides, this Duncan
Hath borne his faculties so meek, hath been
So clear in his great office, that his virtues
Will plead like angels, trumpet-tongued, against
The deep damnation of his taking off;   20
And pity, like a naked new-born babe,
Striding the blast, or heaven's cherubin, horsed
Upon the sightless couriers of the air,
Shall blow the horrid deed in every eye,
That tears shall drown the wind. I have no spur   25
To prick the sides of my intent, but only
Vaulting ambition, which o'er-leaps itself,
And falls on th'other.

Enter LADY.

How now? What news?

LADY
He has almost supped. Why have you left the
chamber?

MACBETH   Hath he asked for me?

LADY   Know you not, he has?   30

MACBETH   We will proceed no further in this business:
He hath honoured me of late, and I have bought
Golden opinions from all sorts of people,
Which would be worn now in their newest gloss,
Not cast aside so soon.

LADY   Was the hope drunk   35
Wherein you dressed yourself? Hath it slept since?
And wakes it now to look so green and pale,
At what it did so freely? From this time
Such I account thy love. Art thou afeared
To be the same in thine own act and valour,   40
As thou art in desire? Wouldst thou have that
Which thou esteem'st the ornament of life,
And live a coward in thine own esteem,
Letting 'I dare not' wait upon 'I would',
Like the poor cat i'th' adage?

MACBETH   Prithee, peace.   45
I dare do all that may become a man,
Who dares do more, is none.

LADY   What beast was't then
That made you break this enterprise to me?
When you durst do it, then you were a man;
And to be more than what you were, you would   50
Be so much more the man. Nor time nor place
Did then adhere, and yet you would make both:
They have made themselves, and that their fitness now
Does unmake you. I have given suck, and know
How tender 'tis to love the babe that milks me: 55
I would, while it was smiling in my face,

Have plucked the nipple from his boneless gums,
And dashed the brains out, had I so sworn
As you have done to this.

MACBETH   If we should fail?

60 LADY   We fail?
But screw your courage to the sticking place,
And we'll not fail. When Duncan is asleep,
Whereto the rather shall his day's hard journey
Soundly invite him, his two chamberlains
65 Will I with wine and wassail so convince,
That memory, the warder of the brain,
Shall be a fume, and the receipt of reason
A limbeck only. When in swinish sleep
Their drenched natures lies as in a death,
70 What cannot you and I perform upon
Th'unguarded Duncan? What not put upon
His spongy officers, who shall bear the guilt
Of our great quell?

MACBETH   Bring forth men-children only;
For thy undaunted mettle should compose
75 Nothing but males. Will it not be received,
When we have marked with blood those sleepy two
Of his own chamber, and used their very daggers,
That they have done't?

LADY   Who dares receive it other,
As we shall make our griefs and clamour roar,
Upon his death?

80 MACBETH   I am settled, and bend up
Each corporal agent to this terrible feat.
Away, and mock the time with fairest show:
False face must hide what the false heart doth know.

                        Exeunt.

2.1   *Enter* BANQUO, *and* FLEANCE,
           with a torch before him.

BANQUO   How goes the night, boy?

FLEANCE
The moon is down; I have not heard the clock.

BANQUO   And she goes down at twelve.

FLEANCE   I take't 'tis later, sir.

BANQUO
Hold, take my sword. There's husbandry in heaven,
5 Their candles are all out; take thee that too.
A heavy summons lies like lead upon me,
And yet I would not sleep. Merciful powers,
Restrain in me the cursed thoughts that nature
Gives way to in repose.

       Enter MACBETH *and a Servant with a torch.*

10   Give me my sword; who's there?

MACBETH   A friend.

BANQUO   What, sir, not yet at rest? The King's abed.
He hath been in unusual pleasure
And sent forth great largess to your offices.
15 This diamond he greets your wife withal,
By the name of most kind hostess, and shut up

In measureless content.

MACBETH   Being unprepared,
Our will became the servant to defect,
Which else should free have wrought.

BANQUO   All's well.

                        Exit Fleance.

I dreamt last night of the three weird sisters: 20
To you they have showed some truth.

MACBETH   I think not of them;
Yet, when we can entreat an hour to serve,
We would spend it in some words upon that business
If you would grant the time.

BANQUO   At your kind'st leisure.

MACBETH   If you shall cleave to my consent when 'tis,   25
It shall make honour for you.

BANQUO   So I lose none
In seeking to augment it, but still keep
My bosom franchised and allegiance clear,
I shall be counselled.

MACBETH   Good repose the while.

BANQUO   Thanks, sir, the like to you.   *Exit Banquo.*   30

MACBETH
Go bid thy mistress, when my drink is ready,
She strike upon the bell. Get thee to bed.

                    Exit Servant.

Is this a dagger which I see before me,
The handle toward my hand? Come, let me clutch
   thee.
I have thee not, and yet I see thee still.   35
Art thou not, fatal vision, sensible
To feeling as to sight? Or art thou but
A dagger of the mind, a false creation,
Proceeding from the heat-oppressed brain?
I see thee yet, in form as palpable   40
As this which now I draw.
Thou marshall'st me the way that I was going,
And such an instrument I was to use.
Mine eyes are made the fools o'th' other senses,
Or else worth all the rest. I see thee still,   45
And on thy blade, and dudgeon, gouts of blood,
Which was not so before. There's no such thing.
It is the bloody business which informs
Thus to mine eyes. Now o'er the one half-world
Nature seems dead, and wicked dreams abuse   50
The curtained sleep; Witchcraft celebrates
Pale Hecate's offerings; and withered Murder,
Alarumed by his sentinel, the wolf,
Whose howl's his watch, thus with his stealthy pace,
With Tarquin's ravishing strides, towards his design   55
Moves like a ghost. Thou sure and firm-set earth,
Hear not my steps, which way they walk, for fear
Thy very stones prate of my whereabout,
And take the present horror from the time,
Which now suits with it. Whiles I threat, he lives;   60
Words to the heat of deeds too cold breath gives.

                    [A bell rings.]

I go, and it is done; the bell invites me.

Hear it not, Duncan, for it is a knell
That summons thee to heaven, or to hell. *Exit.*

2.2 *Enter* LADY.

LADY
That which hath made them drunk, hath made me
    bold;
What hath quenched them, hath given me fire.
Hark, peace; it was the owl that shrieked,
The fatal bellman, which gives the stern'st good
    night.
He is about it. The doors are open, 5
And the surfeited grooms do mock their charge
With snores. I have drugged their possets
That death and nature do contend about them,
Whether they live, or die.

Enter MACBETH.

MACBETH   Who's there? What ho?
LADY   Alack, I am afraid they have awaked, 10
And 'tis not done. The attempt and not the deed
Confounds us. Hark. I laid their daggers ready;
He could not miss 'em. Had he not resembled
My father as he slept, I had done't.
My husband?
MACBETH   I have done the deed. 15
Didst thou not hear a noise?
LADY   I heard the owl scream and the crickets cry.
Did not you speak?
MACBETH   When?
LADY   Now.
MACBETH   As I descended?
LADY Ay.
MACBETH   Hark, who lies i'the second chamber?
LADY   Donalbain.
MACBETH   This is a sorry sight. 20
LADY   A foolish thought, to say a sorry sight.
MACBETH   There's one did laugh in 's sleep,
And one cried, 'Murder', that they did wake each other.
I stood and heard them; but they did say their prayers
And addressed them again to sleep. 25
LADY   There are two lodged together.
MACBETH
One cried, 'God bless us', and 'Amen' the other,
As they had seen me with these hangman's hands.
Listening their fear, I could not say 'Amen'
When they did say, 'God bless us'. 30
LADY   Consider it not so deeply.
MACBETH
But wherefore could not I pronounce 'Amen'?
I had most need of blessing, and 'Amen'
Stuck in my throat.
LADY   These deeds must not be thought
After these ways; so, it will make us mad. 35
MACBETH
Methought I heard a voice cry, 'Sleep no more.

Macbeth does murder sleep' – the innocent sleep,
Sleep that knits up the ravelled sleave of care,
The death of each day's life, sore labour's bath,
Balm of hurt minds, great Nature's second course, 40
Chief nourisher in life's feast –
LADY   What do you mean?
MACBETH
Still it cried, 'Sleep no more' to all the house;
'Glamis hath murdered sleep, and therefore Cawdor
Shall sleep no more. Macbeth shall sleep no more.'
LADY   Who was it that thus cried? Why, worthy thane, 45
You do unbend your noble strength, to think
So brainsickly of things. Go, get some water
And wash this filthy witness from your hand.
Why did you bring these daggers from the place?
They must lie there. Go, carry them, and smear 50
The sleepy grooms with blood.
MACBETH   I'll go no more.
I am afraid to think what I have done;
Look on't again, I dare not.
LADY   Infirm of purpose,
Give me the daggers. The sleeping and the dead
Are but as pictures; 'tis the eye of childhood 55
That fears a painted devil. If he do bleed,
I'll gild the faces of the grooms withal,
For it must seem their guilt. *Exit. Knock within*
MACBETH   Whence is that knocking?
How is't with me, when every noise appals me?
What hands are here? Ha: they pluck out mine eyes. 60
Will all great Neptune's ocean wash this blood
Clean from my hand? No, this my hand will rather
The multitudinous seas incarnadine,
Making the green, one red.

Enter LADY.

LADY   My hands are of your colour, but I shame 65
To wear a heart so white. I hear a knocking   [*Knock*]
At the south entry. Retire we to our chamber;
A little water clears us of this deed.
How easy is it then. Your constancy
Hath left you unattended.   [*Knock*]
                Hark, more knocking. 70
Get on your nightgown, lest occasion call us
And show us to be watchers. Be not lost
So poorly in your thoughts.
MACBETH
To know my deed, 'twere best not know myself.
                   [*Knock*]
Wake Duncan with thy knocking. I would thou
    couldst.   *Exeunt.* 75

2.3 *Enter a Porter. Knocking within.*

PORTER   Here's a knocking indeed: if a man were porter
of Hell Gate, he should have old turning the key.
[*Knock*] Knock, knock, knock. Who's there, i'th' name
of Belzebub? Here's a farmer that hanged himself on

th'expectation of plenty. Come in time. Have napkins
enow about you; here you'll sweat for't. [*Knock*]
Knock, knock. Who's there, in th'other devil's name?
Faith, here's an equivocator that could swear in both
the scales against either scale, who committed treason
enough for God's sake, yet could not equivocate to
heaven. O, come in, equivocator. [*Knock*] Knock,
knock, knock. Who's there? Faith, here's an English
tailor come hither, for stealing out of a French hose.
Come in, tailor; here you may roast your goose. [*Knock*]
Knock, knock. Never at quiet. What are you? But this
place is too cold for hell. I'll devil-porter it no further.
I had thought to have let in some of all professions that
go the primrose way to the everlasting bonfire. [*Knock*]
Anon, anon, I pray you, remember the porter.

Enter MACDUFF *and* LENNOX.

MACDUFF   Was it so late, friend, ere you went to bed,
That you do lie so late?
PORTER   Faith, sir, we were carousing till the second
cock; and drink, sir, is a great provoker of three things.
MACDUFF   What three things does drink especially
provoke?
PORTER   Marry, sir, nose-painting, sleep and urine.
Lechery, sir, it provokes and unprovokes: it provokes
the desire, but it takes away the performance.
Therefore much drink may be said to be an equivocator
with lechery: it makes him, and it mars him; it sets him
on, and it takes him off; it persuades him, and
disheartens him; makes him stand to, and not stand to;
in conclusion, equivocates him in a sleep and, giving
him the lie, leaves him.
MACDUFF   I believe drink gave thee the lie last night.
PORTER   That it did, sir, i'the very throat on me; but I
requited him for his lie, and, I think, being too strong
for him, though he took up my legs sometime, yet I
made a shift to cast him.

Enter MACBETH.

MACDUFF   Is thy master stirring?
Our knocking has awaked him; here he comes.
                                    Exit Porter.
LENNOX   Good morrow, noble sir.
MACBETH   Good morrow both.
MACDUFF   Is the King stirring, worthy thane?
MACBETH   Not yet.
MACDUFF   He did command me to call timely on him;
I have almost slipped the hour.
MACBETH   I'll bring you to him.
MACDUFF   I know this is a joyful trouble to you;
But yet 'tis one.
MACBETH   The labour we delight in physics pain;
This is the door.
MACDUFF
I'll make so bold to call, for 'tis my limited service.
                                    Exit Macduff.
LENNOX   Goes the King hence today?

MACBETH   He does: he did appoint so.
LENNOX   The night has been unruly: where we lay
Our chimneys were blown down and, as they say,
Lamentings heard i'th' air, strange screams of death,
And prophesying, with accents terrible,
Of dire combustion, and confused events
New hatched to th' woeful time. The obscure bird
Clamoured the livelong night. Some say the earth
Was feverous and did shake.
MACBETH   'Twas a rough night.
LENNOX   My young remembrance cannot parallel
A fellow to it.

Enter MACDUFF.

MACDUFF   O horror, horror, horror.
Tongue nor heart cannot conceive nor name thee.
MACBETH, LENNOX   What's the matter?
MACDUFF   Confusion now hath made his masterpiece.
Most sacrilegious murder hath broke ope
The Lord's anointed temple, and stole thence
The life o'th' building.
MACBETH   What is't you say? the life?
LENNOX   Mean you his majesty?
MACDUFF
Approach the chamber, and destroy your sight
With a new Gorgon. Do not bid me speak –
See, and then speak yourselves.
                    Exeunt Macbeth and Lennox.
                        Awake, awake!
Ring the alarum bell! Murder and treason.
Banquo and Donalbain, Malcolm, awake,
Shake off this downy sleep, death's counterfeit,
And look on death itself. Up, up, and see
The great doom's image. Malcolm, Banquo,
As from your graves rise up, and walk like sprites
To countenance this horror. Ring the bell! [*Bell rings.*]

Enter LADY.

LADY   What's the business,
That such a hideous trumpet calls to parley
The sleepers of the house? Speak, speak.
MACDUFF   O gentle lady,
'Tis not for you to hear what I can speak:
The repetition in a woman's ear
Would murder as it fell.

Enter BANQUO.

                    O Banquo, Banquo,
Our royal master's murdered.
LADY   Woe, alas.
What, in our house?
BANQUO   Too cruel anywhere.
Dear Duff, I prithee contradict thyself
And say it is not so.

Enter MACBETH, LENNOX *and* ROSS.

MACBETH   Had I but died an hour before this chance,
I had lived a blessed time, for from this instant

There's nothing serious in mortality;
All is but toys; renown and grace is dead,
95 The wine of life is drawn, and the mere lees
Is left this vault to brag of.

Enter MALCOLM *and* DONALBAIN.

DONALBAIN　　What is amiss?
MACBETH　　　　　　　　　You are, and do not know't:
The spring, the head, the fountain of your blood
Is stopped, the very source of it is stopped.
100 MACDUFF　　Your royal father's murdered.
MALCOLM　　　　　　　　　　　　　O, by whom?
LENNOX
Those of his chamber, as it seemed, had done't.
Their hands and faces were all badged with blood;
So were their daggers, which unwiped we found
Upon their pillows. They stared, and were distracted;
105 No man's life was to be trusted with them.
MACBETH　　O, yet I do repent me of my fury,
That I did kill them.
MACDUFF　　　　　　　Wherefore did yóu so?
MACBETH
Who can be wise, amazed, temperate and furious,
Loyal and neutral, in a moment? No man.
110 The expedition of my violent love
Outran the pauser, reason. Here lay Duncan,
His silver skin laced with his golden blood,
And his gashed stabs looked like a breach in nature
For ruin's wasteful entrance; there, the murderers,
115 Steeped in the colours of their trade, their daggers
Unmannerly breeched with gore. Who could refrain,
That had a heart to love, and in that heart
Courage to make 's love known?
LADY　　　　　　　　　　　　Help me hence, ho.
MACDUFF　　Look to the lady.
MALCOLM
120 Why do we hold our tongues, that most may claim
This argument for ours?
DONALBAIN　　　　　　　What should be spoken
Here, where our fate, hid in an auger hole,
May rush and seize us? Let's away,
Our tears are not yet brewed.
MALCOLM　　　　　　　　Nor our strong sorrow
Upon the foot of motion.
125 BANQUO　　　　　　　Look to the lady. *Exit Lady.*
And when we have our naked frailties hid,
That suffer in exposure, let us meet
And question this most bloody piece of work
To know it further. Fears and scruples shake us.
130 In the great hand of God I stand, and thence
Against the undivulged pretence I fight
Of treasonous malice.
MACDUFF　　　　　　And so do I.
ALL　　　　　　　　　　So all.
MACBETH　　Let's briefly put on manly readiness
And meet i'the hall together.
ALL　　　　　　　　　Well contented.

Exeunt all but Malcolm and Donalbain.

MALCOLM
What will you do? Let's not consort with them.　　135
To show an unfelt sorrow is an office
Which the false man does easy. I'll to England.
DONALBAIN　　To Ireland, I; our separated fortune
Shall keep us both the safer. Where we are,
There's daggers in men's smiles; the near in blood,　　140
The nearer bloody.
MALCOLM　　　　　This murderous shaft that's shot
Hath not yet lighted, and our safest way
Is to avoid the aim. Therefore to horse;
And let us not be dainty of leave-taking,
But shift away. There's warrant in that theft　　145
Which steals itself, when there's no mercy left.

Exeunt.

2.4　　　*Enter* ROSS, *with an* Old Man.

OLD MAN　　Threescore and ten I can remember well,
Within the volume of which time I have seen
Hours dreadful and things strange; but this sore night
Hath trifled former knowings.
ROSS　　　　　　　　　　Ha, good father,
Thou seest the heavens, as troubled with man's act,　　5
Threatens his bloody stage. By th' clock 'tis day,
And yet dark night strangles the travelling lamp.
Is't night's predominance, or the day's shame,
That darkness does the face of earth entomb
When living light should kiss it?
OLD MAN　　　　　　　　　'Tis unnatural,　　10
Even like the deed that's done. On Tuesday last
A falcon towering in her pride of place
Was by a mousing owl hawked at and killed.
ROSS
And Duncan's horses, a thing most strange and
　　certain,
Beauteous and swift, the minions of their race,　　15
Turned wild in nature, broke their stalls, flung out
Contending 'gainst obedience, as they would
Make war with mankind.
OLD MAN　　　　　　　'Tis said they eat each other.
ROSS　　They did so, to th'amazement of mine eyes
That looked upon't.

Enter MACDUFF.

　　　　　　　　　　Here comes the good Macduff.　　20
How goes the world, sir, now?
MACDUFF　　　　　　　　Why, see you not?
ROSS　　Is't known who did this more than bloody deed?
MACDUFF　　Those that Macbeth hath slain.
ROSS　　　　　　　　　　　　Alas, the day.
What good could they pretend?
MACDUFF　　　　　　　　They were suborned.
Malcolm and Donalbain, the King's two sons,　　25
Are stolen away and fled, which puts upon them
Suspicion of the deed.

ROSS   'Gainst nature still,
Thriftless ambition, that will raven up
Thine own life's means. Then 'tis most like
30   The sovereignty will fall upon Macbeth.
MACDUFF   He is already named, and gone to Scone
To be invested.
ROSS   Where is Duncan's body?
MACDUFF   Carried to Colmekill,
The sacred storehouse of his predecessors
And guardian of their bones.
35   ROSS   Will you to Scone?
MACDUFF   No, cousin, I'll to Fife.
ROSS   Well, I will thither.
MACDUFF
  Well may you see things well done there. Adieu,
  Lest our old robes sit easier than our new.
ROSS   Farewell, father.
40   OLD MAN   God's benison go with you, and with those
That would make good of bad and friends of foes.
                        Exeunt omnes.

3.1   *Enter* BANQUO.

BANQUO   Thou hast it now, King, Cawdor, Glamis, all,
As the weïrd women promised, and I fear
Thou played'st most foully for't. Yet it was said
It should not stand in thy posterity,
5   But that myself should be the root and father
Of many kings. If there comes truth from them,
As upon thee, Macbeth, their speeches shine,
Why, by the verities on thee made good,
May they not be my oracles as well
10   And set me up in hope? But hush, no more.

    Sennet sounded. Enter MACBETH *as King,* LADY,
    LENNOX, ROSS, *Lords and Attendants.*

MACBETH   Here's our chief guest.
LADY   If he had been forgotten,
It had been as a gap in our great feast
And all thing unbecoming.
MACBETH   Tonight we hold a solemn supper, sir,
And I'll request your presence.
15   BANQUO   Let your highness
Command upon me, to the which my duties
Are with a most indissoluble tie
For ever knit.
MACBETH   Ride you this afternoon?
BANQUO   Ay, my good lord.
MACBETH
20   We should have else desired your good advice,
Which still hath been both grave and prosperous,
In this day's council: but we'll take tomorrow.
Is't far you ride?
BANQUO   As far, my lord, as will fill up the time
25   'Twixt this, and supper. Go not my horse the better,
I must become a borrower of the night
For a dark hour or twain.

MACBETH   Fail not our feast.
BANQUO   My lord, I will not.
MACBETH   We hear our bloody cousins are bestowed
In England and in Ireland, not confessing   30
Their cruel parricide, filling their hearers
With strange invention. But of that tomorrow,
When therewithal we shall have cause of state,
Craving us jointly. Hie you to horse. Adieu,
Till you return at night. Goes Fleance with you?   35
BANQUO   Ay, my good lord; our time does call upon's.
MACBETH   I wish your horses swift, and sure of foot;
And so I do commend you to their backs.
Farewell.   *Exit Banquo.*
Let every man be master of his time   40
Till seven at night; to make society
The sweeter welcome, we will keep ourself
Till supper time alone. While then, God be with you.
    Exeunt all except Macbeth and a Servant.
Sirrah, a word with you: attend those men our
  pleasure?
SERVANT   They are, my lord, without the palace gate.   45
MACBETH   Bring them before us.   *Exit Servant.*
To be thus is nothing, but to be safely thus:
Our fears in Banquo stick deep,
And in his royalty of nature reigns that
Which would be feared. 'Tis much he dares,   50
And to that dauntless temper of his mind,
He hath a wisdom that doth guide his valour
To act in safety. There is none but he
Whose being I do fear; and under him
My genius is rebuked, as it is said   55
Mark Antony's was by Caesar. He chid the sisters
When first they put the name of king upon me,
And bade them speak to him. Then, prophet-like,
They hailed him father to a line of kings.
Upon my head they placed a fruitless crown   60
And put a barren sceptre in my gripe,
Thence to be wrenched with an unlineal hand,
No son of mine succeeding. If't be so,
For Banquo's issue have I filed my mind;
For them, the gracious Duncan have I murdered;   65
Put rancours in the vessel of my peace
Only for them; and mine eternal jewel
Given to the common enemy of man,
To make them kings, the seeds of Banquo kings.
Rather than so, come fate into the list,   70
And champion me to th'utterance. Who's there?

    Enter Servant *and two* MURDERERS.

Now go to the door and stay there till we call.
                        Exit Servant.
Was it not yesterday we spoke together?
MURDERERS   It was, so please your highness.
MACBETH   Well then,
Now have you considered of my speeches?   75
Know, that it was he, in the times past,
Which held you so under fortune,

Which you had thought had been our innocent self.
This I made good to you, in our last conference,
80 Passed in probation with you:
How you were borne in hand, how crossed;
The instruments, who wrought with them,
And all things else, that might
To half a soul, and to a notion crazed,
Say, 'Thus did Banquo'.
85 1 MURDERER   You made it known to us.
MACBETH I did so; and went further, which is now
Our point of second meeting. Do you find
Your patience so predominant in your nature
That you can let this go? Are you so gospelled
90 To pray for this good man, and for his issue,
Whose heavy hand hath bowed you to the grave,
And beggared yours for ever?
1 MURDERER   We are men, my liege.
MACBETH Ay, in the catalogue ye go for men:
As hounds and greyhounds, mongrels, spaniels, curs,
95 Shoughs, water-rugs and demi-wolves are clept
All by the name of dogs. The valued file
Distinguishes the swift, the slow, the subtle,
The housekeeper, the hunter, every one
According to the gift which bounteous nature
100 Hath in him closed, whereby he does receive
Particular addition, from the bill
That writes them all alike: and so of men.
Now, if you have a station in the file
Not i'th' worst rank of manhood, say't,
105 And I will put that business in your bosoms
Whose execution takes your enemy off,
Grapples you to the heart and love of us,
Who wear our health but sickly in his life,
Which in his death were perfect.
110 2 MURDERER   I am one, my liege
Whom the vile blows and buffets of the world
Hath so incensed, that I am reckless what I do
To spite the world.
1 MURDERER   And I another
So weary with disasters, tugged with fortune,
That I would set my life on any chance,
115 To mend it, or be rid on't.
MACBETH Both of you know Banquo was your enemy.
MURDERERS True, my lord.
MACBETH So is he mine; and in such bloody distance
That every minute of his being thrusts
120 Against my near'st of life: and though I could
With bare-faced power sweep him from my sight
And bid my will avouch it, yet I must not,
For certain friends that are both his and mine,
Whose loves I may not drop, but wail his fall
125 Who I myself struck down. And thence it is,
That I to your assistance do make love,
Masking the business from the common eye
For sundry weighty reasons.
2 MURDERER   We shall, my lord,
Perform what you command us.

1 MURDERER   Though our lives –
MACBETH
Your spirits shine through you. Within this hour at
most,   130
I will advise you where to plant yourselves,
Acquaint you with the perfect spy o'th' time,
The moment on't – for't must be done tonight,
And something from the palace: always thought
That I require a clearness – and with him,   135
To leave no rubs nor botches in the work,
Fleance, his son, that keeps him company,
Whose absence is no less material to me
Than is his father's, must embrace the fate
Of that dark hour. Resolve yourselves apart;   140
I'll come to you anon.
MURDERERS   We are resolved, my lord.
MACBETH I'll call upon you straight: abide within.
                                    Exeunt Murderers.
It is concluded: Banquo, thy soul's flight
If it find heaven, must find it out tonight.   *Exit.*

3.2   *Enter Macbeth's* LADY *and a* Servant.

LADY Is Banquo gone from court?
SERVANT Ay, madam, but returns again tonight.
LADY Say to the King I would attend his leisure
For a few words.
SERVANT   Madam, I will.   *Exit.*
LADY Naught's had, all's spent,   5
Where our desire is got without content.
'Tis safer to be that which we destroy,
Than by destruction dwell in doubtful joy.

Enter MACBETH.

How now, my lord, why do you keep alone?
Of sorriest fancies your companions making,   10
Using those thoughts which should indeed have died
With them they think on? Things without all remedy
Should be without regard: what's done, is done.
MACBETH We have scorched the snake, not killed it:
She'll close, and be herself, whilst our poor malice 15
Remains in danger of her former tooth.
But let the frame of things disjoint, both the worlds
suffer,
Ere we will eat our meal in fear, and sleep
In the affliction of these terrible dreams
That shake us nightly. Better be with the dead,   20
Whom we, to gain our peace, have sent to peace,
Than on the torture of the mind to lie
In restless ecstasy. Duncan is in his grave.
After life's fitful fever, he sleeps well;
Treason has done his worst: nor steel, nor poison, 25
Malice domestic, foreign levy, nothing,
Can touch him further.
LADY   Come on. Gentle my lord,
Sleek o'er your rugged looks, be bright and jovial
Among your guests tonight.

30   MACBETH   So shall I, love, and so I pray be you.
     Let your remembrance apply to Banquo,
     Present him eminence, both with eye and tongue.
     Unsafe the while, that we must lave
35   Our honours in these flattering streams,
     And make our faces vizards to our hearts,
     Disguising what they are.
   LADY   You must leave this.
   MACBETH   O, full of scorpions is my mind, dear wife:
     Thou knowst that Banquo and his Fleance lives.
   LADY   But in them nature's copy's not eterne.
40   MACBETH   There's comfort yet: they are assailable.
     Then be thou jocund; ere the bat hath flown
     His cloistered flight, ere to black Hecate's summons
     The shard-born beetle, with his drowsy hums,
     Hath rung night's yawning peal, there shall be done
     A deed of dreadful note.
45   LADY   What's to be done?
   MACBETH
     Be innocent of the knowledge, dearest chuck,
     Till thou applaud the deed. Come, seeling night,
     Scarf up the tender eye of pitiful day
     And with thy bloody and invisible hand
50   Cancel and tear to pieces that great bond
     Which keeps me pale. Light thickens,
     And the crow makes wing to th' rooky wood.
     Good things of day begin to droop and drowse,
     Whiles night's black agents to their preys do rouse.
55   Thou marvell'st at my words: but hold thee still;
     Things bad begun, make strong themselves by ill.
     So prithee, go with me.   *Exeunt.*

3.3   *Enter three* MURDERERS.

   1 MURDERER   But who did bid thee join with us?
   3 MURDERER   Macbeth.
   2 MURDERER
     He needs not our mistrust, since he delivers
     Our offices, and what we have to do,
     To the direction just.
   1 MURDERER   Then stand with us.
5   The west yet glimmers with some streaks of day.
     Now spurs the lated traveller apace
     To gain the timely inn, and near approaches
     The subject of our watch.
   3 MURDERER   Hark, I hear horses.
   BANQUO [*within*]   Give us a light there, ho!
   2 MURDERER   Then 'tis he: the rest,
10   That are within the note of expectation,
     Already are i'th' court.
   1 MURDERER   His horses go about.
   3 MURDERER   Almost a mile; but he does usually,
     So all men do, from hence to the palace gate
     Make it their walk.

      Enter BANQUO *and* FLEANCE, *with a torch.*

   2 MURDERER   A light, a light.

   3 MURDERER   'Tis he.
   1 MURDERER   Stand to't.
   BANQUO   It will be rain tonight.
   1 MURDERER   Let it come down.   15
   BANQUO   O treachery!
     [*The Murderers attack. First Murderer strikes out the*
     light.]   Fly, good Fleance, fly, fly, fly.
     Thou mayst revenge –   *Exit Fleance.*
               O slave!   [*Dies.*]
   3 MURDERER   Who did strike out the light?
   1 MURDERER   Was't not the way?
   3 MURDERER   There's but one down: the son is fled.
   2 MURDERER   We have lost
     Best half of our affair.
   1 MURDERER   Well, let's away,   20
     And say how much is done.   *Exeunt.*

3.4   *Banquet prepared. Enter* MACBETH, LADY,
       ROSS, LENNOX, Lords *and Attendants.*

   MACBETH
     You know your own degrees, sit down. At first and
       last,
     The hearty welcome.
   LORDS   Thanks to your majesty.
   MACBETH   Ourself will mingle with society
     And play the humble host. Our hostess keeps her state,
     But in best time we will require her welcome.   5
   LADY
     Pronounce it for me, sir, to all our friends,
     For my heart speaks, they are welcome.

      Enter First MURDERER.

   MACBETH
     See, they encounter thee with their hearts' thanks.
     Both sides are even: here I'll sit i'th' midst.
     Be large in mirth; anon we'll drink a measure   10
     The table round. – There's blood upon thy face.
   1 MURDERER   'Tis Banquo's then.
   MACBETH   'Tis better thee without, than he within.
     Is he dispatched?
   1 MURDERER
     My lord, his throat is cut; that I did for him.
   MACBETH   Thou art the best o'th' cut-throats;   15
     Yet he's good that did the like for Fleance.
     If thou didst it, thou art the nonpareil.
   1 MURDERER   Most royal sir, Fleance is scaped.
   MACBETH
     Then comes my fit again: I had else been perfect;
     Whole as the marble, founded as the rock,   20
     As broad and general as the casing air:
     But now I am cabined, cribbed, confined, bound in
     To saucy doubts and fears. But Banquo's safe?
   1 MURDERER
     Ay, my good lord: safe in a ditch he bides,
     With twenty trenched gashes on his head,   25
     The least a death to nature.

MACBETH   Thanks for that.
There the grown serpent lies; the worm that's fled
Hath nature that in time will venom breed,
No teeth for th' present. Get thee gone, tomorrow
We'll hear ourselves again.   *Exit First Murderer.*

30 LADY   My royal lord,
You do not give the cheer: the feast is sold
That is not often vouched, while 'tis a-making,
'Tis given with welcome. To feed were best at home:
From thence, the sauce to meat is ceremony,
Meeting were bare without it.

Enter the Ghost of BANQUO, *and sits in Macbeth's place.*

35 MACBETH   Sweet remembrancer.
Now good digestion wait on appetite,
And health on both.
LENNOX   May't please your highness sit.
MACBETH
Here had we now our country's honour roofed,
40 Were the graced person of our Banquo present,
Who may I rather challenge for unkindness
Than pity for mischance.
ROSS   His absence, sir,
Lays blame upon his promise. Please't your highness
To grace us with your royal company?
MACBETH   The table's full.
LENNOX   Here is a place reserved, sir.
MACBETH   Where?
LENNOX
45 Here my good lord. What is't that moves your
           highness?
MACBETH   Which of you have done this?
LORDS   What, my good lord?
MACBETH   Thou canst not say I did it: never shake
Thy gory locks at me.
ROSS   Gentlemen, rise; his highness is not well.
50 LADY   Sit, worthy friends; my lord is often thus,
And hath been from his youth. Pray you, keep seat,
The fit is momentary; upon a thought
He will again be well. If much you note him
You shall offend him, and extend his passion.
55 Feed, and regard him not. [*to Macbeth*] Are you a man?
MACBETH   Ay, and a bold one, that dare look on that
Which might appal the devil.
LADY   O, proper stuff.
This is the very painting of your fear:
This is the air-drawn dagger which you said
60 Led you to Duncan. O, these flaws and starts,
Imposters to true fear, would well become
A woman's story at a winter's fire,
Authorized by her grandam. Shame itself.
Why do you make such faces? When all's done
You look but on a stool.
65 MACBETH   Prithee see there.
Behold, look, lo, how say you?
[*to Ghost*] Why, what care I? If thou canst nod, speak
           too.

If charnel-houses and our graves must send
Those that we bury back, our monuments
Shall be the maws of kites.   *Exit Ghost.*   70
LADY   What? Quite unmanned in folly.
MACBETH   If I stand here, I saw him.
LADY   Fie, for shame.
MACBETH
Blood hath been shed ere now, i'th' olden time,
Ere humane statute purged the gentle weal;
Ay, and since too, murders have been performed   75
Too terrible for the ear. The times have been,
That when the brains were out, the man would die,
And there an end. But now they rise again
With twenty mortal murders on their crowns,
And push us from our stools. This is more strange   80
Than such a murder is.
LADY   My worthy lord,
Your noble friends do lack you.
MACBETH   I do forget.
Do not muse at me, my most worthy friends,
I have a strange infirmity, which is nothing
To those that know me. Come, love and health to all,   85
Then I'll sit down. Give me some wine, fill full.

Enter Ghost.

I drink to the general joy o'the whole table,
And to our dear friend Banquo, whom we miss –
Would he were here. To all, and him we thirst,
And all to all.
LORDS   Our duties, and the pledge.   90
MACBETH
Avaunt, and quit my sight! Let the earth hide thee.
Thy bones are marrowless, thy blood is cold;
Thou hast no speculation in those eyes
Which thou dost glare with.
LADY   Think of this, good peers,
But as a thing of custom; 'tis no other,   95
Only it spoils the pleasure of the time.
MACBETH   What man dare, I dare.
Approach thou like the rugged Russian bear,
The armed rhinoceros, or the Hyrcan tiger,
Take any shape but that, and my firm nerves   100
Shall never tremble. Or be alive again,
And dare me to the desert with thy sword;
If trembling I inhabit then, protest me
The baby of a girl. Hence, horrible shadow,
Unreal mockery, hence.   *Exit Ghost.*
                       Why so, being gone   105
I am a man again. [*to Lords*] Pray you, sit still.
LADY
You have displaced the mirth, broke the good meeting
With most admired disorder.
MACBETH   Can such things be,
And overcome us like a summer's cloud,
Without our special wonder? You make me strange   110
Even to the disposition that I owe,
When now I think you can behold such sights

And keep the natural ruby of your cheeks
When mine is blanched with fear.

ROSS   What sights, my lord?

115   LADY   I pray you speak not; he grows worse and worse;
Question enrages him. At once, goodnight.
Stand not upon the order of your going
But go at once.

LENNOX   Goodnight, and better health
Attend his majesty.

LADY   A kind goodnight to all.   *Exeunt Lords.*

MACBETH

120   It will have blood they say: blood will have blood:
Stones have been known to move, and trees to speak;
Augures, and understood relations, have
By maggot-pies and choughs and rooks brought forth
The secret'st man of blood. What is the night?

125   LADY   Almost at odds with morning, which is which.

MACBETH

How sayst thou that Macduff denies his person
At our great bidding?

LADY   Did you send to him, sir?

MACBETH   I hear it by the way; but I will send.
There's not a one of them but in his house

130   I keep a servant fee'd. I will tomorrow,
And betimes I will, to the weïrd sisters.
More shall they speak: for now I am bent to know
By the worst means, the worst; for mine own good,
All causes shall give way. I am in blood

135   Stepped in so far, that should I wade no more,
Returning were as tedious as go o'er.
Strange things I have in head, that will to hand,
Which must be acted, ere they may be scanned.

LADY   You lack the season of all natures, sleep.

MACBETH

140   Come we'll to sleep. My strange and self-abuse
Is the initiate fear, that wants hard use.
We are yet but young in deed.   *Exeunt.*

3.5   *Thunder. Enter the three WITCHES, meeting HECATE.*

1 WITCH   Why how now Hecate? You look angerly.

HECATE   Have I not reason, beldams as you are,
Saucy and over-bold? How did you dare
To trade and traffic with Macbeth

5   In riddles and affairs of death;
And I, the mistress of your charms,
The close contriver of all harms,
Was never called to bear my part
Or show the glory of our art?

10   And, which is worse, all you have done
Hath been but for a wayward son,
Spiteful and wrathful, who, as others do,
Loves for his own ends, not for you.
But make amends now; get you gone,

15   And at the pit of Acheron
Meet me i'th' morning; thither he

Will come, to know his destiny.
Your vessels and your spells provide,
Your charms, and every thing beside.
I am for th'air: this night I'll spend   20
Unto a dismal and a fatal end.
Great business must be wrought ere noon.
Upon the corner of the moon
There hangs a vaporous drop profound,
I'll catch it ere it come to ground;   25
And that, distilled by magic sleights,
Shall raise such artificial sprites
As by the strength of their illusion,
Shall draw him on to his confusion.
He shall spurn fate, scorn death, and bear   30
His hopes 'bove wisdom, grace and fear;
And you all know, security
Is mortals' chiefest enemy.   [*Music, and a song*]
Hark, I am called: my little spirit, see,
Sits in a foggy cloud, and stays for me.   *Exit.*   35
   [*Sing within.* 'Come away, come away, *etc.*']

1 WITCH
Come, let's make haste, she'll soon be back again.
                                Exeunt.

3.6   *Enter LENNOX and another* Lord.

LENNOX
My former speeches have but hit your thoughts
Which can interpret further. Only I say
Things have been strangely borne. The gracious
    Duncan
Was pitied of Macbeth; marry, he was dead.
And the right-valiant Banquo walked too late,   5
Whom you may say, if't please you, Fleance killed,
For Fleance fled: men must not walk too late.
Who cannot want the thought how monstrous
It was for Malcolm and for Donalbain
To kill their gracious father? Damned fact,   10
How it did grieve Macbeth! Did he not straight,
In pious rage, the two delinquents tear,
That were the slaves of drink and thralls of sleep?
Was not that nobly done? Ay, and wisely too:
For 'twould have angered any heart alive   15
To hear the men deny't. So that I say,
He has borne all things well, and I do think
That had he Duncan's sons under his key,
As, an't please heaven, he shall not, they should find
What 'twere to kill a father; so should Fleance.   20
But peace; for from broad words, and 'cause he failed
His presence at the tyrant's feast, I hear
Macduff lives in disgrace. Sir, can you tell
Where he bestows himself?

LORD   The son of Duncan,
From whom this tyrant holds the due of birth,   25
Lives in the English court, and is received
Of the most pious Edward with such grace
That the malevolence of fortune nothing

Takes from his high respect. Thither Macduff
Is gone, to pray the holy king, upon his aid
To wake Northumberland, and warlike Siward,
That by the help of these, with Him above
To ratify the work, we may again
Give to our tables meat, sleep to our nights,
Free from our feasts and banquets bloody knives;
Do faithful homage, and receive free honours,
All which we pine for now. And this report
Hath so exasperate their king, that he
Prepares for some attempt of war.

LENNOX   Sent he to Macduff?

LORD   He did. And with an absolute, 'Sir, not I'
The cloudy messenger turns me his back
And hums, as who should say, 'You'll rue the time
That clogs me with this answer'.

LENNOX   And that well might
Advise him to a caution, t'hold what distance
His wisdom can provide. Some holy angel
Fly to the court of England and unfold
His message ere he come, that a swift blessing
May soon return to this our suffering country,
Under a hand accursed.

LORD   I'll send my prayers with him.
                                                              Exeunt.

4.1   *Thunder. Enter the three* WITCHES.

1 WITCH   Thrice the brinded cat hath mewed.

2 WITCH   Thrice, and once the hedge-pig whined.

3 WITCH   Harpier cries, ''Tis time, 'tis time.'

1 WITCH   Round about the cauldron go;
In the poisoned entrails throw.
Toad, that under cold stone
Days and nights has thirty-one,
Sweltered venom sleeping got,
Boil thou first i'th' charmed pot.

ALL   Double, double, toil and trouble;
Fire burn, and cauldron bubble.

2 WITCH   Fillet of a fenny snake,
In the cauldron boil and bake;
Eye of newt and toe of frog,
Wool of bat and tongue of dog,
Adder's fork and blind-worm's sting,
Lizard's leg and howlet's wing,
For a charm of powerful trouble,
Like a hell-broth boil and bubble.

ALL   Double, double, toil and trouble;
Fire burn, and cauldron bubble.

3 WITCH   Scale of dragon, tooth of wolf,
Witch's mummy, maw and gulf
Of the ravined salt-sea shark,
Root of hemlock digged i'th' dark,
Liver of blaspheming Jew,
Gall of goat and slips of yew
Slivered in the moon's eclipse,
Nose of Turk and Tartar's lips,

Finger of birth-strangled babe
Ditch-delivered by a drab,
Make the gruel thick and slab.
Add thereto a tiger's chawdron,
For th'ingredience of our cauldron.

ALL   Double, double, toil and trouble;
Fire burn, and cauldron bubble.

2 WITCH   Cool it with a baboon's blood,
Then the charm is firm and good.

Enter HECATE *and the other three* WITCHES.

HECATE   O, well done. I commend your pains,
And everyone shall share i'th' gains.
And now about the cauldron sing,
Like elves and fairies in a ring,
Enchanting all that you put in.
    [*Music and a song. 'Black spirits, etc.'*]
            Exeunt Hecate and the three other Witches.

2 WITCH   By the pricking of my thumbs,
Something wicked this way comes.
Open locks, whoever knocks.

Enter MACBETH.

MACBETH
How now, you secret, black and midnight hags?
What is't you do?

ALL   A deed without a name.

MACBETH   I conjure you, by that which you profess,
Howe'er you come to know it, answer me;
Though you untie the winds and let them fight
Against the churches, though the yeasty waves
Confound and swallow navigation up,
Though bladed corn be lodged and trees blown down,
Though castles topple on their warders' heads,
Though palaces and pyramids do slope
Their heads to their foundations, though the treasure
Of Nature's germen tumble altogether
Even till destruction sicken, answer me
To what I ask you.

1 WITCH   Speak.

2 WITCH   Demand.

3 WITCH   We'll answer.

1 WITCH
Say, if thou'dst rather hear it from our mouths,
Or from our masters?

MACBETH   Call 'em, let me see 'em.

1 WITCH   Pour in sow's blood that hath eaten
Her nine farrow; grease that's sweaten
From the murderer's gibbet, throw
Into the flame.

ALL   Come, high or low,
Thy self and office deftly show.   [*Thunder*]

Enter FIRST APPARITION: *an armed head.*

MACBETH   Tell me, thou unknown power –

1 WITCH   He knows thy thought:
Hear his speech, but say thou nought.

30
35
40
45
50
55
60
65

909

1 APPARITION

70   Macbeth, Macbeth, Macbeth. Beware Macduff,
     Beware the Thane of Fife. Dismiss me. Enough.
                                        He descends.

MACBETH
     Whate'er thou art, for thy good caution, thanks;
     Thou hast harped my fear aright. But one word more –
1 WITCH   He will not be commanded. Here's another,
75   More potent than the first.   [*Thunder*]

          Enter SECOND APPARITION: *a bloody child.*

2 APPARITION   Macbeth, Macbeth, Macbeth.
MACBETH   Had I three ears, I'd hear thee.
2 APPARITION
     Be bloody, bold and resolute: laugh to scorn
     The power of man, for none of woman born
80   Shall harm Macbeth.   *Descends.*
MACBETH
     Then live, Macduff: what need I fear of thee?
     But yet I'll make assurance double sure,
     And take a bond of fate: thou shalt not live,
     That I may tell pale-hearted fear it lies
     And sleep in spite of thunder.   [*Thunder*]

          Enter THIRD APPARITION: *a child crowned,*
               with a tree in his hand.

85   What is this,
     That rises like the issue of a king
     And wears upon his baby-brow the round
     And top of sovereignty?
ALL   Listen, but speak not to't.
3 APPARITION
     Be lion-mettled, proud, and take no care
90   Who chafes, who frets, or where conspirers are.
     Macbeth shall never vanquished be, until
     Great Birnam Wood to high Dunsinane Hill
     Shall come against him.   *Descends.*
MACBETH   That will never be.
     Who can impress the forest, bid the tree
95   Unfix his earth-bound root? Sweet bodements, good.
     Rebellious dead, rise never till the Wood
     Of Birnam rise, and our high-placed Macbeth
     Shall live the lease of nature, pay his breath
     To time, and mortal custom. Yet my heart
100   Throbs to know one thing: tell me, if your art
     Can tell so much, shall Banquo's issue ever
     Reign in this kingdom?
ALL   Seek to know no more.
MACBETH   I will be satisfied. Deny me this,
     And an eternal curse fall on you. Let me know.
105   Why sinks that cauldron, and what noise is this?
                                        [*Hautboys*]
1 WITCH   Show.
2 WITCH   Show.
3 WITCH   Show.
ALL   Show his eyes, and grieve his heart;
110   Come like shadows, so depart.

A show of eight kings, the last with a glass in
     his hand; and BANQUO.

MACBETH
     Thou art too like the spirit of Banquo; down:
     Thy crown does sear mine eyeballs. And thy hair,
     Thou other gold-bound brow, is like the first.
     A third is like the former. Filthy hags,
     Why do you show me this? – A fourth? Start, eyes!   115
     What, will the line stretch out to th' crack of doom?
     Another yet? A seventh? I'll see no more;
     And yet the eighth appears, who bears a glass
     Which shows me many more; and some I see
     That twofold balls and treble sceptres carry.   120
     Horrible sight. Now I see 'tis true;
     For the blood-boltered Banquo smiles upon me
     And points at them for his.   *Exeunt kings and Banquo.*
                    What? Is this so?
1 WITCH   Ay, sir, all this is so. But why
     Stands Macbeth thus amazedly?   125
     Come, sisters, cheer we up his sprites,
     And show the best of our delights.
     I'll charm the air to give a sound,
     While you perform your antique round,
     That this great king may kindly say   130
     Our duties did his welcome pay.
               Music. The Witches dance and vanish.
MACBETH
     Where are they? Gone? Let this pernicious hour
     Stand ay accursed in the calendar.
     Come in, without there.

               Enter LENNOX.

LENNOX   What's your grace's will?
MACBETH   Saw you the weïrd sisters?
LENNOX   No, my lord.   135
MACBETH   Came they not by you?
LENNOX   No indeed, my lord.
MACBETH   Infected be the air whereon they ride,
     And damned all those that trust them. I did hear
     The galloping of horse. Who was't came by?
LENNOX
     'Tis two or three, my lord, that bring you word   140
     Macduff is fled to England.
MACBETH   Fled to England?
LENNOX   Ay, my good lord.
MACBETH   Time, thou anticipat'st my dread exploits.
     The flighty purpose never is o'ertook
     Unless the deed go with it. From this moment   145
     The very firstlings of my heart shall be
     The firstlings of my hand. And even now,
     To crown my thoughts with acts, be it thought and
          done.
     The castle of Macduff I will surprise,
     Seize upon Fife, give to th'edge o'th' sword   150
     His wife, his babes and all unfortunate souls
     That trace him in his line. No boasting like a fool;

This deed I'll do before this purpose cool.
But no more sights. Where are these gentlemen?
155   Come, bring me where they are.   *Exeunt.*

4.2   *Enter Macduff's* WIFE, *her* SON *and* ROSS.

WIFE   What had he done, to make him fly the land?

ROSS   You must have patience, madam.

WIFE   He had none;
His flight was madness. When our actions do not,
Our fears do make us traitors.

ROSS   You know not
5   Whether it was his wisdom or his fear.

WIFE   Wisdom? To leave his wife, to leave his babes,
His mansion and his titles in a place
From whence himself does fly? He loves us not;
He wants the natural touch. For the poor wren,
10   The most diminutive of birds, will fight,
Her young ones in her nest, against the owl.
All is the fear and nothing is the love;
As little is the wisdom, where the flight
So runs against all reason.

ROSS   My dearest coz,
15   I pray you, school yourself. But for your husband,
He is noble, wise, judicious, and best knows
The fits o'th' season. I dare not speak much further;
But cruel are the times when we are traitors
And do not know ourselves; when we hold rumour
20   From what we fear, yet know not what we fear,
But float upon a wild and violent sea
Each way and move. I take my leave of you;
Shall not be long but I'll be here again.
Things at the worst will cease, or else climb upward
25   To what they were before. My pretty cousin,
Blessing upon you.

WIFE   Fathered he is, and yet he's fatherless.

ROSS   I am so much a fool, should I stay longer,
It would be my disgrace and your discomfort.
30   I take my leave at once.   *Exit Ross.*

WIFE   Sirrah, your father's dead. And what will you do
now? How will you live?

SON   As birds do, mother.

WIFE   What, with worms and flies?

35 SON   With what I get, I mean; and so do they.

WIFE   Poor bird. Thou'dst never fear the net nor lime,
the pitfall nor the gin.

SON   Why should I, mother? Poor birds they are not set
for. My father is not dead, for all your saying.

40 WIFE   Yes, he is dead. How wilt thou do for a father?

SON   Nay, how will you do for a husband?

WIFE   Why, I can buy me twenty at any market.

SON   Then you'll buy 'em to sell again.

WIFE   Thou speak'st with all thy wit, and yet, i'faith,
45   with wit enough for thee.

SON   Was my father a traitor, mother?

WIFE   Ay, that he was.

SON   What is a traitor?

WIFE   Why one that swears and lies.

50 SON   And be all traitors, that do so?

WIFE   Every one that does so is a traitor and must be
hanged.

SON   And must they all be hanged that swear and lie?

WIFE   Every one.

55 SON   Who must hang them?

WIFE   Why, the honest men.

SON   Then the liars and swearers are fools, for there are
liars and swearers enow to beat the honest men, and
hang up them.

60 WIFE   Now, God help thee, poor monkey. But how wilt
thou do for a father?

SON   If he were dead, you'd weep for him; if you would
not, it were a good sign that I should quickly have a
new father.

65 WIFE   Poor prattler, how thou talk'st.

               Enter a Messenger.

MESSENGER
Bless you, fair dame. I am not to you known,
Though in your state of honour I am perfect.
I doubt some danger does approach you nearly.
If you will take a homely man's advice,
70   Be not found here; hence, with your little ones.
To fright you thus, methinks I am too savage;
To do worse to you were fell cruelty,
Which is too nigh your person. Heaven preserve you.
I dare abide no longer.   *Exit Messenger.*

75 WIFE   Whither should I fly?
I have done no harm. But I remember now
I am in this earthly world, where to do harm
Is often laudable, to do good sometime
Accounted dangerous folly. Why, then, alas,
80   Do I put up that womanly defence,
To say I have done no harm?

               Enter MURDERERS.

                         What are these faces?

1 MURDERER   Where is your husband?

WIFE   I hope in no place so unsanctified
Where such as thou mayst find him.

1 MURDERER   He's a traitor.

SON   Thou liest, thou shag-haired villain.

1 MURDERER   What, you egg! 85
Young fry of treachery!   [*Strikes him.*]

SON   He has killed me, mother.
Run away, I pray you.   *Exit Wife crying* 'Murder'.
              Exeunt Murderers, carrying the Son.

4.3   *Enter* MALCOLM *and* MACDUFF.

MALCOLM
Let us seek out some desolate shade and there
Weep our sad bosoms empty.

MACDUFF   Let us rather
Hold fast the mortal sword, and like good men

Bestride our downfall birthdom. Each new morn
5   New widows howl, new orphans cry, new sorrows
Strike heaven on the face, that it resounds
As if it felt with Scotland and yelled out
Like syllable of dolour.

MALCOLM   What I believe, I'll wail;
What know, believe; and what I can redress,
10   As I shall find the time to friend, I will.
What you have spoke, it may be so, perchance.
This tyrant, whose sole name blisters our tongues,
Was once thought honest: you have loved him well;
He hath not touched you yet. I am young, but
    something
15   You may discern of him through me, and wisdom
To offer up a weak, poor, innocent lamb
T'appease an angry god.

MACDUFF   I am not treacherous.

MALCOLM   But Macbeth is.
A good and virtuous nature may recoil
20   In an imperial charge. But I shall crave your pardon;
That which you are, my thoughts cannot transpose.
Angels are bright still, though the brightest fell.
Though all things foul would wear the brows of grace,
Yet grace must still look so.

MACDUFF   I have lost my hopes.

MALCOLM
25   Perchance even there where I did find my doubts.
Why in that rawness left you wife and child –
Those precious motives, those strong knots of love –
Without leave-taking? I pray you,
Let not my jealousies be your dishonours,
30   But mine own safeties. You may be rightly just,
Whatever I shall think.

MACDUFF   Bleed, bleed, poor country.
Great tyranny, lay thou thy basis sure,
For goodness dare not check thee. Wear thou thy
    wrongs;
The title is affeered. Fare thee well, lord.
35   I would not be the villain that thou think'st
For the whole space that's in the tyrant's grasp
And the rich East to boot.

MALCOLM   Be not offended;
I speak not as in absolute fear of you.
I think our country sinks beneath the yoke;
40   It weeps, it bleeds, and each new day a gash
Is added to her wounds. I think withal
There would be hands uplifted in my right;
And here from gracious England have I offer
Of goodly thousands. But for all this,
45   When I shall tread upon the tyrant's head,
Or wear it on my sword, yet my poor country
Shall have more vices than it had before,
More suffer, and more sundry ways than ever,
By him that shall succeed.

MACDUFF   What should he be?
50   MALCOLM   It is myself I mean, in whom I know
All the particulars of vice so grafted

That, when they shall be opened, black Macbeth
Will seem as pure as snow, and the poor state
Esteem him as a lamb, being compared
With my confineless harms.

MACDUFF   Not in the legions   55
Of horrid hell can come a devil more damned
In evils to top Macbeth.

MALCOLM   I grant him bloody,
Luxurious, avaricious, false, deceitful,
Sudden, malicious, smacking of every sin
That has a name. But there's no bottom, none,   60
In my voluptuousness. Your wives, your daughters,
Your matrons and your maids could not fill up
The cistern of my lust; and my desire
All continent impediments would o'erbear
That did oppose my will. Better Macbeth   65
Than such an one to reign.

MACDUFF   Boundless intemperance
In nature is a tyranny. It hath been
Th'untimely emptying of the happy throne,
And fall of many kings. But fear not yet
To take upon you what is yours. You may   70
Convey your pleasures in a spacious plenty
And yet seem cold. The time you may so hoodwink.
We have willing dames enough; there cannot be
That vulture in you to devour so many
As will to greatness dedicate themselves,   75
Finding it so inclined.

MALCOLM   With this there grows
In my most ill-composed affection such
A stanchless avarice that, were I king,
I should cut off the nobles for their lands,
Desire his jewels and this other's house,   80
And my more-having would be as a sauce
To make me hunger more, that I should forge
Quarrels unjust against the good and loyal,
Destroying them for wealth.

MACDUFF   This avarice
Sticks deeper, grows with more pernicious root   85
Than summer-seeming lust, and it hath been
The sword of our slain kings. Yet do not fear;
Scotland hath foisons to fill up your will
Of your mere own. All these are portable,
With other graces weighed.   90

MALCOLM
But I have none. The king-becoming graces,
As justice, verity, temperance, stableness,
Bounty, perseverance, mercy, lowliness,
Devotion, patience, courage, fortitude,
I have no relish of them, but abound   95
In the division of each several crime,
Acting it many ways. Nay, had I power, I should
Pour the sweet milk of concord into hell,
Uproar the universal peace, confound
All unity on earth.

MACDUFF   O Scotland, Scotland.   100

MALCOLM   If such a one be fit to govern, speak.

I am as I have spoken.

MACDUFF   Fit to govern?
No, not to live. O nation miserable!
With an untitled tyrant bloody-sceptred,
105 When shalt thou see thy wholesome days again,
Since that the truest issue of thy throne
By his own interdiction stands accursed
And does blaspheme his breed? Thy royal father
Was a most sainted king; the queen that bore thee,
110 Oft'ner upon her knees than on her feet,
Died every day she lived. Fare thee well.
These evils thou repeat'st upon thyself
Hath banished me from Scotland. O my breast,
Thy hope ends here.

MALCOLM   Macduff, this noble passion,
115 Child of integrity, hath from my soul
Wiped the black scruples, reconciled my thoughts
To thy good truth and honour. Devilish Macbeth
By many of these trains hath sought to win me
Into his power, and modest wisdom plucks me
120 From over-credulous haste. But God above
Deal between thee and me. For even now
I put myself to thy direction and
Unspeak mine own detraction. Here abjure
The taints and blames I laid upon myself,
125 For strangers to my nature. I am yet
Unknown to woman, never was forsworn,
Scarcely have coveted what was mine own,
At no time broke my faith, would not betray
The devil to his fellow, and delight
130 No less in truth than life. My first false speaking
Was this upon myself. What I am truly
Is thine and my poor country's to command.
Whither indeed, before thy here-approach,
Old Siward, with ten thousand warlike men
135 Already at a point, was setting forth.
Now we'll together, and the chance of goodness
Be like our warranted quarrel. Why are you silent?

MACDUFF
Such welcome and unwelcome things at once
'Tis hard to reconcile.

Enter a Doctor.

MALCOLM   Well, more anon.
140 Comes the King forth, I pray you?

DOCTOR Ay, sir; there are a crew of wretched souls
That stay his cure. Their malady convinces
The great assay of art, but at his touch,
Such sanctity hath heaven given his hand,
145 They presently amend.

MALCOLM   I thank you, Doctor.

Exit Doctor.

MACDUFF What's the disease he means?

MALCOLM   'Tis called the Evil:
A most miraculous work in this good king,
Which often, since my here-remain in England,
I have seen him do. How he solicits heaven,

Himself best knows; but strangely-visited people, 150
All swol'n and ulcerous, pitiful to the eye,
The mere despair of surgery, he cures,
Hanging a golden stamp about their necks
Put on with holy prayers; and 'tis spoken,
To the succeeding royalty he leaves 155
The healing benediction. With this strange virtue
He hath a heavenly gift of prophecy,
And sundry blessings hang about his throne
That speak him full of grace.

Enter ROSS.

MACDUFF   See who comes here.

MALCOLM My countryman, but yet I know him not. 160

MACDUFF My ever gentle cousin, welcome hither.

MALCOLM
I know him now. Good God, betimes remove
The means that makes us strangers.

ROSS   Sir, amen.

MACDUFF Stands Scotland where it did?

ROSS   Alas, poor country,
Almost afraid to know itself. It cannot 165
Be called our mother, but our grave. Where nothing,
But who knows nothing, is once seen to smile;
Where sighs, and groans, and shrieks that rend the
air,
Are made, not marked; where violent sorrow seems
A modern ecstasy. The deadman's knell 170
Is there scarce asked for who, and good men's lives
Expire before the flowers in their caps,
Dying or ere they sicken.

MACDUFF O, relation too nice, and yet too true.

MALCOLM What's the newest grief? 175

ROSS That of an hour's age doth hiss the speaker;
Each minute teems a new one.

MACDUFF   How does my wife?

ROSS Why, well.

MACDUFF   And all my children?

ROSS   Well too.

MACDUFF The tyrant has not battered at their peace?

ROSS
No, they were well at peace, when I did leave 'em. 180

MACDUFF
Be not a niggard of your speech. How goes't?

ROSS When I came hither to transport the tidings,
Which I have heavily borne, there ran a rumour
Of many worthy fellows that were out,
Which was to my belief witnessed the rather 185
For that I saw the tyrant's power afoot.
Now is the time of help: your eye in Scotland
Would create soldiers, make our women fight
To doff their dire distresses.

MALCOLM   Be't their comfort
We are coming thither. Gracious England hath 190
Lent us good Siward, and ten thousand men;
An older and a better soldier, none
That Christendom gives out.

ROSS   Would I could answer
This comfort with the like. But I have words
That would be howled out in the desert air,
Where hearing should not latch them.

MACDUFF   What concern they:
The general cause? Or is it a fee-grief
Due to some single breast?

ROSS   No mind that's honest
But in it shares some woe, though the main part
Pertains to you alone.

MACDUFF   If it be mine,
Keep it not from me, quickly let me have it.

ROSS   Let not your ears despise my tongue for ever,
Which shall possess them with the heaviest sound
That ever yet they heard.

MACDUFF   H'm: I guess at it.

ROSS   Your castle is surprised; your wife and babes
Savagely slaughtered. To relate the manner
Were on the quarry of these murdered deer
To add the death of you.

MALCOLM   Merciful heaven.
What, man; ne'er pull your hat upon your brows:
Give sorrow words. The grief that does not speak
Whispers the o'erfraught heart and bids it break.

MACDUFF   My children too?

ROSS   Wife, children, servants, all that could be found.

MACDUFF
And I must be from thence? My wife killed too?

ROSS   I have said.

MALCOLM   Be comforted.
Let's make us medicines of our great revenge,
To cure this deadly grief.

MACDUFF   He has no children. All my pretty ones?
Did you say all? O hell-kite. All?
What, all my pretty chickens, and their dam
At one fell swoop?

MALCOLM   Dispute it like a man.

MACDUFF   I shall do so,
But I must also feel it as a man:
I cannot but remember such things were
That were most precious to me. Did heaven look on,
And would not take their part? Sinful Macduff,
They were all struck for thee. Naught that I am,
Not for their own demerits, but for mine,
Fell slaughter on their souls. Heaven rest them now.

MALCOLM
Be this the whetstone of your sword. Let grief
Convert to anger; blunt not the heart, enrage it.

MACDUFF   O, I could play the woman with mine eyes,
And braggart with my tongue. But gentle heavens,
Cut short all intermission. Front to front
Bring thou this fiend of Scotland and myself;
Within my sword's length set him. If he scape,
Heaven forgive him too.

MALCOLM   This time goes manly.
Come, go we to the King: our power is ready,
Our lack is nothing but our leave. Macbeth

Is ripe for shaking, and the powers above
Put on their instruments. Receive what cheer you may,
The night is long that never finds the day.   *Exeunt.*

5.1   *Enter a* Doctor of Physic, *and a*
                     Waiting Gentlewoman.

DOCTOR   I have two nights watched with you, but can
perceive no truth in your report. When was it she last
walked?

GENTLEWOMAN   Since his majesty went into the field,
I have seen her rise from her bed, throw her nightgown
upon her, unlock her closet, take forth paper, fold it,
write upon't, read it, afterwards seal it, and again
return to bed, yet all this while in a most fast sleep.

DOCTOR   A great perturbation in nature, to receive at
once the benefit of sleep and do the effects of watching.
In this slumbery agitation, besides her walking and
other actual performances, what, at any time, have you
heard her say?

GENTLEWOMAN   That, sir, which I will not report after
her.

DOCTOR   You may to me, and 'tis most meet you should.

GENTLEWOMAN   Neither to you, nor anyone, having
no witness to confirm my speech.

                Enter LADY, *with a taper.*

Lo you, here she comes. This is her very guise, and
upon my life, fast asleep. Observe her, stand close.

DOCTOR   How came she by that light?

GENTLEWOMAN   Why, it stood by her: she has light by
her continually; 'tis her command.

DOCTOR   You see her eyes are open.

GENTLEWOMAN   Ay, but their sense are shut.

DOCTOR   What is it she does now? Look how she rubs
her hands.

GENTLEWOMAN   It is an accustomed action with her, to
seem thus washing her hands. I have known her
continue in this a quarter of an hour.

LADY   Yet here's a spot.

DOCTOR   Hark, she speaks. I will set down what comes
from her, to satisfy my remembrance the more
strongly.

LADY   Out, damned spot: out, I say. One; two. Why then
'tis time to do't. Hell is murky. Fie, my lord, fie, a soldier
and afeared? What need we fear? Who knows it when
none can call our power to account? Yet who would have
thought the old man to have had so much blood in him?

DOCTOR   Do you mark that?

LADY   The Thane of Fife had a wife. Where is she now?
What, will these hands ne'er be clean? No more o'that,
my lord, no more o'that. You mar all with this
starting.

DOCTOR   Go to, go to. You have known what you should
not.

GENTLEWOMAN   She has spoke what she should not, I
am sure of that. Heaven knows what she has known.

LADY Here's the smell of the blood still. All the perfumes
    of Arabia will not sweeten this little hand. Oh, oh, oh. 50

DOCTOR What a sigh is there. The heart is sorely
    charged.

GENTLEWOMAN I would not have such a heart in my
    bosom, for the dignity of the whole body.

DOCTOR Well, well, well. 55

GENTLEWOMAN Pray God it be, sir.

DOCTOR This disease is beyond my practice: yet I have
    known those which have walked in their sleep, who
    have died holily in their beds.

LADY Wash your hands, put on your nightgown, look 60
    not so pale. I tell you yet again, Banquo's buried; he
    cannot come out on's grave.

DOCTOR Even so?

LADY To bed, to bed: there's knocking at the gate.
    Come, come, come, come, give me your hand. What's 65
    done, cannot be undone. To bed, to bed, to bed.

    Exit Lady.

DOCTOR Will she go now to bed?

GENTLEWOMAN Directly.

DOCTOR Foul whisperings are abroad. Unnatural deeds
    Do breed unnatural troubles. Infected minds 70
    To their deaf pillows will discharge their secrets.
    More needs she the divine than the physician.
    God, God forgive us all. Look after her,
    Remove from her the means of all annoyance,
    And still keep eyes upon her. So, goodnight. 75
    My mind she has mated and amazed my sight.
    I think, but dare not speak.

GENTLEWOMAN   Good night, good doctor.

    Exeunt.

5.2   *Drum and Colours. Enter* MENTEITH,
        CAITHNESS, ANGUS, LENNOX, Soldiers.

MENTEITH
    The English power is near, led on by Malcolm,
    His uncle Siward and the good Macduff.
    Revenges burn in them, for their dear causes
    Would to the bleeding and the grim alarm
    Excite the mortified man. 5

ANGUS   Near Birnam Wood
    Shall we well meet them; that way are they coming.

CAITHNESS
    Who knows if Donalbain be with his brother?

LENNOX For certain, sir, he is not; I have a file
    Of all the gentry. There is Siward's son,
    And many unrough youths, that even now 10
    Protest their first of manhood.

MENTEITH   What does the tyrant?

CAITHNESS Great Dunsinane he strongly fortifies.
    Some say he's mad; others, that lesser hate him,
    Do call it valiant fury; but for certain,
    He cannot buckle his distempered cause 15
    Within the belt of rule.

ANGUS   Now does he feel

His secret murders sticking on his hands;
Now minutely revolts upbraid his faith-breach;
Those he commands move only in command,
Nothing in love. Now does he feel his title 20
Hang loose about him, like a giant's robe
Upon a dwarfish thief.

MENTEITH   Who then shall blame
His pestered senses to recoil and start,
When all that is within him does condemn
Itself for being there.

CAITHNESS   Well, march we on, 25
To give obedience where 'tis truly owed.
Meet we the medicine of the sickly weal,
And with him pour we in our country's purge,
Each drop of us.

LENNOX   Or so much as it needs
To dew the sovereign flower, and drown the weeds. 30
Make we our march towards Birnam.

    Exeunt marching.

5.3   *Enter* MACBETH, Doctor *and Attendants.*

MACBETH Bring me no more reports, let them fly all;
    Till Birnam Wood remove to Dunsinane,
    I cannot taint with fear. What's the boy Malcolm?
    Was he not born of woman? The spirits that know
    All mortal consequences have pronounced me thus: 5
    'Fear not, Macbeth, no man that's born of woman
    Shall e'er have power upon thee.' Then fly, false
        thanes,
    And mingle with the English epicures;
    The mind I sway by, and the heart I bear,
    Shall never sag with doubt, nor shake with fear. 10

    Enter Servant.

The devil damn thee black, thou cream-faced loon.
Where got'st thou that goose-look?

SERVANT There is ten thousand.

MACBETH   Geese, villain?

SERVANT   Soldiers, sir.

MACBETH Go prick thy face, and over-red thy fear,
    Thou lily-livered boy. What soldiers, patch? 15
    Death of thy soul, those linen cheeks of thine
    Are counsellors to fear. What soldiers, whey-face?

SERVANT The English force, so please you.

MACBETH Take thy face hence.   *Exit Servant.*
                Seyton, I am sick at heart,
When I behold – Seyton, I say – this push 20
Will cheer me ever, or disseat me now.
I have lived long enough: my way of life
Is fallen into the sere, the yellow leaf,
And that which should accompany old age,
As honour, love, obedience, troops of friends, 25
I must not look to have; but in their stead,
Curses not loud but deep, mouth-honour, breath
Which the poor heart would fain deny, and dare not.
Seyton?

Enter SEYTON.

SEYTON   What's your gracious pleasure?

30 MACBETH   What news more?

SEYTON
All is confirmed, my lord, which was reported.

MACBETH
I'll fight, till from my bones my flesh be hacked.
Give me my armour.

SEYTON   'Tis not needed yet.

MACBETH   I'll put it on.

35   Send out more horses, skirr the country round,
Hang those that talk of fear. Give me mine armour.
How does your patient, doctor?

DOCTOR   Not so sick, my lord,
As she is troubled with thick-coming fancies
That keep her from her rest.

MACBETH   Cure her of that.

40   Canst thou not minister to a mind diseased,
Pluck from the memory a rooted sorrow,
Raze out the written troubles of the brain,
And with some sweet oblivious antidote
Cleanse the stuffed bosom of that perilous stuff
Which weighs upon the heart?

45 DOCTOR   Therein the patient
Must minister to himself.

MACBETH   Throw physic to the dogs, I'll none of it.
Come, put mine armour on; give me my staff;
Seyton, send out. Doctor, the thanes fly from me –

50   Come, sir, dispatch. – If thou couldst, doctor, cast
The water of my land, find her disease,
And purge it to a sound and pristine health,
I would applaud thee to the very echo,
That should applaud again. – Pull't off, I say.

55   What rhubarb, senna, or what purgative drug
Would scour these English hence? Hear'st thou of them?

DOCTOR   Ay, my good lord: your royal preparation
Makes us hear something.

MACBETH   Bring it after me.
I will not be afraid of death and bane

60   Till Birnam forest come to Dunsinane.

Exeunt all except Doctor.

DOCTOR   Were I from Dunsinane away and clear,
Profit again should hardly draw me here.   *Exit.*

5.4   *Drum and Colours. Enter* MALCOLM,
SIWARD, MACDUFF, *Siward's* Son,
MENTEITH, CAITHNESS, ANGUS *and*
Soldiers *marching.*

MALCOLM   Cousins, I hope the days are near at hand
That chambers will be safe.

MENTEITH   We doubt it nothing.

SIWARD   What wood is this before us?

MENTEITH   The Wood of Birnam.

MALCOLM   Let every soldier hew him down a bough

5   And bear't before him; thereby shall we shadow
The numbers of our host, and make discovery

Err in report of us.

SOLDIER   It shall be done.

SIWARD   We learn no other but the confident tyrant
Keeps still in Dunsinane, and will endure
Our setting down before't.

MALCOLM   'Tis his main hope. 10
For where there is advantage to be given,
Both more and less have given him the revolt,
And none serve with him but constrained things,
Whose hearts are absent too.

MACDUFF   Let our just censures
Attend the true event, and put we on   15
Industrious soldiership.

SIWARD   The time approaches,
That will with due decision make us know
What we shall say we have, and what we owe.
Thoughts speculative their unsure hopes relate,
But certain issue, strokes must arbitrate: 20
Towards which, advance the war.   *Exeunt marching.*

5.5   *Enter* MACBETH, SEYTON *and* Soldiers,
with Drum and Colours.

MACBETH   Hang out our banners on the outward walls;
The cry is still, 'They come'. Our castle's strength
Will laugh a siege to scorn. Here let them lie,
Till famine and the ague eat them up.
Were they not forced with those that should be ours,   5
We might have met them dareful, beard to beard,
And beat them backward home.

[A cry within of women]
What is that noise?

SEYTON   It is the cry of women, my good lord.

MACBETH   I have almost forgot the taste of fears.
The time has been, my senses would have cooled   10
To hear a night-shriek, and my fell of hair
Would at a dismal treatise rouse and stir
As life were in't. I have supped full with horrors;
Direness familiar to my slaughterous thoughts
Cannot once start me. Wherefore was that cry?   15

SEYTON   The Queen, my lord, is dead.

MACBETH   She should have died hereafter;
There would have been a time for such a word.
Tomorrow, and tomorrow, and tomorrow,
Creeps in this petty pace from day to day,
To the last syllable of recorded time;   20
And all our yesterdays have lighted fools
The way to dusty death. Out, out, brief candle,
Life's but a walking shadow, a poor player,
That struts and frets his hour upon the stage,
And then is heard no more. It is a tale   25
Told by an idiot, full of sound and fury
Signifying nothing.

Enter a Messenger.

Thou com'st to use thy tongue: thy story, quickly.

MESSENGER   Gracious my lord,

30   I should report that which I say I saw,
    But know not how to do't.
MACBETH   Well, say, sir.
MESSENGER   As I did stand my watch upon the hill,
    I looked toward Birnam, and anon methought
    The wood began to move.
MACBETH   Liar and slave.
35 MESSENGER   Let me endure your wrath, if't be not so.
    Within this three mile may you see it coming.
    I say, a moving grove.
MACBETH   If thou speak'st false,
    Upon the next tree shalt thou hang alive
    Till famine cling thee. If thy speech be sooth,
40   I care not if thou dost for me as much.
    I pull in resolution, and begin
    To doubt th'equivocation of the fiend,
    That lies like truth: 'Fear not, till Birnam Wood
    Do come to Dunsinane', and now a wood
45   Comes toward Dunsinane. Arm, arm, and out.
    If this which he avouches does appear,
    There is nor flying hence, nor tarrying here.
    I 'gin to be aweary of the sun,
    And wish th'estate o'th' world were now undone.
50   Ring the alarum bell. Blow wind, come wrack,
    At least we'll die with harness on our back.   *Exeunt.*

5.6   *Drum and Colours. Enter* MALCOLM, SIWARD,
      MACDUFF *and their Army, with boughs.*

MALCOLM
  Now near enough. Your leafy screens throw down,
  And show like those you are. You, worthy uncle,
  Shall with my cousin, your right noble son,
  Lead our first battle. Worthy Macduff and we
  Shall take upon's what else remains to do,
  According to our order.
SIWARD   Fare you well.
  Do we but find the tyrant's power tonight,
  Let us be beaten if we cannot fight.
MACDUFF
  Make all our trumpets speak, give them all breath,
  Those clamorous harbingers of blood and death.
              Exeunt. Alarums continued.

5.7   *Enter* MACBETH.

MACBETH   They have tied me to a stake; I cannot fly,
  But bear-like I must fight the course. What's he
  That was not born of woman? Such a one
  Am I to fear, or none.

       Enter YOUNG SIWARD.

YOUNG SIWARD   What is thy name?
MACBETH   Thou'lt be afraid to hear it.
YOUNG SIWARD
  No, though thou call'st thyself a hotter name
  Than any is in hell.

MACBETH   My name's Macbeth.
YOUNG SIWARD
  The devil himself could not pronounce a title
  More hateful to mine ear.
MACBETH   No, nor more fearful.
YOUNG SIWARD
  Thou liest, abhorred tyrant; with my sword   10
  I'll prove the lie thou speak'st.
     [*Fight, and Young Siward slain.*]
MACBETH   Thou wast born of woman.
  But swords I smile at, weapons laugh to scorn,
  Brandished by man that's of a woman born.   *Exit.*

       Alarums. Enter MACDUFF.

MACDUFF
  That way the noise is. Tyrant, show thy face,   15
  If thou be'st slain, and with no stroke of mine,
  My wife and children's ghosts will haunt me still.
  I cannot strike at wretched kerns, whose arms
  Are hired to bear their staves. Either thou, Macbeth,
  Or else my sword with an unbattered edge   20
  I sheathe again undeeded. There thou shouldst be;
  By this great clatter, one of greatest note
  Seems bruited. Let me find him, Fortune,
  And more I beg not.   *Exit.*

     Alarums. Enter MALCOLM *and* SIWARD.

SIWARD
  This way, my lord, the castle's gently rendered.   25
  The tyrant's people on both sides do fight;
  The noble thanes do bravely in the war;
  The day almost itself professes yours
  And little is to do.
MALCOLM   We have met with foes
  That strike beside us.
SIWARD   Enter, sir, the castle.   *Exeunt.*   30

5.8   *Alarum. Enter* MACBETH.

MACBETH   Why should I play the Roman fool, and die
  On mine own sword? Whiles I see lives, the gashes
  Do better upon them.

        Enter MACDUFF.

MACDUFF   Turn, hell-hound, turn.
MACBETH   Of all men else I have avoided thee.
  But get thee back, my soul is too much charged   5
  With blood of thine already.
MACDUFF   I have no words.
  My voice is in my sword, thou bloodier villain
  Than terms can give thee out.   [*Fight. Alarum.*]
MACBETH   Thou losest labour;
  As easy mayst thou the intrenchant air
  With thy keen sword impress, as make me bleed.   10
  Let fall thy blade on vulnerable crests;
  I bear a charmed life, which must not yield
  To one of woman born.

MACDUFF   Despair thy charm,
  And let the angel whom thou still hast served
15   Tell thee, Macduff was from his mother's womb
  Untimely ripped.
MACBETH   Accursed be that tongue that tells me so,
  For it hath cowed my better part of man.
  And be these juggling fiends no more believed
20   That palter with us in a double sense,
  That keep the word of promise to our ear,
  And break it to our hope. I'll not fight with thee.
MACDUFF   Then yield thee, coward,
  And live to be the show and gaze o'th' time.
25   We'll have thee, as our rarer monsters are,
  Painted upon a pole, and underwrit,
  'Here may you see the tyrant'.
MACBETH   I will not yield
  To kiss the ground before young Malcolm's feet,
  And to be baited with the rabble's curse.
30   Though Birnam Wood be come to Dunsinane,
  And thou opposed, being of no woman born,
  Yet I will try the last. Before my body
  I throw my warlike shield. Lay on, Macduff,
  And damned be him, that first cries, 'Hold, enough'.
                 Exeunt fighting. Alarums.

Enter fighting, and Macbeth slain.

Exit Macduff with Macbeth's body.

5.9   *Retreat and Flourish. Enter with Drum and*
       Colours MALCOLM, SIWARD, ROSS,
           Thanes *and* Soldiers.

MALCOLM
  I would the friends we miss were safe arrived.
SIWARD   Some must go off; and yet by these I see,
  So great a day as this is cheaply bought.
MALCOLM   Macduff is missing, and your noble son.
5 ROSS   Your son, my lord, has paid a soldier's debt:
  He only lived but till he was a man,
  The which no sooner had his prowess confirmed,
  In the unshrinking station where he fought,
  But like a man he died.
SIWARD   Then he is dead?

ROSS
  Aye, and brought off the field. Your cause of
     sorrow   10
  Must not be measured by his worth, for then
  It hath no end.
SIWARD   Had he his hurts before?
ROSS   Aye, on the front.
SIWARD   Why then, God's soldier be he.
  Had I as many sons as I have hairs,
  I would not wish them to a fairer death.   15
  And so his knell is knolled.
MALCOLM   He's worth more sorrow,
  And that I'll spend for him.
SIWARD   He's worth no more;
  They say he parted well and paid his score,
  And so God be with him. Here comes newer comfort.

Enter MACDUFF *with Macbeth's head.*

MACDUFF
  Hail King, for so thou art. Behold where stands   20
  Th'usurper's cursed head: the time is free.
  I see thee compassed with thy kingdom's pearl,
  That speak my salutation in their minds;
  Whose voices I desire aloud with mine.
  Hail, King of Scotland.
ALL   Hail, King of Scotland.   [*Flourish*]   25
MALCOLM   We shall not spend a large expense of time
  Before we reckon with your several loves
  And make us even with you. My thanes and kinsmen,
  Henceforth be earls, the first that ever Scotland
  In such an honour named. What's more to do,   30
  Which would be planted newly with the time,
  As calling home our exiled friends abroad,
  That fled the snares of watchful tyranny,
  Producing forth the cruel ministers
  Of this dead butcher, and his fiend-like queen,   35
  Who, as 'tis thought, by self and violent hands
  Took off her life – this, and what needful else
  That calls upon us, by the grace of grace,
  We will perform in measure, time and place.
  So thanks to all at once, and to each one,   40
  Whom we invite to see us crowned at Scone.
                 Flourish. Exeunt omnes.

Measure for Measure

Measure for Measure was first printed in the First Folio in 1623 as the fourth of the comedies, but it was performed at the Court of James I on 26 December 1604; it had probably been written and acted at the Globe earlier that year. Possibly the first play Shakespeare wrote after the accession of James I, it deals with many moral and political issues discussed by James in his *Basilicon Doron* (1599, reprinted 1603). Composed later than most of the comedies and at a time when Shakespeare was turning increasingly to tragedy, it has been seen as having particular affinities with *All's Well That Ends Well*, with which it is sometimes classified as a 'problem comedy'. *All's Well* is difficult to date, but it shares with *Measure for Measure* a darker tone than the other comedies, a strong, outspoken (and for some, dislikeable) heroine, and a plot resolved by a 'bed-trick' – the substitution of one woman for another in bed.

Shakespeare's sources were Giraldi Cinthio and George Whetstone, each of whom wrote two versions of the story of the magistrate who demands sexual favours in return for mercy: Cinthio told the story first in his *Hecatommithi* (1565) and dramatized it as *Epitia* (1573); Whetstone wrote a two-part play, *Promos and Cassandra* (1578), and a prose version in his *Heptameron of Civil Discourses* (1582). *Promos and Cassandra* seems to have been the main source, but Shakespeare also used the *Hecatommithi* for the source of *Othello* which was written close in time to *Measure for Measure*. In all the previous versions of the story the character who is the equivalent of Isabella does agree to have sex with the magistrate to save her brother's (or in some versions her husband's) life, but in none of them is she about to take vows as a nun; and Mariana is Shakespeare's invention, though the bed-trick was familiar from folklore and romance. The presence throughout of the disguised ruler is also Shakespeare's invention.

There are some anomalies and dislocations in the text which have been explained in various ways: some scholars have seen them as evidence of authorial revision, the Arden 2 editor ascribed them to oversights and changes of plan, while the editors of the Oxford *Complete Works* argue for adaptation after Shakespeare's death, most likely by Thomas Middleton, who may also have had a revising hand in *Macbeth* and a larger share in *Timon of Athens*. The passages affected are the opening of 1.2, where there is a noticeable inconsistency over Mistress Overdone's knowledge of Claudio's arrest, and the Duke's brief soliloquy at 4.1.58–63, which seems to have been transferred from his earlier speech at 3.1.443–6 in order to cover the conversation between Isabella and Mariana. The evidence adduced for Middleton is persuasive rather than compelling.

William Davenant adapted *Measure for Measure* in 1662 as *The Law Against Lovers*, a play which also took characters and situations from *Much Ado About Nothing*. Many in the eighteenth and nineteenth centuries found its subject-matter distasteful and its conclusion arbitrary: Charlotte Lennox, for example, compared Shakespeare's version with Cinthio's and roundly condemned the former for altering the story for the worse and introducing 'low Contrivance, absurd intrigue and improbable incidents . . . in order to bring about three or four Weddings instead of one good Beheading' (*Shakespeare Illustrated*, 1753). Coleridge called it 'a hateful work', and twentieth-century attempts to rehabilitate it by interpreting it as a Christian parable (with the Duke as 'power divine') have not convinced everyone. It has, however, appealed to modern performers and critics as a play about repressed desire and sexual decadence set, prophetically, in Freud's city of Vienna, and some powerful productions have emphasized the claustrophobia of its containment within the walls of convent, brothel and prison. In the theatre there is often a degree of suspense as to how Isabella will react to the Duke's proposal of marriage in the final scene: Shakespeare gives her no verbal response.

The Arden text is based on the 1623 First Folio.

DUKE	*Vincentio*
ANGELO	*the Deputy*
ESCALUS	*an ancient lord*
CLAUDIO	*a young gentleman*
LUCIO	*a fantastic*
Two other like GENTLEMEN	
PROVOST	
THOMAS	} *two friars*
PETER	
ELBOW	*a simple constable*
FROTH	*a foolish gentleman*
POMPEY Bum	*Clown*
ABHORSON	*an executioner*
BARNARDINE	*a dissolute prisoner*
ISABELLA	*sister to Claudio*
MARIANA	*betrothed to Angelo*
JULIET	*beloved of Claudio*
FRANCISCA	*a nun*
Mistress OVERDONE	*a bawd*
Varrius	*a gentleman*
JUSTICE	
MESSENGER	
SERVANT	
Boy	*a singer*

Attendants, Guards, Lords, Officers, Citizens

1.1 *Enter* DUKE, ESCALUS, *Lords.*

DUKE Escalus.

ESCALUS My lord.

DUKE Of government the properties to unfold
Would seem in me t'affect speech and discourse,
Since I am put to know that your own science
Exceeds in that the lists of all advice
My strength can give you. Then no more remains
But that, to your sufficiency, as your worth is able,
And let them work. The nature of our people,
Our city's institutions and the terms
For common justice, you're as pregnant in
As art and practice hath enriched any
That we remember. There is our commission,
From which we would not have you warp. – Call
    hither,
I say, bid come before us Angelo. –   *Exit a Lord.*
What figure of us think you he will bear?
For you must know, we have with special soul
Elected him our absence to supply;
Lent him our terror, dressed him with our love
And given his deputation all the organs
Of our own power. What think you of it?

ESCALUS If any in Vienna be of worth
To undergo such ample grace and honour,
It is Lord Angelo.

Enter ANGELO.

DUKE   Look where he comes.

ANGELO Always obedient to your grace's will,
I come to know your pleasure.

DUKE   Angelo,
There is a kind of character in thy life
That to th'observer doth thy history
Fully unfold. Thyself and thy belongings
Are not thine own so proper as to waste
Thyself upon thy virtues, they on thee.
Heaven doth with us as we with torches do,
Not light them for themselves; for if our virtues
Did not go forth of us, 'twere all alike
As if we had them not. Spirits are not finely touched
But to fine issues, nor nature never lends
The smallest scruple of her excellence,
But like a thrifty goddess she determines
Herself the glory of a creditor:
Both thanks and use. But I do bend my speech
To one that can my part in him advertise.
Hold therefore, Angelo:
In our remove, be thou at full ourself.
Mortality and mercy in Vienna
Live in thy tongue and heart; old Escalus,
Though first in question, is thy secondary.
Take thy commission.

ANGELO   Now, good my lord,
Let there be some more test made of my metal
Before so noble and so great a figure

Be stamped upon it.

DUKE   No more evasion.   50
We have with a leavened and prepared choice
Proceeded to you; therefore take your honours.
Our haste from hence is of so quick condition
That it prefers itself and leaves unquestioned
Matters of needful value. We shall write to you, 55
As time and our concernings shall importune,
How it goes with us, and do look to know
What doth befall you here. So fare you well.
To th' hopeful execution do I leave you
Of your commissions.

ANGELO   Yet give leave, my lord,   60
That we may bring you something on the way.

DUKE My haste may not admit it.
Nor need you, on mine honour, have to do
With any scruple: your scope is as mine own,
So to enforce or qualify the laws   65
As to your soul seems good. Give me your hand.
I'll privily away. I love the people,
But do not like to stage me to their eyes;
Though it do well, I do not relish well
Their loud applause and aves vehement;   70
Nor do I think the man of safe discretion
That does affect it. Once more, fare you well.

ANGELO The heavens give safety to your purposes.

ESCALUS Lead forth and bring you back in happiness.

DUKE I thank you, fare you well.   *Exit.*   75

ESCALUS I shall desire you, sir, to give me leave
To have free speech with you; and it concerns me
To look into the bottom of my place.
A power I have, but of what strength and nature
I am not yet instructed.   80

ANGELO 'Tis so with me. Let us withdraw together,
And we may soon our satisfaction have
Touching that point.

ESCALUS   I'll wait upon your honour. *Exeunt.*

1.2 *Enter* LUCIO *and two other* Gentlemen.

LUCIO If the Duke, with the other dukes, come not to
composition with the King of Hungary, why then all
the dukes fall upon the King.

1 GENTLEMAN Heaven grant us its peace, but not the
King of Hungary's.   5

2 GENTLEMAN Amen.

LUCIO Thou conclud'st like the sanctimonious pirate
that went to sea with the ten commandments, but
scraped one out of the table.

1 GENTLEMAN Thou shalt not steal?   10

LUCIO Ay, that he razed.

1 GENTLEMAN Why, 'twas a commandment to
command the captain and all the rest from their
functions: they put forth to steal. There's not a soldier
of us all that in the thanksgiving before meat do relish 15
the petition well that prays for peace.

2 GENTLEMAN I never heard any soldier dislike it.

LUCIO   I believe thee, for I think thou never wast where
grace was said.

20   2 GENTLEMAN   No? A dozen times at least.

1 GENTLEMAN   What? In metre?

LUCIO   In any proportion, or in any language.

1 GENTLEMAN   I think, or in any religion.

LUCIO   Ay, why not? Grace is grace, despite of all
25   controversy, as for example, thou thyself art a wicked
villain, despite of all grace.

1 GENTLEMAN   Well. There went but a pair of shears
between us.

LUCIO   I grant – as there may between the lists and the
30   velvet. Thou art the list.

1 GENTLEMAN   And thou the velvet; thou art good
velvet, thou'rt a three-piled piece, I warrant thee. I had
as lief be a list of an English kersey as be piled as thou
art piled for a French velvet. Do I speak feelingly now?

35   LUCIO   I think thou dost. And indeed with most painful
feeling of thy speech, I will, out of thine own
confession, learn to begin thy health but, whilst I live,
forget to drink after thee.

1 GENTLEMAN   I think I have done myself wrong, have
40   I not?

2 GENTLEMAN   Yes, that thou hast; whether thou art
tainted or free.

Enter OVERDONE, *a bawd.*

LUCIO   Behold, behold, where Madam Mitigation
comes. I have purchased as many diseases under her
45   roof, as come to –

2 GENTLEMAN   To what, I pray?

LUCIO   Judge.

2 GENTLEMAN   To three thousand dolours a year.

1 GENTLEMAN   Ay, and more.

50   LUCIO   A French crown more.

1 GENTLEMAN   Thou art always figuring diseases in me,
but thou art full of error, I am sound.

LUCIO   Nay, not, as one would say, healthy, but so
sound, as things that are hollow – thy bones are hollow.
55   Impiety has made a feast of thee.

1 GENTLEMAN   How now, which of your hips has the
most profound sciatica?

OVERDONE   Well, well. There's one yonder arrested and
carried to prison was worth five thousand of you all.

60   2 GENTLEMAN   Who's that, I prithee?

OVERDONE   Marry, sir, that's Claudio, Signior Claudio.

1 GENTLEMAN   Claudio to prison? 'Tis not so.

OVERDONE   Nay, but I know 'tis so. I saw him arrested,
saw him carried away. And which is more, within these
65   three days his head to be chopped off.

LUCIO   But, after all this fooling, I would not have it so.
Art thou sure of this?

OVERDONE   I am too sure of it, and it is for getting
Madam Julietta with child.

70   LUCIO   Believe me, this may be. He promised to meet
me two hours since, and he was ever precise in
promise-keeping.

2 GENTLEMAN   Besides, you know, it draws something
near to the speech we had to such a purpose.

75   1 GENTLEMAN   But most of all agreeing with the
proclamation.

LUCIO   Away: let's go learn the truth of it.

                          Exeunt Lucio and Gentlemen.

OVERDONE   Thus, what with the war, what with the
sweat, what with the gallows, and what with poverty, I
80   am custom-shrunk.

Enter POMPEY.

How now? What's the news with you?

POMPEY   Yonder man is carried to prison.

OVERDONE   Well, what has he done?

POMPEY   A woman.

85   OVERDONE   But what's his offence?

POMPEY   Groping for trouts in a peculiar river.

OVERDONE   What? Is there a maid with child by him?

POMPEY   No, but there's a woman with maid by him.
You have not heard of the proclamation, have you?

90   OVERDONE   What proclamation, man?

POMPEY   All houses in the suburbs of Vienna must be
plucked down.

OVERDONE   And what shall become of those in the city?

POMPEY   They shall stand for seed. They had gone
95   down too, but that a wise burgher put in for them.

OVERDONE   But shall all our houses of resort in the
suburbs be pulled down?

POMPEY   To the ground, mistress.

OVERDONE   Why here's a change indeed in the
100   commonwealth. What shall become of me?

POMPEY   Come, fear not you. Good counsellors lack no
clients; though you change your place, you need not
change your trade. I'll be your tapster still. Courage,
there will be pity taken on you; you that have worn
105   your eyes almost out in the service, you will be
considered.

Enter PROVOST, CLAUDIO, JULIET *and Officers.*

OVERDONE   What's to do here, Thomas Tapster? Let's
withdraw.

POMPEY   Here comes Signior Claudio, led by the
110   provost to prison, and there's Madam Juliet.   *Exeunt.*

CLAUDIO
Fellow, why dost thou show me thus to th' world?
Bear me to prison, where I am committed.

PROVOST   I do it not in evil disposition,
But from Lord Angelo by special charge.

115   CLAUDIO   Thus can the demigod, Authority,
Make us pay down for our offence by weight.
The words of heaven – on whom it will, it will,
On whom it will not, so; yet still 'tis just.

Enter LUCIO.

LUCIO
Why, how now, Claudio! Whence comes this restraint?

CLAUDIO   From too much liberty, my Lucio. Liberty, 120
As surfeit, is the father of much fast,
So every scope by the immoderate use
Turns to restraint. Our natures do pursue,
Like rats that ravin down their proper bane,
A thirsty evil, and when we drink, we die. 125

LUCIO   If I could speak so wisely under an arrest, I
would send for certain of my creditors. And yet, to say
the truth, I had as lief have the foppery of freedom as
the mortality of imprisonment. What's thy offence,
Claudio? 130

CLAUDIO   What but to speak of would offend again.

LUCIO   What, is't murder?

CLAUDIO   No.

LUCIO   Lechery?

CLAUDIO   Call it so. 135

PROVOST   Away, sir, you must go.

CLAUDIO
One word, good friend – Lucio, a word with you.

LUCIO   A hundred, if they'll do you any good. Is lechery
so looked after?

CLAUDIO
Thus stands it with me: upon a true contract 140
I got possession of Julietta's bed.
You know the lady; she is fast my wife,
Save that we do the denunciation lack
Of outward order. This we came not to
Only for propagation of a dower 145
Remaining in the coffer of her friends,
From whom we thought it meet to hide our love
Till time had made them for us. But it chances
The stealth of our most mutual entertainment
With character too gross is writ on Juliet. 150

LUCIO   With child, perhaps?

CLAUDIO   Unhappily, even so.
And the new deputy now for the Duke –
Whether it be the fault and glimpse of newness,
Or whether that the body public be
A horse whereon the governor doth ride, 155
Who newly in the seat, that it may know
He can command, lets it straight feel the spur.
Whether the tyranny be in his place
Or in his eminence that fills it up
I stagger in – but this new governor 160
Awakes me all the enrolled penalties
Which have like unscoured armour hung by th'wall
So long that nineteen zodiacs have gone round
And none of them been worn, and for a name
Now puts the drowsy and neglected act 165
Freshly on me. 'Tis surely for a name.

LUCIO   I warrant it is. And thy head stands so tickle on
thy shoulders that a milkmaid, if she be in love, may
sigh it off. Send after the Duke and appeal to him.

CLAUDIO   I have done so, but he's not to be found. 170
I prithee, Lucio, do me this kind service –
This day, my sister should the cloister enter
And there receive her approbation.

Acquaint her with the danger of my state;
Implore her in my voice that she make friends 175
To the strict deputy; bid herself assay him.
I have great hope in that, for in her youth
There is a prone and speechless dialect
Such as move men; beside, she hath prosperous art
When she will play with reason and discourse, 180
And well she can persuade.

LUCIO   I pray she may, as well for the encouragement of
the like, which else would stand under grievous
imposition, as for the enjoying of thy life, who I would
be sorry should be thus foolishly lost at a game of 185
ticktack. I'll to her –

CLAUDIO   I thank you, good friend Lucio.

LUCIO   Within two hours –

CLAUDIO   Come, officer, away.   *Exeunt.*

1.3   *Enter* DUKE *and Friar* THOMAS.

DUKE   No, holy father, throw away that thought.
Believe not that the dribbling dart of love
Can pierce a complete bosom. Why I desire thee
To give me secret harbour hath a purpose
More grave and wrinkled than the aims and ends 5
Of burning youth.

THOMAS   May your grace speak of it?

DUKE   My holy sir, none better knows than you
How I have ever loved the life removed
And held in idle price to haunt assemblies
Where youth and cost witless bravery keeps. 10
I have delivered to Lord Angelo,
A man of stricture and firm abstinence,
My absolute power and place here in Vienna,
And he supposes me travelled to Poland,
For so I have strewed it in the common ear, 15
And so it is received. Now, pious sir,
You will demand of me why I do this.

THOMAS   Gladly, my lord.

DUKE   We have strict statutes and most biting laws,
The needful bits and curbs to headstrong weeds, 20
Which for this fourteen years we have let slip,
Even like an o'ergrown lion in a cave
That goes not out to prey. Now, as fond fathers,
Having bound up the threatening twigs of birch,
Only to stick it in their children's sight 25
For terror, not to use, in time the rod
More mocked than feared; so our decrees,
Dead to infliction, to themselves are dead,
And liberty plucks justice by the nose,
The baby beats the nurse, and quite athwart 30
Goes all decorum.

THOMAS   It rested in your grace
To unloose this tied-up justice when you pleased,
And it in you more dreadful would have seemed
Than in Lord Angelo.

DUKE   I do fear too dreadful.
Sith 'twas my fault to give the people scope, 35

'Twould be my tyranny to strike and gall them
For what I bid them do – for we bid this be done
When evil deeds have their permissive pass
And not the punishment. Therefore, indeed, my
   father,
40   I have on Angelo imposed the office,
Who may in th'ambush of my name strike home,
And yet my nature never in the fight
To do in slander. And to behold his sway,
I will, as 'twere a brother of your order,
45   Visit both prince and people. Therefore, I prithee,
Supply me with the habit and instruct me
How I may formally in person bear
Like a true friar. Mo reasons for this action
At our more leisure shall I render you;
50   Only this one: Lord Angelo is precise,
Stands at a guard with envy, scarce confesses
That his blood flows, or that his appetite
Is more to bread than stone. Hence shall we see,
If power change purpose, what our seemers be.

                          Exeunt.

1.4   *Enter* ISABELLA *and* FRANCISCA, *a Nun.*

ISABELLA   And have you nuns no farther privileges?
FRANCISCA   Are not these large enough?
ISABELLA   Yes, truly; I speak not as desiring more,
But rather wishing a more strict restraint
5   Upon the sisterhood, the votarists of Saint Clare.
LUCIO [*within*]
Ho! Peace be in this place.
ISABELLA   Who's that which calls?
FRANCISCA   It is a man's voice. Gentle Isabella,
Turn you the key and know his business of him;
You may; I may not. You are yet unsworn.
10   When you have vowed, you must not speak with men
But in the presence of the prioress.
Then if you speak, you must not show your face;
Or if you show your face, you must not speak.
    [*Lucio calls within.*]
He calls again. I pray you, answer him.   *Exit.*
15   ISABELLA   Peace and prosperity. Who is't that calls?

            Enter LUCIO.

LUCIO   Hail, virgin, if you be, as those cheek-roses
Proclaim you are no less. Can you so stead me
As bring me to the sight of Isabella,
A novice of this place and the fair sister
20   To her unhappy brother Claudio?
ISABELLA   Why 'her unhappy brother'? Let me ask,
The rather for I now must make you know
I am that Isabella and his sister.
LUCIO   Gentle and fair, your brother kindly greets you;
25   Not to be weary with you, he's in prison.
ISABELLA   Woe me! For what?
LUCIO   For that which, if myself might be his judge,
He should receive his punishment in thanks:

He hath got his friend with child.
ISABELLA   Sir, make me not your story.
LUCIO   'Tis true.   30
I would not, though 'tis my familiar sin
With maids to seem the lapwing and to jest,
Tongue far from heart, play with all virgins so.
I hold you as a thing enskied and sainted
By your renouncement, an immortal spirit,   35
And to be talked with in sincerity
As with a saint.
ISABELLA   You do blaspheme the good in mocking me.
LUCIO   Do not believe it. Fewness and truth, 'tis thus:
Your brother and his lover have embraced;   40
As those that feed grow full, as blossoming time
That from the seedness the bare fallow brings
To teeming foison, even so her plenteous womb
Expresseth his full tilth and husbandry.
ISABELLA
Someone with child by him? My cousin Juliet?   45
LUCIO   Is she your cousin?
ISABELLA
Adoptedly, as schoolmaids change their names
By vain though apt affection.
LUCIO   She it is.
ISABELLA   O, let him marry her.
LUCIO   This is the point.
The Duke is very strangely gone from hence;   50
Bore many gentlemen, myself being one,
In hand and hope of action, but we do learn
By those that know the very nerves of state,
His giving out were of an infinite distance
From his true meant design. Upon his place   55
And with full line of his authority
Governs Lord Angelo, a man whose blood
Is very snowbroth; one who never feels
The wanton stings and motions of the sense,
But doth rebate and blunt his natural edge   60
With profits of the mind, study and fast.
He, to give fear to use and liberty,
Which have for long run by the hideous law
As mice by lions, hath picked out an act
Under whose heavy sense your brother's life   65
Falls into forfeit. He arrests him on it
And follows close the rigour of the statute
To make him an example; all hope is gone
Unless you have the grace by your fair prayer
To soften Angelo. And that's my pith of business   70
'Twixt you and your poor brother.
ISABELLA   Doth he so seek his life?
LUCIO   H'as censured him already, and as I hear,
The provost hath a warrant for's execution.
ISABELLA   Alas, what poor ability's in me   75
To do him good?
LUCIO   Assay the power you have.
ISABELLA   My power? Alas, I doubt.
LUCIO   Our doubts are traitors
And makes us lose the good we oft might win,

By fearing to attempt. Go to Lord Angelo
And let him learn to know when maidens sue
Men give like gods, but when they weep and kneel,
All their petitions are as freely theirs
As they themselves would owe them.

ISABELLA   I'll see what I can do.

LUCIO   But speedily.

ISABELLA   I will about it straight,
No longer staying but to give the Mother
Notice of my affair. I humbly thank you;
Commend me to my brother; soon at night
I'll send him certain word of my success.

LUCIO   I take my leave of you.

ISABELLA   Good sir, adieu.   *Exeunt.*

2.1   *Enter* ANGELO, ESCALUS,
               and Servants, JUSTICE.

ANGELO   We must not make a scarecrow of the law,
Setting it up to fear the birds of prey,
And let it keep one shape, till custom make it
Their perch and not their terror.

ESCALUS   Ay, but yet
Let us be keen, and rather cut a little
Than fall and bruise to death. Alas, this gentleman
Whom I would save had a most noble father.
Let but your honour know,
Whom I believe to be most strait in virtue,
That in the working of your own affections,
Had time cohered with place, or place with wishing,
Or that the resolute acting of your blood
Could have attained th'effect of your own purpose,
Whether you had not sometime in your life
Erred in this point which now you censure him
And pulled the law upon you.

ANGELO   'Tis one thing to be tempted, Escalus,
Another thing to fall. I not deny
The jury passing on the prisoner's life
May in the sworn twelve have a thief or two
Guiltier than him they try: what's open made to justice,
That justice seizes. What knows the laws
That thieves do pass on thieves? 'Tis very pregnant:
The jewel that we find, we stoop and take't
Because we see it, but what we do not see
We tread upon and never think of it.
You may not so extenuate his offence
For I have had such faults, but rather tell me
When I that censure him do so offend,
Let mine own judgement pattern out my death,
And nothing come in partial. Sir, he must die.

                   Enter PROVOST.

ESCALUS   Be it as your wisdom will.

ANGELO   Where is the provost?

PROVOST   Here, if it like your honour.

ANGELO   See that Claudio
Be executed by nine tomorrow morning.

Bring him his confessor, let him be prepared,   35
For that's the utmost of his pilgrimage.

                                   Exit Provost.

ESCALUS [*aside*]
Well, heaven forgive him, and forgive us all:
Some rise by sin and some by virtue fall,
Some run from breaks of ice and answer none,
And some condemned for a fault alone.   40

     Enter ELBOW, FROTH, POMPEY, *Officers.*

ELBOW   Come, bring them away: if these be good
people in a commonweal, that do nothing but use their
abuses in common houses, I know no law. Bring them
away.

ANGELO   How now, sir, what's your name? And what's   45
the matter?

ELBOW   If it please your honour, I am the poor Duke's
constable, and my name is Elbow. I do lean upon
justice, sir, and do bring in here before your good
honour two notorious benefactors.   50

ANGELO   Benefactors? Well, what benefactors are they?
Are they not malefactors?

ELBOW   If it please your honour, I know not well what
they are, but precise villains they are, that I am sure of,
and void of all profanation in the world that good   55
Christians ought to have.

ESCALUS   This comes off well. Here's a wise officer.

ANGELO   Go to. What quality are they of? 'Elbow' is
your name? Why dost thou not speak, Elbow?

POMPEY   He cannot, sir; he's out at elbow.   60

ANGELO [*to Pompey*]   What are you, sir?

ELBOW   He, sir, a tapster, sir, parcel bawd, one that
serves a bad woman whose house, sir, was, as they say,
plucked down in the suburbs, and now she professes a
hothouse, which I think is a very ill house too.   65

ESCALUS   How know you that?

ELBOW   My wife, sir, whom I detest before heaven and
your honour –

ESCALUS   How? Thy wife?

ELBOW   Ay, sir, whom I thank heaven is an honest   70
woman –

ESCALUS   Dost thou detest her therefore?

ELBOW   I say, sir, I will detest myself, also, as well as she,
that this house, if it be not a bawd's house, it is pity of
her life, for it is a naughty house.   75

ESCALUS   How dost thou know that, constable?

ELBOW   Marry sir, by my wife, who, if she had been a
woman cardinally given, might have been accused in
fornication, adultery and all uncleanliness there.

ESCALUS   By the woman's means?   80

ELBOW   Ay, sir, by Mistress Overdone's means. But as
she spit in his face, so she defied him.

POMPEY   Sir, if it please your honour, this is not so.

ELBOW   Prove it before these varlets here, thou
honourable man, prove it.   85

ESCALUS [*to Angelo*]   Do you hear how he misplaces?

POMPEY   Sir, she came in great with child, and longing,

saving your honour's reverence, for stewed prunes; sir,
we had but two in the house, which at that very distant
time stood, as it were, in a fruit dish – a dish of some
threepence – your honours have seen such dishes –
they are not china dishes, but very good dishes.

ESCALUS   Go to, go to. No matter for the dish, sir.

POMPEY   No indeed sir, not of a pin; you are therein in
the right, but to the point. As I say, this Mistress
Elbow, being, as I say, with child, and being great
bellied, and longing, as I said, for prunes, and having
but two in the dish, as I said – Master Froth here, this
very man, having eaten the rest, as I said, and, as I say,
paying for them very honestly. For, as you know,
Master Froth, I could not give you threepence again.

FROTH   No, indeed.

POMPEY   Very well. You being then, if you be
remembered, cracking the stones of the foresaid
prunes.

FROTH   Ay, so I did indeed.

POMPEY   Why, very well. I telling you then, if you be
remembered, that such a one and such a one were past
cure of the thing you wot of, unless they kept very good
diet, as I told you.

FROTH   All this is true.

POMPEY   Why, very well then.

ESCALUS   Come, you are a tedious fool; to the purpose.
What was done to Elbow's wife that he hath cause to
complain of? Come me to what was done to her.

POMPEY   Sir, your honour cannot come to that yet.

ESCALUS   No sir, nor I mean it not.

POMPEY   Sir, but you shall come to it, by your honour's
leave. And I beseech you, look into Master Froth here,
sir, a man of fourscore pound a year, whose father
died at Hallowmas – was't not at Hallowmas, Master
Froth?

FROTH   All-hallow Eve.

POMPEY   Why, very well. I hope here be truths. He, sir,
sitting, as I say, in a lower chair, sir – 'twas in the
Bunch of Grapes, where indeed you have a delight to
sit, have you not?

FROTH   I have so, because it is an open room, and good
for winter.

POMPEY   Why, very well then. I hope here be truths.

ANGELO   This will last out a night in Russia
When nights are longest there. I'll take my leave
And leave you to the hearing of the cause,
Hoping you'll find good cause to whip them all.

ESCALUS   I think no less. Good morrow to your lordship.

Exit Angelo.

Now, sir, come on. What was done to Elbow's wife,
once more?

POMPEY   Once, sir? There was nothing done to her
once.

ELBOW   I beseech you, sir, ask him what this man did to
my wife.

POMPEY   I beseech your honour, ask me.

ESCALUS   Well, sir, what did this gentleman to her?

POMPEY   I beseech you, sir, look in this gentleman's
face – good Master Froth, look upon his honour, 'tis
for a good purpose – doth your honour mark his face?

ESCALUS   Ay, sir, very well.

POMPEY   Nay, I beseech you, mark it well.

ESCALUS   Well, I do so.

POMPEY   Doth your honour see any harm in his face?

ESCALUS   Why, no.

POMPEY   I'll be supposed upon a book his face is the
worst thing about him. Good then, if his face be the
worst thing about him, how could Master Froth do
the constable's wife any harm? I would know that of
your honour.

ESCALUS   He's in the right, constable. What say you to
it?

ELBOW   First, an it like you, the house is a respected
house; next, this is a respected fellow; and his mistress
is a respected woman.

POMPEY   By this hand, sir, his wife is a more respected
person than any of us all.

ELBOW   Varlet, thou liest; thou liest, wicked varlet. The
time is yet to come that she was ever respected with
man, woman or child.

POMPEY   Sir, she was respected with him before he
married with her.

ESCALUS   Which is the wiser here, Justice or Iniquity?
Is this true?

ELBOW   O thou caitiff, O thou varlet, O thou wicked
Hannibal! I respected with her before I was married to
her? If ever I was respected with her, or she with me,
let not your worship think me the poor Duke's officer
– prove this, thou wicked Hannibal, or I'll have mine
action of battery on thee.

ESCALUS   If he took you a box o'th' ear, you might have
your action of slander too.

ELBOW   Marry, I thank your good worship for it. What
is't your worship's pleasure I shall do with this wicked
caitiff?

ESCALUS   Truly, officer, because he hath some offences
in him that thou wouldst discover if thou couldst, let
him continue in his courses, till thou knowst what they
are.

ELBOW   Marry, I thank your worship for it – thou seest,
thou wicked varlet now, what's come upon thee. Thou
art to continue now, thou varlet, thou art to continue.

ESCALUS   [*to Froth*]   Where were you born, friend?

FROTH   Here in Vienna, sir.

ESCALUS   Are you of fourscore pounds a year?

FROTH   Yes, an't please you, sir.

ESCALUS   So. [*to Pompey*] What trade are you of, sir?

POMPEY   A tapster, a poor widow's tapster.

ESCALUS   Your mistress' name?

POMPEY   Mistress Overdone.

ESCALUS   Hath she had any more than one husband?

POMPEY   Nine, sir; Overdone by the last.

ESCALUS   Nine? Come hither to me, Master Froth.
Master Froth, I would not have you acquainted with

tapsters; they will draw you, Master Froth, and you
will hang them. Get you gone, and let me hear no more
of you.

FROTH I thank your worship. For mine own part, I
never come into any room in a tap-house, but I am
drawn in.

ESCALUS Well, no more of it, Master Froth. Farewell.
Exit Froth.
Come you hither to me, Master Tapster. What's your
name, Master Tapster?

POMPEY Pompey.

ESCALUS What else?

POMPEY Bum, sir.

ESCALUS Troth, and your bum is the greatest thing
about you, so that in the beastliest sense, you are
Pompey the Great. Pompey, you are partly a bawd,
Pompey, howsoever you colour it in being a tapster, are
you not? Come, tell me true, it shall be the better for
you.

POMPEY Truly sir, I am a poor fellow that would live.

ESCALUS How would you live, Pompey? By being a
bawd? What do you think of the trade, Pompey? Is it a
lawful trade?

POMPEY If the law would allow it, sir.

ESCALUS But the law will not allow it, Pompey, nor it
shall not be allowed in Vienna.

POMPEY Does your worship mean to geld and splay all
the youth of the city?

ESCALUS No, Pompey.

POMPEY Truly, sir, in my poor opinion they will to't
then. If your worship will take order for the drabs and
the knaves, you need not to fear the bawds.

ESCALUS There is pretty orders beginning, I can tell
you: it is but heading and hanging.

POMPEY If you head and hang all that offend that way
but for ten year together, you'll be glad to give out a
commission for more heads. If this law hold in Vienna
ten year, I'll rent the fairest house in it after threepence
a bay. If you live to see this come to pass, say Pompey
told you so.

ESCALUS Thank you, good Pompey, and in requital of
your prophecy, hark you. I advise you let me not find
you before me again upon any complaint whatsoever
– no, not for dwelling where you do. If I do, Pompey, I
shall beat you to your tent and prove a shrewd Caesar
to you. In plain dealing, Pompey, I shall have you
whipped. So for this time, Pompey, fare you well.

POMPEY I thank your worship for your good counsel;
[*aside*] but I shall follow it as the flesh and fortune shall
better determine.
Whip me? No, no, let carman whip his jade,
The valiant heart's not whipped out of his trade. *Exit.*

ESCALUS Come hither to me, Master Elbow, come
hither, Master Constable. How long have you been in
this place of constable?

ELBOW Seven year, and a half, sir.

ESCALUS I thought, by the readiness in the office, you

had continued in it some time: you say seven years
together.

ELBOW And a half, sir.

ESCALUS Alas, it hath been great pains to you; they do   260
you wrong to put you so oft upon't. Are there not men
in your ward sufficient to serve it?

ELBOW 'Faith, sir, few of any wit in such matters; as
they are chosen, they are glad to choose me for them.
I do it for some piece of money and go through with   265
all.

ESCALUS Look you bring me in the names of some six
or seven, the most sufficient of your parish.

ELBOW To your worship's house, sir?

ESCALUS To my house. Fare you well.   *Exit Elbow.*   270
What's o'clock, think you?

JUSTICE Eleven, sir.

ESCALUS I pray you home to dinner with me.

JUSTICE I humbly thank you.

ESCALUS It grieves me for the death of Claudio,   275
But there's no remedy.

JUSTICE Lord Angelo is severe.

ESCALUS It is but needful.
Mercy is not itself, that oft looks so;
Pardon is still the nurse of second woe.   280
But yet, poor Claudio! There is no remedy.
Come, sir.   *Exeunt.*

2.2   *Enter* PROVOST *and a* Servant.

SERVANT
He's hearing of a cause; he will come straight,
I'll tell him of you.

PROVOST   'Pray you do.   *Exit Servant.*
I'll know
His pleasure, maybe he will relent; alas,
He hath but as offended in a dream.
All sects, all ages smack of this vice, and he   5
To die for't?

Enter ANGELO.

ANGELO Now, what's the matter, Provost?

PROVOST Is it your will Claudio shall die tomorrow?

ANGELO
Did not I tell thee yea? Hadst thou not order?
Why dost thou ask again?

PROVOST   Lest I might be too rash: 10
Under your good correction I have seen
When after execution, judgement hath
Repented o'er his doom.

ANGELO   Go to; let that be mine,
Do you your office or give up your place,
And you shall well be spared.   15

PROVOST I crave your honour's pardon:
What shall be done, sir, with the groaning Juliet?
She's very near her hour.

ANGELO   Dispose of her
To some more fitter place; and that with speed.

	Enter Servant.	

20 SERVANT   Here is the sister of the man condemned
      Desires access to you.
    ANGELO   Hath he a sister?
    PROVOST   Ay, my good lord, a very virtuous maid,
      And to be shortly of a sisterhood,
      If not already.
    ANGELO   Well, let her be admitted.
                                   Exit Servant.
25   See you the fornicatress be removed.
      Let her have needful but not lavish means.
      There shall be order for't.

                    Enter LUCIO *and* ISABELLA.

    PROVOST   'Save your honour.
    ANGELO
      Stay a little while. [*to Isabella*] You're welcome: what's
        your will?
    ISABELLA   I am a woeful suitor to your honour,
      'Please but your honour hear me.
30 ANGELO   Well, what's your suit?
    ISABELLA   There is a vice that most I do abhor,
      And most desire should meet the blow of justice;
      For which I would not plead, but that I must,
      For which I must not plead, but that I am
      At war 'twixt will and will not.
35 ANGELO   Well, the matter?
    ISABELLA   I have a brother is condemned to die;
      I do beseech you let it be his fault,
      And not my brother.
    PROVOST [*aside*]   Heaven give thee moving graces.
    ANGELO   Condemn the fault, and not the actor of it?
40   Why every fault's condemned ere it be done.
      Mine were the very cipher of a function
      To fine the faults, whose fine stands in record,
      And let go by the actor.
    ISABELLA   O just but severe law!
      I had a brother then; heaven keep your honour.
    LUCIO [*aside to Isabella*]
45   Give't not o'er so. To him again, entreat him,
      Kneel down before him, hang upon his gown.
      You are too cold; if you should need a pin,
      You could not with more tame a tongue desire it:
      To him, I say.
    ISABELLA   Must he needs die?
50 ANGELO   Maiden, no remedy.
    ISABELLA   Yes, I do think that you might pardon him,
      And neither heaven nor man grieve at the mercy.
    ANGELO   I will not do't.
    ISABELLA   But can you if you would?
    ANGELO   Look what I will not, that I cannot do.
    ISABELLA
55   But might you do't and do the world no wrong
      If so your heart were touched with that remorse
      As mine is to him?
    ANGELO   He's sentenced, 'tis too late.

    LUCIO [*aside to Isabella*]
      You are too cold.
    ISABELLA   Too late? Why, no. I that do speak a word   60
      May call it again. Well, believe this,
      No ceremony that to great ones longs,
      Not the king's crown, nor the deputed sword,
      The marshal's truncheon, nor the judge's robe,
      Become them with one half so good a grace   65
      As mercy does. If he had been as you
      And you as he, you would have slipped like him.
      But he, like you, would not have been so stern.
    ANGELO   Pray you be gone.
    ISABELLA   I would to heaven I had your potency,   70
      And you were Isabel. Should it then be thus?
      No. I would tell what 'twere to be a judge,
      And what a prisoner.
    LUCIO [*aside*]   Ay, touch him: there's the vein.
    ANGELO   Your brother is a forfeit of the law,   75
      And you but waste your words.
    ISABELLA   Alas, alas.
      Why, all the souls that were were forfeit once,
      And he that might the vantage best have took
      Found out the remedy. How would you be,
      If he, which is the top of judgement, should   80
      But judge you as you are? O, think on that,
      And mercy then will breathe within your lips
      Like man new made.
    ANGELO   Be you content, fair maid,
      It is the law, not I, condemn your brother.
      Were he my kinsman, brother, or my son,   85
      It should be thus with him: he must die tomorrow.
    ISABELLA
      Tomorrow? O, that's sudden! Spare him, spare him!
      He's not prepared for death. Even for our kitchens
      We kill the fowl of season. Shall we serve heaven
      With less respect than we do minister   90
      To our gross selves? Good, good, my lord, bethink you;
      Who is it that hath died for this offence?
      There's many have committed it.
    LUCIO [*aside*]   Ay, well said.
    ANGELO
      The law hath not been dead, though it hath slept.
      Those many had not dared to do that evil,   95
      If the first that did th'edict infringe
      Had answered for his deed. Now 'tis awake,
      Takes note of what is done, and like a prophet
      Looks in a glass that shows what future evils
      Either now, or by remissness new conceived,   100
      And so in progress to be hatched and born,
      Are now to have no successive degrees,
      But ere they live, to end.
    ISABELLA   Yet show some pity.
    ANGELO   I show it most of all when I show justice,
      For then I pity those I do not know,   105
      Which a dismissed offence would after gall,
      And do him right, that answering one foul wrong
      Lives not to act another. Be satisfied;

Your brother dies tomorrow; be content.

ISABELLA
10 So you must be the first that gives this sentence,
    And he that suffers. O, it is excellent
    To have a giant's strength, but it is tyrannous
    To use it like a giant.

LUCIO [*aside*]   That's well said.

ISABELLA   Could great men thunder
15 As Jove himself does, Jove would never be quiet,
    For every pelting, petty officer
    Would use his heaven for thunder,
    Nothing but thunder. Merciful heaven,
    Thou rather with thy sharp and sulphurous bolt
20 Splits the unwedgeable and gnarled oak
    Than the soft myrtle; but man, proud man,
    Dressed in a little brief authority,
    Most ignorant of what he's most assured,
    His glassy essence, like an angry ape
25 Plays such fantastic tricks before high heaven
    As makes the angels weep, who with our spleens
    Would all themselves laugh mortal.

LUCIO [*aside to Isabella*]
    O, to him, to him, wench. He will relent,
    He's coming: I perceive't.

PROVOST [*aside*]   Pray heaven she win him.

ISABELLA We cannot weigh our brother with ourself.
30 Great men may jest with saints; 'tis wit in them,
    But in the less, foul profanation.

LUCIO [*aside*]   Thou'rt i'th' right, girl, more o'that.

ISABELLA   That in the captain's but a choleric word,
    Which in the soldier is flat blasphemy.

35 LUCIO [*aside to Isabella*]   Art advised o'that? More on't.

ANGELO   Why do you put these sayings upon me?

ISABELLA   Because authority, though it err like others,
    Hath yet a kind of medicine in itself
    That skins the vice o'th' top. Go to your bosom,
40 Knock there, and ask your heart what it doth know
    That's like my brother's fault. If it confess
    A natural guiltiness, such as is his,
    Let it not sound a thought upon your tongue
    Against my brother's life.

ANGELO [*aside*]   She speaks, and 'tis such sense
45 That my sense breeds with it. – Fare you well.

ISABELLA   Gentle my lord, turn back.

ANGELO   I will bethink me: come again tomorrow.

ISABELLA
    Hark, how I'll bribe you; good my lord, turn back.

ANGELO   How? Bribe me?

ISABELLA
50 Ay, with such gifts that heaven shall share with you.

LUCIO [*aside*]   You had marred all else.

ISABELLA   Not with fond sicles of the tested gold,
    Or stones whose rate are either rich or poor
    As fancy values them, but with true prayers
55 That shall be up at heaven and enter there
    Ere sunrise – prayers from preserved souls,
    From fasting maids, whose minds are dedicate

To nothing temporal.

ANGELO   Well, come to me tomorrow.

LUCIO [*aside to Isabella*] Go to, 'tis well; away.

ISABELLA Heaven keep your honour safe.

ANGELO   Amen. 160
    [*aside*] For I am that way going to temptation,
    Where prayers cross.

ISABELLA   At what hour tomorrow
    Shall I attend your lordship?

ANGELO   At any time 'fore noon.

ISABELLA 'Save your honour.

            Exeunt Isabella, Lucio and Provost.

ANGELO   From thee, even from thy virtue.
    What's this? What's this? Is this her fault or mine? 165
    The tempter, or the tempted, who sins most, ha?
    Not she, nor doth she tempt, but it is I
    That, lying by the violet in the sun,
    Do as the carrion does, not as the flower,
    Corrupt with virtuous season. Can it be, 170
    That modesty may more betray our sense
    Than woman's lightness? Having waste ground enough,
    Shall we desire to raze the sanctuary
    And pitch our evils there? O fie, fie, fie,
    What dost thou, or what art thou, Angelo? 175
    Dost thou desire her foully for those things
    That make her good? O, let her brother live.
    Thieves for their robbery have authority,
    When judges steal themselves. What, do I love her,
    That I desire to hear her speak again 180
    And feast upon her eyes? What is't I dream on?
    O cunning enemy that, to catch a saint,
    With saints dost bait thy hook! Most dangerous
    Is that temptation that doth goad us on
    To sin in loving virtue. Never could the strumpet 185
    With all her double vigour, art and nature,
    Once stir my temper; but this virtuous maid
    Subdues me quite. Ever till now
    When men were fond, I smiled and wondered how.
                                        Exit.

2.3   *Enter* DUKE *disguised as a friar and* PROVOST.

DUKE   Hail to you, Provost, so I think you are.

PROVOST
    I am the provost. What's your will, good friar?

DUKE   Bound by my charity and my blessed order,
    I come to visit the afflicted spirits
    Here in the prison. Do me the common right 5
    To let me see them and to make me know
    The nature of their crimes, that I may minister
    To them accordingly.

PROVOST
    I would do more than that, if more were needful.

                Enter JULIET.

    Look here comes one: a gentlewoman of mine, 10
    Who falling in the flaws of her own youth

Hath blistered her report. She is with child,
And he that got it, sentenced – a young man,
More fit to do another such offence
15   Than die for this.
DUKE   When must he die?
PROVOST   As I do think, tomorrow –
[*to Juliet*] I have provided for you, stay awhile
And you shall be conducted.
DUKE   Repent you, fair one, of the sin you carry?
20   JULIET   I do, and bear the shame most patiently.
DUKE
I'll teach you how you shall arraign your conscience
And try your penitence, if it be sound,
Or hollowly put on.
JULIET   I'll gladly learn.
DUKE   Love you the man that wronged you?
25   JULIET   Yes, as I love the woman that wronged him.
DUKE   So then it seems your most offenceful act
Was mutually committed.
JULIET   Mutually.
DUKE   Then was your sin of heavier kind than his.
JULIET   I do confess it and repent it, father.
30   DUKE   'Tis meet so, daughter, but lest you do repent
As that the sin hath brought you to this shame,
Which sorrow is always toward ourselves, not heaven,
Showing we would not spare heaven as we love it,
But as we stand in fear –
35   JULIET   I do repent me, as it is an evil,
And take the shame with joy.
DUKE   There rest.
Your partner, as I hear, must die tomorrow,
And I am going with instruction to him.
Grace go with you, *benedicite*.   *Exit.*
40   JULIET   Must die tomorrow? O injurious love
That respites me a life, whose very comfort
Is still a dying horror.
PROVOST   'Tis pity of him.   *Exeunt.*

2.4   *Enter* ANGELO.

ANGELO
When I would pray and think, I think and pray
To several subjects. Heaven hath my empty words,
Whilst my invention, hearing not my tongue,
Anchors on Isabel. Heaven in my mouth,
5   As if I did but only chew his name,
And in my heart the strong and swelling evil
Of my conception. The state whereon I studied
Is like a good thing, being often read,
Grown sere and tedious; yea, my gravity
10   Wherein, let no man hear me, I take pride,
Could I with boot change for an idle plume
Which the air beats for vain. O place, O form,
How often dost thou with thy case, thy habit,
Wrench awe from fools and tie the wiser souls
15   To thy false seeming? Blood, thou art blood,
Let's write good angel on the devil's horn,

'Tis not the devil's crest. – How now, who's there?

Enter Servant.

SERVANT   One Isabel, a sister, desires access to you.
ANGELO   Teach her the way.   *Exit Servant.*
        O heavens,
Why does my blood thus muster to my heart,   20
Making both it unable for itself
And dispossessing all my other parts
Of necessary fitness?
So play the foolish throngs with one that swoons,
Come all to help him, and so stop the air   25
By which he should revive, and even so
The general subject to a well-wished king
Quit their own part and in obsequious fondness
Crowd to his presence, where their untaught love
Must needs appear offence.

Enter ISABELLA.

        How now, fair maid?   30
ISABELLA   I am come to know your pleasure.
ANGELO
That you might know it would much better please me
Than to demand what 'tis. Your brother cannot live.
ISABELLA   Even so. Heaven keep your honour.
ANGELO   Yet may he live a while, and it may be   35
As long as you or I. Yet he must die.
ISABELLA   Under your sentence?
ANGELO   Yea.
ISABELLA   When, I beseech you: that in his reprieve,
Longer, or shorter, he may be so fitted
That his soul sicken not?   40
ANGELO   Ha? Fie, these filthy vices: it were as good
To pardon him that hath from nature stolen
A man already made, as to remit
Their saucy sweetness that do coin heaven's image
In stamps that are forbid. 'Tis all as easy   45
Falsely to take away a life true made,
As to put metal in restrained means
To make a false one.
ISABELLA   'Tis set down so in heaven, but not in earth.
ANGELO   Say you so? Then I shall pose you quickly.   50
Which had you rather, that the most just law
Now took your brother's life, or to redeem him
Give up your body to such sweet uncleanness
As she that he hath stained?
ISABELLA   Sir, believe this:
I had rather give my body than my soul.   55
ANGELO   I talk not of your soul; our compelled sins
Stand more for number than for account.
ISABELLA   How say you?
ANGELO   Nay, I'll not warrant that, for I can speak
Against the thing I say. Answer to this:
I, now the voice of the recorded law,   60
Pronounce a sentence on your brother's life.
Might there not be a charity in sin
To save this brother's life?

ISABELLA   Please you to do't,
  I'll take it as a peril to my soul,
  It is no sin at all, but charity.

ANGELO   Pleased you to do't at peril of your soul
  Were equal poise of sin and charity.

ISABELLA   That I do beg his life, if it be sin,
  Heaven let me bear it. You granting of my suit,
  If that be sin, I'll make it my morn prayer
  To have it added to the faults of mine
  And nothing of your answer.

ANGELO   Nay, but hear me.
  Your sense pursues not mine: either you are ignorant,
  Or seem so, crafty; and that's not good.

ISABELLA   Let me be ignorant, and in nothing good,
  But graciously to know I am no better.

ANGELO   Thus wisdom wishes to appear most bright
  When it doth tax itself, as these black masks
  Proclaim an enshield beauty ten times louder
  Than beauty could, displayed. But mark me,
  To be received plain, I'll speak more gross:
  Your brother is to die.

ISABELLA   So.

ANGELO   And his offence is so, as it appears,
  Accountant to the law upon that pain.

ISABELLA   True.

ANGELO   Admit no other way to save his life,
  As I subscribe not that, nor any other,
  But in the loss of question, that you, his sister,
  Finding yourself desired of such a person
  Whose credit with the judge, or own great place,
  Could fetch your brother from the manacles
  Of the all-binding law, and that there were
  No earthly mean to save him, but that either
  You must lay down the treasures of your body
  To this supposed, or else to let him suffer:
  What would you do?

ISABELLA   As much for my poor brother as myself:
  That is, were I under the terms of death,
  Th'impression of keen whips I'd wear as rubies,
  And strip myself to death, as to a bed
  That longing have been sick for, ere I'd yield
  My body up to shame.

ANGELO   Then must your brother die.

ISABELLA   And 'twere the cheaper way:
  Better it were a brother died at once,
  Than that a sister by redeeming him
  Should die forever.

ANGELO   Were not you then as cruel as the sentence
  That you have slandered so?

ISABELLA   Ignomy in ransom and free pardon
  Are of two houses: lawful mercy
  Is nothing kin to foul redemption.

ANGELO   You seemed of late to make the law a tyrant,
  And rather proved the sliding of your brother
  A merriment than a vice.

ISABELLA   O, pardon me, my lord; it oft falls out
  To have what we would have, we speak not what we
    mean.

I something do excuse the thing I hate
For his advantage that I dearly love.

ANGELO   We are all frail.

ISABELLA   Else let my brother die,
  If not a feodary, but only he
  Owe and succeed thy weakness.

ANGELO   Nay, women are frail too.

ISABELLA
  Ay, as the glasses where they view themselves,
  Which are as easy broke as they make forms.
  Women? Help heaven, men their creation mar
  In profiting by them. Nay, call us ten times frail,
  For we are soft as our complexions are
  And credulous to false prints.

ANGELO   I think it well.
  And from this testimony of your own sex,
  Since I suppose we are made to be no stronger
  Than faults may shake our frames, let me be bold;
  I do arrest your words. Be that you are,
  That is, a woman; if you be more, you're none.
  If you be one, as you are well expressed
  By all external warrants, show it now
  By putting on the destined livery.

ISABELLA   I have no tongue but one; gentle my lord,
  Let me entreat you speak the former language.

ANGELO   Plainly conceive I love you.

ISABELLA   My brother did love Juliet,
  And you tell me that he shall die for't.

ANGELO   He shall not, Isabel, if you give me love.

ISABELLA   I know your virtue hath a licence in't,
  Which seems a little fouler than it is
  To pluck on others.

ANGELO   Believe me, on mine honour,
  My words express my purpose.

ISABELLA   Ha! Little honour, to be much believed,
  And most pernicious purpose. Seeming, seeming!
  I will proclaim thee, Angelo; look for't.
  Sign me a present pardon for my brother,
  Or with an outstretched throat I'll tell the world
    aloud
  What man thou art.

ANGELO   Who will believe thee, Isabel?
  My unsoiled name, th'austereness of my life,
  My vouch against you and my place i'th' state
  Will so your accusation overweigh
  That you shall stifle in your own report
  And smell of calumny. I have begun,
  And now I give my sensual race the rein;
  Fit thy consent to my sharp appetite,
  Lay by all nicety and prolixious blushes
  That banish what they sue for, redeem thy brother
  By yielding up thy body to my will,
  Or else he must not only die the death,
  But thy unkindness shall his death draw out
  To lingering sufferance. Answer me tomorrow,
  Or by the affection that now guides me most,
  I'll prove a tyrant to him. As for you,
  Say what you can, my false o'erweighs your true.   *Exit.*

ISABELLA To whom should I complain? Did I tell this,
Who would believe me? O perilous mouths
That bear in them one and the selfsame tongue
Either of condemnation or approof,
175 Bidding the law make curtsy to their will,
Hooking both right and wrong to th'appetite,
To follow as it draws. I'll to my brother;
Though he hath fallen by prompture of the blood,
Yet hath he in him such a mind of honour
180 That had he twenty heads to tender down
On twenty bloody blocks, he'd yield them up
Before his sister should her body stoop
To such abhorred pollution.
Then Isabel live chaste, and brother die:
185 More than our brother is our chastity.
I'll tell him yet of Angelo's request
And fit his mind to death for his soul's rest.   *Exit.*

3.1   *Enter* DUKE *disguised as a friar,*
             CLAUDIO *and* PROVOST.

DUKE So then you hope of pardon from Lord Angelo?
CLAUDIO The miserable have no other medicine
But only hope:
I've hope to live, and am prepared to die.
5 DUKE Be absolute for death: either death or life
Shall thereby be the sweeter. Reason thus with life:
If I do lose thee, I do lose a thing
That none but fools would keep; a breath thou art,
Servile to all the skyey influences
10 That dost this habitation where thou keepst
Hourly afflict. Merely, thou art death's fool,
For him thou labour'st by thy flight to shun
And yet run'st toward him still. Thou art not noble,
For all th'accommodations that thou bear'st
15 Are nursed by baseness. Thou'rt by no means valiant,
For thou dost fear the soft and tender fork
Of a poor worm. Thy best of rest is sleep,
And that thou oft provok'st, yet grossly fear'st
Thy death, which is no more. Thou art not thyself,
20 For thou exists on many a thousand grains
That issue out of dust. Happy thou art not,
For what thou hast not still thou striv'st to get,
And what thou hast, forget'st. Thou art not certain,
For thy complexion shifts to strange effects
25 After the moon. If thou art rich, thou'rt poor,
For like an ass, whose back with ingots bows,
Thou bear'st thy heavy riches but a journey,
And death unloads thee. Friend hast thou none,
For thine own bowels which do call thee sire,
30 The mere effusion of thy proper loins,
Do curse the gout, serpigo and the rheum
For ending thee no sooner. Thou hast nor youth nor age,
But as it were an after-dinner's sleep,
Dreaming on both, for all thy blessed youth
35 Becomes as aged and doth beg the alms
Of palsied eld; and when thou art old and rich

Thou hast neither heat, affection, limb nor beauty
To make thy riches pleasant. What's yet in this
That bears the name of life? Yet in this life
Lie hid mo thousand deaths; yet death we fear   40
That makes these odds all even.
CLAUDIO   I humbly thank you.
To sue to live, I find I seek to die,
And seeking death, find life. Let it come on.
ISABELLA [*within*]
What ho? Peace here; grace and good company.
PROVOST
Who's there? Come in, the wish deserves a welcome.   45
DUKE [*to Claudio*]
Dear sir, ere long I'll visit you again.
CLAUDIO   Most holy sir, I thank you.

              Enter ISABELLA.

ISABELLA   My business is a word or two with Claudio.
PROVOST   And very welcome. Look, signior, here's your
sister.   50
DUKE   Provost, a word with you.
PROVOST   As many as you please.
DUKE   Bring me to hear them speak, where I may be
concealed.   *Exeunt Duke and Provost.*
CLAUDIO   Now sister, what's the comfort?
ISABELLA   Why,
As all comforts are: most good, most good indeed: 55
Lord Angelo, having affairs to heaven,
Intends you for his swift ambassador,
Where you shall be an everlasting lieger.
Therefore your best appointment make with speed,
Tomorrow you set on.
CLAUDIO   Is there no remedy?   60
ISABELLA   None, but such remedy as to save a head
To cleave a heart in twain.
CLAUDIO   But is there any?
ISABELLA   Yes, brother, you may live;
There is a devilish mercy in the judge,   65
If you'll implore it, that will free your life
But fetter you till death.
CLAUDIO   Perpetual durance?
ISABELLA   Ay, just, perpetual durance, a restraint,
Though all the world's vastidity you had,
To a determined scope.
CLAUDIO   But in what nature?   70
ISABELLA   In such a one as, you consenting to't,
Would bark your honour from that trunk you bear
And leave you naked.
CLAUDIO   Let me know the point.
ISABELLA   O, I do fear thee, Claudio, and I quake,
Lest thou a feverous life shouldst entertain   75
And six or seven winters more respect
Than a perpetual honour. Dar'st thou die?
The sense of death is most in apprehension,
And the poor beetle that we tread upon
In corporal sufferance finds a pang as great   80
As when a giant dies.

CLAUDIO   Why give you me this shame?
  Think you I can a resolution fetch
  From flowery tenderness? If I must die,
85 I will encounter darkness as a bride
  And hug it in mine arms.
ISABELLA
  There spake my brother. There my father's grave
  Did utter forth a voice. Yes, thou must die;
  Thou art too noble to conserve a life
90 In base appliances. This outward-sainted deputy,
  Whose settled visage and deliberate word
  Nips youth i'th' head and follies doth enew
  As falcon doth the fowl, is yet a devil;
  His filth within being cast, he would appear
  A pond as deep as hell.
95 CLAUDIO   The prenzie Angelo?
ISABELLA   O, 'tis the cunning livery of hell,
  The damned'st body to invest and cover
  In prenzie guards; dost thou think, Claudio,
  If I would yield him my virginity
  Thou might'st be freed?
100 CLAUDIO   O heavens, it cannot be.
ISABELLA
  Yes, he would give't thee; from this rank offence
  So to offend him still. This night's the time
  That I should do what I abhor to name,
  Or else thou diest tomorrow.
105 CLAUDIO   Thou shalt not do't.
ISABELLA   O, were it but my life,
  I'd throw it down for your deliverance
  As frankly as a pin.
CLAUDIO   Thanks, dear Isabel.
110 ISABELLA   Be ready, Claudio, for your death tomorrow.
CLAUDIO   Yes. Has he affections in him
  That thus can make him bite the law by th' nose
  When he would force it? Sure it is no sin,
  Or of the deadly seven it is the least.
115 ISABELLA   Which is the least?
CLAUDIO   If it were damnable, he being so wise,
  Why would he for the momentary trick
  Be perdurably fined? O Isabel!
ISABELLA   What says my brother?
120 CLAUDIO   Death is a fearful thing.
ISABELLA   And shamed life a hateful.
CLAUDIO   Ay, but to die and go we know not where,
  To lie in cold obstruction and to rot,
  This sensible warm motion to become
125 A kneaded clod, and the delighted spirit
  To bathe in fiery floods or to reside
  In thrilling region of thick-ribbed ice,
  To be imprisoned in the viewless winds
  And blown with restless violence round about
130 The pendent world: or to be worse than worst
  Of those that lawless and incertain thought
  Imagine howling; 'tis too horrible.
  The weariest and most loathed worldly life
  That age, ache, penury and imprisonment

  Can lay on nature is a paradise   135
  To what we fear of death.
ISABELLA   Alas, alas.
CLAUDIO   Sweet sister, let me live.
  What sin you do to save a brother's life,
  Nature dispenses with the deed so far   140
  That it becomes a virtue.
ISABELLA   O you beast,
  O faithless coward, O dishonest wretch,
  Wilt thou be made a man out of my vice?
  Is't not a kind of incest to take life
  From thine own sister's shame? What should I think?   145
  Heaven shield my mother played my father fair,
  For such a warped slip of wilderness
  Ne'er issued from his blood. Take my defiance,
  Die, perish. Might but my bending down
  Reprieve thee from thy fate, it should proceed.   150
  I'll pray a thousand prayers for thy death,
  No word to save thee.
CLAUDIO   Nay, hear me, Isabel.
ISABELLA   O fie, fie, fie:
  Thy sin's not accidental, but a trade;   155
  Mercy to thee would prove itself a bawd.
  'Tis best that thou diest quickly.
CLAUDIO   O hear me, Isabella.

Enter DUKE *and* PROVOST.

DUKE   Vouchsafe a word, young sister, but one word.
ISABELLA   What is your will?   160
DUKE   Might you dispense with your leisure, I would by
  and by have some speech with you. The satisfaction I
  would require is likewise your own benefit.
ISABELLA   I have no superfluous leisure, my stay must
  be stolen out of other affairs, but I will attend you a   165
  while.
DUKE   Son, I have overheard what hath passed between
  you and your sister. Angelo had never the purpose to
  corrupt her; only he hath made an assay of her virtue,
  to practise his judgement with the disposition of   170
  natures. She, having the truth of honour in her, hath
  made him that gracious denial which he is most glad to
  receive. I am confessor to Angelo, and I know this to be
  true; therefore prepare yourself to death. Do not
  satisfy your resolution with hopes that are fallible,   175
  tomorrow you must die. Go to your knees and make
  ready.
CLAUDIO   Let me ask my sister pardon. I am so out of
  love with life that I will sue to be rid of it.
DUKE   Hold you there. Farewell. Provost, a word with   180
  you.
PROVOST   What's your will, father?
DUKE   That now you are come, you will be gone. Leave
  me a while with the maid; my mind promises with my
  habit no loss shall touch her by my company.   185
PROVOST   In good time.   *Exit with Claudio.*
DUKE [*to Isabella*]   The hand that hath made you fair
  hath made you good; the goodness that is cheap in

190 beauty makes beauty brief in goodness, but grace
being the soul of your complexion shall keep the body
of it ever fair. The assault that Angelo hath made to
you fortune hath conveyed to my understanding, and,
but that frailty hath examples for his falling, I should
195 wonder at Angelo. How will you do to content this
substitute and to save your brother?

ISABELLA　　I am now going to resolve him. I had rather
my brother die by the law than my son should be
unlawfully born. But, O, how much is the good Duke
200 deceived in Angelo; if ever he return and I can speak to
him, I will open my lips in vain, or discover his
government.

DUKE　　That shall not be much amiss, yet as the matter
now stands, he will avoid your accusation: he made
205 trial of you only. Therefore, fasten your ear on my
advisings. To the love I have in doing good a remedy
presents itself. I do make myself believe that you may
most uprighteously do a poor wronged lady a merited
benefit; redeem your brother from the angry law; do
210 no stain to your own gracious person; and much please
the absent Duke, if peradventure he shall ever return
to have hearing of this business.

ISABELLA　　Let me hear you speak farther. I have spirit
to do anything that appears not foul in the truth of my
spirit.

215 DUKE　　Virtue is bold, and goodness never fearful. Have
you not heard speak of Mariana, the sister of Frederick,
the great soldier who miscarried at sea?

ISABELLA　　I have heard of the lady, and good words
went with her name.

220 DUKE　　She should this Angelo have married, was
affianced to her by oath, and the nuptial appointed.
Between which time of the contract and limit of the
solemnity, her brother Frederick was wrecked at sea,
having in that perished vessel the dowry of his sister.
225 But mark how heavily this befell to the poor
gentlewoman. There she lost a noble and renowned
brother, in his love toward her ever most kind and
natural; with him, the portion and sinew of her
fortune, her marriage dowry; with both, her combinate
230 husband, this well-seeming Angelo.

ISABELLA　　Can this be so? Did Angelo so leave her?

DUKE　　Left her in her tears and dried not one of them
with his comfort; swallowed his vows whole, pretending
in her discoveries of dishonour; in few, bestowed her
235 on her own lamentation, which she yet wears for his
sake; and he, a marble to her tears, is washed with them
but relents not.

ISABELLA　　What a merit were it in death to take this
poor maid from the world! What corruption in this life
240 that it will let this man live! But how out of this can she
avail?

DUKE　　It is a rupture that you may easily heal, and the
cure of it not only saves your brother, but keeps you
from dishonour in doing it.

245 ISABELLA　　Show me how, good father.

DUKE　　This fore-named maid hath yet in her the
continuance of her first affection; his unjust
unkindness – that in all reason should have quenched
her love – hath, like an impediment in the current,
250 made it more violent and unruly. Go you to Angelo,
answer his requiring with a plausible obedience, agree
with his demands to the point, only refer yourself to
this advantage: first, that your stay with him may not
be long; that the time may have all shadow and silence
255 in it; and the place answer to convenience. This being
granted in course – and now follows all – we shall
advise this wronged maid to stead up your appointment,
go in your place. If the encounter acknowledge itself
hereafter, it may compel him to her recompense; and
260 here, by this is your brother saved, your honour
untainted, the poor Mariana advantaged and the
corrupt deputy scaled. The maid will I frame and
make fit for his attempt. If you think well to carry this
as you may, the doubleness of the benefit defends the
265 deceit from reproof. What think you of it?

ISABELLA　　The image of it gives me content already, and
I trust it will grow to a most prosperous perfection.

DUKE　　It lies much in your holding up. Haste you
speedily to Angelo. If for this night he entreat you to
270 his bed, give him promise of satisfaction. I will
presently to Saint Luke's. There at the moated grange
resides this dejected Mariana; at that place call upon
me, and dispatch with Angelo that it may be quickly.

ISABELLA　　I thank you for this comfort. Fare you well,
good father.　　　　　　　　　　　　　　　　*Exit.*　275

Enter ELBOW, POMPEY, *Officers.*

ELBOW　　Nay, if there be no remedy for it but that you
will needs buy and sell men and women like beasts, we
shall have all the world drink brown and white bastard.

DUKE　　O heavens, what stuff is here.

POMPEY　　'Twas never merry world since of two usuries　280
the merriest was put down, and the worser allowed by
order of law a furred gown to keep him warm; and
furred with fox- and lamb-skins too, to signify that
craft, being richer than innocency, stands for the facing.

ELBOW　　Come your way, sir. 'Bless you, good father　285
friar.

DUKE　　And you, good brother father. What offence hath
this man made you, sir?

ELBOW　　Marry, sir, he hath offended the law; and, sir,
we take him to be a thief too, sir: for we have found　290
upon him, sir, a strange picklock, which we have sent
to the deputy.

DUKE　　Fie, sirrah, a bawd, a wicked bawd!
The evil that thou causest to be done,
That is thy means to live. Do thou but think　295
What 'tis to cram a maw or clothe a back
From such a filthy vice. Say to thyself,
From their abominable and beastly touches
I drink, I eat, array myself and live.
Canst thou believe thy living is a life,　300

So stinkingly depending? Go mend, go mend.

POMPEY   Indeed, it does stink in some sort, sir, but yet,
sir, I would prove –

DUKE   Nay, if the devil have given thee proofs for sin
Thou wilt prove his. Take him to prison, officer.
Correction and instruction must both work
Ere this rude beast will profit.

ELBOW   He must before the deputy, sir; he has given
him warning. The deputy cannot abide a whoremaster;
if he be a whoremonger and comes before him, he were
as good go a mile on his errand.

DUKE   That we were all, as some would seem to be,
From our faults, as faults from seeming, free.

Enter LUCIO.

ELBOW   His neck will come to your waist, a cord, sir.

POMPEY   I spy comfort, I cry bail. Here's a gentleman
and a friend of mine.

LUCIO   How now, noble Pompey? What, at the wheels of
Caesar? Art thou led in triumph? What, is there none
of Pygmalion's images newly-made woman to be had
now, for putting the hand in the pocket and extracting
clutched? What reply? Ha? What sayst thou to this
tune, matter and method? Is't not drowned i'th' last
rain? Ha? What sayst thou, trot? Is the world as it was,
man? Which is the way? Is it sad and few words? Or
how? The trick of it?

DUKE   Still thus and thus: still worse!

LUCIO   How doth my dear morsel, thy mistress?
Procures she still? Ha?

POMPEY   Troth, sir, she hath eaten up all her beef and
she is herself in the tub.

LUCIO   Why, 'tis good. It is the right of it; it must be so.
Ever your fresh whore and your powdered bawd, an
unshunned consequence, it must be so. Art going to
prison, Pompey?

POMPEY   Yes, faith, sir.

LUCIO   Why 'tis not amiss, Pompey. Farewell; go say I
sent thee thither. For debt, Pompey? Or how?

ELBOW   For being a bawd, for being a bawd.

LUCIO   Well, then imprison him. If imprisonment be
the due of a bawd, why 'tis his right. Bawd is he
doubtless, and of antiquity too. Bawd born. Farewell,
good Pompey. Commend me to the prison, Pompey,
you will turn good husband now, Pompey – you will
keep the house.

POMPEY   I hope, sir, your good worship will be my bail?

LUCIO   No indeed will I not, Pompey, it is not the wear.
I will pray, Pompey, to increase your bondage; if you
take it not patiently, why, your mettle is the more.
Adieu, trusty Pompey. – Bless you, friar.

DUKE   And you.

LUCIO   Does Bridget paint still, Pompey? Ha?

ELBOW   Come your ways, sir, come.

POMPEY   You will not bail me then, sir?

LUCIO   Then, Pompey, nor now. – What news abroad,
friar? What news?

ELBOW   Come your ways, sir, come.

LUCIO   Go to kennel, Pompey, go.

Exeunt Elbow, Pompey and Officers.

What news, friar, of the Duke?

DUKE   I know none. Can you tell me of any?

LUCIO   Some say he is with the Emperor of Russia;
other some, he is in Rome. But where is he, think you?

DUKE   I know not where, but wheresoever, I wish him well.

LUCIO   It was a mad fantastical trick of him to steal from
the state and usurp the beggary he was never born to.
Lord Angelo dukes it well in his absence; he puts
transgression to't.

DUKE   He does well in't.

LUCIO   A little more lenity to lechery would do no harm
in him: something too crabbed that way, friar.

DUKE   It is too general a vice and severity must cure it.

LUCIO   Yes, in good sooth, the vice is of a great kindred;
it is well allied, but it is impossible to extirp it quite,
friar, till eating and drinking be put down. They say
this Angelo was not made by man and woman, after
this downright way of creation. Is it true, think you?

DUKE   How should he be made, then?

LUCIO   Some report a sea-maid spawned him. Some,
that he was begot between two stockfishes. But it is
certain that when he makes water his urine is congealed
ice, that I know to be true. And he is a motion
generative, that's infallible.

DUKE   You are pleasant, sir, and speak apace.

LUCIO   Why, what a ruthless thing is this in him, for the
rebellion of a codpiece to take away the life of a man!
Would the Duke that is absent have done this? Ere he
would have hanged a man for the getting a hundred
bastards, he would have paid for the nursing a
thousand. He had some feeling of the sport; he knew
the service, and that instructed him to mercy.

DUKE   I never heard the absent Duke much detected for
women; he was not inclined that way.

LUCIO   O sir, you are deceived.

DUKE   'Tis not possible.

LUCIO   Who, not the Duke? Yes, your beggar of fifty,
and his use was to put a ducat in her clack-dish; the
Duke had crotchets in him. He would be drunk too,
that let me inform you.

DUKE   You do him wrong, surely.

LUCIO   Sir, I was an inward of his: a shy fellow was the
Duke, and I believe I know the cause of his withdrawing.

DUKE   What, I prithee, might be the cause?

LUCIO   No, pardon: 'tis a secret must be locked within
the teeth and the lips, but this I can let you understand,
the greater file of the subject held the Duke to be wise.

DUKE   Wise? Why, no question but he was.

LUCIO   A very superficial, ignorant, unweighing fellow.

DUKE   Either this is envy in you, folly or mistaking. The
very stream of his life and the business he hath helmed
must, upon a warranted need, give him a better
proclamation. Let him be but testimonied in his own
bringings forth, and he shall appear to the envious a

scholar, a statesman and a soldier. Therefore you speak unskilfully, or, if your knowledge be more, it is much darkened in your malice.

415 LUCIO   Sir, I know him, and I love him.

DUKE   Love talks with better knowledge, and knowledge with dearer love.

LUCIO   Come, sir, I know what I know.

DUKE   I can hardly believe that, since you know not
420 what you speak. But if ever the Duke return (as our prayers are he may), let me desire you to make your answer before him. If it be honest you have spoke, you have courage to maintain it. I am bound to call upon you, and I pray you, your name?

425 LUCIO   Sir, my name is Lucio, well known to the Duke.

DUKE   He shall know you better, sir, if I may live to report you.

LUCIO   I fear you not.

DUKE   O, you hope the Duke will return no more, or you
430 imagine me too unhurtful an opposite. But indeed I can do you little harm. You'll forswear this again!

LUCIO   I'll be hanged first. Thou art deceived in me, friar. But no more of this. Canst thou tell if Claudio die tomorrow, or no?

435 DUKE   Why should he die, sir?

LUCIO   Why? For filling a bottle with a tundish. I would the Duke we talk of were returned again; this ungenitured agent will unpeople the province with continency. Sparrows must not build in his house
440 eaves because they are lecherous. The Duke yet would have dark deeds darkly answered; he would never bring them to light. Would he were returned. Marry, this Claudio is condemned for untrussing. Farewell, good friar, I prithee pray for me. The Duke (I say to
445 thee again) would eat mutton on Fridays. He's now past it, yet (and I say to thee) he would mouth with a beggar, though she smelt brown bread and garlic. Say that I said so. Farewell.   *Exit.*

DUKE   No might nor greatness in mortality
450 Can censure scape; back-wounding calumny
The whitest virtue strikes. What king so strong
Can tie the gall up in the slanderous tongue?

Enter ESCALUS, PROVOST, *Officers and* OVERDONE.

But who comes here?

ESCALUS   Go, away with her to prison.

455 OVERDONE   Good my lord, be good to me, your honour is accounted a merciful man, good my lord –

ESCALUS   Double and treble admonition, and still forfeit in the same kind? This would make mercy swear and play the tyrant.

460 PROVOST   A bawd of eleven years' continuance, may it please your honour.

OVERDONE   My lord, this is one Lucio's information against me. Mistress Kate Keepdown was with child by him in the Duke's time, he promised her marriage.
465 His child is a year and a quarter old come Philip and Jacob – I have kept it myself – and see how he goes about to abuse me.

ESCALUS   That fellow is a fellow of much licence. Let him be called before us. Away with her to prison. – Go
to, no more words.   *Exeunt Overdone and Officers.*   470
Provost, my brother Angelo will not be altered, Claudio must die tomorrow. Let him be furnished with divines and have all charitable preparation. If my brother wrought by my pity, it should not be so with him.

PROVOST   So please you, this friar hath been with him   475
and advised him for th'entertainment of death.

ESCALUS   Good e'en, good father.

DUKE   Bliss and goodness on you.

ESCALUS   Of whence are you?

DUKE   Not of this country, though my chance is now   480
To use it for my time. I am a brother
Of gracious order, late come from the See
In special business from his holiness.

ESCALUS   What news abroad i'th' world?

DUKE   None, but that there is so great a fever on   485
goodness that the dissolution of it must cure it.
Novelty is only in request, and it is as dangerous to be
aged in any kind of course as it is virtuous to be
constant in any undertaking. There is scarce truth
enough alive to make societies secure, but security   490
enough to make fellowships accursed. Much upon this
riddle runs the wisdom of the world; this news is old
enough, yet it is every day's news. I pray you, sir, of
what disposition was the Duke?

ESCALUS   One that above all other strifes contended   495
especially to know himself.

DUKE   What pleasure was he given to?

ESCALUS   Rather rejoicing to see another merry than
merry at anything which professed to make him
rejoice. A gentleman of all temperance. But leave we   500
him to his events, with a prayer they may prove
prosperous, and let me desire to know how you find
Claudio prepared? I am made to understand that you
have lent him visitation.

DUKE   He professes to have received no sinister measure   505
from his judge, but most willingly humbles himself to
the determination of justice: yet had he framed to
himself (by the instruction of his frailty) many
deceiving promises of life, which I by my good leisure
have discredited to him, and now is he resolved to die.   510

ESCALUS   You have paid the heavens your function, and
the prisoner the very debt of your calling. I have
laboured for the poor gentleman to the extremest shore
of my modesty, but my brother justice have I found so
severe that he hath forced me to tell him, he is indeed   515
Justice.

DUKE   If his own life answer the straitness of his
proceeding, it shall become him well; wherein if he
chance to fail he hath sentenced himself.

ESCALUS   I am going to visit the prisoner, fare you well.   520

DUKE   Peace be with you.   *Exeunt Escalus and Provost.*
He who the sword of heaven will bear
Should be as holy as severe;
Pattern in himself to know,
Grace to stand and virtue go;   525

More nor less to others paying
Than by self-offences weighing.
Shame to him, whose cruel striking
Kills for faults of his own liking:
530   Twice treble shame on Angelo,
To weed my vice and let his grow.
O, what may man within him hide,
Though angel on the outward side?
How may likeness made in crimes,
535   Making practice on the times,
To draw with idle spiders' strings
Most ponderous and substantial things?
Craft against vice I must apply.
With Angelo tonight shall lie
540   His old betrothed but despised:
So disguise shall by th' disguised
Pay with falsehood, false exacting,
And perform an old contracting.   *Exit.*

4.1   *Enter* MARIANA, *and* Boy *singing.*

BOY [*Sings.*]
Take, O take, those lips away,
  That so sweetly were forsworn,
And those eyes, the break of day,
  Lights that do mislead the morn.
5   But my kisses bring again, bring again,
Seals of love, but sealed in vain, sealed in vain.

Enter DUKE *disguised as a friar.*

MARIANA
Break off thy song and haste thee quick away.
                      Exit Boy.
Here comes a man of comfort, whóse advice
Hath often stilled my brawling discontent. –
10   I cry you mercy, sir, and well could wish
You had not found me here so musical.
Let me excuse me, and believe me so,
My mirth it much displeased, but pleased my woe.
DUKE   'Tis good; though music oft hath such a charm
15   To make bad good, and good provoke to harm.
I pray you tell me, hath anybody inquired for me here
today? Much upon this time have I promised here to
meet.
MARIANA   You have not been inquired after; I have sat
20   here all day.

Enter ISABELLA.

DUKE   I do constantly believe you; the time is come even
now. I shall crave your forbearance a little; maybe I will
call upon you anon for some advantage to yourself.
MARIANA   I am always bound to you.   *Exit.*
25   DUKE   Very well met, and welcome.
What is the news from this good deputy?
ISABELLA   He hath a garden circummured with brick,
Whose western side is with a vineyard backed;
And to that vineyard is a planched gate

That makes his opening with this bigger key;   30
This other doth command a little door
Which from the vineyard to the garden leads.
There have I made my promise
Upon the heavy middle of the night
To call upon him.   35
DUKE   But shall you on your knowledge find this way?
ISABELLA   I have ta'en a due and wary note upon't.
With whispering and most guilty diligence
In action all of precept, he did show me
The way twice o'er.
DUKE   Are there no other tokens   40
Between you 'greed, concerning her observance?
ISABELLA   No, none but only a repair i'th' dark,
And that I have possessed him my most stay
Can be but brief; for I have made him know
I have a servant comes with me along   45
That stays upon me, whose persuasion is
I come about my brother.
DUKE   'Tis well borne up.
I have not yet made known to Mariana
A word of this. What ho, within; come forth.

Enter MARIANA.

I pray you be acquainted with this maid.   50
She comes to do you good.
ISABELLA   I do desire the like.
DUKE   Do you persuade yourself that I respect you?
MARIANA
Good friar, I know you do, and so have found it.
DUKE   Take then this your companion by the hand,
Who hath a story ready for your ear.   55
I shall attend your leisure, but make haste;
The vaporous night approaches.
MARIANA [*to Isabella*]
Will't please you walk aside?
                Exeunt Mariana and Isabella.
DUKE   O place and greatness, millions of false eyes
Are stuck upon thee; volumes of report   60
Run with these false and most contrarious quests
Upon thy doings; thousand escapes of wit
Make thee the father of their idle dream
And rack thee in their fancies.

Enter MARIANA *and* ISABELLA.

                  Welcome, how agreed?
ISABELLA   She'll take the enterprise upon her, father,   65
If you advise it.
DUKE   It is not my consent,
But my entreaty too.
ISABELLA   Little have you to say
When you depart from him, but soft and low,
'Remember now my brother'.
MARIANA   Fear me not.
DUKE   Nor, gentle daughter, fear you not at all.   70
He is your husband on a pre-contract;
To bring you thus together, 'tis no sin,

Sith that the justice of your title to him
Doth flourish the deceit. Come, let us go:
75   Our corn's to reap, for yet our tithe's to sow.   *Exeunt.*

4.2   *Enter* PROVOST *and* POMPEY.

PROVOST   Come hither, sirrah. Can you cut off a man's
head?

POMPEY   If the man be a bachelor, sir, I can, but if he be
a married man, he's his wife's head, and I can never cut
5   off a woman's head.

PROVOST   Come, sir, leave me your snatches and yield
me a direct answer. Tomorrow morning are to die
Claudio and Barnardine. Here is in our prison a
common executioner who in his office lacks a helper. If
10   you will take it on you to assist him, it shall redeem you
from your gyves; if not, you shall have your full time of
imprisonment and your deliverance with an unpitied
whipping, for you have been a notorious bawd.

POMPEY   Sir, I have been an unlawful bawd, time out of
15   mind, but yet I will be content to be a lawful hangman.
I would be glad to receive some instruction from my
fellow partner.

PROVOST   What ho, Abhorson! Where's Abhorson
there?

Enter ABHORSON.

20   ABHORSON   Do you call, sir?

PROVOST   Sirrah, here's a fellow will help you tomorrow
in your execution. If you think it meet, compound
with him by the year and let him abide here with you;
if not, use him for the present and dismiss him. He
25   cannot plead his estimation with you; he hath been a
bawd.

ABHORSON   A bawd, sir? Fie upon him, he will discredit
our mystery.

PROVOST   Go to, sir, you weigh equally; a feather will
30   turn the scale.   *Exit.*

POMPEY   Pray, sir, by your good favour – for surely, sir,
a good favour you have, but that you have a hanging
look – do you call, sir, your occupation a mystery?

ABHORSON   Ay, sir, a mystery.

35   POMPEY   Painting, sir, I have heard say, is a mystery;
and your whores, sir, being members of my occupation,
using painting, do prove my occupation a mystery. But
what mystery there should be in hanging, if I should be
hanged, I cannot imagine.

40   ABHORSON   Sir, it is a mystery.

POMPEY   Proof.

ABHORSON   Every true man's apparel fits your thief. If
it be too little for your thief, your true man thinks it big
enough. If it be too big for your thief, your thief thinks
45   it little enough. So every true man's apparel fits your
thief.

Enter PROVOST.

PROVOST   Are you agreed?

POMPEY   Sir, I will serve him, for I do find your
hangman is a more penitent trade than your bawd; he
doth oftener ask forgiveness.   50

PROVOST   You, sirrah, provide your block and your axe
tomorrow, four o'clock.

ABHORSON   Come on, bawd, I will instruct thee in my
trade; follow.

POMPEY   I do desire to learn, sir, and I hope, if you have   55
occasion to use me for your own turn, you shall find
me yare. For truly, sir, for your kindness, I owe you a
good turn.   *Exeunt Pompey and Abhorson.*

PROVOST   Call hither Barnardine and Claudio;
Th'one has my pity; not a jot the other,   60
Being a murderer, though he were my brother.

Enter CLAUDIO.

Look, here's the warrant, Claudio, for thy death;
'Tis now dead midnight, and by eight tomorrow
Thou must be made immortal. Where's Barnardine?

CLAUDIO   As fast locked up in sleep, as guiltless labour   65
When it lies starkly in the traveller's bones.
He will not wake.

PROVOST   Who can do good on him?
Well, go, prepare yourself.   [*Knocking within*]
                          But hark, what noise?
Heaven give your spirits comfort.   *Exit Claudio.*
                          By and by, –
I hope it is some pardon or reprieve   70
For the most gentle Claudio.

Enter DUKE *disguised as a friar.*

                          Welcome, father.

DUKE   The best and wholesom'st spirits of the night
Envelop you, good Provost. Who called here of late?

PROVOST   None since the curfew rung.

DUKE   Not Isabel?

PROVOST   No.

DUKE   They will then, ere't be long.   75

PROVOST   What comfort is for Claudio?

DUKE   There's some in hope.

PROVOST   It is a bitter deputy.

DUKE   Not so, not so. His life is paralleled
Even with the stroke and line of his great justice:
He doth with holy abstinence subdue   80
That in himself which he spurs on his power
To qualify in others. Were he mealed with that
Which he corrects, then were he tyrannous,
But this being so, he's just.   [*Knocking within*]
                          Now are they come.

[*aside*] This is a gentle provost, seldom-when   85
The steeled gaoler is the friend of men. – [*Knocking*]
How now? What noise? That spirit's possessed with
haste
That wounds th'unsisting postern with these strokes.

PROVOST   There he must stay until the officer
Arise to let him in. He is called up.   90

DUKE   Have you no countermand for Claudio yet,

But he must die tomorrow?
PROVOST   None, sir, none.
DUKE   As near the dawning, Provost, as it is,
You shall hear more ere morning.
PROVOST   Happily
95   You something know, yet I believe there comes
No countermand; no such example have we.
Besides, upon the very siege of justice
Lord Angelo hath to the public ear
Professed the contrary.

Enter a Messenger.

                     This is his lordship's man.
100 DUKE   And here comes Claudio's pardon.
MESSENGER   My lord hath sent you this note and by me
this further charge: that you swerve not from the smallest
article of it, neither in time, matter or other circumstance.
Good morrow, for as I take it, it is almost day.
105 PROVOST   I shall obey him.   *Exit Messenger.*
DUKE *[aside]*
This is his pardon purchased by such sin
For which the pardoner himself is in.
Hence hath offence his quick celerity,
When it is borne in high authority.
110 When vice makes mercy, mercy's so extended
That for the fault's love is th'offender friended.
Now, sir, what news?
PROVOST   I told you: Lord Angelo, belike thinking me
remiss in mine office, awakens me with this unwonted
115 putting on, methinks strangely, for he hath not used it
before.
DUKE   Pray you, let's hear.
PROVOST *[Reads.]* *Whatsoever you may hear to the*
contrary, let Claudio be executed by four of the clock, and
120 *in the afternoon Barnardine. For my better satisfaction, let*
me have Claudio's head sent me by five. Let this be duly
performed with a thought that more depends on it than we
must yet deliver. Thus fail not to do your office, as you will
answer it at your peril. What say you to this, sir?
125 DUKE   What is that Barnardine who is to be executed in
th'afternoon?
PROVOST   A Bohemian born, but here nursed up and
bred; one that is a prisoner nine years old.
DUKE   How came it that the absent Duke had not either
130 delivered him to his liberty or executed him? I have
heard it was ever his manner to do so.
PROVOST   His friends still wrought reprieves for him,
and indeed his fact till now in the government of Lord
Angelo came not to an undoubtful proof.
135 DUKE   It is now apparent?
PROVOST   Most manifest, and not denied by himself.
DUKE   Hath he borne himself penitently in prison? How
seems he to be touched?
PROVOST   A man that apprehends death no more
140 dreadfully but as a drunken sleep; careless, reckless
and fearless of what's past, present or to come;
insensible of mortality and desperately mortal.

DUKE   He wants advice.
PROVOST   He will hear none. He hath evermore had the
liberty of the prison; give him leave to escape hence, he   145
would not. Drunk many times a day, if not many days
entirely drunk. We have very oft awaked him as if to
carry him to execution, and showed him a seeming
warrant for it. It hath not moved him at all.
DUKE   More of him anon. There is written in your brow,   150
Provost, honesty and constancy. If I read it not truly,
my ancient skill beguiles me, but in the boldness of my
cunning, I will lay myself in hazard. Claudio, whom
here you have warrant to execute, is no greater forfeit
to the law than Angelo who hath sentenced him. To   155
make you understand this in a manifested effect, I
crave but four days' respite; for the which you are to do
me both a present and a dangerous courtesy.
PROVOST   Pray, sir, in what?
DUKE   In the delaying death.   160
PROVOST   Alack, how may I do it? Having the hour
limited and an express command, under penalty, to
deliver his head in the view of Angelo? I may make my
case as Claudio's to cross this in the smallest.
DUKE   By the vow of mine order, I warrant you, if my   165
instructions may be your guide: let this Barnardine be
this morning executed, and his head borne to Angelo.
PROVOST   Angelo hath seen them both and will discover
the favour.
DUKE   O, death's a great disguiser, and you may add   170
to it: shave the head and tie the beard and say it was the
desire of the penitent to be so bared before his death.
You know the course is common. If anything fall to
you upon this more than thanks and good fortune, by
the saint whom I profess, I will plead against it with   175
my life.
PROVOST   Pardon me, good father, it is against my oath.
DUKE   Were you sworn to the Duke or to the deputy?
PROVOST   To him and to his substitutes.
DUKE   You will think you have made no offence if the   180
Duke avouch the justice of your dealing?
PROVOST   But what likelihood is in that?
DUKE   Not a resemblance, but a certainty. Yet since I see
you fearful, that neither my coat, integrity nor persuasion
can with ease attempt you, I will go further than I meant   185
to pluck all fears out of you. Look you, sir, here is the
hand and seal of the Duke; you know the character, I
doubt not, and the signet is not strange to you.
PROVOST   I know them both.
DUKE   The contents of this is the return of the Duke.   190
You shall anon over-read it at your pleasure, where you
shall find within these two days he will be here. This is
a thing that Angelo knows not, for he this very day
receives letters of strange tenor, perchance of
the Duke's death, perchance entering into some   195
monastery, but by chance nothing of what is writ.
Look, th'unfolding star calls up the shepherd. Put not
yourself into amazement how these things should be;
all difficulties are but easy when they are known. Call

200   your executioner and off with Barnardine's head. I will
      give him a present shrift and advise him for a better
      place. Yet you are amazed, but this shall absolutely
      resolve you. Come away, it is almost clear dawn.

                                                    Exeunt.

4.3   *Enter* POMPEY.

POMPEY   I am as well acquainted here as I was in our
      house of profession; one would think it were Mistress
      Overdone's own house, for here be many of her old
      customers. First, here's young Master Rash, he's in for
5   a commodity of brown paper and old ginger, nine score
      and seventeen pounds, of which he made five marks
      ready money: marry, then ginger was not much in
      request, for the old women were all dead. Then is there
      here one Master Caper, at the suit of Master Threepile
10   the mercer, for some four suits of peach-coloured
      satin, which now peaches him a beggar. Then have we
      here young Dizzy, and young Master Deepvow, and
      Master Copperspur, and Master Starvelackey the
      rapier and dagger man, and young Dropheir that killed
15   lusty Pudding, and Master Forthright the tilter, and
      brave Master Shoetie the great traveller, and wild
      Halfcan that stabbed Pots – and I think forty more, all
      great doers in our trade, and are now 'for the Lord's sake'.

                   Enter ABHORSON.

ABHORSON   Sirrah, bring Barnardine hither.
20   POMPEY   Master Barnardine, you must rise and be
      hanged, Master Barnardine.
ABHORSON   What ho, Barnardine.
BARNARDINE   [*within*] A pox o'your throats. Who
      makes that noise there? What are you?
25   POMPEY   Your friends, sir, the hangman. You must be
      so good, sir, to rise and be put to death.
BARNARDINE   [*within*] Away, you rogue, away, I am
      sleepy.
ABHORSON   Tell him he must awake, and that quickly
30   too.
POMPEY   Pray, Master Barnardine, awake till you are
      executed and sleep afterwards.
ABHORSON   Go in to him and fetch him out.
POMPEY   He is coming, sir, he is coming. I hear his
35   straw rustle.

                   Enter BARNARDINE.

ABHORSON   Is the axe upon the block, sirrah?
POMPEY   Very ready, sir.
BARNARDINE   How now, Abhorson? What's the news
      with you?
40   ABHORSON   Truly, sir, I would desire you to clap into
      your prayers: for look you, the warrant's come.
BARNARDINE   You rogue, I have been drinking all night.
      I am not fitted for't.
POMPEY   O, the better, sir, for he that drinks all night
45   and is hanged betimes in the morning may sleep the
      sounder all the next day.

                   Enter DUKE *disguised as a friar.*

ABHORSON   Look you, sir, here comes your ghostly
      father. Do we jest now, think you?
DUKE   Sir, induced by my charity and hearing how
      hastily you are to depart, I am come to advise you,   50
      comfort you and pray with you.
BARNARDINE   Friar, not I. I have been drinking hard all
      night, and I will have more time to prepare me, or they
      shall beat out my brains with billets. I will not consent
      to die this day, that's certain.   55
DUKE
      O, sir, you must, and therefore I beseech you
      Look forward on the journey you shall go.
BARNARDINE   I swear I will not die today for any man's
      persuasion.
DUKE   But hear you –   60
BARNARDINE   Not a word. If you have anything to say
      to me, come to my ward, for thence will not I today.
                                                    Exit.

                   Enter PROVOST.

DUKE   Unfit to live or die. O gravel heart!
      After him, fellows, bring him to the block.
                          Exeunt Abhorson and Pompey.
PROVOST   Now, sir, how do you find the prisoner?   65
DUKE   A creature unprepared, unmeet for death,
      And to transport him in the mind he is
      Were damnable.
PROVOST   Here in the prison, father,
      There died this morning of a cruel fever
      One Ragozine, a most notorious pirate,   70
      A man of Claudio's years, his beard and head
      Just of his colour. What if we do omit
      This reprobate till he were well inclined
      And satisfy the deputy with the visage
      Of Ragozine, more like to Claudio?   75
DUKE   O, 'tis an accident that heaven provides!
      Dispatch it presently; the hour draws on
      Prefixed by Angelo. See this be done
      And sent according to command, whiles I
      Persuade this rude wretch willingly to die.   80
PROVOST   This shall be done, good father, presently;
      But Barnardine must die this afternoon,
      And how shall we continue Claudio
      To save me from the danger that might come
      If he were known alive?
DUKE   Let this be done: 85
      Put them in secret holds, both Barnardine and
          Claudio;
      Ere twice the sun hath made his journal greeting
      To yonder generation, you shall find
      Your safety manifested.
PROVOST   I am your free dependant.   90
DUKE
      Quick, dispatch, and send the head to Angelo.
                                          Exit Provost.

Now will I write letters to Angelo –
The provost, he shall bear them – whose contents
Shall witness to him I am near at home,
95 And that by great injunctions I am bound
To enter publicly. Him I'll desire
To meet me at the consecrated fount
A league below the city, and from thence
By cold gradation and weal-balanced form
100 We shall proceed with Angelo.

Enter PROVOST *with Ragozine's head.*

PROVOST   Here is the head; I'll carry it myself.
DUKE   Convenient is it. Make a swift return,
For I would commune with you of such things
That want no ear but yours.
PROVOST   I'll make all speed.   *Exit.*
ISABELLA [*within*]
105   Peace, ho, be here.
DUKE   The tongue of Isabel. She's come to know
If yet her brother's pardon be come hither,
But I will keep her ignorant of her good
To make her heavenly comforts of despair
When it is least expected.

Enter ISABELLA.

110 ISABELLA   Ho, by your leave.
DUKE
Good morning to you, fair and gracious daughter.
ISABELLA   The better given me by so holy a man.
Hath yet the deputy sent my brother's pardon?
DUKE   He hath released him, Isabel, from the world;
115 His head is off and sent to Angelo.
ISABELLA
Nay, but it is not so.
DUKE   It is no other.
Show your wisdom, daughter, in your close patience.
ISABELLA   O, I will to him and pluck out his eyes.
DUKE   You shall not be admitted to his sight.
120 ISABELLA   Unhappy Claudio, wretched Isabel,
Injurious world, most damnèd Angelo!
DUKE   This nor hurts him, nor profits you a jot.
Forbear it therefore; give your cause to heaven.
Mark what I say, which you shall find
125 By every syllable a faithful verity.
The Duke comes home tomorrow – nay, dry your eyes –
One of our covent, and his confessor,
Gives me this instance; already he hath carried
Notice to Escalus and Angelo,
130 Who do prepare to meet him at the gates,
There to give up their power. If you can, pace your
wisdom
In that good path that I would wish it go,
And you shall have your bosom on this wretch,
Grace of the Duke, revenges to your heart
135 And general honour.
ISABELLA   I am directed by you.
DUKE   This letter then to Friar Peter give –

'Tis that he sent me of the Duke's return –
Say, by this token, I desire his company
At Mariana's house tonight. Her cause and yours
I'll perfect him withal, and he shall bring you   140
Before the Duke, and to the head of Angelo
Accuse him home and home. For my poor self,
I am combined by a sacred vow
And shall be absent. Wend you with this letter.
Command these fretting waters from your eyes   145
With a light heart; trust not my holy order
If I pervert your course.

Enter LUCIO.

Who's here?
LUCIO   Good e'en;
Friar, where's the provost?
DUKE   Not within, sir.
LUCIO   O, pretty Isabella, I am pale at mine heart to see   150
thine eyes so red: thou must be patient. I am fain to
dine and sup with water and bran; I dare not for my
head fill my belly. One fruitful meal would set me to't.
But they say the Duke will be here tomorrow. By my
troth, Isabel, I loved thy brother; if the old fantastical   155
duke of dark corners had been at home, he had lived.
Exit Isabella.
DUKE   Sir, the Duke is marvelous little beholding to
your reports, but the best is he lives not in them.
LUCIO   Friar, thou knowest not the Duke so well as I do;
he's a better woodman than thou tak'st him for.
DUKE   Well, you'll answer this one day. Fare ye well.   160
LUCIO   Nay, tarry, I'll go along with thee. I can tell thee
pretty tales of the Duke.
DUKE   You have told me too many of him already, sir, if
they be true: if not true, none were enough.
LUCIO   I was once before him for getting a wench with   165
child.
DUKE   Did you such a thing?
LUCIO   Yes, marry, did I, but I was fain to forswear it;
they would else have married me to the rotten medlar.
DUKE   Sir, your company is fairer than honest. Rest you   170
well.
LUCIO   By my troth, I'll go with thee to the lane's end; if
bawdy talk offend you, we'll have very little of it. Nay,
friar, I am a kind of burr, I shall stick.   *Exeunt.*

4.4   *Enter* ANGELO *and* ESCALUS.

ESCALUS   Every letter he hath writ hath disvouched
other.
ANGELO   In most uneven and distracted manner. His
actions show much like to madness; pray heaven his
wisdom be not tainted. And why meet him at the gates   5
and reliver our authorities there?
ESCALUS   I guess not.
ANGELO   And why should we proclaim it in an hour
before his entering, that if any crave redress of injustice,
they should exhibit their petitions in the street?   10

ESCALUS   He shows his reason for that: to have a
   dispatch of complaints and to deliver us from devices
   hereafter, which shall then have no power to stand
   against us.

15 ANGELO   Well, I beseech you let it be proclaimed
   betimes i'th' morn. I'll call you at your house. Give
   notice to such men of sort and suit as are to meet him.

ESCALUS   I shall, sir: fare you well.

ANGELO   Good night.   *Exit Escalus.*

20   This deed unshapes me quite, makes me unpregnant
   And dull to all proceedings. A deflowered maid,
   And by an eminent body that enforced
   The law against it! But that her tender shame
   Will not proclaim against her maiden loss,
25   How might she tongue me! Yet reason dares her no,
   For my authority bears a credent bulk
   That no particular scandal once can touch
   But it confounds the breather. He should have lived,
   Save that his riotous youth with dangerous sense
30   Might in the times to come have ta'en revenge
   By so receiving a dishonoured life
   With ransom of such shame. Would yet he had lived.
   Alack, when once our grace we have forgot,
   Nothing goes right; we would, and we would not.
                                   Exit.

4.5   *Enter* DUKE *in his own robes and* Friar PETER.

DUKE   These letters at fit time deliver me.
   The provost knows our purpose and our plot;
   The matter being afoot, keep your instruction
   And hold you ever to our special drift,
5   Though sometimes you do blench from this to that
   As cause doth minister. Go, call at Flavius' house
   And tell him where I stay. Give the like notice
   To Valencius, Rowland and to Crassus,
   And bid them bring the trumpets to the gate.
   But send me Flavius first.

10 PETER   It shall be speeded well.   *Exit.*

Enter Varrius.

DUKE
   I thank thee, Varrius, thou hast made good haste;
   Come, we will walk. There's other of our friends
   Will greet us here anon, my gentle Varrius.   *Exeunt.*

4.6   *Enter* ISABELLA *and* MARIANA.

ISABELLA   To speak so indirectly I am loath.
   I would say the truth, but to accuse him so,
   That is your part; yet I am advised to do it,
   He says, to veil full purpose.

MARIANA   Be ruled by him.

5 ISABELLA   Besides, he tells me that, if peradventure
   He speak against me on the adverse side,
   I should not think it strange, for 'tis a physic
   That's bitter to sweet end.

MARIANA   I would Friar Peter –

Enter PETER.

ISABELLA   O peace, the friar is come.

PETER   Come, I have found you out a stand most fit,   10
   Where you may have such vantage on the Duke
   He shall not pass you. Twice have the trumpets sounded.
   The generous and gravest citizens
   Have hent the gates, and very near upon
   The Duke is entering. Therefore hence away.   *Exeunt.*   15

5.1   *Enter* DUKE *in his robes,* Varrius, Lords,
      ANGELO, ESCALUS, LUCIO, PROVOST,
      Officers, Citizens at several doors.

DUKE   My very worthy cousin, fairly met.
   Our old and faithful friend, we are glad to see you.

ANGELO, ESCALUS
   Happy return be to your royal grace.

DUKE   Many and hearty thankings to you both.
   We have made enquiry of you, and we hear   5
   Such goodness of your justice that our soul
   Cannot but yield you forth to public thanks
   Forerunning more requital.

ANGELO   You make my bonds still greater.

DUKE
   O, your desert speaks loud, and I should wrong it
   To lock it in the wards of covert bosom   10
   When it deserves with characters of brass
   A forted residence 'gainst the tooth of time
   And razure of oblivion. Give me your hand,
   And let the subject see, to make them know
   That outward courtesies would fain proclaim   15
   Favours that keep within. Come, Escalus,
   You must walk by us on our other hand,
   And good supporters are you.

Enter Friar PETER *and* ISABELLA.

PETER
   Now is your time: speak loud, and kneel before him.

ISABELLA   Justice, O royal Duke, vail your regard   20
   Upon a wronged – I would fain have said, a maid.
   O worthy prince, dishonour not your eye
   By throwing it on any other object
   Till you have heard me in my true complaint
   And given me justice, justice, justice, justice.   25

DUKE
   Relate your wrongs. In what? By whom? Be brief.
   Here is Lord Angelo shall give you justice.
   Reveal yourself to him.

ISABELLA   O worthy Duke,
   You bid me seek redemption of the devil.
   Hear me yourself, for that which I must speak   30
   Must either punish me, not being believed,
   Or wring redress from you. Hear me, O hear me, hear!

ANGELO   My lord, her wits I fear me are not firm.
   She hath been a suitor to me, for her brother

Cut off by course of justice.

35 ISABELLA   By course of justice!

ANGELO   And she will speak most bitterly and strange.

ISABELLA
     Most strange, but yet most truly will I speak.
     That Angelo's forsworn, is it not strange?
     That Angelo's a murderer, is't not strange?
40   That Angelo is an adulterous thief,
     An hypocrite, a virgin-violator,
     Is it not strange and strange?

DUKE   Nay, it is ten times strange.

ISABELLA   It is not truer he is Angelo,
     Than this is all as true as it is strange;
45   Nay, it is ten times true, for truth is truth
     To th'end of reckoning.

DUKE   Away with her. Poor soul,
     She speaks this in th'infirmity of sense.

ISABELLA   O prince, I conjure thee, as thou believ'st
     There is another comfort than this world,
50   That thou neglect me not with that opinion
     That I am touched with madness. Make not impossible
     That which but seems unlike. 'Tis not impossible
     But one the wicked'st caitiff on the ground
     May seem as shy, as grave, as just, as absolute
55   As Angelo; even so may Angelo,
     In all his dressings, characts, titles, forms,
     Be an arch-villain. Believe it, royal prince,
     If he be less, he's nothing, but he's more,
     Had I more name for badness.

DUKE   By mine honesty
60   If she be mad, as I believe no other,
     Her madness hath the oddest frame of sense;
     Such a dependency of thing on thing,
     As e'er I heard in madness.

ISABELLA   O gracious Duke,
     Harp not on that, nor do not banish reason
65   For inequality, but let your reason serve
     To make the truth appear where it seems hid,
     And hide the false seems true.

DUKE   Many that are not mad
     Have sure more lack of reason. What would you say?

ISABELLA   I am the sister of one Claudio,
70   Condemned upon the act of fornication
     To lose his head, condemned by Angelo.
     I, in probation of a sisterhood,
     Was sent to by my brother; one Lucio,
     As then the messenger –

LUCIO   That's I, an't like your grace.
75   I came to her from Claudio and desired her
     To try her gracious fortune with Lord Angelo
     For her poor brother's pardon.

ISABELLA   That's he indeed.

DUKE [*to Lucio*]
     You were not bid to speak.

LUCIO   No, my good lord,
     Nor wished to hold my peace.

DUKE   I wish you now, then.

Pray you take note of it, and when you have   80
     A business for yourself, pray heaven you then
     Be perfect.

LUCIO   I warrant your honour.

DUKE   The warrant's for yourself: take heed to't.

ISABELLA   This gentleman told somewhat of my tale.

LUCIO   Right.   85

DUKE   It may be right, but you are i'the wrong
     To speak before your time. – Proceed.

ISABELLA   I went
     To this pernicious caitiff deputy –

DUKE   That's somewhat madly spoken.

ISABELLA   Pardon it,
     The phrase is to the matter.   90

DUKE   Mended again. The matter: proceed.

ISABELLA   In brief, to set the needless process by –
     How I persuaded, how I prayed and kneeled,
     How he refelled me and how I replied,
     For this was of much length – the vile conclusion   95
     I now begin with grief and shame to utter.
     He would not, but by gift of my chaste body
     To his concupiscible intemperate lust,
     Release my brother; and after much debatement
     My sisterly remorse confutes mine honour,   100
     And I did yield to him. But the next morn betimes,
     His purpose surfeiting, he sends a warrant
     For my poor brother's head.

DUKE   This is most likely.

ISABELLA   O that it were as like as it is true.

DUKE
     By heaven, fond wretch, thou knowst not what thou
          speak'st,   105
     Or else thou art suborned against his honour
     In hateful practice. First, his integrity
     Stands without blemish; next, it imports no reason
     That with such vehemency he should pursue
     Faults proper to himself. If he had so offended   110
     He would have weighed thy brother by himself
     And not have cut him off. Someone hath set you on.
     Confess the truth and say by whose advice
     Thou cam'st here to complain.

ISABELLA   And is this all?
     Then, O you blessed ministers above,   115
     Keep me in patience and with ripened time
     Unfold the evil which is here wrapped up
     In countenance. Heaven shield your grace from woe,
     As I, thus wronged, hence unbelieved go.

DUKE   I know you'd fain be gone. – An officer!   120
     To prison with her. – Shall we thus permit
     A blasting and a scandalous breath to fall
     On him so near us? This needs must be a practice. –
     Who knew of your intent and coming hither?

ISABELLA
     One that I would were here, Friar Lodowick.   125

                               Exit guarded.

DUKE
     A ghostly father, belike. Who knows that Lodowick?

LUCIO My lord, I know him, 'tis a meddling friar,
 I do not like the man. Had he been lay, my lord,
 For certain words he spake against your grace
130 In your retirement, I had swinged him soundly.
DUKE Words against me? This' a good friar belike:
 And to set on this wretched woman here
 Against our substitute. Let this friar be found.
LUCIO But yesternight, my lord, she and that friar,
135 I saw them at the prison: a saucy friar,
 A very scurvy fellow.
PETER   Blessed be your royal grace!
 I have stood by, my lord, and I have heard
 Your royal ear abused. First hath this woman
 Most wrongfully accused your substitute,
140 Who is as free from touch or soil with her
 As she from one ungot.
DUKE   We did believe no less.
 Know you that Friar Lodowick that she speaks of?
PETER I know him for a man divine and holy,
 Not scurvy nor a temporary meddler
145 As he's reported by this gentleman,
 And, on my trust, a man that never yet
 Did, as he vouches, misreport your grace.
LUCIO My lord, most villainously, believe it.
PETER Well, he in time may come to clear himself,
150 But at this instant he is sick, my lord,
 Of a strange fever. Upon his mere request,
 Being come to knowledge that there was complaint
 Intended 'gainst Lord Angelo, came I hither
 To speak as from his mouth what he doth know
155 Is true and false, and what he with his oath
 And all probation will make up full clear
 Whensoever he's convented. First, for this woman:
 To justify this worthy nobleman
 So vulgarly and personally accused,
160 Her shall you hear disproved to her eyes,
 Till she herself confess it.
DUKE   Good friar, let's hear it.
         Exit Friar Peter.
 Do you not smile at this, Lord Angelo?
 O heaven, the vanity of wretched fools.
 Give us some seats. Come, cousin Angelo,
165 In this I'll be impartial: be you judge
 Of your own cause.

   Enter MARIANA *veiled, with* Friar PETER.

     Is this the witness, friar?
 First, let her show her face and after speak.
MARIANA Pardon, my lord, I will not show my face
 Until my husband bid me.
170 DUKE What, are you married?
MARIANA No, my lord.
DUKE Are you a maid?
MARIANA No, my lord.
DUKE A widow then?
175 MARIANA Neither, my lord.
DUKE Why, you are nothing then: neither maid, widow
 nor wife!

LUCIO My lord, she may be a punk, for many of them
 are neither maid, widow nor wife.
DUKE Silence that fellow. I would he had some cause to 180
 prattle for himself.
LUCIO Well, my lord.
MARIANA My lord, I do confess I ne'er was married,
 And I confess besides I am no maid;
 I have known my husband, yet my husband 185
 Knows not that ever he knew me.
LUCIO He was drunk then, my lord, it can be no better.
DUKE
 For the benefit of silence, would thou wert so too.
LUCIO Well, my lord.
DUKE This is no witness for Lord Angelo. 190
MARIANA Now I come to't, my lord.
 She that accuses him of fornication
 In self-same manner doth accuse my husband
 And charges him, my lord, with such a time
 When I'll depose I had him in mine arms 195
 With all th'effect of love.
ANGELO Charges she mo than me?
MARIANA   Not that I know.
DUKE No? You say your husband.
MARIANA Why just, my lord, and that is Angelo,
 Who thinks he knows that he ne'er knew my body, 200
 But knows, he thinks, that he knows Isabel's.
ANGELO This is a strange abuse. Let's see thy face.
MARIANA [*Unveils.*]
 My husband bids me, now I will unmask.
 This is that face, thou cruel Angelo,
 Which once thou swor'st was worth the looking on. 205
 This is the hand, which with a vowed contract
 Was fast belocked in thine. This is the body
 That took away the match from Isabel
 And did supply thee at thy garden-house
 In her imagined person.
DUKE   Know you this woman? 210
LUCIO Carnally, she says.
DUKE Sirrah, no more.
LUCIO Enough, my lord.
ANGELO My lord, I must confess, I know this woman,
 And five years since there was some speech of marriage 215
 Betwixt myself and her – which was broke off,
 Partly for that her promised proportions
 Came short of composition, but in chief
 For that her reputation was disvalued
 In levity. Since which time of five years 220
 I never spoke with her, saw her nor heard from her
 Upon my faith and honour.
MARIANA [*Kneels.*]   Noble prince,
 As there comes light from heaven and words from
  breath,
 As there is sense in truth and truth in virtue,
 I am affianced this man's wife as strongly 225
 As words could make up vows. And, my good lord,
 But Tuesday night last gone, in's garden-house,
 He knew me as a wife. As this is true,
 Let me in safety raise me from my knees,

230   Or else for ever be confixed here
      A marble monument.

ANGELO   I did but smile till now.
      Now, good my lord, give me the scope of justice,
      My patience here is touched. I do perceive
      These poor informal women are no more

235   But instruments of some more mightier member
      That sets them on. Let me have way, my lord,
      To find this practice out.

DUKE   Ay, with my heart,
      And punish them to your height of pleasure.
      Thou foolish friar, and thou pernicious woman
      Compact with her that's gone: think'st thou thy

240   oaths,
      Though they would swear down each particular saint,
      Were testimonies against his worth and credit
      That's sealed in approbation? You, Lord Escalus,
      Sit with my cousin, lend him your kind pains

245   To find out this abuse, whence 'tis derived.
      There is another friar that set them on.
      Let him be sent for.

PETER
      Would he were here, my lord, for he indeed
      Hath set the women on to this complaint.

250   Your provost knows the place where he abides
      And he may fetch him.

DUKE   Go, do it instantly. –
                          Exit Provost.
      And you, my noble and well-warranted cousin,
      Whom it concerns to hear this matter forth,
      Do with your injuries as seems you best

255   In any chastisement. I for a while will leave you,
      But stir not you till you have well determined
      Upon these slanderers.

ESCALUS   My lord, we'll do it throughly.   *Exit Duke.*
      Signior Lucio, did not you say you knew that Friar

260   Lodowick to be a dishonest person?

LUCIO   *Cucullus non facit monachum.* Honest in nothing
      but in his clothes, and one that hath spoke most
      villainous speeches of the Duke.

ESCALUS   We shall entreat you to abide here till he come

265   and enforce them against him. We shall find this friar a
      notable fellow.

LUCIO   As any in Vienna, on my word.

ESCALUS   Call that same Isabel here once again, I would
      speak with her.   *Exit an Officer.*

270   Pray you, my lord, give me leave to question; you shall
      see how I'll handle her.

LUCIO   Not better than he, by her own report.

ESCALUS   Say you?

LUCIO   Marry, sir, I think if you handled her privately

275   she would sooner confess; perchance publicly she'll be
      ashamed.

           Enter DUKE *as friar with* PROVOST;
              ISABELLA *and Officer.*

ESCALUS   I will go darkly to work with her.

LUCIO   That's the way, for women are light at midnight.

ESCALUS   Come on, mistress, here's a gentlewoman
      denies all that you have said.   280

LUCIO   My lord, here comes the rascal I spoke of; here,
      with the provost.

ESCALUS   In very good time. Speak not you to him till
      we call upon you.

LUCIO   Mum.   285

ESCALUS   Come, sir, did you set these women on to
      slander Lord Angelo? They have confessed you did.

DUKE   'Tis false.

ESCALUS   How? Know you where you are?

DUKE   Respect to your great place, and let the devil   290
      Be sometime honoured for his burning throne.
      Where is the Duke? 'Tis he should hear me speak.

ESCALUS
      The Duke's in us, and we will hear you speak.
      Look you speak justly.

DUKE   Boldly, at least. But O, poor souls,   295
      Come you to seek the lamb here of the fox?
      Good night to your redress. Is the Duke gone?
      Then is your cause gone too. The Duke's unjust
      Thus to retort your manifest appeal
      And put your trial in the villain's mouth   300
      Which here you come to accuse.

LUCIO   This is the rascal; this is he I spoke of.

ESCALUS
      Why, thou unreverent and unhallowed friar!
      Is't not enough thou hast suborned these women
      To accuse this worthy man, but in foul mouth   305
      And in the witness of his proper ear
      To call him villain? And then to glance from him
      To th' Duke himself, to tax him with injustice?
      Take him hence. To th' rack with him. We'll touse you
      Joint by joint, but we will know his purpose.   310
      What? 'Unjust'!

DUKE   Be not so hot. The Duke dare no more stretch
      This finger of mine than he dare rack his own.
      His subject am I not, nor here provincial.
      My business in this state   315
      Made me a looker-on here in Vienna,
      Where I have seen corruption boil and bubble
      Till it o'errun the stew. Laws for all faults,
      But faults so countenanced that the strong statutes
      Stand like the forfeits in a barber's shop,   320
      As much in mock as mark.

ESCALUS   Slander to th' state. Away with him to prison.

ANGELO
      What can you vouch against him, Signior Lucio?
      Is this the man that you did tell us of?

LUCIO   'Tis he, my lord. Come hither, goodman   325
      Baldpate. Do you know me?

DUKE   I remember you, sir, by the sound of your voice.
      I met you at the prison, in the absence of the Duke.

LUCIO   O, did you so? And do you remember what you
      said of the Duke?   330

DUKE   Most notedly, sir.

LUCIO   Do you so, sir? And was the Duke a fleshmonger, a fool and a coward, as you then reported him to be?

335   DUKE   You must, sir, change persons with me ere you make that my report. You indeed spoke so of him, and much more, much worse.

LUCIO   O, thou damnable fellow! Did not I pluck thee by the nose for thy speeches?

340   DUKE   I protest, I love the Duke as I love myself.

ANGELO   Hark how the villain would close now after his treasonable abuses.

ESCALUS   Such a fellow is not to be talked withal. Away with him to prison! Where is the provost? Away with
345   him to prison; lay bolts enough upon him; let him speak no more. Away with those giglets too, and with the other confederate companion.

DUKE   Stay, sir; stay awhile.

ANGELO   What, resists he? Help him, Lucio.

350   LUCIO   Come sir, come sir, come sir! Faugh, sir, why you baldpated, lying rascal, you must be hooded, must you? Show your knave's visage, with a pox to you. Show your sheep-biting face and be hanged an hour. Will't not off? [*Pulls off the Friar's hood and reveals the Duke. Angelo and Escalus stand.*]

355   DUKE   Thou art the first knave that e'er mad'st a duke. First, Provost, let me bail these gentle three. Sneak not away, sir, for the friar and you Must have a word anon. Lay hold on him.

LUCIO   This may prove worse than hanging.

DUKE [*to Escalus*]
360   What you have spoke, I pardon; sit you down. We'll borrow place of him. [*to Angelo*] Sir, by your leave.
Hast thou or word, or wit, or impudence That yet can do thee office? If thou hast, Rely upon it till my tale be heard And hold no longer out.

365   ANGELO   O, my dread lord, I should be guiltier than my guiltiness To think I can be undiscernible, When I perceive your grace, like power divine, Hath looked upon my passes. Then, good prince,
370   No longer session hold upon my shame, But let my trial be mine own confession. Immediate sentence, then, and sequent death Is all the grace I beg.

DUKE   Come hither, Mariana. – Say: wast thou e'er contracted to this woman?

375   ANGELO   I was, my lord.

DUKE   Go, take her hence and marry her instantly. Do you the office, friar, which consummate, Return him here again. Go with him, Provost.
Exeunt Friar Peter, Angelo, Mariana and Provost.

ESCALUS   My lord, I am more amazed at his dishonour Than at the strangeness of it.

380   DUKE   Come hither, Isabel. Your friar is now your prince. As I was then,

Advertising and holy to your business, Not changing heart with habit, I am still Attorneyed at your service.

ISABELLA   O, give me pardon
385   That I, your vassal, have employed and pained Your unknown sovereignty.

DUKE   You are pardoned, Isabel. And now, dear maid, be you as free to us. Your brother's death I know sits at your heart,
And you may marvel why I obscured myself
390   Labouring to save his life, and would not rather Make rash remonstrance of my hidden power Than let him so be lost. O, most kind maid, It was the swift celerity of his death, Which I did think with slower foot came on,
395   That brained my purpose. But peace be with him. That life is better life past fearing death Than that which lives to fear. Make it your comfort, So happy is your brother.

ISABELLA   I do, my lord.

Enter ANGELO, MARIANA,
Friar PETER, PROVOST.

DUKE   For this new-married man approaching here,
400   Whose salt imagination yet hath wronged Your well-defended honour, you must pardon For Mariana's sake. But as he adjudged your brother, Being criminal in double violation, Of sacred chastity and of promise-breach
405   Thereon dependent for your brother's life, The very mercy of the law cries out Most audible, even from his proper tongue: 'An Angelo for Claudio, death for death; Haste still pays haste and leisure answers leisure;
410   Like doth quit like and measure still for measure.' Then, Angelo, thy faults thus manifested, Which though thou wouldst deny denies thee vantage, We do condemn thee to the very block Where Claudio stooped to death, and with like haste.
Away with him.

MARIANA   O, my most gracious lord,
415   I hope you will not mock me with a husband?

DUKE
It is your husband mocked you with a husband. Consenting to the safeguard of your honour I thought your marriage fit; else imputation,
420   For that he knew you, might reproach your life And choke your good to come. For his possessions, Although by confiscation they are ours, We do instate and widow you with all To buy you a better husband.

MARIANA   O my dear lord,
425   I crave no other nor no better man.

DUKE   Never crave him, we are definitive.

MARIANA   Gentle my liege –

DUKE   You do but lose your labour. Away with him to death. [*to Lucio*] Now, sir, to you.

MARIANA [*Kneels.*]
  O, my good lord – sweet Isabel, take my part;
430   Lend me your knees, and all my life to come
  I'll lend you all my life to do you service.
DUKE   Against all sense you do importune her:
  Should she kneel down in mercy of this fact,
  Her brother's ghost his paved bed would break
  And take her hence in horror.
435 MARIANA   Isabel!
  Sweet Isabel, do yet but kneel by me.
  Hold up your hands; say nothing: I'll speak all –
  They say best men are moulded out of faults
  And for the most become much more the better
440   For being a little bad. So may my husband –
  O Isabel, will you not lend a knee?
DUKE   He dies for Claudio's death.
ISABELLA [*Kneels.*]   Most bounteous sir,
  Look, if it please you, on this man condemned
  As if my brother lived. I partly think
445   A due sincerity governed his deeds
  Till he did look on me. Since it is so,
  Let him not die. My brother had but justice,
  In that he did the thing for which he died.
  For Angelo,
450   His act did not o'ertake his bad intent
  And must be buried but as an intent
  That perished by the way. Thoughts are no subjects;
  Intents, but merely thoughts.
MARIANA   Merely, my lord.
DUKE   Your suit's unprofitable: stand up, I say. –
455   I have bethought me of another fault:
  Provost, how came it Claudio was beheaded
  At an unusual hour?
PROVOST   It was commanded so.
DUKE   Had you a special warrant for the deed?
PROVOST   No, my good lord; it was by private message.
460 DUKE   For which I do discharge you of your office.
  Give up your keys.
PROVOST   Pardon me, noble lord,
  I thought it was a fault, but knew it not,
  Yet did repent me after more advice.
  For testimony whereof, one in the prison
465   That should by private order else have died,
  I have reserved alive.
DUKE   What's he?
PROVOST   His name is Barnardine.
DUKE   I would thou hadst done so by Claudio.
470   Go, fetch him hither, let me look upon him.
                    Exit Provost.
ESCALUS   I am sorry one so learned and so wise
  As you, Lord Angelo, have still appeared
  Should slip so grossly, both in the heat of blood
  And lack of tempered judgement afterward.
475 ANGELO   I am sorry that such sorrow I procure,
  And so deep sticks it in my penitent heart
  That I crave death more willingly than mercy.
  'Tis my deserving, and I do entreat it.

Enter BARNARDINE *and* PROVOST,
    CLAUDIO *muffled,* JULIET.

DUKE   Which is that Barnardine?
PROVOST   This, my lord.
DUKE   There was a friar told me of this man. –   480
  Sirrah, thou art said to have a stubborn soul
  That apprehends no further than this world
  And squar'st thy life according. Thou'rt condemned:
  But for those earthly faults, I quit them all,
  And pray thee take this mercy to provide   485
  For better times to come. – Friar, advise him,
  I leave him to your hand. What muffled fellow's that?
PROVOST   This is another prisoner that I saved,
  Who should have died when Claudio lost his head,
  As like almost to Claudio as himself.   490
    [*Unmuffles Claudio.*]
DUKE [*to Isabella*]
  If he be like your brother, for his sake
  Is he pardoned, and for your lovely sake
  Give me your hand and say you will be mine,
  He is my brother too. But fitter time for that.
  By this Lord Angelo perceives he's safe –   495
  Methinks I see a quickening in his eye.
  Well, Angelo, your evil quits you well.
  Look that you love your wife: her worth, worth
    yours.
  I find an apt remission in myself;
  And yet here's one in place I cannot pardon.   500
  [*to Lucio*] You, sirrah, that knew me for a fool, a coward,
  One all of luxury, an ass, a madman:
  Wherein have I so deserved of you
  That you extol me thus?
LUCIO   'Faith, my lord, I spoke it but according to the   505
  trick. If you will hang me for it you may, but I had
  rather it would please you I might be whipped.
DUKE   Whipped first, sir, and hanged after.
  Proclaim it, Provost, round about the city,
  If any woman wronged by this lewd fellow –   510
  As I have heard him swear himself there's one
  Whom he begot with child – let her appear,
  And he shall marry her. The nuptial finished,
  Let him be whipped and hanged.
LUCIO   I beseech your highness do not marry me to a   515
  whore. Your highness said even now I made you a
  duke; good my lord, do not recompense me in making
  me a cuckold.
DUKE   Upon mine honour, thou shalt marry her.
  Thy slanders I forgive and therewithal   520
  Remit thy other forfeits. Take him to prison,
  And see our pleasure herein executed.
LUCIO   Marrying a punk, my lord, is pressing to death,
  whipping and hanging.
DUKE   Slandering a prince deserves it.   525
  She, Claudio, that you wronged, look you restore.
  Joy to you, Mariana; love her, Angelo,
  I have confessed her and I know her virtue.

Thanks, good friend Escalus, for thy much
    goodness,
530   There's more behind that is more gratulate.
Thanks, Provost, for thy care and secrecy;
We shall employ thee in a worthier place.
Forgive him, Angelo, that brought you home
The head of Ragozine for Claudio's;

Th'offence pardons itself. Dear Isabel,   535
I have a motion much imports your good,
Whereto if you'll a willing ear incline,
What's mine is yours, and what is yours is mine.
So bring us to our palace, where we'll show
What's yet behind that's meet you all should know.   540
                    Exeunt.

The Merchant of Venice

This play first appeared in print in 1600 as a Quarto entitled *The Comical History of the Merchant of Venice*. An alternative early title of a now lost play seems to have been *The Jew of Venice*, focusing attention on Shylock the Jew, a role which has since proved to be popular with actors but controversial with readers and audiences. *The Merchant of Venice* is one of the six comedies by Shakespeare listed by Francis Meres in his *Palladis Tamia* (1598), and it is generally thought to have been written between 1596 and 1597, after *Love's Labour's Lost* and *A Midsummer Night's Dream* but before *Much Ado About Nothing*, *As You Like It* and *Twelfth Night*. At much the same time Shakespeare was writing the *King Henry IV* plays, which also contain a comic character who threatens to upset their moral and aesthetic balance: Falstaff.

The main plot is very similar to one found in *Il Pecorone*, a fourteenth-century collection of stories first printed in Italian in 1558, in which a merchant called Ansaldo borrows money from a Jew on the surety of a pound of flesh so that his godson, Giannetto, can go to sea to seek his fortune. Instead, Giannetto courts and wins the Lady of Belmont, returning to find his godfather's life at risk. The Lady disguises herself as a lawyer, defeats the Jew and begs her own ring from Giannetto as payment. Scholars think that Shakespeare must have known an English version of this story, now lost, and that he (or the author of the lost version) added the story of the three caskets which is found in various medieval sources including John Gower's *Confessio Amantis* (late 1380s) and Giovanni Boccaccio's *Decameron* (1353). He was also influenced by Christopher Marlowe's play *The Jew of Malta* (c. 1591), in which the Jew's daughter elopes with a Christian. Officially, Jews had been expelled from England during the reign of Edward I, but if they conformed outwardly they were not persecuted. Officially, lending money for interest was condemned, but the Globe theatre was built on borrowed money and Shakespeare himself lent money. Nonetheless, at the heart of the play is the issue of usury and the ethical and religious questions that it raised for Elizabethan culture as a whole.

The 1600 Quarto claims that *The Merchant of Venice* had been 'divers times acted by the Lord Chamberlain his servants', Shakespeare's regular company, but there are no specific records of early performances apart from two at Court before James I in 1605. An adaptation by George Granville called *The Jew of Venice* displaced Shakespeare's version on the stage from 1701 until 1741, when Charles Macklin restored Shakespeare's *Merchant* but continued to play Shylock partly as a comic villain. Edmund Kean, who first played Shylock in 1814, broke with the tradition of presenting him in this way and made him a sympathetic and ultimately tragic figure – an interpretation which was followed by actors from Henry Irving and Edwin Booth to Laurence Olivier and beyond. While Shylock generally dominated the play, several actresses triumphed as Portia, including Sarah Siddons, Helen Faucit, Ellen Terry and Peggy Ashcroft. In the many books and essays on Shakespeare's heroines written by women in the nineteenth century (including Faucit's memoirs) Portia receives pride of place, and is held up as a demonstration that a woman can (at least in fiction) be an intellectual and a professional without losing her femininity. Modern feminist critics have emphasised this element of the play, and the subsidiary role of Jessica has also drawn some attention.

The Merchant of Venice became something of a problem play in the twentieth century, the systematic massacre of Jews in the Holocaust making it impossible for us to take the anti-semitism of the Christian characters lightly. Although many modern performances have aroused sympathy for Shylock, the play makes it clear that his behaviour cannot be endorsed beyond a certain point: he makes his claim for humanity ('Hath not a Jew eyes?' in 3.1), but he does so as a sanction for vindictiveness, albeit that the desire for revenge is ascribed to him in imitation of his Christian adversaries. He remains an adversary who seeks the life of his enemy, and even though the play requires us to celebrate his defeat and to see his involuntary conversion as an opportunity for salvation, Venice and its formal structures are also exposed. The final act of the play returns the action to Belmont, and attempts awkwardly to compensate for its attitude to strangers and outsiders.

The Arden text is based on the 1600 First Quarto.

ANTONIO	*a Christian merchant of Venice and friend of Bassanio*
BASSANIO	*a Venetian lord, friend of Antonio, and suitor to Portia*
LEONARDO	*servant to Bassanio*
GRATIANO	*a gentleman of Venice, friend of Antonio and Bassanio, and suitor to Nerissa*
LORENZO	*a gentleman friend of Bassanio and suitor to Jessica*
SALANIO	*gentlemen of Venice and friends of Bassanio and Antonio*
SALARINO	
DUKE of Venice	
SALERIO	*a Venetian emissary*
PORTIA	*a rich heiress of Belmont and beloved of Bassanio*
NERISSA	*Portia's waiting-woman*
Stephano, a MESSENGER	*a servant in Portia's household*
BALTHAZAR	*another of Portia's servants*
SERVINGMAN	*a menial in Portia's household*
Prince of MOROCCO	*a suitor to Portia*
Prince of ARRAGON	*a second suitor to Portia*
Shylock the JEW	*a Venetian usurer*
JESSICA	*daughter of the Jew and beloved of Lorenzo*
TUBAL	*a fellow Jew and his friend*
Lancelet Giobbe, a CLOWN	*a menial, first in the house of the Jew and later in the house of Antonio*
GIOBBE	*the father of the Clown*
MESSENGER	*a member of Portia's household*
MAN	*a menial in Antonio's household*

Jailer, Magnificoes, Attendants, Followers, Court Officials, Musicians, Servitor

1.1 *Enter* ANTONIO, SALARINO *and* SALANIO.

ANTONIO   In sooth I know not why I am so sad.
  It wearies me; you say it wearies you;
  But how I caught it, found it or came by it,
  What stuff 'tis made of, whereof it is born,
5 I am to learn; and such a want-wit sadness makes of me,
  That I have much ado to know myself.
SALARINO   Your mind is tossing on the ocean,
  There where your argosies with portly sail
  Like signiors and rich burghers on the flood,
10 Or, as it were, the pageants of the sea,
  Do overpeer the petty traffickers
  That curtsy to them, do them reverence
  As they fly by them with their woven wings.
SALANIO   Believe me, sir, had I such venture forth,
15 The better part of my affections would
  Be with my hopes abroad. I should be still
  Plucking the grass to know where sits the wind,
  Peering in maps for ports and piers and roads;
  And every object that might make me fear
20 Misfortune to my ventures, out of doubt,
  Would make me sad.
SALARINO   My wind, cooling my broth,
  Would blow me to an ague when I thought
  What harm a wind too great might do at sea.
  I should not see the sandy hour-glass run
25 But I should think of shallows and of flats,
  And see my wealthy *Andrew* docked in sand,
  Vailing her high top lower than her ribs
  To kiss her burial. Should I go to church
  And see the holy edifice of stone
30 And not bethink me straight of dangerous rocks,
  Which, touching but my gentle vessel's side,
  Would scatter all her spices on the stream,
  Enrobe the roaring waters with my silks,
  And in a word, but even now worth this,
35 And now worth nothing? Shall I have the thought
  To think on this, and shall I lack the thought
  That such a thing bechanced would make me sad?
  But tell not me; I know Antonio
  Is sad to think upon his merchandise.
40 ANTONIO   Believe me, no. I thank my fortune for it,
  My ventures are not in one bottom trusted,
  Nor to one place; nor is my whole estate
  Upon the fortune of this present year:
  Therefore my merchandise makes me not sad.
45 SALANIO   Why then, you are in love.
ANTONIO   Fie, fie.
SALANIO
  Not in love neither? Then let us say you are sad
  Because you are not merry; and 'twere as easy
  For you to laugh and leap and say you are merry
50 Because you are not sad. Now, by two-headed Janus,
  Nature hath framed strange fellows in her time:
  Some that will evermore peep through their eyes
  And laugh like parrots at a bagpiper;

  And other of such vinegar aspect
  That they'll not show their teeth in way of smile   55
  Though Nestor swear the jest be laughable.

      Enter BASSANIO, LORENZO *and* GRATIANO.

  Here comes Bassanio, your most noble kinsman,
  Gratiano and Lorenzo. Fare ye well,
  We leave you now with better company.
SALARINO
  I would have stayed till I had made you merry,   60
  If worthier friends had not prevented me.
ANTONIO   Your worth is very dear in my regard.
  I take it your own business calls on you,
  And you embrace th'occasion to depart.
SALARINO   Good morrow, my good lords.   65
BASSANIO
  Good signiors both, when shall we laugh? Say, when?
  You grow exceeding strange: must it be so?
SALARINO   We'll make our leisures to attend on yours.
        Exeunt Salarino and Salanio.
LORENZO
  My lord Bassanio, since you have found Antonio
  We two will leave you, but at dinner-time   70
  I pray you have in mind where we must meet.
BASSANIO   I will not fail you.
GRATIANO   You look not well, Signior Antonio;
  You have too much respect upon the world:
  They lose it that do buy it with much care.   75
  Believe me, you are marvellously changed.
ANTONIO   I hold the world but as the world, Gratiano,
  A stage, where every man must play a part,
  And mine a sad one.
GRATIANO   Let me play the fool.
  With mirth and laughter let old wrinkles come,   80
  And let my liver rather heat with wine
  Than my heart cool with mortifying groans.
  Why should a man whose blood is warm within
  Sit like his grandsire cut in alabaster?
  Sleep when he wakes? And creep into the jaundice   85
  By being peevish? I tell thee what, Antonio –
  I love thee, and 'tis my love that speaks –
  There are a sort of men whose visages
  Do cream and mantle like a standing pond,
  And do a wilful stillness entertain   90
  With purpose to be dressed in an opinion
  Of wisdom, gravity, profound conceit,
  As who should say, 'I am Sir Oracle,
  And when I ope my lips, let no dog bark.'
  O, my Antonio, I do know of these   95
  That therefore only are reputed wise
  For saying nothing; when, I am very sure,
  If they should speak, would almost damn those ears
  Which, hearing them, would call their brothers fools.
  I'll tell thee more of this another time.   100
  But fish not with this melancholy bait
  For this fool gudgeon, this opinion.
  Come, good Lorenzo. – Fare ye well awhile,

I'll end my exhortation after dinner.

105 LORENZO   Well, we will leave you, then, till dinner-time.
I must be one of these same dumb wise men,
For Gratiano never lets me speak.

GRATIANO   Well, keep me company but two years more
Thou shalt not know the sound of thine own tongue.

110 ANTONIO   Fare you well, I'll grow a talker for this gear.

GRATIANO
Thanks, i'faith, for silence is only commendable
In a neat's tongue dried and a maid not vendible.
Exeunt Gratiano and Lorenzo.

ANTONIO   Is that anything now?

BASSIANO   Gratiano speaks an infinite deal of nothing,
115   more than any man in all Venice. His reasons are as two
grains of wheat hid in two bushels of chaff: you shall
seek all day ere you find them, and, when you have
them, they are not worth the search.

ANTONIO   Well, tell me now, what lady is the same
120   To whom you swore a secret pilgrimage,
That you today promised to tell me of?

BASSANIO   'Tis not unknown to you, Antonio,
How much I have disabled mine estate
By something showing a more swelling port
125   Than my faint means would grant continuance.
Nor do I now make moan to be abridged
From such a noble rate, but my chief care
Is to come fairly off from the great debts
Wherein my time, something too prodigal,
130   Hath left me gaged. To you, Antonio,
I owe the most in money and in love,
And from your love I have a warranty
To unburden all my plots and purposes
How to get clear of all the debts I owe.

135 ANTONIO   I pray you, good Bassanio, let me know it,
And if it stand, as you yourself still do,
Within the eye of honour, be assured
My purse, my person, my extremest means
Lie all unlocked to your occasions.

BASSANIO
140   In my schooldays, when I had lost one shaft,
I shot his fellow of the selfsame flight
The selfsame way, with more advised watch
To find the other forth, and by adventuring both
I oft found both. I urge this childhood proof
145   Because what follows is pure innocence.
I owe you much, and like a wilful youth
That which I owe is lost; but if you please
To shoot another arrow that self way
Which you did shoot the first, I do not doubt,
150   As I will watch the aim, or to find both,
Or bring your latter hazard back again
And thankfully rest debtor for the first.

ANTONIO
You know me well, and herein spend but time
To wind about my love with circumstance,
155   And out of doubt you do me now more wrong
In making question of my uttermost

Than if you had made waste of all I have.
Then do but say to me what I should do
That in your knowledge may by me be done,
And I am pressed unto it: therefore speak.   160

BASSANIO   In Belmont is a lady richly left,
And she is fair and, fairer than that word,
Of wondrous virtues. Sometimes from her eyes
I did receive fair speechless messages.
Her name is Portia, nothing undervalued   165
To Cato's daughter, Brutus' Portia.
Nor is the wide world ignorant of her worth,
For the four winds blow in from every coast
Renowned suitors, and her sunny locks
Hang on her temples like a golden fleece,   170
Which makes her seat of Belmont Colchis' strand,
And many Jasons come in quest of her.
O my Antonio, had I but the means
To hold a rival place with one of them,
I have a mind presages me such thrift   175
That I should questionless be fortunate.

ANTONIO   Thou knowst that all my fortunes are at sea;
Neither have I money, nor commodity
To raise a present sum; therefore go forth:
Try what my credit can in Venice do,   180
That shall be racked even to the uttermost
To furnish thee to Belmont to fair Portia.
Go presently enquire, and so will I,
Where money is, and I no question make
To have it of my trust, or for my sake.   *Exeunt.*   185

1.2   *Enter* PORTIA *with her waiting-woman* NERISSA.

PORTIA   By my troth, Nerissa, my little body is aweary
of this great world.

NERISSA   You would be, sweet madam, if your miseries
were in the same abundance as your good fortunes are;
and yet, for aught I see, they are as sick that surfeit   5
with too much as they that starve with nothing. It
is no mean happiness, therefore, to be seated in the
mean; superfluity comes sooner by white hairs, but
competency lives longer.

PORTIA   Good sentences, and well pronounced.   10

NERISSA   They would be better if well followed.

PORTIA   If to do were as easy as to know what were good
to do, chapels had been churches, and poor men's
cottages princes' palaces. It is a good divine that follows
his own instructions: I can easier teach twenty what   15
were good to be done than to be one of the twenty to
follow mine own teaching. The brain may devise laws
for the blood, but a hot temper leaps o'er a cold decree;
such a hare is madness the youth, to skip o'er the
meshes of good counsel the cripple. But this reasoning   20
is not in the fashion to choose me a husband. O me, the
word 'choose'! I may neither choose who I would, nor
refuse who I dislike, so is the will of a living daughter
curbed by the will of a dead father. Is it not hard,
Nerissa, that I cannot choose one, nor refuse none?   25

NERISSA Your father was ever virtuous, and holy men at their death have good inspirations. Therefore the lottery that he hath devised in these three chests of gold, silver and lead, whereof who chooses his meaning chooses you, will no doubt never be chosen by any rightly but one who you shall rightly love. But what warmth is there in your affection towards any of these princely suitors that are already come?

PORTIA I pray thee over-name them and, as thou namest them, I will describe them, and according to my description level at my affection.

NERISSA First there is the Neapolitan prince.

PORTIA Ay, that's a colt indeed, for he doth nothing but talk of his horse, and he makes it a great appropriation to his own good parts that he can shoe him himself. I am much afeard my lady his mother played false with a smith.

NERISSA Then is there the County Palatine.

PORTIA He doth nothing but frown, as who should say, 'An you will not have me, choose.' He hears merry tales and smiles not; I fear he will prove the weeping philosopher when he grows old, being so full of unmannerly sadness in his youth. I had rather be married to a death's head with a bone in his mouth than to either of these. God defend me from these two.

NERISSA How say you by the French lord, Monsieur Le Bon?

PORTIA God made him, and therefore let him pass for a man. In truth, I know it is a sin to be a mocker, but he! – why, he hath a horse better than the Neapolitan's, a better bad habit of frowning than the Count Palatine. He is every man in no man: if a throstle sing, he falls straight a-capering. He will fence with his own shadow. If I should marry him, I should marry twenty husbands. If he would despise me I would forgive him, for if he love me to madness I shall never requite him.

NERISSA What say you then to Falconbridge, the young baron of England?

PORTIA You know I say nothing to him, for he understands not me, nor I him. He hath neither Latin, French nor Italian, and you will come into the court and swear that I have a poor pennyworth in the English. He is a proper man's picture, but, alas, who can converse with a dumb-show? How oddly he is suited! I think he bought his doublet in Italy, his round hose in France, his bonnet in Germany and his behaviour everywhere.

NERISSA What think you of the Scottish lord, his neighbour?

PORTIA That he hath a neighbourly charity in him, for he borrowed a box of the ear of the Englishman and swore he would pay him again when he was able. I think the Frenchman became his surety and sealed under for another.

NERISSA How like you the young German, the Duke of Saxony's nephew?

PORTIA Very vilely in the morning, when he is sober, and most vilely in the afternoon, when he is drunk. When he is best, he is a little worse than a man, and when he is worst he is little better than a beast. An the worst fall that ever fell, I hope I shall make shift to go without him. 85

NERISSA If he should offer to choose and choose the right casket, you should refuse to perform your father's will if you should refuse to accept him. 90

PORTIA Therefore, for fear of the worst, I pray thee set a deep glass of Rhenish wine on the contrary casket, for if the devil be within, and that temptation without, I know he will choose it. I will do anything, Nerissa, ere I will be married to a sponge. 95

NERISSA You need not fear, lady, the having any of these lords. They have acquainted me with their determinations, which is indeed to return to their home and to trouble you with no more suit, unless you 100 may be won by some other sort than your father's imposition, depending on the caskets.

PORTIA If I live to be as old as Sibylla, I will die as chaste as Diana, unless I be obtained by the manner of my father's will. I am glad this parcel of wooers are so 105 reasonable, for there is not one among them but I dote on his very absence, and I pray God grant them a fair departure.

NERISSA Do you not remember, lady, in your father's time, a Venetian, a scholar and a soldier, that came 110 hither in company of the Marquis of Montferrat?

PORTIA Yes, yes, it was Bassanio, as I think, so was he called.

NERISSA True, madam. He, of all the men that ever my foolish eyes looked upon, was the best deserving a fair 115 lady.

PORTIA I remember him well, and I remember him worthy of thy praise.

Enter a Servingman.

How now, what news?

SERVINGMAN The four strangers seek for you, madam, 120 to take their leave; and there is a forerunner come from a fifth, the Prince of Morocco, who brings word the prince his master will be here tonight.

PORTIA If I could bid the fifth welcome with so good heart as I can bid the other four farewell, I should be 125 glad of his approach. If he have the condition of a saint and the complexion of a devil, I had rather he should shrive me than wive me. Come, Nerissa. – Sirrah, go before.   *Exit Servingman.*

Whiles we shut the gate upon one wooer, another 130 knocks at the door.   *Exeunt.*

1.3   *Enter* BASSANIO *with* Shylock the JEW.

JEW Three thousand ducats, well.

BASSANIO Ay, sir, for three months.

JEW For three months, well.

BASSANIO   For the which, as I told you, Antonio shall be
5   bound.
JEW   Antonio shall become bound, well.
BASSANIO   May you stead me? Will you pleasure me?
   Shall I know your answer?
JEW   Three thousand ducats for three months, and
10   Antonio bound.
BASSANIO   Your answer to that.
JEW   Antonio is a good man.
BASSANIO   Have you heard any imputation to the
   contrary?
15   JEW   Ho, no, no, no, no. My meaning in saying he is a
   good man is to have you understand me that he is
   sufficient, yet his means are in supposition. He hath an
   argosy bound to Tripoli, another to the Indies; I
   understand moreover upon the Rialto, he hath a third
20   at Mexico, a fourth for England, and other ventures he
   hath squandered abroad. But ships are but boards,
   sailors but men; there be land rats, and water rats,
   water thieves, and land thieves – I mean pirates – and
   then there is the peril of waters, winds and rocks. The
25   man is notwithstanding sufficient. Three thousand
   ducats: I think I may take his bond.
BASSANIO   Be assured you may.
JEW   I will be assured I may; and, that I may be assured,
   I will bethink me. May I speak with Antonio?
30   BASSANIO   If it please you to dine with us.
JEW   Yes, to smell pork, to eat of the habitation which
   your prophet the Nazarite conjured the devil into. I
   will buy with you, sell with you, talk with you, walk
   with you and so following. But I will not eat with you,
35   drink with you nor pray with you. What news on the
   Rialto? Who is he comes here?

Enter ANTONIO.

BASSANIO [*to the Jew*]   This is Signior Antonio.
JEW [*aside*]   How like a fawning publican he looks.
   I hate him for he is a Christian;
40   But more, for that in low simplicity
   He lends out money gratis, and brings down
   The rate of usance here with us in Venice.
   If I can catch him once upon the hip,
   I will feed fat the ancient grudge I bear him.
45   He hates our sacred nation, and he rails,
   Even there where merchants most do congregate,
   On me, my bargains and my well-won thrift,
   Which he calls 'interest'. Cursed be my tribe
   If I forgive him.
BASSANIO   Shylock, do you hear?
JEW [*to Bassanio*]
50   I am debating of my present store,
   And, by the near guess of my memory,
   I cannot instantly raise up the gross
   Of full three thousand ducats. What of that?
   Tubal, a wealthy Hebrew of my tribe,
55   Will furnish me. But soft, how many months
   Do you desire? [*to Antonio*] Rest you fair, good signior,

Your worship was the last man in our mouths.
ANTONIO   Shylock, albeit I neither lend nor borrow
   By taking nor by giving of excess,
   Yet, to supply the ripe wants of my friend,   60
   I'll break a custom. [*to Bassanio*] Is he yet possessed
   How much ye would?
JEW   Ay, ay, three thousand ducats.
ANTONIO   And for three months.
JEW
   I had forgot, three months, [*to Bassanio*] you told me so.   65
   [*to Antonio*] Well then, your bond. And let me see
      – but hear you:
   Me thoughts you said you neither lend nor borrow
   Upon advantage.
ANTONIO   I do never use it.
JEW   When Jacob grazed his uncle Laban's sheep,
   This Jacob from our holy Abram was,   70
   As his wise mother wrought in his behalf,
   The third possessor; ay, he was the third.
ANTONIO   And what of him, did he take interest?
JEW   No, not take 'interest', not as you would say
   Directly 'interest'. Mark what Jacob did: 75
   When Laban and himself were compromised
   That all the eanlings which were streaked and pied
   Should fall as Jacob's hire, the ewes, being rank,
   In end of autumn turned to the rams;
   And when the work of generation was   80
   Between these woolly breeders in the act,
   The skilful shepherd peeled me certain wands,
   And, in the doing of the deed of kind,
   He stuck them up before the fulsome ewes,
   Who, then conceiving, did in eaning time   85
   Fall parti-coloured lambs, and those were Jacob's.
   This was a way to thrive, and he was blest:
   And thrift is blessing, if men steal it not.
ANTONIO
   This was a venture, sir, that Jacob served for,
   A thing not in his power to bring to pass,   90
   But swayed and fashioned by the hand of heaven.
   Was this inserted to make interest good?
   Or is your gold and silver ewes and rams?
JEW   I cannot tell, I make it breed as fast.
   But note me, signior.
ANTONIO [*aside*]   Mark you this, Bassanio,   95
   The devil can cite Scripture for his purpose.
   An evil soul producing holy witness
   Is like a villain with a smiling cheek,
   A goodly apple, rotten at the heart.
   O, what a goodly outside falsehood hath!   100
JEW   Three thousand ducats, 'tis a good round sum.
   Three months from twelve, then let me see the rate.
ANTONIO   Well, Shylock, shall we be beholding to you?
JEW   Signior Antonio, many a time and oft
   In the Rialto you have rated me   105
   About my moneys and my usances.
   Still have I borne it with a patient shrug,
   For sufferance is the badge of all our tribe.

You call me misbeliever, cut-throat dog,
10 And spit upon my Jewish gaberdine,
And all for use of that which is mine own.
Well, then, it now appears you need my help.
Go to, then, you come to me, and you say,
'Shylock, we would have moneys.' You say so.
15 You, that did void your rheum upon my beard
And foot me as you spurn a stranger cur
Over your threshold, moneys is your suit.
What should I say to you? Should I not say,
'Hath a dog money? Is it possible
20 A cur can lend three thousand ducats?' Or
Shall I bend low and in a bondman's key,
With bated breath and whispering humbleness,
Say this: 'Fair sir, you spat on me on Wednesday last,
You spurned me such a day; another time,
25 You called me dog: and, for these courtesies,
I'll lend you thus much moneys.'
ANTONIO I am as like to call thee so again,
To spit on thee again, to spurn thee too.
If thou wilt lend this money, lend it not
30 As to thy friends, for when did friendship take
A breed for barren metal of his friend?
But lend it rather to thine enemy,
Who, if he break, thou mayst with better face
Exact the penalty.
35 JEW Why, look you, how you storm.
I would be friends with you and have your love,
Forget the shames that you have stained me with,
Supply your present wants and take no doit
Of usance for my moneys, and you'll not hear me.
40 This is kind I offer.
BASSANIO This were kindness.
JEW This kindness will I show.
Go with me to a notary, seal me there
Your single bond, and, in a merry sport,
If you repay me not on such a day,
45 In such a place, such sum, or sums, as are
Expressed in the condition, let the forfeit
Be nominated for an equal pound
Of your fair flesh, to be cut off and taken
In what part of your body pleaseth me.
50 ANTONIO Content, in faith: I'll seal to such a bond
And say there is much kindness in the Jew.
BASSANIO You shall not seal to such a bond for me;
I'll rather dwell in my necessity.
ANTONIO Why, fear not, man, I will not forfeit it;
55 Within these two months, that's a month before
This bond expires, I do expect return
Of thrice three times the value of this bond.
JEW O, father Abram, what these Christians are,
Whose own hard dealings teaches them suspect
The thoughts of others. [*to Bassanio*] Pray you tell
60 me this:
If he should break his day, what should I gain
By the exaction of the forfeiture?
A pound of a man's flesh, taken from a man,

Is not so estimable, profitable neither,
As flesh of muttons, beeves or goats. I say 165
To buy his favour I extend this friendship;
If he will take it, so; if not, adieu,
And for my love, I pray you, wrong me not.
ANTONIO Yes, Shylock, I will seal unto this bond.
JEW Then meet me forthwith at the notary's; 170
Give him direction for this merry bond,
And I will go and purse the ducats straight,
See to my house, left in the fearful guard
Of an unthrifty knave, and presently
I'll be with you.   *Exit.*
ANTONIO   Hie thee, gentle Jew. 175
The Hebrew will turn Christian, he grows kind.
BASSANIO I like not fair terms and a villain's mind.
ANTONIO Come on, in this there can be no dismay,
My ships come home a month before the day.
                                                       Exeunt.

2.1 *Enter the* Prince of MOROCCO, *a tawny*
Moor, all in white, and three or four Followers
accordingly, with PORTIA, NERISSA *and their train.*

MOROCCO Mislike me not for my complexion,
The shadowed livery of the burnished sun,
To whom I am a neighbour and near bred.
Bring me the fairest creature northward born,
Where Phoebus' fire scarce thaws the icicles, 5
And let us make incision for your love,
To prove whose blood is reddest, his or mine.
I tell thee, lady, this aspect of mine
Hath feared the valiant; by my love I swear,
The best-regarded virgins of our clime 10
Have loved it too. I would not change this hue
Except to steal your thoughts, my gentle queen.
PORTIA In terms of choice I am not solely led
By nice direction of a maiden's eyes.
Besides, the lott'ry of my destiny 15
Bars me the right of voluntary choosing.
But, if my father had not scanted me
And hedged me, by his wit, to yield myself
His wife who wins me by that means I told you,
Yourself, renowned prince, then stood as fair 20
As any comer I have looked on yet
For my affection.
MOROCCO   Even for that I thank you.
Therefore, I pray you, lead me to the caskets
To try my fortune. By this scimitar,
That slew the Sophy and a Persian prince, 25
That won three fields of Sultan Solyman,
I would o'erstare the sternest eyes that look,
Outbrave the heart most daring on the earth,
Pluck the young sucking cubs from the she-bear,
Yea, mock the lion when 'a roars for prey, 30
To win the lady. But, alas the while,
If Hercules and Lichas play at dice
Which is the better man, the greater throw

May turn by fortune from the weaker hand.
35 So is Alcides beaten by his rage,
And so may I, blind Fortune leading me,
Miss that which one unworthier may attain,
And die with grieving.

PORTIA   You must take your chance,
And either not attempt to choose at all,
40 Or swear, before you choose, if you choose wrong
Never to speak to lady afterward
In way of marriage; therefore be advised.

MOROCCO
Nor will not. Come, bring me unto my chance.

PORTIA   First, forward to the temple; after dinner
Your hazard shall be made.

45 MOROCCO   Good fortune, then,
To make me blest or cursed'st among men.   *Exeunt.*

2.2   *Enter the* CLOWN, Lancelet Giobbe, *alone.*

CLOWN   Certainly, my conscience will serve me to run
from this Jew, my master. The fiend is at mine elbow and
tempts me, saying to me, 'Giobbe, Lancelet Giobbe,
good Lancelet', or 'Good Giobbe', or 'Good Lancelet
5 Giobbe, use your legs, take the start, run away.' My
conscience says, 'No; take heed, honest Lancelet, take
heed, honest Giobbe', or, as aforesaid, 'Honest Lancelet
Giobbe, do not run, scorn running with thy heels.'
Well, the most courageous fiend bids me pack. '*Via*,'
10 says the fiend, 'away,' says the fiend, 'for the heavens,
rouse up a brave mind,' says the fiend, 'and run.' Well,
my conscience, hanging about the neck of my heart, says
very wisely to me: 'My honest friend Lancelet', being an
honest man's son, or rather an honest woman's son, for
15 indeed my father did something smack, something grow
to – he had a kind of taste – well, my conscience says,
'Lancelet, budge not.' 'Budge,' says the fiend. 'Budge
not,' says my conscience. 'Conscience,' say I, 'you
counsel well. Fiend,' say I, 'you counsel well.' To be
20 ruled by my conscience, I should stay with the Jew my
master, who, God bless the mark, is a kind of devil; and,
to run away from the Jew, I should be ruled by the fiend,
who, saving your reverence, is the devil himself.
Certainly the Jew is the very devil incarnation, and, in
25 my conscience, my conscience is but a kind of hard
conscience, to offer to counsel me to stay with the Jew.
The fiend gives the more friendly counsel: I will run,
fiend, my heels are at your commandment; I will run.

Enter Old GIOBBE *with a basket.*

GIOBBE   Master young man, you, I pray you, which is
30 the way to Master Jew's?

CLOWN   [*aside*] O, heavens, this is my true-begotten
father, who, being more than sand-blind, high gravel-
blind, knows me not. I will try confusions with him.

GIOBBE   Master young gentleman, I pray you, which is
35 the way to Master Jew's?

CLOWN   Turn up on your right hand at the next turning,

but, at the next turning of all, on your left. Marry, at
the very next turning, turn of no hand, but turn down
indirectly to the Jew's house.

GIOBBE   By God's sonties, 'twill be a hard way to hit.   40
Can you tell me whether one Lancelet, that dwells with
him, dwell with him or no?

CLOWN   Talk you of young Master Lancelet? [*aside*]
Mark me now, now will I raise the waters. [*to Giobbe*]
Talk you of young Master Lancelet?   45

GIOBBE   No master, sir, but a poor man's son. His
father, though I say't, is an honest, exceeding poor
man, and, God be thanked, well to live.

CLOWN   Well, let his father be what 'a will, we talk of
young Master Lancelet.   50

GIOBBE   Your worship's friend and Lancelet, sir.

CLOWN   But, I pray you, ergo, old man, ergo, I beseech
you, talk you of young Master Lancelet.

GIOBBE   Of Lancelet, an't please your mastership.

CLOWN   Ergo, Master Lancelet. Talk not of Master   55
Lancelet, father, for the young gentleman, according
to Fates and Destinies and such odd sayings, the
Sisters Three and such branches of learning, is indeed
deceased, or, as you would say in plain terms, gone to
heaven.   60

GIOBBE   Marry, God forbid, the boy was the very staff
of my age, my very prop.

CLOWN   [*aside*] Do I look like a cudgel, or a hovel
post, a staff, or a prop? [*to Giobbe*] Do you know me,
Father?   65

GIOBBE   Alack the day, I know you not, young gentleman!
But I pray you tell me, is my boy – God rest his soul –
alive, or dead?

CLOWN   Do you not know me, Father?

GIOBBE   Alack, sir, I am sand-blind, I know you not.   70

CLOWN   Nay, indeed, if you had your eyes you might
fail of the knowing me: it is a wise father that knows his
own child. Well, old man, I will tell you news of your
son. [*Kneels.*] Give me your blessing, truth will come
to light, murder cannot be hid long; a man's son may,   75
but in the end truth will out.

GIOBBE   Pray you, sir, stand up. I am sure you are not
Lancelet my boy.

CLOWN   Pray you, let's have no more fooling about it,
but give me your blessing. I am Lancelet, your boy that   80
was, your son that is, your child that shall be.

GIOBBE   I cannot think you are my son.

CLOWN   I know not what I shall think of that. But I am
Lancelet, the Jew's man, and I am sure Margery your
wife is my mother.   85

GIOBBE   Her name is Margery indeed. I'll be sworn, if
thou be Lancelet, thou art mine own flesh and blood.
Lord worshipped might he be, what a beard hast thou
got! Thou hast got more hair on thy chin than Dobbin,
my thill-horse, has on his tail.   90

CLOWN   It should seem, then, that Dobbin's tail grows
backward. I am sure he had more hair of his tail than I
have of my face when I last saw him. [*Stands up.*]

GIOBBE   Lord, how art thou changed! How dost thou
and thy master agree? I have brought him a present;
how 'gree you now?

CLOWN   Well, well: but, for mine own part, as I have
set up my rest to run away, so I will not rest till I have
run some ground. My master's a very Jew. Give him a
present? Give him a halter! I am famished in his
service. You may tell every finger I have with my ribs.
Father, I am glad you are come. Give me your present
to one Master Bassanio, who indeed gives rare new
liveries: if I serve not him, I will run as far as God
has any ground. O, rare fortune, here comes the man.
To him, Father, for I am a Jew if I serve the Jew any
longer.

Enter BASSANIO *with a Follower or
two,* LEONARDO *among them.*

BASSANIO [*to a Follower*]   You may do so, but let it be so
hasted that supper be ready at the farthest by five of
the clock. [*Gives him letters.*] See these letters delivered,
put the liveries to making and desire Gratiano to come
anon to my lodging.   *Exit Follower.*

CLOWN   To him, Father.

GIOBBE [*to Bassanio*]   God bless your worship.

BASSANIO   Gramercy. Wouldst thou aught with me?

GIOBBE   Here's my son, sir, a poor boy –

CLOWN [*to Bassanio*]   Not a poor boy, sir, but the rich
Jew's man that would, sir, as my father shall specify –

GIOBBE   He hath a great infection, sir, as one would say,
to serve.

CLOWN   Indeed the short and long is, I serve the Jew,
and have a desire, as my father shall specify –

GIOBBE   His master and he, saving your worship's
reverence, are scarce cater-cousins.

CLOWN   To be brief, the very truth is that the Jew,
having done me wrong, doth cause me, as my father –
being, I hope, an old man – shall frutify unto you –

GIOBBE   I have here a dish of doves that I would bestow
upon your worship, and my suit is –

CLOWN   In very brief, the suit is impertinent to myself,
as your worship shall know by this honest old man,
and – though I say it, though old man, yet poor man – my
father.

BASSANIO   One speak for both. What would you?

CLOWN   Serve you, sir.

GIOBBE   That is the very defect of the matter, sir.

BASSANIO [*to Clown*]
I know thee well. Thou hast obtained thy suit.
Shylock thy master spoke with me this day
And hath preferred thee, if it be preferment
To leave a rich Jew's service, to become
The follower of so poor a gentleman.

CLOWN   The old proverb is very well parted between
my master Shylock and you, sir: you have the grace of
God, sir, and he hath enough.

BASSANIO
Thou speak'st it well. Go, father, with thy son.

[*to Clown*] Take leave of thy old master and enquire
My lodging out. [*to a Follower*] Give him a livery
More guarded than his fellows': see it done.
                              Exit Follower.

CLOWN   Father, in. I cannot get a service, no! I have
ne'er a tongue in my head! [*Looks at the palm of his* 150
hand.] Well, if any man in Italy have a fairer table,
which doth offer to swear upon a book, I shall have
good fortune. Go to, here's a simple line of life; here's
a small trifle of wives. Alas, fifteen wives is nothing:
eleven widows and nine maids is a simple coming-in 155
for one man, and then to scape drowning thrice,
and to be in peril of my life with the edge of a feather-
bed. Here are simple scapes. Well, if Fortune be a
woman, she's a good wench for this gear.
Father, come; I'll take my leave of the Jew in the 160
twinkling.   *Exeunt Clown and Giobbe.*

BASSANIO [*Gives Leonardo a shopping list.*]
I pray thee, good Leonardo, think on this:
These things being bought and orderly bestowed,
Return in haste, for I do feast tonight
My best esteemed acquaintance. Hie thee, go.   165

LEONARDO   My best endeavours shall be done herein.

Enter GRATIANO.

GRATIANO [*to Leonardo*]   Where's your master?

LEONARDO   Yonder, sir, he walks.   *Exit.*

GRATIANO   Signior Bassanio!

BASSANIO   Gratiano!   170

GRATIANO   I have suit to you.

BASSANIO   You have obtained it.

GRATIANO   You must not deny me; I must go with you
to Belmont.

BASSIANO
Why then, you must. But hear thee, Gratiano,   175
Thou art too wild, too rude and bold of voice:
Parts that become thee happily enough
And in such eyes as ours appear not faults.
But where thou art not known, why, there they
    show
Something too liberal. Pray thee, take pain   180
To allay with some cold drops of modesty
Thy skipping spirit, lest through thy wild behaviour
I be misconstered in the place I go to
And lose my hopes.

GRATIANO   Signior Bassanio, hear me:
If I do not put on a sober habit,   185
Talk with respect, and swear but now and then,
Wear prayer-books in my pocket, look demurely,
Nay more, while grace is saying, hood mine eyes
Thus with my hat, and sigh and say 'amen',
Use all the observance of civility,   190
Like one well studied in a sad ostent
To please his grandam, never trust me more.

BASSANIO   Well, we shall see your bearing.

GRATIANO
Nay, but I bar tonight; you shall not gauge me

By what we do tonight.

195 BASSANIO   No, that were pity.
I would entreat you rather to put on
Your boldest suit of mirth, for we have friends
That purpose merriment. But fare you well;
I have some business.

200 GRATIANO   And I must to Lorenzo and the rest,
But we will visit you at supper-time.   *Exeunt.*

2.3   *Enter* JESSICA *and* Lancelet *the* CLOWN.

JESSICA   I am sorry thou wilt leave my father so.
Our house is hell and thou, a merry devil,
Didst rob it of some taste of tediousness.
But fare thee well; there is a ducat for thee.
5 And, Lancelet, soon at supper shalt thou see
Lorenzo, who is thy new master's guest.
Give him this letter, do it secretly.
And so farewell. I would not have my father
See me in talk with thee.

10 CLOWN   Adieu. Tears exhibit my tongue. Most beautiful
pagan, most sweet Jew! If a Christian do not play the
knave and get thee, I am much deceived. But adieu;
these foolish drops do something drown my manly
spirit. Adieu!   *Exit.*

15 JESSICA   Farewell, good Lancelet.
Alack, what heinous sin is it in me
To be ashamed to be my father's child!
But, though I am a daughter to his blood,
I am not to his manners. O, Lorenzo,
20 If thou keep promise I shall end this strife,
Become a Christian, and thy loving wife.   *Exit.*

2.4   *Enter* GRATIANO, LORENZO, SALARINO
and SALANIO.

LORENZO   Nay, we will slink away in supper-time,
Disguise us at my lodging, and return,
All in an hour.

GRATIANO   We have not made good preparation.

5 SALARINO   We have not spoke us yet of torch-bearers.

SALANIO   'Tis vile unless it may be quaintly ordered,
And better in my mind not undertook.

LORENZO   'Tis now but four of clock; we have two hours
To furnish us.

Enter LANCELET *the* CLOWN, *with a letter.*

Friend Lancelet,
10 What's the news?

CLOWN   An it shall please you to break up this, [*handing
letter to Lorenzo*] it shall seem to signify.

LORENZO   I know the hand; in faith, 'tis a fair hand,
And whiter than the paper it writ on
Is the fair hand that writ.

15 GRATIANO   Love news, in faith!

CLOWN   By your leave, sir.

LORENZO   Whither goest thou?

CLOWN   Marry, sir, to bid my old master, the Jew, to sup
tonight with my new master, the Christian.

LORENZO   Hold here; take this. [*Gives money.*]
Tell gentle Jessica   20
I will not fail her; speak it privately.   *Exit Clown.*
Go, gentlemen,
Will you prepare you for this masque tonight?
I am provided of a torch-bearer.

SALARINO   Ay, marry, I'll be gone about it straight.   25

SALANIO   And so will I.

LORENZO   Meet me and Gratiano
At Gratiano's lodging some hour hence.

SALARINO   'Tis good we do so.
Exeunt Salarino and Salanio.

GRATIANO   Was not that letter from fair Jessica?

LORENZO   I must needs tell thee all. She hath directed   30
How I shall take her from her father's house,
What gold and jewels she is furnished with,
What page's suit she hath in readiness.
If e'er the Jew her father come to heaven,
It will be for his gentle daughter's sake;   35
And never dare misfortune cross her foot
Unless she do it under this excuse:
That she is issue to a faithless Jew.
Come, go with me, peruse this as thou goest.
[*Hands letter to Gratiano.*]
Fair Jessica shall be my torch-bearer.   *Exeunt.*   40

2.5   *Enter* Shylock the JEW *and his man that
was,* Lancelet *the* CLOWN.

JEW   Well, thou shalt see, thy eyes shall be thy judge,
The difference of old Shylock and Bassanio.
[*Calls.*] What, Jessica! [*to Clown*] Thou shalt not
gormandize
As thou hast done with me. –
[*Calls.*]   What, Jessica! –
[*to Clown*] And sleep, and snore, and rend apparel out.   5
[*Calls again.*] Why, Jessica, I say!

CLOWN   Why, Jessica!

JEW   Who bids thee call? I do not bid thee call.

CLOWN   Your worship was wont to tell me I could do
nothing without bidding.

Enter JESSICA.

JESSICA   Call you? What is your will?   10

JEW   I am bid forth to supper, Jessica.
There are my keys. But wherefore should I go?
I am not bid for love; they flatter me,
But yet I'll go in hate, to feed upon
The prodigal Christian. Jessica, my girl,   15
Look to my house. I am right loath to go;
There is some ill a-brewing towards my rest,
For I did dream of money-bags tonight.

CLOWN   I beseech you, sir, go. My young master doth
expect your reproach.   20

JEW   So do I his.

CLOWN   And they have conspired together. I will not say
you shall see a masque, but, if you do, then it was not for
nothing that my nose fell a-bleeding on Black Monday
last, at six o'clock i'th' morning, falling out that year on
Ash Wednesday was four year in th'afternoon.

JEW   What, are there masques? Hear you me, Jessica,
Lock up my doors, and when you hear the drum
And the vile squealing of the wry-necked fife,
Clamber not you up to the casements then,
Nor thrust your head into the public street
To gaze on Christian fools with varnished faces;
But stop my house's ears – I mean my casements –
Let not the sound of shallow foppery enter
My sober house. By Jacob's staff, I swear,
I have no mind of feasting forth tonight.
But I will go. Go you before me, sirrah:
Say I will come.

CLOWN   I will go before, sir.
[*aside to Jessica*] Mistress, look out at window for all
this;
There will come a Christian by
Will be worth a Jewess' eye.   *Exit.*

JEW   What says that fool of Hagar's offspring, ha?

JESSICA
His words were 'Farewell, mistress', nothing else.

JEW   The patch is kind enough, but a huge feeder,
Snail-slow in profit, and he sleeps by day
More than the wildcat. Drones hive not with me,
Therefore I part with him, and part with him
To one that I would have him help to waste
His borrowed purse. Well, Jessica, go in;
Perhaps I will return immediately.
Do as I bid you; shut doors after you.
'Fast bind, fast find.'
A proverb never stale in thrifty mind.   *Exit.*

JESSICA   Farewell, and if my fortune be not crossed,
I have a father, you a daughter, lost.   *Exit.*

2.6   *Enter the masquers* GRATIANO *and* SALARINO.

GRATIANO   This is the penthouse under which Lorenzo
desired us to make stand.

SALARINO   His hour is almost past.

GRATIANO   And it is marvel he outdwells his hour,
For lovers ever run before the clock.

SALARINO   O, ten times faster Venus' pigeons fly
To seal love's bonds new made than they are wont
To keep obliged faith unforfeited.

GRATIANO   That ever holds: who riseth from a feast
With that keen appetite that he sits down?
Where is the horse that doth untread again
His tedious measures with the unbated fire
That he did pace them first? All things that are,
Are with more spirit chased than enjoyed.
How like a younger, or a prodigal,
The scarfed bark puts from her native bay,

Hugged and embraced by the strumpet wind!
How like the prodigal doth she return,
With overweathered ribs and ragged sails,
Lean, rent and beggared by the strumpet wind!   20

Enter LORENZO.

SALARINO
Here comes Lorenzo; more of this hereafter.

LORENZO
Sweet friends, your patience for my long abode.
Not I but my affairs have made you wait.
When you shall please to play the thieves for wives,
I'll watch as long for you then. Approach;   25
Here dwells my father Jew. Ho! who's within?

Enter JESSICA *above, in boy's clothes.*

JESSICA   Who are you? Tell me for more certainty,
Albeit I'll swear that I do know your tongue.

LORENZO   Lorenzo, and thy love.

JESSICA   Lorenzo certain, and my love indeed,   30
For who love I so much? And now, who knows
But you, Lorenzo, whether I am yours?

LORENZO
Heaven and thy thoughts are witness that thou art.

JESSICA   Here, catch this casket; it is worth the pains.
I am glad 'tis night you do not look on me,   35
For I am much ashamed of my exchange.
But love is blind, and lovers cannot see
The pretty follies that themselves commit,
For, if they could, Cupid himself would blush
To see me thus transformed to a boy.   40

LORENZO   Descend, for you must be my torch-bearer.

JESSICA   What, must I hold a candle to my shames?
They, in themselves, good sooth, are too too light.
Why, 'tis an office of discovery, love,
And I should be obscured.

LORENZO   So are you, sweet,   45
Even in the lovely garnish of a boy.
But come at once,
For the close night doth play the runaway,
And we are stayed for at Bassanio's feast.

JESSICA   I will make fast the doors and gild myself   50
With some moe ducats, and be with you straight.
Exit above.

GRATIANO   Now, by my hood, a gentle, and no Jew.

LORENZO   Beshrew me but I love her heartily,
For she is wise, if I can judge of her,
And fair she is, if that mine eyes be true,   55
And true she is, as she hath proved herself:
And therefore like herself, wise, fair and true,
Shall she be placed in my constant soul.

Enter JESSICA.

What, art thou come? On, gentleman, away,
Our masquing mates by this time for us stay.   60
Exeunt all but Gratiano.

Enter ANTONIO.

ANTONIO   Who's there?

GRATIANO   Signior Antonio?

ANTONIO   Fie, fie, Gratiano. Where are all the rest?
'Tis nine o'clock; our friends all stay for you.
65   No masque tonight, the wind is come about.
Bassanio presently will go aboard;
I have sent twenty out to seek for you.

GRATIANO   I am glad on't. I desire no more delight
Than to be under sail and gone tonight.   *Exeunt.*

2.7   *Enter* PORTIA *and* NERISSA *with*
the Prince of MOROCCO, *and both their trains.*

PORTIA [*to Attendant*]
Go, draw aside the curtains and discover
The several caskets to this noble prince.
[*to Morocco*] Now make your choice.

MOROCCO
This first of gold, who this inscription bears:
5   'Who chooseth me shall gain what many men desire.'
The second, silver, which this promise carries:
'Who chooseth me shall get as much as he deserves.'
This third, dull lead, with warning all as blunt:
'Who chooseth me must give and hazard all he hath.'
10   How shall I know if I do choose the right?

PORTIA   The one of them contains my picture, prince.
If you choose that, then I am yours withal.

MOROCCO
Some god direct my judgement! Let me see,
I will survey th'inscriptions back again.
15   What says this leaden casket?
'Who chooseth me must give and hazard all he hath.'
'Must give', for what? For lead? Hazard for lead?
This casket threatens: men that hazard all
Do it in hope of fair advantages.
20   A golden mind stoops not to shows of dross;
I'll then nor give nor hazard aught for lead.
What says the silver with her virgin hue?
'Who chooseth me shall get as much as he deserves.'
'As much as he deserves.' Pause there, Morocco,
25   And weigh thy value with an even hand.
If thou be'st rated by thy estimation
Thou dost deserve enough; and yet, enough
May not extend so far as to the lady.
And yet, to be afeard of my deserving
30   Were but a weak disabling of myself.
As much as I deserve: why, that's the lady.
I do in birth deserve her, and in fortunes,
In graces and in qualities of breeding.
But more than these, in love I do deserve.
35   What if I strayed no farther, but chose here?
Let's see once more this saying graved in gold:
'Who chooseth me shall gain what many men desire.'
Why, that's the lady; all the world desires her.
From the four corners of the earth they come
40   To kiss this shrine, this mortal breathing saint.

The Hyrcanian deserts and the vasty wilds
Of wide Arabia are as throughfares now
For princes to come view fair Portia.
The watery kingdom, whose ambitious head
45   Spits in the face of heaven, is no bar
To stop the foreign spirits, but they come,
As o'er a brook, to see fair Portia.
One of these three contains her heavenly picture.
Is't like that lead contains her? 'Twere damnation
50   To think so base a thought; it were too gross
To rib her cerecloth in the obscure grave.
Or shall I think in silver she's immured,
Being ten times undervalued to tried gold?
O, sinful thought! Never so rich a gem
55   Was set in worse than gold. They have in England
A coin that bears the figure of an angel
Stamped in gold: but that's insculped upon.
But here, an angel in a golden bed
Lies all within. Deliver me the key.
60   Here do I choose, and thrive I as I may.

PORTIA
There, take it, prince, [*giving him the key*] and if my
    form lie there
Then I am yours!
      [*Morocco unlocks the golden casket.*]

MOROCCO   O, hell! What have we here?
A carrion death, within whose empty eye
There is a written scroll. I'll read the writing.
[*Reads.*]
      All that glisters is not gold,   65
      Often have you heard that told.
      Many a man his life hath sold
      But my outside to behold.
      Gilded timber do worms infold.
      Had you been as wise as bold,   70
      Young in limbs, in judgement old,
      Your answer had not been inscrolled,
      Fare you well, your suit is cold.
Cold indeed, and labour lost,
Then farewell, heat, and welcome frost.   75
Portia, adieu. I have too grieved a heart
To take a tedious leave: thus losers part.
                                        Exit with his train.

PORTIA   A gentle riddance. Draw the curtains, go.
Let all of his complexion choose me so.   *Exeunt.*

2.8   *Enter* SALARINO *and* SALANIO.

SALARINO   Why, man, I saw Bassanio under sail.
With him is Gratiano gone along,
And in their ship I am sure Lorenzo is not.

SALANIO
The villain Jew with outcries raised the Duke,
Who went with him to search Bassanio's ship.   5

SALARINO   He came too late, the ship was under sail.
But there the Duke was given to understand
That in a gondola were seen together

Lorenzo and his amorous Jessica.
Besides, Antonio certified the Duke   10
They were not with Bassanio in his ship.

SALANIO   I never heard a passion so confused,
So strange, outrageous, and so variable
As the dog Jew did utter in the streets: 15
'My daughter! O, my ducats! O, my daughter!
Fled with a Christian! O, my Christian ducats!
Justice, the law, my ducats and my daughter!
A sealed bag, two sealed bags of ducats,
Of double ducats, stol'n from me by my daughter!   20
And jewels, two stones, two rich and precious stones,
Stol'n by my daughter! Justice! Find the girl;
She hath the stones upon her, and the ducats.'

SALARINO   Why, all the boys in Venice follow him,
Crying 'His stones, his daughter and his ducats!'

SALANIO   Let good Antonio look he keep his day,   25
Or he shall pay for this.

SALARINO   Marry, well remembered.
I reasoned with a Frenchman yesterday
Who told me, in the narrow seas that part
The French and English, there miscarried   30
A vessel of our country richly fraught.
I thought upon Antonio when he told me,
And wished in silence that it were not his.

SALANIO   You were best to tell Antonio what you hear.
Yet do not suddenly, for it may grieve him.

SALARINO   A kinder gentleman treads not the earth.   35
I saw Bassanio and Antonio part;
Bassanio told him he would make some speed
Of his return. He answered, 'Do not so,
Slubber not business for my sake, Bassanio,
But stay the very riping of the time;   40
And for the Jew's bond, which he hath of me,
Let it not enter in your mind of love.
Be merry, and employ your chiefest thoughts
To courtship, and such fair ostents of love
As shall conveniently become you there.'   45
And even there, his eye being big with tears,
Turning his face, he put his hand behind him,
And, with affection wondrous sensible,
He wrung Bassanio's hand, and so they parted.

SALANIO   I think he only loves the world for him.   50
I pray thee, let us go and find him out,
And quicken his embraced heaviness
With some delight or other.

SALARINO   Do we so.   *Exeunt.*

2.9   *Enter* NERISSA *and a Servitor.*

NERISSA
Quick, quick, I pray thee, draw the curtain straight;
The Prince of Arragon hath ta'en his oath,
And comes to his election presently.

Enter the Prince of ARRAGON, *his train and* PORTIA.

PORTIA   Behold, there stand the caskets, noble prince.

If you choose that wherein I am contained,   5
Straight shall our nuptial rites be solemnized.
But if you fail, without more speech, my lord,
You must be gone from hence immediately.

ARRAGON
I am enjoined by oath to observe three things:
First, never to unfold to anyone   10
Which casket 'twas I chose; next, if I fail
Of the right casket, never in my life
To woo a maid in way of marriage;
Lastly, if I do fail in fortune of my choice,
Immediately to leave you and be gone.   15

PORTIA   To these injunctions everyone doth swear
That comes to hazard for my worthless self.

ARRAGON   And so I have addressed me. Fortune now
To my heart's hope! Gold, silver and base lead.
'Who chooseth me must give and hazard all he hath.'   20
You shall look fairer e'er I give or hazard.
What says the golden chest? Ha, let me see:
'Who chooseth me shall gain what many men desire.'
'What many men desire': that 'many' may be meant
By the fool multitude that choose by show,   25
Not learning more than the fond eye doth teach,
Which pries not to th'interior, but like the martlet
Builds in the weather on the outward wall,
Even in the force and road of casualty.
I will not choose what many men desire,   30
Because I will not jump with common spirits
And rank me with the barbarous multitudes.
Why then, to thee, thou silver treasure house:
Tell me once more what title thou dost bear:
'Who chooseth me shall get as much as he deserves.'   35
And well said too; for who shall go about
To cozen Fortune and be honourable
Without the stamp of merit? Let none presume
To wear an undeserved dignity.
O, that estates, degrees and offices   40
Were not derived corruptly, and that clear honour
Were purchased by the merit of the wearer!
How many then should cover that stand bare?
How many be commanded that command?
How much low peasantry would then be gleaned   45
From the true seed of honour? And how much honour
Picked from the chaff and ruin of the times
To be new varnished? Well, but to my choice.
'Who chooseth me shall get as much as he deserves.'
I will assume desert; give me a key for this,   50
And instantly unlock my fortunes here.
    [*Unlocks the silver casket.*]

PORTIA   Too long a pause for that which you find there.

ARRAGON
What's here? The portrait of a blinking idiot
Presenting me a schedule! I will read it.
How much unlike art thou to Portia!   55
How much unlike my hopes and my deservings.
'Who chooseth me shall have as much as he deserves!'
Did I deserve no more than a fool's head?

Is that my prize? Are my deserts no better?

60 PORTIA   To offend and judge are distinct offices,
And of opposed natures.

ARRAGON   What is here?

[*Reads.*]

        The fire seven times tried this;
        Seven times tried that judgement is,
        That did never choose amiss.
65   *Some there be that shadows kiss;*
        Such have but a shadow's bliss.
        There be fools alive iwis
        Silvered o'er, and so was this.
        Take what wife you will to bed,
70   *I will ever be your head.*
        So be gone: you are sped.

Still more fool I shall appear
By the time I linger here.
With one fool's head I came to woo,
75 But I go away with two.
Sweet, adieu. I'll keep my oath,
Patiently to bear my wroth.   *Exit with his train.*

PORTIA   Thus hath the candle singed the moth.
O, these deliberate fools! When they do choose,
80 They have the wisdom by their wit to lose.

NERISSA   The ancient saying is no heresy:
'Hanging and wiving goes by destiny.'

PORTIA   Come, draw the curtain, Nerissa.

Enter Messenger.

MESSENGER   Where is my lady?

PORTIA   Here. What would my lord?

85 MESSENGER   Madam, there is alighted at your gate
A young Venetian, one that comes before
To signify th'approaching of his lord,
From whom he bringeth sensible regreets:
To wit, besides commends and courteous breath,
90 Gifts of rich value. Yet I have not seen
So likely an ambassador of love.
A day in April never came so sweet
To show how costly summer was at hand,
As this forespurrer comes before his lord.

95 PORTIA   No more, I pray thee; I am half afeard
Thou wilt say anon he is some kin to thee,
Thou spend'st such high-day wit in praising him.
Come, come, Nerissa, for I long to see
Quick Cupid's post that comes so mannerly.

100 NERISSA   Bassanio, lord, love, if thy will it be.   *Exeunt.*

3.1   *Enter* SALANIO *and* SALARINO.

SALANIO   Now, what news on the Rialto?

SALARINO   Why, yet it lives there unchecked that
Antonio hath a ship of rich lading wracked on the
narrow seas. The Goodwins, I think, they call the place:
5 a very dangerous flat, and fatal, where the carcasses of
many a tall ship lie buried, as they say, if my gossip
Report be an honest woman of her word.

SALANIO   I would she were as lying a gossip in that as ever
knapped ginger, or made her neighbours believe she wept
for the death of a third husband. But it is true, without   10
any slips of prolixity, or crossing the plain highway of
talk, that the good Antonio, the honest Antonio – O, that
I had a title good enough to keep his name company! –

SALARINO   Come, the full stop.

SALANIO   Ha, what sayest thou? Why, the end is, he   15
hath lost a ship.

SALARINO   I would it might prove the end of his losses.

SALANIO   Let me say 'amen' betimes, lest the devil
cross my prayer, for here he comes in the likeness of a
Jew.   20

Enter Shylock the JEW.

How now, Shylock, what news among the merchants?

JEW   You knew, none so well, none so well as you, of my
daughter's flight.

SALARINO   That's certain; I, for my part, knew the
tailor that made the wings she flew withal.   25

SALANIO   And Shylock, for his own part, knew the bird
was fledge, and then it is the complexion of them all to
leave the dam.

JEW   She is damned for it.

SALARINO   That's certain, if the devil may be her judge.   30

JEW   My own flesh and blood to rebel!

SALANIO   Out upon it, old carrion, rebels it at these
years?

JEW   I say my daughter is my flesh and my blood.

SALARINO   There is more difference between thy flesh   35
and hers than between jet and ivory, more between
your bloods than there is between red wine and
Rhenish. But tell us, do you hear whether Antonio
have had any loss at sea or no?

JEW   There I have another bad match: a bankrupt, a   40
prodigal, who dare scarce show his head on the Rialto, a
beggar that was used to come so smug upon the mart.
Let him look to his bond. He was wont to call me usurer;
let him look to his bond. He was wont to lend money for
a Christian courtesy; let him look to his bond.   45

SALARINO   Why, I am sure if he forfeit, thou wilt not
take his flesh. What's that good for?

JEW   To bait fish withal; if it will feed nothing else, it will
feed my revenge. He hath disgraced me and hindered
me half a million, laughed at my losses, mocked at   50
my gains, scorned my nation, thwarted my bargains,
cooled my friends, heated mine enemies, and what's
his reason? I am a Jew. Hath not a Jew eyes? Hath not a
Jew hands, organs, dimensions, senses, affections,
passions? Fed with the same food, hurt with the same   55
weapons, subject to the same diseases, healed by the
same means, warmed and cooled by the same winter
and summer as a Christian is? If you prick us do we not
bleed? If you tickle us do we not laugh? If you poison
us do we not die? And if you wrong us shall we not   60
revenge? If we are like you in the rest, we will resemble
you in that. If a Jew wrong a Christian, what is his

humility? Revenge! If a Christian wrong a Jew, what
should his sufferance be by Christian example? Why,
revenge! The villainy you teach me I will execute, and 65
it shall go hard but I will better the instruction.

Enter a MAN *from Antonio.*

MAN   Gentlemen, my master Antonio is at his house
and desires to speak with you both.
SALARINO   We have been up and down to seek him.

Enter TUBAL.

SALANIO   Here comes another of the tribe; a third 70
cannot be matched, unless the devil himself turn Jew.
Exeunt Gentlemen, Salanio and Salarino,
with Antonio's Man.
JEW   How now, Tubal, what news from Genoa? Hast
thou found my daughter?
TUBAL   I often came where I did hear of her, but cannot 75
find her.
JEW   Why, there, there, there, there! A diamond gone
cost me two thousand ducats in Frankfurt. The curse
never fell upon our nation till now; I never felt it till
now. Two thousand ducats in that, and other precious, 80
precious jewels. I would my daughter were dead at my
foot, and the jewels in her ear; would she were hearsed
at my foot, and the ducats in her coffin. No news of
them? Why so? And I know not what's spent in the
search. Why, thou loss upon loss! The thief gone with 85
so much, and so much to find the thief, and no
satisfaction, no revenge, nor no ill luck stirring but
what lights o'my shoulders, no sighs but o'my
breathing, no tears but o'my shedding.
TUBAL   Yes, other men have ill luck too. Antonio, as I 90
heard in Genoa –
JEW   What, what, what? Ill luck, ill luck?
TUBAL   Hath an argosy cast away coming from Tripoli.
JEW   I thank God, I thank God! Is it true, is it true?
TUBAL   I spoke with some of the sailors that escaped the 95
wreck.
JEW   I thank thee, good Tubal: good news, good news!
Ha, ha, heard in Genoa!
TUBAL   Your daughter spent in Genoa, as I heard, one
night fourscore ducats.
JEW   Thou stick'st a dagger in me; I shall never see my 100
gold again. Fourscore ducats at a sitting? Fourscore
ducats!
TUBAL   There came divers of Antonio's creditors in my
company to Venice, that swear he cannot choose but
break. 105
JEW   I am very glad of it. I'll plague him; I'll torture
him. I am glad of it.
TUBAL   One of them showed me a ring that he had of
your daughter for a monkey.
JEW   Out upon her! Thou torturest me, Tubal. It was 110
my turquoise; I had it of Leah when I was a bachelor. I
would not have given it for a wilderness of monkeys.
TUBAL   But Antonio is certainly undone.

JEW   Nay, that's true; that's very true. Go, Tubal, fee me
an officer; bespeak him a fortnight before. I will have 115
the heart of him if he forfeit, for, were he out of Venice,
I can make what merchandise I will. Go, Tubal, and
meet me at our synagogue. Go, good Tubal, at our
synagogue, Tubal.   *Exeunt.*

3.2   *Enter* BASSANIO, PORTIA *with* NERISSA,
GRATIANO and all their trains.

PORTIA   I pray you tarry. Pause a day or two
Before you hazard, for in choosing wrong
I lose your company; therefore, forbear awhile.
There's something tells me – but it is not love –
I would not lose you, and, you know yourself, 5
Hate counsels not in such a quality.
But, lest you should not understand me well –
And yet, a maiden hath no tongue but thought –
I would detain you here some month or two
Before you venture for me. I could teach you 10
How to choose right, but then I am forsworn.
So will I never be, so may you miss me.
But if you do, you'll make me wish a sin,
That I had been forsworn. Beshrew your eyes,
They have o'erlooked me and divided me: 15
One half of me is yours, the other half yours.
Mine own, I would say: but, if mine, then yours,
And so, all yours. O, these naughty times
Puts bars between the owners and their rights:
And so, though yours, not yours. Prove it so, 20
Let Fortune go to hell for it, not I.
I speak too long, but 'tis to peise the time,
To eke it and to draw it out in length,
To stay you from election.
BASSANIO   Let me choose,
For, as I am, I live upon the rack. 25
PORTIA   Upon the rack, Bassanio? Then confess
What treason there is mingled with your love.
BASSANIO   None but that ugly treason of mistrust,
Which makes me fear th'enjoying of my love.
There may as well be amity and life 30
'Tween snow and fire, as treason and my love.
PORTIA   Ay, but I fear you speak upon the rack,
Where men enforced do speak anything.
BASSANIO   Promise me life and I'll confess the truth.
PORTIA   Well then, confess and live.
BASSANIO   Confess and love 35
Had been the very sum of my confession.
O happy torment, when my torturer
Doth teach me answers for deliverance!
But let me to my fortune and the caskets.
PORTIA   Away, then! I am locked in one of them: 40
If you do love me, you will find me out.
Nerissa and the rest, stand all aloof.
Let music sound while he doth make his choice;
Then, if he lose, he makes a swan-like end,
Fading in music. That the comparison 45

May stand more proper, my eye shall be the stream
And wat'ry death-bed for him. He may win,
And what is music then? Then music is
Even as the flourish, when true subjects bow
50 To a new-crowned monarch. Such it is,
As are those dulcet sounds in break of day,
That creep into the dreaming bridegroom's ear
And summon him to marriage. Now he goes
With no less presence, but with much more love,
55 Than young Alcides, when he did redeem
The virgin tribute paid by howling Troy
To the sea monster. I stand for sacrifice.
The rest, aloof, are the Dardanian wives,
With bleared visages come forth to view
60 The issue of th'exploit. Go, Hercules!
Live thou, I live. With much, much more dismay
I view the fight, than thou that mak'st the fray.
       [*Musicians from Portia's train perform a song the whilst*
       Bassanio comments on the caskets to himself.]
              Tell me where is fancy bred,
              Or in the heart, or in the head,
65   How begot, how nourished?
ALL   Reply, reply.
              It is engendered in the eye,
              With gazing fed, and fancy dies
              In the cradle where it lies.
70   Let us all ring fancy's knell.
              I'll begin it. Ding, dong, bell.
ALL   Ding, dong, bell.
BASSANIO
    So may the outward shows be least themselves,
    The world is still deceived with ornament.
75 In law, what plea so tainted and corrupt,
    But, being seasoned with a gracious voice,
    Obscures the show of evil? In religion,
    What damned error but some sober brow
    Will bless it and approve it with a text,
80 Hiding the grossness with fair ornament?
    There is no voice so simple but assumes
    Some mark of virtue on his outward parts.
    How many cowards, whose hearts are all as false
    As stairs of sand, wear yet upon their chins
85 The beards of Hercules and frowning Mars,
    Who, inward searched, have livers white as milk;
    And these assume but valour's excrement
    To render them redoubted. Look on beauty,
    And you shall see 'tis purchased by the weight,
90 Which therein works a miracle in nature,
    Making them lightest that wear most of it:
    So are those crisped snaky golden locks,
    Which maketh such wanton gambols with the wind
    Upon supposed fairness, often known
95 To be the dowry of a second head,
    The skull that bred them in the sepulchre.
    Thus, ornament is but the guiled shore
    To a most dangerous sea; the beauteous scarf
    Veiling an Indian beauty; in a word,

The seeming truth, which cunning times put on   100
To entrap the wisest. Therefore, then, thou gaudy gold,
Hard food for Midas, I will none of thee;
Nor none of thee, thou pale and common drudge
'Tween man and man. But thou, thou meagre lead,
Which rather threaten'st than dost promise aught,   105
Thy paleness moves me more than eloquence,
And here choose I; joy be the consequence.
PORTIA [*aside*]
How all the other passions fleet to air,
As doubtful thoughts, and rash-embraced despair,
And shuddering fear, and green-eyed jealousy.   110
O, love, be moderate, allay thy ecstasy,
In measure rain thy joy, scant this excess.
I feel too much thy blessing; make it less
For fear I surfeit.
BASSANIO [*Opens the leaden casket.*]
              What find I here?
Fair Portia's counterfeit! What demigod   115
Hath come so near creation? Move these eyes?
Or whether riding on the balls of mine
Seem they in motion? Here are severed lips
Parted with sugar breath; so sweet a bar
Should sunder such sweet friends. Here, in her hairs, 120
The painter plays the spider and hath woven
A golden mesh t'entrap the hearts of men
Faster than gnats in cobwebs. But her eyes!
How could he see to do them? Having made one,
Methinks it should have power to steal both his   125
And leave itself unfurnished. Yet look how far
The substance of my praise doth wrong this shadow
In underprizing it, so far this shadow
Doth limp behind the substance. Here's the scroll,
The continent and summary of my fortune.   130
[*Reads.*]
       You that choose not by the view
       Chance as fair and choose as true.
       Since this fortune falls to you,
       Be content and seek no new.
       If you be well pleased with this   135
       And hold your fortune for your bliss,
       Turn you where your lady is,
       And claim her with a loving kiss.
A gentle scroll. Fair lady, by your leave,
I come by note to give and to receive.   [*Kisses Portia.*] 140
Like one of two contending in a prize
That thinks he hath done well in people's eyes,
Hearing applause and universal shout,
Giddy in spirit, still gazing in a doubt
Whether those peals of praise be his or no,   145
So, thrice-fair lady, stand I even so,
As doubtful whether what I see be true,
Until confirmed, signed, ratified by you.
[*Portia kisses him.*]
PORTIA   You see me, Lord Bassanio, where I stand,
Such as I am. Though for myself alone   150
I would not be ambitious in my wish

To wish myself much better, yet, for you,
I would be trebled twenty times myself,
A thousand times more fair, ten thousand times
    more rich,
155 That only to stand high in your account
I might in virtues, beauties, livings, friends
Exceed account. But the full sum of me
Is sum of something: which to term in gross,
Is an unlessoned girl, unschooled, unpractised.
160 Happy in this, she is not yet so old
But she may learn; happier than this,
She is not bred so dull but she can learn.
Happiest of all is that her gentle spirit
Commits itself to yours to be directed,
165 As from her lord, her governor, her king.
Myself, and what is mine, to you and yours
Is now converted. But now, I was the lord
Of this fair mansion, master of my servants,
Queen o'er myself; and even now, but now,
170 This house, these servants and this same myself,
Are yours, my lord's. I give them with this ring
    [*giving him a ring*]
Which, when you part from, lose or give away,
Let it presage the ruin of your love,
And be my vantage to exclaim on you.
175 BASSANIO Madam, you have bereft me of all words.
Only my blood speaks to you in my veins,
And there is such confusion in my powers,
As, after some oration fairly spoke
By a beloved prince, there doth appear
180 Among the buzzing pleased multitude,
Where every something, being blent together,
Turns to a wild of nothing, save of joy,
Expressed and not expressed. But when this ring
Parts from this finger, then parts life from hence;
185 O, then be bold to say, 'Bassanio's dead.'
NERISSA My lord and lady, it is now our time,
That have stood by and seen our wishes prosper,
To cry, 'Good joy, good joy, my lord and lady!'
GRATIANO My lord Bassanio, and my gentle lady,
190 I wish you all the joy that you can wish,
For I am sure you can wish none from me;
And when your honours mean to solemnize
The bargain of your faith, I do beseech you
Even at that time I may be married too.
195 BASSANIO With all my heart, so thou canst get a wife.
GRATIANO I thank your lordship; you have got me one.
My eyes, my lord, can look as swift as yours.
You saw the mistress; I beheld the maid.
You loved, I loved, for intermission
200 No more pertains to me, my lord, than you.
Your fortune stood upon the caskets there,
And so did mine too as the matter falls.
For wooing here until I sweat again,
And swearing till my very roof was dry
205 With oaths of love, at last, if promise last,
I got a promise of this fair one here

To have her love, provided that your fortune
Achieved her mistress.
PORTIA   Is this true, Nerissa?
NERISSA Madam, it is, so you stand pleased withal.
BASSANIO And do you, Gratiano, mean good faith? 210
GRATIANO Yes, faith, my lord.
BASSANIO
Our feast shall be much honoured in your marriage.
GRATIANO We'll play with them the first boy for a
thousand ducats.
NERISSA What, and stake down? 215
GRATIANO
No, we shall ne'er win at that sport and stake down.

      Enter LORENZO, JESSICA *and* SALERIO,
         a messenger from Venice.

But who comes here? Lorenzo and his infidel!
What, and my old Venetian friend Salerio!
BASSANIO Lorenzo and Salerio, welcome hither,
If that the youth of my new interest here 220
Have power to bid you welcome. By your leave,
I bid my very friends and countrymen,
Sweet Portia, welcome.
PORTIA   So do I, my lord.
They are entirely welcome.
LORENZO I thank your honour. For my part, my lord, 225
My purpose was not to have seen you here,
But, meeting with Salerio by the way,
He did entreat me, past all saying nay,
To come with him along.
SALERIO   I did, my lord,
And I have reason for it. Signior Antonio 230
Commends him to you. [*Gives Bassanio a letter.*]
BASSANIO   E'er I ope his letter,
I pray you tell me how my good friend doth.
SALERIO Not sick, my lord, unless it be in mind,
Nor well, unless in mind. His letter there
Will show you his estate. [*Bassanio opens the letter.*] 235
GRATIANO
Nerissa, cheer yond stranger; bid her welcome.
Your hand, Salerio; what's the news from Venice?
How doth that royal merchant, good Antonio?
I know he will be glad of our success:
We are the Jasons; we have won the fleece. 240
SALERIO
I would you had won the fleece that he hath lost.
PORTIA
There are some shrewd contents in yond same paper
That steals the colour from Bassanio's cheek:
Some dear friend dead, else nothing in the world
Could turn so much the constitution 245
Of any constant man. What, worse and worse?
With leave, Bassanio, I am half yourself,
And I must freely have the half of anything
That this same paper brings you.
BASSANIO   O, sweet Portia,
Here are a few of the unpleasant'st words 250

That ever blotted paper. Gentle lady,
When I did first impart my love to you,
I freely told you all the wealth I had
Ran in my veins – I was a gentleman –
255 And then I told you true. And yet, dear lady,
Rating myself at nothing, you shall see
How much I was a braggart. When I told you
My state was nothing, I should then have told you
That I was worse than nothing; for, indeed,
260 I have engaged myself to a dear friend,
Engaged my friend to his mere enemy,
To feed my means. Here is a letter, lady,
The paper as the body of my friend,
And every word in it a gaping wound
265 Issuing life-blood. But is it true, Salerio?
Hath all his ventures failed? What, not one hit,
From Tripoli, from Mexico and England,
From Lisbon, Barbary and India,
And not one vessel scape the dreadful touch
Of merchant-marring rocks?
270 SALERIO   Not one, my lord.
Besides, it should appear that if he had
The present money to discharge the Jew
He would not take it. Never did I know
A creature that did bear the shape of man
275 So keen and greedy to confound a man.
He plies the Duke at morning and at night,
And doth impeach the freedom of the state
If they deny him justice. Twenty merchants,
The Duke himself and the magnificoes
280 Of greatest port have all persuaded with him,
But none can drive him from the envious plea
Of forfeiture, of justice and his bond.
JESSICA   When I was with him, I have heard him swear
To Tubal and to Chus, his countrymen,
285 That he would rather have Antonio's flesh
Than twenty times the value of the sum
That he did owe him; and I know, my lord,
If law, authority and power deny not,
It will go hard with poor Antonio.
290 PORTIA   Is it your dear friend that is thus in trouble?
BASSANIO   The dearest friend to me, the kindest man,
The best-conditioned and unwearied spirit
In doing courtesies; and one in whom
The ancient Roman honour more appears
295 Than any that draws breath in Italy.
PORTIA   What sum owes he the Jew?
BASSANIO   For me three thousand ducats.
PORTIA   What, no more?
Pay him six thousand and deface the bond.
Double six thousand, and then treble that,
300 Before a friend of this description
Shall lose a hair through Bassanio's fault.
First go with me to church and call me wife,
And then away to Venice to your friend,
For never shall you lie by Portia's side
305 With an unquiet soul. You shall have gold

To pay the petty debt twenty times over.
When it is paid, bring your true friend along;
My maid Nerissa and myself meantime
Will live as maids and widows. Come away,
For you shall hence upon your wedding day.   310
Bid your friends welcome, show a merry cheer;
Since you are dear bought, I will love you dear.
But let me hear the letter of your friend.
BASSANIO [*Reads.*]   *Sweet Bassanio, my ships have all
miscarried, my creditors grow cruel, my estate is very low,*   315
*my bond to the Jew is forfeit, and, since, in paying it, it is
impossible I should live, all debts are cleared between you
and I if I might but see you at my death. Notwithstanding,
use your pleasure; if your love do not persuade you to
come, let not my letter.*   320
PORTIA   O, love! Dispatch all business and be gone.
BASSANIO   Since I have your good leave to go away,
I will make haste. But, till I come again,
No bed shall e'er be guilty of my stay,
Nor rest be interposer 'twixt us twain.   *Exeunt.*   325

3.3   *Enter* Shylock the JEW, SALANIO,
                ANTONIO *and the Jailer.*

JEW   Jailer, look to him. Tell not me of mercy.
This is the fool that lent out money gratis.
Jailer, look to him.
ANTONIO   Hear me yet, good Shylock.
JEW   I'll have my bond. Speak not against my bond;
I have sworn an oath that I will have my bond.   5
Thou call'dst me dog before thou hadst a cause,
But, since I am a dog, beware my fangs.
The Duke shall grant me justice. I do wonder,
Thou naughty jailer, that thou art so fond
To come abroad with him at his request.   10
ANTONIO   I pray thee, hear me speak.
JEW   I'll have my bond. I will not hear thee speak.
I'll have my bond, and therefore speak no more.
I'll not be made a soft and dull-eyed fool,
To shake the head, relent, and sigh and yield   15
To Christian intercessors. Follow not;
I'll have no speaking; I will have my bond.   *Exit.*
SALANIO   It is the most impenetrable cur
That ever kept with men.
ANTONIO   Let him alone.
I'll follow him no more with bootless prayers.   20
He seeks my life. His reason well I know:
I oft delivered from his forfeitures
Many that have at times made moan to me;
Therefore he hates me.
SALANIO   I am sure the Duke
Will never grant this forfeiture to hold.   25
ANTONIO   The Duke cannot deny the course of law;
For the commodity that strangers have
With us in Venice, if it be denied,
Will much impeach the justice of the state,
Since that the trade and profit of the city   30

Consisteth of all nations. Therefore, go;
These griefs and losses have so bated me
That I shall hardly spare a pound of flesh
Tomorrow to my bloody creditor.   *Exit Salanio.*
35   Well, jailer, on. Pray God Bassanio come
To see me pay his debt, and then I care not.   *Exeunt.*

3.4   *Enter* PORTIA, NERISSA, LORENZO,
        JESSICA *and* BALTHAZAR, *a man of Portia's.*

LORENZO
Madam, although I speak it in your presence,
You have a noble and a true conceit
Of godlike amity, which appears most strongly
In bearing thus the absence of your lord.
5   But, if you knew to whom you show this honour,
How true a gentleman you send relief,
How dear a lover of my lord, your husband,
I know you would be prouder of the work
Than customary bounty can enforce you.
10 PORTIA   I never did repent for doing good,
Nor shall not now; for in companions
That do converse and waste the time together,
Whose souls do bear an equal yoke of love,
There must be needs a like proportion
15   Of lineaments, of manners and of spirit;
Which makes me think that this Antonio,
Being the bosom lover of my lord,
Must needs be like my lord. If it be so,
How little is the cost I have bestowed
20   In purchasing the semblance of my soul
From out the state of hellish cruelty.
This comes too near the praising of myself;
Therefore, no more of it. Hear other things:
Lorenzo, I commit into your hands
25   The husbandry and manage of my house
Until my lord's return. For mine own part,
I have toward heaven breathed a secret vow
To live in prayer and contemplation,
Only attended by Nerissa here,
30   Until her husband and my lord's return.
There is a monastery two miles off,
And there we will abide. I do desire you
Not to deny this imposition,
The which my love and some necessity
Now lays upon you.
35 LORENZO   Madam, with all my heart,
I shall obey you in all fair commands.
PORTIA   My people do already know my mind
And will acknowledge you and Jessica
In place of Lord Bassanio and myself.
40   So fare you well till we shall meet again.
LORENZO
Fair thoughts and happy hours attend on you.
JESSICA   I wish your ladyship all heart's content.
PORTIA   I thank you for your wish, and am well pleased
To wish it back on you. Fare you well, Jessica.

                    Exeunt Jessica and Lorenzo.
Now, Balthazar,   45
As I have ever found thee honest true,
So let me find thee still. Take this same letter,
And use thou all th'endeavour of a man,
In speed to Mantua. See thou render this
Into my cousin's hand, Doctor Bellario;   50
   [*Gives Balthazar a letter.*]
And look what notes and garments he doth give thee,
Bring them, I pray thee, with imagined speed
Unto the traject, to the common ferry,
Which trades to Venice. Waste no time in words
But get thee gone; I shall be there before thee.   55
BALTHAZAR
Madam, I go, with all convenient speed.   *Exit.*
PORTIA   Come on, Nerissa; I have work in hand
That you yet know not of. We'll see our husbands
Before they think of us!
NERISSA   Shall they see us?
PORTIA   They shall, Nerissa, but in such a habit   60
That they shall think we are accomplished
With that we lack. I'll hold thee any wager,
When we are both accoutred like young men,
I'll prove the prettier fellow of the two,
And wear my dagger with the braver grace,   65
And speak between the change of man and boy
With a reed voice, and turn two mincing steps
Into a manly stride, and speak of frays
Like a fine bragging youth, and tell quaint lies
How honourable ladies sought my love,   70
Which I denying, they fell sick and died.
I could not do withal; then I'll repent,
And wish, for all that, that I had not killed them.
And twenty of these puny lies I'll tell,
That men shall swear I have discontinued school   75
Above a twelvemonth. I have within my mind
A thousand raw tricks of these bragging jacks
Which I will practise.
NERISSA   Why, shall we turn to men?
PORTIA   Fie, what a question's that,
If thou wert near a lewd interpreter.   80
But come, I'll tell thee all my whole device
When I am in my coach, which stays for us
At the park gate; and therefore haste away,
For we must measure twenty miles today.   *Exeunt.*

3.5   *Enter* Lancelet *the* CLOWN *and* JESSICA.

CLOWN   Yes, truly, for, look you, the sins of the
father are to be laid upon the children; therefore, I
promise you, I fear you. I was always plain with you,
and so now I speak my agitation of the matter.
Therefore be of good cheer, for, truly, I think you   5
are damned. There is but one hope in it that can do
you any good, and that is but a kind of bastard hope
neither.

JESSICA   And what hope is that, I pray thee?

10   CLOWN   Marry, you may partly hope that your father
got you not, that you are not the Jew's daughter.

JESSICA   That were a kind of bastard hope indeed, so
the sins of my mother should be visited upon me.

CLOWN   Truly, then, I fear you are damned both by
15   father and mother: thus, when I shun Scylla your
father, I fall into Charybdis your mother; well, you are
gone both ways.

JESSICA   I shall be saved by my husband; he hath made
me a Christian!

20   CLOWN   Truly, the more to blame he; we were Christians
enow before, e'en as many as could well live one by
another. This making of Christians will raise the price
of hogs: if we grow all to be pork eaters, we shall not
shortly have a rasher on the coals for money.

Enter LORENZO.

25   JESSICA   I'll tell my husband, Lancelet, what you say.
Here he comes.

LORENZO   I shall grow jealous of you shortly, Lancelet,
if you thus get my wife into corners!

JESSICA   Nay, you need not fear us, Lorenzo; Lancelet and
30   I are out. He tells me flatly there's no mercy for me in
heaven, because I am a Jew's daughter; and he says you
are no good member of the commonwealth, for, in
converting Jews to Christians, you raise the price of pork.

LORENZO   I shall answer that better to the common-
35   wealth than you can the getting up of the negro's belly:
the Moor is with child by you, Lancelet!

CLOWN   It is much that the Moor should be more than
reason; but if she be less than an honest woman, she is
indeed more than I took her for.

40   LORENZO   How every fool can play upon the word. I
think the best grace of wit will shortly turn into
silence, and discourse grow commendable in none
only but parrots. Go in, sirrah; bid them prepare for
dinner!

45   CLOWN   That is done, sir: they have all stomachs!

LORENZO   Goodly lord, what a wit-snapper are you!
Then bid them prepare dinner.

CLOWN   That is done too, sir; only 'cover' is the word.

LORENZO   Will you cover then, sir?

50   CLOWN   Not so, sir, neither; I know my duty.

LORENZO   Yet more quarrelling with occasion. Wilt
thou show the whole wealth of thy wit in an instant? I
pray thee, understand a plain man in his plain meaning:
go to thy fellows, bid them cover the table, serve in the
55   meat, and we will come in to dinner.

CLOWN   For the table, sir, it shall be served in; for the
meat, sir, it shall be covered; for your coming in to
dinner, sir, why, let it be as humours and conceits
shall govern.   *Exit.*

60   LORENZO   O, dear discretion, how his words are suited.
The fool hath planted in his memory
An army of good words, and I do know
A many fools that stand in better place,

Garnished like him, that for a tricksy word
Defy the matter. How cheer'st thou, Jessica?   65
And now, good sweet, say thy opinion:
How dost thou like the Lord Bassanio's wife?

JESSICA   Past all expressing. It is very meet
The Lord Bassanio live an upright life,
For, having such a blessing in his lady,   70
He finds the joys of heaven here on earth,
And, if on earth he do not mean it, it
Is reason he should never come to heaven.
Why, if two gods should play some heavenly match
And on the wager lay two earthly women,   75
And Portia one, there must be something else
Pawned with the other, for the poor rude world
Hath not her fellow.

LORENZO   Even such a husband
Hast thou of me, as she is for a wife.

JESSICA   Nay, but ask my opinion too of that!   80

LORENZO   I will anon; first let us go to dinner.

JESSICA   Nay, let me praise you while I have a stomach.

LORENZO   No, pray thee, let it serve for table talk,
Then howsome'er thou speak'st, 'mong other things
I shall digest it.

JESSICA   Well, I'll set you forth.   *Exeunt.*   85

4.1   *Enter the* DUKE *of* Venice, *the Magnificoes,*
ANTONIO, BASSANIO, SALERIO, *who*
remains near the door, and GRATIANO *and*
three or four Attendants.

DUKE   What, is Antonio here?

ANTONIO   Ready, so please your grace.

DUKE   I am sorry for thee. Thou art come to answer
A stony adversary, an inhumane wretch,
Uncapable of pity, void and empty
From any dram of mercy.

ANTONIO   I have heard   5
Your grace hath ta'en great pains to qualify
His rigorous course; but, since he stands obdurate,
And that no lawful means can carry me
Out of his envy's reach, I do oppose
My patience to his fury, and am armed   10
To suffer with a quietness of spirit,
The very tyranny and rage of his.

DUKE   Go one and call the Jew into the court.

SALERIO   He is ready at the door; he comes, my lord.

Enter Shylock the JEW.

DUKE   Make room, and let him stand before our face.   15
Shylock, the world thinks, and I think so too,
That thou but leadest this fashion of thy malice
To the last hour of act, and then 'tis thought
Thou'lt show thy mercy and remorse more strange
Than is thy strange apparent cruelty;   20
And where thou now exacts the penalty,
Which is a pound of this poor merchant's flesh,
Thou wilt not only loose the forfeiture,

But, touched with humane gentleness and love,
25 Forgive a moiety of the principal,
Glancing an eye of pity on his losses
That have of late so huddled on his back,
Enough to press a royal merchant down,
And pluck commiseration of his state
30 From brassy bosoms and rough hearts of flint,
From stubborn Turks, and Tartars never trained
To offices of tender courtesy.
We all expect a gentle answer, Jew!

JEW   I have possessed your grace of what I purpose,
35 And by our holy Sabbath have I sworn
To have the due and forfeit of my bond.
If you deny it, let the danger light
Upon your charter and your city's freedom!
You'll ask me why I rather choose to have
40 A weight of carrion flesh than to receive
Three thousand ducats. I'll not answer that!
But say it is my humour. Is it answered?
What if my house be troubled with a rat,
And I be pleased to give ten thousand ducats
45 To have it baned? What, are you answered yet?
Some men there are love not a gaping pig!
Some that are mad if they behold a cat!
And others, when the bagpipe sings i'th' nose,
Cannot contain their urine: for affection,
50 Maistrice of passion, sways it to the mood
Of what it likes or loathes. Now, for your answer:
As there is no firm reason to be rendered
Why he cannot abide a gaping pig,
Why he a harmless necessary cat,
55 Why he a woollen bagpipe, but of force
Must yield to such inevitable shame
As to offend himself being offended;
So can I give no reason, nor I will not,
More than a lodged hate and a certain loathing
60 I bear Antonio, that I follow thus
A losing suit against him! Are you answered?

BASSANIO   This is no answer, thou unfeeling man,
To excuse the current of thy cruelty!

JEW   I am not bound to please thee with my answers!

65 BASSANIO   Do all men kill the things they do not love?

JEW   Hates any man the thing he would not kill?

BASSANIO   Every offence is not a hate at first!

JEW
What, wouldst thou have a serpent sting thee twice?

ANTONIO   I pray you, think you question with the Jew.
70 You may as well go stand upon the beach
And bid the main flood bate his usual height;
You may as well use question with the wolf
Why he hath made the ewe bleat for the lamb;
You may as well forbid the mountain pines
75 To wag their high tops, and to make no noise
When they are fretten with the gusts of heaven;
You may as well do anything most hard
As seek to soften that, than which what's harder –
His Jewish heart! Therefore, I do beseech you,

Make no moe offers, use no farther means,   80
But with all brief and plain conveniency
Let me have judgement, and the Jew his will!

BASSANIO   For thy three thousand ducats here is six!

JEW   If every ducat in six thousand ducats
Were in six parts, and every part a ducat,   85
I would not draw them; I would have my bond!

DUKE   How shalt thou hope for mercy, rendering none?

JEW   What judgement shall I dread, doing no wrong?
You have among you many a purchased slave,
Which, like your asses, and your dogs and mules,   90
You use in abject and in slavish parts,
Because you bought them. Shall I say to you,
'Let them be free, marry them to your heirs.
Why sweat they under burdens? Let their beds
Be made as soft as yours, and let their palates   95
Be seasoned with such viands?' You will answer:
'The slaves are ours.' So do I answer you.
The pound of flesh which I demand of him
Is dearly bought; 'tis mine, and I will have it.
If you deny me, fie upon your law: 100
There is no force in the decrees of Venice.
I stand for judgement: answer, shall I have it?

DUKE   Upon my power I may dismiss this court,
Unless Bellario, a learned doctor,
Whom I have sent for to determine this,   105
Come here today!

SALERIO   My lord, here stays without
A messenger with letters from the doctor,
New come from Padua!

DUKE   Bring us the letters! Call the messenger!

Exit Salerio.

BASSANIO
Good cheer, Antonio! What, man, courage yet: 110
The Jew shall have my flesh, blood, bones and all,
Ere thou shalt lose for me one drop of blood!

ANTONIO   I am a tainted wether of the flock,
Meetest for death; the weakest kind of fruit
Drops earliest to the ground, and so let me.   115
You cannot better be employed, Bassanio,
Than to live still and write mine epitaph!

Enter SALERIO *and* NERISSA, *disguised as
a lawyer's clerk.*

DUKE   Came you from Padua from Bellario?

NERISSA [*Presents a letter to the Duke.*]
From both! My lord, Bellario greets your grace!

BASSANIO   Why dost thou whet thy knife so earnestly?   120

JEW   To cut the forfeiture from that bankrupt there.

GRATIANO   Not on thy sole, but on thy soul, harsh Jew,
Thou mak'st thy knife keen. But no metal can,
No, not the hangman's axe, bear half the keenness
Of thy sharp envy. Can no prayers pierce thee?   125

JEW   No, none that thou hast wit enough to make.

GRATIANO   O, be thou damned, inexecrable dog,
And for thy life let justice be accused!
Thou almost mak'st me waver in my faith,

130	To hold opinion with Pythagoras
	That souls of animals infuse themselves
	Into the trunks of men. Thy currish spirit
	Governed a wolf, who, hanged for human slaughter,
	Even from the gallows did his fell soul fleet,
135	And whilst thou layest in thy unhallowed dam,
	Infused itself in thee; for thy desires
	Are wolvish, bloody, starved and ravenous.

JEW   Till thou canst rail the seal from off my bond
Thou but offend'st thy lungs to speak so loud.

140 Repair thy wit, good youth, or it will fall
To cureless ruin. I stand here for law.

DUKE   This letter from Bellario doth commend
A young and learned doctor to our court.
Where is he?

NERISSA   He attendeth here hard by

145 To know your answer whether you'll admit him.

DUKE   With all my heart. Some three or four of you
Go give him courteous conduct to this place.

Exeunt Attendants.

Meantime the court shall hear Bellario's letter.

[*Reads.*] *Your grace shall understand that at the receipt of*

150 *your letter I am very sick, but, in the instant that your*
messenger came, in loving visitation was with me a young
doctor of Rome: his name is Balthazar. I acquainted him with
the cause in controversy between the Jew and Antonio the
merchant. We turned o'er many books together; he is furnished

155 *with my opinion, which, bettered with his own learning, the*
greatness whereof I cannot enough commend, comes with him
at my importunity to fill up your grace's request in my stead. I
beseech you, let his lack of years be no impediment to let him
lack a reverend estimation, for I never knew so young a body

160 *with so old a head. I leave him to your gracious acceptance,*
whose trial shall better publish his commendation.

Enter PORTIA *as Balthazar, with three*
or four Attendants.

DUKE   You hear the learned Bellario what he writes,
And here, I take it, is the doctor come.
Give me your hand. Come you from old Bellario?

PORTIA   I did, my lord.

165 DUKE   You are welcome: take your place.
Are you acquainted with the difference
That holds this present question in the court?

PORTIA   I am informed throughly of the cause.
Which is the merchant here, and which the Jew?

170 DUKE   Antonio and old Shylock, both stand forth.

PORTIA   Is your name Shylock?

JEW   Shylock is my name.

PORTIA   Of a strange nature is the suit you follow,
Yet in such rule that the Venetian law
Cannot impugn you as you do proceed.

175 [*to Antonio*] You stand within his danger, do you not?

ANTONIO   Ay, so he says.

PORTIA   Do you confess the bond?

ANTONIO   I do.

PORTIA   Then must the Jew be merciful.

JEW   On what compulsion must I? Tell me that.

PORTIA   The quality of mercy is not strained:
It droppeth as the gentle rain from heaven   180
Upon the place beneath. It is twice blest:
It blesseth him that gives and him that takes.
'Tis mightiest in the mightiest; it becomes
The throned monarch better than his crown.
His sceptre shows the force of temporal power,   185
The attribute to awe and majesty,
Wherein doth sit the dread and fear of kings.
But mercy is above this sceptred sway;
It is enthroned in the hearts of kings,
It is an attribute to God himself,   190
And earthly power doth then show likest God's
When mercy seasons justice. Therefore, Jew,
Though justice be thy plea, consider this:
That in the course of justice none of us
Should see salvation. We do pray for mercy,   195
And that same prayer doth teach us all to render
The deeds of mercy. I have spoke thus much
To mitigate the justice of thy plea,
Which, if thou follow, this strict court of Venice
Must needs give sentence 'gainst the merchant
there.   200

JEW   My deeds upon my head, I crave the law,
The penalty and forfeit of my bond.

PORTIA   Is he not able to discharge the money?

BASSANIO   Yes, here I tender it for him in the court,
Yea, twice the sum. If that will not suffice,   205
I will be bound to pay it ten times o'er,
On forfeit of my hands, my head, my heart.
If this will not suffice, it must appear
That malice bears down truth. [*to the Duke*] And, I
beseech you,
Wrest once the law to your authority;   210
To do a great right, do a little wrong
And curb this cruel devil of his will.

PORTIA   It must not be: there is no power in Venice
Can alter a decree established.
'Twill be recorded for a precedent,   215
And many an error by the same example
Will rush into the state. It cannot be.

JEW   A Daniel come to judgement; yea, a Daniel!
O, wise young judge, how I do honour thee.

PORTIA   I pray you, let me look upon the bond.   220

JEW   Here 'tis, most reverend doctor; here it is.

PORTIA   Shylock, there's thrice thy money offered thee.

JEW   An oath, an oath, I have an oath in heaven!
Shall I lay perjury upon my soul?
No, not for Venice.

PORTIA   Why, this bond is forfeit,   225
And lawfully by this the Jew may claim
A pound of flesh, to be by him cut off
Nearest the merchant's heart. [*to the Jew*] Be
merciful:
Take thrice thy money; bid me tear the bond.

JEW   When it is paid according to the tenor.   230

It doth appear you are a worthy judge,
You know the law; your exposition
Hath been most sound. I charge you by the law,
Whereof you are a well-deserving pillar,
235 Proceed to judgement. By my soul I swear,
There is no power in the tongue of man
To alter me. I stay here on my bond.
ANTONIO   Most heartily I do beseech the court
To give the judgement.
PORTIA   Why then, thus it is:
240 You must prepare your bosom for his knife.
JEW   O noble judge! O excellent young man!
PORTIA   For the intent and purpose of the law
Hath full relation to the penalty
Which here appeareth due upon the bond.
245 JEW   'Tis very true. O wise and upright judge,
How much more elder art thou than thy looks!
PORTIA [*to Antonio*]
Therefore lay bare your bosom.
JEW   Ay, his breast.
So says the bond, doth it not, noble judge?
'Nearest his heart': those are the very words.
250 PORTIA   It is so. Are there balance here to weigh
The flesh?
JEW   I have them ready.
PORTIA
Have by some surgeon, Shylock, on your charge,
To stop his wounds, lest he do bleed to death.
JEW   Is it so nominated in the bond?
255 PORTIA   It is not so expressed, but what of that?
'Twere good you do so much for charity.
JEW   I cannot find it; 'tis not in the bond.
PORTIA [*to Antonio*]
You, merchant, have you anything to say?
ANTONIO   But little. I am armed and well prepared.
260 Give me your hand, Bassanio. Fare you well,
Grieve not that I am fall'n to this for you:
For herein Fortune shows herself more kind
Than is her custom. It is still her use
To let the wretched man outlive his wealth,
265 To view with hollow eye and wrinkled brow
An age of poverty, from which lingering penance
Of such misery doth she cut me off.
Commend me to your honourable wife;
Tell her the process of Antonio's end,
270 Say how I loved you, speak me fair in death,
And, when the tale is told, bid her be judge
Whether Bassanio had not once a love.
Repent but you that you shall lose your friend
And he repents not that he pays your debt.
275 For if the Jew do cut but deep enough
I'll pay it instantly with all my heart.
BASSANIO   Antonio, I am married to a wife
Which is as dear to me as life itself;
But life itself, my wife and all the world
280 Are not with me esteemed above thy life.
I would lose all, ay, sacrifice them all

Here to this devil, to deliver you.
PORTIA   Your wife would give you little thanks for that
If she were by to hear you make the offer.
285 GRATIANO   I have a wife who I protest I love.
I would she were in heaven, so she could
Entreat some power to change this currish Jew.
NERISSA   'Tis well you offer it behind her back,
The wish would make else an unquiet house.
JEW
290 These be the Christian husbands! I have a daughter:
Would any of the stock of Barabbas
Had been her husband rather than a Christian.
We trifle time; I pray thee, pursue sentence.
PORTIA
A pound of that same merchant's flesh is thine;
295 The court awards it, and the law doth give it.
JEW   Most rightful judge!
PORTIA   And you must cut this flesh from off his breast;
The law allows it, and the court awards it.
JEW
Most learned judge! A sentence! [*to Antonio*] Come,
prepare.
300 PORTIA   Tarry a little, there is something else.
This bond doth give thee here no jot of blood:
The words expressly are 'a pound of flesh'.
Take then thy bond: take thou thy pound of flesh.
But in the cutting it, if thou dost shed
305 One drop of Christian blood, thy lands and goods
Are by the laws of Venice confiscate
Unto the state of Venice.
GRATIANO   O upright judge!
Mark, Jew – O learned judge!
JEW   Is that the law?
PORTIA   Thyself shalt see the act,
310 For, as thou urgest justice, be assured
Thou shalt have justice more than thou desir'st.
GRATIANO
O learned judge! Mark, Jew: a learned judge!
JEW   I take this offer, then; pay the bond thrice
And let the Christian go.
BASSANIO   Here is the money.
315 PORTIA   Soft!
The Jew shall have all justice. Soft, no haste,
He shall have nothing but the penalty.
GRATIANO   O, Jew, an upright judge, a learned judge!
PORTIA   Therefore, prepare thee to cut off the flesh.
320 Shed thou no blood, nor cut thou less nor more
But just a pound of flesh. If thou tak'st more
Or less than a just pound, be it but so much
As makes it light or heavy in the substance
Or the division of the twentieth part
325 Of one poor scruple: nay, if the scale do turn
But in the estimation of a hair,
Thou diest, and all thy goods are confiscate.
GRATIANO   A second Daniel, a Daniel, Jew!
Now, infidel, I have you on the hip.
330 PORTIA   Why doth the Jew pause? Take thy forfeiture.

JEW   Give me my principal, and let me go.

BASSANIO   I have it ready for thee; here it is.

PORTIA   He hath refused it in the open court;
He shall have merely justice and his bond.

335   GRATIANO   A Daniel still, say I, a second Daniel!
I thank thee, Jew, for teaching me that word.

JEW   Shall I not have barely my principal?

PORTIA   Thou shalt have nothing but the forfeiture,
To be so taken at thy peril, Jew.

340   JEW   Why then, the devil give him good of it!
I'll stay no longer question.   [*Begins to leave.*]

PORTIA   Tarry, Jew,
The law hath yet another hold on you.
It is enacted in the laws of Venice,
If it be proved against an alien

345   That by direct, or indirect, attempts
He seek the life of any citizen,
The party 'gainst the which he doth contrive
Shall seize one-half his goods. The other half
Comes to the privy coffer of the state,

350   And the offender's life lies in the mercy
Of the Duke only, 'gainst all other voice.
In which predicament I say thou stand'st,
For it appears by manifest proceeding
That indirectly, and directly too,

355   Thou hast contrived against the very life
Of the defendant, and thou hast incurred
The danger formerly by me rehearsed.
Down, therefore, and beg mercy of the Duke.

GRATIANO
Beg that thou mayst have leave to hang thyself,

360   And yet, thy wealth being forfeit to the state,
Thou hast not left the value of a cord;
Therefore thou must be hanged at the state's charge.

DUKE   That thou shalt see the difference of our spirit,
I pardon thee thy life before thou ask it.

365   For half thy wealth, it is Antonio's;
The other half comes to the general state,
Which humbleness may drive unto a fine.

PORTIA   Ay, for the state, not for Antonio.

JEW   Nay, take my life and all, pardon not that.

370   You take my house when you do take the prop
That doth sustain my house. You take my life
When you do take the means whereby I live.

PORTIA   What mercy can you render him, Antonio?

GRATIANO
A halter gratis, nothing else, for God's sake!

ANTONIO
375   So please my lord the Duke, and all the court,
To quit the fine for one-half of his goods,
I am content, so he will let me have
The other half in use, to render it
Upon his death unto the gentleman

380   That lately stole his daughter.
Two things provided more: that for this favour
He presently become a Christian;
The other, that he do record a gift

Here in the court of all he dies possessed
Unto his son Lorenzo and his daughter.   385

DUKE   He shall do this, or else I do recant
The pardon that I late pronounced here.

PORTIA   Art thou contented, Jew? What dost thou say?

JEW   I am content.

PORTIA   Clerk, draw a deed of gift.

JEW   I pray you, give me leave to go from hence.   390
I am not well. Send the deed after me
And I will sign it.

DUKE   Get thee gone, but do it.

GRATIANO
In christening shalt thou have two godfathers.
Had I been judge, thou shouldst have had ten more,
To bring thee to the gallows, not to the font.   395
                                            Exit Jew.

DUKE [*to Portia*]
Sir, I entreat you home with me to dinner.

PORTIA   I humbly do desire, your grace, of pardon;
I must away this night toward Padua,
And it is meet I presently set forth.

DUKE   I am sorry that your leisure serves you not.   400
Antonio, gratify this gentleman,
For in my mind you are much bound to him.
                            Exeunt Duke and his train.

BASSANIO   Most worthy gentleman, I and my friend
Have, by your wisdom, been this day acquitted
Of grievous penalties, in lieu whereof   405
Three thousand ducats due unto the Jew
We freely cope your courteous pains withal.

ANTONIO   And stand indebted, over and above,
In love and service to you evermore.

PORTIA   He is well paid that is well satisfied,   410
And I, delivering you, am satisfied,
And therein do account myself well paid;
My mind was never yet more mercenary.
I pray you, know me when we meet again.
I wish you well, and so I take my leave.   415

BASSANIO
Dear sir, of force I must attempt you further.
Take some remembrance of us as a tribute,
Not as fee. Grant me two things, I pray you:
Not to deny me, and to pardon me.

PORTIA   You press me far, and therefore I will yield.   420
Give me your gloves; I'll wear them for your sake,
And, for your love, I'll take this ring from you.
Do not draw back your hand; I'll take no more,
And you, in love, shall not deny me this!

BASSANIO   This ring, good sir? Alas, it is a trifle;   425
I will not shame myself to give you this!

PORTIA   I will have nothing else but only this,
And now, methinks, I have a mind to it!

BASSANIO
There's more depends on this than on the value.
The dearest ring in Venice will I give you,   430
And find it out by proclamation;
Only for this, I pray you, pardon me!

PORTIA I see, sir, you are liberal in offers.
You taught me first to beg, and now, methinks,
435 You teach me how a beggar should be answered.
BASSANIO
Good sir, this ring was given me by my wife,
And when she put it on she made me vow
That I should neither sell, nor give, nor lose it.
PORTIA
That 'scuse serves many men to save their gifts!
440 An if your wife be not a mad woman,
And know how well I have deserved this ring,
She would not hold out enemy for ever
For giving it to me. Well, peace be with you.

Exeunt Portia and Nerissa.

ANTONIO   My lord Bassanio, let him have the ring.
445 Let his deservings and my love withal
Be valued 'gainst your wife's commandement.
BASSANIO   Go, Gratiano, run and overtake him;
Give him the ring, and bring him, if thou canst,
Unto Antonio's house. Away, make haste.

Exit Gratiano.

450 Come, you and I will thither presently,
And in the morning early will we both
Fly toward Belmont. Come, Antonio.   *Exeunt.*

4.2   *Enter* PORTIA *and* NERISSA *still disguised.*

PORTIA
Enquire the Jew's house out, give him this deed,
  [*giving paper to Nerissa*]
And let him sign it. We'll away tonight,
And be a day before our husbands home.
This deed will be well welcome to Lorenzo!

Enter GRATIANO.

5 GRATIANO   Fair sir, you are well o'erta'en.
My lord Bassanio, upon more advice,
Hath sent you here this ring and doth entreat
Your company at dinner.
PORTIA   That cannot be.
His ring I do accept most thankfully,
10 And so, I pray you, tell him. Furthermore,
I pray you, show my youth old Shylock's house.
GRATIANO   That will I do.
NERISSA   Sir, I would speak with you.
[*aside to Portia*] I'll see if I can get my husband's ring,
Which I did make him swear to keep for ever.
PORTIA [*aside to Nerissa*]
15 Thou mayst, I warrant. We shall have old swearing
That they did give the rings away to men,
But we'll outface them and outswear them too.
Away, make haste, thou knowst where I will tarry.

Exit.

NERISSA
Come, good sir, will you show me to this house?

Exeunt.

5.1   *Enter* LORENZO *and* JESSICA.

LORENZO
The moon shines bright. In such a night as this,
When the sweet wind did gently kiss the trees,
And they did make no noise, in such a night
Troilus, methinks, mounted the Trojan walls
And sighed his soul toward the Grecian tents,   5
Where Cressid lay that night.
JESSICA   In such a night
Did Thisbe fearfully o'ertrip the dew,
And saw the lion's shadow ere himself,
And ran dismayed away.
LORENZO   In such a night
Stood Dido with a willow in her hand   10
Upon the wild sea banks and waft her love
To come again to Carthage.
JESSICA   In such a night
Medea gathered the enchanted herbs
That did renew old Aeson.
LORENZO   In such a night
Did Jessica steal from the wealthy Jew,   15
And with an unthrift love did run from Venice
As far as Belmont.
JESSICA   In such a night
Did young Lorenzo swear he loved her well,
Stealing her soul with many vows of faith,
And ne'er a true one.
LORENZO   In such a night   20
Did pretty Jessica, like a little shrew,
Slander her love, and he forgave it her.
JESSICA   I would out-night you did nobody come;
But hark, I hear the footing of a man.

Enter Stephano, a Messenger.

LORENZO   Who comes so fast in silence of the night? 25
MESSENGER   A friend.
LORENZO
A friend? What friend? Your name, I pray you,
  friend?
MESSENGER   Stephano is my name, and I bring word
My mistress will, before the break of day,
Be here at Belmont. She doth stray about   30
By holy crosses, where she kneels and prays
For happy wedlock hours.
LORENZO   Who comes with her?
MESSENGER   None but a holy hermit and her maid.
I pray you, is my master yet returned?
LORENZO   He is not, nor we have not heard from him.   35
But go we in, I pray thee, Jessica,
And ceremoniously let us prepare
Some welcome for the mistress of the house.

Enter Lancelet *the* CLOWN.

CLOWN   Sola, sola! Wo ha ho! sola, sola!
LORENZO   Who calls?   40

CLOWN Sola! Did you see Master Lorenzo and
      Mistress Lorenza! Sola, sola!
LORENZO Leave holloaing, man! Here.
CLOWN Sola! Where, where?
45 LORENZO Here!
CLOWN Tell him there's a post come from my master,
      with his horn full of good news. My master will be
      here ere morning.   *Exit.*
LORENZO
      Sweet soul, let's in, and there expect their coming.
50   And yet, no matter. Why should we go in?
      My friend Stephano, signify, I pray you,
      Within the house, your mistress is at hand,
      And bring your music forth into the air.
                                      Exit Messenger.
      How sweet the moonlight sleeps upon this bank!
55   Here will we sit, and let the sounds of music
      Creep in our ears. Soft stillness and the night
      Become the touches of sweet harmony.
      Sit, Jessica. Look how the floor of heaven
      Is thick inlaid with patens of bright gold.
60   There's not the smallest orb which thou behold'st
      But in his motion like an angel sings,
      Still choiring to the young-eyed cherubins.
      Such harmony is in immortal souls,
      But, whilst this muddy vesture of decay
65   Doth grossly close it in, we cannot hear it.

                  Enter Musicians.

      Come, ho, and wake Diana with a hymn,
      With sweetest touches pierce your mistress' ear,
      And draw her home with music.   *[They play music.]*
JESSICA I am never merry when I hear sweet music.
70 LORENZO The reason is your spirits are attentive.
      For do but note a wild and wanton herd,
      Or race, of youthful and unhandled colts
      Fetching mad bounds, bellowing and neighing loud,
      Which is the hot condition of their blood;
75   If they but hear, perchance, a trumpet sound,
      Or any air of music touch their ears,
      You shall perceive them make a mutual stand,
      Their savage eyes turned to a modest gaze
      By the sweet power of music. Therefore the poet
80   Did feign that Orpheus drew trees, stones and floods,
      Since naught so stockish, hard and full of rage
      But music for the time doth change his nature.
      The man that hath no music in himself,
      Nor is not moved with concord of sweet sounds,
85   Is fit for treasons, stratagems and spoils;
      The motions of his spirit are dull as night
      And his affections dark as Erebus.
      Let no such man be trusted. Mark the music.

              Enter PORTIA *and* NERISSA.

PORTIA That light we see is burning in my hall.
90   How far that little candle throws his beams!
      So shines a good deed in a naughty world.

NERISSA
      When the moon shone we did not see the candle!
PORTIA So doth the greater glory dim the less.
      A substitute shines brightly as a king
      Until a king be by, and then his state   95
      Empties itself, as doth an inland brook
      Into the main of waters. Music, hark!
NERISSA It is your music, madam, of the house!
PORTIA Nothing is good, I see, without respect.
      Methinks it sounds much sweeter than by day!   100
NERISSA Silence bestows that virtue on it, madam.
PORTIA The crow doth sing as sweetly as the lark
      When neither is attended; and, I think,
      The nightingale, if she should sing by day
      When every goose is cackling, would be thought   105
      No better a musician than the wren.
      How many things by season seasoned are
      To their right praise and true perfection.
      Peace! How the moon sleeps with Endymion
      And would not be awaked.   *[Music ceases.]*
LORENZO   That is the voice,   110
      Or I am much deceived, of Portia.
PORTIA
      He knows me as the blind man knows the cuckoo:
      By the bad voice!
LORENZO   Dear lady, welcome home.
PORTIA
      We have been praying for our husbands' welfare,
      Which speed, we hope, the better for our words.   115
      Are they returned?
LORENZO   Madam, they are not yet,
      But there is come a messenger before
      To signify their coming!
PORTIA   Go in, Nerissa.
      Give order to my servants, that they take
      No note at all of our being absent hence,   120
      Nor you, Lorenzo; Jessica, nor you. *[A tucket sounds.]*
LORENZO Your husband is at hand, I hear his trumpet.
      We are no tell-tales, madam, fear you not.
PORTIA This night, methinks, is but the daylight sick;
      It looks a little paler. 'Tis a day   125
      Such as the day is when the sun is hid.

              Enter BASSANIO, ANTONIO,
              GRATIANO *and their Followers.*

BASSANIO We should hold day with the Antipodes,
      If you would walk in absence of the sun.
PORTIA Let me give light, but let me not be light;
      For a light wife doth make a heavy husband,   130
      And never be Bassanio so for me.
      But God sort all. You are welcome home, my lord.
BASSANIO
      I thank you, madam. Give welcome to my friend.
      This is the man, this is Antonio,
      To whom I am so infinitely bound.   135
PORTIA
      You should in all sense be much bound to him,

For, as I hear, he was much bound for you.
ANTONIO   No more than I am well acquitted of.
PORTIA   Sir, you are very welcome to our house.
140   It must appear in other ways than words:
Therefore I scant this breathing courtesy.
GRATIANO [*to Nerissa*]
By yonder moon, I swear you do me wrong!
In faith, I gave it to the judge's clerk.
Would he were gelt that had it, for my part,
145   Since you do take it, love, so much at heart.
PORTIA   A quarrel ho! Already! What's the matter?
GRATIANO   About a hoop of gold, a paltry ring
That she did give me, whose posy was
For all the world like cutler's poetry
150   Upon a knife: 'Love me and leave me not.'
NERISSA   What talk you of the posy or the value?
You swore to me when I did give it you
That you would wear it till your hour of death,
And that it should lie with you in your grave.
155   Though not for me, yet, for your vehement oaths,
You should have been respective and have kept it.
Gave it a judge's clerk! No, God's my judge,
The clerk will ne'er wear hair on's face that had it.
GRATIANO   He will, an if he live to be a man.
160   NERISSA   Ay, if a woman live to be a man.
GRATIANO   Now, by this hand, I gave it to a youth,
A kind of boy, a little scrubbed boy,
No higher than thyself, the judge's clerk,
A prating boy that begged it as a fee;
165   I could not, for my heart, deny it him.
PORTIA   You were to blame, I must be plain with you,
To part so slightly with your wife's first gift,
A thing stuck on with oaths upon your finger
And so riveted with faith unto your flesh.
170   I gave my love a ring and made him swear
Never to part with it, and here he stands.
I dare be sworn for him he would not leave it,
Nor pluck it from his finger, for the wealth
That the world masters. Now, in faith, Gratiano,
175   You give your wife too unkind a cause of grief.
An 'twere to me, I should be mad at it.
BASSANIO [*aside*]
Why, I were best to cut my left hand off
And swear I lost the ring defending it.
GRATIANO   My lord Bassanio gave his ring away
180   Unto the judge that begged it, and, indeed,
Deserved it too, and then the boy, his clerk,
That took some pains in writing, he begged mine,
And neither man nor master would take aught
But the two rings.
PORTIA   What ring gave you, my lord?
185   Not that, I hope, which you received of me.
BASSANIO   If I could add a lie unto a fault,
I would deny it: but you see my finger
[*holding up his hand*]
Hath not the ring upon it: it is gone.
PORTIA   Even so void is your false heart of truth.

By heaven, I will ne'er come in your bed   190
Until I see the ring.
NERISSA [*to Gratiano*]   Nor I in yours
Till I again see mine!
BASSANIO   Sweet Portia,
If you did know to whom I gave the ring,
If you did know for whom I gave the ring,
And would conceive for what I gave the ring,   195
And how unwillingly I left the ring,
When naught would be accepted but the ring,
You would abate the strength of your displeasure!
PORTIA   If you had known the virtue of the ring,
Or half her worthiness that gave the ring,   200
Or your own honour to contain the ring,
You would not then have parted with the ring.
What man is there so much unreasonable,
If you had pleased to have defended it
With any terms of zeal, wanted the modesty   205
To urge the thing held as a ceremony?
Nerissa teaches me what to believe.
I'll die for't, but some woman had the ring!
BASSANIO   No, by my honour, madam, by my soul,
No woman had it, but a civil doctor,   210
Which did refuse three thousand ducats of me
And begged the ring, the which I did deny him
And suffered him to go displeased away:
Even he that had held up the very life
Of my dear friend. What should I say, sweet lady?   215
I was enforced to send it after him,
I was beset with shame and courtesy,
My honour would not let ingratitude
So much besmear it. Pardon me, good lady,
For, by these blessed candles of the night,   220
Had you been there, I think you would have begged
The ring of me to give the worthy doctor.
PORTIA   Let not that doctor e'er come near my house!
Since he hath got the jewel that I loved
And that which you did swear to keep for me,   225
I will become as liberal as you;
I'll not deny him anything I have,
No, not my body, nor my husband's bed.
Know him I shall, I am well sure of it.
Lie not a night from home; watch me like Argus.   230
If you do not, if I be left alone,
Now, by mine honour, which is yet mine own,
I'll have that doctor for my bedfellow.
NERISSA   And I his clerk. Therefore be well advised
How you do leave me to mine own protection.   235
GRATIANO
Well, do you so; let not me take him then,
For if I do I'll mar the young clerk's pen.
ANTONIO   I am th'unhappy subject of these quarrels.
PORTIA
Sir, grieve not you. You are welcome notwithstanding.
BASSANIO   Portia, forgive me this enforced wrong,   240
And in the hearing of these many friends
I swear to thee, even by thine own fair eyes

975

Wherein I see myself –
PORTIA   Mark you but that!
In both my eyes he doubly sees himself,
245   In each eye one. Swear by your double self,
And there's an oath of credit!
BASSANIO   Nay, but hear me.
Pardon this fault, and, by my soul, I swear
I never more will break an oath with thee.
ANTONIO   I once did lend my body for his wealth,
250   Which, but for him that had your husband's ring,
Had quite miscarried. I dare be bound again:
My soul upon the forfeit, that your lord
Will never more break faith advisedly.
PORTIA   Then you shall be his surety. Give him this,
        [*giving Antonio the ring*]
255   And bid him keep it better than the other.
ANTONIO
Here, Lord Bassanio, swear to keep this ring.
BASSANIO   By heaven, it is the same I gave the doctor!
PORTIA   I had it of him. Pardon me, Bassanio,
For by this ring the doctor lay with me.
260   NERISSA   And pardon me, my gentle Gratiano,
For that same scrubbed boy, the doctor's clerk,
In lieu of this, [*showing Gratiano the ring*] last night
        did lie with me.
GRATIANO   Why, this is like the mending of highways
In summer where the ways are fair enough!
265   What, are we cuckolds ere we have deserved it?
PORTIA   Speak not so grossly. You are all amazed.
Here is a letter, read it at your leisure;
It comes from Padua, from Bellario.
There you shall find that Portia was the doctor,
270   Nerissa there, her clerk. Lorenzo here
Shall witness I set forth as soon as you
And even but now returned; I have not yet
Entered my house. Antonio, you are welcome,
And I have better news in store for you
275   Than you expect. Unseal this letter soon;
        [*giving Antonio a letter*]
There you shall find three of your argosies

Are richly come to harbour suddenly.
You shall not know by what strange accident
I chanced on this letter.
ANTONIO   I am dumb!
BASSANIO [*to Portia*]
Were you the doctor, and I knew you not?   280
GRATIANO [*to Nerissa*]
Were you the clerk that is to make me cuckold?
NERISSA   Ay, but the clerk that never means to do it,
Unless he live until he be a man.
BASSANIO [*to Portia*]
Sweet doctor, you shall be my bedfellow.
When I am absent, then lie with my wife!   285
ANTONIO
Sweet lady, you have given me life and living,
For here I read for certain that my ships
Are safely come to road.
PORTIA   How now, Lorenzo?
My clerk hath some good comforts too for you.
NERISSA   Ay, and I'll give them him without a fee.   290
There do I give to you and Jessica
        [*giving the document to Lorenzo*]
From the rich Jew, a special deed of gift,
After his death, of all he dies possessed of.
LORENZO   Fair ladies, you drop manna in the way
Of starved people.
PORTIA   It is almost morning;   295
And yet I am sure you are not satisfied
Of these events at full. Let us go in,
And charge us there upon inter'gatories,
And we will answer all things faithfully.
GRATIANO   Let it be so. The first inter'gatory   300
That my Nerissa shall be sworn on is:
Whether till the next night she had rather stay,
Or go to bed now, being two hours to day.
But, were the day come, I should wish it dark
Till I were couching with the doctor's clerk!   305
Well, while I live, I'll fear no other thing
So sore as keeping safe Nerissa's ring.   *Exeunt.*

The Merry Wives of Windsor

The Merry Wives of Windsor, despite the fact that it uses some characters from the King Henry IV plays which are set in the early fifteenth century, seems to come as close as Shakespeare ever gets to depicting his own contemporary society. The tavern scenes in the histories are moving in this direction, but in Merry Wives the political context has disappeared altogether and the result feels more like the 'city comedies' written by Shakespeare's contemporaries such as Ben Jonson and Thomas Middleton than like his own usual style of romantic comedy with its more remote settings and upper-class characters. Shakespeare's only comedy set in England (if we exclude Cymbeline with its setting in Ancient Britain) is very much a bourgeois play, with 'Sir John' having to adapt to his provincial environment. The main theme is still courtship, and the plot has many precedents in folklore, but the tone is very different from that of Shakespeare's recent comedies, Love's Labour's Lost, A Midsummer Night's Dream and The Merchant of Venice, or the possibly contemporaneous Much Ado About Nothing. Although jokes about cuckolds are a standard element in many plays, it is unusual to find the jealous husband treated as the figure of fun he is here: in Othello, The Winter's Tale and Cymbeline Shakespeare treats him very differently. Merry Wives may date from 1597; if, however, it was written about 1599, as the most recent Arden editor, Giorgio Melchiori, argues, Shakespeare would have had a model in the comic Thorello in Jonson's Every Man in His Humour (1598), a play Shakespeare himself acted in.

An early eighteenth-century story claims that Queen Elizabeth encouraged the composition of the play because she wanted to see 'Falstaff in love'; modern scholars still relate this story while questioning its veracity. Certainly Merry Wives seems to be an Elizabethan play, written after the King Henry IV plays (1596–8) and having some direct connection with the installation of George Carey, the Lord Chamberlain and patron of Shakespeare's company, as a Knight of the Garter in Windsor in 1597:

the Garter ceremonies are referred to quite specifically in Mistress Quickly's speech at 5.5.54–75. If Merry Wives is to be related to the chronology of the histories, Falstaff's penury and the absence of Prince Hal might suggest the period of his reported disgrace between King Henry IV, Part 2 and his reported death in King Henry V. Its tone is of course much lighter: despite Falstaff's attempts to win his way into the Wives' favours and their husbands' fortunes, we remain confident of the basic affability and good sense of most of the people of Windsor. Shakespeare does not seem to be aiming for strict consistency with the history plays: it is difficult, for example, to reconcile the Mistress Quickly here with the character in the Henry IV and Henry V plays.

The earliest published text of this play, the First Quarto of 1602 (Q1), is only about half the length of the version in the 1623 First Folio (F) (where it is the third of the comedies), and has generally been dismissed as a 'bad' quarto, or, less judgementally, as a reported text put together from memory of an acting version of the play. The appearance of five further quartos during the seventeenth century (one based on Q1, the others on F) attests to the popularity of the play. There are records of revivals in 1604, 1613, 1638, 1661 and 1667. Merry Wives continued to be popular in the eighteenth and nineteenth centuries, although it was often abridged in performance. It has been used as the basis for the libretti of at least nine operas, including Giuseppe Verdi's Falstaff (1893) and Ralph Vaughan Williams's Sir John in Love (1929). Twentieth-century productions often revelled in the particularity of the Windsor setting which allowed them to celebrate a 'merry England' not otherwise notably associated with Shakespeare; the fact that the play was chosen for presentation at the Festival of Britain in 1951 testifies to this tendency.

The Arden text is based on the 1623 First Folio.

AT THE GARTER INN

HOST	*of the Garter Inn*
Sir John FALSTAFF	*a Crown pensioner, lodging at the Inn*
ROBIN	*his page-boy*
'Corporal' BARDOLPH	*Falstaff's attendant, later a drawer in the Inn*
'Ancient' PISTOL	
Corporal NIM	*Falstaff's other attendants*
Robert SHALLOW	*a justice of the peace*
Abraham SLENDER	*a young gentleman, his relative*
Peter SIMPLE	*Slender's servant*
FENTON	*a gentleman, former companion of the Prince of Wales*

TOWNSPEOPLE

George PAGE	*a citizen*
MISTRESS Margaret (Meg) PAGE	*his wife*
ANNE (Nan) Page	*their daughter*
WILLIAM Page	*a schoolboy, their son*
Frank FORD	*another citizen*
MISTRESS Alice FORD	*his wife*
JOHN	
ROBERT	*servants in Ford's household*
Sir Hugh EVANS	*a Welsh parson*
Doctor CAIUS	*a French physician*
Mistress QUICKLY	*his housekeeper*
John RUGBY	*his servant*

Children, *disguised as Fairies, instructed by Parson Evans*

1.1   *Enter* Justice SHALLOW, SLENDER *and*
Sir Hugh EVANS.

SHALLOW   Sir Hugh, persuade me not: I will make a
Star Chamber matter of it. If he were twenty Sir John
Falstaffs, he shall not abuse Robert Shallow esquire.

SLENDER   In the County of Gloucester, Justice of Peace
5   and Coram.

SHALLOW   Ay, cousin Slender, and Cust-a-lorum.

SLENDER   Ay, and Rato lorum too; and a gentleman
born, master parson, who writes himself *Armigero*, in
any bill, warrant, quittance, or obligation – *Armigero*.

10   SHALLOW   Ay, that I do, and have done any time these
three hundred years.

SLENDER   All his successors – gone before him – hath
done't; and all his ancestors – that come after him –
may. They may give the dozen white luces in their
15   coat.

SHALLOW   It is an old coat.

EVANS   The dozen white louses do become an old coat
well. It agrees well passant. It is a familiar beast to
man, and signifies love.

20   SHALLOW   The luce is the fresh fish – the salt fish is an
old coat.

SLENDER   I may quarter, coz.

SHALLOW   You may, by marrying.

EVANS   It is marring indeed, if he quarter it.

25   SHALLOW   Not a whit.

EVANS   Yes, py'r lady: if he has a quarter of your coat,
there is but three skirts for yourself, in my simple
conjectures. But that is all one: if Sir John Falstaff have
committed disparagements unto you, I am of the
30   Church, and will be glad to do my benevolence, to
make atonements and comprimises between you.

SHALLOW   The Council shall hear it, it is a riot.

EVANS   It is not meet the Council hear a riot. There is
no fear of Got in a riot. The Council, look you, shall
35   desire to hear the fear of Got, and not to hear a riot.
Take your vizaments in that.

SHALLOW   Ha, o'my life, if I were young again, the
sword should end it.

EVANS   It is petter that friends is the sword, and end it;
40   and there is also another device in my prain, which
peradventure prings goot discretions with it. There is
Anne Page, which is daughter to Master George Page
– which is pretty virginity.

SLENDER   Mistress Anne Page? She has brown hair, and
45   speaks small like a woman?

EVANS   It is that ferry person for all the 'orld, as just as
you will desire, and seven hundred pounds of moneys,
and gold, and silver, is her grandsire upon his
death's-bed – Got deliver to a joyful resurrections! –
50   give, when she is able to overtake seventeen years old.
It were a goot motion, if we leave our pribbles and
prabbles, and desire a marriage between Master
Abraham and Mistress Anne Page.

SLENDER   Did her grandsire leave her seven hundred
55   pound?

EVANS   Ay, and her father is make her a petter penny.

SHALLOW   I know the young gentlewoman, she has
good gifts.

EVANS   Seven hundred pounds, and possibilities, is goot
gifts.   60

SHALLOW   Well, let us see honest Master Page. Is
Falstaff there?

EVANS   Shall I tell you a lie? I do despise a liar, as I do
despise one that is false, or as I despise one that is not
true: the knight Sir John is there, and I beseech you be   65
ruled by your well-willers. I will peat the door for
Master Page. [*Knocks.*] What ho! Got pless your house
here!

PAGE [*within*]   Who's there?

Enter PAGE.

EVANS   Here is Got's plessing and your friend, and   70
Justice Shallow, and here young Master Slender, that
peradventures shall tell you another tale, if matters
grow to your likings.

PAGE   I am glad to see your worships well. I thank you
for my venison, Master Shallow.   75

SHALLOW   Master Page, I am glad to see you, much
good do it your good heart. I wished your venison
better, it was ill killed. How doth good Mistress Page?
And I thank you always with my heart, la – with my
heart.   80

PAGE   Sir, I thank you.

SHALLOW   Sir, I thank you; by yea and no I do.

PAGE   I am glad to see you, good Master Slender.

SLENDER   How does your fallow greyhound, sir? I
heard say he was outrun on Cotsall.   85

PAGE   It could not be judged, sir.

SLENDER   You'll not confess, you'll not confess!

SHALLOW   That he will not 'tis your fault, 'tis your
fault. 'Tis a good dog.

PAGE   A cur, sir.   90

SHALLOW   Sir, he's a good dog, and a fair dog, can there
be more said? He is good, and fair. – Is Sir John Falstaff
here?

PAGE   Sir, he is within; and I would I could do a good
office between you.   95

EVANS   It is spoke as a Christians ought to speak.

SHALLOW   He hath wronged me, Master Page.

PAGE   Sir, he doth in some sort confess it.

SHALLOW   If it be confessed, it is not redressed. Is not
that so, Master Page? He hath wronged me, indeed he   100
hath, at a word he hath. Believe me: Robert Shallow
esquire saith he is wronged.

PAGE   Here comes Sir John.

Enter Sir John FALSTAFF, PISTOL,
BARDOLPH *and* NIM.

FALSTAFF   Now, Master Shallow, you'll complain of me
to the King?   105

SHALLOW   Knight, you have beaten my men, killed my
deer and broke open my lodge.

FALSTAFF But not kissed your keeper's daughter!

SHALLOW Tut, a pin! This shall be answered.

110 FALSTAFF I will answer it straight: I have done all this.
That is now answered.

SHALLOW The Council shall know this.

FALSTAFF 'Twere better for you if it were known in
counsel: you'll be laughed at.

115 EVANS *Pauca verba*, Sir John, good worts.

FALSTAFF Good worts? Good cabbage! – Slender, I
broke your head: what matter have you against me?

SLENDER Marry, sir, I have matter in my head against
you, and against your cony-catching rascals, Bardolph,
120 Nim and Pistol. They carried me to the tavern and
made me drunk, and afterward picked my pocket.

BARDOLPH You Banbury cheese!

SLENDER Ay, it is no matter.

PISTOL How now, Mephostophilus?

125 SLENDER Ay, it is no matter.

NIM Slice, I say! *Pauca, pauca*, slice, that's my humour.

SLENDER Where's Simple, my man? Can you tell,
cousin?

EVANS Peace, I pray you! Now let us understand: there
130 is three umpires in this matter, as I understand. That
is, Master Page, *fidelicet* Master Page; and there is
myself, *fidelicet* myself; and the three party is, lastly
and finally, mine host of the Garter.

PAGE We three to hear it, and end it between them.

135 EVANS Ferry goot, I will make a prief of it in my
notebook, and we will afterwards 'ork upon the cause
with as great discreetly as we can.

FALSTAFF Pistol!

PISTOL He hears with ears.

140 EVANS The tevil and his tam, what phrase is this? He
hears with ears! Why, it is affectations!

FALSTAFF Pistol, did you pick Master Slender's purse?

SLENDER Ay, by these gloves did he, or I would I might
never come in mine own great chamber again else! Of
145 seven groats in mill-sixpences, and two Edward
shovel-boards, that cost me two shilling and two pence
a-piece of Ed miller – by these gloves!

FALSTAFF Is this true, Pistol?

EVANS No, it is false, if it is a pick-purse.

150 PISTOL Ha, thou mountain-foreigner! –
Sir John and master mine,
I combat challenge of this latten bilbo. –
Word of denial in thy *labras* here!
Word of denial! Froth and scum, thou liest!

155 SLENDER [*Points at Nim.*] By these gloves, then 'twas
he.

NIM Be advised, sir, and pass good humours. I will say
'marry trap with you', if you run the nuthook's humour
on me – that is the very note of it.

160 SLENDER By this hat, then he in the red face had it. For,
though I cannot remember what I did when you made
me drunk, yet I am not altogether an ass.

FALSTAFF What say you, Scarlet and John?

BARDOLPH Why, sir, for my part, I say the gentleman
had drunk himself out of his five sentences 165

EVANS It is 'his five senses'. Fie, what the ignorance is!

BARDOLPH And being fap, sir, was, as they say,
cashiered; and so conclusions passed the careers.

SLENDER Ay, you spake in Latin then too; but 'tis no
matter. I'll ne'er be drunk whilst I live again, but in 170
honest, civil, godly company, for this trick. If I be
drunk, I'll be drunk with those that have the fear of
God, and not with drunken knaves.

EVANS So Got 'udge me, that is a virtuous mind.

FALSTAFF You hear all these matters denied, gentlemen; 175
you hear it.

Enter MISTRESS FORD, MISTRESS PAGE *and her daughter*
ANNE, *with wine.*

PAGE Nay, daughter, carry the wine in, we'll drink
within.   *Exit Anne Page.*

SLENDER O heaven, this is Mistress Anne Page.

PAGE How now, Mistress Ford? 180

FALSTAFF Mistress Ford, by my troth you are very well
met. By your leave, good mistress. [*Kisses her.*]

PAGE Wife, bid these gentlemen welcome. – Come, we
have a hot venison pasty to dinner. Come, gentlemen,
I hope we shall drink down all unkindness. 185

                              Exeunt all except Slender.

SLENDER I had rather than forty shillings I had my
book of *Songs and Sonnets* here.

Enter SIMPLE.

How now, Simple, where have you been? I must wait
on myself, must I? You have not the *Book of Riddles*
about you, have you? 190

SIMPLE *Book of Riddles*? Why, did you not lend it to
Alice Shortcake upon Allhallowmas last, a fortnight
afore Michaelmas?

Enter SHALLOW *and* EVANS.

SHALLOW Come, coz, come, coz, we stay for you. A
word with you, coz. Marry, this, coz: there is, as 'twere, 195
a tender, a kind of tender, made afar off by Sir Hugh
here. Do you understand me?

SLENDER Ay, sir, you shall find me reasonable. If it be
so, I shall do that that is reason.

SHALLOW Nay, but understand me. 200

SLENDER So I do, sir.

EVANS Give ear to his motions. Master Slender, I will
description the matter to you, if you be capacity of it.

SLENDER Nay, I will do as my cousin Shallow says. I
pray you pardon me, he's a Justice of Peace in his 205
country, simple though I stand here.

EVANS But that is not the question. The question is
concerning your marriage.

SHALLOW Ay, there's the point, sir.

EVANS Marry, is it, the very point of it – to Mistress 210
Anne Page.

SLENDER   Why, if it be so, I will marry her upon any reasonable demands.

EVANS   But can you affection the 'oman? Let us command to know that of your mouth, or of your lips – for diverse philosophers hold that the lips is parcel of the mouth. Therefore precisely, can you carry your good will to the maid?

SHALLOW   Cousin Abraham Slender, can you love her?

SLENDER   I hope, sir, I will do as it shall become one that would do reason.

EVANS   Nay, Got's lords, and his ladies, you must speak possitable if you can carry-her your desires towards her.

SHALLOW   That you must: will you, upon good dowry, marry her?

SLENDER   I will do a greater thing than that, upon your request, cousin, in any reason.

SHALLOW   Nay, conceive me, conceive me, sweet coz. What I do is to pleasure you, coz. Can you love the maid?

SLENDER   I will marry her, sir, at your request. But if there be no great love in the beginning, yet heaven may decrease it upon better acquaintance, when we are married, and have more occasion to know one another. I hope upon familiarity will grow more contempt. But if you say marry her, I will marry her – that I am freely dissolved, and dissolutely.

EVANS   It is a fery discretion answer. Save the faul' is in the 'ord 'dissolutely' – the 'ort is, according to our meaning, 'resolutely' – his meaning is good.

SHALLOW   Ay, I think my cousin meant well.

SLENDER   Ay, or else I would I might be hanged, la!

Enter ANNE *Page.*

SHALLOW   Here comes fair Mistress Anne. – Would I were young for your sake, Mistress Anne.

ANNE   The dinner is on the table, my father desires your worships' company.

SHALLOW   I will wait on him, fair Mistress Anne.

EVANS   'Od's plessed will! I will not be absence at the grace.   *Exeunt Shallow and Evans.*

ANNE   Will't please your worship to come in, sir?

SLENDER   No, I thank you, forsooth, heartily; I am very well.

ANNE   The dinner attends you, sir.

SLENDER   I am not a-hungry, I thank you, forsooth. [*to Simple*] Go, sirrah, for all you are my man, go wait upon my cousin Shallow.   *Exit Simple.*
A justice of peace sometime may be beholding to his friend for a man. I keep but three men and a boy yet, till my mother be dead. But what though, yet I live like a poor gentleman born.

ANNE   I may not go in without your worship: they will not sit till you come.

SLENDER   I'faith, I'll eat nothing. I thank you as much as though I did.

ANNE   I pray you, sir, walk in.

SLENDER   I had rather walk here, I thank you. I bruised my shin th'other day with playing at sword and dagger with a master of fence – three venues for a dish of stewed prunes – and, by my troth, I cannot abide the smell of hot meat since. – Why do your dogs bark so? Be there bears i'the town?

ANNE   I think there are, sir; I heard them talked of.

SLENDER   I love the sport well, but I shall as soon quarrel at it, as any man in England. You are afraid if you see the bear loose, are you not?

ANNE   Ay indeed, sir.

SLENDER   That's meat and drink to me now. I have seen Sackerson loose twenty times, and have taken him by the chain; but, I warrant you, the women have so cried and shrieked at it that it passed. But women, indeed, cannot abide 'em: they are very ill-favoured rough things.

Enter PAGE.

PAGE   Come, gentle Master Slender, come: we stay for you.

SLENDER   I'll eat nothing, I thank you, sir.

PAGE   By cock and pie, you shall not choose, sir. Come, come.

SLENDER   Nay, pray you, lead the way.

PAGE   Come on, sir.

SLENDER   Mistress Anne, yourself shall go first.

ANNE   Not I, sir; pray you, keep on.

SLENDER   Truly, I will not go first; truly – la! I will not do you that wrong.

ANNE   I pray you, sir.

SLENDER   I'll rather be unmannerly than troublesome. You do yourself wrong, indeed – la!

Exeunt, Slender leading.

1.2   *Enter* Sir Hugh EVANS *and* SIMPLE, *from dinner.*

EVANS   Go your ways, and ask of Doctor Caius' house, which is the way. And there dwells one Mistress Quickly, which is in the manner of his nurse, or his dry nurse, or his cook, or his laundry, his washer and his wringer.

SIMPLE   Well, sir.

EVANS   Nay, it is petter yet: give her this letter. For it is a 'oman that altogether's acquaintance with Mistress Anne Page, and the letter is to desire, and require her, to solicit your master's desires to Mistress Anne Page. I pray you be gone; I will make an end of my dinner, there's pippins and cheese to come.   *Exeunt.*

1.3   *Enter* FALSTAFF, HOST, BARDOLPH, NIM, PISTOL *and* ROBIN.

FALSTAFF   Mine host of the Garter –

HOST   What says my bully rook? Speak scholarly and wisely.

FALSTAFF   Truly, mine host, I must turn away some of my followers.

HOST   Discard, bully Hercules, cashier! Let them wag; trot, trot!

FALSTAFF   I sit at ten pounds a week.

HOST   Thou'rt an emperor – Caesar, Kaiser and Vizier.
10 I will entertain Bardolph: he shall draw, he shall tap. Said I well, bully Hector?

FALSTAFF   Do so, good mine host.

HOST   I have spoke, let him follow. – Let me see thee froth and lime. I am at a word, follow.   *Exit.*

15 FALSTAFF   Bardolph, follow him. A tapster is a good trade: an old cloak makes a new jerkin; a withered servingman, a fresh tapster. Go, adieu.

BARDOLPH   It is a life that I have desired. I will thrive.   *Exit.*

PISTOL   O base Hungarian wight, wilt thou the spigot
20 wield?

NIM   He was gotten in drink. Is not the humour conceited?

FALSTAFF   I am glad I am so acquit of this tinderbox. His thefts were too open: his filching was like an
25 unskilful singer, he kept not time.

NIM   The good humour is to steal at a minute's rest.

PISTOL   'Convey', the wise it call. 'Steal'? Foh! A fico for the phrase!

FALSTAFF   Well, sirs, I am almost out at heels.

30 PISTOL   Why then, let kibes ensue.

FALSTAFF   There is no remedy, I must cony-catch, I must shift.

PISTOL   Young ravens must have food.

FALSTAFF   Which of you know Ford of this town?

35 PISTOL   I ken the wight, he is of substance good.

FALSTAFF   My honest lads, I will tell you what I am about.

PISTOL   Two yards, and more.

FALSTAFF   No quips now, Pistol. – Indeed I am in the
40 waist two yards about, but I am now about no waste: I am about thrift. Briefly, I do mean to make love to Ford's wife. I spy entertainment in her: she discourses, she carves, she gives the leer of invitation. I can construe the action of her familiar style, and the
45 hardest voice of her behaviour – to be Englished rightly – is: 'I am Sir John Falstaff's'.

PISTOL   He hath studied her well, and translated her will – out of honesty into English.

NIM   The anchor is deep: will that humour pass?

50 FALSTAFF   Now, the report goes she has all the rule of her husband's purse: he hath a legion of angels.

PISTOL   As many devils attend her! And 'To her, boy!' say I.

NIM   The humour rises: it is good. Humour me the
55 angels.

FALSTAFF   I have writ me here a letter to her; and here another to Page's wife, who even now gave me good eyes too, examined my parts with most judicious oeillades. Sometimes the beam of her view gilded my
60 foot, sometimes my portly belly.

PISTOL   Then did the sun on dunghill shine.

NIM   I thank thee for that humour.

FALSTAFF   O, she did so course o'er my exteriors, with such a greedy intention, that the appetite of her eye did seem to scorch me up like a burning glass. 65 Here's another letter to her. She bears the purse too: she is a region in Guiana, all gold and bounty. I will be cheaters to them both, and they shall be exchequers to me. They shall be my East and West Indies, and I will trade to them both. [*to Nim*] Go, bear 70 thou this letter to Mistress Page; [*to Pistol*] and thou this to Mistress Ford. – We will thrive, lads, we will thrive.

PISTOL   Shall I Sir Pandarus of Troy become, And by my side wear steel? Then Lucifer take all! 75

NIM   I will run no base humour. Here, take the humour-letter – I will keep the 'haviour of reputation.

FALSTAFF [*to Robin*]
Hold, sirrah, bear you these letters titely, Sail like my pinnace to these golden shores. – Rogues, hence, avaunt! Vanish like hailstones, go! 80 Trudge, plod away o'th' hoof, seek shelter, pack! Falstaff will learn the humour of this age: French thrift, you rogues – myself and skirted page!
                    Exit with Robin.

PISTOL
Let vultures gripe thy guts! For gourd and fullam holds, And high and low beguiles the rich and poor. 85 Tester I'll have in pouch when thou shalt lack, Base Phrygian Turk!

NIM   I have operations In my head, which be humours of revenge.

PISTOL   Wilt thou revenge?

NIM   By welkin and her stars!

PISTOL   With wit, or steel?

NIM   With both the humours, I. 90 I will discuss the humour of this love to Ford.

PISTOL   And I to Page shall eke unfold How Falstaff, varlet vile, His dove will prove, his gold will hold, And his soft couch defile. 95

NIM   My humour shall not cool: I will incense Ford to deal with poison, I will possess him with yellowness, for this revolt of mine is dangerous. That is my true humour.

PISTOL   Thou art the Mars of malcontents. I second 100 thee – troop on.   *Exeunt.*

1.4   *Enter* Mistress QUICKLY *and* SIMPLE.

QUICKLY   What, John Rugby!

Enter RUGBY.

I pray thee go to the casement, and see if you can see my master, Master Doctor Caius, coming. If he do, i'faith, and find anybody in the house, here will be an old abusing of God's patience and the King's English. 5

RUGBY   I'll go watch.

QUICKLY   Go; and we'll have a posset for't soon at night, in faith, at the latter end of a sea-coal fire.

Exit Rugby.

An honest, willing, kind fellow, as ever servant shall come in house withal; and I warrant you, no tell-tale, nor no breed-bate. His worst fault is that he is given to prayer; he is something peevish that way, but nobody but has his fault. But let that pass. – Peter Simple, you say your name is?

SIMPLE   Ay, for fault of a better.

QUICKLY   And Master Slender's your master?

SIMPLE   Ay, forsooth.

QUICKLY   Does he not wear a great round beard, like a glover's paring-knife?

SIMPLE   No, forsooth, he hath but a little wee face, with a little yellow beard: a Cain-coloured beard.

QUICKLY   A softly-sprighted man, is he not?

SIMPLE   Ay, forsooth. But he is as tall a man of his hands, as any is between this and his head. He hath fought with a warrener.

QUICKLY   How, say you? – O, I should remember him: does he not hold up his head, as it were, and strut in his gait?

SIMPLE   Yes, indeed, does he.

QUICKLY   Well, heaven send Anne Page no worse fortune. Tell Master Parson Evans I will do what I can for your master. Anne is a good girl, and I wish –

Enter RUGBY.

RUGBY   Out, alas! Here comes my master!   *Exit.*

QUICKLY   We shall all be shent. Run in here, good young man, go into this closet – he will not stay long. [*Simple steps into the closet.*] What, John Rugby! John! What, John, I say! Go, John, go inquire for my master. I doubt he be not well, that he comes not home. [*Sings.*]   And down, down, adown-a (*etc.*)

Enter Doctor CAIUS.

CAIUS   Vat is you sing? I do not like dese toys. Pray you go and vetch me in my closet *une boîtine verte* – a box, a green-a-box. Do intend vat I speak? A green-a-box.

QUICKLY   Ay, forsooth, I'll fetch it you. – [*aside*] I am glad he went not in himself: if he had found the young man he would have been horn-mad.

CAIUS   *Fe, fe, fe, fe, ma foi, il fait fort chaud. Je m'en vais voir à la cour la grande affaire.*

QUICKLY   Is it this, sir?

CAIUS   *Oui, mette-le au mon* pocket. *Dépêche* quickly. Vere is dat knave Rugby?

QUICKLY   What, John Rugby! John!

Enter RUGBY.

RUGBY   Here, sir.

CAIUS   You are John Rugby, and you are Jack Rugby. Come take-a your rapier, and come after my heel to the court.

RUGBY   'Tis ready, sir, here in the porch.

CAIUS   By my trot, I tarry too long. 'Od's me, *qu'ai-je oublié*! Dere is some simples in my closet dat I will not for the varld I shall leave behind.

QUICKLY   Ay me, he'll find the young man there, and be mad!

CAIUS [*Pulls Simple out.*]   O *diable, diable*, vat is in my closet? Villainy, *larron*! – Rugby, my rapier!

QUICKLY   Good master, be content.

CAIUS   Wherefore shall I be content-a?

QUICKLY   The young man is an honest man.

CAIUS   What shall de honest man do in my closet? Dere is no honest man dat shall come in my closet.

QUICKLY   I beseech you, be not so phlegmatic, hear the truth of it. He came of an errand to me, from Parson Hugh.

CAIUS   Vell?

SIMPLE   Ay, forsooth, to desire her to –

QUICKLY   Peace, I pray you.

CAIUS   Peace-a your tongue! [*to Simple*] Speak-a your tale.

SIMPLE   To desire this honest gentlewoman, your maid, to speak a good word to Mistress Anne Page for my master in the way of marriage.

QUICKLY   This is all indeed, la! But I'll ne'er put my finger in the fire, an't need not.

CAIUS   Sir Hugh send-a you? – Rugby, *baille* me some paper. – Tarry you a little-a-while. [*Writes.*]

QUICKLY [*aside to Simple*]   I am glad he is so quiet. If he had been throughly moved, you should have heard him so loud and so melancholy. But notwithstanding, man, I'll do you your master what good I can; and the very yea and the no is, the French doctor my master – I may call him my master, look you, for I keep his house, and I wash, wring, brew, bake, scour, dress meat and drink, make the beds and do all myself –

SIMPLE [*aside to Mistress Quickly*]   'Tis a great charge to come under one body's hand.

QUICKLY [*aside to Simple*]   Are you avised o'that? You shall find it a great charge, and to be up early and down late; but notwithstanding – to tell you in your ear, I would have no words of it – my master himself is in love with Mistress Anne Page; but notwithstanding that, I know Anne's mind – that's neither here nor there.

CAIUS   You, Jack'nape: give-a this letter to Sir Hugh. By gar, it is a shallenge: I will cut his troat in de park, and I will teach a scurvy jackanape priest to meddle or make. – You may be gone, it is not good you tarry here. – By gar, I will cut all his two stones. By gar, he shall not have a stone to throw at his dog.   *Exit Simple.*

QUICKLY   Alas, he speaks but for his friend.

CAIUS   It is no matter-a ver dat. Do not you tell-a-me dat I shall have Anne Page for myself? By gar, I vill kill de Jack-priest; and I have appointed mine host of de Jarteer to measure our weapon. By gar, I will myself have Anne Page.

QUICKLY   Sir, the maid loves you, and all shall be well.
We must give folks leave to prate, what the good-year!

CAIUS   Rugby, come to the court with me. [*to Mistress
Quickly*] By gar, if I have not Anne Page, I shall turn
your head out of my door. – Follow my heels, Rugby.
                                        Exit with Rugby.

QUICKLY   You shall have An – fool's head of your own.
No, I know Anne's mind for that. Never a woman in
Windsor knows more of Anne's mind than I do, nor
can do more than I do with her, I thank heaven.

FENTON [*within*]   Who's within there, ho?

QUICKLY   Who's there, I trow? Come near the house, I
pray you.

Enter FENTON.

FENTON   How now, good woman, how dost thou?

QUICKLY   The better that it pleases your good worship
to ask.

FENTON   What news? How does pretty Mistress Anne?

QUICKLY   In truth, sir, and she is pretty, and honest,
and gentle, and one that is your friend – I can tell you
that by the way, I praise heaven for it.

FENTON   Shall I do any good, thinkst thou? Shall I not
lose my suit?

QUICKLY   Troth, sir, all is in His hands above. But
notwithstanding, Master Fenton, I'll be sworn on a
book she loves you. Have not your worship a wart
above your eye?

FENTON   Yes, marry, have I; what of that?

QUICKLY   Well, thereby hangs a tale. Good faith, it is
such another Nan – but, I detest, an honest maid as
ever broke bread. We had an hour's talk of that wart. I
shall never laugh but in that maid's company. But,
indeed, she is given too much to allicholy and musing.
But for you – well – go to –

FENTON   Well, I shall see her today. Hold, there's
money for thee: let me have thy voice in my behalf. If
thou seest her before me, commend me –

QUICKLY   Will I? I'faith, that we will! And I will tell
your worship more of the wart the next time we have
confidence, and of other wooers.

FENTON   Well, farewell, I am in great haste now.

QUICKLY   Farewell to your worship.   *Exit Fenton.*
Truly an honest gentleman – but Anne loves him not.
For I know Anne's mind as well as another does. – Out
upon't, what have I forgot?   *Exit.*

2.1   *Enter* MISTRESS PAGE *reading of a letter.*

MISTRESS PAGE   What, have I scaped love-letters in the
holiday-time of my beauty, and am I now a subject for
them? Let me see:
[*Reads.*] *Ask me no reason why I love you, for, though
Love use Reason for his precisian, he admits him not for
his counsellor. You are not young, no more am I: go to,
then, there's sympathy; you are merry, so am I: ha, ha,
then there's more sympathy; you love sack, and so do I:*

*would you desire better sympathy? Let it suffice thee,
Mistress Page, at the least if the love of soldier can suffice,
that I love thee. I will not say 'pity me' – 'tis not a soldier-
like phrase – but I say 'love me'.
By me, thine own true knight, by day or night,
Or any kind of light, with all his might,
For thee to fight. John Falstaff.*

What a Herod of Jewry is this? O wicked, wicked world!
One that is well-nigh worn to pieces with age, to show
himself a young gallant? What an unweighed behaviour
hath this Flemish drunkard picked – with the devil's
name! – out of my conversation, that he dares in this
manner assay me? Why, he hath not been thrice in my
company! What should I say to him? I was then frugal
of my mirth – heaven forgive me! – Why, I'll exhibit a
bill in the parliament for the putting down of men.
How shall I be revenged on him? For revenged I will
be, as sure as his guts are made of puddings.

Enter MISTRESS FORD.

MISTRESS FORD   Mistress Page, trust me, I was going to
your house.

MISTRESS PAGE   And trust me, I was coming to you.
You look very ill.

MISTRESS FORD   Nay, I'll ne'er believe that. I have to
show to the contrary.

MISTRESS PAGE   'Faith, but you do, in my mind.

MISTRESS FORD   Well, I do, then. Yet I say I could show
you to the contrary. O, Mistress Page, give me some
counsel!

MISTRESS PAGE   What's the matter, woman?

MISTRESS FORD   O, woman, if it were not for one
trifling respect, I could come to such honour!

MISTRESS PAGE   Hang the trifle, woman, take the
honour! What is it? Dispense with trifles: what is it?

MISTRESS FORD   If I would but go to hell for an eternal
moment or so, I could be knighted.

MISTRESS PAGE   What? Thou liest! Sir Alice Ford?
These knights will hack, and so thou shouldst not alter
the article of thy gentry.

MISTRESS FORD   We burn daylight. Here, read, read:
perceive how I might be knighted. I shall think the
worse of fat men as long as I have an eye to make
difference of men's liking. And yet he would not swear,
praised women's modesty, and gave such orderly and
well-behaved reproof to all uncomeliness, that I would
have sworn his disposition would have gone to the
truth of his words. But they do no more adhere and
keep place together than the hundred psalms to the
tune of 'Greensleeves'. What tempest, I trow, threw
this whale, with so many tuns of oil in his belly, ashore
at Windsor? How shall I be revenged on him? I think
the best way were to entertain him with hope, till the
wicked fire of lust have melted him in his own grease.
Did you ever hear the like?

MISTRESS PAGE   Letter for letter, but that the name of
Page and Ford differs! To thy great comfort in this

mystery of ill opinions, here's the twin brother of thy letter. But let thine inherit first, for I protest mine never shall. I warrant he hath a thousand of these letters, writ with blank space for different names – sure, more, and these are of the second edition. He will print them, out of doubt; for he cares not what he puts into the press, when he would put us two. I had rather be a giantess, and lie under Mount Pelion. Well, I will find you twenty lascivious turtles ere one chaste man.

MISTRESS FORD Why, this is the very same – the very hand, the very words! What doth he think of us?

MISTRESS PAGE Nay, I know not. It makes me almost ready to wrangle with mine own honesty. I'll entertain myself like one that I am not acquainted withal. For, sure, unless he know some strain in me that I know not myself, he would never have boarded me in this fury.

MISTRESS FORD Boarding, call you it? I'll be sure to keep him above deck.

MISTRESS PAGE So will I. If he come under my hatches, I'll never to sea again. Let's be revenged on him. Let's appoint him a meeting, give him a show of comfort in his suit, and lead him on with a fine-baited delay, till he hath pawned his horses to mine host of the Garter.

MISTRESS FORD Nay, I will consent to act any villainy against him, that may not sully the chariness of our honesty. O, that my husband saw this letter! It would give eternal food to his jealousy.

Enter FORD *with* PISTOL *and* PAGE *with* NIM.

MISTRESS PAGE Why, look where he comes; and my good man too – he's as far from jealousy as I am from giving him cause, and that, I hope, is an unmeasurable distance.

MISTRESS FORD You are the happier woman.

MISTRESS PAGE Let's consult together against this greasy knight. Come hither. *They withdraw.*

FORD Well, I hope it be not so.

PISTOL Hope is a curtal dog in some affairs.
Sir John affects thy wife.

FORD Why, sir, my wife is not young.

PISTOL He woos both high and low, both rich and poor,
Both young and old, one with another, Ford.
He loves the gallimaufry, Ford: perpend.

FORD Love my wife?

PISTOL With liver burning hot.
Prevent, or go thou like Sir Actaeon he,
With Ringwood at thy heels.
O, odious is the name!

FORD What name, sir?

PISTOL The horn, I say. Farewell.
Take heed, have open eye, for thieves do foot by night.
Take heed, ere summer comes, or cuckoo-birds do sing. – Away, Sir Corporal Nim! – Believe it, Page, he speaks sense. *Exit.*

FORD [*aside*] I will be patient, I will find out this.

NIM [*to Page*] And this is true, I like not the humour of lying. He hath wronged me in some humours. I should have borne the humoured letter to her, but I have a sword, and it shall bite upon my necessity. He loves your wife, there's the short and the long. My name is Corporal Nim. I speak, and I avouch 'tis true: my name is Nim and Falstaff loves your wife. Adieu. I love not the humour of bread and cheese. Adieu. *Exit.*

PAGE The humour of it, quoth 'a! Here's a fellow frights English out of his wits.

FORD [*aside*] I will seek out Falstaff.

PAGE [*aside*] I never heard such a drawling-affecting rogue.

FORD [*aside*] If I do find it – well.

PAGE [*aside*] I will not believe such a Cathayan, though the priest o'the town commend him for a true man.

FORD [*aside*] 'Twas a good sensible fellow – well.

MISTRESS PAGE *and* MISTRESS FORD *come forward.*

PAGE How now, Meg?

MISTRESS PAGE Whither go you, George? Hark you.

MISTRESS FORD How now, sweet Frank, why art thou melancholy?

FORD I melancholy? I am not melancholy. Get you home, go.

MISTRESS FORD Faith, thou hast some crotchets in thy head now. – Will you go, Mistress Page?

MISTRESS PAGE Have with you. You'll come to dinner, George? [*aside to Mistress Ford*] Look who comes yonder: she shall be our messenger to this paltry knight.

MISTRESS FORD [*aside to Mistress Page*] Trust me, I thought on her: she'll fit it.

Enter Mistress QUICKLY.

MISTRESS PAGE You are come to see my daughter Anne?

QUICKLY Ay, forsooth. And I pray, how does good Mistress Anne?

MISTRESS PAGE Go in with us and see. We have an hour's talk with you.

*Exeunt Mistress Ford, Mistress Page and
Mistress Quickly.*

PAGE How now, Master Ford?

FORD You heard what this knave told me, did you not?

PAGE Yes, and you heard what the other told me?

FORD Do you think there is truth in them?

PAGE Hang 'em, slaves! I do not think the knight would offer it, but these that accuse him in his intent towards our wives are a yoke of his discarded men – very rogues, now they be out of service.

FORD Were they his men?

PAGE Marry, were they.

FORD I like it never the better for that. – Does he lie at the Garter?

PAGE Ay, marry, does he. If he should intend this voyage toward my wife, I would turn her loose to him, and

what he gets more of her than sharp words, let it lie on
my head.

FORD   I do not misdoubt my wife, but I would be loath
to turn them together. A man may be too confident. I
would have nothing lie on my head: I cannot be thus
satisfied.

Enter HOST.

PAGE   Look where my ranting host of the Garter comes.
There is either liquor in his pate or money in his
purse, when he looks so merrily. – How now, mine
host?

HOST   How now, bully rook? Thou'rt a gentleman. –
Cavaliero Justice, I say!

Enter SHALLOW.

SHALLOW   I follow, mine host, I follow. – Good even
and twenty, good Master Page. Master Page, will you
go with us? We have sport in hand.

HOST   Tell him, Cavaliero Justice, tell him, bully rook!

SHALLOW   Sir, there is a fray to be fought between Sir
Hugh the Welsh priest and Caius the French doctor.

FORD   Good mine host o' the Garter, a word with you.

HOST   What sayst thou, my bully rook? [*Ford and the
Host talk apart.*]

SHALLOW   Will you go with us to behold it? My merry
host hath had the measuring of their weapons, and, I
think, hath appointed them contrary places; for, I
believe me, I hear the parson is no jester. Hark, I will
tell you what our sport shall be. [*Shallow and Page talk
apart, Ford and Host come forward.*]

HOST   Hast thou no suit against my knight, my guest
cavaliero?

FORD   None, I protest. But I'll give you a pottle of burnt
sack to give me recourse to him – and tell him my
name is Brook, only for a jest.

HOST   My hand, bully: thou shalt have egress and
regress – said I well? – and thy name shall be Brook. It
is a merry knight. [*to all*] Will you go, myn-heers?

SHALLOW   Have with you, mine host.

PAGE   I have heard the Frenchman hath good skill in his
rapier.

SHALLOW   Tut, sir, I could have told you more. In these
times you stand on distance – your passes, stoccadoes,
and I know not what. 'Tis the heart, Master Page, 'tis
here, 'tis here. I have seen the time, with my long sword,
I would have made you four tall fellows skip like rats.

HOST   Here, boys, here, here! Shall we wag?

PAGE   Have with you; I had rather hear them scold than
fight.   *Exeunt Host, Shallow and Page.*

FORD   Though Page be a secure fool, and stands so
firmly on his wife's frailty, yet I cannot put off my
opinion so easily. She was in his company at Page's
house, and what they made there I know not. Well, I
will look further into't, and I have a disguise to sound
Falstaff. If I find her honest I lose not my labour. If she
be otherwise, 'tis labour well bestowed.   *Exit.*

2.2   *Enter* FALSTAFF *and* PISTOL.

FALSTAFF   I will not lend thee a penny.

PISTOL   Why then, the world's mine oyster,
Which I with sword will open.

FALSTAFF   Not a penny. I have been content, sir, you
should lay my countenance to pawn; I have grated
upon my good friends for three reprieves for you and
your coach-fellow Nim, or else you had looked through
the grate like a gemini of baboons. I am damned in hell
for swearing to gentlemen my friends you were good
soldiers and tall fellows. And when Mistress Bridget
lost the handle of her fan, I took't upon mine honour
thou hadst it not.

PISTOL   Didst not thou share? Hadst thou not fifteen
pence?

FALSTAFF   Reason, you rogue, reason. Thinkst thou I'll
endanger my soul gratis? At a word: hang no more
about me, I am no gibbet for you. Go – a short knife
and a throng – to your manor of Picked-hatch, go!
You'll not bear a letter for me, you rogue? You stand
upon your honour! Why, thou unconfinable baseness,
it is as much as I can do to keep the terms of my honour
precise. Ay, ay, I myself, sometimes, leaving the fear of
God on the left hand, and hiding mine honour in my
necessity, am fain to shuffle, to hedge, and to lurch; and
yet, you rogue, will ensconce your rags, your cat-amountain looks, your red-lattice phrases, and your
bold beating oaths, under the shelter of your honour!
You will not do it! You!

PISTOL   I do relent. What would thou more of man?

Enter ROBIN.

ROBIN   Sir, here's a woman would speak with you.

FALSTAFF   Let her approach.

Enter Mistress QUICKLY.

QUICKLY   Give your worship good morrow.

FALSTAFF   Good morrow, goodwife.

QUICKLY   Not so, an't please your worship.

FALSTAFF   Good maid, then.

QUICKLY   That I am, I'll be sworn, as my mother was
the first hour I was born.

FALSTAFF   I do believe the swearer. What with me?

QUICKLY   Shall I vouchsafe your worship a word or
two?

FALSTAFF   Two thousand, fair woman; and I'll vouchsafe
thee the hearing.

QUICKLY   There is one Mistress Ford, sir – I pray come
a little nearer this ways – I myself dwell with Master
Doctor Caius –

FALSTAFF   Well, on; Mistress Ford, you say –

QUICKLY   Your worship says very true. – I pray your
worship come a little nearer this ways.

FALSTAFF   I warrant you, nobody hears. – Mine own
people, mine own people.

QUICKLY   Are they so? Now God bless them, and make
them his servants.

FALSTAFF Well, Mistress Ford – What of her?

QUICKLY Why, sir, she's a good creature – Lord, Lord, your worship's a wanton! Well, God forgive you, and all of us, I pray –

FALSTAFF Mistress Ford, come, Mistress Ford.

QUICKLY Marry, this is the short and the long of it: you have brought her into such a canary as 'tis wonderful. The best courtier of them all, when the court lay at Windsor, could never have brought her to such a canary – yet there has been knights, and lords, and gentlemen, with their coaches, I warrant you – coach after coach, letter after letter, gift after gift, smelling so sweetly, all musk, and so rushling, I warrant you, in silk and gold, and in such alligant terms, and in such wine and sugar of the best and the fairest, that would have won any woman's heart; and, I warrant you, they could never get an eye-wink of her. I had myself twenty angels given me this morning, but I defy all angels in any such sort, as they say, but in the way of honesty; and, I warrant you, they could never get her so much as sip on a cup with the proudest of them all – and yet there has been earls – nay, which is more, pensioners – but, I warrant you, all is one with her.

FALSTAFF But what says she to me? Be brief, my good she-Mercury.

QUICKLY Marry, she hath received your letter, for the which she thanks you a thousand times; and she gives you to notify that her husband will be absence from his house between ten and eleven.

FALSTAFF Ten and eleven.

QUICKLY Ay, forsooth; and then you may come and see the picture, she says, that you wot of. Master Ford her husband will be from home. Alas, the sweet woman leads an ill life with him: he's a very jealousy man; she leads a very frampold life with him, good heart.

FALSTAFF Ten and eleven. Woman, commend me to her; I will not fail her.

QUICKLY Why, you say well. But I have another messenger to your worship. Mistress Page hath her hearty commendations to you too; and let me tell you in your ear she's as fartuous a civil modest wife, and one – I tell you – that will not miss you morning nor evening prayer, as any is in Windsor, whoe'er be the other; and she bade me tell your worship that her husband is seldom from home, but she hopes there will come a time. I never knew a woman so dote upon a man – surely I think you have charms, la; yes, in truth.

FALSTAFF Not I, I assure thee. Setting the attraction of my good parts aside, I have no other charms.

QUICKLY Blessing on your heart for't.

FALSTAFF But I pray thee, tell me this: has Ford's wife and Page's wife acquainted each other how they love me?

QUICKLY O God, no, sir: that were a jest indeed! They have not so little grace, I hope; that were a trick indeed! But Mistress Page would desire you to send her your little page, of all loves: her husband has a marvellous

infection to the little page; and truly Master Page is an honest man – never a wife in Windsor leads a better life than she does: do what she will, say what she will, take all, pay all, go to bed when she list, rise when she list, all is as she will, and truly she deserves it, for if there be a kind woman in Windsor, she is one. You must send her your page, no remedy.

FALSTAFF Why, I will.

QUICKLY Nay, but do so then, and, look you, he may come and go between you both; and in any case have a nay-word, that you may know one another's mind, and the boy never need to understand anything; for 'tis not good that children should know any wickedness. Old folks, you know, have discretion, as they say, and know the world.

FALSTAFF Fare thee well, commend me to them both. There's my purse; I am yet thy debtor. – Boy, go along with this woman. – This news distracts me.

Exeunt Mistress Quickly and Robin.

PISTOL This punk is one of Cupid's carriers.
Clap on more sails, pursue, up with your fights,
Give fire! She is my prize, or ocean whelm them all!

Exit.

FALSTAFF Sayst thou so, old Jack? Go thy ways, I'll make more of thy old body than I have done. Will they yet look after thee? Wilt thou, after the expense of so much money, be now a gainer? Good body, I thank thee. Let them say 'tis grossly done – so it be fairly done, no matter.

Enter BARDOLPH.

BARDOLPH Sir John, there's one Master Brook below would fain speak with you and be acquainted with you – and hath sent your worship a morning's draught of sack.

FALSTAFF Brook is his name?

BARDOLPH Ay, sir.

FALSTAFF Call him in. *Exit Bardolph.*
Such brooks are welcome to me, that o'erflows such liquor. Ah ha, Mistress Ford and Mistress Page, have I encompassed you? Go to, *via!*

Enter FORD as Brook, introduced by BARDOLPH.

FORD God bless you, sir.

FALSTAFF And you, sir. Would you speak with me?

FORD I make bold, to press with so little preparation upon you.

FALSTAFF You're welcome. What's your will? – Give us leave, drawer. *Exit Bardolph.*

FORD Sir, I am a gentleman that have spent much; my name is Brook.

FALSTAFF Good Master Brook, I desire more acquaintance of you.

FORD Good Sir John, I sue for yours; not to charge you, for I must let you understand I think myself in better plight for a lender than you are, the which hath something emboldened me to this unseasoned intrusion; for they say if money go before, all ways do lie open.

FALSTAFF Money is a good soldier, sir, and will on.

FORD Truth, and I have a bag of money here troubles me. If you will help to bear it, Sir John, take all, or half, for easing me of the carriage.

FALSTAFF Sir, I know not how I may deserve to be your porter.

FORD I will tell you, sir, if you will give me the hearing.

FALSTAFF Speak, good Master Brook; I shall be glad to be your servant.

FORD Sir, I hear you are a scholar – I will be brief with you – and you have been a man long known to me, though I had never so good means as desire to make myself acquainted with you. I shall discover a thing to you, wherein I must very much lay open mine own imperfection. But, good Sir John, as you have one eye upon my follies, as you hear them unfolded, turn another into the register of your own, that I may pass with a reproof the easier, sith you yourself know how easy it is to be such an offender.

FALSTAFF Very well, sir, proceed.

FORD There is a gentlewoman in this town, her husband's name is Ford.

FALSTAFF Well, sir.

FORD I have long loved her, and, I protest to you, bestowed much on her, followed her with a doting observance, engrossed opportunities to meet her, fee'd every slight occasion that could but niggardly give me sight of her: not only bought many presents to give her, but have given largely to many, to know what she would have given. Briefly, I have pursued her as love hath pursued me, which hath been on the wing of all occasions. But whatsoever I have merited, either in my mind or in my means, meed, I am sure, I have received none – unless experience be a jewel, that I have purchased at an infinite rate, and that hath taught me to say this:

Love like a shadow flies, when substance love pursues,
Pursuing that that flies, and flying what pursues.

FALSTAFF Have you received no promise of satisfaction at her hands?

FORD Never.

FALSTAFF Have you importuned her to such a purpose?

FORD Never.

FALSTAFF Of what quality was your love, then?

FORD Like a fair house built on another man's ground, so that I have lost my edifice by mistaking the place where I erected it.

FALSTAFF To what purpose have you unfolded this to me?

FORD When I have told you that I have told you all. Some say that, though she appear honest to me, yet in other places she enlargeth her mirth so far that there is shrewd construction made of her. Now, Sir John, here is the heart of my purpose: you are a gentleman of excellent breeding, admirable discourse, of great

admittance, authentic in your place and person, generally allowed for your many warlike, courtlike and learned preparations –

FALSTAFF O, sir!

FORD Believe it, for you know it. [*Points to the bag.*] There is money: spend it, spend it, spend more, spend all I have; only give me so much of your time in exchange of it, as to lay an amiable siege to the honesty of this Ford's wife. Use your art of wooing, win her to consent to you: if any man may, you may as soon as any.

FALSTAFF Would it apply well to the vehemency of your affection that I should win what you would enjoy? Methinks you prescribe to yourself very preposterously.

FORD O, understand my drift. She dwells so securely on the excellency of her honour, that the folly of my soul dares not present itself; she is too bright to be looked against. Now, could I come to her with any detection in my hand, my desires had instance and argument to commend themselves. I could drive her then from the ward of her purity, her reputation, her marriage vow and a thousand other her defences, which now are too too strongly embattled against me. What say you to't, Sir John?

FALSTAFF Master Brook, I will first make bold with your money. Next, give me your hand. And last, as I am a gentleman, you shall, if you will, enjoy Ford's wife.

FORD O good sir!

FALSTAFF I say you shall.

FORD Want no money, Sir John, you shall want none.

FALSTAFF Want no Mistress Ford, Master Brook, you shall want none. I shall be with her, I may tell you, by her own appointment; even as you came in to me, her assistant, or go-between, parted from me. I say I shall be with her between ten and eleven, for at that time the jealous rascally knave her husband will be forth. Come you to me at night: you shall know how I speed.

FORD I am blessed in your acquaintance. Do you know Ford, sir?

FALSTAFF Hang him, poor cuckoldly knave, I know him not. Yet I wrong him to call him poor: they say the jealous wittolly knave hath masses of money, for the which his wife seems to me well-favoured. I will use her as the key of the cuckoldly rogue's coffer, and there's my harvest-home.

FORD I would you knew Ford, sir, that you might avoid him if you saw him.

FALSTAFF Hang him, mechanical salt-butter rogue! I will stare him out of his wits, I will awe him with my cudgel: it shall hang like a meteor o'er the cuckold's horns. Master Brook, thou shalt know I will predominate over the peasant, and thou shalt lie with his wife. Come to me soon at night: Ford's a knave, and I will aggravate his style. Thou, Master Brook, shalt know him for knave and cuckold. Come to me soon at night. *Exit.*

FORD What a damned epicurean rascal is this? My heart is ready to crack with impatience. Who says this is improvident jealousy? My wife hath sent to him, the hour is fixed, the match is made: would any man have thought this? See the hell of having a false woman: my bed shall be abused, my coffers ransacked, my reputation gnawn at; and I shall not only receive this villainous wrong, but stand under the adoption of abominable terms, and by him that does me this wrong. Terms, names! Amaimon sounds well; Lucifer, well; Barbason, well; yet they are devils' additions, the names of fiends. But cuckold? Wittol? Cuckold! The devil himself hath not such a name! Page is an ass, a secure ass; he will trust his wife, he will not be jealous. I will rather trust a Fleming with my butter, Parson Hugh the Welshman with my cheese, an Irishman with my aquavitae bottle, or a thief to walk my ambling gelding, than my wife with herself. Then she plots, then she ruminates, then she devises; and what they think in their hearts they may effect – they will break their hearts but they will effect. God be praised for my jealousy! Eleven o'clock the hour – I will prevent this, detect my wife, be revenged on Falstaff and laugh at Page. I will about it: better three hours too soon than a minute too late. Fie, fie, fie! Cuckold, cuckold, cuckold!   *Exit.*

2.3   *Enter* Doctor CAIUS *and* RUGBY.

CAIUS   Jack Rugby!
RUGBY   Sir?
CAIUS   Vat is the clock, Jack?
RUGBY   'Tis past the hour, sir, that Sir Hugh promised to meet.
CAIUS   By gar, he has save his soul, dat he is no-come. He has pray his Pible well, dat he is no-come. By gar, Jack Rugby, he is dead already, if he be come.
RUGBY   He is wise, sir; he knew your worship would kill him if he came.
CAIUS   By gar, de herring is no dead, so as I vill kill him. Take your rapier, Jack; I vill tell you how I vill kill him.
RUGBY   Alas, sir, I cannot fence.
CAIUS   Villainy, take your rapier.
RUGBY   Forbear; here's company.

Enter SHALLOW, PAGE, HOST *and* SLENDER.

HOST   God bless thee, bully Doctor.
SHALLOW   God save you, Master Doctor Caius.
PAGE   Now, good Master Doctor.
SLENDER   'Give you good morrow, sir.
CAIUS   Vat be all you one, two, tree, four, come for?
HOST   To see thee fight, to see thee foin, to see thee traverse; to see thee here, to see thee there; to see thee pass thy punto, thy stock, thy reverse, thy distance, thy montant. Is he dead, my Ethiopian? Is he dead, my François? Ha, bully? What says my Esculapius, my

Galen, my heart of elder, ha? Is he dead, bully stale, is he dead?
CAIUS   By gar, he is de coward Jack-priest of de vorld: he is not show his face.
HOST   Thou art a castalian king urinal – Hector of Greece, my boy!
CAIUS   I pray you bear witness that me have stay – six or seven – two, tree hours for him, and he is no-come.
SHALLOW   He is the wiser man, Master Doctor: he is a curer of souls and you a curer of bodies. If you should fight, you go against the hair of your professions. Is it not true, Master Page?
PAGE   Master Shallow, you have yourself been a great fighter, though now a man of peace.
SHALLOW   Bodykins, Master Page, though I now be old, and of the peace, if I see a sword out, my finger itches to make one. Though we are justices and doctors and churchmen, Master Page, we have some salt of our youth in us – we are the sons of women, Master Page.
PAGE   'Tis true, Master Shallow.
SHALLOW   It will be found so, Master Page. – Master Doctor Caius, I am come to fetch you home. I am sworn of the peace: you have showed yourself a wise physician, and Sir Hugh hath shown himself a wise and patient churchman. You must go with me, Master Doctor.
HOST   Pardon, guest justice. – A word, Monsieur Mockwater.
CAIUS   Mockvater? Vat is dat?
HOST   Mockwater, in our English tongue, is valour, bully.
CAIUS   By gar, then I have as much mockvater as de Englishman. Scurvy Jack-dog priest! By gar, me vill cut his ears.
HOST   He will clapper-claw thee titely, bully.
CAIUS   Clapper-de-claw? Vat is dat?
HOST   That is, he will make thee amends.
CAIUS   By gar, me do look he shall clapper-de-claw me, for, by gar, me vill have it.
HOST   And I will provoke him to't, or let him wag.
CAIUS   Me tank you for dat.
HOST   And moreover, bully – but first, Master guest and Master Page, and eke Cavaliero Slender, go you through the town to Frogmore.
PAGE   [*aside to Host*]   Sir Hugh is there, is he?
HOST   [*aside to Page*]   He is there. See what humour he is in; and I will bring the Doctor about by the fields. Will it do well?
SHALLOW   [*aside to Host*]   We will do it.
PAGE, SHALLOW, SLENDER   Adieu, good Master Doctor.   *Exeunt all but Host, Caius and Rugby.*
CAIUS   By gar, me vill kill de priest, for he speak for a jackanape to Anne Page.
HOST   Let him die. Sheathe thy impatience. Throw cold water on thy choler. Go about the fields with me through Frogmore. I will bring thee where Mistress

Anne Page is, at a farmhouse a-feasting, and thou shalt
woo her. Cried game; said I well?

CAIUS   By gar, me dank you vor dat; by gar, I love you;
85   and I shall procure-a you de good guest: de earl, de
knight, de lords, de gentlemen, my patients.

HOST   For the which I will be thy adversary toward
Anne Page. Said I well?

CAIUS   By gar, 'tis good; vell said.

90   HOST   Let us wag then.

CAIUS   Come at my heels, Jack Rugby.   *Exeunt.*

3.1   *Enter* EVANS *and* SIMPLE.

EVANS   I pray you now, good Master Slender's servingman, and friend Simple by your name, which way have
you looked for Master Caius, that calls himself Doctor
of Physic?

5   SIMPLE   Marry, sir, the Petty-ward, the Park-ward,
every way: Old Windsor way, and every way but the
town way.

EVANS   I most fehemently desire you, you will also look
that way.

10   SIMPLE   I will, sir. [*Stands aside on the lookout.*]

EVANS   Jeshu pless my soul, how full of cholers I am,
and trempling of mind. I shall be glad if he have
deceived me. How melancholies I am. I will knog his
urinals about his knave's costard when I have good
15   opportunities for the 'ork. Pless my soul!
[*Sings.*]   To shallow rivers, to whose falls
Melodious birds sings madrigals –
There will we make our peds of roses
And a thousand fragrant posies.
20   To shallow –
Mercy on me, I have a great dispositions to cry.
[*Sings.*]   Melodious birds sing madrigals –
Whenas I sat in Pabylon –
And a thousand vagram posies.
25   To shallow, etc.

SIMPLE   Yonder he is coming, this way, Sir Hugh.

EVANS   He's welcome.
[*Sings.*]   To shallow rivers, to whose falls –
God prosper the right. What weapons is he?

30   SIMPLE   No weapons, sir. There comes my master,
Master Shallow, and another gentleman; from Frogmore, over the stile, this way.

EVANS   Pray you, give me my gown – or else keep it in
your arms.

Enter PAGE, SHALLOW *and* SLENDER.

35   SHALLOW   How now, Master Parson? Good morrow,
good Sir Hugh. Keep a gamester from the dice and a
good student from his book, and it is wonderful.

SLENDER   Ah, sweet Anne Page!

PAGE   God save you, good Sir Hugh.

40   EVANS   God pless you from his mercy's sake, all of you.

SHALLOW   What, the sword and the word? Do you
study them both, Master Parson?

PAGE   And youthful still – in your doublet and hose, this
raw-rheumatic day?

EVANS   There is reasons and causes for it.   45

PAGE   We are come to you to do a good office, Master
Parson.

EVANS   Fery well; what is it?

PAGE   Yonder is a most reverend gentleman who, belike,
having received wrong by some person, is at most odds   50
with his own gravity and patience that ever you saw.

SHALLOW   I have lived fourscore years and upward; I
never heard a man of his place, gravity and learning so
wide of his own respect.

EVANS   What is he?   55

PAGE   I think you know him: Master Doctor Caius, the
renowned French physician.

EVANS   Got's will and his passion of my heart, I had as
lief you would tell me of a mess of porridge.

PAGE   Why?   60

EVANS   He has no more knowledge in Hibocrates and
Galen, and he is a knave besides – a cowardly knave as
you would desires to be acquainted withal.

PAGE   I warrant you, he's the man should fight with
him.   65

SLENDER   O sweet Anne Page!

SHALLOW   It appears so by his weapons.

Enter CAIUS *and* HOST *followed by* RUGBY.

Keep them asunder: here comes Doctor Caius. [*They
offer to fight.*]

PAGE   Nay, good Master Parson, keep in your weapon.

SHALLOW   So do you, good Master Doctor.   70

HOST   Disarm them, and let them question. Let them
keep their limbs whole and hack our English.

CAIUS   I pray you let-a me speak a word with your ear.
Vherefore vill you not meet-a me?

EVANS   Pray you, use your patience. In good time!   75

CAIUS   By gar, you are de coward, de Jack-dog, John
ape.

EVANS   [*aside to Caius*]   Pray you, let us not be laughing
stocks to other men's humours. I desire you in
friendship, and I will one way or other make you   80
amends. [*aloud*] By Jeshu, I will knog your urinal about
your knave's cogscomb.

CAIUS   *Diable!* Jack Rugby, mine host de Jarteer, have I
not stay for him to kill him? Have I not, at de place I
did appoint?   85

EVANS   As I am a Christians soul, now look you: this is
the place appointed, I'll be judgement by mine host of
the Garter.

HOST   Peace, I say, Gallia and Gaul, French and Welsh,
soul-curer and body-curer.   90

CAIUS   Ay, dat is very good, *excellent.*

HOST   Peace, I say, hear mine host of the Garter. Am I
politic? Am I subtle? Am I a Machiavel? Shall I lose my
doctor? No, he gives me the potions and the motions.
Shall I lose my parson? My priest? My Sir Hugh? No,   95
he gives me the proverbs and the no-verbs. [*to Caius*]

Give me thy hand, terrestrial; so. [*to Evans*] Give me
thy hand, celestial; so. – Boys of art, I have deceived
you both: I have directed you to wrong places. Your
hearts are mighty, your skins are whole, and let burnt
sack be the issue. – Come, lay their swords to pawn.
Follow me, lads of peace, follow, follow, follow.   *Exit.*

SHALLOW   Afore God, a mad host. Follow, gentlemen,
follow.

SLENDER   O sweet Anne Page!
                              Exeunt Shallow, Slender and Page.

CAIUS   Ha, do I perceive dat? Have you make-a de sot of
us, ha, ha?

EVANS   This is well, he has made us his vlouting-stog. I
desire you that we may be friends, and let us knog our
prains together to be revenge on this same scall, scurvy,
cogging companion, the host of the Garter.

CAIUS   By gar, with all my heart. He promise to bring
me where is Anne Page; by gar, he deceive me too.

EVANS   Well, I will smite his noddles. Pray you follow.
                                                        Exeunt.

3.2   *Enter* MISTRESS PAGE, *following* ROBIN.

MISTRESS PAGE   Nay, keep your way, little gallant; you
were wont to be a follower, but now you are a leader.
Whether had you rather, lead mine eyes or eye your
master's heels?

ROBIN   I had rather, forsooth, go before you like a man
than follow him like a dwarf.

MISTRESS PAGE   O, you are a flattering boy: now I see
you'll be a courtier.

Enter FORD.

FORD   Well met, Mistress Page. Whither go you?

MISTRESS PAGE   Truly, sir, to see your wife. Is she at
home?

FORD   Ay, and as idle as she may hang together, for want
of company. I think if your husbands were dead you
two would marry.

MISTRESS PAGE   Be sure of that – two other husbands.

FORD   Where had you this pretty weathercock?

MISTRESS PAGE   I cannot tell what the dickens his name
is my husband had him of. – What do you call your
knight's name, sirrah?

ROBIN   Sir John Falstaff.

FORD   Sir John Falstaff?

MISTRESS PAGE   He, he; I can never hit on's name.
There is such a league between my goodman and he! Is
your wife at home indeed?

FORD   Indeed she is.

MISTRESS PAGE   By your leave, sir, I am sick till I see her.
                                        Exit with Robin.

FORD   Hath Page any brains? Hath he any eyes? Hath he
any thinking? Sure they sleep, he hath no use of them.
Why, this boy will carry a letter twenty mile, as easy as
a cannon will shoot point-blank twelve score. He
pieces out his wife's inclination, he gives her folly

motion and advantage. And now she's going to my
wife, and Falstaff's boy with her. A man may hear this
shower sing in the wind: and Falstaff's boy with her!
Good plots they are laid, and our revolted wives share
damnation together. Well, I will take him, then torture
my wife, pluck the borrowed veil of modesty from the
so-seeming Mistress Page, divulge Page himself for a
secure and wilful Actaeon, and to these violent
proceedings all my neighbours shall cry aim. [*Clock
strikes.*] The clock gives me my cue, and my assurance
bids me search: there I shall find Falstaff. I shall be
rather praised for this than mocked, for it is as positive
as the earth is firm that Falstaff is there. I will go.

Enter SHALLOW, PAGE, HOST, SLENDER, CAIUS,
EVANS *and* RUGBY.

SHALLOW, PAGE, *etc.*   Well met, Master Ford.

FORD   Trust me, a good knot. I have good cheer at
home, and I pray you all go with me.

SHALLOW   I must excuse myself, Master Ford.

SLENDER   And so must I, sir. We have appointed to dine
with Mistress Anne, and I would not break with her for
more money than I'll speak of.

SHALLOW   We have lingered about a match between
Anne Page and my cousin Slender, and this day we
shall have our answer.

SLENDER   I hope I have your good will, father Page.

PAGE   You have, Master Slender, I stand wholly for
you. – But my wife, Master Doctor, is for you
altogether.

CAIUS   Ay, be-gar, and de maid is love-a me: my nursh-a
Quickly tell me so mush.

HOST   What say you to young Master Fenton? He
capers, he dances, he has eyes of youth, he writes
verses, he speaks holiday, he smells April and May: he
will carry't, he will carry't – 'tis in his buttons he will
carry't.

PAGE   Not by my consent, I promise you. The gentleman
is of no having, he kept company with the wild Prince
and Poins. He is of too high a region, he knows too
much – no, he shall not knit a knot in his fortunes with
the finger of my substance. If he take her, let him take
her simply: the wealth I have waits on my consent, and
my consent goes not that way.

FORD   I beseech you heartily, some of you go home with
me to dinner. Besides your cheer you shall have sport:
I will show you a monster. Master Doctor, you shall go;
so shall you, Master Page, and you, Sir Hugh.

SHALLOW   Well, fare you well. We shall have the freer
wooing at Master Page's.   *Exeunt Shallow and Slender.*

CAIUS   Go home, John Rugby; I come anon.
                                            Exit Rugby.

HOST   Farewell, my hearts. I will to my honest knight
Falstaff, and drink canary with him.   *Exit.*

FORD [*aside*]   I think I shall drink in pipe-wine first with
him: I'll make him dance. – Will you go, gentles?

ALL   Have with you to see this monster.   *Exeunt.*

3.3 *Enter* MISTRESS FORD *and* MISTRESS PAGE.

MISTRESS FORD   What, John! What, Robert!

MISTRESS PAGE   Quickly, quickly! Is the buck-basket –

MISTRESS FORD   I warrant. – What, Robert, I say!

Enter JOHN *and* ROBERT *with a great buck-basket.*

MISTRESS PAGE   Come, come, come.

5   MISTRESS FORD   Here, set it down.

MISTRESS PAGE   Give your men the charge; we must be brief.

MISTRESS FORD   Marry, as I told you before, John and Robert, be ready here hard by in the brew-house, and,

10   when I suddenly call you, come forth and, without any pause or staggering, take this basket on your shoulders. That done, trudge with it in all haste, and carry it among the whitsters in Datchet Mead, and there empty it in the muddy ditch close by the Thames side.

15   MISTRESS PAGE   You will do it?

MISTRESS FORD   I ha' told them over and over, they lack no direction. – Be gone, and come when you are called.

Exeunt John and Robert.

Enter ROBIN.

MISTRESS PAGE   Here comes little Robin.

MISTRESS FORD   How now, my eyas-musket, what news

20   with you?

ROBIN   My master, Sir John, is come in at your back door, Mistress Ford, and requests your company.

MISTRESS PAGE   You little Jack-a-Lent, have you been true to us?

25   ROBIN   Ay, I'll be sworn. My master knows not of your being here, and hath threatened to put me into everlasting liberty if I tell you of it; for he swears he'll turn me away.

MISTRESS PAGE   Thou'rt a good boy. This secrecy of

30   thine shall be a tailor to thee, and shall make thee a new doublet and hose. – I'll go hide me.

MISTRESS FORD   Do so. – Go tell thy master I am alone.

Exit Robin.

Mistress Page, remember you your cue.

MISTRESS PAGE   I warrant thee: if I do not act it, hiss

35   me.

MISTRESS FORD   Go to, then. We'll use this unwholesome humidity, this gross watery pumpion; we'll teach him to know turtles from jays.

Exit Mistress Page.

Enter FALSTAFF.

FALSTAFF   Have I caught thee, my heavenly jewel? Why,

40   now let me die, for I have lived long enough: this is the period of my ambition. O this blessed hour!

MISTRESS FORD   O sweet Sir John!

FALSTAFF   Mistress Ford, I cannot cog, I cannot prate, Mistress Ford; now shall I sin in my wish: I would thy

45   husband were dead – I'll speak it before the best lord: I would make thee my lady.

MISTRESS FORD   I your lady, Sir John? Alas, I should be a pitiful lady.

FALSTAFF   Let the court of France show me such

50   another! I see how thine eye would emulate the diamond: thou hast the right arched beauty of the brow that becomes the ship-tire, the tire-valiant, or any tire of Venetian admittance.

MISTRESS FORD   A plain kerchief, Sir John: my brows

55   become nothing else, nor that well neither.

FALSTAFF   By the Lord, thou art a tyrant to say so. Thou wouldst make an absolute courtier, and the firm fixture of thy foot would give an excellent motion to thy gait, in a semi-circled farthingale. I see what thou

60   wert if Fortune thy foe were not, Nature thy friend. Come, thou canst not hide it.

MISTRESS FORD   Believe me, there's no such thing in me.

FALSTAFF   What made me love thee? Let that persuade

65   thee there's something extraordinary in thee. Come, I cannot cog and say thou art this and that, like a many of these lisping hawthorn buds that come like women in men's apparel, and smell like Bucklersbury in simple time. I cannot – but I love thee, none but thee;

70   and thou deservest it.

MISTRESS FORD   Do not betray me, sir; I fear you love Mistress Page.

FALSTAFF   Thou mightst as well say I love to walk by the Counter gate, which is as hateful to me as the reek of a

75   lime-kiln.

MISTRESS FORD   Well, heaven knows how I love you, and you shall one day find it.

FALSTAFF   Keep in that mind, I'll deserve it.

MISTRESS FORD   Nay, I must tell you, so you do; or else

80   I could not be in that mind.

Enter ROBIN.

ROBIN   Mistress Ford, Mistress Ford, here's Mistress Page at the door, sweating, and blowing, and looking wildly, and would needs speak with you presently.

FALSTAFF   She shall not see me; I will ensconce me

85   behind the arras.

MISTRESS FORD   Pray you do so; she's a very tattling woman. [*Falstaff hides behind the arras.*]

Enter MISTRESS PAGE.

What's the matter? How now?

MISTRESS PAGE   O Mistress Ford, what have you done?

90   You're shamed, you're overthrown, you're undone for ever!

MISTRESS FORD   What's the matter, good Mistress Page?

MISTRESS PAGE   O well-a-day, Mistress Ford, having

95   an honest man to your husband, to give him such cause of suspicion!

MISTRESS FORD   What cause of suspicion?

MISTRESS PAGE   What cause of suspicion? Out upon you: how am I mistook in you!

100 MISTRESS FORD Why, alas, what's the matter?

MISTRESS PAGE Your husband's coming hither, woman, with all the officers in Windsor, to search for a gentleman that he says is here now in the house, by your consent, to take an ill advantage of his absence.
105 You are undone.

MISTRESS FORD 'Tis not so, I hope.

MISTRESS PAGE Pray heaven it be not so, that you have such a man here. But 'tis most certain your husband's coming, with half Windsor at his heels, to search for
110 such a one. I come before to tell you. If you know yourself clear, why, I am glad of it; but if you have a friend here, convey, convey him out. Be not amazed, call all your senses to you, defend your reputation, or bid farewell to your good life for ever.

115 MISTRESS FORD What shall I do? There is a gentleman, my dear friend; and I fear not mine own shame so much as his peril. I had rather than a thousand pound he were out of the house.

MISTRESS PAGE For shame, never stand 'you had
120 rather and you had rather'! Your husband's here at hand: bethink you of some conveyance – in the house you cannot hide him. – O, how have you deceived me! – Look, here is a basket: if he be of any reasonable stature, he may creep in here, and throw foul linen
125 upon him, as if it were going to bucking; or – it is whiting time – send him by your two men to Datchet Mead.

MISTRESS FORD He's too big to go in there. What shall I do?

130 FALSTAFF [*Comes out of hiding.*] Let me see't, let me see't, O let me see't! I'll in, I'll in. – Follow your friend's counsel. I'll in.

MISTRESS PAGE What, Sir John Falstaff? [*aside to him*] Are these your letters, knight?

135 FALSTAFF [*aside to her*] I love thee, and none but thee. Help me away. Let me creep in here. I'll never –
[*Goes into the basket, they put clothes over him.*]

MISTRESS PAGE Help to cover your master, boy. – Call your men, Mistress Ford. – You dissembling knight!   *Exit Robin.*

140 MISTRESS FORD What, John! Robert, John!

Enter JOHN *and* ROBERT.

Go, take up these clothes here, quickly. Where's the cowl-staff? – Look how you drumble! Carry them to the laundress in Datchet Mead; quickly, come.

Enter FORD, PAGE, CAIUS
and EVANS.

FORD Pray you, come near. If I suspect without cause,
145 why, then make sport at me, then let me be your jest, I deserve it. – How now? Whither bear you this?

SERVANT To the laundress, forsooth.

MISTRESS FORD Why, what have you to do whither they bear it? You were best meddle with buck-
150 washing!

FORD Buck? I would I could wash myself of the buck! Buck, buck, buck! Ay, buck! I warrant you, buck – and of the season too, it shall appear.

Exeunt John and Robert with the basket.
Gentlemen, I have dreamed tonight; I'll tell you my
155 dream. Here, here, here be my keys: ascend my chambers, search, seek, find out. I'll warrant we'll unkennel the fox. Let me stop this way first. [*Locks the door.*] So, now escape!

PAGE Good Master Ford, be contented; you wrong
160 yourself too much.

FORD True, Master Page. – Up, gentlemen, you shall see sport anon. Follow me, gentlemen.   *Exit.*

EVANS By Jeshu, this is fery fantastical humours and jealousies.

165 CAIUS By gar, 'tis no the fashion of France; it is not jealous in France.

PAGE Nay, follow him, gentlemen; see the issue of his search.   *Exeunt Page, Caius and Evans.*

MISTRESS PAGE Is there not a double excellency in
170 this?

MISTRESS FORD I know not which pleases me better, that my husband is deceived, or Sir John.

MISTRESS PAGE What a taking was he in, when your husband asked who was in the basket!

175 MISTRESS FORD I am half afraid he will have a need of washing: so throwing him into the water will do him a benefit.

MISTRESS PAGE Hang him, dishonest rascal! I would all of the same strain were in the same distress.

180 MISTRESS FORD I think my husband hath some special suspicion of Falstaff's being here, for I never saw him so gross in his jealousy till now.

MISTRESS PAGE I will lay a plot to try that, and we will yet have more tricks with Falstaff. His dissolute disease
185 will scarce obey this medicine.

MISTRESS FORD Shall we send that foolish carrion Mistress Quickly to him, and excuse his throwing into the water, and give him another hope, to betray him to another punishment?

190 MISTRESS PAGE We will do it: let him be sent for tomorrow eight o'clock to have amends.

Enter FORD, PAGE, CAIUS
and EVANS.

FORD I cannot find him. Maybe the knave bragged of that he could not compass.

MISTRESS PAGE [*aside to Mistress Ford*] Heard you that?

MISTRESS FORD You use me well, Master Ford, do
195 you?

FORD Ay, I do so.

MISTRESS FORD Heaven make you better than your thoughts.

FORD Amen.
200 MISTRESS PAGE You do yourself mighty wrong, Master Ford.

FORD Ay, ay; I must bear it.

EVANS   By Jeshu, if there be anypody in the house, and
in the chambers, and in the coffers, and in the presses,
heaven forgive my sins at the day of judgement!

CAIUS   Be gar, nor I too; there is nobodies.

PAGE   Fie, fie, Master Ford, are you not ashamed? What
spirit, what devil, suggests this imagination? I would
not ha' your distemper in this kind, for the wealth of
Windsor Castle.

FORD   'Tis my fault, Master Page, I suffer for it.

EVANS   You suffer for a pad conscience. Your wife is as
honest a 'omans as I will desires among five thousand,
and five hundred too.

CAIUS   By gar, I see 'tis an honest woman.

FORD   Well, I promised you a dinner. Come, come, walk
in the park, I pray you pardon me; I will hereafter
make known to you why I have done this. Come, wife,
come, Mistress Page, I pray you pardon me, pray
heartily pardon me.

PAGE   [*to Caius and Evans*]   Let's go in, gentlemen; but
trust me, we'll mock him. [*to all*] I do invite you
tomorrow morning to my house to breakfast; after,
we'll a-birding together, I have a fine hawk for the
bush. Shall it be so?

FORD   Anything.

EVANS   If there is one, I shall make two in the company.

CAIUS   If there be one or two, I shall make-a the turd.

FORD   Pray you go, Master Page.

Exeunt all but Evans and Caius.

EVANS   I pray you now remembrance tomorrow on the
lousy knave, mine host.

CAIUS   Dat is good, by gar, with all my heart.

EVANS   A lousy knave, to have his gibes and his
mockeries!   *Exeunt.*

3.4   *Enter* FENTON *and* ANNE Page.

FENTON   I see I cannot get thy father's love,
Therefore no more turn me to him, sweet Nan.

ANNE   Alas, how then?

FENTON   Why, thou must be thyself.
He doth object I am too great of birth,
And that, my state being galled with my expense,
I seek to heal it only by his wealth.
Besides these, other bars he lays before me:
My riots past, my wild societies –
And tells me 'tis a thing impossible
I should love thee, but as a property.

ANNE   Maybe he tells you true.

FENTON   No, God so speed me in my time to come!
Albeit I will confess thy father's wealth
Was the first motive that I wooed thee, Anne,
Yet, wooing thee, I found thee of more value
Than stamps in gold or sums in sealed bags.
And 'tis the very riches of thyself
That now I aim at.

ANNE   Gentle Master Fenton,
Yet seek my father's love, still seek it, sir.

If opportunity and humblest suit
Cannot attain it, why then – hark you hither –
[*They talk apart.*]

Enter SHALLOW, SLENDER *and* Mistress QUICKLY.

SHALLOW   Break their talk, Mistress Quickly. My
kinsman shall speak for himself.

SLENDER   I'll make a shaft or a bolt on't. 'Slid, 'tis but
venturing.

SHALLOW   Be not dismayed.

SLENDER   No, she shall not dismay me: I care not for
that, but that I am afeard.

QUICKLY   [*to Anne*]   Hark ye, Master Slender would
speak a word with you.

ANNE   I come to him. – [*aside*] This is my father's
choice.
O, what a world of vile ill-favoured faults
Looks handsome in three hundred pounds a year!

QUICKLY   And how does good Master Fenton? Pray
you, a word with you. [*Draws Fenton aside.*]

SHALLOW   [*to Slender*]   She's coming; to her, coz. O boy,
thou hadst a father!

SLENDER   I had a father, Mistress Anne, my uncle can
tell you good jests of him. – Pray you, uncle, tell
Mistress Anne the jest how my father stole two geese
out of a pen, good uncle.

SHALLOW   Mistress Anne, my cousin loves you.

SLENDER   Ay, that I do, as well as I love any woman in
Gloucestershire.

SHALLOW   He will maintain you like a gentlewoman.

SLENDER   Ay, that I will, come cut and long-tail, under
the degree of a squire.

SHALLOW   He will make you a hundred and fifty
pounds jointure.

ANNE   Good Master Shallow, let him woo for himself.

SHALLOW   Marry, I thank you for it, I thank you for that
good comfort. – She calls you, coz; I'll leave you.

ANNE   Now, Master Slender.

SLENDER   Now, good Mistress Anne.

ANNE   What is your will?

SLENDER   My will? 'Od's heartlings, that's a pretty jest
indeed! I ne'er made my will yet, I thank God: I am not
such a sickly creature, I give God praise.

ANNE   I mean, Master Slender, what would you with me?

SLENDER   Truly, for mine own part, I would little or
nothing with you. Your father and my uncle hath made
motions: if it be my luck, so; if not, happy man be his
dole. They can tell you how things go better than I can.
– You may ask your father: here he comes.

Enter PAGE *and* MISTRESS PAGE.

PAGE
Now, Master Slender, – love him, daughter Anne –
Why, how now? What does Master Fenton here?
You wrong me, sir, thus still to haunt my house.
I told you, sir, my daughter is disposed of.

FENTON   Nay, Master Page, be not impatient.

MISTRESS PAGE
  Good Master Fenton, come not to my child.
PAGE   She is no match for you.
FENTON   Sir, will you hear me?
PAGE   No, good Master Fenton. –
  Come, Master Shallow; come, son Slender, in. –
75 Knowing my mind, you wrong me, Master Fenton.
                    Exit with Shallow and Slender.
QUICKLY [*to Fenton*]   Speak to Mistress Page.
FENTON
  Good Mistress Page, for that I love your daughter
  In such a righteous fashion as I do,
  Perforce, against all checks, rebukes and manners,
80 I must advance the colours of my love
  And not retire. Let me have your good will.
ANNE   Good mother, do not marry me to yond fool.
MISTRESS PAGE   I mean it not, I seek you a better
  husband.
85 QUICKLY [*aside*]   That's my master, Master Doctor.
ANNE   Alas, I had rather be set quick i'th' earth,
  And bowled to death with turnips.
MISTRESS PAGE
  Come, trouble not yourself, good Master Fenton,
  I will not be your friend, nor enemy.
90 My daughter will I question how she loves you,
  And as I find her, so am I affected.
  Till then, farewell, sir; she must needs go in,
  Her father will be angry.
FENTON   Farewell, gentle mistress; farewell, Nan.
                    Exeunt Mistress Page and Anne.
95 QUICKLY   This is my doing, now. 'Nay,' said I, 'will you
  cast away your child on a fool, and a physician? Look
  on Master Fenton!' This is my doing.
FENTON   I thank thee, and I pray thee once tonight
  Give my sweet Nan this ring. – There's for thy pains.
100 QUICKLY   Now heaven send thee good fortune!
                                        Exit Fenton.
  A kind heart he hath: a woman would run through fire
  and water for such a kind heart. But yet I would my
  master had Mistress Anne, or I would Master Slender
  had her; or, in sooth, I would Master Fenton had her.
105 I will do what I can for them all three, for so I have
  promised and I'll be as good as my word – but
  speciously for Master Fenton. Well, I must of another
  errand to Sir John Falstaff from my two mistresses –
  what a beast am I to slack it!   *Exit.*

3.5   *Enter* FALSTAFF.

FALSTAFF   Bardolph, I say!

                    Enter BARDOLPH.

BARDOLPH   Here, sir.
FALSTAFF   Go fetch me a quart of sack; put a toast in't.
                                        Exit Bardolph.
  Have I lived to be carried in a basket like a barrow of
  butcher's offal, and to be thrown in the Thames? Well,

if I be served such another trick, I'll have my brains
ta'en out and buttered, and give them to a dog for a
New Year's gift. 'Sblood, the rogues slighted me into
the river with as little remorse as they would have
drowned a blind bitch's puppies, fifteen i'the litter;   10
and you may know by my size that I have a kind of
alacrity in sinking: if the bottom were as deep as hell, I
should down. I had been drowned, but that the shore
was shelvy and shallow – a death that I abhor, for the
water swells a man – and what a thing should I have   15
been, when I had been swelled? I should have been a
mountain of mummy!

                    Enter BARDOLPH *with sack.*

BARDOLPH   Here's Mistress Quickly, sir, to speak with
  you.
FALSTAFF   Come, let me pour in some sack to the   20
  Thames water, for my belly's as cold as if I had
  swallowed snowballs for pills to cool the reins. – Call
  her in.
BARDOLPH   Come in, woman.

                    Enter Mistress QUICKLY.

QUICKLY   By your leave, I cry you mercy! Give your   25
  worship good morrow.
FALSTAFF   Take away these chalices. Go, brew me a
  pottle of sack finely.
BARDOLPH   With eggs, sir?
FALSTAFF   Simple of itself. I'll no pullet sperm in my 30
  brewage.   *Exit Bardolph.*
  How now?
QUICKLY   Marry, sir, I come to your worship from
  Mistress Ford.
FALSTAFF   Mistress Ford? I have had ford enough. I was 35
  thrown into the ford, I have my belly full of ford.
QUICKLY   Alas the day, good heart, that was not her
  fault. She does so take on with her men: they mistook
  their erection.
FALSTAFF   So did I mine, to build upon a foolish   40
  woman's promise.
QUICKLY   Well, she laments, sir, for it, that it would
  yearn your heart to see it. Her husband goes this
  morning a-birding. She desires you once more to come
  to her, between eight and nine. I must carry her word   45
  quickly; she'll make you amends, I warrant you.
FALSTAFF   Well, I will visit her; tell her so, and bid her
  think what a man is. Let her consider his frailty, and
  then judge of my merit.
QUICKLY   I will tell her.   50
FALSTAFF   Do so. Between nine and ten, sayst thou?
QUICKLY   Eight and nine, sir.
FALSTAFF   Well, be gone. I will not miss her.
QUICKLY   Peace be with you, sir.   *Exit.*
FALSTAFF   I marvel I hear not of Master Brook; he sent 55
  me word to stay within. I like his money well. – By the
  mass, here he comes.

                    Enter FORD *as Brook.*

FORD   God save you, sir.

FALSTAFF   Now, Master Brook, you come to know what
60   hath passed between me and Ford's wife.

FORD   That indeed, Sir John, is my business.

FALSTAFF   Master Brook, I will not lie to you. I was at
her house the hour she appointed me.

FORD   And how sped you, sir?

65   FALSTAFF   Very ill-favouredly, Master Brook.

FORD   How so, sir? Did she change her determination?

FALSTAFF   No, Master Brook, but the peaking cornuto
her husband, Master Brook, dwelling in a continual
'larum of jealousy, comes me in the instant of our
70   encounter, after we had embraced, kissed, protested,
and, as it were, spoke the prologue of our comedy; and
at his heels a rabble of his companions, thither
provoked and instigated by his distemper, and,
forsooth, to search his house for his wife's love.

75   FORD   What, while you were there?

FALSTAFF   While I was there.

FORD   And did he search for you, and could not find
you?

FALSTAFF   You shall hear. As good luck would have it,
80   comes in one Mistress Page, gives intelligence of
Ford's approach; and in her invention, and Ford's
wife's distraction, they conveyed me into a
buck-basket.

FORD   A buck-basket?

85   FALSTAFF   By the Lord, a buck-basket! Rammed me in
with foul shirts and smocks, socks, foul stockings,
greasy napkins, that, Master Brook, there was the
rankest compound of villainous smell that ever
offended nostril.

90   FORD   And how long lay you there?

FALSTAFF   Nay, you shall hear, Master Brook, what I
have suffered to bring this woman to evil for your
good. Being thus crammed in the basket, a couple of
Ford's knaves, his hinds, were called forth by their
95   mistress, to carry me in the name of foul clothes to
Datchet Lane. They took me on their shoulders, met
the jealous knave their master in the door, who asked
them once or twice what they had in their basket. I
quaked for fear lest the lunatic knave would have
100   searched it; but Fate, ordaining he should be a cuckold,
held his hand. Well, on went he for a search, and away
went I for foul clothes. But mark the sequel, Master
Brook. I suffered the pangs of three several deaths:
first, an intolerable fright to be detected with a jealous
105   rotten bell-wether; next, to be compassed like a good
bilbo in the circumference of a peck, hilt to point, heel
to head; and then, to be stopped in like a strong
distillation with stinking clothes that fretted in their
own grease. Think of that, a man of my kidney, think
110   of that – that am as subject to heat as butter – a man of
continual dissolution and thaw: it was a miracle to
scape suffocation. And in the height of this bath –
when I was more than half stewed in grease, like a
Dutch dish – to be thrown into the Thames and

cooled, glowing hot, in that surge like a horseshoe –   115
think of that – hissing hot – think of that, Master
Brook.

FORD   In good sadness, sir, I am sorry that for my sake
you have suffered all this. My suit, then, is desperate:
you'll undertake her no more?   120

FALSTAFF   Master Brook, I will be thrown into Etna, as
I have been into Thames, ere I will leave her thus. Her
husband is this morning gone a-birding; I have
received from her another embassy of meeting: 'twixt
eight and nine is the hour, Master Brook.   125

FORD   'Tis past eight already, sir.

FALSTAFF   Is it? I will then address me to my
appointment. Come to me at your convenient leisure,
and you shall know how I speed; and the conclusion
shall be crowned with your enjoying her. Adieu. You   130
shall have her, Master Brook. Master Brook, you shall
cuckold Ford.   *Exit.*

FORD   Hum – ha! Is this a vision? Is this a dream? Do I
sleep? Master Ford, awake; awake, Master Ford!
There's a hole made in your best coat, Master Ford.   135
This 'tis to be married, this 'tis to have linen and buck-
baskets! Well, I will proclaim myself what I am. I will
now take the lecher. He is at my house, he cannot scape
me – 'tis impossible he should. He cannot creep into a
half-penny purse, nor into a pepperbox. But, lest the   140
devil that guides him should aid him, I will search
impossible places. Though what I am I cannot avoid,
yet to be what I would not shall not make me tame. If I
have horns to make one mad, let the proverb go with
me: I'll be horn-mad.   *Exit.*   145

4.1   *Enter* MISTRESS PAGE, Mistress
                        QUICKLY *and* WILLIAM.

MISTRESS PAGE   Is he at Master Ford's already, thinkst
thou?

QUICKLY   Sure he is by this, or will be presently. But
truly he is very courageous mad about his throwing
into the water. Mistress Ford desires you to come   5
suddenly.

MISTRESS PAGE   I'll be with her by and by: I'll but bring
my young man here to school. Look where his master
comes; 'tis a playing day, I see.

Enter EVANS.

How now, Sir Hugh, no school today?   10

EVANS   No, Master Slender is let the boys leave to play.

QUICKLY   God's blessing of his heart!

MISTRESS PAGE   Sir Hugh, my husband says my son
profits nothing in the world at his book. I pray you, ask
him some questions in his accidence.   15

EVANS   Come hither, William. Hold up your head,
come.

MISTRESS PAGE   Come on, sirrah, hold up your head.
Answer your master, be not afraid.

EVANS   William, how many numbers is in nouns?   20

WILLIAM Two.

QUICKLY Truly, I thought there had been one number more, because they say "Od's nouns'.

EVANS Peace your tattlings. What is 'fair', William?

WILLIAM *Pulcher.*

QUICKLY Polecats? There are fairer things than polecats, sure.

EVANS You are a very simplicity 'oman; I pray you, peace. – What is *lapis*, William?

WILLIAM A stone.

EVANS And what is 'a stone', William?

WILLIAM A pebble.

EVANS No, it is *lapis*; I pray you remember in your prain.

WILLIAM *Lapis.*

EVANS That is a good William. What is he, William, that does lend articles?

WILLIAM Articles are borrowed of the pronoun, and be thus declined: *Singulariter nominativo hic, haec, hoc.*

EVANS *Nominativo hig, haeg, hog,* pray you mark. *Genitivo huius.* Well, what is your accusative case?

WILLIAM *Accusativo hinc –*

EVANS I pray you have your remembrance, child: *accusativo hing, hang, hog.*

QUICKLY 'Hang-hog' is Latin for bacon, I warrant you.

EVANS Leave your prabbles, 'oman. – What is the focative case, William?

WILLIAM O – *vocativo* – O –

EVANS Remember, William; focative is caret.

QUICKLY And that's a good root.

EVANS 'Oman, forbear.

MISTRESS PAGE Peace.

EVANS What is your genitive case plural, William?

WILLIAM Genitive case?

EVANS Ay.

WILLIAM *Genitivo horum, harum, horum.*

QUICKLY 'Vengeance of Jenny's case, fie on her! Never name her, child, if she be a whore.

EVANS For shame, 'oman.

QUICKLY You do ill to teach the child such words. – He teaches him to hick and to hack, which they'll do fast enough of themselves, and to call 'whore 'm'! – Fie upon you!

EVANS 'Oman, art thou lunatics? Hast thou no understandings for thy cases, and the numbers of the genders? Thou art as foolish Christian creatures as I would desires.

MISTRESS PAGE [*to Quickly*] Prithee hold thy peace.

EVANS Show me now, William, some declensions of your pronouns.

WILLIAM Forsooth, I have forgot.

EVANS It is *qui, quae, quod.* If you forget your *quis*, your *quaes*, and your *quods*, you must be preeches. Go your ways and play, go.

MISTRESS PAGE He is a better scholar than I thought he was.

EVANS He is a good sprag memory. Farewell, Mistress Page.

MISTRESS PAGE Adieu, good Sir Hugh. *Exit Evans.*
Get you home, boy. *Exit William.*
Come, we stay too long. *Exeunt.*

4.2 *Enter* FALSTAFF *and* MISTRESS FORD.

FALSTAFF Mistress Ford, your sorrow hath eaten up my sufferance. I see you are obsequious in your love and I profess requital to a hair's breadth, not only, Mistress Ford, in the simple office of love, but in all the accoutrement, compliment and ceremony of it. But are you sure of your husband now?

MISTRESS FORD He's a-birding, sweet Sir John.

MISTRESS PAGE [*within*] What ho, gossip Ford, what ho!

MISTRESS FORD Step into the chamber, Sir John.
Exit Falstaff.

Enter MISTRESS PAGE.

MISTRESS PAGE How now, sweetheart, who's at home besides yourself?

MISTRESS FORD Why, none but mine own people.

MISTRESS PAGE Indeed?

MISTRESS FORD No, certainly. – [*Whispers.*] Speak louder.

MISTRESS PAGE Truly, I am so glad you have nobody here.

MISTRESS FORD Why?

MISTRESS PAGE Why, woman, your husband is in his old lines again: he so takes on yonder with my husband, so rails against all married mankind, so curses all Eve's daughters, of what complexion soever, and so buffets himself on the forehead, crying 'peer out, peer out!', that any madness I ever yet beheld seemed but tameness, civility and patience to this his distemper he is in now. I am glad the fat knight is not here.

MISTRESS FORD Why, does he talk of him?

MISTRESS PAGE Of none but him, and swears he was carried out, the last time he searched for him, in a basket; protests to my husband he is now here, and hath drawn him and the rest of their company from their sport, to make another experiment of his suspicion. But I am glad the knight is not here: now he shall see his own foolery.

MISTRESS FORD How near is he, Mistress Page?

MISTRESS PAGE Hard by, at street end. He will be here anon.

MISTRESS FORD I am undone: the knight is here.

MISTRESS PAGE Why, then you are utterly shamed and he's but a dead man. What a woman are you! Away with him, away with him: better shame than murder.

MISTRESS FORD Which way should he go? How should I bestow him? Shall I put him into the basket again?

Enter FALSTAFF.

FALSTAFF No, I'll come no more i'the basket. May I not go out ere he come?

MISTRESS PAGE Alas, three of Master Ford's brothers watch the door with pistols, that none shall issue out, otherwise you might slip away ere he came. – But what make you here?

FALSTAFF What shall I do? I'll creep up into the chimney.

MISTRESS FORD There they always use to discharge their birding-pieces.

MISTRESS PAGE Creep into the kiln-hole.

FALSTAFF Where is it?

MISTRESS FORD He will seek there, on my word. Neither press, coffer, chest, trunk, well, vault, but he hath an abstract for the remembrance of such places and goes to them by his note. There is no hiding you in the house.

FALSTAFF I'll go out, then.

MISTRESS PAGE If you go out in your own semblance you die, Sir John – unless you go out disguised.

MISTRESS FORD How might we disguise him?

MISTRESS PAGE Alas the day, I know not: there is no woman's gown big enough for him. Otherwise he might put on a hat, a muffler and a kerchief, and so escape.

FALSTAFF Good hearts, devise something; any extremity rather than a mischief.

MISTRESS FORD My maid's aunt, the fat woman of Brentford, has a gown above.

MISTRESS PAGE On my word, it will serve him. She's as big as he is – and there's her thrummed hat and her muffler too. – Run up, Sir John.

MISTRESS FORD Go, go, sweet Sir John. Mistress Page and I will look some linen for your head.

MISTRESS PAGE Quick, quick! We'll come dress you straight; put on the gown the while.   *Exit Falstaff.*

MISTRESS FORD I would my husband would meet him in this shape! He cannot abide the old woman of Brentford; he swears she's a witch, forbade her my house and hath threatened to beat her.

MISTRESS PAGE Heaven guide him to thy husband's cudgel and the devil guide his cudgel afterwards.

MISTRESS FORD But is my husband coming?

MISTRESS PAGE Ay, in good sadness is he, and talks of the basket too, howsoever he hath had intelligence.

MISTRESS FORD We'll try that; for I'll appoint my men to carry the basket again to meet him at the door with it, as they did last time.

MISTRESS PAGE Nay, but he'll be here presently. Let's go dress him like the witch of Brentford.

MISTRESS FORD I'll first direct my men what they shall do with the basket. Go up, I'll bring linen for him straight.

MISTRESS PAGE Hang him, dishonest varlet! We cannot misuse him enough.   *Exit Mistress Ford.*
We'll leave a proof, by that which we will do,
Wives may be merry and yet honest too.

We do not act that often jest and laugh;
'Tis old but true: 'Still swine eats all the draff'.   *Exit.*

Enter MISTRESS FORD *with* JOHN *and* ROBERT.

MISTRESS FORD Go, sirs, take the basket again on your shoulders. Your master is hard at door; if he bid you set it down, obey him. Quickly, dispatch.   *Exit.*

JOHN Come, come, take it up.

ROBERT Pray heaven it be not full of knight again.

JOHN I hope not, I had as lief bear so much lead.

Enter FORD, PAGE, SHALLOW, CAIUS *and* EVANS *at one door, and* JOHN *and* ROBERT *go and fetch in the basket at another.*

FORD Ay, but if it prove true, Master Page, have you any way then to unfool me again? – Set down the basket, villains. Somebody call my wife. Youth in a basket! O you panderly rascals, there's a knot, a gin, a pack, a conspiracy against me. Now shall the devil be shamed. – What, wife, I say! Come, come forth: behold what honest clothes you send forth to bleaching!

PAGE Why, this passes, Master Ford! You are not to go loose any longer, you must be pinioned.

EVANS Why, this is lunatics, this is mad as a mad dog.

SHALLOW Indeed, Master Ford, this is not well indeed.

FORD So say I too, sir.

Enter MISTRESS FORD.

Come hither, Mistress Ford – Mistress Ford, the honest woman, the modest wife, the virtuous creature that hath the jealous fool to her husband! I suspect without cause, mistress, do I?

MISTRESS FORD God be my witness you do, if you suspect me in any dishonesty.

FORD Well said, brazen-face, hold it out! – Come forth, sirrah! [*Pulls clothes from the basket.*]

PAGE This passes.

MISTRESS FORD Are you not ashamed? Let the clothes alone.

FORD I shall find you anon.

EVANS 'Tis unreasonable! Will you take up your wife's clothes? Come, away!

FORD Empty the basket, I say.

PAGE Why, man, why?

FORD Master Page, as I am a man, there was one conveyed out of my house yesterday in this basket. Why may not he be there again? In my house I am sure he is: my intelligence is true, my jealousy is reasonable. – Pluck me out all the linen.

MISTRESS FORD If you find a man there, he shall die a flea's death. [*They empty the basket.*]

PAGE Here's no man.

SHALLOW By my fidelity, this is not well, Master Ford, this wrongs you.

EVANS Master Ford, you must pray, and not follow the imaginations of your own heart: this is jealousies.

FORD Well, he's not here I seek for.

PAGE   No, nor nowhere else but in your brain.

FORD   Help to search my house this one time. If I find
not what I seek, show no colour for my extremity, let
me for ever be your table-sport. Let them say of me 'As
jealous as Ford, that searched a hollow walnut for his
wife's leman'. Satisfy me once more, once more search
with me.   *Exeunt John and Robert with basket.*

MISTRESS FORD   What ho, Mistress Page, come you
and the old woman down; my husband will come into
the chamber.

FORD   Old woman? What old woman's that?

MISTRESS FORD   Why, it is my maid's aunt of
Brentford.

FORD   A witch, a quean, an old cozening quean! Have I
not forbid her my house? She comes of errands, does
she? We are simple men, we do not know what's
brought to pass under the profession of fortune-
telling. She works by charms, by spells, by the figure,
and such daubery as this is, beyond our element: we
know nothing. – Come down, you witch, you hag, you!
Come down, I say!

MISTRESS FORD   Nay, good sweet husband – good
gentlemen, let him not strike the old woman.

Enter FALSTAFF, *disguised like an old woman, and*
MISTRESS PAGE.

MISTRESS PAGE   Come, mother Prat, come, give me
your hand.

FORD   I'll prat her! [*Beats him.*] Out of my door, you
witch, you rag, you baggage, you polecat, you runnion,
out, out! I'll conjure you, I'll fortune-tell you!
                                      Exit Falstaff.

MISTRESS PAGE   Are you not ashamed? I think you have
killed the poor woman.

MISTRESS FORD   Nay, he will do it. 'Tis a goodly credit
for you!

FORD   Hang her, witch!

EVANS   By yea and no, I think the 'oman is a witch
indeed. I like not when a 'oman has a great peard – I
spy a great peard under her muffler.

FORD   Will you follow, gentlemen? I beseech you, follow,
see but the issue of my jealousy. If I cry out thus upon
no trail, never trust me when I open again.

PAGE   Let's obey his humour a little further. Come,
gentlemen.

Exeunt all but Mistress Ford and Mistress Page.

MISTRESS PAGE   By my troth, he beat him most
pitifully.

MISTRESS FORD   Nay, by th'mass, that he did not: he
beat him most unpitifully, methought.

MISTRESS PAGE   I'll have the cudgel hallowed and hung
o'er the altar: it hath done meritorious service.

MISTRESS FORD   What think you? May we, with the
warrant of womanhood and the witness of a good
conscience, pursue him with any further revenge?

MISTRESS PAGE   The spirit of wantonness is sure scared
out of him. If the devil have him not in fee-simple,

with fine and recovery, he will never, I think, in the way
of waste, attempt us again.

MISTRESS FORD   Shall we tell our husbands how we
have served him?

MISTRESS PAGE   Yes, by all means, if it be but to scrape
the figures out of your husband's brains. If they can find
in their hearts the poor unvirtuous fat knight shall be
any further afflicted, we two will still be the ministers.

MISTRESS FORD   I'll warrant they'll have him publicly
shamed, and methinks there would be no period to the
jest should he not be publicly shamed.

MISTRESS PAGE   Come, to the forge with it, then shape
it: I would not have things cool.   *Exeunt.*

4.3   *Enter* HOST *and* BARDOLPH.

BARDOLPH   Sir, the German desires to have three of
your horses. The Duke himself will be tomorrow at
court, and they are going to meet him.

HOST   What duke should that be comes so secretly? I
hear not of him in the court. Let me speak with the
gentlemen – they speak English?

BARDOLPH   Ay, sir. I'll call him to you.

HOST   They shall have my horses, but I'll make them
pay, I'll sauce them. They have had my house a week at
command. I have turned away my other guests: they
must come off, I'll sauce them. Come.   *Exeunt.*

4.4   *Enter* PAGE, FORD, MISTRESS PAGE,
              MISTRESS FORD *and* EVANS.

EVANS   'Tis one of the best discretions of a 'oman as
ever I did look upon.

PAGE   And did he send you both these letters at an
instant?

MISTRESS PAGE   Within a quarter of an hour.

FORD   Pardon me, wife. Henceforth do what thou wilt:
I rather will suspect the sun with cold
Than thee with wantonness. Now doth thy honour
     stand,
In him that was of late an heretic,
As firm as faith.

PAGE   'Tis well, 'tis well, no more.
Be not as extreme in submission as in offence.
But let our plot go forward. Let our wives
Yet once again, to make us public sport,
Appoint a meeting with this old fat fellow,
Where we may take him and disgrace him for it.

FORD   There is no better way than that they spoke of.

PAGE   How? To send him word they'll meet him in the
park at midnight? Fie, fie, he'll never come.

EVANS   You say he has been thrown in the rivers, and has
been grievously peaten, as an old 'oman. Methinks
there should be terrors in him, that he should not
come. Methinks his flesh is punished, he shall have no
desires.

PAGE   So think I too.

MISTRESS FORD

25   Devise but how you'll use him when he comes
        And let us two devise to bring him thither.

MISTRESS PAGE

        There is an old tale goes that Herne the hunter,
        Sometime a keeper here in Windsor Forest,
        Doth, all the winter time, at still midnight,
30   Walk round about an oak, with great ragg'd horns,
        And there he blasts the trees, and takes the cattle,
        And makes milch-kine yield blood and shakes a chain
        In a most hideous and dreadful manner.
        You have heard of such a spirit, and well you know
35   The superstitious idle-headed eld
        Received and did deliver to our age
        This tale of Herne the hunter for a truth.

PAGE

        Why, yet there want not many that do fear
        In deep of night to walk by this Herne's oak.
        But what of this?

40   MISTRESS FORD   Marry, this is our device:
        That Falstaff at that oak shall meet with us,
        Disguised like Herne, with huge horns on his head.

     PAGE   Well, let it not be doubted but he'll come,
        And in this shape; when you have brought him
            thither,
45   What shall be done with him? What is your plot?

MISTRESS PAGE

        That likewise have we thought upon, and thus:
        Nan Page my daughter, and my little son,
        And three or four more of their growth, we'll dress
        Like urchins, oafs and fairies, green and white,
50   With rounds of waxen tapers on their heads
        And rattles in their hands. Upon a sudden,
        As Falstaff, she and I are newly met,
        Let them from forth a sawpit rush at once
        With some diffused song; upon their sight
55   We two in great amazedness will fly;
        Then let them all encircle him about,
        And fairy-like to pinch the unclean knight,
        And ask him why, that hour of fairy revel,
        In their so sacred paths he dares to tread
        In shape profane.

60   MISTRESS FORD   And till he tell the truth
        Let the supposed fairies pinch him sound
        And burn him with their tapers.

     MISTRESS PAGE   The truth being known,
        We'll all present ourselves, dishorn the spirit,
        And mock him home to Windsor.

     FORD   The children must
65   Be practised well to this, or they'll ne'er do't.

     EVANS   I will teach the children their behaviours, and I
        will be like a jackanapes also, to burn the knight with
        my taber.

     FORD   That will be excellent, I'll go buy them vizards.

MISTRESS PAGE

70   My Nan shall be the queen of all the fairies,
        Finely attired in a robe of white.

PAGE   That silk will I go buy – [*aside*] and in that time
        Shall Master Slender steal my Nan away,
        And marry her at Eton. – Go, send to Falstaff straight.

FORD   Nay, I'll to him again in name of Brook: 75
        He'll tell me all his purpose. Sure, he'll come.

MISTRESS PAGE   Fear not you that. Go get us properties
        And tricking for our fairies.

EVANS   Let us about it. – It is admirable pleasures and
        ferry honest knaveries.   *Exeunt Page, Ford and Evans.*   80

MISTRESS PAGE   Go, Mistress Ford,
        Send quickly to Sir John to know his mind.

                                    Exit Mistress Ford.

        I'll to the Doctor: he hath my good will,
        And none but he, to marry with Nan Page.
        That Slender, though well landed, is an idiot –   85
        And he my husband best of all affects.
        The Doctor is well moneyed, and his friends
        Potent at court: he, none but he, shall have her,
        Though twenty thousand worthier come to crave her.

                                                    Exit.

4.5   *Enter* HOST *and* SIMPLE.

HOST   What wouldst thou have, boor? What, thick-skin?
        Speak, breathe, discuss – brief, short, quick, snap.

SIMPLE   Marry, sir, I come to speak with Sir John
        Falstaff from Master Slender.

HOST   There's his chamber, his house, his castle, his   5
        standing-bed, and truckle-bed: 'tis painted about with
        the story of the Prodigal, fresh and new. Go, knock and
        call: he'll speak like an anthropophaginian unto thee.
        Knock, I say.

SIMPLE   There's an old woman, a fat woman, gone up   10
        into his chamber. I'll be so bold as stay, sir, till she
        come down. I come to speak with her indeed.

HOST   Ha? A fat woman? The knight may be robbed, I'll
        call. – Bully knight, bully Sir John! Speak from thy
        lungs military: art thou there? It is thine host, thine   15
        Ephesian, calls.

FALSTAFF [*above*]   How now, mine host?

HOST   Here's a Bohemian-Tartar tarries the coming down
        of thy fat woman. Let her descend, bully, let her descend.
        My chambers are honourable. Fie! Privacy? Fie!   20

                        Enter FALSTAFF.

FALSTAFF   There was, mine host, an old fat woman even
        now with me, but she's gone.

SIMPLE   Pray you, sir, was't not the wise woman of
        Brentford?

FALSTAFF   Ay, marry, was it, mussel-shell. What would   25
        you with her?

SIMPLE   My master, sir, my master, Master Slender,
        sent to her, seeing her go thorough the streets, to know,
        sir, whether one Nim, sir, that beguiled him of a chain,
        had the chain, or no.   30

FALSTAFF   I spake with the old woman about it.

SIMPLE   And what says she, I pray, sir?

FALSTAFF Marry, she says that the very same man that beguiled Master Slender of his chain – cozened him of it.

35

SIMPLE I would I could have spoken with the woman herself. I had other things to have spoken with her too, from him.

FALSTAFF What are they? Let us know.

40

HOST Ay, come. Quick!

SIMPLE I may not conceal them, sir.

HOST Conceal them, or thou diest.

SIMPLE Why, sir, they were nothing but about Mistress Anne Page, to know if it were my master's fortune to have her, or no.

45

FALSTAFF 'Tis, 'tis his fortune.

SIMPLE What, sir?

FALSTAFF To have her, or no. Go, say the woman told me so.

SIMPLE May I be bold to say so, sir?

50

FALSTAFF Ay, sir Tike; who more bold?

SIMPLE I thank your worship; I shall make my master glad with these tidings.   *Exit.*

HOST Thou art clerkly, thou art clerkly, Sir John. Was there a wise woman with thee?

55

FALSTAFF Ay, that there was, mine host; one that hath taught me more wit than ever I learnt before in my life; and I paid nothing for it neither, but was paid for my learning.

Enter BARDOLPH.

60

BARDOLPH Out alas, sir: cozenage, mere cozenage!

HOST Where be my horses? Speak well of them, varletto.

BARDOLPH Run away with the cozeners: for so soon as I came beyond Eton, they threw me off from behind one of them, in a slough of mire, and set spurs and away, like three German devils, three Doctor Faustasses.

65

HOST They are gone but to meet the Duke, villain, do not say they be fled. Germans are honest men.

Enter EVANS.

70

EVANS Where is mine host?

HOST What is the matter, sir?

EVANS Have a care of your entertainments. There is a friend of mine come to town tells me there is three sorts of Cozen-Garmombles, that has cozened all the hosts of Readings, of Maidenhead, of Colebrook, of horses and money. I tell you for good will, look you: you are wise, and full of gibes and vlouting-stocks, and 'tis not convenient you should be cozened. Fare you well.

75

Exit.

Enter CAIUS.

CAIUS Vere is mine host de Jarteer?

80

HOST Here, master Doctor, in perplexity and doubtful dilemma.

CAIUS I cannot tell vat is dat, but, by gar, it is tell-a me dat you make grand preparation for a Duke de Jarmany. By my trot, der is no Duke that the court is know to come. By gar, I tell you for good will. Adieu.

85

Exit.

HOST Hue and cry, villain, go! – Assist me, knight, I am undone! – Fly, run, hue and cry, villain, I am undone!

Exit with Bardolph.

FALSTAFF I would all the world might be cozened, for I have been cozened and beaten too. If it should come to the ear of the court how I have been transformed, and how my transformation hath been washed and cudgelled, they would melt me out of my fat drop by drop, and liquor fishermen's boots with me. I warrant they would whip me with their fine wits till I were as crestfallen as a dried pear. I never prospered since I forswore myself at primero. Well, if my wind were but long enough, I would repent.

90

95

Enter Mistress QUICKLY.

Now, whence come you?

QUICKLY From the two parties, forsooth.

FALSTAFF The devil take one party and his dam the other, and so they shall be both bestowed. I have suffered more for their sakes, more than the villainous inconstancy of man's disposition is able to bear.

100

QUICKLY And have not they suffered? Yes, I warrant, speciously one of them. Mistress Ford, good heart, is beaten black and blue, that you cannot see a white spot about her.

105

FALSTAFF What tellst thou me of black and blue? I was beaten myself into all the colours of the rainbow, and I was like to be apprehended for the witch of Brentford. But that my admirable dexterity of wit, my counterfeiting the action of an old woman, delivered me, the knave constable had set me i'the stocks, i'the common stocks, for a witch.

110

QUICKLY Sir, let me speak with you in your chamber, you shall hear how things go, and, I warrant, to your content. Here is a letter will say somewhat – good hearts, what ado is here to bring you together! Sure, one of you does not serve heaven well, that you are so crossed.

115

FALSTAFF Come up into my chamber.   *Exeunt.*

120

4.6   *Enter* HOST *and* FENTON.

HOST Master Fenton, talk not to me: my mind is heavy – I will give over all.

FENTON Yet hear me speak. Assist me in my purpose,
And, as I am a gentleman, I'll give thee
A hundred pound in gold more than your loss.

5

HOST I will hear you, Master Fenton, and I will, at the least, keep your counsel.

FENTON From time to time I have acquainted you
With the dear love I bear to fair Anne Page,
Who mutually hath answered my affection –
So far forth as herself might be her chooser –

10

Even to my wish. I have a letter from her
Of such contents as you will wonder at,
The mirth whereof so larded with my matter
15 That neither singly can be manifested
Without the show of both, wherein fat Falstaff
Hath a great scene; the image of the jest
I'll show you here at large. Hark, good mine host:
Tonight at Herne's oak, just 'twixt twelve and one,
20 Must my sweet Nan present the Fairy Queen –
The purpose why is here – in which disguise,
While other jests are something rank on foot,
Her father hath commanded her to slip
Away with Slender, and with him at Eton
25 Immediately to marry – she hath consented. Now, sir,
Her mother – ever strong against that match
And firm for Doctor Caius – hath appointed
That he shall likewise shuffle her away
While other sports are tasking of their minds,
30 And at the dean'ry, where a priest attends,
Straight marry her: to this her mother's plot
She, seemingly obedient, likewise hath
Made promise to the Doctor. Now thus it rests:
Her father means she shall be all in white
35 And, in that habit, when Slender sees his time
To take her by the hand and bid her go,
She shall go with him. Her mother hath intended –
The better to denote her to the Doctor,
For they must all be masked and vizarded –
40 That quaint in green she shall be loose enrobed,
With ribbons pendant flaring 'bout her head;
And when the Doctor spies his vantage ripe,
To pinch her by the hand, and on that token
The maid hath given consent to go with him.
45 HOST   Which means she to deceive, father or mother?
FENTON   Both, my good host, to go along with me.
And here it rests: that you'll procure the vicar
To stay for me at church, 'twixt twelve and one,
And, in the lawful name of marrying,
50 To give our hearts united ceremony.
HOST   Well, husband your device; I'll to the vicar.
Bring you the maid, you shall not lack a priest.
FENTON   So shall I evermore be bound to thee;
Besides, I'll make a present recompense.   *Exeunt.*

5.1   *Enter* FALSTAFF *and* Mistress QUICKLY.

FALSTAFF   Prithee, no more prattling. Go, I'll hold: this
is the third time – I hope good luck lies in odd numbers.
Away, go! They say there is divinity in odd numbers,
either in nativity, chance or death. Away!
5 QUICKLY   I'll provide you a chain, and I'll do what I can
to get you a pair of horns.
FALSTAFF   Away, I say; time wears. Hold up your head,
and mince.   *Exit Mistress Quickly.*

Enter FORD *as Brook.*

How now, Master Brook? Master Brook, the matter will

be known tonight or never. Be you in the park about   10
midnight, at Herne's oak, and you shall see wonders.
FORD   Went you not to her yesterday, sir, as you told me
you had appointed?
FALSTAFF   I went to her, Master Brook, as you see, like a
poor old man, but I came from her, Master Brook, like   15
a poor old woman. That same knave, Ford her husband,
hath the finest mad devil of jealousy in him, Master
Brook, that ever governed frenzy. I will tell you he beat
me grievously, in the shape of a woman; for in the
shape of man, Master Brook, I fear not Goliath with a   20
weaver's beam, because I know also life is a shuttle. I
am in haste: go along with me, I'll tell you all, Master
Brook. Since I plucked geese, played truant and
whipped top, I knew not what 'twas to be beaten till
lately. Follow me, I'll tell you strange things of this   25
knave Ford, on whom tonight I will be revenged, and I
will deliver his wife into your hand. Follow – strange
things in hand, Master Brook! – Follow.   *Exeunt.*

5.2   *Enter* PAGE, SHALLOW *and* SLENDER.

PAGE   Come, come: we'll couch i'the castle ditch till we
see the lights of our fairies. Remember, son Slender,
my daughter –
SLENDER   Ay, forsooth. I have spoke with her and we
have a nay-word how to know one another. I come to   5
her in white, and cry 'mum'; she cries 'budget'; and by
that we know one another.
SHALLOW   That's good too. But what needs either your
'mum' or her 'budget'? The white will decipher her
well enough. – It hath struck ten o'clock.   10
PAGE   The night is dark: lights and spirits will become it
well. God prosper our sport. No man means evil but
the devil, and we shall know him by his horns. Let's
away; follow me.   *Exeunt.*

5.3   *Enter* MISTRESS PAGE, MISTRESS FORD
and CAIUS.

MISTRESS PAGE   Master Doctor, my daughter is in
green: when you see your time, take her by the hand,
away with her to the deanery and dispatch it quickly.
Go before into the park. – We two must go together.
CAIUS   I know vat I have to do. Adieu.   5
MISTRESS PAGE   Fare you well, sir.   *Exit Caius.*
My husband will not rejoice so much at the abuse of
Falstaff as he will chafe at the Doctor's marrying my
daughter. But 'tis no matter: better a little chiding than
a great deal of heartbreak.   10
MISTRESS FORD   Where is Nan now, and her troop of
fairies? And the Welsh devil Hugh?
MISTRESS PAGE   They are all couched in a pit hard by
Herne's oak, with obscured lights, which, at the very
instant of Falstaff's and our meeting, they will at once   15
display to the night.
MISTRESS FORD   That cannot choose but amaze him.

MISTRESS PAGE   If he be not amazed, he will be mocked;
  if he be amazed, he will every way be mocked.
20 MISTRESS FORD   We'll betray him finely.
MISTRESS PAGE
  Against such lewdsters and their lechery
  Those that betray them do no treachery.
MISTRESS FORD   The hour draws on. To the oak, to the
  oak!   *Exeunt.*

5.4   *Enter* EVANS, *disguised, and* Children *as fairies.*

EVANS   Trib, trib, fairies. Come, and remember your
  parts: be pold, I pray you, follow me into the pit, and
  when I give the watch-'ords do as I pid you. Come,
  come, trib, trib.   *Exeunt.*

5.5   *Enter* FALSTAFF *with buck's horns on his head.*

FALSTAFF   The Windsor bell hath struck twelve, the
  minute draws on. Now the hot-blooded gods assist me!
  Remember, Jove, thou wast a bull for thy Europa: love set
  on thy horns. O powerful love, that in some respects
5 makes a beast a man, in some other a man a beast!
  You were also, Jupiter, a swan for the love of Leda:
  O omnipotent love, how near the god drew to the
  complexion of a goose! A fault done first in the form of a
  beast – O Jove, a beastly fault! – and then another fault in
10 the semblance of a fowl: think on't, Jove, a foul fault!
  When gods have hot backs, what shall poor men do? For
  me, I am here a Windsor stag, and the fattest, I think,
  i'the forest. Send me a cool rut-time, Jove, or who can
  blame me to piss my tallow? – Who comes here? My doe?

Enter MISTRESS FORD *and* MISTRESS PAGE.

15 MISTRESS FORD   Sir John, art thou there, my deer, my
  male deer?
FALSTAFF   My doe with the black scut! Let the sky rain
  potatoes, let it thunder to the tune of 'Greensleeves',
  hail kissing-comfits and snow eringoes. Let there come
20 a tempest of provocation, I will shelter me here.
MISTRESS FORD   Mistress Page is come with me,
  sweetheart.
FALSTAFF   Divide me like a bribed buck, each a haunch.
  I will keep my sides to myself, my shoulders for the
25 fellow of this walk, – and my horns I bequeath your
  husbands. Am I a woodman, ha? Speak I like Herne the
  hunter? Why, now is Cupid a child of conscience: he
  makes restitution. As I am a true spirit, welcome!
                       [*A noise of horns within*]
MISTRESS PAGE   Alas, what noise?
30 MISTRESS FORD   Heaven forgive our sins!
FALSTAFF   What should this be?
MISTRESS FORD, MISTRESS PAGE   Away, away!
                                    They run away.
FALSTAFF   I think the devil will not have me damned,
  lest the oil that's in me should set hell on fire; he would
35 never else cross me thus.

Enter EVANS *as a Satyr,* ANNE *and* Children *as fairies,*
  Mistress QUICKLY *as the Queen of Fairies,*
              PISTOL *as Hobgoblin.*

QUICKLY   Fairies black, grey, green and white,
  You moonshine revellers and shades of night,
  You orphan heirs of fixed destiny,
  Attend your office and your quality.
  Crier Hobgoblin, make the fairy oyez.   40
PISTOL   Elves, list your names; silence, you airy toys.
  Cricket, to Windsor chimneys shalt thou leap:
  Where fires thou find'st unraked and hearths
    unswept,
  There pinch the maids as blue as bilberry –
  Our radiant queen hates sluts and sluttery.   45
FALSTAFF
  They are fairies, he that speaks to them shall die.
  I'll wink and couch: no man their works must eye.
EVANS
  Where's Pead? Go you, and where you find a maid
  That ere she sleep has thrice her prayers said,
  Raise up the organs of her fantasy.   50
  Sleep she as sound as careless infancy.
  But those as sleep and think not on their sins,
  Pinch them, arms, legs, backs, shoulders, sides and
    shins.
QUICKLY   About, about!
  Search Windsor Castle, elves, within and out.   55
  Strew good luck, oafs, on every sacred room,
  That it may stand till the perpetual doom
  In state as wholesome as in state 'tis fit,
  Worthy the owner and the owner it.
  The several chairs of Order look you scour   60
  With juice of balm and every precious flower;
  Each fair instalment, coat and several crest,
  With loyal blazon, evermore be blest.
  And nightly, meadow-fairies, look you sing,
  Like to the Garter compass, in a ring.   65
  Th'expressure that it bears, green let it be,
  More fertile-fresh than all the field to see;
  And *Honi soit qui mal y pense* write
  In em'rald tufts, flowers purple, blue and white,
  Like sapphire, pearl and rich embroidery,   70
  Buckled below fair knighthood's bending knee:
  Fairies use flowers for their charactery.
  Away, disperse. But till 'tis one o'clock,
  Our dance of custom round about the oak
  Of Herne the hunter let us not forget.   75
EVANS
  Pray you, lock hand in hand, yourselves in order set;
  And twenty glow-worms shall our lanterns be
  To guide our measure round about the tree. –
  But stay, I smell a man of middle earth.
FALSTAFF   Heavens defend me from that Welsh fairy,   80
  lest he transform me to a piece of cheese!
PISTOL
  Vile worm, thou wast o'erlooked even in thy birth.

QUICKLY   With trial fire touch me his finger end:
   If he be chaste, the flame will back descend
85   And turn him to no pain; but if he start,
   It is the flesh of a corrupted heart.
PISTOL   A trial, come.
EVANS   Come, will this wood take fire?
   [*They put the tapers to his fingers, and he starts.*]
FALSTAFF   O, o, o!
QUICKLY   Corrupt, corrupt, and tainted in desire!
90   About him, fairies, sing a scornful rhyme,
   And, as you trip, still pinch him to your time.

          The fairies' song.
     Fie on sinful fantasy,
     Fie on lust and luxury!
     Lust is but a bloody fire,
95   Kindled with unchaste desire,
     Fed in heart, whose flames aspire,
     As thoughts do blow them, higher and higher.
     Pinch him, fairies, mutually,
     Pinch him for his villainy.
100 Pinch him and burn him and turn him about,
   Till candles and starlight and moonshine be out.

   During the song they pinch him, and CAIUS *comes one*
   way and steals away a boy in green, and SLENDER
   another way takes a boy in white; FENTON *comes in and*
   steals Mistress Anne. A noise of hunting is heard within,
   and all the fairies run away. Falstaff pulls off his buck's
   head, and rises up.

   Enter PAGE, FORD, MISTRESS PAGE *and*
           MISTRESS FORD

PAGE
   Nay, do not fly – I think we have watched you now.
   Will none but Herne the hunter serve your turn?
MISTRESS PAGE
   I pray you, come, hold up the jest no higher. –
105 Now, good Sir John, how like you Windsor wives?
   See you these, husband?   [*Points to the horns.*]
              Do not these fair yokes
   Become the forest better than the town?
FORD   Now, sir, who's a cuckold now? Master Brook,
   Falstaff's a knave, a cuckoldly knave. Here are his
110 horns, Master Brook. And, Master Brook, he hath
   enjoyed nothing of Ford's but his buck-basket, his
   cudgel and twenty pounds of money, which must be
   paid to Master Brook. His horses are arrested for it,
   Master Brook.
115 MISTRESS FORD   Sir John, we have had ill luck, we
   could never meet. I will never take you for my love
   again, but I will always count you my deer.
FALSTAFF   I do begin to perceive that I am made an ass.
FORD   Ay, and an ox too: both the proofs are extant.
120 FALSTAFF   And these are not fairies. I was three or four
   times in the thought they were not fairies, and yet the
   guiltiness of my mind, the sudden surprise of my
   powers, drove the grossness of the foppery into a

received belief, in despite of the teeth of all rhyme and
reason, that they were fairies. See now how wit may be   125
made a Jack-a-Lent when 'tis upon ill employment!
EVANS   Sir John Falstaff, serve Got, and leave your
   desires, and fairies will not pinse you.
FORD   Well said, fairy Hugh.
EVANS   And leave you your jealousies too, I pray you.   130
FORD   I will never mistrust my wife again, till thou art
   able to woo her in good English.
FALSTAFF   Have I laid my brain in the sun and dried it,
   that it wants matter to prevent so gross o'erreaching as
   this? Am I ridden with a Welsh goat too? Shall I have a   135
   coxcomb of frieze? 'Tis time I were choked with a
   piece of toasted cheese.
EVANS   Seese is not good to give putter – your belly is all
   putter.
FALSTAFF   'Seese' and 'putter'? Have I lived to stand at   140
   the taunt of one that makes fritters of English? This is
   enough to be the decay of lust and late-walking
   through the realm.
MISTRESS PAGE   Why, Sir John, do you think, though
   we would have thrust virtue out of our hearts by the   145
   head and shoulders, and have given ourselves without
   scruple to hell, that ever the devil could have made you
   our delight?
FORD   What, a hodge-pudding? A bag of flax?
MISTRESS PAGE   A puffed man?   150
PAGE   Old, cold, withered and of intolerable entrails?
FORD   And one that is as slanderous as Satan?
PAGE   And as poor as Job?
FORD   And as wicked as his wife?
EVANS   And given to fornication, and to taverns, and   155
   sack, and wine, and metheglins, and to drinkings, and
   swearings, and starings; pribbles and prabbles?
FALSTAFF   Well, I am your theme: you have the start of
   me. I am dejected, I am not able to answer the Welsh
   flannel, ignorance itself is a plummet o'er me. Use me   160
   as you will.
FORD   Marry, sir, we'll bring you to Windsor to one
   Master Brook that you have cozened of money, to
   whom you should have been a pander. Over and above
   that you have suffered, I think to repay that money will   165
   be a biting affliction.
PAGE   Yet be cheerful, knight: thou shalt eat a posset
   tonight at my house, where I will desire thee to laugh at
   my wife that now laughs at thee. Tell her Master
   Slender hath married her daughter.   170
MISTRESS PAGE [*aside*]   Doctors doubt that: if Anne
   Page be my daughter, she is, by this, Doctor Caius's wife.

           Enter SLENDER.

SLENDER   Whoa, ho, ho, father Page!
PAGE   Son, how now? How now, son, have you
   dispatched?   175
SLENDER   Dispatched? I'll make the best in
   Gloucestershire know on't – would I were hanged, la,
   else!

PAGE Of what, son?

180 SLENDER I came yonder at Eton to marry Mistress Anne Page – and she's a great lubberly boy! If it had not been i'the church, I would have swinged him – or he should have swinged me. If I did not think it had been Anne Page, would I might never stir. – And 'tis a
185 postmaster's boy.

PAGE Upon my life, then, you took the wrong.

SLENDER What need you tell me that? I think so, when I took a boy for a girl! If I had been married to him, for all he was in woman's apparel, I would not have had
190 him.

PAGE Why, this is your own folly. Did not I tell you how you should know my daughter by her garments?

SLENDER I went to her in white, and cried 'mum', and she cried 'budget', as Anne and I had appointed. – And
195 yet it was not Anne, but a postmaster's boy.

MISTRESS PAGE Good George, be not angry: I knew of your purpose, turned my daughter into green, and indeed she is now with the Doctor at the deanery, and there married.

Enter CAIUS.

200 CAIUS Vere is Mistress Page? By gar, I am cozened, I ha' married *un garçon*, a boy, *un paysan*, by gar! A boy it is not Anne Page. By gar, I am cozened.

MISTRESS PAGE Why, did you take her in green?

CAIUS Ay, by gar, and 'tis a boy! By gar, I'll raise all
205 Windsor.

FORD This is strange. Who hath got the right Anne?

Enter FENTON *and* ANNE PAGE.

PAGE My heart misgives me. – Here comes Master Fenton. – How now, Master Fenton?

ANNE Pardon, good father – good my mother, pardon.

PAGE Now, mistress, how chance you went not with 210
Master Slender?

MISTRESS PAGE
Why went you not with Master Doctor, maid?

FENTON You do amaze her. Hear the truth of it:
You would have married her most shamefully
Where there was no proportion held in love. 215
The truth is, she and I, long since contracted,
Are now so sure that nothing can dissolve us.
Th'offence is holy that she hath committed,
And this deceit loses the name of craft,
Of disobedience, and unduteous title, 220
Since therein she doth evitate and shun
A thousand irreligious cursed hours
Which forced marriage would have brought upon her

FORD Stand not amazed, here is no remedy.
In love the heavens themselves do guide the state: 225
Money buys lands, and wives are sold by fate.

FALSTAFF I am glad, though you have ta'en a special stand to strike at me, that your arrow hath glanced.

PAGE Well, what remedy? Fenton, God give thee joy!
What cannot be eschewed must be embraced. 230

FALSTAFF
When night-dogs run, all sorts of deer are chased.

MISTRESS PAGE
Well, I will muse no further. – Master Fenton,
God give you many, many merry days!
Good husband, let us every one go home,
And laugh this sport o'er by a country fire, 235
Sir John and all.

FORD   Let it be so, Sir John.
To Master Brook you yet shall hold your word,
For he tonight shall lie with Mistress Ford. *Exeunt.*

A Midsummer Night's Dream

A Midsummer Night's Dream first appeared in print in 1600. The text might be based on an authorial manuscript, since it contains a number of spellings which are considered Shakespearean, along with other signs of a working copy. A second Quarto followed in 1619 (falsely dated 1600, perhaps as a marketing strategy), and the First Folio in 1623. The play is listed amongst Shakespeare's comedies by Francis Meres in *Palladis Tamia* (1598). It is generally dated between 1594 and 1596, probably after *Love's Labour's Lost* and almost certainly before *The Merchant of Venice*. It also appears to be close in time to *Romeo and Juliet*; the play-within-the-play of 'Pyramus and Thisbe' provides a comic counterpoint to the ending of that love-tragedy. More surprisingly, perhaps, the lyrical language of *Dream* has affinities with that of *King Richard II*, also written around this time.

A Midsummer Night's Dream is relatively unusual among Shakespeare's plays in not having a readily identifiable main source; it works heterogeneous materials into a multi-strand narrative and thematic design. Shakespeare could have read about Theseus in Thomas North's translation of Plutarch's *Lives of the Noble Grecians and Romans* (1579), as well as in Chaucer's *Knight's Tale* (*c*. 1385), which he also adapted loosely for the plot of the four young lovers. (He used this poem again for *The Two Noble Kinsmen* towards the end of his career.) Ovid's *Metamorphoses* inspired the general ambience of the forest scenes and provided the story of Pyramus and Thisbe in the play-within-the-play. For Robin Goodfellow (Puck) and the fairies, Shakespeare drew on folklore tinged with classical elements. *A Midsummer Night's Dream* is his first play with openly supernatural material on any scale. It is also the first where he addresses the nature of artistic illusion itself, notably in Theseus' speech about 'The lunatic, the lover and the poet' at the beginning of 5.1 and the presentation of the play-within-the-play. This theme may often strike the spectator or reader negotiating the many worlds of the play: natural and supernatural; romantic and comic; aristocratic, proletarian and non-human.

The play is often thought to have been performed privately at an aristocratic wedding, but there is no external evidence to support this theory. The title-page of the 1600 Quarto states it was 'sundry times publickely acted' by the Lord Chamberlain's Men, Shakespeare's regular company. It was popular in the eighteenth and nineteenth centuries, usually in adapted form with much music, dancing and spectacle. It has inspired many operas, including Henry Purcell's *The Fairy Queen* (1692) and Benjamin Britten's *A Midsummer Night's Dream* (1960). Felix Mendelssohn wrote extensive music for it (1826, 1843). The lavish productions of earlier times gave way in the twentieth century to less elaborate ones, closer to the text but variously innovative in staging and interpretation. The most celebrated was Peter Brook's revolutionary staging in 1970 for the Royal Shakespeare Company, with its 'white box' set, varied comic tones and unflagging theatrical energy. Films include a 1935 Hollywood version directed by Max Reinhardt, later ones by Peter Hall (1968), Adrian Noble (1996) and Michael Hoffman (1999), and a more drastic reworking by David Kerr (2016). The play has been adapted for productions round the world, from a Nazi concentration camp in Czechia (1943) to a forest near troubled Beirut (1990), from Indian tribal actors (1993) to a joint cast of Vietnamese and American members (2000).

The Arden text is based on the 1600 First Quarto. .

THE COURTIERS

THESEUS	*Duke of Athens*
HIPPOLYTA	*Queen of the Amazons, now Theseus' bride*
EGEUS	*a courtier, Hermia's father*
HERMIA	*Egeus' daughter, in love with Lysander*
HELENA	*in love with Demetrius*
LYSANDER	*in love at different times with Hermia and Helena*
DEMETRIUS	*in love at different times with Helena and Hermia*
PHILOSTRATE	*a courtier, in charge of court entertainments*

Other Lords and Courtiers

THE ARTISANS

Nick BOTTOM	*a weaver; Pyramus in the play-within-the-play*
Peter QUINCE	*a carpenter; producer and Prologue of the play-within-the-play*
Francis FLUTE	*a bellows-mender; Thisbe in the play-within-the-play*
Tom SNOUT	*a tinker; Wall in the play-within-the-play*
SNUG	*a joiner; the Lion in the play-within-the-play*
Robin STARVELING	*a tailor; Moonshine in the play-within-the-play*

THE FAIRIES

OBERON	*King of the Fairies*
TITANIA	*Queen of the Fairies*
ROBIN GOODFELLOW	*a puck*
PEASEBLOSSOM	
COBWEB	
MOTE	*fairies in Titania's train*
MUSTARDSEED	
Another FAIRY	

Other Fairies in Oberon's and Titania's trains

A Midsummer Night's Dream

1.1   *Enter* THESEUS, HIPPOLYTA,
    PHILOSTRATE, *with others.*

THESEUS   Now, fair Hippolyta, our nuptial hour
  Draws on apace. Four happy days bring in
  Another moon; but O, methinks, how slow
  This old moon wanes! She lingers my desires,
  Like to a stepdame or a dowager
  Long withering out a young man's revenue.
HIPPOLYTA
  Four days will quickly steep themselves in night,
  Four nights will quickly dream away the time;
  And then the moon, like to a silver bow
  Now bent in heaven, shall behold the night
  Of our solemnities.
THESEUS   Go, Philostrate,
  Stir up the Athenian youth to merriments;
  Awake the pert and nimble spirit of mirth,
  Turn melancholy forth to funerals.
  The pale companion is not for our pomp.
                    Exit Philostrate.
  Hippolyta, I wooed thee with my sword,
  And won thy love doing thee injuries;
  But I will wed thee in another key,
  With pomp, with triumph, and with revelling.

    Enter EGEUS, HERMIA, LYSANDER
      and DEMETRIUS.

EGEUS   Happy be Theseus, our renowned duke.
THESEUS
  Thanks, good Egeus. What's the news with thee?
EGEUS   Full of vexation come I, with complaint
  Against my child, my daughter Hermia.
  Stand forth, Demetrius. My noble lord,
  This man hath my consent to marry her.
  Stand forth, Lysander. And my gracious duke,
  This man hath bewitched the bosom of my child.
  Thou, thou, Lysander, thou hast given her rhymes
  And interchanged love-tokens with my child;
  Thou hast, by moonlight, at her window sung,
  With faining voice, verses of feigning love,
  And stolen the impression of her fantasy;
  With bracelets of thy hair, rings, gauds, conceits,
  Knacks, trifles, nosegays, sweetmeats (messengers
  Of strong prevailment in unhardened youth),
  With cunning hast thou filched my daughter's heart,
  Turned her obedience, which is due to me,
  To stubborn harshness. And, my gracious duke,
  Be it so she will not here before your grace
  Consent to marry with Demetrius,
  I beg the ancient privilege of Athens:
  As she is mine, I may dispose of her,
  Which shall be either to this gentleman,
  Or to her death, according to our law
  Immediately provided in that case.
THESEUS   What say you, Hermia? Be advised, fair maid.
  To you your father should be as a god,

One that composed your beauties; yea, and one
  To whom you are but as a form in wax,
  By him imprinted, and within his power
  To leave the figure, or disfigure it.
  Demetrius is a worthy gentleman.
HERMIA   So is Lysander.
THESEUS   In himself he is;
  But in this kind, wanting your father's voice,
  The other must be held the worthier.
HERMIA   I would my father looked but with my eyes.
THESEUS
  Rather your eyes must with his judgement look.
HERMIA   I do entreat your grace to pardon me.
  I know not by what power I am made bold,
  Nor how it may concern my modesty
  In such a presence here to plead my thoughts,
  But I beseech your grace that I may know
  The worst that may befall me in this case
  If I refuse to wed Demetrius.
THESEUS   Either to die the death, or to abjure
  For ever the society of men.
  Therefore, fair Hermia, question your desires,
  Know of your youth, examine well your blood
  Whether, if you yield not to your father's choice,
  You can endure the livery of a nun,
  For aye to be in shady cloister mewed
  To live a barren sister all your life,
  Chanting faint hymns to the cold fruitless moon.
  Thrice blessed they that master so their blood
  To undergo such maiden pilgrimage;
  But earthlier happy is the rose distilled
  Than that which, withering on the virgin thorn,
  Grows, lives and dies in single blessedness.
HERMIA   So will I grow, so live, so die, my lord,
  Ere I will yield my virgin patent up
  Unto his lordship whose unwished yoke
  My soul consents not to give sovereignty.
THESEUS
  Take time to pause, and by the next new moon,
  The sealing day betwixt my love and me
  For everlasting bond of fellowship,
  Upon that day either prepare to die
  For disobedience to your father's will,
  Or else to wed Demetrius as he would,
  Or on Diana's altar to protest,
  For aye, austerity and single life.
DEMETRIUS   Relent, sweet Hermia; and Lysander, yield
  Thy crazed title to my certain right.
LYSANDER   You have her father's love, Demetrius.
  Let me have Hermia's: do you marry him.
EGEUS   Scornful Lysander, true, he hath my love,
  And what is mine, my love shall render him;
  And she is mine, and all my right of her
  I do estate unto Demetrius.
LYSANDER   I am, my lord, as well derived as he,
  As well possessed; my love is more than his,

My fortunes every way as fairly ranked
(If not with vantage) as Demetrius';
And (which is more than all these boasts can be)
I am belov'd of beauteous Hermia.
105   Why should not I then prosecute my right?
Demetrius, I'll avouch it to his head,
Made love to Nedar's daughter Helena
And won her soul; and she, sweet lady, dotes,
Devoutly dotes, dotes in idolatry
110   Upon this spotted and inconstant man.
THESEUS   I must confess that I have heard so much,
And with Demetrius thought to have spoke thereof;
But being over-full of self-affairs,
My mind did lose it. But Demetrius, come,
115   And come, Egeus; you shall go with me.
I have some private schooling for you both.
For you, fair Hermia, look you arm yourself
To fit your fancies to your father's will;
Or else, the law of Athens yields you up
120   (Which by no means we may extenuate)
To death, or to a vow of single life.
Come, my Hippolyta. What cheer, my love?
Demetrius and Egeus, go along.
I must employ you in some business
125   Against our nuptial, and confer with you
Of something nearly that concerns yourselves.
EGEUS   With duty and desire we follow you.
                    Exeunt all but Lysander and Hermia.
LYSANDER
How now, my love? Why is your cheek so pale?
How chance the roses there do fade so fast?
130   HERMIA   Belike for want of rain, which I could well
Beteem them from the tempest of my eyes.
LYSANDER   Ay me! for aught that I could ever read,
Could ever hear by tale or history,
The course of true love never did run smooth;
135   But either it was different in blood –
HERMIA   O cross, too high to be enthralled to low!
LYSANDER   Or else misgrafted in respect of years –
HERMIA   O spite, too old to be engaged to young!
LYSANDER   Or else it stood upon the choice of friends –
140   HERMIA   O hell, to choose love by another's eyes!
LYSANDER   Or, if there were a sympathy in choice,
War, death or sickness did lay siege to it,
Making it momentany as a sound,
Swift as a shadow, short as any dream,
145   Brief as the lightning in the collied night
That, in a spleen, unfolds both heaven and earth,
And ere a man hath power to say 'Behold',
The jaws of darkness do devour it up:
So quick bright things come to confusion.
150   HERMIA   If then true lovers have been ever crossed,
It stands as an edict in destiny.
Then let us teach our trial patience
Because it is a customary cross,
As due to love as thoughts and dreams and sighs,
155   Wishes and tears, poor fancy's followers.

LYSANDER
A good persuasion; therefore hear me, Hermia.
I have a widow aunt, a dowager,
Of great revenue, and she hath no child.
From Athens is her house remote seven leagues,
160   And she respects me as her only son.
There, gentle Hermia, may I marry thee,
And to that place the sharp Athenian law
Cannot pursue us. If thou lov'st me, then
Steal forth thy father's house tomorrow night;
165   And in the wood a league without the town,
Where I did meet thee once with Helena
To do observance to a morn of May,
There will I stay for thee.
HERMIA   My good Lysander,
I swear to thee by Cupid's strongest bow,
170   By his best arrow with the golden head,
By the simplicity of Venus' doves,
By that which knitteth souls and prospers loves,
And by that fire which burned the Carthage queen
When the false Trojan under sail was seen,
175   By all the vows that ever men have broke
(In number more than ever women spoke),
In that same place thou hast appointed me,
Tomorrow truly will I meet with thee.
LYSANDER
Keep promise, love. Look, here comes Helena.

                    Enter HELENA.

HERMIA   God speed, fair Helena. Whither away?   180
HELENA   Call you me fair? That fair again unsay.
Demetrius loves your fair: O happy fair!
Your eyes are lodestars, and your tongue's sweet air
More tunable than lark to shepherd's ear
When wheat is green, when hawthorn buds appear.   185
Sickness is catching; O, were favour so!
Your words I catch, fair Hermia; ere I go,
My ear should catch your voice, my eye your eye,
My tongue should catch your tongue's sweet melody.
Were the world mine, Demetrius being bated,   190
The rest I'll give to be to you translated.
O teach me how you look, and with what art
You sway the motion of Demetrius' heart.
HERMIA   I frown upon him, yet he loves me still.
HELENA
O that your frowns would teach my smiles such skill!   195
HERMIA   I give him curses, yet he gives me love.
HELENA   O that my prayers could such affection move!
HERMIA   The more I hate, the more he follows me.
HELENA   The more I love, the more he hateth me.
HERMIA   His folly, Helena, is no fault of mine.   200
HELENA
None but your beauty. Would that fault were mine!
HERMIA   Take comfort: he no more shall see my face.
Lysander and myself will fly this place.
Before the time I did Lysander see,
Seemed Athens as a paradise to me.   205

O then, what graces in my love do dwell,
That he hath turned a heaven unto a hell!
LYSANDER   Helen, to you our minds we will unfold.
Tomorrow night, when Phoebe doth behold
210 Her silver visage in the watery glass,
Decking with liquid pearl the bladed grass
(A time that lovers' flights doth still conceal),
Through Athens' gates have we devised to steal.
HERMIA   And in the wood, where often you and I
215 Upon faint primrose beds were wont to lie
Emptying our bosoms of their counsel sweet,
There my Lysander and myself shall meet,
And thence from Athens turn away our eyes,
To seek new friends and strange companies.
220 Farewell, sweet playfellow. Pray thou for us,
And good luck grant thee thy Demetrius.
Keep word, Lysander. We must starve our sight
From lovers' food till morrow deep midnight.   *Exit.*
LYSANDER   I will, my Hermia. Helena, adieu.
225 As you on him, Demetrius dote on you.   *Exit.*
HELENA   How happy some o'er other some can be!
Through Athens I am thought as fair as she,
But what of that? Demetrius thinks not so;
He will not know what all but he do know.
230 And as he errs, doting on Hermia's eyes,
So I, admiring of his qualities.
Things base and vile, holding no quantity,
Love can transpose to form and dignity.
Love looks not with the eyes but with the mind,
235 And therefore is winged Cupid painted blind.
Nor hath love's mind of any judgement taste:
Wings and no eyes figure unheedy haste.
And therefore is love said to be a child,
Because in choice he is so oft beguiled.
240 As waggish boys in game themselves forswear,
So the boy Love is perjured everywhere.
For ere Demetrius looked on Hermia's eyne,
He hailed down oaths that he was only mine;
And when this hail some heat from Hermia felt,
245 So he dissolved, and showers of oaths did melt.
I will go tell him of fair Hermia's flight.
Then to the wood will he tomorrow night
Pursue her; and for this intelligence
If I have thanks, it is a dear expense.
250 But herein mean I to enrich my pain,
To have his sight thither and back again.   *Exit.*

1.2   *Enter* QUINCE, SNUG, BOTTOM,
              FLUTE, SNOUT *and* STARVELING.

QUINCE   Is all our company here?
BOTTOM   You were best to call them generally, man by
man, according to the scrip.
QUINCE   Here is the scroll of every man's name, which
is thought fit through all Athens to play in our interlude
before the duke and the duchess on his wedding day at
night.

BOTTOM   First, good Peter Quince, say what the play
treats on; then read the names of the actors; and so
grow to a point.   10
QUINCE   Marry, our play is 'The most lamentable
comedy and most cruel death of Pyramus and Thisbe'.
BOTTOM   A very good piece of work, I assure you, and a
merry. Now good Peter Quince, call forth your actors
by the scroll. Masters, spread yourselves.   15
QUINCE   Answer as I call you. Nick Bottom, the weaver?
BOTTOM   Ready. Name what part I am for, and proceed.
QUINCE   You, Nick Bottom, are set down for Pyramus.
BOTTOM   What is Pyramus? A lover, or a tyrant?
QUINCE   A lover that kills himself most gallant for love. 20
BOTTOM   That will ask some tears in the true
performing of it. If I do it, let the audience look to
their eyes. I will move storms; I will condole, in some
measure. To the rest yet, my chief humour is for a
tyrant. I could play Ercles rarely, or a part to tear a cat 25
in, to make all split.
                    The raging rocks
                    And shivering shocks
                    Shall break the locks
                       Of prison gates,   30
                    And Phibbus' car
                    Shall shine from far,
                    And make and mar
                       The foolish Fates.
This was lofty. Now name the rest of the players.   35
This is Ercles' vein, a tyrant's vein. A lover is more
condoling.
QUINCE   Francis Flute, the bellows-mender?
FLUTE   Here, Peter Quince.
QUINCE   Flute, you must take Thisbe on you.   40
FLUTE   What is Thisbe? A wandering knight?
QUINCE   It is the lady that Pyramus must love.
FLUTE   Nay, faith, let not me play a woman. I have a
beard coming.
QUINCE   That's all one. You shall play it in a mask, and 45
you may speak as small as you will.
BOTTOM   And I may hide my face, let me play Thisbe
too. I'll speak in a monstrous little voice: 'Thisne,
Thisne!' – 'Ah, Pyramus, my lover dear! Thy Thisbe
dear, and lady dear.'   50
QUINCE   No, no. You must play Pyramus; and Flute,
you Thisbe.
BOTTOM   Well, proceed.
QUINCE   Robin Starveling, the tailor?
STARVELING   Here, Peter Quince.   55
QUINCE   Robin Starveling, you must play Thisbe's
mother. Tom Snout, the tinker?
SNOUT   Here, Peter Quince.
QUINCE   You, Pyramus' father; myself, Thisbe's father;
Snug the joiner, you the Lion's part; and I hope here is   60
a play fitted.
SNUG   Have you the Lion's part written? Pray you, if it
be, give it me, for I am slow of study.

QUINCE You may do it extempore, for it is nothing but
65 roaring.

BOTTOM Let me play the Lion too. I will roar that I will do
any man's heart good to hear me. I will roar that I will
make the duke say, 'Let him roar again, let him roar again.'

QUINCE And you should do it too terribly, you would
70 fright the duchess and the ladies, that they would
shriek, and that were enough to hang us all.

ALL That would hang us, every mother's son.

BOTTOM I grant you, friends, if you should fright the
ladies out of their wits, they would have no more
75 discretion but to hang us. But I will aggravate my voice
so, that I will roar you as gently as any sucking dove; I
will roar you and 'twere any nightingale.

QUINCE You can play no part but Pyramus; for Pyramus
is a sweet-faced man, a proper man as one shall see in
80 a summer's day, a most lovely gentlemanlike man:
therefore you must needs play Pyramus.

BOTTOM Well, I will undertake it. What beard were I
best to play it in?

QUINCE Why, what you will.

85 BOTTOM I will discharge it in either your straw-colour
beard, your orange-tawny beard, your purple-in-grain
beard, or your French-crown-colour beard, your perfit
yellow.

QUINCE Some of your French crowns have no hair at
90 all, and then you will play bare-faced. But masters,
here are your parts; and I am to intreat you, request
you and desire you to con them by tomorrow night,
and meet me in the palace wood a mile without the
town by moonlight. There will we rehearse; for if we
95 meet in the city, we shall be dogged with company, and
our devices known. In the meantime, I will draw a bill
of properties such as our play wants. I pray you, fail me
not.

BOTTOM We will meet, and there we may rehearse
100 most obscenely and courageously. Take pains, be perfit.
Adieu.

QUINCE At the duke's oak we meet.

BOTTOM Enough. Hold, or cut bowstrings. *Exeunt.*

2.1 *Enter a* FAIRY *at one door, and* ROBIN
GOODFELLOW *at another.*

ROBIN How now, spirit, whither wander you?

FAIRY Over hill, over dale,
Thorough bush, thorough brier,
Over park, over pale,
5 Thorough flood, thorough fire,
I do wander everywhere
Swifter than the moon's sphere,
And I serve the Fairy Queen
To dew her orbs upon the green.
10 The cowslips tall her pensioners be.
In their gold coats, spots you see:
Those be rubies, fairy favours;
In those freckles live their savours.

I must go seek some dew drops here,
And hang a pearl in every cowslip's ear.
15 Farewell, thou lob of spirits; I'll be gone.
Our queen and all her elves come here anon.

ROBIN The king doth keep his revels here tonight.
Take heed the queen come not within his sight;
For Oberon is passing fell and wrath
20 Because that she, as her attendant, hath
A lovely boy stolen, from an Indian king:
She never had so sweet a changeling.
And jealous Oberon would have the child
Knight of his train, to trace the forests wild.
25 But she perforce withholds the loved boy,
Crowns him with flowers, and makes him all her joy.
And now, they never meet in grove or green,
By fountain clear or spangled starlight sheen,
But they do square, that all their elves, for fear,
30 Creep into acorn cups and hide them there.

FAIRY Either I mistake your shape and making quite,
Or else you are that shrewd and knavish sprite
Called Robin Goodfellow. Are not you he
That frights the maidens of the villagery,
35 Skim milk, and sometimes labour in the quern,
And bootless make the breathless housewife churn,
And sometime make the drink to bear no barm,
Mislead night-wanderers, laughing at their harm?
Those that Hobgoblin call you, and sweet Puck,
40 You do their work, and they shall have good luck.
Are not you he?

ROBIN   Thou speak'st aright:
I am that merry wanderer of the night.
I jest to Oberon, and make him smile
When I a fat and bean-fed horse beguile,
45 Neighing in likeness of a filly foal.
And sometime lurk I in a gossip's bowl
In very likeness of a roasted crab,
And when she drinks, against her lips I bob,
And on her withered dewlap pour the ale.
50 The wisest aunt telling the saddest tale
Sometime for three-foot stool mistaketh me;
Then slip I from her bum, down topples she,
And 'Tailor' cries, and falls into a cough;
And then the whole choir hold their hips and laugh,
55 And waxen in their mirth, and neeze, and swear
A merrier hour was never wasted there.
But room, fairy. Here comes Oberon.

FAIRY And here my mistress. Would that he were gone.

Enter OBERON *at one door with his train, and*
TITANIA *at another with hers.*

OBERON Ill met by moonlight, proud Titania. 60

TITANIA What, jealous Oberon? Fairies, skip hence.
I have forsworn his bed and company.

OBERON Tarry, rash wanton. Am not I thy lord?

TITANIA Then I must be thy lady; but I know
When thou hast stolen away from fairy land 65
And in the shape of Corin, sat all day

Playing on pipes of corn, and versing love
To amorous Phillida. Why art thou here
Come from the farthest steep of India,
70   But that, forsooth, the bouncing Amazon,
Your buskined mistress and your warrior love,
To Theseus must be wedded; and you come
To give their bed joy and prosperity.
OBERON   How canst thou thus for shame, Titania,
75   Glance at my credit with Hippolyta,
Knowing I know thy love to Theseus?
Didst not thou lead him through the glimmering
     night
From Perigenia, whom he ravished?
And make him with fair Aegles break his faith,
80   With Ariadne, and Antiopa?
TITANIA   These are the forgeries of jealousy;
And never, since the middle summer's spring,
Met we on hill, in dale, forest or mead,
By paved fountain or by rushy brook,
85   Or in the beached margin of the sea
To dance our ringlets to the whistling wind,
But with thy brawls thou hast disturbed our sport.
Therefore the winds, piping to us in vain,
As in revenge have sucked up from the sea
90   Contagious fogs, which, falling in the land,
Hath every pelting river made so proud
That they have overborne their continents.
The ox hath therefore stretched his yoke in vain,
The ploughman lost his sweat, and the green corn
95   Hath rotted ere his youth attained a beard.
The fold stands empty in the drowned field,
And crows are fatted with the murrain flock.
The nine men's morris is filled up with mud,
And the quaint mazes in the wanton green,
100   For lack of tread, are undistinguishable.
The human mortals want their winter here;
No night is now with hymn or carol blest.
Therefore the moon, the governess of floods,
Pale in her anger, washes all the air
105   That rheumatic diseases do abound.
And thorough this distemperature, we see
The seasons alter: hoary-headed frosts
Fall in the fresh lap of the crimson rose,
And on old Hiems' thin and icy crown
110   An odorous chaplet of sweet summer buds
Is, as in mockery, set. The spring, the summer,
The childing autumn, angry winter change
Their wonted liveries; and the mazed world,
By their increase, now knows not which is which.
115   And this same progeny of evils comes
From our debate, from our dissension:
We are their parents and original.
OBERON   Do you amend it then; it lies in you.
Why should Titania cross her Oberon?
120   I do but beg a little changeling boy
To be my henchman.
TITANIA   Set your heart at rest.

The fairy land buys not the child of me.
His mother was a votaress of my order;
And in the spiced Indian air by night,
Full often hath she gossiped by my side,   125
And sat with me on Neptune's yellow sands
Marking th'embarked traders on the flood,
When we have laughed to see the sails conceive
And grow big-bellied with the wanton wind,
Which she with pretty and with swimming gait   130
Following (her womb then rich with my young
     squire)
Would imitate, and sail upon the land
To fetch me trifles and return again
As from a voyage, rich with merchandise.
But she, being mortal, of that boy did die,   135
And for her sake do I rear up her boy;
And for her sake, I will not part with him.
OBERON   How long within this wood intend you stay?
TITANIA
Perchance till after Theseus' wedding day.
If you will patiently dance in our round   140
And see our moonlight revels, go with us;
If not, shun me, and I will spare your haunts.
OBERON   Give me that boy, and I will go with thee.
TITANIA   Not for thy fairy kingdom. Fairies, away.
We shall chide downright if I longer stay.   145
     Exeunt Titania and her train,
                    and Oberon's train.
OBERON
Well, go thy way. Thou shalt not from this grove
Till I torment thee for this injury.
My gentle puck, come hither. Thou rememberest
Since once I sat upon a promontory,
And heard a mermaid on a dolphin's back   150
Uttering such dulcet and harmonious breath
That the rude sea grew civil at her song,
And certain stars shot madly from their spheres
To hear the sea-maid's music.
ROBIN   I remember.
OBERON   That very time I saw (but thou couldst not) 155
Flying between the cold moon and the earth
Cupid, all armed. A certain aim he took
At a fair vestal, throned by west,
And loosed his love-shaft smartly from his bow
As it should pierce a hundred thousand hearts.   160
But I might see young Cupid's fiery shaft
Quenched in the chaste beams of the watery moon,
And the imperial votaress passed on
In maiden meditation, fancy free.
Yet marked I where the bolt of Cupid fell: 165
It fell upon a little western flower,
Before milk-white, now purple with love's wound,
And maidens call it love-in-idleness.
Fetch me that flower: the herb I showed thee once.
The juice of it, on sleeping eyelids laid,   170
Will make or man or woman madly dote
Upon the next live creature that it sees.

Fetch me this herb, and be thou here again
Ere the Leviathan can swim a league.

175 ROBIN   I'll put a girdle round about the earth
In forty minutes.   *Exit.*

OBERON   Having once this juice,
I'll watch Titania when she is asleep
And drop the liquor of it in her eyes.
The next thing then she, waking, looks upon,
180 Be it on lion, bear, or wolf, or bull,
On meddling monkey or on busy ape,
She shall pursue it with the soul of love.
And ere I take this charm from off her sight
(As I can take it with another herb),
185 I'll make her render up her page to me.
But who comes here? I am invisible,
And I will overhear their conference.

Enter DEMETRIUS, HELENA *following him.*
Oberon stands apart.

DEMETRIUS   I love thee not, therefore pursue me not.
Where is Lysander and fair Hermia?
190 The one I'll stay; the other stayeth me.
Thou toldst me they were stolen unto this wood;
And here am I, and wood within this wood,
Because I cannot meet my Hermia.
Hence, get thee gone, and follow me no more.

195 HELENA   You draw me, you hard-hearted adamant;
But yet you draw not iron, for my heart
Is true as steel. Leave you your power to draw,
And I shall have no power to follow you.

DEMETRIUS   Do I entice you? Do I speak you fair?
200 Or rather do I not in plainest truth
Tell you I do not, nor I cannot love you?

HELENA   And even for that do I love you the more.
I am your spaniel, and Demetrius,
The more you beat me, I will fawn on you.
205 Use me but as your spaniel: spurn me, strike me,
Neglect me, loose me; only give me leave,
Unworthy as I am, to follow you.
What worser place can I beg in your love
(And yet a place of high respect with me)
210 Than to be used as you use your dog?

DEMETRIUS
Tempt not too much the hatred of my spirit;
For I am sick when I do look on thee.

HELENA   And I am sick when I look not on you.

DEMETRIUS   You do impeach your modesty too much,
215 To leave the city and commit yourself
Into the hands of one that loves you not,
To trust the opportunity of night
And the ill counsel of a desert place
With the rich worth of your virginity.

220 HELENA   Your virtue is my privilege, for that
It is not night when I do see your face.
Therefore I think I am not in the night,
Nor doth this wood lack worlds of company,
For you in my respect are all the world.

Then how can it be said I am alone,   225
When all the world is here to look on me?

DEMETRIUS
I'll run from thee and hide me in the brakes,
And leave thee to the mercy of wild beasts.

HELENA   The wildest hath not such a heart as you.
Run when you will, the story shall be changed: 230
Apollo flies, and Daphne holds the chase;
The dove pursues the griffon; the mild hind
Makes speed to catch the tiger: bootless speed,
When cowardice pursues, and valour flies.

DEMETRIUS   I will not stay thy questions. Let me go;   235
Or if thou follow me, do not believe
But I shall do thee mischief in the wood.   *Exit.*

HELENA   Ay, in the temple, in the town, the field
You do me mischief. Fie, Demetrius!
Your wrongs do set a scandal on my sex.   240
We cannot fight for love as men may do;
We should be wooed, and were not made to woo.
I'll follow thee, and make a heaven of hell,
To die upon the hand I love so well.   *Exit.*

OBERON
Fare thee well, nymph. Ere he do leave this grove,   245
Thou shalt fly him, and he shall seek thy love.

Enter ROBIN GOODFELLOW. *Oberon advances.*

Hast thou the flower there? Welcome, wanderer.

ROBIN   Ay, there it is.

OBERON   I pray thee give it me.
I know a bank where the wild thyme blows,
Where oxlips and the nodding violet grows,   250
Quite over-canopied with luscious woodbine,
With sweet musk-roses and with eglantine.
There sleeps Titania sometime of the night,
Lulled in these flowers with dances and delight;
And there the snake throws her enamelled skin,   255
Weed wide enough to wrap a fairy in.
And with the juice of this I'll streak her eyes,
And make her full of hateful fantasies.
Take thou some of it, and seek through this grove:
A sweet Athenian lady is in love   260
With a disdainful youth. Anoint his eyes,
But do it when the next thing he espies
May be the lady. Thou shalt know the man
By the Athenian garments he hath on.
Effect it with some care, that he may prove   265
More fond on her, than she upon her love;
And look thou meet me ere the first cock crow.

ROBIN   Fear not, my lord; your servant shall do so.
Exit Robin. Oberon remains onstage at the back.

2.2   *Enter* TITANIA *with her train*, OBERON
hiding on one side.

TITANIA   Come, now a roundel and a fairy song;
Then for the third part of a minute, hence:
Some to kill cankers in the musk-rose buds;

Some war with rearmice for their leathern wings
To make my small elves coats; and some keep back
The clamorous owl, that nightly hoots and wonders
At our quaint spirits. Sing me now asleep;
Then to your offices, and let me rest.

Fairies sing.

1 FAIRY   You spotted snakes with double tongue,
   Thorny hedgehogs, be not seen.
  Newts and blindworms, do no wrong,
   Come not near our Fairy Queen.
CHORUS
   Philomel, with melody,
   Sing in our sweet lullaby,
  Lulla, lulla, lullaby; lulla, lulla, lullaby.
   Never harm, nor spell, nor charm,
   Come our lovely lady nigh.
   So good night, with lullaby.
2 FAIRY   Weaving spiders, come not here –
   Hence, you long-legged spinners, hence.
  Beetles black, approach not near,
   Worm nor snail do no offence.
CHORUS
   Philomel, with melody,
   Sing in our sweet lullaby,
  Lulla, lulla, lullaby; lulla, lulla, lullaby.
   Never harm, nor spell, nor charm,
   Come our lovely lady nigh.
   So good night, with lullaby.   [*Titania sleeps.*]
1 FAIRY   Hence, away; now all is well.
  One aloof stand sentinel.   *Exeunt Fairies.*

OBERON *advances.*

OBERON [*Squeezes the flower on Titania's eyelids.*]
  What thou seest when thou dost wake,
  Do it for thy true love take;
  Love and languish for his sake.
  Be it ounce or cat or bear,
  Pard, or boar with bristled hair
  In thy eye that shall appear
  When thou wak'st, it is thy dear.
  Wake when some vile thing is near.   *Exit.*

Enter LYSANDER *and* HERMIA.

LYSANDER
Fair love, you faint with wandering in the wood,
And to speak troth, I have forgot our way.
We'll rest us, Hermia, if you think it good,
And tarry for the comfort of the day.
HERMIA   Be it so, Lysander. Find you out a bed,
For I upon this bank will rest my head.
LYSANDER   One turf shall serve as pillow for us both,
One heart, one bed, two bosoms, and one troth.
HERMIA   Nay, good Lysander; for my sake, my dear,
Lie further off, yet. Do not lie so near.
LYSANDER   O take the sense, sweet, of my innocence:

Love takes the meaning in love's conference.   50
I mean that my heart unto yours it knit,
So that but one heart we can make of it:
Two bosoms interchained with an oath,
So then two bosoms, and a single troth.
Then by your side no bed-room me deny;   55
For lying so, Hermia, I do not lie.
HERMIA   Lysander riddles very prettily.
Now much beshrew my manners and my pride
If Hermia meant to say Lysander lied.
But gentle friend, for love and courtesy,   60
Lie further off, in human modesty:
Such separation as may well be said
Becomes a virtuous bachelor and a maid,
So far be distant, and good night, sweet friend.
Thy love ne'er alter till thy sweet life end.   65
LYSANDER   Amen, amen, to that fair prayer say I,
And then end life, when I end loyalty.
Here is my bed; sleep give thee all his rest.
HERMIA
With half that wish the wisher's eyes be pressed.
  [*They sleep.*]

Enter ROBIN GOODFELLOW.

ROBIN   Through the forest have I gone,   70
But Athenian found I none
On whose eyes I might approve
This flower's force in stirring love.
Night and silence! Who is here?
Weeds of Athens he doth wear.   75
This is he, my master said,
Despised the Athenian maid;
And here the maiden, sleeping sound
On the dank and dirty ground.
Pretty soul, she durst not lie   80
Near this lack-love, this kill-courtesy.
Churl, upon thy eyes I throw
All the power this charm doth owe.
  [*Squeezes the flower on Lysander's eyelids.*]
When thou wak'st, let love forbid
Sleep his seat on thy eyelid.   85
So awake, when I am gone;
For I must now to Oberon.   *Exit.*

Enter DEMETRIUS *and* HELENA *running.*

HELENA   Stay, though thou kill me, sweet Demetrius.
DEMETRIUS
I charge thee, hence, and do not haunt me thus.
HELENA   O, wilt thou darkling leave me? Do not so.   90
DEMETRIUS   Stay, on thy peril. I alone will go.   *Exit.*
HELENA   O, I am out of breath in this fond chase.
The more my prayer, the lesser is my grace.
Happy is Hermia, wheresoe'er she lies,
For she hath blessed and attractive eyes.   95
How came her eyes so bright? Not with salt tears;
If so, my eyes are oftener washed than hers.

No, no: I am as ugly as a bear,
For beasts that meet me run away for fear;
100 Therefore no marvel though Demetrius
Do, as a monster, fly my presence thus.
What wicked and dissembling glass of mine
Made me compare with Hermia's sphery eyne?
But who is here? Lysander, on the ground?
105 Dead, or asleep? I see no blood, no wound.
Lysander, if you live, good sir, awake.

LYSANDER [*Wakes.*]
And run through fire I will for thy sweet sake.
Transparent Helena, nature shows art,
That through thy bosom makes me see thy heart.
110 Where is Demetrius? O, how fit a word
Is that vile name to perish on my sword!

HELENA   Do not say so, Lysander, say not so.
What though he love your Hermia? Lord, what
though?
Yet Hermia still loves you; then be content.

115 LYSANDER   Content with Hermia? No, I do repent
The tedious minutes I with her have spent.
Not Hermia, but Helena I love.
Who will not change a raven for a dove?
The will of man is by his reason swayed,
120 And reason says you are the worthier maid.
Things growing are not ripe until their season;
So I, being young, till now ripe not to reason.
And touching now the point of human skill,
Reason becomes the marshal to my will
125 And leads me to your eyes, where I o'erlook
Love's stories, written in love's richest book.

HELENA   Wherefore was I to this keen mockery born?
When at your hands did I deserve this scorn?
Is't not enough, is't not enough, young man,
130 That I did never, no nor never can
Deserve a sweet look from Demetrius' eye,
But you must flout my insufficiency?
Good troth, you do me wrong; good sooth, you do,
In such disdainful manner me to woo.
135 But fare you well. Perforce I must confess
I thought you lord of more true gentleness.
O that a lady of one man refused
Should of another therefore be abused!   *Exit.*

LYSANDER
She sees not Hermia. Hermia, sleep thou there,
140 And never mayst thou come Lysander near.
For as a surfeit of the sweetest things
The deepest loathing to the stomach brings,
Or as the heresies that men do leave
Are hated most of those they did deceive,
145 So thou, my surfeit and my heresy,
Of all be hated, but the most of me;
And all my powers, address your love and might
To honour Helen, and to be her knight.   *Exit.*

HERMIA [*starting*]
Help me, Lysander, help me: do thy best

To pluck this crawling serpent from my breast. 150
Ay me, for pity! What a dream was here!
Lysander, look how I do quake with fear.
Methought a serpent ate my heart away,
And you sat smiling at his cruel prey.
Lysander – what, removed? Lysander, lord – 155
What, out of hearing, gone? No sound, no word?
Alack, where are you? Speak, an if you hear;
Speak, of all loves! I swoon almost with fear.
No, then I well perceive you are not nigh.
Either death or you I'll find immediately. 160

Exit. Titania remains lying asleep.

3.1   *Enter* QUINCE, SNUG, BOTTOM, FLUTE, SNOUT
and STARVELING. *Titania lying asleep.*

BOTTOM   Are we all met?

QUINCE   Pat, pat; and here's a marvellous convenient
place for our rehearsal. This green plot shall be
our stage, this hawthorn brake our tiring-house;
and we will do it in action, as we will do it before 5
the duke.

BOTTOM   Peter Quince!

QUINCE   What sayst thou, bully Bottom?

BOTTOM   There are things in this comedy of Pyramus
and Thisbe that will never please. First, Pyramus must 10
draw a sword to kill himself, which the ladies cannot
abide. How answer you that?

SNOUT   Byrlakin, a parlous fear.

STARVELING   I believe we must leave the killing out,
when all is done. 15

BOTTOM   Not a whit. I have a device to make all well.
Write me a prologue, and let the prologue seem to say
we will do no harm with our swords, and that Pyramus
is not killed indeed; and for the more better assurance,
tell them that I, Pyramus, am not Pyramus, but Bottom 20
the weaver. This will put them out of fear.

QUINCE   Well, we will have such a prologue, and it shall
be written in eight and six.

BOTTOM   No, make it two more. Let it be written in
eight and eight. 25

SNOUT   Will not the ladies be afeared of the Lion?

STARVELING   I fear it, I promise you.

BOTTOM   Masters, you ought to consider with yourself:
to bring in (God shield us) a lion among ladies is a most
dreadful thing; for there is not a more fearful wild-fowl 30
than your lion living, and we ought to look to't.

SNOUT   Therefore another prologue must tell he is not a
lion.

BOTTOM   Nay, you must name his name, and half his
face must be seen through the lion's neck, and he 35
himself must speak through, saying thus, or to the
same defect: 'Ladies', or 'Fair ladies, I would wish
you', or 'I would request you', or 'I would entreat you,
not to fear, not to tremble: my life for yours. If you
think I come hither as a lion, it were pity of my life. No, 40

I am no such thing. I am a man as other men are.' And there, indeed, let him name his name, and tell them plainly he is Snug the joiner.

QUINCE   Well, it shall be so. But there is two hard
45   things: that is, to bring the moonlight into a chamber; for you know Pyramus and Thisbe meet by moonlight.

SNOUT   Doth the moon shine that night we play our play?

BOTTOM   A calendar, a calendar: look in the almanac.
50   Find out moonshine, find out moonshine.

Enter ROBIN GOODFELLOW *behind.*

QUINCE   [*consulting an almanac*]   Yes, it doth shine that night.

BOTTOM   Why, then may you leave a casement of the great chamber window, where we play, open; and the
55   moon may shine in at the casement.

QUINCE   Ay, or else one must come in with a bush of thorns and a lantern, and say he comes to disfigure or to present the person of Moonshine. Then there is another thing: we must have a wall in the great
60   chamber; for Pyramus and Thisbe, says the story, did talk through the chink of a wall.

SNOUT   You can never bring in a wall. What say you, Bottom?

BOTTOM   Some man or other must present Wall; and let
65   him have some plaster, or some loam, or some roughcast about him, to signify Wall; and let him hold his fingers thus, and through that cranny shall Pyramus and Thisbe whisper.

QUINCE   If that may be, then all is well. Come, sit down
70   every mother's son, and rehearse your parts. Pyramus, you begin. When you have spoken your speech, enter into that brake; and so every one according to his cue.

ROBIN   [*aside*]
75   What hempen homespuns have we swaggering here, So near the cradle of the Fairy Queen? What, a play toward? I'll be an auditor; An actor too, perhaps, if I see cause.

QUINCE   Speak, Pyramus. Thisbe, stand forth.

BOTTOM
Thisbe, the flowers of odious savours sweet.

QUINCE   Odours, odours.

BOTTOM
. . . odours savours sweet.
So hath thy breath, my dearest Thisbe dear.
But hark, a voice. Stay thou but here a while,
And by and by I will to thee appear.   *Exit.*

ROBIN   [*aside*]
85   *. . . A stranger Pyramus than ere played here.*   *Exit.*

FLUTE   Must I speak now?

QUINCE   Ay, marry, must you. For you must understand he goes but to see a noise that he heard, and is to come again.

FLUTE
90   *Most radiant Pyramus, most lily-white of hue,*

Of colour like the red rose on triumphant brier,
Most brisky juvenal, and eke most lovely jew,
As true as truest horse that yet would never tire,
I'll meet thee, Pyramus, at Ninny's tomb.

QUINCE   Ninus' tomb, man. Why, you must not speak
95   that yet. That you answer to Pyramus. You speak all your part at once, cues and all. Pyramus, enter; your cue is past. It is 'never tire'.

FLUTE   O!

As true as truest horse, that yet would never tire.
100

Enter BOTTOM *with an ass's head,* ROBIN
GOODFELLOW *following.*

BOTTOM
If I were, fair Thisbe, I were only thine.

QUINCE   O monstrous! O strange! We are haunted. Pray, masters; fly, masters. Help!

Exeunt all except Robin.

ROBIN   I'll follow you; I'll lead you about a round, Through bog, through bush, through brake, through brier.
105
Sometime a horse I'll be, sometime a hound, A hog, a headless bear, sometime a fire, And neigh, and bark, and grunt, and roar, and burn, Like horse, hound, hog, bear, fire, at every turn.   *Exit.*

Enter BOTTOM.

BOTTOM   Why do they run away? This is a knavery of
110   them to make me afeard.

Enter SNOUT.

SNOUT   O Bottom, thou art changed. What do I see on thee?

BOTTOM   What do you see? You see an ass-head of your own, do you?   *Exit Snout.*
115

Enter QUINCE.

QUINCE   Bless thee Bottom, bless thee! Thou art translated.   *Exit.*

BOTTOM   I see their knavery. This is to make an ass of me, to fright me if they could; but I will not stir from
120   this place, do what they can. I will walk up and down here, and I will sing, that they shall hear I am not afraid.
   The ousel cock so black of hue
      With orange-tawny bill,
   The throstle with his note so true,
125
      The wren with little quill.

TITANIA   [*Wakes.*]
What angel wakes me from my flowery bed?

BOTTOM
   The finch, the sparrow and the lark,
      The plainsong cuckoo gray,
   Whose note full many a man doth mark,
130
      And dares not answer nay.
For indeed, who would set his wit to so foolish a bird? Who would give a bird the lie, though he cry cuckoo never so?

135 TITANIA   I pray thee, gentle mortal, sing again:
Mine ear is much enamoured of thy note.
So is mine eye enthrallèd to thy shape,
And thy fair virtue's force perforce doth move me
On the first view to say, to swear, I love thee.

140 BOTTOM   Methinks, mistress, you should have little
reason for that. And yet to say the truth, reason and
love keep little company together nowadays; the more
the pity that some honest neighbours will not make
them friends. Nay, I can gleek upon occasion.

145 TITANIA   Thou art as wise as thou art beautiful.

BOTTOM   Not so neither; but if I had wit enough to get
out of this wood, I have enough to serve mine own turn.

TITANIA   Out of this wood do not desire to go.
Thou shalt remain here, whether thou wilt or no.
150 I am a spirit of no common rate:
The summer still doth tend upon my state,
And I do love thee; therefore go with me.
I'll give thee fairies to attend on thee,
And they shall fetch thee jewels from the deep,
155 And sing while thou on pressèd flowers dost sleep;
And I will purge thy mortal grossness so,
That thou shalt like an airy spirit go.
Peaseblossom, Cobweb, Mote, and Mustardseed!

Enter four Fairies: PEASEBLOSSOM, COBWEB,
MOTE *and* MUSTARDSEED.

PEASEBLOSSOM   Ready.
COBWEB   And I.
MOTE   And I.
MUSTARDSEED   And I.
ALL   Where shall we go?
160 TITANIA   Be kind and courteous to this gentleman.
Hop in his walks, and gambol in his eyes.
Feed him with apricots and dewberries,
With purple grapes, green figs and mulberries.
The honey-bags steal from the humble-bees,
165 And for night-tapers, crop their waxen thighs
And light them at the fiery glow-worms' eyes,
To have my love to bed and to arise;
And pluck the wings from painted butterflies
To fan the moonbeams from his sleeping eyes.
170 Nod to him, elves, and do him courtesies.
PEASEBLOSSOM   Hail, mortal.
COBWEB   Hail.
MOTE   Hail.
MUSTARDSEED   Hail.
BOTTOM   I cry your worships mercy, heartily. I beseech
your worship's name.
COBWEB   Cobweb.
175 BOTTOM   I shall desire you of more acquaintance, good
Master Cobweb. If I cut my finger, I shall make bold
with you. Your name, honest gentleman?
PEASEBLOSSOM   Peaseblossom.
BOTTOM   I pray you commend me to Mistress Squash,
180 your mother, and to Master Peascod, your father.

Good Master Peaseblossom, I shall desire you of more
acquaintance too. Your name, I beseech you, sir?
MUSTARDSEED   Mustardseed.
BOTTOM   Good Master Mustardseed, I know your
patience well. That same cowardly giantlike Ox-beef   185
hath devoured many a gentleman of your house. I
promise you, your kindred hath made my eyes water
ere now. I desire you more acquaintance, good Master
Mustardseed.
TITANIA   Come, wait upon him; lead him to my bower.   190
The moon, methinks, looks with a watery eye;
And when she weeps, weeps every little flower,
Lamenting some enforcèd chastity.
Tie up my lover's tongue, bring him silently.

                                                              Exeunt.

3.2   *Enter* OBERON.

OBERON   I wonder if Titania be awaked;
Then what it was that next came in her eye,
Which she must dote on in extremity.

Enter ROBIN GOODFELLOW.

Here comes my messenger. How now, mad spirit?
What night-rule now about this haunted grove?   5
ROBIN   My mistress with a monster is in love.
Near to her close and consecrated bower,
While she was in her dull and sleeping hour,
A crew of patches, rude mechanicals
That work for bread upon Athenian stalls,   10
Were met together to rehearse a play
Intended for great Theseus' nuptial day.
The shallowest thickskin of that barren sort,
Who Pyramus presented in their sport,
Forsook his scene and entered in a brake,   15
When I did him at this advantage take:
An ass's nole I fixed on his head.
Anon his Thisbe must be answered,
And forth my minic comes. When they him spy,
As wild geese that the creeping fowler eye,   20
Or russet-pated choughs, many in sort
Rising and cawing at the gun's report,
Sever themselves and madly sweep the sky,
So at his sight away his fellows fly;
And at our stamp, here o'er and o'er one falls,   25
He 'Murder' cries, and help from Athens calls.
Their sense, thus weak, lost with their fears thus strong,
Made senseless things begin to do them wrong;
For briers and thorns at their apparel snatch –
Some sleeves, some hats; from yielders, all things catch. 30
I led them on in this distracted fear,
And left sweet Pyramus translated there;
When in that moment, so it came to pass,
Titania waked, and straightway loved an ass.
OBERON   This falls out better than I could devise.   35
But hast thou latched the Athenian's eyes

With the love-juice, as I did bid thee do?
ROBIN   I took him sleeping (that is finished too)
And the Athenian woman by his side,
That when he waked, of force she must be eyed.

Enter DEMETRIUS *and* HERMIA. *Oberon and
Robin stand apart.*

OBERON   Stand close. This is the same Athenian.
ROBIN   This is the woman, but not this the man.
DEMETRIUS   O, why rebuke you him that loves you so?
Lay breath so bitter on your bitter foe.
HERMIA
Now I but chide; but I should use thee worse,
For thou, I fear, hast given me cause to curse.
If thou hast slain Lysander in his sleep,
Being o'er shoes in blood, plunge in the deep
And kill me too.
The sun was not so true unto the day
As he to me. Would he have stolen away
From sleeping Hermia? I'll believe as soon
This whole earth may be bored, and that the moon
May through the centre creep, and so displease
Her brother's noontide with th'antipodes.
It cannot be but thou hast murdered him.
So should a murderer look: so dead, so grim.
DEMETRIUS
So should the murdered look, and so should I,
Pierced through the heart with your stern cruelty.
Yet you, the murderer, look as bright, as clear
As yonder Venus in her glimmering sphere.
HERMIA   What's this to my Lysander? Where is he?
Ah, good Demetrius, wilt thou give him me?
DEMETRIUS
I had rather give his carcass to my hounds.
HERMIA
Out, dog, out, cur! Thou driv'st me past the bounds
Of maiden's patience. Hast thou slain him then?
Henceforth be never numbered among men.
O, once tell true: tell true, even for my sake,
Durst thou have looked upon him, being awake,
And hast thou killed him sleeping? O brave touch!
Could not a worm, an adder do so much?
An adder did it; for with doubler tongue
Than thine, thou serpent, never adder stung.
DEMETRIUS
You spend your passion on a misprised mood.
I am not guilty of Lysander's blood,
Nor is he dead, for aught that I can tell.
HERMIA   I pray thee, tell me then that he is well.
DEMETRIUS   And if I could, what should I get therefor?
HERMIA   A privilege never to see me more.
And from thy hated presence part I so.
See me no more, whether he be dead or no.   *Exit.*
DEMETRIUS
There is no following her in this fierce vein;
Here, therefore, for a while I will remain.
So sorrow's heaviness doth heavier grow

For debt that bankrupt sleep doth sorrow owe,   85
Which now in some slight measure it will pay,
If for his tender here I make some stay.
[*Lies down and sleeps*].

OBERON *and* ROBIN *come forward.*

OBERON
What hast thou done? Thou hast mistaken quite,
And laid the love-juice on some true love's sight.
Of thy misprision must perforce ensue   90
Some true love turned, and not a false turned
    true.
ROBIN
Then fate o'errules, that one man holding troth,
A million fail, confounding oath on oath.
OBERON
About the wood go swifter than the wind,
And Helena of Athens look thou find.   95
All fancy-sick she is and pale of cheer,
With sighs of love that costs the fresh blood dear.
By some illusion see thou bring her here.
I'll charm his eyes, against she do appear.
ROBIN   I go, I go, look how I go,   100
Swifter than arrow from the Tartar's bow.   *Exit.*
OBERON [*Squeezes the flower on Demetrius' eyelids.*]
            Flower of this purple dye,
            Hit with Cupid's archery,
            Sink in apple of his eye.
            When his love he doth espy,   105
            Let her shine as gloriously
            As the Venus of the sky.
            When thou wak'st, if she be by,
            Beg of her for remedy.

Enter ROBIN GOODFELLOW.

ROBIN   Captain of our fairy band,   110
            Helena is here at hand,
            And the youth mistook by me
            Pleading for a lover's fee.
            Shall we their fond pageant see?
            Lord, what fools these mortals be!   115
OBERON   Stand aside. The noise they make
            Will cause Demetrius to awake.
ROBIN   Then will two at once woo one:
            That must needs be sport alone.
            And those things do best please me   120
            That befall preposterously.

Enter LYSANDER *and* HELENA. *Oberon and
Robin stand apart.*

LYSANDER
Why should you think that I should woo in scorn?
    Scorn and derision never come in tears.
Look when I vow, I weep; and vows so born,
    In their nativity all truth appears.   125
How can these things in me seem scorn to you,
Bearing the badge of faith to prove them true?

HELENA   You do advance your cunning more and more.
When truth kills truth, O devilish holy fray!
130   These vows are Hermia's: will you give her o'er?
Weigh oath with oath, and you will nothing weigh.
Your vows to her and me, put in two scales,
Will even weigh, and both as light as tales.
LYSANDER   I had no judgement when to her I swore.
135   HELENA   Nor none, in my mind, now you give her o'er.
LYSANDER   Demetrius loves her, and he loves not you.
DEMETRIUS [*Wakes.*]
O Helen, goddess, nymph, perfect, divine,
To what, my love, shall I compare thine eyne?
Crystal is muddy. O, how ripe in show
140   Thy lips, those kissing cherries, tempting grow!
That pure congealed white, high Taurus' snow,
Fanned with the eastern wind, turns to a crow
When thou hold'st up thy hand. O let me kiss
This impress of pure white, this seal of bliss!
145   HELENA   O spite! O hell! I see you all are bent
To set against me for your merriment.
If you were civil and knew courtesy,
You would not do me thus much injury.
Can you not hate me, as I know you do,
150   But you must join in souls to mock me too?
If you were men, as men you are in show,
You would not use a gentle lady so,
To vow and swear and superpraise my parts
When I am sure you hate me with your hearts.
155   You both are rivals and love Hermia,
And now both rivals to mock Helena.
A trim exploit, a manly enterprise,
To conjure tears up in a poor maid's eyes
With your derision! None of noble sort
160   Would so offend a virgin, and extort
A poor soul's patience, all to make you sport.
LYSANDER   You are unkind, Demetrius; be not so,
For you love Hermia: this you know I know.
And here with all good will, with all my heart,
165   In Hermia's love I yield you up my part;
And yours of Helena to me bequeath,
Whom I do love, and will do till my death.
HELENA   Never did mockers waste more idle breath.
DEMETRIUS   Lysander, keep thy Hermia; I will none.
170   If e'er I loved her, all that love is gone.
My heart to her but as guestwise sojourned,
And now to Helen is it home returned,
There to remain.
LYSANDER   Helen, it is not so.
DEMETRIUS
Disparage not the faith thou dost not know,
175   Lest, to thy peril, thou abye it dear.
Look where thy love comes: yonder is thy dear.

Enter HERMIA.

HERMIA
Dark night, that from the eye his function takes,
The ear more quick of apprehension makes;

Wherein it doth impair the seeing sense,
It pays the hearing double recompense.   180
Thou art not by mine eye, Lysander, found;
Mine ear, I thank it, brought me to thy sound.
But why, unkindly, didst thou leave me so?
LYSANDER
Why should he stay, whom love doth press to go?
HERMIA
What love could press Lysander from my side?   185
LYSANDER
Lysander's love, that would not let him bide:
Fair Helena, who more engilds the night
Than all yon fiery oes and eyes of light.
Why seek'st thou me? Could not this make thee know,
The hate I bare thee made me leave thee so?   190
HERMIA   You speak not as you think. It cannot be.
HELENA   Lo, she is one of this confederacy.
Now I perceive, they have conjoined all three
To fashion this false sport in spite of me.
Injurious Hermia, most ungrateful maid,   195
Have you conspired, have you with these contrived
To bait me with this foul derision?
Is all the counsel that we two have shared,
The sisters' vows, the hours that we have spent,
When we have chid the hasty-footed time   200
For parting us – O, is all forgot?
All schooldays' friendship, childhood innocence?
We, Hermia, like two artificial gods,
Have with our needles created both one flower,
Both on one sampler, sitting on one cushion,   205
Both warbling of one song, both in one key,
As if our hands, our sides, voices and minds
Had been incorporate. So we grew together
Like to a double cherry, seeming parted
But yet an union in partition,   210
Two lovely berries moulded on one stem;
So with two seeming bodies but one heart,
Two of the first, like coats in heraldry,
Due but to one, and crowned with one crest.
And will you rent our ancient love asunder   215
To join with men in scorning your poor friend?
It is not friendly, 'tis not maidenly.
Our sex, as well as I, may chide you for it,
Though I alone do feel the injury.
HERMIA   I am amazed at your passionate words.   220
I scorn you not; it seems that you scorn me.
HELENA   Have you not set Lysander, as in scorn,
To follow me and praise my eyes and face?
And made your other love Demetrius,
Who even but now did spurn me with his foot,   225
To call me goddess, nymph, divine and rare,
Precious, celestial? Wherefore speaks he this
To her he hates? And wherefore doth Lysander
Deny your love, so rich within his soul,
And tender me, forsooth, affection,   230
But by your setting on, by your consent?
What though I be not so in grace as you,

So hung upon with love, so fortunate,
But miserable most, to love unloved?
35 This you should pity rather than despise.
HERMIA I understand not what you mean by this.
HELENA I do. Persevere, counterfeit sad looks,
Make mouths upon me when I turn my back,
Wink each at other, hold the sweet jest up.
40 This sport, well carried, shall be chronicled.
If you have any pity, grace or manners,
You would not make me such an argument.
But fare ye well. 'Tis partly my own fault,
Which death or absence soon shall remedy.
45 LYSANDER Stay, gentle Helena; hear my excuse,
My love, my life, my soul, fair Helena.
HELENA O excellent!
HERMIA [*to Lysander*] Sweet, do not scorn her so.
DEMETRIUS [*to Lysander*]
If she cannot entreat, I can compel.
LYSANDER Thou canst compel no more than she entreat.
Thy threats have no more strength than her weak
50   prayers.
Helen, I love thee, by my life I do.
I swear by that which I will lose for thee
To prove him false that says I love thee not.
DEMETRIUS [*to Helena*]
I say, I love thee more than he can do.
LYSANDER [*to Demetrius*]
55 If thou say so, withdraw, and prove it too.
DEMETRIUS Quick, come.
HERMIA   Lysander, whereto tends all this?
LYSANDER Away, you Ethiop.
DEMETRIUS [*to Hermia*]   No, no: he'll seem
To break loose, take on as you would follow,
But yet come not. [*to Lysander*] You are a tame man,
    go.
LYSANDER
60 Hang off, thou cat, thou burr, vile thing let loose,
Or I will shake thee from me like a serpent.
HERMIA
Why are you grown so rude? What change is this,
Sweet love?
LYSANDER   Thy love? Out, tawny Tartar, out!
Out, loathed medicine; O hated potion, hence.
HERMIA Do you not jest?
HELENA   Yes, sooth, and so do you.
65 LYSANDER Demetrius, I will keep my word with thee.
DEMETRIUS I would I had your bond; for I perceive
A weak bond holds you. I'll not trust your word.
LYSANDER
What, should I hurt her, strike her, kill her dead?
70 Although I hate her, I'll not harm her so.
HERMIA What, can you do me greater harm than hate?
Hate me, wherefore? O me, what news, my love?
Am not I Hermia? Are not you Lysander?
I am as fair now as I was erewhile.
Since night you loved me, yet since night you
75   left me.

Why then, you left me (O the gods forbid)
In earnest, shall I say?
LYSANDER   Ay, by my life,
And never did desire to see thee more.
Therefore be out of hope, of question, of doubt;
Be certain, nothing truer: 'tis no jest   280
That I do hate thee, and love Helena.
HERMIA [*to Helena*]
O me, you juggler, you canker-blossom,
You thief of love! What, have you come by night
And stolen my love's heart from him?
HELENA   Fine, i' faith.
Have you no modesty, no maiden shame,   285
No touch of bashfulness? What, will you tear
Impatient answers from my gentle tongue?
Fie, fie, you counterfeit, you puppet, you!
HERMIA
Puppet? Why so? Aye, that way goes the game.
Now I perceive that she hath made compare   290
Between our statures: she hath urged her height,
And with her personage, her tall personage,
Her height, forsooth, she hath prevailed with him.
And are you grown so high in his esteem
Because I am so dwarfish and so low?   295
How low am I, thou painted maypole? Speak,
How low am I? I am not yet so low
But that my nails can reach unto thine eyes.
HELENA I pray you, though you mock me, gentlemen,
Let her not hurt me. I was never curst;   300
I have no gift at all in shrewishness.
I am a right maid for my cowardice:
Let her not strike me. You perhaps may think
Because she is something lower than myself,
That I can match her.
HERMIA   Lower? Hark again.   305
HELENA Good Hermia, do not be so bitter with me.
I evermore did love you, Hermia,
Did ever keep your counsels, never wronged you,
Save that in love unto Demetrius,
I told him of your stealth unto this wood.   310
He followed you; for love, I followed him.
But he hath chid me hence, and threatened me
To strike me, spurn me, nay to kill me too.
And now, so you will let me quiet go,
To Athens will I bear my folly back,   315
And follow you no further. Let me go.
You see how simple and how fond I am.
HERMIA Why, get you gone. Who is't that hinders you?
HELENA A foolish heart, that I leave here behind.
HERMIA What, with Lysander?
HELENA   With Demetrius.   320
LYSANDER
Be not afraid. She shall not harm thee, Helena.
DEMETRIUS
No, sir, she shall not, though you take her part.
HELENA O, when she is angry, she is keen and shrewd.
She was a vixen when she went to school;

325   And though she be but little, she is fierce.
HERMIA   Little again? Nothing but low and little?
    Why will you suffer her to flout me thus?
    Let me come to her.
LYSANDER   Get you gone, you dwarf,
    You minimus, of hindering knot-grass made,
    You bead, you acorn.
330 DEMETRIUS   You are too officious
    In her behalf that scorns your services.
    Let her alone. Speak not of Helena,
    Take not her part. For if thou dost intend
    Never so little show of love to her,
    Thou shalt abye it.
335 LYSANDER   Now she holds me not.
    Now follow, if thou dar'st, to try whose right,
    Of thine or mine, is most in Helena.
DEMETRIUS
    Follow? Nay, I'll go with thee, cheek by jowl.
        Exeunt Lysander and Demetrius.
HERMIA   You, mistress, all this coil is long of you.
    Nay, go not back.
340 HELENA   I will not trust you, I,
    Nor longer stay in your curst company.
    Your hands than mine are quicker for a fray;
    My legs are longer, though, to run away.   *Exit.*
HERMIA   I am amazed, and know not what to say.   *Exit.*

        OBERON *and* ROBIN *come forward.*

345 OBERON   This is thy negligence. Still thou mistak'st,
    Or else commit'st thy knaveries wilfully.
ROBIN   Believe me, king of shadows, I mistook.
    Did not you tell me I should know the man
    By the Athenian garments he had on?
350   And so far blameless proves my enterprise,
    That I have 'nointed an Athenian's eyes;
    And so far am I glad it so did sort,
    As this their jangling I esteem a sport.
OBERON   Thou seest these lovers seek a place to fight.
355   Hie therefore, Robin, overcast the night;
    The starry welkin cover thou anon
    With drooping fog as black as Acheron,
    And lead these testy rivals so astray
    As one come not within another's way.
360   Like to Lysander sometime frame thy tongue,
    Then stir Demetrius up with bitter wrong,
    And sometime rail thou like Demetrius,
    And from each other look thou lead them thus
    Till o'er their brows, death-counterfeiting, sleep
365   With leaden legs and batty wings doth creep.
    Then crush this herb into Lysander's eye,
    Whose liquor hath this virtuous property
    To take from thence all error with his might,
    And make his eyeballs roll with wonted sight.
370   When they next wake, all this derision
    Shall seem a dream and fruitless vision,
    And back to Athens shall the lovers wend
    With league whose date till death shall never end.

    Whiles I in this affair do thee employ,
    I'll to my queen and beg her Indian boy;   375
    And then I will her charmed eye release
    From monster's view, and all things shall be peace.
ROBIN   My fairy lord, this must be done with haste,
    For night's swift dragons cut the clouds full fast
    And yonder shines Aurora's harbinger,   380
    At whose approach ghosts, wandering here and
        there,
    Troop home to churchyards. Damned spirits all,
    That in cross-ways and floods have burial,
    Already to their wormy beds are gone.
    For fear lest day should look their shames upon,   385
    They wilfully themselves exile from light,
    And must for ay consort with black-browed night.
OBERON   But we are spirits of another sort.
    I with the morning's love have oft made sport,
    And like a forester the groves may tread   390
    Even till the eastern gate, all fiery red,
    Opening on Neptune with fair blessed beams,
    Turns into yellow gold his salt green streams.
    But notwithstanding, haste, make no delay.
    We may effect this business yet ere day.   *Exit.*   395
ROBIN
    Up and down, up and down,
    I will lead them up and down.
    I am feared in field and town.
    Goblin, lead them up and down.
Here comes one.   400

        Enter LYSANDER.

LYSANDER
    Where art thou, proud Demetrius? Speak thou now.
ROBIN   Here, villain, drawn and ready. Where art thou?
LYSANDER   I will be with thee straight.
ROBIN   Follow me then
    To plainer ground.
        Exit Lysander, as though following Demetrius.

        Enter DEMETRIUS.

DEMETRIUS   Lysander, speak again.
    Thou runaway, thou coward, art thou fled?   405
    Speak: in some bush? Where dost thou hide thy head?
ROBIN   Thou coward, art thou bragging to the stars,
    Telling the bushes that thou look'st for wars,
    And wilt not come? Come, recreant, come, thou child.
    I'll whip thee with a rod: he is defiled   410
    That draws a sword on thee.
DEMETRIUS   Yea, art thou there?
ROBIN
    Follow my voice. We'll try no manhood here.   *Exeunt.*

        Enter LYSANDER.

LYSANDER   He goes before me, and still dares me on;
    When I come where he calls, then he is gone.
    The villain is much lighter heeled than I: 415
    I followed fast, but faster he did fly,

That fallen am I in dark uneven way,
And here will rest me.   [*Lies down.*]
               Come, thou gentle day,
For if but once thou show me thy gray light,
420   I'll find Demetrius, and revenge this spite.   [*Sleeps.*]

       Enter ROBIN *and* DEMETRIUS, *shifting places.*

ROBIN   Ho, ho, ho! Coward, why com'st thou not?
DEMETRIUS   Abide me, if thou dar'st. For well I wot,
Thou run'st before me, shifting every place,
And dar'st not stand nor look me in the face.
Where art thou now?
425   ROBIN   Come hither. I am here.
DEMETRIUS
Nay then, thou mockst me. Thou shalt buy this dear
If ever I thy face by daylight see;
Now go thy way. Faintness constraineth me
To measure out my length on this cold bed.
     [*Lies down.*]
430   By day's approach look to be visited.   [*Sleeps.*]

             Enter HELENA.

HELENA   O weary night, O long and tedious night,
Abate thy hours. Shine, comforts, from the east,
That I may back to Athens by daylight
From these that my poor company detest;
435   And sleep, that sometimes shuts up sorrow's eye,
Steal me a while from mine own company.
     [*Lies down and sleeps.*]
ROBIN
     Yet but three? Come one more.
     Two of both kinds makes up four.
     Here she comes, curst and sad.
440   Cupid is a knavish lad,
     Thus to make poor females mad.

             Enter HERMIA.

HERMIA   Never so weary, never so in woe,
Bedabbled with the dew, and torn with briers,
I can no further crawl, no further go;
445   My legs can keep no pace with my desires.
Here will I rest me till the break of day.   [*Lies down.*]
Heavens shield Lysander, if they mean a fray.   [*Sleeps.*]
ROBIN [*Squeezes the juice on Lysander's eyelids.*]
     On the ground
     Sleep sound.
450   I'll apply
     To your eye,
     Gentle lover, remedy.
     When thou wak'st,
     Thou tak'st
455   True delight
     In the sight
     Of thy former lady's eye;
     And the country proverb known,
     That every man should take his own,
460   In your waking shall be shown.

     Jack shall have Jill,
     Nought shall go ill,
     The man shall have his mare again, and all shall be
     well.
       Exit Robin. The lovers remain onstage, sleeping.

4.1   *Enter* TITANIA, BOTTOM *and* FAIRIES,
            and OBERON *behind them.*

TITANIA   Come sit thee down upon this flowery bed
     While I thy amiable cheeks do coy,
And stick musk-roses in thy sleek smooth head,
     And kiss thy fair large ears, my gentle joy.
BOTTOM   Where's Peaseblossom?   5
PEASEBLOSSOM   Ready.
BOTTOM   Scratch my head, Peaseblossom. Where's
Monsieur Cobweb?
COBWEB   Ready.
BOTTOM   Monsieur Cobweb, good Monsieur, get you   10
your weapons in your hand, and kill me a red-hipped
humble-bee on the top of a thistle; and good Monsieur,
bring me the honey-bag. Do not fret yourself too much
in the action, Monsieur; and good Monsieur, have a
care the honey-bag break not. I would be loath to have   15
you overflown with a honey-bag, Signor. Where's
Monsieur Mustardseed?
MUSTARDSEED   Ready.
BOTTOM   Give me your neaf, Monsieur Mustardseed.
Pray you, leave your courtesy, good Monsieur.   20
MUSTARDSEED   What's your will?
BOTTOM   Nothing, good Monsieur, but to help
Cavalery Cobweb to scratch. I must to the barber's,
Monsieur, for methinks I am marvellous hairy about
the face; and I am such a tender ass, if my hair do but   25
tickle me, I must scratch.
TITANIA
What, wilt thou hear some music, my sweet love?
BOTTOM   I have a reasonable good ear in music. Let's
have the tongs and the bones.
            [*Music: tongs, rural music*]
TITANIA   Or say, sweet love, what thou desirest to eat.   30
BOTTOM   Truly, a peck of provender. I could munch
your good dry oats. Methinks I have a great desire to a
bottle of hay. Good hay, sweet hay, hath no fellow.
TITANIA   I have a venturous fairy, that shall seek
The squirrel's hoard, and fetch thee new nuts.   35
BOTTOM   I had rather have a handful or two of dried
peas. But I pray you, let none of your people stir me. I
have an exposition of sleep come upon me.
TITANIA   Sleep thou, and I will wind thee in my arms.
Fairies, be gone, and be always away.   40
            Music stops. Exeunt Fairies.
So doth the woodbine the sweet honeysuckle
Gently entwist; the female ivy so
Enrings the barky fingers of the elm.
O how I love thee! How I dote on thee!   [*They sleep.*]

     Oberon advances. Enter ROBIN GOODFELLOW.

OBERON

45   Welcome, good Robin. Seest thou this sweet sight?
      Her dotage now I do begin to pity.
      For meeting her of late behind the wood,
      Seeking sweet favours for this hateful fool,
      I did upbraid her, and fall out with her;
50   For she his hairy temples then had rounded
      With coronet of fresh and fragrant flowers,
      And that same dew, which sometime on the buds
      Was wont to swell like round and orient pearls,
      Stood now within the pretty flowerets' eyes
55   Like tears that did their own disgrace bewail.
      When I had at my pleasure taunted her,
      And she, in mild terms, begged my patience,
      I then did ask of her her changeling child,
      Which straight she gave me, and her fairy sent
60   To bear him to my bower in fairy land.
      And now I have the boy, I will undo
      This hateful imperfection of her eyes.
      And gentle puck, take this transformed scalp
      From off the head of this Athenian swain,
65   That he, awaking when the other do,
      May all to Athens back again repair,
      And think no more of this night's accidents
      But as the fierce vexation of a dream.
      But first I will release the Fairy Queen.
           [*Squeezes the juice on her eyelids.*]
70   Be as thou wast wont to be.
                See as thou wast wont to see.
                Dian's bud o'er Cupid's flower
                Hath such force and blessed power.
      Now, my Titania, wake you, my sweet queen.
      TITANIA [*Wakes.*]
75   My Oberon, what visions have I seen!
      Methought I was enamoured of an ass.
      OBERON   There lies your love.
      TITANIA   How came these things to pass?
      O, how mine eyes do loathe his visage now!
      OBERON   Silence a while. Robin, take off this head.
80   Titania, music call, and strike more dead
      Than common sleep of all these five the sense.
      TITANIA
      Music, ho, music, such as charmeth sleep.   [*Music still*]
      ROBIN [*Takes the ass-head off Bottom.*]
      Now, when thou wak'st, with thine own fool's eyes peep.
      OBERON
      Sound music. Come, my queen, take hands with me,
85   And rock the ground whereon these sleepers be.
           [*They dance.*]
      Now thou and I are new in amity,
      And will tomorrow midnight solemnly
      Dance in Duke Theseus' house triumphantly,
      And bless it to all fair prosperity.
90   There shall the pairs of faithful lovers be
      Wedded, with Theseus, all in jollity.
      ROBIN
         Fairy king, attend and mark:

      I do hear the morning lark.
      OBERON
         Then, my queen, in silence sad,
         Trip we after night's shade.   95
         We the globe can compass soon,
         Swifter than the wandering moon.
      TITANIA
         Come, my lord, and in our flight,
         Tell me how it came this night
         That I sleeping here was found   100
         With these mortals on the ground
              *Exeunt Oberon, Titania and Robin. The lovers
                          and Bottom remain sleeping.*

      Wind horns. Enter THESEUS, HIPPOLYTA,
              EGEUS *and the Duke's train.*

      THESEUS   Go one of you, find out the forester;
      For now our observation is performed,
      And since we have the vaward of the day,
      My love shall hear the music of my hounds.   105
      Uncouple in the western valley, let them go.
      Dispatch, I say, and find the forester.
                                    Exit an Attendant.
      We will, fair queen, up to the mountain's top,
      And mark the musical confusion
      Of hounds and echo in conjunction.   110
      HIPPOLYTA   I was with Hercules and Cadmus once
      When in a wood of Crete they bayed the bear
      With hounds of Sparta. Never did I hear
      Such gallant chiding; for besides the groves,
      The skies, the fountains, every region near   115
      Seemed all one mutual cry. I never heard
      So musical a discord, such sweet thunder.
      THESEUS
      My hounds are bred out of the Spartan kind:
      So flewed, so sanded, and their heads are hung
      With ears that sweep away the morning dew;   120
      Crook-kneed, and dewlapped like Thessalian bulls,
      Slow in pursuit, but matched in mouth like bells,
      Each under each. A cry more tunable
      Was never holloed to nor cheered with horn
      In Crete, in Sparta, nor in Thessaly.   125
      Judge when you hear. But soft: what nymphs are these?
      EGEUS   My lord, this my daughter here asleep,
      And this Lysander, this Demetrius is,
      This Helena, old Nedar's Helena.
      I wonder of their being here together.   130
      THESEUS   No doubt they rose up early, to observe
      The rite of May; and hearing our intent,
      Came here in grace of our solemnity.
      But speak, Egeus, is not this the day
      That Hermia should give answer of her choice?   135
      EGEUS   It is, my lord.
      THESEUS
      Go, bid the huntsmen wake them with their horns.
              Exit an Attendant. Shout within. Wind horns.
           [*The lovers all start up.*]

THESEUS
Good morrow, friends. Saint Valentine is past.
Begin these wood-birds but to couple now?

LYSANDER
Pardon, my lord. [*The lovers kneel.*]

140 THESEUS   I pray you all, stand up.
I know you two are rival enemies.
How comes this gentle concord in the world,
That hatred is so far from jealousy
To sleep by hate, and fear no enmity?

145 LYSANDER   My lord, I shall reply amazedly,
Half sleep, half waking; but as yet, I swear,
I cannot truly say how I came here.
But as I think (for truly would I speak),
And now I do bethink me, so it is,

150 I came with Hermia hither. Our intent
Was to be gone from Athens, where we might
Without the peril of the Athenian law –

EGEUS   Enough, enough, my lord; you have enough.
I beg the law, the law, upon his head.

155 They would have stolen away, they would, Demetrius,
Thereby to have defeated you and me:
You of your wife, and me of my consent,
Of my consent that she should be your wife.

DEMETRIUS   My lord, fair Helen told me of their stealth,
160 Of this their purpose hither to this wood,
And I in fury hither followed them,
Fair Helena in fancy following me.
But my good lord, I wot not by what power
(But by some power it is) my love to Hermia,

165 Melted as the snow, seems to me now
As the remembrance of an idle gaud,
Which in my childhood I did dote upon;
And all the faith, the virtue of my heart,
The object and the pleasure of mine eye,

170 Is only Helena. To her, my lord,
Was I betrothed ere I see Hermia;
But like in sickness did I loathe this food,
But as in health, come to my natural taste,
Now I do wish it, love it, long for it,

175 And will for evermore be true to it.

THESEUS   Fair lovers, you are fortunately met.
Of this discourse we more will hear anon.
Egeus, I will overbear your will;
For in the temple, by and by, with us,

180 These couples shall eternally be knit.
And for the morning now is something worn,
Our purposed hunting shall be set aside.
Away with us to Athens. Three and three,
We'll hold a feast in great solemnity.

185 Come, Hippolyta.

            Exeunt Theseus, Hippolyta, Egeus and train.

DEMETRIUS
These things seem small and undistinguishable,
Like far-off mountains turned into clouds.

HERMIA   Methinks I see these things with parted eye,
When everything seems double.

HELENA   So methinks;
And I have found Demetrius, like a jewel   190
Mine own, and not mine own.

DEMETRIUS   Are you sure
That we are awake? It seems to me
That yet we sleep, we dream. Do not you think
The duke was here, and bid us follow him?

HERMIA   Yea, and my father.

HELENA   And Hippolyta.   195

LYSANDER   And he did bid us follow to the temple.

DEMETRIUS   Why then, we are awake. Let's follow him,
And by the way let us recount our dreams.

                        Exeunt lovers.

[*Bottom wakes.*]

BOTTOM   When my cue comes, call me, and I will
answer. My next is, 'Most fair Pyramus'. Heigh-ho!   200
Peter Quince? Flute the bellows-mender? Snout the
tinker? Starveling? Gods my life! Stolen hence, and
left me asleep? I have had a most rare vision. I have had
a dream, past the wit of man to say what dream it was.
Man is but an ass if he go about to expound this dream.   205
Methought I was – there is no man can tell what.
Methought I was – and methought I had – but man is
but a patched fool if he will offer to say what methought
I had. The eye of man hath not heard, the ear of man
hath not seen, man's hand is not able to taste, his   210
tongue to conceive, nor his heart to report what my
dream was. I will get Peter Quince to write a ballad of
this dream. It shall be called 'Bottom's Dream',
because it hath no bottom; and I will sing it in the latter
end of a play, before the duke. Peradventure, to make it   215
the more gracious, I shall sing it at her death.   *Exit.*

4.2   *Enter* QUINCE, FLUTE, SNOUT *and* STARVELING.

QUINCE   Have you sent to Bottom's house? Is he come
home yet?

STARVELING   He cannot be heard of. Out of doubt he is
transported.

FLUTE   If he come not, then the play is marred. It goes   5
not forward. Doth it?

QUINCE   It is not possible. You have not a man in all
Athens able to discharge Pyramus but he.

FLUTE   No, he hath simply the best wit of any
handicraftman in Athens.   10

QUINCE   Yea, and the best person too, and he is a very
paramour for a sweet voice.

FLUTE   You must say paragon. A paramour is (God bless
us) a thing of naught.

                        Enter SNUG.

SNUG   Masters, the duke is coming from the temple,   15
and there is two or three lords and ladies more
married. If our sport had gone forward, we had all been
made men.

FLUTE   O sweet bully Bottom! Thus hath he lost sixpence
a day during his life: he could not have scaped sixpence   20

a day. And the duke had not given him sixpence a day
for playing Pyramus, I'll be hanged. He would have
deserved it. Sixpence a day in Pyramus, or nothing.

Enter BOTTOM.

BOTTOM   Where are these lads? Where are these hearts?

25 QUINCE   Bottom! O most courageous day! O most
happy hour!

BOTTOM   Masters, I am to discourse wonders; but ask
me not what. For if I tell you, I am not true Athenian.
I will tell you everything right as it fell out.

30 QUINCE   Let us hear, sweet Bottom.

BOTTOM   Not a word of me. All that I will tell you is that
the duke hath dined. Get your apparel together: good
strings to your beards, new ribands to your pumps.
Meet presently at the palace, every man look o'er his

35 part; for the short and the long is, our play is preferred.
In any case let Thisbe have clean linen; and let not him
that plays the Lion pare his nails, for they shall hang out
for the Lion's claws. And most dear actors, eat no
onions nor garlic, for we are to utter sweet breath; and I

40 do not doubt but to hear them say, it is a sweet comedy.
No more words. Away, go away.   *Exeunt.*

5.1   *Enter* THESEUS, HIPPOLYTA,
            PHILOSTRATE *and Lords.*

HIPPOLYTA
'Tis strange, my Theseus, that these lovers speak of.

THESEUS
More strange than true. I never may believe
These antique fables, nor these fairy toys.
Lovers and madmen have such seething brains,

5   Such shaping fantasies, that apprehend
More than cool reason ever comprehends.
The lunatic, the lover, and the poet
Are of imagination all compact.
One sees more devils than vast hell can hold:

10 That is the madman. The lover, all as frantic,
Sees Helen's beauty in a brow of Egypt.
The poet's eye, in a fine frenzy rolling,
Doth glance from heaven to earth, from earth to heaven;
And as imagination bodies forth

15 The forms of things unknown, the poet's pen
Turns them to shapes, and gives to airy nothing
A local habitation and a name.
Such tricks hath strong imagination
That if it would but apprehend some joy,

20 It comprehends some bringer of that joy;
Or in the night, imagining some fear,
How easy is a bush supposed a bear!

HIPPOLYTA   But all the story of the night told over,
And all their minds transfigured so together,

25 More witnesseth than fancy's images
And grows to something of great constancy,
But howsoever strange and admirable.

Enter LYSANDER, DEMETRIUS, HERMIA *and* HELENA.

THESEUS   Here come the lovers, full of joy and mirth.
Joy, gentle friends, joy and fresh days of love
Accompany your hearts.

LYSANDER   More than to us   30
Wait in your royal walks, your board, your bed.

THESEUS
Come now, what masques, what dances shall we
have
To wear away this long age of three hours
Between our after-supper and bed-time?
Where is our usual manager of mirth?   35
What revels are in hand? Is there no play
To ease the anguish of a torturing hour?
Call Philostrate.

PHILOSTRATE   Here, mighty Theseus.

THESEUS
Say, what abridgement have you for this evening?
What masque, what music? How shall we beguile   40
The lazy time, if not with some delight?

PHILOSTRATE [*Gives him a paper.*]
There is a brief how many sports are ripe.
Make choice of which your highness will see first.

THESEUS [*Reads.*]
'The battle with the Centaurs, to be sung
By an Athenian eunuch to the harp'?   45
We'll none of that. That have I told my love
In glory of my kinsman Hercules.
'The riot of the tipsy Bacchanals
Tearing the Thracian singer in their rage'?
That is an old device, and it was played   50
When I from Thebes came last a conqueror.
'The thrice three Muses mourning for the death
Of learning, late deceased in beggary'?
That is some satire keen and critical,
Not sorting with a nuptial ceremony.   55
'A tedious brief scene of young Pyramus
And his love Thisbe; very tragical mirth'?
Merry and tragical? Tedious and brief?
That is hot ice and wondrous swarthy snow.
How shall we find the concord of this discord?   60

PHILOSTRATE
A play there is, my lord, some ten words long,
Which is as brief as I have known a play.
But by ten words, my lord, it is too long,
Which makes it tedious; for in all the play
There is not one word apt, one player fitted.   65
And tragical, my noble lord, it is,
For Pyramus therein doth kill himself;
Which when I saw rehearsed, I must confess,
Made mine eyes water, but more merry tears
The passion of loud laughter never shed.   70

THESEUS   What are they that do play it?

PHILOSTRATE
Hard-handed men that work in Athens here,
Which never laboured in their minds till now,
And now have toiled their unbreathed memories
With this same play, against your nuptial.   75

THESEUS   And we will hear it.

PHILOSTRATE   No, my noble lord,
It is not for you. I have heard it over,
And it is nothing, nothing in the world,
Unless you can find sport in their intents,
80   Extremely stretched and conned with cruel pain
To do you service.

THESEUS   I will hear that play;
For never anything can be amiss
When simpleness and duty tender it.
Go bring them in, and take your places, ladies.
                                Exit Philostrate.

HIPPOLYTA
85   I love not to see wretchedness o'ercharged,
And duty in his service perishing.

THESEUS
Why, gentle sweet, you shall see no such thing.

HIPPOLYTA   He says they can do nothing in this kind.

THESEUS
The kinder we, to give them thanks for nothing.
90   Our sport shall be to take what they mistake.
And what poor duty cannot do,
Noble respect takes it in might, not merit.
Where I have come, great clerks have purposed
To greet me with premeditated welcomes
95   Where I have seen them shiver and look pale,
Make periods in the midst of sentences,
Throttle their practised accent in their fears,
And in conclusion dumbly have broke off,
Not paying me a welcome. Trust me, sweet,
100 Out of this silence, yet I picked a welcome;
And in the modesty of fearful duty,
I read as much as from the rattling tongue
Of saucy and audacious eloquence.
Love, therefore, and tongue-tied simplicity
105 In least speak most, to my capacity.

                    Enter PHILOSTRATE.

PHILOSTRATE
So please your grace, the Prologue is addressed.

THESEUS   Let him approach.

        Flourish of trumpets. Enter QUINCE as the Prologue.

QUINCE
If we offend, it is with our good will.
    That you should think, we come not to offend,
110 *But with good will. To show our simple skill,*
    That is the true beginning of our end.
Consider then, we come but in despite.
    We do not come, as minding to content you,
Our true intent is. All for your delight,
115   *We are not here. That you should here repent you,*
The actors are at hand; and, by their show,
You shall know all, that you are like to know.

THESEUS   This fellow doth not stand upon points.

LYSANDER   He hath rid his prologue like a rough colt:
120 he knows not the stop. A good moral, my lord. It is not

enough to speak, but to speak true.

HIPPOLYTA   Indeed, he hath played on this prologue
like a child on a recorder: a sound, but not in
government.

THESEUS   His speech was like a tangled chain: nothing   125
impaired, but all disordered. Who is next?

        Enter BOTTOM as Pyramus, FLUTE as Thisbe,
          SNOUT as Wall, STARVELING as Moonshine,
              and SNUG as Lion; a Trumpeter
                      before them.

QUINCE
Gentles, perchance you wonder at this show;
    But wonder on, till truth make all things plain.
This man is Pyramus, if you would know.
    This beauteous lady Thisbe is certain.   130
This man, with lime and roughcast, doth present
    Wall, that vile Wall which did these lovers sunder,
And through Wall's chink, poor souls, they are content
    To whisper; at the which, let no man wonder.
This man, with lantern, dog and bush of thorn,   135
    Presenteth Moonshine. For if you will know,
By moonshine did these lovers think no scorn
    To meet at Ninus' tomb, there, there to woo.
This grisly beast, which Lion hight by name,
    The trusty Thisbe, coming first by night,   140
    Did scare away, or rather did affright;
And as she fled, her mantle she did fall,
    Which Lion vile with bloody mouth did stain.
Anon comes Pyramus, sweet youth and tall,
    And finds his trusty Thisbe's mantle slain;   145
Whereat, with blade, with bloody blameful blade,
    He bravely broached his boiling bloody breast,
And Thisbe, tarrying in mulberry shade,
    His dagger drew, and died. For all the rest,
Let Lion, Moonshine, Wall and lovers twain   150
At large discourse, while here they do remain.
                            Exeunt all but Wall.

THESEUS   I wonder if the lion be to speak.

DEMETRIUS   No wonder, my lord. One lion may, when
many asses do.

SNOUT
In this same interlude it doth befall   155
That I, one Snout by name, present a Wall;
And such a Wall, as I would have you think,
That had in it a crannied hole or chink,
Through which the lovers Pyramus and Thisbe
Did whisper often, very secretly.   160
This loam, this roughcast and this stone doth show
That I am that same Wall: the truth is so.
And this the cranny is, right and sinister,
Through which the fearful lovers are to whisper.

THESEUS   Would you desire lime and hair to speak   165
better?

DEMETRIUS   It is the wittiest partition that ever I heard
discourse, my lord.

                    Enter Pyramus.

THESEUS   Pyramus draws near the wall: silence.
BOTTOM

170   *O grim-looked night, O night, with hue so black,*
     O night, which ever art when day is not,
     O night, O night, alack, alack, alack,
     I fear my Thisbe's promise is forgot.
     And thou, O Wall, O sweet, O lovely Wall,
175   *That stand'st between her father's ground and mine,*
     Thou Wall, O Wall, O sweet and lovely Wall,
     Show me thy chink, to blink through with mine eyne.
     [*Wall parts his fingers.*]
     Thanks, courteous Wall. Jove shield thee well for this.
     But what see I? No Thisbe do I see.
180   *O wicked Wall, through whom I see no bliss,*
     Curst be thy stones for thus deceiving me.

THESEUS   The wall, methinks, being sensible, should
curse again.
BOTTOM   No, in truth, sir, he should not. 'Deceiving
185   me' is Thisbe's cue. She is to enter now, and I am to
spy her through the wall. You shall see it will fall.
[*Enter Thisbe.*] Pat as I told you: yonder she comes.
FLUTE

   O Wall, full often hast thou heard my moans
     For parting my fair Pyramus and me.
190   *My cherry lips have often kissed thy stones,*
     Thy stones with lime and hair knit up in thee.
BOTTOM

   I see a voice. Now will I to the chink,
     To spy and I can hear my Thisbe's face.
     Thisbe?
FLUTE   *My love thou art, my love I think.*
BOTTOM

195   *Think what thou wilt, I am thy lover's grace;*
     And like Limander, am I trusty still.
FLUTE

   And I, like Helen, till the Fates me kill.
BOTTOM

   Not Shafalus to Procrus was so true.
FLUTE

   As Shafalus to Procrus, I to you.
BOTTOM

200   *O kiss me through the hole of this vile Wall.*
FLUTE

   I kiss the Wall's hole, not your lips at all.
BOTTOM

   Wilt thou at Ninny's tomb meet me straightway?
FLUTE

   Tide life, tide death, I come without delay.
SNOUT

   Thus have I, Wall, my part discharged so;
205   *And being done, thus Wall away doth go.*
           Exeunt Wall, Pyramus and Thisbe.
THESEUS   Now is the more use between the two
neighbours.
DEMETRIUS   No remedy, my lord, when walls are so
wilful, to hear without warning.
210 HIPPOLYTA   This is the silliest stuff that ever I heard.

THESEUS   The best in this kind are but shadows; and the
worst are no worse, if imagination amend them.
HIPPOLYTA   It must be your imagination, then, and not
theirs.
THESEUS   If we imagine no worse of them than they of   215
themselves, they may pass for excellent men. Here
come two noble beasts, in a man and a lion.

           Enter Lion.

SNUG

   You ladies, you whose gentle hearts do fear
     The smallest monstrous mouse that creeps on floor,
     May now perchance both quake and tremble here,   220
     When Lion rough in wildest rage doth roar.
     Then know that I, as Snug the joiner, am
     No lion fell, nor else no lion's dam.
     For if I should, as Lion, come in strife
     Into this place, 'twere pity on my life.   225
THESEUS   A very gentle beast, and of a good conscience.
DEMETRIUS   The very best at a beast, my lord, that e'er
I saw.
LYSANDER   This Lion is a very fox for his valour.
THESEUS   True, and a goose for his discretion.   230
DEMETRIUS   Not so, my lord. For his valour cannot
carry his discretion, and the fox carries the goose.
THESEUS   His discretion, I am sure, cannot carry his
valour, for the goose carries not the fox. It is well.
Leave it to his discretion, and let us listen to the Moon.   235

           Enter Moonshine.

STARVELING

   This lanthorn doth the horned moon present.
DEMETRIUS   He should have worn the horns on his head.
THESEUS   He is no crescent, and his horns are invisible,
within the circumference.
STARVELING

   This lanthorn doth the horned moon present.   240
     Myself, the man i'th' moon do seem to be.
THESEUS   This is the greatest error of all the rest. The
man should be put into the lanthorn; how is it else the
man i'th' moon?
DEMETRIUS   He dares not come there for the candle; for   245
you see, it is already in snuff.
HIPPOLYTA   I am aweary of this moon. Would he would
change.
THESEUS   It appears, by his small light of discretion,
that he is in the wane; but yet in courtesy, in all reason,   250
we must stay the time.
LYSANDER   Proceed, moon.
STARVELING   All that I have to say is to tell you that the
lanthorn is the moon, I the man i'th' moon, this thorn-
bush my thorn-bush, and this dog my dog.   255
DEMETRIUS   Why, all these should be in the lanthorn;
for all these are in the moon. But silence: here comes
Thisbe.

           Enter Thisbe.

FLUTE
> *This is old Ninny's tomb. Where is my love?*

260 SNUG   *O.*

> [*The Lion roars. Thisbe runs off, dropping her mantle.*]

DEMETRIUS   Well roared, Lion.

THESEUS   Well run, Thisbe.

HIPPOLYTA   Well shone, Moon. Truly, the Moon shines
with a good grace.

> [*Lion shakes Thisbe's mantle.*]

265 THESEUS   Well moused, Lion.

> *Enter Pyramus.*

DEMETRIUS   And then came Pyramus.   *Exit Lion.*

LYSANDER   And so the Lion vanished.

BOTTOM
> *Sweet Moon, I thank thee for thy sunny beams.*
> *I thank thee, Moon, for shining now so bright.*
270 > *For by thy gracious, golden, glittering gleams,*
> *I trust to take of truest Thisbe sight.*
> > *But stay: O spite!*
> > *But mark, poor knight,*
> > > *What dreadful dole is here?*
275 > *Eyes, do you see?*
> *How can it be?*
> > *O dainty duck, O dear!*
> *Thy mantle good,*
> *What, stained with blood?*
280 > > *Approach, ye Furies fell.*
> *O Fates, come, come,*
> *Cut thread and thrum,*
> > *Quail, crush, conclude, and quell.*

THESEUS   This passion, and the death of a dear friend,
285 would go near to make a man look sad.

HIPPOLYTA   Beshrew my heart, but I pity the man.

BOTTOM
> *O wherefore, Nature, didst thou lions frame?*
> *Since Lion vile hath here deflowered my dear.*
> *Which is – no, no, which was – the fairest dame*
290 > *That lived, that loved, that liked, that looked with*
> > *cheer.*
> *Come, tears, confound;*
> *Out, sword, and wound*
> > *The pap of Pyramus:*
295 > *Ay, that left pap,*
> *Where heart doth hop.*
> > *Thus die I, thus, thus, thus.*   [*Stabs himself.*]
> *Now am I dead,*
> *Now am I fled;*
300 > > *My soul is in the sky.*
> *Tongue, lose thy light.*
> *Moon, take thy flight.*   *Exit Moonshine.*
> > *Now die, die, die, die, die.*   [*Dies.*]

DEMETRIUS   No die but an ace for him; for he is but
one.

305 LYSANDER   Less than an ace, man; for he is dead, he is
nothing.

THESEUS   With the help of a surgeon, he might yet
recover, and yet prove an ass.

HIPPOLYTA   How chance Moonshine is gone before
Thisbe comes back and finds her lover?   310

THESEUS   She will find him by starlight. Here she
comes, and her passion ends the play.

> *Enter Thisbe.*

HIPPOLYTA   Methinks she should not use a long one for
such a Pyramus. I hope she will be brief.

DEMETRIUS   A mote will turn the balance, which   315
Pyramus, which Thisbe is the better: he for a man,
God warrant us; she for a woman, God bless us.

LYSANDER   She hath spied him already, with those
sweet eyes.

DEMETRIUS   And thus she means, *videlicet.*   320

FLUTE
> *Asleep, my love?*
> *What, dead, my dove?*
> > *O Pyramus, arise.*
> *Speak, speak. Quite dumb?*
> *Dead, dead? A tomb*   325
> > *Must cover thy sweet eyes.*
> *These lily lips,*
> *This cherry nose,*
> > *These yellow cowslip cheeks*
> *Are gone, are gone:*   330
> *Lovers make moan.*
> > *His eyes were green as leeks.*
> *O sisters three,*
> *Come, come to me,*
> > *With hands as pale as milk;*   335
> *Lay them in gore,*
> *Since you have shore*
> > *With shears his thread of silk.*
> *Tongue, not a word.*
> *Come, trusty sword,*   340
> > *Come, blade, my breast imbrue.*
> > [*Stabs herself.*]
> *And farewell, friends;*
> *Thus Thisbe ends.*
> > *Adieu, adieu, adieu.*   [*Dies.*]

THESEUS   Moonshine and Lion are left to bury the   345
dead.

DEMETRIUS   Ay, and Wall too.

BOTTOM   No, I assure you, the wall is down that parted
their fathers. Will it please you to see the epilogue, or
to hear a Bergomask dance between two of our   350
company?

THESEUS   No epilogue, I pray you; for your play needs
no excuse. Never excuse; for when the players are all
dead, there need none to be blamed. Marry, if he that
writ it had played Pyramus and hanged himself in   355
Thisbe's garter, it would have been a fine tragedy; and
so it is truly, and very notably discharged. But come,
your Bergomask; let your epilogue alone.

> *Dance, and exeunt actors.*

360 The iron tongue of midnight hath told twelve.
Lovers, to bed; 'tis almost fairy time.
I fear we shall outsleep the coming morn,
As much as we this night have overwatched.
This palpable gross play hath well beguiled
The heavy gait of night. Sweet friends, to bed.
365 A fortnight hold we this solemnity,
In nightly revels and new jollity.   *Exeunt.*

Enter ROBIN GOODFELLOW *with a broom.*

ROBIN
       Now the hungry lion roars
          And the wolf behowls the moon,
       Whilst the heavy ploughman snores,
370   All with weary task fordone.
       Now the wasted brands do glow,
          Whilst the screech-owl, screeching loud,
       Puts the wretch that lies in woe
          In remembrance of a shroud.
375   Now it is the time of night
          That the graves, all gaping wide,
       Every one lets forth his sprite
          In the churchway paths to glide.
       And we fairies, that do run
380   By the triple Hecate's team
       From the presence of the sun,
          Following darkness like a dream,
       Now are frolic. Not a mouse
       Shall disturb this hallowed house.
385   I am sent with broom before,
       To sweep the dust behind the door.

Enter OBERON *and* TITANIA, *with all their train.*

OBERON
       Through the house give glimmering light
          By the dead and drowsy fire.
       Every elf and fairy sprite
390   Hop as light as bird from brier,
       And this ditty after me
       Sing, and dance it trippingly.
TITANIA
       First rehearse your song by rote,

       To each word a warbling note.
       Hand in hand, with fairy grace,   395
       Will we sing and bless this place.
OBERON   THE SONG
       Now, until the break of day,
       Through this house each fairy stray.
       To the best bride-bed will we,
       Which by us shall blessed be,   400
       And the issue there create
       Ever shall be fortunate.
       So shall all the couples three
       Ever true in loving be,
       And the blots of nature's hand   405
       Shall not in their issue stand.
       Never mole, hare-lip, nor scar
       Nor mark prodigious, such as are
       Despised in nativity,
       Shall upon their children be.   410
       With this field-dew consecrate,
       Every fairy take his gate
       And each several chamber bless
       Through this palace with sweet peace;
       And the owner of it blest   415
       Ever shall in safety rest.
       Trip away, make no stay.
       Meet me all, by break of day.   *Exeunt all but Robin.*
ROBIN
       If we shadows have offended,
       Think but this, and all is mended: 420
       That you have but slumbered here
       While these visions did appear.
       And this weak and idle theme,
       No more yielding but a dream,
       Gentles, do not reprehend: 425
       If you pardon, we will mend.
       And as I am an honest puck,
       If we have unearned luck
       Now to scape the serpent's tongue,
       We will make amends ere long;   430
       Else the puck a liar call.
       So, good night unto you all.
       Give me your hands, if we be friends;
       And Robin shall restore amends.   *Exit.*

Much Ado About Nothing

A Quarto edition of *Much Ado About Nothing* appeared in 1600, and the play was not reprinted until it was included in the First Folio in 1623 in a text based on the Quarto. A number of relatively minor inconsistencies in the text have been variously explained as errors in transmission or authorial loose ends. The title-page of the Quarto claims that the play had been 'sundry times publicly acted' by the Lord Chamberlain's Men, Shakespeare's regular company. Unless it is identified with the mysterious *Love's Labour's Won*, it does not occur in Francis Meres's list of Shakespeare's comedies in 1598; this has caused scholars to believe that it was written in the second half of 1598 or 1599. It cannot have been written later than 1599 as the Quarto sometimes uses the name of Will Kemp instead of Dogberry in speech headings, and this famous comic actor left the company in that year. It probably came after *A Midsummer Night's Dream* and before *As You Like It* and *Twelfth Night*. Although we do not have records of early performances of the play, allusions to it indicate that it must have been well known, and it was revived for a Court performance at Whitehall before King James I's daughter Princess Elizabeth and her husband Frederick, the Elector Palatine, in May 1613.

The plot of the play combines the tragicomic story of the courtship of Hero and Claudio (in scenes written mainly in verse) with the witty sparring of Beatrice and Benedick (in scenes written mainly in prose). The latter pair are tricked into acknowledging that their posture of disliking each other conceals their love. Leonard Digges referred to the popularity of Beatrice and Benedick in his prefatory tribute to the 1640 edition of Shakespeare's poems, and King Charles I wrote 'Benedik and Betrice' as a kind of alternative title in his copy of the 1632 Second Folio; the 'merry war' between these two characters (reminiscent of that between Berowne and Rosaline in *Love's Labour's Lost*) usually dominates productions. *Much Ado* is also, however, of particular interest in that it contains Shakespeare's earliest version of the more serious story of the man who mistakenly believes his partner has been unfaithful to him. This story is an ancient one, and Shakespeare could have used a number of Renaissance versions as his source(s). The triangle of Don John (deceiving villain), Claudio (credulous lover or husband) and Hero (slandered fiancée or wife) reappears in Iago, Othello and Desdemona and again in Iachimo, Posthumus and Innogen (in *Cymbeline*). Like Othello and Posthumus, Claudio is held responsible for the death (or apparent death) of the woman, although he at least does not mean to kill her. Not surprisingly recent critics, especially feminists, have found it difficult to forgive such behaviour.

In the Restoration William Davenant amalgamated parts of *Much Ado* with parts of *Measure for Measure* to produce an adaptation called *The Law Against Lovers* (1662), and Shakespeare's play was performed only sporadically until David Garrick's acclaimed revival in 1748. Thereafter it continued to be popular on stage with actors such as Charles Kemble, Henry Irving and John Gielgud starring as Benedick, partnered respectively by Helen Faucit, Ellen Terry and Peggy Ashcroft as Beatrice. The most widely seen films of the play include the 1993 version directed by Kenneth Branagh and another in 2012 directed by Josh Whedon.

The Arden text is based on the 1600 Quarto.

THE SOLDIERS

DON PEDRO	*Prince of Aragon*
DON JOHN	*illegitimate brother to Don Pedro*
Signor BENEDICK	*a lord of Padua*
Signor CLAUDIO	*a lord of Florence*
BALTHASAR	*an attendant to Don Pedro*
CONRADE	
BORACHIO	*companions to Don John*
LORD	

THE HOUSEHOLD OF THE GOVERNOR OF MESSINA

LEONATO	*Governor of Messina*
ANTONIO	*brother to Leonato*
HERO	*daughter to Leonato*
BEATRICE	*niece to Leonato*
MARGARET	
URSULA	*waiting women to Hero*
BOY	

TOWNSPEOPLE OF MESSINA

FRIAR Francis	
DOGBERRY	*master constable*
VERGES	*a headborough*
Members of the WATCH	
George SEACOAL	
Hugh Oatcake	*members of the Watch*
Francis Seacoal, *a* SEXTON	

OTHERS

MESSENGERS

Attendants, Musicians

1.1   *Enter* LEONATO, *Governor of Messina,*
       HERO *his daughter and* BEATRICE *his niece,*
               with a Messenger.

LEONATO   I learn in this letter that Don Pedro of
  Aragon comes this night to Messina.
MESSENGER   He is very near by this. He was not three
  leagues off when I left him.
LEONATO   How many gentlemen have you lost in this
  action?
MESSENGER   But few of any sort, and none of name.
LEONATO   A victory is twice itself when the achiever
  brings home full numbers. I find here that Don Pedro
  hath bestowed much honour on a young Florentine
  called Claudio.
MESSENGER   Much deserved on his part, and equally
  remembered by Don Pedro. He hath borne himself
  beyond the promise of his age, doing in the figure of a
  lamb the feats of a lion; he hath indeed better bettered
  expectation than you must expect of me to tell you
  how.
LEONATO   He hath an uncle here in Messina will be
  very much glad of it.
MESSENGER   I have already delivered him letters, and
  there appears much joy in him, even so much that joy
  could not show itself modest enough without a badge
  of bitterness.
LEONATO   Did he break out into tears?
MESSENGER   In great measure.
LEONATO   A kind overflow of kindness; there are no
  faces truer than those that are so washed. How much
  better is it to weep at joy than to joy at weeping!
BEATRICE   I pray you, is Signor Mountanto returned
  from the wars or no?
MESSENGER   I know none of that name, lady; there was
  none such in the army of any sort.
LEONATO   What is he that you ask for, niece?
HERO   My cousin means Signor Benedick of Padua.
MESSENGER   O, he's returned, and as pleasant as ever
  he was.
BEATRICE   He set up his bills here in Messina and
  challenged Cupid at the flight; and my uncle's fool,
  reading the challenge, subscribed for Cupid and
  challenged him at the bird-bolt. I pray you, how many
  hath he killed and eaten in these wars? But how many
  hath he killed? For indeed I promised to eat all of his
  killing.
LEONATO   Faith, niece, you tax Signor Benedick too
  much, but he'll be meet with you, I doubt it not.
MESSENGER   He hath done good service, lady, in these
  wars.
BEATRICE   You had musty victual, and he hath holp to
  eat it. He is a very valiant trencher-man: he hath an
  excellent stomach.
MESSENGER   And a good soldier too, lady.
BEATRICE   And a good soldier to a lady; but what is he to
  a lord?

MESSENGER   A lord to a lord, a man to a man, stuffed
  with all honourable virtues.   55
BEATRICE   It is so indeed, he is no less than a stuffed
  man; but for the stuffing – well, we are all mortal.
LEONATO   You must not, sir, mistake my niece; there is
  a kind of merry war betwixt Signor Benedick and her.
  They never meet but there's a skirmish of wit between   60
  them.
BEATRICE   Alas, he gets nothing by that. In our last
  conflict, four of his five wits went halting off, and now
  is the whole man governed with one, so that if he have
  wit enough to keep himself warm, let him bear it for a 65
  difference between himself and his horse, for it is all
  the wealth that he hath left to be known a reasonable
  creature. Who is his companion now? He hath every
  month a new sworn brother.
MESSENGER   Is't possible?   70
BEATRICE   Very easily possible. He wears his faith but as
  the fashion of his hat: it ever changes with the next
  block.
MESSENGER   I see, lady, the gentleman is not in your
  books.   75
BEATRICE   No; an he were, I would burn my study. But
  I pray you, who is his companion? Is there no young
  squarer now that will make a voyage with him to the
  devil?
MESSENGER   He is most in the company of the right   80
  noble Claudio.
BEATRICE   O Lord, he will hang upon him like a disease!
  He is sooner caught than the pestilence, and the taker
  runs presently mad. God help the noble Claudio! If he
  have caught the Benedick, it will cost him a thousand   85
  pound ere 'a be cured.
MESSENGER   I will hold friends with you, lady.
BEATRICE   Do, good friend.
LEONATO   You will never run mad, niece.
BEATRICE   No, not till a hot January.   90
MESSENGER   Don Pedro is approached.

       Enter DON PEDRO, CLAUDIO, BENEDICK,
        BALTHASAR *and* DON JOHN *the bastard.*

DON PEDRO   Good Signor Leonato, are you come to
  meet your trouble? The fashion of the world is to avoid
  cost, and you encounter it.
LEONATO   Never came trouble to my house in the   95
  likeness of your grace, for, trouble being gone, comfort
  should remain; but when you depart from me, sorrow
  abides, and happiness takes his leave.
DON PEDRO   You embrace your charge too willingly. I
  think this is your daughter.   100
LEONATO   Her mother hath many times told me so.
BENEDICK   Were you in doubt, sir, that you asked her?
LEONATO   Signor Benedick, no, for then were you a child.
DON PEDRO   You have it full, Benedick; we may guess
  by this what you are, being a man. Truly, the lady   105
  fathers herself. Be happy, lady, for you are like an
  honourable father. [*Don Pedro and Leonato walk apart.*]

BENEDICK   If Signor Leonato be her father, she would
not have his head on her shoulders for all Messina, as
110   like him as she is.

BEATRICE   I wonder that you will still be talking, Signor
Benedick; nobody marks you.

BENEDICK   What, my dear Lady Disdain! Are you yet
living?

115   BEATRICE   Is it possible Disdain should die, while she
hath such meet food to feed it as Signor Benedick?
Courtesy itself must convert to Disdain if you come in
her presence.

BENEDICK   Then is Courtesy a turncoat. But it is
120   certain I am loved of all ladies, only you excepted; and
I would I could find in my heart that I had not a hard
heart, for truly I love none.

BEATRICE   A dear happiness to women – they would
else have been troubled with a pernicious suitor. I
125   thank God and my cold blood, I am of your humour
for that: I had rather hear my dog bark at a crow, than
a man swear he loves me.

BENEDICK   God keep your ladyship still in that mind,
so some gentleman or other shall scape a predestinate
130   scratched face.

BEATRICE   Scratching could not make it worse, an
'twere such a face as yours were.

BENEDICK   Well, you are a rare parrot-teacher.

BEATRICE   A bird of my tongue is better than a beast of
135   yours.

BENEDICK   I would my horse had the speed of your
tongue, and so good a continuer. But keep your way,
o'God's name; I have done.

BEATRICE   You always end with a jade's trick; I know
140   you of old.

DON PEDRO   That is the sum of all, Leonato. [*Addresses
the company*.] Signor Claudio and Signor Benedick,
my dear friend Leonato hath invited you all. I tell him
we shall stay here at the least a month, and he heartily
145   prays some occasion may detain us longer. I dare swear
he is no hypocrite, but prays from his heart.

LEONATO   If you swear, my lord, you shall not be
forsworn. [*to Don John*] Let me bid you welcome, my
lord, being reconciled to the prince your brother. I owe
150   you all duty.

DON JOHN   I thank you. I am not of many words, but I
thank you.

LEONATO [*to Don Pedro*]   Please it your grace lead on?

DON PEDRO   Your hand, Leonato; we will go together.

Exeunt all but Benedick and Claudio.

155   CLAUDIO   Benedick, didst thou note the daughter of
Signor Leonato?

BENEDICK   I noted her not, but I looked on her.

CLAUDIO   Is she not a modest young lady?

BENEDICK   Do you question me as an honest man
160   should do, for my simple true judgement? Or would
you have me speak after my custom, as being a
professed tyrant to their sex?

CLAUDIO   No, I pray thee, speak in sober judgement.

BENEDICK   Why, i'faith methinks she's too low for a
high praise, too brown for a fair praise and too little for   165
a great praise. Only this commendation I can afford
her: that were she other than she is, she were
unhandsome; and being no other but as she is, I do not
like her.

CLAUDIO   Thou thinkest I am in sport. I pray thee tell   170
me truly how thou lik'st her.

BENEDICK   Would you buy her that you inquire after
her?

CLAUDIO   Can the world buy such a jewel?

BENEDICK   Yea, and a case to put it into. But speak you   175
this with a sad brow? Or do you play the flouting jack,
to tell us Cupid is a good hare-finder and Vulcan a rare
carpenter? Come, in what key shall a man take you to
go in the song?

CLAUDIO   In mine eye, she is the sweetest lady that ever   180
I looked on.

BENEDICK   I can see yet without spectacles, and I see no
such matter. There's her cousin, an she were not
possessed with a fury, exceeds her as much in beauty as
the first of May doth the last of December. But I hope   185
you have no intent to turn husband – have you?

CLAUDIO   I would scarce trust myself, though I had
sworn the contrary, if Hero would be my wife.

BENEDICK   Is't come to this? In faith, hath not the
world one man but he will wear his cap with suspicion?   190
Shall I never see a bachelor of threescore again? Go to,
i'faith. An thou wilt needs thrust thy neck into a yoke,
wear the print of it and sigh away Sundays. Look, Don
Pedro is returned to seek you.

Enter DON PEDRO.

DON PEDRO   What secret hath held you here that you   195
followed not to Leonato's?

BENEDICK   I would your grace would constrain me to
tell.

DON PEDRO   I charge thee on thy allegiance.

BENEDICK   You hear, Count Claudio? I can be secret as   200
a dumb man; I would have you think so. But on my
allegiance – mark you this, on my allegiance – he is in
love. With who? Now, that is your grace's part. Mark
how short his answer is: with Hero, Leonato's short
daughter.   205

CLAUDIO   If this were so, so were it uttered.

BENEDICK   Like the old tale, my lord: 'it is not so, nor
'twas not so'; but indeed, God forbid it should be so!

CLAUDIO   If my passion change not shortly, God forbid
it should be otherwise.   210

DON PEDRO   Amen, if you love her, for the lady is very
well worthy.

CLAUDIO   You speak this to fetch me in, my lord.

DON PEDRO   By my troth, I speak my thought.

CLAUDIO   And in faith, my lord, I spoke mine.   215

BENEDICK   And by my two faiths and troths, my lord, I
spoke mine.

CLAUDIO   That I love her, I feel.

DON PEDRO   That she is worthy, I know.

220 BENEDICK   That I neither feel how she should be loved
nor know how she should be worthy is the opinion that
fire cannot melt out of me; I will die in it at the stake.

DON PEDRO   Thou wast ever an obstinate heretic in the
despite of beauty.

225 CLAUDIO   And never could maintain his part but in the
force of his will.

BENEDICK   That a woman conceived me, I thank her;
that she brought me up, I likewise give her most
humble thanks; but that I will have a recheat winded in
230 my forehead, or hang my bugle in an invisible baldrick,
all women shall pardon me. Because I will not do them
the wrong to mistrust any, I will do myself the right to
trust none. And the fine is – for the which I may go the
finer – I will live a bachelor.

235 DON PEDRO   I shall see thee, ere I die, look pale with love.

BENEDICK   With anger, with sickness, or with hunger,
my lord, not with love. Prove that ever I lose more
blood with love than I will get again with drinking, pick
out mine eyes with a ballad-maker's pen and hang me
240 up at the door of a brothel-house for the sign of blind
Cupid.

DON PEDRO   Well, if ever thou dost fall from this faith,
thou wilt prove a notable argument.

BENEDICK   If I do, hang me in a bottle like a cat and
245 shoot at me, and he that hits me, let him be clapped on
the shoulder and called Adam.

DON PEDRO   Well, as time shall try. 'In time the savage
bull doth bear the yoke.'

BENEDICK   The savage bull may, but if ever the sensible
250 Benedick bear it, pluck off the bull's horns and set
them in my forehead; and let me be vilely painted, and
in such great letters as they write 'Here is good horse
to hire', let them signify under my sign, 'Here you may
see Benedick, the married man.'

255 CLAUDIO   If this should ever happen, thou wouldst be
horn-mad.

DON PEDRO   Nay, if Cupid have not spent all his quiver
in Venice, thou wilt quake for this shortly.

BENEDICK   I look for an earthquake too, then.

260 DON PEDRO   Well, you will temporize with the hours.
In the meantime, good Signor Benedick, repair to
Leonato's, commend me to him and tell him I will not
fail him at supper, for indeed he hath made great
preparation.

265 BENEDICK   I have almost matter enough in me for such
an embassage. And so, I commit you –

CLAUDIO   'To the tuition of God. From my house' – if I
had it –

DON PEDRO   'The sixth of July. Your loving friend,
270 Benedick.'

BENEDICK   Nay, mock not, mock not. The body of your
discourse is sometime guarded with fragments, and
the guards are but slightly basted on neither. Ere you
flout old ends any further, examine your conscience.
275 And so I leave you.

CLAUDIO
My liege, your highness now may do me good.

DON PEDRO
My love is thine to teach; teach it but how,
And thou shalt see how apt it is to learn
Any hard lesson that may do thee good.

CLAUDIO   Hath Leonato any son, my lord?   280

DON PEDRO
No child but Hero; she's his only heir.
Dost thou affect her, Claudio?

CLAUDIO   O my lord,
When you went onward on this ended action
I looked upon her with a soldier's eye,
That liked, but had a rougher task in hand   285
Than to drive liking to the name of love.
But now I am returned, and that war-thoughts
Have left their places vacant, in their rooms
Come thronging soft and delicate desires,
All prompting me how fair young Hero is,   290
Saying I liked her ere I went to wars.

DON PEDRO   Thou wilt be like a lover presently
And tire the hearer with a book of words.
If thou dost love fair Hero, cherish it,
And I will break with her and with her father,   295
And thou shalt have her. Was't not to this end
That thou began'st to twist so fine a story?

CLAUDIO   How sweetly you do minister to love,
That know love's grief by his complexion!
But lest my liking might too sudden seem,   300
I would have salved it with a longer treatise.

DON PEDRO
What need the bridge much broader than the flood?
The fairest grant is the necessity;
Look what will serve is fit. 'Tis once, thou lovest,
And I will fit thee with the remedy.   305
I know we shall have revelling tonight;
I will assume thy part in some disguise
And tell fair Hero I am Claudio;
And in her bosom I'll unclasp my heart
And take her hearing prisoner with the force   310
And strong encounter of my amorous tale.
Then after, to her father will I break,
And the conclusion is: she shall be thine.
In practice let us put it presently.   *Exeunt.*

1.2   *Enter* LEONATO *and* ANTONIO, *an
old man, brother to Leonato, meeting.*

LEONATO   How now, brother, where is my cousin your
son? Hath he provided this music?

ANTONIO   He is very busy about it. But brother, I can
tell you strange news that you yet dreamt not of.

LEONATO   Are they good?   5

ANTONIO   As the event stamps them, but they have a
good cover: they show well outward. The prince and
Count Claudio, walking in a thick-pleached alley in
mine orchard, were thus much overheard by a man of

10 mine: the prince discovered to Claudio that he loved
my niece your daughter, and meant to acknowledge it
this night in a dance; and if he found her accordant, he
meant to take the present time by the top and instantly
break with you of it.

15 LEONATO   Hath the fellow any wit that told you this?

ANTONIO   A good sharp fellow; I will send for him, and
question him yourself.

LEONATO   No, no; we will hold it as a dream till it
appear itself. But I will acquaint my daughter withal,
20 that she may be the better prepared for an answer, if
peradventure this be true. Go you and tell her of it.

Exit Antonio.

Enter Attendants, and cross the stage.

Cousins, you know what you have to do. O, I cry you
mercy, friend: go you with me and I will use your skill.
Good cousin, have a care this busy time!   *Exeunt.*

1.3   *Enter* DON JOHN *the bastard and*
           CONRADE *his companion.*

CONRADE   What the goodyear, my lord! Why are you
thus out of measure sad?

DON JOHN   There is no measure in the occasion that
breeds, therefore the sadness is without limit.

5 CONRADE   You should hear reason.

DON JOHN   And when I have heard it, what blessing
brings it?

CONRADE   If not a present remedy, at least a patient
sufferance.

10 DON JOHN   I wonder that thou – being as thou sayst
thou art, born under Saturn – goest about to apply a
moral medicine to a mortifying mischief. I cannot hide
what I am. I must be sad when I have cause, and smile
at no man's jests; eat when I have stomach, and wait for
15 no man's leisure; sleep when I am drowsy, and tend on
no man's business; laugh when I am merry, and claw
no man in his humour.

CONRADE   Yea, but you must not make the full show of
this till you may do it without controlment. You have
20 of late stood out against your brother, and he hath
ta'en you newly into his grace, where it is impossible
you should take true root but by the fair weather that
you make yourself. It is needful that you frame the
season for your own harvest.

25 DON JOHN   I had rather be a canker in a hedge than a
rose in his grace, and it better fits my blood to be
disdained of all than to fashion a carriage to rob love
from any. In this, though I cannot be said to be a
flattering honest man, it must not be denied but I am a
30 plain-dealing villain. I am trusted with a muzzle and
enfranchised with a clog. Therefore I have decreed not
to sing in my cage. If I had my mouth I would bite; if I
had my liberty I would do my liking. In the meantime,
let me be that I am, and seek not to alter me.

35 CONRADE   Can you make no use of your discontent?

DON JOHN   I make all use of it, for I use it only. Who
comes here?

Enter BORACHIO.

What news, Borachio?

BORACHIO   I came yonder from a great supper. The
prince your brother is royally entertained by Leonato,   40
and I can give you intelligence of an intended marriage.

DON JOHN   Will it serve for any model to build mischief
on? What is he for a fool that betroths himself to
unquietness?

BORACHIO   Marry, it is your brother's right hand.   45

DON JOHN   Who, the most exquisite Claudio?

BORACHIO   Even he.

DON JOHN   A proper squire! And who, and who? Which
way looks he?

BORACHIO   Marry, on Hero, the daughter and heir of   50
Leonato.

DON JOHN   A very forward March chick! How came
you to this?

BORACHIO   Being entertained for a perfumer, as I was
smoking a musty room comes me the prince and   55
Claudio, hand in hand in sad conference. I whipped
me behind the arras, and there heard it agreed upon
that the prince should woo Hero for himself, and
having obtained her, give her to Count Claudio.

DON JOHN   Come, come, let us thither; this may prove   60
food to my displeasure. That young start-up hath all the
glory of my overthrow. If I can cross him any way, I bless
myself every way. You are both sure, and will assist me?

CONRADE   To the death, my lord.

DON JOHN   Let us to the great supper; their cheer is the   65
greater that I am subdued. Would the cook were o'my
mind. Shall we go prove what's to be done?

BORACHIO   We'll wait upon your lordship.   *Exeunt.*

2.1   *Enter* LEONATO, *his brother* ANTONIO,
           HERO *his daughter and* BEATRICE *his niece.*

LEONATO   Was not Count John here at supper?

ANTONIO   I saw him not.

BEATRICE   How tartly that gentleman looks! I never can
see him but I am heart-burned an hour after.

HERO   He is of a very melancholy disposition.   5

BEATRICE   He were an excellent man that were made
just in the midway between him and Benedick: the one
is too like an image and says nothing, and the other too
like my lady's eldest son, evermore tattling.

LEONATO   Then half Signor Benedick's tongue in   10
Count John's mouth, and half Count John's melancholy
in Signor Benedick's face –

BEATRICE   With a good leg and a good foot, uncle, and
money enough in his purse, such a man would win any
woman in the world – if 'a could get her good will.   15

LEONATO   By my troth, niece, thou wilt never get thee a
husband, if thou be so shrewd of thy tongue.

ANTONIO   In faith, she's too curst.

BEATRICE   Too curst is more than curst. I shall lessen
20   God's sending that way; for it is said 'God sends a
         curst cow short horns' – but to a cow too curst he sends
         none.

LEONATO   So, by being too curst, God will send you no
         horns.

BEATRICE   Just, if he send me no husband. For the
25   which blessing I am at him upon my knees every
         morning and evening. Lord, I could not endure a
         husband with a beard on his face! I had rather lie in the
         woollen.

LEONATO   You may light on a husband that hath no
30   beard.

BEATRICE   What should I do with him? Dress him in
         my apparel and make him my waiting-gentlewoman?
         He that hath a beard is more than a youth, and he that
35   hath no beard is less than a man; and he that is more
         than a youth is not for me, and he that is less than a
         man, I am not for him. Therefore I will even take
         sixpence in earnest of the bearward and lead his apes
         into hell.

40 LEONATO   Well then, go you into hell?

BEATRICE   No, but to the gate, and there will the devil
         meet me like an old cuckold with horns on his head,
         and say, 'Get you to heaven, Beatrice, get you to
         heaven. Here's no place for you maids!' So deliver I up
45   my apes and away to Saint Peter fore the heavens. He
         shows me where the bachelors sit, and there live we as
         merry as the day is long.

ANTONIO *[to Hero]*   Well, niece, I trust you will be ruled
         by your father.

50 BEATRICE   Yes, faith, it is my cousin's duty to make
         curtsy, and say, 'Father, as it please you.' But yet for all
         that, cousin, let him be a handsome fellow, or else make
         another curtsy, and say, 'Father, as it please me'.

LEONATO   Well, niece, I hope to see you one day fitted
55   with a husband.

BEATRICE   Not till God make men of some other metal
         than earth. Would it not grieve a woman to be over-
         mastered with a piece of valiant dust? To make an
         account of her life to a clod of wayward marl? No,
60   uncle, I'll none. Adam's sons are my brethren, and
         truly, I hold it a sin to match in my kindred.

LEONATO   Daughter, remember what I told you. If the
         prince do solicit you in that kind, you know your
         answer.

65 BEATRICE   The fault will be in the music, cousin, if you
         be not wooed in good time. If the prince be too
         important, tell him there is measure in everything, and
         so dance out the answer. For hear me, Hero; wooing,
         wedding and repenting is as a Scotch jig, a measure
70   and a cinque-pace. The first suit is hot and hasty, like a
         Scotch jig, and full as fantastical; the wedding
         mannerly-modest as a measure, full of state and
         ancientry; and then comes Repentance, and with his
         bad legs falls into the cinque-pace faster and faster, till
75   he sink into his grave.

LEONATO   Cousin, you apprehend passing shrewdly.

BEATRICE   I have a good eye, uncle; I can see a church
         by daylight.

LEONATO *[to Antonio]*   The revellers are entering,
         brother. Make good room. *[Antonio steps aside, and*   80
         masks.]

Enter DON PEDRO, CLAUDIO, BENEDICK,
BALTHASAR, *masked, with a Drum*, MARGARET *and*
URSULA, *and* DON JOHN, BORACHIO *and others.*
Music and dancing begin.

DON PEDRO *[to Hero]*   Lady, will you walk a bout with
         your friend?

HERO   So you walk softly, and look sweetly, and say
         nothing, I am yours for the walk; and especially when I
         walk away.   85

DON PEDRO   With me in your company?

HERO   I may say so, when I please.

DON PEDRO   And when please you to say so?

HERO   When I like your favour – for God defend the
         lute should be like the case!   90

DON PEDRO   My visor is Philemon's roof: within the
         house is Jove.

HERO   Why then, your visor should be thatched.

DON PEDRO   Speak low if you speak love. *[They move*
         aside; Balthasar and Margaret come forward.]

BALTHASAR   Well, I would you did like me.   95

MARGARET   So would not I, for your own sake, for I
         have many ill qualities.

BALTHASAR   Which is one?

MARGARET   I say my prayers aloud.

BALTHASAR   I love you the better; the hearers may cry   100
         amen!

MARGARET   God match me with a good dancer!

BALTHASAR   Amen!

MARGARET   And God keep him out of my sight when
         the dance is done! Answer, clerk.   105

BALTHASAR   No more words; the clerk is answered.
         [They move aside; Ursula and Antonio come forward.]

URSULA   I know you well enough; you are Signor
         Antonio.

ANTONIO   At a word, I am not.

URSULA   I know you by the waggling of your head.   110

ANTONIO   To tell you true, I counterfeit him.

URSULA   You could never do him so ill-well, unless you
         were the very man. Here's his dry hand up and down.
         You are he, you are he!

ANTONIO   At a word, I am not.   115

URSULA   Come, come, do you think I do not know you
         by your excellent wit? Can virtue hide itself? Go to,
         mum; you are he; graces will appear, and there's an
         end. *[They move aside; Benedick and Beatrice come*
         forward.]

BEATRICE   Will you not tell me who told you so?   120

BENEDICK   No, you shall pardon me.

BEATRICE   Nor will you not tell me who you are?

BENEDICK   Not now.

BEATRICE   That I was disdainful, and that I had my
good wit out of *The Hundred Merry Tales*! Well, this
was Signor Benedick that said so.

BENEDICK   What's he?

BEATRICE   I am sure you know him well enough.

BENEDICK   Not I, believe me.

BEATRICE   Did he never make you laugh?

BENEDICK   I pray you, what is he?

BEATRICE   Why he is the prince's jester, a very dull fool;
only his gift is in devising impossible slanders. None but
libertines delight in him, and the commendation is not
in his wit but in his villainy, for he both pleases men and
angers them, and then they laugh at him and beat him.
I am sure he is in the fleet; I would he had boarded me.

BENEDICK   When I know the gentleman, I'll tell him
what you say.

BEATRICE   Do, do. He'll but break a comparison or two
on me, which, peradventure not marked, or not
laughed at, strikes him into melancholy, and then
there's a partridge wing saved, for the fool will eat no
supper that night. We must follow the leaders.

BENEDICK   In every good thing.

BEATRICE   Nay, if they lead to any ill I will leave them at
the next turning.

Dance. Exeunt all but Don John, Borachio
and Claudio.

DON JOHN   Sure my brother is amorous on Hero and
hath withdrawn her father to break with him about it.
The ladies follow her, and but one visor remains.

BORACHIO [*aside to Don John*]   And that is Claudio; I
know him by his bearing.

DON JOHN   Are not you Signor Benedick?

CLAUDIO   You know me well. I am he.

DON JOHN   Signor, you are very near my brother in his
love. He is enamoured on Hero. I pray you, dissuade
him from her; she is no equal for his birth. You may do
the part of an honest man in it.

CLAUDIO   How know you he loves her?

DON JOHN   I heard him swear his affection.

BORACHIO   So did I too, and he swore he would marry
her tonight.

DON JOHN   Come, let us to the banquet.

Exeunt all but Claudio.

CLAUDIO   Thus answer I in name of Benedick,
But hear these ill news with the ears of Claudio.
'Tis certain so; the prince woos for himself.
Friendship is constant in all other things,
Save in the office and affairs of love.
Therefore all hearts in love use their own tongues:
Let every eye negotiate for itself,
And trust no agent; for Beauty is a witch
Against whose charms faith melteth into blood.
This is an accident of hourly proof
Which I mistrusted not. Farewell, therefore, Hero!

Enter BENEDICK.

BENEDICK   Count Claudio.

CLAUDIO   Yea, the same.

BENEDICK   Come, will you go with me?

CLAUDIO   Whither?

BENEDICK   Even to the next willow, about your own
business, county. What fashion will you wear the
garland of? About your neck, like an usurer's chain?
Or under your arm, like a lieutenant's scarf? You must
wear it one way, for the prince hath got your Hero.

CLAUDIO   I wish him joy of her.

BENEDICK   Why, that's spoken like an honest drover; so
they sell bullocks. But did you think the prince would
have served you thus?

CLAUDIO   I pray you leave me.

BENEDICK   Ho, now you strike like the blindman! 'Twas
the boy that stole your meat, and you'll beat the post.

CLAUDIO   If it will not be, I'll leave you.   *Exit.*

BENEDICK   Alas, poor hurt fowl, now will he creep into
sedges. But that my Lady Beatrice should know me,
and not know me! The prince's fool – hah! It may be I
go under that title because I am merry. Yea, but so I am
apt to do myself wrong. I am not so reputed; it is the
base, though bitter, disposition of Beatrice that puts
the world into her person and so gives me out. Well,
I'll be revenged as I may.

Enter DON PEDRO, HERO and LEONATO.

DON PEDRO   Now, signor, where's the count? Did you
see him?

BENEDICK   Troth, my lord, I have played the part of
Lady Fame. I found him here as melancholy as a lodge
in a warren. I told him, and I think I told him true, that
your grace had got the good will of this young lady, and
I offered him my company to a willow tree, either to
make him a garland, as being forsaken, or to bind him
up a rod, as being worthy to be whipped.

DON PEDRO   To be whipped? What's his fault?

BENEDICK   The flat transgression of a schoolboy, who,
being overjoyed with finding a bird's nest, shows it his
companion, and he steals it.

DON PEDRO   Wilt thou make a trust a transgression?
The transgression is in the stealer.

BENEDICK   Yet it had not been amiss the rod had been
made, and the garland too; for the garland he might
have worn himself, and the rod he might have bestowed
on you, who, as I take it, have stolen his bird's nest.

DON PEDRO   I will but teach them to sing, and restore
them to the owner.

BENEDICK   If their singing answer your saying, by my
faith you say honestly.

DON PEDRO   The Lady Beatrice hath a quarrel to you.
The gentleman that danced with her told her she is
much wronged by you.

BENEDICK   O, she misused me past the endurance of a
block! An oak but with one green leaf on it would have
answered her; my very visor began to assume life and
scold with her! She told me, not thinking I had been
myself, that I was the prince's jester, that I was duller

than a great thaw, huddling jest upon jest with such
impossible conveyance upon me that I stood like a man
at a mark, with a whole army shooting at me. She
speaks poniards, and every word stabs. If her breath
235 were as terrible as her terminations there were no
living near her, she would infect to the North Star. I
would not marry her though she were endowed with all
that Adam had left him before he transgressed. She
would have made Hercules have turned spit, yea, and
240 have cleft his club to make the fire too. Come, talk not
of her, you shall find her the infernal Ate in good
apparel. I would to God some scholar would conjure
her, for certainly while she is here a man may live as
quiet in hell as in a sanctuary, and people sin upon
245 purpose because they would go thither – so indeed all
disquiet, horror and perturbation follows her.

Enter CLAUDIO *and* BEATRICE.

DON PEDRO   Look, here she comes.

BENEDICK   Will your grace command me any service to
the world's end? I will go on the slightest errand now to
250 the Antipodes that you can devise to send me on. I will
fetch you a toothpicker now from the furthest inch of
Asia; bring you the length of Prester John's foot; fetch
you a hair off the Great Cham's beard; do you any
embassage to the Pygmies, rather than hold three
255 words' conference with this harpy. You have no
employment for me?

DON PEDRO   None, but to desire your good company.

BENEDICK   O God, sir, here's a dish I love not; I cannot
endure my Lady Tongue!

260 DON PEDRO   Come, lady, come; you have lost the heart
of Signor Benedick.

BEATRICE   Indeed, my lord, he lent it me awhile, and I
gave him use for it, a double heart for his single one.
Marry, once before he won it of me with false dice;
265 therefore your grace may well say I have lost it.

DON PEDRO   You have put him down, lady, you have
put him down.

BEATRICE   So I would not he should do me, my lord,
lest I should prove the mother of fools. I have brought
270 Count Claudio, whom you sent me to seek.

DON PEDRO   Why, how now, Count? Wherefore are you
sad?

CLAUDIO   Not sad, my lord.

DON PEDRO   How then? Sick?

275 CLAUDIO   Neither, my lord.

BEATRICE   The count is neither sad, nor sick, nor
merry, nor well – but civil count, civil as an orange, and
something of that jealous complexion.

DON PEDRO   I'faith, lady, I think your blazon to be true;
280 though I'll be sworn if he be so his conceit is false.
Here, Claudio, I have wooed in thy name, and fair
Hero is won. I have broke with her father, and his good
will obtained. Name the day of marriage, and God give
thee joy!

285 LEONATO   Count, take of me my daughter, and with her

my fortunes. His grace hath made the match, and all
grace say amen to it.

BEATRICE   Speak, Count, 'tis your cue.

CLAUDIO   Silence is the perfectest herald of joy; I were
but little happy if I could say how much. Lady, as you   290
are mine, I am yours. I give away myself for you, and
dote upon the exchange.

BEATRICE   Speak, cousin, or, if you cannot, stop his
mouth with a kiss and let not him speak neither.

DON PEDRO   In faith, lady, you have a merry heart.   295

BEATRICE   Yea, my lord, I thank it, poor fool, it keeps on
the windy side of care. My cousin tells him in his ear
that he is in her heart.

CLAUDIO   And so she doth, cousin.

BEATRICE   Good Lord, for alliance! Thus goes everyone   300
to the world but I, and I am sunburnt. I may sit in a
corner and cry 'Hey-ho for a husband'.

DON PEDRO   Lady Beatrice, I will get you one.

BEATRICE   I would rather have one of your father's
getting. Hath your grace ne'er a brother like you? Your   305
father got excellent husbands, if a maid could come by
them.

DON PEDRO   Will you have me, lady?

BEATRICE   No, my lord, unless I might have another for
working days. Your grace is too costly to wear every   310
day. But I beseech your grace pardon me, I was born to
speak all mirth and no matter.

DON PEDRO   Your silence most offends me, and to be
merry best becomes you, for out o'question, you were
born in a merry hour.   315

BEATRICE   No, sure, my lord, my mother cried; but then
there was a star danced, and under that was I born. [*to
Hero and Claudio*] Cousins, God give you joy!

LEONATO   Niece, will you look to those things I told
you of?   320

BEATRICE   I cry you mercy, uncle. [*to Don Pedro*] By
your grace's pardon.   *Exit.*

DON PEDRO   By my troth, a pleasant-spirited lady.

LEONATO   There's little of the melancholy element in
her, my lord. She is never sad but when she sleeps, and   325
not ever sad then; for I have heard my daughter say she
hath often dreamt of unhappiness and waked herself
with laughing.

DON PEDRO   She cannot endure to hear tell of a
husband.   330

LEONATO   O, by no means. She mocks all her wooers
out of suit.

DON PEDRO   She were an excellent wife for Benedick.

LEONATO   O Lord, my lord, if they were but a week
married, they would talk themselves mad.   335

DON PEDRO   County Claudio, when mean you to go to
church?

CLAUDIO   Tomorrow, my lord. Time goes on crutches
till Love have all his rites.

LEONATO   Not till Monday, my dear son, which is   340
hence a just sennight – and a time too brief, too, to
have all things answer my mind.

DON PEDRO   Come, you shake the head at so long a
breathing, but I warrant thee, Claudio, the time shall
not go dully by us. I will, in the interim, undertake
345 one of Hercules' labours, which is to bring Signor
Benedick and the Lady Beatrice into a mountain of
affection th'one with th'other. I would fain have it a
match, and I doubt not but to fashion it, if you three
350 will but minister such assistance as I shall give you
direction.
LEONATO   My lord, I am for you, though it cost me ten
nights' watchings.
CLAUDIO   And I, my lord.
355 DON PEDRO   And you too, gentle Hero?
HERO   I will do any modest office, my lord, to help my
cousin to a good husband.
DON PEDRO   And Benedick is not the unhopefullest
husband that I know. Thus far can I praise him: he is of
360 a noble strain, of approved valour and confirmed
honesty. I will teach you how to humour your cousin
that she shall fall in love with Benedick; [*to Claudio and
Leonato*] and I, with your two helps, will so practise on
Benedick that, in despite of his quick wit and his
365 queasy stomach, he shall fall in love with Beatrice. If
we can do this, Cupid is no longer an archer; his glory
shall be ours, for we are the only love-gods. Go in with
me and I will tell you my drift.   *Exeunt.*

2.2　　　*Enter* DON JOHN *and* BORACHIO.

DON JOHN   It is so; the Count Claudio shall marry the
daughter of Leonato.
BORACHIO   Yea, my lord, but I can cross it.
DON JOHN   Any bar, any cross, any impediment will
5 be medicinable to me. I am sick in displeasure to him,
and whatsoever comes athwart his affection ranges
evenly with mine. How canst thou cross this marriage?
BORACHIO   Not honestly, my lord, but so covertly that
no dishonesty shall appear in me.
10 DON JOHN   Show me briefly how.
BORACHIO   I think I told your lordship, a year since,
how much I am in the favour of Margaret, the waiting-
gentlewoman to Hero.
DON JOHN   I remember.
15 BORACHIO   I can, at any unseasonable instant of the
night, appoint her to look out at her lady's chamber
window.
DON JOHN   What life is in that to be the death of this
marriage?
20 BORACHIO   The poison of that lies in you to temper. Go
you to the prince your brother; spare not to tell him
that he hath wronged his honour in marrying the
renowned Claudio – whose estimation do you mightily
hold up – to a contaminated stale, such a one as Hero.
25 DON JOHN   What proof shall I make of that?
BORACHIO   Proof enough to misuse the prince, to vex
Claudio, to undo Hero and kill Leonato. Look you for
any other issue?

DON JOHN   Only to despite them I will endeavour
anything.   30
BORACHIO   Go, then. Find me a meet hour to draw
Don Pedro and the Count Claudio alone. Tell them
that you know that Hero loves me. Intend a kind of zeal
both to the prince and Claudio – as in love of your
brother's honour, who hath made this match, and his   35
friend's reputation, who is thus like to be cozened with
the semblance of a maid – that you have discovered
thus. They will scarcely believe this without trial; offer
them instances, which shall bear no less likelihood than
to see me at her chamber window, hear me call   40
Margaret 'Hero', hear Margaret term me 'Claudio'.
And bring them to see this the very night before the
intended wedding (for in the meantime I will so
fashion the matter that Hero shall be absent), and
there shall appear such seeming truth of Hero's   45
disloyalty that jealousy shall be called assurance, and
all the preparation overthrown.
DON JOHN   Grow this to what adverse issue it can, I will
put it in practice. Be cunning in the working this and
thy fee is a thousand ducats.   50
BORACHIO   Be you constant in the accusation and my
cunning shall not shame me.
DON JOHN   I will presently go learn their day of marriage.
                                                   Exeunt.

2.3　　　*Enter* BENEDICK *alone.*

BENEDICK   Boy!

Enter Boy.

BOY   Signor.
BENEDICK   In my chamber window lies a book. Bring it
hither to me in the orchard.
BOY   I am here already, sir.   5
BENEDICK   I know that, but I would have thee hence and
here again.   *Exit Boy.*
I do much wonder that one man, seeing how much
another man is a fool when he dedicates his behaviours
to love, will, after he hath laughed at such shallow follies 10
in others, become the argument of his own scorn by
falling in love. And such a man is Claudio. I have known
when there was no music with him but the drum and the
fife, and now had he rather hear the tabor and the pipe. I
have known when he would have walked ten mile afoot   15
to see a good armour, and now will he lie ten nights
awake carving the fashion of a new doublet. He was wont
to speak plain and to the purpose, like an honest man
and a soldier, and now is he turned ortography; his
words are a very fantastical banquet, just so many   20
strange dishes. May I be so converted and see with these
eyes? I cannot tell; I think not. I will not be sworn but
love may transform me to an oyster, but I'll take my oath
on it, till he have made an oyster of me he shall never
make me such a fool. One woman is fair, yet I am well.   25
Another is wise, yet I am well. Another virtuous, yet I am

well. But till all graces be in one woman, one woman shall not come in my grace. Rich she shall be, that's certain; wise, or I'll none; virtuous, or I'll never cheapen her; fair, or I'll never look on her; mild, or come not near me; noble, or not I for an angel. Of good discourse, an excellent musician, and her hair shall be of what colour it please God. Hah! The prince and Monsieur Love. I will hide me in the arbour. [*Withdraws.*]

Enter DON PEDRO, LEONATO, CLAUDIO *and* BALTHASAR, *with Music.*

DON PEDRO   Come, shall we hear this music?

CLAUDIO   Yea, my good lord. How still the evening is,
As hushed on purpose to grace harmony!

DON PEDRO [*aside to Claudio and Leonato*]
See you where Benedick hath hid himself?

CLAUDIO [*aside*]
O, very well, my lord. The music ended,
We'll fit the kid-fox with a pennyworth.

DON PEDRO
Come, Balthasar, we'll hear that song again.

BALTHASAR   O good my lord, tax not so bad a voice
To slander music any more than once.

DON PEDRO   It is the witness still of excellency
To put a strange face on his own perfection.
I pray thee sing, and let me woo no more.

BALTHASAR   Because you talk of wooing I will sing,
Since many a wooer doth commence his suit
To her he thinks not worthy, yet he woos,
Yet will he swear he loves.

DON PEDRO   Nay, pray thee, come,
Or if thou wilt hold longer argument,
Do it in notes.

BALTHASAR   Note this before my notes:
There's not a note of mine that's worth the noting.

DON PEDRO
Why, these are very crotchets that he speaks.
Note notes forsooth, and nothing!   [*Balthasar plays.*]

BENEDICK   Now, divine air! Now is his soul ravished!
Is it not strange that sheep's guts should hale souls out
of men's bodies? Well, a horn for my money, when all's
done.

BALTHASAR [*Sings.*]
    Sigh no more, ladies, sigh no more,
        Men were deceivers ever;
    One foot in sea, and one on shore,
        To one thing constant never.
    Then sigh not so, but let them go,
        And be you blithe and bonny,
    Converting all your sounds of woe
        Into 'Hey, nonny, nonny'.

    Sing no more ditties, sing no more,
        Of dumps so dull and heavy;
    The fraud of men was ever so,
        Since summer first was leavy.
    Then sigh not so, but let them go,

    And be you blithe and bonny,
        Converting all your sounds of woe
        Into 'Hey, nonny, nonny'.

DON PEDRO   By my troth, a good song.

BALTHASAR   And an ill singer, my lord.

DON PEDRO   Ha? No, no, faith; thou sing'st well enough
for a shift.

BENEDICK [*aside*]   An he had been a dog that should
have howled thus, they would have hanged him. And I
pray God his bad voice bode no mischief. I had as lief
have heard the night-raven, come what plague could
have come after it.

DON PEDRO   Yea, marry, – dost thou hear, Balthasar? I
pray thee get us some excellent music, for tomorrow
night we would have it at the Lady Hero's chamber
window.

BALTHASAR   The best I can, my lord.

DON PEDRO   Do so. Farewell.   *Exit Balthasar.*
Come hither, Leonato. What was it you told me of
today? That your niece Beatrice was in love with
Signor Benedick?

CLAUDIO [*aside*]   O ay, stalk on, stalk on, the fowl sits.
[*Raises his voice.*] I did never think that lady would
have loved any man.

LEONATO   No, nor I neither. But most wonderful that
she should so dote on Signor Benedick, whom she
hath in all outward behaviours seemed ever to abhor.

BENEDICK   Is't possible? Sits the wind in that corner?

LEONATO   By my troth, my lord, I cannot tell what to
think of it. But that she loves him with an enraged
affection, it is past the infinite of thought.

DON PEDRO   Maybe she doth but counterfeit.

CLAUDIO   Faith, like enough.

LEONATO   O God! Counterfeit? There was never
counterfeit of passion came so near the life of passion
as she discovers it.

DON PEDRO   Why, what effects of passion shows she?

CLAUDIO [*aside*]   Bait the hook well, this fish will bite!

LEONATO   What effects, my lord? She will sit you – you
heard my daughter tell you how.

CLAUDIO   She did indeed.

DON PEDRO   How, how, I pray you? You amaze me! I
would have thought her spirit had been invincible
against all assaults of affection.

LEONATO   I would have sworn it had, my lord; especially
against Benedick.

BENEDICK   I should think this a gull, but that the
white-bearded fellow speaks it. Knavery cannot, sure,
hide himself in such reverence.

CLAUDIO [*aside*]   He hath ta'en th'infection; hold it up!

DON PEDRO   Hath she made her affection known to
Benedick?

LEONATO   No, and swears she never will. That's her
torment.

CLAUDIO   'Tis true indeed, so your daughter says.
'Shall I,' says she, 'that have so oft encountered him
with scorn, write to him that I love him?'

30

35

40

45

50

55

60

65

75

80

85

90

95

100

105

110

115

120

125

LEONATO This says she now, when she is beginning to
write to him; for she'll be up twenty times a night, and
there will she sit in her smock till she have writ a sheet
of paper. My daughter tells us all.

CLAUDIO Now you talk of a sheet of paper, I remember
a pretty jest your daughter told us of.

LEONATO O, when she had writ it, and was reading it
over, she found 'Benedick' and 'Beatrice' between the
sheet?

CLAUDIO That.

LEONATO O, she tore the letter into a thousand
halfpence, railed at herself that she should be so
immodest to write to one that she knew would flout
her. 'I measure him', says she, 'by my own spirit; for I
should flout him, if he writ to me – yea, though I loved
him I should.'

CLAUDIO Then down upon her knees she falls, weeps,
sobs, beats her heart, tears her hair, prays, curses, 'O
sweet Benedick! God give me patience!'

LEONATO She doth indeed; my daughter says so. And
the ecstasy hath so much overborne her that my
daughter is sometime afeard she will do a desperate
outrage to herself. It is very true.

DON PEDRO It were good that Benedick knew of it by
some other, if she will not discover it.

CLAUDIO To what end? He would make but a sport of it
and torment the poor lady worse.

DON PEDRO An he should, it were an alms to hang him.
She's an excellent sweet lady, and, out of all suspicion,
she is virtuous.

CLAUDIO And she is exceeding wise.

DON PEDRO In everything but in loving Benedick.

LEONATO O my lord, wisdom and blood combating in
so tender a body, we have ten proofs to one that blood
hath the victory. I am sorry for her, as I have just cause,
being her uncle and her guardian.

DON PEDRO I would she had bestowed this dotage on
me. I would have doffed all other respects and made
her half myself. I pray you tell Benedick of it and hear
what 'a will say.

LEONATO Were it good, think you?

CLAUDIO Hero thinks surely she will die, for she says
she will die if he love her not, and she will die ere she
make her love known, and she will die if he woo her,
rather than she will bate one breath of her accustomed
crossness.

DON PEDRO She doth well. If she should make tender
of her love 'tis very possible he'll scorn it, for the man,
as you know all, hath a contemptible spirit.

CLAUDIO He is a very proper man.

DON PEDRO He hath indeed a good outward happiness.

CLAUDIO Before God, and in my mind very wise.

DON PEDRO He doth indeed show some sparks that are
like wit.

CLAUDIO And I take him to be valiant.

DON PEDRO As Hector, I assure you. And in the
managing of quarrels you may say he is wise, for either

he avoids them with great discretion, or undertakes
them with a most Christian-like fear.

LEONATO If he do fear God, 'a must necessarily keep
peace; if he break the peace, he ought to enter into a
quarrel with fear and trembling.

DON PEDRO And so will he do, for the man doth fear
God, howsoever it seems not in him by some large jests
he will make. Well, I am sorry for your niece. Shall we
go seek Benedick and tell him of her love?

CLAUDIO Never tell him, my lord. Let her wear it out
with good counsel.

LEONATO Nay, that's impossible; she may wear her
heart out first.

DON PEDRO Well, we will hear further of it by your
daughter. Let it cool the while. I love Benedick well,
and I could wish he would modestly examine himself
to see how much he is unworthy so good a lady.

LEONATO My lord, will you walk? Dinner is ready.

CLAUDIO [*to Don Pedro and Leonato*] If he do not dote
on her upon this, I will never trust my expectation.

DON PEDRO [*to Leonato and Claudio*] Let there be the
same net spread for her, and that must your daughter
and her gentlewomen carry. The sport will be when
they hold one an opinion of another's dotage, and no
such matter. That's the scene that I would see, which
will be merely a dumb-show. Let us send her to call
him in to dinner.   *Exeunt all but Benedick.*

BENEDICK [*Emerges.*] This can be no trick. The
conference was sadly borne; they have the truth of this
from Hero. They seem to pity the lady. It seems her
affections have their full bent. Love me? Why, it must
be requited. I hear how I am censured: they say I will
bear myself proudly if I perceive the love come from
her. They say too that she will rather die than give any
sign of affection. I did never think to marry. I must not
seem proud; happy are they that hear their detractions
and can put them to mending. They say the lady is fair
– 'tis a truth, I can bear them witness. And virtuous –
'tis so, I cannot reprove it. And wise, but for loving me.
By my troth, it is no addition to her wit – nor no great
argument of her folly, for I will be horribly in love with
her. I may chance have some odd quirks and remnants
of wit broken on me because I have railed so long
against marriage. But doth not the appetite alter? A
man loves the meat in his youth that he cannot endure
in his age. Shall quips and sentences and these paper
bullets of the brain awe a man from the career of his
humour? No, the world must be peopled. When I said
I would die a bachelor, I did not think I should live till
I were married.

Enter BEATRICE.

Here comes Beatrice. By this day, she's a fair lady! I do
spy some marks of love in her.

BEATRICE Against my will I am sent to bid you come in
to dinner.

BENEDICK Fair Beatrice, I thank you for your pains.

BEATRICE   I took no more pains for those thanks than
    you take pains to thank me. If it had been painful I
    would not have come.

245 BENEDICK   You take pleasure, then, in the message?

BEATRICE   Yea, just so much as you may take upon a
    knife's point and choke a daw withal. You have no
    stomach, signor? Fare you well.   *Exit.*

BENEDICK   Ha! 'Against my will I am sent to bid you

250   come in to dinner' – there's a double meaning in that.
    'I took no more pains for those thanks than you took
    pains to thank me' – that's as much as to say, 'Any pains
    that I take for you is as easy as thanks.' If I do not take
    pity of her I am a villain; if I do not love her I am a Jew.

255 I will go get her picture.   *Exit.*

3.1   *Enter* HERO *and two gentlewomen,*
           MARGARET *and* URSULA.

HERO   Good Margaret, run thee to the parlour;
    There shalt thou find my cousin Beatrice
    Proposing with the prince and Claudio;
    Whisper her ear and tell her I and Ursley

5   Walk in the orchard, and our whole discourse
    Is all of her. Say that thou overheard'st us,
    And bid her steal into the pleached bower
    Where honeysuckles ripened by the sun
    Forbid the sun to enter, like favourites

10   Made proud by princes that advance their pride
    Against that power that bred it; there will she hide
        her
    To listen our propose. This is thy office,
    Bear thee well in it, and leave us alone.

MARGARET   I'll make her come, I warrant you,

15   presently.   *Exit.*

HERO   Now, Ursula, when Beatrice doth come,
    As we do trace this alley up and down
    Our talk must only be of Benedick.
    When I do name him, let it be thy part

20   To praise him more than ever man did merit;
    My talk to thee must be how Benedick
    Is sick in love with Beatrice. Of this matter
    Is little Cupid's crafty arrow made,
    That only wounds by hearsay.

           Enter BEATRICE, *who hides.*

                        Now begin,

25   For look where Beatrice like a lapwing runs
    Close by the ground to hear our conference.

URSULA [*to Hero*]
    The pleasant'st angling is to see the fish
    Cut with her golden oars the silver stream
    And greedily devour the treacherous bait;

30   So angle we for Beatrice, who even now
    Is couched in the woodbine coverture.
    Fear you not my part of the dialogue.

HERO [*to Ursula*]
    Then go we near her, that her ear lose nothing

Of the false sweet bait that we lay for it.
    [*They approach Beatrice's hiding place.*]
    – No, truly, Ursula, she is too disdainful.   35
    I know her spirits are as coy and wild
    As haggards of the rock.

URSULA   But are you sure
    That Benedick loves Beatrice so entirely?

HERO   So says the prince and my new-trothed lord.

URSULA
    And did they bid you tell her of it, madam?   40

HERO   They did entreat me to acquaint her of it;
    But I persuaded them, if they loved Benedick,
    To wish him wrestle with affection
    And never to let Beatrice know of it.

URSULA   Why did you so? Doth not the gentleman   45
    Deserve at full as fortunate a bed
    As ever Beatrice shall couch upon?

HERO   O god of love! I know he doth deserve
    As much as may be yielded to a man.
    But Nature never framed a woman's heart   50
    Of prouder stuff than that of Beatrice.
    Disdain and Scorn ride sparkling in her eyes,
    Misprising what they look on, and her wit
    Values itself so highly that to her
    All matter else seems weak. She cannot love,   55
    Nor take no shape nor project of affection,
    She is so self-endeared.

URSULA   Sure, I think so.
    And therefore certainly it were not good
    She knew his love, lest she'll make sport at it.

HERO   Why, you speak truth. I never yet saw man –   60
    How wise, how noble, young, how rarely featured –
    But she would spell him backward. If fair-faced,
    She would swear the gentleman should be her
        sister;
    If black, why Nature, drawing of an antic,
    Made a foul blot; if tall, a lance ill-headed;   65
    If low, an agate very vilely cut;
    If speaking, why, a vane blown with all winds;
    If silent, why, a block moved with none.
    So turns she every man the wrong side out,
    And never gives to truth and virtue that   70
    Which simpleness and merit purchaseth.

URSULA   Sure, sure, such carping is not commendable.

HERO   No, not to be so odd and from all fashions
    As Beatrice is cannot be commendable.
    But who dare tell her so? If I should speak,   75
    She would mock me into air. O, she would laugh me
    Out of myself, press me to death with wit!
    Therefore let Benedick, like covered fire,
    Consume away in sighs, waste inwardly.
    It were a better death than die with mocks,   80
    Which is as bad as die with tickling.

URSULA   Yet tell her of it; hear what she will say.

HERO   No, rather I will go to Benedick
    And counsel him to fight against his passion.
    And truly, I'll devise some honest slanders   85

To stain my cousin with: one doth not know
How much an ill word may empoison liking.

URSULA   O, do not do your cousin such a wrong!
She cannot be so much without true judgement,
90   Having so swift and excellent a wit
As she is prized to have, as to refuse
So rare a gentleman as Signor Benedick.

HERO   He is the only man of Italy –
Always excepted my dear Claudio.

95   URSULA   I pray you, be not angry with me, madam,
Speaking my fancy. Signor Benedick,
For shape, for bearing, argument and valour,
Goes foremost in report through Italy.

HERO   Indeed, he hath an excellent good name.

100   URSULA   His excellence did earn it ere he had it.
When are you married, madam?

HERO   Why, every day, tomorrow! Come, go in,
I'll show thee some attires, and have thy counsel
Which is the best to furnish me tomorrow.

URSULA [*to Hero*]
105   She's limed, I warrant you! We have caught her, madam!

HERO [*to Ursula*]
If it prove so, then loving goes by haps;
Some Cupid kills with arrows, some with traps.
Exeunt all but Beatrice.

BEATRICE   What fire is in mine ears? Can this be true?
Stand I condemned for pride and scorn so much?
110   Contempt, farewell; and maiden pride, adieu;
No glory lives behind the back of such.
And Benedick, love on, I will requite thee,
Taming my wild heart to thy loving hand.
If thou dost love, my kindness shall incite thee
115   To bind our loves up in a holy band.
For others say thou dost deserve, and I
Believe it better than reportingly.   *Exit.*

3.2   *Enter* DON PEDRO, CLAUDIO,
           BENEDICK *and* LEONATO.

DON PEDRO   I do but stay till your marriage be
consummate, and then go I toward Aragon.

CLAUDIO   I'll bring you thither, my lord, if you'll
vouchsafe me.

5   DON PEDRO   Nay, that would be as great a soil in the
new gloss of your marriage as to show a child his new
coat and forbid him to wear it. I will only be bold with
Benedick for his company, for from the crown of his
head to the sole of his foot, he is all mirth. He hath
10   twice or thrice cut Cupid's bowstring, and the little
hangman dare not shoot at him. He hath a heart as
sound as a bell, and his tongue is the clapper: for what
his heart thinks, his tongue speaks.

BENEDICK   Gallants, I am not as I have been.

15   LEONATO   So say I; methinks you are sadder.

CLAUDIO   I hope he be in love.

DON PEDRO   Hang him, truant! There's no true drop of

blood in him to be truly touched with love. If he be sad,
he wants money.

BENEDICK   I have the toothache.   20

DON PEDRO   Draw it.

BENEDICK   Hang it!

CLAUDIO   You must hang it first and draw it afterwards.

DON PEDRO   What? Sigh for the toothache?

LEONATO   Where is but a humour or a worm.   25

BENEDICK   Well, everyone can master a grief but he
that has it.

CLAUDIO   Yet, say I, he is in love.

DON PEDRO   There is no appearance of fancy in him,
unless it be a fancy that he hath to strange disguises: as   30
to be a Dutchman today, a Frenchman tomorrow – or
in the shape of two countries at once, as a German
from the waist downward, all slops, and a Spaniard
from the hip upward, no doublet. Unless he have a
fancy to this foolery – as it appears he hath – he is no   35
fool for fancy, as you would have it appear he is.

CLAUDIO   If he be not in love with some woman there is
no believing old signs. 'A brushes his hat o'mornings:
what should that bode?

DON PEDRO   Hath any man seen him at the barber's?   40

CLAUDIO   No, but the barber's man hath been seen with
him, and the old ornament of his cheek hath already
stuffed tennis balls.

LEONATO   Indeed, he looks younger than he did by the
loss of a beard.   45

DON PEDRO   Nay, 'a rubs himself with civet. Can you
smell him out by that?

CLAUDIO   That's as much as to say the sweet youth's in
love.

DON PEDRO   The greatest note of it is his melancholy.   50

CLAUDIO   And when was he wont to wash his face?

DON PEDRO   Yea, or to paint himself? For the which I
hear what they say of him.

CLAUDIO   Nay, but his jesting spirit, which is now crept
into a lute-string and now governed by stops.   55

DON PEDRO   Indeed, that tells a heavy tale for him.
Conclude, conclude: he is in love.

CLAUDIO   Nay, but I know who loves him.

DON PEDRO   That would I know too; I warrant one that
knows him not.   60

CLAUDIO   Yes, and his ill conditions, and in despite of
all dies for him.

DON PEDRO   She shall be buried with her face upwards.

BENEDICK   Yet is this no charm for the toothache. [*to
Leonato*] Old signor, walk aside with me. I have studied   65
eight or nine wise words to speak to you which these
hobby-horses must not hear.
Exeunt Benedick and Leonato.

DON PEDRO   For my life, to break with him about
Beatrice!

CLAUDIO   'Tis even so. Hero and Margaret have by this   70
played their parts with Beatrice, and then the two bears
will not bite one another when they meet.

Enter DON JOHN *the bastard.*

DON JOHN My lord and brother, God save you!

DON PEDRO Good e'en, brother.

75 DON JOHN If your leisure served, I would speak with you.

DON PEDRO In private?

DON JOHN If it please you; yet Count Claudio may hear, for what I would speak of concerns him.

80 DON PEDRO What's the matter?

DON JOHN [*to Claudio*] Means your lordship to be married tomorrow?

DON PEDRO You know he does.

DON JOHN I know not that when he knows what I know.

85 CLAUDIO If there be any impediment, I pray you discover it.

DON JOHN You may think I love you not. Let that appear hereafter, and aim better at me by that I now will manifest. For my brother – I think he holds you

90 well and in dearness of heart – hath holp to effect your ensuing marriage; surely suit ill spent and labour ill bestowed.

DON PEDRO Why, what's the matter?

DON JOHN I came hither to tell you; and, circumstances

95 shortened – for she has been too long a-talking of – the lady is disloyal.

CLAUDIO Who, Hero?

DON JOHN Even she: Leonato's Hero, your Hero, every man's Hero.

100 CLAUDIO Disloyal?

DON JOHN The word is too good to paint out her wickedness; I could say she were worse. Think you of a worse title, and I will fit her to it. Wonder not till further warrant. Go but with me, tonight you shall see

105 her chamber window entered, even the night before her wedding day. If you love her then, tomorrow wed her. But it would better fit your honour to change your mind.

CLAUDIO May this be so?

110 DON PEDRO I will not think it.

DON JOHN If you dare not trust that you see, confess not that you know. If you will follow me I will show you enough, and when you have seen more and heard more, proceed accordingly.

115 CLAUDIO If I see anything tonight why I should not marry her, tomorrow in the congregation where I should wed, there will I shame her.

DON PEDRO And as I wooed for thee to obtain her, I will join with thee to disgrace her.

120 DON JOHN I will disparage her no farther till you are my witnesses. Bear it coldly but till midnight, and let the issue show itself.

DON PEDRO O day untowardly turned!

CLAUDIO O mischief strangely thwarting!

125 DON JOHN O plague right well prevented! So will you say when you have seen the sequel. *Exeunt.*

3.3 *Enter* DOGBERRY, *the constable, and his compartner* VERGES, *with the* Watch, *among them* George SEACOAL *and Hugh Oatcake.*

DOGBERRY Are you good men and true?

VERGES Yea, or else it were pity but they should suffer salvation, body and soul.

DOGBERRY Nay, that were a punishment too good for them, if they should have any allegiance in them, being 5 chosen for the prince's watch.

VERGES Well, give them their charge, neighbour Dogberry.

DOGBERRY First, who think you the most desertless man to be constable? 10

1 WATCHMAN Hugh Oatcake, sir, or George Seacoal, for they can write and read.

DOGBERRY Come hither, neighbour Seacoal; [*Seacoal steps forward.*] God hath blest you with a good name. To be a well-favoured man is the gift of fortune, but to 15 write and read comes by nature.

SEACOAL Both which, master constable –

DOGBERRY You have. I knew it would be your answer. Well, for your favour, sir, why, give God thanks, and make no boast of it; and for your writing 20 and reading, let that appear when there is no need of such vanity. You are thought here to be the most senseless and fit man for the constable of the watch, therefore bear you the lantern. [*Hands Seacoal the lantern.*] This is your charge: you shall comprehend all 25 vagrom men. You are to bid any man stand, in the prince's name.

SEACOAL How if 'a will not stand?

DOGBERRY Why then, take no note of him, but let him go, and presently call the rest of the watch together, 30 and thank God you are rid of a knave.

VERGES If he will not stand when he is bidden, he is none of the prince's subjects.

DOGBERRY True, and they are to meddle with none but the prince's subjects. You shall also make no noise in 35 the streets, for for the watch to babble and to talk is most tolerable, and not to be endured.

WATCHMAN We will rather sleep than talk; we know what belongs to a watch.

DOGBERRY Why, you speak like an ancient and most 40 quiet watchman. For I cannot see how sleeping should offend. Only have a care that your bills be not stolen. Well, you are to call at all the alehouses, and bid those that are drunk get them to bed.

WATCHMAN How if they will not? 45

DOGBERRY Why then, let them alone till they are sober. If they make you not then the better answer, you may say they are not the men you took them for.

WATCHMAN Well, sir.

DOGBERRY If you meet a thief, you may suspect him, 50 by virtue of your office, to be no true man. And for such kind of men, the less you meddle or make with them, why, the more is for your honesty.

WATCHMAN   If we know him to be a thief, shall we not
lay hands on him?

DOGBERRY   Truly, by your office you may; but I think
they that touch pitch will be defiled. The most peaceable
way for you, if you do take a thief, is to let him show
himself what he is, and steal out of your company.

VERGES   You have been always called a merciful man,
partner.

DOGBERRY   Truly, I would not hang a dog by my will,
much more a man who hath any honesty in him.

VERGES   If you hear a child cry in the night you must
call to the nurse and bid her still it.

WATCHMAN   How if the nurse be asleep and will not
hear us?

DOGBERRY   Why then, depart in peace, and let the child
wake her with crying; for the ewe that will not hear her
lamb when it baas will never answer a calf when he
bleats.

VERGES   'Tis very true.

DOGBERRY   This is the end of the charge. You,
constable, are to present the prince's own person. If
you meet the prince in the night you may stay him.

VERGES   Nay, by'r Lady, that I think 'a cannot.

DOGBERRY   Five shillings to one on't with any man that
knows the statutes. He may stay him – marry, not
without the prince be willing, for indeed the watch
ought to offend no man, and it is an offence to stay a
man against his will.

VERGES   By'r Lady, I think it be so.

DOGBERRY   Ha, ah ha! Well, masters, good night; an
there be any matter of weight chances, call up me.
Keep your fellows' counsels, and your own, and good
night. [*to Verges*] Come, neighbour. [*Dogberry and
Verges begin to exit.*]

SEACOAL   Well, masters, we hear our charge. Let us go
sit here upon the church bench till two, and then all to
bed.

DOGBERRY [*Returns.*]   One word more, honest neighbours. I pray you watch about Signor Leonato's door,
for the wedding being there tomorrow, there is a great
coil tonight. Adieu. Be vigitant, I beseech you.

Exeunt Dogberry and Verges.

Enter BORACHIO *and* CONRADE.

BORACHIO   What, Conrade!

SEACOAL [*aside*]   Peace, stir not.

BORACHIO   Conrade, I say!

CONRADE   Here, man, I am at thy elbow.

BORACHIO   Mass, and my elbow itched; I thought there
would a scab follow!

CONRADE   I will owe thee an answer for that. And now,
forward with thy tale.

BORACHIO   Stand thee close, then, under this
penthouse, for it drizzles rain, and I will, like a true
drunkard, utter all to thee.

SEACOAL [*aside*]   Some treason, masters. Yet stand
close.

BORACHIO   Therefore, know I have earned of Don John
a thousand ducats.

CONRADE   Is it possible that any villainy should be so
dear?

BORACHIO   Thou shouldst rather ask if it were possible
any villainy should be so rich. For when rich villains
have need of poor ones, poor ones may make what
price they will.

CONRADE   I wonder at it.

BORACHIO   That shows thou art unconfirmed. Thou
knowest that the fashion of a doublet, or a hat, or a
cloak, is nothing to a man.

CONRADE   Yes, it is apparel.

BORACHIO   I mean the fashion.

CONRADE   Yes, the fashion is the fashion.

BORACHIO   Tush, I may as well say the fool's the
fool. But seest thou not what a deformed thief this
fashion is?

WATCHMAN [*aside*]   I know that Deformed. 'A has been
a vile thief this seven year; 'a goes up and down like a
gentleman; I remember his name.

BORACHIO   Didst thou not hear somebody?

CONRADE   No, 'twas the vane on the house.

BORACHIO   Seest thou not, I say, what a deformed
thief this fashion is, how giddily 'a turns about all the
hot-bloods between fourteen and five-and-thirty,
sometimes fashioning them like Pharaoh's soldiers in
the reechy painting, sometime like god Bel's priests in
the old church window, sometime like the shaven
Hercules in the smirched worm-eaten tapestry, where
his codpiece seems as massy as his club.

CONRADE   All this I see, and I see that the fashion
wears out more apparel than the man. But art not
thou thyself giddy with the fashion, too, that thou hast
shifted out of thy tale into telling me of the fashion?

BORACHIO   Not so neither. But know that I have tonight
wooed Margaret, the Lady Hero's gentlewoman, by
the name of Hero; she leans me out at her mistress'
chamber window, bids me a thousand times goodnight
– I tell this tale vilely. I should first tell thee how the
prince, Claudio and my master, planted and placed and
possessed by my master Don John, saw afar off in the
orchard this amiable encounter.

CONRADE   And thought they Margaret was Hero?

BORACHIO   Two of them did, the prince and Claudio,
but the devil my master knew she was Margaret. And
partly by his oaths, which first possessed them, partly
by the dark night, which did deceive them, but chiefly
by my villainy, which did confirm any slander that Don
John had made, away went Claudio enraged, swore he
would meet her as he was appointed next morning at
the temple, and there, before the whole congregation,
shame her with what he saw o'ernight, and send her
home again without a husband.

1 WATCHMAN [*Starts out upon them.*]   We charge you in
the prince's name, stand!

SEACOAL   Call up the right master constable! We have

here recovered the most dangerous piece of lechery
that ever was known in the commonwealth!

1 WATCHMAN   And one Deformed is one of them. I
know him, 'a wears a lock.

CONRADE   Masters, masters –

SEACOAL   You'll be made bring Deformed forth, I
warrant you.

CONRADE   Masters –

SEACOAL   Never speak, we charge you! Let us obey you
to go with us.

BORACHIO [*to Conrade*]   We are like to prove a goodly
commodity, being taken up of these men's bills.

CONRADE   A commodity in question, I warrant you.
Come, we'll obey you.   *Exeunt.*

3.4   *Enter* HERO, MARGARET *and* URSULA.

HERO   Good Ursula, wake my cousin Beatrice and
desire her to rise.

URSULA   I will, lady.

HERO   And bid her come hither.

URSULA   Well.   *Exit.*

MARGARET   Troth, I think your other rebato were better.

HERO   No, pray thee, good Meg, I'll wear this.

MARGARET   By my troth, 's not so good, and I warrant
your cousin will say so.

HERO   My cousin's a fool, and thou art another. I'll wear
none but this.

MARGARET   I like the new tire within excellently, if the
hair were a thought browner. And your gown's a most
rare fashion, i'faith. I saw the Duchess of Milan's
gown that they praise so.

HERO   O, that exceeds, they say.

MARGARET   By my troth, 's but a night-gown in respect
of yours – cloth o'gold, and cuts, and laced with silver,
set with pearls, down sleeves, side sleeves and skirts
round underborne with a bluish tinsel. But for a fine,
quaint, graceful and excellent fashion, yours is worth
ten on't.

HERO   God give me joy to wear it, for my heart is
exceeding heavy.

MARGARET   'Twill be heavier soon by the weight of a
man.

HERO   Fie upon thee! Art not ashamed?

MARGARET   Of what, lady? Of speaking honourably? Is
not marriage honourable in a beggar? Is not your lord
honourable without marriage? I think you would have
me say, saving your reverence, 'a husband'. An bad
thinking do not wrest true speaking, I'll offend nobody.
Is there any harm in 'the heavier for a husband'? None,
I think, an it be the right husband and the right wife;
otherwise 'tis light and not heavy.

Enter BEATRICE.

Ask my lady Beatrice else; here she comes.

HERO   Good morrow, coz.

BEATRICE   Good morrow, sweet Hero.

HERO   Why, how now? Do you speak in the sick tune?

BEATRICE   I am out of all other tune, methinks.

MARGARET   Clap's into 'Light o'love', that goes without
a burden. Do you sing it, and I'll dance it.

BEATRICE   Ye light o'love with your heels? Then if your
husband have stables enough, you'll see he shall lack
no barns.

MARGARET   O illegitimate construction! I scorn that
with my heels.

BEATRICE   'Tis almost five o'clock, cousin; 'tis time you
were ready. By my troth, I am exceeding ill. Hey-ho!

MARGARET   For a hawk, a horse, or a husband?

BEATRICE   For the letter that begins them all: H.

MARGARET   Well, an you be not turned Turk, there's no
more sailing by the star.

BEATRICE   What means the fool, trow?

MARGARET   Nothing, I, but God send everyone their
heart's desire.

HERO   These gloves the count sent me, they are an
excellent perfume.

BEATRICE   I am stuffed, cousin, I cannot smell.

MARGARET   A maid and stuffed! There's goodly
catching of cold.

BEATRICE   O God help me, God help me, how long
have you professed apprehension?

MARGARET   Ever since you left it. Doth not my wit
become me rarely?

BEATRICE   It is not seen enough; you should wear it in
your cap. By my troth, I am sick.

MARGARET   Get you some of this distilled *carduus
benedictus*, and lay it to your heart; it is the only thing
for a qualm.

HERO   There thou prick'st her with a thistle.

BEATRICE   *Benedictus*? Why *benedictus*? You have some
moral in this *benedictus*.

MARGARET   Moral? No, by my troth, I have no moral
meaning, I meant plain holy-thistle. You may think
perchance that I think you are in love? Nay, by'r Lady,
I am not such a fool to think what I list, nor I list not to
think what I can, nor indeed I cannot think, if I would
think my heart out of thinking, that you are in love, or
that you will be in love, or that you can be in love. Yet
Benedick was such another, and now is he become a
man. He swore he would never marry, and yet now
in despite of his heart he eats his meat without
grudging. And how you may be converted I know
not, but methinks you look with your eyes as other
women do.

BEATRICE   What pace is this that thy tongue keeps?

MARGARET   Not a false gallop.

Enter URSULA.

URSULA   Madam, withdraw! The prince, the count,
Signor Benedick, Don John and all the gallants of the
town are come to fetch you to church.

HERO   Help to dress me, good coz, good Meg, good
Ursula.   *Exeunt.*

3.5   *Enter* LEONATO, DOGBERRY, *the constable, and* VERGES, *the headborough.*

LEONATO   What would you with me, honest neighbour?

DOGBERRY   Marry, sir, I would have some confidence with you, that discerns you nearly.

LEONATO   Brief, I pray you, for you see it is a busy time with me.

DOGBERRY   Marry, this it is, sir.

VERGES   Yes, in truth it is, sir.

LEONATO   What is it, my good friends?

DOGBERRY   Goodman Verges, sir, speaks a little off the matter. An old man, sir, and his wits are not so blunt as, God help, I would desire they were; but, in faith, honest as the skin between his brows.

VERGES   Yes, I thank God, I am as honest as any man living, that is an old man and no honester than I.

DOGBERRY   Comparisons are odorous; *palabras*, neighbour Verges.

LEONATO   Neighbours, you are tedious.

DOGBERRY   It pleases your worship to say so, but we are the poor duke's officers. But truly, for mine own part, if I were as tedious as a king I could find in my heart to bestow it all of your worship.

LEONATO   All thy tediousness on me, ah?

DOGBERRY   Yea, an 'twere a thousand pound more than 'tis, for I hear as good exclamation on your worship as of any man in the city, and though I be but a poor man, I am glad to hear it.

VERGES   And so am I.

LEONATO   I would fain know what you have to say.

VERGES   Marry, sir, our watch tonight, excepting your worship's presence, ha' ta'en a couple of as arrant knaves as any in Messina.

DOGBERRY   A good old man, sir, he will be talking. As they say, 'When the age is in, the wit is out.' God help us, it is a world to see! Well said, i'faith, neighbour Verges. Well, God's a good man. An two men ride of a horse, one must ride behind. An honest soul, i'faith, sir, by my troth, he is, as ever broke bread. But, God is to be worshipped, all men are not alike. Alas, good neighbour!

LEONATO   Indeed, neighbour, he comes too short of you.

DOGBERRY   Gifts that God gives.

LEONATO   I must leave you.

DOGBERRY   One word, sir. Our watch, sir, have indeed comprehended two aspicious persons, and we would have them this morning examined before your worship.

LEONATO   Take their examination yourself, and bring it me. I am now in great haste, as it may appear unto you.

DOGBERRY   It shall be suffigance.

LEONATO   Drink some wine ere you go. Fare you well!

Enter Messenger.

MESSENGER   My lord, they stay for you to give your daughter to her husband.

LEONATO   I'll wait upon them; I am ready.

Exit with Messenger.

DOGBERRY   Go, good partner, go get you to Francis Seacoal. Bid him bring his pen and inkhorn to the jail; we are now to examination these men.

VERGES   And we must do it wisely.

DOGBERRY   We will spare for no wit, I warrant you. Here's that shall drive some of them to a noncome. Only get the learned writer to set down our excommunication, and meet me at the jail.   *Exeunt.*

4.1   *Enter* DON PEDRO, DON JOHN *the bastard,* LEONATO, FRIAR Francis, CLAUDIO, BENEDICK, HERO *and* BEATRICE, *with others.*

LEONATO   Come, Friar Francis, be brief: only to the plain form of marriage, and you shall recount their particular duties afterwards.

FRIAR   You come hither, my lord, to marry this lady?

CLAUDIO   No.

LEONATO   To be married to her, Friar; you come to marry her.

FRIAR   Lady, you come hither to be married to this count?

HERO   I do.

FRIAR   If either of you know any inward impediment why you should not be conjoined, I charge you on your souls to utter it.

CLAUDIO   Know you any, Hero?

HERO   None, my lord.

FRIAR   Know you any, Count?

LEONATO   I dare make his answer: none.

CLAUDIO   O, what men dare do! What men may do! What men daily do, not knowing what they do!

BENEDICK   How now? Interjections? Why then, some be of laughing, as ha, ha, he.

CLAUDIO
Stand thee by, Friar. [*to Leonato*] Father, by your leave:
Will you with free and unconstrained soul
Give me this maid, your daughter?

LEONATO   As freely, son, as God did give her me.

CLAUDIO
And what have I to give you back whose worth
May counterpoise this rich and precious gift?

DON PEDRO   Nothing, unless you render her again.

CLAUDIO
Sweet Prince, you learn me noble thankfulness.
There, Leonato, take her back again.
Give not this rotten orange to your friend;
She's but the sign and semblance of her honour.
Behold how like a maid she blushes here!
O, what authority and show of truth
Can cunning sin cover itself withal!
Comes not that blood as modest evidence
To witness simple virtue? Would you not swear,
All you that see her, that she were a maid,
By these exterior shows? But she is none;

She knows the heat of a luxurious bed.
Her blush is guiltiness, not modesty.
LEONATO   What do you mean, my lord?
CLAUDIO   Not to be married, not to knit my soul
To an approved wanton.
LEONATO   Dear my lord, if you, in your own proof,
Have vanquished the resistance of her youth
And made defeat of her virginity –
CLAUDIO
I know what you would say: if I have known her,
You will say she did embrace me as a husband
And so extenuate the forehand sin.
No, Leonato,
I never tempted her with word too large,
But as a brother to his sister showed
Bashful sincerity and comely love.
HERO   And seemed I ever otherwise to you?
CLAUDIO   Out on thee, seeming! I will write against it:
You seem to me as Dian in her orb,
As chaste as is the bud ere it be blown;
But you are more intemperate in your blood
Than Venus, or those pampered animals
That rage in savage sensuality.
HERO   Is my lord well that he doth speak so wide?
LEONATO *[to Don Pedro]*
Sweet Prince, why speak not you?
DON PEDRO   What should I speak?
I stand dishonoured that have gone about
To link my dear friend to a common stale.
LEONATO   Are these things spoken, or do I but dream?
DON JOHN
Sir, they are spoken, and these things are true.
BENEDICK   This looks not like a nuptial.
HERO   True? O God!
CLAUDIO   Leonato, stand I here?
Is this the prince? Is this the prince's brother?
Is this face Hero's? Are our eyes our own?
LEONATO   All this is so, but what of this, my lord?
CLAUDIO
Let me but move one question to your daughter,
And by that fatherly and kindly power
That you have in her bid her answer truly.
LEONATO   I charge thee do so, as thou art my child.
HERO   O, God defend me, how am I beset!
What kind of catechizing call you this?
CLAUDIO   To make you answer truly to your name.
HERO   Is it not Hero? Who can blot that name
With any just reproach?
CLAUDIO   Marry, that can Hero;
Hero itself can blot out Hero's virtue.
What man was he talked with you yesternight
Out at your window betwixt twelve and one?
Now, if you are a maid, answer to this.
HERO   I talked with no man at that hour, my lord.
DON PEDRO   Why, then are you no maiden. Leonato,
I am sorry you must hear. Upon mine honour,
Myself, my brother and this grieved count

Did see her, hear her, at that hour last night,
Talk with a ruffian at her chamber window,
Who hath indeed, most like a liberal villain,
Confessed the vile encounters they have had
A thousand times in secret.   95
DON JOHN   Fie, fie, they are not to be named, my lord,
Not to be spoke of!
There is not chastity enough in language
Without offence to utter them. Thus, pretty lady,
I am sorry for thy much misgovernment.   100
CLAUDIO   O Hero! What a Hero hadst thou been
If half thy outward graces had been placed
About thy thoughts and counsels of thy heart!
But fare thee well, most foul, most fair. Farewell
Thou pure impiety and impious purity.   105
For thee I'll lock up all the gates of love,
And on my eyelids shall conjecture hang
To turn all beauty into thoughts of harm,
And never shall it more be gracious.
LEONATO   Hath no man's dagger here a point for me?   110
[Hero falls.]
BEATRICE
Why, how now, cousin! Wherefore sink you down?
DON JOHN
Come, let us go; these things come thus to light
Smother her spirits up.
              Exeunt Don Pedro, Claudio and Don John.
BENEDICK   How doth the lady?
BEATRICE   Dead, I think. Help, uncle!
Hero! Why Hero! Uncle, Signor Benedick, Friar!   115
LEONATO   O Fate, take not away thy heavy hand!
Death is the fairest cover for her shame
That may be wished for.
BEATRICE   How now, cousin Hero?
[Hero stirs.]
FRIAR   Have comfort, lady.
LEONATO   Dost thou look up?
FRIAR   Yea, wherefore should she not?   120
LEONATO
Wherefore? Why, doth not every earthly thing
Cry shame upon her? Could she here deny
The story that is printed in her blood?
Do not live, Hero; do not ope thine eyes!
For did I think thou wouldst not quickly die,   125
Thought I thy spirits were stronger than thy shames,
Myself would on the rearward of reproaches
Strike at thy life. Grieved I, I had but one?
Chid I for that at frugal Nature's frame?
O, one too much by thee! Why had I one?   130
Why ever wast thou lovely in my eyes?
Why had I not with charitable hand
Took up a beggar's issue at my gates,
Who smirched thus, and mired with infamy,
I might have said: 'No part of it is mine;   135
This shame derives itself from unknown loins.'
But mine, and mine I loved, and mine I praised,
And mine that I was proud on – mine so much

That I myself was to myself not mine
140 Valuing of her. Why she – O, she is fallen
Into a pit of ink that the wide sea
Hath drops too few to wash her clean again,
And salt too little which may season give
To her foul-tainted flesh.

BENEDICK   Sir, sir, be patient.
145 For my part, I am so attired in wonder
I know not what to say.

BEATRICE   O, on my soul, my cousin is belied!

BENEDICK   Lady, were you her bedfellow last night?

BEATRICE   No, truly, not – although until last night
150 I have this twelvemonth been her bedfellow.

LEONATO
Confirmed, confirmed! O, that is stronger made
Which was before barred up with ribs of iron.
Would the two princes lie, and Claudio lie
Who loved her so, that speaking of her foulness
155 Washed it with tears? Hence from her, let her die.

FRIAR   Hear me a little:
For I have only been silent so long,
And given way unto this course of fortune,
By noting of the lady. I have marked
160 A thousand blushing apparitions
To start into her face, a thousand innocent shames
In angel whiteness beat away those blushes;
And in her eye there hath appeared a fire
To burn the errors that these princes hold
165 Against her maiden truth. Call me a fool,
Trust not my reading nor my observations,
Which with experimental seal doth warrant
The tenor of my book; trust not my age,
My reverence, calling nor divinity,
170 If this sweet lady lie not guiltless here
Under some biting error.

LEONATO   Friar, it cannot be.
Thou seest that all the grace that she hath left
Is that she will not add to her damnation
A sin of perjury. She not denies it.
175 Why seek'st thou then to cover with excuse
That which appears in proper nakedness?

FRIAR   Lady, what man is he you are accused of?

HERO   They know that do accuse me. I know none.
If I know more of any man alive
180 Than that which maiden modesty doth warrant,
Let all my sins lack mercy! – O my father,
Prove you that any man with me conversed
At hours unmeet, or that I yesternight
Maintained the change of words with any creature,
185 Refuse me, hate me, torture me to death!

FRIAR
There is some strange misprision in the princes.

BENEDICK   Two of them have the very bent of honour.
And if their wisdoms be misled in this,
The practice of it lives in John the bastard,
190 Whose spirits toil in frame of villainies.

LEONATO   I know not. If they speak but truth of her,

These hands shall tear her; if they wrong her honour,
The proudest of them shall well hear of it.
Time hath not yet so dried this blood of mine,
Nor age so eat up my invention,   195
Nor fortune made such havoc of my means,
Nor my bad life reft me so much of friends
But they shall find awaked in such a kind
Both strength of limb and policy of mind,
Ability in means and choice of friends   200
To quit me of them throughly.

FRIAR   Pause awhile,
And let my counsel sway you in this case.
Your daughter here the princes left for dead.
Let her awhile be secretly kept in,
And publish it that she is dead indeed.   205
Maintain a mourning ostentation,
And on your family's old monument
Hang mournful epitaphs, and do all rites
That appertain unto a burial.

LEONATO
What shall become of this? What will this do?   210

FRIAR   Marry, this well carried shall on her behalf
Change slander to remorse; that is some good.
But not for that dream I on this strange course,
But on this travail look for greater birth:
She, dying, as it must be so maintained,   215
Upon the instant that she was accused,
Shall be lamented, pitied and excused
Of every hearer. For it so falls out
That what we have we prize not to the worth
Whiles we enjoy it, but being lacked and lost,   220
Why, then we rack the value, then we find
The virtue that possession would not show us
Whiles it was ours. So will it fare with Claudio:
When he shall hear she died upon his words,
Th'idea of her life shall sweetly creep   225
Into his study of imagination,
And every lovely organ of her life
Shall come apparelled in more precious habit,
More moving, delicate and full of life,
Into the eye and prospect of his soul   230
Than when she lived indeed. Then shall he mourn –
If ever love had interest in his liver –
And wish he had not so accused her;
No, though he thought his accusation true.
Let this be so, and doubt not but success   235
Will fashion the event in better shape
Than I can lay it down in likelihood.
But if all aim but this be levelled false,
The supposition of the lady's death
Will quench the wonder of her infamy.   240
And if it sort not well, you may conceal her,
As best befits her wounded reputation,
In some reclusive and religious life,
Out of all eyes, tongues, minds and injuries.

BENEDICK   Signor Leonato, let the friar advise you,   245
And though you know my inwardness and love

Is very much unto the prince and Claudio,
Yet, by mine honour, I will deal in this
As secretly and justly as your soul
Should with your body.

250 LEONATO   Being that I flow in grief,
The smallest twine may lead me.

FRIAR
'Tis well consented. Presently away,
For to strange sores strangely they strain the cure.
Come, lady, die to live. This wedding day
255 Perhaps is but prolonged. Have patience and endure.
        Exeunt all but Beatrice and Benedick.

BENEDICK   Lady Beatrice, have you wept all this while?
BEATRICE   Yea, and I will weep awhile longer.
BENEDICK   I will not desire that.
BEATRICE   You have no reason; I do it freely.
260 BENEDICK   Surely I do believe your fair cousin is wronged.
BEATRICE   Ah, how much might the man deserve of me
that would right her!
BENEDICK   Is there any way to show such friendship?
BEATRICE   A very even way, but no such friend.
265 BENEDICK   May a man do it?
BEATRICE   It is a man's office, but not yours.
BENEDICK   I do love nothing in the world so well as you.
Is not that strange?
BEATRICE   As strange as the thing I know not. It were as
270 possible for me to say I loved nothing so well as you.
But believe me not – and yet I lie not. I confess
nothing, nor I deny nothing. I am sorry for my cousin.
BENEDICK   By my sword, Beatrice, thou lovest me.
BEATRICE   Do not swear and eat it.
275 BENEDICK   I will swear by it that you love me, and I will
make him eat it that says I love not you.
BEATRICE   Will you not eat your word?
BENEDICK   With no sauce that can be devised to it. I
protest I love thee.
280 BEATRICE   Why then, God forgive me.
BENEDICK   What offence, sweet Beatrice?
BEATRICE   You have stayed me in a happy hour; I was
about to protest I loved you.
BENEDICK   And do it, with all thy heart.
285 BEATRICE   I love you with so much of my heart that
none is left to protest.
BENEDICK   Come, bid me do anything for thee.
BEATRICE   Kill Claudio.
BENEDICK   Ha, not for the wide world.
290 BEATRICE   You kill me to deny it. Farewell. [*Moves as if
to leave.*]
BENEDICK   Tarry, sweet Beatrice. [*Stays her.*]
BEATRICE   I am gone, though I am here. There is no
love in you; nay, I pray you, let me go.
BENEDICK   Beatrice –
295 BEATRICE   In faith, I will go.
BENEDICK   We'll be friends first.
BEATRICE   You dare easier be friends with me than fight
with mine enemy.
BENEDICK   Is Claudio thine enemy?

BEATRICE   Is 'a not approved in the height a villain, that   300
hath slandered, scorned, dishonoured my kinswoman?
O, that I were a man! What, bear her in hand until they
come to take hands, and then with public accusation,
uncovered slander, unmitigated rancour? O God,
that I were a man! I would eat his heart in the   305
marketplace.
BENEDICK   Hear me, Beatrice –
BEATRICE   Talk with a man out at a window! A proper
saying!
BENEDICK   Nay, but Beatrice –   310
BEATRICE   Sweet Hero! She is wronged, she is
slandered, she is undone.
BENEDICK   Beat –
BEATRICE   Princes and counties! Surely a princely
testimony, a goodly count! Count Comfit, a sweet   315
gallant surely. O that I were a man for his sake! Or
that I had any friend would be a man for my sake!
But manhood is melted into curtsies, valour into
compliment, and men are only turned into tongue, and
trim ones, too. He is now as valiant as Hercules that   320
only tells a lie and swears it. I cannot be a man with
wishing, therefore I will die a woman with grieving.
BENEDICK   Tarry, good Beatrice. By this hand, I love thee.
BEATRICE   Use it for my love some other way than
swearing by it.   325
BENEDICK   Think you in your soul the Count Claudio
hath wronged Hero?
BEATRICE   Yea, as sure as I have a thought or a soul.
BENEDICK   Enough, I am engaged. I will challenge him.
I will kiss your hand, and so I leave you. By this hand,   330
Claudio shall render me a dear account. As you hear of
me, so think of me. Go comfort your cousin. I must say
she is dead, and so farewell.

        Exeunt by different doors.

4.2   *Enter the constables,* DOGBERRY *and*
        VERGES, *and the* Sexton *as town clerk, in gowns,*
        with the Watch, BORACHIO *and* CONRADE.

DOGBERRY   Is our whole dissembly appeared?
VERGES   O, a stool and a cushion for the sexton.
SEXTON [*Sits.*]   Which be the malefactors?
DOGBERRY   Marry, that am I, and my partner.
VERGES   Nay, that's certain; we have the exhibition to   5
examine.
SEXTON   But which are the offenders that are to be
examined? [*to Dogberry*] Let them come before, master
constable.
DOGBERRY   Yea, marry, let them come before me.   10
[*Watch lead Borachio and Conrade forward, then step back.*]
[*to Borachio*] What is your name, friend?
BORACHIO   Borachio.
DOGBERRY [*to the Sexton*]   Pray write down 'Borachio'.
[*to Conrade*] Yours, sirrah?
CONRADE   I am a gentleman, sir, and my name is   15
Conrade.

DOGBERRY   Write down 'master gentleman Conrade'.
Masters, do you serve God?

CONRADE, BORACHIO   Yea, sir, we hope.

20   DOGBERRY   Write down, that they hope they serve
God; and write God first, for God defend but God
should go before such villains. Masters, it is proved
already that you are little better than false knaves, and
it will go near to be thought so shortly. How answer

25   you for yourselves?

CONRADE   Marry, sir, we say we are none.

DOGBERRY   A marvellous witty fellow, I assure you. But
I will go a bout with him. [*to Borachio*] Come you
hither, sirrah. A word in your ear. Sir, I say to you, it is

30   thought you are false knaves.

BORACHIO   Sir, I say to you, we are none.

DOGBERRY   Well, stand aside. 'Fore God, they are both
in a tale. [*to the Sexton*] Have you writ down, that they
are none?

35   SEXTON   Master constable, you go not the way to
examine. You must call forth the watch that are their
accusers.

DOGBERRY   Yea, marry, that's the eftest way. Let the
watch come forth. [*Watch come forward.*] Masters, I

40   charge you in the prince's name, accuse these men.

1 WATCHMAN [*Indicates Borachio.*]   This man said, sir,
that Don John the prince's brother was a villain.

DOGBERRY   Write down 'Prince John a villain'. Why,
this is flat perjury, to call a prince's brother villain!

45   BORACHIO   Master constable –

DOGBERRY   Pray thee, fellow, peace! I do not like thy
look, I promise thee.

SEXTON   What heard you him say else?

2 WATCHMAN   Marry, that he had received a thousand

50   ducats of Don John for accusing the Lady Hero
wrongfully.

DOGBERRY   Flat burglary as ever was committed!

VERGES   Yea, by mass, that it is.

SEXTON   What else, fellow?

55   1 WATCHMAN   And that Count Claudio did mean, upon
his words, to disgrace Hero before the whole assembly,
and not marry her.

DOGBERRY   O villain! Thou wilt be condemned into
everlasting redemption for this.

60   SEXTON   What else?

WATCH   This is all.

SEXTON   And this is more, masters, than you can deny.
Prince John is this morning secretly stolen away; Hero
was in this manner accused, in this very manner

65   refused and, upon the grief of this, suddenly died.
Master constable, let these men be bound and brought
to Leonato's. I will go before and show him their
examination.   *Exit.*

DOGBERRY   Come, let them be opinioned.

70   VERGES   Let them be in the hands – [*Watch move to bind
them.*]

CONRADE   Off, coxcomb!

DOGBERRY   God's my life, where's the sexton? Let him
write down the prince's officer coxcomb! Come, bind
them. [*to Conrade, who resists*] Thou naughty varlet!

CONRADE   Away! You are an ass, you are an ass!   75

DOGBERRY   Dost thou not suspect my place? Dost thou
not suspect my years? O, that he were here to write me
down an ass! But masters, remember that I am an ass;
though it be not written down, yet forget not that I am
an ass. No, thou villain, thou art full of piety, as shall be   80
proved upon thee by good witness. I am a wise fellow,
and which is more, an officer, and which is more, a
householder, and which is more, as pretty a piece of
flesh as any is in Messina, and one that knows the law
– go to! – and a rich fellow enough – go to! – and a   85
fellow that hath had losses, and one that hath two
gowns, and everything handsome about him. – Bring
him away. – O, that I had been writ down an ass!

Exeunt.

5.1   *Enter* LEONATO *and his brother* ANTONIO.

ANTONIO   If you go on thus you will kill yourself,
And 'tis not wisdom thus to second grief
Against yourself.

LEONATO   I pray thee cease thy counsel,
Which falls into mine ears as profitless
As water in a sieve. Give not me counsel,   5
Nor let no comforter delight mine ear
But such a one whose wrongs do suit with mine.
Bring me a father that so loved his child,
Whose joy of her is overwhelmed like mine,
And bid him speak of patience.   10
Measure his woe the length and breadth of mine,
And let it answer every strain for strain,
As thus for thus, and such a grief for such,
In every lineament, branch, shape and form.
If such a one will smile, and stroke his beard   15
And sorrow; wag, cry 'hem', when he should groan,
Patch grief with proverbs, make misfortune drunk
With candle-wasters, bring him yet to me,
And I of him will gather patience.
But there is no such man. For, brother, men   20
Can counsel and speak comfort to that grief
Which they themselves not feel. But tasting it,
Their counsel turns to passion which before
Would give preceptial medicine to rage,
Fetter strong madness in a silken thread,   25
Charm ache with air and agony with words.
No, no, 'tis all men's office to speak patience
To those that wring under the load of sorrow,
But no man's virtue nor sufficiency
To be so moral when he shall endure   30
The like himself. Therefore give me no counsel;
My griefs cry louder than advertisement.

ANTONIO
Therein do men from children nothing differ.

LEONATO   I pray thee peace; I will be flesh and blood.
For there was never yet philosopher   35

That could endure the toothache patiently,
However they have writ the style of gods
And made a push at chance and sufferance.

ANTONIO
Yet bend not all the harm upon yourself;
40 Make those that do offend you suffer too.

LEONATO
There thou speak'st reason. Nay, I will do so:
My soul doth tell me Hero is belied,
And that shall Claudio know, so shall the prince
And all of them that thus dishonour her.

Enter DON PEDRO *and* CLAUDIO.

45 ANTONIO Here comes the prince and Claudio hastily.
DON PEDRO Good e'en, good e'en.
CLAUDIO   Good day to both of you.
LEONATO Hear you, my lords?
DON PEDRO   We have some haste, Leonato.
LEONATO
Some haste, my lord! Well, fare you well, my lord.
Are you so hasty now? Well, all is one.

DON PEDRO
50 Nay, do not quarrel with us, good old man.
ANTONIO If he could right himself with quarrelling,
Some of us would lie low.
CLAUDIO   Who wrongs him?

LEONATO
Marry, thou dost wrong me, thou dissembler, thou!
Nay, never lay thy hand upon thy sword;
I fear thee not.

55 CLAUDIO   Marry, beshrew my hand
If it should give your age such cause of fear.
In faith, my hand meant nothing to my sword.

LEONATO
Tush, tush, man, never fleer and jest at me!
I speak not like a dotard nor a fool,
60 As under privilege of age to brag
What I have done being young, or what would do
Were I not old. Know, Claudio, to thy head,
Thou hast so wronged mine innocent child and me
That I am forced to lay my reverence by,
65 And with grey hairs and bruise of many days
Do challenge thee to trial of a man.
I say thou hast belied mine innocent child.
Thy slander hath gone through and through her
    heart,
And she lies buried with her ancestors –
70 O, in a tomb where never scandal slept,
Save this of hers, framed by thy villainy.
CLAUDIO My villainy?
LEONATO   Thine, Claudio; thine, I say.
DON PEDRO You say not right, old man.
LEONATO   My lord, my lord,
I'll prove it on his body, if he dare,
75 Despite his nice fence and his active practice,
His May of youth and bloom of lustihood.
CLAUDIO Away! I will not have to do with you.

LEONATO
Canst thou so doff me? Thou hast killed my child;
If thou kill'st me, boy, thou shalt kill a man.

ANTONIO He shall kill two of us, and men indeed. 80
But that's no matter, let him kill one first.
Win me and wear me! Let him answer me.
Come, follow me, boy. Come, sir boy, come, follow me,
Sir boy! I'll whip you from your foining fence!
Nay, as I am a gentleman, I will. 85
LEONATO Brother –

ANTONIO
Content yourself. God knows, I loved my niece,
And she is dead, slandered to death by villains
That dare as well answer a man indeed
As I dare take a serpent by the tongue. 90
Boys, apes, braggarts, jacks, milksops!
LEONATO   Brother Anthony –

ANTONIO
Hold you content. What, man? I know them, yea,
And what they weigh, even to the utmost scruple.
Scambling, outfacing, fashion-monging boys,
That lie, and cog, and flout, deprave and slander, 95
Go anticly and show outward hideousness,
And speak off half a dozen dangerous words
How they might hurt their enemies, if they durst –
And this is all.
LEONATO But brother Anthony –
ANTONIO   Come, 'tis no matter. 100
Do not you meddle; let me deal in this.

DON PEDRO
Gentlemen both, we will not wake your patience.
My heart is sorry for your daughter's death,
But on my honour she was charged with nothing
But what was true and very full of proof. 105
LEONATO My lord, my lord –
DON PEDRO   I will not hear you.
LEONATO   No?
– Come, brother, away. I will be heard.
ANTONIO And shall, or some of us will smart for it.

Exeunt Leonato and Antonio.

Enter BENEDICK.

DON PEDRO See, see: here comes the man we went to
seek. 110
CLAUDIO Now, signor, what news?
BENEDICK [*to Don Pedro*] Good day, my lord.
DON PEDRO Welcome, signor. You are almost come to
part almost a fray.
CLAUDIO We had liked to have had our two noses 115
snapped off with two old men without teeth.
DON PEDRO Leonato and his brother. What think'st
thou? Had we fought, I doubt we should have been too
young for them.
BENEDICK In a false quarrel there is no true valour. I 120
came to seek you both.
CLAUDIO We have been up and down to seek thee, for
we are high-proof melancholy and would fain have it

BENEDICK   It is in my scabbard. Shall I draw it?

DON PEDRO   Dost thou wear thy wit by thy side?

CLAUDIO   Never any did so, though very many have
been beside their wit. I will bid thee draw as we do the
minstrels – draw to pleasure us.

DON PEDRO   As I am an honest man, he looks pale. Art
thou sick, or angry?

CLAUDIO   What, courage, man! What though care killed
a cat, thou hast mettle enough in thee to kill care.

BENEDICK   Sir, I shall meet your wit in the career an
you charge it against me. I pray you choose another
subject.

CLAUDIO   Nay, then, give him another staff; this last was
broke cross.

DON PEDRO   By this light, he changes more and more.
I think he be angry indeed.

CLAUDIO   If he be, he knows how to turn his girdle.

BENEDICK   Shall I speak a word in your ear?

CLAUDIO   God bless me from a challenge.

BENEDICK [*aside to Claudio*]   You are a villain. I jest not.
I will make it good how you dare, with what you dare
and when you dare. Do me right, or I will protest your
cowardice. You have killed a sweet lady, and her death
shall fall heavy on you. Let me hear from you.

CLAUDIO   Well, I will meet you, so I may have good
cheer.

DON PEDRO   What, a feast, a feast?

CLAUDIO   I'faith, I thank him, he hath bid me to a calf's
head and a capon, the which if I do not carve most
curiously, say my knife's naught. Shall I not find a
woodcock too?

BENEDICK   Sir, your wit ambles well; it goes easily.

DON PEDRO   I'll tell thee how Beatrice praised thy wit
the other day. I said thou hadst a fine wit. 'True,' said
she, 'a fine little one.' 'No,' said I, 'a great wit.' 'Right,'
says she, 'a great gross one.' 'Nay,' said I, 'a good wit.'
'Just,' said she, 'it hurts nobody.' 'Nay,' said I, 'the
gentleman is wise.' 'Certain,' said she, 'a wise
gentleman.' 'Nay,' said I, 'he hath the tongues.' 'That
I believe,' said she, 'for he swore a thing to me on
Monday night, which he forswore on Tuesday
morning. There's a double tongue; there's two
tongues.' Thus did she an hour together trans-shape
thy particular virtues. Yet at last she concluded, with a
sigh, thou wast the properest man in Italy.

CLAUDIO   For the which she wept heartily and said she
cared not.

DON PEDRO   Yea, that she did, but yet for all that, an if
she did not hate him deadly, she would love him dearly.
The old man's daughter told us all.

CLAUDIO   All, all. And moreover, God saw him when he
was hid in the garden.

DON PEDRO   But when shall we set the savage bull's
horns on the sensible Benedick's head?

CLAUDIO   Yea, and text underneath: 'Here dwells
Benedick the married man.'

BENEDICK   Fare you well. Boy, you know my mind. I
will leave you now to your gossip-like humour. You
break jests as braggarts do their blades, which, God be
thanked, hurt not. My lord, for your many courtesies,
I thank you. I must discontinue your company. Your
brother the bastard is fled from Messina; you have
among you killed a sweet and innocent lady. For my
Lord Lack-beard there, he and I shall meet, and till
then peace be with him.   *Exit.*

DON PEDRO   He is in earnest.

CLAUDIO   In most profound earnest. And, I'll warrant
you, for the love of Beatrice.

DON PEDRO   And hath challenged thee?

CLAUDIO   Most sincerely.

DON PEDRO   What a pretty thing man is when he goes
in his doublet and hose, and leaves off his wit!

CLAUDIO   He is then a giant to an ape; but then is an ape
a doctor to such a man.

DON PEDRO   But soft you, let me be. Pluck up, my
heart, and be sad – did he not say my brother was
fled?

Enter Constables DOGBERRY *and* VERGES, *with the*
Watch, CONRADE *and* BORACHIO.

DOGBERRY   Come you, sir. If justice cannot tame you,
she shall ne'er weigh more reasons in her balance.
Nay, an you be a cursing hypocrite once, you must be
looked to.

DON PEDRO   How now? Two of my brother's men
bound? Borachio one.

CLAUDIO   Hearken after their offence, my lord.

DON PEDRO   Officers, what offence have these men
done?

DOGBERRY   Marry, sir, they have committed false
report. Moreover they have spoken untruths,
secondarily they are slanders, sixth and lastly, they
have belied a lady, thirdly they have verified unjust
things, and, to conclude, they are lying knaves.

DON PEDRO   First I ask thee what they have done,
thirdly I ask thee what's their offence, sixth and lastly
why they are committed, and, to conclude, what you
lay to their charge?

CLAUDIO   Rightly reasoned and in his own division;
and, by my troth, there's one meaning well suited.

DON PEDRO   Who have you offended, masters, that you
are thus bound to your answer? This learned constable
is too cunning to be understood. What's your offence?

BORACHIO   Sweet Prince, let me go no farther to mine
answer. Do you hear me, and let this count kill me. I
have deceived even your very eyes. What your wisdoms
could not discover, these shallow fools have brought to
light, who in the night overheard me confessing to this
man how Don John your brother incensed me to
slander the lady Hero; how you were brought into the
orchard and saw me court Margaret in Hero's
garments; how you disgraced her when you should
marry her. My villainy they have upon record, which I

had rather seal with my death than repeat over to my
shame. The lady is dead upon mine and my master's
false accusation, and, briefly, I desire nothing but the
reward of a villain.

DON PEDRO
Runs not this speech like iron through your blood?

CLAUDIO   I have drunk poison whiles he uttered it.

DON PEDRO   But did my brother set thee on to this?

BORACHIO
Yea, and paid me richly for the practice of it.

DON PEDRO   He is composed and framed of treachery,
And fled he is upon this villainy.

CLAUDIO   Sweet Hero! Now thy image doth appear
In the rare semblance that I loved it first.

DOGBERRY   Come, bring away the plaintiffs. By this
time our sexton hath reformed Signor Leonato of the
matter. And masters, do not forget to specify, when
time and place shall serve, that I am an ass.

VERGES   Here, here comes master Signor Leonato, and
the sexton too.

Enter LEONATO, *his brother*
ANTONIO *and the* Sexton.

LEONATO   Which is the villain? Let me see his eyes,
That when I note another man like him
I may avoid him. Which of these is he?

BORACHIO
If you would know your wronger, look on me.

LEONATO
Art thou the slave that with thy breath hast killed
Mine innocent child?

BORACHIO   Yea, even I alone.

LEONATO   No, not so, villain, thou beliest thyself.
Here stand a pair of honourable men;
A third is fled that had a hand in it.
I thank you, princes, for my daughter's death;
Record it with your high and worthy deeds.
'Twas bravely done, if you bethink you of it.

CLAUDIO   I know not how to pray your patience.
Yet I must speak. Choose your revenge yourself.
Impose me to what penance your invention
Can lay upon my sin. Yet sinned I not
But in mistaking.

DON PEDRO   By my soul, nor I.
And yet to satisfy this good old man
I would bend under any heavy weight
That he'll enjoin me to.

LEONATO   I cannot bid you bid my daughter live –
That were impossible. But I pray you both,
Possess the people in Messina here
How innocent she died. [*to Claudio*] And if your
    love
Can labour aught in sad invention,
Hang her an epitaph upon her tomb
And sing it to her bones. Sing it tonight.
Tomorrow morning come you to my house,
And since you could not be my son-in-law,

Be yet my nephew. My brother hath a daughter,
Almost the copy of my child that's dead,
And she alone is heir to both of us.
Give her the right you should have given her cousin,
And so dies my revenge.

CLAUDIO   O noble sir!
Your over-kindness doth wring tears from me.
I do embrace your offer, and dispose
For henceforth of poor Claudio.

LEONATO   Tomorrow, then, I will expect your coming;
Tonight I take my leave. This naughty man
Shall face to face be brought to Margaret,
Who I believe was packed in all this wrong,
Hired to it by your brother.

BORACHIO   No, by my soul she was not,
Nor knew not what she did when she spoke to me,
But always hath been just and virtuous
In anything that I do know by her.

DOGBERRY   Moreover, sir, which indeed is not under
white and black, this plaintiff here, the offender, did
call me ass. I beseech you let it be remembered in his
punishment. And also the watch heard them talk of
one Deformed; they say he wears a key in his ear and a
lock hanging by it, and borrows money in God's
name, the which he hath used so long, and never
paid, that now men grow hard-hearted and will lend
nothing for God's sake. Pray you examine him upon
that point.

LEONATO   I thank thee for thy care and honest pains.

DOGBERRY   Your worship speaks like a most thankful
and reverent youth, and I praise God for you.

LEONATO [*Gives him money.*]   There's for thy pains.

DOGBERRY   God save the foundation!

LEONATO   Go, I discharge thee of thy prisoner, and I
thank thee.

DOGBERRY   I leave an arrant knave with your worship,
which I beseech your worship to correct yourself, for
the example of others. God keep your worship! I wish
your worship well! God restore you to health! I humbly
give you leave to depart, and if a merry meeting may
be wished, God prohibit it! Come, neighbour.

                    Exeunt Dogberry and Verges.

LEONATO   Until tomorrow morning, lords, farewell.

ANTONIO
Farewell, my lords. We look for you tomorrow.

DON PEDRO   We will not fail.

CLAUDIO   Tonight I'll mourn with Hero.

LEONATO [*to the Watch*]
Bring you these fellows on. We'll talk with Margaret,
How her acquaintance grew with this lewd fellow.

                    Exeunt.

5.2   *Enter* BENEDICK *and* MARGARET.

BENEDICK   Pray thee, sweet mistress Margaret, deserve
well at my hands by helping me to the speech of
Beatrice.

235

240

245

250

255

60

65

70

75

80

285

290

295

300

305

310

315

320

325

MARGARET   Will you then write me a sonnet in praise of
5   my beauty?

BENEDICK   In so high a style, Margaret, that no man
living shall come over it; for in most comely truth thou
deservest it.

MARGARET   To have no man come over me? Why, shall
10   I always keep below stairs?

BENEDICK   Thy wit is as quick as the greyhound's
mouth, it catches.

MARGARET   And yours as blunt as the fencer's foils,
which hit, but hurt not.

15 BENEDICK   A most manly wit, Margaret, it will not hurt
a woman. And so, I pray thee, call Beatrice. I give thee
the bucklers.

MARGARET   Give us the swords; we have bucklers of
our own.

20 BENEDICK   If you use them, Margaret, you must put in
the pikes with a vice, and they are dangerous weapons
for maids.

MARGARET   Well, I will call Beatrice to you, who I think
hath legs.   *Exit.*

25 BENEDICK   And therefore will come.

    [*Sings.*]   The God of love
               That sits above,
      And knows me, and knows me,
         How pitiful I deserve –

30 I mean in singing; but in loving, Leander the good
swimmer, Troilus the first employer of pandars and a
whole bookful of these quondam carpet-mongers,
whose names yet run smoothly in the even road of a
blank verse, why, they were never so truly turned over
35 and over as my poor self in love. Marry, I cannot show it
in rhyme. I have tried; I can find out no rhyme to 'lady'
but 'baby' – an innocent rhyme; for 'scorn', 'horn' – a
hard rhyme; for 'school', 'fool', a babbling rhyme: very
ominous endings. No, I was not born under a rhyming
40 planet nor I cannot woo in festival terms.

               Enter BEATRICE.

Sweet Beatrice, wouldst thou come when I called
thee?

BEATRICE   Yea, signor, and depart when you bid me.

BENEDICK   O, stay but till then.

45 BEATRICE   'Then' is spoken; fare you well now. And yet,
ere I go, let me go with that I came for, which is, with
knowing what hath passed between you and Claudio.

BENEDICK   Only foul words – and thereupon I will kiss
thee.

50 BEATRICE   Foul words is but foul wind, and foul wind is
but foul breath, and foul breath is noisome, therefore I
will depart unkissed.

BENEDICK   Thou hast frighted the word out of his right
sense, so forcible is thy wit. But I must tell thee plainly:
55 Claudio undergoes my challenge, and either I must
shortly hear from him, or I will subscribe him a
coward. And I pray thee now tell me, for which of my
bad parts didst thou first fall in love with me?

BEATRICE   For them all together, which maintained so
60 politic a state of evil that they will not admit any good
part to intermingle with them. But for which of my
good parts did you first suffer love for me?

BENEDICK   'Suffer love'! A good epithet. I do suffer love
indeed, for I love thee against my will.

65 BEATRICE   In spite of your heart, I think. Alas, poor
heart! If you spite it for my sake, I will spite it for
yours, for I will never love that which my friend hates.

BENEDICK   Thou and I are too wise to woo peaceably.

BEATRICE   It appears not in this confession: there's not
70 one wise man among twenty that will praise himself.

BENEDICK   An old, an old instance, Beatrice, that lived
in the time of good neighbours. If a man do not erect
in this age his own tomb ere he dies, he shall live no
longer in monument than the bell rings and the widow
75 weeps.

BEATRICE   And how long is that, think you?

BENEDICK   Question: why, an hour in clamour and a
quarter in rheum. Therefore is it most expedient for
the wise, if Don Worm – his conscience – find no
80 impediment to the contrary, to be the trumpet of his
own virtues, as I am to myself. So much for praising
myself, who I myself will bear witness is praiseworthy.
And now tell me, how doth your cousin?

BEATRICE   Very ill.

85 BENEDICK   And how do you?

BEATRICE   Very ill too.

BENEDICK   Serve God, love me and mend. There will I
leave you too, for here comes one in haste.

               Enter URSULA.

URSULA   Madam, you must come to your uncle.
90 Yonder's old coil at home. It is proved my lady Hero
hath been falsely accused, the prince and Claudio
mightily abused, and Don John is the author of all,
who is fled and gone. Will you come presently?

BEATRICE   Will you go hear this news, signor?

95 BENEDICK   I will live in thy heart, die in thy lap, and be
buried in thy eyes – and moreover, I will go with thee
to thy uncle's.   *Exeunt.*

5.3   *Enter* CLAUDIO, DON PEDRO, *and three*
         or four Attendants, including a Lord *and*
            Musicians, *with tapers.*

CLAUDIO   Is this the monument of Leonato?

LORD   It is, my lord. [*Reads the epitaph.*]
       Done to death by slanderous tongues
        Was the Hero that here lies;
       Death, in guerdon of her wrongs,
5   *Gives her fame which never dies;*
         So the life that died with shame,
         Lives in death with glorious fame.
    [*Hangs scroll.*]
         Hang thou there upon the tomb,
         Praising her when I am dumb.
10

CLAUDIO
Now music sound, and sing your solemn hymn.

[*Music*]

ONE OR MORE SINGERS [*Sing.*]
　　　Pardon, goddess of the night,
　　　Those that slew thy virgin knight,
　　　　For the which with songs of woe
　　　　Round about her tomb they go.
　　　Midnight, assist our moan,
　　　Help us to sigh and groan,
　　　　Heavily, heavily,
　　　Graves yawn and yield your dead,
　　　Till death be uttered,
　　　　Heavily, heavily.

LORD　　Now unto thy bones good night;
Yearly will I do this rite.

DON PEDRO
Good morrow, masters. Put your torches out.
The wolves have preyed, and look, the gentle day,
Before the wheels of Phoebus, round about
Dapples the drowsy east with spots of grey.
Thanks to you all, and leave us. Fare you well.

CLAUDIO　　Good morrow, masters; each his several way.

DON PEDRO
Come, let us hence and put on other weeds,
And then to Leonato's we will go.

CLAUDIO　　And Hymen now with luckier issue speed's
Than this for whom we rendered up this woe.

Exeunt.

5.4　　*Enter* LEONATO, BENEDICK, MARGARET,
　　　　URSULA, ANTONIO, FRIAR Francis, HERO
　　　　and BEATRICE.

FRIAR　　Did I not tell you she was innocent?

LEONATO
So are the prince and Claudio who accused her,
Upon the error that you heard debated.
But Margaret was in some fault for this,
Although against her will, as it appears
In the true course of all the question.

ANTONIO　　Well, I am glad that all things sorts so well.

BENEDICK　　And so am I, being else by faith enforced
To call young Claudio to a reckoning for it.

LEONATO　　Well, daughter, and you gentlewomen all,
Withdraw into a chamber by yourselves,
And when I send for you, come hither masked.
The prince and Claudio promised by this hour
To visit me. You know your office, brother:
You must be father to your brother's daughter
And give her to young Claudio.　　*Exeunt Ladies.*

ANTONIO　　Which I will do with confirmed countenance.

BENEDICK　　Friar, I must entreat your pains, I think.

FRIAR　　To do what, signor?

BENEDICK　　To bind me, or undo me, one of them.
Signor Leonato – truth it is, good signor,
Your niece regards me with an eye of favour.

LEONATO
That eye my daughter lent her? 'Tis most true.

BENEDICK　　And I do with an eye of love requite her.

LEONATO　　The sight whereof I think you had from me, 25
From Claudio and the prince. But what's your will?

BENEDICK　　Your answer, sir, is enigmatical.
But for my will, my will is your good will
May stand with ours this day to be conjoined
In the estate of honourable marriage; 30
In which, good Friar, I shall desire your help.

LEONATO　　My heart is with your liking.

FRIAR　　　　　　　　　　　　And my help.
Here comes the prince and Claudio.

Enter DON PEDRO *and* CLAUDIO, *with Attendants.*

DON PEDRO　　Good morrow to this fair assembly.

LEONATO
Good morrow, Prince, good morrow, Claudio. 35
We here attend you. Are you yet determined
Today to marry with my brother's daughter?

CLAUDIO　　I'll hold my mind were she an Ethiope.

LEONATO
Call her forth, brother. Here's the friar ready.

Exit Antonio.

DON PEDRO
Good morrow, Benedick. Why, what's the matter 40
That you have such a February face,
So full of frost, of storm and cloudiness?

CLAUDIO　　I think he thinks upon the savage bull.
Tush, fear not, man: we'll tip thy horns with gold,
And all Europa shall rejoice at thee, 45
As once Europa did at lusty Jove
When he would play the noble beast in love.

BENEDICK　　Bull Jove, sir, had an amiable low,
And some such strange bull leaped your father's cow
And got a calf in that same noble feat 50
Much like to you, for you have just his bleat.

Enter ANTONIO, HERO, BEATRICE, MARGARET
and URSULA, *the women masked.*

CLAUDIO
For this I owe you. Here comes other reckonings.
Which is the lady I must seize upon?

[*Antonio leads Hero forward.*]

LEONATO　　This same is she, and I do give you her.

CLAUDIO
Why then she's mine. [*to Hero*] Sweet, let me see your
　　face. 55

LEONATO　　No, that you shall not till you take her hand
Before this friar and swear to marry her.

CLAUDIO　　Give me your hand before this holy friar.
I am your husband, if you like of me.

HERO [*Unmasks.*]
And when I lived I was your other wife; 60
And when you loved, you were my other husband.

CLAUDIO　　Another Hero!

HERO　　　　　　　　Nothing certainer.

One Hero died defiled, but I do live,
And surely as I live, I am a maid.
65 DON PEDRO   The former Hero! Hero that is dead!
LEONATO
   She died, my lord, but whiles her slander lived.
FRIAR   All this amazement can I qualify,
   When after that the holy rites are ended,
   I'll tell you largely of fair Hero's death.
70 Meantime, let wonder seem familiar,
   And to the chapel let us presently.
BENEDICK
   Soft and fair, Friar. [*to Antonio*] Which is Beatrice?
BEATRICE [*Unmasks.*]
   I answer to that name. What is your will?
BENEDICK   Do not you love me?
BEATRICE   Why no, no more than reason.
BENEDICK
75 Why then your uncle and the prince and Claudio
   Have been deceived – they swore you did.
BEATRICE   Do not you love me?
BENEDICK   Troth no, no more than reason.
BEATRICE
   Why then my cousin, Margaret and Ursula
   Are much deceived, for they did swear you did.
BENEDICK
80 They swore that you were almost sick for me.
BEATRICE
   They swore that you were well-nigh dead for me.
BENEDICK
   'Tis no such matter. Then you do not love me?
BEATRICE   No truly, but in friendly recompense.
LEONATO
   Come, cousin, I am sure you love the gentleman.
85 CLAUDIO   And I'll be sworn upon't that he loves her,
   For here's a paper written in his hand,
   A halting sonnet of his own pure brain
   Fashioned to Beatrice.
HERO   And here's another,
   Writ in my cousin's hand, stolen from her pocket,
90 Containing her affection unto Benedick.
BENEDICK   A miracle! Here's our own hands against

our hearts. Come, I will have thee, but by this light I
take thee for pity.
BEATRICE   I would not deny you, but by this good day I
   yield upon great persuasion – and partly to save your   95
   life, for I was told you were in a consumption.
LEONATO   Peace! [*to Beatrice*] I will stop your mouth.
   [*Hands her to Benedick.*]
DON PEDRO
   How dost thou, Benedick, the married man?
BENEDICK   I'll tell thee what, Prince; a college of wit-
   crackers cannot flout me out of my humour. Dost thou   100
   think I care for a satire or an epigram? No, if a man will
   be beaten with brains, 'a shall wear nothing handsome
   about him. In brief, since I do purpose to marry, I will
   think nothing to any purpose that the world can say
   against it; and therefore never flout at me for what I   105
   have said against it. For man is a giddy thing, and this
   is my conclusion. For thy part, Claudio, I did think to
   have beaten thee, but in that thou art like to be my
   kinsman, live unbruised and love my cousin.
CLAUDIO   I had well hoped thou wouldst have denied   110
   Beatrice, that I might have cudgelled thee out of thy
   single life, to make thee a double-dealer – which out of
   question thou wilt be, if my cousin do not look
   exceeding narrowly to thee.
BENEDICK   Come, come, we are friends. Let's have a   115
   dance ere we are married, that we may lighten our own
   hearts and our wives' heels.
LEONATO   We'll have dancing afterward.
BENEDICK   First, of my word! Therefore play, music!
   Prince, thou art sad – get thee a wife, get thee a wife!   120
   There is no staff more reverend than one tipped with
   horn.

Enter Messenger.

MESSENGER
   My lord, your brother John is ta'en in flight
   And brought with armed men back to Messina.
BENEDICK   Think not on him till tomorrow; I'll devise   125
   thee brave punishments for him. Strike up, pipers!
                              Dance. Exeunt.

Othello

The traditional date for the composition of *Othello* is 1603–4, though the editor of the 1997 Arden 3 text puts it in 1601–2, mainly on the basis of some echoes of *Othello* in the 1603 'bad' quarto of *Hamlet*. It was performed in the Banqueting House at Whitehall before King James I on 1 November 1604 and had been performed earlier at the Globe. Two early texts of the play were published after Shakespeare's death, the Quarto in 1622 and the First Folio in 1623 (as the ninth of the tragedies). They differ from each other in many hundreds of readings. The Folio text is about 160 lines longer than the Quarto; it alone contains Desdemona's willow song (4.3), and it has a more extensive role for Emilia in the final scenes. Editors have generally assumed that both versions are 'authorial'; the Arden 3 editor argues that the Quarto broadly represents Shakespeare's first thoughts and the Folio his second thoughts, but that some variants can be ascribed to textual corruption rather than to authorial revision.

Whatever the precise date, it is generally agreed that *Othello* is one of a sequence of tragedies Shakespeare wrote between 1599 and 1608, coming after *Julius Caesar* and *Hamlet* and before *King Lear* and *Macbeth*. The main narrative source is a short story in Giraldi Cinthio's *Hecatommithi* (1565), a collection Shakespeare also drew on for the plot of *Measure for Measure*. For *Othello* he seems also to have used John Pory's 1600 translation of John Leo's *A Geographical History of Africa*, Philemon Holland's 1601 translation of Pliny's *History of the World* and Lewis Lewkenor's 1599 *The Commonwealth and Government of Venice*, mainly translated from a Latin text by Cardinal Contarini.

Unlike the other great tragedies written during the same time period, *Othello* opens with a comic structure: a young woman runs away from her father and elopes, a plot element which Shakespeare used in *A Midsummer Night's Dream*, and an older husband is afraid that his younger wife is being unfaithful, which Geoffrey Chaucer popularized in 'The Merchant's Tale' and 'The Miller's Tale' in *The Canterbury Tales*. Moreover, *Othello* is unique among Shakespeare's eponymous tragic figures as a character who knows less than the audience. Because Iago stems from the medieval morality Vice tradition, he reveals his schemes directly to the audience, making us somewhat complicit because we know that Desdemona is innocent. One of the things that makes *Othello* so powerful is the way it morphs and transitions from a play about state affairs that has a comedic structure (Venice needs its Moorish General to defend the island of Cyprus from the Turks) to a very tightly focused domestic tragedy in which state affairs are almost completely erased (the Turks have been vanquished by a storm at sea).

The play has consistently been one of Shakespeare's most popular tragedies on the stage. The portrayal of race, sexuality, homosocialism, gender roles and relations and power as being complicatedly enmeshed remains distressingly relevant. In the twenty-first century, for example, many countries and societies struggle to define who counts as an insider, especially as many rely on militaries staffed by racial and ethnic minorities.

Starting with Richard Burbage and continuing for more than 300 years, the title-role was performed by white actors in racial prosthetics, a mixture of make-up, wigs, visors, gloves, stockings and costuming. When black actors began to perform as Othello, starting with Ira Aldridge in the nineteenth century and culminating with Paul Robeson in the mid-twentieth century, critics claimed that it was like seeing the play for the first time. While black actors now dominate performing the title-role, many question whether this is a real benefit. After all, the role was created to be an impersonation of black masculinity and not a true embodiment of it. The role of Iago is actually larger than that of Othello, and some leading actors have preferred it; Iago has the soliloquies, and a good actor can steal the show from the title-role. There has also been a stage tradition of two 'stars' alternating in the roles; this was most famously done by Henry Irving and Edwin Booth in 1881. The power of the women in *Othello* should not be underestimated, however. Strong performances by Desdemona, Emilia and Bianca can render the homosocial relations depicted in the play as examples of the problems with toxic masculinity.

The Arden text is based on the 1623 First Folio but adopts readings from the 1622 Quarto.

LIST OF ROLES

OTHELLO	*the Moor, a general in the service of Venice*
BRABANTIO	*father to Desdemona, a Venetian senator*
CASSIO	*an honourable lieutenant, who serves under Othello*
IAGO	*a villain, Othello's ancient or ensign*
RODERIGO	*a gulled gentleman, of Venice*
DUKE	*of Venice*
SENATORS	*of Venice*
MONTANO	*governor of Cyprus, replaced by Othello*
GENTLEMEN	*of Cyprus*
LODOVICO	
GRATIANO	*two noble Venetians, Desdemona's cousin and uncle*
SAILOR	
CLOWN	
DESDEMONA	*wife to Othello, and Brabantio's daughter*
EMILIA	*wife to Iago*
BIANCA	*a courtesan, and Cassio's mistress*

Messenger, Herald, Officers, Gentlemen, Musicians and Attendants

1.1   *Enter* RODERIGO *and* IAGO.

RODERIGO
  Tush, never tell me, I take it much unkindly
  That thou, Iago, who hast had my purse
  As if the strings were thine, shouldst know of this.

IAGO
  'Sblood, but you'll not hear me. If ever I did dream
  Of such a matter, abhor me.

RODERIGO   Thou told'st me
  Thou didst hold him in thy hate.

IAGO   Despise me
  If I do not. Three great ones of the city,
  In personal suit to make me his lieutenant,
  Off-capped to him, and by the faith of man
  I know my price, I am worth no worse a place.
  But he, as loving his own pride and purposes,
  Evades them, with a bombast circumstance
  Horribly stuffed with epithets of war,
  And in conclusion
  Nonsuits my mediators. For 'Certes,' says he,
  'I have already chose my officer.'
  And what was he?
  Forsooth, a great arithmetician,
  One Michael Cassio, a Florentine,
  A fellow almost damned in a fair wife
  That never set a squadron in the field
  Nor the division of a battle knows
  More than a spinster – unless the bookish theoric,
  Wherein the toged consuls can propose
  As masterly as he. Mere prattle without practice
  Is all his soldiership – but he, sir, had th'election
  And I, of whom his eyes had seen the proof
  At Rhodes, at Cyprus and on other grounds,
  Christian and heathen, must be be-leed and calmed
  By debitor and creditor. This counter-caster
  He, in good time, must his lieutenant be
  And I, God bless the mark, his Moorship's ancient!

RODERIGO
  By heaven, I rather would have been his hangman.

IAGO
  Why, there's no remedy, 'tis the curse of service:
  Preferment goes by letter and affection
  And not by old gradation, where each second
  Stood heir to th' first. Now sir, be judge yourself
  Whether I in any just term am affined
  To love the Moor.

RODERIGO   I would not follow him then.

IAGO   O sir, content you!
  I follow him to serve my turn upon him.
  We cannot all be masters, nor all masters
  Cannot be truly followed. You shall mark
  Many a duteous and knee-crooking knave
  That, doting on his own obsequious bondage,
  Wears out his time much like his master's ass
  For nought but provender, and, when he's old,
    cashiered.

Whip me such honest knaves! Others there are
Who, trimmed in forms and visages of duty,
Keep yet their hearts attending on themselves   50
And, throwing but shows of service on their lords,
Do well thrive by them, and, when they have lined
  their coats,
Do themselves homage: these fellows have some soul
And such a one do I profess myself. For, sir,
It is as sure as you are Roderigo,   55
Were I the Moor, I would not be Iago.
In following him I follow but myself:
Heaven is my judge, not I for love and duty
But seeming so, for my peculiar end,
For when my outward action doth demonstrate   60
The native act and figure of my heart
In complement extern, 'tis not long after
But I will wear my heart upon my sleeve
For daws to peck at: I am not what I am.

RODERIGO   What a full fortune does the thicklips owe   65
  If he can carry't thus!

IAGO   Call up her father,
  Rouse him, make after him, poison his delight,
  Proclaim him in the streets, incense her kinsmen,
  And, though he in a fertile climate dwell,
  Plague him with flies! Though that his joy be joy   70
  Yet throw such changes of vexation on't
  As it may lose some colour.

RODERIGO   Here is her father's house, I'll call aloud.

IAGO   Do, with like timorous accent and dire yell
  As when by night and negligence the fire   75
  Is spied in populous cities.

RODERIGO   What ho! Brabantio, Signior Brabantio ho!

IAGO
  Awake, what ho, Brabantio! thieves, thieves, thieves!
  Look to your house, your daughter and your bags!
  Thieves, thieves!   80

BRABANTIO *appears above at a window.*

BRABANTIO
  What is the reason of this terrible summons?
  What is the matter there?

RODERIGO   Signior, is all your family within?

IAGO   Are your doors locked?

BRABANTIO   Why? Wherefore ask you this?

IAGO
  Zounds, sir, you're robbed, for shame put on your
    gown!   85
  Your heart is burst, you have lost half your soul,
  Even now, now, very now, an old black ram
  Is tupping your white ewe! Arise, arise,
  Awake the snorting citizens with the bell
  Or else the devil will make a grandsire of you,   90
  Arise I say!

BRABANTIO   What, have you lost your wits?

RODERIGO
  Most reverend signior, do you know my voice?

BRABANTIO   Not I, what are you?

RODERIGO   My name is Roderigo.

BRABANTIO   The worser welcome!

95   I have charged thee not to haunt about my doors:
     In honest plainness thou hast heard me say
     My daughter is not for thee; and now in madness,
     Being full of supper and distempering draughts,
     Upon malicious bravery dost thou come

100 To start my quiet?

RODERIGO   Sir, sir, sir –

BRABANTIO   But thou must needs be sure
     My spirit and my place have in them power
     To make this bitter to thee.

RODERIGO   Patience, good sir!

BRABANTIO
     What tell'st thou me of robbing? This is Venice:
     My house is not a grange.

105 RODERIGO   Most grave Brabantio,
     In simple and pure soul I come to you –

IAGO   Zounds, sir, you are one of those that will not
     serve God, if the devil bid you. Because we come to do
     you service, and you think we are ruffians, you'll have

110 your daughter covered with a Barbary horse; you'll
     have your nephews neigh to you, you'll have coursers
     for cousins and jennets for germans!

BRABANTIO   What profane wretch art thou?

IAGO   I am one, sir, that comes to tell you your daughter

115 and the Moor are now making the beast with two backs.

BRABANTIO   Thou art a villain!

IAGO   You are a senator!

BRABANTIO
     This thou shalt answer. I know thee, Roderigo!

RODERIGO
     Sir, I will answer anything. But I beseech you,
     If 't be your pleasure and most wise consent,

120 As partly I find it is, that your fair daughter
     At this odd-even and dull watch o'th' night,
     Transported with no worse nor better guard
     But with a knave of common hire, a gondolier,
     To the gross clasps of a lascivious Moor –

125 If this be known to you, and your allowance,
     We then have done you bold and saucy wrongs.
     But if you know not this, my manners tell me
     We have your wrong rebuke. Do not believe
     That from the sense of all civility

130 I thus would play and trifle with your reverence.
     Your daughter, if you have not given her leave,
     I say again, hath made a gross revolt,
     Tying her duty, beauty, wit and fortunes
     In an extravagant and wheeling stranger

135 Of here and everywhere. Straight satisfy yourself:
     If she be in her chamber or your house
     Let loose on me the justice of the state
     For thus deluding you.

BRABANTIO   Strike on the tinder, ho!
     Give me a taper, call up all my people.

140 This accident is not unlike my dream,
     Belief of it oppresses me already.

Light, I say, light!   *Exit above.*

IAGO   Farewell, for I must leave you.
     It seems not meet, nor wholesome to my place,
     To be produced, as, if I stay, I shall,
     Against the Moor. For I do know the state,   145
     However this may gall him with some check,
     Cannot with safety cast him, for he's embarked
     With such loud reason to the Cyprus wars,
     Which even now stands in act, that for their souls
     Another of his fathom they have none   150
     To lead their business – in which regard,
     Though I do hate him as I do hell-pains,
     Yet for necessity of present life
     I must show out a flag and sign of love,
     Which is indeed but sign. That you shall surely find
     him,   155
     Lead to the Sagittary the raised search,
     And there will I be with him. So farewell.   *Exit.*

Enter BRABANTIO *in his night-gown and
Servants with torches.*

BRABANTIO   It is too true an evil, gone she is,
     And what's to come of my despised time
     Is nought but bitterness. Now Roderigo,   160
     Where didst thou see her? – O unhappy girl! –
     With the Moor, say'st thou? – Who would be a father? –
     How didst thou know 'twas she? – O, she deceives me
     Past thought! – What said she to you? – Get more
     tapers,
     Raise all my kindred. Are they married, think you?   165

RODERIGO   Truly I think they are.

BRABANTIO
     O heaven, how got she out? O treason of the blood!
     – Fathers, from hence trust not your daughters' minds
     By what you see them act. – Is there not charms
     By which the property of youth and maidhood   170
     May be abused? Have you not read, Roderigo,
     Of some such thing?

RODERIGO   Yes sir, I have indeed.

BRABANTIO
     Call up my brother. – O, would you had had her!
     Some one way, some another. – Do you know
     Where we may apprehend her and the Moor?   175

RODERIGO   I think I can discover him, if you please
     To get good guard and go along with me.

BRABANTIO   Pray you lead on. At every house I'll call,
     I may command at most: get weapons, ho!
     And raise some special officers of night.   180
     On, good Roderigo, I'll deserve your pains.   *Exeunt.*

1.2   *Enter* OTHELLO, IAGO *and
Attendants with torches.*

IAGO   Though in the trade of war I have slain men
     Yet do I hold it very stuff o'th' conscience
     To do no contrived murder: I lack iniquity
     Sometimes to do me service. Nine or ten times

5   I had thought t'have yerked him here, under the ribs.

OTHELLO   'Tis better as it is.

IAGO   Nay, but he prated
    And spoke such scurvy and provoking terms
    Against your honour,
    That with the little godliness I have
10   I did full hard forbear him. But I pray, sir,
    Are you fast married? Be assured of this,
    That the magnifico is much beloved
    And hath in his effect a voice potential
    As double as the duke's: he will divorce you
15   Or put upon you what restraint or grievance
    The law, with all his might to enforce it on,
    Will give him cable.

OTHELLO   Let him do his spite;
    My services, which I have done the signiory,
    Shall out-tongue his complaints. 'Tis yet to know –
20   Which, when I know that boasting is an honour,
    I shall promulgate – I fetch my life and being
    From men of royal siege, and my demerits
    May speak unbonneted to as proud a fortune
    As this that I have reached. For know, Iago,
25   But that I love the gentle Desdemona
    I would not my unhoused free condition
    Put into circumscription and confine
    For the sea's worth. But look, what lights come yond?

Enter CASSIO, *with Officers and torches.*

IAGO   Those are the raised father and his friends,
    You were best go in.

OTHELLO   Not I, I must be found.
30   My parts, my title and my perfect soul
    Shall manifest me rightly. Is it they?

IAGO   By Janus, I think no.

OTHELLO
    The servants of the Duke? and my lieutenant?
35   The goodness of the night upon you, friends.
    What is the news?

CASSIO   The duke does greet you, general,
    And he requires your haste-post-haste appearance,
    Even on the instant.

OTHELLO   What's the matter, think you?

CASSIO   Something from Cyprus, as I may divine;
40   It is a business of some heat. The galleys
    Have sent a dozen sequent messengers
    This very night, at one another's heels,
    And many of the consuls, raised and met,
    Are at the duke's already. You have been hotly called for,
45   When, being not at your lodging to be found,
    The Senate hath sent about three several quests
    To search you out.

OTHELLO   'Tis well I am found by you:
    I will but spend a word here in the house
    And go with you.   *Exit.*

CASSIO   Ancient, what makes he here?

IAGO   Faith, he tonight hath boarded a land carrack:
    If it prove lawful prize, he's made for ever.

CASSIO   I do not understand.

IAGO   He's married.

CASSIO   To whom?

IAGO   Marry, to –

Enter OTHELLO.

               Come, captain, will you go?

OTHELLO   Ha' with you.

CASSIO   Here comes another troop to seek for you.

Enter BRABANTIO, RODERIGO, *with Officers*
and torches and weapons.

IAGO   It is Brabantio: general, be advised,   55
    He comes to bad intent.

OTHELLO   Holla, stand there!

RODERIGO   Signior, it is the Moor.

BRABANTIO   Down with him, thief!

    [*They draw on both sides.*]

IAGO   You, Roderigo! come sir, I am for you.

OTHELLO
    Keep up your bright swords, for the dew will rust them.
    Good signior, you shall more command with years   60
    Than with your weapons.

BRABANTIO
    O thou foul thief, where hast thou stowed my daughter?
    Damned as thou art, thou hast enchanted her,
    For I'll refer me to all things of sense,
    If she in chains of magic were not bound,   65
    Whether a maid so tender, fair and happy,
    So opposite to marriage that she shunned
    The wealthy, curled darlings of our nation,
    Would ever have, t'incur a general mock,
    Run from her guardage to the sooty bosom   70
    Of such a thing as thou? to fear, not to delight.
    Judge me the world if 'tis not gross in sense
    That thou hast practised on her with foul charms,
    Abused her delicate youth with drugs or minerals
    That weakens motion: I'll have't disputed on,   75
    'Tis probable and palpable to thinking.
    I therefore apprehend and do attach thee
    For an abuser of the world, a practiser
    Of arts inhibited and out of warrant.
    Lay hold upon him; if he do resist   80
    Subdue him at his peril!

OTHELLO   Hold your hands,
    Both you of my inclining and the rest:
    Were it my cue to fight, I should have known it
    Without a prompter. Where will you that I go
    To answer this your charge?

BRABANTIO   To prison, till fit time   85
    Of law, and course of direct session
    Call thee to answer.

OTHELLO   What if I do obey?
    How may the duke be therewith satisfied,
    Whose messengers are here about my side
    Upon some present business of the state,   90

To bring me to him?

OFFICER   'Tis true, most worthy signior,
The duke's in council, and your noble self
I am sure is sent for.

BRABANTIO   How? the duke in council?
In this time of the night? Bring him away:
95   Mine's not an idle cause, the duke himself,
Or any of my brothers of the state,
Cannot but feel this wrong as 'twere their own.
For if such actions may have passage free
Bond-slaves and pagans shall our statesmen be.
                               Exeunt.

1.3   Enter DUKE *and* Senators, *set at a table,*
        with lights and Attendants.

DUKE   There is no composition in these news
That gives them credit.

1 SENATOR   Indeed, they are disproportioned.
My letters say a hundred and seven galleys.

DUKE   And mine a hundred forty.

2 SENATOR   And mine two hundred.
5   But though they jump not on a just account –
As in these cases, where the aim reports,
'Tis oft with difference – yet do they all confirm
A Turkish fleet, and bearing up to Cyprus.

DUKE   Nay, it is possible enough to judgement:
10   I do not so secure me in the error
But the main article I do approve
In fearful sense.

SAILOR [*within*]   What ho, what ho, what ho!

Enter Sailor.

OFFICER   A messenger from the galleys.

DUKE   Now? what's the business?

15 SAILOR   The Turkish preparation makes for Rhodes,
So was I bid report here to the state
By Signior Angelo.

DUKE   How say you by this change?

1 SENATOR   This cannot be,
By no assay of reason: 'tis a pageant
20   To keep us in false gaze. When we consider
Th'importancy of Cyprus to the Turk,
And let ourselves again but understand
That as it more concerns the Turk than Rhodes
So may he with more facile question bear it,
25   For that it stands not in such warlike brace
But altogether lacks th'abilities
That Rhodes is dressed in. If we make thought of
    this
We must not think the Turk is so unskilful
To leave that latest which concerns him first,
30   Neglecting an attempt of ease and gain
To wake and wage a danger profitless.

DUKE   Nay, in all confidence, he's not for Rhodes.

OFFICER   Here is more news.

Enter a Messenger.

MESSENGER   The Ottomites, reverend and gracious,
Steering with due course toward the isle of Rhodes,   35
Have there injointed with an after fleet –

1 SENATOR   Ay, so I thought; how many, as you guess?

MESSENGER   Of thirty sail; and now they do re-stem
Their backward course, bearing with frank appearance
Their purposes toward Cyprus. Signior Montano,   40
Your trusty and most valiant servitor,
With his free duty recommends you thus
And prays you to relieve him.

DUKE   'Tis certain then for Cyprus.
Marcus Luccicos, is not he in town?   45

1 SENATOR   He's now in Florence.

DUKE   Write from us to him; post-post-haste, dispatch.

1 SENATOR
Here comes Brabantio and the valiant Moor.

Enter BRABANTIO, OTHELLO, CASSIO, IAGO,
    RODERIGO *and Officers.*

DUKE   Valiant Othello, we must straight employ you
Against the general enemy Ottoman.   50
[*to Brabantio*] I did not see you: welcome, gentle signior,
We lacked your counsel and your help tonight.

BRABANTIO
So did I yours. Good your grace, pardon me,
Neither my place nor aught I heard of business
Hath raised me from my bed, nor doth the general care   55
Take hold on me, for my particular grief
Is of so flood-gate and o'erbearing nature
That it engluts and swallows other sorrows
And it is still itself.

DUKE   Why? What's the matter?

BRABANTIO   My daughter, O my daughter!

1 SENATOR   Dead?

BRABANTIO   Ay, to me: 60
She is abused, stolen from me and corrupted
By spells and medicines bought of mountebanks,
For nature so preposterously to err
Being not deficient, blind, or lame of sense,
Sans witchcraft could not.   65

DUKE   Whoe'er he be, that in this foul proceeding
Hath thus beguiled your daughter of herself,
And you of her, the bloody book of law
You shall yourself read, in the bitter letter,
After your own sense, yea, though our proper son   70
Stood in your action.

BRABANTIO   Humbly I thank your grace.
Here is the man, this Moor, whom now it seems
Your special mandate for the state affairs
Hath hither brought.

ALL   We are very sorry for't.

DUKE [*to Othello*]
What in your own part can you say to this?   75

BRABANTIO   Nothing, but this is so.

OTHELLO   Most potent, grave, and reverend signiors,

My very noble and approved good masters:
That I have ta'en away this old man's daughter
80 It is most true; true, I have married her.
The very head and front of my offending
Hath this extent, no more. Rude am I in my speech
And little blest with the soft phrase of peace,
For since these arms of mine had seven years' pith
85 Till now some nine moons wasted, they have used
Their dearest action in the tented field,
And little of this great world can I speak
More than pertains to feats of broil and battle,
And therefore little shall I grace my cause
90 In speaking for myself. Yet, by your gracious patience,
I will a round unvarnished tale deliver
Of my whole course of love, what drugs, what charms,
What conjuration and what mighty magic –
For such proceeding I am charged withal –
I won his daughter.
95 BRABANTIO   A maiden never bold,
Of spirit so still and quiet that her motion
Blushed at herself; and she, in spite of nature,
Of years, of country, credit, everything,
To fall in love with what she feared to look on?
100 It is a judgement maimed and most imperfect
That will confess perfection so could err
Against all rules of nature, and must be driven
To find out practices of cunning hell
Why this should be. I therefore vouch again
105 That with some mixtures powerful o'er the blood
Or with some dram conjured to this effect
He wrought upon her.
DUKE   To vouch this is no proof,
Without more certain and more overt test
Than these thin habits and poor likelihoods
110 Of modern seeming do prefer against him.
1 SENATOR   But, Othello, speak:
Did you by indirect and forced courses
Subdue and poison this young maid's affections?
Or came it by request and such fair question
As soul to soul affordeth?
115 OTHELLO   I do beseech you,
Send for the lady to the Sagittary,
And let her speak of me before her father.
If you do find me foul in her report
The trust, the office I do hold of you
120 Not only take away, but let your sentence
Even fall upon my life.
DUKE   Fetch Desdemona hither.
OTHELLO
Ancient, conduct them, you best know the place.
And till she come, as truly as to heaven
                              Exeunt Iago and two or three.
125 I do confess the vices of my blood
So justly to your grave ears I'll present
How I did thrive in this fair lady's love
And she in mine.
DUKE   Say it, Othello.

OTHELLO   Her father loved me, oft invited me,
Still questioned me the story of my life   130
From year to year – the battles, sieges, fortunes
That I have passed.
I ran it through, even from my boyish days
To th' very moment that he bade me tell it,
Wherein I spake of most disastrous chances,   135
Of moving accidents by flood and field,
Of hair-breadth scapes i'th' imminent deadly breach,
Of being taken by the insolent foe
And sold to slavery; of my redemption thence
And portance in my travailous history;   140
Wherein of antres vast and deserts idle,
Rough quarries, rocks and hills whose heads touch
     heaven
It was my hint to speak – such was my process –
And of the cannibals that each other eat,
The Anthropophagi, and men whose heads   145
Do grow beneath their shoulders. This to hear
Would Desdemona seriously incline,
But still the house affairs would draw her thence,
Which ever as she could with haste dispatch
She'd come again, and with a greedy ear   150
Devour up my discourse; which I, observing,
Took once a pliant hour and found good means
To draw from her a prayer of earnest heart
That I would all my pilgrimage dilate,
Whereof by parcels she had something heard   155
But not intentively. I did consent,
And often did beguile her of her tears
When I did speak of some distressful stroke
That my youth suffered. My story being done
She gave me for my pains a world of sighs,   160
She swore in faith 'twas strange, 'twas passing strange,
'Twas pitiful, 'twas wondrous pitiful;
She wished she had not heard it, yet she wished
That heaven had made her such a man. She thanked
     me
And bade me, if I had a friend that loved her,   165
I should but teach him how to tell my story
And that would woo her. Upon this hint I spake:
She loved me for the dangers I had passed
And I loved her that she did pity them.
This only is the witchcraft I have used: 170
          Enter DESDEMONA, IAGO, Attendants.
Here comes the lady, let her witness it.
DUKE   I think this tale would win my daughter too.
Good Brabantio, take up this mangled matter at the
     best:
Men do their broken weapons rather use
Than their bare hands.
BRABANTIO   I pray you, hear her speak.   175
If she confess that she was half the wooer,
Destruction on my head if my bad blame
Light on the man. Come hither, gentle mistress:
Do you perceive, in all this noble company,

Where most you owe obedience?

180 DESDEMONA   My noble father,
I do perceive here a divided duty.
To you I am bound for life and education:
My life and education both do learn me
How to respect you; you are the lord of duty,
185 I am hitherto your daughter. But here's my husband:
And so much duty as my mother showed
To you, preferring you before her father,
So much I challenge that I may profess
Due to the Moor my lord.

190 BRABANTIO   God be with you, I have done.
Please it your grace, on to the state affairs;
I had rather to adopt a child than get it.
Come hither, Moor:
I here do give thee that with all my heart
195 Which, but thou hast already, with all my heart
I would keep from thee. For your sake, jewel,
I am glad at soul I have no other child,
For thy escape would teach me tyranny
To hang clogs on them. I have done, my lord.

200 DUKE   Let me speak like yourself, and lay a sentence
Which as a grise or step may help these lovers
Into your favour.
When remedies are past the griefs are ended
By seeing the worst which late on hopes depended.
205 To mourn a mischief that is past and gone
Is the next way to draw new mischief on.
What cannot be preserved when fortune takes,
Patience her injury a mockery makes.
The robbed that smiles steals something from the thief,
210 He robs himself that spends a bootless grief.

BRABANTIO   So let the Turk of Cyprus us beguile,
We lose it not so long as we can smile;
He bears the sentence well that nothing bears
But the free comfort which from thence he hears.
215 But he bears both the sentence and the sorrow
That, to pay grief, must of poor patience borrow.
These sentences to sugar or to gall,
Being strong on both sides, are equivocal.
But words are words: I never yet did hear
220 That the bruised heart was pierced through the ear.
I humbly beseech you, proceed to th'affairs of state.

DUKE   The Turk with a most mighty preparation makes
for Cyprus. Othello, the fortitude of the place is best
known to you, and, though we have there a substitute
225 of most allowed sufficiency, yet opinion, a sovereign
mistress of effects, throws a more safer voice on you.
You must therefore be content to slubber the gloss of
your new fortunes with this more stubborn and
boisterous expedition.

230 OTHELLO   The tyrant custom, most grave senators,
Hath made the flinty and steel couch of war
My thrice-driven bed of down. I do agnize
A natural and prompt alacrity
I find in hardness, and do undertake
235 This present war against the Ottomites.

Most humbly therefore, bending to your state,
I crave fit disposition for my wife,
Due reverence of place, and exhibition,
With such accommodation and besort
As levels with her breeding.   240

DUKE   Why, at her father's.

BRABANTIO   I'll not have it so.

OTHELLO   Nor I.

DESDEMONA   Nor would I there reside
To put my father in impatient thoughts
By being in his eye. Most gracious duke,
To my unfolding lend your prosperous ear   245
And let me find a charter in your voice
T'assist my simpleness.

DUKE   What would you, Desdemona?

DESDEMONA   That I did love the Moor to live with him
My downright violence and scorn of fortunes   250
May trumpet to the world. My heart's subdued
Even to the very quality of my lord:
I saw Othello's visage in his mind,
And to his honours and his valiant parts
Did I my soul and fortunes consecrate,   255
So that, dear lords, if I be left behind,
A moth of peace, and he go to the war,
The rites for which I love him are bereft me,
And I a heavy interim shall support
By his dear absence. Let me go with him.   260

OTHELLO   Let her have your voice.
Vouch with me, heaven, I therefore beg it not
To please the palate of my appetite,
Nor to comply with heat, the young affects
In me defunct, and proper satisfaction,   265
But to be free and bounteous to her mind.
And heaven defend your good souls that you think
I will your serious and great business scant
When she is with me. No, when light-winged toys
Of feathered Cupid seel with wanton dullness   270
My speculative and officed instrument,
That my disports corrupt and taint my business,
Let housewives make a skillet of my helm
And all indign and base adversities
Make head against my estimation.   275

DUKE   Be it as you shall privately determine,
Either for her stay or going: th'affair cries haste
And speed must answer it.

1 SENATOR   You must away tonight.

DESDEMONA   Tonight, my lord?

DUKE   This night.

OTHELLO   With all my heart.

DUKE   At nine i'th' morning here we'll meet again.   280
Othello, leave some officer behind
And he shall our commission bring to you,
And such things else of quality and respect
As doth import you.

OTHELLO   So please your grace, my ancient:
A man he is of honesty and trust.   285
To his conveyance I assign my wife,

With what else needful your good grace shall think
To be sent after me.

DUKE   Let it be so.
Good-night to everyone. And, noble signior,
290 If virtue no delighted beauty lack
Your son-in-law is far more fair than black.

1 SENATOR   Adieu, brave Moor, use Desdemona well.

BRABANTIO
Look to her, Moor, if thou hast eyes to see:
She has deceived her father, and may thee.

Exeunt Duke, Brabantio, Senators, Officers.

295 OTHELLO   My life upon her faith. Honest Iago,
My Desdemona must I leave to thee:
I prithee, let thy wife attend on her
And bring them after in the best advantage.
Come, Desdemona, I have but an hour
300 Of love, of worldly matter and direction
To spend with thee. We must obey the time.

Exeunt Othello and Desdemona.

RODERIGO   Iago!

IAGO   What sayst thou, noble heart?

RODERIGO   What will I do, think'st thou?

305 IAGO   Why, go to bed and sleep.

RODERIGO   I will incontinently drown myself.

IAGO   If thou dost, I shall never love thee after. Why,
thou silly gentleman?

RODERIGO   It is silliness to live when to live is torment;
310 and then have we a prescription to die, when death is
our physician.

IAGO   O villainous! I have looked upon the world for
four times seven years, and since I could distinguish
betwixt a benefit and an injury I never found a man
315 that knew how to love himself. Ere I would say I would
drown myself for the love of a guinea-hen I would
change my humanity with a baboon.

RODERIGO   What should I do? I confess it is my shame
to be so fond, but it is not in my virtue to amend it.

320 IAGO   Virtue? a fig! 'tis in ourselves that we are thus, or
thus. Our bodies are gardens, to the which our wills are
gardeners. So that if we will plant nettles or sow
lettuce, set hyssop and weed up thyme, supply it with
one gender of herbs or distract it with many, either to
325 have it sterile with idleness or manured with industry
– why, the power and corrigible authority of this lies in
our wills. If the balance of our lives had not one scale
of reason to poise another of sensuality, the blood and
baseness of our natures would conduct us to most
330 preposterous conclusions. But we have reason to cool
our raging motions, our carnal stings, our unbitted
lusts; whereof I take this, that you call love, to be a sect
or scion.

RODERIGO   It cannot be.

335 IAGO   It is merely a lust of the blood and a permission of
the will. Come, be a man! drown thyself? drown cats
and blind puppies. I have professed me thy friend, and
I confess me knit to thy deserving with cables of
perdurable toughness. I could never better stead thee

340 than now. Put money in thy purse, follow thou the
wars, defeat thy favour with an usurped beard; I say,
put money in thy purse. It cannot be that Desdemona
should long continue her love to the Moor – put
money in thy purse – nor he his to her. It was a violent
345 commencement in her, and thou shalt see an
answerable sequestration – put but money in thy
purse. These Moors are changeable in their wills – fill
thy purse with money. The food that to him now is as
luscious as locusts shall be to him shortly as acerb as
350 coloquintida. She must change for youth; when she is
sated with his body she will find the error of her
choice: she must have change, she must. Therefore,
put money in thy purse. If thou wilt needs damn
thyself, do it a more delicate way than drowning –
355 make all the money thou canst. If sanctimony, and a
frail vow betwixt an erring Barbarian and a supersubtle
Venetian, be not too hard for my wits and all the tribe
of hell, thou shalt enjoy her – therefore make money.
A pox of drowning thyself, it is clean out of the way:
360 seek thou rather to be hanged in compassing thy joy
than to be drowned and go without her.

RODERIGO   Wilt thou be fast to my hopes, if I depend
on the issue?

IAGO   Thou art sure of me – go, make money. I have told
365 thee often, and I re-tell thee again and again, I hate the
Moor. My cause is hearted, thine hath no less reason:
let us be conjunctive in our revenge against him. If
thou canst cuckold him, thou dost thyself a pleasure,
me a sport. There are many events in the womb of
370 time, which will be delivered. Traverse, go, provide thy
money: we will have more of this tomorrow. Adieu!

RODERIGO   Where shall we meet i'th' morning?

IAGO   At my lodging.

RODERIGO   I'll be with thee betimes.

375 IAGO   Go to, farewell. – Do you hear, Roderigo?

RODERIGO   What say you?

IAGO   No more of drowning, do you hear?

RODERIGO   I am changed. I'll sell all my land.   *Exit.*

IAGO   Go to, farewell, put money enough in your purse.
380 Thus do I ever make my fool my purse:
For I mine own gained knowledge should profane
If I would time expend with such a snipe
But for my sport and profit. I hate the Moor
And it is thought abroad that 'twixt my sheets
385 He's done my office. I know not if 't be true,
But I for mere suspicion in that kind
Will do as if for surety. He holds me well,
The better shall my purpose work on him.
Cassio's a proper man: let me see now,
390 To get his place, and to plume up my will
In double knavery. How? How? let's see:
After some time to abuse Othello's ear
That he is too familiar with his wife.
He hath a person and a smooth dispose
395 To be suspected, framed to make women false.
The Moor is of a free and open nature

That thinks men honest that but seem to be so,
And will as tenderly be led by th' nose
As asses are.
400 I have't, it is engendered! Hell and night
Must bring this monstrous birth to the world's light.

Exit.

2.1 *Enter* MONTANO *and two* Gentlemen.

MONTANO   What from the cape can you discern at sea?
1 GENTLEMAN   Nothing at all, it is a high-wrought flood:
I cannot 'twixt the haven and the main
Descry a sail.
5 MONTANO   Methinks the wind hath spoke aloud at land,
A fuller blast ne'er shook our battlements:
If it hath ruffianed so upon the sea
What ribs of oak, when mountains melt on them,
Can hold the mortise? What shall we hear of this?
10 2 GENTLEMAN   A segregation of the Turkish fleet:
For do but stand upon the foaming shore,
The chidden billow seems to pelt the clouds,
The wind-shaked surge, with high and monstrous mane,
Seems to cast water on the burning bear
15 And quench the guards of th'ever-fired pole.
I never did like molestation view
On the enchafed flood.
MONTANO   If that the Turkish fleet
Be not ensheltered and embayed, they are drowned.
It is impossible to bear it out.

Enter a Third Gentleman.

20 3 GENTLEMAN   News, lads: our wars are done!
The desperate tempest hath so banged the Turks
That their designment halts. A noble ship of Venice
Hath seen a grievous wrack and sufferance
On most part of their fleet.
MONTANO   How? Is this true?
25 3 GENTLEMAN   The ship is here put in,
A Veronessa; Michael Cassio,
Lieutenant to the warlike Moor, Othello,
Is come on shore; the Moor himself at sea,
And is in full commission here for Cyprus.
30 MONTANO   I am glad on't, 'tis a worthy governor.
3 GENTLEMAN
But this same Cassio, though he speak of comfort

Enter CASSIO.

Touching the Turkish loss, yet he looks sadly
And prays the Moor be safe, for they were parted
With foul and violent tempest.
MONTANO   Pray heavens he be,
35 For I have served him, and the man commands
Like a full soldier. Let's to the seaside, ho!
As well to see the vessel that's come in
As to throw out our eyes for brave Othello,
Even till we make the main and th'aerial blue
An indistinct regard.

40 3 GENTLEMAN   Come, let's do so,
For every minute is expectancy
Of more arrivance.
CASSIO   Thanks, you the valiant of this warlike isle
That so approve the Moor. O, let the heavens
45 Give him defence against the elements,
For I have lost him on a dangerous sea.
MONTANO   Is he well shipped?
CASSIO   His bark is stoutly timbered, and his pilot
Of very expert and approved allowance,
50 Therefore my hopes, not surfeited to death,
Stand in bold cure.
A VOICE [*within*]   A sail! a sail! a sail!
CASSIO   What noise?
2 GENTLEMAN
The town is empty: on the brow o'th' sea
Stand ranks of people, and they cry 'A sail!'
CASSIO
55 My hopes do shape him for the governor.   [*a shot*]
2 GENTLEMAN
They do discharge their shot of courtesy,
Our friends at least.
CASSIO   I pray you sir, go forth
And give us truth who 'tis that is arrived.
2 GENTLEMAN   I shall.   *Exit.*
60 MONTANO   But, good lieutenant, is your general wived?
CASSIO   Most fortunately: he hath achieved a maid
That paragons description and wild fame;
One that excels the quirks of blazoning pens
And in th'essential vesture of creation
Does tire the inginer.

Enter Second Gentleman.

65   How now? Who has put in?
2 GENTLEMAN   'Tis one Iago, ancient to the general.
CASSIO   He's had most favourable and happy speed.
Tempests themselves, high seas, and howling winds,
The guttered rocks and congregated sands,
70 Traitors ensteeped to clog the guiltless keel,
As having sense of beauty, do omit
Their mortal natures, letting go safely by
The divine Desdemona.
MONTANO   What is she?
CASSIO   She that I spake of, our great captain's captain,
75 Left in the conduct of the bold Iago,
Whose footing here anticipates our thoughts
A se'nnight's speed. Great Jove, Othello guard,
And swell his sail with thine own powerful breath
That he may bless this bay with his tall ship,
80 Make love's quick pants in Desdemona's arms,
Give renewed fire to our extinct spirits
And bring all Cyprus comfort! –

Enter DESDEMONA, IAGO, RODERIGO *and* EMILIA.

                        O, behold,
The riches of the ship is come on shore:
You men of Cyprus, let her have your knees!

85   Hail to thee, lady, and the grace of heaven,
     Before, behind thee, and on every hand
     Enwheel thee round!
DESDEMONA   I thank you, valiant Cassio.
     What tidings can you tell me of my lord?
CASSIO   He is not yet arrived, nor know I aught
90   But that he's well, and will be shortly here.
DESDEMONA   O, but I fear . . . how lost you company?
CASSIO   The great contention of the sea and skies
     Parted our fellowship.
                [*A voice within:* 'A sail! a sail!']
             But hark! a sail!   [*A shot is heard.*]
2 GENTLEMAN   They give their greeting to the citadel:
     This likewise is a friend.
95 CASSIO   See for the news.
                    Exit Gentleman.
     Good ancient, you are welcome.
     [*to Emilia*]   Welcome, mistress.
     Let it not gall your patience, good Iago,
     That I extend my manners; 'tis my breeding
     That gives me this bold show of courtesy.
     [*He kisses Emilia.*]
100 IAGO   Sir, would she give you so much of her lips
     As of her tongue she oft bestows on me
     You'd have enough.
DESDEMONA   Alas! she has no speech.
IAGO   In faith, too much!
     I find it still when I have list to sleep.
105   Marry, before your ladyship, I grant,
     She puts her tongue a little in her heart
     And chides with thinking.
EMILIA   You have little cause to say so.
IAGO
     Come on, come on, you are pictures out of doors,
110   Bells in your parlours, wild-cats in your kitchens,
     Saints in your injuries, devils being offended,
     Players in your housewifery, and housewives in . . .
     Your beds!
DESDEMONA   O, fie upon thee, slanderer!
IAGO   Nay, it is true, or else I am a Turk:
115   You rise to play, and go to bed to work.
EMILIA   You shall not write my praise.
IAGO   No, let me not.
DESDEMONA
     What wouldst thou write of me, if thou shouldst
         praise me?
IAGO   O, gentle lady, do not put me to't,
     For I am nothing if not critical.
DESDEMONA
120   Come on, assay. There's one gone to the harbour?
IAGO   Ay, madam.
DESDEMONA   I am not merry, but I do beguile
     The thing I am by seeming otherwise.
     Come, how wouldst thou praise me?
125 IAGO   I am about it, but indeed my invention
     Comes from my pate as birdlime does from frieze,
     It plucks out brains and all; but my muse labours

     And thus she is delivered:
     If she be fair and wise, fairness and wit,
     The one's for use, the other useth it.   130
DESDEMONA
     Well praised. How if she be black and witty?
IAGO   If she be black, and thereto have a wit,
     She'll find a white that shall her blackness fit.
DESDEMONA   Worse and worse.
EMILIA   How if fair and foolish?   135
IAGO   She never yet was foolish that was fair,
     For even her folly helped her to an heir.
DESDEMONA   These are old fond paradoxes to make
     fools laugh i'th' alehouse. What miserable praise hast
     thou for her that's foul and foolish?   140
IAGO   There's none so foul, and foolish thereunto,
     But does foul pranks which fair and wise ones do.
DESDEMONA   O heavy ignorance, thou praisest the
     worst best. But what praise couldst thou bestow on a
     deserving woman indeed? One that in the authority of   145
     her merit did justly put on the vouch of very malice
     itself?
IAGO   She that was ever fair and never proud,
     Had tongue at will, and yet was never loud,
     Never lacked gold, and yet went never gay,   150
     Fled from her wish, and yet said 'now I may',
     She that, being angered, her revenge being nigh,
     Bade her wrong stay, and her displeasure fly,
     She that in wisdom never was so frail
     To change the cod's head for the salmon's tail,   155
     She that could think, and ne'er disclose her mind,
     See suitors following, and not look behind,
     She was a wight, if ever such wights were –
DESDEMONA   To do what?
IAGO   To suckle fools, and chronicle small beer.   160
DESDEMONA   O, most lame and impotent conclusion!
     Do not learn of him, Emilia, though he be thy husband.
     How say you, Cassio, is he not a most profane and
     liberal counsellor?
CASSIO   He speaks home, madam, you may relish him   165
     more in the soldier than in the scholar.
IAGO [*aside*]   He takes her by the palm; ay, well said,
     whisper. With as little a web as this will I ensnare as
     great a fly as Cassio. Ay, smile upon her, do: I will gyve
     thee in thine own courtesies. You say true, 'tis so   170
     indeed. If such tricks as these strip you out of your
     lieutenantry, it had been better you had not kissed
     your three fingers so oft, which now again you are
     most apt to play the sir in. Very good, well kissed, and
     excellent courtesy: 'tis so indeed! Yet again, your   175
     fingers to your lips? would they were clyster-pipes for
     your sake!   [*Trumpets within*]
     The Moor! I know his trumpet!
CASSIO   'Tis truly so.
DESDEMONA   Let's meet him and receive him.

            Enter OTHELLO *and Attendants.*

CASSIO   Lo, where he comes!

OTHELLO   O my fair warrior!

180 DESDEMONA   My dear Othello!

OTHELLO   It gives me wonder great as my content
To see you here before me! O my soul's joy,
If after every tempest come such calms
May the winds blow till they have wakened death,
185 And let the labouring bark climb hills of seas,
Olympus-high, and duck again as low
As hell's from heaven. If it were now to die
'Twere now to be most happy, for I fear
My soul hath her content so absolute
190 That not another comfort like to this
Succeeds in unknown fate.

DESDEMONA   The heavens forbid
But that our loves and comforts should increase
Even as our days do grow.

OTHELLO   Amen to that, sweet powers!
I cannot speak enough of this content,
195 It stops me here, it is too much of joy.
And this, and this the greatest discords be [*They kiss.*]
That e'er our hearts shall make.

IAGO [*aside*]
O, you are well tuned now: but I'll set down
The pegs that make this music, as honest
As I am.

200 OTHELLO   Come, let us to the castle.
News, friends, our wars are done, the Turks are
drowned.
How does my old acquaintance of this isle?
Honey, you shall be well desired in Cyprus,
I have found great love amongst them. O my sweet,
205 I prattle out of fashion, and I dote
In mine own comforts. I prithee, good Iago,
Go to the bay and disembark my coffers.
Bring thou the master to the citadel,
He is a good one, and his worthiness
210 Does challenge much respect. Come, Desdemona;
Once more, well met at Cyprus.

Exeunt all but Iago and Roderigo.

IAGO   Do thou meet me presently at the harbour. Come
hither: if thou be'st valiant – as, they say, base men
being in love have then a nobility in their natures, more
215 than is native to them – list me. The lieutenant tonight
watches on the court of guard. First I must tell thee
this: Desdemona is directly in love with him.

RODERIGO   With him? why, 'tis not possible.

IAGO   Lay thy finger thus, and let thy soul be instructed.
220 Mark me with what violence she first loved the Moor,
but for bragging and telling her fantastical lies – and
will she love him still for prating? let not thy discreet
heart think it. Her eye must be fed, and what delight
shall she have to look on the devil? When the blood is
225 made dull with the act of sport, there should be, again
to inflame it, and to give satiety a fresh appetite,
loveliness in favour, sympathy in years, manners and
beauties, all which the Moor is defective in. Now for
want of these required conveniences, her delicate

tenderness will find itself abused, begin to heave the 230
gorge, disrelish and abhor the Moor – very nature will
instruct her in it and compel her to some second
choice. Now sir, this granted – as it is a most pregnant
and unforced position – who stands so eminent in the
degree of this fortune as Cassio does? a knave very 235
voluble, no farther conscionable than in putting on the
mere form of civil and humane seeming, for the better
compassing of his salt and most hidden loose affection.
Why none, why none: a slipper and subtle knave, a
finder out of occasions, that has an eye, can stamp and 240
counterfeit advantages, though true advantage never
present itself – a devilish knave; besides, the knave is
handsome, young, and hath all those requisites in him
that folly and green minds look after. A pestilent
complete knave, and the woman hath found him 245
already.

RODERIGO   I cannot believe that in her, she's full of
most blest condition.

IAGO   Blest fig's-end! The wine she drinks is made of
grapes. If she had been blest she would never have 250
loved the Moor. Blest pudding! Didst thou not see her
paddle with the palm of his hand? Didst not mark
that?

RODERIGO   Yes, that I did, but that was but courtesy.

IAGO   Lechery, by this hand: an index and obscure 255
prologue to the history of lust and foul thoughts. They
met so near with their lips that their breaths embraced
together. Villainous thoughts, Roderigo: when these
mutualities so marshal the way, hard at hand comes
the master and main exercise, th'incorporate 260
conclusion. Pish! But, sir, be you ruled by me. I have
brought you from Venice: watch you tonight. For the
command, I'll lay't upon you. Cassio knows you not,
I'll not be far from you, do you find some occasion to
anger Cassio, either by speaking too loud or tainting 265
his discipline, or from what other cause you please
which the time shall more favourably minister.

RODERIGO   Well.

IAGO   Sir, he's rash and very sudden in choler, and haply
with his truncheon may strike at you: provoke him 270
that he may, for even out of that will I cause these
of Cyprus to mutiny, whose qualification shall come
into no true trust again but by the displanting of
Cassio. So shall you have a shorter journey to your
desires, by the means I shall then have to prefer 275
them, and the impediment most profitably removed,
without the which there were no expectation of our
prosperity.

RODERIGO   I will do this, if you can bring it to any
opportunity. 280

IAGO   I warrant thee. Meet me by and by at the citadel:
I must fetch his necessaries ashore. Farewell.

RODERIGO   Adieu.   *Exit.*

IAGO   That Cassio loves her, I do well believe it,
That she loves him, 'tis apt and of great credit. 285
The Moor, howbeit that I endure him not,

Is of a constant, loving, noble nature,
And I dare think he'll prove to Desdemona
A most dear husband. Now I do love her too,
Not out of absolute lust – though peradventure
I stand accountant for as great a sin –
But partly led to diet my revenge,
For that I do suspect the lusty Moor
Hath leaped into my seat, the thought whereof
Doth like a poisonous mineral gnaw my inwards . . .
And nothing can or shall content my soul
Till I am evened with him, wife for wife . . .
Or, failing so, yet that I put the Moor
At least into a jealousy so strong
That judgement cannot cure; which thing to do,
If this poor trash of Venice, whom I trash
For his quick hunting, stand the putting on,
I'll have our Michael Cassio on the hip,
Abuse him to the Moor in the rank garb –
For I fear Cassio with my night-cap too –
Make the Moor thank me, love me, and reward me
For making him egregiously an ass,
And practising upon his peace and quiet
Even to madness. 'Tis here, but yet confused:
Knavery's plain face is never seen, till used.   *Exit.*

2.2   *Enter Othello's* Herald, *with a proclamation.*

HERALD [*Reads.*]   *It is Othello's pleasure, our noble and
valiant general, that, upon certain tidings now arrived,
importing the mere perdition of the Turkish fleet, every
man put himself into triumph: some to dance, some to
make bonfires, each man to what sport and revels his
addiction leads him. For besides these beneficial news, it is
the celebration of his nuptial.* – So much was his pleasure
should be proclaimed. All offices are open, and there is
full liberty of feasting from this present hour of five till
the bell have told eleven. Heaven bless the isle of
Cyprus and our noble general Othello!   *Exit.*

2.3   *Enter* OTHELLO, CASSIO *and* DESDEMONA.

OTHELLO
Good Michael, look you to the guard tonight.
Let's teach ourselves that honourable stop
Not to outsport discretion.
CASSIO   Iago hath direction what to do,
But notwithstanding with my personal eye
Will I look to't.
OTHELLO   Iago is most honest.
Michael, good night. Tomorrow with your earliest
Let me have speech with you. Come, my dear love,
The purchase made, the fruits are to ensue:
That profit's yet to come 'tween me and you.
Good-night.   *Exeunt Othello and Desdemona.*

Enter IAGO.

CASSIO   Welcome, Iago, we must to the watch.

IAGO   Not this hour, lieutenant, 'tis not yet ten o'th'
clock. Our general cast us thus early for the love of his
Desdemona – whom let us not therefore blame; he
hath not yet made wanton the night with her, and she
is sport for Jove.
CASSIO   She's a most exquisite lady.
IAGO   And I'll warrant her full of game.
CASSIO   Indeed she's a most fresh and delicate creature.
IAGO   What an eye she has! methinks it sounds a parley
to provocation.
CASSIO   An inviting eye; and yet methinks right modest.
IAGO   And when she speaks is it not an alarum to love?
CASSIO   She is indeed perfection.
IAGO   Well: happiness to their sheets! Come, lieutenant,
I have a stoup of wine, and here without are a brace of
Cyprus gallants that would fain have a measure to the
health of black Othello.
CASSIO   Not tonight, good Iago, I have very poor and
unhappy brains for drinking. I could well wish courtesy
would invent some other custom of entertainment.
IAGO   O, they are our friends. But one cup, I'll drink for
you.
CASSIO   I have drunk but one cup tonight, and that was
craftily qualified too, and behold what innovation it
makes here! I am unfortunate in the infirmity, and dare
not task my weakness with any more.
IAGO   What, man, 'tis a night of revels, the gallants
desire it.
CASSIO   Where are they?
IAGO   Here, at the door, I pray you call them in.
CASSIO   I'll do't, but it dislikes me.   *Exit.*
IAGO   If I can fasten but one cup upon him,
With that which he hath drunk tonight already
He'll be as full of quarrel and offence
As my young mistress' dog. Now my sick fool, Roderigo,
Whom love hath turned almost the wrong side out,
To Desdemona hath tonight caroused
Potations pottle-deep, and he's to watch.
Three else of Cyprus, noble swelling spirits
That hold their honours in a wary distance,
The very elements of this warlike isle,
Have I tonight flustered with flowing cups,
And the watch too. Now 'mongst this flock of drunkards
Am I to put our Cassio in some action
That may offend the isle.

Enter CASSIO, MONTANO *and* Gentlemen.

                              But here they come.
If consequence do but approve my dream
My boat sails freely, both with wind and stream.
CASSIO   'Fore God, they have given me a rouse already.
MONTANO   Good faith, a little one, not past a pint, as I
am a soldier.
IAGO   Some wine, ho!
[*Sings.*]
              And let me the cannikin clink, clink,
              And let me the cannikin clink.

A soldier's a man,
O, man's life's but a span,
Why then let a soldier drink!
Some wine, boys!

70 CASSIO 'Fore God, an excellent song!

IAGO I learned it in England, where indeed they are most potent in potting. Your Dane, your German, and your swag-bellied Hollander – drink, ho! – are nothing to your English.

75 CASSIO Is your Englishman so exquisite in his drinking?

IAGO Why, he drinks you with facility your Dane dead drunk; he sweats not to overthrow your Almain; he gives your Hollander a vomit ere the next pottle can be filled.

80 CASSIO To the health of our general!

MONTANO I am for it, lieutenant, and I'll do you justice.

IAGO O sweet England!
[*Sings.*]
King Stephen was and-a worthy peer,
His breeches cost him but a crown,
85 He held them sixpence all too dear,
With that he called the tailor lown.
He was a wight of high renown
And thou art but of low degree,
'Tis pride that pulls the country down,
90 Then take thine auld cloak about thee.
Some wine, ho!

CASSIO 'Fore God, this is a more exquisite song than the other!

IAGO Will you hear't again?

95 CASSIO No, for I hold him to be unworthy of his place that does . . . those things. Well, God's above all, and there be souls must be saved, and there be souls must not be saved.

IAGO It's true, good lieutenant.

100 CASSIO For mine own part, no offence to the general nor any man of quality, I hope to be saved.

IAGO And so do I too, lieutenant.

CASSIO Ay, but, by your leave, not before me. The lieutenant is to be saved before the ancient. Let's have
105 no more of this, let's to our affairs. God forgive us our sins! Gentlemen, let's look to our business. Do not think, gentlemen, I am drunk: this is my ancient, this is my right hand, and this is my left. I am not drunk now: I can stand well enough, and I speak well enough.

110 GENTLEMAN Excellent well.

CASSIO Why, very well then; you must not think then that I am drunk. *Exit.*

MONTANO
To th' platform, masters, come, let's set the watch.

IAGO You see this fellow that is gone before,
115 He is a soldier fit to stand by Caesar
And give direction. And do but see his vice,
'Tis to his virtue a just equinox,
The one as long as th'other. 'Tis pity of him:
I fear the trust Othello puts him in
120 On some odd time of his infirmity

Will shake this island.

MONTANO But is he often thus?

IAGO 'Tis evermore the prologue to his sleep:
He'll watch the horologe a double set
If drink rock not his cradle.

MONTANO It were well
The general were put in mind of it. 125
Perhaps he sees it not, or his good nature
Prizes the virtue that appears in Cassio
And looks not on his evils: is not this true?

Enter RODERIGO.

IAGO [*aside*] How now, Roderigo?
I pray you, after the lieutenant, go! *Exit Roderigo.* 130

MONTANO And 'tis great pity that the noble Moor
Should hazard such a place as his own second
With one of an ingraft infirmity.
It were an honest action to say so
To the Moor.

IAGO Not I, for this fair island. 135
I do love Cassio well, and would do much
[*A cry within:* 'Help! help!']
To cure him of this evil. But hark, what noise?

Enter CASSIO *pursuing* RODERIGO.

CASSIO Zounds, you rogue! you rascal!

MONTANO What's the matter, lieutenant?

CASSIO A knave teach me my duty? I'll beat the knave 140
into a twiggen bottle!

RODERIGO Beat me?

CASSIO Dost thou prate, rogue?

MONTANO Nay, good lieutenant! I pray you, sir, hold
your hand. 145

CASSIO Let me go, sir, or I'll knock you o'er the mazzard.

MONTANO Come, come, you're drunk.

CASSIO Drunk? [*They fight.*]

IAGO [*aside to Roderigo*]
Away, I say, go out and cry a mutiny. *Exit Roderigo.*
Nay, good lieutenant! God's will, gentlemen – 150
Help ho! Lieutenant! sir – Montano – sir –
Help, masters, here's a goodly watch indeed.
[*A bell rings.*]
Who's that which rings the bell? Diablo, ho!
The town will rise, God's will, lieutenant, hold,
You will be shamed for ever! 155

Enter OTHELLO *and Attendants.*

OTHELLO What is the matter here?

MONTANO Zounds, I bleed still;
I am hurt to th' death: he dies! [*Lunges at Cassio.*]

OTHELLO Hold, for your lives!

IAGO
Hold, ho! Lieutenant! sir – Montano – gentlemen –
Have you forgot all sense of place and duty?
Hold, the general speaks to you: hold, for shame! 160

OTHELLO
  Why, how now, ho? From whence ariseth this?
  Are we turned Turks? and to ourselves do that
  Which heaven hath forbid the Ottomites?
  For Christian shame, put by this barbarous brawl;
165 He that stirs next, to carve for his own rage,
  Holds his soul light: he dies upon his motion.
  Silence that dreadful bell, it frights the isle
  From her propriety. What is the matter, masters?
  Honest Iago, that look'st dead with grieving,
170 Speak: who began this? on thy love I charge thee.

IAGO   I do not know, friends all, but now, even now,
  In quarter and in terms like bride and groom
  Divesting them for bed; and then, but now,
  As if some planet had unwitted men,
175 Swords out, and tilting one at other's breasts
  In opposition bloody. I cannot speak
  Any beginning to this peevish odds,
  And would in action glorious I had lost
  Those legs that brought me to a part of it.

180 OTHELLO   How comes it, Michael, you are thus forgot?

CASSIO   I pray you pardon me, I cannot speak.

OTHELLO   Worthy Montano, you were wont to be civil:
  The gravity and stillness of your youth
  The world hath noted, and your name is great
185 In mouths of wisest censure. What's the matter
  That you unlace your reputation thus
  And spend your rich opinion for the name
  Of a night-brawler? Give me answer to it.

MONTANO   Worthy Othello, I am hurt to danger:
190 Your officer Iago can inform you,
  While I spare speech, which something now offends
      me,
  Of all that I do know; nor know I aught
  By me that's said or done amiss this night
195 Unless self-charity be sometimes a vice,
  And to defend ourselves it be a sin
  When violence assails us.

OTHELLO   Now, by heaven,
  My blood begins my safer guides to rule
  And passion, having my best judgement collied,
  Assays to lead the way. Zounds, if I once stir,
200 Or do but lift this arm, the best of you
  Shall sink in my rebuke. Give me to know
  How this foul rout began, who set it on,
  And he that is approved in this offence,
  Though he had twinned with me, both at a birth,
205 Shall lose me. What, in a town of war
  Yet wild, the people's hearts brimful of fear,
  To manage private and domestic quarrel?
  In night, and on the court and guard of safety?
  'Tis monstrous. Iago, who began't?

210 MONTANO   If partially affined or leagued in office
  Thou dost deliver more or less than truth
  Thou art no soldier.

IAGO   Touch me not so near.
  I had rather have this tongue cut from my mouth

  Than it should do offence to Michael Cassio,
215 Yet I persuade myself to speak the truth
  Shall nothing wrong him. Thus it is, general:
  Montano and myself being in speech,
  There comes a fellow crying out for help
  And Cassio following him with determined sword
220 To execute upon him. Sir, this gentleman
  Steps in to Cassio and entreats his pause,
  Myself the crying fellow did pursue
  Lest by his clamour, as it so fell out,
  The town might fall in fright. He, swift of foot,
225 Outran my purpose, and I returned the rather
  For that I heard the clink and fall of swords
  And Cassio high in oath, which till tonight
  I ne'er might say before. When I came back,
  For this was brief, I found them close together
230 At blow and thrust, even as again they were
  When you yourself did part them.
  More of this matter cannot I report.
  But men are men, the best sometimes forget;
  Though Cassio did some little wrong to him,
235 As men in rage strike those that wish them best,
  Yet surely Cassio, I believe, received
  From him that fled some strange indignity
  Which patience could not pass.

OTHELLO   I know, Iago,
  Thy honesty and love doth mince this matter,
240 Making it light to Cassio. Cassio, I love thee,

Enter DESDEMONA, *attended.*

  But never more be officer of mine.
  Look if my gentle love be not raised up!
  I'll make thee an example.

DESDEMONA   What is the matter, dear?

OTHELLO   All's well now, sweeting,
245 Come away to bed. – Sir, for your hurts
  Myself will be your surgeon. Lead him off.

                        Montano is led off.
  Iago, look with care about the town
  And silence those whom this vile brawl distracted.
  Come, Desdemona: 'tis the soldier's life
250 To have their balmy slumbers waked with strife.

                  Exeunt all but Iago and Cassio.

IAGO   What, are you hurt, lieutenant?

CASSIO   Ay, past all surgery.

IAGO   Marry, God forbid!

CASSIO   Reputation, reputation, reputation! O, I have
255 lost my reputation, I have lost the immortal part of
  myself – and what remains is bestial. My reputation,
  Iago, my reputation!

IAGO   As I am an honest man I thought you had received
  some bodily wound; there is more of sense in that than
260 in reputation. Reputation is an idle and most false
  imposition, oft got without merit and lost without
  deserving. You have lost no reputation at all, unless you
  repute yourself such a loser. What, man, there are ways
  to recover the general again. You are but now cast in his

265 mood, a punishment more in policy than in malice,
even so as one would beat his offenceless dog to affright
an imperious lion. Sue to him again, and he's yours.

CASSIO   I will rather sue to be despised, than to deceive
270 so good a commander with so slight, so drunken, and
so indiscreet an officer. Drunk? and speak parrot? and
squabble? swagger? swear? and discourse fustian with
one's own shadow? O thou invisible spirit of wine, if
thou hast no name to be known by, let us call thee
devil!

275 IAGO   What was he that you followed with your sword?
What had he done to you?

CASSIO   I know not.

IAGO   Is't possible?

CASSIO   I remember a mass of things, but nothing
280 distinctly; a quarrel, but nothing wherefore. O God,
that men should put an enemy in their mouths, to steal
away their brains! that we should with joy, pleasance,
revel and applause, transform ourselves into beasts!

IAGO   Why, but you are now well enough: how came you
285 thus recovered?

CASSIO   It hath pleased the devil drunkenness to give
place to the devil wrath; one unperfectness shows me
another, to make me frankly despise myself.

IAGO   Come, you are too severe a moraler. As the time,
290 the place and the condition of this country stands, I
could heartily wish this had not befallen; but since it is
as it is, mend it for your own good.

CASSIO   I will ask him for my place again, he shall tell
me I am a drunkard: had I as many mouths as Hydra,
295 such an answer would stop them all. To be now a
sensible man, by and by a fool, and presently a beast! O
strange! – Every inordinate cup is unblest, and the
ingredience is a devil.

IAGO   Come, come, good wine is a good familiar
300 creature, if it be well used: exclaim no more against it.
And, good lieutenant, I think you think I love you.

CASSIO   I have well approved it, sir. I drunk?

IAGO   You, or any man living, may be drunk at some
time, man. I'll tell you what you shall do. Our general's
305 wife is now the general. I may say so in this respect, for
that he hath devoted and given up himself to the
contemplation, mark and denotement of her parts and
graces. Confess yourself freely to her, importune her
help to put you in your place again. She is of so free, so
310 kind, so apt, so blest a disposition that she holds it a
vice in her goodness not to do more than she is
requested. This broken joint between you and her
husband entreat her to splinter – and my fortunes
against any lay worth naming, this crack of your love
315 shall grow stronger than it was before.

CASSIO   You advise me well.

IAGO   I protest, in the sincerity of love and honest
kindness.

CASSIO   I think it freely, and betimes in the morning I will
320 beseech the virtuous Desdemona to undertake for me. I
am desperate of my fortunes if they check me here.

IAGO   You are in the right. Good-night, lieutenant, I
must to the watch.

CASSIO   Good-night, honest Iago.   *Exit.*

325 IAGO   And what's he then that says I play the villain?
When this advice is free I give and honest,
Probal to thinking and indeed the course
To win the Moor again? For 'tis most easy
Th'inclining Desdemona to subdue
330 In any honest suit. She's framed as fruitful
As the free elements: and then for her
To win the Moor, were't to renounce his baptism,
All seals and symbols of redeemed sin,
His soul is so enfettered to her love
335 That she may make, unmake, do what she list,
Even as her appetite shall play the god
With his weak function. How am I then a villain
To counsel Cassio to this parallel course
Directly to his good? Divinity of hell!
340 When devils will the blackest sins put on
They do suggest at first with heavenly shows
As I do now. For whiles this honest fool
Plies Desdemona to repair his fortune,
And she for him pleads strongly to the Moor,
345 I'll pour this pestilence into his ear:
That she repeals him for her body's lust.
And by how much she strives to do him good
She shall undo her credit with the Moor –
So will I turn her virtue into pitch
350 And out of her own goodness make the net
That shall enmesh them all.

Enter RODERIGO.

                              How now, Roderigo?

RODERIGO   I do follow here in the chase not like a hound
that hunts, but one that fills up the cry. My money is
almost spent, I have been tonight exceedingly well
355 cudgelled, and I think the issue will be I shall have so
much experience for my pains: and so, with no money
at all, and a little more wit, return again to Venice.

IAGO   How poor are they that have not patience!
What wound did ever heal but by degrees?
360 Thou know'st we work by wit and not by witchcraft,
And wit depends on dilatory time.
Does't not go well? Cassio hath beaten thee
And thou by that small hurt hast cashiered Cassio.
Though other things grow fair against the sun
365 Yet fruits that blossom first will first be ripe;
Content thyself a while. By the mass, 'tis morning:
Pleasure and action make the hours seem short.
Retire thee, go where thou art billeted,
Away, I say, thou shalt know more hereafter:
Nay, get thee gone.   *Exit Roderigo.*
370   Two things are to be done:
My wife must move for Cassio to her mistress,
I'll set her on.
Myself the while to draw the Moor apart
And bring him jump when he may Cassio find

375 Soliciting his wife: ay, that's the way!
Dull not device by coldness and delay!   *Exit.*

3.1   *Enter* CASSIO *and some* Musicians.

CASSIO   Masters, play here, I will content your pains;
Something that's brief, and bid 'Good morrow, general'.

They play. Enter Clown.

CLOWN   Why, masters, have your instruments been in
Naples, that they speak i'th' nose thus?
5 1 MUSICIAN   How, sir? how?
CLOWN   Are these, I pray you, wind instruments?
1 MUSICIAN   Ay marry are they, sir.
CLOWN   O, thereby hangs a tail.
1 MUSICIAN   Whereby hangs a tail, sir?
10 CLOWN   Marry, sir, by many a wind instrument that I
know. But, masters, here's money for you, and the
general so likes your music that he desires you, for
love's sake, to make no more noise with it.
1 MUSICIAN   Well, sir, we will not.
15 CLOWN   If you have any music that may not be heard,
to't again. But, as they say, to hear music the general
does not greatly care.
1 MUSICIAN   We have none such, sir.
CLOWN   Then put up your pipes in your bag, for I'll
20 away. Go, vanish into air, away!   *Exeunt Musicians.*
CASSIO   Dost thou hear, mine honest friend?
CLOWN   No, I hear not your honest friend, I hear you.
CASSIO   Prithee keep up thy quillets; there's a poor
25 piece of gold for thee – if the gentlewoman that attends
the general's wife be stirring, tell her there's one Cassio
entreats her a little favour of speech. Wilt thou do this?
CLOWN   She is stirring, sir; if she will stir hither, I shall
seem to notify unto her.

Enter IAGO.

CASSIO   Do, good my friend.   *Exit Clown.*
In happy time, Iago.
30 IAGO   You have not been a-bed then?
CASSIO   Why no, the day had broke before we parted.
I have made bold, Iago, to send in
To your wife: my suit to her is that she will
To virtuous Desdemona procure me
Some access.
35 IAGO   I'll send her to you presently,
And I'll devise a mean to draw the Moor
Out of the way, that your converse and business
May be more free.
CASSIO   I humbly thank you for't.   *Exit Iago.*
I never knew
40 A Florentine more kind and honest.

Enter EMILIA.

EMILIA   Good morrow, good lieutenant. I am sorry
For your displeasure, but all will sure be well.
The general and his wife are talking of it,

And she speaks for you stoutly; the Moor replies
45 That he you hurt is of great fame in Cyprus
And great affinity,
And that in wholesome wisdom he might not but
Refuse you; but he protests he loves you
And needs no other suitor but his likings
50 To take the safest occasion by the front
To bring you in again.
CASSIO   Yet I beseech you,
If you think fit, or that it may be done,
Give me advantage of some brief discourse
With Desdemon alone.
EMILIA   Pray you come in,
55 I will bestow you where you shall have time
To speak your bosom freely.
CASSIO   I am much bound to you.
Exeunt.

3.2   *Enter* OTHELLO, IAGO *and* Gentlemen.

OTHELLO   These letters give, Iago, to the pilot,
And by him do my duties to the Senate;
That done, I will be walking on the works,
Repair there to me.
IAGO   Well, my good lord, I'll do't.
5 OTHELLO   This fortification, gentlemen, shall we see't?
1 GENTLEMAN   We'll wait upon your lordship.
Exeunt.

3.3   *Enter* DESDEMONA, CASSIO *and* Emilia.

DESDEMONA   Be thou assured, good Cassio, I will do
All my abilities in thy behalf.
EMILIA
Good madam, do, I warrant it grieves my husband
As if the cause were his.
DESDEMONA
5 O, that's an honest fellow. Do not doubt, Cassio,
But I will have my lord and you again
As friendly as you were.
CASSIO   Bounteous madam,
Whatever shall become of Michael Cassio,
He's never anything but your true servant.
DESDEMONA
10 I know't, I thank you. You do love my lord,
You have known him long, and be you well assured
He shall in strangeness stand no farther off
Than in a politic distance.
CASSIO   Ay, but, lady,
That policy may either last so long,
15 Or feed upon such nice and waterish diet,
Or breed itself so out of circumstance,
That, I being absent and my place supplied,
My general will forget my love and service.
DESDEMONA   Do not doubt that: before Emilia here
20 I give thee warrant of thy place. Assure thee,
If I do vow a friendship I'll perform it

To the last article. My lord shall never rest,
I'll watch him tame and talk him out of patience,
His bed shall seem a school, his board a shrift,
25   I'll intermingle everything he does
With Cassio's suit: therefore be merry, Cassio,
For thy solicitor shall rather die
Than give thy cause away.

Enter OTHELLO *and* IAGO.

EMILIA   Madam, here comes my lord.
30   CASSIO   Madam, I'll take my leave.
DESDEMONA   Why, stay and hear me speak.
CASSIO   Madam, not now; I am very ill at ease,
Unfit for mine own purposes.
DESDEMONA   Well, do your discretion.   *Exit Cassio.*
IAGO   Ha, I like not that.
35   OTHELLO   What dost thou say?
IAGO   Nothing, my lord; or if – I know not what.
OTHELLO   Was not that Cassio parted from my wife?
IAGO   Cassio, my lord? no, sure, I cannot think it
That he would steal away so guilty-like
Seeing you coming.
40   OTHELLO   I do believe 'twas he.
DESDEMONA   How now, my lord?
I have been talking with a suitor here,
A man that languishes in your displeasure.
OTHELLO   Who is't you mean?
DESDEMONA
45   Why, your lieutenant, Cassio. Good my lord,
If I have any grace or power to move you
His present reconciliation take:
For if he be not one that truly loves you,
That errs in ignorance and not in cunning,
50   I have no judgement in an honest face.
I prithee, call him back.
OTHELLO   Went he hence now?
DESDEMONA   Yes, faith, so humbled
That he hath left part of his grief with me
To suffer with him. Good love, call him back.
55   OTHELLO   Not now, sweet Desdemon, some other time.
DESDEMONA   But shall't be shortly?
OTHELLO   The sooner, sweet, for you.
DESDEMONA   Shall't be tonight, at supper?
OTHELLO   No, not tonight.
DESDEMONA   Tomorrow dinner then?
OTHELLO   I shall not dine at home.
I meet the captains at the citadel.
DESDEMONA
60   Why then, tomorrow night, or Tuesday morn;
On Tuesday, noon or night; on Wednesday morn!
I prithee name the time, but let it not
Exceed three days: i'faith, he's penitent,
And yet his trespass, in our common reason
65   – Save that they say the wars must make examples
Out of their best – is not, almost, a fault
T'incur a private check. When shall he come?
Tell me, Othello. I wonder in my soul

What you would ask me that I should deny
Or stand so mamm'ring on? What, Michael Cassio   70
That came a-wooing with you? and so many a time
When I have spoke of you dispraisingly
Hath ta'en your part, to have so much to do
To bring him in? By'r lady, I could do much! –
OTHELLO
Prithee, no more. Let him come when he will,   75
I will deny thee nothing.
DESDEMONA   Why, this is not a boon,
'Tis as I should entreat you wear your gloves,
Or feed on nourishing dishes, or keep you warm,
Or sue to you to do a peculiar profit
To your own person. Nay, when I have a suit   80
Wherein I mean to touch your love indeed
It shall be full of poise and difficult weight
And fearful to be granted.
OTHELLO   I will deny thee nothing.
Whereon I do beseech thee, grant me this,
To leave me but a little to myself.   85
DESDEMONA   Shall I deny you? No, farewell, my lord.
OTHELLO
Farewell, my Desdemona, I'll come to thee straight.
DESDEMONA
Emilia, come. – Be as your fancies teach you:
Whate'er you be, I am obedient.
                        Exeunt Desdemona and Emilia.
OTHELLO   Excellent wretch! perdition catch my soul   90
But I do love thee! and when I love thee not
Chaos is come again.
IAGO   My noble lord –
OTHELLO   What dost thou say, Iago?
IAGO   Did Michael Cassio, when you wooed my lady,
Know of your love?
OTHELLO   He did, from first to last.   95
Why dost thou ask?
IAGO   But for a satisfaction of my thought,
No further harm.
OTHELLO   Why of thy thought, Iago?
IAGO   I did not think he had been acquainted with her.
OTHELLO   O yes, and went between us very oft.   100
IAGO   Indeed?
OTHELLO
Indeed? Ay, indeed. Discern'st thou aught in that?
Is he not honest?
IAGO   Honest, my lord?
OTHELLO   Honest? Ay, honest.   105
IAGO   My lord, for aught I know.
OTHELLO   What dost thou think?
IAGO   Think, my lord?
OTHELLO   Think, my lord! By heaven, thou echo'st me
As if there were some monster in thy thought   110
Too hideous to be shown. Thou dost mean something,
I heard thee say even now thou lik'st not that
When Cassio left my wife: what didst not like?
And when I told thee he was of my counsel
In my whole course of wooing, thou criedst 'Indeed?'   115

And didst contract and purse thy brow together
As if thou then hadst shut up in thy brain
Some horrible conceit. If thou dost love me
Show me thy thought.

IAGO   My lord, you know I love you.

120 OTHELLO   I think thou dost.
And for I know thou'rt full of love and honesty
And weigh'st thy words before thou giv'st them
    breath,
Therefore these stops of thine fright me the more.
For such things in a false disloyal knave
125 Are tricks of custom, but in a man that's just
They're close delations, working from the heart,
That passion cannot rule.

IAGO   For Michael Cassio,
I dare be sworn, I think, that he is honest.

OTHELLO   I think so too.

IAGO   Men should be what they seem,
130 Or those that be not, would they might seem none.

OTHELLO   Certain, men should be what they seem.

IAGO   Why then I think Cassio's an honest man.

OTHELLO   Nay, yet there's more in this:
I prithee speak to me, as to thy thinkings,
135 As thou dost ruminate, and give thy worst of thoughts
The worst of words.

IAGO   Good my lord, pardon me;
Though I am bound to every act of duty
I am not bound to that all slaves are free to –
Utter my thoughts? Why, say they are vile and false?
140 As where's that palace whereinto foul things
Sometimes intrude not? Who has a breast so pure
But some uncleanly apprehensions
Keep leets and law-days and in session sit
With meditations lawful?

OTHELLO   Thou dost conspire against thy friend, Iago,
45 If thou but think'st him wronged and mak'st his ear
A stranger to thy thoughts.

IAGO   I do beseech you,
Though I perchance am vicious in my guess
– As I confess it is my nature's plague
50 To spy into abuses, and oft my jealousy
Shapes faults that are not – that your wisdom
From one that so imperfectly conceits
Would take no notice, nor build yourself a trouble
Out of his scattering and unsure observance:
55 It were not for your quiet nor your good
Nor for my manhood, honesty and wisdom
To let you know my thoughts.

OTHELLO   Zounds! What dost thou mean?

IAGO   Good name in man and woman, dear my lord,
Is the immediate jewel of their souls:
Who steals my purse steals trash – 'tis something-
    nothing,
60 'Twas mine, 'tis his, and has been slave to thousands –
But he that filches from me my good name
Robs me of that which not enriches him
And makes me poor indeed.

OTHELLO   By heaven, I'll know thy thoughts!

IAGO   You cannot, if my heart were in your hand,   165
Nor shall not whilst 'tis in my custody.

OTHELLO   Ha!

IAGO   O beware, my lord, of jealousy!
It is the green-eyed monster, which doth mock
The meat it feeds on. That cuckold lives in bliss
Who, certain of his fate, loves not his wronger,   170
But O, what damned minutes tells he o'er
Who dotes yet doubts, suspects yet strongly loves!

OTHELLO   O misery!

IAGO   Poor and content is rich, and rich enough,
But riches fineless is as poor as winter   175
To him that ever fears he shall be poor.
Good God, the souls of all my tribe defend
From jealousy.

OTHELLO   Why – why is this?
Think'st thou I'd make a life of jealousy   180
To follow still the changes of the moon
With fresh suspicions? No: to be once in doubt
Is once to be resolved. Exchange me for a goat
When I shall turn the business of my soul
To such exsufflicate and blown surmises,   185
Matching thy inference. 'Tis not to make me jealous
To say my wife is fair, feeds well, loves company,
Is free of speech, sings, plays and dances well:
Where virtue is, these are more virtuous.
Nor from mine own weak merits will I draw   190
The smallest fear or doubt of her revolt,
For she had eyes and chose me. No, Iago,
I'll see before I doubt, when I doubt, prove,
And on the proof there is no more but this:
Away at once with love or jealousy!   195

IAGO   I am glad of this, for now I shall have reason
To show the love and duty that I bear you
With franker spirit: therefore, as I am bound,
Receive it from me. I speak not yet of proof:
Look to your wife, observe her well with Cassio.   200
Wear your eyes thus, not jealous nor secure;
I would not have your free and noble nature
Out of self-bounty be abused: look to't.
I know our country disposition well –
In Venice they do let God see the pranks   205
They dare not show their husbands; their best
    conscience
Is not to leave't undone, but keep't unknown.

OTHELLO   Dost thou say so?

IAGO   She did deceive her father, marrying you,
And when she seemed to shake, and fear your looks,   210
She loved them most.

OTHELLO   And so she did.

IAGO   Why, go to then:
She that so young could give out such a seeming
To seel her father's eyes up, close as oak –
He thought 'twas witchcraft. But I am much to blame,
I humbly do beseech you of your pardon   215
For too much loving you.

OTHELLO   I am bound to thee for ever.
IAGO   I see this hath a little dashed your spirits.
OTHELLO   Not a jot, not a jot.
IAGO   I'faith, I fear it has.
220   I hope you will consider what is spoke
Comes from my love. But I do see you're moved;
I am to pray you not to strain my speech
To grosser issues nor to larger reach
Than to suspicion.
OTHELLO   I will not.
225   IAGO   Should you do so, my lord,
My speech should fall into such vile success
As my thoughts aimed not at: Cassio's my worthy
   friend.
My lord, I see you're moved.
OTHELLO   No, not much moved.
I do not think but Desdemona's honest.
230   IAGO   Long live she so; and long live you to think so.
OTHELLO   And yet how nature, erring from itself –
IAGO   Ay, there's the point: as, to be bold with you,
Not to affect many proposed matches
Of her own clime, complexion and degree,
235   Whereto we see, in all things, nature tends –
Foh! one may smell in such a will most rank,
Foul disproportion, thoughts unnatural.
But pardon me, I do not in position
Distinctly speak of her, though I may fear
240   Her will, recoiling to her better judgement,
May fall to match you with her country forms,
And happily repent.
OTHELLO   Farewell, farewell.
If more thou dost perceive, let me know more:
Set on thy wife to observe. Leave me, Iago.
IAGO   My lord, I take my leave.
245   OTHELLO   Why did I marry?
This honest creature doubtless
Sees and knows more – much more – than he unfolds.
IAGO   My lord, I would I might entreat your honour
To scan this thing no farther. Leave it to time;
250   Although 'tis fit that Cassio have his place,
For sure he fills it up with great ability,
Yet if you please to hold him off a while
You shall by that perceive him, and his means:
Note if your lady strain his entertainment
255   With any strong or vehement importunity,
Much will be seen in that. In the meantime
Let me be thought too busy in my fears
– As worthy cause I have to fear I am –
And hold her free, I do beseech your honour.
260   OTHELLO   Fear not my government.
IAGO   I once more take my leave.   *Exit.*
OTHELLO   This fellow's of exceeding honesty
And knows all qualities, with a learned spirit,
Of human dealings. If I do prove her haggard,
265   Though that her jesses were my dear heart-strings,
I'd whistle her off and let her down the wind
To prey at fortune. Haply for I am black

And have not those soft parts of conversation
That chamberers have, or for I am declined
Into the vale of years – yet that's not much –   270
She's gone, I am abused, and my relief
Must be to loathe her. O curse of marriage
That we can call these delicate creatures ours
And not their appetites! I had rather be a toad
And live upon the vapour of a dungeon   275
Than keep a corner in the thing I love
For others' uses. Yet 'tis the plague of great ones,
Prerogatived are they less than the base;
'Tis destiny unshunnable, like death –
Even then this forked plague is fated to us   280
When we do quicken.

Enter DESDEMONA *and* EMILIA.

                                    Look where she comes:
If she be false, O then heaven mocks itself,
I'll not believe't.
DESDEMONA   How now, my dear Othello?
Your dinner, and the generous islanders
By you invited, do attend your presence.   285
OTHELLO   I am to blame.
DESDEMONA   Why do you speak so faintly?
Are you not well?
OTHELLO   I have a pain upon my forehead, here.
DESDEMONA
Faith, that's with watching, 'twill away again.
Let me but bind it hard, within this hour   290
It will be well.
OTHELLO   Your napkin is too little.
   [*She drops her handkerchief.*]
Let it alone. Come, I'll go in with you.
DESDEMONA   I am very sorry that you are not well.
                          Exeunt Othello and Desdemona.
EMILIA   I am glad I have found this napkin,
This was her first remembrance from the Moor.   295
My wayward husband hath a hundred times
Wooed me to steal it, but she so loves the token
– For he conjured her she should ever keep it –
That she reserves it evermore about her
To kiss and talk to. I'll have the work ta'en out   300
And give't Iago: what he will do with it
Heaven knows, not I,
I nothing, but to please his fantasy.

Enter IAGO.

IAGO   How now! What do you here alone?
EMILIA   Do not you chide, I have a thing for you –   305
IAGO   You have a thing for me? it is a common thing –
EMILIA   Ha?
IAGO   To have a foolish wife.
EMILIA   O, is that all? What will you give me now
For that same handkerchief?
IAGO   What handkerchief?   310
EMILIA   What handkerchief?
Why, that the Moor first gave to Desdemona,

That which so often you did bid me steal.

IAGO   Hast stolen it from her?

315 EMILIA   No, faith, she let it drop by negligence
And, to th'advantage, I being here, took't up.
Look, here it is.

IAGO   A good wench, give it me.

EMILIA
What will you do with't, that you have been so earnest
To have me filch it?

IAGO [*snatching it*]   Why, what's that to you?

320 EMILIA   If it be not for some purpose of import
Give't me again. Poor lady, she'll run mad
When she shall lack it.

IAGO   Be not acknown on't,
I have use for it. Go, leave me.   *Exit Emilia.*
I will in Cassio's lodging lose this napkin

325 And let him find it. Trifles light as air
Are to the jealous confirmations strong
As proofs of holy writ. This may do something.
The Moor already changes with my poison:
Dangerous conceits are in their natures poisons

330 Which at the first are scarce found to distaste
But with a little art upon the blood
Burn like the mines of sulphur.

Enter OTHELLO.

I did say so:
Look where he comes. Not poppy nor mandragora
Nor all the drowsy syrups of the world

335 Shall ever medicine thee to that sweet sleep
Which thou owedst yesterday.

OTHELLO   Ha! Ha! false to me?

IAGO   Why, how now, general? No more of that.

OTHELLO
Avaunt, be gone, thou hast set me on the rack!
I swear 'tis better to be much abused
Than but to know't a little.

340 IAGO   How now, my lord?

OTHELLO
What sense had I of her stolen hours of lust?
I saw't not, thought it not, it harmed not me,
I slept the next night well, fed well, was free and
merry;
I found not Cassio's kisses on her lips;

345 He that is robbed, not wanting what is stolen,
Let him not know't, and he's not robbed at all.

IAGO   I am sorry to hear this.

OTHELLO   I had been happy if the general camp,
Pioneers and all, had tasted her sweet body,

350 So I had nothing known. O now for ever
Farewell the tranquil mind, farewell content!
Farewell the plumed troops and the big wars
That makes ambition virtue! O farewell,
Farewell the neighing steed and the shrill trump,

355 The spirit-stirring drum, th'ear-piercing fife,
The royal banner, and all quality,
Pride, pomp and circumstance of glorious war!

And, O you mortal engines whose rude throats
Th'immortal Jove's dread clamours counterfeit,
Farewell: Othello's occupation's gone.   360

IAGO   Is't possible? my lord?

OTHELLO   Villain, be sure thou prove my love a whore,
Be sure of it, give me the ocular proof,
[*catching hold of him*]
Or by the worth of man's eternal soul
Thou hadst been better have been born a dog   365
Than answer my waked wrath!

IAGO   Is't come to this?

OTHELLO   Make me to see't, or at the least so prove it
That the probation bear no hinge nor loop
To hang a doubt on, or woe upon thy life!

IAGO   My noble lord –   370

OTHELLO   If thou dost slander her and torture me
Never pray more, abandon all remorse;
On horror's head horrors accumulate,
Do deeds to make heaven weep, all earth amazed,
For nothing canst thou to damnation add   375
Greater than that!

IAGO   O grace! O heaven forgive me!
Are you a man? have you a soul, or sense?
God buy you, take mine office. O wretched fool
That lov'st to make thine honesty a vice!
O monstrous world! Take note, take note, O world,   380
To be direct and honest is not safe.
I thank you for this profit, and from hence
I'll love no friend, sith love breeds such offence.

OTHELLO   Nay, stay, thou shouldst be honest.

IAGO   I should be wise, for honesty's a fool   385
And loses that it works for.

OTHELLO   By the world,
I think my wife be honest, and think she is not,
I think that thou art just, and think thou art not.
I'll have some proof. Her name, that was as fresh
As Dian's visage, is now begrimed and black   390
As mine own face. If there be cords or knives,
Poison, or fire, or suffocating streams,
I'll not endure it. Would I were satisfied!

IAGO   I see, sir, you are eaten up with passion.
I do repent me that I put it to you.   395
You would be satisfied?

OTHELLO   Would? nay, and I will!

IAGO   And may – but how? how satisfied, my lord?
Would you, the supervisor, grossly gape on?
Behold her topped?

OTHELLO   Death and damnation! O!

IAGO   It were a tedious difficulty, I think,   400
To bring them to that prospect. Damn them then
If ever mortal eyes do see them bolster
More than their own. What then? how then?
What shall I say? where's satisfaction?
It is impossible you should see this   405
Were they as prime as goats, as hot as monkeys,
As salt as wolves in pride, and fools as gross
As ignorance made drunk. But yet, I say,

If imputation and strong circumstances
410 Which lead directly to the door of truth
Will give you satisfaction, you may have't.
OTHELLO   Give me a living reason she's disloyal.
IAGO   I do not like the office.
But sith I am entered in this cause so far,
415 Pricked to't by foolish honesty and love,
I will go on. I lay with Cassio lately
And being troubled with a raging tooth
I could not sleep. There are a kind of men
So loose of soul that in their sleeps will mutter
420 Their affairs – one of this kind is Cassio.
In sleep I heard him say 'Sweet Desdemona,
Let us be wary, let us hide our loves,'
And then, sir, would he gripe and wring my hand,
Cry 'O sweet creature!' and then kiss me hard
425 As if he plucked up kisses by the roots
That grew upon my lips, lay his leg o'er my
   thigh,
And sigh, and kiss, and then cry 'Cursed fate
That gave thee to the Moor!'
OTHELLO   O monstrous! monstrous!
IAGO   Nay, this was but his dream.
430 OTHELLO   But this denoted a foregone conclusion.
IAGO   'Tis a shrewd doubt, though it be but a dream,
And this may help to thicken other proofs
That do demonstrate thinly.
OTHELLO   I'll tear her all to pieces!
435 IAGO   Nay, yet be wise, yet we see nothing done,
She may be honest yet. Tell me but this,
Have you not sometimes seen a handkerchief
Spotted with strawberries, in your wife's hand?
OTHELLO   I gave her such a one, 'twas my first gift.
440 IAGO   I know not that, but such a handkerchief,
I am sure it was your wife's, did I today
See Cassio wipe his beard with.
OTHELLO   If it be that –
IAGO   If it be that, or any that was hers,
It speaks against her with the other proofs.
445 OTHELLO   O that the slave had forty thousand lives!
One is too poor, too weak for my revenge.
Now do I see 'tis true. Look here, Iago,
All my fond love thus do I blow to heaven:
'Tis gone!
450 Arise, black vengeance, from the hollow hell,
Yield up, O love, thy crown and hearted throne
To tyrannous hate! Swell, bosom, with thy fraught,
For 'tis of aspics' tongues!
IAGO   Yet be content!
OTHELLO   O blood, blood, blood!   [*Othello kneels.*]
455 IAGO   Patience, I say, your mind perhaps may change.
OTHELLO   Never, Iago. Like to the Pontic sea
Whose icy current and compulsive course
Ne'er keeps retiring ebb but keeps due on
To the Propontic and the Hellespont:
460 Even so my bloody thoughts with violent pace
Shall ne'er look back, ne'er ebb to humble love

Till that a capable and wide revenge
Swallow them up. Now by yond marble heaven
In the due reverence of a sacred vow
I here engage my words.
IAGO   Do not rise yet.   [*Iago kneels.*]   465
Witness, you ever-burning lights above,
You elements that clip us round about,
Witness that here Iago doth give up
The execution of his wit, hands, heart,
To wronged Othello's service. Let him command   470
And to obey shall be in me remorse
What bloody business ever.
OTHELLO   I greet thy love
Not with vain thanks but with acceptance
   bounteous,
And will upon the instant put thee to't.
Within these three days let me hear thee say   475
That Cassio's not alive.
IAGO   My friend is dead,
'Tis done – at your request. But let her live.
OTHELLO
Damn her, lewd minx: O damn her, damn her!
Come, go with me apart; I will withdraw
To furnish me with some swift means of death   480
For the fair devil. Now art thou my lieutenant.
IAGO   I am your own for ever.   *Exeunt.*

3.4   Enter DESDEMONA, EMILIA *and* Clown.

DESDEMONA   Do you know, sirrah, where lieutenant
Cassio lies?
CLOWN   I dare not say he lies anywhere.
DESDEMONA   Why, man?
CLOWN   He's a soldier, and for me to say a soldier lies,   5
'tis stabbing.
DESDEMONA   Go to, where lodges he?
CLOWN   To tell you where he lodges is to tell you where
I lie.
DESDEMONA   Can anything be made of this?   10
CLOWN   I know not where he lodges, and for me to
devise a lodging and say he lies here, or he lies there,
were to lie in mine own throat.
DESDEMONA   Can you enquire him out and be edified
by report?   15
CLOWN   I will catechize the world for him, that is, make
questions and by them answer.
DESDEMONA   Seek him, bid him come hither, tell him I
have moved my lord on his behalf, and hope all will be
well.   20
CLOWN   To do this is within the compass of man's wit,
and therefore I will attempt the doing it.   *Exit.*
DESDEMONA
Where should I lose that handkerchief, Emilia?
EMILIA   I know not, madam.
DESDEMONA
Believe me, I had rather have lost my purse   25
Full of crusadoes; and but my noble Moor

Is true of mind, and made of no such baseness
As jealous creatures are, it were enough
30 To put him to ill-thinking.

EMILIA   Is he not jealous?

DESDEMONA
Who, he? I think the sun where he was born
Drew all such humours from him.

EMILIA   Look where he comes.

Enter OTHELLO.

DESDEMONA   I will not leave him now till Cassio
Be called to him. How is't with you, my lord?

OTHELLO
Well, my good lady. [*aside*] O hardness to
    dissemble! –
How do you, Desdemona?

35 DESDEMONA   Well, my good lord.

OTHELLO
Give me your hand. This hand is moist, my lady.

DESDEMONA
It yet hath felt no age, nor known no sorrow.

OTHELLO
This argues fruitfulness and liberal heart:
Hot, hot, and moist. This hand of yours requires
40 A sequester from liberty, fasting and prayer,
Much castigation, exercise devout,
For here's a young and sweating devil, here,
That commonly rebels. 'Tis a good hand,
A frank one.

DESDEMONA   You may indeed say so,
45 For 'twas that hand that gave away my heart.

OTHELLO
A liberal hand. The hearts of old gave hands
But our new heraldry is hands, not hearts.

DESDEMONA
I cannot speak of this. Come, now, your promise.

OTHELLO   What promise, chuck?

DESDEMONA
50 I have sent to bid Cassio come speak with you.

OTHELLO
I have a salt and sullen rheum offends me,
Lend me thy handkerchief.

DESDEMONA   Here, my lord.

OTHELLO   That which I gave you.

55 DESDEMONA   I have it not about me.

OTHELLO   Not?

DESDEMONA   No, faith, my lord.

OTHELLO   That's a fault. That handkerchief
Did an Egyptian to my mother give,
She was a charmer and could almost read
60 The thoughts of people. She told her, while she kept it
'Twould make her amiable and subdue my father
Entirely to her love; but if she lost it
Or made a gift of it, my father's eye
Should hold her loathed and his spirits should hunt
65 After new fancies. She, dying, gave it me
And bid me, when my fate would have me wive,

To give it her. I did so, and – take heed on't! –
Make it a darling, like your precious eye! –
To lose't or give't away were such perdition
As nothing else could match.

DESDEMONA   Is't possible?   70

OTHELLO   'Tis true, there's magic in the web of it.
A sibyl that had numbered in the world
The sun to course two hundred compasses,
In her prophetic fury sewed the work;
The worms were hallowed that did breed the silk,   75
And it was dyed in mummy, which the skilful
Conserved of maidens' hearts.

DESDEMONA   I'faith, is't true?

OTHELLO   Most veritable, therefore look to't well.

DESDEMONA
Then would to God that I had never seen't!

OTHELLO   Ha! wherefore?   80

DESDEMONA   Why do you speak so startingly and rash?

OTHELLO   Is't lost? Is't gone? Speak, is't out o'the way?

DESDEMONA   Heaven bless us!

OTHELLO   Say you?

DESDEMONA   It is not lost, but what an if it were?   85

OTHELLO   How?

DESDEMONA   I say it is not lost.

OTHELLO   Fetch't, let me see't.

DESDEMONA   Why, so I can, sir; but I will not now.
This is a trick to put me from my suit.
Pray you, let Cassio be received again.   90

OTHELLO
Fetch me the handkerchief, my mind misgives.

DESDEMONA   Come, come,
You'll never meet a more sufficient man.

OTHELLO   The handkerchief!

DESDEMONA   I pray, talk me of Cassio.

OTHELLO   The handkerchief!

DESDEMONA   A man that all his time   95
Hath founded his good fortunes on your love,
Shared dangers with you –

OTHELLO   The handkerchief!

DESDEMONA   I'faith, you are to blame.

OTHELLO   Zounds!   *Exit.*

EMILIA   Is not this man jealous?   100

DESDEMONA   I ne'er saw this before,
Sure there's some wonder in this handkerchief;
I am most unhappy in the loss of it.

EMILIA   'Tis not a year or two shows us a man.
They are all but stomachs, and we all but food: 105
They eat us hungerly, and when they are full
They belch us.

Enter IAGO *and* CASSIO.

                    Look you, Cassio and my husband.

IAGO   There is no other way, 'tis she must do't,
And lo, the happiness! go and importune her.

DESDEMONA
How now, good Cassio, what's the news with you?   110

CASSIO   Madam, my former suit. I do beseech you

That by your virtuous means I may again
Exist, and be a member of his love
Whom I, with all the office of my heart
115 Entirely honour. I would not be delayed:
If my offence be of such mortal kind
That nor my service past nor present sorrows
Nor purposed merit in futurity
Can ransom me into his love again,
120 But to know so must be my benefit;
So shall I clothe me in a forced content
And shut myself up in some other course
To fortune's alms.

DESDEMONA　　　　　　Alas, thrice-gentle Cassio,
My advocation is not now in tune;
125 My lord is not my lord, nor should I know him
Were he in favour as in humour altered.
So help me every spirit sanctified
As I have spoken for you all my best
And stood within the blank of his displeasure
130 For my free speech. You must awhile be patient:
What I can do I will, and more I will
Than for myself I dare. Let that suffice you.

IAGO　　Is my lord angry?

EMILIA　　　　　　He went hence but now,
And certainly in strange unquietness.

135 IAGO　　Can he be angry? I have seen the cannon
When it hath blown his ranks into the air
And like the devil, from his very arm,
Puffed his own brother – and can he be angry?
Something of moment then. I will go meet him,
140 There's matter in't indeed, if he be angry.

DESDEMONA　　I prithee do so.　　　　　　*Exit Iago.*
Something sure of state
Either from Venice, or some unhatched practice
Made demonstrable here in Cyprus to him,
Hath puddled his clear spirit, and in such cases
145 Men's natures wrangle with inferior things
Though great ones are their object. 'Tis even so,
For let our finger ache and it indues
Our other healthful members even to that sense
Of pain. Nay, we must think men are not gods
150 Nor of them look for such observancy
As fits the bridal. Beshrew me much, Emilia,
I was, unhandsome warrior as I am,
Arraigning his unkindness with my soul,
But now I find I had suborned the witness
155 And he's indicted falsely.

EMILIA　　　　　　Pray heaven it be
State matters, as you think, and no conception
Nor no jealous toy, concerning you.

DESDEMONA　　Alas the day, I never gave him cause.

EMILIA　　But jealous souls will not be answered so:
160 They are not ever jealous for the cause,
But jealous for they're jealous. It is a monster
Begot upon itself, born on itself.

DESDEMONA
Heaven keep that monster from Othello's mind!

EMILIA　　Lady, amen.

DESDEMONA
I will go seek him. Cassio, walk here about, 165
If I do find him fit I'll move your suit
And seek to effect it to my uttermost.

CASSIO　　I humbly thank your ladyship.
　　　　　　Exeunt Desdemona and Emilia.

Enter BIANCA.

BIANCA　　Save you, friend Cassio!

CASSIO　　　　　　What make you from home?
How is't with you, my most fair Bianca? 170
I'faith, sweet love, I was coming to your house.

BIANCA　　And I was going to your lodging, Cassio.
What, keep a week away? seven days and nights?
Eight score eight hours? and lovers' absent hours
More tedious than the dial, eight score times! 175
O weary reckoning!

CASSIO　　　　　　Pardon me, Bianca,
I have this while with leaden thoughts been pressed,
But I shall in a more continuate time
Strike off this score of absence. Sweet Bianca,
　　[*giving her Desdemona's handkerchief*]
Take me this work out.

BIANCA　　　　　　O Cassio, whence came this? 180
This is some token from a newer friend!
To the felt absence now I feel a cause:
Is't come to this? Well, well.

CASSIO　　　　　　Go to, woman,
Throw your vile guesses in the devil's teeth
From whence you have them! You are jealous now 185
That this is from some mistress, some remembrance:
No, by my faith, Bianca.

BIANCA　　　　　　Why, whose is it?

CASSIO　　I know not neither, I found it in my chamber.
I like the work well: ere it be demanded,
As like enough it will, I'd have it copied. 190
Take it, and do't, and leave me for this time.

BIANCA　　Leave you? Wherefore?

CASSIO　　I do attend here on the general
And think it no addition, nor my wish,
To have him see me womaned.

BIANCA　　　　　　Why, I pray you? 195

CASSIO　　Not that I love you not.

BIANCA　　But that you do not love me.
I pray you, bring me on the way a little,
And say if I shall see you soon at night.

CASSIO　　'Tis but a little way that I can bring you 200
For I attend here, but I'll see you soon.

BIANCA　　'Tis very good: I must be circumstanced.
　　　　　　　　　　　　　Exeunt.

4.1　　　　　　*Enter* OTHELLO *and* IAGO.

IAGO　　Will you think so?

OTHELLO　　　　　　Think so, Iago?

IAGO　　　　　　　　What,

To kiss in private?

OTHELLO   An unauthorized kiss!

IAGO   Or to be naked with her friend in bed
An hour or more, not meaning any harm?

OTHELLO

5   Naked in bed, Iago, and not mean harm?
It is hypocrisy against the devil:
They that mean virtuously, and yet do so,
The devil their virtue tempts, and they tempt heaven.

IAGO   So they do nothing, 'tis a venial slip;

10   But if I give my wife a handkerchief –

OTHELLO   What then?

IAGO   Why, then 'tis hers, my lord, and being hers
She may, I think, bestow't on any man.

OTHELLO   She is protectress of her honour too:

15   May she give that?

IAGO   Her honour is an essence that's not seen,
They have it very oft that have it not.
But for the handkerchief –

OTHELLO
By heaven, I would most gladly have forgot it!

20   Thou said'st – O, it comes o'er my memory
As doth the raven o'er the infectious house
Boding to all – he had my handkerchief.

IAGO   Ay, what of that?

OTHELLO   That's not so good now.

IAGO
What if I had said I had seen him do you wrong?

25   Or heard him say – as knaves be such abroad
Who, having by their own importunate suit
Or voluntary dotage of some mistress
Convinced or supplied them, cannot choose
But they must blab –

OTHELLO   Hath he said anything?

30 IAGO   He hath, my lord, but be you well assured
No more than he'll unswear.

OTHELLO   What hath he said?

IAGO   Faith, that he did – I know not what. He did –

OTHELLO   What? what?

IAGO   Lie.

OTHELLO   With her?

IAGO   With her, on her, what you will.

35 OTHELLO   Lie with her? lie on her? We say lie on her
when they belie her! Lie with her, zounds, that's
fulsome! – Handkerchief! confessions! handkerchief!
– To confess, and be hanged for his labour! First to be
hanged, and then to confess: I tremble at it. Nature

40 would not invest herself in such shadowing passion
without some instruction. It is not words that shakes
me thus. Pish! Noses, ears, and lips. Is't possible?
Confess! handkerchief! O devil! [*He falls in a trance.*]

IAGO   Work on,

45 My medicine, work! Thus credulous fools are
    caught,
And many worthy and chaste dames even thus,
All guiltless, meet reproach. – What ho! my lord!
My lord, I say! Othello!

Enter CASSIO.

                      How now, Cassio?

CASSIO   What's the matter?

IAGO   My lord is fallen into an epilepsy;   50
This is his second fit, he had one yesterday.

CASSIO   Rub him about the temples.

IAGO   No, forbear:
The lethargy must have his quiet course,
If not, he foams at mouth, and by and by
Breaks out to savage madness. Look, he stirs;   55
Do you withdraw yourself a little while,
He will recover straight. When he is gone
I would on great occasion speak with you.

                        Exit Cassio.

How is it, general? have you not hurt your head?

OTHELLO   Dost thou mock me?

IAGO   I mock you? no, by heaven!   60
Would you would bear your fortune like a man!

OTHELLO   A horned man's a monster, and a beast.

IAGO   There's many a beast then in a populous city,
And many a civil monster.

OTHELLO   Did he confess it?

IAGO   Good sir, be a man,   65
Think every bearded fellow that's but yoked
May draw with you. There's millions now alive
That nightly lie in those unproper beds
Which they dare swear peculiar: your case is better.
O, 'tis the spite of hell, the fiend's arch-mock,   70
To lip a wanton in a secure couch
And to suppose her chaste. No, let me know,
And, knowing what I am, I know what she shall be.

OTHELLO   O, thou art wise, 'tis certain.

IAGO   Stand you a while apart,   75
Confine yourself but in a patient list.
Whilst you were here o'erwhelmed with your grief
– A passion most unsuiting such a man –
Cassio came hither. I shifted him away
And laid good 'scuse upon your ecstasy,   80
Bade him anon return and here speak with me,
The which he promised. Do but encave yourself
And mark the fleers, the gibes and notable scorns
That dwell in every region of his face;
For I will make him tell the tale anew   85
Where, how, how oft, how long ago, and when
He hath and is again to cope your wife.
I say, but mark his gesture; marry, patience,
Or I shall say you're all in all in spleen
And nothing of a man.

OTHELLO   Dost thou hear, Iago?   90
I will be found most cunning in my patience
But – dost thou hear? – most bloody.

IAGO   That's not amiss,
But yet keep time in all. Will you withdraw?
    [*Othello withdraws.*]
Now will I question Cassio of Bianca,
A housewife that by selling her desires   95

Buys herself bread and clothes: it is a creature
That dotes on Cassio – as 'tis the strumpet's plague
To beguile many and be beguiled by one.
He, when he hears of her, cannot refrain
100 From the excess of laughter. Here he comes.

Enter CASSIO.

As he shall smile, Othello shall go mad.
And his unbookish jealousy must construe
Poor Cassio's smiles, gestures and light behaviour
Quite in the wrong. How do you now, lieutenant?

105 CASSIO   The worser, that you give me the addition
Whose want even kills me.
IAGO   Ply Desdemona well, and you are sure on't.
[*speaking lower*] Now if this suit lay in Bianca's power
How quickly should you speed!
CASSIO   Alas, poor caitiff!
110 OTHELLO   Look how he laughs already!
IAGO   I never knew a woman love man so.
CASSIO   Alas, poor rogue, I think i'faith she loves me.
OTHELLO   Now he denies it faintly, and laughs it out.
IAGO   Do you hear, Cassio?
OTHELLO   Now he importunes him
115 To tell it o'er; go to, well said, well said.
IAGO   She gives it out that you shall marry her;
Do you intend it?
CASSIO   Ha, ha, ha!
OTHELLO   Do ye triumph, Roman, do you triumph?
120 CASSIO   I marry! What, a customer! prithee bear some
charity to my wit, do not think it so unwholesome. Ha,
ha, ha!
OTHELLO   So, so, so, so: they laugh that win.
IAGO   Faith, the cry goes that you shall marry her.
125 CASSIO   Prithee say true!
IAGO   I am a very villain else.
OTHELLO   Have you stored me? Well.
CASSIO   This is the monkey's own giving out. She is
persuaded I will marry her, out of her own love and
130 flattery, not out of my promise.
OTHELLO   Iago beckons me: now he begins the story.
CASSIO   She was here even now, she haunts me in every
place. I was the other day talking on the sea-bank with
certain Venetians, and thither comes the bauble and, by
135 this hand, falls me thus about my neck –
OTHELLO   Crying 'O dear Cassio!' as it were: his
gesture imports it.
CASSIO   So hangs and lolls and weeps upon me, so
shakes and pulls me! Ha, ha, ha!
140 OTHELLO   Now he tells how she plucked him to my
chamber. O, I see that nose of yours, but not that dog I
shall throw it to.
CASSIO   Well, I must leave her company.
IAGO   Before me! look where she comes!

Enter BIANCA.

145 CASSIO   'Tis such another fitchew; marry, a perfumed
one. What do you mean by this haunting of me?

BIANCA   Let the devil and his dam haunt you! What did
you mean by that same handkerchief you gave me even
now? I was a fine fool to take it – I must take out the
work! A likely piece of work, that you should find it in 150
your chamber and know not who left it there! This is
some minx's token, and I must take out the work?
There, give it your hobby-horse; wheresoever you had
it, I'll take out no work on't!
CASSIO   How now, my sweet Bianca, how now, how now? 155
OTHELLO   By heaven, that should be my handkerchief!
BIANCA   If you'll come to supper tonight, you may; if
you will not, come when you are next prepared for.
                                                                Exit.
IAGO   After her, after her!
CASSIO   Faith, I must, she'll rail in the streets else. 160
IAGO   Will you sup there?
CASSIO   Faith, I intend so.
IAGO   Well, I may chance to see you, for I would very
fain speak with you.
CASSIO   Prithee come, will you? 165
IAGO   Go to, say no more.   *Exit Cassio.*
OTHELLO   How shall I murder him, Iago?
IAGO   Did you perceive how he laughed at his vice?
OTHELLO   O Iago!
IAGO   And did you see the handkerchief? 170
OTHELLO   Was that mine?
IAGO   Yours, by this hand: and to see how he prizes the
foolish woman your wife! She gave it him, and he hath
given it his whore.
OTHELLO   I would have him nine years a-killing. A fine 175
woman, a fair woman, a sweet woman!
IAGO   Nay, you must forget that.
OTHELLO   Ay, let her rot and perish and be damned
tonight, for she shall not live. No, my heart is turned to
stone: I strike it, and it hurts my hand. O, the world 180
hath not a sweeter creature: she might lie by an
emperor's side and command him tasks.
IAGO   Nay, that's not your way.
OTHELLO   Hang her, I do but say what she is: so delicate
with her needle, an admirable musician. O, she will 185
sing the savageness out of a bear! of so high and
plenteous wit and invention!
IAGO   She's the worse for all this.
OTHELLO   O, a thousand, a thousand times: and then of
so gentle a condition. 190
IAGO   Ay, too gentle.
OTHELLO   Nay, that's certain. But yet the pity of it, Iago
– O, Iago, the pity of it, Iago!
IAGO   If you are so fond over her iniquity, give her patent
to offend, for if it touch not you it comes near nobody. 195
OTHELLO   I will chop her into messes! Cuckold me!
IAGO   O, 'tis foul in her.
OTHELLO   With mine officer!
IAGO   That's fouler.
OTHELLO   Get me some poison, Iago, this night. I'll not 200
expostulate with her, lest her body and beauty
unprovide my mind again. This night, Iago.

IAGO   Do it not with poison, strangle her in her bed –
even the bed she hath contaminated.

205   OTHELLO   Good, good, the justice of it pleases; very
good!

IAGO   And for Cassio, let me be his undertaker. You shall
hear more by midnight.

210   OTHELLO   Excellent good. [*A trumpet within.*] What
trumpet is that same?

IAGO   I warrant something from Venice.

Enter LODOVICO, DESDEMONA *and Attendants.*

'Tis Lodovico, this, comes from the duke.
See, your wife's with him.

215   LODOVICO   God save you, worthy general.

OTHELLO   With all my heart, sir.

LODOVICO
The duke and senators of Venice greet you.
[*Gives him a letter.*]

OTHELLO   I kiss the instrument of their pleasures.
[*Opens the letter and reads.*]

DESDEMONA
And what's the news, good cousin Lodovico?

IAGO   I am very glad to see you, signior.

220   Welcome to Cyprus.

LODOVICO   I thank you. How does Lieutenant Cassio?

IAGO   Lives, sir.

DESDEMONA
Cousin, there's fallen between him and my lord
An unkind breach, but you shall make all well –

225   OTHELLO   Are you sure of that?

DESDEMONA   My lord?

OTHELLO [*Reads.*]   *This fail you not to do, as you will –*

LODOVICO   He did not call, he's busy in the paper.
Is there division 'twixt my lord and Cassio?

230   DESDEMONA   A most unhappy one: I would do much
T'atone them, for the love I bear to Cassio.

OTHELLO   Fire and brimstone!

DESDEMONA   My lord?

OTHELLO   Are you wise?

DESDEMONA   What, is he angry?

LODOVICO   Maybe the letter moved him.
For, as I think, they do command him home,

235   Deputing Cassio in his government.

DESDEMONA   By my troth, I am glad on't.

OTHELLO   Indeed!

DESDEMONA   My lord?

OTHELLO   I am glad . . . to see you mad.

DESDEMONA   Why, sweet Othello?

OTHELLO   Devil! [*striking her*]

DESDEMONA   I have not deserved this.

LODOVICO

240   My lord, this would not be believed in Venice
Though I should swear I saw't. 'Tis very much;
Make her amends, she weeps.

OTHELLO   O devil, devil!
If that the earth could teem with woman's tears

Each drop she falls would prove a crocodile:
Out of my sight!

DESDEMONA   I will not stay to offend you.   245

LODOVICO   Truly, an obedient lady.
I do beseech your lordship, call her back.

OTHELLO   Mistress!

DESDEMONA   My lord?

OTHELLO   What would you with her, sir?

LODOVICO   Who, I, my lord?   250

OTHELLO
Ay, you did wish that I would make her turn.
Sir, she can turn, and turn, and yet go on
And turn again. And she can weep, sir, weep.
And she's obedient: as you say, obedient,
Very obedient. – Proceed you in your tears. –   255
Concerning this, sir – O well-painted passion! –
I am commanded home. – Get you away.
I'll send for you anon. – Sir, I obey the mandate
And will return to Venice. – Hence, avaunt! –
                                    Exit Desdemona.
Cassio shall have my place. And, sir, tonight   260
I do entreat that we may sup together.
You are welcome, sir, to Cyprus. Goats and monkeys!
                                    Exit.

LODOVICO
Is this the noble Moor whom our full senate
Call all in all sufficient? This the nature
Whom passion could not shake? whose solid virtue   265
The shot of accident nor dart of chance
Could neither graze nor pierce?

IAGO   He is much changed.

LODOVICO   Are his wits safe? Is he not light of brain?

IAGO   He's that he is: I may not breathe my censure
What he might be; if what he might, he is not,   270
I would to heaven he were!

LODOVICO   What! strike his wife!

IAGO   Faith, that was not so well; yet would I knew
That stroke would prove the worst.

LODOVICO   Is it his use?
Or did the letters work upon his blood
And new-create this fault?

IAGO   Alas, alas!   275
It is not honesty in me to speak
What I have seen and known. You shall observe him,
And his own courses will denote him so
That I may save my speech. Do but go after
And mark how he continues.   280

LODOVICO
I am sorry that I am deceived in him.   *Exeunt.*

4.2   *Enter* OTHELLO *and* EMILIA.

OTHELLO   You have seen nothing, then?

EMILIA   Nor ever heard, nor ever did suspect.

OTHELLO
Yes, you have seen Cassio and . . . she together.

EMILIA   But then I saw no harm, and then I heard
5   Each syllable that breath made up between them.
OTHELLO   What, did they never whisper?
EMILIA   Never, my lord.
OTHELLO   Nor send you out o'th' way?
EMILIA   Never.
OTHELLO
     To fetch her fan, her gloves, her mask, nor nothing?
10 EMILIA   Never, my lord.
OTHELLO   That's strange.
EMILIA   I durst, my lord, to wager she is honest,
     Lay down my soul at stake: if you think other
     Remove your thought, it doth abuse your bosom.
15   If any wretch have put this in your head
     Let heaven requite it with the serpent's curse,
     For if she be not honest, chaste and true
     There's no man happy: the purest of their wives
     Is foul as slander.
OTHELLO   Bid her come hither; go.
                                        Exit Emilia.
20   She says enough; yet she's a simple bawd
     That cannot say as much. This is a subtle whore,
     A closet, lock and key, of villainous secrets;
     And yet she'll kneel and pray, I have seen her do't.

          Enter DESDEMONA *and* EMILIA.

DESDEMONA   My lord, what is your will?
OTHELLO   Pray, chuck, come hither.
DESDEMONA   What is your pleasure?
25 OTHELLO   Let me see your eyes.
     Look in my face.
DESDEMONA   What horrible fancy's this?
OTHELLO [*to Emilia*]   Some of your function, mistress,
     Leave procreants alone and shut the door;
     Cough, or cry hem, if anybody come.
30   Your mystery, your mystery: nay, dispatch!
                                        Exit Emilia.
DESDEMONA
     Upon my knees, what doth your speech import?
     I understand a fury in your words
     But not the words.
OTHELLO   Why, what art thou?
DESDEMONA
35   Your wife, my lord: your true and loyal wife.
OTHELLO   Come, swear it, damn thyself,
     Lest, being like one of heaven, the devils themselves
     Should fear to seize thee: therefore be double-damned,
     Swear thou art honest!
DESDEMONA   Heaven doth truly know it.
OTHELLO
40   Heaven truly knows that thou art false as hell.
DESDEMONA
     To whom, my lord? with whom? how am I false?
OTHELLO   Ah, Desdemon, away, away, away!
DESDEMONA   Alas the heavy day, why do you weep?
     Am I the motive of these tears, my lord?
45   If haply you my father do suspect

An instrument of this your calling back,
Lay not your blame on me: if you have lost him
Why, I have lost him too.
OTHELLO   Had it pleased heaven
To try me with affliction, had they rained
All kinds of sores and shames on my bare head,   50
Steeped me in poverty to the very lips,
Given to captivity me and my utmost hopes,
I should have found in some place of my soul
A drop of patience; but, alas, to make me
The fixed figure for the time of scorn   55
To point his slow and moving finger at!
Yet could I bear that too, well, very well:
But there where I have garnered up my heart,
Where either I must live or bear no life,
The fountain from the which my current runs   60
Or else dries up – to be discarded thence!
Or keep it as a cistern for foul toads
To knot and gender in! Turn thy complexion
     there,
Patience, thou young and rose-lipped cherubin,
Ay, here look, grim as hell!   65
DESDEMONA   I hope my noble lord esteems me honest.
OTHELLO   O, ay, as summer flies are in the shambles,
That quicken even with blowing. O thou weed
Who art so lovely fair and smell'st so sweet
That the sense aches at thee, would thou hadst ne'er
     been born!   70
DESDEMONA
Alas, what ignorant sin have I committed?
OTHELLO   Was this fair paper, this most goodly book
Made to write 'whore' upon? What committed!
Committed? O thou public commoner!
I should make very forges of my cheeks   75
That would to cinders burn up modesty
Did I but speak thy deeds. What committed!
Heaven stops the nose at it, and the moon winks,
The bawdy wind that kisses all it meets
Is hushed within the hollow mine of earth   80
And will not hear't. What committed!
Impudent strumpet!
DESDEMONA   By heaven, you do me wrong.
OTHELLO   Are not you a strumpet?
DESDEMONA   No, as I am a Christian.
If to preserve this vessel for my lord   85
From any hated foul unlawful touch
Be not to be a strumpet, I am none.
OTHELLO   What, not a whore?
DESDEMONA   No, as I shall be saved.
OTHELLO   Is't possible?
DESDEMONA   O heaven, forgive us!
OTHELLO   I cry you mercy then,   90
I took you for that cunning whore of Venice
That married with Othello. You! Mistress!

          Enter EMILIA.

That have the office opposite to Saint Peter

And keep the gates of hell – you, you, ay you!

We have done our course, there's money for your
  pains,

I pray you turn the key and keep our counsel.   *Exit.*

95

EMILIA   Alas, what does this gentleman conceive?

How do you, madam? how do you, my good lady?

DESDEMONA   Faith, half asleep.

100 EMILIA   Good madam, what's the matter with my lord?

DESDEMONA   With whom?

EMILIA   Why, with my lord, madam.

DESDEMONA   Who is thy lord?

EMILIA   He that is yours, sweet lady.

DESDEMONA   I have none. Do not talk to me, Emilia;

105

I cannot weep, nor answers have I none

But what should go by water. Prithee, tonight

Lay on my bed my wedding sheets; remember,

And call thy husband hither.

EMILIA   Here's a change indeed!

                                                                          Exit.

110 DESDEMONA   'Tis meet I should be used so, very meet.

How have I been behaved that he might stick

The small'st opinion on my greatest misuse?

Enter IAGO *and* EMILIA.

IAGO

What is your pleasure, madam? How is't with you?

DESDEMONA

I cannot tell. Those that do teach young babes

Do it with gentle means and easy tasks.

115

He might have chid me so, for, in good faith,

I am a child to chiding.

IAGO   What is the matter, lady?

EMILIA   Alas, Iago, my lord hath so bewhored her,

Thrown such despite and heavy terms upon her

That true hearts cannot bear it.

DESDEMONA   Am I that name, Iago?

120 IAGO   What name, fair lady?

DESDEMONA   Such as she said my lord did say I was.

EMILIA   He called her whore. A beggar in his drink

Could not have laid such terms upon his callat.

IAGO   Why did he so?

125 DESDEMONA   I do not know; I am sure I am none such.

IAGO   Do not weep, do not weep: alas the day!

EMILIA   Hath she forsook so many noble matches,

Her father, and her country, and her friends,

To be called whore? would it not make one weep?

130 DESDEMONA   It is my wretched fortune.

IAGO   Beshrew him for't,

How comes this trick upon him?

DESDEMONA   Nay, heaven doth know.

EMILIA   I will be hanged if some eternal villain

Some busy and insinuating rogue,

Some cogging, cozening slave, to get some office,

135

Have not devised this slander, I'll be hanged else!

IAGO   Fie, there is no such man, it is impossible.

DESDEMONA   If any such there be, heaven pardon him.

EMILIA   A halter pardon him, and hell gnaw his bones!

Why should he call her whore? who keeps her company?

What place, what time, what form, what likelihood?   140

The Moor's abused by some most villainous knave,

Some base notorious knave, some scurvy fellow.

O heaven, that such companions thou'dst unfold

And put in every honest hand a whip

To lash the rascals naked through the world   145

Even from the east to th' west.

IAGO   Speak within doors.

EMILIA   O fie upon them! some such squire he was

That turned your wit the seamy side without

And made you to suspect me with the Moor.

IAGO   You are a fool, go to.

DESDEMONA   O God, Iago,   150

What shall I do to win my lord again?

Good friend, go to him, for, by this light of heaven,

I know not how I lost him. Here I kneel:

If e'er my will did trespass 'gainst his love

Either in discourse of thought or actual deed,   155

Or that mine eyes, mine ears or any sense

Delighted them in any other form,

Or that I do not yet, and ever did,

And ever will – though he do shake me off

To beggarly divorcement – love him dearly,   160

Comfort forswear me! Unkindness may do much,

And his unkindness may defeat my life

But never taint my love. I cannot say whore:

It does abhor me now I speak the word;

To do the act that might the addition earn   165

Not the world's mass of vanity could make me.

IAGO   I pray you, be content, 'tis but his humour;

The business of the state does him offence

And he does chide with you.

DESDEMONA   If 'twere no other –

IAGO   'Tis but so, I warrant.   170

                                                                    [*Trumpets*]

Hark how these instruments summon to supper:

The messengers of Venice stay the meat,

Go in, and weep not; all things shall be well.

                                        Exeunt Desdemona and Emilia.

Enter RODERIGO.

How now, Roderigo?

RODERIGO   I do not find that thou deal'st justly with me.   175

IAGO   What in the contrary?

RODERIGO   Every day thou doff'st me with some

device, Iago, and rather, as it seems to me now, keep'st

from me all conveniency than suppliest me with the

least advantage of hope. I will indeed no longer endure   180

it; nor am I yet persuaded to put up in peace what

already I have foolishly suffered.

IAGO   Will you hear me, Roderigo?

RODERIGO   Faith, I have heard too much; and your

words and performances are no kin together.   185

IAGO   You charge me most unjustly.

RODERIGO   With nought but truth. I have wasted

myself out of my means. The jewels you have had from

190 me to deliver to Desdemona would half have corrupted
a votarist. You have told me she hath received them,
and returned me expectations and comforts of sudden
respect and acquittance, but I find none.

IAGO Well, go to; very well.

195 RODERIGO 'Very well,' 'go to'! I cannot go to, man, nor
'tis not very well. By this hand, I think it is scurvy, and
begin to find myself fopped in it.

IAGO Very well.

RODERIGO I tell you, 'tis not very well! I will make
200 myself known to Desdemona: if she will return me my
jewels I will give over my suit and repent my unlawful
solicitation; if not, assure yourself I will seek
satisfaction of you.

IAGO You have said now.

205 RODERIGO Ay, and said nothing but what I protest
intendment of doing.

IAGO Why, now I see there's mettle in thee, and even
from this instant do build on thee a better opinion
than ever before. Give me thy hand, Roderigo.
210 Thou hast taken against me a most just exception –
but yet I protest I have dealt most directly in thy
affair.

RODERIGO It hath not appeared.

IAGO I grant indeed it hath not appeared, and your
215 suspicion is not without wit and judgement. But,
Roderigo, if thou hast that in thee indeed which I have
greater reason to believe now than ever – I mean
purpose, courage, and valour – this night show it. If
thou the next night following enjoy not Desdemona,
220 take me from this world with treachery and devise
engines for my life.

RODERIGO Well – what is it? Is it within reason and
compass?

IAGO Sir, there is especial commission come from
Venice to depute Cassio in Othello's place.

225 RODERIGO Is that true? Why, then Othello and
Desdemona return again to Venice.

IAGO O no, he goes into Mauretania and taketh away
with him the fair Desdemona, unless his abode be
lingered here by some accident – wherein none can be
230 so determinate as the removing of Cassio.

RODERIGO How do you mean, removing of him?

IAGO Why, by making him uncapable of Othello's
place: knocking out his brains.

RODERIGO And that you would have me to do!

235 IAGO Ay, if you dare do yourself a profit and a right. He
sups tonight with a harlotry, and thither will I go to
him. He knows not yet of his honourable fortune: if
you will watch his going thence – which I will fashion
to fall out between twelve and one – you may take him
240 at your pleasure. I will be near to second your attempt,
and he shall fall between us. Come, stand not amazed
at it, but go along with me: I will show you such a
necessity in his death that you shall think yourself
bound to put it on him. It is now high supper time, and
245 the night grows to waste: about it.

RODERIGO I will hear further reason for this.

IAGO And you shall be satisfied.   *Exeunt.*

4.3 Enter OTHELLO, LODOVICO, DESDEMONA,
EMILIA *and Attendants.*

LODOVICO
I do beseech you, sir, trouble yourself no further.

OTHELLO O, pardon me, 'twill do me good to walk.

LODOVICO
Madam, good night: I humbly thank your ladyship.

DESDEMONA Your honour is most welcome.

OTHELLO   Will you walk, sir?
O, Desdemona –

DESDEMONA My lord?

OTHELLO   Get you to bed   5
On th'instant, I will be returned forthwith.
Dismiss your attendant there: look't be done.

DESDEMONA I will, my lord.
Exeunt Othello, Lodovico and Attendants.

EMILIA
How goes it now? He looks gentler than he did.

DESDEMONA He says he will return incontinent,   10
And hath commanded me to go to bed
And bid me to dismiss you.

EMILIA   Dismiss me?

DESDEMONA
It was his bidding; therefore, good Emilia,
Give me my nightly wearing, and adieu.
We must not now displease him.   15

EMILIA Ay. – Would you had never seen him!

DESDEMONA
So would not I: my love doth so approve him
That even his stubbornness, his checks, his frowns
– Prithee unpin me – have grace and favour.

EMILIA
I have laid those sheets you bade me on the bed.   20

DESDEMONA
All's one. Good faith, how foolish are our minds!
If I do die before thee, prithee shroud me
In one of these same sheets.

EMILIA   Come, come, you talk.

DESDEMONA My mother had a maid called Barbary,
She was in love, and he she loved proved mad   25
And did forsake her. She had a song of 'willow',
An old thing 'twas, but it expressed her fortune
And she died singing it. That song tonight
Will not go from my mind. I have much to do
But to go hang my head all at one side   30
And sing it like poor Barbary. Prithee dispatch.

EMILIA Shall I go fetch your night-gown?

DESDEMONA No, unpin me here.

EMILIA This Lodovico is a proper man. A very
handsome man.   35

DESDEMONA He speaks well.

EMILIA I know a lady in Venice would have walked
barefoot to Palestine for a touch of his nether lip.

DESDEMONA [*Sings.*]

> The poor soul sat sighing by a sycamore tree,
> > Sing all a green willow:
40
> Her hand on her bosom, her head on her knee,
> > Sing willow, willow, willow.
> The fresh streams ran by her and murmured her
> > moans,
> > Sing willow, willow, willow:
45
> Her salt tears fell from her and softened the stones,
> > Sing willow, willow, willow.

[*Speaks.*] Lay by these.

> > Willow, willow –

[*Speaks.*] Prithee hie thee: he'll come anon.

50
> Sing all a green willow must be my garland.
> Let nobody blame him, his scorn I approve –

[*Speaks.*] Nay, that's not next. Hark, who is't that
knocks?

EMILIA   It's the wind.

DESDEMONA [*Sings.*]

> I called my love false love; but what said he then?
55
> > Sing willow, willow, willow:
> If I court moe women, you'll couch with moe men.

[*Speaks.*] So, get thee gone; good night. Mine eyes do
itch,
Doth that bode weeping?

EMILIA   'Tis neither here nor there.

DESDEMONA

I have heard it said so. O, these men, these men!
60 Dost thou in conscience think – tell me, Emilia –
That there be women do abuse their husbands
In such gross kind?

EMILIA   There be some such, no question.

DESDEMONA

Wouldst thou do such a deed for all the world?

EMILIA   Why, would not you?

DESDEMONA   No, by this heavenly light!
65 EMILIA   Nor I neither, by this heavenly light:
I might do't as well i'th' dark.

DESDEMONA

Wouldst thou do such a deed for all the world?

EMILIA   The world's a huge thing: it is a great price
For a small vice.

DESDEMONA   Good troth, I think thou wouldst not.

70 EMILIA   By my troth, I think I should, and undo't when
I had done. Marry, I would not do such a thing for a
joint-ring, nor for measures of lawn, nor for gowns,
petticoats, nor caps, nor any petty exhibition. But for
all the whole world? 'ud's pity, who would not make her
75 husband a cuckold to make him a monarch? I should
venture purgatory for't.

DESDEMONA   Beshrew me, if I would do such a wrong
For the whole world!

EMILIA   Why, the wrong is but a wrong i'th' world; and
80 having the world for your labour, 'tis a wrong in your
own world, and you might quickly make it right.

DESDEMONA   I do not think there is any such woman.

EMILIA   Yes, a dozen, and as many to th' vantage as

would store the world they played for.
But I do think it is their husbands' faults   85
If wives do fall. Say that they slack their duties
And pour our treasures into foreign laps;
Or else break out in peevish jealousies,
Throwing restraint upon us; or say they strike us,
Or scant our former having in despite,   90
Why, we have galls: and though we have some grace
Yet have we some revenge. Let husbands know
Their wives have sense like them: they see, and smell,
And have their palates both for sweet and sour
As husbands have. What is it that they do   95
When they change us for others? Is it sport?
I think it is. And doth affection breed it?
I think it doth. Is't frailty that thus errs?
It is so too. And have not we affections?
Desires for sport? and frailty, as men have?   100
Then let them use us well: else let them know,
The ills we do, their ills instruct us so.

DESDEMONA

Good night, good night. God me such usage send
Not to pick bad from bad, but by bad mend! *Exeunt.*

5.1   *Enter* IAGO *and* RODERIGO.

IAGO

Here, stand behind this bulk, straight will he come.
Wear thy good rapier bare, and put it home;
Quick, quick, fear nothing, I'll be at thy elbow.
It makes us or it mars us, think on that
And fix most firm thy resolution.   5

RODERIGO   Be near at hand, I may miscarry in't.

IAGO   Here, at thy hand: be bold, and take thy stand.
[*Retires.*]

RODERIGO   I have no great devotion to the deed
And yet he hath given me satisfying reasons:
'Tis but a man gone. Forth, my sword: he dies.   10

IAGO   I have rubbed this young quat almost to the sense
And he grows angry. Now, whether he kill Cassio
Or Cassio him, or each do kill the other,
Every way makes my gain. Live Roderigo,
He calls me to a restitution large   15
Of gold and jewels that I bobbed from him
As gifts to Desdemona:
It must not be. If Cassio do remain
He hath a daily beauty in his life
That makes me ugly; and besides, the Moor   20
May unfold me to him – there stand I in much peril.
No, he must die. Be't so! I hear him coming.

Enter CASSIO.

RODERIGO   I know his gait, 'tis he. Villain, thou diest!
[*Makes a thrust at Cassio.*]

CASSIO   That thrust had been mine enemy indeed
But that my coat is better than thou know'st: 25
I will make proof of thine.
[*Draws, and wounds Roderigo.*]

RODERIGO   O, I am slain!

Iago from behind wounds Cassio in the leg, and exit.

CASSIO

     I am maimed for ever! Help, ho! murder! murder!

Enter OTHELLO.

OTHELLO   The voice of Cassio. Iago keeps his word.

RODERIGO   O, villain that I am!

OTHELLO   It is even so.

30   CASSIO   O, help ho! light! a surgeon!

OTHELLO   'Tis he. O brave Iago, honest and just,

     That hast such noble sense of thy friend's wrong!

     Thou teachest me. Minion, your dear lies dead,

     And your unblest fate hies; strumpet, I come.

     Forth of my heart those charms, thine eyes, are

35   blotted,

     Thy bed, lust-stained, shall with lust's blood be

     spotted.   *Exit.*

Enter LODOVICO *and* GRATIANO.

CASSIO

     What ho, no watch, no passage? murder, murder!

GRATIANO

     'Tis some mischance, the voice is very direful.

CASSIO   O help!

40   LODOVICO   Hark!

RODERIGO   O wretched villain!

LODOVICO   Two or three groan. It is a heavy night;

     These may be counterfeits, let's think't unsafe

     To come in to the cry without more help.

45   RODERIGO   Nobody come? then shall I bleed to death.

Enter IAGO, *with a light.*

LODOVICO   Hark!

GRATIANO

     Here's one comes in his shirt, with light and weapons.

IAGO

     Who's there? Whose noise is this that cries on

     murder?

LODOVICO   We do not know.

IAGO   Did not you hear a cry?

CASSIO   Here, here! for heaven's sake help me!

50   IAGO   What's the matter?

GRATIANO   This is Othello's ancient, as I take it.

LODOVICO   The same indeed, a very valiant fellow.

IAGO   What are you here that cry so grievously?

CASSIO   Iago? O, I am spoiled, undone by villains!

55   Give me some help.

IAGO   O me, lieutenant! What villains have done this?

CASSIO   I think that one of them is hereabout

     And cannot make away.

IAGO   O treacherous villains!

     What are you there? Come in, and give some help.

60   RODERIGO   O, help me here!

CASSIO   That's one of them.

IAGO   O murderous slave! O villain!

[*Stabs Roderigo.*]

RODERIGO   O damned Iago! O inhuman dog!

IAGO

     Kill men i'th' dark? Where be these bloody thieves?

     How silent is this town! Ho, murder, murder!

     What may you be? Are you of good or evil?   65

LODOVICO   As you shall prove us, praise us.

IAGO   Signior Lodovico?

LODOVICO   He, sir.

IAGO   I cry you mercy: here's Cassio hurt by villains.

GRATIANO   Cassio?   70

IAGO   How is't, brother?

CASSIO   My leg is cut in two.

IAGO   Marry, heaven forbid!

     Light, gentlemen, I'll bind it with my shirt.

Enter BIANCA.

BIANCA   What is the matter, ho? who is't that cried?

IAGO   Who is't that cried?

BIANCA   O my dear Cassio!   75

     My sweet Cassio! O Cassio, Cassio, Cassio!

IAGO   O notable strumpet! Cassio, may you suspect

     Who they should be that have thus mangled you?

CASSIO   No.

GRATIANO   I am sorry to find you thus;   80

     I have been to seek you.

IAGO   Lend me a garter. So. – O for a chair

     To bear him easily hence!

BIANCA   Alas, he faints! O Cassio, Cassio, Cassio!

IAGO   Gentlemen all, I do suspect this trash   85

     To be a party in this injury.

     Patience awhile, good Cassio. Come, come,

     Lend me a light. Know we this face, or no?

     Alas, my friend and my dear countryman,

     Roderigo? No – yes sure! – O heaven, Roderigo!   90

GRATIANO   What, of Venice?

IAGO   Even he, sir. Did you know him?

GRATIANO   Know him? Ay.

IAGO   Signior Gratiano? I cry you gentle pardon:

     These bloody accidents must excuse my manners

     That so neglected you.

GRATIANO   I am glad to see you.   95

IAGO   How do you, Cassio? O, a chair, a chair!

GRATIANO   Roderigo?

IAGO   He, he, 'tis he.   [*A chair is brought in.*]

               O, that's well said, the chair.

     Some good man bear him carefully from hence,

     I'll fetch the general's surgeon. [*to Bianca.*] For you,

     mistress,   100

     Save you your labour. – He that lies slain here, Cassio,

     Was my dear friend. What malice was between you?

CASSIO

     None in the world, nor do I know the man.

IAGO [*to Bianca*]

     What, look you pale? – O, bear him out o'th' air.

     – Stay you, good gentlemen. – Look you pale, mistress?   105

     – Do you perceive the gastness of her eye?

     – Nay, if you stare we shall hear more anon.

– Behold her well, I pray you, look upon her:
Do you see, gentlemen? nay, guiltiness will speak
Though tongues were out of use.

Enter EMILIA.

110 EMILIA   'Las, what's the matter?
What's the matter, husband?

IAGO   Cassio hath here been set on in the dark
By Roderigo and fellows that are 'scaped:
He's almost slain, and Roderigo dead.

115 EMILIA   Alas, good gentleman! alas, good Cassio!

IAGO   This is the fruits of whoring. Prithee, Emilia,
Go know of Cassio where he supped tonight.
What, do you shake at that?

BIANCA
He supped at my house, but I therefore shake not.

120 IAGO   O, did he so? I charge you, go with me.

EMILIA   O fie upon thee, strumpet!

BIANCA
I am no strumpet, but of life as honest
As you, that thus abuse me.

EMILIA   As I? Foh, fie upon thee!

IAGO
125 Kind gentlemen, let's go see poor Cassio dressed.
Come, mistress, you must tell's another tale.
Emilia, run you to the citadel
And tell my lord and lady what hath happed.
– Will you go on afore? – This is the night
130 That either makes me or fordoes me quite.   *Exeunt.*

5.2   *Enter* OTHELLO, *with a light.* DESDEMONA
in her bed asleep.

OTHELLO   It is the cause, it is the cause, my soul!
Let me not name it to you, you chaste stars,
It is the cause. Yet I'll not shed her blood
Nor scar that whiter skin of hers than snow
And smooth as monumental alabaster:
Yet she must die, else she'll betray more men.
Put out the light, and then put out the light!
If I quench thee, thou flaming minister,
I can again thy former light restore
0 Should I repent me. But once put out thy light,
Thou cunning'st pattern of excelling nature,
I know not where is that Promethean heat
That can thy light relume: when I have plucked the rose
I cannot give it vital growth again,
5 It needs must wither. I'll smell thee on the tree;
O balmy breath, that dost almost persuade
Justice to break her sword! Once more, once more:
Be thus when thou art dead and I will kill thee
And love thee after. Once more, and that's the last.
[*He smells, then kisses her.*]
0 So sweet was ne'er so fatal. I must weep,
But they are cruel tears. This sorrow's heavenly,
It strikes where it doth love. She wakes.

DESDEMONA   Who's there? Othello?

OTHELLO   Ay, Desdemona.

DESDEMONA   Will you come to bed, my lord?

OTHELLO   Have you prayed tonight, Desdemon?

DESDEMONA   Ay, my lord.   25

OTHELLO   If you bethink yourself of any crime
Unreconciled as yet to heaven and grace,
Solicit for it straight.

DESDEMONA
Alack, my lord, what may you mean by that?

OTHELLO   Well, do it, and be brief; I will walk by.   30
I would not kill thy unprepared spirit,
No, heaven forfend, I would not kill thy soul.

DESDEMONA   Talk you of killing?

OTHELLO   Ay, I do.

DESDEMONA   Then, heaven,
Have mercy on me!

OTHELLO   Amen, with all my heart.

DESDEMONA   If you say so, I hope you will not kill me.   35

OTHELLO   Hum!

DESDEMONA   And yet I fear you, for you're fatal then
When your eyes roll so. Why I should fear I know not,
Since guiltiness I know not. But yet I feel I fear.

OTHELLO   Think on thy sins.

DESDEMONA   They are loves I bear to you.   40

OTHELLO   Ay, and for that thou diest.

DESDEMONA
That death's unnatural that kills for loving.
Alas, why gnaw you so your nether lip?
Some bloody passion shakes your very frame,
These are portents: but yet I hope, I hope   45
They do not point on me.

OTHELLO   Peace, and be still.

DESDEMONA   I will. So: what's the matter?

OTHELLO   That handkerchief
Which I so loved and gave thee, thou gavest
To Cassio.

DESDEMONA   No, by my life and soul:
Send for the man and ask him.

OTHELLO   Sweet soul, take heed,   50
Take heed of perjury. Thou art on thy death-bed.

DESDEMONA   I? – but not yet to die!

OTHELLO   Yes, presently.
Therefore confess thee freely of thy sin,
For to deny each article with oath
Cannot remove nor choke the strong conception   55
That I do groan withal. Thou art to die.

DESDEMONA   Then Lord have mercy on me.

OTHELLO   I say amen.

DESDEMONA   And have you mercy too. I never did
Offend you in my life, never loved Cassio
But with such general warranty of heaven   60
As I might love: I never gave him token.

OTHELLO
By heaven, I saw my handkerchief in's hand!
O perjured woman, thou dost stone my heart
And makest me call what I intend to do
A murder, which I thought a sacrifice!   65

I saw the handkerchief.

DESDEMONA   He found it then,
I never gave it him. Send for him hither,
Let him confess the truth.

OTHELLO   He hath confessed.

DESDEMONA   What, my lord?

OTHELLO   That he hath – ud's death! – used thee.

DESDEMONA   How? unlawfully?

OTHELLO   Ay.

70 DESDEMONA   He will not say so.

OTHELLO   No, his mouth is stopped. Honest Iago
Hath ta'en order for't.

DESDEMONA   O, my fear interprets!
What, is he dead?

OTHELLO   Had all his hairs been lives
My great revenge had stomach for them all.

75 DESDEMONA   Alas, he is betrayed, and I undone.

OTHELLO
Out, strumpet, weep'st thou for him to my face?

DESDEMONA   O, banish me, my lord, but kill me not!

OTHELLO   Down, strumpet!

DESDEMONA   Kill me tomorrow, let me live tonight!

80 OTHELLO   Nay, if you strive –

DESDEMONA   But half an hour!

OTHELLO   Being done, there is no pause –

DESDEMONA   But while I say one prayer!

OTHELLO   It is too late.

DESDEMONA   O Lord! Lord! Lord!   [*He smothers her.*]

EMILIA [*within*]
My lord, my lord! what ho, my lord, my lord!

OTHELLO

85 What noise is this? Not dead? not yet quite dead?
I that am cruel am yet merciful,
I would not have thee linger in thy pain.
So, so.

EMILIA [*within*]   What ho! my lord! my lord!

OTHELLO   Who's there?

EMILIA [*within*]
O good my lord, I'd speak a word with you.

OTHELLO   Yes. 'Tis Emilia. –

90 [*to Emilia*]   By and by. – She's dead.
'Tis like she comes to speak of Cassio's death,
The noise was high. Ha, no more moving?
Still as the grave. Shall she come in? were't good?
I think she stirs again. No – what's best to do?

95 If she come in, she'll sure speak to my wife.
My wife, my wife! what wife? I have no wife.
O insupportable, O heavy hour!
Methinks it should be now a huge eclipse
Of sun and moon, and that th'affrighted globe
Should yawn at alteration.

100 EMILIA [*within*]   I do beseech you
That I may speak with you! O good my lord!

OTHELLO   I had forgot thee: O come in, Emilia.
Soft, by and by. Let me the curtains draw.
Where art thou? What's the matter with thee now?
[*He unlocks the door.*]

Enter EMILIA.

EMILIA   O my good lord, yonder's foul murders done!   105

OTHELLO   What? Now?

EMILIA   But now, my lord.

OTHELLO   It is the very error of the moon,
She comes more nearer earth than she was wont
And makes men mad.

EMILIA   Cassio, my lord, hath killed   110
A young Venetian, called Roderigo.

OTHELLO   Roderigo killed? and Cassio killed?

EMILIA   No, Cassio is not killed.

OTHELLO   Not Cassio killed?
Then murder's out of tune, and sweet revenge
Grows harsh.

DESDEMONA   O falsely, falsely murdered!   115

EMILIA   O lord, what cry is that?

OTHELLO   That? what?

EMILIA   Out and alas, that was my lady's voice:
[*She draws the bed-curtains.*]
Help, help, ho, help! O lady, speak again,
Sweet Desdemona, O sweet mistress, speak!   120

DESDEMONA   A guiltless death I die.

EMILIA   O, who hath done
This deed?

DESDEMONA   Nobody. I myself. Farewell.
Commend me to my kind lord – O, farewell!
[*She dies.*]

OTHELLO   Why, how should she be murdered?

EMILIA   Alas, who knows?

OTHELLO   You heard her say herself it was not I.   125

EMILIA   She said so; I must needs report the truth.

OTHELLO   She's like a liar gone to burning hell:
'Twas I that killed her.

EMILIA   O, the more angel she,
And you the blacker devil!

OTHELLO   She turned to folly, and she was a whore.   130

EMILIA   Thou dost belie her, and thou art a devil.

OTHELLO   She was false as water.

EMILIA   Thou art rash as fire to say
That she was false. O, she was heavenly true!

OTHELLO   Cassio did top her: ask thy husband else.
O, I were damned beneath all depth in hell   135
But that I did proceed upon just grounds
To this extremity. Thy husband knew it all.

EMILIA   My husband?

OTHELLO   Thy husband.

EMILIA   That she was false?
To wedlock?

OTHELLO   Ay, with Cassio. Had she been true,
If heaven would make me such another world   140
Of one entire and perfect chrysolite,
I'd not have sold her for it.

EMILIA   My husband?

OTHELLO   Ay, 'twas he that told me on her first;
An honest man he is, and hates the slime
That sticks on filthy deeds.

EMILIA My husband!

145 OTHELLO What needs
This iterance, woman? I say thy husband.

EMILIA
O mistress, villainy hath made mocks with love!
My husband say she was false?

OTHELLO He, woman;
I say thy husband: dost understand the word?

150 My friend thy husband, honest, honest Iago.

EMILIA If he say so, may his pernicious soul
Rot half a grain a day! he lies to th' heart:
She was too fond of her most filthy bargain!

OTHELLO Ha!

155 EMILIA Do thy worst:
This deed of thine is no more worthy heaven
Than thou wast worthy her.

OTHELLO Peace, you were best!

EMILIA Thou hast not half that power to do me harm.
As I have to be hurt. O gull, O dolt,
160 As ignorant as dirt! Thou hast done a deed
    [*He threatens her with his sword.*]
– I care not for thy sword, I'll make thee known
Though I lost twenty lives. Help, help, ho, help!
The Moor hath killed my mistress! Murder, murder!

Enter MONTANO, GRATIANO *and* IAGO.

MONTANO What is the matter? How now, general?

165 EMILIA O, are you come, Iago? you have done well
That men must lay their murders on your neck.

GRATIANO What is the matter?

EMILIA Disprove this villain, if thou be'st a man;
He says thou told'st him that his wife was false,
170 I know thou didst not, thou'rt not such a villain.
Speak, for my heart is full.

IAGO I told him what I thought, and told no more
Than what he found himself was apt and true.

EMILIA But did you ever tell him she was false?

175 IAGO I did.

EMILIA You told a lie, an odious, damned lie!
Upon my soul, a lie, a wicked lie!
She false with Cassio? Did you say with Cassio?

IAGO
With Cassio, mistress. Go to, charm your tongue.

180 EMILIA
I will not charm my tongue, I am bound to speak:
My mistress here lies murdered in her bed.

ALL O heavens forfend!

EMILIA And your reports have set the murder on.

OTHELLO Nay, stare not, masters, it is true indeed.

185 GRATIANO 'Tis a strange truth.

MONTANO O monstrous act!

EMILIA Villainy, villainy, villainy!
I think upon't, I think I smell't, O villainy!
I thought so then: I'll kill myself for grief!
190 O villainy, villainy!

IAGO
What, are you mad? I charge you, get you home.

EMILIA Good gentlemen, let me have leave to speak.
'Tis proper I obey him – but not now.
Perchance, Iago, I will ne'er go home.

195 OTHELLO O! O! O! [*Othello falls on the bed.*]

EMILIA Nay, lay thee down and roar
For thou hast killed the sweetest innocent
That e'er did lift up eye.

OTHELLO O, she was foul.
I scarce did know you, uncle: there lies your niece
Whose breath, indeed, these hands have newly
    stopped;   200
I know this act shows horrible and grim.

GRATIANO
Poor Desdemon, I am glad thy father's dead;
Thy match was mortal to him, and pure grief
Shore his old thread in twain. Did he live now
This sight would make him do a desperate turn,   205
Yea, curse his better angel from his side
And fall to reprobance.

OTHELLO 'Tis pitiful; but yet Iago knows
That she with Cassio hath the act of shame
A thousand times committed. Cassio confessed it,   210
And she did gratify his amorous works
With that recognizance and pledge of love
Which I first gave her: I saw it in his hand,
It was a handkerchief, an antique token
My father gave my mother.   215

EMILIA O God, O heavenly God!

IAGO Zounds, hold your peace!

EMILIA 'Twill out, 'twill out! I peace?
No, I will speak as liberal as the north.
Let heaven and men and devils, let them all,
All, all cry shame against me, yet I'll speak.   220

IAGO Be wise, and get you home.

EMILIA I will not. [*Iago tries to stab Emilia.*]

GRATIANO Fie! Your sword upon a woman?

EMILIA
O thou dull Moor, that handkerchief thou speak'st of
I found by fortune and did give my husband,
For often, with a solemn earnestness   225
– More than indeed belonged to such a trifle –
He begged of me to steal't.

IAGO Villainous whore!

EMILIA She give it Cassio? No, alas, I found it
And I did give't my husband.

IAGO Filth, thou liest!

EMILIA By heaven I do not, I do not, gentlemen!   230
O murderous coxcomb, what should such a fool
Do with so good a wife?
    [*Othello runs at Iago. Iago stabs his wife.*]

OTHELLO Are there no stones in heaven
But what serves for the thunder? Precious villain!

GRATIANO
The woman falls, sure he hath killed his wife.

EMILIA
Ay, ay; O lay me by my mistress' side. *Exit Iago.*   235

GRATIANO He's gone, but his wife's killed.

MONTANO
'Tis a notorious villain. Take you this weapon
Which I have here recovered from the Moor;
Come, guard the door without, let him not pass
But kill him rather. I'll after that same villain,
For 'tis a damned slave.

240

                    Exeunt Montano and Gratiano.

OTHELLO   I am not valiant neither,
But every puny whipster gets my sword.
But why should honour outlive honesty?
Let it go all.

EMILIA   What did thy song bode, lady?
Hark, canst thou hear me? I will play the swan
And die in music. [*Sings.*] Willow, willow, willow.
– Moor, she was chaste, she loved thee, cruel Moor,
So come my soul to bliss as I speak true!
So speaking as I think, alas, I die.   [*She dies.*]

245

OTHELLO
I have another weapon in this chamber,
It is a sword of Spain, the ice-brook's temper;
O, here it is. Uncle, I must come forth.

250

GRATIANO [*within*]
If thou attempt it it will cost thee dear;
Thou hast no weapon, and perforce must suffer.

OTHELLO   Look in upon me then, and speak with me,
Or, naked as I am, I will assault thee.

255

                  Enter GRATIANO.

GRATIANO   What is the matter?

OTHELLO   Behold, I have a weapon,
A better never did itself sustain
Upon a soldier's thigh. I have seen the day
That with this little arm and this good sword
I have made my way through more impediments
Than twenty times your stop: but, O vain boast,
Who can control his fate? 'Tis not so now.
Be not afraid, though you do see me weaponed:
Here is my journey's end, here is my butt
And very sea-mark of my utmost sail.
Do you go back dismayed? 'tis a lost fear:
Man but a rush against Othello's breast
And he retires. Where should Othello go?
Now: how dost thou look now? O ill-starred wench,
Pale as thy smock. When we shall meet at compt
This look of thine will hurl my soul from heaven
And fiends will snatch at it. Cold, cold, my girl,
Even like thy chastity. O cursed, cursed slave!
Whip me, ye devils,
From the possession of this heavenly sight!
Blow me about in winds, roast me in sulphur,
Wash me in steep-down gulfs of liquid fire!
O Desdemon! dead, Desdemon. Dead! O, O!

260

265

270

275

       Enter LODOVICO, MONTANO, *Officers with*
         IAGO, *prisoner, and* CASSIO *in a chair.*

LODOVICO
Where is this rash and most unfortunate man?

280

OTHELLO   That's he that was Othello? here I am.

LODOVICO   Where is that viper? bring the villain forth.

OTHELLO
I look down towards his feet, but that's a fable.
If that thou be'st a devil, I cannot kill thee.
    [*Wounds Iago.*]

LODOVICO   Wrench his sword from him.

IAGO   I bleed, sir, but not killed.

285

OTHELLO   I am not sorry neither, I'd have thee live:
For in my sense 'tis happiness to die.

LODOVICO   O thou Othello, that wert once so good,
Fallen in the practice of a cursed slave,
What shall be said to thee?

OTHELLO   Why, anything;
An honourable murderer, if you will,
For nought I did in hate, but all in honour.

290

LODOVICO
This wretch hath part confessed his villainy.
Did you and he consent in Cassio's death?

OTHELLO   Ay.

295

CASSIO   Dear general, I never gave you cause.

OTHELLO   I do believe it, and I ask your pardon.
Will you, I pray, demand that demi-devil
Why he hath thus ensnared my soul and body?

IAGO   Demand me nothing. What you know, you know.
From this time forth I never will speak word.

300

LODOVICO   What, not to pray?

GRATIANO   Torments will ope your lips.

OTHELLO   Well, thou dost best.

LODOVICO
Sir, you shall understand what hath befallen,
Which, as I think, you know not. Here is a letter
Found in the pocket of the slain Roderigo,
And here another: the one of them imports
The death of Cassio, to be undertook
By Roderigo.

305

OTHELLO   O villain!

CASSIO   Most heathenish and most gross!

310

LODOVICO   Now here's another discontented paper
Found in his pocket too, and this, it seems,
Roderigo meant t'have sent this damned villain
But that, belike, Iago in the nick
Came in, and satisfied him.

315

OTHELLO   O thou pernicious caitiff!
How came you, Cassio, by that handkerchief
That was my wife's?

CASSIO   I found it in my chamber,
And he himself confessed but even now
That there he dropped it for a special purpose
Which wrought to his desire.

320

OTHELLO   O fool, fool, fool!

CASSIO   There is besides in Roderigo's letter
How he upbraids Iago, that he made him
Brave me upon the watch, whereon it came
That I was cast; and even but now he spake,
After long seeming dead, Iago hurt him,
Iago set him on.

325

LODOVICO [*to Othello*]
You must forsake this room and go with us.

Your power and your command is taken off
330   And Cassio rules in Cyprus. For this slave,
If there be any cunning cruelty
That can torment him much and hold him long,
It shall be his. You shall close prisoner rest
Till that the nature of your fault be known
335   To the Venetian state. Come, bring him away.
OTHELLO   Soft you, a word or two before you go.
I have done the state some service, and they
           know't:
No more of that. I pray you, in your letters,
When you shall these unlucky deeds relate,
340   Speak of me as I am. Nothing extenuate,
Nor set down aught in malice. Then must you speak
Of one that loved not wisely, but too well;
Of one not easily jealous, but, being wrought,
Perplexed in the extreme; of one whose hand,
345   Like the base Indian, threw a pearl away
Richer than all his tribe; of one whose subdued eyes,
Albeit unused to the melting mood,
Drops tears as fast as the Arabian trees
Their medicinable gum. Set you down this,
350   And say besides that in Aleppo once,

Where a malignant and a turbanned Turk
Beat a Venetian and traduced the state,
I took by th' throat the circumcised dog
And smote him – thus!   [*He stabs himself.*]
LODOVICO   O bloody period!
GRATIANO   All that's spoke is marred.   355
OTHELLO
I kissed thee ere I killed thee: no way but this,
Killing myself, to die upon a kiss.
           [*Kisses Desdemona, and dies.*]
CASSIO   This did I fear, but thought he had no weapon,
For he was great of heart.
LODOVICO [*to Iago*]   O Spartan dog,
More fell than anguish, hunger, or the sea,   360
Look on the tragic loading of this bed:
This is thy work. The object poisons sight,
Let it be hid. Gratiano, keep the house
And seize upon the fortunes of the Moor
For they succeed to you. To you, lord governor,   365
Remains the censure of this hellish villain,
The time, the place, the torture: O, enforce it!
Myself will straight aboard, and to the state
This heavy act with heavy heart relate.   *Exeunt.*

Pericles

Pericles, Prince of Tyre had been performed before 20 May 1608, when Edward Blount entered it for publication in the Register of the Stationers' Company. The earliest two known Quartos are both dated 1609, and the play reached a sixth edition by 1635. Yet despite its popularity, *Pericles* was not included in the First Folio in 1623. The King's Men who put the Folio together may have known it was only partly by Shakespeare, or they have may have hesitated to reprint its unsatisfactory text. In fact, *Pericles* is the one Shakespeare play that survives only in a clearly corrupt text. (George Wilkins, the minor dramatist who was Shakespeare's probable collaborator, wrote a narrative account of the play in 1608 that may fill in some details of the original.) *Pericles* was the first of seven plays attributed to Shakespeare that were added as a supplement to a reissue of the 1663 Third Folio. Alone of the seven, it was gradually accepted into the Shakespeare canon, partly because of unmistakable signs of Shakespeare's late style, especially in Acts 3–5, but also because of its resemblance to his late romances. Apparently a great success in its own time (as late as 1629 Ben Jonson complained of the continued popularity of such a 'mouldy tale', and *Pericles* was the first Shakespeare play revived at the Restoration), after a long hiatus the play has become a favourite on the modern stage.

In his opening speech, the Chorus, in the person of the fourteenth-century poet John Gower, introduces the story with the claim that '*bonum quo antiquius eo melius*', the older a good thing is the better it is. The romance of Apollonius of Tyre is indeed old, originating in the eastern Mediterranean in the fifth century CE or even earlier. Its many English retellings stretch from a fragmentary Old English translation, by way of Gower's *Confessio Amantis* (late 1380s), through a prose novel by Laurence Twyne, *The Pattern of Painful Adventures . . . that Befell unto Prince Apollonius*, written in the 1570s.

Shakespeare had earlier adapted the tale as the frame for *The Comedy of Errors*. In *Pericles* he changed the hero's name, possibly for metrical reasons, or to recall either Pyrocles from Sidney's *Arcadia* or the Greek statesman whose life he could read in Thomas North's *Plutarch,* also the source of *Coriolanus* and other plays.

Pericles tells its old story with fidelity to the sequence of events in Gower and Twyne but leavened with spectacular moments like Pericles' discovery of incest at Antiochus' court as well as comedy in the prose scenes of fishermen and brothel keepers. The travels and tribulations of Pericles are echoed, fourteen years later, by those of his lost (and supposedly dead) daughter, Marina, so named because she was born in a storm at sea in which her mother, Thaisa, died. The name Marina originates in the play, and strikingly resembles those of other heroines of late Shakespearean romance – Perdita, 'the lost one', and Miranda, 'wonderful'. As in those romances, the play presents a fantasy of recovery from loss: the child presumed dead is miraculously recovered, the broken family is reunited, both Tyre and Pentapolis regain rulers. The Job-like despair and catatonic withdrawal of Pericles are cured, in the play's climactic scene, by reunion with his daughter, a cure effected both by the example of her patience in extremity and by their discovery of each other's identity. As a bonus, a supernatural vision of the goddess Diana, the play's presiding deity, leads Pericles and Marina to Ephesus where the family restoration is completed by the discovery of Thaisa, long supposed dead but providentially resuscitated by the sage Cerimon and preserved as a nun in the temple of Diana. In the epilogue, Gower summarizes the play's romance pattern: 'Virtue preserved from fell destruction's blast, / Led on by heaven and crowned with joy at last'.

The Arden text is based on the 1609 First Quarto.

GOWER	*the chorus*
PERICLES	*Prince of Tyre*
DIANA	*a goddess*
MARINA	*daughter to Pericles and Thaisa, foster child to Cleon and Dionyza*

IN ANTIOCH

ANTIOCHUS	*King of Antioch*
DAUGHTER to Antiochus	
THALIARD	*of Antiochus' chamber*
MESSENGER	

IN TYRE

HELICANUS	*a grave and noble counsellor*
ESCANES	*an elderly counsellor*
Three LORDS	
GENTLEMEN	

IN TARSUS

CLEON	*governor of Tarsus*
DIONYZA	*wife to Cleon*
LEONINE	*servant to Dionyza*
LORD	
OTHER TARSIANS	
Three PIRATES	

IN PENTAPOLIS

SIMONIDES	*King of Pentapolis*
THAISA	*daughter to Simonides*
MARSHAL	
Three FISHERMEN	
FIRST KNIGHT	*of Sparta*
SECOND KNIGHT	*of Macedon*
THIRD KNIGHT	*of Antioch*
FOURTH KNIGHT	
FIFTH KNIGHT	
Three LORDS	
LYCHORIDA	*a nurse*
MASTER	*a mariner*
SAILOR	

IN EPHESUS

Lord CERIMON	
Two GENTLEMEN	
PHILEMON	*servant to Cerimon*
VISITING SERVANT	
Poor Man	
SERVANTS	*to Cerimon*
Maiden Priests	

IN MYTILENE

LYSIMACHUS	*governor of Mytilene*
PANDER	
BAWD	*wife to Pander*
BOLT	*servant to Pander and Bawd*
Two GENTLEMEN	
LORDS	
SAILOR OF TYRE	
SAILOR OF MYTILENE	
Companion to Marina	

Attendants, Ladies, Messengers, Squires

Pericles

1 Chorus/1.0   *Enter* GOWER.

GOWER   To sing a song that old was sung
     From ashes ancient Gower is come,
     Assuming man's infirmities
     To glad your ear and please your eyes.
5   It hath been sung at festivals,
     On ember eves and holy ales,
     And lords and ladies in their lives
     Have read it for restoratives.
     The purchase is to make men glorious,
10   *Et bonum quo antiquius eo melius.*
     If you, born in these latter times
     When wit's more ripe, accept my rhymes,
     And that to hear an old man sing
     May to your wishes pleasure bring,
15   I life would wish, and that I might
     Waste it for you like taper light.
     This Antioch, then.   [*Gestures.*]
           Antiochus the Great
     Built up this city for his chiefest seat –
     The fairest in all Syria.
20   I tell you what mine authors say:
     This king unto him took a fere,
     Who died and left a female heir
     So buxom, blithe and full of face
     As heaven had lent her all his grace,
25   With whom the father liking took
     And her to incest did provoke.
     Bad child, worse father, to entice his own
     To evil should be done by none.
     By custom what they did begin
30   Was with long use account' no sin.
     The beauty of this sinful dame
     Made many princes thither frame
     To seek her as a bedfellow,
     In marriage pleasures playfellow.
35   Which to prevent he made a law
     To keep her still and men in awe:
     That whoso asked her for his wife,
     His riddle told not, lost his life.
     So for her many a wight did die,
40   As yon grim looks do testify.
     [*Points to the heads displayed above.*]
     What now ensues, to the judgement of your eye
     I give, my cause who best can justify.   *Exit.*

1.1   *Enter* ANTIOCHUS, *Prince* PERICLES *and Followers, including Musicians.*

ANTIOCHUS
     Young Prince of Tyre, you have at large received
     The danger of the task you undertake.
PERICLES   I have, Antiochus, and with a soul
     Emboldened with the glory of her praise
5   Think death no hazard in this enterprise.
ANTIOCHUS   Music!   [*Music plays.*]
     Bring in our daughter, clothed like a bride

     For the embracements even of Jove himself,
     At whose conception, till Lucina reigned,
     Nature this dowry gave: to glad her presence,   10
     The senate house of planets all did sit
     To knit in her their best perfections.

     Enter DAUGHTER *to Antiochus with Attendants,*
     as the music continues to play.

PERICLES
     See where she comes, apparelled like the spring,
     Graces her subjects, and her thoughts the king
     Of every virtue gives renown to men;   15
     Her face the book of praises, where is read
     Nothing but curious pleasures, as from thence
     Sorrow were ever razed, and testy wrath
     Could never be her mild companion.
     You gods that made me man and sway in love,   20
     That have inflamed desire in my breast
     To taste the fruit of yon celestial tree
     Or die in the adventure, be my helps,
     As I am son and servant to your will,
     To compass such a boundless happiness.   25
ANTIOCHUS   Prince Pericles –
PERICLES   That would be son to great Antiochus –
ANTIOCHUS   Before thee stands this fair Hesperides,
     With golden fruit, but dangerous to be touched,
     For death-like dragons here affright thee hard.   30
     [*Gestures towards the heads.*]
     Her face, like heaven, enticeth thee to view
     Her countless glory, which desert must gain,
     And which without desert because thine eye
     Presumes to reach, all the whole heap must die.
     Yon sometimes famous princes [*indicating the heads*],
        like thyself,   35
     Drawn by report, adventurous by desire,
     Tell thee with speechless tongues and semblance pale
     That without covering save yon field of stars
     Here they stand, martyrs slain in Cupid's wars,
     And with dead cheeks advise thee to desist   40
     From going on death's net, whom none resist.
PERICLES   Antiochus, I thank thee, who hath taught
     My frail mortality to know itself,
     And by those fearful objects to prepare
     This body, like to them, to what I must.   45
     For death remembered should be like a mirror,
     Who tells us life's but breath, to trust it error.
     I'll make my will then, and, as sick men do
     Who know the world, see heaven, but feeling woe
     Grip not at earthly joys as erst they did,   50
     So I bequeath a happy peace to you
     And all good men, as every prince should do,
     My riches to the earth from whence they came,
     [*to Daughter*] But my unspotted fire of love to you.
     [*to Antiochus*] Thus ready for the way of life or death,   55
     I wait the sharpest blow, Antiochus.
ANTIOCHUS   Scorning advice, read the conclusion then.
     [*Gives him the riddle.*]

Which read and not expounded, 'tis decreed,
As these before thee, thou thyself shalt bleed.
DAUGHTER
60 Of all 'ssayed yet, mayst thou prove prosperous;
Of all 'ssayed yet, I wish thee happiness.
PERICLES   Like a bold champion I assume the lists,
Nor ask advice of any other thought
But faithfulness and courage.
[*Opens riddle and reads.*]
65   *I am no viper, yet I feed*
On mother's flesh which did me breed.
I sought a husband, in which labour
I found that kindness in a father.
He's father, son, and husband mild;
70   *I mother, wife, and yet his child.*
How they may be, and yet in two,
As you will live resolve it you.
[*aside*] Sharp physic is the last. But O, you powers
That gives heaven countless eyes to view men's acts,
75 Why cloud they not their sights perpetually
If this be true, which makes me pale to read it?
[*to Daughter*] Fair glass of light, I loved you, and
could still,
Were not this glorious casket stored with ill.
But I must tell you, now my thoughts revolt;
80 For he's no man on whom perfections wait
That knowing sin within will touch the gate.
You are a fair viol, and your sense the strings,
Who, fingered to make man his lawful music,
Would draw heaven down and all the gods to hearken;
85 But, being played upon before your time,
Hell only danceth at so harsh a chime.
Good sooth, I care not for you.   [*Waves his hand.*]
ANTIOCHUS   Prince Pericles, touch not, upon thy life,
For that's an article within our law
90 As dangerous as the rest. Your time's expired.
Either expound now or receive your sentence.
PERICLES   Great king,
Few love to hear the sins they love to act.
'Twould braid yourself too near for me to tell it.
95 Who has a book of all that monarchs do,
He's more secure to keep it shut than shown.
For vice repeated is like the wandering wind
Blows dust in others' eyes to spread itself;
And yet the end of all is bought thus dear:
100 The breath is gone, and the sore eyes see clear,
To stop the air would hurt them. The blind mole
casts
Copped hills towards heaven, to tell the earth is
thronged
By man's oppression, and the poor worm doth die for't.
Kings are earth's gods; in vice their law's their will;
105 And, if Jove stray, who dares say Jove doth ill?
It is enough you know, and it is fit,
What being more known grows worse, to smother it.
All love the womb that their first being bred;
Then give my tongue like leave to love my head.

ANTIOCHUS [*aside*]
Heaven, that I had thy head! He has found the meaning, 110
But I will gloze with him. – Young Prince of Tyre,
Though by the tenor of our strict edict,
Your exposition misinterpreting,
We might proceed to cancel of your days,
Yet hope, succeeding from so fair a tree 115
As your fair self, doth tune us otherwise.
Forty days longer we do respite you;
If by which time our secret be undone,
This mercy shows we'll joy in such a son.
And until then your entertain shall be 120
As doth befit our honour and your worth.
                                Exeunt all but Pericles.
PERICLES   How courtesy would seem to cover sin,
When what is done is like an hypocrite,
The which is good in nothing but in sight.
If it be true that I interpret false, 125
Then were it certain you were not so bad
As with foul incest to abuse your soul:
Where now you're both a father and a son
By your untimely claspings with your child,
Which pleasures fits a husband, not a father; 130
And she an eater of her mother's flesh,
By the defiling of her parents' bed;
And both like serpents are who, though they feed
On sweetest flowers, yet they poison breed.
Antioch, farewell! For wisdom sees, those men 135
Blush not in actions blacker than the night
Will 'schew no course to keep them from the light.
One sin, I know, another doth provoke;
Murder's as near to lust as flame to smoke.
Poison and treason are the hands of sin, 140
Ay, and the targets to put off the shame.
Then lest my life be cropped to keep you clear
By flight I'll shun the danger which I fear.   *Exit.*

                    Enter ANTIOCHUS.

ANTIOCHUS
He hath found the meaning, for the which
We mean to have his head. 145
He must not live to trumpet forth my infamy,
Nor tell the world Antiochus doth sin
In such a loathed manner;
And therefore instantly this prince must die,
For by his fall my honour must keep high. 150
Who attends us there?

                    Enter THALIARD.

THALIARD   Doth your highness call?
ANTIOCHUS
Thaliard, you are of our chamber, Thaliard, and our
mind
Partakes her private actions to your secrecy;
And for your faithfulness we will advance you.
Thaliard, behold, here's poison and here's gold: 155
We hate the Prince of Tyre, and thou must kill him.

It fits thee not to ask the reason why:
Because we bid it.
Say, is it done?
THALIARD   My lord, 'tis done.
ANTIOCHUS   Enough.

       Enter a Messenger.

160   Let your breath cool yourself, telling your haste.
MESSENGER   My lord, Prince Pericles is fled.   *Exit.*
ANTIOCHUS
As thou wilt live, fly after, and like an arrow
Shot from a well-experienced archer hits
The mark his eye doth level at,
165   So thou never return unless thou say,
'Prince Pericles is dead.'
THALIARD   My lord, if I can get him within my pistol's
length, I'll make him sure enough. So farewell to your
highness.
ANTIOCHUS
Thaliard, adieu.   *Exit Thaliard.*
170   Till Pericles be dead,
My heart can lend no succour to my head.   *Exit.*

1.2   *Enter* PERICLES *with his* Lords.

PERICLES
Let none disturb us.   *Exeunt Lords.*
       Why should this change of thoughts,
The sad companion, dull-eyed melancholy,
Be my so used a guest as not an hour
In the day's glorious walk or peaceful night,
5   The tomb where grief should sleep, can breed me quiet?
Here pleasures court mine eyes and mine eyes shun
   them,
And danger, which I feared, is at Antioch,
Whose arm seems far too short to hit me here.
Yet neither pleasure's art can joy my spirits,
10   Nor yet the other's distance comfort me.
Then it is thus: the passions of the mind,
That have their first conception by misdread,
Have after-nourishment and life by care;
And what was first but fear what might be done
15   Grows elder now, and cares it be not done.
And so with me. The great Antiochus,
'Gainst whom I am too little to contend,
Since he's so great can make his will his act,
Will think me speaking though I swear to silence.
20   Nor boots it me to say I honour him
If he suspect I may dishonour him.
And what may make him blush in being known
He'll stop the course by which it might be known.
With hostile forces he'll o'erspread the land,
25   And with th'ostent of war will look so huge,
Amazement shall drive courage from the state,
Our men be vanquished ere they do resist,
And subjects punished that ne'er thought offence.
Which care of them, not pity of myself,

Who am no more but as the tops of trees   30
Which fence the roots they grow by and defend them,
Makes both my body pine and soul to languish,
And punish that before that he would punish.

    Enter HELICANUS *and all the* Lords *to Pericles.*

1 LORD   Joy and all comfort in your sacred breast.
2 LORD   And keep your mind peaceful and comfortable.   35
HELICANUS   Peace! Peace, and give experience tongue.
They do abuse the king that flatter him,
For flattery is the bellows blows up sin;
The thing the which is flattered, but a spark
To which that wind gives heat and stronger glowing;   40
Whereas reproof, obedient and in order,
Fits kings as they are men, for they may err.
When Signior Sooth here does proclaim 'peace',
He flatters you, makes war upon your life.
Prince, pardon me, or strike me if you please,   45
I cannot be much lower than my knees.   [*Kneels.*]
PERICLES   All leave us else, but let your cares o'erlook
What shipping and what lading's in our haven,
And then return to us.   *Exeunt Lords.*
       Helicanus, thou
Hast moved us. What seest thou in our looks?   50
HELICANUS   An angry brow, dread lord.
PERICLES   If there be such a dart in princes' frowns,
How durst thy tongue move anger to our face?
HELICANUS
How dares the plants look up to heaven, from whence
They have their nourishment?
PERICLES   Thou knowest I have power   55
To take thy life from thee.
HELICANUS   I have ground the axe myself;
Do but you strike the blow.
PERICLES   Rise, prithee rise.
   [*Raises him.*]
Sit down; thou art no flatterer,
I thank thee for't; and heaven forbid
That kings should let their ears hear their faults hid.   60
Fit counsellor and servant for a prince,
Who by thy wisdom makes a prince thy servant,
What wouldst thou have me do?
HELICANUS   To bear with patience
Such griefs as you do lay upon yourself.
PERICLES   Thou speak'st like a physician, Helicanus,   65
That ministers a potion unto me
That thou wouldst tremble to receive thyself.
Attend me then: I went to Antioch,
Where, as thou knowst, against the face of death
I sought the purchase of a glorious beauty   70
From whence an issue I might propagate,
Are arms to princes and bring joys to subjects.
Her face was to mine eye beyond all wonder,
The rest – hark in thine ear – as black as incest.
Which by my knowledge found, the sinful father   75
Seemed not to strike but smooth. But thou knowst this,
'Tis time to fear when tyrants seems to kiss.

Which fear so grew in me I hither fled
Under the covering of a careful night,
80 Who seemed my good protector, and, being here,
Bethought me what was past, what might succeed.
I knew him tyrannous, and tyrants' fears
Decrease not, but grow faster than the years.
And should he doubt, as doubt no doubt he doth,
85 That I should open to the listening air
How many worthy princes' bloods were shed
To keep his bed of blackness unlaid ope,
To lop that doubt he'll fill this land with arms,
And make pretence of wrong that I have done him,
90 When all for mine – if I may call't – offence
Must feel war's blow, who spares not innocence.
Which love to all, of which thyself art one,
Who now reproved'st me for't –

HELICANUS   Alas, sir.

PERICLES
Drew sleep out of mine eyes, blood from my cheeks,
95 Musings into my mind, with thousand doubts
How I might stop this tempest ere it came,
And, finding little comfort to relieve them,
I thought it princely charity to grieve for them.

HELICANUS
Well, my lord, since you have given me leave to speak,
100 Freely will I speak. Antiochus you fear –
And justly too, I think, you fear the tyrant,
Who either by public war or private treason
Will take away your life.
Therefore, my lord, go travel for a while,
105 Till that his rage and anger be forgot,
Or the destinies do cut his thread of life.
Your rule direct to any; if to me,
Day serves not light more faithful than I'll be.

PERICLES   I do not doubt thy faith.
110 But should he wrong my liberties in my absence?

HELICANUS
We'll mingle our bloods together in the earth,
From whence we had our being and our birth.

PERICLES
Tyre, I now look from thee then, and to Tarsus
Intend my travel, where I'll hear from thee,
115 And by whose letters I'll dispose myself.
The care I had and have of subjects' good
On thee I lay, whose wisdom's strength can bear it.
I'll take thy word for faith, not ask thine oath:
Who shuns not to break one will sure crack both.
120 But in our orbs we'll live so round and safe
That time of both this truth shall ne'er convince:
Thou showed'st a subject's shine, I a true prince.
                                                  Exeunt.

1.3   *Enter* THALIARD.

THALIARD   So this is Tyre, and this the court. Here
must I kill King Pericles, and, if I do it not, I am sure
to be hanged at home: 'tis dangerous. Well, I perceive

he was a wise fellow and had good discretion that,
being bid to ask what he would of the king, desired he   5
might know none of his secrets. Now do I see he had
some reason for't: for, if a king bid a man be a villain,
he's bound by the indenture of his oath to be one.
Husht, here comes the lords of Tyre. [*Stands aside.*]

          Enter HELICANUS, ESCANES, *with other Lords.*

HELICANUS
You shall not need, my fellow peers of Tyre,   10
Further to question me of your king's departure.
His sealed commission left in trust with me
Does speak sufficiently he's gone to travel.

THALIARD [*aside*]   How? The king gone?

HELICANUS   If further yet you will be satisfied   15
Why, as it were unlicensed of your loves,
He would depart, I'll give some light unto you.
Being at Antioch –

THALIARD [*aside*]   What from Antioch?

HELICANUS
Royal Antiochus, on what cause I know not,
Took some displeasure at him – at least he judged so – 20
And, doubting lest he had erred or sinned,
To show his sorrow he'd correct himself;
So puts himself unto the shipman's toil,
With whom each minute threatens life or death.

THALIARD [*aside*]   Well, I perceive   25
I shall not be hanged now, although I would.
But, since he's gone, the king's ears it must please:
He scaped the land to perish at the seas.
I'll present myself.
– Peace to the lords of Tyre!

HELICANUS   Lord Thaliard   30
From Antiochus is welcome.

THALIARD   From him I come
With message unto princely Pericles,
But since my landing I have understood
Your lord has betook himself to unknown travels.
Now message must return from whence it came.   35

HELICANUS   We have no reason to desire it,
Commended to our master, not to us.
Yet, ere you shall depart, this we desire:
As friends to Antioch we may feast in Tyre.   *Exeunt.*

1.4   *Enter* CLEON *the governor of Tarsus, with*
        DIONYZA *his wife and* Other Tarsians.

CLEON   My Dionyza, shall we rest us here
And by relating tales of others' griefs
See if 'twill teach us to forget our own?

DIONYZA
That were to blow at fire in hope to quench it,
For who digs hills because they do aspire   5
Throws down one mountain to cast up a higher.
O my distressed lord, even such our griefs are;
Here they are but felt and seen with mischief's eyes,
But like to groves, being topped they higher rise.

10 CLEON   O Dionyza,
    Who wanteth food and will not say he wants it,
    Or can conceal his hunger till he famish?
    Our tongues our sorrows do sound deep,
    Our woes into the air our eyes do weep,
15   Till lungs fetch breath that may proclaim them louder
    That, if heaven slumber while their creatures want,
    They may awake their helps to comfort them.
    I'll then discourse our woes, felt several years,
    And, wanting breath to speak, help me with tears.
20 DIONYZA   I'll do my best, sir.
  CLEON   This Tarsus, o'er which I have the government,
    A city o'er whom plenty held full hand,
    For riches strewed herself even in her streets;
    Whose towers bore heads so high they kissed the clouds,
25   And strangers ne'er beheld but wondered at;
    Whose men and dames so jetted and adorned,
    Like one another's glass to trim them by;
    Their tables were stored full to glad the sight,
    And not so much to feed on as delight.
30   All poverty was scorned, and pride so great
    The name of help grew odious to repeat.
  DIONYZA   O, 'tis too true.
  CLEON   But see what heaven can do by this our change.
    These mouths who but of late earth, sea and air
35   Were all too little to content and please,
    Although they gave their creatures in abundance,
    As houses are defiled for want of use,
    They are now starved for want of exercise.
    Those palates who, not yet two summers younger,
40   Must have inventions to delight the taste
    Would now be glad of bread and beg for it.
    Those mothers, who to nuzzle up their babes
    Thought naught too curious, are ready now
    To eat those little darlings whom they loved.
45   So sharp are hunger's teeth that man and wife
    Draw lots who first shall die to lengthen life.
    Here stands a lord, and there a lady, weeping;
    Here many sink, yet those which see them fall
    Have scarce strength left to give them burial.
50   Is not this true?
  DIONYZA   Our cheeks and hollow eyes do witness it.
  CLEON   O, let those cities that of plenty's cup
    And her prosperities so largely taste
    With their superfluous riots heed these tears.
55   The misery of Tarsus may be theirs.

            Enter a Lord.

  LORD   Where's the lord governor?
  CLEON   Here.
    Speak out thy sorrows which thou bring'st in haste,
    For comfort is too far for us to expect.
  LORD   We have descried upon our neighbouring shore
60   A portly sail of ships make hitherward.
  CLEON   I thought as much.
    One sorrow never comes but brings an heir
    That may succeed as his inheritor;

    And so in ours. Some neighbouring nation,
65   Taking advantage of our misery,
    Hath stuffed the hollow vessels with their power
    To beat us down, the which are down already,
    And make a conquest of unhappy me,
    Whereas no glory's got to overcome.
70 LORD   That's the least fear for, by the semblance
    Of their white flags displayed, they bring us peace,
    And come to us as favourers, not as foes.
  CLEON   Thou speak'st like him's untutored to repeat:
    Who makes the fairest show means most deceit.
75   But bring they what they will and what they can,
    What need we fear?
    The ground's the lowest, and we are halfway there.
    Go tell their general we attend him here
    To know from whence he comes and what he craves.
80 LORD   I go, my lord.   *Exit.*
  CLEON   Welcome is peace, if he on peace consist,
    If wars, we are unable to resist.

       Enter PERICLES *with Attendants.*

  PERICLES   Lord governor, for so we hear you are,
    Let not our ships and number of our men
85   Be like a beacon fired t'amaze your eyes.
    We have heard your miseries as far as Tyre
    And seen the desolation of your streets;
    Nor come we to add sorrow to your hearts,
    But to relieve them of their heavy load;
90   And these our ships – you happily may think
    Are like the Trojan horse was stuffed within
    With bloody veins expecting overthrow –
    Are stored with corn to make your needy bread
    And give them life whom hunger starved half dead.
  ALL TARSIANS [*Kneel.*]
    The gods of Greece protect you,
95
    And we'll pray for you.
  PERICLES   Arise, I pray you, rise.
    [*They rise.*]
    We do not look for reverence but for love,
    And harbourage for ourself, our ships and men.
  CLEON   The which when any shall not gratify,
100   Or pay you with unthankfulness in thought,
    Be it our wives, our children or ourselves,
    The curse of heaven and men succeed their evils!
    Till when – the which I hope shall ne'er be seen –
    Your grace is welcome to our town and us.
  PERICLES
    Which welcome we'll accept, feast here awhile,
105   Until our stars that frown lend us a smile.   *Exeunt.*

2 Chorus/2.0   *Enter* GOWER.

GOWER   Here have you seen a mighty king
    His child, iwis, to incest bring;
    A better prince and benign lord
    That will prove awful both in deed and word.
    Be quiet then, as men should be,   5

Till he hath passed necessity.
I'll show you those in troubles reign,
Losing a mite, a mountain gain.
The good in conversation,
10 To whom I give my benison,
Is still at Tarsus, where each man
Thinks all is writ he speken can,
And to remember what he does
Build his statue to make him glorious.
15 But tidings to the contrary
Are brought your eyes; what need speak I?

Dumb-show. Enter at one door PERICLES *talking with*
CLEON, *all the train with them. Enter at another door a*
Gentleman with a letter to Pericles. Pericles shows the letter
to Cleon; Pericles gives the Messenger a reward and knights
him. Exeunt Pericles and Attendants at one door and Cleon
and Attendants at another.

Good Helicane that stayed at home
Not to eat honey like a drone
From others' labours, though he strive
20 To killen bad, keeps good alive
And to fulfil his prince' desire
Sends word of all that haps in Tyre:
How Thaliard came full bent with sin
And hid intent to murder him,
25 And that in Tarsus was not best
Longer for him to make his rest.
He doing so put forth to seas,
Where when men been there's seldom ease.
For now the wind begins to blow;
30 Thunder above and deeps below
Makes such unquiet that the ship
Should house him safe is wracked and split,
And he, good prince, having all lost,
By waves from coast to coast is tossed.
35 All perishen of man, of pelf,
Ne aught escapend but himself;
Till Fortune, tired with doing bad,
Threw him ashore to give him glad.
And here he comes. What shall be next,
40 Pardon old Gower: this 'longs the text.   *Exit.*

2.1   *Enter* PERICLES *wet.*

PERICLES
Yet cease your ire, you angry stars of heaven!
Wind, rain and thunder, remember earthly man
Is but a substance that must yield to you,
And I, as fits my nature, do obey you.
5 Alas, the seas hath cast me on the rocks,
Washed me from shore to shore, and left me breath
Nothing to think on but ensuing death.
Let it suffice the greatness of your powers
To have bereft a prince of all his fortunes,
10 And, having thrown him from your watery grave,
Here to have death in peace is all he'll crave.

Enter three Fishermen.

1 FISHERMAN   What ho, Pilch!
2 FISHERMAN   Ha, come and bring away the nets.
1 FISHERMAN   What, Patchbreech, I say!
3 FISHERMAN   What say you, master?   15
1 FISHERMAN   Look how thou stirrest now! Come away,
or I'll fetch'ee with a wanion.
3 FISHERMAN   Faith, master, I am thinking of the poor
men that were cast away before us even now.
1 FISHERMAN   Alas, poor souls, it grieved my heart to   20
hear what pitiful cries they made to us to help them
when, well-a-day, we could scarce help ourselves.
3 FISHERMAN   Nay, master, said not I as much when I
saw the porpoise, how he bounced and tumbled? They
say they're half fish, half flesh. A plague on them, they   25
ne'er come but I look to be washed. Master, I marvel
how the fishes live in the sea.
1 FISHERMAN   Why, as men do a-land: the great ones
eat up the little ones. I can compare our rich misers to
nothing so fitly as to a whale: 'a plays and tumbles,   30
driving the poor fry before him, and at last devours
them all at a mouthful. Such whales have I heard on
o'th' land, who never leave gaping till they swallowed
the whole parish, church, steeple, bells and all.
PERICLES [*aside*]   A pretty moral.   35
3 FISHERMAN   But, master, if I had been the sexton, I
would have been that day in the belfry.
2 FISHERMAN   Why, man?
3 FISHERMAN   Because he should have swallowed me
too, and when I had been in his belly I would have kept   40
such a jangling of the bells that he should never have
left till he cast bells, steeple, church and parish up
again. But if the good King Simonides were of my
mind –
PERICLES [*aside*]   Simonides?   45
3 FISHERMAN   We would purge the land of these drones
that rob the bee of her honey.
PERICLES [*aside*]
How from the finny subject of the sea
These fishers tell the infirmities of men
And from their watery empire recollect   50
All that may men approve or men detect.
[*to Fishermen*] Peace be at your labour, honest fishermen.
2 FISHERMAN   Honest! Good fellow, what's that? If it
be a day fits you, search't out of the calendar and
nobody'll look after it!   55
PERICLES   May see the sea hath cast upon your coast –
2 FISHERMAN   What a drunken knave was the sea to cast
thee in our way!
PERICLES   A man, whom both the waters and the wind
In that vast tennis-court hath made the ball   60
For them to play upon, entreats you pity him.
He asks of you that never used to beg.
1 FISHERMAN   No, friend, cannot you beg? Here's them
in our country of Greece gets more with begging than
we can do with working.   65

2 FISHERMAN   Canst thou catch any fishes then?

PERICLES   I never practised it.

2 FISHERMAN   Nay, then thou wilt starve, sure; for
here's nothing to be got nowadays unless thou canst
70 fish for't.

PERICLES   What I have been I have forgot to know;
But what I am want teaches me to think on:
A man thronged up with cold. My veins are chill,
And have no more of life than may suffice
75 To give my tongue that heat to ask your help,
Which if you shall refuse, when I am dead,
For that I am a man, pray see me buried.

1 FISHERMAN   Die, quotha? Now gods forbid't, an I
have a gown here! Come, put it on, keep thee warm.
80 Now, afore me, a handsome fellow! Come, thou shalt
go home, and we'll have flesh for holidays, fish for
fasting-days, and moreo'er puddings and flapjacks,
and thou shalt be welcome.

PERICLES   I thank you, sir.

85 2 FISHERMAN   Hark you, my friend. You said you could
not beg?

PERICLES   I did but crave.

2 FISHERMAN   But crave? Then I'll turn craver too, and
so I shall scape whipping.

90 PERICLES   Why, are your beggars whipped then?

2 FISHERMAN   O, not all, my friend, not all; for if all
your beggars were whipped I would wish no better
office than to be beadle. But, master, I'll go draw up the
net.   *Exeunt Second and Third Fishermen.*

PERICLES [*aside*]
95 How well this honest mirth becomes their labour!

1 FISHERMAN   Hark you, sir, do you know where ye are?

PERICLES   Not well.

1 FISHERMAN   Why, I'll tell you. This is called
Pentapolis, and our king, the good Simonides.

100 PERICLES   The good Simonides do you call him?

1 FISHERMAN   Ay, sir, and he deserves so to be called for
his peaceable reign and good government.

PERICLES   He is a happy king, since he gains from his
subjects the name of good by his government. How far
105 is his court distant from this shore?

1 FISHERMAN   Marry, sir, half a day's journey. And I'll
tell you, he hath a fair daughter, and tomorrow is her
birthday, and there are princes and knights come from
all parts of the world to joust and tourney for her love.

110 PERICLES   Were my fortunes equal to my desires, I
could wish to make one there.

1 FISHERMAN   O, sir, things must be as they may, and
what a man cannot get he may lawfully deal for with
his wife's soul.

Enter Second *and* Third Fishermen, *drawing up a net.*

115 2 FISHERMAN   Help, master, help! Here's a fish hangs in
the net like a poor man's right in the law; 'twill hardly
come out. Ha, bots on't, 'tis come at last, and 'tis
turned to a rusty armour. [*They pull a piece of Pericles'
armour from the net.*]

PERICLES   An armour, friends! I pray you let me see it.
Thanks, Fortune, yet, that after all thy crosses   120
Thou givest me somewhat to repair myself.
And though it was mine own, part of my heritage,
Which my dead father did bequeath to me
With this strict charge, even as he left his life:
'Keep it, my Pericles, it hath been a shield   125
'Twixt me and death', and pointed to this brace,
'For that it saved me, keep it; in like necessity,
The which the gods protect thee from, may't defend
     thee.'
It kept where I kept, I so dearly loved it,
Till the rough seas, that spares not any man,   130
Took it in rage, though calmed have given't again.
I thank thee for't. My shipwreck now's no ill,
Since I have here my father gave in his will.

1 FISHERMAN   What mean you, sir?

PERICLES
To beg of you, kind friends, this coat of worth,
For it was sometime target to a king;   135
I know it by this mark. He loved me dearly,
And for his sake I wish the having of it,
And that you'd guide me to your sovereign's court,
Where with it I may appear a gentleman.
And if that ever my low fortune's better   140
I'll pay your bounties, till then rest your debtor.

1 FISHERMAN   Why, wilt thou tourney for the lady?

PERICLES   I'll show the virtue I have borne in arms.

1 FISHERMAN   Why, d'ye take it, and the gods give thee
good on't.   145

2 FISHERMAN   Ay, but hark you, my friend, 'twas we
that made up this garment through the rough seams of
the waters. There are certain condolements, certain
vails. I hope, sir, if you thrive you'll remember from
whence you had them.   150

PERICLES   Believe't, I will.
By your furtherance I am clothed in steel,
And spite of all the rapture of the sea
This jewel holds his biding on my arm.
Unto thy value I will mount myself   155
Upon a courser, whose delightful steps
Shall make the gazer joy to see him tread.
Only, my friend, I yet am unprovided
Of a pair of bases.

2 FISHERMAN   We'll sure provide. Thou shalt have my   160
best gown to make thee a pair, and I'll bring thee to the
court myself.

PERICLES   Then honour be but equal to my will,
This day I'll rise, or else add ill to ill.   *Exeunt.*

2.2   *Sennet. Enter* SIMONIDES, THAISA,
          Lords *and Attendants.*

SIMONIDES
Are the knights ready to begin the triumph?

1 LORD   They are, my liege,
And stay your coming to present themselves.

SIMONIDES

Return them we are ready, and our daughter,

In honour of whose birth these triumphs are,

Sits here like beauty's child, whom Nature gat

For men to see and, seeing, wonder at.

Exit First Lord.

THAISA It pleaseth you, my royal father, to express

My commendations great, whose merit's less.

SIMONIDES It's fit it should be so, for princes are

A model which heaven makes like to itself;

As jewels lose their glory if neglected,

So princes their renowns if not respected.

'Tis now your honour, daughter, to entertain

The labour of each knight in his device.

THAISA Which to preserve mine honour I'll perform.

Enter First Lord.

The first Knight passes by; his Squire presents
his shield to Thaisa.

SIMONIDES Who is the first that doth prefer himself?

THAISA A knight of Sparta, my renowned father,

And the device he bears upon his shield

Is a black Ethiop reaching at the sun,

The word, *Lux tua vita mihi.*

SIMONIDES

He loves you well that holds his life of you.

The second Knight passes by; his Squire presents
his shield to Thaisa.

Who is the second that presents himself?

THAISA A prince of Macedon, my royal father,

And the device he bears upon his shield

Is an armed knight that's conquered by a lady,

The motto thus in Spanish, *Più per dolcezza che per*
forza.

The third Knight passes by; his Squire presents
his shield to Thaisa.

SIMONIDES And what's the third?

THAISA   The third of Antioch;

And his device a wreath of chivalry.

The word, *Me pompae provexit apex.*

The fourth Knight passes by; his Squire presents
his shield to Thaisa.

SIMONIDES What is the fourth?

THAISA A burning torch that's turned upside down;

The word, *Qui me alit me extinguit.*

SIMONIDES

Which shows that beauty hath her power and will,

Which can as well inflame as it can kill.

The fifth Knight passes by; his Squire presents
his shield to Thaisa.

THAISA The fifth, an hand environed with clouds

Holding out gold that's by the touchstone tried.

The motto thus, *Sic spectanda fides.*

The sixth Knight, PERICLES, *passes in rusty armour*
with bases, and unaccompanied. He presents his
device directly to Thaisa.

SIMONIDES

And what's the sixth and last, the which the knight
himself

With such a graceful courtesy delivered?

THAISA He seems to be a stranger, but his present is

A withered branch that's only green at top,

The motto, *In hac spe vivo.*

SIMONIDES   A pretty moral.

From the dejected state wherein he is

He hopes by you his fortunes yet may flourish.

1 LORD

He had need mean better than his outward show

Can any way speak in his just commend,

For by his rusty outside he appears

To have practised more the whipstock than the lance.

2 LORD He well may be a stranger, for he comes

To an honoured triumph strangely furnished.

3 LORD And on set purpose let his armour rust

Until this day, to scour it in the dust.

SIMONIDES Opinion's but a fool, that makes us scan

The outward habit for the inward man.

But stay, the knights are coming.

We will withdraw into the gallery.

Exeunt. Great shouts offstage, and all cry,
'The mean Knight!'

2.3   *Enter* SIMONIDES, THAISA, *Marshal,*
Ladies, Attendants and Knights *from tilting.*

SIMONIDES Knights,

To say you're welcome were superfluous.

To place upon the volume of your deeds,

As in a title-page, your worth in arms,

Were more than you expect, or more than's fit,

Since every worth in show commends itself.

Prepare for mirth, for mirth becomes a feast.

You are princes and my guests.

THAISA   But you my knight and guest,

To whom this wreath of victory I give

And crown you king of this day's happiness.

[*Offers Pericles a wreath.*]

PERICLES 'Tis more by fortune, lady, than my merit.

SIMONIDES Call it by what you will, the day is yours,

And here, I hope, is none that envies it.

In framing artists art hath thus decreed,

To make some good but others to exceed,

And you are her laboured scholar. Come, queen o'th'
feast,

For daughter so you are, here take your place.

[*to Marshal*] Marshal the rest as they deserve their
grace.

KNIGHTS We are honoured much by good Simonides.

SIMONIDES
20 Your presence glads our days; honour we love,
    For who hates honour hates the gods above.
MARSHAL   Sir, yonder is your place.
PERICLES   Some other is more fit.
1 KNIGHT   Contend not, sir, for we are gentlemen
    Have neither in our hearts nor outward eyes
25 Envied the great, nor shall the low despise.
PERICLES   You are right courteous knights.
SIMONIDES   Sit, sir, sit.
    [*aside*] By Jove I wonder, that is king of thoughts,
    These cates resist me, he but thought upon.
THAISA [*aside*]   By Juno, that is queen of marriage,
30 All viands that I eat do seem unsavoury,
    Wishing him my meat. [*to Simonides*] Sure he's a
        gallant gentleman.
SIMONIDES   He's but a country gentleman.
    Has done no more than other knights have done,
    Has broken a staff or so; so let it pass.
35 THAISA   To me he seems like diamond to glass.
PERICLES   Yon king's to me like to my father's picture,
    Which tells me in that glory once he was,
    Had princes sit like stars about his throne,
    And he the sun for them to reverence.
40 None that beheld him, but like lesser lights
    Did vail their crowns to his supremacy;
    Where now his son's like a glow-worm in the night,
    The which hath fire in darkness, none in light.
    Whereby I see that time's the king of men,
45 He's both their parent and he is their grave,
    And gives them what he will, not what they crave.
SIMONIDES   What, are you merry, knights?
KNIGHTS   Who can be other in this royal presence?
SIMONIDES
    Here, with a cup that's stored unto the brim,
50 As you do love, fill to your mistress' lips.
    We drink this health to you.
KNIGHTS   We thank your grace.
SIMONIDES
    Yet pause awhile. Yon knight doth sit too melancholy,
    As if the entertainment in our court
    Had not a show might countervail his worth.
55 Note it not you, Thaisa?
THAISA   What is't to me, my father?
SIMONIDES   O, attend, my daughter.
    Princes in this should live like gods above,
    Who freely give to everyone that come to honour
        them,
60 And princes not doing so are like to gnats,
    Which make a sound, but killed are wondered at.
    Therefore, to make his entertain more sweet,
    Here, say we drink this standing bowl of wine to
        him.
THAISA   Alas, my father, it befits not me
65 Unto a stranger knight to be so bold.
    He may my proffer take for an offence,
    Since men take women's gifts for impudence.

SIMONIDES
    How? Do as I bid you, or you'll move me else.
THAISA [*aside*]
    Now, by the gods, he could not please me better.
SIMONIDES   And, further, tell him we desire to know   70
    Of whence he is, his name and parentage.
THAISA [*to Pericles*]
    The king my father, sir, has drunk to you –
PERICLES   I thank him.
THAISA   Wishing it so much blood unto your life.
PERICLES
    I thank both him and you, and pledge him freely.   75
        [*Drinks.*]
THAISA   And, further, he desires to know of you
    Of whence you are, your name and parentage.
PERICLES   A gentleman of Tyre, my name Pericles,
    My education's been in arts and arms,
    Who looking for adventures in the world   80
    Was by the rough seas reft of ships and men,
    And after shipwreck driven upon this shore.
THAISA [*Returns to Simonides.*]
    He thanks your grace, names himself Pericles,
    A gentleman of Tyre,
    Who, only by misfortune of the seas   85
    Bereft of ships and men, cast on this shore –
SIMONIDES   Now, by the gods, I pity his misfortune
    And will awake him from his melancholy.
    Come, gentlemen, we sit too long on trifles
    And waste the time which looks for other revels.   90
    Even in your armours as you are addressed
    Will well become a soldiers' dance.
    I will not have excuse with saying this,
    'Loud music is too harsh for ladies' heads',
    Since they love men in arms as well as beds.   95
        [*The Knights dance.*]
    So, this was well asked, 'twas so well performed.
    [*to Pericles*] Come, sir, here's a lady that wants
        breathing too,
    And I have heard you knights of Tyre
    Are excellent in making ladies trip
    And that their measures are as excellent.   100
PERICLES
    In those that practise them they are, my lord.
SIMONIDES   O, that's as much as you would be denied
    Of your fair courtesy.
        [*The Knights and Ladies, Pericles and Thaisa among
        them, dance.*]   Unclasp, unclasp!
    Thanks, gentlemen, to all. All have done well,
    [*to Pericles*] But you the best. Pages and lights, to
        conduct   105
    These knights unto their several lodgings.
    Yours, sir, we have given order be next our own.
PERICLES   I am at your grace's pleasure.
SIMONIDES   Princes, it is too late to talk of love,
    And that's the mark I know you level at.   110
    Therefore each one betake him to his rest;
    Tomorrow all for speeding do their best.   *Exeunt.*

2.4　*Enter* HELICANUS *and* ESCANES.

HELICANUS　No, Escanes, know this of me:
Antiochus from incest lived not free,
For which the most high gods, not minding longer
To withhold the vengeance that they had in store
Due to this heinous capital offence, 5
Even in the height and pride of all his glory,
When he was seated in a chariot
Of inestimable value, and his daughter with him,
A fire from heaven came and shrivelled up
Their bodies even to loathing, for they so stunk 10
That all those eyes adored them ere their fall
Scorn now their hand should give them burial.
ESCANES　'Twas very strange.
HELICANUS　　　　　And yet but justice; for,
Though this king were great, his greatness was no
　　guard
To bar heaven's shaft, but sin had his reward. 15
ESCANES　'Tis very true.

　　　　Enter three Lords.

1 LORD
See, not a man in private conference
Or council has respect with him but he.
2 LORD　It shall no longer grieve without reproof.
3 LORD　And cursed be he that will not second it. 20
1 LORD　Follow me then. – Lord Helicane, a word.
HELICANUS
With me? And welcome. Happy day, my lords.
1 LORD
Know that our griefs are risen to the top
And now at length they overflow their banks.
HELICANUS
Your griefs, for what? Wrong not your prince you love. 25
1 LORD　Wrong not yourself then, noble Helicane,
But if the prince do live let us salute him,
Or know what ground's made happy by his breath.
If in the world he live, we'll seek him out;
If in his grave he rest, we'll find him there. 30
We'll be resolved he lives to govern us,
Or dead, gives cause to mourn his funeral
And leaves us to our free election.
2 LORD
Whose death's indeed the strongest in our censure.
And knowing this kingdom is without a head – 35
Like goodly buildings left without a roof
Soon fall to ruin – your noble self,
That best know how to rule and how to reign,
We thus submit unto – our sovereign!
ALL　Live, noble Helicane! 40
HELICANUS
Try honour's cause. Forbear your suffrages.
If that you love Prince Pericles, forbear.
Take I your wish, I leap into the seas,
Where's hourly trouble for a minute's ease.
A twelvemonth longer let me entreat you 45

To further bear the absence of your king;
If in which time expired he not return,
I shall with aged patience bear your yoke.
But, if I cannot win you to this love,
Go, search like nobles, like noble subjects, 50
And in your search spend your adventurous worth,
Whom if you find and win unto return
You shall like diamonds sit about his crown.
1 LORD　To wisdom he's a fool that will not yield;
And since Lord Helicane enjoineth us, 55
We with our travels will endeavour it.
HELICANUS
Then you love us, we you, and we'll clasp hands.
When peers thus knit, a kingdom ever stands.
　　　　　　　　　　　　　　　Exeunt.

2.5　*Enter* SIMONIDES *reading of a letter at one
　　　door; the* Knights *meet him.*

1 KNIGHT　Good morrow to the good Simonides.
SIMONIDES
Knights, from my daughter this I let you know:
That for this twelvemonth she'll not undertake
A married life.
Her reason to herself is only known, 5
Which from her by no means can I get.
2 KNIGHT　May we not get access to her, my lord?
SIMONIDES
Faith, by no means. She hath so strictly tied
Her to her chamber that 'tis impossible.
One twelvemoons more she'll wear Diana's livery. 10
This by the eye of Cynthia hath she vowed
And on her virgin honour will not break it.
3 KNIGHT　Loath to bid farewell, we take our leaves.
　　　　　　　　　　　　Exeunt Knights.
SIMONIDES
So, they are well dispatched. Now to my daughter's
　　letter.
She tells me here she'll wed the stranger knight, 15
Or never more to view nor day nor light.
'Tis well, mistress, your choice agrees with mine.
I like that well. Nay, how absolute she's in't,
Not minding whether I dislike or no.
Well, I do commend her choice 20
And will no longer have it be delayed.
Soft, here he comes. I must dissemble it.

　　　　Enter PERICLES.

PERICLES　All fortune to the good Simonides.
SIMONIDES
To you as much. Sir, I am beholding to you
For your sweet music this last night. I do 25
Protest, my ears were never better fed
With such delightful pleasing harmony.
PERICLES　It is your grace's pleasure to commend,
Not my desert.
SIMONIDES　　　Sir, you are music's master.

PERICLES   The worst of all her scholars, my good lord.

SIMONIDES   Let me ask you one thing:
What do you think of my daughter, sir?

PERICLES   A most virtuous princess.

SIMONIDES   And she is fair, too, is she not?

PERICLES   As a fair day in summer, wondrous fair.

SIMONIDES   Sir, my daughter thinks very well of you,
Ay, so well that you must be her master
And she will be your scholar; therefore look to it.

PERICLES   I am unworthy for her schoolmaster.

SIMONIDES   She thinks not so. Peruse this writing else.
[*Gives him the letter.*]

PERICLES [*aside*]   What's here?
A letter that she loves the knight of Tyre?
'Tis the king's subtlety to have my life.
– O, seek not to entrap me, gracious lord,
A stranger and distressed gentleman
That never aimed so high to love your daughter,
But bent all offices to honour her.

SIMONIDES   Thou hast bewitched my daughter,
And thou art a villain.

PERICLES   By the gods, I have not;
Never did thought of mine levy offence;
Nor never did my actions yet commence
A deed might gain her love or your displeasure.

SIMONIDES   Traitor, thou liest.

PERICLES   Traitor?

SIMONIDES   Ay, traitor.

PERICLES   Even in his throat, unless it be the king,
That calls me traitor, I return the lie.

SIMONIDES [*aside*]
Now by the gods I do applaud his courage.

PERICLES   My actions are as noble as my thoughts,
That never relished of a base descent.
I came unto your court for honour's cause
And not to be a rebel to her state;
And he that otherwise accounts of me,
This sword shall prove he's honour's enemy.

SIMONIDES   No?
Here comes my daughter; she can witness it.

Enter THAISA.

PERICLES   Then as you are as virtuous as fair,
Resolve your angry father if my tongue
Did e're solicit or my hand subscribe
To any syllable that made love to you?

THAISA   Why, sir, say if you had,
Who takes offence at that would make me glad?

SIMONIDES   Yea, mistress, are you so peremptory?
[*aside*] I am glad on't with all my heart.
– I'll tame you, I'll bring you in subjection.
Will you, not having my consent,
Bestow your love and your affections
Upon a stranger? [*aside*] Who for aught I know
May be (nor can I think the contrary)
As great in blood as I myself.
– Therefore hear you, mistress, either frame your will

To mine, and you, sir, hear you, either be
Ruled by me, or I'll make you – man and wife.
Nay, come, your hands and lips must seal it too,
And, being joined, I'll thus your hopes destroy,
And for further grief – God give you joy!
What, are you both pleased?

THAISA   Yes – if you love me, sir?

PERICLES   Even as my life my blood that fosters it.

SIMONIDES   What, are you both agreed?

BOTH   Yes, if 't please your majesty.

SIMONIDES
It pleaseth me so well that I will see you wed;
Then, with what haste you can, get you to bed.
Exeunt.

3 Chorus/3.0   *Enter* GOWER.

GOWER   Now sleep y-slacked hath the rouse,
No din but snores about the house,
Made louder by the o'erfed breast
Of this most pompous marriage feast.
The cat with eyne of burning coal
Now couches from the mouse's hole,
And crickets sing at the oven's mouth
Are the blither for their drouth.
Hymen hath brought the bride to bed,
Where by the loss of maidenhead
A babe is moulded. Be attent,
And time that is so briefly spent
With your fine fancies quaintly eche.
What's dumb in show I'll plain with speech.

Dumb-show. Enter PERICLES *and* SIMONIDES *at one
door with Attendants; a Messenger meets them, kneels and
gives Pericles a letter. Pericles shows it Simonides, the Lords
kneel to him. Then enter* THAISA *with child, with*
LYCHORIDA, *a nurse. The King shows her the letter; she
rejoices; she and Pericles take leave of her father and depart
with Lychorida and their Attendants. Then exeunt
Simonides and the rest at the other door.*

By many a dern and painful perch
Of Pericles the careful search,
By the four opposing coigns
Which the world together joins,
Is made with all due diligence
That horse and sail and high expense
Can stead the quest. At last from Tyre –
Fame answering the most strange enquire –
To th' court of King Simonides
Are letters brought, the tenor these:
Antiochus and his daughter dead,
The men of Tyrus on the head
Of Helicanus would set on
The crown of Tyre, but he will none.
The mutiny he there hastes t'appease,
Says to 'em, if King Pericles
Come not home in twice six moons,

He, obedient to their dooms,
Will take the crown. The sum of this
Brought hither to Pentapolis
35 Y-ravished the regions round,
And everyone with claps can sound,
'Our heir apparent is a king;
Who dreamt, who thought of such a thing?'
Brief, he must hence depart to Tyre;
40 His queen with child makes her desire –
Which who shall cross? – along to go.
Omit we all their dole and woe.
Lychorida her nurse she takes,
And so to sea. Their vessel shakes
45 On Neptune's billow. Half the flood
Hath their keel cut, but Fortune's mood
Varies again. The grizzled north
Disgorges such a tempest forth
That, as a duck for life that dives,
50 So up and down the poor ship drives.
The lady shrieks and, well-a-near,
Does fall in travail with her fear.
And what ensues in this fell storm
Shall for itself itself perform.
55 I nill relate, action may
Conveniently the rest convey,
Which might not what by me is told.
In your imagination hold
This stage the ship, upon whose deck
60 The sea-tossed Pericles appears to speak.   *Exit.*

3.1   *Enter* PERICLES *on shipboard.*

PERICLES
The god of this great vast, rebuke these surges
Which wash both heaven and hell, and thou that hast
Upon the winds command, bind them in brass,
Having called them from the deep. O, still
5 Thy deafening dreadful thunders; gently quench
Thy nimble sulphurous flashes!   [*Calls.*]
                O how, Lychorida!
How does my queen? – Thou stormest venomously;
Wilt thou spit all thyself? The seaman's whistle
Is as a whisper in the ears of death,
Unheard.   [*Calls.*]
10   Lychorida! – Lucina, O,
Divinest patroness and midwife gentle
To those that cry by night, convey thy deity
Aboard our dancing boat; make swift the pangs
Of my queen's travails! – Now, Lychorida!

Enter LYCHORIDA *with an infant.*

15 LYCHORIDA   Here is a thing too young for such a place,
Who if it had conceit would die, as I
Am like to do. Take in your arms this piece
Of your dead queen.
PERICLES   How! How, Lychorida?
LYCHORIDA   Patience, good sir, do not assist the storm.

Here's all that is left living of your queen,   20
A little daughter. For the sake of it,
Be manly and take comfort.
PERICLES   O you gods!
Why do you make us love your goodly gifts
And snatch them straight away? We here below
Recall not what we give, and therein may   25
Vie honour with you.
LYCHORIDA   Patience, good sir,
Even for this charge.   [*Gives him the babe.*]
PERICLES   Now, mild may be thy life!
For a more blusterous birth had never babe;
Quiet and gentle thy conditions, for
Thou art the rudeliest welcome to this world   30
That ever was prince's child. Happy what follows!
Thou hast as chiding a nativity
As fire, air, water, earth and heaven can make
To herald thee from the womb.
Even at the first thy loss is more than can   35
Thy portage quit, with all thou canst find here.
Now the good gods throw their best eyes upon't!

Enter the ship's Master *and a* Sailor.

MASTER   What courage, sir? God save you!
PERICLES   Courage enough. I do not fear the flaw:
It hath done to me the worst. Yet for the love   40
Of this poor infant, this fresh new seafarer,
I would it would be quiet.
MASTER   Slack the bowlines there! – Thou wilt not, wilt
thou? Blow and split thyself.
SAILOR   But sea-room, an the brine and cloudy billow   45
kiss the moon, I care not.
MASTER   Sir, your queen must overboard. The sea
works high, the wind is loud and will not lie till the
ship be cleared of the dead.
PERICLES   That's your superstition.   50
MASTER   Pardon us, sir; with us at sea it hath been still
observed, and we are strong in custom. Therefore
briefly yield 'er, for she must overboard straight.
PERICLES   As you think meet. Most wretched queen!
LYCHORIDA   Here she lies, sir.   [*Reveals the body.*]   55
PERICLES   A terrible childbed hast thou had, my dear,
No light, no fire. Th'unfriendly elements
Forgot thee utterly, nor have I time
To give thee hallowed to thy grave, but straight
Must cast thee, scarcely coffined, in the ooze,   60
Where, for a monument upon thy bones
And aye-remaining lamps, the belching whale
And humming water must o'erwhelm thy corpse,
Lying with simple shells. O Lychorida,
Bid Nestor bring me spices, ink and paper,   65
My casket and my jewels, and bid Nicander
Bring me the satin coffer.   [*Gives her the babe.*]
                Lay the babe
Upon the pillow. Hie thee, whiles I say
A priestly farewell to her. Suddenly, woman.
                        Exit Lychorida.

70 SAILOR   Sir, we have a chest beneath the hatches,
   caulked and bitumed ready.
PERICLES
   I thank thee. – Mariner, say, what coast is this?
MASTER   We are near Tarsus.
PERICLES   Thither, gentle mariner,
   Alter thy course for Tyre. When canst thou reach it?
MASTER   By break of day, if the wind cease.
75 PERICLES   O, make for Tarsus!
   There will I visit Cleon, for the babe
   Cannot hold out to Tyrus. There I'll leave it
   At careful nursing. Go thy ways, good mariner;
   I'll bring the body presently.
                Exeunt separately, Pericles with Thaisa.

3.2   *Enter* Lord CERIMON *with a* Visiting
        Servant *and a Poor Man.*

CERIMON   Philemon, ho!

        Enter PHILEMON.

PHILEMON   Doth my lord call?
CERIMON   Get fire and meat for these poor men.
                        Exit Philemon.
   'T has been a turbulent and stormy night.
VISITING SERVANT
5   I have been in many, but such a night as this
   Till now I ne'er endured.
CERIMON   Your master will be dead ere you return;
   There's nothing can be ministered to nature
   That can recover him. [*to Poor Man*] Give this to the
      'pothecary,
10   And tell me how it works.
            Exeunt Visiting Servant and Poor Man.

        Enter two Gentlemen.

1 GENTLEMAN   Good morrow.
2 GENTLEMAN   Good morrow to your lordship.
CERIMON   Gentlemen, why do you stir so early?
1 GENTLEMAN
   Sir, our lodgings standing bleak upon the sea
15   Shook as the earth did quake;
   The very principals did seem to rend
   And all to topple. Pure surprise and fear
   Made me to quit the house.
2 GENTLEMAN
   That is the cause we trouble you so early,
20   'Tis not our husbandry.
CERIMON   O, you say well.
1 GENTLEMAN
   But I much marvel that your lordship, having
   Rich tire about you, should at these early hours
   Shake off the golden slumber of repose.
   'Tis most strange
25   Nature should be so conversant with pain,
   Being thereto not compelled.

CERIMON   I hold it ever
   Virtue and cunning were endowments greater
   Than nobleness and riches. Careless heirs
   May the two latter darken and expend,
   But immortality attends the former,   30
   Making a man a god. 'Tis known I ever
   Have studied physic, through which secret art,
   By turning o'er authorities, I have,
   Together with my practice, made familiar
   To me and to my aid the blest infusions   35
   That dwells in vegetives, in metals, stones,
   And I can speak of the disturbances
   That nature works and of her cures, which doth give
      me
   A more content and cause of true delight
   Than to be thirsty after tottering honour,   40
   Or tie my pleasure up in silken bags
   To please the fool and death.
2 GENTLEMAN   Your honour has
   Through Ephesus poured forth your charity,
   And hundreds call themselves your creatures, who
   By you have been restored. And not your knowledge, 45
   Your personal pain, but even your purse still open
   Hath built Lord Cerimon such strong renown
   As time shall never –

        Enter two or three Servants *with a chest.*

1 SERVANT   So, lift there.
1 CERIMON   What's that?
1 SERVANT [*to Cerimon*]   Sir, even now
   Did the sea toss up upon our shore this chest;   50
   'Tis of some wreck.
CERIMON   Set't down. Let's look upon't.
2 GENTLEMAN   'Tis like a coffin, sir.
CERIMON   What e'er it be,
   'Tis wondrous heavy. Did the sea cast it up?
1 SERVANT   I never saw so huge a billow, sir,
   As tossed it upon shore.
CERIMON   Wrench it open straight.   55
        [*The Servants begin to work on the chest.*]
   If the sea's stomach be o'ercharged with gold,
   'Tis a good constraint of fortune
   It belches upon us.
2 GENTLEMAN   'Tis so, my lord.
CERIMON
   How close 'tis caulked and bitumed! Soft! It smells
   Most sweetly in my sense.
2 GENTLEMAN   A delicate odour.   60
CERIMON   As ever hit my nostril. So, up with it.
        [*They open* the *chest.*]
   O you most potent go'ds! What's here, a corpse?
2 GENTLEMAN   Most strange!
CERIMON   Shrouded in cloth of state,
   Balmed and entreasured with full bags of spices!
   A passport too!   65
   Apollo, perfect me in the characters.

[*Reads.*]
    Here I give to understand,
    If e'er this coffin drives a-land,
    I King Pericles have lost
70   *This queen, worth all our mundane cost.*
    Who finds her, give her burying:
    She was the daughter of a king.
    Besides this treasure for a fee,
    The gods requite his charity.
75 If thou livest, Pericles, thou hast a heart
That even cracks for woe. This chanced tonight.

2 GENTLEMAN   Most likely, sir.

CERIMON   Nay, certainly tonight,
For look how fresh she looks. They were too rough
That threw her in the sea. Make a fire within;
80 Fetch hither all my boxes in my closet.
                            Exit First Servant.
Death may usurp on nature many hours
And yet the fire of life kindle again
The o'erpressed spirits. I heard of an Egyptian
That had nine hours lain dead, who was
85 By good appliance recovered.

    Enter First Servant *with napkins and fire.*

Well said, well said; the fire and cloths.
The rough and woeful music that we have,
Cause it to sound, beseech you.
                [*Viol music sounds and stops.*]
The viol once more. How thou stirr'st, thou block!
The music there!   [*Music*]
90   I pray you, give her air.
Gentlemen, this queen will live. Nature awakes;
A warmth breathes out of her! She hath not been
Entranced above five hours. See how she 'gins
To blow into life's flower again.

1 GENTLEMAN   The heavens
95 Through you increase our wonder, and sets up
Your fame for ever.

CERIMON   She is alive! Behold
Her eyelids, cases to those heavenly jewels
Which Pericles hath lost, begin to part
Their fringes of bright gold. The diamonds
100 Of a most praised water doth appear,
To make the world twice rich. Live, and make
Us weep to hear your fate, fair creature,
Rare as you seem to be.   [*She moves.*]

THAISA   O dear Diana, where am I? Where's my lord?
What world is this?

2 GENTLEMAN   Is not this strange?
105 1 GENTLEMAN   Most rare.

CERIMON   Hush, my gentle neighbours.
Lend me your hands. To the next chamber bear her;
Get linen. Now this matter must be looked to,
For her relapse is mortal. Come, come;
110 And Aesculapius guide us.
             They carry her away. Exeunt omnes.

3.3   *Enter* PERICLES *at Tarsus, with* CLEON,
           DIONYZA *and* LYCHORIDA
           carrying baby MARINA.

PERICLES
Most honoured Cleon, I must needs be gone;
My twelve months are expired, and Tyrus stands
In a litigious peace. You and your lady
Take from my heart all thankfulness. The gods
Make up the rest upon you.

CLEON   Your shafts of fortune,   5
Though they hurt you mortally, yet glance
Full wanderingly on us.

DIONYZA   O, your sweet queen!
That the strict fates had pleased you had brought her
   hither
To have blessed mine eyes with her.

PERICLES   We cannot but obey
The powers above us. Could I rage and roar   10
As doth the sea she lies in, yet the end
Must be as 'tis. My gentle babe Marina,
Whom for she was born at sea I have named so,
Here I charge your charity withal,
Leaving her the infant of your care,   15
Beseeching you to give her princely training,
That she may be mannered as she is born.

CLEON   Fear not, my lord, but think
Your grace that fed my country with your corn –
For which the people's prayers still fall upon you –   20
Must in your child be thought on. If neglection
Should therein make me vile, the common body,
By you relieved, would force me to my duty.
But if to that my nature need a spur
The gods revenge it upon me and mine   25
To the end of generation.

PERICLES   I believe you.
Your honour and your goodness teach me to't
Without your vows. Till she be married, madam,
By bright Diana whom we honour all,
Unscissored shall this hair of mine remain,   30
Though I show ill in't. So I take my leave.
Good madam, make me blessed in your care
In bringing up my child.

DIONYZA   I have one myself
Who shall not be more dear to my respect
Than yours, my lord.

PERICLES   Madam, my thanks and prayers.   35

CLEON
We'll bring your grace e'en to the edge o'th' shore,
Then give you up to the masked Neptune and
The gentlest winds of heaven.

PERICLES
I will embrace your offer. Come, dearest madam.
O, no tears, Lychorida, no tears.   40
Look to your little mistress, on whose grace
You may depend hereafter. Come, my lord.   *Exeunt.*

3.4   *Enter* CERIMON *and* THAISA.

CERIMON   Madam, this letter and some certain jewels
    Lay with you in your coffer, which are
    At your command. Know you the character?
THAISA   It is my lord's. That I was shipped at sea
5   I well remember, even on my groaning time,
    But whether there delivered, by the holy gods
    I cannot rightly say. But since King Pericles,
    My wedded lord, I ne'er shall see again,
    A vestal livery will I take me to
10   And never more have joy.
CERIMON   Madam, if this you purpose as ye speak,
    Diana's temple is not distant far,
    Where you may abide till your date expire.
    Moreover, if you please, a niece of mine
15   Shall there attend you.
THAISA   My recompense is thanks, that's all,
    Yet my good will is great, though the gift small.
                           Exeunt.

4 Chorus/4.0   *Enter* GOWER.

GOWER   Imagine Pericles arrived at Tyre,
    Welcomed and settled to his own desire.
    His woeful queen we leave at Ephesus,
    Unto Diana there's a votaress.
5   Now to Marina bend your mind,
    Whom our fast-growing scene must find
    At Tarsus, and by Cleon trained
    In music's letters, who hath gained
    Of education all the grace
10   Which makes her both the heart and place
    Of general wonder. But, alack,
    That monster envy, oft the wrack
    Of earned praise, Marina's life
    Seeks to take off by treason's knife,
15   And in this kind: our Cleon hath
    One daughter and a full-grown wench
    Even ripe for marriage-rite. This maid
    Hight Philoten, and it is said
    For certain in our story she
20   Would ever with Marina be,
    Be't when they weaved the sleided silk
    With fingers long, small, white as milk,
    Or when she would with sharp needle wound
    The cambric which she made more sound
25   By hurting it, or when to th' lute
    She sung, and made the night bird mute
    That still records with moan, or when
    She would with rich and constant pen
    Vail to her mistress Dian; still
30   This Philoten contends in skill
    With absolute Marina. So
    With dove of Paphos might the crow
    Vie feathers white. Marina gets
    All praises, which are paid as debts

And not as given. This so darks   35
In Philoten all graceful marks
That Cleon's wife with envy rare
A present murder does prepare
For good Marina, that her daughter
Might stand peerless by this slaughter.   40
The sooner her vile thoughts to stead,
Lychorida, our nurse, is dead,
And cursed Dionyza hath
The pregnant instrument of wrath
Prest for this blow. The unborn event   45
I do commend to your content,
Only I carry winged time
Post on the lame feet of my rhyme,
Which never could I so convey
Unless your thoughts went on my way.   50
Dionyza does appear
With Leonine, a murderer.   *Exit.*

4.1   *Enter* DIONYZA *with* LEONINE.

DIONYZA
    Thy oath remember. Thou hast sworn to do't.
    'Tis but a blow, which never shall be known.
    Thou canst not do a thing in the world so soon
    To yield thee so much profit. Let not conscience,
    Which is but cold, inflame love in thy bosom,   5
    Nor let pity, which even women have cast off,
    Melt thee, but be a soldier to thy purpose.
LEONINE   I will do't, but yet she is a goodly creature.
DIONYZA   The fitter then the gods should have her.
    Here she comes weeping her only nurse's death.   10
    Thou art resolved?
LEONINE   I am resolved.

    Enter MARINA *with a basket of flowers.*

MARINA   No, I will rob Tellus of her weed
    To strew thy grave with flowers; the yellows, blues,
    The purple violets and marigolds
    Shall as a carpet hang upon the green   15
    While summer days doth last. Ay me, poor maid,
    Born in a tempest when my mother died,
    This world to me is as a lasting storm,
    Whirring me from my friends.
DIONYZA   How now, Marina, why do you keep alone?   20
    How chance my daughter is not with you?
    Do not consume your blood with sorrowing;
    Have you a nurse of me. Lord, how your favour's
    Changed with this unprofitable woe.
    Come, give me your flowers. O'er the sea-margent   25
    Walk with Leonine; the air is quick there
    And it pierces and sharpens the stomach.
    Come, Leonine.
    Take her by the arm, walk with her.
MARINA   No, I pray you.
    I'll not bereave you of your servant.
DIONYZA   Come, come.   30

I love the king your father and yourself
With more than foreign heart. We every day
Expect him here. When he shall come and find
Our paragon to all reports thus blasted,
35 He will repent the breadth of his great voyage,
Blame both my lord and me, that we have taken
No care to your best courses. Go, I pray you,
Walk, and be cheerful once again. Reserve
That excellent complexion, which did steal
40 The eyes of young and old. Care not for me;
I can go home alone.

MARINA   Well, I will go,
But yet I have no desire to it.

DIONYZA   Come, come, I know 'tis good for you.
Walk half an hour, Leonine, at the least.
Remember what I have said.

45 LEONINE   I warrant you, madam.

DIONYZA   I'll leave you, my sweet lady, for a while.
Pray walk softly, do not heat your blood.
What, I must have care of you.

MARINA   My thanks, sweet madam.
                             Exit Dionyza.
Is this wind westerly that blows?

LEONINE   South-west.

MARINA
When I was born the wind was north.

50 LEONINE   Was't so?

MARINA   My father, as nurse says, did never fear,
But cried 'Good seamen!' to the sailors,
Galling his kingly hands with haling ropes,
And clasping to the mast endured a sea
55 That almost burst the deck.

LEONINE   When was this?

MARINA   When I was born.
Never was waves nor wind more violent,
And from the ladder tackle washes off
60 A canvas-climber. 'Ha,' says one, 'wolt out?'
And with a dropping industry they skip
From stem to stern. The boatswain whistles, and
The master calls and trebles their confusion.

LEONINE   Come, say your prayers.

MARINA   What mean you?

65 LEONINE   If you require a little space for prayer,
I grant it. Pray, but be not tedious,
For the gods are quick of ear and I am sworn
To do my work with haste.

MARINA   Why will you kill me?

LEONINE   To satisfy my lady.

MARINA   Why would she have me killed now?
70 As I can remember, by my troth,
I never did her hurt in all my life.
I never spake bad word, nor did ill turn
To any living creature. Believe me, la,
I never killed a mouse nor hurt a fly.
75 I trod upon a worm against my will,
But I wept for't. How have I offended,
Wherein my death might yield her any profit, or

My life imply her danger?

LEONINE   My commission
Is not to reason of the deed, but do't.

MARINA   You will not do't for all the world, I hope.   80
You are well favoured, and your looks foreshow
You have a gentle heart. I saw you lately
When you caught hurt in parting two that fought.
Good sooth, it showed well in you. Do so now.
Your lady seeks my life. Come you between   85
And save poor me, the weaker.

LEONINE   I am sworn
And will dispatch.   [*Seizes her.*]

                Enter Pirates.

1 PIRATE   Hold, villain! [*Leonine releases her.*]

2 PIRATE   A prize, a prize!

3 PIRATE   Half part, mates, half part! Come, let's have   90
her aboard suddenly.   *Exeunt with Marina.*

LEONINE [*Comes forward.*]
These roguing thieves serve the great pirate Valdes,
And they have seized Marina. Let her go.
There's no hope she will return. I'll swear she's
    dead
And thrown into the sea. But I'll see further.   95
Perhaps they will but please themselves upon her,
Not carry her aboard. If she remain,
Whom they have ravished, must by me be slain.

                                Exit.

4.2   *Enter* Pander, Bawd *and* BOLT.

PANDER   Bolt.

BOLT   Sir.

PANDER   Search the market narrowly. Mytilene is full of
gallants. We lost too much money this mart by being
too wenchless.   5

BAWD   We were never so much out of creatures. We
have but poor three, and they can do no more than they
can do, and with continual action they are even as good
as rotten.

PANDER   Therefore let's have fresh ones, whate'er we   10
pay for them. If there be not a conscience to be used in
every trade, we shall never prosper.

BAWD   Thou sayst true. 'Tis not our bringing up of
poor bastards – as I think I have brought up some
eleven –   15

BOLT   Ay, to eleven, and brought them down again – but
shall I search the market?

BAWD   What else, man? The stuff we have, a strong
wind will blow it to pieces, they are so pitifully sodden.

PANDER   Thou sayst true. They're too unwholesome,   20
o'conscience. The poor Transylvanian is dead that lay
with the little baggage.

BOLT   Ay, she quickly pooped him, she made him roast
meat for worms. But I'll go search the market.   *Exit.*

PANDER   Three or four thousand chequins were as   25
pretty a proportion to live quietly, and so give over.

BAWD   Why to give over, I pray you? Is it a shame to get
when we are old?

PANDER   O, our credit comes not in like the commodity,
nor the commodity wages not with the danger.
Therefore, if in our youths we could pick up some
pretty estate, 'twere not amiss to keep our door
hatched. Besides, the sore terms we stand upon with
the gods will be strong with us for giving o'er.

BAWD   Come, other sorts offend as well as we.

PANDER   As well as we, ay, and better too. We offend
worse. Neither is our profession any trade, it's no
calling. But here comes Bolt.

Enter BOLT *with the*
Pirates *and* MARINA.

BOLT [*to Pirates*]   Come your ways, my masters. You say
she's a virgin?

PIRATE   O sir, we doubt it not.

BOLT   Master, I have gone through for this piece you
see. If you like her, so; if not, I have lost my earnest.

BAWD   Bolt, has she any qualities?

BOLT   She has a good face, speaks well and has excellent
good clothes: there's no farther necessity of qualities
can make her be refused.

BAWD   What's her price, Bolt?

BOLT   I cannot be bated one doit of a thousand pieces.

PANDER   Well, follow me, my masters, you shall have
your money presently. Wife, take her in, instruct her
what she has to do, that she may not be raw in her
entertainment.   *Exit with Pirates.*

BAWD   Bolt, take you the marks of her, the colour of
her hair, complexion, height, her age, with warrant of
her virginity, and cry, 'He that will give most shall have
her first.' Such a maidenhead were no cheap thing, if
men were as they have been. Get this done as I
command you.

BOLT   Performance shall follow.   *Exit.*

MARINA   Alack that Leonine was so slack, so slow.
He should have struck, not spoke; or that these
   pirates,
Not enough barbarous, had but o'erboard thrown me
For to seek my mother.

BAWD   Why lament you, pretty one?

MARINA   That I am pretty.

BAWD   Come, the gods have done their part in you.

MARINA   I accuse them not.

BAWD   You are light into my hands, where you are like to
live.

MARINA   The more my fault,
To scape his hands where I was like to die.

BAWD   Ay, and you shall live in pleasure.

MARINA   No.

BAWD   Yes, indeed shall you, and taste gentlemen of all
fashions. You shall fare well; you shall have the
difference of all complexions. What, do you stop your
ears?

MARINA   Are you a woman?

BAWD   What would you have me be, an I be not a   80
woman?

MARINA   An honest woman, or not a woman.

BAWD   Marry, whip the gosling! I think I shall have
something to do with you. Come, you're a young
foolish sapling and must be bowed as I would have you.   85

MARINA   The gods defend me!

BAWD   If it please the gods to defend you by men, then
men must comfort you, men must feed you, men stir
you up.

Enter BOLT.

Bolt's returned. – Now, sir, hast thou cried her through   90
the market?

BOLT   I have cried her almost to the number of her
hairs; I have drawn her picture with my voice.

BAWD   And I prithee tell me, how dost thou find the
inclination of the people, especially of the younger   95
sort?

BOLT   Faith, they listened to me as they would have
hearkened to their father's testament. There was a
Spaniard's mouth watered an he went to bed to her
very description.   100

BAWD   We shall have him here tomorrow with his best
ruff on.

BOLT   Tonight, tonight! But, mistress, do you know the
French knight that cowers i'th' hams?

BAWD   Who, Monsieur Veroles?   105

BOLT   Ay, he; he offered to cut a caper at the
proclamation, but he made a groan at it and swore he
would see her tomorrow.

BAWD   Well, well, as for him, he brought his disease
hither; here he does but repair it. I know he will come   110
in our shadow to scatter his crowns in the sun.

BOLT   Well, if we had of every nation a traveller we
should lodge them with this sign.

BAWD [*to Marina*]   Pray you, come hither awhile. You
have fortunes coming upon you. Mark me, you must   115
seem to do that fearfully which you commit willingly,
despise profit where you have most gain. To weep that
you live as ye do makes pity in your lovers. Seldom but
that pity begets you a good opinion, and that opinion a
mere profit.   120

MARINA   I understand you not.

BOLT   O, take her home, mistress, take her home. These
blushes of hers must be quenched with some present
practice.

BAWD   Thou sayst true i'faith, so they must, for your   125
bride goes to that with shame which is her way to go
with warrant.

BOLT   Faith, some do and some do not. But, mistress, if
I have bargained for the joint –

BAWD   Thou mayst cut a morsel off the spit.   130

BOLT   I may so.

BAWD   Who should deny it? Come, young one, I like the
manner of your garments well.

BOLT   Ay, by my faith they shall not be changed yet.

135 BAWD [*Gives him money.*]   Bolt, spend thou that in the
town. Report what a sojourner we have. You'll lose
nothing by custom. When nature framed this piece,
she meant thee a good turn. Therefore say what a
paragon she is, and thou hast the harvest out of thine
140 own report.

BOLT   I warrant you, mistress, thunder shall not so
awake the beds of eels as my giving out her beauty stirs
up the lewdly inclined. I'll bring home some tonight.
Exit.

BAWD   Come your ways, follow me.

145 MARINA   If fires be hot, knives sharp or waters deep,
Untried I still my virgin knot will keep.
Diana, aid my purpose!

BAWD   What have we to do with Diana? Pray you, will
you go with us?   *Exeunt.*

4.3   *Enter* CLEON *and* DIONYZA.

DIONYZA   Why, are you foolish? Can it be undone?

CLEON   O Dionyza, such a piece of slaughter
The sun and moon ne'er looked upon.

DIONYZA   I think you'll turn a child again.

5 CLEON   Were I chief lord of all this spacious world
I'd give it to undo the deed. A lady
Much less in blood than virtue, yet a princess
To equal any single crown o'th' earth
I'th' justice of compare. O villain Leonine,
10 Whom thou hast poisoned too,
If thou hadst drunk to him 't'ad been a kindness
Becoming well thy face. What canst thou say
When noble Pericles shall demand his child?

DIONYZA   That she is dead. Nurses are not the fates.
15 To foster is not ever to preserve.
She died at night. I'll say so. Who can cross it?
Unless you play the pious innocent
And for an honest attribute cry out,
'She died by foul play.'

CLEON   O, go to. Well, well,
20 Of all the faults beneath the heavens the gods
Do like this worst.

DIONYZA   Be one of those that thinks
The petty wrens of Tarsus will fly hence
And open this to Pericles. I do shame
To think of what a noble strain you are
And of how coward a spirit.

25 CLEON   To such proceeding
Whoever but his approbation added,
Though not his prime consent, he did not flow
From honourable sources.

DIONYZA   Be it so, then.
Yet none does know but you how she came dead,
30 Nor none can know, Leonine being gone.
She did distain my child, and stood between
Her and her fortunes. None would look on her,
But cast their gazes on Marina's face,
Whilst ours was blurted at and held a malkin

Not worth the time of day. It pierced me through, 35
And though you call my course unnatural,
You not your child well loving, yet I find
It greets me as an enterprise of kindness
Performed to your sole daughter.

CLEON   Heavens forgive it!

DIONYZA   And, as for Pericles, what should he say? 40
We wept after her hearse, and yet we mourn.
Her monument is almost finished, and her epitaphs
In glittering golden characters express
A general praise to her and care in us
At whose expense 'tis done.

CLEON   Thou art like the harpy, 45
Which to betray dost use thine angel's face
To seize with thine eagle's talons.

DIONYZA   Ye're like one that superstitiously
Do swear to th' gods that winter kills the flies,
But yet I know you'll do as I advise.   *Exeunt.* 50

5 Chorus/4.4   *Enter* GOWER.

GOWER
Thus time we waste and long leagues make short,
Sail seas in cockles, have and wish but for't,
Making to take our imagination
From bourn to bourn, region to region.
By you being pardoned, we commit no crime 5
To use one language in each several clime
Where our scenes seems to live. I do beseech you
To learn of me, who stand i'th' gaps to teach you
The stages of our story. Pericles
Is now again thwarting the wayward seas, 10
Attended on by many a lord and knight,
To see his daughter, all his life's delight.
Old Helicanus goes along. Behind
Is left to govern, if you bear in mind,
Old Escanes, whom Helicanus late 15
Advanced in time to great and high estate.
Well-sailing ships and bounteous winds have brought
This king to Tarsus – think his pilot thought;
So with his sternage shall your thoughts go on –
To fetch his daughter home, who first is gone. 20
Like motes and shadows see them move awhile;
Your ears unto your eyes I'll reconcile.

Dumb-show. Enter PERICLES *at one door with all his*
train; CLEON *and* DIONYZA *at the other. Cleon shows*
Pericles the tomb, whereat Pericles makes lamentation, puts
on sackcloth and in a mighty passion departs. Exeunt Cleon
and Dionyza at the other door.

See how belief may suffer by foul show.
This borrowed passion stands for true-owed woe,
And Pericles in sorrow all devoured, 25
With sighs shot through and biggest tears
o'ershowered,
Leaves Tarsus and again embarks. He swears
Never to wash his face nor cut his hairs.

He puts on sackcloth and to sea he bears
A tempest which his mortal vessel tears,
And yet he rides it out. Now please you wit
The epitaph is for Marina writ
By wicked Dionyza.
   [*Reads the inscription on Marina's monument.*]
     The fairest, sweetest and best lies here,
     Who withered in her spring of year:
     She was of Tyrus the King's daughter
     On whom foul death hath made this slaughter.
     Marina was she called, and at her birth
     Thetis being proud swallowed some part o'th' earth.
     Therefore the earth, fearing to be o'erflowed,
     Hath Thetis' birth-child on the heavens bestowed;
     Wherefore she does, and swears she'll never stint,
     Make raging battery upon shores of flint.
No vizor does become black villainy
So well as soft and tender flattery.
Let Pericles believe his daughter's dead
And bear his courses to be ordered
By Lady Fortune, while our scene must play
His daughter's woe and heavy well-a-day
In her unholy service. Patience then,
And think you now are all in Mytilene.   *Exit.*

4.5   *Enter two* Gentlemen.

1 GENTLEMAN   Did you ever hear the like?
2 GENTLEMAN   No, nor never shall do in such a place as
this, she being once gone.
1 GENTLEMAN   But to have divinity preached there –
did you ever dream of such a thing?
2 GENTLEMAN   No, no. Come, I am for no more bawdy
houses. Shall's go hear the vestals sing?
1 GENTLEMAN   I'll do anything now that is virtuous,
but I am out of the road of rutting for ever.   *Exeunt.*

         Enter Pander, Bawd *and* BOLT.   [**4.6**]

PANDER   Well, I had rather than twice the worth of her
she had ne'er come here.
BAWD   Fie, fie upon her. She's able to freeze the god
Priapus and undo a whole generation. We must either
get her ravished or be rid of her. When she should do
for clients her fitment, and do me the kindness of our
profession, she has me her quirks, her reasons, her
master reasons, her prayers, her knees, that she would
make a puritan of the devil if he should cheapen a kiss
of her.
BOLT   Faith, I must ravish her, or she'll disfurnish us of
all our *cavalleria* and make our swearers priests.
PANDER   Now the pox upon her green sickness for me.
BAWD   Faith, there's no way to be rid on't but by the
way to the pox.

         Enter LYSIMACHUS.

Here comes the Lord Lysimachus disguised.
BOLT   We should have both lord and loon if the peevish

baggage would but give way to customers.
LYSIMACHUS   [*Unmasks.*]   How now, how a dozen of
virginities?
BAWD   Now the gods to-bless your honour.
BOLT   I am glad to see your honour in good health.
LYSIMACHUS   You may so. 'Tis the better for you that
your resorters stand upon sound legs. How now?
Wholesome iniquity have you, that a man may deal
withal and defy the surgeon?
BAWD   We have here one, sir, if she would – but there
never came her like in Mytilene.
LYSIMACHUS   If she'd do the deeds of darkness, thou
wouldst say.
BAWD   Your honour knows what 'tis to say well enough.
LYSIMACHUS   Well, call forth, call forth.   *Exit Pander.*
BOLT   For flesh and blood, sir, white and red, you shall
see a rose, and she were a rose indeed, if she had but –
LYSIMACHUS   What, prithee?
BOLT   O sir, I can be modest.
LYSIMACHUS   That dignifies the renown of a bawd no
less than it gives a good report to a number to be
chaste.

         Enter Pander *with* MARINA.

BAWD   Here comes that which grows to the stalk; never
plucked yet, I can assure you. Is she not a fair creature?
LYSIMACHUS   Faith, she would serve after a long voyage
at sea. Well, there's for you. [*Gives Bawd money.*]
Leave us.
BAWD   I beseech your honour, give me leave a word, and
I'll have done presently.
LYSIMACHUS   I beseech you, do.
BAWD   [*to Marina*]   First, I would have you note, this is
an honourable man.
MARINA   I desire to find him so, that I may worthily
note him.
BAWD   Next, he's the governor of this country, and a
man whom I am bound to.
MARINA   If he govern the country you are bound to him
indeed, but how honourable he is in that I know not.
BAWD   Pray you, without any more virginal fencing, will
you use him kindly? He will line your apron with gold.
MARINA   What he will do graciously, I will thankfully
receive.
LYSIMACHUS   Ha' you done?
BAWD   My lord, she's not paced yet. You must take some
pains to work her to your manage. – Come, we will
leave his honour and her together. – Go thy ways.
                        Exit with Pander and Bolt.
LYSIMACHUS   Now, pretty one, how long have you been
at this trade?
MARINA   What trade, sir?
LYSIMACHUS   Why, I cannot name't but I shall offend.
MARINA   I cannot be offended with my trade. Please you
to name it.
LYSIMACHUS   How long have you been of this –
profession?

MARINA   E'er since I can remember.

LYSIMACHUS   Did you go to't so young? Were you a
gamester at five, or at seven?

MARINA   Earlier too, sir, if now I be one.

85 LYSIMACHUS   Why, the house you dwell in proclaims
you to be a creature of sale.

MARINA   Do you know this house to be a place of such
resort, and will come into't? I hear say you're of
honourable parts, and are the governor of this place.

90 LYSIMACHUS   Why, hath your principal made known
unto you who I am?

MARINA   Who is my principal?

LYSIMACHUS   Why, your herb-woman, she that sets
seeds and roots of shame and iniquity. O, you have
95 heard something of my power and so stand aloof for
more serious wooing, but I protest to thee, pretty one,
my authority shall not see thee, or else look friendly
upon thee. Come, bring me to some private place.
Come, come.

100 MARINA   If you were born to honour, show it now;
If put upon you, make the judgement good
That thought you worthy of it.

LYSIMACHUS
How's this? How's this? Some more, be sage.

MARINA   For me
That am a maid, though most ungentle Fortune
105 Have placed me in this sty, where since I came
Diseases have been sold dearer than physic –
O, that the gods
Would set me free from this unhallowed place,
Though they did change me to the meanest bird
That flies i'th' purer air!

110 LYSIMACHUS   I did not think
Thou couldst have spoke so well, ne'er dreamt thou
couldst.
Had I brought hither a corrupted mind
Thy speech had altered it. Hold, here's gold for thee.
Persever in that clear way thou goest
115 And the gods strengthen thee.   [*Gives her gold.*]

MARINA   The good gods preserve you.

LYSIMACHUS   For me, be you bethoughted that I came
With no ill intent, for to me the very doors
And windows savour vilely. Fare thee well.
120 Thou art a piece of virtue, and I doubt not
But thy training hath been noble.
Hold, here's more gold for thee.
A curse upon him, die he like a thief,
That robs thee of thy goodness. If thou dost
125 Hear from me it shall be for thy good.

[*Moves towards door.*]

Enter BOLT *from the doorway.*

BOLT   I beseech your honour, one piece for me.

LYSIMACHUS   Avaunt, thou damned doorkeeper!
Your house, but for this virgin that doth prop it,
Would sink and overwhelm you. Away!   *Exit.*

130 BOLT   How's this? We must take another course with

you. If your peevish chastity, which is not worth a
breakfast in the cheapest country under the cope, shall
undo a whole household, let me be gelded like a
spaniel. Come your ways.

MARINA   Whither would you have me?   135

BOLT   I must have your maidenhead taken off, or the
common hangman shall execute it. Come your ways.
We'll have no more gentlemen driven away. Come your
ways, I say.

Enter Bawd *and* Pander.

BAWD   How now, what's the matter?   140

BOLT   Worse and worse, mistress. She has here spoken
holy words to the Lord Lysimachus.

BAWD   O, abominable!

BOLT   She makes our profession as it were to stink afore
the face of the gods.   145

BAWD   Marry, hang her up for ever!

BOLT   The nobleman would have dealt with her like a
nobleman, and she sent him away as cold as a snowball,
saying his prayers too.

BAWD   Bolt, take her away, use her at thy pleasure.   150
Crack the glass of her virginity and make the rest
malleable.

BOLT   An if she were a thornier piece of ground than she
is, she shall be ploughed.

MARINA   Hark, hark, you gods!   155

BAWD   She conjures! Away with her, would she had
never come within my doors. – Marry, hang you! –
She's born to undo us. – Will you not go the way of
womankind? Marry, come up, my dish of chastity with
rosemary and bays!   *Exit with Pander.*   160

BOLT   Come, mistress, come your way with me.

MARINA   Whither wilt thou have me?

BOLT   To take from you the jewel you hold so dear.

MARINA   Prithee, tell me one thing first.

BOLT   Come now, your one thing?   165

MARINA   What canst thou wish thine enemy to be?

BOLT   Why, I could wish him to be my master, or rather
my mistress.

MARINA   Neither of these are so bad as thou art,
Since they do better thee in their command.   170
Thou hold'st a place for which the pained'st fiend
Of hell would not in reputation change.
Thou art the damned doorkeeper to every
Coistrel that comes enquiring for his Tib.
To the choleric fisting of every rogue   175
Thy ear is liable. Thy food is such
As hath been belched on by infected lungs.

BOLT   What would you have me do? Go to the wars,
would you, where a man may serve seven years for the
loss of a leg and have not money enough in the end to 180
buy him a wooden one?

MARINA   Do anything but this thou dost. Empty
Old receptacles or common shores of filth,
Serve by indenture to the common hangman,
Any of these ways are yet better than this.   185

For what thou professest a baboon, could he speak,
Would own a name too dear. O, that the gods
Would safely deliver me from this place!
Here, here's gold for thee.   [*Gives Bolt the money.*]
190   If that thy master would make gain by me,
Proclaim that I can sing, weave, sew and dance,
With other virtues which I'll keep from boast,
And I will undertake all these to teach.
I doubt not but this populous city will
195   Yield many scholars.
BOLT   But can you teach all this you speak of?
MARINA   Prove that I cannot, take me home again
And prostitute me to the basest groom
That doth frequent your house.
200   BOLT   Well, I will see what I can do for thee. If I can
place thee I will.
MARINA   But amongst honest women.
BOLT   Faith, my acquaintance lies little amongst them.
But, since my master and mistress hath bought you,
205   there's no going but by their consent. Therefore I will
make them acquainted with your purpose, and I doubt
not but I shall find them tractable enough. Come, I'll
do for thee what I can. Come your ways.   *Exeunt.*

6 Chorus/5.0   *Enter* GOWER.

GOWER
Marina thus the brothel scapes, and chances
Into an honest house, our story says.
She sings like one immortal and she dances
As goddess-like to her admired lays.
5   Deep clerks she dumbs and with her nee'le composes
Nature's own shape of bud, bird, branch or berry,
That even her art sisters the natural roses.
Her inkle, silk, twin with the rubied cherry,
That pupils lacks she none of noble race,
10   Who pour their bounty on her, and her gain
She gives the cursed Bawd. Here we her place,
And to her father turn our thoughts again,
Where we left him on the sea. We there him lost,
Whence, driven before the winds, he is arrived
15   Here where his daughter dwells, and on this coast
Suppose him now at anchor. The city strived
God Neptune's annual feast to keep, from whence
Lysimachus our Tyrian ship espies,
His banners sable, trimmed with rich expense,
20   And to him in his barge with fervour hies.
In your supposing once more put your sight:
Of heavy Pericles, think this his bark,
Where what is done in action, more if might,
Shall be discovered, please you sit and hark.   *Exit.*

5.1   *Enter* HELICANUS; *to him a* Sailor of Tyre
and a Sailor of Mytilene.

SAILOR OF TYRE [*to Sailor of Mytilene*]
Where is Lord Helicanus? He can resolve you.
O, here he is.

[*to Helicanus*] Sir, there is a barge put off from
Mytilene,
And in it is Lysimachus the governor,
Who craves to come aboard. What is your will?   5
HELICANUS
That he have his.   *Exit Sailor of Mytilene.*
Call up some gentlemen.
SAILOR OF TYRE
Ho, gentlemen, my lord calls.

Enter two or three Gentlemen.

1 GENTLEMAN   Doth your lordship call?
HELICANUS
Gentlemen, there is some of worth would come aboard;
I pray you, greet him fairly.

Enter LYSIMACHUS, *attended, with* Sailor of
Mytilene *and* Lords, *as the Gentlemen go
to meet him.*

SAILOR OF MYTILENE [*to Lysimachus*]   Sir,
This is the man that can in aught you would   10
Resolve you.
LYSIMACHUS   Hail, reverend sir! The gods
Preserve you.
HELICANUS   And you, to outlive the age I am,
And die as I would do.
LYSIMACHUS   You wish me well.
Being on shore, honouring of Neptune's triumphs,
Seeing this goodly vessel ride before us,   15
I made to it to know of whence you are.
HELICANUS   First, what is your place?
LYSIMACHUS
I am the governor of this place you lie before.
HELICANUS   Sir, our vessel is of Tyre, in it the king,
A man who for this three months hath not spoken   20
To anyone, nor taken sustenance
But to prorogue his grief.
LYSIMACHUS   Upon what ground
Is his distemperature?
HELICANUS   'Twould be too tedious
To repeat, but the main grief springs from the loss
Of a beloved daughter and a wife.   25
LYSIMACHUS
May we not see him?
HELICANUS   You may,
But bootless is your sight. He will not speak
To any.
LYSIMACHUS   Yet let me obtain my wish.
HELICANUS   Behold him.

PERICLES is revealed.

This was a goodly person
Till the disaster that one mortal night   30
Drove him to this.
LYSIMACHUS   Sir king, all hail! The gods preserve you!
Hail, royal sir.
HELICANUS   It is in vain. He will not speak to you.

LORD [*to Lysimachus*]

35 Sir, we have a maid in Mytilene, I durst wager
     Would win some words of him.

LYSIMACHUS   'Tis well bethought.
     She questionless, with her sweet harmony
     And other choice attractions, would allure
     And make a battery through his deafened ports
40   Which now are midway stopped.
     She is all happy as the fairest of all,
     And with her fellow maid is now upon
     The leafy shelter that abuts against
     The island's side. Go, fetch her hither.   *Exit Lord.*

HELICANUS

45   Sure all effectless; yet nothing we'll omit
     That bears recovery's name. But, since your
          kindness
     We have stretched thus far, let us beseech you
     That for our gold we may provision have,
     Wherein we are not destitute for want
     But weary for the staleness.

50 LYSIMACHUS   O sir, a courtesy
     Which, if we should deny, the most just gods
     For every graft would send a caterpillar
     And so inflict our province. Yet once more
     Let me entreat to know at large the cause
55   Of your king's sorrow.

HELICANUS   Sit, sir, I will recount it to you. But see,
     I am prevented.

          Enter Lord, MARINA *and her Companion.*

LYSIMACHUS   O, here's the lady
     That I sent for. – Welcome, fair one. – Is't not
     A goodly presence?

HELICANUS   She's a gallant lady.

LYSIMACHUS
60   She's such a one that, were I well assured
     Came of a gentle kind or noble stock,
     I'd wish no better choice and think me rarely wed.
     Fair one, all goodness that consists in bounty
     Expect even here, where is a kingly patient.
65   If that thy prosperous and artificial feat
     Can draw him but to answer thee in aught,
     Thy sacred physic shall receive such pay
     As thy desires can wish.

MARINA   Sir, I will use
     My utmost skill in his recovery, provided
70   That none but I and my companion maid
     Be suffered to come near him.

LYSIMACHUS   Come, let us leave her,
     And the gods make her prosperous.

          [*All the men but Pericles withdraw. Marina sings.*]
          [*Comes forward.*] Marked he your music?

MARINA   No, nor looked on us.

LYSIMACHUS   See, she will speak to him.

                              Exeunt all but Pericles,
                    Marina and her Companion, who sits aside.

MARINA   Hail, sir! My lord, lend ear.

PERICLES   Hum, ha.   [*Pushes her back.*]

MARINA   I am a maid,   75
     My lord, that ne'er before invited eyes,
     But have been gazed on like a comet. She speaks,
     My lord, that may be hath endured a grief
     Might equal yours, if both were justly weighed.
     Though wayward Fortune did malign my state,   80
     My derivation was from ancestors
     Who stood equivalent with mighty kings,
     But time hath rooted out my parentage,
     And to the world and awkward casualties
     Bound me in servitude. [*aside*] I will desist,   85
     But there is something glows upon my cheek
     And whispers in mine ear, 'Go not till he speak.'

PERICLES   My fortunes – parentage – good parentage –
     To equal mine. Was it not thus? What say you?

MARINA   I said, my lord, if you did know my parentage   90
     You would not do me violence.

PERICLES
     I do think so. Pray you, turn your eyes upon me.
     You're like something that – what countrywoman?
     Here of these shores?

MARINA   No, nor of any shores.
     Yet I was mortally brought forth and am   95
     No other than I appear.

PERICLES
     I am great with woe, and shall deliver weeping.
     My dearest wife was like this maid, and such a one
     My daughter might have been. My queen's square
          brows,
     Her stature to an inch, as wand-like straight,   100
     As silver-voiced, her eyes as jewel-like
     And cased as richly, in pace another Juno;
     Who starves the ears she feeds and makes them
          hungry
     The more she gives them speech. Where do you live?

MARINA   Where I am but a stranger. From the deck   105
     You may discern the place.

PERICLES   Where were you bred?
     And how achieved you these endowments which
     You make more rich to owe?

MARINA   If I should tell
     My history, it would seem like lies
     Disdained in the reporting.

PERICLES   Prithee speak.   110
     Falseness cannot come from thee, for thou look'st
     Modest as Justice, and thou seem'st a palace
     For the crowned Truth to dwell in. I will believe thee
     And make my senses credit thy relation
     To points that seem impossible. For thou look'st   115
     Like one I loved indeed. What were thy friends?
     Didst thou not say, when I did push thee back –
     Which was when I perceived thee – that thou cam'st
     From good descending?

MARINA   So indeed I did.

PERICLES   Report thy parentage. I think thou saidst   120
     Thou hadst been tossed from wrong to injury,

And that thou thought'st thy griefs might equal mine
If both were opened.

MARINA   Some such thing I said,
And said no more but what my thoughts
Did warrant me was likely.

125 PERICLES   Tell thy story.
If thine considered prove the thousand part
Of my endurance, thou art a man, and I
Have suffered like a girl. Yet thou dost look
Like Patience gazing on kings' graves and smiling

130 Extremity out of act. What were thy friends?
How lost thou them? Thy name, my most kind virgin?
Recount, I do beseech thee. Come, sit by me.

MARINA [*Sits.*]
My name is Marina.

PERICLES   O, I am mocked,
And thou by some incensed god sent hither
To make the world to laugh at me.

135 MARINA   Patience, good sir,
Or here I'll cease.

PERICLES   Nay, I'll be patient.
Thou little knowst how thou dost startle me
To call thyself Marina.

MARINA   The name
Was given me by one that had some power:
My father, and a king.

140 PERICLES   How! A king's daughter,
And called Marina?

MARINA   You said you would believe me,
But not to be a troubler of your peace
I will end here.

PERICLES   But are you flesh and blood?
Have you a working pulse and are no fairy?

145 Motion as well? Speak on. Where were you born?
And wherefore called Marina?

MARINA   Called Marina
For I was born at sea.

PERICLES   At sea! What mother?

MARINA   My mother was the daughter of a king,
Who died the minute I was born,

50 As my good nurse Lychorida hath oft
Delivered weeping.

PERICLES   O, stop there a little!
[*aside*] This is the rarest dream that e'er dull sleep
Did mock sad fools withal. This cannot be
My daughter, buried. – Well, where were you bred?

55 I'll hear you more, to th' bottom of your story,
And never interrupt you.

MARINA
You scorn. Believe me, 'twere best I did give o'er.

PERICLES   I will believe you by the syllable
Of what you shall deliver. Yet give me leave –

60 How came you in these parts? Where were you bred?

MARINA   The king my father did in Tarsus leave me,
Till cruel Cleon, with his wicked wife,
Did seek to murder me and wooed a villain
To attempt it, who having drawn to do't,

A crew of pirates came and rescued me,   165
Brought me to Mytilene. But, good sir,
Whither will you have me? Why do you weep? It may
be
You think me an impostor. No, good faith.
I am the daughter to King Pericles,
If good King Pericles be.

PERICLES [*Stands.*]   Ho, Helicanus!   170

Enter HELICANUS *and* LYSIMACHUS.

HELICANUS [*Hurries to Pericles.*]
Calls my lord?

PERICLES   Thou art a grave and noble counsellor,
Most wise in general. Tell me if thou canst
What this maid is, or what is like to be,
That thus hath made me weep.

HELICANUS   I know not.   175
But here's the regent, sir, of Mytilene,
Speaks nobly of her.

LYSIMACHUS [*Comes forward.*]   She never would tell
Her parentage. Being demanded that,
She would sit still and weep.

PERICLES   O Helicanus, strike me, honoured sir,   180
Give me a gash, put me to present pain,
Lest this great sea of joys rushing upon me
O'erbear the shores of my mortality
And drown me with their sweetness.
[*to Marina*]   O, come hither,
Thou that beget'st him that did thee beget,   185
Thou that wast born at sea, buried at Tarsus,
And found at sea again! – O Helicanus,
Down on thy knees, thank the holy gods as loud
As thunder threatens us, this is Marina!
[*Helicanus kneels.*]
– What was thy mother's name? Tell me but that,   190
For truth can never be confirmed enough
Though doubts did ever sleep.

MARINA   First, sir, I pray, what is your title?

PERICLES
I am Pericles of Tyre.   [*Marina kneels.*]
                                But tell me now
My drowned queen's name, as in the rest you said   195
Thou hast been godlike perfect, the heir of kingdoms,
And another life to Pericles thy father.

MARINA   Is it no more to be your daughter than
To say my mother's name was Thaisa?
Thaisa was my mother, who did end   200
The minute I began.

PERICLES
Now blessing on thee! Rise. Thou art my child.
[*Marina rises.*]
– Give me fresh garments.   [*Helicanus rises.*]
                                Mine own, Helicanus! She is
Not dead at Tarsus, as she should have been
By savage Cleon. She shall tell thee all,   205
When thou shalt kneel and justify in knowledge
She is thy very princess. Who is this?

HELICANUS   Sir, 'tis the governor of Mytilene,
    Who hearing of your melancholy state
    Did come to see you.
210   PERICLES [*to Lysimachus*]   I embrace you, sir.
    – Give me my robes.   [*They do so.*]
                    I am wild in my beholding.
    O heavens bless my girl!   [*Music*]
               But hark, what music?
    Tell Helicanus, my Marina, tell him
    O'er point by point, for yet he seems to doubt,
    How sure you are my daughter.   [*Music*]
215   But what music?
HELICANUS   My lord, I hear none.
PERICLES   None?
    The music of the spheres. List, my Marina.
LYSIMACHUS
    It is not good to cross him. Give him way.
PERICLES   Rarest sounds. Do ye not hear?
LYSIMACHUS   Music, my lord? I hear –
220   PERICLES   Most heavenly music.
    It nips me unto listening, and thick slumber
    Hangs upon mine eyes. Let me rest.   [*Sleeps.*]
LYSIMACHUS   A pillow for his head. So, leave him all.
    Well, my companion friends,
225   If this but answer to my just belief
    I'll well remember you.
      [*Lysimachus, Helicanus, Marina and Companion*
      withdraw.]

           DIANA *descends.*

DIANA   My temple stands in Ephesus. Hie thee thither,
    And do upon mine altar sacrifice.
    There when my maiden priests are met together,
230   [
                  ] before the people all,
    Reveal how thou at sea didst lose thy wife.
    To mourn thy crosses with thy daughter's, call
    And give them repetition to the life.
235   Perform my bidding, or thou liv'st in woe;
    Do it and happy, by my silver bow.
    Awake and tell thy dream.   *Diana ascends.*
PERICLES   Celestial Dian, goddess argentine,
    I will obey thee. Helicanus!
     [*Helicanus, Lysimachus and Marina come forward.*]
HELICANUS   Sir?
240   PERICLES   My purpose was for Tarsus, there to strike
    The inhospitable Cleon, but I am
    For other service first. Toward Ephesus
    Turn our blown sails; eftsoons I'll tell thee why.
    [*to Lysimachus*] Shall we refresh us, sir, upon your
         shore
245   And give you gold for such provision
    As our intents will need?
LYSIMACHUS   Sir, with all my heart,
    And when you come ashore I have another suit.
PERICLES
    You shall prevail, were it to woo my daughter,

For it seems you have been noble towards her.
LYSIMACHUS   Sir, lend me your arm.
PERICLES   Come, my Marina.   *Exeunt.*   250

7 Chorus/5.2   *Enter* GOWER.

GOWER   Now our sands are almost run,
    More a little, and then dumb.
    This my last boon give me,
    For such kindness must relieve me,
    That you aptly will suppose   5
    What pageantry, what feasts, what shows,
    What minstrelsy and pretty din
    The regent made in Mytilene
    To greet the king. So he thrived
    That he is promised to be wived   10
    To fair Marina, but in no wise
    Till he had done his sacrifice
    As Dian bade, whereto being bound,
    The interim, pray you, all confound.
    In feathered briefness sails are filled,   15
    And wishes fall out as they're willed.
    At Ephesus the temple see
    Our king and all his company.
    That he can hither come so soon
    Is by your fancies' thankful doom.   *Exit.*   20

5.3   *Enter on one side* THAISA *and the Maiden*
        Priests of Diana, and CERIMON*; on the*
        other side PERICLES, MARINA,
        LYSIMACHUS, HELICANUS *and*
        Attendants.

PERICLES   Hail, Dian! To perform
    Thy just command, I here confess myself
    The King of Tyre, who frighted from my country
    Did wed at Pentapolis the fair Thaisa.
    At sea in childbed died she, but brought forth   5
    A maid child called Marina whom, O goddess,
    Wears yet thy silver livery. She at Tarsus
    Was nursed with Cleon, who at fourteen years
    He sought to murder, but her better stars
    Brought her to Mytilene, against whose shore   10
    Riding, her fortunes brought the maid aboard us,
    Where by her own most clear remembrance she
    Made known herself my daughter.
THAISA   Voice and favour!
    You are, you are, O royal Pericles!   [*Faints.*]
PERICLES
    What means the nun? She dies. Help, gentlemen!   15
CERIMON   Noble sir,
    If you have told Diana's altar true,
    This is your wife.
PERICLES   Reverend appearer, no,
    I threw her overboard with these very arms.
CERIMON
    Upon this coast, I warrant you.
PERICLES   'Tis most certain.   20

CERIMON Look to the lady. O, she's but overjoyed.
Early one blustering morn this lady was
Thrown upon this shore. I oped the coffin,
Found there rich jewels, recovered her, and placed her
Here in Diana's temple.

PERICLES May we see them?

CERIMON
Great sir, they shall be brought you to my house,
Whither I invite you. Look, Thaisa is
Recovered.

THAISA [*Rises.*] O, let me look!
If he be none of mine, my sanctity
Will to my sense bend no licentious ear,
But curb it spite of seeing. O my lord,
Are you not Pericles? Like him you spake,
Like him you are. Did you not name a tempest,
A birth and death?

PERICLES The voice of dead Thaisa!

THAISA That Thaisa am I, supposed dead
And drowned.

PERICLES Immortal Dian!

THAISA Now I know you better.
When we with tears parted Pentapolis,
The king my father gave you such a ring.

PERICLES
This, this! No more, you gods! Your present kindness
Makes my past miseries sports. You shall do well
That on the touching of her lips I may
Melt and no more be seen. O, come, be buried
A second time within these arms. [*They embrace.*]

MARINA My heart
Leaps to be gone into my mother's bosom.
[*Kneels to Thaisa.*]

PERICLES
Look who kneels here: flesh of thy flesh, Thaisa,
Thy burden at the sea, and called Marina,
For she was yielded there.

THAISA Blest, and mine own!
[*Embraces Marina.*]

HELICANUS
Hail, madam, and my queen.

THAISA I know you not.

PERICLES
You have heard me say, when I did fly from Tyre
I left behind an ancient substitute.
Can you remember what I called the man?
I have named him oft.

THAISA 'Twas Helicanus then.

PERICLES Still confirmation.
Embrace him, dear Thaisa, this is he.
Now do I long to hear how you were found,
How possibly preserved, and who to thank,
Besides the gods, for this great miracle.

THAISA Lord Cerimon, my lord, this man
Through whom the gods have shown their power,
that can
From first to last resolve you.

PERICLES Reverend sir,
The gods can have no mortal officer
More like a god than you. Will you deliver
How this dead queen relives?

CERIMON I will, my lord.
Beseech you, first go with me to my house,
Where shall be shown you all was found with her,
How she came placed here in the temple,
No needful thing omitted.

PERICLES Pure Dian,
I bless thee for thy vision and will offer
Night-oblations to thee. Dear Thaisa,
This prince, the fair betrothed of your daughter,
At Pentapolis shall marry her.
And now this ornament
Makes me look dismal will I clip to form,
And what this fourteen years no razor touched
To grace thy marriage day I'll beautify.

THAISA Lord Cerimon hath letters of good credit, sir,
My father's dead.

PERICLES
Heavens make a star of him! Yet there, my queen,
We'll celebrate their nuptials, and ourselves
Will in that kingdom spend our following days;
Our son and daughter shall in Tyrus reign.
Lord Cerimon, we do our longing stay
To hear the rest untold. Sir, lead's the way.
Exeunt omnes.

8 Chorus/Epil. *Enter* GOWER.

GOWER In Antiochus and his daughter you have heard
Of monstrous lust the due and just reward;
In Pericles, his queen and daughter seen,
Although assailed with Fortune fierce and keen,
Virtue preserved from fell destruction's blast,
Led on by heaven and crowned with joy at last.
In Helicanus may you well descry
A figure of truth, of faith, of loyalty.
In reverend Cerimon there well appears
The worth that learned charity aye wears.
For wicked Cleon and his wife, when fame
Had spread his cursed deed to th'honoured name
Of Pericles, to rage the city turn,
That him and his they in his palace burn.
The gods for murder seemed so content
To punish, although not done, but meant.
So on your patience evermore attending,
New joy wait on you. Here our play has ending.
Exit.

Romeo and Juliet

Romeo and Juliet was among the first plays Shakespeare wrote as a leading member of the Chamberlain's Men, of which he was a founder member in 1594. A drastically abbreviated text, printed in Quarto in 1597, was superseded in 1599 by a Quarto representing the play, 'Newly corrected, augmented and amended', much as we know it and in the form in which it was reprinted in the 1623 First Folio. *A Midsummer Night's Dream*, written in 1594–5, is usually thought of as following *Romeo*, mainly on the grounds that the mechanicals' play of Pyramus and Thisbe parodies the tragic theme of feuding families and star-crossed lovers.

Unlike most of Shakespeare's tragedies, *Romeo and Juliet* (in common with *Othello*) is based on a fiction, a *novella* written in Italy in the late fifteenth century, that he knew in English versions. It was one of these, Arthur Brooke's pedestrian verse narrative, *Romeus and Juliet* (1562), that Shakespeare transformed into an unrivalled tragedy of young love. The transformation involved abbreviation, increasing sympathy for the lovers by decreasing their ages, building up the contrasting roles of the Nurse and the Friar, inventing that of Mercutio and reducing the element of explicit moralizing. The play is one of several in which Shakespeare openly challenges neoclassical assumptions about genre. It might almost be described as setting its tragic action in the world of comedy.

The celebrity of *Romeo and Juliet* derives largely from the love scenes, but the play that contains them is not confined to lyricism. It includes a wide spectrum of views on love, sex and marriage, so that impulsive adolescent passion gains sympathy by contrast with the prudential arguments of the parents and of Friar Laurence, the obscenity and homosocial jealousy of Mercutio and the

Nurse's moral relativism. Romeo and Juliet's love is acted out against the background of the family feud, which intensifies their love and provides the threat of danger. Despite an emphasis on the lovers' disaster as fated, the outcome of the action as constructed by Shakespeare is as much the result of their own impulsiveness in marrying and in believing the worst as it is of the unexplained feud into which they were born.

Romeo and Juliet is the earliest of Shakespeare's plays to have imparted mythic status to its characters, to the extent that 'Juliet's balcony' (itself an eighteenth-century substitution for the window required by Shakespeare's text) is among the tourist sites of modern Verona. Also in the eighteenth century, David Garrick adapted the ending to allow the revived Juliet a final dialogue with the dying Romeo before her suicide. Nineteenth-century sensibilities were protected by the removal of the play's pervasive sexual jesting and by the suppression of Romeo's initial love for Rosaline. Famous Romeos of that time included the American actress Charlotte Cushman.

The play was a powerful inspiration to composers of the romantic period and since, and is now widely known in the form of Sergei Prokofiev's ballet (1935), or as the source of orchestral compositions by Hector Berlioz (1839) and Pyotr Ilyich Tchaikovsky (1870). It has been reworked in countless other plays, novels and films – most famously in Leonard Bernstein's musical *West Side Story* (1957) – and its theme of love destroyed by irrational inherited hate remains painfully familiar in the events of our own time.

The Arden text is based on the 1599 Second Quarto, with the addition of some stage directions from the 1597 First Quarto.

CAPULETS

JULIET	*a thirteen-year-old girl from Verona, only child of the rich Capulet*
CAPULET	*her father*
CAPULET'S WIFE	*her mother*
COUSIN CAPULET	*a relative of her father's*
NURSE	*Juliet's wet-nurse*
PETER	*Nurse's man*
TYBALT	*Juliet's cousin*
Tybalt's Page	
PETRUCHIO	*a follower of Tybalt*
SAMSON	*a Capulet retainer*
GREGORY	*another Capulet retainer*
SERVINGMEN	*in the Capulet household*

MONTAGUES

ROMEO	*sole son and heir of the Montague family*
MONTAGUE	*Romeo's father*
MONTAGUE'S WIFE	*Romeo's mother*
BENVOLIO	*Romeo's cousin*
BALTHASAR	*Romeo's man*
ABRAHAM	*a Montague retainer*
SERVINGMEN	*in the Montague household*

THE PRINCE'S KINDRED

PRINCE Escalus	*governor of Verona*
MERCUTIO	*his kinsman, and friend of Romeo's*
COUNTY PARIS	*another kinsman, suitor to Juliet*
Paris' Page	
Mercutio's Page	

OTHERS

CHORUS	
CITIZENS	*of Verona*
FRIAR LAURENCE	*a Franciscan*
FRIAR JOHN	*another Franciscan*
Apothecary	*of Mantua*

Three WATCHMEN
Three MUSICIANS,
Simon Catling, Hugh Rebeck
and James Soundpost

Attendants, Masquers, Torchbearers, Guests and Gentlewomen

PROLOGUE

Enter CHORUS.

CHORUS   Two households, both alike in dignity,
In fair Verona, where we lay our scene,
From ancient grudge break to new mutiny,
Where civil blood makes civil hands unclean.
5 From forth the fatal loins of these two foes
A pair of star-crossed lovers take their life,
Whose misadventured piteous overthrows
Doth with their death bury their parents' strife.
The fearful passage of their death-marked love,
10 And the continuance of their parents' rage,
Which but their children's end naught could remove,
Is now the two hours' traffic of our stage;
The which, if you with patient ears attend,
What here shall miss, our toil shall strive to mend.
Exit.

1.1   *Enter* SAMSON *and* GREGORY, *with swords
and bucklers, of the house of Capulet.*

SAMSON   Gregory, on my word, we'll not carry coals.
GREGORY   No, for then we should be colliers.
SAMSON   I mean, an we be in choler, we'll draw.
GREGORY   Ay, while you live, draw your neck out of collar.
5 SAMSON   I strike quickly being moved.
GREGORY   But thou art not quickly moved to strike.
SAMSON   A dog of the house of Montague moves me.
GREGORY   To move is to stir, and to be valiant is to
stand; therefore, if thou art moved, thou runn'st away.
10 SAMSON   A dog of that house shall move me to stand. I
will take the wall of any man or maid of Montague's.
GREGORY   That shows thee a weak slave, for the
weakest goes to the wall.
SAMSON   'Tis true, and therefore women, being the
15 weaker vessels, are ever thrust to the wall; therefore I
will push Montague's men from the wall and thrust his
maids to the wall.
GREGORY   The quarrel is between our masters and us
their men.
20 SAMSON   'Tis all one. I will show myself a tyrant: when
I have fought with the men, I will be civil with the
maids, I will cut off their heads.
GREGORY   The heads of the maids?
SAMSON   Ay, the heads of the maids, or their maidenheads,
25 take it in what sense thou wilt.
GREGORY   They must take it in sense that feel it.
SAMSON   Me they shall feel while I am able to stand,
and 'tis known I am a pretty piece of flesh.
GREGORY   'Tis well thou art not fish; if thou hadst, thou
30 hadst been poor john. Draw thy tool, here comes of the
house of Montagues. [*They draw.*]

Enter two other Servingmen,
one of them ABRAHAM, *of the house of Montague.*

SAMSON   My naked weapon is out. Quarrel, I will back thee.

GREGORY   How, turn thy back and run?
SAMSON   Fear me not.
GREGORY   No, marry, I fear thee!   35
SAMSON   Let us take the law of our sides; let them
begin.
GREGORY   I will frown as I pass by and let them take it
as they list.
SAMSON   Nay, as they dare. I will bite my thumb at   40
them, which is disgrace to them if they bear it.
ABRAHAM   Do you bite your thumb at us, sir?
SAMSON   I do bite my thumb, sir.
ABRAHAM   Do you bite your thumb at us, sir?
SAMSON [*aside to Gregory*]   Is the law of our side if I say   45
'Ay'?
GREGORY [*aside to Samson*]   No.
SAMSON   No, sir, I do not bite my thumb at you, sir, but
I bite my thumb, sir.
GREGORY   Do you quarrel, sir?   50
ABRAHAM   Quarrel, sir? No, sir.
SAMSON   But if you do, sir, I am for you. I serve as good
a man as you.
ABRAHAM   No better.
SAMSON   Well, sir.   55

Enter BENVOLIO.

GREGORY [*aside to Samson*]   Say 'better'. Here comes
one of my master's kinsmen.
SAMSON   Yes, better, sir.
ABRAHAM   You lie.
SAMSON   Draw if you be men. Gregory, remember thy   60
washing blow. [*They fight.*]
BENVOLIO [*Draws.*]   Part, fools!
Put up your swords, you know not what you do.

Enter TYBALT.

TYBALT
What, art thou drawn among these heartless hinds?
[*Draws.*] Turn thee, Benvolio, look upon thy death.   65
BENVOLIO
I do but keep the peace. Put up thy sword,
Or manage it to part these men with me.
TYBALT
What, drawn and talk of peace? I hate the word
As I hate hell, all Montagues and thee.
Have at thee, coward.   [*They fight.*]   70

Enter three or four Citizens *with
clubs or partisans.*

CITIZENS
Clubs, bills and partisans! Strike, beat them down,
Down with the Capulets, down with the Montagues!

Enter old CAPULET *in his gown, and his* WIFE.

CAPULET
What noise is this? Give me my long sword, ho!
CAPULET'S WIFE
A crutch, a crutch! Why call you for a sword?

Enter old MONTAGUE *and his* WIFE.

75   CAPULET   My sword, I say. Old Montague is come,
     And flourishes his blade in spite of me.
   MONTAGUE
     Thou villain Capulet! – Hold me not, let me go.
   MONTAGUE'S WIFE
     Thou shalt not stir one foot to seek a foe.

Enter PRINCE Escalus *with his train.*

   PRINCE   Rebellious subjects, enemies to peace,
80   Profaners of this neighbour-stained steel –
     Will they not hear? What ho, you men, you beasts,
     That quench the fire of your pernicious rage
     With purple fountains issuing from your veins;
     On pain of torture, from those bloody hands
85   Throw your mistempered weapons to the ground
     And hear the sentence of your moved prince.
     Three civil brawls bred of an airy word,
     By thee, old Capulet, and Montague,
     Have thrice disturbed the quiet of our streets
90   And made Verona's ancient citizens
     Cast by their grave-beseeming ornaments,
     To wield old partisans in hands as old,
     Cankered with peace, to part your cankered hate.
     If ever you disturb our streets again,
95   Your lives shall pay the forfeit of the peace.
     For this time all the rest depart away.
     You, Capulet, shall go along with me,
     And, Montague, come you this afternoon,
     To know our farther pleasure in this case,
100   To old Freetown, our common judgement-place.
     Once more, on pain of death, all men depart.

                Exeunt all but Montague, his
                    Wife and Benvolio.

   MONTAGUE
     Who set this ancient quarrel new abroach?
     Speak, nephew, were you by when it began?
   BENVOLIO   Here were the servants of your adversary
105   And yours, close fighting ere I did approach.
     I drew to part them. In the instant came
     The fiery Tybalt, with his sword prepared,
     Which, as he breathed defiance to my ears,
     He swung about his head and cut the winds
110   Who, nothing hurt withal, hissed him in scorn.
     While we were interchanging thrusts and blows
     Came more and more, and fought on part and part,
     Till the Prince came, who parted either part.
   MONTAGUE'S WIFE
     O where is Romeo, saw you him today?
115   Right glad I am he was not at this fray.
   BENVOLIO
     Madam, an hour before the worshipped sun
     Peered forth the golden window of the east,
     A troubled mind drive me to walk abroad,
     Where underneath the grove of sycamore
120   That westward rooteth from this city side,

So early walking did I see your son.
Towards him I made, but he was ware of me
And stole into the covert of the wood.
I, measuring his affections by my own,
Which then most sought where most might not be
     found,   125
Being one too many by my weary self,
Pursued my humour, not pursuing his,
And gladly shunned who gladly fled from me.
   MONTAGUE   Many a morning hath he there been seen,
     With tears augmenting the fresh morning's dew,   130
     Adding to clouds more clouds with his deep sighs.
     But all so soon as the all-cheering sun
     Should in the farthest east begin to draw
     The shady curtains from Aurora's bed,
     Away from light steals home my heavy son,   135
     And private in his chamber pens himself,
     Shuts up his windows, locks fair daylight out
     And makes himself an artificial night.
     Black and portentous must this humour prove,
     Unless good counsel may the cause remove.   140
   BENVOLIO   My noble uncle, do you know the cause?
   MONTAGUE   I neither know it nor can learn of him.
   BENVOLIO   Have you importuned him by any means?
   MONTAGUE   Both by myself and many other friends;
     But he, his own affections' counsellor,   145
     Is to himself – I will not say how true –
     But to himself so secret and so close,
     So far from sounding and discovery
     As is the bud bit with an envious worm
     Ere he can spread his sweet leaves to the air,   150
     Or dedicate his beauty to the same.
     Could we but learn from whence his sorrows grow,
     We would as willingly give cure as know.

Enter ROMEO.

   BENVOLIO
     See where he comes. So please you, step aside.
     I'll know his grievance, or be much denied.   155
   MONTAGUE   I would thou wert so happy by thy stay
     To hear true shrift. Come, madam, let's away.

               Exeunt Montague and his Wife.

   BENVOLIO   Good morrow, cousin.
   ROMEO   Is the day so young?
   BENVOLIO   But new struck nine.
   ROMEO   Ay me, sad hours seem long.
     Was that my father that went hence so fast?   160
   BENVOLIO
     It was. What sadness lengthens Romeo's hours?
   ROMEO
     Not having that which, having, makes them short.
   BENVOLIO   In love?
   ROMEO   Out.
   BENVOLIO   Of love?
   ROMEO   Out of her favour where I am in love.
   BENVOLIO   Alas, that love, so gentle in his view,
     Should be so tyrannous and rough in proof.

ROMEO   Alas, that love, whose view is muffled still,
170   Should without eyes see pathways to his will.
    Where shall we dine? O me, what fray was here?
    Yet tell me not, for I have heard it all.
    Here's much to do with hate, but more with love.
    Why then, O brawling love, O loving hate,
175   O anything of nothing first create,
    O heavy lightness, serious vanity,
    Misshapen chaos of well-seeming forms,
    Feather of lead, bright smoke, cold fire, sick health,
    Still-waking sleep that is not what it is.
180   This love feel I that feel no love in this.
    Dost thou not laugh?

BENVOLIO   No, coz, I rather weep.

ROMEO   Good heart, at what?

BENVOLIO   At thy good heart's oppression.

ROMEO   Why, such is love's transgression.
    Griefs of mine own lie heavy in my breast,
185   Which thou wilt propagate to have it pressed
    With more of thine. This love that thou hast shown
    Doth add more grief to too much of mine own.
    Love is a smoke made with the fume of sighs;
    Being purged, a fire sparkling in lovers' eyes;
190   Being vexed, a sea nourished with loving tears.
    What is it else? A madness most discreet,
    A choking gall and a preserving sweet.
    Farewell, my coz.

BENVOLIO   Soft, I will go along;
    An if you leave me so, you do me wrong.

195   ROMEO   Tut, I have lost myself. I am not here.
    This is not Romeo, he's some otherwhere.

BENVOLIO   Tell me in sadness, who is that you love?

ROMEO   What, shall I groan and tell thee?

BENVOLIO   Groan? Why, no,
    But sadly tell me who.

200   ROMEO   A sick man in sadness makes his will;
    A word ill urged to one that is so ill.
    In sadness, cousin, I do love a woman.

BENVOLIO
    I aimed so near when I supposed you loved.

ROMEO   A right good markman, and she's fair I love.

205   BENVOLIO   A right fair mark, fair coz, is soonest hit.

ROMEO   Well in that hit you miss. She'll not be hit
    With Cupid's arrow. She hath Dian's wit,
    And in strong proof of chastity well armed
    From love's weak childish bow she lives uncharmed.
210   She will not stay the siege of loving terms,
    Nor bide th'encounter of assailing eyes,
    Nor ope her lap to saint-seducing gold.
    O, she is rich in beauty, only poor
    That when she dies, with beauty dies her store.

BENVOLIO
215   Then she hath sworn that she will still live chaste?

ROMEO
    She hath, and in that sparing makes huge waste,
    For beauty starved with her severity,
    Cuts beauty off from all posterity.

    She is too fair, too wise, wisely too fair,
    To merit bliss by making me despair.   220
    She hath forsworn to love, and in that vow
    Do I live dead that live to tell it now.

BENVOLIO   Be ruled by me, forget to think of her.

ROMEO   O teach me how I should forget to think!

BENVOLIO   By giving liberty unto thine eyes.   225
    Examine other beauties.

ROMEO   'Tis the way
    To call hers, exquisite, in question more.
    These happy masks that kiss fair ladies' brows,
    Being black, puts us in mind they hide the fair.
    He that is strucken blind cannot forget   230
    The precious treasure of his eyesight lost.
    Show me a mistress that is passing fair,
    What doth her beauty serve but as a note
    Where I may read who passed that passing fair?
    Farewell, thou canst not teach me to forget.   235

BENVOLIO
    I'll pay that doctrine, or else die in debt.   *Exeunt.*

1.2   *Enter* CAPULET, County PARIS *and a*
                 Servingman.

CAPULET   But Montague is bound as well as I,
    In penalty alike, and 'tis not hard, I think,
    For men so old as we to keep the peace.

PARIS   Of honourable reckoning are you both,
    And pity 'tis you lived at odds so long.   5
    But now, my lord, what say you to my suit?

CAPULET   But saying o'er what I have said before:
    My child is yet a stranger in the world;
    She hath not seen the change of fourteen years.
    Let two more summers wither in their pride   10
    Ere we may think her ripe to be a bride.

PARIS   Younger than she are happy mothers made.

CAPULET
    And too soon marred are those so early married.
    She is the hopeful lady of my earth.
    But woo her, gentle Paris, get her heart.   15
    My will to her consent is but a part,
    And, she agreed, within her scope of choice
    Lies my consent and fair according voice.
    This night I hold an old accustomed feast,
    Whereto I have invited many a guest   20
    Such as I love; and you among the store
    One more, most welcome, makes my number more.
    At my poor house look to behold this night
    Earth-treading stars that make dark heaven light.
    Such comfort as do lusty young men feel   25
    When well-apparelled April on the heel
    Of limping winter treads, even such delight
    Among fresh fennel buds shall you this night
    Inherit at my house. Hear all, all see,
    And like her most whose merit most shall be;   30
    Which, on more view, of many mine being one,
    May stand in number, though in reckoning none.

Come, go with me. [*to Servingman*] Go, sirrah, trudge
about
Through fair Verona; find those persons out
35 Whose names are written there, and to them say
My house and welcome on their pleasure stay.
                                    Exeunt Capulet and Paris.
SERVINGMAN Find them out whose names are written
here! It is written that the shoemaker should meddle
with his yard and the tailor with his last, the fisher
40 with his pencil and the painter with his nets, but
I am sent to find those persons whose names are
here writ, and can never find what names the writing
person hath here writ. I must to the learned. In good
time!

Enter BENVOLIO *and* ROMEO.

BENVOLIO
45 Tut, man, one fire burns out another's burning,
One pain is lessened by another's anguish.
Turn giddy and be holp by backward turning.
One desperate grief cures with another's languish.
Take thou some new infection to thy eye,
50 And the rank poison of the old will die.
ROMEO Your plantain leaf is excellent for that.
BENVOLIO For what, I pray thee?
ROMEO   For your broken shin.
BENVOLIO Why, Romeo, art thou mad?
ROMEO Not mad, but bound more than a madman is;
55 Shut up in prison, kept without my food,
Whipped and tormented and – Good-e'en, good fellow.
SERVINGMAN Godgigoden. I pray, sir, can you read?
ROMEO Ay, mine own fortune in my misery.
SERVINGMAN Perhaps you have learnt it without book.
60 But I pray, can you read anything you see?
ROMEO Ay, if I know the letters and the language.
SERVINGMAN Ye say honestly. Rest you merry.
ROMEO Stay, fellow, I can read. [*He reads the letter.*]
Signor Martino and his wife and daughters;
65 County Anselm and his beauteous sisters;
The lady widow of Vitruvio;
Signor Placentio and his lovely nieces;
Mercutio and his brother Valentine;
Mine uncle Capulet, his wife and daughters;
70 My fair niece Rosaline, and Livia;
Signor Valentio and his cousin Tybalt;
Lucio and the lively Helena.
A fair assembly. Whither should they come?
SERVINGMAN Up.
75 ROMEO Whither? To supper?
SERVINGMAN To our house.
ROMEO Whose house?
SERVINGMAN My master's.
ROMEO Indeed, I should have asked thee that before.
80 SERVINGMAN Now I'll tell you without asking. My
master is the great rich Capulet, and if you be not of
the house of Montagues, I pray come and crush a cup
of wine. Rest you merry.   *Exit.*

BENVOLIO At this same ancient feast of Capulet's
Sups the fair Rosaline whom thou so loves,   85
With all the admired beauties of Verona.
Go thither, and with unattainted eye
Compare her face with some that I shall show,
And I will make thee think thy swan a crow.
ROMEO When the devout religion of mine eye   90
Maintains such falsehood, then turn tears to fires,
And these who, often drowned, could never die,
Transparent heretics, be burnt for liars.
One fairer than my love! The all-seeing sun
Ne'er saw her match since first the world begun.   95
BENVOLIO Tut, you saw her fair none else being by,
Herself poised with herself in either eye.
But in that crystal scales let there be weighed
Your lady's love against some other maid
That I will show you shining at this feast,   100
And she shall scant show well that now seems best.
ROMEO I'll go along no such sight to be shown,
But to rejoice in splendour of mine own.   *Exeunt.*

1.3   *Enter* CAPULET'S WIFE *and* NURSE.

CAPULET'S WIFE
Nurse, where's my daughter? Call her forth to me.
NURSE Now by my maidenhead at twelve year old,
I bade her come. What, lamb! What, ladybird!
God forbid, where's this girl? What, Juliet!

Enter JULIET.

JULIET How now, who calls?   5
NURSE Your mother.
JULIET Madam, I am here. What is your will?
CAPULET'S WIFE
This is the matter. – Nurse, give leave awhile,
We must talk in secret. Nurse, come back again.
I have remembered me, thou's hear our counsel.   10
Thou knowest my daughter's of a pretty age.
NURSE Faith, I can tell her age unto an hour.
CAPULET'S WIFE She's not fourteen.
NURSE   I'll lay fourteen of my teeth,
And yet, to my teen be it spoken, I have but four,
She's not fourteen. How long is it now   15
To Lammastide?
CAPULET'S WIFE A fortnight and odd days.
NURSE Even or odd of all days in the year,
Come Lammas Eve at night shall she be fourteen.
Susan and she, God rest all Christian souls,
Were of an age. Well, Susan is with God;   20
She was too good for me. But as I said,
On Lammas Eve at night shall she be fourteen,
That shall she, marry! I remember it well.
'Tis since the earthquake now eleven years,
And she was weaned, I never shall forget it,   25
Of all the days of the year upon that day.
For I had then laid wormwood to my dug,
Sitting in the sun under the dovehouse wall.

My lord and you were then at Mantua.
30   Nay, I do bear a brain. But as I said,
When it did taste the wormwood on the nipple
Of my dug and felt it bitter, pretty fool,
To see it tetchy and fall out with the dug!
'Shake', quoth the dovehouse. 'Twas no need, I trow,
35   To bid me trudge.
And since that time it is eleven years,
For then she could stand high-lone; nay, by th' rood,
She could have run and waddled all about,
For even the day before she broke her brow.
40   And then my husband – God be with his soul,
'A was a merry man – took up the child:
'Yea,' quoth he, 'dost thou fall upon thy face?
Thou wilt fall backward when thou hast more wit,
Wilt thou not, Jule?' And by my holidam,
45   The pretty wretch left crying and said 'Ay'.
To see now how a jest shall come about!
I warrant, an I should live a thousand years,
I never should forget it. 'Wilt thou not, Jule?' quoth he,
And, pretty fool, it stinted and said 'Ay'.
CAPULET'S WIFE
50   Enough of this, I pray thee, hold thy peace.
NURSE   Yes, madam, yet I cannot choose but laugh,
To think it should leave crying and say 'Ay';
And yet, I warrant, it had upon it brow
A bump as big as a young cockerel's stone;
55   A perilous knock, and it cried bitterly.
'Yea,' quoth my husband, 'fall'st upon thy face?
Thou wilt fall backward when thou comest to age,
Wilt thou not, Jule?' It stinted and said 'Ay'.
JULIET   And stint thou too, I pray thee, Nurse, say I.
60   NURSE   Peace, I have done. God mark thee to his grace,
Thou wast the prettiest babe that e'er I nursed.
An I might live to see thee married once,
I have my wish.
CAPULET'S WIFE   Marry, that 'marry' is the very theme
65   I came to talk of. Tell me, daughter Juliet,
How stands your dispositions to be married?
JULIET   It is an honour that I dream not of.
NURSE   An honour! Were not I thine only nurse,
I would say thou hadst sucked wisdom from thy teat.
CAPULET'S WIFE
70   Well, think of marriage now. Younger than you,
Here in Verona, ladies of esteem,
Are made already mothers. By my count,
I was your mother much upon these years
That you are now a maid. Thus then in brief:
75   The valiant Paris seeks you for his love.
NURSE   A man, young lady; lady, such a man
As all the world – why, he's a man of wax.
CAPULET'S WIFE
Verona's summer has not such a flower.
NURSE   Nay, he's a flower, in faith, a very flower.
CAPULET'S WIFE
80   What say you, can you love the gentleman?
This night you shall behold him at our feast.

Read o'er the volume of young Paris' face,
And find delight writ there with beauty's pen;
Examine every married lineament,
And see how one another lends content;   85
And what obscured in this fair volume lies
Find written in the margent of his eyes.
This precious book of love, this unbound lover,
To beautify him only lacks a cover.
The fish lives in the sea, and 'tis much pride   90
For fair without the fair within to hide.
That book in many's eyes doth share the glory
That in gold clasps locks in the golden story.
So shall you share all that he doth possess,
By having him, making yourself no less.   95
NURSE   No less? Nay, bigger – women grow by men.
CAPULET'S WIFE
Speak briefly, can you like of Paris' love?
JULIET   I'll look to like, if looking liking move,
But no more deep will I endart mine eye
Than your consent gives strength to make it fly.   100

Enter Servingman.

SERVINGMAN   Madam, the guests are come, supper
served up, you called, my young lady asked for, the Nurse
cursed in the pantry, and everything in extremity. I must
hence to wait; I beseech you follow straight.   *Exit.*
CAPULET'S WIFE
We follow thee. Juliet, the County stays.   105
NURSE   Go, girl, seek happy nights to happy days.
Exeunt.

1.4   *Enter* ROMEO, MERCUTIO, BENVOLIO,
with five or six other Masquers,
Torchbearers.

ROMEO
What, shall this speech be spoke for our excuse,
Or shall we on without apology?
BENVOLIO   The date is out of such prolixity.
We'll have no Cupid hoodwinked with a scarf,
Bearing a Tartar's painted bow of lath,   5
Scaring the ladies like a crow-keeper;
Nor no without-book prologue, faintly spoke
After the prompter, for our entrance.
But let them measure us by what they will,
We'll measure them a measure and be gone.   10
ROMEO   Give me a torch. I am not for this ambling,
Being but heavy I will bear the light.
MERCUTIO
Nay, gentle Romeo, we must have you dance.
ROMEO   Not I, believe me. You have dancing shoes
With nimble soles, I have a soul of lead   15
So stakes me to the ground I cannot move.
MERCUTIO   You are a lover; borrow Cupid's wings,
And soar with them above a common bound.
ROMEO   I am too sore empierced with his shaft
To soar with his light feathers, and so bound   20

I cannot bound a pitch above dull woe;
Under love's heavy burden do I sink.
MERCUTIO   And to sink in it should you burden love,
Too great oppression for a tender thing.
25   ROMEO   Is love a tender thing? It is too rough,
Too rude, too boisterous, and it pricks like thorn.
MERCUTIO
If love be rough with you, be rough with love;
Prick love for pricking, and you beat love down.
Give me a case to put my visage in,
30   A visor for a visor! What care I
What curious eye doth quote deformities?
Here are the beetle brows shall blush for me.
BENVOLIO   Come, knock and enter, and no sooner in
But every man betake him to his legs.
35   ROMEO   A torch for me. Let wantons light of heart
Tickle the senseless rushes with their heels,
For I am proverbed with a grandsire phrase:
I'll be a candleholder and look on,
The game was ne'er so fair, and I am dun.
MERCUTIO
40   Tut, dun's the mouse, the constable's own word.
If thou art dun, we'll draw thee from the mire
Or, save your reverence, love, wherein thou stickest
Up to the ears. Come, we burn daylight, ho!
ROMEO   Nay, that's not so.
MERCUTIO   I mean, sir, in delay
45   We waste our lights, in vain light lights by day.
Take our good meaning, for our judgement sits
Five times in that ere once in our five wits.
ROMEO   And we mean well in going to this masque,
But 'tis no wit to go.
MERCUTIO   Why, may one ask?
ROMEO   I dreamt a dream tonight.
50   MERCUTIO   And so did I.
ROMEO   Well, what was yours?
MERCUTIO   That dreamers often lie.
ROMEO
In bed asleep while they do dream things true.
MERCUTIO
O, then I see Queen Mab hath been with you.
She is the fairies' midwife, and she comes
55   In shape no bigger than an agate stone
On the forefinger of an alderman,
Drawn with a team of little atomi
Over men's noses as they lie asleep.
Her chariot is an empty hazelnut
60   Made by the joiner squirrel or old grub,
Time out o'mind the fairies' coachmakers;
Her wagon-spokes made of long spinners' legs,
The cover of the wings of grasshoppers,
Her traces of the smallest spider web,
65   Her collars of the moonshine's watery beams,
Her whip of cricket's bone, the lash of film,
Her wagoner a small grey-coated gnat,
Not half so big as a round little worm
Pricked from the lazy finger of a maid.

And in this state she gallops night by night   70
Through lovers' brains, and then they dream of love;
On courtiers' knees, that dream on curtsies straight;
O'er lawyers' fingers, who straight dream on fees;
O'er ladies lips, who straight on kisses dream,
Which oft the angry Mab with blisters plagues,   75
Because their breaths with sweetmeats tainted are.
Sometime she gallops o'er a courtier's nose,
And then dreams he of smelling out a suit;
And sometime comes she with a tithe-pig's tail,
Tickling a parson's nose as 'a lies asleep;   80
Then he dreams of another benefice.
Sometime she driveth o'er a soldier's neck,
And then dreams he of cutting foreign throats,
Of breaches, ambuscados, Spanish blades,
Of healths five fathom deep; and then anon   85
Drums in his ear, at which he starts and wakes,
And being thus frighted, swears a prayer or two
And sleeps again. This is that very Mab
That plaits the manes of horses in the night,
And bakes the elf-locks in foul sluttish hairs,   90
Which once untangled much misfortune bodes.
This is the hag, when maids lie on their backs,
That presses them and learns them first to bear,
Making them women of good carriage.
This is she –
ROMEO   Peace, peace, Mercutio, peace,   95
Thou talk'st of nothing.
MERCUTIO   True, I talk of dreams,
Which are the children of an idle brain,
Begot of nothing but vain fantasy,
Which is as thin of substance as the air,
And more inconstant than the wind who woos   100
Even now the frozen bosom of the north,
And, being angered, puffs away from thence,
Turning his side to the dew-dropping south.
BENVOLIO
This wind you talk of blows us from ourselves;
Supper is done, and we shall come too late.   105
ROMEO   I fear too early, for my mind misgives;
Some consequence, yet hanging in the stars,
Shall bitterly begin his fearful date
With this night's revels, and expire the term
Of a despised life closed in my breast   110
By some vile forfeit of untimely death.
But he that hath the steerage of my course
Direct my suit. On, lusty gentlemen.
BENVOLIO   Strike, drum.

1.5   *They march about the stage, and*
            Servingmen *come forth with napkins.*

HEAD SERVINGMAN   Where's Potpan, that he helps not
to take away? He shift a trencher! He scrape a trencher!
1 SERVINGMAN   When good manners shall lie all in one
or two men's hands, and they unwashed too, 'tis a foul
thing.   5

HEAD SERVINGMAN   Away with the join-stools, remove
the court-cupboard, look to the plate. Good thou, save
me a piece of marchpane and, as thou loves me, let the
porter let in Susan Grindstone, and Nell, Anthony and
Potpan.

2 SERVINGMAN   Ay, boy, ready.

HEAD SERVINGMAN   You are looked for, and called for,
asked for, and sought for, in the great chamber.

3 SERVINGMAN   We cannot be here and there too.
Cheerly, boys, be brisk awhile, and the longer liver
take all.   *Exeunt.*

Enter CAPULET, CAPULET'S WIFE, JULIET,
TYBALT, NURSE, County PARIS, COUSIN CAPULET,
*Tybalt's Page, Attendants and all the Guests
and Gentlewomen to the Masquers.*

CAPULET
Welcome, gentlemen. Ladies that have their toes
Unplagued with corns will walk a bout with you.
Ah, my mistresses, which of you all
Will now deny to dance? She that makes dainty,
She, I'll swear, hath corns. Am I come near ye now?
Welcome, gentlemen. I have seen the day
That I have worn a visor and could tell
A whispering tale in a fair lady's ear,
Such as would please. 'Tis gone, 'tis gone, 'tis gone.
You are welcome, gentlemen. Come, musicians, play.
                                       [*Music plays and they dance.*]
A hall, a hall! Give room and foot it, girls.
More light, you knaves, and turn the tables up,
And quench the fire, the room is grown too hot.
Ah, sirrah, this unlooked-for sport comes well.
Nay, sit, nay, sit, good cousin Capulet,
For you and I are past our dancing days.
How long is't now since last yourself and I
Were in a masque?

COUSIN CAPULET   By'r Lady, thirty years.

CAPULET
What, man, 'tis not so much, 'tis not so much:
'Tis since the nuptial of Lucentio,
Come Pentecost as quickly as it will,
Some five-and-twenty years, and then we masqued.

COUSIN CAPULET
'Tis more, 'tis more, his son is elder, sir,
His son is thirty.

CAPULET   Will you tell me that?
His son was but a ward two years ago.

ROMEO [*to a Servingman*]
What lady's that which doth enrich the hand
Of yonder knight?

SERVINGMAN   I know not, sir.

ROMEO   O, she doth teach the torches to burn bright.
It seems she hangs upon the cheek of night
As a rich jewel in an Ethiop's ear,
Beauty too rich for use, for earth too dear.
So shows a snowy dove trooping with crows
As yonder lady o'er her fellows shows.

The measure done, I'll watch her place of stand
And, touching hers, make blessed my rude hand.
Did my heart love till now? Forswear it, sight,
For I ne'er saw true beauty till this night.

TYBALT   This by his voice should be a Montague.
Fetch me my rapier, boy.   *Exit Page.*
                                       What, dares the slave
Come hither, covered with an antic face,
To fleer and scorn at our solemnity?
Now by the stock and honour of my kin,
To strike him dead I hold it not a sin.

CAPULET
Why, how now, kinsman, wherefore storm you so?

TYBALT   Uncle, this is a Montague, our foe,
A villain that is hither come in spite
To scorn at our solemnity this night.

CAPULET   Young Romeo is it?

TYBALT   'Tis he, that villain Romeo.

CAPULET   Content thee, gentle coz, let him alone.
'A bears him like a portly gentleman
And, to say truth, Verona brags of him
To be a virtuous and well-governed youth.
I would not for the wealth of all this town
Here in my house do him disparagement.
Therefore be patient, take no note of him.
It is my will, the which if thou respect,
Show a fair presence and put off these frowns,
An ill-beseeming semblance for a feast.

TYBALT   It fits when such a villain is a guest.
I'll not endure him.

CAPULET   He shall be endured.
What, goodman boy, I say he shall, go to!
Am I the master here or you? Go to!
You'll not endure him? God shall mend my soul,
You'll make a mutiny among my guests,
You will set cock-a-hoop, you'll be the man!

TYBALT   Why, uncle, 'tis a shame.

CAPULET   Go to, go to,
You are a saucy boy. Is't so indeed?
This trick may chance to scathe you, I know what.
You must contrary me! – Marry, 'tis time,
Well said, my hearts. – You are a princox, go,
Be quiet, or – More light, more light! – For shame,
I'll make you quiet. – What, cheerly, my hearts!

TYBALT   Patience perforce with wilful choler meeting
Makes my flesh tremble in their different greeting.
I will withdraw, but this intrusion shall,
Now seeming sweet, convert to bitt'rest gall.   *Exit.*

ROMEO   If I profane with my unworthiest hand
This holy shrine, the gentle sin is this:
My lips, two blushing pilgrims, ready stand
To smooth that rough touch with a tender kiss.

JULIET
Good pilgrim, you do wrong your hand too much,
Which mannerly devotion shows in this,
For saints have hands that pilgrims' hands do touch,
And palm to palm is holy palmers' kiss.

ROMEO   Have not saints lips and holy palmers too?

JULIET   Ay, pilgrim, lips that they must use in prayer.

ROMEO   O then, dear saint, let lips do what hands do –
They pray; grant thou, lest faith turn to despair.

JULIET

105   Saints do not move, though grant for prayers' sake.

ROMEO   Then move not while my prayer's effect I take.
      [*Kisses her.*]
Thus from my lips by thine my sin is purged.

JULIET   Then have my lips the sin that they have took.

ROMEO   Sin from my lips? O trespass sweetly urged!
      Give me my sin again.   [*Kisses her.*]

110 JULIET   You kiss by th' book.

NURSE   Madam, your mother craves a word with you.
      [*Juliet moves towards her mother.*]

ROMEO   What is her mother?

NURSE   Marry, bachelor,
Her mother is the lady of the house,
And a good lady, and a wise and virtuous.

115   I nursed her daughter that you talked withal.
I tell you, he that can lay hold of her
Shall have the chinks.

ROMEO   Is she a Capulet?
O dear account! My life is my foe's debt.

BENVOLIO   Away, be gone, the sport is at the best.

120 ROMEO   Ay, so I fear; the more is my unrest.

CAPULET   Nay, gentlemen, prepare not to be gone;
We have a trifling foolish banquet towards.
      [*They whisper in his ear.*]
Is it e'en so? Why then, I thank you all.
I thank you, honest gentlemen, good night.

125   More torches here! Come on then, let's to bed.
Ah, sirrah, by my fay, it waxes late.
I'll to my rest.   *Exeunt all but Juliet and Nurse.*

JULIET   Come hither, Nurse. What is yond gentleman?

NURSE   The son and heir of old Tiberio.

130 JULIET   What's he that now is going out of door?

NURSE   Marry, that I think be young Petruchio.

JULIET
What's he that follows here, that would not dance?

NURSE   I know not.

JULIET   Go ask his name.   [*Nurse moves away.*]
               If he be married,

135   My grave is like to be my wedding bed.

NURSE [*returning*]
His name is Romeo, and a Montague,
The only son of your great enemy.

JULIET   My only love sprung from my only hate,
Too early seen unknown, and known too late!

140   Prodigious birth of love it is to me
That I must love a loathed enemy.

NURSE   What's tis, what's tis?

JULIET   A rhyme I learnt even now
Of one I danced withal.
      [*One calls within* 'Juliet'.]

NURSE   Anon, anon!
Come, let's away, the strangers all are gone.   *Exeunt.*

2.0   *Enter* CHORUS.

CHORUS   Now old desire doth in his deathbed lie,
And young affection gapes to be his heir;
That fair for which love groaned for and would die,
With tender Juliet matched is now not fair.
Now Romeo is beloved and loves again,   5
Alike bewitched by the charm of looks,
But to his foe supposed he must complain,
And she steal love's sweet bait from fearful hooks.
Being held a foe, he may not have access
To breathe such vows as lovers use to swear,   10
And she as much in love, her means much less
To meet her new beloved anywhere.
But passion lends them power, time means, to meet,
Tempering extremities with extreme sweet.   *Exit.*

2.1   *Enter* ROMEO *alone.*

ROMEO   Can I go forward when my heart is here?
Turn back, dull earth, and find thy centre out.
      [*Withdraws.*]

        Enter BENVOLIO *with* MERCUTIO.

BENVOLIO   Romeo, my cousin Romeo, Romeo!

MERCUTIO   He is wise
And, on my life, hath stol'n him home to bed.

BENVOLIO   He ran this way and leapt this orchard wall.   5
Call, good Mercutio.

MERCUTIO   Nay, I'll conjure too.
Romeo, humours, madman, passion, lover,
Appear thou in the likeness of a sigh,
Speak but one rhyme and I am satisfied,
Cry but 'Ay me', pronounce but 'love' and 'dove',   10
Speak to my gossip Venus one fair word,
One nickname for her purblind son and heir,
Young Abraham Cupid, he that shot so trim
When King Cophetua loved the beggar maid –
He heareth not, he stirreth not, he moveth not;   15
The ape is dead and I must conjure him.
I conjure thee by Rosaline's bright eyes,
By her high forehead and her scarlet lip,
By her fine foot, straight leg, and quivering thigh
And the demesnes that there adjacent lie,   20
That in thy likeness thou appear to us.

BENVOLIO   An if he hear thee thou wilt anger him.

MERCUTIO   This cannot anger him. 'Twould anger him
To raise a spirit in his mistress' circle
Of some strange nature, letting it there stand   25
Till she had laid it and conjured it down –
That were some spite. My invocation
Is fair and honest. In his mistress' name
I conjure only but to raise up him.

BENVOLIO
Come, he hath hid himself among these trees   30
To be consorted with the humorous night.
Blind is his love, and best befits the dark.

MERCUTIO   If love be blind, love cannot hit the mark.
Now will he sit under a medlar tree,
35 And wish his mistress were that kind of fruit
As maids call medlars when they laugh alone.
O Romeo, that she were, O, that she were
An open-arse, thou a poperin pear!
Romeo, good night, I'll to my truckle-bed;
40 This field-bed is too cold for me to sleep.
Come, shall we go?
BENVOLIO   Go then, for 'tis in vain
To seek him here that means not to be found.
Exeunt Benvolio and Mercutio.

2.2

ROMEO [*Comes forward.*]
He jests at scars that never felt a wound.
But soft, what light through yonder window breaks?
It is the east, and Juliet is the sun.
Arise, fair sun, and kill the envious moon,
5 Who is already sick and pale with grief
That thou her maid art far more fair than she.
Be not her maid, since she is envious;
Her vestal livery is but sick and green,
And none but fools do wear it. Cast it off.

Enter JULIET *aloft.*

10 It is my lady, O, it is my love!
O, that she knew she were!
She speaks, yet she says nothing. What of that?
Her eye discourses, I will answer it.
I am too bold, 'tis not to me she speaks.
15 Two of the fairest stars in all the heaven,
Having some business, do entreat her eyes
To twinkle in their spheres till they return.
What if her eyes were there, they in her head?
The brightness of her cheek would shame those stars
20 As daylight doth a lamp. Her eyes in heaven
Would through the airy region stream so bright
That birds would sing and think it were not night.
See how she leans her cheek upon her hand.
O, that I were a glove upon that hand,
That I might touch that cheek!
JULIET   Ay me.
25 ROMEO   She speaks.
O speak again, bright angel, for thou art
As glorious to this night, being o'er my head,
As is a winged messenger of heaven
Unto the white-upturned wondering eyes
30 Of mortals that fall back to gaze on him
When he bestrides the lazy-puffing clouds
And sails upon the bosom of the air.
JULIET   O Romeo, Romeo, wherefore art thou Romeo?
Deny thy father and refuse thy name,
35 Or if thou wilt not, be but sworn my love,
And I'll no longer be a Capulet.
ROMEO   Shall I hear more, or shall I speak at this?

JULIET   'Tis but thy name that is my enemy.
Thou art thyself, though not a Montague.
40 What's Montague? It is nor hand nor foot,
Nor arm nor face nor any other part
Belonging to a man. O be some other name!
What's in a name? That which we call a rose
By any other word would smell as sweet;
45 So Romeo would, were he not Romeo called,
Retain that dear perfection which he owes
Without that title. Romeo, doff thy name,
And for thy name, which is no part of thee,
Take all myself.
ROMEO   I take thee at thy word.
Call me but love and I'll be new baptized.
50 Henceforth I never will be Romeo.
JULIET
What man art thou that thus bescreened in night
So stumblest on my counsel?
ROMEO   By a name
I know not how to tell thee who I am.
55 My name, dear saint, is hateful to myself,
Because it is an enemy to thee.
Had I it written, I would tear the word.
JULIET   My ears have yet not drunk a hundred words
Of thy tongue's uttering, yet I know the sound.
60 Art thou not Romeo, and a Montague?
ROMEO   Neither, fair maid, if either thee dislike.
JULIET   How cam'st thou hither, tell me, and wherefore?
The orchard walls are high and hard to climb,
And the place death, considering who thou art,
65 If any of my kinsmen find thee here.
ROMEO
With love's light wings did I o'erperch these walls,
For stony limits cannot hold love out,
And what love can do, that dares love attempt;
Therefore thy kinsmen are no stop to me.
70 JULIET   If they do see thee, they will murder thee.
ROMEO   Alack, there lies more peril in thine eye
Than twenty of their swords. Look thou but sweet,
And I am proof against their enmity.
JULIET   I would not for the world they saw thee here.
75 ROMEO   I have night's cloak to hide me from their eyes,
An but thou love me, let them find me here.
My life were better ended by their hate
Than death prorogued, wanting of thy love.
JULIET
By whose direction found'st thou out this place?
80 ROMEO   By love, that first did prompt me to enquire.
He lent me counsel, and I lent him eyes.
I am no pilot, yet wert thou as far
As that vast shore washed with the farthest sea,
I should adventure for such merchandise.
85 JULIET   Thou knowest the mask of night is on my face,
Else would a maiden blush bepaint my cheek
For that which thou hast heard me speak tonight.
Fain would I dwell on form, fain, fain deny
What I have spoke; but farewell, compliment.

90   Dost thou love me? I know thou wilt say 'Ay',
      And I will take thy word; yet, if thou swear'st,
      Thou mayst prove false. At lovers' perjuries,
      They say, Jove laughs. O gentle Romeo,
      If thou dost love, pronounce it faithfully,
95   Or if thou think'st I am too quickly won,
      I'll frown and be perverse and say thee nay,
      So thou wilt woo, but else not for the world.
      In truth, fair Montague, I am too fond,
      And therefore thou mayst think my haviour light.
100   But trust me, gentleman, I'll prove more true
      Than those that have more cunning to be strange.
      I should have been more strange, I must confess,
      But that thou overheard'st, ere I was ware,
      My true-love passion. Therefore pardon me,
105   And not impute this yielding to light love,
      Which the dark night hath so discovered.
      ROMEO   Lady, by yonder blessed moon I vow,
      That tips with silver all these fruit-tree tops –
      JULIET   O swear not by the moon, th'inconstant moon,
110   That monthly changes in her circled orb,
      Lest that thy love prove likewise variable.
      ROMEO   What shall I swear by?
      JULIET   Do not swear at all,
      Or if thou wilt, swear by thy gracious self,
      Which is the god of my idolatry,
      And I'll believe thee.
115   ROMEO   If my heart's dear love –
      JULIET   Well, do not swear. Although I joy in thee,
      I have no joy of this contract tonight;
      It is too rash, too unadvised, too sudden,
      Too like the lightning which doth cease to be
120   Ere one can say 'it lightens'. Sweet, good night.
      This bud of love by summer's ripening breath
      May prove a beauteous flower when next we meet.
      Good night, good night; as sweet repose and rest
      Come to thy heart as that within my breast.
125   ROMEO   O, wilt thou leave me so unsatisfied?
      JULIET   What satisfaction canst thou have tonight?
      ROMEO
      Th'exchange of thy love's faithful vow for mine.
      JULIET   I gave thee mine before thou didst request it,
      And yet I would it were to give again.
      ROMEO
130   Wouldst thou withdraw it? For what purpose, love?
      JULIET   But to be frank and give it thee again;
      And yet I wish but for the thing I have.
      My bounty is as boundless as the sea,
      My love as deep; the more I give to thee,
135   The more I have, for both are infinite.
      I hear some noise within. Dear love, adieu.
           [*Nurse calls within.*]
      Anon, good Nurse! – Sweet Montague, be true,
      Stay but a little, I will come again.   *Exit.*
      ROMEO   O blessed, blessed night! I am afeared,
140   Being in night, all this is but a dream,
      Too flattering-sweet to be substantial.

Enter JULIET *above.*

JULIET
      Three words, dear Romeo, and good night indeed.
      If that thy bent of love be honourable,
      Thy purpose marriage, send me word tomorrow
      By one that I'll procure to come to thee,   145
      Where and what time thou wilt perform the rite,
      And all my fortunes at thy foot I'll lay,
      And follow thee my lord throughout the world.
NURSE [*within*]   Madam!
JULIET   I come, anon! – But if thou meanest not well,   150
      I do beseech thee –
NURSE [*within*]   Madam!
JULIET   By and by, I come! –
      To cease thy strife and leave me to my grief.
      Tomorrow will I send.
ROMEO   So thrive my soul –
JULIET   A thousand times good night.   *Exit.*
ROMEO   A thousand times the worse to want thy light.   155
      Love goes toward love as schoolboys from their books,
      But love from love toward school with heavy looks.

Enter JULIET *again.*

JULIET   Hist, Romeo, hist! O, for a falconer's voice
      To lure this tassel-gentle back again –
      Bondage is hoarse and may not speak aloud,   160
      Else would I tear the cave where Echo lies
      And make her airy tongue more hoarse than mine
      With repetition of my 'Romeo'.
ROMEO   It is my soul that calls upon my name.
      How silver-sweet sound lovers' tongues by night,   165
      Like softest music to attending ears.
JULIET   Romeo!
ROMEO   My nyas?
JULIET   What o'clock tomorrow
      Shall I send to thee?
ROMEO   By the hour of nine.
JULIET   I will not fail. 'Tis twenty year till then.
      I have forgot why I did call thee back.   170
ROMEO   Let me stand here till thou remember it.
JULIET   I shall forget to have thee still stand there,
      Remembering how I love thy company.
ROMEO   And I'll still stay to have thee still forget,
      Forgetting any other home but this.   175
JULIET   'Tis almost morning. I would have thee gone,
      And yet no farther than a wanton's bird,
      That lets it hop a little from his hand,
      Like a poor prisoner in his twisted gyves,
      And with a silken thread plucks it back again,   180
      So loving-jealous of his liberty.
ROMEO   I would I were thy bird.
JULIET   Sweet, so would I,
      Yet I should kill thee with much cherishing.
      Good night, good night. Parting is such sweet sorrow
      That I shall say goodnight till it be morrow.   185
ROMEO   Sleep dwell upon thine eyes, peace in thy breast;

Would I were sleep and peace, so sweet to rest.

Exit Juliet.

The grey-eyed morn smiles on the frowning night,
Chequering the eastern clouds with streaks of light,
And darkness, fleckled, like a drunkard reels   190
From forth day's pathway made by Titan's wheels.
Hence will I to my ghostly sire's close cell,
His help to crave and my dear hap to tell.   *Exit.*

2.3   *Enter* FRIAR LAURENCE *alone,*
                with a basket.

FRIAR LAURENCE
Now, ere the sun advance his burning eye
The day to cheer and night's dank dew to dry,
I must up-fill this osier cage of ours
With baleful weeds and precious-juiced flowers.
The earth that's nature's mother is her tomb,   5
What is her burying grave, that is her womb;
And from her womb children of divers kind
We sucking on her natural bosom find,
Many for many virtues excellent,
None but for some, and yet all different.   10
O, mickle is the powerful grace that lies
In plants, herbs, stones and their true qualities,
For naught so vile that on the earth doth live
But to the earth some special good doth give,
Nor aught so good but, strained from that fair use,   15
Revolts from true birth, stumbling on abuse.
Virtue itself turns vice, being misapplied,
And vice sometime by action dignified.

                Enter ROMEO.

Within the infant rind of this weak flower
Poison hath residence and medicine power,   20
For this, being smelled, with that part cheers each part,
Being tasted, stays all senses with the heart.
Two such opposed kings encamp them still
In man as well as herbs, grace and rude will,
And where the worser is predominant   25
Full soon the canker death eats up that plant.
ROMEO   Good morrow, father.
FRIAR LAURENCE   *Benedicite.*
What early tongue so sweet saluteth me?
Young son, it argues a distempered head
So soon to bid good morrow to thy bed.   30
Care keeps his watch in every old man's eye,
And where care lodges, sleep will never lie;
But where unbruised youth with unstuffed brain
Doth couch his limbs, there golden sleep doth reign.
Therefore thy earliness doth me assure   35
Thou art uproused with some distemperature;
Or if not so, then here I hit it right,
Our Romeo hath not been in bed tonight.
ROMEO   That last is true, the sweeter rest was mine.
FRIAR LAURENCE
God pardon sin! Wast thou with Rosaline?   40

ROMEO   With Rosaline, my ghostly father? No,
I have forgot that name and that name's woe.
FRIAR LAURENCE
That's my good son; but where hast thou been then?
ROMEO   I'll tell thee ere thou ask it me again.
I have been feasting with mine enemy,   45
Where on a sudden one hath wounded me
That's by me wounded. Both our remedies
Within thy help and holy physic lies.
I bear no hatred, blessed man, for lo,
My intercession likewise steads my foe.   50
FRIAR LAURENCE
Be plain, good son, and homely in thy drift;
Riddling confession finds but riddling shrift.
ROMEO   Then plainly know, my heart's dear love is set
On the fair daughter of rich Capulet.
As mine on hers, so hers is set on mine,   55
And all combined, save what thou must combine
By holy marriage. When, and where, and how
We met, we wooed and made exchange of vow,
I'll tell thee as we pass; but this I pray,
That thou consent to marry us today.   60
FRIAR LAURENCE
Holy Saint Francis, what a change is here!
Is Rosaline, that thou didst love so dear,
So soon forsaken? Young men's love then lies
Not truly in their hearts but in their eyes.
Jesu Maria, what a deal of brine   65
Hath washed thy sallow cheeks for Rosaline!
How much salt water thrown away in waste
To season love that of it doth not taste.
The sun not yet thy sighs from heaven clears,
Thy old groans yet ringing in mine ancient ears.   70
Lo, here upon thy cheek the stain doth sit
Of an old tear that is not washed off yet.
If e'er thou wast thyself and these woes thine,
Thou and these woes were all for Rosaline.
And art thou changed? Pronounce this sentence then: 75
Women may fall when there's no strength in men.
ROMEO   Thou chid'st me oft for loving Rosaline.
FRIAR LAURENCE
For doting, not for loving, pupil mine.
ROMEO   And bad'st me bury love.
FRIAR LAURENCE   Not in a grave
To lay one in, another out to have.   80
ROMEO   I pray thee, chide me not. Her I love now
Doth grace for grace and love for love allow;
The other did not so.
FRIAR LAURENCE   O, she knew well
Thy love did read by rote, that could not spell.
But come, young waverer, come, go with me.   85
In one respect I'll thy assistant be,
For this alliance may so happy prove,
To turn your households' rancour to pure love.
ROMEO   O, let us hence, I stand on sudden haste.
FRIAR LAURENCE
Wisely and slow, they stumble that run fast.   *Exeunt.*   90

    Enter BENVOLIO *and* MERCUTIO.

MERCUTIO   Where the devil should this Romeo be?
Came he not home tonight?

BENVOLIO   Not to his father's; I spoke with his man.

MERCUTIO

5   Why, that same pale, hard-hearted wench, that Rosaline,
Torments him so that he will sure run mad.

BENVOLIO   Tybalt, the kinsman to old Capulet,
Hath sent a letter to his father's house.

MERCUTIO   A challenge, on my life.

BENVOLIO   Romeo will answer it.

10   MERCUTIO   Any man that can write may answer a letter.

BENVOLIO   Nay, he will answer the letter's master, how
he dares being dared.

MERCUTIO   Alas, poor Romeo, he is already dead,
stabbed with a white wench's black eye, run through
15   the ear with a love song, the very pin of his heart cleft
with the blind bow-boy's butt-shaft – and is he a man
to encounter Tybalt?

BENVOLIO   Why, what is Tybalt!

MERCUTIO   More than Prince of Cats. O, he's the
20   courageous captain of compliments: he fights as you
sing pricksong, keeps time, distance and proportion.
He rests his minim rests, one, two, and the third in
your bosom; the very butcher of a silk button, a
duellist, a duellist, a gentleman of the very first house,
25   of the first and second cause. Ah, the immortal *passado*,
the *punto reverso*, the hay!

BENVOLIO   The what?

MERCUTIO   The pox of such antic, lisping, affecting
fantasticoes, these new tuners of accent! By Jesu, a
30   very good blade, a very tall man, a very good whore!
Why, is not this a lamentable thing, grandsire, that we
should be thus afflicted with these strange flies, these
fashion-mongers, these pardon-me's who stand so
much on the new form that they cannot sit at ease on
35   the old bench? O, their bones, their bones!

Enter ROMEO.

BENVOLIO   Here comes Romeo, here comes Romeo!

MERCUTIO   Without his roe, like a dried herring. O
flesh, flesh, how art thou fishified! Now is he for the
numbers that Petrarch flowed in. Laura to his lady was
40   a kitchen wench – marry, she had a better love to
berhyme her – Dido a dowdy, Cleopatra a gypsy, Helen
and Hero hildings and harlots, Thisbe a grey eye or so,
but not to the purpose. Signor Romeo, *bonjour*: there's
a French salutation to your French slop. You gave us
45   the counterfeit fairly last night.

ROMEO   Good morrow to you both. What counterfeit
did I give you?

MERCUTIO   The slip, sir, the slip, can you not conceive?

ROMEO   Pardon, good Mercutio, my business was great,
50   and in such a case as mine a man may strain courtesy.

MERCUTIO   That's as much as to say, such a case as
yours constrains a man to bow in the hams.

ROMEO   Meaning to curtsy.

MERCUTIO   Thou hast most kindly hit it.

ROMEO   A most courteous exposition.   55

MERCUTIO   Nay, I am the very pink of courtesy.

ROMEO   Pink for flower.

MERCUTIO   Right.

ROMEO   Why, then is my pump well flowered.

MERCUTIO   Sure wit, follow me this jest now till thou   60
hast worn out thy pump, that when the single sole of it
is worn, the jest may remain, after the wearing, solely
singular.

ROMEO   O single-soled jest, solely singular for the
singleness!   65

MERCUTIO   Come between us, good Benvolio, my wits
faints.

ROMEO   Swits and spurs, swits and spurs, or I'll cry a
match.

MERCUTIO   Nay, if our wits run the wild goose chase, I   70
am done, for thou hast more of the wild goose in one of
thy wits than, I am sure, I have in my whole five. Was I
with you there for the goose?

ROMEO   Thou wast never with me for anything, when
thou wast not there for the goose.   75

MERCUTIO   I will bite thee by the ear for that jest.

ROMEO   Nay, good goose, bite not.

MERCUTIO   Thy wit is a very bitter sweeting, it is a most
sharp sauce.

ROMEO   And is it not then well served in to a sweet   80
goose?

MERCUTIO   O here's a wit of cheveril, that stretches
from an inch narrow to an ell broad.

ROMEO   I stretch it out for that word 'broad' which,
added to the goose, proves thee far and wide – a broad   85
goose.

MERCUTIO   Why, is not this better now than groaning
for love? Now art thou sociable, now art thou Romeo,
now art thou what thou art, by art as well as by nature,
for this drivelling love is like a great natural that runs   90
lolling up and down to hide his bauble in a hole.

BENVOLIO   Stop there, stop there!

MERCUTIO   Thou desirest me to stop in my tale against
the hair.

BENVOLIO   Thou wouldst else have made thy tale large.   95

MERCUTIO   O, thou art deceived. I would have made it
short, for I was come to the whole depth of my tale and
meant indeed to occupy the argument no longer.

ROMEO   Here's goodly gear!

Enter NURSE *and her man* PETER.

A sail, a sail!   100

MERCUTIO   Two, two, a shirt and a smock.

NURSE   Peter!

PETER   Anon.

NURSE   My fan, Peter.

MERCUTIO   Good Peter, to hide her face, for her fan's   105
the fairer face.

NURSE   God ye good morrow, gentlemen.

MERCUTIO   God ye good den, fair gentlewoman.

NURSE   Is it good den?

110 MERCUTIO   'Tis no less, I tell ye, for the bawdy hand of
the dial is now upon the prick of noon.

NURSE   Out upon you! What a man are you?

ROMEO   One, gentlewoman, that God hath made,
himself to mar.

115 NURSE   By my troth, it is well said: 'for himself to mar',
quoth 'a? Gentlemen, can any of you tell me where I
may find the young Romeo?

ROMEO   I can tell you, but young Romeo will be older
when you have found him than he was when you
120 sought him. I am the youngest of that name, for fault
of a worse.

NURSE   You say well.

MERCUTIO   Yea, is the worst well? Very well took, i'faith,
wisely, wisely.

125 NURSE   If you be he, sir, I desire some confidence with
you.

BENVOLIO   She will indite him to some supper.

MERCUTIO   A bawd, a bawd, a bawd! So ho!

ROMEO   What hast thou found?

130 MERCUTIO   No hare, sir, unless a hare, sir, in a lenten
pie, that is something stale and hoar ere it be spent.
[*He walks by them and sings.*]
An old hare hoar, and an old hare hoar
Is very good meat in Lent.
But a hare that is hoar is too much for a score
135 When it hoars ere it be spent.
Romeo, will you come to your father's? We'll to dinner
thither.

ROMEO   I will follow you.

MERCUTIO   Farewell, ancient lady, farewell lady, [*singing*]
140 'lady, lady'.   *Exeunt Mercutio and Benvolio.*

NURSE   I pray you, sir, what saucy merchant was this
that was so full of his ropery?

ROMEO   A gentleman, Nurse, that loves to hear himself
talk and will speak more in a minute than he will stand
145 to in a month.

NURSE   An 'a speak anything against me, I'll take him
down, an 'a were lustier than he is, and twenty such
jacks, and if I cannot, I'll find those that shall. Scurvy
knave! I am none of his flirt-gills, I am none of his
150 skains-mates. [*She turns to Peter, her man.*] And thou
must stand by too and suffer every knave to use me at
his pleasure!

PETER   I saw no man use you at his pleasure; if I had, my
weapon should quickly have been out. I warrant you, I
155 dare draw as soon as another man, if I see occasion in a
good quarrel and the law on my side.

NURSE   Now, afore God, I am so vexed that every part
about me quivers. Scurvy knave! Pray you, sir, a word;
and, as I told you, my young lady bid me enquire you
160 out. What she bid me say I will keep to myself. But first
let me tell ye, if ye should lead her in a fool's paradise,
as they say, it were a very gross kind of behaviour, as
they say, for the gentlewoman is young and therefore,

if you should deal double with her, truly it were an ill
165 thing to be offered to any gentlewoman, and very weak
dealing.

ROMEO   Nurse, commend me to thy lady and mistress.
I protest unto thee –

NURSE   Good heart, and i'faith I will tell her as much.
170 Lord, Lord, she will be a joyful woman.

ROMEO   What wilt thou tell her, Nurse? Thou dost not
mark me.

NURSE   I will tell her, sir, that you do protest, which, as
I take it, is a gentlemanlike offer.

ROMEO
Bid her devise some means to come to shrift this
175 afternoon,
And there she shall at Friar Laurence' cell
Be shrived and married. Here is for thy pains.

NURSE   No, truly, sir, not a penny.

ROMEO   Go to, I say you shall.

NURSE   This afternoon, sir? Well, she shall be there.   180

ROMEO   And stay, good Nurse, behind the abbey wall.
Within this hour my man shall be with thee
And bring thee cords made like a tackled stair,
Which to the high topgallant of my joy
Must be my convoy in the secret night.   185
Farewell, be trusty, and I'll quit thy pains.
Farewell, commend me to thy mistress.

NURSE   Now God in heaven bless thee! Hark you, sir.

ROMEO   What sayst thou, my dear Nurse?

NURSE   Is your man secret? Did you ne'er hear say   190
'Two may keep counsel, putting one away'?

ROMEO   'Warrant thee, my man's as true as steel.

NURSE   Well, sir, my mistress is the sweetest lady. Lord,
Lord, when 'twas a little prating thing – O, there is a
nobleman in town, one Paris, that would fain lay knife 195
aboard, but she, good soul, had as lief see a toad, a very
toad, as see him. I anger her sometimes and tell her that
Paris is the properer man, but I'll warrant you, when I
say so she looks as pale as any clout in the versal world.
Doth not rosemary and Romeo begin both with a letter? 200

ROMEO   Ay, Nurse, what of that, both with an 'R'.

NURSE   Ah, mocker, that's the dog's name. 'R' is for the
– no, I know it begins with some other letter, and she
hath the prettiest sententious of it, of you and
rosemary, that it would do you good to hear it.   205

ROMEO   Commend me to thy lady.

NURSE   Ay, a thousand times.   *Exit Romeo.*
Peter!

PETER   Anon.

NURSE   Before, and apace.   *Exeunt.*   210

2.5   *Enter* JULIET.

JULIET
The clock struck nine when I did send the Nurse;
In half an hour she promised to return.
Perchance she cannot meet him. That's not so.
O, she is lame! Love's heralds should be thoughts,

5   Which ten times faster glides than the sun's beams,
     Driving back shadows over louring hills.
     Therefore do nimble-pinioned doves draw love,
     And therefore hath the wind-swift Cupid wings.
     Now is the sun upon the highmost hill
10   Of this day's journey, and from nine till twelve
     Is three long hours, yet she is not come.
     Had she affections and warm youthful blood,
     She would be as swift in motion as a ball;
     My words would bandy her to my sweet love,
15   And his to me.
     But old folks, many feign as they were dead,
     Unwieldy, slow, heavy and pale as lead.

                    Enter NURSE *and* PETER.

     O God, she comes. O honey Nurse, what news?
     Hast thou met with him? Send thy man away.
20   NURSE   Peter, stay at the gate.   *Exit Peter.*
     JULIET
     Now, good sweet Nurse – O Lord, why lookest thou
          sad?
     Though news be sad, yet tell them merrily.
     If good, thou shamest the music of sweet news
     By playing it to me with so sour a face.
25   NURSE   I am aweary, give me leave awhile.
     Fie, how my bones ache. What a jaunt have I!
     JULIET   I would thou hadst my bones and I thy news.
     Nay, come, I pray thee, speak, good, good Nurse,
          speak.
     NURSE   Jesu, what haste! Can you not stay a while?
30   Do you not see that I am out of breath?
     JULIET
     How art thou out of breath when thou hast breath
     To say to me that thou art out of breath?
     The excuse that thou dost make in this delay
     Is longer than the tale thou dost excuse.
35   Is thy news good or bad? Answer to that,
     Say either, and I'll stay the circumstance.
     Let me be satisfied, is't good or bad?
     NURSE   Well, you have made a simple choice. You know
     not how to choose a man. Romeo? No, not he. Though
40   his face be better than any man's, yet his leg excels all
     men's; and for a hand and a foot and a body, though
     they be not to be talked on, yet they are past compare.
     He is not the flower of courtesy, but I'll warrant him as
     gentle as a lamb. Go thy ways, wench, serve God.
45   What, have you dined at home?
     JULIET   No, no. But all this did I know before.
     What says he of our marriage, what of that?
     NURSE   Lord, how my head aches! What a head have I!
     It beats as it would fall in twenty pieces.
50   My back a' t'other side, ah, my back, my back!
     Beshrew your heart for sending me about
     To catch my death with jauncing up and down.
     JULIET   I'faith, I am sorry that thou art not well.
     Sweet, sweet, sweet Nurse, tell me, what says my
          love?

     NURSE   Your love says, like an honest gentleman,   55
     And a courteous, and a kind, and a handsome,
     And, I warrant, a virtuous – Where is your mother?
     JULIET   Where is my mother! Why, she is within.
     Where should she be? How oddly thou repliest!
     'Your love says, like an honest gentleman',   60
     'Where is your mother!'
     NURSE   O God's Lady, dear,
     Are you so hot? Marry come up, I trow.
     Is this the poultice for my aching bones?
     Henceforward do your messages yourself.
     JULIET   Here's such a coil! Come, what says Romeo?   65
     NURSE   Have you got leave to go to shrift today?
     JULIET   I have.
     NURSE   Then hie you hence to Friar Laurence' cell;
     There stays a husband to make you a wife.
     Now comes the wanton blood up in your cheeks;   70
     They'll be in scarlet straight at any news.
     Hie you to church; I must another way,
     To fetch a ladder by the which your love
     Must climb a bird's nest soon when it is dark.
     I am the drudge and toil in your delight,   75
     But you shall bear the burden soon at night.
     Go, I'll to dinner. Hie you to the cell.
     JULIET   Hie to high fortune! Honest Nurse, farewell.
                                              Exeunt.

     2.6   *Enter* FRIAR LAURENCE *and* ROMEO.

     FRIAR LAURENCE
     So smile the heavens upon this holy act
     That after-hours with sorrow chide us not.
     ROMEO   Amen, amen, but come what sorrow can,
     It cannot countervail the exchange of joy
     That one short minute gives me in her sight.   5
     Do thou but close our hands with holy words,
     Then love-devouring death do what he dare,
     It is enough I may but call her mine.
     FRIAR LAURENCE
     These violent delights have violent ends
     And in their triumph die, like fire and powder   10
     Which, as they kiss, consume. The sweetest honey
     Is loathsome in his own deliciousness,
     And in the taste confounds the appetite.
     Therefore love moderately; long love doth so;
     Too swift arrives as tardy as too slow.   15

          Enter JULIET *somewhat fast, and embraces Romeo.*

     Here comes the lady. O, so light a foot
     Will ne'er wear out the everlasting flint;
     A lover may bestride the gossamers
     That idles in the wanton summer air,
     And yet not fall, so light is vanity.   20
     JULIET   Good even to my ghostly confessor.
     FRIAR LAURENCE
     Romeo shall thank thee, daughter, for us both.
              [*Romeo kisses her.*]

JULIET As much to him, else is his thanks too much.
    [*She returns his kiss.*]
ROMEO Ah, Juliet, if the measure of thy joy
25   Be heaped like mine, and that thy skill be more
    To blazon it, then sweeten with thy breath
    This neighbour air, and let rich music's tongue
    Unfold the imagined happiness that both
    Receive in either by this dear encounter.
30 JULIET Conceit more rich in matter than in words
    Brags of his substance, not of ornament.
    They are but beggars that can count their worth,
    But my true love is grown to such excess,
    I cannot sum up sum of half my wealth.
FRIAR LAURENCE
35   Come, come with me, and we will make short work,
    For, by your leaves, you shall not stay alone
    Till holy church incorporate two in one.   *Exeunt.*

3.1   *Enter* MERCUTIO, BENVOLIO,
       Mercutio's Page and Men.

BENVOLIO I pray thee, good Mercutio, let's retire;
    The day is hot, the Capels are abroad,
    An if we meet we shall not scape a brawl,
    For now, these hot days, is the mad blood stirring.
5 MERCUTIO Thou art like one of these fellows that,
    when he enters the confines of a tavern, claps me his
    sword upon the table and says 'God send me no need
    of thee!'; and by the operation of the second cup draws
    him on the drawer, when indeed there is no need.
10 BENVOLIO Am I like such a fellow?
MERCUTIO Come, come, thou art as hot a jack in thy
    mood as any in Italy; and as soon moved to be moody,
    and as soon moody to be moved.
BENVOLIO And what to?
15 MERCUTIO Nay, an there were two such, we should
    have none shortly, for one would kill the other. Thou
    – why, thou wilt quarrel with a man that hath a hair
    more or a hair less in his beard than thou hast. Thou
    wilt quarrel with a man for cracking nuts, having no
20   other reason but because thou hast hazel eyes. What
    eye but such an eye would spy out such a quarrel? Thy
    head is as full of quarrels as an egg is full of meat, and
    yet thy head hath been beaten as addle as an egg for
    quarrelling. Thou hast quarrelled with a man for
25   coughing in the street, because he hath wakened thy
    dog that hath lain asleep in the sun. Didst thou not fall
    out with a tailor for wearing his new doublet before
    Easter, with another for tying his new shoes with old
    riband, and yet thou wilt tutor me from quarrelling!
30 BENVOLIO An I were so apt to quarrel as thou art, any
    man should buy the fee-simple of my life for an hour
    and a quarter.
MERCUTIO The fee-simple? O simple!

    Enter TYBALT, PETRUCHIO *and others.*

BENVOLIO By my head, here comes the Capulets.

MERCUTIO By my heel, I care not.   35
TYBALT Follow me close, for I will speak to them.
    Gentlemen, good-e'en, a word with one of you.
MERCUTIO And but one word with one of us? Couple it
    with something, make it a word and a blow.
TYBALT You shall find me apt enough to that, sir, an   40
    you will give me occasion.
MERCUTIO Could you not take some occasion without
    giving?
TYBALT Mercutio, thou consortest with Romeo.
MERCUTIO 'Consort'? What, dost thou make us   45
    minstrels? An thou make minstrels of us, look to hear
    nothing but discords. Here's my fiddlestick, here's that
    shall make you dance. Zounds, 'consort'!
BENVOLIO We talk here in the public haunt of men.
    Either withdraw unto some private place,   50
    Or reason coldly of your grievances,
    Or else depart. Here all eyes gaze on us.
MERCUTIO
    Men's eyes were made to look, and let them gaze.
    I will not budge for no man's pleasure, I.

    Enter ROMEO.

TYBALT
    Well, peace be with you, sir, here comes my man.   55
MERCUTIO
    But I'll be hanged, sir, if he wear your livery.
    Marry, go before to field, he'll be your follower;
    Your worship in that sense may call him 'man'.
TYBALT Romeo, the love I bear thee can afford
    No better term than this: thou art a villain.   60
ROMEO Tybalt, the reason that I have to love thee
    Doth much excuse the appertaining rage
    To such a greeting. Villain am I none,
    Therefore farewell; I see thou knowest me not.
TYBALT Boy, this shall not excuse the injuries   65
    That thou hast done me; therefore turn and draw.
ROMEO I do protest I never injuried thee,
    But love thee better than thou canst devise
    Till thou shalt know the reason of my love.
    And so, good Capulet, which name I tender   70
    As dearly as mine own, be satisfied.
MERCUTIO O calm, dishonourable, vile submission!
    Alla stoccado carries it away.   [*Draws.*]
    Tybalt, you rat-catcher, will you walk?
TYBALT What wouldst thou have with me?   75
MERCUTIO Good King of Cats, nothing but one of
    your nine lives. That I mean to make bold withal and,
    as you shall use me hereafter, dry-beat the rest of the
    eight. Will you pluck your sword out of his pilcher by
    the ears? Make haste, lest mine be about your ears ere   80
    it be out.
TYBALT I am for you. [*Draws.*]
ROMEO Gentle Mercutio, put thy rapier up.
MERCUTIO Come, sir, your *passado*! [*They fight.*]
ROMEO [*Draws.*]
    Draw, Benvolio, beat down their weapons.   85

Gentlemen, for shame, forbear this outrage.
Tybalt, Mercutio, the Prince expressly hath
Forbid this bandying in Verona streets.
Hold, Tybalt! Good Mercutio!

Tybalt under Romeo's arm thrusts
Mercutio in and flies.

90   PETRUCHIO   Away, Tybalt!
MERCUTIO   I am hurt.
A plague a' both houses! I am sped.
Is he gone and hath nothing?
BENVOLIO   What, art thou hurt?
MERCUTIO
Ay, ay, a scratch, a scratch. Marry, 'tis enough.
95   Where is my page? Go, villain, fetch a surgeon.

Exit Page.

ROMEO   Courage, man, the hurt cannot be much.
MERCUTIO   No, 'tis not so deep as a well, nor so wide
as a church door, but 'tis enough, 'twill serve. Ask
for me tomorrow and you shall find me a grave man.
100   I am peppered, I warrant, for this world. A plague
a' both your houses! Zounds, a dog, a rat, a mouse, a
cat, to scratch a man to death! A braggart, a rogue, a
villain, that fights by the book of arithmetic! Why
the devil came you between us? I was hurt under your
105   arm.
ROMEO   I thought all for the best.
MERCUTIO   Help me into some house, Benvolio,
Or I shall faint. A plague a' both your houses!
They have made worms' meat of me.
110   I have it, and soundly too. Your houses!

Exit with Benvolio.

ROMEO   This gentleman, the Prince's near ally,
My very friend, hath got this mortal hurt
In my behalf; my reputation stained
With Tybalt's slander – Tybalt, that an hour
115   Hath been my cousin. O sweet Juliet,
Thy beauty hath made me effeminate
And in my temper softened valour's steel!

Enter BENVOLIO.

BENVOLIO   O Romeo, Romeo, brave Mercutio is dead.
That gallant spirit hath aspired the clouds,
120   Which too untimely here did scorn the earth.
ROMEO
This day's black fate on moe days doth depend,
This but begins the woe others must end.

Enter TYBALT.

BENVOLIO   Here comes the furious Tybalt back again.
ROMEO   Alive, in triumph, and Mercutio slain!
125   Away to heaven, respective lenity,
And fire-eyed fury be my conduct now.
Now, Tybalt, take the 'villain' back again
That late thou gavest me, for Mercutio's soul
Is but a little way above our heads,
130   Staying for thine to keep him company.
Either thou or I, or both, must go with him.

TYBALT
Thou wretched boy, that didst consort him here,
Shalt with him hence.
ROMEO   This shall determine that.

[They fight. Tybalt falls and dies.]

BENVOLIO   Romeo, away, be gone!
The citizens are up and Tybalt slain.   135
Stand not amazed. The Prince will doom thee death
If thou art taken. Hence, be gone, away!
ROMEO   O, I am fortune's fool.
BENVOLIO   Why dost thou stay?   *Exit Romeo.*

Enter CITIZENS.

CITIZENS   Which way ran he that killed Mercutio?
Tybalt, that murderer, which way ran he?   140
BENVOLIO   There lies that Tybalt.
CITIZEN   Up, sir, go with me.
I charge thee in the Prince's name, obey.

Enter PRINCE, *old* MONTAGUE, CAPULET,
their WIVES *and all.*

PRINCE   Where are the vile beginners of this fray?
BENVOLIO   O noble Prince, I can discover all
The unlucky manage of this fatal brawl.   145
There lies the man, slain by young Romeo,
That slew thy kinsman, brave Mercutio.
CAPULET'S WIFE
Tybalt, my cousin, O my brother's child!
O Prince, O cousin, husband, O, the blood is spilled
Of my dear kinsman! Prince, as thou art true,   150
For blood of ours shed blood of Montague.
O cousin, cousin!
PRINCE   Benvolio, who began this bloody fray?
BENVOLIO
Tybalt, here slain, whom Romeo's hand did slay,
Romeo, that spoke him fair, bid him bethink   155
How nice the quarrel was, and urged withal
Your high displeasure. All this, uttered
With gentle breath, calm look, knees humbly bowed,
Could not take truce with the unruly spleen
Of Tybalt deaf to peace, but that he tilts   160
With piercing steel at bold Mercutio's breast,
Who, all as hot, turns deadly point to point
And, with a martial scorn, with one hand beats
Cold death aside, and with the other sends
It back to Tybalt, whose dexterity   165
Retorts it. Romeo, he cries aloud
'Hold, friends, friends, part!', and swifter than his
tongue
His agile arm beats down their fatal points,
And 'twixt them rushes; underneath whose arm
An envious thrust from Tybalt hit the life   170
Of stout Mercutio, and then Tybalt fled.
But by and by comes back to Romeo,
Who had but newly entertained revenge,
And to't they go like lightning, for, ere I
Could draw to part them was stout Tybalt slain,   175

And as he fell did Romeo turn and fly.
This is the truth, or let Benvolio die.

CAPULET'S WIFE   He is a kinsman to the Montague.
Affection makes him false; he speaks not true.
180 Some twenty of them fought in this black strife,
And all those twenty could but kill one life.
I beg for justice, which thou, Prince, must give:
Romeo slew Tybalt, Romeo must not live.

PRINCE   Romeo slew him, he slew Mercutio,
185 Who now the price of his dear blood doth owe?

MONTAGUE
Not Romeo, Prince, he was Mercutio's friend.
His fault concludes but what the law should end,
The life of Tybalt.

PRINCE   And for that offence
Immediately we do exile him hence.
190 I have an interest in your hates' proceeding.
My blood for your rude brawls doth lie a-bleeding,
But I'll amerce you with so strong a fine
That you shall all repent the loss of mine.
I will be deaf to pleading and excuses,
195 Nor tears, nor prayers shall purchase out abuses,
Therefore use none. Let Romeo hence in haste,
Else, when he is found, that hour is his last.
Bear hence this body, and attend our will.
Mercy but murders, pardoning those that kill.

                                                 Exeunt.

3.2   *Enter* JULIET *alone.*

JULIET   Gallop apace, you fiery-footed steeds,
Towards Phoebus' lodging. Such a wagoner
As Phaeton would whip you to the west
And bring in cloudy night immediately.
5 Spread thy close curtain, love-performing night,
That runaways' eyes may wink, and Romeo
Leap to these arms, untalked of and unseen.
Lovers can see to do their amorous rites
By their own beauties; or, if love be blind,
10 It best agrees with night. Come, civil night,
Thou sober-suited matron all in black,
And learn me how to lose a winning match,
Played for a pair of stainless maidenhoods.
Hood my unmanned blood, bating in my cheeks,
15 With thy black mantle, till strange love grow bold,
Think true love acted simple modesty.
Come, night, come, Romeo, come, thou day in night,
For thou wilt lie upon the wings of night
Whiter than new snow upon a raven's back.
20 Come, gentle night, come, loving black-browed night,
Give me my Romeo, and when I shall die
Take him and cut him out in little stars,
And he will make the face of heaven so fine
That all the world will be in love with night
25 And pay no worship to the garish sun.
O, I have bought the mansion of a love
But not possessed it, and though I am sold,

Not yet enjoyed. So tedious is this day
As is the night before some festival
To an impatient child that hath new robes   30
And may not wear them.

Enter NURSE *wringing her hands, with the ladder*
of cords in her lap.

                              O, here comes my Nurse,
And she brings news, and every tongue that speaks
But Romeo's name speaks heavenly eloquence.
Now, Nurse, what news? What hast thou there, the cords
That Romeo bid thee fetch?

NURSE   Ay, ay, the cords.   35

JULIET
Ay me, what news? Why dost thou wring thy hands?

NURSE   Ah weraday, he's dead, he's dead, he's dead!
We are undone, lady, we are undone.
Alack the day, he's gone, he's killed, he's dead.

JULIET   Can heaven be so envious?

NURSE   Romeo can,   40
Though heaven cannot. O Romeo, Romeo,
Whoever would have thought it – Romeo!

JULIET   What devil are thou that dost torment me thus?
This torture should be roared in dismal hell.
Hath Romeo slain himself? Say thou but 'Ay',   45
And that bare vowel 'I' shall poison more
Than the death-darting eye of cockatrice.
I am not I if there be such an 'Ay',
Or those eyes shut that makes thee answer 'Ay'.
If he be slain, say 'Ay', or if not, 'No'.   50
Brief sounds determine of my weal or woe.

NURSE   I saw the wound, I saw it with mine eyes –
God save the mark – here on his manly breast,
A piteous corse, a bloody piteous corse,
Pale, pale as ashes, all bedaubed in blood,   55
All in gore-blood. I sounded at the sight.

JULIET
O break, my heart, poor bankrupt, break at once!
To prison, eyes, ne'er look on liberty.
Vile earth to earth resign, end motion here,
And thou and Romeo press one heavy bier.   60

NURSE   O Tybalt, Tybalt, the best friend I had!
O courteous Tybalt, honest gentleman,
That ever I should live to see thee dead!

JULIET   What storm is this that blows so contrary?
Is Romeo slaughtered and is Tybalt dead,   65
My dearest cousin and my dearer lord?
Then, dreadful trumpet, sound the general doom,
For who is living if those two are gone?

NURSE   Tybalt is gone and Romeo banished,
Romeo that killed him, he is banished.   70

JULIET
O God, did Romeo's hand shed Tybalt's blood?

NURSE   It did, it did, alas the day, it did.

JULIET   O serpent heart hid with a flowering face!
Did ever dragon keep so fair a cave?
Beautiful tyrant, fiend angelical,   75

Dove-feathered raven, wolvish-ravening lamb,
Despised substance of divinest show,
Just opposite to what thou justly seem'st,
A damned saint, an honourable villain.
80   O nature, what hadst thou to do in hell
When thou didst bower the spirit of a fiend
In mortal paradise of such sweet flesh?
Was ever book containing such vile matter
So fairly bound? O, that deceit should dwell
In such a gorgeous palace.

85   NURSE   There's no trust,
No faith, no honesty in men – all perjured,
All forsworn, all naught, all dissemblers.
Ah, where's my man? Give me some aqua vitae.
These griefs, these woes, these sorrows make me old.
Shame come to Romeo!

90   JULIET   Blistered be thy tongue
For such a wish! He was not born to shame;
Upon his brow shame is ashamed to sit
For 'tis a throne where honour may be crowned
Sole monarch of the universal earth.
95   O, what a beast was I to chide at him!

NURSE
Will you speak well of him that killed your cousin?

JULIET   Shall I speak ill of him that is my husband?
Ah, poor my lord, what tongue shall smooth thy name
When I, thy three-hours' wife, have mangled it?
100 But wherefore, villain, didst thou kill my cousin?
That villain cousin would have killed my husband.
Back, foolish tears, back to your native spring,
Your tributary drops belong to woe
Which you, mistaking, offer up to joy.
105 My husband lives that Tybalt would have slain,
And Tybalt's dead that would have slain my husband.
All this is comfort. Wherefore weep I then?
Some word there was, worser than Tybalt's death,
That murdered me. I would forget it fain,
110 But O, it presses to my memory
Like damned guilty deeds to sinners' minds.
Tybalt is dead and Romeo banished;
That 'banished', that one word 'banished'
Hath slain ten thousand Tybalts. Tybalt's death
115 Was woe enough, if it had ended there;
Or, if sour woe delights in fellowship
And needly will be ranked with other griefs,
Why followed not, when she said 'Tybalt's dead',
'Thy father', or 'thy mother', nay, or both,
120 Which modern lamentation might have moved?
But with a rearward following Tybalt's death,
'Romeo is banished' – to speak that word
Is father, mother, Tybalt, Romeo, Juliet,
All slain, all dead. 'Romeo is banished' –
125 There is no end, no limit, measure, bound,
In that word's death; no words can that woe sound.
Where is my father and my mother, Nurse?

NURSE   Weeping and wailing over Tybalt's corse.
Will you go to them? I will bring you thither.

JULIET
Wash they his wounds with tears? Mine shall be
   spent,   130
When theirs are dry, for Romeo's banishment.
Take up those cords. Poor ropes, you are beguiled,
Both you and I, for Romeo is exiled.
He made you for a highway to my bed,
But I, a maid, die maiden-widowed.   135
Come, cords, come, Nurse, I'll to my wedding bed
And death, not Romeo, take my maidenhead.

NURSE   Hie to your chamber. I'll find Romeo
To comfort you. I wot well where he is.
Hark ye, your Romeo will be here at night.   140
I'll to him; he is hid at Laurence' cell.

JULIET   O, find him, give this ring to my true knight
And bid him come to take his last farewell.   *Exeunt.*

3.3   *Enter* FRIAR LAURENCE.

FRIAR LAURENCE
Romeo, come forth, come forth, thou fearful man.
Affliction is enamoured of thy parts,
And thou art wedded to calamity.

                 Enter ROMEO.

ROMEO
Father, what news? What is the Prince's doom?
What sorrow craves acquaintance at my hand   5
That I yet know not?

FRIAR LAURENCE   Too familiar
Is my dear son with such sour company.
I bring thee tidings of the Prince's doom.

ROMEO
What less than doomsday is the Prince's doom?

FRIAR LAURENCE
A gentler judgement vanished from his lips: 10
Not body's death but body's banishment.

ROMEO   Ha, banishment? Be merciful, say 'death',
For exile hath more terror in his look,
Much more, than death. Do not say 'banishment'.

FRIAR LAURENCE
Hence from Verona art thou banished.   15
Be patient, for the world is broad and wide.

ROMEO   There is no world without Verona walls
But purgatory, torture, hell itself.
Hence banished is banished from the world,
And world's exile is death; then 'banished'   20
Is death mistermed. Calling death 'banished',
Thou cutt'st my head off with a golden axe
And smilest upon the stroke that murders me.

FRIAR LAURENCE
O deadly sin, O rude unthankfulness!
Thy fault our law calls death, but the kind Prince,   25
Taking thy part, hath rushed aside the law,
And turned that black word 'death' to banishment.
This is dear mercy, and thou seest it not.

ROMEO   'Tis torture and not mercy. Heaven is here

Where Juliet lives, and every cat and dog
And little mouse, every unworthy thing,
Live here in heaven and may look on her,
But Romeo may not. More validity,
More honourable state, more courtship lives
35 In carrion flies than Romeo. They may seize
On the white wonder of dear Juliet's hand
And steal immortal blessing from her lips,
Who even in pure and vestal modesty
Still blush, as thinking their own kisses sin.
40 But Romeo may not, he is banished.
Flies may do this, but I from this must fly;
They are free men, but I am banished:
And sayest thou yet that exile is not death?
Hadst thou no poison mixed, no sharp-ground knife,
45 No sudden mean of death, though ne'er so mean,
But 'banished' to kill me? Banished!
O Friar, the damned use that word in hell;
Howling attends it. How hast thou the heart,
Being a divine, a ghostly confessor,
0 A sin-absolver, and my friend professed,
To mangle me with that word 'banished'?
FRIAR LAURENCE
Thou fond mad man, hear me a little speak.
ROMEO   O, thou wilt speak again of banishment.
FRIAR LAURENCE
I'll give thee armour to keep off that word,
5 Adversity's sweet milk, philosophy,
To comfort thee though thou art banished
ROMEO   Yet banished? Hang up philosophy!
Unless philosophy can make a Juliet,
Displant a town, reverse a prince's doom,
0 It helps not, it prevails not. Talk no more.
FRIAR LAURENCE
O, then I see that mad men have no ears.
ROMEO
How should they, when that wise men have no eyes?
FRIAR LAURENCE
Let me dispute with thee of thy estate.
ROMEO
Thou canst not speak of that thou dost not feel.
5 Wert thou as young as I, Juliet thy love,
An hour but married, Tybalt murdered,
Doting like me and like me banished,
Then mightst thou speak, then mightst thou tear thy
    hair
And fall upon the ground as I do now,
0 Taking the measure of an unmade grave.   [*Falls.*]
    [*Nurse knocks within.*]
FRIAR LAURENCE
Arise, one knocks. Good Romeo, hide thyself.
ROMEO   Not I, unless the breath of heartsick groans
Mist-like infold me from the search of eyes.   [*Knock*]
FRIAR LAURENCE
Hark how they knock. – Who's there? – Romeo, arise,
Thou wilt be taken. – Stay awhile! – Stand up.
    [*Loud knock*]

30 Run to my study. – By and by! – God's will,
What simpleness is this? – I come, I come!   [*Knock*]
Who knocks so hard? Whence come you? What's
    your will?

    Enter NURSE.

NURSE
Let me come in and you shall know my errand.
I come from Lady Juliet.
FRIAR LAURENCE   Welcome then.   80
NURSE   O holy Friar, O, tell me, holy Friar,
Where is my lady's lord, where's Romeo?
FRIAR LAURENCE
There on the ground, with his own tears made drunk.
NURSE   O, he is even in my mistress' case,
Just in her case. O woeful sympathy,   85
Piteous predicament! Even so lies she,
Blubbering and weeping, weeping and blubbering.
Stand up, stand up, stand an you be a man.
For Juliet's sake, for her sake, rise and stand!
Why should you fall into so deep an O?   90
    [*Romeo rises.*]
ROMEO   Nurse –
NURSE   Ah, sir, ah, sir, death's the end of all.
ROMEO
Spakest thou of Juliet? How is it with her?
Doth not she think me an old murderer,
Now I have stained the childhood of our joy
With blood removed but little from her own?   95
Where is she, and how doth she, and what says
My concealed lady to our cancelled love?
NURSE   O, she says nothing, sir, but weeps and weeps,
And now falls on her bed, and then starts up,
And Tybalt calls, and then on Romeo cries,   100
And then down falls again.
ROMEO   As if that name,
Shot from the deadly level of a gun,
Did murder her, as that name's cursed hand
Murdered her kinsman. O, tell me, Friar, tell me,
In what vile part of this anatomy   105
Doth my name lodge? Tell me, that I may sack
The hateful mansion.
    [*He offers to stab himself, and Nurse snatches the
    dagger away.*]
FRIAR LAURENCE   Hold thy desperate hand!
Art thou a man? Thy form cries out thou art.
Thy tears are womanish, thy wild acts denote
The unreasonable fury of a beast.   110
Unseemly woman in a seeming man,
And ill-beseeming beast in seeming both!
Thou hast amazed me. By my holy order,
I thought thy disposition better tempered.
Hast thou slain Tybalt? Wilt thou slay thyself,   115
And slay thy lady that in thy life lives,
By doing damned hate upon thyself?
Why rail'st thou on thy birth, the heaven and earth,
Since birth, and heaven, and earth, all three do meet

120 In thee at once, which thou at once wouldst lose?
Fie, fie, thou sham'st thy shape, thy love, thy wit,
Which, like a usurer, abound'st in all,
And usest none in that true use indeed
Which should bedeck thy shape, thy love, thy wit.
125 Thy noble shape is but a form of wax,
Digressing from the valour of a man;
Thy dear love sworn but hollow perjury,
Killing that love which thou hast vowed to cherish;
Thy wit, that ornament to shape and love,
130 Misshapen in the conduct of them both,
Like powder in a skilless soldier's flask
Is set afire by thine own ignorance,
And thou dismembered with thine own defence.
What, rouse thee, man! Thy Juliet is alive,
135 For whose dear sake thou wast but lately dead:
There art thou happy. Tybalt would kill thee,
But thou slew'st Tybalt: there art thou happy.
The law that threatened death becomes thy friend
And turns it to exile: there art thou happy.
140 A pack of blessings light upon thy back,
Happiness courts thee in her best array,
But like a mishaved and sullen wench
Thou pouts upon thy fortune and thy love.
Take heed, take heed, for such die miserable.
145 Go, get thee to thy love as was decreed.
Ascend her chamber, hence, and comfort her,
But look thou stay not till the watch be set,
For then thou canst not pass to Mantua,
Where thou shalt live till we can find a time
150 To blaze your marriage, reconcile your friends,
Beg pardon of the Prince and call thee back
With twenty hundred thousand times more joy
Than thou went'st forth in lamentation.
Go before, Nurse. Commend me to thy lady
155 And bid her hasten all the house to bed,
Which heavy sorrow makes them apt unto.
Romeo is coming.
NURSE   O lord, I could have stayed here all the night
To hear good counsel. O, what learning is!
160 My lord, I'll tell my lady you will come.
ROMEO   Do so, and bid my sweet prepare to chide.
    [*Nurse offers to go in and turns again.*]
NURSE   Here, sir, a ring she bid me give you, sir.
Hie you, make haste, for it grows very late.   *Exit.*
ROMEO   How well my comfort is revived by this.
FRIAR LAURENCE
165 Go hence, good night, and here stands all your state:
Either be gone before the watch be set,
Or by the break of day disguised from hence.
Sojourn in Mantua. I'll find out your man,
And he shall signify from time to time
170 Every good hap to you that chances here.
Give me thy hand. 'Tis late. Farewell. Good night.
ROMEO   But that a joy past joy calls out on me,
It were a grief so brief to part with thee.
Farewell.   *Exeunt severally.*

3.4   *Enter old* CAPULET, *his* WIFE *and* PARIS.

CAPULET   Things have fallen out, sir, so unluckily,
That we have had no time to move our daughter.
Look you, she loved her kinsman Tybalt dearly,
And so did I. Well, we were born to die.
5 'Tis very late; she'll not come down tonight.
I promise you, but for your company
I would have been abed an hour ago.
PARIS   These times of woe afford no times to woo.
Madam, good night; commend me to your daughter.
CAPULET'S WIFE
10 I will, and know her mind early tomorrow.
Tonight she's mewed up to her heaviness.
    [*Paris offers to go in and Capulet calls him again.*]
CAPULET   Sir Paris, I will make a desperate tender
Of my child's love. I think she will be ruled
In all respects by me; nay, more, I doubt it not.
15 Wife, go you to her ere you go to bed,
Acquaint her here of my son Paris' love,
And bid her, mark you me, on Wednesday next –
But soft, what day is this?
PARIS   Monday, my lord.
CAPULET
Monday! Ha, ha. Well, Wednesday is too soon.
20 A' Thursday let it be, a' Thursday, tell her,
She shall be married to this noble earl.
Will you be ready? Do you like this haste?
We'll keep no great ado, a friend or two,
For, hark you, Tybalt being slain so late,
25 It may be thought we held him carelessly,
Being our kinsman, if we revel much.
Therefore we'll have some half a dozen friends
And there an end. But what say you to Thursday?
PARIS
My lord, I would that Thursday were tomorrow.
CAPULET   Well, get you gone, a' Thursday be it then.   30
Go you to Juliet ere you go to bed;
Prepare her, wife, against this wedding day.
Farewell, my lord. Light to my chamber, ho!
Afore me, it is so very late that we
May call it early by and by. Good night.   *Exeunt.*   35

3.5   *Enter* ROMEO *and* JULIET *aloft at the window.*

JULIET   Wilt thou be gone? It is not yet near day.
It was the nightingale, and not the lark,
That pierced the fearful hollow of thine ear.
Nightly she sings on yond pomegranate tree.
5 Believe me, love, it was the nightingale.
ROMEO   It was the lark, the herald of the morn,
No nightingale. Look, love, what envious streaks
Do lace the severing clouds in yonder east.
Night's candles are burnt out, and jocund day
10 Stands tiptoe on the misty mountain tops.
I must be gone and live, or stay and die.
JULIET   Yond light is not daylight; I know it, I.

It is some meteor that the sun exhales
To be to thee this night a torchbearer
And light thee on thy way to Mantua.
Therefore stay yet; thou need'st not to be gone.
ROMEO   Let me be ta'en, let me be put to death.
I am content so thou wilt have it so.
I'll say yon grey is not the morning's eye,
'Tis but the pale reflex of Cynthia's brow;
Nor that is not the lark whose notes do beat
The vaulty heaven so high above our heads.
I have more care to stay than will to go.
Come, death, and welcome! Juliet wills it so.
How is't, my soul? Let's talk; it is not day.
JULIET   It is, it is! Hie hence, be gone, away!
It is the lark that sings so out of tune,
Straining harsh discords and unpleasing sharps.
Some say the lark makes sweet division;
This doth not so, for she divideth us.
Some say the lark and loathed toad change eyes.
O, now I would they had changed voices too,
Since arm from arm that voice doth us affray,
Hunting thee hence with hunt's-up to the day.
O, now be gone! More light and light it grows.
ROMEO
More light and light, more dark and dark our woes.

Enter NURSE *hastily.*

NURSE   Madam!
JULIET   Nurse?
NURSE   Your lady mother is coming to your chamber.
The day is broke. Be wary, look about.   *Exit.*
JULIET   Then, window, let day in and let life out.
ROMEO   Farewell, farewell. One kiss, and I'll descend.
   [*He goeth down.*]
JULIET
Art thou gone so, love, lord, ay husband, friend?
I must hear from thee every day in the hour,
For in a minute there are many days.
O, by this count I shall be much in years
Ere I again behold my Romeo.
ROMEO   Farewell.
I will omit no opportunity
That may convey my greetings, love, to thee.
JULIET   O, think'st thou we shall ever meet again?
ROMEO   I doubt it not, and all these woes shall serve
For sweet discourses in our times to come.
JULIET   O God, I have an ill-divining soul!
Methinks I see thee now, thou art so low,
As one dead in the bottom of a tomb.
Either my eyesight fails, or thou look'st pale.
ROMEO   And trust me, love, in my eye so do you.
Dry sorrow drinks our blood. Adieu, adieu!   *Exit.*
JULIET   O Fortune, Fortune, all men call thee fickle.
If thou art fickle, what dost thou with him
That is renowned for faith? Be fickle, Fortune,
For then I hope thou wilt not keep him long,
But send him back.

Enter CAPULET'S WIFE *from within.*

CAPULET'S WIFE   Ho, daughter, are you up?
JULIET   Who is't that calls? It is my lady mother.
Is she not down so late, or up so early?
What unaccustomed cause procures her hither?
   [*She goes down from the window.*]
CAPULET'S WIFE   Why, how now, Juliet?
JULIET   Madam, I am not well.
CAPULET'S WIFE
Evermore weeping for your cousin's death?
What, wilt thou wash him from his grave with tears?
An if thou couldst, thou couldst not make him live;
Therefore have done. Some grief shows much of love,
But much of grief shows still some want of wit.
JULIET   Yet let me weep for such a feeling loss.
CAPULET'S WIFE
So shall you feel the loss, but not the friend
Which you weep for.
JULIET   Feeling so the loss,
I cannot choose but ever weep the friend.
CAPULET'S WIFE
Well, girl, thou weep'st not so much for his death
As that the villain lives which slaughtered him.
JULIET   What villain, madam?
CAPULET'S WIFE   That same villain Romeo.
JULIET [*aside*]   Villain and he be many miles asunder.
– God pardon him! I do, with all my heart,
And yet no man like he doth grieve my heart.
CAPULET'S WIFE
That is because the traitor murderer lives.
JULIET   Ay, madam, from the reach of these my hands.
Would none but I might venge my cousin's death!
CAPULET'S WIFE
We will have vengeance for it, fear thou not.
Then weep no more. I'll send to one in Mantua,
Where that same banished runagate doth live,
Shall give him such an unaccustomed dram
That he shall soon keep Tybalt company;
And then I hope thou wilt be satisfied.
JULIET   Indeed, I never shall be satisfied
With Romeo till I behold him. Dead –
Is my poor heart so for a kinsman vexed.
Madam, if you could find out but a man
To bear a poison, I would temper it,
That Romeo should, upon receipt thereof,
Soon sleep in quiet. O, how my heart abhors
To hear him named and cannot come to him,
To wreak the love I bore my cousin
Upon his body that hath slaughtered him.
CAPULET'S WIFE
Find thou the means and I'll find such a man.
But now I'll tell thee joyful tidings, girl.
JULIET   And joy comes well in such a needy time.
What are they, beseech your ladyship?
CAPULET'S WIFE
Well, well, thou hast a careful father, child,

One who, to put thee from thy heaviness,
Hath sorted out a sudden day of joy
110   That thou expects not, nor I looked not for.
JULIET   Madam, in happy time; what day is that?
CAPULET'S WIFE
Marry, my child, early next Thursday morn,
The gallant, young and noble gentleman,
The County Paris, at Saint Peter's church
115   Shall happily make thee there a joyful bride.
JULIET   Now by Saint Peter's church and Peter too,
He shall not make me there a joyful bride!
I wonder at this haste, that I must wed
Ere he that should be husband comes to woo.
120   I pray you tell my lord and father, madam,
I will not marry yet; and when I do, I swear
It shall be Romeo, whom you know I hate,
Rather than Paris. These are news indeed!
CAPULET'S WIFE
Here comes your father; tell him so yourself,
125   And see how he will take it at your hands.

            Enter CAPULET *and* NURSE.

CAPULET
When the sun sets, the earth doth drizzle dew,
But for the sunset of my brother's son
It rains downright.
How now, a conduit, girl? What, still in tears,
130   Evermore showering? In one little body
Thou counterfeits a bark, a sea, a wind,
For still thy eyes, which I may call the sea,
Do ebb and flow with tears. The bark thy body is,
Sailing in this salt flood; the winds thy sighs,
135   Who, raging with thy tears and they with them,
Without a sudden calm will overset
Thy tempest-tossed body. How now, wife,
Have you delivered to her our decree?
CAPULET'S WIFE
Ay, sir, but she will none, she gives you thanks.
140   I would the fool were married to her grave.
CAPULET
Soft, take me with you, take me with you, wife.
How will she none? Doth she not give us thanks?
Is she not proud? Doth she not count her blessed,
Unworthy as she is, that we have wrought
145   So worthy a gentleman to be her bride?
JULIET
Not proud you have, but thankful that you have.
Proud can I never be of what I hate,
But thankful even for hate that is meant love.
CAPULET
How, how, how, how, chopped logic? What is this?
150   'Proud' and 'I thank you', and 'I thank you not',
And yet 'not proud'? Mistress minion, you,
Thank me no thankings nor proud me no prouds,
But fettle your fine joints 'gainst Thursday next
To go with Paris to Saint Peter's church,
155   Or I will drag thee on a hurdle thither.

Out, you green-sickness carrion! Out, you baggage,
You tallow-face!
CAPULET'S WIFE   Fie, fie, what, are you mad?
JULIET   Good father, I beseech you on my knees,
Hear me with patience but to speak a word.
     [*She kneels down.*]
CAPULET
Hang thee, young baggage, disobedient wretch!   160
I tell thee what: get thee to church a' Thursday
Or never after look me in the face.
Speak not, reply not, do not answer me.
My fingers itch. Wife, we scarce thought us blessed
That God had lent us but this only child,   165
But now I see this one is one too much,
And that we have a curse in having her.
Out on her, hilding!
NURSE   God in heaven bless her!
You are to blame, my lord, to rate her so.
CAPULET
And why, my Lady Wisdom? Hold your tongue,   170
Good Prudence, smatter with your gossips, go.
NURSE   I speak no treason.
CAPULET   O, Godgigoden!
NURSE   May not one speak?
CAPULET   Peace, you mumbling fool!
Utter your gravity o'er a gossip's bowl,
For here we need it not.
CAPULET'S WIFE   You are too hot.   175
CAPULET   God's bread, it makes me mad.
Day, night, hour, tide, time, work, play,
Alone, in company, still my care hath been
To have her matched; and having now provided
A gentleman of noble parentage,   180
Of fair demesnes, youthful and nobly ligned,
Stuffed, as they say, with honourable parts,
Proportioned as one's thought would wish a man,
And then to have a wretched puling fool,
A whining mammet, in her fortune's tender,   185
To answer 'I'll not wed, I cannot love,
I am too young, I pray you pardon me'.
But an you will not wed, I'll pardon you!
Graze where you will, you shall not house with me.
Look to't, think on't; I do not use to jest.   190
Thursday is near. Lay hand on heart, advise.
An you be mine, I'll give you to my friend;
An you be not, hang, beg, starve, die in the streets,
For, by my soul, I'll ne'er acknowledge thee,
Nor what is mine shall never do thee good.   195
Trust to't, bethink you; I'll not be forsworn.   *Exit.*
JULIET   Is there no pity sitting in the clouds
That sees into the bottom of my grief?
O sweet my mother, cast me not away!
Delay this marriage for a month, a week,   200
Or if you do not, make the bridal bed
In that dim monument where Tybalt lies.
CAPULET'S WIFE
Talk not to me, for I'll not speak a word,

Do as thou wilt, for I have done with thee.   *Exit.*

205   JULIET   O God! O Nurse, how shall this be prevented?
My husband is on earth, my faith in heaven.
How shall that faith return again to earth,
Unless that husband send it me from heaven
By leaving earth? Comfort me, counsel me.
210   Alack, alack, that heaven should practise stratagems
Upon so soft a subject as myself.
What sayst thou? Hast thou not a word of joy?
Some comfort, Nurse.

NURSE   Faith, here it is.
Romeo is banished, and all the world to nothing
215   That he dares ne'er come back to challenge you;
Or if he do, it needs must be by stealth.
Then, since the case so stands as now it doth,
I think it best you married with the County.
O, he's a lovely gentleman!
220   Romeo's a dishclout to him. An eagle, madam
Hath not so green, so quick, so fair an eye
As Paris hath. Beshrew my very heart,
I think you are happy in this second match,
For it excels your first; or if it did not,
225   Your first is dead, or 'twere as good he were
As living here and you no use of him.

JULIET   Speak'st thou from thy heart?

NURSE   And from my soul too, else beshrew them both.

JULIET   Amen.

230   NURSE   What?

JULIET
Well, thou hast comforted me marvellous much.
Go in, and tell my lady I am gone,
Having displeased my father, to Laurence' cell,
To make confession and to be absolved.

235   NURSE   Marry, I will, and this is wisely done.   *Exit.*
[*Juliet looks after Nurse.*]

JULIET   Ancient damnation! O most wicked fiend!
Is it more sin to wish me thus forsworn,
Or to dispraise my lord with that same tongue
Which she hath praised him with above compare
240   So many thousand times? Go, counsellor,
Thou and my bosom henceforth shall be twain.
I'll to the Friar to know his remedy.
If all else fail, myself have power to die.   *Exit.*

4.1   *Enter* FRIAR LAURENCE *and*
County PARIS.

FRIAR LAURENCE
On Thursday, sir? The time is very short.

PARIS   My father Capulet will have it so,
And I am nothing slow to slack his haste.

FRIAR LAURENCE
You say you do not know the lady's mind?
Uneven is the course; I like it not.

PARIS   Immoderately she weeps for Tybalt's death,
And therefore have I little talked of love,
For Venus smiles not in a house of tears.

Now, sir, her father counts it dangerous
That she do give her sorrow so much sway,   10
And in his wisdom hastes our marriage
To stop the inundation of her tears,
Which, too much minded by herself alone,
May be put from her by society.
Now do you know the reason of this haste.   15

FRIAR LAURENCE [*aside*]
I would I knew not why it should be slowed.
– Look, sir, here comes the lady toward my cell.

Enter JULIET.

PARIS   Happily met, my lady and my wife.

JULIET   That may be, sir, when I may be a wife.

PARIS   That may be must be, love, on Thursday next.   20

JULIET   What must be shall be.

FRIAR LAURENCE   That's a certain text.

PARIS   Come you to make confession to this father?

JULIET   To answer that, I should confess to you.

PARIS   Do not deny to him that you love me.

JULIET   I will confess to you that I love him.   25

PARIS   So will ye, I am sure, that you love me.

JULIET   If I do so, it will be of more price
Being spoke behind your back than to your face.

PARIS   Poor soul, thy face is much abused with tears.

JULIET   The tears have got small victory by that,   30
For it was bad enough before their spite.

PARIS
Thou wrong'st it more than tears with that report.

JULIET   That is no slander, sir, which is a truth,
And what I spake, I spake it to my face.

PARIS   Thy face is mine, and thou hast slandered it.   35

JULIET   It may be so, for it is not mine own.
Are you at leisure, holy father, now,
Or shall I come to you at evening mass?

FRIAR LAURENCE
My leisure serves me, pensive daughter, now.
My lord, we must entreat the time alone.   40

PARIS   God shield I should disturb devotion!
Juliet, on Thursday early will I rouse ye;
Till then, adieu, and keep this holy kiss.   *Exit.*

JULIET   O, shut the door, and when thou hast done so,
Come weep with me, past hope, past cure, past help.   45

FRIAR LAURENCE   O Juliet, I already know thy grief;
It strains me past the compass of my wits.
I hear thou must, and nothing may prorogue it,
On Thursday next be married to this County.

JULIET   Tell me not, Friar, that thou hearest of this,   50
Unless thou tell me how I may prevent it.
If in thy wisdom thou canst give no help,
Do thou but call my resolution wise,
[*showing her knife*]
And with this knife I'll help it presently.
God joined my heart and Romeo's, thou our hands;   55
And ere this hand, by thee to Romeo's sealed,
Shall be the label to another deed,

Or my true heart with treacherous revolt
Turn to another, this shall slay them both.
60 Therefore, out of thy long-experienced time
Give me some present counsel, or behold,
'Twixt my extremes and me this bloody knife
Shall play the umpire, arbitrating that
Which the commission of thy years and art
65 Could to no issue of true honour bring.
Be not so long to speak. I long to die,
If what thou speak'st speak not of remedy.

FRIAR LAURENCE
Hold, daughter, I do spy a kind of hope,
Which craves as desperate an execution
70 As that is desperate which we would prevent.
If rather than to marry County Paris
Thou hast the strength of will to slay thyself,
Then is it likely thou wilt undertake
A thing like death to chide away this shame,
75 That cop'st with death himself to scape from it;
An if thou dar'st, I'll give thee remedy.

JULIET   O bid me leap, rather than marry Paris,
From off the battlements of any tower,
Or walk in thievish ways, or bid me lurk
80 Where serpents are. Chain me with roaring bears,
Or hide me nightly in a charnel-house,
O'ercovered quite with dead men's rattling bones,
With reeky shanks and yellow chapless skulls;
Or bid me go into a new-made grave,
85 And hide me with a dead man in his shroud,
Things that, to hear them told, have made me tremble,
And I will do it without fear or doubt,
To live an unstained wife to my sweet love.

FRIAR LAURENCE
Hold then: go home, be merry, give consent
90 To marry Paris. Wednesday is tomorrow.
Tomorrow night look that thou lie alone.
Let not the Nurse lie with thee in thy chamber.
Take thou this vial, being then in bed,
And this distilling liquor drink thou off,
95 When presently through all thy veins shall run
A cold and drowsy humour, for no pulse
Shall keep his native progress, but surcease.
No warmth, no breath, shall testify thou livest.
The roses in thy lips and cheeks shall fade
100 To wanny ashes, thy eyes' windows fall
Like death, when he shuts up the day of life.
Each part, deprived of supple government,
Shall stiff and stark and cold appear like death,
And in this borrowed likeness of shrunk death
105 Thou shalt continue two-and-forty hours,
And then awake as from a pleasant sleep.
Now, when the bridegroom in the morning comes
To rouse thee from thy bed, there art thou dead.
Then, as the manner of our country is,
110 In thy best robes, uncovered on the bier,
Thou shalt be borne to that same ancient vault
Where all the kindred of the Capulets lie.

In the meantime, against thou shalt awake,
Shall Romeo by my letters know our drift,
And hither shall he come. And he and I   115
Will watch thy waking, and that very night
Shall Romeo bear thee hence to Mantua.
And this shall free thee from this present shame,
If no inconstant toy nor womanish fear
Abate thy valour in the acting it.   120

JULIET   Give me, give me, O, tell not me of fear!
FRIAR LAURENCE
Hold! Get you gone, be strong and prosperous
In this resolve; I'll send a friar with speed
To Mantua, with my letters to thy lord.

JULIET
Love give me strength, and strength shall help afford. 125
Farewell, dear father.   *Exeunt.*

4.2   *Enter* Father CAPULET, CAPULET'S WIFE,
        NURSE *and* Servingmen, *two or three.*

CAPULET   So many guests invite as here are writ.
                                        Exit Servingman.
Sirrah, go hire me twenty cunning cooks.
SERVINGMAN   You shall have none ill, sir, for I'll try if
they can lick their fingers.
CAPULET   How canst thou try them so?   5
SERVINGMAN   Marry, sir, 'tis an ill cook that cannot lick
his own fingers; therefore, he that cannot lick his
fingers goes not with me.
CAPULET   Go, be gone.   *Exeunt Servingmen.*
We shall be much unfurnished for this time.   10
What, is my daughter gone to Friar Laurence?
NURSE   Ay, forsooth.
CAPULET
Well, he may chance to do some good on her.
A peevish self-willed harlotry it is.

                   Enter JULIET.

NURSE
See where she comes from shrift with merry look.   15
CAPULET
How now, my headstrong, where have you been
gadding?
JULIET   Where I have learnt me to repent the sin
Of disobedient opposition
To you and your behests, and am enjoined
By holy Laurence to fall prostrate here   20
To beg your pardon. Pardon, I beseech you;
Henceforward I am ever ruled by you.
        [*She kneels down.*]
CAPULET   Send for the County, go tell him of this.
I'll have this knot knit up tomorrow morning.
JULIET   I met the youthful lord at Laurence' cell   25
And gave him what becomed love I might,
Not stepping o'er the bounds of modesty.
CAPULET   Why, I am glad on't, this is well. Stand up;
This is as't should be. Let me see – the County!

30   Ay, marry, go, I say, and fetch him hither.
    Now, afore God, this reverend holy friar,
    All our whole city is much bound to him.
    JULIET   Nurse, will you go with me into my closet,
    To help me sort such needful ornaments
35   As you think fit to furnish me tomorrow?
    CAPULET'S WIFE
    No, not till Thursday; there is time enough.
    CAPULET
    Go, Nurse, go with her; we'll to church tomorrow.
                     Exeunt Juliet and Nurse.
    CAPULET'S WIFE   We shall be short in our provision.
    'Tis now near night.
    CAPULET   Tush, I will stir about,
40   And all things shall be well, I warrant thee, wife.
    Go thou to Juliet, help to deck up her.
    I'll not to bed tonight. Let me alone,
    I'll play the housewife for this once.
                    Exit Capulet's Wife.
                            What, ho!
    They are all forth. Well, I will walk myself
45   To County Paris to prepare up him
    Against tomorrow. My heart is wondrous light
    Since this same wayward girl is so reclaimed.   *Exit.*

4.3   *Enter* JULIET *and* NURSE.

    JULIET   Ay, those attires are best. But, gentle Nurse,
    I pray thee leave me to myself tonight,
    For I have need of many orisons
    To move the heavens to smile upon my state,
5   Which, well thou knowest, is cross and full of sin.

           Enter CAPULET'S WIFE.

    CAPULET'S WIFE
    What, are you busy, ho? Need you my help?
    JULIET   No, madam, we have culled such necessaries
    As are behoveful for our state tomorrow.
    So please you, let me now be left alone,
10   And let the Nurse this night sit up with you,
    For I am sure you have your hands full all
    In this so sudden business.
    CAPULET'S WIFE   Good night.
    Get thee to bed and rest, for thou hast need.
    JULIET
    Farewell.   *Exeunt Capulet's Wife and Nurse.*
          God knows when we shall meet again.
15   I have a faint cold fear thrills through my veins,
    That almost freezes up the heat of life.
    I'll call them back again to comfort me.
    Nurse! – What should she do here?
    My dismal scene I needs must act alone.
20   Come, vial.
    What if this mixture do not work at all?
    Shall I be married then tomorrow morning?
    No, no! This shall forbid it. Lie thou there.
        [Lays down a knife.]

    What if it be a poison which the Friar
25   Subtly hath ministered to have me dead,
    Lest in this marriage he should be dishonoured,
    Because he married me before to Romeo?
    I fear it is, and yet methinks it should not,
    For he hath still been tried a holy man.
30   How if, when I am laid into the tomb,
    I wake before the time that Romeo
    Come to redeem me? There's a fearful point.
    Shall I not then be stifled in the vault,
    To whose foul mouth no healthsome air breathes
    in,
35   And there die strangled ere my Romeo comes?
    Or if I live, is it not very like
    The horrible conceit of death and night,
    Together with the terror of the place,
    As in a vault, an ancient receptacle
40   Where for this many hundred years the bones
    Of all my buried ancestors are packed,
    Where bloody Tybalt, yet but green in earth,
    Lies festering in his shroud, where, as they say,
    At some hours in the night spirits resort –
45   Alack, alack, is it not like that I,
    So early waking, what with loathsome smells,
    And shrieks like mandrakes torn out of the earth,
    That living mortals, hearing them, run mad –
    O, if I wake, shall I not be distraught,
50   Environed with all these hideous fears,
    And madly play with my forefathers' joints,
    And pluck the mangled Tybalt from his shroud
    And, in this rage, with some great kinsman's bone,
    As with a club, dash out my desperate brains?
55   O, look, methinks I see my cousin's ghost
    Seeking out Romeo that did spit his body
    Upon a rapier's point. Stay, Tybalt, stay!
    Romeo, Romeo, Romeo, here's drink. I drink to thee.
        [She falls upon her bed within the curtains.]

4.4   *Enter* CAPULET'S WIFE *and*
               NURSE *with herbs.*

    CAPULET'S WIFE
    Hold, take these keys and fetch more spices, Nurse.
    NURSE   They call for dates and quinces in the pastry.

            Enter CAPULET.

    CAPULET
    Come, stir, stir, stir. The second cock hath crowed,
    The curfew bell hath rung, 'tis three o'clock.
5   Look to the baked meats, good Angelica;
    Spare not for cost.
    NURSE   Go, you cotquean, go,
    Get you to bed. Faith, you'll be sick tomorrow
    For this night's watching.
    CAPULET
    No, not a whit. What, I have watched ere now
10   All night for lesser cause, and ne'er been sick.

CAPULET'S WIFE
Ay, you have been a mouse-hunt in your time,
But I will watch you from such watching now.

Exeunt Capulet's Wife and Nurse.

CAPULET A jealous-hood, a jealous-hood!

Enter three or four with spits and logs and baskets.

Now, fellow, what is there?

1 SERVINGMAN
Things for the cook, sir, but I know not what.

CAPULET
Make haste, make haste. *Exit 1 Servingman.*

15 Sirrah, fetch drier logs.
Call Peter; he will show thee where they are.

2 SERVINGMAN
I have a head, sir, that will find out logs
And never trouble Peter for the matter.

CAPULET Mass, and well said! A merry whoreson, ha!
Thou shalt be loggerhead. *Exit 2 Servingman.*

20 Good faith, 'tis day!
The County will be here with music straight,
For so he said he would. [*Play music.*]
I hear him near.
Nurse! Wife! What, ho! What, Nurse, I say!

Enter NURSE.

Go waken Juliet; go and trim her up.
25 I'll go and chat with Paris. Hie, make haste,
Make haste. The bridegroom, he is come already.
Make haste, I say. *Exeunt Capulet and Servingmen.*

4.5

NURSE [*Goes to curtains.*]
Mistress, what, mistress! Juliet! Fast, I warrant her,
she –
Why, lamb, why, lady! Fie, you slug-a-bed!
Why, love, I say! Madam! Sweetheart! Why, bride!
What, not a word? You take your pennyworths now.
5 Sleep for a week, for the next night, I warrant,
The County Paris hath set up his rest
That you shall rest but little. God forgive me,
Marry and amen. How sound is she asleep.
I needs must wake her. Madam, madam, madam!
10 Ay, let the County take you in your bed.
He'll fright you up, i'faith. Will it not be?
What, dressed, and in your clothes, and down again?
I must needs wake you. Lady, lady, lady!
Alas, alas, help, help! My lady's dead!
15 O weraday that ever I was born!
Some aqua vitae, ho! My lord, my lady!

Enter CAPULET'S WIFE.

CAPULET'S WIFE What noise is here?

NURSE O lamentable day!

CAPULET'S WIFE What is the matter?

NURSE Look, look! O heavy day!

CAPULET'S WIFE O me, O me, my child, my only life!
Revive, look up, or I will die with thee. 20
Help, help, call help!

Enter CAPULET.

CAPULET
For shame, bring Juliet forth; her lord is come.

NURSE
She's dead, deceased, she's dead, alack the day!

CAPULET'S WIFE
Alack the day, she's dead, she's dead, she's dead.

CAPULET Ha, let me see her. Out, alas, she's cold. 25
Her blood is settled and her joints are stiff.
Life and these lips have long been separated.
Death lies on her like an untimely frost
Upon the sweetest flower of all the field.

NURSE O lamentable day!

CAPULET'S WIFE O woeful time! 30

CAPULET
Death that hath ta'en her hence to make me wail,
Ties up my tongue and will not let me speak.

Enter FRIAR LAURENCE and the County PARIS.

FRIAR LAURENCE
Come, is the bride ready to go to church?

CAPULET Ready to go, but never to return.
O son, the night before thy wedding day 35
Hath death lain with thy wife. There she lies,
Flower as she was, deflowered by him.
Death is my son-in-law, death is my heir,
My daughter he hath wedded. I will die
And leave him all; life, living, all is death's. 40

PARIS Have I thought long to see this morning's face,
And doth it give me such a sight as this?

CAPULET'S WIFE
Accursed, unhappy, wretched, hateful day!
Most miserable hour that e'er time saw
In lasting labour of his pilgrimage! 45
But one, poor one, one poor and loving child,
But one thing to rejoice and solace in,
And cruel death hath catched it from my sight.

[*All at once cry out and wring their hands.*]

NURSE O woe, O woeful, woeful, woeful day!
Most lamentable day, most woeful day 50
That ever, ever I did yet behold!
O day, O day, O day, O hateful day!
Never was seen so black a day as this.
O woeful day, O woeful day!

PARIS Beguiled, divorced, wronged, spited, slain! 55
Most detestable death, by thee beguiled,
By cruel, cruel thee quite overthrown.
O love, O life, not life but love in death.

CAPULET
Despised, distressed, hated, martyred, killed!
Uncomfortable time, why cam'st thou now 60
To murder, murder our solemnity?
O child, O child, my soul and not my child!

Dead art thou, alack, my child is dead,
And with my child my joys are buried.

FRIAR LAURENCE
Peace, ho, for shame! Confusion's cure lives not
In these confusions. Heaven and yourself
Had part in this fair maid; now heaven hath all,
And all the better is it for the maid.
Your part in her you could not keep from death,
But heaven keeps his part in eternal life.
The most you sought was her promotion,
For 'twas your heaven she should be advanced.
And weep ye now, seeing she is advanced
Above the clouds, as high as heaven itself?
O, in this love you love your child so ill
That you run mad seeing that she is well.
She's not well married that lives married long,
But she's best married that dies married young.
Dry up your tears, and stick your rosemary
On this fair corse, and, as the custom is,
And in her best array, bear her to church;
For though fond nature bids us all lament,
Yet nature's tears are reason's merriment.

CAPULET   All things that we ordained festival
Turn from their office to black funeral:
Our instruments to melancholy bells,
Our wedding cheer to a sad burial feast,
Our solemn hymns to sullen dirges change;
Our bridal flowers serve for a buried corse,
And all things change them to the contrary.

FRIAR LAURENCE
Sir, go you in and, madam, go with him.
And go, Sir Paris. Everyone prepare
To follow this fair corse unto her grave.
The heavens do lour upon you for some ill;
Move them no more by crossing their high will.

They all but the Nurse go forth, casting rosemary on
Juliet and shutting the curtains.

Enter Musicians.

1 MUSICIAN
Faith, we may put up our pipes and be gone.

NURSE   Honest good fellows, ah, put up, put up,
For well you know this is a pitiful case.

1 MUSICIAN
Ay, by my troth, the case may be amended.

Exit Nurse. Musicians make to leave.

Enter PETER.

PETER   Musicians, O musicians, 'Heart's ease', 'Heart's
ease'! O, an you will have me live, play 'Heart's ease'.

1 MUSICIAN   Why 'Heart's ease'?

PETER   O musicians, because my heart itself plays 'My
heart is full'. O, play me some merry dump to comfort
me.

MUSICIANS   Not a dump we! 'Tis no time to play now.

PETER   You will not then?

1 MUSICIAN   No.

PETER   I will then give it you soundly.

1 MUSICIAN   What will you give us?   110

PETER   No money, on my faith, but the gleek. I will give
you the minstrel.

1 MUSICIAN   Then will I give you the serving-creature.

PETER   Then will I lay the serving-creature's dagger on
your pate. I will carry no crotchets. I'll re you, I'll fa   115
you. Do you note me?

1 MUSICIAN   An you re us and fa us, you note us.

2 MUSICIAN   Pray you put up your dagger and put out
your wit.

PETER   Then have at you with my wit! I will dry-beat   120
you with an iron wit and put up my iron dagger.
Answer me like men.

    When griping griefs the heart doth wound
    And doleful dumps the mind oppress,
    Then music with her silver sound –   125

Why 'silver sound'? Why 'music with her silver
sound'? What say you, Simon Catling?

1 MUSICIAN   Marry, sir, because silver hath a sweet
sound.

PETER   Prates! What say you, Hugh Rebeck?   130

2 MUSICIAN   I say 'silver sound', because musicians
sound for silver.

PETER   Prates too! What say you, James Soundpost?

3 MUSICIAN   Faith, I know not what to say.

PETER   O, I cry you mercy! You are the singer. I will say   135
for you. It is 'music with her silver sound' because
musicians have no gold for sounding.

    Then music with her silver sound
    With speedy help doth lend redress.   *Exit.*

1 MUSICIAN   What a pestilent knave is this same!   140

2 MUSICIAN   Hang him, jack! Come, we'll in here, tarry
for the mourners, and stay dinner.   *Exeunt.*

5.1   *Enter* ROMEO.

ROMEO   If I may trust the flattering truth of sleep,
My dreams presage some joyful news at hand.
My bosom's lord sits lightly in his throne,
And all this day an unaccustomed spirit
Lifts me above the ground with cheerful thoughts.   5
I dreamt my lady came and found me dead –
Strange dream that gives a dead man leave to think –
And breathed such life with kisses in my lips
That I revived and was an emperor.
Ah me, how sweet is love itself possessed,   10
When but love's shadows are so rich in joy.

Enter BALTHASAR, *Romeo's man, booted.*

News from Verona! How now, Balthasar,
Dost thou not bring me letters from the Friar?
How doth my lady? Is my father well?
How doth my Juliet? That I ask again,   15
For nothing can be ill if she be well.

BALTHASAR   Then she is well and nothing can be ill.
Her body sleeps in Capel's monument,

And her immortal part with angels lives.
20 I saw her laid low in her kindred's vault,
And presently took post to tell it you.
O, pardon me for bringing these ill news,
Since you did leave it for my office, sir.
ROMEO   Is it e'en so? Then I defy you, stars.
25 Thou knowest my lodging. Get me ink and paper,
And hire post-horses. I will hence tonight.
BALTHASAR   I do beseech you, sir, have patience.
Your looks are pale and wild, and do import
Some misadventure.
ROMEO   Tush, thou art deceived.
30 Leave me, and do the thing I bid thee do.
Hast thou no letters to me from the Friar?
BALTHASAR   No, my good lord.
ROMEO   No matter. Get thee gone,
And hire those horses. I'll be with thee straight.
                                        Exit Balthasar.
Well, Juliet, I will lie with thee tonight.
35 Let's see for means. O mischief, thou art swift
To enter in the thoughts of desperate men.
I do remember an apothecary,
And hereabouts 'a dwells, which late I noted,
In tattered weeds, with overwhelming brows,
40 Culling of simples. Meagre were his looks,
Sharp misery had worn him to the bones,
And in his needy shop a tortoise hung,
An alligator stuffed, and other skins
Of ill-shaped fishes; and about his shelves
45 A beggarly account of empty boxes,
Green earthen pots, bladders and musty seeds,
Remnants of packthread and old cakes of roses
Were thinly scattered to make up a show.
Noting this penury, to myself I said
50 'An if a man did need a poison now,
Whose sale is present death in Mantua,
Here lives a caitiff wretch would sell it him'.
O, this same thought did but forerun my need,
And this same needy man must sell it me.
55 As I remember, this should be the house.
Being holiday, the beggar's shop is shut.
What, ho, apothecary!

                    Enter Apothecary.

APOTHECARY   Who calls so loud?
ROMEO   Come hither, man. I see that thou art poor.
Hold, there is forty ducats. Let me have
60 A dram of poison, such soon-speeding gear
As will disperse itself through all the veins,
That the life-weary taker may fall dead,
And that the trunk may be discharged of breath
As violently as hasty powder fired
65 Doth hurry from the fatal cannon's womb.
APOTHECARY
Such mortal drugs I have, but Mantua's law
Is death to any he that utters them.
ROMEO   Art thou so bare and full of wretchedness,

And fearest to die? Famine is in thy cheeks,
70 Need and oppression starveth in thy eyes,
Contempt and beggary hangs upon thy back,
The world is not thy friend, nor the world's law;
The world affords no law to make thee rich,
Then be not poor, but break it and take this.
APOTHECARY   My poverty but not my will consents. 75
ROMEO   I pay thy poverty and not thy will.
APOTHECARY   Put this in any liquid thing you will
And drink it off; and if you had the strength
Of twenty men, it would dispatch you straight.
ROMEO
There is thy gold, worse poison to men's souls, 80
Doing more murder in this loathsome world
Than these poor compounds that thou mayst not sell.
I sell thee poison; thou hast sold me none.
Farewell, buy food, and get thyself in flesh.
                                        Exit Apothecary.
Come, cordial and not poison, go with me 85
To Juliet's grave, for there must I use thee.   *Exit.*

5.2   *Enter* FRIAR JOHN.

FRIAR JOHN   Holy Franciscan friar, brother, ho!

                    Enter FRIAR LAURENCE.

FRIAR LAURENCE
This same should be the voice of Friar John.
Welcome from Mantua. What says Romeo?
Or if his mind be writ, give me his letter.
FRIAR JOHN   Going to find a barefoot brother out, 5
One of our order, to associate me,
Here in this city visiting the sick,
And finding him, the searchers of the town,
Suspecting that we both were in a house
Where the infectious pestilence did reign, 10
Sealed up the doors and would not let us forth
So that my speed to Mantua there was stayed.
FRIAR LAURENCE   Who bare my letter then to Romeo?
FRIAR JOHN   I could not send it – here it is again –
Nor get a messenger to bring it thee, 15
So fearful were they of infection.
FRIAR LAURENCE
Unhappy fortune! By my brotherhood,
The letter was not nice but full of charge,
Of dear import, and the neglecting it
May do much danger. Friar John, go hence, 20
Get me an iron crow, and bring it straight
Unto my cell.
FRIAR JOHN   Brother, I'll go and bring it thee.   *Exit.*
FRIAR LAURENCE   Now must I to the monument alone.
Within this three hours will fair Juliet wake.
She will beshrew me much that Romeo 25
Hath had no notice of these accidents.
But I will write again to Mantua
And keep her at my cell till Romeo come.
Poor living corse, closed in a dead man's tomb!   *Exit.*

5.3   *Enter* County PARIS *and his* Page *with flowers and sweet water and a torch.*

PARIS   Give me thy torch, boy. Hence, and stand aloof.
Yet put it out, for I would not be seen.
Under yond yew trees lay thee all along,
Holding thy ear close to the hollow ground.
5 So shall no foot upon the churchyard tread,
Being loose, unfirm, with digging up of graves
But thou shalt hear it. Whistle then to me,
As signal that thou hearest something approach.
Give me those flowers. Do as I bid thee, go.
10 PAGE *[aside]*   I am almost afraid to stand alone
Here in the churchyard, yet I will adventure.   *[Retires.]*
[Paris strews the tomb with flowers.]
PARIS   Sweet flower, with flowers thy bridal bed I strew,
O woe, thy canopy is dust and stones,
Which with sweet water nightly I will dew,
15 Or, wanting that, with tears distilled by moans.
The obsequies that I for thee will keep,
Nightly shall be to strew thy grave and weep.
[Page whistles.]
The boy gives warning something doth approach.
What cursed foot wanders this way tonight,
20 To cross my obsequies and true love's rite?
What, with a torch? Muffle me, night, awhile.
[Retires.]

Enter ROMEO *and* BALTHASAR *with a torch,*
a mattock and a crow of iron.

ROMEO   Give me that mattock and the wrenching iron.
Hold, take this letter. Early in the morning
See thou deliver it to my lord and father.
25 Give me the light. Upon thy life I charge thee,
Whate'er thou hearest or seest, stand all aloof,
And do not interrupt me in my course.
Why I descend into this bed of death
Is partly to behold my lady's face,
30 But chiefly to take thence from her dead finger
A precious ring, a ring that I must use
In dear employment. Therefore hence, be gone.
But if thou, jealous, dost return to pry
In what I farther shall intend to do,
35 By heaven, I will tear thee joint by joint
And strew this hungry churchyard with thy limbs.
The time and my intents are savage-wild,
More fierce and more inexorable far
Than empty tigers or the roaring sea.
40 BALTHASAR   I will be gone, sir, and not trouble ye.
ROMEO
So shalt thou show me friendship. Take thou that.
[Gives money.]
Live and be prosperous, and farewell, good fellow.
BALTHASAR *[aside]*
For all this same, I'll hide me hereabout.
His looks I fear, and his intents I doubt.   *[Retires.]*
[Romeo opens the tomb.]

ROMEO   Thou detestable maw, thou womb of death,   45
Gorged with the dearest morsel of the earth,
Thus I enforce thy rotten jaws to open,
And in despite I'll cram thee with more food.
PARIS *[apart]*
This is that banished haughty Montague
That murdered my love's cousin, with which grief   50
It is supposed the fair creature died,
And here is come to do some villainous shame
To the dead bodies. I will apprehend him.
[Steps forward.]
– Stop thy unhallowed toil, vile Montague!
Can vengeance be pursued further than death?   55
Condemned villain, I do apprehend thee.
Obey and go with me, for thou must die.
ROMEO   I must indeed, and therefore came I hither.
Good gentle youth, tempt not a desperate man.
Fly hence and leave me. Think upon these gone,   60
Let them affright thee. I beseech thee, youth,
Put not another sin upon my head
By urging me to fury. O, be gone!
By heaven, I love thee better than myself,
For I come hither armed against myself.   65
Stay not, be gone; live, and hereafter say
A madman's mercy bid thee run away.
PARIS   I do defy thy conjuration
And apprehend thee for a felon here.
ROMEO   Wilt thou provoke me? Then have at thee, boy!   70
[They fight.]
PAGE   O Lord, they fight. I will go call the watch.   *Exit.*
PARIS   O, I am slain! If thou be merciful,
Open the tomb, lay me with Juliet.   *[Dies.]*
ROMEO   In faith, I will. Let me peruse this face.
Mercutio's kinsman, noble County Paris!   75
What said my man when my betossed soul
Did not attend him as we rode? I think
He told me Paris should have married Juliet.
Said he not so? Or did I dream it so?
Or am I mad, hearing him talk of Juliet,   80
To think it was so? O, give me thy hand,
One writ with me in sour misfortune's book.
I'll bury thee in a triumphant grave.
A grave – O, no, a lantern, slaughtered youth,
For here lies Juliet, and her beauty makes   85
This vault a feasting presence full of light.
Death, lie thou there, by a dead man interred.
How oft, when men are at the point of death,
Have they been merry, which their keepers call
A lightening before death. O, how may I   90
Call this a lightening? O my love, my wife,
Death, that hath sucked the honey of thy breath
Hath had no power yet upon thy beauty.
Thou art not conquered. Beauty's ensign yet
Is crimson in thy lips and in thy cheeks,   95
And death's pale flag is not advanced there.
Tybalt, liest thou there in thy bloody sheet?
O, what more favour can I do to thee

Than with that hand that cut thy youth in twain
100   To sunder his that was thine enemy?
Forgive me, cousin! Ah, dear Juliet,
Why art thou yet so fair? Shall I believe
That unsubstantial death is amorous,
And that the lean abhorred monster keeps
105   Thee here in dark to be his paramour?
For fear of that I still will stay with thee
And never from this palace of dim night
Depart again. Here, here will I remain
With worms that are thy chambermaids. O, here
110   Will I set up my everlasting rest,
And shake the yoke of inauspicious stars
From this world-wearied flesh. Eyes, look your last;
Arms, take your last embrace, and lips, O you
The doors of breath, seal with a righteous kiss
115   A dateless bargain to engrossing death.
Come, bitter conduct, come, unsavoury guide.
Thou desperate pilot, now at once run on
The dashing rocks thy seasick weary bark!
Here's to my love.   [*Drinks.*]
            O true apothecary,
120   Thy drugs are quick. Thus with a kiss I die.
   [*Falls and dies.*]

Enter FRIAR LAURENCE *with lantern,*
crow and spade.

FRIAR LAURENCE
   Saint Francis be my speed! How oft tonight
   Have my old feet stumbled at graves. Who's there?
   [*Balthasar comes forward.*]
BALTHASAR
   Here's one, a friend, and one that knows you well.
FRIAR LAURENCE
   Bliss be upon you! Tell me, good my friend,
125   What torch is yond that vainly lends his light
   To grubs and eyeless skulls? As I discern,
   It burneth in the Capels' monument.
BALTHASAR   It doth so, holy sir, and there's my master,
   One that you love.
FRIAR LAURENCE   Who is it?
BALTHASAR   Romeo.
FRIAR LAURENCE   How long hath he been there?
130   BALTHASAR   Full half an hour.
FRIAR LAURENCE   Go with me to the vault.
BALTHASAR   I dare not, sir.
   My master knows not but I am gone hence,
   And fearfully did menace me with death
   If I did stay to look on his intents.
FRIAR LAURENCE
135   Stay then, I'll go alone. Fear comes upon me.
   O, much I fear some ill unthrifty thing.
BALTHASAR   As I did sleep under this yew tree here,
   I dreamt my master and another fought,
   And that my master slew him.   *Exit.*
FRIAR LAURENCE   Romeo!
   [*Friar stoops and looks on the blood and weapons.*]

Alack, alack, what blood is this which stains   140
The stony entrance of this sepulchre?
What mean these masterless and gory swords
To lie discoloured by this place of peace?
Romeo! O, pale! Who else? What, Paris too,
And steeped in blood? Ah, what an unkind hour   145
Is guilty of this lamentable chance!
The lady stirs.   [*Juliet rises.*]
JULIET   O comfortable Friar, where is my lord?
   I do remember well where I should be,
   And there I am. Where is my Romeo?   150
FRIAR LAURENCE
   I hear some noise. Lady, come from that nest
   Of death, contagion and unnatural sleep.
   A greater power than we can contradict
   Hath thwarted our intents. Come, come away.
   Thy husband in thy bosom there lies dead,   155
   And Paris too. Come, I'll dispose of thee
   Among a sisterhood of holy nuns.
   Stay not to question, for the watch is coming.
   Come, go, good Juliet. I dare no longer stay.
JULIET
   Go, get thee hence, for I will not away.   *Exit Friar.*   160
   What's here? A cup closed in my true love's hand?
   Poison, I see, hath been his timeless end.
   O churl, drunk all, and left no friendly drop
   To help me after? I will kiss thy lips.
   Haply some poison yet doth hang on them   165
   To make me die with a restorative.   [*Kisses him.*]
   Thy lips are warm!

Enter PARIS' Page *and* Watchmen.

CHIEF WATCHMAN   Lead, boy. Which way?
JULIET   Yea, noise? Then I'll be brief. O happy dagger!
   [*Takes Romeo's dagger.*]
   This is thy sheath; there rust, and let me die.   170
   [*She stabs herself, falls and dies.*]
PAGE
   This is the place, there where the torch doth burn.
CHIEF WATCHMAN
   The ground is bloody. Search about the churchyard.
   Go, some of you; whoe'er you find, attach.
                   Exeunt some of the Watch.
   Pitiful sight! Here lies the County slain,
   And Juliet bleeding, warm and newly dead,   175
   Who here hath lain this two days buried.
   Go, tell the Prince, run to the Capulets,
   Raise up the Montagues. Some others search.
                  Exeunt others of the Watch.
   We see the ground whereon these woes do lie,
   But the true ground of all these piteous woes   180
   We cannot without circumstance descry.

Enter one of the Watch *with Romeo's man*
BALTHASAR.

2 WATCHMAN
   Here's Romeo's man. We found him in the churchyard.

CHIEF WATCHMAN
Hold him in safety till the Prince come hither.

Enter FRIAR LAURENCE *and another* WATCHMAN.

3 WATCHMAN
Here is a friar that trembles, sighs and weeps.
185 We took this mattock and this spade from him
As he was coming from this churchyard's side.
CHIEF WATCHMAN
A great suspicion! Stay the friar too.

Enter the PRINCE *and Attendants.*

PRINCE   What misadventure is so early up,
That calls our person from our morning rest?

Enter CAPULET *and his* WIFE.

190 CAPULET   What should it be that is so shrieked abroad?
CAPULET'S WIFE
O, the people in the street cry 'Romeo',
Some 'Juliet', and some 'Paris', and all run
With open outcry toward our monument.
PRINCE   What fear is this which startles in your ears?
CHIEF WATCHMAN
195 Sovereign, here lies the County Paris slain,
And Romeo dead, and Juliet, dead before,
Warm and new killed.
PRINCE
Search, seek, and know how this foul murder comes.
CHIEF WATCHMAN
Here is a friar, and slaughtered Romeo's man,
200 With instruments upon them fit to open
These dead men's tombs.
CAPULET
O heavens! O wife, look how our daughter bleeds!
This dagger hath mista'en, for lo, his house
Is empty on the back of Montague,
205 And is mis-sheathed in my daughter's bosom.
CAPULET'S WIFE   O me, this sight of death is as a bell
That warns my old age to a sepulchre.

Enter MONTAGUE *and Attendants.*

PRINCE   Come, Montague, for thou art early up
To see thy son and heir now early down.
210 MONTAGUE   Alas, my liege, my wife is dead tonight;
Grief of my son's exile hath stopped her breath.
What further woe conspires against mine age?
PRINCE   Look, and thou shalt see.
MONTAGUE
O thou untaught! What manners is in this,
215 To press before thy father to a grave?
PRINCE   Seal up the mouth of outrage for a while,
Till we can clear these ambiguities
And know their spring, their head, their true descent,
And then will I be general of your woes
220 And lead you even to death. Meantime forbear,
And let mischance be slave to patience.
Bring forth the parties of suspicion.

FRIAR LAURENCE   I am the greatest, able to do least,
Yet most suspected, as the time and place
Doth make against me, of this direful murder.   225
And here I stand, both to impeach and purge,
Myself condemned and myself excused.
PRINCE   Then say at once what thou dost know in this.
FRIAR LAURENCE
I will be brief, for my short date of breath
Is not so long as is a tedious tale.   230
Romeo, there dead, was husband to that Juliet,
And she, there dead, that's Romeo's faithful wife.
I married them, and their stol'n marriage day
Was Tybalt's doomsday, whose untimely death
Banished the new-made bridegroom from this city;   235
For whom, and not for Tybalt, Juliet pined.
You, to remove that siege of grief from her,
Betrothed and would have married her perforce
To County Paris. Then comes she to me,
And with wild looks bid me devise some mean   240
To rid her from this second marriage,
Or in my cell there would she kill herself.
Then gave I her, so tutored by my art,
A sleeping potion, which so took effect
As I intended, for it wrought on her   245
The form of death. Meantime I writ to Romeo
That he should hither come as this dire night
To help to take her from her borrowed grave,
Being the time the potion's force should cease.
But he which bore my letter, Friar John,   250
Was stayed by accident, and yesternight
Returned my letter back. Then, all alone,
At the prefixed hour of her waking
Came I to take her from her kindred's vault,
Meaning to keep her closely at my cell   255
Till I conveniently could send to Romeo.
But when I came, some minute ere the time
Of her awakening, here untimely lay
The noble Paris and true Romeo dead.
She wakes, and I entreated her come forth   260
And bear this work of heaven with patience.
But then a noise did scare me from the tomb,
And she, too desperate, would not go with me,
But, as it seems, did violence on herself.
All this I know, and to the marriage   265
Her nurse is privy; and if aught in this
Miscarried by my fault, let my old life
Be sacrificed some hour before his time
Unto the rigour of severest law.
PRINCE   We still have known thee for a holy man.   270
Where's Romeo's man? What can he say to this?
BALTHASAR
I brought my master news of Juliet's death,
And then in post he came from Mantua
To this same place, to this same monument.
This letter he early bid me give his father,   275
And threatened me with death, going in the vault,
If I departed not and left him there.

PRINCE   Give me the letter; I will look on it.
Where is the County's page that raised the watch?
280   Sirrah, what made your master in this place?
PAGE   He came with flowers to strew his lady's grave,
And bid me stand aloof, and so I did.
Anon comes one with light to ope the tomb,
And by and by my master drew on him.
285   And then I ran away to call the watch.
PRINCE   This letter doth make good the Friar's words,
Their course of love, the tidings of her death.
And here he writes that he did buy a poison
Of a poor pothecary, and therewithal
290   Came to this vault, to die and lie with Juliet.
Where be these enemies? Capulet, Montague,
See what a scourge is laid upon your hate,
That heaven finds means to kill your joys with love;
And I, for winking at your discords too,

Have lost a brace of kinsmen. All are punished.   295
CAPULET   O brother Montague, give me thy hand.
This is my daughter's jointure, for no more
Can I demand.
MONTAGUE   But I can give thee more,
For I will raise her statue in pure gold,
That whiles Verona by that name is known,   300
There shall no figure at such rate be set
As that of true and faithful Juliet.
CAPULET   As rich shall Romeo's by his lady's lie,
Poor sacrifices of our enmity.
PRINCE   A glooming peace this morning with it brings.   305
The sun for sorrow will not show his head.
Go hence, to have more talk of these sad things.
Some shall be pardoned and some punished,
For never was a story of more woe
Than this of Juliet and her Romeo.   *Exeunt.*   310

Sir Thomas More

Beginning with an insurrection of Londoners and ending with Henry VIII's execution of his former Lord Chancellor, the controversial *Sir Thomas More* was written and revised by several dramatists, Shakespeare among them. Alone of Shakespeare's plays it survives as a manuscript (British Library, Harley MS 7368). Seven identifiable hands are present. The playwright Anthony Munday copied the original play, and he has been credited with its authorship, probably in collaboration with Henry Chettle. Subsequent major revision was co-ordinated by an anonymous theatre scribe labelled as Hand C. It entailed some cancellations as well as additions of various lengths in the hands identified as Chettle, Thomas Dekker, Thomas Heywood and Shakespeare.

The play has three sections, presenting the riots against foreigners living in London as eventually quelled by More (Scenes 1–7), some comic anecdotes about More as Lord Chancellor (consolidated by the revisers into two scenes, Scenes 8 and 9) and More's good-humoured stoicism through his arrest and execution (Scenes 10–17). The account of More is based mainly on the 1587 edition of Raphael Holinshed's *Chronicle*, especially in the later scenes. The authors also drew on manuscript accounts of More by Catholic apologists Nicholas Harpsfield and Thomas Stapleton.

A lost first draft was copied by Munday to establish the original text of the existing manuscript, perhaps in 1599. This was submitted to the Master of the Revels, Edmund Tilney, who was responsible for regulation and control of the drama. He was particularly concerned with the play's expansive treatment of the 1517 'Ill May Day' riots, as a potential threat to law and order. Tilney's annotations ordered major cuts, mainly aimed at removing the insurrection in Scene 1 and perhaps other scenes. The substantial redraft, possibly undertaken in 1603–4, chiefly affected Scenes 4–9, with a further alteration of More's soliloquy in Scene 13. The revisers may have been resigned to losing the inflammatory opening scene, but other insurrection scenes were retained and modified. The manuscript has attracted considerable attention as a theatre document showing direct evidence of authorial drafting, of copying by both the original author and the scribe, of political censorship and of revision to create a new version of the play. Most significant for the present edition, it probably shows us Shakespeare himself in the process of dramatic composition.

Executed by Henry VIII for defying his break with the Catholic Church, More had come to be regarded as a martyr by the Catholic minority in England. The play was daring in its attempt to represent these events, especially in view of its warm portrayal of More as an empathetically humane and humorous civic leader in touch with the people of London and a man of unyielding principle. Unsurprisingly, Tilney deleted key lines relating to More's refusal to sign unspecified 'articles' demanding obedience to the King. The revisers may have hoped that King James, who succeeded Queen Elizabeth in 1603, would have pursued reconciliation with Catholics, and they perhaps imagined the play as instrumental to that end.

Shakespeare took on the key role of rewriting the scene in which the rioters surrender to the King's authority (Scene 6). More calms the crowd skilfully, before urging the doctrine of obedience to the monarch and then moving the citizens to consider how distressful it would be if they found themselves abused and deported as they propose to treat London's foreigners. Two short soliloquies spoken by More at the beginning of Scenes 8 and 9 may also be wholly or partly by Shakespeare, demonstrating his wider involvement in structuring the revised play and developing its interiorized and reflective depiction of More.

Whether the play was performed once its revisions were complete is unknown. The manuscript re-emerged into public view in the nineteenth century when the first edition was prepared by Alexander Dyce (1844). Scattered stage and radio performances in the twentieth century led to Frank Dunlop's full staging at the Nottingham Playhouse in 1964 and Robert Delamere's by the Royal Shakespeare Company in 2005. Ian McKellen, who played More in Nottingham, performed the impressive Shakespearean speeches advocating tolerance to foreigners in his one-man shows 'Acting Shakespeare' and 'A Knight Out'. Videos of McKellen on YouTube have been repeatedly cited in blogs on Shakespeare, migration and tolerance.

This edition is based on the manuscript, and incorporates the manuscript's revisions of the play as attributed to Shakespeare and other dramatists. Headings are provided that show the manuscript sections and the principal hand in each one. Within each section, where a second hand intervenes, the phrase or passage is in sans serif font, and

superscripts identify the hand as follows: 'C': Hand C; Ch: Chettle; Dk: Dekker; H: Heywood; M: Munday; Sh: Shakespeare; T: Tilney. Longer deleted passages are indicated with a marginal line, while deleted single words and short phrases are indicated by underlining; the letters identifying hands are added in subscript where the author of the deletion can be identified. Editorial stage directions are enclosed in square brackets.

Thomas MORE	*a sheriff of London, later Sir Thomas More and Lord Chancellor*
Earl of SHREWSBURY	
Earl of SURREY	
John LINCOLN	*a broker*
DOLL Williamson	
WILLIAMSON	*her husband, a carpenter*
GEORGE BETTS	
CLOWN BETTS	*his brother, called Ralph*
SHERWIN	*a goldsmith*
Francis de BARDE	*a Lombard*
CAVALER	*a Lombard or Frenchman*
LORD MAYOR of London	
LADY MAYORESS	
Justice SURESBY	
LIFTER	*a cutpurse*
Smart	*the plaintiff against him*
RECORDER of London	
Sir Thomas PALMER	
Sir Roger CHOLMLEY	
SIR JOHN Munday	
DOWNES	*a sergeant-at-arms*
CROFTS	*a messenger from the King*
RANDALL	*More's manservant*
JACK FALCONER	*a ruffian*
ERASMUS	*a learned clerk of Rotterdam*
MORRIS	*secretary to the Bishop of Winchester*

THE LORD CARDINAL'S PLAYERS

INCLINATION	
PROLOGUE	
WIT	
Lady VANITY	*played by a boy*
LUGGINS	*player cast as Good Counsel*
William ROPER	*More's son-in-law*
LADY More	*More's wife*
ROPER'S WIFE	*one of More's daughters*
MORE'S OTHER DAUGHTER	
CATESBY	*More's steward*
GOUGH	*More's secretary*
Doctor Fisher, Bishop of ROCHESTER	
LIEUTENANT of the Tower	
GENTLEMAN PORTER of the Tower	
Three WARDERS of the Tower	
HANGMAN	
A poor WOMAN	*a client of More*
Ned BUTLER	
Robin BREWER	*servants in More's household*
Giles PORTER	
Ralph HORSE-KEEPER	
Two SHERIFFS	
MESSENGERS	
CLERK of the Council	
OFFICERS	

Lords, Ladies, Gentlemen, Aldermen, Justices, Citizens, Prentices, Servingmen, Attendants

[Original Text: Munday]

[Tilney]

ᵀ*Leave out the insurrection wholly and the cause thereof,
and begin with Sir Thomas More at the Mayor's sessions,
with a report afterwards of his good service done being
Sheriff of London upon a mutiny against the Lombards –
only by a short report, and not otherwise, at your own perils.*
                                                    *E. Tilney*ᵀ

[Sc. 1] *Enter at one end John* LINCOLN *with
⟨*GEORGE BETTS *[and* CLOWN BETTS*]⟩ *together.*
At the other end enters Francis de ⟨BARDE *and* DOLL⟩,
a lusty woman, he haling her by the arm.

DOLL   Whither wilt thou hale me?

BARDE   Whither I please. Thou art my prize, and I
plead purchase of thee.

DOLL   Purchase of me? Away, ye rascal! I am an honest,
plain carpenter's wife, and, though I have no beauty to
like a husband, yet whatsoever is mine scorns to stoop
to a stranger. Hand off then when I bid thee!

BARDE   Go with me quietly, or I'll compel thee.

DOLL   Compel me, ye dog's face? Thou think'st thou
hast the goldsmith's wife in hand, whom thou
enticed'st from her husband with all his plate, and
when thou turned'st her home to him again mad'st
him, like an ass, pay for his wife's board.

BARDE   So will I make thy husband too, if please me.

Enter CAVALER, *with a pair of doves,* WILLIAMSON
the carpenter and SHERWIN *following him.*

DOLL   Here he comes himself. Tell him so if thou dar'st.

CAVALER [*to Williamson*] Follow me no further. I say
thou shalt not have them.

WILLIAMSON   I bought them in Cheapside, and paid
my money for them.

SHERWIN   He did, sir, indeed, and you offer him wrong,
both to take them from him and not restore him his
money neither.

CAVALER   If he paid for them, let it suffice that I possess
them. Beefs and brewis may serve such hinds. Are
pigeons meat for a coarse carpenter?

LINCOLN [*aside to George Betts*] It is hard when
Englishmen's patience must be thus jetted on by
strangers, and they not dare to revenge their own
wrongs.

GEORGE BETTS [*aside to Lincoln*] Lincoln, let's beat
them down, and bear no more of these abuses.

LINCOLN [*aside to George Betts*] We may not, Betts. Be
patient and hear more.

DOLL   How now, husband? What, one stranger take thy
food from thee, and another thy wife? By'r Lady, flesh
and blood, I think, can hardly brook that.

LINCOLN   Will this gear never be otherwise? Must
these wrongs be thus endured?

GEORGE BETTS   Let us step in, and help to revenge
their injury.

BARDE   What art thou that talkest of revenge? My Lord
Ambassador shall once more make your Mayor have a
check if he punish thee not for this saucy presumption.

WILLIAMSON   Indeed, my Lord Mayor on the
Ambassador's complaint sent me to Newgate one day
because, against my will, I took the wall of a stranger.
You may do anything. The goldsmith's wife, and mine
now, must be at your commandment.

GEORGE BETTS   The more patient fools are ye both to
suffer it.

BARDE   Suffer it? Mend it thou or he if ye can or dare. I
tell thee, fellow, an she were the Mayor of London's
wife, had I her once in my possession I would keep her
in spite of him that durst say nay.

GEORGE BETTS   I tell thee, Lombard, these words
should cost thy best cap, were I not curbed by duty and
obedience. The Mayor of London's wife? O God, shall
it be thus?

DOLL   Why, Betts, am not I as dear to my husband as my
Lord Mayor's wife to him, [*to Williamson*] and wilt
thou so neglectly suffer thine own shame? [*to de Barde*]
Hands off, proud stranger, or, ⟨by⟩ Him that bought
me, if men's milky hearts dare not strike a stranger, yet
women will beat them down ere they bear these abuses.

BARDE   Mistress, I say you shall along with me.

DOLL   Touch not Doll Williamson, lest she lay thee
along on God's dear earth. (*to Cavaler*) And you, sir,
that allow such coarse cates to carpenters, whilst
pigeons which they pay for must serve your dainty
appetite: deliver them back to my husband again, or
I'll call so many women to mine assistance as we'll not
leave one inch untorn of thee. If our husbands must be
bridled by law, and forced to bear your wrongs, their
wives will be a little lawless, and soundly beat ye.

CAVALER   Come away, de Barde, and let us go complain
to my Lord Ambassador.   *Exeunt both.*

DOLL   Ay, go, and send him among us, and we'll give
him his welcome too. I am ashamed that free-born
Englishmen, having beaten strangers within their own
bounds, should thus be braved and abused by them at
home.

SHERWIN   It is not our lack of courage in the cause, but
the strict obedience that we are bound to. I am the
goldsmith whose wrongs you talked of; but how to
redress yours or mine own is a matter beyond all our
abilities.

LINCOLN   Not so, not so, my good friends. I, though
a mean man, a broker by profession, and named John
Lincoln, have long time winked at these vile enormities
with mighty impatience and, as these two brethren
here, Bettses by name, can witness, with loss of mine
own life would gladly remedy them.

GEORGE BETTS   And he is in a good forwardness, I tell
ye, if all hit right.

DOLL   As how, I prithee? Tell it to Doll Williamson.

LINCOLN You know the Spital sermons begin the next
  week. I have drawn a ⟨bill⟩ of our wrongs and the
  strangers' insolencies.
GEORGE BETTS Which he means the preachers shall
100 there openly publish in the pulpit.
WILLIAMSON O, but that they would! I'faith, it would
  tickle our strangers thoroughly.
DOLL Ay, and if you men durst not undertake it, before
  God, we women ⟨will. Take⟩ an honest woman from her
105 husband? Why, it is intolerable.
SHERWIN [*to Lincoln*] But how find ye the preachers
  affected to ⟨our proceeding⟩?
LINCOLN Master Doctor Standish ⟨means not to
  meddle with any such matter in his sermon, but
110 Doctor Beal will do in this matter as much as a priest
  may do to⟩ reform it, and doubts not but happy success
  will ensue ⟨upon⟩ our wrongs. You shall perceive
  there's no hurt in the bill. Here's a copy of it. I pray ye
  hear it.
115 ALL THE REST With all our hearts. For God's sake,
  read it.
LINCOLN (*Reads.*) *To you all the worshipful lords and*
  masters of this city that will take compassion over the poor
  people your neighbours, and also of the great importable
120 *hurts, losses and hindrances whereof proceedeth extreme*
  poverty to all the King's subjects that inhabit within this
  city and suburbs of the same. For so it is that aliens and
  strangers eat the bread from the fatherless children, and
  take the living from all the artificers, and the intercourse
125 *from all merchants, whereby poverty is so much increased*
  that every man bewaileth the misery of other; for
  craftsmen be brought to beggary, and merchants to
  neediness. Wherefore, the premises considered, the redress
  must be of the commons knit and united to one part. And
130 *as the hurt and damage grieveth all men, so must all men*
  set to their willing power for remedy, and not suffer the
  said aliens in their wealth, and the natural-born men of
  this region come to confusion.
DOLL Before God, 'tis excellent, and I'll maintain the
135 suit to be honest.
SHERWIN Well, say 'tis read, what is your further
  meaning in the matter?
GEORGE BETTS What? Marry, list to me. No doubt but
  this will store us with friends enough, whose names we
140 will closely keep in writing, and on May Day next in
  the morning we'll go forth a-Maying, but make it the
  worst May Day for the strangers that ever they saw.
  How say ye? Do ye subscribe, or are ye faint-hearted
  revolters?
145 DOLL Hold thee, George Betts, there's my hand and
  my heart. By the Lord, I'll make a captain among ye,
  and do somewhat to be talk of forever after.
WILLIAMSON My masters, ere we part let's friendly go
  and drink together, and swear true secrecy upon our
150 lives.
GEORGE BETTS There spake an angel. Come, let us
  along then.   *Exeunt.*

[Sc. 2]   *An arras is drawn, and behind it, as in*
  sessions, sit the LORD MAYOR, *Justice* SURESBY
  and other Justices [*and the* Recorder],
  Sheriff MORE *and the other* Sheriff *sitting by.*
  Smart is the plaintiff, LIFTER *the prisoner*
  at the bar.

LORD MAYOR
  Having dispatched our weightier businesses,
  We may give ear to petty felonies.
  Master Sheriff More, what is this fellow?
MORE My lord, he stands indicted for a purse.
  He hath been tried; the jury is together.   5
LORD MAYOR Who sent him in?
SURESBY   That did I, my lord.
  Had he had right, he had been hanged ere this,
  The only captain of the cutpurse crew.
LORD MAYOR What is his name?
SURESBY As his profession is: Lifter, my lord,   10
  One that can lift a purse right cunningly.
LORD MAYOR And is that he accuses him?
SURESBY
  The same, my lord, whom, by your honour's leave,
  I must say somewhat too, because I find
  In some respects he is well worthy blame.   15
LORD MAYOR
  Good Master Justice Suresby, speak your mind.
  We are well pleased to give you audience.
SURESBY Hear me, Smart. Thou art a foolish fellow.
  If Lifter be convicted by the law,
  As I see not how the jury can acquit him,   20
  I'll stand to't thou art guilty of his death.
MORE [*to Lord Mayor*]
  My lord, that's worth the hearing.
LORD MAYOR   Listen then, good Master More.
SURESBY [*to Smart*]
  I tell thee plain, it is a shame for thee
  With such a sum to tempt necessity.
  No less than ten pounds, sir, will serve your turn   25
  To carry in your purse about with ye,
  To crack and brag in taverns of your money?
  I promise ye, a man that goes abroad
  With an intent of truth, meeting such a booty,
  May be provoked to that he never meant.   30
  What makes so many pilferers and felons
  But such fond baits that foolish people lay
  To tempt the needy miserable wretch?
  Ten pounds odd money, this is a pretty sum
  To bear about, which were more safe at home.   35
    Lord Mayor and More whisper.
  'Fore God, 'twere well to fine ye as much more,
  To the relief of the poor prisoners,
  To teach ye be ⟨more careful of⟩ your own.
  ⟨   ⟩ rightly served.
  ⟨   ⟩   40
MORE Good my lord, soothe a ⟨   ⟩ for once,
  Only to try conclusions in this case.

T

LORD MAYOR
 Content, good Master More. We'll rise awhile,
 And till the jury can return their verdict
45 Walk in the garden. How say ye, Justices?
ALL JUSTICES We like it well, my lord; we'll follow ye.
      Exeunt Lord Mayor and Justices.
MORE Nay, plaintiff, go you too.   *Exit Smart.*
     And officers,
 Stand you aside, and leave the prisoner
 To me awhile. [*Exeunt all but More and Lifter.*]
    Lifter, come hither.
50 LIFTER What is your worship's pleasure?
MORE Sirrah, you know that you are known to me,
 And I have often saved ye from this place
 Since first I came in office. Thou seest beside
 That Justice Suresby is thy heavy friend,
55 <u>For all the blame that he pretends to Smart</u>
 <u>For tempting thee with such a sum of money.</u>
 I tell thee what: devise me but a means
 To pick or cut his purse, and, on my credit,
 And as I am a Christian and a man,
60 I will procure thy pardon for that jest.
LIFTER Good Master Shrieve, seek not my overthrow.
 You know, sir, I have many heavy friends,
 And more indictments like to come upon me.
 You are too deep for me to deal withal.
65 You are known to be one of the wisest men
 That is in England. I pray ye, Master Sheriff,
 Go not about to undermine my life.
MORE Lifter, I am true subject to my king.
 Thou much mistak'st me, and for thou shalt not think
70 I mean by this to hurt thy life at all,
 I will maintain the act when thou hast done it.
 Thou knowst there are such matters in my hands
 As, if I pleased to give them to the jury,
 I should not need this way to circumvent thee.
75 All that I aim at is a merry jest.
 Perform it, Lifter, and expect my best.
LIFTER I thank your worship, God preserve your life!
 But Master Justice Suresby is gone in.
 I know not how to come near where he is.
80 MORE Let me alone for that. I'll be thy setter.
 I'll send him hither to thee presently,
 Under the colour of thine own request
 Of private matters to acquaint him with.
LIFTER If ye do so, sir, then let me alone.
85 Forty to one but then his purse is gone.
MORE Well said; but see that thou diminish not
 One penny of the money, but give it me.
 It is the cunning act that credits thee.
LIFTER
 I will, good Master Sheriff, I assure ye. *Exit More.*
90 I see the purpose of this gentleman
 Is but to check the folly of the Justice
 For blaming others in a desperate case
 Wherein himself may fall as soon as any.
 To save my life it is a good adventure.

 Silence there, ho! Now doth the Justice enter. 95

    Enter Justice SURESBY.

SURESBY Now, sirrah, now, what is your will with me?
 Wilt thou discharge thy conscience, like an honest man?
 What sayst to me, sirrah? Be brief, be brief.
LIFTER As brief, sir, as I can.
 (*aside*) If ye stand fair, I will be brief anon. 100
SURESBY
 Speak out and mumble not. What sayst thou, sirrah?
LIFTER Sir, I am charged, as God shall be my comfort,
 With more than's true.
SURESBY Sir, sir, ye are indeed, with more than's true,
 For you are flatly charged with felony. 105
 You're charged with more than truth, and that is theft:
 More than a true man should be charged withal.
 Thou art a varlet; that's no more than true.
 Trifle not with me, do not, do not, sirrah.
 Confess but what thou knowst; I ask no more. 110
LIFTER
 There be, sir – there be, if 't shall please your worship –
SURESBY
 'There be', varlet? What be there? Tell me what there
 be.
 Come off or on. 'There be', what be there, knave?
LIFTER There be, sir, divers very cunning fellows
 That while you stand and look them in the face 115
 Will have your purse.
SURESBY   Th'art an honest knave.
 Tell me what are they, where they may be caught.
 Ay, those are they I look for.
LIFTER   You talk of me, sir –
 Alas, I am a puny. There's one, indeed,
 Goes by my name; he puts down all for purses. 120
 ‹   ›
 ‹   ›
‹SURESBY› ‹Be› as familiar as thou wilt, my knave.
 'Tis this I long to know.
LIFTER (*aside*)
 And you shall have your longing ere ye go. – 125
 This fellow, sir, perhaps will meet ye thus,
  (*action* [*of embracing him as in greeting*])
 Or thus, or thus, and in kind compliment
 Pretend acquaintance, somewhat doubtfully;
 And these embraces serve –
SURESBY (*shrugging gladly*) Ay, marry, Lifter,
 Wherefore serve they?
LIFTER   Only to feel 130
 Whether you go full under sail or no,
 Or that your lading be aboard your barque.
SURESBY In plainer English, Lifter, if my purse
 Be stored or no?
LIFTER Ye have it, sir.
SURESBY   Excellent, excellent!
LIFTER Then, sir, you cannot but for manners' sake 135
 Walk on with him, for he will walk your way,
 Alleging either you have much forgot him,

Or he mistakes you.

SURESBY   But in this time has he my purse or no?

LIFTER

140   Not yet, sir, fie! [*aside*] No, nor I have not yours.
      [*He takes Suresby's purse.*]

    Enter LORD MAYOR[, Justices *and the* Recorder;
      Sheriff MORE *and the other* Sheriff].

    [*to Suresby*] But now we must forbear; my lords return.

SURESBY

    [*aside to Lifter*] A murrain on't! Lifter, we'll more anon.
    [*aloud to Lifter*] Ay, thou sayst true: there are shrewd
      knaves indeed.
      He sits down.

    But let them gull me, widgeon me, rook me, fop me,

145   I'faith, i'faith, they are too short for me.

    Knaves and fools meet when purses go.

    Wise men look to their purses well enough.

MORE (*aside*)   Lifter, is it done?

LIFTER (*aside*)   Done, Master Shrieve, and there it is.
      [*He gives Suresby's purse to More.*]

MORE (*aside*)

    Then build upon my word, I'll save thy life.

150 RECORDER   Lifter, stand to the bar.

    The jury have returned thee guilty; thou must die.

    According to the custom, look to it, Master Shrieve.

LORD MAYOR   Then, gentlemen, as you are wont to do,

    Because as yet we have no burial place,

155   What charity your meaning's to bestow

    Toward burial of the prisoners now condemned,

    Let it be given.   [*Puts money on the table.*]
      There is first for me.

RECORDER [*Adds money.*]   And there's for me.

ANOTHER [*Adds money.*]   And me.

SURESBY   Body of me,

    My purse is gone!

MORE   Gone, sir? What, here? How can that be?

160 LORD MAYOR   Against all reason: sitting on the bench?

SURESBY

    Lifter, I talked with you; you have not lifted me, ha?

LIFTER   Suspect ye me, sir? O, what a world is this!

MORE   But hear ye, Master Suresby. Are ye sure

    Ye had a purse about ye?

165 SURESBY   Sure, Master Shrieve, as sure as you are there;

    And in it seven pounds odd money, on my faith.

MORE

    Seven pounds odd money? What, were you so mad,

    Being a wise man and a magistrate,

    To trust your purse with such a liberal sum?

170   Seven pounds odd money? 'Fore God, it is a shame

    With such a sum to tempt necessity.

    I promise ye, a man that goes abroad

    With an intent of truth, meeting such a booty,

    May be provoked to that he never thought.

175   What makes so many pilferers and felons

    But these fond baits that foolish people lay

    To tempt the needy, miserable wretch?

Should he be taken now that has your purse,

I'd stand to't, you are guilty of his death;

For, questionless, he would be cast by law.   180

'Twere a good deed to fine ye as much more,

To the relief of the poor prisoners,

To teach ye lock your money up at home.

SURESBY   Well, Master More, you are a merry man.

I find ye, sir, I find ye well enough.   185

MORE   Nay, ye shall see, sir, trusting thus your money,

And Lifter here in trial for like case,

But that the poor man is a prisoner,

It would be now suspected that he had it.

Thus may ye see what mischief often comes   190

By the fond carriage of such needless sums.

LORD MAYOR

Believe me, Master Suresby, this is strange,

You being a man so settled in assurance

Will fall in that which you condemned in other.

MORE   Well, Master Suresby, there's your purse again,   195

And all your money. Fear nothing of More.

Wisdom still ‹   › the door.   [*Exeunt.*]

[Sc. 3]   *Enter the* Earls of SHREWSBURY *and*
        SURREY, Sir Thomas PALMER *and*
        Sir Roger CHOLMLEY.

SHREWSBURY

My lord of Surrey, and Sir Thomas Palmer,

Might I with patience tempt your grave advice?

I tell ye true, that in these dangerous times

I do not like this frowning vulgar brow.

My searching eye did never entertain   ᵀ*Mend this.*ᵀ   5

A more distracted countenance of grief

Than I have late observed

In the displeased commons of the City.

SURREY   'Tis strange, that from his princely clemency

So well a tempered mercy and a grace   10

To all the aliens in this fruitful land,

That this high-crested insolence should spring

From them that breathe from his majestic bounty,

That, fattened with the traffic of our country,

Already leap into his subjects' face.   15

PALMER   Yet Sherwin, hindered to commence his suit

Against de Barde by the Ambassador

By supplication made unto the King –

Who, having first enticed away his wife

And got his plate, near worth four hundred pound,   20

To grieve some wronged citizens that found

This vile disgrace oft cast into their teeth,

Of late sues Sherwin, and arrested him

For money for the boarding of his wife.

SURREY

The more knave Barde, that, using Sherwin's goods,   25

Doth ask him interest for the occupation.

I like not that, my lord of Shrewsbury.

He's ill bestead that lends a well-paced horse

Unto a man that will not find him meat.

30 CHOLMLEY   My lord of Surrey will be pleasant still.

PALMER   I being then employed by your honours
　　To stay the broil that fell about the same,
　　Where by persuasion I enforced the wrongs
　　And urged the grief of the displeased City,
35　He answered me, and with a solemn oath,
　　That if he had the Mayor of London's wife
　　He would keep her, in despite of any English ᵀmanᵀ.

SURREY   'Tis good, Sir Thomas, then, for you and me
　　Your wife is dead and I a bachelor.
40　If no man can possess his wife alone,
　　I am glad, Sir Thomas Palmer, I have none.

CHOLMLEY   If 'a take my wife, 'a shall find her meat.

SURREY   And reason good, Sir Roger Cholmley, too:
　　If these hot Frenchmen needsly will have sport,
45　They should in kindness yet defray the charge.
　　'Tis hard when men possess our wives in quiet,
　　And yet leave us in to discharge their diet.

SHREWSBURY
　　My lord, our caters shall not use the market
　　For our provision but some stranger ᵀLombardᵀ now
50　Will take the victuals from him he hath bought.
　　A carpenter, as I was late informed,
　　Who having bought a pair of doves in Cheap,
　　Immediately a Frenchman ᵀLombardᵀ took them
　　　from him,
　　And beat the poor man for resisting him;
55　And when the fellow did complain his wrongs
　　He was severely punished for his labour.

ᵀ SURREY   But if the English blood be once but up,
　　As I perceive their hearts already full,
　　I fear me much, before their spleens be cooled,
60　Some of these saucy aliens for their pride
　　Will pay for't soundly, wheresoe'er it lights.
　　This tide of rage, that with the eddy strives,
　　I fear me much will drown too many lives.

CHOLMLEY
　　Now afore God, your honours, pardon me.
65　Men of your place and greatness are to blame –
　　I tell ye true, my lords – in that his majesty
　　Is not informed of this base abuse,
　　And daily wrongs are offered to his subjects;
　　For if he were, I know his gracious wisdom
70 ᵀ Would soon redress it.

Enter a Messenger.

SHREWSBURY   Sirrah, what news?

CHOLMLEY　　　　　　　None good, I fear.

ᵀ MESSENGER
　　My lord, ill news; and worse, I fear, will follow
　　If speedily it be not looked unto.
　　The City is in an uproar, and the Mayor
75　Is threatened if he come out of his house.
　　A number, poor artificers ⟨　　　　⟩
ᵀ　⟨　　　　　　　　　　　⟩
　⟨CHOLMLEY⟩
　　⟨'Twas to be⟩ feared what this would come unto.

This follows on the doctor's publishing
The bill of wrongs in public at the Spital.　　　　80

SHREWSBURY
　　That Doctor Beal may chance beshrew himself
　　For reading of the bill.

PALMER   Let us go gather forces to the Mayor
　　For quick suppressing this rebellious rout.

SURREY   Now I bethink myself of Master More,　　85
　　One of the sheriffs, a wise and learned gentleman,
　　And in especial favour with the people.
　　He, backed with other grave and sober men,
　　May by his gentle and persuasive speech
　　Perhaps prevail more than we can with power.　90

SHREWSBURY
　　Believe me but your honour well advises.
　　Let us make haste, or I do greatly fear
　　Some to their graves this morning's work will bear.

　　　　　　　　　　　　　　　　　Exeunt.

[Sc. 4]　　　　　ᶜ*Enter* LINCOLN, BETTS,
　　　　　　　　WILLIAMSON, DOLL.ᶜ
Enter LINCOLN, BETTSES [GEORGE *and* CLOWN],
　WILLIAMSON, SHERWIN *and other, armed;*
　　DOLL *in a shirt of mail, a headpiece,*
　　　sword and buckler; a crew attending.

[Original Text: Munday]

[Addition II: Heywood]

CLOWN BETTS   Come, come, we'll tickle their turnips,
　　we'll butter their boxes! Shall strangers rule the roast?
　　Yes, but we'll baste the roast. Come, come, aflaunt,
　　aflaunt!

GEORGE BETTS
　　Brother, give place, and hear John Lincoln speak.　5

CLOWN BETTS
　　　　Ay, Lincoln, my leader,
　　　　And Doll, my true breeder,
　　　　With the rest of our crew
　　　　Shall ran-tan-tarra-ran.
　　　　Do all they what they can,　　　　　　10
　　　　Shall we be bobbed, braved? – No!
　　　　Shall we be held under? – No!
　　　　We are free-born
　　　　And do take scorn
　　　　To be used so.　　　　　　　　　15

DOLL   Peace there, I say! Hear Captain Lincoln speak.
　　Keep silence till we know his mind at large.

CLOWN BETTS [*to Lincoln*]   Then largely deliver. Speak,
　　bully, and he that presumes to interrupt thee in thy
　　oration, this for him!　　　　　　　　20

LINCOLN
　　Then gallant bloods, you whose free souls do scorn
　　To bear the enforced wrongs of aliens,
　　Add rage to resolution! Fire the houses
　　Of these audacious strangers! This is St Martin's,
　　And yonder dwells Meautis, a wealthy Picardy,　25

At the Green Gate;
De Barde, Pieter van Hollak, Adrian Martin,
With many more outlandish fugitives.
Shall these enjoy more privilege than we
30 In our own country? Let's become their slaves.
Since justice keeps not them in greater awe,
We'll be ourselves rough ministers at law.

CLOWN BETTS
    Use no more swords,
    Nor no more words,
35   But fire the houses,
    Brave Captain Courageous,
    Fire me their houses.

DOLL   Ay, for we may as well make bonfires on May Day
as at Midsummer. We'll alter the day in the calendar,
40 and set it down in flaming letters.

SHERWIN
Stay, no, that would much endanger the whole City,
Whereto I would not the least prejudice.

DOLL   No, nor I neither: so may mine own house be
burned for company. I'll tell ye what: we'll drag the
45 strangers into Moorfields, and there bumbaste them
till they stink again.

CLOWN BETTS   And that's soon done, for they smell for
fear already.

GEORGE BETTS
Let some of us enter the strangers' houses,
50 And, if we find them there, then bring them forth.

DOLL   But if ye bring them forth ere ye find them, I'll
ne'er allow of that.

CLOWN BETTS
    Now Mars for thy honour,
    Dutch or French,
55   So it be a wench,
    I'll upon her.
    [*Exeunt Sherwin, Clown Betts and others.*]

LINCOLN `C`WILLIAMSON`C`
Now, lads, how shall we labour in our safety?
I hear the Mayor hath gathered men in arms,
And that Shrieve More an hour ago received
60 Some of the Privy Council in at Ludgate.
Force now must make our peace, or else we fall.
'Twill soon be known we are the principal.

DOLL   And what of that? If thou be'st afraid, husband,
go home again and hide thy head, for, by the Lord, I'll
65 have a little sport now we are at it.

GEORGE BETTS
Let's stand upon our swords, and if they come
Receive them as they were our enemies.

[*Enter* SHERWIN, CLOWN BETTS *and the rest.*]

CLOWN BETTS   A purchase, a purchase! We have found,
we ha' found –

70 DOLL   What?

CLOWN BETTS   Nothing. Not a French Fleming nor a
Fleming French to be found, but all fled, in plain
English.

LINCOLN [*to Sherwin*]   How now, have you found any?

75 SHERWIN   No, not one, they're all fled.

LINCOLN
Then fire the houses, that, the Mayor being busy
About the quenching of them, we may scape.
Burn down their kennels! Let us straight away,
Lest this day prove to us an ill May Day.
    [*Exeunt;*] `C`*manet Clown.*`C`

80 CLOWN BETTS   Fire, fire! I'll be the first.
If hanging come, 'tis welcome; that's the worst. [*Exit.*]

[Addition II: Heywood]

[Addition II: Hand C]

[Sc. 5]   *Enter at one door* Sir Thomas MORE *and*
LORD MAYOR; *at another door* SIR JOHN
Munday, *hurt.*

LORD MAYOR   What, Sir John Munday, are you hurt?

SIR JOHN   A little knock, my lord. There was even now
A sort of prentices playing at cudgels.
I did command them to their masters' houses,
But one of them, backed by the other crew, 5
Wounded me in the forehead with his cudgel;
And now, I fear me, they are gone to join
With Lincoln, Sherwin and their dangerous train.

MORE   The captains of this insurrection
Have ta'en themselves to arms, and came but now 10
To both the Counters, where they have released
Sundry indebted prisoners, and from thence
I hear that they are gone into St Martin's,
Where they intend to offer violence
To the amazed Lombards. Therefore, my lord, 15
If we expect the safety of the City,
'Tis time that force or parley do encounter
With these displeased men.

Enter a Messenger.

LORD MAYOR   How now, what news?

MESSENGER
My lord, the rebels have broke open Newgate,
From whence they have delivered many prisoners, 20
Both felons and notorious murderers,
That desperately cleave to their lawless train.

LORD MAYOR
Up with the drawbridge! Gather some forces
To Cornhill and Cheapside. And, gentlemen,
If diligence be used on every side, 25
A quiet ebb will follow this rough tide.
    [*Exit Messenger.*]

Enter SHREWSBURY, SURREY, PALMER;
CHOLMLEY.

SHREWSBURY
Lord Mayor, his majesty, receiving notice
Of this most dangerous insurrection,
Hath sent my lord of Surrey and myself,

30   Sir Thomas Palmer and our followers
     To add unto your forces our best means
     For pacifying of this mutiny.
     In God's name then, set on with happy speed.
     The King laments if one true subject bleed.

SURREY

35   I hear they mean to fire the Lombards' houses.
     O power, what art thou in a madman's eyes!
     Thou mak'st the plodding idiot bloody-wise.

MORE   My lords, I doubt not but we shall appease
     With a calm breath this flux of discontent.

40 PALMER   To call them to a parley questionless
     May fall out good. 'Tis well said, Master More.

MORE   Let's to these simple men, for many sweat
     Under this act that knows not the law's debt
     Which hangs upon their lives. For silly men

45   Plod on they know not how; like a fool's pen
     That, ending, shows not any sentence writ
     Linked but to common reason or slightest wit.
     These follow for no harm, but yet incur
     Self penalty with those that raised this stir.

50   I'God's name on, to calm our private foes
     With breath of gravity, not dangerous blows.   *Exeunt.*

[Sc. 6]   *Enter* LINCOLN, DOLL, CLOWN
[BETTS], GEORGE BETTS, WILLIAMSON,
[SHERWIN,] *others:* [Citizens *and*
Prentices, *armed*].

[Addition II: Hand C]

[Addition II: Shakespeare]

LINCOLN   Peace, hear me! He that will not see a red
herring at a Harry groat, butter at eleven pence a
pound, meal at nine shillings a bushel and beef at four
nobles a stone, list to me.

5 OTHER ^CGEORGE BETTS^C   It will come to that pass if
strangers be suffered. Mark him.

LINCOLN   Our country is a great eating country;
argo they eat more in our country than they do in their
own.

10 OTHER ^CCLOWN BETTS^C   By a halfpenny loaf a day, troy
weight.

LINCOLN   They bring in strange roots, which is merely
to the undoing of poor prentices. For what's a sorry
parsnip to a good heart?

15 OTHER ^CWILLIAMSON^C   Trash, trash. They breed sore
eyes, and 'tis enough to infect the City with the palsy.

LINCOLN   Nay, it has infected it with the palsy, for these
bastards of dung – as you know, they grow in dung –
have infected us, and it is our infection will make the

20 City shake. Which partly comes through the eating of
parsnips.

OTHER ^CCLOWN BETTS^C   True, and pumpkins together.

      ^C*Enter*^C [DOWNES, *a sergeant-at-arms*].

DOWNES   What say you to the mercy of the King?

     Do you refuse it?

LINCOLN   You would have us upon th' hip, would you?   25
No, marry, do we not. We accept of the King's mercy,
but we will show no mercy upon the strangers.

DOWNES
You are the simplest things that ever stood
In such a question.

LINCOLN   How say you now, prentices? Prentices   30
'simple'? Down with him!

ALL CITIZENS   Prentices simple? Prentices simple?

     Enter the LORD MAYOR, SURREY, SHREWSBURY[,
       MORE *and* PALMER. *They rescue Downes*].

SHREWSBURY ^CMAYOR^C
Hold, in the King's name, hold!

SURREY   Friends, masters, countrymen –

LORD MAYOR
Peace ho, peace! I charge you keep the peace.

SHREWSBURY   My masters, countrymen –   35

SHERWIN ^CWILLIAMSON^C   The noble Earl of Shrewsbury!
Let's hear him.

^CGEORGE^C BETTS   We'll hear the Earl of Surrey.

LINCOLN   The Earl of Shrewsbury!

GEORGE BETTS   We'll hear both.   40

ALL CITIZENS   Both, both, both, both!

LINCOLN   Peace, I say, peace! Are you men of wisdom,
or what are you?

SURREY
What you will have them, but not men of wisdom.

SOME CITIZENS   We'll not hear my lord of Surrey.   45

OTHER CITIZENS   No, no, no, no, no! Shrewsbury,
Shrewsbury!

MORE   Whiles they are o'er the bank of their obedience
Thus will they bear down all things.

LINCOLN   Shrieve More speaks. Shall we hear Shrieve   50
More speak?

DOLL   Let's hear him. 'A keeps a plentiful shrievaltry,
and 'a made my brother, Arthur Watchins, Sergeant
Safe's yeoman. Let's hear Shrieve More!

ALL CITIZENS   Shrieve More, More, More, Shrieve   55
More!

MORE   Even by the rule you have among yourselves,
Command still audience.

SOME CITIZENS   Surrey, Surrey!

OTHER CITIZENS   More, More!   60

LINCOLN, GEORGE BETTS   Peace, peace, silence, peace!

MORE   You that have voice and credit with the number,
Command them to a stillness.

LINCOLN   A plague on them, they will not hold their
peace. The devil cannot rule them.   65

MORE   Then what a rough and riotous charge have you
To lead those that the devil cannot rule.
Good masters, hear me speak.

DOLL   Ay, by th' mass w'ill we, More. Thou'rt a good
housekeeper, and I thank thy good worship for my   70
brother Arthur Watchins.

ALL THE OTHER CITIZENS   Peace, peace!

MORE   Look what you do offend you cry upon;
　　That is, the peace. Not one of you here present,
75　　Had there such fellows lived when you were babes
　　That could have topped the peace as now you would,
　　The peace wherein you have till now grown up
　　Had been ta'en from you, and the bloody times
　　Could not have brought you to the state of men.
80　　Alas, poor things! What is it you have got
　　Although we grant you get the thing you seek?
GEORGE BETTS   Marry, the removing of the strangers,
　　which cannot choose but much advantage the poor
　　handicrafts of the City.
MORE
85　　Grant them removed, and grant that this your noise
　　Hath chid down all the majesty of England.
　　Imagine that you see the wretched strangers,
　　Their babies at their backs, with their poor luggage,
　　Plodding to th' ports and coasts for transportation,
90　　And that you sit as kings in your desires,
　　Authority quite silenced by your brawl,
　　And you in ruff of your opinions clothed:
　　What had you got? I'll tell you: you had taught
　　How insolence and strong hand should prevail,
95　　How order should be quelled. And by this pattern
　　Not one of you should live an aged man;
　　For other ruffians, as their fancies wrought,
　　With selfsame hand, self reasons, and self right,
　　Would shark on you, and men, like ravenous fishes,
100　　Would feed on one another.
DOLL   Before God, that's as true as the gospel.
GEORGE BETTS ᶜLINCOLNᶜ   Nay, this' a sound fellow, I
　　tell you. Let's mark him.
MORE
　　Let me set up before your thoughts, good friends,
105　　One supposition, which if you will mark
　　You shall perceive how horrible a shape
　　Your innovation bears. First, 'tis a sin
　　Which oft th'apostle did forewarn us of,
　　Urging obedience to authority;
110　　And 'twere no error if I told you all
　　You were in arms 'gainst ⟨God⟩.
ALL CITIZENS   Marry, God forbid that!
MORE   Nay, certainly you are.
　　For to the king God hath his office lent
115　　Of dread, of justice, power and command;
　　Hath bid him rule, and willed you to obey.
　　And, to add ampler majesty to this,
　　He hath not only lent the king His figure,
　　His throne and sword, but given him His own name:
120　　Calls him a god on earth. What do you, then,
　　Rising 'gainst him that God Himself installs,
　　But rise 'gainst God? What do you to your souls
　　In doing this? O, desperate as you are,
　　Wash your foul minds with tears, and those same hands
125　　That you, like rebels, lift against the peace,
　　Lift up for peace; and your unreverent knees,
　　Make them your feet. ᶜTo kneel to be forgiven

　　Is safer wars than ever you can make
　　Whose discipline is riot.
　　In, in, to your obedience! Why, even your hurly   130
　　Cannot proceed but by obedience.ᶜ
　　ᶜTell me but this:ᶜ What rebel captain,
　　As mutinies are incident, by his name
　　Can still the rout? Who will obey a traitor?
　　Or how can well that proclamation sound   135
　　When there is no addition but 'a rebel'
　　To qualify a rebel? You'll put down strangers,
　　Kill them, cut their throats, possess their houses
　　And lead the majesty of law in lyam
　　To slip him like a hound. ᶜAlas, alas!ᶜ Say now the
　　　King,   140
　　As he is clement if th'offender mourn,
　　Should so much come too short of your great trespass
　　As but to banish you: whither would you go?
　　What country, by the nature of your error,
　　Should give you harbour? Go you to France or Flanders,   145
　　To any German province, Spain or Portugal,
　　Nay, anywhere that not adheres to England:
　　Why, you must needs be strangers. Would you be pleased
　　To find a nation of such barbarous temper
　　That, breaking out in hideous violence,   150
　　Would not afford you an abode on earth,
　　Whet their detested knives against your throats,
　　Spurn you like dogs, and like as if that God
　　Owed not nor made not you, nor that the elements
　　Were not all appropriate to your comforts   155
　　But chartered unto them? What would you think
　　To be thus used? This is the strangers' case,
　　And this your mountainish inhumanity.
ALL CITIZENS   Faith, 'a says true. Let's do as we may be
　　done by.   160
ALL CITIZENS ᶜLINCOLNᶜ   We'll be ruled by you,
　　Master More, if you'll stand our friend to procure our
　　pardon.
MORE   Submit you to these noble gentlemen,
　　Entreat their mediation to the King,   165
　　Give up yourself to form, obey the magistrate,
　　And there's no doubt but mercy may be found
　　If you so seek it.

[Addition II: Shakespeare]
_____
[Original Text: Munday]

ALL CITIZENS   We yield, and desire his highness' mercy.
　　They lay by their weapons.
MORE   No doubt his majesty will grant it you.   170
　　But you must yield to go to several prisons
　　Till that his highness' will be further known.
ALL CITIZENS   Most willingly, whither you will have us.
SHREWSBURY
　　Lord Mayor, let them be sent to several prisons,
　　And there, in any case, be well entreated.   175
　　My lord of Surrey, please you to take horse
　　And ride to Cheapside, where the aldermen

Are with their several companies in arms.
Will them to go unto their several wards,
180　Both for the stay of further mutiny
And for the apprehending of such persons
As shall contend.
SURREY　　　　　　I go, my noble lord.　　　*Exit.*
SHREWSBURY
We'll straight go tell his highness these good news.
Withal, Shrieve More, I'll tell him how your breath
185　Hath ransomed many a subject from sad death.　*Exit.*
LORD MAYOR
Lincoln and Sherwin, you shall both to Newgate,
The rest unto the Counters.
PALMER
Go, guard them hence. A little breath well spent
Cheats expectation in his fair'st event.
190　DOLL　　Well, Sheriff More, thou hast done more with
thy good words than all they could with their weapons.
Give me thy hand. Keep thy promise now for the
King's pardon, or, by the Lord, I'll call thee a plain
cony-catcher.
LINCOLN
195　Farewell, Shrieve More. And, as we yield by thee,
So make our peace; then thou deal'st honestly.
HCLOWN BETTS　Ay, and save us from the gallows, else
'a deals double honestly.H
　　　　　　　　　　　　[The Citizens] are led away.
LORD MAYOR
Master Shrieve More, you have preserved the City
200　From a most dangerous fierce commotion.
For if this limb of riot here in St Martin's
Had joined with other branches of the City
That did begin to kindle, 'twould have bred
Great rage. That rage much murder would have fed.
PALMER
205　Not steel but eloquence hath wrought this good.
You have redeemed us from much threatened blood.
MORE　　My lord, and brethren, what I here have spoke
My country's love and, next, the City's care
Enjoined me to; which since it thus prevails,
210　Think God hath made weak More His instrument
To thwart sedition's violent intent.
I think 'twere best, my lord, some two hours hence
We meet at the Guildhall, and there determine
That thorough every ward the watch be clad
215　In armour. But especially provide
That at the City gates selected men,
Substantial citizens, do ward tonight,
For fear of further mischief.
LORD MAYOR　　　　　　　　It shall be so.

Enter SHREWSBURY *[with Attendant bearing
a staff of office].*

But yond, methinks, my lord of Shrewsbury.
220　SHREWSBURY　　My lord, his majesty sends loving thanks
To you, your brethren and his faithful subjects
Your careful citizens. But Master More, to you

A rougher yet as kind a salutation.
Your name is yet too short. Nay, you must kneel.
　　[More kneels.]
A knight's creation is this knightly steel.　　225
　　[He knights More.]
Rise up Sir Thomas More.
MORE *[Rises.]*
I thank his highness for thus honouring me.
SHREWSBURY
This is but first taste of his princely favour,
For it hath pleased his high majesty,
Noting your wisdom and deserving merit,　　230
To put this staff of honour in your hand,
For he hath chose you of his Privy Council.
　　[He gives More the staff of office.]
MORE　　My lord, for to deny my sovereign's bounty
Were to drop precious stones into the heaps
Whence first they came.　　　　　　　　235
To urge my imperfections in excuse
Were all as stale as custom. No, my lord,
My service is my king's. Good reason why,
Since life or death hangs on our sovereign's eye.
LORD MAYOR
His majesty hath honoured much the City　　240
In this his princely choice.
MORE　　　　　　　　　My lord and brethren,
Though I depart for ⟨Court,⟩ my love shall rest
⟨　　　　　　　　　　　　　　　　　⟩
I now must sleep in Court, sound sleeps forbear.
The chamberlain to state is public care.　　245
Yet in this rising of my private blood
My studious thoughts shall tend the City's good.

Enter CROFTS.

SHREWSBURY　　How now, Crofts? What news?
CROFTS
My lord, his highness sends express command
That a record be entered of this riot,　　250
And that the chief and capital offenders
Be thereon straight arraigned; for himself intends
To sit in person on the rest tomorrow
At Westminster.
SHREWSBURY　　　Lord Mayor, you hear your charge.
Come, good Sir Thomas More, to Court let's hie.　　255
You are th'appeaser of this mutiny.
MORE *[to Lord Mayor]*
My lord, farewell. New days begets new tides.
Life whirls 'bout fate, then to a grave it slides.
　　　　　　　　　　　　　Exeunt severally.

[Sc. 7]　　　　*Enter* Master Sheriff, *and
meet a* Messenger.

SHERIFF　　Messenger, what news?
MESSENGER　　　　　　　Is execution yet performed?
SHERIFF　　Not yet. The carts stand ready at the stairs,
And they shall presently away to Tyburn.

MESSENGER

Stay, Master Shrieve. It is the Council's pleasure,

5 For more example in so bad a case,

A gibbet be erected in Cheapside

Hard by the Standard, whither you must bring

Lincoln, and those that were the chief with him,

To suffer death, and that immediately.

Enter Officers.

SHERIFF   It shall be done, sir.   *Exit Messenger.*

10   Officers, be speedy.

Call for a gibbet, see it be erected.

Others make haste to Newgate; bid them bring

The prisoners hither, for they here must die.

Away, I say, and see no time be slacked.

15 OFFICERS   We go, sir.

SHERIFF   That's well said, fellows. Now you do your duty.

Exeunt some [Officers], severally.

Others set up the gibbet.

God for his pity help these troublous times!

The streets stopped up with gazing multitudes,

Command our armed officers with halberds

20 Make way for entrance of the prisoners.

Let proclamation once again be made

That every householder, on pain of death,

Keep in his prentices, and every man

Stand with a weapon ready at his door,

25 As he will answer to the contrary.

1 OFFICER   I'll see it done, sir.   *Exit.*

Enter another Officer.

SHERIFF   Bring them away to execution.

The writ is come above two hours since.

The City will be fined for this neglect.

2 OFFICER

30 There's such a press and multitude at Newgate

They cannot bring the carts unto the stairs

To take the prisoners in.

SHERIFF   Then let them come on foot.

We may not dally time with great command.

2 OFFICER   Some of the Bench, sir, think it very fit

35 That stay be made, and give it out abroad

The execution is deferred till morning;

And when the streets shall be a little cleared

To chain them up, and suddenly dispatch it.

The prisoners are brought in, [among them LINCOLN,

DOLL, WILLIAMSON, CLOWN BETTS *and* SHERWIN,]

well guarded, [with the Hangman].

SHERIFF   Stay, meantime methinks they come along.

40 See, they are coming. So, 'tis very well.

Bring Lincoln there the first unto the tree.

ᴴCLOWN BETTS   Ay, for I cry lag, sir.ᴴ

LINCOLN   I knew the first, sir, did belong to me.

This the old proverb now complete doth make:

That 'Lincoln should be hanged for London's sake.'

45 I'God's name, let's to work.

[*to Hangman*]   Fellow, dispatch.

He goes up.

I was the foremost man in this rebellion,

And I the foremost that must die for it.

DOLL   Bravely, John Lincoln, let thy death express

That, as thou lived'st a man, thou died'st no less.   50

LINCOLN

Doll Williamson, thine eyes shall witness it.

Then, to all you that come to view mine end,

I must confess I had no ill intent

But against such as wronged us overmuch.

And now I can perceive it was not fit   55

That private men should carve out their redress

Which way they list. No, learn it now by me:

Obedience is the best in each degree.

And, asking mercy meekly of my king,

I patiently submit me to the law.   60

But God forgive them that were cause of it;

And, as a Christian, truly from my heart,

I likewise crave they would forgive me too,

‹   ›

That others by example of the same   65

Henceforth be warned to attempt the like

'Gainst any alien that repaireth hither,

Fare ye well all. The next time that we meet

I trust in heaven we shall each other greet.

He leaps off.

DOLL   Farewell, John Lincoln. Say all what they can, 70

Thou lived'st a good fellow, and died'st an honest man.

ᴴCLOWN BETTS   Would I were so far on my journey. The

first stretch is the worst, methinks.ᴴ

SHERIFF   Bring Williamson there forward.

DOLL   Good Master Shrieve, I have an earnest suit,   75

And, as you are a man, deny't me not.

SHERIFF   Woman, what is it? Be it in my power,

Thou shalt obtain it.

DOLL   Let me die next, sir, that is all I crave.

You know not what a comfort you shall bring   80

To my poor heart to die before my husband.

SHERIFF   Bring her to death. She shall have her desire.

ᴴCLOWN BETTS   Sir, and I have a suit to you too.

SHERIFF   What is it?

CLOWN BETTS   That, as you have hanged Lincoln first   85

and will hang her next, so you will not hang me at all.

SHERIFF   Nay, you set ope the Counter gates, and you

must hang chiefly.

CLOWN BETTS   Well then, so much for that!ᴴ

DOLL [*to Sheriff*]

Sir, your free bounty much contents my mind.   90

Commend me to that good shrieve Master More,

And tell him, had't not been for his persuasion,

John Lincoln had not hung here as he does.

We would first have locked up in Leadenhall,

And there been burned to ashes with the roof.   95

SHERIFF

Woman, what Master More did was a subject's duty,

And hath so pleased our gracious lord the King

That he is hence removed to higher place
And made of Council to his majesty.

100 DOLL   Well is he worthy of it, by my troth:
An honest, wise, well-spoken gentleman.
Yet would I praise his honesty much more
If he had kept his word and saved our lives.
But let that pass. Men are but men, and so
105 Words are but words, and pays not what men owe.
Now, husband, since perhaps the world may say
That through my means thou com'st thus to thy end,
Here I begin this cup of death to thee,
Because thou shalt be sure to taste no worse
110 Than I have taken that must go before thee.
What though I be a woman? That's no matter.
I do owe God a death, and I must pay him.
Husband, give me thy hand. Be not dismayed.
This chore being chored, then all our debt is paid.
115 Only two little babes we leave behind us,
And all I can bequeath them at this time
Is but the love of some good honest friend
To bring them up in charitable sort.
What, masters? – He goes upright that never halts,
120 And they may live to mend their parents' faults.
WILLIAMSON
Why, well said, wife. I'faith, thou cheer'st my heart.
Give me thy hand. Let's kiss, and so let's part.
      He kisses her on the ladder.
DOLL   The next kiss, Williamson, shall be in heaven.
Now cheerly, lads! George Betts, a hand with thee.
[*to Clown Betts*] And thine too, Ralph. And thine,
125   good honest Sherwin.
Now let me tell the women of this town
No stranger yet brought Doll to lying down.
So long as I an Englishman can see,
Nor French nor Dutch shall get a kiss of me.
130 And when that I am dead, for me yet say
I died in scorn to be a stranger's prey.
      A great shout and noise [*within*].
VOICES WITHIN   Pardon, pardon, pardon, pardon!
Room for the Earl of Surrey! Room there, room!

      Enter SURREY.

SURREY   Save the man's life, if it be possible!
135 SHERIFF   It is too late, my lord, he's dead already.
SURREY   I tell ye, Master Sheriff, you are too forward
To make such haste with men unto their death.
I think your pains will merit little thanks,
Since that his highness is so merciful
140 As not to spill the blood of any subject.
SHERIFF
My noble lord, would we so much had known!
The Council's warrant hastened our dispatch.
It had not else been done so suddenly.
SURREY   Sir Thomas More humbly upon his knee
145 Did beg the lives of all, since on his word
They did so gently yield. The King hath granted it,
And made him Lord High Chancellor of England,

According as he worthily deserves.
Since Lincoln's life cannot be had again,
Then for the rest, from my dread sovereign's lips,   150
I here pronounce free pardon for them all.
ALL (*flinging up caps*)
God save the King! God save the King,
My good Lord Chancellor and the Earl of Surrey!
DOLL   And Doll desires it from her very heart
More's name may live for this right noble part;   155
And whensoe'er we talk of Ill May Day
Praise More, whose ‹   › falls ‹   ›.
SURREY   In hope his highness' clemency and mercy,
Which in the arms of mild and meek compassion
Would rather clip you, as the loving nurse   160
Oft doth the wayward infant, than to leave you
To the sharp rod of justice; so to draw you
To shun such lewd assemblies as beget
Unlawful riots and such traitorous acts
That, striking with the hand of private hate,   165
Maim your dear country with a public wound.
O God, that mercy, whose majestic brow
Should be unwrinkled, and that awe-full justice,
Which looketh through a veil of sufferance
Upon the frailty of the multitude,   170
Should with the clamours of outrageous wrongs
Be stirred and wakened thus to punishment!
But your deserved death he doth forgive.
Who gives you life, pray all he long may live.
ALL   God save the King! God save the King,   175
My good Lord Chancellor, and the Earl of Surrey!
                              Exeunt.

[Sc. 8] *A table being covered with a green carpet, a
state cushion on it, and the purse and mace lying thereon.*

                              [Original Text: Munday]

                              [Addition III: Hand C]

                    Enter MORE.

MORE   It is in heaven that I am thus and thus,
And that which we profanely term our fortunes
Is the provision of the power above,
Fitted and shaped just to that strength of nature
Which we are born with. Good God, good God,   5
That I from such an humble bench of birth
Should step, as 'twere, up to my country's head,
And give the law out there; I, in my father's life,
To take prerogative and tithe of knees
From elder kinsmen, and him bind, by my place,   10
To give the smooth and dexter way to me
That owe it him by nature: sure these things,
Not physicked by respect, might turn our blood
To much corruption. But, More, the more thou hast,
Either of honour, office, wealth and calling,   15
Which might accite thee to embrace and hug them,
The more do thou in serpents' natures think them,

Fear their gay skins with thought of their sharp state,
And let this be thy maxim: to be great
Is, when the thread of hazard is once spun,
A bottom, great wound up, greatly undone.

20

[Addition III: Hand C]

[Addition IV: Hand C]

Enter Sir Thomas More's man [RANDALL],
attired like him.

Come on, sir, are you ready?

RANDALL Yes, my lord. I stand but on a few points. I
shall have done presently. Before God, I have practised
your lordship's shift so well that I think I shall grow
proud, my lord.

25

MORE
'Tis fit thou shouldst wax proud, or else thou'lt ne'er
Be near allied to greatness. Observe me, sirrah.
The learned clerk Erasmus is arrived
Within our English Court. Last night, I hear,
He feasted with our honoured English poet
The Earl of Surrey, and I learned today
The famous clerk of Rotterdam will visit
Sir Thomas More. Therefore, sir, take my seat.
You are Lord Chancellor.   [*Randall sits.*]

30

                              Dress your behaviour
According to my carriage. But beware
You talk not overmuch, for 'twill betray thee.
Who prates not much seems wise, his wit few scan,
While the tongue blabs tales of the imperfect man.
I'll see if great Erasmus can distinguish
Merit and outward ceremony.

35

40

RANDALL   If I do not deserve a share for playing of your
lordship well, let me be yeoman usher to your sumpter
and be banished from wearing of a gold chain forever.

MORE   Well, sir, I'll hide our motion. Act my part
With a firm boldness, and thou winn'st my heart.

45

Enter the Sheriff *with* FALCONER
(*a ruffian*), *and* Officers.

How now, what's the matter?

FALCONER [*to Officers*] Tug me not; I'm no bear.
'Sblood, if all the dogs in Paris Garden hung at my tail,
I'd shake 'em off with this: that I'll appear before no
king christened but my good Lord Chancellor.

50

SHERIFF We'll christen you, sirrah. – Bring him
forward.

MORE [*to Falconer*]   How now, what tumults make you?

FALCONER   The azured heavens protect my noble Lord
Chancellor!

55

MORE [*to Sheriff*]   What fellow's this?

SHERIFF   A ruffian, my lord, that hath set half the City
in an uproar.

FALCONER   My lord –

60

SHERIFF   There was a fray in Paternoster Row, and
because they would not be parted the street was choked
up with carts.

FALCONER   My noble lord, Pannyer Alley's throat was
open.

65

MORE   Sirrah, hold your peace.

FALCONER   I'll prove the street was not choked, but is as
well as ever it was since it was a street.

SHERIFF   This fellow was a principal broacher of the
broil –

70

FALCONER   'Sblood, I broached none. It was broached
and half run out before I had a lick at it.

SHERIFF   – and would be brought before no justice but
your honour.

FALCONER   I am haled, my noble lord.

75

MORE [*to Sheriff*]
No ear to choose for every trivial noise
But mine, and in so full a time? Away.
You wrong me, Master Shrieve. Dispose of him
At your own pleasure. Send the knave to Newgate.

FALCONER   To Newgate? 'Sblood, Sir Thomas More, I
appeal, I appeal: from Newgate to any of the two
worshipful Counters.

80

MORE   Fellow, whose man are you that are thus lusty?

FALCONER   My name's Jack Falconer. I serve, next
under God and my prince, Master Morris, secretary to
my lord of Winchester.

85

MORE   A fellow of your hair is very fit
To be a secretary's follower!

FALCONER   I hope so, my lord. The fray was between
the Bishops' men of Ely and Winchester, and I could
not in honour but part them. I thought it stood not
with my reputation and degree to come to my
questions and answers before a City justice. I knew I
should to the pot.

90

MORE   Thou hast been there, it seems, too late already.

95

FALCONER   I know your honour is wise, and so forth,
and I desire to be only catechized or examined by you,
my noble Lord Chancellor.

MORE   Sirrah, sirrah, you are a busy dangerous ruffian.

FALCONER   Ruffian?

100

MORE   How long have you worn this hair?

FALCONER   I have worn this hair ever since I was born.

MORE   You know that's not my question: but how long
Hath this shag fleece hung dangling on thy head?

FALCONER   How long, my lord? Why, sometimes thus
long, sometimes lower, as the Fates and humours
please.

105

MORE   So quick, sir, with me, ha? I see, good fellow,
Thou lovest plain dealing. Sirrah, tell me now
When were you last at barber's? How long time
Have you upon your head worn this shag hair?

110

FALCONER   My lord, Jack Falconer tells no Aesop's
fables. Troth, I was not at barber's this three years. I
have not been cut, nor will not be cut, upon a foolish
vow which, as the Destinies shall direct, I am sworn to
keep.

115

MORE   When comes that vow out?

FALCONER   Why, when the humours are purged; not
these three years.

120 MORE   Vows are recorded in the court of heaven,
       For they are holy acts. Young man, I charge thee
       And do advise thee start not from that vow.
       And for I will be sure thou shalt not shear,
       Besides because it is an odious sight
125   To see a man thus hairy, thou shalt lie
       In Newgate till thy vow and thy three years
       Be full expired. – Away with him.
       FALCONER   My lord –
       MORE   Cut off this fleece and lie there but a month.
       FALCONER   I'll not lose a hair to be Lord Chancellor of
130   Europe!
       MORE   To Newgate then. Sirrah, great sins are bred
       In all that body where there's a foul head.
       Away with him.   *Exeunt [all but Randall].*

            Enter SURREY, ERASMUS *and Attendants.*

       SURREY
       Now, great Erasmus, you approach the presence
135   Of a most worthy learned gentleman.
       This little isle holds not a truer friend
       Unto the arts; nor doth his greatness add
       A feigned flourish to his worthy parts.
       He's great in study: that's the statist's grace
140   That gains more reverence than the outward place.
       ERASMUS
       Report, my lord, hath crossed the narrow seas,
       And to the several parts of Christendom
       Hath borne the fame of your Lord Chancellor.
       I long to see him whom with loving thoughts
145   I in my study oft have visited.
       Is that Sir Thomas More?
       SURREY   It is, Erasmus.
       Now shall you view the honourablest scholar,
       The most religious politician,
       The worthiest counsellor, that tends our state.
150   That study is the general watch of England.
       In it, the Prince's safety and the peace
       That shines upon our commonwealth are forged
       By loyal industry.
       ERASMUS   I doubt him not
       To be as near the life of excellence
155   As you proclaim him, when his meanest servants
       Are of some weight. You saw, my lord, his porter
       Give entertainment to us at the gate
       In Latin good phrase. What's the master, then,
       When such good parts shine in his meanest men?
160   SURREY   His lordship hath some weighty business,
       For, see, as yet he takes no notice of us.
       ERASMUS   I think 'twere best I did my duty to him
       In a short Latin speech.
            [He takes off his hat and addresses Randall.]
       Qui in celeberrima patria natus est et gloriosa plus habet
165   *negotii ut in lucem veniat quam qui –*
       RANDALL   I prithee, good Erasmus, be covered. I have
       forsworn speaking of Latin, else, as I am true
       councillor, I'd tickle you with a speech. Nay, sit,

       Erasmus. Sit, good my lord of Surrey. I'll make my
       lady come to you anon, if she will, and give you   170
       entertainment.
       ERASMUS   Is this Sir Thomas More?
       SURREY   O good Erasmus,
       You must conceive his vein. He's ever furnished
       With these conceits.
       RANDALL   Yes, faith, my learned poet doth not lie for   175
       that matter. I am neither more nor less than merry Sir
       Thomas always. Wilt sup with me? By God, I love a
       parlous wise fellow that smells of a politician better
       than a long progress.

            Enter Sir Thomas MORE.

       SURREY   We are deluded. This is not his lordship.   180
       RANDALL   I pray you, Erasmus, how long will the
       Holland cheese in your country keep without maggots?
       MORE   Fool, painted barbarism, retire thyself
       Into thy first creation.   *[Exit Randall.]*
                              Thus you see,   185
       My loving learned friends, how far respect
       Waits often on the ceremonious train
       Of base illiterate wealth, whilst men of schools,
       Shrouded in poverty, are counted fools.
       Pardon, thou reverend German, I have mixed
       So slight a jest to the fair entertainment   190
       Of thy most worthy self. For know, Erasmus,
       Mirth wrinkles up my face, and I still crave
       When that forsakes me I may hug my grave.
                    Et tu Erasmus an diabolus.
       ERASMUS   Your honour's merry humour is best physic
       Unto your able body, for we learn,   195
       Where melancholy chokes the passages
       Of blood and breath, the erected spirit still
       Lengthens our days with sportful exercise.
       Study should be the saddest time of life;
       The rest a sport exempt from thought of strife.   200
       MORE   Erasmus preacheth gospel against physic.
       My noble poet –
       SURREY   O my lord, you tax me
       In that word 'poet' of much idleness.
       It is a study that makes poor our fate.
       Poets were ever thought unfit for state.   205
       MORE   O, give not up fair poesy, sweet lord,
       To such contempt. That I may speak my heart,
       It is the sweetest heraldry of art
       That sets a difference 'tween the tough, sharp holly
       And tender bay tree.
       SURREY   Yet, my lord,   210
       It is become the very lag i'number
       To all mechanic sciences.
       MORE   Why I'll show the reason
       This is no age for poets. They should sing
       To the loud canon *heroica facta*:
       Qui faciunt reges heroica carmina laudant;   215
       And, as great subjects of their pen decay,
       Even so, unphysicked, they do melt away.

Enter Master MORRIS.

[*to Surrey*] Come, will your lordship in? – My dear
    Erasmus!
– I'll hear you, Master Morris, presently.

220   [*to Surrey*] My lord, I make you master of my house.
We'll banquet here with fresh and staid delights.
The Muses' music here shall cheer our spirits.
The cates must be but mean where scholars sit;
For they're made all with courses of neat wit.
          [*Exeunt Surrey, Erasmus and Attendants.*]

225   How now, Master Morris?

MORRIS   I am a suitor to your lordship in behalf of a
servant of mine.

MORE   The fellow with long hair, good Master Morris?
Come to me three years hence, and then I'll hear you.

230 MORRIS   I understand your honour; but the foolish
knave has submitted himself to the mercy of a barber,
and is without, ready to make a new vow before your
lordship hereafter to live civil.

MORE   Nay then, let's talk with him; pray call him in.

Enter FALCONER *and* Officers.

235 FALCONER   Bless your honour: a new man, my lord.

MORE   Why sure this' not he.

FALCONER   An your lordship will, the barber shall give
you a sample of my head. I am he, in faith, my lord, ^DI
am *ipse*.^D

240 MORE   Why, now thy face is like an honest man's.
Thou hast played well at this new-cut and won.

FALCONER   No, my lord, lost all that ever God sent me.

MORE   God sent thee into the world as thou art now,
with a short hair. How quickly are three years run out
245 in Newgate!

FALCONER   I think so, my lord, for there was but a hair's
length between my going thither and so long time.

MORE   Because I see some grace in thee, go free.
Discharge him, fellows.   [*Exeunt Officers.*]
        Farewell, Master Morris.

250 [*to Falconer*] Thy head is for thy shoulders now more fit:
Thou hast less hair upon it, but more wit.   *Exit.*

MORRIS   Did not I tell thee always of these locks?

FALCONER   An the locks were on again, all the
goldsmiths in Cheapside should not pick them open.
255 'Sheart, if my hair stand not on end when I look for my
face in a glass, I am a polecat. Here's a lousy jest! But if
I notch not that rogue Tom Barber that makes me look
thus like a Brownist, hang me. I'll be worse to the
nittical knave than ten tooth-drawings. Here's a head
260 with a pox!

[Addition IV: Hand C]

[Addition IV: Dekker]

MORRIS   What ail'st thou? Art thou mad now?

FALCONER   Mad now? Nails, if loss of hair cannot mad
a man – what can? I am deposed: my crown is taken
from me. More had been better a' scoured Moorditch

265 than a' notched me thus. Does he begin sheep-shearing
with Jack Falconer?

MORRIS   Nay, an you feed this vein, sir, fare you well.

FALCONER   Why, farewell, frost! I'll go hang myself out
for the – poll-head. Make a Sar'cen of Jack?

270 MORRIS   Thou desperate knave, for that I see the devil
Wholly gets hold of thee –

FALCONER   The devil's a damned rascal.

MORRIS   I charge thee wait on me no more; no more
Call me thy master.

275 FALCONER   Why then, a word, Master Morris.

MORRIS   I'll hear no words, sir, fare you well.

FALCONER   'Sblood, 'farewell'?

MORRIS   Why dost thou follow me?

FALCONER   Because I'm an ass. Do you set your shavers
280 upon me, and then cast me off? Must I condole? Have
the Fates played the fools? (*Weeps.*) Am I their cut?
Now the poor sconce is taken, must Jack march with
bag and baggage?

MORRIS   You cockscomb!

285 FALCONER   Nay, you ha' poached me. You h'a' given me
a hair, it's here, here.

MORRIS   Away, you kind ass. Come, sir, dry your eyes.
Keep your old place, and mend these fooleries.

FALCONER   I care not to be turned off, an 'twere a
290 ladder, so it be in my humour or the Fates beckon to
me. Nay, pray, sir, if the Destinies spin me a fine
thread, Falconer flies another pitch. And to avoid the
headache, hereafter before I'll be a hairmonger I'll be a
whoremonger.   *Exeunt.*

[Addition IV: Dekker]

[Addition V: Hand C]

[Sc. 9]   *Enter a* Messenger *to* MORE.

              ^C*Messenger: T. Goodale.*^C

MESSENGER   My honourable lord, the Mayor of London
Accompanied with his lady and her train
Are coming hither, and are hard at hand
To feast with you. A sergeant's come before
To tell your lordship of their near approach.
           [*Exit Messenger.*]   5

MORE
Why, this is cheerful news. Friends go and come.
Reverend Erasmus, whose delicious words
Express the very soul and life of wit,
Newly took sad leave of me, with tears
Troubled the silver channel of the Thames,   10
Which, glad of such a burden, proudly swelled
And on her bosom bore him toward the sea.
He's gone to Rotterdam. Peace go with him!
He left me heavy when he went from hence,
But this recomforts me: the kind Lord Mayor,   15
His brethren aldermen, with their fair wives
Will feast this night with us. Why, so't should be.
More's merry heart lives by good company.

[*Enter* Master ROPER *and* Servingmen.]

Good gentlemen, be careful; give great charge
20 Our diet be made dainty for the taste.
For, of all people that the earth affords,
The Londoners fare richest at their boards.

[Addition V: Hand C]

[Original Text: Munday]

Come, my good fellows, stir, be diligent.
Sloth is an idle fellow. Leave him now.
25 The time requires your expeditious service.
Place me here stools to set the ladies on.
    [*Servingmen set stools.*]
Son Roper, you have given order for the banquet?
ROPER   I have, my lord, and everything is ready.

Enter [*More's*] LADY.

MORE   O welcome, wife. Give you direction
30 How women should be placed; you know it best.
For my Lord Mayor, his brethren and the rest,
Let me alone. Men best can order men.
LADY   I warrant ye, my lord, all shall be well.
There's one without that stays to speak with ye,
35 And bade me tell ye that he is a player.
MORE   A player, wife? – One of ye bid him come in.
              Exit one[, *a Servingman*].
Nay, stir there, fellows. Fie, ye are too slow!
See that your lights be in a readiness.
The banquet shall be here. – God's me, madam,
Leave my Lady Mayoress? Both of us from the
40   board?
And my son Roper too? What may our guests think?
LADY   My lord, they are risen, and sitting by the fire.
MORE   Why, yet go you, and keep them company.
It is not meet we should be absent both.   *Exit Lady.*

Enter PLAYER.

45 Welcome, good friend. What is your will with me?
PLAYER   My lord, my fellows and myself
Are come to tender ye our willing service,
So please you to command us.
MORE   What, for a play, you mean?
Whom do ye serve?
PLAYER   My Lord Cardinal's grace.
MORE
50 My Lord Cardinal's players? Now trust me, welcome.
You happen hither in a lucky time
To pleasure me and benefit yourselves.
The Mayor of London and some aldermen,
His lady and their wives are my kind guests
55 This night at supper. Now, to have a play
Before the banquet will be excellent.
How think you, son Roper?
ROPER   'Twill do well, my lord,
And be right pleasing pastime to your guests.
MORE   I prithee tell me, what plays have ye?

PLAYER   Diverse, my lord: *The Cradle of Security*,   60
Hit Nail o'th' Head, Impatient Poverty,
The Play of Four Ps, Dives and Lazarus,
Lusty Juventus and *The Marriage of Wit and Wisdom.*
MORE
The Marriage of Wit and Wisdom? That, my lads,
I'll none but that. The theme is very good,   65
And may maintain a liberal argument.
To marry wit to wisdom asks some cunning.
Many have wit that may come short of wisdom.
We'll see how Master Poet plays his part,
And whether wit or wisdom grace his art.   70
[*to Servingmen*] Go, make him drink, and all his
   fellows too.
[*to Player*] How many are ye?
PLAYER   Four men and a boy, sir.
MORE   But one boy?
Then I see there's but few women in the play.
PLAYER   Three, my lord: Dame Science, Lady Vanity   75
And Wisdom she herself.
MORE
And one boy play them all? By'r Lady, he's loaden!
Well, my good fellow, get ye straight together
And make ye ready with what haste ye may.
[*to Servingmen*] Provide their supper 'gainst the play
   be done,   80
Else shall we stay our guests here overlong.
[*to Player*] Make haste, I pray ye.
PLAYER   We will, my lord.
           Exeunt Servingmen and Player.
MORE
Where are the waits? [*to Roper*] Go, bid them play,
To spend the time awhile.

Enter [*his*] LADY.

           How now, madam?
LADY   My lord, they're coming hither.   85
MORE   They're welcome. Wife, I'll tell ye one thing.
Our sport is somewhat mended: we shall have
A play tonight, *The Marriage of Wit and Wisdom*,
And acted by my good Lord Cardinal's players.
How like ye that, wife?
LADY   My lord, I like it well.   90
See, they are coming.

The waits plays hautboys. Enters LORD MAYOR,
so many Aldermen *as may, the* LADY MAYORESS,
in scarlet, with other Ladies *and Sir Thomas More's*
DAUGHTERS, [*one of them* ROPER'S WIFE,] Servants
carrying lighted torches by them.

MORE
Once again, welcome, welcome, my good Lord Mayor,
And brethren all – for once I was your brother,
And so am still in heart. It is not state
That can our love from London separate.   95
⟨   ⟩
⟨   ⟩ naught but pride;

But they that cast an eye still whence they came
Know how they rose, and how to use the same.

LORD MAYOR

100 My lord, you set a gloss on London's fame,
And make it happy ever by your name.
Needs must we say when we remember More,
'Twas he that drove rebellion from our door,
With grave discretion's mild and gentle breath
105 Shielding a many subjects' lives from death.
O, how our City is by you renowned,
And with your virtues our endeavours crowned!

MORE

No more, my good Lord Mayor; but thanks to all,
That on so short a summons you would come
110 To visit him that holds your kindness dear.
[*to his Lady*] Madam, you are not merry with my
    Lady Mayoress
And these fair ladies. Pray ye, seat them all.
[*to Lord Mayor*] And here, my lord, let me appoint
    your place;
The rest to seat themselves. Nay, I'll weary ye;
115 You will not long in haste to visit me.

LADY   Good madam, sit. In sooth, you shall sit here.

LADY MAYORESS

Good madam, pardon me, it may not be.

LADY   In troth, I'll have it so. I'll sit here by ye.
Good ladies, sit. – More stools here, ho!

LADY MAYORESS

120 It is your favour, madam, makes me thus
Presume above my merit.

LADY   When we come to you,
Then shall you rule us as we rule you here.
    [*They sit.*]
Now must I tell ye, madam, we have a play
To welcome ye withal. How good soe'er
125 That know not I; my lord will have it so.

MORE

[*aside to her*] Wife, hope the best; I am sure they'll do
    their best.
They that would better comes not at our feast.
[*aloud*] My good Lord Cardinal's players, I thank
    them for it,
Play us a play, to lengthen out your welcome,
130 My good Lord Mayor and all my other friends.
They say it is *The Marriage of Wit and Wisdom* –
A theme of some import, howe'er it prove.
But if art fail, we'll inch it out with love.
What, are they ready?

SERVANT

135 My lord, one of the players craves to speak with you.

MORE   With me? Where is he?

Enter [the PLAYER *of*] INCLINATION, *the Vice,
ready[, with a bridle in his hand*].

PLAYER *of* INCLINATION   Here, my lord.

MORE   How now, what's the matter?

PLAYER *of* INCLINATION   We would desire your honour

but to stay a little. One of my fellows is but run to   140
Ogle's for a long beard for young Wit, and he'll be here
presently.

MORE   A long beard for young Wit? Why, man, he may
be without a beard till he come to marriage, for wit
goes not all by the hair. When comes Wit in?   145

PLAYER *of* INCLINATION   In the second scene, next to
the Prologue, my lord.

MORE   Why, play on till that scene come, and by that
time Wit's beard will be grown, or else the fellow
returned with it. And what part play'st thou?   150

PLAYER *of* INCLINATION   Inclination, the Vice, my
lord.

MORE   Gramercies, now I may take the Vice if I list. And
wherefore hast thou that bridle in thy hand?

PLAYER *of* INCLINATION   I must be bridled anon, my   155
lord.

MORE   An thou be'st not saddled too it makes no matter,
for then Wit's Inclination may gallop so fast that he
will outstrip wisdom and fall to folly.

PLAYER *of* INCLINATION   Indeed, so he does, to Lady   160
Vanity; but we have no Folly in our play.

MORE   Then there's no wit in't, I'll be sworn. Folly waits
on wit as the shadow on the body, and where wit is
ripest, there folly still is readiest. But begin, I prithee.
We'll rather allow a beardless Wit than Wit, all beard,   165
to have no brain.

PLAYER *of* INCLINATION   Nay, he has his apparel on
too, my lord, and therefore he is the readier to enter.

MORE

Then, good Inclination, begin at a venture.
                        Exit [*Player of Inclination*].
My Lord Mayor, Wit lacks a beard, or else they would
begin.   170
I'd lend him mine, but that it is too thin.
Silence, they come.

The trumpet sounds. Enter the PROLOGUE.

PROLOGUE

Now forasmuch as in these latter days
    Throughout the whole world in every land
Vice doth increase and virtue decays,   175
    Iniquity having the upper hand,
We therefore intend, good gentle audience,
    A pretty, short interlude to play at this present,
Desiring your leave and quiet silence
    To show the same as is meet and expedient.   180
It is called The Marriage of Wit and Wisdom,
    A matter right pithy and pleasing to hear,
Whereof in brief we will show the whole sum.
    But I must be gone, for Wit doth appear.   *Exit.*

Enter WIT, *ruffling, and* INCLINATION, *the Vice.*

WIT [*Sings.*]

    In an arbour green, asleep whereas I lay –   185
    The birds sang sweetly in the midst of the day –
    I dreamed fast of mirth and play.

In youth is pleasure, in youth is pleasure.

190
    Methought I walked still to and fro,
    And from her company I could not go;
    But when I waked it was not so.
In youth is pleasure, in youth is pleasure.

    Therefore my heart is surely plight
    Of her alone to have a sight
195
    Which is my joy and heart's delight.
In youth is pleasure, in youth is pleasure.

MORE [*to Lord Mayor*]   Mark ye, my lord, this is Wit without a beard. What will he be by that time he comes to the commodity of a beard?

INCLINATION [*to Wit*]

200
    O sir, the ground is the better on which she doth go,
    For she will make better cheer with a little she can get
    Than many a one can with a great banquet of meat.

WIT   *And is her name Wisdom?*

INCLINATION   *Ay, sir, a wife most fit*
    For you, my good master, my dainty sweet Wit.

205
WIT   *To be in her company my heart it is set.*
    Therefore I prithee to let us be gone,
    For unto Wisdom Wit hath inclination.

INCLINATION   *O sir, she will come herself even anon,*
    For I told her before where we would stand,
210
    And then she said she would beck us with her hand.
        (*flourishing his dagger*)
    Back with those boys and saucy great knaves.
    What, stand ye here so big in your braves?
    My dagger about your cockscombs shall walk
    If I may but so much as hear ye chat or talk.

215
WIT   *But will she take pains to come for us hither?*

INCLINATION
    I warrant ye, therefore you must be familiar with her.
        When she cometh in place
        You must her embrace
            Somewhat handsomely,
220
        Lest she think it danger
        Because you are a stranger
            To come in your company.

WIT   *I warrant thee, Inclination, I will be busy.*
    O, how Wit longs to be in Wisdom's company!

Enter Lady VANITY, *singing, and beckoning with her hand.*

225
VANITY   *Come hither, come hither, come hither, come.*
    Such cheer as I have, thou shalt have some.

MORE   This is Lady Vanity, I'll hold my life.
    Beware, good Wit, you take not her to wife.

INCLINATION [*to Lady Vanity*]
    What, Unknown Honesty, a word in your ear.
        ([*Lady Vanity*] *offers to depart.*)
230
    You shall not be gone as yet, I swear.
    Here's none but your friends; you need not to fray.
    This young gentleman loves ye, therefore you must stay.

WIT
    I trust in me she will think no danger;
    For I love well the company of fair women

    – And, though to you I am a stranger,
235
    Yet Wit may pleasure you now and then.

VANITY
    Who, you? Nay, you are such a holy man
    That to touch one you dare not be bold.
    I think you would not kiss a young woman
240
    If one would give ye twenty pound in gold.

WIT
    Yes, in good sadness, lady, that I would.
    I could find in my heart to kiss you in your smock.

VANITY   *My back is broad enough to bear that mock;*
    For it hath been told me many a time
245
    That you would be seen in no such company as mine.

WIT   *Not Wit in the company of Lady Wisdom?*
    O Jove, for what do I hither come?

INCLINATION   *Sir, she did this nothing else but to prove*
    Whether a little thing would you move
250
    To be angry and fret.
        What an if one said so?
        Let such trifling matters go,
    And with a kind kiss come out of her debt.

Enter another PLAYER.

PLAYER *of* INCLINATION   Is Luggins come yet with the beard?
255

2 PLAYER   No, faith, he is not come. Alas, what shall we do?

PLAYER *of* INCLINATION [*to More*]   Forsooth, we can go no further till our fellow Luggins come, for he plays Good Counsel, and now he should enter to admonish
260
Wit that this is Lady Vanity and not Lady Wisdom.

MORE   Nay, an it be no more but so, ye shall not tarry at a stand for that. We'll not have our play marred for lack of a little good counsel. Till your fellow come I'll give him the best counsel that I can. Pardon me, my
265
Lord Mayor, I love to be merry.
    [*He rises and joins the Players.*]

MORE [*as Good Counsel*]
    O ⟨good Master⟩ Wit, thou art now on the bow hand,
    And blindly in thine own opinion dost stand.
    I tell thee, this naughty lewd Inclination
270
    Does lead thee amiss in a very strange fashion.
    This is not Wisdom, but Lady Vanity.
    Therefore list to Good Counsel, and be ruled by me.

PLAYER *of* INCLINATION   In troth, my lord, it is as right to Luggins's part as can be. Speak, Wit.

275
MORE   Nay, we will not have our audience disappointed if I can help it.

WIT   *Art thou Good Counsel, and wilt tell me so?*
    Wouldst thou have Wit from Lady Wisdom to go?
    Thou art some deceiver, I tell thee verily,
    In saying that this is Lady Vanity.
280

MORE [*as Good Counsel*]
    Wit, judge not things by the outward show.
    The eye oft mistakes, right well you do know.
    Good Counsel assures thee upon his honesty
    That this is not Wisdom, but Lady Vanity.

Enter LUGGINS, *with the beard.*

285 PLAYER *of* INCLINATION   O my lord, he is come. Now
we shall go forward.

MORE [*to Luggins*]   Art thou come? Well, fellow, I have
help to save thine honesty a little. Now, if thou canst
give Wit any better counsel than I have done, spare
290 not. There I leave him to thy mercy.
But by this time I am sure our banquet's ready.
My lord and ladies, we will taste that first,
And then they shall begin the play again,
Which through the fellow's absence, and by me,
295 Instead of helping, hath been hindered.
[*to Servants*] Prepare against we come. Lights there, I
say.
– Thus fools oft-times do help to mar the play.
Exeunt. Players remain.

PLAYER *of* WIT   Fie, fellow Luggins, you serve us
handsomely, do ye not, think ye?

300 LUGGINS   Why, Ogle was not within, and his wife would
not let me have the beard, and, by my troth, I ran so
fast that I sweat again.

PLAYER *of* INCLINATION   Do ye hear, fellows? Would
not my lord make a rare player? O, he would uphold a
305 company beyond all ho, better than Mason among the
King's players. Did ye mark how extemp'rically he fell
to the matter, and spake Luggins's part almost as it is
in the very book set down?

PLAYER *of* WIT   Peace, do ye know what ye say? My lord
310 a player? Let us not meddle with any such matters. Yet
I may be a little proud that my lord hath answered me
in my part. But come, let us go and be ready to begin
the play again.

LUGGINS   Ay, that's the best, for now we lack nothing.

ᶜ*Enter a* Servingman *to the Players, with a reward.*ᶜ

[Original Text: Munday]

[Addition VI: Heywood]

315 SERVINGMAN   Where be these players?

ALL THE PLAYERS   Here, sir.

SERVINGMAN   My lord is sent for to the Court,
And all the guests do after supper part;
And, for he will not trouble you again,
320 By me for your reward 'a sends eight angels,
With many thanks. But sup before you go.
It is his will you should be fairly entreated.
Follow, I pray ye.   [*Exit.*]

PLAYER *of* WIT   This, Luggins, is your negligence.
Wanting Wit's beard brought things into dislike;
325 For otherwise the play had been all seen,
Where now some curious citizen disgraced it,
And, discommending it, all is dismissed.

PLAYER *of* INCLINATION   'Fore God, 'a says true. But
hear ye, sirs; eight angels, ha! My lord would never
330 give's eight angels. More or less, for twelve pence:
either it should be three pounds, five pounds or ten
pounds. There're twenty shillings wanting, sure.

PLAYER *of* WIT   Twenty to one, 'tis so. I have a trick. My
lord comes; stand aside.

ᶜ*Enter* MORE *with Attendants, with
purse and mace.*ᶜ

MORE   In haste, to Council? What's the business now   335
That all so late his highness sends for me?
– What seek'st thou, fellow?

PLAYER *of* WIT
Nay, nothing. Your lordship sent eight angels by your
man,
And I have lost two of them in the rushes.

MORE
Wit, look to that! Eight angels? I did send them ten.   340
Who gave it them?

SERVINGMAN   I, my lord. I had no more about me;
But by and by they shall receive the rest.

MORE
Well, Wit, 'twas wisely done. Thou play'st Wit well
indeed
Not to be thus deceived of thy right.   345
Am I a man by office truly ordained
Equally to divide true right his own,
And shall I have deceivers in my house?
Then what avails my bounty, when such servants
Deceive the poor of what the master gives?   350
Go one and pull his coat over his ears.
There are too many such. Give them their right.
Wit, let thy fellows thank thee; 'twas well done.
Thou now deservest to match with Lady Wisdom.
[*Exeunt More and Attendants.*]

PLAYER *of* INCLINATION   God-a-mercy, Wit. [*to the*   355
Servingman] Sir, you had a master, Sir Thomas More.
More? But now we shall have more.

LUGGINS   God bless him, I would there were more of
his mind! 'A loves our quality, and yet he's a learned
man and knows what the world is.   360

PLAYER *of* INCLINATION   Well, a kind man, and more
loving than many other, but I think we ha' met with the
first –

LUGGINS   First served his man that had our angels; and
he may chance dine with Duke Humphrey tomorrow,   365
being turned away today. Come, let's go.

PLAYER *of* INCLINATION   And many such rewards
would make us all ride, and horse us with the best nags
in Smithfield.   [*Exeunt.*]

[Addition VI: Heywood]

[Original Text: Munday]

[Sc. 10]   *Enter the* Earls of SHREWSBURY,
SURREY, Bishop of ROCHESTER *and other*
Lords, [*attended,*] *severally, doing courtesy to*
each other, Clerk of the Council *waiting bare-headed.*

SURREY   Good morrow to my lord of Shrewsbury.

SHREWSBURY
The like unto the honoured Earl of Surrey.

Yond comes my lord of Rochester.

ROCHESTER   Good morrow, my good lords.

SURREY   Clerk of the Council,
What time is't of day?

5   CLERK   Past eight of clock, my lord.

SHREWSBURY   I wonder that my good Lord Chancellor
Doth stay so long, considering there's matters
Of high importance to be scanned upon.

SURREY   Clerk of the Council, certify his lordship
The lords expect him here.

10   ROCHESTER   It shall not need.
Yond comes his lordship.

       Enter Sir Thomas MORE, *with purse and mace*
               borne before him.

MORE   Good morrow to this fair assembly.
Come, my good lords, let's sit.
     They sit. [Purse and mace are laid on the table.]
                   O serious square!
Upon this little board is daily scanned

15   The health and preservation of the land,
We the physicians that effect this good,
Now by choice diet, anon by letting blood.
Our toil and careful watching brings the King
In league with slumbers to which peace doth sing.

20   – Avoid the room there!   *[Exeunt Attendants.]*
– What business, lords, today?

SHREWSBURY   This, my good lord:
About the entertainment of the Emperor
'Gainst the perfidious French into our pay.

SURREY   My lords, as 'tis the custom in this place

25   The youngest should speak first, so if I chance
In this case to speak youngly, pardon me.
I will agree France now hath her full strength,
As having new recovered the pale blood
Which war sluiced forth; and I consent to this:

30   That the conjunction of our English forces
With arms of Germany may sooner bring
This prize of conquest in. But then, my lords,
As, in the moral hunting 'twixt the lion
And other beasts, force joined ⟨   ⟩

35   Frighted the weaker sharers from their parts,
So, if the Empire's sovereign chance to put
His plea of partnership into war's court,
Swords should decide the difference, and our blood
In private tears lament his entertainment.

SHREWSBURY

40   To doubt the worst is still the wise man's shield
That arms him safely, but the world knows this:
The Emperor is a man of royal faith.
His love unto our sovereign brings him down
From his imperial seat, to march in pay

45   Under our English flag, and wear the cross
Like some high order on his manly breast.
Thus serving, he's not master of himself,
But, like a colonel, commanding other,
Is by the general overawed himself.

ROCHESTER   Yet, my good lord –

SHREWSBURY   Let me conclude my speech.   50
As subjects share no portion in the conquest
Of their true sovereign other than the merit
That from the sovereign guerdons the true subject,
So the good Emperor in a friendly league
Of amity with England will not soil   55
His honour with the theft of English spoil.

MORE   There is no question but this entertainment
Will be most honourable, most commodious.
I have oft heard good captains wish to have
Rich soldiers to attend them, such as would fight   60
Both for their lives and livings. Such a one
Is the good Emperor. I would to God
We had ten thousand of such able men.
Ha, then there would appear no court, no city,
But, where the wars were, they would pay
     themselves.   65
Then, to prevent in French wars England's loss,
Let German flags wave with our English cross.

           Enter Sir Thomas PALMER.

PALMER   My lords, his majesty hath sent by me
These articles enclosed, first to be viewed,
And then to be subscribed to. (*with great reverence*) I
     tender them   70
In that due reverence which befits this place.

MORE   Subscribe these articles? Stay, let us pause.
Our conscience first shall parley with our laws.
My lord of Rochester, view you the paper.

ROCHESTER
Subscribe to these? Now good Sir Thomas Palmer,   75
Beseech the King that he will pardon me.
My heart will check my hand whilst I do write.
Subscribing so, I were an hypocrite.

PALMER   Do you refuse it then, my lord?

ROCHESTER   I do, Sir Thomas.

PALMER   Then here I summon you forthwith t'appear   ^T 80
Before his majesty, to answer there
This capital contempt.

ROCHESTER   I rise, and part,
In lieu of this, to tender him my heart.   *He riseth.*

PALMER
Will't please your honour to subscribe, my lord?

MORE   Sir, tell his highness, I entreat   85
Some time for to bethink me of this task.
In the meanwhile, I do resign mine office
Into my sovereign's hands.   ^T*All alter.*^T
     [He hands over the purse, mace and chain of office.]

PALMER   Then, my lord,
Hear the prepared order from the King.
On your refusal you shall straight depart   90
Unto your house at Chelsea, till you know
Our sovereign's further pleasure.

MORE   Most willingly I go.
My lords, if you will visit me at Chelsea
We'll go a-fishing, and with a cunning net,

95 Not like weak film, we'll catch none but the great.
Farewell, my noble lords. Why, this is right:
Good morrow to the sun, to state good night.   *Exit.*
PALMER   Will you subscribe, my lords?
SURREY   Instantly, good Sir Thomas.
They write.
100 We'll bring the writing unto our sovereign.
PALMER   My lord of Rochester,
You must with me, to answer this contempt.
ROCHESTER   This is the worst.
Who's freed from life is from all care exempt.
Exeunt Rochester and Palmer.
T   SURREY   Now let us ⟨hasten⟩ to our sovereign.
105 'Tis strange that my Lord Chancellor should refuse
The duty that the law of God bequeaths
Unto the king.
SHREWSBURY   Come, let us in. No doubt
His mind will alter, and the Bishop's too.
Error in learned heads hath much to do.   [*Exeunt.*]

[Sc. 11]   *Enter the* LADY *More, her two*
DAUGHTERS, [*one of them* ROPER'S WIFE,]
and Master ROPER, *as walking.*

ROPER   Madam, what ails ye for to look so sad?
LADY   Troth, son, I know not what. I am not sick,
And yet I am not well. I would be merry,
But somewhat lies so heavy on my heart
5   I cannot choose but sigh. You are a scholar.
I pray ye tell me, may one credit dreams?
ROPER   Why ask you that, dear madam?
LADY   Because tonight I had the strangest dream
That e'er my sleep was troubled with.
10 Methought 'twas night,
And that the King and Queen went on the Thames
In barges to hear music. My lord and I
Were in a little boat, methought – Lord, Lord,
What strange things live in slumbers! – and being near,
15 We grappled to the barge that bare the King;
But after many pleasing voices spent
In that still-moving music house, methought
The violence of the stream did sever us
Quite from the golden fleet, and hurried us
20 Unto the Bridge which, with unused horror,
We entered at full tide; thence some flight-shoot
Being carried by the waves, our boat stood still
Just opposite the Tower; and there it turned
And turned about, as when a whirlpool sucks
25 The circled waters. Methought that we both cried,
Till that we sunk, where arm in arm we died.
ROPER   Give no respect, dear madam, to fond dreams.
They are but slight illusions of the blood.
LADY   Tell me not all are so, for often dreams
30 Are true diviners, either of good or ill.
I cannot be in quiet till I hear
How my lord fares.

ROPER   (*aside*)   Nor I. [*aside to his wife*] Come
hither, wife.
I will not fright thy mother to interpret
The nature of a dream; but, trust me, sweet,
35 This night I have been troubled with thy father
Beyond all thought.
ROPER'S WIFE [*aside to Roper*]   Truly, and so have I.
Methought I saw him here in Chelsea church,
Standing upon the rood-loft, now defaced;
And whilst he kneeled and prayed before the image
40 It fell with him into the upper choir,
Where my poor father lay all stained in blood.
ROPER [*aside to his wife*]
Our dreams all meet in one conclusion,
Fatal, I fear.
LADY   What's that you talk? I pray ye let me know it.
ROPER'S WIFE   Nothing, good mother.
45 LADY   This is your fashion still: I must know nothing.
Call Master Catesby; he shall straight to Court
And see how my lord does. I shall not rest
Until my heart lean panting on his breast.

Enter Sir Thomas MORE, *merrily, Servants attending.*

MORE'S OTHER DAUGHTER
See where my father comes, joyful and merry.   50
MORE   As seamen, having passed a troubled storm,
Dance on the pleasant shore, so I – O, I could speak
Now like a poet! – now afore God, I am passing light.
Wife, give me kind welcome.   [*He kisses her.*]
Thou wast wont to blame
55 My kissing when my beard was in the stubble;
But I have been trimmed of late: I have had
A smooth Court shaving, in good faith, I have.
Daughters kneel.
[*to Daughters*] God bless ye. – Son Roper, give me
your hand.
ROPER   Your honour's welcome home.
MORE   Honour? Ha, ha!
And how dost, wife?
ROPER [*aside*]   He bears himself most strangely.   60
LADY   Will your lordship in?
MORE   Lordship? No, wife, that's gone.
The ground was slight that we did lean upon.
LADY
Lord, that your honour ne'er will leave these jests!
In faith, it ill becomes ye.
MORE   O good wife,
Honour and jests are both together fled.   65
The merriest councillor of England's dead.
LADY   Who's that, my lord?
MORE   Still 'lord'? The Lord Chancellor, wife.
LADY   That's you.
MORE   Certain, but I have changed my life.
Am I not leaner than I was before?
The fat is gone. My title's only 'More'.   70
Contented with one style, I'll live at rest.

They that have many names are not still best.
I have resigned mine office. Count'st me not wise?

75 LADY   O God!

MORE   Come, breed not female children in your eyes.
The King will have it so.

LADY   What's the offence?

MORE   Tush, let that pass; we'll talk of that anon.
The King seems a physician to my fate:
His princely mind would train me back to state.

80 ROPER   Then be his patient, my most honoured father.

MORE   O son Roper,
    Ubi turpis est medicina, sanari piget.
No, wife, be merry, and be merry all.
You smiled at rising; weep not at my fall.

85 Let's in, and here joy like to private friends,
Since days of pleasure have repentant ends.
The light of greatness is with triumph borne;
It sets at midday oft, with public scorn.   *Exeunt.*

[Sc. 12]   *Enter the* Bishop of ROCHESTER,
        SURREY, SHREWSBURY, LIEUTENANT of the
        Tower *and* Warders *with weapons.*

ROCHESTER   Your kind persuasions, honourable lords,
I can but thank ye for, but in this breast
There lives a soul that aims at higher things
Than temporary pleasing earthly kings.

5 God bless his highness, even with all my heart.
We shall meet one day, though that now we part.

SURREY   We not misdoubt your wisdom can discern
What best befits it; yet in love and zeal
We could entreat it might be otherwise.

10 SHREWSBURY [*to Rochester*]
No doubt your fatherhood will by yourself
Consider better of the present case,
And grow as great in favour as before.

ROCHESTER
For that, as pleaseth God. In my restraint
From worldly causes I shall better see

15 Into myself than at proud liberty.
The Tower and I will privately confer
Of things wherein at freedom I may err.
But I am troublesome unto your honours,
And hold ye longer than becomes my duty.

20 Master Lieutenant, I am now your charge;
And, though you keep my body, yet my love
Waits on my king and you while Fisher lives.

SURREY   Farewell, my lord of Rochester. We'll pray
For your release, and labour't as we may.

SHREWSBURY [*to Rochester*]

25 Thereof assure yourself. So do we leave ye,
And to your happy private thoughts bequeath ye.
                Exeunt [*Surrey and Shrewsbury*].

ROCHESTER
Now, Master Lieutenant, on; i'God's name, go;
And with as glad a mind go I with you
As ever truant bade the school adieu.   *Exeunt.*

[Sc. 13]   *Enter* Sir Thomas MORE, *his* LADY,
    DAUGHTERS, [*one of them* ROPER'S WIFE,] Master
    ROPER, *Gentlemen and Servants* [*among them*
    CATESBY *and* GOUGH], *as in his house at Chelsea.*
                    Low stools.

MORE
Good morrow, good son Roper. [*to his Lady*] Sit, good
    madam,
Upon an humble seat; the time so craves.
Rest your good heart on earth, the roof of graves.
You see the floor of greatness is uneven,

5 The cricket and high throne alike near heaven.
Now, daughters, you that like to branches spread
And give best shadow to a private house:
Be comforted, my girls. Your hopes stand fair.
Virtue breeds gentry; she makes the best heir.

BOTH DAUGHTERS
Good morrow to your honour.

10 MORE   Nay, good night rather.
Your honour's crest-fall'n with your happy father.

ROPER   O, what formality, what square observance,
Lives in a little room! Here public care
Gags not the eyes of slumber. Here fierce riot

15 Ruffles not proudly in a coat of trust
Whilst, like a pawn at chess, he keeps in rank
With kings and mighty fellows. Yet indeed,
Those men that stand on tiptoe smile to see
Him pawn his fortunes.

MORE   True, son, here's ⟨no strife,⟩

20 Nor does the wanton tongue here screw itself
Into the ear, that like a vice drinks up
The iron instrument.

LADY   We are here at peace.

MORE   Then peace, good wife.

LADY   For keeping still in compass – a strange point

25 In time's new navigation – we have sailed
Beyond our course.

MORE   Have done!

LADY   We are exiled the Court.

MORE   Still thou harp'st on that.
'Tis sin for to deserve that banishment;
But he that ne'er knew Court courts sweet content.

LADY   O, but dear husband –

MORE   I will not hear thee, wife.

30 The winding labyrinth of thy strange discourse
Will ne'er have end. Sit still, and, my good wife,
Entreat thy tongue be still, or, credit me,
Thou shalt not understand a word we speak.
We'll talk in Latin.

35 [*to Roper*] _Humida vallis raros patitur fulminis ictus._
More rest enjoys the subject meanly bred
Than he that bears the kingdom in his head.
Great men are still musicians, else the world lies:
They learn low strains after the notes that rise.

40 ROPER   Good sir, be still yourself, and but remember
How in this general court of short-lived pleasure,

The world, creation is the ample food
That is digested in the maw of time.
45 If man himself be subject to such ruin,
How shall his garment then, or the loose points
That tie respect unto his awe-full place,
Avoid destruction? Most honoured father-in-law,
The blood you have bequeathed these several hearts
50 To nourish your posterity stands firm;
And as with joy you led us first to rise,
So with like hearts we'll lock preferment's eyes.

[Original Text: Munday]

[Addition I: Chettle]

MORE Now will I speak like More in melancholy;
For if grief's power could with her sharpest darts
55 Pierce my firm bosom, here's sufficient cause
To take my farewell of mirth's hurtless laws.
Poor humbled lady, thou that wert of late
Placed with the noblest women of the land,
Invited to their angel companies,
60 Seeming a bright star in the courtly sphere:
Why shouldst thou like a widow sit thus low,
And all thy fair consorts move from the clouds
That overdrip thy beauty and thy worth?
I'll tell thee the true cause. The Court, like heaven,
65 Examines not the anger of the prince,
And, being more frail-composed of gilded earth,
Shines upon them on whom the King doth shine,
Smiles if he smile, declines if he decline.
Yet, seeing both are mortal – Court and King –
70 Shed not one tear for any earthly thing;
For, so God pardon me in my saddest hour,
Thou hast no more occasion to lament –
Nor these, nor those – my exile from the Court,
No, nor this body's torture, were't imposed –
75 As commonly disgraces of great men
Are the forewarnings of a hasty death –
Than to behold me after many a toil
Honoured with endless rest. Perchance the King,
Seeing the Court is full of vanity,
80 Has pity lest our souls should be misled,
And sends us to a life contemplative.
O, happy banishment from worldly pride
When souls by private life are sanctified!
WIFE O, but I fear some plot against your life.
85 MORE Why then, 'tis thus: the King, of his high grace,
Seeing my faithful service to his state,
Intends to send me to the King of Heaven
For a rich present; where my soul shall prove
A true rememberer of his majesty.
90 Come, prithee, mourn not. The worst chance is death,
And that brings endless joy for fickle breath.
WIFE Ah, but your children.
MORE   Tush, let them alone.
Say they be stripped from this poor painted cloth,
This outside of the earth, left houseless, bare;
95 They have minds instructed how to gather more.

There's no man that's ingenious can be poor.
And therefore do not weep, my little ones.
Though you lose all the earth, keep your souls even,
And you shall find inheritance in heaven.
But for my servants: there's my chiefest care.   100
[*to Catesby*] Come hither, faithful steward. Be not
   grieved
That in thy person I discharge both thee
And all thy other fellow officers;
For my great master hath discharged me.
If thou by serving me hast suffered loss,   105
Then benefit thyself by leaving me.
I hope thou hast not; for such times as these
Bring gain to officers, whoever leese.
Great lords have only name; but in the fall
Lord Spend-All's steward's Master Gathers-All.   110
But I suspect not thee. Admit thou hast.
It's good the servants save when masters waste.
– But you, poor gentlemen, that had no place
T'enrich yourselves but by loathed bribery,
Which I abhorred, and never found you loved: 115
Think, when an oak falls, underwood shrinks down,
And yet may live, though bruised. I pray ye strive
To shun my ruin; for the axe is set
Even at my root, to fell me to the ground.
The best I can do to prefer you all   120
With my mean store expect; for heaven can tell
That More loves all his followers more than well.

[Addition I: Chettle]

[Original Text: Munday]

Enter a Servant.

SERVANT My lord, there are new lighted at the gate
The Earls of Surrey and of Shrewsbury,
And they expect you in the inner court.   125
MORE Entreat their lordships come into the hall.
LADY O God, what news with them?
MORE   Why, how now, wife?
They are but come to visit their old friend.
LADY O God, I fear, I fear.
MORE   What shouldst thou fear, fond woman?
Iustum, si fractus illabatur orbis, impavidum ferient
   ruinae.   130
Here let me live estranged from great men's looks.
They are like golden flies on leaden hooks.

Enter the Earls [*of* SURREY *and* SHREWSBURY],
   DOWNES, *with his mace, and Attendants.*

SHREWSBURY Good morrow, good Sir Thomas.
SURREY [*to More's Lady*]
Good day, good madam. (*Kind salutations.*)
MORE   Welcome, my good lords.
What ails your lordships look so melancholy?   135
O, I know: you live in Court, and the Court diet
Is only friend to physic.
SURREY   O Sir Thomas,

Our words are now the King's, and our sad looks
The interest of your love. We are sent to you
140 From our mild sovereign, once more to demand
If you'll subscribe unto those articles
He sent ye th'other day. Be well advised,
For, on mine honour, lord, grave Doctor Fisher,
Bishop of Rochester, at the selfsame instant
145 Attached with you, is sent unto the Tower
For the like obstinacy. His majesty
Hath only sent you prisoner to your house,
But, if you now refuse for to subscribe,
A stricter course will follow.
LADY   O dear husband –
BOTH DAUGHTERS (*kneeling and weeping*)
Dear father –
150 MORE   See, my lords,
This partner and these subjects to my flesh
Prove rebels to my conscience. But, my good lords,
If I refuse, must I unto the Tower?
SHREWSBURY
You must, my lord.   [*Gestures to Downes.*]
Here is an officer
155 Ready for to arrest you of high treason.
LADY, DAUGHTERS   O God, O God!
ROPER   Be patient, good madam.
MORE   Ay, Downes, is't thou? I once did save thy life,
When else by cruel riotous assault
Thou hadst been torn in pieces. Thou art reserved
160 To be my summoner to yond spiritual court.
Give me thy hand, good fellow. Smooth thy face.
The diet that thou drink'st is spiced with mace,
And I could ne'er abide it. 'Twill not digest,
'Twill lie too heavy, man, on my weak breast.
165 SHREWSBURY   Be brief, my lord, for we are limited
Unto an hour.
MORE   Unto an hour? 'Tis well.
The bell, earth's thunder, soon shall toll my knell.
LADY (*kneeling*)
Dear loving husband, if you respect not me,
Yet think upon your daughters.
MORE (*pondering to himself*)   Wife, stand up.
170 I have bethought me;
And I'll now satisfy the King's good pleasure.
BOTH DAUGHTERS   O happy alteration!
SHREWSBURY   Come then, subscribe, my lord.
SURREY   I am right glad of this your fair conversion.
MORE   O pardon me,
175 I will subscribe to go unto the Tower
With all submissive willingness, and thereto add
My bones to strengthen the foundation
Of Julius Caesar's palace. Now, my lord,
I'll satisfy the King even with my blood.
Nor will I wrong your patience.
180 [*to Downes*]   Friend, do thine office.
DOWNES   Sir Thomas More, Lord Chancellor of
England, I arrest you in the King's name of high treason.
MORE   Gramercies, friend.

To a great prison, to discharge the strife
Commenced 'twixt conscience and my frailer life,   185
More now must march. Chelsea, adieu, adieu.
Strange farewell: thou shalt ne'er more see More
true,
For I shall ne'er see thee more. – Servants, farewell.
– Wife, mar not thine indifferent face. Be wise.
More's widow's husband, he must make thee rise.   190
– Daughters, ‹   › what's here, what's here?
Mine eye had almost parted with a tear.
– Dear son, possess my virtue; that I ne'er gave.
Grave More thus lightly walks to a quick grave.
ROPER   *Curae leves loquuntur, ingentes stupent.*   195
MORE
You that way in. Mind you my course in prayer.
By water I to prison, to heaven through air.
            Exeunt [More, Shrewsbury, Surrey, Downes and
                Attendants at one door, the rest at another].

[Sc. 14]   *Enter the* Warders of the Tower,
                        with halberds.

1 WARDER   Ho, make a guard there!
2 WARDER   Master Lieutenant gives a strait command
The people be avoided from the bridge.
3 WARDER
From whence is he committed, who can tell?
1 WARDER   From Durham House, I hear.   5
2 WARDER   The guard were waiting there an hour ago.
3 WARDER   If he stay long, he'll not get near the wharf,
There's such a crowd of boats upon the Thames.
1 WARDER   Well, be it spoken without offence to any,
A wiser or more virtuous gentleman   10
Was never bred in England.
2 WARDER   I think the poor will bury him in tears.
I never heard a man since I was born
So generally bewailed of everyone.

            Enter a poor Woman [*from a crowd*].

3 WARDER
What means this woman? – Whither dost thou press?   15
1 WARDER   This woman will be trod to death anon.
2 WARDER [*to the Woman*]
What makest thou here?
WOMAN
To speak with that good man Sir Thomas More.
1 WARDER
To speak with him? He's not Lord Chancellor.
WOMAN   The more's the pity, sir, if it pleased God.   20
1 WARDER   Therefore if thou hast a petition to deliver,
Thou mayst keep it now, for anything I know.
WOMAN
I am a poor woman, and have had, God knows,
A suit this two year in the Chancery,
And he hath all the evidence I have,   25
Which should I lose I am utterly undone.

1 WARDER

  Faith, and I fear thou'lt hardly come by 'em now.
  I am sorry for thee even with all my heart.

  Enter the Lords [*of* SHREWSBURY *and* SURREY],
  with Sir Thomas MORE *and Attendants; and enter*
  LIEUTENANT *and* GENTLEMAN PORTER.

2 WARDER

30 Woman, stand back. You must avoid this place.
    The lords must pass this way into the Tower.

MORE   I thank your lordships for your pains thus far
       To my strong-house.

WOMAN

    Now good Sir Thomas More, for Christ's dear sake
    Deliver me my writings back again
35 That do concern my title.

MORE   What, my old client, are thou got hither too?
       Poor silly wretch, I must confess indeed
       I had such writings as concern thee near,
       But the King
40   Has ta'en the matter into his own hand;
       He has all I had. Then, woman, sue to him.
       I cannot help thee. Thou must bear with me.

WOMAN   Ah, gentle heart, my soul for thee is sad.
        Farewell, the best friend that the poor e'er had.   *Exit.*

GENTLEMAN PORTER

45   Before you enter through the Tower gate,
     Your upper garment, sir, belongs to me.

MORE   Sir, you shall have it. There it is.
          He gives him his cap.

GENTLEMAN PORTER

     The upmost on your back, sir. You mistake me.

MORE   Sir, now I understand ye very well.
          [*He gives him his cloak.*]
50   But that you name my back,
     Sure else my cap had been the uppermost.

SHREWSBURY

     Farewell, kind lord. God send us merry meeting.

MORE   Amen, my lord.

SURREY   Farewell, dear friend. I hope your safe return.

MORE   My lord, and my dear fellow in the Muses,
55   Farewell. Farewell, most noble poet.

LIEUTENANT

     Adieu, most honoured lords.   *Exeunt Lords.*

MORE   Fair prison, welcome. Yet methinks
       For thy fair building 'tis too foul a name.
60   Many a guilty soul, and many an innocent,
       Have breathed their farewell to thy hollow rooms.
       I oft have entered into thee this way,
       Yet, I thank God, ne'er with a clearer conscience
       Than at this hour.
65   This is my comfort yet: how hard soe'er
       My lodging prove, the cry of the poor suitor,
       Fatherless orphan or distressed widow
       Shall not disturb me in my quiet sleep.
       On then, i'God's name, to our close abode.
70   God is as strong here as he is abroad.   *Exeunt.*

[Sc. 15]   *Enter* BUTLER, BREWER, PORTER *and*
                HORSE-KEEPER, *several ways.*

BUTLER   Robin Brewer, how now, man? What cheer,
         what cheer?

BREWER   Faith, Ned Butler, sick of thy disease, and these
         our other fellows here, Ralph Horse-keeper and Giles
         Porter: sad, sad. They say my lord goes to his trial today.   5

HORSE-KEEPER   To it, man? Why, he is now at it. God
               send him well to speed!

PORTER   Amen. Even as I wish to mine own soul, so
         speed it with my honourable lord and master Sir
         Thomas More!   10

BUTLER   I cannot tell – I have nothing to do with
         matters above my capacity – but, as God judge me, if I
         might speak my mind, I think there lives not a more
         harmless gentleman in the universal world.

BREWER   Nor a wiser, nor a merrier, nor an honester.   15
         Go to, I'll put that in upon mine own knowledge.

PORTER   Nay, an ye bate him his due of his
         housekeeping, hang ye all! Ye have many lord chancellors
         comes in debt at the year's end, and for very housekeeping!

HORSE-KEEPER   Well, he was too good a lord for us, and   20
               therefore, I fear, God himself will take him. But I'll be
               hanged if ever I have such another service.

BREWER   Soft, man, we are not discharged yet. My lord
         may come home again, and all will be well.

BUTLER   I much mistrust it. When they go to 'raigning   25
         once, there's ever foul weather for a great while after.

          Enter GOUGH *and* CATESBY, *with a paper.*

         But soft, here comes Master Gough and Master
         Catesby. Now we shall hear more.

HORSE-KEEPER   Before God, they are very sad. I doubt
               my lord is condemned.   30

PORTER   God bless his soul, and a fig then for all worldly
         condemnation!

GOUGH   Well said, Giles Porter, I commend thee for it.
        'Twas spoken like a well-affected servant
        Of him that was a kind lord to us all.   35

CATESBY

        Which now no more he shall be, for, dear fellows,
        Now we are masterless. Though he may live
        So long as please the King, but law hath made him
        A dead man to the world, and given the axe his head,
        But his sweet soul to live among the saints.   40

GOUGH   Let us entreat ye to go call together
        The rest of your sad fellows – by the roll
        You're just seven score – and tell them what ye hear
        A virtuous, honourable lord hath done
        Even for the meanest follower that he had.   45
        This writing found my lady in his study
        This instant morning, wherein is set down
        Each servant's name, according to his place
        And office in the house. On every man
        He frankly hath bestown twenty nobles,   50
        The best and worst together, all alike,

Which Master Catesby here forth will pay ye.
CATESBY   Take it as it is meant, a kind remembrance
Of a far kinder lord, with whose sad fall
55   He gives up house, and farewell to us all.
Thus the fair-spreading oak falls not alone,
But all the neighbour plants and under-trees
Are crushed down with his weight. No more of this.
Come and receive your due, and after go
60   Fellow-like hence, co-partners of one woe.   *Exeunt.*

[Sc. 16]   *Enter* Sir Thomas MORE, *the*
             LIEUTENANT, *and a* Servant *attending,*
                as in his chamber in the Tower.

MORE   Master Lieutenant, is the warrant come?
If it be so, i'God's name let us know it.
LIEUTENANT   My lord, it is.
MORE   'Tis welcome, sir, to me with all my heart.
5   His blessed will be done.
LIEUTENANT
Your wisdom, sir, hath been so well approved,
And your fair patience in imprisonment
Hath ever shown such constancy of mind
And Christian resolution in all troubles,
10   As warrants us you are not unprepared.
MORE   No, Master Lieutenant.
I thank my God I have peace of conscience,
Though the world and I are at a little odds.
But we'll be even now, I hope, ere long.
15   When is the execution of your warrant?
LIEUTENANT   Tomorrow morning.
MORE   So, sir, I thank ye.
I have not lived so ill I fear to die.
Master Lieutenant,
I have had a sore fit of the stone tonight;
20   But the King hath sent me such a rare receipt,
I thank him, as I shall not need to fear it much.
LIEUTENANT
In life and death, still merry Sir Thomas More.
MORE [*to Servant*]   Sirrah fellow, reach me the urinal.
      He gives it him.
Ha, let me see. ⟨There's⟩ gravel in the water.
25   ⟨And yet, in very sober truth I swear,⟩
The man were likely to live long enough,
So pleased the King. Here, fellow, take it.
SERVANT   Shall I go with it to the doctor, sir?
MORE   No, save thy labour. We'll cozen him of a fee.
30   Thou shalt see me take a dram tomorrow morning
Shall cure the stone, I warrant, doubt it not.
– Master Lieutenant, what news of my lord of
      Rochester?
LIEUTENANT   Yesterday morning was he put to death.
MORE   The peace of soul sleep with him!
35   He was a learned and a reverend prelate,
And a rich man, believe me.
LIEUTENANT
If he were rich, what is Sir Thomas More,

That all this while hath been Lord Chancellor?
MORE
Say ye so, Master Lieutenant? What do you think
A man that with my time had held my place   40
Might purchase?
LIEUTENANT
Perhaps, my lord, two thousand pound a year.
MORE   Master Lieutenant, I protest to you,
I never had the means in all my life
To purchase one poor hundred pound a year.   45
I think I am the poorest chancellor
That ever was in England, though I could wish,
For credit of the place, that my estate were better.
LIEUTENANT   It's very strange.
MORE   It will be found as true.
I think, sir, that with most part of my coin   50
I have purchased as strange commodities
As ever you heard tell of in your life.
LIEUTENANT   Commodities, my lord?
Might I without offence enquire of them?
MORE   Crutches, Master Lieutenant, and bare cloaks,   55
For halting soldiers and poor needy scholars,
Have had my gettings in the Chancery.
To think but what achete the crown shall have
By my attainder!
I prithee, if thou be'st a gentleman,   60
Get but a copy of my inventory.
That part of poet that was given me
Made me a very unthrift;
For this is the disease attends us all:
Poets were never thrifty, never shall.   65

Enter Lady MORE, *mourning*, DAUGHTERS, [*one of them*
      ROPER'S WIFE,] Master ROPER.

LIEUTENANT   O noble More!
My lord, your wife, your son-in-law and daughters.
MORE   Son Roper, welcome. Welcome, wife and girls.
Why do you weep? Because I live at ease?
Did you not see, when I was Chancellor   70
I was so cloyed with suitors every hour
I could not sleep nor dine nor sup in quiet.
Here's none of this. Here I can sit and talk
With my honest keeper half a day together,
Laugh and be merry. Why then should you weep?   75
ROPER
These tears, my lord, for this your long restraint
Hope had dried up, with comfort that we yet,
Although imprisoned, might have had your life.
MORE   To live in prison: what a life were that?
The King, I thank him, loves me more than so.   80
Tomorrow I shall be at liberty
To go even whither I can,
After I have dispatched my business.
LADY   Ah husband, husband, yet submit yourself.
Have care of your poor wife and children.   85
MORE   Wife, so I have, and I do leave you all
To His protection hath the power to keep

You safer than I can,
The father of the widow and the orphan.

90 ROPER   The world, my lord, hath ever held you wise,
And't shall be no distaste unto your wisdom
To yield to the opinion of the state.

MORE   I have deceived myself, I must acknowledge;
And as you say, son Roper, to confess the same
95 It will be no disparagement at all.

LADY (*offering to depart*)
His highness shall be certified thereof, immediately.

MORE   Nay, hear me, wife. First let me tell ye how
I thought to have had a barber for my beard;
Now I remember that were labour lost:
100 The headsman now shall cut off head and all.

ROPER'S WIFE
Father, his majesty, upon your meek submission,
Will yet, they say, receive you to his grace,
In as great credit as you were before.

MORE   ‹   › wench. Faith, my lord the King
105 Has appointed me to do a little business.
If that were past, my girl, thou then shouldst see
What I would say to him about that matter.
But I shall be so busy until then
I shall not tend it.

BOTH DAUGHTERS   Ah, my dear father!
110 LADY   Dear lord and husband!

MORE
Be comforted, good wife, to live and love my children,
For with thee leave I all my care of them.
Son Roper, for my sake that have loved thee well,
And for her virtue's sake, cherish my child.
115 – Girl, be not proud, but of thy husband's love.
Ever retain thy virtuous modesty.
That modesty is such a comely garment
As it is never out of fashion, sits as fair
Upon the meaner woman as the empress.
120 No stuff that gold can buy is half so rich,
Nor ornament that so becomes a woman.
Live all, and love together, and thereby
You give your father a rich obsequy.

BOTH DAUGHTERS   Your blessing, dear father.

MORE   I must be gone –
125 God bless you – to talk with God, who now doth call.

LADY   Ah, my dear husband –

MORE   Sweet wife, goodnight, goodnight.
God send us all his everlasting light.

ROPER   I think before this hour
More heavy hearts ne'er parted in the Tower.
Exeunt [More's Lady, Daughters and Roper one way;
More, Lieutenant and Servant another].

[Sc. 17]   [*A scaffold is set forth.*] *Enter the* [*two*]
Sheriffs of London *and their* Officers *at one door, the*
Warders *with their halberds at another.*

1 SHERIFF   Officers, what time of day is't?
OFFICER   Almost eight o'clock.

2 SHERIFF
We must make haste then, lest we stay too long.

1 WARDER
Good morrow, Master Shrieves of London. Master
Lieutenant
Wills ye repair to the limits of the Tower,
There to receive your prisoner.   5

1 SHERIFF [*to Officer*]
Go back and tell his worship we are ready.

2 SHERIFF   Go bid the officers make clear the way,
There may be passage for the prisoner.

Enter LIEUTENANT *and his Guard, with* MORE.

MORE   Yet God be thanked, here's a fair day toward
To take our journey in. Master Lieutenant,   10
It were fair walking on the Tower leads.

LIEUTENANT
An so it might have liked my sovereign lord,
I would to God you might have walked there still.
He weeps.

MORE   Sir, we are walking to a better place.
O sir, your kind and loving tears   15
Are like sweet odours to embalm your friend.
Thank your good lady; since I was your guest
She has made me a very wanton, in good sooth.

LIEUTENANT
O, I had hoped we should not yet have parted!

MORE   But I must leave ye for a little while.   20
Within an hour or two you may look for me.
But there will be so many come to see me
That I shall be so proud I will not speak;
And sure my memory is grown so ill
I fear I shall forget my head behind me.   25

LIEUTENANT   God and his blessed angels be about ye!
– Here, Master Shrieves, receive your prisoner.

MORE
Good morrow, Master Shrieves of London, to ye both.
I thank ye that ye will vouchsafe to meet me.
I see by this you have not quite forgot   30
That I was in times past as you are now,
A sheriff of London.

1 SHERIFF   Sir, then you know our duty doth require it.

MORE   I know it well, sir, else I would have been glad
You might have saved a labour at this time.   35
[*to 2 Sheriff*] Ah, Master Sheriff,
You and I have been of old acquaintance.
You were a patient auditor of mine
When I read the divinity lecture at St Lawrence's.

2 SHERIFF   Sir Thomas More,   40
I have heard you oft, as many other did,
To our great comfort.

MORE   Pray God you may so now, with all my heart.
And, as I call to mind,
When I studied the law in Lincoln's Inn   45
I was of counsel with ye in a cause.

2 SHERIFF   I was about to say so, good Sir Thomas.
‹   ›

[They pass over the stage. Enter the Hangman.*]*

MORE   O, is this the place?

50   I promise ye, it is a goodly scaffold.

In sooth, I am come about a headless errand,

For I have not much to say, now I am here.

Well, let's ascend, i'God's name.

[to the Hangman] In troth, methinks your stair is
    somewhat weak.

55   I prithee, honest friend, lend me thy hand

To help me up. As for my coming down,

Let me alone, I'll look to that myself.

As he is going up the stairs, enters the Earls of
SURREY *and* SHREWSBURY.

My lords of Surrey and of Shrewsbury, give me your
hands yet before we ‹part›. Ye see, though it pleaseth

60   the King to raise me thus high, yet I am not proud; for
the higher I mount the better I can see my friends
about me. I am now ‹on a› far voyage, and this strange
wooden horse must bear me thither. Yet I perceive by
your looks you like my bargain so ill that there's not

65   one of ye all dare venture with me. *(walking)* Truly,
here's a most sweet gallery. I like the air of it better
than my garden at Chelsea. By your patience, good
people that have pressed thus into my bedchamber, if
you'll not trouble me I'll take a sound sleep here.

SHREWSBURY

70   My lord, 'twere good you'd publish to the world

Your great offence unto his majesty.

MORE   My lord, I'll bequeath this legacy to the
hangman, and do it instantly. *(Gives him his gown.)* I
confess his majesty hath been ever good to me, and my

75   offence to his highness makes me, of a state pleader, a
stage player – though I am old and have a bad voice –
to act this last scene of my tragedy. I'll send him, for
my trespass, a reverent head: somewhat bald, for it is
not requisite any head should stand covered to so high

80   majesty. If that content him not, because I think my
body will then do me small pleasure, let him but bury
it and take it.

SURREY

My lord, my lord, hold conference with your soul.

You see, my lord, the time of life is short.

85 MORE   I see it, my good lord. I dispatched that business
the last night. I come hither only to be let blood by the
hangman. My doctor here tells me it is good for the
headache.

HANGMAN   I beseech ye, my lord, forgive me.

90 MORE   Forgive thee, honest fellow? Why?

HANGMAN   For your death, my lord.

MORE   O, my death! I had rather it were in thy power to
forgive me, for thou hast the sharpest action against
me. The law, my honest friend, lies in thy hands now.

95   *([Gives him] his purse.)* Here's thy fee. And, my good
fellow, let my suit be dispatched presently; for 'tis all
one pain to die a lingering death and to live in the
continual mill of a lawsuit. But I can tell thee, my neck
is so short that if thou shouldst behead an hundred

100   noblemen like myself, thou wouldst ne'er get credit by
it. Therefore – look ye, sir – do it handsomely, or, of my
word, thou shalt never deal with me hereafter.

HANGMAN   I'll take an order for that, my lord.

MORE   One thing more: take heed thou cutt'st not off

105   my beard. O, I forgot, execution passed upon that last
night, and the body of it lies buried in the Tower. Stay,
is't not possible to make a scape from all this strong
guard? It is.

There is a thing within me that will raise

110   And elevate my better part 'bove sight

Of these same weaker eyes. And Master Shrieves,

For all this troop of steel that tends my death,

I shall break from you and fly up to heaven.

Let's seek the means for this.

115 HANGMAN   My lord, I pray ye put off your doublet.

MORE   Speak not so coldly to me; I am hoarse already.

I would be loath, good fellow, to take more.

Point me the block; I ne'er was here before.

HANGMAN   To the east side, my lord.

MORE   Then to the east.

120   We go to sigh; that o'er, to sleep in rest.

Here More forsakes all mirth. Good reason why:

The fool of flesh must, with her frail life, die.

No eye salute my trunk with a sad tear.

Our birth to heaven should be thus: void of fear.

                            Exit [with Hangman].

125 SURREY   A very learned worthy gentleman

Seals error with his blood. Come, we'll to Court.

Let's sadly hence to perfect unknown fates,

Whilst he tends progress to the state of states.

                              [Exeunt.]

[Original Text: Munday]

The Taming of the Shrew

The text of *The Taming of the Shrew* printed in the First Folio in 1623 as the eleventh of the comedies stands in close, but ill-defined, relation to a play printed in 1594 with the similar title of *The Taming of a Shrew*. Once regarded as Shakespeare's source for *The Shrew*, *A Shrew* is perhaps better understood as a garbled and abbreviated adaptation of it in which the 'taming' plot follows very similar lines and includes verbal reminiscences; the 'Bianca' plot is radically rewritten and draws heavily on quotations from Marlowe's plays; and the framing device of Sly is sustained to the end of the play, where it affords an ironic epilogue in which Sly, sober, sets off home to tame his wife too. The likely period of composition of *The Shrew* is between about 1590 and 1594.

Shrew-taming stories and ballads, originating in folk-tales, were widely known in the sixteenth century and no single original for the play has been identified. Similarly, the device of gulling a beggar into the belief that he is a king or lord is an ancient and widespread narrative motif, best known today from *The Arabian Nights' Entertainment*. The story of Bianca and her suitors has an immediate dramatic source in *Supposes* (1566), George Gascoigne's English version of a prose comedy, *I Suppositi* (1509), by Lodovico Ariosto. The skilful weaving of these three into a complex action is among the play's notable achievements.

The Taming of the Shrew has had a long and successful stage history, both in its full form and in successive adaptations and abridgements, of which David Garrick's *Catherine and Petruchio* (1756) had the longest life. The play shares with *The Merchant of Venice* the unhappy distinction of giving general offence to modern sensibilities. However, Shakespeare's portrayal of the 'taming' of Katherina tones down the coarseness and physical violence of contemporary analogues, substituting a course of psychological homoeopathy to cure her of her shrewishness. A feminist response was delivered as early as 1610 by John Fletcher in his comedy *The Woman's Prize, or the Tamer Tamed*. In it, Petruchio is subjected to four acts of frustration and humiliation by a second wife, Maria (who is evidently acquainted with the *Lysistrata* of Aristophanes), before wounded male pride is restored at the end by her voluntary reversion to wifely good behaviour.

The modern response of indignation at the taming plot is understandable – even inevitable – but it runs the risk of ignoring the wholly speculative and fictional scheme of things in which Shakespeare's 'supposes' – hypothetical propositions about men and women as much as disguised or substituted characters – are presented for the entertainment of Sly and of ourselves. Katherina and Petruchio are at once differentiated from the rest of the characters by force of personality and by an evident emotional compatibility: the roles have been relished by generations of star performers, among them Richard Burton and Elizabeth Taylor on film. Their interchanges anticipate the 'merry war' of Beatrice and Benedick, both in their witty surface and in the underlying seriousness of the tussle for power in marriage. Sly's disappearance at the end of the first act of the Folio text is perplexing: some modern productions have made effective use of his later interventions borrowed from *A Shrew*. The disappearance of Sly leaves the end of the play more open to the various reactions of an audience, whereas his epilogue can increase a sense of that ending as no more than a male fantasy of unattainable control.

The Arden text is based on the 1623 First Folio.

THE INDUCTION

Christopher SLY	*a tinker*
HOSTESS	*an alewife*
LORD	
BARTHOLOMEW	*the Lord's page*
HUNTSMEN	
SERVANTS	*attending the Lord*
PLAYERS	

THE PLAY-WITHIN-THE-PLAY

BAPTISTA Minola	*a rich citizen of Padua*
KATHERINA	*his elder daughter*
BIANCA	*his younger daughter*
PETRUCCIO	*a gentleman of Verona*
GRUMIO	*his groom*
HORTENSIO	*Petruccio's friend, suitor to Bianca*
LUCENTIO	*a gentleman of Pisa, suitor to Bianca*
TRANIO	
BIONDELLO	*Lucentio's servants*
GREMIO	*a rich old man, suitor to Bianca*
VINCENTIO	*Lucentio's father*
MERCHANT	*from Mantua*
WIDOW	*Hortensio's wife*
CURTIS	*Petruccio's steward*
NATHANIEL	
PHILIP	
JOSEPH	*Petruccio's servants*
NICHOLAS	
PETER	
TAILOR	
HABERDASHER	

Attendants, Servants (Walter, Sugarsop, Gregory, Gabriel, Adam, Rafe), Officer

The Taming of the Shrew

Induction 1   *Enter* Christopher SLY
and Hostess.

SLY   I'll feeze you, in faith.

HOSTESS   A pair of stocks, you rogue!

SLY   You're a baggage, the Slys are no rogues. Look in
the Chronicles; we came in with Richard Conqueror:
therefore *paucas pallabris*, let the world slide. Sessa!   5

HOSTESS   You will not pay for the glasses you have
burst?

SLY   No, not a denier. Go by, Saint Jeronimy, go to thy
cold bed and warm thee.

HOSTESS   I know my remedy; I must go fetch the   10
headborough.   *Exit.*

SLY   Third, or fourth, or fifth borough, I'll answer him
by law. I'll not budge an inch, boy. Let him come, and
kindly. [*Falls asleep.*]

Wind horns. Enter Lord *from hunting, two*
Huntsmen *and others.*

LORD
Huntsman, I charge thee, tender well my hounds: 15
Breathe Merriman – the poor cur is embossed –
And couple Clowder with the deep-mouthed brach.
Sawst thou not, boy, how Silver made it good
At the hedge corner, in the coldest fault?
I would not lose the dog for twenty pound.   20

1 HUNTSMAN   Why, Belman is as good as he, my lord:
He cried upon it at the merest loss,
And twice today picked out the dullest scent.
Trust me, I take him for the better dog.

LORD   Thou art a fool. If Echo were as fleet   25
I would esteem him worth a dozen such.
But sup them well, and look unto them all:
Tomorrow I intend to hunt again.

1 HUNTSMAN   I will, my lord.

LORD
What's here? One dead, or drunk? See, doth he
breathe?   30

2 HUNTSMAN
He breathes, my lord. Were he not warmed with ale,
This were a bed but cold to sleep so soundly.

LORD   O monstrous beast, how like a swine he lies!
Grim death, how foul and loathsome is thine image.
Sirs, I will practise on this drunken man.   35
What think you, if he were conveyed to bed,
Wrapped in sweet clothes, rings put upon his fingers,
A most delicious banquet by his bed
And brave attendants near him when he wakes,
Would not the beggar then forget himself?   40

1 HUNTSMAN
Believe me, lord, I think he cannot choose.

2 HUNTSMAN
It would seem strange unto him when he waked.

LORD
Even as a flattering dream or worthless fancy.
Then take him up, and manage well the jest:
Carry him gently to my fairest chamber,   45

And hang it round with all my wanton pictures;
Balm his foul head in warm distilled waters
And burn sweet wood to make the lodging sweet;
Procure me music ready when he wakes
To make a dulcet and a heavenly sound;   50
An if he chance to speak, be ready straight
And with a low submissive reverence
Say, 'What is it your honour will command?'
Let one attend him with a silver basin
Full of rose-water and bestrewed with flowers;   55
Another bear the ewer, the third a diaper,
And say, 'Will't please your lordship cool your
hands?'
Some one be ready with a costly suit
And ask him what apparel he will wear;
Another tell him of his hounds and horse   60
And that his lady mourns at his disease.
Persuade him that he hath been lunatic,
And when he says he is, say that he dreams,
For he is nothing but a mighty lord.
This do, and do it kindly, gentle sirs,   65
It will be pastime passing excellent,
If it be husbanded with modesty.

1 HUNTSMAN
My lord, I warrant you we will play our part
As he shall think by our true diligence
He is no less than what we say he is.   70

LORD   Take him up gently and to bed with him,
And each one to his office when he wakes.
Some carry Sly out. Sound trumpets.
Sirrah, go see what trumpet 'tis that sounds.
Exit a Servant.
Belike some noble gentleman that means,
Travelling some journey, to repose him here.   75

Enter Servant.

How now? Who is it?

SERVANT   An't please your honour,
Players that offer service to your lordship.

Enter Players.

LORD   Bid them come near. –
Now, fellows, you are welcome.

PLAYERS   We thank your honour.

LORD   Do you intend to stay with me tonight?   80

1 PLAYER   So please your lordship to accept our duty.

LORD   With all my heart. This fellow I remember
Since once he played a farmer's eldest son –
'Twas where you wooed the gentlewoman so well.
I have forgot your name, but sure that part   85
Was aptly fitted and naturally performed.

2 PLAYER   I think 'twas Soto that your honour means.

LORD   'Tis very true; thou didst it excellent.
– Well, you are come to me in happy time,
The rather for I have some sport in hand   90
Wherein your cunning can assist me much.
There is a lord will hear you play tonight;

But I am doubtful of your modesties
Lest, over-eyeing of his odd behaviour –
For yet his honour never heard a play –   95
You break into some merry passion
And so offend him; for I tell you, sirs,
If you should smile, he grows impatient.
1 PLAYER   Fear not, my lord, we can contain ourselves
    Were he the veriest antic in the world.   100
LORD   Go, sirrah, take them to the buttery
    And give them friendly welcome every one;
    Let them want nothing that my house affords.
                                    Exit one with the Players.
    – Sirrah, go you to Barthol'mew my page
    And see him dressed in all suits like a lady.   105
    That done, conduct him to the drunkard's chamber,
    And call him 'Madam', do him obeisance.
    Tell him from me, as he will win my love,
    He bear himself with honourable action
    Such as he hath observed in noble ladies   110
    Unto their lords by them accomplished.
    Such duty to the drunkard let him do,
    With soft low tongue and lowly courtesy,
    And say, 'What is't your honour will command,
    Wherein your lady and your humble wife   115
    May show her duty and make known her love?'
    And then with kind embracements, tempting kisses
    And with declining head into his bosom,
    Bid him shed tears, as being overjoyed
    To see her noble lord restored to health,   120
    Who for this seven years hath esteemed him
    No better than a poor and loathsome beggar.
    And if the boy have not a woman's gift
    To rain a shower of commanded tears,
    An onion will do well for such a shift,   125
    Which in a napkin being close conveyed
    Shall in despite enforce a watery eye.
    See this dispatched with all the haste thou canst;
    Anon I'll give thee more instructions.
                                    Exit a Servant.
    I know the boy will well usurp the grace,   130
    Voice, gait and action of a gentlewoman.
    I long to hear him call the drunkard 'husband',
    And how my men will stay themselves from laughter
    When they do homage to this simple peasant.
    I'll in to counsel them: haply my presence   135
    May well abate the over-merry spleen
    Which otherwise would grow into extremes.   *Exeunt.*

Induction 2   *Enter aloft SLY*
    the drunkard and three Servants – *with apparel,*
    basin and ewer, and other appurtenances – and Lord.

SLY   For God's sake, a pot of small ale.
1 SERVANT
    Will't please your lordship drink a cup of sack?
2 SERVANT
    Will't please your honour taste of these conserves?

3 SERVANT
    What raiment will your honour wear today?
SLY   I am Christophero Sly – call not me 'honour' nor   5
    'lordship'. I ne'er drank sack in my life, and if you give
    me any conserves, give me conserves of beef. Ne'er
    ask me what raiment I'll wear, for I have no more
    doublets than backs, no more stockings than legs,
    nor no more shoes than feet – nay, sometime more feet   10
    than shoes, or such shoes as my toes look through the
    over-leather.
LORD   Heaven cease this idle humour in your honour!
    O, that a mighty man of such descent,
    Of such possessions and so high esteem,   15
    Should be infused with so foul a spirit.
SLY   What, would you make me mad? Am not I
    Christopher Sly, old Sly's son of Burton Heath,
    by birth a pedlar, by education a cardmaker, by
    transmutation a bear-herd and now by present   20
    profession a tinker? Ask Marian Hacket, the fat ale-
    wife of Wincot, if she know me not. If she say I am not
    fourteen pence on the score for sheer ale, score me up
    for the lying'st knave in Christendom. What, I am not
    bestraught: here's –   25
3 SERVANT   O, this it is that makes your lady mourn.
2 SERVANT   O, this is it that makes your servants droop.
LORD
    Hence comes it that your kindred shuns your house,
    As beaten hence by your strange lunacy.
    O noble lord, bethink thee of thy birth,   30
    Call home thy ancient thoughts from banishment
    And banish hence these abject lowly dreams.
    Look how thy servants do attend on thee,
    Each in his office ready at thy beck.
    Wilt thou have music?   [*Music*]
                    Hark, Apollo plays,   35
    And twenty caged nightingales do sing.
    Or wilt thou sleep? We'll have thee to a couch
    Softer and sweeter than the lustful bed
    On purpose trimmed up for Semiramis.
    Say thou wilt walk, we will bestrew the ground.   40
    Or wilt thou ride? Thy horses shall be trapped,
    Their harness studded all with gold and pearl.
    Dost thou love hawking? Thou hast hawks will soar
    Above the morning lark. Or wilt thou hunt?
    Thy hounds shall make the welkin answer them   45
    And fetch shrill echoes from the hollow earth.
1 SERVANT
    Say thou wilt course, thy greyhounds are as swift
    As breathed stags – ay, fleeter than the roe.
2 SERVANT
    Dost thou love pictures? We will fetch thee straight
    Adonis painted by a running brook   50
    And Cytherea all in sedges hid,
    Which seem to move and wanton with her breath
    Even as the waving sedges play with wind.
LORD   We'll show thee Io as she was a maid,
    And how she was beguiled and surprised,   55

As lively painted as the deed was done.

3 SERVANT

Or Daphne roaming through a thorny wood,
Scratching her legs that one shall swear she bleeds,
And at that sight shall sad Apollo weep,
60   So workmanly the blood and tears are drawn.

LORD   Thou art a lord, and nothing but a lord.
Thou hast a lady far more beautiful
Than any woman in this waning age.

1 SERVANT

And till the tears that she hath shed for thee
65   Like envious floods o'er-ran her lovely face
She was the fairest creature in the world –
And yet she is inferior to none.

SLY   Am I a lord, and have I such a lady?
Or do I dream? Or have I dreamed till now?
70   I do not sleep. I see, I hear, I speak,
I smell sweet savours and I feel soft things.
Upon my life, I am a lord indeed,
And not a tinker, nor Christopher Sly.
Well, bring our lady hither to our sight,
75   And once again a pot o'th' smallest ale.

2 SERVANT

Will't please your mightiness to wash your hands?
O, how we joy to see your wit restored;
O, that once more you knew but what you are.
These fifteen years you have been in a dream,
80   Or when you waked, so waked as if you slept.

SLY   These fifteen years – by my fay, a goodly nap.
But did I never speak of all that time?

1 SERVANT   O yes, my lord, but very idle words;
For though you lay here in this goodly chamber,
85   Yet would you say ye were beaten out of door,
And rail upon the hostess of the house
And say you would present her at the leet
Because she brought stone jugs and no sealed quarts.
Sometimes you would call out for Cicely Hacket.

90   SLY   Ay, the woman's maid of the house.

3 SERVANT

Why, sir, you know no house nor no such maid
Nor no such men as you have reckoned up –
As Stephen Sly and old John Naps of Greet,
And Peter Turph and Henry Pimpernell –
95   And twenty more such names and men as these,
Which never were, nor no man ever saw.

SLY   Now Lord be thanked for my good amends.

ALL   Amen.

SLY   I thank thee, thou shalt not lose by it.

Enter BARTHOLOMEW *the Page as
Lady, with Attendants.*

BARTHOLOMEW   How fares my noble lord?

100   SLY   Marry, I fare well, for here is cheer enough.
Where is my wife?

BARTHOLOMEW

Here, noble lord. What is thy will with her?

SLY   Are you my wife, and will not call me 'husband'?

My men should call me 'lord'; I am your goodman.

BARTHOLOMEW

My husband and my lord, my lord and husband,   105
I am your wife in all obedience.

SLY   I know it well. – What must I call her?

LORD   'Madam.'

SLY   'Al'ce madam'? Or 'Joan madam'?

LORD   'Madam', and nothing else. So lords call ladies.   110

SLY   Madam wife, they say that I have dreamed
And slept above some fifteen year or more.

BARTHOLOMEW

Ay, and the time seems thirty unto me,
Being all this time abandoned from your bed.

SLY   'Tis much. Servants, leave me and her alone.   115
Exeunt Lord and Servants.
Madam, undress you and come now to bed.

BARTHOLOMEW

Thrice-noble lord, let me entreat of you
To pardon me yet for a night or two,
Or if not so, until the sun be set.
For your physicians have expressly charged,   120
In peril to incur your former malady,
That I should yet absent me from your bed.
I hope this reason stands for my excuse.

SLY   Ay, it stands so that I may hardly tarry so long; but
I would be loath to fall into my dreams again. I will   125
therefore tarry in despite of the flesh and the blood.

Enter a Servant.

SERVANT

Your honour's players, hearing your amendment,
Are come to play a pleasant comedy;
For so your doctors hold it very meet,
Seeing too much sadness hath congealed your blood –   130
And melancholy is the nurse of frenzy –
Therefore they thought it good you hear a play
And frame your mind to mirth and merriment,
Which bars a thousand harms and lengthens life.

SLY   Marry, I will. Let them play it. Is not a comonty a   135
Christmas gambol or a tumbling trick?

BARTHOLOMEW

No, my good lord, it is more pleasing stuff.

SLY   What, household stuff?

BARTHOLOMEW   It is a kind of history.

SLY   Well, we'll see't. Come, madam wife, sit by my side
And let the world slip: we shall ne'er be younger.   140

1.1   *Flourish. Enter* LUCENTIO *and
his man* TRANIO.

LUCENTIO   Tranio, since for the great desire I had
To see fair Padua, nursery of arts,
I am arrived for fruitful Lombardy,
The pleasant garden of great Italy,
And by my father's love and leave am armed   5
With his good will and thy good company –
My trusty servant, well approved in all –

Here let us breathe and haply institute
A course of learning and ingenious studies.
10 Pisa, renowned for grave citizens,
Gave me my being and my father first –
A merchant of great traffic through the world –
Vincentio, come of the Bentivogli.
Vincentio's son, brought up in Florence,
15 It shall become to serve all hopes conceived
To deck his fortune with his virtuous deeds:
And therefore, Tranio, for the time I study,
Virtue and that part of philosophy
Will I apply that treats of happiness
20 By virtue specially to be achieved.
Tell me thy mind, for I have Pisa left
And am to Padua come, as he that leaves
A shallow plash to plunge him in the deep,
And with satiety seeks to quench his thirst.
25 TRANIO   *Mi perdonato*, gentle master mine,
I am in all affected as yourself,
Glad that you thus continue your resolve
To suck the sweets of sweet philosophy.
Only, good master, while we do admire
30 This virtue and this moral discipline,
Let's be no stoics nor no stocks, I pray,
Or so devote to Aristotle's checks
As Ovid be an outcast quite abjured.
Balk logic with acquaintance that you have
35 And practise rhetoric in your common talk;
Music and poesy use to quicken you;
The mathematics and the metaphysics,
Fall to them as you find your stomach serves you.
No profit grows where is no pleasure ta'en:
40 In brief, sir, study what you most affect.
LUCENTIO   Gramercies, Tranio, well dost thou advise.
If, Biondello, thou wert come ashore,
We could at once put us in readiness
And take a lodging fit to entertain
45 Such friends as time in Padua shall beget.
But stay awhile, what company is this?
TRANIO   Master, some show to welcome us to town.

Enter BAPTISTA *with his two daughters,* KATHERINA
and BIANCA; GREMIO, *a pantaloon;* HORTENSIO,
suitor to Bianca. Lucentio and Tranio stand by.

BAPTISTA   Gentlemen, importune me no farther,
For how I firmly am resolved you know:
50 That is, not to bestow my youngest daughter
Before I have a husband for the elder.
If either of you both love Katherina,
Because I know you well and love you well,
Leave shall you have to court her at your pleasure.
55 GREMIO   To cart her, rather. She's too rough for me.
There, there, Hortensio, will you any wife?
KATHERINA   I pray you, sir, is it your will
To make a stale of me amongst these mates?
HORTENSIO
'Mates', maid? How mean you that? No mates for you

Unless you were of gentler, milder mould.   60
KATHERINA
I'faith, sir, you shall never need to fear.
Iwis it is not half-way to her heart:
But if it were, doubt not her care should be
To comb your noddle with a three-legged stool
And paint your face and use you like a fool.   65
HORTENSIO
From all such devils, good Lord deliver us!
GREMIO   And me too, good Lord.
TRANIO
Husht, master, here's some good pastime toward;
That wench is stark mad or wonderful froward.
LUCENTIO   But in the other's silence do I see   70
Maids' mild behaviour and sobriety.
Peace, Tranio.
TRANIO   Well said, master. Mum, and gaze your fill.
BAPTISTA   Gentlemen, that I may soon make good
What I have said – Bianca, get you in;   75
And let it not displease thee, good Bianca,
For I will love thee ne'er the less, my girl.
KATHERINA   A pretty peat. It is best put finger in the
eye, an she knew why.
BIANCA   Sister, content you in my discontent.   80
– Sir, to your pleasure humbly I subscribe:
My books and instruments shall be my company,
On them to look and practise by myself.
LUCENTIO
Hark, Tranio, thou mayst hear Minerva speak.
HORTENSIO   Signor Baptista, will you be so strange?   85
Sorry am I that our good will effects
Bianca's grief.
GREMIO   Why will you mew her up,
Signor Baptista, for this fiend of hell,
And make her bear the penance of her tongue?
BAPTISTA   Gentlemen, content ye: I am resolved.   90
Go in, Bianca.   *Exit Bianca.*
And for I know she taketh most delight
In music, instruments and poetry,
Schoolmasters will I keep within my house
Fit to instruct her youth. If you, Hortensio,   95
Or, Signor Gremio, you know any such,
Prefer them hither; for to cunning men
I will be very kind, and liberal
To mine own children in good bringing up.
And so farewell. – Katherina, you may stay,   100
For I have more to commune with Bianca.   *Exit.*
KATHERINA   Why, and I trust I may go too, may I not?
What, shall I be appointed hours, as though, belike,
I knew not what to take and what to leave? Ha!   *Exit.*
GREMIO   You may go to the devil's dam! Your gifts are so   105
good here's none will hold you. Their love is not so
great, Hortensio, but we may blow our nails together
and fast it fairly out. Our cake's dough on both sides.
Farewell. Yet for the love I bear my sweet Bianca, if I
can by any means light on a fit man to teach her that   110
wherein she delights, I will wish him to her father.

HORTENSIO So will I, Signor Gremio. But a word, I
pray: though the nature of our quarrel yet never
brooked parle, know now, upon advice, it toucheth us
both – that we may yet again have access to our fair
mistress and be happy rivals in Bianca's love – to
labour and effect one thing specially.

GREMIO What's that, I pray?

HORTENSIO Marry, sir, to get a husband for her sister.

GREMIO A husband? A devil.

HORTENSIO I say a husband.

GREMIO I say a devil. Think'st thou, Hortensio, though
her father be very rich, any man is so very a fool to be
married to hell?

HORTENSIO Tush, Gremio: though it pass your
patience and mine to endure her loud alarums, why,
man, there be good fellows in the world, an a man
could light on them, would take her with all faults, and
money enough.

GREMIO I cannot tell, but I had as lief take her dowry
with this condition: to be whipped at the high cross
every morning.

HORTENSIO Faith, as you say, there's small choice in
rotten apples. But come, since this bar in law makes us
friends, it shall be so far forth friendly maintained till
by helping Baptista's eldest daughter to a husband we
set his youngest free for a husband – and then have to't
afresh. Sweet Bianca! Happy man be his dole. He that
runs fastest gets the ring. How say you, Signor
Gremio?

GREMIO I am agreed, and would I had given him the
best horse in Padua to begin his wooing that would
thoroughly woo her, wed her, and bed her, and rid the
house of her. Come on.

Exeunt Gremio and Hortensio.

TRANIO I pray, sir, tell me, is it possible
That love should of a sudden take such hold?

LUCENTIO O Tranio, till I found it to be true
I never thought it possible or likely.
But see, while idly I stood looking on,
I found the effect of love-in-idleness,
And now in plainness do confess to thee
That art to me as secret and as dear
As Anna to the Queen of Carthage was:
Tranio, I burn, I pine; I perish, Tranio,
If I achieve not this young modest girl.
Counsel me, Tranio, for I know thou canst;
Assist me, Tranio, for I know thou wilt.

TRANIO Master, it is no time to chide you now;
Affection is not rated from the heart.
If love have touched you, naught remains but so:
Redime te captum quam queas minimo.

LUCENTIO
Gramercies, lad. Go forward, this contents;
The rest will comfort, for thy counsel's sound.

TRANIO Master, you looked so longly on the maid,
Perhaps you marked not what's the pith of all.

LUCENTIO O yes, I saw sweet beauty in her face,

Such as the daughter of Agenor had
That made great Jove to humble him to her hand
When with his knees he kissed the Cretan strand.

TRANIO
Saw you no more? Marked you not how her sister
Began to scold and raise up such a storm
That mortal ears might hardly endure the din?

LUCENTIO Tranio, I saw her coral lips to move,
And with her breath she did perfume the air;
Sacred and sweet was all I saw in her.

TRANIO Nay, then 'tis time to stir him from his trance.
– I pray, awake, sir. If you love the maid,
Bend thoughts and wits to achieve her. Thus it
stands:
Her elder sister is so curst and shrewd
That till the father rid his hands of her,
Master, your love must live a maid at home,
And therefore has he closely mewed her up
Because she will not be annoyed with suitors.

LUCENTIO Ah, Tranio, what a cruel father's he.
But art thou not advised he took some care
To get her cunning schoolmasters to instruct her?

TRANIO Ay, marry am I, sir – and now 'tis plotted.

LUCENTIO I have it, Tranio.

TRANIO   Master, for my hand,
Both our inventions meet and jump in one.

LUCENTIO Tell me thine first.

TRANIO   You will be schoolmaster
And undertake the teaching of the maid:
That's your device.

LUCENTIO   It is. May it be done?

TRANIO Not possible: for who shall bear your part
And be in Padua here Vincentio's son,
Keep house and ply his book, welcome his friends,
Visit his countrymen and banquet them?

LUCENTIO *Basta*, content thee, for I have it full.
We have not yet been seen in any house,
Nor can we be distinguished by our faces
For man or master. Then it follows thus:
Thou shalt be master, Tranio, in my stead,
Keep house and port and servants as I should;
I will some other be – some Florentine,
Some Neapolitan, or meaner man of Pisa.
'Tis hatched, and shall be so. Tranio, at once
Uncase thee; take my coloured hat and cloak.

[They exchange outer clothing.]

When Biondello comes, he waits on thee,
But I will charm him first to keep his tongue.

TRANIO So had you need.
In brief, sir, sith it your pleasure is,
And I am tied to be obedient –
For so your father charged me at our parting:
'Be serviceable to my son,' quoth he,
Although I think 'twas in another sense –
I am content to be Lucentio,
Because so well I love Lucentio.

LUCENTIO Tranio, be so, because Lucentio loves,

And let me be a slave to achieve that maid
Whose sudden sight hath thralled my wounded eye.

Enter BIONDELLO.

220   Here comes the rogue. Sirrah, where have you been?
BIONDELLO   Where have I been? Nay, how now, where
are you? Master, has my fellow Tranio stolen your
clothes, or you stolen his, or both? Pray, what's the news?
LUCENTIO   Sirrah, come hither. 'Tis no time to jest,
225   And therefore frame your manners to the time.
Your fellow Tranio here, to save my life,
Puts my apparel and my countenance on,
And I for my escape have put on his;
For in a quarrel since I came ashore
230   I killed a man, and fear I was descried.
Wait you on him, I charge you, as becomes,
While I make way from hence to save my life.
You understand me?
BIONDELLO   I, sir? Ne'er a whit.
LUCENTIO   And not a jot of 'Tranio' in your mouth:
235   Tranio is changed into Lucentio.
BIONDELLO   The better for him; would I were so too.
TRANIO
So could I, faith, boy, to have the next wish after:
That Lucentio indeed had Baptista's youngest daughter.
But sirrah, not for my sake but your master's, I advise
You use your manners discreetly in all kind of
240   companies.
When I am alone, why then I am Tranio,
But in all places else, your master Lucentio.
LUCENTIO   Tranio, let's go.
One thing more rests that thyself execute:
245   To make one among these wooers. If thou ask me why,
Sufficeth my reasons are both good and weighty.

Exeunt.

The Presenters above speak.

SERVANT   My lord, you nod; you do not mind the play.
SLY   Yes, by Saint Anne do I – a good matter, surely.
Comes there any more of it?
250   BARTHOLOMEW   My lord, 'tis but begun.
SLY   'Tis a very excellent piece of work, madam lady.
Would 'twere done. [*They sit and mark.*]

1.2   *Enter* PETRUCCIO *and his man* GRUMIO.

PETRUCCIO   Verona, for a while I take my leave
To see my friends in Padua, but of all
My best-beloved and approved friend
Hortensio – and I trow this is his house.
5   Here, sirrah Grumio, knock, I say.
GRUMIO   Knock, sir? Whom should I knock? Is there
any man has rebused your worship?
PETRUCCIO   Villain, I say, knock me here soundly.
GRUMIO   Knock you here, sir? Why, sir, what am I, sir,
10   that I should knock you here, sir?
PETRUCCIO   Villain, I say, knock me at this gate,
And rap me well or I'll knock your knave's pate.

GRUMIO
My master is grown quarrelsome. I should knock you
first,
And then I know after who comes by the worst.
PETRUCCIO   Will it not be?   15
Faith, sirrah, an you'll not knock, I'll ring it.
I'll try how you can *sol-fa* and sing it.
[*Wrings him by the ears.*]
GRUMIO   Help, masters, help! My master is mad.
PETRUCCIO   Now knock when I bid you, sirrah villain.

Enter HORTENSIO.

HORTENSIO   How now, what's the matter? My old   20
friend Grumio and my good friend Petruccio? How do
you all at Verona?
PETRUCCIO
Signor Hortensio, come you to part the fray?
Con tutto il cuore ben trovato, may I say.
HORTENSIO   *Alla nostra casa ben venuto, molto honorato*   25
signor mio Petruccio.
Rise, Grumio, rise; we will compound this quarrel.
GRUMIO   Nay, 'tis no matter, sir, what he 'lleges in
Latin. If this be not a lawful cause for me to leave his
service – look you, sir: he bid me knock him and rap   30
him soundly, sir. Well, was it fit for a servant to use his
master so, being perhaps, for aught I see, two-and-
thirty, a pip out?
Whom would to God I had well knocked at first,
Then had not Grumio come by the worst.   35
PETRUCCIO   A senseless villain. Good Hortensio,
I bade the rascal knock upon your gate,
And could not get him for my heart to do it.
GRUMIO   Knock at the gate? O heavens, spake you not
these words plain: 'Sirrah, knock me here, rap me   40
here, knock me well and knock me soundly'?
And come you now with knocking at the gate?
PETRUCCIO   Sirrah, be gone, or talk not, I advise you.
HORTENSIO
Petruccio, patience, I am Grumio's pledge.
Why this' a heavy chance 'twixt him and you –   45
Your ancient, trusty, pleasant servant Grumio.
And tell me now, sweet friend, what happy gale
Blows you to Padua here from old Verona?
PETRUCCIO
Such wind as scatters young men through the
world
To seek their fortunes farther than at home,   50
Where small experience grows. But in a few,
Signor Hortensio, thus it stands with me:
Antonio my father is deceased,
And I have thrust myself into this maze,
Haply to wive and thrive as best I may;   55
Crowns in my purse I have and goods at home,
And so am come abroad to see the world.
HORTENSIO
Petruccio, shall I then come roundly to thee
And wish thee to a shrewd, ill-favoured wife?

60　　　Thou'dst thank me but a little for my counsel:
　　　　And yet I'll promise thee she shall be rich,
　　　　And very rich. But thou'rt too much my friend,
　　　　And I'll not wish thee to her.

PETRUCCIO
　　　　Signor Hortensio, 'twixt such friends as we
65　　　Few words suffice; and therefore, if thou know
　　　　One rich enough to be Petruccio's wife –
　　　　As wealth is burden of my wooing dance –
　　　　Be she as foul as was Florentius' love,
　　　　As old as Sibyl, and as curst and shrewd
70　　　As Socrates' Xanthippe or a worse,
　　　　She moves me not – or not removes at least
　　　　Affection's edge in me – were she as rough
　　　　As are the swelling Adriatic seas.
　　　　I come to wive it wealthily in Padua;
75　　　If wealthily, then happily in Padua.

GRUMIO　　Nay, look you, sir, he tells you flatly what his
　　　　mind is. Why, give him gold enough and marry him to
　　　　a puppet or an aglet-baby, or an old trot with ne'er a
　　　　tooth in her head, though she have as many diseases as
80　　　two and fifty horses, why, nothing comes amiss – so
　　　　money comes withal.

HORTENSIO
　　　　Petruccio, since we are stepped thus far in,
　　　　I will continue that I broached in jest.
　　　　I can, Petruccio, help thee to a wife
85　　　With wealth enough, and young and beauteous,
　　　　Brought up as best becomes a gentlewoman.
　　　　Her only fault – and that is faults enough –
　　　　Is that she is intolerable curst,
　　　　And shrewd and froward so beyond all measure
90　　　That, were my state far worser than it is,
　　　　I would not wed her for a mine of gold.

PETRUCCIO
　　　　Hortensio, peace; thou knowst not gold's effect.
　　　　Tell me her father's name and 'tis enough,
　　　　For I will board her though she chide as loud
95　　　As thunder when the clouds in autumn crack.

HORTENSIO　　Her father is Baptista Minola,
　　　　An affable and courteous gentleman;
　　　　Her name is Katherina Minola,
　　　　Renowned in Padua for her scolding tongue.

100　PETRUCCIO　I know her father, though I know not her,
　　　　And he knew my deceased father well.
　　　　I will not sleep, Hortensio, till I see her,
　　　　And therefore let me be thus bold with you
　　　　To give you over at this first encounter –
105　　　Unless you will accompany me thither.

GRUMIO　　I pray you, sir, let him go while the humour
　　　　lasts. O'my word, an she knew him as well as I do, she
　　　　would think scolding would do little good upon him.
　　　　She may perhaps call him half a score knaves or so –
110　　　why, that's nothing; an he begin once, he'll rail in his
　　　　rope-tricks. I'll tell you what, sir, an she stand him but
　　　　a little, he will throw a figure in her face and so disfigure
　　　　her with it that she shall have no more eyes to see

withal than a cat. You know him not, sir.

HORTENSIO　Tarry, Petruccio, I must go with thee,　　115
　　　　For in Baptista's keep my treasure is.
　　　　He hath the jewel of my life in hold,
　　　　His youngest daughter, beautiful Bianca,
　　　　And her withholds from me and other more –
　　　　Suitors to her and rivals in my love –　　　　　120
　　　　Supposing it a thing impossible,
　　　　For those defects I have before rehearsed,
　　　　That ever Katherina will be wooed.
　　　　Therefore this order hath Baptista ta'en:
　　　　That none shall have access unto Bianca　　　125
　　　　Till Katherine the Curst have got a husband.

GRUMIO　　'Katherine the Curst' –
　　　　A title for a maid of all titles the worst.

HORTENSIO
　　　　Now shall my friend Petruccio do me grace
　　　　And offer me disguised in sober robes　　　　130
　　　　To old Baptista as a schoolmaster
　　　　Well seen in music, to instruct Bianca,
　　　　That so I may by this device at least
　　　　Have leave and leisure to make love to her
　　　　And unsuspected court her by herself.　　　　135

Enter GREMIO *with a paper and* LUCENTIO
disguised as Cambio, a schoolmaster.

GRUMIO　　Here's no knavery. See, to beguile the old
　　　　folks, how the young folks lay their heads together.
　　　　Master, master, look about you. Who goes there, ha?

HORTENSIO　Peace, Grumio, it is the rival of my love.
　　　　Petruccio, stand by awhile.　　　　　　　　140

GRUMIO　　A proper stripling and an amorous.
　　　　[*Petruccio, Hortensio and Grumio stand aside.*]

GREMIO　　O, very well; I have perused the note.
　　　　Hark you, sir, I'll have them very fairly bound
　　　　(All books of love, see that at any hand)
　　　　And see you read no other lectures to her:　　145
　　　　You understand me. Over and beside
　　　　Signor Baptista's liberality,
　　　　I'll mend it with a largess. Take your paper too,
　　　　And let me have them very well perfumed,
　　　　For she is sweeter than perfume itself　　　　150
　　　　To whom they go to. What will you read to her?

LUCENTIO　Whate'er I read to her I'll plead for you
　　　　As for my patron, stand you so assured,
　　　　As firmly as yourself were still in place;
　　　　Yea, and perhaps with more successful words　155
　　　　Than you – unless you were a scholar, sir.

GREMIO　　O, this learning, what a thing it is!

GRUMIO　　O, this woodcock, what an ass it is!

PETRUCCIO　Peace, sirrah.

HORTENSIO　Grumio, mum. – God save you, Signor　160
　　　　Gremio.

GREMIO　　And you're well met, Signor Hortensio.
　　　　Trow you whither I am going? To Baptista Minola.
　　　　I promised to inquire carefully
　　　　About a schoolmaster for the fair Bianca,　　165

And by good fortune I have lighted well
On this young man, for learning and behaviour
Fit for her turn, well read in poetry
And other books – good ones, I warrant ye.

170 HORTENSIO   'Tis well, and I have met a gentleman
Hath promised me to help me to another,
A fine musician to instruct our mistress.
So shall I no whit be behind in duty
To fair Bianca, so beloved of me.

175 GREMIO   Beloved of me, and that my deeds shall prove.

GRUMIO   And that his bags shall prove.

HORTENSIO   Gremio, 'tis now no time to vent our love.
Listen to me, and if you speak me fair,
I'll tell you news indifferent good for either.

180 Here is a gentleman whom by chance I met,
Upon agreement from us to his liking
Will undertake to woo curst Katherine,
Yea, and to marry her, if her dowry please.

GREMIO   So said, so done, is well.

185 Hortensio, have you told him all her faults?

PETRUCCIO   I know she is an irksome brawling scold.
If that be all, masters, I hear no harm.

GREMIO   No, sayst me so, friend? What countryman?

PETRUCCIO   Born in Verona, old Antonio's son.

190 My father dead, my fortune lives for me,
And I do hope good days and long to see.

GREMIO
O sir, such a life with such a wife were strange.
But if you have a stomach, to't o'God's name;
You shall have me assisting you in all.
But will you woo this wildcat?

195 PETRUCCIO   Will I live?

GRUMIO   Will he woo her? Ay, or I'll hang her.

PETRUCCIO   Why came I hither but to that intent?
Think you a little din can daunt mine ears?
Have I not in my time heard lions roar?

200 Have I not heard the sea, puffed up with winds,
Rage like an angry boar chafed with sweat?
Have I not heard great ordnance in the field,
And heaven's artillery thunder in the skies?
Have I not in a pitched battle heard

205 Loud 'larums, neighing steeds and trumpets' clang?
And do you tell me of a woman's tongue,
That gives not half so great a blow to hear
As will a chestnut in a farmer's fire?
Tush, tush, fear boys with bugs.

GRUMIO   For he fears none.

210 GREMIO   Hortensio, hark:
This gentleman is happily arrived,
My mind presumes, for his own good and yours.

HORTENSIO   I promised we would be contributors
And bear his charge of wooing, whatsoe'er.

215 GREMIO   And so we will – provided that he win her.

GRUMIO   I would I were as sure of a good dinner.

Enter TRANIO *brave as Lucentio, and* BIONDELLO.

TRANIO   Gentlemen, God save you. If I may be bold,

tell me, I beseech you, which is the readiest way to the
house of Signor Baptista Minola?

220 BIONDELLO   He that has the two fair daughters – is't he
you mean?

TRANIO   Even he, Biondello.

GREMIO   Hark you, sir, you mean not her to –

TRANIO
Perhaps him and her, sir: what have you to do?

PETRUCCIO
225 Not her that chides, sir, at any hand, I pray.

TRANIO   I love no chiders, sir: Biondello, let's away.

LUCENTIO [*aside*]
Well begun, Tranio.

HORTENSIO   Sir, a word ere you go:
Are you a suitor to the maid you talk of – yea or no?

TRANIO   And if I be, sir, is it any offence?

GREMIO
230 No, if without more words you will get you hence.

TRANIO   Why, sir, I pray, are not the streets as free
For me as for you?

GREMIO   But so is not she.

TRANIO   For what reason, I beseech you?

GREMIO   For this reason, if you'll know:
235 That she's the choice love of Signor Gremio.

HORTENSIO
That she's the chosen of Signor Hortensio.

TRANIO   Softly, my masters. If you be gentlemen,
Do me this right: hear me with patience.
Baptista is a noble gentleman
240 To whom my father is not all unknown,
And were his daughter fairer than she is
She may more suitors have, and me for one.
Fair Leda's daughter had a thousand wooers,
Then well one more may fair Bianca have.
245 And so she shall: Lucentio shall make one,
Though Paris came in hope to speed alone.

GREMIO   What, this gentleman will out-talk us all.

LUCENTIO
Sir, give him head, I know he'll prove a jade.

PETRUCCIO
Hortensio, to what end are all these words?

HORTENSIO   Sir, let me be so bold as ask you,
250 Did you yet ever see Baptista's daughter?

TRANIO   No, sir, but hear I do that he hath two;
The one as famous for a scolding tongue
As is the other for beauteous modesty.

PETRUCCIO   Sir, sir, the first's for me; let her go by.

255 GREMIO   Yea, leave that labour to great Hercules,
And let it be more than Alcides' twelve.

PETRUCCIO   Sir, understand you this of me in sooth:
The youngest daughter whom you hearken for
Her father keeps from all access of suitors,
260 And will not promise her to any man
Until the elder sister first be wed.
The younger then is free, and not before.

TRANIO   If it be so, sir, that you are the man
Must stead us all, and me amongst the rest,
265

An if you break the ice and do this feat –
Achieve the elder, set the younger free
For our access – whose hap shall be to have her
Will not so graceless be to be ingrate.

HORTENSIO
270 Sir, you say well, and well you do conceive;
And since you do profess to be a suitor
You must, as we do, gratify this gentleman,
To whom we all rest generally beholding.

TRANIO Sir, I shall not be slack; in sign whereof,
275 Please ye we may contrive this afternoon
And quaff carouses to our mistress' health,
And do as adversaries do in law,
Strive mightily, but eat and drink as friends.

GRUMIO, BIONDELLO
O excellent motion! Fellows, let's be gone.

280 HORTENSIO The motion's good indeed, and be it so.
Petruccio, I shall be your *ben venuto.*   *Exeunt.*

2.1   *Enter* KATHERINA *and* BIANCA.

BIANCA
Good sister, wrong me not, nor wrong yourself
To make a bondmaid and a slave of me –
That I disdain; but for these other goods,
Unbind my hands, I'll pull them off myself,
5 Yea, all my raiment to my petticoat,
Or what you will command me will I do,
So well I know my duty to my elders.

KATHERINA Of all thy suitors here I charge thee tell
Whom thou lov'st best. See thou dissemble not.

10 BIANCA Believe me, sister, of all the men alive
I never yet beheld that special face
Which I could fancy more than any other.

KATHERINA Minion, thou liest. Is't not Hortensio?

BIANCA If you affect him, sister, here I swear
15 I'll plead for you myself but you shall have him.

KATHERINA O then, belike you fancy riches more:
You will have Gremio to keep you fair.

BIANCA Is it for him you do envy me so?
Nay then, you jest, and now I well perceive
20 You have but jested with me all this while.
I prithee, sister Kate, untie my hands.

KATHERINA
If that be jest, then all the rest was so.   [*Strikes her.*]

Enter BAPTISTA.

BAPTISTA
Why, how now, dame, whence grows this insolence?
Bianca, stand aside. Poor girl, she weeps.
25 Go ply thy needle, meddle not with her.
For shame, thou hilding of a devilish spirit,
Why dost thou wrong her that did ne'er wrong
   thee?
When did she cross thee with a bitter word?

KATHERINA
Her silence flouts me, and I'll be revenged.
   [*Flies after Bianca.*]

BAPTISTA
What, in my sight? – Bianca, get thee in.   30
                     Exit Bianca.

KATHERINA
What, will you not suffer me? Nay, now I see
She is your treasure, she must have a husband,
I must dance barefoot on her wedding day
And, for your love to her, lead apes in hell.
Talk not to me, I will go sit and weep   35
Till I can find occasion of revenge.   *Exit.*

BAPTISTA Was ever gentleman thus grieved as I?
But who comes here?

Enter GREMIO, LUCENTIO *as Cambio, in the habit
of a mean man,* PETRUCCIO *with* HORTENSIO
as Licio, TRANIO *as Lucentio, with his boy*
BIONDELLO *bearing a lute and books.*

GREMIO Good morrow, neighbour Baptista.

BAPTISTA Good morrow, neighbour Gremio. God save   40
you, gentlemen.

PETRUCCIO
And you, good sir. Pray, have you not a daughter
Called Katherina, fair and virtuous?

BAPTISTA I have a daughter, sir, called Katherina.

GREMIO You are too blunt; go to it orderly.   45

PETRUCCIO
You wrong me, Signor Gremio, give me leave.
– I am a gentleman of Verona, sir,
That hearing of her beauty and her wit,
Her affability and bashful modesty,
Her wondrous qualities and mild behaviour,   50
Am bold to show myself a forward guest
Within your house to make mine eye the witness
Of that report which I so oft have heard,
And for an entrance to my entertainment
I do present you with a man of mine,   55
Cunning in music and the mathematics,
To instruct her fully in those sciences,
Whereof I know she is not ignorant.
Accept of him or else you do me wrong.
His name is Licio, born in Mantua.   60

BAPTISTA
You're welcome, sir, and he for your good sake.
But for my daughter Katherine, this I know:
She is not for your turn – the more my grief.

PETRUCCIO I see you do not mean to part with her,
Or else you like not of my company.   65

BAPTISTA Mistake me not, I speak but as I find.
Whence are you, sir? What may I call your name?

PETRUCCIO Petruccio is my name, Antonio's son,
A man well known throughout all Italy.

BAPTISTA
I know him well. You are welcome for his sake.   70

GREMIO Saving your tale, Petruccio, I pray let us that
are poor petitioners speak too. *Baccare*, you are
marvellous forward.

PETRUCCIO
O, pardon me, Signor Gremio, I would fain be doing.
GREMIO
75   I doubt it not, sir. But you will curse your wooing.
Neighbour, this is a gift very grateful, I am sure of it.
To express the like kindness, myself, that have been
more kindly beholding to you than any, freely give unto
you this young scholar that hath been long studying at
80   Rheims, as cunning in Greek, Latin and other
languages as the other in music and mathematics. His
name is Cambio. Pray accept his service.
BAPTISTA A thousand thanks, Signor Gremio.
Welcome, good Cambio. [*to Tranio*] But, gentle sir,
85   methinks you walk like a stranger. May I be so bold to
know the cause of your coming?
TRANIO   Pardon me, sir, the boldness is mine own
That, being a stranger in this city here,
Do make myself a suitor to your daughter,
90   Unto Bianca, fair and virtuous;
Nor is your firm resolve unknown to me
In the preferment of the eldest sister.
This liberty is all that I request:
That upon knowledge of my parentage
95   I may have welcome 'mongst the rest that woo,
And free access and favour as the rest.
And toward the education of your daughters
I here bestow a simple instrument
And this small packet of Greek and Latin
books;
100   If you accept them, then their worth is great.
BAPTISTA   Lucentio is your name – of whence, I pray?
TRANIO   Of Pisa, sir, son to Vincentio.
BAPTISTA   A mighty man of Pisa – by report
I know him well. You are very welcome, sir.
[*to Hortensio*] Take you the lute [*to Lucentio*] and you
105   the set of books;
You shall go see your pupils presently.
Holla, within!

Enter a Servant.

Sirrah, lead these gentlemen
To my daughters and tell them both
These are their tutors. Bid them use them well.
Exeunt Servant, Lucentio and Hortensio,
Biondello following.
110   We will go walk a little in the orchard,
And then to dinner. You are passing welcome,
And so I pray you all to think yourselves.
PETRUCCIO   Signor Baptista, my business asketh haste,
And every day I cannot come to woo.
115   You knew my father well, and in him me,
Left solely heir to all his lands and goods,
Which I have bettered rather than decreased.
Then tell me, if I get your daughter's love,
What dowry shall I have with her to wife?
120   BAPTISTA   After my death, the one half of my lands,
And in possession twenty thousand crowns.

PETRUCCIO   And for that dowry I'll assure her of
Her widowhood, be it that she survive me,
In all my lands and leases whatsoever.
Let specialties be therefore drawn between us,   125
That covenants may be kept on either hand.
BAPTISTA   Ay, when the special thing is well obtained –
That is, her love, for that is all in all.
PETRUCCIO   Why, that is nothing, for I tell you, father,
I am as peremptory as she proud-minded,   130
And where two raging fires meet together
They do consume the thing that feeds their fury.
Though little fire grows great with little wind,
Yet extreme gusts will blow out fire and all:
So I to her, and so she yields to me,   135
For I am rough and woo not like a babe.
BAPTISTA
Well mayst thou woo, and happy be thy speed.
But be thou armed for some unhappy words.
PETRUCCIO
Ay, to the proof, as mountains are for winds,
That shakes not though they blow perpetually.   140

Enter HORTENSIO *as Licio with his head broke.*

BAPTISTA
How now, my friend, why dost thou look so pale?
HORTENSIO   For fear, I promise you, if I look pale.
BAPTISTA
What, will my daughter prove a good musician?
HORTENSIO   I think she'll sooner prove a soldier;
Iron may hold with her, but never lutes.   145
BAPTISTA
Why then, thou canst not break her to the lute?
HORTENSIO
Why no, for she hath broke the lute to me.
I did but tell her she mistook her frets
And bowed her hand to teach her fingering
When, with a most impatient devilish spirit,   150
'Frets call you these?' quoth she, 'I'll fume with them,'
And with that word she struck me on the head,
And through the instrument my pate made way,
And there I stood amazed for a while,
As on a pillory, looking through the lute,   155
While she did call me 'rascal', 'fiddler',
And 'twangling Jack', with twenty such vile terms,
As had she studied to misuse me so.
PETRUCCIO   Now, by the world, it is a lusty wench;
I love her ten times more than e'er I did.   160
O, how I long to have some chat with her!
BAPTISTA [*to Hortensio*]
Well, go with me, and be not so discomfited.
Proceed in practice with my younger daughter;
She's apt to learn and thankful for good turns.
Signor Petruccio, will you go with us,   165
Or shall I send my daughter Kate to you?
PETRUCCIO   I pray you, do.   *Exeunt all but Petruccio.*
I'll attend her here,
And woo her with some spirit when she comes.

Say that she rail, why then I'll tell her plain
170　She sings as sweetly as a nightingale;
Say that she frown, I'll say she looks as clear
As morning roses newly washed with dew;
Say she be mute and will not speak a word,
Then I'll commend her volubility
175　And say she uttereth piercing eloquence.
If she do bid me pack, I'll give her thanks
As though she bid me stay by her a week;
If she deny to wed, I'll crave the day
When I shall ask the banns, and when be married.

　　　　　　　Enter KATHERINA.

180　But here she comes, and now, Petruccio, speak.
Good morrow, Kate, for that's your name, I hear.

KATHERINA
Well have you heard, but something hard of hearing:
They call me Katherine that do talk of me.

PETRUCCIO
You lie, in faith, for you are called plain Kate,
185　And bonny Kate, and sometimes 'Kate the Curst';
But Kate, the prettiest Kate in Christendom,
Kate of Kate Hall, my super-dainty Kate –
For dainties are all cates, and therefore 'Kate' –
Take this of me, Kate of my consolation:
190　Hearing thy mildness praised in every town,
Thy virtues spoke of and thy beauty sounded –
Yet not so deeply as to thee belongs –
Myself am moved to woo thee for my wife.

KATHERINA
'Moved'. In good time, let him that moved you hither
195　Re-move you hence. I knew you at the first
You were a movable.

PETRUCCIO　Why, what's a movable?

KATHERINA　A joint-stool.

PETRUCCIO　Thou hast hit it: come, sit on me.

200　KATHERINA　Asses are made to bear, and so are you.

PETRUCCIO　Women are made to bear, and so are you.

KATHERINA　No such jade as you, if me you mean.

PETRUCCIO　Alas, good Kate, I will not burden thee,
For, knowing thee to be but young and light –

205　KATHERINA　Too light for such a swain as you to catch,
And yet as heavy as my weight should be.

PETRUCCIO　'Should be'? Should – buzz.

KATHERINA　　　　　　　Well ta'en, and like a buzzard.

PETRUCCIO
O slow-winged turtle, shall a buzzard take thee?

KATHERINA　Ay, for a turtle, as he takes a buzzard.

PETRUCCIO
210　Come, come, you wasp, i'faith you are too angry.

KATHERINA　If I be waspish, best beware my sting.

PETRUCCIO　My remedy is then to pluck it out.

KATHERINA　Ay, if the fool could find it where it lies.

PETRUCCIO
Who knows not where a wasp does wear his sting?
215　In his tail.

KATHERINA　In his tongue.

PETRUCCIO　Whose tongue?

KATHERINA　Yours, if you talk of tails, and so farewell.

PETRUCCIO　What, with my tongue in your tail?
Nay, come again, good Kate, I am a gentleman –　220

KATHERINA　That I'll try. [*Strikes him.*]

PETRUCCIO　I swear I'll cuff you if you strike again.

KATHERINA　So may you lose your arms.
If you strike me you are no gentleman,
And if no gentleman, why then, no arms.　225

PETRUCCIO　A herald, Kate? O, put me in thy books.

KATHERINA　What is your crest – a coxcomb?

PETRUCCIO　A combless cock, so Kate will be my hen.

KATHERINA
No cock of mine: you crow too like a craven.

PETRUCCIO
Nay, come, Kate, come; you must not look so sour.　230

KATHERINA　It is my fashion when I see a crab.

PETRUCCIO
Why, here's no crab, and therefore look not sour.

KATHERINA　There is, there is.

PETRUCCIO　Then show it me.

KATHERINA　Had I a glass, I would.　235

PETRUCCIO　What, you mean my face?

KATHERINA　Well aimed of such a young one.

PETRUCCIO
Now, by Saint George, I am too young for you.

KATHERINA　Yet you are withered.

PETRUCCIO　'Tis with cares.　240

KATHERINA　I care not.

PETRUCCIO
Nay, hear you, Kate. In sooth, you scape not so.

KATHERINA　I chafe you if I tarry. Let me go.

PETRUCCIO　No, not a whit; I find you passing gentle.
'Twas told me you were rough and coy and sullen,　245
And now I find report a very liar,
For thou art pleasant, gamesome, passing courteous,
But slow in speech, yet sweet as springtime flowers;
Thou canst not frown, thou canst not look askance,
Nor bite the lip, as angry wenches will,　250
Nor hast thou pleasure to be cross in talk;
But thou with mildness entertain'st thy wooers
With gentle conference, soft and affable.
Why does the world report that Kate doth limp?
O slanderous world! Kate like the hazel twig　255
Is straight and slender, and as brown in hue
As hazelnuts, and sweeter than the kernels.
O, let me see thee walk. Thou dost not halt.

KATHERINA
Go, fool, and whom thou keep'st command.

PETRUCCIO　Did ever Dian so become a grove　260
As Kate this chamber with her princely gait?
O, be thou Dian, and let her be Kate,
And then let Kate be chaste and Dian sportful.

KATHERINA
Where did you study all this goodly speech?

PETRUCCIO　It is extempore, from my mother-wit.　265

KATHERINA　A witty mother, witless else her son.

PETRUCCIO   Am I not wise?

KATHERINA   Yes, keep you warm.

PETRUCCIO

Marry, so I mean, sweet Katherine, in thy bed.

270 And therefore, setting all this chat aside,

Thus in plain terms: your father hath consented

That you shall be my wife, your dowry 'greed on,

And will you, nill you, I will marry you.

Now, Kate, I am a husband for your turn,

275 For, by this light whereby I see thy beauty –

Thy beauty that doth make me like thee well –

Thou must be married to no man but me,

Enter BAPTISTA, GREMIO *and* TRANIO *as Lucentio.*

For I am he am born to tame you, Kate,

And bring you from a wild Kate to a Kate

280 Conformable as other household Kates.

Here comes your father. Never make denial:

I must and will have Katherine to my wife.

BAPTISTA   Now, Signor Petruccio, how speed you with

my daughter?

285 PETRUCCIO   How but well, sir? How but well?

It were impossible I should speed amiss.

BAPTISTA

Why, how now, daughter Katherine, in your dumps?

KATHERINA

Call you me daughter? Now I promise you

You have showed a tender fatherly regard

290 To wish me wed to one half lunatic,

A madcap ruffian and a swearing Jack

That thinks with oaths to face the matter out.

PETRUCCIO   Father, 'tis thus: yourself and all the world

That talked of her have talked amiss of her.

295 If she be curst, it is for policy,

For she's not froward, but modest as the dove;

She is not hot, but temperate as the morn;

For patience she will prove a second Grissel,

And Roman Lucrece for her chastity;

300 And to conclude, we have 'greed so well together

That upon Sunday is the wedding day.

KATHERINA   I'll see thee hanged on Sunday first.

GREMIO   Hark, Petruccio, she says she'll see thee

hanged first.

TRANIO

Is this your speeding? Nay, then, goodnight our

305 part.

PETRUCCIO

Be patient, gentlemen. I choose her for myself;

If she and I be pleased, what's that to you?

'Tis bargained 'twixt us twain, being alone,

That she shall still be curst in company.

310 I tell you, 'tis incredible to believe

How much she loves me. O, the kindest Kate,

She hung about my neck, and kiss on kiss

She vied so fast, protesting oath on oath,

That in a twink she won me to her love.

315 O, you are novices! 'Tis a world to see

How tame, when men and women are alone,

A meacock wretch can make the curstest shrew.

– Give my thy hand, Kate, I will unto Venice

To buy apparel 'gainst the wedding day;

320 – Provide the feast, father, and bid the guests.

I will be sure my Katherine shall be fine.

BAPTISTA

I know not what to say, but give me your hands.

God send you joy, Petruccio, 'tis a match.

GREMIO, TRANIO

Amen, say we. We will be witnesses.

325 PETRUCCIO   Father, and wife, and gentlemen, adieu.

I will to Venice. Sunday comes apace.

We will have rings, and things, and fine array,

And kiss me, Kate, 'We will be married o'Sunday.'

Exeunt Petruccio and Katherina.

GREMIO   Was ever match clapped up so suddenly?

BAPTISTA

330 Faith, gentlemen, now I play a merchant's part

And venture madly on a desperate mart.

TRANIO   'Twas a commodity lay fretting by you;

'Twill bring you gain, or perish on the seas.

BAPTISTA   The gain I seek is quiet in the match.

335 GREMIO   No doubt but he hath got a quiet catch.

But now, Baptista, to your younger daughter:

Now is the day we long have looked for.

I am your neighbour, and was suitor first.

TRANIO   And I am one that love Bianca more

340 Than words can witness, or your thoughts can guess.

GREMIO   Youngling, thou canst not love so dear as I.

TRANIO   Greybeard, thy love doth freeze.

GREMIO   But thine doth fry.

Skipper, stand back. 'Tis age that nourisheth.

TRANIO   But youth in ladies' eyes that flourisheth.

BAPTISTA

345 Content you, gentlemen, I will compound this strife.

'Tis deeds must win the prize, and he of both

That can assure my daughter greatest dower

Shall have my Bianca's love.

Say, Signor Gremio, what can you assure her?

GREMIO   First, as you know, my house within the city

350 Is richly furnished with plate and gold,

Basins and ewers to lave her dainty hands;

My hangings all of Tyrian tapestry;

In ivory coffers I have stuffed my crowns,

355 In cypress chests my arras counterpoints,

Costly apparel, tents and canopies,

Fine linen, Turkey cushions bossed with pearl,

Valance of Venice gold in needlework,

Pewter and brass, and all things that belongs

360 To house or housekeeping; then at my farm

I have a hundred milch-kine to the pail,

Six score fat oxen standing in my stalls,

And all things answerable to this portion.

Myself am struck in years, I must confess,

365 And if I die tomorrow this is hers,

If whilst I live she will be only mine.

TRANIO   That 'only' came well in. Sir, list to me:
   I am my father's heir and only son;
   If I may have your daughter to my wife,
370   I'll leave her houses three or four as good
   Within rich Pisa walls as any one
   Old Signor Gremio has in Padua,
   Besides two thousand ducats by the year
   Of fruitful land, all which shall be her jointure.
375   – What, have I pinched you, Signor Gremio?
GREMIO   Two thousand ducats by the year of land?
   [*aside*] My land amounts not to so much in all.
   – That she shall have, besides an argosy
   That now is lying in Marsellis' road.
380   – What, have I choked you with an argosy?
TRANIO   Gremio, 'tis known my father hath no less
   Than three great argosies, besides two galliasses
   And twelve tight galleys. These I will assure her,
   And twice as much whate'er thou offer'st next.
385 GREMIO   Nay, I have offered all. I have no more,
   And she can have no more than all I have.
   If you like me, she shall have me and mine.
TRANIO   Why, then the maid is mine from all the world
   By your firm promise; Gremio is out-vied.
390 BAPTISTA   I must confess your offer is the best,
   And, let your father make her the assurance,
   She is your own; else – you must pardon me –
   If you should die before him, where's her dower?
TRANIO   That's but a cavil: he is old, I young.
395 GREMIO   And may not young men die as well as old?
BAPTISTA
   Well, gentlemen, I am thus resolved: on Sunday next
   You know, my daughter Katherine is to be married.
   – Now, on the Sunday following shall Bianca
400   Be bride to you, if you make this assurance;
   If not, to Signor Gremio.
   And so I take my leave, and thank you both.   *Exit.*
GREMIO
   Adieu, good neighbour. – Now I fear thee not.
   Sirrah, young gamester, your father were a fool
405   To give thee all and in his waning age
   Set foot under thy table. Tut, a toy,
   An old Italian fox is not so kind, my boy.   *Exit.*
TRANIO   A vengeance on your crafty withered hide!
   Yet I have faced it with a card of ten.
410   'Tis in my head to do my master good:
   I see no reason but supposed Lucentio
   Must get a father called supposed Vincentio;
   And that's a wonder – fathers commonly
   Do get their children, but in this case of wooing
   A child shall get a sire, if I fail not of my cunning.
   Exit.

3.1   *Enter* LUCENTIO *as Cambio,*
   HORTENSIO *as Licio and* BIANCA.

LUCENTIO
   Fiddler, forbear – you grow too forward, sir;

   Have you so soon forgot the entertainment
   Her sister Katherine welcomed you withal?
HORTENSIO   But, wrangling pedant, this is
   The patroness of heavenly harmony.   5
   Then give me leave to have prerogative,
   And when in music we have spent an hour,
   Your lecture shall have leisure for as much.
LUCENTIO   Preposterous ass, that never read so far
   To know the cause why music was ordained!   10
   Was it not to refresh the mind of man
   After his studies or his usual pain?
   Then give me leave to read philosophy
   And, while I pause, serve in your harmony.
HORTENSIO
   Sirrah, I will not bear these braves of thine.   15
BIANCA   Why, gentlemen, you do me double wrong
   To strive for that which resteth in my choice.
   I am no breeching scholar in the schools:
   I'll not be tied to hours nor 'pointed times
   But learn my lessons as I please myself;   20
   And to cut off all strife, here sit we down.
   – Take you your instrument, play you the whiles;
   His lecture will be done ere you have tuned.
HORTENSIO   You'll leave his lecture when I am in tune?
LUCENTIO   That will be never. Tune your instrument.   25
BIANCA   Where left we last?
LUCENTIO   Here, Madam:
   [*Reads.*] *Hic ibat Simois, hic est Sigeia tellus,*
      Hic steterat Priami regia celsa senis.
BIANCA   Conster them.   30
LUCENTIO   *Hic ibat*, as I told you before; *Simois*, I am
   Lucentio; *hic est*, son unto Vincentio of Pisa; *Sigeia
   tellus*, disguised thus to get your love; *hic steterat*, and
   that Lucentio that comes a-wooing; *Priami*, is my man
   Tranio; *regia*, bearing my port; *celsa senis*, that we   35
   might beguile the old pantaloon.
HORTENSIO   Madam, my instrument's in tune.
BIANCA   Let's hear. O fie, the treble jars.
LUCENTIO   Spit in the hole, man, and tune again.
BIANCA   Now let me see if I can conster it. *Hic ibat*   40
   Simois, I know you not; *hic est Sigeia tellus*, I trust you
   not; *hic steterat Priami*, take heed he hear us not; *regia*,
   presume not; *celsa senis*, despair not.
HORTENSIO   Madam, 'tis now in tune.
LUCENTIO   All but the bass.
HORTENSIO
   The bass is right; 'tis the base knave that jars.   45
   How fiery and forward our pedant is!
   [*aside*] Now, for my life, the knave doth court my love.
   Pedascule, I'll watch you better yet.
BIANCA   In time I may believe, yet I mistrust.
LUCENTIO   Mistrust it not, for sure Aeacides   50
   Was Ajax, called so from his grandfather.
BIANCA   I must believe my master; else, I promise you,
   I should be arguing still upon that doubt.
   But let it rest. – Now, Licio, to you:
   Good master, take it not unkindly, pray,   55

That I have been thus pleasant with you both.

HORTENSIO
You may go walk, and give me leave awhile;
My lessons make no music in three parts.

LUCENTIO   Are you so formal, sir? Well, I must wait –
60   And watch withal, for, but I be deceived,
Our fine musician groweth amorous.

HORTENSIO   Madam, before you touch the instrument,
To learn the order of my fingering,
I must begin with rudiments of art,
65   To teach you gamut in a briefer sort,
More pleasant, pithy and effectual
Than hath been taught by any of my trade;
And there it is in writing fairly drawn.

BIANCA   Why, I am past my gamut long ago.

70 HORTENSIO   Yet read the gamut of Hortensio.

BIANCA [*Reads.*]   *Gamut* I am, the ground of all accord:
    A re, to plead Hortensio's passion;
    B mi, Bianca, take him for thy lord;
    C fa, ut, that loves with all affection;
75   *D sol, re*, one clef, two notes have I;
    E la, mi, show pity, or I die.
Call you this gamut? Tut, I like it not.
Old fashions please me best; I am not so nice
To change true rules for odd inventions.

Enter a Servant.

SERVANT
80   Mistress, your father prays you leave your books
And help to dress your sister's chamber up;
You know tomorrow is the wedding day.

BIANCA   Farewell, sweet masters both, I must be gone.

Exeunt Bianca and Servant.

LUCENTIO
Faith, mistress, then I have no cause to stay.   *Exit.*
85 HORTENSIO   But I have cause to pry into this pedant:
Methinks he looks as though he were in love.
Yet if thy thoughts, Bianca, be so humble
To cast thy wandering eyes on every stale,
Seize thee that list; if once I find thee ranging,
90   Hortensio will be quit with thee by changing.   *Exit.*

3.2   *Enter* BAPTISTA, GREMIO, TRANIO
as Lucentio, KATHERINA, BIANCA, LUCENTIO
as Cambio and others, Attendants.

BAPTISTA   Signor Lucentio, this is the 'pointed day
That Katherine and Petruccio should be married,
And yet we hear not of our son-in-law.
What will be said? What mockery will it be
5   To want the bridegroom when the priest attends
To speak the ceremonial rites of marriage?
What says Lucentio to this shame of ours?

KATHERINA
No shame but mine. I must forsooth be forced
To give my hand opposed against my heart
10   Unto a mad-brain rudesby full of spleen

Who wooed in haste and means to wed at leisure.
I told you, I, he was a frantic fool,
Hiding his bitter jests in blunt behaviour,
And to be noted for a merry man,
He'll woo a thousand, 'point the day of marriage,   15
Make feast, invite friends, and proclaim the banns,
Yet never means to wed where he hath wooed.
Now must the world point at poor Katherine
And say, 'Lo, there is mad Petruccio's wife,
If it would please him come and marry her.'   20

TRANIO   Patience, good Katherine, and Baptista too.
Upon my life, Petruccio means but well;
Whatever fortune stays him from his word,
Though he be blunt, I know him passing wise;
Though he be merry, yet withal he's honest.   25

KATHERINA
Would Katherine had never seen him though.

Exit weeping, Bianca following.

BAPTISTA
Go, girl, I cannot blame thee now to weep,
For such an injury would vex a very saint,
Much more a shrew of impatient humour.

Enter BIONDELLO.

BIONDELLO   Master, master, news – old news, and such   30
news as you never heard of!

BAPTISTA   Is it new and old too? How may that be?

BIONDELLO   Why, is it not news to hear of Petruccio's
coming?

BAPTISTA   Is he come?   35

BIONDELLO   Why no, sir.

BAPTISTA   What then?

BIONDELLO   He is coming.

BAPTISTA   When will he be here?

BIONDELLO   When he stands where I am and sees you   40
there.

TRANIO   But say, what to thine old news?

BIONDELLO   Why, Petruccio is coming in a new hat and
an old jerkin, a pair of old breeches thrice-turned; a
pair of boots that have been candle-cases, one buckled,   45
another laced with two broken points; an old rusty
sword ta'en out of the town armoury with a broken hilt
and chapeless; his horse hipped – with an old mothy
saddle and stirrups of no kindred – besides, possessed
with the glanders and like to mose in the chine;   50
troubled with the lampass, infected with the fashions,
full of windgalls, sped with spavins, rayed with the
yellows, past cure of the fives, stark spoiled with the
staggers, begnawn with the bots, weighed in the back
and shoulder-shotten, near-legged before and with a   55
half-cheeked bit and a headstall of sheep's leather
which, being restrained to keep him from stumbling,
hath been often burst and now repaired with knots;
one girth six times pieced, and a woman's crupper of
velour which hath two letters for her name fairly set   60
down in studs, and here and there pieced with
packthread.

BAPTISTA   Who comes with him?

BIONDELLO   O sir, his lackey, for all the world
caparisoned like the horse: with a linen stock on one
leg and a kersey boot-hose on the other, gartered with
a red and blue list; an old hat, and the humour of forty
fancies pricked in't for a feather – a monster, a very
monster in apparel, and not like a Christian footboy or
a gentleman's lackey.

TRANIO
'Tis some odd humour pricks him to this fashion,
Yet oftentimes he goes but mean-apparelled.

BAPTISTA   I am glad he's come, howsoe'er he comes.

BIONDELLO   Why sir, he comes not.

BAPTISTA   Didst thou not say he comes?

BIONDELLO   Who? That Petruccio came?

BAPTISTA   Ay, that Petruccio came.

BIONDELLO   No sir, I say his horse comes with him on
his back.

BAPTISTA   Why, that's all one.

BIONDELLO   Nay, by Saint Jamy,
I hold you a penny,
A horse and a man
Is more than one,
And yet not many.

Enter PETRUCCIO *and* GRUMIO.

PETRUCCIO   Come, where be these gallants? Who's at
home?

BAPTISTA   You are welcome, sir.

PETRUCCIO   And yet I come not well.

BAPTISTA   And yet you halt not.

TRANIO   Not so well apparelled as I wish you were.

PETRUCCIO   Were it better I should rush in thus?
But where is Kate? Where is my lovely bride?
How does my father? Gentles, methinks you frown,
And wherefore gaze this goodly company
As if they saw some wondrous monument,
Some comet or unusual prodigy?

BAPTISTA   Why sir, you know this is your wedding day.
First were we sad, fearing you would not come,
Now sadder that you come so unprovided.
Fie, doff this habit, shame to your estate,
An eyesore to our solemn festival.

TRANIO   And tell us what occasion of import
Hath all so long detained you from your wife
And sent you hither so unlike yourself?

PETRUCCIO   Tedious it were to tell, and harsh to hear.
Sufficeth I am come to keep my word,
Though in some part enforced to digress,
Which at more leisure I will so excuse
As you shall well be satisfied with all.
But where is Kate? I stay too long from her,
The morning wears, 'tis time we were at church.

TRANIO   See not your bride in these unreverent robes;
Go to my chamber; put on clothes of mine.

PETRUCCIO   Not I, believe me; thus I'll visit her.

BAPTISTA   But thus, I trust, you will not marry her.

PETRUCCIO
Good sooth, even thus. Therefore ha' done with words:
To me she's married, not unto my clothes.
Could I repair what she will wear in me
As I can change these poor accoutrements,
'Twere well for Kate and better for myself.
But what a fool am I to chat with you
When I should bid good morrow to my bride
And seal the title with a lovely kiss.
                                 Exit with Grumio.

TRANIO   He hath some meaning in his mad attire;
We will persuade him, be it possible,
To put on better ere he go to church.

BAPTISTA   I'll after him, and see th'event of this.
             Exit with Gremio, Biondello and Attendants.

TRANIO   But sir, to love concerneth us to add
Her father's liking, which to bring to pass,
As I before imparted to your worship,
I am to get a man, whate'er he be –
It skills not much, we'll fit him to our turn –
And he shall be 'Vincentio of Pisa',
And make assurance here in Padua
Of greater sums than I have promised.
So shall you quietly enjoy your hope
And marry sweet Bianca with consent.

LUCENTIO   Were it not that my fellow schoolmaster
Doth watch Bianca's steps so narrowly,
'Twere good, methinks, to steal our marriage,
Which once performed, let all the world say no,
I'll keep mine own, despite of all the world.

TRANIO   That by degrees we mean to look into
And watch our vantage in this business:
We'll overreach the greybeard Gremio,
The narrow-prying father Minola,
The quaint musician, amorous Licio,
All for my master's sake, Lucentio.

Enter GREMIO.

Signor Gremio, came you from the church?

GREMIO   As willingly as e'er I came from school.

TRANIO
And is the bride and bridegroom coming home?

GREMIO   A bridegroom, say you? 'Tis a groom indeed –
A grumbling groom, and that the girl shall find.

TRANIO   Curster than she? Why, 'tis impossible.

GREMIO   Why, he's a devil, a devil, a very fiend.

TRANIO   Why, she's a devil, a devil, the devil's dam.

GREMIO   Tut, she's a lamb, a dove, a fool, to him.
I'll tell you, Sir Lucentio: when the priest
Should ask if Katherine should be his wife,
'Ay, by gog's wounds,' quoth he, and swore so loud
That, all amazed, the priest let fall the book,
And as he stooped again to take it up,
This mad-brained bridegroom took him such a cuff
That down fell priest and book, and book and priest.
'Now take them up,' quoth he, 'if any list.'

TRANIO   What said the wench when he rose up again?

GREMIO
    Trembled and shook; for why he stamped and swore
    As if the vicar meant to cozen him.
170   But after many ceremonies done
    He calls for wine: 'A health,' quoth he, as if
    He had been aboard, carousing to his mates
    After a storm; quaffed off the muscadel
    And threw the sops all in the sexton's face,
175   Having no other reason
    But that his beard grew thin and hungerly
    And seemed to ask him sops as he was drinking.
    This done, he took the bride about the neck
    And kissed her lips with such a clamorous smack
180   That at the parting all the church did echo.
    And I seeing this came thence for very shame,
    And after me, I know, the rout is coming.
    Such a mad marriage never was before. *[Music plays.]*
    Hark, hark, I hear the minstrels play.

Enter PETRUCCIO, KATHERINA, BIANCA, HORTENSIO
    as Licio, BAPTISTA, GRUMIO *and others.*

PETRUCCIO
185   Gentlemen and friends, I thank you for your pains.
    I know you think to dine with me today
    And have prepared great store of wedding cheer,
    But so it is my haste doth call me hence
    And therefore here I mean to take my leave.
190 BAPTISTA   Is't possible you will away tonight?
PETRUCCIO   I must away today before night come.
    Make it no wonder: if you knew my business
    You would entreat me rather go than stay.
    And, honest company, I thank you all
195   That have beheld me give away myself
    To this most patient, sweet and virtuous wife.
    Dine with my father, drink a health to me,
    For I must hence, and farewell to you all.
TRANIO   Let us entreat you stay till after dinner.
200 PETRUCCIO   It may not be.
GREMIO   Let me entreat you.
PETRUCCIO   It cannot be.
KATHERINA   Let me entreat you.
PETRUCCIO   I am content.
KATHERINA   Are you content to stay?
205 PETRUCCIO   I am content you shall entreat me stay –
    But yet not stay, entreat me how you can.
KATHERINA   Now, if you love me, stay.
PETRUCCIO   Grumio, my horse.
GRUMIO   Ay, sir, they be ready: the oats have eaten the
    horses.
210 KATHERINA   Nay then –
    Do what thou canst, I will not go today,
    No, nor tomorrow – not till I please myself.
    The door is open, sir, there lies your way;
    You may be jogging whiles your boots are green:
215   For me, I'll not be gone till I please myself.
    'Tis like you'll prove a jolly surly groom
    That take it on you at the first so roundly.

PETRUCCIO
    O Kate, content thee; prithee be not angry.
KATHERINA   I will be angry; what hast thou to do?
220   – Father, be quiet; he shall stay my leisure.
GREMIO   Ay, marry, sir, now it begins to work.
KATHERINA   Gentlemen, forward to the bridal dinner.
    I see a woman may be made a fool
    If she had not a spirit to resist.
PETRUCCIO
225   They shall go forward, Kate, at thy command.
    – Obey the bride, you that attend on her.
    Go to the feast, revel and domineer,
    Carouse full measure to her maidenhead,
    Be mad and merry, or go hang yourselves;
230   But for my bonny Kate, she must with me.
    – Nay, look not big, nor stamp, nor stare, nor fret,
    I will be master of what is mine own.
    She is my goods, my chattels; she is my house,
    My household-stuff, my field, my barn,
235   My horse, my ox, my ass, my anything,
    And here she stands. Touch her whoever dare,
    I'll bring mine action on the proudest he
    That stops my way in Padua. – Grumio,
    Draw forth thy weapon, we are beset with thieves;
240   Rescue thy mistress, if thou be a man.
    – Fear not, sweet wench, they shall not touch thee, Kate;
    I'll buckler thee against a million.
            Exeunt Petruccio, Katherina and Grumio.
BAPTISTA   Nay, let them go – a couple of quiet ones.
GREMIO
    Went they not quickly, I should die with laughing.
TRANIO   Of all mad matches never was the like.   245
LUCENTIO
    Mistress, what's your opinion of your sister?
BIANCA   That being mad herself, she's madly mated.
GREMIO   I warrant him, Petruccio is Kated.
BAPTISTA
    Neighbours and friends, though bride and bridegroom
      wants
    For to supply the places at the table,   250
    You know there wants no junkets at the feast.
    Lucentio, you shall supply the bridegroom's place,
    And let Bianca take her sister's room.
TRANIO   Shall sweet Bianca practise how to bride it?
BAPTISTA
    She shall, Lucentio. Come gentlemen, let's go. *Exeunt.*   255

4.1   *Enter* GRUMIO.

GRUMIO   Fie, fie on all tired jades, on all mad masters,
    and all foul ways! Was ever man so beaten? Was ever
    man so rayed? Was ever man so weary? I am sent before
    to make a fire, and they are coming after to warm them.
    Now were not I a little pot and soon hot, my very lips   5
    might freeze to my teeth, my tongue to the roof of my
    mouth, my heart in my belly, ere I should come by a
    fire to thaw me; but I with blowing the fire shall warm

myself, for considering the weather, a taller man than I
will take cold. Holla, ho, Curtis!

Enter CURTIS.

CURTIS   Who is that calls so coldly?

GRUMIO   A piece of ice. If thou doubt it, thou mayst
slide from my shoulder to my heel with no greater a
run but my head and my neck. A fire, good Curtis.

CURTIS   Is my master and his wife coming, Grumio?

GRUMIO   O ay, Curtis, ay – and therefore fire, fire, cast
on no water.

CURTIS   Is she so hot a shrew as she's reported?

GRUMIO   She was, good Curtis, before this frost; but
thou knowst winter tames man, woman and beast, for
it hath tamed my old master, and my new mistress, and
myself, fellow Curtis.

CURTIS   Away, you three-inch fool, I am no beast.

GRUMIO   Am I but three inches? Why, thy horn is a foot,
and so long am I at the least. But wilt thou make a fire,
or shall I complain on thee to our mistress, whose hand
– she being now at hand – thou shalt soon feel, to thy
cold comfort, for being slow in thy hot office?

CURTIS   I prithee, good Grumio, tell me, how goes the
world?

GRUMIO   A cold world, Curtis, in every office but thine
– and therefore fire. Do thy duty, and have thy duty, for
my master and mistress are almost frozen to death.

CURTIS   There's fire ready, and therefore, good Grumio,
the news.

GRUMIO   Why, 'Jack boy, ho boy!' and as much news as
wilt thou.

CURTIS   Come, you are so full of cony-catching.

GRUMIO   Why, therefore, fire, for I have caught extreme
cold. Where's the cook, is supper ready, the house
trimmed, rushes strewed, cobwebs swept, the
servingmen in their new fustian, their white stockings,
and every officer his wedding garment on? Be the Jacks
fair within, the Jills fair without, the carpets laid, and
everything in order?

CURTIS   All ready, and therefore, I pray thee, news.

GRUMIO   First, know my horse is tired, my master and
mistress fallen out.

CURTIS   How?

GRUMIO   Out of their saddles into the dirt, and thereby
hangs a tale.

CURTIS   Let's ha't, good Grumio.

GRUMIO   Lend thine ear.

CURTIS   Here.

GRUMIO   [*Cuffs him.*] There.

CURTIS   This 'tis to feel a tale, not to hear a tale.

GRUMIO   And therefore 'tis called a sensible tale; and
this cuff was but to knock at your ear and beseech
listening. Now I begin: *Inprimis*, we came down a foul
hill, my master riding behind my mistress –

CURTIS   Both of one horse?

GRUMIO   What's that to thee?

CURTIS   Why, a horse.

GRUMIO   Tell thou the tale. But hadst thou not crossed
me, thou shouldst have heard how her horse fell, and
she under her horse; thou shouldst have heard in how
miry a place, how she was bemoiled, how he left her
with the horse upon her, how he beat me because her
horse stumbled, how she waded through the dirt to
pluck him off me, how he swore, how she prayed that
never prayed before, how I cried, how the horses ran
away, how her bridle was burst, how I lost my crupper
– with many things of worthy memory which now shall
die in oblivion, and thou return unexperienced to thy
grave.

CURTIS   By this reckoning he is more shrew than she.

GRUMIO   Ay, and that thou and the proudest of you all
shall find when he comes home. But what talk I of this?
Call forth Nathaniel, Joseph, Nicholas, Philip, Walter,
Sugarsop and the rest. Let their heads be sleekly
combed, their blue coats brushed, and their garters of
an indifferent knit; let them curtsy with their left legs,
and not presume to touch a hair of my master's horse-
tail till they kiss their hands. Are they all ready?

CURTIS   They are.

GRUMIO   Call them forth.

CURTIS   Do you hear, ho? You must meet my master to
countenance my mistress.

GRUMIO   Why, she hath a face of her own.

CURTIS   Who knows not that?

GRUMIO   Thou, it seems, that calls for company to
countenance her.

CURTIS   I call them forth to credit her.

Enter four or five Servants.

GRUMIO   Why, she comes to borrow nothing of them.

NATHANIEL   Welcome home, Grumio.

PHILIP   How now, Grumio.

JOSEPH   What, Grumio.

NICHOLAS   Fellow Grumio.

NATHANIEL   How now, old lad.

GRUMIO   Welcome you; how now you; what you; fellow
you; and thus much for greeting. Now, my spruce
companions, is all ready, and all things neat?

NATHANIEL   All things is ready. How near is our
master?

GRUMIO   E'en at hand, alighted by this; and therefore
be not – Cock's passion, silence, I hear my master.

Enter PETRUCCIO *and* KATHERINA.

PETRUCCIO
Where be these knaves? What, no man at door
To hold my stirrup nor to take my horse?
Where is Nathaniel, Gregory, Philip?

ALL SERVANTS   Here, here sir, here sir.

PETRUCCIO   'Here sir, here sir, here sir, here sir'!
You logger-headed and unpolished grooms.
What, no attendance? No regard? No duty?
Where is the foolish knave I sent before?

GRUMIO   Here sir, as foolish as I was before.

PETRUCCIO
You peasant swain, you whoreson malthorse drudge,
Did I not bid thee meet me in the park
And bring along these rascal knaves with thee?

GRUMIO Nathaniel's coat, sir, was not fully made,
120 And Gabriel's pumps were all unpinked i'th' heel;
There was no link to colour Peter's hat,
And Walter's dagger was not come from sheathing;
There were none fine but Adam, Rafe and Gregory,
The rest were ragged, old and beggarly.
125 Yet, as they are, here are they come to meet you.

PETRUCCIO Go, rascals, go, and fetch my supper in.
Exeunt Servants.
[*Sings.*] Where is the life that late I led?
Where are those –?
Sit down, Kate, and welcome. Soud, soud, soud, soud.

Enter Servants with supper.

130 Why, when, I say? – Nay, good sweet Kate, be merry.
– Off with my boots, you rogues, you villains: when?
[*Sings.*] It was the friar of orders grey,
As he forth walked on his way –
Out, you rogue, you pluck my foot awry.
135 Take that, and mend the plucking off the other.
– Be merry, Kate. – Some water here. What ho!

Enter one with water.

Where's my spaniel Troilus? Sirrah, get you hence
And bid my cousin Ferdinand come hither –
One, Kate, that you must kiss and be acquainted with.
140 – Where are my slippers? Shall I have some water?
Come, Kate, and wash, and welcome heartily.
– You whoreson villain, will you let it fall?

KATHERINA
Patience, I pray you, 'twas a fault unwilling.

PETRUCCIO
A whoreson beetle-headed, flap-eared knave.
145 Come, Kate, sit down, I know you have a stomach.
Will you give thanks, sweet Kate, or else shall I?
– What's this – mutton?

1 SERVANT Ay.

PETRUCCIO Who brought it?

150 PETER I.

PETRUCCIO 'Tis burnt, and so is all the meat.
What dogs are these? Where is the rascal cook?
How durst you villains bring it from the dresser
And serve it thus to me that love it not?
155 There, take it to you, trenchers, cups and all;
You heedless jolt-heads and unmannered slaves.
What, do you grumble? I'll be with you straight.
Exeunt Grumio and Servants.

KATHERINA I pray you, husband, be not so disquiet.
The meat was well, if you were so contented.

PETRUCCIO
160 I tell thee, Kate, 'twas burnt and dried away,
And I expressly am forbid to touch it;
For it engenders choler, planteth anger,

And better 'twere that both of us did fast,
Since, of ourselves, ourselves are choleric,
Than feed it with such over-roasted flesh. 165
Be patient, tomorrow't shall be mended,
And for this night we'll fast for company.
Come, I will bring thee to thy bridal chamber. *Exeunt.*

Enter GRUMIO *and* Servants *severally.*

NATHANIEL Peter, didst ever see the like?
PETER He kills her in her own humour. 170

Enter CURTIS, *a Servant.*

GRUMIO Where is he?
CURTIS In her chamber,
Making a sermon of continency to her;
And rails, and swears, and rates, that she, poor soul,
Knows not which way to stand, to look, to speak, 175
And sits as one new risen from a dream.
Away, away, for he is coming hither.
Exeunt Grumio and Servants.

Enter PETRUCCIO.

PETRUCCIO Thus have I politicly begun my reign,
And 'tis my hope to end successfully.
My falcon now is sharp and passing empty, 180
And till she stoop she must not be full-gorged,
For then she never looks upon her lure.
Another way I have to man my haggard,
To make her come and know her keeper's call:
That is, to watch her, as we watch these kites 185
That bate, and beat, and will not be obedient.
She ate no meat today, nor none shall eat;
Last night she slept not, nor tonight she shall not.
As with the meat, some undeserved fault
I'll find about the making of the bed, 190
And here I'll fling the pillow, there the bolster,
This way the coverlet, another way the sheets.
Ay, and amid this hurly I intend
That all is done in reverend care of her;
And in conclusion she shall watch all night, 195
And if she chance to nod I'll rail and brawl
And with the clamour keep her still awake.
This is a way to kill a wife with kindness,
And thus I'll curb her mad and headstrong humour.
He that knows better how to tame a shrew, 200
Now let him speak; 'tis charity to show. *Exit.*

4.2   *Enter* TRANIO *as Lucentio and*
HORTENSIO *as Licio.*

TRANIO
Is't possible, friend Licio, that mistress Bianca
Doth fancy any other but Lucentio?
I tell you, sir, she bears me fair in hand.
HORTENSIO Sir, to satisfy you in what I have said,
Stand by, and mark the manner of his teaching. 5

Enter BIANCA *and* LUCENTIO *as Cambio.*

LUCENTIO Now, mistress, profit you in what you read?
BIANCA What master read you? First resolve me that.
LUCENTIO I read that I profess, *The Art to Love.*
BIANCA And may you prove, sir, master of your art.
LUCENTIO
10 While you, sweet dear, prove mistress of my heart.
HORTENSIO
Quick proceeders, marry! Now tell me, I pray,
You that durst swear that your mistress Bianca
Loved none in the world so well as Lucentio –
TRANIO O despiteful love, unconstant womankind!
15 I tell thee, Licio, this is wonderful.
HORTENSIO Mistake no more, I am not Licio,
Nor a musician, as I seem to be,
But one that scorn to live in this disguise
For such a one as leaves a gentleman
20 And makes a god of such a cullion.
Know, sir, that I am called Hortensio.
TRANIO Signor Hortensio, I have often heard
Of your entire affection to Bianca;
And since mine eyes are witness of her lightness
25 I will with you, if you be so contented,
Forswear Bianca and her love forever.
HORTENSIO
See how they kiss and court. Signor Lucentio,
Here is my hand, and here I firmly vow
Never to woo her more, but do forswear her
30 As one unworthy all the former favours
That I have fondly flattered her withal.
TRANIO And here I take the like unfeigned oath
Never to marry with her though she would entreat.
Fie on her! See how beastly she doth court him.
HORTENSIO
35 Would all the world but he had quite forsworn.
For me, that I may surely keep mine oath,
I will be married to a wealthy widow
Ere three days pass, which hath as long loved me
As I have loved this proud disdainful haggard.
40 And so farewell, Signor Lucentio.
Kindness in women, not their beauteous looks,
Shall win my love; and so I take my leave,
In resolution as I swore before.   *Exit.*
TRANIO Mistress Bianca, bless you with such grace
45 As 'longeth to a lover's blessed case.
Nay, I have ta'en you napping, gentle love,
And have forsworn you with Hortensio.
BIANCA
Tranio, you jest – but have you both forsworn me?
TRANIO Mistress, we have.
LUCENTIO   Then we are rid of Licio.
50 TRANIO I'faith, he'll have a lusty widow now
That shall be wooed and wedded in a day.
BIANCA God give him joy.
TRANIO Ay, and he'll tame her.
BIANCA He says so, Tranio?

TRANIO Faith, he is gone unto the taming school.   55
BIANCA
The taming school? What, is there such a place?
TRANIO Ay, mistress, and Petruccio is the master
That teacheth tricks eleven-and-twenty long
To tame a shrew and charm her chattering tongue.

Enter BIONDELLO.

BIONDELLO O, master, master, I have watched so long   60
That I am dog-weary, but at last I spied
An ancient angel coming down the hill
Will serve the turn.
TRANIO   What is he, Biondello?
BIONDELLO Master, a marcantant or a pedant,
I know not what, but formal in apparel,   65
In gait and countenance surely like a father.
LUCENTIO And what of him, Tranio?
TRANIO If he be credulous and trust my tale,
I'll make him glad to seem Vincentio
And give assurance to Baptista Minola   70
As if he were the right Vincentio.
Take in your love, and then let me alone.
Exeunt Lucentio and Bianca.

Enter a Merchant.

MERCHANT God save you, sir.
TRANIO   And you, sir. You are welcome.
Travel you far on, or are you at the farthest?
MERCHANT Sir, at the farthest for a week or two,   75
But then up farther, and as far as Rome,
And so to Tripoli, if God lend me life.
TRANIO What countryman, I pray?
MERCHANT   Of Mantua.
TRANIO Of Mantua, sir? Marry, God forbid!
And come to Padua, careless of your life?   80
MERCHANT
My life, sir? How, I pray? For that goes hard.
TRANIO 'Tis death for anyone in Mantua
To come to Padua. Know you not the cause?
Your ships are stayed at Venice, and the Duke,
For private quarrel 'twixt your Duke and him,   85
Hath published and proclaimed it openly.
'Tis marvel, but that you are but newly come,
You might have heard it else proclaimed about.
MERCHANT Alas, sir, it is worse for me than so,
For I have bills for money by exchange   90
From Florence, and must here deliver them.
TRANIO Well, sir, to do you courtesy,
This will I do, and this I will advise you –
First tell me, have you ever been at Pisa?
MERCHANT Ay, sir, in Pisa have I often been,   95
Pisa renowned for grave citizens.
TRANIO Among them know you one Vincentio?
MERCHANT I know him not, but I have heard of him,
A merchant of incomparable wealth.
TRANIO He is my father, sir, and sooth to say,   100
In countenance somewhat doth resemble you.

BIONDELLO   As much as an apple doth an oyster, and
   all one.

TRANIO   To save your life in this extremity,
105   This favour will I do you for his sake –
   And think it not the worst of all your fortunes
   That you are like to Sir Vincentio.
   His name and credit shall you undertake,
   And in my house you shall be friendly lodged.
110   Look that you take upon you as you should –
   You understand me, sir? So shall you stay
   Till you have done your business in the city.
   If this be courtesy, sir, accept of it.

MERCHANT   O sir, I do, and will repute you ever
115   The patron of my life and liberty.

TRANIO   Then go with me to make the matter good.
   This, by the way, I let you understand:
   My father is here looked for every day
   To pass assurance of a dower in marriage
120   'Twixt me and one Baptista's daughter here.
   In all these circumstances I'll instruct you.
   Go with me to clothe you as becomes you.   *Exeunt.*

4.3   *Enter* KATHERINA *and* GRUMIO.

GRUMIO   No, no, forsooth, I dare not for my life.

KATHERINA
   The more my wrong, the more his spite appears.
   What, did he marry me to famish me?
   Beggars that come unto my father's door
5   Upon entreaty have a present alms;
   If not, elsewhere they meet with charity.
   But I, who never knew how to entreat,
   Nor never needed that I should entreat,
   Am starved for meat, giddy for lack of sleep,
10   With oaths kept waking and with brawling fed;
   And that which spites me more than all these wants,
   He does it under name of perfect love,
   As who should say, if I should sleep or eat
   'Twere deadly sickness or else present death.
15   I prithee, go and get me some repast –
   I care not what, so it be wholesome food.

GRUMIO   What say you to a neat's foot?

KATHERINA
   'Tis passing good; I prithee, let me have it.

GRUMIO   I fear it is too choleric a meat.
20   How say you to a fat tripe finely broiled?

KATHERINA   I like it well; good Grumio, fetch it me.

GRUMIO   I cannot tell, I fear 'tis choleric.
   What say you to a piece of beef and mustard?

KATHERINA   A dish that I do love to feed upon.
25   GRUMIO   Ay, but the mustard is too hot a little.

KATHERINA
   Why then, the beef, and let the mustard rest.

GRUMIO
   Nay then, I will not: you shall have the mustard
   Or else you get no beef of Grumio.

KATHERINA   Then both, or one, or anything thou wilt.

GRUMIO   Why then, the mustard without the beef.   30

KATHERINA
   Go, get thee gone, thou false deluding slave
    [*Beats him.*]
   That feed'st me with the very name of meat.
   Sorrow on thee and all the pack of you
   That triumph thus upon my misery.
   Go, get thee gone, I say.   35

Enter PETRUCCIO *and* HORTENSIO *with meat.*

PETRUCCIO
   How fares my Kate? What, sweeting, all amort?

HORTENSIO   Mistress, what cheer?

KATHERINA   Faith, as cold as can be.

PETRUCCIO
   Pluck up thy spirits, look cheerfully upon me.
   Here, love, thou seest how diligent I am   40
   To dress thy meat myself and bring it thee.
   I am sure, sweet Kate, this kindness merits thanks.
   What, not a word? Nay then, thou lov'st it not,
   And all my pains is sorted to no proof.
   Here, take away this dish.   45

KATHERINA   I pray you, let it stand.

PETRUCCIO   The poorest service is repaid with thanks,
   And so shall mine before you touch the meat.

KATHERINA   I thank you, sir.

HORTENSIO   Signor Petruccio, fie, you are to blame.   50
   Come, Mistress Kate, I'll bear you company.

PETRUCCIO [*to Hortensio*]
   Eat it up all, Hortensio, if thou lovest me.
   – Much good do it unto thy gentle heart.
   Kate, eat apace; and now, my honey love,
   Will we return unto thy father's house   55
   And revel it as bravely as the best,
   With silken coats and caps, and golden rings,
   With ruffs and cuffs, and farthingales and things,
   With scarves and fans, and double change of bravery,
   With amber bracelets, beads and all this knavery.   60
   What, hast thou dined? The tailor stays thy leisure,
   To deck thy body with his ruffling treasure.

Enter Tailor.

   Come, tailor, let us see these ornaments.
   Lay forth the gown.

Enter Haberdasher.

            What news with you, sir?

HABERDASHER
   Here is the cap your worship did bespeak.   65

PETRUCCIO   Why, this was moulded on a porringer –
   A velvet dish. Fie, fie, 'tis lewd and filthy.
   Why, 'tis a cockle, or a walnut-shell,
   A knack, a toy, a trick, a baby's cap.
   Away with it; come, let me have a bigger.   70

KATHERINA   I'll have no bigger: this doth fit the time,
   And gentlewomen wear such caps as these.

PETRUCCIO
    When you are gentle you shall have one too,
    And not till then.
HORTENSIO   That will not be in haste.
75 KATHERINA   Why, sir, I trust I may have leave to speak,
    And speak I will. I am no child, no babe;
    Your betters have endured me say my mind,
    And if you cannot, best you stop your ears.
    My tongue will tell the anger of my heart,
80   Or else my heart concealing it will break,
    And, rather than it shall, I will be free
    Even to the uttermost, as I please, in words.
PETRUCCIO   Why, thou sayst true – it is a paltry cap,
    A custard-coffin, a bauble, a silken pie;
85   I love thee well in that thou lik'st it not.
KATHERINA   Love me or love me not, I like the cap,
    And it I will have, or I will have none.
PETRUCCIO
    Thy gown? Why, ay: come, tailor, let us see't.
                    Exit Haberdasher.
    O mercy, God, what masking stuff is here?
90   What's this? A sleeve? 'Tis like a demi-cannon.
    What, up and down carved like an apple tart?
    Here's snip, and nip, and cut, and slish and slash,
    Like to a cithern in a barber's shop.
    Why, what i'devil's name, tailor, call'st thou this?
HORTENSIO
95   I see she's like to have neither cap nor gown.
TAILOR   You bid me make it orderly and well,
    According to the fashion and the time.
PETRUCCIO
    Marry, and did; but if you be remembered,
    I did not bid you mar it to the time.
100   Go, hop me over every kennel home,
    For you shall hop without my custom, sir:
    I'll none of it. Hence, make your best of it.
KATHERINA   I never saw a better-fashioned gown,
    More quaint, more pleasing, nor more commendable.
105   Belike you mean to make a puppet of me.
PETRUCCIO
    Why true, he means to make a puppet of thee.
TAILOR   She says your worship means to make a puppet
    of her.
PETRUCCIO
    O monstrous arrogance. Thou liest, thou thread, thou
      thimble,
110   Thou yard, three-quarters, half-yard, quarter, nail,
    Thou flea, thou nit, thou winter-cricket, thou!
    Braved in mine own house with a skein of thread?
    Away, thou rag, thou quantity, thou remnant,
    Or I shall so bemete thee with thy yard
115   As thou shalt think on prating whilst thou liv'st.
    I tell thee, I, that thou hast marred her gown.
TAILOR   Your worship is deceived; the gown is made
    Just as my master had direction.
    Grumio gave order how it should be done.
120 GRUMIO   I gave him no order; I gave him the stuff.

TAILOR   But how did you desire it should be made?
GRUMIO   Marry, sir, with needle and thread.
TAILOR   But did you not request to have it cut?
GRUMIO   Thou hast faced many things.
125 TAILOR   I have.
GRUMIO   Face not me. Thou has braved many men;
    brave not me. I will neither be faced nor braved. I say
    unto thee, I bid thy master cut out the gown, but I did
    not bid him cut it to pieces. *Ergo*, thou liest.
130 TAILOR   Why, here is the note of the fashion to testify.
PETRUCCIO   Read it.
GRUMIO   The note lies in's throat if he say I said so.
TAILOR   'Inprimis, a loose-bodied gown.'
GRUMIO   Master, if ever I said 'loose-bodied gown', sew
135   me in the skirts of it and beat me to death with a
    bottom of brown thread. I said 'a gown'.
PETRUCCIO   Proceed.
TAILOR   'With a small-compassed cape.'
GRUMIO   I confess the cape.
140 TAILOR   'With a trunk sleeve.'
GRUMIO   I confess two sleeves.
TAILOR   'The sleeves curiously cut.'
PETRUCCIO   Ay, there's the villainy.
GRUMIO   Error i'th' bill, sir, error i'th' bill! I
145   commanded the sleeves should be cut out and sewed
    up again, and that I'll prove upon thee though thy little
    finger be armed in a thimble.
TAILOR   This is true that I say; an I had thee in place
    where, thou shouldst know it.
150 GRUMIO   I am for thee straight. Take thou the bill, give
    me thy mete-yard and spare not me.
HORTENSIO   God-a-mercy, Grumio, then he shall have
    no odds.
PETRUCCIO   Well sir, in brief, the gown is not for me.
155 GRUMIO   You are i'th' right, sir, 'tis for my mistress.
PETRUCCIO   Go, take it up unto thy master's use.
GRUMIO   Villain, not for thy life! Take up my mistress'
    gown for thy master's use?
PETRUCCIO   Why sir, what's your conceit in that?
160 GRUMIO   O sir, the conceit is deeper than you think for.
    'Take up my mistress' gown to his master's use'? O fie,
    fie, fie!
PETRUCCIO [*aside to Hortensio*]
    Hortensio, say thou wilt see the tailor paid.
    – Go, take it hence; be gone, and say no more.
HORTENSIO
165   Tailor, I'll pay thee for thy gown tomorrow –
    Take no unkindness of his hasty words.
    Away, I say, commend me to thy master.   *Exit Tailor.*
PETRUCCIO
    Well, come, my Kate, we will unto your father's,
    Even in these honest mean habiliments:
170   Our purses shall be proud, our garments poor,
    For 'tis the mind that makes the body rich,
    And as the sun breaks through the darkest clouds,
    So honour peereth in the meanest habit.
    What is the jay more precious than the lark

175 Because his feathers are more beautiful?
Or is the adder better than the eel
Because his painted skin contents the eye?
O no, good Kate; neither art thou the worse
For this poor furniture and mean array.
180 If thou account'st it shame, lay it on me,
And therefore frolic: we will hence forthwith
To feast and sport us at thy father's house.
– Go call my men, and let us straight to him,
And bring our horses unto Long-lane end.
185 There will we mount, and thither walk on foot.
Let's see, I think 'tis now some seven o'clock,
And well we may come there by dinner-time.
KATHERINA   I dare assure you, sir, 'tis almost two,
And 'twill be supper-time ere you come there.
190 PETRUCCIO   It shall be seven ere I go to horse.
Look what I speak, or do, or think to do,
You are still crossing it. Sirs, let 't alone.
I will not go today, and ere I do,
It shall be what o'clock I say it is.
HORTENSIO
195 Why so, this gallant will command the sun.   *Exeunt.*

4.4   *Enter* TRANIO *as Lucentio and the* Merchant,
booted and dressed like Vincentio.

TRANIO   Sir, this is the house; please it you that I call?
MERCHANT   Ay, what else? And but I be deceived,
Signor Baptista may remember me.
Near twenty years ago in Genoa –
5 TRANIO   Where we were lodgers at the Pegasus.
'Tis well, and hold your own, in any case,
With such austerity as 'longeth to a father.

Enter BIONDELLO.

MERCHANT
I warrant you. But, sir, here comes your boy;
'Twere good he were schooled.
10 TRANIO   Fear you not him. Sirrah Biondello,
Now do your duty throughly, I advise you.
Imagine 'twere the right Vincentio.
BIONDELLO   Tut, fear not me.
TRANIO   But hast thou done thy errand to Baptista?
15 BIONDELLO   I told him that your father was at Venice,
And that you looked for him this day in Padua.
TRANIO   Thou'rt a tall fellow; hold thee that to drink.
– Here comes Baptista. Set your countenance, sir.

Enter BAPTISTA *and* LUCENTIO *as Cambio.*
Merchant stands bare-headed.

TRANIO   Signor Baptista, you are happily met.
20 – Sir, this is the gentleman I told you of.
I pray you stand good father to me now:
Give me Bianca for my patrimony.
MERCHANT
Soft, son. – Sir, by your leave, having come to Padua
To gather in some debts, my son Lucentio

Made me acquainted with a weighty cause   25
Of love between your daughter and himself;
And for the good report I hear of you,
And for the love he beareth to your daughter –
And she to him – to stay him not too long,
I am content, in a good father's care,   30
To have him matched; and if you please to like
No worse than I, upon some agreement
Me shall you find ready and willing
With one consent to have her so bestowed;
For curious I cannot be with you,   35
Signor Baptista, of whom I hear so well.
BAPTISTA   Sir, pardon me in what I have to say;
Your plainness and your shortness please me well.
Right true it is your son Lucentio here
Doth love my daughter, and she loveth him –   40
Or both dissemble deeply their affections –
And therefore if you say no more than this,
That like a father you will deal with him
And pass my daughter a sufficient dower,
The match is made and all is done: 45
Your son shall have my daughter with consent.
TRANIO
I thank you, sir. Where, then, do you know best
We be affied and such assurance ta'en
As shall with either part's agreement stand?
BAPTISTA   Not in my house, Lucentio, for you know   50
Pitchers have ears, and I have many servants;
Besides, old Gremio is hearkening still,
And happily we might be interrupted.
TRANIO   Then at my lodging, an it like you;
There doth my father lie, and there this night   55
We'll pass the business privately and well.
Send for your daughter by your servant here;
My boy shall fetch the scrivener presently.
The worst is this, that at so slender warning
You are like to have a thin and slender pittance.   60
BAPTISTA   It likes me well. Cambio, hie you home,
And bid Bianca make her ready straight;
And if you will, tell what hath happened:
Lucentio's father is arrived in Padua,
And how she's like to be Lucentio's wife.   65
Exit Lucentio.
BIONDELLO
I pray the gods she may, with all my heart.
TRANIO   Dally not with the gods, but get thee gone.
Exit Biondello.
– Signor Baptista, shall I lead the way?
Welcome: one mess is like to be your cheer.
Come, sir, we will better it in Pisa.   70
BAPTISTA   I follow you.   *Exeunt.*

Enter LUCENTIO *as Cambio and* BIONDELLO.

BIONDELLO   Cambio.
LUCENTIO   What sayst thou, Biondello?
BIONDELLO   You saw my master wink and laugh upon
you?   75

LUCENTIO   Biondello, what of that?

BIONDELLO   Faith, nothing, but h'as left me here behind to expound the meaning or moral of his signs and tokens.

80 LUCENTIO   I pray thee moralize them.

BIONDELLO   Then thus: Baptista is safe, talking with the deceiving father of a deceitful son.

LUCENTIO   And what of him?

BIONDELLO   His daughter is to be brought by you to 85 the supper.

LUCENTIO   And then?

BIONDELLO   The old priest at Saint Luke's church is at your command at all hours.

LUCENTIO   And what of all this?

90 BIONDELLO   I cannot tell, except they are busied about a counterfeit assurance. Take you assurance of her, *cum privilegio ad imprimendum solum*: to th' church take the priest, clerk and some sufficient honest witnesses.

95   If this be not that you look for, I have no more to say, But bid Bianca farewell for ever and a day.

LUCENTIO   Hear'st thou, Biondello?

BIONDELLO   I cannot tarry. I knew a wench married in an afternoon as she went to the garden for parsley to 100 stuff a rabbit; and so may you, sir; and so adieu, sir. My master hath appointed me to go to Saint Luke's to bid the priest be ready to come against you come with your appendix.   *Exit.*

LUCENTIO

I may and will, if she be so contented.

105 She will be pleased, then wherefore should I doubt? Hap what hap may, I'll roundly go about her: It shall go hard if Cambio go without her.   *Exit.*

4.5   *Enter* PETRUCCIO, KATHERINA,
                HORTENSIO *and* GRUMIO.

PETRUCCIO

Come on, i'God's name, once more toward our father's.

Good Lord, how bright and goodly shines the moon!

KATHERINA

The moon? The sun; it is not moonlight now.

PETRUCCIO   I say it is the moon that shines so bright.

5 KATHERINA   I know it is the sun that shines so bright.

PETRUCCIO

Now by my mother's son – and that's myself –

It shall be moon or star or what I list

Or e'er I journey to your father's house.

[*to Grumio*] Go on and fetch our horses back again.

10 – Evermore crossed and crossed, nothing but crossed.

HORTENSIO [*to Katherina*]

Say as he says, or we shall never go.

KATHERINA

Forward, I pray, since we have come so far,

And be it moon or sun or what you please,

And if you please to call it a rush-candle,

Henceforth I vow it shall be so for me.   15

PETRUCCIO   I say it is the moon.

KATHERINA   I know it is the moon.

PETRUCCIO   Nay then, you lie; it is the blessed sun.

KATHERINA   Then God be blest, it is the blessed sun,

But sun it is not, when you say it is not,   20

And the moon changes even as your mind.

What you will have it named, even that it is,

And so it shall be so for Katherine.

HORTENSIO   Petruccio, go thy ways, the field is won.

PETRUCCIO

Well, forward, forward, thus the bowl should run,   25

And not unluckily against the bias.

Enter VINCENTIO.

But soft, what company is coming here?

Good morrow, gentle mistress, where away?

– Tell me, sweet Kate, and tell me truly too,

Hast thou beheld a fresher gentlewoman,   30

Such war of white and red within her cheeks?

What stars do spangle heaven with such beauty

As those two eyes become that heavenly face?

– Fair lovely maid, once more good day to thee.

– Sweet Kate, embrace her for her beauty's sake.   35

HORTENSIO   'A will make the man mad, to make the woman of him.

KATHERINA

Young budding virgin, fair, and fresh, and sweet,

Whither away, or where is thy abode?

Happy the parents of so fair a child;

Happier the man whom favourable stars   40

Allots thee for his lovely bedfellow.

PETRUCCIO

Why, how now, Kate, I hope thou art not mad.

This is a man – old, wrinkled, faded, withered –

And not a maiden, as thou sayst he is.   45

KATHERINA   Pardon, old father, my mistaking eyes

That have been so bedazzled with the sun

That everything I look on seemeth green.

Now I perceive thou art a reverend father.

Pardon, I pray thee, for my mad mistaking.   50

PETRUCCIO

Do, good old grandsire, and withal make known

Which way thou travell'st – if along with us,

We shall be joyful of thy company.

VINCENTIO   Fair sir, and you, my merry mistress,

That with your strange encounter much amazed me,   55

My name is called Vincentio, my dwelling Pisa,

And bound I am to Padua, there to visit

A son of mine which long I have not seen.

PETRUCCIO   What is his name?

VINCENTIO   Lucentio, gentle sir.

PETRUCCIO   Happily met – the happier for thy son.   60

And now by law, as well as reverend age,

I may entitle thee my loving father.

The sister to my wife, this gentlewoman,

Thy son by this hath married. Wonder not,

65   Nor be not grieved: she is of good esteem,
     Her dowry wealthy, and of worthy birth;
     Beside, so qualified as may beseem
     The spouse of any noble gentleman.
     Let me embrace with old Vincentio,
70   And wander we to see thy honest son,
     Who will of thy arrival be full joyous.
VINCENTIO   But is this true, or is it else your pleasure,
     Like pleasant travellers, to break a jest
     Upon the company you overtake?
75 HORTENSIO   I do assure thee, father, so it is.
PETRUCCIO
     Come, go along and see the truth hereof,
     For our first merriment hath made thee jealous.
                              Exeunt all but Hortensio.
HORTENSIO
     Well, Petruccio, this has put me in heart.
     Have to my widow, and if she be froward,
80   Then hast thou taught Hortensio to be untoward.
                                            Exit.

5.1   *Enter* GREMIO; *then, unseen by him,*
      BIONDELLO, LUCENTIO *and* BIANCA.

BIONDELLO   Softly and swiftly, sir, for the priest is
     ready.
LUCENTIO   I fly, Biondello; but they may chance to
     need thee at home, therefore leave us.
                              Exeunt Lucentio and Bianca.
5 BIONDELLO   Nay, faith, I'll see the church o'your back,
     and then come back to my master's as soon as I can.
                                            Exit.
GREMIO   I marvel Cambio comes not all this while.

      Enter PETRUCCIO, KATHERINA, VINCENTIO,
      GRUMIO *with Attendants.*

PETRUCCIO
     Sir, here's the door, this is Lucentio's house.
     My father's bears more toward the market-place;
10   Thither must I, and here I leave you, sir.
VINCENTIO
     You shall not choose but drink before you go:
     I think I shall command your welcome here,
     And by all likelihood some cheer is toward.   [*Knocks*]
GREMIO   They're busy within; you were best knock
15   louder.

      Merchant *looks out of the window.*

MERCHANT   What's he that knocks as he would beat
     down the gate?
VINCENTIO   Is Signor Lucentio within, sir?
MERCHANT   He's within, sir, but not to be spoken
20   withal.
VINCENTIO   What if a man bring him a hundred pound
     or two to make merry withal?
MERCHANT   Keep your hundred pounds to yourself; he
     shall need none so long as I live.

PETRUCCIO   Nay, I told you your son was well beloved   25
     in Padua. – Do you hear, sir? To leave frivolous
     circumstances, I pray you tell Signor Lucentio that his
     father is come from Pisa and is here at the door to
     speak with him.
MERCHANT   Thou liest. His father is come to Padua   30
     and here looking out at the window.
VINCENTIO   Art thou his father?
MERCHANT   Ay, sir, so his mother says, if I may believe
     her.
PETRUCCIO   Why, how now, gentleman! Why, this is flat   35
     knavery, to take upon you another man's name.
MERCHANT   Lay hands on the villain. I believe 'a means
     to cozen somebody in this city under my countenance.

      Enter BIONDELLO.

BIONDELLO [*aside*]   I have seen them in the church
     together, God send 'em good shipping. But who is here   40
     – mine old master Vincentio? Now we are undone and
     brought to nothing.
VINCENTIO   Come hither, crackhemp.
BIONDELLO   I hope I may choose, sir.
VINCENTIO   Come hither, you rogue. What, have you   45
     forgot me?
BIONDELLO   Forgot you? No, sir. I could not forget
     you, for I never saw you before in all my life.
VINCENTIO   What, you notorious villain, didst thou
     never see thy master's father, Vincentio?   50
BIONDELLO   What, my old worshipful old master? Yes,
     marry, sir, see where he looks out of the window.
VINCENTIO   Is't so indeed? [*Beats Biondello.*]
BIONDELLO   Help, help, help! Here's a madman will
     murder me.   *Exit.*   55
MERCHANT   Help, son! Help, Signor Baptista!
     [*Leaves the window.*]
PETRUCCIO   Prithee, Kate, let's stand aside and see the
     end of this controversy.

      Enter Merchant *below with Servants,* BAPTISTA
      and TRANIO *as Lucentio.*

TRANIO   Sir, what are you that offer to beat my servant?
VINCENTIO   What am I, sir? Nay, what are you, sir? O   60
     immortal gods! O fine villain! A silken doublet, a
     velvet hose, a scarlet cloak and a copatain hat! O, I am
     undone, I am undone. While I play the good husband
     at home, my son and my servant spend all at the
     university.   65
TRANIO   How now, what's the matter?
BAPTISTA   What, is the man lunatic?
TRANIO   Sir, you seem a sober ancient gentleman by
     your habit, but your words show you a madman. Why,
     sir, what 'cerns it you if I wear pearl and gold? I thank   70
     my good father, I am able to maintain it.
VINCENTIO   Thy father! O villain, he is a sailmaker in
     Bergamo.
BAPTISTA   You mistake, sir; you mistake, sir. Pray, what
     do you think is his name?   75

VINCENTIO   His name? As if I knew not his name: I
  have brought him up ever since he was three years old,
  and his name is Tranio.
MERCHANT   Away, away, mad ass. His name is Lucentio,
  and he is mine only son, and heir to the lands of me,
  Signor Vincentio.
VINCENTIO   Lucentio? O, he hath murdered his master!
  Lay hold on him, I charge you, in the Duke's name. O
  my son, my son! Tell me, thou villain, where is my son
  Lucentio?
TRANIO   Call forth an officer.

Enter an Officer.

  Carry this mad knave to the jail. Father Baptista, I
  charge you see that he be forthcoming.
VINCENTIO   Carry me to the jail?
GREMIO   Stay, officer; he shall not go to prison.
BAPTISTA   Talk not, Signor Gremio; I say he shall go to
  prison.
GREMIO   Take heed, Signor Baptista, lest you be cony-
  catched in this business. I dare swear this is the right
  Vincentio.
MERCHANT   Swear, if thou dar'st.
GREMIO   Nay, I dare not swear it.
TRANIO   Then thou wert best say that I am not Lucentio.
GREMIO   Yes, I know thee to be Signor Lucentio.
BAPTISTA   Away with the dotard; to the jail with him.

Enter BIONDELLO, LUCENTIO *and* BIANCA.

VINCENTIO   Thus strangers may be haled and abused.
  O monstrous villain!
BIONDELLO   O, we are spoiled, and – yonder he is.
  Deny him, forswear him, or else we are all undone.
  Exeunt Biondello, Tranio and Merchant as fast as may be.
LUCENTIO   Pardon, sweet father. [*Kneels.*]
VINCENTIO   Lives my sweet son?
BIANCA   Pardon, dear father.
BAPTISTA
  How hast thou offended? Where is Lucentio?
LUCENTIO
  Here's Lucentio, right son to the right Vincentio,
  That have by marriage made thy daughter mine
  While counterfeit supposes bleared thine eyne.
GREMIO   Here's packing, with a witness, to deceive us
  all.
VINCENTIO   Where is that damned villain, Tranio,
  That faced and braved me in this matter so?
BAPTISTA   Why, tell me, is not this my Cambio?
BIANCA   Cambio is changed into Lucentio.
LUCENTIO   Love wrought these miracles. Bianca's love
  Made me exchange my state with Tranio
  While he did bear my countenance in the town,
  And happily I have arrived at the last
  Unto the wished haven of my bliss.
  What Tranio did, myself enforced him to;
  Then pardon him, sweet father, for my sake.

VINCENTIO   I'll slit the villain's nose that would have   125
  sent me to the jail.
BAPTISTA   But do you hear, sir? Have you married my
  daughter without asking my good will?
VINCENTIO   Fear not, Baptista, we will content you – go
  to. But I will in to be revenged for this villainy.   *Exit.*   130
BAPTISTA   And I, to sound the depth of this knavery.
                                                        Exit.
LUCENTIO   Look not pale, Bianca, thy father will not
  frown.   *Exeunt Lucentio and Bianca.*
GREMIO   My cake is dough, but I'll in among the rest,
  Out of hope of all but my share of the feast.   *Exit.*   135
KATHERINA   Husband, let's follow to see the end of this
  ado.
PETRUCCIO   First kiss me, Kate, and we will.
KATHERINA   What, in the midst of the street?
PETRUCCIO   What, art thou ashamed of me?   140
KATHERINA   No sir, God forbid – but ashamed to kiss.
PETRUCCIO
  Why then, let's home again. – Come, sirrah, let's away.
KATHERINA
  Nay, I will give thee a kiss. [*Kisses him.*] Now pray
  thee love, stay.
PETRUCCIO   Is not this well? Come, my sweet Kate.
  Better once than never, for never too late.   *Exeunt.*   145

5.2   *Enter* BAPTISTA, VINCENTIO, GREMIO, *the*
        Merchant, LUCENTIO *and* BIANCA, PETRUCCIO,
        KATHERINA, HORTENSIO *and* Widow, GRUMIO,
        BIONDELLO *and* TRANIO *with Servants*
        bringing in a banquet.

LUCENTIO
  At last, though long, our jarring notes agree,
  And time it is when raging war is done
  To smile at scapes and perils overblown.
  My fair Bianca, bid my father welcome,
  While I with selfsame kindness welcome thine.   5
  Brother Petruccio, sister Katherina,
  And thou, Hortensio, with thy loving widow,
  Feast with the best, and welcome to my house.
  My banquet is to close our stomachs up
  After our great good cheer. Pray you, sit down,   10
  For now we sit to chat as well as eat.
PETRUCCIO   Nothing but sit and sit, and eat and eat.
BAPTISTA   Padua affords this kindness, son Petruccio.
PETRUCCIO   Padua affords nothing but what is kind.
HORTENSIO
  For both our sakes I would that word were true.   15
PETRUCCIO
  Now, for my life, Hortensio fears his widow.
WIDOW   Then never trust me if I be afeared.
PETRUCCIO
  You are very sensible, and yet you miss my sense:
  I mean Hortensio is afeard of you.
WIDOW   He that is giddy thinks the world turns round.   20
PETRUCCIO   Roundly replied.

KATHERINA　Mistress, how mean you that?

WIDOW　Thus I conceive by him.

PETRUCCIO

Conceives by me – how likes Hortensio that?

HORTENSIO

25　My widow says, thus she conceives her tale.

PETRUCCIO

Very well mended. Kiss him for that, good widow.

KATHERINA

'He that is giddy thinks the world turns round' –

I pray you tell me what you meant by that.

WIDOW　Your husband, being troubled with a shrew,

30　Measures my husband's sorrow by his woe:

And now you know my meaning.

KATHERINA　A very mean meaning.

WIDOW　　　　　　　　　　　Right, I mean you.

KATHERINA　And I am mean indeed, respecting you.

PETRUCCIO　To her, Kate!

35　HORTENSIO　To her, widow!

PETRUCCIO

A hundred marks my Kate does put her down.

HORTENSIO　That's my office.

PETRUCCIO　Spoke like an officer. Ha' to thee, lad.

　　　　[*Drinks to Hortensio.*]

BAPTISTA　How likes Gremio these quick-witted folks?

40　GREMIO　Believe me, sir, they butt together well.

BIANCA　Head and butt? An hasty-witted body

Would say your head and butt were head and horn.

VINCENTIO

Ay, mistress bride, hath that awakened you?

BIANCA

Ay, but not frighted me; therefore I'll sleep again.

PETRUCCIO

45　Nay, that you shall not. Since you have begun,

Have at you for a better jest or two.

BIANCA　Am I your bird? I mean to shift my bush,

And then pursue me as you draw your bow.

You are welcome all.

　　　　Exeunt Bianca, Katherina and Widow.

PETRUCCIO

50　She hath prevented me. Here, Signor Tranio,

This bird you aimed at, though you hit her not;

Therefore a health to all that shot and missed.

TRANIO

O sir, Lucentio slipped me like his greyhound,

Which runs himself and catches for his master.

PETRUCCIO

55　A good swift simile, but something currish.

TRANIO　'Tis well, sir, that you hunted for yourself –

'Tis thought your deer does hold you at a bay.

BAPTISTA　O, O, Petruccio, Tranio hits you now.

LUCENTIO　I thank thee for that gird, good Tranio.

HORTENSIO

60　Confess, confess, hath he not hit you here?

PETRUCCIO　'A has a little galled me, I confess,

And as the jest did glance away from me,

'Tis ten to one it maimed you two outright.

BAPTISTA　Now in good sadness, son Petruccio,

65　I think thou hast the veriest shrew of all.

PETRUCCIO

Well, I say no: and therefore, Sir Assurance,

Let's each one send unto his wife,

And he whose wife is most obedient

To come at first when he doth send for her

70　Shall win the wager which we will propose.

HORTENSIO　Content. What's the wager?

LUCENTIO　Twenty crowns.

PETRUCCIO　Twenty crowns!

I'll venture so much of my hawk or hound,

75　But twenty times so much upon my wife.

LUCENTIO　A hundred then.

HORTENSIO　　　　　　　Content.

PETRUCCIO　　　　　　　　　　A match – 'tis done.

HORTENSIO　Who shall begin?

LUCENTIO　That will I. Go, Biondello, bid your mistress

come to me.

BIONDELLO　I go.　　　　　　　　*Exit.*　80

BAPTISTA　Son, I'll be your half Bianca comes.

LUCENTIO　I'll have no halves; I'll bear it all myself.

　　　　Enter BIONDELLO.

How now, what news?

BIONDELLO　Sir, my mistress sends you word that she is

busy, and she cannot come.　85

PETRUCCIO　How? 'She's busy and she cannot come'?

Is that an answer?

GREMIO　　　　　　Ay, and a kind one too:

Pray God, sir, your wife send you not a worse.

PETRUCCIO　I hope better.

HORTENSIO　Sirrah Biondello, go and entreat my wife　90

to come to me forthwith.　　　*Exit Biondello.*

PETRUCCIO

O ho, 'entreat' her – nay then, she must needs come.

HORTENSIO　I am afraid sir, do what you can,

　　　　Enter BIONDELLO.

Yours will not be entreated. Now, where's my wife?

BIONDELLO

She says you have some goodly jest in hand.　95

She will not come; she bids you come to her.

PETRUCCIO

Worse and worse: 'She will not come' – O vile,

Intolerable, not to be endured.

Sirrah Grumio, go to your mistress;

Say I command her come to me.　*Exit Grumio.*　100

HORTENSIO　I know her answer.

PETRUCCIO　What?

HORTENSIO　She will not.

PETRUCCIO

The fouler fortune mine, and there an end.

　　　　Enter KATHERINA.

BAPTISTA

Now, by my halidom, here comes Katherina.　105

KATHERINA

    What is your will, sir, that you send for me?

PETRUCCIO

    Where is your sister, and Hortensio's wife?

KATHERINA   They sit conferring by the parlour fire.

PETRUCCIO

    Go fetch them hither; if they deny to come,

110   Swinge me them soundly forth unto their husbands.

    Away, I say, and bring them hither straight.

                           Exit Katherina.

LUCENTIO   Here is a wonder, if you talk of a wonder.

HORTENSIO   And so it is. I wonder what it bodes.

PETRUCCIO

    Marry, peace it bodes, and love, and quiet life,

115   An awful rule and right supremacy

    And, to be short, what not that's sweet and happy.

BAPTISTA   Now fair befall thee, good Petruccio!

    The wager thou hast won, and I will add

    Unto their losses twenty thousand crowns,

120   Another dowry to another daughter,

    For she is changed as she had never been.

PETRUCCIO   Nay, I will win my wager better yet

    And show more sign of her obedience –

    Her new-built virtue and obedience.

        Enter KATHERINA, BIANCA *and* Widow.

125   See where she comes, and brings your froward wives

    As prisoners to her womanly persuasion.

    Katherine, that cap of yours becomes you not:

    Off with that bauble – throw it underfoot.

WIDOW   Lord, let me never have a cause to sigh

130   Till I be brought to such a silly pass.

BIANCA   Fie, what a foolish duty call you this?

LUCENTIO   I would your duty were as foolish too:

    The wisdom of your duty, fair Bianca,

    Hath cost me five hundred crowns since supper time.

135   BIANCA   The more fool you for laying on my duty.

PETRUCCIO

    Katherine, I charge thee tell these headstrong women

    What duty they do owe their lords and husbands.

WIDOW

    Come, come, you're mocking: we will have no telling.

PETRUCCIO   Come on, I say, and first begin with her.

140   WIDOW   She shall not.

PETRUCCIO   I say she shall: 'and first begin with her'.

KATHERINA

    Fie, fie, unknit that threatening unkind brow,

    And dart not scornful glances from those eyes

    To wound thy lord, thy king, thy governor.

145   It blots thy beauty as frosts do bite the meads,

    Confounds thy fame as whirlwinds shake fair buds

    And in no sense is meet or amiable.

    A woman moved is like a fountain troubled,

    Muddy, ill-seeming, thick, bereft of beauty

    And while it is so, none so dry or thirsty   150

    Will deign to sip or touch one drop of it.

    Thy husband is thy lord, thy life, thy keeper,

    Thy head, thy sovereign: one that cares for thee

    And for thy maintenance; commits his body

    To painful labour both by sea and land,   155

    To watch the night in storms, the day in cold,

    Whilst thou liest warm at home, secure and safe,

    And craves no other tribute at thy hands

    But love, fair looks and true obedience –

    Too little payment for so great a debt.   160

    Such duty as the subject owes the prince,

    Even such a woman oweth to her husband;

    And when she is froward, peevish, sullen, sour,

    And not obedient to his honest will,

    What is she but a foul contending rebel   165

    And graceless traitor to her loving lord?

    I am ashamed that women are so simple

    To offer war where they should kneel for peace,

    Or seek for rule, supremacy and sway

    When they are bound to serve, love and obey.   170

    Why are our bodies soft, and weak, and smooth,

    Unapt to toil and trouble in the world,

    But that our soft conditions and our hearts

    Should well agree with our external parts?

    Come, come, you froward and unable worms,   175

    My mind hath been as big as one of yours,

    My heart as great, my reason haply more,

    To bandy word for word and frown for frown.

    But now I see our lances are but straws,

    Our strength as weak, our weakness past compare,   180

    That seeming to be most which we indeed least are.

    Then vail your stomachs, for it is no boot,

    And place your hands below your husband's foot:

    In token of which duty, if he please,

    My hand is ready, may it do him ease.   185

PETRUCCIO

    Why, there's a wench. Come on, and kiss me, Kate.

LUCENTIO

    Well, go thy ways, old lad, for thou shalt ha't.

VINCENTIO

    'Tis a good hearing when children are toward.

LUCENTIO

    But a harsh hearing, when women are froward.

PETRUCCIO   Come Kate, we'll to bed.   190

    We three are married, but you two are sped.

    – 'Twas I won the wager, though you hit the white,

    And being a winner, God give you good night.

                           Exit Petruccio.

HORTENSIO

    Now go thy ways; thou hast tamed a curst shrew.

LUCENTIO

    'Tis a wonder, by your leave, she will be tamed so.   195

                              Exeunt.

The Tempest

The Tempest was printed as the first comedy, and consequently the first play, in the Folio of 1623. It may have been granted such prominence as the last non-collaborative play Shakespeare wrote, but it must in any event have been highly regarded by the publishers of the Folio, and by his former colleagues John Heminges and Henry Condell, who vouched for the authority and completeness of the volume, to appear first in it. Its full, descriptive stage directions may have been amplified by the scribe Ralph Crane, who transcribed the manuscript copy used by the printer. Its date of composition is fixed as 1610–11 by a performance at Court on 1 November 1611 and by its use of William Strachey's account (dated from Virginia on 15 July 1610 and known to have reached London no earlier than September) of the shipwreck of Sir George Somers on Bermuda in the summer of 1609. The play may have been designed for the Blackfriars playhouse, but no record of performance there or at the Globe has survived.

Like other plays from *Hamlet* onwards, *The Tempest* reflects Shakespeare's knowledge of the *Essays* of Michel de Montaigne, in John Florio's English version (1603). The essay 'Of the Cannibals' underlies Gonzalo's vision of an ideal commonwealth, raises questions about the distinction between civilization and barbarism and probably suggested Caliban's name. Virgil's *Aeneid* is a further influence, while Prospero's renunciation of magic at 5.1.33–57 is closely modelled on Medea's invocation in Ovid's *Metamorphoses*, 7.179–219.

The Tempest, in which Shakespeare observed the unities of place and time for the first time since *The Comedy of Errors*, is a work of synthesis and retrospection. The controlling role of Prospero may recall the Duke in *Measure for Measure*, who also prefers forgiveness to vindictive justice at the end. His magic harks back to Oberon in *A Midsummer Night's Dream*, just as Ariel's role recalls that of Puck. Its presentation of the pursuit of political power is equally reminiscent of the English histories and political tragedies. Stephano is the last, and most sinister, of Shakespeare's comic drunkards.

The Tempest was among the first of Shakespeare's plays to be adapted for the changed theatrical conditions of the Restoration. The version by John Dryden and William Davenant (1667) supplied it with a busier action, introducing sisters for Miranda and Caliban, a female counterpart for Ariel, and Hippolyto, a man who has never seen a woman (a travesty role for an actress). The dreamlike quality of its action and the mythic symmetries of its cast have led to a wide and increasingly various array of interpretations of *The Tempest*. Nineteenth-century interest found its focus in Prospero, who was increasingly identified with Shakespeare; in the late twentieth century, attention shifted towards Caliban and colonialism, or towards Miranda and the oppressions of patriarchy. The play has inspired many later literary and musical compositions, among them Hector Berlioz's symphonic fantasy *Lélio* (1832), Robert Browning's 'Caliban upon Setebos' (1864), Jean Sibelius's incidental music for the play (1926), W.H. Auden's *The Sea and the Mirror* (1944) and Sir Michael Tippett's opera *The Knot Garden* (1970).

The Arden text is based on the 1623 First Folio.

LIST OF ROLES

ALONSO	*King of Naples*
SEBASTIAN	*his brother*
PROSPERO	*the right Duke of Milan*
ANTONIO	*his brother, the usurping Duke of Milan*
FERDINAND	*son to the King of Naples*
GONZALO	*an honest old councillor*
ADRIAN *and* FRANCISCO	*lords*
CALIBAN	*a savage and deformed slave*
TRINCULO	*a jester*
STEPHANO	*a drunken butler*
MASTER	*of a ship*
BOATSWAIN	
MARINERS	
MIRANDA	*daughter to Prospero*
ARIEL	*an airy spirit*
IRIS	
CERES	
JUNO	*spirits*
Nymphs	
Reapers	

1.1 *A tempestuous noise of thunder and lightning heard; enter a* Shipmaster *and a* Boatswain.

MASTER   Boatswain!

BOATSWAIN   Here master. What cheer?

MASTER   Good, speak to th' mariners. Fall to't yarely or we run ourselves aground. Bestir, bestir!   *Exit.*

Enter Mariners.

BOATSWAIN   Heigh, my hearts; cheerly, cheerly, my hearts! Yare! Yare! Take in the topsail. Tend to the master's whistle! [*to the storm*] Blow till thou burst thy wind, if room enough.

Enter ALONSO, SEBASTIAN, ANTONIO, FERDINAND, GONZALO *and others.*

ALONSO   Good boatswain, have care. Where's the master? Play the men!

BOATSWAIN   I pray now, keep below!

ANTONIO   Where is the master, boatswain?

BOATSWAIN   Do you not hear him? You mar our labour. Keep your cabins! You do assist the storm.

GONZALO   Nay, good, be patient.

BOATSWAIN   When the sea is! Hence. What cares these roarers for the name of king? To cabin! Silence! Trouble us not.

GONZALO   Good, yet remember whom thou hast aboard.

BOATSWAIN   None that I more love than myself. You are a councillor; if you can command these elements to silence and work the peace of the present, we will not hand a rope more. Use your authority! If you cannot, give thanks you have lived so long and make yourself ready in your cabin for the mischance of the hour, if it so hap. – Cheerly, good hearts. – Out of our way, I say!   *Exit.*

GONZALO   I have great comfort from this fellow. Methinks he hath no drowning mark upon him – his complexion is perfect gallows. Stand fast, good fate, to his hanging; make the rope of his destiny our cable, for our own doth little advantage. If he be not born to be hanged, our case is miserable.   *Exeunt.*

Enter Boatswain.

BOATSWAIN   Down with the topmast! Yare! Lower, lower! Bring her to try with main course. [*A cry within*] A plague upon this howling. They are louder than the weather or our office.

Enter SEBASTIAN, ANTONIO *and* GONZALO.

Yet again? What do you here? Shall we give o'er and drown? Have you a mind to sink?

SEBASTIAN   A pox o'your throat, you bawling, blasphemous, incharitable dog.

BOATSWAIN   Work you, then.

ANTONIO   Hang, cur! Hang, you whoreson, insolent noise-maker! We are less afraid to be drowned than thou art.

GONZALO   I'll warrant him for drowning, though the ship were no stronger than a nutshell and as leaky as an unstanched wench.   45

BOATSWAIN   Lay her a-hold, a-hold! Set her two courses off to sea again! Lay her off!

Enter Mariners, *wet.*

MARINERS   All lost! To prayers, to prayers! All lost!   50

BOATSWAIN   What, must our mouths be cold?

GONZALO   The King and prince at prayers, let's assist them, for our case is as theirs.

SEBASTIAN   I'm out of patience.

ANTONIO   We are merely cheated of our lives by   55
drunkards. This wide-chopped rascal – would thou mightst lie drowning the washing of ten tides!

GONZALO   He'll be hanged yet, though every drop of water swear against it and gape at widest to glut him. [*A confused noise within*] Mercy on us! – We split, we   60
split! – Farewell my wife and children! – Farewell brother! – We split, we split, we split!

ANTONIO   Let's all sink wi'th' King.

SEBASTIAN   Let's take leave of him.   *Exit with Antonio.*

GONZALO   Now would I give a thousand furlongs of sea   65
for an acre of barren ground – long heath, brown furze, anything. The wills above be done, but I would fain die a dry death.   *Exit.*

1.2   *Enter* PROSPERO *and* MIRANDA.

MIRANDA   If by your art, my dearest father, you have
Put the wild waters in this roar, allay them.
The sky, it seems, would pour down stinking pitch
But that the sea, mounting to th' welkin's cheek,
Dashes the fire out. O, I have suffered   5
With those that I saw suffer – a brave vessel
(Who had no doubt some noble creature in her)
Dashed all to pieces. O, the cry did knock
Against my very heart! Poor souls, they perished.
Had I been any god of power, I would   10
Have sunk the sea within the earth or ere
It should the good ship so have swallowed and
The fraughting souls within her.

PROSPERO   Be collected;
No more amazement. Tell your piteous heart
There's no harm done.

MIRANDA   O woe the day.

PROSPERO   No harm!   15
I have done nothing but in care of thee,
Of thee, my dear one, thee my daughter, who
Art ignorant of what thou art, naught knowing
Of whence I am, nor that I am more better
Than Prospero, master of a full poor cell,   20
And thy no greater father.

MIRANDA   More to know
Did never meddle with my thoughts.

PROSPERO   'Tis time
I should inform thee further. Lend thy hand

And pluck my magic garment from me. So,

25 Lie there my art. Wipe thou thine eyes, have comfort;
The direful spectacle of the wreck which touched
The very virtue of compassion in thee,
I have with such provision in mine art
So safely ordered, that there is no soul –

30 No, not so much perdition as an hair,
Betid to any creature in the vessel
Which thou heard'st cry, which thou sawst sink. Sit down,
For thou must now know further.

MIRANDA   You have often
Begun to tell me what I am, but stopped

35 And left me to a bootless inquisition,
Concluding, 'Stay, not yet'.

PROSPERO   The hour's now come;
The very minute bids thee ope thine ear.
Obey and be attentive. Canst thou remember
A time before we came unto this cell?

40 I do not think thou canst, for then thou wast not
Out three years old.

MIRANDA   Certainly, sir, I can.

PROSPERO   By what? By any other house or person?
Of any thing the image, tell me, that
Hath kept with thy remembrance.

MIRANDA   'Tis far off,

45 And rather like a dream than an assurance
That my remembrance warrants. Had I not
Four or five women once, that tended me?

PROSPERO
Thou hadst, and more, Miranda. But how is it
That this lives in thy mind? What seest thou else

50 In the dark backward and abysm of time?
If thou rememb'rest aught ere thou cam'st here,
How thou cam'st here thou mayst.

MIRANDA   But that I do not.

PROSPERO
Twelve year since, Miranda, twelve year since,
Thy father was the Duke of Milan and
A prince of power.

55 MIRANDA   Sir, are not you my father?

PROSPERO   Thy mother was a piece of virtue, and
She said thou wast my daughter; and thy father
Was Duke of Milan, and his only heir
And princess, no worse issued.

MIRANDA   O, the heavens!

60 What foul play had we that we came from thence?
Or blessed wast we did?

PROSPERO   Both, both, my girl.
By foul play, as thou sayst, were we heaved thence,
But blessedly holp hither.

MIRANDA   O, my heart bleeds
To think o'th' teen that I have turned you to,

65 Which is from my remembrance. Please you, farther.

PROSPERO   My brother and thy uncle, called Antonio –
I pray thee mark me, that a brother should
Be so perfidious – he, whom next thyself

Of all the world I loved, and to him put
The manage of my state, as at that time   70
Through all the signories it was the first,
And Prospero the prime Duke, being so reputed
In dignity, and for the liberal arts
Without a parallel; those being all my study,
The government I cast upon my brother   75
And to my state grew stranger, being transported
And rapt in secret studies. Thy false uncle –
Dost thou attend me?

MIRANDA   Sir, most heedfully.

PROSPERO   Being once perfected how to grant suits,
How to deny them, who t'advance and who   80
To trash for overtopping, new created
The creatures that were mine, I say, or changed 'em,
Or else new formed 'em; having both the key
Of officer and office, set all hearts i'th' state
To what tune pleased his ear, that now he was   85
The ivy which had hid my princely trunk
And sucked my verdure out on't. Thou attend'st not!

MIRANDA   O, good sir, I do.

PROSPERO   I pray thee, mark me.
I thus neglecting worldly ends, all dedicated
To closeness and the bettering of my mind   90
With that which, but by being so retired,
O'er-prized all popular rate, in my false brother
Awaked an evil nature, and my trust,
Like a good parent, did beget of him
A falsehood in its contrary as great   95
As my trust was, which had indeed no limit,
A confidence sans bound. He being thus lorded,
Not only with what my revenue yielded
But what my power might else exact, like one
Who, having into truth by telling of it,   100
Made such a sinner of his memory
To credit his own lie, he did believe
He was indeed the duke, out o'th' substitution
And executing th'outward face of royalty
With all prerogative. Hence his ambition growing –   105
Dost thou hear?

MIRANDA   Your tale, sir, would cure deafness.

PROSPERO
To have no screen between this part he played
And him he played it for, he needs will be
Absolute Milan. Me, poor man, my library
Was dukedom large enough. Of temporal royalties   110
He thinks me now incapable; confederates,
So dry he was for sway, wi'th' King of Naples
To give him annual tribute, do him homage,
Subject his coronet to his crown, and bend
The dukedom yet unbowed (alas, poor Milan)   115
To most ignoble stooping.

MIRANDA   O, the heavens!

PROSPERO
Mark his condition and th'event, then tell me
If this might be a brother.

MIRANDA   I should sin

To think but nobly of my grandmother;
Good wombs have borne bad sons.

120 PROSPERO   Now the condition.
This King of Naples, being an enemy
To me inveterate, hearkens my brother's suit,
Which was that he, in lieu o'th' premises
Of homage, and I know not how much tribute,
125 Should presently extirpate me and mine
Out of the dukedom and confer fair Milan,
With all the honours, on my brother. Whereon –
A treacherous army levied – one midnight
Fated to th' purpose did Antonio open
130 The gates of Milan and i'th' dead of darkness
The ministers for th' purpose hurried thence
Me and thy crying self.

MIRANDA   Alack, for pity.
I, not rememb'ring how I cried out then,
Will cry it o'er again. It is a hint
That wrings mine eyes to't.

135 PROSPERO   Hear a little further,
And then I'll bring thee to the present business
Which now's upon's, without the which this story
Were most impertinent.

MIRANDA   Wherefore did they not
That hour destroy us?

PROSPERO   Well demanded, wench:
140 My tale provokes that question. Dear, they durst not,
So dear the love my people bore me, nor set
A mark so bloody on the business, but
With colours fairer painted their foul ends.
In few, they hurried us aboard a bark,
145 Bore us some leagues to sea, where they prepared
A rotten carcass of a butt, not rigged,
Nor tackle, sail, nor mast – the very rats
Instinctively have quit it. There they hoist us
To cry to th' sea that roared to us, to sigh
150 To th' winds, whose pity, sighing back again,
Did us but loving wrong.

MIRANDA   Alack, what trouble
Was I then to you?

PROSPERO   O, a cherubin
Thou wast that did preserve me. Thou didst smile,
Infused with a fortitude from heaven,
155 When I have decked the sea with drops full salt,
Under my burden groaned, which raised in me
An undergoing stomach to bear up
Against what should ensue.

MIRANDA   How came we ashore?

PROSPERO   By providence divine.
160 Some food we had, and some fresh water, that
A noble Neapolitan, Gonzalo,
Out of his charity – who, being then appointed
Master of this design – did give us, with
Rich garments, linens, stuffs and necessaries,
165 Which since have steaded much; so of his gentleness,
Knowing I loved my books, he furnished me
From mine own library with volumes that

I prize above my dukedom.

MIRANDA   Would I might
But ever see that man!

PROSPERO   Now I arise.
Sit still and hear the last of our sea-sorrow.   170
Here in this island we arrived, and here
Have I, thy schoolmaster, made thee more profit
Than other princes can that have more time
For vainer hours, and tutors not so careful.

MIRANDA
Heavens thank you for't. And now I pray you, sir,   175
For still 'tis beating in my mind, your reason
For raising this sea-storm?

PROSPERO   Know thus far forth:
By accident most strange, bountiful fortune
(Now, my dear lady) hath mine enemies
Brought to this shore; and by my prescience   180
I find my zenith doth depend upon
A most auspicious star, whose influence
If now I court not, but omit, my fortunes
Will ever after droop. Here cease more questions.
Thou art inclined to sleep; 'tis a good dullness,   185
And give it way. I know thou canst not choose.
[*to Ariel*] Come away, servant, come; I am ready now.
Approach, my Ariel. Come.

Enter ARIEL.

ARIEL   All hail, great master; grave sir, hail! I come
To answer thy best pleasure, be't to fly,   190
To swim, to dive into the fire, to ride
On the curled clouds. To thy strong bidding, task
Ariel and all his quality.

PROSPERO   Hast thou, spirit,
Performed to point the tempest that I bade thee?

ARIEL   To every article.   195
I boarded the King's ship: now on the beak,
Now in the waist, the deck, in every cabin
I flamed amazement. Sometime I'd divide
And burn in many places – on the topmast,
The yards and bowsprit would I flame distinctly,   200
Then meet and join. Jove's lightning, the precursors
O'th' dreadful thunderclaps, more momentary
And sight-outrunning were not; the fire and cracks
Of sulphurous roaring, the most mighty Neptune
Seem to besiege and make his bold waves tremble,   205
Yea, his dread trident shake.

PROSPERO   My brave spirit,
Who was so firm, so constant, that this coil
Would not infect his reason?

ARIEL   Not a soul
But felt a fever of the mad and played
Some tricks of desperation. All but mariners   210
Plunged in the foaming brine and quit the vessel;
Then all afire with me, the King's son Ferdinand,
With hair up-staring (then like reeds, not hair),
Was the first man that leapt, cried 'Hell is empty,
And all the devils are here'.

215 PROSPERO   Why, that's my spirit!
But was not this nigh shore?
ARIEL   Close by, my master.
PROSPERO   But are they, Ariel, safe?
ARIEL   Not a hair perished;
On their sustaining garments not a blemish,
But fresher than before; and, as thou bad'st me,
220 In troops I have dispersed them 'bout the isle.
The King's son have I landed by himself,
Whom I left cooling of the air with sighs,
In an odd angle of the isle, and sitting,
His arms in this sad knot.
PROSPERO   Of the King's ship,
225 The mariners, say how thou hast disposed,
And all the rest o'th' fleet?
ARIEL   Safely in harbour
Is the King's ship, in the deep nook where once
Thou called'st me up at midnight to fetch dew
From the still-vexed Bermudas; there she's hid,
230 The mariners all under hatches stowed,
Who, with a charm joined to their suffered labour,
I have left asleep. And for the rest o'th' fleet,
Which I dispersed, they all have met again,
And are upon the Mediterranean float,
235 Bound sadly home for Naples,
Supposing that they saw the King's ship wrecked
And his great person perish.
PROSPERO   Ariel, thy charge
Exactly is performed; but there's more work.
What is the time o'th' day?
ARIEL   Past the mid-season.
PROSPERO
240 At least two glasses. The time 'twixt six and now
Must by us both be spent most preciously.
ARIEL
Is there more toil? Since thou dost give me pains,
Let me remember thee what thou hast promised,
Which is not yet performed me.
PROSPERO   How now? Moody?
What is't thou canst demand?
245 ARIEL   My liberty.
PROSPERO   Before the time be out? No more!
ARIEL   I prithee
Remember I have done thee worthy service,
Told thee no lies, made thee no mistakings, served
Without or grudge or grumblings. Thou did promise
250 To bate me a full year.
PROSPERO   Dost thou forget
From what a torment I did free thee?
ARIEL   No.
PROSPERO
Thou dost, and think'st it much to tread the ooze
Of the salt deep,
To run upon the sharp wind of the north,
255 To do me business in the veins o'th' earth
When it is baked with frost.
ARIEL   I do not, sir.

PROSPERO
Thou liest, malignant thing; hast thou forgot
The foul witch Sycorax, who with age and envy
Was grown into a hoop? Hast thou forgot her?
ARIEL   No, sir.
PROSPERO   Thou hast! Where was she born? Speak;
tell me.   260
ARIEL   Sir, in Algiers.
PROSPERO   O, was she so? I must
Once in a month recount what thou hast been,
Which thou forget'st. This damned witch Sycorax,
For mischiefs manifold and sorceries terrible
To enter human hearing, from Algiers,   265
Thou knowst, was banished. For one thing she did
They would not take her life; is not this true?
ARIEL   Ay, sir.
PROSPERO
This blue-eyed hag was hither brought with child,
And here was left by th' sailors. Thou, my slave,   270
As thou report'st thyself, was then her servant,
And – for thou wast a spirit too delicate
To act her earthy and abhorred commands,
Refusing her grand hests – she did confine thee,
By help of her more potent ministers   275
And in her most unmitigable rage,
Into a cloven pine, within which rift
Imprisoned thou didst painfully remain
A dozen years, within which space she died
And left thee there, where thou didst vent thy groans   280
As fast as millwheels strike. Then was this island
(Save for the son that she did litter here,
A freckled whelp, hag-born) not honoured with
A human shape.
ARIEL   Yes, Caliban, her son.
PROSPERO   Dull thing, I say so – he, that Caliban,   285
Whom now I keep in service. Thou best knowst
What torment I did find thee in: thy groans
Did make wolves howl and penetrate the breasts
Of ever-angry bears. It was a torment
To lay upon the damned, which Sycorax   290
Could not again undo. It was mine art,
When I arrived and heard thee, that made gape
The pine and let thee out.
ARIEL   I thank thee, master.
PROSPERO   If thou more murmur'st, I will rend an oak
And peg thee in his knotty entrails till   295
Thou hast howled away twelve winters.
ARIEL   Pardon, master,
I will be correspondent to command
And do my spriting gently.
PROSPERO   Do so, and after two days
I will discharge thee.
ARIEL   That's my noble master.   300
What shall I do? Say what? What shall I do?
PROSPERO   Go make thyself like a nymph o'th' sea;
Be subject to no sight but thine and mine, invisible
To every eyeball else. Go take this shape

305 And hither come in't. Go! Hence with diligence.

Exit Ariel.

[*to Miranda*] Awake, dear heart, awake; thou hast
slept well.
Awake.

MIRANDA   The strangeness of your story put
Heaviness in me.

PROSPERO   Shake it off. Come on,
We'll visit Caliban, my slave, who never
Yields us kind answer.

310 MIRANDA   'Tis a villain, sir,
I do not love to look on.

PROSPERO   But as 'tis,
We cannot miss him; he does make our fire,
Fetch in our wood, and serves in offices
That profit us. – What ho, slave! Caliban,
Thou earth, thou: speak!

315 CALIBAN [*within*]   There's wood enough within.

PROSPERO
Come forth I say, there's other business for thee.
Come, thou tortoise, when?

Enter ARIEL, *like a water nymph.*

Fine apparition, my quaint Ariel,
Hark in thine ear.

ARIEL   My lord, it shall be done.   *Exit.*

PROSPERO
320 Thou poisonous slave, got by the devil himself
Upon thy wicked dam; come forth!

Enter CALIBAN.

CALIBAN   As wicked dew as e'er my mother brushed
With raven's feather from unwholesome fen
Drop on you both. A southwest blow on ye
325 And blister you all o'er.

PROSPERO
For this, be sure, tonight thou shalt have cramps,
Side-stitches, that shall pen thy breath up; urchins
Shall forth at vast of night that they may work
All exercise on thee; thou shalt be pinched
330 As thick as honeycomb, each pinch more stinging
Than bees that made 'em.

CALIBAN   I must eat my dinner.
This island's mine by Sycorax, my mother,
Which thou tak'st from me. When thou cam'st first
Thou strok'st me and made much of me; wouldst give
me
335 Water with berries in't, and teach me how
To name the bigger light and how the less
That burn by day and night. And then I loved thee
And showed thee all the qualities o'th' isle:
The fresh springs, brine pits, barren place and fertile.
340 Cursed be I that did so! All the charms
Of Sycorax – toads, beetles, bats – light on you,
For I am all the subjects that you have,
Which first was mine own king; and here you sty me
In this hard rock, whiles you do keep from me

The rest o'th' island.

PROSPERO   Thou most lying slave, 345
Whom stripes may move, not kindness; I have used
thee
(Filth as thou art) with humane care and lodged thee
In mine own cell, till thou didst seek to violate
The honour of my child.

CALIBAN   O ho, O ho! Would't had been done; 350
Thou didst prevent me, I had peopled else
This isle with Calibans.

MIRANDA   Abhorred slave,
Which any print of goodness wilt not take,
Being capable of all ill; I pitied thee,
Took pains to make thee speak, taught thee each hour 355
One thing or other. When thou didst not, savage,
Know thine own meaning, but wouldst gabble like
A thing most brutish, I endowed thy purposes
With words that made them known. But thy vile race
(Though thou didst learn) had that in't which good
natures 360
Could not abide to be with; therefore wast thou
Deservedly confined into this rock,
Who hadst deserved more than a prison.

CALIBAN   You taught me language, and my profit on't
Is I know how to curse. The red plague rid you 365
For learning me your language.

PROSPERO   Hag-seed, hence:
Fetch us in fuel, and be quick – thou'rt best –
To answer other business. Shrug'st thou, malice?
If thou neglect'st, or dost unwillingly
What I command, I'll rack thee with old cramps, 370
Fill all thy bones with aches, make thee roar,
That beasts shall tremble at thy din.

CALIBAN   No, pray thee.
[*aside*] I must obey; his art is of such power
It would control my dam's god Setebos,
And make a vassal of him.

PROSPERO   So, slave, hence.   *Exit Caliban.* 375

Enter FERDINAND, *and* ARIEL, *invisible,*
playing and singing.

ARIEL [*Sings.*]
Come unto these yellow sands,
And then take hands;
Curtsied when you have, and kissed
The wild waves whist;
Foot it featly here and there, 380
And sweet sprites bear
The burden.
[*Burden dispersedly*]

SPIRITS   Hark, hark! Bow-wow,
The watch dogs bark, bow-wow.

ARIEL   Hark hark, I hear, 385
The strain of strutting chanticleer
Cry cock a diddle dow.

FERDINAND
Where should this music be? I'th' air, or th'earth?

It sounds no more, and sure it waits upon
Some god o'th' island. Sitting on a bank,
Weeping again the King my father's wreck,
This music crept by me upon the waters,
Allaying both their fury and my passion
With its sweet air. Thence I have followed it
(Or it hath drawn me, rather) but 'tis gone.
No, it begins again.

ARIEL [*Sings.*]
    Full fathom five thy father lies,
    Of his bones are coral made;
    Those are pearls that were his eyes,
    Nothing of him that doth fade
    But doth suffer a sea-change
    Into something rich and strange.
    Sea nymphs hourly ring his knell.

SPIRITS   Ding dong.
ARIEL   Hark, now I hear them.
SPIRITS   Ding dong bell.

FERDINAND
The ditty does remember my drowned father;
This is no mortal business nor no sound
That the earth owes. I hear it now above me.

PROSPERO [*to Miranda*]
The fringed curtains of thine eye advance,
And say what thou seest yond.

MIRANDA   What is't, a spirit?
Lord, how it looks about. Believe me, sir,
It carries a brave form. But 'tis a spirit.

PROSPERO
No, wench, it eats and sleeps and hath such senses
As we have – such. This gallant which thou seest
Was in the wreck, and but he's something stained
With grief (that's beauty's canker) thou mightst call
   him
A goodly person. He hath lost his fellows
And strays about to find 'em.

MIRANDA   I might call him
A thing divine, for nothing natural
I ever saw so noble.

PROSPERO [*aside*]   It goes on, I see,
As my soul prompts it. [*to Ariel*] Spirit, fine spirit, I'll
   free thee
Within two days for this.

FERDINAND   Most sure the goddess
On whom these airs attend! – Vouchsafe my prayer
May know if you remain upon this island,
And that you will some good instruction give
How I may bear me here. My prime request,
Which I do last pronounce, is (O, you wonder!)
If you be maid or no?

MIRANDA   No wonder, sir,
But certainly a maid.

FERDINAND   My language? Heavens!
I am the best of them that speak this speech,
Were I but where 'tis spoken.

PROSPERO   How? The best?

What wert thou if the King of Naples heard thee?

FERDINAND   A single thing, as I am now, that wonders
To hear thee speak of Naples. He does hear me,
And that he does, I weep. Myself am Naples,
Who, with mine eyes, never since at ebb, beheld
The King my father wrecked.

MIRANDA   Alack, for mercy!

FERDINAND
Yes, faith, and all his lords – the Duke of Milan
And his brave son being twain.

PROSPERO [*aside*]   The Duke of Milan
And his more braver daughter could control thee
If now 'twere fit to do't. At the first sight
They have changed eyes. [*to Ariel*] Delicate Ariel,
I'll set thee free for this. [*to Ferdinand*] A word, good sir;
I fear you have done yourself some wrong. A word.

MIRANDA [*aside*]
Why speaks my father so ungently? This
Is the third man that e'er I saw, the first
That e'er I sighed for. Pity move my father
To be inclined my way.

FERDINAND   O, if a virgin,
And your affection not gone forth, I'll make you
The Queen of Naples.

PROSPERO   Soft, sir, one word more.
[*aside*] They are both in either's powers, but this swift
   business
I must uneasy make, lest too light winning
Make the prize light. [*to Ferdinand*] One word more. I
   charge thee
That thou attend me. Thou dost here usurp
The name thou ow'st not and hast put thyself
Upon this island as a spy, to win it
From me, the lord on't.

FERDINAND   No, as I am a man.

MIRANDA
There's nothing ill can dwell in such a temple.
If the ill spirit have so fair a house,
Good things will strive to dwell with't.

PROSPERO [*to Ferdinand*]   Follow me. –
Speak not you for him; he's a traitor. – Come,
I'll manacle thy neck and feet together;
Sea water shalt thou drink; thy food shall be
The fresh-brook mussels, withered roots, and husks
Wherein the acorn cradled. Follow!

FERDINAND   No,
I will resist such entertainment till
Mine enemy has more power.

[*He draws and is charmed from moving.*]

MIRANDA   O dear father,
Make not too rash a trial of him, for
He's gentle and not fearful.

PROSPERO   What, I say,
My foot my tutor? Put thy sword up, traitor,
Who mak'st a show but dar'st not strike, thy conscience
Is so possessed with guilt. Come from thy ward,
For I can here disarm thee with this stick

And make thy weapon drop.

MIRANDA   Beseech you, father –

PROSPERO   Hence; hang not on my garments.

475   MIRANDA   Sir, have pity;
I'll be his surety.

PROSPERO   Silence! One word more
Shall make me chide thee, if not hate thee. What,
An advocate for an impostor? Hush.
Thou think'st there is no more such shapes as he,
480   Having seen but him and Caliban. Foolish wench,
To th' most of men, this is a Caliban,
And they to him are angels.

MIRANDA   My affections
Are then most humble. I have no ambition
To see a goodlier man.

PROSPERO [*to Ferdinand*]   Come on, obey:
485   Thy nerves are in their infancy again
And have no vigour in them.

FERDINAND   So they are!
My spirits, as in a dream, are all bound up.
My father's loss, the weakness which I feel,
The wreck of all my friends, nor this man's threats
490   (To whom I am subdued) are but light to me,
Might I but through my prison once a day
Behold this maid. All corners else o'th' earth
Let liberty make use of; space enough
Have I in such a prison.

PROSPERO [*aside*]   It works. [*to Ferdinand*] Come on. –
495   Thou hast done well, fine Ariel. – Follow me; –
Hark what thou else shalt do me.

MIRANDA [*to Ferdinand*]   Be of comfort;
My father's of a better nature, sir,
Than he appears by speech. This is unwonted
Which now came from him.

PROSPERO [*to Ariel*]   Thou shalt be as free
500   As mountain winds, but then exactly do
All points of my command.

ARIEL   To th' syllable.

PROSPERO [*to Ferdinand*]
Come, follow; – speak not for him.   *Exeunt.*

2.1   *Enter* ALONSO, SEBASTIAN, ANTONIO,
GONZALO, ADRIAN, FRANCISCO *and others.*

GONZALO   Beseech you, sir, be merry. You have cause
(So have we all) of joy, for our escape
Is much beyond our loss. Our hint of woe
Is common: every day some sailor's wife,
5   The masters of some merchant, and the merchant,
Have just our theme of woe. But for the miracle,
I mean our preservation, few in millions
Can speak like us. Then wisely, good sir, weigh
Our sorrow with our comfort.

ALONSO   Prithee, peace.

10   SEBASTIAN [*to Antonio*]   He receives comfort like cold
porridge.

ANTONIO [*to Sebastian*]   The visitor will not give him
o'er so.

SEBASTIAN   Look, he's winding up the watch of his wit;
by and by it will strike –   15

GONZALO [*to Alonso*]   Sir –

SEBASTIAN   One. Tell.

GONZALO   When every grief is entertained that's
offered, comes to th'entertainer –

SEBASTIAN   A dollar.   20

GONZALO   Dolour comes to him, indeed. You have
spoken truer than you purposed.

SEBASTIAN   You have taken it wiselier than I meant you
should.

GONZALO   Therefore, my lord –   25

ANTONIO   Fie, what a spendthrift is he of his tongue!

ALONSO   I prithee, spare.

GONZALO   Well, I have done; but yet –

SEBASTIAN   He will be talking.

ANTONIO   Which, of he or Adrian, for a good wager,   30
first begins to crow?

SEBASTIAN   The old cock.

ANTONIO   The cockerel.

SEBASTIAN   Done! The wager?

ANTONIO   A laughter.   35

SEBASTIAN   A match!

ADRIAN   Though this island seem to be desert –

ANTONIO   Ha, ha, ha.

SEBASTIAN   So, you're paid.

ADRIAN   Uninhabitable and almost inaccessible –   40

SEBASTIAN   Yet –

ADRIAN   Yet –

ANTONIO   He could not miss't.

ADRIAN   It must needs be of subtle, tender and delicate
temperance.   45

ANTONIO   Temperance was a delicate wench.

SEBASTIAN   Ay, and a subtle, as he most learnedly
delivered.

ADRIAN   The air breathes upon us here most sweetly.

SEBASTIAN   As if it had lungs, and rotten ones.   50

ANTONIO   Or, as 'twere perfumed by a fen.

GONZALO   Here is everything advantageous to life.

ANTONIO   True, save means to live.

SEBASTIAN   Of that there's none, or little.

GONZALO   How lush and lusty the grass looks! How   55
green!

ANTONIO   The ground indeed is tawny.

SEBASTIAN   With an eye of green in't.

ANTONIO   He misses not much.

SEBASTIAN   No; he doth but mistake the truth totally.   60

GONZALO   But the rarity of it is, which is indeed almost
beyond credit –

SEBASTIAN   As many vouched rarities are.

GONZALO   That our garments being, as they were,
drenched in the sea, hold notwithstanding their   65
freshness and gloss, being rather new-dyed than
stained with salt water.

ANTONIO   If but one of his pockets could speak, would it not say he lies?

70 SEBASTIAN   Ay, or very falsely pocket up his report.

GONZALO   Methinks our garments are now as fresh as when we put them on first in Africa, at the marriage of the King's fair daughter Claribel to the King of Tunis.

SEBASTIAN   'Twas a sweet marriage, and we prosper
75   well in our return.

ADRIAN   Tunis was never graced before with such a paragon to their queen.

GONZALO   Not since widow Dido's time.

ANTONIO   Widow? A pox o'that. How came that widow
80   in? Widow Dido!

SEBASTIAN   What if he had said widower Aeneas too? Good lord, how you take it!

ADRIAN   Widow Dido, said you? You make me study of that. She was of Carthage, not of Tunis.

85 GONZALO   This Tunis, sir, was Carthage.

ADRIAN   Carthage?

GONZALO   I assure you, Carthage.

ANTONIO   His word is more than the miraculous harp.

SEBASTIAN   He hath raised the wall, and houses too.

90 ANTONIO   What impossible matter will he make easy next?

SEBASTIAN   I think he will carry this island home in his pocket and give it his son for an apple.

ANTONIO   And sowing the kernels of it in the sea, bring
95   forth more islands!

GONZALO   I —

ANTONIO   Why, in good time.

GONZALO   Sir, we were talking that our garments seem now as fresh as when we were at Tunis at the marriage
100   of your daughter, who is now Queen.

ANTONIO   And the rarest that e'er came there.

SEBASTIAN   Bate, I beseech you, widow Dido.

ANTONIO   O, widow Dido? Ay, widow Dido.

GONZALO   Is not, sir, my doublet as fresh as the first day
105   I wore it? I mean, in a sort.

ANTONIO   That sort was well fished for.

GONZALO   When I wore it at your daughter's marriage.

ALONSO   You cram these words into mine ears, against The stomach of my sense. Would I had never
110   Married my daughter there, for coming thence My son is lost and (in my rate) she too, Who is so far from Italy removed I ne'er again shall see her. O thou mine heir Of Naples and of Milan, what strange fish Hath made his meal on thee?

115 FRANCISCO   Sir, he may live. I saw him beat the surges under him And ride upon their backs. He trod the water, Whose enmity he flung aside, and breasted The surge most swoll'n that met him. His bold head
120   'Bove the contentious waves he kept and oared Himself with his good arms in lusty stroke To th' shore, that o'er his wave-worn basis bowed, As stooping to relieve him. I not doubt

He came alive to land.

ALONSO   No, no, he's gone.

SEBASTIAN
  Sir, you may thank yourself for this great loss,   125
  That would not bless our Europe with your daughter
  But rather loose her to an African,
  Where she at least is banished from your eye,
  Who hath cause to wet the grief on't.

ALONSO   Prithee, peace.

SEBASTIAN
  You were kneeled to and importuned otherwise   130
  By all of us, and the fair soul herself
  Weighed between loathness and obedience, at
  Which end o'th' beam should bow. We have lost your son,
  I fear, for ever. Milan and Naples have
  More widows in them of this business' making   135
  Than we bring men to comfort them.
  The fault's your own.

ALONSO   So is the dear'st o'th' loss.

GONZALO   My lord Sebastian,
  The truth you speak doth lack some gentleness,
  And time to speak it in. You rub the sore   140
  When you should bring the plaster.

SEBASTIAN   Very well.

ANTONIO   And most chirurgeonly!

GONZALO   It is foul weather in us all, good sir,
  When you are cloudy.

SEBASTIAN   Foul weather?

ANTONIO   Very foul.

GONZALO   Had I plantation of this isle, my lord –   145

ANTONIO   He'd sow't with nettle-seed.

SEBASTIAN   Or docks, or mallows.

GONZALO   And were the king on't, what would I do?

SEBASTIAN   'Scape being drunk, for want of wine.

GONZALO   I'th' commonwealth I would by contraries
  Execute all things, for no kind of traffic   150
  Would I admit; no name of magistrate;
  Letters should not be known; riches, poverty
  And use of service, none; contract, succession,
  Bourn, bound of land, tilth, vineyard – none;
  No use of metal, corn, or wine or oil;   155
  No occupation, all men idle, all;
  And women, too, but innocent and pure;
  No sovereignty –

SEBASTIAN   Yet he would be king on't.

ANTONIO   The latter end of his commonwealth forgets
  the beginning.   160

GONZALO
  All things in common nature should produce
  Without sweat or endeavour; treason, felony,
  Sword, pike, knife, gun, or need of any engine
  Would I not have; but nature should bring forth
  Of its own kind all foison, all abundance,   165
  To feed my innocent people.

SEBASTIAN   No marrying 'mong his subjects?

ANTONIO   None, man, all idle – whores and knaves.

GONZALO   I would with such perfection govern, sir,
170   T'excel the Golden Age.
SEBASTIAN   'Save his majesty!
ANTONIO   Long live Gonzalo!
GONZALO   And – do you mark me, sir? –
ALONSO   Prithee, no more.
Thou dost talk nothing to me.
GONZALO   I do well believe your highness, and did it to
175   minister occasion to these gentlemen, who are of such
sensible and nimble lungs that they always use to laugh
at nothing.
ANTONIO   'Twas you we laughed at.
GONZALO   Who, in this kind of merry fooling, am
180   nothing to you, so you may continue and laugh at
nothing still.
ANTONIO   What a blow was there given!
SEBASTIAN   An it had not fallen flat-long.
GONZALO   You are gentlemen of brave mettle. You
185   would lift the moon out of her sphere, if she would
continue in it five weeks without changing.

Enter ARIEL *playing solemn music.*

SEBASTIAN   We would so, and then go a bat-fowling.
ANTONIO   Nay, good my lord, be not angry.
GONZALO   No, I warrant you, I will not adventure my
190   discretion so weakly. Will you laugh me asleep, for I am
very heavy.
ANTONIO   Go sleep, and hear us.
        [*All sleep except Alonso, Sebastian and Antonio.*]
ALONSO   What, all so soon asleep? I wish mine eyes
Would, with themselves, shut up my thoughts. I find
They are inclined to do so.
195   SEBASTIAN   Please you, sir,
Do not omit the heavy offer of it.
It seldom visits sorrow; when it doth,
It is a comforter.
ANTONIO   We two, my lord,
Will guard your person while you take your rest,
And watch your safety.
200   ALONSO   Thank you. Wondrous heavy.
                              Alonso sleeps. Exit Ariel.
SEBASTIAN   What a strange drowsiness possesses them!
ANTONIO   It is the quality o'th' climate.
SEBASTIAN   Why
Doth it not then our eyelids sink? I find not
Myself disposed to sleep.
ANTONIO   Nor I. My spirits are nimble.
205   They fell together all, as by consent;
They dropped, as by a thunderstroke. What might,
Worthy Sebastian, O, what might – ? No more;
And yet, methinks I see it in thy face
What thou shouldst be. Th'occasion speaks thee, and
210   My strong imagination sees a crown
Dropping upon thy head.
SEBASTIAN   What, art thou waking?
ANTONIO   Do you not hear me speak?
SEBASTIAN   I do, and surely

It is a sleepy language, and thou speak'st
Out of thy sleep. What is it thou didst say?
This is a strange repose, to be asleep   215
With eyes wide open – standing, speaking, moving,
And yet so fast asleep.
ANTONIO   Noble Sebastian,
Thou let'st thy fortune sleep – die rather; wink'st
Whiles thou art waking.
SEBASTIAN   Thou dost snore distinctly.
There's meaning in thy snores.   220
ANTONIO   I am more serious than my custom. You
Must be so too, if heed me, which to do
Trebles thee o'er.
SEBASTIAN   Well, I am standing water.
ANTONIO   I'll teach you how to flow.
SEBASTIAN   Do so. To ebb
Hereditary sloth instructs me.
ANTONIO   O,   225
If you but knew how you the purpose cherish
Whiles thus you mock it, how in stripping it
You more invest it. Ebbing men, indeed,
Most often do so near the bottom run
By their own fear or sloth.
SEBASTIAN   Prithee, say on;   230
The setting of thine eye and cheek proclaim
A matter from thee, and a birth, indeed,
Which throes thee much to yield.
ANTONIO   Thus, sir:
Although this lord of weak remembrance – this
Who shall be of as little memory   235
When he is earthed – hath here almost persuaded
(For he's a spirit of persuasion, only
Professes to persuade) the King his son's alive,
'Tis as impossible that he's undrowned
As he that sleeps here swims.
SEBASTIAN   I have no hope   240
That he's undrowned.
ANTONIO   O, out of that 'no hope',
What great hope have you! No hope that way is
Another way so high a hope that even
Ambition cannot pierce a wink beyond,
But doubt discovery there. Will you grant with me   245
That Ferdinand is drowned?
SEBASTIAN   He's gone.
ANTONIO   Then tell me,
Who's the next heir of Naples?
SEBASTIAN   Claribel.
ANTONIO   She that is Queen of Tunis; she that dwells
Ten leagues beyond man's life; she that from Naples
Can have no note unless the sun were post –   250
The man i'th' moon's too slow – till newborn chins
Be rough and razorable; she that from whom
We all were sea-swallowed, though some cast again,
And by that destiny to perform an act
Whereof what's past is prologue, what to come   255
In yours and my discharge!
SEBASTIAN   What stuff is this? How say you?

'Tis true my brother's daughter's Queen of Tunis,
So is she heir of Naples, 'twixt which regions
There is some space.

260 ANTONIO   A space whose every cubit
Seems to cry out, 'How shall that Claribel
Measure us back to Naples? Keep in Tunis,
And let Sebastian wake.' Say this were death
That now hath seized them; why, they were no worse
265 Than now they are. There be that can rule Naples
As well as he that sleeps; lords that can prate
As amply and unnecessarily
As this Gonzalo. I myself could make
A chough of as deep chat. O that you bore
270 The mind that I do! What a sleep were this
For your advancement! Do you understand me?

SEBASTIAN   Methinks I do.

ANTONIO   And how does your content
Tender your own good fortune?

SEBASTIAN   I remember
You did supplant your brother Prospero.

ANTONIO   True:
275 And look how well my garments sit upon me
Much feater than before. My brother's servants
Were then my fellows; now they are my men.

SEBASTIAN   But for your conscience?

ANTONIO   Ay, sir, where lies that? If 'twere a kibe
280 'Twould put me to my slipper, but I feel not
This deity in my bosom. Twenty consciences
That stand 'twixt me and Milan, candied be they
And melt ere they molest! Here lies your brother,
No better than the earth he lies upon.
285 If he were that which now he's like (that's dead)
Whom I with this obedient steel – three inches of it –
Can lay to bed forever (whiles you, doing thus,
To the perpetual wink for aye might put
This ancient morsel, this Sir Prudence, who
290 Should not upbraid our course) – for all the rest
They'll take suggestion as a cat laps milk;
They'll tell the clock to any business that
We say befits the hour.

SEBASTIAN   Thy case, dear friend,
Shall be my precedent. As thou got'st Milan,
295 I'll come by Naples. Draw thy sword! One stroke
Shall free thee from the tribute which thou payest,
And I the king shall love thee.

ANTONIO   Draw together,
And when I rear my hand, do you the like
To fall it on Gonzalo.

SEBASTIAN   O, but one word –

Enter ARIEL *with music and song.*

ARIEL
300 My master through his art foresees the danger
That you, his friend, are in, and sends me forth
(For else his project dies) to keep them living.
[*Sings in Gonzalo's ear.*]
While you here do snoring lie,

Open-eyed conspiracy
His time doth take.   305
If of life you keep a care,
Shake off slumber and beware.
Awake, awake!

ANTONIO   Then let us both be sudden.

GONZALO [*Wakes.*]
Now, good angels preserve the King!   310

ALONSO [*Wakes.*]
Why, how now, ho! Awake! Why are you drawn?
Wherefore this ghastly looking?

GONZALO   What's the matter?

SEBASTIAN
Whiles we stood here securing your repose,
Even now we heard a hollow burst of bellowing,
Like bulls, or rather lions. Did't not wake you?   315
It struck mine ear most terribly.

ALONSO   I heard nothing.

ANTONIO   O, 'twas a din to fright a monster's ear –
To make an earthquake! Sure it was the roar
Of a whole herd of lions.

ALONSO   Heard you this, Gonzalo?

GONZALO   Upon mine honour, sir, I heard a humming,   320
And that a strange one too, which did awake me.
I shaked you, sir, and cried. As mine eyes opened,
I saw their weapons drawn. There was a noise,
That's verily. 'Tis best we stand upon our guard,
Or that we quit this place. Let's draw our weapons.   325

ALONSO
Lead off this ground, and let's make further search
For my poor son.

GONZALO   Heavens keep him from these beasts,
For he is, sure, i'th' island.

ALONSO   Lead away.

ARIEL   Prospero, my lord, shall know what I have done;
So, King, go safely on to seek thy son.   *Exeunt.*   330

2.2   *Enter* CALIBAN, *with a burden of wood;*
a noise of thunder heard.

CALIBAN   All the infections that the sun sucks up
From bogs, fens, flats, on Prosper fall, and make him
By inchmeal a disease! His spirits hear me,
And yet I needs must curse. But they'll nor pinch,
Fright me with urchin-shows, pitch me i'th' mire,   5
Nor lead me, like a firebrand in the dark,
Out of my way unless he bid 'em. But
For every trifle are they set upon me:
Sometime like apes that mow and chatter at me
And after bite me, then like hedgehogs which   10
Lie tumbling in my barefoot way and mount
Their pricks at my footfall. Sometime am I
All wound with adders, who with cloven tongues
Do hiss me into madness. Lo now, lo,

Enter TRINCULO.

Here comes a spirit of his, and to torment me   15

For bringing wood in slowly. I'll fall flat;
Perchance he will not mind me.

TRINCULO   Here's neither bush nor shrub to bear off
any weather at all, and another storm brewing; I hear
it sing i'th' wind. Yond same black cloud, yond huge
one, looks like a foul bombard that would shed his
liquor. If it should thunder as it did before, I know
not where to hide my head. Yond same cloud cannot
choose but fall by pailfuls. [*Sees Caliban.*] What have
we here, a man or a fish? Dead or alive? A fish: he
smells like a fish, a very ancient and fish-like smell, a
kind of – not of the newest – poor-John. A strange
fish! Were I in England now (as once I was) and had
but this fish painted, not a holiday fool there but
would give a piece of silver. There would this monster
make a man; any strange beast there makes a man.
When they will not give a doit to relieve a lame beggar,
they will lay out ten to see a dead Indian. Legged like a
man and his fins like arms! Warm, o'my troth! I do now
let loose my opinion, hold it no longer: this is no fish,
but an islander that hath lately suffered by a
thunderbolt. Alas, the storm is come again. My best
way is to creep under his gaberdine; there is no other
shelter hereabout. Misery acquaints a man with
strange bedfellows! I will here shroud till the dregs
of the storm be past.

Enter STEPHANO *singing.*

STEPHANO   I shall no more to sea, to sea,
 Here shall I die ashore.
This is a very scurvy tune to sing at a man's funeral.
Well, here's my comfort.
 [*Drinks and then sings.*]
 The master, the swabber, the boatswain and I;
  The gunner and his mate,
 Loved Mall, Meg, and Marian, and Margery,
  But none of us cared for Kate.
 For she had a tongue with a tang,
 Would cry to a sailor, 'Go hang!'
 She loved not the savour of tar nor of pitch,
 Yet a tailor might scratch her where'er she did itch.
 Then to sea, boys, and let her go hang!
This is a scurvy tune too, but here's my comfort.
 [*Drinks.*]

CALIBAN   Do not torment me! O!

STEPHANO   What's the matter? Have we devils here?
Do you put tricks upon's with savages and men of
Ind? Ha! I have not 'scaped drowning to be afeard now
of your four legs; for it hath been said, 'As proper a
man as ever went on four legs cannot make him give
ground'. And it shall be said so again while Stephano
breathes at' nostrils.

CALIBAN   The spirit torments me! O!

STEPHANO   This is some monster of the isle, with four
legs, who hath got, as I take it, an ague. Where the devil
should he learn our language? I will give him some
relief, if it be but for that. If I can recover him and keep

him tame, and get to Naples with him, he's a present
for any emperor that ever trod on neat's leather.

CALIBAN   Do not torment me, prithee. I'll bring my
wood home faster.

STEPHANO   He's in his fit now and does not talk after
the wisest. He shall taste of my bottle; if he have never
drunk wine afore, it will go near to remove his fit. If I
can recover him and keep him tame, I will not take too
much for him! He shall pay for him that hath him, and
that soundly.

CALIBAN   Thou dost me yet but little hurt. Thou wilt
anon, I know it by thy trembling. Now Prosper works
upon thee.

STEPHANO   Come on your ways; open your mouth.
Here is that which will give language to you, cat. Open
your mouth! This will shake your shaking, I can tell
you, and that soundly. [*Pours into Caliban's mouth.*] You
cannot tell who's your friend. Open your chaps again.

TRINCULO   I should know that voice. It should be – but
he is drowned, and these are devils. O, defend me!

STEPHANO   Four legs and two voices – a most delicate
monster! His forward voice now is to speak well of his
friend; his backward voice is to utter foul speeches and
to detract. If all the wine in my bottle will recover him,
I will help his ague. Come. Amen! I will pour some in
thy other mouth.

TRINCULO   Stephano!

STEPHANO   Doth thy other mouth call me? Mercy,
mercy! This is a devil and no monster. I will leave him;
I have no long spoon.

TRINCULO   Stephano? If thou be'st Stephano, touch me
and speak to me, for I am Trinculo! Be not afeard – thy
good friend Trinculo.

STEPHANO   If thou be'st Trinculo, come forth. I'll pull
thee by the lesser legs. If any be Trinculo's legs, these
are they. [*Pulls him from under the cloak.*] Thou art very
Trinculo indeed! How cam'st thou to be the siege of
this mooncalf? Can he vent Trinculos?

TRINCULO   I took him to be killed with a thunderstroke.
But art thou not drowned, Stephano? I hope now thou
art not drowned. Is the storm overblown? I hid me
under the dead mooncalf's gaberdine for fear of the
storm. And art thou living, Stephano? O Stephano,
two Neapolitans 'scaped?

STEPHANO   Prithee, do not turn me about; my stomach
is not constant.

CALIBAN
These be fine things, an if they be not sprites;
That's a brave god and bears celestial liquor.
I will kneel to him.

STEPHANO   How didst thou scape? How cam'st thou
hither? Swear by this bottle how thou cam'st hither. I
escaped upon a butt of sack, which the sailors heaved
o'erboard – by this bottle, which I made of the bark of
a tree with mine own hands since I was cast ashore.

CALIBAN   I'll swear upon that bottle to be thy true
subject, for the liquor is not earthly.

125 STEPHANO   Here, swear then how thou escaped'st.

TRINCULO   Swum ashore, man, like a duck. I can swim
     like a duck, I'll be sworn.

STEPHANO   Here, kiss the book. [*Trinculo drinks.*]
     Though thou canst swim like a duck, thou art made
130 like a goose.

TRINCULO   O Stephano, hast any more of this?

STEPHANO   The whole butt, man. My cellar is in a rock
     by th' seaside, where my wine is hid. How now,
     mooncalf, how does thine ague?

135 CALIBAN   Hast thou not dropped from heaven?

STEPHANO   Out o'th' moon, I do assure thee. I was the
     man i'th' moon when time was.

CALIBAN
     I have seen thee in her, and I do adore thee!
     My mistress showed me thee, and thy dog and thy bush.

140 STEPHANO   Come, swear to that. Kiss the book. I will
     furnish it anon with new contents. Swear! [*Caliban
     drinks.*]

TRINCULO   By this good light, this is a very shallow
     monster. I afeard of him? A very weak monster. The
     man i'th' moon? A most poor credulous monster! Well
145 drawn, monster, in good sooth.

CALIBAN   I'll show thee every fertile inch o'th' island,
     And I will kiss thy foot. I prithee, be my god.

TRINCULO   By this light, a most perfidious and drunken
     monster; when's god's asleep, he'll rob his bottle.

150 CALIBAN   I'll kiss thy foot. I'll swear myself thy subject.

STEPHANO   Come on, then, down and swear.

TRINCULO   I shall laugh myself to death at this puppy-
     headed monster. A most scurvy monster. I could find
     in my heart to beat him –

155 STEPHANO   Come, kiss.

TRINCULO   But that the poor monster's in drink. An
     abominable monster!

CALIBAN
     I'll show thee the best springs; I'll pluck thee berries;
     I'll fish for thee, and get thee wood enough.
160 A plague upon the tyrant that I serve!
     I'll bear him no more sticks but follow thee,
     Thou wondrous man.

TRINCULO   A most ridiculous monster – to make a
     wonder of a poor drunkard!

165 CALIBAN   I prithee, let me bring thee where crabs grow,
     And I with my long nails will dig thee pignuts,
     Show thee a jay's nest, and instruct thee how
     To snare the nimble marmoset. I'll bring thee
     To clust'ring filberts, and sometimes I'll get thee
170 Young scamels from the rock. Wilt thou go with me?

STEPHANO   I prithee, now, lead the way without any
     more talking. Trinculo, the King and all our company
     else being drowned, we will inherit here. Here, bear
     my bottle. Fellow Trinculo, we'll fill him by and by
175 again.

CALIBAN [*Sings drunkenly.*]
     Farewell, master; farewell, farewell!

TRINCULO   A howling monster, a drunken monster!

CALIBAN
     No more dams I'll make for fish,
     Nor fetch in firing at requiring,
     Nor scrape trenchering, nor wash dish.   180
     Ban' ban' Ca-caliban,
     Has a new master, get a new man.
     Freedom, high-day; high-day freedom; freedom
     highday, freedom.

STEPHANO   O brave monster, lead the way.   *Exeunt.*   185

3.1   *Enter* FERDINAND, *bearing a log.*

FERDINAND
     There be some sports are painful, and their labour
     Delight in them sets off. Some kinds of baseness
     Are nobly undergone; and most poor matters
     Point to rich ends. This my mean task
     Would be as heavy to me as odious, but   5
     The mistress which I serve quickens what's dead,
     And makes my labours pleasures. O, she is
     Ten times more gentle than her father's crabbed,
     And he's composed of harshness. I must remove
     Some thousands of these logs and pile them up,   10
     Upon a sore injunction. My sweet mistress
     Weeps when she sees me work and says such baseness
     Had never like executor. I forget;
     But these sweet thoughts do even refresh my labours
     Most busiest when I do it.

Enter MIRANDA, *and* PROSPERO *at a distance, unseen.*

MIRANDA   Alas now, pray you,   15
     Work not so hard. I would the lightning had
     Burnt up those logs that you are enjoined to pile!
     Pray set it down and rest you. When this burns,
     'Twill weep for having wearied you. My father
     Is hard at study; pray now, rest yourself.   20
     He's safe for these three hours.

FERDINAND   O most dear mistress,
     The sun will set before I shall discharge
     What I must strive to do.

MIRANDA   If you'll sit down,
     I'll bear your logs the while. Pray give me that;
     I'll carry it to the pile.

FERDINAND   No, precious creature,   25
     I had rather crack my sinews, break my back,
     Than you should such dishonour undergo
     While I sit lazy by.

MIRANDA   It would become me
     As well as it does you, and I should do it
     With much more ease, for my good will is to it,   30
     And yours it is against.

PROSPERO [*aside*]   Poor worm, thou art infected!
     This visitation shows it.

MIRANDA   You look wearily.

FERDINAND
     No, noble mistress, 'tis fresh morning with me
     When you are by at night. I do beseech you –

35 Chiefly that I might set it in my prayers –
What is your name?
MIRANDA   Miranda. – O my father,
I have broke your hest to say so!
FERDINAND   Admired Miranda!
Indeed the top of admiration, worth
What's dearest to the world! Full many a lady
40 I have eyed with best regard, and many a time
Th' harmony of their tongues hath into bondage
Brought my too diligent ear. For several virtues
Have I liked several women; never any
With so full soul but some defect in her
45 Did quarrel with the noblest grace she owed
And put it to the foil. But you, O you,
So perfect and so peerless, are created
Of every creature's best.
MIRANDA   I do not know
One of my sex, no woman's face remember –
50 Save, from my glass, mine own. Nor have I seen
More that I may call men than you, good friend,
And my dear father. How features are abroad
I am skilless of, but by my modesty
(The jewel in my dower), I would not wish
55 Any companion in the world but you,
Nor can imagination form a shape,
Besides yourself, to like of. But I prattle
Something too wildly, and my father's precepts
I therein do forget.
FERDINAND   I am, in my condition,
60 A prince, Miranda; I do think a king
(I would not so!) and would no more endure
This wooden slavery than to suffer
The flesh-fly blow my mouth! Hear my soul speak:
The very instant that I saw you did
65 My heart fly to your service, there resides
To make me slave to it, and for your sake
Am I this patient log-man.
MIRANDA   Do you love me?
FERDINAND
O heaven, O earth, bear witness to this sound,
And crown what I profess with kind event
70 If I speak true; if hollowly, invert
What best is boded me to mischief! I,
Beyond all limit of what else i'th' world,
Do love, prize, honour you.
MIRANDA   I am a fool
To weep at what I am glad of.
PROSPERO [*aside*]   Fair encounter
75 Of two most rare affections! Heavens rain grace
On that which breeds between 'em.
FERDINAND   Wherefore weep you?
MIRANDA   At mine unworthiness that dare not offer
What I desire to give, and much less take
What I shall die to want. But this is trifling,
80 And all the more it seeks to hide itself,
The bigger bulk it shows. Hence, bashful cunning,
And prompt me, plain and holy innocence!

I am your wife, if you will marry me;
If not, I'll die your maid. To be your fellow
You may deny me, but I'll be your servant   85
Whether you will or no.
FERDINAND   My mistress, dearest,
And I thus humble ever.
MIRANDA   My husband, then?
FERDINAND   Ay, with a heart as willing
As bondage e'er of freedom. Here's my hand.
MIRANDA
And mine, with my heart in't. And now farewell   90
Till half an hour hence.
FERDINAND   A thousand thousand!
                    Exeunt Miranda and Ferdinand.
PROSPERO   So glad of this as they I cannot be,
Who are surprised withal, but my rejoicing
At nothing can be more. I'll to my book,
For yet ere suppertime must I perform   95
Much business appertaining.   *Exit.*

3.2   *Enter* CALIBAN, STEPHANO *and* TRINCULO.

STEPHANO   Tell not me. When the butt is out, we will
drink water; not a drop before. Therefore bear up and
board 'em. Servant monster, drink to me.
TRINCULO   Servant monster? The folly of this island!
They say there's but five upon this isle; we are three of   5
them. If th'other two be brained like us, the state totters.
STEPHANO   Drink, servant monster, when I bid thee.
Thy eyes are almost set in thy head.
TRINCULO   Where should they be set else? He were a
brave monster, indeed, if they were set in his tail.   10
STEPHANO   My man-monster hath drowned his tongue
in sack. For my part, the sea cannot drown me. I swam,
ere I could recover the shore, five and thirty leagues off
and on. By this light, thou shalt be my lieutenant,
monster, or my standard.   15
TRINCULO   Your lieutenant, if you list; he's no standard.
STEPHANO   We'll not run, Monsieur Monster.
TRINCULO   Nor go, neither; but you'll lie like dogs and
yet say nothing, neither.
STEPHANO   Mooncalf, speak once in thy life, if thou   20
be'st a good mooncalf.
CALIBAN   How does thy honour? Let me lick thy shoe.
I'll not serve him; he is not valiant.
TRINCULO   Thou liest, most ignorant monster. I am in
case to jostle a constable. Why thou deboshed fish,   25
thou, was there ever man a coward that hath drunk so
much sack as I today? Wilt thou tell a monstrous lie,
being but half a fish and half a monster?
CALIBAN   Lo, how he mocks me. Wilt thou let him, my
lord?   30
TRINCULO   'Lord', quoth he? That a monster should be
such a natural!
CALIBAN   Lo, lo again! Bite him to death, I prithee.
STEPHANO   Trinculo, keep a good tongue in your head.
If you prove a mutineer – the next tree! The poor   35

monster's my subject, and he shall not suffer indignity.

CALIBAN   I thank my noble lord. Wilt thou be pleased to
hearken once again to the suit I made to thee?

STEPHANO   Marry, will I. Kneel and repeat it; I will
40 stand, and so shall Trinculo.

Enter ARIEL, *invisible.*

CALIBAN   As I told thee before, I am subject to a tyrant,
A sorcerer, that by his cunning hath
Cheated me of the island.

ARIEL [*in Trinculo's voice*]   Thou liest.

CALIBAN   Thou liest, thou jesting monkey, thou.
45 I would my valiant master would destroy thee.
I do not lie.

STEPHANO   Trinculo, if you trouble him any more in's
tale, by this hand, I will supplant some of your teeth.

TRINCULO   Why, I said nothing.

50 STEPHANO   Mum, then, and no more. Proceed.

CALIBAN   I say, by sorcery he got this isle.
From me he got it. If thy greatness will
Revenge it on him – for I know thou dar'st,
But this thing dare not –

55 STEPHANO   That's most certain.

CALIBAN   Thou shalt be lord of it, and I'll serve thee.

STEPHANO   How now shall this be compassed? Canst
thou bring me to the party?

CALIBAN   Yea, yea, my lord, I'll yield him thee asleep,
60 Where thou mayst knock a nail into his head.

ARIEL [*in Trinculo's voice*]   Thou liest, thou canst not.

CALIBAN
What a pied ninny's this? Thou scurvy patch!
I do beseech thy greatness, give him blows,
And take his bottle from him. When that's gone,
65 He shall drink nought but brine, for I'll not show him
Where the quick freshes are.

STEPHANO   Trinculo, run into no further danger.
Interrupt the monster one word further, and by this
hand I'll turn my mercy out o'doors and make a
70 stockfish of thee.

TRINCULO   Why, what did I? I did nothing. I'll go
farther off.

STEPHANO   Didst thou not say he lied?

ARIEL [*in Trinculo's voice*]   Thou liest.

75 STEPHANO   Do I so? Take thou that! [*Hits Trinculo.*] As
you like this, give me the lie another time!

TRINCULO   I did not give thee the lie. Out o'your wits
and hearing too? A pox o'your bottle! This can sack
and drinking do. A murrain on your monster, and the
80 devil take your fingers.

CALIBAN   Ha, ha, ha!

STEPHANO   Now, forward with your tale. [*to Trinculo*]
Prithee, stand farther off.

CALIBAN   Beat him enough; after a little time,
85 I'll beat him too.

STEPHANO [*to Trinculo*]   Stand farther. [*to Caliban*]
Come, proceed.

CALIBAN   Why, as I told thee, 'tis a custom with him
I'th' afternoon to sleep. There thou mayst brain him,

Having first seized his books, or with a log   90
Batter his skull, or paunch him with a stake,
Or cut his wezand with thy knife. Remember
First to possess his books, for without them
He's but a sot, as I am, nor hath not
One spirit to command. They all do hate him   95
As rootedly as I. Burn but his books.
He has brave utensils (for so he calls them)
Which, when he has a house, he'll deck withal.
And that most deeply to consider is
The beauty of his daughter; he himself   100
Calls her a nonpareil. I never saw a woman
But only Sycorax, my dam, and she;
But she as far surpasseth Sycorax
As great'st does least.

STEPHANO   Is it so brave a lass?

CALIBAN   Ay, lord, she will become thy bed, I warrant,   105
And bring thee forth brave brood.

STEPHANO   Monster, I will kill this man. His daughter
and I will be king and queen – save our graces – and
Trinculo and thyself shall be viceroys. Dost thou like
the plot, Trinculo?   110

TRINCULO   Excellent.

STEPHANO   Give me thy hand. I am sorry I beat thee,
but while thou livest, keep a good tongue in thy head.

CALIBAN   Within this half hour will he be asleep.
Wilt thou destroy him then?

STEPHANO   Ay, on mine honour.   115

ARIEL [*aside*]   This will I tell my master.

CALIBAN   Thou mak'st me merry; I am full of pleasure.
Let us be jocund. Will you troll the catch
You taught me but whilere?

STEPHANO   At thy request, monster. I will do reason,   120
any reason. Come on, Trinculo, let us sing.
[*Sings.*]   Flout 'em and scout 'em,
                And scout 'em and flout 'em,
                Thought is free.

CALIBAN   That's not the tune.   125

[*Ariel plays the tune on a tabor and pipe.*]

STEPHANO   What is this same?

TRINCULO   This is the tune of our catch, played by the
picture of Nobody.

STEPHANO   If thou be'st a man, show thyself in thy
likeness. If thou be'st a devil, take't as thou list.   130

TRINCULO   O, forgive me my sins!

STEPHANO   He that dies pays all debts. I defy thee.
Mercy upon us!

CALIBAN   Art thou afeard?

STEPHANO   No, monster, not I.   135

CALIBAN   Be not afeard. The isle is full of noises,
Sounds and sweet airs that give delight and hurt not.
Sometimes a thousand twangling instruments
Will hum about mine ears; and sometimes voices,
That if I then had waked after long sleep,   140
Will make me sleep again; and then in dreaming,
The clouds, methought, would open and show riches
Ready to drop upon me, that when I waked
I cried to dream again.

STEPHANO   This will prove a brave kingdom to me,
  where I shall have my music for nothing.

CALIBAN   When Prospero is destroyed.

STEPHANO   That shall be by and by. I remember the
  story.

TRINCULO   The sound is going away. Let's follow it,
  and after do our work.

STEPHANO   Lead, monster, we'll follow. I would I could
  see this taborer; he lays it on.

TRINCULO [*to Caliban*]   Wilt come? I'll follow Stephano.
                               Exeunt.

3.3   *Enter* ALONSO, SEBASTIAN,
          ANTONIO, GONZALO, ADRIAN,
          FRANCISCO *and others.*

GONZALO   By'r lakin, I can go no further, sir;
  My old bones aches. Here's a maze trod, indeed,
  Through forthrights and meanders! By your patience,
  I needs must rest me.

ALONSO   Old lord, I cannot blame thee,
  Who am myself attached with weariness
  To th' dulling of my spirits. Sit down and rest.
  Even here I will put off my hope and keep it
  No longer for my flatterer. He is drowned
  Whom thus we stray to find, and the sea mocks
  Our frustrate search on land. Well, let him go.

ANTONIO [*aside to Sebastian*]
  I am right glad that he's so out of hope.
  Do not, for one repulse, forgo the purpose
  That you resolved t'effect.

SEBASTIAN [*aside to Antonio*]   The next advantage
  Will we take throughly.

ANTONIO   Let it be tonight,
  For now they are oppressed with travail; they
  Will not, nor cannot, use such vigilance
  As when they are fresh.

SEBASTIAN   I say tonight. No more.

Solemn and strange music, and PROSPERO *on the top,*
invisible. Enter several strange shapes, bringing in a
banquet, and dance about it with gentle actions of
salutations, and inviting the King etc. to eat, they depart.

ALONSO
  What harmony is this? My good friends, hark!

GONZALO   Marvellous sweet music!

ALONSO
  Give us kind keepers, heavens! What were these?

SEBASTIAN   A living drollery! Now I will believe
  That there are unicorns; that in Arabia
  There is one tree, the phoenix' throne, one phoenix
  At this hour reigning there.

ANTONIO   I'll believe both;
  And what does else want credit, come to me
  And I'll be sworn 'tis true. Travellers ne'er did lie,
  Though fools at home condemn 'em.

GONZALO   If in Naples
  I should report this now, would they believe me?

If I should say I saw such islanders
(For certes, these are people of the island),
Who, though they are of monstrous shape, yet note
Their manners are more gentle, kind, than of
Our human generation you shall find
Many – nay, almost any.

PROSPERO [*aside*]   Honest lord,
Thou hast said well, for some of you there present
Are worse than devils.

ALONSO   I cannot too much muse
Such shapes, such gesture and such sound, expressing
(Although they want the use of tongue) a kind
Of excellent dumb discourse.

PROSPERO [*aside*]   Praise in departing.

FRANCISCO   They vanished strangely!

SEBASTIAN   No matter, since
They have left their viands behind, for we have
  stomachs.
Will't please you taste of what is here?

ALONSO   Not I.

GONZALO
Faith, sir, you need not fear. When we were boys,
Who would believe that there were mountaineers
Dewlapped like bulls, whose throats had hanging at 'em
Wallets of flesh? Or that there were such men
Whose heads stood in their breasts, which now we find
Each putter-out of five for one will bring us
Good warrant of?

ALONSO   I will stand to and feed,
Although my last; no matter, since I feel
The best is past. Brother, my lord the Duke,
Stand to and do as we.

Thunder and lightning. Enter ARIEL, *like a harpy,*
claps his wings upon the table, and with a quaint
device the banquet vanishes.

ARIEL   You are three men of sin, whom destiny,
That hath to instrument this lower world
And what is in't, the never-surfeited sea
Hath caused to belch up you, and on this island
Where man doth not inhabit – you 'mongst men
Being most unfit to live – I have made you mad;
And even with such-like valour, men hang and drown
Their proper selves.
  [*Alonso, Sebastian and Antonio draw their swords.*]
             You fools! I and my fellows
Are ministers of fate. The elements
Of whom your swords are tempered may as well
Wound the loud winds, or with bemocked-at stabs
Kill the still-closing waters, as diminish
One dowl that's in my plume. My fellow ministers
Are like invulnerable. If you could hurt,
Your swords are now too massy for your strengths
And will not be uplifted. But remember
(For that's my business to you) that you three
From Milan did supplant good Prospero,
Exposed unto the sea, which hath requit it,
Him and his innocent child; for which foul deed,

145

150

5

10

15

20

25

30

35

40

45

50

55

60

65

70

The powers delaying, not forgetting, have
Incensed the seas and shores – yea, all the creatures –
75 Against your peace. Thee of thy son, Alonso,
They have bereft, and do pronounce by me
Ling'ring perdition, worse than any death
Can be at once, shall step by step attend
You and your ways, whose wraths to guard you from –
80 Which here, in this most desolate isle, else falls
Upon your heads – is nothing but heart's sorrow
And a clear life ensuing.

He vanishes in thunder. Then, to soft music, enter
the shapes again and dance with mocks and mows,
and carry out the table.

PROSPERO   Bravely the figure of this harpy hast thou
Performed, my Ariel; a grace it had, devouring.
85 Of my instruction hast thou nothing bated
In what thou hadst to say. So, with good life
And observation strange, my meaner ministers
Their several kinds have done. My high charms work,
And these, mine enemies, are all knit up
90 In their distractions. They now are in my power;
And in these fits I leave them while I visit
Young Ferdinand (whom they suppose is drowned)
And his, and mine, loved darling.   *Exit.*
GONZALO
I'th' name of something holy, sir, why stand you
In this strange stare?
95 ALONSO   O, it is monstrous, monstrous!
Methought the billows spoke and told me of it;
The winds did sing it to me, and the thunder –
That deep and dreadful organpipe – pronounced
The name of Prosper. It did bass my trespass.
100 Therefore my son i'th' ooze is bedded, and
I'll seek him deeper than e'er plummet sounded,
And with him there lie mudded.   *Exit.*
SEBASTIAN   But one fiend at a time,
I'll fight their legions o'er.
ANTONIO   I'll be thy second.
Exeunt Sebastian and Antonio.
GONZALO
105 All three of them are desperate: their great guilt,
Like poison given to work a great time after,
Now 'gins to bite the spirits. I do beseech you
That are of suppler joints, follow them swiftly,
And hinder them from what this ecstasy
May now provoke them to.
110 ADRIAN   Follow, I pray you. *Exeunt omnes.*

4.1 *Enter* PROSPERO, FERDINAND *and* MIRANDA.

PROSPERO [*to Ferdinand*]
If I have too austerely punished you,
Your compensation makes amends, for I
Have given you here a third of mine own life,
Or that for which I live, who once again
5 I tender to thy hand. All thy vexations

Were but my trials of thy love, and thou
Hast strangely stood the test. Here, afore heaven,
I ratify this my rich gift. O Ferdinand,
Do not smile at me that I boast her off,
For thou shalt find she will outstrip all praise   10
And make it halt behind her.
FERDINAND   I do believe it
Against an oracle.
PROSPERO   Then as my gift and thine own acquisition
Worthily purchased, take my daughter. But
If thou dost break her virgin-knot before   15
All sanctimonious ceremonies may
With full and holy rite be ministered,
No sweet aspersion shall the heavens let fall
To make this contract grow; but barren hate,
Sour-eyed disdain and discord shall bestrew   20
The union of your bed with weeds so loathly
That you shall hate it both. Therefore take heed,
As Hymen's lamps shall light you.
FERDINAND   As I hope
For quiet days, fair issue and long life,
With such love as 'tis now, the murkiest den,   25
The most opportune place, the strong'st suggestion
Our worser genius can, shall never melt
Mine honour into lust to take away
The edge of that day's celebration,
When I shall think or Phoebus' steeds are foundered   30
Or night kept chained below.
PROSPERO   Fairly spoke.
Sit then and talk with her; she is thine own.
What, Ariel! My industrious servant Ariel!

Enter ARIEL.

ARIEL   What would my potent master? Here I am.
PROSPERO
Thou and thy meaner fellows your last service   35
Did worthily perform, and I must use you
In such another trick. Go bring the rabble
(O'er whom I give thee power) here to this place.
Incite them to quick motion, for I must
Bestow upon the eyes of this young couple   40
Some vanity of mine art. It is my promise,
And they expect it from me.
ARIEL   Presently?
PROSPERO   Ay, with a twink.
ARIEL   Before you can say 'come' and 'go',
And breathe twice and cry 'so, so',   45
Each one tripping on his toe,
Will be here with mop and mow.
Do you love me, master? No?
PROSPERO   Dearly, my delicate Ariel. Do not approach
Till thou dost hear me call.
ARIEL   Well, I conceive.   *Exit.*   50
PROSPERO [*to Ferdinand*]
Look thou be true. Do not give dalliance
Too much the rein. The strongest oaths are straw
To th' fire i'th' blood. Be more abstemious

Or else good night your vow!

FERDINAND   I warrant you, sir,
  The white cold virgin snow upon my heart
  Abates the ardour of my liver.

PROSPERO   Well! –
  Now come, my Ariel; bring a corollary
  Rather than want a spirit. Appear, and pertly.

                      [*Soft music*]

  No tongue, all eyes. Be silent!

Enter IRIS.

IRIS   Ceres, most bounteous lady, thy rich leas
  Of wheat, rye, barley, vetches, oats and peas;
  Thy turfy mountains where live nibbling sheep,
  And flat meads thatched with stover them to keep;
  Thy banks with pioned and twilled brims,
  Which spongy April at thy hest betrims
  To make cold nymphs chaste crowns; and thy
      broomgroves
  Whose shadow the dismissed bachelor loves,
  Being lass-lorn; thy pole-clipped vineyard,
  And thy sea-marge, sterile and rocky-hard,
  Where thou thyself dost air – the queen o'th' sky,
  Whose watery arch and messenger am I,
  Bids thee leave these, and with her sovereign grace,

JUNO *descends.*

  Here on this grass-plot, in this very place,
  To come and sport. Her peacocks fly amain.
  Approach, rich Ceres, her to entertain.

Enter CERES.

CERES   Hail, many-coloured messenger, that ne'er
  Dost disobey the wife of Jupiter;
  Who, with thy saffron wings, upon my flowers
  Diffusest honey-drops, refreshing showers,
  And with each end of thy blue bow dost crown
  My bosky acres and my unshrubbed down,
  Rich scarf to my proud earth. Why hath thy queen
  Summoned me hither to this short-grassed green?

IRIS   A contract of true love to celebrate,
  And some donation freely to estate
  On the blessed lovers.

CERES   Tell me, heavenly bow,
  If Venus or her son, as thou dost know,
  Do now attend the queen? Since they did plot
  The means that dusky Dis my daughter got,
  Her and her blind boy's scandaled company
  I have forsworn.

IRIS   Of her society
  Be not afraid. I met her deity
  Cutting the clouds towards Paphos, and her son
  Dove-drawn with her. Here thought they to have done
  Some wanton charm upon this man and maid,
  Whose vows are that no bed-right shall be paid
  Till Hymen's torch be lighted, but in vain.
  Mars's hot minion is returned again;

Her waspish-headed son has broke his arrows,
Swears he will shoot no more, but play with sparrows
And be a boy right out.

CERES   Highest queen of state,
  Great Juno comes; I know her by her gait.

JUNO   How does my bounteous sister? Go with me
  To bless this twain that they may prosperous be,
  And honoured in their issue.

[*They sing.*]

JUNO   Honour, riches, marriage-blessing,
  Long continuance and increasing,
  Hourly joys be still upon you;
  Juno sings her blessings on you.

CERES   Earth's increase, foison plenty,
  Barns and garners never empty.
  Vines with clustering bunches growing,
  Plants with goodly burden bowing;
  Spring come to you at the farthest,
  In the very end of harvest.
  Scarcity and want shall shun you,
  Ceres' blessing so is on you.

FERDINAND   This is a most majestic vision, and
  Harmonious charmingly. May I be bold
  To think these spirits?

PROSPERO   Spirits, which by mine art
  I have from their confines called to enact
  My present fancies.

FERDINAND   Let me live here ever!
  So rare a wondered father and a wise
  Makes this place paradise.

[*Juno and Ceres whisper, and send Iris on employment.*]

PROSPERO   Sweet now, silence!
  Juno and Ceres whisper seriously.
  There's something else to do. Hush and be mute,
  Or else our spell is marred.

IRIS
  You nymphs, called naiads, of the windring brooks,
  With your sedged crowns and ever-harmless looks,
  Leave your crisp channels, and on this green land
  Answer your summons; Juno does command.
  Come, temperate nymphs, and help to celebrate
  A contract of true love. Be not too late.

Enter certain Nymphs.

  You sunburned sicklemen, of August weary,
  Come hither from the furrow and be merry;
  Make holiday! Your rye-straw hats put on,
  And these fresh nymphs encounter every one
  In country footing.

Enter certain Reapers, properly habited. They join with
the Nymphs in a graceful dance, towards the end whereof
Prospero starts suddenly and speaks; after which, to a
strange hollow and confused noise, they heavily vanish.

PROSPERO [*aside*]   I had forgot that foul conspiracy
  Of the beast Caliban and his confederates
  Against my life. The minute of their plot

Is almost come. [*to the Spirits*] Well done. Avoid, no
more! *Spirits depart.*

FERDINAND [*to Miranda*]
This is strange. Your father's in some passion
That works him strongly.

MIRANDA   Never till this day
145   Saw I him touched with anger so distempered!

PROSPERO   You do look, my son, in a moved sort,
As if you were dismayed. Be cheerful, sir.
Our revels now are ended. These our actors,
As I foretold you, were all spirits and
150   Are melted into air, into thin air;
And – like the baseless fabric of this vision –
The cloud-capped towers, the gorgeous palaces,
The solemn temples, the great globe itself,
Yea, all which it inherit, shall dissolve,
155   And like this insubstantial pageant faded,
Leave not a rack behind. We are such stuff
As dreams are made on, and our little life
Is rounded with a sleep. Sir, I am vexed;
Bear with my weakness; my old brain is troubled.
160   Be not disturbed with my infirmity.
If you be pleased, retire into my cell
And there repose. A turn or two I'll walk
To still my beating mind.

FERDINAND, MIRANDA   We wish your peace.
Exeunt.

PROSPERO
Come with a thought, I thank thee, Ariel. Come!

Enter ARIEL.

165   ARIEL   Thy thoughts I cleave to. What's thy pleasure?

PROSPERO
Spirit, we must prepare to meet with Caliban.

ARIEL   Ay, my commander. When I presented Ceres,
I thought to have told thee of it, but I feared
Lest I might anger thee.

PROSPERO
170   Say again, where didst thou leave these varlets?

ARIEL   I told you, sir, they were red-hot with drinking,
So full of valour that they smote the air
For breathing in their faces, beat the ground
For kissing of their feet, yet always bending
175   Towards their project. Then I beat my tabor,
At which like unbacked colts they pricked their ears,
Advanced their eyelids, lifted up their noses
As they smelt music; so I charmed their ears
That calf-like they my lowing followed, through
180   Toothed briars, sharp furzes, pricking gorse and thorns,
Which entered their frail shins. At last I left them
I'th' filthy-mantled pool beyond your cell,
There dancing up to th' chins, that the foul lake
O'erstunk their feet.

PROSPERO   This was well done, my bird.
185   Thy shape invisible retain thou still.
The trumpery in my house: go bring it hither,
For stale to catch these thieves.

ARIEL   I go, I go.   *Exit.*

PROSPERO   A devil, a born devil, on whose nature
Nurture can never stick; on whom my pains
Humanely taken – all, all lost, quite lost!   190
And, as with age his body uglier grows,
So his mind cankers. I will plague them all,
Even to roaring. Come, hang them on this line.

Enter ARIEL, *loaden with glistering apparel, etc.*
Enter CALIBAN, STEPHANO *and* TRINCULO, *all wet.*

CALIBAN
Pray you tread softly, that the blind mole may
Not hear a footfall. We now are near his cell.   195

STEPHANO   Monster, your fairy, which you say is a
harmless fairy, has done little better than played the
jack with us.

TRINCULO   Monster, I do smell all horse piss, at which
my nose is in great indignation.   200

STEPHANO   So is mine. Do you hear, monster? If I
should take a displeasure against you, look you!

TRINCULO   Thou wert but a lost monster.

CALIBAN   Good my lord, give me thy favour still.
Be patient, for the prize I'll bring thee to   205
Shall hoodwink this mischance. Therefore speak softly;
All's hushed as midnight yet.

TRINCULO   Ay, but to lose our bottles in the pool –

STEPHANO   There is not only disgrace and dishonour
in that, monster, but an infinite loss.   210

TRINCULO   That's more to me than my wetting, yet this
is your harmless fairy, monster.

STEPHANO   I will fetch off my bottle, though I be o'er
ears for my labour.

CALIBAN   Prithee, my king, be quiet. Seest thou here;   215
This is the mouth o'th' cell. No noise, and enter.
Do that good mischief which may make this island
Thine own forever, and I, thy Caliban,
For aye thy foot-licker.

STEPHANO   Give me thy hand. I do begin to have   220
bloody thoughts.

TRINCULO [*Sees the clothes.*]   O King Stephano! O peer! O
worthy Stephano! Look what a wardrobe here is for thee!

CALIBAN   Let it alone, thou fool; it is but trash.

TRINCULO   O ho, monster; we know what belongs to a   225
frippery! O King Stephano! [*Puts on a garment.*]

STEPHANO   Put off that gown, Trinculo. By this hand,
I'll have that gown.

TRINCULO   Thy grace shall have it.

CALIBAN
The dropsy drown this fool! What do you mean   230
To dote thus on such luggage? Let't alone
And do the murder first. If he awake,
From toe to crown he'll fill our skins with pinches,
Make us strange stuff.

STEPHANO   Be you quiet, monster. Mistress Line, is   235
not this my jerkin? Now is the jerkin under the line!
Now jerkin you are like to lose your hair and prove a
bald jerkin.

TRINCULO   Do, do. We steal by line and level, an't like
240   your grace.
STEPHANO   I thank thee for that jest; here's a garment
  for't. Wit shall not go unrewarded while I am king of
  this country. 'Steal by line and level' is an excellent
  pass of pate. There's another garment for't.
245   TRINCULO   Monster, come put some lime upon your
  fingers and away with the rest.
CALIBAN   I will have none on't. We shall lose our time,
  And all be turned to barnacles, or to apes
  With foreheads villainous low.
250   STEPHANO   Monster, lay to your fingers. Help to bear
  this away where my hogshead of wine is, or I'll turn
  you out of my kingdom! Go to; carry this.
TRINCULO   And this.
STEPHANO   Ay, and this.

A noise of hunters heard. Enter diverse Spirits in
shape of dogs and hounds, hunting them about,
Prospero and Ariel setting them on.

255   PROSPERO   Hey, Mountain, hey!
ARIEL   Silver! There it goes, Silver!
PROSPERO
  Fury, Fury! There, Tyrant, there! Hark, hark!
The Spirits chase Caliban, Stephano and Trinculo off stage.
  Go, charge my goblins that they grind their joints
  With dry convulsions, shorten up their sinews
260   With aged cramps, and more pinch-spotted make them
  Than pard or cat o'mountain.
ARIEL   Hark, they roar!
PROSPERO   Let them be hunted soundly. At this hour
  Lies at my mercy all mine enemies.
  Shortly shall all my labours end, and thou
265   Shalt have the air at freedom. For a little,
  Follow and do me service.   *Exeunt.*

5.1   *Enter* PROSPERO, *in his magic robes, and* ARIEL.

PROSPERO   Now does my project gather to a head.
  My charms crack not; my spirits obey; and time
  Goes upright with his carriage. How's the day?
ARIEL   On the sixth hour, at which time, my lord,
  You said our work should cease.
5   PROSPERO   I did say so,
  When first I raised the tempest. Say, my spirit,
  How fares the King and's followers?
ARIEL   Confined together
  In the same fashion as you gave in charge,
  Just as you left them; all prisoners, sir,
10   In the line grove which weather-fends your cell.
  They cannot budge till your release. The King,
  His brother and yours abide all three distracted,
  And the remainder mourning over them,
  Brimful of sorrow and dismay; but chiefly
15   Him that you termed, sir, the good old Lord Gonzalo.
  His tears run down his beard like winter's drops
  From eaves of reeds. Your charm so strongly works 'em

That, if you now beheld them, your affections
Would become tender.
PROSPERO   Dost thou think so, spirit?
ARIEL   Mine would, sir, were I human.
PROSPERO   And mine shall.   20
  Hast thou, which art but air, a touch, a feeling
  Of their afflictions, and shall not myself
  (One of their kind, that relish all as sharply,
  Passion as they) be kindlier moved than thou art?
  Though with their high wrongs I am struck to th' quick,   25
  Yet with my nobler reason 'gainst my fury
  Do I take part. The rarer action is
  In virtue than in vengeance. They being penitent,
  The sole drift of my purpose doth extend
  Not a frown further. Go, release them, Ariel.   30
  My charms I'll break; their senses I'll restore;
  And they shall be themselves.
ARIEL   I'll fetch them, sir.   *Exit.*
PROSPERO [*Traces a circle.*]
  Ye elves of hills, brooks, standing lakes and groves,
  And ye that on the sands with printless foot
  Do chase the ebbing Neptune, and do fly him   35
  When he comes back; you demi-puppets that
  By moonshine do the green sour ringlets make,
  Whereof the ewe not bites; and you whose pastime
  Is to make midnight-mushrooms, that rejoice
  To hear the solemn curfew, by whose aid –   40
  Weak masters though ye be – I have bedimmed
  The noontide sun, called forth the mutinous winds,
  And 'twixt the green sea and the azured vault
  Set roaring war; to the dread-rattling thunder
  Have I given fire and rifted Jove's stout oak   45
  With his own bolt: the strong-based promontory
  Have I made shake, and by the spurs plucked up
  The pine and cedar; graves at my command
  Have waked their sleepers, ope'd and let 'em forth
  By my so potent art. But this rough magic   50
  I here abjure; and when I have required
  Some heavenly music (which even now I do)
  To work mine end upon their senses that
  This airy charm is for, I'll break my staff,
  Bury it certain fathoms in the earth,   55
  And deeper than did ever plummet sound
  I'll drown my book.   [*Solemn music*]

Here enters ARIEL *before; then* ALONSO *with a frantic*
gesture, attended by GONZALO; SEBASTIAN *and* ANTONIO
in like manner, attended by ADRIAN *and* FRANCISCO.
They all enter the circle which Prospero had made and there
stand charmed, which Prospero observing, speaks:

  A solemn air and the best comforter
  To an unsettled fancy, cure thy brains
  (Now useless) boiled within thy skull. There stand,   60
  For you are spell-stopped. –
  Holy Gonzalo, honourable man,
  Mine eyes, ev'n sociable to the show of thine,
  Fall fellowly drops. [*aside*] The charm dissolves apace,

65   And as the morning steals upon the night,
    Melting the darkness, so their rising senses
    Begin to chase the ignorant fumes that mantle
    Their clearer reason. – O good Gonzalo,
    My true preserver and a loyal sir
70   To him thou follow'st, I will pay thy graces
    Home, both in word and deed. – Most cruelly
    Didst thou, Alonso, use me and my daughter.
    Thy brother was a furtherer in the act. –
    Thou art pinched for't now, Sebastian! – Flesh and
      blood,
75   You, brother mine, that entertained ambition,
    Expelled remorse and nature, whom with Sebastian
    (Whose inward pinches therefore are most strong)
    Would here have killed your king, I do forgive thee,
    Unnatural though thou art. [*aside*] Their understanding
80   Begins to swell, and the approaching tide
    Will shortly fill the reasonable shore
    That now lies foul and muddy. Not one of them
    That yet looks on me or would know me. – Ariel,
    Fetch me the hat and rapier in my cell;
             Exit Ariel and returns immediately.
85 I will discase me and myself present
    As I was sometime Milan. Quickly, spirit,
    Thou shalt ere long be free.
    ARIEL [*Sings and helps to attire him.*]
      Where the bee sucks, there suck I,
      In a cowslip's bell I lie;
      There I couch when owls do cry.
90   On the bat's back I do fly
      After summer merrily.
      Merrily, merrily, shall I live now,
      Under the blossom that hangs on the bough.
    PROSPERO
95   Why, that's my dainty Ariel! I shall miss thee,
    But yet thou shalt have freedom. – So, so, so. –
    To the King's ship, invisible as thou art;
    There shalt thou find the mariners asleep
    Under the hatches. The master and the boatswain
100   Being awake, enforce them to this place,
    And presently, I prithee.
    ARIEL   I drink the air before me and return
    Or ere your pulse twice beat.   *Exit.*
    GONZALO
    All torment, trouble, wonder and amazement
105   Inhabits here. Some heavenly power guide us
    Out of this fearful country.
    PROSPERO   Behold, sir King,
    The wronged Duke of Milan, Prospero!
    For more assurance that a living prince
    Does now speak to thee, I embrace thy body,
110   And to thee and thy company I bid
    A hearty welcome.
    ALONSO   Whe'er thou be'st he or no,
    Or some enchanted trifle to abuse me
    (As late I have been), I not know. Thy pulse
    Beats as of flesh and blood; and since I saw thee,

    Th'affliction of my mind amends, with which   115
    I fear a madness held me. This must crave –
    An if this be at all – a most strange story.
    Thy dukedom I resign and do entreat
    Thou pardon me my wrongs. But how should Prospero
    Be living, and be here?
    PROSPERO [*to Gonzalo*]   First, noble friend,   120
    Let me embrace thine age, whose honour cannot
    Be measured or confined.
    GONZALO   Whether this be
    Or be not, I'll not swear.
    PROSPERO   You do yet taste
    Some subtleties o'th' isle that will not let you
    Believe things certain. Welcome, my friends all;   125
      [*aside to Sebastian and Antonio*] But you, my brace of
        lords, were I so minded,
    I here could pluck his highness' frown upon you
    And justify you traitors! At this time
    I will tell no tales.
    SEBASTIAN   The devil speaks in him.
    PROSPERO   No.
    For you, most wicked sir, whom to call brother   130
    Would even infect my mouth, I do forgive
    Thy rankest fault – all of them; and require
    My dukedom of thee, which perforce I know
    Thou must restore.
    ALONSO   If thou be'st Prospero,
    Give us particulars of thy preservation,   135
    How thou hast met us here, whom three hours since
    Were wrecked upon this shore, where I have lost
    (How sharp the point of this remembrance is!)
    My dear son Ferdinand.
    PROSPERO   I am woe for't, sir.
    ALONSO   Irreparable is the loss, and patience   140
    Says it is past her cure.
    PROSPERO   I rather think
    You have not sought her help, of whose soft grace
    For the like loss I have her sovereign aid
    And rest myself content.
    ALONSO   You the like loss?
    PROSPERO   As great to me as late; and supportable   145
    To make the dear loss have I means much weaker
    Than you may call to comfort you, for I
    Have lost my daughter.
    ALONSO   A daughter?
    O heavens, that they were living both in Naples,
    The king and queen there! That they were, I wish   150
    Myself were mudded in that oozy bed
    Where my son lies. When did you lose your daughter?
    PROSPERO   In this last tempest. – I perceive these lords
    At this encounter do so much admire
    That they devour their reason and scarce think   155
    Their eyes do offices of truth, their words
    Are natural breath. – But howsoe'er you have
    Been jostled from your senses, know for certain
    That I am Prospero and that very duke
    Which was thrust forth of Milan, who most strangely   160

Upon this shore where you were wrecked, was landed
To be the lord on't. No more yet of this,
For 'tis a chronicle of day by day,
Not a relation for a breakfast, nor
165 Befitting this first meeting. – Welcome, sir.
This cell's my court; here have I few attendants,
And subjects none abroad. Pray you, look in.
My dukedom since you have given me again,
I will requite you with as good a thing,
170 At least bring forth a wonder to content ye
As much as me my dukedom.

Here Prospero discovers Ferdinand and Miranda,
playing at chess.

MIRANDA   Sweet lord, you play me false.
FERDINAND   No, my dearest love,
     I would not for the world.
MIRANDA
     Yes, for a score of kingdoms you should wrangle,
     And I would call it fair play.
175 ALONSO   If this prove
     A vision of the island, one dear son
     Shall I twice lose.
SEBASTIAN   A most high miracle!
FERDINAND [*Sees Alonso and the others.*]
     Though the seas threaten, they are merciful.
     I have cursed them without cause.   [*Kneels.*]
ALONSO   Now all the blessings
180 Of a glad father compass thee about!
     Arise and say how thou cam'st here.
MIRANDA   O wonder!
     How many goodly creatures are there here!
     How beauteous mankind is! O brave new world
     That has such people in't.
PROSPERO   'Tis new to thee.
ALONSO
185 What is this maid with whom thou wast at play?
     Your eld'st acquaintance cannot be three hours.
     Is she the goddess that hath severed us
     And brought us thus together?
FERDINAND   Sir, she is mortal,
     But by immortal providence she's mine;
190 I chose her when I could not ask my father
     For his advice, nor thought I had one. She
     Is daughter to this famous Duke of Milan –
     Of whom so often I have heard renown
     But never saw before – of whom I have
195 Received a second life; and second father
     This lady makes him to me.
ALONSO   I am hers.
     But O, how oddly will it sound that I
     Must ask my child forgiveness.
PROSPERO   There, sir, stop.
     Let us not burden our remembrances with
     A heaviness that's gone.
200 GONZALO   I have inly wept,
     Or should have spoke ere this. Look down, you gods,

And on this couple drop a blessed crown,
For it is you that have chalked forth the way
Which brought us hither.
ALONSO   I say 'amen', Gonzalo.
GONZALO   Was Milan thrust from Milan that his issue   205
     Should become kings of Naples? O, rejoice
     Beyond a common joy, and set it down
     With gold on lasting pillars: in one voyage
     Did Claribel her husband find at Tunis;
     And Ferdinand, her brother, found a wife   210
     Where he himself was lost; Prospero his dukedom
     In a poor isle; and all of us ourselves,
     When no man was his own.
ALONSO [*to Ferdinand and Miranda*]
                         Give me your hands.
     Let grief and sorrow still embrace his heart
     That doth not wish you joy.
GONZALO   Be it so; amen.   215

Enter ARIEL, *with the* Master *and* Boatswain
amazedly following.

     O look, sir, look, sir; here is more of us!
     I prophesied, if a gallows were on land
     This fellow could not drown. [*to Boatswain*] Now,
          blasphemy,
     That swear'st grace o'erboard, not an oath on shore?
     Hast thou no mouth by land? What is the news?   220
BOATSWAIN   The best news is that we have safely found
     Our King and company. The next: our ship,
     Which but three glasses since we gave out split,
     Is tight and yare and bravely rigged as when
     We first put out to sea.
ARIEL [*to Prospero*]   Sir, all this service   225
     Have I done since I went.
PROSPERO   My tricksy spirit!
ALONSO   These are not natural events; they strengthen
     From strange to stranger. Say, how came you hither?
BOATSWAIN   If I did think, sir, I were well awake,
     I'd strive to tell you. We were dead of sleep   230
     And – how we know not – all clapped under hatches,
     Where but even now with strange and several noises
     Of roaring, shrieking, howling, jingling chains
     And more diversity of sounds, all horrible,
     We were awaked; straightway at liberty,   235
     Where we, in all our trim, freshly beheld
     Our royal, good and gallant ship; our master
     Cap'ring to eye her. On a trice, so please you,
     Even in a dream, were we divided from them
     And were brought moping hither.
ARIEL [*to Prospero*]   Was't well done?   240
PROSPERO   Bravely, my diligence. Thou shalt be free.
ALONSO   This is as strange a maze as e'er men trod,
     And there is in this business more than nature
     Was ever conduct of. Some oracle
     Must rectify our knowledge.
PROSPERO   Sir, my liege,   245
     Do not infest your mind with beating on

The strangeness of this business. At picked leisure,
Which shall be shortly, single I'll resolve you
(Which to you shall seem probable) of every
250 These happened accidents. Till when, be cheerful
And think of each thing well.
[*aside to Ariel*]   Come hither, spirit.
Set Caliban and his companions free;
Untie the spell.   *Exit Ariel.*
[*to Alonso*]   How fares my gracious sir?
There are yet missing of your company
255 Some few odd lads that you remember not.

Enter ARIEL, *driving in* CALIBAN, STEPHANO
and TRINCULO *in their stolen apparel.*

STEPHANO   Every man shift for all the rest, and let no
man take care for himself, for all is but fortune.
Coraggio, bully monster, *coraggio*.
TRINCULO   If these be true spies which I wear in my
260 head, here's a goodly sight.
CALIBAN   O Setebos, these be brave spirits indeed!
How fine my master is! I am afraid
He will chastise me.
SEBASTIAN   Ha, ha!
What things are these, my lord Antonio?
Will money buy 'em?
265 ANTONIO   Very like. One of them
Is a plain fish and no doubt marketable.
PROSPERO
Mark but the badges of these men, my lords,
Then say if they be true. This misshapen knave,
His mother was a witch, and one so strong
270 That could control the moon, make flows and ebbs,
And deal in her command without her power.
These three have robbed me, and this demi-devil
(For he's a bastard one) had plotted with them
To take my life. Two of these fellows you
275 Must know and own; this thing of darkness I
Acknowledge mine.
CALIBAN   I shall be pinched to death.
ALONSO   Is not this Stephano, my drunken butler?
SEBASTIAN   He is drunk now. Where had he wine?
ALONSO
And Trinculo is reeling ripe! Where should they
280 Find this grand liquor that hath gilded 'em?
How cam'st thou in this pickle?
TRINCULO   I have been in such a pickle since I saw you
last, that I fear me will never out of my bones. I shall
not fear fly-blowing.
285 SEBASTIAN   Why, how now, Stephano?
STEPHANO   O touch me not; I am not Stephano, but a
cramp!
PROSPERO   You'd be king o'the isle, sirrah?
STEPHANO   I should have been a sore one then.
290 ALONSO   This is a strange thing as e'er I looked on.
PROSPERO   He is as disproportioned in his manners
As in his shape. Go, sirrah, to my cell;
Take with you your companions. As you look

To have my pardon, trim it handsomely.
CALIBAN   Ay, that I will; and I'll be wise hereafter   295
And seek for grace. What a thrice-double ass
Was I to take this drunkard for a god,
And worship this dull fool!
PROSPERO   Go to, away.
ALONSO [*to Stephano and Trinculo*]
Hence, and bestow your luggage where you found it.
SEBASTIAN   Or stole it, rather.   300
Exeunt Caliban, Stephano and Trinculo.
PROSPERO   Sir, I invite your highness and your train
To my poor cell, where you shall take your rest
For this one night, which (part of it) I'll waste
With such discourse as, I not doubt, shall make it
Go quick away – the story of my life,   305
And the particular accidents gone by
Since I came to this isle – and in the morn
I'll bring you to your ship, and so to Naples,
Where I have hope to see the nuptial
Of these our dear-beloved solemnized;   310
And thence retire me to my Milan, where
Every third thought shall be my grave.
ALONSO   I long
To hear the story of your life, which must
Take the ear strangely.
PROSPERO   I'll deliver all,
And promise you calm seas, auspicious gales   315
And sail so expeditious that shall catch
Your royal fleet far off. [*aside to Ariel*] My Ariel, chick,
That is thy charge. Then to the elements
Be free, and fare thou well!
[*to the others*]   Please you, draw near.
Exeunt omnes.

EPILOGUE
spoken by PROSPERO

Now my charms are all o'erthrown,
And what strength I have's mine own,
Which is most faint. Now, 'tis true
I must be here confined by you,
Or sent to Naples. Let me not,   5
Since I have my dukedom got
And pardoned the deceiver, dwell
In this bare island by your spell;
But release me from my bands
With the help of your good hands.   10
Gentle breath of yours my sails
Must fill, or else my project fails,
Which was to please. Now I want
Spirits to enforce, art to enchant;
And my ending is despair,   15
Unless I be relieved by prayer,
Which pierces so that it assaults
Mercy itself, and frees all faults.
    As you from crimes would pardoned be,
Let your indulgence set me free.   *Exit.*   20

Timon of Athens

No reference to *Timon of Athens* survives from the years before its appearance in the First Folio of 1623. It is even questionable whether the play would have been included in the Folio at all, had not need arisen to fill, at short notice, an unplanned gap between *Romeo and Juliet* and *Julius Caesar*. When it was written is uncertain, though recent scholars have tended to date *Timon* to 1606, following shortly after *King Lear* (1605–6), with which it has clear thematic and linguistic affinities. It is probable that, like *Antony and Cleopatra* (1606–7) and *Coriolanus* (1608), *Timon* grew out of Shakespeare's intense reading of Plutarch at this time. *Coriolanus* in particular is built on a structure similar to the Alcibiades plot in *Timon*; and Timon's self-banishment, like that of Coriolanus, is a reaction to the cruel ingratitude of the city that nourished him.

Timon is a peculiar and for many readers an unpalatable piece of work: the plot is rather more allegorical than is typical of Shakespeare; there are many loose ends and insufficiently integrated episodes; several of the characters have generic rather than personal names; the verse is frequently uneven; and the main character is hard to sympathize with – he starts as pathologically generous and ends a misanthrope. Unlike the classic Shakespearean tragic hero, he dies offstage (exactly what kills him remains a mystery) and leaves behind only an ambiguous epitaph. But the play turns what might seem like disadvantages into assets; its sheer ferocity, its intense concentration on the destructiveness of economic relations and its virulent critique of human ingratitude have (under Marx's influence) won it a valued place among present-day performers and playgoers.

The anomalous features of the text probably derive from the fact that it is the result of a collaboration between two writers, Shakespeare and Thomas Middleton, the former older and more established, the latter a brash newcomer who was beginning to make his mark with a series of satirical London comedies and the brilliantly bitter *The Revenger's Tragedy*. Middleton's hand is confidently identified in 1.2, 3.1–3 and much of 3.4–6, as well as parts of Act 4, especially those involving the steward, Flavius.

The Alcibiades subplot, seemingly shared between the two writers, is never integrated with the main plot. A parallel figure to Timon, Alcibiades, once the darling of the city, is banished and turns on Athens in retaliation for its crimes. His plea before the senate in favour of his unnamed friend (3.6) is rejected, but nothing more comes of that, so that by the end Alcibiades seems to have forgotten his friend and to be motivated mainly by his anger at the Athenian treatment of Timon.

Other loose ends include inconsistent naming and the spelling of characters' names, erratic plotting and the presence of two somewhat contradictory epitaphs for Timon at the finish. The unusual features of the text raise the question of genre – what kind of play is this? Although it appears in the tragedies section of the Folio, it arrived there by an anomalous sequence of events. As a tragedy, it is pessimistic, almost nihilistic, laced throughout with satire and carrying an allegorical message about greed and selfishness. The play thus pulls in multiple directions, towards tragedy, allegory and satire; this is due, at least partly, to Shakespeare and Middleton's two hands.

Such a mixture is exemplified in Timon's final moments onstage, when he moves deftly from comic unmasking of the fretful and sycophantic Senators to lines like 'My long sickness / Of health and living now begins to mend / And nothing brings me all things' (5.2.71–3). This is a nihilistic but powerful stance, reminiscent of Macbeth and Lear. The play briefly pulls away from satire and yet remains tied to it. There is a certain strain in the final act that hints at the fault-lines in the hybrid structure. But that gives the play its modernity. Though it may never have been staged in Shakespeare's day and was rarely produced before the twentieth century, since the 1980s it has proved to be not only relevant but brilliantly effective in performance.

The Arden text is based on the 1623 First Folio.

TIMON	*a wealthy Athenian*
APEMANTUS	*a churlish philosopher*
ALCIBIADES	*an Athenian captain*
FLAVIUS	*Timon's steward*
LUCILIUS	
FLAMINIUS	*Timon's servants*
SERVILIUS	
VENTIDIUS	
LUCULLUS	*flattering lords and false*
LUCIUS	*friends of Timon*
SEMPRONIUS	
POET	
PAINTER	
JEWELLER	
MERCHANT	

Other LORDS and SENATORS of Athens
Three STRANGERS, one called HOSTILIUS
OLD ATHENIAN

CAPHIS	
SERVANT of ISIDORE	
Two SERVANTS of VARRO	
TITUS	*servants of creditors*
HORTENSIUS	
LUCIUS	
PHILOTUS	
FOOL	
PAGE	
CUPID	
LADIES dressed as Amazons	*figures in the masque*
TIMANDRA	
PHRYNIA	*prostitutes accompanying Alcibiades*
THIEVES	
SERVANTS	
SOLDIERS	
MESSENGERS	

Attendants

1.1   *Enter* POET, PAINTER, JEWELLER *and*
           MERCHANT *at several doors.*

POET   Good day, sir.
PAINTER   I am glad you're well.
POET   I have not seen you long – how goes the world?
PAINTER   It wears, sir, as it grows.
POET   Ay, that's well known.
   But what particular rarity? What strange,
5   Which manifold record not matches? See,
   Magic of bounty, all these spirits thy power
   Hath conjured to attend. I know the merchant.
PAINTER   I know them both – th'other's a jeweller.
MERCHANT   O, 'tis a worthy lord!
JEWELLER   Nay, that's most fixed.
MERCHANT
10   A most incomparable man, breathed as it were
   To an untireable and continuate goodness –
   He passes.
JEWELLER   I have a jewel here.
MERCHANT   O, pray let's see't.
   For the Lord Timon, sir?
15   JEWELLER   If he will touch the estimate. But for that –
POET *[to himself]*
   When we for recompense have praised the vile,
   It stains the glory in that happy verse
   Which aptly sings the good.
MERCHANT   'Tis a good form.
JEWELLER   And rich – here is a water, look ye.
PAINTER
20   You are rapt, sir, in some work, some dedication
   To the great lord?
POET   A thing slipped idly from me.
   Our poesy is as a gum which oozes
   From whence 'tis nourished. The fire i'th' flint
   Shows not till it be struck, our gentle flame
25   Provokes itself and, like the current, flies
   Each bound it chases. What have you there?
PAINTER   A picture, sir. When comes your book forth?
POET   Upon the heels of my presentment, sir.
   Let's see your piece.
PAINTER   'Tis a good piece.
30   POET   So 'tis; this comes off well and excellent.
PAINTER   Indifferent.
POET   Admirable! How this grace
   Speaks his own standing! What a mental power
   This eye shoots forth! How big imagination
   Moves in this lip! To th' dumbness of the gesture
35   One might interpret.
PAINTER   It is a pretty mocking of the life;
   Here is a touch – is't good?
POET   I will say of it
   It tutors nature; artificial strife
   Lives in these touches livelier than life.

       Enter certain Senators *and pass over the stage.*

40   PAINTER   How this lord is followed!

POET   The senators of Athens, happy men!
PAINTER   Look, more!
POET
   You see this confluence, this great flood of visitors –
   I have in this rough work shaped out a man
   Whom this beneath world doth embrace and hug   45
   With amplest entertainment. My free drift
   Halts not particularly, but moves itself
   In a wide sea of wax; no levelled malice
   Infects one comma in the course I hold,
   But flies an eagle flight, bold and forth on,   50
   Leaving no tract behind.
PAINTER   How shall I understand you?
POET   I will unbolt to you.
   You see how all conditions, how all minds,
   As well of glib and slippery creatures as   55
   Of grave and austere quality, tender down
   Their services to Lord Timon? His large fortune,
   Upon his good and gracious nature hanging,
   Subdues and properties to his love and tendance
   All sorts of hearts; yea, from the glass-faced flatterer   60
   To Apemantus that few things loves better
   Than to abhor himself – even he drops down
   The knee before him and returns in peace,
   Most rich in Timon's nod.
PAINTER   I saw them speak together.
POET   Sir, I have upon a high and pleasant hill   65
   Feigned Fortune to be throned. The base o'th' mount
   Is ranked with all deserts, all kind of natures
   That labour on the bosom of this sphere
   To propagate their states. Amongst them all
   Whose eyes are on this sovereign Lady fixed,   70
   One do I personate of Lord Timon's frame,
   Whom Fortune with her ivory hand wafts to her,
   Whose present grace to present slaves and servants
   Translates his rivals.
PAINTER   'Tis conceived to scope.
   This throne, this Fortune and this hill, methinks,   75
   With one man beckoned from the rest below
   Bowing his head against the steepy mount
   To climb his happiness, would be well expressed
   In our condition.
POET   Nay, sir, but hear me on:
   All those which were his fellows but of late –   80
   Some better than his value – on the moment
   Follow his strides, his lobbies fill with tendance,
   Rain sacrificial whisperings in his ear,
   Make sacred even his stirrup and through him
   Drink the free air.
PAINTER   Ay, marry, what of these?   85
POET   When Fortune in her shift and change of mood
   Spurns down her late beloved, all his dependants,
   Which laboured after him to the mountain's top
   Even on their knees and hands, let him slip down,
   Not one accompanying his declining foot.   90
PAINTER   'Tis common:
   A thousand moral paintings I can show

That shall demonstrate these quick blows of Fortune's
More pregnantly than words. Yet you do well
95 To show Lord Timon that mean eyes have seen
The foot above the head.

Trumpets sound. Enter Lord TIMON, *addressing
himself courteously to every suitor and speaking with a*
Messenger *from Ventidius;* LUCILIUS *and other
Servants follow.*

TIMON Imprisoned is he, say you?
MESSENGER Ay, my good lord, five talents is his debt,
His means most short, his creditors most strait.
100 Your honourable letter he desires
To those have shut him up, which failing,
Periods his comfort.
TIMON   Noble Ventidius, well!
I am not of that feather to shake off
My friend when he most needs me. I do know him
105 A gentleman that well deserves a help,
Which he shall have. I'll pay the debt and free him.
MESSENGER Your lordship ever binds him.
TIMON Commend me to him, I will send his ransom
And, being enfranchised, bid him come to me;
110 'Tis not enough to help the feeble up,
But to support him after. Fare you well.
MESSENGER All happiness to your honour!   *Exit.*

Enter an OLD ATHENIAN.

OLD ATHENIAN Lord Timon, hear me speak.
TIMON   Freely, good father.
OLD ATHENIAN Thou hast a servant named Lucilius.
115 TIMON I have so. What of him?
OLD ATHENIAN
Most noble Timon, call the man before thee.
TIMON Attends he here or no? Lucilius!
LUCILIUS Here, at your lordship's service.
OLD ATHENIAN
This fellow here, Lord Timon, this thy creature,
120 By night frequents my house. I am a man
That from my first have been inclined to thrift,
And my estate deserves an heir more raised
Than one which holds a trencher.
TIMON   Well, what further?
OLD ATHENIAN One only daughter have I, no kin else
125 On whom I may confer what I have got.
The maid is fair, o'th' youngest for a bride,
And I have bred her at my dearest cost
In qualities of the best. This man of thine
Attempts her love – I prithee, noble lord,
130 Join with me to forbid him her resort;
Myself have spoke in vain.
TIMON   The man is honest.
OLD ATHENIAN Therefore he will be, Timon.
His honesty rewards him in itself,
It must not bear my daughter.
TIMON   Does she love him?
135 OLD ATHENIAN She is young and apt:

Our own precedent passions do instruct us
What levity's in youth.
TIMON [*to Lucilius*]   Love you the maid?
LUCILIUS Ay, my good lord, and she accepts of it.
OLD ATHENIAN
If in her marriage my consent be missing,
140 I call the gods to witness, I will choose
Mine heir from forth the beggars of the world
And dispossess her all.
TIMON How shall she be endowed
If she be mated with an equal husband?
OLD ATHENIAN
145 Three talents on the present; in future, all.
TIMON This gentleman of mine hath served me long;
To build his fortune, I will strain a little,
For 'tis a bond in men. Give him thy daughter,
What you bestow, in him I'll counterpoise
And make him weigh with her.
OLD ATHENIAN   Most noble lord,
150 Pawn me to this your honour, she is his.
TIMON My hand to thee, mine honour on my promise.
LUCILIUS Humbly I thank your lordship. Never may
That state or fortune fall into my keeping
Which is not owed to you.   *Exit with Old Athenian.*
155 POET Vouchsafe my labour and long live your lordship.
TIMON I thank you, you shall hear from me anon,
Go not away. [*Poet stands aside.*]
                  – What have you there, my friend?
PAINTER A piece of painting, which I do beseech
Your lordship to accept.
TIMON   Painting is welcome.
160 The painting is almost the natural man,
For since dishonour traffics with man's nature,
He is but outside; these pencilled figures are
Even such as they give out. I like your work,
And you shall find I like it – wait attendance
165 Till you hear further from me.
PAINTER   The gods preserve ye.
TIMON Well fare you, gentleman, give me your hand.
We must needs dine together. Sir, your jewel
Hath suffered under praise.
JEWELLER   What, my lord, dispraise?
170 TIMON A mere satiety of commendations –
If I should pay you for't as 'tis extolled,
It would unclew me quite.
JEWELLER   My lord, 'tis rated
As those which sell would give. But you well know
Things of like value differing in the owners
175 Are prized by their masters. Believe't, dear lord,
You mend the jewel by the wearing it.
TIMON   Well mocked.

Enter APEMANTUS.

MERCHANT
No, my good lord, he speaks the common tongue
Which all men speak with him.
TIMON Look who comes here – will you be chid?

JEWELLER	We'll bear it with your lordship.	
180	MERCHANT	He'll spare none.

TIMON   Good morrow to thee, gentle Apemantus.

APEMANTUS
Till I be gentle, stay thou for thy good morrow –
When thou art Timon's dog, and these knaves honest.

TIMON
Why dost thou call them knaves? Thou knowst them
not.

185 APEMANTUS   Are they not Athenians?

TIMON   Yes.

APEMANTUS   Then I repent not.

JEWELLER   You know me, Apemantus?

190 APEMANTUS   Thou knowst I do, I called thee by thy
name.

TIMON   Thou art proud, Apemantus.

APEMANTUS   Of nothing so much as that I am not like
Timon.

TIMON   Whither art going?

195 APEMANTUS   To knock out an honest Athenian's brains.

TIMON   That's a deed thou'lt die for.

APEMANTUS   Right, if doing nothing be death by th'
law.

TIMON   How lik'st thou this picture, Apemantus?

200 APEMANTUS   The best for the innocence.

TIMON   Wrought he not well that painted it?

APEMANTUS   He wrought better that made the painter,
and yet he's but a filthy piece of work.

PAINTER   You're a dog!

205 APEMANTUS   Thy mother's of my generation – what's
she, if I be a dog?

TIMON   Wilt dine with me, Apemantus?

APEMANTUS   No, I eat not lords.

TIMON   An thou shouldst, thou'dst anger ladies.

210 APEMANTUS   O, they eat lords – so they come by great
bellies.

TIMON   That's a lascivious apprehension.

APEMANTUS   So thou apprehend'st it, take it for thy
labour.

215 TIMON   How dost thou like this jewel, Apemantus?

APEMANTUS   Not so well as plain-dealing, which will
not cost a man a doit.

TIMON   What dost thou think 'tis worth?

APEMANTUS   Not worth my thinking. How now, poet?

220 POET   How now, philosopher?

APEMANTUS   Thou liest.

POET   Art not one?

APEMANTUS   Yes.

POET   Then I lie not.

225 APEMANTUS   Art not a poet?

POET   Yes.

APEMANTUS   Then thou liest: look in thy last work,
where thou hast feigned him a worthy fellow.

POET   That's not feigned, he is so.

230 APEMANTUS   Yes, he is worthy of thee, and to pay thee
for thy labour. He that loves to be flattered is worthy
o'th' flatterer. Heavens, that I were a lord!

TIMON   What wouldst do then, Apemantus?

APEMANTUS   E'en as Apemantus does now, hate a lord
with my heart.   235

TIMON   What, thyself?

APEMANTUS   Ay.

TIMON   Wherefore?

APEMANTUS   That I had no angry wit to be a lord. Art
not thou a merchant?   240

MERCHANT   Ay, Apemantus.

APEMANTUS   Traffic confound thee, if the gods will not.

MERCHANT   If traffic do it, the gods do it.

APEMANTUS   Traffic's thy god, and thy god confound
thee!   245

Trumpet sounds. Enter a Messenger.

TIMON   What trumpet's that?

MESSENGER   'Tis Alcibiades, and some twenty horse,
All of companionship.

TIMON   Pray entertain them, give them guide to us.
Exit one or two Attendants.
You must needs dine with me. Go not you hence   250
Till I have thanked you; when dinner's done,
Show me this piece. I am joyful of your sights.

Enter ALCIBIADES *with his company.*

Most welcome, sir.

APEMANTUS   [*aside*]   So, so – there! Aches contract and
starve your supple joints! That there should be small   255
love amongst these sweet knaves, and all this courtesy.
The strain of man's bred out into baboon and monkey.

ALCIBIADES
Sir, you have saved my longing, and I feed
Most hungrily on your sight.

TIMON   Right welcome, sir!
Ere we depart we'll share a bounteous time   260
In different pleasures. Pray you, let us in.
Exeunt all but Apemantus.

Enter two Lords.

1 LORD   What time o'day is't, Apemantus?

APEMANTUS   Time to be honest.

1 LORD   That time serves still.

APEMANTUS
The most accursed thou, that still omitt'st it.   265

2 LORD   Thou art going to Lord Timon's feast?

APEMANTUS   Ay, to see meat fill knaves and wine heat
fools.

2 LORD   Fare thee well, fare thee well.

APEMANTUS   Thou art a fool to bid me farewell twice.   270

2 LORD   Why, Apemantus?

APEMANTUS   Shouldst have kept one to thyself, for I
mean to give thee none.

1 LORD   Hang thyself!

APEMANTUS   No, I will do nothing at thy bidding –   275
make thy requests to thy friend.

2 LORD   Away, unpeaceable dog, or I'll spurn thee
hence.

APEMANTUS   I will fly like a dog the heels o'th' ass.

                                           Exit.

280   1 LORD   He's opposite to humanity.
       Come, shall we in and taste Lord Timon's bounty?
       He outgoes the very heart of kindness.

     2 LORD   He pours it out; Plutus, the god of gold,
       Is but his steward: no meed but he repays
285   Sevenfold above itself, no gift to him
       But breeds the giver a return exceeding
       All use of quittance.

     1 LORD   The noblest mind he carries
       That ever governed man.

     2 LORD   Long may he live in fortunes. Shall we in?
290   1 LORD   I'll keep you company.   *Exeunt.*

1.2   *Oboes playing loud music. A great banquet*
        served in, FLAVIUS *and* Servants *attending;*
        and then enter Lord TIMON, *the* Senators,
         the Athenian Lords, ALCIBIADES
          and VENTIDIUS, *which Timon redeemed*
        from prison. Then comes, dropping after
        all, APEMANTUS, *discontentedly, like himself.*

VENTIDIUS   Most honoured Timon,
       It hath pleased the gods to remember
       My father's age and call him to long peace.
       He is gone happy and has left me rich.
5   Then, as in grateful virtue I am bound
       To your free heart, I do return those talents,
       Doubled with thanks and service, from whose help
       I derived liberty.

TIMON   O, by no means,
       Honest Ventidius, you mistake my love:
10   I gave it freely ever, and there's none
       Can truly say he gives if he receives.
       If our betters play at that game, we must not dare
       To imitate them; faults that are rich are fair.

VENTIDIUS   A noble spirit!

TIMON   Nay my lords,
15   Ceremony was but devised at first
       To set a gloss on faint deeds, hollow welcomes,
       Recanting goodness, sorry ere 'tis shown.
       But where there is true friendship there needs none.
       Pray sit, more welcome are ye to my fortunes
20   Than my fortunes to me.

1 LORD   My lord, we always have confessed it.

APEMANTUS
       Ho ho, confessed it? Hanged it, have you not?

TIMON   O Apemantus, you are welcome.

APEMANTUS   No,
       You shall not make me welcome –
25   I come to have thee thrust me out of doors.

TIMON   Fie, thou'rt a churl, you've got a humour there
       Does not become a man; 'tis much to blame.
       They say, my lords, *ira furor brevis est,*
       But yon man is ever angry.
30   Go, let him have a table by himself,

For he does neither affect company
    Nor is he fit for't indeed.

APEMANTUS   Let me stay at thine apperil, Timon.
    I come to observe, I give thee warning on't.

TIMON   I take no heed of thee: thou'rt an Athenian,   35
    therefore welcome. I myself would have no power,
    prithee let my meat make thee silent.

APEMANTUS   I scorn thy meat, 'twould choke me 'fore I
    should e'er flatter thee. O you gods, what a number of
    men eats Timon and he sees 'em not! It grieves me to   40
    see so many dip their meat in one man's blood, and all
    the madness is, he cheers them up too.
    I wonder men dare trust themselves with men,
    Methinks they should invite them without knives –
    Good for their meat and safer for their lives.   45
    There's much example for't: the fellow that sits next
    him, now parts bread with him, pledges the breath
    of him in a divided draft, is the readiest man to kill
    him – 't has been proved. If I were a huge man I should
    fear to drink at meals,   50
    Lest they should spy my windpipe's dangerous notes;
    Great men should drink with harness on their throats.

TIMON   My lord, in heart, and let the health go round.

2 LORD   Let it flow this way, my good lord.

APEMANTUS   Flow this way? A brave fellow! He keeps   55
    his tides well; those healths will make thee and thy
    state look ill, Timon.
    Here's that which is too weak to be a sinner,
    Honest water, which ne'er left man i'th' mire;
    This and my food are equals, there's no odds,   60
    Feasts are too proud to give thanks to the gods.

                  Apemantus' grace

      Immortal gods, I crave no pelf,
      I pray for no man but myself;
      Grant I may never prove so fond
      To trust man on his oath or bond,   65
      Or a harlot for her weeping,
      Or a dog that seems a-sleeping,
      Or a keeper with my freedom,
      Or my friends if I should need 'em,
      Amen. So fall to't.   70
      Rich men sin and I eat root.

Much good dich thy good heart, Apemantus.

TIMON   Captain Alcibiades, your heart's in the field
    now.

ALCIBIADES   My heart is ever at your service, my lord.   75

TIMON   You had rather be at a breakfast of enemies than
    a dinner of friends.

ALCIBIADES   So they were bleeding new, my lord,
    there's no meat like 'em; I could wish my best friend at
    such a feast.   80

APEMANTUS   Would all those flatterers were thine
    enemies then, that then thou mightst kill 'em, and bid
    me to 'em.

1 LORD   Might we but have that happiness, my lord,
    that you would once use our hearts, whereby we might   85

express some part of our zeals, we should think ourselves forever perfect.

TIMON   O no doubt, my good friends, but the gods themselves have provided that I shall have much help from you – how had you been my friends else? Why have you that charitable title from thousands, did not you chiefly belong to my heart? I have told more of you to myself than you can with modesty speak in your own behalf. And thus far I confirm you. O you gods, think I, what need we have any friends, if we should ne'er have need of 'em? They were the most needless creatures living should we ne'er have use for 'em, and would most resemble sweet instruments hung up in cases that keeps their sounds to themselves. Why, I have often wished myself poorer that I might come nearer to you. We are born to do benefits, and what better or properer can we call our own than the riches of our friends? O, what a precious comfort 'tis to have so many like brothers commanding one another's fortunes. O, joy's e'en made away ere't can be born – mine eyes cannot hold out water, methinks. To forget their faults, I drink to you.

APEMANTUS   Thou weep'st to make them drink, Timon.

2 LORD   Joy had the like conception in our eyes
And at that instant like a babe sprung up.

APEMANTUS
Ho ho, I laugh to think that babe a bastard.

3 LORD   I promise you, my lord, you moved me much.

APEMANTUS   Much.   [*A tucket sounds.*]

TIMON   What means that trump?

Enter a Servant.

How now?

SERVANT   Please you my lord, there are certain ladies most desirous of admittance.

TIMON   Ladies? What are their wills?

SERVANT   There comes with them a forerunner, my lord, which bears that office to signify their pleasures.

TIMON   I pray let them be admitted.   *Exit Servant.*

Enter CUPID.

CUPID   Hail to thee, worthy Timon, and to all that of his bounties taste! The five best senses acknowledge thee their patron and come freely to gratulate thy plenteous bosom.
There taste, touch, all, pleased from thy table rise,
They only now come but to feast thine eyes.

TIMON
They're welcome all, let 'em have kind admittance.
Music, make their welcome.

1 LORD   You see, my lord, how ample you're beloved.

Enter a masque of Ladies *dressed as Amazons,
with lutes in their hands, dancing and playing.*

APEMANTUS   Hoy-day,
What a sweep of vanity comes this way.

They dance? They are madwomen;
Like madness is the glory of this life,   135
As this pomp shows to a little oil and root.
We make ourselves fools to disport ourselves,
And spend our flatteries to drink those men
Upon whose age we void it up again
With poisonous spite and envy.   140
Who lives that's not depraved or depraves?
Who dies that bears not one spurn to their graves
Of their friends' gift?
I should fear those that dance before me now
Would one day stamp upon me. 'T has been done,   145
Men shut their doors against a setting sun.

[*The Lords rise from table, with much adoring of
Timon, and to show their loves each single out an
Amazon and all dance, men with women, a lofty strain
or two to the oboes and cease.*]

TIMON
You have done our pleasures much grace, fair ladies,
Set a fair fashion on our entertainment,
Which was not half so beautiful and kind.
You have added worth unto't and lustre,   150
And entertained me with mine own device.
I am to thank you for't.

1 LADY   My lord, you take us even at the best.

APEMANTUS   Faith, for the worst is filthy and would not
hold taking, I doubt me.   155

TIMON   Ladies, there is an idle banquet attends you,
Please you to dispose yourselves.

LADIES   Most thankfully, my lord.   *Exeunt with Cupid.*

TIMON   Flavius!

FLAVIUS   My lord?   160

TIMON   The little casket bring me hither.

FLAVIUS   Yes, my lord. [*aside*] More jewels yet?
There is no crossing him in's humour,
Else I should tell him well, i'faith I should;
When all's spent, he'd be crossed then, an he could.   165
'Tis pity bounty had not eyes behind
That man might ne'er be wretched for his mind.

                                                        Exit.

1 LORD   Where be our men?

SERVANT   Here, my lord, in readiness.

2 LORD   Our horses!

Enter FLAVIUS *with the casket.*

TIMON   O my friends, I have one word   170
To say to you – look you, my good lord,
I must entreat you honour me so much
As to advance this jewel –
Accept it and wear it, kind my lord.

1 LORD   I am so far already in your gifts –   175

ALL   So are we all.

Enter a Servant.

SERVANT   My lord, there are certain nobles of the senate
newly alighted and come to visit you.

TIMON   They are fairly welcome.   *Exit Servant.*

180 FLAVIUS I beseech your honour, vouchsafe me a word
       – it does concern you near.
    TIMON Near? Why then, another time I'll hear thee. I
       prithee let's be provided to show them entertainment.
    FLAVIUS [*aside*] I scarce know how.

                  Enter another Servant.

185 2 SERVANT May it please your honour, Lord Lucius,
       out of his free love, hath presented to you four milk-
       white horses, trapped in silver.
    TIMON I shall accept them fairly; let the presents be
       worthily entertained.   *Exit Servant.*

                  Enter a third Servant.

190   How now, what news?
    3 SERVANT Please you, my lord, that honourable
       gentleman, Lord Lucullus, entreats your company
       tomorrow to hunt with him and has sent your honour
       two brace of greyhounds.
195 TIMON I'll hunt with him, and let them be received
       Not without fair reward.   *Exit Servant.*
    FLAVIUS [*aside*]   What will this come to?
       He commands us to provide and give great gifts,
       And all out of an empty coffer;
       Nor will he know his purse or yield me this:
200   To show him what a beggar his heart is,
       Being of no power to make his wishes good.
       His promises fly so beyond his state
       That what he speaks is all in debt – he owes
       For every word. He is so kind that he now
205   Pays interest for't; his land's put to their books.
       Well, would I were gently put out of office
       Before I were forced out.
       Happier is he that has no friend to feed,
       Than such that do e'en enemies exceed.
210   I bleed inwardly for my lord.   *Exit.*
    TIMON You do yourselves much wrong,
       You bate too much of your own merits.
       Here, my lord, a trifle of our love.
    2 LORD
       With more than common thanks I will receive it.
215 3 LORD O, he's the very soul of bounty.
    TIMON And now I remember, my lord, you gave good
       words the other day of a bay courser I rode on. 'Tis
       yours because you liked it.
    3 LORD O, I beseech you pardon me, my lord, in that.
    TIMON
220   You may take my word, my lord; I know no man
       Can justly praise but what he does affect.
       I weigh my friend's affection with mine own.
       I tell you true, I'll call to you.
    ALL LORDS O, none so welcome!
225 TIMON I take all and your several visitations
       So kind to heart, 'tis not enough to give;
       Methinks I could deal kingdoms to my friends,
       And ne'er be weary. Alcibiades,
       Thou art a soldier, therefore seldom rich –

       It comes in charity to thee, for all thy living   230
       Is 'mongst the dead and all the lands thou hast
       Lie in a pitched field.
    ALCIBIADES Ay, defiled land, my lord.
    1 LORD We are so virtuously bound –
    TIMON And so am I to you.   235
    2 LORD So infinitely endeared –
    TIMON All to you. Lights, more lights!
    1 LORD The best of happiness, honour and fortunes
       keep with you, Lord Timon.
    TIMON Ready for his friends.
              Exeunt Lords and others. Apemantus
                           and Timon remain.
    APEMANTUS   What a coil's here!   240
       Serving of becks and jutting out of bums!
       I doubt whether their legs be worth the sums
       That are given for 'em. Friendship's full of dregs;
       Methinks false hearts should never have sound legs.
       Thus honest fools lay out their wealth on curtsies. 245
    TIMON Now Apemantus, if thou wert not sullen
       I would be good to thee.
    APEMANTUS No, I'll nothing – for if I should be bribed
       too, there would be none left to rail upon thee and then
       thou wouldst sin the faster. Thou giv'st so long, Timon, 250
       I fear me thou wilt give away thyself in paper shortly.
       What needs these feasts, pomps and vainglories?
    TIMON Nay, an you begin to rail on society once, I am
       sworn not to give regard to you.
       Farewell, and come with better music.   *Exit.*
    APEMANTUS   So,   255
       Thou wilt not hear me now, thou shalt not then.
       I'll lock thy heaven from thee.
       O, that men's ears should be
       To counsel deaf, but not to flattery.   *Exit.*

    2.1   *Enter a* Senator.

    SENATOR
       And late five thousand; to Varro and to Isidore
       He owes nine thousand, besides my former sum,
       Which makes it five and twenty. Still in motion
       Of raging waste? It cannot hold, it will not.
       If I want gold, steal but a beggar's dog   5
       And give it Timon, why, the dog coins gold.
       If I would sell my horse and buy twenty more
       Better than he, why, give my horse to Timon –
       Ask nothing, give it him – it foals me straight
       And able horses. No porter at his gate,   10
       But rather one that smiles and still invites
       All that pass by. It cannot hold; no reason
       Can sound his state in safety. Caphis, ho!
       Caphis, I say!

                       Enter CAPHIS.

    CAPHIS   Here, sir, what is your pleasure?
    SENATOR
       Get on your cloak and haste you to Lord Timon.   15

Importune him for my moneys; be not ceased
With slight denial, nor then silenced when
'Commend me to your master', and the cap
Plays in the right hand, thus. But tell him
My uses cry to me, I must serve my turn   20
Out of mine own, his days and times are past,
And my reliances on his fracted dates
Have smit my credit. I love and honour him,
But must not break my back to heal his finger.
Immediate are my needs, and my relief   25
Must not be tossed and turned to me in words,
But find supply immediate. Get you gone,
Put on a most importunate aspect,
A visage of demand, for I do fear
When every feather sticks in his own wing,   30
Lord Timon will be left a naked gull
Which flashes now a phoenix. Get you gone.
CAPHIS   I go, sir.
SENATOR   Take the bonds along with you,
And have the dates in. Come.
CAPHIS   I will, sir.
SENATOR   Go.   *Exeunt.*

2.2   *Enter* FLAVIUS, *with many bills in his hand.*

FLAVIUS   No care, no stop, so senseless of expense
That he will neither know how to maintain it
Nor cease his flow of riot. Takes no account
How things go from him, nor resumes no care
Of what is to continue; never mind   5
Was to be so unwise, to be so kind.
What shall be done? He will not hear till feel.
I must be round with him, now he comes from
    hunting.
Fie, fie, fie, fie.   [*Retires.*]

Enter CAPHIS, ISIDORE SERVANT *and*
First VARRO SERVANT.

CAPHIS   Good even, Varro. What, you come for money?   10
1 VARRO SERVANT   Is't not your business too?
CAPHIS   It is, and yours too, Isidore?
ISIDORE SERVANT   It is so.
CAPHIS   Would we were all discharged.
1 VARRO SERVANT   I fear it.   15
CAPHIS   Here comes the lord.

Enter TIMON *and his train*
with ALCIBIADES.

TIMON   So soon as dinner's done, we'll forth again,
My Alcibiades. – With me? What is your will?
CAPHIS   My lord, here is a note of certain dues.
TIMON   Dues? Whence are you?
CAPHIS   Of Athens here, my lord.   20
TIMON   Go to my steward.
CAPHIS   Please it your lordship, he hath put me off
To the succession of new days this month.
My master is awaked by great occasion

To call upon his own and humbly prays you   25
That with your other noble parts you'll suit
In giving him his right.
TIMON   Mine honest friend,
I prithee but repair to me next morning.
CAPHIS   Nay, good my lord –
TIMON   Contain thyself, good friend.
1 VARRO SERVANT
One Varro's servant, my good lord –
ISIDORE SERVANT   From Isidore,   30
He humbly prays your speedy payment –
CAPHIS   If you did know, my lord, my master's wants –
1 VARRO SERVANT
'Twas due on forfeiture, my lord, six weeks and past –
ISIDORE SERVANT
Your steward puts me off, my lord, and I
Am sent expressly to your lordship –
TIMON   Give me breath.   35
I do beseech you, good my lords, keep on,
I'll wait upon you instantly.
            Exeunt Timon's train and Alcibiades.
[*to Flavius, who comes forward*] Come hither. Pray you
How goes the world, that I am thus encountered
With clamorous demands of broken bonds
And the detention of long-since-due debts   40
Against my honour?
FLAVIUS [*to Servants*]   Please you gentlemen,
The time is unagreeable to this business.
Your importunacy cease till after dinner,
That I may make his lordship understand
Wherefore you are not paid.
TIMON   Do so, my friends.   45
– See them well entertained.   *Exit.*
FLAVIUS   Pray draw near.   *Exit.*

Enter APEMANTUS *and* FOOL.

CAPHIS   Stay, stay, here comes the fool with Apemantus;
let's ha' some sport with 'em.
1 VARRO SERVANT   Hang him, he'll abuse us.
ISIDORE SERVANT   A plague upon him – dog!   50
1 VARRO SERVANT   How dost, Fool?
APEMANTUS   Dost dialogue with thy shadow?
1 VARRO SERVANT   I speak not to thee.
APEMANTUS   No, 'tis to thyself. [*to Fool*] Come away.
ISIDORE SERVANT [*to 1 Varro Servant*]   There's the fool   55
hangs on your back already.
APEMANTUS   No, thou stand'st single, thou'rt not on
him yet.
CAPHIS   Where's the fool now?
APEMANTUS   He last asked the question. Poor rogues   60
and usurers' men, bawds between gold and want.
ALL SERVANTS   What are we, Apemantus?
APEMANTUS   Asses.
ALL SERVANTS   Why?
APEMANTUS   That you ask me what you are and do not   65
know yourselves. Speak to 'em, Fool.
FOOL   How do you, gentlemen?

ALL SERVANTS   Gramercies, good Fool. How does your
    mistress?

70 FOOL   She's e'en setting on water to scald such chickens
    as you are. Would we could see you at Corinth.

APEMANTUS   Good, gramercy.

Enter PAGE.

FOOL   Look you, here comes my mistress's page.

PAGE [*to Fool*]   Why how now, captain, what do you in
75   this wise company? How dost thou, Apemantus?

APEMANTUS   Would I had a rod in my mouth that I
    might answer thee profitably.

PAGE   Prithee, Apemantus, read me the superscription
    of these letters, I know not which is which.

80 APEMANTUS   Canst not read?

PAGE   No.

APEMANTUS   There will little learning die, then, that
    day thou art hanged. This is to Lord Timon, this to
    Alcibiades. Go, thou wast born a bastard and thou'lt
85   die a bawd.

PAGE   Thou wast whelpt a dog and thou shalt famish a
    dog's death. Answer not, I am gone.   *Exit.*

APEMANTUS   E'en so thou out-runn'st grace. Fool, I
    will go with you to Lord Timon's.

90 FOOL   Will you leave me there?

APEMANTUS   If Timon stay at home. – You three serve
    three usurers?

ALL SERVANTS   Ay, would they served us.

APEMANTUS   So would I – as good a trick as ever
95   hangman served thief.

FOOL   Are you three usurers' men?

ALL SERVANTS   Ay, Fool.

FOOL   I think no usurer but has a fool to his servant. My
    mistress is one, and I am her fool. When men come to
100   borrow of your masters, they approach sadly and go
    away merry, but they enter my mistress's house merrily
    and go away sad. The reason of this?

1 VARRO SERVANT   I could render one.

APEMANTUS   Do it then, that we may account thee a
105   whoremaster and a knave, which notwithstanding thou
    shalt be no less esteemed.

1 VARRO SERVANT   What is a whoremaster, Fool?

FOOL   A fool in good clothes, and something like thee.
    'Tis a spirit: sometime 't appears like a lord, sometime
110   like a lawyer, sometime like a philosopher, with two
    stones more than's artificial one. He is very often like a
    knight; and generally, in all shapes that man goes up and
    down in from fourscore to thirteen, this spirit walks in.

1 VARRO SERVANT   Thou art not altogether a fool.

115 FOOL   Nor thou altogether a wise man. As much foolery
    as I have, so much wit thou lack'st.

APEMANTUS   That answer might have become
    Apemantus.

ALL SERVANTS   Aside, aside, here comes Lord Timon.

Enter TIMON and FLAVIUS.

120 APEMANTUS   Come with me, Fool, come.

FOOL   I do not always follow lover, elder brother and
    woman, sometime the philosopher.
                        Exeunt Apemantus and Fool.

FLAVIUS
    Pray you walk near, I'll speak with you anon.
                                Exeunt Servants.

TIMON
    You make me marvel wherefore ere this time
    Had you not fully laid my state before me,   125
    That I might so have rated my expense
    As I had leave of means.

FLAVIUS   You would not hear me:
    At many leisures I proposed –

TIMON   Go to,
    Perchance some single vantages you took
    When my indisposition put you back,   130
    And that unaptness made your minister
    Thus to excuse yourself.

FLAVIUS   O my good lord,
    At many times I brought in my accounts,
    Laid them before you; you would throw them off
    And say you found them in mine honesty.   135
    When for some trifling present you have bid me
    Return so much, I have shook my head and wept,
    Yea, 'gainst th'authority of manners, prayed you
    To hold your hand more close. I did endure
    Not seldom nor no slight checks, when I have   140
    Prompted you in the ebb of your estate
    And your great flow of debts. My loved lord,
    Though you hear now, too late, yet now's a time:
    The greatest of your having lacks a half
    To pay your present debts.

TIMON   Let all my land be sold.   145

FLAVIUS   'Tis all engaged, some forfeited and gone,
    And what remains will hardly stop the mouth
    Of present dues; the future comes apace.
    What shall defend the interim, and at length
    How goes our reckoning?   150

TIMON   To Lacedaemon did my land extend.

FLAVIUS   O my good lord, the world is but a word;
    Were it all yours to give it in a breath,
    How quickly were it gone.

TIMON   You tell me true.

FLAVIUS   If you suspect my husbandry of falsehood,   155
    Call me before th'exactest auditors
    And set me on the proof. So the gods bless me,
    When all our offices have been oppressed
    With riotous feeders, when our vaults have wept
    With drunken spilth of wine, when every room   160
    Hath blazed with lights and brayed with minstrelsy,
    I have retired me to a wasteful cock
    And set mine eyes at flow.

TIMON   Prithee, no more.

FLAVIUS
    'Heavens,' have I said, 'the bounty of this lord!
    How many prodigal bits have slaves and peasants   165
    This night englutted? Who is not Timon's,

What heart, head, sword, force, means, but is Lord
   Timon's?
"Great Timon, noble, worthy, royal Timon!" '
Ah, when the means are gone that buy this praise,
170 The breath is gone whereof this praise is made.
Feast-won, fast-lost; one cloud of winter showers,
These flies are couched.
TIMON   Come, sermon me no further.
No villainous bounty yet hath passed my heart –
Unwisely, not ignobly, have I given.
175 Why dost thou weep? Canst thou the conscience lack
To think I shall lack friends? Secure thy heart –
If I would broach the vessels of my love
And try the argument of hearts by borrowing,
Men and men's fortunes could I frankly use
As I can bid thee speak.
180 FLAVIUS   Assurance bless your thoughts.
TIMON
And in some sort these wants of mine are crowned,
That I account them blessings. For by these
Shall I try friends. You shall perceive how you
Mistake my fortunes: I am wealthy in my friends.
185 – Within there, Flaminius, Servilius?

      Enter FLAMINIUS, SERVILIUS *and*
         a third Servant.

SERVANTS   My lord, my lord.
TIMON   I will dispatch you severally: [*to Servilius*] you
to Lord Lucius; [*to Flaminius*] to Lord Lucullus you, I
hunted with his honour today; [*to Third Servant*] you
190 to Sempronius. Commend me to their loves; and I am
proud, say, that my occasions have found time to use
'em toward a supply of money: let the request be fifty
talents.
FLAMINIUS   As you have said, my lord.
                          Exeunt Servants.
195 FLAVIUS [*aside*]   Lord Lucius and Lucullus? Humh!
TIMON   Go you, sir, to the senators,
Of whom, even to the state's best health, I have
Deserved this hearing: bid 'em send o'th' instant
A thousand talents to me.
FLAVIUS   I have been bold
200 (For that I knew it the most general way)
To them to use your signet and your name,
But they do shake their heads, and I am here
No richer in return.
TIMON   Is't true? Can't be?
FLAVIUS   They answer in a joint and corporate voice
205 That now they are at fall, want treasure, cannot
Do what they would, are sorry. You are honourable,
But yet they could have wished – they know not –
Something hath been amiss – a noble nature
May catch a wrench – would all were well – 'tis pity –
210 And so intending other serious matters,
After distasteful looks and these hard fractions,
With certain half-caps and cold-moving nods
They froze me into silence.

TIMON   You gods, reward them!
Prithee, man, look cheerly. These old fellows
Have their ingratitude in them hereditary.   215
Their blood is caked, 'tis cold, it seldom flows,
'Tis lack of kindly warmth they are not kind;
And nature as it grows again toward earth
Is fashioned for the journey, dull and heavy.
Go to Ventidius – prithee be not sad,   220
Thou art true and honest, ingeniously I speak,
No blame belongs to thee. Ventidius lately
Buried his father, by whose death he's stepped
Into a great estate. When he was poor,
Imprisoned and in scarcity of friends,   225
I cleared him with five talents. Greet him from me,
Bid him suppose some good necessity
Touches his friend which craves to be remembered
With those five talents; that had, give't these fellows
To whom 'tis instant due. Ne'er speak, or think,   230
That Timon's fortunes 'mong his friends can sink.
                             Exit.
FLAVIUS   I would I could not think it:
That thought is bounty's foe;
Being free itself, it thinks all others so.   *Exit.*

3.1   *Enter* FLAMINIUS *who waits to speak*
       with LUCULLUS *from his Master; enter*
          a Servant *to him.*

SERVANT   I have told my lord of you; he is coming down
to you.
FLAMINIUS   I thank you, sir.

         Enter LUCULLUS.

SERVANT   Here's my lord.
LUCULLUS [*aside*]   One of Lord Timon's men? A gift, I   5
warrant. Why this hits right: I dreamt of a silver basin
and ewer tonight. – Flaminius, honest Flaminius, you
are very respectively welcome, sir. [*to Servant*] Fill me
some wine.   *Exit Servant.*
And how does that honourable, complete, free-hearted   10
gentleman of Athens, thy very bountiful good lord and
master?
FLAMINIUS   His health is well, sir.
LUCULLUS   I am right glad that his health is well, sir.
And what hast thou there under thy cloak, pretty   15
Flaminius?
FLAMINIUS   Faith, nothing but an empty box, sir, which
in my lord's behalf I come to entreat your honour to
supply – who, having great and instant occasion to use
fifty talents, hath sent to your lordship to furnish him,   20
nothing doubting your present assistance therein.
LUCULLUS   La, la, la, la! Nothing doubting, says he?
Alas, good lord, a noble gentleman 'tis, if he would not
keep so good a house. Many a time and often I ha'
dined with him, and told him on't, and come again to   25
supper to him of purpose to have him spend less, and
yet he would embrace no counsel, take no warning by

my coming – every man has his fault, and honesty is
his. I ha' told him on't, but I could ne'er get him
from't.

Enter Servant *with wine.*

SERVANT   Please your lordship, here is the wine.

LUCULLUS   Flaminius, I have noted thee always wise.
Here's to thee!

FLAMINIUS   Your lordship speaks your pleasure.

LUCULLUS   I have observed thee always for a towardly
prompt spirit, give thee thy due, and one that knows
what belongs to reason, and canst use the time well if
the time use thee well – good parts in thee. [*to Servant*]
Get you gone, sirrah.   *Exit Servant.*
Draw nearer, honest Flaminius. Thy lord's a bountiful
gentleman, but thou art wise and thou knowst well
enough, although thou com'st to me, that this is no
time to lend money, especially upon bare friendship
without security. Here's three solidares for thee; good
boy, wink at me, and say thou sawst me not. Fare thee
well.

FLAMINIUS
Is't possible the world should so much differ,
And we alive that lived? Fly, damned baseness,
To him that worships thee.   [*Throws the money back.*]

LUCULLUS   Ha? Now I see
Thou art a fool and fit for thy master.   *Exit Lucullus.*

FLAMINIUS
May these add to the number that may scald thee!
Let molten coin be thy damnation,
Thou disease of a friend, and not himself.
Has friendship such a faint and milky heart
It turns in less than two nights? O you gods,
I feel my master's passion. This slave
Unto this hour has my lord's meat in him:
Why should it thrive and turn to nutriment,
When he is turned to poison?
O, may diseases only work upon't,
And when he's sick to death, let not that part of
    nature
Which my lord paid for be of any power
To expel sickness, but prolong his hour!   *Exit.*

3.2   *Enter* LUCIUS, *with three* Strangers.

LUCIUS   Who, the Lord Timon? He is my very good
friend and an honourable gentleman.

1 STRANGER   We know him for no less, though we are
but strangers to him. But I can tell you one thing, my
lord, and which I hear from common rumours: now
Lord Timon's happy hours are done and past, and his
estate shrinks from him.

LUCIUS   Fie, no, do not believe it; he cannot want for
money.

2 STRANGER   But believe you this, my lord, that not
long ago one of his men was with the Lord Lucullus to
borrow so many talents, nay urged extremely for't and

showed what necessity belonged to't, and yet was
denied.

LUCIUS   How?

2 STRANGER   I tell you, denied, my lord.

LUCIUS   What a strange case was that! Now, before the
gods I am ashamed on't. Denied that honourable man?
There was very little honour showed in't. For my own
part, I must needs confess I have received some small
kindnesses from him, as money, plate, jewels and such
like trifles – nothing comparing to his. Yet had he
mistook him, and sent to me, I should ne'er have
denied his occasion so many talents.

Enter SERVILIUS.

SERVILIUS   See, by good hap yonder's my lord; I have
sweat to see his honour. – My honoured lord!

LUCIUS   Servilius? You are kindly met, sir. Fare thee
well, commend me to thy honourable virtuous lord,
my very exquisite friend.

SERVILIUS   May it please your honour, my lord hath
sent –

LUCIUS   Ha, what has he sent? I am so much endeared
to that lord, he's ever sending. How shall I thank him,
think'st thou? And what has he sent now?

SERVILIUS   He's only sent his present occasion now, my
lord, requesting your lordship to supply his instant use
with so many talents.   [*Hands Lucius a note.*]

LUCIUS   I know his lordship is but merry with me;
He cannot want fifty – five hundred talents.

SERVILIUS
But in the mean time, he wants less, my lord.
If his occasion were not virtuous
I should not urge it half so faithfully.

LUCIUS   Dost thou speak seriously, Servilius?

SERVILIUS   Upon my soul 'tis true, sir.

LUCIUS   What a wicked beast was I to disfurnish myself
against such a good time, when I might ha' shown
myself honourable! How unluckily it happened that I
should purchase the day before for a little part and
undo a great deal of honour! Servilius, now before the
gods, I am not able to do – the more beast I, I say – I
was sending to use Lord Timon myself, these
gentlemen can witness. But I would not for the wealth
of Athens I had done't now. Commend me bountifully
to his good lordship, and I hope his honour will
conceive the fairest of me, because I have no power to
be kind. And tell him this from me: I count it one of
my greatest afflictions, say, that I cannot pleasure such
an honourable gentleman. Good Servilius, will you
befriend me so far as to use mine own words to him?

SERVILIUS   Yes sir, I shall.

LUCIUS
I'll look you out a good turn, Servilius. *Exit Servilius.*
[*to the Strangers*] True as you said, Timon is shrunk
    indeed,
And he that's once denied will hardly speed.   *Exit.*

1 STRANGER   Do you observe this, Hostilius?

65　2 STRANGER　Ay, too well.

1 STRANGER　Why this is the world's soul,
　And just of the same piece is every
　Flatterer's spirit. Who can call him his friend
　That dips in the same dish? For in my knowing
70　Timon has been this lord's father and kept
　His credit with his purse,
　Supported his estate, nay, Timon's money
　Has paid his men their wages. He ne'er drinks,
　But Timon's silver treads upon his lip,
75　And yet – O, see the monstrousness of man
　When he looks out in an ungrateful shape –
　He does deny him, in respect of his,
　What charitable men afford to beggars.

3 STRANGER　Religion groans at it.

1 STRANGER　　　　　　　　For mine own part,
80　I never tasted Timon in my life,
　Nor came any of his bounties over me
　To mark me for his friend. Yet I protest,
　For his right noble mind, illustrious virtue
　And honourable carriage,
85　Had his necessity made use of me,
　I would have put my wealth into donation
　And the best half should have returned to him,
　So much I love his heart. But I perceive
　Men must learn now with pity to dispense,
90　For policy sits above conscience.　　　*Exeunt.*

3.3　　*Enter Timon's* Third Servant *with*
　　　SEMPRONIUS, *another of Timon's friends.*

SEMPRONIUS
　Must he needs trouble me in't, hmm? 'Bove all
　　others?
　He might have tried Lord Lucius or Lucullus –
　And now Ventidius is wealthy too,
　Whom he redeemed from prison. All these
　Owe their estates unto him.

5　3 SERVANT　　　　　　　My lord,
　They have all been touched and found base metal,
　For they have all denied him.

SEMPRONIUS　How? Have they denied him,
　Has Ventidius and Lucullus denied him
10　And does he send to me? Three – hmm?
　It shows but little love or judgement in him.
　Must I be his last refuge? His friends, like physicians,
　Thrive, give him over – must I take th' cure upon me?
　He's much disgraced me in't: I'm angry at him,
15　That might have known my place. I see no sense for't
　But his occasions might have wooed me first,
　For in my conscience I was the first man
　That ere received gift from him –
　And does he think so backwardly of me now
20　That I'll requite it last? No;
　So it may prove an argument of laughter
　To th'rest, and 'mongst lords I be thought a fool.
　I'd rather than the worth of thrice the sum

He'd sent to me first, but for my mind's sake,
I'd such a courage to do him good. But now return　25
And with their faint reply this answer join:
Who bates mine honour shall not know my coin.
　　　　　　　　　　　　　　Exit.

SERVANT　Excellent! Your lordship's a goodly villain.
　The devil knew not what he did when he made man
　politic; he crossed himself by't, and I cannot think but　30
　in the end the villainies of man will set him clear. How
　fairly this lord strives to appear foul, takes virtuous
　copies to be wicked! Like those that under hot ardent
　zeal would set whole realms on fire, of such a nature is
　his politic love.　　35
　This was my lord's best hope, now all are fled
　Save only the gods. Now his friends are dead,
　Doors that were ne'er acquainted with their wards
　Many a bounteous year must be employed
　Now to guard sure their master.　　40
　And this is all a liberal course allows,
　Who cannot keep his wealth, must keep his house.
　　　　　　　　　　　　　　Exit.

3.4　　*Enter two of Varro's* Servants,
　　　meeting TITUS *and* HORTENSIUS, *and*
　　　then LUCIUS, *all Servants of Timon's creditors,*
　　　to wait for his coming out.

1 VARRO SERVANT
　Well met, good morrow Titus and Hortensius.

TITUS　The like to you, kind Varro.

HORTENSIUS　　　　　　　Lucius!
　What, do we meet together?

LUCIUS　　　　　　　　　Ay, and I think
　One business does command us all; for mine
　Is money.

TITUS　　So is theirs and ours.

　　　　　　Enter PHILOTUS.

LUCIUS　　　　　　　　And, sir,　5
　Philotus' too.

PHILOTUS　　Good day at once.

LUCIUS
　Welcome, good brother, what do you think the hour?

PHILOTUS　Labouring for nine.

LUCIUS　So much?

PHILOTUS　　　　　Is not my lord seen yet?

LUCIUS　　　　　　　　　　Not yet.

PHILOTUS
　I wonder on't, he was wont to shine at seven.　10

LUCIUS　Ay, but the days are waxed shorter with him.
　You must consider that a prodigal course
　Is like the sun's, but not like his recoverable.
　I fear 'tis deepest winter in Lord Timon's purse –
　That is, one may reach deep enough and yet　15
　Find little.

PHILOTUS　I am of your fear for that.

TITUS　I'll show you how t'observe a strange event:

Your lord sends now for money?

HORTENSIUS   Most true, he does.

TITUS   And he wears jewels now of Timon's gift,
20   For which I wait for money.

HORTENSIUS   It is against my heart.

LUCIUS   Mark how strange it shows,
        Timon in this should pay more than he owes:
        And e'en as if your lord should wear rich jewels
        And send for money for 'em.

HORTENSIUS
25   I'm weary of this charge, the gods can witness;
        I know my lord hath spent of Timon's wealth,
        And now ingratitude makes it worse than stealth.

1 VARRO SERVANT
        Yes, mine's three thousand crowns. What's yours?

LUCIUS   Five thousand mine.

1 VARRO SERVANT
30   'Tis much deep, and it should seem by th' sum
        Your master's confidence was above mine,
        Else surely his had equalled.

                Enter FLAMINIUS.

TITUS   One of Lord Timon's men.

LUCIUS   Flaminius? Sir, a word! Pray, is my lord ready
35   to come forth?

FLAMINIUS   No, indeed he is not.

TITUS   We attend his lordship; pray signify so much.

FLAMINIUS   I need not tell him that, he knows you are
        too diligent.   *Exit.*

                Enter FLAVIUS *in a cloak, muffled.*

40   LUCIUS   Ha, is not that his steward muffled so?
        He goes away in a cloud. Call him, call him.

TITUS   Do you hear, sir?

2 VARRO SERVANT   By your leave, sir.

FLAVIUS   What do ye ask of me, my friend?

TITUS   We wait for certain money here, sir.

FLAVIUS   Ay,
45   If money were as certain as your waiting,
        'Twere sure enough.
        Why then preferred you not your sums and bills
        When your false masters ate of my lord's meat?
        Then they could smile and fawn upon his debts,
50   And take down th'interest into their gluttonous maws.
        You do yourselves but wrong to stir me up,
        Let me pass quietly.
        Believe't, my lord and I have made an end,
        I have no more to reckon, he to spend.

55   LUCIUS   Ay, but this answer will not serve.

FLAVIUS   If 'twill not serve 'tis not so base as you,
        For you serve knaves.   *Exit.*

1 VARRO SERVANT   How? What does his cashiered
        worship mutter?

60   2 VARRO SERVANT   No matter what, he's poor, and
        that's revenge enough. Who can speak broader than he
        that has no house to put his head in? Such may rail
        against great buildings.

                Enter SERVILIUS.

TITUS   O, here's Servilius; now we shall know some
        answer.   65

SERVILIUS   If I might beseech you gentlemen to repair
        some other hour, I should derive much from't. For
        take't of my soul, my lord leans wondrously to
        discontent; his comfortable temper has forsook him,
        he's much out of health and keeps his chamber.   70

LUCIUS   Many do keep their chambers are not sick.
        And if it be so far beyond his health,
        Methinks he should the sooner pay his debts
        And make a clear way to the gods.

SERVILIUS   Good gods!

TITUS   We cannot take this for answer, sir.   75

FLAMINIUS [*within*]   Servilius, help! My lord, my lord!

                Enter TIMON *in a rage.*

TIMON
        What, are my doors opposed against my passage?
        Have I been ever free, and must my house
        Be my retentive enemy, my jail?
        The place which I have feasted, does it now,   80
        Like all mankind, show me an iron heart?

LUCIUS   Put in now, Titus.

TITUS   My lord, here is my bill.

LUCIUS   Here's mine.

HORTENSIUS   And mine, my lord.   85

BOTH VARRO SERVANTS   And ours, my lord.

PHILOTUS   All our bills.

TIMON
        Knock me down with 'em, cleave me to the girdle.

LUCIUS   Alas, my lord –

TIMON   Cut my heart in sums –   90

TITUS   Mine, fifty talents –

TIMON   Tell out my blood.

LUCIUS   Five thousand crowns, my lord.

TIMON
        Five thousand drops pays that. What yours, and yours?

1 VARRO SERVANT   My lord –   95

2 VARRO SERVANT   My lord –

TIMON
        Tear me, take me, and the gods fall upon you.   *Exit.*

HORTENSIUS   Faith, I perceive our masters may throw
        their caps at their money; these debts may well be
        called desperate ones, for a madman owes 'em.   100

                                                Exeunt.

3.5   *Enter* TIMON *and* FLAVIUS.

TIMON
        They have e'en put my breath from me, the slaves.
        Creditors? Devils!

FLAVIUS   My dear lord –

TIMON   What if it should be so?

FLAVIUS   My lord –

TIMON   I'll have it so. [*calling*] My steward!

FLAVIUS   Here, my lord.

5 TIMON   So fitly? Go, bid all my friends again,
Lucius, Lucullus and Sempronius, all,
I'll once more feast the rascals.

FLAVIUS   O my lord,
You only speak from your distracted soul;
There's not so much left to furnish out
A moderate table.

10 TIMON   Be it not in thy care.
Go, I charge thee, invite them all, let in the tide
Of knaves once more: my cook and I'll provide.

                                            Exeunt.

3.6   *Enter three* Senators *at one door,*
ALCIBIADES meeting them, with Attendants.

1 SENATOR   My lord, you have my voice to't, the fault's
Bloody: 'tis necessary he should die.
Nothing emboldens sin so much as mercy.

2 SENATOR   Most true, the law shall bruise 'em.

ALCIBIADES
5   Honour, health and compassion to the senate!

1 SENATOR   Now, captain?

ALCIBIADES   I am an humble suitor to your virtues,
For pity is the virtue of the law
And none but tyrants use it cruelly.
10   It pleases time and fortune to lie heavy
Upon a friend of mine, who in hot blood
Hath stepped into the law, which is past depth
To those that without heed do plunge into't.
He is a man, setting his fate aside,
15   Of comely virtues,
Nor did he soil the fact with cowardice –
An honour in him which buys out his fault –
But with a noble fury and fair spirit,
Seeing his reputation touched to death,
20   He did oppose his foe.
And with such sober and unnoted passion
He did behave his anger ere 'twas spent,
As if he had but proved an argument.

1 SENATOR   You undergo too strict a paradox
25   Striving to make an ugly deed look fair.
Your words have took such pains as if they laboured
To bring manslaughter into form and set quarrelling
Upon the head of valour, which indeed
Is valour misbegot and came into the world
30   When sects and factions were newly born.
He's truly valiant that can wisely suffer
The worst that man can breathe, and make his wrongs
His outsides to wear them like his raiment, carelessly,
And ne'er prefer his injuries to his heart,
35   To bring it into danger.
If wrongs be evils and enforce us kill,
What folly 'tis to hazard life for ill!

ALCIBIADES   My lord –

1 SENATOR   You cannot make gross sins look clear:
To revenge is no valour, but to bear.

ALCIBIADES   My lords, then, under favour, pardon me   40
If I speak like a captain.
Why do fond men expose themselves to battle
And not endure all threats, sleep upon't
And let the foes quietly cut their throats
Without repugnancy? If there be   45
Such valour in the bearing, what make we
Abroad? Why then, women are more valiant
That stay at home, if bearing carry it,
And the ass more captain than the lion, the felon
Loaden with irons wiser than the judge,   50
If wisdom be in suffering. O my lords,
As you are great, be pitifully good.
Who cannot condemn rashness in cold blood?
To kill, I grant, is sin's extremest gust,
But in defence, by mercy, 'tis most just.   55
To be in anger is impiety,
But who is man that is not angry?
Weigh but the crime with this.

2 SENATOR   You breathe in vain.

ALCIBIADES   In vain? His service done
At Lacedaemon and Byzantium,   60
Were a sufficient briber for his life.

1 SENATOR   What's that?

ALCIBIADES
Why, I say, my lords, he's done fair service
And slain in fight many of your enemies.
How full of valour did he bear himself   65
In the last conflict and made plenteous wounds!

2 SENATOR   He has made too much plenty with 'em.
He's a sworn rioter: he has a sin
That often drowns him and takes his valour prisoner.
If there were no foes, that were enough   70
To overcome him. In that beastly fury,
He has been known to commit outrages
And cherish factions. 'Tis inferred to us
His days are foul and his drink dangerous.

1 SENATOR   He dies.

ALCIBIADES   Hard fate! He might have died in war.   75
My lords, if not for any parts in him,
Though his right arm might purchase his own time
And be in debt to none, yet more to move you,
Take my deserts to his and join 'em both.
And for I know your reverend ages love   80
Security, I'll pawn my victories, all
My honour, to you upon his good returns.
If by this crime, he owes the law his life,
Why, let the war receive't in valiant gore,
For law is strict and war is nothing more.   85

1 SENATOR   We are for law. He dies, urge it no more
On height of our displeasure. Friend or brother,
He forfeits his own blood that spills another.

ALCIBIADES   Must it be so? It must not be.
My lords, I do beseech you, know me.

2 SENATOR   How?   90

ALCIBIADES   Call me to your remembrances.

3 SENATOR   What?

ALCIBIADES   I cannot think but your age has forgot me,
It could not else be I should prove so base
To sue and be denied such common grace.
My wounds ache at you.

95   1 SENATOR   Do you dare our anger?
'Tis in few words, but spacious in effect:
We banish thee forever.

ALCIBIADES   Banish me?
Banish your dotage, banish usury
That makes the senate ugly.

1 SENATOR   If after two days' shine,

100   Athens contain thee, attend our weightier judgement.
And not to swell our spirit, he shall be
Executed presently.   *Exeunt Senators.*

ALCIBIADES   Now the
Gods keep you old enough, that you may live
Only in bone, that none may look on you!

105   I'm worse than mad: I have kept back their foes
While they have told their money and let out
Their coin upon large interest – I myself
Rich only in large hurts. All those, for this?
Is this the balsam that the usuring senate

110   Pours into captains' wounds? Banishment.
It comes not ill: I hate not to be banished,
It is a cause worthy my spleen and fury,
That I may strike at Athens. I'll cheer up
My discontented troops and lay for hearts.

115   'Tis honour with most lands to be at odds,
Soldiers should brook as little wrongs as gods.   *Exit.*

3.7   *Music. Enter divers of Timon's Friends*
         at several doors, among them LUCIUS,
       LUCULLUS, VENTIDIUS, SEMPRONIUS *and*
            other Lords.

1 LORD   The good time of day to you, sir.

2 LORD   I also wish it to you. I think this honourable
lord did but try us this other day.

1 LORD   Upon that were my thoughts tiring when we
5   encountered. I hope it is not so low with him as he
made it seem in the trial of his several friends.

2 LORD   It should not be, by the persuasion of his new
feasting.

1 LORD   I should think so. He hath sent me an earnest
10   inviting, which many my near occasions did urge me to
put off; but he hath conjured me beyond them and I
must needs appear.

2 LORD   In like manner was I in debt to my importunate
business, but he would not hear my excuse. I am sorry
15   when he sent to borrow of me that my provision was
out.

1 LORD   I am sick of that grief too, as I understand how
all things go.

2 LORD   Every man here's so. What would he have
20   borrowed of you?

1 LORD   A thousand pieces.

2 LORD   A thousand pieces?

1 LORD   What of you?

2 LORD   He sent to me sir – here he comes.

Enter TIMON *and Attendants who prepare
a table and seats for a banquet.*

TIMON   With all my heart, gentlemen both, and how   25
fare you?

1 LORD   Ever at the best, hearing well of your lordship.

2 LORD   The swallow follows not summer more willing
than we your lordship.

TIMON   Nor more willingly leaves winter – such   30
summer birds are men. Gentlemen, our dinner will
not recompense this long stay. Feast your ears with the
music awhile, if they will fare so harshly o' th' trumpets'
sound; we shall to't presently.

1 LORD   I hope it remains not unkindly with your   35
lordship that I returned you an empty messenger.

TIMON   O sir, let it not trouble you.

2 LORD   My noble lord –

TIMON   Ah my good friend, what cheer?

2 LORD   My most honourable lord, I am e'en sick of   40
shame that when your lordship this other day sent to
me I was so unfortunate a beggar.

TIMON   Think not on't, sir.

2 LORD   If you had sent but two hours before –

TIMON   Let it not cumber your better remembrance. [*to*   45
Attendants] Come, bring in all together.

The banquet is brought in.

2 LORD   All covered dishes!

1 LORD   Royal cheer, I warrant you.

3 LORD   Doubt not that, if money and the season can
yield it.   50

1 LORD   How do you? What's the news?

3 LORD   Alcibiades is banished, hear you of it?

1, 2 LORDS   Alcibiades banished?

3 LORD   'Tis so, be sure of it.

1 LORD   How, how?   55

2 LORD   I pray you, upon what?

TIMON   My worthy friends, will you draw near?

3 LORD   I'll tell you more anon. Here's a noble feast
toward.

2 LORD   This is the old man still.   60

3 LORD   Will't hold, will't hold?

2 LORD   It does, but time will – and so –

3 LORD   I do conceive.

TIMON   Each man to his stool with that spur as he
would to the lip of his mistress – your diet shall be in   65
all places alike. Make not a city feast of it to let the meat
cool ere we can agree upon the first place. Sit, sit.
The gods require our thanks:
     You great benefactors, sprinkle our society with
thankfulness. For your own gifts, make yourselves   70
praised, but reserve still to give, lest your deities be
despised. Lend to each man enough, that one need

not lend to another, for were your godheads to
borrow of men, men would forsake the gods. Make
75 the meat be beloved more than the man that gives it.
Let no assembly of twenty be without a score of
villains. If there sit twelve women at the table, let a
dozen of them be as they are. The rest of your foes,
O gods – the senators of Athens, together with the
80 common lag of people – what is amiss in them, you
gods, make suitable for destruction. For these my
present friends, as they are to me nothing, so in
nothing bless them and to nothing are they welcome.
Uncover, dogs, and lap! [*The dishes are uncovered and
prove to be full of lukewarm water.*]

85 A LORD   What does his lordship mean?

ANOTHER LORD   I know not.

TIMON   May you a better feast never behold,
You knot of mouth-friends! Smoke and lukewarm
        water
Is your perfection. This is Timon's last,
90 Who, stuck and spangled with your flatteries,
Washes it off and sprinkles in your faces
Your reeking villainy.   [*Throws water in their faces.*]
                        Live loathed and long,
Most smiling, smooth, detested parasites,
Courteous destroyers, affable wolves, meek bears –
95 You fools of fortune, trencher-friends, time's flies,
Cap-and-knee slaves, vapours and minute-jacks!
Of man and beast the infinite malady
Crust you quite o'er!
        [*as one is trying to leave*] What, dost thou go?
Soft, take thy physic first [*throwing things at him and
others*]; thou too, and thou!
100 Stay, I will lend thee money, borrow none.
                        Exeunt Lords in disarray.
What, all in motion? Henceforth be no feast
Whereat a villain's not a welcome guest.
Burn house, sink Athens, henceforth hated be
Of Timon man and all humanity!   *Exit.*

        Enter the Senators, *with* Lords.

105 1 LORD   How now, my lords?

2 LORD   Know you the quality of Lord Timon's fury?

3 LORD   Push, did you see my cap?

4 LORD   I have lost my gown.

1 LORD   He's but a mad lord, and naught but humours
110 sways him. He gave me a jewel th'other day, and now
he has beat it out of my hat.
Did you see my jewel?

3 LORD   Did you see my cap?

2 LORD   Here 'tis.

4 LORD   Here lies my gown.

1 LORD   Let's make no stay.

2 LORD   Lord Timon's mad.

3 LORD   I feel't upon my bones.

4 LORD
115 One day he gives us diamonds, next day stones.
                        Exeunt Lords and Senators.

4.1   *Enter* TIMON.

TIMON   Let me look back upon thee. O thou wall
That girdles in those wolves, dive in the earth
And fence not Athens! Matrons, turn incontinent;
Obedience, fail in children; slaves and fools,
Pluck the grave wrinkled senate from the bench   5
And minister in their steads. To general filths
Convert o'th' instant, green virginity,
Do't in your parents' eyes. Bankrupts, hold fast;
Rather than render back, out with your knives
And cut your trusters' throats! Bound servants,
        steal: 10
Large-handed robbers your grave masters are
And pill by law. Maid, to thy master's bed,
Thy mistress is o'th' brothel. Son of sixteen,
Pluck the lined crutch from thy old limping sire,
With it beat out his brains. Piety and fear,   15
Religion to the gods, peace, justice, truth,
Domestic awe, night-rest and neighbourhood,
Instruction, manners, mysteries and trades,
Degrees, observances, customs and laws,
Decline to your confounding contraries –   20
And let confusion live! Plagues incident to men,
Your potent and infectious fevers heap
On Athens, ripe for stroke. Thou cold sciatica,
Cripple our senators that their limbs may halt
As lamely as their manners; lust and liberty,   25
Creep in the minds and marrows of our youth
That 'gainst the stream of virtue they may strive
And drown themselves in riot. Itches, blains,
Sow all th'Athenian bosoms, and their crop
Be general leprosy; breath, infect breath,   30
That their society, as their friendship, may
Be merely poison. Nothing I'll bear from thee
But nakedness, thou detestable town.
Take thou that too, with multiplying bans.
Timon will to the woods, where he shall find   35
Th'unkindest beast more kinder than mankind.
The gods confound – hear me, you good gods all! –
Th'Athenians both within and out that wall,
And grant as Timon grows his hate may grow
To the whole race of mankind, high and low!   40
Amen.   *Exit.*

4.2   *Enter* FLAVIUS *with two or three* Servants.

1 SERVANT
Hear you, master steward, where's our master?
Are we undone, cast off, nothing remaining?

FLAVIUS   Alack, my fellows, what should I say to you?
Let me be recorded by the righteous gods,
I am as poor as you.

1 SERVANT   Such a house broke?   5
So noble a master fallen? All gone, and not
One friend to take his fortune by the arm
And go along with him?

2 SERVANT   As we do turn our backs
From our companion thrown into his grave,
10 So his familiars to his buried fortunes
Slink all away, leave their false vows with him
Like empty purses picked; and his poor self,
A dedicated beggar to the air,
With his disease of all-shunned poverty,
15 Walks, like contempt, alone. – More of our fellows.

Enter other Servants.

FLAVIUS   All broken implements of a ruined house.
3 SERVANT   Yet do our hearts wear Timon's livery –
That see I by our faces. We are fellows still,
Serving alike in sorrow; leaked is our bark,
20 And we poor mates stand on the dying deck
Hearing the surges threat – we must all part
Into this sea of air.
FLAVIUS   Good fellows all,
The latest of my wealth I'll share amongst you.
Wherever we shall meet, for Timon's sake
25 Let's yet be fellows. Let's shake our heads and say,
As 'twere a knell unto our master's fortunes,
'We have seen better days'. Let each take some,
        [*offering them money*]
Nay, put out all your hands – not one word more,
Thus part we rich in sorrow, parting poor.
        They embrace and part several ways.
30 O, the fierce wretchedness that glory brings us!
Who would not wish to be from wealth exempt,
Since riches point to misery and contempt?
Who would be so mocked with glory, or to live
But in a dream of friendship –
35 To have his pomp and all what state compounds
But only painted, like his varnished friends?
Poor honest lord, brought low by his own heart,
Undone by goodness! Strange unusual blood
When man's worst sin is he does too much good.
40 Who then dares to be half so kind again?
For bounty that makes gods do still mar men.
My dearest lord, blessed to be most accursed,
Rich only to be wretched, thy great fortunes
Are made thy chief afflictions. Alas, kind lord,
45 He's flung in rage from this ungrateful seat
Of monstrous friends;
Nor has he with him to supply his life,
Or that which can command it.
I'll follow and inquire him out.
50 I'll ever serve his mind with my best will:
Whilst I have gold, I'll be his steward still.   *Exit.*

4.3   *Enter* TIMON *in the woods.*

TIMON   O blessed breeding sun, draw from the earth
Rotten humidity, below thy sister's orb
Infect the air! Twinned brothers of one womb
Whose procreation, residence and birth
5 Scarce is dividant, touch them with several fortunes,

The greater scorns the lesser. Not nature,
To whom all sores lay siege, can bear great fortune
But by contempt of nature.
Raise me this beggar and deject that lord:
10 The senator shall bear contempt hereditary,
The beggar native honour.
It is the pasture lards the rother's sides,
The want that makes him lean. Who dares – who
        dares
In purity of manhood stand upright
15 And say, 'This man's a flatterer'? If one be,
So are they all, for every grece of fortune
Is smoothed by that below. The learned pate
Ducks to the golden fool. All's obliquy,
There's nothing level in our cursed natures
20 But direct villainy. Therefore be abhorred
All feasts, societies and throngs of men!
His semblable, yea himself, Timon disdains.
Destruction fang mankind! Earth, yield me roots.
        [*Digs in the earth.*]
Who seeks for better of thee, sauce his palate
25 With thy most operant poison. – What is here?
Gold? Yellow, glittering, precious gold?
No, gods, I am no idle votarist –
Roots, you clear heavens! Thus much of this will
        make
Black white, foul fair, wrong right,
30 Base noble, old young, coward valiant.
Ha, you gods, why this? What this, you gods? Why,
        this
Will lug your priests and servants from your sides,
Pluck stout men's pillows from below their heads.
This yellow slave
35 Will knit and break religions, bless th'accursed,
Make the hoar leprosy adored, place thieves
And give them title, knee and approbation
With senators on the bench. This is it
That makes the wappered widow wed again,
40 She whom the spittle-house and ulcerous sores
Would cast the gorge at, this embalms and spices
To th'April day again. Come, damned earth,
Thou common whore of mankind that puts odds
Among the rout of nations, I will make thee
Do thy right nature.   [*March afar off*]
45   Ha? A drum? Thou'rt quick
But yet I'll bury thee. Thou'lt go, strong thief,
When gouty keepers of thee cannot stand.
Nay, stay thou out for earnest.   [*Keeps some gold.*]

Enter ALCIBIADES *with drum and fife*
in warlike manner, and PHRYNIA *and* TIMANDRA.

ALCIBIADES   What art thou there? Speak.
TIMON   A beast, as thou art. The canker gnaw thy heart
50 For showing me again the eyes of man!
ALCIBIADES
What is thy name? Is man so hateful to thee
That art thyself a man?

TIMON   I am Misanthropos and hate mankind.
55   For thy part, I do wish thou wert a dog
         That I might love thee something.
ALCIBIADES   I know thee well,
         But in thy fortunes am unlearned and strange.
TIMON
         I know thee too, and more than that I know thee
         I not desire to know. Follow thy drum,
60   With man's blood paint the ground gules, gules.
         Religious canons, civil laws are cruel,
         Then what should war be? This fell whore of thine
         Hath in her more destruction than thy sword,
         For all her cherubin look.
PHRYNIA   Thy lips rot off!
65   TIMON   I will not kiss thee, then the rot returns
         To thine own lips again.
ALCIBIADES
         How came the noble Timon to this change?
TIMON   As the moon does, by wanting light to give;
         But then renew I could not like the moon –
         There were no suns to borrow of.
70   ALCIBIADES   Noble Timon,
         What friendship may I do thee?
TIMON   None but to
         Maintain my opinion.
ALCIBIADES   What is it, Timon?
TIMON   Promise me friendship, but perform none.
         If thou wilt not promise, the gods plague thee,
75   For thou art a man; if thou dost perform,
         Confound thee, for thou art a man.
ALCIBIADES   I have heard in some sort of thy miseries.
TIMON   Thou sawst them when I had prosperity.
ALCIBIADES   I see them now; then was a blessed time.
80   TIMON   As thine is now, held with a brace of harlots.
TIMANDRA
         Is this th'Athenian minion whom the world
         Voiced so regardfully?
TIMON   Art thou Timandra?
TIMANDRA   Yes.
TIMON
         Be a whore still, they love thee not that use thee;
         Give them diseases, leaving with thee their lust.
85   Make use of thy salt hours: season the slaves
         For tubs and baths, bring down rose-cheeked youth
         To the tub-fast and the diet.
TIMANDRA   Hang thee, monster!
ALCIBIADES   Pardon him, sweet Timandra, for his wits
         Are drowned and lost in his calamities.
90   I have but little gold of late, brave Timon,
         The want whereof doth daily make revolt
         In my penurious band. I have heard and grieved
         How cursed Athens, mindless of thy worth,
         Forgetting thy great deeds when neighbour states
95   But for thy sword and fortune trod upon them –
TIMON   I prithee, beat thy drum and get thee gone.
ALCIBIADES
         I am thy friend and pity thee, dear Timon.

TIMON
         How dost thou pity him whom thou dost trouble?
         I had rather be alone.
ALCIBIADES   Why fare thee well.
         Here is some gold for thee.
TIMON   Keep it, I cannot eat it.   100
ALCIBIADES   When I have laid proud Athens on a heap –
TIMON   Warr'st thou 'gainst Athens?
ALCIBIADES   Ay Timon, and have cause.
TIMON   The gods confound them all in thy conquest,
         And thee after when thou hast conquered!
ALCIBIADES   Why me, Timon?
TIMON   That by killing of villains   105
         Thou wast born to conquer my country.
         Put up thy gold. Go on, here's gold, go on.
         Be as a planetary plague when Jove
         Will o'er some high-viced city hang his poison
         In the sick air. Let not thy sword skip one: 110
         Pity not honoured age for his white beard,
         He is an usurer; strike me the counterfeit matron,
         It is her habit only that is honest,
         Herself's a bawd; let not the virgin's cheek
         Make soft thy trenchant sword, for those milk-paps   115
         That through the window-bars bore at men's eyes
         Are not within the leaf of pity writ,
         But set them down horrible traitors; spare not the
            babe
         Whose dimpled smiles from fools exhaust their mercy,
         Think it a bastard whom the oracle   120
         Hath doubtfully pronounced thy throat shall cut
         And mince it sans remorse. Swear against objects,
         Put armour on thine ears and on thine eyes,
         Whose proof nor yells of mothers, maids nor babes,
         Nor sight of priests in holy vestments bleeding,   125
         Shall pierce a jot. There's gold to pay thy soldiers –
         Make large confusion and, thy fury spent,
         Confounded be thyself. Speak not, be gone!
ALCIBIADES
         Hast thou gold yet? I'll take the gold thou givest me,
         Not all thy counsel.   130
TIMON
         Dost thou or dost thou not, heaven's curse upon thee!
TIMANDRA, PHRYNIA
         Give us some gold, good Timon, hast thou more?
TIMON   Enough to make a whore forswear her trade
         And, to make whores, a bawd. Hold up, you sluts,
         Your aprons mountant; you are not oathable,   135
         Although I know you'll swear – terribly swear
         Into strong shudders and to heavenly agues –
         Th'immortal gods that hear you. Spare your oaths,
         I'll trust to your conditions. Be whores still,
         And he whose pious breath seeks to convert you,   140
         Be strong in whore, allure him, burn him up;
         Let your close fire predominate his smoke
         And be no turncoats. Yet may your pain-sick months
         Be quite contrary. And thatch your poor thin roofs
         With burdens of the dead – some that were hanged –   145

No matter, wear them, betray with them. Whore still,
Paint till a horse may mire upon your face.
A pox of wrinkles!
TIMANDRA, PHRYNIA   Well, more gold, what then?
Believe't that we'll do anything for gold.
150   TIMON   Consumptions sow
In hollow bones of man, strike their sharp shins
And mar men's spurring. Crack the lawyer's voice
That he may never more false title plead
Nor sound his quillets shrilly. Hoar the flamen
155   That scolds against the quality of flesh
And not believes himself. Down with the nose,
Down with it flat, take the bridge quite away
Of him that, his particular to foresee,
Smells from the general weal. Make curled-pate
ruffians bald
160   And let the unscarred braggarts of the war
Derive some pain from you. Plague all,
That your activity may defeat and quell
The source of all erection. There's more gold.
Do you damn others and let this damn you,
165   And ditches grave you all!
TIMANDRA, PHRYNIA
More counsel with more money, bounteous Timon!
TIMON
More whore, more mischief first – I have given you
earnest.
ALCIBIADES
Strike up the drum towards Athens. Farewell, Timon;
If I thrive well, I'll visit thee again.
170   TIMON   If I hope well, I'll never see thee more.
ALCIBIADES   I never did thee harm.
TIMON   Yes, thou spok'st well of me.
ALCIBIADES   Call'st thou that harm?
TIMON   Men daily find it. Get thee away, and take
Thy beagles with thee.
ALCIBIADES   We but offend him, strike.
       Drum beats. Exeunt Alcibiades, Phrynia and Timandra.
TIMON
175   That nature, being sick of man's unkindness,
Should yet be hungry!   [*Digs.*]
                Common mother – thou
Whose womb unmeasurable and infinite breast
Teems and feeds all, whose selfsame mettle
Whereof thy proud child, arrogant man, is puffed,
180   Engenders the black toad and adder blue,
The gilded newt and eyeless venomed worm,
With all th'abhorred births below crisp heaven
Whereon Hyperion's quickening fire doth shine –
Yield him who all the human sons do hate
185   From forth thy plenteous bosom one poor root.
Ensear thy fertile and conceptious womb,
Let it no more bring out ungrateful man.
Go great with tigers, dragons, wolves and bears,
Teem with new monsters whom thy upward face
190   Hath to the marbled mansion all above
Never presented. – O, a root, dear thanks! –

Dry up thy marrows, vines and plough-torn leas,
Whereof ungrateful man with liquorish draughts
And morsels unctuous greases his pure mind,
That from it all consideration slips –   195

                Enter APEMANTUS.

More man? Plague, plague!
APEMANTUS   I was directed hither. Men report
Thou dost affect my manners and dost use them.
TIMON   'Tis then because thou dost not keep a dog
Whom I would imitate. Consumption catch thee!   200
APEMANTUS   This is in thee a nature but affected,
A poor unmanly melancholy sprung
From change of fortune. Why this spade, this place,
This slave-like habit and these looks of care?
Thy flatterers yet wear silk, drink wine, lie soft,   205
Hug their diseased perfumes and have forgot
That ever Timon was. Shame not these woods
By putting on the cunning of a carper.
Be thou a flatterer now and seek to thrive
By that which has undone thee: hinge thy knee   210
And let his very breath whom thou'lt observe
Blow off thy cap; praise his most vicious strain
And call it excellent. Thou wast told thus;
Thou gav'st thine ears, like tapsters that bade
welcome,
To knaves and all approachers. 'Tis most just   215
That thou turn rascal; had'st thou wealth again,
Rascals should have't. Do not assume my likeness.
TIMON   Were I like thee, I'd throw away myself.
APEMANTUS
Thou hast cast away thyself, being like thyself
A madman so long, now a fool. What, think'st   220
That the bleak air, thy boisterous chamberlain,
Will put thy shirt on warm? Will these mossed trees
That have outlived the eagle page thy heels
And skip when thou point'st out? Will the cold brook,
Candied with ice, caudle thy morning taste   225
To cure thy o'ernight's surfeit? Call the creatures
Whose naked natures live in all the spite
Of wreakful heaven, whose bare unhoused trunks
To the conflicting elements exposed
Answer mere nature, bid them flatter thee.   230
O, thou shalt find –
TIMON   A fool of thee. Depart.
APEMANTUS   I love thee better now than e'er I did.
TIMON   I hate thee worse.
APEMANTUS   Why?
TIMON   Thou flatter'st misery.
APEMANTUS   I flatter not, but say thou art a caitiff.
TIMON   Why dost thou seek me out?
APEMANTUS   To vex thee.   235
TIMON   Always a villain's office, or a fool's.
Dost please thyself in't?
APEMANTUS   Ay.
TIMON   What, a knave too?
APEMANTUS   If thou didst put this sour cold habit on

To castigate thy pride, 'twere well; but thou
240 Dost it enforcedly. Thou'dst courtier be again,
Wert thou not beggar. Willing misery
Outlives uncertain pomp, is crowned before –
The one is filling still, never complete,
The other, at high wish. Best state, contentless,
245 Hath a distracted and most wretched being,
Worse than the worst, content.
Thou shouldst desire to die, being miserable.
TIMON   Not by his breath that is more miserable.
Thou art a slave whom fortune's tender arm
250 With favour never clasped, but bred a dog.
Hadst thou like us from our first swath proceeded
The sweet degrees that this brief world affords
To such as may the passive drudges of it
Freely command, thou wouldst have plunged thyself
255 In general riot, melted down thy youth
In different beds of lust and never learned
The icy precepts of respect, but followed
The sugared game before thee. But myself –
Who had the world as my confectionary,
260 The mouths, the tongues, the eyes and hearts of men
At duty more than I could frame employment,
That numberless upon me stuck as leaves
Do on the oak, have with one winter's brush
Fell from their boughs and left me open, bare
265 For every storm that blows – I to bear this,
That never knew but better, is some burden.
Thy nature did commence in sufferance, time
Hath made thee hard in't. Why shouldst thou hate
    men?
They never flattered thee. What hast thou given?
270 If thou wilt curse, thy father, that poor rogue,
Must be thy subject, who in spite put stuff
To some she-beggar and compounded thee
Poor rogue hereditary. Hence, be gone!
If thou hadst not been born the worst of men,
275 Thou hadst been a knave and flatterer.
APEMANTUS   Art thou proud yet?
TIMON   Ay, that I am not thee.
APEMANTUS   Ay, that I was no prodigal.
TIMON   Ay, that I am one now.
Were all the wealth I have shut up in thee,
280 I'd give thee leave to hang it. Get thee gone.
That the whole life of Athens were in this!
Thus would I eat it.   [*Eats a root.*]
APEMANTUS   Here, I will mend thy feast.
    [*Offers food.*]
TIMON   First mend my company, take away thyself.
APEMANTUS
So I shall mend mine own by th'lack of thine.
285 TIMON   'Tis not well mended so, it is but botched;
If not, I would it were.
APEMANTUS   What wouldst thou have to Athens?
TIMON   Thee thither in a whirlwind. If thou wilt,
Tell them there I have gold – look, so I have.
APEMANTUS   Here is no use for gold.

TIMON   The best and truest,
For here it sleeps and does no hired harm.   290
APEMANTUS   Where liest a-nights, Timon?
TIMON   Under that's above me. Where feed'st thou
a-days, Apemantus?
APEMANTUS   Where my stomach finds meat, or rather
where I eat it.   295
TIMON   Would poison were obedient and knew my
mind.
APEMANTUS   Where wouldst thou send it?
TIMON   To sauce thy dishes.
APEMANTUS   The middle of humanity thou never   300
knewst, but the extremity of both ends. When thou
wast in thy gilt and thy perfume, they mocked thee for
too much curiosity; in thy rags thou knowst none but
art despised for the contrary. There's a medlar for thee
– eat it.   305
TIMON   On what I hate I feed not.
APEMANTUS   Dost hate a medlar?
TIMON   Ay, though it look like thee.
APEMANTUS   An thou'dst hated meddlers sooner, thou
shouldst have loved thyself better now. What man   310
didst thou ever know unthrift that was beloved after
his means?
TIMON   Who, without those means thou talk'st of, didst
thou ever know beloved?
APEMANTUS   Myself.   315
TIMON   I understand thee: thou hadst some means to
keep a dog.
APEMANTUS   What things in the world canst thou
nearest compare to thy flatterers?
TIMON   Women nearest; but men – men are the things   320
themselves. What wouldst thou do with the world,
Apemantus, if it lay in thy power?
APEMANTUS   Give it the beasts, to be rid of the men.
TIMON   Wouldst thou have thyself fall in the confusion
of men and remain a beast with the beasts?   325
APEMANTUS   Ay, Timon.
TIMON   A beastly ambition, which the gods grant thee
t'attain to. If thou wert the lion, the fox would beguile
thee; if thou wert the lamb, the fox would eat thee; if
thou wert the fox, the lion would suspect thee when   330
peradventure thou wert accused by the ass; if thou
wert the ass, thy dullness would torment thee, and still
thou lived'st but as a breakfast to the wolf; if thou wert
the wolf, thy greediness would afflict thee and oft thou
shouldst hazard thy life for thy dinner. Wert thou the   335
unicorn, pride and wrath would confound thee and
make thine own self the conquest of thy fury; wert
thou a bear, thou wouldst be killed by the horse; wert
thou a horse, thou wouldst be seized by the leopard;
wert thou a leopard, thou wert germane to the lion,   340
and the spots of thy kindred were jurors on thy life – all
thy safety were remotion and thy defence absence.
What beast couldst thou be that were not subject to a
beast? And what a beast art thou already that seest not
thy loss in transformation!   345

APEMANTUS   If thou couldst please me with speaking to me, thou mightst have hit upon it here. The commonwealth of Athens is become a forest of beasts.

TIMON   How! Has the ass broke the wall, that thou art out of the city?

APEMANTUS   Yonder comes a poet and a painter. The plague of company light upon thee! I will fear to catch it, and give way. When I know not what else to do, I'll see thee again.

TIMON   When there is nothing living but thee, thou shalt be welcome. I had rather be a beggar's dog than Apemantus.

APEMANTUS   Thou art the cap of all the fools alive.

TIMON   Would thou wert clean enough to spit upon!

APEMANTUS
A plague on thee, thou art too bad to curse.

TIMON   All villains that do stand by thee are pure.

APEMANTUS
There is no leprosy but what thou speak'st.

TIMON   If I name thee.
I'll beat thee, but I should infect my hands.

APEMANTUS   I would my tongue could rot them off!

TIMON   Away, thou issue of a mangy dog!
Choler does kill me that thou art alive –
I swoon to see thee.

APEMANTUS   Would thou wouldst burst!

TIMON   Away, thou tedious rogue!
I am sorry I shall lose a stone by thee!   [*Throws a stone.*]

APEMANTUS   Beast!

TIMON   Slave!

APEMANTUS   Toad!

TIMON   Rogue, rogue, rogue!
I am sick of this false world and will love naught
But even the mere necessities upon't.
Then, Timon, presently prepare thy grave:
Lie where the light foam of the sea may beat
Thy gravestone daily; make thine epitaph,
That death in me at others' lives may laugh.
[*to the gold*] O thou sweet king-killer and dear divorce
'Twixt natural son and sire; thou bright defiler
Of Hymen's purest bed, thou valiant Mars;
Thou ever young, fresh, loved and delicate wooer
Whose blush doth thaw the consecrated snow
That lies on Dian's lap; thou visible god,
That solder'st close impossibilities
And mak'st them kiss, that speak'st with every tongue
To every purpose. O thou touch of hearts,
Think thy slave man rebels, and by thy virtue
Set them into confounding odds, that beasts
May have the world in empire!

APEMANTUS   Would 'twere so,
But not till I am dead. I'll say thou'st gold:
Thou wilt be thronged to shortly.

TIMON   Thronged to?

APEMANTUS   Ay.

TIMON   Thy back, I prithee.

APEMANTUS   Live and love thy misery.

TIMON
Long live so and so die! I am quit.   [*Withdraws.*]

APEMANTUS
More things like men. Eat, Timon, and abhor them.
Exit.

Enter Thieves.

1 THIEF   Where should he have this gold? It is some poor fragment, some slender ort of his remainder. The mere want of gold and the falling-from of his friends drove him into this melancholy.

2 THIEF   It is noised he hath a mass of treasure.

3 THIEF   Let us make the assay upon him. If he care not for't, he will supply us easily; if he covetously reserve it, how shall's get it?

2 THIEF   True, for he bears it not about him: 'tis hid.

1 THIEF   Is not this he?

2, 3 THIEVES   Where?

2 THIEF   'Tis his description.

3 THIEF   He; I know him.

ALL THIEVES   Save thee, Timon.

TIMON   Now thieves.

ALL THIEVES   Soldiers, not thieves.

TIMON   Both too, and women's sons.

ALL THIEVES
We are not thieves, but men that much do want.

TIMON   Your greatest want is you want much of meat.
Why should you want? Behold, the earth hath roots,
Within this mile break forth a hundred springs,
The oaks bear mast, the briars scarlet hips,
The bounteous housewife Nature on each bush
Lays her full mess before you. Want? Why want?

1 THIEF
We cannot live on grass, on berries, water,
As beasts and birds and fishes.

TIMON
Nor on the beasts themselves, the birds and fishes –
You must eat men. Yet thanks I must you con
That you are thieves professed, that you work not
In holier shapes, for there is boundless theft
In limited professions. Rascal thieves,
Here's gold. Go, suck the subtle blood o'th' grape
Till the high fever seethe your blood to froth,
And so scape hanging. Trust not the physician –
His antidotes are poison and he slays
More than you rob. Take wealth and lives together,
Do villainy, do, since you protest to do't
Like workmen. I'll example you with thievery:
The sun's a thief and with his great attraction
Robs the vast sea; the moon's an arrant thief
And her pale fire she snatches from the sun;
The sea's a thief whose liquid surge resolves
The moon into salt tears; the earth's a thief
That feeds and breeds by a composture stol'n
From general excrement. Each thing's a thief.
The laws, your curb and whip, in their rough power
Has unchecked theft. Love not yourselves; away!

Rob one another – there's more gold. Cut throats,
All that you meet are thieves. To Athens go,
Break open shops, nothing can you steal
But thieves do lose it. Steal less for this I give you,
445 And gold confound you howsoe'er. Amen.
    [*Withdraws.*]
3 THIEF   He's almost charmed me from my profession
    by persuading me to it.
1 THIEF   'Tis in the malice of mankind that he thus
    advises us, not to have us thrive in our mystery.
450 2 THIEF   I'll believe him as an enemy and give over my
    trade.
1 THIEF   Let us first see peace in Athens; there is no
    time so miserable but a man may be true.
                                    Exeunt Thieves.

        Enter FLAVIUS *to* TIMON.

FLAVIUS   O you gods!
455   Is yon despised and ruinous man my lord,
    Full of decay and failing? O monument
    And wonder of good deeds evilly bestowed!
    What an alteration of honour has desperate want made.
    What viler thing upon the earth than friends
460   Who can bring noblest minds to basest ends?
    How rarely does it meet with this time's guise,
    When man was wished to love his enemies.
    Grant I may ever love and rather woo
    Those that would mischief me than those that do.
465   He's caught me in his eye; I will present
    My honest grief unto him and as my lord
    Still serve him with my life. – My dearest master!
TIMON   Away! What art thou?
FLAVIUS   Have you forgot me, sir?
TIMON   Why dost ask that? I have forgot all men.
    Then, if thou grant'st thou'rt a man, I have forgot
470   thee.
FLAVIUS   An honest poor servant of yours –
TIMON   Then I know thee not.
    I never had honest man about me, I; all
    I kept were knaves to serve in meat to villains.
475 FLAVIUS   The gods are witness,
    Ne'er did poor steward wear a truer grief
    For his undone lord than mine eyes for you.
TIMON
    What, dost thou weep? Come nearer then. I love thee
    Because thou art a woman and disclaim'st
480   Flinty mankind, whose eyes do never give
    But thorough lust and laughter. Pity's sleeping.
    Strange times that weep with laughing, not with
        weeping.
FLAVIUS   I beg of you to know me, good my lord,
    T'accept my grief and whilst this poor wealth lasts
485   To entertain me as your steward still.
TIMON   Had I a steward
    So true, so just and now so comfortable?
    It almost turns my dangerous nature mild.
    Let me behold thy face. Surely this man

490 Was born of woman.
    Forgive my general and exceptless rashness,
    You perpetual sober gods! I do proclaim
    One honest man. Mistake me not: but one,
    No more I pray, and he's a steward.
495   How fain would I have hated all mankind,
    And thou redeem'st thyself. But all save thee
    I fell with curses.
    Methinks thou art more honest now than wise,
    For by oppressing and betraying me
500   Thou mightst have sooner got another service,
    For many so arrive at second masters
    Upon their first lord's neck. But tell me true
    (For I must ever doubt, though ne'er so sure)
    Is not thy kindness subtle, covetous,
505   A usuring kindness and, as rich men deal gifts,
    Expecting in return twenty for one?
FLAVIUS   No, my most worthy master, in whose breast
    Doubt and suspect, alas, are placed too late;
    You should have feared false times when you did feast,
510   Suspect still comes where an estate is least.
    That which I show heaven knows is merely love,
    Duty and zeal to your unmatched mind,
    Care of your food and living. And believe it,
    My most honoured lord,
515   For any benefit that points to me,
    Either in hope or present, I'd exchange
    For this one wish: that you had power and wealth
    To requite me by making rich yourself.
TIMON   Look thee, 'tis so. Thou singly honest man,
520   Here, take; the gods out of my misery
    Has sent thee treasure. Go, live rich and happy,
    But thus conditioned: thou shalt build from men.
    Hate all, curse all, show charity to none,
    But let the famished flesh slide from the bone
525   Ere thou relieve the beggar. Give to dogs
    What thou deniest to men. Let prisons swallow 'em,
    Debts wither 'em to nothing; be men like blasted
        woods,
    And may diseases lick up their false bloods!
    And so farewell and thrive.
FLAVIUS   O, let me stay
    And comfort you, my master.
TIMON   If thou hat'st curses,
530   Stay not. Fly whilst thou art blest and free,
    Ne'er see thou man, and let me ne'er see thee.
                        Exit Flavius. Timon withdraws.

5.1   *Enter* POET *and* PAINTER, TIMON
              in his cave.

PAINTER   As I took note of the place, it cannot be far
    where he abides.
POET   What's to be thought of him? Does the rumour
    hold for true that he's so full of gold?
PAINTER   Certain. Alcibiades reports it; Phrynia and
5   Timandra had gold of him. He likewise enriched poor

straggling soldiers with great quantity. 'Tis said he
gave unto his steward a mighty sum.

POET   Then this breaking of his has been but a try for
10   his friends?

PAINTER   Nothing else. You shall see him a palm in
Athens again and flourish with the highest. Therefore
'tis not amiss we tender our loves to him in this
supposed distress of his: it will show honestly in us and
15   is very likely to load our purposes with what they
travail for, if it be a just and true report that goes of his
having.

POET   What have you now to present unto him?

PAINTER   Nothing at this time but my visitation; only I
20   will promise him an excellent piece.

POET   I must serve him so too, tell him of an intent
that's coming toward him.

PAINTER   Good as the best. Promising is the very air
o'th' time; it opens the eyes of expectation.
25   Performance is ever the duller for his act and, but in
the plainer and simpler kind of people, the deed of
saying is quite out of use. To promise is most courtly
and fashionable; performance is a kind of will or
testament which argues a great sickness in his
30   judgement that makes it.

Enter TIMON *from his cave.*

TIMON [*aside*]   Excellent workman, thou canst not paint
a man so bad as is thyself.

POET   I am thinking what I shall say I have provided for
him. It must be a personating of himself, a satire
35   against the softness of prosperity, with a discovery of
the infinite flatteries that follow youth and opulency.

TIMON [*aside*]   Must thou needs stand for a villain in
thine own work? Wilt thou whip thine own faults in
other men? Do so, I have gold for thee.

40   PAINTER   Nay, let's seek him.
Then do we sin against our own estate
When we may profit meet and come too late.

POET   True.
When the day serves, before black-cornered night,
45   Find what thou want'st by free and offered light.
Come.

TIMON [*aside*]   I'll meet you at the turn:
What a god's gold, that he is worshipped
In a baser temple than where swine feed!
50   'Tis thou that rigg'st the bark and plough'st the foam,
Settlest admired reverence in a slave –
To thee be worship, and thy saints for aye
Be crowned with plagues that thee alone obey.
Fit I meet them.

POET   Hail worthy Timon!

55   PAINTER   Our late noble master!

TIMON   Have I once lived to see two honest men?

POET   Sir,
Having often of your open bounty tasted,
Hearing you were retired, your friends fall'n off,
60   Whose thankless natures (O abhorred spirits)

Not all the whips of heaven are large enough –
What, to you,
Whose star-like nobleness gave life and influence
To their whole being? I am rapt and cannot cover
The monstrous bulk of this ingratitude   65
With any size of words.

TIMON   Let it go naked – men may see't the better.
You that are honest, by being what you are,
Make them best seen and known.

PAINTER   He and myself
Have travelled in the great shower of your gifts,   70
And sweetly felt it.

TIMON   Ay, you are honest men.

PAINTER   We are hither come to offer you our service.

TIMON   Most honest men! Why, how shall I requite you?
Can you eat roots and drink cold water – no?

BOTH   What we can do we'll do, to do you service.   75

TIMON
You're honest men. You've heard that I have gold,
I am sure you have, speak truth, you're honest men.

PAINTER   So it is said, my noble lord; but therefore
Came not my friend nor I.

TIMON
Good honest men! [*to Painter*] Thou draw'st a
    counterfeit   80
Best in all Athens; thou'rt indeed the best,
Thou counterfeit'st most lively.

PAINTER   So so, my lord.

TIMON
E'en so, sir, as I say. [*to Poet*] And for thy fiction,
Why, thy verse swells with stuff so fine and smooth
That thou art even natural in thine art.   85
But for all this, my honest-natured friends,
I must needs say you have a little fault;
Marry, 'tis not monstrous in you, neither wish I
You take much pains to mend.

BOTH   Beseech your honour
To make it known to us.

TIMON   You'll take it ill.   90

BOTH   Most thankfully, my lord.

TIMON   Will you indeed?

BOTH   Doubt it not, worthy lord.

TIMON   There's never a one of you but trusts a knave
That mightily deceives you.

BOTH   Do we, my lord?

TIMON   Ay, and you hear him cog, see him dissemble,   95
Know his gross patchery, love him, feed him,
Keep in your bosom, yet remain assured
That he's a made-up villain.

PAINTER   I know none such, my lord.

POET   Nor I.

TIMON   Look you, I love you well. I'll give you gold –   100
Rid me these villains from your companies;
Hang them or stab them, drown them in a draught,
Confound them by some course and come to me,
I'll give you gold enough.

BOTH   Name them, my lord, let's know them.   105

TIMON   You that way and you this, but two in company:
Each man apart, all single and alone,
Yet an arch-villain keeps him company.
[*to one*] If where thou art, two villains shall not be,
Come not near him.
110   [*to the other*]   If thou wouldst not reside
But where one villain is, then him abandon.
Hence, pack! [*throws stones*] There's gold – you came
for gold, ye slaves!
[*to one*] You have work for me, there's payment, hence!
[*to the other*] You are an alchemist, make gold of that.
115   Out, rascal dogs!   *Exeunt Poet and Painter, driven*
out by Timon, who retires to his cave.

5.2   *Enter* FLAVIUS *and two* Senators.

FLAVIUS   It is vain that you would speak with Timon,
For he is set so only to himself
That nothing but himself which looks like man
Is friendly with him.
5   1 SENATOR   Bring us to his cave.
It is our part and promise to th'Athenians
To speak with Timon.
2 SENATOR   At all times alike
Men are not still the same: 'twas time and griefs
That framed him thus. Time, with his fairer hand,
Offering the fortunes of his former days,
10   The former man may make him. Bring us to him
And chance it as it may.
FLAVIUS   Here is his cave.
Peace and content be here! Lord Timon! Timon,
Look out and speak to friends. Th'Athenians
By two of their most reverend senate greet thee.
15   Speak to them, noble Timon.

Enter TIMON *out of his cave.*

TIMON
Thou sun that comforts, burn! Speak and be hanged!
For each true word, a blister, and each false
Be as a cantherizing to the root o'th' tongue,
Consuming it with speaking.
1 SENATOR   Worthy Timon –
20   TIMON   Of none but such as you, and you of Timon.
1 SENATOR   The senators of Athens greet thee, Timon.
TIMON [*aside*]
I thank them and would send them back the plague,
Could I but catch it for them.
1 SENATOR   O, forget
What we are sorry for ourselves in thee.
25   The senators with one consent of love
Entreat thee back to Athens, who have thought
On special dignities, which vacant lie
For thy best use and wearing.
2 SENATOR   They confess
Toward thee forgetfulness too general gross,
30   Which now the public body, which doth seldom
Play the recanter, feeling in itself

A lack of Timon's aid, hath sense withal
Of its own fall, restraining aid to Timon,
And send forth us to make their sorrowed render,
Together with a recompense more fruitful   35
Than their offence can weigh down by the dram,
Ay, even such heaps and sums of love and wealth,
As shall to thee blot out what wrongs were theirs,
And write in thee the figures of their love,
Ever to read them thine.
TIMON   You witch me in it,   40
Surprise me to the very brink of tears.
Lend me a fool's heart and a woman's eyes
And I'll beweep these comforts, worthy senators.
1 SENATOR   Therefore so please thee to return with us,
And of our Athens, thine and ours, to take   45
The captainship, thou shalt be met with thanks,
Allowed with absolute power, and thy good name
Live with authority. So soon we shall drive back
Of Alcibiades th'approaches wild,
Who like a boar too savage doth root up   50
His country's peace.
2 SENATOR   And shakes his threatening sword
Against the walls of Athens.
1 SENATOR   Therefore, Timon –
TIMON   Well, sir, I will. Therefore I will, sir, thus:
If Alcibiades kill my countrymen,
Let Alcibiades know this of Timon,   55
That Timon cares not. But if he sack fair Athens
And take our goodly aged men by th' beards,
Giving our holy virgins to the stain
Of contumelious, beastly, mad-brained war,
Then let him know, and tell him Timon speaks it   60
In pity of our aged and our youth,
I cannot choose but tell him that I care not;
And – let him take't at worst – for their knives care not
While you have throats to answer. For myself,
There's not a whittle in th'unruly camp   65
But I do prize it at my love before
The reverend'st throat in Athens. So I leave you
To the protection of the prosperous gods,
As thieves to keepers.
FLAVIUS   Stay not, all's in vain.
TIMON   Why, I was writing of my epitaph;   70
It will be seen tomorrow. My long sickness
Of health and living now begins to mend
And nothing brings me all things. Go, live still,
Be Alcibiades your plague, you his,
And last so long enough.
1 SENATOR   We speak in vain.   75
TIMON   But yet I love my country and am not
One that rejoices in the common wrack,
As common bruit doth put it.
1 SENATOR   That's well spoke.
TIMON   Commend me to my loving countrymen.
1 SENATOR
These words become your lips as they pass through
them.   80

2 SENATOR   And enter in our ears like great triumphers
    In their applauding gates.
TIMON   Commend me to them,
    And tell them that to ease them of their griefs,
    Their fears of hostile strokes, their aches, losses,
85   Their pangs of love, with other incident throes
    That nature's fragile vessel doth sustain
    In life's uncertain voyage, I will some kindness do them;
    I'll teach them to prevent wild Alcibiades' wrath.
1 SENATOR [*aside*]   I like this well, he will return again.
90 TIMON   I have a tree which grows here in my close
    That mine own use invites me to cut down,
    And shortly must I fell it. Tell my friends,
    Tell Athens, in the sequence of degree
    From high to low throughout, that whoso please
95   To stop affliction, let him take his haste,
    Come hither ere my tree hath felt the axe
    And hang himself. I pray you do my greeting.
FLAVIUS
    Trouble him no further; thus you still shall find him.
TIMON   Come not to me again, but say to Athens
100   Timon hath made his everlasting mansion
    Upon the beached verge of the salt flood,
    Who once a day with his embossed froth
    The turbulent surge shall cover; thither come,
    And let my gravestone be your oracle.
105   Lips, let sour words go by, and language end:
    What is amiss, plague and infection mend;
    Graves only be men's works and death their gain,
    Sun, hide thy beams, Timon hath done his reign.
                           Exit.
1 SENATOR   His discontents are unremoveably
110   Coupled to nature.
2 SENATOR   Our hope in him is dead. Let us return
    And strain what other means is left unto us
    In our dear peril.
1 SENATOR   It requires swift foot.   *Exeunt.*

5.3   *Enter two other* Senators,
            with a Messenger.

3 SENATOR
    Thou hast painfully discovered. Are his files
    As full as thy report?
MESSENGER   I have spoke the least.
    Besides his expedition promises
    Present approach.
4 SENATOR
5   We stand much hazard if they bring not Timon.
MESSENGER   I met a courier, one mine ancient friend,
    Whom, though in general part we were opposed,
    Yet our old love made a particular force
    And made us speak like friends. This man was riding
10   From Alcibiades to Timon's cave,
    With letters of entreaty, which imported
    His fellowship i'th' cause against your city,
    In part for his sake moved.

Enter the other Senators *from* TIMON.

3 SENATOR   Here come our brothers.
1 SENATOR   No talk of Timon, nothing of him expect,
    The enemy's drum is heard and fearful scouring   15
    Doth choke the air with dust. In, and prepare;
    Ours is the fall, I fear, our foe's the snare.   *Exeunt.*

5.4   *Enter a* Soldier *in the woods,*
            seeking TIMON.

SOLDIER   By all description this should be the place.
    Who's here? Speak, ho! No answer? What is this?
    Timon is dead, who hath outstretched his span,
    Some beast read this, there does not live a man.
    Dead, sure, and this his grave; what's on this tomb   5
    I cannot read. The character I'll take with wax;
    Our captain hath in every figure skill,
    An aged interpreter though young in days.
    Before proud Athens he's set down by this,
    Whose fall the mark of his ambition is.   *Exit.*   10

5.5   *Trumpets sound. Enter* ALCIBIADES
            with his powers before Athens.

ALCIBIADES   Sound to this coward and lascivious town
    Our terrible approach.   [*A parley sounds.*]

      The Senators *appear upon the walls.*

    Till now you have gone on and filled the time
    With all licentious measure, making your wills
    The scope of justice. Till now myself and such   5
    As slept within the shadow of your power
    Have wandered with our traversed arms, and breathed
    Our sufferance vainly. Now the time is flush,
    When crouching marrow in the bearer strong
    Cries of itself 'no more'. Now breathless wrong   10
    Shall sit and pant in your great chairs of ease,
    And pursy insolence shall break his wind
    With fear and horrid flight.
1 SENATOR   Noble and young,
    When thy first griefs were but a mere conceit,
    Ere thou hadst power or we had cause of fear,   15
    We sent to thee to give thy rages balm,
    To wipe out our ingratitude with loves
    Above their quantity.
2 SENATOR   So did we woo
    Transformed Timon to our city's love
    By humble message and by promised means.   20
    We were not all unkind, nor all deserve
    The common stroke of war.
1 SENATOR   These walls of ours
    Were not erected by their hands from whom
    You have received your griefs; nor are they such
    That these great towers, trophies and schools should
        fall   25
    For private faults in them.

2 SENATOR   Nor are they living
  Who were the motives that you first went out:
  Shame that they wanted, coming in excess,
  Hath broke their hearts. March, noble lord,
30 Into our city with thy banners spread;
  By decimation and a tithed death,
  If thy revenges hunger for that food
  Which nature loathes, take thou the destined tenth,
  And by the hazard of the spotted die
35 Let die the spotted.

1 SENATOR   All have not offended.
  For those that were, it is not square to take
  On those that are, revenge; crimes like lands
  Are not inherited. Then, dear countryman,
  Bring in thy ranks but leave without thy rage;
40 Spare thy Athenian cradle and those kin
  Which in the bluster of thy wrath must fall
  With those that have offended; like a shepherd,
  Approach the fold and cull th'infected forth,
  But kill not all together.

2 SENATOR   What thou wilt,
45 Thou rather shalt enforce it with thy smile,
  Than hew to't with thy sword.

1 SENATOR   Set but thy foot
  Against our rampired gates and they shall ope,
  So thou wilt send thy gentle heart before
  To say thou'lt enter friendly.

2 SENATOR   Throw thy glove,
50 Or any token of thine honour else,
  That thou wilt use the wars as thy redress
  And not as our confusion. All thy powers
  Shall make their harbour in our town, till we
  Have sealed thy full desire.

ALCIBIADES   Then there's my glove;
55 Descend and open your uncharged ports;

  Those enemies of Timon's and mine own
  Whom you yourselves shall set out for reproof
  Fall, and no more; and, to atone your fears
  With my more noble meaning, not a man
60 Shall pass his quarter or offend the stream
  Of regular justice in your city's bounds,
  But shall be remedied to your public laws
  At heaviest answer.

BOTH   'Tis most nobly spoken.

ALCIBIADES
  Descend, and keep your words.
  Exeunt Senators from above and, after a time, enter below.

Enter a Soldier.

SOLDIER   My noble general, Timon is dead,   65
  Entombed upon the very hem o'th' sea,
  And on his gravestone this insculpture, which
  With wax I brought away, whose soft impression
  Interprets for my poor ignorance.

ALCIBIADES [*Reads the epitaph.*]
  Here lie I, Timon, who alive all living men did hate,   70
  Pass by and curse thy fill, but pass and stay not here thy gait.
  These well express in thee thy latter spirits.
  Though thou abhorred'st in us our human griefs,
  Scorned'st our brains' flow and those our droplets
    which
  From niggard nature fall, yet rich conceit   75
  Taught thee to make vast Neptune weep for aye
  On thy low grave, on faults forgiven. Dead
  Is noble Timon, of whose memory
  Hereafter more. Bring me into your city,
  And I will use the olive with my sword,   80
  Make war breed peace, make peace stint war, make each
  Prescribe to other, as each other's leech.
  Let our drums strike.   *Exeunt.*

Titus Andronicus

The only recorded copy of a 1594 Quarto edition of *The Most Lamentable Roman Tragedy of Titus Andronicus* was found in Sweden in 1904. It survives as the earliest known printed edition of any of Shakespeare's plays and is now a treasured item in the collection of the Folger Shakespeare Library. Before its discovery, the play was known from the Quartos of 1600 and 1611 and from the First Folio of 1623, where it is the second of the tragedies and gains a whole scene, 3.2, not present in the Quartos. This scene, whose authorship is disputed, may well have been added at some date later than 1594. The 1594 title-page records performance by the Earl of Derby's, Earl of Pembroke's and Earl of Sussex's Men, whether consecutively or in combination (the play makes heavy casting demands). Five performances at the Rose playhouse between 23 January and 12 June 1594 are recorded in Philip Henslowe's accounts, three by Sussex's Men, two by the Lord Chamberlain's (i.e. Derby's) Men. Proposed dates of composition range from 1589 to 1593–4: the Arden 3 editor puts forward arguments for the later date. Long regarded as a play of dubious authorship, *Titus* is now generally accepted as mainly Shakespeare's, although Act 1, which shows signs of revision to incorporate the killings of Alarbus and Mutius, is generally thought to be the work of George Peele. A drawing by Henry Peacham of characters from the play (see p. 6) appears to combine moments from different scenes, if indeed it relates directly to performance at all. Once dated 1595, this well-known drawing may in fact have been made as late as 1615 (the date on it admitting of more than one interpretation).

Despite the presence of many motifs familiar from Ovid's *Metamorphoses* (a book used in its action), Seneca's tragedies and the plays of Christopher Marlowe, the plot of *Titus* appears to be original. A ballad and prose history once identified as its sources are better accounted for as derivative spin-offs, occasioned by the sustained success of the play (whose continued popularity Ben Jonson mocked as late as 1614).

A long period of infrequent revival and generally low esteem followed the attempt of Edward Ravenscroft to rewrite *Titus* for audiences in the Restoration. Modern theatrical interest began in the 1920s and received much stimulus from the worldwide success of Peter Brook's production starring Laurence Olivier and Vivien Leigh, which was first presented at Stratford-upon-Avon in 1955. Recent productions have used a less thoroughly rearranged text than that of Brook, who cut it heavily and reordered its action to inhibit intrusive laughter.

It is easy to caricature *Titus* as violent melodrama, but it exercises great power in the theatre and shows Shakespeare already engaged with tragic characters and situations to which he would return as late as *Antony and Cleopatra* and *Coriolanus* (alluded to at 4.4.62–8), which again dramatize the opposition of the values of an ostensibly civilized and honourable Rome to those of threatening barbarians. Titus adumbrates both the crafty madness of Hamlet and the passionate madness of Lear; the villainous Moor, Aaron, combines qualities which were to separate into Othello and Iago; but it is supremely Lavinia, mutilated and mute, who first realizes the pathos of female victims of violence that is so distinctive a feature of Shakespeare's tragic writing.

The Arden text is based on the unique copy of the 1594 First Quarto, with a few corrections from the 1600 Second Quarto and the addition of 3.2 from the 1623 First Folio, designated by superscript Q2 or F at the beginning and end of them. Braces { } identify three passages, 1.1.35–8, 3.1.36 and 4.3.94–100, that Q1 should probably have deleted.

ROMANS

SATURNINUS	*eldest son of the recently deceased Emperor of Rome, later Emperor*
BASSIANUS	*younger brother of Saturninus*
TITUS Andronicus	*a Roman nobleman, general against the Goths*
MARCUS Andronicus	*a tribune of the people, brother of Titus*
LUCIUS	
QUINTUS	*the surviving sons of Titus Andronicus*
MARTIUS	*(in descending order of age)*
MUTIUS	
LAVINIA	*only daughter of Titus Andronicus, betrothed to Bassianus*
Young Lucius, *a* BOY	*son of Lucius*
PUBLIUS	*son of Marcus Andronicus*
SEMPRONIUS	
CAIUS	*kinsmen of the Andronici*
VALENTINE	
EMILLIUS	*a Roman*
CAPTAIN	
MESSENGER	
NURSE	
CLOWN	
Other ROMANS	*including Senators, Tribunes, Soldiers and Attendants*

GOTHS

TAMORA	*Queen of the Goths and later Empress of Rome by marriage to Saturninus*
ALARBUS	
DEMETRIUS	*the sons of Tamora (in descending order of age)*
CHIRON	
AARON	*a Moor in the service of Tamora, her lover*
Other GOTHS	*forming an army*

Titus Andronicus

1.1 *Flourish. Enter the* Tribunes *including*
MARCUS Andronicus *and Senators aloft. And then enter*
below SATURNINUS *and his followers at one door, and*
BASSIANUS *and his followers at the other, with*
drums and colours.

SATURNINUS   Noble patricians, patrons of my right,
Defend the justice of my cause with arms.
And countrymen, my loving followers,
Plead my successive title with your swords.
5 I am his first-born son that was the last
That wore the imperial diadem of Rome:
Then let my father's honours live in me,
Nor wrong mine age with this indignity.

BASSIANUS
Romans, friends, followers, favourers of my right,
10 If ever Bassianus, Caesar's son,
Were gracious in the eyes of royal Rome,
Keep then this passage to the Capitol,
And suffer not dishonour to approach
The imperial seat, to virtue consecrate,
15 To justice, continence and nobility;
But let desert in pure election shine,
And, Romans, fight for freedom in your choice.

MARCUS [*aloft, with the crown*]
Princes, that strive by factions and by friends
Ambitiously for rule and empery,
Know that the people of Rome, for whom we
20 stand
A special party, have by common voice
In election for the Roman empery
Chosen Andronicus, surnamed Pius
For many good and great deserts to Rome.
25 A nobler man, a braver warrior,
Lives not this day within the city walls.
He by the senate is accited home
From weary wars against the barbarous Goths,
That with his sons, a terror to our foes,
30 Hath yoked a nation strong, trained up in arms.
Ten years are spent since first he undertook
This cause of Rome and chastised with arms
Our enemies' pride; five times he hath returned
Bleeding to Rome, bearing his valiant sons
35 In coffins from the field {and at this day
To the monument of the Andronici
Done sacrifice of expiation,
And slain the noblest prisoner of the Goths}.
And now at last, laden with honour's spoils,
40 Returns the good Andronicus to Rome,
Renowned Titus, flourishing in arms.
Let us entreat, by honour of his name
Whom worthily you would have now succeed,
And in the Capitol and senate's right,
45 Whom you pretend to honour and adore,
That you withdraw you and abate your strength,
Dismiss your followers and, as suitors should,
Plead your deserts in peace and humbleness.

SATURNINUS
How fair the tribune speaks to calm my thoughts.

BASSIANUS   Marcus Andronicus, so I do affy   50
In thy uprightness and integrity,
And so I love and honour thee and thine,
Thy noble brother Titus and his sons,
And her to whom my thoughts are humbled all,
Gracious Lavinia, Rome's rich ornament,   55
That I will here dismiss my loving friends
And to my fortune's and the people's favour
Commit my cause in balance to be weighed.
                    Exeunt his Soldiers.

SATURNINUS
Friends that have been thus forward in my right,
I thank you all and here dismiss you all,   60
And to the love and favour of my country
Commit myself, my person and the cause.
                    Exeunt his Soldiers.
Rome, be as just and gracious unto me
As I am confident and kind to thee.
Open the gates and let me in.   65

BASSIANUS   Tribunes, and me, a poor competitor.
          Flourish. They go up into the Senate House.

          Enter a Captain.

CAPTAIN   Romans, make way: the good Andronicus,
Patron of virtue, Rome's best champion,
Successful in the battles that he fights,
With honour and with fortune is returned   70
From where he circumscribed with his sword
And brought to yoke the enemies of Rome.

Sound drums and trumpets, and then enter two of Titus'
Sons, and then two men bearing a coffin covered with
black, then two other Sons, then TITUS ANDRONICUS,
and then, as prisoners, TAMORA, the Queen of Goths,
and her three sons, ALARBUS, CHIRON and DEMETRIUS,
with AARON the Moor, and others as many as can be.
Then set down the coffin and Titus speaks.

TITUS   Hail, Rome, victorious in thy mourning weeds!
Lo, as the bark that hath discharged his freight
Returns with precious lading to the bay   75
From whence at first she weighed her anchorage,
Cometh Andronicus, bound with laurel boughs,
To resalute his country with his tears,
Tears of true joy for his return to Rome.
Thou great defender of this Capitol,   80
Stand gracious to the rites that we intend.
Romans, of five-and-twenty valiant sons,
Half of the number that King Priam had,
Behold the poor remains, alive and dead:
These that survive, let Rome reward with love;   85
These that I bring unto their latest home,
With burial amongst their ancestors.
Here Goths have given me leave to sheathe my sword.
Titus, unkind and careless of thine own,
Why suffer'st thou thy sons unburied yet   90

To hover on the dreadful shore of Styx?
Make way to lay them by their brethren.
   [*They open the tomb.*]
There greet in silence, as the dead are wont,
And sleep in peace, slain in your country's wars.
95   O sacred receptacle of my joys,
Sweet cell of virtue and nobility,
How many sons hast thou of mine in store
That thou wilt never render to me more!
LUCIUS   Give us the proudest prisoner of the Goths,
100   That we may hew his limbs and on a pile
Ad manes fratrum sacrifice his flesh
Before this earthly prison of their bones,
That so the shadows be not unappeased,
Nor we disturbed with prodigies on earth.
105   TITUS   I give him you, the noblest that survives,
The eldest son of this distressed queen.
TAMORA [*kneeling*]
   Stay, Roman brethren, gracious conqueror,
Victorious Titus, rue the tears I shed,
A mother's tears in passion for her son!
110   And if thy sons were ever dear to thee,
O, think my son to be as dear to me.
Sufficeth not that we are brought to Rome
To beautify thy triumphs, and return
Captive to thee and to thy Roman yoke?
115   But must my sons be slaughtered in the streets
For valiant doings in their country's cause?
O, if to fight for king and commonweal
Were piety in thine, it is in these.
Andronicus, stain not thy tomb with blood.
120   Wilt thou draw near the nature of the gods?
Draw near them then in being merciful.
Sweet mercy is nobility's true badge:
Thrice noble Titus, spare my first-born son.
TITUS   Patient yourself, madam, and pardon me.
125   These are their brethren whom your Goths beheld
Alive and dead, and for their brethren slain,
Religiously they ask a sacrifice.
To this your son is marked, and die he must,
T'appease their groaning shadows that are gone.
130   LUCIUS   Away with him, and make a fire straight,
And with our swords upon a pile of wood
Let's hew his limbs till they be clean consumed.
   Exeunt Titus' Sons with Alarbus.
TAMORA [*rising*]   O cruel, irreligious piety!
CHIRON   Was never Scythia half so barbarous!
135   DEMETRIUS   Oppose not Scythia to ambitious Rome.
Alarbus goes to rest and we survive
To tremble under Titus' threatening look.
Then, madam, stand resolved, but hope withal
The self-same gods that armed the queen of Troy
140   With opportunity of sharp revenge
Upon the Thracian tyrant in his tent
May favour Tamora, the queen of Goths
(When Goths were Goths and Tamora was queen),
To quit the bloody wrongs upon her foes.

   Enter the Sons *of Andronicus again.*
LUCIUS   See, lord and father, how we have performed   145
Our Roman rites: Alarbus' limbs are lopped
And entrails feed the sacrificing fire,
Whose smoke like incense doth perfume the sky.
Remaineth nought but to inter our brethren
And with loud 'larums welcome them to Rome.   150
TITUS   Let it be so, and let Andronicus
Make this his latest farewell to their souls.
   [*Sound trumpets, and lay the coffin in the tomb.*]
In peace and honour rest you here, my sons;
Rome's readiest champions, repose you here in rest,
Secure from worldly chances and mishaps.   155
Here lurks no treason, here no envy swells,
Here grow no damned drugs, here are no storms,
No noise, but silence and eternal sleep:
In peace and honour rest you here, my sons.

   Enter LAVINIA.
LAVINIA   In peace and honour, live Lord Titus long: 160
My noble lord and father, live in fame!
Lo, at this tomb my tributary tears
I render for my brethren's obsequies,
[*kneeling*] And at thy feet I kneel with tears of joy
Shed on this earth for thy return to Rome.   165
O bless me here with thy victorious hand,
Whose fortunes Rome's best citizens applaud.
TITUS   Kind Rome, that hast thus lovingly reserved
The cordial of mine age to glad my heart.
Lavinia live, outlive thy father's days   170
And fame's eternal date, for virtue's praise.
   [*Lavinia rises.*]

   Enter MARCUS *below.*
MARCUS   Long live Lord Titus, my beloved brother,
Gracious triumpher in the eyes of Rome!
TITUS   Thanks, gentle tribune, noble brother Marcus.
MARCUS   And welcome, nephews, from successful wars,   175
You that survive and you that sleep in fame.
Fair lords, your fortunes are alike in all
That in your country's service drew your swords;
But safer triumph is this funeral pomp
That hath aspired to Solon's happiness   180
And triumphs over chance in honour's bed.
Titus Andronicus, the people of Rome,
Whose friend in justice thou hast ever been,
Send thee by me, their tribune and their trust,
This palliament of white and spotless hue,   185
And name thee in election for the empire
With these our late-deceased emperor's sons.
Be *candidatus* then and put it on,
And help to set a head on headless Rome.
   [*Offers robe.*]
TITUS   A better head her glorious body fits   190
Than his that shakes for age and feebleness.
What, should I don this robe and trouble you?

Be chosen with proclamations today,
Tomorrow yield up rule, resign my life
195   And set abroad new business for you all?
Rome, I have been thy soldier forty years,
And led my country's strength successfully,
And buried one-and-twenty valiant sons,
Knighted in field, slain manfully in arms
200   In right and service of their noble country:
Give me a staff of honour for mine age,
But not a sceptre to control the world.
Upright he held it, lords, that held it last.
MARCUS   Titus, thou shalt obtain and ask the empery.
205   SATURNINUS [*aloft*]
Proud and ambitious tribune, canst thou tell?
TITUS   Patience, prince Saturninus.
SATURNINUS [*aloft*]   Romans, do me right.
Patricians, draw your swords and sheathe them not
Till Saturninus be Rome's emperor.
210   Andronicus, would thou were shipped to hell
Rather than rob me of the people's hearts.
LUCIUS   Proud Saturnine, interrupter of the good
That noble-minded Titus means to thee.
TITUS   Content thee, prince, I will restore to thee
215   The people's hearts, and wean them from themselves.
BASSIANUS [*aloft*]   Andronicus, I do not flatter thee,
But honour thee, and will do till I die.
My faction if thou strengthen with thy friends,
I will most thankful be, and thanks to men
220   Of noble minds is honourable meed.
TITUS   People of Rome, and people's tribunes here,
I ask your voices and your suffrages.
Will ye bestow them friendly on Andronicus?
TRIBUNES [*aloft*]   To gratify the good Andronicus
225   And gratulate his safe return to Rome,
The people will accept whom he admits.
TITUS   Tribunes, I thank you, and this suit I make,
That you create our emperor's eldest son,
Lord Saturnine, whose virtues will, I hope,
230   Reflect on Rome as Titan's rays on earth,
And ripen justice in this commonweal –
Then if you will elect by my advice,
Crown him and say, 'Long live our emperor!'
MARCUS   With voices and applause of every sort,
235   Patricians and plebeians, we create
Lord Saturninus Rome's great emperor,
And say, 'Long live our emperor Saturnine!'
[*A long flourish till they come down*]
SATURNINUS   Titus Andronicus, for thy favours done
To us in our election this day,
240   I give thee thanks in part of thy deserts,
And will with deeds requite thy gentleness.
And for an onset, Titus, to advance
Thy name and honourable family,
Lavinia will I make my empress,
245   Rome's royal mistress, mistress of my heart,
And in the sacred Pantheon her espouse.
Tell me, Andronicus, doth this motion please thee?

TITUS   It doth, my worthy lord, and in this match
I hold me highly honoured of your grace,
250   And here in sight of Rome to Saturnine,
King and commander of our commonweal,
The wide world's emperor, do I consecrate
My sword, my chariot and my prisoners,
Presents well worthy Rome's imperious lord:
255   Receive them then, the tribute that I owe,
Mine honour's ensigns humbled at thy feet.
[*Titus' sword and prisoners are handed over to*
Saturninus.]
SATURNINUS   Thanks, noble Titus, father of my life.
How proud I am of thee and of thy gifts,
Rome shall record, and when I do forget
260   The least of these unspeakable deserts,
Romans forget your fealty to me.
TITUS [*to Tamora*]
Now, madam, are you prisoner to an emperor,
To him that for your honour and your state
Will use you nobly and your followers.
265   SATURNINUS   A goodly lady, trust me, of the hue
That I would choose were I to choose anew.
[*to Tamora*] Clear up, fair queen, that cloudy
countenance:
Though chance of war hath wrought this change of
cheer,
Thou com'st not to be made a scorn in Rome;
270   Princely shall be thy usage every way.
Rest on my word, and let not discontent
Daunt all your hopes; madam, he comforts you
Can make you greater than the queen of Goths.
Lavinia, you are not displeased with this?
275   LAVINIA   Not I, my lord, sith true nobility
Warrants these words in princely courtesy.
SATURNINUS   Thanks, sweet Lavinia. Romans, let us go.
Ransomless here we set our prisoners free;
Proclaim our honours, lords, with trump and drum.
[*Sound drums and trumpets. Tamora, Chiron,*
Demetrius and Aaron are released.]
BASSIANUS [*seizing Lavinia*]
Lord Titus, by your leave, this maid is mine.
280   TITUS   How, sir? Are you in earnest then, my lord?
BASSIANUS   Ay, noble Titus, and resolved withal
To do myself this reason and this right.
MARCUS   *Suum cuique* is our Roman justice:
This prince in justice seizeth but his own.
285   LUCIUS [*joining Bassianus*]
And that he will, and shall, if Lucius live.
TITUS   Traitors, avaunt! Where is the emperor's guard?
Treason, my lord – Lavinia is surprised.
SATURNINUS   Surprised? By whom?
BASSIANUS   By him that justly may
Bear his betrothed from all the world away.
290   MUTIUS   Brothers, help to convey her hence away,
And with my sword I'll keep this door safe.
Bassianus, Marcus and Titus' Sons
bear Lavinia out of one door.

TITUS   Follow, my lord, and I'll soon bring her back.
*Saturninus does not follow, but exit at the other door
with Tamora, her two Sons and Aaron the Moor.*
MUTIUS   My lord, you pass not here.
295   TITUS   What, villain boy, barr'st me my way in Rome?
[He kills him.]
MUTIUS   Help, Lucius, help!
LUCIUS *[returning]*
My lord, you are unjust, and more than so:
In wrongful quarrel you have slain your son.
TITUS   Nor thou, nor he, are any sons of mine:
300   My sons would never so dishonour me.
Traitor, restore Lavinia to the emperor.
LUCIUS   Dead if you will, but not to be his wife
That is another's lawful promised love.   *Exit.*

Enter aloft the Emperor *with* TAMORA *and her
two* Sons *and* AARON *the Moor.*

SATURNINUS *[aloft]*
No, Titus, no, the emperor needs her not,
305   Nor her, nor thee, nor any of thy stock.
I'll trust by leisure him that mocks me once,
Thee never, nor thy traitorous haughty sons,
Confederates all thus to dishonour me.
Was none in Rome to make a stale
310   But Saturnine? Full well, Andronicus,
Agree these deeds with that proud brag of thine
That saidst I begged the empire at thy hands.
TITUS
O monstrous! What reproachful words are these?
SATURNINUS *[aloft]*
But go thy ways, go give that changing piece
315   To him that flourished for her with his sword.
A valiant son-in-law thou shalt enjoy,
One fit to bandy with thy lawless sons,
To ruffle in the commonwealth of Rome.
TITUS   These words are razors to my wounded heart.
SATURNINUS *[aloft]*
320   And therefore, lovely Tamora, queen of Goths,
That like the stately Phoebe 'mongst her nymphs
Dost overshine the gallant'st dames of Rome,
If thou be pleased with this my sudden choice,
Behold, I choose thee, Tamora, for my bride,
325   And will create thee empress of Rome.
Speak, queen of Goths, dost thou applaud my choice?
And here I swear by all the Roman gods,
Sith priest and holy water are so near,
And tapers burn so bright, and everything
330   In readiness for Hymenaeus stand,
I will not resalute the streets of Rome,
Or climb my palace, till from forth this place
I lead espoused my bride along with me.
TAMORA *[aloft]*
And here in sight of heaven to Rome I swear,
335   If Saturnine advance the queen of Goths,
She will a handmaid be to his desires,
A loving nurse, a mother to his youth.

SATURNINUS *[aloft]*
Ascend, fair queen, Pantheon. Lords, accompany
Your noble emperor and his lovely bride,
Sent by the heavens for prince Saturnine,   340
Whose wisdom hath her fortune conquered.
There shall we consummate our spousal rites.
Exeunt omnes except Titus.
TITUS   I am not bid to wait upon this bride.
Titus, when wert thou wont to walk alone,
Dishonoured thus and challenged of wrongs?   345

Enter MARCUS *and Titus' three remaining* Sons.

MARCUS   O Titus, see! O see what thou hast done!
In a bad quarrel slain a virtuous son.
TITUS   No, foolish tribune, no. No son of mine,
Nor thou, nor these, confederates in the deed
That hath dishonoured all our family –   350
Unworthy brother and unworthy sons.
LUCIUS   But let us give him burial as becomes;
Give Mutius burial with our brethren.
TITUS   Traitors, away! He rests not in this tomb.
This monument five hundred years hath stood,   355
Which I have sumptuously re-edified.
Here none but soldiers and Rome's servitors
Repose in fame; none basely slain in brawls.
Bury him where you can, he comes not here.
MARCUS   My lord, this is impiety in you;   360
My nephew Mutius' deeds do plead for him,
He must be buried with his brethren.
2, 3 SONS   And shall, or him we will accompany.
TITUS   And shall? What villain was it spake that word?
2 SON   He that would vouch it in any place but here.   365
TITUS   What, would you bury him in my despite?
MARCUS   No, noble Titus, but entreat of thee
To pardon Mutius and to bury him.
TITUS   Marcus, even thou hast struck upon my crest,
And with these boys mine honour thou hast wounded.   370
My foes I do repute you every one,
So trouble me no more, but get you gone.
3 SON   He is not with himself, let us withdraw.
2 SON   Not I, till Mutius' bones be buried.
[The Brother and the Sons kneel.]
MARCUS   Brother, for in that name doth nature plead –   375
2 SON   Father, and in that name doth nature speak –
TITUS   Speak thou no more, if all the rest will speed.
MARCUS   Renowned Titus, more than half my soul –
LUCIUS   Dear father, soul and substance of us all –
MARCUS   Suffer thy brother Marcus to inter   380
His noble nephew here in virtue's nest,
That died in honour and Lavinia's cause.
Thou art a Roman, be not barbarous.
The Greeks upon advice did bury Ajax
That slew himself, and wise Laertes' son   385
Did graciously plead for his funerals:
Let not young Mutius then, that was thy joy,
Be barred his entrance here.
TITUS   Rise, Marcus, rise. *[They rise.]*

The dismall'st day is this that e'er I saw: 390
To be dishonoured by my sons in Rome!
Well, bury him, and bury me the next.
> [*They put him in the tomb.*]

LUCIUS
There lie thy bones, sweet Mutius, with thy friends',
Till we with trophies do adorn thy tomb.

MARCUS & TITUS' SONS [*kneeling*]
No man shed tears for noble Mutius: 395
He lives in fame that died in virtue's cause.
> *Exeunt all but Marcus and Titus.*

MARCUS   My lord – to step out of these dreary dumps –
How comes it that the subtle queen of Goths
Is of a sudden thus advanced in Rome?

TITUS   I know not, Marcus, but I know it is – 400
Whether by device or no, the heavens can tell.
Is she not then beholden to the man
That brought her for this high good turn so far?

ᶠMARCUS   Yes – and will nobly him remunerate.

*Flourish.*ᶠ *Enter the* Emperor, TAMORA *and her two*
Sons, *with the Moor at one door. Enter at the other door*
BASSIANUS *and* LAVINIA, *with Titus' three* Sons.

SATURNINUS
So, Bassianus, you have played your prize.
God give you joy, sir, of your gallant bride. 405

BASSIANUS   And you of yours, my lord. I say no more,
Nor wish no less, and so I take my leave.

SATURNINUS
Traitor, if Rome have law or we have power,
Thou and thy faction shall repent this rape.

BASSIANUS
'Rape' call you it, my lord, to seize my own, 410
My true betrothed love, and now my wife?
But let the laws of Rome determine all;
Meanwhile am I possessed of that is mine.

SATURNINUS
'Tis good, sir. You are very short with us.
But if we live we'll be as sharp with you. 415

BASSIANUS   My lord, what I have done, as best I may,
Answer I must, and shall do with my life.
Only thus much I give your grace to know:
By all the duties that I owe to Rome,
This noble gentleman, Lord Titus here, 420
Is in opinion and in honour wronged,
That in the rescue of Lavinia
With his own hand did slay his youngest son
In zeal to you, and highly moved to wrath
To be controlled in that he frankly gave. 425
Receive him then to favour, Saturnine,
That hath expressed himself in all his deeds
A father and a friend to thee and Rome.

TITUS   Prince Bassianus, leave to plead my deeds;
'Tis thou and those that have dishonoured me. 430
> [*Kneels.*]
Rome and the righteous heavens be my judge
How I have loved and honoured Saturnine!

TAMORA [*to Saturninus*]
My worthy lord, if ever Tamora
Were gracious in those princely eyes of thine,
Then hear me speak indifferently for all, 435
And at my suit, sweet, pardon what is past.

SATURNINUS   What, madam, be dishonoured openly,
And basely put it up without revenge?

TAMORA   Not so, my lord. The gods of Rome forfend
I should be author to dishonour you. 440
But on mine honour dare I undertake
For good Lord Titus' innocence in all,
Whose fury not dissembled speaks his griefs.
Then at my suit look graciously on him;
Lose not so noble a friend on vain suppose, 445
Nor with sour looks afflict his gentle heart.
[*aside to Saturninus*] My lord, be ruled by me, be won
    at last,
Dissemble all your griefs and discontents.
You are but newly planted in your throne;
Lest then the people, and patricians too, 450
Upon a just survey take Titus' part,
And so supplant you for ingratitude,
Which Rome reputes to be a heinous sin,
Yield at entreats – and then let me alone:
I'll find a day to massacre them all, 455
And raze their faction and their family,
The cruel father and his traitorous sons
To whom I sued for my dear son's life,
And make them know what 'tis to let a queen
Kneel in the streets and beg for grace in vain. 460
[*aloud*] Come, come, sweet emperor – come,
    Andronicus –
Take up this good old man, and cheer the heart
That dies in tempest of thy angry frown.

SATURNINUS
Rise, Titus, rise: my empress hath prevailed.

TITUS [*rising*]   I thank your majesty and her, my lord; 465
These words, these looks, infuse new life in me.

TAMORA   Titus, I am incorporate in Rome,
A Roman now adopted happily,
And must advise the emperor for his good.
This day all quarrels die, Andronicus; 470
And let it be mine honour, good my lord,
That I have reconciled your friends and you.
For you, Prince Bassianus, I have passed
My word and promise to the emperor
That you will be more mild and tractable. 475
And fear not, lords, and you, Lavinia:
By my advice, all humbled on your knees,
You shall ask pardon of his majesty.
> [*Titus' Sons kneel.*]

LUCIUS   We do, and vow to heaven and to his highness
That what we did was mildly as we might, 480
Tendering our sister's honour and our own.

MARCUS [*kneeling*]
That on mine honour here do I protest.

SATURNINUS   Away, and talk not; trouble us no more.

TAMORA
　　Nay, nay, sweet emperor, we must all be friends;
485　　The tribune and his nephews kneel for grace;
　　I will not be denied: sweet heart, look back.

SATURNINUS
　　Marcus, for thy sake, and thy brother's here,
　　And at my lovely Tamora's entreats,
　　I do remit these young men's heinous faults.
　　　　[*Marcus and Titus' Sons stand up.*]
490　　Lavinia, though you left me like a churl,
　　I found a friend, and sure as death I swore
　　I would not part a bachelor from the priest.
　　Come, if the emperor's court can feast two brides,
　　You are my guest, Lavinia, and your friends.
495　　This day shall be a love-day, Tamora.

TITUS　Tomorrow, and it please your majesty
　　To hunt the panther and the hart with me,
　　With horn and hound we'll give your grace *bonjour*.

SATURNINUS　Be it so, Titus, and gramercy too.
　　　　Sound trumpets. Exeunt all except the Moor.

[2.1]

500　AARON　Now climbeth Tamora Olympus' top,
　　Safe out of fortune's shot, and sits aloft,
　　Secure of thunder's crack or lightning flash,
　　Advanced above pale envy's threatening reach.
　　As when the golden sun salutes the morn
505　　And, having gilt the ocean with his beams,
　　Gallops the zodiac in his glistering coach
　　And overlooks the highest-peering hills,
　　So Tamora.
　　Upon her wit doth earthly honour wait,
510　　And virtue stoops and trembles at her frown.
　　Then, Aaron, arm thy heart and fit thy thoughts
　　To mount aloft with thy imperial mistress,
　　And mount her pitch whom thou in triumph long
　　Hast prisoner held, fettered in amorous chains
515　　And faster bound to Aaron's charming eyes
　　Than is Prometheus tied to Caucasus.
　　Away with slavish weeds and servile thoughts!
　　I will be bright, and shine in pearl and gold
　　To wait upon this new-made empress.
520　　To wait, said I? – to wanton with this queen,
　　This goddess, this Semiramis, this nymph,
　　This siren that will charm Rome's Saturnine
　　And see his shipwreck and his commonweal's.
　　Hallo, what storm is this?

　　　　Enter CHIRON *and* DEMETRIUS, *braving.*

DEMETRIUS
525　　Chiron, thy years want wit, thy wits want edge
　　And manners to intrude where I am graced
　　And may, for aught thou knowest, affected be.

CHIRON　Demetrius, thou dost overween in all,
　　And so in this, to bear me down with braves.
530　　'Tis not the difference of a year or two

Makes me less gracious, or thee more fortunate:
　　I am as able and as fit as thou
　　To serve, and to deserve my mistress' grace,
　　And that my sword upon thee shall approve,
　　And plead my passions for Lavinia's love.　535

AARON [*aside*]
　　Clubs, clubs! These lovers will not keep the peace.

DEMETRIUS　Why, boy, although our mother, unadvised,
　　Gave you a dancing-rapier by your side,
　　Are you so desperate grown to threat your friends?
　　Go to, have your lath glued within your sheath　540
　　Till you know better how to handle it.

CHIRON　Meanwhile, sir, with the little skill I have,
　　Full well shalt thou perceive how much I dare.

DEMETRIUS　Ay boy, grow ye so brave?　[*They draw.*]

AARON　　　　　　　　Why, how now, lords?
　　So near the emperor's palace dare ye draw　545
　　And maintain such a quarrel openly?
　　Full well I wot the ground of all this grudge.
　　I would not for a million of gold
　　The cause were known to them it most concerns,
　　Nor would your noble mother for much more　550
　　Be so dishonoured in the court of Rome.
　　For shame, put up.

DEMETRIUS　　　　　　Not I, till I have sheathed
　　My rapier in his bosom, and withal
　　Thrust those reproachful speeches down his throat
　　That he hath breathed in my dishonour here.　555

CHIRON　For that I am prepared and full resolved,
　　Foul-spoken coward, that thunderest with thy tongue,
　　And with thy weapon nothing dar'st perform.

AARON　Away, I say.
　　Now, by the gods that warlike Goths adore,　560
　　This petty brabble will undo us all.
　　Why, lords, and think you not how dangerous
　　It is to jet upon a prince's right?
　　What, is Lavinia then become so loose,
　　Or Bassianus so degenerate,　565
　　That for her love such quarrels may be broached
　　Without controlment, justice, or revenge?
　　Young lords, beware – and should the empress know
　　This discord's ground, the music would not please.

CHIRON　I care not, I, knew she and all the world:　570
　　I love Lavinia more than all the world.

DEMETRIUS
　　Youngling, learn thou to make some meaner choice;
　　Lavinia is thine elder brother's hope.

AARON　Why, are ye mad? Or know ye not in Rome
　　How furious and impatient they be,　575
　　And cannot brook competitors in love?
　　I tell you, lords, you do but plot your deaths
　　By this device.

CHIRON　Aaron, a thousand deaths would I propose
　　T'achieve her whom I love.

AARON　　　　　　T'achieve her how?　580

DEMETRIUS　Why makes thou it so strange?
　　She is a woman, therefore may be wooed;

She is a woman, therefore may be won;
She is Lavinia, therefore must be loved.
585 What, man, more water glideth by the mill
Than wots the miller of, and easy it is
Of a cut loaf to steal a shive, we know.
Though Bassianus be the emperor's brother,
Better than he have worn Vulcan's badge.

590 AARON [*aside*] Ay, and as good as Saturninus may.

DEMETRIUS
Then why should he despair that knows to court it
With words, fair looks and liberality?
What, hast not thou full often struck a doe
And borne her cleanly by the keeper's nose?

595 AARON Why then, it seems some certain snatch or so
Would serve your turns.

CHIRON   Ay, so the turn were served.

DEMETRIUS   Aaron, thou hast hit it.

AARON   Would you had hit it too,
Then should not we be tired with this ado.
Why, hark ye, hark ye, and are you such fools
600 To square for this? Would it offend you then
That both should speed?

CHIRON   Faith, not me.

DEMETRIUS   Nor me, so I were one.

AARON   For shame, be friends, and join for that you jar.
'Tis policy and stratagem must do
605 That you affect, and so must you resolve
That what you cannot as you would achieve,
You must perforce accomplish as you may.
Take this of me: Lucrece was not more chaste
Than this Lavinia, Bassianus' love.
610 A speedier course than lingering languishment
Must we pursue, and I have found the path.
My lords, a solemn hunting is in hand;
There will the lovely Roman ladies troop.
The forest walks are wide and spacious,
615 And many unfrequented plots there are,
Fitted by kind for rape and villainy.
Single you thither then this dainty doe,
And strike her home by force, if not by words:
This way or not at all stand you in hope.
620 Come, come, our empress, with her sacred wit
To villainy and vengeance consecrate,
Will we acquaint withal what we intend,
And she shall file our engines with advice
That will not suffer you to square yourselves,
625 But to your wishes' height advance you both.
The emperor's court is like the house of Fame,
The palace full of tongues, of eyes and ears;
The woods are ruthless, dreadful, deaf and dull:
There speak and strike, brave boys, and take your turns;
630 There serve your lust, shadowed from heaven's eye,
And revel in Lavinia's treasury.

CHIRON   Thy counsel, lad, smells of no cowardice.

DEMETRIUS   *Sit fas aut nefas*, till I find the stream
To cool this heat, a charm to calm these fits,
635 *Per Stygia, per manes vehor.*   *Exeunt.*

2.1   *Enter* TITUS ANDRONICUS *and his*   [2.2]
      three Sons, *and* MARCUS, *making a noise with*
                        hounds and horns.

TITUS   The hunt is up, the morn is bright and grey,
The fields are fragrant and the woods are green.
Uncouple here, and let us make a bay
And wake the emperor and his lovely bride,
And rouse the prince, and ring a hunter's peal,   5
That all the court may echo with the noise.
Sons, let it be your charge, as it is ours,
To attend the emperor's person carefully.
I have been troubled in my sleep this night,
But dawning day new comfort hath inspired.   10

Here a cry of hounds, and wind horns in a peal; then enter
SATURNINUS, TAMORA, BASSIANUS, LAVINIA, CHIRON,
           DEMETRIUS *and their Attendants.*

Many good morrows to your majesty;
Madam, to you as many and as good.
I promised your grace a hunter's peal.

SATURNINUS   And you have rung it lustily, my lords,
Somewhat too early for new-married ladies.   15

BASSIANUS   Lavinia, how say you?

LAVINIA   I say no:
I have been broad awake two hours and more.

SATURNINUS
Come on then, horse and chariots let us have,
And to our sport. [*to Tamora*] Madam, now shall
      ye see
Our Roman hunting.

MARCUS   I have dogs, my lord,   20
Will rouse the proudest panther in the chase
And climb the highest promontory top.

TITUS   And I have horse will follow where the game
Makes way and runs like swallows o'er the plain.

DEMETRIUS [*aside*]
Chiron, we hunt not, we, with horse nor hound,   25
But hope to pluck a dainty doe to ground.   *Exeunt.*

2.2   *Enter* AARON *alone, with a money-bag.*   [2.3]

AARON   He that had wit would think that I had none,
To bury so much gold under a tree
And never after to inherit it.
Let him that thinks of me so abjectly
Know that this gold must coin a stratagem   5
Which, cunningly effected, will beget
A very excellent piece of villainy.
And so repose, sweet gold, for their unrest
That have their alms out of the empress' chest.
      [*Hides the money-bag.*]

             Enter TAMORA *alone, to the Moor.*

TAMORA
My lovely Aaron, wherefore look'st thou sad   10
When everything doth make a gleeful boast?

The birds chant melody on every bush,
The snakes lies rolled in the cheerful sun,
The green leaves quiver with the cooling wind
15 And make a chequered shadow on the ground.
Under their sweet shade, Aaron, let us sit,
And whilst the babbling echo mocks the hounds,
Replying shrilly to the well-tuned horns
As if a double hunt were heard at once,
20 Let us sit down and mark their yellowing noise;
And after conflict such as was supposed
The wandering prince and Dido once enjoyed,
When with a happy storm they were surprised
And curtained with a counsel-keeping cave,
25 We may, each wreathed in the other's arms,
Our pastimes done, possess a golden slumber,
Whiles hounds and horns and sweet melodious birds
Be unto us as is a nurse's song
Of lullaby to bring her babe asleep.

30 AARON   Madam, though Venus govern your desires,
Saturn is dominator over mine.
What signifies my deadly-standing eye,
My silence and my cloudy melancholy,
My fleece of woolly hair that now uncurls
35 Even as an adder when she doth unroll
To do some fatal execution?
No, madam, these are no venereal signs;
Vengeance is in my heart, death in my hand,
Blood and revenge are hammering in my head.
40 Hark, Tamora, the empress of my soul,
Which never hopes more heaven than rests in thee,
This is the day of doom for Bassianus,
His Philomel must lose her tongue today,
Thy sons make pillage of her chastity
45 And wash their hands in Bassianus' blood.
Seest thou this letter? Take it up, I pray thee,
     [*Gives letter.*]
And give the king this fatal-plotted scroll.
Now question me no more: we are espied.
Here comes a parcel of our hopeful booty,
50 Which dreads not yet their lives' destruction.

Enter BASSIANUS *and* LAVINIA.

TAMORA   Ah, my sweet Moor, sweeter to me than life!
AARON   No more, great empress: Bassianus comes.
Be cross with him, and I'll go fetch thy sons
To back thy quarrels, whatsoe'er they be.   *Exit.*
55 BASSIANUS   Who have we here? Rome's royal empress,
Unfurnished of her well-beseeming troop?
Or is it Dian, habited like her,
Who hath abandoned her holy groves
To see the general hunting in this forest?
60 TAMORA   Saucy controller of my private steps,
Had I the power that some say Dian had,
Thy temples should be planted presently
With horns, as was Actaeon's, and the hounds
Should drive upon thy new-transformed limbs,
65 Unmannerly intruder as thou art.

LAVINIA   Under your patience, gentle empress,
'Tis thought you have a goodly gift in horning,
And to be doubted that your Moor and you
Are singled forth to try experiments.
70 Jove shield your husband from his hounds today:
'Tis pity they should take him for a stag.

BASSIANUS   Believe me, queen, your swart Cimmerian
Doth make your honour of his body's hue,
Spotted, detested and abominable.
75 Why are you sequestered from all your train,
Dismounted from your snow-white goodly steed,
And wandered hither to an obscure plot,
Accompanied but with a barbarous Moor,
If foul desire had not conducted you?

80 LAVINIA   And being intercepted in your sport,
Great reason that my noble lord be rated
For sauciness. [*to Bassianus*] I pray you, let us hence,
And let her joy her raven-coloured love.
This valley fits the purpose passing well.

85 BASSIANUS   The king my brother shall have note of this.
LAVINIA   Ay, for these slips have made him noted long:
Good king, to be so mightily abused!
TAMORA   Why, I have patience to endure all this.

Enter CHIRON *and* DEMETRIUS.

DEMETRIUS
How now, dear sovereign and our gracious mother,
90 Why doth your highness look so pale and wan?

TAMORA   Have I not reason, think you, to look pale?
These two have 'ticed me hither to this place:
A barren detested vale you see it is;
The trees, though summer, yet forlorn and lean,
95 O'ercome with moss and baleful mistletoe;
Here never shines the sun, here nothing breeds
Unless the nightly owl or fatal raven.
And when they showed me this abhorred pit,
They told me here at dead time of the night
100 A thousand fiends, a thousand hissing snakes,
Ten thousand swelling toads, as many urchins,
Would make such fearful and confused cries
As any mortal body hearing it
Should straight fall mad, or else die suddenly.
105 No sooner had they told this hellish tale,
But straight they told me they would bind me here
Unto the body of a dismal yew
And leave me to this miserable death.
And then they called me foul adulteress,
110 Lascivious Goth, and all the bitterest terms
That ever ear did hear to such effect.
And had you not by wondrous fortune come,
This vengeance on me had they executed.
Revenge it as you love your mother's life,
115 Or be ye not henceforth called my children.

DEMETRIUS   This is a witness that I am thy son.
     [*Stabs him.*]
CHIRON
And this for me, struck home to show my strength.

[He also stabs Bassianus, who dies.]

LAVINIA Ay, come, Semiramis, nay, barbarous Tamora,
For no name fits thy nature but thy own.

TAMORA
120 Give me the poniard. You shall know, my boys,
Your mother's hand shall right your mother's wrong.

DEMETRIUS Stay, madam, here is more belongs to her:
First thrash the corn, then after burn the straw.
This minion stood upon her chastity,
125 Upon her nuptial vow, her loyalty,
And with that quaint hope braves your mightiness.
And shall she carry this unto her grave?

CHIRON And if she do, I would I were an eunuch.
Drag hence her husband to some secret hole
130 And make his dead trunk pillow to our lust.

TAMORA But when ye have the honey we desire,
Let not this wasp outlive, us both to sting.

CHIRON I warrant you, madam, we will make that sure.
Come, mistress, now perforce we will enjoy
135 That nice-preserved honesty of yours.

LAVINIA O Tamora, thou bearest a woman's face –

TAMORA I will not hear her speak; away with her!

LAVINIA Sweet lords, entreat her hear me but a word.

DEMETRIUS *[to Tamora]*
Listen, fair madam, let it be your glory
140 To see her tears, but be your heart to them
As unrelenting flint to drops of rain.

LAVINIA
When did the tiger's young ones teach the dam?
O, do not learn her wrath: she taught it thee.
The milk thou suckst from her did turn to marble;
145 Even at thy teat thou hadst thy tyranny.
Yet every mother breeds not sons alike:
[to Chiron] Do thou entreat her show a woman's pity.

CHIRON
What, wouldst thou have me prove myself a bastard?

LAVINIA 'Tis true, the raven doth not hatch a lark.
150 Yet have I heard – O, could I find it now –
The lion, moved with pity, did endure
To have his princely paws pared all away.
Some say that ravens foster forlorn children
The whilst their own birds famish in their nests.
155 O be to me, though thy hard heart say no,
Nothing so kind, but something pitiful.

TAMORA I know not what it means; away with her!

LAVINIA O, let me teach thee for my father's sake,
That gave thee life when well he might have slain thee.
160 Be not obdurate, open thy deaf ears.

TAMORA Hadst thou in person ne'er offended me,
Even for his sake am I pitiless.
Remember, boys, I poured forth tears in vain
To save your brother from the sacrifice,
165 But fierce Andronicus would not relent.
Therefore away with her and use her as you will:
The worse to her, the better loved of me.

LAVINIA *[clinging to Tamora]*
O Tamora, be called a gentle queen,

And with thine own hands kill me in this place.
For 'tis not life that I have begged so long;   170
Poor I was slain when Bassianus died.

TAMORA
What begg'st thou then, fond woman? Let me go!

LAVINIA 'Tis present death I beg, and one thing more
That womanhood denies my tongue to tell.
O, keep me from their worse-than-killing lust,   175
And tumble me into some loathsome pit
Where never man's eye may behold my body.
Do this, and be a charitable murderer.

TAMORA So should I rob my sweet sons of their fee.
No, let them satisfy their lust on thee.   180

DEMETRIUS *[to Lavinia]*
Away, for thou hast stayed us here too long.

LAVINIA
No grace? No womanhood? Ah, beastly creature,
The blot and enemy to our general name,
Confusion fall –

CHIRON   Nay then, I'll stop your mouth.
[Grabs her, covering her mouth.]
[to Demetrius] Bring thou her husband: 185
This is the hole where Aaron bid us hide him.

Demetrius throws Bassianus' body into the pit, he and
Chiron then exeunt, dragging Lavinia.

TAMORA
Farewell, my sons; see that you make her sure.
Ne'er let my heart know merry cheer indeed
Till all the Andronici be made away.
Now will I hence to seek my lovely Moor,   190
And let my spleenful sons this trull deflower. *Exit.*

Enter AARON *with two of Titus' sons,* QUINTUS *and*
MARTIUS.

AARON Come on, my lords, the better foot before.
Straight will I bring you to the loathsome pit
Where I espied the panther fast asleep.

QUINTUS My sight is very dull, whate'er it bodes.   195

MARTIUS
And mine, I promise you; were it not for shame,
Well could I leave our sport to sleep awhile.
[Falls into the pit.]

QUINTUS
What, art thou fallen? What subtle hole is this,
Whose mouth is covered with rude-growing briers
Upon whose leaves are drops of new-shed blood   200
As fresh as morning dew distilled on flowers?
A very fatal place it seems to me.
Speak, brother, hast thou hurt thee with the fall?

MARTIUS *[from below]*
O brother, with the dismall'st object hurt
That ever eye with sight made heart lament.   205

AARON *[aside]*
Now will I fetch the king to find them here,
That he thereby may have a likely guess
How these were they that made away his brother.
Exit.

MARTIUS [*from below*]
　　Why dost not comfort me and help me out
210　From this unhallowed and bloodstained hole?
QUINTUS　I am surprised with an uncouth fear;
　　A chilling sweat o'erruns my trembling joints;
　　My heart suspects more than mine eye can see.
MARTIUS [*from below*]
215　To prove thou hast a true-divining heart,
　　Aaron and thou look down into this den,
　　And see a fearful sight of blood and death.
QUINTUS　Aaron is gone and my compassionate heart
　　Will not permit mine eyes once to behold
　　The thing whereat it trembles by surmise.
220　O tell me who it is, for ne'er till now
　　Was I a child to fear I know not what.
MARTIUS [*from below*]
　　Lord Bassianus lies berayed in blood
　　All on a heap, like to a slaughtered lamb,
　　In this detested, dark, blood-drinking pit.
225 QUINTUS　If it be dark, how dost thou know 'tis he?
MARTIUS [*from below*]
　　Upon his bloody finger he doth wear
　　A precious ring that lightens all this hole,
　　Which like a taper in some monument
　　Doth shine upon the dead man's earthy cheeks
230　And shows the ragged entrails of this pit.
　　So pale did shine the moon on Pyramus
　　When he by night lay bathed in maiden blood.
　　O brother, help me with thy fainting hand –
　　If fear hath made thee faint, as me it hath –
235　Out of this fell devouring receptacle,
　　As hateful as Cocytus' misty mouth.
QUINTUS [*Reaches into pit.*]
　　Reach me thy hand that I may help thee out
　　Or, wanting strength to do thee so much good,
　　I may be plucked into the swallowing womb
240　Of this deep pit, poor Bassianus' grave.
　　I have no strength to pluck thee to the brink –
MARTIUS [*from below*]
　　Nor I no strength to climb without thy help.
QUINTUS　Thy hand once more; I will not loose again
　　Till thou art here aloft or I below.
245　Thou canst not come to me – I come to thee.
　　　　[*Falls into the pit.*]

Enter the Emperor *and* AARON *the Moor, with Attendants.*

SATURNINUS　Along with me! I'll see what hole is here
　　And what he is that now is leapt into it.
　　　　[*Speaks into the pit.*]
　　Say, who art thou that lately didst descend
　　Into this gaping hollow of the earth?
MARTIUS [*from below*]
250　The unhappy sons of old Andronicus,
　　Brought hither in a most unlucky hour
　　To find thy brother Bassianus dead.
SATURNINUS
　　My brother dead? I know thou dost but jest;

　　He and his lady both are at the lodge
　　Upon the north side of this pleasant chase.   255
　　'Tis not an hour since I left them there.
MARTIUS [*from below*]
　　We know not where you left them all alive,
　　But, out alas, here have we found him dead.

Enter TAMORA, TITUS ANDRONICUS
and LUCIUS.

TAMORA　Where is my lord the king?
SATURNINUS
　　Here, Tamora, though gride with killing grief.   260
TAMORA　Where is thy brother Bassianus?
SATURNINUS
　　Now to the bottom dost thou search my wound:
　　Poor Bassianus here lies murdered.
TAMORA　Then all too late I bring this fatal writ,
　　The complot of this timeless tragedy,   265
　　And wonder greatly that man's face can fold
　　In pleasing smiles such murderous tyranny.
　　　　[*She giveth Saturnine a letter.*]
SATURNINUS [*Reads.*]
　　And if we miss to meet him handsomely,
　　Sweet huntsman – Bassianus 'tis we mean –
　　Do thou so much as dig the grave for him.   270
　　Thou know'st our meaning. Look for thy reward
　　Among the nettles at the elder tree
　　Which overshades the mouth of that same pit
　　Where we decreed to bury Bassianus.
　　Do this, and purchase us thy lasting friends.   275
　　O Tamora, was ever heard the like?
　　This is the pit and this the elder tree.
　　Look, sirs, if you can find the huntsman out
　　That should have murdered Bassianus here.
AARON [*finding the money-bag*]
　　My gracious lord, here is the bag of gold.   280
SATURNINUS [*to Titus*]
　　Two of thy whelps, fell curs of bloody kind,
　　Have here bereft my brother of his life.
　　Sirs, drag them from the pit unto the prison.
　　There let them bide until we have devised
　　Some never-heard-of torturing pain for them.   285
TAMORA　What, are they in this pit? O wondrous thing!
　　How easily murder is discovered.
　　　　[*Attendants pull Quintus, Martius and Bassianus'*
　　　　body from the pit.]
TITUS [*kneeling*]　High emperor, upon my feeble knee
　　I beg this boon with tears not lightly shed:
　　That this fell fault of my accursed sons,   290
　　Accursed if the fault be proved in them –
SATURNINUS　If it be proved? You see it is apparent.
　　Who found this letter? Tamora, was it you?
TAMORA　Andronicus himself did take it up.
TITUS　I did, my lord, yet let me be their bail,   295
　　For by my fathers' reverend tomb I vow
　　They shall be ready at your highness' will
　　To answer their suspicion with their lives.

SATURNINUS

  Thou shalt not bail them. See thou follow me.

300   Some bring the murdered body, some the murderers.

  Let them not speak a word: the guilt is plain;

  For, by my soul, were there worse end than death

  That end upon them should be executed.

TAMORA   Andronicus, I will entreat the king;

305   Fear not thy sons, they shall do well enough.

TITUS [*rising*]

  Come, Lucius, come; stay not to talk with them.

  Exeunt, some taking the body, some guarding the prisoners.

2.3   *Enter* the *Empress' Sons with* LAVINIA,   [2.4]
     her hands cut off and her tongue cut out, and ravished.

DEMETRIUS   So, now go tell, and if thy tongue can speak,

  Who 'twas that cut thy tongue and ravished thee.

CHIRON   Write down thy mind, bewray thy meaning so,

  And if thy stumps will let thee, play the scribe.

DEMETRIUS

5   See how with signs and tokens she can scrawl.

CHIRON   Go home, call for sweet water, wash thy hands.

DEMETRIUS

  She hath no tongue to call, nor hands to wash,

  And so let's leave her to her silent walks.

CHIRON   And 'twere my cause, I should go hang myself.

DEMETRIUS

10   If thou hadst hands to help thee knit the cord.

         Exeunt Chiron and Demetrius.

    Wind horns. Enter MARCUS *from hunting.*
      Lavinia runs away.

MARCUS   Who is this – my niece that flies away so fast?

  Cousin, a word. Where is your husband?

    [*Lavinia turns.*]

  If I do dream, would all my wealth would wake me;

  If I do wake, some planet strike me down

15   That I may slumber an eternal sleep.

  Speak, gentle niece, what stern ungentle hands

  Hath lopped and hewed and made thy body bare

  Of her two branches, those sweet ornaments

  Whose circling shadows kings have sought to sleep in

20   And might not gain so great a happiness

  As half thy love. Why dost not speak to me?

    [*Lavinia opens her mouth.*]

  Alas, a crimson river of warm blood,

  Like to a bubbling fountain stirred with wind,

  Doth rise and fall between thy rosed lips,

25   Coming and going with thy honey breath.

  But sure some Tereus hath deflowered thee

  And, lest thou shouldst detect him, cut thy tongue.

  Ah, now thou turn'st away thy face for shame,

  And notwithstanding all this loss of blood,

30   As from a conduit with three issuing spouts,

  Yet do thy cheeks look red as Titan's face,

  Blushing to be encountered with a cloud.

  Shall I speak for thee? Shall I say 'tis so?

O that I knew thy heart, and knew the beast,

That I might rail at him to ease my mind!   35

Sorrow concealed, like an oven stopped,

Doth burn the heart to cinders where it is.

Fair Philomela, why she but lost her tongue,

And in a tedious sampler sewed her mind;

But, lovely niece, that mean is cut from thee.   40

A craftier Tereus, cousin, hast thou met,

And he hath cut those pretty fingers off,

That could have better sewed than Philomel.

O, had the monster seen those lily hands

Tremble like aspen leaves upon a lute   45

And make the silken strings delight to kiss them,

He would not then have touched them for his life.

Or had he heard the heavenly harmony

Which that sweet tongue hath made,

He would have dropped his knife and fell asleep,   50

As Cerberus at the Thracian poet's feet.

Come, let us go and make thy father blind,

For such a sight will blind a father's eye.

One hour's storm will drown the fragrant meads:

What will whole months of tears thy father's eyes?   55

Do not draw back, for we will mourn with thee;

O, could our mourning ease thy misery!   *Exeunt.*

3.1   *Enter the Tribunes as judges and the Senators,*
    with Titus' two Sons QUINTUS *and* MARTIUS
    bound, passing to the place of execution, and
     TITUS *going before pleading.*

TITUS   Hear me, grave fathers; noble tribunes, stay!

  For pity of mine age, whose youth was spent

  In dangerous wars whilst you securely slept;

  For all my blood in Rome's great quarrel shed,

  For all the frosty nights that I have watched,   5

  And for these bitter tears which now you see

  Filling the aged wrinkles in my cheeks,

  Be pitiful to my condemned sons,

  Whose souls is not corrupted as 'tis thought.

  For two-and-twenty sons I never wept,   10

  Because they died in honour's lofty bed.

    [*Andronicus lieth down, and the judges pass by him.*]

  For these two, tribunes, in the dust I write

  My heart's deep languor and my soul's sad tears.

  Let my tears staunch the earth's dry appetite;

  My sons' sweet blood will make it shame and blush.   15

        Exeunt all but Titus.

  O earth, I will befriend thee more with rain

  That shall distil from these two ancient ruins

  Than youthful April shall with all his showers.

  In summer's drought I'll drop upon thee still;

  In winter with warm tears I'll melt the snow   20

  And keep eternal springtime on thy face,

  So thou refuse to drink my dear sons' blood.

    Enter LUCIUS *with his weapon drawn.*

  O reverend tribunes, O gentle aged men,

Unbind my sons, reverse the doom of death,
25 And let me say, that never wept before,
My tears are now prevailing orators.

LUCIUS   O noble father, you lament in vain:
The tribunes hear you not, no man is by,
And you recount your sorrows to a stone.

30 TITUS   Ah Lucius, for thy brothers let me plead.
Grave tribunes, once more I entreat of you –

LUCIUS   My gracious lord, no tribune hears you speak.

TITUS   Why, 'tis no matter, man: if they did hear,
They would not mark me, or if they did mark,
35 They would not pity me; yet plead I must,
{And bootless unto them.}
Therefore I tell my sorrows to the stones,
Who, though they cannot answer my distress,
Yet in some sort they are better than the tribunes
40 For that they will not intercept my tale.
When I do weep, they humbly at my feet
Receive my tears and seem to weep with me,
And were they but attired in grave weeds
Rome could afford no tribunes like to these.
45 A stone is soft as wax, tribunes more hard than stones;
A stone is silent and offendeth not,
And tribunes with their tongues doom men to death.
But wherefore stand'st thou with thy weapon drawn?

LUCIUS   To rescue my two brothers from their death,
50 For which attempt the judges have pronounced
My everlasting doom of banishment.

TITUS [*rising*]
O happy man, they have befriended thee!
Why, foolish Lucius, dost thou not perceive
That Rome is but a wilderness of tigers?
55 Tigers must prey, and Rome affords no prey
But me and mine. How happy art thou then
From these devourers to be banished.
But who comes with our brother Marcus here?

Enter MARCUS *with* LAVINIA.

MARCUS   Titus, prepare thy aged eyes to weep,
60 Or if not so, thy noble heart to break:
I bring consuming sorrow to thine age.

TITUS   Will it consume me? Let me see it then.

MARCUS   This was thy daughter.

TITUS   Why, Marcus, so she is.

65 LUCIUS [*falling to his knees*] Ay me, this object kills me.

TITUS   Faint-hearted boy, arise and look upon her.
[*Lucius rises.*]
Speak, Lavinia, what accursed hand
Hath made thee handless in thy father's sight?
What fool hath added water to the sea?
70 Or brought a faggot to bright-burning Troy?
My grief was at the height before thou cam'st,
And now like Nilus it disdaineth bounds.
Give me a sword, I'll chop off my hands too,
For they have fought for Rome, and all in vain;
75 And they have nursed this woe in feeding life;
In bootless prayer have they been held up,

And they have served me to effectless use.
Now all the service I require of them
Is that the one will help to cut the other.
'Tis well, Lavinia, that thou hast no hands, 80
For hands to do Rome service is but vain.

LUCIUS   Speak, gentle sister: who hath martyred thee?

MARCUS   O, that delightful engine of her thoughts,
That blabbed them with such pleasing eloquence,
Is torn from forth that pretty hollow cage 85
Where, like a sweet melodious bird, it sung
Sweet varied notes, enchanting every ear.

LUCIUS   O, say thou for her: who hath done this deed?

MARCUS   O, thus I found her, straying in the park,
Seeking to hide herself, as doth the deer 90
That hath received some unrecuring wound.

TITUS   It was my dear, and he that wounded her
Hath hurt me more than had he killed me dead.
For now I stand as one upon a rock,
Environed with a wilderness of sea, 95
Who marks the waxing tide grow wave by wave,
Expecting ever when some envious surge
Will in his brinish bowels swallow him.
This way to death my wretched sons are gone;
Here stands my other son, a banished man, 100
And here my brother, weeping at my woes.
But that which gives my soul the greatest spurn
Is dear Lavinia, dearer than my soul.
Had I but seen thy picture in this plight,
It would have madded me; what shall I do 105
Now I behold thy lively body so?
Thou hast no hands to wipe away thy tears,
Nor tongue to tell me who hath martyred thee;
Thy husband he is dead, and for his death
Thy brothers are condemned, and dead by this. 110
Look, Marcus, ah, son Lucius, look on her!
When I did name her brothers, then fresh tears
Stood on her cheeks, as doth the honey-dew
Upon a gathered lily almost withered.

MARCUS
Perchance she weeps because they killed her husband, 115
Perchance because she knows them innocent.

TITUS   If they did kill thy husband, then be joyful,
Because the law hath ta'en revenge on them.
No, no, they would not do so foul a deed:
Witness the sorrow that their sister makes. 120
Gentle Lavinia, let me kiss thy lips
Or make some sign how I may do thee ease.
Shall thy good uncle and thy brother Lucius
And thou and I sit round about some fountain,
Looking all downwards to behold our cheeks, 125
How they are stained like meadows yet not dry,
With miry slime left on them by a flood?
And in the fountain shall we gaze so long
Till the fresh taste be taken from that clearness
And made a brine pit with our bitter tears? 130
Or shall we cut away our hands like thine?
Or shall we bite our tongues and in dumb shows

Pass the remainder of our hateful days?
What shall we do? Let us that have our tongues
135 Plot some device of further misery
To make us wondered at in time to come.
LUCIUS   Sweet father, cease your tears, for at your grief
See how my wretched sister sobs and weeps.
MARCUS
Patience, dear niece; good Titus, dry thine eyes.
    [*Gives handkerchief.*]
140 TITUS   Ah Marcus, Marcus, brother, well I wot
Thy napkin cannot drink a tear of mine,
For thou, poor man, hast drowned it with thine own.
LUCIUS   Ah, my Lavinia, I will wipe thy cheeks.
TITUS   Mark, Marcus, mark! I understand her signs:
145 Had she a tongue to speak, now would she say
That to her brother which I said to thee.
His napkin with his true tears all bewet
Can do no service on her sorrowful cheeks.
O, what a sympathy of woe is this;
150 As far from help as limbo is from bliss.

Enter AARON *the Moor alone.*

AARON   Titus Andronicus, my lord the emperor
Sends thee this word: that if thou love thy sons,
Let Marcus, Lucius, or thyself, old Titus,
Or any one of you, chop off your hand
155 And send it to the king, he for the same
Will send thee hither both thy sons alive –
And that shall be the ransom for their fault.
TITUS   O gracious emperor, O gentle Aaron!
Did ever raven sing so like a lark
160 That gives sweet tidings of the sun's uprise?
With all my heart I'll send the emperor my hand.
Good Aaron, wilt thou help to chop it off?
LUCIUS   Stay, father, for that noble hand of thine
That hath thrown down so many enemies
165 Shall not be sent. My hand will serve the turn.
My youth can better spare my blood than you,
And therefore mine shall save my brothers' lives.
MARCUS
Which of your hands hath not defended Rome
And reared aloft the bloody battleaxe,
170 Writing destruction on the enemy's casque?
O, none of both but are of high desert.
My hand hath been but idle: let it serve
To ransom my two nephews from their death,
Then have I kept it to a worthy end.
175 AARON   Nay, come, agree whose hand shall go along,
For fear they die before their pardon come.
MARCUS   My hand shall go.
LUCIUS   By heaven it shall not go.
TITUS
Sirs, strive no more. Such withered herbs as these
Are meet for plucking up – and therefore mine.
180 LUCIUS   Sweet father, if I shall be thought thy son,
Let me redeem my brothers both from death.
MARCUS   And for our father's sake and mother's care,

Now let me show a brother's love to thee.
TITUS   Agree between you: I will spare my hand.
LUCIUS   Then I'll go fetch an axe.   185
MARCUS   But I will use the axe.
                    Exeunt Lucius and Marcus.
TITUS   Come hither, Aaron. I'll deceive them both:
Lend me thy hand and I will give thee mine.
AARON [*aside*]   If that be called deceit, I will be honest
And never whilst I live deceive men so.   190
But I'll deceive you in another sort,
And that you'll say ere half an hour pass.
    [*He cuts off Titus' hand.*]

Enter LUCIUS *and* MARCUS *again.*

TITUS
Now stay your strife; what shall be is dispatched.
Good Aaron, give his majesty my hand.
Tell him it was a hand that warded him   195
From thousand dangers, bid him bury it:
More hath it merited; that let it have.
As for my sons, say I account of them
As jewels purchased at an easy price,
And yet dear too, because I bought mine own.   200
AARON   I go, Andronicus, and for thy hand
Look by and by to have thy sons with thee.
    [*aside*] Their heads I mean. O, how this villainy
Doth fat me with the very thoughts of it.
Let fools do good and fair men call for grace,   205
Aaron will have his soul black like his face.   *Exit.*
TITUS   O, here I lift this one hand up to heaven
And bow this feeble ruin to the earth.   [*Kneels.*]
If any power pities wretched tears,
To that I call.   [*Lavinia kneels.*]
                    What, wouldst thou kneel with me?   210
Do then, dear heart, for heaven shall hear our prayers,
Or with our sighs we'll breathe the welkin dim
And stain the sun with fog, as sometime clouds
When they do hug him in their melting bosoms.
MARCUS   O brother, speak with possibility,   215
And do not break into these deep extremes.
TITUS   Is not my sorrows deep, having no bottom?
Then be my passions bottomless with them.
MARCUS   But yet let reason govern thy lament.
TITUS   If there were reason for these miseries,   220
Then into limits could I bind my woes.
When heaven doth weep, doth not the earth o'erflow?
If the winds rage, doth not the sea wax mad,
Threatening the welkin with his big-swollen face?
And wilt thou have a reason for this coil?   225
I am the sea. Hark how her sighs doth blow.
She is the weeping welkin, I the earth.
Then must my sea be moved with her sighs,
Then must my earth with her continual tears
Become a deluge overflowed and drowned,   230
For why my bowels cannot hide her woes,
But like a drunkard must I vomit them.
Then give me leave, for losers will have leave

To ease their stomachs with their bitter tongues.

Enter a Messenger *with two heads and a hand.*

[*Titus and Lavinia may rise here.*]

235 MESSENGER Worthy Andronicus, ill art thou repaid
For that good hand thou sent'st the emperor.
Here are the heads of thy two noble sons,
And here's thy hand in scorn to thee sent back:
Thy grief their sports, thy resolution mocked,
240 That woe is me to think upon thy woes
More than remembrance of my father's death.
                    Sets down heads and hand, exit.

MARCUS Now let hot Etna cool in Sicily,
And be my heart an ever-burning hell!
These miseries are more than may be borne.
245 To weep with them that weep doth ease some deal,
But sorrow flouted at is double death.

LUCIUS
Ah, that this sight should make so deep a wound
And yet detested life not shrink thereat!
That ever death should let life bear his name,
250 Where life hath no more interest but to breathe!
[*Lavinia kisses the heads.*]

MARCUS Alas, poor heart, that kiss is comfortless
As frozen water to a starved snake.

TITUS When will this fearful slumber have an end?

MARCUS Now farewell flattery, die Andronicus.
255 Thou dost not slumber. See thy two sons' heads,
Thy warlike hand, thy mangled daughter here,
Thy other banished son with this dear sight
Struck pale and bloodless, and thy brother, I,
Even like a stony image, cold and numb.
260 Ah, now no more will I control thy griefs:
Rend off thy silver hair, thy other hand
Gnawing with thy teeth, and be this dismal sight
The closing up of our most wretched eyes.
Now is a time to storm. Why art thou still?

265 TITUS Ha, ha, ha!

MARCUS Why dost thou laugh? It fits not with this hour.

TITUS Why? I have not another tear to shed.
Besides, this sorrow is an enemy
And would usurp upon my watery eyes
270 And make them blind with tributary tears.
Then which way shall I find Revenge's cave?
For these two heads do seem to speak to me
And threat me I shall never come to bliss
Till all these mischiefs be returned again
275 Even in their throats that hath committed them.
Come, let me see what task I have to do.
You heavy people, circle me about,
That I may turn me to each one of you
And swear unto my soul to right your wrongs.
[*They make a vow.*]
280 The vow is made. Come, brother, take a head,
And in this hand the other will I bear.
And, Lavinia, thou shalt be employed:
Bear thou my hand, sweet wench, between thy teeth.

As for thee, boy, go get thee from my sight:
Thou art an exile and thou must not stay;   285
Hie to the Goths and raise an army there,
And if ye love me, as I think you do,
Let's kiss and part, for we have much to do.
                    They kiss. Exeunt. Lucius remains.

LUCIUS Farewell, Andronicus, my noble father,
The woefull'st man that ever lived in Rome.   290
Farewell, proud Rome, till Lucius come again;
He loves his pledges dearer than his life.
Farewell, Lavinia, my noble sister,
O would thou wert as thou tofore hast been!
But now nor Lucius nor Lavinia lives   295
But in oblivion and hateful griefs.
If Lucius live, he will requite your wrongs
And make proud Saturnine and his empress
Beg at the gates like Tarquin and his queen.
Now will I to the Goths and raise a power,   300
To be revenged on Rome and Saturnine. *Exit Lucius.*

ᶠ3.2   *A banquet. Enter* TITUS ANDRONICUS,
            MARCUS, LAVINIA *and the* BOY, Young Lucius.

TITUS So, so, now sit, and look you eat no more
Than will preserve just so much strength in us
As will revenge these bitter woes of ours. [*They sit.*]
Marcus, unknit that sorrow-wreathen knot.
Thy niece and I, poor creatures, want our hands   5
And cannot passionate our tenfold grief
With folded arms. This poor right hand of mine
Is left to tyrannize upon my breast,
Who, when my heart, all mad with misery,
Beats in this hollow prison of my flesh,   10
Then thus I thump it down.
[*to Lavinia*] Thou map of woe, that thus dost talk in
    signs,
When thy poor heart beats with outrageous beating,
Thou canst not strike it thus to make it still.
Wound it with sighing, girl, kill it with groans,   15
Or get some little knife between thy teeth
And just against thy heart make thou a hole,
That all the tears that thy poor eyes let fall
May run into that sink and, soaking in,
Drown the lamenting fool in sea-salt tears.   20

MARCUS Fie, brother, fie! Teach her not thus to lay
Such violent hands upon her tender life.

TITUS How now, has sorrow made thee dote already?
Why, Marcus, no man should be mad but I.
What violent hands can she lay on her life?   25
Ah, wherefore dost thou urge the name of hands
To bid Aeneas tell the tale twice o'er
How Troy was burnt and he made miserable?
O handle not the theme, to talk of hands,
Lest we remember still that we have none.   30
Fie, fie, how franticly I square my talk,
As if we should forget we had no hands
If Marcus did not name the word of hands.

Come, let's fall to, and, gentle girl, eat this.

35   Here is no drink! Hark, Marcus, what she says:
I can interpret all her martyred signs –
She says she drinks no other drink but tears,
Brewed with her sorrow, mashed upon her cheeks.
Speechless complainer, I will learn thy thought.

40   In thy dumb action will I be as perfect
As begging hermits in their holy prayers.
Thou shalt not sigh, nor hold thy stumps to heaven,
Nor wink, nor nod, nor kneel, nor make a sign,
But I of these will wrest an alphabet

45   And by still practice learn to know thy meaning.

BOY   Good grandsire, leave these bitter deep laments;
Make my aunt merry with some pleasing tale.

MARCUS   Alas, the tender boy in passion moved
Doth weep to see his grandsire's heaviness.

50 TITUS   Peace, tender sapling, thou art made of tears,
And tears will quickly melt thy life away.
    [*Marcus strikes the dish with a knife.*]
What dost thou strike at, Marcus, with thy knife?

MARCUS   At that that I have killed, my lord – a fly.

TITUS   Out on thee, murderer. Thou kill'st my heart.

55   Mine eyes are cloyed with view of tyranny;
A deed of death done on the innocent
Becomes not Titus' brother. Get thee gone;
I see thou art not for my company.

MARCUS   Alas, my lord, I have but killed a fly.

60 TITUS   'But'?
How if that fly had a father and a mother?
How would he hang his slender gilded wings
And buzz lamenting doings in the air.
Poor harmless fly,

65   That with his pretty buzzing melody
Came here to make us merry, and thou hast killed
    him.

MARCUS   Pardon me, sir, it was a black ill-favoured fly,
Like to the empress' Moor. Therefore I killed him.

TITUS   Oh, Oh, Oh!

70   Then pardon me for reprehending thee,
For thou hast done a charitable deed.
Give me thy knife; I will insult on him,
Flattering myself as if it were the Moor
Come hither purposely to poison me.
    [*Takes knife and strikes.*]

75   There's for thyself, and that's for Tamora.
Ah, sirrah!
Yet I think we are not brought so low
But that between us we can kill a fly
That comes in likeness of a coal-black Moor.

80 MARCUS   Alas, poor man! Grief has so wrought on him
He takes false shadows for true substances.

TITUS   Come, take away. Lavinia, go with me;
I'll to thy closet and go read with thee
Sad stories chanced in the times of old.

85   Come, boy, and go with me; thy sight is young,
And thou shalt read when mine begin to dazzle.
    *Exeunt.*ᵛ

4.1   *Enter Lucius' son* Young Lucius *and* LAVINIA
running after him, and the BOY *flies from her with his
books under his arm. He drops the books. Enter* TITUS
and MARCUS.

BOY   Help, grandsire, help! My aunt Lavinia
Follows me everywhere, I know not why.
Good uncle Marcus, see how swift she comes.
Alas, sweet aunt, I know not what you mean.

MARCUS   Stand by me, Lucius; do not fear thine aunt.   5

TITUS   She loves thee, boy, too well to do thee harm.

BOY   Ay, when my father was in Rome she did.

MARCUS   What means my niece Lavinia by these signs?

TITUS
Fear her not, Lucius – somewhat doth she mean.

MARCUS   See, Lucius, see how much she makes of thee;   10
Somewhither would she have thee go with her.
Ah, boy, Cornelia never with more care
Read to her sons than she hath read to thee
Sweet poetry and Tully's *Orator*.
Canst thou not guess wherefore she plies thee thus?   15

BOY   My lord, I know not, I, nor can I guess,
Unless some fit or frenzy do possess her.
For I have heard my grandsire say full oft
Extremity of griefs would make men mad,
And I have read that Hecuba of Troy   20
Ran mad for sorrow. That made me to fear,
Although, my lord, I know my noble aunt
Loves me as dear as e'er my mother did,
And would not but in fury fright my youth,
Which made me down to throw my books and fly,   25
Causeless perhaps. But pardon me, sweet aunt,
And, madam, if my uncle Marcus go,
I will most willingly attend your ladyship.

MARCUS   Lucius, I will. [*Lavinia turns over the books.*]

TITUS   How now, Lavinia? Marcus, what means this?   30
Some book there is that she desires to see.
Which is it, girl, of these? Open them, boy.
[*to Lavinia*] But thou art deeper read and better
    skilled:
Come and take choice of all my library,
And so beguile thy sorrow till the heavens   35
Reveal the damned contriver of this deed.
Why lifts she up her arms in sequence thus?

MARCUS
I think she means that there were more than one
Confederate in the fact. Ay, more there was –
Or else to heaven she heaves them for revenge.   40

TITUS   Lucius, what book is that she tosseth so?

BOY   Grandsire, 'tis Ovid's *Metamorphosis*;
My mother gave it me.

MARCUS   For love of her that's gone,
Perhaps she culled it from among the rest.

TITUS   Soft, so busily she turns the leaves! [*Helps her.*]   45
What would she find? Lavinia, shall I read?
This is the tragic tale of Philomel,
And treats of Tereus' treason and his rape –

And rape, I fear, was root of thy annoy.
MARCUS
50   See, brother, see: note how she quotes the leaves.
TITUS   Lavinia, wert thou thus surprised, sweet girl,
  Ravished and wronged as Philomela was,
  Forced in the ruthless, vast and gloomy woods?
  [*Lavinia nods.*] See, see!
55   Ay, such a place there is where we did hunt –
  O, had we never, never hunted there! –
  Patterned by that the poet here describes,
  By nature made for murders and for rapes.
MARCUS   O, why should nature build so foul a den,
60   Unless the gods delight in tragedies?
TITUS
  Give signs, sweet girl – for here are none but friends –
  What Roman lord it was durst do the deed.
  Or slunk not Saturnine, as Tarquin erst,
  That left the camp to sin in Lucrece' bed?
MARCUS
65   Sit down, sweet niece. Brother, sit down by me.
  [*They sit.*] Apollo, Pallas, Jove or Mercury
  Inspire me, that I may this treason find.
  My lord, look here; look here, Lavinia.
    [*He writes his name with his staff,*
    and guides it with feet and mouth.]
  This sandy plot is plain. Guide, if thou canst,
70   This after me. I here have writ my name
  Without the help of any hand at all.
  Cursed be that heart that forced us to this shift.
  Write thou, good niece, and here display at last
  What God will have discovered for revenge.
75   Heaven guide thy pen to print thy sorrows plain,
  That we may know the traitors and the truth.
    [*She takes the staff in her mouth,*
    and guides it with her stumps, and writes.]
  O do ye read, my lord, what she hath writ?
TITUS   *Stuprum – Chiron – Demetrius.*
MARCUS   What, what? The lustful sons of Tamora
80   Performers of this heinous bloody deed?
TITUS   *Magni dominator poli,*
  Tam lentus audis scelera, tam lentus vides?
MARCUS   O calm thee, gentle lord, although I know
  There is enough written upon this earth
85   To stir a mutiny in the mildest thoughts
  And arm the minds of infants to exclaims.
  My lord, kneel down with me; Lavinia, kneel;
  And kneel, sweet boy, the Roman Hector's hope,
    [*They kneel.*]
  And swear with me – as, with the woeful fere
90   And father of that chaste dishonoured dame,
  Lord Junius Brutus swore for Lucrece' rape –
  That we will prosecute by good advice
  Mortal revenge upon these traitorous Goths,
  And see their blood, or die with this reproach.
    [*They rise.*]
95 TITUS   'Tis sure enough, and you knew how.
  But if you hunt these bear-whelps, then beware:

The dam will wake, and if she wind ye once
She's with the lion deeply still in league,
And lulls him whilst she playeth on her back,
And when he sleeps will she do what she list.   100
You are a young huntsman, Marcus. Let alone,
And come, I will go get a leaf of brass
And with a gad of steel will write these words,
And lay it by. The angry northern wind
Will blow these sands like Sibyl's leaves abroad,   105
And where's our lesson then? Boy, what say you?
BOY   I say, my lord, that if I were a man
  Their mother's bedchamber should not be safe
  For these base bondmen to the yoke of Rome.
MARCUS   Ay, that's my boy! Thy father hath full oft   110
  For his ungrateful country done the like.
BOY   And, uncle, so will I, and if I live.
TITUS   Come, go with me into mine armoury:
  Lucius, I'll fit thee, and withal my boy
  Shall carry from me to the empress' sons   115
  Presents that I intend to send them both.
  Come, come, thou'lt do my message, wilt thou not?
BOY   Ay, with my dagger in their bosoms, grandsire.
TITUS   No, boy, not so; I'll teach thee another course.
  Lavinia, come; Marcus, look to my house;   120
  Lucius and I'll go brave it at the court.
  Ay, marry, will we, sir, and we'll be waited on.
      Exeunt all but Marcus.
MARCUS   O heavens, can you hear a good man groan
  And not relent or not compassion him?
  Marcus, attend him in his ecstasy   125
  That hath more scars of sorrow in his heart
  Than foemen's marks upon his battered shield,
  But yet so just that he will not revenge.
  Revenge the heavens for old Andronicus!   *Exit.*

4.2   *Enter* AARON, CHIRON *and* DEMETRIUS
    at one door, and at the other door Young Lucius
    and another, with a bundle of weapons, and verses
    writ upon them.

CHIRON   Demetrius, here's the son of Lucius:
  He hath some message to deliver us.
AARON
  Ay, some mad message from his mad grandfather.
BOY   My lords, with all the humbleness I may,
  I greet your honours from Andronicus –   5
  [*aside*] And pray the Roman gods confound you both.
DEMETRIUS
  Gramercy, lovely Lucius. What's the news?
BOY [*aside*]
  That you are both deciphered, that's the news,
  For villains marked with rape.
  [*to them*]   May it please you,
  My grandsire, well advised, hath sent by me   10
  The goodliest weapons of his armoury
  To gratify your honourable youth,
  The hope of Rome, for so he bid me say,

And so I do, and with his gifts present
15 Your lordships that, whenever you have need,
You may be armed and appointed well.
[*Attendant presents the weapons.*]
And so I leave you both [*aside*] like bloody villains.
Exit with Attendant.
DEMETRIUS
What's here? A scroll, and written round about?
Let's see:
20 [*Reads.*] *Integer vitae, scelerisque purus,*
Non eget Mauri iaculis, nec arcu.
CHIRON O, 'tis a verse in Horace, I know it well:
I read it in the grammar long ago.
AARON Ay, just – a verse in Horace, right, you have it.
25 [*aside*] Now what a thing it is to be an ass.
Here's no sound jest! The old man hath found their
guilt,
And sends them weapons wrapped about with lines
That wound beyond their feeling to the quick.
But were our witty empress well afoot
30 She would applaud Andronicus' conceit.
But let her rest in her unrest awhile.
[*to them*] And now, young lords, was't not a happy star
Led us to Rome, strangers and, more than so,
Captives, to be advanced to this height?
35 It did me good before the palace gate
To brave the tribune in his brother's hearing.
DEMETRIUS But me more good to see so great a lord
Basely insinuate and send us gifts.
AARON Had he not reason, Lord Demetrius?
40 Did you not use his daughter very friendly?
DEMETRIUS I would we had a thousand Roman dames
At such a bay, by turn to serve our lust.
CHIRON A charitable wish, and full of love.
AARON Here lacks but your mother for to say amen.
CHIRON
45 And that would she, for twenty thousand more.
DEMETRIUS Come, let us go and pray to all the gods
For our beloved mother in her pains.
AARON Pray to the devils; the gods have given us over.
[*Trumpets sound.*]
DEMETRIUS
Why do the emperor's trumpets flourish thus?
50 CHIRON Belike for joy the emperor hath a son.
DEMETRIUS Soft, who comes here?

Enter Nurse *with a blackamoor child.*

NURSE Good morrow, lords.
O tell me, did you see Aaron the Moor?
AARON Well, more or less, or ne'er a whit at all:
55 Here Aaron is, and what with Aaron now?
NURSE O gentle Aaron, we are all undone.
Now help, or woe betide thee evermore!
AARON Why, what a caterwauling dost thou keep!
What dost thou wrap and fumble in thy arms?
60 NURSE O, that which I would hide from heaven's eye,
Our empress' shame and stately Rome's disgrace:

She is delivered, lords, she is delivered.
AARON To whom?
NURSE I mean she is brought abed.
AARON
Well, God give her good rest. What hath he sent her? 65
NURSE A devil.
AARON Why then, she is the devil's dam: a joyful issue.
NURSE A joyless, dismal, black and sorrowful issue.
Here is the babe, as loathsome as a toad
Amongst the fair-faced breeders of our clime. 70
The empress sends it thee, thy stamp, thy seal,
And bids thee christen it with thy dagger's point.
AARON Zounds, ye whore, is black so base a hue?
[*to the baby*] Sweet blowze, you are a beauteous
blossom, sure.
DEMETRIUS Villain, what hast thou done? 75
AARON That which thou canst not undo.
CHIRON Thou hast undone our mother.
AARON Villain, I have done thy mother.
DEMETRIUS
And therein, hellish dog, thou hast undone her.
Woe to her chance and damned her loathed choice, 80
Accursed the offspring of so foul a fiend.
CHIRON It shall not live.
AARON It shall not die.
NURSE Aaron, it must: the mother wills it so.
AARON What, must it, nurse? Then let no man but I 85
Do execution on my flesh and blood.
DEMETRIUS
I'll broach the tadpole on my rapier's point.
Nurse, give it me; my sword shall soon dispatch it.
AARON Sooner this sword shall plough thy bowels up.
[*Draws his sword and takes the child.*]
Stay, murderous villains, will you kill your brother? 90
Now, by the burning tapers of the sky
That shone so brightly when this boy was got,
He dies upon my scimitar's sharp point
That touches this, my first-born son and heir.
I tell you, younglings, not Enceladus 95
With all his threatening band of Typhon's brood,
Nor great Alcides, nor the god of war,
Shall seize this prey out of his father's hands.
What, what, ye sanguine, shallow-hearted boys,
Ye white-limed walls, ye alehouse painted signs! 100
Coal-black is better than another hue
In that it scorns to bear another hue;
For all the water in the ocean
Can never turn the swan's black legs to white,
Although she lave them hourly in the flood. 105
Tell the empress from me I am of age
To keep mine own, excuse it how she can.
DEMETRIUS Wilt thou betray thy noble mistress thus?
AARON My mistress is my mistress, this myself,
The vigour and the picture of my youth. 110
This before all the world do I prefer,
This maugre all the world will I keep safe,
Or some of you shall smoke for it in Rome.

DEMETRIUS   By this our mother is for ever shamed.
115   CHIRON   Rome will despise her for this foul escape.
       NURSE   The emperor in his rage will doom her death.
       CHIRON   I blush to think upon this ignomy.
       AARON   Why, there's the privilege your beauty bears.
            Fie, treacherous hue, that will betray with blushing
120   The close enacts and counsels of thy heart.
            Here's a young lad framed of another leer:
            Look how the black slave smiles upon the father,
            As who should say, 'Old lad, I am thine own.'
            He is your brother, lords, sensibly fed
125   Of that self blood that first gave life to you,
            And from that womb where you imprisoned were
            He is enfranchised and come to light.
            Nay, he is your brother by the surer side,
            Although my seal be stamped in his face.
130   NURSE   Aaron, what shall I say unto the empress?
       DEMETRIUS   Advise thee, Aaron, what is to be done
            And we will all subscribe to thy advice.
            Save thou the child, so we may all be safe.
       AARON   Then sit we down and let us all consult.
135   My son and I will have the wind of you.
            Keep there.   [*They sit.*]
                       Now talk at pleasure of your safety.
       DEMETRIUS [*to the Nurse*]
            How many women saw this child of his?
       AARON   Why, so, brave lords, when we join in league
            I am a lamb – but if you brave the Moor,
140   The chafed boar, the mountain lioness,
            The ocean, swells not so as Aaron storms.
            [*to the Nurse*] But say again, how many saw the child?
       NURSE   Cornelia the midwife, and myself,
            And no one else but the delivered empress.
145   AARON   The empress, the midwife and yourself.
            Two may keep counsel when the third's away.
            Go to the empress, tell her this I said: [*He kills her.*]
            'Wheak, wheak!' – so cries a pig prepared to the spit.
            [*All stand up.*]
       DEMETRIUS
            What mean'st thou, Aaron? Wherefore didst thou this?
150   AARON   O Lord, sir, 'tis a deed of policy:
            Shall she live to betray this guilt of ours?
            A long-tongued, babbling gossip? No, lords, no.
            And now be it known to you, my full intent.
            Not far one Muly lives, my countryman:
155   His wife but yesternight was brought to bed;
            His child is like to her, fair as you are.
            Go pack with him and give the mother gold,
            And tell them both the circumstance of all,
            And how by this their child shall be advanced
160   And be received for the emperor's heir,
            And substituted in the place of mine,
            To calm this tempest whirling in the court;
            And let the emperor dandle him for his own.
            Hark ye, lords, you see I have given her physic,
165   And you must needs bestow her funeral;
            The fields are near and you are gallant grooms.

            This done, see that you take no longer days,
            But send the midwife presently to me.
            The midwife and the nurse well made away,
            Then let the ladies tattle what they please.   170
       CHIRON   Aaron, I see thou wilt not trust the air
            With secrets.
       DEMETRIUS   For this care of Tamora,
            Herself and hers are highly bound to thee.
                Exeunt Chiron and Demetrius, with the Nurse's body.
       AARON   Now to the Goths, as swift as swallow flies,
            There to dispose this treasure in mine arms   175
            And secretly to greet the empress' friends.
            Come on, you thick-lipped slave, I'll bear you hence,
            For it is you that puts us to our shifts.
            I'll make you feed on berries and on roots,
            And fat on curds and whey, and suck the goat,   180
            And cabin in a cave, and bring you up
            To be a warrior and command a camp.   *Exit.*

4.3   *Enter* TITUS, OLD MARCUS, *Young Lucius,*
            and other Gentlemen, Marcus' son PUBLIUS;
            kinsmen of the Andronici, CAIUS *and* SEMPRONIUS
            with bows; and Titus bears the arrows with letters
                       on the ends of them.

       TITUS   Come, Marcus, come; kinsmen, this is the way.
            Sir Boy, let me see your archery.
            Look ye draw home enough, and 'tis there straight.
            Terras Astraea reliquit: be you remembered, Marcus,
            She's gone, she's fled. Sirs, take you to your tools.   5
            You, cousins, shall go sound the ocean
            And cast your nets:
            Happily you may catch her in the sea;
            Yet there's as little justice as at land.
            No, Publius and Sempronius, you must do it,   10
            'Tis you must dig with mattock and with spade,
            And pierce the inmost centre of the earth.
            Then, when you come to Pluto's region,
            I pray you deliver him this petition.
            Tell him it is for justice and for aid,   15
            And that it comes from old Andronicus,
            Shaken with sorrows in ungrateful Rome.
            Ah, Rome! Well, well, I made thee miserable
            What time I threw the people's suffrages
            On him that thus doth tyrannize o'er me.   20
            Go, get you gone, and pray be careful all,
            And leave you not a man-of-war unsearched:
            This wicked emperor may have shipped her hence,
            And, kinsmen, then we may go pipe for justice.
       MARCUS   O Publius, is not this a heavy case,   25
            To see thy noble uncle thus distract?
       PUBLIUS   Therefore, my lords, it highly us concerns
            By day and night t'attend him carefully
            And feed his humour kindly as we may,
            Till time beget some careful remedy.   30
       MARCUS   Kinsmen, his sorrows are past remedy,
            But let us live in hope that Lucius will

Join with the Goths and with revengeful war
Take wreak on Rome for this ingratitude,
35 And vengeance on the traitor Saturnine.
TITUS   Publius, how now? How now, my masters?
What, have you met with her?
PUBLIUS   No, my good lord, but Pluto sends you word
If you will have Revenge from hell, you shall.
40 Marry, for Justice, she is so employed,
He thinks with Jove in heaven or somewhere else,
So that perforce you must needs stay a time.
TITUS   He doth me wrong to feed me with delays.
I'll dive into the burning lake below
45 And pull her out of Acheron by the heels.
Marcus, we are but shrubs, no cedars we,
No big-boned men framed of the Cyclops' size,
But metal, Marcus, steel to the very back,
Yet wrung with wrongs more than our backs can bear.
50 And sith there's no justice in earth nor hell,
We will solicit heaven and move the gods
To send down Justice for to wreak our wrongs.
Come, to this gear. You are a good archer, Marcus:
  [*He gives them the arrows.*]
'Ad Jovem', that's for you; here, 'ad Apollinem';
55 'Ad Martem', that's for myself;
Here, boy, 'to Pallas'; here, 'to Mercury';
'To Saturn', Caius – not to Saturnine:
You were as good to shoot against the wind.
To it, boy; Marcus, loose when I bid.
60 Of my word, I have written to effect:
There's not a god left unsolicited.
MARCUS
Kinsmen, shoot all your shafts into the court;
We will afflict the emperor in his pride.
TITUS   Now, masters, draw.   [*They shoot.*]
             O, well said, Lucius,
65 Good boy: in Virgo's lap! Give it Pallas.
MARCUS   My lord, I aimed a mile beyond the moon:
Your letter is with Jupiter by this.
TITUS   Ha, ha! Publius, Publius, what hast thou done?
See, see, thou hast shot off one of Taurus' horns.
MARCUS
70 This was the sport, my lord: when Publius shot,
The Bull, being galled, gave Aries such a knock
That down fell both the Ram's horns in the court,
And who should find them but the empress' villain!
She laughed and told the Moor he should not choose
75 But give them to his master for a present.
TITUS   Why, there it goes; God give his lordship joy.

Enter the Clown *with a basket and two pigeons in it.*

News, news, from heaven! Marcus, the post is come.
Sirrah, what tidings? Have you any letters?
Shall I have justice? What says Jupiter?
80 CLOWN   Ho, the gibbet-maker? He says that he hath
taken them down again, for the man must not be
hanged till the next week.
TITUS   But what says Jupiter, I ask thee?

CLOWN   Alas, sir, I know not Jubiter, I never drank with
him in all my life.   85
TITUS   Why, villain, art not thou the carrier?
CLOWN   Ay, of my pigeons, sir – nothing else.
TITUS   Why, didst thou not come from heaven?
CLOWN   From heaven? Alas, sir, I never came there.
God forbid I should be so bold to press to heaven in   90
my young days. Why, I am going with my pigeons to
the tribunal plebs to take up a matter of brawl betwixt
my uncle and one of the emperal's men.
{MARCUS [*to Titus*]   Why, sir, that is as fit as can be to
serve for your oration, and let him deliver the pigeons to 95
the emperor from you.
TITUS   Tell me, can you deliver an oration to the
emperor with a grace?
CLOWN   Nay, truly, sir, I could never say grace in all
my life.}   100
TITUS   Sirrah, come hither; make no more ado,
But give your pigeons to the emperor.
By me thou shalt have justice at his hands.
Hold, hold – meanwhile here's money for thy charges.
Give me pen and ink.   [*Writes.*]   105
Sirrah, can you with a grace deliver up a supplication?
CLOWN   Ay, sir.
TITUS [*Gives letter.*]   Then here is a supplication for you,
and when you come to him, at the first approach you
must kneel, then kiss his foot, then deliver up your   110
pigeons, and then look for your reward. I'll be at hand,
sir; see you do it bravely.
CLOWN   I warrant you, sir, let me alone.
TITUS   Sirrah, hast thou a knife? Come, let me see it.
Here, Marcus, fold it in the oration;   115
[*to the Clown*] For thou must hold it like an humble
  suppliant,
And when thou hast given it to the emperor,
Knock at my door and tell me what he says.
CLOWN   God be with you, sir. I will.   *Exit.*
TITUS   Come, Marcus, let us go; Publius, follow me.   120
                                                         Exeunt.

4.4   *Enter* Emperor *and* Empress *and her two*
        Sons, *and Attendants. The Emperor brings the*
        arrows in his hand that Titus shot at him.

SATURNINUS
Why, lords, what wrongs are these! Was ever seen
An emperor in Rome thus overborne,
Troubled, confronted thus, and for the extent
Of equal justice used in such contempt?
My lords, you know, as know the mightful gods,   5
However these disturbers of our peace
Buzz in the people's ears, there nought hath passed
But even with law against the wilful sons
Of old Andronicus. And what and if
His sorrows have so overwhelmed his wits?   10
Shall we be thus afflicted in his wreaks,
His fits, his frenzy and his bitterness?

And now he writes to heaven for his redress.
See, here's 'to Jove', and this 'to Mercury',
15 This 'to Apollo', this 'to the god of war':
Sweet scrolls to fly about the streets of Rome!
What's this but libelling against the senate
And blazoning our injustice everywhere?
A goodly humour, is it not, my lords?
20 As who would say, in Rome no justice were.
But if I live, his feigned ecstasies
Shall be no shelter to these outrages,
But he and his shall know that justice lives
In Saturninus' health, whom, if she sleep,
25 He'll so awake as she in fury shall
Cut off the proud'st conspirator that lives.

TAMORA   My gracious lord, my lovely Saturnine,
Lord of my life, commander of my thoughts,
Calm thee and bear the faults of Titus' age,
30 Th'effects of sorrow for his valiant sons
Whose loss hath pierced him deep and scarred his heart;
And rather comfort his distressed plight
Than prosecute the meanest or the best
For these contempts.
[*aside*]   Why, thus it shall become
35 High-witted Tamora to gloze withal.
But, Titus, I have touched thee to the quick;
Thy life-blood out, if Aaron now be wise,
Then is all safe, the anchor in the port.

Enter Clown.

How now, good fellow, wouldst thou speak with us?
CLOWN
40 Yea, forsooth, and your mistress-ship be emperial.
TAMORA   Empress I am, but yonder sits the emperor.
CLOWN   'Tis he. God and Saint Stephen give you good
e'en. I have brought you a letter and a couple of
pigeons here. [*Saturninus reads the letter.*]
45 SATURNINUS   Go, take him away and hang him presently!
CLOWN   How much money must I have?
TAMORA   Come, sirrah, you must be hanged.
CLOWN   Hanged, by'Lady? Then I have brought up a
neck to a fair end.   *Exit under guard.*
50 SATURNINUS   Despiteful and intolerable wrongs!
Shall I endure this monstrous villainy?
I know from whence this same device proceeds.
May this be borne as if his traitorous sons,
That died by law for murder of our brother,
55 Have by my means been butchered wrongfully?
Go, drag the villain hither by the hair:
Nor age nor honour shall shape privilege.
For this proud mock I'll be thy slaughterman,
Sly frantic wretch that holp'st to make me great
60 In hope thyself should govern Rome and me.

Enter EMILLIUS, *a messenger.*

What news with thee, Emillius?
EMILLIUS
Arm, arm, my lords! Rome never had more cause:

The Goths have gathered head, and with a power
Of high-resolved men bent to the spoil
They hither march amain under conduct   65
Of Lucius, son to old Andronicus,
Who threats in course of this revenge to do
As much as ever Coriolanus did.
SATURNINUS   Is warlike Lucius general of the Goths?
These tidings nip me and I hang the head   70
As flowers with frost or grass beat down with storms.
Ay, now begins our sorrows to approach.
'Tis he the common people love so much;
Myself hath often heard them say,
When I have walked like a private man,   75
That Lucius' banishment was wrongfully,
And they have wished that Lucius were their emperor.
TAMORA   Why should you fear? Is not your city strong?
SATURNINUS   Ay, but the citizens favour Lucius
And will revolt from me to succour him.   80
TAMORA   King, be thy thoughts imperious like thy name.
Is the sun dimmed, that gnats do fly in it?
The eagle suffers little birds to sing,
And is not careful what they mean thereby,
Knowing that with the shadow of his wings   85
He can at pleasure stint their melody:
Even so mayst thou the giddy men of Rome.
Then cheer thy spirit, for know thou, emperor,
I will enchant the old Andronicus
With words more sweet and yet more dangerous   90
Than baits to fish or honey-stalks to sheep,
When as the one is wounded with the bait,
The other rotted with delicious feed.
SATURNINUS   But he will not entreat his son for us.
TAMORA   If Tamora entreat him, then he will,   95
For I can smooth and fill his aged ears
With golden promises that, were his heart
Almost impregnable, his old ears deaf,
Yet should both ear and heart obey my tongue.
[*to Emillius*] Go thou before to be our ambassador: 100
Say that the emperor requests a parley
Of warlike Lucius, and appoint the meeting
Even at his father's house, the old Andronicus.
SATURNINUS   Emillius, do this message honourably,
And if he stand in hostage for his safety,   105
Bid him demand what pledge will please him best.
EMILLIUS   Your bidding shall I do effectually.   *Exit.*
TAMORA   Now will I to that old Andronicus,
And temper him with all the art I have
To pluck proud Lucius from the warlike Goths.   110
And now, sweet emperor, be blithe again
And bury all thy fear in my devices.
SATURNINUS   Then go incessantly and plead to him.
                                Exeunt by different doors.

5.1   *Flourish. Enter* LUCIUS *with an army of*
            Goths *with Drums and Soldiers.*

LUCIUS   Approved warriors and my faithful friends,

I have received letters from great Rome
Which signifies what hate they bear their emperor,
And how desirous of our sight they are.
5   Therefore, great lords, be as your titles witness,
Imperious, and impatient of your wrongs,
And wherein Rome hath done you any scath
Let him make treble satisfaction.
1 GOTH   Brave slip sprung from the great Andronicus,
10   Whose name was once our terror, now our comfort,
Whose high exploits and honourable deeds
Ingrateful Rome requites with foul contempt,
Be bold in us. We'll follow where thou lead'st,
Like stinging bees in hottest summer's day
15   Led by their master to the flowered fields,
And be avenged on cursed Tamora.
ALL GOTHS   And as he saith, so say we all with him.
LUCIUS   I humbly thank him, and I thank you all.
But who comes here, led by a lusty Goth?

Enter a Goth, *leading of* AARON *with his child in his arms.*

20   2 GOTH   Renowned Lucius, from our troops I strayed
To gaze upon a ruinous monastery,
And as I earnestly did fix mine eye
Upon the wasted building, suddenly
I heard a child cry underneath a wall.
25   I made unto the noise, when soon I heard
The crying babe controlled with this discourse:
'Peace, tawny slave, half me and half thy dame!
Did not thy hue bewray whose brat thou art,
Had nature lent thee but thy mother's look,
30   Villain, thou mightst have been an emperor.
But where the bull and cow are both milk-white,
They never do beget a coal-black calf.
Peace, villain, peace,' – even thus he rates the babe –
'For I must bear thee to a trusty Goth
35   Who, when he knows thou art the empress' babe,
Will hold thee dearly for thy mother's sake.'
With this my weapon drawn, I rushed upon him,
Surprised him suddenly, and brought him hither
To use as you think needful of the man.
40   LUCIUS   O worthy Goth, this is the incarnate devil
That robbed Andronicus of his good hand;
This is the pearl that pleased your empress' eye,
And here's the base fruit of her burning lust.
[*to Aaron*] Say, wall-eyed slave, whither wouldst thou
          convey
45   This growing image of thy fiend-like face?
Why dost not speak? What, deaf? Not a word?
A halter, soldiers! Hang him on this tree,
And by his side his fruit of bastardy.
AARON   Touch not the boy, he is of royal blood.
50   LUCIUS   Too like the sire for ever being good.
First hang the child, that he may see it sprawl:
A sight to vex the father's soul withal.
Get me a ladder.
          [*A Goth brings a ladder, which Aaron is made to climb;
          another Goth takes the child.*]

AARON   Lucius, save the child,
And bear it from me to the empress.
If thou do this, I'll show thee wondrous things   55
That highly may advantage thee to hear.
If thou wilt not, befall what may befall,
I'll speak no more but 'Vengeance rot you all!'
LUCIUS
Say on, and if it please me which thou speak'st,
Thy child shall live and I will see it nourished.   60
AARON   And if it please thee? Why, assure thee, Lucius,
'Twill vex thy soul to hear what I shall speak:
For I must talk of murders, rapes and massacres,
Acts of black night, abominable deeds,
Complots of mischief, treasons, villainies,   65
Ruthful to hear yet piteously performed;
And this shall all be buried in my death
Unless thou swear to me my child shall live.
LUCIUS   Tell on thy mind; I say thy child shall live.
AARON   Swear that he shall and then I will begin.   70
LUCIUS
Who should I swear by? Thou believest no god.
That granted, how canst thou believe an oath?
AARON   What if I do not? as indeed I do not –
Yet for I know thou art religious
And hast a thing within thee called conscience,   75
With twenty popish tricks and ceremonies
Which I have seen thee careful to observe,
Therefore I urge thy oath; for that I know
An idiot holds his bauble for a god,
And keeps the oath which by that god he swears,   80
To that I'll urge him, therefore thou shalt vow
By that same god, what god soe'er it be
That thou adorest and hast in reverence,
To save my boy, to nurse and bring him up,
Or else I will discover nought to thee.   85
LUCIUS   Even by my god I swear to thee I will.
AARON   First know thou I begot him on the empress.
LUCIUS   O most insatiate and luxurious woman!
AARON   Tut, Lucius, this was but a deed of charity
To that which thou shalt hear of me anon.   90
'Twas her two sons that murdered Bassianus;
They cut thy sister's tongue and ravished her
And cut her hands and trimmed her as thou sawest.
LUCIUS
O detestable villain, call'st thou that trimming?
AARON
Why, she was washed and cut and trimmed, and 'twas   95
Trim sport for them which had the doing of it.
LUCIUS   O barbarous, beastly villains, like thyself!
AARON   Indeed, I was their tutor to instruct them.
That codding spirit had they from their mother,
As sure a card as ever won the set.   100
That bloody mind I think they learned of me,
As true a dog as ever fought at head.
Well, let my deeds be witness of my worth:
I trained thy brethren to that guileful hole
Where the dead corpse of Bassianus lay;   105

I wrote the letter that thy father found,
And hid the gold within that letter mentioned,
Confederate with the queen and her two sons;
And what not done that thou hast cause to rue
110   Wherein I had no stroke of mischief in it?
I played the cheater for thy father's hand,
And when I had it, drew myself apart
And almost broke my heart with extreme laughter;
I pried me through the crevice of a wall
115   When for his hand he had his two sons' heads,
Beheld his tears and laughed so heartily
That both mine eyes were rainy like to his;
And when I told the empress of this sport,
She sounded almost at my pleasing tale
120   And for my tidings gave me twenty kisses.
1 GOTH   What, canst thou say all this and never blush?
AARON   Ay, like a black dog, as the saying is.
LUCIUS   Art thou not sorry for these heinous deeds?
AARON   Ay, that I had not done a thousand more.
125   Even now I curse the day – and yet I think
Few come within the compass of my curse –
Wherein I did not some notorious ill,
As kill a man or else devise his death,
Ravish a maid or plot the way to do it,
130   Accuse some innocent and forswear myself,
Set deadly enmity between two friends,
Make poor men's cattle break their necks,
Set fire on barns and haystacks in the night
And bid the owners quench them with their tears.
135   Oft have I digged up dead men from their graves
And set them upright at their dear friends' door,
Even when their sorrows almost was forgot,
And on their skins, as on the bark of trees,
Have with my knife carved in Roman letters,
140   'Let not your sorrow die though I am dead'.
Tut, I have done a thousand dreadful things
As willingly as one would kill a fly,
And nothing grieves me heartily indeed
But that I cannot do ten thousand more.
145   LUCIUS   Bring down the devil, for he must not die
So sweet a death as hanging presently.
        [*Aaron is made to climb down.*]
AARON   If there be devils, would I were a devil,
To live and burn in everlasting fire,
So I might have your company in hell
150   But to torment you with my bitter tongue.
LUCIUS   Sirs, stop his mouth and let him speak no more.
        [*Aaron is gagged.*]

                Enter EMILLIUS.

A GOTH   My lord, there is a messenger from Rome
Desires to be admitted to your presence.
LUCIUS   Let him come near.
155   Welcome, Emillius: what's the news from Rome?
EMILLIUS   Lord Lucius and you princes of the Goths,
The Roman emperor greets you all by me,
And for he understands you are in arms,

He craves a parley at your father's house,
Willing you to demand your hostages   160
And they shall be immediately delivered.
1 GOTH   What says our general?
LUCIUS   Emillius, let the emperor give his pledges
Unto my father and my uncle Marcus,
And we will come.   *Flourish. They march away.*   165

5.2   *Enter* TAMORA *and her two* Sons, *disguised.*

TAMORA   Thus, in this strange and sad habiliment,
I will encounter with Andronicus
And say I am Revenge, sent from below
To join with him and right his heinous wrongs.
Knock at his study, where they say he keeps   5
To ruminate strange plots of dire revenge;
Tell him Revenge is come to join with him
And work confusion on his enemies.

    They knock, and TITUS *aloft with papers, opens
                his study door.*

TITUS [*aloft*]   Who doth molest my contemplation?
Is it your trick to make me ope the door,   10
That so my sad decrees may fly away
And all my study be to no effect?
You are deceived, for what I mean to do
See here in bloody lines I have set down,
And what is written shall be executed.   15
TAMORA   Titus, I am come to talk with thee.
TITUS [*aloft*]   No, not a word. How can I grace my talk,
Wanting a hand to give it action?
Thou hast the odds of me, therefore no more.
TAMORA
If thou didst know me, thou wouldst talk with me.   20
TITUS [*aloft*]   I am not mad, I know thee well enough:
Witness this wretched stump, witness these crimson
    lines,
Witness these trenches made by grief and care,
Witness the tiring day and heavy night,
Witness all sorrow, that I know thee well   25
For our proud empress, mighty Tamora.
Is not thy coming for my other hand?
TAMORA   Know, thou sad man, I am not Tamora:
She is thy enemy and I thy friend.
I am Revenge, sent from th'infernal kingdom   30
To ease the gnawing vulture of thy mind
By working wreakful vengeance on thy foes.
Come down and welcome me to this world's light,
Confer with me of murder and of death.
There's not a hollow cave or lurking place,   35
No vast obscurity or misty vale
Where bloody murder or detested rape
Can couch for fear, but I will find them out,
And in their ears tell them my dreadful name,
Revenge, which makes the foul offender quake.   40
TITUS [*aloft*]
Art thou Revenge? And art thou sent to me

To be a torment to mine enemies?

TAMORA   I am, therefore come down and welcome me.

TITUS [*aloft*]

Do me some service ere I come to thee.

45   Lo by thy side where Rape and Murder stands;
Now give some surance that thou art Revenge:
Stab them or tear them on thy chariot wheels,
And then I'll come and be thy waggoner,
And whirl along with thee about the globe,

50   Provide thee two proper palfreys, black as jet,
To hale thy vengeful waggon swift away
And find out murderers in their guilty caves;
And when thy car is loaden with their heads,
I will dismount and by thy waggon wheel

55   Trot like a servile footman all day long,
Even from Hyperion's rising in the east
Until his very downfall in the sea.
And day by day I'll do this heavy task,
So thou destroy Rapine and Murder there.

60   TAMORA   These are my ministers, and come with me.

TITUS [*aloft*]

Are these thy ministers? What are they called?

TAMORA   Rape and Murder, therefore called so
'Cause they take vengeance of such kind of men.

TITUS [*aloft*]

Good Lord, how like the empress' sons they are,

65   And you the empress! But we worldly men
Have miserable, mad, mistaking eyes.
O sweet Revenge, now do I come to thee,
And if one arm's embracement will content thee,
I will embrace thee in it by and by.   *Exit aloft.*

70   TAMORA   This closing with him fits his lunacy.
Whate'er I forge to feed his brainsick humours
Do you uphold and maintain in your speeches,
For now he firmly takes me for Revenge,
And, being credulous in this mad thought,

75   I'll make him send for Lucius his son,
And whilst I at a banquet hold him sure,
I'll find some cunning practice out of hand
To scatter and disperse the giddy Goths,
Or at the least make them his enemies.

80   See, here he comes, and I must ply my theme.

Enter TITUS, *below.*

TITUS   Long have I been forlorn, and all for thee.
Welcome, dread Fury, to my woeful house;
Rapine and Murder, you are welcome too.
How like the empress and her sons you are!

85   Well are you fitted, had you but a Moor;
Could not all hell afford you such a devil?
For well I wot the empress never wags
But in her company there is a Moor,
And would you represent our queen aright

90   It were convenient you had such a devil.
But welcome as you are. What shall we do?

TAMORA   What wouldst thou have us do, Andronicus?

DEMETRIUS   Show me a murderer, I'll deal with him.

CHIRON   Show me a villain that hath done a rape,
And I am sent to be revenged on him.   95

TAMORA

Show me a thousand that hath done thee wrong,
And I will be revenged on them all.

TITUS [*to Demetrius*]

Look round about the wicked streets of Rome,
And when thou find'st a man that's like thyself,
Good Murder, stab him: he's a murderer.   100

[*to Chiron*] Go thou with him, and when it is thy hap
To find another that is like to thee,
Good Rapine, stab him: he is a ravisher.

[*to Tamora*] Go thou with them, and in the emperor's
court,
There is a queen attended by a Moor –   105
Well shalt thou know her by thine own proportion,
For up and down she doth resemble thee –
I pray thee, do on them some violent death:
They have been violent to me and mine.

TAMORA   Well hast thou lessoned us; this shall we do.   110
But would it please thee, good Andronicus,
To send for Lucius, thy thrice-valiant son,
Who leads towards Rome a band of warlike Goths,
And bid him come and banquet at thy house?
When he is here, even at thy solemn feast,   115
I will bring in the empress and her sons,
The emperor himself and all thy foes,
And at thy mercy shall they stoop and kneel,
And on them shalt thou ease thy angry heart.
What says Andronicus to this device?   120

TITUS   Marcus, my brother! 'Tis sad Titus calls.

Enter MARCUS.

Go, gentle Marcus, to thy nephew Lucius;
Thou shalt enquire him out among the Goths.
Bid him repair to me and bring with him
Some of the chiefest princes of the Goths.   125
Bid him encamp his soldiers where they are.
Tell him the emperor and the empress too
Feast at my house, and he shall feast with them.
This do thou for my love, and so let him,
As he regards his aged father's life.   130

MARCUS   This will I do, and soon return again.   *Exit.*

TAMORA   Now will I hence about thy business,
And take my ministers along with me.

TITUS   Nay, nay, let Rape and Murder stay with me –
Or else I'll call my brother back again   135
And cleave to no revenge but Lucius.

TAMORA [*aside to her Sons*]

What say you, boys, will you abide with him
Whiles I go tell my lord the emperor
How I have governed our determined jest?
Yield to his humour, smooth and speak him fair,   140
And tarry with him till I turn again.

TITUS [*aside*]

I knew them all, though they supposed me mad,
And will o'erreach them in their own devices –

A pair of cursed hellhounds and their dam.

145 DEMETRIUS Madam, depart at pleasure, leave us here.

TAMORA Farewell, Andronicus: Revenge now goes
To lay a complot to betray thy foes.

TITUS I know thou dost – and sweet Revenge, farewell.
Exit Tamora.

CHIRON Tell us, old man, how shall we be employed?

150 TITUS Tut, I have work enough for you to do.
Publius, come hither; Caius and Valentine.

Enter PUBLIUS, CAIUS and VALENTINE.

PUBLIUS What is your will?

TITUS Know you these two?

PUBLIUS
The empress' sons I take them: Chiron, Demetrius.

155 TITUS Fie, Publius, fie, thou art too much deceived.
The one is Murder and Rape is the other's name,
And therefore bind them, gentle Publius;
Caius and Valentine, lay hands on them.
Oft have you heard me wish for such an hour,

160 And now I find it; therefore bind them sure,
And stop their mouths if they begin to cry. *Exit.*

CHIRON Villains, forbear! We are the empress' sons.

PUBLIUS
And therefore do we what we are commanded.
[They bind and gag them.]
Stop close their mouths; let them not speak a word.

165 Is he sure bound? Look that you bind them fast.

*Enter TITUS ANDRONICUS with a knife, and
LAVINIA with a basin.*

TITUS Come, come, Lavinia: look, thy foes are bound.
Sirs, stop their mouths; let them not speak to me,
But let them hear what fearful words I utter.
O villains, Chiron and Demetrius,
Here stands the spring whom you have stained with

170 mud,
This goodly summer with your winter mixed.
You killed her husband, and for that vile fault
Two of her brothers were condemned to death,
My hand cut off and made a merry jest,

175 Both her sweet hands, her tongue, and that more dear
Than hands or tongue, her spotless chastity,
Inhuman traitors, you constrained and forced.
What would you say if I should let you speak?
Villains, for shame you could not beg for grace.

180 Hark, wretches, how I mean to martyr you:
This one hand yet is left to cut your throats,
Whiles that Lavinia 'tween her stumps doth hold
The basin that receives your guilty blood.
You know your mother means to feast with me,

185 And calls herself Revenge and thinks me mad.
Hark, villains, I will grind your bones to dust,
And with your blood and it I'll make a paste,
And of the paste a coffin I will rear,
And make two pasties of your shameful heads,

190 And bid that strumpet, your unhallowed dam,

Like to the earth swallow her own increase.
This is the feast that I have bid her to,
And this the banquet she shall surfeit on:
For worse than Philomel you used my daughter,
And worse than Progne I will be revenged. 195
And now, prepare your throats. Lavinia, come,
Receive the blood, and when that they are dead
Let me go grind their bones to powder small,
And with this hateful liquor temper it,
And in that paste let their vile heads be baked. 200
Come, come, be everyone officious
To make this banquet, which I wish may prove
More stern and bloody than the Centaurs' feast.
[He cuts their throats.]
So, now bring them in, for I'll play the cook,
And see them ready against their mother comes. 205
Exeunt with the bodies.

5.3 *Enter LUCIUS, MARCUS and the Goths,
with AARON prisoner and one carrying his child.*

LUCIUS Uncle Marcus, since 'tis my father's mind
That I repair to Rome, I am content.

1 GOTH And ours with thine, befall what fortune will.

LUCIUS Good uncle, take you in this barbarous Moor,
This ravenous tiger, this accursed devil; 5
Let him receive no sustenance, fetter him
Till he be brought unto the empress' face
For testimony of her foul proceedings.
And see the ambush of our friends be strong:
I fear the emperor means no good to us. 10

AARON Some devil whisper curses in my ear,
And prompt me that my tongue may utter forth
The venomous malice of my swelling heart.

LUCIUS Away, inhuman dog, unhallowed slave!
Sirs, help our uncle to convey him in. 15
Exit Aaron under guard. Sound trumpets.
The trumpets show the emperor is at hand.

*Enter Emperor and Empress, with Tribunes and
others including EMILLIUS.*

SATURNINUS
What, hath the firmament more suns than one?

LUCIUS What boots it thee to call thyself a sun?

MARCUS Rome's emperor, and nephew, break the parle;
These quarrels must be quietly debated. 20
The feast is ready which the careful Titus
Hath ordained to an honourable end,
For peace, for love, for league and good to Rome,
Please you therefore, draw nigh and take your places.

SATURNINUS Marcus, we will. 25

*Trumpets sounding, a table brought in. They sit. Enter
TITUS like a cook, placing the dishes, and LAVINIA with a
veil over her face and Young Lucius.*

TITUS
Welcome, my gracious lord; welcome, dread queen;

Welcome, ye warlike Goths; welcome, Lucius;
And welcome, all. Although the cheer be poor,
'Twill fill your stomachs. Please you, eat of it.

30 SATURNINUS Why art thou thus attired, Andronicus?

TITUS Because I would be sure to have all well
To entertain your highness and your empress.

TAMORA We are beholden to you, good Andronicus.

TITUS And if your highness knew my heart you were.

35 My lord the emperor, resolve me this:
Was it well done of rash Virginius
To slay his daughter with his own right hand,
Because she was enforced, stained and deflowered?

SATURNINUS It was, Andronicus.

TITUS   Your reason, mighty lord?

SATURNINUS

40 Because the girl should not survive her shame,
And by her presence still renew his sorrows.

TITUS A reason mighty, strong, and effectual;
A pattern, precedent, and lively warrant
For me, most wretched, to perform the like.
[*Unveils Lavinia.*]

45 Die, die, Lavinia, and thy shame with thee,
And with thy shame thy father's sorrow die.
[*He kills her.*]

SATURNINUS

What hast thou done, unnatural and unkind?

TITUS

Killed her for whom my tears have made me blind.
I am as woeful as Virginius was,
50 And have a thousand times more cause than he
To do this outrage, and it now is done.

SATURNINUS

What, was she ravished? Tell who did the deed.

TITUS

Will't please you eat? Will't please your highness feed?

TAMORA Why hast thou slain thine only daughter thus?

55 TITUS Not I, 'twas Chiron and Demetrius:
They ravished her and cut away her tongue,
And they, 'twas they, that did her all this wrong.

SATURNINUS Go, fetch them hither to us presently.

TITUS Why, there they are, both baked in this pie,
60 Whereof their mother daintily hath fed,
Eating the flesh that she herself hath bred.
'Tis true, 'tis true, witness my knife's sharp point.
[*He stabs the Empress.*]

SATURNINUS Die, frantic wretch, for this accursed deed.
[*He kills Titus.*]

LUCIUS Can the son's eye behold his father bleed?
65 There's meed for meed, death for a deadly deed.
[*He kills Saturninus. Uproar. The Goths protect the
Andronici, who go aloft.*]

MARCUS [*aloft*]

You sad-faced men, people and sons of Rome,
By uproars severed, as a flight of fowl
Scattered by winds and high tempestuous gusts,
O let me teach you how to knit again
70 This scattered corn into one mutual sheaf,

These broken limbs again into one body.

A ROMAN LORD Let Rome herself be bane unto herself,
And she whom mighty kingdoms curtsy to,
Like a forlorn and desperate castaway,
Do shameful execution on herself!   75
But if my frosty signs and chaps of age,
Grave witnesses of true experience,
Cannot induce you to attend my words,
Speak, Rome's dear friend, as erst our ancestor
When with his solemn tongue he did discourse   80
To lovesick Dido's sad-attending ear
The story of that baleful burning night
When subtle Greeks surprised King Priam's Troy.
Tell us what Sinon hath bewitched our ears,
Or who hath brought the fatal engine in   85
That gives our Troy, our Rome, the civil wound.

MARCUS [*aloft*]

My heart is not compact of flint nor steel,
Nor can I utter all our bitter grief,
But floods of tears will drown my oratory
And break my utterance even in the time   90
When it should move ye to attend me most,
And force you to commiseration.
Here's Rome's young captain: let him tell the tale,
While I stand by and weep to hear him speak.

LUCIUS [*aloft*]

Then, gracious auditory, be it known to you   95
That Chiron and the damned Demetrius
Were they that murdered our emperor's brother,
And they it were that ravished our sister;
For their fell faults our brothers were beheaded,
Our father's tears despised and basely cozened 100
Of that true hand that fought Rome's quarrel out
And sent her enemies unto the grave;
Lastly myself, unkindly banished,
The gates shut on me, and turned weeping out
To beg relief among Rome's enemies,   105
Who drowned their enmity in my true tears
And oped their arms to embrace me as a friend.
I am the turned-forth, be it known to you,
That have preserved her welfare in my blood,
And from her bosom took the enemy's point,   110
Sheathing the steel in my adventurous body.
Alas, you know I am no vaunter, I;
My scars can witness, dumb although they are,
That my report is just and full of truth.
But soft, methinks I do digress too much,   115
Citing my worthless praise. O pardon me,
For when no friends are by, men praise themselves.

MARCUS [*aloft*] Now is my turn to speak.
[*Points to Aaron's baby.*]   Behold the child:
Of this was Tamora delivered,
The issue of an irreligious Moor,   120
Chief architect and plotter of these woes.
The villain is alive in Titus' house,
And as he is to witness this is true,
Now judge what cause had Titus to revenge

125	These wrongs unspeakable, past patience,	

125 These wrongs unspeakable, past patience,
    Or more than any living man could bear.
    Now have you heard the truth: what say you, Romans?
    Have we done aught amiss, show us wherein,
    And from the place where you behold us pleading,
130 The poor remainder of Andronici
    Will hand in hand all headlong hurl ourselves
    And on the ragged stones beat forth our souls
    And make a mutual closure of our house.
    Speak, Romans, speak, and if you say, we shall,
135 Lo, hand in hand, Lucius and I will fall.
    EMILLIUS Come, come, thou reverend man of Rome,
    And bring our emperor gently in thy hand,
    Lucius, our emperor, for well I know
    The common voice do cry it shall be so.
140 MARCUS [*aloft*] Lucius, all hail, Rome's royal emperor!
    [*to others*] Go, go into old Titus' sorrowful house
    And hither hale that misbelieving Moor
    To be adjudged some direful slaughtering death
    As punishment for his most wicked life.
            Exeunt some into the house. A long flourish
                    till the Andronici come down.
145 ALL ROMANS Lucius, all hail, Rome's gracious governor!
    LUCIUS Thanks, gentle Romans. May I govern so
    To heal Rome's harms and wipe away her woe.
    But, gentle people, give me aim awhile,
    For nature puts me to a heavy task.
150 Stand all aloof, but, uncle, draw you near
    To shed obsequious tears upon this trunk.
        [*Kisses Titus.*]
    O, take this warm kiss on thy pale cold lips,
    These sorrowful drops upon thy bloodstained face,
    The last true duties of thy noble son.
    MARCUS [*Kisses Titus.*]
155 Tear for tear and loving kiss for kiss,
    Thy brother Marcus tenders on thy lips.
    O, were the sum of these that I should pay
    Countless and infinite, yet would I pay them.
    LUCIUS [*to his son*]
    Come hither, boy, come, come and learn of us
160 To melt in showers. Thy grandsire loved thee well:
    Many a time he danced thee on his knee,
    Sung thee asleep, his loving breast thy pillow;
    Many a story hath he told to thee,

And bid thee bear his pretty tales in mind
And talk of them when he was dead and gone.   165
MARCUS
    How many thousand times hath these poor lips,
    When they were living, warmed themselves on thine!
    O now, sweet boy, give them their latest kiss:
    Bid him farewell, commit him to the grave;
    Do them that kindness and take leave of them.   170
BOY [*Kisses Titus.*]
    O grandsire, grandsire, e'en with all my heart
    Would I were dead, so you did live again.
    O Lord, I cannot speak to him for weeping,
    My tears will choke me if I ope my mouth.

            Enter AARON *under guard.*

A ROMAN You sad Andronici, have done with woes,   175
    Give sentence on this execrable wretch
    That hath been breeder of these dire events.
LUCIUS Set him breast-deep in earth and famish him;
    There let him stand and rave and cry for food.
    If anyone relieves or pities him,   180
    For the offence he dies. This is our doom;
    Some stay to see him fastened in the earth.
AARON
    Ah, why should wrath be mute and fury dumb?
    I am no baby, I, that with base prayers
    I should repent the evils I have done.   185
    Ten thousand worse than ever yet I did
    Would I perform if I might have my will.
    If one good deed in all my life I did
    I do repent it from my very soul.
LUCIUS
    Some loving friends convey the emperor hence,   190
    And give him burial in his fathers' grave;
    My father and Lavinia shall forthwith
    Be closed in our household's monument;
    As for that ravenous tiger, Tamora,
    No funeral rite, nor man in mourning weed,   195
    No mournful bell shall ring her burial,
    But throw her forth to beasts and birds to prey:
    Her life was beastly and devoid of pity,
    And being dead, let birds on her take pity.
                            Exeunt with the bodies.

Troilus and Cressida

Published in quarto in 1609 as *The Famous History of Troilus and Cressida*, the play was to have followed *Romeo and Juliet* as the fourth of the tragedies in the First Folio of 1623, and its first three pages had been printed before it was removed and replaced by *Timon of Athens*. It does not appear in the table of contents, and some copies of the Folio had already gone on sale without it before it was hastily printed and inserted between *King Henry VIII*, last of the histories, and *Coriolanus*, first of the tragedies, in a text which adds the Prologue and shows minor but frequent variation of word or phrase from that of the Quarto, of which the version printed in the Folio is possibly a revision. The play was written about 1601–2, in the aftermath of the abortive rising of the Earl of Essex and his execution in February 1601. It may be in part the Chamberlain's Men's response to an earlier play on the subject by Thomas Dekker and Henry Chettle performed by the rival Admiral's Men in 1599 (now known only from a damaged stage 'plot').

A first setting of the title-page of the 1609 Quarto claimed that the play had been acted by the King's Men at the Globe – a claim retracted when that title-page was cancelled and replaced, deleting all reference to performance, and an epistle from 'A never writer to an ever reader' was added, in which the play, 'never clapper-clawed with the palms of the vulgar', is praised as a comedy which readers are lucky to see in print, contrary its 'grand possessors' wills'. This epistle has given rise to the hypothesis that the play was written for a private occasion, although no positive evidence exists for such a performance. The Epilogue, which may not have been included in all performances, has struck some scholars as more appropriate to an audience of lawyers at one of the Inns of Court than to public performance at the Globe. This chequered history of publication may result from disputes over copyright, or it may reflect the political sensitivity of its subject at a time when the association of Essex with Achilles was commonplace.

Many English plays (now lost) had been written on the 'matter of Troy' before *Troilus and Cressida*, which presents a sour, minor-key variation on familiar themes and characters. Shakespeare himself had often alluded to Troy in earlier works, notably *Lucrece*, which contains a lengthy discourse on a painting of the Fall of Troy; *The Merchant of Venice*, which alludes to the separation of Troilus and Cressida; and *Hamlet*, where it supplies apt and familiar material for the Player's tragic speech. Medieval mythology derived the British people from the Trojan line of Aeneas, and London could still be popularly referred to as Troynovant or New Troy. The Troy story reached Shakespeare in part through George Chapman's translation of seven books of the *Iliad* (1598) but more importantly through medieval retellings and expansions. The play makes use of at least two of them. For the love story, itself a medieval addition to the 'matter of Troy', he adapted Chaucer's *Troilus and Criseyde* (c. 1385) (earlier a minor source for *Romeo and Juliet*, whose love story is sourly parodied by that of *Troilus and Cressida*) and, for the war plot, William Caxton's *Recuyell of the Histories of Troy* (1474). Shakespeare was the first to balance the war story against the love story, although unevenly, as the war story occupies two thirds of his action and the love story only one third. Whether history, tragedy or comedy, the play offers a destructive analysis of chivalric honour and romantic love that culminates in the double shock to Troilus of the infidelity of Cressida with Diomedes and of the murder of Hector by Achilles' Myrmidons.

After an adaptation by John Dryden which attempted to turn it into an exemplary tragedy, *Troilus and Cressida* disappeared from the stage for some 200 years. Its disillusioned tone and inconclusive action recommended it to the twentieth century and it has been regularly revived in productions many of which have urged its topicality by setting it in the historical periods of all the major wars since the Crimean War and the American Civil War.

The Arden text is based on the 1623 First Folio, supplemented and corrected from the 1609 Quarto.

PROLOGUE

THE TROJANS

PRIAM	*King of Troy*
HECTOR	
PARIS	
DEIPHOBUS	
HELENUS	*his sons*
TROILUS	
MARGARETON	
AENEAS	
Antenor	*Trojan commanders*
CASSANDRA	*Priam's daughter, a prophetess*
ANDROMACHE	*Hector's wife*
CRESSIDA	*Calchas' daughter*
CALCHAS	*Cressida's father, a Trojan priest, a defector to the Greeks*
PANDARUS	*a lord, Cressida's uncle*
ALEXANDER	*Cressida's servant*
BOY	*Troilus' servant*
SERVANT	*attending on Paris*

Attendants, Soldiers, Musicians, Torchbearers

THE GREEKS

AGAMEMNON	*general commander of the Greeks*
MENELAUS	*King of Sparta, his brother*
HELEN	*Menelaus' wife, living with Paris in Troy*
ACHILLES	
AJAX	
ULYSSES	*Greek commanders*
NESTOR	
DIOMEDES	
PATROCLUS	*Achilles' companion*
THERSITES	*a deformed and scurrilous Greek*
SERVANT	*attending on Diomedes*
MYRMIDONS	

Attendants, Soldiers, Trumpeter

1300

PROLOGUE

Enter Speaker of the Prologue, *in armour.*

PROLOGUE
In Troy there lies the scene. From isles of Greece
The princes orgulous, their high blood chafed,
Have to the port of Athens sent their ships
Fraught with the ministers and instruments
5 Of cruel war. Sixty and nine, that wore
Their crownets regal, from th'Athenian bay
Put forth toward Phrygia, and their vow is made
To ransack Troy, within whose strong immures
The ravished Helen, Menelaus' queen,
10 With wanton Paris sleeps; and that's the quarrel.
To Tenedos they come,
And the deep-drawing barks do there disgorge
Their warlike freightage. Now on Dardan plains
The fresh and yet unbruised Greeks do pitch
15 Their brave pavilions. Priam's six-gated city –
Dardan and Timbria, Helias, Chetas, Troien
And Antenorides – with massy staples
And corresponsive and fulfilling bolts,
Spar up the sons of Troy.
20 Now expectation, tickling skittish spirits
On one and other side, Trojan and Greek,
Sets all on hazard. And hither am I come,
A Prologue armed, but not in confidence
Of author's pen or actor's voice, but suited
25 In like conditions as our argument,
To tell you, fair beholders, that our play
Leaps o'er the vaunt and firstlings of those broils,
Beginning in the middle, starting thence away
To what may be digested in a play.
30 Like or find fault; do as your pleasures are;
Now good or bad, 'tis but the chance of war. *Exit.*

1.1 *Enter* PANDARUS *and* TROILUS.

TROILUS Call here my varlet; I'll unarm again.
Why should I war without the walls of Troy,
That find such cruel battle here within?
Each Trojan that is master of his heart,
5 Let him to field; Troilus, alas, hath none.
PANDARUS Will this gear ne'er be mended?
TROILUS
The Greeks are strong, and skilful to their strength,
Fierce to their skill, and to their fierceness valiant;
But I am weaker than a woman's tear,
10 Tamer than sleep, fonder than ignorance,
Less valiant than the virgin in the night,
And skilless as unpractised infancy.
PANDARUS Well, I have told you enough of this; for my
part, I'll not meddle nor make no farther. He that will
15 have a cake out of the wheat must tarry the grinding.
TROILUS Have I not tarried?
PANDARUS Ay, the grinding; but you must tarry the
bolting.

TROILUS Have I not tarried?
PANDARUS Ay, the bolting; but you must tarry the 20
leavening.
TROILUS Still have I tarried.
PANDARUS Ay, to the leavening; but here's yet in the
word hereafter the kneading, the making of the cake,
the heating the oven, and the baking. Nay, you must 25
stay the cooling too, or ye may chance burn your lips.
TROILUS Patience herself, what goddess e'er she be,
Doth lesser blench at suff'rance than I do.
At Priam's royal table do I sit,
And when fair Cressid comes into my thoughts – 30
So, traitor! 'When she comes'! When is she thence?
PANDARUS Well, she looked yesternight fairer than ever
I saw her look, or any woman else.
TROILUS I was about to tell thee – when my heart,
As wedged with a sigh, would rive in twain, 35
Lest Hector or my father should perceive me,
I have, as when the sun doth light a-scorn,
Buried this sigh in wrinkle of a smile;
But sorrow that is couched in seeming gladness
Is like that mirth fate turns to sudden sadness. 40
PANDARUS An her hair were not somewhat darker than
Helen's – well, go to – there were no more comparison
between the women. But, for my part, she is my
kinswoman; I would not, as they term it, praise her. But
I would somebody had heard her talk yesterday, as I did. 45
I will not dispraise your sister Cassandra's wit, but –
TROILUS O Pandarus! I tell thee, Pandarus –
When I do tell thee there my hopes lie drowned,
Reply not in how many fathoms deep
They lie indrenched. I tell thee I am mad 50
In Cressid's love. Thou answer'st 'She is fair',
Pour'st in the open ulcer of my heart
Her eyes, her hair, her cheek, her gait, her voice;
Handlest in thy discourse, O, that her hand,
In whose comparison all whites are ink 55
Writing their own reproach; to whose soft seizure
The cygnet's down is harsh, and spirit of sense
Hard as the palm of ploughman. This thou tell'st me –
As true thou tell'st me – when I say I love her;
But, saying thus, instead of oil and balm, 60
Thou lay'st in every gash that love hath given me
The knife that made it.
PANDARUS I speak no more than truth.
TROILUS Thou dost not speak so much.
PANDARUS Faith, I'll not meddle in it. Let her be as she 65
is. If she be fair, 'tis the better for her; an she be not,
she has the mends in her own hands.
TROILUS Good Pandarus – how now, Pandarus?
PANDARUS I have had my labour for my travail, ill
thought on of her, and ill thought on of you; gone 70
between and between, but small thanks for my labour.
TROILUS What, art thou angry, Pandarus? What, with
me?
PANDARUS Because she's kin to me, therefore she's not
so fair as Helen; an she were not kin to me, she would 75

be as fair o' Friday as Helen is on Sunday. But what
care I? I care not an she were a blackamoor; 'tis all one
to me.

TROILUS   Say I she is not fair?

80   PANDARUS   I do not care whether you do or no. She's a
fool to stay behind her father; let her to the Greeks,
and so I'll tell her the next time I see her. For my part,
I'll meddle nor make no more i'th' matter.

TROILUS   Pandarus –

85   PANDARUS   Not I.

TROILUS   Sweet Pandarus –

PANDARUS   Pray you, speak no more to me; I will leave
all as I found it, and there an end.   *Exit.*
[*Sound alarum.*]

TROILUS
Peace, you ungracious clamours! Peace, rude sounds!
90   Fools on both sides! Helen must needs be fair,
When with your blood you daily paint her thus.
I cannot fight upon this argument;
It is too starved a subject for my sword.
But Pandarus – O gods, how do you plague me!
95   I cannot come to Cressid but by Pandar,
And he's as tetchy to be wooed to woo
As she is stubborn-chaste against all suit.
Tell me, Apollo, for thy Daphne's love,
What Cressid is, what Pandar, and what we?
100   Her bed is India; there she lies, a pearl.
Between our Ilium and where she resides,
Let it be called the wild and wand'ring flood,
Ourself the merchant, and this sailing Pandar
Our doubtful hope, our convoy and our bark.

Alarum. Enter AENEAS.

AENEAS
105   How now, Prince Troilus, wherefore not afield?

TROILUS
Because not there. This woman's answer sorts,
For womanish it is to be from thence.
What news, Aeneas, from the field today?

AENEAS   That Paris is returned home, and hurt.

TROILUS   By whom, Aeneas?

110   AENEAS   Troilus, by Menelaus.

TROILUS   Let Paris bleed. 'Tis but a scar to scorn;
Paris is gored with Menelaus' horn.   [*Alarum*]

AENEAS   Hark, what good sport is out of town today!

TROILUS
Better at home, if 'would I might' were 'may'.
115   But to the sport abroad. Are you bound thither?

AENEAS   In all swift haste.

TROILUS   Come, go we then together.   *Exeunt.*

1.2   *Enter* CRESSIDA *and her man* ALEXANDER.

CRESSIDA   Who were those went by?

ALEXANDER   Queen Hecuba and Helen.

CRESSIDA   And whither go they?

ALEXANDER   Up to the eastern tower,

Whose height commands as subject all the vale,
To see the battle. Hector, whose patience
Is as a virtue fixed, today was moved.   5
He chid Andromache and struck his armourer;
And, like as there were husbandry in war,
Before the sun rose he was harnessed light,
And to the field goes he, where every flower
Did as a prophet weep what it foresaw   10
In Hector's wrath.

CRESSIDA   What was his cause of anger?

ALEXANDER
The noise goes, this: there is among the Greeks
A lord of Trojan blood, nephew to Hector;
They call him Ajax.

CRESSIDA   Good, and what of him?

ALEXANDER   They say he is a very man *per se,*   15
And stands alone.

CRESSIDA   So do all men, unless they are drunk, sick or
have no legs.

ALEXANDER   This man, lady, hath robbed many beasts
of their particular additions. He is as valiant as the lion,   20
churlish as the bear, slow as the elephant; a man into
whom nature hath so crowded humours that his valour
is crushed into folly, his folly sauced with discretion.
There is no man hath a virtue that he hath not a
glimpse of, nor any man an attaint but he carries some   25
stain of it. He is melancholy without cause, and merry
against the hair; he hath the joints of everything, but
everything so out of joint that he is a gouty Briareus,
many hands and no use, or purblind Argus, all eyes and
no sight.   30

CRESSIDA   But how should this man, that makes me
smile, make Hector angry?

ALEXANDER   They say he yesterday coped Hector in the
battle and struck him down, the disdain and shame
whereof hath ever since kept Hector fasting and   35
waking.

Enter PANDARUS.

CRESSIDA   Who comes here?

ALEXANDER   Madam, your uncle Pandarus.

CRESSIDA   Hector's a gallant man.

ALEXANDER   As may be in the world, lady.   40

PANDARUS   What's that? What's that?

CRESSIDA   Good morrow, uncle Pandarus.

PANDARUS   Good morrow, cousin Cressid. What do you
talk of? – Good morrow, Alexander. – How do you,
cousin? When were you at Ilium?   45

CRESSIDA   This morning, uncle.

PANDARUS   What were you talking of when I came? Was
Hector armed and gone ere ye came to Ilium? Helen
was not up, was she?

CRESSIDA   Hector was gone, but Helen was not up?   50

PANDARUS   E'en so. Hector was stirring early.

CRESSIDA   That were we talking of, and of his anger.

PANDARUS   Was he angry?

CRESSIDA   So he says here.

PANDARUS   True, he was so. I know the cause too. He'll lay about him today, I can tell them that; and there's Troilus will not come far behind him; let them take heed of Troilus, I can tell them that too.

CRESSIDA   What, is he angry too?

PANDARUS   Who, Troilus? Troilus is the better man of the two.

CRESSIDA   O Jupiter, there's no comparison.

PANDARUS   What, not between Troilus and Hector? Do you know a man if you see him?

CRESSIDA   Ay, if I ever saw him before and knew him.

PANDARUS   Well, I say Troilus is Troilus.

CRESSIDA   Then you say as I say, for I am sure he is not Hector.

PANDARUS   No, nor Hector is not Troilus in some degrees.

CRESSIDA   'Tis just to each of them; he is himself.

PANDARUS   Himself? Alas, poor Troilus, I would he were.

CRESSIDA   So he is.

PANDARUS   Condition I had gone barefoot to India!

CRESSIDA   He is not Hector.

PANDARUS   Himself? No, he's not himself, would 'a were himself! Well, the gods are above; time must friend or end. Well, Troilus, well, I would my heart were in her body. No, Hector is not a better man than Troilus.

CRESSIDA   Excuse me.

PANDARUS   He is elder.

CRESSIDA   Pardon me, pardon me.

PANDARUS   Th'other's not come to't; you shall tell me another tale when th'other's come to't. Hector shall not have his wit this year.

CRESSIDA   He shall not need it, if he have his own.

PANDARUS   Nor his qualities.

CRESSIDA   No matter.

PANDARUS   Nor his beauty.

CRESSIDA   'Twould not become him; his own's better.

PANDARUS   You have no judgement, niece. Helen herself swore th'other day that Troilus, for a brown favour – for so 'tis, I must confess – not brown neither –

CRESSIDA   No, but brown.

PANDARUS   Faith, to say truth, brown and not brown.

CRESSIDA   To say the truth, true and not true.

PANDARUS   She praised his complexion above Paris'.

CRESSIDA   Why, Paris hath colour enough.

PANDARUS   So he has.

CRESSIDA   Then Troilus should have too much. If she praised him above, his complexion is higher than his; he having colour enough, and the other higher, is too flaming a praise for a good complexion. I had as lief Helen's golden tongue had commended Troilus for a copper nose.

PANDARUS   I swear to you, I think Helen loves him better than Paris.

CRESSIDA   Then she's a merry Greek indeed.

PANDARUS   Nay, I am sure she does. She came to him th'other day into the compassed window – and you know he has not past three or four hairs on his chin –

CRESSIDA   Indeed, a tapster's arithmetic may soon bring his particulars therein to a total.

PANDARUS   Why, he is very young, and yet will he within three pound lift as much as his brother Hector.

CRESSIDA   Is he so young a man, and so old a lifter?

PANDARUS   But to prove to you that Helen loves him: she came and puts me her white hand to his cloven chin –

CRESSIDA   Juno have mercy, how came it cloven?

PANDARUS   Why, you know 'tis dimpled. I think his smiling becomes him better than any man in all Phrygia.

CRESSIDA   O, he smiles valiantly.

PANDARUS   Does he not?

CRESSIDA   O, yes, an 'twere a cloud in autumn.

PANDARUS   Why, go to, then. But to prove to you that Helen loves Troilus –

CRESSIDA   Troilus will stand to the proof, if you'll prove it so.

PANDARUS   Troilus? Why, he esteems her no more than I esteem an addle egg.

CRESSIDA   If you love an addle egg as well as you love an idle head, you would eat chickens i'th' shell.

PANDARUS   I cannot choose but laugh, to think how she tickled his chin. Indeed, she has a marvellous white hand, I must needs confess –

CRESSIDA   Without the rack.

PANDARUS   And she takes upon her to spy a white hair on his chin.

CRESSIDA   Alas, poor chin! Many a wart is richer.

PANDARUS   But there was such laughing! Queen Hecuba laughed that her eyes ran o'er –

CRESSIDA   With millstones.

PANDARUS   And Cassandra laughed –

CRESSIDA   But there was a more temperate fire under the pot of her eyes. Did her eyes run o'er too?

PANDARUS   And Hector laughed.

CRESSIDA   At what was all this laughing?

PANDARUS   Marry, at the white hair that Helen spied on Troilus' chin.

CRESSIDA   An 't had been a green hair I should have laughed too.

PANDARUS   They laughed not so much at the hair as at his pretty answer.

CRESSIDA   What was his answer?

PANDARUS   Quoth she, 'Here's but two-and-fifty hairs on your chin, and one of them is white'.

CRESSIDA   This is her question.

PANDARUS   That's true, make no question of that. 'Two-and-fifty hairs', quoth he, 'and one white: that white hair is my father, and all the rest are his sons.' 'Jupiter!', quoth she, 'which of these hairs is Paris, my husband?' 'The forked one', quoth he; 'pluck't out, and give it him.' But there was such laughing, and Helen so blushed, and Paris so chafed, and all the rest so laughed, that it passed.

CRESSIDA So let it now, for it has been a great while going by.

PANDARUS Well, cousin, I told you a thing yesterday. Think on't.

CRESSIDA So I do.

PANDARUS I'll be sworn 'tis true. He will weep you an 'twere a man born in April.

CRESSIDA And I'll spring up in his tears, an 'twere a nettle against May. [*Sound a retreat.*]

PANDARUS Hark, they are coming from the field. Shall we stand up here and see them as they pass toward Ilium? Good niece, do, sweet niece Cressida.

CRESSIDA At your pleasure.

PANDARUS Here, here, here's an excellent place; here we may see most bravely. I'll tell you them all by their names as they pass by, but mark Troilus above the rest.

Enter AENEAS *and passes over the stage.*

CRESSIDA Speak not so loud.

PANDARUS That's Aeneas; is not that a brave man? He's one of the flowers of Troy, I can tell you, but mark Troilus; you shall see anon.

Enter Antenor and passes over the stage.

CRESSIDA Who's that?

PANDARUS That's Antenor. He has a shrewd wit, I can tell you, and he's a man good enough; he's one o'th' soundest judgements in Troy whosoever, and a proper man of person. When comes Troilus? I'll show you Troilus anon; if he see me, you shall see him nod at me.

CRESSIDA Will he give you the nod?

PANDARUS You shall see.

CRESSIDA If he do, the rich shall have more.

Enter HECTOR *and passes over the stage.*

PANDARUS That's Hector, that, that, look you, that; there's a fellow! Go thy way, Hector! There's a brave man, niece. O brave Hector! Look how he looks! There's a countenance! Is't not a brave man?

CRESSIDA O, a brave man!

PANDARUS Is 'a not? It does a man's heart good. Look you what hacks are on his helmet, look you yonder, do you see? Look you there, there's no jesting; there's laying on, take't off who will, as they say; there be hacks.

CRESSIDA Be those with swords?

PANDARUS Swords, anything, he cares not; an the devil come to him, it's all one. By God's lid, it does one's heart good. Yonder comes Paris, yonder comes Paris!

Enter PARIS *and passes over the stage.*

Look ye yonder, niece, is't not a gallant man too, is't not? Why, this is brave now. Who said he came hurt home today? He's not hurt. Why, this will do Helen's heart good now, ha? Would I could see Troilus now. You shall see Troilus anon.

Enter HELENUS *and passes over the stage.*

CRESSIDA Who's that?

PANDARUS That's Helenus. I marvel where Troilus is. That's Helenus. I think he went not forth today. That's Helenus.

CRESSIDA Can Helenus fight, uncle?

PANDARUS Helenus? No – yes, he'll fight indifferent well. I marvel where Troilus is. Hark, do you not hear the people cry 'Troilus'? Helenus is a priest.

CRESSIDA What sneaking fellow comes yonder?

Enter TROILUS *and passes over the stage.*

PANDARUS Where? Yonder? That's Deiphobus. – 'Tis Troilus! There's a man, niece! Hem! Brave Troilus, the prince of chivalry!

CRESSIDA Peace, for shame, peace!

PANDARUS Mark him, note him. O brave Troilus! Look well upon him, niece, look you how his sword is bloodied, and his helm more hacked than Hector's, and how he looks, and how he goes! O admirable youth! He ne'er saw three-and-twenty. Go thy way, Troilus, go thy way! Had I a sister were a grace, or a daughter a goddess, he should take his choice. O admirable man! Paris? Paris is dirt to him, and I warrant Helen, to change, would give money to boot.

Enter Common Soldiers and pass over the stage.

CRESSIDA Here comes more.

PANDARUS Asses, fools, dolts; chaff and bran, chaff and bran; porridge after meat. I could live and die i'th' eyes of Troilus. Ne'er look, ne'er look, the eagles are gone; crows and daws, crows and daws! I had rather be such a man as Troilus than Agamemnon and all Greece.

CRESSIDA There is among the Greeks Achilles, a better man than Troilus.

PANDARUS Achilles? A drayman, a porter, a very camel.

CRESSIDA Well, well.

PANDARUS 'Well, well'! Why, have you any discretion? Have you any eyes? Do you know what a man is? Is not birth, beauty, good shape, discourse, manhood, learning, gentleness, virtue, youth, liberality and so forth the spice and salt that season a man?

CRESSIDA Ay, a minced man; and then to be baked with no date in the pie, for then the man's date is out.

PANDARUS You are such another woman! One knows not at what ward you lie.

CRESSIDA Upon my back to defend my belly, upon my wit to defend my wiles, upon my secrecy to defend mine honesty, my mask to defend my beauty, and you to defend all these; and at all these wards I lie, at a thousand watches.

PANDARUS Say one of your watches.

CRESSIDA Nay, I'll watch you for that; and that's one of the chiefest of them too. If I cannot ward what I would not have hit, I can watch you for telling how I took the blow – unless it swell past hiding, and then it's past watching.

PANDARUS You are such another!

Enter Troilus' Boy.

BOY Sir, my lord would instantly speak with you.

270 PANDARUS Where?

BOY At your own house. There he unarms him.

PANDARUS Good boy, tell him I come. *Exit Boy.*
I doubt he be hurt. Fare ye well, good niece.

CRESSIDA Adieu, uncle.

275 PANDARUS I'll be with you, niece, by and by.

CRESSIDA To bring, uncle?

PANDARUS Ay, a token from Troilus.

CRESSIDA By the same token, you are a bawd.

Exit Pandarus.
Words, vows, gifts, tears and love's full sacrifice

280 He offers in another's enterprise;
But more in Troilus thousandfold I see
Than in the glass of Pandar's praise may be.
Yet hold I off. Women are angels, wooing;
Things won are done; joy's soul lies in the doing.

285 That she beloved knows naught that knows not this:
Men prize the thing ungained more than it is.
That she was never yet that ever knew
Love got so sweet as when desire did sue.
Therefore this maxim out of love I teach:

290 'Achievement is command; ungained, beseech'.
Then, though my heart's contents firm love doth bear,
Nothing of that shall from mine eyes appear.

Exit with Alexander.

1.3 *Sennet. Enter* AGAMEMNON, NESTOR,
ULYSSES, DIOMEDES, MENELAUS, *with others.*

AGAMEMNON Princes,
What grief hath set the jaundice on your cheeks?
The ample proposition that hope makes
In all designs begun on earth below

5 Fails in the promised largeness. Checks and disasters
Grow in the veins of actions highest reared,
As knots, by the conflux of meeting sap,
Infects the sound pine and diverts his grain
Tortive and errant from his course of growth.

10 Nor, princes, is it matter new to us
That we come short of our suppose so far
That after seven years' siege yet Troy walls stand,
Sith every action that hath gone before,
Whereof we have record, trial did draw

15 Bias and thwart, not answering the aim
And that unbodied figure of the thought
That gave't surmised shape. Why then, you princes,
Do you with cheeks abashed behold our works
And think them shames, which are indeed naught
else

20 But the protractive trials of great Jove
To find persistive constancy in men?
The fineness of which metal is not found
In Fortune's love; for then the bold and coward,

The wise and fool, the artist and unread,
25 The hard and soft, seem all affined and kin.
But in the wind and tempest of her frown,
Distinction, with a broad and powerful fan,
Puffing at all, winnows the light away,
And what hath mass or matter by itself
30 Lies rich in virtue and unmingled.

NESTOR With due observance of thy godly seat,
Great Agamemnon, Nestor shall apply
Thy latest words. In the reproof of chance
Lies the true proof of men. The sea being smooth,
35 How many shallow bauble boats dare sail
Upon her patient breast, making their way
With those of nobler bulk!
But let the ruffian Boreas once enrage
The gentle Thetis, and anon behold
40 The strong-ribbed bark through liquid mountains cut,
Bounding between the two moist elements
Like Perseus' horse. Where's then the saucy boat
Whose weak untimbered sides but even now
Co-rivalled greatness? Either to harbour fled
45 Or made a toast for Neptune. Even so
Doth valour's show and valour's worth divide
In storms of fortune. For in her ray and brightness
The herd hath more annoyance by the breese
Than by the tiger; but when the splitting wind
50 Makes flexible the knees of knotted oaks
And flies flee under shade, why then the thing of
courage,
As roused with rage, with rage doth sympathize,
And with an accent tuned in selfsame key
Retorts to chiding fortune.

ULYSSES Agamemnon,
55 Thou great commander, nerve and bone of Greece,
Heart of our numbers, soul and only spirit,
In whom the tempers and the minds of all
Should be shut up: hear what Ulysses speaks.
Besides th'applause and approbation
60 The which, [*to Agamemnon*] most mighty for thy place
and sway,
[*to Nestor*] And thou most reverend for thy
stretched-out life,
I give to both your speeches, which were such
As, Agamemnon, every hand of Greece
Should hold up high in brass; and such again
65 As venerable Nestor, hatched in silver,
Should with a bond of air, strong as the axletree
On which the heavens ride, knit all Greeks' ears
To his experienced tongue, yet let it please both,
Thou great, and wise, to hear Ulysses speak.

AGAMEMNON
70 Speak, Prince of Ithaca; and be't of less expect
That matter needless, of importless burden,
Divide thy lips, than we are confident,
When rank Thersites opes his mastic jaws,
We shall hear music, wit and oracle.

ULYSSES Troy, yet upon his basis, had been down, 75

And the great Hector's sword had lacked a master,
But for these instances:
The specialty of rule hath been neglected;
And look how many Grecian tents do stand
80 Hollow upon this plain, so many hollow factions.
When that the general is not like the hive
To whom the foragers shall all repair,
What honey is expected? Degree being vizarded,
Th'unworthiest shows as fairly in the mask.
85 The heavens themselves, the planets and this centre
Observe degree, priority and place,
Insisture, course, proportion, season, form,
Office and custom, in all line of order.
And therefore is the glorious planet Sol
90 In noble eminence enthroned and sphered
Amidst the other, whose med'cinable eye
Corrects the ill aspects of planets evil
And posts, like the commandment of a king,
Sans check, to good and bad. But when the planets
95 In evil mixture to disorder wander,
What plagues and what portents, what mutiny,
What raging of the sea, shaking of earth,
Commotion in the winds, frights, changes, horrors,
Divert and crack, rend and deracinate
100 The unity and married calm of states
Quite from their fixure! O, when degree is shaked,
Which is the ladder to all high designs,
The enterprise is sick. How could communities,
Degrees in schools and brotherhoods in cities,
105 Peaceful commerce from dividable shores,
The primogeneity and due of birth,
Prerogative of age, crowns, sceptres, laurels,
But by degree stand in authentic place?
Take but degree away, untune that string,
110 And hark what discord follows. Each thing meets
In mere oppugnancy. The bounded waters
Should lift their bosoms higher than the shores
And make a sop of all this solid globe;
Strength should be lord of imbecility,
115 And the rude son should strike his father dead;
Force should be right; or rather, right and wrong,
Between whose endless jar justice resides,
Should lose their names, and so should justice too.
Then everything includes itself in power,
120 Power into will, will into appetite;
And appetite, an universal wolf,
So doubly seconded with will and power,
Must make perforce an universal prey
And last eat up himself. Great Agamemnon,
125 This chaos, when degree is suffocate,
Follows the choking.
And this neglection of degree it is
That by a pace goes backward in a purpose
It hath to climb. The general's disdained
130 By him one step below, he by the next,
That next by him beneath; so every step,
Exampled by the first pace that is sick

Of his superior, grows to an envious fever
Of pale and bloodless emulation.
And 'tis this fever that keeps Troy on foot, 135
Not her own sinews. To end a tale of length,
Troy in our weakness lives, not in her strength.

NESTOR Most wisely hath Ulysses here discovered
The fever whereof all our power is sick.

AGAMEMNON
The nature of the sickness found, Ulysses, 140
What is the remedy?

ULYSSES The great Achilles, whom opinion crowns
The sinew and the forehand of our host,
Having his ear full of his airy fame,
Grows dainty of his worth and in his tent 145
Lies mocking our designs. With him Patroclus,
Upon a lazy bed, the livelong day
Breaks scurril jests,
And with ridiculous and awkward action –
Which, slanderer, he imitation calls – 150
He pageants us. Sometime, great Agamemnon,
Thy topless deputation he puts on,
And, like a strutting player, whose conceit
Lies in his hamstring, and doth think it rich
To hear the wooden dialogue and sound 155
'Twixt his stretched footing and the scaffoldage,
Such to-be-pitied and o'erwrested seeming
He acts thy greatness in; and when he speaks,
'Tis like a chime a-mending, with terms unsquared,
Which from the tongue of roaring Typhon dropped 160
Would seem hyperboles. At this fusty stuff
The large Achilles, on his pressed bed lolling,
From his deep chest laughs out a loud applause,
Cries 'Excellent! 'Tis Agamemnon just.
Now play me Nestor; hem, and stroke thy beard, 165
As he being dressed to some oration.'
That's done, as near as the extremest ends
Of parallels, as like as Vulcan and his wife;
Yet god Achilles still cries, 'Excellent!
'Tis Nestor right. Now play him me, Patroclus, 170
Arming to answer in a night-alarm.'
And then, forsooth, the faint defects of age
Must be the scene of mirth; to cough and spit,
And with a palsy fumbling on his gorget
Shake in and out the rivet. And at this sport 175
Sir Valour dies; cries, 'O, enough, Patroclus,
Or give me ribs of steel! I shall split all
In pleasure of my spleen.' And in this fashion,
All our abilities, gifts, natures, shapes,
Severals and generals of grace exact, 180
Achievements, plots, orders, preventions,
Excitements to the field, or speech for truce,
Success or loss, what is or is not, serves
As stuff for these two to make paradoxes.

NESTOR And in the imitation of these twain, 185
Who, as Ulysses says, opinion crowns
With an imperial voice, many are infect.
Ajax is grown self-willed and bears his head

In such a rein, in full as proud a place
190 As broad Achilles; keeps his tent like him,
Makes factious feasts, rails on our state of war,
Bold as an oracle, and sets Thersites –
A slave whose gall coins slanders like a mint –
To match us in comparisons with dirt,
195 To weaken and discredit our exposure,
How rank soever rounded in with danger.
ULYSSES   They tax our policy and call it cowardice,
Count wisdom as no member of the war,
Forestall prescience, and esteem no act
200 But that of hand. The still and mental parts,
That do contrive how many hands shall strike,
When fitness calls them on, and know by measure
Of their observant toil the enemy's weight –
Why, this hath not a finger's dignity.
205 They call this bed-work, mapp'ry, closet war;
So that the ram that batters down the wall,
For the great swinge and rudeness of his poise,
They place before his hand that made the engine
Or those that with the fineness of their souls
210 By reason guide his execution.
NESTOR   Let this be granted, and Achilles' horse
Makes many Thetis' sons.   [*Tucket*]
AGAMEMNON   What trumpet? Look, Menelaus.
MENELAUS   From Troy.

Enter AENEAS *with a Trumpeter.*

215 AGAMEMNON   What would you 'fore our tent?
AENEAS   Is this great Agamemnon's tent, I pray you?
AGAMEMNON   Even this.
AENEAS   May one that is a herald and a prince
Do a fair message to his kingly ears?
220 AGAMEMNON   With surety stronger than Achilles' arm
'Fore all the Greekish lords, which with one voice
Call Agamemnon head and general.
AENEAS   Fair leave and large security. How may
A stranger to those most imperial looks
Know them from eyes of other mortals?
225 AGAMEMNON   How?
AENEAS   Ay.
I ask, that I might waken reverence,
And bid the cheek be ready with a blush
Modest as morning when she coldly eyes
230 The youthful Phoebus.
Which is that god in office, guiding men?
Which is the high and mighty Agamemnon?
AGAMEMNON [*to the Greeks*]
This Trojan scorns us, or the men of Troy
Are ceremonious courtiers.
235 AENEAS   Courtiers as free, as debonair, unarmed,
As bending angels – that's their fame in peace.
But when they would seem soldiers, they have galls,
Good arms, strong joints, true swords, and – Jove's
      accord –
Nothing so full of heart. But peace, Aeneas,

Peace, Trojan; lay thy finger on thy lips!   240
The worthiness of praise distains his worth
If that the praised himself bring the praise forth.
But what the repining enemy commends,
That breath Fame blows; that praise, sole pure,
      transcends.
AGAMEMNON   Sir, you of Troy, call you yourself Aeneas?   245
AENEAS   Ay, Greek, that is my name.
AGAMEMNON   What's your affair, I pray you?
AENEAS   Sir, pardon, 'tis for Agamemnon's ears.
AGAMEMNON
He hears naught privately that comes from Troy.
AENEAS   Nor I from Troy come not to whisper him.   250
I bring a trumpet to awake his ear,
To set his sense on the attentive bent,
And then to speak.
AGAMEMNON   Speak frankly as the wind;
It is not Agamemnon's sleeping hour.
That thou shalt know, Trojan, he is awake,   255
He tells thee so himself.
AENEAS   Trumpet, blow loud!
Send thy brass voice through all these lazy tents;
And every Greek of mettle, let him know
What Troy means fairly shall be spoke aloud.
                              [*The trumpet sounds.*]
We have, great Agamemnon, here in Troy   260
A prince called Hector – Priam is his father –
Who in this dull and long-continued truce
Is resty grown. He bade me take a trumpet,
And to this purpose speak: 'Kings, princes, lords,
If there be one among the fair'st of Greece   265
That holds his honour higher than his ease,
That seeks his praise more than he fears his peril,
That knows his valour and knows not his fear,
That loves his mistress more than in confession
With truant vows to her own lips he loves,   270
And dare avow her beauty and her worth
In other arms than hers; to him this challenge:
Hector, in view of Trojans and of Greeks,
Shall make it good, or do his best to do it,
He hath a lady, wiser, fairer, truer,   275
Than ever Greek did compass in his arms;
And will tomorrow with his trumpet call,
Midway between your tents and walls of Troy,
To rouse a Grecian that is true in love.
If any come, Hector shall honour him;   280
If none, he'll say in Troy when he retires,
The Grecian dames are sunburnt, and not worth
The splinter of a lance.' Even so much.
AGAMEMNON
This shall be told our lovers, Lord Aeneas.
If none of them have soul in such a kind,   285
We left them all at home; but we are soldiers,
And may that soldier a mere recreant prove
That means not, hath not, or is not in love.
If then one is, or hath, or means to be,
That one meets Hector; if none else, I'll be he.   290

NESTOR [*to Aeneas*]
Tell him of Nestor, one that was a man
When Hector's grandsire sucked. He is old now;
But if there be not in our Grecian mould
One noble man that hath one spark of fire
295 To answer for his love, tell him from me,
I'll hide my silver beard in a gold beaver
And in my vambrace put this withered brawn;
And, meeting him, will tell him that my lady
Was fairer than his grandam and as chaste
300 As may be in the world. His youth in flood,
I'll prove this truth with my three drops of blood.

AENEAS Now heavens forfend such scarcity of youth!

ULYSSES Amen.

AGAMEMNON Fair Lord Aeneas, let me touch your hand;
305 To our pavilion shall I lead you first.
Achilles shall have word of this intent;
So shall each lord of Greece, from tent to tent.
Yourself shall feast with us before you go
And find the welcome of a noble foe.

As all are leaving, Ulysses detains Nestor.

310 ULYSSES Nestor!

NESTOR What says Ulysses?

ULYSSES I have a young conception in my brain;
Be you my time to bring it to some shape.

NESTOR What is't?

315 ULYSSES This 'tis:
Blunt wedges rive hard knots; the seeded pride
That hath to this maturity blown up
In rank Achilles must or now be cropped
Or, shedding, breed a nursery of like evil
320 To overbulk us all.

NESTOR Well, and how?

ULYSSES This challenge that the gallant Hector sends,
However it is spread in general name,
Relates in purpose only to Achilles.

325 NESTOR The purpose is perspicuous even as substance
Whose grossness little characters sum up;
And in the publication make no strain
But that Achilles, were his brain as barren
As banks of Libya – though, Apollo knows,
330 'Tis dry enough – will with great speed of judgement,
Ay, with celerity, find Hector's purpose
Pointing on him.

ULYSSES And wake him to the answer, think you?

NESTOR Yes, 'tis most meet. Who may you else oppose,
335 That can from Hector bring his honour off,
If not Achilles? Though't be a sportful combat,
Yet in this trial much opinion dwells;
For here the Trojans taste our dear'st repute
With their fin'st palate. And trust to me, Ulysses,
340 Our imputation shall be oddly poised
In this wild action; for the success,
Although particular, shall give a scantling
Of good or bad unto the general,
And in such indexes, although small pricks
345 To their subsequent volumes, there is seen

The baby figure of the giant mass
Of things to come at large. It is supposed
He that meets Hector issues from our choice;
And choice, being mutual act of all our souls,
350 Makes merit her election and doth boil,
As 'twere from forth us all, a man distilled
Out of our virtues; who miscarrying,
What heart from hence receives the conqu'ring part,
To steel a strong opinion to themselves!
355 Which entertained, limbs are his instruments,
In no less working than are swords and bows
Directive by the limbs.

ULYSSES Give pardon to my speech:
Therefore 'tis meet Achilles meet not Hector.
360 Let us, like merchants, show our foulest wares,
And think perchance they'll sell; if not,
The lustre of the better yet to show
Shall show the better. Do not consent
That ever Hector and Achilles meet,
365 For both our honour and our shame in this
Are dogged with two strange followers.

NESTOR
I see them not with my old eyes. What are they?

ULYSSES What glory our Achilles shares from Hector,
Were he not proud, we all should wear with him.
370 But he already is too insolent;
And we were better parch in Afric sun
Than in the pride and salt scorn of his eyes
Should he scape Hector fair. If he were foiled,
Why then we did our main opinion crush
375 In taint of our best man. No, make a lott'ry,
And by device let blockish Ajax draw
The sort to fight with Hector; among ourselves
Give him allowance as the worthier man,
For that will physic the great Myrmidon,
380 Who broils in loud applause, and make him fall
His crest that prouder than blue Iris bends.
If the dull brainless Ajax come safe off,
We'll dress him up in voices; if he fail,
Yet go we under our opinion still
385 That we have better men. But, hit or miss,
Our project's life this shape of sense assumes:
Ajax employed plucks down Achilles' plumes.

NESTOR Now, Ulysses, I begin to relish thy advice,
And I will give a taste of it forthwith
390 To Agamemnon. Go we to him straight.
Two curs shall tame each other; pride alone
Must tar the mastiffs on, as 'twere their bone.

Exeunt.

2.1 *Enter* THERSITES, *followed by* AJAX.
Ajax is having trouble getting the attention of
Thersites, who is no doubt pretending not to hear.

AJAX Thersites!

THERSITES Agamemnon — how if he had boils, full, all
over, generally?

AJAX   Thersites!

5   THERSITES   And those boils did run (say so), did not the general run, then? Were not that a botchy core?

AJAX   Dog!

THERSITES   Then there would come some matter from him. I see none now.

10   AJAX   Thou bitch-wolf's son, canst thou not hear? Feel, then. [*Strikes him.*]

THERSITES   The plague of Greece upon thee, thou mongrel beef-witted lord!

AJAX   Speak, then, thou vinewed'st leaven, speak. I will
15   beat thee into handsomeness.

THERSITES   I shall sooner rail thee into wit and holiness; but I think thy horse will sooner con an oration than thou learn a prayer without book. Thou canst strike, canst thou? A red murrain o'thy jade's tricks!

20   AJAX   Toadstool, learn me the proclamation.

THERSITES   Dost thou think I have no sense, thou strik'st me thus?

AJAX   The proclamation!

THERSITES   Thou art proclaimed a fool, I think.

25   AJAX   Do not, porcupine, do not. My fingers itch.

THERSITES   I would thou didst itch from head to foot. An I had the scratching of thee, I would make thee the loathsomest scab in Greece. When thou art forth in the incursions, thou strikest as slow as another.

30   AJAX   I say, the proclamation!

THERSITES   Thou grumblest and railest every hour on Achilles, and thou art as full of envy at his greatness as Cerberus is at Proserpina's beauty, ay, that thou bark'st at him.

35   AJAX   Mistress Thersites!

THERSITES   Thou shouldst strike him –

AJAX   Cobloaf!

THERSITES   He would pun thee into shivers with his fist, as a sailor breaks a biscuit.

40   AJAX   [*Beats him.*]   You whoreson cur!

THERSITES   Do, do.

AJAX   Thou stool for a witch!

THERSITES   Ay, do, do! Thou sodden-witted lord, thou hast no more brain than I have in mine elbows; an
45   asinico may tutor thee. Thou scurvy-valiant ass, thou art here but to thrash Trojans, and thou art bought and sold among those of any wit, like a barbarian slave. If thou use to beat me, I will begin at thy heel and tell what thou art by inches, thou thing of no bowels,
50   thou!

AJAX   You dog!

THERSITES   You scurvy lord!

AJAX   [*Beats him.*]   You cur!

THERSITES   Mars his idiot! Do, rudeness, do, camel;
55   do, do!

Enter ACHILLES *and* PATROCLUS.

ACHILLES
Why, how now, Ajax, wherefore do ye thus? –
How now, Thersites, what's the matter, man?

THERSITES   You see him there, do you?

ACHILLES   Ay, what's the matter?

THERSITES   Nay, look upon him.   60

ACHILLES   So I do. What's the matter?

THERSITES   Nay, but regard him well.

ACHILLES   Well, why, I do so.

THERSITES   But yet you look not well upon him; for, whosomever you take him to be, he is Ajax.   65

ACHILLES   I know that, fool.

THERSITES   Ay, but that fool knows not himself.

AJAX   Therefore I beat thee.

THERSITES   Lo, lo, lo, lo, what modicums of wit he utters! His evasions have ears thus long. I have bobbed   70
his brain more than he has beat my bones. I will buy nine sparrows for a penny, and his pia mater is not worth the ninth part of a sparrow. This lord, Achilles – Ajax, who wears his wit in his belly and his guts in his head – I'll tell you what I say of him.   75

ACHILLES   What?

THERSITES   I say, this Ajax –

[*Ajax threatens to beat him; Achilles intervenes.*]

ACHILLES   Nay, good Ajax.

THERSITES   Has not so much wit –

ACHILLES   [*to Ajax*]   Nay, I must hold you.   80

THERSITES   As will stop the eye of Helen's needle, for whom he comes to fight.

ACHILLES   Peace, fool!

THERSITES   I would have peace and quietness, but the fool will not – he there, that he. Look you there.   85

AJAX   O thou damned cur, I shall –

ACHILLES   [*to Ajax*]   Will you set your wit to a fool's?

THERSITES   No, I warrant you, for a fool's will shame it.

PATROCLUS   Good words, Thersites.

ACHILLES   What's the quarrel?   90

AJAX   I bade the vile owl go learn me the tenor of the proclamation, and he rails upon me.

THERSITES   I serve thee not.

AJAX   Well, go to, go to.

THERSITES   I serve here voluntary.   95

ACHILLES   Your last service was sufferance, 'twas not voluntary; no man is beaten voluntary. Ajax was here the voluntary, and you as under an impress.

THERSITES   E'en so. A great deal of your wit, too, lies in your sinews, or else there be liars. Hector shall have a   100
great catch an 'a knock out either of your brains. 'A were as good crack a fusty nut with no kernel.

ACHILLES   What, with me too, Thersites?

THERSITES   There's Ulysses and old Nestor – whose wit was mouldy ere your grandsires had nails on their toes   105
– yoke you like draught-oxen and make you plough up the war.

ACHILLES   What? What?

THERSITES   Yes, good sooth. To, Achilles! To, Ajax, to!

AJAX   I shall cut out your tongue.   110

THERSITES   'Tis no matter. I shall speak as much as thou afterwards.

PATROCLUS   No more words, Thersites. Peace!

THERSITES　I will hold my peace when Achilles' brach
115　　bids me, shall I?
ACHILLES　There's for you, Patroclus.
THERSITES　I will see you hanged like clotpolls ere I
　　come any more to your tents. I will keep where there is
　　wit stirring and leave the faction of fools.　　　　*Exit.*
120　PATROCLUS　A good riddance.
ACHILLES [*to Ajax*]
　　Marry, this, sir, is proclaimed through all our host:
　　That Hector, by the fifth hour of the sun,
　　Will with a trumpet 'twixt our tents and Troy
　　Tomorrow morning call some knight to arms
125　　That hath a stomach, and such a one that dare
　　Maintain – I know not what; 'tis trash. Farewell.
AJAX　Farewell. Who shall answer him?
ACHILLES　I know not. 'Tis put to lottery. Otherwise
　　He knew his man.
130　AJAX　O, meaning you? I will go learn more of it.
　　　　　　　　　　　　　　　　　　　　　　Exeunt.

2.2　　　*Enter* PRIAM, HECTOR, TROILUS,
　　　　　　　PARIS *and* HELENUS.

PRIAM　After so many hours, lives, speeches spent,
　　Thus once again says Nestor from the Greeks:
　　'Deliver Helen, and all damage else –
　　As honour, loss of time, travail, expense,
5　　Wounds, friends, and what else dear that is consumed
　　In hot digestion of this cormorant war –
　　Shall be struck off.' Hector, what say you to't?
HECTOR　Though no man lesser fears the Greeks than I
　　As far as toucheth my particular,
10　　Yet, dread Priam,
　　There is no lady of more softer bowels,
　　More spongy to suck in the sense of fear,
　　More ready to cry out 'Who knows what follows?'
　　Than Hector is. The wound of peace is surety,
15　　Surety secure; but modest doubt is called
　　The beacon of the wise, the tent that searches
　　To th' bottom of the worst. Let Helen go.
　　Since the first sword was drawn about this question,
　　Every tithe soul 'mongst many thousand dismes
20　　Hath been as dear as Helen – I mean, of ours.
　　If we have lost so many tenths of ours
　　To guard a thing not ours, nor worth to us
　　(Had it our name) the value of one ten,
　　What merit's in that reason which denies
　　The yielding of her up?
25　TROILUS　　　　　　　Fie, fie, my brother!
　　Weigh you the worth and honour of a king
　　So great as our dread father in a scale
　　Of common ounces? Will you with counters sum
　　The past-proportion of his infinite
30　　And buckle in a waist most fathomless
　　With spans and inches so diminutive
　　As fears and reasons? Fie, for godly shame!
HELENUS　No marvel though you bite so sharp at reasons,

You are so empty of them. Should not our father
Bear the great sway of his affairs with reason,　　　35
Because your speech hath none that tell him so?
TROILUS
You are for dreams and slumbers, brother priest;
You fur your gloves with reason. Here are your reasons:
You know an enemy intends you harm;
You know a sword employed is perilous,　　　40
And reason flies the object of all harm.
Who marvels, then, when Helenus beholds
A Grecian and his sword, if he do set
The very wings of reason to his heels,
And fly like chidden Mercury from Jove,　　　45
Or like a star disorbed? Nay, if we talk of reason,
Let's shut our gates and sleep. Manhood and honour
Should have hare hearts, would they but fat their
　　thoughts
With this crammed reason; reason and respect
Make livers pale and lustihood deject.　　　50
HECTOR　Brother, she is not worth what she doth cost
　　The holding.
TROILUS　　　　What's aught but as 'tis valued?
HECTOR　But value dwells not in particular will;
　　It holds his estimate and dignity
　　As well wherein 'tis precious of itself　　　55
　　As in the prizer. 'Tis mad idolatry
　　To make the service greater than the god;
　　And the will dotes that is inclinable
　　To what infectiously itself affects,
　　Without some image of th'affected merit.　　　60
TROILUS　I take today a wife, and my election
　　Is led on in the conduct of my will,
　　My will enkindled by mine eyes and ears,
　　Two traded pilots 'twixt the dangerous shores
　　Of will and judgement. How may I avoid,　　　65
　　Although my will distaste what it elected,
　　The wife I chose? There can be no evasion
　　To blench from this, and to stand firm by honour.
　　We turn not back the silks upon the merchant
　　When we have soiled them; nor the remainder viands　　　70
　　We do not throw in unrespective sieve
　　Because we now are full. It was thought meet
　　Paris should do some vengeance on the Greeks.
　　Your breath of full consent bellied his sails;
　　The seas and winds, old wranglers, took a truce,　　　75
　　And did him service; he touched the ports desired;
　　And for an old aunt whom the Greeks held captive
　　He brought a Grecian queen, whose youth and freshness
　　Wrinkles Apollo's, and makes stale the morning.
　　Why keep we her? The Grecians keep our aunt.　　　80
　　Is she worth keeping? Why, she is a pearl
　　Whose price hath launched above a thousand ships
　　And turned crowned kings to merchants.
　　If you'll avouch 'twas wisdom Paris went –
　　As you must needs, for you all cried 'Go, go!';　　　85
　　If you'll confess he brought home noble prize –
　　As you must needs, for you all clapped your hands

And cried 'Inestimable!' – why do you now
The issue of your proper wisdoms rate
90   And do a deed that never Fortune did,
Beggar the estimation which you prized
Richer than sea and land? O theft most base,
That we have stol'n what we do fear to keep!
But thieves unworthy of a thing so stol'n,
95   That in their country did them that disgrace
We fear to warrant in our native place!

Enter CASSANDRA, *with her hair about her ears.*

CASSANDRA   Cry, Trojans, cry!
PRIAM   What noise? What shriek is this?
TROILUS   'Tis our mad sister. I do know her voice.
CASSANDRA   Cry, Trojans!
100 HECTOR   It is Cassandra.
CASSANDRA
Cry, Trojans, cry! Lend me ten thousand eyes,
And I will fill them with prophetic tears.
HECTOR   Peace, sister, peace!
CASSANDRA
Virgins and boys, mid-age and wrinkled old,
105 Soft infancy, that nothing canst but cry,
Add to my clamour! Let us pay betimes
A moiety of that mass of moan to come.
Cry, Trojans, cry! Practise your eyes with tears!
Troy must not be, nor goodly Ilium stand;
110 Our firebrand brother Paris burns us all.
Cry, Trojans, cry! A Helen and a woe!
Cry, cry! Troy burns, or else let Helen go.   *Exit.*
HECTOR
Now, youthful Troilus, do not these high strains
Of divination in our sister work
115 Some touches of remorse? Or is your blood
So madly hot that no discourse of reason,
Nor fear of bad success in a bad cause,
Can qualify the same?
TROILUS   Why, brother Hector,
We may not think the justness of each act
120 Such and no other than th'event doth form it,
Nor once deject the courage of our minds
Because Cassandra's mad. Her brain-sick raptures
Cannot distaste the goodness of a quarrel
Which hath our several honours all engaged
125 To make it gracious. For my private part,
I am no more touched than all Priam's sons;
And Jove forbid there should be done amongst us
Such things as might offend the weakest spleen
To fight for and maintain.
130 PARIS   Else might the world convince of levity
As well my undertakings as your counsels.
But I attest the gods, your full consent
Gave wings to my propension, and cut off
All fears attending on so dire a project.
135 For what, alas, can these my single arms?
What propugnation is in one man's valour
To stand the push and enmity of those

This quarrel would excite? Yet I protest,
Were I alone to pass the difficulties
And had as ample power as I have will,   140
Paris should ne'er retract what he hath done
Nor faint in the pursuit.
PRIAM   Paris, you speak
Like one besotted on your sweet delights.
You have the honey still, but these the gall;
So to be valiant is no praise at all.   145
PARIS   Sir, I propose not merely to myself
The pleasures such a beauty brings with it;
But I would have the soil of her fair rape
Wiped off in honourable keeping her.
What treason were it to the ransacked queen,   150
Disgrace to your great worths, and shame to me,
Now to deliver her possession up
On terms of base compulsion! Can it be
That so degenerate a strain as this
Should once set footing in your generous bosoms?   155
There's not the meanest spirit on our party
Without a heart to dare, or sword to draw,
When Helen is defended, nor none so noble
Whose life were ill bestowed, or death unfamed,
Where Helen is the subject. Then, I say,   160
Well may we fight for her whom, we know well,
The world's large spaces cannot parallel.
HECTOR   Paris and Troilus, you have both said well
And on the cause and question now in hand
Have glozed – but superficially, not much   165
Unlike young men, whom Aristotle thought
Unfit to hear moral philosophy.
The reasons you allege do more conduce
To the hot passion of distempered blood
Than to make up a free determination   170
'Twixt right and wrong; for pleasure and revenge
Have ears more deaf than adders to the voice
Of any true decision. Nature craves
All dues be rendered to their owners. Now,
What nearer debt in all humanity   175
Than wife is to the husband? If this law
Of nature be corrupted through affection,
And that great minds, of partial indulgence
To their benumbed wills, resist the same,
There is a law in each well-ordered nation   180
To curb those raging appetites that are
Most disobedient and refractory.
If Helen then be wife to Sparta's king,
As it is known she is, these moral laws
Of nature and of nations speak aloud   185
To have her back returned. Thus to persist
In doing wrong extenuates not wrong,
But makes it much more heavy. Hector's opinion
Is this in way of truth; yet, ne'ertheless,
My sprightly brethren, I propend to you   190
In resolution to keep Helen still;
For 'tis a cause that hath no mean dependence
Upon our joint and several dignities.

TROILUS
Why, there you touched the life of our design!
195   Were it not glory that we more affected
Than the performance of our heaving spleens,
I would not wish a drop of Trojan blood
Spent more in her defence. But, worthy Hector,
She is a theme of honour and renown,
200   A spur to valiant and magnanimous deeds,
Whose present courage may beat down our foes
And fame in time to come canonize us.
For I presume brave Hector would not lose
So rich advantage of a promised glory
205   As smiles upon the forehead of this action
For the wide world's revenue.
HECTOR   I am yours,
You valiant offspring of great Priamus.
I have a roisting challenge sent amongst
The dull and factious nobles of the Greeks
210   Will strike amazement to their drowsy spirits.
I was advertised their great general slept,
Whilst emulation in the army crept.
This, I presume, will wake him.   *Exeunt.*

2.3   *Enter* THERSITES, *alone.*

THERSITES   How now, Thersites? What, lost in the
labyrinth of thy fury? Shall the elephant Ajax carry it
thus? He beats me, and I rail at him. O worthy
satisfaction! Would it were otherwise – that I could
5   beat him whilst he railed at me. 'Sfoot, I'll learn to
conjure and raise devils but I'll see some issue of my
spiteful execrations. Then there's Achilles – a rare
engineer! If Troy be not taken till these two undermine
it, the walls will stand till they fall of themselves. O
10   thou great thunder-darter of Olympus, forget that
thou art Jove, the king of gods; and Mercury, lose all
the serpentine craft of thy caduceus, if ye take not that
little, little, less than little wit from them that they
have! – which short-armed ignorance itself knows is so
15   abundant scarce it will not in circumvention deliver a
fly from a spider without drawing their massy irons
and cutting the web. After this, the vengeance on the
whole camp! Or rather, the Neapolitan bone-ache! For
that, methinks, is the curse dependent on those that
20   war for a placket. I have said my prayers, and devil
Envy say 'Amen'. – What ho! My Lord Achilles!

Enter PATROCLUS *at the entrance of Achilles' tent.*

PATROCLUS   Who's there? Thersites? Good Thersites,
come in and rail.   *Disappears briefly.*
THERSITES   If I could ha' remembered a gilt counterfeit,
25   thou wouldst not have slipped out of my contemplation;
but it is no matter. Thyself upon thyself! The common
curse of mankind, folly and ignorance, be thine in
great revenue! Heaven bless thee from a tutor, and
discipline come not near thee! Let thy blood be thy
30   direction till thy death; then if she that lays thee out

says thou art a fair corpse, I'll be sworn and sworn
upon't she never shrouded any but lazars.

PATROCLUS *reappears.*

Amen. – Where's Achilles?
PATROCLUS   What, art thou devout? Wast thou in
prayer?   35
THERSITES   Ay. The heavens hear me!
PATROCLUS   Amen.

Enter ACHILLES.

ACHILLES   Who's there?
PATROCLUS   Thersites, my lord.
ACHILLES   Where? Where? O, where? – Art thou come?   40
Why, my cheese, my digestion, why hast thou not
served thyself in to my table so many meals? Come,
what's Agamemnon?
THERSITES   Thy commander, Achilles. Then tell me,
Patroclus, what's Achilles?   45
PATROCLUS   Thy lord, Thersites. Then tell me, I pray
thee, what's thyself?
THERSITES   Thy knower, Patroclus. Then tell me,
Patroclus, what art thou?
PATROCLUS   Thou mayst tell that knowest.   50
ACHILLES   O, tell, tell.
THERSITES   I'll decline the whole question. Agamemnon
commands Achilles, Achilles is my lord, I am Patroclus'
knower, and Patroclus is a fool.
PATROCLUS   You rascal!   55
THERSITES   Peace, fool, I have not done.
ACHILLES   He is a privileged man. – Proceed, Thersites.
THERSITES   Agamemnon is a fool, Achilles is a fool,
Thersites is a fool, and, as aforesaid, Patroclus is a fool.
ACHILLES   Derive this. Come.   60
THERSITES   Agamemnon is a fool to offer to command
Achilles, Achilles is a fool to be commanded of
Agamemnon, Thersites is a fool to serve such a fool,
and Patroclus is a fool positive.
PATROCLUS   Why am I a fool?   65
THERSITES   Make that demand to the creator; it suffices
me thou art. Look you, who comes here?

Enter at a distance AGAMEMNON, ULYSSES,
NESTOR, DIOMEDES, AJAX *and* CALCHAS.

ACHILLES   Patroclus, I'll speak with nobody. – Come in
with me, Thersites.   *Exit.*
THERSITES   Here is such patchery, such juggling and   70
such knavery! All the argument is a whore and a
cuckold; a good quarrel to draw emulous factions and
bleed to death upon. Now the dry serpigo on the
subject, and war and lechery confound all!   *Exit.*
AGAMEMNON [*to Patroclus*]   Where is Achilles?   75
PATROCLUS   Within his tent, but ill-disposed, my lord.
AGAMEMNON   Let it be known to him that we are here.
He shent our messengers, and we lay by
Our appertainments, visiting of him.
Let him be told so, lest perchance he think   80

We dare not move the question of our place
Or know not what we are.

PATROCLUS   I shall so say to him.   *Exit.*

ULYSSES   We saw him at the opening of his tent.
85   He is not sick.

AJAX   Yes, lion-sick, sick of proud heart. You may call it
    melancholy, if you will favour the man, but, by my
    head, 'tis pride. But why, why? Let him show us the
    cause. – A word, my lord. [*Takes Agamemnon aside.*]

90 NESTOR   What moves Ajax thus to bay at him?

ULYSSES   Achilles hath inveigled his fool from him.

NESTOR   Who? Thersites?

ULYSSES   He.

NESTOR   Then will Ajax lack matter, if he have lost his
95   argument.

ULYSSES   No. You see, he is his argument that has his
    argument: Achilles.

NESTOR   All the better; their fraction is more our wish
    than their faction. But it was a strong composure a fool
100   could disunite.

ULYSSES   The amity that wisdom knits not, folly may
    easily untie.

Enter PATROCLUS.

Here comes Patroclus.

NESTOR   No Achilles with him.

ULYSSES
105   The elephant hath joints, but none for courtesy;
    His legs are legs for necessity, not for flexure.

PATROCLUS   Achilles bids me say he is much sorry
    If anything more than your sport and pleasure
    Did move your greatness, and this noble state,
110   To call upon him; he hopes it is no other
    But for your health and your digestion sake,
    An after-dinner's breath.

AGAMEMNON   Hear you, Patroclus:
    We are too well acquainted with these answers;
    But his evasion, winged thus swift with scorn,
115   Cannot outfly our apprehensions.
    Much attribute he hath, and much the reason
    Why we ascribe it to him; yet all his virtues,
    Not virtuously on his own part beheld,
    Do in our eyes begin to lose their gloss,
120   Yea, like fair fruit in an unwholesome dish,
    Are like to rot untasted. Go and tell him
    We come to speak with him. And you shall not sin
    If you do say we think him over-proud
    And under-honest, in self-assumption greater
125   Than in the note of judgement; and worthier than
    himself
    Here tend the savage strangeness he puts on,
    Disguise the holy strength of their command,
    And underwrite in an observing kind
    His humorous predominance – yea, watch
130   His pettish lunes, his ebbs, his flows, as if
    The passage and whole carriage of this action
    Rode on his tide. Go tell him this, and add

That if he overhold his price so much,
We'll none of him, but let him, like an engine
Not portable, lie under this report: 135
'Bring action hither; this cannot go to war'.
A stirring dwarf we do allowance give
Before a sleeping giant. Tell him so.

PATROCLUS   I shall, and bring his answer presently.

AGAMEMNON   In second voice we'll not be satisfied;   140
We come to speak with him. – Ulysses, enter you.

Exit Ulysses following Patroclus.

AJAX   What is he more than another?

AGAMEMNON   No more than what he thinks he is.

AJAX   Is he so much? Do you not think he thinks himself
a better man than I am?   145

AGAMEMNON   No question.

AJAX   Will you subscribe his thought, and say he is?

AGAMEMNON   No, noble Ajax. You are as strong, as
valiant, as wise, no less noble, much more gentle, and
altogether more tractable.   150

AJAX   Why should a man be proud? How doth pride
grow? I know not what pride is.

AGAMEMNON   Your mind is the clearer, Ajax, and your
virtues the fairer. He that is proud eats up himself.
Pride is his own glass, his own trumpet, his own   155
chronicle; and whatever praises itself but in the deed
devours the deed in the praise.

Enter ULYSSES.

AJAX   I do hate a proud man as I hate the engendering of
toads.

NESTOR [*aside*]   Yet he loves himself. Is't not strange? 160

ULYSSES   Achilles will not to the field tomorrow.

AGAMEMNON   What's his excuse?

ULYSSES   He doth rely on none,
But carries on the stream of his dispose,
Without observance or respect of any,
In will peculiar and in self-admission.   165

AGAMEMNON   Why, will he not, upon our fair request,
Untent his person and share the air with us?

ULYSSES
Things small as nothing, for request's sake only,
He makes important. Possessed he is with greatness
And speaks not to himself but with a pride   170
That quarrels at self-breath. Imagined worth
Holds in his blood such swoll'n and hot discourse
That 'twixt his mental and his active parts
Kingdomed Achilles in commotion rages
And batters down himself. What should I say?   175
He is so plaguy proud that the death-tokens of it
Cry 'No recovery'.

AGAMEMNON   Let Ajax go to him. –
Dear lord, go you and greet him in his tent.
'Tis said he holds you well and will be led,
At your request, a little from himself.   180

ULYSSES   O Agamemnon, let it not be so!
We'll consecrate the steps that Ajax makes
When they go from Achilles. Shall the proud lord

That bastes his arrogance with his own seam
185 And never suffers matter of the world
     Enter his thoughts, save such as doth revolve
     And ruminate himself – shall he be worshipped
     Of that we hold an idol more than he?
     No; this thrice-worthy and right valiant lord
190 Must not so stale his palm, nobly acquired,
     Nor, by my will, assubjugate his merit,
     As amply titled as Achilles' is,
     By going to Achilles.
     That were to enlard his fat-already pride,
195 And add more coals to Cancer when he burns
     With entertaining great Hyperion.
     This lord go to him? Jupiter forbid,
     And say in thunder: 'Achilles, go to him'.

NESTOR [*aside to Diomedes*]
     O, this is well. He rubs the vein of him.

DIOMEDES [*aside to Nestor*]
200 And how his silence drinks up this applause!

AJAX   If I go to him, with my armed fist
       I'll pash him o'er the face.

AGAMEMNON   O, no, you shall not go.

AJAX   An 'a be proud with me, I'll feeze his pride.
205   Let me go to him.

ULYSSES
       Not for the worth that hangs upon our quarrel.

AJAX   A paltry, insolent fellow!

NESTOR [*aside*]   How he describes himself!

AJAX   Can he not be sociable?

210 ULYSSES [*aside*]   The raven chides blackness.

AJAX   I'll let his humorous blood.

AGAMEMNON [*aside*]   He will be the physician that
       should be the patient.

AJAX   An all men were o' my mind –

215 ULYSSES [*aside*]   Wit would be out of fashion.

AJAX   – 'a should not bear it so. 'A should eat swords
       first. Shall pride carry it?

NESTOR [*aside*]   An 'twould, you'd carry half.

ULYSSES [*aside*]   'A would have ten shares.

220 AJAX   I will knead him; I'll make him supple.

NESTOR [*aside*]   He's not yet through warm. Farce him
       with praises. Pour in, pour in! His ambition is dry.

ULYSSES [*to Agamemnon*]
       My lord, you feed too much on this dislike.

NESTOR [*to Agamemnon*]
       Our noble general, do not do so.

DIOMEDES [*to Agamemnon*]
225   You must prepare to fight without Achilles.

ULYSSES   Why, 'tis this naming of him does him harm.
       Here is a man – but 'tis before his face;
       I will be silent.

NESTOR   Wherefore should you so?
       He is not emulous, as Achilles is.

230 ULYSSES   Know the whole world, he is as valiant –

AJAX   A whoreson dog, that shall palter thus with us!
       Would he were a Trojan!

NESTOR   What a vice were it in Ajax now –

ULYSSES   If he were proud –

DIOMEDES   Or covetous of praise –

ULYSSES   Ay, or surly borne –

DIOMEDES   Or strange, or self-affected.   235

ULYSSES [*to Ajax*]
       Thank the heavens, lord, thou art of sweet composure.
       Praise him that got thee, she that gave thee suck;
       Famed be thy tutor, and thy parts of nature
       Thrice-famed beyond, beyond all erudition!
       But he that disciplined thine arms to fight,   240
       Let Mars divide eternity in twain
       And give him half; and for thy vigour,
       Bull-bearing Milo his addition yield
       To sinewy Ajax! I will not praise thy wisdom,
       Which, like a bourn, a pale, a shore, confines   245
       Thy spacious and dilated parts. Here's Nestor,
       Instructed by the antiquary times;
       He must, he is, he cannot but be wise.
       But pardon, father Nestor, were your days
       As green as Ajax' and your brain so tempered,   250
       You should not have the eminence of him,
       But be as Ajax.

AJAX   Shall I call you father?

ULYSSES   Ay, my good son.

DIOMEDES   Be ruled by him, Lord Ajax.

ULYSSES   There is no tarrying here; the hart Achilles
       Keeps thicket. Please it our great general   255
       To call together all his state of war.
       Fresh kings are come to Troy; tomorrow
       We must with all our main of power stand fast.
       And here's a lord – come knights from east to west,
       And cull their flower, Ajax shall cope the best.   260

AGAMEMNON   Go we to council. Let Achilles sleep.
       Light boats sail swift, though greater hulks draw deep.
                                               Exeunt.

3.1   *Music sounds within. Enter* PANDARUS
             and a Servant.

PANDARUS   Friend, you, pray you, a word. Do not you
       follow the young Lord Paris?

SERVANT   Ay, sir, when he goes before me.

PANDARUS   You depend upon him, I mean.

SERVANT   Sir, I do depend upon the Lord.   5

PANDARUS   You depend upon a notable gentleman; I
       must needs praise him.

SERVANT   The Lord be praised!

PANDARUS   You know me, do you not?

SERVANT   Faith, sir, superficially.   10

PANDARUS   Friend, know me better: I am the Lord
       Pandarus.

SERVANT   I hope I shall know your honour better.

PANDARUS   I do desire it.

SERVANT   You are in the state of grace?   15

PANDARUS   Grace? Not so, friend. 'Honour' and
       'lordship' are my titles. What music is this?

SERVANT   I do but partly know, sir: it is music in parts.

PANDARUS   Know you the musicians?

20 SERVANT   Wholly, sir.

PANDARUS   Who play they to?

SERVANT   To the hearers, sir.

PANDARUS   At whose pleasure, friend?

SERVANT   At mine, sir, and theirs that love music.

25 PANDARUS   'Command', I mean, friend.

SERVANT   Who shall I command, sir?

PANDARUS   Friend, we understand not one another: I am too courtly and thou too cunning. At whose request do these men play?

30 SERVANT   That's to't indeed, sir. Marry, sir, at the request of Paris my lord, who is there in person; with him, the mortal Venus, the heart-blood of beauty, love's visible soul –

PANDARUS   Who, my cousin Cressida?

35 SERVANT   No, sir, Helen. Could not you find out that by her attributes?

PANDARUS   It should seem, fellow, thou hast not seen the Lady Cressid. I come to speak with Paris from the Prince Troilus. I will make a complimental assault

40 upon him, for my business seethes.

SERVANT   Sodden business! There's a stewed phrase indeed.

Enter PARIS *and* HELEN *attended by Musicians.*

PANDARUS   Fair be to you, my lord, and to all this fair company! Fair desires, in all fair measure, fairly guide

45 them! – especially to you, fair queen. Fair thoughts be your fair pillow!

HELEN   Dear lord, you are full of fair words.

PANDARUS   You speak your fair pleasure, sweet queen. [*to Paris*] Fair prince, here is good broken music.

50 PARIS   You have broke it, cousin, and, by my life, you shall make it whole again; you shall piece it out with a piece of your performance. – Nell, he is full of harmony.

PANDARUS   Truly, lady, no.

HELEN   O, sir!

55 PANDARUS   Rude, in sooth; in good sooth, very rude.

PARIS   Well said, my lord. Well, you say so in fits.

PANDARUS   I have business to my lord, dear queen. – My lord, will you vouchsafe me a word?

HELEN   Nay, this shall not hedge us out. We'll hear you

60 sing, certainly.

PANDARUS   Well, sweet queen, you are pleasant with me. – But, marry, thus, my lord: my dear lord and most esteemed friend, your brother Troilus –

HELEN   My Lord Pandarus, honey-sweet lord –

65 PANDARUS   Go to, sweet queen, go to – commends himself most affectionately to you.

HELEN   You shall not bob us out of our melody. If you do, our melancholy upon your head!

PANDARUS   Sweet queen, sweet queen, that's a sweet

70 queen, i'faith –

HELEN   And to make a sweet lady sad is a sour offence.

PANDARUS   Nay, that shall not serve your turn, that shall it not, in truth, la. Nay, I care not for such words,

no, no. – And, my lord, he desires you that if the King call for him at supper, you will make his excuse. 75

HELEN   My Lord Pandarus –

PANDARUS   What says my sweet queen, my very very sweet queen?

PARIS   What exploit's in hand? Where sups he tonight?

HELEN   Nay, but, my lord – 80

PANDARUS   What says my sweet queen? My cousin will fall out with you.

HELEN   [*to Paris*]   You must not know where he sups.

PARIS   I'll lay my life, with my disposer Cressida.

PANDARUS   No, no, no such matter, you are wide. Come, 85

your disposer is sick.

PARIS   Well, I'll make 's excuse.

PANDARUS   Ay, good my lord. Why should you say Cressida? No, your poor disposer's sick.

PARIS   I spy. 90

PANDARUS   You spy? What do you spy? – Come, give me an instrument. [*He is handed a musical instrument.*] Now, sweet queen.

HELEN   Why, this is kindly done.

PANDARUS   My niece is horribly in love with a thing you 95

have, sweet queen.

HELEN   She shall have it, my lord, if it be not my Lord Paris.

PANDARUS   He? No, she'll none of him. They two are twain. 100

HELEN   Falling in after falling out may make them three.

PANDARUS   Come, come, I'll hear no more of this. I'll sing you a song now.

HELEN   Ay, ay, prithee. Now by my troth, sweet lord, thou hast a fine forehead. 105

PANDARUS   Ay, you may, you may.

HELEN   Let thy song be love. 'This love will undo us all.' O Cupid, Cupid, Cupid!

PANDARUS   Love? Ay, that it shall, i'faith.

PARIS   Ay, good now, 'Love, love, nothing but love'. 110

PANDARUS   In good truth, it begins so.

[*Sings.*]
Love, love, nothing but love, still love, still more!
    For, O, love's bow
    Shoots buck and doe.
    The shaft confounds 115
    Not that it wounds,
But tickles still the sore.

These lovers cry, 'O! O!', they die!
Yet that which seems the wound to kill
Doth turn 'O! O!' to 'Ha, ha, he!' 120
    So dying love lives still.
    'O! O!' a while, but 'Ha, ha, ha!'
    'O! O!' groans out for 'Ha, ha, ha!' –
Heigh-ho!

HELEN   In love, i'faith, to the very tip of the nose. 125

PARIS   He eats nothing but doves, love, and that breeds hot blood, and hot blood begets hot thoughts, and hot thoughts beget hot deeds, and hot deeds is love.

PANDARUS   Is this the generation of love? Hot blood, hot
130   thoughts and hot deeds? Why, they are vipers. Is love a
generation of vipers? – Sweet lord, who's afield today?
PARIS   Hector, Deiphobus, Helenus, Antenor and all the
gallantry of Troy. I would fain have armed today, but
my Nell would not have it so. How chance my brother
135   Troilus went not?
HELEN   He hangs the lip at something. – You know all,
Lord Pandarus.
PANDARUS   Not I, honey-sweet queen. I long to hear
how they sped today. – You'll remember your brother's
140   excuse?
PARIS   To a hair.
PANDARUS   Farewell, sweet queen.
HELEN   Commend me to your niece.
PANDARUS   I will, sweet queen.   *Exit. Sound a retreat.*
145 PARIS   They're come from field. Let us to Priam's hall
To greet the warriors. Sweet Helen, I must woo you
To help unarm our Hector. His stubborn buckles,
With these your white enchanting fingers touched,
Shall more obey than to the edge of steel
150   Or force of Greekish sinews. You shall do more
Than all the island kings: disarm great Hector.
HELEN   'Twill make us proud to be his servant, Paris.
Yea, what he shall receive of us in duty
Gives us more palm in beauty than we have,
155   Yea, overshines ourself.
PARIS   Sweet, above thought I love thee.   *Exeunt.*

3.2   *Enter* PANDARUS *and Troilus'* Boy, *meeting.*

PANDARUS   How now, where's thy master? At my cousin
Cressida's?
BOY   No, sir, he stays for you to conduct him thither.

Enter TROILUS.

PANDARUS   O, here he comes. – How now, how now?
5 TROILUS [*to his Boy*]   Sirrah, walk off.   *Exit Boy.*
PANDARUS   Have you seen my cousin?
TROILUS   No, Pandarus. I stalk about her door
Like a strange soul upon the Stygian banks
Staying for waftage. O, be thou my Charon,
10   And give me swift transportation to those fields
Where I may wallow in the lily-beds
Proposed for the deserver! O gentle Pandar,
From Cupid's shoulder pluck his painted wings
And fly with me to Cressid!
15 PANDARUS   Walk here i'th' orchard. I'll bring her straight.
Exit.
TROILUS   I am giddy; expectation whirls me round.
Th'imaginary relish is so sweet
That it enchants my sense. What will it be,
When that the wat'ry palates taste indeed
20   Love's thrice-repured nectar? Death, I fear me,
Swooning destruction, or some joy too fine,
Too subtle-potent, tuned too sharp in sweetness,
For the capacity of my ruder powers.

I fear it much; and I do fear besides
That I shall lose distinction in my joys,   25
As doth a battle, when they charge on heaps
The enemy flying.

Enter PANDARUS.

PANDARUS   She's making her ready; she'll come straight.
You must be witty now. She does so blush, and fetches
her wind so short, as if she were frayed with a sprite.   30
I'll fetch her. It is the prettiest villain! She fetches her
breath as short as a new-ta'en sparrow.   *Exit.*
TROILUS   Even such a passion doth embrace my bosom.
My heart beats thicker than a feverous pulse,
And all my powers do their bestowing lose,   35
Like vassalage at unawares encount'ring
The eye of majesty.

Enter PANDARUS, *and* CRESSIDA *veiled.*

PANDARUS   Come, come, what need you blush? Shame's
a baby. [*to Troilus*] Here she is now. Swear the oaths
now to her that you have sworn to me. [*Cressida draws*   40
back.] What, are you gone again? You must be watched
ere you be made tame, must you? Come your ways,
come your ways; an you draw backward, we'll put you
i'th' thills. [*to Troilus*] Why do you not speak to her? [*to*
Cressida] Come, draw this curtain, and let's see your   45
picture. [*She is unveiled.*] Alas the day, how loath you
are to offend daylight! An 'twere dark, you'd close
sooner. [*to Troilus*] So, so, rub on, and kiss the mistress.
[*They kiss.*] How now, a kiss in fee-farm? Build there,
carpenter, the air is sweet. Nay, you shall fight your   50
hearts out ere I part you. The falcon as the tercel, for
all the ducks i'the river. Go to, go to.
TROILUS   You have bereft me of all words, lady.
PANDARUS   Words pay no debts; give her deeds. But
she'll bereave you o'the deeds too, if she call your   55
activity in question. [*They kiss.*] What, billing again?
Here's 'In witness whereof the parties interchangeably'.
Come in, come in. I'll go get a fire.   *Exit.*
CRESSIDA   Will you walk in, my lord?
TROILUS   O Cressida, how often have I wished me thus!   60
CRESSIDA   Wished, my lord? The gods grant – O my
lord!
TROILUS   What should they grant? What makes this
pretty abruption? What too-curious dreg espies my
sweet lady in the fountain of our love?   65
CRESSIDA   More dregs than water, if my fears have eyes.
TROILUS   Fears make devils of cherubims; they never
see truly.
CRESSIDA   Blind fear, that seeing reason leads, finds
safer footing than blind reason, stumbling without   70
fear. To fear the worst oft cures the worse.
TROILUS   O, let my lady apprehend no fear. In all
Cupid's pageant there is presented no monster.
CRESSIDA   Nor nothing monstrous neither?
TROILUS   Nothing but our undertakings, when we vow   75
to weep seas, live in fire, eat rocks, tame tigers, thinking

it harder for our mistress to devise imposition enough
than for us to undergo any difficulty imposed. This is
the monstruosity in love, lady, that the will is infinite
and the execution confined; that the desire is boundless
and the act a slave to limit.

CRESSIDA   They say all lovers swear more performance
than they are able, and yet reserve an ability that they
never perform, vowing more than the perfection of ten
and discharging less than the tenth part of one. They
that have the voice of lions and the act of hares, are
they not monsters?

TROILUS   Are there such? Such are not we. Praise us as
we are tasted, allow us as we prove. Our head shall go
bare till merit crown it. No perfection in reversion shall
have a praise in present. We will not name desert before
his birth, and, being born, his addition shall be humble.
Few words to fair faith. Troilus shall be such to Cressid
as what envy can say worst shall be a mock for his truth,
and what truth can speak truest not truer than Troilus.

CRESSIDA   Will you walk in, my lord?

Enter PANDARUS.

PANDARUS   What, blushing still? Have you not done
talking yet?

CRESSIDA   Well, uncle, what folly I commit, I dedicate
to you.

PANDARUS   I thank you for that. If my lord get a boy of
you, you'll give him me. Be true to my lord. If he
flinch, chide me for it.

TROILUS *[to Cressida]*   You know now your hostages:
your uncle's word and my firm faith.

PANDARUS   Nay, I'll give my word for her too. Our
kindred, though they be long ere they be wooed, they
are constant being won. They are burs, I can tell you;
they'll stick where they are thrown.

CRESSIDA
Boldness comes to me now, and brings me heart.
Prince Troilus, I have loved you night and day
For many weary months.

TROILUS   Why was my Cressid then so hard to win?

CRESSIDA   Hard to seem won; but I was won, my lord,
With the first glance that ever – pardon me;
If I confess much, you will play the tyrant.
I love you now, but till now not so much
But I might master it. In faith, I lie;
My thoughts were like unbridled children, grown
Too headstrong for their mother. See, we fools!
Why have I blabbed? Who shall be true to us
When we are so unsecret to ourselves?
But though I loved you well, I wooed you not;
And yet, good faith, I wished myself a man,
Or that we women had men's privilege
Of speaking first. Sweet, bid me hold my tongue,
For in this rapture I shall surely speak
The thing I shall repent. See, see, your silence,
Cunning in dumbness, in my weakness draws
My soul of counsel from me! Stop my mouth.

TROILUS   And shall, albeit sweet music issues thence.
[Kisses her.]

PANDARUS   Pretty, i'faith.

CRESSIDA *[to Troilus]*
My lord, I do beseech you, pardon me;
'Twas not my purpose thus to beg a kiss.
I am ashamed. O heavens, what have I done?
For this time will I take my leave, my lord.

TROILUS   Your leave, sweet Cressid?

PANDARUS   Leave? An you take leave till tomorrow
morning –

CRESSIDA   Pray you, content you.

TROILUS   What offends you, lady?

CRESSIDA   Sir, mine own company.

TROILUS   You cannot shun yourself.

CRESSIDA   Let me go and try.
I have a kind of self resides with you,
But an unkind self that itself will leave
To be another's fool. Where is my wit?
I would be gone. I speak I know not what.

TROILUS
Well know they what they speak that speak so wisely.

CRESSIDA
Perchance, my lord, I show more craft than love
And fell so roundly to a large confession
To angle for your thoughts. But you are wise,
Or else you love not, for to be wise and love
Exceeds man's might; that dwells with gods above.

TROILUS   O, that I thought it could be in a woman –
As, if it can, I will presume in you –
To feed for aye her lamp and flames of love,
To keep her constancy in plight and youth,
Outliving beauty's outward, with a mind
That doth renew swifter than blood decays!
Or that persuasion could but thus convince me
That my integrity and truth to you
Might be affronted with the match and weight
Of such a winnowed purity in love;
How were I then uplifted! But alas,
I am as true as truth's simplicity,
And simpler than the infancy of truth.

CRESSIDA   In that I'll war with you.

TROILUS   O virtuous fight,
When right with right wars who shall be most right!
True swains in love shall in the world to come
Approve their truth by Troilus. When their rhymes,
Full of protest, of oath and big compare,
Wants similes, truth tired with iteration –
'As true as steel, as plantage to the moon,
As sun to day, as turtle to her mate,
As iron to adamant, as earth to th' centre' –
Yet, after all comparisons of truth,
As truth's authentic author to be cited,
'As true as Troilus' shall crown up the verse
And sanctify the numbers.

CRESSIDA   Prophet may you be!
If I be false, or swerve a hair from truth,

When time is old and hath forgot itself,
When waterdrops have worn the stones of Troy,
And blind oblivion swallowed cities up,
And mighty states characterless are grated
185 To dusty nothing, yet let memory,
From false to false, among false maids in love,
Upbraid my falsehood! When they've said 'As false
As air, as water, wind, or sandy earth,
As fox to lamb, or wolf to heifer's calf,
190 Pard to the hind, or stepdame to her son',
Yea, let them say, to stick the heart of falsehood,
'As false as Cressid'.
PANDARUS   Go to, a bargain made. Seal it, seal it; I'll be
the witness. Here I hold your hand, here my cousin's.
195 If ever you prove false one to another, since I have
taken such pains to bring you together, let all pitiful
goers-between be called to the world's end after my
name: call them all panders. Let all constant men be
Troiluses, all false women Cressids, and all brokers
200 between panders! Say 'Amen'.
TROILUS   Amen.
CRESSIDA   Amen.
PANDARUS   Amen. Whereupon I will show you a
chamber with a bed; which bed, because it shall not
205 speak of your pretty encounters, press it to death. Away!
                    Exeunt Troilus and Cressida.
And Cupid grant all tongue-tied maidens here
Bed, chamber, pander to provide this gear!   *Exit.*

3.3   *Flourish. Enter* ULYSSES, DIOMEDES,
NESTOR, AGAMEMNON, AJAX, MENELAUS
and CALCHAS.

CALCHAS
Now, princes, for the service I have done you,
Th'advantage of the time prompts me aloud
To call for recompense. Appear it to your mind
That, through the sight I bear in things to come,
5 I have abandoned Troy, left my possessions,
Incurred a traitor's name, exposed myself,
From certain and possessed conveniences,
To doubtful fortunes, sequest'ring from me all
That time, acquaintance, custom and condition
10 Made tame and most familiar to my nature;
And here, to do you service, am become
As new into the world, strange, unacquainted.
I do beseech you, as in way of taste,
To give me now a little benefit
15 Out of those many registered in promise
Which, you say, live to come in my behalf.
AGAMEMNON
What wouldst thou of us, Trojan, make demand?
CALCHAS   You have a Trojan prisoner, called Antenor,
Yesterday took. Troy holds him very dear.
20 Oft have you – often have you thanks therefor –
Desired my Cressid in right great exchange,

Whom Troy hath still denied; but this Antenor,
I know, is such a wrest in their affairs
That their negotiations all must slack,
Wanting his manage; and they will almost   25
Give us a prince of blood, a son of Priam,
In change of him. Let him be sent, great princes,
And he shall buy my daughter; and her presence
Shall quite strike off all service I have done
In most accepted pain.
AGAMEMNON   Let Diomedes bear him,   30
And bring us Cressid hither; Calchas shall have
What he requests of us. Good Diomed,
Furnish you fairly for this interchange;
Withal, bring word if Hector will tomorrow
Be answered in his challenge. Ajax is ready.   35
DIOMEDES   This shall I undertake, and 'tis a burden
Which I am proud to bear.   *Exit with Calchas.*

ACHILLES *and* PATROCLUS *stand in their tent.*

ULYSSES   Achilles stands i'th' entrance of his tent.
Please it our general pass strangely by him,
As if he were forgot; and, princes all,   40
Lay negligent and loose regard upon him.
I will come last. 'Tis like he'll question me
Why such unplausive eyes are bent, why turned on him.
If so, I have derision medicinable
To use between your strangeness and his pride,   45
Which his own will shall have desire to drink.
It may do good. Pride hath no other glass
To show itself but pride; for supple knees
Feed arrogance, and are the proud man's fees.
AGAMEMNON   We'll execute your purpose, and put on   50
A form of strangeness as we pass along.
So do each lord, and either greet him not
Or else disdainfully, which shall shake him more
Than if not looked on. I will lead the way.
          [They proceed in turn past Achilles' tent.]
ACHILLES   What, comes the general to speak with me?   55
You know my mind: I'll fight no more 'gainst Troy.
AGAMEMNON *[to Nestor]*
What says Achilles? Would he aught with us?
NESTOR *[to Achilles]*
Would you, my lord, aught with the general?
ACHILLES   No.
NESTOR *[to Agamemnon]* Nothing, my lord.   60
AGAMEMNON   The better.
                    Exeunt Agamemnon and Nestor.
ACHILLES *[to Menelaus]*   Good day, good day.
MENELAUS   How do you? How do you?   *Exit.*
ACHILLES *[to Patroclus]*   What, does the cuckold scorn
me?   65
AJAX   How now, Patroclus?
ACHILLES   Good morrow, Ajax.
AJAX   Ha?
ACHILLES   Good morrow.
AJAX   Ay, and good next day too.   *Exit.*   70
          [Ulysses remains behind, reading.]

ACHILLES [*to Patroclus*]
    What mean these fellows? Know they not Achilles?
PATROCLUS
    They pass by strangely. They were used to bend,
    To send their smiles before them to Achilles,
    To come as humbly as they use to creep
    To holy altars.
75 ACHILLES   What, am I poor of late?
    'Tis certain, greatness, once fall'n out with
        fortune,
    Must fall out with men too. What the declined is
    He shall as soon read in the eyes of others
    As feel in his own fall; for men, like butterflies,
80   Show not their mealy wings but to the summer,
    And not a man, for being simply man,
    Hath any honour, but honour for those honours
    That are without him – as place, riches and favour,
    Prizes of accident as oft as merit;
85   Which when they fall, as being slippery standers,
    The love that leaned on them as slippery too
    Doth one pluck down another and together
    Die in the fall. But 'tis not so with me;
    Fortune and I are friends. I do enjoy
90   At ample point all that I did possess,
    Save these men's looks, who do, methinks, find out
    Something not worth in me such rich beholding
    As they have often given. Here is Ulysses;
    I'll interrupt his reading. – How now, Ulysses?
95 ULYSSES   Now, great Thetis' son!
ACHILLES   What are you reading?
ULYSSES   A strange fellow here
    Writes me that man, how dearly ever parted,
    How much in having, or without or in,
100   Cannot make boast to have that which he hath,
    Nor feels not what he owes, but by reflection;
    As when his virtues, shining upon others,
    Heat them, and they retort that heat again
    To the first givers.
ACHILLES   This is not strange, Ulysses.
105   The beauty that is borne here in the face
    The bearer knows not, but commends itself
    To others' eyes; nor doth the eye itself,
    That most pure spirit of sense, behold itself,
    Not going from itself, but eye to eye opposed
110   Salutes each other with each other's form.
    For speculation turns not to itself
    Till it hath travelled and is mirrored there
    Where it may see itself. This is not strange at all.
ULYSSES   I do not strain at the position –
115   It is familiar – but at the author's drift,
    Who in his circumstance expressly proves
    That no man is the lord of anything,
    Though in and of him there be much consisting,
    Till he communicate his parts to others;
120   Nor doth he of himself know them for aught
    Till he behold them formed in th'applause
    Where they're extended – who, like an arch, reverb'rate

    The voice again, or, like a gate of steel
    Fronting the sun, receives and renders back
    His figure and his heat. I was much rapt in this,   125
    And apprehended here immediately
    Th'unknown Ajax. Heavens, what a man is there!
    A very horse, that has he knows not what.
    Nature, what things there are
    Most abject in regard and dear in use!   130
    What things again most dear in the esteem
    And poor in worth! Now shall we see tomorrow
    An act that very chance doth throw upon him.
    Ajax renowned? O heavens, what some men do,
    While some men leave to do!   135
    How some men creep in skittish Fortune's hall,
    Whiles others play the idiots in her eyes!
    How one man eats into another's pride,
    While pride is fasting in his wantonness!
    To see these Grecian lords! Why, even already   140
    They clap the lubber Ajax on the shoulder,
    As if his foot were on brave Hector's breast,
    And great Troy shrinking.
ACHILLES   I do believe it; for they passed by me
    As misers do by beggars, neither gave to me   145
    Good word nor look. What, are my deeds forgot?
ULYSSES   Time hath, my lord, a wallet at his back,
    Wherein he puts alms for oblivion,
    A great-sized monster of ingratitudes.
    Those scraps are good deeds past, which are   150
    Devoured as fast as they are made, forgot
    As soon as done. Perseverance, dear my lord,
    Keeps honour bright; to have done is to hang
    Quite out of fashion, like a rusty mail
    In monumental mock'ry. Take the instant way,   155
    For honour travels in a strait so narrow
    Where one but goes abreast. Keep then the path,
    For emulation hath a thousand sons,
    That one by one pursue. If you give way,
    Or hedge aside from the direct forthright,   160
    Like to an entered tide they all rush by
    And leave you hindmost;
    Or, like a gallant horse fall'n in first rank,
    Lie there for pavement to the abject rear,
    O'er-run and trampled on. Then what they do in
        present,   165
    Though less than yours in past, must o'ertop yours;
    For Time is like a fashionable host
    That slightly shakes his parting guest by th' hand,
    And, with his arms outstretched as he would fly,
    Grasps in the comer. Welcome ever smiles,   170
    And Farewell goes out sighing. O, let not virtue seek
    Remuneration for the thing it was;
    For beauty, wit,
    High birth, vigour of bone, desert in service,
    Love, friendship, charity, are subjects all   175
    To envious and calumniating Time.
    One touch of nature makes the whole world kin,
    That all with one consent praise new-born gauds,

Though they are made and moulded of things past,
180　And give to dust that is a little gilt
More laud than gilt o'er-dusted.
The present eye praises the present object.
Then marvel not, thou great and complete man,
That all the Greeks begin to worship Ajax,
185　Since things in motion sooner catch the eye
Than what not stirs. The cry went once on thee,
And still it might, and yet it may again,
If thou wouldst not entomb thyself alive
And case thy reputation in thy tent,
190　Whose glorious deeds but in these fields of late
Made emulous missions 'mongst the gods themselves
And drave great Mars to faction.

ACHILLES　　　　　　　　　　　　Of this my privacy
I have strong reasons.

ULYSSES　　　　　　　　　　But 'gainst your privacy
The reasons are more potent and heroical.
195　'Tis known, Achilles, that you are in love
With one of Priam's daughters.

ACHILLES　　Ha? Known?

ULYSSES　　Is that a wonder?
The providence that's in a watchful state
200　Knows almost every grain of Pluto's gold,
Finds bottom in th'uncomprehensive deeps,
Keeps place with thought, and almost, like the gods,
Do thoughts unveil in their dumb cradles.
There is a mystery – with whom relation
205　Durst never meddle – in the soul of state,
Which hath an operation more divine
Than breath or pen can give expressure to.
All the commerce that you have had with Troy
As perfectly is ours as yours, my lord;
210　And better would it fit Achilles much
To throw down Hector than Polyxena.
But it must grieve young Pyrrhus now at home,
When Fame shall in our islands sound her trump
And all the Greekish girls shall tripping sing:
215　'Great Hector's sister did Achilles win,
But our great Ajax bravely beat down him'.
Farewell, my lord. I as your lover speak;
The fool slides o'er the ice that you should break.　*Exit.*

PATROCLUS　To this effect, Achilles, have I moved you.
220　A woman impudent and mannish grown
Is not more loathed than an effeminate man
In time of action. I stand condemned for this;
They think my little stomach to the war,
And your great love to me, restrains you thus.
225　Sweet, rouse yourself, and the weak wanton Cupid
Shall from your neck unloose his amorous fold
And, like a dew-drop from the lion's mane,
Be shook to air.

ACHILLES　　　　　　　Shall Ajax fight with Hector?

PATROCLUS
Ay, and perhaps receive much honour by him.
230　ACHILLES　I see my reputation is at stake.
My fame is shrewdly gored.

PATROCLUS　　　　　　　　　O, then, beware!
Those wounds heal ill that men do give themselves.
Omission to do what is necessary
Seals a commission to a blank of danger,
And danger, like an ague, subtly taints　　　　　235
Even then when we sit idly in the sun.

ACHILLES　Go call Thersites hither, sweet Patroclus.
I'll send the fool to Ajax and desire him
T'invite the Trojan lords after the combat
To see us here unarmed. I have a woman's longing,　240
An appetite that I am sick withal,
To see great Hector in his weeds of peace,

Enter THERSITES.

To talk with him, and to behold his visage
Even to my full of view. – A labour saved.

THERSITES　A wonder!　　　　　　　　　　　　245

ACHILLES　What?

THERSITES　Ajax goes up and down the field, asking for
himself.

ACHILLES　How so?

THERSITES　He must fight singly tomorrow with　250
Hector, and is so prophetically proud of an heroical
cudgelling that he raves in saying nothing.

ACHILLES　How can that be?

THERSITES　Why, 'a stalks up and down like a peacock –
a stride and a stand; ruminates like an hostess that hath　255
no arithmetic but her brain to set down her reckoning;
bites his lip with a politic regard, as who should say,
'There were wit in this head, an 'twould out' – and so
there is, but it lies as coldly in him as fire in a flint,
which will not show without knocking. The man's　260
undone for ever, for if Hector break not his neck i'th'
combat, he'll break't himself in vainglory. He knows
not me. I said, 'Good morrow, Ajax', and he replies,
'Thanks, Agamemnon'. What think you of this man,
that takes me for the general? He's grown a very　265
landfish, languageless, a monster. A plague of opinion!
A man may wear it on both sides, like a leather jerkin.

ACHILLES　Thou must be my ambassador to him,
Thersites.

THERSITES　Who, I? Why, he'll answer nobody. He　270
professes not-answering; speaking is for beggars. He
wears his tongue in's arms. I will put on his presence.
Let Patroclus make demands to me. You shall see the
pageant of Ajax.

ACHILLES　To him, Patroclus. Tell him I humbly desire　275
the valiant Ajax to invite the most valorous Hector to
come unarmed to my tent, and to procure safe-conduct
for his person of the magnanimous and most illustrious
six-or-seven-times-honoured captain-general of the
Grecian army, Agamemnon, *et cetera*. Do this.　　　280

PATROCLUS [*to Thersites, as though addressing Ajax*]　Jove
bless great Ajax!

THERSITES [*Mimics Ajax' manner.*]　H'm!

PATROCLUS　I come from the worthy Achilles –

THERSITES　Ha?　　　　　　　　　　　　　　　285

PATROCLUS   Who most humbly desires you to invite
    Hector to his tent –
THERSITES   H'm!
PATROCLUS   And to procure safe-conduct from
290   Agamemnon.
THERSITES   Agamemnon?
PATROCLUS   Ay, my lord.
THERSITES   Ha!
PATROCLUS   What say you to't?
295 THERSITES   God b'wi' you, with all my heart.
PATROCLUS   Your answer, sir.
THERSITES   If tomorrow be a fair day, by eleven o'clock
    it will go one way or other. Howsoever, he shall pay for
    me ere he has me.
300 PATROCLUS   Your answer, sir.
THERSITES   Fare ye well, with all my heart.
                [A pretended exit. Achilles applauds
                    their concluded pantomime.]
ACHILLES   Why, but he is not in this tune, is he?
THERSITES   No, but he's out o' tune thus. What music
    will be in him when Hector has knocked out his brains,
305   I know not; but I am sure, none, unless the fiddler
    Apollo get his sinews to make catlings on.
ACHILLES   Come, thou shalt bear a letter to him straight.
THERSITES   Let me carry another to his horse, for that's
    the more capable creature.
310 ACHILLES   My mind is troubled, like a fountain stirred,
    And I myself see not the bottom of it.
                    Exeunt Achilles and Patroclus.
THERSITES   Would the fountain of your mind were clear
    again, that I might water an ass at it! I had rather be a
    tick in a sheep than such a valiant ignorance.   *Exit.*

4.1   *Enter, at one door,* AENEAS *and a*
            Torchbearer with a torch; at another,
            PARIS, DEIPHOBUS, *Antenor,*
        DIOMEDES *the Grecian and others with torches.*

PARIS   See, ho! Who is that there?
DEIPHOBUS   It is the Lord Aeneas.
AENEAS   Is the prince there in person?
    Had I so good occasion to lie long
5   As you, Prince Paris, nothing but heavenly business
    Should rob my bed-mate of my company.
DIOMEDES
    That's my mind too. – Good morrow, Lord Aeneas.
PARIS   A valiant Greek, Aeneas; take his hand.
    Witness the process of your speech, wherein
10   You told how Diomed, e'en a whole week by days,
    Did haunt you in the field.
AENEAS   Health to you, valiant sir,
    During all question of the gentle truce;
    But when I meet you armed, as black defiance
15   As heart can think or courage execute.
DIOMEDES   The one and other Diomed embraces.
    Our bloods are now in calm; and, so long, health;
    But when contention and occasion meet,

By Jove, I'll play the hunter for thy life
    With all my force, pursuit and policy.   20
AENEAS   And thou shalt hunt a lion that will fly
    With his face backward. – In human gentleness,
    Welcome to Troy! Now by Anchises' life,
    Welcome indeed! By Venus' hand I swear,
    No man alive can love in such a sort   25
    The thing he means to kill more excellently.
DIOMEDES   We sympathize. Jove, let Aeneas live,
    If to my sword his fate be not the glory,
    A thousand complete courses of the sun!
    But in mine emulous honour let him die,   30
    With every joint a wound, and that tomorrow!
AENEAS   We know each other well.
DIOMEDES   We do, and long to know each other worse.
PARIS   This is the most despiteful'st gentle greeting,
    The noblest hateful love, that e'er I heard of.   35
    [to Aeneas] What business, lord, so early?
AENEAS
    I was sent for to the King; but why, I know not.
PARIS
    His purpose meets you. 'Twas to bring this Greek
    To Calchas' house and there to render him,
    For the enfreed Antenor, the fair Cressid.   40
    Let's have your company, or, if you please,
    Haste there before us.
    [aside to Aeneas]   I constantly do think –
    Or rather, call my thought a certain knowledge –
    My brother Troilus lodges there tonight.
    Rouse him and give him note of our approach,   45
    With the whole quality wherefore. I fear
    We shall be much unwelcome.
AENEAS *[aside to Paris]*   That I assure you.
    Troilus had rather Troy were borne to Greece
    Than Cressid borne from Troy.
PARIS *[aside to Aeneas]*   There is no help.
    The bitter disposition of the time   50
    Will have it so. – On, lord; we'll follow you.
AENEAS   Good morrow, all.   *Exit with Torchbearer.*
PARIS   And tell me, noble Diomed, faith, tell me true,
    Even in the soul of sound good fellowship,
    Who, in your thoughts, merits fair Helen most,   55
    Myself or Menelaus?
DIOMEDES   Both alike.
    He merits well to have her that doth seek her,
    Not making any scruple of her soilure,
    With such a hell of pain and world of charge;
    And you as well to keep her that defend her,   60
    Not palating the taste of her dishonour,
    With such a costly loss of wealth and friends.
    He, like a puling cuckold, would drink up
    The lees and dregs of a flat 'tamed piece;
    You, like a lecher, out of whorish loins   65
    Are pleased to breed out your inheritors.
    Both merits poised, each weighs nor less nor more,
    But he as he. Which heavier for a whore?
PARIS   You are too bitter to your country woman.

DIOMEDES   She's bitter to her country. Hear me, Paris: 70
For every false drop in her bawdy veins
A Grecian's life hath sunk; for every scruple
Of her contaminated carrion weight
A Trojan hath been slain. Since she could speak,
She hath not given so many good words breath 75
As for her Greeks and Trojans suffered death.
PARIS   Fair Diomed, you do as chapmen do,
Dispraise the thing that you desire to buy.
But we in silence hold this virtue well:
We'll not commend what we intend to sell. 80
Here lies our way.   *Exeunt.*

4.2   *Enter* TROILUS *and* CRESSIDA.

TROILUS   Dear, trouble not yourself. The morn is cold.
CRESSIDA
Then, sweet my lord, I'll call mine uncle down.
He shall unbolt the gates.
TROILUS   Trouble him not.
To bed, to bed! Sleep kill those pretty eyes
And give as soft attachment to thy senses 5
As infants' empty of all thought!
CRESSIDA   Good morrow, then.
TROILUS   I prithee now, to bed.
CRESSIDA   Are you aweary of me?
TROILUS   O Cressida! But that the busy day,
Waked by the lark, hath roused the ribald crows, 10
And dreaming night will hide our joys no longer,
I would not from thee.
CRESSIDA   Night hath been too brief.
TROILUS
Beshrew the witch! With venomous wights she stays
As tediously as hell, but flies the grasps of love
With wings more momentary-swift than thought. 15
You will catch cold and curse me.
CRESSIDA   Prithee, tarry. You men will never tarry.
O foolish Cressid, I might have still held off,
And then you would have tarried! – Hark, there's one
up.
PANDARUS [*within*]   What's all the doors open here? 20
TROILUS   It is your uncle.

Enter PANDARUS.

CRESSIDA
A pestilence on him! Now will he be mocking.
I shall have such a life!
PANDARUS   How now, how now, how go maidenheads?
Here, you maid! Where's my cousin Cressid? 25
CRESSIDA
Go hang yourself, you naughty mocking uncle!
You bring me to do – and then you flout me too.
PANDARUS   To do what, to do what? – Let her say what.
– What have I brought you to do?
CRESSIDA
Come, come, beshrew your heart! You'll ne'er be good, 30
Nor suffer others.

PANDARUS   Ha, ha! Alas, poor wretch! Ah, poor
capocchia, has 't not slept tonight? Would he not – ah,
naughty man – let it sleep? A bugbear take him!
CRESSIDA [*to Troilus*]
Did not I tell you? Would he were knocked i'th' head! 35
[*One knocks.*]
Who's that at door? Good uncle, go and see. –
My lord, come you again into my chamber.
You smile and mock me, as if I meant naughtily.
TROILUS   Ha, ha!
CRESSIDA
Come, you are deceived. I think of no such thing. 40
[*Knock*]
How earnestly they knock! Pray you, come in.
I would not for half Troy have you seen here.
Exeunt Troilus and Cressida.
PANDARUS   Who's there? What's the matter? Will you
beat down the door? [*Opens the door.*] How now, what's
the matter? 45

Enter AENEAS.

AENEAS   Good morrow, lord, good morrow.
PANDARUS   Who's there? My Lord Aeneas? By my troth,
I knew you not. What news with you so early?
AENEAS   Is not Prince Troilus here?
PANDARUS   Here? What should he do here? 50
AENEAS   Come, he is here, my lord. Do not deny him.
It doth import him much to speak with me.
PANDARUS   Is he here, say you? It's more than I know,
I'll be sworn. For my own part, I came in late. What
should he do here? 55
AENEAS
Ho, nay, then! Come, come, you'll do him wrong
Ere you are ware. You'll be so true to him
To be false to him. Do not you know of him,
But yet go fetch him hither. Go.

Enter TROILUS.

TROILUS   How now, what's the matter? 60
AENEAS   My lord, I scarce have leisure to salute you,
My matter is so rash. There is at hand
Paris your brother and Deiphobus,
The Grecian Diomed, and our Antenor
Delivered to us; and for him forthwith, 65
Ere the first sacrifice, within this hour,
We must give up to Diomedes' hand
The Lady Cressida.
TROILUS   Is it concluded so?
AENEAS   By Priam and the general state of Troy.
They are at hand and ready to effect it. 70
TROILUS   How my achievements mock me! –
I will go meet them. And, my Lord Aeneas,
We met by chance; you did not find me here.
AENEAS   Good, good my lord, the secrets of nature
Have not more gift in taciturnity. 75
Exeunt Troilus and Aeneas.
PANDARUS   Is 't possible? No sooner got but lost? The

devil take Antenor! The young prince will go mad. A
plague upon Antenor! I would they had broke 's neck!

Enter CRESSIDA.

CRESSIDA
How now? What's the matter? Who was here?

80 PANDARUS   Ah, ah!

CRESSIDA
Why sigh you so profoundly? Where's my lord?
Gone? Tell me, sweet uncle, what's the matter?

PANDARUS   Would I were as deep under the earth as I
am above!

85 CRESSIDA   O the gods! What's the matter?

PANDARUS   Pray thee, get thee in. Would thou hadst
ne'er been born! I knew thou wouldst be his death. O,
poor gentleman! A plague upon Antenor!

CRESSIDA   Good uncle, I beseech you, on my knees I
90 beseech you, what's the matter?

PANDARUS   Thou must be gone, wench, thou must be
gone. Thou art changed for Antenor. Thou must to thy
father and be gone from Troilus. 'Twill be his death,
'twill be his bane; he cannot bear it.

95 CRESSIDA   O you immortal gods! I will not go.

PANDARUS   Thou must.

CRESSIDA   I will not, uncle. I have forgot my father.
I know no touch of consanguinity;
No kin, no love, no blood, no soul so near me
100 As the sweet Troilus. O you gods divine,
Make Cressid's name the very crown of falsehood
If ever she leave Troilus! Time, force and death,
Do to this body what extremes you can;
But the strong base and building of my love
105 Is as the very centre of the earth,
Drawing all things to it. I'll go in and weep –

PANDARUS   Do, do.

CRESSIDA
Tear my bright hair and scratch my praised cheeks,
Crack my clear voice with sobs, and break my heart
110 With sounding 'Troilus'. I will not go from Troy.

Exeunt.

4.3   *Enter* PARIS, TROILUS, AENEAS,
           DEIPHOBUS, *Antenor and* DIOMEDES.

PARIS   It is great morning, and the hour prefixed
Of her delivery to this valiant Greek
Comes fast upon. Good my brother Troilus,
Tell you the lady what she is to do
5 And haste her to the purpose.

TROILUS   Walk into her house.
I'll bring her to the Grecian presently;
And to his hand when I deliver her,
Think it an altar and thy brother Troilus
A priest, there off'ring to it his own heart.

10 PARIS   I know what 'tis to love;
And would, as I shall pity, I could help!
Please you walk in, my lords.   *Exeunt.*

4.4   *Enter* PANDARUS *and* CRESSIDA.

PANDARUS   Be moderate, be moderate.

CRESSIDA   Why tell you me of moderation?
The grief is fine, full, perfect that I taste,
And violenteth in a sense as strong
As that which causeth it. How can I moderate it?   5
If I could temporize with my affection,
Or brew it to a weak and colder palate,
The like allayment could I give my grief.
My love admits no qualifying dross;
No more my grief, in such a precious loss.   10

Enter TROILUS.

PANDARUS   Here, here, here he comes. Ah, sweet ducks!

CRESSIDA [*Embraces Troilus.*]   O Troilus! Troilus!

PANDARUS   What a pair of spectacles is here! Let me
embrace, too. 'O heart', as the goodly saying is,
    'O heart, heavy heart,   15
    Why sigh'st thou without breaking?'
where he answers again:
    'Because thou canst not ease thy smart
    By friendship nor by speaking.'
There was never a truer rhyme. Let us cast away   20
nothing, for we may live to have need of such a verse.
We see it, we see it. How now, lambs?

TROILUS   Cressid, I love thee in so strained a purity
That the blest gods, as angry with my fancy –
More bright in zeal than the devotion which   25
Cold lips blow to their deities – take thee from me.

CRESSIDA   Have the gods envy?

PANDARUS   Ay, ay, ay, ay, 'tis too plain a case.

CRESSIDA   And is it true that I must go from Troy?

TROILUS   A hateful truth.

CRESSIDA   What, and from Troilus too?   30

TROILUS   From Troy and Troilus.

CRESSIDA   Is't possible?

TROILUS   And suddenly, where injury of chance
Puts back leave-taking, jostles roughly by
All time of pause, rudely beguiles our lips
Of all rejoindure, forcibly prevents   35
Our locked embrasures, strangles our dear vows
Even in the birth of our own labouring breath.
We two, that with so many thousand sighs
Did buy each other, must poorly sell ourselves
With the rude brevity and discharge of one.   40
Injurious Time now with a robber's haste
Crams his rich thiev'ry up, he knows not how.
As many farewells as be stars in heaven,
With distinct breath and consigned kisses to them,
He fumbles up into a loose adieu   45
And scants us with a single famished kiss,
Distasted with the salt of broken tears.

AENEAS [*within*]   My lord, is the lady ready?

TROILUS
Hark, you are called. Some say the Genius so
Cries 'Come!' to him that instantly must die. –   50

Bid them have patience. She shall come anon.

PANDARUS   Where are my tears? Rain, to lay this wind,
or my heart will be blown up by the root.   *Exit.*

CRESSIDA   I must, then, to the Grecians?

TROILUS   No remedy.

55   CRESSIDA   A woeful Cressid 'mongst the merry Greeks!
When shall we see again?

TROILUS   Hear me, my love. Be thou but true of heart –

CRESSIDA   I true? How now, what wicked deem is this?

TROILUS   Nay, we must use expostulation kindly,
60   For it is parting from us.
I speak not 'Be thou true' as fearing thee,
For I will throw my glove to Death himself
That there's no maculation in thy heart;
But 'Be thou true', say I, to fashion in
65   My sequent protestation: Be thou true,
And I will see thee.

CRESSIDA   O, you shall be exposed, my lord, to dangers
As infinite as imminent! But I'll be true.

TROILUS
And I'll grow friend with danger. Wear this sleeve.

CRESSIDA [*as they exchange favours*]
70   And you this glove. When shall I see you?

TROILUS   I will corrupt the Grecian sentinels,
To give thee nightly visitation.
But yet, be true.

CRESSIDA   O heavens! 'Be true' again?

TROILUS   Hear why I speak it, love.
75   The Grecian youths are full of quality;
Their loving well composed with gifts of nature,
And flowing o'er with arts and exercise.
How novelty may move and parts with person,
Alas, a kind of godly jealousy –
80   Which, I beseech you, call a virtuous sin –
Makes me afeard.

CRESSIDA   O heavens, you love me not!

TROILUS   Die I a villain then!
In this I do not call your faith in question
So mainly as my merit. I cannot sing,
85   Nor heel the high lavolt, nor sweeten talk,
Nor play at subtle games – fair virtues all,
To which the Grecians are most prompt and
pregnant.
But I can tell that in each grace of these
There lurks a still and dumb-discoursive devil
90   That tempts most cunningly. But be not tempted.

CRESSIDA   Do you think I will?

TROILUS   No.
But something may be done that we will not;
And sometimes we are devils to ourselves,
95   When we will tempt the frailty of our powers,
Presuming on their changeful potency.

AENEAS [*within*]   Nay, good my lord –

TROILUS   Come, kiss, and let us part.

PARIS [*within*]   Brother Troilus!

TROILUS [*Calls out.*]   Good brother, come you hither,
And bring Aeneas and the Grecian with you.

CRESSIDA   My lord, will you be true?   100

TROILUS   Who, I? Alas, it is my vice, my fault.
Whiles others fish with craft for great opinion,
I with great truth catch mere simplicity;
Whilst some with cunning gild their copper crowns,
With truth and plainness I do wear mine bare.   105

Enter AENEAS, PARIS, *Antenor,*
DEIPHOBUS *and* DIOMEDES.

Fear not my truth. The moral of my wit
Is 'plain and true'; there's all the reach of it. –
Welcome, Sir Diomed. Here is the lady
Which for Antenor we deliver you.
At the port, lord, I'll give her to thy hand   110
And by the way possess thee what she is.
Entreat her fair and, by my soul, fair Greek,
If e'er thou stand at mercy of my sword,
Name Cressid, and thy life shall be as safe
As Priam is in Ilium.

DIOMEDES   Fair Lady Cressid,   115
So please you, save the thanks this prince expects.
The lustre in your eye, heaven in your cheek,
Pleads your fair usage; and to Diomed
You shall be mistress and command him wholly.

TROILUS   Grecian, thou dost not use me courteously,   120
To shame the zeal of my petition to thee
In praising her. I tell thee, lord of Greece,
She is as far high-soaring o'er thy praises
As thou unworthy to be called her servant.
I charge thee use her well, even for my charge;   125
For, by the dreadful Pluto, if thou dost not,
Though the great bulk Achilles be thy guard,
I'll cut thy throat.

DIOMEDES   O, be not moved, Prince Troilus.
Let me be privileged by my place and message
To be a speaker free. When I am hence,   130
I'll answer to my lust. And know you, lord,
I'll nothing do on charge. To her own worth
She shall be prized; but that you say 'Be't so',
I'll speak it in my spirit and honour: 'No'.

TROILUS   Come, to the port. – I'll tell thee, Diomed, 135
This brave shall oft make thee to hide thy head. –
Lady, give me your hand and, as we walk,
To our own selves bend we our needful talk.
Exeunt Troilus, Cressida and Diomedes.
[*Sound trumpet within.*]

PARIS   Hark, Hector's trumpet!

AENEAS   How have we spent this morning!
The prince must think me tardy and remiss,   140
That swore to ride before him in the field.

PARIS
'Tis Troilus' fault. Come, come, to field with him.

DEIPHOBUS   Let us make ready straight.

AENEAS   Yea, with a bridegroom's fresh alacrity,
Let us address to tend on Hector's heels.   145
The glory of our Troy doth this day lie
On his fair worth and single chivalry.   *Exeunt.*

4.5   *Enter* AJAX, *armed,* ACHILLES,
     PATROCLUS, AGAMEMNON, MENELAUS,
     ULYSSES, NESTOR, *etc. and Trumpeter.*

AGAMEMNON [*to Ajax*]
     Here art thou in appointment fresh and fair,
     Anticipating time with starting courage.
     Give with thy trumpet a loud note to Troy,
     Thou dreadful Ajax, that the appalled air
5   May pierce the head of the great combatant
     And hale him hither.
AJAX [*Gives money.*]   Thou, trumpet, there's my purse.
     Now crack thy lungs and split thy brazen pipe.
     Blow, villain, till thy sphered bias cheek
     Outswell the colic of puffed Aquilon.
10   Come, stretch thy chest, and let thy eyes spout blood;
     Thou blowest for Hector.   [*Trumpet sounds.*]
ULYSSES   No trumpet answers.
ACHILLES   'Tis but early days.

          Enter DIOMEDES *with* CRESSIDA.

AGAMEMNON
     Is not yond Diomed, with Calchas' daughter?
15   ULYSSES   'Tis he. I ken the manner of his gait;
     He rises on the toe. That spirit of his
     In aspiration lifts him from the earth.
AGAMEMNON   Is this the Lady Cressid?
DIOMEDES   Even she.
AGAMEMNON
     Most dearly welcome to the Greeks, sweet lady.
          [*Kisses her.*]
20   NESTOR   Our general doth salute you with a kiss.
ULYSSES   Yet is the kindness but particular;
     'Twere better she were kissed in general.
NESTOR
     And very courtly counsel. I'll begin.   [*Kisses her.*]
     So much for Nestor.
25   ACHILLES   I'll take that winter from your lips, fair lady.
     Achilles bids you welcome.   [*Kisses her.*]
MENELAUS   I had good argument for kissing once.
PATROCLUS   But that's no argument for kissing now;
     For thus popped Paris in his hardiment,
30   And parted thus you and your argument.   [*Kisses her.*]
ULYSSES   O deadly gall and theme of all our scorns,
     For which we lose our heads to gild his horns!
PATROCLUS   The first was Menelaus' kiss; this, mine.
     Patroclus kisses you.   [*Kisses her again.*]
MENELAUS   O, this is trim!
35   PATROCLUS   Paris and I kiss evermore for him.
MENELAUS   I'll have my kiss, sir. – Lady, by your leave.
CRESSIDA   In kissing, do you render or receive?
MENELAUS   Both take and give.
CRESSIDA   I'll make my match to live,
     The kiss you take is better than you give;
40   Therefore no kiss.
MENELAUS
     I'll give you boot; I'll give you three for one.

CRESSIDA   You are an odd man; give even, or give none.
MENELAUS   An odd man, lady? Every man is odd.
CRESSIDA   No, Paris is not, for you know 'tis true
     That you are odd, and he is even with you.   45
MENELAUS   You fillip me o'th' head.
CRESSIDA   No, I'll be sworn.
ULYSSES   It were no match, your nail against his horn.
     May I, sweet lady, beg a kiss of you?
CRESSIDA   You may.
ULYSSES   I do desire it.
CRESSIDA   Why, beg too.
ULYSSES   Why then, for Venus' sake, give me a kiss,   50
     When Helen is a maid again, and his –
CRESSIDA   I am your debtor; claim it when 'tis due.
ULYSSES   Never's my day, and then a kiss of you.
DIOMEDES
     Lady, a word. I'll bring you to your father.
          [*They talk apart.*]
NESTOR   A woman of quick sense.
ULYSSES   Fie, fie upon her!   55
     There's language in her eye, her cheek, her lip,
     Nay, her foot speaks; her wanton spirits look out
     At every joint and motive of her body.
     O, these encounterers, so glib of tongue,
     That give accosting welcome ere it comes,   60
     And wide unclasp the tables of their thoughts
     To every tickling reader! Set them down
     For sluttish spoils of opportunity
     And daughters of the game.
          Exeunt Diomedes and Cressida.

     Flourish. Enter all of Troy: HECTOR *armed,* PARIS,
          AENEAS, HELENUS, TROILUS *and Attendants.*

ALL   The Trojan's trumpet.
AGAMEMNON   Yonder comes the troop.   65
AENEAS
     Hail, all you state of Greece! What shall be done
     To him that victory commands? Or do you purpose
     A victor shall be known? Will you the knights
     Shall to the edge of all extremity
     Pursue each other, or shall they be divided   70
     By any voice or order of the field?
     Hector bade ask.
AGAMEMNON   Which way would Hector have it?
AENEAS   He cares not; he'll obey conditions.
AGAMEMNON   'Tis done like Hector.
ACHILLES   But securely done,
     A little proudly, and great deal disprizing   75
     The knight opposed.
AENEAS   If not Achilles, sir,
     What is your name?
ACHILLES   If not Achilles, nothing.
AENEAS   Therefore Achilles. But whate'er, know this:
     In the extremity of great and little,
     Valour and pride excel themselves in Hector,   80
     The one almost as infinite as all,
     The other blank as nothing. Weigh him well,

And that which looks like pride is courtesy.
This Ajax is half made of Hector's blood,
85   In love whereof half Hector stays at home;
Half heart, half hand, half Hector comes to seek
This blended knight, half Trojan and half Greek.
ACHILLES   A maiden battle, then? O, I perceive you.

Enter DIOMEDES.

AGAMEMNON   Here is Sir Diomed. – Go, gentle knight;
90   Stand by our Ajax. As you and Lord Aeneas
Consent upon the order of their fight,
So be it, either to the uttermost
Or else a breath. The combatants being kin
Half stints their strife before their strokes begin.
        [*Hector and Ajax enter the lists.*]
95   ULYSSES   They are opposed already.
AGAMEMNON [*to Ulysses*]
What Trojan is that same that looks so heavy?
ULYSSES   The youngest son of Priam, a true knight,
Not yet mature, yet matchless firm of word,
Speaking in deeds and deedless in his tongue;
100   Not soon provoked, nor being provoked soon calmed;
His heart and hand both open and both free.
For what he has he gives; what thinks, he shows;
Yet gives he not till judgement guide his bounty,
Nor dignifies an impair thought with breath;
105   Manly as Hector, but more dangerous,
For Hector in his blaze of wrath subscribes
To tender objects, but he in heat of action
Is more vindicative than jealous love.
They call him Troilus, and on him erect
110   A second hope, as fairly built as Hector.
Thus says Aeneas, one that knows the youth
Even to his inches, and with private soul
Did in great Ilium thus translate him to me.
        [*Alarum. Hector and Ajax fight.*]
AGAMEMNON   They are in action.
115   NESTOR   Now, Ajax, hold thine own!
TROILUS   Hector, thou sleep'st. Awake thee!
AGAMEMNON
His blows are well disposed. – There, Ajax!
                [*Trumpets cease.*]
DIOMEDES   You must no more.
AENEAS   Princes, enough, so please you.
AJAX   I am not warm yet. Let us fight again.
DIOMEDES   As Hector pleases.
120   HECTOR   Why, then will I no more.
Thou art, great lord, my father's sister's son,
A cousin-german to great Priam's seed.
The obligation of our blood forbids
A gory emulation 'twixt us twain.
125   Were thy commixtion Greek and Trojan so
That thou couldst say, 'This hand is Grecian all,
And this is Trojan; the sinews of this leg
All Greek, and this all Troy; my mother's blood
Runs on the dexter cheek, and this sinister
130   Bounds in my father's', by Jove multipotent,

Thou shouldst not bear from me a Greekish member
Wherein my sword had not impressure made
Of our rank feud. But the just gods gainsay
That any drop thou borrowed'st from thy mother,
My sacred aunt, should by my mortal sword   135
Be drained. Let me embrace thee, Ajax.
By him that thunders, thou hast lusty arms!
Hector would have them fall upon him thus.
Cousin, all honour to thee!   [*They embrace.*]
AJAX   I thank thee, Hector.
Thou art too gentle and too free a man.   140
I came to kill thee, cousin, and bear hence
A great addition earned in thy death.
HECTOR   Not Neoptolemus so mirable,
On whose bright crest Fame with her loud'st 'Oyez'
Cries, 'This is he', could promise to himself   145
A thought of added honour torn from Hector.
AENEAS   There is expectance here from both the sides
What further you will do.
HECTOR   We'll answer it:
The issue is embracement. – Ajax, farewell.
        [*They embrace again.*]
AJAX   If I might in entreaties find success –   150
As seld I have the chance – I would desire
My famous cousin to our Grecian tents.
DIOMEDES   'Tis Agamemnon's wish; and great Achilles
Doth long to see unarmed the valiant Hector.
HECTOR   Aeneas, call my brother Troilus to me,   155
And signify this loving interview
To the expecters of our Trojan part;
Desire them home. [*to Ajax*] Give me thy hand, my
        cousin.
I will go eat with thee, and see your knights.
        [*Agamemnon and the rest come forward.*]
AJAX   Great Agamemnon comes to meet us here.   160
HECTOR [*to Aeneas*]
The worthiest of them tell me name by name;
But for Achilles, mine own searching eyes
Shall find him by his large and portly size.
AGAMEMNON   Worthy of arms! As welcome as to one
That would be rid of such an enemy –   165
But that's no welcome. Understand more clear:
What's past and what's to come is strewed with husks
And formless ruin of oblivion;
But in this extant moment, faith and troth,
Strained purely from all hollow bias-drawing,   170
Bids thee, with most divine integrity,
From heart of very heart, great Hector, welcome.
HECTOR   I thank thee, most imperious Agamemnon.
AGAMEMNON [*to Troilus*]
My well-famed lord of Troy, no less to you.
MENELAUS
Let me confirm my princely brother's greeting.   175
You brace of warlike brothers, welcome hither.
        [*Embraces Hector and Troilus.*]
HECTOR [*to Aeneas*]   Who must we answer?
AENEAS   The noble Menelaus.

HECTOR   O, you, my lord? By Mars his gauntlet, thanks!
Mock not that I affect th'untraded oath;
180   Your quondam wife swears still by Venus' glove.
She's well, but bade me not commend her to you.
MENELAUS   Name her not now, sir; she's a deadly theme.
HECTOR   O, pardon! I offend.
NESTOR   I have, thou gallant Trojan, seen thee oft,
185   Labouring for destiny, make cruel way
Through ranks of Greekish youth; and I have seen
        thee,
As hot as Perseus, spur thy Phrygian steed,
And seen thee scorning forfeits and subduements,
When thou hast hung thy advanced sword i'th' air,
190   Not letting it decline on the declined,
That I have said to some my standers-by:
'Lo, Jupiter is yonder, dealing life!'
And I have seen thee pause and take thy breath,
When that a ring of Greeks have hemmed thee in,
195   Like an Olympian, wrestling. This have I seen;
But this thy countenance, still locked in steel,
I never saw till now. I knew thy grandsire,
And once fought with him. He was a soldier good,
But by great Mars, the captain of us all,
200   Never like thee. Let an old man embrace thee;
And, worthy warrior, welcome to our tents.
        [*They embrace.*]
AENEAS [*to Hector*]   'Tis the old Nestor.
HECTOR   Let me embrace thee, good old chronicle,
That hast so long walked hand in hand with time.
205   Most reverend Nestor, I am glad to clasp thee.
NESTOR
I would my arms could match thee in contention
As they contend with thee in courtesy.
HECTOR   I would they could.
NESTOR
Ha! By this white beard, I'd fight with thee tomorrow.
210   Well, welcome, welcome. I have seen the time!
ULYSSES   I wonder now how yonder city stands
When we have here her base and pillar by us.
HECTOR   I know your favour, Lord Ulysses, well.
Ah, sir, there's many a Greek and Trojan dead
215   Since first I saw yourself and Diomed
In Ilium, on your Greekish embassy.
ULYSSES   Sir, I foretold you then what would ensue.
My prophecy is but half his journey yet;
For yonder walls, that pertly front your town,
220   Yon towers, whose wanton tops do buss the clouds,
Must kiss their own feet.
HECTOR   I must not believe you.
There they stand yet, and modestly I think
The fall of every Phrygian stone will cost
A drop of Grecian blood. The end crowns all,
225   And that old common arbitrator, Time,
Will one day end it.
ULYSSES   So to him we leave it.
Most gentle and most valiant Hector, welcome.
After the general, I beseech you next

To feast with me and see me at my tent.
ACHILLES   I shall forestall thee, Lord Ulysses, thou!   230
Now, Hector, I have fed mine eyes on thee;
I have with exact view perused thee, Hector,
And quoted joint by joint.
HECTOR   Is this Achilles?
ACHILLES   I am Achilles.
HECTOR   Stand fair, I pray thee. Let me look on thee.   235
ACHILLES   Behold thy fill.
HECTOR   Nay, I have done already.
ACHILLES   Thou art too brief. I will the second time,
As I would buy thee, view thee limb by limb.
HECTOR   O, like a book of sport thou'lt read me o'er;
But there's more in me than thou understand'st.   240
Why dost thou so oppress me with thine eye?
ACHILLES
Tell me, you heavens, in which part of his body
Shall I destroy him? Whether there, or there, or
        there?
That I may give the local wound a name
And make distinct the very breach whereout   245
Hector's great spirit flew. Answer me, heavens!
HECTOR   It would discredit the blest gods, proud man,
To answer such a question. Stand again.
Think'st thou to catch my life so pleasantly
As to prenominate in nice conjecture   250
Where thou wilt hit me dead?
ACHILLES   I tell thee, yea.
HECTOR   Wert thou the oracle to tell me so,
I'd not believe thee. Henceforth guard thee well;
For I'll not kill thee there, nor there, nor there,
But, by the forge that stithied Mars his helm,   255
I'll kill thee everywhere, yea, o'er and o'er. –
You wisest Grecians, pardon me this brag;
His insolence draws folly from my lips.
But I'll endeavour deeds to match these words,
Or may I never –
AJAX   Do not chafe thee, cousin.   260
And you, Achilles, let these threats alone,
Till accident or purpose bring you to't.
You may have every day enough of Hector,
If you have stomach. The general state, I fear,
Can scarce entreat you to be odd with him.   265
HECTOR [*to Achilles*]
I pray you, let us see you in the field.
We have had pelting wars since you refused
The Grecians' cause.
ACHILLES   Dost thou entreat me, Hector?
Tomorrow do I meet thee, fell as death;
Tonight all friends.
HECTOR   Thy hand upon that match.   270
AGAMEMNON
First, all you peers of Greece, go to my tent;
There in the full convive we. Afterwards,
As Hector's leisure and your bounties shall
Concur together, severally entreat him.
Beat loud the taborins, let the trumpets blow,   275

That this great soldier may his welcome know.
            Flourish. Exeunt all but Troilus and Ulysses.
TROILUS   My Lord Ulysses, tell me, I beseech you,
In what place of the field doth Calchas keep?
ULYSSES   At Menelaus' tent, most princely Troilus.
280   There Diomed doth feast with him tonight,
Who neither looks on heaven nor on earth,
But gives all gaze and bent of amorous view
On the fair Cressid.
TROILUS   Shall I, sweet lord, be bound to you so much,
285   After we part from Agamemnon's tent,
To bring me thither?
ULYSSES   You shall command me, sir.
As gentle tell me, of what honour was
This Cressida in Troy? Had she no lover there
That wails her absence?
290   TROILUS   O sir, to such as boasting show their scars
A mock is due. Will you walk on, my lord?
She was beloved, she loved; she is, and doth;
But still sweet love is food for Fortune's tooth.
                                    Exeunt.

5.1   *Enter* ACHILLES *and* PATROCLUS.

ACHILLES
I'll heat his blood with Greekish wine tonight,
Which with my scimitar I'll cool tomorrow.
Patroclus, let us feast him to the height.
PATROCLUS   Here comes Thersites.

            Enter THERSITES.

ACHILLES   How now, thou core of envy?
5   Thou crusty batch of nature, what's the news?
THERSITES   Why, thou picture of what thou seemest
and idol of idiot-worshippers, here's a letter for thee.
ACHILLES   From whence, fragment?
THERSITES   Why, thou full dish of fool, from Troy.
    [*Gives a letter. Achilles stands aside to read it.*]
10   PATROCLUS   Who keeps the tent now?
THERSITES   The surgeon's box, or the patient's wound.
PATROCLUS   Well said, adversity. And what need these
tricks?
THERSITES   Prithee, be silent, boy. I profit not by thy
15   talk. Thou art thought to be Achilles' male varlet.
PATROCLUS   Male varlet, you rogue? What's that?
THERSITES   Why, his masculine whore. Now, the rotten
diseases of the south, guts-griping, ruptures, catarrhs,
loads o' gravel i'th' back, lethargies, cold palsies, raw
20   eyes, dirt-rotten livers, wheezing lungs, bladders full of
imposthume, sciaticas, limekilns i'th' palm, incurable
bone-ache and the rivelled fee-simple of the tetter, take
and take again such preposterous discoveries!
PATROCLUS   Why, thou damnable box of envy, thou,
25   what mean'st thou to curse thus?
THERSITES   Do I curse thee?
PATROCLUS   Why, no, you ruinous butt, you whoreson
indistinguishable cur, no.

THERSITES   No? Why art thou then exasperate, thou
idle immaterial skein of sleave-silk, thou green sarsenet   30
flap for a sore eye, thou tassel of a prodigal's purse,
thou? Ah, how the poor world is pestered with such
waterflies, diminutives of nature!
PATROCLUS   Out, gall!
THERSITES   Finch egg!   35
ACHILLES   My sweet Patroclus, I am thwarted quite
From my great purpose in tomorrow's battle.
Here is a letter from Queen Hecuba,
A token from her daughter, my fair love,
Both taxing me and gaging me to keep   40
An oath that I have sworn. I will not break it.
Fall, Greeks; fail, fame; honour, or go or stay;
My major vow lies here; this I'll obey.
Come, come, Thersites, help to trim my tent;
This night in banqueting must all be spent.   45
Away, Patroclus!   *Exit with Patroclus.*
THERSITES   With too much blood and too little brain,
these two may run mad; but if with too much brain and
too little blood they do, I'll be a curer of madmen.
Here's Agamemnon, an honest fellow enough, and one   50
that loves quails, but he has not so much brain as earwax.
And the goodly transformation of Jupiter there, his
brother, the bull – the primitive statue and oblique
memorial of cuckolds, a thrifty shoeing-horn in a
chain, hanging at his brother's leg – to what form but   55
that he is should wit larded with malice and malice
farced with wit turn him to? To an ass were nothing; he
is both ass and ox. To an ox were nothing; he is both ox
and ass. To be a dog, a mule, a cat, a fitchew, a toad, a
lizard, an owl, a puttock, or a herring without a roe, I   60
would not care; but to be Menelaus! I would conspire
against destiny. Ask me not what I would be, if I were
not Thersites, for I care not to be the louse of a lazar so
I were not Menelaus. – Heyday! Sprites and fires!

        Enter HECTOR, TROILUS, AJAX, AGAMEMNON,
        ULYSSES, NESTOR, MENELAUS *and* DIOMEDES,
                    with lights.

AGAMEMNON   We go wrong, we go wrong.
AJAX   No, yonder 'tis –   65
There, where we see the light.
HECTOR   I trouble you.
AJAX   No, not a whit.

            Enter ACHILLES.

ULYSSES   Here comes himself to guide you.
ACHILLES
Welcome, brave Hector. Welcome, princes all.
AGAMEMNON
So now, fair prince of Troy, I bid good night.
Ajax commands the guard to tend on you.   70
HECTOR
Thanks, and good night to the Greeks' general.
MENELAUS   Good night, my lord.
HECTOR   Good night, sweet Lord Menelaus.

THERSITES [*aside*] Sweet draught. 'Sweet', quoth 'a?
Sweet sink, sweet sewer.

ACHILLES

75   Good night and welcome both at once to those
That go or tarry.

AGAMEMNON   Good night.

Exeunt Agamemnon and Menelaus.

ACHILLES   Old Nestor tarries; and you too, Diomed,
Keep Hector company an hour or two.

80   DIOMEDES   I cannot, lord. I have important business,
The tide whereof is now. – Good night, great Hector.

HECTOR   Give me your hand.

ULYSSES [*aside to Troilus*]
Follow his torch; he goes to Calchas' tent.
I'll keep you company.

TROILUS [*aside to Ulysses*]   Sweet sir, you honour me.

HECTOR   And so, good night.

Exit Diomedes; Ulysses and Troilus following.

85   ACHILLES   Come, come, enter my tent.

Exeunt Achilles, Hector, Ajax and Nestor.

THERSITES   That same Diomed's a false-hearted rogue,
a most unjust knave. I will no more trust him when he
leers than I will a serpent when he hisses. He will
spend his mouth and promise, like Brabbler the hound,

90   but when he performs, astronomers foretell it; it is
prodigious, there will come some change. The sun
borrows of the moon when Diomed keeps his word. I
will rather leave to see Hector than not to dog him.
They say he keeps a Trojan drab, and uses the traitor

95   Calchas his tent. I'll after. Nothing but lechery! All
incontinent varlets!   *Exit.*

5.2   *Enter* DIOMEDES.

DIOMEDES   What, are you up here, ho? Speak.

CALCHAS [*within*]   Who calls?

DIOMEDES   Diomed. Calchas, I think? Where's your
daughter?

5   CALCHAS [*within*]   She comes to you.

Enter TROILUS *and* ULYSSES *at a distance, and,
separate from them,* THERSITES.

ULYSSES [*aside to Troilus*]
Stand where the torch may not discover us.

Enter CRESSIDA.

TROILUS [*aside to Ulysses*]
Cressid comes forth to him.

DIOMEDES [*to Cressida*]   How now, my charge?

CRESSIDA
Now, my sweet guardian. Hark, a word with you.
[*Whispers to him.*]

TROILUS [*aside*]   Yea, so familiar?

10   ULYSSES [*aside to Troilus*]   She will sing any man at first
sight.

THERSITES [*aside*]   And any man may sing her, if he can
take her clef. She's noted.

DIOMEDES   Will you remember?

CRESSIDA   Remember? Yes.   15

DIOMEDES   Nay, but do, then,
And let your mind be coupled with your words.

TROILUS [*aside*]   What should she remember?

ULYSSES [*aside to Troilus*]   List!

CRESSIDA
Sweet honey Greek, tempt me no more to folly.   20

THERSITES [*aside*]   Roguery!

DIOMEDES   Nay then –

CRESSIDA   I'll tell you what –

DIOMEDES
Foh, foh, come, tell a pin! You are forsworn.

CRESSIDA
In faith, I cannot. What would you have me do?   25

THERSITES [*aside*]   A juggling trick: to be secretly open.

DIOMEDES
What did you swear you would bestow on me?

CRESSIDA   I prithee, do not hold me to mine oath.
Bid me do anything but that, sweet Greek.

DIOMEDES   Good night. [*Starts to leave.*]   30

TROILUS [*aside*]   Hold, patience!

ULYSSES [*aside to Troilus*]   How now, Trojan?

CRESSIDA   Diomed –

DIOMEDES
No, no, good night. I'll be your fool no more.

TROILUS [*aside*]   Thy better must.   35

CRESSIDA   Hark, one word in your ear. [*Whispers to
him.*]

TROILUS [*aside*]   O plague and madness!

ULYSSES [*aside to Troilus*]
You are moved, Prince. Let us depart, I pray you,
Lest your displeasure should enlarge itself
To wrathful terms. This place is dangerous,   40
The time right deadly. I beseech you, go.

TROILUS [*aside to Ulysses*]
Behold, I pray you.

ULYSSES [*aside to Troilus*]   Nay, good my lord, go off.
You flow to great distraction. Come, my lord.

TROILUS [*aside to Ulysses*]
I prithee, stay.

ULYSSES [*aside to Troilus*]   You have not patience. Come.

TROILUS [*aside to Ulysses*]
I pray you, stay. By hell and all hell's torments,   45
I will not speak a word.

DIOMEDES [*Starts to leave.*]
And so, good night.

CRESSIDA   Nay, but you part in anger.

TROILUS [*aside*]
Doth that grieve thee? O withered truth!

ULYSSES [*aside to Troilus*]   Why, how now, lord?

TROILUS [*aside to Ulysses*]   By Jove, I will be patient.

CRESSIDA   Guardian! Why, Greek!

DIOMEDES
Foh, foh! Adieu. You palter.   50

CRESSIDA   In faith, I do not. Come hither once again.

ULYSSES [*aside to Troilus*]
You shake, my lord, at something. Will you go?

You will break out.

TROILUS [*aside*]   She strokes his cheek!

ULYSSES [*aside to Troilus*]   Come, come.

TROILUS [*aside to Ulysses*]

55   Nay, stay. By Jove, I will not speak a word.
        There is between my will and all offences
        A guard of patience. Stay a little while.

THERSITES [*aside*]   How the devil Luxury, with his fat
        rump and potato finger, tickles these together! Fry,
        lechery, fry.

60   DIOMEDES [*to Cressida*]   But will you, then?

CRESSIDA   In faith I will, la. Never trust me else.

DIOMEDES   Give me some token for the surety of it.

CRESSIDA   I'll fetch you one.   *Exit.*

ULYSSES [*aside to Troilus*]
        You have sworn patience.

TROILUS [*aside to Ulysses*]   Fear me not, sweet lord.

65   I will not be myself, nor have cognition
        Of what I feel. I am all patience.

        Enter CRESSIDA *with Troilus' sleeve.*

THERSITES [*aside*]   Now the pledge; now, now, now!

CRESSIDA   Here, Diomed, keep this sleeve.
        [*Gives him the sleeve.*]

TROILUS [*aside*]   O beauty, where is thy faith?

70   ULYSSES [*aside to Troilus*]   My lord –

TROILUS [*aside to Ulysses*]
        I will be patient; outwardly I will.

CRESSIDA   You look upon that sleeve? Behold it well.
        He loved me – O false wench! – Give't me again.
        [*Snatches the sleeve.*]

DIOMEDES   Whose was't?

75   CRESSIDA   It is no matter, now I have't again.
        I will not meet with you tomorrow night.
        I prithee, Diomed, visit me no more.

THERSITES [*aside*]   Now she sharpens. Well said,
        whetstone!

80   DIOMEDES   I shall have it.

CRESSIDA   What, this?

DIOMEDES   Ay, that.

CRESSIDA
        O all you gods! – O pretty, pretty pledge!
        Thy master now lies thinking on his bed

85   Of thee and me, and sighs, and takes my glove,
        And gives memorial dainty kisses to it –
        As I kiss thee.
        [*He grabs the sleeve; she tries to get it back.*]

DIOMEDES   Nay, do not snatch it from me.

CRESSIDA
        He that takes that doth take my heart withal.

DIOMEDES   I had your heart before. This follows it.

90   TROILUS [*aside*]   I did swear patience.

CRESSIDA
        You shall not have it, Diomed, faith, you shall not.
        I'll give you something else.

DIOMEDES   I will have this. Whose was it?

CRESSIDA   It is no matter.

DIOMEDES   Come, tell me whose it was.   95

CRESSIDA
        'Twas one's that loved me better than you will.
        But now you have it, take it.

DIOMEDES   Whose was it?

CRESSIDA   By all Diana's waiting-women yond,
        And by herself, I will not tell you whose.

DIOMEDES   Tomorrow will I wear it on my helm   100
        And grieve his spirit that dares not challenge it.

TROILUS [*aside*]
        Wert thou the devil, and wor'st it on thy horn,
        It should be challenged.

CRESSIDA
        Well, well, 'tis done, 'tis past. And yet it is not;
        I will not keep my word.

DIOMEDES   Why then, farewell.   105
        Thou never shalt mock Diomed again.
        [*Starts to leave.*]

CRESSIDA   You shall not go. One cannot speak a word
        But it straight starts you.

DIOMEDES   I do not like this fooling.

TROILUS [*aside*]
        Nor I, by Pluto; but that that likes not you
        Pleases me best.

DIOMEDES   What, shall I come? The hour? 110

CRESSIDA
        Ay, come. – O Jove! – Do, come. – I shall be plagued.

DIOMEDES   Farewell till then.   *Exit.*

CRESSIDA   Good night. I prithee, come. –
        Troilus, farewell! One eye yet looks on thee,
        But with my heart the other eye doth see.
        Ah, poor our sex! This fault in us I find: 115
        The error of our eye directs our mind.
        What error leads must err. O, then conclude:
        Minds swayed by eyes are full of turpitude.   *Exit.*

THERSITES [*aside*]
        A proof of strength she could not publish more,
        Unless she said, 'My mind is now turned whore'. 120

ULYSSES   All's done, my lord.

TROILUS   It is.

ULYSSES   Why stay we, then?

TROILUS   To make a recordation to my soul
        Of every syllable that here was spoke.
        But if I tell how these two did co-act,
        Shall I not lie in publishing a truth?   125
        Sith yet there is a credence in my heart,
        An esperance so obstinately strong,
        That doth invert th'attest of eyes and ears,
        As if those organs had deceptious functions,
        Created only to calumniate.   130
        Was Cressid here?

ULYSSES   I cannot conjure, Trojan.

TROILUS   She was not, sure.

ULYSSES   Most sure she was.

TROILUS   Why, my negation hath no taste of madness.

ULYSSES
        Nor mine, my lord. Cressid was here but now.

TROILUS   Let it not be believed, for womanhood!
 Think, we had mothers. Do not give advantage
 To stubborn critics, apt, without a theme
 For depravation, to square the general sex
 By Cressid's rule. Rather think this not Cressid. 135

ULYSSES
 What hath she done, Prince, that can soil our mothers? 140

TROILUS   Nothing at all, unless that this were she.

THERSITES [*aside*]   Will 'a swagger himself out on 's own
 eyes?

TROILUS   This she? No, this is Diomed's Cressida.
 If beauty have a soul, this is not she; 145
 If souls guide vows, if vows be sanctimonies,
 If sanctimony be the gods' delight,
 If there be rule in unity itself,
 This is not she. O, madness of discourse,
 That cause sets up with and against itself! 150
 Bifold authority, where reason can revolt
 Without perdition, and loss assume all reason
 Without revolt! This is and is not Cressid.
 Within my soul there doth conduce a fight
 Of this strange nature, that a thing inseparate 155
 Divides more wider than the sky and earth,
 And yet the spacious breadth of this division
 Admits no orifex for a point as subtle
 As Ariachne's broken woof to enter.
 Instance, O instance, strong as Pluto's gates, 160
 Cressid is mine, tied with the bonds of heaven;
 Instance, O instance, strong as heaven itself,
 The bonds of heaven are slipped, dissolved and
  loosed,
 And with another knot, five-finger-tied,
 The fractions of her faith, orts of her love, 165
 The fragments, scraps, the bits and greasy relics
 Of her o'ereaten faith, are bound to Diomed.

ULYSSES   May worthy Troilus be half attached
 With that which here his passion doth express?

TROILUS   Ay, Greek, and that shall be divulged well 170
 In characters as red as Mars his heart
 Inflamed with Venus. Never did young man fancy
 With so eternal and so fixed a soul.
 Hark, Greek: as much as I do Cressid love,
 So much by weight hate I her Diomed. 175
 That sleeve is mine that he'll bear in his helm.
 Were it a casque composed by Vulcan's skill,
 My sword should bite it. Not the dreadful spout
 Which shipmen do the hurricano call,
 Constringed in mass by the almighty sun, 180
 Shall dizzy with more clamour Neptune's ear
 In his descent than shall my prompted sword
 Falling on Diomed.

THERSITES [*aside*]   He'll tickle it for his concupy.

TROILUS   O Cressid! O false Cressid! False, false, false! 185
 Let all untruths stand by thy stained name,
 And they'll seem glorious.

ULYSSES   O, contain yourself.
 Your passion draws ears hither.

Enter AENEAS.

AENEAS [*to Troilus*]
 I have been seeking you this hour, my lord.
 Hector, by this, is arming him in Troy. 190
 Ajax, your guard, stays to conduct you home.

TROILUS
 Have with you, Prince. – My courteous lord, adieu. –
 Farewell, revolted fair! – And, Diomed,
 Stand fast, and wear a castle on thy head!

ULYSSES   I'll bring you to the gates. 195

TROILUS   Accept distracted thanks.
    Exeunt Troilus, Aeneas and Ulysses.

THERSITES   Would I could meet that rogue Diomed! I
 would croak like a raven; I would bode, I would bode.
 Patroclus will give me anything for the intelligence of
 this whore. The parrot will not do more for an almond 200
 than he for a commodious drab. Lechery, lechery, still
 wars and lechery; nothing else holds fashion. A
 burning devil take them!   *Exit.*

5.3   *Enter* HECTOR, *armed, and* ANDROMACHE.

ANDROMACHE
 When was my lord so much ungently tempered
 To stop his ears against admonishment?
 Unarm, unarm, and do not fight today.

HECTOR   You train me to offend you. Get you in.
 By all the everlasting gods, I'll go! 5

ANDROMACHE
 My dreams will sure prove ominous to the day.

HECTOR   No more, I say.

Enter CASSANDRA.

CASSANDRA   Where is my brother Hector?

ANDROMACHE
 Here, sister, armed, and bloody in intent.
 Consort with me in loud and dear petition;
 Pursue we him on knees. For I have dreamt 10
 Of bloody turbulence, and this whole night
 Hath nothing been but shapes and forms of slaughter.

CASSANDRA   O, 'tis true.

HECTOR [*Calls out.*]   Ho! Bid my trumpet sound!

CASSANDRA
 No notes of sally, for the heavens, sweet brother.

HECTOR   Begone, I say. The gods have heard me swear. 15

CASSANDRA
 The gods are deaf to hot and peevish vows.
 They are polluted off'rings, more abhorred
 Than spotted livers in the sacrifice.

ANDROMACHE [*to Hector*]
 O, be persuaded! Do not count it holy
 To hurt by being just. It is as lawful, 20
 For we would give much, to use violent thefts,
 And rob in the behalf of charity.

CASSANDRA
 It is the purpose that makes strong the vow,

But vows to every purpose must not hold.
Unarm, sweet Hector.

25 HECTOR   Hold you still, I say.
Mine honour keeps the weather of my fate.
Life every man holds dear, but the dear man
Holds honour far more precious-dear than life.

Enter TROILUS *armed.*

How now, young man, mean'st thou to fight today?
30 ANDROMACHE   Cassandra, call my father to persuade.
Exit Cassandra.
HECTOR
No, faith, young Troilus, doff thy harness, youth.
I am today i'th' vein of chivalry.
Let grow thy sinews till their knots be strong,
And tempt not yet the brushes of the war.
35 Unarm thee, go, and doubt thou not, brave boy,
I'll stand today for thee and me and Troy.
TROILUS   Brother, you have a vice of mercy in you,
Which better fits a lion than a man.
HECTOR
What vice is that? Good Troilus, chide me for it.
40 TROILUS   When many times the captive Grecian falls,
Even in the fan and wind of your fair sword,
You bid them rise and live.
HECTOR   O, 'tis fair play.
TROILUS   Fool's play, by heaven, Hector.
HECTOR   How now, how now?
TROILUS   For th' love of all the gods,
45 Let's leave the hermit Pity with our mothers,
And when we have our armours buckled on,
The venomed vengeance ride upon our swords,
Spur them to ruthful work, rein them from ruth.
HECTOR   Fie, savage, fie!
TROILUS   Hector, then 'tis wars.
50 HECTOR   Troilus, I would not have you fight today.
TROILUS   Who should withhold me?
Not fate, obedience, nor the hand of Mars
Beck'ning with fiery truncheon my retire;
Not Priamus and Hecuba on knees,
55 Their eyes o'ergalled with recourse of tears;
Nor you, my brother, with your true sword drawn
Opposed to hinder me, should stop my way,
But by my ruin.

Enter PRIAM *and* CASSANDRA.

CASSANDRA
Lay hold upon him, Priam, hold him fast;
60 He is thy crutch. Now if thou loose thy stay,
Thou on him leaning, and all Troy on thee,
Fall all together.
PRIAM   Come, Hector, come. Go back.
Thy wife hath dreamt, thy mother hath had visions,
Cassandra doth foresee, and I myself
65 Am like a prophet suddenly enrapt
To tell thee that this day is ominous.
Therefore, come back.

HECTOR   Aeneas is afield,
And I do stand engaged to many Greeks,
Even in the faith of valour, to appear
This morning to them.
70 PRIAM   Ay, but thou shalt not go.
HECTOR   I must not break my faith.
You know me dutiful; therefore, dear sir,
Let me not shame respect, but give me leave
To take that course by your consent and voice
75 Which you do here forbid me, royal Priam.
CASSANDRA   O Priam, yield not to him!
ANDROMACHE   Do not, dear father.
HECTOR   Andromache, I am offended with you.
Upon the love you bear me, get you in.
Exit Andromache.
TROILUS   This foolish, dreaming, superstitious girl
Makes all these bodements.
CASSANDRA   O, farewell, dear Hector!   80
Look how thou diest! Look how thy eye turns
    pale!
Look how thy wounds do bleed at many vents!
Hark, how Troy roars, how Hecuba cries out,
How poor Andromache shrills her dolour forth!
85 Behold, distraction, frenzy and amazement,
Like witless antics, one another meet,
And all cry, 'Hector! Hector's dead! O, Hector!'
TROILUS   Away! Away!
CASSANDRA   Farewell. Yet soft! Hector, I take my leave.
90 Thou dost thyself and all our Troy deceive.   *Exit.*
HECTOR [*to Priam*]
You are amazed, my liege, at her exclaim.
Go in and cheer the town. We'll forth and fight,
Do deeds of praise, and tell you them at night.
PRIAM
Farewell. The gods with safety stand about thee!
Exeunt Priam and Hector at different doors. Alarum.
TROILUS
They are at it, hark! – Proud Diomed, believe,   95
I come to lose my arm or win my sleeve.

Enter PANDARUS *with a letter.*

PANDARUS   Do you hear, my lord? Do you hear?
TROILUS   What now?
PANDARUS   Here's a letter come from yond poor girl.
TROILUS   Let me read. [*Reads.*]   100
PANDARUS   A whoreson phthisic, a whoreson rascally
phthisic so troubles me, and the foolish fortune of this
girl, and what one thing, what another, that I shall
leave you one o'these days. And I have rheum in mine
eyes too, and such an ache in my bones that, unless a   105
man were cursed, I cannot tell what to think on't. –
What says she there?
TROILUS
Words, words, mere words, no matter from the heart;
Th'effect doth operate another way.
[*Tears the letter and tosses it away.*]
Go, wind, to wind! There turn and change together.   110

My love with words and errors still she feeds,
But edifies another with her deeds.   *Exeunt severally.*

5.4   *Alarum; excursions. Enter* THERSITES.

THERSITES   Now they are clapper-clawing one another.
I'll go look on. That dissembling abominable varlet,
Diomed, has got that same scurvy doting foolish young
knave's sleeve of Troy there in his helm. I would fain see
them meet, that that same young Trojan ass that loves   5
the whore there might send that Greekish whoremasterly
villain with the sleeve back to the dissembling luxurious
drab, of a sleeveless errand. O'th' t'other side, the policy
of those crafty swearing rascals – that stale old mouse-
eaten dry cheese, Nestor, and that same dog-fox,   10
Ulysses – is proved not worth a blackberry. They set me
up, in policy, that mongrel cur, Ajax, against that dog of
as bad a kind, Achilles. And now is the cur Ajax prouder
than the cur Achilles, and will not arm today, whereupon
the Grecians began to proclaim barbarism, and policy   15
grows into an ill opinion.

Enter DIOMEDES, *wearing Cressida's sleeve on
his helmet, and* TROILUS *following.*

Soft! Here comes sleeve and t'other. [*Stands aside.*]
TROILUS [*to Diomedes*]
Fly not, for shouldst thou take the river Styx
I would swim after.
DIOMEDES   Thou dost miscall retire.
I do not fly, but advantageous care   20
Withdrew me from the odds of multitude.
Have at thee!   [*They fight.*]
THERSITES   Hold thy whore, Grecian! Now for thy
whore, Trojan! Now the sleeve, now the sleeve!
Exeunt Troilus and Diomedes, fighting.

Enter HECTOR.

HECTOR
What art thou, Greek? Art thou for Hector's match?   25
Art thou of blood and honour?
THERSITES   No, no, I am a rascal, a scurvy railing knave,
a very filthy rogue.
HECTOR   I do believe thee. Live.   *Exit.*
THERSITES   God-a-mercy, that thou wilt believe me; but   30
a plague break thy neck for frighting me! What's
become of the wenching rogues? I think they have
swallowed one another. I would laugh at that miracle –
yet, in a sort, lechery eats itself. I'll seek them.   *Exit.*

5.5   *Enter* DIOMEDES *and* Servant.

DIOMEDES
Go, go, my servant, take thou Troilus' horse;
Present the fair steed to my Lady Cressid.
Fellow, commend my service to her beauty;
Tell her I have chastised the amorous Trojan
And am her knight by proof.
SERVANT   I go, my lord.   *Exit.*   5

Enter AGAMEMNON.

AGAMEMNON   Renew, renew! The fierce Polydamas
Hath beat down Menon; bastard Margareton
Hath Doreus prisoner,
And stands colossus-wise, waving his beam
Upon the pashed corpses of the kings   10
Epistrophus and Cedius. Polyxenes is slain,
Amphimachus and Thoas deadly hurt,
Patroclus ta'en or slain, and Palamedes
Sore hurt and bruised. The dreadful Sagittary
Appals our numbers. Haste we, Diomed,   15
To reinforcement, or we perish all.

Enter NESTOR *with Soldiers bearing Patroclus' body.*

NESTOR [*to his Soldiers*]
Go, bear Patroclus' body to Achilles,
And bid the snail-paced Ajax arm for shame.
Exeunt some Soldiers with the body.
There is a thousand Hectors in the field.
Now here he fights on Galathe his horse,   20
And there lacks work; anon he's there afoot,
And there they fly or die, like scaled schools
Before the belching whale; then is he yonder,
And there the strawy Greeks, ripe for his edge,
Fall down before him, like the mower's swath.   25
Here, there and everywhere he leaves and takes,
Dexterity so obeying appetite
That what he will he does, and does so much
That proof is called impossibility.

Enter ULYSSES.

ULYSSES   O, courage, courage, princes! Great Achilles   30
Is arming, weeping, cursing, vowing vengeance.
Patroclus' wounds have roused his drowsy blood,
Together with his mangled Myrmidons,
That noseless, handless, hacked and chipped, come
to him,
Crying on Hector. Ajax hath lost a friend   35
And foams at mouth, and he is armed and at it,
Roaring for Troilus, who hath done today
Mad and fantastic execution,
Engaging and redeeming of himself
With such a careless force and forceless care   40
As if that luck, in very spite of cunning,
Bade him win all.

Enter AJAX.

AJAX   Troilus! Thou coward Troilus!   *Exit.*
DIOMEDES   Ay, there, there!   *Exit.*
NESTOR   So, so, we draw together.   45

Enter ACHILLES.

ACHILLES   Where is this Hector?
Come, come, thou boy-queller, show thy face!
Know what it is to meet Achilles angry.

Hector! Where's Hector? I will none but Hector.

Exit with others.

5.6   *Enter* AJAX.

AJAX   Troilus, thou coward Troilus, show thy head!

Enter DIOMEDES.

DIOMEDES   Troilus, I say! Where's Troilus?
AJAX   What wouldst thou?
DIOMEDES   I would correct him.
5   AJAX   Were I the general, thou shouldst have my office
Ere that correction. – Troilus, I say! What, Troilus!

Enter TROILUS.

TROILUS
O traitor Diomed! Turn thy false face, thou traitor,
And pay the life thou owest me for my horse!
DIOMEDES   Ha, art thou there?
10   AJAX   I'll fight with him alone. Stand, Diomed.
DIOMEDES   He is my prize. I will not look upon.
TROILUS
Come, both you cogging Greeks. Have at you both!

Enter HECTOR.

Exit Troilus fighting with Ajax and Diomedes.

HECTOR
Yea, Troilus? O, well fought, my youngest brother!

Enter ACHILLES.

ACHILLES
Now do I see thee. Ha! Have at thee, Hector!
[*They fight.*]
15   HECTOR   Pause, if thou wilt.
ACHILLES   I do disdain thy courtesy, proud Trojan.
Be happy that my arms are out of use.
My rest and negligence befriends thee now,
But thou anon shalt hear of me again;
Till when, go seek thy fortune.   *Exit.*
20   HECTOR   Fare thee well.
I would have been much more a fresher man,
Had I expected thee.

Enter TROILUS.

How now, my brother!
TROILUS   Ajax hath ta'en Aeneas. Shall it be?
No, by the flame of yonder glorious heaven,
25   He shall not carry him. I'll be ta'en too,
Or bring him off. Fate, hear me what I say!
I reck not though thou end my life today.   *Exit.*

Enter one in Greek armour.

HECTOR
Stand, stand, thou Greek! Thou art a goodly mark.
No? Wilt thou not? I like thy armour well;
30   I'll frush it and unlock the rivets all,
But I'll be master of it.   *Exit one in armour.*

Wilt thou not, beast, abide?
Why then, fly on. I'll hunt thee for thy hide.

Exit in pursuit.

5.7   *Enter* ACHILLES, *with* Myrmidons.

ACHILLES   Come here about me, you my Myrmidons;
Mark what I say. Attend me where I wheel.
Strike not a stroke, but keep yourselves in breath,
And when I have the bloody Hector found,
Empale him with your weapons round about;   5
In fellest manner execute your arms.
Follow me, sirs, and my proceedings eye.
It is decreed Hector the great must die.   *Exeunt.*

5.8   *Enter* THERSITES; MENELAUS *and*
PARIS *fighting.*

THERSITES   The cuckold and the cuckold-maker are at it.
Now, bull! Now, dog! 'Loo, Paris, 'loo! Now, my
double-horned Spartan! 'Loo, Paris, 'loo! – The bull
has the game. Ware horns, ho!

Exeunt Paris and Menelaus.

Enter Bastard MARGARETON.

MARGARETON   Turn, slave, and fight.   5
THERSITES   What art thou?
MARGARETON   A bastard son of Priam's.
THERSITES   I am a bastard too; I love bastards. I am
bastard begot, bastard instructed, bastard in mind,
bastard in valour, in everything illegitimate. One bear   10
will not bite another, and wherefore should one
bastard? Take heed, the quarrel's most ominous to us.
If the son of a whore fight for a whore, he tempts
judgement. Farewell, bastard.   *Exit.*
MARGARETON   The devil take thee, coward!   *Exit.*   15

5.9   *Enter* HECTOR *dragging the Greek in armour.*

HECTOR   Most putrefied core, so fair without,
Thy goodly armour thus hath cost thy life.
Now is my day's work done. I'll take good breath.
Rest, sword; thou hast thy fill of blood and death.
[*Starts to disarm.*]

Enter ACHILLES *and his* Myrmidons.

ACHILLES   Look, Hector, how the sun begins to set,   5
How ugly night comes breathing at his heels.
Even with the vail and dark'ning of the sun
To close the day up, Hector's life is done.
HECTOR   I am unarmed. Forgo this vantage, Greek.
ACHILLES   Strike, fellows, strike! This is the man I seek.   10
[*They fall upon Hector and kill him.*]
So, Ilium, fall thou! Now, Troy, sink down!
Here lies thy heart, thy sinews and thy bone. –
On, Myrmidons, and cry you all amain,
'Achilles hath the mighty Hector slain'.

[*Retreat sounded from both sides.*]

15 Hark! A retire upon our Grecian part.

MYRMIDON
The Trojan trumpets sound the like, my lord.

ACHILLES
The dragon wing of night o'erspreads the earth
And, stickler-like, the armies separates.
My half-supped sword, that frankly would have fed,
20 Pleased with this dainty bait, thus goes to bed.
 [*Sheathes his sword.*]
Come, tie his body to my horse's tail;
Along the field I will the Trojan trail.
 Exeunt with the bodies.

5.10 *Sound retreat. Enter* AGAMEMNON,
 AJAX, MENELAUS, NESTOR, DIOMEDES
 and the rest, marching to the sound of drums.
 Shout within.

AGAMEMNON Hark, hark, what shout is that?
NESTOR Peace, drums! [*Drums cease.*]
SOLDIERS [*within*]
 Achilles! Achilles! Hector's slain! Achilles!
DIOMEDES The bruit is, Hector's slain, and by Achilles.
5 AJAX If it be so, yet bragless let it be;
Great Hector was as good a man as he.
AGAMEMNON March patiently along. Let one be sent
To pray Achilles see us at our tent.
If in his death the gods have us befriended,
10 Great Troy is ours, and our sharp wars are ended.
 Exeunt marching.

5.11 *Enter* AENEAS, PARIS, *Antenor*
 and DEIPHOBUS.

AENEAS Stand, ho! Yet are we masters of the field.
Never go home; here starve we out the night.

 Enter TROILUS.

TROILUS Hector is slain.
ALL Hector! The gods forbid!
TROILUS He's dead, and at the murderer's horse's tail,
5 In beastly sort, dragged through the shameful field.
Frown on, you heavens, effect your rage with speed!
Sit, gods, upon your thrones and smite at Troy!
I say at once: let your brief plagues be mercy,
And linger not our sure destructions on!
10 AENEAS My lord, you do discomfort all the host.
TROILUS You understand me not that tell me so.
I do not speak of flight, of fear, of death,
But dare all imminence that gods and men
Address their dangers in. Hector is gone.

15 Who shall tell Priam so, or Hecuba?
Let him that will a screech-owl aye be called
Go into Troy, and say their Hector's dead.
There is a word will Priam turn to stone,
Make wells and Niobes of the maids and wives,
20 Cold statues of the youth, and, in a word,
Scare Troy out of itself. But march away.
Hector is dead. There is no more to say.
Stay yet. – You vile abominable tents,
Thus proudly pitched upon our Phrygian plains,
25 Let Titan rise as early as he dare,
I'll through and through you! And, thou great-sized
 coward,
No space of earth shall sunder our two hates.
I'll haunt thee like a wicked conscience still,
That mouldeth goblins swift as frenzy's thoughts.
30 Strike a free march to Troy! With comfort go.
Hope of revenge shall hide our inward woe.

 Enter PANDARUS.

PANDARUS But hear you, hear you!
TROILUS Hence, broker-lackey! Ignomy and shame
Pursue thy life, and live aye with thy name!
 Exeunt all but Pandarus.

PANDARUS A goodly medicine for my aching bones! O
35 world, world, world! Thus is the poor agent despised.
O traitors and bawds, how earnestly are you set a-work
and how ill requited! Why should our endeavour be so
desired and the performance so loathed? What verse
40 for it? What instance for it? Let me see:

 Full merrily the humble-bee doth sing,
 Till he hath lost his honey and his sting;
 And being once subdued in armed tail,
 Sweet honey and sweet notes together fail.

45 Good traders in the flesh, set this in your painted
cloths:

As many as be here of Panders' hall,
Your eyes, half out, weep out at Pandar's fall;
Or if you cannot weep, yet give some groans,
50 Though not for me, yet for your aching bones.
Brethren and sisters of the hold-door trade,
Some two months hence my will shall here be
 made.
It should be now, but that my fear is this:
Some galled goose of Winchester would hiss.
55 Till then I'll sweat and seek about for eases,
And at that time bequeath you my diseases. *Exit.*

Twelfth Night

Twelfth Night, or What You Will was first printed in 1623 as the thirteenth of the comedies in the First Folio. It was probably written in 1601, but the first known performance took place in the hall of the Middle Temple on 2 February 1602, Candlemas Day, the end of the Christmas season of revels. A law student, John Manningham, noted in his diary that it was 'much like the *Comedy of Errors*, or *Menaechmi* in Plautus, but most like and near to that in Italian called *Inganni*'. *Gl'Ingannati* (*The Deceived Ones*), an Italian comedy acted in Siena (1531), provides the main lines of the love plot, whether directly or through sixteenth-century imitations and rewritings, one of which, the tale of Apolonius and Silla in Barnaby Rich's *Rich his Farewell to Military Profession* (1581), Shakespeare knew. The play was revived at Court, under the title of 'Malvolio', on Candlemas Day 1623. Despite Samuel Pepys's affirmation in 1663 that *Twelfth Night* 'is not related at all to the name or day', several of the comedy's themes are pertinent to its festive title: revelry under the aegis of Sir Toby; the giving of presents such as money and pictures; disguise, typical of Christmas revels; the songs of the clown Feste; and – the main theme of the Epiphany – revelation, especially in the final scene.

Twelfth Night is the last of the so-called romantic comedies, and is also the last of Shakespeare's four cross-dressing comedies. Viola, however, is the only Shakespeare heroine to lament – unlike Julia, Portia and Rosalind – the difficulties of performing her role as Duke Orsino's male servant Cesario ('Disguise, I see thou art a wickedness', 2.2.27), thereby drawing attention to the play's emphasis on gender identity and androgyny. The theme of the separated twins recalls, as Manningham notes, *The Comedy of Errors*, but here it is treated in far greater psychological depth, as Viola endeavours to keep her lost brother 'alive' by recreating his image. Antonio's love for Sebastian, with its possible homoerotic implications, parallels the love of another Antonio for Bassanio in *The Merchant of Venice*. Desire is difficult to keep in check in this play, as its weave of gender-crossing infatuations suggests. Desire is also related to class and social mobility. The steward Malvolio's supposed passion for Olivia is at least in part dictated by his ambition to improve his status ('To be count Malvolio', 2.5.34); where he fails, Olivia's waiting-gentlewoman Maria succeeds through her secret marriage to Sir Toby.

Twelfth Night is full of enigmas calling for interpretation: some of these are verbal, such as the 'fustian riddle' of the false love letter from Olivia that traps Malvolio in 2.5; others are visual, notably Feste's teasing invocation of 'the picture of "we three"' (2.3.15–16). The latter is one of several allusions to pictures, including the miniature portrait Olivia gives to Cesario in 3.4. The twin topics of enigmas and pictures come together in the comedy's abiding interest in optical illusion, most explicitly so in the finale, in which the sight of the reunited twins is perceived by Orsino as a visual trick ('A natural perspective, that is and is not' (5.1.213). Optical illusion is one of the many forms of deception at work in the comedy, the most important of which is self-deception, which affects all the characters, with the possible exception of Feste.

Twelfth Night remains among Shakespeare's best loved and most frequently revived plays. In the 1602 performance, it is almost certain that the great comic actor and writer Robert Armin played Feste, and probable that Richard Burbage played the romantic lead Orsino. Performance history is particularly marked by a series of notable Violas, from Peg Woffington and Dorothy Jordan to Ellen Terry and Judi Dench. The role of Malvolio has likewise been a vehicle for memorable comic performances, from those of Charles Macklin and Robert Bensley to those of Laurence Olivier, Donald Sinden and Stephen Fry. Among the many important productions of the play over the centuries, mention might be made of Herbert Beerbohm Tree's spectacular 1901 revival with its ornate Italianate garden set; Harley Granville-Barker's legendary modernist and art deco version in 1912; John Barton's melancholy autumnal staging for the Royal Shakespeare Company in 1969; and more recently, Tim Carroll's brilliant all-male Shakespeare's Globe Theatre production at the Middle Temple in 2002, on the occasion of the fourth centenary of the performance witnessed by Manningham. In this staging, revived in 2012, the true protagonist was Mark Rylance's superb Queen-Elizabeth-like Olivia. The most significant version for cinema is Trevor Nunn's 1996 feature film.

The Arden text is based on the 1623 First Folio.

| VIOLA | *a shipwrecked lady, later disguised as Cesario* |
| CAPTAIN | *of the wrecked ship, who befriends Viola* |

| SEBASTIAN | *Viola's twin brother, also shipwrecked* |
| ANTONIO | *a sea-captain, who befriends Sebastian* |

ORSINO	*Duke of Illyria*
CURIO	
VALENTINE	*gentlemen attending on Orsino*
Two OFFICERS	

OLIVIA	*a countess*
MARIA	*Olivia's waiting-gentlewoman*
SIR TOBY Belch	*Olivia's kinsman*
SIR ANDREW Aguecheek	*companion to Sir Toby*
MALVOLIO	*Olivia's steward*
FESTE	*clown, Olivia's jester*
FABIAN	*a member of Olivia's household*
PRIEST	
SERVANT	*in Olivia's household*

Musicians, Lords, Sailors, Attendants

1.1 *Music. Enter* ORSINO, *Duke of Illyria,*
CURIO *and other Lords.*

ORSINO If music be the food of love, play on,
Give me excess of it, that surfeiting
The appetite may sicken and so die.
That strain again, it had a dying fall.
O, it came o'er my ear like the sweet south
That breathes upon a bank of violets,
Stealing and giving odour. Enough, no more,
'Tis not so sweet now as it was before. [*Music ceases.*]
O spirit of love, how quick and fresh art thou
That, notwithstanding thy capacity
Receiveth as the sea, naught enters there
Of what validity and pitch soe'er
But falls into abatement and low price
Even in a minute. So full of shapes is fancy
That it alone is high fantastical.

CURIO Will you go hunt, my lord?

ORSINO   What, Curio?

CURIO   The hart.

ORSINO Why so I do, the noblest that I have.
O, when mine eyes did see Olivia first
Methought she purged the air of pestilence;
That instant was I turned into a hart,
And my desires, like fell and cruel hounds,
E'er since pursue me.

Enter VALENTINE.

                    How now, what news from her?

VALENTINE So please my lord, I might not be admitted,
But from her handmaid do return this answer:
The element itself till seven years' heat
Shall not behold her face at ample view,
But like a cloistress she will veiled walk
And water once a day her chamber round
With eye-offending brine – all this to season
A brother's dead love, which she would keep fresh
And lasting in her sad remembrance.

ORSINO O, she that hath a heart of that fine frame
To pay this debt of love but to a brother,
How will she love when the rich golden shaft
Hath killed the flock of all affections else
That live in her – when liver, brain and heart,
These sovereign thrones, are all supplied, and filled
Her sweet perfections with one self king!
Away before me to sweet beds of flowers:
Love-thoughts lie rich when canopied with bowers.
                                        Exeunt.

1.2 *Enter* VIOLA, *a* Captain *and Sailors.*

VIOLA What country, friends, is this?

CAPTAIN   This is Illyria, lady.

VIOLA And what should I do in Illyria?
My brother he is in Elysium.
Perchance he is not drowned. What think you, sailors?

CAPTAIN It is perchance that you yourself were saved.

VIOLA
O my poor brother! And so perchance may he be.

CAPTAIN
True, madam, and to comfort you with chance,
Assure yourself, after our ship did split,
When you and those poor number saved with you
Hung on our driving boat, I saw your brother,
Most provident in peril, bind himself –
Courage and hope both teaching him the practice –
To a strong mast that lived upon the sea,
Where, like Arion on the dolphin's back,
I saw him hold acquaintance with the waves
So long as I could see.

VIOLA   For saying so, there's gold.
Mine own escape unfoldeth to my hope –
Whereto thy speech serves for authority –
The like of him. Knowst thou this country?

CAPTAIN Ay, madam, well, for I was bred and born
Not three hours' travel from this very place.

VIOLA Who governs here?

CAPTAIN   A noble duke
In nature as in name.

VIOLA   What is his name?

CAPTAIN Orsino.

VIOLA Orsino: I have heard my father name him.
He was a bachelor then.

CAPTAIN And so is now, or was so very late,
For but a month ago I went from hence,
And then 'twas fresh in murmur – as you know
What great ones do the less will prattle of –
That he did seek the love of fair Olivia.

VIOLA What's she?

CAPTAIN A virtuous maid, the daughter of a count
That died some twelvemonth since, then leaving her
In the protection of his son, her brother,
Who shortly also died, for whose dear love,
They say, she hath abjured the company
And sight of men.

VIOLA   O that I served that lady,
And might not be delivered to the world –
Till I had made mine own occasion mellow –
What my estate is.

CAPTAIN   That were hard to compass,
Because she will admit no kind of suit,
No, not the duke's.

VIOLA There is a fair behaviour in thee, captain,
And though that nature with a beauteous wall
Doth oft close in pollution, yet of thee
I will believe thou hast a mind that suits
With this thy fair and outward character.
I pray thee – and I'll pay thee bounteously –
Conceal me what I am, and be my aid
For such disguise as haply shall become
The form of my intent. I'll serve this duke.
Thou shalt present me as an eunuch to him.
It may be worth thy pains, for I can sing

55 And speak to him in many sorts of music,
That will allow me very worth his service.
What else may hap to time I will commit;
Only shape thou thy silence to my wit.

CAPTAIN   Be you his eunuch, and your mute I'll be.
60 When my tongue blabs then let mine eyes not see.

VIOLA   I thank thee. Lead me on.   *Exeunt.*

1.3   *Enter* SIR TOBY Belch *and* MARIA.

SIR TOBY   What a plague means my niece to take the
death of her brother thus? I am sure care's an enemy to
life.

MARIA   By my troth, Sir Toby, you must come in earlier
5   o'nights. Your cousin, my lady, takes great exceptions
to your ill hours.

SIR TOBY   Why, let her except, before excepted.

MARIA   Ay, but you must confine yourself within the
modest limits of order.

10 SIR TOBY   Confine? I'll confine myself no finer than I
am. These clothes are good enough to drink in, and so
be these boots too; an they be not, let them hang
themselves in their own straps.

MARIA   That quaffing and drinking will undo you. I
15   heard my lady talk of it yesterday, and of a foolish
knight that you brought in one night here to be her
wooer.

SIR TOBY   Who, Sir Andrew Aguecheek?

MARIA   Ay, he.

20 SIR TOBY   He's as tall a man as any's in Illyria.

MARIA   What's that to th' purpose?

SIR TOBY   Why, he has three thousand ducats a year.

MARIA   Ay, but he'll have but a year in all these ducats.
He's a very fool and a prodigal.

25 SIR TOBY   Fie that you'll say so! He plays o'th' viol-de-
gamboys, and speaks three or four languages word for
word without book and hath all the good gifts of
nature.

MARIA   He hath indeed, almost natural, for, besides that
30   he's a fool, he's a great quarreller, and, but that he hath
the gift of a coward to allay the gust he hath in
quarrelling, 'tis thought among the prudent he would
quickly have the gift of a grave.

SIR TOBY   By this hand they are scoundrels and
35   substractors that say so of him. Who are they?

MARIA   They that add, moreover, he's drunk nightly in
your company.

SIR TOBY   With drinking healths to my niece. I'll drink
to her as long as there is a passage in my throat and
40   drink in Illyria. He's a coward and a coistrel that will
not drink to my niece till his brains turn o'th' toe, like
a parish top.

Enter SIR ANDREW Aguecheek.

What, wench, *Castiliano vulgo*, for here comes Sir
Andrew Agueface.

SIR ANDREW   Sir Toby Belch! How now, Sir Toby Belch?   45

SIR TOBY   Sweet Sir Andrew.

SIR ANDREW [*to Maria*]   Bless you, fair shrew.

MARIA   And you too, sir.

SIR TOBY   Accost, Sir Andrew, accost.

SIR ANDREW   What's that?   50

SIR TOBY   My niece's chambermaid.

SIR ANDREW   Good Mistress Accost, I desire better
acquaintance.

MARIA   My name is Mary, sir.

SIR ANDREW   Good Mistress Mary Accost.   55

SIR TOBY   You mistake, knight. 'Accost' is front her,
board her, woo her, assail her.

SIR ANDREW   By my troth I would not undertake her in
this company. Is that the meaning of 'accost'?

MARIA   Fare you well, gentlemen.   60

SIR TOBY   An thou let part so, Sir Andrew, would thou
mightst never draw sword again.

SIR ANDREW   An you part so, mistress, I would I might
never draw sword again. Fair lady, do you think you
have fools in hand?   65

MARIA   Sir, I have not you by th' hand.

SIR ANDREW   Marry, but you shall have, and here's my
hand.

MARIA [*Takes his hand.*]   Now, sir, thought is free. I pray
you, bring your hand to th' buttery-bar, and let it drink.   70
[*Brings his hand to her breast.*]

SIR ANDREW   Wherefore, sweetheart? What's your
metaphor?

MARIA   It's dry, sir.

SIR ANDREW   Why, I think so. I am not such an ass but
I can keep my hand dry. But what's your jest?   75

MARIA   A dry jest, sir.

SIR ANDREW   Are you full of them?

MARIA   Ay, sir, I have them at my fingers' ends. [*Lets go of
his hand.*] Marry, now I let go your hand I am barren.
          Exit.

SIR TOBY   O knight, thou lack'st a cup of canary. When   80
did I see thee so put down?

SIR ANDREW   Never in your life, I think, unless you see
canary put me down. Methinks sometimes I have no
more wit than a Christian or an ordinary man has; but
I am a great eater of beef, and I believe that does harm   85
to my wit.

SIR TOBY   No question.

SIR ANDREW   An I thought that, I'd forswear it. I'll ride
home tomorrow, Sir Toby.

SIR TOBY   *Pourquoi*, my dear knight?   90

SIR ANDREW   What is 'pourquoi'? Do, or not do? I
would I had bestowed that time in the tongues that
I have in fencing, dancing and bear-baiting. O, had I
but followed the arts.

SIR TOBY   Then hadst thou had an excellent head of   95
hair.

SIR ANDREW   Why, would that have mended my hair?

SIR TOBY   Past question, for thou seest it will not curl
by nature.

100 SIR ANDREW But it becomes me well enough, does't not?

SIR TOBY Excellent, it hangs like flax on a distaff, and I hope to see a housewife take thee between her legs and spin it off.

105 SIR ANDREW Faith, I'll home tomorrow, Sir Toby. Your niece will not be seen or, if she be, it's four to one she'll none of me. The count himself here hard by woos her.

SIR TOBY She'll none o'th' count. She'll not match
110 above her degree, neither in estate, years nor wit – I have heard her swear't. Tut, there's life in't, man.

SIR ANDREW I'll stay a month longer. I am a fellow o'th' strangest mind i'th' world. I delight in masques and revels sometimes altogether.

115 SIR TOBY Art thou good at these kickshawses, knight?

SIR ANDREW As any man in Illyria whatsoever he be, under the degree of my betters; and yet I will not compare with an old man.

SIR TOBY What is thy excellence in a galliard, knight?

120 SIR ANDREW Faith, I can cut a caper.

SIR TOBY And I can cut the mutton to't.

SIR ANDREW And I think I have the back-trick simply as strong as any man in Illyria. [*Dances.*]

SIR TOBY Wherefore are these things hid? Wherefore
125 have these gifts a curtain before 'em? Are they like to take dust, like Mistress Mall's picture? Why dost thou not go to church in a galliard and come home in a coranto? My very walk should be a jig. I would not so much as make water but in a sink-apace. What dost
130 thou mean? Is it a world to hide virtues in? I did think by the excellent constitution of thy leg it was formed under the star of a galliard.

SIR ANDREW Ay, 'tis strong, and it does indifferent well in a flame-coloured stock. Shall we set about some
135 revels?

SIR TOBY What shall we do else? Were we not born under Taurus?

SIR ANDREW Taurus? That's sides and heart.

SIR TOBY No, sir, it is legs and thighs – let me see thee
140 caper. [*Sir Andrew capers.*] Ha, higher! Ha, ha, excellent.

Exeunt.

1.4 *Enter* VALENTINE, *and* VIOLA *in man's attire as Cesario.*

VALENTINE If the duke continue these favours towards you, Cesario, you are like to be much advanced. He hath known you but three days, and already you are no stranger.

5 VIOLA You either fear his humour or my negligence that you call in question the continuance of his love. Is he inconstant, sir, in his favours?

VALENTINE No, believe me.

Enter ORSINO, CURIO *and Attendants.*

VIOLA I thank you. Here comes the count.

ORSINO Who saw Cesario, ho? 10

VIOLA On your attendance, my lord; here.

ORSINO [*to Valentine, Curio and Attendants*]
Stand you awhile aloof. [*to Viola*] Cesario,
Thou knowst no less but all: I have unclasped
To thee the book even of my secret soul.
Therefore, good youth, address thy gait unto her, 15
Be not denied access, stand at her doors
And tell them there thy fixed foot shall grow
Till thou have audience.

VIOLA   Sure, my noble lord,
If she be so abandoned to her sorrow
As it is spoke, she never will admit me. 20

ORSINO Be clamorous and leap all civil bounds
Rather than make unprofited return.

VIOLA Say I do speak with her, my lord, what then?

ORSINO O then unfold the passion of my love,
Surprise her with discourse of my dear faith. 25
It shall become thee well to act my woes.
She will attend it better in thy youth
Than in a nuncio's of more grave aspect.

VIOLA I think not so, my lord.

ORSINO   Dear lad, believe it,
For they shall yet belie thy happy years 30
That say thou art a man. Diana's lip
Is not more smooth and rubious. Thy small pipe
Is as the maiden's organ, shrill and sound,
And all is semblative a woman's part.
I know thy constellation is right apt 35
For this affair.
[*to Valentine, Curio and Attendants*]
                               Some four or five attend him –
All, if you will – for I myself am best
When least in company. [*to Viola*] Prosper well in this
And thou shalt live as freely as thy lord,
To call his fortunes thine.

VIOLA   I'll do my best 40
To woo your lady. [*aside*] Yet a barful strife:
Whoe'er I woo, myself would be his wife. *Exeunt.*

1.5 *Enter* MARIA *and* FESTE.

MARIA Nay, either tell me where thou hast been or I will not open my lips so wide as a bristle may enter in way of thy excuse. My lady will hang thee for thy absence.

FESTE Let her hang me. He that is well hanged in this 5
world needs to fear no colours.

MARIA Make that good.

FESTE He shall see none to fear.

MARIA A good lenten answer. I can tell thee where that saying was born of 'I fear no colours'. 10

FESTE Where, good Mistress Mary?

MARIA In the wars, and that may you be bold to say in your foolery.

FESTE Well, God give them wisdom that have it; and those that are fools, let them use their talents. 15

MARIA   Yet you will be hanged for being so long absent. Or to be turned away – is not that as good as a hanging to you?

FESTE   Many a good hanging prevents a bad marriage; and for turning away let summer bear it out.

MARIA   You are resolute then?

FESTE   Not so neither, but I am resolved on two points.

MARIA   That if one break the other will hold; or if both break your gaskins fall.

FESTE   Apt in good faith, very apt. Well, go thy way. If Sir Toby would leave drinking, thou wert as witty a piece of Eve's flesh as any in Illyria.

MARIA   Peace, you rogue, no more o'that.

Enter Lady OLIVIA *with* MALVOLIO *and Attendants.*

Here comes my lady; make your excuse wisely you were best.   *Exit.*

FESTE   Wit, an't be thy will, put me into good fooling! Those wits that think they have thee do very oft prove fools, and I that am sure I lack thee may pass for a wise man. For what says Quinapalus? 'Better a witty fool than a foolish wit.' [*to Olivia*] God bless thee, lady.

OLIVIA   Take the fool away.

FESTE   Do you not hear, fellows? Take away the lady.

OLIVIA   Go to, you're a dry fool, I'll no more of you. Besides, you grow dishonest.

FESTE   Two faults, madonna, that drink and good counsel will amend: for give the dry fool drink, then is the fool not dry; bid the dishonest man mend himself – if he mend, he is no longer dishonest, if he cannot, let the botcher mend him. Anything that's mended is but patched: virtue that transgresses is but patched with sin, and sin that amends is but patched with virtue. If that this simple syllogism will serve, so; if it will not, what remedy? As there is no true cuckold but calamity, so beauty's a flower. – The lady bade take away the fool, therefore I say again, take her away.

OLIVIA   Sir, I bade them take away you.

FESTE   Misprision in the highest degree! Lady, *cucullus non facit monachum* – that's as much to say as I wear not motley in my brain. Good madonna, give me leave to prove you a fool.

OLIVIA   Can you do it?

FESTE   Dexteriously, good madonna.

OLIVIA   Make your proof.

FESTE   I must catechize you for it, madonna. Good my mouse of virtue, answer me.

OLIVIA   Well, sir, for want of other idleness I'll bide your proof.

FESTE   Good madonna, why mourn'st thou?

OLIVIA   Good fool, for my brother's death.

FESTE   I think his soul is in hell, madonna.

OLIVIA   I know his soul is in heaven, fool.

FESTE   The more fool, madonna, to mourn for your brother's soul being in heaven. – Take away the fool, gentlemen.

OLIVIA   What think you of this fool, Malvolio, doth he not mend?

MALVOLIO   Yes, and shall do till the pangs of death shake him. Infirmity, that decays the wise, doth ever make the better fool.

FESTE   God send you, sir, a speedy infirmity, for the better increasing your folly. Sir Toby will be sworn that I am no fox, but he will not pass his word for twopence that you are no fool.

OLIVIA   How say you to that, Malvolio?

MALVOLIO   I marvel your ladyship takes delight in such a barren rascal. I saw him put down the other day with an ordinary fool that has no more brain than a stone. Look you now, he's out of his guard already. Unless you laugh and minister occasion to him, he is gagged. I protest I take these wise men that crow so at these set kind of fools no better than the fools' zanies.

OLIVIA   O, you are sick of self-love, Malvolio, and taste with a distempered appetite. To be generous, guiltless and of free disposition is to take those things for bird-bolts that you deem cannon bullets. There is no slander in an allowed fool though he do nothing but rail; nor no railing in a known discreet man though he do nothing but reprove.

FESTE   Now Mercury endue thee with leasing, for thou speak'st well of fools.

Enter MARIA.

MARIA   Madam, there is at the gate a young gentleman much desires to speak with you.

OLIVIA   From the Count Orsino, is it?

MARIA   I know not, madam. 'Tis a fair young man, and well attended.

OLIVIA   Who of my people hold him in delay?

MARIA   Sir Toby, madam, your kinsman.

OLIVIA   Fetch him off, I pray you, he speaks nothing but madman. Fie on him.   *Exit Maria.* Go you, Malvolio. If it be a suit from the count, I am sick, or not at home. What you will to dismiss it.   *Exit Malvolio.* Now you see, sir, how your fooling grows old and people dislike it.

FESTE   Thou hast spoke for us, madonna, as if thy eldest son should be a fool,

Enter SIR TOBY.

whose skull Jove cram with brains, for here comes one of thy kin has a most weak pia mater.

OLIVIA   By mine honour, half drunk. [*to Sir Toby*] What is he at the gate, cousin?

SIR TOBY   A gentleman.

OLIVIA   A gentleman? What gentleman?

SIR TOBY   'Tis a gentleman here. [*Belches.*] A plague o'these pickle herring! [*to Feste*] How now, sot?

FESTE   Good Sir Toby.

OLIVIA   Cousin, cousin, how have you come so early by this lethargy?

SIR TOBY   Lechery? I defy lechery. There's one at the gate.

OLIVIA   Ay, marry, what is he?

125 SIR TOBY   Let him be the devil an he will, I care not. Give me faith, say I. Well, it's all one.   *Exit.*

OLIVIA   What's a drunken man like, fool?

FESTE   Like a drowned man, a fool and a madman: one draught above heat makes him a fool, the second mads 130 him and a third drowns him.

OLIVIA   Go thou and seek the crowner, and let him sit o'my coz, for he's in the third degree of drink – he's drowned. Go look after him.

FESTE   He is but mad yet, madonna, and the fool shall 135 look to the madman.   *Exit.*

Enter MALVOLIO.

MALVOLIO   Madam, yon young fellow swears he will speak with you. I told him you were sick. He takes on him to understand so much, and therefore comes to speak with you. I told him you were asleep. He seems 140 to have a foreknowledge of that too, and therefore comes to speak with you. What is to be said to him, lady? He's fortified against any denial.

OLIVIA   Tell him he shall not speak with me.

MALVOLIO   Has been told so, and he says he'll stand at 145 your door like a sheriff's post and be the supporter to a bench, but he'll speak with you.

OLIVIA   What kind o'man is he?

MALVOLIO   Why, of mankind.

OLIVIA   What manner of man?

150 MALVOLIO   Of very ill manner: he'll speak with you, will you or no.

OLIVIA   Of what personage and years is he?

MALVOLIO   Not yet old enough for a man, nor young enough for a boy, as a squash is before 'tis a peascod, 155 or a codling when 'tis almost an apple. 'Tis with him in standing water between boy and man. He is very well favoured, and he speaks very shrewishly. One would think his mother's milk were scarce out of him.

160 OLIVIA   Let him approach. Call in my gentlewoman.

MALVOLIO [*Goes to door.*]   Gentlewoman, my lady calls.
                                                    Exit.

Enter MARIA.

OLIVIA   Give me my veil; come throw it o'er my face. We'll once more hear Orsino's embassy.

Enter VIOLA *as Cesario.*

VIOLA   The honourable lady of the house, which is 165 she?

OLIVIA   Speak to me, I shall answer for her. Your will?

VIOLA   Most radiant, exquisite and unmatchable beauty – I pray you, tell me if this be the lady of the house, for I never saw her. I would be loath to cast away my 170 speech, for, besides that it is excellently well penned, I have taken great pains to con it. Good beauties, let me

sustain no scorn: I am very comptible, even to the least sinister usage.

OLIVIA   Whence came you, sir?

VIOLA   I can say little more than I have studied, and that 175 question's out of my part. Good gentle one, give me modest assurance if you be the lady of the house, that I may proceed in my speech.

OLIVIA   Are you a comedian?

VIOLA   No, my profound heart. And yet – by the very 180 fangs of malice, I swear – I am not that I play. Are you the lady of the house?

OLIVIA   If I do not usurp myself, I am.

VIOLA   Most certain if you are she you do usurp yourself, for what is yours to bestow is not yours to 185 reserve. But this is from my commission. I will on with my speech in your praise, and then show you the heart of my message.

OLIVIA   Come to what is important in't – I forgive you the praise.   190

VIOLA   Alas, I took great pains to study it, and 'tis poetical.

OLIVIA   It is the more like to be feigned, I pray you keep it in. I heard you were saucy at my gates, and allowed your approach rather to wonder at you than to hear 195 you. If you be not mad, be gone. If you have reason, be brief. 'Tis not that time of moon with me to make one in so skipping a dialogue.

MARIA   Will you hoist sail, sir? Here lies your way.

VIOLA   No, good swabber, I am to hull here a little 200 longer. – Some mollification for your giant, sweet lady. Tell me your mind, I am a messenger.

OLIVIA   Sure you have some hideous matter to deliver when the courtesy of it is so fearful. Speak your office.   205

VIOLA   It alone concerns your ear. I bring no overture of war, no taxation of homage. I hold the olive in my hand: my words are as full of peace as matter.

OLIVIA   Yet you began rudely. What are you? What would you?   210

VIOLA   The rudeness that hath appeared in me have I learned from my entertainment. What I am and what I would are as secret as maidenhead: to your ears, divinity; to any other's, profanation.

OLIVIA [*to Maria and Attendants*] Give us the place alone, 215 we will hear this divinity.

                          Exeunt Maria and Attendants.

Now sir, what is your text?

VIOLA   Most sweet lady –

OLIVIA   A comfortable doctrine, and much may be said of it. Where lies your text?   220

VIOLA   In Orsino's bosom.

OLIVIA   In his bosom? In what chapter of his bosom?

VIOLA

To answer by the method, in the first of his heart.

OLIVIA   O, I have read it, it is heresy. Have you no more to say?   225

VIOLA   Good madam, let me see your face.

OLIVIA   Have you any commission from your lord to
negotiate with my face? You are now out of your text.
But we will draw the curtain and show you the picture.
230   [*Unveils.*] Look you, sir, such a one I was this present.
Is't not well done?

VIOLA   Excellently done, if God did all.

OLIVIA
'Tis in grain, sir, 'twill endure wind and weather.

VIOLA   'Tis beauty truly blent, whose red and white
235   Nature's own sweet and cunning hand laid on.
Lady, you are the cruell'st she alive
If you will lead these graces to the grave
And leave the world no copy.

OLIVIA   O sir, I will not be so hard-hearted. I will give
240   out diverse schedules of my beauty. It shall be
inventoried, and every particle and utensil labelled to
my will, as, item, two lips, indifferent red; item, two
grey eyes, with lids to them; item, one neck, one chin
and so forth. Were you sent hither to praise me?

245   VIOLA   I see you what you are, you are too proud;
But if you were the devil you are fair.
My lord and master loves you. O, such love
Could be but recompensed, though you were crowned
The nonpareil of beauty.

OLIVIA   How does he love me?

250   VIOLA   With adoration's fertile tears,
With groans that thunder love, with sighs of fire.

OLIVIA
Your lord does know my mind: I cannot love him.
Yet I suppose him virtuous, know him noble,
Of great estate, of fresh and stainless youth,
255   In voices well divulged, free, learn'd and valiant,
And in dimension and the shape of nature
A gracious person; but yet I cannot love him.
He might have took his answer long ago.

VIOLA   If I did love you in my master's flame,
260   With such a suffering, such a deadly life,
In your denial I would find no sense,
I would not understand it.

OLIVIA   Why, what would you?

VIOLA   Make me a willow cabin at your gate
And call upon my soul within the house;
265   Write loyal cantons of contemned love
And sing them loud even in the dead of night;
Hallow your name to the reverberate hills
And make the babbling gossip of the air
Cry out 'Olivia!' O, you should not rest
270   Between the elements of air and earth
But you should pity me.

OLIVIA   You might do much.
What is your parentage?

VIOLA   Above my fortunes, yet my state is well:
I am a gentleman.

OLIVIA   Get you to your lord.
275   I cannot love him; let him send no more,
Unless perchance you come to me again
To tell me how he takes it. Fare you well.

I thank you for your pains.   [*Offers money.*]
Spend this for me.

VIOLA   I am no fee'd post, lady; keep your purse.
280   My master, not myself, lacks recompense.
Love make his heart of flint that you shall love,
And let your fervour like my master's be
Placed in contempt. Farewell, fair cruelty.   *Exit.*

OLIVIA   'What is your parentage?'
285   'Above my fortunes, yet my state is well:
I am a gentleman.' I'll be sworn thou art –
Thy tongue, thy face, thy limbs, actions and spirit
Do give thee fivefold blazon. Not too fast, soft, soft –
Unless the master were the man. How now?
290   Even so quickly may one catch the plague?
Methinks I feel this youth's perfections
With an invisible and subtle stealth
To creep in at mine eyes. Well, let it be.
What ho, Malvolio.

Enter MALVOLIO.

MALVOLIO   Here, madam, at your service.

OLIVIA   Run after that same peevish messenger   295
The county's man. He left this ring behind him,
Would I or not. Tell him I'll none of it.
Desire him not to flatter with his lord,
Nor hold him up with hopes: I am not for him.
If that the youth will come this way tomorrow,   300
I'll give him reasons for't. Hie thee, Malvolio.

MALVOLIO   Madam, I will.   *Exit.*

OLIVIA   I do I know not what, and fear to find
Mine eye too great a flatterer for my mind.
Fate, show thy force, ourselves we do not owe.   305
What is decreed must be – and be this so.   *Exit.*

2.1   *Enter* ANTONIO *and* SEBASTIAN.

ANTONIO   Will you stay no longer, nor will you not that
I go with you?

SEBASTIAN   By your patience, no. My stars shine darkly
over me, the malignancy of my fate might perhaps
distemper yours. Therefore I shall crave of you your   5
leave that I may bear my evils alone. It were a bad
recompense for your love to lay any of them on you.

ANTONIO   Let me yet know of you whither you are
bound.

SEBASTIAN   No, sooth, sir. My determinate voyage is   10
mere extravagancy. But I perceive in you so excellent a
touch of modesty that you will not extort from me what
I am willing to keep in, therefore it charges me in
manners the rather to express myself. You must know
of me then, Antonio, my name is Sebastian, which I   15
called Roderigo. My father was that Sebastian of
Messaline whom I know you have heard of. He left
behind him myself and a sister, both born in an hour. If
the heavens had been pleased, would we had so ended.
But you, sir, altered that, for some hour before you took   20
me from the breach of the sea was my sister drowned.

ANTONIO   Alas the day!

SEBASTIAN   A lady, sir, though it was said she much resembled me, was yet of many accounted beautiful. But though I could not with such estimable wonder over-far believe that, yet thus far I will boldly publish her: she bore a mind that envy could not but call fair. She is drowned already, sir, with salt water, though I seem to drown her remembrance again with more.

ANTONIO   Pardon me, sir, your bad entertainment.

SEBASTIAN   O good Antonio, forgive me your trouble.

ANTONIO   If you will not murder me for my love, let me be your servant.

SEBASTIAN   If you will not undo what you have done, that is kill him whom you have recovered, desire it not. Fare ye well at once. My bosom is full of kindness, and I am yet so near the manners of my mother that upon the least occasion more mine eyes will tell tales of me. I am bound to the Count Orsino's court. Farewell.

Exit.

ANTONIO   The gentleness of all the gods go with thee.
I have many enemies in Orsino's court,
Else would I very shortly see thee there.
But come what may I do adore thee so
That danger shall seem sport, and I will go.   *Exit.*

2.2   *Enter* VIOLA *as Cesario and* MALVOLIO *at separate doors.*

MALVOLIO   Were not you e'en now with the Countess Olivia?

VIOLA   Even now, sir; on a moderate pace I have since arrived but hither.

MALVOLIO   She returns this ring to you, sir. [*Shows ring.*] You might have saved me my pains to have taken it away yourself. She adds, moreover, that you should put your lord into a desperate assurance she will none of him. And one thing more: that you be never so hardy to come again in his affairs, unless it be to report your lord's taking of this. [*Offers ring.*] Receive it so.

VIOLA   She took the ring of me, I'll none of it.

MALVOLIO   Come, sir, you peevishly threw it to her, and her will is it should be so returned. [*Throws down ring.*] If it be worth stooping for, there it lies, in your eye; if not, be it his that finds it.   *Exit.*

VIOLA [*Picks up ring.*]
I left no ring with her. What means this lady?
Fortune forbid my outside have not charmed her.
She made good view of me, indeed so much
That methought her eyes had lost her tongue,
For she did speak in starts, distractedly.
She loves me sure. The cunning of her passion
Invites me in this churlish messenger.
None of my lord's ring? Why, he sent her none.
I am the man. If it be so, as 'tis,
Poor lady, she were better love a dream.
Disguise, I see thou art a wickedness,
Wherein the pregnant enemy does much.

How easy is it for the proper false
In women's waxen hearts to set their forms.
Alas, our frailty is the cause, not we,
For such as we are made of, such we be.
How will this fadge? My master loves her dearly,
And I, poor monster, fond as much on him,
And she, mistaken, seems to dote on me.
What will become of this? As I am man,
My state is desperate for my master's love;
As I am woman, now alas the day,
What thriftless sighs shall poor Olivia breathe?
O time, thou must untangle this, not I.
It is too hard a knot for me t'untie.   *Exit.*

2.3   *Enter* SIR TOBY *and* SIR ANDREW.

SIR TOBY   Approach, Sir Andrew. Not to be abed after midnight is to be up betimes, and *diluculo surgere*, thou knowst.

SIR ANDREW   Nay, by my troth I know not; but I know to be up late is to be up late.

SIR TOBY   A false conclusion. I hate it as an unfilled can. To be up after midnight and to go to bed then is early, so that to go to bed after midnight is to go to bed betimes. Does not our life consist of the four elements?

SIR ANDREW   Faith, so they say, but I think it rather consists of eating and drinking.

SIR TOBY   Thou'rt a scholar; let us therefore eat and drink. [*Calls.*] Marian, I say, a stoup of wine.

Enter FESTE.

SIR ANDREW   Here comes the fool, i'faith.

FESTE   How now, my hearts? Did you never see the picture of 'we three'?

SIR TOBY   Welcome, ass. Now let's have a catch.

SIR ANDREW   By my troth the fool has an excellent breast. I had rather than forty shillings I had such a leg, and so sweet a breath to sing, as the fool has. In sooth, thou wast in very gracious fooling last night, when thou spok'st of Pigrogromitus, of the Vapians passing the equinoctial of Queubus. 'Twas very good, i'faith. I sent thee sixpence for thy leman. Hadst it?

FESTE   I did impeticos thy gratility – for Malvolio's nose is no whipstock, my lady has a white hand and the Myrmidons are no bottle-ale houses.

SIR ANDREW   Excellent! Why, this is the best fooling, when all is done. Now a song.

SIR TOBY [*to Feste*]   Come on, there is sixpence for you. Let's have a song.

SIR ANDREW [*to Feste*]   There's a testril of me too. If one knight give a –

FESTE   Would you have a love-song, or a song of good life?

SIR TOBY   A love-song, a love-song.

SIR ANDREW   Ay, ay. I care not for good life.

FESTE [*Sings.*]
O mistress mine, where are you roaming?

O stay and hear, your true love's coming,
    That can sing both high and low.
40   Trip no further, pretty sweeting;
    Journeys end in lovers meeting,
      Every wise man's son doth know.

SIR ANDREW   Excellent good, i'faith.
45 SIR TOBY   Good, good.

FESTE [*Sings.*]
    What is love? 'Tis not hereafter,
    Present mirth hath present laughter.
      What's to come is still unsure.
    In delay there lies no plenty,
50   Then come kiss me, sweet and twenty.
      Youth's a stuff will not endure.

SIR ANDREW   A mellifluous voice, as I am true knight.
SIR TOBY   A contagious breath.
SIR ANDREW   Very sweet and contagious, i'faith.
55 SIR TOBY   To hear by the nose it is dulcet in contagion!
But shall we make the welkin dance indeed? Shall we
rouse the night-owl in a catch that will draw three souls
out of one weaver? Shall we do that?
SIR ANDREW   An you love me, let's do't. I am dog at a
60 catch.
FESTE   By'r Lady, sir, and some dogs will catch well.
SIR ANDREW   Most certain. Let our catch be 'Thou
knave'.
FESTE   'Hold thy peace, thou knave', knight? I shall be
65 constrained in't to call thee knave, knight.
SIR ANDREW   'Tis not the first time I have constrained
one to call me knave. Begin, fool. It begins 'Hold thy
peace'.
FESTE   I shall never begin if I hold my peace.
70 SIR ANDREW   Good, i'faith. Come, begin.
      [*They sing the catch.*]

Enter MARIA.

MARIA   What a caterwauling do you keep here! If my
lady have not called up her steward Malvolio and bid
him turn you out of doors, never trust me.
75 SIR TOBY   My lady's a Cathayan, we are politicians,
Malvolio's a Peg-o'-Ramsey and [*singing*] 'Three
merry men be we'. Am not I consanguineous? Am I
not of her blood? Tilly-vally, lady! [*Sings.*] 'There
dwelt a man in Babylon, lady, lady.'
FESTE   Beshrew me, the knight's in admirable fooling.
80 SIR ANDREW   Ay, he does well enough if he be disposed,
and so do I too. He does it with a better grace, but I do
it more natural.
SIR TOBY [*Sings.*]   O'the twelfth day of December –
MARIA   For the love o'God, peace.

Enter MALVOLIO.

85 MALVOLIO   My masters, are you mad or what are you?
Have you no wit, manners nor honesty but to gabble
like tinkers at this time of night? Do ye make an
alehouse of my lady's house that ye squeak out your
coziers' catches without any mitigation or remorse of
90 voice? Is there no respect of place, persons nor time in
you?
SIR TOBY   We did keep time, sir, in our catches. Sneck
up!
MALVOLIO   Sir Toby, I must be round with you. My
95 lady bade me tell you that though she harbours you as
her kinsman she's nothing allied to your disorders. If
you can separate yourself and your misdemeanours,
you are welcome to the house; if not, an it would please
you to take leave of her, she is very willing to bid you
100 farewell.
SIR TOBY [*Sings.*]
    Farewell, dear heart, since I must needs be gone.
MARIA   Nay, good Sir Toby.
FESTE [*Sings.*]
    His eyes do show his days are almost done.
MALVOLIO   Is't even so?
105 SIR TOBY [*Sings.*]   But I will never die.
FESTE [*Sings.*]   Sir Toby, there you lie.
MALVOLIO   This is much credit to you.
SIR TOBY [*Sings.*]   Shall I bid him go?
FESTE [*Sings.*]   What an if you do?
110 SIR TOBY [*Sings.*]   Shall I bid him go, and spare not?
FESTE [*Sings.*]   O no, no, no, no, you dare not.
SIR TOBY [*to Feste*]   Out o'tune, sir – ye lie. [*to Malvolio*]
Art any more than a steward? Dost thou think because
thou art virtuous there shall be no more cakes and
115 ale?
FESTE   Yes, by Saint Anne, and ginger shall be hot i'th'
mouth too.
SIR TOBY   Thou'rt i'th' right. [*to Malvolio*] Go, sir, rub
your chain with crumbs. – A stoup of wine, Maria.
120 MALVOLIO   Mistress Mary, if you prized my lady's
favour at anything more than contempt, you would not
give means for this uncivil rule. She shall know of it,
by this hand.   *Exit.*
MARIA   Go shake your ears.
125 SIR ANDREW   'Twere as good a deed as to drink when a
man's a-hungry to challenge him the field and then to
break promise with him and make a fool of him.
SIR TOBY   Do't, knight. I'll write thee a challenge, or
I'll deliver thy indignation to him by word of mouth.
130 MARIA   Sweet Sir Toby, be patient for tonight. Since the
youth of the count's was today with my lady, she is
much out of quiet. For Monsieur Malvolio, let me
alone with him. If I do not gull him into a nayword and
make him a common recreation, do not think I have
135 wit enough to lie straight in my bed. I know I can do it.
SIR TOBY   Possess us, possess us. Tell us something of
him.
MARIA   Marry, sir, sometimes he is a kind of Puritan.
SIR ANDREW   O, if I thought that, I'd beat him like a
140 dog.
SIR TOBY   What, for being a Puritan? Thy exquisite
reason, dear knight?
SIR ANDREW   I have no exquisite reason for't, but I
have reason good enough.

145 MARIA The devil a Puritan that he is, or anything
constantly but a time-pleaser; an affectioned ass that
cons state without book and utters it by great swathes;
the best persuaded of himself, so crammed, as he
thinks, with excellencies that it is his grounds of faith
150 that all that look on him love him, and on that vice in
him will my revenge find notable cause to work.

SIR TOBY What wilt thou do?

MARIA I will drop in his way some obscure epistles of
love, wherein by the colour of his beard, the shape of
155 his leg, the manner of his gait, the expressure of his
eye, forehead and complexion he shall find himself
most feelingly personated. I can write very like my lady
your niece. On a forgotten matter we can hardly make
distinction of our hands.

160 SIR TOBY Excellent, I smell a device.

SIR ANDREW I have't in my nose too.

SIR TOBY He shall think by the letters that thou wilt
drop that they come from my niece, and that she's in
love with him.

165 MARIA My purpose is indeed a horse of that colour.

SIR ANDREW And your horse now would make him an
ass.

MARIA As I doubt not.

SIR ANDREW O, 'twill be admirable.

170 MARIA Sport royal, I warrant you. I know my physic
will work with him. I will plant you two – and let the
fool make a third – where he shall find the letter.
Observe his construction of it. For this night, to bed
and dream on the event. Farewell.   *Exit.*

175 SIR TOBY Good night, Penthesilea.

SIR ANDREW Before me, she's a good wench.

SIR TOBY She's a beagle true bred, and one that adores
me. What o'that?

SIR ANDREW I was adored once too.

180 SIR TOBY Let's to bed, knight. Thou hadst need send
for more money.

SIR ANDREW If I cannot recover your niece, I am a foul
way out.

SIR TOBY Send for money, knight. If thou hast her not
185 i'th' end, call me cut.

SIR ANDREW If I do not, never trust me, take it how you
will.

SIR TOBY Come, come, I'll go burn some sack; 'tis too
late to go to bed now. Come, knight, come, knight.
                                             Exeunt.

2.4   *Enter* ORSINO, VIOLA *as Cesario,*
            CURIO *and others.*

ORSINO
Give me some music. Now good morrow, friends.
Now good Cesario, but that piece of song,
That old and antic song we heard last night:
Methought it did relieve my passion much,
5 More than light airs and recollected terms
Of these most brisk and giddy-paced times.

Come, but one verse.

CURIO He is not here, so please your lordship, that
should sing it.

ORSINO Who was it?   10

CURIO Feste the jester, my lord, a fool that the Lady
Olivia's father took much delight in. He is about the
house.

ORSINO Seek him out, and play the tune the while.
                          Music plays. Exit Curio.
[*to Viola*] Come hither, boy. If ever thou shalt love,   15
In the sweet pangs of it remember me;
For such as I am all true lovers are,
Unstaid and skittish in all motions else
Save in the constant image of the creature
That is beloved. How dost thou like this tune?   20

VIOLA It gives a very echo to the seat
Where love is throned.

ORSINO   Thou dost speak masterly.
My life upon't, young though thou art, thine eye
Hath stayed upon some favour that it loves.
Hath it not, boy?

VIOLA   A little, by your favour.   25

ORSINO What kind of woman is't?

VIOLA   Of your complexion.

ORSINO
She is not worth thee then. What years, i'faith?

VIOLA About your years, my lord.

ORSINO Too old, by heaven. Let still the woman take
An elder than herself; so wears she to him,   30
So sways she level in her husband's heart.
For, boy, however we do praise ourselves,
Our fancies are more giddy and unfirm,
More longing wavering, sooner lost and worn
Than women's are.

VIOLA   I think it well, my lord.   35

ORSINO Then let thy love be younger than thyself,
Or thy affection cannot hold the bent;
For women are as roses, whose fair flower
Being once displayed doth fall that very hour.

VIOLA And so they are. Alas that they are so,   40
To die even when they to perfection grow.

            Enter CURIO *and* FESTE.

ORSINO [*to Feste*]
O fellow, come, the song we had last night.
Mark it, Cesario, it is old and plain.
The spinsters, and the knitters in the sun
And the free maids that weave their thread with bones 45
Do use to chant it. It is silly sooth
And dallies with the innocence of love
Like the old age.

FESTE Are you ready, sir?

ORSINO I prithee sing.   50

FESTE [*Sings.*]
Come away, come away death,
And in sad cypress let me be laid.
Fie away, fie away breath,

I am slain by a fair cruel maid.
55 My shroud of white, stuck all with yew,
O prepare it.
My part of death no one so true
Did share it.

60 Not a flower, not a flower sweet
On my black coffin let there be strewn.
Not a friend, not a friend greet
My poor corpse, where my bones shall be thrown.
A thousand thousand sighs to save,
Lay me, O where
65 Sad true love never find my grave,
To weep there.

ORSINO   There's for thy pains.   [*Gives money.*]
FESTE   No pains, sir. I take pleasure in singing, sir.
ORSINO   I'll pay thy pleasure then.
70 FESTE   Truly, sir, and pleasure will be paid, one time or
another.
ORSINO   Give me now leave to leave thee.
FESTE   Now the melancholy god protect thee, and the
tailor make thy doublet of changeable taffeta, for thy
75 mind is a very opal. I would have men of such
constancy put to sea, that their business might be
everything and their intent everywhere, for that's it
that always makes a good voyage of nothing. Farewell.
Exit.
ORSINO   Let all the rest give place.
Exeunt all but Orsino and Viola.
Once more, Cesario,
80 Get thee to yon same sovereign cruelty.
Tell her my love, more noble than the world,
Prizes not quantity of dirty lands.
The parts that fortune hath bestowed upon her
Tell her I hold as giddily as fortune;
85 But 'tis that miracle and queen of gems
That nature pranks her in attracts my soul.
VIOLA   But if she cannot love you, sir?
ORSINO   I cannot be so answered.
VIOLA   Sooth, but you must.
Say that some lady, as perhaps there is,
90 Hath for your love as great a pang of heart
As you have for Olivia. You cannot love her;
You tell her so. Must she not then be answered?
ORSINO   There is no woman's sides
Can bide the beating of so strong a passion
95 As love doth give my heart; no woman's heart
So big to hold so much – they lack retention.
Alas, their love may be called appetite,
No motion of the liver but the palate,
That suffer surfeit, cloyment and revolt.
100 But mine is all as hungry as the sea,
And can digest as much. Make no compare
Between that love a woman can bear me
And that I owe Olivia.
VIOLA   Ay, but I know –
ORSINO   What dost thou know?
105 VIOLA   Too well what love women to men may owe.

In faith, they are as true of heart as we.
My father had a daughter loved a man,
As it might be, perhaps, were I a woman,
I should your lordship.
ORSINO   And what's her history?
VIOLA   A blank, my lord. She never told her love,   110
But let concealment like a worm i'th' bud
Feed on her damask cheek. She pined in thought,
And with a green and yellow melancholy
She sat like Patience on a monument,
Smiling at grief. Was not this love indeed?   115
We men may say more, swear more, but indeed
Our shows are more than will, for still we prove
Much in our vows, but little in our love.
ORSINO   But died thy sister of her love, my boy?
VIOLA   I am all the daughters of my father's house,   120
And all the brothers too; and yet I know not.
Sir, shall I to this lady?
ORSINO   Ay, that's the theme:
To her in haste. Give her this jewel; say
My love can give no place, bide no denay.   *Exeunt.*

2.5 *Enter* SIR TOBY, SIR ANDREW *and* FABIAN.

SIR TOBY   Come thy ways, Signor Fabian.
FABIAN   Nay, I'll come. If I lose a scruple of this sport
let me be boiled to death with melancholy.
SIR TOBY   Wouldst thou not be glad to have the
niggardly, rascally sheep-biter come by some notable   5
shame?
FABIAN   I would exult, man. You know he brought me
out o'favour with my lady about a bear-baiting here.
SIR TOBY   To anger him we'll have the bear again, and
we will fool him black and blue, shall we not, Sir   10
Andrew?
SIR ANDREW   An we do not, it is pity of our lives.

Enter MARIA *with a letter.*

SIR TOBY   Here comes the little villain. How now, my
metal of India?
MARIA   Get ye all three into the box-tree. Malvolio's   15
coming down this walk. He has been yonder i'the sun
practising behaviour to his own shadow this half-hour.
Observe him for the love of mockery, for I know this
letter will make a contemplative idiot of him. Close, in
the name of jesting! [*The men hide. Maria drops letter.*]   20
Lie thou there, for here comes the trout that must be
caught with tickling.   *Exit.*

Enter MALVOLIO.

MALVOLIO   'Tis but fortune, all is fortune. Maria once
told me she did affect me, and I have heard herself
come thus near, that should she fancy it should be one   25
of my complexion. Besides, she uses me with a more
exalted respect than anyone else that follows her. What
should I think on't?
SIR TOBY   Here's an overweening rogue.

30 FABIAN O peace. Contemplation makes a rare turkey-cock of him. How he jets under his advanced plumes.

SIR ANDREW 'Slight, I could so beat the rogue!

SIR TOBY Peace, I say.

MALVOLIO To be count Malvolio.

35 SIR TOBY Ah, rogue!

SIR ANDREW Pistol him, pistol him!

SIR TOBY Peace, peace.

MALVOLIO There is example for't: the Lady of the Strachy married the yeoman of the wardrobe.

40 SIR ANDREW Fie on him, Jezebel!

FABIAN O peace, now he's deeply in. Look how imagination blows him.

MALVOLIO Having been three months married to her, sitting in my state –

45 SIR TOBY O for a stone-bow to hit him in the eye!

MALVOLIO Calling my officers about me, in my branched velvet gown, having come from a day-bed where I have left Olivia sleeping –

SIR TOBY Fire and brimstone!

50 FABIAN O peace, peace.

MALVOLIO And then to have the humour of state, and after a demure travail of regard – telling them I know my place, as I would they should do theirs – to ask for my kinsman Toby.

55 SIR TOBY Bolts and shackles!

FABIAN O peace, peace, peace! Now, now!

MALVOLIO Seven of my people, with an obedient start, make out for him. I frown the while and perchance wind up my watch, or play with my [*touching his chain*] – some rich jewel. Toby approaches, curtsies there to me.

SIR TOBY Shall this fellow live?

FABIAN Though our silence be drawn from us with cars, yet peace!

65 MALVOLIO I extend my hand to him thus, quenching my familiar smile with an austere regard of control –

SIR TOBY And does not Toby take you a blow o'the lips then?

MALVOLIO Saying 'Cousin Toby, my fortunes, having cast me on your niece, give me this prerogative of speech' –

SIR TOBY What, what?

MALVOLIO 'You must amend your drunkenness.'

SIR TOBY Out, scab!

75 FABIAN Nay, patience, or we break the sinews of our plot.

MALVOLIO 'Besides, you waste the treasure of your time with a foolish knight' –

SIR ANDREW That's me, I warrant you.

80 MALVOLIO 'One Sir Andrew.'

SIR ANDREW I knew 'twas I, for many do call me fool.

MALVOLIO [*Sees letter.*] What employment have we here?

FABIAN Now is the woodcock near the gin.

85 SIR TOBY O peace, and the spirit of humours intimate reading aloud to him.

MALVOLIO [*Takes up letter.*] By my life, this is my lady's hand. These be her very c's, her u's and her t's, and thus makes she her great P's. It is in contempt of question her hand.

90 SIR ANDREW Her c's, her u's and her t's. Why that?

MALVOLIO [*Reads.*] *To the unknown beloved, this, and my good wishes.* Her very phrases! By your leave, wax. Soft – and the impressure her Lucrece, with which she uses to seal. 'Tis my lady. To whom should this be? [*Opens letter.*]

95 FABIAN This wins him, liver and all.

MALVOLIO [*Reads.*]
    Jove knows I love,
      But who?
    Lips, do not move,
      No man must know.

100 'No man must know.' What follows? The numbers altered. 'No man must know.' If this should be thee, Malvolio?

105 SIR TOBY Marry, hang thee, brock!

MALVOLIO [*Reads.*]
    I may command where I adore,
      But silence, like a Lucrece knife,
      With bloodless stroke my heart doth gore.
      M.O.A.I. doth sway my life.

110 FABIAN A fustian riddle.

SIR TOBY Excellent wench, say I.

MALVOLIO [*Reads.*] *M.O.A.I. doth sway my life.* Nay, but first let me see, let me see, let me see.

FABIAN What dish o'poison has she dressed him!

115 SIR TOBY And with what wing the staniel checks at it!

MALVOLIO [*Reads.*] *I may command where I adore.* Why, she may command me. I serve her, she is my lady. Why, this is evident to any formal capacity. There is no obstruction in this. And the end – what should that alphabetical position portend? If I could make that resemble something in me! Softly – [*reading*] *M.O.A.I.*

120 SIR TOBY O ay, make up that! He is now at a cold scent.

FABIAN Sowter will cry upon't for all this, though it be as rank as a fox.

125 MALVOLIO 'M.' Malvolio. 'M' – why, that begins my name!

FABIAN Did not I say he would work it out? The cur is excellent at faults.

MALVOLIO 'M.' But then there is no consonancy in the sequel. That suffers under probation: 'A' should follow, but 'O' does.

130 FABIAN And 'O' shall end, I hope.

SIR TOBY Ay, or I'll cudgel him and make him cry 'O!'

MALVOLIO And then 'I' comes behind.

135 FABIAN Ay, an you had any eye behind you, you might see more detraction at your heels than fortunes before you.

MALVOLIO [*Reads.*] *M.O.A.I.* This simulation is not as the former. And yet to crush this a little it would bow to me, for every one of these letters are in my name. Soft, here follows prose.

140

[*Reads.*] *If this fall into thy hand, revolve. In my stars I am above thee, but be not afraid of greatness. Some are born great, some achieve greatness and some have greatness thrust upon them. Thy fates open their hands: let thy blood and spirit embrace them, and, to inure thyself to what thou art like to be, cast thy humble slough and appear fresh. Be opposite with a kinsman, surly with servants. Let thy tongue tang arguments of state; put thyself into the trick of singularity. She thus advises thee that sighs for thee. Remember who commended thy yellow stockings and wished to see thee ever cross-gartered – I say remember. Go to, thou art made if thou desir'st to be so; if not, let me see thee a steward still, the fellow of servants and not worthy to touch Fortune's fingers. Farewell. She that would alter services with thee,*

The Fortunate Unhappy.

Daylight and champaign discovers not more. This is open. I will be proud, I will read politic authors, I will baffle Sir Toby, I will wash off gross acquaintance, I will be point-device the very man. I do not now fool myself to let imagination jade me; for every reason excites to this, that my lady loves me. She did commend my yellow stockings of late, she did praise my leg being cross-gartered, and in this she manifests herself to my love and with a kind of injunction drives me to these habits of her liking. I thank my stars, I am happy. I will be strange, stout, in yellow stockings and cross-gartered even with the swiftness of putting on. Jove and my stars be praised! Here is yet a postscript.

[*Reads.*] *Thou canst not choose but know who I am. If thou entertain'st my love, let it appear in thy smiling – thy smiles become thee well. Therefore in my presence still smile, dear my sweet, I prithee.* Jove, I thank thee. I will smile, I will do everything that thou wilt have me.

Exit.

FABIAN   I will not give my part of this sport for a pension of thousands to be paid from the Sophy.

SIR TOBY   I could marry this wench for this device –

SIR ANDREW   So could I too.

SIR TOBY   And ask no other dowry with her but such another jest.

Enter MARIA.

SIR ANDREW   Nor I neither.

FABIAN   Here comes my noble gull-catcher.

SIR TOBY [*to Maria*]   Wilt thou set thy foot o'my neck?

SIR ANDREW   Or o'mine either?

SIR TOBY   Shall I play my freedom at tray-trip and become thy bondslave?

SIR ANDREW   I'faith, or I either?

SIR TOBY   Why, thou hast put him in such a dream that when the image of it leaves him he must run mad.

MARIA   Nay, but say true, does it work upon him?

SIR TOBY   Like aqua vitae with a midwife.

MARIA   If you will then see the fruits of the sport, mark his first approach before my lady. He will come to her in yellow stockings – and 'tis a colour she abhors – and

cross-gartered – a fashion she detests – and he will smile upon her, which will now be so unsuitable to her disposition, being addicted to a melancholy as she is, that it cannot but turn him into a notable contempt. If you will see it, follow me.

SIR TOBY   To the gates of Tartar, thou most excellent devil of wit.

SIR ANDREW   I'll make one too.   *Exeunt.*

3.1   *Enter* VIOLA *as Cesario and* FESTE
playing on pipe and tabor.

VIOLA   Save thee, friend, and thy music. Dost thou live by thy tabor?

FESTE   No, sir, I live by the church.

VIOLA   Art thou a churchman?

FESTE   No such matter, sir. I do live by the church, for I do live at my house, and my house doth stand by the church.

VIOLA   So thou mayst say the king lies by a beggar if a beggar dwell near him, or the church stands by thy tabor if thy tabor stand by the church.

FESTE   You have said, sir. To see this age! A sentence is but a cheverel glove to a good wit: how quickly the wrong side may be turned outward.

VIOLA   Nay, that's certain. They that dally nicely with words may quickly make them wanton.

FESTE   I would therefore my sister had had no name, sir.

VIOLA   Why, man?

FESTE   Why, sir, her name's a word, and to dally with that word might make my sister wanton. But indeed words are very rascals, since bonds disgraced them.

VIOLA   Thy reason, man?

FESTE   Troth sir, I can yield you none without words, and words are grown so false I am loath to prove reason with them.

VIOLA   I warrant thou art a merry fellow, and car'st for nothing.

FESTE   Not so, sir, I do care for something; but in my conscience, sir, I do not care for you. If that be to care for nothing, sir, I would it would make you invisible.

VIOLA   Art not thou the Lady Olivia's fool?

FESTE   No indeed, sir, the Lady Olivia has no folly. She will keep no fool, sir, till she be married, and fools are as like husbands as pilchards are to herrings – the husband's the bigger. I am indeed not her fool, but her corrupter of words.

VIOLA   I saw thee late at the Count Orsino's.

FESTE   Foolery, sir, does walk about the orb like the sun, it shines everywhere. I would be sorry, sir, but the fool should be as oft with your master as with my mistress. I think I saw your wisdom there.

VIOLA   Nay, an thou pass upon me, I'll no more with thee. Hold, there's expenses for thee. [*Gives coin.*]

FESTE   Now Jove in his next commodity of hair send thee a beard.

VIOLA   By my troth I'll tell thee, I am almost sick for

one, though I would not have it grow on my chin. Is
thy lady within?

FESTE   Would not a pair of these have bred, sir?

VIOLA   Yes, being kept together and put to use.

50 FESTE   I would play Lord Pandarus of Phrygia, sir, to
bring a Cressida to this Troilus.

VIOLA   I understand you, sir, 'tis well begged. [*Gives
another coin.*]

FESTE   The matter, I hope, is not great, sir, begging but
55 a beggar: Cressida was a beggar. My lady is within, sir.
I will conster to them whence you come. Who you are
and what you would are out of my welkin. I might say
'element', but the word is overworn.   *Exit.*

VIOLA   This fellow is wise enough to play the fool,
60 And to do that well craves a kind of wit.
He must observe their mood on whom he jests,
The quality of persons and the time,
And, like the haggard, check at every feather
That comes before his eye. This is a practice
65 As full of labour as a wise man's art;
For folly that he wisely shows is fit,
But wise men, folly-fallen, quite taint their wit.

Enter SIR TOBY *and* SIR ANDREW.

SIR TOBY   Save you, gentleman.

VIOLA   And you, sir.

70 SIR ANDREW   *Dieu vous garde, monsieur.*

VIOLA   *Et vous aussi; votre serviteur.*

SIR ANDREW   I hope, sir, you are, and I am yours.

SIR TOBY   Will you encounter the house? My niece is
desirous you should enter if your trade be to her.

75 VIOLA   I am bound to your niece, sir – I mean, she is the
list of my voyage.

SIR TOBY   Taste your legs, sir, put them to motion.

VIOLA   My legs do better understand me, sir, than I
understand what you mean by bidding me taste my
80 legs.

SIR TOBY   I mean to go, sir, to enter.

VIOLA   I will answer you with gait and entrance.

Enter OLIVIA *and* MARIA.

But we are prevented. [*to Olivia*] Most excellent
accomplished lady, the heavens rain odours on you.

85 SIR ANDREW [*aside*]   That youth's a rare courtier; 'rain
odours' – well!

VIOLA   My matter hath no voice, lady, but to your own
most pregnant and vouchsafed ear.

SIR ANDREW [*aside*]   'Odours', 'pregnant' and 'vouchsafed'
90 – I'll get 'em all three all ready.

OLIVIA   Let the garden door be shut and leave me to my
hearing.   *Exeunt Sir Toby, Sir Andrew and Maria.*
Give me your hand, sir.

VIOLA   My duty, madam, and most humble service.

95 OLIVIA   What is your name?

VIOLA   Cesario is your servant's name, fair princess.

OLIVIA   My servant, sir? 'Twas never merry world
Since lowly feigning was called compliment.

You're servant to the Count Orsino, youth.

VIOLA   And he is yours, and his must needs be yours.   100
Your servant's servant is your servant, madam.

OLIVIA   For him, I think not on him. For his thoughts,
Would they were blanks rather than filled with me.

VIOLA   Madam, I come to whet your gentle thoughts
On his behalf.   105

OLIVIA   O by your leave, I pray you;
I bade you never speak again of him.
But would you undertake another suit,
I had rather hear you to solicit that
Than music from the spheres.

VIOLA   Dear lady –

OLIVIA   Give me leave, beseech you. I did send,   110
After the last enchantment you did here,
A ring in chase of you. So did I abuse
Myself, my servant and, I fear me, you.
Under your hard construction must I sit,
To force that on you in a shameful cunning   115
Which you knew none of yours. What might you
    think?
Have you not set mine honour at the stake
And baited it with all th'unmuzzled thoughts
That tyrannous heart can think? To one of your
    receiving
Enough is shown: a cypress, not a bosom,   120
Hides my heart. So let me hear you speak.

VIOLA   I pity you.

OLIVIA   That's a degree to love.

VIOLA   No, not a grize, for 'tis a vulgar proof
That very oft we pity enemies.

OLIVIA   Why then, methinks 'tis time to smile again.   125
O world, how apt the poor are to be proud!
If one should be a prey, how much the better
To fall before the lion than the wolf!   [*Clock strikes.*]
The clock upbraids me with the waste of time.
Be not afraid, good youth, I will not have you,   130
And yet when wit and youth is come to harvest,
Your wife is like to reap a proper man.
There lies your way, due west.

VIOLA   Then westward ho.
Grace and good disposition attend your ladyship.
You'll nothing, madam, to my lord by me?   135

OLIVIA   Stay –
I prithee tell me what thou think'st of me.

VIOLA   That you do think you are not what you are.

OLIVIA   If I think so, I think the same of you.

VIOLA   Then think you right: I am not what I am.   140

OLIVIA   I would you were as I would have you be.

VIOLA   Would it be better, madam, than I am?
I wish it might, for now I am your fool.

OLIVIA [*aside*]   O, what a deal of scorn looks beautiful
In the contempt and anger of his lip.   145
A murderous guilt shows not itself more soon
Than love that would seem hid. Love's night is noon.
– Cesario, by the roses of the spring,
By maidhood, honour, truth and everything,

150 I love thee so that maugre all thy pride
Nor wit nor reason can my passion hide.
Do not extort thy reasons from this clause:
For that I woo, thou therefore hast no cause.
But rather reason thus with reason fetter:
155 Love sought is good, but given unsought is better.
VIOLA   By innocence I swear, and by my youth,
I have one heart, one bosom and one truth,
And that no woman has, nor never none
Shall mistress be of it save I alone.
160 And so adieu, good madam; never more
Will I my master's tears to you deplore.
OLIVIA   Yet come again, for thou perhaps mayst move
That heart which now abhors to like his love.   *Exeunt.*

3.2   *Enter* SIR TOBY, SIR ANDREW *and* FABIAN.

SIR ANDREW   No, faith, I'll not stay a jot longer.
SIR TOBY   Thy reason, dear venom, give thy reason.
FABIAN   You must needs yield your reason, Sir Andrew.
SIR ANDREW   Marry, I saw your niece do more favours
5   to the count's servingman than ever she bestowed
upon me. I saw't i'th' orchard.
SIR TOBY   Did she see thee the while, old boy? Tell me
that.
SIR ANDREW   As plain as I see you now.
10 FABIAN   This was a great argument of love in her toward
you.
SIR ANDREW   'Slight! Will you make an ass o'me?
FABIAN   I will prove it legitimate, sir, upon the oaths of
judgement and reason.
15 SIR TOBY   And they have been grand-jurymen since
before Noah was a sailor.
FABIAN   She did show favour to the youth in your sight
only to exasperate you, to awake your dormouse valour,
to put fire in your heart and brimstone in your liver.
20 You should then have accosted her and, with some
excellent jests, fire-new from the mint, you should
have banged the youth into dumbness. This was looked
for at your hand and this was balked. The double gilt of
this opportunity you let time wash off, and you are now
25 sailed into the north of my lady's opinion, where you
will hang like an icicle on a Dutchman's beard, unless
you do redeem it by some laudable attempt either of
valour or policy.
SIR ANDREW   An't be any way, it must be with valour, for
30 policy I hate. I had as lief be a Brownist as a politician.
SIR TOBY   Why then, build me thy fortunes upon the
basis of valour. Challenge me the count's youth to fight
with him. Hurt him in eleven places – my niece shall
take note of it. And assure thyself there is no love-
35 broker in the world can more prevail in man's
commendation with woman than report of valour.
FABIAN   There is no way but this, Sir Andrew.
SIR ANDREW   Will either of you bear me a challenge to
him?

SIR TOBY   Go write it in a martial hand, be curst and   40
brief. It is no matter how witty, so it be eloquent and
full of invention. Taunt him with the licence of ink. If
thou thou'st him some thrice, it shall not be amiss; and
as many lies as will lie in thy sheet of paper, although
the sheet were big enough for the bed of Ware in   45
England, set 'em down. Go, about it. Let there be gall
enough in thy ink – though thou write with a goose-
pen, no matter. About it.
SIR ANDREW   Where shall I find you?
SIR TOBY   We'll call thee at the cubiculo. Go.   50
Exit Sir Andrew.
FABIAN   This is a dear manikin to you, Sir Toby.
SIR TOBY   I have been dear to him, lad, some two
thousand strong or so.
FABIAN   We shall have a rare letter from him; but you'll
not deliver't?   55
SIR TOBY   Never trust me then; and by all means stir on
the youth to an answer. I think oxen and wain-ropes
cannot hale them together. For Andrew, if he were
opened and you find so much blood in his liver as will
clog the foot of a flea, I'll eat the rest of th'anatomy.   60
FABIAN   And his opposite, the youth, bears in his visage
no great presage of cruelty.

Enter MARIA.

SIR TOBY   Look where the youngest wren of nine
comes.
MARIA   If you desire the spleen, and will laugh   65
yourselves into stitches, follow me. Yon gull Malvolio
is turned heathen, a very renegado, for there is no
Christian that means to be saved by believing rightly
can ever believe such impossible passages of grossness.
He's in yellow stockings.   70
SIR TOBY   And cross-gartered?
MARIA   Most villainously, like a pedant that keeps a
school i'th' church. I have dogged him like his
murderer. He does obey every point of the letter that I
dropped to betray him. He does smile his face into   75
more lines than is in the new map with the
augmentation of the Indies. You have not seen such a
thing as 'tis. I can hardly forbear hurling things at him;
I know my lady will strike him. If she do, he'll smile
and take't for a great favour.   80
SIR TOBY   Come, bring us, bring us where he is.
Exeunt.

3.3   *Enter* SEBASTIAN *and* ANTONIO.

SEBASTIAN   I would not by my will have troubled you,
But since you make your pleasure of your pains
I will no further chide you.
ANTONIO   I could not stay behind you. My desire,
More sharp than filed steel, did spur me forth,   5
And not all love to see you – though so much
As might have drawn me to a longer voyage –

But jealousy what might befall your travel,
Being skill-less in these parts, which to a stranger,
Unguided and unfriended, often prove
Rough and unhospitable. My willing love,
The rather by these arguments of fear,
Set forth in your pursuit.

SEBASTIAN   My kind Antonio,
I can no other answer make but thanks,
And thanks, and ever thanks; and oft good turns
Are shuffled off with such uncurrent pay.
But were my worth as is my conscience firm,
You should find better dealing. What's to do?
Shall we go see the relics of this town?

ANTONIO
Tomorrow, sir; best first go see your lodging.

SEBASTIAN   I am not weary, and 'tis long to night.
I pray you, let us satisfy our eyes
With the memorials and the things of fame
That do renown this city.

ANTONIO   Would you'd pardon me.
I do not without danger walk these streets.
Once in a sea-fight 'gainst the count his galleys
I did some service, of such note indeed
That were I ta'en here it would scarce be answered.

SEBASTIAN
Belike you slew great number of his people?

ANTONIO   Th'offence is not of such a bloody nature,
Albeit the quality of the time and quarrel
Might well have given us bloody argument.
It might have since been answered in repaying
What we took from them, which for traffic's sake
Most of our city did. Only myself stood out,
For which if I be lapsed in this place
I shall pay dear.

SEBASTIAN   Do not then walk too open.

ANTONIO
It doth not fit me. Hold, sir, here's my purse.
In the south suburbs, at the Elephant,
Is best to lodge. I will bespeak our diet
Whiles you beguile the time and feed your knowledge
With viewing of the town. There shall you have me.

SEBASTIAN   Why I your purse?

ANTONIO   Haply your eye shall light upon some toy
You have desire to purchase; and your store,
I think, is not for idle markets, sir.

SEBASTIAN
I'll be your purse-bearer, and leave you for an hour.

ANTONIO   To th'Elephant.

SEBASTIAN   I do remember.   *Exeunt.*

3.4   *Enter* OLIVIA *and* MARIA.

OLIVIA [*aside*]
I have sent after him; he says he'll come.
How shall I feast him? What bestow of him?
For youth is bought more oft than begged or borrowed.
I speak too loud.

[*to Maria*] Where's Malvolio? He is sad and civil,
And suits well for a servant with my fortunes.
Where is Malvolio?

MARIA   He's coming, madam, but in very strange
manner. He is sure possessed, madam.

OLIVIA   Why, what's the matter? Does he rave?

MARIA   No, madam, he does nothing but smile. Your
ladyship were best to have some guard about you if he
come, for sure the man is tainted in's wits.

OLIVIA   Go call him hither.   *Exit Maria.*
                    I am as mad as he,
If sad and merry madness equal be.

Enter MALVOLIO, *in yellow stockings and
cross-gartered, with* MARIA.

How now, Malvolio?

MALVOLIO   Sweet lady, ho, ho!

OLIVIA   Smil'st thou? I sent for thee upon a sad
occasion.

MALVOLIO   Sad, lady? I could be sad. This does make
some obstruction in the blood, this cross-gartering, but
what of that? If it please the eye of one, it is with me as
the very true sonnet is: 'Please one, and please all.'

OLIVIA   Why, how dost thou, man? What is the matter
with thee?

MALVOLIO   Not black in my mind, though yellow in my
legs. It did come to his hands, and commands shall be
executed. I think we do know the sweet Roman hand.

OLIVIA   Wilt thou go to bed, Malvolio?

MALVOLIO   To bed? Ay, sweetheart, and I'll come to
thee.

OLIVIA   God comfort thee. Why dost thou smile so and
kiss thy hand so oft?

MARIA   How do you, Malvolio?

MALVOLIO   At your request? Yes, nightingales answer
daws.

MARIA   Why appear you with this ridiculous boldness
before my lady?

MALVOLIO   'Be not afraid of greatness' – 'twas well
writ.

OLIVIA   What mean'st thou by that, Malvolio?

MALVOLIO   'Some are born great' –

OLIVIA   Ha?

MALVOLIO   'Some achieve greatness' –

OLIVIA   What sayst thou?

MALVOLIO   'And some have greatness thrust upon
them.'

OLIVIA   Heaven restore thee!

MALVOLIO   'Remember who commended thy yellow
stockings' –

OLIVIA   Thy yellow stockings?

MALVOLIO   'And wished to see thee cross-gartered.'

OLIVIA   Cross-gartered?

MALVOLIO   'Go to, thou art made if thou desir'st to be
so.'

OLIVIA   Am I made?

MALVOLIO   'If not, let me see thee a servant still.'

OLIVIA Why, this is very midsummer madness.

Enter Servant.

SERVANT Madam, the young gentleman of the Count
60   Orsino's is returned. I could hardly entreat him back.
       He attends your ladyship's pleasure.

OLIVIA I'll come to him.   *Exit Servant.*
       Good Maria, let this fellow be looked to. Where's my
       cousin Toby? Let some of my people have a special
65   care of him; I would not have him miscarry for the half
       of my dowry.   *Exeunt Olivia and Maria.*

MALVOLIO O ho, do you come near me now? No worse
       man than Sir Toby to look to me! This concurs directly
       with the letter. She sends him on purpose that I may
70   appear stubborn to him, for she incites me to that in
       the letter. 'Cast thy humble slough,' says she, 'be
       opposite with a kinsman, surly with servants. Let thy
       tongue tang with arguments of state; put thyself into
       the trick of singularity', and consequently sets down
75   the manner how, as a sad face, a reverend carriage, a
       slow tongue, in the habit of some sir of note and so
       forth. I have limed her, but it is Jove's doing and Jove
       make me thankful! And when she went away now, 'Let
       this fellow be looked to.' 'Fellow', not 'Malvolio', nor
80   after my degree, but 'fellow'! Why, everything adheres
       together that no dram of a scruple, no scruple of a
       scruple, no obstacle, no incredulous or unsafe
       circumstance – what can be said? – nothing that can be
       can come between me and the full prospect of my
85   hopes. Well, Jove, not I, is the doer of this, and he is to
       be thanked.

Enter SIR TOBY, FABIAN *and* MARIA.

SIR TOBY Which way is he, in the name of sanctity? If
       all the devils of hell be drawn in little, and Legion
       himself possessed him, yet I'll speak to him.

90 FABIAN Here he is, here he is. [*to Malvolio*] How is't
       with you, sir? How is't with you, man?

MALVOLIO Go off, I discard you. Let me enjoy my
       private. Go off.

MARIA Lo, how hollow the fiend speaks within him.
95   Did not I tell you? Sir Toby, my lady prays you to have
       a care of him.

MALVOLIO Aha! Does she so?

SIR TOBY Go to, go to. Peace, peace, we must deal
       gently with him. Let me alone. How do you, Malvolio?
100   How is't with you? What, man, defy the devil!
       Consider, he's an enemy to mankind.

MALVOLIO Do you know what you say?

MARIA La you, an you speak ill of the devil, how he
       takes it at heart. Pray God he be not bewitched.

105 FABIAN Carry his water to th' wise woman.

MARIA Marry, and it shall be done tomorrow morning,
       if I live. My lady would not lose him for more than I'll
       say.

MALVOLIO How now, mistress?

110 MARIA O Lord!

SIR TOBY Prithee hold thy peace, this is not the way.
       Do you not see you move him? Let me alone with him.

FABIAN No way but gentleness, gently, gently. The
       fiend is rough, and will not be roughly used.

SIR TOBY Why how now, my bawcock? How dost thou,   115
       chuck?

MALVOLIO Sir!

SIR TOBY Ay, biddy, come with me. What, man, 'tis not
       for gravity to play at cherry-pit with Satan. Hang him,
       foul collier!   120

MARIA Get him to say his prayers, good Sir Toby, get
       him to pray.

MALVOLIO My prayers, minx?

MARIA No, I warrant you, he will not hear of godliness.

MALVOLIO Go hang yourselves, all. You are idle shallow   125
       things; I am not of your element. You shall know more
       hereafter.   *Exit.*

SIR TOBY Is't possible?

FABIAN If this were played upon a stage now, I could
       condemn it as an improbable fiction.   130

SIR TOBY His very genius hath taken the infection of
       the device, man.

MARIA Nay, pursue him now, lest the device take air
       and taint.

FABIAN Why, we shall make him mad indeed.   135

MARIA The house will be the quieter.

SIR TOBY Come, we'll have him in a dark room and
       bound. My niece is already in the belief that he's mad.
       We may carry it thus for our pleasure and his penance
       till our very pastime, tired out of breath, prompt us to 140
       have mercy on him; at which time we will bring the
       device to the bar and crown thee for a finder of madmen.

Enter SIR ANDREW *with a letter.*

But see, but see.

FABIAN More matter for a May morning.

SIR ANDREW Here's the challenge, read it. I warrant   145
       there's vinegar and pepper in't.

FABIAN Is't so saucy?

SIR ANDREW Ay, is't, I warrant him. Do but read.

SIR TOBY Give me. [*Reads.*] *Youth, whatsoever thou art,
       thou art but a scurvy fellow.*   150

FABIAN Good, and valiant.

SIR TOBY [*Reads.*] *Wonder not nor admire not in thy mind
       why I do call thee so, for I will show thee no reason for't.*

FABIAN A good note, that keeps you from the blow of
       the law.   155

SIR TOBY [*Reads.*] *Thou com'st to the Lady Olivia, and in
       my sight she uses thee kindly. But thou liest in thy throat;
       that is not the matter I challenge thee for.*

FABIAN Very brief, and to exceeding good sense [*aside*]
       -less.   160

SIR TOBY [*Reads.*] *I will waylay thee going home, where
       if it be thy chance to kill me –*

FABIAN Good.

SIR TOBY [*Reads.*] *Thou kill'st me like a rogue and a
       villain.*   165

FABIAN   Still you keep o'th' windy side of the law –
good.

SIR TOBY   [*Reads.*]   *Fare thee well, and God have mercy*
upon one of our souls. He may have mercy upon mine, but
my hope is better, and so look to thyself. Thy friend as thou
usest him, and thy sworn enemy,

Andrew Aguecheek.

If this letter move him not, his legs cannot. I'll give't
him.

MARIA   You may have very fit occasion for't. He is now
in some commerce with my lady, and will by and by
depart.

SIR TOBY   Go, Sir Andrew. Scout me for him at the
corner of the orchard like a bumbaily. So soon as ever
thou seest him, draw and, as thou draw'st, swear
horrible, for it comes to pass oft that a terrible oath,
with a swaggering accent sharply twanged off, gives
manhood more approbation than ever proof itself
would have earned him. Away!

SIR ANDREW   Nay, let me alone for swearing.   *Exit.*

SIR TOBY   Now will not I deliver his letter, for the
behaviour of the young gentleman gives him out to be of
good capacity and breeding. His employment between
his lord and my niece confirms no less. Therefore this
letter, being so excellently ignorant, will breed no terror
in the youth. He will find it comes from a clod-pole.
But, sir, I will deliver his challenge by word of mouth,
set upon Aguecheek a notable report of valour and drive
the gentleman – as I know his youth will aptly receive it
– into a most hideous opinion of his rage, skill, fury and
impetuosity. This will so fright them both that they will
kill one another by the look, like cockatrices.

Enter OLIVIA *and* VIOLA *as Cesario.*

FABIAN   Here he comes with your niece. Give them way
till he take leave, and presently after him.

SIR TOBY   I will meditate the while upon some horrid
message for a challenge.

Exeunt Sir Toby, Fabian and Maria.

OLIVIA   I have said too much unto a heart of stone
And laid mine honour too unchary on't.
There's something in me that reproves my fault,
But such a headstrong potent fault it is
That it but mocks reproof.

VIOLA   With the same haviour that your passion bears
Goes on my master's griefs.

OLIVIA   Here, wear this jewel for me: 'tis my picture.
Refuse it not, it hath no tongue to vex you;
And I beseech you come again tomorrow.
What shall you ask of me that I'll deny
That honour saved may upon asking give?

VIOLA   Nothing but this: your true love for my master.

OLIVIA   How with mine honour may I give him that
Which I have given to you?

VIOLA   I will acquit you.

OLIVIA   Well, come again tomorrow. Fare thee well.
A fiend like thee might bear my soul to hell.   *Exit.*

Enter SIR TOBY *and* FABIAN.

SIR TOBY   Gentleman, God save thee.

VIOLA   And you, sir.

SIR TOBY   That defence thou hast, betake thee to't. Of
what nature the wrongs are thou hast done him, I know
not, but thy intercepter, full of despite, bloody as the
hunter, attends thee at the orchard end. Dismount thy
tuck, be yare in thy preparation, for thy assailant is
quick, skilful and deadly.

VIOLA   You mistake, sir. I am sure no man hath any
quarrel to me. My remembrance is very free and clear
from any image of offence done to any man.

SIR TOBY   You'll find it otherwise, I assure you.
Therefore, if you hold your life at any price, betake you
to your guard, for your opposite hath in him what
youth, strength, skill and wrath can furnish man
withal.

VIOLA   I pray you, sir, what is he?

SIR TOBY   He is knight, dubbed with unhatched rapier
and on carpet consideration, but he is a devil in private
brawl. Souls and bodies hath he divorced three, and
his incensement at this moment is so implacable that
satisfaction can be none but by pangs of death and
sepulchre. 'Hob-nob' is his word: give't or take't.

VIOLA   I will return again into the house and desire
some conduct of the lady. I am no fighter. I have heard
of some kind of men that put quarrels purposely on
others to taste their valour. Belike this is a man of that
quirk.

SIR TOBY   Sir, no. His indignation derives itself out of a
very competent injury, therefore get you on and give
him his desire. Back you shall not to the house, unless
you undertake that with me which with as much safety
you might answer him. Therefore on, or strip your
sword stark naked, for meddle you must, that's certain,
or forswear to wear iron about you.

VIOLA   This is as uncivil as strange. I beseech you do me
this courteous office as to know of the knight what my
offence to him is. It is something of my negligence,
nothing of my purpose.

SIR TOBY   I will do so. Signor Fabian, stay you by this
gentleman till my return.   *Exit.*

VIOLA   Pray you, sir, do you know of this matter?

FABIAN   I know the knight is incensed against you even
to a mortal arbitrament, but nothing of the
circumstance more.

VIOLA   I beseech you, what manner of man is he?

FABIAN   Nothing of that wonderful promise to read him
by his form as you are like to find him in the proof of
his valour. He is indeed, sir, the most skilful, bloody
and fatal opposite that you could possibly have found
in any part of Illyria. Will you walk towards him, I will
make your peace with him – if I can.

VIOLA   I shall be much bound to you for't. I am one that
had rather go with Sir Priest than Sir Knight. I care
not who knows so much of my mettle.   *Exeunt.*

Enter SIR TOBY *and* SIR ANDREW.

275 SIR TOBY   Why, man, he's a very devil. I have not seen
such a firago. I had a pass with him, rapier, scabbard
and all, and he gives me the stuck in with such a mortal
motion that it is inevitable; and on the answer, he pays
you as surely as your feet hits the ground they step on.
280 They say he has been fencer to the Sophy.

SIR ANDREW   Pox on't, I'll not meddle with him.

SIR TOBY   Ay, but he will not now be pacified. Fabian
can scarce hold him yonder.

SIR ANDREW   Plague on't, an I thought he had been
285 valiant, and so cunning in fence, I'd have seen him
damned ere I'd have challenged him. Let him let the
matter slip and I'll give him my horse, grey Capulet.

SIR TOBY   I'll make the motion. Stand here, make a
good show on't. This shall end without the perdition
290 of souls. [*aside*] Marry, I'll ride your horse as well as I
ride you.

Enter FABIAN *and* VIOLA *as Cesario.*

[*aside to Fabian*] I have his horse to take up the quarrel.
I have persuaded him the youth's a devil.

FABIAN [*aside to Sir Toby*]   He is as horribly conceited of
295 him, and pants and looks pale as if a bear were at his
heels.

SIR TOBY [*aside to Viola*]   There's no remedy, sir, he will
fight with you for's oath' sake. Marry, he hath better
bethought him of his quarrel and he finds that now
300 scarce to be worth talking of. Therefore draw for the
supportance of his vow. He protests he will not hurt
you.

VIOLA [*aside*]   Pray God defend me! A little thing would
make me tell them how much I lack of a man.

FABIAN [*aside to Sir Andrew*]   Give ground if you see
305 him furious.

SIR TOBY [*aside to Sir Andrew*]   Come, Sir Andrew,
there's no remedy. The gentleman will for his honour's
sake have one bout with you; he cannot by the duello
avoid it. But he has promised me, as he is a gentleman
310 and a soldier, he will not hurt you. Come on, to't.

SIR ANDREW [*aside*]   Pray God he keep his oath!

Enter ANTONIO.

VIOLA [*to Sir Andrew*]   I do assure you 'tis against my
will. [*Sir Andrew and Viola draw swords.*]

ANTONIO [*Draws sword.*]
[*to Sir Andrew*] Put up your sword. If this young
gentleman
315 Have done offence, I take the fault on me.
If you offend him, I for him defy you.

SIR TOBY   You, sir? Why, what are you?

ANTONIO   One, sir, that for his love dares yet do more
Than you have heard him brag to you he will.

320 SIR TOBY [*Draws sword.*]   Nay, if you be an undertaker,
I am for you.

Enter Officers.

FABIAN   O good Sir Toby, hold. Here come the officers.

SIR TOBY [*to Antonio*]   I'll be with you anon.

VIOLA [*to Sir Andrew*]   Pray, sir, put your sword up, if
you please.   325

SIR ANDREW   Marry, will I, sir. And for that I promised
you I'll be as good as my word. He will bear you easily,
and reins well.

1 OFFICER [*Indicates Antonio.*]   This is the man; do thy
office.   330

2 OFFICER   Antonio, I arrest thee at the suit
Of Count Orsino.

ANTONIO   You do mistake me, sir.

1 OFFICER   No, sir, no jot. I know your favour well,
Though now you have no sea-cap on your head.
[*to Second Officer*] Take him away; he knows I know
him well.   335

ANTONIO
I must obey. [*to Viola*] This comes with seeking you.
But there's no remedy; I shall answer it.
What will you do now my necessity
Makes me to ask you for my purse? It grieves me
Much more for what I cannot do for you   340
Than what befalls myself. You stand amazed,
But be of comfort.

2 OFFICER   Come, sir, away.

ANTONIO [*to Viola*]
I must entreat of you some of that money.

VIOLA   What money, sir?   345
For the fair kindness you have showed me here,
And part being prompted by your present trouble,
Out of my lean and low ability
I'll lend you something. My having is not much.
I'll make division of my present with you.   350
Hold, [*offering money*] there's half my coffer.

ANTONIO [*Refuses money.*]   Will you deny me now?
Is't possible that my deserts to you
Can lack persuasion? Do not tempt my misery,
Lest that it make me so unsound a man
As to upbraid you with those kindnesses   355
That I have done for you.

VIOLA   I know of none,
Nor know I you by voice or any feature.
I hate ingratitude more in a man
Than lying vainness, babbling drunkenness
Or any taint of vice whose strong corruption   360
Inhabits our frail blood.

ANTONIO   O heavens themselves!

2 OFFICER   Come, sir, I pray you go.

ANTONIO
Let me speak a little. This youth that you see here
I snatched one half out of the jaws of death,
Relieved him with such sanctity of love,   365
And to his image, which methought did promise
Most venerable worth, did I devotion.

1 OFFICER   What's that to us? The time goes by. Away!

ANTONIO   But O, how vile an idol proves this god!
Thou hast, Sebastian, done good feature shame.   370

In nature there's no blemish but the mind:
None can be called deformed but the unkind.
Virtue is beauty, but the beauteous evil
Are empty trunks o'erflourished by the devil.

1 OFFICER
375   The man grows mad, away with him. Come, come, sir.

ANTONIO   Lead me on.   *Exit with Officers.*

VIOLA [*aside*]
Methinks his words do from such passion fly
That he believes himself. So do not I.
Prove true, imagination, O prove true,
380   That I, dear brother, be now ta'en for you!

SIR TOBY   Come hither, knight; come hither, Fabian.
We'll whisper o'er a couplet or two of most sage saws.
[*They stand aside.*]

VIOLA   He named Sebastian. I my brother know
Yet living in my glass. Even such and so
385   In favour was my brother, and he went
Still in this fashion, colour, ornament,
For him I imitate. O, if it prove,
Tempests are kind, and salt waves fresh in love!   *Exit.*

SIR TOBY [*to Sir Andrew*]   A very dishonest, paltry boy,
390   and more a coward than a hare. His dishonesty appears
in leaving his friend here in necessity and denying
him; and, for his cowardship, ask Fabian.

FABIAN   A coward, a most devout coward, religious in it.

SIR ANDREW   'Slid, I'll after him again and beat him.

SIR TOBY   Do, cuff him soundly, but never draw thy
395   sword.

SIR ANDREW   An I do not –   *Exit.*

FABIAN   Come, let's see the event.

SIR TOBY   I dare lay any money 'twill be nothing yet.
        Exeunt.

4.1   *Enter* SEBASTIAN *and* FESTE.

FESTE   Will you make me believe that I am not sent for
you?

SEBASTIAN   Go to, go to, thou art a foolish fellow.
Let me be clear of thee.

5   FESTE   Well held out, i'faith! No, I do not know you, nor
I am not sent to you by my lady to bid you come speak
with her, nor your name is not Master Cesario, nor this
is not my nose neither. Nothing that is so is so.

SEBASTIAN   I prithee vent thy folly somewhere else,
10   Thou knowst not me.

FESTE   Vent my folly! He has heard that word of some
great man and now applies it to a fool. Vent my folly! I
am afraid this great lubber the world will prove a
cockney. I prithee now ungird thy strangeness, and tell
15   me what I shall vent to my lady. Shall I vent to her that
thou art coming?

SEBASTIAN   I prithee, foolish Greek, depart from me.
There's money for thee. If you tarry longer
I shall give worse payment.

20   FESTE   By my troth thou hast an open hand. These wise

men that give fools money get themselves a good
report, after fourteen years' purchase.

Enter SIR ANDREW, SIR TOBY *and* FABIAN.

SIR ANDREW [*to Sebastian*]   Now, sir, have I met you
again. [*Strikes him.*] There's for you.

SEBASTIAN
Why, [*striking Sir Andrew*] there's for thee,   25
And there, and there. Are all the people mad?

SIR TOBY [*Restrains Sebastian.*]   Hold, sir, or I'll throw
your dagger o'er the house.

FESTE   This will I tell my lady straight. I would not be in
some of your coats for twopence.   *Exit.*   30

SIR TOBY   Come on, sir, hold!

SIR ANDREW   Nay, let him alone, I'll go another way to
work with him. I'll have an action of battery against
him if there be any law in Illyria. Though I struck him
first, yet it's no matter for that.   35

SEBASTIAN [*to Sir Toby*]   Let go thy hand.

SIR TOBY   Come, sir, I will not let you go. Come, my
young soldier, put up your iron. You are well fleshed.
Come on.

SEBASTIAN   I will be free from thee.   [*Frees himself.*]
        What wouldst thou now?   40
If thou dar'st tempt me further, draw thy sword.
[*Draws sword.*]

SIR TOBY   What, what? Nay then, I must have an ounce
or two of this malapert blood from you. [*Draws sword.*]

Enter OLIVIA.

OLIVIA   Hold, Toby! On thy life I charge thee hold.

SIR TOBY   Madam.   45

OLIVIA   Will it be ever thus? Ungracious wretch,
Fit for the mountains and the barbarous caves,
Where manners ne'er were preached. Out of my sight!
[*to Sebastian*] Be not offended, dear Cesario.
[*to Sir Toby*] Rudesby, be gone!
        Exeunt Sir Toby, Sir Andrew and Fabian.
        I prithee, gentle friend,   50
Let thy fair wisdom, not thy passion, sway
In this uncivil and unjust extent
Against thy peace. Go with me to my house
And hear thou there how many fruitless pranks
This ruffian hath botched up, that thou thereby   55
Mayst smile at this. Thou shalt not choose but go.
Do not deny. Beshrew his soul for me,
He started one poor heart of mine in thee.

SEBASTIAN
What relish is in this? How runs the stream?
Or I am mad or else this is a dream.   60
Let fancy still my sense in Lethe steep:
If it be thus to dream, still let me sleep.

OLIVIA
Nay, come, I prithee, would thou'dst be ruled by me.

SEBASTIAN   Madam, I will.

OLIVIA   O say so, and so be.   *Exeunt.*

4.2   *Enter* MARIA, *carrying a gown*
                and false beard, and FESTE.

MARIA Nay, I prithee put on this gown and this beard;
make him believe thou art Sir Topas the curate. Do it
quickly. I'll call Sir Toby the whilst.   *Exit.*

FESTE Well, I'll put it on, and I will dissemble myself
5   in't, and I would I were the first that ever dissembled in
such a gown. I am not tall enough to become the
function well, nor lean enough to be thought a good
student, but to be said an honest man and a good
housekeeper goes as fairly as to say a careful man and a
10   great scholar.

            Enter SIR TOBY *and* MARIA.

The competitors enter.

SIR TOBY Jove bless thee, Master Parson.

FESTE [*as Sir Topas*] *Bonos dies*, Sir Toby. For as the old
hermit of Prague, that never saw pen and ink, very
15   wittily said to a niece of King Gorboduc, 'That that is
is'; so I being Master Parson am Master Parson, for
what is 'that' but 'that' and 'is' but 'is'?

SIR TOBY To him, Sir Topas.

FESTE What ho, I say, peace in this prison.

20 SIR TOBY The knave counterfeits well – a good knave.

MALVOLIO [*within*] Who calls there?

FESTE Sir Topas the curate, who comes to visit Malvolio
the lunatic.

MALVOLIO Sir Topas, Sir Topas, good Sir Topas, go to
25   my lady.

FESTE Out, hyperbolical fiend, how vexest thou this
man! Talkest thou nothing but of ladies?

SIR TOBY Well said, Master Parson.

MALVOLIO Sir Topas, never was man thus wronged.
30   Good Sir Topas, do not think I am mad. They have
laid me here in hideous darkness.

FESTE Fie, thou dishonest Satan! I call thee by the most
modest terms, for I am one of those gentle ones that
will use the devil himself with courtesy. Sayst thou
35   that house is dark?

MALVOLIO As hell, Sir Topas.

FESTE Why, it hath bay-windows transparent as
barricadoes, and the clerestories toward the south-
north are as lustrous as ebony, and yet complainest
40   thou of obstruction?

MALVOLIO I am not mad, Sir Topas. I say to you this
house is dark.

FESTE Madman, thou errest. I say there is no darkness
but ignorance, in which thou art more puzzled than the
45   Egyptians in their fog.

MALVOLIO I say this house is as dark as ignorance,
though ignorance were as dark as hell; and I say there
was never man thus abused. I am no more mad
than you are. Make the trial of it in any constant
50   question.

FESTE What is the opinion of Pythagoras concerning
wildfowl?

MALVOLIO That the soul of our grandam might haply
inhabit a bird.

FESTE What think'st thou of his opinion?   55

MALVOLIO I think nobly of the soul, and no way
approve his opinion.

FESTE Fare thee well. Remain thou still in darkness.
Thou shalt hold th'opinion of Pythagoras ere I will
allow of thy wits, and fear to kill a woodcock lest thou 60
dispossess the soul of thy grandam. Fare thee well.

MALVOLIO Sir Topas, Sir Topas!

SIR TOBY My most exquisite Sir Topas.

FESTE Nay, I am for all waters.

MARIA Thou mightst have done this without thy beard 65
and gown. He sees thee not.

SIR TOBY [*to Feste*] To him in thine own voice, and
bring me word how thou find'st him. I would we were
well rid of this knavery. If he may be conveniently
delivered, I would he were, for I am now so far in 70
offence with my niece that I cannot pursue with any
safety this sport to the upshot. Come by and by to my
chamber.   *Exit with Maria.*

FESTE [*As himself; sings.*]
          Hey Robin, jolly Robin,
          Tell me how thy lady does.   75

MALVOLIO Fool!

FESTE [*Sings.*]
          My lady is unkind, pardie.

MALVOLIO Fool!

FESTE [*Sings.*]
          Alas, why is she so?

MALVOLIO Fool, I say!   80

FESTE [*Sings.*]
          She loves another –
Who calls, ha?

MALVOLIO Good fool, as ever thou wilt deserve well at
my hand, help me to a candle, and pen, ink and paper. As
I am a gentleman, I will live to be thankful to thee for't. 85

FESTE Master Malvolio?

MALVOLIO Ay, good fool.

FESTE Alas, sir, how fell you besides your five wits?

MALVOLIO Fool, there was never man so notoriously
abused. I am as well in my wits, fool, as thou art. 90

FESTE But as well? Then you are mad indeed, if you be
no better in your wits than a fool.

MALVOLIO They have here propertied me: keep me in
darkness, send ministers to me, asses, and do all they
can to face me out of my wits. 95

FESTE Advise you what you say, the minister is here. [*as
Sir Topas*] Malvolio, Malvolio, thy wits the heavens
restore. Endeavour thyself to sleep and leave thy vain
bibble babble.

MALVOLIO Sir Topas!   100

FESTE [*as Sir Topas*] Maintain no words with him, good
fellow. [*as himself*] Who, I, sir? Not I, sir! God b'wi'
you, good Sir Topas. [*as Sir Topas*] Marry, amen. [*as
himself*] I will, sir, I will.

MALVOLIO Fool, fool, fool, I say!   105

FESTE   Alas, sir, be patient. What say you, sir? I am
shent for speaking to you.

MALVOLIO   Good fool, help me to some light and some
paper. I tell thee I am as well in my wits as any man in
110   Illyria.

FESTE   Welladay that you were, sir.

MALVOLIO   By this hand, I am. Good fool, some ink,
paper and light, and convey what I will set down to my
lady. It shall advantage thee more than ever the bearing
115   of letter did.

FESTE   I will help you to't. But tell me true, are you not
mad indeed, or do you but counterfeit?

MALVOLIO   Believe me, I am not, I tell thee true.

FESTE   Nay, I'll ne'er believe a madman till I see his
120   brains. I will fetch you light, and paper, and ink.

MALVOLIO   Fool, I'll requite it in the highest degree. I
prithee be gone.

FESTE [*Sings.*]
  I am gone, sir, and anon, sir,
    I'll be with you again,
125   In a trice, like to the old Vice,
    Your need to sustain,
  Who with dagger of lath, in his rage and his wrath,
    Cries 'Aha!' to the devil,
  Like a mad lad, 'Pare thy nails, dad.
130   Adieu, goodman devil.'   *Exit.*

4.3   *Enter* SEBASTIAN.

SEBASTIAN   This is the air, that is the glorious sun;
  This pearl she gave me, I do feel't and see't,
  And though 'tis wonder that enwraps me thus,
  Yet 'tis not madness. Where's Antonio, then?
5   I could not find him at the Elephant;
  Yet there he was, and there I found this credit,
  That he did range the town to seek me out.
  His counsel now might do me golden service,
  For though my soul disputes well with my sense
10   That this may be some error but no madness,
  Yet doth this accident and flood of fortune
  So far exceed all instance, all discourse,
  That I am ready to distrust mine eyes
  And wrangle with my reason that persuades me
15   To any other trust but that I am mad,
  Or else the lady's mad. Yet if 'twere so
  She could not sway her house, command her
    followers,
  Take and give back affairs and their dispatch
  With such a smooth, discreet and stable bearing
20   As I perceive she does. There's something in't
  That is deceivable.

Enter OLIVIA *and* Priest.

  But here the lady comes.

OLIVIA   Blame not this haste of mine. If you mean well,
  Now go with me and with this holy man
  Into the chantry by. There before him,

And underneath that consecrated roof,   25
  Plight me the full assurance of your faith,
  That my most jealous and too doubtful soul
  May live at peace. He shall conceal it
  Whiles you are willing it shall come to note,
  What time we will our celebration keep   30
  According to my birth. What do you say?

SEBASTIAN   I'll follow this good man and go with you,
  And, having sworn truth, ever will be true.

OLIVIA
  Then lead the way, good father, and heavens so shine
  That they may fairly note this act of mine.   *Exeunt.*   35

5.1   *Enter* FESTE, *with a letter, and* FABIAN.

FABIAN   Now, as thou lov'st me, let me see his letter.

FESTE   Good Master Fabian, grant me another request.

FABIAN   Anything.

FESTE   Do not desire to see this letter.

FABIAN   This is to give a dog and, in recompense, desire   5
my dog again.

Enter ORSINO, VIOLA *as Cesario,* CURIO *and Lords.*

ORSINO   Belong you to the Lady Olivia, friends?

FESTE   Ay, sir, we are some of her trappings.

ORSINO
I know thee well. How dost thou, my good fellow?

FESTE   Truly, sir, the better for my foes, and the worse   10
for my friends.

ORSINO   Just the contrary: the better for thy friends.

FESTE   No, sir, the worse.

ORSINO   How can that be?

FESTE   Marry, sir, they praise me and make an ass of me.   15
Now my foes tell me plainly I am an ass, so that by my
foes, sir, I profit in the knowledge of myself, and by my
friends I am abused. So that, conclusions to be as
kisses, if your four negatives make your two
affirmatives, why then, the worse for my friends and   20
the better for my foes.

ORSINO   Why, this is excellent.

FESTE   By my troth, sir, no, though it please you to be
one of my friends.

ORSINO
Thou shalt not be the worse for me: there's gold.   25
  [*Gives coin.*]

FESTE   But that it would be double-dealing, sir, I would
you could make it another.

ORSINO   O, you give me ill counsel.

FESTE   Put your grace in your pocket, sir, for this once,   30
and let your flesh and blood obey it.

ORSINO   Well, I will be so much a sinner to be a double-
dealer. There's another. [*Gives coin.*]

FESTE   *Primo, secundo, tertio* is a good play, and the old
saying is 'The third pays for all.' The triplex, sir, is a   35
good tripping measure, as the bells of Saint Bennet,
sir, may put you in mind – one, two, three.

ORSINO   You can fool no more money out of me at this

throw. If you will let your lady know I am here to speak
with her, and bring her along with you, it may awake
40   my bounty further.

FESTE   Marry, sir, lullaby to your bounty till I come
again. I go, sir, but I would not have you to think that
my desire of having is the sin of covetousness. But as
you say, sir, let your bounty take a nap, I will awake it
45   anon.   *Exit.*

Enter ANTONIO *and* Officers.

VIOLA   Here comes the man, sir, that did rescue me.
ORSINO   That face of his I do remember well,
Yet when I saw it last it was besmeared
As black as Vulcan in the smoke of war.
50   A baubling vessel was he captain of,
For shallow draught and bulk unprizable,
With which such scatheful grapple did he make
With the most noble bottom of our fleet
That very envy and the tongue of loss
55   Cried fame and honour on him. – What's the matter?
1 OFFICER   Orsino, this is that Antonio
That took the Phoenix and her fraught from Candy,
And this is he that did the Tiger board,
When your young nephew Titus lost his leg.
60   Here in the streets, desperate of shame and state,
In private brabble did we apprehend him.
VIOLA   He did me kindness, sir, drew on my side,
But in conclusion put strange speech upon me.
I know not what 'twas but distraction.
ORSINO [*to Antonio*]
65   Notable pirate, thou salt-water thief,
What foolish boldness brought thee to their mercies
Whom thou in terms so bloody and so dear
Hast made thine enemies?
ANTONIO   Orsino, noble sir,
Be pleased that I shake off these names you give me.
70   Antonio never yet was thief or pirate,
Though I confess on base and ground enough
Orsino's enemy. A witchcraft drew me hither:
That most ingrateful boy there by your side
From the rude sea's enraged and foamy mouth
75   Did I redeem. A wreck past hope he was.
His life I gave him and did thereto add
My love, without retention or restraint,
All his in dedication. For his sake
Did I expose myself – pure for his love –
80   Into the danger of this adverse town,
Drew to defend him when he was beset,
Where, being apprehended, his false cunning,
Not meaning to partake with me in danger,
Taught him to face me out of his acquaintance,
85   And grew a twenty years' removed thing
While one would wink, denied me mine own purse,
Which I had recommended to his use
Not half an hour before.
VIOLA   How can this be?
ORSINO   When came he to this town?

ANTONIO   Today, my lord, and for three months before,   90
No interim, not a minute's vacancy,
Both day and night did we keep company.

Enter OLIVIA *and Attendants.*

ORSINO
Here comes the countess; now heaven walks on earth.
But for thee, fellow – fellow, thy words are madness.
Three months this youth hath tended upon me.   95
But more of that anon. – Take him aside.
OLIVIA
What would my lord, but that he may not have,
Wherein Olivia may seem serviceable?
Cesario, you do not keep promise with me.
VIOLA   Madam –   100
ORSINO   Gracious Olivia –
OLIVIA   What do you say, Cesario? Good my lord –
VIOLA   My lord would speak, my duty hushes me.
OLIVIA   If it be aught to the old tune, my lord,
It is as fat and fulsome to mine ear   105
As howling after music.
ORSINO   Still so cruel?
OLIVIA   Still so constant, lord.
ORSINO   What, to perverseness? You uncivil lady,
To whose ingrate and unauspicious altars
My soul the faithfull'st offerings hath breathed out   110
That e'er devotion tendered – what shall I do?
OLIVIA
Even what it please my lord that shall become him.
ORSINO   Why should I not, had I the heart to do it,
Like to th'Egyptian thief at point of death,
Kill what I love – a savage jealousy   115
That sometime savours nobly? But hear me this:
Since you to non-regardance cast my faith,
And that I partly know the instrument
That screws me from my true place in your favour,
Live you the marble-breasted tyrant still.   120
But this your minion, whom I know you love,
And whom, by heaven I swear, I tender dearly,
Him will I tear out of that cruel eye
Where he sits crowned in his master's spite.
[*to Viola*] Come, boy, with me. My thoughts are ripe
       in mischief.   125
I'll sacrifice the lamb that I do love
To spite a raven's heart within a dove.   [*Goes to door.*]
VIOLA   And I most jocund, apt and willingly
To do you rest a thousand deaths would die.
[*Follows Orsino.*]
OLIVIA   Where goes Cesario?
VIOLA   After him I love   130
More than I love these eyes, more than my life,
More by all mores than e'er I shall love wife.
If I do feign, you witnesses above
Punish my life for tainting of my love.
OLIVIA   Ay me detested, how am I beguiled!   135
VIOLA
Who does beguile you? Who does do you wrong?

OLIVIA   Hast thou forgot thyself? Is it so long?
  [*to Attendant*] Call forth the holy father.

                                  Exit Attendant.

ORSINO [*to Viola*]   Come, away.
OLIVIA   Whither, my lord? Cesario, husband, stay!
ORSINO   Husband?

140   OLIVIA   Ay, husband. Can he that deny?
ORSINO   Her husband, sirrah?
VIOLA   No, my lord, not I.
OLIVIA   Alas, it is the baseness of thy fear
  That makes thee strangle thy propriety.
  Fear not, Cesario, take thy fortunes up,

145   Be that thou knowst thou art, and then thou art
  As great as that thou fear'st.

         Enter Priest *and Attendant.*

                O welcome, father.
  Father, I charge thee by thy reverence
  Here to unfold – though lately we intended
  To keep in darkness what occasion now

150   Reveals before 'tis ripe – what thou dost know
  Hath newly passed between this youth and me.
PRIEST   A contract of eternal bond of love,
  Confirmed by mutual joinder of your hands,
  Attested by the holy close of lips,

155   Strengthened by interchangement of your rings,
  And all the ceremony of this compact
  Sealed in my function, by my testimony.
  Since when, my watch hath told me, toward my grave
  I have travelled but two hours.
ORSINO [*to Viola*]

160   O thou dissembling cub! What wilt thou be
  When time hath sowed a grizzle on thy case?
  Or will not else thy craft so quickly grow
  That thine own trip shall be thine overthrow?
  Farewell, and take her, but direct thy feet

165   Where thou and I henceforth may never meet.
VIOLA   My lord, I do protest –
OLIVIA   O do not swear!
  Hold little faith, though thou hast too much fear.

             Enter SIR ANDREW.

SIR ANDREW   For the love of God, a surgeon! Send one
  presently to Sir Toby.

170   OLIVIA   What's the matter?
SIR ANDREW   Has broke my head across, and has given
  Sir Toby a bloody coxcomb too. For the love of God,
  your help! I had rather than forty pound I were at home.
OLIVIA   Who has done this, Sir Andrew?

175   SIR ANDREW   The count's gentleman, one Cesario. We
  took him for a coward, but he's the very devil
  incardinate.
ORSINO   My gentleman Cesario?
SIR ANDREW   'Od's lifelings, here he is! [*to Viola*] You

180   broke my head for nothing, and that that I did I was set
  on to do't by Sir Toby.
VIOLA   Why do you speak to me? I never hurt you.

You drew your sword upon me without cause,
  But I bespake you fair and hurt you not.

         Enter SIR TOBY *and* FESTE.

SIR ANDREW   If a bloody coxcomb be a hurt, you have   185
  hurt me. I think you set nothing by a bloody coxcomb.
  Here comes Sir Toby halting. You shall hear more; but
  if he had not been in drink he would have tickled you
  othergates than he did.
ORSINO [*to Sir Toby*]   How now, gentleman? How is't   190
  with you?
SIR ANDREW   That's all one, has hurt me, and there's
  th'end on't. [*to Feste*] Sot, didst see Dick Surgeon, sot?
FESTE   O he's drunk, Sir Toby, an hour agone. His eyes
  were set at eight i'th' morning.   195
SIR TOBY   Then he's a rogue, and a passy-measures
  pavan. I hate a drunken rogue.
OLIVIA   Away with him! Who hath made this havoc with
  them?
SIR ANDREW   I'll help you, Sir Toby, because we'll be   200
  dressed together.
SIR TOBY   Will you help? An ass-head and a coxcomb
  and a knave, a thin-faced knave, a gull?
OLIVIA   Get him to bed, and let his hurt be looked to.

    Exeunt Sir Toby, Sir Andrew, Fabian and Feste.

              Enter SEBASTIAN.

SEBASTIAN [*to Olivia*]
  I am sorry, madam, I have hurt your kinsman,   205
  But had it been the brother of my blood
  I must have done no less with wit and safety.
  You throw a strange regard upon me, and by that
  I do perceive it hath offended you.
  Pardon me, sweet one, even for the vows   210
  We made each other but so late ago.
ORSINO
  One face, one voice, one habit and two persons:
  A natural perspective, that is and is not.
SEBASTIAN   Antonio! O my dear Antonio,
  How have the hours racked and tortured me   215
  Since I have lost thee!
ANTONIO   Sebastian are you?
SEBASTIAN   Fear'st thou that, Antonio?
ANTONIO   How have you made division of yourself?
  An apple cleft in two is not more twin
  Than these two creatures. Which is Sebastian?   220
OLIVIA   Most wonderful!
SEBASTIAN [*Sees Viola.*]
  Do I stand there? I never had a brother,
  Nor can there be that deity in my nature
  Of here and everywhere. I had a sister,
  Whom the blind waves and surges have devoured.   225
  [*to Viola*] Of charity, what kin are you to me?
  What countryman? What name? What parentage?
VIOLA   Of Messaline. Sebastian was my father.
  Such a Sebastian was my brother too;
  So went he suited to his watery tomb.   230

If spirits can assume both form and suit,
You come to fright us.

SEBASTIAN   A spirit I am indeed,
But am in that dimension grossly clad
Which from the womb I did participate.
235   Were you a woman, as the rest goes even,
I should my tears let fall upon your cheek
And say, 'Thrice welcome, drowned Viola.'
VIOLA   My father had a mole upon his brow.
SEBASTIAN   And so had mine.
240   VIOLA   And died that day when Viola from her birth
Had numbered thirteen years.
SEBASTIAN   O, that record is lively in my soul!
He finished indeed his mortal act
That day that made my sister thirteen years.
245   VIOLA   If nothing lets to make us happy both
But this my masculine usurped attire,
Do not embrace me till each circumstance
Of place, time, fortune do cohere and jump
That I am Viola – which to confirm
250   I'll bring you to a captain in this town,
Where lie my maiden weeds, by whose gentle help
I was preserved to serve this noble count.
All the occurrence of my fortune since
Hath been between this lady and this lord.
SEBASTIAN [*to Olivia*]
255   So comes it, lady, you have been mistook;
But nature to her bias drew in that.
You would have been contracted to a maid,
Nor are you therein, by my life, deceived.
You are betrothed both to a maid and man.
ORSINO [*to Olivia*]
260   Be not amazed, right noble is his blood.
If this be so, as yet the glass seems true,
I shall have share in this most happy wreck.
[*to Viola*] Boy, thou hast said to me a thousand times
Thou never shouldst love woman like to me.
265   VIOLA   And all those sayings will I overswear,
And all those swearings keep as true in soul
As doth that orbed continent the fire
That severs day from night.
ORSINO   Give me thy hand,
And let me see thee in thy woman's weeds.
270   VIOLA   The captain that did bring me first on shore
Hath my maid's garments. He upon some action
Is now in durance, at Malvolio's suit,
A gentleman and follower of my lady's.
OLIVIA   He shall enlarge him – fetch Malvolio hither.
275   And yet, alas, now I remember me,
They say, poor gentleman, he's much distract.

Enter FESTE, *with a letter, and* FABIAN.

A most extracting frenzy of mine own
From my remembrance clearly banished his.
[*to Feste*] How does he, sirrah?
280   FESTE   Truly, madam, he holds Beelzebub at the stave's
end as well as a man in his case may do. Has here writ

a letter to you. I should have given't you today
morning, but, as a madman's epistles are no gospels, so
it skills not much when they are delivered.
OLIVIA   Open't and read it.   285
FESTE   Look then to be well edified, when the fool
delivers the madman. [*Reads madly.*] *By the Lord,*
madam –
OLIVIA   How now, art thou mad?
FESTE   No, madam, I do but read madness. An your   290
ladyship will have it as it ought to be, you must allow
vox.
OLIVIA   Prithee read i'thy right wits.
FESTE   So I do, madonna, but to read his right wits is to
read thus. Therefore, perpend, my princess, and give   295
ear.
OLIVIA [*to Fabian*]   Read it you, sirrah.
FABIAN [*Reads.*]   *By the Lord, madam, you wrong me, and*
the world shall know it. Though you have put me into
darkness and given your drunken cousin rule over me, yet   300
have I the benefit of my senses as well as your ladyship. I
have your own letter that induced me to the semblance I put
on, with the which I doubt not but to do myself much right
or you much shame. Think of me as you please. I leave my
duty a little unthought of, and speak out of my injury.   305
                    The madly used Malvolio.
OLIVIA   Did he write this?
FESTE   Ay, madam.
ORSINO   This savours not much of distraction.
OLIVIA   See him delivered, Fabian; bring him hither.   310
                                    Exit Fabian.
My lord, so please you, these things further thought
    on,
To think me as well a sister as a wife,
One day shall crown th'alliance on't, so please you,
Here at my house and at my proper cost.
ORSINO   Madam, I am most apt t'embrace your offer.   315
[*to Viola*] Your master quits you, and for your service
    done him –
So much against the mettle of your sex,
So far beneath your soft and tender breeding –
And, since you called me master for so long,
Here is my hand; you shall from this time be   320
Your master's mistress.
OLIVIA   A sister – you are she.

Enter MALVOLIO, *with a letter, and* FABIAN.

ORSINO   Is this the madman?
OLIVIA   Ay, my lord, this same.
How now, Malvolio?
MALVOLIO   Madam, you have done me wrong,
Notorious wrong.
OLIVIA   Have I, Malvolio? No.
MALVOLIO   Lady, you have. Pray you peruse that letter.   325
You must not now deny it is your hand.
Write from it, if you can, in hand or phrase,
Or say 'tis not your seal, not your invention.
You can say none of this. Well, grant it then,

330 And tell me in the modesty of honour
Why you have given me such clear lights of favour,
Bade me come smiling and cross-gartered to you,
To put on yellow stockings, and to frown
Upon Sir Toby and the lighter people;
335 And acting this in an obedient hope,
Why have you suffered me to be imprisoned,
Kept in a dark house, visited by the priest,
And made the most notorious geck and gull
That e'er invention played on! Tell me why!
340 OLIVIA Alas, Malvolio, this is not my writing –
Though I confess much like the character –
But out of question 'tis Maria's hand.
And now I do bethink me, it was she
First told me thou wast mad; then cam'st in smiling
345 And in such forms which here were presupposed
Upon thee in the letter. Prithee be content;
This practice hath most shrewdly passed upon thee,
But when we know the grounds and authors of it,
Thou shalt be both the plaintiff and the judge
Of thine own cause.
350 FABIAN   Good madam, hear me speak,
And let no quarrel nor no brawl to come
Taint the condition of this present hour,
Which I have wondered at. In hope it shall not,
Most freely I confess myself and Toby
355 Set this device against Malvolio here,
Upon some stubborn and uncourteous parts
We had conceived against him. Maria writ
The letter, at Sir Toby's great importance,
In recompense whereof he hath married her.
360 How with a sportful malice it was followed
May rather pluck on laughter than revenge,
If that the injuries be justly weighed
That have on both sides passed.
OLIVIA [*to Malvolio*]
Alas, poor fool, how have they baffled thee!
365 FESTE Why, 'Some are born great, some achieve
greatness and some have greatness thrown upon
them.' I was one, sir, in this interlude, one Sir Topas,
sir, but that's all one. 'By the Lord, fool, I am not
mad.' But do you remember, 'Madam, why laugh

370 you at such a barren rascal, an you smile not, he's
gagged'? And thus the whirligig of time brings in his
revenges.
MALVOLIO
I'll be revenged on the whole pack of you!   *Exit.*
OLIVIA   He hath been most notoriously abused.
ORSINO [*to Fabian*]
375 Pursue him, and entreat him to a peace.   *Exit Fabian.*
He hath not told us of the captain yet;
When that is known, and golden time convents,
A solemn combination shall be made
Of our dear souls. Meantime, sweet sister,
380 We will not part from hence. Cesario, come –
For so you shall be while you are a man;
But when in other habits you are seen,
Orsino's mistress and his fancy's queen.
                              Exeunt all but Feste.
FESTE [*Sings.*]
When that I was and a little tiny boy,
With hey, ho, the wind and the rain,
385 A foolish thing was but a toy,
For the rain it raineth every day.

But when I came to man's estate,
With hey, ho, the wind and the rain,
390 'Gainst knaves and thieves men shut their gate,
For the rain it raineth every day.

But when I came, alas, to wive,
With hey, ho, the wind and the rain,
By swaggering could I never thrive,
395 For the rain it raineth every day.

But when I came unto my beds,
With hey, ho, the wind and the rain,
With tosspots still had drunken heads,
For the rain it raineth every day.

A great while ago the world begun,
400 With hey, ho, the wind and the rain,
But that's all one, our play is done,
And we'll strive to please you every day.   *Exit.*

The Two Gentlemen of Verona

The Two Gentlemen of Verona occupies a prominent position in the First Folio of 1623, where it was first printed. It is the second play, following The Tempest, though it seems to have been written around 1594 (some scholars believe it is earlier). Francis Meres grouped it among six of Shakespeare's comedies as examples to show that he 'is the most excellent' author of both comedy and tragedy. The play's primary sources include the Spanish romance Diana by George of Montemayor, translated into English by Bartholomew Yong; the tale of Titus and Gisippus in Sir Thomas Elyot's The Boke Named the Governour; and Arthur Brooke's poem The Tragical History of Romeus and Juliet.

Shakespeare added Valentine to Montemayor's tragicomic love-triangle of two women and a faithless man, creating two couples, complex in different ways, who exit to a double wedding at the end. Shakespeare's other major change was to add the servants Speed and Lance, and Lance's dog, Crab, the only animal role in Shakespeare and an important source of the play's theatrical appeal (real dogs on the stage have often misbehaved in various ways, or just not responded as intended). Lance and Crab, moreover, parody the main plot's romantic story. Julia is the first of Shakespeare's heroines in male disguise, a device that took advantage of the skilful boy actors in Shakespeare's company; he continued to exploit this blurring of traditional gender stereotypes in his later comedies, with Portia (Merchant of Venice), Rosalind (As You Like It), Viola (Twelfth Night) and Innogen (Cymbeline).

The most controversial moments of the play come in the final scene with a sequence of events that modern readers often find difficult to accept: Proteus's attempted rape of Silvia, Valentine's intervention, Proteus's psychologically implausible sudden penitence and Valentine's forgiveness of Proteus and his offer to 'give' Silvia to his now-reformed friend. While these melodramatic events can be (partly) justified as a critique of the discourse of male friendship (which Shakespeare would later treat more directly in The Two Noble Kinsmen), they have nevertheless motivated attempts to rewrite the play's ending for performance, beginning with Benjamin Victor (1763), who simply omitted Valentine's offer of Silvia and rearranged some of the lines to produce a more general reconciliation. While Shakespeare's text formally resolves the predicaments of its characters, it also usually leaves viewers unsettled and not quite satisfied. The play emphasizes metamorphosis – especially through love and role-playing – as an invigorating source of energy but one that also destabilizes identity.

The play has a fairly continuous stage history, and although it is not performed as often as many of the comedies, The Two Gentlemen of Verona was chosen, in the summer of 1996, as the first play to be staged at the reconstructed Shakespeare's Globe in London, and was the play being performed in the opening scenes of the Oscar-winning Best Picture of 1998, Shakespeare in Love, in which the 'Henslowe' character says, 'Love and a bit with a dog, that's what they like'. Shakespeare's original audience no doubt agreed..

The Arden text is based on the 1623 First Folio.

LIST OF ROLES

DUKE	*father to Silvia*
VALENTINE	
PROTEUS	*the two gentlemen*
ANTONIO	*father to Proteus*
TURIO	*a foolish rival to Valentine*
EGLAMOUR	*agent for Silvia in her escape*
HOST	*where Julia lodges*
OUTLAWS	*with Valentine*
SPEED	*a clownish servant to Valentine*
LANCE	*the like to Proteus*
PANTINO	*servant to Antonio*
JULIA	*beloved of Proteus*
SILVIA	*beloved of Valentine*
LUCETTA	*waiting-woman to Julia*
SERVANT	*to the Duke*

Attendants and Musicians

1.1 *Enter* VALENTINE *and* PROTEUS.

VALENTINE   Cease to persuade, my loving Proteus;
  Home-keeping youth have ever homely wits.
  Were't not affection chains thy tender days
  To the sweet glances of thy honoured love,
5 I rather would entreat thy company
  To see the wonders of the world abroad
  Than, living dully sluggardized at home,
  Wear out thy youth with shapeless idleness.
  But since thou lov'st, love still, and thrive therein,
10 Even as I would when I to love begin.
  PROTEUS   Wilt thou be gone? Sweet Valentine, adieu.
  Think on thy Proteus when thou haply seest
  Some rare noteworthy object in thy travel.
  Wish me partaker in thy happiness
15 When thou dost meet good hap; and in thy danger,
  If ever danger do environ thee,
  Commend thy grievance to my holy prayers,
  For I will be thy beadsman, Valentine.
VALENTINE   And on a love-book pray for my success?
20 PROTEUS   Upon some book I love I'll pray for thee.
VALENTINE   That's on some shallow story of deep love –
  How young Leander crossed the Hellespont.
PROTEUS   That's a deep story of a deeper love,
  For he was more than over-shoes in love.
25 VALENTINE   'Tis true; for you are over-boots in love
  And yet you never swam the Hellespont.
PROTEUS   Over the boots? Nay, give me not the boots.
VALENTINE   No, I will not, for it boots thee not.
PROTEUS   What?
VALENTINE
  To be in love, where scorn is bought with groans,
  Coy looks with heart-sore sighs, one fading
30   moment's mirth
  With twenty watchful, weary, tedious nights.
  If haply won, perhaps a hapless gain;
  If lost, why then a grievous labour won;
  However, but a folly bought with wit,
35 Or else a wit by folly vanquished.
PROTEUS   So, by your circumstance, you call me fool.
VALENTINE
  So, by your circumstance, I fear you'll prove.
PROTEUS   'Tis Love you cavil at. I am not Love.
VALENTINE   Love is your master, for he masters you;
40 And he that is so yoked by a fool
  Methinks should not be chronicled for wise.
PROTEUS   Yet writers say, as in the sweetest bud
  The eating canker dwells, so doting love
  Inhabits in the finest wits of all.
45 VALENTINE   And writers say, as the most forward bud
  Is eaten by the canker ere it blow,
  Even so by love the young and tender wit
  Is turned to folly, blasting in the bud,
  Losing his verdure, even in the prime,
50 And all the fair effects of future hopes.
  But wherefore waste I time to counsel thee

  That art a votary to fond desire?
  Once more, adieu. My father at the road
  Expects my coming, there to see me shipped.
PROTEUS   And thither will I bring thee, Valentine.   55
VALENTINE   Sweet Proteus, no. Now let us take our leave.
  To Milan let me hear from thee by letters
  Of thy success in love, and what news else
  Betideth here in absence of thy friend;
  And I likewise will visit thee with mine.   60
PROTEUS   All happiness bechance to thee in Milan.
VALENTINE
  As much to you at home, and so farewell.   *Exit.*
PROTEUS   He after honour hunts, I after love:
  He leaves his friends to dignify them more;
  I leave myself, my friends and all, for love.   65
  Thou, Julia, thou hast metamorphosed me:
  Made me neglect my studies, lose my time,
  War with good counsel, set the world at naught;
  Made wit with musing weak, heart sick with thought.

Enter SPEED.

SPEED   Sir Proteus, 'save you. Saw you my master?   70
PROTEUS
  But now he parted hence to embark for Milan.
SPEED   Twenty to one, then, he is shipped already,
  And I have played the sheep in losing him.
PROTEUS   Indeed, a sheep doth very often stray,
  An if the shepherd be awhile away.   75
SPEED
  You conclude that my master is a shepherd then, and
    I a sheep?
PROTEUS   I do.
SPEED
  Why then, my horns are his horns, whether I wake or
    sleep.
PROTEUS   A silly answer, and fitting well a sheep.
SPEED   This proves me still a sheep.   80
PROTEUS   True, and thy master a shepherd.
SPEED   Nay, that I can deny by a circumstance.
PROTEUS   It shall go hard but I'll prove it by another.
SPEED   The shepherd seeks the sheep, and not the sheep
  the shepherd; but I seek my master, and my master   85
  seeks not me. Therefore I am no sheep.
PROTEUS   The sheep for fodder follow the shepherd,
  the shepherd for food follows not the sheep; thou for
  wages followest thy master, thy master for wages
  follows not thee. Therefore thou art a sheep.   90
SPEED   Such another proof will make me cry 'baa'.
PROTEUS   But dost thou hear? Gav'st thou my letter to
  Julia?
SPEED   Ay, sir. I, a lost mutton, gave your letter to her, a
  laced mutton, and she, a laced mutton, gave me, a lost   95
  mutton, nothing for my labour.
PROTEUS   Here's too small a pasture for such store of
  muttons.
SPEED   If the ground be overcharged, you were best
  stick her.   100

PROTEUS   Nay, in that you are astray; 'twere best pound
　　you.
SPEED   Nay, sir, less than a pound shall serve me for
　　carrying your letter.
105   PROTEUS   You mistake; I mean the pound – a pinfold.
SPEED   From a pound to a pin? Fold it over and over,
　　'Tis threefold too little for carrying a letter to your
　　lover.
PROTEUS   But what said she?
SPEED   [*Nods his head.*] Ay.
110   PROTEUS   Nod-ay – why, that's 'noddy'.
SPEED   You mistook, sir. I say she did nod, and you ask
　　me if she did nod, and I say 'Ay'.
PROTEUS   And that set together is 'noddy'.
SPEED   Now you have taken the pains to set it together,
115   　　take it for your pains.
PROTEUS   No, no, you shall have it for bearing the letter.
SPEED   Well, I perceive I must be fain to bear with you.
PROTEUS   Why, sir, how do you bear with me?
SPEED   Marry, sir, the letter, very orderly, having
120   　　nothing but the word 'noddy' for my pains.
PROTEUS   Beshrew me, but you have a quick wit.
SPEED   And yet it cannot overtake your slow purse.
PROTEUS   Come, come, open the matter; in brief, what
　　said she?
125   SPEED   Open your purse, that the money and the matter
　　may be both at once delivered.
PROTEUS   [*Gives him a coin.*]   Well, sir, here is for your
　　pains. What said she?
SPEED   [*Examines coin.*]   Truly, sir, I think you'll hardly
130   　　win her.
PROTEUS   Why? Couldst thou perceive so much from
　　her?
SPEED   Sir, I could perceive nothing at all from her;
　　No, not so much as a ducat for delivering your letter.
135   　　And being so hard to me that brought your mind,
　　I fear she'll prove as hard to you in telling your mind.
　　Give her no token but stones, for she's as hard as steel.
PROTEUS   What said she, nothing?
SPEED   No, not so much as 'Take this for thy pains.' To
140   　　testify your bounty, I thank you, you have testerned
　　me; in requital whereof, henceforth carry your letters
　　yourself. And so, sir, I'll commend you to my master.
　　　　　　　　　　　　　　　　　　　　　　　Exit.
PROTEUS   Go, go, begone, to save your ship from wreck,
　　Which cannot perish having thee aboard,
145   　　Being destined to a drier death on shore.
　　I must go send some better messenger.
　　I fear my Julia would not deign my lines,
　　Receiving them from such a worthless post.   *Exit.*

1.2   *Enter* JULIA *and* LUCETTA.

JULIA   But say, Lucetta, now we are alone,
　　Wouldst thou then counsel me to fall in love?
LUCETTA   Ay, madam, so you stumble not unheedfully.
JULIA   Of all the fair resort of gentlemen

That every day with parle encounter me,   5
In thy opinion which is worthiest love?
LUCETTA
Please you repeat their names, I'll show my mind
According to my shallow simple skill.
JULIA   What think'st thou of the fair Sir Eglamour?
LUCETTA   As of a knight well-spoken, neat and fine;   10
But, were I you, he never should be mine.
JULIA   What think'st thou of the rich Mercatio?
LUCETTA   Well of his wealth; but of himself, so-so.
JULIA   What think'st thou of the gentle Proteus?
LUCETTA   Lord, Lord, to see what folly reigns in us!   15
JULIA   How now? What means this passion at his name?
LUCETTA   Pardon, dear madam, 'tis a passing shame
That I, unworthy body as I am,
Should censure thus on lovely gentlemen.
JULIA   Why not on Proteus, as of all the rest?   20
LUCETTA   Then thus: of many good, I think him best.
JULIA   Your reason?
LUCETTA   I have no other but a woman's reason:
I think him so because I think him so.
JULIA   And wouldst thou have me cast my love on him?   25
LUCETTA   Ay, if you thought your love not cast away.
JULIA   Why, he of all the rest hath never moved me.
LUCETTA   Yet he of all the rest I think best loves ye.
JULIA   His little speaking shows his love but small.
LUCETTA   Fire that's closest kept burns most of all.   30
JULIA   They do not love that do not show their love.
LUCETTA   O, they love least that let men know their love.
JULIA   I would I knew his mind.
LUCETTA   Peruse this paper, madam.
　　[*Gives her a letter.*]
JULIA   *To Julia.* Say, from whom?   35
LUCETTA   That the contents will show.
JULIA   Say, say, who gave it thee?
LUCETTA
Sir Valentine's page; and sent, I think, from Proteus.
He would have given it you, but I, being in the way,
Did in your name receive it. Pardon the fault, I pray.   40
JULIA   Now, by my modesty, a goodly broker!
Dare you presume to harbour wanton lines?
To whisper and conspire against my youth?
Now trust me, 'tis an office of great worth,
And you an officer fit for the place.   45
There, take the paper. See it be returned,
Or else return no more into my sight.
LUCETTA   To plead for love deserves more fee than hate.
JULIA   Will ye be gone?
LUCETTA   That you may ruminate.   *Exit.*
JULIA   And yet I would I had o'erlooked the letter;   50
It were a shame to call her back again
And pray her to a fault for which I chid her.
What fool is she, that knows I am a maid
And would not force the letter to my view,
Since maids in modesty say 'No' to that   55
Which they would have the profferer construe 'Ay'.
Fie, fie, how wayward is this foolish love

That, like a testy babe, will scratch the nurse
And presently, all humbled, kiss the rod!
60 How churlishly I chid Lucetta hence,
When willingly I would have had her here!
How angerly I taught my brow to frown,
When inward joy enforced my heart to smile!
My penance is to call Lucetta back
65 And ask remission for my folly past.
What ho! Lucetta!

Enter LUCETTA.

LUCETTA   What would your ladyship?
JULIA   Is't near dinner-time?
LUCETTA   I would it were,
That you might kill your stomach on your meat
And not upon your maid.
          [*Drops and picks up the letter.*]
70 JULIA   What is't that you took up so gingerly?
LUCETTA   Nothing.
JULIA   Why didst thou stoop then?
LUCETTA   To take a paper up that I let fall.
JULIA   And is that paper nothing?
75 LUCETTA   Nothing concerning me.
JULIA   Then let it lie for those that it concerns.
LUCETTA   Madam, it will not lie where it concerns,
Unless it have a false interpreter.
JULIA   Some love of yours hath writ to you in rhyme.
80 LUCETTA   That I might sing it, madam, to a tune.
Give me a note, your ladyship can set –
JULIA   As little by such toys as may be possible.
Best sing it to the tune of 'Light o'love'.
LUCETTA   It is too heavy for so light a tune.
85 JULIA   Heavy? Belike it hath some burden then?
LUCETTA   Ay, and melodious were it, would you sing it.
JULIA   And why not you?
LUCETTA   I cannot reach so high.
JULIA   Let's see your song.   [*Takes the letter.*]
                    How now, minion!
LUCETTA   Keep tune there still, so you will sing it out.
90 And yet methinks I do not like this tune.
JULIA   You do not?
LUCETTA   No, madam, 'tis too sharp.
JULIA   You, minion, are too saucy.
LUCETTA   Nay, now you are too flat,
And mar the concord with too harsh a descant.
95 There wanteth but a mean to fill your song.
JULIA   The mean is drowned with your unruly bass.
LUCETTA   Indeed, I bid the base for Proteus.
JULIA   This babble shall not henceforth trouble me;
Here is a coil with protestation.   [*Tears the letter.*]
100 Go, get you gone, and let the papers lie.
You would be fingering them to anger me.
LUCETTA
She makes it strange, but she would be best pleased
To be so angered with another letter.   *Exit.*
JULIA   Nay, would I were so angered with the same.
105 O hateful hands, to tear such loving words!

Injurious wasps, to feed on such sweet honey
And kill the bees that yield it with your stings!
I'll kiss each several paper for amends.
Look, here is writ *kind Julia*. Unkind Julia!
As in revenge of thy ingratitude,   110
I throw thy name against the bruising stones,
Trampling contemptuously on thy disdain.
And here is writ *love-wounded Proteus*.
Poor wounded name, my bosom as a bed
Shall lodge thee till thy wound be throughly healed;   115
And thus I search it with a sovereign kiss.
But twice or thrice was *Proteus* written down.
Be calm, good wind, blow not a word away
Till I have found each letter in the letter,
Except mine own name. That, some whirlwind bear   120
Unto a ragged, fearful, hanging rock,
And throw it thence into the raging sea.
Lo, here in one line is his name twice writ,
Poor forlorn Proteus, passionate Proteus,
To the sweet Julia – that I'll tear away;   125
And yet I will not, sith so prettily
He couples it to his complaining names.
Thus will I fold them, one upon another;
Now kiss, embrace, contend, do what you will.

Enter LUCETTA.

LUCETTA
Madam, dinner is ready, and your father stays.   130
JULIA   Well, let us go.
LUCETTA
What, shall these papers lie like tell-tales here?
JULIA   If you respect them, best to take them up.
LUCETTA   Nay, I was taken up for laying them down.
Yet here they shall not lie, for catching cold.   135
          [*Picks up pieces of the letter.*]
JULIA   I see you have a month's mind to them.
LUCETTA   Ay, madam, you may say what sights you see;
I see things too, although you judge I wink.
JULIA   Come, come, will't please you go?   *Exeunt.*

1.3   *Enter* ANTONIO *and* PANTINO.

ANTONIO   Tell me, Pantino, what sad talk was that
Wherewith my brother held you in the cloister?
PANTINO   'Twas of his nephew, Proteus your son.
ANTONIO   Why? What of him?
PANTINO   He wondered that your lordship
Would suffer him to spend his youth at home   5
While other men, of slender reputation,
Put forth their sons to seek preferment out –
Some to the wars to try their fortune there;
Some to discover islands far away;
Some to the studious universities.   10
For any or for all these exercises
He said that Proteus your son was meet,
And did request me to importune you
To let him spend his time no more at home,

15   Which would be great impeachment to his age
      In having known no travel in his youth.
  ANTONIO
      Nor need'st thou much importune me to that
      Whereon this month I have been hammering.
      I have considered well his loss of time,
20   And how he cannot be a perfect man
      Not being tried and tutored in the world.
      Experience is by industry achieved
      And perfected by the swift course of time.
      Then tell me, whither were I best to send him?
25 PANTINO   I think your lordship is not ignorant
      How his companion, youthful Valentine,
      Attends the Emperor in his royal court.
  ANTONIO   I know it well.
  PANTINO
      'Twere good, I think, your lordship sent him thither.
30   There shall he practise tilts and tournaments,
      Hear sweet discourse, converse with noblemen
      And be in eye of every exercise
      Worthy his youth and nobleness of birth.
  ANTONIO   I like thy counsel; well hast thou advised.
35   And that thou mayst perceive how well I like it,
      The execution of it shall make known;
      Even with the speediest expedition
      I will dispatch him to the Emperor's court.
  PANTINO   Tomorrow, may it please you, Don Alfonso
40   With other gentlemen of good esteem
      Are journeying to salute the Emperor
      And to commend their service to his will.
  ANTONIO
      Good company – with them shall Proteus go.

                  Enter PROTEUS *reading a letter.*

      And in good time! Now will we break with him.
45 PROTEUS   Sweet love, sweet lines, sweet life!
      Here is her hand, the agent of her heart;
      Here is her oath for love, her honour's pawn.
      O, that our fathers would applaud our loves
      To seal our happiness with their consents.
50   O heavenly Julia!
  ANTONIO
      How now? What letter are you reading there?
  PROTEUS
      May't please your lordship, 'tis a word or two
      Of commendations sent from Valentine,
      Delivered by a friend that came from him.
55 ANTONIO   Lend me the letter. Let me see what news.
  PROTEUS   There is no news, my lord, but that he writes
      How happily he lives, how well beloved
      And daily graced by the Emperor,
      Wishing me with him, partner of his fortune.
60 ANTONIO   And how stand you affected to his wish?
  PROTEUS   As one relying on your lordship's will,
      And not depending on his friendly wish.
  ANTONIO   My will is something sorted with his wish.
      Muse not that I thus suddenly proceed,

      For what I will, I will, and there an end.   65
      I am resolved that thou shalt spend some time
      With Valentinus in the Emperor's court.
      What maintenance he from his friends receives,
      Like exhibition thou shalt have from me.
      Tomorrow be in readiness to go.   70
      Excuse it not, for I am peremptory.
  PROTEUS   My lord, I cannot be so soon provided;
      Please you deliberate a day or two.
  ANTONIO
      Look what thou want'st shall be sent after thee.
      No more of stay: tomorrow thou must go.   75
      Come on, Pantino, you shall be employed
      To hasten on his expedition.
                          Exeunt Antonio and Pantino.
  PROTEUS
      Thus have I shunned the fire for fear of burning
      And drenched me in the sea where I am drowned.
      I feared to show my father Julia's letter   80
      Lest he should take exceptions to my love,
      And with the vantage of mine own excuse
      Hath he excepted most against my love.
      O, how this spring of love resembleth
      The uncertain glory of an April day,   85
      Which now shows all the beauty of the sun,
      And by and by a cloud takes all away.

                          Enter PANTINO.

  PANTINO   Sir Proteus, your father calls for you.
      He is in haste, therefore I pray you go.
  PROTEUS   Why this it is: my heart accords thereto,   90
      And yet a thousand times it answers 'No'.   *Exeunt.*

2.1   *Enter* VALENTINE *and* SPEED.

  SPEED   Sir, your glove.
  VALENTINE   Not mine – my gloves are on.
  SPEED   Why then, this may be yours, for this is but one.
  VALENTINE   Ha? Let me see. Ay, give it me, it's mine.
      Sweet ornament that decks a thing divine.
      Ah, Silvia, Silvia!   5
  SPEED [*Calls.*]   Madam Silvia! Madam Silvia!
  VALENTINE   How now, sirrah?
  SPEED   She is not within hearing, sir.
  VALENTINE   Why sir, who bade you call her?
  SPEED   Your worship, sir, or else I mistook.   10
  VALENTINE   Well, you'll still be too forward.
  SPEED   And yet I was last chidden for being too slow.
  VALENTINE   Go to, sir. Tell me, do you know Madam
      Silvia?
  SPEED   She that your worship loves?   15
  VALENTINE   Why, how know you that I am in love?
  SPEED   Marry, by these special marks: first, you have
      learned, like Sir Proteus, to wreathe your arms, like a
      malcontent; to relish a love-song, like a robin redbreast;
      to walk alone, like one that had the pestilence; to sigh,   20

like a schoolboy that had lost his *A B C*; to weep, like a
young wench that had buried her grandam; to fast, like
one that takes diet; to watch, like one that fears
robbing; to speak puling, like a beggar at Hallowmas.
25   You were wont, when you laughed, to crow like a cock;
when you walked, to walk like one of the lions; when
you fasted, it was presently after dinner; when you
looked sadly, it was for want of money. And now you
are metamorphosed with a mistress, that when I look
30   on you, I can hardly think you my master.
VALENTINE   Are all these things perceived in me?
SPEED   They are all perceived without ye.
VALENTINE   Without me? They cannot.
SPEED   Without you? Nay, that's certain, for without
35   you were so simple, none else would. But you are so
without these follies, that these follies are within you,
and shine through you like the water in an urinal, that
not an eye that sees you but is a physician to comment
on your malady.
40   VALENTINE   But tell me, dost thou know my lady Silvia?
SPEED   She that you gaze on so, as she sits at supper?
VALENTINE   Hast thou observed that? Even she I mean.
SPEED   Why sir, I know her not.
VALENTINE   Dost thou know her by my gazing on her,
45   and yet knowst her not?
SPEED   Is she not hard-favoured, sir?
VALENTINE   Not so fair, boy, as well-favoured.
SPEED   Sir, I know that well enough.
VALENTINE   What dost thou know?
50   SPEED   That she is not so fair as – of you – well favoured.
VALENTINE   I mean that her beauty is exquisite but her
favour infinite.
SPEED   That's because the one is painted and the other
out of all count.
55   VALENTINE   How painted? And how out of count?
SPEED   Marry, sir, so painted to make her fair that no
man counts of her beauty.
VALENTINE   How esteem'st thou me? I account of her
beauty.
60   SPEED   You never saw her since she was deformed.
VALENTINE   How long hath she been deformed?
SPEED   Ever since you loved her.
VALENTINE   I have loved her ever since I saw her, and
still I see her beautiful.
65   SPEED   If you love her, you cannot see her.
VALENTINE   Why?
SPEED   Because Love is blind. O, that you had mine
eyes, or your own eyes had the lights they were wont
to have when you chid at Sir Proteus for going
70   ungartered.
VALENTINE   What should I see then?
SPEED   Your own present folly and her passing
deformity; for he, being in love, could not see to garter
his hose; and you, being in love, cannot see to put on
75   your hose.
VALENTINE   Belike, boy, then you are in love, for last
morning you could not see to wipe my shoes.

SPEED   True, sir, I was in love with my bed. I thank you,
you swinged me for my love, which makes me the
bolder to chide you for yours.   80
VALENTINE   In conclusion, I stand affected to her.
SPEED   I would you were set, so your affection would
cease.
VALENTINE   Last night she enjoined me to write some
lines to one she loves.   85
SPEED   And have you?
VALENTINE   I have.
SPEED   Are they not lamely writ?
VALENTINE   No, boy, but as well as I can do them.

Enter SILVIA.

Peace, here she comes.   90
SPEED [*aside*]   O excellent motion! O exceeding puppet!
Now will he interpret to her.
VALENTINE
    Madam and mistress, a thousand good-morrows.
SPEED [*aside*]   O, give ye good e'en! Here's a million of
manners.   95
SILVIA   Sir Valentine and servant, to you two thousand.
SPEED [*aside*]   He should give her interest, and she gives
it him.
VALENTINE   As you enjoined me, I have writ your letter
    Unto the secret, nameless friend of yours,   100
    Which I was much unwilling to proceed in
    But for my duty to your ladyship.   [*Gives her a letter.*]
SILVIA
    I thank you, gentle servant, 'tis very clerkly done.
VALENTINE   Now trust me, madam, it came hardly off,
    For being ignorant to whom it goes   105
    I writ at random, very doubtfully.
SILVIA
    Perchance you think too much of so much pains?
VALENTINE   No, madam; so it stead you, I will write,
    Please you command, a thousand times as much.
    And yet –   110
SILVIA   A pretty period. Well, I guess the sequel;
    And yet I will not name it. And yet I care not.
    And yet take this again.   [*Offers him the letter.*]
                        And yet I thank you,
    Meaning henceforth to trouble you no more.
SPEED [*aside*]   And yet you will, and yet another 'yet'!   115
VALENTINE
    What means your ladyship? Do you not like it?
SILVIA   Yes, yes, the lines are very quaintly writ,
    But, since unwillingly, take them again.
        [*Offers the letter again.*]
    Nay, take them.
VALENTINE   Madam, they are for you.
SILVIA   Ay, ay, you writ them, sir, at my request,   120
    But I will none of them. They are for you.
    I would have had them writ more movingly.
VALENTINE
    Please you, I'll write your ladyship another.
SILVIA   And when it's writ, for my sake read it over,

125 And if it please you, so. If not, why, so.
VALENTINE   If it please me, madam? What then?
SILVIA   Why, if it please you, take it for your labour.
And so, good morrow, servant.   *Exit.*
SPEED [*aside*]   O jest unseen, inscrutable, invisible
As a nose on a man's face, or a weathercock on a
130   steeple!
My master sues to her, and she hath taught her suitor,
He being her pupil, to become her tutor.
O excellent device, was there ever heard a better?
That my master, being scribe, to himself should write
the letter?
135 VALENTINE   How now, sir? What, are you reasoning
with yourself?
SPEED   Nay, I was rhyming; 'tis you that have the
reason.
VALENTINE   To do what?
140 SPEED   To be a spokesman from Madam Silvia.
VALENTINE   To whom?
SPEED   To yourself. Why, she woos you by a figure.
VALENTINE   What figure?
SPEED   By a letter, I should say.
145 VALENTINE   Why, she hath not writ to me.
SPEED   What need she, when she hath made you write to
yourself? Why, do you not perceive the jest?
VALENTINE   No, believe me.
SPEED   No believing you indeed, sir. But did you
150   perceive her earnest?
VALENTINE   She gave me none, except an angry word.
SPEED   Why, she hath given you a letter.
VALENTINE   That's the letter I writ to her friend.
SPEED   And that letter hath she delivered, and there an
155   end.
VALENTINE   I would it were no worse.
SPEED   I'll warrant you, 'tis as well.
For often have you writ to her, and she, in modesty
Or else for want of idle time, could not again reply,
Or fearing else some messenger that might her mind
160   discover,
Herself hath taught her love himself to write unto her
lover.
All this I speak in print, for in print I found it. Why
muse you, sir? 'Tis dinner-time.
VALENTINE   I have dined.
165 SPEED   Ay, but hearken, sir: though the chameleon Love
can feed on the air, I am one that am nourished by my
victuals, and would fain have meat. O, be not like your
mistress – be moved, be moved!   *Exeunt.*

2.2   *Enter* PROTEUS *and* JULIA.

PROTEUS   Have patience, gentle Julia.
JULIA   I must, where is no remedy.
PROTEUS   When possibly I can, I will return.
JULIA   If you turn not, you will return the sooner.
5 Keep this remembrance for thy Julia's sake.
[*Gives him a ring.*]

PROTEUS
Why then, we'll make exchange: here, take you this.
[*Gives her a ring.*]
JULIA   And seal the bargain with a holy kiss.
[*They kiss.*]
PROTEUS
Here is my hand for my true constancy.
And when that hour o'erslips me in the day
Wherein I sigh not, Julia, for thy sake,   10
The next ensuing hour some foul mischance
Torment me for my love's forgetfulness.
My father stays my coming; answer not.
The tide is now – nay, not thy tide of tears,
That tide will stay me longer than I should.   15
Julia, farewell.   *Exit Julia.*
What, gone without a word?
Ay, so true love should do: it cannot speak,
For truth hath better deeds than words to grace it.

Enter PANTINO.

PANTINO
Sir Proteus, you are stayed for.
PROTEUS   Go, I come, I come.
Alas, this parting strikes poor lovers dumb.   *Exeunt.*   20

2.3   *Enter* LANCE *with his dog Crab.*

LANCE   Nay, 'twill be this hour ere I have done weeping;
all the kind of the Lances have this very fault. I have
received my proportion, like the prodigious son, and
am going with Sir Proteus to the Imperial's court. I
think Crab my dog be the sourest-natured dog that   5
lives: my mother weeping, my father wailing, my sister
crying, our maid howling, our cat wringing her hands
and all our house in a great perplexity, yet did not this
cruel-hearted cur shed one tear. He is a stone, a very
pebblestone, and has no more pity in him than a dog. A   10
Jew would have wept to have seen our parting. Why,
my grandam, having no eyes, look you, wept herself
blind at my parting. Nay, I'll show you the manner of
it. This shoe is my father. No, this left shoe is my
father. No, no, this left shoe is my mother. Nay, that   15
cannot be so neither. Yes, it is so, it is so: it hath the
worser sole. This shoe with the hole in it is my mother,
and this my father. A vengeance on't – there 'tis. Now,
sir, this staff is my sister; for, look you, she is as white
as a lily and as small as a wand. This hat is Nan, our   20
maid. I am the dog. No, the dog is himself, and I am
the dog. O, the dog is me, and I am myself. Ay, so, so.
Now come I to my father: 'Father, your blessing.' Now
should not the shoe speak a word for weeping. Now
should I kiss my father – well, he weeps on. Now come   25
I to my mother: O, that she could speak now, like a
wood woman! Well, I kiss her. Why there 'tis – here's
my mother's breath up and down. Now come I to my
sister: mark the moan she makes. Now the dog all this

30 while sheds not a tear nor speaks a word; but see how I
lay the dust with my tears.

Enter PANTINO.

PANTINO Lance, away, away! Aboard! Thy master is
shipped, and thou art to post after with oars. What's
35 the matter? Why weep'st thou, man? Away, ass, you'll
lose the tide if you tarry any longer.
LANCE It is no matter if the tied were lost, for it is the
unkindest tied that ever any man tied.
PANTINO What's the unkindest tide?
LANCE Why, he that's tied here, Crab, my dog.
40 PANTINO Tut, man, I mean thou'lt lose the flood, and
in losing the flood, lose thy voyage, and in losing thy
voyage, lose thy master, and in losing thy master, lose
thy service, and in losing thy service – why dost thou
stop my mouth?
45 LANCE For fear thou shouldst lose thy tongue.
PANTINO Where should I lose my tongue?
LANCE In thy tale.
PANTINO In thy tail!
LANCE Lose the tide, and the voyage, and the master,
50 and the service, and the tied? Why, man, if the river
were dry, I am able to fill it with my tears; if the
wind were down, I could drive the boat with my
sighs.
PANTINO Come, come away, man. I was sent to call
55 thee.
LANCE Sir, call me what thou dar'st.
PANTINO Wilt thou go?
LANCE Well, I will go. *Exeunt.*

2.4 *Enter* VALENTINE, SILVIA,
TURIO *and* SPEED.

SILVIA Servant!
VALENTINE Mistress?
SPEED Master, Sir Turio frowns on you.
VALENTINE Ay, boy, it's for love.
5 SPEED Not of you.
VALENTINE Of my mistress then.
SPEED 'Twere good you knocked him. *Exit.*
SILVIA Servant, you are sad.
VALENTINE Indeed, madam, I seem so.
10 TURIO Seem you that you are not?
VALENTINE Haply I do.
TURIO So do counterfeits.
VALENTINE So do you.
TURIO What seem I that I am not?
15 VALENTINE Wise.
TURIO What instance of the contrary?
VALENTINE Your folly.
TURIO And how quote you my folly?
VALENTINE I quote it in your jerkin.
20 TURIO My jerkin is a doublet.
VALENTINE Well, then, I'll double your folly.
TURIO How!

SILVIA What, angry, Sir Turio? Do you change colour?
VALENTINE Give him leave, madam, he is a kind of
chameleon. 25
TURIO That hath more mind to feed on your blood than
live in your air.
VALENTINE You have said, sir.
TURIO Ay, sir, and done too, for this time.
VALENTINE I know it well, sir. You always end ere you 30
begin.
SILVIA A fine volley of words, gentlemen, and quickly
shot off.
VALENTINE 'Tis indeed, madam, we thank the giver.
SILVIA Who is that, servant? 35
VALENTINE Yourself, sweet lady, for you gave the fire.
Sir Turio borrows his wit from your ladyship's looks,
and spends what he borrows kindly in your company.
TURIO Sir, if you spend word for word with me, I shall
make your wit bankrupt. 40
VALENTINE I know it well, sir. You have an exchequer
of words and, I think, no other treasure to give your
followers, for it appears by their bare liveries that they
live by your bare words.

Enter DUKE.

SILVIA No more, gentlemen, no more. Here comes my 45
father.
DUKE Now, daughter Silvia, you are hard beset.
Sir Valentine, your father is in good health;
What say you to a letter from your friends
Of much good news?
VALENTINE   My lord, I will be thankful 50
To any happy messenger from thence.
DUKE Know ye Don Antonio, your countryman?
VALENTINE Ay, my good lord, I know the gentleman
To be of worth, and worthy estimation,
And not without desert so well reputed. 55
DUKE Hath he not a son?
VALENTINE Ay, my good lord, a son that well deserves
The honour and regard of such a father.
DUKE You know him well?
VALENTINE
I knew him as myself, for from our infancy 60
We have conversed and spent our hours together.
And though myself have been an idle truant,
Omitting the sweet benefit of time
To clothe mine age with angel-like perfection,
Yet hath Sir Proteus, for that's his name, 65
Made use and fair advantage of his days:
His years but young, but his experience old;
His head unmellowed, but his judgement ripe;
And in a word, for far behind his worth
Comes all the praises that I now bestow, 70
He is complete in feature and in mind,
With all good grace to grace a gentleman.
DUKE Beshrew me, sir, but if he make this good,
He is as worthy for an empress' love,
As meet to be an emperor's counsellor. 75

Well, sir, this gentleman is come to me
With commendation from great potentates,
And here he means to spend his time awhile.
I think 'tis no unwelcome news to you.

VALENTINE
80   Should I have wished a thing, it had been he.

DUKE   Welcome him then according to his worth.
Silvia, I speak to you, and you, Sir Turio;
For Valentine, I need not cite him to it.
I will send him hither to you presently.   *Exit.*

85 VALENTINE   This is the gentleman I told your ladyship
Had come along with me, but that his mistress
Did hold his eyes locked in her crystal looks.

SILVIA   Belike that now she hath enfranchised them
Upon some other pawn for fealty.

VALENTINE
90   Nay, sure, I think she holds them prisoners still.

SILVIA   Nay, then he should be blind, and being blind
How could he see his way to seek out you?

VALENTINE   Why, lady, Love hath twenty pair of eyes.

TURIO   They say that Love hath not an eye at all.

95 VALENTINE   To see such lovers, Turio, as yourself;
Upon a homely object, Love can wink.

Enter PROTEUS.

SILVIA
Have done, have done. Here comes the gentleman.

VALENTINE
Welcome, dear Proteus! Mistress, I beseech you
Confirm his welcome with some special favour.

100 SILVIA   His worth is warrant for his welcome hither,
If this be he you oft have wished to hear from.

VALENTINE   Mistress, it is. Sweet lady, entertain him
To be my fellow-servant to your ladyship.

SILVIA   Too low a mistress for so high a servant.

105 PROTEUS   Not so, sweet lady, but too mean a servant
To have a look of such a worthy mistress.

VALENTINE   Leave off discourse of disability.
Sweet lady, entertain him for your servant.

PROTEUS   My duty will I boast of, nothing else.

110 SILVIA   And duty never yet did want his meed.
Servant, you are welcome to a worthless mistress.

PROTEUS   I'll die on him that says so but yourself.

SILVIA   That you are welcome?

PROTEUS   That you are worthless.

Enter Servant.

SERVANT
Madam, my lord your father would speak with you.

SILVIA   I wait upon his pleasure.   *Exit Servant.*
115   – Come, Sir Turio,
Go with me. – Once more, new servant, welcome.
I'll leave you to confer of home affairs;
When you have done, we look to hear from you.

PROTEUS   We'll both attend upon your ladyship.
                        Exeunt Silvia and Turio.

VALENTINE
Now tell me: how do all from whence you came?   120

PROTEUS
Your friends are well and have them much
  commended.

VALENTINE   And how do yours?

PROTEUS   I left them all in health.

VALENTINE
How does your lady? And how thrives your love?

PROTEUS   My tales of love were wont to weary you;
I know you joy not in a love-discourse.   125

VALENTINE   Ay, Proteus, but that life is altered now.
I have done penance for contemning Love,
Whose high imperious thoughts have punished me
With bitter fasts, with penitential groans,
With nightly tears and daily heart-sore sighs;   130
For in revenge of my contempt of love,
Love hath chased sleep from my enthrallèd eyes,
And made them watchers of mine own heart's sorrow.
O gentle Proteus, Love's a mighty lord,
And hath so humbled me as I confess   135
There is no woe to his correction,
Nor to his service no such joy on earth.
Now, no discourse, except it be of love;
Now can I break my fast, dine, sup and sleep
Upon the very naked name of love.   140

PROTEUS   Enough; I read your fortune in your eye.
Was this the idol that you worship so?

VALENTINE   Even she; and is she not a heavenly saint?

PROTEUS   No, but she is an earthly paragon.

VALENTINE   Call her divine.

PROTEUS   I will not flatter her.   145

VALENTINE   O, flatter me, for love delights in praises.

PROTEUS   When I was sick, you gave me bitter pills,
And I must minister the like to you.

VALENTINE   Then speak the truth by her; if not divine,
Yet let her be a principality,   150
Sovereign to all the creatures on the earth.

PROTEUS   Except my mistress.

VALENTINE   Sweet, except not any,
Except thou wilt except against my love.

PROTEUS   Have I not reason to prefer mine own?

VALENTINE   And I will help thee to prefer her too: 155
She shall be dignified with this high honour,
To bear my lady's train, lest the base earth
Should from her vesture chance to steal a kiss,
And of so great a favour growing proud
Disdain to root the summer-swelling flower   160
And make rough winter everlastingly.

PROTEUS   Why, Valentine, what braggartism is this?

VALENTINE   Pardon me, Proteus, all I can is nothing
To her, whose worth makes other worthies nothing;
She is alone.

PROTEUS   Then let her alone.   165

VALENTINE
Not for the world! Why, man, she is mine own,
And I as rich in having such a jewel

As twenty seas, if all their sand were pearl,
The water nectar and the rocks pure gold.
170 Forgive me that I do not dream on thee,
Because thou seest me dote upon my love.
My foolish rival, that her father likes
Only for his possessions are so huge,
Is gone with her along, and I must after;
175 For love, thou knowst, is full of jealousy.

PROTEUS   But she loves you?
VALENTINE
Ay, and we are betrothed; nay more, our marriage
    hour,
With all the cunning manner of our flight,
Determined of: how I must climb her window,
180 The ladder made of cords, and all the means
Plotted and 'greed on for my happiness.
Good Proteus, go with me to my chamber
In these affairs to aid me with thy counsel.

PROTEUS   Go on before; I shall enquire you forth.
185 I must unto the road to disembark
Some necessaries that I needs must use,
And then I'll presently attend you.

VALENTINE   Will you make haste?
PROTEUS   I will.   *Exit Valentine.*
Even as one heat another heat expels,
190 Or as one nail by strength drives out another,
So the remembrance of my former love
Is by a newer object quite forgotten.
Is it mine eye, or Valentine's praise,
Her true perfection, or my false transgression
195 That makes me reasonless to reason thus?
She is fair; and so is Julia that I love –
That I did love, for now my love is thawed,
Which like a waxen image 'gainst a fire
Bears no impression of the thing it was.
200 Methinks my zeal to Valentine is cold,
And that I love him not as I was wont.
O, but I love his lady too too much,
And that's the reason I love him so little.
How shall I dote on her with more advice
205 That thus without advice begin to love her?
'Tis but her picture I have yet beheld,
And that hath dazzled my reason's light;
But when I look on her perfections,
There is no reason but I shall be blind.
210 If I can check my erring love, I will;
If not, to compass her I'll use my skill.   *Exit.*

2.5   *Enter* SPEED, *and* LANCE *with his dog Crab.*

SPEED   Lance, by mine honesty, welcome to Milan.
LANCE   Forswear not thyself, sweet youth, for I am not
welcome. I reckon this always, that a man is never undone
till he be hanged, nor never welcome to a place till some
5 certain shot be paid and the hostess say 'Welcome'.
SPEED   Come on, you madcap. I'll to the alehouse with
you presently, where, for one shot of fivepence, thou

shalt have five thousand welcomes. But, sirrah, how
did thy master part with Madam Julia?
LANCE   Marry, after they closed in earnest, they parted   10
very fairly in jest.
SPEED   But shall she marry him?
LANCE   No.
SPEED   How then? Shall he marry her?
LANCE   No, neither.   15
SPEED   What, are they broken?
LANCE   No, they are both as whole as a fish.
SPEED   Why then, how stands the matter with them?
LANCE   Marry, thus: when it stands well with him, it
stands well with her.   20
SPEED   What an ass art thou! I understand thee not.
LANCE   What a block art thou that thou canst not! My
staff understands me.
SPEED   What thou sayst?
LANCE   Ay, and what I do too. Look thee, I'll but lean,   25
and my staff understands me.
SPEED   It stands under thee indeed.
LANCE   Why, stand-under and under-stand is all one.
SPEED   But tell me true, will't be a match?
LANCE   Ask my dog. If he say 'Ay', it will; if he say 'No',   30
it will; if he shake his tail and say nothing, it will.
SPEED   The conclusion is, then, that it will.
LANCE   Thou shalt never get such a secret from me but
by a parable.
SPEED   'Tis well that I get it so. But Lance, how sayst   35
thou that my master is become a notable lover?
LANCE   I never knew him otherwise.
SPEED   Than how?
LANCE   A notable lubber, as thou reportest him to be.
SPEED   Why, thou whoreson ass, thou mistak'st me.   40
LANCE   Why, fool, I meant not thee, I meant thy master.
SPEED   I tell thee, my master is become a hot lover.
LANCE   Why, I tell thee, I care not, though he burn
himself in love. If thou wilt, go with me to the alehouse;
if not, thou art an Hebrew, a Jew, and not worth the   45
name of a Christian.
SPEED   Why?
LANCE   Because thou hast not so much charity in thee
as to go to the ale with a Christian. Wilt thou go?
SPEED   At thy service.   *Exeunt.*   50

2.6   *Enter* PROTEUS *alone.*

PROTEUS   To leave my Julia shall I be forsworn;
To love fair Silvia shall I be forsworn;
To wrong my friend, I shall be much forsworn.
And e'en that power which gave me first my oath
Provokes me to this threefold perjury.   5
Love bade me swear, and Love bids me forswear.
O sweet-suggesting Love, if thou hast sinned,
Teach me, thy tempted subject, to excuse it.
At first I did adore a twinkling star,
But now I worship a celestial sun.   10
Unheedful vows may heedfully be broken,

And he wants wit that wants resolved will
To learn his wit t'exchange the bad for better.
Fie, fie, unreverent tongue, to call her bad
15 Whose sovereignty so oft thou hast preferred
With twenty thousand soul-confirming oaths.
I cannot leave to love, and yet I do;
But there I leave to love where I should love.
Julia I lose, and Valentine I lose;
20 If I keep them, I needs must lose myself.
If I lose them, thus find I by their loss,
For Valentine, myself, for Julia, Silvia.
I to myself am dearer than a friend,
For love is still most precious in itself,
25 And Silvia – witness heaven that made her fair –
Shows Julia but a swarthy Ethiope.
I will forget that Julia is alive,
Remembering that my love to her is dead.
And Valentine I'll hold an enemy,
30 Aiming at Silvia as a sweeter friend.
I cannot now prove constant to myself
Without some treachery used to Valentine.
This night he meaneth with a corded ladder
To climb celestial Silvia's chamber-window,
35 Myself in counsel, his competitor.
Now presently I'll give her father notice
Of their disguising and pretended flight,
Who, all enraged, will banish Valentine,
For Turio he intends shall wed his daughter.
40 But Valentine being gone, I'll quickly cross
By some sly trick blunt Turio's dull proceeding.
Love, lend me wings to make my purpose swift,
As thou hast lent me wit to plot this drift.   *Exit.*

2.7   *Enter* JULIA *and* LUCETTA.

JULIA   Counsel, Lucetta; gentle girl, assist me,
And e'en in kind love I do conjure thee,
Who art the table wherein all my thoughts
Are visibly charactered and engraved,
5   To lesson me and tell me some good mean
How with my honour I may undertake
A journey to my loving Proteus.

LUCETTA   Alas, the way is wearisome and long.

JULIA   A true-devoted pilgrim is not weary
10   To measure kingdoms with his feeble steps;
Much less shall she that hath Love's wings to fly,
And when the flight is made to one so dear,
Of such divine perfection as Sir Proteus.

LUCETTA   Better forbear till Proteus make return.

JULIA   15 O, knowst thou not his looks are my soul's food?
Pity the dearth that I have pined in
By longing for that food so long a time.
Didst thou but know the inly touch of love
Thou wouldst as soon go kindle fire with snow
20   As seek to quench the fire of love with words.

LUCETTA   I do not seek to quench your love's hot fire,
But qualify the fire's extreme rage,

Lest it should burn above the bounds of reason.

JULIA
The more thou damm'st it up, the more it burns.
25 The current that with gentle murmur glides,
Thou knowst, being stopped, impatiently doth rage;
But when his fair course is not hindered,
He makes sweet music with th'enamelled stones,
Giving a gentle kiss to every sedge
30 He overtaketh in his pilgrimage;
And so by many winding nooks he strays
With willing sport to the wild ocean.
Then let me go and hinder not my course,
I'll be as patient as a gentle stream
35 And make a pastime of each weary step
Till the last step have brought me to my love,
And there I'll rest as after much turmoil
A blessed soul doth in Elysium.

LUCETTA   But in what habit will you go along?

JULIA   Not like a woman, for I would prevent   40
The loose encounters of lascivious men.
Gentle Lucetta, fit me with such weeds
As may beseem some well-reputed page.

LUCETTA   Why then, your ladyship must cut your hair.

JULIA   No, girl, I'll knit it up in silken strings   45
With twenty odd-conceited true-love knots.
To be fantastic may become a youth
Of greater time than I shall show to be.

LUCETTA
What fashion, madam, shall I make your breeches?

JULIA   That fits as well as 'Tell me, good my lord,   50
What compass will you wear your farthingale?'
Why, e'en what fashion thou best likes, Lucetta.

LUCETTA
You must needs have them with a codpiece, madam.

JULIA   Out, out, Lucetta, that will be ill-favoured.

LUCETTA   A round hose, madam, now's not worth a pin   55
Unless you have a codpiece to stick pins on.

JULIA   Lucetta, as thou lov'st me, let me have
What thou think'st meet and is most mannerly.
But tell me, wench, how will the world repute me
For undertaking so unstaid a journey?   60
I fear me it will make me scandalized.

LUCETTA   If you think so, then stay at home and go not.

JULIA   Nay, that I will not.

LUCETTA   Then never dream on infamy, but go.
If Proteus like your journey when you come,   65
No matter who's displeased when you are gone.
I fear me he will scarce be pleased withal.

JULIA   That is the least, Lucetta, of my fear.
A thousand oaths, an ocean of his tears,
And instances of infinite of love   70
Warrant me welcome to my Proteus.

LUCETTA   All these are servants to deceitful men.

JULIA   Base men, that use them to so base effect!
But truer stars did govern Proteus' birth.
His words are bonds, his oaths are oracles,   75
His love sincere, his thoughts immaculate,

His tears pure messengers sent from his heart,
His heart as far from fraud as heaven from earth.

LUCETTA
Pray heaven he prove so when you come to him.

80 JULIA Now, as thou lov'st me, do him not that wrong
To bear a hard opinion of his truth.
Only deserve my love by loving him,
And presently go with me to my chamber
To take a note of what I stand in need of
85 To furnish me upon my longing journey.
All that is mine I leave at thy dispose,
My goods, my lands, my reputation;
Only, in lieu thereof, dispatch me hence.
Come, answer not, but to it presently;
90 I am impatient of my tarriance.   *Exeunt.*

3.1   *Enter* DUKE, TURIO *and* PROTEUS.

DUKE   Sir Turio, give us leave, I pray, awhile;
We have some secrets to confer about.   *Exit Turio.*
Now tell me, Proteus, what's your will with me?

PROTEUS
My gracious lord, that which I would discover
5 The law of friendship bids me to conceal,
But when I call to mind your gracious favours
Done to me, undeserving as I am,
My duty pricks me on to utter that
Which else no worldly good should draw from me.
10 Know, worthy prince, Sir Valentine my friend
This night intends to steal away your daughter;
Myself am one made privy to the plot.
I know you have determined to bestow her
On Turio, whom your gentle daughter hates,
15 And should she thus be stol'n away from you,
It would be much vexation to your age.
Thus, for my duty's sake, I rather chose
To cross my friend in his intended drift
Than, by concealing it, heap on your head
20 A pack of sorrows which would press you down,
Being unprevented, to your timeless grave.

DUKE   Proteus, I thank thee for thine honest care,
Which to requite command me while I live.
This love of theirs myself have often seen,
25 Haply when they have judged me fast asleep,
And oftentimes have purposed to forbid
Sir Valentine her company and my court.
But fearing lest my jealous aim might err
And so unworthily disgrace the man –
30 A rashness that I ever yet have shunned –
I gave him gentle looks, thereby to find
That which thyself hast now disclosed to me.
And that thou mayst perceive my fear of this,
Knowing that tender youth is soon suggested,
35 I nightly lodge her in an upper tower,
The key whereof myself have ever kept;
And thence she cannot be conveyed away.

PROTEUS   Know, noble lord, they have devised a mean

How he her chamber-window will ascend
And with a corded ladder fetch her down;   40
For which the youthful lover now is gone,
And this way comes he with it presently,
Where, if it please you, you may intercept him.
But, good my lord, do it so cunningly
That my discovery be not aimed at;   45
For love of you, not hate unto my friend,
Hath made me publisher of this pretence.

DUKE   Upon mine honour, he shall never know
That I had any light from thee of this.

Enter VALENTINE.

PROTEUS   Adieu, my lord, Sir Valentine is coming.   50
                                                        Exit.

DUKE   Sir Valentine, whither away so fast?

VALENTINE   Please it your grace, there is a messenger
That stays to bear my letters to my friends,
And I am going to deliver them.

DUKE   Be they of much import?   55

VALENTINE   The tenor of them doth but signify
My health and happy being at your court.

DUKE   Nay then, no matter. Stay with me awhile;
I am to break with thee of some affairs
That touch me near, wherein thou must be secret.   60
'Tis not unknown to thee that I have sought
To match my friend Sir Turio to my daughter.

VALENTINE   I know it well, my lord, and sure the match
Were rich and honourable. Besides, the gentleman
Is full of virtue, bounty, worth and qualities   65
Beseeming such a wife as your fair daughter.
Cannot your grace win her to fancy him?

DUKE   No, trust me, she is peevish, sullen, froward,
Proud, disobedient, stubborn, lacking duty,
Neither regarding that she is my child   70
Nor fearing me as if I were her father.
And, may I say to thee, this pride of hers,
Upon advice, hath drawn my love from her,
And where I thought the remnant of mine age
Should have been cherished by her childlike duty,   75
I now am full resolved to take a wife
And turn her out to who will take her in.
Then let her beauty be her wedding dower,
For me and my possessions she esteems not.

VALENTINE
What would your grace have me to do in this?   80

DUKE   There is a lady of Verona here
Whom I affect, but she is nice and coy,
And naught esteems my aged eloquence.
Now therefore would I have thee to my tutor –
For long agone I have forgot to court;   85
Besides, the fashion of the time is changed –
How and which way I may bestow myself
To be regarded in her sun-bright eye.

VALENTINE   Win her with gifts if she respect not words;
Dumb jewels often in their silent kind   90
More than quick words do move a woman's mind.

DUKE   But she did scorn a present that I sent her.

VALENTINE

    A woman sometime scorns what best contents her.

    Send her another; never give her o'er,

95   For scorn at first makes after-love the more.

    If she do frown, 'tis not in hate of you,

    But rather to beget more love in you.

    If she do chide, 'tis not to have you gone,

    Forwhy the fools are mad if left alone.

100   Take no repulse, whatever she doth say,

    For 'Get you gone' she doth not mean 'Away!'

    Flatter and praise, commend, extol their graces;

    Though ne'er so black, say they have angels' faces.

    That man that hath a tongue, I say, is no man

105   If with his tongue he cannot win a woman.

DUKE   But she I mean is promised by her friends

    Unto a youthful gentleman of worth,

    And kept severely from resort of men,

    That no man hath access by day to her.

110 VALENTINE   Why then, I would resort to her by night.

DUKE   Ay, but the doors be locked and keys kept safe,

    That no man hath recourse to her by night.

VALENTINE

    What lets but one may enter at her window?

DUKE   Her chamber is aloft, far from the ground,

115   And built so shelving that one cannot climb it

    Without apparent hazard of his life.

VALENTINE

    Why then, a ladder quaintly made of cords

    To cast up, with a pair of anchoring hooks,

    Would serve to scale another Hero's tower,

120   So bold Leander would adventure it.

DUKE   Now, as thou art a gentleman of blood,

    Advise me where I may have such a ladder.

VALENTINE

    When would you use it? Pray, sir, tell me that.

DUKE   This very night; for Love is like a child

125   That longs for everything that he can come by.

VALENTINE   By seven o'clock I'll get you such a ladder.

DUKE   But hark thee: I will go to her alone.

    How shall I best convey the ladder thither?

VALENTINE

    It will be light, my lord, that you may bear it

130   Under a cloak that is of any length.

DUKE   A cloak as long as thine will serve the turn?

VALENTINE   Ay, my good lord.

DUKE   Then let me see thy cloak;

    I'll get me one of such another length.

VALENTINE

    Why, any cloak will serve the turn, my lord.

135 DUKE   How shall I fashion me to wear a cloak?

    I pray thee let me feel thy cloak upon me.

      [*Takes Valentine's cloak and finds a letter and a rope*

      ladder concealed under it.]

    What letter is this same? What's here? *To Silvia*?

    And here an engine fit for my proceeding.

    I'll be so bold to break the seal for once.

[*Reads.*] *My thoughts do harbour with my Silvia nightly,*   140

And slaves they are to me that send them flying.

O, could their master come and go as lightly,

Himself would lodge where, senseless, they are lying.

My herald thoughts in thy pure bosom rest them,

While I, their king, that thither them importune,   145

Do curse the grace that with such grace hath blessed them,

Because myself do want my servants' fortune.

    I curse myself for they are sent by me,

    That they should harbour where their lord should be.

What's here?   150

    Silvia, this night I will enfranchise thee.

'Tis so; and here's the ladder for the purpose.

Why, Phaëton, for thou art Merops' son,

Wilt thou aspire to guide the heavenly car,

And with thy daring folly burn the world?   155

Wilt thou reach stars because they shine on thee?

Go, base intruder, overweening slave,

Bestow thy fawning smiles on equal mates,

And think my patience, more than thy desert,

Is privilege for thy departure hence.   160

Thank me for this more than for all the favours

Which, all too much, I have bestowed on thee.

But if thou linger in my territories

Longer than swiftest expedition

Will give thee time to leave our royal court,   165

By heaven, my wrath shall far exceed the love

I ever bore my daughter or thyself.

Begone, I will not hear thy vain excuse,

But, as thou lov'st thy life, make speed from hence.

                               Exit.

VALENTINE

    And why not death, rather than living torment?   170

    To die is to be banished from myself,

    And Silvia is myself; banished from her

    Is self from self – a deadly banishment.

    What light is light, if Silvia be not seen?

    What joy is joy, if Silvia be not by?   175

    Unless it be to think that she is by

    And feed upon the shadow of perfection.

    Except I be by Silvia in the night,

    There is no music in the nightingale.

    Unless I look on Silvia in the day,   180

    There is no day for me to look upon.

    She is my essence, and I leave to be

    If I be not by her fair influence

    Fostered, illumined, cherished, kept alive.

    I fly not death to fly his deadly doom: 185

    Tarry I here, I but attend on death,

    But fly I hence, I fly away from life.

Enter PROTEUS *and* LANCE.

PROTEUS   Run, boy, run, run and seek him out.

LANCE   So-ho, so-ho!

PROTEUS   What seest thou?   190

LANCE   Him we go to find. There's not a hair on's head

    but 'tis a Valentine.

PROTEUS   Valentine?

VALENTINE   No.

195 PROTEUS   Who then? His spirit?

VALENTINE   Neither.

PROTEUS   What then?

VALENTINE   Nothing.

LANCE   Can nothing speak? Master, shall I strike?

200 PROTEUS   Who wouldst thou strike?

LANCE   Nothing.

PROTEUS   Villain, forbear.

LANCE   Why, sir, I'll strike nothing. I pray you –

PROTEUS

   Sirrah, I say forbear. Friend Valentine, a word.

VALENTINE

205   My ears are stopped and cannot hear good news,
   So much of bad already hath possessed them.

PROTEUS   Then in dumb silence will I bury mine,
   For they are harsh, untuneable and bad.

VALENTINE   Is Silvia dead?

PROTEUS   No, Valentine.

210 VALENTINE   No Valentine indeed for sacred Silvia.
   Hath she forsworn me?

PROTEUS   No, Valentine.

VALENTINE   No Valentine, if Silvia have forsworn me.
   What is your news?

LANCE   Sir, there is a proclamation that you are
215   vanished.

PROTEUS   That thou art banished – O, that's the news –
   From hence, from Silvia, and from me thy friend.

VALENTINE   O, I have fed upon this woe already,
   And now excess of it will make me surfeit.

220   Doth Silvia know that I am banished?

PROTEUS   Ay, ay; and she hath offered to the doom,
   Which unreversed stands in effectual force,
   A sea of melting pearl, which some call tears;
   Those at her father's churlish feet she tendered,

225   With them, upon her knees, her humble self,
   Wringing her hands, whose whiteness so became them
   As if but now they waxed pale for woe.
   But neither bended knees, pure hands held up,
   Sad sighs, deep groans, nor silver-shedding tears

230   Could penetrate her uncompassionate sire,
   But Valentine, if he be ta'en, must die.
   Besides, her intercession chafed him so,
   When she for thy repeal was suppliant,
   That to close prison he commanded her,

235   With many bitter threats of biding there.

VALENTINE

   No more, unless the next word that thou speak'st
   Have some malignant power upon my life;
   If so, I pray thee breathe it in mine ear,
   As ending anthem of my endless dolour.

240 PROTEUS   Cease to lament for that thou canst not help
   And study help for that which thou lament'st.
   Time is the nurse and breeder of all good.
   Here if thou stay, thou canst not see thy love;
   Besides, thy staying will abridge thy life.

Hope is a lover's staff; walk hence with that   245
And manage it against despairing thoughts.
Thy letters may be here, though thou art hence,
Which, being writ to me, shall be delivered
Even in the milk-white bosom of thy love.
The time now serves not to expostulate.   250
Come, I'll convey thee through the city-gate,
And ere I part with thee confer at large
Of all that may concern thy love affairs.
As thou lov'st Silvia, though not for thyself,
Regard thy danger and along with me.   255

VALENTINE

   I pray thee, Lance, an if thou seest my boy,
   Bid him make haste and meet me at the North Gate.

PROTEUS   Go, sirrah, find him out. Come, Valentine.

VALENTINE   O, my dear Silvia! Hapless Valentine!

                              Exeunt Valentine and Proteus.

LANCE   I am but a fool, look you, and yet I have the wit to   260
think my master is a kind of a knave; but that's all one,
if he be but one knave. He lives not now that knows me
to be in love, yet I am in love, but a team of horse shall
not pluck that from me, nor who 'tis I love; and yet 'tis
a woman, but what woman I will not tell myself; and yet   265
'tis a milkmaid; yet 'tis not a maid, for she hath had
gossips; yet 'tis a maid, for she is her master's maid and
serves for wages. She hath more qualities than a water-
spaniel, which is much in a bare Christian. [*Pulls out a
paper.*] Here is the cate-log of her condition. [*Reads.*]   270
Inprimis, she can fetch and carry. Why, a horse can do no
more; nay, a horse cannot fetch but only carry, therefore
is she better than a jade. *Item, she can milk.* Look you, a
sweet virtue in a maid with clean hands.

                              Enter SPEED.

SPEED   How now, Signior Lance? What news with your   275
mastership?

LANCE   With my master's ship? Why, it is at sea.

SPEED   Well, your old vice still: mistake the word. What
news, then, in your paper?

LANCE   The blackest news that ever thou heard'st.   280

SPEED   Why, man? How black?

LANCE   Why, as black as ink.

SPEED   Let me read them.

LANCE   Fie on thee, jolt-head, thou canst not read.

SPEED   Thou liest: I can.   285

LANCE   I will try thee. Tell me this: who begot thee?

SPEED   Marry, the son of my grandfather.

LANCE   O illiterate loiterer! It was the son of thy
grandmother. This proves that thou canst not read.

SPEED   Come, fool, come; try me in thy paper.   290

LANCE [*Gives him the paper.*]   There, and Saint Nicholas
be thy speed.

SPEED   *Inprimis, she can milk.*

LANCE   Ay, that she can.

SPEED   *Item, she brews good ale.*   295

LANCE   And thereof comes the proverb, 'Blessing of
your heart, you brew good ale.'

SPEED   *Item, she can sew.*

LANCE   That's as much as to say, 'Can she so?'

300   SPEED   *Item, she can knit.*

LANCE   What need a man care for a stock with a wench, when she can knit him a stock?

SPEED   *Item, she can wash and scour.*

LANCE   A special virtue, for then she need not be washed

305   and scoured.

SPEED   *Item, she can spin.*

LANCE   Then may I set the world on wheels, when she can spin for her living.

SPEED   *Item, she hath many nameless virtues.*

310   LANCE   That's as much as to say 'bastard virtues', that indeed know not their fathers, and therefore have no names.

SPEED   Here follow her vices.

LANCE   Close at the heels of her virtues.

315   SPEED   *Item, she is not to be kissed fasting in respect of her breath.*

LANCE   Well, that fault may be mended with a breakfast. Read on.

SPEED   *Item, she hath a sweet mouth.*

320   LANCE   That makes amends for her sour breath.

SPEED   *Item, she doth talk in her sleep.*

LANCE   It's no matter for that, so she sleep not in her talk.

SPEED   *Item, she is slow in words.*

325   LANCE   O villain, that set this down among her vices! To be slow in words is a woman's only virtue. I pray thee out with't, and place it for her chief virtue.

SPEED   *Item, she is proud.*

LANCE   Out with that too; it was Eve's legacy and

330   cannot be ta'en from her.

SPEED   *Item, she hath no teeth.*

LANCE   I care not for that neither, because I love crusts.

SPEED   *Item, she is curst.*

LANCE   Well, the best is, she hath no teeth to bite.

335   SPEED   *Item, she will often praise her liquor.*

LANCE   If her liquor be good, she shall; if she will not, I will, for good things should be praised.

SPEED   *Item, she is too liberal.*

LANCE   Of her tongue she cannot, for that's writ down

340   she is slow of; of her purse, she shall not, for that I'll keep shut. Now, of another thing she may, and that cannot I help. Well, proceed.

SPEED   *Item, she hath more hair than wit, and more faults than hairs, and more wealth than faults.*

345   LANCE   Stop there; I'll have her. She was mine and not mine twice or thrice in that last article. Rehearse that once more.

SPEED   *Item, she hath more hair than wit –*

LANCE   More hair than wit. It may be; I'll prove it: the

350   cover of the salt hides the salt, and therefore it is more than the salt; the hair that covers the wit is more than the wit, for the greater hides the less. What's next?

SPEED   *And more faults than hairs –*

LANCE   That's monstrous. O, that that were out!

SPEED   *And more wealth than faults.*   355

LANCE   Why, that word makes the faults gracious. Well, I'll have her; and if it be a match, as nothing is impossible –

SPEED   What then?

LANCE   Why, then will I tell thee that thy master stays   360 for thee at the North Gate.

SPEED   For me?

LANCE   For thee? Ay, who art thou? He hath stayed for a better man than thee.

SPEED   And must I go to him?   365

LANCE   Thou must run to him, for thou hast stayed so long that going will scarce serve the turn.

SPEED   Why didst not tell me sooner? Pox of your love letters!   *Exit.*

LANCE   Now will he be swinged for reading my letter;   370 an unmannerly slave, that will thrust himself into secrets. I'll after, to rejoice in the boy's correction.

  Exit.

3.2   *Enter* DUKE *and* TURIO.

DUKE   Sir Turio, fear not but that she will love you
Now Valentine is banished from her sight.

TURIO   Since his exile she hath despised me most,
Forsworn my company and railed at me,
That I am desperate of obtaining her.   5

DUKE   This weak impress of love is as a figure
Trenched in ice, which with an hour's heat
Dissolves to water and doth lose his form.
A little time will melt her frozen thoughts,
And worthless Valentine shall be forgot.   10

        Enter PROTEUS.

How now, Sir Proteus, is your countryman,
According to our proclamation, gone?

PROTEUS   Gone, my good lord.

DUKE   My daughter takes his going grievously.

PROTEUS   A little time, my lord, will kill that grief.   15

DUKE   So I believe, but Turio thinks not so.
Proteus, the good conceit I hold of thee –
For thou hast shown some sign of good desert –
Makes me the better to confer with thee.

PROTEUS   Longer than I prove loyal to your grace   20
Let me not live to look upon your grace.

DUKE   Thou knowst how willingly I would effect
The match between Sir Turio and my daughter?

PROTEUS   I do, my lord.

DUKE   And also, I think, thou art not ignorant   25
How she opposes her against my will?

PROTEUS   She did, my lord, when Valentine was here.

DUKE   Ay, and perversely she persevers so.
What might we do to make the girl forget
The love of Valentine, and love Sir Turio?   30

PROTEUS   The best way is to slander Valentine
With falsehood, cowardice and poor descent,
Three things that women highly hold in hate.

DUKE   Ay, but she'll think that it is spoke in hate.
35 PROTEUS   Ay, if his enemy deliver it.
    Therefore it must with circumstance be spoken
    By one whom she esteemeth as his friend.
    DUKE   Then you must undertake to slander him.
    PROTEUS   And that, my lord, I shall be loath to do;
40 'Tis an ill office for a gentleman,
    Especially against his very friend.
    DUKE   Where your good word cannot advantage him,
    Your slander never can endamage him;
    Therefore the office is indifferent,
45 Being entreated to it by your friend.
    PROTEUS   You have prevailed, my lord. If I can do it
    By aught that I can speak in his dispraise,
    She shall not long continue love to him.
    But say this weed her love from Valentine,
50 It follows not that she will love Sir Turio.
    TURIO   Therefore, as you unwind her love from him,
    Lest it should ravel and be good to none,
    You must provide to bottom it on me,
    Which must be done by praising me as much
55 As you in worth dispraise Sir Valentine.
    DUKE   And, Proteus, we dare trust you in this kind
    Because we know, on Valentine's report,
    You are already Love's firm votary,
    And cannot soon revolt and change your mind.
60 Upon this warrant shall you have access
    Where you with Silvia may confer at large –
    For she is lumpish, heavy, melancholy,
    And, for your friend's sake, will be glad of you –
    Where you may temper her by your persuasion
65 To hate young Valentine and love my friend.
    PROTEUS   As much as I can do, I will effect.
    But you, Sir Turio, are not sharp enough.
    You must lay lime to tangle her desires
    By wailful sonnets, whose composed rhymes
70 Should be full-fraught with serviceable vows.
    DUKE   Ay, much is the force of heaven-bred poesy.
    PROTEUS   Say that upon the altar of her beauty
    You sacrifice your tears, your sighs, your heart.
    Write till your ink be dry, and with your tears
75 Moist it again, and frame some feeling line
    That may discover such integrity;
    For Orpheus' lute was strung with poets' sinews,
    Whose golden touch could soften steel and stones,
    Make tigers tame and huge leviathans
80 Forsake unsounded deeps to dance on sands.
    After your dire-lamenting elegies,
    Visit by night your lady's chamber-window
    With some sweet consort; to their instruments
    Tune a deploring dump. The night's dead silence
85 Will well become such sweet-complaining grievance.
    This, or else nothing, will inherit her.
    DUKE   This discipline shows thou hast been in love.
    TURIO   And thy advice this night I'll put in practice.
    Therefore, sweet Proteus, my direction-giver,
90 Let us into the city presently

To sort some gentlemen well skilled in music.
I have a sonnet that will serve the turn
To give the onset to thy good advice.
DUKE   About it, gentlemen!
PROTEUS   We'll wait upon your grace till after supper,   95
And afterward determine our proceedings.
DUKE   Even now about it. I will pardon you.   *Exeunt.*

4.1   *Enter* VALENTINE, SPEED *and certain* Outlaws.

1 OUTLAW   Fellows, stand fast. I see a passenger.
2 OUTLAW
    If there be ten, shrink not, but down with 'em.
3 OUTLAW
    Stand, sir, and throw us that you have about ye.
    If not, we'll make you sit and rifle you.
SPEED   Sir, we are undone; these are the villains   5
    That all the travellers do fear so much.
VALENTINE   My friends –
1 OUTLAW   That's not so, sir. We are your enemies.
2 OUTLAW   Peace! We'll hear him.
3 OUTLAW   Ay, by my beard will we; for he is a proper   10
    man.
VALENTINE
    Then know that I have little wealth to lose.
    A man I am crossed with adversity;
    My riches are these poor habiliments,
    Of which if you should here disfurnish me,   15
    You take the sum and substance that I have.
2 OUTLAW   Whither travel you?
VALENTINE   To Verona.
1 OUTLAW   Whence came you?
VALENTINE   From Milan.   20
3 OUTLAW   Have you long sojourned there?
VALENTINE
    Some sixteen months, and longer might have stayed
    If crooked fortune had not thwarted me.
1 OUTLAW   What, were you banished thence?
VALENTINE   I was.   25
2 OUTLAW   For what offence?
VALENTINE
    For that which now torments me to rehearse:
    I killed a man, whose death I much repent,
    But yet I slew him manfully in fight,
    Without false vantage or base treachery.   30
1 OUTLAW   Why, ne'er repent it, if it were done so.
    But were you banished for so small a fault?
VALENTINE   I was, and held me glad of such a doom.
2 OUTLAW   Have you the tongues?
VALENTINE
    My youthful travel therein made me happy,   35
    Or else I often had been miserable.
3 OUTLAW   By the bare scalp of Robin Hood's fat friar,
    This fellow were a king for our wild faction.
1 OUTLAW
    We'll have him. Sirs, a word.   [*Outlaws talk apart.*]
SPEED   Master, be one of them.

40   It's an honourable kind of thievery.

VALENTINE   Peace, villain.

2 OUTLAW   Tell us this: have you anything to take to?

VALENTINE   Nothing but my fortune.

3 OUTLAW   Know then that some of us are gentlemen,

45   Such as the fury of ungoverned youth

Thrust from the company of awful men.

Myself was from Verona banished

For practising to steal away a lady,

An heir, and near allied unto the Duke.

50   2 OUTLAW   And I from Mantua, for a gentleman

Who, in my mood, I stabbed unto the heart.

1 OUTLAW   And I for suchlike petty crimes as these.

But to the purpose, for we cite our faults

That they may hold excused our lawless lives;

55   And partly, seeing you are beautified

With goodly shape, and by your own report

A linguist, and a man of such perfection

As we do in our quality much want –

2 OUTLAW   Indeed because you are a banished man,

60   Therefore above the rest we parley to you.

Are you content to be our general?

To make a virtue of necessity

And live as we do in this wilderness?

3 OUTLAW

What sayst thou? Wilt thou be of our consort?

65   Say 'Ay', and be the captain of us all,

We'll do thee homage and be ruled by thee,

Love thee as our commander and our king.

1 OUTLAW   But if thou scorn our courtesy, thou diest.

2 OUTLAW

Thou shalt not live to brag what we have offered.

70   VALENTINE   I take your offer and will live with you,

Provided that you do no outrages

On silly women or poor passengers.

3 OUTLAW   No, we detest such vile base practices.

Come, go with us. We'll bring thee to our crews

75   And show thee all the treasure we have got,

Which, with ourselves, all rest at thy dispose.   *Exeunt.*

4.2   *Enter* PROTEUS.

PROTEUS   Already have I been false to Valentine,

And now I must be as unjust to Turio.

Under the colour of commending him

I have access my own love to prefer.

5   But Silvia is too fair, too true, too holy

To be corrupted with my worthless gifts.

When I protest true loyalty to her,

She twits me with my falsehood to my friend;

When to her beauty I commend my vows,

10   She bids me think how I have been forsworn

In breaking faith with Julia, whom I loved.

And notwithstanding all her sudden quips,

The least whereof would quell a lover's hope,

Yet, spaniel-like, the more she spurns my love,

15   The more it grows and fawneth on her still.

Enter TURIO *and Musicians.*

But here comes Turio. Now must we to her window,

And give some evening music to her ear.

TURIO

How now, Sir Proteus, are you crept before us?

PROTEUS   Ay, gentle Turio, for you know that love

Will creep in service where it cannot go.   20

TURIO   Ay, but I hope, sir, that you love not here.

PROTEUS   Sir, but I do, or else I would be hence.

TURIO   Who? Silvia?

PROTEUS   Ay, Silvia – for your sake.

TURIO   I thank you for your own. Now, gentlemen,

Let's tune, and to it lustily awhile.   25

Enter Host, *and* JULIA *in boy's clothes as Sebastian.*

HOST   Now, my young guest, methinks you're allicholy.

I pray you, why is it?

JULIA   Marry, mine host, because I cannot be merry.

HOST   Come, we'll have you merry. I'll bring you where

you shall hear music, and see the gentleman that you   30

asked for.

JULIA   But shall I hear him speak?

HOST   Ay, that you shall.

JULIA   That will be music.   [*Music plays.*]

HOST   Hark, hark!   35

JULIA   Is he among these?

HOST   Ay; but peace, let's hear 'em.

SONG

Who is Silvia? What is she,

That all our swains commend her?

Holy, fair and wise is she;   40

The heaven such grace did lend her,

That she might admired be.

Is she kind as she is fair?

For beauty lives with kindness.

Love doth to her eyes repair   45

To help him of his blindness,

And, being helped, inhabits there.

Then to Silvia let us sing,

That Silvia is excelling;

She excels each mortal thing   50

Upon the dull earth dwelling.

To her let us garlands bring.

HOST   How now, are you sadder than you were before?

How do you, man? The music likes you not.

JULIA   You mistake; the musician likes me not.   55

HOST   Why, my pretty youth?

JULIA   He plays false, father.

HOST   How, out of tune on the strings?

JULIA   Not so; but yet so false that he grieves my very

heart-strings.   60

HOST   You have a quick ear.

JULIA   Ay, I would I were deaf; it makes me have a slow
  heart.
HOST   I perceive you delight not in music.
65 JULIA   Not a whit, when it jars so.
HOST   Hark, what fine change is in the music!
JULIA   Ay, that change is the spite.
HOST   You would have them always play but one thing?
JULIA   I would always have one play but one thing.
70   But, host, doth this Sir Proteus that we talk on
  Often resort unto this gentlewoman?
HOST   I tell you what Lance, his man, told me: he loved
  her out of all nick.
JULIA   Where is Lance?
75 HOST   Gone to seek his dog, which tomorrow, by his
  master's command, he must carry for a present to his
  lady.
JULIA   Peace, stand aside; the company parts.
PROTEUS   Sir Turio, fear not you; I will so plead
80   That you shall say my cunning drift excels.
TURIO   Where meet we?
PROTEUS   At Saint Gregory's well.
TURIO   Farewell.
            Exeunt Turio and Musicians.

        Enter SILVIA *above.*

PROTEUS   Madam, good even to your ladyship.
SILVIA   I thank you for your music, gentlemen.
  Who is that that spake?
85 PROTEUS   One, lady, if you knew his pure heart's truth,
  You would quickly learn to know him by his voice.
SILVIA   Sir Proteus, as I take it.
PROTEUS   Sir Proteus, gentle lady, and your servant.
SILVIA   What's your will?
PROTEUS   That I may compass yours.
90 SILVIA   You have your wish. My will is even this,
  That presently you hie you home to bed.
  Thou subtle, perjured, false, disloyal man,
  Think'st thou I am so shallow, so conceitless,
  To be seduced by thy flattery
95   That hast deceived so many with thy vows?
  Return, return, and make thy love amends.
  For me – by this pale queen of night I swear –
  I am so far from granting thy request
  That I despise thee for thy wrongful suit,
100   And by and by intend to chide myself
  Even for this time I spend in talking to thee.
PROTEUS   I grant, sweet love, that I did love a lady,
  But she is dead.
JULIA [*aside*]   'Twere false, if I should speak it,
  For I am sure she is not buried.
105 SILVIA   Say that she be; yet Valentine thy friend
  Survives, to whom, thyself art witness,
  I am betrothed. And art thou not ashamed
  To wrong him with thy importunacy?
PROTEUS   I likewise hear that Valentine is dead.
110 SILVIA   And so suppose am I, for in his grave
  Assure thyself, my love is buried.

PROTEUS   Sweet lady, let me rake it from the earth.
SILVIA   Go to thy lady's grave and call hers thence,
  Or, at the least, in hers sepulchre thine.
JULIA [*aside*]   He heard not that.   115
PROTEUS   Madam, if your heart be so obdurate,
  Vouchsafe me yet your picture for my love,
  The picture that is hanging in your chamber.
  To that I'll speak, to that I'll sigh and weep;
  For since the substance of your perfect self   120
  Is else devoted, I am but a shadow,
  And to your shadow will I make true love.
JULIA [*aside*]
  If 'twere a substance you would sure deceive it
  And make it but a shadow, as I am.
SILVIA   I am very loath to be your idol, sir.   125
  But, since your falsehood shall become you well
  To worship shadows and adore false shapes,
  Send to me in the morning, and I'll send it.
  And so, good rest.   *Exit.*
PROTEUS   As wretches have o'ernight
  That wait for execution in the morn.   *Exit.*   130
JULIA   Host, will you go?
HOST   By my halidom, I was fast asleep.
JULIA   Pray you, where lies Sir Proteus?
HOST   Marry, at my house. Trust me, I think 'tis almost
  day.   135
JULIA   Not so; but it hath been the longest night
  That e'er I watched, and the most heaviest.   *Exeunt.*

4.3   *Enter* EGLAMOUR.

EGLAMOUR   This is the hour that Madam Silvia
  Entreated me to call and know her mind;
  There's some great matter she'd employ me in.
  Madam, madam!

        Enter SILVIA *above.*

SILVIA   Who calls?
EGLAMOUR   Your servant and your friend;
  One that attends your ladyship's command.   5
SILVIA   Sir Eglamour, a thousand times good morrow.
EGLAMOUR   As many, worthy lady, to yourself.
  According to your ladyship's impose,
  I am thus early come to know what service
  It is your pleasure to command me in.   10
SILVIA   O Eglamour, thou art a gentleman –
  Think not I flatter, for I swear I do not –
  Valiant, wise, remorseful, well accomplished.
  Thou art not ignorant what dear good will
  I bear unto the banished Valentine,   15
  Nor how my father would enforce me marry
  Vain Turio, whom my very soul abhorred.
  Thyself hast loved, and I have heard thee say
  No grief did ever come so near thy heart
  As when thy lady and thy true love died,   20
  Upon whose grave thou vowed'st pure chastity.
  Sir Eglamour, I would to Valentine,

To Mantua, where I hear he makes abode;
And for the ways are dangerous to pass
25   I do desire thy worthy company,
Upon whose faith and honour I repose.
Urge not my father's anger, Eglamour,
But think upon my grief, a lady's grief,
And on the justice of my flying hence
30   To keep me from a most unholy match,
Which heaven and fortune still rewards with
        plagues.
I do desire thee, even from a heart
As full of sorrows as the sea of sands,
To bear me company and go with me;
35   If not, to hide what I have said to thee,
That I may venture to depart alone.
EGLAMOUR   Madam, I pity much your grievances,
Which, since I know they virtuously are placed,
I give consent to go along with you,
40   Recking as little what betideth me
As much I wish all good befortune you.
When will you go?
SILVIA   This evening coming.
EGLAMOUR   Where shall I meet you?
SILVIA   At Friar Patrick's cell,
Where I intend holy confession.
45   EGLAMOUR   I will not fail your ladyship:
Good morrow, gentle lady.
SILVIA   Good morrow, kind Sir Eglamour.   *Exeunt.*

4.4   *Enter* LANCE *with his dog Crab.*

LANCE   When a man's servant shall play the cur with
him, look you, it goes hard: one that I brought up of a
puppy; one that I saved from drowning when three or
four of his blind brothers and sisters went to it. I have
5   taught him even as one would say precisely, 'Thus I
would teach a dog.' I was sent to deliver him as a
present to Mistress Silvia from my master, and I came
no sooner into the dining-chamber but he steps me to
her trencher and steals her capon's leg. O, 'tis a foul
10   thing when a cur cannot keep himself in all companies!
I would have, as one should say, one that takes upon
him to be a dog indeed, to be, as it were, a dog at all
things. If I had not had more wit than he, to take a fault
upon me that he did, I think verily he had been hanged
15   for't; sure as I live, he had suffered for't. You shall
judge. He thrusts me himself into the company of three
or four gentleman-like dogs under the Duke's table. He
had not been there – bless the mark! – a pissing-while
but all the chamber smelt him. 'Out with the dog', says
20   one; 'What cur is that?', says another; 'Whip him out',
says the third; 'Hang him up', says the Duke. I, having
been acquainted with the smell before, knew it was
Crab, and goes me to the fellow that whips the dogs.
'Friend,' quoth I, 'you mean to whip the dog?' 'Ay,
25   marry do I', quoth he. 'You do him the more wrong,'
quoth I, ''twas I did the thing you wot of.' He makes me

no more ado but whips me out of the chamber. How
many masters would do this for his servant? Nay, I'll be
sworn I have sat in the stocks for puddings he hath
stolen, otherwise he had been executed. I have stood on   30
the pillory for geese he hath killed, otherwise he had
suffered for't. [*to Crab*] Thou think'st not of this now.
Nay, I remember the trick you served me when I took
my leave of Madam Silvia. Did not I bid thee still mark
me, and do as I do? When didst thou see me heave up   35
my leg and make water against a gentlewoman's
farthingale? Didst thou ever see me do such a trick?

Enter PROTEUS, *and* JULIA *as Sebastian.*

PROTEUS   Sebastian is thy name? I like thee well,
And will employ thee in some service presently.
JULIA   In what you please; I'll do what I can.   40
PROTEUS
I hope thou wilt. [*to Lance*] How now, you whoreson
        peasant,
Where have you been these two days loitering?
LANCE   Marry, sir, I carried Mistress Silvia the dog you
bade me.
PROTEUS   And what says she to my little jewel?   45
LANCE   Marry, she says your dog was a cur, and tells you
currish thanks is good enough for such a present.
PROTEUS   But she received my dog?
LANCE   No, indeed, did she not. Here have I brought
him back again.   50
PROTEUS   What, didst thou offer her this from me?
LANCE   Ay, sir, the other squirrel was stolen from me by
the hangman's boys in the market-place, and then I
offered her mine own, who is a dog as big as ten of
yours, and therefore the gift the greater.   55
PROTEUS   Go, get thee hence, and find my dog again,
Or ne'er return again into my sight.
Away, I say! Stayest thou to vex me here?
A slave that still an end turns me to shame.
                                Exit Lance with Crab.
Sebastian, I have entertained thee   60
Partly that I have need of such a youth
That can with some discretion do my business –
For 'tis no trusting to yond foolish lout –
But chiefly for thy face and thy behaviour,
Which, if my augury deceive me not,   65
Witness good bringing-up, fortune and truth.
Therefore know thou, for this I entertain thee.
Go presently, and take this ring with thee,
Deliver it to Madam Silvia.
She loved me well delivered it to me.   70
JULIA   It seems you loved not her, to leave her token.
She is dead belike?
PROTEUS   Not so; I think she lives.
JULIA   Alas!
PROTEUS   Why dost thou cry 'Alas'?
JULIA   I cannot choose
But pity her.
PROTEUS   Wherefore shouldst thou pity her?   75

JULIA   Because methinks that she loved you as well
   As you do love your lady Silvia.
   She dreams on him that has forgot her love;
   You dote on her that cares not for your love.
80 'Tis pity love should be so contrary;
   And thinking on it makes me cry 'Alas'.
PROTEUS   Well, give her that ring, and therewithal
   This letter. That's her chamber. Tell my lady
   I claim the promise for her heavenly picture.
85 Your message done, hie home unto my chamber,
   Where thou shalt find me sad and solitary. *Exit.*
JULIA   How many women would do such a message?
   Alas, poor Proteus, thou hast entertained
   A fox to be the shepherd of thy lambs.
90 Alas, poor fool, why do I pity him
   That with his very heart despiseth me?
   Because he loves her, he despiseth me;
   Because I love him, I must pity him.
   This ring I gave him when he parted from me
95 To bind him to remember my good will.
   And now am I, unhappy messenger,
   To plead for that which I would not obtain,
   To carry that which I would have refused,
   To praise his faith which I would have dispraised.
100 I am my master's true confirmed love,
   But cannot be true servant to my master
   Unless I prove false traitor to myself.
   Yet will I woo for him, but yet so coldly
   As, heaven it knows, I would not have him speed.

     Enter SILVIA *attended.*

105 Gentlewoman, good day. I pray you, be my mean
   To bring me where to speak with Madam Silvia.
SILVIA   What would you with her, if that I be she?
JULIA   If you be she, I do entreat your patience
   To hear me speak the message I am sent on.
110 SILVIA   From whom?
JULIA   From my master, Sir Proteus, madam.
SILVIA   O, he sends you for a picture?
JULIA   Ay, madam.
SILVIA   Ursula, bring my picture there. [*She brings it.*]
115 Go, give your master this. Tell him from me,
   One Julia, that his changing thoughts forget,
   Would better fit his chamber than this shadow.
JULIA   Madam, please you peruse this letter.
    [*Gives her a letter.*]
   Pardon me, madam, I have unadvised
120 Delivered you a paper that I should not.
   This is the letter to your ladyship.
    [*Takes back the letter and gives her another.*]
SILVIA   I pray thee let me look on that again.
JULIA   It may not be. Good madam, pardon me.
SILVIA   There, hold.
125 I will not look upon your master's lines.
   I know they are stuffed with protestations
   And full of new-found oaths, which he will break
   As easily as I do tear his paper. [*Tears the letter.*]

JULIA   Madam, he sends your ladyship this ring.
SILVIA   The more shame for him that he sends it me, 130
   For I have heard him say a thousand times
   His Julia gave it him at his departure.
   Though his false finger have profaned the ring,
   Mine shall not do his Julia so much wrong.
JULIA   She thanks you. 135
SILVIA   What sayst thou?
JULIA   I thank you, madam, that you tender her.
   Poor gentlewoman, my master wrongs her much.
SILVIA   Dost thou know her?
JULIA   Almost as well as I do know myself. 140
   To think upon her woes I do protest
   That I have wept a hundred several times.
SILVIA   Belike she thinks that Proteus hath forsook her?
JULIA   I think she doth, and that's her cause of sorrow.
SILVIA   Is she not passing fair? 145
JULIA   She hath been fairer, madam, than she is.
   When she did think my master loved her well,
   She, in my judgement, was as fair as you.
   But since she did neglect her looking-glass
   And threw her sun-expelling mask away, 150
   The air hath starved the roses in her cheeks
   And pinched the lily-tincture of her face,
   That now she is become as black as I.
SILVIA   How tall was she?
JULIA   About my stature; for at Pentecost, 155
   When all our pageants of delight were played,
   Our youth got me to play the woman's part,
   And I was trimmed in Madam Julia's gown,
   Which served me as fit, by all men's judgements,
   As if the garment had been made for me; 160
   Therefore I know she is about my height.
   And at that time I made her weep a-good,
   For I did play a lamentable part.
   Madam, 'twas Ariadne, passioning
   For Theseus' perjury and unjust flight, 165
   Which I so lively acted with my tears
   That my poor mistress, moved therewithal,
   Wept bitterly; and would I might be dead
   If I in thought felt not her very sorrow.
SILVIA   She is beholding to thee, gentle youth. 170
   Alas, poor lady, desolate and left!
   I weep myself to think upon thy words.
   Here, youth, there is my purse. I give thee this
   For thy sweet mistress' sake, because thou lov'st her.
   Farewell. *Exeunt Silvia and Attendants.* 175
JULIA
   And she shall thank you for't, if e'er you know her.
   A virtuous gentlewoman, mild and beautiful.
   I hope my master's suit will be but cold,
   Since she respects my mistress' love so much.
   Alas, how love can trifle with itself! 180
   Here is her picture. Let me see, I think
   If I had such a tire, this face of mine
   Were full as lovely as is this of hers;
   And yet the painter flattered her a little,

185   Unless I flatter with myself too much.
        Her hair is auburn, mine is perfect yellow;
        If that be all the difference in his love,
        I'll get me such a coloured periwig.
        Her eyes are grey as glass, and so are mine.
190   Ay, but her forehead's low, and mine's as high.
        What should it be that he respects in her
        But I can make respective in myself,
        If this fond Love were not a blinded god?
        Come, shadow, come, and take this shadow up,
        For 'tis thy rival.   [*Looks at the picture.*]
195   O thou senseless form,
        Thou shalt be worshipped, kissed, loved and adored;
        And were there sense in his idolatry
        My substance should be statue in thy stead.
        I'll use thee kindly for thy mistress' sake
200   That used me so; or else, by Jove I vow,
        I should have scratched out your unseeing eyes
        To make my master out of love with thee.   *Exit.*

5.1   *Enter* EGLAMOUR.

EGLAMOUR   The sun begins to gild the western sky,
        And now it is about the very hour
        That Silvia at Friar Patrick's cell should meet me.
        She will not fail, for lovers break not hours,
5   Unless it be to come before their time,
        So much they spur their expedition.

                  Enter SILVIA.

        See where she comes. Lady, a happy evening!
SILVIA Amen, amen. Go on, good Eglamour,
        Out at the postern by the abbey wall;
10   I fear I am attended by some spies.
EGLAMOUR
        Fear not. The forest is not three leagues off;
        If we recover that, we are sure enough.   *Exeunt.*

5.2   *Enter* TURIO, PROTEUS, *and*
                     JULIA *as Sebastian.*

TURIO   Sir Proteus, what says Silvia to my suit?
PROTEUS O, sir, I find her milder than she was,
        And yet she takes exceptions at your person.
TURIO   What? That my leg is too long?
5   PROTEUS No, that it is too little.
TURIO   I'll wear a boot, to make it somewhat rounder.
JULIA [*aside*]
        But love will not be spurred to what it loathes.
TURIO   What says she to my face?
PROTEUS She says it is a fair one.
10   TURIO   Nay then, the wanton lies; my face is black.
PROTEUS But pearls are fair; and the old saying is,
        'Black men are pearls in beauteous ladies' eyes.'
JULIA [*aside*]
        'Tis true, such pearls as put out ladies' eyes,
        For I had rather wink than look on them.
15   TURIO   How likes she my discourse?

PROTEUS   Ill, when you talk of war.
TURIO   But well when I discourse of love and peace.
JULIA [*aside*]
        But better, indeed, when you hold your peace.
TURIO   What says she to my valour?
PROTEUS   O, sir, she makes no doubt of that.   20
JULIA [*aside*]
        She needs not when she knows it cowardice.
TURIO   What says she to my birth?
PROTEUS   That you are well derived.
JULIA [*aside*]   True, from a gentleman to a fool.
TURIO   Considers she my possessions?   25
PROTEUS   O, ay, and pities them.
TURIO   Wherefore?
JULIA [*aside*]   That such an ass should owe them.
PROTEUS   That they are out by lease.

                  Enter DUKE.

JULIA   Here comes the Duke.
DUKE   How now, Sir Proteus! How now, Turio!   30
        Which of you saw Eglamour of late?
TURIO   Not I.
PROTEUS   Nor I.
DUKE   Saw you my daughter?
PROTEUS   Neither.
DUKE   Why then, she's fled unto that peasant Valentine,
        And Eglamour is in her company.
        'Tis true, for Friar Laurence met them both   35
        As he in penance wandered through the forest.
        Him he knew well, and guessed that it was she,
        But, being masked, he was not sure of it.
        Besides, she did intend confession
        At Patrick's cell this even, and there she was not. 40
        These likelihoods confirm her flight from hence.
        Therefore, I pray you, stand not to discourse,
        But mount you presently and meet with me
        Upon the rising of the mountain foot
        That leads toward Mantua, whither they are fled.   45
        Dispatch, sweet gentlemen, and follow me.   *Exit.*
TURIO   Why, this it is to be a peevish girl
        That flies her fortune when it follows her.
        I'll after, more to be revenged on Eglamour
        Than for the love of reckless Silvia.   *Exit.* 50
PROTEUS   And I will follow, more for Silvia's love
        Than hate of Eglamour that goes with her.   *Exit.*
JULIA   And I will follow, more to cross that love
        Than hate for Silvia, that is gone for love. *Exit.*

5.3   *Enter* SILVIA *and* Outlaws.

1 OUTLAW   Come, come, be patient. We must bring you
        to our captain.
SILVIA   A thousand more mischances than this one
        Have learned me how to brook this patiently.
2 OUTLAW   Come, bring her away.   5
1 OUTLAW   Where is the gentleman that was with her?
3 OUTLAW   Being nimble-footed, he hath outrun us.

	But Moses and Valerius follow him.
	Go thou with her to the west end of the wood;
10	There is our captain. We'll follow him that's fled.
	The thicket is beset, he cannot scape.

Exeunt Second and Third Outlaws.

1 OUTLAW
Come, I must bring you to our captain's cave.
Fear not, he bears an honourable mind
And will not use a woman lawlessly.

15 SILVIA　O Valentine, this I endure for thee!　*Exeunt.*

5.4　　　*Enter* VALENTINE.

VALENTINE　How use doth breed a habit in a man!
This shadowy desert, unfrequented woods,
I better brook than flourishing peopled towns.
Here can I sit alone, unseen of any,
5　And to the nightingale's complaining notes
Tune my distresses and record my woes.
O thou that dost inhabit in my breast,
Leave not the mansion so long tenantless,
Lest, growing ruinous, the building fall
10　And leave no memory of what it was.
Repair me with thy presence, Silvia;
Thou gentle nymph, cherish thy forlorn swain.
　　　　　　　　　　　[Shouts within]
What hallowing and what stir is this today?
These are my mates, that make their wills their law,
15　Have some unhappy passenger in chase.
They love me well; yet I have much to do
To keep them from uncivil outrages.

Enter PROTEUS, SILVIA, *and* JULIA *as Sebastian.*

Withdraw thee, Valentine.　*[Steps aside.]*
　　　　　　　　　　Who's this comes here?
PROTEUS　Madam, this service I have done for you
20　(Though you respect not aught your servant doth),
To hazard life and rescue you from him
That would have forced your honour and your love.
Vouchsafe me for my meed but one fair look;
A smaller boon than this I cannot beg,
25　And less than this, I am sure, you cannot give.
VALENTINE *[aside]*
How like a dream is this I see and hear!
Love, lend me patience to forbear awhile.
SILVIA　O miserable, unhappy that I am!
PROTEUS　Unhappy were you, madam, ere I came;
30　But by my coming I have made you happy.
SILVIA　By thy approach thou mak'st me most unhappy.
JULIA *[aside]*
And me, when he approacheth to your presence.
SILVIA　Had I been seized by a hungry lion
I would have been a breakfast to the beast
35　Rather than have false Proteus rescue me.
O heaven, be judge how I love Valentine,
Whose life's as tender to me as my soul!
And full as much, for more there cannot be,

I do detest false perjured Proteus.
Therefore be gone, solicit me no more.　　　40
PROTEUS
What dangerous action, stood it next to death,
Would I not undergo for one calm look?
O, 'tis the curse in love, and still approved,
When women cannot love where they're beloved.
SILVIA　When Proteus cannot love where he's beloved.　45
Read over Julia's heart, thy first, best love,
For whose dear sake thou didst then rend thy faith
Into a thousand oaths, and all those oaths
Descended into perjury to love me.
Thou hast no faith left now, unless thou'dst two,　50
And that's far worse than none; better have none
Than plural faith, which is too much by one.
Thou counterfeit to thy true friend!
PROTEUS　　　　　　　　　In love
Who respects friend?
SILVIA　　　　　　　All men but Proteus.
PROTEUS　Nay, if the gentle spirit of moving words　55
Can no way change you to a milder form,
I'll woo you like a soldier, at arms' end,
And love you 'gainst the nature of love – force ye.
　　　[Seizes her.]
SILVIA　O heaven!
PROTEUS　　　　I'll force thee yield to my desire.
VALENTINE *[Comes forward.]*
Ruffian, let go that rude uncivil touch,　　　60
Thou friend of an ill fashion!
PROTEUS　　　　　　　　Valentine!
VALENTINE
Thou common friend, that's without faith or love,
For such is a friend now! Treacherous man,
Thou hast beguiled my hopes. Naught but mine eye
Could have persuaded me. Now I dare not say　65
I have one friend alive; thou wouldst disprove me.
Who should be trusted, when one's right hand
Is perjured to the bosom? Proteus,
I am sorry I must never trust thee more,
But count the world a stranger for thy sake.　70
The private wound is deepest. O time most accurst,
'Mongst all foes that a friend should be the worst!
PROTEUS　My shame and guilt confounds me.
Forgive me, Valentine; if hearty sorrow
Be a sufficient ransom for offence,　　　75
I tender't here. I do as truly suffer
As e'er I did commit.
VALENTINE　　　　Then I am paid,
And once again I do receive thee honest.
Who by repentance is not satisfied
Is nor of heaven nor earth, for these are pleased;　80
By penitence th'Eternal's wrath's appeased.
And that my love may appear plain and free,
All that was mine in Silvia I give thee.
JULIA　O me unhappy!　*[Faints.]*
PROTEUS　　　　　Look to the boy.
VALENTINE　　　　　　　　Why, boy!

85 Why, wag! How now? What's the matter? Look up;
speak.

JULIA   O good sir, my master charged me to deliver a
ring to Madam Silvia, which out of my neglect was
never done.

90 PROTEUS   Where is that ring, boy?

JULIA   Here 'tis; this is it. [*Gives him a ring.*]

PROTEUS   How? Let me see.
Why, this is the ring I gave to Julia.

JULIA   O, cry you mercy, sir, I have mistook.

95 This is the ring you sent to Silvia.
[*Shows another ring.*]

PROTEUS
But how cam'st thou by this ring? At my depart
I gave this unto Julia.

JULIA   And Julia herself did give it me –
And Julia herself hath brought it hither.
[*Reveals herself.*]

100 PROTEUS   How? Julia?

JULIA   Behold her that gave aim to all thy oaths
And entertained 'em deeply in her heart.
How oft hast thou with perjury cleft the root!
O Proteus, let this habit make thee blush.

105 Be thou ashamed that I have took upon me
Such an immodest raiment, if shame live
In a disguise of love.
It is the lesser blot, modesty finds,
Women to change their shapes than men their minds.

PROTEUS

110 Than men their minds? 'Tis true. O heaven, were man
But constant, he were perfect. That one error
Fills him with faults, makes him run through all th'
sins;
Inconstancy falls off ere it begins.
What is in Silvia's face but I may spy

115 More fresh in Julia's, with a constant eye?

VALENTINE   Come, come, a hand from either.
Let me be blest to make this happy close.
'Twere pity two such friends should be long foes.

PROTEUS   Bear witness, heaven, I have my wish forever.

JULIA   And I mine.

Enter Outlaws *with* DUKE *and* TURIO.

120 OUTLAWS   A prize, a prize, a prize!

VALENTINE
Forbear, forbear, I say! It is my lord the Duke.
Your grace is welcome to a man disgraced,
Banished Valentine.

DUKE   Sir Valentine!

TURIO   Yonder is Silvia, and Silvia's mine.

125 VALENTINE   Turio, give back, or else embrace thy death;

Come not within the measure of my wrath.
Do not name Silvia thine; if once again,
Verona shall not hold thee. Here she stands;
Take but possession of her with a touch –
I dare thee but to breathe upon my love.   130

TURIO   Sir Valentine, I care not for her, I.
I hold him but a fool that will endanger
His body for a girl that loves him not.
I claim her not, and therefore she is thine.

DUKE   The more degenerate and base art thou   135
To make such means for her as thou hast done,
And leave her on such slight conditions. –
Now, by the honour of my ancestry,
I do applaud thy spirit, Valentine,
And think thee worthy of an empress' love.   140
Know then, I here forget all former griefs,
Cancel all grudge, repeal thee home again,
Plead a new state in thy unrivalled merit,
To which I thus subscribe: Sir Valentine,
Thou art a gentleman, and well derived;   145
Take thou thy Silvia, for thou hast deserved her.

VALENTINE
I thank your grace; the gift hath made me happy.
I now beseech you, for your daughter's sake,
To grant one boon that I shall ask of you.

DUKE   I grant it for thine own, whate'er it be.   150

VALENTINE
These banished men, that I have kept withal,
Are men endued with worthy qualities.
Forgive them what they have committed here,
And let them be recalled from their exile.
They are reformed, civil, full of good   155
And fit for great employment, worthy lord.

DUKE   Thou hast prevailed; I pardon them and thee.
Dispose of them as thou knowst their deserts.
Come, let us go. We will include all jars
With triumphs, mirth and rare solemnity.   160

VALENTINE   And as we walk along, I dare be bold
With our discourse to make your grace to smile.
What think you of this page, my lord?

DUKE   I think the boy hath grace in him; he blushes.

VALENTINE
I warrant you, my lord, more grace than boy.   165

DUKE   What mean you by that saying?

VALENTINE   Please you, I'll tell you as we pass along,
That you will wonder what hath fortuned.
Come, Proteus, 'tis your penance but to hear
The story of your loves discovered.   170
That done, our day of marriage shall be yours,
One feast, one house, one mutual happiness.

Exeunt.

The Two Noble Kinsmen

The Two Noble Kinsmen was printed in 1634 as the joint work of 'the memorable Worthies of their time' John Fletcher and William Shakespeare, performed by the King's Men at the Blackfriars theatre. These claims fit the likely date of composition, 1613–14, making it the latest surviving play in which Shakespeare had a hand. A dance from *The Masque of the Inner Temple and Gray's Inn*, by Fletcher's regular collaborator Francis Beaumont, which was presented at Court on 20 February 1613 during the wedding celebrations of Princess Elizabeth and Frederick, the Elector Palatine, supplied the characters (and presumably the costumes) for the morris dance in 3.5. Fletcher's major share in the authorship meant that until the nineteenth century the play remained within the printed canon of 'Beaumont and Fletcher' rather than Shakespeare. Interest in *The Two Noble Kinsmen* revived after collaborative authorship of *King Henry VIII* began to be seriously proposed in the mid-nineteenth century, and since the 1970s it has regularly appeared in collected editions of Shakespeare. The mode of collaboration is uncertain but the scenes in which Shakespeare's hand is most evident are mainly in the first and last acts (1.1–5; 2.1, 3[?]; 3.1–2; 4.3[?]; 5.1, 3–4), leaving to Fletcher the bulk of the central action and almost all of the subplot of the Jailer's Daughter.

Though the story of the siege of Thebes is pervasive in classical Greek and Latin literature, the playwrights relied on a medieval accretion to it. Chaucer's version of the perplexities of the Theban cousins Palamon and Arcite in their rivalry for the love of Emilia, sister of the Amazon queen Hippolyta, bride of Theseus, is assigned to the Knight in *The Canterbury Tales* (dating from the 1390s). Chaucer got the story from the *Teseida* of Giovanni Boccaccio (?late 1340s), behind which lies the *Thebaid* of Statius. Shakespeare had earlier used *The Knight's Tale* for his treatment of Theseus and Hippolyta in *A Midsummer Night's Dream*.

Like Chaucer's tale, the play sets up a series of moral and emotional dilemmas for its characters. Should Theseus proceed with his wedding, or postpone it until he has avenged the widowed queens? Should Palamon and Arcite fight for their native Thebes, or flee from the corruptions of its king, their uncle Creon? Should their friendship prevail over their rivalry in love for Emilia? Should the Jailer's Daughter free Palamon at the risk of her father's life? Should Emilia choose between marriage and virginity – or between her equally unknown and unwelcome suitors? The struggles of the characters to resolve these dilemmas culminate in a scene, adapted from Chaucer, in which Arcite, Palamon and Emilia in turn invoke their tutelary gods, Mars, Venus and Diana. Thereafter, we increasingly see them as pawns in a divine chess-game. The outcome, in which accidental death robs Arcite of his victory in combat and leaves Emilia to the disconsolate Palamon, is well characterized by Emilia's cry, 'Is this winning?' (5.3.138). Meanwhile the destructive passion of the Jailer's Daughter for Palamon moves through suicidal despair and madness to the apparent possibility of transference to her faithful Wooer by a therapy involving sexual relations with him under the pretence that he is Palamon. It is unclear how fully audiences are invited to endorse Theseus' statement that 'in the passage / The gods have been most equal' (5.4.114–15), or his determinist conclusion: 'Let us be thankful / For that which is, and with you leave dispute / That are above our question' (5.4.134–6).

The tone of the play varies sharply between elegaic solemnity and a brittle, even cynical, detachment. Since the 1970s, stage productions have proliferated after centuries of relative neglect. The play offers a powerful portrayal of the predicaments of women in a male-dominated world, and its unhappy open-endedness is congruous with the chastened mood of the turn of the century.

The Arden text is based on the 1634 Quarto.

Speaker of the Prologue

BOY	*singer in the wedding procession*
HYMEN	
Nymphs	*figures in the wedding procession*

ATHENIANS

THESEUS	*Duke of Athens*
PIRITHOUS	*friend of Theseus*
HIPPOLYTA	*bride of Theseus, an Amazon*
EMILIA	*sister of Hippolyta*
OFFICER (Artesius)	*officer of Theseus*
HERALD	
WAITING WOMAN	*to Emilia*
JAILER	
DAUGHTER	*to Jailer*
WOOER	*to Jailer's Daughter*
BROTHER	*to Jailer*
Two FRIENDS	*of Jailer*
DOCTOR	
MAID	*companion to Jailer's Daughter*
SCHOOLMASTER (Gerald)	
Five COUNTRYMEN	*(among them Arcas, Rycas, Sennois)*
TABORER (Timothy)	
Actor playing BAVIAN	
Five COUNTRYWOMEN	Barbary, Friz, Luce, Maudlin, Nell
GENTLEMEN	
EXECUTIONER	
Two MESSENGERS	

THEBANS

Three QUEENS	*widows of besiegers of Thebes*
ARCITE	
PALAMON	*cousins, nephews to Creon, King of Thebes*
VALERIUS	
Three KNIGHTS	*supporters of Arcite*
Three KNIGHTS	*supporters of Palamon*

Speaker of the Epilogue

Servants, Guards, Attendants, *etc.*

PROLOGUE

Flourish. Enter Speaker of the Prologue.

New plays and maidenheads are near akin:
Much followed both, for both much money gi'en,
If they stand sound and well. And a good play,
Whose modest scenes blush on his marriage day
5 And shake to lose his honour, is like her
That after holy tie and first night's stir
Yet still is Modesty and still retains
More of the maid, to sight, than husband's pains.
We pray our play may be so, for I am sure
10 It has a noble breeder and a pure,
A learned, and a poet never went
More famous yet 'twixt Po and silver Trent.
Chaucer, of all admired, the story gives;
There, constant to eternity, it lives.
15 If we let fall the nobleness of this
And the first sound this child hear be a hiss,
How will it shake the bones of that good man
And make him cry from under ground, 'Oh, fan
From me the witless chaff of such a writer
20 That blasts my bays and my famed works makes lighter
Than Robin Hood!' This is the fear we bring;
For, to say truth, it were an endless thing
And too ambitious to aspire to him,
Weak as we are, and, almost breathless, swim
25 In this deep water. Do but you hold out
Your helping hands and we shall tack about
And something do to save us. You shall hear
Scenes, though below his art, may yet appear
Worth two hours' travel. To his bones sweet sleep;
30 Content to you. If this play do not keep
A little dull time from us, we perceive
Our losses fall so thick, we must needs leave.
Flourish. Exit.

1.1 *Music. Enter Hymen with a torch burning; a Boy,*
in a white robe, before, singing and strewing flowers; after
Hymen, a Nymph encompassed in her tresses, bearing a
wheaten garland. Then THESEUS *between two other*
nymphs with wheaten chaplets on their heads. Then
HIPPOLYTA *the bride, led by* PIRITHOUS *and another*
holding a garland over her head (her tresses likewise
hanging). After her, EMILIA, *holding up her train;*
Artesius; Attendants; Musicians.

BOY [*Sings.*]
Roses, their sharp spines being gone,
Not royal in their smells alone
But in their hue;
Maiden pinks of odour faint,
5 Daisies smell-less yet most quaint,
And sweet thyme true;

Primrose, first-born child of Ver,
Merry springtime's harbinger,
With harebells dim,

Oxlips in their cradles growing, 10
Marigolds on deathbeds blowing,
Lark's-heels trim: [*Strews flowers.*]

All dear Nature's children sweet
Lie 'fore bride and bridegroom's feet,
Blessing their sense. 15
Not an angel of the air,
Bird melodious, or bird fair,
Is absent hence.

The crow, the sland'rous cuckoo, nor
The boding raven, nor chough hoar, 20
Nor chatt'ring 'pie,
May on our bride-house perch or sing,
Or with them any discord bring,
But from it fly.

Enter three QUEENS *in black, with veils stained, with*
imperial crowns. The First Queen falls down at the foot
of Theseus; the Second falls down at the foot of
Hippolyta; the Third before Emilia.

1 QUEEN [*to Theseus*]
For pity's sake and true gentility's, 25
Hear and respect me.
2 QUEEN [*to Hippolyta*]   For your mother's sake
And as you wish your womb may thrive with fair ones,
Hear and respect me.
3 QUEEN [*to Emilia*]
Now, for the love of him whom Jove hath marked
The honour of your bed and for the sake 30
Of clear virginity, be advocate
For us and our distresses. This good deed
Shall raze you out o'th' book of trespasses
All you are set down there.
THESEUS   Sad lady, rise.
HIPPOLYTA   Stand up.
EMILIA   No knees to me! 35
What woman I may stead that is distressed
Does bind me to her.
THESEUS
What's your request?
[*to First Queen*]   Deliver you for all.
1 QUEEN
We are three queens whose sovereigns fell before
The wrath of cruel Creon, who endure 40
The beaks of ravens, talons of the kites
And pecks of crows, in the foul fields of Thebes.
He will not suffer us to burn their bones,
To urn their ashes, nor to take th'offence
Of mortal loathsomeness from the blest eye 45
Of holy Phoebus, but infects the winds
With stench of our slain lords. O pity, Duke;
Thou purger of the earth, draw thy feared sword
That does good turns to th' world; give us the bones
Of our dead kings that we may chapel them; 50
And of thy boundless goodness take some note

That for our crowned heads we have no roof,
Save this which is the lion's and the bear's
And vault to every thing.

THESEUS   Pray you, kneel not:
55   I was transported with your speech and suffered
Your knees to wrong themselves. I have heard the
        fortunes
Of your dead lords, which gives me such lamenting
As wakes my vengeance and revenge for 'em.
[*to First Queen*] King Capaneus was your lord. The day
60   That he should marry you, at such a season
As now it is with me, I met your groom.
By Mars's altar, you were that time fair!
Not Juno's mantle fairer than your tresses
Nor in more bounty spread her. Your wheaten wreath
65   Was then nor threshed nor blasted; Fortune at you
Dimpled her cheek with smiles. Hercules our kinsman,
Then weaker than your eyes, laid by his club;
He tumbled down upon his Nemean hide
And swore his sinews thawed. O, grief and time,
70   Fearful consumers, you will all devour!

1 QUEEN   O, I hope some god,
Some god hath put his mercy in your manhood,
Whereto he'll infuse power, and press you forth
Our undertaker.

THESEUS   O, no knees, none, widow.
75   Unto the helmeted Bellona use them,
And pray for me, your soldier.
Troubled I am.   [*Turns away.*]

2 QUEEN   Honoured Hippolyta,
Most dreaded Amazonian, that hast slain
The scythe-tusked boar; that with thy arm, as strong
80   As it is white, wast near to make the male
To thy sex captive, but that this thy lord,
Born to uphold creation in that honour
First nature styled it in, shrunk thee into
The bound thou wast o'erflowing, at once subduing
85   Thy force and thy affection; soldieress,
That equally canst poise sternness with pity,
Whom now I know hast much more power on him
Than ever he had on thee, who ow'st his strength
And his love too, who is a servant for
90   The tenor of thy speech; dear glass of ladies:
Bid him that we, whom flaming war doth scorch,
Under the shadow of his sword may cool us.
Require him he advance it o'er our heads.
Speak't in a woman's key; like such a woman
95   As any of us three; weep ere you fail.
Lend us a knee;
But touch the ground for us no longer time
Than a dove's motion, when the head's plucked off.
Tell him, if he i'th' blood-sized field lay swollen,
100   Showing the sun his teeth, grinning at the moon,
What you would do.

HIPPOLYTA   Poor lady, say no more.
I had as lief trace this good action with you
As that whereto I am going, and never yet

Went I so willing way. My lord is taken
Heart-deep with your distress. Let him consider: 105
I'll speak anon.   [*Second Queen rises.*]

3 QUEEN   O, my petition was
Set down in ice, which by hot grief uncandied
Melts into drops; so sorrow, wanting form,
Is pressed with deeper matter.

EMILIA   Pray, stand up;
Your grief is written in your cheek.

3 QUEEN   O, woe,   110
You cannot read it there.   [*Rises.*]
                      There, through my tears,
Like wrinkled pebbles in a glassy stream,
You may behold 'em. Lady, lady, alack,
He that will all the treasure know o'th' earth
Must know the centre too; he that will fish   115
For my least minnow, let him lead his line
To catch one at my heart. O, pardon me;
Extremity, that sharpens sundry wits,
Makes me a fool.

EMILIA   Pray you, say nothing, pray you:
Who cannot feel nor see the rain, being in't,   120
Knows neither wet nor dry. If that you were
The ground-piece of some painter, I would buy you
T'instruct me 'gainst a capital grief, indeed
Such heart-pierced demonstration; but, alas,
Being a natural sister of our sex,   125
Your sorrow beats so ardently upon me
That it shall make a counter-reflect 'gainst
My brother's heart and warm it to some pity,
Though it were made of stone. Pray, have good comfort.

THESEUS   Forward to th' temple! Leave not out a jot   130
O'th' sacred ceremony.

1 QUEEN   O, this celebration
Will longer last and be more costly than
Your suppliants' war! Remember that your fame
Knolls in the ear o'th' world: what you do quickly
Is not done rashly; your first thought is more   135
Than others' laboured meditance; your premeditating
More than their actions; but, O Jove, your actions,
Soon as they move, as ospreys do the fish,
Subdue before they touch. Think, dear Duke, think
What beds our slain kings have!

2 QUEEN   What griefs our beds,   140
That our dear lords have none!

3 QUEEN   None fit for th' dead.
Those that with cords, knives, drams' precipitance,
Weary of this world's light, have to themselves
Been death's most horrid agents, human grace
Affords them dust and shadow –

1 QUEEN   But our lords   145
Lie blistering 'fore the visiting sun,
And were good kings when living.

THESEUS   It is true.
And I will give you comfort,
To give your dead lords graves – the which to do,
Must make some work with Creon.

1 QUEEN   And that work
    Presents itself to th' doing.
    Now 'twill take form; the heats are gone tomorrow.
    Then, bootless toil must recompense itself
    With its own sweat; now, he's secure,
    Nor dreams we stand before your puissance
    Rinsing our holy begging in our eyes
    To make petition clear.
2 QUEEN   Now you may take him,
    Drunk with his victory –
3 QUEEN   And his army full
    Of bread and sloth.
THESEUS [*to Officer*]   Artesius, that best knowest
    How to draw out fit to this enterprise
    The prim'st for this proceeding and the number
    To carry such a business – forth and levy
    Our worthiest instruments, whilst we dispatch
    This grand act of our life, this daring deed
    Of fate in wedlock.
1 QUEEN [*to Second and Third Queens*]
                              Dowagers, take hands.
    Let us be widows to our woes; delay
    Commends us to a famishing hope.
QUEENS   Farewell!
2 QUEEN
    We come unseasonably; but when could grief
    Cull forth, as unpanged judgement can, fitt'st time
    For best solicitation?
THESEUS   Why, good ladies,
    This is a service, whereto I am going,
    Greater than any war; it more imports me
    Than all the actions that I have foregone,
    Or futurely can cope.
1 QUEEN   The more proclaiming
    Our suit shall be neglected when her arms,
    Able to lock Jove from a synod, shall
    By warranting moonlight corslet thee. O, when
    Her twinning cherries shall their sweetness fall
    Upon thy taste-full lips, what wilt thou think
    Of rotten kings or blubbered queens? What care
    For what thou feel'st not, what thou feel'st being able
    To make Mars spurn his drum? O, if thou couch
    But one night with her, every hour in't will
    Take hostage of thee for a hundred and
    Thou shalt remember nothing more than what
    That banquet bids thee to.
HIPPOLYTA   Though much unlike
    You should be so transported, as much sorry
    I should be such a suitor, yet I think,
    Did I not, by th'abstaining of my joy
    Which breeds a deeper longing, cure their surfeit
    That craves a present med'cine, I should pluck
    All ladies' scandal on me. Therefore, sir, [*Kneels.*]
    As I shall here make trial of my prayers,
    Either presuming them to have some force,
    Or sentencing for aye their vigour dumb,
    Prorogue this business we are going about and hang

Your shield afore your heart, about that neck
    Which is my fee and which I freely lend
    To do these poor queens service.
QUEENS [*to Emilia*]   Oh, help now.
    Our cause cries for your knee.
EMILIA [*Kneels, to Theseus*]   If you grant not
    My sister her petition in that force,
    With that celerity and nature, which
    She makes it in, from henceforth I'll not dare
    To ask you anything nor be so hardy
    Ever to take a husband.
THESEUS   Pray, stand up.
    I am entreating of my self to do
    That which you kneel to have me. [*They rise.*]
                              Pirithous,
    Lead on the bride; get you and pray the gods
    For success and return; omit not anything
    In the pretended celebration. – Queens,
    Follow your soldier.
    [*to Officer*]   As before – hence, you,
    And at the banks of Aulis meet us with
    The forces you can raise, where we shall find
    The moiety of a number for a business
    More bigger-looked.   *Exit Officer.*
    [*to Hippolyta*]   Since that our theme is haste,
    I stamp this kiss upon thy current lip;
    Sweet, keep it as my token. Set you forward,
    For I will see you gone.
        [*Procession moves toward the temple.*]
    – Farewell, my beauteous sister. – Pirithous,
    Keep the feast full; bate not an hour on't.
PIRITHOUS   Sir,
    I'll follow you at heels; the feast's solemnity
    Shall want till your return.
THESEUS   Cousin, I charge you,
    Budge not from Athens. We shall be returning
    Ere you can end this feast, of which I pray you
    Make no abatement. Once more, farewell all.
                Exeunt all except Theseus and Queens.
1 QUEEN
    Thus dost thou still make good the tongue o'th' world –
2 QUEEN   And earn'st a deity equal with Mars –
3 QUEEN   If not above him, for
    Thou, being but mortal, mak'st affections bend
    To godlike honours; they themselves, some say,
    Groan under such a mast'ry.
THESEUS   As we are men,
    Thus should we do; being sensually subdued,
    We lose our human title. Good cheer, ladies:
    Now turn we towards your comforts.
                              Flourish. Exeunt.

1.2   *Enter* PALAMON *and* ARCITE.

ARCITE   Dear Palamon, dearer in love than blood
    And our prime cousin: yet unhardened in
    The crimes of nature, let us leave the city

Thebes and the temptings in't, before we further

5   Sully our gloss of youth
And here to keep in abstinence we shame
As in incontinence; for not to swim
I'th' aid o'th' current, were almost to sink,
At least to frustrate striving, and to follow

10   The common stream, 'twould bring us to an eddy
Where we should turn or drown; if labour through,
Our gain but life and weakness.

PALAMON   Your advice
Is cried up with example. What strange ruins,
Since first we went to school, may we perceive

15   Walking in Thebes! Scars and bare weeds
The gain o'th' martialist, who did propound
To his bold ends honour and golden ingots,
Which, though he won, he had not – and now flurted
By Peace for whom he fought! Who then shall offer

20   To Mars's so scorned altar? I do bleed
When such I meet and wish great Juno would
Resume her ancient fit of jealousy
To get the soldier work, that Peace might purge
For her repletion and retain anew

25   Her charitable heart, now hard and harsher
Than strife or war could be.

ARCITE   Are you not out?
Meet you no ruin but the soldier in
The cranks and turns of Thebes? You did begin
As if you met decays of many kinds.

30   Perceive you none that do arouse your pity
But th'unconsidered soldier?

PALAMON   Yes, I pity
Decays where'er I find them, but such most
That, sweating in an honourable toil,
Are paid with ice to cool 'em.

ARCITE   'Tis not this

35   I did begin to speak of. This is virtue
Of no respect in Thebes. I spake of Thebes –
How dangerous, if we will keep our honours,
It is for our residing, where every evil
Hath a good colour; where every seeming good's

40   A certain evil; where not to be e'en jump
As they are here were to be strangers, and,
Such things to be, mere monsters.

PALAMON   'Tis in our power,
Unless we fear that apes can tutor's, to
Be masters of our manners. What need I

45   Affect another's gait, which is not catching
Where there is faith, or to be fond upon
Another's way of speech when by mine own
I may be reasonably conceived, saved too,
Speaking it truly? Why am I bound

50   By any generous bond to follow him
Follows his tailor, haply so long until
The followed make pursuit? Or let me know
Why mine own barber is unblessed, with him
My poor chin too, for 'tis not scissored just

55   To such a favourite's glass? What canon is there

That does command my rapier from my hip
To dangle't in my hand, or to go tiptoe
Before the street be foul? Either I am
The fore-horse in the team or I am none

60   That draw i'th' sequent trace. These poor slight sores
Need not a plantain; that which rips my bosom
Almost to th' heart's –

ARCITE   Our uncle Creon.

PALAMON   He.
A most unbounded tyrant, whose successes
Makes heaven unfeared and villainy assured

65   Beyond its power there's nothing; almost puts
Faith in a fever and deifies alone
Voluble Chance; who only attributes
The faculties of other instruments
To his own nerves and act; commands men service

70   And what they win in't, boot and glory; one
That fears not to do harm; good, dares not. Let
The blood of mine that's sib to him be sucked
From me with leeches, let them break and fall
Off me with that corruption.

ARCITE   Clear-spirited cousin,

75   Let's leave his court, that we may nothing share
Of his loud infamy; for our milk
Will relish of the pasture and we must
Be vile or disobedient: not his kinsmen
In blood unless in quality.

PALAMON   Nothing truer:

80   I think the echoes of his shames have deafed
The ears of heavenly Justice. Widows' cries
Descend again into their throats and have not
Due audience of the gods.

Enter VALERIUS.

                       Valerius!

VALERIUS   The king calls for you; yet be leaden-footed

85   Till his great rage be off him. Phoebus, when
He broke his whipstock and exclaimed against
The horses of the sun, but whispered to
The loudness of his fury.

PALAMON   Small winds shake him.
But what's the matter?

VALERIUS

90   Theseus, who, where he threats, appals, hath sent
Deadly defiance to him and pronounces
Ruin to Thebes, who is at hand to seal
The promise of his wrath.

ARCITE   Let him approach.
But that we fear the gods in him, he brings not

95   A jot of terror to us. Yet what man
Thirds his own worth (the case is each of ours)
When that his action's dregged with mind assured
'Tis bad he goes about?

PALAMON   Leave that unreasoned.
Our services stand now for Thebes, not Creon.

100   Yet to be neutral to him were dishonour,
Rebellious to oppose; therefore we must

With him stand to the mercy of our fate,
Who hath bounded our last minute.
ARCITE   So we must.
[*to Valerius*] Is't said this war's afoot, or, it shall be,
On fail of some condition?
105 VALERIUS   'Tis in motion.
The intelligence of state came in the instant
With the defier.
PALAMON   Let's to the king – who, were he
A quarter-carrier of that honour which
His enemy come in, the blood we venture
110 Should be as for our health, which were not spent,
Rather laid out for purchase; but, alas,
Our hands advanced before our hearts, what will
The fall o'th' stroke do damage?
ARCITE   Let th'event,
That never-erring arbitrator, tell us
115 When we know all ourselves – and let us follow
The becking of our chance.   *Exeunt.*

1.3 *Enter* PIRITHOUS, HIPPOLYTA *and* EMILIA.

PIRITHOUS   No further.
HIPPOLYTA   Sir, farewell; repeat my wishes
To our great lord, of whose success I dare not
Make any timorous question; yet I wish him
Excess and overflow of power, an't might be
5 To dure ill-dealing fortune. Speed to him!
Store never hurts good governors.
PIRITHOUS   Though I know
His ocean needs not my poor drops, yet they
Must yield their tribute there.
[*to Emilia*]   My precious maid,
Those best affections that the heavens infuse
10 In their best-tempered pieces keep enthroned
In your dear heart.
EMILIA   Thanks, sir. Remember me
To our all-royal brother, for whose speed
The great Bellona I'll solicit; and,
Since in our terrene state petitions are not
15 Without gifts understood, I'll offer to her
What I shall be advised she likes. Our hearts
Are in his army, in his tent –
HIPPOLYTA   In's bosom.
We have been soldiers and we cannot weep
When our friends don their helms, or put to sea,
20 Or tell of babes broached on the lance, or women
That have sod their infants in (and after eat them)
The brine they wept at killing 'em. Then, if
You stay to see of us such spinsters, we
Should hold you here forever.
PIRITHOUS   Peace be to you
25 As I pursue this war, which shall be then
Beyond further requiring.   *Exit.*
EMILIA   How his longing
Follows his friend! Since his depart, his sports,
Though craving seriousness and skill, passed slightly

His careless execution, where nor gain
Made him regard or loss consider, but,   30
Playing one business in his hand, another
Directing in his head, his mind nurse equal
To these so-differing twins. Have you observed him,
Since our great lord departed?
HIPPOLYTA   With much labour,
And I did love him for't. They two have cabined   35
In many as dangerous as poor a corner,
Peril and want contending; they have skiffed
Torrents whose roaring tyranny and power
I'th' least of these was dreadful; and they have
Sought out together where Death's self was lodged;   40
Yet fate hath brought them off. Their knot of love,
Tied, weaved, entangled, with so true, so long,
And with a finger of so deep a cunning,
May be outworn, never undone. I think
Theseus cannot be umpire to himself,   45
Cleaving his conscience into twain and doing
Each side like justice, which he loves best.
EMILIA   Doubtless,
There is a best and reason has no manners
To say it is not you. I was acquainted
Once with a time when I enjoyed a play-fellow.   50
You were at wars when she the grave enriched,
Who made too proud the bed – took leave o'th' moon
(Which then looked pale at parting) when our count
Was each eleven.
HIPPOLYTA   'Twas Flavina.
EMILIA   Yes.
You talk of Pirithous' and Theseus' love.   55
Theirs has more ground, is more maturely seasoned,
More buckled with strong judgement, and their needs
The one of th'other may be said to water
Their intertangled roots of love – but I
And she I sigh and spoke of were things innocent,   60
Loved for we did and like the elements
That know not what nor why, yet do effect
Rare issues by their operance; our souls
Did so to one another. What she liked
Was then of me approved; what not, condemned –   65
No more arraignment. The flower that I would pluck
And put between my breasts (then but beginning
To swell about the blossom), O, she would long
Till she had such another, and commit it
To the like innocent cradle, where phoenix-like   70
They died in perfume. On my head no toy
But was her pattern; her affections – pretty,
Though happily her careless wear – I followed
For my most serious decking; had mine ear
Stol'n some new air or at adventure hummed one   75
From musical coinage, why, it was a note
Whereon her spirits would sojourn – rather, dwell on,
And sing it in her slumbers. This rehearsal,
Which fury-innocent wots well, comes in
Like old importment's bastard, has this end: 80
That the true love 'tween maid and maid may be

More than in sex dividual.

HIPPOLYTA   You're out of breath!
And this high-speeded pace is but to say
That you shall never, like the maid Flavina,
Love any that's called man.

85 EMILIA   I am sure I shall not.

HIPPOLYTA   Now, alack, weak sister,
I must no more believe thee in this point,
Though in't I know thou dost believe thy self,
Than I will trust a sickly appetite

90 That loathes even as it longs. But sure, my sister,
If I were ripe for your persuasion, you
Have said enough to shake me from the arm
Of the all-noble Theseus – for whose fortunes
I will now in and kneel, with great assurance

95 That we, more than his Pirithous, possess
The high throne in his heart.

EMILIA   I am not
Against your faith, yet I continue mine.   *Exeunt.*

1.4   *Cornets. A battle struck within; then a retreat.*
Flourish. Then enter THESEUS *as victor, with a Herald,*
other Lords, and Soldiers, PALAMON *and* ARCITE *on*
hearses. The three QUEENS *meet him and fall on their*
faces before him.

1 QUEEN   To thee no star be dark!

2 QUEEN   Both heaven and earth
Friend thee forever!

3 QUEEN   All the good that may
Be wished upon thy head, I cry 'Amen' to't!

THESEUS
Th'impartial gods, who from the mounted heavens
5 View us, their mortal herd, behold who err
And, in their time, chastise. Go and find out
The bones of your dead lords and honour them
With treble ceremony, rather than a gap
Should be in their dear rites. We would supply't,
10 But those we will depute, which shall invest
You in your dignities and even each thing
Our haste does leave imperfect. So adieu,
And heaven's good eyes look on you.   *Exeunt Queens.*
[*Theseus notices the two hearses.*]   What are those?

HERALD   Men of great quality, as may be judged
15 By their appointment. Some of Thebes have told's
They are sisters' children, nephews to the King.

THESEUS   By th' helm of Mars, I saw them in the war,
Like to a pair of lions, smeared with prey,
Make lanes in troops aghast. I fixed my note
20 Constantly on them, for they were a mark
Worth a god's view. What prisoner was't that told me
When I enquired their names?

HERALD   Wi' leave, they're called
Arcite and Palamon.

THESEUS   'Tis right; those, those.
They are not dead?

25 HERALD   Nor in a state of life. Had they been taken

When their last hurts were given, 'twas possible
They might have been recovered; yet they breathe
And have the name of men.

THESEUS   Then like men use 'em.
The very lees of such, millions of rates,
Exceed the wine of others. All our surgeons   30
Convent in their behoof; our richest balms,
Rather than niggard, waste; their lives concern us
Much more than Thebes is worth. Rather than
    have 'em
Freed of this plight and in their morning state,
Sound and at liberty, I would 'em dead;   35
But forty-thousandfold we had rather have 'em
Prisoners to us than death. Bear 'em speedily
From our kind air, to them unkind, and minister
What man to man may do, for our sake – more,
Since I have known frights, fury, friends' behests,   40
Love's provocations, zeal, a mistress' task,
Desire of liberty, a fever, madness,
Hath set a mark which nature could not reach to
Without some imposition, sickness in will
O'er-wrestling strength in reason. For our love   45
And great Apollo's mercy, all our best
Their best skill tender. Lead into the city,
Where having bound things scattered, we will post
To Athens 'fore our army.   *Flourish. Exeunt.*

1.5   *Music. Enter the* QUEENS *with the hearses of*
their knights, in a funeral solemnity.

The Dirge

Urns and odours bring away;
Vapours, sighs, darken the day;
Our dole more deadly looks than dying –
Balms and gums and heavy cheers,
Sacred vials fill'd with tears,   5
And clamours through the wild air flying.
Come, all sad and solemn shows
That are quick-eyed Pleasure's foes;
We convent naught else but woes.
We convent naught else but woes.   10

3 QUEEN
This funeral path brings to your household's grave:
Joy seize on you again; peace sleep with him.

2 QUEEN   And this to yours.

1 QUEEN   Yours this way. Heavens lend
A thousand differing ways to one sure end.

3 QUEEN   This world's a city full of straying streets,   15
And death's the market-place where each one meets.
    Exeunt severally.

2.1   *Enter* Jailer *and* Wooer.

JAILER   I may depart with little while I live; something I
may cast to you, not much. Alas, the prison I keep,
though it be for great ones, yet they seldom come;

before one salmon, you shall take a number of
minnows. I am given out to be better lined than it can
appear to me report is a true speaker. I would I were
really that I am delivered to be. Marry, what I have, be
it what it will, I will assure upon my daughter at the
day of my death.

WOOER   Sir, I demand no more than your own offer and
I will estate your daughter in what I have promised.

JAILER   Well, we will talk more of this when the
solemnity is past. But have you a full promise of her?

Enter the Jailer's Daughter *carrying rushes.*

When that shall be seen, I tender my consent.

WOOER   I have, sir. Here she comes.

JAILER [*to his Daughter*]   Your friend and I have chanced
to name you here, upon the old business. But no more
of that now; so soon as the court hurry is over, we will
have an end of it. I'th' meantime, look tenderly to the
two prisoners. I can tell you, they are princes.

DAUGHTER   These strewings are for their chamber. 'Tis
pity they are in prison and 'twere pity they should be
out. I do think they have patience to make any adversity
ashamed. The prison itself is proud of 'em and they
have all the world in their chamber.

JAILER   They are famed to be a pair of absolute men.

DAUGHTER   By my troth, I think Fame but stammers
'em; they stand a grise above the reach of report.

JAILER   I heard them reported in the battle to be the
only doers.

DAUGHTER   Nay, most likely, for they are noble
sufferers. I marvel how they would have looked had
they been victors, that with such a constant nobility
enforce a freedom out of bondage, making misery their
mirth and affliction a toy to jest at.

JAILER   Do they so?

DAUGHTER   It seems to me they have no more sense of
their captivity than I of ruling Athens. They eat well,
look merrily, discourse of many things, but nothing of
their own restraint and disasters. Yet sometime a
divided sigh, martyred, as 'twere, i'th' deliverance,
will break from one of them – when the other
presently gives it so sweet a rebuke that I could wish
myself a sigh to be so chid, or at least a sigher to be
comforted.

WOOER   I never saw 'em.

JAILER   The Duke himself came privately in the night
and so did they.

Enter PALAMON and ARCITE, *above.*

What the reason of it is, I know not. Look, yonder they
are; that's Arcite looks out.

DAUGHTER   No, sir, no, that's Palamon. Arcite is the
lower of the twain; you may perceive a part of him.

JAILER   Go to, leave your pointing; they would not make
us their object. Out of their sight.

DAUGHTER   It is a holiday to look on them. Lord, the
difference of men!   *Exeunt.*

2.2   *Enter PALAMON and ARCITE in prison.*

PALAMON   How do you, noble cousin?

ARCITE   How do you, sir?

PALAMON   Why, strong enough to laugh at misery
And bear the chance of war; yet we are prisoners,
I fear, forever, cousin.

ARCITE   I believe it
And to that destiny have patiently
Laid up my hour to come.

PALAMON   O, cousin Arcite,
Where is Thebes now? Where is our noble country?
Where are our friends and kindreds? Never more
Must we behold those comforts, never see
The hardy youths strive for the games of honour,
Hung with the painted favours of their ladies,
Like tall ships under sail – then start amongst 'em,
And as an east wind leave 'em all behind us,
Like lazy clouds, whilst Palamon and Arcite,
Even in the wagging of a wanton leg,
Outstripped the people's praises, won the garlands,
Ere they have time to wish 'em ours. O, never
Shall we two exercise, like twins of honour,
Our arms again and feel our fiery horses
Like proud seas under us; our good swords now
(Better the red-eyed god of war ne'er wore),
Ravished our sides, like age must run to rust
And deck the temples of those gods that hate us.
These hands shall never draw 'em out like lightning
To blast whole armies more.

ARCITE   No, Palamon,
Those hopes are prisoners with us. Here we are,
And here the graces of our youths must wither
Like a too-timely spring; here age must find us
And, which is heaviest, Palamon, unmarried.
The sweet embraces of a loving wife,
Loaden with kisses, armed with thousand Cupids,
Shall never clasp our necks; no issue know us;
No figures of ourselves shall we e'er see,
To glad our age, and like young eagles teach 'em
Boldly to gaze against bright arms and say,
'Remember what your fathers were, and conquer!'
The fair-eyed maids shall weep our banishments
And in their songs curse ever-blinded Fortune
Till she for shame see what a wrong she has done
To youth and nature. This is all our world.
We shall know nothing here but one another,
Hear nothing but the clock that tells our woes.
The vine shall grow but we shall never see it;
Summer shall come and with her all delights,
But dead-cold winter must inhabit here still.

PALAMON   'Tis too true, Arcite. To our Theban hounds
That shook the aged forest with their echoes
No more now must we hallow, no more shake
Our pointed javelins whilst the angry swine
Flies like a Parthian quiver from our rages,
Struck with our well-steeled darts. All valiant uses,

The food and nourishment of noble minds,
In us two here shall perish; we shall die,
Which is the curse of honour, lastly,
Children of grief and ignorance.

55 ARCITE   Yet, cousin,
Even from the bottom of these miseries,
From all that Fortune can inflict upon us,
I see two comforts rising, two mere blessings,
If the gods please: to hold here a brave patience
60 And the enjoying of our griefs together.
While Palamon is with me, let me perish
If I think this our prison!

PALAMON   Certainly,
'Tis a main goodness, cousin, that our fortunes
Were twined together; 'tis most true, two souls
65 Put in two noble bodies, let 'em suffer
The gall of hazard, so they grow together,
Will never sink; they must not, say they could.
A willing man dies sleeping and all's done.

ARCITE   Shall we make worthy uses of this place
That all men hate so much?

70 PALAMON   How, gentle cousin?

ARCITE   Let's think this prison holy sanctuary,
To keep us from corruption of worse men.
We are young and yet desire the ways of honour,
That liberty and common conversation,
75 The poison of pure spirits, might, like women,
Woo us to wander from. What worthy blessing
Can be but our imaginations
May make it ours? And here being thus together,
We are an endless mine to one another;
80 We are one another's wife, ever begetting
New births of love; we are father, friends, acquaintance,
We are, in one another, families;
I am your heir and you are mine. This place
Is our inheritance; no hard oppressor
85 Dare take this from us; here, with a little patience,
We shall live long and loving. No surfeits seek us;
The hand of war hurts none here, nor the seas
Swallow their youth. Were we at liberty,
A wife might part us lawfully, or business;
90 Quarrels consume us; envy of ill men
Crave our acquaintance. I might sicken, cousin,
Where you should never know it, and so perish
Without your noble hand to close mine eyes,
Or prayers to the gods. A thousand chances,
Were we from hence, would sever us.

95 PALAMON   You have made me –
I thank you, cousin Arcite – almost wanton
With my captivity: what a misery
It is to live abroad and everywhere!
'Tis like a beast, methinks. I find the court here –
100 I am sure, a more content; and all those pleasures
That woo the wills of men to vanity,
I see through now and am sufficient
To tell the world 'tis but a gaudy shadow
That old Time as he passes by takes with him.

What had we been, old in the court of Creon,   105
Where sin is justice, lust and ignorance
The virtues of the great ones? Cousin Arcite,
Had not the loving gods found this place for us,
We had died as they do, ill old men, unwept,
And had their epitaphs, the people's curses.   110
Shall I say more?

ARCITE   I would hear you still.

PALAMON   You shall.
Is there record of any two that loved
Better than we do, Arcite?

ARCITE   Sure there cannot.

PALAMON   I do not think it possible our friendship
Should ever leave us.

ARCITE   Till our deaths it cannot.   115

Enter EMILIA *and her* Woman.

And after death our spirits shall be led
To those that love eternally.   [*Palamon sees Emilia.*]
                                        Speak on, sir.

EMILIA   This garden has a world of pleasures in't.
What flower is this?

WOMAN   'Tis called narcissus, madam.

EMILIA   That was a fair boy, certain, but a fool   120
To love himself. Were there not maids enough?

ARCITE [*to Palamon*]   Pray, forward.

PALAMON   Yes –

EMILIA   Or were they all hard-hearted?

WOMAN   They could not be to one so fair.

EMILIA   Thou wouldst not.

WOMAN   I think I should not, madam.

EMILIA   That's a good wench.
But take heed to your kindness, though.

WOMAN   Why, madam?   125

EMILIA   Men are mad things.

ARCITE   Will ye go forward, cousin?

EMILIA
Canst not thou work such flowers in silk, wench?

WOMAN   Yes.

EMILIA   I'll have a gown full o' 'em, and of these.
This is a pretty colour; will't not do
Rarely upon a skirt, wench?

WOMAN   Dainty, madam.   130

ARCITE
Cousin, cousin! how do you, sir? Why, Palamon!

PALAMON   Never till now was I in prison, Arcite.

ARCITE   Why, what's the matter, man?

PALAMON [*Indicates Emilia.*]   Behold, and wonder!
By heaven, she is a goddess.

ARCITE [*Sees Emilia.*]   Ha!

PALAMON   Do reverence.
She is a goddess, Arcite.

EMILIA   Of all flowers   135
Methinks a rose is best.

WOMAN   Why, gentle madam?

EMILIA   It is the very emblem of a maid.
For, when the west wind courts her gently,

How modestly she blows and paints the sun
With her chaste blushes! When the north comes near
140   her,
Rude and impatient, then, like chastity,
She locks her beauties in her bud again
And leaves him to base briars.
WOMAN   Yet, good madam,
Sometimes her modesty will blow so far
145 She falls for't. A maid,
If she have any honour, would be loath
To take example by her.
EMILIA   Thou art wanton.
ARCITE   She is wondrous fair.
PALAMON   She is all the beauty extant.
EMILIA
The sun grows high; let's walk in. Keep these flowers.
150 We'll see how near art can come near their colours.
I am wondrous merry-hearted; I could laugh now.
WOMAN   I could lie down, I am sure.
EMILIA   And take one with you?
WOMAN   That's as we bargain, madam.
EMILIA   Well, agree then.
               Exeunt Emilia and Woman.
PALAMON   What think you of this beauty?
ARCITE   'Tis a rare one.
PALAMON   Is't but a rare one?
155 ARCITE   Yes, a matchless beauty.
PALAMON
Might not a man well lose himself and love her?
ARCITE   I cannot tell what you have done; I have,
Beshrew mine eyes for't; now I feel my shackles.
PALAMON   You love her then?
ARCITE   Who would not?
PALAMON   And desire her?
ARCITE   Before my liberty.
160 PALAMON   I saw her first.
ARCITE   That's nothing.
PALAMON   But it shall be.
ARCITE   I saw her too.
PALAMON   Yes, but you must not love her.
ARCITE   I will not as you do, to worship her
As she is heavenly and a blessed goddess.
165 I love her as a woman, to enjoy her:
So both may love.
PALAMON   You shall not love at all.
ARCITE   Not love at all!
Who shall deny me?
PALAMON   I that first saw her, I that took possession
170 First with mine eye of all those beauties in her
Revealed to mankind! If thou lovest her,
Or entertain'st a hope to blast my wishes,
Thou art a traitor, Arcite, and a fellow
False as thy title to her. Friendship, blood,
175 And all the ties between us, I disclaim,
If thou once think upon her.
ARCITE   Yes, I love her
And, if the lives of all my name lay on it,

I must do so; I love her with my soul:
If that will lose ye, farewell, Palamon.
180 I say again,
I love her and in loving her maintain
I am as worthy and as free a lover,
And have as just a title to her beauty,
As any Palamon, or any living
That is a man's son.
185 PALAMON   Have I called thee friend?
ARCITE
Yes, and have found me so; why are you moved thus?
Let me deal coldly with you: am not I
Part of your blood, part of your soul? you have told me
That I was Palamon and you were Arcite.
PALAMON   Yes.
190 ARCITE   Am not I liable to those affections,
Those joys, griefs, angers, fears, my friend shall suffer?
PALAMON   Ye may be.
ARCITE   Why then would you deal so cunningly,
So strangely, so unlike a noble kinsman,
To love alone? Speak truly: do you think me
Unworthy of her sight?
195 PALAMON   No, but unjust
If thou pursue that sight.
ARCITE   Because another
First sees the enemy, shall I stand still
And let mine honour down, and never charge?
PALAMON   Yes, if he be but one.
ARCITE   But say that one
Had rather combat me?
200 PALAMON   Let that one say so,
And use thy freedom. Else, if thou pursuest her,
Be as that cursed man that hates his country,
A branded villain.
ARCITE   You are mad.
PALAMON   I must be,
Till thou art worthy, Arcite; it concerns me.
205 And, in this madness, if I hazard thee
And take thy life, I deal but truly.
ARCITE   Fie, sir!
You play the child extremely. I will love her;
I must, I ought, to do so, and I dare,
And all this justly.
PALAMON   O that now, that now,
210 Thy false self and thy friend had but this fortune:
To be one hour at liberty and grasp
Our good swords in our hands! I would quickly teach
   thee
What 'twere to filch affection from another;
Thou art baser in it than a cutpurse.
215 Put but thy head out of this window more
And, as I have a soul, I'll nail thy life to't.
ARCITE
Thou dar'st not, fool, thou canst not, thou art feeble.
Put my head out? I'll throw my body out
And leap the garden, when I see her next,
220 And pitch between her arms, to anger thee.

Enter Jailer.

PALAMON   No more; the keeper's coming. I shall live
        To knock thy brains out with my shackles.
ARCITE   Do!
JAILER   By your leave, gentlemen.
PALAMON   Now, honest keeper?
JAILER   Lord Arcite, you must presently to th' Duke;
        The cause I know not yet.
225   ARCITE   I am ready, keeper.
JAILER   Prince Palamon, I must awhile bereave you
        Of your fair cousin's company.
                        Exeunt Arcite and Jailer.
PALAMON   And me too,
        Even when you please, of life. – Why is he sent for?
        It may be he shall marry her; he's goodly
230   And like enough the Duke hath taken notice
        Both of his blood and body. But his falsehood –
        Why should a friend be treacherous? If that
        Get him a wife so noble and so fair,
        Let honest men ne'er love again. Once more
235   I would but see this fair one. Blessed garden
        And fruit and flowers more blessed that still
            blossom
        As her bright eyes shine on ye: would I were
        For all the fortune of my life hereafter
        Yon little tree, yon blooming apricock!
240   How I would spread and fling my wanton arms
        In at her window! I would bring her fruit
        Fit for the gods to feed on; youth and pleasure
        Still as she tasted should be doubled on her
        And, if she be not heavenly, I would make her
245   So near the gods in nature, they should fear her,

Enter Jailer.

        And then I am sure she would love me. – How now,
            keeper?
        Where's Arcite?
JAILER   Banished. Prince Pirithous
        Obtained his liberty, but never more
        Upon his oath and life must he set foot
        Upon this kingdom.
250   PALAMON   He's a blessed man.
        He shall see Thebes again and call to arms
        The bold young men that, when he bids 'em charge,
        Fall on like fire. Arcite shall have a fortune,
        If he dare make himself a worthy lover,
255   Yet in the field to strike a battle for her
        And, if he lose her then, he's a cold coward;
        How bravely may he bear himself to win her
        If he be noble Arcite – thousand ways!
        Were I at liberty, I would do things
260   Of such a virtuous greatness that this lady,
        This blushing virgin, should take manhood to her
        And seek to ravish me.
JAILER   My lord, for you
        I have this charge to –

PALAMON   To discharge my life.
JAILER
        No, but from this place to remove your lordship;
        The windows are too open.
PALAMON   Devils take 'em   265
        That are so envious to me! Prithee, kill me.
JAILER   And hang for't afterward!
PALAMON   By this good light,
        Had I a sword I would kill thee.
JAILER   Why, my lord?
PALAMON
        Thou bringst such pelting, scurvy news continually,
        Thou art not worthy life. I will not go.   270
JAILER   Indeed you must, my lord.
PALAMON   May I see the garden?
JAILER   No.
PALAMON   Then I am resolved; I will not go.
JAILER
        I must constrain you then and, for you are dangerous,
        I'll clap more irons on you.
PALAMON   Do, good keeper!
        I'll shake 'em so, ye shall not sleep;   275
        I'll make ye a new morris. – Must I go?
JAILER   There is no remedy.
PALAMON   Farewell, kind window.
        May rude winds never hurt thee! – O, my lady,
        If ever thou hast felt what sorrow was,
        Dream how I suffer! – Come, now bury me.   280
                        Exeunt Palamon and Jailer.

2.3   *Enter* ARCITE.

ARCITE   Banished the kingdom? 'Tis a benefit,
        A mercy I must thank 'em for; but banished
        The free enjoying of that face I die for –
        Oh, 'twas a studied punishment, a death
        Beyond imagination, such a vengeance   5
        That, were I old and wicked, all my sins
        Could never pluck upon me. Palamon,
        Thou hast the start now; thou shalt stay and see
        Her bright eyes break each morning 'gainst thy
            window
        And let in life into thee; thou shalt feed   10
        Upon the sweetness of a noble beauty
        That nature ne'er exceeded nor ne'er shall.
        Good gods, what happiness has Palamon!
        Twenty to one, he'll come to speak to her
        And, if she be as gentle as she's fair,   15
        I know she's his; he has a tongue will tame
        Tempests and make the wild rocks wanton.
        Come what can come,
        The worst is death; I will not leave the kingdom.
        I know mine own is but a heap of ruins   20
        And no redress there. If I go, he has her.
        I am resolved another shape shall make me
        Or end my fortunes. Either way I am happy:
        I'll see her and be near her, or no more.

Enter four Countrymen, *and one with a garland before them.* ARCITE *stands aside.*

25 1 COUNTRYMAN   My masters, I'll be there, that's certain.

2 COUNTRYMAN   And I'll be there.

3 COUNTRYMAN   And I.

4 COUNTRYMAN
Why then, have with ye, boys. 'Tis but a chiding.
Let the plough play today; I'll tickl't out
Of the jades' tails tomorrow.

30 1 COUNTRYMAN   I am sure
To have my wife as jealous as a turkey –
But that's all one: I'll go through; let her mumble.

2 COUNTRYMAN
Clap her aboard tomorrow night and stow her,
And all's made up again.

3 COUNTRYMAN   Ay, do but put

35 A fescue in her fist and you shall see her
Take a new lesson out and be a good wench.
Do we all hold against the Maying?

4 COUNTRYMAN   Hold?
What should ail us?

3 COUNTRYMAN   Arcas will be there.

2 COUNTRYMAN   And Sennois

40 And Rycas – and three better lads ne'er danced
Under green tree – and ye know what wenches, ha?
But will the dainty dominie, the schoolmaster,
Keep touch, do you think? For he does all, ye know.

3 COUNTRYMAN   He'll eat a hornbook ere he fail. Go to;

45 The matter's too far driven between him
And the tanner's daughter to let slip now;
And she must see the Duke and she must dance too.

4 COUNTRYMAN   Shall we be lusty?

2 COUNTRYMAN   All the boys in Athens
Blow wind i'th' breech on's. And here I'll be,

50 And there I'll be for our town and here again,
And there again – ha, boys, hey for the weavers!

1 COUNTRYMAN   This must be done i'th' woods.

4 COUNTRYMAN   O, pardon me.

2 COUNTRYMAN
By any means; our thing of learning says so –
Where he himself will edify the Duke
Most parlously in our behalfs. He's excellent i'th'

55 woods;
Bring him to th' plains, his learning makes no cry.

3 COUNTRYMAN
We'll see the sports, then every man to's tackle;
And, sweet companions, let's rehearse, by any means,
Before the ladies see us and do sweetly

60 And God knows what may come on't.

4 COUNTRYMAN
Content; the sports once ended, we'll perform.
Away, boys – and hold.   [*Arcite comes forward.*]

ARCITE   By your leaves, honest friends:
Pray you, whither go you?

4 COUNTRYMAN   Whither?
Why, what a question's that?

ARCITE   Yes, 'tis a question,
To me that know not.

3 COUNTRYMAN   To the games, my friend.   65

2 COUNTRYMAN
Where were you bred, you know it not?

ARCITE   Not far, sir;
Are there such games today?

1 COUNTRYMAN   Yes, marry, are there
And such as you never saw; the Duke himself
Will be in person there.

ARCITE   What pastimes are they?

2 COUNTRYMAN
Wrestling and running. – 'Tis a pretty fellow.   70

3 COUNTRYMAN   Thou wilt not go along?

ARCITE   Not yet, sir.

4 COUNTRYMAN   Well, sir,
Take your own time. Come, boys.

1 COUNTRYMAN [*aside to the others*]
                My mind misgives me,
This fellow has a vengeance trick o'th' hip;
Mark how his body's made for't.

2 COUNTRYMAN   I'll be hanged, though,
If he dare venture. Hang him, plum porridge!   75
He wrestle? He roast eggs! Come, let's be gone, lads.
                Exeunt Countrymen.

ARCITE   This is an offered opportunity
I durst not wish for. Well I could have wrestled –
The best men called it excellent – and run
Swifter than wind upon a field of corn,   80
Curling the wealthy ears, never flew. I'll venture
And in some poor disguise be there; who knows
Whether my brows may not be girt with garlands
And happiness prefer me to a place,
Where I may ever dwell in sight of her?   *Exit.*   85

2.4   *Enter Jailer's* Daughter *alone.*

DAUGHTER
Why should I love this gentleman? 'Tis odds
He never will affect me: I am base,
My father the mean keeper of his prison,
And he a prince. To marry him is hopeless;
To be his whore is witless. Out upon't,   5
What pushes are we wenches driven to
When fifteen once has found us! – First, I saw him;
I, seeing, thought he was a goodly man;
He has as much to please a woman in him,
If he please to bestow it so, as ever   10
These eyes yet looked on. Next, I pitied him –
And so would any young wench, o' my conscience,
That ever dreamed, or vowed her maidenhead
To a young handsome man. Then, I loved him,
Extremely loved him, infinitely loved him!   15
And yet he had a cousin fair as he too,
But in my heart was Palamon and there,
Lord, what a coil he keeps! To hear him
Sing in an evening, what a heaven it is!

20   And yet his songs are sad ones. Fairer spoken
       Was never gentleman. When I come in
       To bring him water in a morning, first
       He bows his noble body, then salutes me, thus:
       'Fair, gentle maid, good morrow; may thy goodness
25   Get thee a happy husband.' Once, he kissed me.
       I loved my lips the better ten days after:
       Would he would do so every day! He grieves much –
       And me as much to see his misery.
       What should I do to make him know I love him?
30   For I would fain enjoy him. Say I ventured
       To set him free? What says the law then?
       Thus much for law or kindred! I will do it!
       And this night, or tomorrow, he shall love me.   *Exit.*

2.5   *A short flourish of cornets and shouts within.*
      Enter THESEUS, HIPPOLYTA, PIRITHOUS, EMILIA;
       ARCITE, *disguised as a countryman, with a garland;*
         Attendants and Spectators.

THESEUS   You have done worthily; I have not seen,
       Since Hercules, a man of tougher sinews.
       Whate'er you are, you run the best and wrestle,
       That these times can allow.
ARCITE   I am proud to please you.
THESEUS   What country bred you?
5   ARCITE   This; but far off, Prince.
THESEUS   Are you a gentleman?
ARCITE   My father said so
       And to those gentle uses gave me life.
THESEUS   Are you his heir?
ARCITE   His youngest, sir.
THESEUS   Your father
       Sure is a happy sire then. What profess you?
10   ARCITE   A little of all noble qualities.
       I could have kept a hawk and well have hallowed
       To a deep cry of dogs. I dare not praise
       My feat in horsemanship, yet they that knew me
       Would say it was my best piece; last and greatest,
       I would be thought a soldier.
15   THESEUS   You are perfect.
PIRITHOUS [*to Emilia*]   Upon my soul, a proper man.
EMILIA   He is so.
PIRITHOUS [*to Hippolyta*]   How do you like him, lady?
HIPPOLYTA   I admire him.
       I have not seen so young a man so noble,
       If he say true, of his sort.
EMILIA   Believe,
20   His mother was a wondrous handsome woman;
       His face, methinks, goes that way.
HIPPOLYTA   But his body
       And fiery mind illustrate a brave father.
PIRITHOUS   Mark how his virtue, like a hidden sun,
       Breaks through his baser garments.
HIPPOLYTA   He's well got, sure.
THESEUS [*to Arcite*]   What made you seek this place, sir?
25   ARCITE   Noble Theseus,

To purchase name and do my ablest service
To such a well-found wonder as thy worth,
For only in thy court, of all the world,
Dwells fair-eyed Honour.
PIRITHOUS   All his words are worthy.
THESEUS [*to Arcite*]
       Sir, we are much indebted to your travel,   30
       Nor shall you lose your wish. Pirithous,
       Dispose of this fair gentleman.
PIRITHOUS   Thanks, Theseus.
       [*to Arcite*] Whate'er you are, you're mine, and I shall
         give you
       To a most noble service: to this lady,
         [*Leads him to Emilia.*]
       This bright young virgin; pray observe her goodness.   35
       You have honoured her fair birthday with your
         virtues
       And, as your due, you're hers; kiss her fair hand, sir.
ARCITE   Sir, you're a noble giver. – Dearest beauty,
       Thus let me seal my vowed faith.   [*Kisses her hand.*]
                    When your servant,
       Your most unworthy creature, but offends you,   40
       Command him die: he shall.
EMILIA   That were too cruel.
       If you deserve well, sir, I shall soon see't.
       You're mine and somewhat better than your rank I'll
         use you.
PIRITHOUS   I'll see you furnished and, because you say
       You are a horseman, I must needs entreat you   45
       This afternoon to ride, but 'tis a rough one.
ARCITE   I like him better, Prince; I shall not then
       Freeze in my saddle.
THESEUS [*to Hippolyta*]   Sweet, you must be ready;
       And you, Emelia, and [*to Pirithous*] you, friend,
         and all,
       Tomorrow by the sun, to do observance   50
       To flowery May, in Dian's wood.
       [*to Arcite*]   Wait well, sir,
       Upon your mistress. – Emily, I hope
       He shall not go afoot.
EMILIA   That were a shame, sir,
       While I have horses. [*to Arcite*] Take your choice and
         what
       You want at any time, let me but know it;   55
       If you serve faithfully, I dare assure you
       You'll find a loving mistress.
ARCITE   If I do not,
       Let me find that my father ever hated,
       Disgrace and blows.
THESEUS   Go lead the way; you have won it
       It shall be so: you shall receive all dues   60
       Fit for the honour you have won; 'twere wrong else.
       – Sister, beshrew my heart, you have a servant,
       That, if I were a woman, would be a master.
       But you are wise.
EMILIA   I hope, too wise for that, sir.
                            Flourish. Exeunt.

2.6   *Enter Jailer's* Daughter *alone.*

DAUGHTER   Let all the dukes and all the devils roar,
He is at liberty! I have ventured for him
And out I have brought him; to a little wood
A mile hence I have sent him, where a cedar
5 Higher than all the rest spreads like a plane
Fast by a brook, and there he shall keep close
Till I provide him files and food, for yet
His iron bracelets are not off. O, Love,
What a stout-hearted child thou art! My father
10 Durst better have endured cold iron than done it.
I love him beyond love and beyond reason,
Or wit, or safety; I have made him know it;
I care not, I am desperate. If the law
Find me and then condemn me for't, some wenches,
15 Some honest-hearted maids, will sing my dirge
And tell to memory my death was noble,
Dying almost a martyr. That way he takes,
I purpose, is my way too. Sure he cannot
Be so unmanly as to leave me here;
20 If he do, maids will not so easily
Trust men again. And yet he has not thanked me
For what I have done, no, not so much as kissed me,
And that methinks is not so well; nor scarcely
Could I persuade him to become a free man,
25 He made such scruples of the wrong he did
To me and my father. Yet I hope,
When he considers more, this love of mine
Will take more root within him. Let him do
What he will with me, so he use me kindly –
30 For use me so he shall, or I'll proclaim him,
And to his face, no man. I'll presently
Provide him necessaries and pack my clothes up
And where there is a path of ground I'll venture,
So he be with me; by him, like a shadow,
35 I'll ever dwell. Within this hour the hubbub
Will be all o'er the prison: I am then
Kissing the man they look for. Farewell, father!
Get many more such prisoners and such daughters
And shortly you may keep yourself. Now to him.
Exit.

3.1   *Cornets in sundry places. Noise and hallooing as
people a–Maying. Enter* ARCITE *alone.*

ARCITE   The Duke has lost Hippolyta; each took
A several laund. This is a solemn rite
They owe bloomed May and the Athenians pay it
To th' heart of ceremony. O, Queen Emilia,
5 Fresher than May, sweeter
Than her gold buttons on the boughs, or all
Th'enamelled knacks o'th' mead, or garden – yea,
We challenge too the bank of any nymph
That makes the stream seem flowers: thou, oh jewel
10 O'th' wood, o'th' world, hast likewise blest a pace
With thy sole presence. In thy rumination,
That I, poor man, might eftsoons come between

And chop on some cold thought! Thrice blessed chance
To drop on such a mistress, expectation
Most guiltless on't! Tell me, O Lady Fortune   15
(Next, after Emily, my sovereign), how far
I may be proud. She takes strong note of me,
Hath made me near her and, this beauteous morn,
The prim'st of all the year, presents me with
A brace of horses: two such steeds might well   20
Be by a pair of kings backed, in a field
That their crowns' titles tried. Alas, alas,
Poor cousin Palamon, poor prisoner, thou
So little dream'st upon my fortune, that
Thou thinkst thyself the happier thing, to be   25
So near Emilia; me thou deem'st at Thebes,
And therein wretched, although free. But if
Thou knew'st my mistress breathed on me, and that
I eared her language, lived in her eye; O, coz,
What passion would enclose thee!

Enter PALAMON *as out of a bush, with his shackles; he
bends his fist at Arcite.*

PALAMON   Traitor kinsman,   30
Thou shouldst perceive my passion, if these signs
Of prisonment were off me and this hand
But owner of a sword! By all oaths in one,
I and the justice of my love would make thee
A confessed traitor! O, thou most perfidious   35
That ever gently looked, the void'st of honour
That e'er bore gentle token, falsest cousin
That ever blood made kin: call'st thou her thine?
I'll prove it in my shackles, with these hands,
Void of appointment, that thou liest, and art   40
A very thief in love, a chaffy lord
Not worth the name of villain. Had I a sword
And these house-clogs away –
ARCITE   Dear cousin Palamon –
PALAMON   Cozener Arcite, give me language such
As thou hast showed me feat.
ARCITE   Not finding in   45
The circuit of my breast any gross stuff
To form me like your blazon holds me to
This gentleness of answer. 'Tis your passion
That thus mistakes, the which to you being enemy,
Cannot to me be kind: honour and honesty   50
I cherish and depend on, howsoe'er
You skip them in me, and with them, fair coz,
I'll maintain my proceedings. Pray be pleased
To show in generous terms your griefs, since that
Your question's with your equal, who professes   55
To clear his own way with the mind and sword
Of a true gentleman.
PALAMON   That thou durst, Arcite!
ARCITE   My coz, my coz, you have been well advertised
How much I dare; you've seen me use my sword
Against th'advice of fear. Sure, of another   60
You would not hear me doubted, but your silence
Should break out, though i'th' sanctuary.

PALAMON   Sir,
I have seen you move in such a place, which well
Might justify your manhood; you were called
A good knight and a bold. But the whole week's not
65   fair
If any day it rain: their valiant temper
Men lose when they incline to treachery
And then they fight like compelled bears, would fly
Were they not tied.

ARCITE   Cousin, you might as well
70 Speak this and act it in your glass as to
His ear which now disdains you.

PALAMON   Come up to me;
Quit me of those cold gyves; give me a sword,
Though it be rusty, and the charity
Of one meal lend me. Come before me then,
75   A good sword in thy hand, and do but say
That Emily is thine – I will forgive
The trespass thou hast done me, yea, my life,
If then thou carry't, and brave souls in shades
That have died manly, which will seek of me
80   Some news from earth, they shall get none but this:
That thou art brave and noble.

ARCITE   Be content.
Again betake you to your hawthorn house.
With counsel of the night, I will be here
With wholesome viands. These impediments
85   Will I file off; you shall have garments and
Perfumes to kill the smell o'th' prison. After,
When you shall stretch yourself and say but, 'Arcite,
I am in plight', there shall be at your choice
Both sword and armour.

PALAMON   O you heavens, dares any
90 So nobly bear a guilty business? None
But only Arcite; therefore none but Arcite
In this kind is so bold.

ARCITE   Sweet Palamon.   [*Offers to embrace him.*]

PALAMON
I do embrace you and your offer; for
Your offer do't I only, sir; your person
95   Without hypocrisy I may not wish
More than my sword's edge on't.

ARCITE   You hear the horns;   [*Horns*]
Enter your musit, lest this match between's
Be crossed ere met. Give me your hand; farewell.
I'll bring you every needful thing. I pray you
Take comfort and be strong.

100 PALAMON   Pray hold your promise
And do the deed with a bent brow. Most certain
You love me not; be rough with me and pour
This oil out of your language. By this air,
I could for each word give a cuff, my stomach
Not reconciled by reason.

105 ARCITE   Plainly spoken.
Yet pardon me hard language. When I spur
My horse I chide him not; content and anger
In me have but one face.   [*Horns again*]

Hark, sir, they call
The scattered to the banquet. You must guess
I have an office there.

PALAMON   Sir, your attendance   110
Cannot please heaven and I know your office
Unjustly is achieved.

ARCITE   'Tis a good title.
I am persuaded, this question, sick between 's,
By bleeding must be cured. I am a suitor
That to your sword you will bequeath this plea   115
And talk of it no more.

PALAMON   But this one word:
You are going now to gaze upon my mistress –
For, note you, mine she is –

ARCITE   Nay, then –

PALAMON   Nay, pray you!
You talk of feeding me to breed me strength.
You are going now to look upon a sun   120
That strengthens what it looks on; there
You have a vantage on me. But enjoy't till
I may enforce my remedy. Farewell.   *Exeunt.*

3.2   *Enter Jailer's* Daughter *alone.*

DAUGHTER
He has mistook the brake I meant, is gone
After his fancy. 'Tis now well-nigh morning.
No matter: would it were perpetual night,
And darkness lord o'th' world! – Hark, 'tis a wolf!
In me hath grief slain fear and but for one thing   5
I care for nothing and that's Palamon.
I reck not if the wolves would jaw me, so
He had this file. What if I hallooed for him?
I cannot hallow. If I whooped – what then?
If he not answered, I should call a wolf,   10
And do him but that service. I have heard
Strange howls this livelong night; why may't not be
They have made prey of him? He has no weapons;
He cannot run: the jangling of his gyves
Might call fell things to listen, who have in them   15
A sense to know a man unarmed and can
Smell where resistance is. I'll set it down,
He's torn to pieces; they howled many together
And then they fed on him. So much for that:
Be bold to ring the bell. How stand I then?   20
All's chared when he is gone – no, no, I lie.
My father's to be hanged for his escape,
Myself to beg, if I prized life so much
As to deny my act – but that I would not,
Should I try death by dozens. I am moped.   25
Food took I none these two days;
Sipped some water. I have not closed mine eyes,
Save when my lids scoured off their brine. Alas,
Dissolve, my life! Let not my sense unsettle,
Lest I should drown, or stab, or hang myself.   30
Oh, state of nature, fail together in me,
Since thy best props are warped! – So, which way now?

The best way is the next way to a grave:
Each errant step beside is torment. Lo,
35 The moon is down, the crickets chirp, the screech-owl
Calls in the dawn; all offices are done
Save what I fail in. But the point is this:
An end, and that is all. *Exit.*

3.3 *Enter* ARCITE *with meat, wine and files.*

ARCITE
I should be near the place. Ho! Cousin Palamon?

PALAMON [*from the bush*]
Arcite?

ARCITE The same. I have brought you food and files.
Come forth and fear not; here's no Theseus.

Enter PALAMON.

PALAMON Nor none so honest, Arcite.

ARCITE That's no matter.
5 We'll argue that hereafter. Come, take courage!
You shall not die thus beastly; here, sir, drink –
I know you are faint – then I'll talk further with you.

PALAMON Arcite, thou mightst now poison me.

ARCITE I might,
But I must fear you first. Sit down and, good now,
10 No more of these vain parleys; let us not,
Having our ancient reputation with us,
Make talk for fools and cowards. To your health –
[*Drinks.*]

PALAMON Do!

ARCITE Pray sit down then, and let me entreat you,
By all the honesty and honour in you,
15 No mention of this woman; 'twill disturb us.
We shall have time enough.

PALAMON Well, sir, I'll pledge you. [*Drinks.*]

ARCITE Drink a good hearty draught: it breeds good
blood, man.
Do not you feel it thaw you?

PALAMON Stay, I'll tell you
After a draught or two more.

ARCITE Spare it not;
The Duke has more, coz. Eat now.

PALAMON Yes.

20 ARCITE I am glad
You have so good a stomach.

PALAMON I am gladder
I have so good meat to't.

ARCITE Is't not mad lodging,
Here in the wild woods, cousin?

PALAMON Yes, for them
That have wild consciences.

ARCITE How tastes your victuals?
Your hunger needs no sauce, I see.

25 PALAMON Not much.
But if it did, yours is too tart, sweet cousin.
What is this?

ARCITE Venison.

PALAMON 'Tis a lusty meat.
Give me more wine. – Here, Arcite, to the wenches
We have known in our days. The Lord Steward's
daughter –
Do you remember her?

ARCITE After you, coz. 30

PALAMON She loved a black-haired man –

ARCITE She did so; well, sir?

PALAMON And I have heard some call him Arcite, and –

ARCITE Out with't, faith.

PALAMON She met him in an arbour.
What did she there, coz? play o'th' virginals?

ARCITE Something she did, sir –

PALAMON Made her groan a month for't. 35
Or two, or three, or ten.

ARCITE The Marshall's sister
Had her share too, as I remember, cousin;
Else there be tales abroad. You'll pledge her?

PALAMON Yes.

ARCITE A pretty brown wench 'tis. There was a time
When young men went a-hunting, and a wood, 40
And a broad beech; and thereby hangs a tale –
Hey ho.

PALAMON For Emily, upon my life! Fool,
Away with this strained mirth! I say again,
That sigh was breathed for Emily; base cousin,
Dar'st thou break first?

ARCITE You are wide.

PALAMON By heaven and earth, 45
There's nothing in thee honest.

ARCITE Then I'll leave you;
You are a beast now.

PALAMON As thou mak'st me, traitor.

ARCITE
There's all things needful – files and shirts, and
perfumes;
I'll come again some two hours hence, and bring
That that shall quiet all –

PALAMON A sword and armour. 50

ARCITE Fear me not. You are now too foul; farewell.
Get off your trinkets. You shall want nought.

PALAMON Sirrah –

ARCITE I'll hear no more. *Exit.*

PALAMON If he keep touch, he dies for't. *Exit.*

3.4 *Enter Jailer's Daughter.*

DAUGHTER I am very cold and all the stars are out too,
The little stars and all, that look like aglets;
The sun has seen my folly. – Palamon! –
Alas, no, he's in heaven; where am I now?
Yonder's the sea and there's a ship; how't tumbles! 5
And there's a rock lies watching under water;
Now, now, it beats upon it; now, now, now!
There's a leak sprung, a sound one! How they cry!
Run her before the wind, you'll lose all else.
Up with a course or two and tack about, boys! 10

Good night, good night, you're gone. – I am very
    hungry.
Would I could find a fine frog; he would tell me
News from all parts o'th' world. Then would I make
A carrack of a cockle shell and sail
15   By east and north-east to the king of pygmies,
For he tells fortunes rarely. Now, my father
Twenty to one is trussed up in a trice
Tomorrow morning; I'll say never a word.
[*Sings.*]
    For I'll cut my green coat, a foot above my knee
20   And I'll clip my yellow locks, an inch below mine eye.
        Hey, nonny, nonny, nonny,
    He's buy me a white cut, forth for to ride,
    And I'll go seek him through the world that is so
        wide,
        Hey, nonny, nonny, nonny.
25   O, for a prick now, like a nightingale,
To put my breast against. I shall sleep like a top else.
                              Exit.

3.5   *Enter* SCHOOLMASTER Gerald *and five*
               Countrymen.

SCHOOLMASTER   Fie, fie,
    What tediosity and disinsanity
    Is here among ye! Have my rudiments
    Been laboured so long with ye, milked unto ye
5   And, by a figure, even the very plum-broth
    And marrow of my understanding laid upon ye,
    And do ye still cry 'Where?' and 'How?' and
        'Wherefore?'
    You most coarse-frieze capacities, ye jean judgements,
    Have I said, 'Thus let be' and 'There let be'
10   And 'Then let be', and no man understand me?
    Proh Deum! Medius Fidius! Ye are all dunces.
    For why?
    Here stand I. Here the Duke comes; there are you,
    Close in the thicket; the Duke appears; I meet him
15   And unto him I utter learned things
    And many figures; he hears and nods and hums
    And then cries, 'Rare!' and I go forward. At length,
    I fling my cap up – mark there! Then do you,
    As once did Meleager and the boar,
20   Break comely out before him; like true lovers,
    Cast yourselves in a body decently
    And sweetly, by a figure, trace and turn, boys.
1 COUNTRYMAN
    And sweetly we will do it, Master Gerald.
2 COUNTRYMAN
    Draw up the company. Where's the taborer?
3 COUNTRYMAN   Why, Timothy!

             Enter TABORER.

25   TABORER   Here, my mad boys, have at ye!
SCHOOLMASTER   But, I say, where's these women?
4 COUNTRYMAN   Here's Friz and Maudlin.

        Enter five Countrywomen.

2 COUNTRYMAN
    And little Luce with the white legs and bouncing
    Barbary.
1 COUNTRYMAN
    And freckled Nell that never failed her master.
SCHOOLMASTER
    Where be your ribbons, maids? Swim with your bodies
    And carry it sweetly and deliverly   30
    And now and then a favour and a frisk.
NELL   Let us alone, sir.
SCHOOLMASTER   Where's the rest o'th' music?
3 COUNTRYMAN   Dispersed, as you commanded.
SCHOOLMASTER   Couple then
    And see what's wanting; where's the Bavian?
    – My friend, carry your tail without offence   35
    Or scandal to the ladies and be sure
    You tumble with audacity and manhood
    And, when you bark, do it with judgement.
BAVIAN   Yes, sir.
SCHOOLMASTER
    Quo usque tandem! Here's a woman wanting.
4 COUNTRYMAN
    We may go whistle; all the fat's i'th' fire.   40
SCHOOLMASTER
    We have, as learned authors utter, washed a tile.
    We have been *fatuus* and laboured vainly.
2 COUNTRYMAN
    This is that scornful piece, that scurvy hilding
    That gave her promise faithfully, she would be here –
    Cicely, the sempster's daughter.   45
    The next gloves that I give her shall be dogskin!
    Nay, an she fail me once – you can tell, Arcas,
    She swore by wine and bread, she would not break.
SCHOOLMASTER   An eel and woman,
    A learned poet says, unless by th' tail   50
    And with thy teeth thou hold, will either fail.
    In manners this was false position.
1 COUNTRYMAN   A fire ill take her; does she flinch now?
3 COUNTRYMAN   What
    Shall we determine, sir?
SCHOOLMASTER   Nothing.
    Our business is become a nullity,   55
    Yea, and a woeful and a piteous nullity.
4 COUNTRYMAN
    Now, when the credit of our town lay on it,
    Now to be frampul, now to piss o'th' nettle!
    Go thy ways, I'll remember thee, I'll fit thee.

        Enter the Jailer's Daughter.

DAUGHTER [*Sings.*]
    The George Alow came from the south   60
    From the coast of Barbary-a
    And there he met with brave gallants of war,
    By one, by two, by three-a.

    'Well hailed, well hailed, you jolly gallants,
    And whither now are you bound-a?   65
    O let me have your company

Till we come to the sound-a.'

There was three fools fell out about an howlet:
    The one he said it was an owl,
70   The other he said nay,
    The third he said it was a hawk,
    And her bells were cut away.

3 COUNTRYMAN
    There's a dainty madwoman, Master,
    Comes i'th' nick, as mad as a March hare.
75 If we can get her dance, we are made again;
    I warrant her, she'll do the rarest gambols.
1 COUNTRYMAN   A madwoman? We are made, boys.
SCHOOLMASTER   And are you mad, good woman?
DAUGHTER   I would be sorry else.
    Give me your hand.
SCHOOLMASTER   Why?
DAUGHTER   I can tell your fortune.
80 You are a fool. Tell ten. – I have posed him. Buzz!
    – Friend, you must eat no white bread; if you do,
    Your teeth will bleed extremely. – Shall we dance, ho?
    – I know you, you're a tinker; sirrah tinker,
    Stop no more holes but what you should.
SCHOOLMASTER   *Dii boni,*
    A tinker, damsel?
85 DAUGHTER   Or a conjurer.
    Raise me a devil now and let him play
    Chi passa o'th' bells and bones.
SCHOOLMASTER   Go take her
    And fluently persuade her to a peace.
    Et opus exegi quod nec Jovis ira, nec ignis –
    Strike up and lead her in.   [*Taborer plays.*]
90 2 COUNTRYMAN   Come, lass, let's trip it.
DAUGHTER   I'll lead. [*Dances.*]
3 COUNTRYMAN   Do, do!   [*Horns*]
SCHOOLMASTER   Persuasively and cunningly.
    Away, boys; I hear the horns. Give me some meditation –
    And mark your cue.   *Exeunt all but Schoolmaster.*
          Pallas inspire me!

    Enter THESEUS, PIRITHOUS, HIPPOLYTA,
        EMILIA *and train.*

THESEUS   This way the stag took.
SCHOOLMASTER   Stay and edify!
95 THESEUS   What have we here?
PIRITHOUS   Some country sport, upon my life, sir.
THESEUS [*to Schoolmaster*]
    Well, sir, go forward; we will 'edify'.
    [*Chair and stools brought out.*]
    Ladies, sit down; we'll stay it.
    [*Theseus, Hippolyta and Emilia sit.*]
SCHOOLMASTER
    Then, doughty Duke, all hail; all hail, sweet ladies –
100 THESEUS This is a cold beginning.
SCHOOLMASTER
    If you but favour, our country pastime made is.
    We are a few of those collected here

That ruder tongues distinguish 'villager'.
And to say verity, and not to fable,
We are a merry rout, or else a *rable,*   105
Or company, or, by a figure, *chorus,*
That 'fore thy dignity will dance a morris.
And I that am the rectifier of all,
By title *pedagogus,* that let fall
The birch upon the breeches of the small ones 110
And humble with a ferula the tall ones,
Do here present this machine, or this frame,
And, dainty Duke, whose doughty dismal fame
From Dis to Daedalus, from post to pillar,
Is blown abroad, help me, thy poor well-willer, 115
And with thy twinkling eyes look right and straight
Upon this mighty 'Moor' of mickle weight.
'Is' now comes in, which, being glued together,
Makes 'Morris' and the cause that we came hither:
The body of our sport, of no small study.   120
I first appear, though rude and raw and muddy,
To speak before thy noble grace this tenor:
At whose great feet I offer up my penner.
The next the Lord of May and Lady bright;
The Chambermaid and Servingman, by night 125
That seek out silent hanging; then mine Host
And his fat Spouse that welcomes to their cost
The galled traveller and with a beck'ning
Informs the tapster to inflame the reck'ning.
Then the beest-eating Clown and next the Fool, 130
The Bavian with long tail and eke long tool,
Cum multis aliis that make a dance.
Say, 'Ay,' and all shall presently advance.
THESEUS   Ay, ay, by any means, dear *Domine.*
PIRITHOUS   Produce.   135
SCHOOLMASTER   *Intrate filii!* Come forth and foot it.
    [*Music. The villagers, with the Jailer's Daughter,*
    perform a morris dance.]
SCHOOLMASTER   Ladies, if we have been merry
    And have pleased ye with a derry,
    And a derry, and a down,
    Say the schoolmaster's no clown;   140
    Duke, if we have pleased thee too
    And have done as good boys should do,
    Give us but a tree or twain
    For a Maypole and again,
    Ere another year run out,   145
    We'll make thee laugh and all this rout.
THESEUS
    Take twenty, *Domine.* – How does my sweetheart?
HIPPOLYTA   Never so pleased, sir.
EMILIA   'Twas an excellent dance
    And, for a preface, I never heard a better.
THESEUS
    Schoolmaster, I thank you. One see 'em all rewarded. 150
PIRITHOUS
    And here's something to paint your pole withall.
    [*Gives Schoolmaster money.*]
THESEUS   Now to our sports again.

SCHOOLMASTER

    May the stag thou hunt'st stand long,

    And thy dogs be swift and strong;

155   May they kill him without lets

    And the ladies eat his dowsets.

                Theseus and his party depart. Horns.

Come, we are all made, *dii deaeque omnes.* Ye have

danced rarely, wenches.   *Exeunt.*

3.6   *Enter* PALAMON *from the bush.*

PALAMON   About this hour my cousin gave his faith

    To visit me again and with him bring

    Two swords and two good armours. If he fail

    He's neither man nor soldier. When he left me

5   I did not think a week could have restored

    My lost strength to me, I was grown so low

    And crest-fall'n with my wants. I thank thee, Arcite:

    Thou art yet a fair foe; and I feel myself,

    With this refreshing, able once again

10   To outdure danger. To delay it longer

    Would make the world think, when it comes to hearing,

    That I lay fatting like a swine to fight

    And not a soldier. Therefore this blest morning

    Shall be the last and that sword he refuses,

15   If it but hold, I kill him with: 'tis justice.

    So love and fortune for me!

        Enter ARCITE *with armours and swords.*

               O, good morrow.

ARCITE   Good morrow, noble kinsman.

PALAMON   I have put you

    To too much pains, sir.

ARCITE   That too much, fair cousin,

    Is but a debt to honour, and my duty.

PALAMON

20   Would you were so in all, sir; I could wish ye

    As kind a kinsman as you force me find

    A beneficial foe, that my embraces

    Might thank ye, not my blows.

ARCITE   I shall think either,

    Well done, a noble recompense.

PALAMON   Then I shall quit you.

25 ARCITE   Defy me in these fair terms, and you show

    More than a mistress to me. No more anger,

    As you love anything that's honourable!

    We were not bred to talk, man; when we are armed

    And both upon our guards, then let our fury,

30   Like meeting of two tides, fly strongly from us;

    And then to whom the birthright of this beauty

    Truly pertains (without upbraidings, scorns,

    Despisings of our persons, and such poutings

    Fitter for girls and schoolboys) will be seen

35   And quickly, yours or mine. Will't please you arm, sir?

    Or, if you feel yourself not fitting yet

    And furnished with your old strength, I'll stay, cousin,

    And every day discourse you into health,

    As I am spared. Your person I am friends with

    And I could wish I had not said I loved her,   40

    Though I had died; but, loving such a lady

    And justifying my love, I must not fly from't.

PALAMON   Arcite, thou art so brave an enemy

    That no man but thy cousin's fit to kill thee.

    I am well and lusty; choose your arms.

ARCITE   Choose you, sir.   45

PALAMON   Wilt thou exceed in all, or dost thou do it

    To make me spare thee?

ARCITE   If you think so, cousin,

    You are deceived, for, as I am a soldier,

    I will not spare you.

PALAMON   That's well said.

ARCITE   You'll find it.

PALAMON   Then, as I am an honest man and love,   50

    With all the justice of affection

    I'll pay thee soundly.   [*Chooses armour.*]

            This I'll take.

ARCITE [*Takes the other.*]   That's mine then.

    I'll arm you first.

PALAMON   Do.   [*Arcite begins to arm him.*]

              Pray thee tell me, cousin,

    Where got'st thou this good armour?

ARCITE   'Tis the Duke's

    And, to say true, I stole it. Do I pinch you?

PALAMON   No.   55

ARCITE   Is't not too heavy?

PALAMON   I have worn a lighter,

    But I shall make it serve.

ARCITE   I'll buckl't close.

PALAMON   By any means.

ARCITE   You care not for a grand guard?

PALAMON   No, no, we'll use no horses; I perceive

    You would fain be at that fight.

ARCITE   I am indifferent.   60

PALAMON

    Faith, so am I. Good cousin, thrust the buckle

    Through far enough.

ARCITE   I warrant you.

PALAMON   My casque now.

ARCITE   Will you fight bare-armed?

PALAMON   We shall be the nimbler.

ARCITE

    But use your gauntlets, though. Those are o'th' least;

    Prithee take mine, good cousin.

PALAMON   Thank you, Arcite.   65

    How do I look? Am I fall'n much away?

ARCITE   Faith, very little; love has used you kindly.

PALAMON   I'll warrant thee, I'll strike home.

ARCITE   Do and spare not.

    I'll give you cause, sweet cousin.

PALAMON   Now to you, sir.   [*Begins to arm Arcite.*]

    Methinks this armour's very like that, Arcite,   70

    Thou wor'st that day the three kings fell, but lighter.

ARCITE   That was a very good one. And that day,

    I well remember, you outdid me, cousin;

I never saw such valour. When you charged
Upon the left wing of the enemy,
I spurred hard to come up and under me
I had a right good horse.

PALAMON   You had indeed:
A bright bay, I remember.

ARCITE   Yes, but all
Was vainly laboured in me; you outwent me,
Nor could my wishes reach you. Yet a little
I did by imitation.

PALAMON   More by virtue.
You are modest, cousin.

ARCITE   When I saw you charge first,
Methought I heard a dreadful clap of thunder
Break from the troop.

PALAMON   But still before that flew
The lightning of your valour. – Stay a little:
Is not this piece too strait?

ARCITE   No, no, 'tis well.

PALAMON
I would have nothing hurt thee but my sword:
A bruise would be dishonour.

ARCITE   Now I am perfect.

PALAMON   Stand off then.

ARCITE   Take my sword; I hold it better.

PALAMON   I thank ye, no; keep it, your life lies on it.
Here's one: if it but hold, I ask no more
For all my hopes. My cause and honour guard me!

ARCITE   And me my love!
        [*They bow several ways, then advance and stand.*]
                    Is there aught else to say?

PALAMON
This only, and no more. Thou art mine aunt's son
And that blood we desire to shed is mutual,
In me thine and in thee mine; my sword
Is in my hand and if thou killest me
The gods and I forgive thee. If there be
A place prepared for those that sleep in honour,
I wish his weary soul that falls may win it.
Fight bravely, cousin; give me thy noble hand.

ARCITE   Here, Palamon. This hand shall never more
Come near thee with such friendship.

PALAMON   I commend thee.

ARCITE   If I fall, curse me, and say I was a coward,
For none but such dare die in these just trials.
Once more farewell, my cousin.

PALAMON   Farewell, Arcite.
        [*They fight. Horns within. They stand.*]

ARCITE   Lo, cousin, lo, our folly has undone us!

PALAMON   Why?

ARCITE   This is the Duke, a-hunting as I told you;
If we be found, we are wretched. O, retire,
For honour's sake and safety, presently
Into your bush again. Sir, we shall find
Too many hours to die in! Gentle cousin,
If you be seen you perish instantly
For breaking prison and I, if you reveal me,

For my contempt. Then all the world will scorn us
And say we had a noble difference,
But base disposers of it.

PALAMON   No, no, cousin:
I will no more be hidden, nor put off
This great adventure to a second trial;
I know your cunning and I know your cause.
He that faints now, shame take him! Put thyself
Upon thy present guard –

ARCITE   You are not mad?

PALAMON   Or I will make the advantage of this hour
Mine own, and what to come shall threaten me
I fear less than my fortune. Know, weak cousin,
I love Emilia and in that I'll bury
Thee and all crosses else.

ARCITE   Then come what can come.
Thou shalt know, Palamon, I dare as well
Die as discourse or sleep. Only this fears me:
The law will have the honour of our ends.
Have at thy life!

PALAMON   Look to thine own well, Arcite.
        [*They fight again.*]

        Horns. Enter THESEUS, HIPPOLYTA, EMILIA,
                PIRITHOUS *and train.*

THESEUS   What ignorant and mad malicious traitors
Are you, that 'gainst the tenor of my laws
Are making battle, thus like knights appointed,
Without my leave and officers of arms?
By Castor, both shall die!

PALAMON   Hold thy word, Theseus.
We are certainly both traitors, both despisers
Of thee and of thy goodness. I am Palamon
That cannot love thee, he that broke thy prison –
Think well what that deserves – and this is Arcite:
A bolder traitor never trod thy ground;
A falser ne'er seemed friend. This is the man
Was begged and banished; this is he contemns thee
And what thou dar'st do and in this disguise
Against thine own edict follows thy sister,
That fortunate bright star, the fair Emilia –
Whose servant, if there be a right in seeing
And first bequeathing of the soul to, justly
I am – and, which is more, dares think her his.
This treachery, like a most trusty lover,
I called him now to answer. If thou be'st
As thou art spoken, great and virtuous,
The true decider of all injuries,
Say, 'Fight again' and thou shalt see me, Theseus,
Do such a justice thou thyself wilt envy.
Then take my life; I'll woo thee to't.

PIRITHOUS   O heaven,
What more than man is this!

THESEUS   I have sworn.

ARCITE   We seek not
Thy breath of mercy, Theseus; 'tis to me
A thing as soon to die as thee to say it

160 And no more moved. Where this man calls me traitor,
Let me say thus much: if in love be treason,
In service of so excellent a beauty,
As I love most, and in that faith will perish,
As I have brought my life here to confirm it,
165 As I have served her truest, worthiest,
As I dare kill this cousin that denies it,
So let me be most traitor and ye please me.
For scorning thy edict, Duke: ask that lady
Why she is fair, and why her eyes command me
170 Stay here to love her and, if she say 'traitor',
I am a villain fit to lie unburied.

PALAMON   Thou shalt have pity of us both, O Theseus,
If unto neither thou show mercy. Stop,
As thou art just, thy noble ear against us;
175 As thou art valiant – for thy cousin's soul,
Whose twelve strong labours crown his memory –
Let's die together, at one instant, Duke.
Only a little let him fall before me,
That I may tell my soul, he shall not have her.

THESEUS
180 I grant your wish, for, to say true, your cousin
Has ten times more offended, for I gave him
More mercy than you found, sir, your offences
Being no more than his. None here speak for 'em,
For, ere the sun set, both shall sleep for ever.

185 HIPPOLYTA   Alas the pity! Now or never, sister,
Speak not to be denied. That face of yours
Will bear the curses else of after ages
For these lost cousins.

EMILIA   In my face, dear sister,
I find no anger to 'em, nor no ruin.
190 The misadventure of their own eyes kill 'em.
Yet that I will be woman and have pity,
My knees shall grow to th' ground but I'll get mercy.
Help me, dear sister; in a deed so virtuous,
The powers of all women will be with us.   [*Kneels.*]
Most royal brother –

195 HIPPOLYTA [*Kneels.*] Sir, by our tie of marriage –

EMILIA   By your own spotless honour –

HIPPOLYTA   By that faith,
That fair hand and that honest heart you gave me –

EMILIA   By that you would have pity in another,
By your own virtues infinite –

HIPPOLYTA   By valour,
200 By all the chaste nights I have ever pleased you –

THESEUS   These are strange conjurings.

PIRITHOUS   Nay, then, I'll in too.   [*Kneels.*]
By all our friendship, sir, by all our dangers,
By all you love most: wars, and this sweet lady –

EMILIA   By that you would have trembled to deny
A blushing maid –
205 HIPPOLYTA   By your own eyes, by strength,
In which you swore I went beyond all women,
Almost all men, and yet I yielded, Theseus –

PIRITHOUS   To crown all this, by your most noble soul,
Which cannot want due mercy, I beg first –

HIPPOLYTA   Next hear my prayers –

EMILIA   Last, let me entreat, sir –   210

PIRITHOUS   For mercy!

HIPPOLYTA   Mercy!

EMILIA   Mercy on these princes!

THESEUS   Ye make my faith reel. Say I felt
Compassion to 'em both, how would you place it?
[*Emilia, Hippolyta and Pirithous rise.*]

EMILIA   Upon their lives. But with their banishments.

THESEUS   You are a right woman, sister: you have pity   215
But want the understanding where to use it.
If you desire their lives, invent a way
Safer than banishment. Can these two live
And have the agony of love about 'em
And not kill one another? Every day   220
They'd fight about you; hourly bring your honour
In public question with their swords. Be wise then
And here forget 'em; it concerns your credit
And my oath equally. I have said they die.
Better they fall by th' law than one another.   225
Bow not my honour.

EMILIA   O, my noble brother,
That oath was rashly made and in your anger.
Your reason will not hold it; if such vows
Stand for express will, all the world must perish.
Besides, I have another oath 'gainst yours,   230
Of more authority, I am sure more love,
Not made in passion neither but good heed.

THESEUS   What is it, sister?

PIRITHOUS   Urge it home, brave lady.

EMILIA   That you would ne'er deny me anything
Fit for my modest suit and your free granting.   235
I tie you to your word now; if ye fail in't,
Think how you maim your honour. Tell me not
(For now I am set a-begging, sir, I am deaf
To all but your compassion) how their lives
Might breed the ruin of my name. Opinion!   240
Shall anything that loves me perish for me?
That were a cruel wisdom. Do men prune
The straight young boughs that blush with thousand
    blossoms,
Because they may be rotten? O, Duke Theseus,
The goodly mothers that have groaned for these   245
And all the longing maids that ever loved,
If your vow stand, shall curse me and my beauty
And in their funeral songs for these two cousins
Despise my cruelty and cry woe worth me,
Till I am nothing but the scorn of women.   250
For heaven's sake, save their lives and banish 'em.

THESEUS   On what conditions?

EMILIA   Swear 'em never more
To make me their contention, or to know me,
To tread upon thy dukedom, and to be,
Wherever they shall travel, ever strangers   255
To one another.

PALAMON   I'll be cut a-pieces
Before I take this oath! Forget I love her?

O, all ye gods, despise me then! Thy banishment
I not mislike, so we may fairly carry
260   Our swords and cause along; else, never trifle,
But take our lives, Duke; I must love and will
And, for that love, must and dare kill this cousin
On any piece the earth has.

THESEUS   Will you, Arcite,
Take these conditions?

PALAMON   He's a villain then.

265 PIRITHOUS   These are men!

ARCITE
No, never, Duke. 'Tis worse to me than begging
To take my life so basely. Though I think
I never shall enjoy her, yet I'll preserve
The honour of affection and die for her,
270   Make death a devil.

THESEUS
What may be done? For now I feel compassion.

PIRITHOUS   Let it not fall again, sir.

THESEUS   Say, Emilia,
If one of them were dead, as one must, are you
Content to take the other as your husband?
275   They cannot both enjoy you. They are princes
As goodly as your own eyes and as noble
As ever fame yet spoke of. Look upon 'em
And, if you can love, end this difference;
I give consent. Are you content too, princes?

PALAMON, ARCITE   With all our hearts.

280 THESEUS   He that she refuses
Must die then.

PALAMON, ARCITE
        Any death thou canst invent, Duke.

PALAMON   If I fall from that mouth, I fall with favour
And lovers yet unborn shall bless my ashes.

ARCITE   If she refuse me, yet my grave will wed me
And soldiers sing my epitaph.

285 THESEUS [*to Emilia*]   Make choice, then.

EMILIA   I cannot, sir; they are both too excellent;
For me, a hair shall never fall of these men.

HIPPOLYTA   What will become of 'em?

THESEUS   Thus I ordain it
And by mine honour, once again, it stands,
290   Or both shall die. You shall both to your country
And each, within this month, accompanied
With three fair knights, appear again in this place,
In which I'll plant a pyramid; and whether,
Before us that are here, can force his cousin,
295   By fair and knightly strength, to touch the pillar,
He shall enjoy her; th'other lose his head,
And all his friends. Nor shall he grudge to fall,
Nor think he dies with interest in this lady.
Will this content ye?

PALAMON   Yes. There, cousin Arcite,
     [*Offers his hand.*]
I am friends again, till that hour.

300 ARCITE   I embrace ye.

THESEUS   Are you content, sister?

EMILIA   Yes, I must, sir,
Else both miscarry.

THESEUS   Come, shake hands again, then,
And take heed, as you are gentlemen, this quarrel
Sleep till the hour prefixed, and hold your course.
     [*Palamon and Arcite shake hands.*]

PALAMON   We dare not fail thee, Theseus.

THESEUS   Come, I'll give ye   305
Now usage like to princes and to friends.
When ye return, who wins, I'll settle here;
Who loses, yet I'll weep upon his bier.   *Exeunt.*

4.1   *Enter* Jailer *and* First Friend.

JAILER   Heard you no more? Was nothing said of me
Concerning the escape of Palamon?
Good sir, remember!

1 FRIEND   Nothing that I heard,
For I came home before the business
Was fully ended. Yet I might perceive,   5
Ere I departed, a great likelihood
Of both their pardons. For Hippolyta
And fair-eyed Emily, upon their knees,
Begged with such handsome pity that the Duke
Methought stood staggering whether he should follow   10
His rash oath or the sweet compassion
Of those two ladies; and, to second them,
That truly noble Prince Pirithous,
Half his own heart, set in too, that I hope
All shall be well. Neither heard I one question   15
Of your name or his 'scape.

             Enter Second Friend.

JAILER   Pray heaven it hold so.

2 FRIEND   Be of good comfort, man; I bring you news,
Good news!

JAILER   They are welcome.

2 FRIEND   Palamon has cleared you,
And got your pardon, and discovered how
And by whose means he 'scaped – which was your
     daughter's,   20
Whose pardon is procured too; and the prisoner,
Not to be held ungrateful to her goodness,
Has given a sum of money to her marriage:
A large one, I'll assure you.

JAILER   You're a good man
And ever bring good news.

1 FRIEND   How was it ended?   25

2 FRIEND
Why, as it should be. They that never begged
But they prevailed had their suits fairly granted:
The prisoners have their lives.

1 FRIEND   I knew 'twould be so.

2 FRIEND
But there be new conditions, which you'll hear of
At better time.

JAILER   I hope they are good.

2 FRIEND   They are honourable;
How good they'll prove, I know not.

Enter Wooer.

1 FRIEND   'Twill be known.
WOOER [*to Jailer*]   Alas, sir, where's your daughter?
JAILER   Why do you ask?
WOOER   O, sir, when did you see her?
2 FRIEND   How he looks!
JAILER   This morning.
WOOER   Was she well? Was she in health? Sir,
When did she sleep?
1 FRIEND   These are strange questions.
JAILER   I do not think she was very well, for now
You make me mind her: but this very day
I asked her questions, and she answered me
So far from what she was, so childishly,
So sillily, as if she were a fool,
An innocent, and I was very angry.
But what of her, sir?
WOOER   Nothing but my pity.
But you must know it, and as good by me
As by another that less loves her.
JAILER   Well, sir?
1 FRIEND   Not right?
2 FRIEND   Not well?
WOOER   No sir, not well:
'Tis too true: she is mad.
1 FRIEND   It cannot be!
WOOER   Believe, you'll find it so.
JAILER   I half suspected
What you have told me. The gods comfort her!
Either this was her love to Palamon,
Or fear of my miscarrying on his 'scape,
Or both.
WOOER   'Tis likely.
JAILER   But why all this haste, sir?
WOOER   I'll tell you quickly. As I late was angling
In the great lake that lies behind the palace,
From the far shore, thick set with reeds and sedges,
As patiently I was attending sport,
I heard a voice, a shrill one, and attentive
I gave my ear, when I might well perceive
'Twas one that sung and, by the smallness of it,
A boy or woman. I then left my angle
To his own skill, came near, but yet perceived not
Who made the sound, the rushes and the reeds
Had so encompassed it. I laid me down
And listened to the words she sung, for then,
Through a small glade cut by the fishermen,
I saw it was your daughter.
JAILER   Pray go on, sir.
WOOER   She sung much, but no sense; only I heard her
Repeat this often: 'Palamon is gone,
Is gone to th' wood to gather mulberries;
I'll find him out tomorrow.'
1 FRIEND   Pretty soul!

WOOER   'His shackles will betray him, he'll be taken;
And what shall I do then? I'll bring a bevy,
A hundred black-eyed maids that love as I do,
With chaplets on their heads of daffadillies,
With cherry-lips and cheeks of damask roses,
And all we'll dance an antic 'fore the Duke
And beg his pardon.' Then she talked of you, sir:
That you must lose your head tomorrow morning,
And she must gather flowers to bury you,
And see the house made handsome. Then she sung
Nothing but 'Willow, willow, willow' and, between,
Ever was 'Palamon, fair Palamon'
And 'Palamon was a tall young man'. The place
Was knee-deep where she sat; her careless tresses
A wreath of bullrush rounded; about her stuck
Thousand fresh water-flowers of several colours,
That methought she appeared like the fair nymph
That feeds the lake with waters, or as Iris
Newly dropped down from heaven. Rings she made
Of rushes that grew by and to 'em spoke
The prettiest posies: 'Thus our true love's tied',
'This you may loose, not me', and many a one.
And then she wept, and sung again, and sighed,
And with the same breath smiled and kissed her hand.
2 FRIEND   Alas, what pity it is!
WOOER   I made in to her.
She saw me, and straight sought the flood; I saved
    her,
And set her safe to land, when presently
She slipped away and to the city made,
With such a cry and swiftness that, believe me,
She left me far behind her. Three or four
I saw from far off cross her – one of 'em
I knew to be your brother – where she stayed
And fell, scarce to be got away. I left them with her,

Enter Jailer's Brother, *Jailer's* Daughter *and others.*

And hither came to tell you. Here they are.
DAUGHTER [*Sings.*]
        May you never more enjoy the light, (*etc.*)
    Is not this a fine song?
BROTHER   O, a very fine one.
DAUGHTER   I can sing twenty more.
BROTHER   I think you can.
DAUGHTER   Yes, truly, can I. I can sing 'The Broom'
And 'Bonny Robin'. Are not you a tailor?
BROTHER   Yes.
DAUGHTER   Where's my wedding gown?
BROTHER   I'll bring it tomorrow.
DAUGHTER   Do, very early. I must be abroad else
To call the maids and pay the minstrels,
For I must lose my maidenhead by cocklight;
'Twill never thrive else.
[*Sings.*]   O fair, O sweet, (*etc.*)
BROTHER [*to Jailer*]
You must e'en take it patiently.
JAILER   'Tis true.

30
35
40
45
50
55
60
65
70
75
80
85
90
95
100
105
110
115

DAUGHTER
  Good ev'n, good men; pray, did you ever hear
  Of one young Palamon?
JAILER   Yes, wench, we know him.
DAUGHTER   Is't not a fine young gentleman?
JAILER   'Tis, love.
BROTHER
  By no means cross her, she is then distempered
  Far worse than now she shows.
120 1 FRIEND [*to Daughter*]   Yes, he's a fine man.
DAUGHTER   O, is he so? You have a sister.
1 FRIEND   Yes.
DAUGHTER   But she shall never have him – tell her so –
  For a trick that I know; you'd best look to her,
  For if she see him once, she's gone; she's done,
125 And undone, in an hour. All the young maids
  Of our town are in love with him, but I laugh at 'em
  And let 'em all alone; is't not a wise course?
1 FRIEND   Yes.
DAUGHTER
  There is at least two hundred now with child by him –
  There must be four – yet I keep close for all this,
130 Close as a cockle; and all these must be boys
  (He has the trick on't) and at ten years old
  They must be all gelt for musicians
  And sing the wars of Theseus.
2 FRIEND   This is strange.
DAUGHTER   As ever you heard, but say nothing.
1 FRIEND   No.
DAUGHTER
135 They come from all parts of the dukedom to him.
  I'll warrant ye, he had not so few last night
  As twenty to dispatch – he'll tickle't up
  In two hours, if his hand be in.
JAILER   She's lost
  Past all cure.
BROTHER   Heaven forbid, man!
DAUGHTER [*to Jailer*]   Come hither!
  You are a wise man.
1 FRIEND [*aside*]   Does she know him?
140 2 FRIEND [*aside*]   No.
  Would she did!
DAUGHTER   You are master of a ship?
JAILER   Yes.
DAUGHTER   Where's your compass?
JAILER   Here.
DAUGHTER   Set it to th' north.
  And now direct your course to th' wood, where
      Palamon
  Lies longing for me. For the tackling,
145 Let me alone; come, weigh, my hearts, cheerily!
ALL [*severally*]
  Ugh! Ugh! Ugh!
  'Tis up! – The wind's fair! – Top the bowline! –
  Out with the mainsail! – Where's your whistle, master?
BROTHER   Let's get her in.
JAILER   Up to the top, boy.

BROTHER   Where's the pilot?
1 FRIEND   Here.   150
DAUGHTER   What kenn'st thou?
2 FRIEND   A fair wood.
DAUGHTER   Bear for it, master;
  Tack about!
  [*Sings.*] When Cynthia with her borrowed light, (*etc.*)
                                              Exeunt.

4.2   *Enter* EMILIA *alone, with two pictures.*

EMILIA
  Yet I may bind those wounds up, that must open
  And bleed to death for my sake else; I'll choose,
  And end their strife. Two such young, handsome men
  Shall never fall for me; their weeping mothers,
  Following the dead cold ashes of their sons,   5
  Shall never curse my cruelty.
    [*Looks at one of the pictures.*] Good heaven,
  What a sweet face has Arcite! If wise Nature,
  With all her best endowments, all those beauties
  She sows into the births of noble bodies,
  Were here a mortal woman and had in her   10
  The coy denials of young maids, yet, doubtless,
  She would run mad for this man. What an eye,
  Of what a fiery sparkle and quick sweetness,
  Has this young prince! Here Love himself sits smiling;
  Just such another wanton Ganymede   15
  Set Jove afire with, and enforced the god
  Snatch up the goodly boy and set him by him,
  A shining constellation. What a brow,
  Of what a spacious majesty, he carries,
  Arched like the great-eyed Juno's, but far sweeter,   20
  Smoother than Pelops' shoulder! Fame and Honour,
  Methinks, from hence, as from a promontory
  Pointed in heaven, should clap their wings and sing,
  To all the under-world, the loves and fights
  Of gods and such men near 'em.
    [*Looks at the other picture.*]   Palamon   25
  Is but his foil; to him, a mere dull shadow;
  He's swart and meagre, of an eye as heavy
  As if he had lost his mother; a still temper;
  No stirring in him, no alacrity;
  Of all this sprightly sharpness, not a smile.   30
  Yet these that we count errors may become him:
  Narcissus was a sad boy, but a heavenly.
  – 'O, who can find the bent of woman's fancy?'
  I am a fool, my reason is lost in me,
  I have no choice, and I have lied so lewdly   35
  That women ought to beat me. On my knees,
  I ask thy pardon, Palamon: thou art alone
  And only beautiful, and these the eyes,
  These the bright lamps of beauty, that command
  And threaten love, and what young maid dare cross 'em? 40
  What a bold gravity, and yet inviting,
  Has this brown manly face! O Love, this only,
  From this hour, is complexion!

[*Lays Arcite's picture down.*] Lie there, Arcite;
Thou art a changeling to him, a mere gypsy,
45 And this the noble body. – I am sotted,
Utterly lost. My virgin's faith has fled me.
For if my brother but even now had asked me
Whether I loved, I had run mad for Arcite;
Now, if my sister, more for Palamon.
50 Stand both together. Now, come ask me, brother.
'Alas, I know not!' Ask me now, sweet sister.
'I may go look.' What a mere child is Fancy,
That, having two fair gauds of equal sweetness,
Cannot distinguish, but must cry for both!

Enter Gentleman.

How now, sir?
55 GENTLEMAN   From the noble Duke your brother,
Madam, I bring you news. The knights are come.
EMILIA   To end the quarrel?
GENTLEMAN   Yes.
EMILIA   Would I might end first!
What sins have I committed, chaste Diana,
That my unspotted youth must now be soiled
60 With blood of princes, and my chastity
Be made the altar where the lives of lovers –
Two greater and two better never yet
Made mothers joy – must be the sacrifice
To my unhappy beauty?

Enter THESEUS, HIPPOLYTA, PIRITHOUS *and Attendants.*

THESEUS   Bring 'em in
65 Quickly, by any means; I long to see 'em.
[*to Emilia*] Your two contending lovers are returned,
And with them their fair knights. Now, my fair sister,
You must love one of them.
EMILIA   I had rather both;
So neither for my sake should fall untimely.
THESEUS   Who saw 'em?
PIRITHOUS   I a while.
70 GENTLEMAN   And I.

Enter Messenger.

THESEUS   From whence come you, sir?
MESSENGER   From the knights.
THESEUS   Pray speak,
You that have seen them, what they are.
MESSENGER   I will, sir,
And truly what I think. Six braver spirits
Than these they have brought, if we judge by the
        outside,
75 I never saw nor read of. He that stands
In the first place with Arcite, by his seeming
Should be a stout man, by his face a prince,
His very looks so say him: his complexion
Nearer a brown than black, stern, and yet noble,
80 Which shows him hardy, fearless, proud of dangers.
The circles of his eyes show fire within him,
And as a heated lion so he looks.

His hair hangs long behind him, black and shining
Like ravens' wings; his shoulders broad and strong;
85 Armed long and round, and on his thigh a sword,
Hung by a curious baldrick, when he frowns,
To seal his will with. Better o' my conscience
Was never soldier's friend.
THESEUS   Thou hast well described him.
PIRITHOUS   Yet a great deal short,
90 Methinks, of him that's first with Palamon.
THESEUS   Pray, speak him, friend.
PIRITHOUS   I guess he is a prince too,
And, if it may be, greater; for his show
Has all the ornament of honour in't.
He's somewhat bigger than the knight he spoke of,
95 But of a face far sweeter. His complexion
Is, as a ripe grape, ruddy; he has felt
Without doubt what he fights for, and so apter
To make this cause his own. In's face appears
All the fair hopes of what he undertakes
100 And, when he's angry, then a settled valour,
Not tainted with extremes, runs through his body
And guides his arm to brave things. Fear he cannot;
He shows no such soft temper. His head's yellow,
Hard-haired, and curled, thick-twined like ivy tods,
105 Not to undo with thunder. In his face
The livery of the warlike maid appears,
Pure red and white, for yet no beard has blessed him;
And in his rolling eyes sits Victory,
As if she ever meant to court his valour.
110 His nose stands high, a character of honour;
His red lips, after fights, are fit for ladies.
EMILIA   Must these men die too?
PIRITHOUS   When he speaks, his tongue
Sounds like a trumpet. All his lineaments
Are as a man would wish 'em, strong and clean;
115 He wears a well-steeled axe, the staff of gold;
His age some five-and-twenty.
MESSENGER   There's another,
A little man, but of a tough soul, seeming
As great as any; fairer promises
In such a body yet I never looked on.
PIRITHOUS   O, he that's freckle-faced?
MESSENGER   The same, my lord. 120
Are they not sweet ones?
PIRITHOUS   Yes, they are well.
MESSENGER   Methinks,
Being so few and well disposed, they show
Great and fine art in nature. He's white-haired,
Not wanton white, but such a manly colour,
125 Next to an auburn; tough and nimble set,
Which shows an active soul; his arms are brawny,
Lined with strong sinews. To the shoulder piece,
Gently they swell, like women new-conceived,
Which speaks him prone to labour, never fainting
130 Under the weight of arms; stout-hearted, still,
But when he stirs, a tiger. He's grey-eyed,
Which yields compassion where he conquers; sharp

To spy advantages and, where he finds 'em,
He's swift to make 'em his. He does no wrongs,
135 Nor takes none; he's round-faced and when he smiles
He shows a lover; when he frowns, a soldier.
About his head he wears the winner's oak
And in it stuck the favour of his lady.
His age, some six-and-thirty. In his hand
140 He bears a charging-staff, embossed with silver.
THESEUS   Are they all thus?
PIRITHOUS   They are all the sons of honour.
THESEUS   Now, as I have a soul, I long to see 'em.
[*to Hippolyta*] Lady, you shall see men fight now.
HIPPOLYTA   I wish it,
But not the cause, my lord. They would show bravely
145 Fighting about the titles of two kingdoms.
'Tis pity love should be so tyrannous.
– O, my soft-hearted sister, what think you?
Weep not, till they weep blood. Wench, it must be.
THESEUS
You have steeled 'em with your beauty.
[*to Pirithous*]   Honoured friend,
150 To you I give the field; pray order it
Fitting the persons that must use it.
PIRITHOUS   Yes, sir.
THESEUS   Come, I'll go visit 'em! I cannot stay –
Their fame has fir'd me so; till they appear,
Good friend, be royal.
PIRITHOUS   There shall want no bravery.
                              Exeunt all but Emilia.
155 EMILIA   Poor wench, go weep, for whosoever wins
Loses a noble cousin, for thy sins.   *Exit.*

4.3   *Enter* Jailer, Wooer *and* Doctor.

DOCTOR   Her distraction is more at some time of the
moon than at other some, is it not?
JAILER   She is continually in a harmless distemper:
sleeps little; altogether without appetite, save often
5   drinking; dreaming of another world and a better; and,
what broken piece of matter soe'er she's about, the
name Palamon lards it, that she farces every business
withall, fits it to every question.

            Enter Jailer's Daughter.

Look where she comes; you shall perceive her
10   behaviour.
DAUGHTER   I have forgot it quite. The burden on't was
'Down-a, down-a' and penned by no worse man than
Giraldo, Emilia's Schoolmaster; he's as fantastical too
as ever he may go upon's legs – for in the next world
15   will Dido see Palamon, and then will she be out of love
with Aeneas.
DOCTOR   What stuff's here? Poor soul!
JAILER   Even thus all day long.
DAUGHTER   Now for this charm that I told you of: you
20   must bring a piece of silver on the tip of your tongue,
or no ferry. Then if it be your chance to come where

the blessed spirits are, there's a sight now! We maids
that have our livers perished, cracked to pieces with
love, we shall come there and do nothing all day long
but pick flowers with Proserpine. Then will I make   25
Palamon a nosegay; then let him mark me – then.
DOCTOR   How prettily she's amiss! Note her a little
further.
DAUGHTER   Faith, I'll tell you, sometime we go to
barley-break, we of the blessed. Alas, 'tis a sore life   30
they have i'th' other place – such burning, frying,
boiling, hissing, howling, chattering, cursing: oh, they
have shrewd measure; take heed! If one be mad, or
hang or drown themselves, there they go – Jupiter
bless us! – and there shall we be put in a cauldron of   35
lead and usurers' grease, amongst a whole million of
cutpurses, and there boil like a gammon of bacon that
will never be enough.
DOCTOR   How her brain coins!
DAUGHTER   Lords and courtiers that have got maids   40
with child, they are in this place. They shall stand in
fire up to the navel and in ice up to the heart, and there
th'offending part burns and the deceiving part freezes.
In troth, a very grievous punishment, as one would
think, for such a trifle. Believe me, one would marry a   45
leprous witch to be rid on't, I'll assure you.
DOCTOR   How she continues this fancy! 'Tis not an
engrafted madness but a most thick and profound
melancholy.
DAUGHTER   To hear there a proud lady and a proud city   50
wife, howl together! I were a beast an I'd call it good
sport. One cries, 'O, this smoke!', another, 'This fire!'
One cries, 'O, that ever I did it behind the arras!' and
then howls; th'other curses a suing fellow and her
garden house.   55
[*Sings.*] I will be true, my stars, my fate, (*etc.*)   *Exit.*
JAILER   What think you of her, sir?
DOCTOR   I think she has a perturbed mind, which I
cannot minister to.
JAILER   Alas, what then?   60
DOCTOR   Understand you she ever affected any man ere
she beheld Palamon?
JAILER   I was once, sir, in great hope she had fixed her
liking on this gentleman, my friend.
WOOER   I did think so too, and would account I had a   65
great penn'orth on't, to give half my state that both she
and I at this present stood unfeignedly on the same
terms.
DOCTOR   That intemperate surfeit of her eye hath
distempered the other senses; they may return and   70
settle again to execute their preordained faculties, but
they are now in a most extravagant vagary. This you
must do. Confine her to a place where the light may
rather seem to steal in than be permitted. Take upon
you, young sir her friend, the name of Palamon; say   75
you come to eat with her and to commune of love. This
will catch her attention, for this her mind beats upon;
other objects that are inserted 'tween her mind and eye

become the pranks and friskins of her madness. Sing
to her such green songs of love as she says Palamon
hath sung in prison. Come to her stuck in as sweet
flowers as the season is mistress of and thereto make an
addition of some other compounded odours which are
grateful to the sense. All this shall become Palamon,
for Palamon can sing, and Palamon is sweet and every
good thing. Desire to eat with her, carve her, drink to
her and, still among, intermingle your petition of
grace and acceptance into her favour. Learn what
maids have been her companions and play-feres and
let them repair to her with Palamon in their mouths,
and appear with tokens, as if they suggested for him. It
is a falsehood she is in, which is with falsehoods to be
combated. This may bring her to eat, to sleep, and
reduce what's now out of square in her into their
former law and regiment. I have seen it approved, how
many times I know not, but to make the number more
I have great hope in this. I will, between the passages of
this project, come in with my appliance. Let us put it
in execution and hasten the success, which, doubt not,
will bring forth comfort. *Exeunt.*

5.1 *Flourish. Enter* THESEUS, PIRITHOUS,
HIPPOLYTA, *Attendants.*

THESEUS Now let 'em enter and before the gods
  Tender their holy prayers. Let the temples
  Burn bright with sacred fires and the altars
  In hallowed clouds commend their swelling incense
  To those above us. Let no due be wanting.
  They have a noble work in hand, will honour
  The very powers that love 'em.

  Flourish of cornets. Enter PALAMON *and* ARCITE
  and their Knights.

PIRITHOUS   Sir, they enter.
THESEUS You valiant and strong-hearted enemies,
  You royal german foes, that this day come
  To blow that nearness out that flames between ye:
  Lay by your anger for an hour and, dove-like,
  Before the holy altars of your helpers,
  The all-feared gods, bow down your stubborn bodies.
  Your ire is more than mortal; so your help be;
  And, as the gods regard ye, fight with justice.
  I'll leave you to your prayers and betwixt ye
  I part my wishes.
PIRITHOUS   Honour crown the worthiest.
                    Exeunt Theseus and his train.
PALAMON The glass is running now that cannot finish
  Till one of us expire. Think you but thus:
  That were there aught in me which strove to show
  Mine enemy in this business, were't one eye
  Against another, arm oppressed by arm,
  I would destroy th'offender, coz, I would,
  Though parcel of myself. Then from this gather
  How I should tender you.

ARCITE   I am in labour
  To push your name, your ancient love, our kindred
  Out of my memory and i'th' selfsame place
  To seat something I would confound. So hoist we
  The sails that must these vessels port, even where
  The heavenly limiter pleases.
PALAMON   You speak well.
  Before I turn, let me embrace thee, cousin.
  This I shall never do again.
ARCITE   One farewell.
PALAMON Why, let it be so. Farewell, coz.
ARCITE   Farewell, sir.
          Exeunt Palamon and his Knights.
          [*Arcite addresses his three Knights.*]
  Knights, kinsmen, lovers – yea, my sacrifices –
  True worshippers of Mars, whose spirit in you
  Expels the seeds of fear and th'apprehension
  Which still is father of it: go with me
  Before the god of our profession; there
  Require of him the hearts of lions and
  The breath of tigers, yea the fierceness too,
  Yea, the speed also – to go on, I mean:
  Else wish we to be snails. You know my prize
  Must be dragged out of blood; force and great feat
  Must put my garland on, where she sticks
  The queen of flowers. Our intercession then
  Must be to him that makes the camp a cistern
  Brimmed with the blood of men. Give me your aid
  And bend your spirits towards him.
          [*They prostrate themselves before the altar, then
          kneel.*]
  Thou mighty one, that with thy power hast turned
  Green Neptune into purple; whose approach
  Comets prewarn; whose havoc in vast field
  Unearthed skulls proclaim; whose breath blows
          down
  The teeming Ceres' foison; who dost pluck
  With hand armipotent from forth blue clouds
  The masoned turrets; that both mak'st and break'st
  The stony girths of cities: me thy pupil,
  Youngest follower of thy drum, instruct this day
  With military skill, that to thy laud
  I may advance my streamer and by thee
  Be styled the lord o'th' day. Give me, great Mars,
  Some token of thy pleasure.
          [*Here they fall on their faces, as formerly, and there is
          heard clanging of armour, with a short thunder, as
          the burst of a battle, whereupon they all rise and bow
          to the altar.*]
  O great corrector of enormous times;
  Shaker of o'er-rank states; thou grand decider
  Of dusty and old titles, that heal'st with blood
  The earth when it is sick and cur'st the world
  O'th' pleurisy of people: I do take
  Thy signs auspiciously and in thy name
  To my design march boldly. Let us go.
          Exeunt Arcite and his Knights.

Enter PALAMON *and his Knights, with the
former observance.*

PALAMON   Our stars must glister with new fire or be
70   Today extinct. Our argument is love,
     Which, if the goddess of it grant, she gives
     Victory too; then blend your spirits with mine,
     You whose free nobleness do make my cause
     Your personal hazard. To the goddess Venus
75   Commend we our proceeding and implore
     Her power unto our party.
       [*Here they kneel as formerly.*]
     Hail, sovereign queen of secrets, who hast power
     To call the fiercest tyrant from his rage
     And weep unto a girl; that hast the might,
80   Even with an eye-glance, to choke Mars's drum
     And turn th'alarm to whispers; that canst make
     A cripple flourish with his crutch and cure him
     Before Apollo; that mayst force the king
     To be his subject's vassal and induce
85   Stale gravity to dance! The polled bachelor –
     Whose youth, like wanton boys through bonfires,
     Have skipped thy flame – at seventy, thou canst catch
     And make him, to the scorn of his hoarse throat,
     Abuse young lays of love. What godlike power
90   Hast thou not power upon? To Phoebus thou
     Add'st flames hotter than his: the heavenly fires
     Did scorch his mortal son, thine him; the huntress
     All moist and cold, some say, began to throw
     Her bow away and sigh. Take to thy grace
95   Me thy vowed soldier, who do bear thy yoke
     As 'twere a wreath of roses, yet is heavier
     Than lead itself, stings more than nettles.
     I have never been foul-mouthed against thy law;
     Ne'er revealed secret, for I knew none – would not,
100   Had I kenned all there were. I never practised
     Upon man's wife nor would the libels read
     Of liberal wits. I never at great feasts
     Sought to betray a beauty, but have blushed
     At simpering sirs that did. I have been harsh
105   To large confessors and have hotly asked them
     If they had mothers – I had one, a woman,
     And women 'twere they wronged. I knew a man
     Of eighty winters, this I told them, who
     A lass of fourteen brided. 'Twas thy power
110   To put life into dust: the aged cramp
     Had screwed his square foot round;
     The gout had knit his fingers into knots;
     Torturing convulsions from his globy eyes
     Had almost drawn their spheres, that what was life
115   In him seemed torture. This anatomy
     Had by his young fair fere a boy, and I
     Believed it was his, for she swore it was –
     And who would not believe her? Brief, I am,
     To those that prate and have done, no companion;
120   To those that boast and have not, a defier;
     To those that would and cannot, a rejoicer.

     Yea, him I do not love that tells close offices
     The foulest way nor names concealments in
     The boldest language. Such a one I am
     And vow that lover never yet made sigh   125
     Truer than I. O, then, most soft sweet goddess,
     Give me the victory of this question, which
     Is true love's merit, and bless me with a sign
     Of thy great pleasure.
       [*Here music is heard; doves are seen to flutter. They
       fall again upon their faces, then rise to their knees.*]
     O thou that from eleven to ninety reign'st   130
     In mortal bosoms, whose chase is this world
     And we in herds thy game: I give thee thanks
     For this fair token, which, being laid unto
     Mine innocent true heart, arms in assurance
     My body to this business. Let us rise   135
     And bow before the goddess.   [*They rise and bow.*]
                       Time comes on.

Exeunt Palamon and his Knights.

Still music of recorders. Enter EMILIA *in white, her hair
about her shoulders, wearing a wheaten wreath. One Maid
in white holding up her train, her hair stuck with flowers.
One Maid before her carrying a silver hind, in which is
conveyed incense and sweet odours, which being set upon
the altar, her maids standing aloof, she sets fire to it.
Then they curtsey and kneel.*

EMILIA   O sacred, shadowy, cold and constant queen,
     Abandoner of revels, mute contemplative,
     Sweet, solitary, white as chaste, and pure
     As wind-fanned snow, who to thy female knights   140
     Allow'st no more blood than will make a blush,
     Which is their order's robe: I here, thy priest,
     Am humbled 'fore thine altar. O, vouchsafe
     With that thy rare green eye, which never yet
     Beheld thing maculate, look on thy virgin;   145
     And, sacred silver mistress, lend thine ear,
     Which ne'er heard scurrile term, into whose port
     Ne'er entered wanton sound, to my petition
     Seasoned with holy fear. This is my last
     Of vestal office. I am bride-habited,   150
     But maiden-hearted; a husband I have 'pointed,
     But do not know him. Out of two, I should
     Choose one and pray for his success, but I
     Am guiltless of election. Of mine eyes,
     Were I to lose one, they are equal precious;   155
     I could doom neither: that which perished should
     Go to't unsentenced. Therefore, most modest Queen,
     He of the two pretenders that best loves me
     And has the truest title in't, let him
     Take off my wheaten garland, or else grant   160
     The file and quality I hold I may
     Continue in thy band.
       [*Here the hind vanishes under the altar and in
       the place ascends a rose tree, having one rose upon it.*]
     See what our general of ebbs and flows,

165   Out from the bowels of her holy altar,
With sacred art advances: but one rose!
If well inspired, this battle shall confound
Both these brave knights and I, a virgin flower,
Must grow alone, unplucked.
> [*Here is heard a sudden twang of instruments, and the*
> *rose falls from the tree, which then descends.*]

170   The flower is fall'n; the tree descends. O, mistress,
Thou here dischargest me; I shall be gathered –
I think so – but I know not thine own will;
Unclasp thy mystery! – I hope she's pleased;
Her signs were gracious.   *They curtsey and exeunt.*

5.2   *Enter* Doctor, Jailer *and* Wooer *in the*
           habit of Palamon.

DOCTOR
   Has this advice I told you done any good upon her?
WOOER
   O, very much. The maids that kept her company
Have half persuaded her that I am Palamon.
Within this half hour she came smiling to me
And asked me what I would eat and when I would
5   kiss her.
I told her, 'Presently!' and kissed her twice.
DOCTOR
   'Twas well done. Twenty times had been far better,
For there the cure lies mainly.
WOOER   Then she told me
She would watch with me tonight, for well she knew
What hour my fit would take me.
10 DOCTOR   Let her do so.
And, when your fit comes, fit her home, and presently.
WOOER   She would have me sing.
DOCTOR   You did so?
WOOER   No.
DOCTOR   'Twas very ill-done then;
You should observe her every way.
WOOER   Alas,
15 I have no voice, sir, to confirm her that way.
DOCTOR   That's all one, if ye make a noise.
If she entreat again, do anything.
Lie with her if she ask you.
JAILER   Whoa there, Doctor!
DOCTOR   Yes, in the way of cure.
JAILER   But first, by your leave,
I'th' way of honesty.
20 DOCTOR   That's but a niceness.
Ne'er cast your child away for honesty.
Cure her first this way; then if she will be honest,
She has the path before her.
JAILER   Thank ye, Doctor.
DOCTOR   Pray bring her in and let's see how she is.
25 JAILER   I will, and tell her
Her Palamon stays for her. But, Doctor,
Methinks you are i'th' wrong still.   *Exit Jailer.*
DOCTOR   Go, go,

You fathers are fine fools. Her honesty?
An we should give her physic till we find *that*!
WOOER   Why, do you think she is not honest, sir?   30
DOCTOR   How old is she?
WOOER   She's eighteen.
DOCTOR   She may be,
But that's all one, 'tis nothing to our purpose.
Whate'er her father says, if you perceive
Her mood inclining that way that I spoke of,
Videlicet, the 'way of flesh' – you have me?   35
WOOER   Yes, very well, sir.
DOCTOR   Please her appetite
And do it home, it cures her, *ipso facto*,
The melancholy humour that infects her.
WOOER   I am of your mind, Doctor.

       Enter Jailer, Daughter *and Maid.*

DOCTOR   You'll find it so. She comes; pray, humour her.   40
JAILER   Come, your love Palamon stays for you, child,
And has done this long hour, to visit you.
DAUGHTER   I thank him for his gentle patience;
He's a kind gentleman and I am much bound to him.
Did you ne'er see the horse he gave me?
JAILER   Yes.   45
DAUGHTER   How do you like him?
JAILER   He's a very fair one.
DAUGHTER   You never saw him dance?
JAILER   No.
DAUGHTER   I have, often.
He dances very finely, very comely,
And for a jig, come cut and long tail to him,
He turns ye like a top.
JAILER   That's fine indeed.   50
DAUGHTER
He'll dance the morris twenty mile an hour –
And that will founder the best hobby-horse,
If I have any skill, in all the parish –
And gallops to the tune of 'Light o' love'.
What think you of this horse?
JAILER   Having these virtues,   55
I think he might be brought to play at tennis.
DAUGHTER   Alas, that's nothing.
JAILER   Can he read and write too?
DAUGHTER
A very fair hand, and casts himself th'accounts
Of all his hay and provender. That ostler
Must rise betimes that cozens him. You know   60
The chestnut mare the Duke has?
JAILER   Very well.
DAUGHTER
She is horribly in love with him, poor beast!
But he is like his master, coy and scornful.
JAILER   What dowry has she?
DAUGHTER   Some two hundred bottles
And twenty strike of oats – but he'll ne'er have her.   65
He lisps in's neighing, able to entice
A miller's mare. He'll be the death of her.

DOCTOR   What stuff she utters!

JAILER   Make curtsey, here your love comes.

[*Wooer comes forward and bows.*]

WOOER   Pretty soul,
How do ye?   [*She curtseys.*]

70   That's a fine maid! There's a curtsey!

DAUGHTER   Yours to command i'th' way of honesty.
How far is't now to th'end o'th' world, my masters?

DOCTOR   Why, a day's journey, wench.

DAUGHTER [*to Wooer*]   Will you go with me?

WOOER   What shall we do there, wench?

DAUGHTER   Why, play at stool-ball;
What is there else to do?

75   WOOER   I am content,
If we shall keep our wedding there.

DAUGHTER   'Tis true,
For there, I will assure you, we shall find
Some blind priest for the purpose, that will venture
To marry us, for here they are nice and foolish.

80   Besides, my father must be hanged tomorrow
And that would be a blot i'th' business.
Are not you Palamon?

WOOER   Do not you know me?

DAUGHTER   Yes, but you care not for me. I have nothing
But this poor petticoat and two coarse smocks.

WOOER   That's all one; I will have you.

85   DAUGHTER   Will you surely?

WOOER   Yes, by this fair hand, will I.   [*Takes her hand.*]

DAUGHTER   We'll to bed then.

WOOER   E'en when you will.   [*Kisses her.*]

DAUGHTER [*Rubs off the kiss.*]
                    O, sir, you would fain be nibbling.

WOOER   Why do you rub my kiss off?

DAUGHTER   'Tis a sweet one
And will perfume me finely against the wedding.
Is not this your cousin Arcite?   [*Indicates the Doctor.*]

90   DOCTOR   Yes, sweetheart,
And I am glad my cousin Palamon
Has made so fair a choice.

DAUGHTER [*to Doctor*]   Do you think he'll have me?

DOCTOR   Yes, without doubt.

DAUGHTER [*to Jailer*]   Do you think so too?

JAILER   Yes.

DAUGHTER   We shall have many children.
[*to Doctor*]   Lord, how you're grown!

95   My Palamon, I hope, will grow too, finely,
Now he's at liberty. Alas, poor chicken,
He was kept down with hard meat and ill lodging!
But I'll kiss him up again.

Enter Messenger.

MESSENGER
What do you here? You'll lose the noblest sight
That e'er was seen.

JAILER   Are they i'th' field?

100   MESSENGER   They are.
You bear a charge there too.

JAILER   I'll away straight.
I must e'en leave you here.

DOCTOR   Nay, we'll go with you;
I will not lose the sight.

JAILER [*to Doctor*]   How did you like her?

DOCTOR
I'll warrant you, within these three or four days
I'll make her right again.   *Exit Jailer with Messenger.*
[*to Wooer*]   You must not from her,   105
But still preserve her in this way.

WOOER   I will.

DOCTOR   Let's get her in.

WOOER [*to Daughter*]   Come, sweet, we'll go to dinner
And then we'll play at cards.

DAUGHTER   And shall we kiss too?

WOOER   An hundred times.

DAUGHTER   And twenty?

WOOER   Ay, and twenty.

DAUGHTER   And then we'll sleep together.

DOCTOR   Take her offer.   110

WOOER [*to Daughter*]   Yes, marry, will we.

DAUGHTER   But you shall not hurt me.

WOOER   I will not, sweet.

DAUGHTER   If you do, love, I'll cry.   *Exeunt.*

5.3   *Flourish. Enter* THESEUS, HIPPOLYTA, EMILIA,
                PIRITHOUS *and Attendants.*

EMILIA   I'll no step further.

PIRITHOUS   Will you lose this sight?

EMILIA   I had rather see a wren hawk at a fly
Than this decision. Every blow that falls
Threats a brave life; each stroke laments
The place whereon it falls and sounds more like   5
A bell than blade. I will stay here.
It is enough my hearing shall be punished
With what shall happen, 'gainst the which there is
No deafing, but to hear, not taint mine eye
With dread sights it may shun.

PIRITHOUS [*to Theseus*]   Sir, my good lord,   10
Your sister will no further.

THESEUS   O, she must.
She shall see deeds of honour in their kind,
Which sometime show well, pencilled. Nature now
Shall make and act the story, the belief
Both sealed with eye and ear.
[*to Emilia*]   You must be present: 15
You are the victor's meed, the prize and garland
To crown the question's title.

EMILIA   Pardon me;
If I were there, I'd wink.

THESEUS   You must be there:
This trial is as 'twere i'th' night, and you
The only star to shine.

EMILIA   I am extinct.   20
There is but envy in that light which shows
The one the other. Darkness, which ever was

The dam of horror, who does stand accursed
Of many mortal millions, may even now,
25 By casting her black mantle over both
That neither could find other, get herself
Some part of a good name and many a murder
Set off whereto she's guilty.
HIPPOLYTA   You must go.
EMILIA   In faith, I will not.
THESEUS   Why, the knights must kindle
30 Their valour at your eye. Know, of this war
You are the treasure and must needs be by
To give the service pay.
EMILIA   Sir, pardon me;
The title of a kingdom may be tried
Out of itself.
THESEUS   Well, well, then, at your pleasure.
35 Those that remain with you could wish their office
To any of their enemies.
HIPPOLYTA   Farewell, sister.
I am like to know your husband 'fore yourself
By some small start of time; he whom the gods
Do of the two know best, I pray them he
40 Be made your lot.   *Exeunt all but Emilia.*
EMILIA   Arcite is gently visaged, yet his eye
Is like an engine bent, or a sharp weapon
In a soft sheath; mercy and manly courage
Are bedfellows in his visage. Palamon
45 Has a most menacing aspect; his brow
Is graved and seems to bury what it frowns on,
Yet sometime 'tis not so, but alters to
The quality of his thoughts. Long time his eye
Will dwell upon his object. Melancholy
50 Becomes him nobly. So does Arcite's mirth.
But Palamon's sadness is a kind of mirth,
So mingled as if mirth did make him sad
And sadness merry. Those darker humours that
Stick misbecomingly on others, on them
55 Live in fair dwelling.
               [*Cornets. Trumpets sound as to a charge.*]
Hark how yon spurs to spirit do incite
The princes to their proof! Arcite may win me
And yet may Palamon wound Arcite to
The spoiling of his figure. O, what pity
60 Enough for such a chance? If I were by
I might do hurt, for they would glance their eyes
Toward my seat and in that motion might
Omit a ward or forfeit an offence
Which craved that very time. It is much better
I am not there.
               [*Cornets; a great cry and noise within, crying,*
                                    '*A Palamon!*']
65   O, better never born
Than minister to such harm!

               Enter Servant.

                         What is the chance?
SERVANT   The cry's 'A Palamon!'

EMILIA   Then he has won.
'Twas ever likely.
He looked all grace and success and he is
Doubtless the prim'st of men. I prithee, run 70
And tell me how it goes.
               [*Shout, and cornets; cries of* '*A Palamon!*']
SERVANT   Still 'Palamon'!
EMILIA   Run and enquire.   *Exit Servant.*
                         Poor servant, thou hast lost.
Upon my right side still I wore thy picture,
Palamon's on the left. Why so, I know not;
I had no end in't else; chance would have it so. 75
On the sinister side the heart lies. Palamon
Had the best-boding chance.
               [*Another cry and shout within, and cornets*]
                         This burst of clamour
Is sure th'end o'th' combat.

               Enter Servant.

SERVANT   They said that Palamon had Arcite's body
Within an inch o'th' pyramid, that the cry 80
Was general, 'A Palamon!' But anon
Th'assistants made a brave redemption and
The two bold titlers at this instant are
Hand to hand at it.
EMILIA   Were they metamorphosed
Both into one! – O, why? There were no woman 85
Worth so composed a man: their single share,
Their nobleness peculiar to them, gives
The prejudice of disparity, value's shortness,
To any lady breathing.
               [*Cornets. Cry within,* '*Arcite! Arcite!*']
                         More exulting?
'Palamon' still?
SERVANT   Nay, now the sound is 'Arcite!' 90
EMILIA   I prithee, lay attention to the cry.
               [*Cornets; a great shout and cry,* '*Arcite! Victory!*']
Set both thine ears to th' business.
SERVANT   The cry is
'Arcite and victory!' Hark! 'Arcite! Victory!'
The combat's consummation is proclaim'd
By the wind instruments.
EMILIA   Half-sights saw 95
That Arcite was no babe. God's lid, his richness
And costliness of spirit looked through him; it
   could
No more be hid in him than fire in flax,
Than humble banks can go to law with waters
That drift winds force to raging. I did think 100
Good Palamon would miscarry, yet I knew not
Why I did think so. Our reasons are not prophets
When oft our fancies are.   [*Cornets*]
                         They are coming off.
Alas, poor Palamon!

               Enter THESEUS, HIPPOLYTA, PIRITHOUS, ARCITE
                    (*as victor*) *and Attendants.*

THESEUS Lo, where our sister is in expectation, 105
Yet quaking and unsettled. – Fairest Emily,
The gods by their divine arbitrament
Have given you this knight; he is a good one
As ever struck at head. Give me your hands:
Receive you her, you him, be plighted with 110
A love that grows as you decay.

ARCITE   Emilia,
To buy you, I have lost what's dearest to me,
Save what is bought; and yet I purchase cheaply,
As I do rate your value.

THESEUS   O, loved sister,
He speaks now of as brave a knight as e'er 115
Did spur a noble steed. Surely the gods
Would have him die a bachelor, lest his race
Should show i'th world too godlike. His behaviour
So charmed me that methought Alcides was
To him a sow of lead. If I could praise 120
Each part of him to th'all I have spoke, your
      Arcite
Did not lose by't. For he that was thus good
Encountered yet his better. I have heard
Two emulous Philomels beat the ear o'th' night
With their contentious throats, now one the higher, 125
Anon the other, then again the first,
And by and by out-breasted, that the sense
Could not be judge between 'em. So it fared
Good space between these kinsmen, till heavens did
Make hardly one the winner.

[*to Arcite*]   Wear the garland 130
With joy that you have won. – For the subdued,
Give them our present justice, since I know
Their lives but pinch 'em. Let it here be done.
The scene's not for our seeing; go we hence,
Right joyful, with some sorrow.

[*to Arcite*]   Arm your prize; 135
I know you will not loose her. – Hippolyta,
I see one eye of yours conceives a tear,
The which it will deliver.   [*Flourish*]

EMILIA   Is this winning?
O, all you heavenly powers, where is your mercy?
But that your wills have said it must be so, 140
And charge me live to comfort this unfriended,
This miserable prince, that cuts away
A life more worthy from him than all women,
I should and would die too.

HIPPOLYTA   Infinite pity 145
That four such eyes should be so fixed on one
That two must needs be blind for't.

THESEUS   So it is.   *Exeunt.*

5.4   *Enter* PALAMON *and his* Knights, *pinioned;*
Jailer, *Executioner, Guard and others, carrying a
block and axe.*

PALAMON   There's many a man alive that has outlived
The love o'th' people; yea, i'th' selfsame state

Stands many a father with his child. Some comfort
We have by so considering. We expire
And not without men's pity; to live still, 5
Have their good wishes. We prevent
The loathsome misery of age, beguile
The gout and rheum that in lag hours attend
For grey approachers; we come towards the gods
Young and unwappered, not halting under crimes 10
Many and stale. That sure shall please the gods,
Sooner than such, to give us nectar with 'em,
For we are more clear spirits.

[*to Knights*]   My dear kinsmen,
Whose lives for this poor comfort are laid down,
You have sold 'em too, too cheap.

1 KNIGHT   What ending could be 15
Of more content? O'er us the victors have
Fortune, whose title is as momentary
As to us death is certain. A grain of honour
They not o'erweigh us.

2 KNIGHT   Let us bid farewell
And with our patience anger tottering Fortune, 20
Who at her certain'st reels.   [*They embrace.*]

3 KNIGHT   Come, who begins?

PALAMON   E'en he that led you to this banquet shall
Taste to you all. [*to Jailer*] Aha, my friend, my friend,
Your gentle daughter gave me freedom once;
You'll see't done now forever. Pray, how does she? 25
I heard she was not well; her kind of ill
Gave me some sorrow.

JAILER   Sir, she's well restored
And to be married shortly.

PALAMON   By my short life,
I am most glad on't. 'Tis the latest thing
I shall be glad of; prithee, tell her so. 30
Commend me to her and, to piece her portion,
Tender her this.   [*Gives him his purse.*]

1 KNIGHT   Nay, let's be offerers all.

2 KNIGHT   Is it a maid?

PALAMON   Verily I think so.
A right good creature, more to me deserving
Than I can 'quite or speak of.

THE KNIGHTS [*to Jailer*]   Commend us to her. 35
      [*They give their purses.*]

JAILER
The gods requite you all and make her thankful.

PALAMON   Adieu; and let my life be now as short
As my leave-taking.   [*He lays his head on the block.*]

1 KNIGHT   Lead, courageous cousin.

2, 3 KNIGHT   We'll follow cheerfully.
      [*A great noise within, crying,* 'Run, save, hold!']

Enter in haste a Messenger.

MESSENGER   Hold, hold! O, hold, hold, hold! 40

Enter PIRITHOUS *in haste.*

PIRITHOUS   Hold, ho! It is a cursed haste you made
If you have done so quickly! – Noble Palamon,

The gods will show their glory in a life
That thou art yet to lead.
PALAMON   Can that be,
45 When Venus, I have said, is false? How do things fare?
PIRITHOUS   Arise, great sir, and give the tidings ear
That are most rarely sweet and bitter.
PALAMON   What
Hath waked us from our dream?
PIRITHOUS   List, then. Your cousin,
Mounted upon a steed that Emily
50 Did first bestow on him, a black one, owing
Not a hair-worth of white, which some will say
Weakens his price and many will not buy
His goodness with this note – which superstition
Here finds allowance – on this horse is Arcite
55 Trotting the stones of Athens, which the calkins
Did rather tell than trample; for the horse
Would make his length a mile, if 't pleased his rider
To put pride in him. As he thus went counting
The flinty pavement, dancing as 'twere to th' music
60 His own hoofs made (for, as they say, from iron
Came music's origin), what envious flint,
Cold as old Saturn and, like him, possessed
With fire malevolent, darted a spark,
Or what fierce sulphur else, to this end made,
65 I comment not. The hot horse, hot as fire,
Took toy at this and fell to what disorder
His power could give his will; bounds, comes on end,
Forgets school-doing, being therein trained
And of kind manage; pig-like he whines
70 At the sharp rowell, which he frets at rather
Than any jot obeys; seeks all foul means
Of boist'rous and rough jad'ry to disseat
His lord, that kept it bravely. When nought served –
When neither curb would crack, girth break, nor
     diff'ring plunges
75 Disroot his rider whence he grew, but that
He kept him 'tween his legs – on his hind hoofs
On end he stands,
That Arcite's legs, being higher than his head,
Seemed with strange art to hang. His victor's
     wreath
80 Even then fell off his head and presently
Backward the jade comes o'er and his full poise
Becomes the rider's load. Yet is he living,
But such a vessel 'tis, that floats but for
The surge that next approaches. He much desires
85 To have some speech with you. Lo, he appears.

            Enter THESEUS, HIPPOLYTA, EMILIA,
                 ARCITE *carried in a chair.*

PALAMON   O miserable end of our alliance!
The gods are mighty. Arcite, if thy heart,
Thy worthy, manly heart, be yet unbroken,
Give me thy last words. I am Palamon,
One that yet loves thee dying.

ARCITE   Take Emilia   90
And, with her, all the world's joy. Reach thy hand;
Farewell. I have told my last hour. I was false
Yet never treacherous. Forgive me, cousin.
One kiss from fair Emilia.   [*Emilia kisses Arcite.*]
                              'Tis done.
Take her. I die.
PALAMON   Thy brave soul seek Elysium!   95
     [*Arcite dies.*]
EMILIA
I'll close thine eyes, Prince; blessed souls be with thee.
Thou art a right good man and, while I live,
This day I give to tears.
PALAMON   And I to honour.
THESEUS   In this place first you fought: e'en very here
I sundered you. Acknowledge to the gods   100
Our thanks that you are living.
His part is played and, though it were too short,
He did it well; your day is lengthened and
The blissful dew of heaven does arrose you.
The powerful Venus well hath graced her altar   105
And given you your love. Our master Mars
Hath vouched his oracle and to Arcite gave
The grace of the contention. So the deities
Have showed due justice. Bear this hence.
PALAMON   O, cousin!   110
That we should things desire, which do cost us
The loss of our desire! That nought could buy
Dear love, but loss of dear love!
     [*Arcite's body is carried out.*]
THESEUS   Never Fortune
Did play a subtler game. The conquered triumphs;
The victor has the loss; yet in the passage
The gods have been most equal. – Palamon,   115
Your kinsman hath confessed the right o'th' lady
Did lie in you, for you first saw her and
Even then proclaimed your fancy. He restored her
As your stol'n jewel and desired your spirit
To send him hence forgiven. The gods my justice   120
Take from my hand and they themselves become
The executioners. Lead your lady off
And call your lovers from the stage of death,
Whom I adopt my friends. A day or two
Let us look sadly and give grace unto   125
The funeral of Arcite, in whose end
The visages of bridegrooms we'll put on
And smile with Palamon – for whom an hour,
But one hour since, I was as dearly sorry
As glad of Arcite, and am now as glad   130
As for him sorry. O, you heavenly charmers,
What things you make of us! For what we lack
We laugh, for what we have are sorry, still
Are children in some kind. Let us be thankful
For that which is, and with you leave dispute   135
That are above our question. Let's go off
And bear us like the time.   *Flourish. Exeunt.*

EPILOGUE

Enter Speaker of the Epilogue.

I would now ask ye how ye like the play,
But, as it is with schoolboys, cannot say.
I am cruel fearful! Pray yet, stay a while,
And let me look upon ye. No man smile?
Then it goes hard, I see. He that has   5
Loved a young handsome wench, then, show his face –
'Tis strange if none be here – and, if he will,
Against his conscience let him hiss, and kill
Our market. 'Tis in vain, I see, to stay ye:
Have at the worst can come then! Now, what say ye?   10
And yet mistake me not: I am not bold;
We have no such cause. If the tale we have told
(For 'tis no other) any way content ye –
For to that honest purpose it was meant ye –
We have our end; and ye shall have ere long,   15
I dare say, many a better, to prolong
Your old loves to us. We, and all our might,
Rest at your service. Gentlemen, goodnight!

Flourish. Exit.

The Winter's Tale

Shakespeare's imagination is at full throttle in *The Winter's Tale*. It is an innovative, experimental and highly sophisticated play – what we might expect from Shakespeare in almost the last phase of his writing. It plumbs the depths of grief, despair and shame but finds a way out of them, unbelievably – and this is the point – into reconciliation and heart-stopping joy. The play was most likely written in late 1610 or early 1611, a short while after *Cymbeline* and a few months before *The Tempest*. These are the last plays that Shakespeare wrote by himself, and there is every sign he intended them to be taken together as a group, all designed for performance by the King's Men at their public outdoor theatre, the Globe, their upscale indoor theatre, the Blackfriars, and at the Court. The audiences Shakespeare was writing for could not have been more diverse in outlook and tastes. The three plays have generic features in common – for example, royal children who are lost and believed to be dead, but who have survived and are made stronger and rewarded by their ordeals (Innogen and her brothers in *Cymbeline*, Ferdinand in *The Tempest*, Perdita in *The Winter's Tale*). The storyline in each play pushes its audience to the edge of what it can believe, and beyond: the king told a nobleman to do away with the baby princess and he took the baby to expose her on the shore but a storm came and his ship sank and all the sailors died and a bear came and ate the nobleman but not the princess, and a shepherd and his son made the baby part of the family. And the king learnt that the baby was not a bastard, but his true child and the queen died and his son the prince died. This is just a portion of the story of Act 3 of *The Winter's Tale*. One member of the Globe audience in 1611 remembered the action in these terms, and in exactly this sort of simple language, though he did not mention other things equally improbable – most noticeably the statute of the dead queen that comes to life in Act 5 – or rather rather not a statue but Hermione in the flesh, who has been no less improbably kept secretly alive by Paulina for sixteen years. The implausible sequence is that of a fairy tale or a 'winter's tale', which is what the Elizabethans called stories like this.

Fairy and folk tales are often recapitulative, as are chivalric romances (such as *Don Quixote*, which Shakespeare later drew on for *Cardenio*, the lost Shakespeare–Fletcher collaboration that underlies *Double Falsehood*). What happens in the first half of the tale – a crime or dreadful deed – is retraced in some benign way that ends in a happy outcome, though never without loss. *The Winter's Tale* is organized like this, on many levels. In Act 1, Leontes, the king, fantasizes grossly about his wife Hermione's infidelity, to the point where he denies, madly and wickedly, everything that is natural and true (she is innocent). Because of this, the play is set to be a tragedy, a perpetual winter, and Leontes' young son does indeed die. Sixteen years later, however, the king's wickedness is undone, symbolically and emotionally, in the festival in Act 4 by his lost daughter Perdita (the baby princess). She brings back the spring in an exquisite classical mythology, which Shakespeare drew from his favourite writer, the Roman poet Ovid. The mythology is that 'great creating Nature' (Perdita's description at 4.4.88) will not allow unnatural male thoughts to pervert and overwhelm it. Because of Nature's counter-story, tragedy is superseded by tragicomedy and romance, the two generic terms most favoured by modern critics of the play.

It is Shakespeare's integration of the disparate elements in *The Winter's Tale* that makes it a masterpiece. He places folk culture and rough-and-tumble vignettes of ordinary lives – men getting drunk, rustic girls on the lookout for husbands, a backroads conman cheating, thieving and whoring – alongside high-born high culture, with royalty in disguise and predatory. It was a story that another writer, Robert Greene, had already told in outline more than twenty years earlier in his prose romance *Pandosto*, though without the classical infusions (from Ovid and Euripides, and Aristotle's *Poetics*) and without Shakespeare's *almost* happy outcome. (It is worth remembering that Hermione never speaks to Leontes after she steps down from the plinth.) And it is perhaps of more than passing interest that it was Greene, on his deathbed in 1592, who wrote a wounding attack on Shakespeare – that he was an uneducated, jumped-up hack, who stole his good bits from better writers. Perhaps for Shakespeare, repurposing Greene's novella as *The Winter's Tale* became another way of undoing old hurt and sorrow, the second half of a personal story.

The Arden text is based on the 1623 First Folio.

LIST OF ROLES

SICILIA

LEONTES	*King of Sicilia*
MAMILLIUS	*young prince of Sicilia*
CAMILLO	
ANTIGONUS	*four lords of Sicilia*
CLEOMENES	
DION	
HERMIONE	*queen to Leontes*
PERDITA	*daughter to Leontes and Hermione*
PAULINA	*wife to Antigonus*
EMILIA	*a lady-in-waiting to Hermione*
GAOLER	
GENTLEMAN	
ROGERO	*a gentleman*
STEWARD	*servant to Paulina*
MARINER	
OFFICERS	*at Hermione's trial*
SERVANT	*to Mamillius*
LORDS	
LADIES	

BOHEMIA

POLIXENES	*King of Bohemia*
FLORIZEL	*prince of Bohemia, at first under the assumed name of Doricles*
SHEPHERD	*reputed father of Perdita*
CLOWN	*his son*
AUTOLYCUS	*a rogue*
ARCHIDAMUS	*a lord of Bohemia*
SERVANT	
MOPSA	
DORCAS	*shepherdesses*
TIME	*as Chorus*

Other Lords, Ladies and Gentlemen, Servants, Attendants

Shepherds and Shepherdesses, Twelve rustic Dancers dressed as satyrs, Bear

1.1 *Enter* CAMILLO *and* ARCHIDAMUS.

ARCHIDAMUS If you shall chance, Camillo, to visit
Bohemia on the like occasion whereon my services are
now on foot, you shall see, as I have said, great
difference betwixt our Bohemia and your Sicilia.

CAMILLO I think this coming summer the King of
Sicilia means to pay Bohemia the visitation which he
justly owes him.

ARCHIDAMUS Wherein our entertainment shall shame
us, we will be justified in our loves; for indeed –

CAMILLO Beseech you –

ARCHIDAMUS Verily, I speak it in the freedom of my
knowledge. We cannot with such magnificence – in so
rare – I know not what to say. We will give you sleepy
drinks, that your senses, unintelligent of our
insufficience, may, though they cannot praise us, as
little accuse us.

CAMILLO You pay a great deal too dear for what's given
freely.

ARCHIDAMUS Believe me, I speak as my understanding
instructs me, and as mine honesty puts it to utterance.

CAMILLO Sicilia cannot show himself over-kind to
Bohemia. They were trained together in their
childhoods, and there rooted betwixt them then such
an affection which cannot choose but branch now.
Since their more mature dignities and royal necessities
made separation of their society, their encounters –
though not personal – hath been royally attorneyed
with interchange of gifts, letters, loving embassies, that
they have seemed to be together, though absent; shook
hands as over a vast; and embraced as it were from the
ends of opposed winds. The heavens continue their
loves.

ARCHIDAMUS I think there is not in the world either
malice or matter to alter it. You have an unspeakable
comfort of your young prince, Mamillius. It is a
gentleman of the greatest promise that ever came into
my note.

CAMILLO I very well agree with you in the hopes of
him. It is a gallant child; one that, indeed, physics the
subject, makes old hearts fresh. They that went on
crutches ere he was born desire yet their life to see him
a man.

ARCHIDAMUS Would they else be content to die?

CAMILLO Yes, if there were no other excuse why they
should desire to live.

ARCHIDAMUS If the king had no son they would desire
to live on crutches till he had one. *Exeunt.*

1.2 *Enter* LEONTES, HERMIONE, MAMILLIUS,
    POLIXENES *and* CAMILLO.

POLIXENES Nine changes of the watery star hath been
The shepherd's note since we have left our throne
Without a burden. Time as long again
Would be filled up, my brother, with our thanks,
And yet we should for perpetuity
Go hence in debt. And therefore, like a cipher,
Yet standing in rich place, I multiply
With one 'we thank you' many thousands moe
That go before it.

LEONTES   Stay your thanks a while,
And pay them when you part.

POLIXENES   Sir, that's tomorrow.
I am questioned by my fears of what may chance
Or breed upon our absence, that may blow
No sneaping winds at home to make us say
This is put forth too truly. Besides, I have stayed
To tire your royalty.

LEONTES   We are tougher, brother,
Than you can put us to't.

POLIXENES   No longer stay.

LEONTES One sev'night longer.

POLIXENES   Very sooth, tomorrow.

LEONTES
We'll part the time between's then; and in that
I'll no gainsaying.

POLIXENES   Press me not, beseech you, so.
There is no tongue that moves, none, none i'th' world
So soon as yours, could win me. So it should now,
Were there necessity in your request, although
'Twere needful I denied it. My affairs
Do even drag me homeward; which to hinder
Were, in your love, a whip to me; my stay,
To you a charge and trouble. To save both,
Farewell, our brother.

LEONTES   Tongue-tied, our queen? Speak you.

HERMIONE
I had thought, sir, to have held my peace until
You had drawn oaths from him not to stay. You, sir,
Charge him too coldly. Tell him you are sure
All in Bohemia's well; this satisfaction
The bygone day proclaimed. Say this to him,
He's beat from his best ward.

LEONTES   Well said, Hermione.

HERMIONE To tell he longs to see his son were strong;
But let him say so then, and let him go;
But let him swear so and he shall not stay,
We'll thwack him hence with distaffs.
[*to Polixenes*] Yet of your royal presence I'll adventure
The borrow of a week. When at Bohemia
You take my lord, I'll give him my commission
To let him there a month behind the gest
Prefixed for's parting: yet, good deed, Leontes,
I love thee not a jar o'th' clock behind
What lady she her lord. You'll stay?

POLIXENES   No, madam.

HERMIONE Nay, but you will.

POLIXENES   I may not, verily.

HERMIONE Verily?
You put me off with limber vows. But I,
Though you would seek t'unsphere the stars with oaths,
Should yet say 'Sir, no going'. Verily

50 You shall not go. A lady's 'verily' is
   As potent as a lord's. Will you go yet?
   Force me to keep you as a prisoner,
   Not like a guest: so you shall pay your fees
   When you depart, and save your thanks. How say you?
55 My prisoner? Or my guest? By your dread 'verily',
   One of them you shall be.
POLIXENES   Your guest then, madam.
   To be your prisoner should import offending,
   Which is for me less easy to commit
   Than you to punish.
HERMIONE   Not your gaoler then,
60 But your kind hostess. Come, I'll question you
   Of my lord's tricks and yours when you were boys.
   You were pretty lordings then?
POLIXENES   We were, fair queen,
   Two lads that thought there was no more behind
   But such a day tomorrow as today,
   And to be boy eternal.
65 HERMIONE   Was not my lord
   The verier wag o'th' two?
POLIXENES
   We were as twinned lambs that did frisk i'th' sun
   And bleat the one at th'other: what we changed
   Was innocence for innocence; we knew not
70 The doctrine of ill-doing, nor dreamed
   That any did. Had we pursued that life,
   And our weak spirits ne'er been higher reared
   With stronger blood, we should have answered heaven
   Boldly, 'not guilty', the imposition cleared
   Hereditary ours.
75 HERMIONE   By this we gather
   You have tripped since.
POLIXENES   O my most sacred lady,
   Temptations have since then been born to's, for
   In those unfledged days was my wife a girl;
   Your precious self had then not crossed the eyes
   Of my young playfellow.
80 HERMIONE   Grace to boot!
   Of this make no conclusion, lest you say
   Your queen and I are devils. Yet go on.
   Th'offences we have made you do we'll answer,
   If you first sinned with us, and that with us
85 You did continue fault, and that you slipped not
   With any but with us.
LEONTES   Is he won yet?
HERMIONE   He'll stay, my lord.
LEONTES   At my request he would not.
   Hermione, my dearest, thou never spok'st
   To better purpose.
HERMIONE   Never?
LEONTES   Never, but once.
HERMIONE
90 What? Have I twice said well? When was't before?
   I prithee tell me; cram's with praise, and make's
   As fat as tame things. One good deed, dying
      tongueless,

Slaughters a thousand waiting upon that.
Our praises are our wages. You may ride's
With one soft kiss a thousand furlongs ere   95
With spur we heat an acre. But to th' goal:
My last good deed was to entreat his stay.
What was my first? It has an elder sister,
Or I mistake you. O, would her name were Grace!
But once before I spoke to th' purpose? When?   100
Nay, let me have't – I long.
LEONTES   Why, that was when
Three crabbed months had soured themselves to
   death
Ere I could make thee open thy white hand
And clap thyself my love. Then didst thou utter,
'I am yours for ever.'
HERMIONE   'Tis grace indeed.   105
Why, lo you now, I have spoke to th' purpose twice.
The one for ever earned a royal husband;
Th'other for some while a friend.
   [*Gives her hand to Polixenes.*]
LEONTES [*aside*]   Too hot, too hot!
To mingle friendship far is mingling bloods.
I have *tremor cordis* on me. My heart dances,   110
But not for joy, not joy. This entertainment
May a free face put on, derive a liberty
From heartiness, from bounty, fertile bosom,
And well become the agent – 't may, I grant –
But to be paddling palms and pinching fingers,   115
As now they are, and making practised smiles
As in a looking-glass; and then to sigh, as 'twere
The mort o'th' deer – O, that is entertainment
My bosom likes not, nor my brows. – Mamillius,
Art thou my boy?
MAMILLIUS   Ay, my good lord.
LEONTES   I'fecks;   120
Why, that's my bawcock. What? Hast smutched thy
   nose?
They say it is a copy out of mine. Come, captain,
We must be neat – not neat, but cleanly, captain.
   [*Wipes Mamillius' face.*]
And yet the steer, the heifer and the calf
Are all called neat. – Still virginalling   125
Upon his palm? – How now, you wanton calf!
Art thou my calf?
MAMILLIUS   Yes, if you will, my lord.
LEONTES
Thou want'st a rough pash and the shoots that I have
To be full like me. Yet they say we are
Almost as like as eggs – women say so,   130
That will say anything. But were they false
As o'erdyed blacks, as wind, as waters, false
As dice are to be wished by one that fixes
No bourn 'twixt his and mine, yet were it true
To say this boy were like me. Come, sir page,   135
Look on me with your welkin eye. Sweet villain,
Most dearest, my collop! Can thy dam? May't be
Affection? – Thy intention stabs the centre,

Thou dost make possible things not so held,
Communicat'st with dreams – how can this be? –
With what's unreal thou coactive art,
And fellow'st nothing. Then 'tis very credent
Thou mayst co-join with something, and thou dost,
And that beyond commission, and I find it,
And that to the infection of my brains
And hard'ning of my brows.

POLIXENES   What means Sicilia?

HERMIONE
He something seems unsettled.

POLIXENES   How? My lord?

LEONTES
What cheer? How is't with you, best brother?

HERMIONE   You look
As if you held a brow of much distraction.
Are you moved, my lord?

LEONTES   No, in good earnest.
How sometimes nature will betray its folly,
Its tenderness, and make itself a pastime
To harder bosoms. Looking on the lines
Of my boy's face, methoughts I did recoil
Twenty-three years, and saw myself unbreeched,
In my green velvet coat; my dagger muzzled,
Lest it should bite its master, and so prove,
As ornaments oft does, too dangerous.
How like, methought, I then was to this kernel,
This squash, this gentleman. Mine honest friend,
Will you take eggs for money?

MAMILLIUS   No, my lord, I'll fight.

LEONTES
You will? Why, happy man be's dole! My brother,
Are you so fond of your young prince as we
Do seem to be of ours?

POLIXENES   If at home, sir,
He's all my exercise, my mirth, my matter;
Now my sworn friend, and then mine enemy;
My parasite, my soldier, statesman, all.
He makes a July's day short as December,
And with his varying childness cures in me
Thoughts that would thick my blood.

LEONTES   So stands this squire
Officed with me. We two will walk, my lord,
And leave you to your graver steps. Hermione,
How thou lov'st us show in our brother's welcome.
Let what is dear in Sicily be cheap.
Next to thyself and my young rover, he's
Apparent to my heart.

HERMIONE   If you would seek us,
We are yours i'th' garden. Shall's attend you there?

LEONTES
To your own bents dispose you. You'll be found,
Be you beneath the sky. [*aside*] I am angling now,
Though you perceive me not how I give line.
Go to, go to!
How she holds up the neb, the bill to him,
And arms her with the boldness of a wife

To her allowing husband.

                              Exeunt Polixenes and Hermione.
                              Gone already.
Inch-thick, knee-deep, o'er head and ears a forked one!
Go play, boy, play. Thy mother plays, and I
Play too; but so disgraced a part, whose issue
Will hiss me to my grave. Contempt and clamour
Will be my knell. Go play, boy, play. There have been,
Or I am much deceived, cuckolds ere now,
And many a man there is even at this present,
Now, while I speak this, holds his wife by th'arm,
That little thinks she has been sluiced in's absence,
And his pond fished by his next neighbour, by
Sir Smile, his neighbour. Nay, there's comfort in't,
Whiles other men have gates, and those gates opened,
As mine, against their will. Should all despair
That have revolted wives, the tenth of mankind
Would hang themselves. Physic for't there's none:
It is a bawdy planet, that will strike
Where 'tis predominant; and 'tis powerful, think it,
From east, west, north and south; be it concluded,
No barricado for a belly. Know't,
It will let in and out the enemy
With bag and baggage. Many thousand on's
Have the disease and feel't not. How now, boy?

MAMILLIUS   I am like you, they say.

LEONTES   Why, that's some comfort.
What, Camillo there!

CAMILLO [*Comes forward.*] Ay, my good lord.

LEONTES   Go play, Mamillius; thou'rt an honest man.
                              Exit Mamillius.
Camillo, this great sir will yet stay longer.

CAMILLO   You had much ado to make his anchor hold;
When you cast out, it still came home.

LEONTES   Didst note it?

CAMILLO   He would not stay at your petitions, made
His business more material.

LEONTES   Didst perceive it?
[*aside*] They're here with me already, whispering,
     rounding,
'Sicilia is a so-forth.' 'Tis far gone
When I shall gust it last. – How came't, Camillo,
That he did stay?

CAMILLO   At the good queen's entreaty.

LEONTES
'At the queen's' be't; 'good' should be pertinent,
But so it is, it is not. Was this taken
By any understanding pate but thine?
For thy conceit is soaking, will draw in
More than the common blocks. Not noted, is't,
But of the finer natures? By some severals
Of head-piece extraordinary? Lower messes
Perchance are to this business purblind? Say.

CAMILLO   Business, my lord? I think most understand
Bohemia stays here longer.

LEONTES   Ha?

CAMILLO   Stays here longer.

LEONTES   Ay, but why?

230   CAMILLO   To satisfy your highness, and the entreaties
Of our most gracious mistress.

LEONTES   Satisfy?
Th'entreaties of your mistress? Satisfy?
Let that suffice. I have trusted thee, Camillo,
With all the nearest things to my heart, as well

235   My chamber-counsels, wherein, priest-like, thou
Hast cleansed my bosom; I from thee departed
Thy penitent reformed. But we have been
Deceived in thy integrity, deceived
In that which seems so.

CAMILLO   Be it forbid, my lord.

240   LEONTES   To bide upon't: thou art not honest; or
If thou inclin'st that way, thou art a coward,
Which hoxes honesty behind, restraining
From course required. Or else thou must be counted
A servant grafted in my serious trust,

245   And therein negligent; or else a fool,
That seest a game played home, the rich stake drawn,
And tak'st it all for jest.

CAMILLO   My gracious lord,
I may be negligent, foolish and fearful;
In every one of these no man is free,

250   But that his negligence, his folly, fear,
Among the infinite doings of the world
Sometime puts forth. In your affairs, my lord,
If ever I were wilful-negligent,
It was my folly; if industriously

255   I played the fool, it was my negligence,
Not weighing well the end; if ever fearful
To do a thing where I the issue doubted,
Whereof the execution did cry out
Against the non-performance, 'twas a fear

260   Which oft infects the wisest. These, my lord,
Are such allowed infirmities that honesty
Is never free of. But beseech your grace
Be plainer with me, let me know my trespass
By its own visage. If I then deny it,
'Tis none of mine.

265   LEONTES   Ha' not you seen, Camillo –
But that's past doubt; you have, or your eye-glass
Is thicker than a cuckold's horn – or heard –
For, to a vision so apparent, rumour
Cannot be mute – or thought – for cogitation

270   Resides not in that man that does not think –
My wife is slippery? If thou wilt confess –
Or else be impudently negative
To have nor eyes, nor ears, nor thought – then say
My wife's a hobby-horse, deserves a name

275   As rank as any flax-wench that puts to
Before her troth-plight. Say't, and justify't.

CAMILLO   I would not be a stander-by to hear
My sovereign mistress clouded so without
My present vengeance taken. 'Shrew my heart,

280   You never spoke what did become you less
Than this; which to reiterate were sin

As deep as that, though true.

LEONTES   Is whispering nothing?
Is leaning cheek to cheek? Is meeting noses?
Kissing with inside lip? Stopping the career
Of laughter with a sigh? – A note infallible   285
Of breaking honesty. Horsing foot on foot?
Skulking in corners? Wishing clocks more swift?
Hours, minutes? Noon, midnight? And all eyes
Blind with the pin and web but theirs, theirs only,
That would unseen be wicked? Is this nothing?   290
Why then the world and all that's in't is nothing,
The covering sky is nothing, Bohemia nothing,
My wife is nothing, nor nothing have these nothings,
If this be nothing.

CAMILLO   Good my lord, be cured
Of this diseased opinion, and betimes,   295
For 'tis most dangerous.

LEONTES   Say it be, 'tis true.

CAMILLO   No, no, my lord.

LEONTES   It is – you lie, you lie!
I say thou liest, Camillo, and I hate thee,
Pronounce thee a gross lout, a mindless slave,
Or else a hovering temporizer, that   300
Canst with thine eyes at once see good and evil,
Inclining to them both. Were my wife's liver
Infected as her life, she would not live
The running of one glass.

CAMILLO   Who does infect her?

LEONTES
Why, he that wears her like her medal, hanging   305
About his neck, Bohemia – who, if I
Had servants true about me, that bare eyes
To see alike mine honour as their profits,
Their own particular thrifts, they would do that
Which should undo more doing. Ay, and thou   310
His cupbearer – whom I from meaner form
Have benched, and reared to worship, who mayst see
Plainly as heaven sees earth and earth sees heaven,
How I am galled – mightst bespice a cup
To give mine enemy a lasting wink,   315
Which draught to me were cordial.

CAMILLO   Sir, my lord,
I could do this, and that with no rash potion,
But with a lingering dram that should not work
Maliciously, like poison. But I cannot
Believe this crack to be in my dread mistress,   320
So sovereignly being honourable.
I have loved thee –

LEONTES   Make that thy question, and go rot!
Dost think I am so muddy, so unsettled,
To appoint myself in this vexation? Sully
The purity and whiteness of my sheets –   325
Which to preserve is sleep; which being spotted
Is goads, thorns, nettles, tails of wasps –
Give scandal to the blood o'th' prince, my son,
Who I do think is mine, and love as mine,
Without ripe moving to't? Would I do this?   330

Could man so blench?

CAMILLO   I must believe you, sir.
I do, and will fetch off Bohemia for't,
Provided that when he's removed your highness
Will take again your queen as yours at first,
Even for your son's sake, and thereby for sealing   335
The injury of tongues in courts and kingdoms
Known and allied to yours.

LEONTES   Thou dost advise me
Even so as I mine own course have set down.
I'll give no blemish to her honour, none.

CAMILLO   My lord,
Go then, and, with a countenance as clear   340
As friendship wears at feasts, keep with Bohemia
And with your queen. I am his cupbearer.
If from me he have wholesome beverage,
Account me not your servant.

LEONTES   This is all.
Do't, and thou hast the one half of my heart;   345
Do't not, thou splitt'st thine own.

CAMILLO   I'll do't, my lord.

LEONTES   I will seem friendly, as thou hast advised me.
                                                      Exit.

CAMILLO   O miserable lady. But for me,
What case stand I in? I must be the poisoner
Of good Polixenes, and my ground to do't   350
Is the obedience to a master – one
Who in rebellion with himself will have
All that are his so too. To do this deed,
Promotion follows. If I could find example
Of thousands that had struck anointed kings   355
And flourished after, I'd not do't. But since
Nor brass, nor stone, nor parchment bears not one,
Let villainy itself forswear't. I must
Forsake the court. To do't or no is certain
To me a break-neck. Happy star reign now!   360

              Enter POLIXENES.

Here comes Bohemia.

POLIXENES [*aside*]   This is strange. Methinks
My favour here begins to warp. Not speak?
– Good day, Camillo.

CAMILLO   Hail, most royal sir.

POLIXENES   What is the news i'th' court?

CAMILLO   None rare, my lord.

POLIXENES   The king hath on him such a countenance   365
As he had lost some province, and a region
Loved as he loves himself. Even now I met him
With customary compliment, when he,
Wafting his eyes to th' contrary and falling
A lip of much contempt, speeds from me, and   370
So leaves me to consider what is breeding
That changes thus his manners.

CAMILLO   I dare not know, my lord.

POLIXENES
How, dare not? Do not? Do you know, and dare not?
Be intelligent to me – 'tis thereabouts;

For to yourself what you do know you must,   375
And cannot say you dare not. Good Camillo,
Your changed complexions are to me a mirror
Which shows me mine changed too; for I must be
A party in this alteration, finding
Myself thus altered with't.

CAMILLO   There is a sickness   380
Which puts some of us in distemper, but
I cannot name the disease, and it is caught
Of you that yet are well.

POLIXENES   How caught of me?
Make me not sighted like the basilisk.
I have looked on thousands who have sped the better   385
By my regard, but killed none so. Camillo,
As you are certainly a gentleman, thereto
Clerk-like experienced, which no less adorns
Our gentry than our parents' noble names,
In whose success we are gentle; I beseech you,   390
If you know aught which does behove my knowledge
Thereof to be informed, imprison't not
In ignorant concealment.

CAMILLO   I may not answer.

POLIXENES   A sickness caught of me, and yet I 'well'.
I must be answered. Dost thou hear, Camillo?   395
I conjure thee, by all the parts of man
Which honour does acknowledge, whereof the least
Is not this suit of mine, that thou declare
What incidency thou dost guess of harm
Is creeping toward me; how far off, how near,   400
Which way to be prevented, if to be;
If not, how best to bear it.

CAMILLO   Sir, I will tell you,
Since I am charged in honour, and by him
That I think honourable. Therefore mark my counsel,
Which must be ev'n as swiftly followed as   405
I mean to utter it, or both yourself and me
Cry lost, and so good night!

POLIXENES   On, good Camillo.

CAMILLO   I am appointed him to murder you.

POLIXENES   By whom, Camillo?

CAMILLO   By the king.

POLIXENES   For what?

CAMILLO
He thinks – nay, with all confidence he swears,   410
As he had seen't, or been an instrument
To vice you to't – that you have touched his queen
Forbiddenly.

POLIXENES   O, then my best blood turn
To an infected jelly and my name
Be yoked with his that did betray the best!   415
Turn then my freshest reputation to
A savour that may strike the dullest nostril
Where I arrive, and my approach be shunned,
Nay hated too, worse than the great'st infection
That e'er was heard or read.

CAMILLO   Swear his thought over   420
By each particular star in heaven and

By all their influences, you may as well
Forbid the sea for to obey the moon
As or by oath remove or counsel shake
425 The fabric of his folly, whose foundation
Is piled upon his faith and will continue
The standing of his body.

POLIXENES   How should this grow?

CAMILLO   I know not, but I am sure 'tis safer to
Avoid what's grown than question how 'tis born.
430 If therefore you dare trust my honesty,
That lies enclosed in this trunk which you
Shall bear along impawned, away tonight!
Your followers I will whisper to the business,
And will by twos and threes at several posterns
435 Clear them o'th' city. For myself, I'll put
My fortunes to your service, which are here
By this discovery lost. Be not uncertain,
For, by the honour of my parents, I
Have uttered truth – which, if you seek to prove,
440 I dare not stand by; nor shall you be safer
Than one condemned by the king's own mouth,
Thereon his execution sworn.

POLIXENES   I do believe thee,
I saw his heart in's face. Give me thy hand.
Be pilot to me, and thy places shall
445 Still neighbour mine. My ships are ready, and
My people did expect my hence departure
Two days ago. This jealousy
Is for a precious creature. As she's rare,
Must it be great; and, as his person's mighty,
450 Must it be violent, and as he does conceive
He is dishonoured by a man which ever
Professed to him, why, his revenges must
In that be made more bitter. Fear o'ershades me.
Good expedition be my friend, and comfort
455 The gracious queen, part of his theme, but nothing
Of his ill-ta'en suspicion. Come, Camillo,
I will respect thee as a father if
Thou bear'st my life off. Hence! Let us avoid.

CAMILLO   It is in mine authority to command
460 The keys of all the posterns. Please your highness
To take the urgent hour. Come, sir, away.   *Exeunt.*

2.1   *Enter* HERMIONE, MAMILLIUS *and* Ladies.

HERMIONE   Take the boy to you. He so troubles me,
'Tis past enduring.

1 LADY   Come, my gracious lord,
Shall I be your playfellow?

MAMILLIUS   No, I'll none of you.

1 LADY   Why, my sweet lord?

5 MAMILLIUS   You'll kiss me hard, and speak to me as if
I were a baby still. [*to Second Lady*] I love you better.

2 LADY   And why so, my lord?

MAMILLIUS   Not for because
Your brows are blacker – yet black brows they say
Become some women best, so that there be not

Too much hair there, but in a semicircle,   10
Or a half-moon made with a pen.

2 LADY   Who taught this?

MAMILLIUS
I learned it out of women's faces. Pray now,
What colour are your eyebrows?

1 LADY   Blue, my lord.

MAMILLIUS
Nay, that's a mock. I have seen a lady's nose
That has been blue, but not her eyebrows.

1 LADY   Hark ye,   15
The queen, your mother, rounds apace. We shall
Present our services to a fine new prince
One of these days, and then you'd wanton with us
If we would have you.

2 LADY   She is spread of late
Into a goodly bulk: good time encounter her!   20

HERMIONE
What wisdom stirs amongst you? Come, sir, now
I am for you again. Pray you sit by us,
And tell's a tale.

MAMILLIUS   Merry or sad shall't be?

HERMIONE   As merry as you will.

MAMILLIUS   A sad tale's best for winter. I have one   25
Of sprites and goblins.

HERMIONE   Let's have that, good sir.
Come on, sit down, come on, and do your best
To fright me with your sprites. You're powerful at it.

MAMILLIUS   There was a man –

HERMIONE   Nay, come sit down; then on.

MAMILLIUS
Dwelt by a churchyard – I will tell it softly,   30
Yon crickets shall not hear it.

HERMIONE   Come on then,
And give't me in mine ear.

Enter LEONTES, ANTIGONUS *and* Lords.

LEONTES
Was he met there? His train? Camillo with him?

LORD   Behind the tuft of pines I met them. Never
Saw I men scour so on their way. I eyed them   35
Even to their ships.

LEONTES   How blest am I
In my just censure, in my true opinion!
Alack, for lesser knowledge – how accursed
In being so blest. There may be in the cup
A spider steeped, and one may drink, depart,   40
And yet partake no venom, for his knowledge
Is not infected; but if one present
Th'abhorred ingredient to his eye, make known
How he hath drunk, he cracks his gorge, his sides,
With violent hefts. I have drunk, and seen the spider.   45
Camillo was his help in this, his pander.
There is a plot against my life, my crown;
All's true that is mistrusted. That false villain
Whom I employed was pre-employed by him.
He has discovered my design, and I   50

Remain a pinched thing – yea, a very trick
For them to play at will. How came the posterns
So easily open?
LORD   By his great authority,
Which often hath no less prevailed than so
On your command.
55 LEONTES   I know't too well.
[*to Hermione*] Give me the boy. I am glad you did not
    nurse him.
Though he does bear some signs of me, yet you
Have too much blood in him.
HERMIONE   What is this? Sport?
LEONTES
Bear the boy hence: he shall not come about her.
60 Away with him, and let her sport herself
With that she's big with, [*to Hermione*] for 'tis Polixenes
Has made thee swell thus.   *Mamillius is taken away.*
HERMIONE   But I'd say he had not,
And I'll be sworn you would believe my saying,
Howe'er you lean to th' nayward.
LEONTES   You, my lords,
65 Look on her, mark her well. Be but about
To say she is a goodly lady, and
The justice of your hearts will thereto add
'Tis pity she's not honest, honourable.
Praise her but for this her without-door form –
70 Which on my faith deserves high speech – and straight
The shrug, the hum or ha, these petty brands
That calumny doth use – O, I am out! –
That mercy does, for calumny will sear
Virtue itself – these shrugs, these hums and ha's,
75 When you have said she's goodly, come between
Ere you can say she's honest. But be't known
From him that has most cause to grieve it should be,
She's an adulteress!
HERMIONE   Should a villain say so,
The most replenished villain in the world,
80 He were as much more villain – you, my lord,
Do but mistake.
LEONTES   You have mistook, my lady,
Polixenes for Leontes. O thou thing,
Which I'll not call a creature of thy place,
Lest barbarism, making me the precedent,
85 Should a like language use to all degrees,
And mannerly distinguishment leave out
Betwixt the prince and beggar. I have said
She's an adulteress, I have said with whom.
More, she's a traitor, and Camillo is
90 A federary with her, and one that knows
What she should shame to know herself,
But with her most vile principal, that she's
A bed-swerver, even as bad as those
That vulgars give bold'st titles; ay, and privy
To this their late escape.
95 HERMIONE   No, by my life,
Privy to none of this. How will this grieve you
When you shall come to clearer knowledge, that

You thus have published me? Gentle my lord,
You scarce can right me throughly then to say
You did mistake.
LEONTES   No. If I mistake   100
In those foundations which I build upon,
The centre is not big enough to bear
A schoolboy's top. Away with her, to prison.
He who shall speak for her is afar off guilty,
But that he speaks!
HERMIONE   There's some ill planet reigns.   105
I must be patient till the heavens look
With an aspect more favourable. Good my lords,
I am not prone to weeping, as our sex
Commonly are, the want of which vain dew
Perchance shall dry your pities; but I have   110
That honourable grief lodged here which burns
Worse than tears drown. Beseech you all, my lords,
With thoughts so qualified as your charities
Shall best instruct you, measure me; and so
The king's will be performed.
LEONTES   Shall I be heard?   115
HERMIONE
Who is't that goes with me? Beseech your highness
My women may be with me, for you see
My plight requires it. Do not weep, good fools,
There is no cause. When you shall know your mistress
Has deserved prison, then abound in tears   120
As I come out; this action I now go on
Is for my better grace. Adieu, my lord.
I never wished to see you sorry; now
I trust I shall. My women, come, you have leave.
LEONTES Go, do our bidding. Hence!   125
                    Exit Hermione, as a prisoner, with Ladies.
LORD Beseech your highness, call the queen again.
ANTIGONUS
Be certain what you do, sir, lest your justice
Prove violence, in the which three great ones suffer:
Yourself, your queen, your son.
LORD   For her, my lord,
I dare my life lay down, and will do't, sir,   130
Please you t'accept it, that the queen is spotless
I'th' eyes of heaven and to you – I mean
In this which you accuse her.
ANTIGONUS   If it prove
She's otherwise, I'll keep my stables where
I lodge my wife; I'll go in couples with her;   135
Than when I feel and see her, no farther trust her;
For every inch of woman in the world,
Ay, every dram of woman's flesh, is false
If she be.
LEONTES Hold your peaces.
LORD   Good my lord –
ANTIGONUS It is for you we speak, not for ourselves.   140
You are abused, and by some putter-on
That will be damned for't. Would I knew the villain,
I would land-damn him. Be she honour-flawed,
I have three daughters – the eldest is eleven;

145   The second and the third, nine and some five.
    If this prove true, they'll pay for't. By mine honour,
    I'll geld 'em all. Fourteen they shall not see,
    To bring false generations. They are co-heirs,
    And I had rather glib myself than they
    Should not produce fair issue.

150 LEONTES   Cease, no more!
    You smell this business with a sense as cold
    As is a dead man's nose. But I do see't and feel't
    As you feel doing thus [*laying hold of Antigonus*] – and
      see withal
    The instruments that feel.

ANTIGONUS   If it be so,
155   We need no grave to bury honesty;
    There's not a grain of it the face to sweeten
    Of the whole dungy earth.

LEONTES   What! Lack I credit?

LORD   I had rather you did lack than I, my lord,
    Upon this ground; and more it would content me
160   To have her honour true than your suspicion,
    Be blamed for't how you might.

LEONTES   Why, what need we
    Commune with you of this, but rather follow
    Our forceful instigation? Our prerogative
    Calls not your counsels, but our natural goodness
165   Imparts this; which if you, or stupefied
    Or seeming so in skill, cannot or will not
    Relish a truth like us, inform yourselves
    We need no more of your advice. The matter,
    The loss, the gain, the ordering on't, is all
    Properly ours.

170 ANTIGONUS   And I wish, my liege,
    You had only in your silent judgement tried it
    Without more overture.

LEONTES   How could that be?
    Either thou art most ignorant by age,
    Or thou wert born a fool. Camillo's flight,
175   Added to their familiarity –
    Which was as gross as ever touched conjecture
    That lacked sight only, naught for approbation
    But only seeing, all other circumstances
    Made up to th' deed – doth push on this proceeding.
180   Yet for a greater confirmation –
    For in an act of this importance 'twere
    Most piteous to be wild – I have dispatched in post
    To sacred Delphos, to Apollo's temple,
    Cleomenes and Dion, whom you know
185   Of stuffed sufficiency. Now from the oracle
    They will bring all, whose spiritual counsel had,
    Shall stop or spur me. Have I done well?

LORD   Well done, my lord.

LEONTES   Though I am satisfied, and need no more
190   Than what I know, yet shall the oracle
    Give rest to th' minds of others; such as he
    Whose ignorant credulity will not
    Come up to th' truth. So have we thought it good
    From our free person she should be confined,

    Lest that the treachery of the two fled hence   195
    Be left her to perform. Come, follow us,
    We are to speak in public; for this business
    Will raise us all.

ANTIGONUS [*aside*]   To laughter, as I take it,
    If the good truth were known.   *Exeunt.*

2.2   *Enter* PAULINA, *a Gentleman and Attendants.*

PAULINA   The keeper of the prison, call to him.
    Let him have knowledge who I am.   *Exit Gentleman.*
                   Good lady,
    No court in Europe is too good for thee;
    What dost thou then in prison?

        Enter the GAOLER *and the Gentleman.*

                    Now, good sir,
    You know me, do you not?

GAOLER   For a worthy lady,   5
    And one who much I honour.

PAULINA   Pray you then,
    Conduct me to the queen.

GAOLER   I may not, madam,
    To the contrary I have express commandment.

PAULINA
    Here's ado, to lock up honesty and honour from
    Th'access of gentle visitors. Is't lawful, pray you,   10
    To see her women? Any of them? Emilia?

GAOLER   So please you, madam,
    To put apart these your attendants, I
    Shall bring Emilia forth.

PAULINA   I pray now call her. –
    Withdraw yourselves.   *Exeunt Gentleman and*
                              Attendants.

GAOLER   And, madam,   15
    I must be present at your conference.

PAULINA   Well, be't so; prithee.   *Exit Gaoler.*
    Here's such ado to make no stain a stain
    As passes colouring.

        Enter the GAOLER *with* EMILIA.

                   Dear gentlewoman,
    How fares our gracious lady?   20

EMILIA   As well as one so great and so forlorn
    May hold together. On her frights and griefs –
    Which never tender lady hath borne greater –
    She is, something before her time, delivered.

PAULINA   Aboy?

EMILIA   A daughter, and a goodly babe,   25
    Lusty, and like to live. The queen receives
    Much comfort in't; says, 'My poor prisoner,
    I am innocent as you.'

PAULINA   I dare be sworn.
    These dangerous, unsafe lunes i'th' king, beshrew them!
    He must be told on't, and he shall. The office   30
    Becomes a woman best; I'll take't upon me.
    If I prove honey-mouthed, let my tongue blister

And never to my red-looked anger be
The trumpet any more. Pray you, Emilia,
35   Commend my best obedience to the queen.
If she dares trust me with her little babe,
I'll show't the king, and undertake to be
Her advocate to th' loudest. We do not know
How he may soften at the sight o'th' child.
40   The silence often of pure innocence
Persuades when speaking fails.

EMILIA   Most worthy madam,
Your honour and your goodness is so evident
That your free undertaking cannot miss
A thriving issue; there is no lady living
45   So meet for this great errand. Please your ladyship
To visit the next room, I'll presently
Acquaint the queen of your most noble offer,
Who but today hammered of this design,
But durst not tempt a minister of honour
Lest she should be denied.

50   PAULINA   Tell her, Emilia,
I'll use that tongue I have. If wit flow from't
As boldness from my bosom, let't not be doubted
I shall do good.

EMILIA   Now be you blest for it!
I'll to the queen. Please you come something nearer.

GAOLER
55   Madam, if't please the queen to send the babe
I know not what I shall incur to pass it,
Having no warrant.

PAULINA   You need not fear it, sir.
This child was prisoner to the womb, and is
By law and process of great Nature thence
60   Freed and enfranchised, not a party to
The anger of the king, nor guilty of –
If any be – the trespass of the queen.

GAOLER   I do believe it.

PAULINA   Do not you fear. Upon mine honour, I
Will stand betwixt you and danger.   *Exeunt.*

2.3   *Enter* LEONTES.

LEONTES
Nor night nor day, no rest. It is but weakness
To bear the matter thus, mere weakness. If
The cause were not in being – part o'th' cause,
She, th'adulteress; for the harlot king
5   Is quite beyond mine arm, out of the blank
And level of my brain, plot-proof; but she
I can hook to me – say that she were gone,
Given to the fire, a moiety of my rest
Might come to me again. Who's there?

Enter a Servant.

SERVANT   My lord.

LEONTES   How does the boy?
10   SERVANT   He took good rest tonight; 'tis hoped
His sickness is discharged.

LEONTES   To see his nobleness
Conceiving the dishonour of his mother!
He straight declined, drooped, took it deeply,
Fastened and fixed the shame on't in himself,
Threw off his spirit, his appetite, his sleep,   15
And downright languished. Leave me solely. Go,
See how he fares.   *Exit Servant.*
                    Fie, fie, no thought of him.
The very thought of my revenges that way
Recoil upon me; in himself too mighty,
And in his parties, his alliance; let him be   20
Until a time may serve. For present vengeance,
Take it on her. Camillo and Polixenes
Laugh at me, make their pastime at my sorrow.
They should not laugh if I could reach them, nor
Shall she, within my power.

Enter PAULINA *carrying a baby, with* ANTIGONUS,
Lords *and the* Servant.

LORD   You must not enter.   25
PAULINA   Nay rather, good my lords, be second to me.
Fear you his tyrannous passion more, alas,
Than the queen's life? A gracious, innocent soul,
More free than he is jealous.

ANTIGONUS   That's enough.

SERVANT
Madam, he hath not slept tonight, commanded   30
None should come at him.

PAULINA   Not so hot, good sir.
I come to bring him sleep. 'Tis such as you,
That creep like shadows by him and do sigh
At each his needless heavings – such as you
Nourish the cause of his awaking. I   35
Do come with words as medicinal as true,
Honest as either, to purge him of that humour
That presses him from sleep.

LEONTES   What noise there, ho?

PAULINA   No noise, my lord, but needful conference
About some gossips for your highness.

LEONTES   How?   40
Away with that audacious lady! Antigonus,
I charged thee that she should not come about me.
I knew she would.

ANTIGONUS   I told her so, my lord,
On your displeasure's peril and on mine,
She should not visit you.

LEONTES   What, canst not rule her?   45

PAULINA   From all dishonesty he can; in this –
Unless he take the course that you have done,
Commit me for committing honour – trust it,
He shall not rule me.

ANTIGONUS   La you now, you hear,
When she will take the rein I let her run,   50
But she'll not stumble.

PAULINA [*to Leontes*]   Good my liege, I come –
And I beseech you hear me, who professes
Myself your loyal servant, your physician,

Your most obedient counsellor; yet that dares
55 Less appear so in comforting your evils
Than such as most seem yours – I say, I come
From your good queen.

LEONTES   Good queen?

PAULINA
Good queen, my lord, good queen, I say good queen,
And would by combat make her good, so were I
A man, the worst about you.

60 LEONTES   Force her hence.

PAULINA   Let him that makes but trifles of his eyes
First hand me. On mine own accord, I'll off.
But first I'll do my errand. The good queen –
For she is good – hath brought you forth a daughter;
Here 'tis; [*laying the baby down*] commends it to your
blessing.

65 LEONTES   Out!
A mankind witch! Hence with her, out o' door;
A most intelligencing bawd.

PAULINA   Not so.
I am as ignorant in that as you
In so entitling me, and no less honest
70 Than you are mad, which is enough, I'll warrant,
As this world goes, to pass for honest.

LEONTES   Traitors!
Will you not push her out? [*to Antigonus*] Give her
the bastard,
Thou dotard; thou art woman-tired, unroosted
By thy Dame Partlet here. Take up the bastard,
Take't up, I say; give't to thy crone.

75 PAULINA [*to Antigonus*]   For ever
Unvenerable be thy hands if thou
Tak'st up the princess by that forced baseness
Which he has put upon't.

LEONTES   He dreads his wife.

PAULINA
So I would you did. Then 'twere past all doubt
You'd call your children yours.

80 LEONTES   A nest of traitors!

ANTIGONUS   I am none, by this good light.

PAULINA   Nor I, nor any
But one that's here, and that's himself; for he
The sacred honour of himself, his queen's,
His hopeful son's, his babe's, betrays to slander,
85 Whose sting is sharper than the sword's; and will not –
For, as the case now stands, it is a curse
He cannot be compelled to't – once remove
The root of his opinion, which is rotten
As ever oak or stone was sound.

LEONTES   A callat
90 Of boundless tongue, who late hath beat her husband,
And now baits me! This brat is none of mine.
It is the issue of Polixenes.
Hence with it, and together with the dam
Commit them to the fire.

PAULINA   It is yours,
95 And might we lay th'old proverb to your charge,

So like you, 'tis the worse. Behold, my lords,
Although the print be little, the whole matter
And copy of the father – eye, nose, lip,
The trick of's frown, his forehead, nay, the valley,
The pretty dimples of his chin and cheek, his smiles,   100
The very mould and frame of hand, nail, finger.
And thou, good goddess Nature, which hast made it
So like to him that got it, if thou hast
The ordering of the mind too, 'mongst all colours,
No yellow in't, lest she suspect, as he does,   105
Her children not her husband's.

LEONTES   A gross hag!
[*to Antigonus*] And, lozel, thou art worthy to be hanged,
That wilt not stay her tongue.

ANTIGONUS   Hang all the husbands
That cannot do that feat, you'll leave yourself
Hardly one subject.

LEONTES   Once more, take her hence!   110

PAULINA   A most unworthy and unnatural lord
Can do no more.

LEONTES   I'll ha' thee burnt.

PAULINA   I care not.
It is an heretic that makes the fire,
Not she which burns in't. I'll not call you tyrant;
But this most cruel usage of your queen,   115
Not able to produce more accusation
Than your own weak-hinged fancy, something
savours
Of tyranny, and will ignoble make you,
Yea, scandalous to the world.

LEONTES   On your allegiance,
Out of the chamber with her! Were I a tyrant,   120
Where were her life? She durst not call me so
If she did know me one. Away with her!

PAULINA   I pray you do not push me, I'll be gone.
Look to your babe, my lord, 'tis yours – Jove send her
A better guiding spirit. What needs these hands?   125
You that are thus so tender o'er his follies
Will never do him good, not one of you.
So, so; farewell, we are gone.   *Exit.*

LEONTES [*to Antigonus*]
Thou, traitor, hast set on thy wife to this.
My child? Away with't! Even thou, that hast   130
A heart so tender o'er it, take it hence,
And see it instantly consumed with fire.
Even thou, and none but thou. Take it up straight.
Within this hour bring me word 'tis done,
And by good testimony, or I'll seize thy life,   135
With what thou else call'st thine. If thou refuse,
And wilt encounter with my wrath, say so;
The bastard brains with these my proper hands
Shall I dash out. Go, take it to the fire,
For thou set'st on thy wife.

ANTIGONUS   I did not, sir.   140
These lords, my noble fellows, if they please,
Can clear me in't.

LORDS   We can. My royal liege,

He is not guilty of her coming hither.

LEONTES   You're liars all!

145 LORD   Beseech your highness, give us better credit.
We have always truly served you, and beseech
So to esteem of us; and on our knees we beg,
As recompense of our dear services
Past and to come, that you do change this purpose,

150 Which, being so horrible, so bloody, must
Lead on to some foul issue. We all kneel.

LEONTES   I am a feather for each wind that blows.
Shall I live on, to see this bastard kneel
And call me father? Better burn it now

155 Than curse it then. But be it; let it live.
It shall not neither. [*to Antigonus*] You, sir, come you
hither,
You that have been so tenderly officious
With Lady Margery, your midwife there,
To save this bastard's life – for 'tis a bastard,

160 So sure as this beard's grey. What will you adventure
To save this brat's life?

ANTIGONUS   Anything, my lord,
That my ability may undergo,
And nobleness impose – at least thus much:
I'll pawn the little blood which I have left

165 To save the innocent – anything possible.

LEONTES   It shall be possible. Swear by this sword
Thou wilt perform my bidding.

ANTIGONUS   I will, my lord.

LEONTES
Mark, and perform it, seest thou? For the fail
Of any point in't shall not only be

170 Death to thyself but to thy lewd-tongued wife,
Whom for this time we pardon. We enjoin thee,
As thou art liegeman to us, that thou carry
This female bastard hence, and that thou bear it
To some remote and desert place, quite out

175 Of our dominions; and that there thou leave it,
Without more mercy, to it own protection
And favour of the climate. As by strange fortune
It came to us, I do in justice charge thee,
On thy soul's peril and thy body's torture,

180 That thou commend it strangely to some place
Where chance may nurse or end it. Take it up.

ANTIGONUS   I swear to do this, though a present death
Had been more merciful. [*Picks up the baby*.] Come
on, poor babe,
Some powerful spirit instruct the kites and ravens

185 To be thy nurses. Wolves and bears, they say,
Casting their savageness aside, have done
Like offices of pity. [*to Leontes*] Sir, be prosperous
In more than this deed does require; [*to the baby*] and
blessing
Against this cruelty, fight on thy side,
Poor thing, condemned to loss.
                              Exit with the baby.

190 LEONTES   No, I'll not rear
Another's issue.

Enter a Servant.

SERVANT   Please your highness, posts
From those you sent to th'oracle are come
An hour since. Cleomenes and Dion,
Being well arrived from Delphos, are both landed,
Hasting to th' court.

LORD   So please you, sir, their speed   195
Hath been beyond account.

LEONTES   Twenty-three days
They have been absent; 'tis good speed, foretells
The great Apollo suddenly will have
The truth of this appear. Prepare you, lords,
Summon a session, that we may arraign   200
Our most disloyal lady; for, as she hath
Been publicly accused, so shall she have
A just and open trial. While she lives
My heart will be a burden to me. Leave me,
And think upon my bidding.   *Exeunt.*   205

3.1   *Enter* CLEOMENES *and* DION.

CLEOMENES
The climate's delicate, the air most sweet,
Fertile the isle, the temple much surpassing
The common praise it bears.

DION   I shall report,
For most it caught me, the celestial habits –
Methinks I so should term them – and the reverence   5
Of the grave wearers. O, the sacrifice,
How ceremonious, solemn and unearthly
It was i'th' offering!

CLEOMENES   But of all, the burst
And the ear-deafening voice o'th' oracle,
Kin to Jove's thunder, so surprised my sense   10
That I was nothing.

DION   If th'event o'th' journey
Prove as successful to the queen – O, be't so –
As it hath been to us rare, pleasant, speedy,
The time is worth the use on't.

CLEOMENES   Great Apollo
Turn all to th' best. These proclamations,   15
So forcing faults upon Hermione,
I little like.

DION   The violent carriage of it
Will clear or end the business. When the oracle,
Thus by Apollo's great divine sealed up,
Shall the contents discover, something rare   20
Even then will rush to knowledge. Go. Fresh horses!
And gracious be the issue.   *Exeunt.*

3.2   *Enter* LEONTES, Lords *and* Officers.

LEONTES
This sessions, to our great grief we pronounce,
Even pushes 'gainst our heart; the party tried,
The daughter of a king, our wife, and one

Of us too much beloved. Let us be cleared
5   Of being tyrannous, since we so openly
Proceed in justice, which shall have due course
Even to the guilt or the purgation.
Produce the prisoner.

OFFICER   It is his highness' pleasure that the queen
Appear in person here in court.

Enter HERMIONE *as a prisoner, with* PAULINA
and Ladies.

10   Silence.

LEONTES   Read the indictment.

OFFICER [*Reads.*]   *Hermione, queen to the worthy Leontes,*
King of Sicilia, thou art here accused and arraigned of
high treason in committing adultery with Polixenes, King
15   *of Bohemia, and conspiring with Camillo to take away the*
life of our sovereign lord the king, thy royal husband; the
pretence whereof being by circumstances partly laid open,
thou, Hermione, contrary to the faith and allegiance of a
true subject, didst counsel and aid them for their better
20   *safety to fly away by night.*

HERMIONE   Since what I am to say must be but that
Which contradicts my accusation, and
The testimony on my part no other
But what comes from myself, it shall scarce boot me
25   To say 'Not guilty'. Mine integrity
Being counted falsehood shall, as I express it,
Be so received. But thus: if powers divine
Behold our human actions – as they do –
I doubt not then but innocence shall make
30   False accusation blush and tyranny
Tremble at patience. You, my lord, best know,
Whom least will seem to do so, my past life
Hath been as continent, as chaste, as true
As I am now unhappy; which is more
35   Than history can pattern, though devised
And played to take spectators. For behold me,
A fellow of the royal bed, which owe
A moiety of the throne; a great king's daughter,
The mother to a hopeful prince, here standing
40   To prate and talk for life and honour, 'fore
Who please to come and hear. For life, I prize it
As I weigh grief, which I would spare. For honour,
'Tis a derivative from me to mine,
And only that I stand for. I appeal
45   To your own conscience, sir, before Polixenes
Came to your court how I was in your grace,
How merited to be so; since he came,
With what encounter so uncurrent I
Have strained t'appear thus. If one jot beyond
50   The bound of honour, or in act, or will
That way inclining, hardened be the hearts
Of all that hear me, and my nearest of kin
Cry fie upon my grave.

LEONTES   I ne'er heard yet
That any of these bolder vices wanted
55   Less impudence to gainsay what they did

Than to perform it first.

HERMIONE   That's true enough,
Though 'tis a saying, sir, not due to me.

LEONTES   You will not own it.

HERMIONE   More than mistress of
Which comes to me in name of fault, I must not
At all acknowledge. For Polixenes,   60
With whom I am accused, I do confess
I loved him as in honour he required;
With such a kind of love as might become
A lady like me; with a love, even such,
So, and no other, as yourself commanded;   65
Which not to have done, I think, had been in me
Both disobedience and ingratitude
To you and toward your friend, whose love had spoke
Even since it could speak, from an infant, freely
That it was yours. Now, for conspiracy,   70
I know not how it tastes, though it be dished
For me to try how. All I know of it
Is that Camillo was an honest man;
And why he left your court the gods themselves,
Wotting no more than I, are ignorant.   75

LEONTES   You knew of his departure, as you know
What you have underta'en to do in's absence.

HERMIONE   Sir,
You speak a language that I understand not.
My life stands in the level of your dreams,
Which I'll lay down.

LEONTES   Your actions are my dreams.   80
You had a bastard by Polixenes,
And I but dreamed it. As you were past all shame –
Those of your fact are so – so past all truth;
Which to deny concerns more than avails; for as
Thy brat hath been cast out, like to itself,   85
No father owning it – which is indeed
More criminal in thee than it – so thou
Shalt feel our justice, in whose easiest passage
Look for no less than death.

HERMIONE   Sir, spare your threats.
The bug which you would fright me with I seek.   90
To me can life be no commodity;
The crown and comfort of my life, your favour,
I do give lost, for I do feel it gone
But know not how it went. My second joy,
And first fruits of my body, from his presence   95
I am barred, like one infectious. My third comfort,
Starred most unluckily, is from my breast,
The innocent milk in it most innocent mouth,
Haled out to murder; myself on every post
Proclaimed a strumpet; with immodest hatred   100
The childbed privilege denied, which 'longs
To women of all fashion; lastly, hurried
Here, to this place, i'th' open air, before
I have got strength of limit. Now, my liege,
Tell me what blessings I have here alive,   105
That I should fear to die. Therefore proceed.
But yet hear this – mistake me not – no life,

I prize it not a straw, but for mine honour,
Which I would free – if I shall be condemned
110 Upon surmises, all proofs sleeping else
But what your jealousies awake, I tell you
'Tis rigour, and not law. Your honours all,
I do refer me to the oracle.
Apollo be my judge.

LORD   This your request
115 Is altogether just. Therefore bring forth,
And in Apollo's name, his oracle.

                        Exeunt certain Officers.

HERMIONE   The Emperor of Russia was my father.
O that he were alive, and here beholding
His daughter's trial; that he did but see
120 The flatness of my misery; yet with eyes
Of pity, not revenge.

       Enter Officers *with* CLEOMENES *and* DION.

OFFICER
You here shall swear upon this sword of justice,
That you, Cleomenes and Dion, have
Been both at Delphos, and from thence have brought
125 This sealed-up oracle, by the hand delivered
Of great Apollo's priest; and that since then
You have not dared to break the holy seal,
Nor read the secrets in't.

CLEOMENES, DION   All this we swear.

LEONTES   Break up the seals and read.

130 OFFICER [*Reads.*]   *Hermione is chaste, Polixenes blameless,*
Camillo a true subject, Leontes a jealous tyrant, his
innocent babe truly begotten, and the king shall live
without an heir if that which is lost be not found.

LORDS   Now blessed be the great Apollo!

HERMIONE   Praised!

LEONTES   Hast thou read truth?

135 OFFICER   Ay, my lord, even so
As it is here set down.

LEONTES   There is no truth at all i'th' oracle.
The sessions shall proceed – this is mere falsehood.

                Enter a Servant.

SERVANT   My lord the king! The king!

LEONTES   What is the business?

140 SERVANT   O sir, I shall be hated to report it.
The prince your son, with mere conceit and fear
Of the queen's speed, is gone.

LEONTES   How, 'gone'?

SERVANT   Is dead.

LEONTES   Apollo's angry, and the heavens themselves
Do strike at my injustice.   [*Hermione faints.*]
                   How now there?

PAULINA
145 This news is mortal to the queen. Look down
And see what death is doing.

LEONTES   Take her hence.
Her heart is but o'ercharged. She will recover.
I have too much believed mine own suspicion.

Beseech you, tenderly apply to her
Some remedies for life.   *Exeunt Paulina and Ladies,*
                 carrying Hermione, and Servant.
                  Apollo, pardon 150
My great profaneness 'gainst thine oracle.
I'll reconcile me to Polixenes,
New woo my queen, recall the good Camillo,
Whom I proclaim a man of truth, of mercy;
For being transported by my jealousies 155
To bloody thoughts and to revenge, I chose
Camillo for the minister to poison
My friend Polixenes, which had been done,
But that the good mind of Camillo tardied
My swift command. Though I with death and with 160
Reward did threaten and encourage him,
Not doing it and being done, he, most humane
And filled with honour, to my kingly guest
Unclasped my practice, quit his fortunes here –
Which you knew great – and to the certain hazard 165
Of all incertainties himself commended,
No richer than his honour. How he glisters
Through my rust! And how his piety
Does my deeds make the blacker!

              Enter PAULINA.

PAULINA   Woe the while!
O cut my lace, lest my heart, cracking it, 170
Break too.

LORD   What fit is this, good lady?

PAULINA   What studied torments, tyrant, hast for me?
What wheels, racks, fires? What flaying, boiling
In leads or oils? What old or newer torture
Must I receive, whose every word deserves 175
To taste of thy most worst? Thy tyranny,
Together working with thy jealousies –
Fancies too weak for boys, too green and idle
For girls of nine – O think what they have done,
And then run mad indeed, stark mad, for all 180
Thy bygone fooleries were but spices of it.
That thou betrayed'st Polixenes, 'twas nothing;
That did but show thee, of a fool, inconstant,
And damnable ingrateful. Nor was't much
Thou wouldst have poisoned good Camillo's honour, 185
To have him kill a king – poor trespasses,
More monstrous standing by; whereof I reckon
The casting forth to crows thy baby daughter
To be or none or little, though a devil
Would have shed water out of fire ere done't. 190
Nor is't directly laid to thee the death
Of the young prince, whose honourable thoughts –
Thoughts high for one so tender – cleft the heart
That could conceive a gross and foolish sire
Blemished his gracious dam. This is not, no, 195
Laid to thy answer. But the last – O lords,
When I have said, cry woe! The queen, the queen,
The sweetest, dearest creature's dead, and vengeance
   for't

Not dropped down yet.

LORD   The higher powers forbid!

PAULINA

200 I say she's dead – I'll swear't. If word nor oath
     Prevail not, go and see. If you can bring
     Tincture or lustre in her lip, her eye,
     Heat outwardly or breath within, I'll serve you
     As I would do the gods. But O thou tyrant,
205 Do not repent these things, for they are heavier
     Than all thy woes can stir. Therefore betake thee
     To nothing but despair. A thousand knees,
     Ten thousand years together, naked, fasting,
     Upon a barren mountain, and still winter
210 In storm perpetual, could not move the gods
     To look that way thou wert.

LEONTES   Go on, go on.
     Thou canst not speak too much. I have deserved
     All tongues to talk their bitterest.

LORD [*to Paulina*]   Say no more;
     Howe'er the business goes, you have made fault
     I'th' boldness of your speech.

215 PAULINA   I am sorry for't.
     All faults I make, when I shall come to know them,
     I do repent. Alas, I have showed too much
     The rashness of a woman. He is touched
     To th' noble heart. What's gone and what's past help
     Should be past grief. [*to Leontes*] Do not receive
220   affliction
     At my petition; I beseech you, rather
     Let me be punished, that have minded you
     Of what you should forget. Now, good my liege,
     Sir, royal sir, forgive a foolish woman.
225 The love I bore your queen – lo, fool again!
     I'll speak of her no more, nor of your children.
     I'll not remember you of my own lord,
     Who is lost too. Take your patience to you,
     And I'll say nothing.

LEONTES   Thou didst speak but well
230 When most the truth, which I receive much better
     Than to be pitied of thee. Prithee bring me
     To the dead bodies of my queen and son.
     One grave shall be for both. Upon them shall
     The causes of their death appear, unto
235 Our shame perpetual. Once a day I'll visit
     The chapel where they lie, and tears shed there
     Shall be my recreation. So long as nature
     Will bear up with this exercise, so long
     I daily vow to use it. Come, and lead me
240 To these sorrows.   *Exeunt.*

3.3   *Enter* ANTIGONUS, *carrying the baby,*
          with a Mariner.

ANTIGONUS
     Thou art perfect, then, our ship hath touched upon
     The deserts of Bohemia?

MARINER   Ay, my lord, and fear

We have landed in ill time. The skies look grimly
And threaten present blusters. In my conscience,
The heavens with that we have in hand are angry,   5
And frown upon's.

ANTIGONUS   Their sacred wills be done. Go get aboard;
     Look to thy barque; I'll not be long before
     I call upon thee.

MARINER   Make your best haste, and go not
     Too far i'th' land; 'tis like to be loud weather.   10
     Besides, this place is famous for the creatures
     Of prey that keep upon't.

ANTIGONUS   Go thou away;
     I'll follow instantly.

MARINER   I am glad at heart
     To be so rid o'th' business.   *Exit.*

ANTIGONUS   Come, poor babe.
     I have heard, but not believed, the spirits o'th' dead   15
     May walk again. If such thing be, thy mother
     Appeared to me last night, for ne'er was dream
     So like a waking. To me comes a creature,
     Sometimes her head on one side, some another;
     I never saw a vessel of like sorrow,   20
     So filled and so becoming. In pure white robes,
     Like very sanctity, she did approach
     My cabin where I lay, thrice bowed before me,
     And, gasping to begin some speech, her eyes
     Became two spouts; the fury spent, anon   25
     Did this break from her: 'Good Antigonus,
     Since fate, against thy better disposition,
     Hath made thy person for the thrower-out
     Of my poor babe according to thine oath,
     Places remote enough are in Bohemia;   30
     There weep, and leave it crying; and for the babe
     Is counted lost for ever, Perdita
     I prithee call't. For this ungentle business
     Put on thee by my lord, thou ne'er shalt see
     Thy wife Paulina more.' And so, with shrieks,   35
     She melted into air. Affrighted much,
     I did in time collect myself, and thought
     This was so and no slumber. Dreams are toys,
     Yet for this once, yea superstitiously,
     I will be squared by this. I do believe   40
     Hermione hath suffered death, and that
     Apollo would – this being indeed the issue
     Of King Polixenes – it should here be laid,
     Either for life or death, upon the earth
     Of its right father. Blossom, speed thee well!   45
          [*Lays the baby down in a mantle, with a box and letters.*]
     There lie, and there thy character. There these,
     Which may, if Fortune please, both breed thee, pretty,
     And still rest thine.   [*Thunder*]
                         The storm begins. Poor wretch,
     That for thy mother's fault art thus exposed
     To loss, and what may follow! Weep I cannot,   50
     But my heart bleeds, and most accursed am I
     To be by oath enjoined to this. Farewell.
     The day frowns more and more. Thou'rt like to have

A lullaby too rough. I never saw
The heavens so dim by day.
[*Thunder, and the sounds of dogs barking and hunting horns*]
55   A savage clamour!
Well may I get aboard. This is the chase.
I am gone for ever!   *Exit, pursued by a bear.*

Enter SHEPHERD.

SHEPHERD   I would there were no age between ten and
three-and-twenty, or that youth would sleep out the rest;
60   for there is nothing in the between but getting wenches
with child, wronging the ancientry, stealing, fighting –
hark you now, would any but these boiled-brains of
nineteen and two-and-twenty hunt this weather? They
have scared away two of my best sheep, which I fear the
65   wolf will sooner find than the master. If anywhere I have
them, 'tis by the seaside, browsing of ivy. Good luck,
an't be thy will! [*Sees the baby.*] What have we here?
Mercy on's, a bairn! A very pretty bairn. A boy or a
child, I wonder? A pretty one, a very pretty one – sure
70   some scape; though I am not bookish, yet I can read
waiting-gentlewoman in the scape. This has been some
stair-work, some trunk-work, some behind-door-work.
They were warmer that got this than the poor thing is
here. I'll take it up for pity; yet I'll tarry till my son come.
75   He hallooed but even now. Whoa-ho-hoa!

Enter CLOWN.

CLOWN   Hilloa, loa!
SHEPHERD   What, art so near? If thou'lt see a thing to
talk on when thou art dead and rotten, come hither.
What ail'st thou, man?
80   CLOWN   I have seen two such sights, by sea and by land!
But I am not to say it is a sea, for it is now the sky;
betwixt the firmament and it you cannot thrust a
bodkin's point.
SHEPHERD   Why, boy, how is it?
85   CLOWN   I would you did but see how it chafes, how it
rages, how it takes up the shore; but that's not to the
point. O, the most piteous cry of the poor souls!
Sometimes to see 'em, and not to see 'em; now the ship
boring the moon with her mainmast, and anon
90   swallowed with yeast and froth, as you'd thrust a cork
into a hogshead. And then for the land-service, to see
how the bear tore out his shoulder-bone, how he cried
to me for help, and said his name was Antigonus, a
nobleman! But to make an end of the ship – to see how
95   the sea flapdragoned it! But first, how the poor souls
roared, and the sea mocked them, and how the poor
gentleman roared, and the bear mocked him, both
roaring louder than the sea or weather.
SHEPHERD   Name of mercy, when was this, boy?
100   CLOWN   Now, now. I have not winked since I saw these
sights. The men are not yet cold under water, nor the
bear half dined on the gentleman – he's at it now.
SHEPHERD   Would I had been by to have helped the old
man!

CLOWN   I would you had been by the ship side, to have   105
helped her; there your charity would have lacked
footing.
SHEPHERD   Heavy matters, heavy matters. But look thee
here, boy. Now bless thyself; thou met'st with things
dying, I with things newborn. Here's a sight for thee.   110
Look thee, a bearing-cloth for a squire's child. [*Points to
the box.*] Look thee here, take up, take up, boy, open't. So,
let's see. It was told me I should be rich by the fairies.
This is some changeling; open't. What's within, boy?
CLOWN [*Opens the box.*]   You're a made old man. If the   115
sins of your youth are forgiven you, you're well to live.
Gold, all gold!
SHEPHERD   This is fairy gold, boy, and 'twill prove so.
Up with't, keep it close. Home, home, the next way. We
are lucky, boy, and to be so still requires nothing but   120
secrecy. Let my sheep go. Come, good boy, the next
way home.
CLOWN   Go you the next way with your findings. I'll go
see if the bear be gone from the gentleman, and how
much he hath eaten. They are never curst but when   125
they are hungry. If there be any of him left, I'll bury it.
SHEPHERD   That's a good deed. If thou mayst discern
by that which is left of him what he is, fetch me to th'
sight of him.
CLOWN   Marry, will I; and you shall help to put him   130
i'th' ground.
SHEPHERD   'Tis a lucky day, boy, and we'll do good
deeds on't.   *Exeunt.*

4.1   *Enter* TIME, *the Chorus.*

TIME   I, that please some, try all; both joy and terror
Of good and bad, that makes and unfolds error,
Now take upon me, in the name of Time,
To use my wings. Impute it not a crime
To me or my swift passage that I slide   5
O'er sixteen years, and leave the growth untried
Of that wide gap, since it is in my power
To o'erthrow law, and in one self-born hour
To plant and o'erwhelm custom. Let me pass
The same I am ere ancient'st order was,   10
Or what is now received. I witness to
The times that brought them in; so shall I do
To th' freshest things now reigning, and make stale
The glistering of this present as my tale
Now seems to it. Your patience this allowing,   15
I turn my glass, and give my scene such growing
As you had slept between. Leontes leaving –
Th'effects of his fond jealousies so grieving
That he shuts up himself – imagine me,
Gentle spectators, that I now may be   20
In fair Bohemia, and remember well
I mentioned a son o'th' king's, which Florizel
I now name to you; and with speed so pace
To speak of Perdita, now grown in grace
Equal with wondering. What of her ensues   25

I list not prophesy, but let Time's news
Be known when 'tis brought forth. A shepherd's
    daughter,
And what to her adheres, which follows after,
Is th'argument of Time. Of this allow,
30   If ever you have spent time worse ere now;
If never, yet that Time himself doth say
He wishes earnestly you never may.   *Exit.*

4.2   *Enter* POLIXENES *and* CAMILLO.

POLIXENES   I pray thee, good Camillo, be no more
    importunate. 'Tis a sickness denying thee anything, a
    death to grant this.
CAMILLO   It is fifteen years since I saw my country.
5   Though I have for the most part been aired abroad, I
    desire to lay my bones there. Besides, the penitent
    king, my master, hath sent for me, to whose feeling
    sorrows I might be some allay – or I o'erween to think
    so – which is another spur to my departure.
10 POLIXENES   As thou lov'st me, Camillo, wipe not out
    the rest of thy services by leaving me now. The need I
    have of thee thine own goodness hath made. Better not
    to have had thee than thus to want thee. Thou, having
    made me businesses which none without thee can
15   sufficiently manage, must either stay to execute them
    thyself, or take away with thee the very services thou
    hast done; which if I have not enough considered – as
    too much I cannot – to be more thankful to thee shall
    be my study, and my profit therein the heaping
20   friendships. Of that fatal country Sicilia, prithee speak
    no more, whose very naming punishes me with the
    remembrance of that penitent – as thou call'st him –
    and reconciled king my brother, whose loss of his most
    precious queen and children are even now to be afresh
25   lamented. Say to me, when saw'st thou the Prince
    Florizel, my son? Kings are no less unhappy, their
    issue not being gracious, than they are in losing them
    when they have approved their virtues.
CAMILLO   Sir, it is three days since I saw the prince.
30   What his happier affairs may be are to me unknown;
    but I have missingly noted he is of late much retired
    from court, and is less frequent to his princely exercises
    than formerly he hath appeared.
POLIXENES   I have considered so much, Camillo, and
35   with some care, so far that I have eyes under my service
    which look upon his removedness, from whom I have
    this intelligence: that he is seldom from the house of a
    most homely shepherd, a man, they say, that from very
    nothing, and beyond the imagination of his neighbours,
40   is grown into an unspeakable estate.
CAMILLO   I have heard, sir, of such a man, who hath a
    daughter of most rare note. The report of her is
    extended more than can be thought to begin from such
    a cottage.
45 POLIXENES   That's likewise part of my intelligence;
    but, I fear, the angle that plucks our son thither. Thou

shalt accompany us to the place, where we will, not
appearing what we are, have some question with the
shepherd, from whose simplicity I think it not uneasy
to get the cause of my son's resort thither. Prithee, be   50
my present partner in this business, and lay aside the
thoughts of Sicilia.
CAMILLO   I willingly obey your command.
POLIXENES   My best Camillo! We must disguise
    ourselves.   *Exeunt.*   55

4.3   *Enter* AUTOLYCUS *singing.*

AUTOLYCUS
    When daffodils begin to peer,
    With heigh, the doxy over the dale,
    Why then comes in the sweet o'the year,
    For the red blood reigns in the winter's pale.

    The white sheet bleaching on the hedge,   5
    With heigh, the sweet birds, O how they sing!
    Doth set my pugging tooth an edge,
    For a quart of ale is a dish for a king.

    The lark, that tirra-lirra chants,
    With heigh, with heigh, the thrush and the jay,   10
    Are summer songs for me and my aunts
    While we lie tumbling in the hay.

I have served Prince Florizel, and in my time wore
three-pile, but now I am out of service.

    But shall I go mourn for that, my dear?   15
    The pale moon shines by night,
    And when I wander here and there
    I then do most go right.

    If tinkers may have leave to live,
    And bear the sow-skin budget,   20
    Then my account I well may give,
    And in the stocks avouch it.

My traffic is sheets – when the kite builds, look to
lesser linen. My father named me Autolycus, who
being, as I am, littered under Mercury, was likewise a   25
snapper-up of unconsidered trifles. With die and drab
I purchased this caparison, and my revenue is the silly
cheat. Gallows and knock are too powerful on the
highway. Beating and hanging are terrors to me. For
the life to come, I sleep out the thought of it. A prize, a   30
prize!

Enter CLOWN.

CLOWN   Let me see. Every 'leven wether tods, every tod
    yields pound and odd shilling. Fifteen hundred shorn,
    what comes the wool to?
AUTOLYCUS [*aside*]   If the springe hold, the cock's mine.   35
CLOWN   I cannot do't without counters. Let me see,

what am I to buy for our sheep-shearing feast? Three
pound of sugar, five pound of currants, rice – what will
this sister of mine do with rice? But my father hath
made her mistress of the feast, and she lays it on. She
hath made me four-and-twenty nosegays for the
shearers – three-man songmen, all, and very good ones
– but they are most of them means and basses, but one
Puritan amongst them, and he sings psalms to
hornpipes. I must have saffron to colour the warden
pies; mace; dates, none – that's out of my note; nutmegs,
seven; a race or two of ginger – but that I may beg; four
pound of prunes, and as many of raisins o'th' sun.

AUTOLYCUS [*Grovels on the ground.*]   O, that ever I was
born!

CLOWN   I'th' name of me!

AUTOLYCUS   O help me, help me! Pluck but off these
rags, and then death, death!

CLOWN   Alack, poor soul, thou hast need of more rags
to lay on thee rather than have these off.

AUTOLYCUS   O sir, the loathsomeness of them offend
me more than the stripes I have received, which are
mighty ones and millions.

CLOWN   Alas, poor man, a million of beating may come
to a great matter.

AUTOLYCUS   I am robbed, sir, and beaten; my money
and apparel ta'en from me, and these detestable things
put upon me.

CLOWN   What, by a horseman, or a footman?

AUTOLYCUS   A footman, sweet sir, a footman.

CLOWN   Indeed, he should be a footman, by the
garments he has left with thee. If this be a horseman's
coat, it hath seen very hot service. Lend me thy hand,
I'll help thee. Come, lend me thy hand. [*Helps
Autolycus up.*]

AUTOLYCUS   O, good sir, tenderly. O!

CLOWN   Alas, poor soul!

AUTOLYCUS   O, good sir, softly, good sir! I fear, sir, my
shoulder-blade is out.

CLOWN   How now? Canst stand?

AUTOLYCUS   Softly, dear sir. Good sir, softly. [*Picks the
Clown's pocket.*] You ha' done me a charitable office.

CLOWN   Dost lack any money? I have a little money for
thee.

AUTOLYCUS   No, good sweet sir, no, I beseech you, sir. I
have a kinsman not past three-quarters of a mile hence,
unto whom I was going. I shall there have money, or
anything I want. Offer me no money, I pray you – that
kills my heart.

CLOWN   What manner of fellow was he that robbed
you?

AUTOLYCUS   A fellow, sir, that I have known to go about
with troll-madams. I knew him once a servant of the
prince. I cannot tell, good sir, for which of his virtues it
was, but he was certainly whipped out of the court.

CLOWN   His vices, you would say – there's no virtue
whipped out of the court. They cherish it to make it
stay there, and yet it will no more but abide.

AUTOLYCUS   Vices, I would say, sir. I know this man
well. He hath been since an ape-bearer, then a process-
server – a bailiff – then he compassed a motion of the
Prodigal Son, and married a tinker's wife within a mile
where my land and living lies, and, having flown over
many knavish professions, he settled only in rogue.
Some call him Autolycus.

CLOWN   Out upon him! Prig, for my life, prig! He
haunts wakes, fairs and bear-baitings.

AUTOLYCUS   Very true, sir. He, sir, he. That's the rogue
that put me into this apparel.

CLOWN   Not a more cowardly rogue in all Bohemia. If
you had but looked big and spit at him, he'd have run.

AUTOLYCUS   I must confess to you, sir, I am no fighter.
I am false of heart that way, and that he knew, I warrant
him.

CLOWN   How do you now?

AUTOLYCUS   Sweet sir, much better than I was. I can
stand and walk. I will even take my leave of you, and
pace softly towards my kinsman's.

CLOWN   Shall I bring thee on the way?

AUTOLYCUS   No, good-faced sir; no, sweet sir.

CLOWN   Then fare thee well. I must go buy spices for
our sheep-shearing.

AUTOLYCUS   Prosper you, sweet sir.   *Exit Clown.*
Your purse is not hot enough to purchase your spice.
I'll be with you at your sheep-shearing, too. If I make
not this cheat bring out another and the shearers prove
sheep, let me be unrolled and my name put in the book
of virtue.
[*Sings.*]   Jog on, jog on, the footpath way,
            And merrily hent the stile-a.
            A merry heart goes all the day,
            Your sad tires in a mile-a.   *Exit.*

4.4   *Enter* FLORIZEL, *disguised as Doricles a
countryman, and* PERDITA *as Queen of the Feast.*

FLORIZEL
These your unusual weeds to each part of you
Does give a life; no shepherdess, but Flora
Peering in April's front. This your sheep-shearing
Is as a meeting of the petty gods,
And you the queen on't.

PERDITA   Sir, my gracious lord,
To chide at your extremes it not becomes me –
O, pardon that I name them. Your high self,
The gracious mark o'th' land, you have obscured
With a swain's wearing, and me, poor lowly maid,
Most goddess-like pranked up. But that our feasts
In every mess have folly, and the feeders
Digest it with a custom, I should blush
To see you so attired; swoon, I think,
To show myself a glass.

FLORIZEL   I bless the time
When my good falcon made her flight across
Thy father's ground.

PERDITA   Now Jove afford you cause!
To me the difference forges dread; your greatness
Hath not been used to fear. Even now I tremble
To think your father by some accident
20 Should pass this way, as you did. O, the fates!
How would he look to see his work, so noble,
Vilely bound up? What would he say? Or how
Should I, in these my borrowed flaunts, behold
The sternness of his presence?

FLORIZEL   Apprehend
25 Nothing but jollity. The gods themselves,
Humbling their deities to love, have taken
The shapes of beasts upon them. Jupiter
Became a bull and bellowed; the green Neptune
A ram and bleated; and the fire-robed god,
30 Golden Apollo, a poor humble swain,
As I seem now. Their transformations
Were never for a piece of beauty rarer,
Nor in a way so chaste, since my desires
Run not before mine honour, nor my lusts
Burn hotter than my faith.

PERDITA   O, but sir,
35 Your resolution cannot hold when 'tis
Opposed, as it must be, by th' power of the king.
One of these two must be necessities,
Which then will speak that you must change this
    purpose,
Or I my life.

FLORIZEL   Thou dearest Perdita,
40 With these forced thoughts I prithee darken not
The mirth o'th' feast – or I'll be thine, my fair,
Or not my father's. For I cannot be
Mine own, nor anything to any, if
45 I be not thine. To this I am most constant,
Though destiny say no. Be merry, gentle;
Strangle such thoughts as these with anything
That you behold the while. Your guests are coming.
Lift up your countenance as it were the day
50 Of celebration of that nuptial which
We two have sworn shall come.

PERDITA   O Lady Fortune,
Stand you auspicious!

FLORIZEL   See, your guests approach.
Address yourself to entertain them sprightly,
And let's be red with mirth.

      Enter SHEPHERD, *with* POLIXENES *and*
      CAMILLO, *both disguised,* CLOWN, MOPSA,
      DORCAS, *Shepherds and Shepherdesses.*

55 SHEPHERD   Fie, daughter, when my old wife lived, upon
This day she was both pantler, butler, cook;
Both dame and servant, welcomed all, served all,
Would sing her song and dance her turn, now here
At upper end o'th' table, now i'th' middle;
60 On his shoulder and his, her face o'fire
With labour, and the thing she took to quench it

She would to each one sip. You are retired
As if you were a feasted one and not
The hostess of the meeting. Pray you, bid
These unknown friends to's welcome, for it is   65
A way to make us better friends, more known.
Come, quench your blushes and present yourself
That which you are, mistress o'th' feast. Come on,
And bid us welcome to your sheep-shearing,
As your good flock shall prosper.

PERDITA [*to Polixenes*]   Sir, welcome.   70
It is my father's will I should take on me
The hostess-ship o'th' day. [*to Camillo*] You're
    welcome, sir.
Give me those flowers there, Dorcas. Reverend sirs,
For you there's rosemary and rue; these keep
Seeming and savour all the winter long.   75
Grace and remembrance be to you both,
And welcome to our shearing.

POLIXENES   Shepherdess,
A fair one are you. Well you fit our ages
With flowers of winter.

PERDITA   Sir, the year growing ancient,
Not yet on summer's death, nor on the birth   80
Of trembling winter, the fairest flowers o'th' season
Are our carnations and streaked gillyvors,
Which some call Nature's bastards; of that kind
Our rustic garden's barren, and I care not
To get slips of them.

POLIXENES   Wherefore, gentle maiden,   85
Do you neglect them?

PERDITA   For I have heard it said
There is an art which in their piedness shares
With great creating Nature.

POLIXENES   Say there be,
Yet Nature is made better by no mean
But Nature makes that mean. So over that art,   90
Which you say adds to Nature, is an art
That Nature makes. You see, sweet maid, we marry
A gentler scion to the wildest stock,
And make conceive a bark of baser kind
By bud of nobler race. This is an art   95
Which does mend Nature – change it rather – but
The art itself is Nature.

PERDITA   So it is.

POLIXENES   Then make your garden rich in gillyvors,
And do not call them bastards.

PERDITA   I'll not put
The dibble in earth to set one slip of them;   100
No more than, were I painted, I would wish
This youth should say 'twere well, and only therefore
Desire to breed by me. Here's flowers for you:
Hot lavender, mints, savory, marjoram,
The marigold, that goes to bed wi'th' sun,   105
And with him rises, weeping. These are flowers
Of middle summer, and I think they are given
To men of middle age. You're very welcome.
    [*Gives them flowers.*]

CAMILLO   I should leave grazing were I of your flock,
And only live by gazing.

110 PERDITA   Out, alas,
You'd be so lean that blasts of January
Would blow you through and through.
[*to Florizel*]   Now, my fair'st friend,
I would I had some flowers o'th' spring that might
Become your time of day; [*to Mopsa and Dorcas*] and
      yours, and yours,
115 That wear upon your virgin branches yet
Your maidenheads growing. O Proserpina,
For the flowers now that, frighted, thou let'st fall
From Dis's wagon! Daffodils,
That come before the swallow dares, and take
120 The winds of March with beauty; violets, dim,
But sweeter than the lids of Juno's eyes
Or Cytherea's breath; pale primroses,
That die unmarried ere they can behold
Bright Phoebus in his strength – a malady
125 Most incident to maids; bold oxlips, and
The crown imperial; lilies of all kinds,
The flower-de-luce being one. O, these I lack
To make you garlands of, and my sweet friend
To strew him o'er and o'er.
FLORIZEL   What, like a corpse?
130 PERDITA   No, like a bank, for love to lie and play on,
Not like a corpse – or if, not to be buried,
But quick and in mine arms. Come, take your flowers.
Methinks I play as I have seen them do
In Whitsun pastorals; sure this robe of mine
135 Does change my disposition.
FLORIZEL   What you do
Still betters what is done. When you speak, sweet,
I'd have you do it ever; when you sing,
I'd have you buy and sell so, so give alms,
Pray so, and for the ordering your affairs,
140 To sing them too. When you do dance, I wish you
A wave o'th' sea, that you might ever do
Nothing but that, move still, still so,
And own no other function. Each your doing,
So singular in each particular,
145 Crowns what you are doing in the present deeds,
That all your acts are queens.
PERDITA   O Doricles,
Your praises are too large. But that your youth
And the true blood which peeps fairly through't
Do plainly give you out an unstained shepherd,
150 With wisdom I might fear, my Doricles,
You wooed me the false way.
FLORIZEL   I think you have
As little skill to fear as I have purpose
To put you to't. But come, our dance, I pray;
Your hand, my Perdita – so turtles pair,
That never mean to part.
155 PERDITA   I'll swear for 'em.
POLIXENES [*to Camillo*]
This is the prettiest low-born lass that ever

Ran on the greensward. Nothing she does or seems
But smacks of something greater than herself,
Too noble for this place.
CAMILLO   He tells her something
That makes her blood look out. Good sooth, she is   160
The queen of curds and cream.
CLOWN   Come on, strike up!
DORCAS   Mopsa must be your mistress. Marry, garlic to
mend her kissing with!
MOPSA   Now, in good time!   165
CLOWN   Not a word, a word, we stand upon our manners.
Come, strike up!   [*Music*]
    [*Here a dance of Shepherds and Shepherdesses,
    including Florizel and Perdita*]
                    Exeunt Shepherds and Shepherdesses.
POLIXENES
Pray, good shepherd, what fair swain is this
Which dances with your daughter?
SHEPHERD
They call him Doricles, and boasts himself   170
To have a worthy feeding; but I have it
Upon his own report, and I believe it –
He looks like sooth. He says he loves my daughter;
I think so, too, for never gazed the moon
Upon the water as he'll stand and read,   175
As 'twere, my daughter's eyes; and, to be plain,
I think there is not half a kiss to choose
Who loves another best.
POLIXENES   She dances featly.
SHEPHERD
So she does anything, though I report it
That should be silent. If young Doricles   180
Do light upon her, she shall bring him that
Which he not dreams of.

                    Enter Servant.

SERVANT   O, master, if you did but hear the pedlar at the
door, you would never dance again after a tabor and
pipe. No, the bagpipe could not move you. He sings   185
several tunes faster than you'll tell money. He utters
them as he had eaten ballads, and all men's ears grew
to his tunes.
CLOWN   He could never come better. He shall come in.
I love a ballad but even too well, if it be doleful matter 190
merrily set down, or a very pleasant thing indeed and
sung lamentably.
SERVANT   He hath songs for man or woman of all sizes.
No milliner can so fit his customers with gloves. He
has the prettiest love songs for maids, so without   195
bawdry, which is strange, with such delicate burdens of
dildos and fadings, 'jump her and thump her'; and
where some stretch-mouthed rascal would, as it were,
mean mischief and break a foul gap into the matter, he
makes the maid to answer, 'Whoop, do me no harm,   200
good man'; puts him off, slights him, with 'Whoop, do
me no harm, good man!'
POLIXENES   This is a brave fellow.

CLOWN Believe me, thou talkest of an admirable
conceited fellow. Has he any unbraided wares?

SERVANT He hath ribbons of all the colours i'th'
rainbow; points more than all the lawyers in Bohemia
can learnedly handle, though they come to him by th'
gross; inkles, caddisses, cambrics, lawns, why, he sings
'em over as they were gods or goddesses. You would
think a smock were a she-angel, he so chants to the
sleeve-hand and the work about the square on't.

CLOWN Prithee bring him in, and let him approach
singing.

PERDITA Forewarn him that he use no scurrilous words
in's tunes.   *Exit Servant.*

CLOWN You have of these pedlars that have more in
them than you'd think, sister.

PERDITA Ay, good brother, or go about to think.

Enter AUTOLYCUS, *disguised, carrying
his pack and singing.*

AUTOLYCUS
  Lawn as white as driven snow,
  Cypress black as e'er was crow,
  Gloves as sweet as damask roses,
  Masks for faces and for noses;
  Bugle-bracelet, necklace-amber,
  Perfume for a lady's chamber;
  Golden coifs and stomachers
  For my lads to give their dears;
  Pins and poking-sticks of steel,
  What maids lack from head to heel –
  Come, buy of me, come; come buy, come buy,
  Buy, lads, or else your lasses cry. Come buy!

CLOWN If I were not in love with Mopsa, thou shouldst
take no money of me, but, being enthralled as I am,
it will also be the bondage of certain ribbons and
gloves.

MOPSA I was promised them against the feast, but they
come not too late now.

DORCAS He hath promised you more than that, or there
be liars.

MOPSA He hath paid you all he promised you. Maybe
he has paid you more, which will shame you to give
him again.

CLOWN Is there no manners left among maids? Will
they wear their plackets where they should bear their
faces? Is there not milking-time, when you are going to
bed, or kiln-hole, to whistle of these secrets, but you
must be tittle-tattling before all our guests? 'Tis well
they are whispering. Clammer your tongues and not a
word more.

MOPSA I have done. Come, you promised me a tawdry-
lace and a pair of sweet gloves.

CLOWN Have I not told thee how I was cozened by the
way and lost all my money?

AUTOLYCUS And indeed, sir, there are cozeners abroad,
therefore it behoves men to be wary.

CLOWN Fear not thou, man, thou shalt lose nothing here.

AUTOLYCUS I hope so, sir, for I have about me many
parcels of charge.

CLOWN What hast here? Ballads?

MOPSA Pray now, buy some. I love a ballad in print,
a-life, for then we are sure they are true.

AUTOLYCUS Here's one to a very doleful tune, how a
usurer's wife was brought to bed of twenty money-
bags at a burden, and how she longed to eat adders'
heads and toads carbonadoed.

MOPSA Is it true, think you?

AUTOLYCUS Very true, and but a month old.

DORCAS Bless me from marrying a usurer!

AUTOLYCUS Here's the midwife's name to't, one
Mistress Tale-Porter, and five or six honest wives' that
were present. Why should I carry lies abroad?

MOPSA [*to Clown*] Pray you now, buy it.

CLOWN Come on, lay it by, and let's first see moe
ballads. We'll buy the other things anon.

AUTOLYCUS Here's another ballad, of a fish that
appeared upon the coast on Wednesday the fourscore
of April, forty thousand fathom above water, and sung
this ballad against the hard hearts of maids. It was
thought she was a woman and was turned into a cold
fish for she would not exchange flesh with one that
loved her. The ballad is very pitiful, and as true.

DORCAS Is it true too, think you?

AUTOLYCUS Five justices' hands at it, and witnesses
more than my pack will hold.

CLOWN Lay it by, too. Another.

AUTOLYCUS This is a merry ballad, but a very pretty one.

MOPSA Let's have some merry ones.

AUTOLYCUS Why, this is a passing merry one, and goes
to the tune of 'Two Maids Wooing a Man'. There's
scarce a maid westward but she sings it. 'Tis in request,
I can tell you.

MOPSA We can both sing it. If thou'lt bear a part thou
shalt hear; 'tis in three parts.

DORCAS We had the tune on't a month ago.

AUTOLYCUS I can bear my part, you must know 'tis my
occupation. Have at it with you.
  [*They sing.*]

AUTOLYCUS Get you hence, for I must go
        Where it fits not you to know.

DORCAS Whither?

MOPSA O whither?

DORCAS Whither?

MOPSA It becomes thy oath full well,
        Thou to me thy secrets tell.

DORCAS Me too. Let me go thither.

MOPSA Or thou goest to th' grange or mill,

DORCAS If to either, thou dost ill.

AUTOLYCUS Neither.

DORCAS What neither?

AUTOLYCUS Neither.

DORCAS Thou hast sworn my love to be.

MOPSA Thou hast sworn it more to me.
        Then whither goest? Say, whither?

CLOWN   We'll have this song out anon by ourselves. My
father and the gentlemen are in sad talk, and we'll not
315   trouble them. Come, bring away thy pack after me.
Wenches, I'll buy for you both. Pedlar, let's have the
first choice. Follow me, girls.
                                            Exit with Dorcas and Mopsa.
AUTOLYCUS   And you shall pay well for 'em.
[*Sings.*] Will you buy any tape,
320   Or lace for your cape,
        My dainty duck, my dear-a?
        Any silk, any thread,
        Any toys for your head,
        Of the new'st and fin'st, fin'st wear-a?
325   Come to the pedlar,
        Money's a meddler,
        That doth utter all men's ware-a.   *Exit.*

                    Enter the Servant.

SERVANT   Master, there is three carters, three
shepherds, three neatherds, three swineherds that have
330   made themselves all men of hair. They call themselves
saultiers, and they have a dance which the wenches say
is a gallimaufry of gambols, because they are not in't.
But they themselves are o'th' mind, if it be not too
rough for some that know little but bowling, it will
335   please plentifully.
SHEPHERD   Away! We'll none on't. Here has been too
much homely foolery already. [*to Polixenes*] I know, sir,
we weary you.
POLIXENES   You weary those that refresh us. Pray, let's
340   see these four threes of herdsmen.
SERVANT   One three of them, by their own report, sir,
hath danced before the king, and not the worst of the
three but jumps twelve foot and a half by th' square.
SHEPHERD   Leave your prating. Since these good men
345   are pleased, let them come in – but quickly, now.
SERVANT   Why, they stay at door, sir.

        *The Servant admits twelve rustic Dancers
        dressed as satyrs, who dance to music.*

                        Exeunt Servant and Dancers.
POLIXENES [*to Shepherd*]
   O, father, you'll know more of that hereafter.
   [*to Camillo*] Is it not too far gone? 'Tis time to part
      them.
   He's simple, and tells much. [*to Florizel*] How now,
      fair shepherd,
350   Your heart is full of something that does take
   Your mind from feasting. Sooth, when I was young
   And handed love as you do, I was wont
   To load my she with knacks. I would have ransacked
   The pedlar's silken treasury, and have poured it
355   To her acceptance. You have let him go,
   And nothing marted with him. If your lass
   Interpretation should abuse and call this
   Your lack of love or bounty, you were straited
   For a reply, at least if you make a care

Of happy holding her.
FLORIZEL   Old sir, I know   360
   She prizes not such trifles as these are.
   The gifts she looks from me are packed and locked
   Up in my heart, which I have given already,
   But not delivered. [*to Perdita*] O, hear me breathe my
      life
   Before this ancient sir, whom, it should seem,   365
   Hath sometime loved. I take thy hand, this hand
   As soft as dove's down and as white as it,
   Or Ethiopian's tooth, or the fanned snow that's bolted
   By th' northern blasts twice o'er.
POLIXENES   What follows this?
   [*to Camillo*] How prettily th' young swain seems to wash   370
   The hand was fair before! [*to Florizel*] I have put you
      out.
   But to your protestation. Let me hear
   What you profess.
FLORIZEL   Do, and be witness to't.
POLIXENES   And this my neighbour too?
FLORIZEL   And he, and more
   Than he, and men, the earth, the heavens and all –   375
   That were I crowned the most imperial monarch,
   Thereof most worthy, were I the fairest youth
   That ever made eye swerve, had force and knowledge
   More than was ever man's, I would not prize them
   Without her love, for her employ them all,   380
   Commend them and condemn them to her service
   Or to their own perdition.
POLIXENES   Fairly offered.
CAMILLO   This shows a sound affection.
SHEPHERD   But, my daughter,
   Say you the like to him?
PERDITA   I cannot speak
   So well, nothing so well, no, nor mean better.   385
   By th' pattern of mine own thoughts I cut out
   The purity of his.
SHEPHERD   Take hands, a bargain;
   And, friends unknown, you shall bear witness to't.
   I give my daughter to him, and will make
   Her portion equal his.
FLORIZEL   O, that must be   390
   I'th' virtue of your daughter. One being dead,
   I shall have more than you can dream of yet,
   Enough then for your wonder. But come on,
   Contract us 'fore these witnesses.
SHEPHERD   Come, your hand;
   And, daughter, yours.
POLIXENES   Soft, swain, awhile, beseech you.   395
   Have you a father?
FLORIZEL   I have. But what of him?
POLIXENES   Knows he of this?
FLORIZEL   He neither does nor shall.
POLIXENES   Methinks a father
   Is at the nuptial of his son a guest
   That best becomes the table. Pray you once more,   400
   Is not your father grown incapable

Of reasonable affairs? Is he not stupid
With age and altering rheums? Can he speak? Hear?
Know man from man? Dispute his own estate?
405 Lies he not bed-rid? And again does nothing
But what he did being childish?
SHEPHERD   No, good sir.
He has his health and ampler strength indeed
Than most have of his age.
POLIXENES   By my white beard,
You offer him, if this be so, a wrong
410 Something unfilial. Reason my son
Should choose himself a wife, but as good reason
The father, all whose joy is nothing else
But fair posterity, should hold some counsel
In such a business.
FLORIZEL   I yield all this;
415 But for some other reasons, my grave sir,
Which 'tis not fit you know, I not acquaint
My father of this business.
POLIXENES   Let him know't.
FLORIZEL   He shall not.
POLIXENES   Prithee let him.
FLORIZEL   No, he must not.
SHEPHERD
Let him, my son. He shall not need to grieve
At knowing of thy choice.
420 FLORIZEL   Come, come, he must not.
Mark our contract.
POLIXENES [*Removes his disguise.*]
                         Mark your divorce, young sir,
Whom son I dare not call. Thou art too base
To be acknowledged. Thou a sceptre's heir,
That thus affects a sheep-hook? [*to Shepherd*] Thou,
      old traitor,
425 I am sorry that by hanging thee I can
But shorten thy life one week. [*to Perdita*] And thou,
      fresh piece
Of excellent witchcraft, whom of force must know
The royal fool thou cop'st with –
SHEPHERD   O, my heart!
POLIXENES
I'll have thy beauty scratched with briars and made
More homely than thy state. [*to Florizel*] For thee,
430   fond boy,
If I may ever know thou dost but sigh
That thou no more shalt see this knack, as never
I mean thou shalt, we'll bar thee from succession,
Not hold thee of our blood, no, not our kin,
435 Far than Deucalion off. Mark thou my words.
Follow us to the court. [*to Shepherd*] Thou churl, for
      this time,
Though full of our displeasure, yet we free thee
From the dead blow of it. [*to Perdita*] And you,
      enchantment,
Worthy enough a herdsman – yea, him too,
440 That makes himself, but for our honour therein,
Unworthy thee – if ever henceforth thou

These rural latches to his entrance open,
Or hoop his body more with thy embraces,
I will devise a death as cruel for thee
As thou art tender to't.   *Exit.*
PERDITA   Even here undone.   445
I was not much afeard, for once or twice
I was about to speak and tell him plainly,
The selfsame sun that shines upon his court
Hides not his visage from our cottage, but
Looks on alike. [*to Florizel*] Will't please you, sir, be
      gone?   450
I told you what would come of this. Beseech you,
Of your own state take care. This dream of mine
Being now awake, I'll queen it no inch farther,
But milk my ewes and weep.
CAMILLO [*to Shepherd*]   Why, how now, father?
Speak ere thou diest.
SHEPHERD   I cannot speak, nor think,   455
Nor dare to know that which I know. [*to Florizel*] O sir,
You have undone a man of fourscore-three,
That thought to fill his grave in quiet, yea,
To die upon the bed my father died,
To lie close by his honest bones; but now   460
Some hangman must put on my shroud and lay me
Where no priest shovels in dust. [*to Perdita*] O cursed
      wretch,
That knewst this was the prince and wouldst adventure
To mingle faith with him. Undone, undone!
If I might die within this hour, I have lived   465
To die when I desire.   *Exit.*
FLORIZEL [*to Perdita*]   Why look you so upon me?
I am but sorry, not afeard; delayed,
But nothing altered. What I was, I am,
More straining on for plucking back, not following
My leash unwillingly.
CAMILLO   Gracious my lord,   470
You know your father's temper. At this time
He will allow no speech, which I do guess
You do not purpose to him; and as hardly
Will he endure your sight as yet, I fear;
Then till the fury of his highness settle,   475
Come not before him.
FLORIZEL   I not purpose it.
I think Camillo?
CAMILLO   Even he, my lord.
PERDITA [*to Florizel*]
How often have I told you 'twould be thus?
How often said my dignity would last
But till 'twere known?
FLORIZEL   It cannot fail but by   480
The violation of my faith, and then
Let Nature crush the sides o'th' earth together,
And mar the seeds within. Lift up thy looks.
From my succession wipe me, father! I
Am heir to my affection.
CAMILLO   Be advised.   485
FLORIZEL   I am, and by my fancy; if my reason

Will thereto be obedient, I have reason.
If not, my senses, better pleased with madness,
Do bid it welcome.

CAMILLO   This is desperate, sir.

490 FLORIZEL   So call it; but it does fulfil my vow;
I needs must think it honesty. Camillo,
Not for Bohemia, nor the pomp that may
Be thereat gleaned; for all the sun sees, or
The close earth wombs, or the profound seas hides
495 In unknown fathoms, will I break my oath
To this my fair beloved. Therefore, I pray you,
As you have ever been my father's honoured friend,
When he shall miss me – as, in faith, I mean not
To see him any more – cast your good counsels
500 Upon his passion. Let myself and Fortune
Tug for the time to come. This you may know,
And so deliver: I am put to sea
With her who here I cannot hold on shore,
And, most opportune to our need, I have
505 A vessel rides fast by, but not prepared
For this design. What course I mean to hold
Shall nothing benefit your knowledge, nor
Concern me the reporting.

CAMILLO   O my lord,
I would your spirit were easier for advice,
Or stronger for your need.

510 FLORIZEL   Hark, Perdita –   [*Takes Perdita aside.*]
[*to Camillo*] I'll hear you by and by.

CAMILLO [*aside*]   He's irremovable,
Resolved for flight. Now were I happy if
His going I could frame to serve my turn,
Save him from danger, do him love and honour,
515 Purchase the sight again of dear Sicilia
And that unhappy king, my master, whom
I so much thirst to see.

FLORIZEL   Now, good Camillo,
I am so fraught with curious business that
I leave out ceremony.

CAMILLO   Sir, I think
520 You have heard of my poor services i'th' love
That I have borne your father?

FLORIZEL   Very nobly
Have you deserved. It is my father's music
To speak your deeds, not little of his care
To have them recompensed as thought on.

CAMILLO   Well, my lord,
525 If you may please to think I love the king,
And through him what's nearest to him, which is
Your gracious self, embrace but my direction,
If your more ponderous and settled project
May suffer alteration. On mine honour,
530 I'll point you where you shall have such receiving
As shall become your highness, where you may
Enjoy your mistress – from the whom I see
There's no disjunction to be made but by,
As heavens forfend, your ruin – marry her,
535 And with my best endeavours in your absence,

Your discontenting father strive to qualify,
And bring him up to liking.

FLORIZEL   How, Camillo,
May this, almost a miracle, be done?
That I may call thee something more than man,
And after that trust to thee.

CAMILLO   Have you thought on   540
A place whereto you'll go?

FLORIZEL   Not any yet.
But as th'unthought-on accident is guilty
To what we wildly do, so we profess
Ourselves to be the slaves of chance, and flies
Of every wind that blows.

CAMILLO   Then list to me.   545
This follows, if you will not change your purpose
But undergo this flight: make for Sicilia,
And there present yourself and your fair princess,
For so I see she must be, 'fore Leontes;
She shall be habited as it becomes   550
The partner of your bed. Methinks I see
Leontes opening his free arms and weeping
His welcomes forth; asks thee there, 'Son,
     forgiveness!'
As 'twere i'th' father's person; kisses the hands
Of your fresh princess; o'er and o'er divides him   555
'Twixt his unkindness and his kindness. Th'one
He chides to hell, and bids the other grow
Faster than thought or time.

FLORIZEL   Worthy Camillo,
What colour for my visitation shall I
Hold up before him?

CAMILLO   Sent by the king your father   560
To greet him and to give him comforts. Sir,
The manner of your bearing towards him, with
What you, as from your father, shall deliver –
Things known betwixt us three – I'll write you down,
The which shall point you forth at every sitting   565
What you must say, that he shall not perceive
But that you have your father's bosom there
And speak his very heart.

FLORIZEL   I am bound to you.
There is some sap in this.

CAMILLO   A course more promising
Than a wild dedication of yourselves   570
To unpathed waters, undreamed shores; most certain
To miseries enough – no hope to help you,
But as you shake off one to take another;
Nothing so certain as your anchors, who
Do their best office if they can but stay you   575
Where you'll be loath to be. Besides, you know
Prosperity's the very bond of love,
Whose fresh complexion and whose heart together
Affliction alters.

PERDITA   One of these is true.
I think affliction may subdue the cheek,   580
But not take in the mind.

CAMILLO   Yea? Say you so?

There shall not at your father's house these seven years
Be born another such.

FLORIZEL　　　　　　　　My good Camillo,
She's as forward of her breeding as
She is i'th' rear our birth.

585 CAMILLO　　　　　　　　I cannot say 'tis pity
She lacks instructions, for she seems a mistress
To most that teach.

PERDITA　　　　　　　　Your pardon, sir; for this
I'll blush you thanks.

FLORIZEL　　　　　　　　My prettiest Perdita!
But O, the thorns we stand upon! Camillo,
590 Preserver of my father, now of me,
The medicine of our house, how shall we do?
We are not furnished like Bohemia's son,
Nor shall appear in Sicilia –

CAMILLO　　　　　　　　　My lord,
Fear none of this. I think you know my fortunes
595 Do all lie there. It shall be so my care
To have you royally appointed, as if
The scene you play were mine. For instance, sir –
That you may know you shall not want – one word.

　　　[They speak apart.]

　　　Enter AUTOLYCUS.

AUTOLYCUS　Ha, ha! What a fool honesty is, and trust
600 – his sworn brother – a very simple gentleman! I have
sold all my trumpery; not a counterfeit stone, not a
ribbon, glass, pomander, brooch, table-book, ballad,
knife, tape, glove, shoe-tie, bracelet, horn-ring to keep
my pack from fasting. They throng who should buy
605 first, as if my trinkets had been hallowed and brought a
benediction to the buyer; by which means I saw whose
purse was best in picture; and what I saw, to my good
use I remembered. My clown, who wants but
something to be a reasonable man, grew so in love with
610 the wenches' song that he would not stir his pettitoes
till he had both tune and words, which so drew the rest
of the herd to me that all their other senses stuck in
ears. You might have pinched a placket, it was senseless.
'Twas nothing to geld a codpiece of a purse. I could
615 have filed keys off that hung in chains. No hearing, no
feeling, but my sir's song, and admiring the nothing of
it. So that, in this time of lethargy, I picked and cut
most of their festival purses, and, had not the old man
come in with a hubbub against his daughter and the
620 king's son, and scared my choughs from the chaff, I
had not left a purse alive in the whole army.

　　　[Camillo, Florizel and Perdita come forward.]

CAMILLO
Nay, but my letters, by this means being there
So soon as you arrive, shall clear that doubt.

FLORIZEL
And those that you'll procure from King Leontes?

CAMILLO　Shall satisfy your father.

625 PERDITA　　　　　　　　Happy be you.
All that you speak shows fair.

CAMILLO *[Sees Autolycus.]*　　　Who have we here?
We'll make an instrument of this, omit
Nothing may give us aid.

AUTOLYCUS *[aside]*
If they have overheard me now – why, hanging!

CAMILLO　How now, good fellow? Why shakest thou so?　630
Fear not, man. Here's no harm intended to thee.

AUTOLYCUS　I am a poor fellow, sir.

CAMILLO　Why, be so still. Here's nobody will steal that
from thee. Yet, for the outside of thy poverty, we must
make an exchange. Therefore discase thee instantly –　635
thou must think there's a necessity in't – and change
garments with this gentleman. Though the pennyworth on his side be the worst, yet hold thee, there's
some boot. *[Gives him money.]*

AUTOLYCUS　I am a poor fellow, sir. *[aside]* I know ye　640
well enough.

CAMILLO　Nay prithee, dispatch – the gentleman is half
flayed already.

AUTOLYCUS　Are you in earnest, sir? *[aside]* I smell the
trick on't.　　　　　　　　　　　　　　　　　645

FLORIZEL　Dispatch, I prithee.

AUTOLYCUS　Indeed, I have had earnest, but I cannot
with conscience take it.

CAMILLO　Unbuckle, unbuckle. *[Florizel and Autolycus
exchange clothes.]*
[to Perdita] Fortunate mistress – let my prophecy　650
Come home to ye! – you must retire yourself
Into some covert; take your sweetheart's hat
And pluck it o'er your brows, muffle your face,
Dismantle you and, as you can, disliken
The truth of your own seeming, that you may –　　655
For I do fear eyes over – to shipboard
Get undescried.

PERDITA　　　　　　　　I see the play so lies
That I must bear a part.

CAMILLO　　　　　　　　　No remedy.
– Have you done there?

FLORIZEL　　　　　　　　Should I now meet my father,
He would not call me son.

CAMILLO　　　　　　　　　Nay, you shall have no hat.　660
　　　[Gives the hat to Perdita.]
Come, lady, come. – Farewell, my friend.

AUTOLYCUS　　　　　　　　　　　Adieu, sir.

FLORIZEL　O Perdita, what have we twain forgot!
Pray you, a word.　　*[They talk apart.]*

CAMILLO *[aside]*
What I do next shall be to tell the king
Of this escape, and whither they are bound;　　665
Wherein my hope is I shall so prevail
To force him after, in whose company
I shall re-view Sicilia, for whose sight
I have a woman's longing.

FLORIZEL　　　　　　　　Fortune speed us!
Thus we set on, Camillo, to th' seaside.　　670

CAMILLO　The swifter speed the better.

　　　Exeunt Florizel, Perdita and Camillo.

AUTOLYCUS   I understand the business, I hear it. To have an open ear, a quick eye and a nimble hand is necessary for a cutpurse. A good nose is requisite also, to smell out work for th'other senses. I see this is the time that the unjust man doth thrive. What an exchange had this been without boot! What a boot is here with this exchange! Sure the gods do this year connive at us, and we may do anything extempore. The prince himself is about a piece of iniquity, stealing away from his father with his clog at his heels. If I thought it were a piece of honesty to acquaint the king withal, I would not do't. I hold it the more knavery to conceal it, and therein am I constant to my profession.

Enter CLOWN *and* SHEPHERD *carrying a bundle and a box.*

Aside, aside! Here is more matter for a hot brain. Every lane's end, every shop, church, session, hanging, yields a careful man work.

CLOWN   See, see, what a man you are now! There is no other way but to tell the king she's a changeling, and none of your flesh and blood.

SHEPHERD   Nay, but hear me.

CLOWN   Nay, but hear me.

SHEPHERD   Go to, then.

CLOWN   She being none of your flesh and blood, your flesh and blood has not offended the king, and so your flesh and blood is not to be punished by him. Show those things you found about her, those secret things, all but what she has with her. This being done, let the law go whistle, I warrant you.

SHEPHERD   I will tell the king all, every word, yea, and his son's pranks, too – who, I may say, is no honest man, neither to his father nor to me, to go about to make me the king's brother-in-law.

CLOWN   Indeed, brother-in-law was the farthest off you could have been to him, and then your blood had been the dearer by I know not how much an ounce.

AUTOLYCUS [*aside*]   Very wisely, puppies.

SHEPHERD   Well, let us to the king. There is that in this fardel will make him scratch his beard.

AUTOLYCUS [*aside*]   I know not what impediment this complaint may be to the flight of my master.

CLOWN   Pray heartily he be at palace.

AUTOLYCUS [*aside*]   Though I am not naturally honest, I am so sometimes by chance. Let me pocket up my pedlar's excrement. [*Removes his false beard.*] How now, rustics, whither are you bound?

SHEPHERD   To th' palace, an it like your worship.

AUTOLYCUS   Your affairs there? What? With whom? The condition of that fardel? The place of your dwelling? Your names? Your ages? Of what having, breeding, and anything that is fitting to be known, discover!

CLOWN   We are but plain fellows, sir.

AUTOLYCUS   A lie – you are rough and hairy. Let me have no lying; it becomes none but tradesmen, and they often give us soldiers the lie, but we pay them for it with stamped coin, not stabbing steel, therefore they do not give us the lie.

CLOWN   Your worship had like to have given us one if you had not taken yourself with the manner.

SHEPHERD   Are you a courtier, an't like you, sir?

AUTOLYCUS   Whether it like me or no, I am a courtier. Seest thou not the air of the court in these enfoldings? Hath not my gait in it the measure of the court? Receives not thy nose court-odour from me? Reflect I not on thy baseness court-contempt? Think'st thou, for that I insinuate to toze from thee thy business, I am therefore no courtier? I am courtier cap-a-pie, and one that will either push on or pluck back thy business there. Whereupon I command thee to open thy affair.

SHEPHERD   My business, sir, is to the king.

AUTOLYCUS   What advocate hast thou to him?

SHEPHERD   I know not, an't like you.

CLOWN [*aside to Shepherd*]   Advocate's the court word for a pheasant. Say you have none.

SHEPHERD   None, sir. I have no pheasant, cock nor hen.

AUTOLYCUS   How blessed are we that are not simple men! Yet Nature might have made me as these are. Therefore I will not disdain.

CLOWN   This cannot be but a great courtier.

SHEPHERD   His garments are rich, but he wears them not handsomely.

CLOWN   He seems to be the more noble in being fantastical. A great man, I'll warrant. I know by the picking on's teeth.

AUTOLYCUS   The fardel there, what's i'th' fardel? Wherefore that box?

SHEPHERD   Sir, there lies such secrets in this fardel and box which none must know but the king, and which he shall know within this hour, if I may come to th' speech of him.

AUTOLYCUS   Age, thou hast lost thy labour.

SHEPHERD   Why, sir?

AUTOLYCUS   The king is not at the palace; he is gone aboard a new ship to purge melancholy and air himself; for, if thou beest capable of things serious, thou must know the king is full of grief.

SHEPHERD   So 'tis said, sir: about his son, that should have married a shepherd's daughter.

AUTOLYCUS   If that shepherd be not in handfast, let him fly; the curses he shall have, the tortures he shall feel, will break the back of man, the heart of monster.

CLOWN   Think you so, sir?

AUTOLYCUS   Not he alone shall suffer what wit can make heavy and vengeance bitter, but those that are germane to him, though removed fifty times, shall all come under the hangman, which, though it be great pity, yet it is necessary. An old sheep-whistling rogue, a ram-tender, to offer to have his daughter come into grace! Some say he shall be stoned; but that death is too soft for him, say I. Draw our throne into a sheepcote? All deaths are too few, the sharpest too easy.

CLOWN Has the old man e'er a son, sir, do you hear, an't like you, sir?

785 AUTOLYCUS He has a son, who shall be flayed alive, then 'nointed over with honey, set on the head of a wasps' nest, then stand till he be three-quarters-and-a-dram dead, then recovered again with aqua

790 vitae, or some other hot infusion, then, raw as he is, and in the hottest day prognostication proclaims, shall he be set against a brick wall, the sun looking with a southward eye upon him, where he is to behold him with flies blown to death. But what talk we of these traitorly rascals, whose miseries are to be smiled at,

795 their offences being so capital? Tell me – for you seem to be honest plain men – what you have to the king. Being something gently considered, I'll bring you where he is aboard, tender your persons to his presence, whisper him in your behalfs, and if it be in

800 man, besides the king, to effect your suits, here is man shall do it.

CLOWN [*aside to Shepherd*] He seems to be of great authority. Close with him, give him gold; and, though authority be a stubborn bear, yet he is oft led by the

805 nose with gold. Show the inside of your purse to the outside of his hand, and no more ado. Remember, 'stoned', and 'flayed alive'.

SHEPHERD An't please you, sir, to undertake the business for us, here is that gold I have. I'll make it as

810 much more, and leave this young man in pawn till I bring it you.

AUTOLYCUS After I have done what I promised?

SHEPHERD Ay, sir.

AUTOLYCUS Well, give me the moiety. [*to Clown*] Are

815 you a party in this business?

CLOWN In some sort, sir. But, though my case be a pitiful one, I hope I shall not be flayed out of it.

AUTOLYCUS O, that's the case of the shepherd's son. Hang him, he'll be made an example.

820 CLOWN [*aside to Shepherd*] Comfort, good comfort. We must to the king and show our strange sights. He must know 'tis none of your daughter, nor my sister. We are gone else. – Sir, I will give you as much as this old man does when the business is performed, and remain, as

825 he says, your pawn till it be brought you.

AUTOLYCUS I will trust you. Walk before toward the seaside; go on the right hand – I will but look upon the hedge, and follow you.

CLOWN [*aside to Shepherd*] We are blessed in this man,

830 as I may say, even blessed.

SHEPHERD Let's before, as he bids us. He was provided to do us good. *Exit with Clown.*

AUTOLYCUS If I had a mind to be honest, I see Fortune would not suffer me – she drops booties in my mouth.

835 I am courted now with a double occasion: gold, and a means to do the prince my master good, which who knows how that may turn back to my advancement? I will bring these two moles, these blind ones, aboard him. If he think it fit to shore them again, and that the

complaint they have to the king concerns him nothing, 840 let him call me rogue for being so far officious; for I am proof against that title and what shame else belongs to't. To him will I present them. There may be matter in it. *Exit.*

5.1 *Enter* LEONTES, CLEOMENES, DION *and* PAULINA.

CLEOMENES [*to Leontes*]
Sir, you have done enough, and have performed
A saint-like sorrow. No fault could you make
Which you have not redeemed; indeed, paid down
More penitence than done trespass. At the last
Do as the heavens have done, forget your evil; 5
With them, forgive yourself.

LEONTES   Whilst I remember
Her and her virtues, I cannot forget
My blemishes in them, and so still think of
The wrong I did myself, which was so much
That heirless it hath made my kingdom, and 10
Destroyed the sweet'st companion that e'er man
Bred his hopes out of. True?

PAULINA   Too true, my lord.
If one by one you wedded all the world,
Or from the all that are took something good
To make a perfect woman, she you killed 15
Would be unparalleled.

LEONTES   I think so. Killed?
She I killed? I did so. But thou strik'st me
Sorely, to say I did; it is as bitter
Upon thy tongue as in my thought. Now, good now,
Say so but seldom.

CLEOMENES   Not at all, good lady. 20
You might have spoken a thousand things that would
Have done the time more benefit and graced
Your kindness better.

PAULINA   You are one of those
Would have him wed again.

DION   If you would not so,
You pity not the state, nor the remembrance 25
Of his most sovereign name, consider little
What dangers, by his highness' fail of issue,
May drop upon his kingdom and devour
Incertain lookers-on. What were more holy
Than to rejoice the former queen is well? 30
What holier, than for royalty's repair,
For present comfort and for future good,
To bless the bed of majesty again
With a sweet fellow to't?

PAULINA   There is none worthy,
Respecting her that's gone. Besides, the gods 35
Will have fulfilled their secret purposes.
For has not the divine Apollo said?
Is't not the tenor of his oracle
That King Leontes shall not have an heir
Till his lost child be found? Which that it shall 40

Is all as monstrous to our human reason
As my Antigonus to break his grave
And come again to me; who, on my life,
Did perish with the infant. 'Tis your counsel
45 My lord should to the heavens be contrary,
Oppose against their wills. [*to Leontes*] Care not for
    issue;
The crown will find an heir. Great Alexander
Left his to th' worthiest, so his successor
Was like to be the best.
LEONTES   Good Paulina,
50 Who hast the memory of Hermione,
I know, in honour – O, that ever I
Had squared me to thy counsel! Then even now
I might have looked upon my queen's full eyes,
Have taken treasure from her lips.
PAULINA   And left them
More rich for what they yielded.
55 LEONTES   Thou speak'st truth.
No more such wives, therefore no wife. One worse,
And better used, would make her sainted spirit
Again possess her corpse, and on this stage,
Were we offenders now, appear soul-vexed,
And begin, 'Why to me?'
60 PAULINA   Had she such power,
She had just cause.
LEONTES   She had, and would incense me
To murder her I married.
PAULINA   I should so.
Were I the ghost that walked, I'd bid you mark
Her eye, and tell me for what dull part in't
65 You chose her. Then I'd shriek that even your ears
Should rift to hear me, and the words that followed
Should be, 'Remember mine.'
LEONTES   Stars, stars,
And all eyes else, dead coals! Fear thou no wife;
I'll have no wife, Paulina.
PAULINA   Will you swear
70 Never to marry but by my free leave?
LEONTES   Never, Paulina, so be blest my spirit.
PAULINA
Then, good my lords, bear witness to his oath.
CLEOMENES   You tempt him over-much.
PAULINA   Unless another
As like Hermione as is her picture
Affront his eye –
CLEOMENES   Good madam –
75 PAULINA   I have done.
Yet if my lord will marry – if you will, sir,
No remedy but you will – give me the office
To choose you a queen. She shall not be so young
As was your former, but she shall be such
80 As, walked your first queen's ghost, it should take joy
To see her in your arms.
LEONTES   My true Paulina,
We shall not marry till thou bidd'st us.
PAULINA   That

Shall be when your first queen's again in breath.
Never till then.

                    Enter a Gentleman.

GENTLEMAN
One that gives out himself Prince Florizel,   85
Son of Polixenes, with his princess – she
The fairest I have yet beheld – desires access
To your high presence.
LEONTES   What with him? He comes not
Like to his father's greatness. His approach,
So out of circumstance and sudden, tells us   90
'Tis not a visitation framed, but forced
By need and accident. What train?
GENTLEMAN   But few,
And those but mean.
LEONTES   His princess, say you, with him?
GENTLEMAN
Ay, the most peerless piece of earth, I think,
That e'er the sun shone bright on.
PAULINA   O, Hermione,   95
As every present time doth boast itself
Above a better, gone, so must thy grave
Give way to what's seen now. [*to the Gentleman*] Sir,
    you yourself
Have said and writ so; but your writing now
Is colder than that theme. She had not been   100
Nor was not to be equalled – thus your verse
Flowed with her beauty once; 'tis shrewdly ebbed
To say you have seen a better.
GENTLEMAN   Pardon, madam.
The one I have almost forgot – your pardon –
The other, when she has obtained your eye,   105
Will have your tongue too. This is a creature,
Would she begin a sect, might quench the zeal
Of all professors else, make proselytes
Of who she but bid follow.
PAULINA   How? Not women!
GENTLEMAN
Women will love her, that she is a woman   110
More worth than any man; men, that she is
The rarest of all women.
LEONTES   Go, Cleomenes.
Yourself, assisted with your honoured friends,
Bring them to our embracement.
                    Exit Cleomenes with Gentleman.
                                        Still 'tis strange
He thus should steal upon us.
PAULINA   Had our prince,   115
Jewel of children, seen this hour, he had paired
Well with this lord; there was not full a month
Between their births.
LEONTES   Prithee no more; cease. Thou knowest
He dies to me again when talked of. Sure,
When I shall see this gentleman, thy speeches   120
Will bring me to consider that which may
Unfurnish me of reason. They are come.

Enter FLORIZEL, PERDITA, CLEOMENES *and others.*

Your mother was most true to wedlock, prince,
For she did print your royal father off,
125 Conceiving you. Were I but twenty-one,
Your father's image is so hit in you,
His very air, that I should call you brother,
As I did him, and speak of something wildly
By us performed before. Most dearly welcome,
130 And your fair princess – goddess – O, alas,
I lost a couple that 'twixt heaven and earth
Might thus have stood, begetting wonder, as
You, gracious couple, do; and then I lost –
All mine own folly – the society,
135 Amity too, of your brave father, whom,
Though bearing misery, I desire my life
Once more to look on him.

FLORIZEL   By his command
Have I here touched Sicilia, and from him
Give you all greetings that a king at friend
140 Can send his brother; and but infirmity,
Which waits upon worn times, hath something seized
His wished ability, he had himself
The lands and waters 'twixt your throne and his
Measured to look upon you, whom he loves –
145 He bade me say so – more than all the sceptres,
And those that bear them, living.

LEONTES   O, my brother!
Good gentleman, the wrongs I have done thee stir
Afresh within me, and these thy offices,
So rarely kind, are as interpreters
150 Of my behindhand slackness. Welcome hither,
As is the spring to th'earth! And hath he too
Exposed this paragon to th' fearful usage –
At least ungentle – of the dreadful Neptune,
To greet a man not worth her pains, much less
Th'adventure of her person?

FLORIZEL   Good my lord,
155 She came from Libya.

LEONTES   Where the warlike Smalus,
That noble honoured lord, is feared and loved?

FLORIZEL
Most royal sir, from thence; from him whose daughter
His tears proclaimed his, parting with her. Thence,
160 A prosperous south wind friendly, we have crossed,
To execute the charge my father gave me
For visiting your highness. My best train
I have from your Sicilian shores dismissed;
Who for Bohemia bend, to signify
165 Not only my success in Libya, sir,
But my arrival and my wife's, in safety
Here where we are.

LEONTES   The blessed gods
Purge all infection from our air whilst you
Do climate here. You have a holy father,
170 A graceful gentleman, against whose person,
So sacred as it is, I have done sin,

For which the heavens, taking angry note,
Have left me issueless; and your father's blessed,
As he from heaven merits it, with you,
Worthy his goodness. What might I have been, 175
Might I a son and daughter now have looked on,
Such goodly things as you?

Enter a Lord.

LORD   Most noble sir,
That which I shall report will bear no credit
Were not the proof so nigh. Please you, great sir,
Bohemia greets you from himself, by me; 180
Desires you to attach his son, who has,
His dignity and duty both cast off,
Fled from his father, from his hopes, and with
A shepherd's daughter.

LEONTES   Where's Bohemia? Speak.

LORD   Here in your city. I now came from him. 185
I speak amazedly, and it becomes
My marvel and my message. To your court
Whiles he was hastening – in the chase, it seems,
Of this fair couple – meets he on the way
The father of this seeming lady and 190
Her brother, having both their country quitted
With this young prince.

FLORIZEL   Camillo has betrayed me,
Whose honour and whose honesty till now
Endured all weathers.

LORD   Lay't so to his charge.
He's with the king your father.

LEONTES   Who? Camillo? 195

LORD   Camillo, sir. I spake with him, who now
Has these poor men in question. Never saw I
Wretches so quake. They kneel, they kiss the earth,
Forswear themselves as often as they speak.
Bohemia stops his ears, and threatens them 200
With divers deaths in death.

PERDITA   O, my poor father!
The heaven sets spies upon us, will not have
Our contract celebrated.

LEONTES   You are married?

FLORIZEL   We are not, sir, nor are we like to be.
The stars, I see, will kiss the valleys first; 205
The odds for high and low's alike.

LEONTES   My lord,
Is this the daughter of a king?

FLORIZEL   She is,
When once she is my wife.

LEONTES
That 'once', I see, by your good father's speed
Will come on very slowly. I am sorry, 210
Most sorry, you have broken from his liking,
Where you were tied in duty, and as sorry
Your choice is not so rich in worth as beauty,
That you might well enjoy her.

FLORIZEL [*to Perdita*]   Dear, look up.
Though Fortune, visible an enemy, 215

Should chase us with my father, power no jot
Hath she to change our loves. Beseech you, sir,
Remember since you owed no more to time
Than I do now. With thought of such affections,
220 Step forth mine advocate; at your request,
My father will grant precious things as trifles.

LEONTES
Would he do so, I'd beg your precious mistress,
Which he counts but a trifle.

PAULINA   Sir, my liege,
Your eye hath too much youth in't. Not a month
225 'Fore your queen died, she was more worth such gazes
Than what you look on now.

LEONTES   I thought of her
Even in these looks I made. [*to Florizel*] But your
    petition
Is yet unanswered. I will to your father.
Your honour not o'erthrown by your desires,
230 I am friend to them and you; upon which errand
I now go toward him; therefore follow me,
And mark what way I make. Come, good my lord.

                                Exeunt.

5.2   *Enter* AUTOLYCUS *and a* Gentleman.

AUTOLYCUS   Beseech you, sir, were you present at this
    relation?

GENTLEMAN   I was by at the opening of the fardel,
    heard the old shepherd deliver the manner how he
5   found it; whereupon, after a little amazedness, we were
    all commanded out of the chamber. Only this,
    methought I heard the shepherd say he found the
    child.

AUTOLYCUS   I would most gladly know the issue of it.

10 GENTLEMAN   I make a broken delivery of the business,
    but the changes I perceived in the king and Camillo
    were very notes of admiration. They seemed almost,
    with staring on one another, to tear the cases of their
    eyes. There was speech in their dumbness, language in
15   their very gesture. They looked as they had heard of a
    world ransomed, or one destroyed. A notable passion
    of wonder appeared in them, but the wisest beholder,
    that knew no more but seeing, could not say if
    th'importance were joy or sorrow; but in the extremity
20   of the one it must needs be.

                Enter ROGERO.

Here comes a gentleman that happily knows more.
The news, Rogero?

ROGERO   Nothing but bonfires. The oracle is fulfilled,
    the king's daughter is found. Such a deal of wonder is
25   broken out within this hour that ballad-makers cannot
    be able to express it.

                Enter the Steward.

Here comes the Lady Paulina's steward; he can deliver
you more. How goes it now, sir? This news which is
called true is so like an old tale that the verity of it is in
strong suspicion. Has the king found his heir?   30

STEWARD   Most true, if ever truth were pregnant by
    circumstance. That which you hear you'll swear you
    see; there is such unity in the proofs. The mantle of
    Queen Hermione's; her jewel about the neck of it; the
    letters of Antigonus found with it, which they know to   35
    be his character; the majesty of the creature, in
    resemblance of the mother; the affection of nobleness
    which nature shows above her breeding, and many
    other evidences proclaim her with all certainty to be
    the king's daughter. Did you see the meeting of the   40
    two kings?

ROGERO   No.

STEWARD   Then have you lost a sight which was to be
    seen, cannot be spoken of. There might you have
    beheld one joy crown another, so and in such manner   45
    that it seemed sorrow wept to take leave of them, for
    their joy waded in tears. There was casting up of eyes,
    holding up of hands, with countenance of such
    distraction that they were to be known by garment,
    not by favour. Our king being ready to leap out of   50
    himself for joy of his found daughter, as if that joy were
    now become a loss, cries, 'O, thy mother, thy mother!',
    then asks Bohemia forgiveness, then embraces his son-
    in-law, then again worries he his daughter with
    clipping her. Now he thanks the old shepherd, which   55
    stands by like a weather-bitten conduit of many
    kings' reigns. I never heard of such another encounter,
    which lames report to follow it, and undoes description
    to do it.

ROGERO   What, pray you, became of Antigonus, that   60
    carried hence the child?

STEWARD   Like an old tale still, which will have matter
    to rehearse though credit be asleep and not an ear open
    – he was torn to pieces with a bear. This avouches the
    shepherd's son, who has not only his innocence, which 65
    seems much, to justify him, but a handkerchief and
    rings of his, that Paulina knows.

GENTLEMAN   What became of his barque and his
    followers?

STEWARD   Wrecked the same instant of their master's   70
    death, and in the view of the shepherd; so that all the
    instruments which aided to expose the child were even
    then lost when it was found. But O, the noble combat
    that 'twixt joy and sorrow was fought in Paulina! She
    had one eye declined for the loss of her husband,   75
    another elevated that the oracle was fulfilled. She lifted
    the princess from the earth, and so locks her in
    embracing as if she would pin her to her heart, that she
    might no more be in danger of losing.

GENTLEMAN   The dignity of this act was worth the   80
    audience of kings and princes, for by such was it acted.

STEWARD   One of the prettiest touches of all, and that
    which angled for mine eyes – caught the water, though
    not the fish – was when at the relation of the queen's
    death, with the manner how she came to't bravely   85

confessed and lamented by the king, how attentiveness wounded his daughter till from one sign of dolour to another she did, with an 'Alas', I would fain say bleed tears; for I am sure my heart wept blood. Who was most marble there changed colour. Some swooned, all sorrowed. If all the world could have seen't, the woe had been universal.

GENTLEMAN   Are they returned to the court?

STEWARD   No. The princess, hearing of her mother's statue, which is in the keeping of Paulina, a piece many years in doing and now newly performed by that rare Italian master Giulio Romano, who, had he himself eternity and could put breath into his work, would beguile Nature of her custom, so perfectly he is her ape. He so near to Hermione hath done Hermione that they say one would speak to her and stand in hope of answer. Thither with all greediness of affection are they gone, and there they intend to sup.

ROGERO   I thought she had some great matter there in hand, for she hath privately twice or thrice a day, ever since the death of Hermione, visited that removed house. Shall we thither, and with our company piece the rejoicing?

GENTLEMAN   Who would be thence, that has the benefit of access? Every wink of an eye some new grace will be born. Our absence makes us unthrifty to our knowledge. Let's along.

Exeunt Gentleman, Rogero and Steward

AUTOLYCUS   Now, had I not the dash of my former life in me, would preferment drop on my head. I brought the old man and his son aboard the prince; told him I heard them talk of a fardel, and I know not what; but he at that time over-fond of the shepherd's daughter – so he then took her to be – who began to be much seasick and himself little better, extremity of weather continuing, this mystery remained undiscovered. But 'tis all one to me, for had I been the finder-out of this secret it would not have relished among my other discredits.

Enter SHEPHERD *and* CLOWN *dressed as gentlemen.*

Here come those I have done good to against my will, and already appearing in the blossoms of their fortune.

SHEPHERD   Come, boy, I am past moe children, but thy sons and daughters will be all gentlemen born.

CLOWN [*to Autolycus*]   You are well met, sir. You denied to fight with me this other day because I was no gentleman born. See you these clothes? Say you see them not, and think me still no gentleman born. You were best say these robes are not gentlemen born. Give me the lie, do, and try whether I am not now a gentleman born.

AUTOLYCUS   I know you are now, sir, a gentleman born.

CLOWN   Ay, and have been so any time these four hours.

SHEPHERD   And so have I, boy.

CLOWN   So you have; but I was a gentleman born before my father, for the king's son took me by the hand and called me brother, and then the two kings called my father brother, and then the prince my brother and the princess my sister called my father father, and so we wept; and there was the first gentleman-like tears that ever we shed.

SHEPHERD   We may live, son, to shed many more.

CLOWN   Ay, or else 'twere hard luck, being in so preposterous estate as we are.

AUTOLYCUS   I humbly beseech you, sir, to pardon me all the faults I have committed to your worship, and to give me your good report to the prince my master.

SHEPHERD   Prithee, son, do; for we must be gentle now we are gentlemen.

CLOWN   Thou wilt amend thy life?

AUTOLYCUS   Ay, an it like your good worship.

CLOWN   Give me thy hand. I will swear to the prince thou art as honest a true fellow as any is in Bohemia.

SHEPHERD   You may say it, but not swear it.

CLOWN   Not swear it, now I am a gentleman? Let boors and franklins say it; I'll swear it.

SHEPHERD   How if it be false, son?

CLOWN   If it be ne'er so false, a true gentleman may swear it in the behalf of his friend. [*to Autolycus*] And I'll swear to the prince thou art a tall fellow of thy hands, and that thou wilt not be drunk; but I know thou art no tall fellow of thy hands, and that thou wilt be drunk; but I'll swear it, and I would thou wouldst be a tall fellow of thy hands.

AUTOLYCUS   I will prove so, sir, to my power.

CLOWN   Ay, by any means prove a tall fellow. If I do not wonder how thou dar'st venture to be drunk, not being a tall fellow, trust me not.   [*Flourish sounded within.*] Hark, the kings and the princes, our kindred, are going to see the queen's picture. Come, follow us. We'll be thy good masters.   *Exeunt.*

5.3   *Enter* LEONTES, POLIXENES, FLORIZEL,
   PERDITA, CAMILLO, PAULINA, *Lords and others.*

LEONTES   O grave and good Paulina, the great comfort
That I have had of thee!

PAULINA   What, sovereign sir,
I did not well, I meant well. All my services
You have paid home, but that you have vouchsafed
With your crowned brother, and these your contracted
Heirs of your kingdoms, my poor house to visit,
It is a surplus of your grace which never
My life may last to answer.

LEONTES   O Paulina,
We honour you with trouble. But we came
To see the statue of our queen. Your gallery
Have we passed through, not without much content
In many singularities, but we saw not
That which my daughter came to look upon,
The statue of her mother.

PAULINA   As she lived peerless,
So her dead likeness I do well believe

Excels whatever yet you looked upon,
Or hand of man hath done. Therefore I keep it
Lonely, apart. But here it is: prepare
To see the life as lively mocked as ever
20   Still sleep mocked death. Behold, and say 'tis well.
        [*Draws a curtain and reveals the figure of Hermione,
         standing like a statue.*]
I like your silence; it the more shows off
Your wonder. But yet speak – first you, my liege.
Comes it not something near?
LEONTES   Her natural posture.
Chide me, dear stone, that I may say indeed
25   Thou art Hermione – or, rather, thou art she
In thy not chiding; for she was as tender
As infancy and grace. But yet, Paulina,
Hermione was not so much wrinkled, nothing
So aged as this seems.
POLIXENES   O, not by much.
30 PAULINA   So much the more our carver's excellence,
Which lets go by some sixteen years and makes her
As she lived now.
LEONTES   As now she might have done,
So much to my good comfort as it is
Now piercing to my soul. O, thus she stood,
35   Even with such life of majesty – warm life,
As now it coldly stands – when first I wooed her.
I am ashamed. Does not the stone rebuke me
For being more stone than it? O royal piece!
There's magic in thy majesty, which has
40   My evils conjured to remembrance, and
From thy admiring daughter took the spirits,
Standing like stone with thee.
PERDITA   And give me leave,
And do not say 'tis superstition, that
I kneel and then implore her blessing. Lady,
45   Dear queen, that ended when I but began,
Give me that hand of yours to kiss.
PAULINA   O patience!
The statue is but newly fixed; the colour's
Not dry.
CAMILLO [*to Leontes*]
My lord, your sorrow was too sore laid on,
50   Which sixteen winters cannot blow away,
So many summers dry. Scarce any joy
Did ever so long live; no sorrow
But killed itself much sooner.
POLIXENES [*to Leontes*]   Dear my brother,
Let him that was the cause of this have power
55   To take off so much grief from you as he
Will piece up in himself.
PAULINA [*to Leontes*]   Indeed, my lord,
If I had thought the sight of my poor image
Would thus have wrought you – for the stone is mine –
I'd not have showed it.   [*Makes to draw the curtain.*]
LEONTES   Do not draw the curtain.
PAULINA
60   No longer shall you gaze on't, lest your fancy

May think anon it moves.
LEONTES   Let be, let be!
Would I were dead but that methinks already –
What was he that did make it? See, my lord,
Would you not deem it breathed, and that those veins
Did verily bear blood?
POLIXENES   Masterly done.   65
The very life seems warm upon her lip.
LEONTES   The fixure of her eye has motion in't,
As we are mocked with art.
PAULINA   I'll draw the curtain.
My lord's almost so far transported that
He'll think anon it lives.
LEONTES   O sweet Paulina,   70
Make me to think so twenty years together.
No settled senses of the world can match
The pleasure of that madness. Let't alone.
PAULINA   I am sorry, sir, I have thus far stirred you; but
I could afflict you farther.
LEONTES   Do, Paulina,   75
For this affliction has a taste as sweet
As any cordial comfort. Still methinks
There is an air comes from her. What fine chisel
Could ever yet cut breath? Let no man mock me,
For I will kiss her.
PAULINA   Good my lord, forbear;   80
The ruddiness upon her lip is wet.
You'll mar it if you kiss it, stain your own
With oily painting. Shall I draw the curtain?
LEONTES   No, not these twenty years.
PERDITA   So long could I
Stand by, a looker-on.
PAULINA   Either forbear,   85
Quit presently the chapel, or resolve you
For more amazement. If you can behold it,
I'll make the statue move indeed, descend
And take you by the hand. But then you'll think –
Which I protest against – I am assisted   90
By wicked powers.
LEONTES   What you can make her do
I am content to look on; what to speak
I am content to hear; for 'tis as easy
To make her speak as move.
PAULINA   It is required
You do awake your faith. Then all stand still.   95
Or those that think it is unlawful business
I am about, let them depart.
LEONTES   Proceed.
No foot shall stir.
PAULINA   Music, awake her; strike!   [*Music*]
[*to Hermione*] 'Tis time; descend; be stone no more;
    approach.
Strike all that look upon with marvel. Come,   100
I'll fill your grave up. Stir – nay, come away;
Bequeath to death your numbness, for from him
Dear life redeems you. You perceive she stirs.
    [*Hermione steps down.*]

Start not. Her actions shall be holy as
You hear my spell is lawful. [*to Leontes*] Do not shun
105　　her
Until you see her die again, for then
You kill her double. Nay, present your hand.
When she was young, you wooed her; now in age,
Is she become the suitor?

LEONTES　　　　　　　　　　O, she's warm!
110　If this be magic, let it be an art
Lawful as eating.

POLIXENES　　　　　She embraces him.

CAMILLO　She hangs about his neck;
If she pertain to life, let her speak too!

POLIXENES
Ay, and make it manifest where she has lived,
Or how stolen from the dead.

PAULINA　　　　　　　　　That she is living,
115　Were it but told you, should be hooted at
Like an old tale. But it appears she lives,
Though yet she speak not. Mark a little while.
[*to Perdita*] Please you to interpose, fair madam.
　　Kneel,
And pray your mother's blessing.
120　[*to Hermione*]　　　　　Turn, good lady,
Our Perdita is found.

HERMIONE　　　　You gods, look down,
And from your sacred vials pour your graces
Upon my daughter's head! Tell me, mine own,
Where hast thou been preserved? Where lived? How
　　found
125　Thy father's court? For thou shalt hear that I,
Knowing by Paulina that the oracle

Gave hope thou wast in being, have preserved
Myself to see the issue.

PAULINA　　　　　　　There's time enough for that,
Lest they desire upon this push to trouble
Your joys with like relation. Go together,　　　130
You precious winners all; your exultation
Partake to everyone. I, an old turtle,
Will wing me to some withered bough, and there
My mate, that's never to be found again,
Lament till I am lost.

LEONTES　　　　　　　O peace, Paulina!　　　135
Thou shouldst a husband take by my consent,
As I by thine a wife. This is a match,
And made between's by vows. Thou hast found mine,
But how is to be questioned, for I saw her,
As I thought, dead, and have in vain said many　　140
A prayer upon her grave. I'll not seek far –
For him, I partly know his mind – to find thee
An honourable husband. Come, Camillo,
And take her by the hand, whose worth and honesty
Is richly noted, and here justified　　　145
By us, a pair of kings. Let's from this place.
[*to Hermione*] What? Look upon my brother. Both
　　your pardons,
That e'er I put between your holy looks
My ill suspicion. This your son-in-law,
And son unto the king, whom heavens directing,　　150
Is troth-plight to your daughter. Good Paulina,
Lead us from hence, where we may leisurely
Each one demand and answer to his part
Performed in this wide gap of time since first
We were dissevered. Hastily lead away.　　*Exeunt.*　155

Bibliography

SHAKESPEARE'S LIFE

Bentley, G.E., *Shakespeare: A Biographical Handbook*, New Haven: Yale University Press, 1961
Chambers, E.K., *William Shakespeare: A Study of Facts and Problems*, 2 vols, Oxford: Clarendon Press, 1930
Duncan-Jones, Katherine, *Shakespeare: An Ungentle Life*, London: A & C Black, 2010
Dutton, Richard, *William Shakespeare: A Literary Life*, Basingstoke, Hants: Macmillan, 1989
Eccles, Mark, *Shakespeare in Warwickshire*, Madison: University of Wisconsin Press, 1961
Fraser, Russell, *Shakespeare, the Later Years*, New York: Columbia University Press, 1992
Fraser, Russell, *Young Shakespeare*, New York: Columbia University Press, 1988
Honan, Park, *Shakespeare: A Life*, Oxford: Oxford University Press, 1999
Schoenbaum, Samuel, *Shakespeare's Lives*, new edn, Oxford: Clarendon Press, 1991
Schoenbaum, Samuel, *William Shakespeare: A Compact Documentary Life*, rev. edn, Oxford: Oxford University Press, 1987
Schoenbaum, Samuel, *William Shakespeare: A Documentary Life*, Oxford: Oxford University Press, 1975
Schoenbaum, Samuel, *William Shakespeare: Records and Images*, Oxford: Oxford University Press, 1981
Shapiro, James, *1599: A Year in the Life of William Shakespeare*, London: Faber & Faber, 2005
Shapiro, James, *1606: William Shakespeare and the Year of Lear*, London: Faber & Faber, 2016
Shapiro, James, *Contested Will: Who Wrote Shakespeare?*, London: Faber & Faber, 2010

SHAKESPEARE IN PERFORMANCE

Shakespeare on the stage

Astington, John H., *Actors and Acting in Shakespeare's Time: The Art of Stage Playing*, Cambridge: Cambridge University Press, 2010
Bate, Jonathan, *Shakespeare: An Illustrated Stage History*, Oxford: Oxford University Press, 1996
Beckerman, Bernard, *Shakespeare at the Globe, 1599–1609*, New York: Macmillan, 1962
Berry, Herbert, *Shakespeare's Playhouses*, New York: AMS Press, 1987
Bevington, David, *Action Is Eloquence: Shakespeare's Language of Gesture*, Cambridge, Mass.: Harvard University Press, 1984
Bulman, J.C., and H.R. Coursen, eds, *Shakespeare on Television*, Hanover, N.H.: University Press of New England, 1988
Callow, Simon, *Orson Welles: Hello Americans*, London: Jonathan Cape, 2015
Carson, Christie, and Farah Karim-Cooper, eds, *Shakespeare's Globe: A Theatrical Experiment*, Cambridge, Cambridge University Press, 2008
Dessen, Alan C., *Recovering Shakespeare's Theatrical Vocabulary*, Cambridge: Cambridge University Press, 1995
Dessen, Alan C., and Leslie Thomson, *A Dictionary of Stage Directions in English Drama, 1580–1642*, Cambridge: Cambridge University Press, 1999
Dobson, Michael, *Shakespeare and Amateur Performance: A Cultural History*, Cambridge: Cambridge University Press, 2011
Duncan-Jones, K., *Shakespeare: Upstart Crow to Sweet Swan, 1592–1623*, London: Arden Shakespeare, 2011
Edmondson, Paul, and Stanley Wells, *The Shakespeare Circle*, Cambridge: Cambridge University Press, 2015
Escolme, Bridget, *Talking to the Audience: Shakespeare, Performance, Self*, Abingdon and New York: Routledge, 2005
Gurr, Andrew, *Playgoing in Shakespeare's London*, Cambridge: Cambridge University Press, 1989
Gurr, Andrew, *Shakespearian Playing Companies*, Oxford: Clarendon Press, 1996
Gurr, Andrew, *The Shakespearean Stage, 1574–1642*, 3rd edn, Cambridge: Cambridge University Press, 1992
Gurr, Andrew, and Mariko Ichikawa, *Staging in Shakespeare's Theatres*, Oxford Shakespeare Topics, Oxford: Oxford University Press, 2000
Gurr, Andrew, and Farah Karim-Cooper, eds, *Moving Shakespeare Indoors: Performance and Repertoire in the Jacobean Playhouse*, Cambridge: Cambridge University Press, 2015
Gurr, Andrew, and John Orrell, *Rebuilding Shakespeare's Globe*, London: Weidenfeld & Nicolson, 1989
Hodgdon, Barbara, and W.B. Worthen, *A Companion to Shakespeare and Performance*, Oxford: Oxford University Press, 2005
Hogan, Charles B., *Shakespeare in the Theatre, 1701–1800*, 2 vols, Oxford: Clarendon Press, 1952–7
Holland, Peter, *English Shakespeares: Shakespeare on the English Stage in the 1990s*, Cambridge: Cambridge University Press, 1997
Keenan, Siobhan, *Acting Companies and their Plays in Shakespeare's London*, London: Bloomsbury, 2014
Kennedy, Dennis, and Yong Li Lan, eds, *Shakespeare in Asia: Contemporary Performance*, Cambridge: Cambridge University Press, 2010
King, T.J., *Casting Shakespeare's Plays: London Actors and Their Roles, 1590–1642*, Cambridge: Cambridge University Press, 1992
Knutson, Roslyn L., *The Repertory of Shakespeare's Company, 1594–1613*, Fayetteville: University of Arkansas Press, 1991
Mulryne, J.R., and Margaret Shewring, eds, *Shakespeares' Globe Rebuilt*, Cambridge: Cambridge University Press, 1997
Nungezer, Edwin, *A Dictionary of Actors and Other Persons Associated with Public Representation of Plays in England before 1642*, New Haven: Yale University Press, 1929
Orrell, John, *The Quest for Shakespeare's Globe*, Cambridge: Cambridge University Press, 1983

Pollard, Tanya, *Shakespeare's Theater: A Sourcebook*, Oxford: Blackwell, 2004

Raw, Laurence, *Theatre of the People: Donald Wolfit's Shakespearean Productions 1937–1953*, Lanham, Md.: Rowman & Littlefield, 2016

Sasayama, Takashi, J.R. Mulryne and Margaret Shewring, *Shakespeare and the Japanese Stage*, Cambridge: Cambridge University Press, 1998

Schafer, Elizabeth J., *Shakespeare in Production: 'The Taming of the Shrew'*, Cambridge: Cambridge University Press, 2002

Shattuck, Charles H., *Shakespeare on the American Stage: From the Hallams to Edwin Booth*, Washington: Folger Shakespeare Library, 1976

Sprague, Arthur Colby, *Shakespeare and the Actors: The Stage Business in His Plays, 1660–1905*, Cambridge, Mass.: Harvard University Press, 1944

Stern, Tiffany, *Rehearsal from Shakespeare to Sheridan*, Oxford: Oxford University Press, 2000

Thomson, Peter, *Shakespeare's Theatre*, 2nd edn, London: Routledge, 1992

Trewin, J.C., *Shakespeare on the English Stage, 1900–1964*, London: Barrie & Rockliff, 1964

Warren, Roger, *Staging Shakespeare's Late Plays*, Oxford: Clarendon Press, 1990

Wells, Stanley, *Great Shakespearian Actors: Burbage to Branagh*, Oxford: Oxford University Press, 2015

Wells, Stanley, *Shakespeare and Company*, London: Allen Lane, 2006

Wells, Stanley, and Sarah Stanton, *The Cambridge Companion to Shakespeare on Stage*, Cambridge: Cambridge University Press, 2002

Wiles, David, *Shakespeare's Clown: Actor and Text in the Elizabethan Playhouse*, Cambridge: Cambridge University Press, 1987

Ziegler, Philip, *Olivier*, London: MacLehose, 2013

Shakespeare on film, television and radio

Boose, Lynda E., and Richard Burt, eds, *Shakespeare, The Movie* and *Shakespeare, The Movie II*, London and New York: Routledge, 1997 and 2003

Buchanan, Judith, *Shakespeare on Film*, Harlow: Longman-Pearson, 2005

Buchanan, Judith, *Shakespeare on Silent Film*, Cambridge: Cambridge University Press, 2009

Bulman, J.C., and H.R. Coursen, eds, *Shakespeare on Television*, Hanover, N.H.: University Press of New England, 1988

Burnett, Mark Thornton, *Filming Shakespeare in the Global Marketplace*, Basingstoke: Palgrave Macmillan, 2007

Burnett, Mark Thornton, *Shakespeare and World Cinema*, Cambridge: Cambridge University Press, 2013

Holland, Peter, ed., *Shakespeare, Sound and Screen: Shakespeare Survey 61*, Cambridge: Cambridge University Press, 2008

Jackson, Russell, ed., *The Cambridge Companion to Shakespeare on Film*, Cambridge: Cambridge University Press, 2000

Jorgens, Jack J., *Shakespeare on Film*, Bloomington: Indiana University Press, 1976

McKernan, Luke, and Olwen Terris, eds, *Walking Shadows: Shakespeare in the National Film and Television Archive*, London: British Film Institute Publishing, 1994

Rothwell, Kenneth, *A History of Shakespeare on Screen*, Cambridge: Cambridge University Press, 1999

Terris, Olwen, Eve-Marie Oesterlen and Luke McKernan, eds, *Shakespeare on Film, Television and Radio: The Researcher's Guide*, London: British Universities Film and Video Council, 2009

SHAKESPEARE ONLINE RESOURCES

British Book Trade Index, ed. Peter Isaac, University of Oxford, *http://bbti.bodleian.ox.ac.uk*

Database of Early English Playbooks (DEEP), ed. Alan Farmer and Zachary Lesser, University of Pennsylvania, *http://deep.sas.upenn.edu*

Early English Books Online (EEBO), *http://eebo.chadwyck.com/home*

Global Shakespeares Video and Performance Archive, ed. Peter Donaldson, MIT, *https://globalshakespeares.mit.edu*

Henslowe-Alleyn Digitisation Project, Dulwich College, *http://www.henslowe-alleyn.org.uk/index.html*

LUNA: Folger Digital Image Collection, Folger Shakespeare Library, *https://luna.folger.edu/luna/servlet/FOLGERCM1~6~6*

MIT Global Shakespeares: Video and Performance Archive, *https://globalshakespeares.mit.edu*

REED Online, Records of Early English Drama, University of Toronto, *https://ereed.library.utoronto.ca*

Shakespeare in Quarto, British Library, *https://www.bl.uk/treasures/shakespeare/homepage.html*

Shakespeare's Plays, Folger Digital Texts, ed. Barbara Mowat, Paul Werstine, Michael Poston and Rebecca Niles, Folger Shakespeare Library, *www.folgerdigitaltexts.org*

Shakespearean Promptbooks of the Seventeenth Century, ed. G. Blakemore Evans, Bibliographical Society of the University of Virginia, *http://bsuva.org/bsuva/promptbook*

GLOBAL SHAKESPEARE

Dionne, Craig, and Parmita Kapadia, eds, *Bollywood Shakespeares*, London: Palgrave Macmillan, 2014

Dionne, Craig, and Parmita Kapadia, eds, *Native Shakespeares: Indigenous Appropriations on a Global Stage*, Farnham: Ashgate, 2008

Drouin, Jennifer, *Shakespeare in Quebec: Nation, Gender, and Adaptation*, Toronto: University of Toronto Press, 2014

Hennessey, Katherine, *Shakespeare on the Arabian Peninsula*, London: Palgrave Macmillan, 2018

Huang, Alexa, *Chinese Shakespeares: Two Centuries of Cultural Exchange*, New York: Columbia University Press, 2009

Kennedy, Dennis, *Global Shakespeare and Globalized Performance*, Oxford: Oxford University Press, 2017

Kliman, Bernice, and Rick Santos, eds, *Latin American Shakespeares*, Madison: Fairleigh Dickinson University Press, 2005

McMullan, Gordon, and Philip Mead, *Antipodal Shakespeare: Remembering and Forgetting in Britain, Australia and New Zealand, 1916–2016*, Arden Shakespeare, London: Bloomsbury, 2018

Massai, Sonia, ed., *World-Wide Shakespeares: Local Appropriations in Film and Performance*, London and New York: Routledge, 2005

Prescott, Paul, and Erin Sullivan, eds, *Shakespeare on the Global Stage: Performance and Festivity in the Olympic Year*, Arden Shakespeare, London: Bloomsbury, 2015

Wilson-Lee, Edward, *Shakespeare in Swahililand: In Search of a Global Poet*, New York: Farrar, Straus & Giroux, 2016

THE EARLY TEXTS

BL Quartos: https://www.bl.uk/treasures/shakespeare

First Folio: https://first.folio.bodleian.ox.ac.uk

Sir Thomas More: examples of what may be Shakespeare's handwriting at https://www.bl.uk/collection-items/shakespeares-handwriting-in-the-book-of-sir-thomas-more

Allen, Michael J.B., and Kenneth Muir, *Shakespeare's Plays in Quarto: A Facsimile Edition of Copies Primarily in the Henry E. Huntington Library*, Berkeley and Los Angeles: University of California Press, 1981

Bourus, Terri, *Young Shakespeare's Young Hamlet: Print, Piracy, and Performance*, New York: Palgrave Macmillan, 2014

Egan, Gabriel, *The Struggle for Shakespeare's Text: Twentieth-Century Editorial Theory and Practice*, Cambridge: Cambridge University Press, 2011

Grant, Stephen H., *Collecting Shakespeare: The Story of Henry and Emily Folger*, Baltimore, Md.: Johns Hopkins University Press, 2016

Hinman, Charlton, ed., *The Norton Facsimile: The First Folio of Shakespeare*, 2nd edn, New York: Norton, 1996

Jowett, John, *Shakespeare and the Text*, rev. edn, Oxford: Oxford University Press, 2019

Kidnie, M.J., and Sonia Massai, eds, *Shakespeare and Textual Studies*, Cambridge: Cambridge University Press, 2015

Lesser, Zachary, *Hamlet after Q1: An Uncanny History of the Shakespearean Text*, Philadelphia: University of Pennsylvania Press, 2014

Miller, Stephen R., ed., *The Taming of a Shrew*, Cambridge: Cambridge University Press, 1998

Rasmussen, Eric, and Anthony J. West, *The Shakespeare First Folios: A Descriptive Catalogue*, New York: Palgrave Macmillan, 2012

Smith, Emma, *The Making of Shakespeare's First Folio*, Oxford: Bodleian Library, 2016

Smith, Emma, *Shakespeare's First Folio: Four Centuries of an Iconic Book*, Oxford: Oxford University Press, 2016

Werstine, Paul, *Early Playhouse Manuscripts and the Editing of Shakespeare*, Cambridge: Cambridge University Press, 2013

TEXTUAL STUDIES

Blayney, Peter W.M., *The First Folio of Shakespeare*, Washington: Folger Library Publications, 1991

Blayney, Peter W.M., *The Texts of King Lear and Their Origins*, Vol. 1: *Nicholas Okes and the First Quarto*, Cambridge: Cambridge University Press, 1982

Bowers, Fredson, *On Editing Shakespeare*, Charlottesville: University of Virginia Press, 1966

Brooks, Douglas A., *From Playhouse to Printing House: Drama and Authorship in Early Modern England*, Cambridge: Cambridge University Press, 2000

De Grazia, Margreta, *Shakespeare Verbatim: The Reproduction of Authenticity and the 1790 Apparatus*, Oxford: Clarendon Press, 1991

Erne, Lukas, *Shakespeare and the Book Trade*, Cambridge: Cambridge University Press, 2013

Erne, Lukas, *Shakespeare as Literary Dramatist*, 2nd edn, Cambridge: Cambridge University Press, 2013

Greg, W.W., *The Editorial Problem in Shakespeare*, 3rd edn, Oxford: Clarendon Press, 1954

Greg, W.W., *The Shakespeare First Folio: Its Bibliographical and Textual History*, Oxford: Clarendon Press, 1955

Hinman, Charlton, *The Printing and Proof-reading of the First Folio Shakespeare*, 2 vols, Oxford: Clarendon Press, 1963

Honigmann, E.A.J., *The Stability of Shakespeare's Text*, London: Edward Arnold, 1965

Honigmann, E.A.J., *The Texts of 'Othello' and Shakespearian Revision*, London and New York: Routledge, 1996

Kastan, David Scott, *Shakespeare and the Book*, Cambridge: Cambridge University Press, 2001

Lesser, Zachary, *Renaissance Drama and the Politics of Publication: Readings in the English Book Trade*, Cambridge: Cambridge University Press, 2004

Maguire, Laurie, *Shakespearean Suspect Texts: The 'Bad' Quartos and Their Contexts*, Cambridge: Cambridge University Press, 1996

Pollard, Alfred W., *Shakespeare Folios and Quartos: A Study in the Bibliography of Shakespeare's Plays, 1594–1685*, London: Methuen, 1909

Taylor, Gary, and John Jowett, *Shakespeare Reshaped 1606–1623*, Oxford: Clarendon Press, 1993

Walker, Alice, *Textual Problems of the First Folio*, Cambridge: Cambridge University Press, 1953

Wells, Stanley, and Gary Taylor, eds, *Modernizing Shakespeare's Spelling: With Three Studies of the Text of 'Henry V'*, Oxford: Clarendon Press, 1979

Wells, Stanley, and Gary Taylor, eds, *Re-editing Shakespeare for the Modern Reader*, Oxford: Clarendon Press, 1984

Wells, Stanley, and Gary Taylor, eds, *William Shakespeare: A Textual Companion*, Oxford: Clarendon Press, 1987

Wilson, F.P., *Shakespeare and the New Bibliography*, ed. Helen Gardner, Oxford: Clarendon Press, 1970

LANGUAGE AND STYLE

Dictionaries and concordances

Crystal, David, and Ben Crystal, *Shakespeare's Words: A Glossary and Language Companion*, London and New York: Penguin, 2004

Dent, R.W., *Shakespeare's Proverbial Language: An Index*, Berkeley and Los Angeles: University of California Press, 1981

Onions, Charles T., *A Shakespeare Glossary*, 3rd edn, ed. Robert D. Eagleson, Oxford: Clarendon Press, 1986

Partridge, Eric, *Shakespeare's Bawdy: A Literary and Psychological Essay and a Comprehensive Glossary*, 3rd edn, London and New York: Routledge, 1991

Schmidt, Alexander, *Shakespeare Lexicon: A Complete Dictionary of all the English Words, Phrases, and Constructions in the Work of the Poet*, 2 vols, 3rd edn, rev. and enl. by Gregor Sarrazin, New York: Dover, 1971

Spevack, Martin, ed., *A Complete and Systematic Concordance to the Works of Shakespeare*, 9 vols, Hildesheim, Germany: George Olms, 1968–80

Williams, Gordon, *A Dictionary of Sexual Language and Imagery in Shakespearean and Stuart Literature*, 3 vols, London: Athlone Press, 1994

Studies

Abbott, E.A., *A Shakespearian Grammar*, New York: Dover, 1966

Adamson, Sylvia, Lynette Hunter, Lynne Magnusson, Ann Thompson and Katie Wales, eds, *Reading Shakespeare's Dramatic Language: A Guide*, London: Thomson Learning, 2000

Alexander, Catherine, ed, *Shakespeare and Language*, Cambridge: Cambridge University Press, 2004

Blake, N.F., *Shakespeare's Language: An Introduction*, New York: St Martin's Press, 1983

Cercignani, Fausto, *Shakespeare's Works and Elizabethan Pronunciation*, Oxford: Clarendon Press, 1981

Donawerth, Jane, *Shakespeare and the Sixteenth-Century Study of Language*, Urbana: University of Illinois Press, 1984

Doran, Madeleine, *Shakespeare's Dramatic Language*, Madison: University of Wisconsin Press, 1976

Edwards, Philip, Inga-Stina Ewbank and G.K. Hunter, *Shakespeare's Styles: Essays in Honour of Kenneth Muir,* Cambridge: Cambridge University Press, 1980

Greene, Roland, *Five Words: Critical Semantics in the Age of Shakespeare and Cervantes*, Chicago: University of Chicago Press, 2013

Hope, Jonathan, *Shakespeare and Language: Reason, Eloquence and Artifice in the Renaissance*, London: Bloomsbury, 2010

Hussey, S.S., *The Literary Language of Shakespeare*, 2nd edn, London and New York: Longman, 1992

Kermode, Frank, *Shakespeare's Language*, London: Allen Lane, 2000

MacDonald, Russ, *Shakespeare and the Arts of Language*, Oxford: Oxford University Press, 2001

Parker, Patricia, *Shakespearean Intersections: Language, Contexts, Critical Keywords*, Philadelphia, Pa.: University of Pennsylvania Press, 2018

Thompson, Ann, and John O. Thompson, *Shakespeare: Meaning and Metaphor*, Iowa City: University of Iowa Press, 1987

Vickers, Brian, *The Artistry of Shakespeare's Prose*, London: Methuen, 1968

Wright, George T., *Shakespeare's Metrical Art*, Berkeley and Los Angeles: University of California Press, 1988

SHAKESPEARE'S SOURCES

Bate, Jonathan, *Shakespeare and Ovid*, Oxford: Oxford University Press, 1993

Britton, Dennis Austin, and Melissa Walter, eds, *Rethinking Shakespeare Source Study: Audience, Authors, and Digital Technologies*, New York: Routledge, 2018

Bullough, Geoffrey, ed., *Narrative and Dramatic Sources of Shakespeare*, 8 vols, London: Routledge & Kegan Paul; New York: Columbia University Press, 1957–75

Burrow, Colin, *Shakespeare and Classical Antiquity*, Oxford: Oxford University Press, 2013

Cooper, Helen, *Shakespeare and the Medieval World*, London: Bloomsbury, 2010

Donaldson, E. Talbot, *The Swan at the Well: Shakespeare Reading Chaucer*, New Haven: Yale University Press, 1985

Ellrodt, Robert, *Montaigne and Shakespeare: The Emergence of Modern Self-Consciousness*, Manchester: Manchester University Press, 2015

Gillespie, Stuart, ed., *Shakespeare's Books: A Dictionary of Shakespeare's Sources*, 2nd edn, London: Bloomsbury, 2016

Hadfield, Andrew, *Shakespeare, Spenser and the Matter of Britain*, Basingstoke: Palgrave Macmillan, 2004

Kerrigan, John, *Shakespeare's Originality*, Oxford: Oxford University Press, 2018

Miola, Robert S., *Shakespeare and Classical Tragedy: The Influence of Seneca*, Oxford: Clarendon Press, 1993

Miola, Robert S., *Shakespeare's Reading*, Oxford: Oxford University Press, 2000

Morse, Ruth, Helen Cooper and Peter Holland, eds, *Medieval Shakespeare: Pasts and Presents*, Cambridge: Cambridge University Press, 2013

Shaheen, Naseeb, *Biblical References in Shakespeare's Plays*, Newark, Del.: University of Delaware Press, 1999

Thompson, Ann, *Shakespeare's Chaucer: A Study in Literary Origins*, Liverpool: Liverpool University Press, 1978

GENERAL CRITICISM

Anthologies of criticism

Barclay, Bill, and David Lindley, eds, *Shakespeare, Music and Performance*, Cambridge: Cambridge University Press, 2017

Bulman, James C., ed., *Shakespeare, Theory, and Performance*, London: Routledge, 1996

De Grazia, Margreta, Maureen Quilligan and Peter Stallybrass, eds, *Subject and Object in Renaissance Culture*, Cambridge: Cambridge University Press, 1996

Desmet, Christy, and Robert Sawyer, eds, *Shakespeare and Appropriation*, London: Routledge, 1999

Dollimore, Jonathan, and Alan Sinfield, eds, *Political Shakespeare: New Essays in Cultural Materialism*, Manchester: Manchester University Press, 1985

Loomba, Ania, and Martin Orkin, eds, *Post-colonial Shakespeares*, London: Routledge, 1998

McDonald, Russ, ed., *Shakespeare: An Anthology of Criticism and Theory 1945–2000*, Oxford: Wiley Blackwell, 2004

Parker, Patricia, and Geoffrey Hartman, eds, *Shakespeare and the Question of Theory*, London and New York: Methuen, 1985

Smith, Bruce R., ed., *The Cambridge Guide to the Worlds of Shakespeare*, 2 vols, Cambridge: Cambridge University Press, 2016

Individual critical studies

Coleridge, Samuel Taylor, *Samuel Taylor Coleridge: Shakespearean Criticism*, 2 vols, ed. T.M. Raysor, London: Constable & Co., 1930

Cooper, Farah Karim, and Tiffany Stern, *Shakespeare's Theatre and the Effects of Performance*, London: Bloomsbury, 2013

Dusinberre, Juliet, *Shakespeare and the Nature of Women*, 2nd edn, New York: St Martin's Press, 1996

Erne, Lukas, *Shakespeare as Literary Dramatist*, Cambridge: Cambridge University Press, 2013

Freinkel, Lisa, *Shakespeare's Will: The Theology of Figure from Augustine to the Sonnets*, New York: Columbia University Press, 2001

Garber, Marjorie, *Shakespeare After All*, New York: Anchor, 2005

Greenblatt, Stephen, *Shakespearean Negotiations: The Circulation of Social Energy in Renaissance England*, Berkeley and Los Angeles: University of California Press, 1988

Hooks, Adam, *Selling Shakespeare: Biography, Bibliography, and the Book Trade*, Cambridge: Cambridge University Press, 2018

James, Heather, *Shakespeare's Troy: Drama, Politics, and the Translation of Empire*, Cambridge: Cambridge University Press, 2007

Johnson, Samuel, *Samuel Johnson on Shakespeare*, ed. H.R. Woudhuysen, London: Penguin, 1989

Kahn, Coppélia, *Man's Estate: Masculine Identity in Shakespeare*, Berkeley and Los Angeles: University of California Press, 1981

Kastan, David Scott, *A Will to Believe: Shakespeare and Religion*, Oxford: Oxford University Press, 2014

Kott, Jan, *Shakespeare Our Contemporary*, trans. Boleslaw Taborski, Garden City, N.Y.: Anchor Doubleday, 1966

Lupton, Julia Reinhard, *Citizen-Saints: Shakespeare and Political Theology*, Chicago and London: University of Chicago Press, 2005

Lyne, Raphael, *Shakespeare, Rhetoric, and Cognition*, Cambridge: Cambridge University Press, 2012

McEachern, Claire, *Believing in Shakespeare: Studies in Longing*, Cambridge: Cambridge University Press, 2018

Marcus, Leah, *Puzzling Shakespeare: Local Reading and Its Discontents*, Berkeley and Los Angeles: University of California Press, 1988

Mullaney, Steven, *The Reformation of Emotions in the Age of Shakespeare*, Chicago: University of Chicago Press, 2015

Orgel, Stephen, *Imagining Shakespeare: A History of Texts and Visions*, Basingstoke: Palgrave Macmillan, 2003

Patterson, Annabel, *Shakespeare and the Popular Voice*, Oxford: Basil Blackwell, 1989

Rackin, Phyllis, *Shakespeare and Women*, Oxford: Oxford University Press, 2005

Schwartz, Regina, *Loving Justice, Living Shakespeare*, Oxford: Oxford University Press, 2016

Schwarz, Katherine, *What You Will: Gender, Contract, and Social Space*, Philadelphia: University of Pennsylvania Press, 2011

Shapiro, James, *1599: A Year in the Life of William Shakespeare*, London: Faber & Faber, 2005

Shaw, George Bernard, *Shaw on Shakespeare*, ed. Edwin Wilson, New York: Dutton, 1961

Smith, Emma, *This Is Shakespeare*, London: Penguin Random House, 2019

Stern, Tiffany, *Making Shakespeare: From Page to Stage*, London: Routledge, 2004

Syme, Holger, *Theatre and Testimony in Shakespeare's England*, Cambridge: Cambridge University Press, 2011

Traub, Valerie, *Desire and Anxiety: Circulations of Sexuality in Shakespearean Drama*, London and New York: Routledge, 1992

Weimann, Robert, *Author's Pen and Actor's Voice: Playing and Writing in Shakespeare's Theatre*, ed. Helen Higbee and William West, Cambridge: Cambridge University Press, 2000

Criticism of the comedies and romances

Alexander, Catherine, ed., *The Cambridge Companion to Shakespeare's Last Plays*, Cambridge: Cambridge University Press, 2009

Butler, Martin, ed., *Cymbeline*, Cambridge: Cambridge University Press, 2005

Carnegie, David, and Gary Taylor, eds, *The Quest for Cardenio: Shakespeare, Fletcher, Cervantes, and the Lost Play*, Oxford: Oxford University Press, 2012

Collins, Michael, *Shakespeare's Sweet Thunder: Essays on the Early Comedies*, Newark, Del.: University of Delaware Press; London: Associated University Presses, 1997

Cooper, Helen, *The English Romance in Time: Transforming Motifs from Geoffrey of Monmouth to the Death of Shakespeare*, Oxford: Oxford University Press, 2004

Danson, Lawrence, *Shakespeare's Dramatic Genres*, Oxford: Oxford University Press, 2000

Hulme, Peter, and William T. Sherman, eds, *'The Tempest' and its Travels*, London: Reaktion, 2000

Jones, Emrys, 'Reclaiming early Shakespeare', *Essays in Criticism*, 51 (2001), 35–50

Lindley, David, ed., *The Tempest*, 2nd edn, Cambridge: Cambridge University Press, 2013

Lyne, Raphael, *Shakespeare's Late Work*, Oxford: Oxford University Press, 2007

McDonald, Russ, *Shakespeare's Late Style*, Cambridge, Cambridge University Press, 2006

McMullan Gordon, *Shakespeare and the Idea of Late Writing: Authorship in the Proximity of Death*, Cambridge: Cambridge University Press, 2007

Mahon, John W., and Ellen MacLeod Mahon, eds, *The Merchant of Venice: New Critical Essays*, New York: London: Routledge, 2002

Mahood, M.M., *Playing Bit Parts in Shakespeare*, London and New York: Routledge, 1998

Maslen, R.W., *Shakespeare and Comedy*, London: Arden Shakespeare, 2005

Miola, Robert S., ed., *The Comedy of Errors: Critical Essays*, New York and London: Garland, 1997

Richards, Jennifer, and James Knowles, eds, *Shakespeare's Late Plays: New Readings*, Edinburgh: Edinburgh University Press, 1999

Ryan, Kiernan, *Shakespeare's Comedies*, Basingstoke: Palgrave Macmillan, 2009

Schiffer, James, ed., *Twelfth Night: New Critical Essays*, New York and London: Routledge, 2010

Shakespeare Survey 56: Shakespeare and Comedy, ed. Peter Holland, Cambridge: Cambridge University Press, 2003

Watson, Robert N., *Back to Nature: The Green and the Real in the Late Renaissance*, Philadelphia, Pa.: University of Pennsylvania Press, 2006: chapters on *As You Like It*, *The Merchant of Venice*

White, Martin, *A Midsummer Night's Dream*, Basingstoke: Palgrave Macmillan, 2009

Criticism of the history plays

Dutton, Richard, and Jean Howard, eds, *A Companion to Shakespeare's Work: Volume II: The Histories*, Malden, Mass.: Wiley-Blackwell, 2003

Goy-Blanquet, Dominique, *Shakespeare's Early History Plays: from Chronicle to Stage*, Oxford: Oxford University Press, 2000

Grene, Nicholas, *Shakespeare's Serial History Plays*, Cambridge: Cambridge University Press, 2002

Hattaway, Michael, ed., *The Cambridge Companion to Shakespeare's History Plays*, Cambridge: Cambridge University Press, 2002

Hogdon, Barbara, *The End Crowns All: Closure and Contradiction in Shakespeare's History*, Princeton, N.J.: Princeton University Press, 1991

Howard, Jean, and Phyllis Rackin, *Engendering a Nation: A Feminist Account of Shakespeare's English Histories*, London and New York: Routledge, 1997

Kastan, David Scott, *Shakespeare and the Shapes of Time*, Hanover, N.H.: University Press of New England, 1982

Parvini, Neema, *Shakespeare's History Plays: Rethinking Historicism*, Edinburgh: Edinburgh University Press, 2012

Pugliatti, Paola, *Shakespeare the Historian*, London: Macmillan, 2002

Rackin, Phyllis, *Stages of History: Shakespeare's English Chronicles*, Ithaca, N.Y.: Cornell University Press, 1990

Saccio, Peter, *Shakespeare's English Kings*, Oxford: Oxford University Press, 1977

Watt, R.J.C., ed., *Shakespeare's History Plays*, London: Longman, 2002

Criticism of the tragedies

Aebischer, Pascale, *Shakespeare's Violated Bodies: Stage and Screen Performance*, Cambridge: Cambridge University Press, 2004

Berry, Philippa, *Shakespeare's Feminine Endings*, London: Routledge, 1999

Booth, Stephen, *'King Lear', 'Macbeth', Indefinition, and Tragedy*, New Haven: Yale University Press, 1983

Dollimore, Jonathan, *Radical Tragedy: Religion, Ideology and Power in the Drama of Shakespeare and his Contemporaries*, Brighton: Harvester Press, 1984

Foakes, R.A., *'Hamlet' versus 'Lear': Cultural Politics and Shakespeare's Art*, Cambridge: Cambridge University Press, 1993

Kahn, Coppélia, *Roman Shakespeare: Warriors, Wounds, and Women*, London, Routledge, 1997

Kerrigan, John, *Revenge Tragedy: Aeschylus to Armageddon*, Oxford: Oxford University Press, 1996

Neill, Michael, and David Schalkwyk, eds, *The Oxford Handbook of Shakespearean Tragedy*, Oxford: Oxford University Press, 2017

Hamlet criticism

Burnett, Mark Thornton, *'Hamlet' and World Cinema*, Cambridge: Cambridge University Press, 2019

Callaghan, Dympna, *'Hamlet', Language and Writing*, London: Bloomsbury, 2015

Clayton, Thomas, ed., *The 'Hamlet' First Published (Q1, 1603): Origins, Form, Intertextuality*, Newark, Del.: University of Delaware Press, 1992

Croall, Jonathan, *Performing Hamlet: Actors in the Modern Age*, London: Bloomsbury, 2018

De Grazia, Margreta, *'Hamlet' without Hamlet*, Cambridge: Cambridge University Press, 2007

Greenblatt, Stephen, *Hamlet in Purgatory*, Princeton, N.J.: Princeton University Press, 2001

Howard, Tony, *Women as Hamlet: Performance and Interpretation in Theatre, Film and Fiction*, Cambridge: Cambridge University Press, 2007

Lavender, Andy, *'Hamlet' in Pieces: Shakespeare Reworked by Peter Brook, Robert Lepage, Robert Wilson*, London: Nick Hern Books, 2001

Lee, John, *Shakespeare's 'Hamlet' and the Controversies of Self*, Oxford: Oxford University Press, 2000

Lesser, Zachary, *'Hamlet' After Q1: An Uncanny History of the Shakespearean Text*, Philadelphia, Pa.: University of Philadelphia Press, 2015

Loftis, Sonya Freeman, Allison Kellar and Lisa Ulevich, eds, *Shakespeare's 'Hamlet' in an Era of Textual Exhaustion*, New York: Routledge, 2018

Maher, Mary Z., *Modern Hamlets and Their Soliloquies* (expanded edn), Iowa City: Iowa University Press, 2003

Peterson, Kaara L., and Deanne Williams, eds, *The Afterlife of Ophelia*, London: Palgrave Macmillan, 2012

Scofield, Martin, *The Ghosts of 'Hamlet': The Play and Modern Writers*, Cambridge: Cambridge University Press, 1980

Thompson, Ann, and Neil Taylor, eds, *'Hamlet': A Critical Reader*, London: Bloomsbury, 2016

Young, Alan, *'Hamlet' and the Visual Arts, 1709–1900*, Newark, Del.: University of Delaware Press, 2002

King Lear criticism

Blayney, Peter, *The Texts of 'King Lear' and their Origins*, Cambridge: Cambridge University Press, 1982
Croall, Jonathan, *Performing King Lear: Gielgud to Russell Beale*, London: Bloomsbury, 2015
Davidson, Adele, *Shakespeare in Shorthand: The Textual Mystery of King Lear*, Newark: University of Delaware Press, 2009
Elton, William R., *'King Lear' and the Gods*, Lexington: University of Kentucky Press, 1988
Foakes, R.A., *'Hamlet' Versus 'Lear': Cultural Politics and Shakespeare's Art*, Cambridge: Cambridge University Press, 1993
Kahan, Jeffrey, ed., *'King Lear': New Critical Essays*, New York: Routledge, 2008
Kronefield, Judy, *'King Lear' and The Naked Truth: Rethinking the Language of Religion and Resistance*, Durham, N.C.: Duke University Press, 1998
Lusardi, James P., and June Schuleter, *Reading Shakespeare in Performance: 'King Lear'*, Rutherford, N.J.: Fairleigh Dickinson, 1991
Mack, Maynard, *'King Lear' in Our Time*, Berkeley and Los Angeles: University of California Press, 1965
Shapiro, James, *1606: Shakespeare and the Year of Lear*, London: Faber & Faber, 2016
Sun, Emily, *Succeeding King Lear: Literature, Exposure, and the Possibilities of Politics*, New York: Fordham University Press, 2010
Taylor, Gary, and Michael Warren, eds., *Division of the Kingdoms: Shakespeare's Two Versions of 'King Lear'*, Oxford: Clarendon Press, 1983
Vickers, Brian, *The One 'King Lear'*, Cambridge, Mass.: Harvard University Press, 2016

Macbeth criticism

Braunmuller, A.R., 'How farre is't called to Soris? Or, Where was Mr. Hobbs when Charles II died?', in Laurie E. Maguire and Thomas L. Berger, eds, *Textual Formations and Reformations*, Newark, Del.: University of Delaware Press; London: Associated University Presses, 1998
Coursen, Herbert R., *Macbeth: A Guide to the Play*, Westport and London: Greenwood Press, 1997
Hodgdon, Barbara, '*Macbeth* at the turn of the millenium', in Jay L. Halio and Hugh Richmond, eds, *Shakespearean Illuminations: Essays in Honor of Marvin Rosenberg*, Newark, Del.: University of Delaware Press; London: Associated University Presses, 1998
Kinney, Arthur F., *Lies Like Truth: Shakespeare, 'Macbeth', and the Cultural Moment*, Detroit: Wayne State University Press, 2001
Leggatt, Alexander, ed., *William Shakespeare's Macbeth: A Sourcebook*, London: Routledge, 2006
Macbeth, ed. A.R. Braunmuller, 2nd edn, Cambridge: Cambridge University Press, 1997
McLuskie, Kathleen E., *William Shakespeare: Macbeth*, Writers and their Work, Horndon: Northcote House, 2009
Newstok, Scott L., and Ayanna Thompson, eds, *Weyward Macbeth: Intersections of Race and Performance*, Basingstoke: Palgrave Macmillan, 2010
Shakespeare Survey 57, 'Macbeth' and Its Afterlife, ed. Peter Holland, Cambridge: Cambridge University Press, 2004
Smith, Emma, *Macbeth: Language and Writing*, London: Bloomsbury, 2013
Walter, Harriet, *Macbeth*, Actors on Shakespeare, London: Faber & Faber, 2002
Wilders, John, *Macbeth*, Shakespeare in Production, Cambridge: Cambridge University Press, 2004

Othello criticism

Altman, Joel B., *The Improbability of 'Othello'*, Chicago and London: University of Chicago Press, 2010
Bartels, Emily C., *Speaking the Moor: from 'Alcazar' to 'Othello'*, Philadelphia: University of Pennsylvania Press, 2008
Cowhig, Ruth M., *Ira Aldridge: The African Roscius*, Rochester, N.Y.: University of Rochester Press, 2007
Daileader, Celia R., *Racism, Misogyny, and the Othello Myth: Inter-racial Couples from Shakespeare to Spike Lee,* Cambridge: Cambridge University Press, 2005
Erickson, Peter, and Maurice Hunt, eds, *Approaches to Teaching Shakespeare's 'Othello'*, New York: Modern Language Association of America, 2005
Hankey, J., *Shakespeare in Production: Othello*, 2nd edn, Cambridge: Cambridge University Press, 2005
Hatchuel, Sarah, and Nathalie Vienne-Guerin, eds, *Shakespeare on Screen: 'Othello'*, Cambridge: Cambridge University Press, 2015
Heilman, Robert B., *Magic in the Web: Action and Language in 'Othello'*, Lexington: University of Kentucky Press, 1956
Jones, Eldred, *Othello's Countrymen: The African in English Renaissance Drama*, Oxford: Oxford University Press, 1965
McMillin, Scott, ed., *The First Quarto of 'Othello'*, Cambridge Early Quartos, Cambridge: Cambridge University Press, 2001
Maguire, Laurie, *Othello, Language and Writing*, London: Bloomsbury, 2014
Marcus, Leah, 'The two texts of *Othello* and early modern constructions of race', in L. Erne and M.J. Kidnie, eds, *Textual Performances: The Modern Reproduction of Shakespeare's Drama*, Cambridge: Cambridge University Press, 2004
Massai, Sonia., ed., *World-Wide Shakespeares: Local Appropriation in Film and Performance*, Abingdon and New York: Routledge, 2005
Neil, Michael, '"Mulattos", "Blacks", and "Indian Moors": Othello and early modern constructions of human difference', *Shakespeare Quarterly*, 49 (1998), 361–72
Neil, Michael, ed., *Othello*, Oxford: Oxford University Press, 2006
Pechter, Edward, '"Have you not read of some such thing": sex and sexual stories in *Othello*', *Shakespeare Survey 49* (1996), 201–16
Pechter, Edward, *'Othello' and Interpretative Traditions*, Iowa City: University of Iowa Press, 1999
Potter, L., *'Othello': Shakespeare in Performance*, Manchester: Manchester University Press, 2002
Rosenberg, Marvin, *The Masks of 'Othello': The Search for the Identity of Othello, Iago, and Desdemona by Three Centuries of Actors and Critics*, 1961, reissued Newark: University of Delaware Press, 1992
Thompson, Ayanna, *Passing Strange: Shakespeare, Race and Contemporary America*, New York, Oxford: Oxford University Press, 2011
Vitkus, D.J., 'Turning Turk in *Othello*: the conversion and damnation of the Moor', *Shakespeare Quarterly*, 48 (1997), 145–76

Criticism of the non-dramatic poetry

Belsey, Catherine, 'Tarquin dispossessed: expropriation and consent in *The Rape of Lucrece*', *Shakespeare Quarterly*, 52 (2001), 315–35
Cheney, Patrick, '"O, let my books be . . . dumb presagers": poetry and theater in Shakespeare's *Sonnets*', *Shakespeare Quarterly*, 52 (2001), 222–54
Cheney, Patrick, *Shakespeare: National Poet-Playwright*, Cambridge: Cambridge University Press, 2004
Duncan-Jones, Katherine, 'What are Shakespeare's Sonnets called?', *Essays in Criticism*, 47 (1997), 1–12
Hyland, Peter, *An Introduction to Shakespeare's Poems*, Basingstoke: Palgrave Macmillan, 2003
Kahn, Coppélia, *Roman Shakespeare: Warriors, Wounds, and Women*, London: Routledge, 1997
Kolin, Philip C., ed., *Venus and Adonis: Critical Essays*, New York: Garland Publishers, 1997
Martindale, C., and A.B. Taylor, eds, *Shakespeare and the Classics*, Cambridge: Cambridge University Press, 2004
Monsarrat, G.D., '*A Funeral Elegy*, Ford, W.S. and Shakespeare', *Review of English Studies*, 53 (2002), 186–203
Post, Jonathan F.S., *Shakespeare's Sonnets and Poems: A Very Short Introduction*, Oxford: Oxford University Press, 2017

Roberts, Sasha, *Reading Shakespeare's Poems in Early Modern England*, Basingstoke: Palgrave Macmillan, 2003

Schalkwyk, David, 'What may words do? The performative of praise in Shakespeare's Sonnets', *Shakespeare Quarterly*, 49 (1998), 251–68

Schoenfeldt, Michael Carl, ed., *A Companion to Shakespeare's Sonnets*, Malden and Oxford: Blackwell, 2007

Sharon-Zisser, Shirley, ed., *Critical Essays on Shakespeare's 'A Lover's Complaint': Suffering Ecstasy*, Aldershot: Ashgate, 2006

Taylor, A.B., *Shakespeare's Ovid: The 'Metamorphoses' in the Plays and Poems*, Cambridge: Cambridge University Press, 2000

Vendler, Helen, *The Art of Shakespeare's Sonnets*, Cambridge, Mass., and London: Belknap Press of Harvard University Press, 1997

Vickers, Brian, *Shakespeare, 'A Lover's Complaint', and John Davies of Hereford*, Cambridge: Cambridge University Press, 2007

Wilson, Richard, 'A "Bloody Question": the politics of *Venus and Adonis*', in Jean-Marie Maguin and Charles Whitworth, eds, *William Shakespeare: Venus and Adonis: Nouvelles Perspectives Critiques*, Astrea, 9, Montpellier: Université Paul-Valéry, 1999

Index of First Lines of Sonnets

Index of First Lines of Songs

Glossary

'a, a he

a life on (my) life (an oath)

abate blunt; beat; shorten; deprive; except

abatement diminished amount; depreciation

Abel *see* **Cain**

abhor disgust; reject

abide stay temporarily; withstand, stand up to; pay the penalty for (*cf.* **aby**)

abject *n.* servile person; *adj.* base, servile

able empower

abode *n.* staying; *v.* forebode

abortive *n.* premature birth; *adj.* deformed, horrible

abram auburn

abridgement shortening; passing of time, entertainment

abroad on the move; apart

abrook bear, tolerate

abruption interruption of speech

Absey book introductory book, primer

absolute perfect, complete, without limitation; determined

absonant harsh, discordant; abhorrent to reason

abuse *n.* deception; *v.* deceive

aby, abye pay the penalty for (*cf.* **abide**)

abysm abyss

accident incident

accite cite, call up; excite

accommodate equip

accommodation provision, delicacy

accomplice colleague

accomplish equip

accountant responsible

accoutred dressed

accusativo 'in the accusative case' (*Lat.*)

acerb bitter

ache *see* **H**

Acheron a river of the underworld

achete escheat: confiscation, reversion to feudal lord

achieve win

Achilles' spear spear able both to wound and to cure those wounds with its rust

acknown aware, in the know

aconitum wolf's bane, a poisonous plant

acquit pay back; free

Actaeon hunter in myth who, seeing Diana bathing, was turned by her into a stag (creating connotations of cuckoldry, *see* **horn**) and hunted to death by his hounds

action-taking taking legal action, litigious

acture action

ad manes fratrum to our brothers' spirits (*Lat.*)

Adam fallen man, wickedness; Adam Bell, an archer in folklore

adamant exceedingly hard metal; magnet

adder's sense *see* **sense**

addiction propensity

addition title granted in honour of some excellence

address prepare

admiral flagship

admiration amazement, wonder

admire wonder

admittance admissibility, fashion

adoptious bestowed

adsum here I am (*Lat.*)

advantage *n.* addition; interest; *v.* help, benefit

adventure *n.* risk; *v.* take a risk

advertise make known, notify

advertisement advice, admonition; news

advice thought, reflection

advised careful

aedile Roman public officer

Aeneas Trojan prince who carried his father, Anchises, out of burning Troy and became the lover of Dido (*see* **Dido**) before abandoning her to found the Roman state

Aeolus god of the winds

aery *see* **eyrie**

Aesculapius *see* **Esculapius**

affect *n.* passion, appetite; affection; *v.* admire, have affection for, favour; impersonate, put on

affectedly affectionately

affection feeling, disposition, propensity; passion; affectation

affeered assured

affiance trust

affined connected, bound

affront *n.* attack; *v.* come face to face with, meet

affy affiance, betroth; place trust

aflaunt with a swagger

after in the manner of

after-eye look after

again back, reciprocally

against before; in preparation for (when)

agate jewel sometimes carved with a small figure

Agenor father of Europa (*see* **Europa**)

aglet-baby (?) baby dressed with aglets (tags attached to clothes); (?) aglet in the shape of a small figure

agnize acknowledge

a-hold close to the wind

aidance help

aim *n.* conjecture, idea; *v.* conjecture; **cry aim** = applaud, cheer; **give aim** = observe an archer's shots

Aio te, Aeacida, Romanos vincere posse the ambiguous answer Apollo gave Pyrrhus when he enquired whether he would vanquish Rome (*Lat.* = 'I affirm that thou, descendant of Aeacus, canst conquer the Romans' or 'I affirm that the Romans can vanquish thee, descendant of Aeacus')

Ajax Greek hero in the Trojan war

alarm noise; attack; *see* **alarum**

alarum call to arms

Alcides Hercules (*see* **Hercules**)

alderliefest dearest of all

Alecto one of the Furies, mythological hags with serpents in their hair

all amort downcast

all hid the game of hide and seek

all to altogether, utterly

Alla nostra casa ben venuto, molto honorato signor mio Petrucio 'Welcome to our house, my much-honoured Signor Petruccio' (*Ital.*)

alla stoccato at the thrust (*Ital.*)

allay *n.* calming influence; *v.* detract from

allegiant loyal

All-hallond Eve Hallowe'en (31 October)

All-hallowmas All Saints' Day (1 November)

All-hallown summer late season of fine weather

allicholy, allycholy melancholy

alligant Quickly's word for either 'elegant' or 'eloquent'

allons 'let's go' (*Fr.*)

allottery something allotted, share

allowance acknowledgement; approval, praise; permission

All-Souls' day 2 November

all-thing entirely

Almain German

alms-drink drink taken as charity

alow *see* **'loo**

alter exchange

Althaea Queen of Calydon who killed her son, Meleager, by burning a firebrand reserved for him by the Fates

although even if

amain aloud; at speed

amerce penalize

ames-ace two aces thrown at dice, the lowest score

an if

anatomize open up for inspection, dissect

anatomy skeleton

Anchises father of Aeneas (*see* **Aeneas**)

anchor religious recluse

ancient standard; standardbearer; Ensign

and *see* **an**

andirons props to support burning logs over a hearth

angel spirit; English gold coin depicting the archangel Michael

Anna sister of Dido (*see* **Dido**)

annexment addition, appendage

annothanize (?) *see* **anatomize**; (?) annotate

annoy *n.* torment, pain, injury; *v.* injure

anon in a moment; **till anon** = until a little later

Anthropophagi cannibals

anthropophaginian cannibal

antic *n.* grotesque figure, fool; grotesque pageant; *adj.* in grotesque disguise, masked; *v.* make grotesque

antre cave

ape mimic; fool; **leading apes in hell** = traditional punishment of old maids

Apollo god of song and music, of the sun, of healing and of the oracle at Delphi; he fell in love with Daphne who was transformed into a laurel as he chased her

appaid satisfied

apparently in open view

appeach impeach, accuse

appeal *n.* formal challenge, accusation; *v.* impeach

appellant formal challenger

apple-john type of apple kept until shrivelled

appliance compliance; service; treatment

appointed equipped, armed

appointment equipment; resolution; direction

apprehensive possessing reason; well-understanding

approof proof, proving; sanction

appropriate made specially

approve prove; put to proof; be to one's credit

apt ready, inclined; probable, likely; impressionable

aqua-vitae strong spirits

Aquilon the North wind

Arabian bird the phoenix, a mythical bird supposed to be unique

arbitrament, arbitrement arbitration, decision

arch lord

argal *see* **ergo**

argo *see* **ergo**

argosy large trading vessel

argument theme, subject of controversy; proof, demonstration

Ariachne = Arachne, a weaver in mythology, metamorphosed to a spider

Ariadne beloved of Theseus, who abandoned her

Arion poet who charmed a dolphin into carrying him over the waves

arm bear, carry

arm-gaunt lean from bearing arms

Armigero from the title '*Armiger*' (*Lat.*), signifying entitlement to a coat of arms

armipotent mighty in arms

aroint thee, aroynt thee be off with you

arras curtain of woven tapestry

arrose sprinkle

Arthur's show an exhibition of archery given by an Arthurian society

articulate negotiate terms; set forth in detail

artificial relating to or skilled in any of the 'arts' (painting, medicine, witchcraft, *etc.*)

artist learned man

Ascanius son of Aeneas (*see* **Aeneas**)

asinico little ass (*Sp.*)

aspect gaze; countenance; image; (in astrology) planetary position

aspersion sprinkling, with connotations of benediction

aspicious Dogberry's word for 'suspicious'

assay *n.* attempt; challenge; trial; *v.* try, test out, make trial of

assubjugate subdue

assurance transfer of property; guarantee, security; certitude; betrothal

assure betroth

Astraea goddess of justice

Atalanta maiden who outsprinted her suitors and put them to death

Ate goddess of confusion and strife

atomy atom, tiny particle; Quickly's word for 'anatomy' (*see* **anatomy**)

atone agree; set in agreement

atonement agreement

Atropos one of the Fates (*see* **Fates**)

attach arrest

attachment arrest

attainder accusation, taint, disgrace; forfeit of estate from the condemned

attaint *n.* disgrace; infection; weariness; *v.* condemn; stain

attasked taken to task

attribute esteem, character, reputation

attribution praise

audacious impudent

auditory audience

aught anything

aunt old woman, crony; female beggar; prostitute

auricular relating to the ear, heard

avise advise

avoid leave; expel, get rid of; (in law) invalidate

awkward oblique, adverse

baby girl's doll

baccare stand back (*pseudo-Lat.*)

back saddle or ride (a horse)

back-friend false friend; police officer

backsword man fencer (backsword = single-stick, used in fencing)

back-trick backward step in dancing

baffle (of a knight) publicly disgrace

baille bring (*Fr.*)

bait *n.* light meal; *v.* harrass, terrorize, as with dogs; offer bait to, tempt, lure

baldrick belt, girdle

bale sorrow, misfortune

balk miss; lay up; **balk logic** = chop logic

ban *n.* curse; *v.* curse

Banbury cheese proverbially thin cheese

band fetter

ban-dog fierce dog

bandy toss, exchange; contend, brawl

bane poison; death, destruction

bank *n.* shore; *v.* sail along the shore

banquet light refreshment; **running banquet** = light refreshment; whipping

Barbary breed of horse

Barbason a devil

barbed (of a horse) armed

barber-monger someone always at the barber's shop, vain person

barful full of difficulties

barge large ceremonial ornamented boat

bark *n.* ship; *v.* strip bark from

barley-break rustic chasing game in which the base was called 'hell'

barm yeast, head of froth

barnacle shellfish supposed to metamorphose into a goose

barne child

Barrabas murderer whose release from prison the Jews demanded instead of Christ's

Barson Barston or Barcheston (Warwickshire towns)

Bartholomew boar-pig roast pig eaten at Bartholomew Fair (*see* **Bartholomew-tide**)

Bartholomew-tide St Bartholomew's day (24 August), date of a popular fair

Basan biblical mountain famous for its bulls

base a chasing game; **bid a base** = challenge to a chase

base-court lower courtyard

bases knight's pleated skirt

Basilisco-like like Basilisco, a boastful knight in the play *Soliman and Perseda* (1592)

basilisk cockatrice (*see* **cockatrice**); large cannon

bass-viol stringed instrument, an early cello

basta enough (*Ital.*)

bastard sweet wine from Spain

baste beat up, cudgel

bastinado cudgelling, hefty wallop

bate *n.* strife; *v.* flutter the wings; abate, diminish; let off; lose; modify

bate-breeding mischief-making

bateless sharp

bat-fowling bird-catching at night by means of a strong light and sticks

batler paddle used to beat clothes being washed

batten gorge and grow fat

bauble toy, thing of trifling value; fool; fool's stick

baubling like a bauble, trifling

bavian baboon

bavin brushwood

bawcock fine chap

bawd hare; pimp

bay *n.* space under the gable of a building; barking; *adj.* (of horses) reddish brown; *v.* chase with barking; trap, corner; **at bay** = cornered

Bayard-like blindly reckless (Bayard was the magic steed given by Charlemagne to Renaud in medieval romance)

bays poet's laurel wreath

beached of the beach

beachy *see* **beached**

beadle parish constable

beadsman person hired to pray for others

beam large piece of wood, mentioned by Christ as a metaphor for grave sinfulness (Matt. 7.3–5; Luke 4.41–2) (*cf.* **mote**)

bear win; **bear in hand** = lead on, deceive; **bear away** get away with

bear-herd *see* **bearward**

bearing-cloth cloth in which a child was carried to be christened

bearward bear-keeper

beated beaten

beaver helmet's visor

beck *n.* beckoning; *v.* beckon

beckles beetles, overhangs

become be appropriate for, suit

bedded lying down

Bedlam hospital for the insane

bedlam *n.* insane person; *adj.* insane, frantic

bed-swerver adulterous person

beest the unpalatable milk of a cow that has just given birth

beetle *n.* sledge-hammer; *v.* jut out

begin drink as a toast, pledge

beldam grandmother; crone

be-leed left without wind, high and dry

bell, book and candle formula used in the ceremony of excommunication

Bellona goddess of war

bell-wether sheep at the head of a flock

belocked locked

bemadding causing madness

be-met met

bemete measure out

bemoiled covered with dirt

be-monster make hideous

bench *n.* authority; *v.* raise to or occupy a position of authority; **King's Bench** (a high court)

bench-hole hole in a privy

bend *n.* look; obeisance; knot; *v.* turn; crease; tense

benetted netted, trapped

benevolence obligatory loan to the sovereign

benison blessing

bent limit, strain; direction, disposition; arch; sight

berayed stained, sullied

Bergomask from Bergamo in Italy, rustic

Bermoothes Bermudas

beshrew curse

besom brush, broom

besonian, bezonian ignoramus, beggarly person

besort *n.* appropriate company; *v.* be appropriate for

beteem grant, allow

betid happened

betime soon, early

bevel oblique, zigzag

Bevis Bevis of Southampton, a legendary hero renowned for feats of arms

bewray betray, reveal, divulge

bezonian *see* **besonian**

bias *adj.* convex; *adv.* crookedly; **of bias** = oblique, roundabout

bias-drawing deceit

bibbing drunken

bide stay, linger; endure

bifold twofold

bigamy marriage with someone previously married

biggen coarse nightcap

bilbo sword with a flexible blade

bilboes shackles used for prisoners on a ship

bill pike or halberd, painted brown to prevent rust; officer carrying a bill; written note; notice

bird-bolt flat-headed arrow for shooting birds

birding-piece gun for shooting birds

bis coctus cooked twice (*Lat.*)

bisson blind; obscuring the sight

bite the thumb make an insulting gesture

bitumed smeared with bitumen, made watertight

Black-Monday Easter Monday

blame blameworthy (in the phrase 'too blame')

blank *n.* range, focus, target; *v.* make pale, drain of colour; **blank charter** = blank cheque

blastment blight

blazon *n.* coat of arms; proclamation; description; *v.* proclaim; describe

blear dim or blur, especially with weeping

blench *n.* sidelong glance; *v.* flinch, turn aside

blind-worm slow-worm

blistered padded

block mould for shaping a hat; mounting-block (for mounting horses)

blood family; gallant man; character, disposition; appetite, passion; **in blood** = active, healthy

blood-boltered having hair caked and matted with blood

blood-sized glazed with blood (*cf.* **size**)

bloody-wise knowledgeable about bloodshed

blot deface

blow swell; (of plants) blossom; (of flies) lay eggs (on); **blow wind i'th' breech** = be unable to keep pace (with); break wind

blowse stocky, rosy-cheeked girl

blubbered with tear-stained face

bluebottle beadle, parish constable

blue-cap Scot

blunt blunt weapons, cudgels

blurt scoff

board draw up alongside; attack

boarding upkeep; sexual mounting

bob *n.* jest; *v.* beat; cheat, diddle

bodement foreboding

bodkin short dagger; hair-pin; **God's bodkin** = by the Eucharist (God's little body) (an oath)

bodykins *see* **bodkin**

boggle take fright, swerve uncertainly

bolins bowlines on a ship

boll'n swollen

bolt *n.* arrow; shackle; *v.* sift, refine; shackle

bolted fastened down

bolter cloth for sifting meal

bolting-hutch sifting-bin

bombard wine vessel

bombast *n.* cotton padding; *adj.* padded; bombastic, verbally over-elaborate

bona terra, mala gens a good land but bad people (*Lat.*)

bona-roba better class of prostitute (*Ital.*)

bones rustic musical instrument accompanied by bells or tongs; bone bobbins for lace-making

book theatre-company playbook

book-man scholar

boot *n.* booty, spoil; something extra; advantage, help; *v.* give as something extra; help; **give the boots** = make a laughing-stock of

boot-hose long over-stocking

bootless useless, pointless

Boreas north wind

borrow *n.* loan; *v.* take, adopt

borrowed taken, feigned, not genuine

bosky shrubby, woody

bosomed close, intimate

botcher one who patches old clothes

botchy carbuncular, ulcerous

both also

bots maggot infection in horses

bottom *n.* valley; ship's hold, ship; bobbin for winding thread; *v.* wind

bought and sold tricked, betrayed

bounce bang

bounden bound, obliged

bourn limit; burn, brook

bow-hand left-hand side of an archer

box vagina

boy endow with the characteristics of a boy

brabble brawl

brace pair; armour to protect the arm; defensive position

brach bitch-hound

bragless without bragging

braid *adj.* false, deceitful *v.* upbraid, reproach

brainish deluded, frenzied

brain-pan skull

brake clump of bushes

branched bearing a pattern of leafy branches

brave *n.* vaunt, boast; *adj.* fine, admirable; finely dressed; fearless, insolent; *v.* make brave, adorn; defy; **brave it** = swagger

bravery finery; flamboyance; defiant attitude

brawl French dance

brawn fattened boar; arm or leg muscle

break break up, disband; communicate; discipline; break across; **break cross** = (of a knight's lance) break awkwardly or unfairly; **break up** = open

break-neck disaster

breast stomach; heart; singing voice

breathe talk, talk of; train, condition, accustom; allow to take a breath

breath'd uttered

breathing voice; excercise, activity; interval

breech breeches, trousers; **i'th' breech on** = behind, following

breed-bate trouble-maker (*cf.* **bate**)

breeding opportunity for development

breese, breeze gadfly

brewage brew

brewis bread soaked in broth

Briareus giant with a hundred arms and fifty heads

bribed (?) stolen; (?) obtained through bribery

bride-house house where a wedding takes place

brief *n.* letter; list, summary; **brief in hand** = in need of attention

brinded patterned with streaks

bring off rescue

Brittain Brittany

Brittish Breton

broach pierce; tap

brock badger

brogues heavy shoes

broke trade

broken fragmented; missing teeth; **broken music** = music played by instruments of different families

broker go-between, pimp

brooch *n.* ornament; *v.* decorate

brooded brooding

Brownist member of an English Puritan sect founded by Robert Browne

bruit *n.* rumour; *v.* announce, report

bubuncle Fluellen's confusion of '*bubo*' (*Lat.* = 'abscess') and 'carbuncle' buck stag; linen in the wash; **buck of the first head** = fully grown stag

bucking laundry

buckle grapple (as in a naval battle)

buckler *n.* shield; *v.* protect, shield; **give the bucklers** = acknowledge defeat

Bucklersbury London street known for its apothecaries

buckram tough, stiff linen

buck-washing washing of linen

budget tinker's bag

buff hard-wearing leather worn by constables

bug bugbear, bogeyman

bugle black glass bead

bulk display stall at the front of a shop

bully fine man, friend

bum-baily bailiff

bumbaste thrash backsides

bung pickpocket

burden load; undersong; refrain; **at a burden** = at one birth

burgonet close-fitting helmet

burn heat up; light up; **burn daylight** = waste time

burthen *see* burden

buss *n.* kiss; *v.* kiss

buttery bar hatch of a buttery (store room) where beer was served

butt-shaft strong, heavy arrow

buzzard insect; fool

by and by immediately; in due course

by-drinkings drinks between meals

by-peeping glancing sidelong

by'r lady by our Lady (an oath)

by'r lakin, byrlakin by our little Lady (an oath)

cabin *n.* hut; den, cave; *v.* dwell, rest

cabinet small lodging

cacodemon malignant spirit

caddis ribbon for a garter

cade large barrel

cadent falling

Cadmus legendary founder of Thebes

caduceus Mercury's staff, wound about with two serpents

cage prison

Cain son of Adam and Eve, who murdered his brother Abel; **Cain-coloured** = red, the imagined colour of Cain's beard

caitiff, caitive *n.* wretch; *adj.* captive; wretched

cake (of roses) compressed block used as perfume; **cake is dough** = plan has failed

calculate forecast by means of a horoscope; speculate upon the future

Caleno custore me Elizabethan version of '*cailin og a' stor*', the refrain of a popular Irish song, for Pistol a specimen of an incomprehensible foreign language

Calipolis character in Peele's *Battle of Alcazar* (1594), there presented with a lioness to eat

caliver light musket

calkins parts of a horse-shoe

call decoy

callat, callet slut

Cambyses a Persian king, subject of an early Elizabethan tragedy

can began

canary wine from the Canaries; Spanish dance

candidatus 'clad in a white robe', hence candidate (*Lat.*)

candied frosted, as if with sugar

candle-mine load of tallow

candle-waster book-worm

canker sore; wild rose; parasitic caterpillar

cannikin small drinking can

canon Church law, *hence* law, edict; musical composition in which voices take up the subject in turn

cantle segment of a circle

canton song

canvas, canvass toss about

canzonet canzonetta, short song

capable responsive, appreciative; capacious; qualified to inherit

capacity mental capacity, mind

cap-a-pe, cap-à-pe 'head to foot' (*Old Fr.*)

capital mortal, fatal; chief, main

Capitol temple of Jupiter in Rome

capitulate come to terms

capocchia fool, simple person (*Ital.*)

capriccio caprice, fancy (*Ital.*)

captious capacious; deceitful

car cart, chariot

caract official marking

carbonado *n.* fish or meat scored and grilled; *v.* score, slash

carcanet jewelled necklace

card *n.* playing card; toothed instrument for combing out wool; compass; model; *v.* adulterate, dilute; **by the card** = correctly; **card of ten** = playing card worth ten points; **cooling card** = playing card that dashes an opponent's hopes; **pack cards with** = shuffle playing cards in favour of

cardecue small French coin (*quart d'écu*)

cardinally Elbow's word for 'carnally'

cardmaker maker of cards for wool (*see* card)

carduus benedictus 'holy thistle' (*Lat.*), a plant credited with healing properties

caret 'it is missing' (*Lat.*); interpreted by Quickly as 'carrot' (penis)

carl churl, rustic person

carlot rustic person

carnation rosy-pink

carpet *n.* cover for chests and tables; **on carpet consideration** = at court rather than on the battle-field

carpet-monger knight more at home at court than in battle

carrack galleon, treasure ship

carriage carrying; ability to carry; conduct; deportment; purport

carry coals endure insults without retaliation

carry out a side fulfil a side of an agreement

carry-tale spy

carve *v.* compliment; **be one's own carver, carve for oneself** = be independent

case *n.* question; body, skin or clothes; *v.* clothe, mask; skin; **in case** = in a position or mood; **on the case** = for some particular offence

cashiered discarded; (?) robbed

cast *adj.* cast off; condemned; *v.* vomit; discharge; examine; calculate; **cast the gorge** = vomit

casted *see* cast (*adj.*)

Castiliano vulgo Sir Toby's attempt to refer in Spanish and (?) Latin to (?) wine, (?) the devil

casual accidental; subject to misfortune

cat o' mountain, cat-amountain leopard

Cataian Cathaian (Chinese), used insultingly

cataplasm plaster

catastrophe final phase of action in classical drama

catch tune for several voices

cate choice foodstuff

cater caterer, household purchaser

cater-cousins close friends

caterpillar parasite

cates choice provisions, delicacies

Catiline traitor, from Lucius Sergius Catilina, a Roman who conspired against his country in 63 BCE

catling catgut for stringed instruments

cautel wile, deception

cautelous deceitful

censer ornamental vessel for burning perfume

censure *n.* judgement; opinion; *v.* judge; express an opinion

centre the earth's mid-point

century one hundred soldiers

Cerberus three-headed dog at the gate of the underworld, fought with by Hercules and charmed to sleep by Orpheus

cerecloth shroud

cerements shroud

Ceres goddess of agriculture and plenty

'cerns concerns

certes truly

cess ceasing, decease; **out of cess** = excessively

cesse cease

chair-days time of rest

chairs of order stalls in St George's Chapel, Windsor, for the Knights of the Order of the Garter

challenge *n.* claim; legal objection; *v.* claim as due

chamberer wooer

chamber-lye urine

chambers small cannon

chamblet rich cloth of silk and goat's hair

champaign open countryside

champion challenge to fight

Chancery court of the Lord Chancellor

changeling turncoat; fairy child swapped for a human one (or vice versa)

chanson song

chanticleer cock

chape metal cap on the end of a scabbard

chapless with the lower jaw gone

chaplets garlands

chapman merchant

chaps chops, jaws

character *n.* handwriting; *v.* write

charactery writing

chare *n.* chore; *v.* accomplish, finish

charge-house school

charging-staff knight's lance

Charles' wain constellation of the Plough

charneco sweet wine

Charon ferryman of the underworld

chase hunt; (in tennis) bouncing ball

chat gossip about

chaudron entrails

che I; che vor ye = I warrant you; ch'ill = I will; ch'ud = I had (*dial.*)

cheapen bargain for

cheater officer in charge of estates forfeited to the crown

check *n.* rebuke; *v.* come to a stop; rebuke

chequin gold coin

cherry-pit children's game of throwing cherry stones into a hole cherubin cherub

cheval volant . . . qui a les narines de feu, le 'the flying horse . . . who has fiery nostrils' (*Fr.*)

cheveril, chev'ril kid leather, known for its stretching capacity

chewet jackdaw; minced-meat pie

Chi passa name of a popular dance tune (*Ital.* = 'Who is passing?')

chide down bring down by quarrelling

chiding din

chien est retourné à son propre vomissement, et la truie lavée au bourbier, le 'The dog has returned to his own vomit and the washed sow to her mud' (*Fr.*, 2 Peter 2.22)

child girl

childe title used by young nobles aspiring to knighthood

childed having children

childing generative, fertile

ch'ill *see* che

chine joint of meat

chirurgeonly in the expert manner of a surgeon

choler one of the four humours (*see* humour); anger

chop *n.* crack; *v.* crack; chop on = burst in on

chopine fashionable platform shoe

chopless *see* chapless

chough jackdaw

christom newly christened

chrysolite white or green gem

ch'ud *see* che

cicatrice mark, scar

cinque-pace quick dance

Cinque-ports five English ports; the barons of these places

cipher *n.* the figure nought, zero; *v.* decipher; represent

Circe sorceress in Homer's *Odyssey* who transformed men into beasts

circummured walled round

circumvent entrap

cisterns water containers for sheep

cite summon, as to court; incite

citizen city-bred

cittern guitar with a carved head

civet perfume derived from a civet cat's anal glands

civil of citizens, urban; well-behaved; civil doctor = doctor of civil law

clack-dish begging bowl

clap pledge with a clasping of hands; clap aboard = board (a ship); clap into = begin promptly; clap i'th' clout = hit the bull's-eye (*cf.* clout); clap up = agree promptly

clapper-claw handle roughly

clefture fissure

clepe call

clept called

clerestories upper windows in halls and churches

clerk cleric, scholar

clew ball of twine

climate *n.* region of the earth or sky; *v.* live in a particular region

climatures inhabitants of a particular region

clime climate; region

cling shrink up, wither

clinquant glittering

clip encircle, embrace

clipper one who trims coins for the metal

close *n.* encounter; (in music) cadence; *adj.* confined; secret; secretive; *adv.* secretly; *v.* come to agreement

closet private inner room

closure containment; conclusion

cloth o' gold, cloth-of-gold sumptuous, top-quality cloth

clothier's yard a 'cloth-yard' length, the length of an arrow (*cf.* yard)

cloud (of horses) facial blemish

clout target in archery; cloth, rag; babe of clouts = rag doll; idiot

clouted patched; hobnailed

clown person from the country

cloyed clogged up

clubs traditional cry for assistance in breaking up a brawl

clyster-pipe syringe inserted into the rectum or vagina

coat coat of arms

coat-armour a velvet vest displaying heraldic devices worn over armour, or the armour itself

cobloaf small loaf

cock rowing boat towed behind a larger ship; weathercock; tap; (in oaths) God; by cock and pie = by God and pie (an oath) (*cf.* pie)

cockatrice legendary creature with a fatal stare

cockle cockleshell; weed; cockle hat = pilgrim's hat

cocklight first light, dawn

cockney person of affected manners

cock'red pampered

cockscomb fool

cockshut twilight

Cocytus a river of the underworld

cod husk

codding lascivious

codpiece prominent pouch at the front of a man's breeches to hold his genitals

coffin pie-crust

cog cheat

cognizance emblem worn by retainers

coif cap

coign corner

coil commotion, fuss

coistrel base person, scoundrel

Colbrand Danish giant in the English romance of Guy of Warwick

collect infer, learn

collection piecing together, understanding

collied darkened

collop slice of flesh

Colme-kill Iona

coloquintida colocynth, a bitter apple

Colossus gigantic statue of Apollo at Rhodes that stood over the harbour entrance

colour *n.* appearance; pretext; sort, type; *v.* disguise

colourable plausible

colours military colours, banner

colt *n.* young and foolish person; *v.* play the fool with, trick; colt's tooth = friskiness

combinate bound by pledge

come off withdraw; pay up; shut up

come on spit it out

come out expire, finish

coming-on compliant

commeddled mingled

commit commit sins

commodious advantageous

commodity supply of merchandise; benefit, advantage; pledge against a loan

commoner prostitute

comonty Sly's word for 'comedy'

companion fellow, used insultingly

company trade guild

comparative *n.* dealer in insults; *adj.* skilled at (insulting) comparisons

comparisons trappings

compeer *n.* peer, companion; *v.* be the peer of, equal

competitor partner

complain bewail

complement outward appearance

complexion constitution, nature; face

complot *n.* design, conspiracy; *v.* conspire

comply behave formally

compose reach agreement

compt account, reckoning; the Day of Judgement

comptible sensitive

con study, memorize; con thanks = acknowledge gratitude

con tutto il cuore ben trovato 'with all my heart well met' (*Ital.*)

conceit *n.* mental, imaginative or artistic conception; wit, intelligence; fancy article; *v.* conceive

conceited witty, inventive; be conceited of = conceive of

conceptious conceiving, fertile

concernancy relevance

conclusion experiment; judgement; riddle

concolinel (?) title of a song; (?) singer's preparatory warble

concupiscible concupiscent, lustful

concupy (?) concupiscence; (?) concubine

condition rank; disposition; compact, contract

condolement grieving; (?) confused with dole, portion

conference conversation, debate

confessors boasters

confiners inhabitants

congee, congie bow, take one's leave

congree agree together

conjunctions sexual unions; alignments of the planets

conjure appeal by an oath or by something held sacred; solemnly appeal to

conscience matter of conscience; mind, thoughts

conscionable governed by conscience

consider reward; (?) appreciate

consign subscribe, endorse

consist stand firm, insist

consolate console

conspectuity power of vision

constring'd drawn together, compressed

contain retain

contemned treated with contempt; despised

contestation contention

continent *n.* container, vessel; sum, summary; *adj.* restraining

continuance period of time

contraction solemn agreement

control *n.* compulsion; *v.* contradict; overpower

controller steward; critic

convenient fit, suitable

convent call together

conventicle secret assembly

conversation dealing; social conduct

converse associate, be in company (with)

conversion promotion; conversation

convert change

convertite penitent

convey manage discreetly; steal

conveyance dishonest dealing; (in law) transfer of property; escort

convict convicted

convince overpower; prove; prove guilty, convict

convive feast together

convoy means of transport

cony rabbit

cony-catch dupe, cheat

copatain hat hat with a high crown

cope *n.* sky; *v.* encounter; have dealings; requite

copesmate companion

copped peaked

copy theme, copiously discussed; exemplar, model; copyhold, tenure

coragio courage (*Ital.*)

coram for 'quorum', justice whose particular presence was necessary for some cases

coranto dance with a running step

cordial medicinal drink

Corinth ancient city known for its licentiousness and partying

Corinthian one from Corinth (*see* **Corinth**)

corky dry, withered

Cornelia mother of the Gracchi (famous early Roman republicans)

cornet body of cavalry

cornuto horned beast, cuckold (*Ital.*) (*cf.* **horn**)

corollary excessive amount

corporal of the body, physical

correctioner one from the 'House of Correction'

corrigible corrective; susceptible of punishment

corroborate strengthened; Pistol's word for 'ruined'

corslet piece of body armour

costard large apple; the head

costermonger fruit seller, petty trader

cote *n.* cottage; *v.* overtake

cot-quean man who meddles in domestic affairs

Cotsall the Cotswold hills

couch lie hidden; cause to shrink back

counsel reflection; secrets

countenance *n.* face, outward appearance, demeanour; approval, patronage; *v.* behold; suit

counter *n.* coin of negligible value; debtors' prison; *adv.* (in hunting) backwards, off course

counterchange exchange, reciprocation

counterfeit *n.* image, reproduction; fake money; *adj.* painted, not real

Counter-gate gate of the Counter prison (*cf.* **counter**)

countermand contradict; prohibit

counterpoint counterpane, tapestry

countervail counterbalance, be equal to

county count

couple a gorge Pistol's version of '*coupe la gorge*' (*Fr.* = 'cut the throat')

courage disposition

course sail of a ship

courser horse; **courser's hair** = horse's hair, supposed to turn into a serpent in water

court of guard guard room; body of soldiers on guard

court-creed manners, behaviour or beliefs of the royal court

court-cupboard sideboard

courthand handwriting used for legal contracts

cousin any near relation

coverture covering, shelter

cowish cowardly

cowl-staff wooden rod for carrying a cowl (tub)

cox cock's (God's) (*see* **cock**)

coxcomb jester's cap; the head

coy caress; show reluctance

coz cousin (*see* **cousin**)

cozen cheat

cozier cobbler

crab crab apple

crack *n.* lad, rascal; partial fracture; *v.* boast; **cracked within the ring** = (of coins) nicked past the ring around the sovereign's head, and so no longer legal tender

crack-hemp one deserving to be hanged

crak'd cracked (*see* **crack**)

crank *n.* winding passage; *v.* twist and turn

cranny narrow

crants garland

crash a cup drink

craven *n.* cock; coward; *v.* make cowardly

craze break, damage

crazy of unsound mind

creation created state

credent believing; believable, plausible

credit credibility; belief, current opinion

crescive growing, having the power of growth

cressets fire-baskets, beacons

crestless not bearing a heraldic crest, not aristocratic

cricket low stool

cringes servile or sycophantic bows

critic fault-finder, satirist

cross *n.* an Elizabethan coin; *adj.* quarrelsome, thwarting; (of lightning) forked

crossed freed from debts

cross-gartered wearing garters above and below the knee (and so crossed behind)

cross-row the alphabet

crow-flower the ragged robin flower

crow-keeper, crowkeeper scarecrow; boy employed to shoo birds off crops

crown coin worth five shillings

crown imperial the fritillary plant

crudy thick

crupper strap fixing the saddle to the horse's back end

crusado Portuguese coin

cry *n.* barking pack of hounds; rumour; *v.* proclaim; **cried in the top of** = loudly exceeded; **cry aim** *see* **aim**; **cry out of** = cry out against; **cry up** = applaud

cubiculo bedroom

cucullus non facit monachum 'the hood does not make the monk' (*Lat.*, proverbial)

cullion rascal

cullison employer's or patron's badge

culverin small cannon

cum privilegio 'with privilege (*i.e.* immunity)' (*Lat.*); *cum privilegio ad imprimendum solum* = 'with the privilege for printing only' (*i.e.* 'with the sole right to print')

cunning *n.* knowledge; skill; *adj.* skilful; ingenious

Cupid son of Venus, a winged boy, sometimes thought of as blind, whose arrows caused people to fall in (and out of) love; **Cupid's flower** = pansy

curae leves loquuntur, ingentes stupent 'small sorrows speak, great ones are silent' (*Lat.*)

curate parish priest

curb strap connected to a horse's bit

curdied congealed

cure take care of

curiosity delicacy, scrupulousness

curious scrupulous, careful; hard to please, critical; elaborate, exquisite; anxious

currence flowing

curst fierce, cantankerous

curtal with a docked tail

curtle-axe short broadsword

cushes thigh-armour

Custalorum for '*Custos Rotulorum*' (*Lat.* = 'keeper of the rolls'), the highest justiciary office in a county

customer prostitute; prostitute's client

cut docked or gelded horse; nag, work-horse; female genitals; share; **cut and longtail** = every kind; in any event; **draw cuts** = draw lots

cut-purse, cutpurse petty thief who snips purses from people's belts

cuttle (?) thief

Cyclops = Cyclopes, one-eyed giants who assisted in the manufacture of armour for the gods

cyme a medicinal plant

cynic foul-mouthed philosopher

Cynthia the goddess Diana when represented as the moon

cypress cypress wood; crape, linen

Cytherea the goddess Venus

Daedalus father of Icarus (*see* **Icarus**)

daff *see* **doff**

Dagonet King Arthur's fool

Daintry Daventry

dainty *adj.* particular, finicky; **make dainty** = hesitate primly

dam mother

Damascus traditional scene of Abel's murder (*see* **Cain**)

dan sir

dancing horse a famous Elizabethan performing horse

dancing-rapier ornamental sword worn when dancing

danger power to harm

Dansker Dane

Daphne *see* **Apollo**

dare (in bird-catching) dazzle, daze

darkling in the dark

darraign set in order, prepare

dash *n.* mark, sign; blow; *v.* crush, dishearten; **at first dash** = at the outset

date fixed term or limit

daub it put on a false show

daubery false pretence, trickery

day-bed couch

day-woman dairymaid

dear important; intense, ardent; grievous

dearth scarcity, *hence* high value

death-practised whose death has been plotted

deathsman executioner

death-token sign of the plague

debate *n.* struggle, contention; *v.* contend; contend about

debile feeble

debitor and creditor account book; book-keeper

Deborah Israelite judge who incited an attack on Sisera, the general of the Canaanite king Jabin

deboshed debauched

decerns Dogberry's word for 'concerns'

decimation execution of one man in ten

deck *n.* deck of cards; *v.* adorn, cover

decoct boil up

deed performance, doing; contract; **deed of saying** = keeping promises deep-fet fetched from deep down

deer animals

default fault, offence; **in the default** = (?) when necessary; (?) when you fail

defeat mar, destroy; defraud

defeature disfigurement

defence armour; fencing, swordplay

defend forbid

definement definition, description

defunct extinct, dead

defunction death

defunctive relating to death, funereal

degree order, hierarchy; step, stage

delations narrations, accusations

deliberate pre-plan

delicate delightful, charming, elegant

delicates luxuries, delicacies

deliverly nimbly

demean conduct, behave

demerit merit; deficiency, sin

demi-cannon large gun

demises intentions

demure *adj.* solemn, modest; *v.* look thoughtfully

denay *n.* denial; *v.* deny

denier small copper coin

denunciation public announcement

depend be dependent; lean; hang, impend

dependency dependants; logical sequence; submissiveness

deplore talk woefully

depose take an oath; examine on oath

deputation appointment or office of a deputy (usually in high office)

deracinate uproot

derived descended

dern dark, wild

derogate *adj.* degenerate, debased; derogatory; *v.* degrade oneself

descant *n.* sung variations; *v.* sing variations

descension descent

descent child

describe discern

descry *n.* discovery; *v.* discover

deserts excellences; good qualities

design *n.* purpose, enterprise; *v.* designate, refer to

designment purpose, enterprise

Destinies Fates

determinate *adj.* at an end; decisive; planned; *v.* put an end to

determination end, expiry; decision

determine end, conclude; put an end to

Deucalion with his wife, the

sole survivors of a great flood sent by Jupiter

deuce-ace a low score at dice

dewlap loose flesh around a cow's throat

dexter right

dey-woman dairy woman

Di faciant laudis summa sit ista tuae 'The gods grant that this may be the peak of thy glory' (*Lat.*, Ovid)

diable devil (*Fr.*)

diablo devil (*Sp.*)

dial clock; sundial

Dian, Diana goddess of chastity, hunting and the moon (*cf.* **Cynthia**)

diapason bass accompaniment to a melody

diaper towel

dich (?) do it

Dickon Dick (Richard)

Dido Queen of Carthage, loved and abandoned by Aeneas (*see* **Aeneas**)

diet *n.* prescribed course; food; *v.* prescribe a course for, condition

difference distinguishing mark in heraldry; distinction; variety; variance, strife

diffidence doubt, mistrust

digression deviation (from right)

dilate extend; relate or set out extensively

dildo artificial phallus, frequently mentioned in ballads

dilemma argument which always catches an opponent out

diluculo surgere 'to rise early [is very healthy]' (*Lat.*, proverbial)

dine with Duke Humphrey go without dinner

dint impression, force; stroke, blow

directitude mistake for (?) discreditude (disrepute); (?) dejectitude (misfortune)

Dis Pluto (*see* **Pluto**)

disable disqualify, disparage

disanimate dishearten

disappointed unprepared

disaster sign of ill-omen, as seen in the stars

disbranch break off, as from a tree trunk

discandy melt, thaw (*cf.* **candied**)

discase undress (*cf.* **case**)

discernings intellect

discharge dismiss; send away

discomfortable having no word of comfort

discommend disapprove of

discontent discontented person, malcontent

discordant inharmonious; jarring

discourse *n.* talk, conversation; process or faculty of reasoning;

v. talk

discover expose, reveal; distinguish

discovery revelation; exploration, reconnaissance

disdained disdainful

disease *n.* unease, distress; *v.* make uneasy, trouble

disedged satisfied, with respect to appetite

disfurnish deprive, leave with nothing

disgrace fall from favour; insult, discredit

disgracious lacking grace, unpleasant

disguise altered appearance, strange fashion; masque; wild drunkenness

dishabited dislodged, stripped

dishonest immodest

dishonesty unchastity

dislike displease; disapprove

disliken disguise

dislimn break up, smudge

disme tenth part

dismission dismissal

dismount (of swords) unsheathe; (of guns) lower

disorbed dislocated from its sphere

dispark put (parkland) to other uses

dispatch settle, conclude; kill; bereave, deprive

dispiteous merciless

displeased angry; *v.* angered

disponge be sponged, drip

dispose *n.* disposal; disposition; *v.* compose, make terms; encamp

disposer one who can do what he or she will with another

disposition arrangements

disprize devalue or undervalue

dispropertied dispossessed

dispursed disbursed, distributed

disputable disputatious, argumentative

dissembly Dogberry's word for 'assembly'

distaff cleft stick for spinning wool

distain make colourless; stain, defile

distance (in fencing) correct space between the opponents

distaste *n.* disrelish, unpleasantness; *v.* be distasteful; make distasteful; find distasteful

distemper *n.* lack of even temper, lack of balance; *v.* upset, disturb

distemperance disorder

distinctly separately, individually

distinguishment distinction

distract *adj.* separate; deranged, confused; *v.* divide; derange,

confuse

distrain confiscate

distressful gained by misery and toil

distrust be wary of

dive-dapper dabchick, little grebe

divers several, various, different; perverse, evil

dividant separable, different

divide apportion

divided unfinished, broken

dividual separable

divine extemporal a clergyman who improvises prayers

division musical notes that elaborate upon a basic melody; military arrangement

divulge openly proclaim

do him dead kill him

doctor cleric

doctrine lesson

document lesson

doff take off; put off, dismiss

dog-apes baboons

dogged dog-like, cruel

doit small coin

dole grief; share; **happy man be his dole** = may his lot be that of a happy man (*i.e.* good luck to him)

dollar silver coin

domineer revel, feast

dominical red letter used to mark Sundays in almanacs

dominie schoolmaster

doom *n.* judgement; day of judgement; *v.* judge, sentence

dotant senile person

double voucher testimony given by two independent parties

double-fatal fatal in two ways, as with the yew which was both poisonous and used for making bows

double-man supernatural apparition

doublet and hose jacket and breeches (basic Elizabethan male dress)

doubt *n.* suspicion; fear; *v.* suspect; fear

dout extinguish

dowl one of the filaments or fibres of a feather

dowlas coarse linen from Brittany

down-gyved fallen down and resembling gyves (fetters)

down-roping falling in long strings

dowsets testicles

doxy female beggar

drab strumpet

drachma silver coin

draff pig-swill

draught sink, privy

draw withdraw; receive; drain; **draw dry-foot** = hunt by the scent

drawer tapster, waiter

dress prepare; adorn, cultivate

dribbling (in archery) weakly shot, ineffective

drift *n.* intention, purpose; shower; *adj.* driving

drinking drunk drinking until drunk

drollery puppet show; comic painting

drum rallying-point

drumble be sluggish, lag

dry-beat bruise, beat

ducat gold coin

ducdame ostensibly nonsense but possibly Cymric ('Come to me') or Italian ('Lead him from me')

dudgeon haft, handle

due endue, grace

duello correct practice of duelling (*Ital.*)

dumb-discoursive quietly seductive

dump tune, usually melancholy

dumps low spirits

dun *n.* horse; log dragged out of an imaginary mire as a Christmas game; *adj.* dull grey-brown; **dun's the mouse** = be still

dung earth, the physical world

dupped opened

durance durable cloth or nature; imprisonment

each, at end to end

eager sharp, bitter

ean (of sheep) give birth

eanling new-born lamb

ear *v.* hear; plough; **by th'ears** = at odds; **in the ear** = in earshot; **shake your ears** = behave like the ass you are

earing ploughing

earn grieve

earnest initial payment of money as a deposit

earth hide, burrow in the earth

earthed laid in a grave

easy easily won over; small, light

eche augment, increase

ecstasy deranged mental state; unconsciousness

Edward shovel-board shilling from the reign of Edward VI later used in shovel-board (*see* **shove-groat**)

effectual conclusive

effigies likeness

effuse effusion

eftest Dogberry's word for 'aptest'

eftsoons afterwards

egall equal

egg worthless thing or person

egma Costard's word for 'enigma'

ego et Rex meus I and my king (*Lat.*)

egregious outstanding, remarkable

eisel, eisell vinegar

eke also

elbow thrust back; **rub the elbow** = express pleasure

eld old age; people of a previous time

elder-gun pop-gun used for firing paper pellets

elect *n.* people specially chosen; *v.* choose, accept

element one of the four universal substances (earth, water, air, fire); sky

elf *n.* fairy, spirit; *v.* tangle or mat together

elf-locks hair tangled or matted together

Elizium, Elysium abode of the virtuous after death in the ancient world

elm tree used to train vines

emballing taking up the orb, a symbol of royalty

embare make bare

embarquements embargos, hindrances

embattail, embattle prepare for battle

embayed sheltered in a bay

emblaze set forth, as in heraldry

embossed hunted down, exhausted; bulging, swollen

embounded enclosed

embowel disembowel

embrasure embrace

eminence superiority, high rank

Emmanuel 'God with us', formula used to begin letters and documents

emmet ant

empale surround, encircle, enclose for defence (used of armour)

empatron be patron to

emperial imperial

empery empire, sovereignty

empiric quack doctor

empiricutic characteristic of quack medicine

emulation envious rivalry

emulator petty rival, disparager

emulous envious

encieled screened

encompassment roundabout course

enew (in falconry) drive (the bird) into water

enfeoff surrender (property)

engage bind; pledge as security

engine plot, device; instrument; military machine

engineer, enginer military engineer, sapper

englut devour

engraffed, engrafted attached; ingrained

engross fatten; amass, gather; monopolize; write large

enlard fatten

enlarge set free

enlargement liberty; liberation

enormous monstrous

enow enough

enround encircle

ensconce hide, tuck away

enseamed greasy (*cf.* **seam**)

ensear dry up, wither

enskied placed in heaven

ensteeped under water

entertain *n.* entertainment; *v.* treat; employ; maintain

entertainment treatment; employment

entitled, entituled called; having a claim

entreat *n.* entertainment; *v.* negotiate, ask; treat

entreatment negotiation

envire hem in

envy *n.* malice, spite; *v.* bear ill will towards

enwheel encircle

Ephesian revelling companion

epicurism gluttony

epithet, epitheton adjective, expression

equal balanced, just, fair

equally justly, impartially

equinox time of the year when day and night are of equal length

Ercles Hercules (*see* **Hercules**)

Erebus place of darkness on the way to the underworld

erected active, attentive

erection Quickly's word for 'direction' (instruction)

ergo therefore (*Lat.*)

eringo root of the sea-holly, a delicacy and aphrodisiac

erst once, formerly

escapes transgressions, sexual lapses

escot provide for

Esculapius god of healing

esperance hope; the motto of the Percy family

espial spy

essay *see* **assay**

estimable esteemed, valuable; esteeming, admiring

estimation rate of esteem, worth; esteemed or valued object; reputation; valuation

estridge ostrich; goshawk

Et bonum quo antiquius eo melius 'And the older a good thing is, the better it is' (*Lat.*, proverbial)

et tu Erasmus an diabolus and you are either Erasmus or the devil (*Lat.*)

eternize immortalize

Europa daughter of Agenor and loved by Jupiter, who transformed himself into a bull and carried her off to Crete

even *n.* the level truth; *adj.* quits, without strife; *v.* make even; keep up with; **even o'er** = make sense of; **go even** = agree

even-Christen fellow Christians

event outcome

ever always; **not ever** = not always; **ever among** = all the while

Evil, the the King's Evil (scrofula), supposed to be cured by the King's touch

evil (?) privy; (?) brothel

evitate avoid

exactly expressly

examine question

except take exception to; set aside; **except, before**

excepted = legal phrase common in leases (*i.e.* 'with the aforesaid exceptions')

exception disapproval, objection

excitement exhortation

exclaim exclamation, outcry

exclamation reproach

excrement outgrowth from the body, particularly hair

excursion (in stage directions) skirmish

exempt separated, far away

exequies funeral ceremonies

exercise devotional exercise; homily

exhalation meteor, falling star

exhale draw out

exhaust draw out, elicit

exhibit submit, introduce; Gobbo's word for 'inhibit'

exhibition gift; allowance, maintenance; Verges' word for 'commission' (authority)

exigent critical moment

exion Quickly's word for 'action'

exorcise conjure up evil spirits

expect aim to achieve

expectancy expectation, hope

expedience speed, expedition

expedient swift

expense expenditure

experimental of experience

expiate *adj.* terminated; *v.* extinguish

expostulate discuss, inquire into, argue

exposture exposure

express *adj.* well formed, well executed; *v.* show forth, make known

expressure expression; impression

exsufflicate (?) inflated, farfetched

extemporal extempore

extemporically with skill in improvisation

extend seize in satisfaction for a debt

extent behaviour; exercise; seizure (*cf.* **extend**)

extenuate mitigate, weaken the force of

extirp extirpate, root out

extracting drawing everything else away with it, absorbing

extraught extracted, derived

extravagancy vagrancy

extravagant straying beyond its proper bounds, vagrant

eyases young hawks, noted for their clamour

eyas-musket young sparrowhawk

eye *n.* spot; hole in a bowling ball; *v.* appear; **in the eye** = in sight

eye-glass lens of the eye

eye-strings muscles or tendons of the eye

eyne eyes

eyrie nest of a bird of prey

face *n.* outward show; *v.* (of garments) trim with braid or velvet; bully; deceive; (in cards) call an opponent's bluff; **face down** = swear blind; **face out** = brazen out, intimidate, bluff

face-royal head depicted on a coin

Facile precor gelida quando pecus omne sub umbra Ruminat Holofernes's misquotation from a pastoral poem by Mantuanus (*Lat.* = '[Faustus], I pray, while all the herd chews the cud in the cold shade')

facinerious facinorous, wicked

fact deed, crime; **in the fact** = red-handed

factious of or forming a faction, rebellious

factor agent, representative

faculty power; quality, nature

fadge turn out, succeed

fading word used in contemporary songs

fail *n.* failure; failure to produce a son; death; *v.* fail in; die

fain *adj.* glad, well pleased, content; *adv.* gladly

fairings gifts bought at a fair

fair-snouted pretty-nosed

faithed believed

falchion curved broadsword

fall *n.* cadence in music; *v.* let fall, bring down; befall; happen, turn out; waste away; **at fall** = at ebb; **fall from** = desert; **fall off** = revolt

falling-sickness epilepsy

falsing deceptive

fame *n.* public image or opinion; news; *v.* make famous

familiar *n.* spirit or demon; close friend; *adj.* native, accustomed

fan sift (*e.g.* grain) by means of an air current

fanatical frantic, outlandish

fancy *n.* love; short piece of poetry or music, fantasia; *v.* love

fancy-free free from love

fancy-monger dealer in love

fangled pretentiously fashionable

fantastic *n.* person given to flights of fancy; fop, gallant; *adj.* of the mind; given to or produced by extravagant flights of fancy, crazy

fantastical *see* **fantastic** (*adj.*).

fantasy imagination; imagining, fancy; self-delusion

fap drunk

farce stuff

fardel pack

fare travel; feed; be, feel

far-fet far-fetched, highly cunning

farm rent; lease out profits from taxes in return for an immediate sum of cash; **in farm** = leased out

farrow pigs of a litter

farthingale petticoat stretched over whalebone hoops

fashions farcy, a disease in horses

fat stuffy; (?) sweating

Fates three deities who span the threads of human lives

fatigate fatigued, weary

faucet-seller seller of taps for wine-barrels

fault sin; misfortune; (in hunting) lost or 'cold' scent; **for fault of** = for want of

favour appearance, face, feature; charm; token of good will; aid, support

fay faith

fazed tattered, frayed

feat *adj.* graceful; *adv.* gracefully, neatly; *v.* (?) make or render graceful

feature appearance of the body

federary *see* **feodary**

fee livestock; estate of a feudal lord; reward for services to a lord; **in fee** = outright; **in fee farm** = permanent

feeder servant; parasite

fee-grief particular grief, suggesting a large estate rented by a single tenant (*cf.* **fee**)

feeze beat

felicitate made happy

fell *n.* skin, fleece; *adj.* terrible, savage

fellies parts of a wheel that form the rim

fence *n.* defence; swordsmanship; *v.* shut in, defend

feodary confederate

fere companion; husband or wife

fern-seed seed supposed both to possess and to impart invisibility

ferret torment; search thoroughly

ferula teacher's cane for beating

fescue teacher's stick for pointing

festinate hurried, hasty

fetch *n.* trick, evasion; *v.* make; strike; **fetch about** = change tack; **fetch in** = surround, catch; **fetch off** = rescue; get the better of, kill

fettle groom, prepare

few, in in short

fewness and truth the truth in short

fia see via

fico fig (*Ital.*) (*see* **fig**)

fidelicet Evans's word for '*videlicet*' (*see* **videlicet**)

field-bed camp bed

fielded in the battle field

fifteens fifteenths (*see* **fifteenth**)

fifteenth tax of one-fifteenth levied on personal property

fig *n.* contemptuous exclamation; obscene gesture sometimes called the 'fig of Spain'; *v.* make the 'fig' gesture; move lasciviously

fights protective screens used on warships

fig's-end *see* **fig**

figure *n.* numeral or letter; esoteric diagram; rhetorical device; imagining; *v.* express, represent; imagine

file *n.* body of men, especially soldiers; list; *v.* defile; keep pace, as in marching

fill-horse horse used to draw a cart

film gossamer

find find out; understand; **find forth** = locate

fine *n.* end; *adj.* refined; *v.* conclude; undertake to pay; make beautiful; **fine and recovery** = transfer of property

fineless boundless

firago virago, female warrior

fire-drake meteor

fire-new brand-new, as if fresh from the forge

firk beat, perhaps with connotations of 'fuck'

firstling first offspring

fisnomy physiognomy, face

fit *n.* spasm; section of poetry or music; *v.* be appropriate (for)

fitchew polecat, known for its foul stench and sexual appetite

fitchook *see* **fitchew**

fitment that which is fitting; device

fives avives, a disease in horses

flamen ancient Roman priest

flanker cannon in a flanking position

flap-dragon small fruit, floating in liquor, set alight and swallowed as a Christmas game

flap-jack pancake

flatness (?) completeness; (?) unrelieved expanse

flaunts fine clothes

flaw *n.* fragment; gust or blast of wind; outburst; *v.* crack, break

fleckled spotted, blotchy

fledge fledged

fleer *n.* sneer; *v.* grin, sneer

flesh (in hunting) awaken an appetite for bloodshed

fleshment first success

fleur-de-luce *see* **flower-de-luce**

flewed big-jowled

flidge *see* **fledge**

flight-shoot distance to which an arrow is shot

flirt-gill easy woman

float sea

flourish *n.* fanfare; decoration; *v.* sound a fanfare; decorate, embellish

flower-de-luce *fleur-de-lis* (iris), French heraldic device also used later by English kings

flurted scorned

flush ripe, full of vigour

flushing redness caused by weeping

flux something that flows

fluxive flowing, fluid

flying at the brook hunting for water-fowl with hawks

foil *n.* defeat, disgrace; complementary setting or background; *v.* defeat, overthrow

foin *n.* thrust of a sword; *v.* thrust or parry with a sword

foison plenty, abundance

fold enclose sheep

fond *adj.* foolish; *v.* dote

fondling foolish person

fool jester; **fool's bolt** = allusion to the proverb 'a fool's bolt is soon shot'; **shrieve's fool** = penniless idiot in the custody of the sherrif (*cf.* **shrieve**)

fool-begged so idiotic that one might request custody of it from the courts

foot be or go on foot; kick; (of an eagle) snatch with the talons

foot-cloth *n.* horse's decorative saddle-cloth; *adj.* equipped with a foot-cloth

foot-landrakers vagabond highwaymen

fop *n.* fool; *v.* make a fool of; *see* **fub**

foppery, fopp'ry folly, foolery; cheating, trickery

foppish foolish

for for lack of; for fear of

foragement prey

forbid under a curse

force strengthen; care; urge, enforce; stuff; **force a straw** = care a straw for; **force perforce** = in spite of opposition, necessarily; **of force** = of importance; of necessity

fordo ruin, destroy

fordone tired out

forecast forethought

fore-end earlier part

foregone done previously

fore-hand, forehand leading position; **forehand shaft** = arrow shot with the target seen above the bow hand; **'forehand sin** = sin of acting prematurely

forehorse leading horse

fore-past previous

foresay determine, decree

forespent previously spent, worn out

forestall prevent, deny in advance

foreward vanguard

forgetive inventive

fork snake's tongue; arrow's head; leg or legs (where the body forks)

forked barbed; horned, cuckolded (*cf.* **horn**)

forlorn desolate, forsaken

formal rational, sane; conventional, regular

formality decorum, regularity

former foremost

forsake give up; deny, decline

forslow delay

forspent wearied, exhausted

fortitude strength

fortuna de la guerra the chance of war (*Sp.?*)

foutre (*Fr.*) ruder version of 'fig' (*cf.* **fig**)

fox sword

foxship qualities of a fox, supposedly ingratitude and cunning

fracted broken

fraction breach, estrangement, quarrel; fragment

frame *n.* systematic form; design; *v.* form, contrive, execute

frampold, frampul badtempered, full of peevishness

franchise freedom from servitude

franchised free

frank *n.* sty for hogs; *adj.* generous; free from restraint; *v.* shut in a sty

franklin freeholder, rich yeoman

fraught *n.* freight, cargo; *adj.* laden, supplied; *v.* burden

fraughtage freight, cargo

fray *n.* affray, riot; *v.* be frightened

frayed frightened

French crown French gold coin; head bald through syphilis

frequent familiar, in company (with)

fresh freshwater spring

fret chafe, wear away; rot; ferment; adorn, ornament; equip with frets (**see frets**)

frets ridges on a lute to guide the fingering

fretten fretted, chafed

friend *n.* family member; lover; *v.* befriend; **at friend, to friend** = friendly, as a friend

friends relatives

frieze coarse cloth

frippery old clothes shop

friskins leapings about

front *n.* forehead, face; *v.* face, oppose; march in front

frontier rampart; border fortress

froward recalcitrant, awkward

frush beat, hammer

fub rob, cheat; **fub off** = fob off

fugitive refugee

fullam kind of false dice

fulsome full, abundant; foul

fumiter the fumitory plant, a weed

Furies mythological fiends who punished crimes

furnishings decorations, trimmings

furniture equipment; horse's gear

fury transcendental state; poetic inspiration

fury-innocent (?) one innocent of fury

fust become musty

fustian *n.* coarse cloth; nonsense; *adj.* bombastic, highflown

fustilarian (?) fustilugs (a gross woman)

gaberdine cloak

gad spike; **upon the gad** = suddenly (as if pricked with a spike)

gag prop or jerk open

gage *n.* pledge, especially to fight; *v.* pledge, engage, bind

gaingiving misgiving

gainsay deny, forbid

Galen famous Greek physician and author of medical textbooks

gall *n.* suffering; indignation; bitterness; *v.* vex, hurt

Gallian Gallic, French

galliard dance punctuated by capers (little leaps)

galliass large ship

gallimaufry jumble, mixture

gallow scare

Gallowglasses axe-wielding Irish soldiers

gallows person who will or should be hanged

gamester gambler

gamut musical scale

Ganymede beautiful youth whom an enamoured Jupiter transported to heaven to be the cupbearer of the gods

garboil uproar, disturbance

Gargantua giant from French folklore, made famous by the work of Rabelais

garland crown; hero

Garmombles Evans's version of 'German nobles', close to 'geremumble', an obscure term of abuse; with probable allusion to Count Mömpelgard, a German noble who aspired to be elected Knight of the Garter

garnish *n.* clothes; *v.* clothe, decorate

gaskins wide breeches

gastness dread; ghastliness

gaud showy ornament, triviality

gaudy bright, ornate, festive

gaze thing gazed at; (in hunting) **at gaze** = distracted

gear purpose; matter, business

geck dupe

gemini pair, as of twins

gender *n.* genus, sort; *v.* procreate, breed

generosity those of noble birth

generous of noble birth

genitivo 'in the genitive case' (*Lat.*)

genius spirit, especially a person's guardian spirit

gentility good birth and breeding; good manners

gentle *n.* gentleman or gentlewoman; *adj.* noble, well bred; *adv.* nobly; *v.* ennoble

gentry nobility; noble behaviour

George badge of St George worn by Knights of the Order of the Garter

german, germane *n.* close relative; *adj.* closely related

germen seed

gest stage in a journey, especially a royal progress; great deed, usually chivalric

get beget, sire

ghasted frightened

ghost *n.* corpse; *v.* haunt

gib male cat

gift giving

gig spinning-top

giglet, giglot dizzy woman; strumpet

gillyvors gillyflowers

gimmaled made with gimbals (**see gimmer**)

gimmer gimmal, mechanical joint

gin snare, trap

gird *n.* taunt, reproof; *v.* sneer or scoff (at)

glaive halberd or sword, especially broadsword

glance *n.* innuendo; *v.* rebound; make an oblique, usually disparaging, hint

glass *n.* mirror; hour-glass; **glass eyes** = spectacles

glaze glare

gleek *n.* scoff, gesture of contempt; *v.* scoff

glib geld, castrate

globe head; name of Shakespeare's theatre

glose, gloze *n.* marginal comment; superficial word-play; *v.* interpret or comment as if with scholastic glosses; use false, attractive language

gloss attractive external appearance

glut swallow hungrily

go walk; **go to** = expression of scorn or disbelief (*cf.* go on, get away)

goatish lecherous, as goats were supposed to be

gobbet chunk of flesh

God dig-you-den, God gi' good e'en, God 'i' good e'en, God ye good e'en, God-den, good den (God give you) good evening

God 'ild (may) God yield (reward)

God-a-mercy thank God

God's lid see **'Slid**

good good for credit, wealthy

good dild see **God 'ild**

goodly handsome

goodman title for people below the rank of gentleman; husband

good-year, what the exclamation of surprise

goose tailor's iron; short for Winchester goose (= prostitute); sore caused by veneral disease

gorbellied big-bellied

Gordian knot according to legend, an impossibly complex knot to be untied only by he who would go on to rule Asia; Alexander the Great cut it with his sword

gore-blood clotted blood

gorge vomit

gorget throat armour

Gorgon one of three monsters, the most famous being Medusa, whose look turned the viewer to stone

gospelled instructed in the precepts of the gospel

gossip *n.* godparent; merry, talkative woman; *v.* stand as a godparent; be merry in company

gothic uncivilized; belonging to the dark ages

gourd kind of false dice

gout drop of liquid

government self-discipline, self-control; **in government** = under control

graceful blessed; favourable

graff, graft *n.* grafted (*i.e.* hybrid) plant; *v.* graft, crossbreed by implanting a shoot into a plant of a different kind

grafter plant from which the shoot is taken for grafting (*see* **graff**)

grain, in fast dyed, ingrained; **purple-in-grain** = red

grained ingrained; bearing or displaying the grains found in timber

gramercy great thanks

grand guard heavy armour worn on horseback

grange farm house sometimes belonging to a religious establishment

grapple fasten onto with iron clamps

grate vex, annoy

grateful pleasing

gratify reward; make pleasant

gratulate *adj.* gratifying; *v.* greet; gratify, satisfy

grave bury, entomb; carve, engrave

gravel urinary crystals

greasily obscenely

great morning broad daylight

'gree agree

greeing suitable

Greek reveller, person with relaxed moral standards

Greensleeves popular English ballad about an inconstant woman

grievance distress, trauma

grieve sorrow; offend; vex, taunt, misuse

gripe *n.* clutch; vulture or eagle; *v.* grip, clutch

grise, grize stair, step

groat coin; **ten groats** = an attorney's fee

gross summary; large letters

gross-daubing coarse or inartistic painting

ground (in heraldry) coloured background; (in music) air on which variations are sung or played

groundlings theatregoers who stood in front of the stage

ground-piece (?) exemplary painting

grow (of a sum of money) grow due; **grow to a point** = come to a stop; **grow upon** = encroach on

guardant guard; **Jack guardant** = petty official (*cf.* **Jack**)

guards trimmings of a garment; stars in the Ursa Minor constellation used for navigation

guidon pennant, flag

guilder gold coin

guiled deceitful, full of guile

guinea-hen (?) cunning woman; (?) prostitute

guise usual practice

gules (in heraldry) red

gull *n.* nestling; credulous fool; hoax; *v.* trick, fool

gummed treated with gum, glossy

gurnet small fish considered a delicacy

gust *n.* taste, appetite; *v.* get a taste of, realize

Guy, Sir Guy of Warwick, hero of an early English romance

gyve *n.* (leg) fetter; *v.* fetter

H letter of the alphabet pronounced 'aitch', so sounding like the Elizabethan pronunciation of the word 'ache'

habiliment attire, dress

habit clothing, garments; bearing, disposition

habited dressed

habitude character, disposition

hack (?) associate with loose women

hackney prostitute

hade land part of the field where the plough turns around, and so planted last

haggard *n.* wild hawk; *adj.* wild

haggled hacked

hag-seed offspring of a hag

hair sort, kind, nature; **against the hair** = against the grain

haircloth man penitent wearing coarse haircloth against skin

hairmonger barber's client

halberd battle-axe on a long pole; one armed with a halberd

halcyon kingfisher, supposed when hung up to turn its beak with the wind; **halcyon days** = period of calm

half partner, wife

half-blooded having only one parent of noble blood

half-caps caps taken only half off, slight salutations

half-cheek profile

half-cheeked (of a horse's bit) giving insufficient control

half-face profile

half-faced showing a face in profile; pinched-faced

half-kirtle skirt portion of a kirtle (*see* **kirtle**)

half-sword very close quarters

halidom state of being holy; anything regarded as holy

halloo, hallow call, shout

Hallowmas All Saints' Day (1 November)

halt limp

hand-fast custody; marriage contract

handicraft artisan, workman

handmaid a small ship that attends a larger one

handsaw small saw; (?) heron

handy-dandy take your choice (from a children's game)

hang upon clasp onto

hanger straps attaching the sword to the girdle

haply by chance

happiness handsomeness

happy lucky

harbinger one who runs on ahead

hard-haired with tightly curled hair

hardiment valour; deeds of valour

hardiness boldness, daring

hardness difficulty

harlot *n.* person of loose life; beggar; *adj.* lewd

harlotry good-for-nothing

Harry ten shillings half-sovereign coined under Henry VII

hatch lower half of a divided door

hatchment tablet displaying a coat of arms

haud credo 'I do not believe' (*Lat.*)

haught haughty, arrogant

haughty high-pitched, ambitious

hautboy oboe

havoc signal for indiscriminate slaughter

hay country dance; (in fencing) thrust reaching the antagonist

hazard *n.* dice game; risk; stake; *v.* risk

head *n.* headland, promontory; subdivision; armed force, advance; *v.* behead; **head and front** = height

headless brainless, stupid

headstall part of the bridle that fits round the head

heady-rash impetuously violent

heap great company, crowd; **on a heap** = prostrate

heat: in the very heat in the heat of the moment

heavy serious, grievous; sad; tiresome

hebenon poison

Hecate goddess of witchcraft

hectic fever

Hector Trojan hero

Hecuba Queen of Troy

hedge-pig hedgehog

hefts heavings, retchings

heirs inherits

Hellespont the narrow strait known as the Dardanelles; in Greek mythology it separated Leander's home, Abydos, in Europe, from Hero's tower at Sestos in Asia; Leander swam it to reach his lover Hero and drowned

hempseed one deserving to be hanged

hent *n.* seized opportunity; *v.* seize; reach

herb of grace rue

herblet small herb

Hercules legendary hero, supposedly a kinsman of

Theseus; **Hercules and his load** = Hercules bearing the world on his shoulders, perhaps the sign at the Globe Theatre

Hero lover of Leander (*see* **Leander**)

Herod biblical tyrant

heroica facta heroic feats (*Lat.*)

he's he shall

Hesperides nymphs in classical mythology, daughters of Hesperus, the evening star, guarding an orchard of golden apples with the help of a dragon; often in the Renaissance the orchard itself was wrongly referred to as the Hesperides

Hesperus the planet Venus

hest behest, command

hey-day, heyday exclamation of surprise or joy

hic et ubique 'here and everywhere' (*Lat.*)

Hic ibat Simois, hic est Sigeia tellus, / Hic steterat Priami regia celsa senis 'Here ran the river Simois; here is the Sigeian land; here stood old Priam's lofty palace' (*Lat.*, Ovid)

hic jacet 'here lies' (*Lat.*)

Hiems Winter (personified)

high and low false dice

high-crested proud, self-assertive

high-day *see* **hey-day**

high-lone alone, without support

high-proof in the highest degree

high-stomached high-spirited, haughty, stubborn

hight is called

hild held

hilding contemptible person of either sex, coward

hind female deer; rustic servant; boor

hindrance injury, damage

hint occasion, opportunity

hipped having a dislocated hipbone

Hiren seductive woman (from the name of a character in a play by Peele)

hit agree; **hit of** = hit on

hive hat

ho cessation, limit

hoar *adj.* mouldy; whitish; *v.* become mouldy; whiten (with disease)

hobby-horse character in the morris-dance; buffoon; loose woman

hodge-pudding pudding or sausage made of hodge (pigs' entrails)

holding consistency; refrain of a song

holidame *see* halidom

holp helped

holy-ales rural festivals on saints' days

holy-rood day feast of the Holy Cross (14 September)

holy-thistle *see carduus benedictus*

home thoroughly

honest worthy, decent; truthful; chaste

honesty uprightness, decency; chastity; generosity

honey-stalks clover flowers

honorificabilitudinitatibus stock comic example of a long (Latin) word

honour honourable deed

hood (of a hawk) blindfold

hoodman-blind blind man's buff

horn deer; sign of a cuckold

horn-book, hornbook child's primer (the alphabet on a leaf of paper protected by a translucent plate of horn)

horn-mad like a furious bull, with connotations of cuckoldry (*cf.* horn)

horologe clock

horrors (*v.*) horrifies

hose breeches; French hose = loose-fitting hose

host *n.* army; *v.* lodge

hot-house brothel

house-clogs shackles

housekeeper domestic woman; guard dog

housewife hussy, prostitute

howlet owlet or owl

hox hamstring

hoy small coasting vessel

hoy-day, hoyday *see* hey-day

hugger-mugger secrecy

hull float with sails furled

Humida vallis raros patitur fulminis ictus 'Rarely is a damp valley struck by thunderbolts' (*Lat.*, Seneca)

humorous damp; temperamental, capricious, whimsical (*see* humour)

humour dampness; one of the four physiological 'elements' (melancholy, blood, choler, phlegm) governing disposition, *hence* temperament, mood, inclination

Humphrey, to dine with Duke to go without dinner; hence Humphrey Hour, perhaps personifies hunger?

Hungarian needy, hungry

hunt's up morning song to awaken a newly married wife

hurricano waterspout

hurry commotion

hurtless harmless, unhurting

husband *n.* one who manages a household, accounts, *etc.*; *v.* cultivate; marry

husbandry management (*cf.* husband), thrift; farming, cultivation

huswife *see* housewife

Hybla mountain in Sicily famous for honey

Hydra legendary snake with many heads which grew back sevenfold when they were cut off

hyen hyena

Hymen, Hymenaeus god of marriage

hyperbole figure of speech used for exaggeration

Hyperion Phoebus, the sun god

Hyrcan, Hyrcanian from Hyrcania, a region on the shore of the Caspian sea famous for tigers

hysterica passio type of hysteria, mainly in women (*Lat.*)

Icarus son of Daedalus who, with his father, used artificial wings to fly from Crete, where King Minos had imprisoned them; flying too near the sun, he melted the wax in his wings and so fell to his death in the sea

ice-brook stream of icy water, used in the tempering of sword blades

Iceland dog lap-dog from Iceland

idea image

ides of March 15 March in the Roman dating system

ignis fatuus (*Lat.*) will o'the wisp

ignominy, ignomy disgrace

Ilion, Ilium Troy; palace of Priam in Troy

ill-favoured ugly, unpleasant (*cf.* favour)

illness evil nature

illo hallo

ill-tempered (of the humours in the blood) badly balanced (*see* humour)

illustrous not lustrous, lacklustre

image archetypal image, perfect example

imaginary imagining, imaginative

imbecility feebleness

imbrue pierce; spill blood

imitari to imitate (*Lat.*)

immanity barbarity, ferocity

immediacy the position of being next in authority

immediate direct; next in succession

imminence impending danger

immoment of no moment, insignificant

immures enclosing walls

imp *n.* young offshoot, *hence* child; *v.* repair (a wing) by grafting on new feathers

impale *see* empale

imparched roasted, encrusted

impare inappropriate, unworthy

impart say, reveal; provide

impartment speech, communication

impasted formed into a crust

impawn pledge, stake

impeach *n.* charge, reproach; *v.* undermine, discredit

impeachment charge; impediment, hindrance

imperator emperor

imperseverant (?) stubborn; (?) imperceptive

impertinency irrelevance, nonsense

impertinent Gobbo's word for 'pertinent'

impeticos (?) pocket

implorators implorers, beseechers

import *n.* weighty significance; *v.* signify; involve, concern

importable unbearable

importance significance, meaning; importunity, urgent request; question at issue

importancy significance, importance

important importunate, urgent

importless without significance, trivial

importment importance, significance

importune demand, urge

imposition command; accusation; penalty, burden

imposthume, impostume abscess

imprese allegorical representations used in heraldic decoration (*Ital.*)

impress *n.* conscription; *v.* press into military service

imputation attribution, reputation

in capite 'at the head' (*Lat.*), used of tenants holding land direct from the king

In hac spe vivo 'In this hope I live' (*Lat.*)

inapproved unproven

incapable unable to take in; unable to understand, unaware

incardinate Aguecheek's word for 'incarnate'

incarnadine turn red

incarnation Gobbo's word for 'incarnate'

inch island; Saint Colme's Inch = Inchcomb, an island in the Firth of Forth

inch out eke out, augment

inchmeal, by inch by inch

inclining *n.* inclination, side; *adj.* ready to be persuaded

income gathering in

incomprehensible limitless

incontinent *adj.* lacking self-restraint; *adv.* immediately

incony darling; delicate

incorporate united in one body

incorpsed united into a single body

incorrect uncorrected, incorrigible

incredulous incredible, unbelievable

Ind, Inde India

indebted debt-laden

indent *n.* indentation; *v.* make an agreement; dart about

index table of contents at the beginning or end of a book

indifferency impartiality; unremarkable nature

indifferent impartial, lacking prejudice or interest; mediocre, moderate; identical

indigest *n.* that which is amorphous; *adj.* crude, amorphous

indign disgraceful

indirect devious, wrongful

indirection injustice; oblique method

indirectly wrongly; obliquely; nonchalantly

indisposition unwillingness

indistinguishable of no recognized kind or function

indistinguished indistinguishable; limitless

individable (?) conforming to the dramatic unity of place; (?) not to be identified by divisions and subdivisions of genre

indrenched drenched, overwhelmed

induction first step; opening scene

infamonize Armado's word for 'infamize' (make infamous, defame)

infect infected

infection Quickly's and Old Gobbo's word for 'affection' (*see* affection)

infer bring in; allege; imply

influence planetary emanation supposed to exert a determining effect upon people

inform take on a form; give form to, fashion, direct; report

informal deranged

infuse pour into or onto

ingenious mentally alert, responsive; crafty; crafted; appropriate

ingeniously ingenuously, candidly

inginer *see* engineer

ingling fondling, caressing

ingraft *see* engraffed

inhabitable uninhabitable

inherit possess, come to possess; put in possession of; take possession of

inhibited prohibited

inhibition prohibition, ban

initiate belonging to a beginner

injurious abusive, offensive

ink-horn small vessel for containing ink; **inkhorn mate** = bookish person

inkle tape or yarn

inland *n.* interior of a land, especially its urban and prosperous parts

innocent *n.* idiot, fool; *adj.* simple, foolish

inoculate graft a new shoot into (a plant)

insane causing insanity

insconce *see* **ensconce**

insensible unable to be sensed

insinuate flatter, wheedle; hint to

insinuation flattery, worming a way in

insisture (?) persistence; (?) moment of stasis

instalment installation; stall

instance proof, sign, evidence; motive

instruction information

insuppressive unable to be suppressed or contained

Integer vitae, scelerisque purus, / Non eget Mauri iaculis, nec arcu 'The man of upright life and free from crime does not need the javelins or bows of the Moor' (*Lat.*, Horace)

intellect message, meaning

intelligence communication; secret information; spies

intelligencer messenger; spy

intelligencing carrying information

intelligent carrying information; intelligible

intendment intention

intentively attentively

intercept interrupt

intercession interval

intercourse commerce, business

interessed given a right to or share in

interest right to or share in

interlude short comedy

intervallum interval, pause

intitled, intituled *see* **entitled**

intreat *see* **entreat**

intrenchant unable to be cut

intrince intricate

intrinsicate intricate

investments robes; seiges

invitis nubibus 'in spite of the opposition of the clouds' (*Lat.*)

inward intimate

ipse he himself (*Lat.*)

ipso facto 'by that very act' (*Lat.*)

Ira furor brevis est 'Anger is a brief madness' (*Lat.*, Horace)

Iris messenger of Juno, represented as a rainbow

irreconciled unreconciled (to God)

irregular lawless, unruly, immoral

irregulous *see* **irregular**

iterance repetition

iustum, si fractus illabatur orbis, impavidum ferient ruinae 'even if the shattered world collapses on to him, the ruins cannot hurt the just and fearless man' (*Lat.*)

iwis truly

Jack, jack term of contempt, meaning fool, knave, trickster, also used in combinations, *e.g.* **Jack-priest, Jack-slave**

jack mechanized human figure that strikes a clock bell; small wooden block in a keyboard (wrongly used of the keys themselves); (in bowls) small bowl aimed at by the players; soldier's padded jacket; drinking vessel

Jack-a-Lent brightly dressed puppet stoned by fun-seeking children during Lent

jack-a-nape, jack-an-ape, jackanape, jackanapes, jack'nape performing monkey; fool

jade *n.* contemptuous term for an inferior or difficult horse; contemptuous term for a woman; *v.* trick; harrass

jad'ry, jadery a horse's difficult behaviour (*cf.* **jade**)

jakes latrine

jaunce *n.* (?) tiring business; *v.* prance

jaw devour

jay glamorous, immoral woman

jealous anxious; suspicious, doubtful

jealous-hood (?) jealous woman

jealousy anxiety; suspicion

jean kind of twilled cotton

jennet Spanish horse

jerk stroke, as of wit

jerkin jacke

jesses straps fastening a hawk's legs to the falconer's wrist

jet strut self-importantly; encroach; jut (*see* **jut**)

jig *n.* merry tune or dance; *v.* sing or move in the manner of a jig

Jockey Jack (John)

jocund joyful

John Drum's entertainment a good beating

jointress widow who inherits her husband's estate

joint-ring ring formed of two interlocking halves

joint-stool stool that has been properly crafted

jollity extravagant clothes

jolt-head, jolthead fool

jordan piss-pot

journal daily

Jove Jupiter (*see* **Jupiter**)

Jovial of Jupiter, *hence* kingly, liberal; **Jovial star** = the planet Jupiter

jowl strike, knock

Judas (Iscariot) apostle who betrayed Christ, identifying him to the authorities by kissing him; popular legend gave him red hair and says he hanged himself

Judas Maccabeus great Jewish warrior and freedom-fighter

Jug Joan

jump *n.* risky move; *adv.* just, exactly; *v.* risk, chance; coincide, agree

junkets sweetmeats, dainties

Juno sister and wife of Jupiter, sometimes associated with marriage, otherwise imagined as formidably jealous and prone to anger

Jupiter principal god in classical mythology, brother and husband of Juno but given to affairs with mortals (*see* **Europa, Leda**)

just *n.* jousting tournament; *adj.* precise; *adv.* precisely, indeed; **just distance** = half-way

justicer judge

justify verify; vindicate

jut overhang, encroach

jutty *n.* part of a building that projects beyond the wall; *v.* overhang

Juventus Youth (*Lat.*)

kam awry, perverse

kecksies kexes, hollow stalks

kee quoth, said

keech rolled lump of fat

keel cool

ken *n.* sight; *v.* see; know

Kendal green coarse cloth

kennel gutter, open drain

kercher cloth, handkerchief

kern, Kerne Irish foot-soldier

kernel little seed

kersey plain, coarse cloth

kettle kettle-drum

key key for tuning a stringed instrument

kibe chilblain, sore on the heel

kickshaws fancy extra, trifle

kicky-wicky (?) lover; *see* **kickshaws**

killen kill

kiln-hole opening of a kiln

kind *n.* nature; lineage, family; way, manner; *adj.* natural; gracious

kindle incite; bring forth young

kindless unnatural

kindly *adj.* natural, in accordance with one's nature; *adv.* naturally; graciously; exactly

kirtle gown consisting of a bodice and skirt

kiss (in bowls) brush (the jack) with one's bowl

kissing-comfits sweetmeats (dried fruits, *etc.*) for sweetening the breath

kite bird of prey; whore

knack knick-knack, pretty artefact

knap knock; bite

knoll toll

knot gang, small group; folded arms; flower-bed

knot-grass plant supposed to inhibit growth

knotted laid with flower-beds (*cf.* **knot**)

knotty-pated block-headed

La fin couronne les oeuvres 'The end crowns the deeds' (*Fr.*, proverbial)

label append, as a codicil

labour work at; take pains over

laboured employed in labour; accomplished with labour

laboursome finely worked; persistent

labras Pistol's word for '*labra*' (*Lat.* = 'lips')

lace interlace, embroider; laced mutton *see* **mutton**

lackey *n.* page, footman; *v.* run around after, like a page

lade drain, bale out

lady-smock (?) cuckoo-flower

lag late, behind; *v.* go last (as in children's games)

Lammas-tide 1 August, an old harvest festival

lampass a disease in horses

land-damn (?) thrash; (?) scold

lank become thin

lantern turret with windows

lap wrap, clad

lapse *n.* fall; *v.* slip, *hence* sin

lapsed (?) fallen; (?) apprehended; **lapsed in** = (?) having let slip by

lard baste, enrich; garnish

large liberal, unrestrained; **at large** = in full; full-size

lark's-heels larkspur

'larum, larum *see* **alarum**

latch catch, grasp; moisten

latest final

lath cheap wood

latten brass or tinplate

laud song of praise

laund cleared space in a wood

lavolt, lavolta dance involving high leaps

law-days court sessions

lay *n.* wager; song; **lay aboard** = board (a ship); **lay by the heels** = put in fetters or stocks; **lay for** = waylay, beset

lazar leper

lead *n.* lining of a wooden coffin; *v.* weight (a fishing line)

leading command

leads roof of a building

leaguer camp

Leander lover of Hero; every night he swam across the Hellespont and climbed up to her window to visit her

leaping-house brothel

learn teach

learned schooled; informed

leash *n.* (of hounds) group of three; *v.* keep (three hounds) on a leash

leasing falsehood, lying

leather-coats russet apples

leathern skin-clad (wearing animal skins, therefore after the Fall of Adam)

lecture lesson

Leda maiden loved by Jupiter, who turned himself into a swan to visit her, and the mother of Helen of Troy

leer cheek, complexion

lees sediment

leese loose; lose

leet court held by a lord of the manor

legion army; multitude; **Legion** name of a host of evil spirits in the Bible (Mark 5.9)

legitimation legitimacy

leiger resident ambassador

leman lover, sweetheart

lendings clothes; advance payment for soldiers

Lent in the Christian calendar, forty days before Easter marked by fasting and abstinence from meat (the slaughter of animals required a special licence)

lenten of Lent, *hence* thin, frugal

l'envoy epilogue of a poem

let *n.* hindrance; *v.* hinder; forbear; (of blood) drain off; **let slip** = let (hounds) loose

Lethe a river of the underworld; its water caused drinkers to forget their past

letter, affect the resort to alliteration

lettered learned

level *n.* line of fire, range; *adj.* unimpeded; *v.* aim; guess; by **line and level** *see* **line**; **level with** = equal

lewd base, wicked

lewdster rake, lecherous person

liable subject; suitable

liberal refined; unrestrained

liberty right, prerogative; licence, licentiousness

lie live, lodge; **lie along** = lie stretched out

lief dear; **have as lief** = hold as dear, be as willing

liege lord

lieger *see* **leiger**

lifter thief

light *n.* inkling; *v.* alight, descend, fall

lighten flash, as lightning; enlighten

like *adj.* likely; *adv.* alike, identically; *v.* please; liken; thrive

liking physique

limbeck alembic, a gourd-shaped vessel used in distillation

limber limp, flabby

Limbo region occupied by the souls of the virtuous who died before Christ (*Limbo Patrum*) or of unbaptized babies; prison

lime *n.* birdlime, a kind of glue used to trap small birds; *v.* flavour with lime; smear or catch with birdlime; bind with mortar

limit *n.* territory, precinct; appointed time; *v.* appoint; **strength of limit** = recovery after childbirth

limitation time allotted

line *n.* equator; category; *v.* picture, draw; strengthen; by **line and level** = according to rule

lined padded; financially provided for

line-grove grove of lime trees

linger protract

link torch, flare

linsey-woolsey mixture of wool and flax

linstock stick which held the lighted match for detonating a cannon

list *n.* inclination; boundary; edge of a piece of cloth; *see* **lists**; *v.* desire; listen; hear

lists arena for a contest

lither unresisting

little, in in miniature

little, in a in brief

livelihood life, liveliness

lively living; lifelike

liver dweller; organ supposedly responsible for intense feeling, especially love; **liver vein** = vein or style of love

livery (in law) delivery or transfer of property

lob *n.* lout, rustic; *v.* droop

lockram linen fabric

lode-star the Pole star

lodge flatten, beat down

loggets game of throwing pieces of wood at a target

London Stone a rounded block of stone in Cannon Street, London

'long, long belong

long purples kind of wild orchis

long-staff sixpenny strikers robbers who attack their victims with long poles

'loo, loo a shout of encouragement to dogs or hounds (*cf.* halloo)

loofed (?) aloof, at a distance

look search out

look how, look what before certain words is an idiomatic equivalent of adding 'ever', *e.g.* **look how** = however; **look what** = whatever

look upon stand by and watch

loon rogue, low-bred person

looped full of holes

loose *n.* firing of an arrow; *adj.* unattached, independent; *v.* fire (an arrow); let loose, release

lop cuttings from a tree

Lord's sake, for the begging cry of prisoners at their windows

lose cause to lose; bring to ruin; let slip, forget

lots to blanks, it is (?) 'the chances are'

love-in-idleness pansy

lover friend

lown *see* **loon**

lozel rogue

lubber oaf; Quickly's word for 'leopard' (*cf.* libbard)

luce pike

Lucina goddess of childbirth, properly a surname of Juno (*see* **Juno**)

lucre gain, acquisition

Lud's town London, after King Lud, Cymbeline's grandfather

luggage baggage, encumbrance

lunes lunatic fits

Lupercal = Lupercalia, an ancient Roman festival at which participants ran around striking the citizens with animal skins

lurch rob

lure apparatus used by a falconer to recall his bird

lust pleasure

lustihood vigorous health

lustique in sprightly fashion

lusty cheerful; lustful

Lux tua vita mihi 'Thy light is life to me' (*Lat.*)

luxurious lecherous

luxury lechery

lyam leash for hounds

Ma foi '(by) my faith' (*Fr.*, an oath); *ma foi, il fait fort chaud. Je m'en vais voir à la court la grande affaire* = 'by my faith, it's very hot. I'm going to court, to see the great business'

Machiavel amoral intriguer, after the Italian politician, Niccolò Machiavelli

maculate spotted, blemished

maculation spot, blemish

madrigal song

magnanimous, magnanimous great-hearted, noble

Magni dominator poli, / Tam lentus audis scelera, tam lentus vides? 'Ruler of the great heavens, are you so slow to hear crimes, so slow to see?' (*Lat.*, after Seneca)

magnifico Venetian of high social standing

magot-pies magpies

Maid Marian a bawdy role in the morris-dance

mail *n.* suit of armour; small bag; *v.* dress in armour; wrap (a hawk) in cloth

main *n.* main part; sea; mainland; army; stake in a dice game; *adj.* strong; important; *v.* maim

main-course mainsail

mainly mightily; greatly

maistrice controller (of passion)

major basic premise in an argument

majority distinction, preeminence

make *n.* partner; *v.* do; make fast, shut; make one's way, move; achieve; **make one** = join in

making bodily form

malapert insolent

malicho iniquity

malkin wench

malmsey strong, sweet wine

malt-horse, malthorse brewer's horse

malt-worms, maltworms beer drinkers

mammet doll

mammock tear into shreds

mamm'ring, mammering hesitating, stuttering

man tame; use as a weapon

manage *n.* management; (of a horse) training, exercise; *v.* take control of (a horse)

mandragora the mandrake plant (*see* **mandrake**)

mandrake poisonous plant supposed to issue a fatal shriek when uprooted

man-entered entered like a man

manhood manliness, masculinity

mankind masculine, savage

manner, taken with the caught red-handed

mansionry dwelling

mantle scum resting on the surface of stagnant water

manu cita with ready hand (*Lat.*)

map image

mapp'ry, mappery map-reading

Marches, marches Welsh or Scottish borders

marchpane marzipan

margent margin, *hence* notes, accompanying explanation

mark marking, observation; (in archery) something aimed at; coin worth 13 shillings and fourpence, or two thirds of a pound market profit

marry a mild oath, from the name of the Virgin Mary

Mars god of war and lover of Venus (*see* Venus)

Martial of Mars, *hence* warlike, *etc.*

Martin's summer, Saint good weather late in the year (St Martin's day = 11 November)

martlemas St Martin's day (*cf.* Martin's summer, Saint)

martlet swift or house-martin

Mary-buds marigolds

mast acorns, chestnuts and similar

master qualified artisan

mastic violently abusive

mate match; check, put at a loss

material of matter, substantial

maugre despite

maund basket

maw belly

mazard, mazzard head

Me pompae provexit apex 'The crown of the triumph has led me on' (*Lat.*)

meacock tame, spiritless

mealed mixed, of a piece

mean *n.* middle position or course; middle voice in vocal or instrumental music; *v.* moan, lament

measurable fit, suitable

measure *n.* dance or piece of music; punishment; *v.* tread, cross

mechanic, mechanical *n.* manual labourer, artisan; *adj.* performing manual labour, common; of science, practical arts, or manual skills

Medea enchantress who rejuvenated her father-in-law Aeson and murdered her children and her brother

med'cinable, medicinable medicinal, curative

med'cine, medicine *n.* doctor; drug, potion; (in alchemy) the elixir reputed to turn base metals into gold; *v.* heal; med'cine potable = drug containing gold

Medice, teipsum physician, (heal) thyself (*Lat.*)

meditance meditating

medlar fruit eaten when almost rotten; prostitute

meed merit; payment

meetly fair, not bad

Mehercle by Hercules (*Lat.*)

meinie, meiny multitude; retinue

melancholy depression, associated with a thickening of the blood

Meleager Calydonian prince who, with Theseus and others, hunted down a local boar

mell associate, have intercourse

mellow ripe, going towards rottenness

memorize make memorable

memory memorial, souvenir

mended improved, repaired

mercatante merchant (*Ital.*)

Mercurial of Mercury, *hence* fleet of foot, *etc.*

Mercury the messenger god, associated with eloquence; he was depicted with winged sandals

mere utter, total

mered defined, marked out

merit reward, desert

mess serving of food; group of diners occupying a ranked position at table

metaphysical supernatural

mete judge; aim or level

metheglin potent spiced mead

method, by the in the same style

mew confine (a bird) in a cage

mi perdonato excuse me (*Ital.*)

micher one who plays truant

miching lurking, stealthy

mickle great

microcosm man as the universe in miniature; map of my microcosm = my face

milch in milk, lactating

Mile-End Green drill-ground east of London for citizens under training and a place for fairs and shows

milk-livered chicken-hearted

milliner seller of gloves and fancy apparel

mill-sixpences silver sixpences

mince trivialize; walk or talk in an affected, gamesome manner

mind have in mind, mean; call to mind; notice

mineral poison; mine

Minerva goddess of wisdom and of arts and crafts

minic actor

minikin high-pitched

minim basic short note-value in Tudor music

minime not in the least (*Lat.*)

minimus tiny creature

minion favourite or mistress; slut

minister administrator

Minotaur a monster, half bull and half man, placed in a labyrinth by Minos, King of Crete

minute-jacks clock figures (*cf.* jack)

minutely very frequent, by the minute

mirable admirable, marvellous

mirror pattern, example

Misanthropos man-hater (*Gr.*)

misbecomingly unfittingly

mischief *n.* evil; misfortune; disease; *v.* harm

mis-dread fear of evil

miser wretched person

misgoverned unrestrained, rebellious

misgovernment misconduct

misgraffed ill-matched

misprision misunderstanding, blunder; disdain; false imprisonment

misproud arrogant, inappropriately proud

missive messenger

mistake take wrongly; misunderstand, misjudge

mistemper disorder; discomposure; indisposition

misthink think badly of, misjudge

mistress (in bowls) the jack

mo, moe plural form of more

mobbled with face muffled

mock insult

mockery, mock'ry semblance, imitation

model pattern; mould

modern trite, commonplace; recent

modest moderate, sober

modestly moderately, restrainedly

modesty moderation

module pattern, image

moiety portion, sometimes a half

moisture water of the sea

moldwarp mole

mome fool, ass

moment significance

momentany momentary

Monarcho the name used by a famously vain contemporary Italian at the English court

Monmouth cap soldier's cap

monster make monstrous

monstruosity monstrosity

montant (in fencing) upward thrust (*Fr.*)

monument sign, omen

monumental serving as a sign or token (of identity, *etc.*)

mood anger; expression of feelings; (in music) scale, mode

mooncalf creature born deformed

Moorditch a notoriously filthy open sewer in London

mop *n.* grimace; *v.* grimace like a monkey

mope be or wander about in a daze, lack awareness

moralize expound morally or symbolically

Morisco morris-dancer

morris morris-dance

mort call of the hunting-horn announcing the death of the deer

Mort Dieu God's death (an oath)

mortified insensate, subdued

mortifying life-depriving

mortise part of a joint in carpentry

mose in the chine (?) display the symptoms of glanders (a disease in horses) in its final stages

mot motto, device

mote speck, mentioned by Christ as a metaphor for trivial sinfulness (*cf.* beam)

mother tenderness; *see* *hysterica passio*

motion *n.* puppet or puppet-show; appeal, proposal; impulse, feeling; *v.* move, propose; upon the foot of motion = at the stage of being expressed

motive mover, cause or instrument

motley pied garments of a jester

mould earth, clay, the mortal human body

moulten having moulted

mountainish hugely overbearing, barbarous

mountebank swindle in the manner of a mountebank (a pedlar of quack medicines)

mouse *n.* term of affection for a woman; *v.* treat as a cat treats a mouse

mouse-hunt one who hunts women, rake (*cf.* mouse)

mow *n.* grimace; *v.* grimace mockingly

mulled dulled

mummer performer in a dumbshow

mummy dried human flesh used as the basis for a medicinal liquid

muniments military supplies or defences

murdering-piece cannon with a spraying shot

mure wall

murrain, murrion *n.* plague in cattle or other animals; *adj.* infected

muscadel sweet wine

muse marvel (at); complain

musit hole in a hedge; hiding place

musk-cat musk-deer

musk-cod perfumed fop

muss game in which children scramble for objects thrown on the ground

mutine *n.* mutineer; *v.* mutiny

mutiny *n.* dispute; *v.* riot

mutton prostitute; laced mutton = prostitute

mutual shared, common; intimate

mutuality familiarity, intimacy

mutually together; reciprocally

myn-heers gentlemen (*Dutch*)

Myrmidons followers of Achilles in the Trojan war; the great Myrmidon = Achilles (*see* Achilles)

mystery art or craft, calling

Nabuchadnezzar = Nebuchadnezzar, Babylonian king whom God punished by driving him into the wilderness where he ate grass like an ox

nail one-sixteenth of a yard

naked unarmed; **in naked bed** = undressed and in bed

napless worn, threadbare

Naso family name of the poet Ovid, from *nasus* (*Lat.* = 'nose')

native *n.* natural source; *adj.* innate, natural; naturally connected

natural *n.* congenital idiot; *adj.* idiotic

natural-born native

naturalize familiarize

naught *n.* wrongdoing; *adj.* bad, worthless; **all to naught** = worthless; **be naught awhile** = petty insult

naughty bad, worthless

nave hub or boss of a wheel; navel

nay-ward direction of disbelief

nay-word, nayword password; byword

Nazarite Nazarene, *i.e.* Christ

ne intelligis domine? 'do you understand, sir?' (*Lat.*)

neaf fist (*dial.*)

Neapolitan bone-ache syphilis

near nearer

near-legged knock-kneed

neat *n.* ox; *adj.* trim, fancy; tasty; unadulterated

neb beak, nose or mouth

necessitous poor; needy

needsly necessarily

neeze sneeze

neglect cause to be neglected

neglectly negligently

Nemean of Nemea, where lived a fearsome lion; Hercules slew it and wore its hide

nephew cousin; descendant

Neptune god of the sea

Nereides benevolent sea-nymphs

Nero Roman emperor who had his mother murdered and was supposed to have played a harp while Rome burned

nerve nerve or sinew

nervy courageous; sinewy

Nessus centaur killed with a poisoned arrow by Hercules for abducting his wife; the bloodied shirt was later worn by Hercules who was driven to suicide by its residual poison

Nestor Hellenic king famed for his advanced age and wisdom

netherland underworld

nether-stocks stockings for the lower legs

new-cut a card game

Newhaven the Elizabethan name for the 16th-century French seaport of Le Havre

next closest

nice easy-going; delicate, particular; refined; slight

nicely subtly; strictly, particularly; daintily

niceness daintiness

nicer more scrupulous

nicety scruples

Nicholas, Saint patron saint of scholars; **Saint Nicholas' clerks** = highway robbers

nick *v.* (?) cut short; (?) emasculate; **in the nick** = at that point; **out of all nick** = beyond measure

nickname miscall; find new names for

niggard act meanly; stint

night-gown dressing-gown

night-rule affairs of the night

nimble quick-witted

nimble-pinioned swift-winged

nine-men's-morris rustic game played on a diagram cut in turf

Niobe mother of fourteen children slain by Apollo and Diana, transformed into stone as she wept

nittical nit-infested, lousy

noble gold coin

noise *n.* concert or small company of musicians; report, rumour; strife; *v.* report, rumour; **noise it** = cry out

nole noddle, head

nonce, for the for the occasion, as the occasion requires

non-come Dogberry's word for '*non plus*' (*Lat.* = 'bewilderment'), confused with '*non compos*' (*Lat.* = 'mentally defective')

nonpareil unrivalled paragon

nonsuit reject, with respect to a suit

nook-shotten full of nooks and corners, misshapen

nose-herbs scented plants

notch slash; roughly haircut

note *n.* mark of disgrace; mark, characteristic; notice, apprehension; record; *v.* mark with disgrace

notedly assuredly

nothing able to be pronounced 'noting' (= observing, tune, *etc.*); *n.* triviality; *adv.* in no way

notion intellect, awareness

nourish bring up, nurture

Novi hominem tanquam te 'I know the man as well as I know you' (*Lat.*)

novum dice game at which nine and five were high scores and perhaps interchangeable

noyance annoyance, harm

number order

nuncio messenger

nursery care, nurturing

nut-hook, nuthook beadle

O spot; spangle, star; the Globe Theatre; vagina; sigh; prayer

oafs children of elves or fairies

oathable able to be placed under oath

ob. for '*obolus*' (*Lat.*), used in England of a halfpenny

objection accusation or criminal charge

obligation contract

obliged bound by contract

obliquy (?) obliquity, perversity; (?) *see* obloquy

oblivious causing oblivion or forgetfulness

obloquy slander, shame

obsequious of obsequies or funeral rites; loyal

observance observation; deference, respect; ritual

observant fawning attendant

observation performance of a rite; respectful attention

observe court; pay due respect to

obstruction lack of movement

occasion matter; need; fault; opportunity, proverbially represented as bearing a forelock (or 'front') which should be seized

occident the west

occulted concealed, secret

occupation labour, trade

occupy have sex

occurrents occurrences

oddly unevenly

odour spiced ointment

'Od's, Od's 'God's' or 'God save' (in oaths)

oeillades meaningful, amorous looks

o'erblow blow away

o'ercount outnumber

o'ercrow triumph over

o'er-dy'd weak with overdyeing

o'er-eaten gnawed at and bitten

o'er-flourished elaborately carved or ornamented

o'er-galled made excessively sore

o'erlook, overlook look over, examine, read; curse, bewitch

o'ermaster make oneself master of

o'erparted assigned a theatrical part above one's capabilities

o'erpeer, over-peer, overpeer look down upon

o'erpicturing outdoing in pictorial qualities

o'erpoize overbalance, outweigh

o'er-posting passing over

o'er-raught, o'erraught o'erreached (*see* o'erreach)

o'erreach cheat; overtake

o'ersized smeared over, as with size (*see* size)

o'erteemed exhausted by bearing children

o'erwatched exhausted through lack of sleep

o'erwhelm hang over

o'er-wrested overdone

off-cap take off one's cap or hat out of respect

offend trouble, injure

offer attempt; threaten violence

office *n.* duty; official or body of officials; *v.* act as a servant; deter by means of one's station

offices servants' quarters, pantry, *etc.*

old plenty of; 'fine old'

omit neglect, disregard; forbear to use

omittance omission

omne bene all's well (*Lat.*)

onyers a grand-sounding title, possibly sherrifs owing debts to the king

ope open

open-arse the medlar fruit (*see* **medlar**)

operant working, effective

operation effective power

opinion reputation; general opinion; (adverse) judgement; (high) opinion of oneself

opposeless unable to be opposed

opposite *n.* opponent; *adj.* opposed, antagonistic

opposition combat

oppress distress

oppression distress

oppugnancy antagonism, opposition

or ere, before; **or . . . or** = either . . . or

orb ring; earth; *see* sphere

ordinance that which is ordained by God, providence, tradition, *etc.*; order; ordnance, artillery

ordinant ordaining, directing

ordinary inn; supper, as served in a tavern

orgulous haughty

orifex orifice, opening

orison prayer

ort leftover, scrap

orthography correct spelling, *hence* pedantic style of speaking

ostent appearance, show

ostentation public display, formal show

ostler groom, stableboy

othergates in another way

Ottomite Ottoman, Turk

ouches gems, brooches

ought owed

ounce lynx

ousel blackbird

outbrave outdo in bravery or splendour (*cf.* brave)

out-crafty outdo in craftiness

outdure outlast

outfly outstrip, overtake

outlandish foreign

out-peer excel

outside outer surface, outer garment

outvied outbidden

outward *n.* outside, exterior; *adj.* on the outside of secret affairs

ovator one who receives ovations

overdrip rain on, overshadow

overhear hear over

overhold value too highly

overlook *see* **o'erlook**

over-peer, overpeer *see* **o'erpeer**

overscutched worn out

overthrow destruction

overture opening, disclosure, declaration

Ovid Roman poet, author of *Metamorphoses*, a long poem telling stories of transformation, and erotic verse which may have contributed to his exile among the Getae (Goths)

owe own; bear

oyez 'hear ye' (*Fr.*), a call for order before a public announcement

pace *n.* horse's trained walk; way, passage; *v.* train or exercise (a horse) in walking

pack *n.* conspiracy; *v.* conspire; be in league; pack off, go; pack cards with *see* **card**

packing intrigue

paddock toad

pageant *n.* spectacular show or float; *v.* mimic, as in a pageant

pain *n.* penalty; labour, pains; *v.* put to pains

painful involving labour; undergoing labour

painted hollow, false; **painted cloth** = decorative wall hanging painted with familiar figures

pair-taunt like as if holding a better hand (at cards)

pajock (?) peacock, supposed to be lecherous; (?) patchock (rogue)

palabras see **paucas pallabris**

pale *n.* pallor; fence; rail; enclosure; *v.* make pale; enclose

palfrey small horse

palisadoes iron-pointed stakes

pall lose force; wrap

Pallas Greek goddess associated with law and wisdom

pallet basic bed

palliament candidate's gown

palmer pilgrim

palmy flourishing, victorious

palter equivocate, use deceit

pandar, pander *n.* pimp, go-between; *v.* serve, as a pandar

Pandion father of Philomel and Progne (*see* **Philomel**)

pantaloon stock figure of the foolish old man in Italian comedy

Pantheon a temple in Rome

pantler servant in charge of the pantry

paper *n.* statement of one's crime worn as a public penance; *v.* send a note to

Paracelsus innovative Swiss physician

paradox improbable or unusual proposition

paragon put forward as a paragon; surpass; parallel

Parca one of the *Parcae*, the Latin name for the Fates (*see* **Fates**)

parcel *n.* group, band; item, part, bit; *v.* particularize

parcel-gilt partly gilded

Paris-balls tennis-balls

Parish top large spinning-top

Parish-garden Paris Garden in London where bear-baiting took place

paritor officer of the Ecclesiastical Courts

parle parley, talk

parlous perilous, dangerous

parmacity spermaceti, used as a medicinal treatment

part *n.* ability, accompishment; quality; action; *v.* depart; **in part** = in part-payment

partake take sides; **partake to** = share with

partaker confederate

part-coloured variegated

parted gifted, accomplished; (of the eyes) unfocused

partial of partiality

partialize make partial

partially by or with partiality

parti-coated dressed in a fool's outfit (*cf.* **motley**)

particular regard; personal concern, duty or motive

partisan pike-like weapon

Partlet traditional name for a hen

party-verdict share in a joint decision

pash *n.* head; *v.* bash

passado forward lunge with a sword

passage that which passed

passages transitions

passant (in heraldry) walking position

passenger traveller

passion *n.* strong emotion; suffering, *esp.* the final sufferings of Christ; passionate speech; *v.* suffer; express passion

passionate *adj.* compassionate; *v.* express passionately

passy measures pavin = passe-measure pavan, a stately dance

patch *n.* jester, clown; *v.* make, as from patches

patchery fool's play, cheating

paten shallow metal dish, as used in Holy Communion

patent entitlement, licence

patience sufferance, permission

patronage patronise, defend

pattern *n.* example, model; *v.* set a precedent (for)

paucas pallabris Sly's version of '*pocas palabras*' (*Sp.* = 'few words')

pauca verba few words (*Lat.*)

Paul's St Paul's Cathedral, London, a centre for trade and the hiring of servingmen

paunch rip or stab the belly

pax representation of Christ kissed by worshippers at Mass

peach *see* **appeach**

peak languish, become emaciated

pearl cataract

peat pet, sweetheart

peck *n.* reasonable-sized vessel; *v. see* **pick**

peculiar own, personal, private

pedant schoolmaster

pedascule from '*pedasculus*' (*pseudo-Lat.* = little pedant)

peeled tonsured

Pegasus winged horse associated with the hero Perseus

peise weigh (down); balance

pelf possessions, booty

pelican bird supposed to feed its young with its own blood

Pelion a famous mountain from Greek antiquity, like Ossa and Olympus

Pelops boy to whom the gods gave an ivory shoulder

pelt scold

pelting trivial, petty, worthless

pencil paintbrush

pencilled painted

pendant pennon or long narrow flag

pendent hanging

pendulous overhanging

Pene gelidus timor occupat artus 'Cold fear almost seizes the limbs' (*Lat.*)

penner pen-holder

penn'orth, pennyworth bargain (often in a bad sense)

pensioner royal attendant

Penthesilea an Amazon queen

Pepin French king of the eighth century

Per Stygia, per manes vehor 'I am carried through the Stygian regions, through the realm of shades' (*Lat.*, after Seneca) (*cf.* **Styx**)

peradventure perhaps

perdie by God (an oath)

perdition loss; ruin

perdu sentinel placed in a fatally exposed position

perdurable everlasting, imperishable

perdy *see* **perdie**

peregrinate like one who travels abroad

peremptorily emphatically

peremptory determined, obstinate, high-handed

perfect *adj.* matured; ripe, prepared; sure; learned; *v.* finish; enlighten, instruct

perfection achievement, fulfilment

perfit perfect, word-perfect

perfumer one who fumigates rooms with pleasant scents

perge continue (*Lat.*)

periapts amulets, charms

period *n.* end-point, goal; full stop, pause at the end of sentence; *v.* end

perjure *n.* perjurer; *v.* force into perjury

perniciously fatally, to the point of death

peroration oration, speech

perpend weigh, consider

Perseus in Greek mythology the slayer of the gorgon Medusa, who turned those who looked at her into stone; Athena gave him a polished shield allowing him to observe Medusa without looking at her directly, and so to behead her

persistive persistent

perspective optical illusion or a glass device for producing one

pert quick, sharp

pervert divert

pester obstruct, trouble

petard bomb

pettish peevish

pew-fellow companion at church

Phaëthon, Phaeton, Phaëton son of Phoebus (*see* **Phoebus**) and stepson of Merops; attempting to drive Phoebus' sun chariot, he failed to control its horses and almost crashed into the earth, whereupon Jupiter killed him with a lightning bolt

phantasma nightmare

phantisime person given to flights of fancy

Philip traditional name for a sparrow; **Philip and Jacob** = feast of SS. Philip and James (1 May)

Philippan from the Battle of Philippi, where Antony and Octavius defeated the republicans

Philomel, Philomela daughter of King Pandion, she was raped and mutilated by her brother-in-law Tereus but revealed her ordeal by depicting it in a tapestry; she was subsequently transformed into a nightingale (*cf.* **Progne**)

philosopher's stone means of transforming base metal into gold

Phoebe the goddess Diana when represented as the moon

Phoebus the god Apollo in his role as sun god and father of Phaeton (*see* **Phaëthon**)

phoenix fabulous bird supposed to be one of a kind and to rise again from its ashes

phraseless that defies the power of language

phthisic consumptive cough

physic *n.* medicine; *v.* mend, heal

physical healthy, therapeutic

pia mater membrane in the brain, *hence* brain

pick hurl

picked select; dandified, refined

Picked-hatch seedy district of London

pickers and stealers hands

pickthanks flatterers

'pie magpie

pie church service book; *see* **'pie**

piece *n.* coin; wine cask; masterpiece, paragon; insulting term for a woman; *v.* supplement; **piece out, piece up** = add to, increase

pigeon-livered incapable of anger

pight pitched; set, determined

pike pitchfork; spike set in the centre of shield

pilcher scabbard

pill pillage, take by force; peel, strip

Pillicock penis; **Pillicock Hill** = female genitals

pin nothing, an irrelevance; (in archery) bullseye; **pin and web** = cataracts

pinch *n.* nip; *v.* vex, irritate; (of an animal) nip with the teeth

pinfold pound for stray animals

pinioned bound

pinked with small holes or slits cut (in material or finished garment)

pioned (?) covered in flowers; (?) dug out

pip spot on a playing card, *hence* one point

pipe-wine wine from a cask

Pippen *see* **Pepin**

pismire ant

pitch *n.* height; **Pitch and pay** = 'cash only'

Più per dolcezza che per forza 'More by gentleness than by force' (*Ital.*)

place *n.* safe place; (in falconry) a hawk's highest pitch; *v.* employ; **take place** = become respectable

placket skirt or slit in a skirt

plain-song basic melody

planched made of planks

plant sole of a foot

plantage plant growing

plantain plant used for basic first aid

plantation planting; colonization

plash puddle

plate *n.* coin; *v.* dress in armour

plausible worthy of applause

plausibly with applause

plausive approved, worthy of applause; plausible

Plautus Roman writer of comedies

pleached intertwined, as the branches of a hedge; hedged

pleasant jesting

please-man flatterer

pleurisy inflamed excess

plight *n.* pledge, promise; *v.* pledge, swear; *adj.* pledged; **in plight** = physically fit

plodding dull, tedious

plume up (?) make a show of, as a bird ruffles its feathers

Pluto god of the underworld

Plutus personification of wealth, sometimes imagined as its god

point *n.* lace for tying garments; sword; signal; pinnacle; *v.* appoint, assign; **at point** = ready, prepared; in every detail; about

point-device, point-devise *adj.* neat, exact; *adv.* exactly

poise *n.* weight; *v.* weigh, consider; counterpoise

poke large bag

poking-sticks rods used for the stiffening of ruffs

Polack *n.* Pole; *adj.* Polish

pole star; standard

polecat whore

pole-clipped hedged in by tall stakes (?); pruned short

policy politics; wisdom; strategy; stratagem

politic political

politician plotter, schemer

poll shaved

polled lopped, cleared; bald

pomander perfume ball

pomewater popular type of apple

Pomgarnet 'Pomegranate', the name of a room

pompous characterized by pomp, magnificent, stately

poop overcome

poor-John dried, salted hake

popinjay parrot

popular common, of the people

popularity the people

porpentine porcupine

porridge soup, broth

porringer fancy hat, shaped like a dish

port *n.* portal, gate; (high) position in life; attitude, behaviour; *v.* bring to port

portable supportable

portage voyage (through life); porthole

portance attitude, behaviour

portion dowry

posied engraved with a posy (*see* **posy**)

position proposition, tenet advanced

possess give possession; tell, give to understand

possessed briefed

posset *n.* drink made by curdling hot milk with wine; *v.* curdle

post *n.* messenger; horse; *adv.* quickly; *v.* hurry; **in post** = quickly; **post off** = defer

poster one who travels quickly

postern small side-gate

post-post-haste urgently

posy short motto engraved on a ring

potable *see* **med'cine**

potato supposed to be an aphrodisiac

potch jab, poke

potency power, authority

potential potent, commanding

potents potentates, rulers

pother uproar, riot

potting drinking

pottle half-gallon tankard

pouncet-box box containing perfume

powder pickle in salt

powdering-tub pickling barrel; Pistol's reference to the sweating tub (*see* **tub**)

power military force; person in authority; faculty

pox syphilis

practic practical

practice trick, machination; doing, performance

practisants accomplices

practise plot

praemunire writ issued against one who prefers papal to sovereign authority

praetor Roman magistrate

praise *n.* virtue, merit; *v.* appraise; **praise in departing** = do not praise too soon

prank offensive act

preambulate walk before

precedence that which has preceded

precedent *n.* example; sign; original; *adj.* earlier, previous

preceptial of precepts or moral instruction

precipitation precipitousness, sharpness of a drop

precise morally scrupulous, puritanical

precisian puritanical guide in religious matters

pre-contract future contract of marriage

precurrer precursor

precurse that which precedes by way of an omen

predicament category; situation

predominance ascendency, predominant influence (*see* **influence**)

predominant in the ascendent, a powerful planetary position

prefer bring forward; bring to attention, recommend; promote

pregnancy sharpness of intellect

pregnant skilful; ready, open; clear

prejudicate judge in advance

prejudice *n.* detriment, disadvantage; *v.* harm

premeditation meditation on the future

premise aforesaid matter

premised predestined

prenominate *adj.* aforenamed; *v.* say in advance

pre-ordinance established rule

preparation military force; quality, gift

preposterous topsy-turvy, perverse

prerogative privilege, precedence

presage prediction, omen

presaging experiencing omens of evil or misfortune

prescript *n.* order, instruction; *adj.* prescribed

prescription claim based on long-standing possession

presence presence chamber, where royalty entertains visitors

present *n.* present moment; document; *adj.* sudden, immediate; ready; *v.* act; lay before a court

presentation representation, image

presently at once

presentment presentation; representation

press *n.* licence for conscription; cupboard; *v.* conscript; torture with crushing weights

pressure image, as if impressed on wax

Prester John legendary ruler of a medieval Eastern kingdom

presupposed previously laid down

pretence intention

pretend intend; claim; propose; show

prevent anticipate, pre-empt

prevention anticipation, forestalling

price value

prick *n.* mark; point aimed at in archery; *v.* mark; urge; clothe

pricket two-year-old male deer

pricksong singing from printed music

pride highest pitch; splendour; lust

prig tinker, thief

prime *n.* spring; *adj.* first, principal; sexually aroused

primero a card game

primogeneity primogeniture, the inheritance rights of the oldest son

principal *n.* accomplice; cornerpost of a house; *adj.* chiefly responsible for the crime

principality one of the orders of angels

princox impertinent youth

Priscian Roman grammarian

pristine original, of old

prithee '(I) pray thee', please

private *n.* privacy; common subject; private communication; *adj.* domestic

privilege *n.* something that bestows a privilege; advantage; *v.* sanction, permit

prize *n.* fight, bout; privilege; plunder; *v.* esteem, care for

prizer prizefighter

pro eris generosis servis gloriosum mori 'dying for generous masters is the servants' glory' (*Lat.*)

probal reasonable

probation proof; testing, trial

proceeders scholars

process sequence of events; relation, story; mandate, summons

procurator proxy, substitute

prodigious ominous; unnatural; Launce's word for 'prodigal'

proditor betrayer

proface an expression of welcome

profit *n.* learning, advancement; *v.* learn, advance

progeny ancestry, lineage

Progne wife of Tereus and sister of Philomel (*see* **Philomel**); after learning of Philomel's rape she obtained revenge by serving Tereus the flesh of their son at dinner

prognostication prophecy; weather forecast

Proh Deum! Medius Fidius! 'By God! Holy Fidius (*i.e.* Jupiter) [help] me!' (*Lat.*)

project *n.* thought, anticipation; *v.* present

projection scale

prolixious time-wasting

prolonged postponed

Promethean of Prometheus (*see* **Prometheus**)

Prometheus legendary figure who stole fire from the gods to give to man and was punished by being shackled to a mountain where an eagle pecked at his liver

promulgate make publicly known

prone prostrate; eager, headstrong

proof testing, trial; tried and tested armour; success; **in proof** has been proved

propend incline

propension propensity, desire

proper personal, own; decent, fine

property *n.* individual quality; instrument; *v.* obtain; exploit, treat as an object

proportion fortune; number, magnitude; **lay the proportions** = estimate the numbers needed

propose *n.* talk; *v.* hold forth, talk

propriety true nature or identity

propugnation protection

prorogue postpone, put off; prolong

prosecution pursuit, attack

Proserpina, Proserpine daughter of Ceres, abducted by Pluto while she gathered flowers and then imprisoned in the underworld

prosperous favourable, leading to a desirable outcome

Proteus mythological figure able to change his shape

protraction delay

protractive delaying

proud resplendent, luxurious

provand *see* **provender**

prove test, try out, put on trial; ascertain; **proved** put to the test

provender food, fodder

provincial subject to provincial jurisdiction; **Provincial rose** = (Provençal) rose with many petals

prude excessively prim person, bordering on a hypocrite

prune preen

psaltery stringed musical instrument

publish proclaim; publicly represent

pudder *see* **pother**

pudding stuffed intestine, sausage

pudency modesty

pueritia boyhood (*Lat.*)

pugging thieving

puissance strength; troops

puissant strong, overpowering

puke-stocking (wearing) heavy dark woollen stockings

pumpion pumpkin

punk whore, slut

punto (in fencing) thrust (*Ital.*); *punto reverso* = back-handed thrust (*Ital.*)

purblind blind or weak-sighted

purchase plunder; marketable value of a property, equal to twelve years' rent

purgation acquittal; confession and absolution

purl curl

purlieus vicinity of a forest

purpose talk; proposal

pursuivant royal messenger

pursy flabby, short of breath

purveyor one who travels ahead of a party on the move to prepare for its arrival

push *n.* crisis; action; *int.* 'pish'; **stand the push** = stand up to, tolerate

push-pin a children's game

put down overdo

putter-off investor who is repaid five-fold upon returning from a foreign voyage

putter-on one who instigates or incites

puttock kite

puzzel slut

pyramid obelisk, pillar

quail *n.* whore; *v.* overpower; slacken

quaint skilful; ingenious, artful; dainty, pretty

qualify pacify; moderate; dilute; designate, define

quality nature; accomplishment; rank; profession; company

quare why (*Lat.*)

quarry game killed in hunting

quarter military location, watch; part of an army; relations

quat pimple

quatch (?) plump

quean slut

queasy dangerous; easily upset; sickened

quench cool down

quern (?) handmill; (?) churn

quest *n.* jury, inquest; search; *v.* bark

question *n.* conversation; trial, examination, consideration; *v.* talk (to), discuss; **in the loss of question** = for the sake of argument; **on the top of question** = with the maximum of contention

questionable which invites questioning

questrist seeker

Qui faciunt reges heroica carmina laudant 'Heroic poems praise what kings do' (*Lat.*)

Qui me alit, me extinguit 'Who feeds me extinguishes me' (*Lat.*)

quick living; pregnant; lively; fresh

quicken bring to life, fertilize; come to life, be conceived; make lively

quiddities quibbles

quietus clearing of accounts

quill, in the (?) in a body; (?) in order

quillets, quillities quibbles

quintain post for tilting practice

quis who (*Lat.*)

quit release from service; acquit; remit; pay; reward, requite

quite *see* **quit**

quiver nimble

quo usque tandem 'how long?' (*Lat.*), expression of impatience

quoif *see* **coif**

quoit throw stones (a quoit was a flat stone disc thrown in an exercise of strength)

quondam former (*Lat.*)

quoniam because (*Lat.*)

quote note; observe; set down

quotidian daily fever; **quotidian tertian** = (?) Quickly's confusion of two types of fever; (?) a severe fever of more than one strain

R letter meant to sound like the growling of a dog

rabbit-sucker baby rabbit

race hereditary nature; course; (of horses) stud; (of ginger) *see* **raze** (*n.*)

rack *n.* cloud or bank of clouds; instrument of torture; *v.* stretch, as on a rack; tax at an extortionate rate; move at a fast, steady pace

racker torturer (*cf.* **rack**)

rage *n.* poetic inspiration (*cf.* **fury**); *v.* enrage

raging-wood crazy with anger

'raigning arraigning, putting on trial

rail abuse; be abusive

raisins o'th' sun grapes dried naturally in the open air

ramp slut

rampallian rogue

ramping as heraldic 'rampant', rearing up in an aggressive stance

rampired barricaded or protected by ramparts

rangers gamekeepers

rank *n.* journey; *adj.* excessively grown or swollen, bloated; sexually excited; *v.* tier

rankle make sore, aggravate

rankness excessive growth or swelling

ransacked stolen, taken as plunder

rap possess, overcome

rapture violent seizure; paroxysm

rarieties rarities

rascal *n.* young, skinny deer; *adj.* common

rash *adj.* sudden, hasty, violent; *adv.* hastily

rate *n.* estimation, value; manner, style; *v.* berate, revile; estimate, evaluate; be valued at; give (a share)

rather, the all the sooner, all the more so

ratified brought into 'rate' or proportion

raught reached

ravel tangle; untangle

raven *see* **ravin** (*v.*)

ravin *adj.* ravenous; *v.* gulp, swallow eagerly

ravined (?) ravenous; (?) having gorged itself

ravish violate; seize, tear; enthrall

ravished seized from

rawness unprotected condition

rayed soiled

raze *n.* (of ginger) root; *v.* scrape, cut

razure erasure, destruction

reach range of understanding

read lecture, tutor

re-answer repay

reason *n.* something reasonable; talk, discourse; way of thinking; just cause; *v.* talk; ask, plead; argue rationally about; explain; **no reason** = nothing for it

reasonable of reason

reave deprive

rebate dampen

rebato type of stiff collar or ruff

rebeck an early ancestor of the violin

receipt something received; receptacle; volume; recipe

receiving apprehension, perception

recheat call on a hunting horn

reck care, take account of

reckless thoughtless, having no care for

reclaim overcome; recall (to better conduct); domesticate (an animal)

recognizance bond acknowledging a debt; badge

recoil fall back, give way

recomfort restore spirits

recomforted comforted, reassured

recommend commend, entrust; report to

record sing

recordation record, memorial

Recorder civil magistrate of a city

recourse access; repeated flowing

recover revive, restore; obtain reach; **recover the wind** = allow the hunted quarry to smell the hunt on the wind (*cf.* **wind**)

recoverable able to be recovered or retraced

recreation repast, refreshment

rectify put right

rector priest; ruler

rectorship sovereignty

recure cure, heal, repair

rede guidance, instruction

red herring cured herring, kipper

Redime te captum quam queas minimo 'Ransom yourself from captivity as cheaply as you can' (*Lat.*)

red-lattice wooden lattices painted red, an alternative to glass windows found in taverns

reduce bring or lead back

reechy grimy with smoke or grease

reed voice breaking, adolescent voice

re-edify rebuild

reek *n.* smoke, fumes; *v.* be exhaled in the form of smoke or fumes

refel reject

reflect shine; look; rebound, throw back

refuge *n.* (last) resort; *v.* screen, comfort

regard *n.* face, expression, look; sight; consideration; heed; *v.* respect, pay attention to; tend

regiment authority

region realm, kingdom; stratum of the atmosphere, sky

regreet *n.* greeting; reciprocal greeting; *v.* greet again

reguerdon *n.* reward; *v.* reward

rehearsal account, repetition

rehearse tell, repeat

reins kidneys

rejoicer (?) encourager

rejoindure union; reunion

rejourn postpone

relation report

relative cogent, material

religion dutifulness, keen attention; superstition

religious dutiful, conscientious, assiduous

relinquish dismiss, abandon

relish *n.* taste, quality; *v.* taste; flavour; please; sing elaborately

relume reignite

remainder someone remaining; money yet to be paid

remediate acting as a remedy

remember commemorate; remind; mention

remission pardon for an offence, *hence* desire or power to pardon; release from an obligation

remit give up

remonstrance manifestation

remorse compassion, sensitivity; (?) obligation

remorseful sensitive, compassionate

remotion relocation

remove raising of a siege

removedness withdrawal, absence

remover person who changes or withdraws

render *n.* surrender; confession; (?) due service; *v.* surrender; report

rendezvous meeting place; home, refuge

renege deny; abandon

renew re-enact, resume; renew a battle

renown make famous

repair *n.* act of making one's way; *v.* make one's way

repairing resilient

repasture food

repeal *n.* recall (from exile); *v.* recall (from exile)

repetition utterance, narration; repetitive talk; talk of former events

repine fretting, vexation

repining grudging

replenished total, consummate

replication reply; repetition for the purposes of elaboration or illustration

reprisal booty

reprobance damnation

reprobate sinful

reproof condemnation; disproof

reprove deny, disprove

repugn repel, reject

repugnancy fighting back

repugnant recalcitrant, rebellious

repured refined

repute judge, hold; make a reputation (of), broadcast

requiring stern commands; request

requit requited

reremice bats

rescue forcible retrieval of a person or goods from custody

resemblance seeming

reserved temporarily kept alive, set apart

resist (?) repel, disgust

resolution certainty

resolve dissolve; solve, provide an answer; satisfy

resolvedly with clarification

respect *n.* consideration; respectablity, worth; *v.* consider; value; **without respect** = absolutely

respective respectful; careful; equivalent, parallel

respectively respectfully

respice finem 'think on your end' (*Lat.*)

respite end of a period of respite

responsive appropriate, matching

'rest arrest

rest *n.* stay, sojourn; *v.* remain; **above the rest** = above all; **in rest** = under arrest, detained; **set up one's rest** = resolve, stake all (from a card game)

resting changeless

restrain restrict, withhold

restrained tightly drawn

resty lethargic, idle

retention detention; record, notebook; holding capacity

retentive restraining, detaining

retire *n.* retreat; *v.* retreat; withdraw; **make retire** = withdraw

retort reject, throw back

retrograde (of a planet) moving backwards, *hence* contrary

retrospection action of looking back upon past time

return *n.* reply; *v.* reply

reverb sound as a reverberation

reverberate reverberating, echoing

reverse '*punto reverso*' (*see* *punto*)

reversion inheritance or restoration of property to an original owner viewed as a future event

re-view, review see once more

revolt change or transfer (of allegiance); disgust; rebel

revolted rebellious, treacherous

revolution turn, as of Fortune's or Time's wheel; turning of the thoughts

revolve consider, dwell on

rhapsody confused heap

Rhenish Rhine wine

rheum catarrhal or lachrymal discharge, seen in chronic cases as a morbid condition and sometimes linked with venereal disease

ribaudred (?) ribald (licentious); (?) 'ribald-rid' (ridden by a ribald man); (?) knackered with ribaldry

rifted torn, split

riggish licentious

right *adv.* straight; correctly; justly; **in right of** = in the name of

right-hand file aristocracy

rigol circle

rim peritoneum, abdominal membrane

ring, cracked within the *see* **crack**

ring-carrier bawd

ringlet fairy ring; fairy dance

riot revelling, partying; **riots** debauchery

ripe *adj.* ready; urgent; of marriageable age; *v.* ripen

rivage shore

rival *n.* fellow, colleague; *v.* compete

rivality equality

rive burst, crack

rivelled wrinkled

rivo a cheer at drinking (*Sp.*)

road raid, inroad; leg of a journey; anchorage, harbour

robustious turbulent

rogue vagrant

roguing roving, vagrant

roguish vagabond's

roisting wild, boisterous

roll register

Roman (of handwriting) italic

rondure circle, sphere (*cf.* **roundure**)

ronyon mangy animal; term of abuse for a woman

rood-loft gallery across a church chancel-arch supporting a cross

rook fool, trick; crouch

ropery lewd jesting

Roscius great Roman actor

roted acquired or learnt by rote

round *n.* earth; ring-dance; circular journey; rung; *adj.* direct; *adv.* thoroughly; *v.* surround; grow round; whisper mysteriously

roundel ring-dance

roundly without fuss or ceremony, directly; fluently; completely

roundure ring, circle (*cf.* **rondure**)

rouse *n.* drink or drinking session; *v.* (in hunting) drive from cover

rowell spur

royal *n.* coin worth ten shillings; **royal merchant** = successful merchant

royalty right granted to a subject by the king; crown

roynish scabby, dirty

rub *n.* (in bowls) something that impedes or deflects the bowl from its course; *v.* sidetrack; annoy, irritate; revive, stir up; **rub on** = roll on

rubious ruby-red

ruddock robin

rude rough, unskilled, unsophisticated

rudeness roughness, lack of skill or sophistication

rudesby ruffian

rue pity

ruff pranked-up vainglory

ruffle *n.* hectic activity and quarrels; *v.* brag; handle roughly; fight; **ruffle up** = enrage

rugged bristling

rug-headed having long, wild hair

ruinous in ruins, damaged

rummage busy activity, as on a ship

rumour confused din; rumoured character

rump-fed (?) fed on choice cuts; (?) having fat buttocks

runagate renegade, apostate

runnion *see* **ronyon**

russet reddish-brown, the colour of a coarse cloth worn by peasants

ruth repentance; pity

Saba the Queen of Sheba

sable *n.* blackness; *adj.* black

sables magnificent dark furs

sack white wine, often sherry

sackbut brass instrument resembling the trombone

Sackerson a famous bear from the London bear-baiting scene

sacring bell small bell used in Protestant times to summon parishoners to prayers

sad serious, solemn; dark-coloured

sadly seriously, soberly

sadness seriousness; **in sadness** = in earnest, truly

safe *adj.* well, sound; *adv.* with regard to security; *v.* make safe

safety custody

saffron a dye used in both clothing and food

Sagittary a centaur that fought against the Greeks in the Trojan war

sail fleet

sain said

salad days youth

salamander species of lizard supposedly able to live in fire

sale-work ready-made goods

Salic law French law blocking females and their descendants from succession to the crown

sallet salad; light piece of armour for the head

sallied assailed, besieged

salt *n.* salt tears; *adj.* bitter; salacious, lustful; (of fish) saltwater

salute cheer, excite

sample example

sanctimonious holy

sanctimony holiness; something holy

sanctuarize provide with sanctuary or immunity from punishment

sand-blind partially blind

sanded sandy-coloured

sandy of sand, as used in an hour-glass

sanguine red, ruddy (the colour of blood); full-blooded

sans without (*Fr.*)

sapient wise

sarcenet, sarsenet thin, delicate silk

Sarum ancient city near Camelot

sate ignored

satis quid sufficit Holofernes's version of '*satis quod sufficit*' (*Lat.* = 'enough is as good as a feast')

Saturn (in astrology) planet associated with old age, coldness, melancholy and evil

sauce season, spice, make hot

saucy highly seasoned; impudent; sexually bold or carefree

saultiers tumblers, acrobats

savagery profuse vegetation

savour *n.* smell; nature; *v.* smack, smell; sense, relish

Savoy a great house on the Strand in London

saw wise saying

say *n.* assay, evidence; kind of silk cloth; *v.* speak; speak truly or aptly

'say'd assayed, tried

'Sblood (by God)'s blood (an oath)

scab rogue

scaffoldage stage

scald scabby, scurvy

scale *n.* mark used for measuring distance, height, *etc.*; *v.* weigh, judge

scamble scramble

scamels an unidentified type of bird, or perhaps shellfish

scan judge, assess; **scanned** scrutinized

scandalized slandered; disgraced

scantling degree of capacity or ability; sample, specimen

scantly resentfully

'scape, scape *n.* escape; escapade; transgression; *v.* escape

scar wound

scarf sling; sash used to indicate rank in the army

scathe *n.* injury, damage; *v.* injure

scattering scattered, disordered

schedule paper, often a list or summary

scholar's prize school-prize match

school *n.* university; *v.* teach (a lesson); govern, control

science (theoretical) knowledge

scion shoot or cutting from a plant

sconce small round fort; protective screen; head

scope target, purpose, aim; permission, opportunity; **scope of nature** = an event permitted by nature, a natural event

scorch cut, gash

score notch on a stick or post to mark an account, *hence* account; *v.* cut a notch, *hence* mark on an account

scorn, take scorn

scot small payment; **scot and lot** = in full

scotch *n.* gash; *v.* gash

scour clean out (a pistol) with a ramrod; hurry

scrimers fencers

scrip script; shepherd's bag

scrippage Touchstone's coinage for 'shepherd's baggage' (*cf.* **scrip**)

scriptures (written) words

scroyles scabby scoundrels

scrubbed dwarfish

scruple doubt; a third of a dram

scrupulous full of scruples, hesitant

scullion kitchen servant of either sex

sculls schools (of fish)

scurril, scurrile scurrilous, filthy

scut tail of a rabbit or deer; female genitals

scutcheon cheap coat of arms used at funerals

Scythian Asiatic nomad, typifying brutality

'Sdeath (by God)'s death (an oath)

se offendendo the Gravedigger's version of '*se defendendo*' (*Lat.* = 'in self-defence')

sea-coal superior type of coal transported to London by sea

seam grease

sea-maid mermaid

sea-monster creature to whom Laomedon, King of Troy, attempted to sacrifice his daughter Hesione; Hercules rescued her thinking to obtain some horses in payment

seamy showing the seams; **seamy side** = inner side (of a garment or glove)

sear *n.* part of a gunlock; *v.* wrap in a cerecloth (shroud); brand; **tickle a'th' sear** = liable to go off (*cf.* **tickle**)

searchers public health officers similar to modern coroners

searching sharp, strong

second *n.* supporter, as in a duel; *adj.* representative

seconds second-rate material

sect cutting; class, profession; political faction; sex

sectary adherent of a sect, disciple; **sectary astronomical** = disciple of astrologers

secure *adj.* over-confident; *v.* comfort; make over-confident; protect

securely with (false) confidence

security over-confidence

See, the the Holy See, the diocese of the Pope

seeded grown, matured

seedness state of being sown

seeing what one sees, appearance

seel sew up (the eyelids of a hawk in training)

seeming *n.* appearance; likelihood; deception, falseness; *adj.* apparent; *adv.* in a seemly manner

seen qualified

seld seldom

self selfsame; relating to oneself, one's own

semblable *n.* likeness; *adj.* matching

semblative similar in appearance to

Seneca Roman Stoic philosopher and writer of tragedies

sennet fanfare of trumpets or cornets

se'nnight, seve'night, sevennight, sev'n-night week

sense senses; sexual awareness; mind; **adder's sense** = senses 'as deaf as an adder' (proverbial); **to the sense** = to the quick

senseless insensate, unresponsive; unconscious

sensible able to sense, having sensation; able to be sensed, material, evident

sensibly perceptibly; being alive and sensitive; with feeling

sentence opinion; decision, ruling; memorable saying

sententious memorable, using choice words; the Nurse's word for 'sentence'

Septentrion north

sequel that which follows

sequent *n.* follower; *adj.* following, subsequent; successive

sequester *n.* sequestration, removal; *v.* remove, divorce

sequestration removal, isolation; loss of property; (?) sequel, result

sere *n.* dried-up condition; *adj.* dry

sergeant arresting officer

serpigo a skin disease popularly linked with venereal disease

servant lover

servanted to in the service of

service food served at table

set *n.* twelve hours on a clock face; *adj.* seated; (of eyes) closed; lacking spontaneous wit; *v.* sit; put up a stake (in gambling); compose music for words; close (the eyes of the dead); **set a match** = plan a robbery; **set hand** = formal handwriting

setter thieves' informant; decoy

several *n.* individual; particular; *adj.* different, various; individual, distinct, separate; personal, (one's) own

severally individually

sewer chief servant, in charge of setting the table

'Sfoot (by God)'s foot (an oath)

shadow shade or shady spot; illusory image, picture; actor; spirit; ghost

shaft or a bolt on't, make a do it somehow

shag rough, untrimmed

shales husks, pods

shame natural modesty

shame-faced, shamefaced shy; full of shame

shard piece of broken pottery; cow-pat

shark prey like a shark; **shark up** snatch indiscriminately, as a shark its food

sharp, at with unbated swords, for real

shavers barbers; extortioners

shearman one involved in the manufacture of cloth

sheaved composed of sheaves (of straw)

sheep-biter dog or wolf that bites sheep, *hence* dangerous, sanctimonious person

sheep-biting dangerous, sanctimonious (*cf.* **sheep-biter**)

sheer pure

shent rebuked, scolded

sherris sherry

shift *n.* expedient, trick; trickery; smock; *v.* make do, improvise, live on one's wits; change (clothing); **make shift** = use tricks or resourcefulness to achieve a purpose

ship-tire elaborate head-dress shaped like a ship or sails

shive slice

shoal area of shallow water

shock throw into confusion, meet force with force

shog be going; **shog off** = come away

shoon shoes

short inadequate

shot payment; account, bill; marksman, gunner

shotten (of a fish) having shot its roe (shed its eggs), lank

shoughs shag-haired dogs

shoulder-shotten having dislocated shoulders

shove-groat shovel-board, a game of propelling coins across a smooth board

shrewd sharp; cunning, mischievous, wicked

shrewdly sharply; sorely

shrievaltry shrievalty, office of sheriff

shrieve sheriff; **shrieve's fool** *see* **fool**

shrift sacrament of Confession, *hence* confession, absolution or confessional

shrill-gorged shrill-sounding

shrine statue, icon

shrink down give way, collapse

shrive hear confession and grant absolution

shroud *n.* guard, protection; ropes of a ship's mast; *v.* hide, take cover

shuffle shift, make do; smuggle; cheat

Si fortuna me tormenta, spero me contenta see Si fortune (etc.)

Si fortune me tormente sperato me contento Pistol's expression, in a mixture of European languages, of the motto 'If fortune torments me, hope contents me'

Sic spectanda fides 'Thus is faithfulness to be shown' (*Lat.*)

sickle shekel, a Hebrew coin

siege seat, *esp.* of office or high rank; rank, status; excrement

sight aperture at the front of helmet; **of one's sight** = seeing one

sightless invisible; unpleasant to look at

silly simple; defenceless; meagre, trifling

simple *n.* herb used as a medicine; ingredient; *adj.* unadulterated, pure

simpleness stupidity, nonsense; plain honesty; purity, state of being unadulterated

simplicity stupidity

simular *n.* simulator, false representative; *adj.* specious

sinfully in a state of sin; **sinfully miscarry** = die without the last rites

single *adj.* alone, unaided; honest, direct; weak; *v.* seek out; (in hunting) select and pursue (an animal from the herd); **single bond** = (?) a contract without conditions; **single ten** = ten at cards

singulariter nominativo 'in the nominative singular' (*Lat.*)

singularity personal qualities; odd behaviour; remarkable object

singuled singled out

sinister left; irregular, wrong

sink *n.* cesspit; *v.* go down to hell

sink-a-pace *see* **cinque-pace**

Sinon Greek who tricked the Trojans into receiving a wooden horse containing soldiers who went on to capture Troy

sirrah term of address to a social inferior

sir-reverence phrase used to apologize for foul talk; a euphemism for dung

sister closely resemble; neighbour

Sisters Three = the Fates (*see* **Fates**)

sit fas aut nefas 'be it right or wrong' (*Lat.*)

sith since

sithence since

size a gelatinous glaze; allowance of food and drink

skains-mates cut-throat companions

skiffed travelled in a skiff (a light boat)

skill *n.* discernment; need, reason; *v.* matter

skilless ignorant

skillet cooking pot

skimble-skamble incoherent, wild

skipper light-brained, skipping person

skirr run hastily

skittish wanton, frivolous

slab thick and slimy

slack spend (time) wastefully

slander *n.* accusation; disgrace; disgraceful person; *v.* charge, accuse; disgrace, abuse

slanderous of accusation; bringing disgrace; ill-reputed

slave enslave

sleave a coarse silk

sledded riding in sledges; or perhaps studded with lead

sleeve-hand cuff of a sleeve

sleided separated into loose threads

'Slid (by God)'s (eye-)lid (an oath)

sliding sin

'Slight (by God)'s light (an oath)

slip *n.* cutting or graft from a plant; counterfeit coin; leash; *v.* unleash (a greyhound)

slipper slippery

slippery unstable, treacherous

slipshod wearing slippers

sliver split off

slobbery muddy, slimy

slop, slops large baggy breeches

slough old snake-skin

slovenry slovenliness, dirty untidiness

slubber smear, stain; carelessly hurry

smatch smack, whiff

smatter prattle, chat

smock petticoat; woman

smoke *n.* fog; *v.* steam; smoke out, as in fox-hunting; beat; disinfect

smooth *n.* flatter, indulge; gloss over; *adj.* flattering

smug spruced-up; smooth, unruffled

snaffle bridle-bit

sneap *n.* snub, reprimand; *v.* bite, chill

sneck up an offensive insult

snipped-taffeta jagged silk (slashed to display the lining underneath)

snuff resentment; candle-end; **in snuff** = (of candles) needing to be snuffed; **take in snuff** = take offence

sob rest, breather

sod sodden, boiled

soiled lively or skittish

soilure sullying, staining

sole singular

solely wholly

solemnity festal occasion, celebration (often of marriage)

solicit *n.* suit, petition; *v.* urge, excite

solidares (?) *solidi* (Roman coins)

sometime, sometimes *adj.* former; *adv.* formerly, once

sonance sonorous sound

sonties, be God's by God's saints (an oath)

sooth *n.* truth; appeasement, flattery; *adv.* truly

soothe flatter; play along with, indulge

soothers flatterers

soothing flattering

sop hunk of bread soaked in wine

sophister clever arguer

sophisticated adulterated, no longer simple or natural

Sophy Shah (king) of Persia

sore four-year-old male deer

sorel three-year-old male deer

sort *n.* rank; dress; lot; *v.* accord; find; conclude; keep company (with)

sortance accordance; **hold sortance** = accord

sotted made a sot (a fool)

sound faint; fathom

souse strike; (in hawking) swoop (upon)

soused pickled

South Sea the Pacific; **South Sea of discovery** = a long, frustrating voyage

sow ingot, block

sowl seize roughly, drag

Sowter 'Cobbler', a dog's name

span-counter a children's game like marbles

spavin tumour on a horse's legjoint

specialty contract; particular distinction

spectacles spyglasses (telescopes); eyes

speculation sight, observation

speculative of sight

sped ruined; *see* **speed**

speed *n.* fate, lot; *v.* fare; meet with success; favour; **be one's speed** = bring one good fortune; **have the speed of** = match in speed; overtake; **speed you** = God speed (favour) you

speeding *n.* fate, lot; success; *adj.* successful

spend speak; use up; **spend the mouth** = be in full cry, as a hunting hound

sphere (in Ptolomaic astronomy) one of the massive crystalline spheres around the earth in which the planets, stars, *etc.* were believed fixed; they

revolved, generating harmonious music, inaudible on earth

spherical of a planet

spigot part of a tap on a barrel

spill destroy

spilth spilling

spin spurt

spines thorns

spinners (?) spiders; (?) craneflies

spinster woman spinning flax or wool

spirit frame of mind

spital hospital, *esp.* for the lower classes

spleen organ supposedly responsible for fierce passion, laughter and melancholy, *hence* the abstract condition or a fit or bout of any of these moods

splinted splintered (*see* **splinter**)

splinter apply splints to (a broken limb)

spoil *n.* sacking, carrying off booty; bloody end of a hunt; *v.* sack, rob, steal

spongy watery, dripping; full of drink

spot piece of embroidery; mark on a list; blemish

sprag smart, quick

spring bud, shoot, sapling

springe snare for catching birds

springhalt muscular disorder in horses causing them to jerk back their legs

spurn *n.* blow, rude rejection; *v.* kick fiercely

square *n.* measuring rule; breastpiece of a dress; *adj.* just, fair; *v.* measure; regulate, direct; square up, adopt a hostile stance; **by the square** = precisely; **square of sense** = (?) part of the body or mind

squarer one who squares for a fight, brawler

squash unripe pea-pod

squier square (measuring rule)

squiny squint

staff quarterstaff, spear or lance; stanza; **set in one's staff** = take up residence

stagger falter, be unsure

staggers disease in horses causing staggering; reeling state

stain *n.* blemish; tincture, hint; one whose superiority casts a shadow (stain) on others; *v.* eclipse

stair-work furtive business on the back stairs

stale *n.* urine; decoy; whore; laughing-stock, *esp.* a risible lover; stalemate; *v.* make stale; cheapen, debase

stall enthrone; lodge, as in an animal's stall; **stall together** = (?) tolerate each other's presence

stamp *n.* something created or minted; seal, official mark; *v.* create, manufacture, (of coins) mint; seal, authenticate

stand stand about; stand still; stand up to; act as, hold good as; **stand in an action** = be a party in a legal action; **stand to** insist on, swear on

standard standard-bearer

standing-bed bed with legs

standing-bowl bowl with a foot or pedestal

staniel kestrel

staple U-shaped rod into which a bolt is shot; pillar (?); fibre from which a thread is made

Star-chamber the heavens; the Tudor Court of Star-chamber, dealing with serious criminal cases

stare *n.* staring state; *v.* stand up stiffly

start *n.* outburst; *v.* (in hunting) drive from cover; frighten

start at pause over; need to investigate

starting-hole bolt-hole, hiding place

starve destroy, *esp.* with cold, freeze; suffer or perish with cold

state standing position, stance; estate (property, condition or social position); chair of state, throne; court

state pleader advocate for the Crown

states men of rank

station standing (still), posture

statist politician, man of affairs

statute document providing security to a creditor

statute-caps (?) academic caps; (?) apprentices' caps

stave's staff's (*see* **staff**)

staves staffs (*see* **staff**)

stay *n.* support; ongoing condition; check, interruption; *v.* support, hold (up); delay; **stay by't** = stand up to things, stand one's ground

stayed waited; was deferred or postponed

stead help, serve the needs of; **stead up** = stand in for

stelled stellar, starry; fixed; (?) portrayed

stern helm

stew brothel

stick stick out; stickle, scruple; pierce, kill

stickler-like in the manner of a moderator, usher or umpire

stigmatic someone criminal (branded) or deformed

stigmatical deformed

still *adj.* constant; *adv.* always, constantly; **still an end** = constantly

stillitory apparatus used for distilling perfumes, *etc.*

stilly quietly

sting passionate urge

stint stop

stithy *n.* smithy, forge; *v.* forge

stoccado (in fencing) thrust with the swordpoint

stock family; dowry; stocking; idiot; stoccado (*see* **stoccado**)

stock-fish, stockfish dried cod, haddock, *etc.*

stockish inanimate, insensible

stole robe, sometimes of religious significance

stomach *n.* part of the body supposedly the seat of pride, ambition and courage; appetite; inclination; *v.* feel indignant (at)

stomacher piece of women's clothing worn over the breast

stone *n.* testicle; kidney stone; thunderbolt; translucent stone used as a mirror; *v.* turn to stone

stone-bow catapult

stool-ball bat and ball game

stoop bow, bend over; (of a bird of prey) swoop down upon prey

stop (in horseriding) rapid switch from a gallop to a halt; point where the finger determines a note on a musical instrument

store *n.* plenty; *v.* fill up

stoup flagon, tankard

stout proud; courageous

stoutness pride; courage

stover winter food for cattle

Strachy, The Lady of the (?) an unidentified lady of the day

straight-pight standing straight, upright

strain *n.* inherited character; pitch, level; *v.* embrace; transgress; pervert; **make no strain** = do not doubt; **strain courtesy** = be unceremonious; hang back

strait narrow; severe

straited hard pushed

strange alien, foreign, unfamiliar; remarkable

strange-achieved (?) got by curious means; (?) got in distant lands

strangely like a foreigner or stranger; remarkably

strangeness aloofness

strappado a form of torture that involves breaking the arms

stratagem trick, plot; violent act; military exploit

stravagant extravagant

stray men wandering aimlessly; **make a stray** stray, deviate

strayers straggling sheep

strength body of soldier

stretch stretching; stage of a journey

strewments strewed flowers

stricture repression; strictness, rigour

strike *n.* quantity of bushels; *v.* strike (lower) sail; (of a planet) ruin with evil influence; fight; **strike vessels** = (?) chink cups, as in a toast; (?) tap casks

strossers trousers

stubborn hard, rigid

stuck *see* **stoccado**

stuffed congested; full (of qualities or accomplishments)

stuprum rape (*Lat.*)

Stygian of the Styx (*see* **Styx**)

style appellation, title

Styx a river of the underworld

subduements men conquered

subjection allegiance, as required of a subject

submission confession

subscribe sign; proclaim; agree; admit

subscription support, allegiance

substractors subtractors, Sir Toby's word for 'detractors' (critics)

subtle deceptive, false

subtleties elaborate sugar sculptures

succeed follow; proceed; inherit; pass by succession

success outcome, upshot, result; succession

successfully potentially successful; successively

succession that which follows; inheritors

successive hereditary

successively through succession or inheritance

sue make a petition, ask; woo

sufferance, suffrance suffering; patience, endurance; permission

suffice feed, nourish; satisfy

sufficient competent; prosperous, well off; qualified to act as a guarantor

suggest tempt, woo, persuade (into sin or discontent)

suggestion prompting; temptation; craftiness

suits pursuits; wooings; garb

sumless countless

summoner officer who cited people to appear in an ecclesiastical court

sumpter horse used for carrying baggage

superflux unnecessary luxuries

supernal celestial, heavenly

superscript superscription, address at the head of a letter

super-serviceable anxious to do any kind of service

superstitious loving, in the manner of a religious worshipper

supervise *n.* inspection, reading; *v.* look over, inspect

suppliance filling-up, occupation

supplies provision of funds

supply military reinforcement

supposal idea, notion

suppose *n.* notion, estimate; *v.* guess at

supposition, in potential, unconfirmed

surcease *n.* end, *hence* death; *v.* cease

sure safe; loyal; **make sure** = dispose of, kill; **surer side** = mother's side

surety *n.* guarantor; guaranteeing; certainty; *v.* act as guarantor for

surprised captured

sur-reined overworked, exhausted

suspect suspicion

suspiration sighing

suspire respire, breath

sutler seller of provisions

suum cuique 'to each his own' (*Lat.*)

swabber sailor in charge of keeping the ship clean

swaddling-clouts *see* **swathing-clothes**

swagger act like a bragging ruffian

swaggerer bragging ruffian

swart swarthy, dark

swarth *see* **swath**

swashers swashbucklers, loud ruffians

swashing swashbuckling, rough

swath swathe, heap (of mown grass); *see* **swathing-clothes**

swathing-clothes, swathling clothes baby clothes

sway *n.* rule, authority, control; *v.* rule, exert influence; control oneself

swayed broken, deformed

swear make swear, exact an oath from; **swear out** = give up; **swear over** = attempt to repudiate with oaths

sweat *n.* plague; *v.* use a sweating tub (*see* **tub**)

sweet *n.* scent; flower; *adj.* scented

sweet-gorged crammed with sweet foods

sweeting sweet apple, used as a term of affection

swim sail

swindged swinged (*see* **swinge**)

swing full scope

swinge beat

swinge-bucklers swashbucklers

Swithold (?) St Withold

swoltery sultry

swoopstake in the manner of a sweepstake (one who takes all the stakes in a game)

sword-and-buckler swashbuckling, boisterous

sworder soldier

swounded fainted (*cf.* **sound**)

'Swounds (by God)'s wounds (an oath)

sympathize agree with or resemble (another) in some quality; share; represent accurately

synod gathering, conference

table *n.* wooden board for painting on; writing-tablet; palm (of the hand); *v.* write down

table-book book of writing-tablets

tables backgammon

tabor type of drum, usually played together with a pipe

taborins military drums, similar to tabors

tack about change direction (at sea)

tackled stair rope-ladder on a ship

taffeta, taffety type of silk

tag common people

tailor traditional exclamation when, upon going to sit down, one falls; (?) penis

taint *n.* fault; discredit; *adj.* tainted; *v.* lose freshness; speak badly of

take take on (a role), feign; take fire; make an impression; encounter; enchant, possess; **take head** = rush away; **take on** = show anger; **take out** = copy; **take the heat** = show anger; act quickly

taking *n.* panic; infection; *adj.* noxious, infectious

tale penis (*cf.* **tailor**); **in a tale** = agreed upon the same story

talent ancient unit of currency; talon

tall courageous; good-looking, dashing; **tall stockings** = long stockings

tally stick notched to keep an account

tamed exposed to the air

tang clang forth, as a bell

Tanta est erga te mentis integritas Regina serenissima 'Such is the honesty of mind towards you, fairest queen' (*Lat.*)

Tantaene animis coelestibus irae? 'Can heavenly spirits such great resentments feel?' (*Lat.*, Virgil)

tar *see* **tarre**

tardy off, come executed inadequately

targe shield; target

tarre urge (a dog) to fight

tarriance waiting

tarry await

Tartar Tartarus, the deepest region of the underworld; Mongol, an archer warrior from the East

task challenge; tax

tasking challenging

tassel-gentle *see* **tercel**

taste sample

tawdry-lace coloured neckcloth

tax *n.* charge; *v.* charge, reproach, condemn

taxation critical attacks; requirement

teem breed, *esp.* abundantly

teen misery, pain

tell count, count up to

temper *n.* character as defined by the humours (*see* **humour**); stability of character, as from a balance of the humours; *v.* mix, concoct; dilute

Temperance a Christian name popular with Puritans

temperate well-tempered, balanced, modest

temporary temporal (rather than spiritual)

tempt attempt, make trial of

tenant someone dependent on a lord

tend attend

tendance attendance

tender *n.* offer, token; concern; *v.* attend to; offer, lay (down); cherish; treat; **tender-hefted** soft and gentle

tenor purport; meaning

tent *n.* probe for a wound; canopy over a bed; *v.* probe (a wound) to clean or explore it

tercel male falcon

Tereus *see* **Philomel** *and* **Progne**

Termagant a blustering, villainous role supposedly in Mystery plays

terminations terms, language

termless that defies the power of language (terms)

Terras Astraea reliquit 'Astraea has left the earth' (*Lat.*, Ovid) (*see* **Astraea**)

tester, testril small coin

tetchy touchy, irritable

tetter *n.* disfiguring skin complaint; *v.* disfigure on the skin

text motto; sermon; **text B** = 'B' in formal script

Thane Scottish nobleman of middling rank

thankful deserving thanks

theoric (military) theory

therefor for that

Thessaly region of Greece terrorized by a fierce boar

Thetis sea-goddess and mother of Achilles

thews sinews, strength

thick *adj.* dull; numerous; *adv.* In a hectic manner, hurriedly

thills shafts of a cart or wagon

thin-belly having a thin waist

thing, a something

think be gloomily introspective

third achieve a third of

thirdborough officer similar to a constable

thought melancholy contemplation; **with a thought** = quick as a thought

Thracian from Thrace; **Thracian poet** = Orpheus, killed by followers of Bacchus; **Thracian tyrant** = Polymestor, blinded by Hecuba for murdering her son

thrasonical like Thraso, a braggart soldier in a comedy by the Roman dramatist Terence

three-farthings coin featuring a rose behind the sovereign's ear

three-man song-men singers of music for three male voices

three-nooked divided into three, as a map of the world divided into Asian, European and African segments

three-pile thick, costly velvet

Threne *threnos* (*Gr.* = 'lament for the dead')

thrice-crowned queen the moon

thrift profit

thriftless unprofitable

throe (of giving birth) pain

thrum tuft of unwoven yarn

thunder-stone thunderbolt, believed to be a stone

thwart *adj.* churlish, obstreperous; *adv.* sideways; *v.* cross

tickle *adj.* unsteady; *v.* flatter; entertain; vex, irritate; beat, thrash (euphemism); **tickle't up** = give sexual pleasure, bring to orgasm

tick-tack board game involving pegs and holes

tide full flood, chance for action; **high tides** = holidays

tidy well-fed

tight water-tight; skilful

tike mongrel

tile, washed a wasted time, as one would by washing an oven tile (proverbial)

tilt spar, thrust

timeless untimely; taking no time, speedy

timely in good time, early

tinct alchemists' potion (*see* **med'cine**); colouring

tincture colour, *esp.* in heraldry; scent

tire *n.* attire, *esp.* for the head; *v.* (of birds of prey) feed by pulling the flesh apart

tiring-house attiring-house, green-room

tisick phthisic, a cough associated with lung disease

Titan the sun

titely quickly, speedily; securely or water-tight

tithe *n.* a tenth of one's produce or income paid to the church; tribute; *v.* take tithes

tithing parish

title entitlement, claim

titlers claimants

tittles little dots and dashes in writing

to cry of encouragement

toast fragment of toasted bread taken in wine

toaze tease

tod *n.* unit of weight in wool-dealing; bush; *v.* amount to a tod of wool

tofore before

toge toga, gown

toil *n.* hunter's snare or net; *v.* exercise, put to work

tokens, the Lord's skin blemishes caused by the plague

toll for put up for sale

tomboys harlots, whores

tool blade; penis

top *n.* height; *v.* cut off; go beyond; topple; mount, have sex with (*cf.* **tup**); **take time by the top** *see* **occasion**

topgallant platform on a ship's mast

topless supreme

tortive contorted

toss carry impaled on a pike; (of a book) (?) leaf through; (?) throw about

tottering swaying; ragged

touch *n.* touchstone; brushstroke; facial feature; *v.* test, as a touchstone tests gold; refer to; **keep touch** = keep one's promise

touse dislocate

toy something trivial or imaginary; **take toy** = be seized by a mad impulse

trace succeed; attend, keep up with; roam

tract track, route; trace

trade traffic, business

traded skilled

trade-fallen out of work

train *n.* bait, snare; *v.* lure, as towards a trap

traject an Italian ferry

trammel up entangle, as in a net

transfix pierce, impale; fix, imprint

translate convert, metamorphose; explain

transport rapture, ecstasy

transpose alter

trapically by a trap or trope

trash keep (an eager hound) in check

travail, travel *n.* labour; journey; *v.* labour

traverse (in fencing) dodge and weave; march

tray-trip a dice game (*cf.* **trey**)

treatise words, account, story

treble-dated long-living

tree gallows

tremor cordis 'trembling of the heart' (*Lat.*), palpitations

trench dig (a trench), gouge, cut

trencher wooden plate

trencher-friends friends won by feeding

trenchering trenchers (*see* **trencher**)

trencher-knight one who is brave only at the dinner table

trey winning throw of three at dice

tribunal platform for Roman magistrates; **tribunal plebs** = Clown's mistake for '*tribuni plebis*' (*Lat.* = 'tribunes of the people' (*see* **tribune**))

tribune Roman magistrate representing the interests of ordinary citizens

trick *n.* trifle; knack; distinctive feature; *v.* (in heraldry) colour; dress

tricking adornments

Trigon triplicity, grouping of three zodiacal signs by element (*e.g.* fire)

trill roll

triple third

triple-turned three times unfaithful

tristful sorrowful

triumph pageant of processions and tournaments

triumphant of a triumph, triumphal

triumphantly in the spirit of a triumph

triumvirate a ruling coalition formed on two occasions in Roman history, first between Julius Caesar, Crassus and Pompey, subsequently between Octavius, Antony and Lepidus

triumviry *see* **triumvirate**

Trojan lad, bloke

troll sing heartily

troll-my-dames game taken round fairs

trophy monument, *esp.* of a battle; ornament; token

tropically metaphorically

trot crone, hag

troth truth; faith

trow suppose, believe; know; wish to know, wonder

troy weight standard of weights (as from Troyes, France)

Troyan *see* **Trojan**

truckle-bed small bed on wheels stored under a normal bed

truepenny good lad

trull whore

truncheon baton, symbol of military command

trundle-tail curly-tailed dog

trunk sleave large, wide sleave

trusted invested in

try *n.* test; *v.* test, prove; **try with main-course** = (of a ship) lie stationary

tub pickling barrel; sweating tub, for the treatment of venereal disease

tuck rapier; **standing tuck** = blade that has lost its resilience

tucket trumpet-call

tuition care

Tully (Marcus Tullius) Cicero, Roman politician, orator and writer of books on oratory

tun-dish type of funnel

tup (of a ram) mount, penetrate

turtle turtle dove, known for its faithfulness

tushes tusks

twiggen made of twigs, wickerwork

twire twinkle, glint

twit find fault with

Tyburn place of public hanging in London

type mark, badge, title

tyrannically fiercely

tyranny violence, fierceness

tyrant fierce; **fowl of tyrant wing** = bird of prey

umber brown earth

umbrage shadow

unable powerless

unaccommodated not provided with the usual clothes or comforts

unacquainted unfamiliar

unadvised *adj.* unintentional; *adv.* carelessly, without thinking

unagreeable inappropriate

unaneled not anointed with the holy oil of the last rites

unapproved false

unaptness unwillingness

unattainted not infected

unattempted unassailed

unavoided unable to be avoided, inevitable

unbarbed uncovered

unbated not blunted; lacking the protective 'button' normally used on the tip of a fencing weapon

unbend slacken; weaken

unbent not frowning; not prepared, as the slack bow of an archer

unbid not asked for or invited

unbitted unrestrained

unblowed cut before fully grown

unbolt open up

unbolted impure; (?) without a penis

unbonneted without one's hat; without having removed one's hat

unbookish ill-informed

unbraided still in good condition

unbreathed unpractised

uncape uncover (? a fox)

uncase take off one's outer garments

uncharge exonerate, remove from suspicion

uncharged unassailed, still standing

unchary unsparingly, lavishly

unchecked not denied or refuted

unclasp open up, reveal

unclew undo, be the end of (*cf.* **clew**)

uncoined in its natural state, like gold bullion

uncomprehensive unimaginable; unfathomable

unconfirmed inexperienced; (?) not having had the sacrament of Confirmation

uncouth unfamiliar, unknown

uncovered without a hat; barefaced

uncrossed with debts not crossed off

unction ointment

uncurrent out of the ordinary

undeeded not having performed any deeds

under beneath the sun, worldly; of the underworld; **go under** = bear; seem; be called

underbear suffer under

underborne edged

undercrest have (a title) above one as one would a crest

undergo go under, bear, be subject to

underhand discreet

underskinker junior tapster (one who serves drink in an inn)

undertake take on; take in one's charge; take responsibility

undertaker one who takes on (a challenge)

under-trees understorey trees

undervalued of less value

underwood woodland understorey

underwrite accept

underwrought undermined

undeserving (?) *n.* that which is undeserving; (?) *adj.* undeserved

undistinguished *see* **indistinguished**

undoubted free from doubt or fear

uneared unsown, as with ears of corn

uneath not easily, hardly

unexperient person without experience

unexpressive unable to be expressed

unfair make no longer fair

unfashionable lacking finished form

unfenced unbounded; unprotected

unfold open up, expose, reveal

unfolding star star at whose rising shepherds let their sheep out of the folds

unfurnished unprovided for, solitary, naked; unprepared

ungalled unwounded, safe

ungenitured sterile; (?) without genitals

ungored unwounded

unguem nail (*Lat.*), as used in the phrase '*ad unguem*' ('to the nail, exactly')

unhaired without (facial) hair

unhandsome unskilful; (?) unsoldierly

unhappily, unhapp'ly unfortunately; adversely; with malice

unhappy unlucky, cursed

unhatched not yet hatched, embryonic

unhearsed released from the grave or tomb

unhoused not occupying or used to occupying a house

unhouseled not having received the eucharist in the last rites

unimproved unchecked, unrestrained

union pearl of fine quality; marriage

unjust false

unkennel unearth, uncover

unkind acting against one's family or the natural order

unlimited observing no dramatic unities

unluckily ominously

unmanned (of a hawk) untrained

unmeet unsuitable

unnerved enfeebled in sinew, strengthless

unowed unowned

unpaved castrated

unpeopled unpopulated

unphysicked lacking exercise or treatment

unpinked with the decorative holes (pinks) either unfinished or worn out

unpitied merciless

unplausive disapproving

unpolicied lacking or outmanoeuvred in political skill

unpractised inexperienced

unpregnant slack, unresponsive

unprevailing pointless

unprivileged unauthorized

unprizable of little value; of great value

unprized unvalued; priceless

unproper shared; indecent

unproportioned unruly, unrestrained

unprovide disarm

unqualitied robbed of one's nature, unmanned

unquestionable irritable when spoken to

unquietness disquiet, perturbation

unraked (of a fire) not kept smouldering overnight

unrecalling irrevocable

unreclaimed untamed

unrecuring past curing, fatal

unrespective confused, without distinction or order; heedless

unrolled dismissed from a fraternity

unroosted knocked off the roost, henpecked

unrough without facial hair, adolescent; of good family

unscanned unconsidered, rash

unseasoned raw, unready; untimely

unseasons deprives of relish

unsecret open, forthcoming

unseminared seedless, castrated

unset unsown

unshape unsettle

unshaped fragmentary, incoherent

unsifted untried, inexperienced

unsisting (?) unresting; (?) insisting; (?) unassisting

unsorted inappropriate

unspeaking speechless, dumbfounded

unsphere knock from a sphere or spheres (*see* **sphere**)

unsquared unsuitable

unstanched *see* **unstaunched**

unstate rid of wealth and status

unstaunched leaking; unquenched

unsured unsure, uncertain

untainted untouched; uninjured; uncharged

untempering unable to melt or soften

untented too deep to be tented (*see* **tent**)

unthrift spendthrift

untoward perverse, unruly

untraded little used, unfamiliar

untrimmed sexually intact; stripped; set off balance

untrussing undoing laces

unused unusual, unexampled

unvalued of no value; of inestimable value

unwappered unexhausted

unwarily unsuspectingly

unweighed unconsidered; light

unwitted made mad

unwrung not chafed by the saddle

unyoked unbridled

up in arms; imprisoned; **game is up** = game is afoot; **kill up** = kill off; **up and down** = absolutely, entirely

upcast (in bowls) throw

upper outer (garment)

uproar turn to uproar or chaos

upshoot (in archery) the best shot until subsequently beaten

upspring wild dance

up-till up against

urchin hedgehog; goblin or elf, *esp.* in the shape of a hedgehog

urinal glass phial used to examine urine; (?) testicle

usance usury

use *n.* custom, habit, way; interest; profit; *v.* be accustomed (to); keep company with; **in use** = in trust

usher assistant schoolmaster

utis holiday merriment; noise, din

utter advertise, sell

utterance furthest point

uttermost, to the (of a fight) to the death

vacancy spare time; air; the vacuum created by a removal of air

vade go away, fade

vagary wandering or erring state

vagrom Dogberry's word for 'vagrant'

vail *n.* setting; *v.* lower, abase (oneself)

vails leftovers given to servants, tips

vain *n.* vanity; *adj.* foolish; flattering

valanced decoratively draped

validity value, worth; strength, efficacy

value evaluate, consider; compare; merit, be worth

valued discriminating, listing individual qualities

valure valour

vambrace defensive armour for the arms

Vanity a female role in the morality plays

vantage advantage; opportunity; **of vantage** = also, in addition

vara very (*dial.*)

varlet servant, page; often a term of abuse with occasional sexual overtones

varletry common people (*cf.* **varlet**)

vastidity vastness

vastures expanses

vaulty vaulted, arched

vaunt *n.* first part; *v.* rejoice

vaunt-couriers forerunners

vaward vanguard, front of an army

vein spirit, style; **rub the vein of** = encourage, flatter

velure velvet

velvet-guards those wearing fine clothes (*cf.* **guards**)

Venetia, Venetia, chi non ti vede, non ti pretia 'Venice, Venice, he who does not see you does not prize you' (*Ital.*, proverbial)

veney *see* **venue**

vengeance *adj.* terrific; *adv.* terrifically

vent venting, discharge; (in hunting) scent, such as makes the hounds bark

ventages holes

ventricle chamber in the brain

venturous adventurous

venue (in fencing) round, assault

Venus goddess of love and lover of Mars (*see* **Mars**)

Ver spring

verbatim in speech

verdict affirmation

verge rim; area surrounding the court

Veronessa ship from Verona

vestal *n.* virgin or nun, as the Roman virgins who tended the fire in the temple of Vesta; *adj.* relating to Vesta or virginity

via an expression of encouragement or impatience (*Ital.*)

viands food

Vice a comic villain in sixteenth-century moral interludes

vice *n.* grasp; screw; *v.* force

vicegerent deputy (a royal title)

vicious wicked; blameworthy; mistaken

videlicet 'that is to say' (*Lat.*)

Videsne quis venit? Video, et gaudeo 'Do you see who comes? I see and rejoice' (*Lat.*)

vie vie with, rival; multiply; (at cards) put down a stake

vigil evening before a feast-day

Vilia miretur vulgus: mihi flavus Apollo / Pocula Castalia plena ministret aqua 'Let the common folk marvel at the everyday: golden Apollo shall serve me cups filled from the Castalian spring' (*Lat.*, Ovid)

villain, villein person of low birth, servant

villiago villain, rascal

vinewed'st mouldiest

viol stringed instrument, an early violin

viol-de-gamboys *see* **bass-viol**

violenteth rages

vir sapit qui pauca loquitur 'he is wise who says little' (*Lat.*, proverbial)

virginalling pressing with the fingers, as one would the keys of a virginal (an early keyboard)

virtue masculine virtue, courage; power; essence

virtuous fertile, breeding; powerful, effective; inherent, lying within

visitation infection

visited punished by God; infected

visitor one who visits the sick and distressed

visor, vizor mask

viva voce orally; speaking out loud (*Lat.*)

vizaments Evans's word for 'advisements'; **take your vizaments in that** = consider that

vizard *see* **visor**

vocativo 'in the vocative case' (*Lat.*)

vocatur '(it) is called' (*Lat.*)

voice *n.* determining say, vote; *v.* vote, choose; **in voices** = reportedly

voiding lobby corridor for entrance or exit

Volquessen Rouen and district

voluble moving smoothly and swiftly, fluent

voluntary volunteer

votaress female votary (*cf.* **votarist**)

votarist, votary one under a vow, *esp.* in a religious order

vouch *n.* allegation, evidence; *v.* testify

voucher corroborative witness

vouchsafe agree

voyage enterprise

Vulcan god of fire and cuckolded husband of Venus, represented as a smith

vulgar *n.* vernacular, native tongue; *adj.* of or among the ordinary people, common

waft wave; turn; carry by boat

waftage passage by boat

wafture waving gesture

wag go, go away, move

wage pay (a wage to); risk; stake; struggle, vie

wainropes wagon-ropes

waist middle of a ship's upper deck; garment for the waist

wait attend

waits group of instrumentalists (maintained by the City of London)

wake *n.* parish festival; *v.* not sleep, stay up

walk move actively

wall-eyed glowering

wanion, with a a phrase used to emphasize a statement

wanned became wan, paled

want lack; feel the lack of

wanton *n.* exuberant joker; delicate youth, pampered child; *adj.* vibrant, skittish; delicate; *v.* play

wappened sexually exhausted

ward *n.* defence, defensive position; room in a prison; lock mechanism; *v.* defend

warden type of pear or apple

warder umpire's baton

ware *adj.* aware; wary; *v.* take heed of, beware

warp turn; change

war-proof, of experienced in war

warrant *n.* licence; assurance; *v.* approve, license; assure, guarantee

warrantise guarantee, pledge

warranty sanction, licence

warren enclosure for rabbits and other game

warrener one who protects rabbits from poachers

washing *see* **swashing**

wassail drinking session; **wassail candle** = thick candle

waste *n.* damage done to a property by a tenant; *v.* consume, destroy

Wat traditional name for a hare

watch *n.* fixed period of time; candle; watchword; *v.* keep watch over, stay awake for; catch by lying in wait for; train (a hawk) through sleep deprivation

watchful sleepless, of sleeplessness

watching wakefulness

water transparency in diamonds, used to grade their quality

water-galls minor types of rainbow

watering drinking

water-rugs rough-haired water dogs

waters, for all versatile, multi-talented

water-standing full of tears

waterwork painted imitation tapestry

wave waver

waxen *adj.* soft as wax; *v.* wax, increase

ways, come your come on your way, come

weal prosperity, well-being; state, society

wealsmen politicians

wealth prosperity, well-being (*cf.* **weal**)

wear *n.* thing worn, fashion; *v.* wear out; be in fashion; adapt; entertain (doubts); **wear the willow** = put on mourning clothes

weather, keep the be upwind, in a superior position

weather-fends defends from the weather

web and pin *see* **pin (pin and web)**

wedding-knives a pair of knives worn at the girdle of a bride, presented by the groom

weed piece of clothing

week, in by the trapped, imprisoned

ween think

weet know, recognize

Weïrd Sisters goddesses of *wyrd* (*OE* = 'fate')

welkin *n.* sky; *adj.* blue as the sky

well to live well off, well-to-do

well-a-day *n.* saying 'alas', lament; *int.* alas

well-a-near alas (*cf.* **well-a-day**)

well-breathed (?) well-trained; (?) breathing well

well-favoured good-looking, attractive

well-liking heavy

well-respected properly considered, not rash

Welsh hook a type of bill-hook or pike (without the 'cross' of a sword)

weraday *see* **well-a-day**

westward ho! Thames watermen's call for passengers heading west

wezand windpipe, throat

wharf river bank

what whatever

wheel *n.* sung refrain; *v.* move in an arc; **on wheels** = giddily; easily; **turn i'th' wheel** = (of dogs) tread a wheel to turn a spit

Wheeson Whitsun (*dial.*)

whelk boil

whelked resembling the shellfish, twisting round

when a cry of impatience

whenas when (first)

whether which (of two)

whey-face one blanching with fear

whiffler one who clears the path of an approaching procession

while until

whileere a short time ago

whiles while (*see* **while**)

whilom once, in the past

whilst while (*see* **while**)

whipping-cheer a bellyful of whipping

whipster whipper-snapper, boy

whip-stock, whipstock whip handle

whirligig spinning-top

whist silent, still

white *n.* (in archery) bullseye; *adj.* afraid, cowardly

white-limed daubed with lime

whiting-time time for bleaching clothes

whitsters professional bleachers

whittle carving-knife

whoo-bub hubbub

whoreson bastard, used technically, offensively or affectionately

wide failing to hit, off course, wrong

widgeon kind of wild duck, *hence* 'fool' (*v.*)

widow provide (the widow) with the estate of the deceased

wight creature, person

Wild, the the Weald, an area of southern England

wild *n.* desert, wasteland; *adj.* headstrong, unthinking; wild mare = boys' game of jumping on each other's backs

wilderness wildness, wild stock

wild-goose chase a type of horse race

wildly chaotically, haphazardly

wildness madness, distraction

wilful-blame blamable for too much self-will

will sexual organ

wimpled muffled, blindfolded

wince kick out

winch wince

Winchester goose *see* goose

Wincot a hamlet near Stratford-upon-Avon

wind *n.* breath; (in hunting) direction of the wind and thus of scent; *v.* get wind of; wheedle; wind up = fill; tune (a stringed instrument) by tightening its pegs

windgalls tumours on the legs of horses

windlasses deviations

window-bars square patterns on a woman's bodice

windring both winding and wandering

wink *n.* shutting the eyes; *v.* shut the eyes; tip the wink = signal slyly

winking with closed eyes

winnow sift, refine

wintered during winter

winter-ground (?) *n.* ground in winter; (?) *v.* insulate, keep warm

wipe branded stigma

wise *n.* way, fashion; *adj.* in one's right mind; wise woman = expert in herbal medicine, witchcraft, *etc.*

wishtly wishfully and/or wistly (*see* wistly)

wisp of straw traditional target of a shrewish woman's hectoring

wistly earnestly, eagerly, attentively

wit *n.* mind, intelligence, cleverness; *v.* know; five wits = five mental faculties; wit, wither wilt? = catchphrase used to shut someone up

wit-crackers teasers, jibers

with along

withal, *prep.* with; *adv.* therewith, with (something specified); do withal = do anything about it

withers ridge between a horse's shoulders

withhold hold back, keep

without outside, beyond

without-door exterior

witting knowing

wittol husband who accepts his being cuckolded

witty mentally sound, intelligent, clever

woe-woman grieving widow

wold open country

woman-tired prey to a woman (*see* tire)

wondered to be wondered at; capable of producing wonders

wond'ring wondering at

wood wild, frantic

woodbine honeysuckle or similar plant

woodcock a stupid, easily

trapped bird

wooden horse wooden contraption; ship

woodman hunter; hunter of women

woollen *adj.* dressed in coarse wool; in the woollen = in scratchy blankets

woolward wearing a woollen shirt without a vest to stop it scratching

woosel *see* ousel

woo't wilt (will you)

working *n.* mental working, perception; deed; *adj.* moving

world *n.* body (*cf.* microcosm); go to the world = reject the cloister, get married

worm snake

worn worn out

worship dignity

worshipped dignified

wort a plant of the cabbage family; unfermented beer

worthy *v.* make seem a hero; the Worthies = nine heroes from history and legend

wot know (*cf.* wit); wilt (*cf.* woo't)

wrack *n.* wreck; wrecking; victim of a wreck; *v.* wreck

wrangler quarreller

wrath *n.* raging passion; *adj.* wroth, furious

wreak *n.* revenge; *v.* revenge

wrest tuning-key; peg for tightening a surgical ligature

wring twist, writhe

writ holy writ, scripture; any document or paper

writhled shrivelled, wrinkled

wroth misfortune, grief

wrying going astray

wry-necked with neck twisted, as was characteristic of fifers

Xanthippe notoriously bad-tempered wife of the philosopher Socrates

yard stick for measuring a yard; penis

yare light; quick; ready

yaw sail unsteadily

y-clad clad, clothed

ycleped cleped, called

Yead Ed (*cf.* Yedward)

yea-forsooth given to using mild oaths in a servile manner

yearn grieve

Yedward Edward

yellowness jealousy

yellows jaundice in horses

yeoman lower-ranking attendant

yerk strike; kick

yest yeast, foam

yield bring forth; report; reward

yoke-devils devils working together

younger younger son, prodigal

youngly as inexperienced youth

younker young man, prodigal

y-ravished ravished, enraptured

y-slacked slacked, reduced to inactivity

zany clown's assistant

'zounds, zounds *see* 'Swounds

zwaggered swaggered (*dial.*) (*see* swagger)